ML

STO

ACPL ITEM
DISCARDED

Y0-ACE-322

025

7030750

OVERSIZE   Oversize

REFERENCE

REFERENCE

Handbook of International Documentation and Information

Volume 16

Museums of the World

3rd Revised Edition

K·G·Saur München·New York·London·Paris 1981

Editorial Staff:

Judy Benson
Barbara Fischer
Harald Gläser
Irmgard Gschwendtner
Dagmar Schäfer
Alexandrina Stegmann

ALLEN COUNTY PUBLIC LIBRARY
EORT WAYNE, INDIANA

CIP-Kurztitelaufnahme der Deutschen Bibliothek

Museums of the world
]. – 3., rev. ed. – München ; New York ;
London ; Paris : Saur, 1981.
(Handbook of international documentation
and information ; Vol. 16)
ISBN 3-598-10118-X

© Copyright 1981
by K. G. Saur Verlag KG, München
Printed and bound in the Federal Republic of Germany
All rights reserved. No part of this publication may be reproduced,
stored in a retrieval system or transmitted in any form or by any means,
electronic, mechanical, photocopying, recording, or otherwise,
without permission in writing from the publisher.

Computer-controlled phototypesetting: Digiset. – Data preparation
and automatic data processing: alphadat/Josef Keller GmbH & Co., Starnberg
Printed by grafik + druck GmbH & Co, München
Bound by WB-Druckanstalt Blasaditsch, Füssen/Allgäu
ISBN 3-598-10118-x

Contents

Foreword

The completely revised 3rd edition of *Museums of the World* incorporates a new typography and layout, a more convenient arrangement of entries, and an improved subject index – not to mention hundreds of additions and corrections.

All entries from the 2nd edition were individually reviewed and, in most cases, updated on the basis of current information received from both new and previously listed museums. In this manner certain countries – Bulgaria, Czechoslovakia, the USSR, and Japan, to mention only a few – could be reworked in entirety. By the same token ten countries could be listed for the very first time: Bhutan, Bahrain, Maldives, Oman, Qatar, São Tomé and Príncipe, Swaziland, United Arab Emirates, Yemen Arab Republic, and People's Democratic Republic of Yemen. The 3rd edition thus lists a total of 163 countries.

While the 2nd edition was arranged by continent, we felt that a straightforward alphabetical arrangement by country would greatly simplify a work of this kind, and the 3rd edition is accordingly so organized. The alphabetical arrangement by site within each country was retained.

This same scheme was carried over into the revised subject index, in which references under a given subject heading are organized first by country, and within each country by site. For the sake of convenience, a list of the subject headings used, together with ample cross-references, precedes the index proper. Altogether the subject index in the 3rd edition is far more detailed and comprehensive than in previous editions.

The list of national and international museum associations, a popular feature of the 2nd edition, has been expaned and updated. Thus in the International Section alone, twenty-two organizations could be added.

A work of this scope would of course not be possible without the active support of countless clerks, secretaries, curators, and administrators in the museum, art, and diplomatic professions. Again we extend our gratitude for their generous response to our various requests for aid and information. They have helped to ensure the continuing popularity of this unique international reference work.

Munich, February 1981
The Editors

Note on Use

Museums of the World is arranged alphabetically by country, and within each country alphabetically by site – usually the town or city in which a given museum is physically located. A second, mailing address is indicated by the note *mail to* or *mail c/o* in the address section of the entry.

A typical entry consists of the following information arranged in the following order:
Entry number
Museum name
Address
Museum type and year of founding
Collections and facilities

In all but a few cases each museum has been typed according to one of the following subject categories:
Agriculture Museum
Anthropology Museum
Archeology Museum
Decorative Arts Museum
Fine Arts Museum
General Museum
History and Public Affairs Museum
Music Museum
Natural History Museum
Performing Arts Museum
Religious Arts Museum
Science and Technology Museum

or one of the following administrative categories:

Historic Site
Junior Museum
Open Air Museum

References in the name and subject indexes are to entry, not page numbers.

Place names are usually given in their native form. Alphabetical arrangements are based on the English alphabet.

Museums of the World

Afghanistan

Ghazni

00001
Ghazni Museum
Ghazni
General Museum

Herat

00002
Herat Museum
Herat
General Museum

Kabul

00003
National Museum of Afghanistan
Darul Aman, Kabul
General Museum - 1922
Local and Far Eastern antiquities and
objects d'art; costumes and jewelery

00004
Pathology Museum
Kabul University, Kabul
Science/Tech Museum

00005
Science Museum
Faculty of Science, Kabul University,
Kabul
Natural History Museum
Zoological collections

Kandahar

00006
Kandahar Museum
Kandahar
General Museum

Maimana

00007
Maimana Museum
Maimana
General Museum

Mazar-e-Sharif

00008
Mazar-e-Sharif Museum
Mazar-e-Sharif
General Museum

Albania

Bérat

00009
Bérat Museum
Bérat
General Museum - 1958
Local history; documents

Durrës

00010
Durrës Museum
Durrës
General Museum
Local archaeology and history

Elbasan

00011
Elbasan Museum
Elbasan
General Museum
Local and military history; natural
history

Fier

00012
Fier Museum
Fier
General Museum
Archaeological finds from Apollonia

Gjirokastër

00013
Gjirokastër Museum
Gjirokastër
General Museum
Local and military history

Korçë

00014
Korçë Museum
Korçë
General Museum
Local history; ethnography

Shkodër

00015
Shkodër Museum
Shkodër
General Museum
History of the town and province from
Neolithic times; ethnography

Tirana

00016
Lenin-Stalin Museum
Tirana
History/Public Affairs Museum - 1954

00017
**Museum of Archaeology and
Ethnography**
Institute of Scientific Research in
History and Linguistics, State
University of Tirana, Tirana
General Museum - 1948
Archaeology (objects from Illyrian
culture); exhibits on Middle Ages in
Albania; household objects; textiles;
costumes; crafts

00018
Museum of Natural Sciences
State University of Tirana, Tirana
Natural History Museum
Biology; geology; botany

00019
**Museum of the Struggle for National
Liberation**
Tirana
History/Public Affairs Museum
History of the Albanian people from
the Ottoman period to the present day

Vlorë

00020
Vlorë Museum
Vlorë
General Museum
Local history

Algeria

Alger

00021
Jardin d'Essai
El Hamma, Alger
Natural History Museum
Plants and flowers

00022
Musée des Antiquités
Parc de la Liberté, Alger
Fine Arts Museum - 1897
Classical and Islamic archaeology;
Islamic art

00023
Musée des Arts Populaires
rue Mohamed Akli Malek, Kasbah,
Alger
Fine Arts Museum - 1962
Popular arts and crafts

00024
Musée du Bardo
3, rue Roosevelt, Alger
General Museum - 1928
Prehistoric and ethnographic
collections; African art

00025
Musée du Mont Riant
Parc Mont-Riant, Alger
Junior Museum - 1966

00026
Musée National de la Revolution
22, rue du 1er Novembre, Alger
History/Public Affairs Museum - 1968
Pictures, documents, weapons and
other objects associated with the
Algerian War of Independence

00027
Musée National des Beaux-Arts
El Hamma, Alger
Fine Arts Museum - 1930
Contemporary and 16th cent painting;
drawing, sculpture and graphics; 19th
cent. Oriental painting - library

Annaba

00028
Musée d'Hippone
Route d'Hippone, Annaba
Fine Arts Museum
Classical antiquities

Béjaia

00029
Musée de Béjaia
Béjaia
General Museum
Archaeology; natural sciences; fine
arts

Beni-Abbes

00030
Centre de la Recherche Scientifique
Beni-Abbes
Natural History Museum
Botanical and zoological gardens

Cherchell

00031
Musée de Cherchell
Cherchell
Archeology Museum
Egyptian, Greek and Roman antiquities

Constantine

00032
Musée de Constantine
Plateau Coudiat, Constantine
Fine Arts Museum
Prehistoric antiquities; Islamic art;
painting

Djemila

00033
Musée de Djemila
Djemila
Fine Arts Museum
Architecture; sculpture; classical
antiquities

El-Oued

00034
Musée d'El-Oued
El-Oued
General Museum - 1954
Prehistory; ethnography; crafts

Ghardaia Oasis

00035
Musée Folklorique de Ghardaia
Ghardaia Oasis
Decorative Arts Museum
crafts; folk arts

Guelma

00036
Musée du Théâtre de Guelma
Guelma
General Museum
Sculpture; numismatics

1

Oran

00037
Musée d'Oran
bd Zabana, Oran
General Museum - 1884
Prehistory; modern art; ethnography;
natural science; classical antiquities;
Roman and Byzantine coins

Ouargla

00038
Musée Saharien de Ouargla
Ouargla
General Museum
Prehistory; ethnography; crafts

Sétif

00039
Musée de Sétif
Route de Bedjaia, Sétif
General Museum - 1968
Classical antiquities; ceramics;
mosaics

Skikda

00040
Musée de Skikda
Skikda
Fine Arts Museum
Punic and Roman antiquities; modern
art

Souk-Ahras

00041
Musée Saint-Augustin
Crypte de l'Eglise Saint-Augustin,
Souk-Ahras
Archeology Museum

Tazoult

00042
Musée de Tazoult
Tazoult
Archeology Museum
Classical antiquities

Tebessa

00043
Musée du Temple de Minerve
Tebessa
General Museum
Local art; prehistoric finds; antiquities

Timgad

00044
Musée de Timgad
Timgad
Fine Arts Museum
Classical antiquities; mosaics; coins

Tipasa

00045
Musée de Tipasa
Tipasa
Archeology Museum
Antique sculpture and archaeology

Tizi-Ouzou

00046
Musée de Tizi-Ouzou
Tizi-Ouzou
Fine Arts Museum
Antiquities, arts and crafts

Tlemcen

00047
Musée de Tlemcen
Mosquée de Sidi Bel Hacine, Tlemcen
General Museum
Islamic arts; natural science; classical
antiquities

Angola

Carmona

00048
Museu de Congo
C.P. 11, Carmona
General Museum - 1965
Items of material culture of the people
of the area; indigenous art; wood
carvings and ivories

Dundo

00049
Museu do Dundo
Companhia de Diamantas de Angola,
Dundo
General Museum
Ethnographic collections including art
of the local Chokwe tribe; tape library
of North Eastern Angola folk music;
local history; photos from the 1880s

Luanda

00050
**Museu de Geológia, Paleontológia e
Mineralógia**
Avenida Paulo Dias de Novais 105,
Luanda
Natural History Museum
Geology and mineralogy;
palaeontology; archaeology

00051
Museu do Café
Empresa Nacional do Café, Av. 4
Fevereiro 101, POB 342, Luanda
Anthropology Museum
Historical and ethnographic artifacts
related to the cultivation and
preparation of coffee

00052
Museu Nacional de História Natural
Rua de Nossa Senhora da Muxima, 1,
C.P. 1267, Luanda
Natural History Museum - 1938
Natural history exhibits - library

00053
National Museum of Anthropology
Avelino Dias No 57-59-61, 1267-C,
Luanda
Anthropology Museum - 1976
Ethnographical exhibits; African arts -
library

Moçamedes

00054
Museu da Pesca
Moçamedes
General Museum
History of local fishing trade and
industry

Nova Lisboa

00055
Museu Municipal
Avenida Paiva Couceiro, Nova Lisboa
Anthropology Museum
Historical and ethnologic collections;
traditional and modern African
sculpture

Sá da Bandeira

00056
Museu da Huíla 2
C.P. 445, Sá da Bandeira
General Museum - 1956
Natural history, history and prehistory
with emphasis on Huíla region; musical
instruments

Argentina

Adrogué

00057
**Museo y Archivo 'Almirante
Guillermo Brown'**
Rosales 1520, Adrogué
History/Public Affairs Museum - 1947
Documents, photographs and
memorabilia of Admiral Brown

Alta Gracia

00058
**Museo Histórico de la Casa del
Virrey Liniers**
Sáenz Peña 41, Alta Gracia
History/Public Affairs Museum - 1969
Memorabilia of Virrey Liniers

00059
Museo 'Manuel de Falla'
Chalet 'Los Espinillos', Carlos
Pellegrini 1.011, Alta Gracia, Córdoba
5186
Music Museum - 1970
Memorabilia of the composer Manuel
de Falla (1876-1946)

Andalgalá

00060
**Museo Arqueológico 'Samuel Lafone
Quevedo'**
Núñez de Prado s/no., Andalgalá
Archeology Museum - 1964
Historical and archeological artifacts

Arrecifes

00061
**Museo y Archivo Histórico de
Arrecifes**
Saavedra 382, Arrecifes
General Museum - 1968
Local history

Avellaneda

00062
**Museo Histórico y Tradicional de
Barracas al Sud**
Beruti 216, Avellaneda
History/Public Affairs Museum - 1962
Regional history

00063
Museo Municipal de Artes Plásticas
San Martín 799, Avellaneda
Fine Arts Museum - 1956
Painting, sculpture, drawing, and
engraving by contemporary Argentine
artists

00064
**Museo Pedagógico 'Bernardino
Rivadavia'**
Av. Mitre 750, Avellaneda
History/Public Affairs Museum - 1963
Educational tools, methods and
techniques

Azul

00065
Museo de Ciencias Naturales
San Martín 620, Azul
Natural History Museum - 1974
Local flora and fauna - library

00066
**Museo Etnográfico y Archivo
Histórico 'Enrique Squirru'**
San Martín esq. Alvear, Azul
General Museum - 1945
Local history and archeology; art and
folklore; crafts

Bahía Blanca

00067
**Museo Histórico y de Ciencias
Naturales**
Dorrego 116, Bahía Blanca
General Museum - 1951
Archeology, anthropology and natural
history

00068
Museo Municipal de Bellas Artes
Alsina 65, Bahía Blanca
Fine Arts Museum - 1951
Painting, sculpture, drawing, engraving

Belén

00069
**Museo Regional 'Condor Huasi' e
Instituto Cultural 'Cesar N. Julián'**
Rivadavia 175, Belén
General Museum - 1944
History, archeology, folklore, colonial
art, numismatics and medals

Bernal

00070
**Museo Histórico Regional 'Almirante
Brown'**
25 de Mayo 198, Bernal
History/Public Affairs Museum - 1952
Memorabilia of Almirante Brown and
national naval war history

Bernasconi

00071
**Museo de Ciencias y Artes 'Lucio V.
Mansilla'**
Urquiza 477, Bernasconi
General Museum - 1965
Local history and culture; arts; Indian
relics

Bolivar

00072
Museo 'Florentino Ameghino'
Av. San Martín 1065, Bolivar
Archeology Museum - 1930
Regional archeology

Buenos Aires

00073
Antiguo Congreso Nacional
Balcarce 139, Buenos Aires
History/Public Affairs Museum - 1949
Documents and memorabilia of the
National Congress (1964-1905) -
library

00074
**Archivo y Museo Historicos del
Banco de la Provincia de Buenos
Aires**
Av. Córdoba 934, piso 1, Buenos Aires
History/Public Affairs Museum - 1903
Exhibits depicting the history of the
bank

00075
Buque-Museo Fragata 'Presidente Sarmiento'
Dársena Norte, Buenos Aires
History/Public Affairs Museum - 1964
Original flags, furnishings, armaments and instruments of the frigate Presidente Sarmiento

00076
Exposición Permanente de Materias Primas Minerales
Av. Julio A. Roca 651, piso 10, Buenos Aires
Natural History Museum - 1960
Minerals

00077
Museo 'Alfredo L. Palacios'
Charcas 4741, Buenos Aires
Historic Site - 1971
Furnishings, documents, library and other personal belongings of A.L. Palacios

00078
Museo Areneo de Estudios Históricos de Nueva Pompeya
Av. Sáenz 1260, Buenos Aires
History/Public Affairs Museum - 1971
Manuscripts, scores, photographs and memorabilia of Argentine artists, poets and musicians

00079
Museo Argentino de Ciencias Naturales 'Bernardino Rivadavia' e Instituto Nacional de Investigaciones de las Ciencias Naturales
Av. Angel Gallardo 470, Buenos Aires
Natural History Museum - 1812
Comprehensive collections in all areas of natural science - library

00080
Museo Argentino para la Escuela Primaria 'Juan B. Teran'
Pedro Echagüe 2750, Buenos Aires
History/Public Affairs Museum - 1931
Argentine history and geography

00081
Museo Arqueológico 'Gaston Maspero'
San Martín 274, Buenos Aires
Archeology Museum - 1971
Classical and Ibero-American archeology

00082
Museo 'Bernardo A. Houssay'
Viamonte 2790, Buenos Aires
Historic Site - 1977
Library, uniforms, documents; medals, correspondence and other memorabilia of B.A. Houssay, displayed in his former residence

00083
Museo Botanico
Av. Las Heras 4102, Buenos Aires
Natural History Museum - 1964
Herbarium; morphology and taxonomy of plants; botany

00084
Museo 'Casa de Ricardo Rojas' e Instituto de Investigaciones
Charcas 2837, Buenos Aires
Historic Site - 1958
Furnishings, works of art, books, documents and memorabilia of Dr. Ricardo Rojas, displayed in his former residence

00085
Museo 'Casa de Yrurtia'
O'Higgins 2390, Buenos Aires
Historic Site - 1942/1949
Furnishings, works of art and memorabilia of the sculptor Rogelio Yrurtia, in original setting

00086
Museo Criollo de los Corrales
Av. de los Corrales 6476, Buenos Aires
General Museum - 1963
Clothing, arms, lassos, domestic utensils, etc. representative of gaucho life

00087
Museo de Aduanas
Azopardo 350, Buenos Aires
History/Public Affairs Museum - 1967
Artifacts and documents illustrating the history of the customs authority from the 16th c. onward

00088
Museo de Armas de la Nacion
Santa Fé 750, Buenos Aires
Anthropology Museum - 1938
Firearms and other weapons from around the world

00089
Museo de Arte Marino
Callao 966, Manzanares 2091, Buenos Aires
Fine Arts Museum - 1964
Painting, sculpture and graphic arts depicting the sea

00090
Museo de Arte Moderno de la Ciudad de Buenos Aires
Av. Corrientes 1530, piso 9, Buenos Aires
Fine Arts Museum - 1956
Painting, sculpture and media displays

00091
Museo de Artes Plásticas 'Eduardo Sivori'
Av. Corrientes 1530, piso 7 y 8, Buenos Aires
Fine Arts Museum - 1934
Argentine painting, sculpture, drawing and graphics (19th and 20th c.)

00092
Museo de Bellas Artes de la Boca
Pedro de Mendoza 1835, Buenos Aires
Fine Arts Museum - 1936
Works of art by contemporary Argentine authors

00093
Museo de Bellas Artes de la Escuela No. 1 del Distrito Escolar XII 'General Urquiza'
Yerbal 2370, Buenos Aires
Fine Arts Museum - 1963
Argentine painting and sculpture

00094
Museo de Botánica y Farmacología 'Juan A. Dominguez'
Junín 956, piso 1, Buenos Aires
Natural History Museum - 1900
Herbarium; useful plants; wood exhibits

00095
Museo de Calcos y Escultura Comparada
Av. Tristán Achával Rodríguez 1701, Buenos Aires
Fine Arts Museum - 1961
Original sculpture and plaster casts (Greek, Roman, Hindu, Gothic, and Renaissance to modern)

00096
Museo de Ciencias Naturales
Azcuénaga 158, Buenos Aires
Natural History Museum - 1970
Biology; zoology; mineralogy and geology

00097
Museo de Ciencias Naturales 'Angel Gallardo'
Pedro Echagüe 2750, Buenos Aires
Natural History Museum - 1929
Prepared specimens (birds, fishes, mammals, reptiles, etc.); comparative displays of Argentine flora and fauna; minerals and elements of human anatomy

00098
Museo de Instituto Antártico Argentino
Av. Angel Gallardo 470, Buenos Aires
Natural History Museum - 1956
Natural history of the Antarctic

00099
Museo de la Basilica del Rosario de la Reconquista y Defensa de Buenos Aires
Defensa 422, Buenos Aires
History/Public Affairs Museum
Indian cult objects and paintings; battle flags (campaign of Gen. Manuel Belgrano)

00100
Museo de la Casa de Gobierno
Hipólito Yrigoyen 219, Buenos Aires
History/Public Affairs Museum
Argentine history; memorabilia and documents of Argentine presidents; furniture, medals and objects of art

00101
Museo de la Casa del Teatro
Santa Fé 1243, Buenos Aires
Performing Arts Museum - 1976
History of the Argentine theater

00102
Museo de la Ciudad
Alsina 412, Buenos Aires
General Museum - 1968
Momentos and artifacts illustrating the history of the city

00103
Museo de la Diplomacia Argentina
Juncal 851, Buenos Aires
History/Public Affairs Museum - 1976
Photographs, documents uniforms and other articles illustrating the history of Argentine diplomacy

00104
Museo de la Farmacia
Junín 956, piso 5, Buenos Aires
Science/Tech Museum - 1969
Pharmacy and drugs

00105
Museo de la Policia Federal Argentina
San Martín 353, piso 7, Buenos Aires
History/Public Affairs Museum - 1899
Weapons, uniforms, documents and other exhibits illustrating the history of the Argentine police force

00106
Museo de Lapiceras Históricas
Charcas 3761, Buenos Aires
History/Public Affairs Museum - 1898
Writing equipment of Argentine statesmen and writers

00107
Museo de las Obras Misionales Pontificias
Medrano 735, Buenos Aires
Anthropology Museum
Handicrafts, musical instruments, textiles, weapons and ethnographic exhibits from Africa and Asia

00108
Museo de los Subterraneos
Matheu y Pavón, Buenos Aires
Science/Tech Museum - 1971
Busses, streetcars, subway trains and other municipal transportation equipment

00109
Museo de Mineralogía y Geología
Santa Fe 1548, piso 3, Buenos Aires
Science/Tech Museum - 1904
Minerals; petrified wood; paleontology; regional geology

00110
Museo de Motivos Populares Argentinos 'José Hernandez'
Av. del Libertador 2373, Buenos Aires
General Museum - 1948
Ceramics; decorative and applied arts; musical instruments; firearms; lithographs and paintings

00111
Museo del Escritor
Uruguay 1371, piso 1, Buenos Aires
History/Public Affairs Museum - 1958
Manuscripts, first editions and memorabilia of Argentine writers and artists from all periods

00112
Museo del Grabado
San Martín 933, P. 2 Dpto. 22, Buenos Aires
Fine Arts Museum - 1960
Engravings by Argentine artists; books with original engravings, lithographs

00113
Museo del Instituto de Hipología
Av. del Libertador 4625, Buenos Aires
Natural History Museum - 1917
Stuffed horses and skeletal displays of prize horses; horseshoe collection; artifacts relating to hippology

00114
Museo del Instituto Nacional Sanmartiniano
Mariscal Ramón Castilla y Av. A.M. de Aguado, Buenos Aires
History/Public Affairs Museum - 1944
Lithographs, engravings, documents and personal belonings of Gen. Jose&1 de San Martín - library

00115
Museo del Regimiento de Granaderos a Caballo 'General San Martín'
Av. Luis María Campos 554, Buenos Aires
History/Public Affairs Museum - 1968
Military uniforms and artifacts used by Gen. San Martín in the Chile campaign; military documents and objects

00116
Museo del Teatro Colón
Arturo Toscanini 1154, Buenos Aires
Performing Arts Museum - 1939
Photographs, documents, programs and personal objects illustrating the history of the Teatro Colon

00117
Museo Entel de Telefonía
Uruguay esq. Bartolomé Mitre, Buenos Aires
Natural History Museum - 1975
Documents, photographs, and equipment illustrating the history of the telephone in Argentina

00118
Museo Etnográfico 'Juán B. Ambrosetti'
Moreno 350, Buenos Aires
Anthropology Museum - 1904
Archeology, ethnography, anthropology and folklore

00119
Museo Farmacobotánico 'José F. Molfino'
Av. Caseros 2161, Buenos Aires
Natural History Museum - 1967
Botany

00120
Museo Forense de la Justicia Nacional
Junín 760, Buenos Aires
History/Public Affairs Museum - 1977
Portraits documents and memorabilia of·Gen. Don Manuel Belgrano - library and archive

00121
Museo 'Hermano Esteban' del Colegio Lasalle
Río Bamba 650, Buenos Aires
Natural History Museum - 1909

00122
Museo Histórico de la Ciudad de Buenos Aires 'Brigadier General Cornelio de Saavedra'
Republiquetas 6309, Buenos Aires
General Museum - 1942
History of Buenos Aires from the 18th c. onward (numismatics, works of art, firearms, costumes, etc.)

00123
Museo Histórico de la Iglesia
San Martín 701, Buenos Aires
Religious Art Museum - 1969
Religious objects and works of art from the colonial period onward

00124
Museo Histórico Nacional
Defensa 1600, Buenos Aires
History/Public Affairs Museum - 1889
Flags, arms, uniforms, medals, documents, etc. illustrating the history of Argentina

00125
Museo Histórico Nacional del Cabildo de la Ciudad de Buenos Aires y de la Revolucion de Mayo
Bolívar 65, Buenos Aires
History/Public Affairs Museum - 1940
Furnishings, arms, documents, religious art

00126
Museo Histórico Nacional del Traje
Chile 832, Buenos Aires
Anthropology Museum - 1972
History of Argentine fashion from Colonial times to the present; military and civilian costume

00127
Museo Histórico Sarmiento
Cuba 2079, Buenos Aires
History/Public Affairs Museum - 1938
Memorabilia of Domingo Faustino Sarmiento - library

00128
Museo Histórico y Numismático del Banco de la Nación Argentina
Bartolomé Mitre 326, piso 1, Buenos Aires
History/Public Affairs Museum - 1966
Artifacts relating to the history of the National Bank of Argentina

00129
Museo Internacional de la Caricatura y Humorismo 'Severo Vaccaro'
Estados Unidos 2162, Buenos Aires
Fine Arts Museum - 1950
Illustrations; national and foreign political caricatures

00130
Museo Judio
Libertad 769, Buenos Aires
Religious Art Museum - 1967
Religious and ceremonial art of Argentine and foreign Jews

00131
Museo 'Maria Antonia de la Paz y Figueroa'
Independencia 1190, Buenos Aires
Religious Art Museum - 1790
Religious and ceremonial art objects

00132
Museo 'Maurice Minkowski'
Pasteur 633, piso 3, Buenos Aires
Fine Arts Museum - 1941
Memorabilia of the painter M. Minkowski

00133
Museo Mitre
San Martín 336, Buenos Aires
Historic Site - 1906
Furnishings, works of art, weapons, uniforms, medals, books, etc. of Gen. Bartolomé Mitre, housed his former residence

00134
Museo Municipal de Arte Español 'Enrique Larreta'
Juramento 2291, Buenos Aires
Fine Arts Museum - 1962
Works of art; furnishings and memorabilia of writer Enrique Larreta

00135
Museo Municipal de Arte Hispanoamericano 'Isaac Fernandez Blanco'
Suipacha 1422, Buenos Aires
Fine Arts Museum - 1922
Spanish and colonial works of art; furnishings; Peruvian sculpture; numismatics

00136
Museo Municipal del Cine 'Palo Cristian Ducros Hicken'
Sarmiento 1551, piso 3, Buenos Aires
Performing Arts Museum - 1972
Documents and relics from the history of motion pictures, especially in Argentina

00137
Museo Nacional de Aeronáutica
Av. Rafael Obligado 4550, Buenos Aires
Science/Tech Museum - 1960
Documents and relics from the history of Argentine and international aeronautics; aircraft exhibit

00138
Museo Nacional de Arte Decorativo
Av. del Libertador 1902, Buenos Aires
Decorative Arts Museum - 1937
Furnishings; procelain; tapestries; painting and sculpture

00139
Museo Nacional de Arte Oriental
Av. del Libertador 1902, piso 1, Buenos Aires
Fine Arts Museum - 1965
Oriental art

00140
Museo Nacional de Bellas Artes
Av. del Libertador 1473, Buenos Aires
Fine Arts Museum - 1895
European painting (16th-20th c.); sculpture; modern Argentine painting - library

00141
Museo Nacional del Hombre
3 de Febrero 1370/1378, Buenos Aires
Anthropology Museum - 1964
Archeology, ethnography, folk art and crafts

00142
Museo Nacional del Teatro
Av. Córdoba 1199, Buenos Aires
Performing Arts Museum - 1938
Documents, original scripts, first editions, autographs, memorabilia, etc. illustrating the history of the theater

00143
Museo Nacional y Centro de Estudios Históricos Ferroviarios
Av. del Libertador 405, Buenos Aires
Science/Tech Museum - 1971
Documents and historic exhibits depicting the development of railway transportation in Argentina

00144
Museo Naval 'Coronel de Marina Tomas Espora'
Av. Caseros 2526, Buenos Aires
History/Public Affairs Museum - 1967
Naval history

00145
Museo Naval de la Corbeta Uruguay
Dársena Norte-Muelle Sur-Capital Federal, Buenos Aires
History/Public Affairs Museum - 1975
Furnishings, instruments and other original equipment on site in a retired corvette

00146
Museo Notarial
Guido 1841, Buenos Aires
History/Public Affairs Museum - 1973
Documents, writing utensils, proclamatins, etc. illustrating the history of the notary public in Argentina

00147
Museo Notarial Argentino
Uruguay 637, Buenos Aires
History/Public Affairs Museum - 1965
History of notary science and the work of the Argentine Scribe General

00148
Museo Numismático del Banco Central de la República Argentina 'Doctor José Evaristo Uriburu'
Reconquista 266, Buenos Aires
History/Public Affairs Museum - 1941
Numismatics and history of banking

00149
Museo Numismático y de Valores del Estado
Av. Antártida Argentina s/no., Puerto Nuevo, Buenos Aires
History/Public Affairs Museum - 1927
Numismatics; history of Argentine money

00150
Museo Postal y Telegráfico 'Doctor Ramon J. Carcano'
Sarmiento 151, piso 2, Buenos Aires
Science/Tech Museum - 1888
History of postal services

00151
Museo 'Roberto Noble'
Piedras 1743, piso 3, Buenos Aires
History/Public Affairs Museum - 1970
Works of art, books, documents, furnishings and memorabilia of the journalist and politician Roberto Noble

00152
Museo Roca Instituto de Investigaciones Históricas
Vicente López 2220, Buenos Aires
History/Public Affairs Museum - 1961
Documents, photographs, books, etc. of Gen. Julio A. Roca

00153
Museo 'San Roque'
Alsina 340, Buenos Aires
Fine Arts Museum - 1967
Classical and contemporary Hispano-American art (18th-19th c.)

00154
Museo Tecnológico 'Ingeniero Eduardo Latzina'
Paseo Colón 650, Buenos Aires
Science/Tech Museum - 1913
History of technology

00155
Museo y Archivo Histórico de la Dirección General Impositiva
Lavalle 1268, piso 1, Buenos Aires
History/Public Affairs Museum - 1974
Customs, taxes, internal revenue

00156
Museo y Biblioteca de la Literature Porteña
Honduras 3784, Buenos Aires
History/Public Affairs Museum - 1977
Memorabilia of the poet Evaristo Carriego - library of Argentine literature

00157
Primer Museo Argentino de Historia Argentina en la Escuela Primaria
Pedro Eshagüe 2750, Buenos Aires
History/Public Affairs Museum - 1939
Documents, numismatics, replicas of historic flags, portraits and other objects pertaining to the history of Argentina

00158
Primer Museo Argentino del Juguete
General Venancio Flores 3450, Buenos Aires
Anthropology Museum - 1974
Antique and modern toys

00159
Primer Museo Permanente del Boxeo Argentino
Bartomomé Mitre 2020, Buenos Aires
Anthropology Museum - 1968
Materials from the history of boxing sport in Argentina

00160
Sala Histórica 'General Savio'
Cabildo 65, Buenos Aires
History/Public Affairs Museum - 1977
Documents and relics pertaining to the life of Gen. don Manuel Nicolás Aristóbulo Savio and the military equipment industry

00161
Serpentario y Museo de Animales Venenosos
Av. Vélez Sarsfield 563, Buenos Aires
Natural History Museum - 1954
Live poisonous animals

Cachi

00162
Museo Arqueológico
Cachi
Archeology Museum - 1971
Regional archeology

Cafayate

00163
Museo de Arqueologia Calchaqui
Colón 191, Cafayate
Decorative Arts Museum
Local crafts

Campana

00164
Museo Municipal de Bellas Artes de Campana
San Martín 383, Campana
Fine Arts Museum - 1970
Painting, sculpture and graphics by Argentine artists

Carhué

00165
Museo Regional 'Adolfo Alsina'
Rivadavia y Laprida, Carhué
General Museum - 1963
Regional archeology; historical documents; weapons

Carlos Tejedor

00166
Museo Histórico Regional de Carlos Tejedor
Esteban y Santiago Garré 513, Carlos Tejedor
General Museum - 1969
Archeology; crafts; 19th and 20th cent. architecture

Carmen de Patagonés

00167
Museo Histórico Regional 'Francisco de Viedma'
Edificio Municipal, calle 7 de Marzo, planta baja, Carmen de Patagonés
General Museum - 1951
Local history, life and customs

Catamarca

00168
Museo Arqueológico 'Adan Quiroga'
Sarmiento 450, Catamarca
General Museum - 1937
Regional archeology; colonial history; natural history; postage stamps

00169
Museo Provincial de Bellas Artes 'Laureano Brizuela'
República 330, Catamarca
Fine Arts Museum - 1935
Argentine art

Chacabuco

00170
Museo de Artes Visuales
Palacio Municipal, Chacabuco
Fine Arts Museum
Contemporary Argentine painting, sculpture, engraving and pottery

00171
Museo Tradicionalista 'El Rancho'
Pueyrredón 139, Chacabuco
History/Public Affairs Museum
Arms, animal specimens, and artifacts of traditional ranch life and culture

Chascomús

00172
Museo Pampeano y Parque 'Los Libres del Sur'
Av. Lastra y Av. Francisco Javier Muñiz, Chascomús
General Museum - 1941
Archeology, history and folklore

Chilecito

00173
Museo 'Samay Huasi'
San Miguel, Chilecito
General Museum - 1962
Archeology; botany and zoology; painting and sculpture; memorabilia of writer Joaquín V. González - library

Chivilcoy

00174
Museo Histórico
Bolívar 319, Chivilcoy
General Museum - 1943
Local history; weapons and uniforms - library

00175
Museo Municipal de Artes Plásticas
Bolívar 319, Chivilcoy
Fine Arts Museum - 1944
Argentine painting, sculpture, drawing, graphics and pottery

Cipolletti

00176
Museo 'Fortin Primera División'
Rutas 22 y 151, Rotonda, Cipolletti
Anthropology Museum - 1968
Crafts and jewelry; local art; documents of a desert expedition (1833-1879)

Colón

00177
Jardin Zoológico y Museo Natural 'Dr. Carlos A. Marelli'
Calles 44 y 24, Colón
Natural History Museum - 1952
Zoology, botany and mineralogy

00178
Museo Municipal de Colón
Calle 12 de Abril 500, Colón
General Museum - 1971
History; painting and sculpture; furnishings; crafts; costume

Comodoro Rivadavia

00179
Museo Histórico Regional Patagónico
Ex-Hotel de Truismo, piso 2, Comodoro Rivadavia
General Museum - 1948
Archeology, history and natural history

Concepción del Uruguay

00180
Museo Entrerriano de Historia y Arqueología
Posadas 1114, Concepción del Uruguay
General Museum - 1920
Archeology and history; natural history

Concordia

00181
Museo Municipal de Artes Visuales
Urquiza 638, Concordia
Fine Arts Museum - 1948
Drawings, painting, sculpture, and engravings by Argentine artists

Córdoba

00182
Instituto de Antropología
Hipólito Yrigoyen 320, Córdoba
General Museum - 1941
Archeology, natural history, folklore and anthropology

00183
Museo Botánico
Av. Vélez Sarsfield y Duarte Quirós, Córdoba
Natural History Museum - 1870
Botany - library

00184
Museo de Arte Religioso 'Juan de Tejeda'
Independencia 122, Córdoba
Religious Art Museum
Religious art and liturgical items; church treasure

00185
Museo de la Escuela Normal 'Alejandro Carbo'
Colón 959, Córdoba
General Museum
History, geography and natural science; firearms and antique weapons

00186
Museo de Mineralogia y Geología 'Dr. Alfredo Stelzner'
Av. Vélez Sársfield 249, Córdoba
Natural History Museum - 1871/1971
Mineralogy; fossils; invertebrates

00187
Museo de Zoologia
Av. Véley Sársfield 249, piso 2, Córdoba
Natural History Museum - 1837
Zoology

00188
Museo del Teatro y la Música de Córdoba 'Cristobal de Aguilar'
Av. Vélez Sársfield 345, Córdoba
Performing Arts Museum - 1970
History of music and theater in Argentina

00189
Museo Histórico Provincial 'Marques de Sobremonte'
Rosario de Santa Fé 218, Córdoba
General Museum - 1887
Regional history; art; weapons; jewelry - library

00190
Museo Municipal de Bellas Artes 'Dr. Genaro Perez'
Av. General Paz 33, Córdoba
Fine Arts Museum - 1943
Argentine painting, sculpture and engraving

00191
Museo Numismático del Banco de la Nación Argentina
San Gerónimo 40, Córdoba
History/Public Affairs Museum - 1970
Colonial Spanish and Argentine numismatics; history of money

00192
Museo Provincial de Bellas Artes 'Emilio A. Caraffa'
Pl. España, Córdoba
Fine Arts Museum - 1914
Argentine painting, drawing, sculpture and engraving (19th-20th c.); foreign painting (17th-19th c.) - library

00193
Museo Provincial de Ciencias Naturales 'Bartolome Mitre'
Av. Hipólito Yrigoyen 115, Córdoba
Natural History Museum - 1919
Zoology; mineralogy; anthropology; botany

00194
Museo Salesiano 'Ceferino Namuncura'
Av. Colón 1055, Córdoba
General Museum - 1957
History; anthropology; archeology; ceramics; natural sciences; numismatics - library

Córdoba 3

00195
Museo 'Diego Salguero y Cabrera'
Obispo Salguero esq. San Jerónimo, Córdoba 3
Natural History Museum - 1970
History of pharmacy; pharmaceutical collections from the 16th to the 18th cent.

Coronel Dorrego

00196
Museo de Historia y Ciencias Naturales 'Florentino Ameghino'
Juan B. Maciel 555, Coronel Dorrego
General Museum - 1964
Historical exhibits; natural science

Coronel Pringles

00197
Museo de Bellas Artes de Coronel Pringles
San Martín 857, Coronel Pringles
Fine Arts Museum - 1959
Contemporary Argentine painting, drawing, engraving and sculpture

00198
Museo Regional Histórico y de Ciencias Naturales
Colón 425, Coronel Pringles
General Museum - 1966
History and natural science

Corrientes

00199
Museo Colonial e Histórico
9 de Julio 1044, Corrientes
General Museum - 1929
Religious and colonial art; weapons; furnishings; numismatics; painting and sculpture; history

00200
Museo de Bellas Artes 'Doctor Juan Ramón Vidal'
San Juan 634, Corrientes
Fine Arts Museum - 1927
Painting, sculpture, and objects d'art

00201
Museo de Ciencias Naturales 'Amado Bonpland'
San Martín 854, Corrientes
Natural History Museum - 1854
Botany, mineralogy, fossils, zoology and birds; geology of Argentina; archeology

00202
Museo 'Fray José de la Quintana'
Fray José de la Quintana y San Juan, Corrientes
Religious Art Museum - 1970
Religious art of the 16th and 17th cent.; memorabilia of Fray José de la Quintana

00203
Museo Odontológico 'Dr. Jorge E. Dunster'
Paraguay 837, Corrientes
Science/Tech Museum - 1969
History of dentistry in Argentina

Dolores

00204
Museo y Parque Evocativo 'Los Libres del Sur'
Ruta Nacional No. 2, Kilómetro 210, Dolores
General Museum - 1940
Local history; natural sciences - library

Dos de Mayo

00205
Museo de Ciencias Naturales
Dos de Mayo
General Museum
Local natural history

El Cadillal

00206
Museo Arqueológico 'Doctor Ernesto Padilla'
Dique 'El Cadillal', El Cadillal
Archeology Museum - 1975
Local archeology and anthropology, particularly items found during construction of the dam

5

El Palomar

00207
Museo Gauchesco
El Rodeo 383, El Palomar
General Museum - 1939
History and folklore

00208
Museo Histórico de 'El Palomar de Caseros'
Colegio Militar de la Nación, El Palomar
History/Public Affairs Museum
History of war; weapons and uniforms; documents and pictures

Ensenada

00209
Museo Naval 'Fuerte de Barragan'
Costanera a Punta Lara y Arroyo Doña Flora, Ensenada
Science/Tech Museum - 1969
Aeronautics

Esperanza

00210
Museo de la Colonización
Lehmann 1566, Esperanza
General Museum - 1968
Local history of colonization

Famatina

00211
Museo de Historia Natural
Famatina
Natural History Museum - 1951
Minerals of the region

Florencio Varela

00212
Museo y Casa Natal 'Guillermo Enrique Hudson'
Av. Hudson a 7 km de la Estación del F.C.G. Belgrano, Florencio Varela
History/Public Affairs Museum - 1957
Exhibits illustrating the life and works of writer Guillermo Enrique Hudson

Gálvez

00213
Museo Pedagógico de Artes Visuales
San Martín 468, Gálvez
Fine Arts Museum - 1971
Painting, sculpture, engraving, and drawing

General Belgrano

00214
Museo Histórico Regional de General Belgrano
Intendencia Municipal, General Belgrano
History/Public Affairs Museum - 1969
Local and regional education

General Paz

00215
Museo Histórico de Ranchos
Calle 68 s/no., General Paz
General Museum - 1967
Regional history; crafts; zoology; botany

General Pico

00216
Museo Regional 'Mara-Co'
Av. San Martín s/no., General Pico
General Museum - 1967
Regional history and archeology

General Pinto

00217
Fuerte y Museo 'General Lavalle'
Fortín Ancaloo, General Pinto
General Museum - 1969
Weapons, documents and other objects related to the history of General Pinto

Godoy Cruz

00218
Museo Municipal de Bellas Artes
Perito Moreno 16, Godoy Cruz
Fine Arts Museum - 1941
Painting, drawings, engravings and sculpture by Argentine artists

Gonnet

00219
Museo del Muñeco y Titere Internacional de Gonnet
República de los Niños-Camino General Belgrano km. 6.5, Gonnet
Anthropology Museum - 1951
Puppets and marionettes; animal specimens

Goya

00220
Museo de Ciencias Naturales 'Carmen Gonzalez de Spinelli'
J.E. Martínez 532, Goya
General Museum - 1949
Archeology; anthropology; mineralogy; zoology

Gualeguay

00221
Museo Histórico Regional 'Juan B. Ambrosetti'
San Antonio Notre 130, Gualeguay
General Museum - 1949
Regional history

Gualeguaychú

00222
Museo del Instituto 'Magnasco'
Camila Nievas 78, Gualeguaychú
General Museum - 1898
History; sculpture; numismatics and medals; weapons; archives

Guaymallén

00223
Museo - Bodega
Av. de Acceso Este y Urquiza, Guaymallén
Agriculture Museum - 1974
Equipment and processes related to wine making

Haedo

00224
Museo Farmacobotánico 'José F. Molfino'
Martíney de Hoz y Marconi, Haedo
Natural History Museum - 1967
Botany and pharmacy

Hernando

00225
Museo Histórico, Galeria de Arte y Biblioteco Estudiantil 'Paul P. Harris'
General Paz 227, Hernando
General Museum
Regional history and arts

Humahuaca

00226
Estudio Museo 'Ramoneda'
Salta 214, Humahuaca
Fine Arts Museum - 1936
Paintings and drawings by Ramoneda, Martín, Alice, Roig, Rimsa, Popof, Pereyra, Lubavsky, Larrañaga, Sevilla, Dufour, Guaragna, Yasaki, Esgrelli

00227
Museo Folklórico Regional
Av. San Martín 55, Humahuaca
Decorative Arts Museum - 1969
Decorative and folk arts; wood sculpture; works from the colonial period; American art

Ingeniero

00228
Museo Regional de Ciencias Naturales e Historia 'Jorge H. Gerhold'
Centro Cultural Municipal, Ingeniero
Natural History Museum - 1949
Anthropology; archeology; ethnography; natural history

Jesús María

00229
Museo Nacional Jesuitico de Jesús María
Convento e Iglesia de San Isidro, Jesús María
General Museum - 1946
Local archaeology; religious art; furnishings (17th-18th c.); ceramics; numismatics

Junín

00230
Museo Municipal de Bellas Artes 'D. Angel Maria de Rosa'
Saavedra 225, Junín
Fine Arts Museum - 1944
Painting and sculpture

La Carlota

00231
Museo Histórico Municipal
Av. Vélez Sársfield 785, La Carlota
History/Public Affairs Museum - 1949
Artifacts relating to the history of Argentina

Laguna de los Padres

00232
Museo Tradicionalista Argentino 'José Hernández'
Ruta 226 altura km. 14, Laguna de los Padres
Anthropology Museum - 1959
Folklore

La Paz

00233
Museo Regional de la Ciudad de la Paz
Parque 'Berón de Astrade', calle 3 de Febrero s/no., La Paz
General Museum - 1972
Documents, armaments, and other artifacts from the early history of the city; ancient religious artifacts; coins and medals; furnishings, agricultural implements, etc.

La Plata

00234
Museo 'Almafuerte'
Calle 66 No. 530, La Plata
History/Public Affairs Museum - 1928
Personal objects, furnishings, manuscripts and memorabilia of the writer Almafuerte

00235
Museo Belgraniano
Calles 13 y 40 (Plaza Belgrano), La Plata
History/Public Affairs Museum - 1971
Portraits, documents and numismatics connected with General Manuel Belgrano

00236
Museo de Ciencias Naturales de la Plata
Paseo del Bosque, La Plata
Natural History Museum - 1884
Archeology; ethnography; botany; geology; minerals; paleontology; Patagonian mammalia - library

00237
Museo de Instrumentos Musicales 'Emilio Azzarini'
Calle 44 No. 775, La Plata
Music Museum - 1973
Antique musical instruments from around the world

00238
Museo de La Plata
Paseo del Bosque, La Plata
Natural History Museum - 1884
Anthropology; ethnography; botany; geology; paleontology, zoology

00239
Museo Histórico Nacional 'Almafuerte'
Calle 66 No. 530, La Plata
General Museum - 1921
Manuscripts; furnishings; paintings; masks - library

00240
Museo Municipal de Bellas Artes
Calle 53 No. 840, La Plata
Fine Arts Museum - 1959
Painting, sculpture, drawing and engraving

00241
Museo Policial 'Juan Vucetich'
Calle 54 No. 393, La Plata
History/Public Affairs Museum - 1951
History of the Argentine police

00242
Museo Provincial de Bellas Artes
Calle 51 No. 525, La Plata
Fine Arts Museum - 1928
Argentine art (17th-19th c.); contemporary American and European painting - library

00243
Museo 'Vucetich' e Instituto de Identidad
Calle 47 No. 522, La Plata
History/Public Affairs Museum - 1923
Dactyloscopy and identification in penal law; memorabioia of Juan Vucetic

00244
Museo y Archivo 'Dardo Rocha'
Calle 50 No. 922, La Plata
General Museum - 1952
Local art, memorabilia of Dardo Roca - library and archive

La Reja

00245
Museo 'Antartida Argentina'
Av. Storni s/no., La Reja
Science/Tech Museum - 1967
Documents and exhibits relating to the
Argentine antarctic

La Rioja

00246
Museo de Bellas Artes 'Octavio de la Colina'
Copiapó 245, La Rioja
Fine Arts Museum - 1951
Contemporary argentine painting and
sculpture

00247
Museo Folklórico
Pelagio B. Luna 811, La Rioja
Anthropology Museum - 1969
Folklore and regional crafts

00248
Museo Histórico de la Rioja
Adolfo E. Fávila 87, La Rioja
History/Public Affairs Museum - 1916
Archeology; numismatics

00249
Museo 'Inca Huasi'
Juan Bautista Alberdi 650, La Rioja
General Museum - 1926
Regional archeology; religious art;
weapons; anthropology; mineralogy;
paleontology - library

00250
Museo Municipal de Bellas Artes 'Octavio de la Colina'
Copiapó 245, La Rioja
Fine Arts Museum - 1951
Paintings, sculpture, and book
illustrations by contemporary artists

La Roja

00251
Museo 'Padre Nardillo'
Juan Manuel de Rosas 547, La Roja
History/Public Affairs Museum
Religious art, weapons and military
uniforms

Las Heras

00252
Museo Municipal de Bellas Artes
San Miguel s/no., Las Heras
Fine Arts Museum - 1968
Painting, drawings, engravings and
sculpture by Argentine artists

Lincoln

00253
Museo de Bellas Artes
Av. Massey 1439, Lincoln
Fine Arts Museum - 1965
Contemporary Argentine art

Lobería

00254
Museo de Historia y Ciencias Naturales 'Club de Pesca Lobería'
Alvear 181, Lobería
Natural History Museum - 1960
Paleontology; archeology; natural
history

Lomas de Zamora

00255
Museo Municipal de Lomas de Zamora
Manuel Castro 254, Lomas de Zamora
General Museum - 1958
Anthropology; history; numismatics;
natural history; archeology;
paleontology

Longchamps

00256
Museo del Tranvia 'Federico Lacroze'
Rivadavia 1256, Longchamps
Science/Tech Museum - 1965
History of street cars around the
world

00257
Museo y Archivo Histórico 'Esteban Adroque'
Rivadavia 1256, Longchamps
History/Public Affairs Museum - 1954
Archeology; postage stamps; coins;
weapons, religious art

Losa Corral

00258
Casa Museo de 'Fernando Fader'
Losa Corral
History/Public Affairs Museum - 1961
Furnishings and memorabilia of the
painter Fernando Fader

Los Toldos

00259
Museo del Indio
Monasterio Benedictino, Los Toldos
General Museum - 1962
Indian culture

00260
Museo Municipal de Arte e Historia
Edificio del ex Concejo Deliberante,
Los Toldos
General Museum - 1975
Historical objects; pictorial art

Luján

00261
Complejo Museo Gráfico 'Enrique Udaondo'
Lavalle y Lezica y Torrezuri, Luján
General Museum - 1923
Regional history (colonial period to
20th c.); furnishings; jewelry; weapons;
fine and applied arts

00262
Museo de Bellas Artes
Parque Ameghino e San Martín y
Lavalle, Luján
Fine Arts Museum - 1961
Contemporary Argentine art

00263
Museo de Cera de la Virgen de Luján
San Martin y Padre Salver, Luján
Religious Art Museum - 1974
Representations of the Virgin of Luján;
votive panels

Luján de Cuyo

00264
Museo Provincial de Bellas Artes
Mayor Drumond, Luján de Cuyo
Fine Arts Museum - 1951
Painting, sculpture and engraving

Mar del Plata

00265
Instituto de Biologia Marina
Playa Grande, Casilla de Correo 175,
Mar del Plata
Natural History Museum - 1960
Maritime botany and zoology

00266
Museo Municipal de Bellas Artes
Av. Luro 2440, piso 7, Mar del Plata
Fine Arts Museum - 1963
Painting, sculpture, engraving and
drawing

00267
Museo Municipal de Ciencias Naturales
Av. Libertad 3099, Mar del Plata
Natural History Museum - 1940
Paleontology; zoology; anthropology;
malacology

Martínez

00268
Museo 'Chavin de Huantar'
Luis Sáenz Peña 2864, Martínez
General Museum - 1967
Archeology of the Americas;
Argentine historical documents;
contemporary Argentine painting;
porcelain, bronze and ivory miniatures

Mendoza

00269
Acuario Municipal
Ituzaingó y Buenos Aires, Mendoza
Natural History Museum - 1945
Specimans from the Río Paraná and
tropical and exotic specimans from
other parts of the world

00270
Museo de Historia Natural 'Juan Cornelio Moyano'
Plaza Independencia, Mendoza
General Museum - 1911
Natural history; archeology;
anthropology; folklore; regional history

00271
Museo del Pasado Cuyano
Montevideo 544, Mendoza
History/Public Affairs Museum - 1961
Numismatics; weapons; religious art;
history of Cuyo province; petroleum

00272
Museo Forestal
Parque San Martín, Mendoza
Science/Tech Museum - 1969
Wood and wood-crafted art works

00273
Museo Histórico de la Policia de Mendoza
Av. Prado Español s/no., Parque San
Martín, Edificio ex-Playas Serranas,
Mendoza
History/Public Affairs Museum - 1961
Weapons and other objects of crime
detection and prevention

00274
Museo Histórico 'General San Martín'
Remedios Escalada de San Martín
1843, Mendoza
History/Public Affairs Museum - 1913
Memorabilia of celebrated
Argentinians; history of aeronautics in
Argentina

00275
Museo Instituto de Arqueologia
Facultad de Filosofía y Letras, Centro
Universitario, Mendoza
General Museum - 1961
Archeology; ethnology; regional
folklore

00276
Museo Municipal de Arte Moderno
San Martin 1143, Mendoza
Fine Arts Museum - 1967
Architecture; painting, sculpture,
engraving, and ceramics; music and
dance; literature; cinema and theatre;
modern art

00277
Museo Privado 'Manuel Tellechea'
Hipólito Yrigoyen 151, Mendoza
Natural History Museum - 1935
Geology and mineralogy;
crystallography

00278
Museo 'Profesor Manuel Tellechea'
Hipólito Yrigoyen 151, Mendoza
Natural History Museum - 1935
Geology and mineralogy, particularly
crystalography

Mercedes

00279
Museo de Bellas Artes
Calle 29 No. 674, Mercedes
General Museum - 1932
Archeology; fossils; history; art -
library

00280
Museo Municipal de Ciencias Naturales 'Carlos Ameghino'
Calle 26 No. 512, Mercedes
Natural History Museum - 1965
Paleontology; geology; archeology;
zoology; botany; art of the Americas

00281
Museo 'Victor E. Miguez'
Calle 12 entre 21 y 23, Mercedes
General Museum - 1973
Municipal history

Monte Hermoso

00282
Museo Municipal de Ciencias Naturales
Monte Hermoso
Natural History Museum - 1969

Moreno

00283
Museo 'Florencio Molina Campos'
Güemes y Av. Victoria, Moreno
History/Public Affairs Museum - 1971
Originals and reproductions of the
works of Molina Campos

00284
Museo Histórico Municipal 'Amancio Alcorta'
Diagonal Coletta Palacio, Moreno
General Museum - 1964
Local history; crafts

Morón

00285
Museo 'Domingo Vittoria'
José M. Torres 518, Morón
Fine Arts Museum
Argentine painting and sculpture

00286
Museo Histórico y de Artes 'General San Martin'
Sarmiento y Casullo, Morón
General Museum - 1951
National, provincial and local history
and art

Necochea

00287
Museo Bromatológico 'Doctor José Squadrone'
Calle 61 No. 2627, Necochea
Agriculture Museum - 1945
Foodstuffs and nutrition

Nueve de Julio

00288
Archivo y Museo Histórico 'General Julio de Vedia'
Edificio de la Intendencia Municipal, 9 de Julio, Nueve de Julio
General Museum - 1956
Local history and culture; medals and seals

Olavarría

00289
Museo Etnográfico Municipal
San Martín 2870, Olavarría
General Museum - 1963
Archeology and ethnography - library

00290
Museo Municipal de Bellas Artes 'Damaso Arce'
San Martín 2862, Olavarría
Fine Arts Museum - 1961
Works of Dámaso Arce; works by Argentine artists

Oliva

00291
Exposición Permanente de Ciencias Naturales y del Hombre
Av. Colón 1055, Oliva
General Museum - 1970
Aquarium; stuffed animals; temporary exhibitions

Paraná

00292
Museo de Ciencias Naturales y Antropológicas
Rivadavia 462, Paraná
General Museum - 1917
Archeology and ethnography; birds, invertebrates; reptiles, and insects; botany, mineralogy and paleontology

00293
Museo de Entre Rios
Rivadavia 224, Paraná
General Museum - 1917
Industry; anthropology; natural science - library

00294
Museo del Colegio Nacional 'Justo José de Urquiza'
General Urquiza e/ General Galarza y 9 de Julio, piso 1, Paraná
Natural History Museum - 1949

00295
Museo Histórico de Entre Rios 'Martiniano Liguizamon'
Buenos Aires y Laprida, Paraná
General Museum - 1948
Archeology; ethnology; numismatics; local history

00296
Museo Provincial de Bellas Artes 'Dr. Pedro E. Martinez'
Laprida y Buenos Aires, Paraná
Fine Arts Museum - 1925
Painting, drawing, engraving and sculpture - library and archive

Pedro Luro

00297
Museo 'Doctor José Luro'
Fortín Mercedes, Pedro Luro
General Museum - 1925
History; paleontology; natural history; Araucan arms and utensils

Pergamino

00298
Museo de la Agricultura Pampeana
Estación Experimental Agropecuaria, Pergamino
Agriculture Museum - 1963
Agricultural history of the Argentine pampa

00299
Museo Municipal de Bellas Artes
San Martín 621, Pergamino
Fine Arts Museum
Painting, engraving and sculpture by Argentine artists

Posadas

00300
Museo de Ciencias Naturales
San Luis 384, Posadas
Natural History Museum
Regional fauna; reptile farm

00301
Museo Municipal de Bellas Artes
Rivadavia 328, Posadas
Fine Arts Museum - 1948
Painting, sculpture and engravings; history and documentation of the local missions

00302
Museo Policial
Departamento de Policía, Posadas
History/Public Affairs Museum - 1977
Antique and modern weapons; historical objects related to law enforcement

00303
Museo Regional de Posadas
Parque República del Paraguay, Posadas
General Museum - 1947
History; archeology; ethnography; natural history

00304
Palacio del Mate
Rivadavia 324, Posadas
General Museum - 1969
Painting and sculpture; regional furniture

Puerto Iguazú

00305
Museo de Ciencias Naturales del Parque Nacional Iguazu
Puerto Iguazú
Natural History Museum - 1946
Flora and fauna of the region

00306
Museo 'Teofilo Rodolfo Allon'
San Martín s/no., Puerto Iguazú
Fine Arts Museum - 1956
Sculpture and wood carving

Puerto Quequén

00307
Estación Hidrobiológica de Puerto Quequen
Puerto Quequén
Natural History Museum - 1928

Quilmes

00308
Museo Municipal de Artes Visuales
Rivadavia 498, Quilmes
Fine Arts Museum - 1965
Painting, sculpture, drawing, engraving

Rafaela

00309
Museo Histórico y Archivo Municipal
San Martín 555, Rafaela
General Museum - 1956
National, regional and local history; weapons

00310
Museo Municipal de Bellas Artes
San Martín 555, Rafaela
Fine Arts Museum - 1969
Sculpture

Ranchos

00311
Museo Histórico de Ranchos
Calle 68 s/no., Ranchos
General Museum - 1964
Local history; artifacts of peasant culture; local fauna

Rauch

00312
Museo Municipal de Arte
Av. San Martín 252, Rauch
Fine Arts Museum - 1962
Painting, drawings, engravings, and sculpture by Argentine artists

Resistencia

00313
El Fogon de los Arrieros
Brown 350, Resistencia
General Museum - 1947
Painting, sculpture and engraving; photographs; crafts; documents - library

00314
Museo de Ciencias Naturales
Bartolomé Mitre esq. Corrientes, Resistencia
Natural History Museum - 1965

00315
Museo Policial de Armas
Julio A. Roca 227, Resistencia
History/Public Affairs Museum - 1968
Weapons

00316
Museo Regional de Antropologia
Av. Las Heras 727, Resistencia
Archeology Museum - 1968
Anthropology and archeology

Rio Cuarto

00317
Museo Municipal de Bellas Artes
Colón 149, Rio Cuarto
Fine Arts Museum - 1933
Argentine sculpture; Argentine, European and North American painting; archeology

00318
Museo Regional de Ciencias Naturales e Historia
Colón 149, Rio Cuarto
General Museum - 1971
Natural history; fossils; weapons; musical instruments

Río Ferrari

00319
Museo del Instituto 'Contardo Ferrari'
Pablo Robert 90, Río Ferrari
General Museum - 1971
Ruins of an antique chapel; coins; stuffed animals

Río Gallegos

00320
Museo Regional Provincial
Belgrano y Tucumán, Río Gallegos
Natural History Museum - 1957
Anthropology; zoology; mineralogy; archeoloy; biology; botany - library

Río Grande

00321
Museo 'Monseñor Jose Fagnano'
Misión Salesiana, Río Grande
General Museum - 1892
Local arts and crafts; weapons; zoology

Río Segundo

00322
Museo Arqueológico Regional Anibal Montes'
Sarmiento 900, Río Segundo
General Museum - 1970
Regional and local archeology and history

Rivadavia 1256

00323
Museo Ferroviario 'Jorge A. Rollings Maddox'
Longchamps, Rivadavia 1256
Science/Tech Museum - 1962
Trains and railroads

Rosario

00324
Museo Acuario del Centro de Investigaciones 'Rosario'
Cordiviola y Parque Alem, Rosario
Science/Tech Museum - 1940
Marine biology

00325
Museo de la Prensa
Santa Fé 620, Rosario
History/Public Affairs Museum - 1972
History of the press, especially in Santa Fe province

00326
Museo del Teatro
Laprida 1235, Rosario
Performing Arts Museum - 1969
Documents and artifacts from the history of the Argentine theater; musical (stringed) instruments

00327
Museo Didáctico Provincial
Laprida 1145, Rosario
History/Public Affairs Museum - 1949
Education and teaching

00328
Museo Histórico Provincial de Rosario 'Dr. Julio Marc'
Parque Independencia, Rosario
General Museum - 1939
Local history; crafts; coins and medals; furnishings; pre-Columbian ceramics and textiles; early Mexican ceramics; colonial art

00329
Museo Municipal de Arte Decorativo 'Firma y Odilo Estevez'
Santa Fé 748, Rosario
Decorative Arts Museum - 1968
Spanish and French furnishings
(16th-18th c.); ivories, glass, porcelain, ceramics; tapestries; Hispano-American jewelry; paintings by Goya, El Greco, David, Boucher, Van Dyck and Ribera

00330
Museo Municipal de Bellas Artes 'Juan B. Castagnino'
Pellegrini 2202, Rosario
Fine Arts Museum - 1937
Argentine art from independence to the present; sculpture; prints; paintings by El Greco, Goya, David and Titian - library

00331
Museo Policial de Rosario
Santa Fe 1950, Rosario
History/Public Affairs Museum - 1952
Crime and criminology

00332
Museo Provincial de Ciencias Naturales 'Dr. Angel Gallardo'
Moreno 750 piso 1, Rosario
Natural History Museum - 1945
Zoology; botany; paleontology; mineralogy - library

Salliqueló

00333
Museo Histórico y Regional
Av. 9 de Julio s/no., Salliqueló
General Museum - 1952
History and archeology; natural history; Indian artifacts

Salta

00334
Museo Arqueológico de Salta
Av. Ejército del Norte y calle Polo Sur, Salta
Archeology Museum - 1974
Archeology of northeast Argentina, espc. Salta province

00335
Museo Colonial, Histórico y de Bellas Artes
Caseros 575, Salta
General Museum - 1930

00336
Museo de Ciencias Naturales
Mendoza 2, Salta
Natural History Museum - 1950
Biology, geology and archeology

00337
Museo 'El Tribuno Pajarito Velarde'
Pueyrredón 106, Salta
General Museum - 1966
Folklore

00338
Museo Histórico del Norte
Caseros 549, Salta
General Museum - 1949
History; numismatics; archeology; religious art; weapons; crafts and folklore

00339
Museo 'Presidente José Evaristo Uriburu'
Caseros 417, Salta
General Museum - 1943
Memorabilia of the generals José Evaristo Uriburu, San Martín y Alvarez de Arenales, Belgrano, and Alvarado; archeological and numismatic collections; books

San Antonio de Areco

00340
Museo Escolar de Ciencias Naturales 'Carlos A. Merti'
Matheu 283, San Antonio de Areco
Natural History Museum - 1942
Paleontology; archeology - library

00341
Museo Gauchesco y Parque Criollo
Camino Ricardo Guiraldes, San Antonio de Areco
General Museum - 1937
History; arts and crafts; folklore
(18th-20th c.); memorabilia of Ricardo Guiraldes

San Carlos de Bariloche

00342
Museo de la Patagonia 'Dr. Francisco P. Moreno'
Centro Cívico, San Carlos de Bariloche
General Museum - 1940
Regional history; natural history; archeology; ethnography

San Fernando del Valle de Catamarca

00343
Museo Arqueológico 'Adan Quiroga'
Sarmiento 450, San Fernando del Valle de Catamarca
General Museum - 1937
Regional archeology; colonial history; natural history; portraits; jewelry

San Francisco

00344
Museo y Salón Municipal
Boulevard 9 de Julio esq. Avellaneda, San Francisco
Fine Arts Museum - 1967
Sculpture by Argentine artists

San Ignacio

00345
Museo Jesuítico
Ruinas Jesuíticas de San Ignacio, San Ignacio
Religious Art Museum - 1953
Architecture; collections of the Jesuits

00346
Museo Jesuítico Numismático 'Domingo F. Sarmiento'
Av. Sarmiento s/no., San Ignacio
Fine Arts Museum - 1969
Sculpture; Pre-Columbian pottery; coins and medals

San Isidro

00347
Casa Museo 'Luis A. Cordiviola'
España 531, San Isidro
Fine Arts Museum - 1933
Paintings, drawings, furnishings, sculpture and other works of art in original Spanish colonial setting

00348
Museo, Biblioteca y Archivo 'General Juan Martín de Pueyrredon'
Rivera Indarte 48, San Isidro
General Museum - 1941
Art; weapons; historical documents and memorabilia of General Pueyrredón - library and archive

00349
Museo de Ciencias Naturales
Av. Libertador General San Martín 17.715, San Isidro
Natural History Museum - 1940
Vertebrates and invertebrates from Argentine regions

San Jorge

00350
Museo Gráfico de los Pueblos
Santa Fé 271, San Jorge
Anthropology Museum - 1961
World cultures; photographic reproductions of works of art; archeology

San José

00351
Museo Histórico Regional
Urquiza 378, San José
General Museum - 1957
History of colonization; carriages and weapons; musical instruments; Argentine folk costumes; religious artifacts

San José de Balcarce

00352
Museo Regional Escolar de Balcarce
paraje El Volcán (altura Km. 61 de la Ruta Nacional 226), San José de Balcarce
General Museum - 1970
History, economics, geography, paleontology of the Balcarce region

San Juan

00353
Museo Arqueológico
Av. Libertador General San Martín 3369, San Juan
Archeology Museum - 1966
Archeological artifacts; mummies

00354
Museo de Ciencias Naturales
Av. Libertador General San Martín y Sarmiento, San Juan
Natural History Museum - 1968
Mining; natural sciences

00355
Museo 'Dorotea Galeano de Sugo'
Dr. Aberastain 872, Sur, San Juan
Decorative Arts Museum - 1949
Local crafts; weapons; ceramics; keys; skulls

00356
Museo 'Franklin Rawson'
Av. San Martín 315, Oeste, San Juan
Fine Arts Museum - 1934
Argentine painting, drawing, sculpture, and engraving

00357
Museo Geográfico 'Einstein' y Biblioteca Especializada 'Hector T. Castro'
Av. Alem 915 Norte, y Catamarca 1468 Norte, San Juan
Natural History Museum - 1965
Astronomy; geology; botany; zoology; anthropology; archeology

00358
Museo Histórico y Biblioteca 'Sarmiento'
Sarmiento 21, Sur, San Juan
History/Public Affairs Museum - 1911
Memorabilia of Domingo Faustino Sarmiento and family

00359
Museo Particular 'Sormani'
Av. 9 de Julio 695, Este, San Juan
Decorative Arts Museum
Jewelry; furnishings; clocks

San Lorenzo

00360
Museo del Convento de San Carlos
Sargento Cabral, San Lorenzo
General Museum - 1969
Religious and secular art; furnishings; postage stamps; coins and medals

San Luís

00361
Museo Histórico, de Bellas Artes y Ciencias Naturales
Ayacucho 941 y 957, San Luis
General Museum - 1955
History, art, and natural history

San Martín

00362
Museo de Artes Plásticas 'Mercedes Tomasa de San Martín de Balcarce'
Pueyrredón 502, San Martín
Fine Arts Museum - 1967
Argentine painting, sculpture, and engraving

San Martín de los Andes

00363
Museo Regional Municipal
Edificio de la Municipalidad, San Martín de los Andes
General Museum - 1961
Araucan art; musical instruments; regional collections - library

San Miguel de Tucumán

00364
Museo Antropología
25 de Mayo 492, San Miguel de Tucumán
Archeology Museum - 1928
Prehistory; archeology; anthropology and ethnography - library

00365
Museo 'Casa Histórica de la Independencia'
Congreso 151, San Miguel de Tucumán
History/Public Affairs Museum - 1943
Historical documents and related paintings, furnishings and art objects

00366
Museo 'Casa Padilla'
Congreso 147, San Miguel de Tucumán
Decorative Arts Museum - 1976
Furnishings and objects d'art
(17th-19th c.) in an 1860 Italianate building

00367
Museo de Arte Religioso
Congreso 147, San Miguel de Tucumán
Religious Art Museum - 1977
liturgical objects, furnishings, items used formerly in the cathedral and churches of Tucumán

00368
Museo de Bellas Artes
9 de Julio 48, San Miguel de Tucumán
Fine Arts Museum - 1916
Painting, sculpture, engravings

00369
Museo de la Casa de los Patricios Tucumanos
San Martín 186, San Miguel de Tucumán
General Museum - 1956
Painting; weapons; crafts; numismatics; tools; military artifacts; ceramics; furnishings; jewelry; folk art; lamps

00370
Museo de la Industria Azucarera
Casa del Obispo Colombres, Parque 9 de Julio, San Miguel de Tucumán
General Museum - 1977
Instruments and machinery used formerly in the sugar industry; domestic utensils and period furnishings displayed in an 18th cent. villa.

00371
Museo Folklórico Provincial
24 de Septiembre 565, San Miguel de Tucumán
General Museum - 1943
Regional history and archeology; crafts; folklore - library

00372
Museo Histórico de la Provincia
Congreso 56, San Miguel de Tucumán
General Museum - 1976
Furniture, documents, weapons, and pictures; memorabilia from the history of the province

00373
Museo 'Iramain'
Entre Ríos 27, San Miguel de Tucumán
Fine Arts Museum - 1937
Painting, drawings, and sculpture by Juan Carlos Iramain

00374
Museo 'Miguel Lillo'
Miguel Lillo 205, San Miguel de Tucumán
Natural History Museum - 1931
Biology; geology; zoology; fossils; minerals

San Nicolás de los Arroyos

00375
Museo de Ciencias Naturales del 'Colegio Don Bosco'
Don Bosco 580, San Nicolás de los Arroyos
Natural History Museum - 1956

00376
Museo Municipal de Bellas Artes
de la Nación 346, San Nicolás de los Arroyos
Fine Arts Museum
Painting, engravings, and sculpture by Argentine artists

00377
Museo y Archivo Histórico de San Nicolas 'Primer Combate Naval Argentino'
Francia 187, San Nicolás de los Arroyos
General Museum - 1971
Regional art and folklore; coins and medals; documents and archives

00378
Museo y Biblioteca de la Casa del Acuerdo
de la Nación 143, San Nicolás de los Arroyos
1937 50 o
19th cent. history; painting; furnishings

San Rafael

00379
Museo de Bellas Artes
Bdo. de Irigoyen 138, San Rafael
Fine Arts Museum - 1948
Painting, drawing, engravings, and sculpture by Argentine artists

00380
Museo de Ciencias Naturales
San Martín 127, San Rafael
Natural History Museum - 1956
Botany; zoology; mineralogy; geology; paleontology; archeology; folklore; regional history

San Salvador de Jujuy

00381
Museo 'Carlos Darwin'
Gorriti 253, San Salvador de Jujuy
Natural History Museum - 1962
Anthropology; archeology; mineralogy; biology

00382
Museo del Instituto de Geología y Mineria
Independencia y Lavalle, San Salvador de Jujuy
Natural History Museum - 1946
Geology and mineralogy

00383
Museo Histórico Provincial
Lavalle 252, San Salvador de Jujuy
General Museum - 1942
Local history, art, and archeology

00384
Museo 'San Francisco'
Lavalle 325, San Salvador de Jujuy
General Museum - 1932
Regional archeology; antique firearms; colonial and religious painting

San Vicente

00385
Museo y Biblioteca del Doctor Ramón de Castro Estevez
Almirante Brown 250, San Vicente
History/Public Affairs Museum - 1960
Postage stamps, books, journals, relics, medals, and paintings from the collection of Dr. Castro Estevez

Santa Clara del Mar

00386
Centro de Artesanias Americanas
Santa Clara del Mar
Decorative Arts Museum - 1967
Contemporary Latin American folklore and crafts

Santa Fé

00387
Museo del Convento de San Francisco
Amenábar 2567, Santa Fé
Fine Arts Museum - 1937
Sculpture, painting, religious art, and historical documents

00388
Museo Etnográfico
25 de Mayo 1470, Santa Fé
Anthropology Museum - 1940
Folklore; ethnography; archeology; historical documents

00389
Museo Histórico Provincial 'Brigadier General Estanislao Lopez'
San Martín y 3 de Febrero, Santa Fé
General Museum - 1943
Peruvian painting (17th-18th c.); colonial furnishings; art; weapons; regional history and memorabilia of celebrated persons

00390
Museo Histórico y de Arte Sagrado
General López y San Jerónimo, Santa Fé
Religious Art Museum - 1970

00391
Museo Municipal de Artes Visuales
San Martín 2068, Santa Fé
Fine Arts Museum - 1936
Painting

00392
Museo Provincial de Bellas Artes 'Rosa Galisteo de Rodriguez'
4 de Enero 1510, Santa Fé
Fine Arts Museum - 1922
Painting, drawings, engravings, and sculpture (contemporary Argentine and modern) - library

00393
Museo Provincial de Ciencias Naturales 'Florentino Ameghino'
Moreno 2557, Santa Fé
1914
Paleontology and other branches of natural history - library

Santa Maria

00394
Museo Arqueológico y Folklórico Provincial
Sarmiento 180, Santa María
General Museum - 1960
Regional and local archeology and folklore

Santa Rosa

00395
Museo Provincial
Pellegrini 258, Santa Rosa
General Museum - 1935
Art and natural history

Santiago del Estero

00396
Casa Museo de 'Andres Chazarreta'
Mitre 127, Santiago del Estero
Anthropology Museum - 1956
Ethnography and folklore

00397
Museo Arqueológico Provincial 'Emilio y Duncan Wagner'
Avellaneda 355 planta baja, Santiago del Estero
General Museum - 1917
Archeological finds from the Chaco-Santiagueno and later cultures; musical instruments and ceremonial objects, paleontology; folklore; anthropology 700 0040; 0130; 1130

00398
Museo de Arte Sacro 'San Francisco Solano'
Av. Roca 716, Santiago del Estero
Religious Art Museum - 1969

00399
Museo Histórico de la Provincia
Urquiza 354, Santiago del Estero
General Museum - 1941
History; art; numismatics; folklore; weapons

00400
Museo Provincial de Bellas Artes 'Ramon Gomez Cornet'
Independencia 222, Santiago del Estero
Fine Arts Museum - 1942
Painting, sculpture, drawings, and engravings

Sarmiento

00401
Museo 'Desiderio Torres'
Av. Ing. Coronel s/no., Sarmiento
General Museum - 1971
Archeology and ethnography

Sinsacate

00402
Museo Rural de la Posta de Sinsacate
Posta de Sinsacate, Sinsacate
General Museum - 1946
Regional history, culture and folklore

Suipacha

00403
Museo Histórico
Balcarce 645, Suipacha
History/Public Affairs Museum - 1932
National and regional history; historical archives

Tandil

00404
Museo 'Fuerte Independencia'
4 de Abril 845, Tandil
General Museum - 1963
National and regional history - library

00405
Museo Rural
Chacabuco 764, Tandil
Fine Arts Museum
Paintings of Impressionist, Cubist, Modern and Classical schools

Tapalqué

00406
Museo y Centro Popular de Cultura
Belgrano 83, Tapalqué
History/Public Affairs Museum - 1969
History; paleontology

Temperley

00407
Museo-Archivo 'Carlos Alberto Laumann'
Av. Meeks 778, Temperley
History/Public Affairs Museum - 1960
Memorabilia of the writer Carlos Alberto Laumann

Tigre

00408
Museo de la Reconquista
Liniers 818, Tigre
History/Public Affairs Museum - 1949
Argentine history

00409
Museo Naval de la Nación
Paseo Victorica 620, Tigre
History/Public Affairs Museum - 1892
Uniforms, weapons, navigation equipment, ship models, maritime paintings, etc.

Tilcara

00410
Museo Arqueológico de Tilcara
Belgrano s/no. (frente a la plaza),
Tilcara
Archeology Museum - 1968
Archeological finds from northeast
Argentina, Chile, Peru and Bolivia;
reproductions of stone paintings from
the same areas

00411
Museo del Pucara de Tilcara
Pucara de Tilcara (situado a 1 km. al
sur del pueblo de Tilcara), Tilcara
Fine Arts Museum - 1968
Argentine art and archeology

00412
Museo 'Ernesto Soto Avendaño'
Belgrano s/no., Tilcara
History/Public Affairs Museum - 1968
Memorabilia of the sculptor Ernesto
Soto Avendaño

00413
**Museo Regional de Pintura 'José
Antonia Terry'**
Rivadavia 459, Tilcara
Fine Arts Museum - 1966
Works of the painter J.A. Terry

Tornquist

00414
Museo Histórico Regional
Edificio de la Municipalidad, Tornquist
General Museum - 1969
Local and regional history

Totoral

00415
Museo 'Casa de Octavio Pintos'
Casa de Octavio Pintos, Totoral
Fine Arts Museum - 1975
Paintings by O. Pintos; related works
of art by Argentine artists

Trenque Lauguen

00416
**Museo Historico de las Campañas al
Desierto 'General Conrado E.
Villegas'**
San Martín 1140, Trenque Lauguen
Trenque Lauquen - 1955
Regional history and culture (16th-20th
c.)

Tres Arroyos

00417
Museo de Bellas Artes
Av. Moreno 232, Tres Arroyos
Fine Arts Museum - 1959
Painting and sculpture

00418
**Museo Regional de Ciencias
Naturales 'Tomás Santa Coloma'**
Lucio V. López 473, Tres Arroyos
Natural History Museum - 1956
Anthropology and archeology

Valentín Alsina

00419
Museo Histórico y de Bellas Artes
Hipólito Yrigoyen 3860, Valentín Alsina
General Museum - 1977
Photographs and documents of local
interest; paintings and engravings

Veinticinco de Mayo

00420
Museo Municipal 'Paula Florido'
Calle 27 entre 8 y 9, Veinticinco de
Mayo
General Museum - 1946
History and natural science

Vicente López

00421
**Museo Escuela de Bellas Artes de
Vicente Lopez**
Agustín Alvarez 1568, Vicente López
Fine Arts Museum - 1961
Painting, sculpture, drawing, and
engraving

Vichigasta

00422
Museo 'Padre Nardillo'
Casa del Padre Nardillo, Vichigasta,
Depto. Chilecito
General Museum
Religious art; archeology; weapons
and uniforms

Villa Ballester

00423
**Museo de Bellas Artes 'Ceferino
Carnacini'**
América 151, Villa Ballester
Fine Arts Museum
Argentine painting and engraving

00424
**Museo Histórico 'Jose Hernandez -
Chacra Pueyrredon de General San
Martin'**
General Roca 1860, Villa Ballester
General Museum - 1966
Memorabilia of the writer José
Hernández (1834-1886) - library

Villa Carlos Paz

00425
**Salón de Artes Plásticas 'Antonia F.
Rizzuto'**
Cárcano 75, Villa Carlos Paz
Fine Arts Museum - 1969
Paintings, drawings, sculpture and
ceramics by contemporary Argentine
and foreign artists

Villa de Maria

00426
**Museo y Biblioteca de la Casa de
Leopoldo Lugones**
Villa de María, Departamento Río Seco
Books and memorabilia of the writer
and poet L. Lugones - 1945

Villa Dolores

00427
**Museo Arqueológico 'Profesor
Ernesto Arrieta'**
Av. San Martín 541, Villa Dolores
General Museum - 1960
Regional history and archeology

Villa Maria

00428
**Museo Municipal 'Fernando
Bonfiglioli'**
Hipólito Yrigoyen 30, Villa María
Fine Arts Museum - 1971
Paintings, sculpture, drawings, and
graphics by Argentine artists

Villa Rivera Indarte

00429
Museo 'Independencia'
Colegio León XIII, Villa Rivera Indarte
General Museum - 1916
Anthropology, history and natural
history

Yatasto

00430
Posta de Yatasto
Yatasto, Departamento Metán
Decorative Arts Museum - 1941
Historic building with period
furnishings

Zapala

00431
Museo Histórico
Frotín Regimiento 21, Zapala
General Museum - 1965
Araucan art; weapons; documents and
historical photos

00432
**Museo 'Professor Doctor Juan
Augusto Olsacher'**
Olascoaga 439, Zapala
Natural History Museum - 1969
Paleontology; mineralogy; archeology;
ethnography

Australia

Adelaide

00433
Art Gallery of South Australia
North Terrace, Adelaide, SA 5000
Fine Arts Museum - 1881
Coll: Australian paintings; Old Master
prints; Thai ceramics; South
Australiana; Master of the Uttenheimer
altarpiece: St.Martin of Tours and
St.Nicholas of Bari(tempera on wood);
Elizabethan Standing Salt, silver-gilt;
Thai Temple Guardian (14th c.),
Sawankhalok stoneware, lifesize

00434
**Constitutional Museum of South
Australia**
North Terrace, Adelaide, SA 5000
History/Public Affairs Museum - 1978
Political history and propaganda -
library

00435
Mile End Railway Museum
Railway Terrace Mile End South,
Adelaide, SA 5001
Open Air Museum - 1963
Locomotives from South Australian
Railways, Commonwealth Railways,
Silverton Tramway Co. and private
railways

00436
South Australian Museum
North Terrace, Adelaide, SA 5000
General Museum - 1856
Australian ethnology and archeology;
zoology; minerals; insects; Pacific
culture; Benin bronzes - library

Adventure Bay

00437
Bligh Museum of Pacific Exploration
Adventure Bay, Tas. 7160
History/Public Affairs Museum - 1954
Historical items relating to the
exploration of the South Pacific; rare
books and journals relating to Cook's
and Bligh's voyages to the South
Pacific - library

Airlie Beach

00438
Heirloom Doll Museum
POB 116, Airlie Beach, Qld. 4800
Decorative Arts Museum - 1970

Albany

00439
Albany Residency Museum Branch
of Western Australian Museum
Port Rd, Albany, WA 6330
General Museum - 1975
Regional natural history and
specimens; pre-colonial history;
aboriginals; relics of the local whaling
industry

Albury

00440
Hotel Turk's Head Museum
Wodonga Place, Albury, NSW 2640
Anthropology Museum - 1967

Alice Springs

00441
Central Australian Aviation Museum
Connellan Hangar, Memorial Drive,
Alice Springs, NT 5750
Science/Tech Museum - 1977
Aircrafts; flying doctor service items -
library

Ararat

00442
Ararat Gallery
Town Hall, Vincent St, POB 72, Ararat,
Vic. 3377
Decorative Arts Museum - 1968
Contemporary textiles and fibers;
'Coraza en dos Colores' by Olga de
Amaral of Bogota, Columbia

Ardross

00443
**Wireless Hill Telecommunications
Museum**
Almondbury Rd, Ardross, POB 130,
Applecross, WA 6153
Science/Tech Museum - 1979
Telecommunications equipment from
the early radio to modern space
exploration; bush pedal radio

Armadale

00444
History House
Off Jull St, Armadale, WA 6112
History/Public Affairs Museum - 1976
Items relating to early settlers in the
district of Armadale-Kelmscott, local
objects and photographs - library

Armidale

00445
Armidale and District Folk Museum
CNR Faulkner and Rusden Streets,
POB 75A, Armidale, NSW 2350
History/Public Affairs Museum - 1955
Coll: domestic, social, and economic
history of 19th century New England

Balaklava

00446
Centenary Hall
May Terrace, Balaklava, SA 5461
General Museum - 1971
Local artifacts

Ballarat

00447
Gold Museum
Bradshaw St, Ballarat, Vic. 3350
History/Public Affairs Museum - 1977
Local history; Paul Simon alluvial gold
and gold coin collection; Ballarat
Historical Society collection - library

00448
Old Curiosity Shop
7 Queen St, Ballarat, Vic. 3350
Decorative Arts Museum - 1855
Victorian furniture, ornaments,
glassware and examples of
needlework

Beachport

00449
**Beachport and District Branch
National Trust of South Australia**
Old Wool Store, Railway Terrace,
Beachport, SA 5280
General Museum
Aboriginal artifacts; relics of local
wrecks; local memorabilia

Beacon

00450
Jangling Farm Museum
POB 12, Beacon, WA 6472
Anthropology Museum - 1975
Bottles; horse gear; farm items;
charcoal and irons

Beechworth

00451
Carriage and Harness Museum
Ford St, behind Tanswell's Hotel,
Beechworth, Vic. 3747
Science/Tech Museum - 1969
Carriages ranging from 1875-1910;
preserved locally made hearse; 21
passenger drags; coaches

00452
Powder Magazine
Gorge Reserve, Beechworth, Vic. 3747
Historic Site - 1965
Completely restored magazine used
for storing explosives during the gold
rush (built 1859)

00453
The Rockcavern
Ford St, Beechworth, Vic. 3747
Natural History Museum - 1971
Coll: stamps of the first white man
born in Fiji; African stone carvings;
fluorescent minerals

Belgrave

00454
Puffing Billy Steam Museum
POB 156, Belgrave, Vic. 3160
Open Air Museum - 1961
Steam locomotives and stationary
engines - the museum is part of a fully
restored 14 km narrow gauge line,
traffic handled by four 1900-1910
vintage locomotives

Bendigo

00455
Bendigo Art Gallery
42 View St, Bendigo, Vic. 3550
Fine Arts Museum - 1887
Australian and European painting (19th
c.); European silver, porcelain and
furniture (18th and 19th c.); Barbizon
School painting

Berkeley Vale

00456
Tuggerah Lakes Military Museum
Cnr Wyong and Chittaway Rds,
Berkeley Vale, NSW 2259
History/Public Affairs Museum - 1976
Coll: military exhibits ranging from the
Maori Wars of 1861 to Vietnam; WW II
Japanese tank in working order;
weapons; uniforms

Beverley

00457
Beverley Aeronautical Museum
Vincent St, POB 20, Beverley, WA
6304
Science/Tech Museum - 1967
Silver centenary biplane (designed by
S.A. Ford, built by Ford and Shackles
in Beverley); models of Comet jet and
Air India Boeing 707 jet; Anson
Cheetah 9 engine; De Havilland
Vampire jet

Bli Bli

00458
Suncoast Pioneer Village
David Low Hwy, Bli Bli, Qld. 4560
History/Public Affairs Museum - 1976
Vintage cars; jugs; fire brigade display;
Australiana

Bothwell

00459
Thorpe Water Mill
Bothwell, Tas. 7411
Science/Tech Museum - 1975
Authentic mill (1823), restored and still
operating

Brisbane

00460
Brisbane G.P.O. Museum
General Post Office Building, Queen
St, POB 6000, Brisbane, Qld. 4001
Science/Tech Museum - 1979
Postal and telecommunications
exhibits; early documents from the
convict days covering 150 years of
postal service in Queensland

00461
Queensland Air Museum
Eagle Farm Aerodrome, Brisbane
Airport, GPOB 2315, Brisbane, Qld.
4001
Science/Tech Museum
Aviation exhibits

00462
Queensland Art Gallery
M.I.M. Bldg, 160 Ann St, Brisbane, Qld.
4000
Fine Arts Museum - 1895
Paintings, drawings and sculpture
including works of Picasso and
Giovanni Bologna; Australian art

00463
Queensland Maritime Museum
South Brisbane Dry Dock, Stanley St,
South Brisbane, POB 197, Hamilton,
Qld. 4007
Science/Tech Museum - 1971
Steam tug 'Forceful' (built 1925,
maintained and operated as part of the
museum); frigate ex HMAS
'Diamantina'; relics from the recently
discovered HMS 'Pandora' - library of
maritime volumes

Broadway

00464
**Museum of Applied Arts and
Sciences**
659 Harris St, Broadway, NSW 2007
Decorative Arts Museum - 1880
Coll: Doulton ceramics; Meissen
portrait bust by Kändler (1739); history
of transportation in New South Wales,
including the first train (1855), the first
Australian airmail aircraft (1911,
Bleriot), an aeronautical steam beam
engine by Boulton and Watt (1785) and
an original Otto-Langen gas engine
(c.1866) - library

Brompton

00465
Sagasco Historical Group Museum
Gas Works, East St, Brompton, GPOB
1199, Adelaide, SA 5001
Science/Tech Museum - 1978
Gas industry objects and data - South
Australian Gas Company facilities

Bullcreek

00466
**Air Force Association Aviation
Museum**
Benningfield Rd, Bullcreek, WA 6153
Science/Tech Museum - 1979
Coll: 60 aero engines; 23 aircraft,
some extremely rare; relics and
photos depicting the development of
aviation - library

Burnie

00467
Burnie Art Gallery
Civic Centre, Wilmot St, POB 62,
Burnie, Tas. 7320
Fine Arts Museum - 1978
Contemporary Australian prints,
drawings, watercolours; small but
growing international collection

Busselton

00468
Prospect Villa
Pries Av, Busselton, WA 6280
General Museum - 1855
Australia's smallest known paddle
steamer 'Juwina'; pioneer tools;
kitchen utensils; aboriginal weapons

Bylands

00469
Victoria's Tramway Museum
Union Lane, Bylands, Vic. 3600
Science/Tech Museum - 1973
Horse, cable and electric tramcars;
ancillary tramway vehicles;
photographs, tickets, uniforms,
tramway equipment; extensive
collection of Melbourne cable trams

Campbell

00470
Australian War Memorial
Cnr Limestone Av and Ansac Parade,
Campbell, POB 345, Canberra City,
ACT 2601
History/Public Affairs Museum - 1941
Coll: military weapons and equipment;
uniforms; decorations and medals;
paintings, drawings and sculptures
relating to both World Wars and to
other conflicts from the Sudan to
Vietnam - library

Cannington

00471
Woodloes Folk Museum
Woodloe St, Cannington, WA 6107
General Museum - 1978
Local Australian history exhibits;
display of 1870-1900 timber industry

Carlton

00472
Gryphon Gallery Melbourne State
College
757 Swanston St, Carlton, Vic. 3053
Fine Arts Museum - 1972
Arts and crafts

Castlemaine

00473
**Castlemaine Art Gallery and
Historical Museum**
Lyttleton St, Castlemaine, Vic. 3450
General Museum - 1913
Australian paintings, prints and
drawings; records and documents;
photographs and articles concerning
the district

Caulfield

00474
Victorian Racing Museum
mail c/o Victoria Amateur Turf Club,
Station St, POB 231, Caulfield, Vic.
3145
History/Public Affairs Museum - 1975

Chinchilla

00475
Chinchilla Folk Museum
Villiers St, POB 250, Chinchilla, Qld.
4413
General Museum - 1970
Steam engines ; authentic operational
saw mill - Library mainly of local
history

Claire

00476
Clare National Trust Museum
Former Police Station, Casualty
Hospital, mail c/o John Haynes, 6
Archer St, Claire, SA 5453
History/Public Affairs Museum - 1970
Cemetery and genealogical records;
aboriginal artifacts - library; town
archives

Cleveland

00477
Redland Museum Foundation
125 Bay St, Cleveland, Qld. 4163
History/Public Affairs Museum - 1970
Horse drawn vehicles; farm
implements; steam engine and
stationary engines; early typewriter;
printing press

Colac

00478
Provan's Mechanical Museum
Princes Hwy, Colac, Vic. 3250
Science/Tech Museum - 1977
Motorcycles 1905-1951, steam
engines 1875-1914, cars and trucks
1906-1930; farm implements; wireless
sets, clocks; wind mills; oil and gas
engines

Coober Pedy

00479
Umoona Opal Mine Museum
Main Rd, POB 372, Coober Pedy, SA
5273
General Museum - 1977
Art and artifacts of Central Australian
desert aboriginal tribes; opal deposits;
preserved opal mine; Coober Pedy
alluvial black opal

Coolangatta

00480
Gilltrap's Yesteryear World
Creek St, POB 131, Coolangatta, Qld.
4225
History/Public Affairs Museum
Veteran, vintage and post-vintage
cars; motorcycles; cycles; horse-
drawn vehicles; commercial vehicles;
home of 'Genevieve' of film fame

Corrigin

00481
Corrigin Museum
Goyder St, POB 203, Corrigin, WA
6375
Anthropology Museum - 1970
Machinery; tools; local items

Corryong

00482
**Man From Snowy River Folk
Museum**
103 Hanson St, POB 127, Corryong,
Vic. 3707
Anthropology Museum - 1963
Ski collection; folk art

Cunderdin

00483
The Cunderdin Municipal Museum
Great Eastern Hwy, Cunderdin, WA
6407
General Museum - 1972
Local rural history and development;
farm tractors and other agricultural
machinery

Daylesford

00484
**Daylesford and District Historical
Museum**
Vincent St, Daylesford, Vic. 3460
History/Public Affairs Museum - 1971
Local history - library

Deloraine

00485
Folk Museum and Cider Bar The
Family and Commercial Inn
98 Emu Bay Rd, Deloraine, Tas. 7304
General Museum
Local artifacts; photographs; 'Jimmy
Possum' chairs

00486
The Military Museum
22 Bass Hwy, Deloraine, Tas. 7304
History/Public Affairs Museum - 1977
Military vehicles and guns used by
Australian forces from World War I to
present days; scale military models
and model soldiers; collection of
propaganda posters, photographs,
documents, newspapers and
magazines, cigarette cards, uniforms
and equipment

Devonport

00487
Devonport Gallery and Arts Centre
46 Steele Street, POB 645, Devonport,
Tas. 7310
Fine Arts Museum - 1966
Glass and ceramics (20th c.)

Dowerin

00488
Dowerin District Museum
16 Cotterell St, Dowerin, WA 6461
General Museum - 1914
Reconstructed pioneer's house with
furniture (1900-1920)

Echuca

00489
The Alambee Auto and Folk Museum
7-11 Warren St, Echuca, Vic. 3625
General Museum - 1976
Vintage and veteran cars; model
railway; folk items; period costumes;
guns, phonographs, wirelesses, bottles
and coins

Elsternwick

00490
Rippon Lea National Trust of Australia
192 Hotham St, Elsternwick,
Elsternwick, Vic. 3185
Historic Site
Historical home (created by Frederick
Thomas Sargood 1860-1887) with
furniture and an extensive garden

Esk

00491
Esk Bottle Museum
POB 29, Esk, Qld. 4312
General Museum - 1968
Handcrafted work; bottles from 2 000
BC to present day; tapestries and
needlework; fossils and petrified wood

Euroa

00492
Farmers Arms Hotel Museum
25 Kirkland Av, Euroa, Vic. 3666
General Museum - 1973
Coll: textiles, irons, kitchen utensils,
mangle and washing boards of
pioneer days; old farm machinery

Ferny Grove

00493
Brisbane Tramway Museum
2 McGinn Rd, Ferny Grove, Qld. 4055
History/Public Affairs Museum - 1968
Brisbane trams and buses; archival
holdings of the Brisbane City Council
Transport Department; 1885 horse
tram truck built by John Stephenson;
1901 Californian combination car; four
motor trams (1938) - library;
photographical archives

Fortitude Valley

00494
Queensland Museum
Gregory Terrace, Fortitude Valley, Qld.
4006
Natural History Museum - 1871
Coll: Girault type of
microhymenoptera (Insecta);
Macgregor collection of Papua New
Guinea ethnography (in part); Thomas
Macleod Queensland aviation
collection; Royal Worcester porcelain
collection, containing 250 pieces from
1860 to the present; Bert Hinkler's
aeroplanes - library and mobile
facilities for country areas

Franklin

00495
**Greg Clark Memorial Apple Industry
Museum**
Weather Board, Saint John's Church
Hall, Main Rd, POB 20, Franklin, Tas.
7113
Agriculture Museum - 1978
Early machinery and implements used
in the processing of apples; historical
documents

Fremantle

00496
**Western Australian Maritime
Museum**
Cliff St, Fremantle, WA 6160
History/Public Affairs Museum - 1979
Coll: maritime archeology;
conservation

Geelong

00497
Geelong Art Gallery
Little Malop St, Geelong, Vic. 3220
Fine Arts Museum - 1900
Australian art (19th and 20th c.);
English paintings (late 19th c.)

Gladstone

00498
Gladstone Gaol Museum
Prison Reserve, Ward St, POB 18,
Gladstone, SA 5473
History/Public Affairs Museum - 1978
Gaol relics; former cells

Grange

00499
**Charles Sturt Memorial Museum
Trust Inc.** 'The Grange'
Jetty St, Grange, SA 5022
Historic Site - 1960
Residence of Captain Charles Sturt,
whose voyage down the river Murray,
1829-30, led to the founding of South
Australia; furniture of the Sturt family;
Union Jacks hoisted during the
voyage and northern expedition

Hahndorf

00500
**Art Galleries and German Folk
Museum** Hahndorf Academy
68 Main St, Hahndorf, SA 5245
General Museum - 1967
German and Australian household
items, literature and tools of the 19th
century; small collection of original
works by Sir Hans Heysen - library

00501
Tinariba Gallery and Museum
77 Main St, Hahndorf, SA 5245
Anthropology Museum - 1955
Mask collection from the Baining tribe
of New Britain (fully documented);
contemporary New Ireland Malangans
(documented with the legend); Tolai
masks and carvings from New Britain;
Australian aboriginal stone artifacts -
library

Hervey Bay

00502
Hervey Bay Historical Society
1-16 Zephyr St, Hervey Bay, Qld. 4656
General Museum
library

Hobart

00503
**Allport Library and Museum of Fine
Arts**
91 Murray St, Hobart, Tas. 7000
Fine Arts Museum

00504
John R. Elliott Classics Museum
University of Tasmania
GPOB 252 C, Hobart, Tas. 7001
Archeology Museum - 1954
Ancient art; archeology; Greek
pottery; Greek and Roman coins

00505
Tasmanian Museum and Art Gallery
5 Argyle St, POB 1164 M, Hobart, Tas.
7001
General Museum - 1829
Tasmanian paintings (particularly 19th
c.); Tasmanian geology, botany,
zoology; aboriginal culture - library

00506
**Van Diemen's Land Memorial Folk
Museum** 'Narryna'
103 Hampden Rd, Battery Point,
Hobart, Tas. 7000
Anthropology Museum - 1957
Ayrshire embroidery; clothing (mainly
19th c.); needlework; colonial furniture

Iondaryan

00507
**Iondaryan Woolshed Museum and
Park Association**
Iondaryan, PO Town Hall Box 3005,
Toowoomba, Qld. 4350
General Museum - 1972
Folklore exhibits

Kadina

00508
Kadina Museum Complex
mail c/o National Trust S.A., Kadina
Branch, 1 1/2 km south Kadina off the
Moonta Rd, Kadina, SA 5554
General Museum - 1967
Curiosities and furniture of the
Victorian era; early agricultural
machinery; native animal enclosure
and native trees; old blacksmith's
shop; printing; mining; domestic
utensils; place where Caroline
Carleton, authoress of the 'Song of
Australia', died

Kalgoorlie

00509
Hainault Tourist Gold Mine
Boulder Block Rd, POB 271,
Kalgoorlie, WA 6430
Science/Tech Museum - 1973
Underground and surface mining
methods used in the 'Golden Mile'

Kelvin Grove

00510
**Ninth Battalion's Association
Museum**
mail c/o Ninth Battalion, The Royal
Queensland Regiment, Gone Barracks,
Kelvin Grove, Qld. 4059
History/Public Affairs Museum - 1967
Weapons and relics from Vietnam, the
Gallipoli Campaign, the Western Front,
the Middle East and exhibits of various
battalions - library

Kimba

00511
**Kimba and Gawler Ranges Historical
Society**
Eyre Hwy, Box 134, Kimba, SA 5641
General Museum - 1978
Local history

Korumburra

00512
Coal Creek Historical Park
Silkstone Rd, POB 193, Korumburra,
Vic. 3950
Historic Site - 1973
History of the South Gippsland area,
black coal mining, railways and early
rural history

Kyneton

00513
Kyneton Historical Centre
67 Piper St, POB 151, Kyneton, Vic.
3444
History/Public Affairs Museum - 1968
Victoriana; dolls; local history

Landsborough

00514
**Shire of Landsborough Historical
Society**
Maleny Rd, Landsborough, Qld. 4550
General Museum - 1973
Local history displays; tools; laundry
and kitchen implements; photographs

Langwarrin

00515
McClelland Gallery
Studio Park, McClelland Drive,
Langwarrin, Vic. 3910
Fine Arts Museum - 1971
Australian painting 1900-1940;
contemporary sculpture - library

Latrobe

00516
Latrobe Court House Museum
mail c/o E.J. Curtis, 10 Hamilton St,
Latrobe, Tas. 7307
General Museum - 1970
Pioneer and aboriginal artifacts;
courtroom furniture; hospital articles

Launceston

00517
Franklin House
POB 711, Launceston, Tas. 7250
General Museum - 1960
Restored house of the early 19th
century; 18th century furniture;
lithographs

00518
**Queen Victoria Museum and Art
Gallery**
Wellington St, Launceston, Tas. 7250
Natural History Museum - 1891
Tasmanian history, botany, geology,
zoology, paleontology; Tasmanian and
general anthropology; primitive and
colonial art; industrial design

Lilydale

00519
**Lilydale and District Historical
Museum**
Castella St, Lilydale, Vic. 3140
Music Museum - 1976
Memorabilia of Helen Porter Mitchell
(Dame Nellie Melba), Australian
operatic soprano; local artifacts

Littlehampton

00520
Baderloo Railway Museum
Balhannah Rd, Littlehampton, SA 5250
History/Public Affairs Museum - 1968
International collection of railway
relics; postal stamps marking special
railway events; express sleeping car
of 1919

Loxton

00521
Loxton District Historical Village
Riverfront Rd, POB 409, Loxton, SA
5333
History/Public Affairs Museum - 1970
History of pioneer settlements; leather
craft

Mahogany Creek

00522
The Old Mahogany Inn
Great Eastern Hwy, Mahogany Creek,
WA 6072
Historic Site - 1842
Early Australian Inn; furniture and local
historical items

Maitlands

00523
Maitland Museum
Former School, Cnr Kilkerran Tce and
Gardiner Tce, POB 106, Maitlands, SA
5573
General Museum - 1972

Manjimup

00524
Manjimup Timber Museum
Barrie St, Manjimup, WA 6258
Science/Tech Museum - 1978
Timber of Western Australia and the
timber industry; dining room suite
(jarrah wood); early paper-making
machine

Maylands

00525
Tranby House The National Trust of
Australia
Johnson St, Maylands, WA 6051
General Museum - 1977
House furnished in the style of the
mid-19th century and depicting an
early colonial farmhouse

Melbourne

00526
Ancient Times House Museum of the
Australian Institute of Archaeology
116 Little Bourke St, mail c/o The
Australian Institute of Archaeology,
174 Collins St, Melbourne, Vic. 3000
Archeology Museum - 1954
Archeology of the ancient Near East
from the Sumerian to the Roman
period, limited aboriginal and
prehistoric artifacts; Cypriot pottery
(BC to Cypro-Roman); pottery and
artifacts from Jericho and Jerusalem
excavations; Alalakh tablets, Akkadian
tablets and archives from Umm-el-Jir

00527
Geological Museum
107 Russell St, Melbourne, Vic. 3000
Natural History Museum - 1910
Geological specimens including typical
rocks, fossils and minerals found in
Victoria; dioramas depicting the
occurrence of groundwater and
brown coal; models of Victorian gold
nuggets - library

00528
National Gallery of Victoria Victorian
Arts Centre
180 St. Kilda Rd, Melbourne, Vic. 3004
Fine Arts Museum - 1859
Old master paintings, prints and
drawings; Asian art; modern European
and American painting and sculpture;
decorative arts; antiquities;
photography; Australian art

00529
National Museum of Victoria
285-321 Russell St, Melbourne, Vic.
3000
Natural History Museum - 1854
Coll: minerals; fossils; Australian and
Oceanic ethnology; Australian
invertebrates; ornithology;
entomology; fishes; reptiles and
amphibians; crustacea - library

00530
**Old Melbourne Gaol and Penal
Museum**
Russell St, Melbourne, Vic. 3000
History/Public Affairs Museum

00531
Performing Arts Museum Victorian
Arts Centre
Melbourne Concert Hall, St. Kilda Rd,
Melbourne, Vic. 3004
Performing Arts Museum - 1978
Dame Nellie Melba Memorial
Collection, including Lohengrin cape
1891; Tait Collection of Costume
Design; J. C. Williamson Program
Collection; archives of St. Martins
Theatre, Melbourne, Emerald Hill
Theatre, South Melbourne, National
Theatre, Melbourne, Melbourne
Repertory Theatre - library

00532
Science Museum of Victoria
304-308 Swanson St, Melbourne, Vic.
3000
Science/Tech Museum - 1870
Div: engineering; transportation and
communication; agriculture; applied
physics; chemistry; biology; geology;
electronics; numismatics; arms;
horology; public health; first
Australian-made motorcar and
aeroplane - library

00533
**The Victorian College of the Arts
Gallery** School of Art
Grounds of the National Gallery of
Victoria, via Nolan St, South
Melbourne, 234 St. Kilda Rd,
Melbourne, Vic. 3004
Fine Arts Museum - 1976
Works by students of the School of
Art from 1890 to present day - the
gallery complements the art-teaching
program of the college

Mildura

00534
Mildura Arts Centre
199 Cureton Av, POB 748, Mildura, Vic.
3500
Fine Arts Museum

Moe

00535
Old Gippstown
Lloyd St, POB 337, Moe, Vic. 3825
Historic Site - 1969
Over 30 original buildings brought to
the site from all over Gippsland, now
fully restored; one of the best
collections of fully restored, horse-
drawn vehicles in Australia; 'Bushy
Park' homestead of Angus Mc Millan,
discoverer of Gippsland

Mornington

00536
Mornington Peninsula Arts Centre
Vancouver St, Mornington, Vic. 3931
Fine Arts Museum - 1969
Australian paintings, drawings and
prints - library

00537
Old Mornington Post Office
Cnr Main St and Esplanade,
Mornington, Vic. 3931
General Museum - 1968
Local history; folklore; photos of
historic homes

Mount Gambier

00538
Lewis' Museum
12 Pick Av, POB 239, Mount Gambier,
SA 5290
General Museum - 1975
Aboriginal artifacts; coins and notes;
kerosene lamps; display of miniature
shoes; guns, swords; minerals; shells;
antiquities (18th-19th c.)

Mundingburra

00539
Thuringowa Aero Museum
Beck's Farm, Beck's Rd, Condon, Thuringowa Shire, PO, Mundingburra, Qld. 4812
Science/Tech Museum - 1971
Coll: Aircraft materials, aero engines, ground trainers; photographic files of Southwest Pacific World War II period; first American fighter aircraft to land in Papua New Guinea 1942

Narrogin

00540
Narrogin Old Courthouse Museum
Old Courthouse Building, Cnr Egerton and Earl Sts, Location No 260, *mail c/o* Town Clerk, POB 198, Narrogin, WA 6312
General Museum - 1976
Local history - library

Nedlands

00541
Anthropology Research Museum
University of Western Australia
Social Science Building, Nedlands, WA 6009
Anthropology Museum - 1976
Berndt collection (Australian aborigines and New Guinea highlands); Lucich collection (North-Western Australian aboriginal); Anderson collection (Sepik region and Australian aboriginal); sacred rangga boards associated with the Elcho Island Adjustment Movement (Northern Australian aboriginal); collection of Arnhem Land post figures (Northern Australian aboriginal) - library

00542
Musical Instruments Collection
Department of Music, University of Western Australia, Nedlands, WA 6009
Music Museum - 1971
Ethnic (mainly Asian) and historical European musical instruments; Javanese gamelan; harpsichord by J. Kirkman (1760)

00543
Stirling House Museum
49 Broadway, Nedlands, WA 6009
General Museum - 1964
Documentation on pioneer families; costumes - library

New Norcia

00544
New Norcia Museum and Art Gallery
Saint Joseph's, 82 miles from Perth
New Norcia, WA 6509
General Museum - 1951
Coll: European oil paintings; ecclesiastical vestments; aboriginal artifacts; rare books; local history - library

Newtown

00545
Camperdown Cemetery
187 Church St, Newtown, NSW 2042
Historic Site - 1848
Victorian funerary decoration and statuary; church of colonial architect Edmund Blacket

Nile

00546
Clarendon National Trust House
Nile, Tas. 7212
General Museum - 1962
Restored country house of the early 19th century; late 18th and early 19th century English furniture; oil painting by John Glover

Norman Park

00547
Earlystreet
75 Mcilwraith Av, Norman Park, Qld. 4170
Open Air Museum - 1965
Early Queensland buildings, artifacts and gardens

Norseman

00548
Norseman Historical and Geological Museum
School of Mines Building, Battery Rd, POB 14, Norseman, WA 6443
Anthropology Museum - 1972
Artifacts from the construction of the Coolgardie-Dundas (Norseman)-Balladonia-Eucla telegraph line (constructed 1896-97); household equipment and mining tools; mining books (1920-1970) - library

Norwood

00549
Kensington and Norwood Historical Society Museum
110 The Parade, Norwood, SA 5067
Anthropology Museum - 1978
library

00550
Performing Arts Collection of South Australia
79 Beulah Rd, Norwood, SA 5067
Performing Arts Museum
Theatre artifacts and ephemera (not yet open to the public)

Oatlands

00551
Tasmanian Old Time Music Parlour
66 High St, Oatlands, Tas. 7205
Science/Tech Museum - 1979
Mechanical musical instruments; music boxes; organettes; phonographs; gramophones; triola (half mechanical zither, 19th c.)

Parkville

00552
Grainger Museum University of Melbourne
Royal Parade, Parkville, Vic. 3052
Music Museum - 1938
Grainger collection of 'free-music' machines (early synthesisers), music (manuscripts and published), sound archives, correspondence, furniture, costumes, works of art, ethnographic material and other personal items from Grainger's lifetime; archival records of the Royal Victorian Liedertafel; music manuscripts of G.W.L. Marshall-Hall, Florence Ewart, Henry Tate, Ian Bonighton; smaller Australian collections; folk music from Great Britain, Denmark and the South Pacific

00553
University Gallery
University of Melbourne, Parkville, Vic. 3052
General Museum - 1972
Leonhard Adam ethnographical collection (mainly Oceanic); Norman Lindsay collection; Australian historical collection; classical coins - library

Parramatta

00554
Royal New South Wales Lancers Memorial Museum
Linden House, Lancer Barracks, Smith St, Parramatta, NSW 2150
History/Public Affairs Museum - 1957

Perth

00555
Army Museum of Western Australia Inc.
2 Bulwer St, Perth, WA 6000
History/Public Affairs Museum - 1977
Memorabilia of Western Australian formations and units

00556
The Art Gallery of Western Autralia
47 James St, Perth, WA 6000
Fine Arts Museum - 1895
Fine art and craft objects

00557
Post and Telecom Museum
78 Murray St, Perth, WA 6000
History/Public Affairs Museum - 1973
Postal and telecommunications history of Western Australia from 1829 to the present; antique telephones; morse equipment; Australian stamps; cancellers; seals; posting boxes; teleprinters; working telephone exchanges; full-size replicas of early post and telegraph offices - library

00558
Western Australian Museum
Francis St, Perth, WA 6000
General Museum - 1891
Zoology; paleontology; anthropology; archeology; regional history; technology; maritime archeology; regional fauna - library

Peterborough

00559
Peterborough Museum Department of Further Education
Main St, POB 146, Peterborough, SA 5422
General Museum - 1877

Pinjarra

00560
Old Blythewood The National Trust of Australia
South West Hwy, Pinjarra, WA 6208
General Museum - 1976
Old Blythewood house furnished in the style of the mid-19th century and depicting an early colonial farm home

Port Lincoln

00561
Rosewall Memorial Shell Museum
Flinders Hwy, Port Lincoln, SA 5606
Natural History Museum - 1978
Shells

Port Pirie

00562
Carn-Brae
32 Florence St, Port Pirie, SA 5540
General Museum - 1971
Antiquities; dolls (since 1850); stained glass windows

00563
National Trust Historical and Folk Museum
Ellen St, Port Pirie, SA 5540
History/Public Affairs Museum - 1970
Display of items from the Lead Smelters at Port Pirie, in a former railway station of unusual architectural design

Port Victoria

00564
Maritime Museum
Former Goods Smed, Main Street, Port Victoria, Box 106, Maitland, SA 5573
History/Public Affairs Museum - 1975
Local maritime history

Redcliffe

00565
Redcliffe Historical Society
Old Bathing Pavillon, Suttons Beach, POB 148, Redcliffe, Qld. 4020
History/Public Affairs Museum - 1969
Australiana; shipwreck relics of Queensland coast; aboriginal relics - library

Renmark

00566
P.S. 'Industry' Museum
POB 730, Renmark, SA 5341
Science/Tech Museum
Former riverboat relics, log books and photographs - Steamer in a specially constructed basin

Richmond

00567
Bridge Inn Antique Autos World of Wheels
Bridge St, Richmond, Tas. 7025
History/Public Affairs Museum - 1977
21 antique Ford automobiles

Rottnest Island

00568
Rottnest Island Museum
Rottnest Island, WA 6161
History/Public Affairs Museum - 1975
Native prison relics

St. Kilda

00569
Australian Electric Transport Museum
St. Kilda Rd, St. Kilda, SA, GPOB 2012, Adelaide, SA 5001
History/Public Affairs Museum - 1958
Tramcars, trolleybuses, motorbuses, horsetram, electric locomotive and associated transportation artifacts; double-deck horsetram (builder: J. Stephenson, 1878); prototype Australian trolleybus (1932); Adelaide's No 1 electric tramcar (1908)

Shepparton

00570
Shepparton Arts Centre
Civic Centre, Welsford St, POB 989,
Shepparton, Vic. 3630
Fine Arts Museum - 1935
Coll: Australian pottery and ceramics
(1820-1980); Australian painting,
drawing and contemporary prints;
Japanese and Asian ceramics - library

Snug

00571
Channel Historical and Folk Museum
'The Rockery', Channel Hwy, POB 559,
Snug, Tas. 7145
General Museum
Settlers' house with original tools and
implements; historical documents

South Nanango

00572
Gem and Historical Museum
Mail Service 396, South Nanango, Qld.
4315
General Museum - 1966
Minerals; gemstones; world wide
general specimens; aboriginal stone
implements; antique bottles; local
historical items in Nanango's first
school; tektites - library

Spalding

00573
Geralka Rural Farm
R.M.D., Spalding, SA 5454
Agriculture Museum - 1972
Copper-mining history; various
ploughs from the earliest to the
modern day machine, likewise
harrows, cultivators, seeding
equipment, harvestors and headers;
Clydesdale working horses; 1908
Daimler road train

Strathalbyn

00574
Strathalbyn Branch National Trust
Museum
Rankine St, Strathalbyn, SA 5255
General Museum - 1970
Farm, industrial, and domestic utensils;
period furniture; costumes

Swan Hill

00575
**Swan Hill Pioneer Settlement
Authority**
Pioneer Settlement Post Office, Swan
Hill, Vic. 3585
General Museum - 1963
Australiana; early agricultural
machinery; Australia's largest inland
paddle steamer P.S. 'Gem';
stereoscopic theatre - library and
education centre

Swanbourne

00576
Tom Collins House
9 Servetus St, Swanbourne, WA 6010
Historic Site - 1949
House built in 1907 by Joseph Furphy
(Tom Collins), a famous Australian
author; Furphy memorabilia; rare
Australian books - library

Sydney

00577
Art Gallery of New South Wales
Art Gallery Rd, Domaine, Sydney,
NSW 2000
Fine Arts Museum - 1874
Australian art; primitive and aboriginal
art, including notable burial posts and
park paintings; Melanesian art; British
painting and sculpture; European
painting, prints and drawings; Oriental
art; British pewter (17th-18th c.);
English porcelain (18th c. and
Victorian); contemporary tapestries

00578
The Australian Museum
Sandstone, 6-8 College St, POB A 285,
Sydney, NSW 2000
General Museum - 1827
Australian and Melanesian
anthropology; Oceanian native
cultures; Polynesian cultures; natural
sciences; Melanesian art; Vickery
stamp collection - library

00579
Geological and Mining Museum
36 George St, Sydney, NSW 2000
Science/Tech Museum - 1876
Minerals; ores; gemstones; rocks and
fossils

00580
**J. L. Shellshear Museum of
Comparative Anatomy and Physical
Anthropology** Dept. of Anatomy,
University of Sydney
Sydney, NSW 2006
Natural History Museum - 1958
Human skulls, skeletons and brains;
marsupials

00581
**J. T. Wilson Museum of Human
Anatomy** Dept. of Anatomy, University
of Sydney
Sydney, NSW 2006
Natural History Museum - 1886
Human anatomy and anthropology

00582
The Macleay Museum The University
of Sidney
Sydney, NSW 2006
Natural History Museum - 1888
Miklouho-Maklai Ethnographical
Collection; Godsall Collection of
Chinese Ceramics and Bronzes; Sir
William Macleay Insect Collection;
Selby Collection of Microscopes;
Louis Pasteur's flask

00583
Nicholson Museum of Antiquities
University of Sydney
Sydney, NSW 2006
Archeology Museum - 1860
Egyptian, Greek, Roman, Cypriot,
Middle Eastern and European
antiquities

00584
Power Gallery of Contemporary Art
Power Institute of Fine Arts, University
of Sydney
Sydney, NSW 2006
Fine Arts Museum - 1979
Australian and contemporary overseas
art

00585
War Memorial Gallery of Fine Arts
University of Sydney
Parramatta Rd, Sydney, NSW 2006
Fine Arts Museum - 1959
Paintings, crafts and sculpture

Tanunda

00586
Barossa Valley Historical Museum
47 Murray St, POB 51, Tanunda, SA
5352
General Museum - 1963
Local history; folk art; hand-made early
pioneer tools and implements - library

Taranna

00587
Norfolk Galleries
Arthur Hwy, Taranna, 178 Macquarie
St, Hobart, Tas. 7180
Fine Arts Museum - 1973
Early artifacts and furniture of the Port
Arthur settlement; primitive paintings
of the period of settlement;
mouthpiece of the trumpet used to
sound the charge of the Inniskilling
Dragoons at Waterloo - library

Tea Tree Gully

00588
Old Highercombe Hotel
3 Perserverance Rd, Tea Tree Gully,
SA 5090
General Museum - 1961
Interior of the old hotel furnished in
the style of the 1850's; historic items of
the district

Toodyay

00589
Old Gaol Museum
Toodyay, WA 6566
History/Public Affairs Museum
Colonial building (1867) containing
artifacts belonging to early settlers;
historical maps; lace and embroidery;
James Drummond botanical collection

Vaucluse

00590
Vaucluse House Historic Site
Wentworth Rd, Olala Av, Vaucluse,
NSW 2030
1911
Home of William C. Wentworth, 'Father
of the Constitution', fully furnished in
mid-19th century style; Wentworth
memorabilia; china collection; antique
arms; 19th century carriages

Wanneroo

00591
Gloucester Lodge Museum
mail c/o Yanchep National Park,
Yanchep St, POB 21, Wanneroo, WA
6065
General Museum - 1979
Colonial artifacts; Gnangara mineral
sands; speleological exhibits;
shipwrecks off the Wanneroo/
Yanchep Coast

Warrnambool

00592
Warrnambool Art Gallery
214 Timor St, Warrnambool, Vic. 3280
Fine Arts Museum - 1887
Contemporary Australian prints; late
19th century Australian and European
paintings

Wauchope

00593
Timbertown
Oxley Hwy, POB 208, Wauchope,
NSW 2446
Open Air Museum - 1976
Operating recreation of an 1880
logging and sawmilling community with
craftsmen

Wellington

00594
Wellington Courthouse Complex
Wellington, SA 5259
History/Public Affairs Museum
Historical police station and
courthouse; local history artifacts;
early aboriginal and gold rush-related
documents - special children's section

Westbury

00595
White House
Village Green, Westbury, Tas. 7303
General Museum - 1970
Coll: English period furniture of the
17th and 18th centuries; early
Tasmanian prints; paintings; copper
and brass ware; toy exhibit; bicycles,
cars, and horsedrawn vehicles

Whyalla Norrie

00596
Mount Laura Homestead Museum
Ekblom St, Whyalla Norrie, SA 5608
General Museum - 1975
Documents of the discovery of the
area by Captain Matthew Flinders in
1802, early local exploration and
pastoral activities following South
Australia's founding in 1836; history of
iron ore mining

Williamstown

00597
**Australian Railway Historical Society
Museum**
Champion Rd, North Williamstown,
GPOB 5177 AA, Melbourne, Vic. 3001
History/Public Affairs Museum - 1961
Victorian railways; locomotives,
carriages, wagons, photographic
display

00598
The Victorian Maritime Museum
HMAS 'Castlemaine', Gem Pier,
Williamstown, POB 139, Port
Melbourne, Vic. 3207
History/Public Affairs Museum - 1974
HMAS 'Castlemaine', Australian built
corvette (length 186 ft, 733 tons,
launched 7.8.41)

00599
Williamstown Historical Museum
Electra St, Williamstown, Vic. 3016
History/Public Affairs Museum - 1963
Model ships; maritime artifacts; model
of turret ship 'Cerberus' (1876);
equipment from HMS 'Nelson' (1805);
local history of European settlement in
1835 - library and education centre

Windsor

00600
Hawkesbury Museum
7 Thompson Square, Windsor, NSW
2756
History/Public Affairs Museum - 1962

Wongan Hills

00601
Wongan Ballidu and District Museum
Old Hospital, Cnr Camm and Mitchell Sts, Wongan Hills, WA 6603
General Museum - 1972
Local history; saddlery and blacksmithing tools including forge and bellows; photographic reproductions; horse-drawn farm machinery; reconstructed settler's hut - library; archives

Zeehan

00602
West Coast Pioneer's Memorial Museum
Main St, POB 70, Zeehan, Tas. 7469
Science/Tech Museum - 1892
Coll: minerals; railway locomotives; mining history

Austria

Admont

00603
Naturhistorisches Museum
Benedektinerstift Admont, A-8911 Admont
Natural History Museum - 1866
Coll: insects; birds; reptiles; amphibians; fish; shells; minerals and stones; fossils

Aigen i.M.

00604
Stiftsmuseum Schlägel
Schlägl 1, Postfach 3, A-4160 Aigen i.M.
Fine Arts Museum - 1902
Painting (late Gothic, Baroque, Danube School); manuscripts and incunabula (1463-1520); paraments; stamps - library

Alpl

00605
Österreichisches Wandermuseum
Waldschule, A-8671 Alpl 2
Anthropology Museum - 1978
Coll: history of hiking; hiking organizations; dress and equipment; symbolism and language; hiking maps; memorial to the writer Peter Rosegger

00606
Peter-Rosegger-Geburtshaus
Kluppenegger Hof, A-8671 Alpl
Historic Site - 1927
Coll: typical Styrian farmstead where the popular writer Peter Rosegger was born; memorabilia of Rosegger; 19th century furnishings; flax hut; historical implements for flax processing

Altaussee

00607
Salzbergwerk Altaussee
Lichtersberg 25, Steinberghaus, A-8992 Altaussee
Natural History Museum - 1929
Coll: salt mine; minerals; fossils; salt-mining tools; exhibits on salt mining

Altenburg

00608
Benediktinerstift und Stiftssammlungen
A-3591 Altenburg
Fine Arts Museum - 1144
Coll: 12th-18th century art, especially Austrian Baroque painting, sculpture, furniture; historic 18th century buildings; manuscripts and documents from the 12th century on - library

Ansfelden

00609
Bruckner-Geburtshaus
A-4052 Ansfelden
Historic Site
Coll: birth house of the composer Anton Bruckner; memorabilia

Arnfels

00610
Uhren-, Musikalien- und Volkskundemuseum
Maltschach 3, A-8454 Arnfels
General Museum - 1945
Coll: prehistory; paleontology; clocks; musical instruments; religious art; weapons; folk customs; stamps; herbarium - botanical garden

Aschau

00611
Hafnermuseum
A-4082 Aschau
Decorative Arts Museum
Coll: potter's workshop; domestic earthenware from 16th-19th centuries

Asparn a.d.Zaya

00612
Museum für Urgeschichte des Landes Niederösterreich
A-2151 Asparn a.d.Zaya
Archeology Museum - 1970
Coll: pre- and ancient history of Lower Austria - library; workshops; park; open air museum on prehistory

00613
Weinlandmuseum
A-2151 Asparn a.d.Zaya
General Museum - 1949
History; history of law; crafts and guilds; religious art (Gothic to present); agricultural implements; peasant furniture and domestic tools; important local personalities; stones; local artists; documentation center on folk customs; archives

Bad Aussee

00614
Salinenspital
Meranplatz 157, A-8990 Bad Aussee
Religious Art Museum
Coll: in 16th century hospital; religious art; liturgical items, paintings, sculpture, liturgical vestments and books

Bad Deutsch-Altenburg

00615
Afrikamuseum
A-2405 Bad Deutsch-Altenburg
Anthropology Museum - 1967
Coll: in 17th century castle with moat; natural history and ethnology of Africa; dioramas of the Serengeti steppe and Kilimanjaro

00616
Museum Carnuntinum
Badgasse 42, A-2405 Bad Deutsch-Altenburg
History/Public Affairs Museum - 1904
Roman art from the 1st to the 4th century - library

Bad Goisern

00617
Freilichtmuseum Anzenaumühle
Anzenaumühle, A-4822 Bad Goisern
Open Air Museum - 1968
Coll: local and regional history; peasant crafts and tools

00618
Heimatmuseum
Gottlieb-Oberhauser-Str., A-4822 Bad Goisern
General Museum - 1946
Coll: literary estate of the peasant philosopher Konrad Deubler; local history; violin construction; handicrafts; markmanship

Bad Ischl

00619
Fotomuseum des Landes Oberösterreich Sammlung Frank
Marmorschlößl, Postfach 117, A-4820 Bad Ischl
Performing Arts Museum - 1978
Coll:history and development of photography; cameras; 19th century photographs; photos of Austrian photographers

00620
Haenel-Pancera-Familien-Museum
Concordiastr. 3, A-4820 Bad Ischl
Fine Arts Museum - 1959
Coll: in early 20th century villa; painting; sculpture; glass; procelain; Oriental art; furniture from the Renaissance and Empire periods; autographs of famous composers; memorabilia of the pianist Ella Pancera

00621
Heimatmuseum
Lehárkai 10, A-4820 Bad Ischl
General Museum - 1874
Coll: in Franz Lehár's villa; pre- and ancient history; local history; religious folk art; mangers; traditional costumes; geology; salt mining; history of the theater; memorabilia of the actor A. Girardi

00622
Kaiser-Villa
Jainzen 38, A-4820 Bad Ischl
Historic Site
Coll: in 19th century villa of Kaiser Franz Josef I; 19th century interiors; paintings; sculpture; porcelain; arts and crafts; hunting trophies of Kaiser Franz Josef I

00623
Lehármuseum
Lehárkai 8, A-4820 Bad Ischl
Historic Site - 1949
Coll: in the residence of the composer Franz Lehár; memorabilia of Lehár; the composer's art collection; original music scores; period furniture

Bad Mitterndorf

00624
Heimatkundliche Privatsammlung
A-8993 Bad Mitterndorf 67
General Museum - 1908
Coll: archeological finds; paleontology; religious folk art; domestic implements; coins; weapons; traditional costumes; masks of the local Nikolaus drama; pewter; archives - library

Bad Tatzmannsdorf

00625
Freilichtmuseum
A-7431 Bad Tatzmannsdorf
Open Air Museum - 1967
Coll: original and reconstructed 17th-20th century farmhouses; stalls; wine cellar; smithy

Bad Vöslau

00626
Stadtmuseum
Altes Rathaus, Kirchenplatz 8, A-2540 Bad Vöslau
General Museum - 1898
Geology of the eastern alpine zone; local industry; local history; general history; domestic implements; hunting trophies; weapons

Bad Wimsbach-Neydharting

00627
Budweiser-Zimmer
A-4654 Bad Wimsbach-Neydharting
General Museum - 1955
Coll: memorabilia of the founding of the Budweiser forestry school; documents; school books; paintings; weapons; antlers; uniforms

00628
Drudenfuß-Sammlung Otto Stöber
A-4654 Bad Wimsbach-Neydharting
Anthropology Museum - 1910
Coll: pentagrams from late Stone Age to the present

00629
Internationales Moor-Museum
A-4654 Bad Wimsbach-Neydharting
Natural History Museum - 1960
Coll: geology of marshland; marshland archeology; uses of marshland and peat in industry and agriculture; marshland as a theme in world literature, history, and heraldry - library

Baden

00630
Kaiser-Franz-Josef-Museum für Handwerk und Volkskunst
Hochstr. 51, A-2500 Baden
Anthropology Museum - 1900
Coll: handicrafts; folk art of Lower Austria; locksmith and forge; lamps; ceramics; wood crafts; coopery; weaving; clocks; musical instruments; religious folk art; weapons

00631
Rollettmuseum Städtische Sammlungen und Archiv
A-2500 Baden
General Museum - 1800
Coll: Roman finds; natural history; local history; ceramics; paintings from the Biedermeier period; maps; skull collection; memorabilia of Grillparzer and Beethoven; archives

Baldramsdorf

00632
Kärntner Handwerksmuseum
A-9805 Baldramsdorf
Anthropology Museum
Arts and crafts

Bärnbach

00633
Burgenkundliches Museum
Schloß Alt-Kainach, A-8572 Bärnbach
History/Public Affairs Museum - 1968
Coll: comparative history of fortresses,
especially the Styrian fortresses;
models, typology, paintings, maps;
stamps with fortresses and castles;
artists, commanders-in-chief,
statesmen, and scientists in Styrian
fortresses

Bernstein

00634
Sammlungen Burg Bernstein
A-7434 Bernstein
History/Public Affairs Museum - 1892
Coll: historical interiors and inventory;
weapons and armor; instruments of
torture; pre- and ancient history;
retorts and 17th century alchemist
laboratory - library

Bleiburg

00635
Werner-Berg-Galerie
Hauptplatz 4, A-9150 Bleiburg
Fine Arts Museum - 1968
Coll: woodprints, paintings, graphics,
and sketches of Werner Berg

Brandhof

00636
Jagdmuseum Erzherzog Johann
Jagdschlößl, A-8601 Brandhof
History/Public Affairs Museum - 1850
Coll: historical inventory of hunting
trophies; memorabilia of Archduke
Johann

Bregenz

00637
Vorarlberger Landesmuseum
Kornmarkt 1, A-6900 Bregenz
General Museum - 1857
Local history; folk art; pre- and early
history; crafts; weapons - library;
workshops

Breitenau

00638
**Votivschatz der Wallfahrtskirche St.
Erhard**
A-2624 Breitenau
Religious Art Museum
Coll: 14th century glass paintings;
votive panels

Bruck a.d.Lafnitz

00639
Kernstock-Museum
Festenburg 1, A-8251 Bruck a.d.Lafnitz
Historic Site - 1928
Coll: memorial to the poet Dr. Ottokar
Kernstock; his former home;
memorabilia

Döllach

00640
Goldbergbaumuseum
Schloß Großkirchheim, A-9843
Döllach
History/Public Affairs Museum - 1956
Coll: in 16th century gold miner's
castle; historical furnishings; sculpture
and paintings; glass; pewter; copper
and bronze; gold mining; minerals, ore
samples, tools, gold amalgamation

Dölsach

00641
Museum Aguntinum
A-9991 Dölsach
Archeology Museum - 1931
Coll: Roman finds from early Roman
towns; Roman ruins; 2nd century city
wall; handicraft area; 1st-5th century
thermae

Dornbirn

00642
Vorarlberger Naturschau
Marktstr. 33, A-6850 Dornbirn
Natural History Museum - 1955
Geology; paleontology; insects;
botany; zoology; ecology; climate;
lakes and rivers - library

Drosendorf

00643
Franz-Kießling-Museum
A-2095 Drosendorf 17
General Museum - 1925
Coll: local and regional history;
handicraft tools; archives and writings
of Franz Kießling

Eggenburg

00644
Krahuletz-Museum
Krahuletz-Platz 1, A-3730 Eggenburg
General Museum - 1866
Coll: geology and paleontology; pre-
and ancient history; Stone Age bone
tools; ceramics; Roman provincial art;
folklore; peasant tools; crafts; glass;
porcelain; clocks; costumes;
armaments; stones; stonemasonry

Eibenstein bei Gmünd

00645
Geologisches Freilichtmuseum
Naturpark Blockheide, A-3950
Eibenstein bei Gmünd
Open Air Museum - 1964
Stones from Lower Austria north of
the Danube

Eibiswald

00646
Kloepfer- und Heimatmuseum
A-8552 Eibiswald 36
General Museum - 1950
Coll: prehistory; local and regional
history; handicrafts and folk art; iron
and coal; agriculture; manuscripts,
letters, and collected works of the
popular writer Hans Kloepfer

Eisbach

00647
**Sammlungen des
Zisterzienserstiftes Rein**
A-8103 Eisbach
History/Public Affairs Museum
Coll: in 12th century Cistercian
cloister; incunabula; musical
instruments; chapel with sepulchers;
treasure items

Eisenerz

00648
Bergmuseum
Tullstr. 17, A-8790 Eisenerz
Natural History Museum - 1931
Coll: ore mining; historical finds;
models; land profiles and maps; tools;
minerals; archives - library

Eisenstadt

00649
Burgenländisches Landesmuseum
Museumgasse 1-5, A-7000 Eisenstadt
General Museum - 1926
Div: geology and paleontology;
archeology; zoology and botany; folk
customs; archives; manuscripts;
Judaica; military arts; medaillons and
orders; clocks - library; workshops;
specimen workshops

00650
Haydn-Museum
Haydngasse 21, A-7000 Eisenstadt
Historic Site - 1935
Haydn memorabilia; scores,
instruments, medals and other artifacts
of the period, housed in the
composer's former residence

00651
Schloss Esterházy
Schlossplatz 1, A-7000 Eisenstadt
Fine Arts Museum
Loan exhibitions of contemporary art;
Baroque interiors and furnishings;
Haydn Concert Hall

Enns

00652
Museum Lauriacum
Hauptplatz 19, A-4470 Enns
General Museum - 1892
Roman art and archaeology;
technology; art history; folk customs;
archives - library

Forchtenstein

00653
Schloß-Sammlungen
Neustift a.d.Rosalia, A-7210
Forchtenstein
History/Public Affairs Museum
Coll: objects, archives, and books
treating the history of the Reformation
in Austria, especially Kärnten

Freistadt

00654
Mühlviertler Heimathaus
Schloßhof 2, A-4240 Freistadt
General Museum - 1926
Coll: pre- and ancient history; geology;
local history; folk customs of the
Mühlviertel; glass paintings; peasant
furniture and tools; history of the
guilds; history of law and defence;
traditional costumes; textiles; jewelry;
archives - library

Fresach

00655
Evangelisches Diözesanmuseum
A-9712 Fresach
Religious Art Museum - 1960
Coll: history of the Reformation and
Protestantism in Austria and countries
of the former K.U.K. Monarchy;
documents; archives; books and
Bibles; hymnals

Friedberg

00656
**Museum der Stadtgemeinde
Friedberg**
Anton-Bauergasse, A-8240 Friedberg
General Museum
History of the Friedberg-Hungarian
border area; crafts and folk art of the
Middle Ages

Frohnleiten

00657
Privatsammlung Schloß Rabenstein
A-8130 Frohnleiten
History/Public Affairs Museum
Coll: historical furnishings; knight halls;
Baroque stucco ceilings; weapons
(16th-19th centuries); in 13th century
fortress

Fulpmes

00658
Schmiedemuseum
A-6166 Fulpmes
History/Public Affairs Museum - 1970
Old tools; ancient hammer smithy

Gleisdorf

00659
Heimatmuseum
Rathaus, Florianiplatz, A-8200
Gleisdorf
General Museum - 1965
Prehistoric and Roman artifacts; local
and regional history; peasant life;
tools; history of the post

Gloggnitz

00660
Dr.-Karl-Renner-Museum
Rennergasse 4, A-2640 Gloggnitz
History/Public Affairs Museum - 1978
Coll: in the former villa of the politician
Dr. Renner; exhibits on his private and
public life; archives

Gmünd

00661
Stadt-, Glas- und Steinmuseum
Stadtplatz 34, A-3950 Gmünd
General Museum
Coll: local history; minerals and
stones; guilds; weapons; handicrafts;
religious art; history of glass
production; glass-making tools;
glasses (16th-19th century); masonry

Gmunden

00662
Kammerhofmuseum
Kammerhofgasse 8, Postfach 74,
A-4810 Gmunden
General Museum - 1907
Local history; history of the salt trade;
local ceramics; Brahms and Hebbel
rooms; Brahms collection

Gobelsburg

00663
Schloßmuseum
Schloß Gobelsburg, Schloßstr. 16,
A-3550 Gobelsburg
General Museum - 1969
Prehistoric artifacts from local
excavations; Austrian peasant
furniture; folk art from the Ausseerland
area

Göttweig-Furth

00664
**Kunstsammlungen und Graphisches
Kabinett Stift Göttweig**
A-3511 Göttweig-Furth
Fine Arts Museum - 1960
Coll: historical rooms and interiors;
Roman art; 16th-18th century German,
Dutch, Italian, and French graphic arts
and drawings; 17th-18th century
copper plaques; numismatics; painting;
weapons; paraments; music archives;
portraits; topography; in 11th century
religious foundation - library

Graz

00665
Alte Galerie Steiermärkisches
Landesmuseum Joanneum
Neutorgasse 45, A-8010 Graz
Fine Arts Museum - 1941
Coll: medieval paintings; Austrian and
Southern German Baroque paintings;
arts and crafts from medieval times to
the present - library; archives;
workshops

00666
Bild- und Tonarchiv Steiermärkisches
Landesmuseum Joanneum
Sackstr. 17, A-8010 Graz
History/Public Affairs Museum
Coll: pictures of Styrian places and
historical buildings; portraits;
documentation of modern times

00667
Jakob-Gschiel-Gedenkstätte
Lorbeergasse 1, A-8020 Graz
Historic Site - 1975
Coll: in former house of the Styrian
sculptor Jakob Gschiel; original
sculptures, carved furniture, wooden
reliefs; documents; drawings; photos;
newspaper articles

00668
Landeszeughaus Steiermärkisches
Landesmuseum Joanneum
Herrengasse 16, A-8010 Graz
History/Public Affairs Museum - 1644
Coll: 16th-17th century weapons;
handarms; armor

00669
Neue Galerie Steiermärkisches
Landesmuseum Joanneum
Palais Eggenberg-Herberstein,
Sackstr. 16, A-8010 Graz
Fine Arts Museum - 1941
Austrian art of the 19th and 20th
centuries; 19th and 20th century
graphic art - library; audiovisual
learning center

00670
**Österreichisches Schloß- und
Schlüsselmuseum**
Griesgasse 14, A-8020 Graz
Decorative Arts Museum - 1973
Coll: historic locks and keys from
antiquity to the present from around
the world; tools; metal mountings

00671
Schloss Eggenberg Steiermärkisches
Landesmuseum Joanneum
Eggenberger Allee 90, A-8020 Graz
History/Public Affairs Museum - 1947
Coll: artifacts, gardens and interiors
from the 17th century; allegorical
paintings by Hans Adam
Weissenkircher, 14th century Gothic
chapel, 18th century church; hunting
illustrated by weapons, paintings,
dioramas, and trophies; pre- and
ancient history, coins from antiquity to
the 20th century, items from ancient
cultures from Egypt to Etruria; Roman
stone collection - library; workshops;
park with animals

00672
Stadtmuseum
Sackstr. 18, A-8010 Graz
General Museum - 1928
Coll: local history; topography;
graphics and photos of Graz; theater;
pharmacy; documentation on the
construction of the Graz castle

00673
**Steiermärkisches Landesmuseum
Joanneum**
Raubergasse 10, A-8010 Graz
General Museum - 1811
Botany Div.: European and
non-European plants, ferns, algea,
mushrooms, European wood types,
fruit and seeds, paintings of Alpine
plants; Geology Div.: paleontology,
and mining; Mineralogy Div.: precious
stones, meteorites, minerals; Zoology
Div.: Styrian animals, extinct animals,
and exotic fauna - library; workshops

00674
Steirisches Volkskundemuseum
Steiermärkisches Landesmuseum
Joanneum
Paulustorgasse 13, A-8010 Graz
Anthropology Museum - 1913
Coll: Styrian furnishings and interiors;
16th century smoke house; household
items and tools; tradition costumes;
customs and folk beliefs - library

00675
Tramway-Museum
Keplerstr. 105, A-8020 Graz
Science/Tech Museum - 1971
Coll: 19 old trollies, wagons, engines
from Graz, Innsbruck, Vienna,
Hungary, and Yugoslavia; wagons
from the Graz Castle mountain cable
railway

Greifenstein

00676
Burg Greifenstein
A-3422 Greifenstein
History/Public Affairs Museum
Coll: in 11th century fortress; historic
period rooms; weapons; folk customs
and art; history of the fortress - library

Greillenstein

00677
Schloßmuseum
Schloß Greillenstein, A-3592
Greillenstein
History/Public Affairs Museum - 1959
Coll: in 16th century castle with
Baroque gardens designed by
Fischer; historic period rooms;
portraits and paintings; weapons;
uniforms; documents; collection of
items on ancient law, including
instruments of torture, documents on
crime and police, court room

Grein a.d.Donau

00678
Österreichisches Schiffahrtsmuseum
mail c/o Coburg'sche FV Greinburg,
Greinburg 1, A-4360 Grein a.d.Donau
History/Public Affairs Museum - 1970
Coll: navigation from antiquity to the
present; Danube, Inn, Salzach, and
Enns ship transportation; rafts; history
of rowboat navigation on the Danube

Großreifling

00679
Österreichisches Forstmuseum
A-8931 Großreifling
Natural History Museum - 1979
Coll: wood types; wood processing;
vehicles for wood transport; exhibits
on forestry; documentation

Gutenstein

00680
Waldbauernmuseum
Alte Hofmühle, Markt 31, Postfach 11,
A-2770 Gutenstein
General Museum - 1965
Woodworking tools and equipment;
1767 sawmill; dioramas; drawings,
paintings, photos, and etchings; wood
production and its by-products

Haag

00681
Haager Heimatstuben
Schloß Starhemberg, A-4680 Haag
General Museum - 1966
Coll: in 12th century fortress and later
Renaissance building; local history;
mining; local handicrafts; guilds;
agriculture; peasant life

Hall in Tirol

00682
Stadtmuseum
Oberer Stadtplatz 1, Postfach 84,
A-6060 Hall in Tirol
General Museum - 1922
history of guilds; mining; fine arts;
coins; arms and armor; prehistoric
artifacts

Hallein

00683
Keltenmuseum
Pflegerplatz 5, A-5400 Hallein
History/Public Affairs Museum
Coll: pre- and ancient history; Latène
findings; prehistoric salt mining;
topography; town history; archives -
library

Hallstatt

00684
**Prähistorisches Museum/
Heimathaus**
Seestr. 56, A-4830 Hallstatt
General Museum - 1844
Coll: folklore; local finds from Hallstatt
and Latène periods; local salt mining;
Roman provincial art; ornithology;
wood cross-sections - library

Haslach

00685
Webereimuseum
Kirchenplatz 3, A-4170 Haslach
History/Public Affairs Museum - 1970
Coll: flax processing; thread; hand and
mechanized weaving; printing and
dying; starch and linseed oil; history of
linen production

Haus

00686
Dekanatsmuseum
A-8967 Haus
History/Public Affairs Museum - 1964
Coll: history of the Upper Inn Valley;
religious customs; Christian art;
Peasant War; Reformation and
Counter-Reformation; folk beliefs;
pilgrimages; ecclesiastical art

Hellmonsödt

00687
Freilichtmuseum Pelmberg
A-4202 Hellmonsödt
Open Air Museum

Hermagor

00688
Gailtaler Heimatmuseum
Bahnhofstraße, A-9620 Hermagor
General Museum - 1900
Coll: pre- and ancient history; natural
history; peasant life during the
Baroque and Biedermeier periods;
glass paintings; traditional costumes;
musical instruments; Hafner ceramics;
painting; Gothic wooden statuettes;
religious books and ancient Bibles -
library

Herzogenburg

00689
**Kunstausstellung Stift
Herzogenburg**
Stiftsgebäude 3, A-3130
Herzogenburg
Fine Arts Museum
Coll: in 12th century cloister; medieval
art; Baroque painting, sculpture, arts
and crafts; paraments; prehistoric
items; coins; incunabula; archives -
library

Hollabrunn

00690
Neues Museum
Hofmühle, A-2020 Hollabrunn
General Museum
Coll: pre- and ancient history; local
history; folk customs and art;
numismatics; medaillons

Horn

00691
Höbarthmuseum
Wienerstr. 4, A-3580 Horn
Natural History Museum - 1973
Local prehistory; geology and
mineralogy; art and folk art

Imst

00692
Heimatmuseum
Ballgasse 1, A-6460 Imst
General Museum - 1911
Prehistoric finds; works of local
artists; manger scenes; country
furniture and utensils

Innsbruck

00693
Archäologische Sammlung der Universität
Innrain 52, A-6020 Innsbruck
Archeology Museum
Original works and casts of Antique sculpture

00694
Berg-Isel-Museum der Tiroler Kaiserjäger
Berg Isel Nr. 3, A-6020 Innsbruck
General Museum - 1880
History of the 1809 War of Independence ; memorabilia of Andreas Hofer; history of the former Tirolian Imperial Regiment

00695
Hofburt, Silberne Kapelle und Hofkirche
Rennweg 1, A-6020 Innsbruck
Historic Site
Late 18th cent. furnishings and decorations in former imperial residence, built by Maximilian I; ceiling paintings, portraits and tapestries

00696
Kunsthistorische Sammlungen
Schloss Ambras
Schlossstrasse 20, A-6020 Innsbruck
Fine Arts Museum - 1580
Painting; weapons; period furnishings

00697
Museum der Tiroler Kaiserschützen
Museumstr. 15, A-6020 Innsbruck
General Museum - 1931
history of the Tirol marksmen

00698
Prämonstratenser Chorherrenstift Wilten
Klostergasse 7, A-6020 Innsbruck
Fine Arts Museum - 1138
Sculpture and painting from Gothic to Baroque, in historic rooms; tin collection

00699
Sammlungen Schloß Ambras
A-6020 Innsbruck
Fine Arts Museum
Art, armor; antiquarium

00700
Tiroler Landeskundliches Museum im Zeughaus
Zeughausgasse, D-6020 Innsbruck
Science/Tech Museum - 1973
Mineralogy and mining; hunting; musical instruments; cartography

00701
Tiroler Landesmuseum Ferdinandeum
Museumsstr. 15, A-6020 Innsbruck
General Museum - 1823
Prehistory; European painting and sculpture (Romanesque to present); decorative arts; coins

00702
Tiroler Volkskunstmuseum
Universitätsstr. 2, A-6020 Innsbruck
Decorative Arts Museum - 1888
Tirolian folk arts

Jedenspeigen

00703
Urgeschichtssammlung und Heimatmuseum
Sierndorf a.d.M., Nr. 80, A-2264 Jedenspeigen
General Museum - 1950
Local history; folklore; wine production; farm implements and household utensils; artworks; weapons; masonry collection - library

Judenburg

00704
Heimatmuseum
Kaserngasse 1, A-8750 Judenburg
General Museum - 1948
Local and regional history; mineralogy; crafts and trades; art works; folklore; coins; contemporary history

Kindberg

00705
Ungarisches Adelskapitel
Schloß Hart, A-8650 Kindberg
General Museum - 1956
Hungarian decorative arts and folklore; Hungarian genealogy and heraldry

Kirchberg am Wechsel

00706
Ludwig-Wittgenstein-Dokumentation
A-2880 Kirchberg am Wechsel 1
History/Public Affairs Museum - 1874
Photos, works and memorabilia of the philosopher Ludwig Wittgenstein

Kitzeck

00707
I. Steirisches Weinmuseum
Steinriegel 16, A-8442 Kitzeck
Science/Tech Museum - 1979
Presses and other implements used in viticulture

Klagenfurt

00708
Bergbaumuseum
Klinkstr. 6, A-9020 Klagenfurt
Science/Tech Museum - 1973
Mining equipment; documentation on history of mining in Kärnten; mineralogy

00709
Diözesanmuseum
Lidmanskygasse 10, A-9020 Klagenfurt
Religious Art Museum - 1917
Religious art from Kärnten (12th-18th cent.)

00710
Kärntner Landesgalerie
Burggasse 8, A-9020 Klagenfurt
Fine Arts Museum - 1933
19th and 20th cent. art from Kärnten; decorative arts

00711
Landesmuseum für Kärnten
Museumgasse 2, A-9010 Klagenfurt
General Museum - 1844/1884
Archeology and prehistory; cultural history; zoology; geology; botany; folklore

Klosterneuburg

00712
Mährisch-Schlesisches Heimatmuseum
Schießstattgasse 2, A-3400 Klosterneuburg
Anthropology Museum - 1957
Folklore of East and West Silesia and Moravia

00713
Museum des Chorherrenstifts Klosterneuburg
Stiftsplatz 1, A-3400 Klosterneuburg
Fine Arts Museum
Medieval panel painting; decorative arts - library

Krems

00714
Historisches Museum und Weinbaumuseum
Dominikanerplatz 8/9, A-3500 Krems
General Museum - 1891/1928
History of the Krems region from prehistoric to modern times; crafts and trades; furnishings and folklore; viticulture; contemporary arts

Kremsmünster

00715
Kunstsammlungen, Fischbehälter u. Naturwissenschaftliche Sammlungen des Stifts Kremsmünster
Benediktinerstift, A-4550 Kremsmünster
General Museum
Zoology, mineralogy, geology, paleontology and anthropology; physics and astronomy; Gothic, Renaissance, Baroque and Biedermeier art works; armor - library

Krieglach

00716
Peter-Rosegger-Museum
Peter-Rosegger-Str. 233, A-8670 Krieglach
Historic Site - 1947
Photos, documents, first editions and memorabilia of Peter Rosegger in rooms he occupied; typical country furniture and furnishings from the Styria region

Kufstein

00717
Heimatmuseum auf der Burg Kufstein
Baumgartnerstr. 5, A-6330 Kufstein
General Museum - a907
Early Bronze Period artifacts; bird collection; peasant rooms; paintings by Kufstein artists

Landsee

00718
Burgenländisches Steinmuseum
Markt St. Martin, A-7341 Landsee
Open Air Museum - 1876
Geology of the Burgenland

Längenfeld

00719
Ötztaler Freilichtmuseum
A-6444 Längenfeld
Open Air Museum - 1968
Historic farmhouses and outbuildings of the Ötztal region; farm implements and household utensils

Langenlois

00720
Schloßmuseum Gobelsburg
Schloßstr. 16, A-3550 Langenlois
Anthropology Museum - 1966
Austrian majolica; peasant furniture and glass; folk arts

Langenzersdorf

00721
Anton-Hanak-Museum
Obere Kirchengasse 23, A-2103 Langenzersdorf
Fine Arts Museum - 1970
Sculpture, sketches and drawings of Anton Hanak (local resident 1901-1923)

Launsdorf

00722
Burg Hochosterwitz
A-9314 Launsdorf
History/Public Affairs Museum
Weapons and armor (16th-17th cent.), family portraits, housed in historic medieval fortress; history of the Khevenhüller family, owners of the fortress since the 16th cent.

Leibnitz

00723
Römermuseum Frauenberg
A-8430 Leibnitz
Archeology Museum - 1955
Roman temple ruins (1st cent. A.D.) and finds from former Roman settlement Flavia Solva (lamps, ceramics, glass, coins, inscriptions)

00724
Römische Steindenkmäler
Schloß Seggau, A-8430 Leibnitz
Archeology Museum
Gravestones, votive panels, and reliefs from the ancient Roman graveyard at Flavia Solva

Lendorf

00725
Museum Teurnia
St. Peter in Holz, A-9811 Lendorf
Fine Arts Museum - 1911
Early Christian mosaics, Roman monuments and inscriptions, and small grave finds from local ancient settlement; preserved early Christian basilica

Leoben

00726
Brauereimuseum
A-8707 Leoben
Science/Tech Museum - 1970
Old brewery tools and implements, housed in former malt house

00727
Museum der Stadt
Kirchgasse 6, A-8700 Leoben
General Museum - 1883/1970
Early history; zoology, mineralogy and mining; art works (Gothic to Baroque); incunabula; old tools; decorative arts; weapons (18th-19th cent.) - library and archive

Lienz

00728
Osttiroler Heimatmuseum Museum der Stadt Lienz
Schloß Bruck, A-9900 Lienz
General Museum - 1907
Natural history; folklore and folk arts; farm implements; costumes and domestic utensils; painting

Linz

00729
Adalbert-Stifter-Institut des Landes Oberösterreich
Stifterhaus, Untere Donaulände 6, A-4020 Linz
History/Public Affairs Museum - 1950
Literature by and about Adalbert Stifter; Upper Austrian literature - library

00730
Neue Galerie der Stadt Linz
Wolfgang-Gurlitt-Museum
Im Lentia 2000, Blütenstr. 15, A-4020
Linz
Fine Arts Museum
19th and 20th century art; works of
Alfred Kubin - library of catalogues

00731
Oberösterreichisches
Landesmuseum
Tummerplatz 10 and Museumstr. 14,
Postfach 91, A-4020 Linz
General Museum - 1833
Worldwide collection of birds of prey;
natural and social history of Upper
Austria - library

Marchegg

00732
Jagdmuseum
Schloß Marchegg, A-2293 Marchegg
Anthropology Museum - 1959
History of hunting in Lower Austria;
hunting in art; hunting customs around
the world; stuffed animals

Maria Saal

00733
Kärntner Freilichtmuseum
Museumweg 1, A-9063 Maria Saal
Open Air Museum - 1960
Kärnten farm houses and interiors

Mariazell

00734
Heimatmuseum
Wienerstr. 35, A-8630 Mariazell
General Museum - 1973
Peasant furniture and household
utensils; votive offerings, glass
paintings, prayer books and other
items of religious folk art; decorative
cast iron works; crafts

00735
Schatzkammer der Basilika
Kardinal-Eugéne-Tisserant-Platz 1,
A-8630 Mariazell
Religious Art Museum
Religious arts and crafts (14th-18th
cent.) including cathedral treasure

Mauterndorf

00736
Sammlungen Schloß Moosham
A-5570 Mauterndorf
Fine Arts Museum
Painting, sculpture, frescoes; faience;
antique stoves; arms and armor; local
folk and decorative arts

Melk

00737
Benediktiner-Stift u. Stifts-
Sammlungen
A-3390 Melk
Religious Art Museum - 1960
Medieval and Baroque religious art
and crafts - library

Mittersill

00738
Heimatmuseum
A-5730 Mittersill
General Museum - 1960
Farm and country culture, including
examples of tools, furnishings and
domestic utensils; minerals; crafts;
skiing exhibit; local and regional
history

Mödling

00739
Missions-Ethnographisches
Museum St. Gabriel
Gabrielerstr. 171, A-2340 Mödling
Anthropology Museum - 1909
medieval Chinese sculpture; artifacts
from Papua New Guinea

00740
Stadtmuseum
Josef-Deutsch-Platz 2, A-2340 Mödling
General Museum - 1901
Artifacts from local Avarian burial site;
folklore; botanical and mineralogical
collections - library

Mondsee

00741
Freilichtmuseum Mondseer
Rauchhaus
Hilfbergstr. 7, A-5310 Mondsee
Anthropology Museum - 1959
Renovated historic smokehouse and
other buildings; peasant furnishings,
tools and implements

00742
Heimatmuseum
Marschall-v.-Wrede-Platz, A-5310
Mondsee
General Museum - 1953
Early local history; art works from the
Mondsee monestary; folk art; book
illumination; costume collection;
hunting collection

Murau

00743
Eisenmuseum
Schloß Murau, A-8850 Murau
Science/Tech Museum - 1957
Local iron ore mining and heavy
industry

Mürzzuschlag

00744
Wintersport- und Heimatmuseum
Wiener Str. 79, A-8680 Mürzzuschlag
General Museum - 1946
History and development of winter
sports; farm implements; folklore

Niederleis

00745
Schloßmuseum
A-2116 Niederleis
Fine Arts Museum - 1964
Sculpture, painting, tapestries, faience,
glass, etc. in Renaissance moated
castle

Oberndorf

00746
Heimatmuseum
Salzburger Str. 88, A-5110 Oberndorf
General Museum - 1960
Local and regional history; crafts and
guilds; costumes; clocks and watches;
Salzach River navigation; weapons; art
works; history of the Christmas carol,
'Silent Night'

Oberperfuss

00747
Peter-Anich-Museum
Schulhaus, A-6173 Oberperfuss
Science/Tech Museum - 1906
Memorabilia of the cartographers
Peter Anich (1723-1766) and Blasius
Heuber (1735-1818); astronomical
instruments, maps and globes

Oberzeiring

00748
Schaubergwerk und Museum
A-8762 Oberzeiring
Science/Tech Museum - 1958
Reconstructed 13th cent. silver mine;
history of mining; minerals; folklore

00749
Silber-Schaubergwerk
A-8762 Oberzeiring
Science/Tech Museum - 1956
12th century silver mining techniques

Orth

00750
Heimatmuseum /
Bienenzuchtmuseum
Schloß, A-2304 Orth
General Museum - 1957
Local and regional history; domestic
utensils; weapons, natural history;
development of beekeeping in Austria
from earliest times to present

00751
Österreichisches Fischereimuseum
Schloß, A-2304 Orth
Science/Tech Museum - 1961
Development of international fresh
water and deep sea fishing industry;
local fishes and fishing; fresh water
aquarium

Perchtoldsdorf

00752
Hugo-Wolf-Gedenkstätte
Brunnergasse 26, A-2380
Perchtoldsdorf
History/Public Affairs Museum
Memorabilia of composer Hugo Wolf
(1860-1903), in originally furnished
rooms

00753
Museum im Rathaus
A-2380 Perchtoldsdorf
General Museum - 1970
Historic late Gothic building; frescos;
portraits; viticulture exhibition

Petronell

00754
Donaumuseum
Schloß Petronell, A-2404 Petronell
General Museum - 1956
Danube River in historical, cultural,
economic, geological and scientific
perspective; models of castles,
fortresses and towns in the Danube
valley

00755
Freilichtmuseum Carnuntum
A-2404 Petronell
Open Air Museum - 1949
Ruins of the ancient Roman town
Carnuntum

00756
Kunstgewerbemuseum
Schloß Petronell, A-2404 Petronell
Decorative Arts Museum - 1963
Furniture, costumes; Venetian glass;
ceramics; metalwork; ivories; frescos
and portrait gallery

Peuerbach

00757
Bauernkriegmuseum
Schloss Peuerbach, Hauptstr. 19,
A-4722 Peuerbach
History/Public Affairs Museum
Artifacts from the period of the
Peasants' War

Pischeldorf

00758
Ausgrabungsmuseum
Magdalensberg
A-9064 Pischeldorf
Archeology Museum - 1948
Early Roman and late Antique art and
architectural remains, housed in
reconstructed antique buildings

Pöchlarn

00759
Heimatmuseum
Regensburgerstr., A-3380 Pöchlarn
General Museum - 1927
Roman and prehistorical artifacts; local
peasant artifacts

Pottenbrunn

00760
Österreichisches Zinnfiguren-
Museum
A-3140 Pottenbrunn
History/Public Affairs Museum - 1969
Austrian history, especially military
history, displayed by 35,000 tin figures
in 26 dioramas

Raiding

00761
Liszt-Museum
Liszt-Str. 42, A-7321 Raiding
Historic Site - 1911
Documents, scores, photos,
autographs and memorabilia of Franz
Liszt (1811-1886), displayed in the
composer's birth place

Reichersberg

00762
Museum des Chorherrenstiftes
A-4981 Reichersberg
Religious Art Museum - 1966
Paintings, sculpture, documents, etc.,
displayed in historic monastery rooms
- library

Reidling

00763
Niederösterreichisches
Barockmuseum
Schloß Heiligenkreuz-Gutenbrunn,
A-3454 Reidling
Fine Arts Museum - 1964
Baroque and Rococo interiors and
furnishings; Baroque decorative arts
(glass, majolica; tin); costume
collection; graphics

Ried im Innkreis

00764
Innviertler Volkskundehaus und
Galerie der Stadt Ried
Kirchenplatz 13, Postfach 100, A-4910
Ried im Innkreis
General Museum - 1933
Religious folk art - library

Riegersburg

00765
Burg Riegersburg
A-8333 Riegersburg
General Museum
Weapons; instruments of torture;
history of the Lichtenstein family;
Asian and African exhibits

00766
Schloßmuseum
A-2092 Riegersburg
Fine Arts Museum - 1957
Original 18th cent. furnishings in a
Baroque palace (Fischer von Erlach,
1736); permanent exhibit on
aristocratic taste in the 18th cent.

Riezlern
00767
Walser Museum
A-6991 Riezlern
General Museum - 1969
History and geology of the Wals
Valley; folk art and customs; farm
implements; sculpture and painting

Rohrau
00768
**Graf Harrach'sche
Familiensammlung**
Schloss, A-2471 Rohrau
Fine Arts Museum - 1850
Spanish and Neapolitan Baroque
painting; 19th century furniture; period
furnishings
00769
Haydn-Museum
A-2471 Rohrau 66
Historic Site - 1959
Pictures, scores and memorabilia of
Joseph Haydn (1732-1809), displayed
in the composer's birthplace

Rosenau
00770
**Österreichisches
Freimaurermuseum**
Schloß Rosenau, A-3924 Rosenau
Anthropology Museum - 1974
History of Freemasonry

Salzburg
00771
Burgmuseum
Festung Hohensalzburg, A-5020
Salzburg
History/Public Affairs Museum - 1959
Weapons and armor; historical
artifacts related to history of law and
order
00772
Dommuseum zu Salzburg
Kapitelplatz 2, A-5010 Salzburg
Fine Arts Museum - 1974
Cathedral treasure; 'Rupertus' cross
(8th century)
00773
Haus der Natur
Museumsplatz 5, A-5020 Salzburg
Natural History Museum - 1924
Mineralogy; geology; paleontology;
human biology; nature and
environment in various continents;
marine biology; man and space
00774
Mozart-Museum
Getreidegasse 9, A-5020 Salzburg
Historic Site - 1880
Portraits, scores, books, musical
instruments and other memorabilia of
W.A. Mozart, displayed in the
composer's birthplace
00775
Mozarts Wohnhaus
Makartplatz 8, A-5020 Salzburg
Historic Site - 1955
Historic music instruments; Mozart
autographs

00776
Rainer-Regiments-Museum
Festung Hohensalzburg, A-5020
Salzburg
History/Public Affairs Museum - 1927
History of the Imperial 'Archduke
Rainer' Regiment; uniforms and
equipment of the Austrian alpine
troops in WW II; history of the
Austrian Army in both world wars
00777
Salzburger Barockmuseum
Mirabellgarten, Orangerie, A-5020
Salzburg
Fine Arts Museum - 1973
Plans and drawings for monumental
works in the European Baroque style
00778
Salzburger Landessammlungen
Residenzgalerie
Residenzplatz 1, A-5020 Salzburg
Fine Arts Museum - 1789/1923
European painting from the 15th to the
19th cent.
00779
**Salzburger Museum Carolino
Augusteum**
Museumsplatz 1-6, Postfach 525,
A-5010 Salzburg
General Museum - 1834
Archaeology; crafts and folk arts; fine
arts - library; projection and film room
00780
Spielzeugmuseum
Bürgerspitalgasse 2, A-5020 Salzburg
Anthropology Museum - 1978
Old and new toys in all materials
(wood, metal, paper, clay, etc.); dolls
and doll houses - playroom; stage
00781
Trakl-Gedenkstätte
Waagplatz 1a, A-5020 Salzburg
Historic Site - 1978
Furnishings, letters, documents, works
and memorabilia of Georg Trakl
(1887-1914), displayed in the poet's
birthplace; secondary literature on
Trakl
00782
Volkskundemuseum
Schloß Hellbrunn, A-5020 Salzburg
Decorative Arts Museum - 1924
Folklore and customs; glass, faience
and porcelain; peasant furnishings;
costumes; weapons

Sankt Florian
00783
Oberösterreichisches Jagdmuseum
Schloß Hohenbrunn, A-4490 Sankt
Florian
Decorative Arts Museum - 1967
Historic weapons; tapestries;
porcelain and faience; glass and silver
with hunting motives; 18th cent.
hunting paintings; memorabilia of
Emperor Franz Joseph I
00784
**Sammlungen des Augustiner
Chorherrenstifts St. Florian**
Stiftstr. 1, A-4490 Sankt Florian
General Museum
Historic rooms; painting and sculpture;
decorative arts; graphic collection;
minerals and natural history collection
00785
Stiftssammlungen Augustiner
Chorherrenstift
Stiftstr. 1, A-4490 Sankt Florian
Fine Arts Museum - 1071
Painting; interiors; sculpture

St. Johann
00786
Schloßmuseum
Herbertstein, A-8222 St. Johann
History/Public Affairs Museum - 1937
Coll: in 13th century castle; historic
period rooms; 14th century frescoes;
arms and armor; saddles and horse
harnesses; Baroque chapel; portraits;
household utensils; agricultural
equipment

**Sankt Johann bei
Herberstein**
00787
**Familienmuseum Schloss
Herberstein**
Buchberg 1, A-8222 Sankt Johann bei
Herberstein
General Museum
Weapons; portrain gallery; saddles;
glass; porcelain

St. Johann i.S.
00788
Rauchstubenhaus
Gündorf 11, A-8453 St. Johann i.S.
History/Public Affairs Museum
Coll: peasant life and furnishings;
tools; in 18th century smoke house

St. Lambrecht
00789
**Sammlungen des Stiftes St.
Lambrecht**
Hauptstr. 1, A-8813 St. Lambrecht
General Museum - 1848
Div: historical period rooms, religious
art, in particular Gothic and 17th-18th
century panel paintings and sculpture;
ornithology, stuffed mammals,
minerals, natural science; religious folk
art, peasant furniture and household
utensils from upper Styria; in 11th
century cloister

St. Martin
00790
**Votivsammlung der Wallfahrtskirche
Maria Kirchental**
A-5092 St. Martin
Religious Art Museum - 1962
Coll: votive tablets donated by pilgrims
since 1690; in 17th century church

St. Paul
00791
Stiftsmuseum
Benediktinerstift, A-9470 St. Paul
Religious Art Museum - 1809
Coll: in 11th century cloister; 17th-18th
century ecclesiastical items; paintings;
graphics; porcelain; coins; paraments;
archives; incunabula - library

Sankt Paul i. Lav.
00792
**Kunstsammlungen des
Benediktinerstiftes**
Benediktinerstift, A-9470 Sankt Paul i.
Lav.
Fine Arts Museum - 1809
Romanesque art - library

St. Pölten
00793
Diözesan-Museum
Domplatz 1, A-3100 St. Pölten
Religious Art Museum - 1888
Coll: panel paintings; sculpture; Gothic
glass painting and copper etchings;
religious art; liturgical items; Baroque
furniture; pre- and ancient history;
ceramics; Roman finds; coins and
medaillons; seals since antiquity;
mineralogy; zoology; botany; fossils;
archives; incunabula
00794
Stadtmuseum
Prandtauerstr. 2, A-3100 St. Pölten
General Museum - 1879
Coll: pre- and ancient history; local
and regional history; economics;
post-1820 theater; coins; late medieval
art in St. Pölten; Baroque sculpture
and painting

Schallaburg
00795
Museum Schloß Schallaburg
A Schallaburg
History/Public Affairs Museum
Coll: history of the castle; period
rooms with historic furnishings; in
Renaissance castle

Schärding
00796
Heimathaus
Schloßgasse, A-4780 Schärding
General Museum - 1906
Coll: town and regional history;
prehistoric finds; folk customs and art;
peasant and town-dweller furnishings;
arts and crafts; Gothic and Baroque
painting and sculpture; superstitions;
memorabilia of the poets M. Denis and
R. Billinger and the chronicler J.E.
Lamprecht

Scharnstein
00797
Strafrechtsmuseum
Schloß, A-4644 Scharnstein
History/Public Affairs Museum
Exhibits on criminal law

Schladming
00798
Stadtmuseum
Reissinger-Behausung,
Vernoulettgasse 68, A-8970
Schladming
General Museum
Minerals; mining equipment; history of
Schladming; folk sagas; geology

Schlaining
00799
Burg Schlaining mit Museum
Rochusplatz 1, A-7461 Schlaining
History/Public Affairs Museum - 1956
Coll: period interiors and domestic
utensils from the Renaissance,
Baroque, and Rococo periods;
17th-19th century painting; weapons;
historical musical instruments;
post-1600 ironwork

Schlierbach

00800
Sammlungen des Zisterzienserstifts
Stift, A-4553 Schlierbach
Religious Art Museum
Coll: historical interiors; religious arts
and crafts; in 14th century Cistercien
cloister - library

Schwarzenberg

00801
Gemeindemuseum
No. 34, A-6867 Schwarzenberg
General Museum - 1913
Coll: local and regional history;
peasant life, furnishings, and
handicrafts, traditional costumes;
weapons; memorial to the painters
Bartle Kleber, Jokob Fink, and
Angelika Kauffmann

Seckau

00802
**Benediktinerabtei und
Abteimuseum**
A-8732 Seckau
History/Public Affairs Museum
Coll: historical interiors; religious art
and liturgical items; coins; in 12th
century cloister - library

Seeboden

00803
Kärntner Fischereimuseum
A-9871 Seeboden
History/Public Affairs Museum
Exhibits on fisheries especially from
the Millstätt sea

Seitenstetten

00804
**Kunstsammlungen Stift
Seitenstetten**
Am Klosterberg 1, A-3353
Seitenstetten
Fine Arts Museum
Coll: historical buildings from 12th-18th
centuries; interiors; sculpture; Gothic
to Baroque painting and sculpture;
natural histor; graphics; manuscripts;
archeology; music archives - library

Siegendorf-Schuschenwald

00805
**Freilichtmuseum
Spätbronzezeitlicher Hügelgräber**
A-7011 Siegendorf-Schuschenwald
Open Air Museum - 1974
Coll: excavated and reconstructed
mound grave of a warrior from 1200
B.C.; grave finds

Solbad Hall

00806
Bergbaumuseum
Oberer Stadtplatz, A-6060 Solbad Hall
Science/Tech Museum
Coll: reconstructed salt mine; minerals

00807
Stadtmuseum
A-6060 Solbad Hall
General Museum - 1933
Coll: prehistory; history; cultural and
economic development of the town as
a center of salt mining, coin and glass
production; handicrafts; religious
crafts (17th-18th centuries); medieval
cloister in Hall Valley

Spital am Pyhrn

00808
Österreichisches Felsbildermuseum
No. 382, A-4582 Spital am Pyhrn
Archeology Museum - 1979
Coll: photos, slides, and graphics of
the prehistoric rock drawings
discovered in Austria in 1958

Spittal

00809
Bezirksheimatmuseum
Edlingerstr., A-9800 Spittal
General Museum - 1958
Coll: period rooms of the 16th century
castle; local and regional history;
fishing and hunting; folk art;
handicrafts; toys; customs; religious
art; paintings of Karl Truppe and
history of his school; glass production
in Upper Carinthia; mining; pottery;
archives - library

Spitz

00810
Schiffahrtsmuseum
Auf der Wehr 21, A-3620 Spitz
Science/Tech Museum - 1969
Coll: history and development of
navigation of the Danube; rowboat and
raft navigation; tools and equipment
used in ship building; models of old
ships and rafts; open air museum with
two historical wooden ships

Stadl-Paura

00811
Schiffleutemuseum
Pfarrhof, A-4651 Stadl-Paura
History/Public Affairs Museum - 1934
Coll: history of navigation of the Traun;
models; local history; peasant
furnishings

Stainz

00812
Steirisches Bauernmuseum
Schloß Stainz, A-8510 Stainz
History/Public Affairs Museum - 1968
Coll: Styrian peasant life; furniture,
domestic utensils, tools; 16th-18th
century peasant rooms; cookbooks;
archives on 'Baumkuchen' - workshop

Stams

00813
**Zisterzienserstift und
Stiftssammlungen**
A-6422 Stams
Religious Art Museum
Coll: ornate historical rooms; religious
art; artistic locks; inlaid work; in 13th
century Cistercian cloister

Stans

00814
Schloß Tratzberg mit Sammlungen
A-6135 Stans
History/Public Affairs Museum
Coll: historic period rooms; furnishings
and crafts (late Gothic to early
Renaissance); painting; armor;
weapons; in 13th century castle

Steyr

00815
Heimathaus
Grünermarkt 26, A-4400 Steyr
General Museum - 1913
Historical armor and weapons;
Baroque interiors; knife collection (500
exhibits from 4 continents); folklore;
local history

Straßburg

00816
Diözesan- und Heimatmuseum 2
Schloß Straßburg, A-9341 Straßburg
General Museum - 1961
Historical interiors; religious folk art;
peasant household and farming
utensils

Stübing bei Graz

00817
Österreichisches Freilichtmuseum
A-8114 Stübing bei Graz
Open Air Museum - 1962
Farm houses and village buildings

Telfs

00818
Heimatmuseum
Untermarktstr. 18, 6410 Telfs
General Museum - 1966
Folk art; tools and domestic utensils;
manger scenes; masks worn in local
folk festival

Villach

00819
Museum der Stadt Villach
Widmanngasse 38, A-9500 Villach
General Museum - 1873
Local archaeology; municipal history;
local landscape painting (19th century);
local minerals and fossils; large-scale
topographical map of Kärnten (in
Schillerpark)

Vöcklamarkt

00820
Kinderweltmuseum
Schloß Walchen, A-4870 Vöcklamarkt
Anthropology Museum - 1979
The world of the child in all its aspects
(education, clothing, play, food, etc.)

Waidhofen an der Thaya

00821
Heimatmuseum
Wienerstr. 14 und Schadekgasse 4,
A-3830 Waidhofen an der Thaya
General Museum
crafts; folk art; glass painting

Warmbad-Villach

00822
Archäologische Sammlung
Kurhaus, Kadischenallee 22, A-9504
Warmbad-Villach
Archeology Museum
Archaeology

Weißenkirchen

00823
Wachaumuseum
Teisenhornerhof, A-3610
Weissenkirchen
Fine Arts Museum - 1965
Painting of the Wachau School (late
19th century)

00824
Wachaumuseum
Teisenhoferhof, A-3610
Weißenkirchen
General Museum - 1965
Paintings of the Wachau school (late
19th c.); Baroque painting; folklore;
press hut with old wine press

Wenigzell

00825
Heimathaus
A-8254 Wenigzell
General Museum - 1964
Functional old grinding mill and
equipment; ceramics; street lamp
collection; religious folk art; peasant
furniture

Wien

00826
Adalbert-Stifter-Museum
Mölkerbastei 8, A-1010 Wien
History/Public Affairs Museum - 1918
Coll: life and works of the writer
Adalbert Stifter; his paintings,
drawings, manuscripts, and first
editions; archives - library

00827
Beethoven-Wohnung
Probusgasse 6, A-1190 Wien
History/Public Affairs Museum - 1970
Photos of the 'Heiligenstädter
Testament' written by Beethoven in
1802 in this apartment; pictures of
Heiligenstadt and environs

00828
Beethoven-Wohnung Pasqualatihaus
Mölkerbastei 8, A-1010 Wien
History/Public Affairs Museum - 1941
Coll: memorabilia of Beethoven; room
in which he died; portraits of
Beethoven and his friends; music
scores

00829
Bezirksmuseum Alsergrund
Währinger Str. 43, A-1090 Wien
General Museum - 1958
Coll: topography; district history;
memorial to the writer Heimito von
Doderer, including his study with
original furnishings; documentation on
Doderer - library

00830
Bezirksmuseum Döbling
Döblinger Hauptstr. 96, A-1190 Wien
General Museum - 1963
Coll: historic interiors in 19th century
Villa Wertheimstein; memorials to the
writers Friedrich von Saar and Eduard
von Bauernfeld; district history
including maps, medaillons, music,
geology, local artists; archives -
library

00831
Bundessammlung Alter Stilmöbel
Mariahilfer Str. 88, A-1070 Wien
Decorative Arts Museum - 1920
Coll: Austrian early Baroque -
Biedermeier period furniture from
imperial estate - workshops

00832
Elektropathologisches Museum
Selzergasse 19, A-1150 Wien
Science/Tech Museum - 1904
Coll: exhibits on damage to organic
and anorganic objects caused by
electricity; protective measures and
first aid; electropathology; archives -
library

00833
Ephesos-Museum, Antikensammlung
Kunsthistorisches Museum Wien
Neue Hofburg, Heldenplatz, A-1010
Wien
Archeology Museum - 1978
Coll: finds from the Austrian
excavations in Ephesos and
Samothrace; Greek and Roman
architecture and sculpture; archives -
library; workshops; photo laboratory

00834
**Erzbischöfliches Dom- und
Diözesanmuseum**
Stephansplatz 6/1, A-1010 Wien
Religious Art Museum - 1932
Sacred art from the Middle Ages to
the present

00835
Feuerwehrmuseum
Zentralfeuerwache
Am Hof 20, A Wien
History/Public Affairs Museum
Coll: fire fighting and civil defense
work

00836
Fiakermuseum
Veronikagasse 12, A-1170 Wien
History/Public Affairs Museum - 1963
Coll: development of the Viennese
coachman profession; models;
pictures; originals; archives - library

00837
Friedrich-Julius-Bieber-Museum
Tuersgasse 21, A-1130 Wien
Anthropology Museum - 1905
Ethnologic collections of Ethiopia and
Tibesti (Sahara)

00838
Galerie Graf Czernin
Friedrich-Schmidt-Platz 4, A-1080
Wien
Fine Arts Museum
Paintings

00839
Gemäldegalerie Akademie der
Bildenden Künste
Schillerplatz 3, A-1010 Wien
Fine Arts Museum - 1829
European master paintings, especially
17th century Dutch painting and 20th
century Viennese painting; archives -
library; photo laboratory; workshop

00840
Geymüller-Schlössel Sammlung
Sobek
Khevenhüllerstr. 2, A-1180 Wien
Decorative Arts Museum - 1965
Coll: Empire and Biedermeier furniture
and paintings (1800-1850); Viennese
clocks of the Biedermeier period

00841
Glockensammlung Pfundner
Troststr. 38, A-1100 Wien
Decorative Arts Museum - 1970
Coll: 7,000 bells; cast bronzes; in
original bell foundry

00842
Graphische Sammlung Albertina
Augustinerstr. 1, A-1010 Wien
Fine Arts Museum - 1822
Drawings and graphics from the 15th
century to the present - library; photo
laboratory; workshops

00843
Gustinus Ambrosi-Museum
Österreichische Galerie
Scherzergasse 1a, A-1020 Wien
Fine Arts Museum
Coll: sculpture and busts by the
Austrian sculptor Gustinus Ambrosi
(1893-1975)

00844
Haus des Meeres
Vivarium Wien, Flakturm,
Esterhazypark, A-1070 Wien
Natural History Museum - 1956
Coll: ethnography of New Guinea;
shells; marine biology

00845
Haydn-Museum Historisches
Museum der Stadt Wien
Haydngasse 19, A-1070 Wien
Historic Site - 1899
Coll: memorabilia of the composer
Joseph Haydn, housed in his former
residence

00846
Heeresgeschichtliches Museum
Militärwissenschaftliches Institut
Arsenal 1, A-1030 Wien
History/Public Affairs Museum - 1869
Military artifacts; history of the
Austrian army; archives; models -
library

00847
**Historisches Museum der Stadt
Wien**
Karlsplatz, A-1040 Wien
General Museum - 1888
Coll: history of art and cultural life of
Vienna from prehistoric to present
times; topography; graphics; portraits;
history of theater; numismatics; arts
and crafts; furniture; folk customs;
painting; sculpture; architecture;
weapons; archives - library;
workshop

00848
Hofburg-Schauräume
Michaelerplatz 1, A-1010 Wien
History/Public Affairs Museum
Coll: secular and religious art
treasures; fortress chapel; imperial
residence with original interiors;
Amalienhof with historical interiors of
Empress Elisabeth I; memorabilia; in
Viennese court fortress (13th-18th
centuries)

00849
Institut für Geschichte der Medizin
Universität Wien
Währinger Str. 25, A-1090 Wien
Natural History Museum - 1920
18th century anatomical and
obstetrical models; history of medicine
in Vienna; manuscripts; coins and
medaillons - library

00850
Internationales Esperanto-Museum
Hofburg, Batthyanstiege, 3. Stock,
A-1010 Wien
History/Public Affairs Museum - 1929
Photos; picture postcards; sound films
in Esperanto; posters; exhibits
depicting Esperanto movement;
archives - library

00851
Jüdisches Museum
Bauernfeldgasse 4, A-1010 Wien
Religious Art Museum
Cultural history of the Jews

00852
Kapuzinergruft
Tegetthoffstr. 2, A-1010 Wien
History/Public Affairs Museum
Family vault of the Habsburg imperial
family; 144 sarcophagi including those
of 12 emperors and 15 empresses

00853
Kunsthistorisches Museum Wien
Burgring 5, A-1010 Wien
Fine Arts Museum - 1918
Coll: Egyptian and Oriental art;
sculpture; arts and crafts; tapestry;
painting and portraits; numismatics;
music instruments

00854
**Kunstsammlungen Palais
Schwarzenberg**
Rennweg 2, A-1030 Wien
Fine Arts Museum
Coll: historic period rooms in late 17th
century palace; Baroque art; sculpture
- park

00855
Kupferstichkabinett Akademie der
bildenden Künste
A-1010 Wien, Schillerplatz 3
Fine Arts Museum - 1773
Coll: drawings and grafic arts (15th -
20th century), gothic architectural
designs - library

00856
Kynologisches Museum
Karl-Schweighofer-Gasse 3, A-1070
Wien
Natural History Museum - 1956
Coll: history and origin of the dog;
breeding; photos, engravings, and
paintings - library

00857
Lehar-Schlössl Schikaneder-Schlössl
Hackhofergasse 18, A Wien
Fine Arts Museum
Coll: historical interors; architecture

00858
Lichtentaler Pfarrmuseum
Marktgasse 40, A-1090 Wien
General Museum - 1978
Coll: local history; paraments;
memorabilia of Franz Schubert and the
parish Lichtental

00859
**Liechtenstein'sche Fürstliche
Sammlungen**
Fürstengasse 1, A Wien
Fine Arts Museum
Paintings

00860
Mozart-Wohnung
Domgasse 5, A-1010 Wien
Historic Site - 1941
Coll: memorabilia of the composer
Wolfgang A. Mozart, housed in his
former residence; exhibits on Mozart
and Vienna; illustrations in Mozart's
works; Mozart's circle of friends

00861
**Museum der Mechitaristen-
Congregation**
Mechitaristengasse 4, A-1070 Wien
Anthropology Museum - 1811
Coll: history of Armenia; numismatics;
philology; ethnology; archives - library

00862
Museum des 20. Jahrhunderts
Schweizergarten, A-1030 Wien
Fine Arts Museum - 1962
International art of the 20th century -
library; film auditorium

00863
Museum des Blindenwesens
Wittelsbachstr. 5, A-1020 Wien
History/Public Affairs Museum - 1910
Coll: development and history of
education for the blind; the Braille
script; Braille book printing,
typewriters; the blind person in art;
historical archives - library

00864
**Museum des Österreichischen
Freiheitskampfes**
Wipplingerstr. 8, Stiege 3, A Wien
History/Public Affairs Museum

00865
**Museum für Beschirrungs- und
Sattelungslehre, Pflege und Wartung
der Haustiere**
Linke Bahngasse 11, A-1030 Wien
Anthropology Museum - 1767
Coll: harnesses for horses and cattle,
saddles, bits and bridles; training and
care; reindeer sleds; trotter and troika
harnesses - library; workshop

00866
Museum für das Bestattungswesen
Goldeggasse 19, Postfach 72, A-1040
Wien
History/Public Affairs Museum - 1967
Coll: funeral ceremonies; palls; orders
and awards; paraments; old Viennese
cemeteries; historic funerals; hearses;
death announcements; uniforms;
cremation; documents on the history
of burials; death mask of Joseph
Haydn; archives - library

00867
**Museum für Orthopädie bei Huf- und
Klauentieren**
Linke Bahngasse 11, A-1020 Wien
Natural History Museum - 1767
Coll: horseshoes; development of
horseshoeing; tools; specimens;
treatment of hoof and claw diseases -
library; workshop

00868
Museum für Völkerkunde
Neue Hofburg, Heldenplatz, A-1014
Wien
Anthropology Museum - 1876
Ancient Mexican archaeology and
ethnology; artifacts from Siberia,
Southeast Asia, India, Australasia;
Africa, North and South America;
archives - library; audiovisual center;
workshops; photo laboratory

00869
Museum Moderner Kunst
Fürstengasse 1, A-1090 Wien
Fine Arts Museum - 1979
Coll: contemporary and current art

00870
Naturhistorisches Museum
Burgring 7, A-1014 Wien
Natural History Museum - 1748
Div: mineralogy and petrography;
geology and paleontology;, botany;
zoology; anthropology; prehistory;
archives - library; laboratories;
workshops; bookbinding

00871
**Niederösterreichisches
Landesmuseum**
Herrengasse 9, A-1014 Wien
General Museum - 1907
Coll: fine arts; contemporary fine arts;
prehistory; numismatics; zoology,
botany, paleontology, geology,
mineralogy; ethnology; archives -
workshops

00872
Österreichische Galerie
Schloß Belvedere, Prinz-Eugen-Str. 27,
A-1030 Wien
Fine Arts Museum - 1903
Div: medieval Austrian art; Baroque
art; 19th-20th century painting

00873
Österreichisches Circus- und Clown-Museum
Karmelitergasse 9, A-1020 Wien
Performing Arts Museum - 1968
International clown collection; circus photos and posters; costumes and props; archives - library

00874
Österreichisches Eisenbahnmuseum
Mariahilferstr. 212, A-1140 Wien
Science/Tech Museum - 1885
Coll: history of the Austrian railway system; transportation archives - library; workshops

00875
Österreichisches Filmmuseum
Augustinerstr. 1, Albertina, A-1010 Wien
Performing Arts Museum
History of Austrian film

00876
Österreichisches Gesellschafts- und Wirtschaftsmuseum
Vogelsanggasse 36, A-1050 Wien
History/Public Affairs Museum - 1925
Contemporary Austrian history; business and economy in Austria

00877
Österreichisches Gesellschafts- und Wirtschaftsmuseum
Vogelsanggasse 36, A-1050 Wien
History/Public Affairs Museum - 1925
Coll: documentation on the political, social, and economic development of Austria from 1900 to the present - library; workshops

00878
Österreichisches Museum für Angewandte Kunst
Stubenring 5, A-1010 Wien
Decorative Arts Museum - 1864
European and East Asian decorative arts; Oriental carpets; textiles; furniture; metal items; glass; ceramics and porcelain; art prints - library; workshops; photo laboratory; bookbinding

00879
Österreichisches Museum für Volkskunde
Palais Schönborn, Laudongasse 15-19, A-1080 Wien
Anthropology Museum - 1895
Furniture; ceramics; masks; religious folk art; folklore glass painting; musical instruments; archives - library; workshops

00880
Österreichisches Tabakmuseum
Mariahilferstr. 2, A-1070 Wien
History/Public Affairs Museum - 1957
Porcelain pipes and snuff boxes; antique pipes - library

00881
Österreichisches Theatermuseum
Hanuschgasse 3, A-1010 Wien
Performing Arts Museum
Manuscripts, photos, books, drawings, paintings, costumes, films, phonograph records, etc. depicting the world of the theater, especially in Austria

00882
Pathologisch-Anatomisches Bundesmuseum
Spitalgasse 2, A-1090 Wien
Science/Tech Museum - 1796
Moulage collection (ca. 2500 exhibits); prepared specimens, mainly human objects; bones and skeletons

00883
Post- und Telegraphenmuseum
Mariahilfer Str. 212, A-1140 Wien
Science/Tech Museum - 1889
History of postal services from Antiquity to the present; mail boxes, stamps, telecommunications and mail processing equipment illustrating work and development of the Austrian Postal Service

00884
Pratermuseum
Prater, Planetarium, A-1020 Wien
General Museum - 1933
History of the Viennese amusement park, Prater

00885
Römische Baureste am Hof
Am Hof 9, A-1010 Wien
Archeology Museum - 1953
Roman remains; sketches, charts and pictures illustrating Vienna's Roman past

00886
Römische Ruinen unter dem Hohen Markt
Hoher Markt 3, A-1010 Wien
Archeology Museum - 1950
Excavations, architectural fragments, casts, and reliefs from Roman times

00887
Sammlung des Franziskaner-Klosters
Franziskanerplatz 4, A-1010 Wien
Religious Art Museum
History of the Franciscan Order; paintings; liturgical items; reliquaries

00888
Sammlung Religiöse Volkskunst
Johannesgasse 8, A-1010 Wien
Decorative Arts Museum - 1966
Historic monastary apothecary; religious folk art (esp. 17th and 18th c.); religious decorative arts and liturgical items

00889
Sammlungen der Gesellschaft der Musikfreunde
Bösendorfer Str. 12, A-1010 Wien
Music Museum
Coll: original manuscripts of Beethoven, Mozart, Schubert, Haydn, Bruckner, and others

00890
Sammlungen des Internationalen Künstlerclubs
Österreich-Haus, Palais Palffy, Josefsplatz 6, A Wien
Fine Arts Museum
Coll: contemporary international art, graphics, and painting

00891
Schatzkammer des Deutschen Ordens
Singerstr. 7, A-1010 Wien
Decorative Arts Museum - 1956
Coll: goldsmith work; crystal; mountings of semi-precious stones especially from the 15th-17th centuries; documents; coins; badges; ornate goblets; tableware; weapons; clocks; portraits

00892
Schausammlung der Hoftafel- und Silberkammer
Batthyanstiege, A-1010 Wien
Decorative Arts Museum - 1919
Coll: 18th-19th century tableware of the former Austrian imperial family

00893
Schloß Schönbrunn
A-1130 Wien
History/Public Affairs Museum
Coll: court furnishings and original interiors; historic coaches for state and everyday occasions

00894
Schubert-Museum Historisches Museum der Stadt Wien
Nußdorfer Str. 54, A-1090 Wien
Historic Site - 1912
Coll: memorabilia of the composer Franz Schubert, housed in his birthplace; portraits of his circle of friends and family; scores and compositions; historical documents

00895
Schuberts Sterbezimmer
Historisches Museum der Stadt Wien
Kettenbrückengasse 6, A-1040 Wien
Historic Site
Coll: memorabilia of the last years of the composer Franz Schubert

00896
Sigmund-Freud-Museum
Berggasse 19/6, A-1090 Wien
Historic Site - 1971
Coll: original furniture, books, antique collection and memorabilia of Freud housed in his appartment and office (1891-1938); archives on the history of psychoanalysis - library

00897
Technisches Museum für Industrie und Gewerbe
Mariahilferstr. 212, A-1140 Wien
Science/Tech Museum - 1908
Coll: development of technology from ancient times to the present; exhibits on chemistry and physics; models - library; workshops

00898
Uhrenmuseum Historisches Museum der Stadt Wien
Schulhof 2, A-1010 Wien
Science/Tech Museum - 1921
Coll: history of measuring time; clocks

00899
Waffensammlung des Kunsthistorischen Museums
Neue Burg, Heldenplatz, A-1010 Wien
History/Public Affairs Museum - 15th century
Imperial armory; imperial hunting cabinet; arms collection of Ambras Castle; late Gothic tournament armor - library

00900
Weinbaumuseum Bezirksmuseum Döbling
Döblinger Hauptstr. 96, A-1190 Wien
Agriculture Museum - 1972
Coll: viticulture; wine cellars with equipment

00901
Weinmuseum Schlumberger
Heiligenstädter Str. 43, A-1190 Wien
Agriculture Museum - 1919
Coll: history of the production of wine and champaigne; Austrian wine trade; history of the family Schlumberger; archives - library

00902
Wiener Ziegelmuseum
Hickelgasse 5, A-1140 Wien
Science/Tech Museum - 1978
Coll: development of masonry

Wiener Neustadt

00903
Sammlung des Bürgerkorps zu Wiener Neustadt 1231 'Allzeit-Getreu'
Schlögelgasse 24, A-2700 Wiener Neustadt
History/Public Affairs Museum - 1231
Coll: history of the civic corps; equipment, weapons, uniforms, flags; photo documentation

00904
Stadtmuseum
Wiener Str. 63, A-2700 Wiener Neustadt
General Museum - 1904
Coll: prehistory; archeology; local history; painting; sculpture; frescoes; arts and crafts; coins

Wieselburg

00905
Stefan-Denk-Sammlung
Hauptplatz 26, A-3250 Wieselburg
Archeology Museum - 1952
Prehistoric finds; artifacts from the Ice Age to the Modern Era

Wildschönau-Oberau

00906
Bergbauernmuseum
A-6311 Wildschönau-Oberau
Agriculture Museum - 1971
Coll: peasant life; wooden machines; tools for flax and hemp production; domestic utensils; furnishings; butter molds; mangers; weapons; traditional costumes; superstition and witchery

Wilhering

00907
Stiftssammlungen
Zisterzienserstift, A-4073 Wilhering
Religious Art Museum - 1146
Coll: Baroque painting; furnishings; coins; religious art; in 12th century cloister

Zwentendorf

00908
Ortsmuseum
Amtshaus, A-3435 Zwentendorf
Archeology Museum - 1962
Coll: Roman finds; early Christian cemetery (10th-11th centuries); medieval finds

Zwettl

00909
Anton-Museum
Landstr. 65, A-3910 Zwettl
General Museum - 1927
Coll: folk art and handicrafts; 18th-19th century sculpture, glass painting, peasant furnishings, tools, and weapons

Bahamas

Hope Town

00910
The Wyannie Malone Historical Museum
Hope Town, Abaco
General Museum - 1977
Coll: chronology of Hope Town's history (1783-1780); daily life of the past; sponging; wreaking; boatbuilding

Nassau

00911
Angelo Roker's Art Centre and Museum
Harold Rd, POB SS 6230, Nassau
General Museum

00912
Bahamas Historical Society Museum
Elizabeth Avenue, POB N 1715, Nassau
General Museum - 1959
maps; prints; photographs; shells; marine salvage collection - library

00913
Bahamia Museum
Blue Hill Road, POB N3913, Nassau
Anthropology Museum - 1973
Folklore

00914
The Nassau Public Library and Museum
POB N-3210, Nassau
General Museum

Bahrain

Muharraq

00915
Bahrain National Museum
Gulf Air Road, Busaitin, POB 43, Muharraq
General Museum
Archaeological display on the rise of the Dilmun civilization; Dilmun seals; costumes, tools, weapons, etc. of historic Bahrain

Bangladesh

Chittagong

00916
Ethnological Museum
Chittagong
General Museum
East Bengal country boat; manikins in costume; textiles; wood and metal work; craft products of Chittagong hill tribes

Comilla

00917
Ram Mala Museum
Comilla
General Museum
Local history

Dacca

00918
Balda Museum of Art and Archaeology
Dacca
General Museum - 1927
Art and archaeology collections

00919
Dacca Museum
Ramna Rd, Dacca
General Museum - 1913
Art and archaeology of Bengal; Buddhist and Brahmanical iconography; coins

00920
Lala Bagh Fort Museum
Dacca
History/Public Affairs Museum
Historical collections housed in 18th cent. pavilion

Mainamati

00921
Temple Museum
Mainamati, East Bengal
Archeology Museum - 1966
Remains of Buddhist monastery; terracotta plaques

Rajshahi

00922
Varendra Research Museum
University of Rajshahi, Rajshahi
General Museum - 1910
Architectural fragments from the Kushan, Gupta, Pala and Sena periods; articles from the Muslim period (c.1200-1857); stone and metal images; paintings; arms; manuscripts and inscriptions; coins - library

Barbados

Saint Michael

00923
Barbados Museum and Historical Society
Saint Ann's Garrison, Saint Michael
General Museum - 1933
Historical collections; natural history; furniture; silver, glass and china; Cunard collection of West Indian prints

Belgium

Aalst

00924
Stedelijk Museum Aalst
Oude Vismarkt 13, B-9300 Aalst
Fine Arts Museum
Works of art; archeology; history of arts and traditions

Aarschot

00925
Stedelijk Museum voor Heemkunde en Folklore
Begijnhof 25, B-3220 Aarschot
General Museum - 1967
Documents on Joseph Cuypers (composer) and the Meulemans family (musicians); iconography; prehistory; local history; folklore

Andenne

00926
Musée Communal de la Céramique
rue Charles Lapierre, B-5220 Andenne
General Museum - 1930
Andenne pottery and porcelain; Roman pottery; Merovingian sarcophagus; earthen pipes

Antwerpen

00927
Antwerps Marionettenmuseum 'Poesje'
Repenstraat 3, B-2000 Antwerpen
Performing Arts Museum
Puppets

00928
Archief en Museum voor het Vlaamse Cultuurleven
Minderbroedersstraat 22, B-2000 Antwerpen
History/Public Affairs Museum - 1933
Flemish literature in documents, letters, portraits, newspaper cuttings, posters; fine arts; music; theatre; 'Flemish Movement' - library

00929
Etnografisch Museum
International Zeemanshuis, Falconrui 21, B-2000 Antwerpen
Anthropology Museum
Arts and crafts of pre-literate and non-European peoples (not open to the public)

00930
Georges Eekhoud-Kabinet
Stadsbibliotheek, H. Conscienceplein 4, B-2000 Antwerpen
History/Public Affairs Museum
Documents on French language writers

00931
Hôtel de Ville
Grote Markt, B-2000 Antwerpen
Fine Arts Museum
Paintings and portraits (16th-19th c.)

00932
Koninklijk Museum voor Schone Kunsten
Leopold de Waelplaats, Plaatsnijdersstraat 2, B-2000 Antwerpen
Fine Arts Museum - 1812
Flemish art (15th-20th) and foreign schools - library

00933
Koninklijke Maatschappij voor Dierkunde van Antwerpen
Koningin Astridplein 26, B-2000 Antwerpen
Natural History Museum - 1843
Zoology; botany; Dr. H. Van Heurck collections - library

00934
Magdenhuismuseum
Lange Gasthuisstraat 33, B-2000 Antwerpen
Decorative Arts Museum - 1930
Antwerpen pottery (16th c.); paintings; sculpture - archives

00935
Maison Rockox
Keizersstraat 10-12, B-2000 Antwerpen
Fine Arts Museum - 1977
Painting (Rubens, Van Dyck, Bruegel); furniture - library

00936
Museum Browershuis
Adriaan Brouwerstraat 20, B-2000 Antwerpen
History/Public Affairs Museum
Installations for the supply of water to breweries (16th c.); rich council chamber

00937
Museum Mayer van den Bergh
Lange Gasthuisstraat 19, B-2000 Antwerpen
Fine Arts Museum - 1904
Gothic painting and sculpture; 17th century painting; Pieter Bruegel I 'Dulle Griet' (Mad Margot); Meester Heinrich te Konstanz 'Jezus-Johannes-groep'

00938
Museum Plantin-Moretus
Vrijdagmarkt 22, B-2000 Antwerpen
Science/Tech Museum - 1876
Old printing office and foundry of Christopher Plantin and his successors (1555-1876), typographical material, old bindings; paintings (including Rubens) - library

00939
Museum Ridder Smidt Van Gelder
Belgiëlei 91, B-2000 Antwerpen
Decorative Arts Museum - 1950
Chinese, Japanese and European porcelain; 18th century interior

00940
Museum Vleeshuis
Vleeshouwersstraat 38-40, B-2000 Antwerpen
General Museum - 1913
Ceramics, sculpture, furniture, musical instruments of Antwerpen manufacture; local history; archeology - library

00941
Museum voor Amateurtoneel
Wolstraat 5, Antwerpen, Weversfabriekstraat 54, B-2200 Borgerhout
Performing Arts Museum - 1976
Drawings, documents and objects from amateur theatre

00942
Museum voor Kerkelijke Kunst
Kammenstraat 73, B-2000 Antwerpen
Religious Art Museum
Works by Rubens, Van Dyck and Jordaens; religious objects

00943
Nationaal Scheepvaartmuseum
Steenplein 1, B-2000 Antwerpen
Science/Tech Museum - 1952
Shipping, maritime history, shipbuilding, yachting, river craft, harbour equipment, boats; ethnology and folklore - library

00944
Open-air Museum for Sculpture Middelheim
Middelheimlaan 61, B-2020 Antwerpen
Fine Arts Museum - 1950
Modern art; contemporary sculpture (including Moore, Rodin, Maillol, Zadkine, Marini) - library

00945
Polder- en Zeemuseum
Tolhuisstraat 10-16, Lillo-Fort, B-2040 Antwerpen
Anthropology Museum - 1959
Costumes; agricultural implements; furniture; kitchen utensils; objects and documents in connection with popular superstition and customs; photographs of old sites and buildings no longer existing

00946
Provinciaal Diamantmuseum
Jezusstraat 28-30, B-2000 Antwerpen
Science/Tech Museum - 1972
Technic of diamond cutting and the craft of diamond jewelry; historical tools for diamond cutting - library

00947
Provinciaal Veiligheidsinstituut
Jezusstraat 28-30, B-2000 Antwerpen
History/Public Affairs Museum - 1942
Exhibition of all kinds of items about work safety - library

00948
Rubenianum Kunsthistorische Musea
Belgiëlei 91, B-2000 Antwerpen
Fine Arts Museum - 1964
Documentation centre for study of 17th century Flemish art

00949
Rubenshuis
Wapper 9-11, B-2000 Antwerpen
Historic Site - 1956
Reconstructed home and studio of
Peter Paul Rubens (1577-1640);
Flemish furniture (17th c.); paintings
and sketches by Rubens and some of
his contemporaries

00950
Stedelijk Prentenkabinet
Vrijdagmarkt 22, B-2000 Antwerpen
Fine Arts Museum - 1938
Prints; photography; graphic arts -
library

00951
Volkskundemuseum
Gildekamersstraat, B-2000 Antwerpen
General Museum - 1907
The Pageants and the Giants;
Antwerpen figures; popular beliefs,
magic, popular medicine (pharmacy);
Flemish folk art; popular prints;
popular customs; puppet theatre; the
head of the Giant Druon Antigon -
library

Arlon

00952
**Musée de la Basilique et des
Thermes Romains**
rue des Thermes Romains, *mail c/o*
Institut Archéologique du Luxembourg,
rue des Martyrs, 13, B-6700 Arlon
Archeology Museum
Remainders of a 4th century basilica,
burial place for christianized
Merovingians; Roman thermae, bath
and canalization

00953
Musée de la Tour Romaine
Grand Place, B-6700 Arlon
Archeology Museum
Remainders of a fortress tower (3rd
c.); Roman sepulchral monuments

00954
Musée Luxembourgeois
rue des Martyrs, 13, B-6700 Arlon
Archeology Museum - 1847
Coll: Prehistory; Gallo-Roman period;
sepulchral monuments; ceramics,
glass and ornaments; Merovingian
period; jewels; weapons; religious art;
Retable of Fisenne

Asse

00955
Heemkundig Museum
mail c/o M.F. De Smedt, Mollestraat 5,
B-1700 Asse
General Museum

Ath

00956
Musée Athois
rue du Bouchain, 16, B-7800 Ath
General Museum - 1966
Prehistoric and Roman archeology;
local history; clay models about
evolution of the town; ceramics,
pottery, lace, furnishings, tapestries,
stitching, crafts (stone,
wood-workings); medieval and
Renaissance sculpture; 'Grablegung
Christi' (Notre-Dame du Refuge, Ath,
1400-1410)

Aubechies

00957
Domus Romana
mail c/o Demarez Leonce, rue de
Leuze, 17, B-7672 Aubechies
Archeology Museum - 1977
Coll: prehistoric and protohistoric
objects; fragments of mural painting

Awirs

00958
Château d'Aigremont
rue du Château, 12, B-4131 Awirs
Historic Site
Painting (18th c.); tapestries (17th c.);
furniture (18th c.)

Bastogne

00959
Bastogne Historical Center
American Memorial Hill of the
Mardasson, B-6650 Bastogne
History/Public Affairs Museum - 1976
Uniforms, guns, vehicles of World War
II in special context with Bastogne -
diorama; audio-visual program; cinema

Battice

00960
Musée du Remoudou
Place du Marché, *mail c/o* Accueil
touristique de Battice, M. Jean
Duysens, 40, rue de Herve, B-4651
Battice
History/Public Affairs Museum - 1962
Weaving; craftmen's instruments; rope
making; kitchen with complete
equipment; cheese production

Beaumont

00961
Musée de la Tour Salamandre
B-6570 Beaumont
General Museum
Regional history; iconography;
regional arts and crafts

Beauraing

00962
Musée Marial de Beauraing
rue de l'Eglise, 21, B-5570 Beauraing
Religious Art Museum - 1964

Bellem

00963
Museum van de Vlaamse Strijd
B-9881 Bellem
History/Public Affairs Museum - 1980
Documentation on the fight of the
Flemish people for political and native-
language rights

Beloeil

00964
Château de Beloeil
rue Durieu, 11, B-7970 Beloeil
History/Public Affairs Museum
Castle with tapestries, furniture (18th
c.), paintings, Chinese porcelain,
archives (since 13th c.) and library with
works of the Belgian writer Ch.-J. de
Ligne (18th c.)

Berneau

00965
Musée Gallo-Romain de Berneau
rue de Visé, 12, *mail c/o* Jean
Polmans, Route de Fairon, 16, B-4541
Berneau
Archeology Museum
Tools; bronze objects; Gallo-Roman
pottery; coins

Beveren

00966
Gemeentelijk Heemkundig Museum
Kasteel Cortewalle
Kloosterstraat 86, B-2750 Beveren
General Museum - 1974
Agricultural items; various crafts; tools;
domestic utensils

Binche

00967
**Musée International du Carnaval et
du Masque**
rue de l'Eglise, 16, B-7130 Binche
History/Public Affairs Museum - 1975
Coll: masks and disguises from Latin
America, Asia (especially India), Africa,
Europe; carnival in Europe, Belgium
and especially at Binche

Blankenberge

00968
**Blankenbergs en Kustfolkloristisch
Museum 't Zeitgat**
Coin Notebaertstraat 20, rue Van
Mulhem, B-8370 Blankenberge
General Museum
Reconstructed fisherman's room
(1900); craftmen's tools; Flemish
ceramics; popular religious art;
paintings; fossils, minerals

Blicquy

00969
Musée du Poitier Gallo-Romain
rue du Couvent, B-7922 Blicquy
Archeology Museum
Iron and bronze objects; gravestones;
vases

Boekhoute

00970
Heemkundig Museum Boekhoute
Dorp 3, B-9961 Boekhoute
General Museum
Crafts; agriculture; folklore; fishing

Bon-Secours

00971
Maison de la Forêt Centre culturel de
Bon-Secours
rue des Sapins, 8, B-7603
Bon-Secours
Natural History Museum - 1979
Coll: exhibits pertaining to ecology -
diorama

Booischot

00972
Vogelmuseum
Lierse Steenweg 15, B-3150 Booischot
Natural History Museum
Taxidermic exhibit of birds

Boom

00973
Gemeentelijk Museum
Tuyaertstraat 19-21, B-2650 Boom
General Museum
Literature; history; folklore; regional
industries; natural history

Borgerhout

00974
Heemmuseum van Borgerhout
Turnhoutsebaan 110, B-2200
Borgerhout
General Museum
Local history; crafts; popular religious
art; costumes

00975
Strijkijzermuseum
Vosstraat 87, B-2200 Borgerhout
General Museum - 1962
Coll: flatirons; religious traditions;
folklore; craftmen's tools

Borsbeek

00976
Vogelkundig Museum
De Robianostraat 179, B-2210
Borsbeek
Natural History Museum
Coll: bird exhibits

Bouillon

00977
Musée Ducal
rue du Petit, 1-3, B-6830 Bouillon
General Museum - 1947
Interiors (18th-19th c.); crafts;
costumes; local history; history of the
crusades; medieval weapons and
documents from the Orient and
Occident; Byzantine goldsmith art;
Limoges enamelware; Persian
ceramics; furniture (15th c.)

Bouvignes

00978
Musée Communal
Maison Espagnole, Pl du Baillage,
B-7803 Bouvignes
General Museum
Arms and weapons; religious art and
objects; arts and crafts; iconography

Braine-l'Alleud

00979
Panorama de la Bataille de Waterloo
rue des Vertes Bornes, 90, B-1420
Braine-l'Alleud
History/Public Affairs Museum - 1911
Documentation on the battle of
Waterloo

Braine-le-Comte

00980
**Musée Communal de la Ville de
Braine-le-Comte**
rue des Dominicains, B-7490 Braine-
le-Comte
General Museum
Local history and folklore; local
writers; documents of the period
1914-1948

Brecht

00981
Kempisch Museum
Mudeusstraat 2, B-2160 Brecht
General Museum - 1904
Ancient crafts; agricultural materials;
prehistory; folklore

Bree

00982
Heemkundig Museum
Ancien Hôtel de Ville, B-3690 Bree
General Museum - 1975
Arts and crafts; local flora and fauna;
photos

Brugge

00983
Archiefmuseum Rijksarchief te
Brugge
Academiestraat 14-18, B-8000 Brugge
History/Public Affairs Museum - 1975
Documents

00984
Arentshuis
Dyver 16, B-6000 Brugge
Fine Arts Museum
Furniture; ceramics; copper; tin;
tapestries; town views (17th-19th c.);
works of the English painter Frank
Brangwyn

00985
Begijnhofmuseum Monasterium de
Wijngaard
Oud-Begijnhof 30, B-8000 Brugge
Religious Art Museum
Reconstruction of a 17th century
Beguine house

00986
Folklore Museum
Balstraat 27, B-8000 Brugge
Decorative Arts Museum
Popular arts and customs

00987
Groeningemuseum
Dijver 12, B-8000 Brugge
Fine Arts Museum
Fine arts; Flemish Primitives

00988
Gruuthusemuseum
Dijver 17, B-8000 Brugge
General Museum
Decorative arts; prehistoric and
medieval archeology; sciences;
manufacturing; lace; musical
instruments; numismatics; weights and
measures; tapestries; textiles; glass

00989
Guido Gezelle Museum
Rolweg 64, B-8000 Brugge
Historic Site - 1926
Birthplace of Guido Gezelle (his library
and all his manuscripts and other
archival documents are held in
safekeeping at the City Library
Brugge)

00990
Historisch Museum Brugge
Langestraat 191, B-8000 Brugge
History/Public Affairs Museum
Local history (1789-1914); documents
relating to World War I and II and the
former Belgian Congo

00991
José Storiehuis
Steenhouwersdijk 2, B-8000 Brugge
Historic Site
House of the portraitist José Storie;
furniture; paintings; lace

00992
**Koninklijk Hoofdgild
Sint-Sebastiaansgilde**
Carmerstraat 178, B-8000 Brugge
History/Public Affairs Museum
Documents and archives relating to
the guild of St. Sebastian (since 1400);
documents on royal families of
Belgium and England

00993
Memlingmuseum
St. Janshospitaal, Mariastraat 38,
B-8000 Brugge
Fine Arts Museum
Paintings by Hans Memling; portraits;
archeology

00994
**Museum van de St.-Salvators-
Kathedraal**
Steen-en Zuidzandstraat, mail c/o
Heer Conservator van het Museum
van de Kathedraal,
St.-Salvatorkoorstraat 8, B-8000
Brugge
Religious Art Museum
Old Flemish painting, sculptures,
embroidery, goldsmith art;
tombstones, frescoes on 13th century
graves

00995
Museum van het Heilig Bloed
Basiliek van het Heilig Bloed, Burg 13,
B-8000 Brugge
Religious Art Museum
Paintings (Pourbus, Van Dyck); works
of goldsmith Jan Crabbe (1617);
tapestries (1637); reliquaries

00996
Potteriemuseum
Potterielei, B-8000 Brugge
Religious Art Museum
Paintings; carpets and furniture (16th
c.); treasury

00997
Sint-Janshuismolen
Kruisvest, B-8000 Brugge
Science/Tech Museum - 1770
Windmill exhibits; demonstration of
cornmilling

00998
Stadhuis
Burg, B-8000 Brugge
History/Public Affairs Museum
Gothic hall; paintings relating to the
history of the town

00999
Stedelijk Museum voor Volkskunde
Balstraat 27, B-8000 Brugge
Anthropology Museum - 1973
Folklore; regional ethnology; folk art;
religious traditions; interiors of a 19th
century inn and drugstore; kitchen
utensils

Bruxelles

01000
Archives et Musée de la Littérature
Bibliothèque Royale Albert I
bd de l'Empereur, 4, B-1000 Bruxelles
History/Public Affairs Museum
Manuscripts and documentation on
Belgian literature in French;
documents on theatre history;
archives of the Royal Academy of
French Language and Literature;
archives of Henry Van de Velde -
library

01001
Atomium
Heysel, B-1000 Bruxelles
Natural History Museum
Physics; chemistry; peaceful use of
nuclear energy

01002
Beguinage d'Anderlecht
rue du Chapelain, 4, B-1070 Bruxelles
Religious Art Museum - 1930
Folklore; religious interiors

01003
Cabinet des Estampes Bibliothèque
Royale Albert I
1, Pl du Musée, B-1000 Bruxelles
Fine Arts Museum - 1876
Engravings; drawings; prints;
woodcuts; documentation

01004
**Exposition Permanente de
Documents d'Archives** Archives
Générales du Royaume
rue de Ruysbroeck, 2-6, B-1000
Bruxelles
History/Public Affairs Museum
Archives of Belgium

01005
Hôtel de Ville
Grand Place, B-1000 Bruxelles
History/Public Affairs Museum
Brussels tapestries (16th-18th c.);
paintings (17th-20th c.); furniture and
wooden decoration (18th-19th c.)

01006
**Institut Royal des Sciences
Naturelles de Belgique**
Rue Vautier 31, B-1040 Bruxelles
Natural History Museum - 1846
Coll: Belgian fossils and vertebrates;
mammals and exotic birds;
paleobotany; dioramas - library

01007
Maison Camille Lemonnier 'Maison
des Ecrivains'
Chaussée de Wawre, 150, B-1050
Bruxelles
Fine Arts Museum - 1946
Reconstruction of Camille Lemonnier's
working room with library,
manuscripts and documents ;
paintings by Belgian masters of the
second half of the 19th century;
drawings

01008
Maison d'Erasme
rue du Chapître, 31, B-1070 Bruxelles
History/Public Affairs Museum - 1932
Art and history of humanism; one
painting by Hieronymus Bosch -
library

01009
Musée Communal Maison du Roi
rue du Poivre, 1, B-1000 Bruxelles
General Museum - 1887
Local history and archeology; 'The
wedding cortege' of Pieter Bruegel the
elder; two altarpieces (16th c.) - library

01010
Musée Constantin Meunier
rue de l'Abbaye, 58, B-1050 Bruxelles
Fine Arts Museum
Works by C. Meunier (sculpture,
paintings, watercolours, drawings);
reconstruction of his studio

01011
Musée d'Art Ancien
rue de la Régence, 3, B-1000 Bruxelles
Fine Arts Museum - 1846
15th-19th century Flemish and foreign
art, painting, sculpture; Peter Bruegel
the elder - library

01012
Musée d'Art Moderne
mail c/o Musée Royaux des Beaux-
Arts de Belgique, Rue du Musée, 9,
B-1000 Bruxelles
Fine Arts Museum
New building in construction until
1984; 19th-20th centuries collections
(paintings, sculptures and drawings)
may be seen at the Musée d'Art
Ancien, 3 rue de la Régence, Bruxelles

01013
Musée de la Brasserie
Grand-Place, 10, B-1000 Bruxelles
History/Public Affairs Museum
Brewery (18th c.) with original
equipment and inn

01014
Musée de la Dynastie
rue Bréderode, 10, B-1000 Bruxelles
History/Public Affairs Museum
Biographical history; documents on
the history of the Belgian dynasty;
prints; iconography

01015
Musée de la Porte de Hal
Porte de Hal, bd de Waterloo, B-1000
Bruxelles
History/Public Affairs Museum
Arms and armors; history of arms and
objects relating to the Belgian dynasty

01016
Musée de l'Assistance Publique
Hôpital Saint-Pierre, rue Haute, 298 A,
B-1000 Bruxelles
Fine Arts Museum
Paintings; sculptures; tin; goldsmith
work; furniture; tapestries;
contemporary painting

01017
Musée de l'Hôtel Bellevue Musée
Royaux d'Art et d'Histoire
Place des Palais, 7, B Bruxelles
Decorative Arts Museum
Furniture; porcelaine; silverware; lace;
painting; costumes

01018
Musée des Chemins de Fer
Gare du Nord, B-1000 Bruxelles
Science/Tech Museum
Railroad history; architecture of
railway stations; uniforms and medals

01019
Le Musée des enfants
rue de Tenbosch, 32, B-1050 Bruxelles
Junior Museum - 1978
Exhibition on housing conditions and
everyday life

01020
**Musée des Postes et
Telecommunications**
Place du Grand Sablon, 40, B-1000
Bruxelles
Science/Tech Museum - 1931
Postal history; stamp collection of
Belgium and foreign countries; K.
Zirkenbach collection;
telecommunications - library

01021
Musée d'Ixelles
rue Jean Van Volsem, 71, B-1050
Bruxelles
Fine Arts Museum - 1892
Art (17th-20th c.); drawings by
Rembrandt, Dürer, Bandinelli,
Fragonard, Boucher; Flemish and
Dutch painting (16th-18th c.); French
and Belgian painting (19th c.) - library

01022
Musée du Cinema
rue Baron Horta, 9, B-1000 Bruxelles
Science/Tech Museum
History of cinema

01023
Musée du Costume et de la Dentelle
rue de la Violette, 6, B-1000 Bruxelles
Decorative Arts Museum - 1977
Traditional and contemporary lace,
passementerie; skirt of Brussels lace,
that probably belonged to the empress
Eugénie, wife of Napoleon III - library

01024
Musée du Jouet Itinérants
av des Azalées, 44, B-1030 Bruxelles
Decorative Arts Museum
Toys; toy trains; games; dolls; model
cars, boats, aeroplanes; garden
railways; steam engines - library

01025
**Musée du Livre et Musée de
l'Imprimerie** Cabinets de Donations
Mont des Arts, B-1000 Bruxelles
History/Public Affairs Museum - 1970
History of books from the early
beginnings

01026
**Musée du Théâtre Royal de la
Monnaie**
rue Leopold, 4, B-1000 Bruxelles
Performing Arts Museum - 1962
Documents about the Théâtre Royal
de la Monnaie and about the opera
and ballet in general

01027
Musée Horta
rue Americaine, 25, B-1060 Bruxelles
Decorative Arts Museum - 1969
Furniture of the architect V. Horta -
library

01028
Musée Instrumental
rue Aus-Laines, 14, B-1000 Bruxelles
Music Museum - 1877
Musical instruments (16th c. to
present) from European and
non-European countries

01029
**Musée Royal de l'Armée et
d'Histoire Militaire**
Parc du Cinquantenaire, 3, B-1040
Bruxelles
History/Public Affairs Museum - 1910
Militaria from the 18th century to
World War II - library; iconographic
service

01030
Musée Schott
rue du Chêne, 27, B-1000 Bruxelles
Fine Arts Museum - 1967
Works and collections of painter
Philippe Schott; sculptures (15th-18th
c.); furniture (16th-18th c.)

01031
Musée Wiertz
rue Vauthier, 62, B-1050 Bruxelles
Historic Site
Works by the 19th century painter
Antoine Wiertz

01032
Musées Royaux d'Art et d'Histoire
Parc du Cinquantenaire, 10, B-1040
Bruxelles
General Museum - 1835
Sculpture; decorative arts; archeology;
history; ethnology; folklore; scientific
material; ceramics; costumes; textiles;
lace; jewelry; stained glass; goldsmith
art; musical instruments; farm tools -
library

01033
Pavillon Chinois
Parc de Laeken, av Van Praet, 44, *mail
c/o* Musées royaux d'art et d'histoire,
Parc du Cinquantenaire, 10, B-1040
Bruxelles
Decorative Arts Museum
Verhaeghe de Naeyer's collection of
Far Eastern porcelain (17th-18th c.),
paintings, European ceramics

01034
Penningkabinet
Keizerslaan 4, B-1000 Bruxelles
History/Public Affairs Museum - 1835
Coins, medals and instruments for
coinage; De Hirsch Collection -
numismatic library

Buzenol

01035
Musée et Parc de Montauban
B-6743 Buzenol
Archeology Museum
Fortresses of the Iron Age and the
Roman period; fortress tower of the
Middle Ages; Roman sculpture found
in situ

Carnières-Morlanwelz

01036
Musée Alexandre-Louis Martin
Place de Carnières, B-6508 Carnières-
Morlanwelz
Fine Arts Museum
Works and personal remembrances of
the painter Alexandre-Louis Martin

Cerfontaine

01037
Musée régional de Cerfontaine
Ancienne Gare, B-6450 Cerfontaine
General Museum - 1973
History; archeology; folklore; crafts;
shoemaker's shop for wooden shoes

Charleroi

01038
Musée Communal des Beaux Arts
Hôtel de Ville, B-6000 Charleroi
Fine Arts Museum - 1953
Works by local artists (19th-20th c.),
paintings by François-Joseph Navez,
Pierre Paulus, Fernand André; works
by foreign artists

01039
**Musée de la Société Royale
d'Archéologie et de Paléontologie de
Charleroi**
bd Defontaine 10, B-6000 Charleroi
Archeology Museum - 1979
Prehistory; Greek and Roman
archeology; medieval and
post-medieval wooden sculptures -
library

01040
Musée du Verre 'Art et Technique'
bd Defontaine, 10, B-6000 Charleroi
Decorative Arts Museum

Chaudfontaine

01041
Musée Hydrogéologique Institut
Thermal de Chaudfontaine
B-4930 Chaudfontaine
Natural History Museum
Geology

Comblain-au-Pont

01042
Musée Ourthe-Ambleve
Grand-Place, 1, B-4170 Comblain-
au-Pont
General Museum - 1933/1977
Prehistory; fossils; history; folklore;
craftmen's tools - library

Cortil-Noirmont

01043
Musée Français
rue Zemsoul, 3, B-5861 Cortil-
Noirmont
History/Public Affairs Museum
Canons, guns and various arms

Cul-des-Sarts

01044
Musée des Riezes et des Sarts
rue de Rocroi, 1, B-6404 Cul-des-Sarts
General Museum
Crafts; arms; furniture

Damme

01045
**Oudheidkundig Museum van het
St.-Janshospitaal**
Kerkstraat 39, B-8340 Damme
Decorative Arts Museum - 1960
Local history; religious history; silver;
tin; furniture

01046
Stedelijk Museum
Stadhuis, Kerkstraat 12, B-8340
Damme
General Museum - 1950
Medieval Archeology; local history
and folklore

01047
Tijl Uilenspiegelmuseum
Huyze de Grote Sterre, Kerkstraat 14,
B-8340 Damme
General Museum - 1977
Collection of paintings, etchings and
statues depicting Uilenspiegel

01048
Zeemuseum Zeeland en het Zwin
Zuidvaartdijk 3, B-8351 Damme
General Museum
Ship models; furniture (in Louis XV
and Flemish Renaissance styles);
maps; paintings by Antoon Devaere

Dampicourt

01049
Museum van het Boerenleven
Montquintin, B-6763 Dampicourt
General Museum
Country life

Deinze

01050
**Museum voor Oudheidkunde,
Folklore en Nijverheid**
Emiel Clausplein, B-9800 Deinze
General Museum - 1929
Crafts and industries; archeology;
Flemish ceramics; arms; furniture

01051
**Museum voor Schone Kunsten van
Latem en Leiestreek**
Emiel Clausplein, B-9800 Deinze
Fine Arts Museum
Paintings and sculptures of the Latem
school and by regional painters

Dendermonde

01052
**Stedelijk Oudheidkundig Museum
Vleeshuis**
Grote Markt 32, B-9330 Dendermonde
General Museum - 1895
Archeology; history; folklore;
iconography

De Panne

01053
Koningin Astridmuseum
Zeelan 9, B-8470 De Panne
History/Public Affairs Museum - 1977
World War I documentation; Royal
Astrid Queen of Belgium and King
Albert collection; Red Cross;
sculptures

Deurle

01054
**Gemeentelijk Museum Gust De
Smet**
Gust De Smetdreef 1, B-9831 Deurle
Historic Site - 1950
House of the painter Gustav De Smet
(1877-1943) and parts of his works;
antiquities

01055
Musée Leon De Smet
Museumlaan 14, B-9831 Deurle
Fine Arts Museum
Works of the painter Léon De Smet
and personal effects

01056
**Museum Mevrouw Jules Dhondt-
Dhaenens**
Museumslaan 12, B-9831 Deurle
Fine Arts Museum - 1967
Paintings of Flemish expressionist and
modern art

Deurne

01057
**Natuurhistorisch Museum
Boekenbergpark**
Boekenbergpark, B-2100 Deurne
Natural History Museum
Div: speleology; mineralogy;
prehistory; archeology; paleontology

01058
Provinciaal Museum Sterckshof
Hooftvunderlei 160, B-2100 Deurne
General Museum - 1954
Historical arts and crafts from the
Flemish part of Belgium; general
history of photography in prints and
cameras; Renaissance painted
wooden ceiling (about 1545); civil
silversmith work (17th-18th c.);
wet-collodion portable field darkroom
(1860) - library; workshop pewter and
photography

01059
Volksmuseum Gallivorde
Koraalplaats 2, B-2100 Deurne
General Museum - 1970
Coll: local history and paleontology
(whalebones); wage earners and the
industrial revolution - library in
preparation

Diest

01060
Stedelijk Museum Diest
Stadhuis, Grote Markt, B-3290 Diest
General Museum - 1957
Local art and history; decorative arts;
painting 'The last Judgement'
(1420-1450) - library

Diksmuide

01061
Stedelijk Museum Diksmuide
Stadhuis, Grote Markt, B-8160
Diksmuide
General Museum - 1927
Coll: Objects recalling Word War I;
rural life; paintings and postcards;
remainders of the Gothic sculptures
'Het Doksaal', destructed in World War
I - library

01062
Vredesmuseum
Yzerdijk 2, B-8160 Diksmuide
History/Public Affairs Museum
Memorials and documents relating to
World Wars I and II; paintings by Sam
De Vriendt and Joe English

Drogenbos

01063
Museum Felix De Boeck
Grande route, 222, B-1620 Drogenbos
Fine Arts Museum
Works of painter F. De Boeck

Durbuy

01064
**Musée Archéologique, Science,
Pêche et Folklore**
Halle aux Blés, Grand-rue, B-5480
Durbuy
General Museum
Archeology; hunting; folklore; local
flora and fauna; religious objects
(15th-18th c.); domestic utensils

Ecaussinnes-Lalaing

01065
Musée du Chateau-Fort
Château, mail c/o M.F. Cartuyvels, rue
de Seneffe, 5, B-7191 Ecaussinnes-
Lalaing
Fine Arts Museum
Furniture; paintings; glasses;
porcelain; sculptures; portraits;
ceramics

Eeklo

01066
Heemmuseum Eeklo
Raamstraat, B-9900 Eeklo
Anthropology Museum
Folklore

Elouges

01067
Musée Communal Georges Mulpas
Square des Combattants, rue du
Commerce, B-7370 Elouges
General Museum - 1968
Local archeology (prehistoric, Gallo-
Roman, Merovingian); documents;
regional industries; numismatics;
folklore

Essen

01068
Folkloremuseum
Heuvelplein 23, B-2190 Essen
General Museum
Rural interiors; farm implements;
crafts; folklore and religious objects -
library

01069
Karrenmuseum
Moerkansebaan 54, B-2190 Essen
Historic Site
Historic farm house; agricultural and
industrial vehicles, vehicles for the
conveyance of passengers

Falmignoul

01070
Musée de la Petite Reine
rue de la Draisienne, 152, B-5511
Falmignoul
History/Public Affairs Museum
Bicycles and motorcycles since 1818

Flobecq

01071
Musée Robert Pollaert
rue Wahier, 6, B 26=7880 Flobecq
General Museum
Ancient crafts; archeological finds

Fontaine-l'Evêque

01072
Musée de la Mine
Château, B-4140 Fontaine-l'Evêque
History/Public Affairs Museum
Mining

Gaasbeek

01073
Staatsdomein van Gaasbeek
Groenstraat 11, B-1682 Gaasbeek
Decorative Arts Museum
Medieval and Renaissance
architecture; antiquities; paintings,
sculptures (15th-18th c.); furniture;
tapestries - library; archives

Geel

01074
St. Dimpna- en Gasthuismuseum
Gasthuisstraat 3 en 5, B-2440 Geel
Anthropology Museum
Folkloristic furniture; household
articles in tin, copper and earthenware;
details about the cult of St. Dimpna
and the boarding out of mental
patients; treasures of the Geel parish
churches

Genk

01075
**Gemeentelijk Museum Emiel Van
Doren**
H. Decleenestraat 21, B-3600 Genk
Fine Arts Museum - 1976
Works of the painter Emiel Van Doren
(1865-1949); studio, furniture and
personal effects

01076
Heemkundig Museum
H. Decleenestraat 21, B-3600 Genk
General Museum - 1977
Folklore; costumes; domestic utensils;
manuscripts; photos; shells and
fossils; mining tools; religious items

01077
Openluchtmuseum Bokrijk
Domein Bokrijk, B-3600 Genk
General Museum - 1953
Popular rural and urban life of Flanders

Gent

01078
**Archeologisch Museum van de
Universiteit**
Blandijnberg 2, B-9000 Gent
Archeology Museum
Prehistory; Gallo-Roman period;
Middle Ages; mainly objects from
Belgium but also from Italy, Spain,
France, Switzerland, the Netherlands
and Germany

01079
**Etnografische Collecties van de
Universiteit**
Sint-Hubertusstraat 2, B-9000 Gent
Anthropology Museum - 1968
Ethnological objects from Africa,
America and Melanesia; archeology;
glass; folklore

01080
Hôtel de Ville
Botermarkt, B-9000 Gent
Historic Site
Historic halls with various art objects;
place of the peace treaty between
Protestants and Catholics in 1576

01081
Krocht van de St.-Baafskathedraal
St.-Baafsplein, B-9000 Gent
Religious Art Museum
Crypt of the former 'St.-Janskerk' with
wall paintings (12th c.); Justus van
Gent 'Calvarie' (15th c.); H. Andreas
Pourbus 'Leven' (16th c.); frescoes
(15th c.)

01082
Meerhemmuseum Instituut Sint-Jan
de Deo
Fraterplein, B-9000 Gent
General Museum
History of the local textile industry and
religious traditions

01083
Museum Arnold van der Haeghen
Veldstraat 82, B-9000 Gent
History/Public Affairs Museum - 1975
History of Gent in the 19th century;
Maurice Maeterlinck (1862-1942)
room; Victor Stuyvaert (1897-1974)
room

01084
Museum van de Sint-Jorisgilde
Vrouwebroederstraat 6a, B-9000 Gent
History/Public Affairs Museum
Archives, documents and arms of the
rifle association of St.George

01085
Museum van Hedendaagse Kunst
De Liemaeckereplein 3, B-9000 Gent
Fine Arts Museum - 1976
Art since 1945

01086
Museum voor Schone Kunsten
Citadelpark, B-9000 Gent
History/Public Affairs Museum - 1902
Old and modern art; painting

01087
Museum voor Sierkunst
Jan Breydelstraat 7, B-9000 Gent
Decorative Arts Museum - 1903
Art objects and decorations (15th-19th
c.); furniture, dining room and lustre by
J.F. Allaert (1703-1779); writing desk of
Louis XVIII - library

01088
Museum voor Volkskunde
Kraanlei 63, B-9000 Gent
General Museum - 1962
Crafts, industries and folklore from
around 1900

01089
Museum Wetenschap en Techniek
Korte Meer 7-9, B-9000 Gent
Science/Tech Museum - 1965
Medicine; biology; thermodynamics
astronomy; chemistry;
telecommunication; Prof. Deneffe
collection of ancient ophthalmological
apparatus - library; films

01090
Natuurmuseum - Michel Thiery
St. Pietersplein 14, B-9000 Gent
Natural History Museum - 1924
Minerals; molluscs; insects; fossils;
birds and mammals; biology of man;
specimen of Conus gloriamaris -
library; educational service for schools
and children

01091
**Oudheidkundig Museum van de
Bijloke**
Godshuizenlaan 2, B-9000 Gent
History/Public Affairs Museum - 1833
Decorative arts; folklore; history;
armaments; ceramics; painting;
sculpture; glass; goldsmith art;
costumes

01092
Sint Baafsabdij
Gandestraat, B-9000 Gent
Religious Art Museum
Ruins of an old abbey; romanesque
refectory; ruins dating back to the 12th
century; wall paintings; archeological
objects; stone sculptures

Geraardsbergen

01093
Museum van het Abtenhuis
Abdijstraat 10, B-9500
Geraardsbergen
Religious Art Museum - 1962
Coll: Japanese and Chinese faience;
Louis XV and Renaissance furniture;
paintings by Dutch masters and the
Laguillère-school; Sèvre vase, once
the property of a French king,
representing the battle of Fontenoy; a
'boudoir', identical to the Salle des
Glaces of Versailles

Gesves

01094
Musée de la Préhistoire Cavernes
Préhistorique de Goyet
Vallée du Samson, B-5132 Gesves
Archeology Museum
Caves; Paleolitic human fossils; traces
of human existence tools; arms;
ornaments; fossils of animals from the
surroundings of Wurm glaciation

Gistel

01095
Sint-Godelievemuseum
Centre provincial, B-8240 Gistel
Religious Art Museum - 1972
Religious objects and traditions

Gomzé-Andoumont

01096
**Petit Musée de la Poupée du XIXe
Siècle**
Château de Mosbeux, route du Rys de
Mosbeux, B-4941 Gomzé-Andoumont
History/Public Affairs Museum
Porcelain puppets

Grobbendonk

01097
Archaeology Museum
Gemeenthuis, *mail c/o* Nete en Aa
VZW, Oude Steenweg 13 A, B-2280
Grobbendonk
Archeology Museum
Results of archeological excavations
1200 BC- 300 AC

01098
Diamantmuseum
Bovenpad 3 A, *mail c/o* Nete en Aa
VZW, Oude Steenweg 13 A, B-2280
Grobbendonk
Decorative Arts Museum
Different kinds of diamonds and
diamond treatment; diamond polishers
at work

Halen

01099
**Museum van de Slag der Zilveren
Helmen**
Rothemstraat 14, B-3460 Halen
History/Public Affairs Museum
Uniforms from 1870 to 1914; arms;
documents

Halle

01100
**Basilique de Notre Dame de
Hal-Crypte**
B-1500 Halle
Religious Art Museum
Religious treasury

01101
Klokkenmuseum
Tour de la Basilique, B-1500 Halle
History/Public Affairs Museum - 1973
Historic bells and chimes

Hamme

01102
**Archeologisch Museum 'Van
Bogaert-Wauters'**
Museumstraat 3, B-9160 Hamme
General Museum - 1955
Archeology; history - library

Han-sur-Lesse

01103
Musée de Monde Souterrain
A proximité des grottes, B-5432
Han-sur-Lesse
Archeology Museum
Archeology; geology

Harelbeke

01104
Peter Benoitmuseum
Marktstraat 55-57, B-8730 Harelbeke
Historic Site
Archives, manuscripts, furniture and
personal effects of the Flemish
composer Peter Benoit

Hastière-par-delà

01105
Musée et Patrimoine Hastière
Tour de l'église romane, rue Moussia,
B-5541 Hastière-par-delà
General Museum
Archeological objects (prehistoric,
Roman and medieval); coins; tools;
religious traditions; photos and
documents

Heist-op-den-Berg

01106
Heemmuseum 'Die Swane'
Gemeentelijk Museumgebouw
Kerkplein, B-3100 Heist-op-den-Berg
General Museum - 1956
Local history and folklore

01107
**Spoorwegmuseum van
Miniaturmodellen** Gemeentelijk
Museumgebouw
Kerkplein, B-3100 Heist-op-den-Berg
History/Public Affairs Museum - 1971
History and models of steam
locomotives

Herentals

01108
Fraikin-Museum
Stadhuis, B-2410 Herentals
Fine Arts Museum - 1893
Works of sculptor Charles-Auguste
Fraikin

Herstal

01109
**Musée Communal Herstalien
d'Archeologie et de Folklore**
Place Licourt, 25, B-4400 Herstal
General Museum - 1971
Arms; folklore; archeology; paintings
and sculpture of local artists;
Merovingian gravestone

Hoegaarden

01110
Musée 't Nieuwhuys Hoegaarden
Fondation Julien van Nerum
Ernest Ourystraat 2-4, B-3320
Hoegaarden
General Museum - 1965
Archeology; local history; folklore;
crafts and industries

Hoeilaart

01111
Musée de Hoeilaart
W. Eggerickxstraat 16, B-1990
Hoeilaart
General Museum
Local history and archeology

Hoogstraten

01112
Stedelijk Ostmuseum
Begijnhof 1, B-2320 Hoogstraten
Fine Arts Museum - 1976
Works by the painter Alfred Ost;
archeological objects; local furniture -
archives

Houthalen

01113
Provinciaal Automuseum
Domein Kelchterhoef, B-3530
Houthalen
Science/Tech Museum - 1970
History of motorcars

Huy

01114
Musée Communal de Huy
rue Vankeerberghen, B-5200 Huy
General Museum
Prehistoric archeology; local history;
sculpture; folklore; medieval pottery;
arts and crafts; religious art

01115
Musée du Fort de Huy
Quai de Namur, B-5200 Huy
History/Public Affairs Museum - 1967
Arms; museum will be reorganized

01116
Tresor de la Collegiale
Quai de Namur, B-5200 Huy
Religious Art Museum
Goldsmith art; reliquary of Gedefroi
De Huy; sculpture

Ieper

01117
Hotel-Museum Merghelynck
Merghelynckstraat 2, B-8900 Ieper
Decorative Arts Museum
Patrician house with period furniture
and decorative art; Chinese and
Japanese porcelain

01118
Museum O.C.M.W. Belle Godshuis
Rijselsestraat 38, B-8900 Ieper
Fine Arts Museum - 1962
Painting; stitching; costumes;
furnishing; goldsmith art; pewter;
madonna of 1420

01119
**Provinciaal Museum voor Moderne
Kunst**
Lakenhalle, B-8900 Ieper
Fine Arts Museum - 1974
Paintings, sculptures, drawings,
etchings from the expressionists up to
the present - children's workshop and
catalogue in preparation

01120
Salient Museum '14-18'
Grote Markt, B-8900 Ieper
History/Public Affairs Museum - 1927
History of World War I

Ingooigem

01121
Provinciaal Museum Stijn Streuvels
'Het Lijsternest'
Stijn Streuvelsstraat 24, B-8561
Ingooigem
Historic Site - 1980
Library, furniture, paintings, household
effects of Streuvels' lifetime;
photographic exhibition about the
author's life; general view of
bookprinting from the 15th to the 20th
century; paintings by Constant
Permeke, Albert Saverys, Rik
Slabbinck

Ivoz-Ramet

01122
**Musée de Préhistoire des
Chercheurs de la Wallonie**
rue des Chercheurs de la Wallonie, 1,
B-4120 Ivoz-Ramet
Natural History Museum - 1907
Prehistoric archeology; paleontology;
mineralogy; biospeleology

Izegem

01123
Stedelijk Schoeiselmuseum
Wijngaardstraat 9, B-8700 Izegem
History/Public Affairs Museum
History of the shoemaking craft and
industry

Izenberge

01124
**Regionale Heemmusea Bachten de
Kupe v.z.w.**
Groenestraat 26, B-8993 Izenberge
General Museum - 1970
Crafts; regional archeology; religious
customs; textile industry; peasant life

Jabbeke

01125
**Provinciaal Museum Constant
Permeke**
Gistelsteenweg 341, B-8220 Jabbeke
Fine Arts Museum - 1969
Paintings, drawings and sculpture by
C. Permeke; documents, photos and
correspondence of Permeke; works
of P. Devos, F. Van den Berghe, O.
Jespers, L. Peire

Jehay-Bodegnée

01126
**Musée Historique et Préhistorique
van den Steen**
Château de et à Jehay, B-5262 Jehay-
Bodegnée
History/Public Affairs Museum
Prehistoric relics; Greek and Roman
objects; Celtic jewelry; memorials of
the Duke and the Duchess of
Malborough

Jette-Saint-Pierre

01127
Musée Communal Musée National de
Figurines Historiques, Musée
Archéologique
Maison abbatiale de Dielegem, rue
Jean Tiebackx 24, B Jette-Saint-Pierre,
Bruxelles
General Museum
Figurines of tin, lead, plastic and other
materials; archeology

Kanne

01128
Musée Souterrain
Avergat, B-3778 Kanne
Natural History Museum
Paintings of prehistoric animals and
plants; fossils; grottos

Keerbergen

01129
De Botermolen
Oudstrijderslaan 21, B-2850
Keerbergen
Anthropology Museum
Folklore; church furniture; toys

Knokke-Heist

01130
Heemkundig Museum 'Sincfala'
Pannestraat 140, B-8390 Knokke-Heist
General Museum - 1960
Archeology; folklore; agricultural
equipment; fishing; German
emergency money and various relics
from 1940-1945 - library

Koksijde

01131
Museum van de Duinenabdij
Koninklijke Prinslaan 8, B-8460
Koksijde
General Museum
Regional history and archeology; flora
and fauna; architecture

01132
Museum van de Westhoek
Strandlaan 295, Sint-Idesbald, B-8460
Koksijde
Fine Arts Museum - 1975
Sculpture

01133
National Museum for Mechanical Organs
R. Vandammestraat 45, B-8460
Koksijde
Science/Tech Museum - 1974

Kontich

01134
Museum voor Heem- en Oudheidkunde
Molenstraat 32, B-2550 Kontich
General Museum - 1959
Folklore; prehistory; pottery and ceramics; textiles; religious art and traditions; craftmen's tools - library

Kortrijk

01135
Begijnhofmuseum
Begijnhofstraat, B-8500 Kortrijk
History/Public Affairs Museum
Buildings, archives and photos relating to the Beguines

01136
Museum voor Schone Kunsten en Museum voor Oudheidkunde en Sierkunst
Broelkaai 6, B-8500 Kortrijk
Fine Arts Museum
Old and modern painting; objects of the Stone and Bronze Ages; Gallo-Roman antiquities; folklore; ceramics; damask collection 'de Béthune'; works by Roeland Savery

01137
Nationaal Vlasmuseum
Stijn Streuvelslaan, B-8500 Kortrijk
History/Public Affairs Museum
Tools and machinery used in the Belgian linen industry; paintings; photos; sculptures

Laarne

01138
Kasteel Slot van Laarne
Eekhoek 5, B-9270 Laarne
Decorative Arts Museum - 1965
Silverware (15th-18th c.); furniture (17th-18th c.); tapestries (15th-17th c.); pictures (16th-17th c.)

Lahamaide

01139
Musée Vivant de Lahamaide
B-7882 Lahamaide
Agriculture Museum
Ancient agricultural methods and rural handicrafts

Lasne

01140
Musée Ribauri
rue du Musée, 4, B-1338 Lasne
Anthropology Museum
Primitive art from Africa, Oceania; Indian and Chinese art; shells

Latour

01141
Musée Baillet-Latour
rue Baillet,, B-6761 Latour
History/Public Affairs Museum - 1964
History of the castle of Latour and its inhabitants

Lavaux-Sainte-Anne

01142
Musée de la Chasse, de la Venerie et de la Protection de la Nature
Château de Lavaux-Sainte-Anne,
B-6926 Lavaux-Sainte-Anne
General Museum - 1958
Castle (14th c.); hunting and hunting costumes; ornithology; botany; furniture; art objects

Lembeke

01143
Musée Bardelaere
Dorp 41, B-9971 Lembeke
General Museum - 1975
Agricultural implements; handicrafts; domestic utensils; religious art; toys

Lessines

01144
Musée d'Histoire de la Ville de Lessines
Hôpital Notre-Dame de la Rose,
B-7860 Lessines
General Museum
Ancient furniture; paintings; tin; porcelain; local industry; military history in preparation

Leuven

01145
Archief en Museum van het Vlaams Studentenleven
Bibliothèque de l'Université, Mgr
Ladeuzeplein 21, B-3000 Leuven
History/Public Affairs Museum - 1925
Archives, documents and manuscripts, books and journals concerning student life

01146
Museum voor Kerkelijke Kunst Sint-Pieterskerk
Grote Markt, B-3000 Leuven
Religious Art Museum
Thierry Bouts: 'The Last Supper'

01147
Provinciaal Van Humbeeck-Pironmuseum
Sint-Jorisdal, Mechelsevest 108,
B-3000 Leuven
Fine Arts Museum
Works of the architects and painters Pierre Van Humbeeck and Maria Piron

01148
Stedelijk Brouwerijmuseum
Hôtel de Ville, B-3000 Leuven
History/Public Affairs Museum
Local economic and social history in connection with the brewing industry

01149
Stedelijk Museum Vander Kelen-Mertens
Savoyestraat 6, B-3000 Leuven
General Museum
Coll: painting of the Leuven school (Albert Bouts, Quentin Metsys, Jan Willems, Jan Rombauts); Brabantine sculpture (15th-16th c.); arts and crafts, goldsmith work, porcelain, ceramics, pottery

Lièege

01150
Musée de la Boverie (Ancien Musée des Beaux-Arts)
Parc de la Boverie, 3, B-4020 Liège
Fine Arts Museum - 1819
Coll: old masters; modern Belgian painting; French painting from Boudin to Picasso; sculpture; Collection Graindorge - library

Liège

01151
Aquarium et Musée de Zoologie de l'Université de Liège Institut de Zoologie
Quai Van Beneden, 22, B-4020 Liège
Natural History Museum
Stuffed animals and skeletons

01152
Cabinet des Estampes et Dessins
Parc de la Boverie, 3, B-4020 Liège
Fine Arts Museum - 1951
Copper engraving and drawings of local artists (16th c.- present days); works of Adrien de Witte, Auguste Donnay, François Maréchal - library

01153
Musée Curtius
Quai de Maestricht 13, B-4000 Liège
General Museum - 1909
Gallo-Roman archeology; Frankish gold jewels; glass; numismatics of Liège from the Merovingian period to the 18th century ; decorative arts; Mosan art (11th-13th c.); furniture (16th-18th c.); silverware; ivory; French miniatures; European and Oriental ceramics (medieval-19th c.)

01154
Musée Curtius-Hypocauste
Place Saint-Lambert, B-4000 Liège
Archeology Museum - 1910
Prehistoric, Gallo-Roman and medieval archeology

01155
Musée d'Ansembourg
Féronstrée 114, B-4000 Liège
Decorative Arts Museum - 1905
Applied and decorative arts of the 18th century at Liège, especially furniture

01156
Musée d'Architecture
Impasse des Ursulines, B-4000 Liège
Decorative Arts Museum

01157
Musée d'Armes de Liège
Quai de Maestricht, 8, B-4000 Liège
History/Public Affairs Museum - 1885
Firearms and mechanism of firearms (14th-20th c.); edged and defensive weapons (Prehistory-20th c.); medals, decorations and orders of Chivalry; only fourteen-barrelled flintlock rifle ever made; only surviving example of Chambers seven-barrelled swivel-gun (224 shots); double wheellock pistol, which belonged to Louis XIII - library

01158
Musée d'Art Religieux et d'Art Mosan (Ancien Musée Diocésain)
Basilique Saint-Martin, rue Mont-Saint-Martin, B-4000 Liège
Religious Art Museum - 1880
Coll: medieval sculpture; textiles; goldsmith art; Flemish and Italian painting (16th c.); German and Dutch painting (15th c.)

01159
Musée de la Vie Vallonne
Cour de Mineurs, B-4000 Liège
Anthropology Museum - 1912
Ethnography; folklore; rural crafts and agriculture; puppets; glass; religion and science; Max Elskamp sun-dials collection - library

01160
Musée du Fer et du Charbon Section du Musée de la Vie Walo010nne
bd R. Poincaré, 17, B-4020 Liège
Science/Tech Museum
Metalworking industries and coal mines; reconstruction of Walloon iron foundry (18th c.); blast furnace using charcoal; melting iron techniques; bar iron production; kitchen utensils; coal miner's tools - library

01161
Musée du Verre
Quai de Maestricht, 13, B-4000 Liège
Decorative Arts Museum - 1959
Glass production from the beginnings to 20th century - library

01162
Musée en Plein Air
Domain universitaire du Sart Tilman,
Bâtiment B5, B-4000 Liège 1
Fine Arts Museum - 1976
Plastic art

01163
Musée et Collections Artistiques de l'Université
Place du XX Août, B-4000 Liège
Natural History Museum
Paleontology; geology; mineralogy; paintings and engravings; medals; musical instruments; arms and masks from Africa

01164
Studio Eugene Ysaye
Impasse des Ursulines, 14, B-4000
Liège
History/Public Affairs Museum
Reconstruction of the studio of Master Ysaye with furniture, music library, works of art and memorials

01165
Trésor de la Cathédrale St. Paul
6, rue Bonne Fortune, mail c/o Ch.
Zeevaert, sacristain, 2a, rue St. Paul,
B-4000 Liège
Religious Art Museum
Goldsmith art; ivory; manuscripts (11th and 13th c.)

Lier

01166
Museum Wuyts-Van Campen en Baron Caroly
Fl. Van Cauwenberghstraat 14, B-2500
Lier
Fine Arts Museum
Paintings, including works by Rubens, Van Dyck, Sneyders, Floris; prints; decorative arts; furnishing; porcelain

01167
Het Timmermans-Opsomer Huis
Netelaan 4, B-2500 Lier
Historic Site
Reconstructed painter's studio of Baron I. Opsomer; paintings, drawings, watercolours, etchings; reconstructed working room of Felix Timmermans; pen drawings, manuscripts, letters; iron works by Lodewijk Van Boeckel; room devoted to musical composer Renaat Veremans

01168
Zimmertoren
Zimmerplein 18, B-2500 Lier
Science/Tech Museum - 1930
Astromical clocks; 'The time and space'

Ligny
01169
Musée Napoleonien
Ancienne Maison Communale de Ligny, B-6338 Ligny
History/Public Affairs Museum
Objects relating to the Emperor and his epoch

Lokeren
01170
Museum van Oudheidkunde en Folklore
Groote Kaai 1, Lokeren, *mail c/o* M. Frans De Vos, Luikstraat 49, B-9100 Lokeren
General Museum
Local history; folklore; ethnology; paintings; sculpture; furnishing; museum is temporarily closed for restauration

Lommel
01171
Lommels Museum
Dorp 14, B-3900 Lommel
General Museum - 1958
Coll: Farmer's stateroom; agriculture; prints; maps; local lore objects; archeology

01172
Prehistorisch Museum Eymard-Instituut
mail c/o P.Henri De Cock, Oude Diestersebaan 5, B-3900 Lommel
Archeology Museum - 1947
Stone objects; urns

Maaseik
01173
Apotheek en Stedelijk Museum
Markt 46, B-3680 Maaseik
General Museum - 1962
Prehistory; weapons; furniture; ivory; folklore; oldest chemistry of Belgium, Delft and tin chemist's pots, old chemist's instruments; spice cultivation

Marche-en-Famenne
01174
Musée de la Tourelle
Rempart des Jésuites, *mail c/o* Syndicat d'initiative, rue de Luxembourg, 52, B-5400 Marche-en-Famenne
General Museum
Arms; prehistorical archeology; ancient documents; craftmen's tools

Marchienne-au-Pont
01175
Musée Marchiennois
Place des Martyrs, 36, B-6030 Marchienne-au-Pont
General Museum - 1976
Local history from Gallo-Roman times to the present; regional industrial development

Maredret
01176
Le Musée du Bois
rue des Artisans, 33a, B Maredret, Anhée
Decorative Arts Museum
All kinds of wooden objects

Mariembourg
01177
Chemin de Fer à Vapeur des Trois Vallées
Remise des locomotives, B-6370 Mariembourg
Science/Tech Museum - 1979
Steam engines and steam locomotives

Martelange
01178
Musée de la Haute Sure
rue du Musée, 244, B-6630 Martelange
General Museum
Reconstruction of the interior of a slater's house of 1600, furniture, kitchen utensils

Massemen
01179
Musée Varekouter
B-9201 Massemen
Agriculture Museum
Ancient agricultural tools and household utensils

Mechelen
01180
Ernest Wijnantsmuseum
Minderbroedersgang 5, B-2800 Mechelen
Fine Arts Museum
Sculptures of Ernest Wijnants

01181
Museum der Oude Mechelse Kunstambachten 'Huis De Zalm'
Zoutwerf 5, B-2800 Mechelen
Decorative Arts Museum
Former Mechlin industrial arts; lace; gold-leather; tin; iron; silver; copper; bronze; history of fishmonger trade

01182
Museum voor Folklore
XII Apostelenstraat 17, B-2800 Mechelen
Anthropology Museum - 1962
Inn; chemist's shop; puppet-show; processions; trades; instruction; chattels; popular devotion

01183
Stedelijk Museum 'Hof van Busleyden'
Fr. De Merodestraat 67, B-2800 Mechelen
General Museum
Gallo-Roman collection; paintings (15th-19th c.); contemporary art; numismatics; history of crafts and guilds

Melle
01184
Gemeentelijk Museum
Brusselsesteenweg 395, B-9230 Melle
General Museum - 1973
Archeology; folklore

Merksem
01185
Hofke van Roosendael
Terlindenhofstraat 265, B-2060 Merksem
General Museum
Folklore; local history

01186
Museum van de Archeologische Stichting 'Petronella'
Terlindehofstraat 206 A, B-2060 Merksem
Archeology Museum - 1971
Archeology; paleontology

Mesen
01187
Gemeentelijk Museum Mesen
Stadhuis, Markt, B-8942 Mesen
General Museum
Folklore; ancient Mesen abbey; history of World War I

Mol
01188
Musée Jakob Smits
Sluis 155, B-2400 Mol
Historic Site - 1977
Graphic art and painting by the Dutch artist Jakob Smits; documentation on his life; works of contemporaries

01189
Natuurhistorisch Museum-Provinciaal Domein 'Zilvermeer'
Zilvermeerlaan, B-2400 Mol
Natural History Museum
Regional flora and fauna; ornithology

Mons
01190
Chapelle et Crypte Saint Calixte
Square du Château, B-7000 Mons
History/Public Affairs Museum
Roman vault; medieval iconography

01191
Musée de la Vie Montoise
Maison Jean Lescarts, rue Neuve, 9, B-7000 Mons
General Museum
Paintings; ancient arms; statues; furniture; weights and measures; folklore especially handicrafts and festivals; archeology

01192
Musée des Beaux-Arts de la Ville de Mons
rue Neuve, 8, B-7000 Mons
Fine Arts Museum - 1913/1970
Coll: primitive painting (Nicolas de Neuchatel, Corneille De Vos); Flemish painting (16th c.); French painting (17th-18th c.); Dutch painting (17th-18th c.); Italian painting (18thc.); contemporary Flemish school; sculpture

01193
Musée d'Histoire Naturelle de Mons
rue des Gaillers, 7, B-7000 Mons
Natural History Museum - 1839
Natural history; skeleton of giant Constantin (2,59 m)

01194
Musée du Chanoine Puissant 'Vieux Logis' - 'Attacat'
rue de Notre-Dame Débonnaire, rue des Sars, B-7000 Mons
Religious Art Museum - 1934
Furniture; crafts objects; wrought iron work; weapons; modern ceramics by Sars-La-Bruyère; drawings; religious objects; goldsmith art; wood sculptures; vestments; old textiles; manuscripts; books (15-18th c.); Gutenberg bible - library

01195
Musée du Vieux Nimy
rue Mouzin, 31, B-7000 Mons
General Museum - 1973
Pipes; ancient tools used in the local crafts; local folklore; history of the battle of Mons in 1914

01196
Musées du Centenaire
Jardins du Maïeur, B-7000 Mons
General Museum - 1930
Coll: archeology; numismatics; ceramics; history of World War I and II

01197
Trésor de la Collegiale Sainte-Waudru
Salle du Chapitre, *mail c/o* Melle Tondreau, rue du Gouvernement, 29, B-7000 Mons
Religious Art Museum - 1958
Goldsmith art; religious vestments; documents

Morlanwelz-Mariemont
01198
Musée Royal de Mariemont
Chaussée de Mariemont, B-6510 Morlanwelz-Mariemont
Archeology Museum - 1920
Antiquities from Egypt, the Middle East, Greece, Rome, China, Japan; local Gallo-Roman and Merovingian archeology; porcelain of Tournai; bookbindings - library

Mortroux
01199
Musée de la Roue et de la Vie Régionale
Relais du Trimlen, rue Nelhein, 115, B-4543 Mortroux
Science/Tech Museum
Reconstructed sirup factory; agricultural implements; vehicles; ancient machinery

Mouscron
01200
Musée Communal de Folklore Léon Maes
rue de la Résistance, B-7700 Mouscron
General Museum
Folklore; arts and crafts

Namur
01201
Musée Archéologique
Halle des Bouchers, rue du Pont, B-5000 Namur
Archeology Museum
Prehistoric, Greek and Roman archeology; history; decorative arts

01202
**Musée d'Armes et d'Histoire
Militaire du Comte de Namur**
Route Merveilleuse, 4, B-5000 Namur
History/Public Affairs Museum - 1957
Military history; arms; hunting and
sports; local history

01203
Musée de Groesbeeck de Croix
rue I. Saintraint, 3, B-5000 Namur
General Museum
Furniture; paintings; history; ceramics;
glasses; art objects

01204
**Musée des Archives de l'Etat à
Namur**
rue d'Arquet, 45, B-5000 Namur
History/Public Affairs Museum - 1931
Historical documents (8th-20th c.)

01205
**Musée des Arts Anciens du
Namurois**
Hôtel de Gaiffier d'Hestroy, rue de Fer,
24, B-5000 Namur
Fine Arts Museum
Regional art objects from the Middle
Ages to Renaissance

01206
Musée Diocésain
Place du Chapitre, 1, B-5000 Namur
Religious Art Museum - 1896
Medieval goldsmith art; portable altar
with ivory decoration; crown reliquary
of Saint Doornen; sculpture (11th-18th
c.); vestments; glass

01207
Musée Felicien Rops
Hôtel de Gaiffier d'Hestroy, rue de Fer,
24, B-5000 Namur
Fine Arts Museum - 1964
Paintings and engravings by Felicien
Rops

01208
Musée Provincial de la Forêt
Route Merveilleuse, 7, B-5000 Namur
Natural History Museum - 1901
Fauna and flora of Walloon forests;
exotic insects; arboretum

01209
Le Tresor d'Hugo d'Oignies
Ecole des Sœurs de Notre Dame, rue
Julie Billiard, B-5000 Namur
Religious Art Museum
Medieval goldsmith art (13th c.)

Neufchâteau

01210
Musée de la Vie Ardennaise
Place du Faubourg, B-6620
Neufchâteau
General Museum
Agricultural machinery and
implements; domestic utensils;
handicrafts

Neufchâteau-Dalhem

01211
Musée du Fort d'Aubin Neufchâteau
rue du Colonel d'Ardenne, 1, B-4561
Neufchâteau-Dalhem
History/Public Affairs Museum - 1977
Arms and ammunition; military history
and archives

Nevele

01212
**Streekmuseum van het Land van
Nevele 'Rietgaverstede'**
A.C. Vander Cruyssenstraat, 60,
B-9850 Nevele
General Museum - 1963
Archeology; local history; crafts and
guilds; transport and industry; military
history; local literature; agriculture;
natural history; folklore

Nieuwpoort

01213
Museum van Vogels en Schaaldieren
Stadshalle, Marktplein, B-8450
Nieuwpoort
Natural History Museum - 1956
Ornithology; shells

01214
**Museum voor Plaatselijke
Geschiedenis**
Stadshalle, Marktplein, B-8450
Nieuwpoort
General Museum - 1974
Maps and plans; local history
documents; folklore; memorabilia of
World War I

Nismes

01215
Maison des Bailles
rue Vieille Eglise, B-6380 Nismes
General Museum - 1972
Local history; folklore; local
archeology; genealogy; works of
painter Fernand Charlier

Nivelles

01216
Musée Charles Gheude
av de la Tour de Guet, BE-1400
Nivelles
Fine Arts Museum - 1968
Paintings and sculptures from Belgium
(19th-20th c.)

01217
Musée d'Archéologie
rue de Bruxelles, 27, B-1400 Nivelles
General Museum - 1956
Art history; archeology; ceramics

Oedelem

01218
Musée de Folklore
Hoogstraat 11, B-8330 Oedelem
General Museum - 1964
Folklore; archeology

Oelegem

01219
Textielmuseum Vrieselhof
Schildesteenweg 79, B-2231 Oelegem
Decorative Arts Museum - 1977
Lace; costumes; textile craft
techniques; recent Flemish textile art -
library

Oevel

01220
**Heemmuseum van de Gemeente
Westerlo en Ambachtsmuseum van
de Zuiderkempen**
St. Michielsstraat 1, B-2431 Oevel
General Museum - 1970
Local history; iconography; tools from
local arts and crafts

Olsene

01221
Gemeentelijk Museum
Kerkstraat 36, B-9870 Olsene
General Museum - 1978
Ancient furniture; porcelain; tapestries;
paintings; tin

Oostduinkerke

01222
Folkloremuseum 'Florishof'
Koksijdesteenweg 24, B-8458
Oostduinkerke
Decorative Arts Museum - 1972
Holy-water vases; Romanesque vases;
ancient documents; tools; crafts; old
inn; chapel (1660); shed with ancient
agricultural implements

01223
**Visserijmuseum Burgemeester H.
Loones**
Pastoor Smitzstraat 2, B-8458
Oostduinkerke
History/Public Affairs Museum - 1975
Tombstones with the names of 352
fishermen; documents on fishery; ship
models since the 8th century;
porcelain with ornaments relating to
fishing; house of a fisherman with
interiors

Oostende

01224
Heemkundig Museum 'De Plate'
Feest- en Cultuurpaleis, Wapenplein,
B-8400 Oostende
General Museum
Folklore; local history

01225
James Ensorhuis
Vlaanderenstraat 27, B-8400 Oostende
Historic Site
Reconstitution of the last home of
James Ensor (1860-1949)

01226
**Museum voor Moderne Religieuze
Kunst**
Sint-Sebastiaanstraat 41, B-8400
Oostende
Religious Art Museum - 1974
Religious art of James Ensor, Constant
Permeke, Léon Spillaert, Jan De
Clerck, Jacob Smits, Gustave Van de
Woestijne, Paul Vermere and others

01227
Museum voor Schone Kunsten
Feest- en Cultuurpaleis
Wapenplein, B-8400 Oostende
Fine Arts Museum
Modern art from Ensor to
contemporary tendencies

Opheylissem

01228
**Musée de Folklore et d'Histoire
Armand Pellegrin**
Ancienne Ecole des garçons, rue du
Moulin, B-5919 Opheylissem
General Museum - 1930
Local history; crafts; pottery; pipes;
ancient machinery; religious
documents

Orp-le-Grand

01229
Musée Archéologique d'Orp
rue Hagnoul, 52, B-5960 Orp-le-Grand
Archeology Museum
Prehistory; Iron Age pottery; Gallo-
Roman and Merovingian finds

Oud-Turnhout

01230
Museum Albert Van Dyck
Priorij Corsendonk, B-2360
Oud-Turnhout
Fine Arts Museum - 1975
Albert Van Dyck Collection

Oudenaarde

01231
Stadsmuseum
Stadhuis, Grote Markt, B-9700
Oudenaarde
General Museum - 19th century
Flemish and Dutch paintings (15th-19th
c.); sculptures; tapestries; weapons;
iron industry; Mechlin leather; local
history and folklore

Oudenburg

01232
Gemeentelijk Museum
Weststraat 33, B-8230 Oudenburg
Archeology Museum
Remains of a fortress from the Roman
period

Overmere

01233
Boerenkrijgmuseum
Gemeentehuis Overmere, Baron
Tibbautstraat 2, B-9280 Overmere
History/Public Affairs Museum - 1960
Memorials of the Peasants' War, which
started at Overmere in 1798; local
folklore

Poperinge

01234
**Nationaal Hopmuseum 'De
Stadsschaal'**
Groothuisstraat 71-73, B-8970
Poperinge
Agriculture Museum
History of hop cultivation

Raeren

01235
Musée de la Poterie
Château de Raeren, B-4730 Raeren
Decorative Arts Museum - 1963
History of local pottery (12th-19th c.)

Rekem

01236
Gemeentelijk Museum
Groenplaats, mail c/o M. Maesen,
Kleinveldlaan 15, B-3620 Rekem
Religious Art Museum - 1956
Church furniture (17th-18zh c.)

Rochefort

01237
Musée du Pays de Rochefort
av d'Alost, 5, B-5430 Rochefort
General Museum - 1965
Cultural history of the region

Roeselare

01238
Pauselijk Zouavenmuseum Stedelijk
Museum voor Volkskunde en
Plaatselijk Geschiedenis
Polenplein, B-8800 Roeselare
Religious Art Museum

01239
Stedelijk Museum voor Volkskunde en Plaatselijke Geschiedenis
Polenplein, B-8800 Roeselare
General Museum
Local history and folklore

Roisin

01240
Maison Emile Verhaeren
rue Bargettes 14, B-7386 Roisin
History/Public Affairs Museum
Study of poet E. Verhaeren
(1855-1916) and affiliated documents

Roly

01241
Musée des Fagnes
Château de Roly, mail c/o
Conservateur M. René Mathot, rue
Basse Cornet, 2, B-6371 Roly
General Museum
Archeology; geology; paleontology;
history; local flora and fauna; folklore

Ronse

01242
Museum voor Folklore en Plaatselijke Geschiedenis St.
Hermeskrypte
Priesterstraat 15, B-9600 Ronse
General Museum - 1937
Local history; folklore; interiors of
middle-class houses; trades and
guilds; archeology of the Roman
period and early Middle Ages; stone
objects

Ruisbroek-Puurs

01243
Museum 'De Bres'
Gemeentehuis, Dorp, B-2658
Ruisbroek-Puurs
History/Public Affairs Museum - 1976
Mementoes of the flood on January
3rd 1976 - library

Rumes

01244
Musée Gallo-Romain A.S.B.L.
Ecole Communale, rue H. Delaisse,
B-7610 Rumes
Archeology Museum - 1965
Prehistoric tools; Gallo-Roman
ceramics; Merovingian vases; Roman
safe

Rupelmonde

01245
Scheldeland-Reinaertmuseum
Mercatoreiland, Kasteelstraat, B-2628
Rupelmonde
General Museum - 1955
Folklore; regional art objects; ship
building, navigation and fishing;
documents on geographer Gerardus
Mercator (16th c.); water mill; statue
'Uilenspiegel groet de Schelde'

Saint-Hubert

01246
Musée de la Vie Rurale en Wallonie
Musée provincial de la Province de
Luxembourg
Fourneau Saint Michel, Palais Abbatial,
B-6900 Saint-Hubert
Open Air Museum - 1971
Peasant houses with furniture and
domestic utensils from different parts
of the region; ancient crafts - library

01247
Musée des Archives Archives de
l'Etat Saint-Hubert
Pl de l'Abbaye, 12, B-6900 Saint-
Hubert
History/Public Affairs Museum - 1978
Regional archives

01248
Musée du Fer Musées Provinciaux
Luxembourgeois
Fourneau Saint Michel, Palais Abbatial,
B-6900 Saint-Hubert
Science/Tech Museum - 1950
Ancient metallurgy (12th-18th c.) -
library

Saint-Vith

01249
Zwischen Venn und Schneifel
Heckingstraße 2, B-4780 Saint-Vith
General Museum - 1967
Coll: ancient habitation and country
life; sacred art; ancient crafts;
historical documents on the region of
Saint-Vith

Schelle

01250
Heemmuseum Bijsterveld
Peperstraat 48, B-2621 Schelle
General Museum
Religious art; interiors (1900-1910);
agricultural implements; machinery
(1900-1910)

Schepdaal

01251
Trammuseum
Ninoofsesteenweg 184, 1750
Schepdaal, mail c/o J. de Meurs, av
G.B. Lebon, 159, B-1150 Bruxelles
Science/Tech Museum - 1962
Urban and suburban railways; photos

Schoten

01252
Mineralogisch Museum
Churchilllaan 59, mail c/o Academy for
Mineralogy, J.Hendrickxstraat 49,
B-2120 Schoten
Natural History Museum - 1979
Minerals; stones; fossils

's-Gravenwezel

01253
Heemkundig Museum 'De Drie Rozen'
Kerkstraat 41, B-2232 's-Gravenwezel
General Museum
Interiors; genealogy; numismatics;
military items; folklore - library

Sint-Amands

01254
Emile Verhaeren Museum
Sint-Amandskaai 22, B-2688
Sint-Amands
History/Public Affairs Museum - 1968
Works, portraits and documents of the
poet E.Verhaeren

Sint-Martens-Latem

01255
Latems Museum voor Moderne Kunst
B-9830 Sint-Martens-Latem
Fine Arts Museum - 1974
Contemporary Flemish painting and
sculpture

Sint-Niklaas

01256
Stedelijk Museum voor Volkskunde, Oude Ambachten, Regionale Geschiedenis, Exlibris en Schone Kunsten
Zamanstraat 49, B-2700 Sint-Niklaas
General Museum - 1861
Crafts; folklore; tin; copper; devotion;
heraldry; maps; engravings; paintings;
regional paleontology; archeology

Sint-Truiden

01257
Brustempoort Museum
Luikerstraat, B-3800 Sint-Truiden
Historic Site - 1969
Medieval gate; ammunition chambers;
weapons; plans and maps

01258
Festraets Studio
Begijnhof, B-3800 Sint-Truiden
Science/Tech Museum - 1974
Restraets clock; the Foucault
pendulum; rotation of the earth round
the sun; ruins of the abbey; reliquary

01259
Provinciaal Museum voor Religieuze Kunst
Begijnhof 59, B-3800 Sint-Truiden
Religious Art Museum - 1979
Cycle of mural paintings (13th-17th c.);
sculpture - library

01260
Sint Franciscusmuseum
Minderbroederstraat 5, B-3800
Sint-Truiden
Fine Arts Museum
Medieval sculpture and painting
(Rubens, Rembrandt)

Soignies

01261
Musée du Vieux-Cimetière
rue Henry Leroy, 17, B-7400 Soignies
Fine Arts Museum - 1895
Prehistoric and medieval archeology;
paintings (16th-18th c.); sculpture
(14th-19th c.); ceramics; porcelain;
'Christ au Golgatha' (sculpture,15th c.);
'Adoration des Mages' (painting, 1520)

Spa

01262
Musée de la Ville d'Eaux
av Reine Astrid, 77, B-4880 Spa
Fine Arts Museum
Drawings; engravings; wood painting

01263
Musée du Cheval
av Reine Astrid, 77, B-4880 Spa
Anthropology Museum
Documents on horse racing

Sprimont

01264
Musée Communal de la Pierre
Place Joseph Wauters, Ancien Hôtel
de Ville, B-4060 Sprimont
Science/Tech Museum
Industrial and artistic treatment of
stone; extracting methods and tools;
fossils; shells; minerals

Stavelot

01265
Musée de l'Ancienne Abbaye
B-4970 Stavelot
General Museum - 1926
History of the tanning industry; local
history documents; painting (17th-18th
c.); sculpture; goldsmith art;
contemporary paintings (Delvaux,
Spilliaert, Mambour, Claus, Tytgat);
works of Degouve de Nuncques

01266
Musée Guillaume Apollinaire
Hôtel de Ville, rue du Châtelet, B-4970
Stavelot
History/Public Affairs Museum - 1954
Works (various editions), manuscripts
and biography of G.Apollinaire
(1880-1918); letters from his friends;
reconstruction of his room; paintings
by Marie Laurencin; bronze figure by
O. Zadkine

01267
Trésor de l'Eglise Primaire de Saint-Sebastien
rue de l'Eglise, B-4970 Stavelot
Religious Art Museum
Religious goldsmith art; sacerdotal
vestment

Temse

01268
Gemeentemuseum
Kasteeldreef 16, B-2690 Temse
General Museum
Archeology; painting and sculpture by
local artists; local history - library

Terhagen

01269
Museum van de Baksteennijverheid
Steenbakkerijk Heylen, Nieuwstraat,
B-2651 Terhagen
Science/Tech Museum - 1978
Briquet manufacturing

Tervuren

01270
Musée Royal de l'Afrique Centrale
Steenweg op Leuven, B-1980
Tervuren
Anthropology Museum - 1898
Coll: ethnography, mainly African art
and technology, musical instruments;
prehistory and archeology of tropical
Africa; zoology, African vertebrates
and invertebrates; wood of tropical
regions; European involvement in
Africa; geology and minerals of Africa;
Statue of King Kata Mbula, Kuba,
Zaire; statue of Ndengeze, Zaire; Luba
helmet-mask, Zaire; wood sculpture of
8th-9th century, Angola - library

Tielt

01271
Hageland Museum
Gemeentehuis, Kruisstraat, B-3211
Tielt
General Museum - 1955
Regional history and folklore;
domestic utensils; tools

Tienen

01272
Stedelijk Museum 'Het Toreke'
Grote Markt, B-3300 Tienen
General Museum - 1978
Gallo-Roman archeology; medieval
and baroque sculpture; silver
ornaments; folklore - library

Tongeren

01273
Moerenpoortmuseum
Leopoldwal, B-3700 Tongeren
History/Public Affairs Museum
Porter's kitchen; print room; guild
room

01274
Provinciaal Gallo-Romeins Museum
Kielenstraat 15, B-3700 Tongeren
Archeology Museum - 1854
Coll: prehistory; Gallo-Roman
archeology; Merovingian archeology

01275
Schatkamer van de Onze-Lieve-Vrouwebasiliek
Grand-Place, B-3700 Tongeren
Religious Art Museum
Goldsmith art; vestments; ivory;
silverware; manuscripts (10th-11th c.)

01276
Stedelijk Museum
Stadhuisplein 9, B-3700 Tongeren
General Museum - 1963
Sculpture; local history; ceramics;
numismatics; goldsmith work; glass;
charters; guilds

Tournai

01277
Musée de Folklore
Réduit des Sions, B-7500 Tournai
General Museum - 1930/1950
Folklore; interiors (19th c.); religious
life; documents of nobility; uniforms;
carnival; crafts; topography; maps

01278
Musée de la Tour Henri VIII
rue des Remparts, B-7500 Tournai
History/Public Affairs Museum
Military history; arms and weapons;
documents of resistence during World
War II

01279
Musée de Paléontologie et de Préhistoire
rue des Carmes, 8, B-7500 Tournai
Natural History Museum
Geology; mineralogy; natural history;
fossils; oceanography

01280
Musée des Beaux Arts
Enclos St.-Martin, 3, B-7500 Tournai
Fine Arts Museum
Old Flemish Masters (including Rogier
van der Weyden, Jaques Danet,
Mabuse, Pieter Huys, Jordaans);
modern art, painting, sculpture,
drawings, prints; French and Belgian
paintings (19th-20th c.); Belgian and
French impressionists

01281
Musée d'Histoire et d'Archéologie et des Arts Decoratives
rue des Carmes, 8, B-7500 Tournai
General Museum - 1953
History and arts and crafts of Tournai;
Gallo-Roman and Merovingian
objects; medieval and Renaissance
sculpture; tapestries (15th-16th c.)
from Tournai; manuscripts; porcelain;
silverware

01282
Musée d'Histoire Naturelle de la Ville de Tournai
Cour de l'Hôtel de Ville, B-7500
Tournai
Natural History Museum - 1829
Zoology; botany; fauna of Madagascar

01283
Trésor de la Cathedrale Notre-Dame
Place de l'Evêché, B-7500 Tournai
Religious Art Museum
Ivory; goldsmith art; tapestries;
vestments; lace; coat of Emperor
Charles; Byzantine cross

Tubize

01284
Musée de la Porte
rue de Bruxelles, 62, B-1360 Tubize
General Museum - 1968
Folklore; art objects; ancient
pharmaceutical laboratory; paintings
by Jules Genthier; religious traditions
crafts; local history

Turnhout

01285
Kempisch Vogelmuseum De
Wielewaal
Graatakker 11, B-2300 Turnhout
Natural History Museum
Stuffed birds in their natural
environment

01286
Nationaal Museum van de Speelkaart
Begijnenstraat 28, B-2300 Turnhout
Decorative Arts Museum - 1965
Playing cards and archives of
Turnhout; engines for the production
of cards - library

01287
Oudheidkundig Museum van het Begijnhof
Béguinage, 56, B-2300 Turnhout
History/Public Affairs Museum
History of the Beguines (12th-17th c.)

01288
Taxandria Stadsmuseum
Mermansstraat 27, B-2300 Turnhout
General Museum - 1913
Regional history; furniture (17th-18th
c.); sculpture; archeology (prehistoric
to 7th c.); folklore; numismatics;
decorative arts; paintings - library

Uccle

01289
Musée David et Alice van Buuren
av Léon Errera, 41, B Uccle, Bruxelles
Fine Arts Museum
Paintings (Pieter Bruegel the elder,
Seghers, Fantin-Latour, Joachim
Patenier, Rik Wouters, Constant
Permeke, James Ensor, Van de
Woestijne, Max Ernst); sculpture;
drawings

Velzeke

01290
Gallo-Romeins Museum
Paddestraat 7A, B-9610 Velzeke
Archeology Museum - 1972
Roman pottery, glasses, ironware;
relics from Merovingian tombs

Verviers

01291
Musée d'Archéologie et de Folklore
rue des Raines, 42, B-4800 Verviers
Archeology Museum - 1959
Prehistoric, Egyptian, Greek, Roman,
Gallo-Roman and Frankish archeology;
folklore; history; furniture (17th-19th
c.); weapons (18th-19th c.); lace;
Roman coins

01292
Musée des Beaux-Arts et de la Ceramique
rue Renier, 17-19, B-4800 Verviers
Fine Arts Museum - 1884
Paintings of Liège, Flemish, Dutch,
French and Italian masters; 19th-20th
century paintings; modern Belgian and
French prints; 15th-16th century
sculptures; porcelain; Raeren
sandstones

Veurne

01293
Baretta-Museum
Grote Markt 1, B-8480 Veurne
Fine Arts Museum
Art and history exhibits

Vieux-Genappe

01294
Musée de la Ferme du Caillou
Chaussée de Bruxelles, B-1472 Vieux-Genappe
History/Public Affairs Museum
Memorials of Napoleon I; documents;
furniture; weapons

Villers-devant-Orval

01295
Musée de l'Abbaye d'Orval
Abbaye Notre-Dame d'Orval, B-6823
Villers-devant-Orval
History/Public Affairs Museum - 1935
Ruins of medieval abbey (from 12th c.
on); sculptures; paintings; manuscripts;
medical utensils; garden of medical
plants

Virton

01296
Musée Gaumais
rue d'Arlon, 38-40, B-6760 Virton
General Museum
Cast-iron hearth plates, wrought iron,
pot hangers, firedogs, stoves, locks;
furniture (17th-19th c.); reconstruction
of 18th and 19th century interiors and
workshops; prehistoric, Gallo-Roman,
Merovingian archeology; watercolours
by Nestor Outer; wood sculpture (16th
c.); Boch faience (18th c.)

Visé

01297
Musée de la Compagnie Royale des Anciens Arquebusiers de Visé
rue Haute, 11, B-4540 Visé
History/Public Affairs Museum
History of firearms; documents on
local history

01298
Musée de la Société Royale des Anciens Arbaletriers Visetois
rue Haute, 44, B-4540 Visé
History/Public Affairs Museum
Folklore; ethnology; history;
armaments

01299
Musée Régional d'Histoire et d'Archéologie
Hôtel de Ville, rue des Récollets, 1,
B-4540 Visé
General Museum
Prehistorical objects; Roman pottery;
Belgian guilds

Vlijtingen

01300
Heemkundig Museum 'Slag van Lafelt'
Oud Gemeentehuis, Mheerplaats,
B-3758 Vlijtingen
Archeology Museum
Prehistory; Iron Age; Roman and
Merovingian period; medieval pottery;
documents on the Battle of Lafelt

Vresse-sur-Semois

01301
Musée du Tabac et du Folklore
rue Grande, 44, B-6869 Vresse-sur-Semois
Anthropology Museum
Local folklore; cultivation and use of
tobacco

Waasmunster

01302
Musée de l'Abbaye de Roosenberg
Roosenberg, Oude Heirweg 20,
B-9170 Waasmunster
History/Public Affairs Museum - 1937
Religious history; documents on the
history of Abbey Roosenberg; maps
(17th-18th c.); iconography; religious
books; paintings; furniture - library

Wachtebeke

01303
Moervarststede
Kalve 70, B-9070 Wachtebeke
General Museum
Historical arms; coins; folklore;
popular religious objects; relics from
World War I and II

01304
Provinciaal Molenmuseum
Puyenbrug 3, B-9070 Wachtebeke
Science/Tech Museum
Water and wind mills; mill
construction; documentation on milling

Waterloo

01305
Musée Wellington
Chaussée de Bruxelles, 147, B-1410
Waterloo
Historic Site
Quarters of General Wellington at the
time of the victory against Napoleon in
June 1815; personal objects of
Wellington and Colonel Gordon; arms;
engravings

Wavre

01306
Musée Cantonnal
rue de l'Escaille, 2, B-1300 Wavre
Archeology Museum - 1964
Archeology (prehistory to Gallo-Roman period)

Weert

01307
Streekmuseum van Klein-Brabant
'De Zilverreiger'
Scheldestraat 14, B-2681 Weert
General Museum - 1969
Crafts; regional flora and fauna

Westerlo

01308
Musée Léonard de Vinci (Abbaye, Tongerlo)
B-3180 Westerlo
Fine Arts Museum - 1966
Replica of L. da Vinci's 'The Last Supper' with documentation

Wetteren

01309
Heemkundig Museum Wetteren
Maison Communale, Markt, B-9200 Wetteren
General Museum
Folklore; popular religious objects; ancient crafts; relics of World War II

01310
Poppenmuseum 'Christus Koning'
Parochiaal, Oude Aardeweg, B-9200 Wetteren
Religious Art Museum
Religious traditions; puppets with religious vestments

Wezemaal

01311
Lampenmuseum
Steenweg Leuven-Aarschot 86, B-3111 Wezemaal
History/Public Affairs Museum
Lamps from various centuries and countries

Wijtschate

01312
Vredesmuseum Wijtschate 1914-1918
Croonaertdomein, Voormezelestraat 2A, B-8940 Wijtschate
History/Public Affairs Museum
Relics of World War I and II

Willebroek

01313
National Memorial Fort Breendonk
B-2660 Willebroek
History/Public Affairs Museum
Fort occupied during World War I and World War II; concentration camp (World War II); Jacques Ockx collection

Woluwe-Saint-Lambert

01314
Musée Communal
rue de la Charrette, 40, B Woluwe-Saint-Lambert, Bruxelles
General Museum
Local flora and fauna; prehistory and history; folklore; ecology; ancient furniture - library

Wommelgem

01315
Heemmuseum 'De Kaeck'
Dasstraat 25, B-2220 Wommelgem
General Museum
Agricultural machinery; domestic utensils; guilds; photos

Xhoris

01316
Musée Local de Xhoris
Maison Communale de Xhoris, B-4183 Xhoris
General Museum
Reconstructed ancient kitchen; tools used in the local handicrafts; agricultural implements

Zeebrugge

01317
Zeebruggemuseum
Pieter Troostlaan 7, B-8380 Zeebrugge
History/Public Affairs Museum - 1923
Objects relating to World Wars I and II

Zichem

01318
Stichting Huize Ernst Claes V.Z.W.
Ernest Claesstraat 152, B-3280 Zichem
History/Public Affairs Museum - 1966
Works of the writer Ernest Claes, manuscripts, photos and personel effects; furniture; domestic utensils

Zillebeke

01319
Sanctuary Wood - Hill 62
Canadalaan 26, B-8902 Zillebeke
History/Public Affairs Museum
Photos and various materials from World War I

Zonhoven

01320
Voorhistorisch Museum
Fraters, Kleine Hemmen 4, B-3520 Zonhoven
Archeology Museum
Prehistory; geology

Zoutleeuw

01321
Sint-Leonardus Kerk
Markt 2, B-3440 Zoutleeuw
Religious Art Museum - 1945
Medieval church, typical Romanesque-Gothic with the features of the Rhine and Meuse style; treasures preserved intact from the 11th century till nowadays; statues (11th-19th c.); Baptismal font (16th c.); stone tabernacle of the holy Sacrament (1550-52 by Cornelis Floris De Vriendt), containing 200 statues

Zulte

01322
Museum Modest Huys
Modest Huyslaan 44, B-9780 Zulte
Fine Arts Museum - 1960
Paintings and drawings of Modest Huys (1874-1932)

Zwijndrecht

01323
Musée Alfred Ost
Maison Communale, B-2730 Zwijndrecht
Fine Arts Museum
Works by the painter Alfred Ost

Benin

Abomey

01324
Musée Historique
Institut français d'Afrique noire, Abomey
History/Public Affairs Museum

Cotonou

01325
Musée de Cotonou
Institut français d'Afrique noire, Cotonou
General Museum
Ethnographic collections

Ouidah

01326
Musée d'Histoire
Ex-Fort Portugais, Ouidah
History/Public Affairs Museum
History of the colonial period (1420-1960) and the discovery of the Gulf of Guinea

Parakou

01327
Musée de Plein Air, d'Ethnographie et de Science Naturelles
Parakou
Natural History Museum
Natural history and ethnography

Porto-Novo

01328
Musée Ethnographique
BP 6, Porto-Novo
General Museum
Exhibits on the tribes of Dahomey

Bermuda

Hamilton

01329
Bermuda Government Aquarium and Museum
Smith's Parish, Hamilton
Natural History Museum - 1926
Live Bermuda fishes and invertebrates in natural environment; Bermuda natural history artifacts and displays; marine animals including corals, shells, sponges, crustacenas, echinoderms; geology; botany and ornithology

01330
Bermuda Historical Society Museum
Par-la-Ville, Hamilton
History/Public Affairs Museum
local history

01331
Verdmont
Collector's Hill, Smith's Parish, Hamilton
General Museum
portraits by Judge Green; old Bermuda cedar furniture

St. George's

01332
Carriage Museum
Water St, St. George's
General Museum
coaches and carriages

01333
The Confederate Museum
The King's Parade, St. George's
General Museum
History of Bermuda's role in the American Civil War; old furniture

01334
President Henry Tucker House
Water St., St. George's
General Museum - 1955
paintings by Blackburn; furniture

01335
St. George's Historical Society Museum
Duke of Kent St., St. George's 1-07
History/Public Affairs Museum - 1920
Bermuda cedar furniture; silver coins; local historical objects

Bhutan

Paro

01336
National Museum of Bhutan
Tag-Dzong, Paro, Rinpung Dzong
General Museum - 1968
Northern Buddhist and Bhutanese art objects

Bolivia

Cochabamba

01337
Museo Arqueológico Universitario
Universidad Mayor de San Simón
Oquendo Esq. Calama, Cochabamba
Archeology Museum
archaeology; paleolithic finds; ceramics; pre-Inca and pre-Columbian cultures; metal

La Paz

01338
Museo 'Casa de Murillo'
Jean 790, La Paz
Anthropology Museum - 1950
archaeology; objects of Kallwaya civilization; pre-Columbian masks; ceramics of Tihuanaco; Inca and Mollo, colonial and Bolivian folk art; silver 18th and 19th century; 18th century painting

01339
Museo Fritz Buck Embajada Alemana
Av. Arce 2395, La Paz
Archeology Museum
archaeology; folklore

01340
Museo Mineralogico
Calle Comercio no. 1290, La Paz
Natural History Museum
Minerals of Bolivia and other countries

01341
Museo Nacional de Arqueologia
Tihuanacu 93, Casilla Oficial 64, La Paz
Archeology Museum - 1846
archaeology; anthropology; ethnology; zoology; numismatics; traditional native arts and crafts; colonial art; Lake Titicaca district exhibitions - library

01342
Museo Nacional de Arte
Socabaya 485, La Paz
Fine Arts Museum - 1961
folklore

Potosi

01343
Museo de la Casa Nacional de la Moneda
Calle Ayacucho s/n, Apdo. 39, Potosí
History/Public Affairs Museum - 1938
Silver mint machinery (1750); history; mineralogy; numismatics; regional ethnography; archaeology; modern art - library, archives

Sucre

01344
Museo Antropologico Palacio de Gran Poder
Bolívar 401, Apdo. 212, Sucre
Anthropology Museum - 1944
ethnography; folklore; archaeology; items of pre-Inca civilization

01345
Museo de Arte Colonial 'Charcas'
Bolívar 401, Sucre
Archeology Museum
colonial art; folklore

01346
Museo del Ateneo de Bellas Artes
Sucre
Fine Arts Museum
fine arts

Botswana

Gaborone

01347
Botswana National Museum and Art Gallery
Independence Av, POB 114, Gaborone
General Museum
Local history and customs; art of Africa south of the Sahara; loan exhibitions

Kanye

01348
Kgosi Bathoen II Museum
Private Bag 2, Kanye
General Museum
Ethnology; archeology and natural history housed in old London Missionary Church

Lobatse

01349
Postal Museum
Lobatse
History/Public Affairs Museum
National historical stamp collection; items related to history of national postal services

Mochudi

01350
Phuthadikobo Museum and Centre
POB 367, Mochudi
General Museum
Photography; ethnography - art training facility

Brazil

Belém

01351
Museu Paraense Emilio Goeldi
Av. Independencia, C.P. 399, Belém
Natural History Museum - 1866
anthropology; ethnography; zoology; botany; natural sciences of the Amazonia - library

Belo Horizonte

01352
Fundação Palácio das Artes
Av. Afonso Pena 1.537, Belo Horizonte
Fine Arts Museum - 2942

01353
Museu de Arte e História Racioppi
Rua Padre Eustáquio 1.442, Belo Horizonte
Fine Arts Museum - 1931
Profane and religious art from Antiquity to the present

01354
Museu Histórico Abilio Barreto
Rua Bernardo Mascarenhas, Belo Horizonte
General Museum - 1941
local history

Botafogo

01355
Casa de Rui Barbosa
Rua São Clemente 134, 22,260 Botafogo, Rio de Janeiro
History/Public Affairs Museum - 1930
Rui Barbosa's personal belongings; furniture; silver; porcelain; sculptures; paintings; ceramics; jewelry; medals; carpets; books; drawing; documents - library

Brasília

01356
Fundação Cultural do Distrito Federal
Av. W-3, 508, lote 47, Brasília
History/Public Affairs Museum
Documentation on the evolution and construction of Brasília

Cachoeira

01357
Museu das Alfaias da Paróquia da Cachoeira
Igreja Matriz de N. Sa. do Rosário da Cachoeira, Cachoeira
Religious Art Museum
Objects of gold, silver and precious stones; paintings (17th and 18th c.)

Caeté

01358
Casa Setecentista de Caeté
Rua Monsenhor Domingos s/no., Caeté, Minas Gerais
General Museum - 1979
Colonial furniture and religious art; musical instruments; objects from the collection of novelist Cornélio Pena

Campanha

01359
Museu Dom Inocencio
Rua João Luiz Alvez 76, Campanha
General Museum
Coins; minerals; books and manuscripts

Campinas

01360
Centro de Ciências, Letras e Artes
Museu Carlos Gomes
Rua Bernardino de Campos 989, Campinas
Music Museum - 1955
Documents and personal belongings of Gomes family

01361
Museu Arquidiocesano de Campinas
Rua Aquidabã 734, Campinas
General Museum - 1964
Art works; historical objects

01362
Museu de Arte Contemporãnea de Campinas
Av. Saudade 1.004, Campinas
Fine Arts Museum - 1965
Brazilian contemporary art

01363
Museu Ferroviário da Cia. Mogiana de Estradas de Ferro
Rua Sales de Oliveira 1.380, Campinas
History/Public Affairs Museum - 1965
Historic photographs, uniforms, furnishings and equipment used by the railroads

01364
Museu Municipal de Campinas
Bosque de Jequitibás, Campinas
Natural History Museum - 1939

Campo Grande

01365
Museu Regional D. Bosco
Av. Pres. Kennedy, Campo Grande
General Museum - 1951
history; ethnography

Campos do Jordão

01366
Coleção do Palácio do Governo de Campos do Jordão
Palácio Boa Vista, Campos do Jordão
General Museum - 1964
Painting and sculpture; antique furniture, porcelain; religious objects; Persian carpets

Carpina

01367
Museu do Instituto Histórico
Praça Carlos Pena 94, Carpina
General Museum - 1962
Antique weapons; numismatics; religious objects

Cataguases

01368
Museu de Belas-Artes
Chácara da Granjaria, Cataguases
Fine Arts Museum

Curitiba

01369
Casa de Alfredo Andersen Museu e Escola de Arte
Rua Mateus Leme 336, Curitiba
Fine Arts Museum - 1971
Paintings, drawings, and personal belongings of Alfredo Andersen

01370
Museu Davi Carneiro
Rua Comendador Araújo, Curitiba
General Museum
history; classical archaeology

01371
Museu do Homem Departamento do Antropologia, Universidade Federal do Praná
Rua General Carneiro 460, s/619, Curitiba
Anthropology Museum - 1957
Indian ethnography; paleontology and prehistoric archeology; folklore

01372
Museum Paranaense
Praça Generoso Marques s/no., POB 1442 80,000 Curitiba, Paraña
General Museum - 1876
history; anthropology; ethnography; prehistory; sculpture; graphic arts; metalwork arms; numismatic - library

Diamantina

01373
Museu do Diamante
Rua Direita 14, Diamantina
General Museum - 1954
Minerals; furniture and altar pieces; paintings and ceramics

Feira de Santana

01374
Museu Regional de Feira de Santana
Rua Geminiano Costa s/no., Feira de Santana
Fine Arts Museum - 1967
Local and national art, particularly contemporary works; English contemporary art

Florianópolis

01375
Museu de Antropológia da Universidade Federal de Santa Catarina
Ciudade Universitaria, C.P. 798, Florianópolis
Anthropology Museum
social anthropology; archaeology; geology; prehistory; folklore

Fortaleza

01376
Arquivo Publico e Museu Historico de Estado de Ceara
Praça da Sé 332, Fortaleza
History/Public Affairs Museum
archives and documents

01377
Museu Artur Ramos
Rua Barão do Rio Branco 1.321, Fortaleza
General Museum
Ethnography (Artur Ramos Collection); popular art; archeology and prehistory

01378
Museu de Arte da Universidade do Ceara
Av. Visconde de Cauipé 2854, Fortaleza
Fine Arts Museum

01379
Museu Gustavo Barroso
Colégio Militar de Fortaleza, Parça da Bandeira, s/no., Fortaleza
History/Public Affairs Museum

Goiânia

01380
Museu de Ornitologia
Avenida Pará 381-395, 74,000 Goiânia, Goiás
Natural History Museum - 1968
ornithology - library; archive; laboratory

01381
Museu de Ornitologia
Av. Pará 393/395, Goiânia
Natural History Museum - 1968
Fauna of the province of Goià and of
Brazil in general

01382
**Museu Estadual do Professor
Zoroastro Artiaza**
Praça Civica, Goiânia
General Museum
Ethnography and anthropology;
natural history; archeology;
numismatics; furniture and paintings;
items of local history

Goiás

01383
Museu das Bandeiras
Praça Dr. Brasil, Goiás
History/Public Affairs Museum - 1950
Artifacts, mostly from the 18th cent.,
from the history of the region; objects
from the local churches; ceramics

Govea

01384
Museu da Cidade
Parque de Cidade, Govea
General Museum

Guaira

01385
Museu Sete Quedas
Av. Joaquim Dornelles Vargas 479,
Guaira
Natural History Museum - 1961
Zoology, botany, archeology,
ethnology, mineralogy, and
numismatics

Guarapuava

01386
**Museu Municipal Visconde de
Guarapuava**
Rua Visconde de Gurarpuava 288,
Guarapuava
General Museum - 1956
Indian agricultural and domestic
utensils; local history

Itatiaia

01387
Museu Parque Nacional do Itatiaia
Itatiaia
Natural History Museum - 1942
local flora

Itú

01388
**Museu Republicano Convenção de
Itú**
Rua Barão de Itaim 69, Itú
General Museum - 1923
history; folklore

João Pessoa

01389
**Museu-Escola Esacro do Estado da
Paraiba**
Praça São Francisco s/no., João
Pessoa
General Museum - 1970
Anthropology and ethnography;
archeology; geography; religious art;
local history;natural history

Juazeiro do Norte

01390
**Museu Civico-Religioso Padre
Cicero**
Rua São José 224, Juazeiro do Norte
1951
Artifacts of Amazon Indians; local
folklore and folk art; natural history

Juiz de Fora

01391
**Museu do Banco de Crédito Real de
Minas Gerais S.A.**
Rua Halfeld 504, Juiz de Fora
History/Public Affairs Museum - 1964
Numismatics and banking

01392
Museu Mariano Procópio
Rua Mariano Procópio, Juiz de Fora
General Museum - 1921
Porcelain, furniture, and painting
(19th-20th c.)

Lavras

01393
Museu Histórico
Escola Superior de Agricultura de
Lavras, Lavras
General Museum - 1949
Local history; furnishings; instruments
of torture; documents and maps

Lençóis

01394
Casa de Cultura Afrânio Peixoto
Praça Afrânio Peixoto, s/no., Lençóis
Historic Site - 1970
Memorabilia of A. Peixoto

Macapá

01395
Museu Territorial do Amapá
Fortaleza de S. José de Macapá,
Macapá
General Museum - 1948
zoology; archaeology; ethnography
and numismatics of Amapá territory

Maceió

01396
**Museu Comercial e Arqueológico do
Sindicato dos Empregados**
Rua João Pessoa 418, Maceió
Archeology Museum

01397
Museu de Arte Sacra Dom Ranulfo
Igreja do Rosário, Rua João Pessoa
270, Maceió
Religious Art Museum - 1966
Paintings and icons; religious books
and objects

Manaus

01398
**Museu e Biblioteca do Instituto
Geográfico e Histórico do Amazonas**
Rua Bernardo Ramos 131, Manaus
General Museum - 1917
history; natural history - library

01399
Museu Indigena Salesiano
Rua Duque de Caxias s/n, 69,000
Manaus, Amazonas
General Museum - 1952
music instruments; hunting and fishing
tools; weaving; ceramics; arts and
crafts - library

01400
**Seção de Numismática do Estado do
Amazonas**
Palácio Rio Branco, Av. Pedro II,
Manaus
History/Public Affairs Museum
World-wide collections of antique
coins

Mariana

01401
Museu Arquidiocesano de Mariana
Rua Frei Durão 49, Mariana
Fine Arts Museum

Natal

01402
Museu Câmara Cascudo
Av. Hermes da Fonseca 1398, Natal,
Rio Grande do Norte
General Museum - 1961
Regional archeology; natural history,
Brazilian ethnology

01403
Museu de Arte e História
Rua da Conceição 601, Natal
General Museum
Fine arts and folk art; Indian art;
domestic utensils characteristic of the
region; arms; various historical
artifacts

01404
**Museu de Artre Popular da Fortaleza
dos Reis Magos**
Fortaleza dos Reis Magos, Rua Trairi
558, Natal
Decorative Arts Museum - 1966
Furnishings, sculpture, applied arts

01405
**Museu do Instituto de Antropologia
Cæmara Cascudo**
Av. Hermes da Fonseca 1.398, Natal
General Museum
Collections in anthropology, natural
history, paleontology, etc.

01406
**Museu do Instituto Histórico e
Geográfico do Rio Grande do Norte**
Rua da Conceição, Natal
General Museum
history; geography

Niteroi

01407
Museu Antonio Parreiras
Rua Tiradentes 47, Niteroi
Fine Arts Museum - 1941
paintings and drawings from Antônio
Parreiras; European paintings;
Brazilian contemporary art

Nova Era

01408
Museu Municipal de Arte e História
Praça da Matriz, Nova Era
Fine Arts Museum - 1965
Profane and sacred art collections
demonstrating the history of art

Olinda

01409
Museu Regional de Olinda
Rua do Amparo 128, Olinda
General Museum - 1934
history; art

Ouro Prêto

01410
Museu da Inconfidência
Praça Tiradentes 139, 35,400 Ouro
Preto, Minos Gerais
General Museum - 1944
colonial art; history; objects related to
the 1789 revolutionaires of Minos
Gerais; wood carvings; furniture;
paintings; religious art; silver - library

01411
Museu de Arte e Historia Casa de
Gonzaga
Rua do Ouvidor 9, Ouro Prêto
General Museum
art; history

Ouru Preto

01412
**Museu da Escola Nacional de Minas
e Matalurgia**
Praça Tiradentes 20, Ouru Preto
Natural History Museum - 1876
mining and metallurgy

Paranaguá

01413
**Museu de Arqueologia e Artes
Populares**
Rua Quinze de Novembro 567,
Paranaguá
Anthropology Museum - 1965
Prehistoric archeology (Brazil, Asia,
Africa and Europe); Brazilian arts and
crafts

Pelotas

01414
**Museu e Biblioteca Pública
Pelotense**
Praça Coronel Pedro Osório 103,
Pelotas
General Museum

Petrópolis

01415
Museu de Armas Ferreira da Cunha
Rodovia Washington Luis, km 40,
Petrópolis
History/Public Affairs Museum - 1957
Brazilian, European, African and
Asiatic arms

01416
Museu Imperial
Av. de Sete de Setembro 94 e 220,
Petrópolis
History/Public Affairs Museum - 1940
Empire 1808-1889; imperial clothing;
jewelry - library

Piratini

01417
Piratini Museu Histórico Farroupilha
Coronel Manoel Pedroso 77, Piratini
General Museum
art; history

Porto Alegre

01418
Museu Anchieta Av. Nilo Peçanha
1.521
Porto Alegre
Natural History Museum - 1908
Entomology and ornithology; local
minerals; fossils; shells; etc. - library

01419
Museu da Curia Metropolitana
Arcebispado, Pôrto Alegre
Fine Arts Museum
religious art

01420
Museu de Arte do Rio Grande do Sul
Praça Mal. Deodoro (altos do Teatro
São Pedro), Porto Alegre
Fine Arts Museum - 1957

01421
Museu do Instituto de Folclore
Rua Carlos Chagas, esquina Av. Júlio
de Castilhos, Porto Alegre
Anthropology Museum

01422
Museu 'Julio de Castilhos'
Rua Duque de Caxias 1231, Pœrto
Alegre
History/Public Affairs Museum - 1931
national history; militaria; Indian
collection; armaments; old furniture;
ethnology

01423
**Museu Particular de Armas de
Arlindo Pedro Zatti**
Av. Mostardeiro 938, Porto Alegre
Science/Tech Museum - 1920
Arms and weapons from various
periods and parts of the world (over
2,000 exhibits)

01424
**Museu Rio-Grandense de Ciências
Naturais**
Av. Mauá 1.855 s/loja, Porto Alegre
Natural History Museum - 1955
Zoology (anthropods, mollusks,
vertebrates and invertebrates, algae,
etc.)

Porto Velho

01425
**Museu da Estrada de Ferro Madeira-
Mamoré**
Praça da EFMM, Porto Velho
Science/Tech Museum - 1971
Restored railroad cars and equipment;
restored railway station

Recife

01426
**Museu de Antropologia do Instituto
Joaquim Nabuco de Pesquisas
Sociais**
Av. 17 de Agosto 2.187, Recife
Anthropology Museum
Ceramics, furnishings domestic and
agricultural utensils and implements,
folklore, etc.

01427
Museu de Arte Popular
Horto Dois Irmãos, Recife
Decorative Arts Museum - 1953
Regional ceramics; folk and popular
art

01428
**Museu de Arte Sacra da Irmandade
de Nossa Senhora da Conceição dos
Militares**
Rua Nova no. 309, Recife, Pernambuco
Religious Art Museum -

01429
Museu de Ciências Naturais
Universidade Federal Rural de
Pernambuco
Dois Irmãos, Recife
Natural History Museum
Brazilian fauna, particularly of the
Amazon and central Brazilian regions;
mineralolgy

01430
Museu do Estado
Av. Rui Barbosa 960, Recife
Fine Arts Museum - 1928
local history; art history; ethnology;
weapons; furniture; paintings from
Estevão, Ribera, Baltar - library

01431
**Museu do Instituto Arqueológico,
Histórico e Geográfico Pernam
Bucano**
Rua do Hospicio 130, Recife
General Museum
history; archaeology

01432
Museu Dom Vital Convento da Penha
Praça Dom Vital, Recife
Fine Arts Museum
religious art

Recôncavo

01433
**Museu do Recôncavo Wanderley
Pinho**
Engenho da Freguesia, Recôncavo
Decorative Arts Museum
Furnishings, porcelain, silver, etc.

Rio de Janeiro

01434
Army Museum
Praça da República 197, Rio de Janeiro
History/Public Affairs Museum
military history

01435
Banco do Brasil Museum
Av. Presidente Vargas 328-160, Rio de
Janeiro
General Museum - 1952
Numismatics; Brazilian coins

01436
Casa Rui Barbosa
Rua São Clemente 134, Rio de Janeiro
Historic Site - 1930
Personal effects and mid-19th cent.
furnishings in original setting occupied
by Rui Barbosa

01437
Centro de Pesquisas Folclóricas
Rua do Passeio 98, 20021 Rio de
Janeiro, Rio de Janeiro
General Museum - 1943
folklore music - library

01438
Chácara do Céu Museum Fundação
Raymundo Ottoni de Castro Maya
Rua Murtinho Nobre 93 - Santa
Teresa, Rio de Janeiro
Fine Arts Museum - 1972
Works by modern masters; Brazilian
and Oriental art

01439
Estrada do Açude Museum Fundação
Raymundo Ottoni de Castro Maya
Estrada do Açude 764, Rio de Janeiro
Fine Arts Museum - 1962
Water colors and drawings by Jean
Baptiste Debret; porcelain and tiles
(18th-20th c.)

01440
**'Laguna e Dourados' Memorial
Monument Museum**
Praça General Tibúrcio 83, Rio de
Janeiro
History/Public Affairs Museum
militaria

01441
**Museo de Nossa Senhora da Glória
do Outeiro**
Praça Nossa Senhora da Glória 135,
Rio de Janeiro
Fine Arts Museum
religious art

01442
Museu Clube dos Caçadores
Rua São Geraldo 38, Rio de Janeiro
Anthropology Museum
hunting

01443
Museu Antonio Lago
rua dos andradas 96, Rio de Janeiro
Science/Tech Museum
pharmacy

01444
**Museu Biblioteca da Academia de
Policia**
Rui Frei Caneca, Rio de Janeiro
History/Public Affairs Museum
jurisdiction; police

01445
Museu Carmen Miranda
Av. Rui Barbosa; Parque do Flamengo,
Rio de Janeiro
Fine Arts Museum

01446
**Museu Carpológico do Jardim
Botânico do Rio de Janeiro**
1.oo8 e Pacheco Leão 915, Rio de
Janeiro
Natural History Museum - 1912
dry fruits of Brazilian and exotic plants

01447
**Museu da Academia Nacional de
Medicina**
Av. General Justo 365, Rio de Janeiro
Science/Tech Museum - 1829
medicine - library

01448
**Museu da Companhia Independente
do Palácio Guanabara - Policia
Militar do Estado do Rio de Janeiro**
Rua Cardoso Junio 479, Rio de Janeiro
History/Public Affairs Museum
police; militaria

01449
**Museu da Divisa‰ de Geologia e
Mineralogia do DNPM do Ministério
das Minas e Energia**
Av. Pasteur 404, Praia Vermelha, Rio
de Janeiro
Natural History Museum
mineralogy; geology; fossils

01450
Museu da Escola Naval
Ilha de Villegaignon, Rio de Janeiro
History/Public Affairs Museum - 1962
marine history - library

01451
Museu da Farmácia Santa Casa da
Misericórdia do Rio de Janeiro
Rua Santa Luzia 206, Rio de Janeiro
Science/Tech Museum
pharmacy

01452
Museu da Fauna
Quinta da Boa Vista, São Christóvão,
Rio de Janeiro
Natural History Museum - 1938
birds and mammals of the Brazilian
fauna

01453
Museu da Fazenda Federal
Av. Pres. Antonio Carlos 375, Rio de
Janeiro
History/Public Affairs Museum - 1970
historical financial documentation;
machines; coins; numismatics - library

01454
Museu da FEB
Rua das Marrecas 35, Rio de Janeiro
History/Public Affairs Museum - 1976
Military weapons, uniforms,
decorations and equipment used by
the Brazilian Expeditionary Force and
other units in World War II

01455
Museu da Imprensa
Setor de Indústrias Gráficas, quadra 6,
lote 800, Rio de Janeiro
General Museum - 1940
Typographic machines; historical
newspapers and artifacts relating to
the history of the press in Argentina

01456
Museu da República
Rua do Catete, Rio de Janeiro
Decorative Arts Museum - 1960
relics of presidents of the republic;
furniture; paintings; engravings;
drawings; watercolours; sculptures;
silverware; jewels; weapons; crystals;
coins; medals; documents

01457
**Museu da Seccao de Tecnologia do
Servico Florestal do Ministerio da
Agricultura**
Rua Major Rubéns Vaz 122, Rio de
Janeiro
Science/Tech Museum - 1938
Wood technology; products of the
wood industry

01458
**Museu da Venrável Ordem Terceira
de São Francisco da Peniténcia**
Largo da Carioca, Rio de Janeiro
Fine Arts Museum
religious art and traditions

01459
**Museu de Arte Moderna do Rio de
Janeiro**
Av. Beira-Mar, Aterno, Rio de Janeiro
Fine Arts Museum - 1948
paintings; engravings; sculptures;
drawings of foreign and national artists
- library

01460
**Museu de Arte Moderna do Rio de
Janeiro**
Av. Infante Don Henrique 85, C.P. 44,
Rio de Janeiro
Fine Arts Museum - 1958
Brazilian and foreign modern art -
library

01461
Museu de Arte Sacra Santa Casa da
Misericórdia do Rio de Janeiro
Rua Santa Luzia 206, Rio de Janeiro
Fine Arts Museum
religious art

01462
Museu de Folclore
Rua do Catete 179, Rio de Janeiro
Anthropology Museum - 1969
wood handicrafts; ceramics; toys;
theatre; folk music; religions - library

01463
**Museu de Patologia do Instituto
Oswaldo Cruz**
Manguinhos, Rio de Janeiro
Science/Tech Museum
public health

01464
**Museu de Valores do Banco Central
do Brasil**
Av. Rio Branco 30, Rio de Janeiro
History/Public Affairs Museum - 1966
Brazilian and foreign countries; coins,
bank notes, medals, documents

01465
Museu do Indio
Rua Mata Machado 127, Rio de
Janeiro
Anthropology Museum - 1953
history; ethnography of Indians;
basket and feather handicrafts;
weapons; garments; ceramics; musical
instruments; pictures; films and
recordings of Indian music

01466
Museu do Instituto Histórico e Geográfico Brasileiro
Av. Augusto Severo 8, Rio de Janeiro
History/Public Affairs Museum - 1838
history; geography; ethnography

01467
Museu do Porto do Rio
Av. Rodrigues Alves, Rio de Janeiro
General Museum

01468
Museu do Serviço de Educação Sanitária
Rua Coronel Gomez Machado 226, Rio de Janeiro
Science/Tech Museum - 1952
public health education; medicine, hygiene

01469
Museu Histórico da Cidade do Rio de Janeiro
Estrada Santa Marinha, Rio de Janeiro
Fine Arts Museum - 1934
Rio de Janeiro art and history; furniture; weapons; coins and medals; paintings; engravings; watercolors; drawings; sculptures; chinaware; religious images; historical documents; banners; flags; jewels; instruments of torture of the black slaves - library

01470
Museu Histórico e Diplomático do Itamaraty
Av. Marechal Floriano 196, Rio de Janeiro
History/Public Affairs Museum

01471
Museu Histórico Nacional
Praça Marechal Âncora, Rio de Janeiro
General Museum - 1922
National history; painting, prints, and ivories; porcelain; arms; numismatics; weapons

01472
Museu Nacional
Quinta da Boa Vista, Rio de Janeiro
Natural History Museum - 1818
archaeology; ethnolgoy; natural history; anthropology; geology; botany; zoology; fossils; Egyptian and American antiquities

01473
Museu Nacional de Belas Artes
Av. Rio Branco 199, Rio de Janeiro
Fine Arts Museum - 1938
Brazilian and European paintings; sculpture; graphic arts; furniture; primitive art; numismatics; posters library

01474
Museu Villa-Lobos
Rua da Imprensa 16, Rio de Janeiro
General Museum - 1960
memorabilia of the composer Heitor Villa-Lobos (1887-1959); books; documents; recordings

01475
Museum da Imagem e do Som
Praça Marechal Âncora 1, Rio de Janeiro
Music Museum - 1965
Brazilian musical heritage

01476
National Produciton Museum
Av. Pasteur 404, Rio de Janeiro
Natural History Museum
mineralogy

01477
Navy Museum
Rua Dom Manual 15, Rio de Janeiro
History/Public Affairs Museum - 1884
maritime history; navigation; maps; archaeological material; weapons; paintings - library

01478
Rio de Janeiro Theater Museum
Teatro Municipal
Av. Rio Branco, Rio de Janeiro
Fine Arts Museum
theater, dance

01479
Second Great War Memorial Museum
Av. Infante D. Henrique 75, Rio de Janeiro
History/Public Affairs Museum
military history

Rio Grande

01480
Museu Oceanografico
Heitor Perdigão s/n, POB 379 96,2000 Rio Grande
Natural History Museum - 1953
largest seashell collection of Latin America; oceanography; ichthyology; malacology; algology; bentology - library

Rio Pardo

01481
Museo Municipal 'Barão de Santo Ângelo'
Rua Andrade Neves 324, 96,640 Rio Pardo, Rio Grande do Sul
General Museum - 1940
costumes and traditions; arms and armor - library

01482
Museu 'Barao de S. Angelo'
Rua Andrade Neves, Rio Pardo
General Museum

01483
Museu da Orden Terceira da Sao Francisco da Penitencia
Largo da Carioca 5, Rio Pardo
Religious Art Museum

Sabará

01484
Museu do Ouro
Rua da Intendência, Sabará
History/Public Affairs Museum - 1946
History and technology of gold mining; 18th cent. silver and furniture; crafts of the mining regions - library

Salvador

01485
Casa dos Sete Candeeiros
Rua São Francisco 32, Salvador
Decorative Arts Museum
Furnishings, goldwork and objects d'art; portraits

01486
Coleçã0 Nelson de Sousa Oliveira
Av. 7 de Setembro 172-174, Salvador
General Museum - 1919
Natural history; fine and decorative arts; folklore

01487
Fundação Museu Carlos Costa Pinto
Avenida Sete de Setembro 389-391, Salvador
Decorative Arts Museum - 1969
Brazilian furnishings (17th-19th c.); Chinese and European porcelain (18th-19th c.); jewelry and objects d'art; painting

01488
Museu Casa de Rui Barbosa
Rua Rui Barbosa 12, Salvador
Historic Site
Books, photographs, documents and personal objects of Rui Barbosa

01489
Museu Castro Alves
Colégio Ipiranga, Rua do Sodré, Salvador
Historic Site
Documents and personal objects of Castro Alves

01490
Museu de Arte Antiga Instituto Feminino da Bahia
Rua Monsenhor Flaviano 2, Salvador
Fine Arts Museum - 1933
Religious and popular art; national art; crafts in gold and silver; costumes; armaments

01491
Museu de Arte da Bahia
Av. Joana Angélica 198, Salvador
Fine Arts Museum - 1918
Furniture and porcelain; Bahian colonial art - library

01492
Museu de Arte Moderna da Bahia
Rua Desembargador Castelo Branco 1, Salvador
Fine Arts Museum
Modern and popular art

01493
Museu de Arte Popular
Rua Desembargador Castelo Branco 1 - Solar do Unhão, Salvador
Decorative Arts Museum - 1966
Popular arts and crafts

01494
Museu de Arte Sacra
Rua do Sodré 25, Salvador
Religious Art Museum
Religious art objects

01495
Museu de Arte Sacra da Catedral-Basilica
Terreiro de Jesus, Salvador
Religious Art Museum
Icons and other religious art and artifacts from the 17th to 18th cent.

01496
Museu do Convento do Carmo
Ladeira do Carmo, Salvador
Religious Art Museum
Sculpture, furnishings and artifacts (17th-19th c.); documents

01497
Museu do Estado da Bahia
Rua do Carmo s/n, Convento do Carmo, Salvador
General Museum - 1918
History and art

01498
Museu do Instituto Geografico e Historico da Bahia
Av. Sete de Setembro 94, Salvador
General Museum - 1894
Geography and history; folklore and mineralogy of Bahia

01499
Museu do Instituto 'Nina Rodrigues'
Rua Alfredo Brito, Salvador
History/Public Affairs Museum - 1896
Anthropology; forensic medicine

01500
Museu Maconico 'Udo Schleusner'
Grande Loja da Bahia, Salvador
History/Public Affairs Museum

Santa Leopoldina

01501
Museu do Colono
Rua Presidente Vargas, s/no., Santa Leopoldina
Fine Arts Museum - 1968
Maps, rare Bibles, furniture, musical instruments, and other items of colonial domestic culture

Santa Maria

01502
Museu Victor Bersani
Rua Venâncio Aires 1934, Santa Maria
General Museum
Local history

Santana do Ipanema

01503
Museu Histórico e de Artes
Av. N. Sa. de Fátima 181, Santana do Ipanema
General Museum - 1959
Popular culture, costumes, and art

Santana do Livramento

01504
Museu Municipal 'Davi Canabarro'
Rua Manduca Rodrigues, Santana do Livramento
General Museum
Weapons and historical documents; minerals

São Cristóvão

01505
Museu Histórico de Sergipe
Praça São Francisco s/n, 49,1000 São Cristóvão
History/Public Affairs Museum - 1960
arms and armor; sculptures; numismatics; furniture; porcelain - library

São Gabriel

01506
Museu 'João Pedro Nunes'
Rua Cel. Sezefredo 536, São Gabriel
General Museum

São João Del-Rei

01507
Museu Municipal
Praça Frei Orlando 90, São João Del-Rei
General Museum - 1959
Antique telephones; lamps; paintings and portraits; period furniture; instruments of torture; natural history exhibits; etc.

São Leopoldo

01508
Museu Histórico 'Visconde de São Leopoldo'
Independência 111, São Leopoldo, Rio Grande do Sul
General Museum - 1959
history; geography; folklore - library

São Paulo

01509
Casa das Civilizações
Pça. N.S. Aparecida 139 (Galerias do Hotel Recreio), São Paulo
Anthropology Museum - 1968
Egyptian collection; archeology of Mesopotamia and Central America; numismatics - library

01510
Museu da Aeronáutica
Parque Ibirapuera, São Paulo
Science/Tech Museum

01511
Museu da Cidade
Rua Roberto Simonsen 136, São Paulo
Anthropology Museum - 1980
Ethnographic objects from Brazilian Indian tribes; 19th cent. household objects

01512
Museu da Curia Metropolitana
Praça Clovis Bevilacqua 37, São Paulo
Religious Art Museum - 1919
Religious artifacts; numismatics

01513
Museu da Imigração Japonesa no Brasil
Rua São Joaquim 381, São Paulo
History/Public Affairs Museum
Documents relating to Japanese in Brasil

01514
Museu de Arqueologia e Etnologia da Universidade de São Paulo
Cidade Universitária, Edificio de Geografia e História, São Paulo
Archeology Museum
Classical, Mesopotamian, and pre-Columbian archeology

01515
Museu de Arte Brasileira Fundação Álvares Penteado
Bairro do Pacaembu, São Paulo
Fine Arts Museum
Contemporary art

01516
Museu de Arte Contemporânea da Universidade de São Paulo
Parque Ibirapuera, Pavilhão da Bienal, São Paulo
Fine Arts Museum - 1963
Painting, sculpture, prints and drawings by modern masters of the international school

01517
Museu de Arte de São Paulo Assis Chateaubriand
Av. Paulista 1578, São Paulo
Fine Arts Museum - 1947
Italian, Spanish, Dutch, Flemish, and French painting (classical and modern)

01518
Museu de Arte Moderna
Rua Sete de Abril 230, São Paulo
Fine Arts Museum - 1946
Painting, sculpture, engravings and drawings; architectural works; crafts

01519
Museu de Arte Moderna de São Paulo
Parque Ibirapuera em Frente à Bienal, São Paulo
Fine Arts Museum - 1946
Modern art

01520
Museu de Arte Sacra de São Paulo
Av. Tiradentes 676, São Paulo
Religious Art Museum

01521
Museu de Artes e Técnicas Populares
Palácio Governador Garcez, Parque Ibirapuera, São Paulo
Anthropology Museum
Folk art; industrial art; folklore

01522
Museu de Etnografia 'Plinio Ayrosa'
Universidade de São Paulo, C.P. 8105, São Paulo
Anthropology Museum - 1934
Relics of Brazilian Indian cultures; Tupi ceramics; Rio Negro wooden signal drums; Canella and Bororo collections

01523
Museu de Pesca
Avenida Bartolomeu de Gusmão 192, São Paulo
Natural History Museum - 1950
Marine and fresh water fish; mammals, birds, crustaceans, and molluscs; fishing gear

01524
Museu de Zoologia Universidade de São Paulo
Av. Nazaré 481, São Paulo
Natural History Museum - 1892
Animals of the neotropical region - library

01525
Museu do Telefone
Rua Martiniano de Carvalho 851, São Paulo
Science/Tech Museum - 1977
Telecommunications, including videophone and facsimile equipment

01526
Museu Florestal 'Octavio Vecchi'
Horto Florestal, São Paulo
Science/Tech Museum - 1931
Forestry science and technology

01527
Museu Folclorico da Divisão de Discoteca e Biblioteca de Música de São Paulo
Rua Catão 611, São Paulo
Anthropology Museum - 1935
Folklore; folk music

01528
Museu José Bonifácio
Rue Benjamin Constant 158, São Paulo
History/Public Affairs Museum - 1958
Weapons and military equipment; decorations; historical documents

01529
Museu Lasal Segall
Rua Afonso Celso 362/388, 04119 São Paulo, São Paulo
History/Public Affairs Museum
books

01530
Museu Paulista da Universidade de São Paulo
Parque da Independência s/n, POB 42,503 01000 São Paulo, São Paulo
General Museum - 1895
history; ethnography; philatelics; numismatics; archaeology; natural history; religious art; furniture; documents; gold collection - library

01531
Museu Plinio Ayrosa
Departamento de Antropologia da Cidade Universitária, São Paulo
Anthropology Museum

01532
Pinacoteca do Estado do São Paulo
Praç da Luz 2, São Paulo
Fine Arts Museum - 1906
Painting

Sobral

01533
Museu Diocesano
Sobral
General Museum - 1952
Furnishings, coins, objects d'art, rare books, religious art, and items of ethnographic interest

Teresina

01534
Museu Histórico do Piaú Casa Anísio de Brito
Rua Coelho Rodrigues 1.016, Teresina
General Museum - 1947
Numismatics (Brazil and Portugal); ethnography; fossils; arms; porcelain, furniture, and objects d'art

Teresopolis

01535
Museu von Martius
Avenida Rotariana s/n, Teresopolis, Rio de Janeiro
Natural History Museum - 1971
botany; manuscripts

Terezina 41 1941

01536
Casa 'Anisio Brito'
Rue Coelho Rodrigues 1016, Terezina 41 1941
General Museum
Regional history; archives and documents

Triunfo

01537
Museu Farroupilha
Av. Luis Barreto 23, Triunfo
General Museum

Vitória

01538
Museu Capela Santa Luzia
Universidade Federal do Espírito Santo
Rua José Marcelino, Vitória
Decorative Arts Museum
Furniture; jewelry; religious art; paintings

01539
Museu de Arte e Historia da Universidade Federal do Espirito Santo
Av. 15 de Novembro, Jucutuquara, Vitória
General Museum - 1939
Religious art; archeology, folklore and history

01540
Museu de Arte Moderna
Escadaria do Rosário 77, C.P. 899, Vitória
Fine Arts Museum
modern art

01541
Museu de Arte Religiosa
Rua José Marcelino s/n, Vitória
Religious Art Museum

01542
Museu Solar Monjardim
Universidade Federal do Espírito Santo
Av. Paulino Muller, Jucutuquara, Vitória
History/Public Affairs Museum - 1939
Furniture; archeology; items of local historical interest; locale folklore; instruments of torture; clocks and watches; etc.

Brunei

Bandar Seri Begawan

01543
Churchill Memorial Museum
Bandar Seri Begawan
Historic Site - 1971

01544
Historical and Cultural Centre
Bandar Seri Begawan
General Museum - 1971

Bolkiah Camp

01545
Project for Royal Brunei Malay Regiment
Bolkiah Camp, Bandar Seri Begawan
History/Public Affairs Museum
Small warships, including the world's fastest patrol boat; helicopters; armored vehicles; small arms; regiment insignia - library

Kota Batu

01546
The Brunei Museum
Kota Batu
General Museum
Archaeology; ethnography; history; natural history - archive and library

Bulgaria

Asenovgrad

01547
Gradski istoričeski muzej (City Museum of History)
ul. Georgi Dimitrov 27, BG Asenovgrad
General Museum
Archeology; history of the 18th-19th century Bulgarian National Revival period and liberation movement; history of capitalism and the revolutionary labour movement

Bačkovo

01548
Bačkovski manastir, muzej (Bačkovo Monastery, Museum)
BG Bačkovo
Religious Art Museum
History of the monastery; religious art; icons; folk art; jewelry

Balčik

01549
Gradski istoričeski muzej (City Historical Museum)
pl. Deveti Septemvri, kulturen dom, BG Balčik
General Museum
Thracian, Greek and Roman archeology; history of the Bulgarian National Revival period (18th-19th century); contemporary history; art

Bansko

01550
Kăšta-muzej 'Nikola Jonkov Vapcarov' (N.J. Vapcarov Memorial House)
pl. Vapcarov 9, BG Bansko
Historic Site
Memorabilia on the poet and revolutionist N.J. Vapcarov (1909-1942) in his birthplace; manuscripts; first editions of his poems; personal possessions; history of the anti-Fascist movement in Bulgaria

Batak

01551
Gradski istoričeski muzej (City Museum of History)
ul. Aprilci 9, BG Batak, Pazardžiški okrăg
History/Public Affairs Museum - 1956
History of the 18th-19th century Bulgarian National Revival period and liberation movement, especially history of the April 1876 Uprising; history of capitalism and the revolutionary labour movement

Belogradčik

01552
Gradski istoričeski muzej (Pašova kăšta)
BG Belogradčik
General Museum
History of the Belogradčik Uprising (1850) and liberation movement; agriculture; animal husbandry; smithwork; tools; copper smithery; pottery; textiles; in a house built 1810

Berkovica

01553
Etnografski muzej
ul. Poručik Grozdanov, BG Berkovica
Anthropology Museum - 1974
Ethnography; folk art; crafts; folk costumes; in a 19th century house

01554
Gradska chudožestvena galerija (City Art Gallery)
BG Berkovica
Fine Arts Museum
Bulgarian fine art

01555
Kăšta-muzej 'Ivan Vazov' (Ivan Vazov Memorial House)
ul. Poručik Grozdanov 2, BG Berkovica, Michajlovgradski okrăg
Historic Site
Memorabilia on the Bulgarian national writer Ivan Vazov (1850-1921) and his stay in Berkovica 1879-1880; in a 19th century house

Bjala

01556
Voenno-istoričeski muzej 'Osvoboditelna Vojna 1877-1878' (Military History Museum 'War of Liberation 1877-1878')
BG Bjala
History/Public Affairs Museum
History of the Russo-Turkish War 1877-1878; documents; uniforms; weapons; banner; lithographs

Blagoevgrad

01557
Okrăžen istoričeski muzej (Regional Historical Museum)
ul. Rajko Daskalov 2, BG Blagoevgrad
General Museum - 1952
Archeology; ethnology; history of the Bulgarian National Revival period (19th century) and national liberation movement; natural history; art; labour movement

Botevgrad

01558
Gradski istoričeski muzej (City Museum of History)
Červen ploštad, BG Botevgrad
General Museum
Div: archeology; history of the Bulgarian National Revival period and liberation movement; ethnography; history of capitalism and the revolutionary labour movement; contemporary history

Boženci

01559
Muzej-rezervat
BG Boženci, Gabrovski okrăg
Open Air Museum
The village is an architectonic and ethnographic reserve, representing the life of the Bulgarian National Revival period; several 18th-19th century houses; original interiors; traditional Bulgarian wood-carved ceilings; ironworks; domestic utensils; carpets; textiles; embroideries

Bracigovo

01560
Gradski istoričeski muzej (City Museum of History)
pl. Deveti septemvri, BG Bracigovo
History/Public Affairs Museum
History of the Bulgarian National Revival period and liberation movement; history of the April 1876 Uprising; weapons; banners; documents; contemporary history

Burgas

01561
Etnografski muzej Okrăžen istoričeski muzej, Burgas
Jana Lăskova 31, BG Burgas
Anthropology Museum
Folk costumes; domestic utensils; interiors; crafts; in a 19th century house

01562
Okrăžen istoričeski muzej (Regional Historical Museum)
ul. Lenin 21, BG Burgas
General Museum - 1947
Archeology of the Black-Sea Greek colonies Apolonia, Messembria and Anchialos; ceramics; gold jewelry; tombstones; history of the national liberation movement; natural history; ethnography

01563
Okrăžna chudožestvena galerija (Regional Art Galery)
ul. Št. Voderičarov 24, BG Burgas
Fine Arts Museum - 1966
Paintings by I. Mrkvička, Z. Todorov, N. Michajlov, V. Dimitrov-Majstora, G. Mitev, G. Baev, T. Atanasov, Jani Christopulos etc.; icon collection

Čepelare

01564
Muzej na rodopskija karst (Museum of the Rhodopian Karst)
BG Čepelare
Natural History Museum - 1980
Geology

Chaskovo

01565
Okrăžen istoričeski muzej (Regional Historical Museum)
ul. Car Osvoboditel 10, BG Chaskovo
General Museum - 1952
Divisions: archeology; Bulgarian National Revival period and liberation movement; ethnography; history of capitalism and the labour movement

Chisarja

01566
Gradski archeologičeski muzej (City Archeological Museum)
ul. Aleksandăr Stambolijski 8, BG Chisarja
Archeology Museum
Prehistoric archeology; Roman finds

Čirpan

01567
Gradski istoričeski muzej (City Museum of History)
ul. Tanjo Peev, BG Čirpan
General Museum
Regional history

Čurek

01568
Muzej na partizanskija otrjad 'Čavdar' (Museum of the Partisan Brigade 'Čavdar')
mestnost Žerkovo, BG Čurek
History/Public Affairs Museum
History of the partisan struggle during World War II; weapons; documents

Dimitrovgrad

01569
Muzej Okrăžen istoričeski muzej, Chaskovo (Branch of the Regional Historical Museum, Chaskovo)
ul. Georgi Sava Rakovski 7, BG Dimitrovgrad
History/Public Affairs Museum
Contemporary history; history of the development of socialism

Drjanovo

01570
Drjanovski manastir, muzej (Drjanovo Monastery, Museum)
BG Drjanovo
History/Public Affairs Museum
History of the monastery; history of the April 1876 Uprising against Ottoman rule; documents; photographs; arms

01571
Muzej Kolju Fičeto
BG Drjanovo
History/Public Affairs Museum
History of Bulgarian architecture during the National Revival period (18th-19th century); tools; models; memorabilia on the architect Nikola Fičev, also known as Kolju Fičeto

Elchovo

01572
Etnografski muzej
ul. Šipka 4, BG Elchovo, Jambolski okrăg
Anthropology Museum - 1959
Ethnography; folk art

Elena

01573
Văzroždendki muzej 'Ilarion Makariopolski' (I. Makariopolski Museum of Bulgarian National Revival Period)
ul. Dojčo Gramatik 2, BG Elena
History/Public Affairs Museum
The museum consists of the following divisions: Kăšta-muzej Ilarion Makariopolski: memorabilia of Ilarion Makariopolski; religious history. Daskalolivnica: local history; history of education. Kăšta-muzej Petko J. Todorov: memorabilia of the poet P.J. Todorov; icon collection; paintings; history of the labour movement

Etăra

01574
Etnografski muzej na otkrito
BG Etăra, Gabrovski okrăg
Open Air Museum - 1963
Old crafts of the Bulgarian National Revival Period (18th-19th century); several workshops, equipped with original tools and still in operation, show the development of various crafts: goldsmithery, weaving, mills, dyeing, pottery, ironwork, cutlery, wooden shoemaking, carpet manufacturing, bakery

Etropole

01575
Gradski istoričeski muzej (City Museumof History)
ul. Christo Botev, BG Etropole
General Museum
Div: archeology; history of the Bulgarian National Revival period and the liberation movement; ethnography; history of capitalism and the revolutionary labour movement; contemporary history

Gabrovo

01576
Kaššta-muzej 'Mitko Palauzov' Okrăžen muzej, Gabrovo (Mitko Palauzov Memorial House)
ul. Veselie 3, BG Gabrovo
Historic Site
Memorabilia of the child partisan Dimităr Trifonov Palauzov, also known as Mitko, who was killed by the fascists at the age of eleven

01577
Muzej na narodnoto obrazovanie (Museum of Public Education)
BG Gabrovo
History/Public Affairs Museum - 1973
History of education in Bulgaria

01578
Okrăžen istoričeski muzej (Regional Museum of History)
pl. Balvan 7, BG Gabrovo
General Museum - 1873
Div: archeology; history of The Bulgarian National Revival Period and liberation movement; ethnography; history of the capitalism and the labour movement; development of socialism

43

Ichtiman

01579
Muzej na revoljucionnoto rabotničesko dviženie (Museum of the Revolutionary Labour Movement)
ul. Georgi Dimitrov 84, BG Ichtiman
History/Public Affairs Museum
Ethnography; local history; history of the revolutionary labour movement; history of the September 1923 Uprising and anti-Fascist struggle (1941-1944)

Jambol

01580
Okrăžen istoričeski muzej (Regional Museum of History)
Izrael Džaldeti 12, BG Jambol
General Museum - 1952
Div: archeology; history of the Bulgarian National Revival period and liberation movement; ethnography; history of capitalism and the revolutionary labour movement; development of socialism; art

01581
Okrăžna chudožestvena galerija (Regional Art Gallery)
ul. M. Rubenova 10, BG Jambol
Fine Arts Museum - 1980
Contemporary Bulgarian fine art

Kărdžali

01582
Okrăžen istoričeski muzej (Regional Museum of History)
BG Kărdžali
General Museum - 1960
Divisions: archeology; Bulgarian National Revival period and liberation movement; ethnography; history of capitalism and the revolutionary labour movement; development of socialism

Kalofer

01583
Kăšta-muzej 'Christo Botev' (Christo Botev Memorial House)
ul. Christo Botev 15, BG Kalofer, Plovdivski okrăg
Historic Site - 1945
Memorabilia on Christo Botev (1849-1976), Bulgarian national poet, publicist and revolutionist; manuscripts; books; documents on his revolutionary activity in Romania; history of the Bulgarian national liberation movement against the Ottoman rule

Karlovo

01584
Gradski istoričeski muzej (City Historical Museum)
Văzroždenska 4, BG Karlovo
General Museum
Archeology; history of the Bulgarian National Revival period and liberation movement; ethnography; contemporary history

01585
Kăšta-muzej 'Vasil Levski' Gradski istoričeski muzej (Vasil Levski Memorial House)
ul. Karl Marks 57, BG Karlovo
Historic Site
The birthplace of Vasil Levski (1837-1873), founder and organizer of the Revolutionary Committee for the liberation of Bulgaria; history of the 19th century liberation movement against Ottoman rule; documents

Karnobat

01586
Gradski istoričeski muzej (City Museum of History)
bul. Lenin 18, BG Karnobat
General Museum
Archeology; local history; ethnography

Kazanlăk

01587
Gradski istoričeski muzej (City Museum of History)
ul. Iskra 15, BG Kazanlăk, Starozagorski okrăg
General Museum - 1901
Divisions: archeology; history of the Bulgarian National Revival period and liberation movement; ethnography; history of capitalism and the labour movement; contemporary history

01588 *
Kazanlăška roza Gradski istoričeski muzej
BG Kazanlăk, Starozagorski okrăg
Science/Tech Museum
History of the production of rose oil, a fragrant essential oil, obtained from special roses and used chiefly in perfumery and in flavoring; old tools; destillation equipment

01589
Nacionalen park-muzej 'Sipka-Buzludža'
ul. Kiril i Metodij 11, BG Kazanlăk, Starozagorski okrăg
Open Air Museum - 1959
National park-museum in the Šipka pass, mountain pass in the Balkan Mts., scene of major battles (1877) during the Russo-Turkish War (1877-1878); history of the national liberation movement against Ottoman rule; history of the foundation of the Bulgarian Workers' Social Democratic Party at Buzludža in 1891; contemporary history

Kjustendil

01590
Okrăžen istoričeski muzej (Regional Museum of History)
ul. Christo Smirnenski 1, BG Kjustendil
General Museum - 1934
Div: archeology; Bulgarian National Revival Period and liberation movement; ethnography; history of the capitalism and the revolutionary labour movement; development of socialism

01591
Okrăžna chudožestvena galerija 'Vladimir Dimitrov-Majstora' (Regional Art Gallery)
ul. Ljuben Karavelov 1, BG Kjustendil
Fine Arts Museum
Bulgarian painting, especially works of Vladimir Dimitrov- Majstora

Klisura

01592
Gradski istoričeski muzej (City Historical Museum)
ul. Christo G. Danov 38, BG Klisura
History/Public Affairs Museum
History of the April 1876 Uprising; documents; maps; arms

Koprivštica

01593
Etnografski muzej Oslekova kăšta (Ethnographic Museum in the Oslekov House)
BG Koprivštica
Anthropology Museum - 1958
Ethnography; folk art; wood carvings; mural paintings; original interiors; in a house built in 1856

01594
Kăšta-muzej 'Dimčo Debeljanov' (Dimčo Debeljanov Memorial House)
BG Koprivštica
Historic Site - 1958
Memorabilia of the poet Dimčo Debeljanov (1887-1916); books; first editions; in his birthplace built in 1830

01595
Kăšta-muzej 'Ljuben Karavelov' (Ljuben Karavelov Memorial House)
BG Koprivštica
Historic Site - 1958
Memorabilia of the writer and revolutionist Ljuben Karavelov (1837-1879); history of the Bulgarian National Revival period; in his birthplace built in 1810

01596
Kăšta-muzej 'Todor Kableškov' (Todor Kableškov Memorial House)
BG Koprivštica
Historic Site - 1958
Memorabilia of the revolutionist Todor Kableškov; history of the Bulgarian National Revival period and the April 1876 Uprising against Ottoman rule; in his birthplace built in 1845

Kotel

01597
Gradski istoričeski muzej (City Museum of History)
ul. Izvorska, BG Kotel, Slivenski okrăg
History/Public Affairs Museum
History of the Bulgarian National Revival period and liberation movement in the 19th century; memorabilia on the revolutionist and publicist Georgi S. Rakovski (1821-1867); exposition on the literary and pedagogic activity of Dr. Petăr Beron; documents on A. Kipilovski, Sofronij Vračanski, Neofit Bozveli etc.; in an old school built in 1869

01598
Kjorpeeva kăšta (Kjorpeev's House)
ul. Kjorpeev, BG Kotel
Anthropology Museum
19th century Kotel architecture; original interiors; Kotel carpets; textiles; jewelry; costumes

01599
Prirodonaučen muzej (Natural History Museum)
ul. Izvorska 12, BG Kotel, Slivenski okrăg
Natural History Museum
Natural history; geological science; insects; birds; mammals

Kovačevci

01600
Kăšta-muzej 'Georgi Dimitrov' (Georgi Dimitrov Memorial House)
BG Kovačevci, Perniški okrăg
Historic Site
Memorabilia on the politician Georgi Dimitrov (1882-1949) in his birthplace, history of the international labour movement

Lom

01601
Gradski istoričeski muzej (City Historical Museum)
ul. Eremija Bălgarov 6, BG Lom
General Museum
Archeology; history of the Bulgarian National Revival Period and liberation movement; ethnography; contemporary history

Loveč

01602
Muzej Vasil Levski (Vasil Levski Memorial House)
ul. Marin Pop Lukanov 14, BG Loveč
Historic Site
Memorabilia on Vasil Levski (1837-1873), founder and organizer of the Revolutionary Committe the for Liberation of Bulgaria; history of the 19th century liberation movement against Ottoman rule

01603
Okrăžen istoričeski muzej
ul. Christo Karpačev 17, BG Loveč
General Museum - 1952
Div: archeology; history of the Bulgarian National Revival Period (18th-19th century) and liberation movement; ethnography; history of capitalism and the revolutionary labour movement; development of socialism

Madan

01604
Muzej na socialističeskoto stroitelstvo (Museum of Socialist Development)
ul. Republika 3, BG Madan
History/Public Affairs Museum
Contemporary history

Madara

01605
Muzej 'R. Popov'
BG Madara, Šumenski okrăg
Archeology Museum

Melnik

01606
Gradski istoričeski muzej (City Museum of History)
BG Melnik
General Museum - 1953
Archeology; ethnography; national liberation movement; history of the Bulgarian National Revival Period (19th century)

Michajlovgrad

01607
Muzej na Septemvrijskoto văstanie (Museum of the September Uprising)
ul. Vasil Kolarov 3, BG Michajlovgrad
History/Public Affairs Museum
History of the September 1923 Uprising; revolutionary movement(1925-1944) and anti-Fascist struggle (1941-1944); documents; photographs; maps; weapons; memorabilia on the politicians Vasil Kolarov (1877-1950) and Georgi Dimitrov (1882-1949)

Nesebăr

01608
Gradski archeologičeski muzej (City Museum of Archeology)
BG Nesebăr, Burgaski okrăg
Archeology Museum - 1956
Archeology; Greek ceramics and statues; tombstones; ethnography; medieval art; icons; finds from the Ottoman period; the revolutionary movement; in an 11th century 'Sveti Ivan' church

Nova Zagora

01609
Gradski istoričeski muzej (City Museum of History)
ul. Ivan Pašov 1, BG Nova Zagora
General Museum
Archeology; contemporary history; fine art

Orjachovo

01610
Gradski istoričeski muzej (City Museum of History)
BG Orjachovo
General Museum
Archeology; ethnography; local history

Panagjurište

01611
Gradski istoričeski muzej (City Museum of History)
ul. Račo Ralčev 1, BG Panagjurište
History/Public Affairs Museum
History of the Bulgarian National Revival period and liberation movement; history of the April 1976 Uprising against Ottoman rule and the Russo-Turkish War (1877-1878); contemporary history

01612
Kăšta-muzej 'Rajna Popgeorgieva'
ul. Oborište 5, BG Panagjurište
Historic Site
History of the Bulgarian National Revival period and liberation movement; memorabilia of the folk heroine Rajna Popgeorgieva, also known as Rajna Knjaginja; history of the April 1876 Uprising; historical banner sewn by R. Popgeorgieva in 1876

Pazardžik

01613
Kăšta-muzej 'Stanislav Dospevski' (Stanislav Dospevski Memorial House)
bul. Georgi Dimitrov 50, BG Pazardžik
Historic Site
Life and work of the painter Stanislav Dospevski (1823-1876) in his former house; documents on the role of the painter in the 19th century National Liberation Movement; personal effects; icons; paintings

01614
Okrăž istoričeski muzej (Regional Historical Museum)
ul. Asen Zlatarov 5, BG Pazardžik
General Museum - 1952
Div: Archeology; Bulgarian National Revival Period (18th-19th century) and liberation movement; history of capitalism and the labour movement; socialist development. Division of Ethnography: folk art; folk costumes; interiors; arts and crafts; folk architecture (ul. Otec Paisij, Pazardžik)

01615
Okrăžna chudožestvena galerija (Regional Art Gallery)
bul. Deveti Septemvri, BG Pazardžik
Fine Arts Museum - 1966
Art works of Bulgarian artists from the Pazardžik region: Stanislav Dospevski, Konstantin Veličkov, Elisaveta Konsulova-Vazova, Georgi Mašev, Stojan Vasilev, Todor Hadžinikolov, Mana Parpulova, Zlatka Dăbova etc.

Pernik

01616
Okrăžen istoričeski muzej (Regional Historical Museum)
ul. Kiril i Metodij 13, BG Pernik
General Museum - 1954
Div: archeology; Bulgarian National Revival Period (18th-19th century) and liberation movement; ethnography; history of capitalism and the revolutionary labour movement; socialist development

Peruštica

01617
Gradski istoričeski muzej (City Museum of History)
Gradski ploštad, BG Peruštica, Plovdivski okrăg
History/Public Affairs Museum
History of 18th-19th century Bulgarian National Revival period and liberation movement, especially history of the April 1876 Uprising; history of capitalism and the revolutionary labour movement

Pleven

01618
Kăšta-muzej Stojan i Vladimir Zaimovi
Skobelev Park, BG Pleven
Historic Site
Memorabilia on the revolutionist and writer Stojan Zaimov (1853-1932) and his son Vladimir Zaimov (1888-1942)

01619
Muzej 'Osvoboždenieto na Pleven 1877' (Museum of the Liberation of Pleven 1877)
BG Pleven
History/Public Affairs Museum
History of the Russo-Turkish War 1877-1878 and the liberation of Pleven; documents on the meeting between the commander of the Turkish army Osman Pasha and the Russian Emperor Alexander the Second; arms; weapons

01620
Okrăžen istoričeski muzej (Regional Museum of History)
bul. Georgi Dimitrov 104, BG Pleven
General Museum - 1952
Div: archeology; history of the Bulgarian National Revival period and liberation movement; ethnography; history of capitalism and the revolutionary labour movement; socialist development

01621
Okrăžna chudožestvena galerija (Regional Art Gallery)
ul. D-r Zamenchov 13, BG Pleven
Fine Arts Museum
Painting; sculpture; graphics; works by I.Mrkvička, S. Spiridonov, I. Lazarov, K. Zonev, D. Uzunov, G. Popov, N. Petkov, S. Rusev, I. Nenov etc.; icon collection

01622
Voennoistoričeski muzej (Museum of Military History)
ul. G. Dimitrov 157, BG Pleven
History/Public Affairs Museum - 1907
History of the Russo-Turkish War 1877/1878 and the liberation of Bulgaria from Ottoman rule

Pliska

01623
Muzej
BG Pliska, Šumenski okrăg
Archeology Museum
History of Pliska, capital city of Bulgaria (681-893); medieval archeology; arms; ceramics

Plovdiv

01624
Kăšta-muzej 'Lamartin' (Alphonse de Lamartine Memorial House)
ul. Zora, BG Plovdiv
Historic Site
Memorabilia on the French poet Alphonse de Lamartine and his stay in Plovdiv; documents; manuscripts; books; in a house where the poet lived 1833

01625
Okrăžen archeologičeski muzej (Regional Archeological Museum)
pl. Săedinenie 1, BG Plovdiv
Archeology Museum - 1882
Prehistoric, classical and medieval archeology; finds from the Thracian, Roman, Byzantine and Bulgarian period; numismatics

01626
Okrăžen etnografski muzej (Regional Ethnographical Museum)
ul. D-r. Čomakov 2, BG Plovdiv
Anthropology Museum - 1917
Agriculture; handicrafts; costumes; textiles; interiors; jewelry; musical instruments; games and customs; architecture; in a 19th century house decorated with frescoes

01627
Okrăžen muzej na istorijata na kapitalizma i rabotničeskoto revoljucionno dviženie i socialističesko stroitelstvo (District Museum of the History of Capitalism , Labour Revolutionary Movement and Socialist Development)
ul. Angel Bukureštliev 14, BG Plovdiv
History/Public Affairs Museum - 1948
Historical documents; contemporary history

01628
Okrăžna chudožestvena galerija (Regional Art Gallery)
ul. Vasil Kolarov 15, BG Plovdiv
Fine Arts Museum - 1950
Art of the Bulgarian National Revival period (18th-19th century); 20th century art; current art; graphics; 18th-19th century icons

01629
Okrăžen muzej na Văzraždaneto i nacionalno-osvoboditelnite borbi (Regional Museum of the Bulgarian National Revival period and Liberation Movement)
ul. Starinna 1, BG Plovdiv
History/Public Affairs Museum - 1956
17th-19th century Bulgarian history; economic history; cultural history; in a house built 1848

01630
Prirodonaučen muzej (Natural History Museum)
ul. General Zaimov 34, BG Plovdiv
Natural History Museum - 1955
Soil science; flora; fauna; history of evolution; invertebrates; reptiles; vertebrates; birds; mammals

Pordim

01631
Muzej 'Glavna kvartira na ruskata armija 1877-1878 (Museum 'Headquaters of the Russian Army 1877-1878')
BG Pordim, Plevenski okrăg
History/Public Affairs Museum
History of the Russo-Turkish War 1877-1878; documents; uniforms; weapons

01632
Muzej 'Rumănskijat vojnik 1877-1878' (Museum of the Romanian Soldier 1877-1878)
BG Pordim, Plevenski okrăg
History/Public Affairs Museum
Headquarters of the Romanian Army during the Russo-Turkish War 1877-1878; documents on the siege of Pleven; weapons; uniforms; medals

Preslav

01633
Muzej 'Veliki Preslav'
BG Preslav
Archeology Museum
History of Preslav, capital city of Bulgaria (893-1018); medieval archeology, especially from the 10th century; pottery; ceramic icons; architectural details, decorations and ornaments; medieval Bulgarian art; metal work; glass; inscriptions

Razgrad

01634
Okrăžen istoričeski muzej (Regional Historical Museum)
BG Razgrad
General Museum - 1950
Div: archeology; history of the Bulgarian National Revival period and liberation movement; ethnography; history of capitalism and the revolutionary labour movement; socialist development

01635
Okrăžna chudožestvena galerija (Regional Art Gallery)
ul. Kiril i Metodij 3, BG Razgrad
Fine Arts Museum - 1962
Contemporary Bulgarian art

Razlog

01636
Kăšta-muzej 'Nikola Parapunov' (Nikola Parapunov Memorial House)
pl. 15. Septemvri 1903, BG Razlog
Historic Site
Memorabilia on the revolutionist Nikola Parapunov (1909-1943); history of the anti-Fascist partisan struggle during World War II

Rilski Manastir

01637
Nacionalen muzej 'Rilski Manastir'
(Rila Monastery National Museum)
BG Rilski Manastir
History/Public Affairs Museum - 1961
History and art history of the Bulgarian
National Revival period; history of the
monastery; architecture; mural
paintings; wood carving; arts and
crafts. The Rila Monastery consists of:
museum, picture gallery, ethnographic
exposition, visitors' rooms, cell of
Paissij Chilendarski (Paissij of
Chilendar 1722-1798), rooms of Neofit
Rilski (1793-1881), monastery library

Ruse

01638
Kăšta-muzej 'Baba Tonka' (Baba
Tonka Memorial House)
ul. Aleksandăr Stambolijski 16, BG
Ruse
Historic Site
History of the Bulgarian National
Revival period and liberation
movement; organization of the
struggle against Ottoman rule in
Bukarest (Romania); memorabilia on
the legendary heroine Baba Tonka

01639
Okrăžen istoričeski muzej (Regional
Historical Museum)
ul. Dimitär Blagoev 5, BG Ruse
General Museum - 1904
Div: archeology; history of the
Bulgarian National Revival period and
liberation movement; ethnography;
history of the capitalism and labour
revolutionary movement; socialist
development; natural history

01640
Okrăžna chudožestvena galerija
(Regional Art Garelly)
ul. Sredec 6, BG Ruse
Fine Arts Museum - 1947
Bulgarian painting especially of the
30's (Ivan Milev, Penčo Georgiev, Ilija
Beškov, Dečko Uzunov, Kiril Conev,
Zlatju Bojadžiev, Danail Dečev;
collection of works of Vladimir
Dimitrov-Majstora); sculpture (Ivan
Lazarov; Ivan Funev)

01641
Transporten muzej (Museum of
transportation)
ul. Bratja Obretenovi 13, BG Ruse
Science/Tech Museum
Railway transportation; Danube River
navigation; communications; post and
telecommunications

Samokov

01642
Gradski istoričeski muzej (City
Museum of History)
ul. Ljuben Barămov 4, BG Samokov
General Museum - 1949
Divisions: archeology; history of
Bulgarian National Revival period and
liberation movement; ethnography;
history of capitalism and labour
revolutionary movement; socialist
development; art (examples of the
famous 18th-19th century Samokov
Art School and Samokov
Wood-Carving School)

Sandanski

01643
Gradski archeologičeski muzej (City
Museum of Archeology)
bul. Georgi Dimitrov 12, BG Sandanski
Archeology Museum
Roman finds from the middle Struma
Valley; mosaics from the Byzantine
period (3rd-4th century)

Sevlievo

01644
Gradski istoričeski muzej (City
Museum of History)
BG Sevlievo
General Museum
History of the region; ethnography

Silistra

01645
Okrăžen istoričeski muzej (Regional
Historical Museum)
ul. Dočo Michajlov 18, BG Silistra
General Museum - 1954
Divisions: archeology; history of the
Bulgarian National Revival period and
liberation movement; ethnography;
history of capitalism and labour
movement; contemporary history
(division of natural history: in the
National Park 'Srebărna' near Silistra)

Sliven

01646
Kăšta-muzej 'Chadži Dimităr'
Okrăžen istoričeski muzej (Chadži
Dimităr Memorial House)
ul. Asenovska 2, BG Sliven
Historic Site
Memorabilia on the revolutionist
Chadži Dimităr (1840-1868) in his
birthplace; history of the Bulgarian
liberation movement against Ottoman
rule in 19th century; documents;
original interiors

01647
Kăšta-muzej 'Dobri Čintulov' (Dobri
Čintulov Memorial House)
ul. Mesta 5, BG Sliven
Historic Site
Memorabilia of the poet and
pedagogue Dobri Čintulov (1822-1886),
author of several popular revolutionary
songs in the 19th century

01648
Kăšta-muzej 'Panajot Chitov'
Okrăžen istoričeski muzej (Panajot
Chitov Memorial House)
ul. Černo more 7, BG Sliven
Historic Site
Memorabilia on the revolutionist
Panajot Chitov in his birthplace;
history of the Bulgarian liberation
movement against Ottoman rule in
19th century

01649
Okrăžen istoričeski muzej (Regional
Historical Museum)
ul. Lenin 6, BG Sliven
General Museum - 1948
Div: archeology; history of the
Bulgarian National Revival period and
liberation movement; ethnography;
history of capitalism and the labour
movement; socialist development

01650
Okrăžna chudožestvena galerija
(Regional Art Gallery)
bul. Lenin 7, BG Sliven
Fine Arts Museum
19th century art of the Bulgarian
National Revival Period (D. Dobrovič,
G. Dančov, N. Pavlovič); 20th century
art (J. Kjuvliev, S. Ivanov, Christo
Stančev, Vladimir Dimitrov-Majstora, Z.
Lavrenov, N. Marinov, D. Dečev, N.
Tanev, I. Beškov, L. Dalčev, K. Zonev
etc.)

Smoljan

01651
Okrăžen istoričeski muzej (Regional
Historical Museum)
bul. Lenin 5, BG Smoljan
General Museum - 1952
Div: archeology; history of the
Bulgarian National Revival period and
liberation movement; ethnography;
history of capitalism and the labour
movement; socialist development

Sofija

01652
Gradska chudožestvena galerija
(Municipal Art Gallery)
ul. Gurko 1, BG Sofija
Fine Arts Museum - 1957
Paintings; sculpture; graphics

01653
**Kăšta-muzej 'Aleksandăr
Stambolijski'** (Aleksandăr Stambolijski
Memorial House)
ul. Suchodol 44, BG Sofija
Historic Site - 1956
Exhibits illustrating the life of the
politician A. Stambolijski (1879-1923),
documents relating to the Agrarian
Union Government of 1920-23 and to
the 1923 Peasant Uprising

01654
Kăšta-muzej 'Christo Smirnenski'
Nacionalen muzej na bălgarskata
literatura (Christo Smirnenski
Memorial House)
ul. Emil Šekerdžijski 116, BG Sofija
Historic Site - 1953
Memorabilia on the revolutionary poet
Christo Smirnenski (1898-1923)

01655
Kăšta-muzej 'Dimităr Blagoev'
(Dimităr Blagoev Memorial House)
ul. Lajoš Košut 34, BG Sofija
Historic Site - 1948
Memorabilia on Dimităr Bladoev
(1856-1924), founder of the Bulgarian
Workers' Social Democratic Party;
history of the Bulgarian labour
movement

01656
Kăšta-muzej 'Georgi Kirkov' (Georgi
Kirkov Memorial Museum)
ul. Bačo Kiro 53, BG Sofija
Historic Site
Memorabilia on the revolutionist and
politician Georgi Kirkov; history of the
Bulgarian labour movement

01657
Kăšta-muzej 'Ivan Vazov' Nacionalen
muzej na bălgarskata literatura (Ivan
Vazov Memorial House)
ul. Ivan Vazov 10, BG Sofija
Historic Site - 1926
Memorabilia on the Bulgarian national
poet and writer Ivan Vazov
(1850-1921) in his former house

01658
Kăšta-muzej 'Nikola Vapcarov'
Nacionalen muzej na bălgarskata
literatura (Nikola Vapcarov Memorial
House)
ul. Angel Kănčev 37, BG Sofija
Historic Site - 1956
Memorabilia on the revolutionary poet
Nikola Vapcarov (1909-1942);
manuscripts; documents; letters

01659
Kăšta-muzej 'Nikolaj Chrelkov'
Nacionalen muzej na bălgarskata
literatura (Nikolaj Chrelkov Memorial
House)
ul. Ochrid 21, BG Sofija
Historic Site - 1954
Memorabilia on the revolutionary poet
Nikolaj Chrelkov

01660
Kăšta-muzej 'Pejo Javorov'
Nacionalen muzej na bălgarskata
literatura (Pejo Javorov Memorial
House)
ul. Rakovski 136, BG Sofija
Historic Site - 1956
Memorabilia on the poet Pejo
Kračolov Javorov (1877-1914) in his
former house

01661
**Kăšta-muzej 'Petko i Penčo
Slavejkovi'** Nacionalen muzej na
bălgarskata literatura (Petko and
Penčo Slavejkov Memorial House)
ul. Rakovski 138, BG Sofija
Historic Site - 1949
Memorabilia on the Bulgarian writers
Petko Račo Slavejkov (1828-1895) and
his son Penčo Slavejkov (1866-1912);
original interiors; documents; library

01662
Kăšta-muzej 'Vasil Kolarov'
ul. Asen Zlatarev 5, BG Sofija
Historic Site - 1956
Memorabilia of the politician Vasil
Kolarov (1877-1950)

01663
Muzej za istorija na Sofija (Museum
of History of the City of Sofija)
ul. Ekzarch Josif 27, BG Sofija
History/Public Affairs Museum - 1952
Archeology; ethnography; local
history; history of the labour
movement; contemporary history (not
open to the public)

01664
**Nacionalen archeologičeski muzej
na Bălgarskata Akademija na
Naukite** (National Archeological
Museum of the Bulgarian Academy of
Sciences)
bul. Aleksandăr Stambolijski 2, BG
Sofija
Archeology Museum - 1879
Prehistoric archeology, finds from the
Neolithic, Copper and Iron Ages;
Thracian period exhibits; collection of
Greek tombstones and ceramics;
Roman sculptures; medieval
archeology; Slav and Bulgarian
material culture and art; epitaphs;
proto-Bulgarian inscriptions; in a 15th
century Bujuk Mosque

01665
**Nacionalen cărkoven istoriko-
archeologičeski muzej** (National
Museum of Ecclesiastical History)
bul. Lenin 19, BG Sofija
Religious Art Museum - 1922
Valuable 15th-19th century Bulgarian
icons; manuscripts; religious history
and art; archeology; crafts; decorative
arts

01666
Nacionalen etnografski muzej na Bălgarskata Akademija na Naukite (National Ethnographic Museum of the Bulgarian Academy of Sciences)
ul. Moskovska 6a, BG Sofija
Anthropology Museum - 1906
18th-20th century folk art; fishing; hunting; apiculture; agriculture; rose-growing; wine-producing; domestic utensils; handicrafts; weaving; textiles; interiors; carpets; folk costumes; embroideries; jewelry; ceramics - library

01667
Nacionalen muzej 'Bojanska cărkva' (Bojana Church Museum)
kvartal Bojana, BG Sofija
Religious Art Museum - 1947
Valuable frescoes from 1259, examples of Bulgarian medieval art in a church built in the 11th-13th centuries; various painted scenes belonging to the precious heritage of Bulgarian painting during the time of the Second Bulgarian Kingdom

01668
Nacionalen muzej 'Georgi Dimitrov' (Georgi Dimitrov Memorial House)
ul. Opălčenska 66, BG Sofija
Historic Site - 1959
Memorabilia on the politician and Communist Party leader G. Dimitrov (1882-1949) in his former house; library; political documents; history of the Bulgarian labour movement

01669
Nacionalen muzej na bălgarosăvetskata družba (Museum of the Bulgarian-Soviet Friendship)
bul. Klement Gotvald 4, BG Sofija
History/Public Affairs Museum - 1975
Archeology; medieval cultural history; old prints; Russian icons; documents on the Bulgarian-Russian relationship in the 19th century, especially on the Russo-Turkish War (1877-1878); 20th century history; paintings - library

01670
Nacionalen muzej na dekorativno-priložnite izkustva (National Museum of Decorated and Applied Arts)
BG Sofija
Decorative Arts Museum - 1976
Not open to the public

01671
Nacionalen muzej na revoljucionnoto dviženie v Bălgarija (Museum of the Revolutionary Movement in Bulgaria)
pl. Narodno Săbranie 11, BG Sofija
History/Public Affairs Museum - 1950
History of the labour movement and foundation of the Bulgarian Workers' Social Democratic Party; history of the 1917 Soldier Revolt and the 1923 September Revolt; documents on the European anti-Fascist movement; memorabilia on the politician Georgi Dimitrov (1882-1949); contemporary history; weapons; photographs; maps

01672
Nacionalen politechničeski muzej (Polytechnic Museum)
ul. Rakovski 108, BG Sofija
Science/Tech Museum - 1957
Non open to the public

01673
Nacionalen voenno-istoričeski muzej (National Museum of Military History)
bul. Skobelev 23, BG Sofija
History/Public Affairs Museum - 1916
Slav and Bulgarian medieval arms from the 7th-14th centuries; national liberation movement against Ottoman rule; documents on the Russo-Turkish War (1877-1878); 20th century military history

01674
Nacionalna chudožestvena galerija (National Art Gallery)
ul. Moskovska 6, BG Sofija
Fine Arts Museum - 1948
19th century art of the Bulgarian National Revival period; 20th century Bulgarian painting, sculpture and graphics; 15th-20th century European art; branch in Alexandăr Nevski Cathedral (museum for icons and medieval ecclesiastical art)

01675
Nationalen prirodonaučen muzej kăm BAN (National Natural History Museum of the Bulgarian Academy of Sciences)
bul. Ruski 1, BG Sofija
Natural History Museum - 1906
Fauna and flora of Bulgaria; mammals; predatory animals; insect collection; natural history

Sopot

01676
Kăšta-muzej 'Ivan Vazov' (Ivan Vazov Memorial House)
pl. Ivan Vazov, BG Sopot
Historic Site - 1947
Memorabilia of the Bulgarian national poet Ivan Vazov (1850-1921) in his birthplace; original interiors; documents on the life and work of the poet; manuscripts; books

Sozopol

01677
Gradski istoričeski muzej (City Museum of History)
BG Sozopol
Archeology Museum - 1961
Archeological finds from the antique Greek town Apollonius (Apolonia); vases; collection of antique and medieval amphorae

Stanke Dimitrov

01678
Gradski muzej (City Museum)
BG Stanke Dimitrov
General Museum
Local history

Stara Zagora

01679
Kăšta-muzej 'Geo Milev' (Geo Milev Memorial House)
ul. Geo Milev 35, BG Stara Zagora
Historic Site
Memorabilia of the poet and revolutionist Geo Milev (1893-1925) in hisbirth place; original interiors; historical documents on the September 1923 Uprising

01680
Okrăžen istoričeski muzej (Regional Museum of History)
bul. Rakovski 42, BG Stara Zagora
General Museum - 1948
Div: archeology; history of the Bulgarian National Revival period and liberation movement; ethnography; history of capitalism and the labour movement; contemporary history

01681
Okrăžna chudožestvena galerija (Regional Art Gallery)
ul. Bajer, BG Stara Zagora
Fine Arts Museum - 1960
Contemporary Bulgarian fine art, paintings by B. Mitov, G. Mitov, N. Kožucharov, D. Gjudženev, A. Michov, M. Žekov etc.

Šumen

01682
Kăšta-muzej 'Lajoš Košuť' (Lajos Kossuth Memorial House)
ul. Car Osvoboditel 35, BG Šumen
Historic Site
Memorabilia on the Hungarian revolutionist and politician Lajos Kossuth (1802-1894) and his stay in Šumen in 1848; historical documents; in a 19th century house

01683
Kăšta-muzej 'Vasil Kolarov' (Vasil Kolarov Memorial House)
ul. I. Ikonomov 11, BG Šumen
Historic Site
Memorabilia of the politician Vasil Kolarov (1877-1950) in his birthplace; personal library

01684
Okrăžen istoričeski muzej (Regional Historical Museum)
ul. Dimităr Blagoev 10, BG Šumen
General Museum - 1857
Division of archeology: prehistoric archeology; finds form Thracian necropolis; medieval Bulgarian burial remains. Division of ethnography: folk art; handicrafts (ul. Rakovski 21). Division of Bulgarian National Revival Period: documents on the development of education in the 19th century; cultural history; guilds and crafts. Division of history of capitalism and revolutionary labour movement: historical documents; photographs; archives (ul. Gen. Zaimov 74)

01685
Okrăžna chudožestvena galerija (Regional Art Gallery)
BG Šumen
Fine Arts Museum - 1969
Contemporary Bulgarian fine art

Svištov

01686
Gradski istoričeski muzej 'Aleko Konstantinov' (City Museum of History)
ul. Klokotnica 6, BG Svištov
General Museum
Local history; memorabilia on the writer Aleko Konstantinov (1863-1897)

Targovište

01687
Okrăžen istoričeski muzej (Regional Historical Museum)
ul. Rakovski 1, BG Targovište
General Museum - 1959
Division of archeology, history of the Bulgarian National Revival period and liberation movement, history of capitalism and the labour movement (ul. Rakovski 1). Division of ethnography: folk arts and crafts; costumes; 19th century interiors (in Chadžiangelova kăšta). Division of art: contemporary Bulgarian art, works by N. Marinov, I. Petrov, S. Venev etc.(in učilište 'Sveti Sedmočislenici')

Teteven

01688
Gradski istoričeski muzej (City Museum of History)
BG Teteven
General Museum
Local history

Tolbuchin

01689
Okrăžen istoričeski muzej (Regional Historical Museum)
bul. Lenin 1, BG Tolbuchin
General Museum - 1960
Div: archeology; history of the Bulgarian National Revival period and liberation movement; ethnography; history of capitalsm and the labour movement; contemporary history; natural history

Trjavna

01690
Muzej na rezbarskoto i zografsko izkustvo (Museum of Wood Carving and Mural Paintings)
ul. Petko Slavejkov 27, BG Trjavna
Decorative Arts Museum - 1959
Valuable examples of the art of the Bulgarian National Revival Period (18th-19th century); exhibits from the 19th century 'Trjavna School' of wood carving and painting; old icons; wood-carved ceilings and altar pieces; original tools; original interiors; in a Daskalov house, built in 1808

Trojan

01691
Muzej na chudožestvenite zanajati i priložni izkustva (Museum of Handicrafts and Applied Arts)
ul. Vasil Vlaskovski 3, BG Trojan, Loveški okrăg
Decorative Arts Museum - 1962
19th century pottery workshop interior; copper, silver and goldsmith work; jewelry; tanners' and furriers' trade; wood working; folk costumes; textiles; Trojan carpets

Tutrakan

01692
Etnografski muzej Okrăžen istoričeski muzej, Silistra (Ethnographical Branch of the Regional Historical Museum in Silistra)
BG Tutrakan, Silistrenski okrăg
Anthropology Museum
Danubian fishing and boatbuilding, ethnography

Varna

01693
Archeologičeski muzej Okräžen
istoričeski muzej, Varna
ul. Šejnovo 5, BG Varna
Archeology Museum
Antique finds; Greek ceramics and
terra cotta; Roman sculpture;
numismatics; medieval art; Byzantine
archeology; lapidarium

01694
Etnografski muzej Okräžen istoričeski
muzej, Varna
ul. 27. Juli 9, BG Varna
Anthropology Museum
Crafts; copper smithery; folk
costumes; embroidery; textiles; 19th
century interiors

01695
Kartinna galerija (Art Gallery)
bul. Lenin 65, BG Varna
Fine Arts Museum
Painting; graphics; sculpture; works by
I. Mrkvička, S. Ivanov, Z. Todorov, Z.
Bojadžiev, D. Usunov, D. Dečev, A.
Michov, A. Mutafov,

01696
Muzej na revoljucionnoto dviženie
Okräžen istorički muzej, Varna
(Museum of the Revolutionary
Movement)
ul. 8. Noemvri 5, BG Varna
History/Public Affairs Museum
History of the revolutionary labour
movement; foundation of the Bulgarian
Workers' Social Democratic Party;
photographs; documents

01697
Muzej na Văzraždaneto Okräžen
istoričeski muzej, Varna (Museum of
the Bulgarian National Revival Period)
ul. 27. Juli 9, BG Varna
History/Public Affairs Museum
19th century Bulgarian religious art;
icons; history of the Bulgarian National
Revival period (18th-19th century)

01698
Muzej na văzroždenskata ikona
Okräžen istoričeski muzej, Varna
(Museum of Icons)
ul. Graf Ignatiev 19, BG Varna
Fine Arts Museum
North Bulgarian icon collection,
especially examples from the 19th
century 'Trjavna School' of
woodcarving and painting; in the
church 'Sveti Anastas'

01699
Okräžen istoričeski muzej (Regional
Historical Museum)
bul. 8. Noemvri 5, BG Varna
History/Public Affairs Museum - 1906
The museum has the following
branches: Archeological Museum;
Ethnographical Museum; Museum of
the Bulgarian National Revival Period;
Museum of Icons; Museum of the
Revolutionary Movement

01700
Prirodonaučen muzej (Museum of
Natural History)
Morska gradina, BG Varna
Natural History Museum
Black Sea flora and fauna; coastal
flora; birds and mammals

01701
Voenno-morski muzej (Museum of
Maritime History)
bul. Červenoarmejski 2, BG Varna
History/Public Affairs Museum - 1885
Navigation history; navigation during
the Ottoman period; Bulgarian
maritime history; documents on World
War II

Veliko Tărnovo

01702
Etnografski musej Okräžen istoričeski
musej
Chadži Nikoli Chan, BG Veliko
Tärnovo
Anthropology Museum
History of the Bulgarian National
Revival period; economical and
cultural history; development of
education; arts and crafts;
ethnography; tools; handicrafts;
architecture; in an inn built 1858 by
Kolju Fičeto

01703
Okräžen istoričeski muzej (Regional
Historical Museum)
ul. Ivanka Boteva 1, BG Veliko Tärnovo
History/Public Affairs Museum - 1871
Thracian period archeological finds;
cermics; gold jewelry; exhibits from
the period of the Second Bulgarian
State (1187-1396); icon collection;
division of history of capitalism and the
revolutionary labour movement (pl.
Säedinenie, Veliko Tärnovo)

01704
Okräžna chudožestvena galerija
(Regional Art Gallery)
ul. Karaminkov 6, BG Veliko Tärnovo
Fine Arts Museum - 1957
Paintings; graphics; sculpture; works
by Ivan Christov, B. Denev, N. Tanev,
A. Terziev, J. Popov etc.

01705
Zatvor-muzej (Prison Museum)
pl. Säedinenie, BG Veliko Tärnovo
History/Public Affairs Museum
History of the 18th-19th century
liberation movement against Ottoman
rule; memorabilia on Vasil Levski, Bačo
Kiro, T. Kableškov, S. Karadža; history
of the anti-Fascist struggle

Velingrad

01706
Muzej 'Vela Peeva'
ul. Georgi Kirkov 2, BG Velingrad
General Museum
Local history; ethnography

Vidin

01707
Okräžen istoričeski muzej (Regional
Historical Museum)
ul. G. Dimitrov 55, BG Vidin
General Museum - 1906
Division of archeology, history of the
Bulgarian National Revival period and
liberation movement; Division of
ethnology, history of capitalism,
revolutionary labour movement and
socialist development (ul. Bojan Čonos
36)

01708
Okräžna chudožestvena galerija
(Regional Art Gallery)
BG Vidin
Fine Arts Museum
Paintings; sculpture; graphics; works
by I. Mrkvička, B. Mitov, Vladimir
Dimitrov-Majstora, Z. Bojadžiev, L.
Dalčev

01709
Peštera Rabiša, muzej (Rabiša Cave,
Museum)
BG Vidin
Archeology Museum
Prehistoric archeology; cave art;
natural history

Vraca

01710
Okräžen istoričeski muzej (Regional
Historical Museum)
ul. Christo Botev 10, BG Vraca
General Museum - 1953
Divisions: archeology; Bulgarian
National Revival period and liberation
movement; ethnography; history of
capitalism and the revolutionary labour
movement; development of socialism

01711
Okräžna chudožestvena galerija
(Regional Art Gallery)
ul. Georgi Dimitrov, BG Vraca
Fine Arts Museum
Contemporary Bulgarian art

01712
Otdel 'Etnografija' Okräžen istoričeski
muzej, Vraca (Regional Historical
Museum, Ethnographic Division)
bul. Lenin 4, BG Vraca
Anthropology Museum - 1953
Goldsmith tools and work; folk
costumes; embroidery; crafts

Žeravna

01713
Kăšta-muzej 'Jordan Jovkov' (Jordan
Jovkov Memorial House)
BG Žeravna
Historic Site
Memorabilia of the writer Jordan
Jovkov in his birthplace; original
interiors; documents; books

Burma

Banbhore

01714
Banbhore Museum
Banbhore
Archeology Museum - 1967
Architectural remains, 8th to 13th cent.

Bassein

01715
Bassein Museum
Bassein
General Museum

Kyaukpyu

01716
State Library and Museum
Kyaukpyu
General Museum - 1955
Silver coins; costumes

Mandalay

01717
National Museum of Mandalay
Glass Palace, Mandalay
General Museum
19th cent. history of Mandalay;
architectural fragments; art objects

01718
State Gallery
Mandalay
Fine Arts Museum

01719
University of Mandalay Collections
Bawdigon, Mandalay
General Museum
Ethnography; art; history

Moulmein

01720
Mon Museum
Moulmein
Fine Arts Museum - 1955

01721
State Library and Museum
Moulmein
General Museum - 1955

Myohaung

01722
Archaeological Museum
Myohaung
Archeology Museum

Pagan

01723
Archaeological Museum
Pagan
Archeology Museum - 1904
Major archaeological site

Pegu

01724
Museum of the Shwenawdaw Pagoda
Pegu
Religious Art Museum
Old bronzes; modern sacral articles

Prome

01725
Prome Museum
High St, Prome, Pecu Division
History/Public Affairs Museum - 1950
Cultural and historical relics of the
Burmese kings

Rangoon

01726
Bogyoke Aung San Museum
25 Tower Lane, Rangoon
History/Public Affairs Museum - 1959
Memorabilia of General Aung San

01727
Health Museum
Municipal Corp. Bldgs., Baar St,
Rangoon
Science/Tech Museum
Medicine and hygiene

01728
Museum in the Peace Pagoda
Institute of Advanced Buddhistic
Studies
Kaba-aye Pagoda Compound,
Rangoon
Religious Art Museum - 1956
Buddhist art and archaeology; history
of pagodas in Burma - library

01729
**National Museum of Art and
Archaeology**
Jubilee Hall, Pagoda Rd, Rangoon
General Museum - 1952
Archaeological finds; contemporary
painting; crafts; ethnology; Mandalay
Lion Throne; regalia of King Thibaw of
Mandalay

01730
Natural History Museum
Rangoon
Natural History Museum - 1968
Mammals; fish; geology; forestry

01731
War Museum
Stewart Rd, Rangoon
History/Public Affairs Museum
Militaria

Shrikshetra

01732
Shrikshetra Museum
Shrikshetra
Archeology Museum
Archaeological site

Taungdwingyi

01733
Forest Museum
Taungdwingyi
Science/Tech Museum - 1964
Forestry

Burundi

Bujumbura

01734
Musée Vivant de Bujumbura
BP 1095, Bujumbura
Natural History Museum
Natural history; zoology

Gitega

01735
Musée National de Gitega
Pl de la Révolution 223, BP 110, Gitega
General Museum - 1955
Musical instruments; weapons;
witchcraft utensils; basket works -
library

Cameroon

Bamenda

01736
Mankon Museum
Bamenda
General Museum

Douala

01737
Musée de Douala
BP 1271, Douala
General Museum
Ethnography; traditional art

Dschang

01738
Foyer Culturel de Dschang
Centre de Jeunesse, BP 10, Dschang
Fine Arts Museum

01739
Musée Bamilike
BP 152, Dschang
General Museum
Sculpture; masks; pottery

Fort Fourreau

01740
Musée du Fort Fourreau
Fort Fourreau
Fine Arts Museum
Traditional art

Foumban

01741
**Musée des Arts et des Traditions
Bamboun**
BP 71, Foumban
General Museum
Art and handicrafts; ethnography

01742
Musée du Palais
Palais du Sultanat Bamoun, BP 50,
Foumban
General Museum
Archaeology; history; ethnology;
handicrafts

Maroua

01743
Musée de Diamare
Maroua
Fine Arts Museum

01744
Musée de Maroua
BP 36, Maroua
General Museum

Mokolo

01745
Musée Municipal de Mokolo
Mokolo
General Museum

Yaoundé

01746
Musée d'Art Negre
Centre Catholique Universitaire de
Yaoundé, BP 876, Yaoundé
Fine Arts Museum
Traditional art; archaeology; Ethiopian
coins; ceramics; African antiquities

01747
Petit Musée d'Art Camerounais
Monastère bénédictin de Mont Fébé,
BP 1178, Yaoundé
Fine Arts Museum - 1979
Works of sacred art

Canada

Abbotsford

01748
Matsqui-Abbotsford Museum
33660 South Fraser Way, Abbotsford,
British Columbia V2S 2B9
General Museum - 1969
Local history; native exhibits -
archives

Adolphustown

01749
United Empire Loyalist Museum
Adolphustown Park, Adolphustown,
mail c/o Ms. Evelyn Drew, East Main
St, Picton, Ontario K0K 2T0
History/Public Affairs Museum - 1962
History of Loyalist settlers; pioneer
tools, costumes, furniture and
documents

Alberta Beach

01750
Alberta Beach Museum
Alberta Beach, Alberta TOE 0A0
General Museum - 1967
Historical artifacts; geological material;
dinosaur bones

Alberton

01751
Alberton Museum
Poplar St, POB 121, Alberton, Prince
Edward Island C0B 1B0
General Museum - 1965
Local history

Alert Bay

01752
Alert Bay Museum
Fir St, POB 208, Alert Bay, British
Columbia V0N 1A0
General Museum - 1958
Local history; ethnography; fishing
industry

Alexandria

01753
Glengarry Pioneer Museum
RR 1, Dunvegan Rd, *mail c/o* Ms.
Harriet MacKinnon, Glengary
Historical Society, POB 416,
Alexandria, Ontario K0C 1A0
History/Public Affairs Museum - 1962
Local history including farm
implements and domestic utensils of
the Scottish settlers

01754
Nor'Wester and Loyalist Museum
Williamstown, POB 416, Alexandria,
Ontario K0C 1A0
General Museum - 1967
Fur trade equipment; Indian and Inuit
artifacts; history of Loyalists;
genealogical records; geology

Alida

01755
Wheels Museum
Alida, Saskatchewan S0C 0B0
History/Public Affairs Museum - 1972
Automobiles of North America,
pioneer artifacts, music boxes

Alix

01756
Wagon Wheel Regional Museum
POB 157, Alix, Alberta T0C 0B0
General Museum - 1970
Local historical artifacts; archives

Alliston

01757
South Simcoe Pioneer Museum
Riverdale Drive, Town Municipal
Office, Alliston, Ontario L0M 1A0
General Museum - 1959
Pioneer history including agricultural
implements and tools, guns, musical
instruments, historical log cabin

Amherstburg

01758
Fort Malden National Historic Site
POB 38, Amherstburg, Ontario N9V
2Z2
History/Public Affairs Museum - 1939
General history including Indian and
military history

Andrew

01759
**Andrew and District Local History
Museum**
POB 180, Andrew, Alberta T0B 0C0
General Museum - 1973
Local historical artifacts and records

Annapolis Royal

01760
Fort Anne National Historic Park
295 St. George St, POB 9, Annapolis
Royal, Nova Scotia B0S 1A0
History/Public Affairs Museum - 1919
Early fortification of the French period
(1606-1710); British fort (1710-1854)

Anola

01761
**Anola and District Community
Museum**
mail c/o Ms. W. Kruchak Anola,
Manitoba R0E 0A0
History/Public Affairs Museum - 1975
Local history

Arichat

01762
Le Noir Forge
POB 239, Arichat, Nova Scotia B0E
1A0
General Museum - 1967
Local crafts and trades; blacksmith
forge and tools

Arkona

01763
**Arkona Lion's Club Indian Artifacts
Museum**
Smith St, Arkona, Ontario N0M 1B0
Anthropology Museum - 1972
Indian artifacts including arrowheads,
skinning stones, ceremonial stones;
fossils and petrified wood; minerals
and semi-precious stones

Arnprior

01764
Arnprior and District Museum
35 Madawaska St, Arnprior, Ontario
K7S 1R6
General Museum - 1967
Indian artifacts; fur trading and
lumbering industry; furnishings;
antique jewelry; documents dating
back to the 1840's

Arthabasca

01765
Musée Laurier
16 ouest, rue Laurier, Arthabasca, CP
306, Victoriaville, Québec G6P 6S9
Historic Site - 1934
Home of Wilfred Laurier from
1867-1896; furniture; paintings;
sculpture; engravings

Ashcroft

01766
Ashcroft Museum
Railway Av and 3rd St, POB 129,
Ashcroft
General Museum - 1960
History; agricultural implements; native
Indian and Chinese items; mineralogy
- archives

Ashville

01767
Drifting River Museum
Farm in Gilbert Plains Municipality, RR
No 2, Ashville, Manitoba R0E A0A
General Museum - 1970
Indian artifacts; rocks and minerals;
fossils; Ukrainian handicrafts

Atikokan

01768
Atikokan Centennial Museum
Civic Square, POB 1330, Atikokan,
Ontario P0T 1C0
General Museum - 1966
Local history; local art; Indian artifacts;
lumbering and mining

Atlin

01769
Atlin Historical Museum
3rd and Trainor Sts, POB 111, Atlin,
British Columbia V0W 1A0
General Museum - 1972
Local history; natural history; material
from the Gold Rush era - archives

Au Lac

01770
**Fort Beausejour National Historic
Park**
RR 3, Au Lac, New Brunswick E0A
3C0
History/Public Affairs Museum - 1936
Documentation on French-British
battles; military items; local history

Austin

01771
Manitoba Agricultural Museum
South of the junction of Hwys 1 and
34, west of Austin, POB 10, Austin,
Manitoba R0H 0C0
Agriculture Museum - 1953
Antique agricultural equipment;
household utensils (1880-1920)

Aylmer

01772
Canadian Golf Museum
Mountain Rd, RR 1, Aylmer, Québec
J9H 5E1
History/Public Affairs Museum - 1967
Golf equipment; books, prints, and
other related artifacts

Baddeck

01773
**Alexander Graham Bell National
Historic Park**
Route 205, Chebucto St, POB 159,
Baddeck, Nova Scotia B0E 1B0
Science/Tech Museum - 1956
Documentation on Dr. A.G. Bell's
experiments and activities including
the visible speach system for the deaf,
development of the telephone, the
hydrofoil, vacuum jacket, early aircraft
engines and an original tetrahedral
shelter

01774
**Victoria County Library Museum and
Archives**
Gilbert Grosvenor Bldg, *mail c/o* Dr.
C.M. Bethune, Chebucto St, Baddeck,
Nova Scotia B0E 1B0
General Museum - 1971
Agricultural implements; domestic
utensils - archives

Baie Comeau

01775
**Musée de la Société Historique de la
Côte Nord**
41 av Mance, CP 258, Baie Comeau,
Québec G4Z 2H1
History/Public Affairs Museum - 1952
Coll: ethnological and archeological
exhibits; domestic utensils; natural
history specimens

Bancroft

01776
Bancroft Historical Museum
Station St, POB 239, Bancroft, Ontario
K0L 1C0
History/Public Affairs Museum - 1967
Original log house (1859) with pioneer
artifacts; historical documents

Banff

01777
**Banff National Park Museum of
Natural History**
POB 900, Banff, Alberta T0L 0C0
Natural History Museum - 1904
Geological specimens with typical
fauna and flora

01778
Luxton Museum
1 Birch Av, Banff, Alberta T0L 0C0
General Museum - 1952
Indian costumes, weapons, tools and
utensils; Inuit material; North American
natural history specimens; paintings

01779
Peter Whyte Gallery
111 Bear St, POB 160, Banff, Alberta
T0L 0C0
Fine Arts Museum - 1968
Paintings, sculptures and artifacts
mainly relevant to the Canadian
Rockies

01780
Walter J. Phillips Gallery
POB 1020, Banff, Alberta T0L 0C0
Fine Arts Museum - 1976
Fine and decorative arts

Barkerville

01781
Barkerville Historic Park
88 km west of Quesnel, Barkerville,
British Columbia V0K 1B0
Open Air Museum - 1958
Buildings including a church, saloon,
store, blacksmith and cabinet makers
shops, bakery, print shop (1858-1900);
mining; commerce and transportation
- archives

01782
**Bowron Lakes Provincial Park
Nature House**
28 km east of Barkerville, POB 33,
Barkerville, British Columbia V0K 1B0
Natural History Museum - 1972
Natural history; park maps; geology;
human history

Barrhead

01783
**Barrhead and District Centennial
Museum**
Sports grounds, Hwy 33, POB 626,
Barrhead, Alberta T0G 0E0
General Museum - 1967
Local historical artifacts and archives

Barrie

01784
Simcoe County Museum
Hwy 26, north of Barrie, RR 2,
Minesing, Ontario L0L 1Y0
General Museum - 1928
Local history; agriculture;
transportation; archeology; costumes;
ethnology; historic buildings - library;
archives

Barrington

01785
Old Woolen Mill
Barrington, Nova Scotia B0W 1E0
History/Public Affairs Museum - 1969
Water-powered woolen mill (1890)
with carding and spinning machinery;
history of wool production before
1900

Basin Head

01786
Basin Head Fisheries Museum
Basin Head, POB 248, Souris, Prince
Edward Island C0A 2B0
Agriculture Museum - 1973
Fishing industry

Batiscan

01787
**Musée du Manoir du Presbytere de
Batiscan**
340 rue Principale, Route 2, Batiscan,
Québec G0X 1A0
History/Public Affairs Museum - 1690
Furniture dating back to the 17th
century; local geological specimens;
manuscripts pertaining to Canada's
history

Batoche

01788
Batoche National Historic Site
Batoche, POB 70, Battleford,
Saskatchewan S0M 0E0
History/Public Affairs Museum - 1961
Métis cultural history; military exhibits;
historic buildings - outdoor
interpretive satellite

Battleford

01789
Battleford National Historic Park
POB 70, Battleford, Saskatchewan
S0M 0E0
History/Public Affairs Museum - 1951
Coll: military buildings; Indian
ethnology; pioneer artifacts;
anthropology; agriculture; Lindemere
paintings

Bear River

01790
Bear River Farmers' Museum
Bear River, Nova Scotia B0S 1B0
General Museum
Farming, logging and shipping
equipment (19th-early 20th c.)

Beausejour

01791
**Broken-Beau Historical Society
Museum Village Complex**
Brokenhead Centennial Park, *mail c/o*
Peter H. Kozyra, POB 222, Beausejour,
Manitoba R0E 0C0
Open Air Museum - 1973
Local pioneer artifacts; agricultural
implements; restored school, railroad
station and community hall

Beauval

01792
Frazier's Museum
Hwy 155 north, 2 miles south of
Beauval Forks, POB 64, Beauval,
Saskatchewan
History/Public Affairs Museum - 1970
Coll: native and pioneer artifacts;
missionary and Métis culture; northern
technology

Beaverlodge

01793
South Peace Centennial Museum
Northwest of Beaverlodge on Hwy 2,
POB 493, Beaverlodge, Alberta T0H
0C0
General Museum - 1967
Pioneer farm equipments; household
artifacts

Belleville

01794
Hastings County Museum
257 Bridge St East, Belleville, Ontario
K8N 1P4
General Museum - 1973
Local history; Couldry collection of
European and Oriental furniture and
paintings; Dr. William A. Paul lighting
collection - archives

Berthierville

01795
Village du Défricheur
1497 Grande Côte, Route 139,
Berthierville, Québec J0K 1A0
History/Public Affairs Museum
Coll: antique liturgical items and
statues; pottery; furniture; medical and
surgical instruments

Beulah

01796
Ulley's Country Store and Museum
Beulah, Manitoba R0M 0B0
General Museum - 1976
Indian artifacts; pioneer utensils and
furniture; store items (1911)

Biggar

01797
Biggar Museum and Gallery
292-3rd Av West, POB 331, Biggar,
Saskatchewan S0K 0M0
General Museum - 1972
Coll: local history from the time of the
native people to the early thirties;
artifacts used in early photography,
medicine and drug stores; applied
arts; clothing

Black Lake

01798
**Musée Minéralogique et Minier de la
Région de L'Amiante**
Thetford Mines, Boulevard Smith, CP
462, Black Lake, Québec G6G 5T3
Science/Tech Museum
All sorts of asbestos specimens from
different countries; history of asbestos
mining; products made of asbestos;
fossils

Blind River

01799
Timber Village Museum
Hwy 17, 13 Michigan Av, Blind River, Ontario
Open Air Museum - 1966
History of lumbering; blacksmith shop; rocks and minerals; agriculture; woodcarvings

Boissevain

01800
Beckoning Hills Museum
mail c/o Mr. C. Deacon Boissevain, Manitoba R0K 0E0
General Museum - 1967
Early agricultural tools; pioneer household utensils; clothing; pictures, books and documents; Indian artifacts

Bonavista

01801
Bonavista Museum
POB 549, Bonavista, Newfoundland A0C 1B0
History/Public Affairs Museum - 1968
Local history

Bonshaw

01802
Car Life Museum
Bonshaw, 45 Oak Dr, Charlottetown, Prince Edward Island C1A 6T6
History/Public Affairs Museum - 1966
Restored early cars, pioneer farm machinery

Borden

01803
Base Borden Military Museum
Worthington Park, Canadian Forces Base, Borden, Ontario L0M 1C0
History/Public Affairs Museum - 1963
Military history and equipment; World War I and II fighting vehicles and guns

Bothwell

01804
Fairfield Museum
Hwy 2, RR 3, Bothwell, Ontario N0P 1C0
Religious Art Museum - 1960
Life of Moravian missionaries; Indian artifacts; Bibles and handbooks translated into the Algonquin language of the Delaware Indians

Bowmanville

01805
Bowmanville Museum
37 Silver St, POB 188, Bowmanville, Ontario L1C 3K9
General Museum - 1961
Local history; trades and crafts before 1900; toys; furnishings; music instruments; textiles; tools

Bowsman

01806
McKays Museum
RR 1, Bowsman, Manitoba R0L 0H0
History/Public Affairs Museum - 1959
Local history

Bracken

01807
Bakken-Wright Museum
mail c/o Laura Wright, 8 1/2 miles north east of Bracken on a farm, POB 34, Bracken, Saskatchewan S0N 0G0
General Museum - 1957
Ammonites; Indian artifacts; household items

Brandon

01808
B.J. Hales Museum of Natural History
A.E. McKenzie Bldg, Brandon University, 18th St, POB 60, Brandon, Manitoba R7A 6A9
Natural History Museum - 1966
Mounted birds and mammals; geology; archeology

01809
Historical Society Museum Brandon Mental Health Centre
POB 420, Brandon, Manitoba R7A 5Z5
History/Public Affairs Museum - 1972
History of mental health

Brantford

01810
Alexander Bell Homestead and Henderson Home
94 Tutela Height Rd, 1 Sherwood Drive, Brantford, Ontario N3T 1W3
Historic Site - 1917
Home of Alexander Graham Bell; period furnishings; Bell's inventions including telephone technology

01811
Art Gallery of Brant
76 Dalhousie St, POB 1747, Brantford, Ontario N3T 5V7
Fine Arts Museum - 1971
Contemporary Canadian prints and drawings; European and American prints; works by Robert Whale of Brant

01812
Brant County Museum
57 Charlotte St, Brantford, Ontario N3T 2W6
General Museum - 1908
Indian and pioneer history; Six Nations Indian collection; paintings and portraits by Robert Whale, George Waite and Alice Pilant; documents on local personalities including A.G. Bell

Bridgewater

01813
Dean Wile Carding Mill
Pearl St at Victoria Rd, POB 353, Bridgewater, Nova Scotia B4V 2W9
History/Public Affairs Museum - 1974
Wool carding mill with waterwheel (1860)

01814
Desbrisay Museum and National Exhibition Centre
130 Jubilee Rd, POB 353, Bridgewater, Nova Scotia B4V 2W9
General Museum - 1974
Local history; Micmac Indian artifacts; French, English and German historic items; arts and crafts; natural history

Brighton

01815
Presqu'ile Provincial Park Museum
Presqu'ile Provincial Park, RR 4, Brighton, Ontario K0K 1H0
Natural History Museum - 1957
Natural history; ecology

Britannia Beach

01816
British Columbia Museum of Mining
POB 155, Britannia Beach, British Columbia V0N 1J0
Science/Tech Museum - 1975
Mining; located in the closed Anaconda Mine

Brooks

01817
Brooks and District Museum
568 Sutherland Drive, POB 1255, Brooks, Alberta T0J 0J0
Anthropology Museum - 1975
History; ethnology; archives

Bruce Mines

01818
Bruce Mines Museum
Hwy 17, Bruce Mines, Ontario P0R 1C0
History/Public Affairs Museum - 1956
Local history - archives

Bulyea

01819
Lakeside Museum
4 miles south and 10 1/2 miles west of Bulyea, R.R. 1, Bulyea, Saskatchewan S0G 0L0
History/Public Affairs Museum - 1945
Pioneer, Indian and war relics; prehistoric bones

Burlington

01820
Joseph Brant Museum
1240 North Shore Bd East, Burlington, Ontario L7S 1G5
General Museum - 1942
Iroquois Indian artifacts; local history; 19th century costumes; mementos of Captain Joseph Brant and the Brant family - library

Burnaby

01821
Burnaby Art Gallery
6344 Gilpin St, Burnaby, British Columbia V5G 2J3
Fine Arts Museum - 1967
Contemporary and historical Canadian works of art; prints

01822
Heritage Village Museum
Century Park, 4900 Deer Lake Av, Burnaby, British Columbia V5G 3T6
General Museum - 1971
Regional history (1890-1925); ethnic history; transportation; industrial machinery; medicine - archives

01823
Museum of Archaeology and Ethnology Simon Fraser University, Dept. of Archaeology
Burnaby, British Columbia V5A 1S6
Anthropology Museum - 1971
Prehistory; ethnography; cultural material from Africa, Asia, Australia, Central and South America

01824
Simon Fraser Gallery Simon Fraser University, Centre for the Arts
Burnaby, British Columbia V5A 1S6
Fine Arts Museum - 1971
Contemporary and eskimo art; international graphics

Caledonia

01825
Chiefswood
Hwy 54, near Caledonia, Post Office, Ohsweken, Ontario N0A 1M0
Historic Site - 1963
Historic Indian mansion from the pre-Confederation period; birthplace of the Indian poetess E. Pauline Johnson

Calgary

01826
Alberta College of Art Gallery
1301-16th Av NW, Calgary, Alberta T2M 0L4
History/Public Affairs Museum - 1958
Works of the students and the staff; Canadian ceramics

01827
Calgary Zoo, Botanical Gardens and Natural History Park
St. George's Island, Calgary, Alberta T2G 3H4
Natural History Museum - 1929
Mammals; birds; reptiles; botany; natural history; models of early dinosaurs

01828
Centennial Planetarium
POB 2100, Calgary, Alberta T2P 2M5
Natural History Museum - 1967
Aircraft and aircraft engines; aviation photographs; electronic devices such as radios, televisions, computers

01829
Fort Calgary
750-9th Av SE, POB 2100, Calgary, Alberta T2P 2M5
Open Air Museum - 1978
Historic buildings

01830
Glenbow-Alberta Institute
Calgary Convention Centre and Palliser Square, 9th Av and 1st St SE, Calgary, Alberta T2G 0P3
General Museum - 1964
Ethnology; cultural history; arms and armor; numismatics; mineralogy; historical paintings, prints, drawings and illustrations; modern and contemporary Canadian art - library; archives

01831
Heritage Park
1900 Heritage Park Drive SW, Calgary, Alberta T2V 2X3
Open Air Museum - 1964
Pioneer life from the days of the Indians and early fur traders to 1914; historic buildings; standard gauge locomotive; passenger paddle wheel steamer

01832
Inglewoog Bird Sanctuary
9th Av and 23rd St SE, POB 2100, Calgary, Alberta T2P 2M5
Natural History Museum - 1970
Mounted birds, butterflies and mammals

01833
Lord Strathcona Horse Museum
Currie Barracks, CFB Calgary,
Calgary, Alberta T3E 1T8
History/Public Affairs Museum - 1970
Military artifacts

01834
Museum of Zoology University of
Calgaray
Dept. of Biology, 2920-24th Av NW,
Calgary, Alberta T2N 1N4
Natural History Museum - 1966
Osteological specimens; skin
collection; vertebrate material

01835
Muttart Gallery
2nd Floor, Memorial Parc Library,
1221, 2nd St SW, Calgary, Alberta T2H
0J1
Fine Arts Museum - 1978
Civic Art collection

01836
**Princess Patricia's Canadian Light
Infantry Museum**
Currie Barracks, Calgary, Alberta T3E
1T8
History/Public Affairs Museum - 1954
Regimental history from 1914 to the
present

01837
**Sam Livingstone Fish Hatchery and
Rearing Station**
1440-17 A St SE, Calgary, Alberta T2G
4Y9
Science/Tech Museum - 1973
Displays and mechanical equipment
related to fish culture

01838
University of Calgary Art Gallery
Main Floor, Library Block, 29th Av and
26th St NW, Calgary, Alberta T2N 1N4
Fine Arts Museum - 1975
Works by Alberta artists, some
American, Italian, French and English
artists, and contemporary Canadian
artists

Campbell River

01839
Campbell River Museum
1235 Island Hwy, Campbell River,
British Columbia V9W 2C7
Anthropology Museum - 1958
Northwest Coast Indian ethnography;
local history - library; archives

Camrose

01840
**Camrose and District Centennial
Museum**
46th Av and 53rd St, 20 Grand Park
Crescent, Camrose, Alberta T2N 1N4
General Museum - 1967
Antique clothing, furniture and home
equipment; business machines and
store equipment; farm equipment

Cape Spear

01841
**Cape Spear Lighthouse National
Historic Park**
Cape Spear, POB 5879, St. John's,
Newfoundland A1C 5X4
Science/Tech Museum - 1968
Historic lighthouse with 1836 period
furniture

Caraquet

01842
Musée Acadien
Caraquet, New Brunswick E0B 1K0
General Museum - 1967
Folklore

01843
Village Historique Acadien
CP 820, Caraquet, New Brunswick
E0B 1K0
Historic Site - 1977
Historical village of the Acadiens
(1780-1880); furnishings; farm
implements; fishing equipment

Cardston

01844
C.O. Card Home and Museum
337 Main St, POB 280, Cardston,
Alberta T0K 0K0
General Museum - 1967
Local history in restored 1887 home

Carillon

01845
Musée d'Argenteuil
Carillon, CP 5, Lachute, Québec J8H
3X2
History/Public Affairs Museum - 1938
Indian artifacts; domestic utensils;
farming equipment; Ranger uniforms;
military equipment - archives

Carleton

01846
Musée Carleton
Route 132, CP 128, Carleton, Québec
G0C 1J9
History/Public Affairs Museum - 1970
Coins and stamps; weapons; domestic
utensils; history of Baie-des-Chaleurs
navigation

Carleton Place

01847
**R. Tait McKenzie Memorial Museum
and Mill of Kintail**
northwest of Almonte, mail c/o
Mississippi Valley Conservation
Authority, POB 419, Carleton Place,
Ontario K7C 3P5
Historic Site - 1952
Memorial to the sculptor R. Tait
McKenzie (1867-1938); works by the
artist and documents on his life

Carlyle

01848
Rusty Relics Museum
mail c/o Mrs. Stella McLeod, POB 396,
Carlyle, Saskatchewan S0C 0R0
General Museum - 1974
Pioneer artifacts; old dentist's office

Carman

01849
Dufferin Historical Museum
King's Park, POB 426, Carman,
Manitoba R0G 0J0
General Museum - 1954
Watercolors depicting rural life about
1900; clothing; Indian artifacts;
household and farm utensils

01850
Heaman's Antique Autorama
POB 105, Carman, Manitoba R0G 0J0
Science/Tech Museum - 1967
Canadian and American automobiles
from 1912 to the present

Cartwright

01851
Badger Creek Museum
Former telephone building, mail c/o
A.E. Thompson Cartwright, Manitoba
R0K 0L0
History/Public Affairs Museum - 1975
Agricultural and domestic tools and
utensils - archives

Castlegar

01852
Castlegar National Exhibition Centre
SS No 1, Site 2, Comp. 10, Castlegar,
British Columbia V1N 3H7
General Museum - 1967
Regional history; ethnography; mining
equipment and tools

01853
Doukhobour Village Museum
East side of Kinnaird Bridge, POB
3081, Castlegar, British Columbia V1N
3H4
Open Air Museum - 1971
Rebuilt village; handmade furniture and
household utensils; handspun clothing;
embroidery; old farm machinery and
tools

01854
**Selkirk College Archives and Local
History Collection**
POB 1200, Castlegar, British Columbia
V1N 3J1
History/Public Affairs Museum - 1970
Printed material, photographs, films
and sound recordings relating to the
Doukhobours of the West

Castor

01855
Castor and District Museum
5101-49th Av, POB 210, Castor,
Alberta T0C 0X0
General Museum - 1969
Local history

Caughnawaga

01856
Musée Kateri Tekakwitha
Mission Saint-François Xavier, CP 70,
Caughnawaga, Québec J0L 1B0
Religious Art Museum - 1925
Exhibits devoted to the only Iroquois
Indian to be declared blessed;
religious relics made of gold; Indian
belts; sculpture

Cayuga

01857
Haldimand County Museum
Court House Park, mail c/o Ms. John
Walker, Secretary, Museum Board
Cayuga, Ontario N0A 1E0
General Museum - 1936
Pioneer history; Indian artifacts;
military equipment; natural history; log
cabin restored to the 1840 period

Centreville

01858
Archelaus Smith Museum
mail c/o Cape Sable Historical
Society, McGray Post Office,
Centreville, Nova Scotia B0W 2G0
History/Public Affairs Museum - 1970
Marine history; fishing industry;
boatbuilding; local history

Cereal

01859
Cereal Prairie Pioneer Museum
Old Railway Station, POB 131, Cereal,
Alberta T0J 0N0
General Museum - 1974
Local history

Chambly

01860
**Parc Historique National du Fort
Chambly**
CP 115, Chambly, Québec J3L 2B9
History/Public Affairs Museum - 1921
Ruins of Fort Chambly; exhibits
concerning military life

Chapleau

01861
Chapleau Historical Museum
Pine St, POB 129, Chapleau, Ontario
P0M 1K0
General Museum - 1967
Mineralogy; mounted animals;
historical pictures and booklets

Charlottetown

01862
Beaconsfield
2 Kent St, mail c/o Prince Edward
Island Heritage Foundation, POB 922,
Charlottetown, Prince Edward Island
C1A 7L9
History/Public Affairs Museum - 1973
Artifacts, displays, and archives
pertaining to local history

01863
**Confederation Centre Art Gallery
and Museum**
Confederation Centre, POB 848,
Charlottetown, Prince Edward Island
C1A 7L9
Decorative Arts Museum - 1964
Canadian paintings, graphics,
decorative arts, porcelain (1780-1880);
Robert Harris collection

Chatham

01864
Miramichi Natural History Museum
149 Wellington St, 13 Henderson St,
Chatham, New Brunswick E1N 1L9
Natural History Museum - 1893
Geology; paleontology; vertebrate
zoology; Indian artifacts - archives

01865
Saint Michael's Museum
12 Howard St, 12 Alexandra St,
Chatham, New Brunswick E1N 1P8
Religious Art Museum - 1975
Church related artifacts; documents
written by the local clergy (1816-1900);
genealogical records from parish
registers (1801)

Chatham

01866
Chatham-Kent Museum
59 William St North, Chatham , Ontario
N7M 4L3
General Museum - 1945
History; natural history; ornithological
collection; Indian artifacts; Australian
and Egyptian displays

Cheticamp

01867
Musée Acadien
CP 98, Cheticamp, Nova Scotia B0E
1H0
General Museum - 1967
History of wool carding; fishing
implements; agricultural tools;
domestic utensils

Chicoutimi

01868
Musée du Saguenay
534 rue Jacques-Cartier est,
Chicoutimi, Québec G7H 1Z6
History/Public Affairs Museum - 1953
Coll: prehistoric and historic
archeology; 18th and 19th century
weapons; antique furniture; Indian
artifacts

Chilliwack

01869
**Canadian Military Engineers
Museum**
Canadian Force Base, Chilliwack,
Keith Wilson Rd Vedder Crossing,
British Columbia V0X 1Z0
History/Public Affairs Museum - 1957
Canadian military engineer uniforms;
medals; weapons; equipment;
documents

01870
Wells Centennial Museum
209 Corbould St South, Chilliwack,
British Columbia V2P 4A6
General Museum - 1971
Pioneer artifacts, household items;
farm machinery; F.W. Lee watercolor
paintings - archives

Churchill

01871
Eskimo Museum
POB 10, Churchill, Manitoba R0B 0E0
Anthropology Museum - 1944
Eskimo material including archeology,
ethnology and fine arts; pre-Dorset,
Thule and Eskimo artifacts

01872
**Fort Prince of Wales National
Historic Park**
Eskimo Point, POB 127, Churchill,
Manitoba R0B 0E0
Open Air Museum - 1922
Restored Hudson Bay Company Fort
(1771)

Claresholm

01873
Claresholm Museum
5126-1st St, Hwy No 2, POB 1000,
Claresholm, Alberta T0L 0T0
General Museum - 1967
Local history; wildlife displays

Clemensport

01874
Old St. Edwards Church
Clemensport, RR No 2, Annapolis
Royal, Nova Scotia B0S 1E0
Religious Art Museum - 1961
18th century Anglican church;
ecclesiastical artifacts

Clinton

01875
South Cariboo Historical Museum
Hwy 97, POB 46, Clinton, British
Columbia V0K 1K0
General Museum - 1953
Local historical artifacts; transportation
equipment used in the Cariboo -
archives

Coaticook

01876
Musée Beaulne
Château Norton, 96 rue Union,
Coaticook, Québec J1A 1Y9
History/Public Affairs Museum - 1964
Clothing; furniture; points of interest
concerning the cinema

Cobalt

01877
**Cobalt's Northern Ontario Mining
Museum**
24 Silver St, POB 215, Cobalt, Ontario
P0J 1C0
Science/Tech Museum - 1963
Mining history; rock samples and
mineral specimens; silver specimens -
archives

Cobourg

01878
**Art Gallery of Cobourg and National
Exhibition Centre**
55 King St West, Cobourg, Ontario
K9A 2M2
Fine Arts Museum - 1961/1977
Canadian, European and American
paintings; arts and crafts; Eskimo
artifacts; ceramics and sculpture

Colinton

01879
Kinnoull Historical Museum
General Delivery, Colinton, Alberta
T0G 0K0
History/Public Affairs Museum - 1963
Local historical artifacts

College Bridge

01880
Keillor House Museum
Dorchester, RR 1, College Bridge,
New Brunswick E0A 1L0
General Museum - 1967
Stone farmhouse (1813) furnished in
the period style of 1813 to 1900;
costumes; tools; maps; antique
vehicles

Collingwood

01881
Collingwood Museum
Memorial Park, St. Paul St, *mail c/o*
Miss Lina Lavers, 9 Victoria Drive,
Collingwood, Ontario L9Y 3B9
History/Public Affairs Museum - 1909
Local history including shipbuilding
industry

Comber

01882
Tilbury West Agricultural Museum
Hwy 77, south of Comber, *mail c/o* Mr.
Don McMillan POB 158 Comber,
Ontario N0P 1J0
Agriculture Museum - 1967
Agricultural development of the region

Cooks Creek

01883
Cook's Creek Heritage Museum
Hwy 212, Cooks Creek, RR 2, Dugald,
Manitoba R0E 0K0
History/Public Affairs Museum - 1969
Slavic pioneer material; religious
artifacts; Galician log house; farm
machinery

Cornwall

01884
United Counties Museum
731 Second St West, POB 773,
Cornwall, Ontario K6H 5T5
General Museum - 1956
Canadiana; household utensils and
furniture; clothing; toys; early pottery -
archives

Coronach

01885
Allan Black Memorial Museum
mail c/o Mrs. Allan Black, Main Street,
POB 15, Coronach, Saskatchewan
S0H 0Z0
History/Public Affairs Museum - 1966
WW 1 artifacts and military equipment
dating back to 1840; archives

Côteau-du-lac

01886
**Parc Historique National de Côteau-
du-lac**
CP 211, Côteau-du-lac, Québec J0P
1B0
History/Public Affairs Museum - 1967
Ruins of a military fort; model of the
fort as it existed in 1812; military
artifacts; exhibits on 19th century
transportation

Cottonwood

01887
Cottonwood House Historic Park
18 miles east of Quesnel, Cottonwood,
Barkerville Historic Park, Barkerville,
British Columbia V0K 1B0
Open Air Museum - 1966
Stage coach shop (1864) on the
Cariboo Wagon Road, restored and
furnished in the style of the gold rush
era; farm machinery

Courtenay

01888
Courtenay and District Museum
360 Cliffe Av, POB 3128, Courtenay,
British Columbia V9N 5N4
Natural History Museum - 1972
Pioneer, Indian, Chinese fossils -
archives

Coutts

01889
Altamont Museum
POB 176, Coutts, Alberta T0K 0N0
General Museum - 1967
Historical artifacts

Cowansville

01890
Centre d'Art de Cowansville
225 rue Principale, Cowansville,
Québec J2K 1J4
Fine Arts Museum - 1967
Canadian paintings

Craik

01891
Prairie Pioneer Museum
mail c/o Mrs. H.D. Anderson, Old No
11 Hwy, POB 273, Craik,
Saskatchewan S0G 0V0
History/Public Affairs Museum - 1967
Restored pioneer house (1904),
furnished in the style of that period;
dolls; jewelry; Elizabethan Bible

Cranbrook

01892
Crownsnest Route Railway Museum
1 Van Horne St North, POB 400,
Cranbrook, British Columbia V1C 4H9
Science/Tech Museum - 1978
Restored dining car and caboose with
artifacts and archival material including
photographs, pamphlets, newspapers,
maps and books

Creighton

01893
Frames Northern Museum
436-1st St West, Creighton, *mail c/o*
Lawrence Frame, POB 473, Flin Flon,
Manitoba R8A 1M3
Natural History Museum - 1966
Mounted animals, birds, and fish
indigenous to the North

Cumberland

01894
**Cumberland Township Heritage
Museum**
Regional Rd 34, east of Cumberland,
POB 159, Cumberland, Ontario K0A
1S0
Open Air Museum - 1976
Local history; historic buildings

Cumberland

01895
Cumberland Museum
Dunsmuir Av and 4th St, POB 289,
Cumberland , British Columbia V0R
1S0
General Museum - 1965
Mining equipment; old hospital
equipment; Chinese items

Czar

01896
Prairie Panorama Museum
Shorncliffe Park, POB 156, Czar,
Alberta T0B 0Z0
Fine Arts Museum - 1962
Fine and decorative arts; local archival
material

Dalhousie

01897
Chaleur History Museum
Court House Square, POB 1717,
Dalhousie, New Brunswick E0K 1B0
History/Public Affairs Museum - 1967
History of the Restigouche County
area including the Inter-colonial
Railway, the Acadian and Scottish
settlers; fossils

Dartmouth

01898
Dartmouth Heritage Museum
100 Wyse Rd, Dartmouth, Nova Scotia
B3A 1M1
History/Public Affairs Museum - 1968
History of the Micmac Indians; local
history; whaling; local industry

Dauphin

01899
Fort Dauphin Museum
140 Jackson Av, POB 181, Dauphin,
Manitoba R7N 2V1
General Museum - 1976
Archeology; fur trade; pioneer artifacts

Dawson City

01900
Dawson City Museum
Old Territorial Administration Building,
5th Ave, POB 303, Dawson City,
Yukon Territory Y0B 1G0
General Museum - 1962
Local history exhibits, especially
concerning the Klondike Gold Rush

Dawson Creek

01901
Dawson Creek Art Gallery
10100-13th St, POB 845, Dawson
Creek, British Columbia V1G 1T8
General Museum - 1962
Fine and decorative arts

01902
**Dawson Creek Museum and Pioneer
Village**
10100-13th St, Dawson Creek, British
Columbia V1G 1T8
Open Air Museum - 1962
Natural history of the region; historical
artifacts of pioneer era

Delaware

01903
Ska-Nah-Doht Indian Village
Longwoods Rd Conservation Area,
west of Delaware on Hwy 2, RR 1,
Mount Brydes, Ontario N0L 1W0
Open Air Museum - 1973
History of the Neutral Nation including
reconstructed historical buildings

Delta

01904
Delta Historical Museum
4858 Delta St, Delta, British Columbia
V4K 2T8
General Museum - 1969
Pioneer, maritime and Indian material;
period rooms; photographs .

Denare Beach

01905
Northern Gateway Museum
Denare Beach, *mail c/o* Mrs. Anne
Wiebe, POB 42, Flin Flon, Manitoba
R8A 1M6
General Museum - 1956
Local beadwork; Inuit carvings; trade
goods; fossils; primitive tools

Dorval

01906
Dorval Cultural Centre
1401 Lakeshore Dr, Dorval, Québec
H9S 2E5
Decorative Arts Museum - 1967
Coll: paintings; sculpture; crafts;
jewelry

Downsview

01907
Art Gallery of York University
Ross Bldg No 145, 4700 Keele St,
Downsview, Ontario M3J 1P3
Fine Arts Museum - 1970
Contemporary Canadian and
international paintings, sculpture,
drawings and prints; historic and
modern carvings

01908
Black Creek Pioneer Village
1000 Murray Ross Parkway, 5
Shoreham Drive, Downsview, Ontario
M3N 1S4
Open Air Museum - 1960
Canadian folklore; agriculture;
furniture; textiles; blacksmith tools;
toys and dolls; handicrafts; restored
Ontario village (1793-1867)

Dresden

01909
Uncle Tom's Cabin Museum
RR 5, Dresden, Ontario N0P 1M0
Open Air Museum - 1963
Negro history

Drumheller

01910
**Drumheller and District Fossil
Museum**
335-1st St East, POB 2135, Drumheller,
Alberta T0J 0Y0
General Museum - 1957
Fossils; Indian artifacts; local history

01911
Newcastle Coalminers Museum
POB 2097, Drumheller, Alberta T0J
0Y0
History/Public Affairs Museum - 1971
Early coal-mining history

Dryden

01912
Dryden and District Museum
284 Government St, Dryden, Ontario
P8N 2P3
General Museum - 1960
Indian and pioneer artifacts; trapping
equipment; minerals

Duck Lake

01913
Duck Lake Historical Museum
POB 370, Duck Lake, Saskatchewan
S0K 1J0
History/Public Affairs Museum - 1960
Indian beadwork; pioneer utensils;
articles pertaining to Louis Riel and the
Indian outlaw 'Almighty Voice'

Dufresne

01914
**Aunt Margaret's Museum of
Childhood**
Dufresne, Manitoba R0A 0J0
Junior Museum - 1968
Toys

Duncan

01915
British Columbia Forest Museum
1 mile north of Duncan on the Trans-
Canada Hwy, R.R. 4, Duncan, British
Columbia V9L 3W8
Open Air Museum - 1964
Forest industry including buildings,
machinery and photos; Indian display;
locomotives and narrow-gauge
operating railroad with steam trains

Dundas

01916
Dundas Historical Society Museum
139 Park St West, Dundas, Ontario
L9H 1X8
General Museum - 1956
Local history; Indian artifacts;
costumes and textiles; porcelain and
glass; furnishings; children's section

01917
Dundas Valley School of Art Gallery
21 Ogilvie St, Dundas, Ontario L9H
2S1
Fine Arts Museum - 1967
Contemporary Canadian sculpture and
works of art

Dunvegan

01918
St. Charles Mission Historic Site
Dunvegan, *mail c/o* Historic Sites
Services, 10158-103rd St, Edmonton,
Alberta T5J 1H7
Historic Site - 1961
Restored home and mission house
with early 20th century furnishings

Durrell

01919
Durrell Museum
Arm Lads' Brigade Armoury, Durrell,
Newfoundland A0G 1Y0
History/Public Affairs Museum - 1978
Fishery

Eastend

01920
Eastend School Museum
First Av, POB 392, Eastend,
Saskatchewan S0N 0T0
General Museum - 1930
Fossils; local history, rocks,
photographs

Eaton

01921 ,
**Compton County Historical and
Museum Society**
mail c/o Mrs. E.S. Heatherington, POB
413, Cookshire, Québec J0B 1M0
History/Public Affairs Museum - 1959
Farm implements, household items; old
medical instruments; wooden articles

Eddystone

01922
Village Site Museum
Eddystone, Manitoba R0L 0S0
General Museum - 1957
Furnishings; Iceland artifacts; cars and
horse-drawn vehicles; farm machinery

Edmonton

01923
**Alberta Pioneer Railway Association
Museum**
Station C, POB 6102, Edmonton,
Alberta T5B 2N0
Science/Tech Museum - 1967
Former railway station with two steam
locomotives; wooden combination
baggage coach and sleeping car;
vintage freight cars

01924
Art Gallery and Museum University
of Alberta
Ring House 1, Edmonton, Alberta T6G
2E2
General Museum - 1929
Fine and decorative arts;
anthropology; human history; natural
history

01925
Aviation Hall of Fame
715, Centennial Bldg, 10015-103rd Av,
Edmonton, Alberta T5J 0H6
Historic Site - 1973
Hall of fame dedicated to individuals
who have made contributions to
aviation history in Canada

01926
Dental Museum University of Alberta,
Faculty of Dentistry
Edmonton, Alberta T6G 2N8
Natural History Museum - 1952
Antique and historic dental
instruments and furniture; natural
history; animal skulls;
palaeoanthropology collection of early
fossil hominids - archives

01927
Edmonton Art Gallery
2 Sir Winston Churchill Sq, Edmonton,
Alberta T5J 2C1
Fine Arts Museum - 1924
Western Canadian art; Canadian art
from Krieghoff and his time to the
present; contemporary international
art

01928
Fort Edmonton Park
Edmonton Parks and Recreation, 10th
Floor, CN Tower, Edmonton, Alberta
T5J 0K1
Open Air Museum - 1974
Historical buildings from the mid-18th
century to the 1940's; reconstruction
of a fur-trading post (1846) and of the
pre-railway settlements

01929
G. McDougall Museum and Shrine
10025-101 St, 10086 Macdonald Drive,
Edmonton, Alberta T5J 2B7
Religious Art Museum - 1946
Historical pictures, portraits, books
and Bibles; communion vessels and
other artifacts pertaining to the
McDougall mission

01930
John Walter Museum
South of 105th St Bridge, Edmonton
Parks and Recreation, 10th Floor, CN
Tower, Edmonton, Alberta T5J 0K1
Open Air Museum - 1961
Houses belonging to John Walter,
early settler and industrialist; period
furnishings

01931
Man and Telecommunications Display Centre
Vista 33, Alberta Telephone Tower, 100020-100 St, POB 2411, Edmonton, Alberta T5J 0N5
Science/Tech Museum - 1972
Development of the telephone industry; antique telephones, switchboards, test gear, tools, insulators, vehicles

01932
Museum of Geology University of Alberta, Dept. of Geology
Edmonton, Alberta T6G 2E1
Natural History Museum - 1913
Geology; paleontology; mineralogy

01933
Museum of Ukrainian Arts and Culture
10951-107th St, 14525-82nd Av, Edmonton, Alberta T5R 3R7
General Museum - 1953
Ethnography; folk art; textiles - library

01934
Provincial Museum of Alberta
12845-102nd Av, Edmonton, Alberta T5N 0M6
General Museum - 1967
Regional historical artifacts from prehistory to the early 20th century; folklore; Plains and Northern Indian material, esp. of the Blackfoot Tribe; fine and decorative arts; natural history

01935
Queen Elizabeth Planetarium
Coronation Park, Edmonton Parks and Recreation, 10th Floor, CN Tower, Edmonton, Alberta T5J 0K1
Natural History Museum - 1960
Goto Venus projector; displays of solar systems; stellar evolution and meteors

01936
Rutherford House
University of Alberta Campus, 11153 Saskatchewan Drive, *mail c/o* Historic Sites Service, 10158-103rd St, Edmonton, Alberta T5J 0X6
Historic Site - 1974
Home of the first Premier of Alberta, A.C. Rutherford, furnished in the style of the early 20th century

01937
Ukrainian Canadian Archives and Museum of Alberta
9543-110th Av, Edmonton, Alberta T5H 1H3
History/Public Affairs Museum - 1974
History of Ukrainians in Alberta; Ukrainian arts and crafts

01938
Ukrainian Catholic Women's League Museum
10825-97th St, Edmonton, Alberta T5H 2M4
History/Public Affairs Museum - 1952
Ukrainian artifacts and textiles; historical costumes

01939
Ukrainian Cultural Heritage Village
East of Elk Island National Park gate, *mail c/o* Historical Resources, Alberta Culture, 14th Floor, CN Tower, Edmonton, Alberta T5J 0K1
Open Air Museum - 1976
Buildings including churches, homesteads, stores restored and furnished in the style of the period from 1890-1930

Edmundston

01940
Galerie Colline de Saint Louis Maillet
165 bd Herbert, Edmundston, New Brunswick
Fine Arts Museum - 1969
Painting; sculpture; graphic arts and decorative arts

Elbow

01941
Elbow Museum
POB 219, Elbow S0H 1J0
General Museum - 1968
Local historical items; Indian artifacts; arrowhead collection; sod house

Eldon

01942
Lord Selkirk Settlement
off Trans-Canada Hwy near Eldon, POB 2003, Charlottetown, Prince Edward Island C1A 7N7
History/Public Affairs Museum - 1973
Replicas of the first shelters of the Selkirk settlers

Elk Point

01943
Fort George Museum
POB 66, Elk Point, Alberta T0A 1A0
History/Public Affairs Museum - 1952
Local history; archeology

Elkhorn

01944
Manitoba Automobile Museum
POB 235, Elkhorn, Manitoba R0M 0N0
Science/Tech Museum - 1966
Automobiles from 1908 to 1958; picture walls; agricultural machinery; household utensils

Elliot Lake

01945
Elliot Lake Nuclear and Mining Museum
Municipal Office Bldg, 45 Hillside Drive North, Elliot Lake, Ontario P5A 1X5
Science/Tech Museum - 1965
Mining equipment; models of uranium mine buildings; natural history

Emerson

01946
Gateway Stopping Place Museum
mail c/o Miss Jessie Johnston
Emerson, Manitoba R0A 0L0
Open Air Museum - 1958
Pioneer artifacts; fur trading; historic jailhouse (1879) and customs house (1870); history of the North West Mounted Police and Plains Indians

Eriksdale

01947
Eriksdale Museum
Railway Av South, POB 13, Eriksdale, Manitoba R0C 0W0
History/Public Affairs Museum - 1974
Pioneer artifacts; local newspapers (1961-present)

Esterhazy

01948
Kaposvar Historic Site Our Lady of Assumption Church Museum
3 miles south of Esterhazy, POB 115, Esterhazy S0A 0X0
History/Public Affairs Museum - 1975
Coll: exhibit concerning the first Hungarian colony in Saskatchewan; habits of local Grey nuns; church artifacts

Estevan

01949
Estevan National Exhibition Centre
1102 Fourth St, Estevan, Saskatchewan S4A 2A8
General Museum - 1978
Local artifacts; paintings; prints; archive

Evansburg

01950
Pembina Lobstick Historical Museum
Evansburg, Alberta T0E 0T0
History/Public Affairs Museum - 1970
Local historical artifacts and archives

Fenelon Falls

01951
Fenelon Falls Museum
50 Oak St, *mail c/o* Ms. Bessie Christian, 18 Francis St East, Fenelon Falls, Ontario K0M 1N0
General Museum - 1963
Local history and folklore; gun collection

Fergus

01952
Wellington County Museum
Wellington Place, RR 1, Fergus, Ontario N1M 2W3
History/Public Affairs Museum - 1952
General history relating to the county - archives

Flesherton

01953
South Grey Museum
Memorial Park on Hwy 10, *mail c/o* Ms. Irene Field, POB 65, Flesherton, Ontario
General Museum - 1973
Hydro development at Lake Eugenia; farm implements; medical instruments; railway exhibit

Foam Lake

01954
Foam Lake Centennial Museum
POB 163, Foam Lake, Saskatchewan S0A 1A0
General Museum - 1967
Local pioneer items; various household articles

Forest

01955
Forest Lambton Museum
59 Broadway, RR 1, Forest, Ontario N0N 1J0
General Museum - 1963
Ornithology; fossils; religious artifacts; lighting and telephone systems; furnishings; local history - library

Fort Erie

01956
Fort Erie Historical Railroad Museum
Cokes Park, Central Av, POB 355, Fort Erie, Ontario L2A 3M9
Science/Tech Museum - 1976
Railroad equipment

01957
Old Fort Erie
Niagara River Parkway, Fort Erie, *mail c/o* Niagara Parks Commission, POB 150, Niagara Falls, Ontario L2E 6T2
History/Public Affairs Museum - 1939
Military equipment in the earliest British fort (1764)

Fort Frances

01958
Fort Frances Museum and Recreational Cultural Centre
259 Scott St, Fort Frances, Ontario P9A 1G8
General Museum - 1978
Logging equipment; Indian artifacts; farm implements

Fort Langley

01959
British Columbia Farm Machinery Museum
9131 King St, POB 279, Fort Langley, British Columbia V0X 1J0
Science/Tech Museum - 1966
Farm machinery used in British Columbia from 1880 to the 1940's - library

01960
Fort Langley National Historic Park
Mavis St, POB 129, Fort Langley, British Columbia V0X 1J0
General Museum - 1955
Artifacts illustrating fur trade and settlement; reconstructed trading fort (1840-1860)

01961
Langley Centennial Museum and National Exhibition Centre
9135 King St, Fort Langley, British Columbia V0X J0
General Museum - 1958/1974
Pioneer artifacts; handiwork and native artifacts

Fort MacLeod

01962
Fort Museum
25th St between 3rd and 4th Av, POB 776, Fort MacLeod, Alberta T0E 0T0
Open Air Museum - 1970
Historic buildings; Indian and pioneer artifacts; transportation machinery and equipment

Fort Qu'appelle

01963
Fort Qu'appelle Museum and Gallery
POB 544, Fort Qu'appelle, Saskatchewan S0G 1S0
History/Public Affairs Museum - 1967
Indian artifacts; pioneer life; items relating to the Anti-Tuberculosis League

Fort St. James

01964
Fort St. James National Historic Park
POB 1148, Fort St. James, British
Columbia V0J 1P0
Open Air Museum - 1977
Historic buildings furnished according
to the 1890 period; history
(pre-European to 1896)

Fort Saskatchewan

01965
Fort Saskatchewan Museum
10104-101 St, 9803-101 St, Fort
Saskatchewan, Alberta T8L 2C7
History/Public Affairs Museum - 1967
History; archeology; archives of the
Historical Society

Fort Smith

01966
**Northern Life Museum and National
Exhibition Centre**
POB 371, Fort Smith, Northwest
Territories X0E 0P0
Natural History Museum - 1974
Natural history; ethnology; minerals
and fossils

Fort Steele

01967
Fort Steele Historic Park
Fort Steele, British Columbia V0B 1N0
Open Air Museum - 1967
History; Kutenai Indians;
transportation; industrial archeology;
Kootenaiana archives

Fredericton

01968
Beaverbrook Art Gallery
703 Queen St, POB 605, Fredericton,
New Brunswick E3B 5A6
Fine Arts Museum - 1959
British and Canadian painting;
paintings by Salvador Dali; English
porcelain; sculpture

01969
The Guard House
Carleton St, Fredericton Military
Compound, POB 6000, Fredericton,
New Brunswick E3B 5H1
History/Public Affairs Museum
Restored British military guard house
with period rooms

01970
**University of New Brunswick Art
Centre**
Memorial Hall, Fredericton, New
Brunswick E3B 5A3
Fine Arts Museum - 1942
Art by university and Atlantic artists

01971
**University of New Brunswick
Electrical Engineering Museum**
Dept. of Electrical Engineering Head
Hall, Fredericton, New Brunswick E3B
5A3
Science/Tech Museum - 1968
Electronic tubes; demonstration
apparatuses; measuring instruments;
radios from the 1920's; old books on
electronical phenomena

01972
**York Sunbury Historical Society
Museum**
Central Queen St, POB 1312,
Fredericton, New Brunswick E3B 5C8
History/Public Affairs Museum - 1950
Military and local history

Freetown

01973
Scales Pond Provincial Historic Park
Hydro Electric Museum
Between Summerside and Borden on
the Trans-Canada Hwy, Freetown, 322
Poplar Av, Summerside, Prince
Edward Island C1N 2B8
Science/Tech Museum - 1973
Hydro-electric plant; machinery used
in the early days of electricity

Frobisher

01974
Frobisher Thresherman's Museum
Frobisher, Saskatchewan S0C 0Y0
Agriculture Museum - 1976
Steam engines; wooden threshing
separators (1912); tractors; 19th
century household items

Gagetown

01975
Queen's County Museum
On Route 102, Gagetown, New
Brunswick E0G 1V0
Historic Site - 1967
Home of Sir Leonard Tilley, 'father of
the confederation'; period rooms; local
history

Gananoque

01976
Gananoque Historical Museum
10 King St, *mail c/o* Derrol Simpson,
POB 293, Gananoque, Ontario K7G
2T7
General Museum - 1964
Indian artifacts; pioneer tools; glass
and china; toys; industrial artifacts;
local art; Victorian furniture

Gander

01977
Aviation Exhibit
Gander Airport, *mail c/o*
Newfoundland Museum, Duckworth
St, St. John's, Newfoundland A1C 1G9
Science/Tech Museum - 1967
Aeronautical models; photographs of
pioneer aviation

Gaspé

01978
**Musée d'Histoire et de Traditions
Populaires**
Baie de Gaspé, CP 680, Gaspé,
Québec G0C 1R0
History/Public Affairs Museum - 1972
Coll: historical, ethnographical, and
archeological exhibits; works of art

Georgetown

01979
Linden Lea Museum
POB 197, Georgetown, Prince Edward
Island C0A 1L0
General Museum - 1960
Victorian memorabilia, local history,
photos, crafts

Gibsons

01980
Elphinstone Pioneer Museum
Winn Rd and Gower Point Rd in
Municipal Hall complex, POB 766,
Gibsons, British Columbia V0N 1V0
General Museum - 1965
Pioneer materials; Salish Indian
artifacts; shells

Girouxville

01981
Musée Girouxville
C.P. 129, Girouxville, Alberta T0H 1S0
General Museum - 1969
History and archives; natural history;
agriculture and industries

Glace Bay

01982
**Cape Breton Miners Museum and
National Exhibition Centre**
Quarry Point, Glace Bay, Nova Scotia
B1A 5T8
History/Public Affairs Museum - 1967
Coal mining in the late 19th to early
20th century; coal formation,
transportation and company history;
steam locomotive

Godbout

01983
**Musée Amérindien et Inuit de
Godbout**
Chemin Pascal Comeau, Godbout, 48
Carillon, Chicoutimi-Nord, Québec
G7G 3J3
Anthropology Museum - 1978
Indian and Inuit artifacts; clothing;
antiques

Goderich

01984
Huron County Pioneer Museum
110 North St, Goderich, Ontario N7A
2T8
General Museum - 1950
Local trades and crafts; Victorian
furnishings and costumes; natural
history; transportation; toys

Golden

01985
Golden and District Museum
11th Av at 13th St, POB 992, Golden,
British Columbia V04 1H0
History/Public Affairs Museum - 1974
Pioneer artifacts from 1865 - archives

Golden Lake

01986
Golden Lake Algonquin Museum
Golden Lake Indian Reserve, *mail c/o*
Mr. Andrew Lavaly, General Delivery,
Golden Lake, Ontario K0J 1X0
General Museum - 1954
Pioneer history and folklore; Indian
artifacts; natural history; costumes;
paintings; mineralogy

Gore Bay

01987
**Manitoulin Historical Society
Museum**
Dawson St, *mail c/o* Ms.H.E. Cook,
POB 145, Gore Bay, Ontario P0P 1H0
General Museum - 1954
Agriculture; archeology; botany; local
history; Indian artifacts; transportation
and industries; medical equipment;
textiles and costumes; ornithology -
library

Gow-Ganda

01988
Gow-Ganda and Area Museum
Gow-Ganda, Ontario P0J 1J0
History/Public Affairs Museum - 1974
History of the silver mining area;
mining equipment; hand tools and
implements used by the early trappers
and loggers - library

Grafton

01989
Barnum House Museum
Hwy 2, west of Grafton, *mail c/o* Ms.
G. Young Grafton, Ontario K0K 2G0
History/Public Affairs Museum - 1940
Historic mansion (1813-17) furnished
to represent the home of a country
gentleman

Grand Bank

01990
**Southern Newfoundland Seamen's
Museum**
Marine Drive, Grand Bank,
Newfoundland A0E 1W0
History/Public Affairs Museum - 1972
Navigation

Grand Falls

01991
Grand Falls Historical Museum
Court St, POB 1572, Grand Falls E0J
1M0
General Museum - 1973
Pioneer and early Victorian artifacts;
farm and lumbering implements;
newspapers

01992
**Mary March Regional Museum and
National Exhibition Centre**
22 Catherine St, POB 545, Grand Falls,
Newfoundland A2A 2J9
General Museum - 1970/1977
Beothuck Indian and Dorset Eskimo
artifacts; natural history; early logging
implements

Grand Forks

01993
Boundary Museum
108-SE 9th St, POB 422, Grand Forks,
British Columbia V0H 1H0
General Museum - 1958
Regional artifacts and history; pictures
of the area and descriptive literature

Grand Manan

01994
Grand Manan Museum
POB 60, Grand Harbour, Grand
Manan, New Brunswick E0G 1X0
General Museum - 1967
Local history; geology; Moses
collection of birds of Grand Manan

Grand Pré

01995
Grand Pré National Historic Park
Grand Pré, Nova Scotia B0P 1M0
General Museum - 1930
Regional history including the
Acadians, New England planters and
United Empire Loyalists; blacksmith
shop; hand-crafted furniture; farm
equipment

Grande Prairie

01996
Grande Prairie Pioneer Museum
Bear Creek Centennial Park, POB 687,
Grande Prairie, Alberta T8V 3A8
General Museum - 1969
Local pioneer artifacts; fossils; wildlife
specimens; minerals

01997
Prairie Gallery
10130-99th St, POB 1097, Grande
Prairie T8V 4B5
Fine Arts Museum - 1975
Works by local and provincial artists

Grandview

01998
Crossley Museum
RR 4, Grandview, Manitoba R0L 0Y0
General Museum - 1937
Polished rocks; fossils; Indian artifacts;
household utensils; machinery

01999
**Watson Crossley Community
Museum**
Railway Av North, Grandview,
Manitoba R0L 0Y0
General Museum - 1975
Human and natural history of the area;
Ukrainian tools and handicrafts; Indian
artifacts; pioneer furnishings

Gravenhurst

02000
Bethune Memorial House
Cnr of John and Hughson Sts, POB
2160, Gravenhurst, Ontario P0C 1G0
Historic Site - 1976
Birthplace of Dr. Norman Bethune with
documentation on his life

02001
Segwun Steamboat Museum
Gravenhurst Bay, POB 1283,
Gravenhurst, Ontario P0C 1G0
History/Public Affairs Museum - 1962
Marine and lumbering history
documented in the last remaining
steamboat on the Muskoka Lakes

Greenspond

02002
Greenspond Museum
Greenspond, Newfoundland A0G 2H0
History/Public Affairs Museum - 1974
Local history

Greenwood

02003
Greenwood Museum
City Hall, 202 Government St, POB
258, Greenwood, British Columbia
V0H 1J0
General Museum - 1967
Pioneer artifacts including mining and
lodging equipment; photographic
archives

Grenfell

02004
Grenfell Community Museum
Wolseley Av, POB 400, Grenfell,
Saskatchewan S0G 2B0
General Museum - 1973
Pioneer artifacts; Victorian house
furnished in a Victorian style

Grimsby

02005
**Grimsby Public Library and Art
Gallery**
25 Adelaide St, Grimsby, Ontario L3M
1X2
Fine Arts Museum - 1975
20th century Canadian art

02006
Stone Shop Museum
271 Main St West, 8 Balmoral Av,
Grimsby, Ontario L3M 1G3
General Museum - 1963
Textiles; glass and china; pottery;
tools; historical pictures - archives

Grondines

02007
Musée des Grondines
215 rue Principale, CP 99, Grondines,
Québec G0A 1W0
Archeology Museum
Coll: archeology; ethnology;
contemporary art

Guelph

02008
**Colonel John McRae Birthplace
Museum**
102 Water St, POB 601, Guelph,
Ontario N1H 6L3
Historic Site - 1968
Home of John McRae; literary works,
drawings and personel articles of J.
McRae

02009
Guelph Civic Museum
6 Gordon St, Guelph, Ontario N1H
4G7
General Museum - 1967
Local history; agricultural and
industrial development; dolls with
historical costumes; music instruments

02010
University of Guelph Art Gallery
University Campus, mail c/o
McLaughlin Library Guelph, Ontario
N1G 2W1
Fine Arts Museum - 1950
Canadian art (18th c.-present);
international prints

Halifax

02011
Army Museum
Halifax Citadel, POB 3666, Halifax,
Nova Scotia South B3J 3K6
History/Public Affairs Museum - 1953
Arms and armour; swords since the
16th century ; uniforms (18th c.);
models of fortifications; paintings and
prints

02012
Art Gallery of Nova Scotia
6152 Coburg Rd, POB 2262, Halifax,
Nova Scotia B3J 3C8
Fine Arts Museum - 1975
Historical and contemporary Nova
Scotian art; folk art

02013
Cavalier Block Halifax Citadel
Halifax Citadel, mail c/o Nova Scotia
Museum, 1747 Summer St, Halifax,
Nova Scotia B3H 3A6
History/Public Affairs Museum - 1960
Human history; Micmac Indian
artifacts; history of explorations and
local history; furniture, silver and glass

02014
Dalhousie University Art Gallery
Arts Centre, Dalhousie University,
Halifax, Nova Scotia B3H 3J5
Fine Arts Museum - 1955
Canadian paintings and drawings;
American paintings and sculpture;
British painting; primitive pottery;
Japanese and Egyptian artifacts;
Eskimo carvings and prints

02015
Halifax Police Department Museum
1975 Gottingen St, Halifax City Police
Headquarters, Halifax, Nova Scotia
B3J 2H1
History/Public Affairs Museum - 1964
Historical police equipment; items
used in unusual crimes

02016
**Mount Saint Vincent University Art
Gallery**
Seton Academic Centre, Halifax, Nova
Scotia B3M 2J6
Fine Arts Museum - 1971
Canadian art, painting, sculpture,
graphics, crafts; ceramics and
paintings by Alice Hagen

02017
Nova Scotia Museum
1747 Summer St, Halifax, Nova Scotia
B3H 3A6
General Museum - 1831
Geology; botany; zoology; marine
history; history; furniture; glass; silver;
agricultural implements

02018
Public Archives of Nova Scotia
Coburg Rd, Halifax, Nova Scotia B3H
1Z9
History/Public Affairs Museum - 1931
Government records; minute books of
clubs and societies; correspondence
of old business firms; maps; general
history - Akins library and archives
library

02019
Telephone Historical Collection
Maritime Centre, POB 880, Halifax,
Nova Scotia B3J 2W3
Science/Tech Museum - 1967
Telephone equipment including Bell's
experimental models as well as the
latest models in use

02020
York Redoubt National Historic Site
Purcello Cove Rd, Halifax, POB 17,
Site 15, RR No 5, Armdale, Nova
Scotia
History/Public Affairs Museum - 1969
Military history from the early 1790's
to World War II

Hamilton

02021
Art Gallery of Hamilton
123 King St West, Hamilton, Ontario
L8P 4S8
Fine Arts Museum - 1914
Historical and contemporary Canadian
art; American, British and European art
- library

02022
Canadian Football Hall of Fame
City Hall Plaza, 58 Jackson St West,
Hamilton, Ontario L8P 1L4
History/Public Affairs Museum - 1972
Development of football over the past
100 years including television replays
and trophies; stained glass window
depicting major uniform changes since
1900

02023
Dundurn Castle
Dundurn Park, York Bd, Hamilton,
Ontario L8R 3H1
Historic Site - 1967
Home of Sir Allan Napier MacNab,
Prime Minister of the United Canadas
1854-56; period furnishings (1836-56)

02024
Hamilton Military Museum
Battery Lodge, Dundurn Castle,
Dundurn Park, York Bd, Hamilton,
Ontario L8R 3H1
History/Public Affairs Museum - 1976
Military history from 1812 to World
War II

02025
McMaster University Art Gallery
Togo Salmon Hall, 1280 Main St West,
McMaster University, Hamilton,
Ontario L8S 4M2
Fine Arts Museum - 1967
Georges Rouault prints; German
expressionist prints; European and
North American paintings

Hamiota

02026
Hamiota Pioneer Club Museum
Centennial Park, POB 44, Hamiota,
Manitoba R0M 0T0
General Museum - 1966
Regional history; farm machinery;
wildlife display

Hampton

02027
**King's County Historical Society
Museum**
Hampton, King's County, mail c/o W.
Harvey Dalling Sussex Corner, New
Brunswick E0G 1Z0
General Museum - 1968
Pioneer artifacts; early handicrafts; old
china; jewelry - archives

Hanna

02028
Hanna Pioneer Museum
East end of Hanna townsite, POB
1137, Hanna, Alberta T0J 1P0
Open Air Museum - 1966
Pioneer village; antique farm
machinery

Harbour Grace

02029
Conception Bay Museum
POB 442, Harbour Grace,
Newfoundland A0E 1W0
General Museum - 1974
Historical pirate fort (1610); 19th
century furniture; history of early
aviation; local art objects

Havelock

02030
Trent River Pioneer Museum
RR 2, Havelock, RR 1, Wooler, Ontario
K0K 3M0
Open Air Museum - 1961
Original pioneer buildings, mainly log
cabins with farm and household
equipment (dating back to 1728)

Havre-Aubert

02031
Musée de la Mer
Havre-Aubert, CP 69, Iles-de-
la-Madelaine, Québec G0B 1J0
General Museum - 1969
Articles pertaining to fishing,
navigation, and shipwrecks; domestic
art - archives

Hazelton

02032
**'Ksan Indian Village and Museum
and Northwestern National
Exhibition Centre**
High Level Rd, Hazelton, British
Columbia V0J 1Y0
Anthropology Museum - 1970/1976
Gitksan regalia and artifacts

High Prairie

02033
**High Prairie and District Centennial
Museum**
POB 629, High Prairie, Alberta T0G
1E0
General Museum - 1967
Indian artifacts; pioneer items; archival
material from the ghost town of
Grouard; geological specimens

High River

02034
Museum of the Highwood
4th Av and 1st St SW, POB 363, High
River, Alberta T0L 1B0
General Museum - 1967
Material related to early trading,
ranching and farming; Indian artifacts;
fossils

Hinton

02035
Alberta Forestry Service Museum
POB 880, Hinton, Alberta T0E 1B0
Agriculture Museum - 1971
Historical collection related to the
management and use of the forest

Hope

02036
Hope Museum
Municipal Hall, Water St, POB 609,
Hope, British Columbia V0X 1L0
General Museum - 1965
Pioneer implements; domestic
utensils; Indian artifacts; historical
photos; native rocks

Hopewell Cape

02037
Albert County Museum
Hopewell Cape, POB 505, Moncton,
New Brunswick E1C 8L9
General Museum - 1962
Restored country gaol (1845); pioneer
artifacts; maps of the French and
English settlements and documents

Horsefly

02038
Horsefly Historical Museum
POB 148, Horsefly, British Columbia
V0L 1L0
General Museum - 1973
Gold mining artifacts; farm implements
and domestic utensils

Hudson's Hope

02039
Hudson's Hope Museum
Beattie Drive and Fredette Av, POB
98, Hudson's Hope, British Columbia
V0C 1V0
General Museum - 1967
Fur trapping; gold panning; pioneer
household goods; tools and
implements; fossils; Indian crafts

Huntsville

02040
**Muskoka Pioneer Village and
Museum**
Huntsville Park, Brunel Rd, Huntsville,
Ontario P0A 1K0
General Museum - 1958
Local history

Ile d'Orléans

02041
Manoir Mauvide-Jenest
1451 avenue Royale, Saint-Jean, Ile
d'Orléans, Québec G0A 3W0
History/Public Affairs Museum - 1928
English Victorian furniture; 18th
century furniture

Imperial

02042
Nels Berggran Museum
POB 125, Imperial, Saskatchewan S0G
2J0
General Museum - 1955
Hanging lamps; musical instruments;
clocks; art

Innisfail

02043
Historical Village
POB 642, Innisfail, Alberta T0M 1A0
Historic Site - 1972
Pioneer buildings furnished to
interpret the history of the locality up
to 1930; farm machinery

Innisville

02044
Innisville and District Museum
Hwy 7, Innisville, *mail c/o* Ms. John H.
Rintoul, RR 1, Carleton Place, Ontario
K0A 1J0
General Museum - 1969
Local history and folklore

Invermere

02045
**Windermere District Historical
Museum**
7th Av and 9th St, POB 784,
Invermere, British Columbia V0A 1K0
General Museum - 1964
Pioneer and Indian artifacts; local
mining and mineral collection;
archeology - archives

Iroquois

02046
Carman House Museum
Carman Rd, POB 249, Iroquois,
Ontario K0E 1K0
General Museum - 1967
Arts and crafts (early 19th century);
original period furnishings

Jerseyside

02047
Castle Hill National Historic Park
POB 10, Jerseyside, Newfoundland
A0B 2G0
History/Public Affairs Museum - 1968
French fortifications (1692-1713);
cannons from the English period;
French and English flags

Joliette

02048
Musée d'Art de Joliette
145 rue Wilfrid Corbeil, CP 132,
Joliette, Québec J6E 3Z3
Fine Arts Museum - 1975
Coll: religious and medieval art;
Canadian and European paintings and
sculpture

Jonquière

02049
Institut des Arts au Saguenay
rue Maisonneuve, CP 605, Jonquière,
Québec G7X 7W4
Fine Arts Museum - 1962
Sculpture; paintings; engravings;
sketches

Jordan

02050
Ball's Falls Conservation Area
RR 1, Jordan, 40 South Pelham St,
POB 460, Fonthill, Ontario L0S 1E0
Open Air Museum - 1963
Buildings and artifacts related to early
industrial activities of the Niagara area
including grist mill (1809), blacksmith
shop (1880), log cabins (1740-1777)

02051
**Jordan Historical Museum of the
Twenty**
Main St, Jordan, POB 698, St.
Catharines, Ontario L2R 7E4
General Museum - 1953
Pioneer history; farm implements;
weapons; kitchenware and furniture;
letters and books

Kamloops

02052
Kamloops Museum
207 Seymour St, Kamloops, British
Columbia V2C 2E7
General Museum - 1937
Prehistory; fur trading; pioneer and
Chinese artifacts; geological
specimens; numismatics - archives;
herbarium

02053
Kamloops Ranch Museum
Riverside Park, 207 Seymour St,
Kamloops, British Columbia V2C 2E7
History/Public Affairs Museum - 1966
Early farm and logging equipment

Kapuskasing

02054
**Kapuskasing Public Historical
Museum**
CNR Station, Hwy 11, North Route, 17
Stewart Av, Kapuskasing, Ontario P5N
1R9
History/Public Affairs Museum - 1967
Railroad history

Kelowna

02055
Father Pandosy Mission
1831 Ethel St, Kelowna, British
Columbia V1Y 2Z2
Open Air Museum - 1958
Restorated buildings of the Oblate
Mission (1859); domestic utensils;
furnishings; farm machinery;
transportation equipment

02056
**Kelowna Centennial Museum and
National Exhibition Centre**
470 Queensway Av, Kelowna, British
Columbia V1Y 6S7
General Museum - 1967/1976
Local history; natural history;
transportation; agricultural equipment

Kenora

02057
Lake of the Woods Museum
Water St, POB 497, Kenora, Ontario
P9N 3X5
General Museum - 1964
Zoology; mineralogy; Indian and
pioneer artifacts; period costumes;
documents

Killarney

02058
J.A. Victor David Museum
414 Williams Av, POB 1047, Killarney,
Manitoba R0K 1G0
General Museum - 1937
Pioneer history and textiles; Indian
artifacts; natural history

Kindersley

02059
Kindersley Plains Museum
First St West and Princess Av, Baker
Park, POB 609, Kindersley,
Saskatchewan S0I 1S0
General Museum - 1968
Local geological specimens; Indian
artifacts; pioneer history; genealogical
records

Kingston

02060
Agnes Etherington Art Centre
Queens University
University Av and Queen's Crescent,
Kingston, Ontario K7L 3H6
Fine Arts Museum - 1957
Coll: Canadian and European
paintings, drawings, and sculpture;
decorative arts; ethnology

02061
**Bellevue House National Historic
Park**
35 Centre St, Kingston, Ontario K7L
4E5
Historic Site - 1967
The home of Canada's first Prime
Minister, Sir John A. MacDonald,
furnished in the style of the 1840's

02062
**Canadian Forces Communications
and Electronics Museum**
Vimy Barracks, Canadian Forces Base,
Kingston, Ontario K7L 2Z2
History/Public Affairs Museum - 1963
Communications equipment; uniforms
- archives

02063
Canadian Penitentiary Service Museum
Adjacent to the Correctional Staff College, *mail c/o* Mr. Murray Millar, Director of Correctional Staff College, 443 Union St, Kingston, Ontario K7L 4Z8
History/Public Affairs Museum - 1969
Coll: contraband items made by prison inmates, such as escape devices and weapons; old restraint devices; drug apparatus and stills - archives

02064
Geological Sciences Museum
Queens University
Millar Hall, Kingston, Ontario K7L 3H6
Natural History Museum - 1841
Minerals; rocks; fossils

02065
International Hockey Hall of Fame and Museum
POB 82, Kingston, Ontario K7L 4V6
History/Public Affairs Museum - 1965
Hockey history displays (1855 to the present day); equipment; mementoes of early teams and hockey stars

02066
Maclachlan Woodworking Museum
1316 Princess St, POB 186, KIngston, Ontario K7L 4V8
History/Public Affairs Museum - 1974
Coll: artifacts made of wood, using wood, or used for harvesting and working wood; 19th century farming and domestic articles; items used in several trades

02067
Old Fort Henry
Junction of Hwys 2 and 15, one mile east of Kingston, POB 213, Kingston, Ontario K7L 4V8
History/Public Affairs Museum - 1938
Coll: an original 19th century fort; military and naval artifacts (1750-1919); displays depicting the life of the British garrison c. 1867

02068
Royal Military College Museum
Martello Tower, Fort Frederick, *mail c/o* Chairman, Royal Military College, Kingston, Ontario K7L 2W3
History/Public Affairs Museum - 1961
Coll: military articles of national interest; Douglas collection of weapons; Naval dockyard Point Frederick artifacts; small arms once the property of General Dias, President of Mexico

Kinistino

02069
Kinistino District Pioneer Museum
POB 433, Kinistino, Saskatchewan S0J 1H0
History/Public Affairs Museum - 1971
Indian artifacts; Hudson Bay Company trade goods; rural life in the 1880's

Kirkland Lake

02070
Museum of Northern History
20 Duncan Av, POB 966, Kirkland Lake, Ontario P2N 3L1
General Museum - 1967
Coll: early trades and crafts; mining exhibits, minerals and ore; agriculture; lumbering; pioneer artifacts

Kitchener

02071
Doon Pioneer Village
RR 2, Kitchener, Ontario N2G 3W5
History/Public Affairs Museum - 1956
Coll: various pioneer homes and buildings, such as a church (1861), general store (1840), and blacksmith's and cooper's shops; Indian and pioneer artifacts

02072
Woodside National Historic Park
528 Wellington St North, Kitchener, Ontario N2H 5L5
Historic Site - 1954
Restored home of William Lyon MacKenzie King; family relics; middle upper-class Victorian furnishings of the era

Kitimat

02073
Kitimat Centennial Museum
293 City Centre, Kitimat, British Columbia V8C 1T6
History/Public Affairs Museum
Indian and pioneer material - archives

Kleinburg

02074
McMicheal Canadian Collection
Kleinburg, Ontario L0J 1C0
Fine Arts Museum - 1965
Coll: works of the Group of Seven, Tom Thomson, Emily Carr, David Milne, J.W. Morrice, Clarence Gagnon and others; art of the West Coast and Woodland Indian; Inuit art

Knowlton

02075
Brome County Historical Society Museum
Lakeshore Rd, POB 690, Knowlton, Québec J0E 1V0
History/Public Affairs Museum - 1903
Coll: pioneer artifacts; Victorian furniture; original 1918 Fokker DVII airfract; nature exhibits - archives

La Prairie

02076
Musée de La Prairie
131 rue Saint-Georges, CP 131, La Prairie, Québec J5R 3Y2
History/Public Affairs Museum - 1974
Photographs and items related to the history of La Prairie; genealogical documents

Lac-à-la-Croix

02077
Musée Lac-à-la-Croix
Sainte-Croix, Lac Saint-Jean est, Route 169, Lac-à-la-Croix, Québec G0S 2H0
General Museum - 1972
Franco-Canadian furniture; ceramics; crockery; domestic items

Lachine

02078
Musée de Lachine
100 chemin LaSalle, Lachine, Québec H8S 2X1
General Museum
Coll: weapons; jewelry; costumes and accessories; furniture; domestic utensils; religious items

La Have Island

02079
La Have Island Marine Museum
mail c/o Mr. C.A. Hirtle La Have Island, Nova Scotia
History/Public Affairs Museum - 1978
Marine artifacts

Lancaster Park

02080
Canadian Airborne Forces Museum
Canadian Forces Base Edmonton, Lancaster Park, Alberta T0A 2H0
History/Public Affairs Museum - 1975
Artifacts, equipment and instruments relating to the airborne history - archives

Lancer

02081
Lancer Centennial Museum
mail c/o Archie W. Murch, POB 64, Lancer, Saskatchewan S0N 1G0
General Museum - 1967
Models of Lancer as it was in 1915 and in 1965; early homestead items

Lang

02082
Century Village
10 miles southeast of Peterbourough, 2 miles north of Keene, Lang RR 3, Keene, Ontario K0L 2G0
History/Public Affairs Museum - 1967
Coll: artifacts from 1820-1899 displayed in their historical setting in a museum village; village homes, store, church blacksmith shop, cider barn, and shingle mill; early farm machinery

La Pocatière

02083
Musée François-Pilote
Collège de la Pocatière, av Painchaud, La Pocatière, Québec G0R 1Z0
General Museum - 1929
Coll: agricultural exhibits; ornithology; mammalia; entomology; local history; antique furniture; crafts

La Rivière

02084
Archibald Historical Museum
2 miles east and 4 miles north of La Rivière La Rivière, Manitoba R0G 1A0
History/Public Affairs Museum - 1973
Local history

La Ronge

02085
Lac La Ronge Museum
City Center, POB 38, La Ronge, Saskatchewan S0J 1L0
Natural History Museum - 1965
Mounted animals, birds and fish; Indian artifacts

La Sarre

02086
Musée d'Histoire et d'Archéologie
Ecole Polyno de La Sarre, CP 115, La Sarre, Québec J9Z 2X4
Archeology Museum - 1969
Prehistoric utensils made of stone

La Tuque

02087
Centre Culturel de La Tuque
rue Saint Eugène, La Tuque, Québec G9X 2T3
Fine Arts Museum - 1969
Pottery, paintings, sculpture

Leamington

02088
Leamington Art Gallery
11 Queens St, POB 148, Leamington, Ontario N8H 3W1
Fine Arts Museum - 1971
Coll: paintings and prints by Anne Fine, T.M. Bidner, John Palchinsky, Deli Sacilotto, Kazys 'Otis' Tamasaukas, and Joy Walker; batik by Patty Woolston

Lennox Island

02089
Lennox Island Museum
Lennox Island, Prince Edward Island
Anthropology Museum - 1973
Artifacts pertaining to the history of the Micmac Indians

Lethbridge

02090
Sir Alexander Galt Museum
West end of 5th Av, Community Services Dept., Lethbridge, Alberta T1J 0P6
History/Public Affairs Museum - 1965
Human history of Southern Alberta - archives

02091
Southern Alberta Art Gallery
601-3rd Av South, Lethbridge, Alberta T1J 0P6
Fine Arts Museum - 1976
Works by local, national and international artists - workshops

Lillooet

02092
Lillooet Museum
Main St, POB 441, Lillooet, British Columbia V0K 1V0
General Museum - 1969
Pioneer history; period room; Indian artifacts; farm machinery

Lindsay

02093
Victoria County Historical Museum
435 Kent St West, 66 Colborne St West, Lindsay, Ontario K9V 3S9
General Museum - 1959
Pioneer home furnishings; clothing; farming tools; Indian artifacts

L'Islet-sur-mer

02094
Musée Maritime de L'Islet-sur-mer
CP 291, L'Islet-sur-mer, Québec G0R 2B0
History/Public Affairs Museum - 1968
Models of ships and of a shipyard; navigational instruments; personal possessions of Capt. J.E. Bernier

Liverpool

02095

Simeon Perkins House
Liverpool, Queen's county, *mail c/o*
Nova Scotia Museum, 1747 Summer
St, Halifax, Nova Scotia B3H 3A6
Historic Site - 1947
Historic house in Cape Cod style
(1766), home of Colonel Simeon
Perkins, the diarist of Liverpool; period
furniture; local history

Lloydminster

02096

Barr Colony Museum
Weaver Park, City Hall, Lloydminster,
Saskatchewan S9V 0T8
General Museum - 1964
Pioneer artifacts; history of the Barr
Colony

London

02097

Eldon House
481 Ridout St North, 325 Queens Av,
London, Ontario N6B 3L7
History/Public Affairs Museum - 1961
House built in 1834 by John Harris;
original Harris furniture

02098

Gratton's Weldwood Museum
Hwy 2 South, RR 4, London, Ontario
History/Public Affairs Museum - 1969
Coll: antique and classic cars
(1914-1940); arms; mounted animals;
musical instruments; Indian and
pioneer artifacts

02099

London Regional Art Gallery
305 Queen's Av, 355 Ridout St North,
London, Ontario N6A 2N8
Fine Arts Museum - 1978
Coll: Canadian paintings, sculpture,
prints, and graphics; architecture;
decorative arts

02100

London Regional Children's Museum
380 Wellington St, City Centre,
London, Ontario N6A 5B5
Junior Museum - 1976
Coll: Indian and Inuit artifacts; clothing,
especially used for cave exploration;
games; Victorian life-style artifacts;
crafts

02101

McIntosh Gallery University of
Western Ontario
London, Ontario N6A 3K7
Fine Arts Museum - 1942
Coll: European Old Masters; 18th-20th
century Canadian paintings, sculpture,
drawings, and prints

02102

Medical Museum University of
Western Ontario
Main Floor of University Hospital,
Health Sciences complex, *mail c/o*
University Hospital, 339 Windemere
Rd, POB 5339, Terminal 'A', London,
Ontario N6A 5A5
History/Public Affairs Museum - 1973
Country doctor's office of the 19th
century; medical instruments and
machines; books dating back to the
17th century

02103

Museum of Indian Archeology
University of Western Ontario
Somerville House London, Ontario
N6A 5B7
Archeology Museum - 1934
Coll: archeological, ethnographic, and
historical artifacts of southwestern
Ontario

02104

**The Royal Canadian Regiment
Museum**
Wolseley Hall, Wolseley Barracks
London, Ontario N5Y 4T7
History/Public Affairs Museum - 1962
Military displays pertaining to the
regiment (1883 to the present)

Longueuil

02105

Musée Historique de l'Electricité
440 chemin de Chambly, Succursale
'A', CP 61, Longueuil, Québec J4H
3W2
Science/Tech Museum - 1973
Industrial and domestic use of
electricity - library

Loretteville

02106

Musée Kio-Warini
Village Huron, Loretteville, Québec
G2B 3W5
Anthropology Museum - 1972
Photographs and artifacts pertaining
to the Huron culture and mythology -
archives

Louisbourg

02107

**Fortress Louisbourg National
Historic Park**
POB 160, Louisbourg, Nova Scotia
B0A 1M0
Open Air Museum - 1928
Partly reconstructed fortress; 18th
century French and provincial
furnishings; history; geography;
geology; industry; archeology;
decorative arts - archives

02108

**Sydney and Louisbourg Railway
Museum**
Main St, Louisbourg, Nova Scotia B0A
1M0
History/Public Affairs Museum - 1972
Restored station (1895); local history;
marine commerce and railroading -
archives

Lunenburg

02109

**Lunenburg Fisheries Museum and
Aquarium**
POB 609, Lunenburg, Nova Scotia B0J
2C0
History/Public Affairs Museum - 1967
History of Nova Scotia schoonermen
including the first draggers and the
'Reo II', a rum runner built in the
American prohibition era

McCord

02110

McCord Museum
POB 62, McCord, Saskatchewan S0H
2T0
History/Public Affairs Museum - 1969
Indian and pioneer artifacts; rock
collection; historical church

Madoc

02111

O'Hara Mill
3 miles north of Hwy 7, northwest of
Madoc, 308 North Front St, Belleville,
Ontario K8P 3C4
General Museum - 1957
Coll: historic buildings; furnished
pioneer farm house (1848); sawmill
(1848); shingle mill; agriculture;
costumes

Magnetawan

02112

Magnetawan Historical Museum
Hwy 520 at Biddy St, *mail c/o* Mr.
Arthur F. Raaflaub, Secretary-
Treasurer, Magnetawan Historical
Museum Board, POB 8, Magnetawan,
Ontario P0A 1P0
History/Public Affairs Museum - 1972
Restored machinery and turbine that
supplied the first electricity for the
village; local artifacts; log cabin (1880)

Maitland

02113

W. D. Lawrence House
Maitland, Hants County, *mail c/o* Nova
Scotia Museum, 1747 Summer St,
Halifax, Nova Scotia B3H 3A6
Historic Site - 1970
Home of W.D. Lawrence, builder of the
largest square-rigged sailing ship ever
built in Canada; period furniture;
shipbuilding in the 'Golden Age of sail'

Malartic

02114

Musée Minier de Malartic
650 rue de la Paix, Abitibi est, CP 4227,
Malartic, Québec J0Y 1Z0
Science/Tech Museum - 1972
Mining specimens and equipment

Manicougan

02115

Musée Forestier de Manic
Base Marine, mille 14, Route 389
Manicougan, Québec G0H 1J0
Agriculture Museum - 1971
Horse stables; a forge; lumbering
equipment; buildings constructed
without nails - archives

Manitowaning

02116

Assiginack Historical Museum
mail c/o Municipal Clerk, Arthur St,
Manitowaning, Ontario P0P 1N0
General Museum - 1955
Former local jail housing historical
artifacts; early farm implements; Indian
artifacts; restored pioneer buildings

Manor

02117

Cannington Manor Historic Park
16 miles east of Moose Mountain
Provincial Park, Manor, *mail c/o*
Supervisor Historic Parks, Dept. of
Culture and Youth, 11th floor Avord
Tower, Regina, Saskatchewan S4P
0M8
History/Public Affairs Museum - 1965
Artifacts used by the English and
Canadian settlers during the 1880's
and 1890's; original photographs

Manotick

02118

**Watson's Mill-Dickenson Square
Conservation Area**
Mill St, POB 599, Manotick, Ontario
K0A 2N0
Agriculture Museum - 1974
Water-powered flour and gristmill
(1860)

Maple Creek

02119

Antique Tractor Museum
3 miles south from Maple Creek on
Hwy 21, Maple Creek, Saskatchewan
S0N 1N0
Agriculture Museum - 1972
Farm machinery; tractors

02120

Fort Walsh National Historic Park
34 miles southwest of Maple Creek in
Cypress Hills, POB 278, Maple Creek,
Saskatchewan S0N 1N0
History/Public Affairs Museum - 1972
Mounted Police fort (1880);
refurnished trader's post (1872)

Maplewood

02121

**Parkdale-Maplewood Community
Museum**
Maplewood, RR1, Barss Corners,
Lunenburg County, Nova Scotia B0R
1A0
History/Public Affairs Museum - 1951
German heritage and local history

Marble Mountain

02122

**Marble Mountain Community
Museum**
Marble Mountain, Nova Scotia B0E
3K0
History/Public Affairs Museum - 1974
Mining tools; marble rock; local history

Marten River

02123

Northern Ontario Trappers Museum
Hwy 11, between North Bay and
Temagami Marten River, Ontario P0H
1T0
General Museum - 1970
Trapper's equipment; beaver house
and dam; mounted animals

Masset

02124

Ed Jones Haida Museum
Masset, British Columbia V0T 1M0
Anthropology Museum - 1974
Ethnography and archives related to
the Haida Indians

Massey

02125

Massey Area Pioneer Museum
Hwy 17 Massey, Ontario P0P 1P0
General Museum - 1968
Pioneer and Indian artifacts;
lumbering; fur-trading; fluorescent
minerals; miniatures; costumes

Mattawa

02126
Voyageur Canoe Exhibit
Samuel de Champlain Provincial Park,
Hwy 17, 8 miles west of Mattawa, POB
147, Mattawa, Ontario P0H 1V0
History/Public Affairs Museum - 1971
Replica of 38 foot Canôt de Maître;
history and construction of birch bark
canoes; fur-trading

Medicine Hat

02127
**Medicine Hat Historical Museum
and National Exhibition Centre**
1302 Bomford Cres. SW, Medicine
Hat, Alberta T1A 5E6
General Museum - 1951/1978
Pioneer home furnishings and clothing
prior to 1900; farm machinery; Indian
artifacts; paleontological material

Melbourne

02128
**Richmond County Historical Society
Museum**
Main St South, POB 280, Melbourne,
Québec J0B 2B0
History/Public Affairs Museum - 1968
Old tools; photographs; newspapers

Melville

02129
Melville Railway Museum
mail c/o Melville Regional Park
Commission, Melville Regional Park,
Melville, Saskatchewan S0A 7P0
History/Public Affairs Museum - 1978
Railway artifacts

Merrickville

02130
Blockhouse Museum
Cnr of Saint Lawrence and Main Sts,
mail c/o Miss Phyllis Walker,
Secretary, Merrickville and District
Historical Society, POB 294,
Merrickville, Ontario K0G 1N0
History/Public Affairs Museum - 1966
Coll: blockhouse built in 1832 as a
defence for the Rideau Canal; military
items; agriculture; local heritage

Miami

02131
Miami Station Museum
3rd St, Miami, POB 1855, Winnipeg,
Manitoba R3C 3R1
General Museum - 1976
Period costumes; local history;
restored railway station

Midland

02132
Huron Indian Village
Little Lake Park, POB 547, Midland,
Ontario L4R 4K9
Open Air Museum - 1954
Huron Village restored to its original
appearance prior to European contact;
17th century Indian artifacts

02133
Huronia Museum
Little Lake Park, POB 638, Midland,
Ontario L4R 4L3
General Museum - 1947
Pioneer and Indian artifacts; art; Great
Lakes shipping photographs

02134
Sainte-Marie Among the Hurons
RR 1, POB 160, Midland, Ontario L4R
4K8
History/Public Affairs Museum - 1967
Coll: archeological artifacts; 16th and
17th century European antiques;
Indian artifacts

Milford

02135
Mariner's Park Museum
mail c/o Mrs. F.W. Dusen, RR 2,
Milford, Ontario K0K 2P0
History/Public Affairs Museum - 1967
Marine artifacts from surrounding
waters and the Great Lakes;
lighthouse; lifeboat; wheel house

Milton

02136
Halton Region Museum
6 miles northwest of Milton in Kelso
Park, RR 3, Milton, Ontario L9T 2X7
General Museum - 1962
History of Halton County from 1808 to
1920; ornithology

02137
Ontario Agricultural Museum
3 miles west of Milton, POB 38, Milton,
Ontario L9T 2Y3
Agriculture Museum - 1975
Agricultural machinery; farm home
equipment and furnishings; tools

Minden

02138
**Kanawa International Museum of
Canoes, Kayaks, and Rowing Craft**
20 miles north of Minden, mail c/o
Prof. K. Wipper, School of Physical
and Health Education, University of
Toronto, Room 7, 121 Saint Joseph St,
Toronto, Ontario M5S 1A1
History/Public Affairs Museum - 1966
Coll: full-size canoes, kayaks, and
rowing craft with associated tools, art,
and artifacts; frontier collections in
restored log cabins

Minesing

02139
Simcoe County Museum
5 miles north of Barrie on Hwy 26,
next to Springwater Provincial Park,
RR 2, Minesing, Ontario L0L 1Y0
General Museum - 1928
Coll: archeology; ethnology; pioneer
and Victorian exhibits; domestic items;
early agricultural material

Minnedosa

02140
**Minnedosa and District
Co-Cooperative Museum**
POB 312, Minnedosa, Manitoba R0J
1E0
History/Public Affairs Museum - 1962
Local history

Miscouche

02141
**Musée Acadien de L'Ile du Prince
Edouard à Miscouche**
Miscouche, Ile du Prince Edouard C0B
1T0
General Museum - 1964
Objects used by the Acadians;
carpentry, blacksmith and kitchen
items; old books; photographs

Mission City

02142
Mission Museum
33201-2nd Av, Mission City, British
Columbia V2V 1J9
General Museum - 1972
Local history; Indian artifacts; minerals;
farm equipment; period rooms -
archives

Mississauga

02143
The Bradley House Museum
Orr Rd at Meadowwood Rd, mail c/o
City of Mississauga, 1 City Centre
Drive, Mississauga, Ontario L5B 1M2
Historic Site - 1967
Home of the Bradley family, one of the
first to settle in Toronto Township, built
in 1830; barn reconstructed; authentic
kitchen

Mistassini

02144
Centre Culturel Confederatif
219 bd Panoramique, Mistassini,
Québec G0W 2C0
Fine Arts Museum - 1967
Art gallery; cultural exhibits

Moncton

02145
Galerie d'Art Université de Moncton
Edifice Champlain, Moncton, New
Brunswick E1A 3E9
Fine Arts Museum - 1965
Contemporary Canadian art

02146
Lutz Mountain Meeting House
3143 Mountain Rd, POB 2952,
Moncton, New Brunswick E1C 8T8
General Museum - 1976
Furniture; clothing; household utensils;
farm implements; genealogical files on
the first settlers (1766)

02147
Moncton Museum
20 Mountain Rd, Moncton, New
Brunswick E1C 2J8
History/Public Affairs Museum - 1973
Human history; local history since
1700

02148
Musée Acadien Université de
Moncton
Edifice Champlain, Moncton, New
Brunswick E1A 3E9
General Museum - 1886
Customs of the Acadians; antique
Bibles; pottery; musical instruments;
tools; furniture; porcelain; coins

Montréal

02149
Alcan Museum and Archives
1 Place Ville Marie, POB 6090,
Montréal, Québec H3C 3H2
History/Public Affairs Museum - 1967
Objects, documents and photographs
related to the company's founding and
growth; early and unusual uses of
aluminum - archives

02150
**The Arthur Pascal Collection of
Antique Woodworking Tools**
301 Saint-Antoine, 901 rue Bleury,
Montréal, Québec H2Z 1M3
History/Public Affairs Museum - 1973
Woodworking tools from all over the
world dating back to the 15th and 16th
centuries

02151
Bank of Montréal Museum
129 Saint James St, POB 6002,
Montréal, Québec H3C 2B1
History/Public Affairs Museum - 1963
Numismatic and banking memorabilia

02152
**Bell Canada Telephone Historical
Collection**
1050 Beaver Hall Hill, Room 1436,
Montréal, Québec H2Z 1S3
Science/Tech Museum - 1936
Telecommunications history

02153
**Black Watch of Canada Regimental
Memorial Museum**
2067 Bleury St, Montréal, Québec H3A
2K2
History/Public Affairs Museum - 1949
Medals; weapons; uniforms; paintings
and other military memorabilia - library

02154
Centre d'Art du Mont-Royal
1260 chemin Remembrance, Montréal,
Québec H3H 1A2
Fine Arts Museum - 1963
Painting; sculpture; engravings

02155
Centre Missionnaire Sainte-Therèse
Musée et Archives
4387 Esplanade, Montréal, Québec
H2W 1T3
Fine Arts Museum - 1967
Coll: mounted animals; arts and crafts;
Indian, African and Ethiopian art -
archives

02156
Château de Ramezay
280 est, rue Notre-Dame, Montréal,
Québec H2Y 1C5
Decorative Arts Museum - 1895
Coll: traditional domestic art; Indian
ethnology; antique furniture; silver,
pewter and ceramic items

02157
Galerie UQAM Université du Québec
CP 8888, Montréal, Québec H3C 3P8
Fine Arts Museum - 1972
Coll: furniture; sculpture; more than
1,000 engravings; Egyptian art; French
ceramics

02158
McCord Museum
690 Sherbrooke St West, Montréal,
Québec H3A 1E9
General Museum - 1919
Coll: ethnological material pertaining to
the Arctic, Prairies and North West
Coast; paintings by well-known artists;
drawings, prints and paintings by
Canadian artists; antique costumes,
accessories, furniture and crafts -
archives

02159
Maison du Calvet
401 rue Bonsecours, Montréal,
Québec H2Y 3C3
History/Public Affairs Museum - 1966
Antique furniture

02160
Musée d'Art Contemporain
Cité du Havre, Montréal, Québec H3C
3R4
Fine Arts Museum - 1965
Coll: Paintings; sculpture; engravings;
graphic art; works by Canadian artists

02161
Musée d'Art Neo-Bysantin
10025 bd l'Acadie, Montréal, Québec
H4N 2S1
Fine Arts Museum - 1975
Icons; wood sculpture; textiles

02162
Musée de l'Eglise Notre-Dame
430 rue Saint-Sulpice, Montréal,
Québec H2Y 2V5
Decorative Arts Museum - 1937
Furniture; silver and ceramic items;
religious ornaments; paintings; statues
- archives

02163
Musée des Beaux-Arts de Montréal
3400 av du Musée, Montréal, Québec
H3G 1K3
Fine Arts Museum - 1860
Coll: European, African and Canadian
sculpture; Asian, European, Islamic,
Pre-Columbian, and American Indian
art; furniture; silver and ceramic items
- library

02164
Musée du Cinéma
360 McGill, Montréal, Québec H2Y
2E9
History/Public Affairs Museum - 1967
Kaleidoscopes; optical tricks; cinema
apparatus such as cameras from
various lands - archives

02165
Musée du Frère André Oratoire
Saint-Joseph
3800 chemin Queen Mary, Montréal,
Québec H3V 1H6
Religious Art Museum - 1952
Church windows; mosaics; frescoes;
sculpture

02166
Musée Marguerite Bourgeois
400 est, rue Saint-Paul, Montréal,
Québec H2Y 1H4
History/Public Affairs Museum - 1951
History of Montréal and of the life of
Marguerite Bourgeois

02167
**Musée Militaire et Maritime de
Montréal**
Le Vieux Fort, Ile Sainte-Hélène,
Succursale 'A', CP 1024, Montréal,
Québec H3C 2W9
History/Public Affairs Museum - 1955
Coll: military, maritime and social
history exhibits; MacDonald-Stewart
collection of domestic utensils; arms
and ammunition

02168
Powerhouse Gallery
3738 Saint Dominique, Montréal,
Québec H2X 2X9
Fine Arts Museum - 1973
A womens co-operative gallery, run by
women, to provide exhibition space
primarily for women artists

02169
**Royal Canadian Ordinance Corps
Museum**
6560 Hochelaga St, Building 108, POB
6109, Montréal, Québec H3C 3H7
History/Public Affairs Museum - 1962
Military items pertaining to the Royal
Canadian Ordinance Corps

02170
**Saidye Bronfman Centre of the
YM-YWHA**
5170 Côte Sainte-Catherine, Montréal,
Québec H3W 1M7
Fine Arts Museum - 1967
Exhibits of national and provincial
works of art

02171
Sir George Williams Art Galleries
1445 ouest, bd de Maisonneuve,
Montréal, Québec H3G 1M8
Fine Arts Museum - 1966
Coll: contemporary Canadian
paintings, drawings, and sculpture;
primitive sculpture

Mooretown
02172
Moore Museum
6th Line, Moore at Mooretown, quarter
mile from Saint Clair Parkway
Mooretown, Ontario N0N 1M0
General Museum - 1974
Coll: history of the Moore Township;
lumbering, agricultural, and carpentry
tools; pioneer toys; dressmaking and
boot making materials

Moose Jaw
02173
**Moose Jaw Art Museum and
National Exhibition Centre**
Crescent Park, Moose Jaw,
Saskatchewan S6H 0X6
General Museum - 1966
Paintings; Plains Indians and local
historical artifacts

02174
Western Development Museum
1770 Hamilton Dr, POB 185, Moose
Jaw, Saskatchewan S6H 4N8
Science/Tech Museum - 1976
Transportation exhibits; aviation;
railway

Moosehorn
02175
Moosehorn Museum
1st Av East, POB 66, Moosehorn,
Manitoba R0C 2E0
General Museum - 1974
History; ethnology - archives

Moosomin
02176
Jamieson Museum
306 Gertie St, POB 236, Moosomin,
Saskatchewan S0G 3N0
History/Public Affairs Museum - 1972
Large military collection; farm
implements; house built before 1900
and furnished in the style of the period

Morden
02177
Morden and District Museum
Cnr Stephen and 8th Sts, POB 728,
Morden, Manitoba R0G 1J0
General Museum - 1971
Marine fossils (paleozoic era); pioneer
artifacts

Morpeth
02178
Rondeau Park Interpretive Centre
RR 1, Morpeth, Ontario N0P 1X0
Natural History Museum - 1965
Coll: herbarium; zoology; entomology;
ornithology; archeology; history -
library

Morrisburg
02179
Upper Canada Village
Hwy 2, seven miles east of
Morrisburg, POB 740, Morrisburg,
Ontario K0C 1X0
Open Air Museum - 1961
Coll: recreated 19th century village of
40 buildings moved from original sites,
portraying an Upper Canadian Saint
Lawrence River Valley community;
furnishings; decorative arts; textiles -
library

Mount Uniacke
02180
Uniacke House
Mount Uniacke, Hant's County, *mail
c/o* Nova Scotia Museum, 1747
Summer St, Halifax, Nova Scotia B3H
3A6
Historic Site - 1949
Home of Richard John Uniacke,
attorney general of Nova Scotia
1797-1830, with original furnishings

Muenster
02181
St. Peter's College Museum
south of St. Peter's Park, college
building, POB 10, Muenster,
Saskatchewan S0K 2Y6
General Museum - 1973
Pioneer and Indian relics; mounted
birds and animals of the area; rocks,
minerals and fossils

Mundare
02182
Basilian Fathers Museum
POB 379, Mundare, Alberta T0B 3H0
General Museum - 1950
Ukrainian folklore including national
costumes, Eastern Church vestments
and paintings - archives

Musgrave Harbour
02183
Fisherman's Museum
Marine Drive, Musgrave Harbour,
Newfoundland A0G 3J0
History/Public Affairs Museum - 1974
Fishery; ship models; engines;
logbooks (1902) containing accounts
of local shipwrecks

Nakusp
02184
Nakusp Museum
POB 86, Nakusp, British Columbia
V0G 1R0
History/Public Affairs Museum - 1968
Local history; Indian artifacts

Nanaimo
02185
The Bastion
Front St, Nanaimo, British Columbia
V9R 5S5
General Museum - 1930
Log fortification (1853) containing
pioneer, mining and nautical material;
ethnography; coins; rifles

02186
Nanaimo Centennial Museum
100 Cameron Rd, Nanaimo, British
Columbia V9R 2X1
General Museum - 1967
Local history; coal mining

Napanee
02187
Allan MacPherson House
180 Elizabeth St, POB 183, Napanee,
Ontario K7R 3M3
General Museum - 1967
Restored home built in 1826 by Allan
MacPherson; period furniture and
furnishings

02188
**Lennox and Addington Historical
Museum**
POB 160, Napanee, Ontario K7R 3M3
General Museum - 1976
Coll: Indian artifacts; furniture; farm
and household tools; pioneer
costumes; china; glass - archives,
library

Neepawa
02189
Murray's Museum of History
POB 489, Neepawa, Manitoba R0J
1H0
Archeology Museum - 1972
Archeology - archives

Nelson
02190
Kootenay Museum
402 Andersom St, Nelson, British
Columbia V1L 3Y3
General Museum - 1957
Indian artifacts; pioneer and explorer
material; Doukhobour arts and crafts;
geology and mining - archives

02191
Kootenay School of Art Gallery
David Thompson University Centre,
POB 480, Nelson, British Columbia
V1L 5R3
Fine Arts Museum - 1965
Fine art; folk craft; photographs;
historical forms of art

New Denmark·
02192
New Denmark Memorial Museum
New Denmark, New Brunswick E0G
2P0
General Museum - 1972
Household articles, tools, machinery
and documents of the Danish settlers

New Glasgow
02193
**Pictou County Historical Society
Museum**
86 Temperance St, New Glasgow,
Nova Scotia B2H 5E5
General Museum - 1964
Agricultural equipment; household
utensils; pictures and documents
relating to the area; early native
glassware

New London
02194
Lucy Maud Montgomery Birthplace
New London, R.R. No. 6, Kensington,
Prince Edward Island C0B 1M0
General Museum - 1965
Furniture of 1870's-1880's, scrapbooks

New Ross
02195
Ross Farm Museum of Agriculture
Route 12, New Ross, Nova Scotia B0J
2M0
Agriculture Museum - 1970
Old agricultural methods and
implements; rural crafts; plow
collection

New Westminster

02196
Irving House Historic Centre and New Westminster Museum
302 Royal Av, New Westminster, British Columbia V3L 1H7
General Museum - 1950/1964
Indian artifacts; general history of the town; furnished pioneer home - archives

02197
Royal Westminster Regimental Museum
The Armoury, 530 Queens Av, New Westminster, British Columbia V3L 1K3
History/Public Affairs Museum - 1973
Military artifacts and memorabilia of the Royal Westminster Regiment and its antecedents (1863)

Niagara Falls

02198
Lundy's lane Historical Museum
5810 Ferry St, Niagara Falls, Ontario L2G 1S9
General Museum - 1961
Pioneer utensils and tools; Indian and military artifacts; children's toys

02199
Oak Hall
mail c/o Mr. M.S. Cushing, Assistant General Manager, Niagara Parks Commission, Portage Rd, POB 150, Niagara Falls, Ontario L2E 6T2
General Museum - 1964
Home and furniture of Sir Harry Oakes; Canadian paintings

Niagara-on-the-Lake

02200
Fort George National Historic Park
POB 787, Niagara-on-the-Lake, Ontario L0S 1J0
History/Public Affairs Museum - 1950
Reconstructed fort built in 1799; furnishings of the period from 1797 to 1812; relics of the War of 1812

02201
The Niagara Apothecary
5 Queens St at King, Niagara-on-the-Lake, mail c/o Ontario College of Pharmacists, 483 Huron St, Toronto, Ontario M5R 2R4
History/Public Affairs Museum - 1971
Restored pharmacy (1866); original glass and ceramic apothecary ware

02202
Niagara Fire Museum
mail c/o Mr. Noel Haines, District Chief, Fire Dept., POB 498, Niagara-on-the-Lake, Ontario
History/Public Affairs Museum - 1972
Exhibits of local firefighting equipment dating back 140 years

Nicolet

02203
Séminaire de Nicolet
700 bd Louis-Fréchette, Nicolet, Québec J0G 1E0
General Museum - 1831
Coll: botany; ornithology; zoology; astronomy; chemistry; physics; furniture; religious accessories - archives; library

Nipawin

02204
Nipawin and District Historical Museum
2nd Av West (Arts Centre) and old No 35 Hwy East (Outdoor Area), POB 1917, Nipawin, Saskatchewan S0E 1E0
Agriculture Museum - 1972
Historical exhibits, especially of regional lumbering industries

North Battleford

02205
North Battleford Art Centre
1301-104th St, POB 460, North Battleford, Saskatchewan S9A 2Y6
Fine Arts Museum - 1973
Paintings by local artists

02206
Western Development Museum
Junction of Hwys 40 and 5 East, POB 183, North Battleford, Saskatchewan S9A 2Y1
History/Public Affairs Museum - 1949
Pioneer village displaying household items and agricultural machinery

North East Margaree

02207
Margaree Salmon Museum
North East Margaree, Nova Scotia B0E 2H0
History/Public Affairs Museum - 1965
Historic fishing tackles and books an angling

02208
Museum of Cape Breton Heritage
North East Margaree, Nova Scotia B0E 2H0
Decorative Arts Museum - 1972
Cape Breton crafts; china and glass; locally-made furniture; hand-hooked rugs

North Vancouver

02209
North Shore Museum and Archives
209 West 4th St, mail c/o W.J. Baker, 617 West 23rd St, North Vancouver, British Columbia V7M 2C2
General Museum - 1976
Indian artifacts; shipbuilding and railroad industries - archives

Norwich

02210
Norwich and District Historical Museum
Stover St North, Norwich, Ontario N0J 1P0
Religious Art Museum - 1969
Former Quaker meeting house; displays portraying pioneer life and Quaker culture; farm implements and machinery

Oakville

02211
Oakville Centennial Gallery
120 Navy St, Oakville, Ontario L6J 2Z4
Fine Arts Museum - 1967
Coll: native Indian art; Keene collection of war, travel, and commercial posters

02212
Taras H. Shevchenko Museum and Memorial Park
1363 Dundas St, Oakville, 42 Roncevalles Av, Toronto, Ontario M6R 2K3
General Museum - 1952
Shevchenko's paintings, literary, and poetical works; Ukrainian ceramics and handcrafts; Ukrainian pioneer life in Western Canada

Odanak

02213
Musée des Abénakis
Réserve Indienne des Abénakis Odanak, Québec J0G 1H0
Anthropology Museum - 1962
Coll: sculpture portraiting the culture of the Abénakis; items made by other Canadian Indian tribes; religious objects made by Québec goldsmiths; baskets

Oil Springs

02214
Oil Museum of Canada
22 miles southeast of Sarnia, RR 2, Oil Springs, Ontario N0N 1P0
History/Public Affairs Museum - 1960
History of the discovery and development of oil in the area; life in an oil town of the 1860's; working wells with antique equipment - library, arcives

Orillia

02215
Stephan Leacock Memorial Home
Old Brewery Bay, POB 625, Orillia, Ontario L3V 6K5
Historic Site - 1958
Furniture belonging to Stephen Leacock; his manuscripts, letters, and personal library - library, archives

Oromocto

02216
CFB Gagetown Military Museum
Base Gagetown, Oromocto, New Brunswick E0G 2P0
History/Public Affairs Museum - 1971
Guns (18th c.-present); uniforms; weapons

02217
Fort Hughes Military Blockhouse
Wharf Rd, POB 37, Oromocto, New Brunswick E2V 2G4
Historic Site - 1970
Fort of Sir Richard Hughes, Lieutenant-Governor of Nova Scotia during the American Revolution

Orwell Corner

02218
Orwell Corner Agricultural Museum
Orwell Corner, POB 1888, Charlottetown, Prince Edward Island C1A 7M4
Agriculture Museum - 1973
Restored rural crossroads, buildings of a late 19th century rural community

Oshawa

02219
Canadian Automotive Museum
99 Simcoe St South, Oshawa, Ontario L1H 4G7
History/Public Affairs Museum - 1962
Coll: antique and classic cars and trucks (1898-1960); related memorabilia - library

02220
Henry House Museum
Lakeview Park, RR 4, POB 17, Oshawa, Ontario L1H 7K6
History/Public Affairs Museum - 1966
One of the three surviving buildings (built in 1848) of Port Sydenham, now Oshawa harbor; household artifacts of the period - library

02221
The Robert McLaughlin Gallery
Queen St at the foot of Bagot, mail c/o Civic Centre Oshawa, Ontario L1H 3Z3
Fine Arts Museum - 1967
Coll: contemporary Canadian collection; works of the 'Painters Eleven'; Japanese wood-block prints; drawings; sculpture - library

Osoyoos

02222
Osoyoos Museum
Main St, Community Park 2, POB 791, Osoyoos, British Columbia V0H 1V0
General Museum - 1963
Reconstructed log cabin furnished in pioneer style; Indian artifacts and handicrafts

Ottawa

02223
Bytown Historical Museum
The Driveway, near Junction of Rideau Canal and Ottawa River, Station 'B', POB 523, Ottawa, Ontario K1P 5P6
General Museum - 1918
Artifacts relating to Colonel By, the rideau Canal, Ottawa, and the vicinity

02224
Canadian Scouting Museum Boy Scouts of Canada National Headquarters
1345 Baseline Rd, POB 5151, Station 'F', Ottawa, Ontario K2C 3G7
History/Public Affairs Museum
Memorabilia of the founder of Scouting, Lord Baden-Powell; Canadian Scouting items, such as badges, equipment, and books

02225
Canadian Ski Museum
457 A Sussex Drive, Ottawa, Ontario K1N 6Z4
History/Public Affairs Museum - 1971
Artifacts and records pertaining to the history of skiing achievements in Canada

02226
Canadian War Museum
330 Sussex Drive, Ottawa, Ontario K1A 0M8
History/Public Affairs Museum - 1880
Coll: weapons, uniforms, photographs, war art, and medals - library

02227
Canadiana Sport Art Collection
333 River Rd, Ottawa, Ontario K1L 8B9
History/Public Affairs Museum - 1971
Combination of Canadian sport and art

02228
Laurier House
335 Laurier Av East, Ottawa, Ontario
K1N 6R4
Historic Site - 1951
House built in 1878, the residence of
two Canadian Prime Ministers;
furnishings; books; paintings;
manuscripts - library

02229
National Aeronautical Collection
Rockcliffe Airport, 1867 Saint Laurent
Bd, Ottawa, Ontario K1A 0M8
1964
Coll: 92 civil and military aircraft
ranging from the pre WW I days to the
supersonic jet; aero engines; artifacts
related to aviation

02230
National Gallery of Canada
Immeuble Lorne Bldg, Elgin St, Ottawa,
Ontario K1A 0M8
Fine Arts Museum - 1880
Coll: Old Masters - Italian, Dutch,
French, Flemish, and German; modern
European and American paintings and
sculptures; medieval art; Canadian art
from the 18th century to the present;
decorative arts - library

02231
National Museum of Man
Victoria Memorial Museum Bldg,
MacLeod at Metcalfe Sts, Ottawa,
Ontario K1A 0M8
Anthropology Museum - 1910
Coll: anthropology; ethnology;
archeology; costumes; folklore; folk
music and linguistics; decorative arts;
Indian and Eskimo artifacts; military
history - library

02232
**National Museum of Natural
Sciences**
Victoria Memorial Museum Bldg,
MacLeod and Metcalfe Sts, Ottawa,
Ontario K1A 0M8
Natural History Museum - 1842
Coll: zoology; ichthyology;
herpetology; mammalia; mollusks;
ornithology; botany; vertebrate
paleontology; mineral sciences -
library

02233
**National Museum of Science and
Technology**
1867 Saint Laurent Bd, Ottawa, Ontario
K1A 0M8
Science/Tech Museum - 1967
Coll: national exhibits in the physical
sciences and all the technologies;
aeronautics; agriculture; astronomy;
industry; transportation - library,
observatory

02234
National Postal Museum
180 Wellington St, Confederation
Heights, Ottawa, Ontario K1A 0B1
History/Public Affairs Museum - 1974
Coll: stamps of all nations; post office
artifacts and equipment; photographs
- library

02235
Photo Gallery National Film Board
150 Kent St, *mail c/o* Canadian
Government Photo Centre, Tunney's
Pasture, Ottawa, Ontario K1A 0M9
Fine Arts Museum - 1967
Coll: creative photography by
Canadian photographers

02236
**Public Information Office and
Community Museum**
122 Murray St, *mail c/o* Pollution
Probe, 53 Queens St, Ottawa, Ontario
Science/Tech Museum - 1977
Graphics, photographs, and artifacts
pertaining to energy conservation;
wind generator; solar collector; heat
pump; fuel- saving furnace

02237
Regimental Museum Governor
General's Foot Guards
Drill Hall, Cartier Square, Ottawa,
Ontario K1A 0K2
History/Public Affairs Museum - 1955
Artifacts of regimental interest over
the past 100 years, located in the Drill
Hall (1879); weapons; uniforms;
medals; war souvenirs - library

02238
Saw Gallery
72 Rideau St, Ottawa, Ontario K1N
5W9
Fine Arts Museum - 1972
Contemporary art

Owen Sound

02239
Owen Sound Museum The County of
Grey
975 6th St East, Owen Sound, Ontario
N4K 1G9
General Museum - 1967
Ojibway Indian and emigrant European
culture artifacts; log cabins; blacksmith
shop - library

02240
**Tom Thomson Memorial Gallery and
Museum of Fine Art**
840 1st Av West, POB 312, Owen
Sound, Ontario N4K 5P5
Fine Arts Museum - 1967
Coll: paintings and drawings by Tom
Thomson; memorabilia of his life;
works of the 'Group of Seven' and
other contemporary Canadian artists;
native Indian paintings; graphics;
crafts - library

Oxbow

02241
Ralph Allen Memorial Museum
802 Railway Av, No 18 Hwy, Oxbow,
Saskatchewan S0C 2B0
General Museum - 1973
Oil field and railway displays; pioneer
and Indian artifacts; early pictures of
the district

Oyen

02242
Crossroads Museum
1st Av, POB 9, Oyen, Alberta T0J 2J0
General Museum - 1973
Local history; farm machinery; settler's
effects; restored prairie home

Parrsboro

02243
**Mineral and Gem Geological
Museum**
1 Eastern Av, POB 297, Parrsboro,
Nova Scotia B0M 1S0
Natural History Museum - 1960
Minerals and ores; agate; jewelry

Patricia

02244
Dinosaur Provincial Park
28 miles northeast from Brooks
Patricia, Alberta T0J 2Ko
Natural History Museum - 1955
Partial dinosaur skeletal remains,
hadrosaurian and young ceratopsian
dinosaur; displays of animal life in the
present; geology; pioneer history

Peace River

02245
Peace River Centennial Museum
POB 747, Peace River, Alberta T0H
2X0
General Museum - 1967
Artifacts relating to the fur trade, early
settlement and agriculture; navigation
on the Peace River - archives; films

Pembroke

02246
Champlain Trail Museum
1032 Pembroke St East, RR 2,
Pembroke, Ontario K8A 6W3
General Museum - 1958
Coll: exhibits pertaining to Chaplain's
exploration (1613); fur trade;
lumbering; pioneer household items;
agricultural implements; costumes;
uniforms; steam engines; pioneer
home (1872) - library, archives

Penetanguishene

02247
**Penetanguishene Centennial
Museum**
8 Burke St, 12 Harriet St,
Penetanguishene, Ontario L0K 1P0
General Museum - 1967
Indian artifacts; general store; local
artifacts from the late 19th century; old
fire hall

Penticton

02248
Penticton Art Gallery
785 Main St, POB 728, Penticton,
British Columbia V2A 6Y7
Fine Arts Museum - 1972
Paintings, drawings and pastels by
Okanagan artists; pottery; sculpture;
photographs

02249
R.N. Atkinson Museum
785 Main St, Penticton, British
Columbia V2A 5E3
General Museum - 1958
Salish artifacts; military insignia and
arms; mineralogy - archives

Percé

02250
**Le Centre d'Histoire Naturelle de
Percé**
Route d'Irlande, CP 190, Percé, Comté
de Gaspé, Québec G0C 2L0
Natural History Museum - 1974
Characteristic biological specimens of
the Altantic coast region

Peribonka

02251
Musée Maria Chapdelaine
Route 169, Peribonka, Québec G0W
2G0
General Museum - 1939
Exhibits portraiting the life of the early
settlers

Perth

02252
**Archibald W. Campbell Memorial
Museum**
Matheson House, 11 Gore St, POB
222, Perth, Ontario K7H 3E4
General Museum - 1067
Matheson House restored to the 1840
period; agriculture; Mexican pottery;
archeology; natural history;
mineralogy; Indian artifacts

Peterborough

02253
Art Gallery of Peterborough
2 Crescent St, Suite 203,
Peterborough Square, Peterborough,
Ontario K9H 7E7
Fine Arts Museum - 1978
European and Canadian paintings and
prints

02254
Peterborough Centennial Museum
Armour Hill, Hunter St East at Armour
Rd, POB 143, Peterborough, Ontario
K9J 6Y5
General Museum - 1967
Pioneer and 19th century furniture,
utensils, clothing, tools, dolls, and toys;
natural history - archives

Pickering

02255
Town of Pickering Museum
Pickering Town Offices, 1710 Kingston
Rd, Pickering, Ontario L0H 1A0
General Museum - 1969
Pioneer farm equipment; early
Canadian gasoline and steam engines;
historic buildings

Pictou

02256
Micmac Museum
RR 1, Pictou, Nova Scotia B0K 1H0
General Museum - 1956
Indian artifacts from burial mounds;
tools, weapons, beads

02257
**Thomas McCulloch House and
Hector National Exhibition Centre**
POB 1210, Pictou, Nova Scotia B0K
1H0
Historic Site - 1974/1973
Home of Thomas McCulloch, founder
of a liberalized system of education;
genealogical material; early 19th
century period furniture

Pilot Mound

02258
Pilot Mound Centennial Museum
Centennial Bldg, Broadway St, Pilot
Mound, Manitoba R0G 1P0
History/Public Affairs Museum - 1967
Historical artifacts and photographs

Plamondon

02259
Plamondon and District Museum
Plamondon, Alberta T0A 2T0
Science/Tech Museum - 1976
Local history and culture

Pointe-au-Pic

02260
Musée Laure Conan
30 rue Saint-André, La Malbaie, CP 667, Pointe-au-Pic, Québec G0T 1M0
General Museum - 1946
Coll: folk art and history; tomahawks and 18th century weapons; photographs and documents retracing the colonization of Charlevoix county

Pointe-Bleue

02261
Société d'Histoire et d'Archéologie de Pointe-Bleue
406 Armisk, Pointe-Bleue, Québec G0W 2H0
Archeology Museum - 1977
Archeology; Indian artifacts

Pointe-Claire

02262
Pointe-Claire Cultural Centre: Stewart Hall Art Gallery
176 Lakeshore Rd, Pointe-Claire, Québec H9S 4J7
Decorative Arts Museum - 1963
Ceramics; weaving; art

Ponoka

02263
Alberta Hospital Museum
POB 1000, Ponoka, Alberta T0C 2H0
Science/Tech Museum - 1969
Artifacts showing changes in the practices of the hospital since 1910 including instruments, clothing and photographs

Porcupine Plain

02264
Porcupine Plain and District Museum
Cultural Centre Bldg, West on Elm St, POB 98, Porcupine Plain, Saskatchewan S0E 1H0
General Museum - 1976
Local historic items; Indian artifacts; Inuit display; lace pillows; pioneer log cabin

Port Alberni

02265
Alberni Valley Museum
4255 Wallace St, Port Alberni, British Columbia V9Y 3Y6
General Museum - 1973
Regional history; Nootkan Indian artifacts; prehistoric artifacts; photographic collection (historical and ethnographical)

Port Carling

02266
Port Carling Pioneer Museum
Island Park, by the Locks, POB 33, Port Carling, Ontario P0B 1J0
General Museum - 1961
Articles used by settlers in the Muskoka area dating back to 1865; locally-built boats; Indian artifacts

Port Colborne

02267
Port Colborne Historical and Marine Museum
280 King St, Port Colborne, Ontario L3K 4H1
General Museum - 1974
Local historical artifacts; exhibits featuring Erie and Foster glass manufacturers; school house (1818)

Port Hill

02268
Green Park Shipbuilding Museum
Port Hill Tyne Valley, Prince Edward Island C0B 2C0
Science/Tech Museum - 1973
Wooden shipbuilding yard

Port Moody

02269
Port Moody Museum
126 Kyle St, Port Moody, British Columbia V3H 3N7
General Museum - 1973
Regional archeology; social and economic material; furniture and furnishings; lumbering and landclearing - archives including early photographs

Port Rowan

02270
Backus Mill and Agricultural Museum
Backus Conservation Area, 3 miles east of Hwy 59 and one mile north of Port Rowan, mail c/o Long Point Region Conservation Authority, POB 525, Simcoe, Ontario N3Y 4N5
Open Air Museum - 1956
Agricultural tools; horse-drawn vehicles; sawmill, windmill, and ciderpress in operation; threshing barn

Port Royal

02271
Port Royal National Historic Park
Port Royal, POB 9, Annapolis Royal, Nova Scotia B0S 1A0
Open Air Museum - 1939
First permanent European settlement north of the Spanish possessions; history of French settlers (1605-1613)

Portage la Prairie

02272
Fort La Reine Museum and Pioneer Village
2 miles east of Portage La Prairie, POB 997, Portage la Prairie, Manitoba R1N 3C4
Open Air Museum - 1967
Late 19th century village with furnishings; vehicles; local history

Pouce Coupe

02273
Pouce Coupe Museum
Railway Station, POB 293, Pouce Coupe, British Columbia V0C 2C0
General Museum - 1972
Pioneer artifacts - archives

Powell River

02274
Powell River Historical Museum
Centennial Bldg, Marine Av, POB 42, Powell River, British Columbia V8A 4Z5
General Museum - 1968
Prehistory; Indian artifacts; pioneer period rooms - archives

Prelate

02275
St. Angela's Museum and Archives
mail c/o St. Angela's Convent, POB 220, Prelate, Saskatchewan S0N 2B0
Religious Art Museum - 1969
History of the Ursuline Order in Saskatchewan and of the district from the pioneer days

Prescott

02276
Fort Wellington National Historic Park
400 Dibble St, POB 479, Prescott, Ontario K0E 1T0
Historic Site - 1926
Restored British fort built in 1838 to guard the Upper Saint Lawrence; period furnishings; small arms; uniforms and accoutrements

Prince George

02277
Fort George Regional Museum
POB 1779, Prince George, British Columbia V2L 4V7
General Museum - 1972
Indian artifacts; local history

Prince Rupert

02278
Museum of Northern British Columbia
McBride St at 1st Av, POB 669, Prince Rupert, British Columbia V8J 3S1
General Museum - 1932
Local history; natural history including Northwest Coast Indian material; fossils and rocks; coins; historic photographs

Prince William

02279
Kings Landing Historical Settlement
Prince William on trans-Canada Hwy, 23 miles west of Fredericton, POB 522, Fredericton, New Brunswick E3B 5A6
Open Air Museum - 1974
History of the Saint John River valley (1790-1870); historical farm; saw mill; various buildings

Princeton

02280
Princeton and District Pioneer Museum
167 Vermilion Av, POB 687, Princeton, British Columbia V0X 1W0
General Museum - 1958
Indian and Chinese material; pioneer items; period rooms

Québec

02281
Centre Marie de l'Incarnation et Musée des Ursulines
12 rue Donacona, CP 760, Québec, Québec G1R 4T1
Religious Art Museum - 1964
Antique furniture; a nun's cell (1686); pewter - archives

02282
Maison Maillou
17 rue Saint-Louis, Québec, Québec G1R 3Y8
History/Public Affairs Museum - 1959
Furniture of the 18th century; military drums

02283
Musée de Québec
Parc des Champs de Bataille, Québec, Québec G1S 1C8
Fine Arts Museum - 1933
Coll: old, modern and contemporary art by Québec artists; works representing all schools of art from the 17th century to the present; furniture; applied and decorative arts - library

02284
Musée des Augustines de l'Hôpital Général de Québec
Monastère des Augustines, 260 bd Langelier, Québec, Québec G1K 5N1
Religious Art Museum - 1930
Paintings, sculpture, gildings and embroidery made by the Jesuits; goldsmith workshop

02285
Musée des Augustines de l'Hôtel-Dieu de Québec
32 rue Charlevoix, Québec, Québec G1R 3R9
History/Public Affairs Museum - 1958
Art and relics pertaining to the first hospital built in the Americas north of Mexico (1639); religious buildings

02286
Musée et Archives du Séminaire de Québec
6 rue de l'Université, CP 460, Québec, Québec G1R 5A6
General Museum - 1874
Paintings; goldsmith work; furniture; porcelain; numismatics; philately - archives

02287
Musée Royal 22e Régiment
La Citadelle Québec, Québec G1R 3R2
History/Public Affairs Museum - 1949
All sorts of military objects; guns, machine guns and canons; uniforms

02288
La Vielle Maison des Jesuites
2320 chemin des Foulons, Québec, Québec G1T 1X4
Religious Art Museum - 1926
Exhibits depicting the work of Jesuits in Québec; old books and engravings; Indian artifacts

Quesnel

02289
Quesnel Historical Museum
Carson Av, 405 Barlow, Quesnel, British Columbia V2J 2C3
General Museum - 1963
Local history; mining; Chinese and Indian artifacts

Rawdon

02290
Earle Moore's Canadiana Village
200 Lake Morgan Rd, Rawdon, 8455
Decarie Bd, Montréal, Québec H4P
2J3
History/Public Affairs Museum - 1970
Restored buildings from various
villages in Québec, furnished with
early Canadian furniture

Readlyn

02291
Thompson Museum
west of Readlyn, POB 40, Readlyn,
Saskatchewan S0H 3N0
History/Public Affairs Museum - 1955
Antique tractors and cars; historical
artifacts

Red Deer

02292
Red Deer and District Museum
45th St and 47A Av, POB 762, Red
Deer, Alberta T4N 5H2
General Museum - 1973
Local natural history; artifacts of native
peoples; agriculture; manufacturing;
trade; transport

Regina

02293
Diefenbaker Homestead House
mail c/o Wascana Centre Authority,
Public Health Bldg No 440, Broad St
and Lakeshore Dr, Regina,
Saskatchewan S4P 0N3
Historic Site - 1967
Restored boyhood home of Canada's
18th Prime Minister; memorabilia of
the family; pioneer artifacts

02294
Dunlop Art Gallery
mail c/o Regina Public Library,
2311-12 Av, Regina, Saskatchewan
S4P 0N3
Fine Arts Museum - 1946
Saskatchewan art; Canadian prints,
drawings, paintings and photographs

02295
Legislative Building Art Galleries
mail c/o Guide Service, Legislative
Building, Corner of Albert and 20th
Sts, Regina, Saskatchewan S4P 0N3
Fine Arts Museum - 1911
Coll: paintings of famous prairie
Indians; pencil sketches of outstanding
persons in Saskatchewan; portraits of
people formerly active in the
government

02296
Museum of Natural History
Wascana Park, Regina, Saskatchewan
S4P 3V7
Natural History Museum - 1955
Coll: Saskatchewan wildlife exhibits;
geology; paleontology; archeology;
human history; conservation; zoology

02297
Norman Mackenzie Art Gallery
University of Regina
Regina, Saskatchewan S4S 0A2
Fine Arts Museum - 1953
Coll: 15th to 19th century European
paintings; drawings and prints;
historical and contemporary Canadian
and American art - library

02298
R.C.M.P. Museum
'Depot' Division of R.C.M.P., POB 6500,
Regina, Saskatchewan S4P 3J7
History/Public Affairs Museum - 1933
Artifacts of the Mounted Police's
influence on the history of Canada

02299
Saskatchewan Arts Board
Centre of the Arts, 200 Lakeshore Dr,
Regina, Saskatchewan S4S 0A4
Fine Arts Museum - 1970
Works by contemporary
Saskatchewan artists (1950 to the
present)

02300
Saskatchewan Sports Hall of Fame
1915 South Railway St, Regina,
Saskatchewan S4P 0B1
History/Public Affairs Museum - 1967
Portraits of regional sports
personalities; sports items

02301
Telorama
2350 Albert St, Regina, Saskatchewan
S4P 2Y4
Science/Tech Museum - 1965
Communications history

Reston

02302
**Reston and District Historical
Museum**
POB 304, Reston, Manitoba R0M 1X0
History/Public Affairs Museum - 1967
Regional history - archives

Revelstoke

02303
Revelstoke Museum
1st St West, POB 410, Revelstoke,
British Columbia V0E 2S0
General Museum - 1964
Local history including lumbering,
mining, farming, railroading and early
settlement

Richibucto

02304
Richibucto River Museum
Old Post Office, Town Hall, Richibucto,
New Brunswick E0A 2M0
General Museum - 1968
Local history

Richmond

02305
Richmond Arts Centre
7671 Minoru Gate, 6911 No 3 Rd,
Richmond, British Columbia V6Y 2C1
General Museum - 1967
Local history; fishing and navigation;
aviation agriculture; religion; education

Richmond Hill

02306
Dunlap Observatory University of
Toronto
mail c/o David Dunlap Observatory,
Hillsview Drive, POB 360, Richmond
Hill, Ontario L4C 4Y6
Science/Tech Museum - 1935
Coll: astronomical research
photographs and spectograms
extending back 40 years - library

Rigaud

02307
Musée du Collège Bourget
65 rue Saint-Pierre, CP 1000, Rigaud,
Québec J0P 1P0
General Museum - 1885
Coll: mammalia, herpetology, marine
biology and other natural sciences;
paintings, sculpture and crafts;
weapons and war relics

Rimbey

02308
Pas-Ka-Poo Historical Park
Rimbey, mail c/o Alvin Goetz Bluffton,
Alberta T0C 0M0
Open Air Museum - 1967
Restored buildings including the first
church, school and town hall in Rimbey
- archives

Riverhurst

02309
F.T. Hill Museum
Riverhurst, Saskatchewan S0H 3P0
General Museum - 1967
Pioneer and Indian artifacts; fossils

Roblin

02310
Keystone Pioneer Museum
east of Roblin on Hwy No 5, POB 10,
Roblin, Manitoba R0L 1O0
Agriculture Museum - 1972
Agricultural equipment

Rocanville

02311
Rocanville and District Museum
Corner of Qu'Appelle Av and St.
Albert St, Rocanville, Saskatchewan
S0A 3L0
History/Public Affairs Museum - 1967
Steam and gas engines; machinery;
tools; pioneer furnishings

Rock Island

02312
Barn Museum
Lee Farm, USA Border, Hwy 143,
Rock Island, mail c/o Stanstead
Historical Society, 110 Main St, Beebe,
Québec J0B 1E0
Agriculture Museum - 1967
Farming equipment; handicraft tools;
exhibits related to pioneer life

Rockton

02313
Wentworth Pioneer Village
Hwy 52, north of Hwy 8, Rockton, mail
c/o Robert Mulholland, Regional
Municipality of Hamilton-Wentworth,
POB 910, Hamilton, Ontario L8N 3V9
Open Air Museum - 1964
Coll: various buildings recreating a mid
19th century rural community in
western Canada including a
blacksmith, harness, and printing and
bookbinding shop; general store;
locomotive; Indian log church

Rockwood

02314
**Ontario Electric Railway Historical
Association**
3 miles south of Rockwood, POB 121,
Station 'A', Scarborough, Ontario M1K
5B9
Science/Tech Museum - 1972
Operating electric railway exhibits
depicting the history of electric
railways in the 19th and 20th
centuries; street railway and
interurban equipment

Rocky Mountain House

02315
**Rocky Mountain House National
HIstoric Park**
POB 2130, Rocky Mountain House,
Alberta
History/Public Affairs Museum - 1970
Fur-trading history (1799-1875); Indian
artifacts

Rocky Point

02316
Fort Amherst National Historic Park
Rocky Point, mail c/o Parks Canada,
POB 487, Charlottetown, Prince
Edward Island C1A 7L1
General Museum - 1967
Social, political and military history of
the vicinity

Rossland

02317
Rossland Historical Museum
Hwy Junction at Rossland, POB 26,
Rossland, British Columbia V0G 1Y0
General Museum - 1967
Regional history; mining industry;
British Columbia Hall of Fame housing
trophies and equipment of Nancy
Green and Olans Jeldness

Rosthern

02318
Rosthern Cultural Museum
Rosthern, Saskatchewan
Religious Art Museum - 1963
German and Russian Mennonite
artifacts dating back to the 1890's

Saanichton

02319
Central Saanich Centennial Museum
POB 73, Saanichton, British Columbia
V0S 1M0
Agriculture Museum - 1967
Agricultural machinery and equipment

Sackville

02320
Owens Art Gallery Mount Allison
University
Sackville, New Brunswick E0A 3C0
Fine Arts Museum - 1893
Graphic arts

St. Albert

02321
Father Lacombe Museum
7 St. Vital Av, POB 98, St. Albert,
Alberta T8N 1N2
Religious Art Museum - 1927
Objects relating to Father A. Lacombe,
Bishop V. Grandin and other
missionaries; paintings; church
furniture; tools

St. Andrews

02322
Red River House Museum
north of junction of Hwys 238 and 410,
St. Andrews, 1705 Croydon Av,
Winnipeg, Manitoba R3N 0J9
Historic Site - 1968
Historic house of Capt. Kennedy, a
Hudson Bay Company fur trader and
arctic explorer; furniture and
furnishings; pictures, maps and
diagrams illustrating the history of
Manitoba

02323
St. Andrews Blockhouse
23 Joes Point Rd, Town Hall, St.
Andrews, New Brunswick E0G 2X0
Open Air Museum - 1967
Restored fortification of the War of
1812

St. Ann's

02324
**Giant Macaskill Highland Pioneers
Museum**
St. Ann's, POB 9, Baddeck, Nova
Scotia B0E 1B0
History/Public Affairs Museum - 1945
Relics of the Cape Breton giant Angus
Macaskill; history of Scottish pioneers
and of Reverend Norman MacLeod;
tartan weaving

St. Basile

02325
Chapel Museum
St. Basile Parish, POB 150, St. Basile,
New Brunswick E0L 1H0
General Museum - 1956
Local history and folklore

St. Boniface

02326
Musée de Saint Boniface
494, rue Tâché, St. Boniface, Manitoba
R2H 3B5
General Museum - 1967
Pioneer history; furnishings of French
Canadians

St. Catherines

02327
**Rodman Hall Art Centre and
National Exhibition Centre**
109 Saint Paul Crescent, St.
Catherines, Ontario L2S 1M3
Fine Arts Museum - 1960
Coll: 19th and 20th century Canadian
paintings, sculpture, prints, and
drawings; American and European art
- library

02328
Saint Catherines Historical Museum
343 Merritt St, St. Catherines, Ontario
L2T 1K7
General Museum - 1967
Coll: historical development of the
Welland Ship Canal; firefighting
equipment; arts and crafts; Indian
artifacts; agricultural and industrial
implements; domestic utensils - library

St. Claude

02329
St. Claude Museum
mail c/o Mr. E. Genest St. Claude,
Manitoba R0G 1Z0
History/Public Affairs Museum
History of the first settlers

St. George

02330
**Adelaide Hunter Hoodless
Homestead**
west of junction of Hwy 5 and 24 at St.
George, mail c/o Mrs. John Charleton,
Secretary, 5 Bayly Drive, Paris,
Ontario N3L 2R1
Historic Site - 1961
Birthplace of the founder of the
Federated Women's Institutes;
furnishings of the 1850-1881 period

St. Jacques

02331
Musée Automobile
Les Jardins, St. Jacques, mail c/o
Administration Branch, Dept. of
Historic Resources, POB 6000,
Fredericton, New Brunswick E3B 5H1
Science/Tech Museum - 1972
Automotive and other mechanical
inventions of the past seventy years

Saint John

02332
Barbour's General Store
King St East and Carmarthen, Dept. of
Economic Development, City Hall,
POB 1971, Saint John, New Brunswick
E2L 4L1
General Museum - 1967
Historical country store with original
furnishings (1867) and equipment; fully
equipped barber shop

02333
Loyalist House Museum
mail c/o New Brunswick Historical
Society, 120 Union St, Saint John,
New Brunswick E2L 1A3
Historic Site - 1960
Georgian mansion (1817) of a Loyalist
family, memorial to the Loyalists in
Canada

02334
New Brunswick Museum
277 Douglas Av, Saint John, New
Brunswick E2K 1E5
General Museum - 1842
Coll: ornithology; mammals; fish;
geology; paintings, especially works
by New Brunswick artists (19th-20th
c.); decorative art; history including
social history - archives; library

St. John's

02335
Maritime Museum and Gallery
Arts and Culture Center, Allandale Rd
and Prince Philip Drive, mail c/o
Newfoundland Museum, 287
Duckworth St, St. John's,
Newfoundland A1C 1G9
History/Public Affairs Museum - 1967
Marine items and photographs

02336
Memorial University Art Gallery
Arts and Culture Centre, Allandale Rd
and Prince Philip Drive, St. John's,
Newfoundland A1C 5S7
Fine Arts Museum - 1961
Contemporary Canadian art; early
Canadian and European art;

02337
Newfoundland Museum
287 Duckworth St, St. John's,
Newfoundland A1C 1G9
General Museum - 1849
History of early settlers; navigation;
whaling, cod and seal fishing; pulp-
and papermaking; aviation;
archeology; Viking, Beothuck and
Nascapi Indian ethnology; Eskimo
artifacts

02338
**Newfoundland Naval and Military
Museum**
Confederation Bldg, 11th floor, mail
c/o Newfoundland Museum, 281
Duckworth St, St. John's,
Newfoundland A1C 1G9
History/Public Affairs Museum - 1962
Naval and military history

02339
Port Au Choix National Historic Park
150 miles north of Deer Lake on the
Great Northern Peninsula, POB 5879,
St. John's, Newfoundland A1C 5X4
Archeology Museum - 1969
Maritime archaic Indian culture (2000
B.C.) including excavations from burial
grounds

02340
Signal Hill National Historic Park
Signal Hill, POB 5879, St. John's,
Newfoundland A1C 5X4
History/Public Affairs Museum - 1968
History of Newfoundland from the
early Vikings (ca 1000) to
Confederation with Canada in 1949

St. Joseph

02341
Musée St. Joseph
mail c/o M. Jean-Louis Perron, CP 47,
St. Joseph, Manitoba R0G 2C0
General Museum - 1977
Minerals; historic house with
furnishings (1915-1925); antiquities;
agricultural implements

Saint Joseph Island

02342
**Fort Saint Joseph National Historic
Park**
St. Joseph Island, POB 179, Richard's
Landing, Ontario
History/Public Affairs Museum - 1972
Ruins of a fort built after 1796 to serve
as a centre for the fur trade, British
military, and the Indian department in
the Upper Great Lakes

St. Martins

02343
Quaco Museum and Library
St. Martins, New Brunswick E0G 2Z0
General Museum - 1978
Historical artifacts; furnishings and
family treasures; lumbering and
farming implements; Indian artifacts -
archives

St. Mary's

02344
St. Mary's District Museum
177 Church St South, mail c/o Mrs.
Edna Fulcher, 130 Church St, St.
Mary's, Ontario N0M 2Y0
General Museum - 1959
Old stone house displays pioneer
women artifacts; antique furniture;
glassware; musical instruments; local
historical artifacts

St. Peters

02345
Nicolas Denys Museum
POB 249, St. Peters, Nova Scotia B0E
3B0
History/Public Affairs Museum - 1967
History of settlement (French including
Huguenots and Acadians, Micman
Indians, Scottish and Irish

St. Thomas

02346
Elgin County Pioneer Museum
32 Talbot St, St. Thomas, Ontario N5P
1A3
General Museum - 1957
Historic building (1848); first medical
school in Upper Canada (1824)

St. Viktor

02347
McGillis Museum
St. Viktor, Saskatchewan S0H 3T0
General Museum - 1972
Log home (1889); furnishings; Indian
and Métis artifacts

St. Walburg

02348
Imhoff Art Gallery
4 miles south, 1 mile west of St.
Walburg, POB 36, St. Walburg,
Saskatchewan S0M 2T0
Fine Arts Museum - 1920
Paintings by Berthold von Imhoff
(1914-1939)

St.-Constant

02349
Canadian Railway Museum
122A Saint-Pierre St, POB 148,
St.-Constant, Québec J0L 1X0
Science/Tech Museum - 1965
Steam and diesel locomotives;
streetcars; model railway; restored
railway station - library; archives

Ste.-Anne de Beaupré

02350
Musée Historial
Basilique Ste.-Anne, bd Ste.-Anne,
Ste.-Anne de Beaupré, Québec G0A
3C0
Religious Art Museum - 1957
Goldsmith work; 17th and 18th
century votive pictures; sculptures -
archives

Ste.-Foy

02351
Musée d'Anthropologie Université
Laval
Ste.-Foy, Québec G1K 7B4
Anthropology Museum - 1974
African items and instruments; South
American Indians; feather ornaments;
Inuit artifacts and clothes

St.-Hyacinthe

02352
**Musee du Seminaire de
St.-Hyacinthe**
450 rue Girouard, CP 370,
St.-Hyacinthe, Québec J2S 7B8
History/Public Affairs Museum - 1875
Coll: ornithology; entomology;
antiques of historical interest;
portraits; stamps; medals

St.-Jean

02353
Muse%oe du Fort St.-Jean
Collège militaire royal, Route 223,
St.-Jean, Québec J0J 1R0
History/Public Affairs Museum - 1966
History of Fort St.-Jean from 1666 to
the present; uniforms; weapons;
archeological discoveries

St.-Joseph de Sorel

02354
Muse%oe du Navigateur Flottant La
Goelette
425 rue Désiré, St.-Joseph de Sorel,
Québec J3I 3E2
History/Public Affairs Museum - 1977
Ship with displays of items once used
by seamen

St.-Paul, Ile-aux-Noix

02355
**Parc Historique National du Fort
Lennox**
St.-Paul, Ile-aux-Noix, Québec J0J 1G0
History/Public Affairs Museum - 1921
Various artifacts from Fort Lennox
such as weapons and ceramics;
several refurnished rooms

Salmon Arm

02356
Salmon Arm Museum and Archives
POB 1642, Salmon Arm, British
Columbia V0E 2T0
General Museum - 1962
Indian and pioneer material - films

Salvage

02357
Salvage Fisherman's Museum
Bishop Drive, Salvage, Newfoundland
A0B 5X0
General Museum - 1969
Local history; tools; ship and fishing
vessel equipment; household utensils
and furniture; crafts; firearms

Sangudo

02358
**Lac Ste. Anne and District Pioneer
Museum**
POB 186, Sangudo, Alberta T0E 2A0
General Museum - 1959
History; ethnology; farm equipment
and tools - archives

Sarnia

02359
Sarnia Public Library and Art Gallery
124 South Christina St, Sarnia, Ontario
N7T 2M6
Fine Arts Museum - 1903
Coll: Canadian paintings, prints, and
sculpture, mainly works of the 'Group
of Seven'; Eskimo carvings

Saskatoon

02360
Art Department Gallery University of
Saskatchewan
Room 181, Murray Memorial Bldg,
Saskatoon, Saskatchewan S7N 0W0
Fine Arts Museum - 1964
Locally organized and traveling
exhibitions of works of art

02361
Biology Museum University of
Saskatchewan
Dept. of Biology Saskatoon,
Saskatchewan S7N 0W0
Natural History Museum - 1969
Fossils; entomology; ornithology; live
animals

02362
Geological Museum University of
Saskatchewan
Dept. of Geological Sciences,
Saskatoon, Saskatchewan S7N 0W0
Natural History Museum - 1977
Fossils, including horse skeletons;
meteorites; rocks and minerals

02363
Memorial Library and Art Gallery
Nutana Collegiate Institute
411-11th St East, Saskatoon,
Saskatchewan S7N 0E9
History/Public Affairs Museum - 1925
Memorial to the collegiate students
who died in WW I; Canadian paintings
- library

02364
Mendel Art Gallery Saskatoon
Gallery and Conservatory Corporation
950 Spadina Crescent East, POB 569,
Saskatoon, Saskatchewan S7K 3L6
Fine Arts Museum - 1964
Coll: Canadian paintings, drawings,
sculpture, prints; Inuit sculpture and
prints

02365
**Museum and Archives of Ukrainian
Culture**
202 Av 'M' South, Saskatoon,
Saskatchewan S7M 2K4
Anthropology Museum - 1951
Coll: displays of the religious and
cultural-ethnic contributions of
Ukrainian immigrants to Canada;
handwork; religious articles - archives

02366
Photographers Gallery
234A Second Av South, Saskatoon,
Saskatchewan S7K 1K9
Fine Arts Museum - 1973
Contemporary Canadian photography

02367
St. Thomas More College Gallery
University of Saskatchewan
Saskatoon, Saskatchewan S7N 0W0
Fine Arts Museum - 1968
Traditional, impressionistic and
abstract art; photography

02368
Shoestring Gallery
220 3rd Av South, Saskatoon,
Saskatchewan S7K 1M1
General Museum - 1971
Paintings, graphics, ceramics and fibre
works of artists from the vicinity

02369
Ukrainian Museum of Canada
1240 Temperance St, Saskatoon,
Saskatchewan S7K 0P1
Anthropology Museum - 1941
Ukrainian heritage objects, especially
textiles - archives

02370
**University of Saskatchewan
Observatory**
Department of Physics, University of
Saskatchewan Saskatoon,
Saskatchewan S7N 0W0
Science/Tech Museum - 1929
Displays on astronomy; Watkins
telescope (1727), sentant and heliostat

02371
Western Development Museum
2610 Lorne Av South, POB 1910,
Saskatoon, Saskatchewan S7K 3S5
General Museum - 1949
Reconstruction of prairie town (1910);
pioneer artifacts; automobiles; farm
implements

02372
W.P. Fraser Herbarium University of
Saskatchewan
University of Saskatchewan Campus
Saskatoon, Saskatchewan S7N 0W0
Natural History Museum - 1925
Dried herbarium specimens of
vascular plants, especially of flora of
Saskatchewan and boreal and arctic
North America

Sault Sainte Marie

02373
Ermatinger Old Stone House
mail c/o Historic Sites Board, 831
Queen St East, POB 580, Sault Ste.
Marie, Ontario P6A 5N1
Historic Site - 1969
Oldest stone house west of Toronto
(1814); period furnishings; exhibits
describing the fur trade and local
historical events

02374
Museum Ship Norgoma
Former Canadian Steamship Line
Dock, *mail c/o* Mr. Harold Brain,
Secretary, Historical Board, POB 580,
Sault Sainte Marie, Ontario P6A 5N1
Science/Tech Museum - 1976
Motor ship Norgoma, 188 foot
passenger vessel built in 1950;
historical artifacts

Scarborough

02375
Cornell House
Thomson Memorial Park, Brinley Rd,
mail c/o Scarborough Historical
Society, POB 593, Station 'A',
Scarborough, Ontario M1K 5C4
General Museum - 1962
Historic house furnished to represent
the era of Scarborough's Centennial in
1896

Selkirk

02376
**Lower Fort Garry National Historic
Park**
POB 7, Selkirk, Manitoba R1A 2A8
General Museum - 1963
Coll: Government collection icluding
Euro-Canadian artifacts, fur trade,
development of Red River settlement,
ethnographic material; Hudson Bay
Company collection, mainly
ethnographic, including Athapaskan
and Algonquian beadwork and
quillwork

02377
Marine Museum of Manitoba
Selkirk Park, 6-305 Mercy Av, Selkirk,
Manitoba R1A 2A8
History/Public Affairs Museum - 1972
Marine history of the Red River and
Lake Winnipeg; fishing; two vessels
on land

Sept-Iles

02378
Musée des Sept-Iles
380 Dequen, Sept-Iles, Québec G4R
2O8
Archeology Museum - 1976
Archeology; antique furniture

Shandro

02379
**Historical Living Village and Pioneer
Museum**
Shandro, POB 147, Willingdon, Alberta
T0B 4R0
Open Air Museum - 1961
Furnished historical buildings, each
typifying one aspect of pioneer rural
living

Sharon

02380
Sharon Temple Museum
18062 Sutton Rd, Sharon, *mail c/o* Dr.
Edwin J. Hunt, 31 Lundy's Lane,
Newmarket, Ontario
Religious Art Museum - 1918
Wooden house built between
1825-1832 by the Children of Peace;
artifacts of this religious sect and the
York County area

Shaunavon

02381
Grand Coteau Museum
POB 1222, Shaunavon, Saskatchewan
S0N 2M0
General Museum - 1932
Natural history; archeology; Indian and
pioneer artifacts

Shawinigan

02382
Centre Culturel de Shawinigan
2100 rue Dessaules, Shawinigan,
Québec G9N 6V3
Fine Arts Museum - 1967
Paintings by local artists; photography

Sheguiandah

02383
**The Little Current-Howland
Centennial Museum**
Hwy 68, south of Little Current, *mail
c/o* Mr. George H. Bishop, RR 1,
Sheguiandah, Ontario P0P 1W0
General Museum
Indian artifacts; history of the pioneers
of Manitoulin Island following the
signing of the Treaty in 1862 permitting
white settlement

Shelburne

02384
Ross-Thompson House
Charlotte Lane, POB 39, Shelburne,
Nova Scotia B0T 1W0
History/Public Affairs Museum - 1957
History of the Loyalists; documents
relating to George and Robert Ross
and Robert Thompson

Sherbrooke

02385
**Centre Culturel et Artistique de
l'Académie de Ballet de Sherbrooke**
167 rue Marquette, Sherbrooke,
Québec J1H 1L6
Performing Arts Museum - 1948
Dance exhibits

02386
Galerie d'Art et Centre Culturel
Université de Sherbrooke
2500 bd Université, Sherbrooke,
Québec J1K 2R1
Fine Arts Museum - 1969
Paintings and engravings by Québec
artists

02387
Musée du Seminaire de Sherbrooke
195 rue Marquette, CP 790,
Sherbrooke, Québec J1H 5K8
Natural History Museum - 1974
Coll: natural history; ethnology;
archeology

Sherbrooke

02388
Sherbrooke Village
POB 285, Sherbrooke , Nova Scotia
B0J 3C0
Open Air Museum - 1971
Restoration of a lumbering and
goldmining town (1860-1890)

Shilo

02389
Royal Canadian Artillery Museum
Buildings C2 and C4, Canadian Forces
Base, Shilo, Manitoba R0K 2A0
History/Public Affairs Museum - 1962
Regimental history; uniforms; medals;
documents and technical books

Shoal Lake

02390
Spruce Haven Museum
Lakeside Park, mail c/o Historical
Society Shoal Lake, Manitoba R0J 1Z0
General Museum - 1970
Pioneer artifacts; prints and paintings;
shells, fossils, petrified wood

Sidney

02391
Sidney Museum
Old Customs House, 2538 Beacon Av,
Sidney, British Columbia V8L 1Y2
General Museum - 1971
Local history

Simcoe

02392
Eva Brook Donly Museum
109 Norfolk St South, Simcoe, Ontario
N3Y 2W3
General Museum - 1946
Brick house with Victorian and pioneer
furnishings; fossils; Indian artifacts;
Van Norman forge exhibit; local
history; paintings by Edgar Cantelon -
archives

Sioux Lookout

02393
Sarah Vaughan Library-Museum
5th Av, POB 1028, Sioux Lookout,
Ontario P0V 2T0
History/Public Affairs Museum - 1967
Early aviation artifacts; paintings by
Carl Roy; Indian crafts; pioneer
displays; replica of skis used by Byrd
on his South Pole exploration

Skidegate

02394
Queen Charlotte Islands Museum
Second Beach, Skidegate, British
Columbia
Anthropology Museum - 1976
Haida ethnology and archeology;
natural history; local history; totem
pole collection - photo archives

Sombra

02395
Sombra Township Museum
146 Saint Clair St, POB 99, Sombra,
Ontario N0P 2H0
General Museum - 1959
Exhibits pertaining to the Saint Clair
River; kitchen utensils; crafts; local
historical artifacts - library

Sooke

02396
Sooke Region Museum
POB 774, Sooke, British Columbia V0S
1N0
General Museum - 1977
Local history - archives

Souris

02397
Hillcrest Museum
26 Crescent East, POB 430, Souris,
Manitoba R0K 2C0
General Museum - 1967
Furnished period rooms (1912);
pioneer artifacts including tools and
toys; Indian artifacts

South Rawdon

02398
South Rawdon Museum
South Rawdon, RR 1, Mount Uniacke,
Nova Scotia B0N 1Z0
History/Public Affairs Museum - 1965
Early local crafts and trades; Victorian
costumes and furnishings

Springhill

02399
Springhill Miner's Museum
Black River Rd, Springhill, Nova Scotia
B0M 1X0
History/Public Affairs Museum - 1972
Mining history

Spy Hill

02400
**Wolverine Hobby and Historical
Society Museum**
mail c/o Mrs. George Barker, Main St
next to Community Hall, POB 187, Spy
Hill, Saskatchewan S0A 3W0
History/Public Affairs Museum - 1954
Local history exhibits; pioneer and
Indian artifacts; violins; early
gramophones

Squamish

02401
Squamish Valley Museum
2nd Av, Squamish, PoB 166, Garibaldi
Highlands, British Columbia V0N 1T0
General Museum - 1975
Pioneer and Indian artifacts; natural
history - archives

Stanbridge East

02402
Missisquoi Museum
2 River St, POB 186, Stanbridge East,
Québec J0J 2H0
General Museum - 1971
Coll: farm machinery; model Victorian
village; workshops of various trades;
Indian artifacts; handicrafts; antique
weapons - library

Steinbach

02403
Mennonite Village Museum
Hwy 12, north of Steinbach, POB,
Steinbach, Manitoba R0A 2A0
Open Air Museum - 1966
Reconstructed Mennonite village
including school, church, windmill,
blacksmith shop, printery; pioneer and
Mennonite artifacts - library; archives

Stellarton

02404
Stellarton Miners Museum
Allan Centennial Park, POB 2200,
Stellarton, Nova Scotia B0K 1S0
History/Public Affairs Museum - 1967
Underground mining

Stettler

02405
Stettler Town and Country Museum
44th Av West, POB 2118, Stettler,
Alberta T0C 2L0
Open Air Museum - 1974
Historic buildings with furnishings and
artifacts from pioneer days

Stewart

02406
Stewart Historical Museum
Columbia and 6th Av, POB 690,
Stewart, British Columbia V0T 1W0
History/Public Affairs Museum - 1975
Mining equipment; mineralogy; natural
history; pioneer items - archives

Stoney Creek

02407
Erland Lee Home
RR 1, Ridge Rd, Stoney Creek, mail
c/o Federated Women's Institute of
Canada, 1200 Bay St, 5th Floor,
Toronto, Ontario M5R 2A6
General Museum - 1972
Typical artifacts of a farm home
occupied through six generations;
relics of the 1900 era

Stony Plain

02408
Multicultural Heritage Centre
5411-51st St, POB 980, Stony Plain,
Alberta T0E 2G0
General Museum - 1974
Art; local history - library

Strasbourg

02409
Strasbourg and District Museum
C.P.R. Station, Railway Av, POB 446,
Strasbourg, Saskatchewan S0G 4V0
General Museum - 1973
Local pioneer and Indian artifacts;
mounted birds and animals indigenous
to Saskatchewan

Stratford

02410
The Gallery
54 Romeo St South, Stratford, Ontario
N5A 4S9
Fine Arts Museum - 1966
Coll: contemporary Canadian and
American prints and drawings;
sculpture - library

02411
Minnie Thomson Memorial Museum
138 Vivian St, Stratford, Ontario
Agriculture Museum - 1060
Coll: household items; antique
automobiles; farm machinery and
tractors; steam caliope (1897); steam
locomotive and coach

Strathroy

02412
Strathroy-Middlesex Museum
84 Oxford St, Strathroy, Ontario N7G
3A5
General Museum - 1971
Local history exhibits; period rooms;
computer room; tools

Sturgeon Falls

02413
Sturgeon River House Museum
Hwy 17 East, POB 1390, Sturgeon
Falls, Ontario P0H 2G0
Agriculture Museum - 1968
Artifacts pertaining to the furtrade;
local history

Sudbury

02414
**Laurentian University Museum and
Arts Centre**
mail c/o Dept. of Cultural Affairs, John
St off Paris-Drinkwater Overpass,
Sudbury, Ontario P3E 2C6
Fine Arts Museum - 1967
Coll: Canadian historical and
contemporary painting; sculpture;
graphics; Eskimo prints, sculpture, and
artifacts

Summerland

02415
Summerland Museum
Former Kettle Valley Railway Station
on Victoria Rd South, POB 1491,
Summerland, British Columbia V0H
1Z0
General Museum - 1976
Historical photos of pioneers and the
district; early 20th century archival
material; household utensils;
agricultural tools; railway history

Summerside

02416
**Eptek Centre, National Exhibition
Centre and Sports Hall of Fame**
130 Water St, POB 1378, Summerside,
Prince Edward Island
General Museum - 1978
Sports, temporary exhibits

Surrey

02417
Surrey Museum
17679-60th Av, POB 1006, Station 'A',
Cloverdale, Surrey, British Columbia
V3S 4P5
General Museum - 1958
Indian artifacts; pioneer furnishings -
archives

Sutton

02418
Communications Hall of Fame
72 Mountain St, POB 430, Sutton,
Québec J0E 2K0
Science/Tech Museum - 1967
Communication artifacts depicting
telegraph, telephone, radio, television,
printing and postal history

02419
Eildon Hall Sibbald Memorial Museum
Sibbald Point Provincial Park, RR 2,
Sutton, Ontario L0E 1R0
History/Public Affairs Museum - 1957
Pioneer home of the Sibbald family
(1837); portraits and military and naval
paraphernalia primarily of the Victorian
era

Swift Current

02420
Swift Current Museum
105 Chaplin St East, POB 1477, Swift
Current, Saskatchewan S9H 3X5
General Museum
Mounted animals indigenous to the
province; pioneer relics; rocks and
minerals - herbarium

02421
Wright Historical Museum
5 miles north of Swift Current on Hwy
No 4, POB 712, Swift Current,
Saskatchewan S9H 3W7
History/Public Affairs Museum - 1967
German WW II items including
uniforms, swords and concentration
camp material; pioneer and Indian
artifacts

Sydney

02422
St. Patrick's Church Museum
North Esplanade, POB 760, Sydney,
Nova Scotia B1P 6J1
General Museum - 1967
Local history; artifacts and pictures of
early Sydney; original steel rail;
clothes - library

Tadoussac

02423
Chapelle des Indiens
Tadoussac, Québec G0T 2A0
Religious Art Museum - 1747
Religious items; missal (1600); Virgin
Mary statue (1760); paintings; Indian
necklace

Tatamagouche

02424
Sunrise Trail Museum
Tatamagouche, Nova Scotia B0K 1V0
General Museum - 1958
Local history; artifacts of early settlers;
household and kitchen utensils;
farming

Tatla Lake

02425
Tatla Lake Centennial Museum
Tatla Lake, British Columbia V0L 1V0
Natural History Museum - 1967
Human history; natural history -
archives

Teeterville

02426
Windham Township Pioneer Museum
POB 45, Teeterville, Ontario N0E 1S0
General Museum - 1967
Agricultural implements; furnished
pioneer log cabin (1867) - archives

Teulon

02427
Teulon and District Museum
Owen Acres Park, *mail c/o* Ms. Mary
Revel Teulon, Manitoba R0C 3B0
History/Public Affairs Museum - 1976
Local history

The Pas

02428
Sam Waller Little Northern Museum
1359 Gordon Av, POB 185, The Pas,
Manitoba R9A 1K4
General Museum - 1958
Indian artifacts; mineralogy; natural
history; numismatics

Thunder Bay

02429
Centennial Park Logging Museum
Centennial Park Rd, *mail c/o* Division
of Parks and Recreation, City Hall
Annex Thunder Bay, Ontario P7E 5V3
Open Air Museum - 1967
Coll: restored typical local logging
camp (1910) including cookery,
bunkhouse, sauna, blacksmith's shop,
and stable; logging artifacts

02430
Old Fort William
mail c/o Vickers Heights Post Office,
King Rd, Thunder Bay, Ontario P0T
2Z9
Open Air Museum - 1973
Coll: reconstruction of Fort William as
it existed in 1816; a living historical
community, including a farm, cottages,
artisan's square, boat-building areas,
jail, and Council House - library

02431
Thunder Bay Historical Society
219 South May St, Thunder Bay,
Ontario P7E 1B5
History/Public Affairs Museum - 1953
Indian and pioneer artifacts; marine
and military items

Tillsonburg

02432
**Tillsonburg and District Historical
Museum**
8 Ross St, Tillsonburg, Ontario N4G
3N8
General Museum - 1972
Prints; clothing; displays pertaining to
local history

Tobermory

02433
**Peninsula and Saint Edmunds
Township Museum**
RR 1, Tobermory, Ontario N0H 2R0
General Museum - 1967
Local historical artifacts; dolls; tools;
furniture; underwater display

Tofield

02434
Tofield Historical Museum
Tofield Agricultural Complex, Tofield,
Alberta T0B 4J0
General Museum - 1962
Indian artifacts; agricultural tools and
implements; minute books; historic
Bibles

Toronto

02435
Art Gallery of Ontario
Grange Park, 317 Dundas St West,
Toronto, Ontario M5T 1G4
Fine Arts Museum - 1900
Coll: Italian 15th-18th century, Dutch
17th century, French 17th-20th
century, British 18th-20th century,
Canadian and American 19th-20th
century paintings, drawing, sculptures,
and prints; Henry Moore sculpture
and graphics - library

02436
The Art Works
50 Bleecker St, Toronto, Ontario M4X
1L8
Fine Arts Museum - 1976
Contemporary Canadian paintings,
sculptures, graphics

02437
Artists Co-operative Toronto Gallery
424 Wellington St West, Toronto,
Ontario M5V 1E3
Fine Arts Museum - 1974
Contemporary art, primarily of Toronto
artists

02438
Baycrest Heritage Museum
3560 Bathurst St, Toronto, Ontario
M6A 2E1
General Museum - 1972
Coll: Judaic ritual items; European and
Asian household furnishings;
sculpture; tapestry; paintings

02439
Beth Tzedec Museum
1700 Bathurst St, Toronto, Ontario
M5P 3K3
Religious Art Museum - 1962
Coll: silver, pewter, and bronze Judaic
objects; torah scroll ornaments in
silver and textiles; illuminated marriage
contracts (17th-19th centuries)

02440
Borough of York Museum
Borough of York Centennial Bldg,
2694 Eglinton Av West, *mail c/o*
Clerk's Dept, 2700 Eglinton Av West,
Toronto, Ontario M6M 1V1
General Museum - 1969
Coll: tools dating back to the pioneer
days in the Old Town of Weston and
vicinity; equipment used by the local
Police Department

02441
Campbell House
160 Queen St West, Toronto, Ontario
M5H 3H3
General Museum - 1974
Home of the Chief Justice of Upper
Canada (1822); furnishings of the
period; model of the Town of York in
1825

02442
**The Canadian Museum of Carpets
and Textiles**
585 Bloor St West, Toronto, Ontario
M6G 1K5
Decorative Arts Museum - 1975
Coll: Canadian hooked rugs; Central
Asian embroidery

02443
Centre for Contemporary Art
155A Roncesvalles Av, Toronto, Ontario
M6R 2L3
Fine Arts Museum - 1969
Contemporary paintings, prints, and
sculptures by Canadian artists

02444
**Centre for Experimental Art and
Communication**
15 Duncan St, Toronto, Ontario M5H
3H1
Fine Arts Museum - 1973
Canadian and international art in the
form of performances, discussions,
interviews and installations; artists'
books - archives

02445
Colborne Lodge
Colborne Lodge Rd, High Park, *mail
c/o* Toronto Historical Board, Stanley
Barracks, Exhibition Place, Toronto,
Ontario M6K 3C3
History/Public Affairs Museum - 1927
House built in 1836 by John Howard,
architect and engineer; original
furnishings; watercolor

02446
**Craven Foundation Automobile
Museum**
760 Lawrence Av West, Toronto,
Ontario M6A 1B8
History/Public Affairs Museum - 1972
Coll: 74 antique automobiles from 1901
to 1933; miniature automobiles from
the former Mortarini collection -
library

02447
Enoch Turner Schoolhouse
106 Trinity St, Toronto, Ontario M5A
3C6
History/Public Affairs Museum - 1971
School articles and textbooks of the
1800's

02448
Hart House
mail c/o University of Toronto Toronto,
Ontario M4S 1A1
Fine Arts Museum - 1919
Canadian art from 1919 to the present

02449
Historic Fort York
Garrison Rd, Strachan Av and Fleet St
West, *mail c/o* Toronto Historical
Board, Exhibition Park, Toronto,
Ontario M6K 3C3
Open Air Museum - 1934
Coll: eight original buildings (1813)
including barracks, officers' quarters,
and gunpowder magazines; uniforms;
military artifacts; displays depicting the
history of Toronto

02450
H.M.C.S. Haida
Ontario Place on Lakeshore Bd, *mail
c/o* Ontario Place Corporation, 955
Lakeshore Bd West, Toronto, Ontario
M6K 3B9
History/Public Affairs Museum
WW II and Korean War Royal
Canadian Navy destroyer

02451
Hockey Hall of Fame National
Hockey League
Exhibition Place, Toronto, Ontario M6K
3C3
History/Public Affairs Museum - 1961
Artifacts relevant to the history of
hockey; trophies; skates, sticks and
other instruments - library

02452
La Chasse-Galerie
204 Saint George St, Toronto, Ontario
Fine Arts Museum
Paintings and sculptures by Franco-
Canadian artists

02453
MacKenzie House
82 Bond St, *mail c/o* Toronto Historical
Board, Stanley Barracks, Exhibition
Park, Toronto, Ontario M6K 3C3
Historic Site - 1946
Home of William MacKenzie, Toronto's
first Mayor and leader of the rebellion
of 1837; furnishings and memorabilia
of the period from 1820-1860

02454
Marine Museum of Upper Canada
Exhibition Place, near Prince's Gate,
mail c/o Toronto Historical Board,
Stanley Barracks, Exhibition Park,
Toronto, Ontario M6K 3C3
History/Public Affairs Museum - 1960
History of shipping and transportation
of the Great Lakes-Saint Lawrence
region; exhibits describing the role of
inland waterways in defence and fur
trade settlement through the days of
paddle, sail, and steam

02455
Museum of the History of Medicine
288 Bloor St West, Toronto, Ontario
M5S 1V8
History/Public Affairs Museum - 1977
Coll: instruments, drugs, and other
artifacts depicting the history of
medical practice in Ontario from the
pioneer days up to the present;
pediatric collection of Dr. Theodore
Drake; rare books

02456
Ontario Crafts Council
346 Dundas St West, Toronto, Ontario
M5T 1G5
Decorative Arts Museum - 1976
Canadian crafts

02457
Patmos Gallery
406 King St East, Toronto, Ontario
M5A 1L4
Fine Arts Museum - 1971
Exhibitions of the works of young
local, Canadian and American artists

02458
**Queen's Own Rifles of Canada
Regimental Museum**
Casa Loma, 1 Austin Terrace, Toronto,
Ontario M4P 2B9
History/Public Affairs Museum - 1970
Artifacts pertaining to the regiment's
activities in times of war and peace;
medals; weapons

02459
Royal Ontario Museum
100 Queen's Park, Toronto, Ontario
M5S 2C6
General Museum - 1912
Greek, Roman, Near and Far Eastern,
European and Canadian art and
applied art; Chinese art and
archeology; ethnology esp. of
American Indians; North American
archeology; entomology; invertebrate
zoology; geology; ichthyology and
herpetology; invertebrate
paleontology; mammalogy; mineralogy;
ornithology; vertebrate paleontology;
music; philately; Canadian textiles and
costumes - library

02460
Scadding Cabin
Canadian National Exhibition Grounds,
Toronto, *mail c/o* Ms. Lina E. Yates,
139 Botany Hill Rd, Scarborough,
Ontario M1G 3K6
General Museum - 1879
Log cabin (1794) containing
furnishings and household utensils of
the period

02461
Todmorden Mills Museum
67 Pottery Rd, 550 Mortimer Av,
Toronto, Ontario M4J 2H2
General Museum - 1967
Local history - archives

02462
Ukrainian Museum of Canada
Eastern Canada Branch
620 Spadina Av, Toronto, Ontario M5S
2H4
Anthropology Museum - 1944
Textiles and costumes; wooden
artifacts; ethnographical books

Tracadie

02463
Musée Historique de Tracadie
rue du Couvent, Académie Sainte-
Famille, CP 1221, Tracadie, New
Brunswick E0C 2B0
History/Public Affairs Museum - 1968
Medical and pharmaceutical
equipment

Trinity

02464
Trinity Museum and Archives
POB 54, Trinity, Newfoundland A0C
2S0
General Museum - 1967
History of early settlers; sealing and
whaling; shipbuilding; sports; English
fire engine (1731) - archives

Trois-Rivières

02465
Musée d'Archéologie Préhistorique
CP 500, Trois-Rivières, Québec G9H
5A5
Archeology Museum - 1963
Coll: prehistoric objects found in the
Mauricie, Lac Abitibi, Lotbinière and
Lanoraie regions; prehistoric items
found in southern France (paleolithic
to Iron Age)

02466
Musée des Ursulines
784 rue Des Ursulines, Trois-Rivières,
Québec G9A 5B5
History/Public Affairs Museum - 1896
Coll: historic and prehistoric relics;
items made at the old forges of Saint
Maurice (1735); sculpture; paintings;
porcelain; embroidery

02467
Musee Pierre Boucher
Séminaire St-Joseph, 858 rue
Laviolette, Trois-Rivières, Québec G9A
1V8
Religious Art Museum - 1934
Exhibits describing the life and
livelihood of the 'petite patrie'; the
forges of Saint Maurice; agricultural
and navigational displays

02468
**Parc Historique National des Forges
du Saint-Maurice**
10150 bd des Forges, Trois-Rivières,
Québec G0X 2X0
History/Public Affairs Museum - 1973
Reproductions of paintings; exhibits of
objects made in forges

02469
Pavillon Saint-Arnaud
Parc Pie XXII, CP 1383, Trois-Rivières,
Québec G9A 5L2
Decorative Arts Museum - 1955
Coll: batiks; gouaches; pottery;
enamels; embroidery

Truro

02470
Colchester Historical Museum
29 Young St, POB 412, Truro, Nova
Scotia
General Museum - 1976
Local history including agriculture,
forestry, shipbuilding, railroading and
education; Micmac Indian culture -
archives

Twillingate

02471
Twillingate Museum
POB 356, Twillingate, Newfoundland
A0G 4M0
General Museum - 1971
Victorian period furniture; medical
instruments; guns; printing press
(1834); Dorset Eskimo and Beothuck
Indian artifacts

Upper Woodstock

02472
Old Carleton County Court House
Upper Woodstock, *mail c/o* Carleton
County Historical Society Woodstock,
New Brunswick E0J 2B0
History/Public Affairs Museum - 1967
Site of the first county council in New
Brunswick (1833); local history

Uxbridge

02473
**Uxbridge-Scott Historical Society
Museum**
mail c/o Ms. Isobel St. John, RR 3,
Uxbridge, Ontario L0C 1K0
General Museum - 1971
Local folklore; Quaker memorabilia;
local papers (1870-1930); local
industries

Valcout

02474
Musée J. Armand Bombardier
1000 rue J.A. Bombardier, CP 370,
Valcout, Québec J0E 2L0
Science/Tech Museum - 1971
Exhibits illustrating M. Bombardier's
industrial life; equipment essential to
the industry's development; wooden
vehicles

Vancouver

02475
**British Columbia Congenital Heart
Museum** University of British
Columbia, Dept. of Paediatrics, Faculty
of Medicine
865 West 10th Av, 715 West 12th Av,
Vancouver, British Columbia V5Z 1M9
Natural History Museum - 1967
Specimens of human hearts with
congenital heart defects

02476
**British Columbia Museum of
Medicine**
Academy of Medicine Bldg, 1807 West
10th Av, Vancouver, British Columbia
V6J 2A9
Science/Tech Museum - 1965
Shaman medicine artifacts of the
Northwest Coast Indians;
pre-Columbia healing figures; African
medical instruments; eye glasses;
surgical instruments from the
battlefield of World War I; 19th and
20th century pharmacy equipment;
x-ray equipment (1914) - archives

02477
**British Columbia Sports Hall of Fame
and Museum**
British Columbia Pavillion, Exhibition
Park, POB 69020, Station 'K',
Vancouver, British Columbia V5K 4W3
Anthropology Museum - 1965
Sports

02478
Cowan Vertebrate Museum
University of British Columbia, Dept. of
Zoology
Vancouver, British Columbia V6T 1W5
Natural History Museum - 1960
Specimens of mammals, birds, reptiles
and amphibians

02479
Ichthyological Collection University
of British Columbia, Institute of
Resource Ecology
Vancouver, British Columbia V6T 1W5
Natural History Museum - 1953
Preserved fish; skeletons; fossils

02480
Museum of Anthropology University
of British Columbia
6393 Northwest Marine Drive,
Vancouver, British Columbia V6T 1W5
Anthropology Museum - 1948
Ethnography; archeology

02481
M.Y. Williams Geological Museum
University of British Columbia
Geological Science Centre,
Vancouver, British Columbia V6T 1W5
Natural History Museum - 1924
Minerals; ore deposits; paleontology;
petrology

02482
Old Hastings Mill Store Museum
Alma Rd and Jericho Beach, 1575
Alma Rd, Vancouver, British Columbia
V6R 3P3
General Museum - 1931
Mill store (1865); pioneer and Indian
artifacts; furniture and furnishings;
textiles; maps and pictures

02483
**Seaforth Highlanders Regimental
Museum**
Seaforth Armoury, 1650 Burrard St,
Vancouver, British Columbia V6J 3G4
History/Public Affairs Museum - 1972
Artifacts, documents and photos
relating to Seaforth Highlanders and
affiliated regiments; uniforms;
weapons

02484
Spencer Entomological Collection
University of British Columbia, Dept. of
Zoology
Vancouver, British Columbia V6T 1W5
Natural History Museum - 1953
Insects

02485
Ukrainian Museum of Canada B.C.
Branch
154 East 10th Av, 102-1540 West 15th
Av, Vancouver, British Columbia V6J
2K6
History/Public Affairs Museum - 1957
Ukrainian costumes; textiles; ceramics;
woodcarvings; embroidery and
embroidery patterns - archives

02486
Vancouver Art Gallery
1145 West Georgia St, Vancouver,
British Columbia V6E 3H2
Fine Arts Museum - 1931
Canadian paintings and graphics;
works by Emily Carr (1871-1945);
modern American prints; British
watercolors; British paintings
(18th-20th c.)

02487
Vancouver Centennial Museum
Vanier Park, 1100 Chestnut St,
Vancouver, British Columbia V6J 3J9
General Museum - 1968
Indian archeology; historical material
relating to Indians, explorers, fur
traders and pioneers; natural history

02488
Vancouver Maritime Museum
Vanier Park at foot of Cypress St,
1905 Ogden St, Vancouver, British
Columbia V6J 3J9
History/Public Affairs Museum - 1959
Maritime history including models,
uniforms, paintings, photographs,
documents, engines, tools,
communications equipment, fishing
gear - archives

Vaudreuil

02489
Musée des Sciences Naturelles
Pavillon Vaudreuil, Cité des Jeunes,
Vaudreuil, Québec J7V 6B1
Natural History Museum - 1972
Coll: mammalia; ornithology;
herpetology; ichthyology; entomology;
mollusks; minerals; fossils; plants

02490
Musée Historique de Vaudreuil
431 bd Roche, Vaudreuil, CP 121,
Dorion, Québec J7V 5W1
Decorative Arts Museum - 1965
Coll: paintings, sculpture and
engravings; armory and locksmith
items; costumes, textiles and
tapestries; furniture; applied arts

Verdun

02491
Centre Culturel de Verdun
4555 av Verdun, Verdun, Québec H4G
1M4
Fine Arts Museum - 1967
Paintings; sculptures; theatre exhibits

Veregin

02492
Doukhoubor Society Museum
Veregin, Saskatchewan S0A 4H0
General Museum - 1969
Tools; handcrafts; costumes and
literature pertaining to Doukhoubor
history

Vernon

02493
O'Keefe Ranch
8 miles north of Vernon on Hwy No
97, POB 955, Vernon, British Columbia
V1T 6M8
Open Air Museum - 1965
Historic ranch (1867); furnishings; farm
equipment

02494
Vernon Museum
3009-32nd Av, Vernon, British
Columbia V1T 2L8
General Museum - 1955
Indian and pioneer artifacts; natural
history - archives

Vernon

02495
Osgoode Township Museum
POB 83, Vernon , Ontario K0A 3J0
General Museum - 1974
Local history; clothing; agricultural
tools; family bibles and books; old
machinery

Victoria

02496
Art Gallery of Greater Victoria
1040 Moss St, Victoria, British
Columbia V8V 4P1
Fine Arts Museum - 1951
Canadian art (1860-present);
contemporary art of British Columbia;
prints and drawings from Europe,
North America and Japan; decorative
arts and textiles; Japanese and
Chinese ceramics

02497
**British Columbia Forest Service
Museum**
mail c/o Information Div, Ministry of
Forests, Legislative Bldgs, Victoria,
British Columbia V8V 1X5
Agriculture Museum - 1951
Forestry; historical books and tools

02498
British Columbia Mineral Museum
mail c/o Ministry of Mines and
Petroleum Resources, Parliament
Buildings, Victoria, British Columbia
V8V 1X4
Natural History Museum - 1896
Rocks and minerals; petrology;
geology

02499
British Columbia Provincial Museum
675 Belleville St, Victoria, British
Columbia V8V 1X4
General Museum - 1886
Natural history; human history
including modern history, ethnology,
archeology and Indian linguistics

02500
Emily Carr Arts Centre
207 Government St, Victoria, British
Columbia V8V 2K8
Fine Arts Museum - 1972
Birthplace of Emily Carr (1871-1945);
reproductions of her paintings;
personal articles and letters

02501
Fort Rodd Hill National Historic Park
501 Belmont Rd, Victoria, British
Columbia V9C 1B5
Open Air Museum - 1966
Coastal artillery installation (1895);
lighthouse (1860); historic photographs

02502
Helmcken House Historical Museum
mail c/o Provincial Archives,
Parliament Buildings, Victoria, British
Columbia V8V 1X4
History/Public Affairs Museum - 1941
Furniture (1860); medical instruments
of Dr. J.S. Helmcken

02503
Maltwood Art Museum and Gallery
University of Victoria
University Campus, POB 1700,
Victoria, British Columbia V8W 2Y2
Fine Arts Museum - 1977
Katherine Maltwood collection; British
Columbia art; decorative arts;
paintings; sculpture; graphics;
archeology; costumes; glass; textiles;
ceramics; furniture - library

02504
**Maritime Museum of British
Columbia**
28 Bastion Square, Victoria, British
Columbia V8W 1H9
History/Public Affairs Museum - 1955
Maritime history including models,
documents and pictures - library;
photographic archives

02505
Point Ellice House Museum
2616 Pleasant St, Victoria, British
Columbia V8T 4V3
History/Public Affairs Museum - 1968
Victorian and Edwardian furniture and
furnishings

02506
Thunderbird Park
Belleville and Douglas Sts, mail c/o
British Columbia Provincial Museum,
601 Belleville St, Victoria, British
Columbia V8V 1X4
Open Air Museum - 1940
Ethnology; Kwaikiut dance house,
poles and carvings of coastal tribes

Viking

02507
Viking Historical Museum
5024-58th Av, POB 232, Viking, Alberta
T0B 4N0
History/Public Affairs Museum - 1967
Local history; land maps of the area
and photographs

Ville des Laurentides

02508
Maison Sir Wilfred Laurier
205 12e av Laurier, CP 70, Ville des
Laurentides, Québec J0R 1C0
History/Public Affairs Museum - 1941
Restored house, furnished in the style
of the period from 1840-1950

Ville Saint-Laurent

02509
Musée d'Art de Saint-Laurent
625 boulevard Sainte-Croix, Ville Saint-
Laurent, Québec H4L 3X7
Fine Arts Museum - 1962
Coll: 18th and 19th century works of
art and artifacts; prehistoric items;
American Indian artifacts; Québec art
and cultural exhibits

Virden

02510
**Pioneer Home Museum of Virden
and Districts**
390 King St West, POB 807, Virden,
Manitoba R0M 2C0
Historic Site - 1969
Historic brick house (1888) furnished
in Victorian style

Wasaga Beach

02511
Museum of the Upper Lakes Nancy
Island Historic Site
mail c/o Wasaga Beach Provincial
Park, Mosley St, POB 183, Wasaga
Beach, Ontario L0L 2P0
History/Public Affairs Museum - 1969
Remains of the British Schooner
Nancy; marine aspects of the War of
1812; replica of an early Upper Lakes
lighthouse

Waskada

02512
Waskada Museum
mail c/o Ms. H. Lowe, Railway Av,
POB 59, Waskada, Manitoba R0M 2E0
Historic Site - 1967
Historic house; local history

Waterloo

02513
Arts Centre Gallery University of
Waterloo
Modern Languages Bldg Waterloo,
Ontario N2L 3G1
Fine Arts Museum - 1962
Contemporary Canadian art;
international works of art

02514
Biology-Earth Sciences Museum
University of Waterloo
Biology Bldg, Waterloo, Ontario N2L
3G1
Natural History Museum - 1968
Coll: ornithology; minerals; fossils;
dinosaur display; African game heads

02515
Museum and Archives of Games
415 Philip St, mail c/o University of
Waterloo Waterloo, Ontario N2L 3G1
History/Public Affairs Museum - 1973
Artifacts depicting the history and
development of games throughout the
world - archives

02516
Optometry Museum University of
Waterloo
Optometry Bldg, Columbia St
Waterloo, Ontario N2L 3G1
Science/Tech Museum - 1974
Early instruments; antique spectacles;
documents on optometry; visual
science and optics

Wawa

02517
Agawa Bay Exhibition Centre
Agawa Campground, 58 miles south of
Wawa on Hwy 17, mail c/o District
Manager, Ministry of Natural
Resources, POB 1160, Wawa, Ontario
P0S 1K0
Natural History Museum - 1965
Mounted mammals, reptiles, birds, and
butterflies

Weekes

02518
Dunwell and Community Museum
Weekes Centennial Community Hall,
POB 120, Weekes, Saskatchewan S0E
1V0
General Museum - 1971
Local pioneer artifacts representing
several countries of origin

Welland

02519
Welland Historical Museum
654 South Pelham St, POB 412,
Welland, Ontario
General Museum - 1977
Local historical artifacts; displays
related to the Welland Canal; Indian,
military, and pioneer relics

Wellington

02520
**Wellington Community Historical
Museum**
Main St, POB 55, Wellington, Ontario
K0K 3L0
General Museum - 1967
Local history; glass; stamps; farm
implements

Wells

02521
Wells Museum and Sunset Theatre
Pooley St, POB 107, Wells, British
Columbia V0K 2R0
General Museum - 1975
Local historical artifacts; mining

Welshpool

02522
**Campobello Island Public Library
and Museum**
Campobello Island, Welshpool, New
Brunswick E0G 3H0
History/Public Affairs Museum
History of Campobello Island and the
early settlers; items pertaining to the
late President Rooosevelt, who spent
his summers on Campobello Island

02523
**Roosevelt Campobello International
Park**
Campobello Island, Welshpool, New
Brunswick E0G 3H0
Historic Site - 1964
Summer home and furnishings of
Franklin Delano Roosevelt

Wesleyville

02524
**Bonavista North Regional Memorial
Museum**
mail c/o Wesleyville Museum
Committee Wesleyville, Newfoundland
A0G 4R0
Fine Arts Museum - 1976
Fine and decorative arts

Westport

02525
Rideau District Museum
Bedford St, Westport, Ontario K0G
1X0
History/Public Affairs Museum - 1961
Pioneer history

Wetaskiwin

02526
Reynolds Museum
4202-57 St, POB 6780, Wetaskiwin,
Alberta T9A 2G4
Science/Tech Museum - 1955
Antique and vintage cars and trucks;
gas tractors; steam engines; gas
engines; fire engines; airplanes;
carriages; motorcycles; sleighs

Weyburn

02527
Allie Griffin Gallery
mail c/o Weyburn Arts Council, 45
Bison Av, POB 1178, Weyburn,
Saskatchewan
Fine Arts Museum - 1970
Realistic art by contemporary artists

02528
Soo Line Historical Museum
411 Industrial Lane, Hwy 39 East, POB
1016, Weyburn, Saskatchewan S4H
2L2
General Museum - 1960
Pioneer and Indian artifacts; farm and
household items; musical instruments

Whitby

02529
Whitby Arts 'Station' Gallery
Henry and Victoria St West, POB 124,
Whitby, Ontario L1N 5R7
Fine Arts Museum - 1970
Historical and contemporary prints
and drawings; contemporary sculpture

White Rock

02530
**City of White Rock Museum and
Archives**
Burlington Northern Railway Station,
14970 Marine Drive, White Rock,
British Columbia V4B 1C4
History/Public Affairs Museum
Regional history - archives

Whitehorse

02531
MacBride Centennial Museum
1st Av and Wood St, POB 4037,
Whitehorse, Yukon Territory Y1A 3S9
History/Public Affairs Museum - 1967
Prehistoric items; Klondike Gold Rush;
pioneer articles; wildlife display

02532
S.S. 'Klondike'
2nd Av and South Access, mail c/o
Parks Canada, No 227, 220 Range Rd,
Whitehorse, Yukon Territory Y1A 3V1
History/Public Affairs Museum - 1971
Restored sternwheeler, one of a
limited number of such vessels, built to
serve transportation purposes on the
Yukon River

Whitemouth

02533
Whitemouth Municipal Museum
Whitemouth Community Grounds,
POB 187, Whitemouth, Manitoba R0E
2G0
General Museum - 1974
Agricultural equipment; blacksmith
shop; pioneer farm artifacts

Williams Lake

02534
Williams Lake Museum
Cariboo Hwy South, mail c/o Reg
Beck, RR No 2, Fox Mountain, Williams
Lake, British Columbia V2G 2P2
General Museum - 1967
Ranching; mining; Shuswap Indian,
Chilcotin and Chinese artifacts -
archives

Willowdale

02535
Gibson House
5172 Yonge St, Willowdale, Ontario
M2N 5P6
History/Public Affairs Museum - 1971
Local history

Windsor

02536
Art Gallery of Windsor
445 Riverside Drive West, Windsor,
Ontario N9A 6T8
Fine Arts Museum - 1943
Paintings, drawings, prints, sculpture
and graphic arts, especially Canadian
art; Inuit art; European 17th century
paintings; Japanese prints (18th-20th
c.)

02537
Haliburton House
Windsor, mail c/o Nova Scotia
Museum, 1747 Summer St, Halifax,
Nova Scotia B3H 3A6
General Museum - 1940
Original Victorian furnishings

02538
Hiram Walker Historical Museum
254 Pitt St West, Windsor, Ontario
N9A 5L5
General Museum - 1958
Arts and crafts of the pioneers;
agricultural implements; furniture;
Indian artifacts; local history -
archives

02539
**Southwestern Ontario Heritage
Village**
County Rd 23, south of Essex, mail c/o
Historic Vehicle Society, POB 788,
Windsor, Ontario N9A 4H7
Open Air Museum - 1974
Historic village including original King
house from Kingsville and station from
Tecumseh

Wingham

02540
**Wingham and District Historical
Museum**
Josephine St, mail c/o Secretary,
Wingham District Heritage and History
Society, POB 586, Wingham, Ontario
N0G 2W0
General Museum - 1977
Pioneer history; paintings of the late
George A. Reid; artifacts from the
early days of a radio and television
station

Winnipeg

02541
**Aquatic Hall of Fame and Museum of
Canada**
Pan-Am Pool, 25 Poseidon Bay, 436
Main St, Winnipeg, Manitoba R3B 1B2
History/Public Affairs Museum - 1967
Aquatic sports - archives

02542
**Fort Garry Horse Regimental
Museum**
McGregor Armoury, Winnipeg,
Manitoba R2W 1A8
History/Public Affairs Museum - 1976
Regimental history including archival
material

02543
Gallery III School of Art, University of
Manitoba
Winnipeg, Manitoba R3T 2N2
Fine Arts Museum - 1965
Contemporary Canadian, American
and European paintings, prints,
drawings and sculptures

02544
**Historical Museum of St. James-
Assiniboia**
3180 Portage Av, Winnipeg, Manitoba
R3K 0Y5
General Museum - 1971
Indian and Eskimo artifacts; pioneer
history

02545
Ivan Franko Museum
603 Pritchard Av, 595 Pritchard Av,
Winnipeg, Manitoba R2W 2K4
Historic Site - 1956
Documents on the life and work of the
Ukrainian writer, poet and statesman
Ivan Franko (1856-1916), including
photocopies of manuscripts; Ukrainian
costumes and embroidery

02546
MacDonald House Museum
61 Carlton St, Winnipeg, Manitoba
R3C 1N7
Historic Site - 1974
House of Hugh John MacDonald with
furniture and furnishings (1840-1905);
English, Canadian, American, Chinese
and German artifacts

02547
**Manitoba Museum of Man and
Nature**
Centennial Centre, 555 Main St, 190
Rupert Av, Winnipeg, Manitoba R3B
0N2
General Museum - 1970
Anthropology; archeology; history;
textiles and costumes; ethnology;
geology; herpetology; entomology;
biology; mineralogy; natural history;
paleontology - herbarium; planetarium

02548
Mineralogy Museum University of
Manitoba, Dept of Earth Sciences
Winnipeg, Manitoba R3T 2N2
Natural History Museum - 1922
Mineralogical specimens

02549
**Queen's own Cameron Highlanders
Museum**
Room 219, Minto Armoury, 969 St.
Matthew's St, Winnipeg, Manitoba
R3G 0J7
History/Public Affairs Museum - 1973
Regimental uniforms and equipment
(1910-present)

02550
Royal Winnipeg Rifles Museum
Room 208 , Minto Armoury, 969 St.
Matthew's Av, Winnipeg, Manitoba
R3G 0J7
History/Public Affairs Museum - 1970
Weapons; medals; bagdes; uniforms;
pictures

02551
St. Volodymyr Ukrainian Catholic Center Museum
418 Aberdeen Av, Winnipeg, Manitoba R2W 1V7
Religious Art Museum - 1967
Church artifacts icluding religious books, icons, crosses, vestments, candleholders; Ukrainian embroidery, woodcarving, ceramics, costumes, paintings

02552
Seven Oaks House Museum
Rupertsland Av, 1760 Main St, West Kildonan, Winnipeg, Manitoba R2V 1Z7
Historic Site - 1976
Historic house (1851) with furniture and household articles, period furnishings

02553
Sounds of Yesteryear
71 De Bourmont Bay, Winnipeg, Manitoba R2J 1K2
Music Museum - 1974
Antique automatic musical istruments including player pianos, nickelodians, orchestrions, music boxes

02554
Transcona Regional History Museum
1121 Wabasha St, 401 Pandora Av West, Winnipeg, Manitoba R2C 1M7
General Museum - 1968
Archeology; ethnology; entomology; local history

02555
Ukrainian Arts and Crafts Museum
1175 Main St, Winnipeg, Manitoba R2W 3S4
Decorative Arts Museum - 1954
Ukrainian national costumes and embroidery; tapestries; ceramics and woodwork

02556
Ukrainian Cultural and Educational Centre
184 Alexander Av, Winnipeg, Manitoba R3C 2K3
General Museum - 1944
Fine and decorative art; history of the Ukrainians in Canada and the Ukrainian Nationalist Movement

02557
Ukrainian Free Academy of Sciences Historical Museum
202-456 Main St, Winnipeg, Manitoba R3B 0N2
History/Public Affairs Museum - 1970
History; ethnology - archives

02558
Western Canada Aviation Museum
Room 215, 190 Rupert Av, POB 99, Station 'C', Winnipeg, Manitoba R3M 3S6
Science/Tech Museum - 1974
Civil and military aircraft - archives

02559
Winnipeg Art Gallery
300 Memorial Boulevard, Winnipeg, Manitoba R3C 1V1
Fine Arts Museum - 1912
Canadian contemporary art; Canadian paintings and prints (19th-20th c.); Eskimo sculpture and prints; Gothic panel painting (15th-16th c.); English porcelain, silver and glass (18th-19th c.)

02560
Zoology Museum University of Manitoba, Dept of Zoology
Duff Roblin Bldg, Winnipeg, Manitoba R3T 2N2
Natural History Museum - 1960
Mammals; birds; fish; reptiles; amphibians; crustaceans; mollusks; casts of fossils; snakes

Wolfville

02561
Acadia University Art Gallery
POB 1269, Wolfville, Nova Scotia B0P 1X0
Fine Arts Museum - 1838
20th century Canadian drawings; maritime paintings; Eskimo sculpture; Southeast Asian and African ethnography

02562
Wolfville Historical Museum
Main St beside William Park, POB 460, Wolfville, Nova Scotia B0P 1X0
History/Public Affairs Museum - 1941
Historic mansion (built 1815-16) with original period furniture and kitchen utensils; toys; portraits

Wood Mountain

02563
Wood Mountain Historic Park
3 miles south of Wood Mountain, *mail c/o* Supervisor Historic Parks, Dept of Culture and Youth, 11th floor Avord Tower, Regina, Saskatchewan S4P 0M8
History/Public Affairs Museum - 1965
Artifacts of the North West Mounted Police and Sioux Indians (c. 1885)

Woodbridge

02564
Kortright Centre Museum
Pine Valley Drive, Woodbridge, 5 Shoreham Drive, Downsview, Ontario M3N 1S4
Science/Tech Museum - 1978
Management of the renewable natural resources land, water, forest and wildlife

Woodstock

02565
Oxford Museum
City Square, Woodstock, Ontario N4S 1C4
General Museum
Local history; natural history

Wynyard

02566
Frank Cameron Museum
POB 734, Wynyard, Saskatchewan S0A 4T0
History/Public Affairs Museum - 1974
Farm and household articles; WW I material; handcar with rails and ties

Yarmouth

02567
Firefighters' Museum of Nova Scotia and National Exhibition Centre
451 Main St, Yarmouth, Nova Scotia B5A 1G9
History/Public Affairs Museum - 1968/1974
Firefighting history - library

02568
Yarmouth County Historical Society Museum
22 Collins St, Yarmouth, Nova Scotia B5A 3C8
General Museum - 1958
Ship models and ship portraits; paintings; dolls; musical istruments; period rooms of the Victorian era; costumes; local industries and local history - library

Yellowknife

02569
Prince of Wales Museum
Frame Lake North, mail c/o Department of Natural and Cultural Affairs, Government of the Northwest Territories Yellowknife, Northwest Territories X1A 2L9
General Museum - 1979
Archeology; ethnology; history; the natural sciences and arts, primarily of the Canadian Arctic and subarctic

Yorkton

02570
Western Development Museum
Hwy No 14 West, on the Yellowhead, POB 1033, Yorkton, Saskatchewan S3N 2X3
History/Public Affairs Museum - 1972
Pioneer history displays of the various nationalities which influenced the development of the west; Ukrainian log house furnished in the style of 1900

02571
Yorkton Art Centre
113-4th Av North, Yorkton, Saskatchewan S3N 1A4
Fine Arts Museum - 1966
Local artists' exhibits; graphics; pottery; serigraphs

Central African Republic

Bangassou

02572
Musée Labasso
Maison des Jeunes, B.P. 89, Bangassou
Anthropology Museum - 1975
Archeology from Nzakara and Zandé districts; historical maps and documents; ethnology

Bangui

02573
Musée Barthelemy Boganda
Rues Languedoc et Industrie, B.P. 349, Bangui
Anthropology Museum - 1964
Ethnography

Bouar

02574
Musée éthnographique regional
Bouar
Anthropology Museum
Ethnography; folklore

Maboké

02575
Musée de Maboké
Maboké
Natural History Museum
Natural history

Mbaïki

02576
Musée botanique de Boukoko
Mbaïki
Natural History Museum
Botany

Chad

Fort Archambault

02577
Musée Musée National, N'Djamena
Fort Archambault
General Museum
Local history; archeology; ethnography

N'Djamena

02578
Musée National Institut National des Sciences Humaines (I.N.S.H.)
1, Place de l'Indépendance, B.P. 503, N'Djamena
General Museum - 1963
Paleontology; archeology; ethnography; handicrafts; natural sciences; arms; musical instruments

Chile

Angol

02579
Museo Dillmann S. Bullock
Angol
Natural History Museum - 1946
local flora and fauna; birds; mammals; reptiles; insects; archaeology; anthropology; colonial weapons; 80 funeral urns of the Kofkeche culture - library

Arica

02580
Museo Arqueologico San Miguel de Azapa Universidad del Norte
18 Septiembre 2222, POB 287, Arica, Arica
Archeology Museum - 1967
archaeology; ceramics; anthropology - library

Calama

02581
Museo Anthropologico de Calama
Ramírez No 2022, Edificio Municipal, Casilla No 151, Calama, Provincia de El Loa
Archeology Museum
Coll: ceramics from northern Chile; archeological finds

Chiu Chiu - Comuna de Calama

02582
Museo Arqueológico de Chiu Chiu
Calle central, Chiu Chiu - Comuna de Calama, Provincia de El Loa
Archeology Museum - 1980
Archeological artifacts found in the Chiu Chiu region

Concepción

02583
Casa del Arte de la Universidad de Concepción
Chacabuco, esq. de Paicavi, Apdo 2737, Concepción
Fine Arts Museum
paintings

02584
Museo de Ciencias Naturales de Concepción
Edmundo Larenas 460, Concepción
General Museum - 1902
archaeology; natural history - library

02585
Pinacoteca de la Universidad de Concepción
Casa del Arte, Barrion Universitario
Frente a Plaza Perú, Concepción
Fine Arts Museum
paintings

La Serena

02586
Museo Arqueológico de La Serena
Cordovez esq. Cienfuego, Apdo. 117, La Serena
General Museum - 1943
archaeology; prehistory; colonial history; ethnography and anthropology; paleontology; pottery of Molle, Diaguita and Inca culture; feather embroided costumes - library

Linares

02587
Museo de Linares
Avda. Valentín Letelier 580, Apdo. 272, Linares
General Museum - 1966
agriculture; birds; weaving; ceramics; Araucan arms and masks

Osorno

02588
Museo Historico de Osorno
M.A.Matta 809, Osorno, Osorno, X Region
History/Public Affairs Museum - 1946
anthropology; arms; ceramics; pictures; fossils; minerals

Punta Arenas

02589
Museo Regional 'Mayorino Borgatello' Instituto 'Don Bosco'
Av. Bulness 374, Punta Arenas
General Museum - 1913
natural history; ethnography; relics of Indian tribes

San Pedro de Atamaca

02590
Museo Arqueológico
San Pedro de Atamaca
General Museum - 1963
archaeology; mummies; stone tools; snuffing boxes; textiles

Santiago

02591
Luis E. Peñà G. Entomology Collection
Apdo. 2974, Santiago
Natural History Museum
Entomology

02592
Museo Arqueológico 'Emilio y Duncan Wagner'
Santiago
Natural History Museum - 1917
archaeology; anthropology; ethnography; mineralogy; paleontology

02593
Museo de Anatomia Humana 'Manual Villela'
Santiago
Natural History Museum - 1930
human anatomy

02594
Museo de Arte Colonial de San Francisco
Alameda esq. Londres, POB 122-D, Santiago, Santiago
Fine Arts Museum
religious art; paintings 17th-19th century - library

02595
Museo de Arte Contemporaneo
Apdo. 5627, Santiago
Fine Arts Museum
contemporary art

02596
Museo de Arte Popular Americano
Cerro Santa Lucía, Santiago
Anthropology Museum - 1944
folk art; crafts; trades; folklore; Araucanian silver - library

02597
Museo de Artes Aplicada
Universidad de Chile
Arturo Prat 1171, Santiago
Decorative Arts Museum

02598
Museo de Historia Natural de San Pedro Nolasco
Huérfanos 669, Apdo. 525, Santiago
Natural History Museum - 1912

02599
Museo Historico Nacional de Chile
Miraflores 50, POB Casilla 9764, Santiago, Santiago
History/Public Affairs Museum - 1911
militaria; arms; painting; furniture; silver; porcelain; textiles; engravings - library

02600
Museo Nacional de Bellas Artes
Casilla 3209, Santiago
Fine Arts Museum - 1880
Coll: history of Chilean painting from colonial times to today; Dutch and Spanish baroque items; Italian drawings of the 15th, 16th, and 17th centuries - library

02601
Museo Nacional de Historia Natural
Quinta Normal, Santiago
Natural History Museum - 1830
vertebrates; invertebrates; entomology; biology; botany; mineralogy; geology; paleontology; anthropology - library

02602
Museo Pedagogico de Chile
Cienfuegos 59, Santiago, Santiago
History/Public Affairs Museum - 1941
history of education in Chile; numismatics - library

Talca

02603
Museo O'Higginiano y de Bellas Artes
Calle Uno Norte No. 875, Talca
Fine Arts Museum - 1925
paintings; stainded glass; armaments

Temuco

02604
Museo Araucano Regional de Temuco
Apdo. 481, Alemanía No. 084, Temuco
General Museum - 1940
arts and crafts of Araucanian Indians; folklore; history; pre-Araucanian ceramics; crania; fossiles trees; lithic tombs - library

Valparaíso

02605
Museo de Historia Natural de Valparaíso
Gran Bretaña, Playa Ancha, Valparaíso
Natural History Museum
invertebrates; mollusks; fishes; birds; vertebrates; minerals; fossils; archaeology - library

02606
Museo Municipal de Bellas Artes de Valparaíso Palacio Baburizza
Paseo Yugoslavo del Cerro Algere, Valparaíso
Fine Arts Museum

Viña del Mar

02607
Museo Comparativo de Zoologia Marina
Av. Borgoño s/n Mar, POB Casilla 13-D, Viña del Mar, V-Region
Natural History Museum - 1948
marine invertebrates; sea birds; fishes; shells

02608
Museo de Bellas Artes Quinta Vergara
Avda. Errázuriz No. 596, Viña del Mar
Fine Arts Museum

China, People's Republic

Anyang

02609
Archeological Museum
Anyang, Henan
Archeology Museum
Coll: bronze ceremonial vessels; jade figures; music instruments; finds from local excavations of tombs from 16th-11th century B.C.

Baoji

02610
Municipal Museum
Baoji, Shaanxi
Archeology Museum
Archeological finds including bronzes

Beijing

02611
Anthropological Museum Institute of Vertebrate Paleontology and Paleoanthropology
Beijing
Anthropology Museum

02612
Beijing Natural History Museum
Tian Qiao Nan Da Jie St, Beijing
Natural History Museum - 1958
Coll: botany; zoology; paleontology; anthropology; fossils; dioramas of fauna

02613
Imperial Palace Museum
Shen Wu Men Gate, Beijing
Fine Arts Museum
Coll: archeological finds including terra cotta figures from the grave of Emperor Quin Shi Huang (259-210 B.C.) near Xian; jade burial dress from Mancheng; furnishings of the Imperial Palace; bronzes of the Shang and Zhou dynasties; scroll paintings; traditional crafts (jade and goldsmith work)

02614
Lu Xun Museum
off Fu Cheng Men St, near Pai-tasi Pagoda, Beijing
History/Public Affairs Museum - 1956
Coll: documents, texts, and memorabilia of the writer Lu Xun (1881-1936)

02615
Museum of Chinese History
Tian An Men Square, Beijing
History/Public Affairs Museum
History of China from the very beginnings to the Opium War of 1840; archeological finds; models and display charts

02616
Museum of Fine Arts
Chaoyan Men St, Beijing
Fine Arts Museum
Coll: modern Chinese painting and graphics

02617
Museum of the Chinese Revolution
Tian-An-Men Square, Beijing
History/Public Affairs Museum
Coll: display charts on the epoch 1840-1960; historical items

02618
Museum of the Cultural Palace of National Minorities
west end of Chang'an St, Beijing
Anthropology Museum
Coll: documents on the national minorities of China; characteristic music instruments, ornaments, costumes; agricultural tools and products; displays, mannequins, and models

02619
National Museum of Music National Music Institute
Xue Yuan St, Beijing
Music Museum
Coll: history of music; music instruments

Changping

02620
Museum near the Ming Tombs
Changping north of Beijing
Archeology Museum
Coll: burial offerings from the 17th century grave of the Emperor Shen Zong (Wan Li) and his two wives Xiao Duan and Xiao Jing; in the tomb complex

Changsha

02621
Museum of the Hunan Province
Dongfeng St, Lieshi Gongyuan Park,
Changsha, Hunan
Archeology Museum
Coll: archeological finds from the
tombs at Mawangdui (2nd century
B.C.); 3,000 items including the mummy
of the wife of the Duke of T'ai, a silk
burial gown, scientific texts, wood
statuettes, lacquer items, bambus texts,
music instruments, and ceramics

Chengde

02622
Pu Le Temple
Chengde, Hebei
Open Air Museum - 1703-1790
Coll: the summer resort of the Qing
emperors; palaces in various
architectural styles; furnishings; stone-
carved poems; lake center pavilions;
sculpture; stone tablets - teahouse;
exhibition hall

Chengdu

02623
Museum of History Chengdu
University
Chengdu, Sichuan
Fine Arts Museum
Tang figures from the Qiong lai area
02624
Museum of Sichuan Province
People's St, southern district,
Chengdu, Sichuan
General Museum
Excavations including Buddhist
sculptures from the Tang and Sung
periods; Shang bronze; Han stone
figures; Sung and Ming porcelain; tile
reliefs from the Han period

Dalian

02625
Museum of Natural History
near to the station, northern district,
Dalian, Liaoning
Natural History Museum - 1950
Mineralogy; fauna and flora; navigation

Fufeng

02626
County Museum
Fufeng, Shaanxi
Archeology Museum
Excavations including Shang bronzes
and a Hu gui bronze vessel (9th c.
B.C.)

Guangzhou

02627
**Institute of the National Peasant
Movement**
in Confucius temple, Zhongshansi St
at Yuexin St, Guangzhou, Guangdong
History/Public Affairs Museum - 1924
Coll: documentation of the activites of
Mao Zedong and Zhou Enlai;
memorabilia of the two statesmen
02628
Lu Xun Museum
Wen Ming St, near the Museum of
Guangdong Province, Guangzhou,
Guangdong
History/Public Affairs Museum
Coll: documentation on the life and
work of the writer Lu Xun (1881-1936)

02629
Museum of Guangdong Province
Guangdong University, Wen Ming St,
Guangzhou, Guangdong
General Museum
Coll: prehistory; bronzes from the
Shang period (16th-11th centuries
B.C.); tomb figures from the Han
period (206 B.C.-220 A.D.); painting;
calligraphy
02630
Museum of History Guangzhou
Museum
Yue Xue Park, Zhen Hai Lou (the
five-storied pagoda), Guangzhou,
Guangdong
History/Public Affairs Museum
Coll: local history; maps; models;
excavation finds; photos; documents
02631
Museum of the Revolution
near the Mausoleum of the Martyrs,
Zhong Shan San St, Guangzhou,
Guangdong
History/Public Affairs Museum
Coll: documentation on the Opium
War up to 1949

Hangzhou

02632
Museum of Zhejiang Province
Gu Shan Island, Hangzhou, Zhejiang
General Museum
History; folk art; geography; botany;
zoology; documents on the Great
Chanel; porcelain; whale skeleton
(13th c.)

Harbin

02633
Museum of Heilongjiang Province
Harbin, Heilongjiang
Natural History Museum - 1923
Coll: development of man and the
animal world; 130,000 historical
artifacts; 100,000 animals

Hefei

02634
Museum of Anhui Province
Hefei, Anhui
General Museum

Jinan

02635
Museum of Shandong
south of Ba Duo Quan Park, in the
former Dao Temple, Jinan, Shandong
Fine Arts Museum
Bronze axes from the Shang period;
Longshan Rhyton vessels; Bamboo
writing (219 B.C.); earthen figures from
a grave of the Western Han dynasty;
grave painting from the Sui dynasty;
burial remains of Prince of Lu, son of
the first Ming Emperor; Buddhist
stone sculptures

Jingdezhen

02636
Jingdezhen Museum of Porcelain
Jingdezhen, Jiangxi
Decorative Arts Museum - 1980
Porcelain and history of porcelain
making

Jiuquan

02637
Municipal Museum
Jiuquan, Gansu
General Museum
Coll: Oriental art; tomb paintings from
the 3rd-4th centuries; archeological
finds

Kunming

02638
Museum of Yünnan Province
Dongfeng St, Yuantong Shan Hill,
Kunming, Yünnan
Archeology Museum
Finds from the Han grave of Shi zhai
shan; Han bronze from graves near
Jinning

Lanzhou

02639
Municipal Museum
near the Friendship Hotel, Lanzhou,
Gansu
Fine Arts Museum
Coll: ceramics from Yangshao; tomb
with paintings from the Han period
(206 B.C.-220 A.D.); the bronze 'Flying
Horse' from the East Han dynasty (2nd
century A.D.)

Lhasa

02640
Museum of the History of Revolution
Lhasa, Xizang autonomous region
History/Public Affairs Museum
History of traditional Tibet and the
period since 1959

Lintong

02641
**Museum of Emperor Qin Shih
Huang's Grave**
6 km from the grave, Lintong, Shaanxi
Archeology Museum - 1979
Hall above the front grave with 6,000
statues of the Emperor's army

Liquan Xian

02642
Zhaoling Museum
Liquan Xian, Shaanxi
Archeology Museum
Archeological finds including Ding
bronze vessel (14th c. B.C.), painted
ceramic figures from the grave of Li
Zhen depicting various officials

Lüda

02643
Museum of Natural History
Lüda, Liaoning
Natural History Museum

Luoyang

02644
Municipal Museum
in Guan Di Miao Tempel, Wang Cheng
Park, north of Zhongzhou St, Luoyang,
Henan
Archeology Museum
Coll: prehistoric finds from Er li tou;
Yangshao ceramics; bronzes from the
Shang and Zhou dynasties (16th c.-771
B.C.); Sung porcelain (960-1279); stone
lions from the Sui dynasty; Han tomb
figures(206 B.C.-220 A.D.); fossils; jade
objects; development of society from
prehistory to feudal times

Nanchang

02645
Museum of Fine Arts
Wujiaotong St, near to the Park of the
People, Nanchang, Jiangxi
Fine Arts Museum
Modern Art

02646
Museum of Jiangxi Province
Bayi Da Dao St, near to the First of
August Memorial, Nanchang, Jiangxi
General Museum - 1952
History; geography; antique ceramics

02647
Museum of the Revolution
Bayi Da Dao St, near to the First of
August Memorial, Nanchang, Jiangxi
History/Public Affairs Museum
Documentation on the rebellion and
battles of 1927/28

Nanjing

02648
Jiangsu Provincial Museum
Zhongshan Dong St, near Zhongshan
Gate, Nanjing, Jiangsu
General Museum - 1950
Archeological finds from prehistory to
the Han dynasty; porcelain; painting;
bronze

02649
Nanjing Museum
Nanjing, Jiangsu
Fine Arts Museum

02650
Taiping Museum
Taiping St, near to the southern gate of
the town, Nanjing, Jiangsu
History/Public Affairs Museum
Documentation on the Taiping
Rebellion

Nanning

02651
Museum of the Guangxi Province
Qiyi Guangdhang Square, Nanning,
Guangxi
General Museum
Coll: excavation finds from the
Guiangxi province; ancient bronze
drums; history of the Taiping Rebellion

Qian Xian

02652
Qianling Museum
besides the grave of Princess Yong
Tai, Qian Xian, Shaanxi
Archeology Museum
Grave findings from Tang period
including ceramic figures

Quanzhou

02653
Museum of Navigation History
Quanzhou, Fujian
History/Public Affairs Museum
History of regional navigation; ship
from the Sung dynasty; Islamic,
Nestorian, Manichean, Brahmanic and
Buddhist inscription stones; Hindu
Vishnu statue

Shanghai

02654
Lu Xun House
Shang Sen St 7, near Hong Kou Park, Shanghai
Historic Site - 1956
Coll: documents, letters, manuscripts, books, photos of the writer Lu Xun (1881-1936); in the house where he spent his last years

02655
Museum Heude
Shanghai
Natural History Museum

02656
Museum of Art and History
Cnr Yan'an St, Henan St, Shanghai
Fine Arts Museum - 1952
Coll: bronzes; ceramics and porcelain; wall paintings from the Tang dynasty; scroll paintings from the Ming (1368-1644) and Ch'ing (1644-1912) periods; statues from the tomb of Qin Shi Huang near Xian

02657
Museum of Natural History
Yan'an St, Shanghai
Natural History Museum
Coll: exhibits on natural history

02658
Royal Asiatic Society Museum
Shanghai
Natural History Museum

02659
Shanghai Museum
Shanghai
Fine Arts Museum
Fine and decorative arts; crafts

Shenyang

02660
Imperial Palace Museum
Former palace of Emperors Nu Er Ha Chi and Huang Tai Ji, Shenyang, Liaoning
History/Public Affairs Museum
Historical objects and arts and crafts from the Qing dynasty

02661
Museum of Liaoning Province
Shenyang, Liaoning
General Museum
Bronze; painting from the Tang to Yüan dynasties

Suzhou

02662
Museum of History
Xi Bei St, northeastern district, Suzhou, Jiangsu
History/Public Affairs Museum
Archeological finds (prehistory to present); history of silk weaving since the Sung dynasty; bronze; porcelain; historic geography of the Great Chanel

Taiyuan

02663
Museum of Shanxi Province
Taiyuan, Shanxi
Fine Arts Museum - 1955
Buddhist sculptures from the Tang period; sitting Guanyin statue from the Yuan period; painting and calligraphy; Sutra texts from the Jin period; Tang grave from Dongrucun near Taiyuan (696)

Tianjin

02664
Museum Hoang-Ho, Pai-Ho
Tianjin
Natural History Museum

02665
Museum of Art and History
Tianjin
Fine Arts Museum - 1957
Coll: Scroll paintings of the Yüan to the Qing periods; Chinese art

Urumqi

02666
Museum of the Autonomous Region of Xinjiang
Urumqi, Xinjiang
Archeology Museum - 1953
Local archeological finds and customs from the Stone Age to the Qing dynasty

Wuhan

02667
Museum of Hubei Province
in Donghu Park, western coast of the East Sea, Wuhan, Hubei
General Museum
Coll: local history following the Opium War; new excavations; ceramics; ancient chimes; burial offerings from Jin Zhou; burial remains from a 5th century grave

Wuxi

02668
Municipal Museum
former Shigong Si Monastery, north Guoqing St, Wuxi, Jiangsu
Archeology Museum
Burial remains from the Han dynasty; sarcophargi from the period of the Fife Dynasties and North Sung dynasty; Tang sculptures from the Shi Kefa grave

02669
Museum of History
Wuxi, Jiangsu
Archeology Museum
Local archeological finds

Xian

02670
Banpo Museum
10 km east of Xian, Xian, Shaanxi
Archeology Museum - 1958
Excavated Neolithic settlement (4,000 B.C.) including residential district, cemetary and pottery; documentation

02671
Museum of Shaanxi Province
Bo Shu Lin St, southwest of Nan Da Jie, Xian, Shaanxi
History/Public Affairs Museum - 1911
Former temple of Confucius; history including excavations and reproductions of the Tang Emperors' graves of Qian Xian; sculptures including animal sculptures and Buddhist sculptures from the Tang period; inscriptions beginning with the Han dynasty, including Confucian classical philosophers (9th c.); gold treasure from Hejiacun (Tang dynasty)

Xianyang

02672
Municipal Museum
Xianyang, Shaanxi
Archeology Museum
Archeological finds including earthen figures of warriors and horsemen from Yangjiawan (Western Han dynasty); jade figures

Xinhui

02673
Regional Museum
behind Confucius Temple, Xinhui, Guangdong
General Museum
Coll: prehistory; ceramics of the Sung to Ming dynasties

Yanan

02674
Museum of the Revolution
at the Yan River, Yanan, Shaanxi
History/Public Affairs Museum
Documentation on Mao Zedong, who lived here for some time

Yao Xian

02675
Yao Xian Museum
east of Yao Xian, Yao Xian, Shaanxi
Archeology Museum
Stelae dating back to the Northern Wei dynasty

Zhengzhou

02676
Museum of the Henan Province
Jinshui St, Dongfang Hong Park, west of the Zhengzhou Hotel, Zhengzhou, Henan
Archeology Museum
Coll: items from the Stone and Bronze Ages; ceramics from the period of the Warring States (475-221 B.C.); Han burial offerings and porcelain; clay model of an ornate tower house from the Han period; bronze vases (4th century B.C.); archeological finds from Anyang; items from a grave of the Warring States period; burial remains from the Sung dynasty

China, Republic

Ali Shan

02677
Ali Shan Museum
Ali Shan
General Museum
Local history collections

Chia-yi

02678
Chia-yi Museum
Chia-yi, Taiwan
General Museum
Local history

Chung-hsing Hsin-ts'un

02679
Chung-hsing Hsin-Ts'un Museum
Chung-hsing Hsin-ts'un, Taiwan
General Museum
Local history

Sintien

02680
Postal Museum
17 Lane 142, Kwang Min St, Sintien, Taiwan
History/Public Affairs Museum - 1966
History of the postal service; stamps; proofs and engravings

Tainan

02681
Chihkan Tower
Tainan, Taiwan
History/Public Affairs Museum
Documents and arms

Taipei

02682
Exhibition Hall Institute of History and Philology, Academia Sinica
Taipei, Taiwan
Archeology Museum
Cabinet records of the Ming and Ch'ing dynasties, factual files of Ming dynasty

02683
Museum of Military History
243 Kwei Yang St, Taipei, Taiwan
History/Public Affairs Museum - 1961
Military documents and history

02684
National Art Gallery of Taiwan
Nan Hai Rd, Taipei, Taiwan
Fine Arts Museum

02685
National Museum of History
49 Nan Hai Rd, Taipei, Taiwan
History/Public Affairs Museum - 1955
Antiques from the province of Honan, objects excavated in the Kinwen and Penghu (Pescadora) Islands; murals; bronzes; musical instruments; pottery; porcelain; weapons; costumes; Buddhist sculpture; copies of murals from the Tun Huang Caves; furniture from the Manchu dynasty; calligraphy; coins; jade; ivory - library

02686
National Museum of Science and Education
Taipei, Taiwan
History/Public Affairs Museum
Education

02687
National Palace Museum
Waishuang-hsi, Shih-lin, Taipei, Taiwan
Fine Arts Museum - 1965
Calligraphy; painting of the Tang and Sung dynasties; jade; bronzes; porcelain from the Sung and Yuan dynasties; sculpture; enamelware; lacquer; carvings; embroidery; miniature crafts; rare books and documents; manuscripts from the Shang period to the 20th century - library; archives

02688
Taiwan Museum
2 Siangyang Rd, Taipei, Taiwan 100
Natural History Museum - 1908
Coll: zoology and botany; fossils; mineral specimens; fishes and other marine organisms; prehistoric culture, ethnology and culture of Taiwan aborigines; local history

Colombia

Armenia

02689
Museo Arqueológico del Quindio
Banco Popular, Calle 21 No. 16-37,
Armenia
Archeology Museum
Regional archaeology

Barranquilla

02690
Museo de Antropologia
Calle 68 No. 5345, Barranquilla
General Museum
Folklore

Belencito

02691
Museo Siderúrgico de Colombia
Calle 15 No. 10-26, Belencito
Natural History Museum - 1969
Mining; metallurgy; geology

Bogotá

02692
Casa-Museo 20 de Julio de 1810
Calle 11 No. 6-94, Bogotá
History/Public Affairs Museum
Documents; printing press; furniture

02693
Casa-Museo Jorge Eliécer Gaitán
Calle 42 No. 15-52, Bogotá
General Museum - 1950
Local history; memorabilia of Jorge
Eliécer Gaitán

02694
**Instituto de Ciencias Naturales -
Museo de Historia Natural-
Universidad Nacional**
Apdo 7495, Bogotá
Natural History Museum - 1936
Anthropology; botany; geology;
zoology

02695
**Museo Arqueológico del Banco
Popular**
Casa del Marqués San Jorge, Carrera
6a No. 7-43, Bogotá
Archeology Museum
Ceramics; relics of Colombian,
Mexican, Peruvian and Ecuadorian
civilization

02696
Museo Arqueológico Nacional
Carrera 7A No. 28-66, Apdo Nacional
407, Bogotá
Archeology Museum

02697
Museo de Arte Colonial
Carrera 6a No. 9-77, Bogotá
Fine Arts Museum - 1942
Paintings, sculptures, decorative
objects and graphic arts fromthe
Spanish colonial period (16th to 18th
century); miniatures; goldsmith work;
furniture

02698
Museo de Arte Contemporáneo
Minuto de Dios, Carrera 73 No. 81-27,
Bogotá
Fine Arts Museum - 1966
Colombian, Latin American, European
contemporary art; paintings;
engravings; sculptures; drawings;
ceramics - library

02699
Museo de Arte Moderno de Bogotá
Calle 26 No. 6-05, Bogotá
Fine Arts Museum - 1958
Colombian art since 1900: graphics;
paintings; sculptures; contemporary
art of Latin America - library

02700
**Museo de Arte y Tradiciones
Populares**
Carrera 8 No. 7-21, Bogotá
Anthropology Museum - 1971
Colombian popular art and traditional
handicrafts

02701
Museo de Artes Gráficas
Carrera 15 No. 56 Sur, Bogotá
Fine Arts Museum
Graphic arts; printing presses

02702
**Museo de Desarollo Urbano de
Bogotá**
Calle 10 No. 4-21, Bogotá
History/Public Affairs Museum
Maps; plans; photography

02703
Museo de Don Antonio Nariño
Calle 10 Sur Carrera 38, Bogotá
History/Public Affairs Museum
Documents, memorabilia of General
Antonio Nariño

02704
Museo de Historia de la Medicina
Facultad de Medicina, Ciudad
Universitaria, Bogotá
Science/Tech Museum
Medical science; medical instruments

02705
**Museo de Historia Natural de
Colombia**
Calle 26 Carrera 7a, Bogotá
Natural History Museum
Colombian flora and fauna

02706
**Museo de Minerales del Instituto
Geofisico**
Carrera 7 No. 40-62, Bogotá
Natural History Museum - 1941
Colombian minerals

02707
Museo de Museos Colsubsidio
Carrera 3a No. 17-23, Bogotá
Fine Arts Museum
Reproductions of engravings

02708
Museo de Numismática
Calle 11 No. 4-93, Bogotá
History/Public Affairs Museum
Numismatics; colonial style furniture

02709
Museo de Santa Clara
Calle 9 No. 8-31, Bogotá
Religious Art Museum
Religious art; painting

02710
Museo del Instituto de la Salle
Calle 11 No. 1-69, Bogotá
General Museum
Natural history; religious art

02711
Museo del Mar
Calle 23 No. 4-47, Bogotá
Natural History Museum - 1969
Marine specimens of the Atlantic and
Pacific coast of Colombia - library

02712
Museo del Oro
Banco de la República, Calle 16 No.
5-41, Bogotá
Anthropology Museum - 1939
Pre-Colombian gold collection; native
Indian tribal culture; history; religions;
customs - library

02713
Museo Etnografico de Colombia
Calle 34 No. 6-61 piso 30, Apdo Aéreo
10511, Bogotá
Anthropology Museum - 1966
Folklore; religious art; applied arts;
relocs of Indian tribes - library

02714
Museo Geológico Nacional
Carrera 30 No. 51-59, Apdo Aéreo
4865, Bogotá
Natural History Museum - 1951
Minerals; fossils; skeletons and
emeralds of Colombia

02715
**Museo Histórico de la Policia
Nacional**
Carrera 7 No. 28-66, Bogotá
History/Public Affairs Museum
Arms; uniforms

02716
**Museo Mercedes Sierra de Pérez 'El
Chico'**
Carrera 7a No. 94-17, Bogotá
General Museum
Art; furniture; applied arts

02717
Museo Nacional
Carrera 7a No. 28-66, Bogotá
General Museum - 1823
Modern art and sculpture; arms;
uniforms; medals; pictures and
documents; Spanish conquest and
colonial period

02718
Museo Nacional de Antropologia
Carrera 7a No. 28-66, Apdo Nacional
407, Bogotá
Anthropology Museum - 1938
Colombian ethnography; archaeology,
anthropology; paintings; folklore;
textiles; carvings; ceramics; crafts

02719
**Museo Organológico Folklórico
Musical**
Conservatorio de Música, Ciudad
Universitaria, Bogotá
Music Museum
Organs

02720
Museo Taurino de Bogotá
Plaza de Toros de Santa Maria,
Bogotá
Anthropology Museum
Bullfighting

02721
Museos de Armas
Escuela de Cadetes, Calle 81, Carrera
38, Bogotá
History/Public Affairs Museum
Arms; uniforms; insignia

02722
Quinta y Museo de Bolivar
Calle 20 No. 3-23, Bogotá
Historic Site - 1922
Memorabilia on Colombian national
hero Simón de Bolívar (1783-1830)

Bucaramanga

02723
Casa de Bolivar
Calle 37 No. 12-15, Bucaramanga
General Museum
Archaeology; history and documents

Cali

02724
Museo de Arte Moderno la Tertulia
Avenida Colombia, Cali, Valle de
Cauca
Fine Arts Museum - 1968
paintings; sculptures; graphic arts;
drawings - library

02725
**Museo Departamental de Ciencias
Natural 'F. Carlos Lehman Valencia'**
Carrera 24 No. 7-18, Apdo 938, Cali
Natural History Museum - 1963
Zoology; geology; Indian ceramics

02726
Museo Manuel Maria Buenaventura
Av 4 No. 10-42, Cali

Cartagena

02727
Museo Antropológico
Plaza de Bolívar, Cartagena
Anthropology Museum
Folklore; natural history

02728
Museo Casa Rafael Núñez
Carrera 2 No. 41-89, El Cabrero,
Cartagena
Historic Site
Memorabilia on president Rafael
Núñez

02729
**Museo de Arte Moderno de
Cartagena**
Plaza de San Pedro Claver, Cartagena
Fine Arts Museum
Modern art

02730
Museo de Arte Religioso
Casa de San Pedro Claver, Carrera 4
No. 30-01, Cartagena
Religious Art Museum
Archaeology; ethnography; paintings
and sculptures; religious art

02731
**Museo Histórico Palacio de la
Inquisición**
Plaza de Bolívar, Cartagena
Anthropology Museum
Folklore; colonial architecture; history
and archaeology

Cartago

02732
Museo de Ciencias y Antropologia
Colegio Nacional Académico, Cartago
Anthropology Museum
Ethnography; natural sciences

02733
**Museo Trajes Regionales de
Colombia**
Calle 13 No. 4-53, Cartago
Anthropology Museum - 1971
Regional costumes

Cúcuta

02734
Museo de la Ciudad
Calle 13 No. 3-67, Cúcuta
Fine Arts Museum
Modern art; paintings; sculptures;
engravings; drawings

Duitama

02735
Museo de Arte Religioso
Palacio Episcopal, Duitama
Fine Arts Museum - 1965
Colonial art; ethnography; religious art

02736
Museo de Ciencias Naturales
Calle 13 No. 14-41, Duitama
Natural History Museum
Botany; zoology

El Retiro

02737
Museo Arqueológico 'La Puma de Oro'
Hacienda Los Potreros, El Retiro, Antioquia
Archeology Museum

Envigado

02738
Museo Colegio de la Salle
Calle 24 Sur No. 42B-45, Envigado
History/Public Affairs Museum
Education

Granada

02739
Museo de Historia Natural de las Hermanas Franciscanas
Granada
History/Public Affairs Museum
Education

Ibagué

02740
Museo de Arte Moderno de Ibagué
Extensión Cultural del Tolima, Ibagué
Fine Arts Museum
Modern art

02741
Museo del Hombre Tolimense
Universidad del Tolima, Ibagué
Archeology Museum - 1967
Pre-Colombian ceramics; goldwork and lithic funeral statuary - library

Ipiales

02742
Museo Arqueológico
Batallón Cabal, Ipiales
General Museum
Archaeology; ethnography

Mamatoco

02743
Museo de San Pedro Alejandrino
Mamatoco
General Museum
Memorabilia on Simón Bolívar; furniture; pictures

Manizales

02744
Exposición Permanente de Cerámica Indígena
Banco de la República 20. piso, Manizales
Anthropology Museum
Indian ceramics; crafts; folklore

02745
Museo Antropológico de Caldas
Escuela de Bellas Artes, Apdo 150, Manizales
Anthropology Museum - 1955
Folklore and regional archaeology

02746
Museo de Historia de Caldas
Colegio de Cristo, Manizales
General Museum
Local history

Medellín

02747
Fundación Jardín Botánico 'Joaquín A. Uribe'
Carrera 52 No. 73-298, Medellín
Natural History Museum
Botany

02748
Museo Club Científico Colombiano
Carrera 50 No. 53-51, Medellín
Natural History Museum
Herpetology; entomology; ornithology; mineralogy

02749
Museo de Ciencias Naturales del Colegio de San José
Apdo Aéreo 1180, Medellín
Natural History Museum - 1913
Natural history; zoology; botany; mineralogy; anthropology - library

02750
Museo de Historia Natural del Colegio de San José
Calle 54 A. No. 30-02, POB 1180, Medellín, Antioquía
Natural History Museum - 1915
zoology; botany; mineralogy; fossils; archaeology; mollusks; insects - library

02751
Museo de Zea
Carrera 52 A Pasaje Veracruz, Medellín
Fine Arts Museum
Modern art

02752
Museo el Castillo Diego Echavarria
El Poblado, Medellín
Fine Arts Museum
Furniture; porcelain; sculptures; European style paintings and tapestries

02753
Museo Etnográfico 'Madre Laura'
Transversal 92 No. 33B-21, Benecito-Medellín
Anthropology Museum - 1964
Ethnography and folklore; archaeology

02754
Museo Etnográfico Miguel Angel Bulnes
Carrera 81 No. 52B-120, Medellín
General Museum
Ethnography

02755
Museo Folklórico Tejicondor
Carrera 65 No.45A-23, Medellín
Anthropology Museum
Folklore; costumes; textiles

02756
Museo Histórico de la Ciudad de Medellín
Carrera 52 No. 20-63, Avenida Guayabal, Medellín
General Museum
History of Medellín

02757
Museo Mineralógico 'Salón Tulio Ospina'
Barrio Robledo, Medellín
Natural History Museum
Minerals

02758
Museo Universitario Universidad de Antioquía
POB A.A. 1226, Medellín, Antioquía
Anthropology Museum - 1932
Anthropology; natural sciences; sculptures; Maya civilization

Meléndez-Cali

02759
Museo Regional de Investigación Arqueológica
Universidad del Valle, Meléndez-Cali
Archeology Museum
Archaeological finds of the region

Pamplona

02760
Museo Casa Colonial
Calle 6 No. 2-56, Pamplona
General Museum
Paleography; history; anthropology; archaeology; folklore

Pasca

02761
Museo Arqueológico
Casa Parroquial, Pasca
Archeology Museum - 1969
Lithic and ceramic objects; colonial paintings, documents, numismatics - library

Pasto

02762
Museo Escobar Maria Goretti
Avenida de 'Las Américas', Pasto, Nariño
General Museum
Archaeology; history; folklore; natural history

02763
Museo Maridiaz
Calle 18, Apdo Aéreo 319, Pasto
General Museum - 1940
Archaeology; ethnography; folklore; mineralogy; botany; zoology; geography; art

Popayán

02764
Museo Arqueológico y Etnográfico
Universidad del Cauca, Popayán
Archeology Museum
Archaeology; folklore

02765
Museo Arquidiocesano de Arte Religioso de Popayán
Calle 4a No. 4-56, Popayán, Cauca
Religious Art Museum
Religious art; vestments

02766
Museo Casa Valencia
Calle 3a, Carrera 6a, Popayán, Cauca
Historic Site
Memorabilia on the poet Guillermo Valencia

02767
Museo de Arte Colonial e Historia 'Casa Mosquera'
Calle 3 No. 5-14, Popayán, Cauca
Fine Arts Museum - 1970
Colonial art; paintings; ceramics; porcelain; furniture; Isis statuette from the Sais excavation

02768
Museo de Historia Natural Universidad del Cauca
Popayán, Cauca
Natural History Museum - 1936
Enthomology; ornithology; zoology; herpetology; ichthyology - library

02769
Museo Efrain Martinez
Carrera 3, Via Sur, El Refugio, Popayán, Cauca
Fine Arts Museum
Works of the painter Efrain Martínez

02770
Museo San Francisco
Calle 4a, Carrera 9a, Popayán, Cauca
Religious Art Museum
Cult objects; colonial art

Ráquira

02771
Museo de Arte Religioso del Desierto de la Candelaria
Ráquira
Religious Art Museum
Objects of religious and colonial art; incunabula

Rionegro

02772
Museo de Arte Religioso
Parque Central, Catedral de San Nicolás, Rionegro, Antioquia
Religious Art Museum

02773
Museo del Banco de Oriente
Carrera 50 No. 50-04, Rionegro, Antioquia
History/Public Affairs Museum
Archives; documents; historical objects

02774
Museo Histórico Casa de la Convención
Calle de la Convención No. 47-67, Rionegro, Antioquia
General Museum
History; paintings

Santa Fé

02775
Museo Colonial Don Juan del Corral
Calle 11 No. 9-77, Santa Fé
General Museum - 1970
Religious art; colonial furnishings; implements; objects of Indian handicraft

Santa Marta

02776
Museo de San Pedro Alejandrino
Calle 17 No. 16 E-36, Santa Marta
General Museum

Socorro

02777
Museo Casa de la Cultura
Calle 14 No. 12-35, Socorro
General Museum
History; archaeology; ethnography; documents

Sogamoso

02778
Museo Arqueológico
Sogamoso
Archeology Museum
Archaeology; anthropology; folklore; botany

Sonsón

02779
Casa de los Abuelos
Calle 9 No. 7-30, Sonsón
Anthropology Museum - 1957
Folklore

02780
Museo de Arte Religioso Tiberio de J. Salazar y Herrera
Catedral de Sonsón, Sonsón
Religious Art Museum
Jewelry; pictures

Tunja

02781
Casa Museo Don Juan de Vargas
Calle 20 Carreras 8 y 9, Tunja, Boyacá
Archeology Museum

02782
Museo de Historia Natural
Carretera Central, salida a Paipa, Tunja
Natural History Museum
Zoology; entomology; botany

02783
Museo de Museos
Carrera 10 No. 19-17, Tunja
Fine Arts Museum
Painting

02784
Museo Eclesiástico Colonial
Carrera 11 No. 16-82, Tunja
Religious Art Museum
Religious items

Usiacurí

02785
Casa-Museo Julio Flórez
Usiacurí
Historic Site
Manuscripts and memorabilia of the
poet Julio Flórez

Valledupar

02786
Museo Histórico del Cesar
Calle 12, Carrera 6, Valledupar
General Museum
Archaeology; ethnography

Villa de Leiva

02787
Museo de Arte Colonial
Alcaldía Municipal, Villa de Leiva
Fine Arts Museum - 1971
Colonial paintings

02788
Museo del Carmen
Plazuela del Carmen, Villa de Leiva
Religious Art Museum
Religious art; cult objects

Congo

Brazzaville

02789
Musée National du Congo
Av. Patrice Lumumba, B.P. 459,
Brazzaville
General Museum - 1965
National history; ethnography; ivory
sculptures - library

Costa Rica

Alajuela

02790
Museo Juan Santamaria
Apartado 785, Alajuela
General Museum

San José

02791
Galeria Facultad de Bellas Artes
Universidad de Costa Rica
San José
Fine Arts Museum

02792
Galeria la Casa del Artista
San José
Fine Arts Museum

02793
Galeria Teatro Nacional
San José
Fine Arts Museum

02794
Museo de Arte Costaricense Sabena
E
San José
General Museum

02795
Museo de Jade Instituto Nacional de
Seguros
San José
General Museum

02796
Museo de Oro Banco Central de
Costa Rica
San José
General Museum

02797
Museo Indigeno Seminario Central
San José
Anthropology Museum
native arts and crafts

02798
Museo Nacional de Costa Rica
Avenidas 0 y 2, Calles 15-17, Apdo.
749, San José
General Museum - 1887
pre-Columbian; colonial and republican
religious art; herbarium and birds -
library

Cuba

Camagüey

02799
Museo Ignacio Agramonte
Camagüey
General Museum
colonial paintings; furniture; history

Cardenas

02800
Museo Oscar Maria Rojas
Calzada esq. Av. José Martí, Cardenas
General Museum
coins; arms; snails; butterflies;
archaeology; history

La Habana

02801
**Museo Agricola y Exposición
Permanente**
La Habana
Science/Tech Museum
agricultural and mining history and
products

02802
Museo Antropológico Montane
Universidad de La Habana
La Habana
Anthropology Museum - 1903
American, Cuban ethnography;
primitive cultures; Asian, African and
Oceanian ethnography; Cuban magic
traditions; folklore; objects of the
Cuban prehistorical cultures Ciboney
and Taino - library

02803
Museo 'Carlos de la Torre y Huerta'
Av. de Italia entre Lagunas y Animas,
La Habana
Natural History Museum
malacology

02804
Museo Colonial de la Habana
Plaza de la Catedral, La Habana
History/Public Affairs Museum

02805
Museo de Arte Popular
Plaza de la Catedral, La Habana
Fine Arts Museum
Cuban and foreign art

02806
Museo de Artes Decorativos
Calle 17 No. 502, Vedado, La Habana
Decorative Arts Museum - 1967
decorative art in gold, silver, bronze
and porcelain; tapestries; European
and Oriental furniture; 15th-19th
century fans; crafts - library

02807
Museo de Etnologia Palacio Aldama
Reina y Amistad, La Habana
Anthropology Museum
folklore, especially in connection with
Africa

02808
Museo de la Ciudad de la Habana
Tacón 1 entre Opispo y O'Reilly, La
Habana
History/Public Affairs Museum - 1938
history of the city since aboriginal
times; memorabilia of Martí Gómez
and Maceo; foundation of La Habana -
library

02809
**Museo del Instituto de Segunda
Enseñanza**
La Habana
Natural History Museum
departments of natural history, botany,
mineralogy, zoology, ornithology

02810
Museo 'Felipe Poey' Capitolo
Nacional
La Habana
Natural History Museum
archaeology; anthropology;
speleology; ichthyology; reptiles;
paleontology; ornithology; mineralogy
- planetarium

02811
Museo Hemingway
Finca La Vigía, San Francisco de Paula,
La Habana
General Museum
personal memorabilia of writer Ernest
Hemingway (1899-1961)

02812
Museo Histórico de Guanabacoa
Martí 108, La Habana, Guanabacoa
History/Public Affairs Museum
19th century relics; Afro-Cuban
collection

02813
**Museo Histórico de las Ciencias
'Carlos J. Finlay'**
Cuba 460, Apdo. 70, La Habana 1
Science/Tech Museum - 1962
history of medical and general
science; pharmaceutical ceramics;
colonial furniture and paintings

02814
Museo Histórico Municipal Palacio
de Lombillo
Plaza de la Catedral, La Habana
General Museum
local history

02815
Museo José Marti
Leonor Pérez 314, La Habana
General Museum - 1925
works, iconography and bibliography
of writer and Cuban hero José Martí
(1853-1895)

02816
Museo Nacional
Palacio de Bellas Artes animas entre
Zulueta y Monserrate, La Habana
Fine Arts Museum - 1913
Egyptian, Greek and Roman art;
Renaissance and 17th-18th century
Italian art; Netherlands, French,
English and Spanish art; Cuban art
since colonial times

02817
**Museo Nacional de la Campana de
Alfabetización** Ciudad Libertad
Mariano, La Habana
History/Public Affairs Museum
history of Cuban literacy campaign

02818
Museo Napoleónico
San Miguel y Ronda, La Habana
Decorative Arts Museum - 1961
artworks; furniture; porcelain;
armaments; costumes; history of
France in Revolutionary, Imperial and
Directorate periods

02819
Museo Poey Facultad de Ciencias,
Universidad de La Habana
La Habana
Natural History Museum
zoology

02820
Museo y Biblioteca de Zoología
Calle 42 No. 3307, Mariano 13, La
Habana
Natural History Museum - 1933
zoology; mollusks - library

Mantanzas

02821
**Museo Arqueológico Francisco
Ximeno**
Mantanzas
Archeology Museum

02822
Museo Municipal de Mantanzas
Mantanzas
General Museum

Pinar del Rio

02823
**Museo de Pesca de la Escuela Naval
del Mariel**
Pinar del Rio
Natural History Museum - 1943
marine biology; rare specimens of
deep-sea fish

Remedios

02824
**Museo de Remedios 'José Maria
Espiñosa'**
Maceo 32, Remedios
General Museum
local art; history; natural history

Santiago de Cuba

02825
**Museo Municipal 'Emilio Bacardi
Moreau'**
Pio Rosado y Aguilera, Santiago de
Cuba
General Museum - 1899
art; archeology; natural history

Cyprus

Episkopi
02826
Episkopi Museum
Episkopi, Limassol District

Kouklia
02827
Palaepaphos Museum
Kouklia, Paphos District
General Museum

Larnaca
02828
Larnaca District Museum
M. Parides Sq, POB 534, Larnaca
General Museum

02829
Pierides Museum
4, Zenon Kitiefs St, POB 25, Larnaca
Anthropology Museum - 1839
Archaeological finds from all periods
of Cypriot history, from Neolithic to
Roman and Byzantine; Minoan and
Mycenaean collections - library

Limassol
02830
Limassol District Museum
Lord Byron St, Limassol
General Museum

Nicosia
02831
Argo Gallery
Princess Zena de Tyras Palace,
Nicosia
Fine Arts Museum

02832
Cyprus Museum
Museum Av, POB 2024, Nicosia
General Museum - 1883
Pottery from the Neolithic and
Chalcolithic periods to the Roman age;
terra cotta figures; limestone and
marble sculpture ; Bronze Age
jewelry; Mycenaean finds; coins;
inscriptions; glass

02833
Cyprus National Struggle Museum
Archbishop Kyprianos Sq, Nicosia
History/Public Affairs Museum

02834
Folk Art Museum
Archbishop Kyprianos Sq, Nicosia
Anthropology Museum
Cypriot arts and crafts from early to
recent times

02835
Icon Museum
Nicosia
Religious Art Museum
Byzantine icons

Paphos
02836
Paphos District Museum
G. Grivas-Dighenis Av, POB 50,
Paphos
General Museum

Yeroskipou
02837
Folk Art Museum
Yeroskipou, Paphos District
General Museum

Czechoslovakia

1884
02838
Okresni muzeum
Leninovo nám.114, CS-397 01 1884
General Museum
Geology; mineralogy; history of gold
mining in the area; archeology; applied
arts; ethnography; cultural history;
history of the labour movement;
contemporary history

Antol
02839
**Lesnicke, Drevárske a Poľovnicke
Múzeum** (Museum of Forestry, Timber
Processing and Hunting)
Hrad, CS-969 72 Antol, okr. Žiar n/Hr.
General Museum - 1954
Original furnishings; history of hunting
in Slovakia; forestry; fauna; flora; in a
18th century palace

Aš
02840
Městské muzeum
U Staré radnice 2, Mikulášská ul. 3,
cs-352 01 Aš
General Museum - 1892
Art; crafts; porcelain; textiles;
mineralogy; ornithology; Oriental arms;
exhibits illustrating the anti-Fashist
struggle in World War II

Banská Bystrica
02841
**Múzeum slovenského narodného
povstania** (Museum of the Slovakian
National Uprising)
CS-974 00 Banská Bystrica
History/Public Affairs Museum - 1955
History of the Slovakian anti-Faschist
struggle in World War II

02842
Oblastná galéria (Regional Art
Gallery)
Nám. CA 25, CS-975 90 Banská
Bystrica
Fine Arts Museum
Modern art; paintings

02843
Stredoslovenské múzeum (Museum
of Central Slovakia)
Nám. SNP 4, CS-974 00 Banská
Bystrica
General Museum - 1889
Archeology; mining; natural sciences;
paintings; ethnography; local history

Banská Štiavnica
02844
Slovenské banské múzeum (Slovak
Mining Museum)
CS-969 00 Banská Štiavnica
General Museum
Geology; mining; metallurgy; tools;
miners' folk art; archeology; local
history; ethnography,

Bardejov
02845
Šarišské múzeum
Radnica, CS-085 01 Bardejov
General Museum
Archeology; Gothic embroidery;
religious art; folk art; ceramics;
painting; local history

Bardejowské Kúpele
02846
Múzeum
CS-086 31 Bardejowské Kúpele
Open Air Museum
Ethnography

Bechyně
02847
Muzeum keramiky (Ceramics
Museum)
Nám. Rudé armády 140, CS-391 65
Bechyně
Decorative Arts Museum - 1911
Ceramics; folk art; local history;
archeology

Bělá pod Bezdězem
02848
Vlastivědné muzeum
Zámek 1, CS-294 21 Bělá pod
Bezdězem
General Museum - 1906
Local geology; ethnography; social
and cultural history of the region

Benátky nad Jizerou
02849
Městské muzeum
Zámek 1, CS-294 71 Benátky nad
Jizerou
General Museum - 1937
Paleontology; botany; ornithology;
archeology; ethnography; local
history; collections illustrating the life
and work of the composer Bedřich
Smetana (1824-1884) and the
astronomer Tycho Brahe (1546-1601)

Beroun
02850
Okresni muzeum
Gottwaldovo nám. 87, CS-266 01
Beroun
General Museum - 1883
Paleontology; mineralogy; archeology;
local history; ethnography;
memorabilia of the conductor Václav
Talich (b.1883)

Betliar
02851
Štátny kultúrny majetok
CS-049 21 Betliar
General Museum - 1949
Furnishings; painting; arms; hunting
trophies; in a 18th century palace -
library

Bilá Třemešná
02852
Památnik Jana Ámose Komenského
CS-544 72 Bílá Třemešná
Historic Site - 1958
Life and work of the pedagogue,
philosopher and theologist Jan Ámos
Komenský (J.A. Comenius, 1592-1670)
in his former house

Bilovec
02853
Městské muzeum
Zámecká ul. 5, CS-743 01 Bílovec
General Museum - 1905
Local history; archeology;
ethnography

Blansko
02854
Vlastivědné muzeum
Zámek 1, CS-678 01 Blansko
General Museum - 1969
Local history; industrial history;
archeology; iron casts

Blovice
02855
Okresni muzeum
Tř. Rudé armády 148, CS-336 01
Blovice
General Museum - 1953
Archeology; history; ethnography;
literature

Bojkovice
02856
Muzeum
zámek Nový Světlov, CS-687 71
Bojkovice
General Museum - 1931
Mineralogy; entomology; history;
ethnography

Bojnice
02857
Múzeum
Hrad, CS-972 01 Bojnice
General Museum - 1950
Nitra Valley geology; geography;
prehistoric archeology; weaving;
furniture; fine arts; in a 13th century
castle

Boskovice
02858
Vlastivědné muzeum
Hradní ul. 6, zámek, CS-680 01
Boskovice
General Museum - 1905
Ornithology; archeology; local history

Bouzov
02859
Státni hrad Krajské vlastivědné
muzeum Olomouc (Castle Museum)
CS-783 25 Bouzov
History/Public Affairs Museum
Interiors in neo-Gothic style; paintings;
handicrafts

Brandýs nad Labem - Stará Boleslav
02860
Okresni muzeum Praha-východ
Zámek 402, CS-250 01 Brandýs nad
Labem - Stará Boleslav
General Museum - 1911
Regional natural history; prehistory;
medieval archeology; ethnography

02861
**Památnik Františka Ondřička a
Českého kvarteta**
CS-250 01 Brandýs nad Labem - Stará
Boleslav
Historic Site - 1962
Memorial to the violinist František
Ondříček and Czech quartet in
Brandýs n.L.

Brandýs nad Orlicí

02862
Památník Jana Ámose Komenského
Náměstí 203, CS-561 12 Brandýs nad
Orlicí
Historic Site - 1957
Memorabilia of the pedagogue,
philosopher and theologist Jan Amos
Komenský (J.A. Comenius 1592-1670)

Bratislava

02863
**Galéria hlavného mesta SSR
Bratislavy** (Gallery of the Capital of
the Slovak Socialist Republic
Bratislava)
Mirbachov palác, Diebrovo nám. 11,
CS-894 16 Bratislava
Fine Arts Museum
Comprises three exhibitions: Ancient
European Art, Primaciálny palác;
18th-to 20th century Art, Mirbachov
palác; Gothic painting and plastic art,
Klarisky - library

02864
Janko Jesenský múzeum Mestske
múzeum
Somolického 4, CS-800 00 Bratislava
Historic Site
Memorabilia of the writer Janko
Jesenský (1874-1945) in his former
home - library

02865
Johann Nepomuk Hummel múzeum
Mestské múzeum
Klobučnická 2, CS-800 00 Bratislava
Historic Site
Life and work of the composer J. N.
Hummel (1778-1837) in his birth house
; original spinets, pianos

02866
Mestské múzeum
Primaciálny palác - Stará Radnica,
CS-800 00 Bratislava
General Museum - 1868
Local history; folk art; crafts;
furnishings; tools; musical instruments;
prehistoric weapons; ceramics;
costumes

02867
Múzeum V. I. Lenina
ul. Obrancov mieru 21a, CS-801 00
Bratislava
History/Public Affairs Museum
Memorial to V.I.Lenin; documents

02868
Slovenská národna galéria
Riečna 1, CS-890 13 Bratislava
Fine Arts Museum - 1948
Paintings; sculpture; prints; drawings;
applied art - library

02869
Slovenské národné múzeum (Slovak
National Museum)
Vajanského nábr. 2, CS-885 36
Bratislava
General Museum - 1924
Archeology; history; natural sciences;
museology

Břeclav

02870
Zahradnické Oddělení
Československé zemědělské
múzeum, Praha (Museum of
Horticulture)
Zámek Lednice u Břeclavi, CS-690 03
Břeclav
Agriculture Museum
Hunting; horticulture; botany

Břeclav-Pohansko

02871
Archeologické muzeum
Pohansko, zámeček, CS-690 00
Břeclav-Pohansko
Archeology Museum - 1964
Prehistoric archeology; exhibits from
local excavations

Březnice

02872
**Městské muzeum a galerie Ludvíka
Kuby**
zámek, CS-262 72 Březnice
General Museum - 1897
Archeology; local history;
ethnography; paintings by Ludvík
Kuba

Brezno

02873
Horehronské Múzeum
Gottwaldovo nám. 1, CS-977 26
Brezno
General Museum - 1960
Ethnography; local history

Brno

02874
**Botanické a entomologické oddělení
Moravského muzea** (Botanical and
Entomological Branch of the Moravian
Museum in Brno)
Preslova ul. 1, CS-600 00 Brno
Science/Tech Museum
Botany; entomology

02875
**Etnografický ústav Moravského
muzea** (Ethnographical Institute of the
Moravian Museum in Brno)
Gagarinova tř. 1, CS-600 00 Brno
Anthropology Museum - 1961
Ethnography; folk art; agricultural
machinery; farm implements

02876
**Hudební oddělení Moravského
múzea** (Music Branch of the Moravian
Museum in Brno)
Smetanova ul. 14, CS-600 00 Brno
Music Museum - 1963
Music; musicology; musical
instruments; manuscripts; memorabilia
of the composer Leoš Janáček
(1854-1928)

02877
Moravská galerie v Brně (Moravian
Gallery in Brno)
Husova 14, CS-600 00 Brno
Fine Arts Museum - 1818
European paintings and graphics from
16th to 19th century; Czech art from
Middle Ages to 20th century; applied
art; oriental art; textiles; jewelry;
ceramics; photography - library

02878
Moravské muzeum v Brně (Moravian
Museum in Brno)
Nám. 25. února 8, CS-600 00 Brno
General Museum - 1818
Geology; mineralogy; Karst
geomorphology; ethnography; botany;
numismatics; museology - music-
theatre, archive

02879
Muzeum dělnického hnutí (Museum
of the Labour Movement)
Nám. Rudé armády 1a, CS-600 00
Brno
History/Public Affairs Museum - 1957
History of the labour movement and
the Communist Party in Southern
Moravia

02880
Muzeum města Brna (Municipal
Museum)
Hrad 1, CS-600 00 Brno
General Museum - 1894
Archeology; applied arts; fine arts;
local history; history of the Italian,
Hungarian and Polish revolutionary
prisoners in the Špilberk fortress;
resistance movement in World War II

02881
Památník Gregoria Mendela
Moravské muzeum v Brně
CS-600 00 Brno
Historic Site
Memorabilia of the geneticist Gregor
Johann Mendel (1822-1884); botany

02882
Pavillon Anthropos Moravské
muzeum v Brně
CS-600 00 Brno
Anthropology Museum - 1965
Anthropology and paleontology of
Moravia

02883
Technické muzeum
Orlí ul. 20, CS-600 00 Brno
Science/Tech Museum - 1953
Machine products; cast iron; internal
combustion motors; hydraulic energy;
geodesy; documents from scientists'
bequests

Broumov

02884
Vlastivědné muzeum
Klášter, CS-550 01 Broumov
General Museum - 1945
History and natural history of the
region; ethnography

Bruntál

02885
Okresní vlastivědné muzeum
Zámecké náměstí 5, cs-685 01 Bruntál
General Museum - 1907
Natural history and history of the
region

Bučovice

02886
Vlastivědné muzeum
Zámek 1, CS-685 01 Bučovice
General Museum - 1914
Local mineralogy and archeology;
history; ethnography; numismatics

Budyně nad Ohří

02887
Městské muzeum
Zámek, cs-411 18 Budyně nad Ohří
General Museum - 1945
Paleontology; archeology; art;
handicrafts; ethnography

Bystřice nad Pernštejnem

02888
Městské muzeum
nám. 9. května 1, CS-593 01 Bystřice
nad Pernštejnem
General Museum - 1955
Local natural history and history in
general; handicrafts; ethnography

Bzenec

02889
Muzeum
Náměstí 75, CS-696 81 Bzenec
General Museum
Local history

Čadca

02890
Kysucke Múzeum
Palárikov dom, CS-022 01 Čadca
General Museum
Local history

Čáslav

02891
Městské muzeum
ul. Protifašistických bojovníků 291,
CS-286 01 Čáslav
General Museum - 1864/1884
Geology; mineralogy; zoology; botany;
archeology; numismatics;
ethnography; art; handicrafts; literary
archives of the writer Jiří Mahen

Čáslavice

02892
Památník Bedřicha Václavka
CS-675 24 Čáslavice
Historic Site - 1942
Memorabilia of the literary historian
Bedřich Václavek in his former home

Čechy pod Kosířem

02893
Památník Josefa Mánesa
Zámek, CS-798 58 Čechy pod
Kosířem
Historic Site
Memorabilia of the painter Josef
Mánes (1820-1871)

Čelákovice

02894
Městské muzeum
CS-250 80 Čelákovice
General Museum - 1911
Local archeology; history; natural
history of the Polabí region; basketry

Červený Hrádek

02895
Památník boje proti fašismu Okresní
muzeum Chomutov
Zámek, CS-281 42 Červený Hrádek
History/Public Affairs Museum - 1969
Historical exhibits on the agreement
between Konrad Henlein and Lord
Runciman (1938) over Sudetenland;
anti-Fascist resistance in World War II

Červený Kameň

02896
Štátny Hrad (Castle Museum)
Hrad, CS-018 56 Červený Kameň
General Museum - 1950
Original furnishing; arms; ceramics;
porcelain; sculpture; paintings;
Slovakian folk art; in a 16th century
castle

Červený Kláštor-Kúpele

02897
Červený Kláštor Východoslovenské
Múzeum, Košice
Pieniny, CS-059 06 Červený Kláštor-
Kúpele
Religious Art Museum
Cloister history; religious art;
furnishing; Hussite armaments;
ethnography; in a 14th century cloister

Červený Kostelec

02898
Památník Boženy Němcové
ul. Boženy Němcové 127, CS-549 41
Červený Kostelec
Historic Site
Memorabilia of the writer Božena
Němcová (1820-1862)

Česká Lípa

02899
Okresni vlastivědné muzeum
Komenského nám. 297, CS-470 01
Česká Lípa
General Museum - 1900
Geology; mineralogy; paleontology;
zoology; archeology; ethnography;
numismatics; applied art; fine art; old
prints; history of labour movement

Česká Skalice

02900
Muzeum Boženy Němcové
ul. Boženy Němcové 9, CS-552 03
Česká Skalice
Historic Site - 1931
Memorabilia of the writer Božena
Němcová (1820-1862); porcelain;
textiles; ethnography; history; painting

Česká Třebová

02901
Městské muzeum
Nám. Sbratření 77, CS-560 02 Česká
Třebová
General Museum - 1887
Folk art; local history; guild relics;
development of railway transportation

České Budějovice

02902
Jihočeské múzeum (Museum of
South Bohemia)
Dukelská ul. 1, CS-370 00 České
Budějovice
General Museum - 1876
Natural sciences; archeology; theatre
and music ; local history; ethnography;
numismatics; regional literature;
manuscripts; prints

02903
**Muzeum dělnického revolučniho
hnuti** (Museum of the Labour
Revolutionary Movement)
Lidická tř., CS-370 00 České
Budějovice
History/Public Affairs Museum - 1975
Labour movement in the region of
South Bohemia

Český Brod

02904
Muzeum Regionální Muzeum Kolín
ul. 5. května 761, CS-282 01 Český
Brod
General Museum - 1896
Local archeology; ethnography;
history of the town

Český Dub

02905
Muzeum Karoliny Světlé
CS-463 43 Český Dub 31/IV
General Museum - 1919
Local ethnography, archeology,
geology and mineralogy; literary
history and memorabilia of the writer
Karolina Světlá

Český Krumlov

02906
Okresni vlastivědné muzeum
Horní ul. 152, CS-381 01 Český
Krumlov
General Museum - 1946
Natural history; archeology; local
history; ethnography; Gothic and
Renaissance sculpture

Český Těšín

02907
Okresni vlastivědné muzeum
Revoluční ul. 13 and 15, CS-737 01
Český Těšín
General Museum - 1948
Local history; ethnography; botany;
geology

Cheb

02908
Chebské muzeum
Nám. Krále Jiřího z Poděbrad 3,
CS-350 01 Cheb
General Museum - 1874
Coll: archeology; ethnography; natural
sciences; history; memorabilia of
Albrecht Valdsten (Albrecht von
Wallenstein, Duke of Friedland,
1583-1634)

02909
Galerie výtvarného umění (Gallery of
Fine Arts)
Nám. Krále Jiřího z Poděbrad 16,
CS-350 01 Cheb
Fine Arts Museum - 1961
Czech Gothic sculpture from 14th to
16th century; 16th-17th century wood
carving; contemporary Czech art

Chlum

02910
Památník Války 1866
post office Všetary 66, CS- Chlum
History/Public Affairs Museum - 1932
Mementoes of the Austro-Prussian
War and the Battle of Hradec Králové
(Königgrätz)

Chlumec nad Cidlinou

02911
**Muzeum selských bouři a V.K.
Klicpery** (Museum of Peasants' Revolt
and V.K. Klicpera Memorial House)
castle Karlova Koruna, CS-503 51
Chlumec nad Cidlinou
History/Public Affairs Museum - 1928
History of the peasants' revolt in the
18th century; development of the
theatre during the rebirth of the
nationalist movement in the 19th
century; memorabilia of Václav Kliment
Klicpera

Chlumec u Ústí nad Labem

02912
Památník Bitvy 1813
CS Chlumec u Ústí nad Labem
History/Public Affairs Museum - 1913
Mementoes of the Battle of Ústí nad
Labem (Aussig) in 1813; historical
documents

Choceň

02913
Orlické muzeum
Pardubická 1, zámek, CS-565 00
Choceň
General Museum - 1909
Ornithology; paleontology;
archeology; ethnography; history of
the Resistance Movement 1939-1945

Chomutov

02914
Okresni muzeum
nám. 1. máje 1, CS-430 00 Chomutov
General Museum - 1923
Geology; mineralogy; archeology;
production of lace and trimmings;
16th-18th century sculpture

Chotěboř

02915
**Městské muzeum a galerie Jindřicha
Průchy**
Riegrova 1, zámek, CS-583 01
Chotěboř
General Museum - 1885
Geology; mineralogy; local history;
applied art; paintings; graphics and
sculpture by Jindřich Průcha, Zdeněk
Rykr and Karel Opatrný

Chrast u Chrudimě

02916
Městské muzeum
Gottwaldovo nám. 1, zámek, CS-538
51 Chrast u Chrudimě
General Museum - 1893
Geology; local history; handicrafts;
paintings

Chropyně

02917
Památník Dr. Emila Axmana
Náměstí 30, zámek, CS-768 11
Chropyně
Historic Site - 1960
Memorabilia of the composer Dr. Emil
Axman and the painter Emil Filla; local
history and ethnography

Chrudim

02918
Vlastivědné muzeum
Obránců míru 86, CS-537 00 Chrudim
IV
General Museum - 1865
Mineralogy; zoology; archeology; local
history and ethnography; applied art

Chudenice

02919
**Muzeum Josefa Dobrovského a
Jaroslava Kvapila**
Starý zámek, CS-340 14 Chudenice
Historic Site - 1952
Memorabilia of the Slavicist Josef
Dobrovský (1753-1829) and the writer
Jaroslav Kvapil; local history

Dačice

02920
Městské muzeum
Jemnická ul. 21, CS-380 01 Dačice
General Museum - 1893
Local and regional archeology; history;
art from the Middle Ages to the 20th
century; contemporary Czech painting
and graphics

Dašice

02921
Památník Josefa Hybeše
Na Zářečí 2, CS-533 03 Dašice
Historic Site - 1971
Memorabilia of the politician and
workers' leader Josef Hybeš

Děčín

02922
Vlastivědné muzeum
Tř. Československé mládeže 1/31,
CS-405 00 Děčín IV
General Museum
Local history; shipping on the Elbe
River; geology; entomology; paintings;
sculpture; graphics; art; handicrafts;
relics and history of the German
concentration camp at Rabštejn

Dědice u Vyškova

02923
Památník Klementa Gottwalda
Revoluční 16, CS Dědice u Vyškova
Historic Site - 1955
Collections illustrating the youth, life
and work of the politician Klement
Gottwald (1896-1953)

Dětřichov u Frýdlantu

02924
**Památník sklářstvi v Jizerských
Horách** Muzeum skla a bižuterie
Jablonec nad Nisou (Glass Museum)
Kristiánov v Jizerských Horách,
CS-463 71 Dětřichov u Frýdlantu
Decorative Arts Museum - 1963
History of the glass manufacture in the
former glass settlement Kristiánov

Diváky

02925
Památník Bratří Mrštíků (Mrštík
Brothers Memorial House)
CS-691 71 Diváky 57
Historic Site - 1960
Memorabilia of the Mrštík brothers,
19th century writers, in their former
house

Dobřív

02926
Starý hamr Okresní muzeum
Rokycany
CS-338 44 Dobřív
Science/Tech Museum
Forge with water-driven hammer (ca
1702)

Dobruška

02927
Městské muzeum
Šubrtovo náměstí 53, CS-518 01
Dobruška
History/Public Affairs Museum - 1931
Local and regional history; documents
on the period of rebirth of the
nationalist movement in the 19th
century

Doksy

02928
Památník Karla Hynka Máchy
Okresni vlastivědné muzeum Česká
Lípa
Lípové náměstí 150, CS-472 01 Doksy
Historic Site - 1960
Memorabilia of the poet Karel Hynek
Mácha (1810-1836)

Dolínek

02929
Památník Vítězslava Hálka
CS Dolínek
Historic Site - 1963
Collection of items about the life and
work of Czech writers, especially of
the poet Vítzeslav Hálek (1835-1874)

Dolná Strehová

02930
**Okresné vlastivedné múzeum Veľký
Krtíš**
CS-991 02 Dolná Strehová
General Museum
Local historyemorial to the writer Imre
Madách (1823-1864)

Dolní Domaslovice

02931
Památník
Škola, CS-739 38 Dolní Domaslovice
Anthropology Museum
Handicrafts; folk furniture; costumes;
local history

Dolný Kubín

02932
**Literárne múzeum Pavla Országha-
Hviezdoslava**
Hviezdoslavovo nám. 44, CS-026 01
Dolný Kubín
Historic Site - 1932
Memorial to the poet Pavol O.
Hviezdoslav (1849-1921)

02933
Oravská galéria
Hviezdoslavovo nám. 43, CS-026 01
Dolný Kubín
Fine Arts Museum - 1965
Painting; sculpture; graphics

Domažlice

02934
Chodské muzeum
Chodské náměstí 96, hrad, CS-344 00
Domažlice
General Museum - 1889
Local history; ethnography; regional
archeology; numismatics; decorative
art; paintings by Karel Špilar;
memorabilia of the poet Jaroslav
Vrchlický (1853-1912)

02935
Muzeum Jindřicha Jindřicha
Nám. Svobody 61, CS-344 00
Domažlice
Historic Site
Ethnography; regional painting; literary
and musical manuscripts by the
musician and ethnography collector
Jindřich Jindřich

Dunajská Streda

02936
Žitnoostrovské múzeum
Malinovského 22, CS-929 01 Dunajská
Streda
General Museum
Local history

Dvůr Králové nad Labem

02937
Městské a textilní muzeum
Nejedlého ul. 1029, CS-544 00 Dvůr
Králové nad Labem
General Museum - 1936
History of textile manufacturing in
Czech lands

Fiľakovo

02938
Novohradské múzeum
Zápotockého 14, CS-986 01 Fiľakovo
General Museum
Local history

Františkovy Lázně

02939
Městské muzeum
ul. Dr. Pohoreckého 8, CS-351 01
Františkovy Lázně
General Museum - 1913
Local history concerning the
development of the town as a spa;
balneology

Frenštát pod Radhoštěm

02940
Městské muzeum
Náměstí Míru 1, CS-744 01 Frenštát
pod Radhoštěm
General Museum - 1951
Local history; folk art; ethnography;
weaving

Frýdek-Místek

02941
Okresni vlastivědné muzeum
Náměstí Míru 1, CS-738 01 Frýdek-
Místek
General Museum - 1929
Natural history; ethnography; folk art;
memorabilia of the composer Leoš
Janáček and the poet Petr Bezruč

Frýdlant v Čechách

02942
Městské muzeum
Stalingradské nám. 12, CS-464 01
Frýdlant v Čechách
General Museum - 1899
Geology; botany; local history; applied
arts; documents of the Peasant Revolt
of 1679 and 1775; history of the labour
movement in the region

Fulnek

02943
Památník Jana Ámose Komenského
Sborová 1, CS-742 45 Fulnek
Historic Site - 1954
Memorabilia of the pedagogue,
philosopher and theologist Jan Ámos
Komenský (Comenius)

Galanta

02944
Okresné vlastivedné múzeum
CS-924 00 Galanta
General Museum
Local history; ethnology

Gelnica

02945
Banícke múzeum (Mining Museum)
Banícke nám. 6, CS-056 01 Gelnica
Science/Tech Museum - 1938
Mineralogy; mining history and
technology; local history

Gottwaldov

02946
Oblastni galerie výtvaného umění
Dům umění, CS-760 00 Gottwaldov
Fine Arts Museum - 1953
Modern Czech art

02947
**Oblastni muzeum Jihovýchodní
Moravy**
Soudní' ul. 1, CS-760 00 Gottwaldov
General Museum - 1953
Coll: natural sciences; archeology;
ethnography; history

02948
Obuvnické muzeum N.P. Svit (Shoe
Museum)
CS-760 00 Gottwaldov
Science/Tech Museum - 1959
History of shoe production and
technology

Habry

02949
Stálá Výstava Okresní muzeum,
Havlíčkuv Brod
Leškovice, CS-582 81 Habry 38
History/Public Affairs Museum - 1962
History of the partisan brigade called
'Brigade of M.J. Hus' during World
War II

Harrachov v Krkonošich

02950
Muzeum Skla (Glass Museum)
CS-512 46 Harrachov v Krkonošich
Decorative Arts Museum
Coll: blown glass from one of the
oldest Czechoslovakian glass works,
founded in 1712; modern glass
examples

Havířov

02951
Muzeum boje proti fašismu (Museum
of the Struggle against Fascism)
CS-736 00 Havířov Životice
History/Public Affairs Museum
History of the German occupation and
the local resistance movement

Havlíčkova Borová

02952
Památník Karla Havlíčka Borovského
CS-582 23 Havlíčkova Borová 163
Historic Site - 1931
Life and work of the journalist and
writer Karel Havlíček Borovský

Havlíčkův Brod

02953
Galerie výtvarného umění (Art
Gallery)
Malinův dům, nám. Čs. armády 50,
CS-580 01 Havlíčkův Brod
Fine Arts Museum - 1965
Czech drawings and graphics

02954
**Okresní muzeum - Památník Karla
Havlíčka Borovského**
Nám. Čs. armády 19, CS-580 01
Havlíčkův Brod
General Museum - 1924
Memorabilia on the life and work of
the journalist and writer Karel Havlíček
Borovský in the house where he lived
in his youth

02955
Památník Otakara Štáfla Okresní
muzeum
Havlíčkovy sady - bašta, CS-580 01
Havlíčkův Brod
Fine Arts Museum - 1957
Memorabilia of the painter Otakar
Štáfl; collection of his paintings

Havýřov

02956
Muzeum socialistické výstavby
(Museum of Socialist Development)
CS-736 00 Havýřov IV, bl. 63
History/Public Affairs Museum
Local contemporary history - 1960

Hlinsko v Čechách

02957
Vlastivědné muzeum a galerie
Havlíčkova 675, CS-539 01 Hlinsko v
Čechách
General Museum
Natural history, especially mineralogy,
geology; regional history;
ethnography; archeology; art

Hlohovec

02958
Okresné múzeum Trnava
Komenského 15, CS-920 01 Hlohovec
General Museum - 1950
Natural sciences; history

Hluboká nad Vltavou

02959
Alšova Jihočeská galerie (Aleš South
Bohemian Gallery)
CS-373 41 Hluboká nad Vltavou
Fine Arts Museum - 1952
Coll: Gothic and Baroque art of South
Bohemia; 17th century Flemish and
Dutch painting; ceramics and modern
20th century Czech art

02960
**Lesnické, myslivecké a rybářské
sbirka** Československé zemědělské
Muzeum, Praha (Museum of Forestry,
Hunting and Fishery)
Zámek Ohrada u Hluboké nad Vltavou,
CS-373 41 Hluboká nad Vltavou
Anthropology Museum - 1961
Coll: forestry; hunting; fishery

Hodonín

02961
Galerie výtvarného uměni (Art
Gallery)
Úprkova 1, CS-695 00 Hodonín
Fine Arts Museum - 1907
Modern Czech art; contemporary
paintings

02962
Okresni Muzeum Hodoninska
Zámecké nám. 9, CS-695 00 Hodonín
General Museum - 1903
Geology; mineralogy; local history;

Hodslavice

02963
Památník Františka Palackého
CS-742 71 Hodslavice 108
Historic Site - 1946
Memorabilia of the historian and
politician František Palacký
(1798-1876) in his former home

Holešov

02964
Městské muzeum Okresní muzeum
Kroměřížska, Kroměříž
Nám. F.X. Richtera 190, CS-769 01
Holešov
General Museum - 1941
Furniture production; local history and
ethnography

Holice v Čechách

02965
Památník Dr. Emila Holuba
Holubova ul. I/768, CS-534 01 Holice v
Čechách
Historic Site - 1970
Memorabilia of the explorer Dr. Emil
Holub; natural history, art and
ethnography of Africa

Horažďovice

02966
Městské muzeum
Zámek, CS-341 00 Horažďovice
General Museum - 1895
Local history; agriculture; archeology;
ethnography

Hořice v Pokrkonoši

02967
Meštské muzeum a galerie
Revoluční nám. 160, CS-508 01 Hořice
v Pokrkonoši
General Museum - 1887
Archeology; ethnography; toy making;
art (especially sculpture and
stonecutting)

Horní Branná

02968
Památník Jana Ámose Komenského
Zámek, CS-512 36 Horní Branná
Historic Site
Collection illustrating life and work of
the pedagogue, philosopher and
theologist Jan Ámos Komenský
(Comenius, 1592-1670)

Horní Planá

02969
Památník Adalberta Stiftera Okresní
muzeum Český Krumlov
CS-382 26 Horní Planá
Historic Site
Memorabilia of the Austrian writer
Adalbert Stifter (1805-1868) in his
former house

Horný Smokovec

02970
Tatranská Galéria
CS-062 01 Horný Smokovec
Fine Arts Museum
Fine art; contemporary art

Hořovice

02971
Okresní muzeum
tzv. Nový zámek 1, CS-268 01
Hořovice II
General Museum - 1912
Geology; paleontology; mineralogy;
zoology; archeology; ethnography;
applied art

Horšovský Týn

02972
Vlastivědné muzeum
Zámecký park 5, CS-346 01
Horšovský Týn
General Museum - 1945
Local history and archeology;
numismatics; ethnography; applied art

Hostinné

02973
Muzeum antického uměni (Museum
of Classical Art)
Františkanský klášter, CS-543 71
Hostinné
Fine Arts Museum - 1969
Casts from Greek and Roman
sculpture

02974
Památník Karla Kliče
Náměstí 1. máje 1, CS-543 71 Hostinné
Historic Site
Memorabilia of Karel Klíč (1841-1926),
inventor of the gravure press

Hradec Králové

02975
Krajská galerie (Regional Gallery)
Žižkovo náměstí 35, CS-500 00
Hradec Králové
Fine Arts Museum - 1953
20th century Czech art

02976
Odděleni archeologické a historické
Krajské muzeum Vychodnych Čech
(Regional Museum of Eastern
Bohemia, Department of Archeology
and History)
Nábř. protifašistických bojovníků 465,
CS-500 00 Hradec Králove
Archeology Museum - 1879
Regional archeology; history; history
of the revolutionary movement;
medieval ceramics; illuminated
manuscripts; numismatics; applied art;
arms

02977
Odděleni přirodovědecké Krajské
muzeum Vychodních Čech (Regional
Museum of Eastern Bohemia,
Department of Natural History)
Husovo náměstí 124, 125, CS-500 00
Hradec Králové
Natural History Museum - 1939
Mineralogy; paleontology; geology;
botany; entomology; zoology

Hranice na Moravě

02978
Muzeum Moravské Brány Okresní
vlastivědné muzeum Přerov
Janáčkova ul. 1, CS Hranice na
Moravě
General Museum - 1905
Local natural history and history in
general; archeology; ethnography;
pottery from the 18th century

Hronov

02979
Muzeum Aloise Jiráska
Jiráskovo divadlo, CS-549 31 Hronov
Historic Site - 1910
Memorabilia of the writer Alois Jirásek
(1851-1930); local and natural history

Hudlice

02980
Památník Leoše Janáčka
Hukvaldy 78, CS-267 03 Hudlice
Historic Site - 1933
Memorabilia of the composer Leoš
Janáček (1854-1928)

Humenné

02981
Okresné vlastivedné múzeum
CS-066 01 Humenné
Anthropology Museum - 1960
Ethnography; folk art; in a 17th century
Renaissance palace

Humpolec

02982
Muzeum Dr. Aleše Hrdličky
Horní náměstí 273, CS-396 01
Humpolec
Historic Site - 1895
Memorabilia of the anthropologist Dr.
Aleš Hrdlička (1869-1943); local
history; textile production;
ethnography

Husinec

02983
Památník Mistra Jana Husa
Rodný domek, CS-384 21 Husinec
Historic Site - 1952
Memorabilia of the reformer Jan Hus
(1370-1415) in his former home

Hynčice-Vražné

02984
Památník Gregora Mendela
CS Hynčice-Vražné 120
Historic Site - 1965
Collections illustrating the life and
work of the botanist Gregor Mendel
(1822-1884)

Ilava

02985
Mestské múzeum
CS-019 01 Ilava
General Museum
Local history

Ivančice

02986
Okresni muzeum
Palackého nám. 6, CS-664 91 Ivančice
General Museum - 1894
Archeology; local history;
ethnography; ceramics

Jabkenice

02987
Památník Bedřicha Smetany Muzeum
české hudby, Praha
CS-294 45 Jabkenice 33
Historic Site - 1937
Memorabilia of the composer Bedřich
Smetana (1824-1857)

Jablonec nad Nisou

02988
Muzeum skla a bižuterie (Museum of
Glass and Jewelry)
Jiráskova ul. 4, CS-466 00 Jablonec
nad Nisou
Decorative Arts Museum - 1900
16th-19th century European, especially
Northern Bohemian glass; glass
products of all kinds; jewelry

Jáchymov

02989
**Muzeum Jáchymovského hornictví a
lázeňstvi** Karlovarské muzeum,
Karlovy Vary (Museum of Mining and
Balneology in Jáchymov)
Nám. Republiky 37, CS-362 51
Jáchymov
History/Public Affairs Museum - 1923
Numismatics; library of the 16th
century Latin school at Jáchymov;
history of the spa; uranium mining

Jaroměř

02990
**Městské muzeum a galerie Otakara
Španiela a Josefa Wágnera**
Husova tř. 259, CS Jaroměř
General Museum - 1883
Archeology; ethnography;
numismatics; exhibits on the life and
work of the sculptor Otakar Španiel;
paintings and sculpture by O. Spaniel
and J. Wágner

Jemnice

02991
Muzeum
Nám. Svobody 31, CS-675 31 Jemnice
General Museum - 1928
Local history; history of mining; old
crafts; medieval ceramics; cultural
history of the town

Jesenice u Rakovníka

02992
Městské muzeum
Mírové nám. 15, CS-270 33 Jesenice u
Rakovníka
General Museum
Archeology; old crafts; ethnography;
natural history

Jeseník

02993
Muzeum Okresní vlastivědné muzeum
Šumperk
Zámecké nám. 1, CS-790 00 Jeseník
General Museum - 1901
Geology; mineralogy; local
archeology; history of the town and
spa

Jičín

02994
Okresni galerie (Regional Art Gallery)
Zámek, Gottwaldovo nám., CS-506 01
Jičín
Fine Arts Museum
Contemporary Czech art, regional art

02995
Okresni muzeum
Gottwaldovo náměstí 1, zámek,
CS-506 01 Jičín
General Museum - 1905
Natural history; archeology;
ethnography; local history

Jihlava

02996
Muzeum Vysočiny v Jihlavě
Nám. Miru 57-58, CS-586 00 Jihlava
General Museum - 1892
Natural history of Czech-Moravian
Highlands; geology; mineralogy;
zoology; archeology; history;
ethnography; applied art; history and
technology of the local mining industry
- library

02997
Oblastní galerie Vysočiny (Regional
Art Gallery)
Komenského 10, CS-586 00 Jihlava
Fine Arts Museum - 1948
Czech modern art

Jilemnice

02998
Krkonošské muzeum (Museum of
Krkonoše Region)
Zámek č. 75, CS-514 01 Jilemnice
General Museum - 1891
Geology of the region of Krkonoše;
old crafts; folk art; history; paintings by
František Kaván

Jílové u Prahy

02999
Muzeum těžby a zpracovaní zlata
(Museum of Gold Mining and
Technology)
Náměstí 16, CS-254 01 Jílové u Prahy
Science/Tech Museum - 1891
History and technology of local gold
mining; archeology; local natural
history

Jindřichův Hradec

03000
Expozice Soudobé Tapiserie
Uměleckoprůmyslové Muzeum, Praha
(Tapestry Museum)
Státní zámek, CS-377 01 Jindřichův
Hradec
Decorative Arts Museum
Coll: contemporary tapestry; wall
decorations; textiles; ceramics

03001
Vlastivědné muzeum
Balbínovo nám. 19/I, CS-377 01
Jindřichův Hradec
General Museum
Local history; memorabilia of Bedřich
Smetana, Ema Destinová, F. Rákoczi;
ethnography; Gothic and baroque
Czech art; Bohemian glass; folk art

Jur pri Bratislave

03002
Mestské Múzeum
ul. Červenej armády, CS-900 21 Jur pri
Bratislave
Archeology Museum
Archeology; local history

03003
Múzeum Petra Jilemnického
Letohradská, CS-900 21 Jur pri
Bratislave
Historic Site - 1952
Memorabilia of the writer Peter
Jilemnický (1901-1949) in his parents'
home

Kačina

03004
Zemědělské muzeum
Československé zemědělské muzeum
Praha
Kačina, CS-285 31 Nové Dvory u
Kutné Hory
Agriculture Museum
History of agriculture in
Czechoslovakia; food production

Kadaň

03005
Muzeum Okresní muzeum Chomutov
Františkánský klášter, Švermova 474,
CS-432 01 Kadaň
General Museum
Local history; ethnography

Kamenice nad Lipou

03006
Vlastivědné muzeum
Palackého ul. 75, CS-394 70 Kamenice
nad Lipou
General Museum - 1940
Mineralogy; zoology; local history;
applied art; ethnography; numismatics;
memorabilia of the composer Vítězslav
Novák

Kamenický Šenov

03007
Muzeum skla Muzeum skla a bižuterie
Jablonec nad Nisou (Glass Museum)
ul. Osvobození 69, CS-471 14
Kamenický Šenov
Decorative Arts Museum - 1893
Old Bohemian glass; modern glass
products

Karlovy Vary

03008
Galerie umění (Art Gallery)
Puškinova strezka 7, CS-360 00
Karlovy Vary
Fine Arts Museum - 1953
20th century Czech and Slovak art

03009
Karlovarské muzeum
Zámecký vrch 22, CS-360 00 Karlovy
Vary
General Museum
Coll: natural sciences; art; applied arts;
industry; history and documents of the
Karlovy Vary Spa

03010
Muzeum Karla Marxe
Marxova ul. 3, CS-360 00 Karlovy Vary
Historic Site - 1960
Collections illustrating the period in
which Karl Marx (1818-1883) lived in
Carlsbad; history of the labour
movement in the region

03011
Muzeum karlovarského porcelánu
(Museum of Porcelain in Carlsbad)
CS-360 08 Karlovy Vary 8
Decorative Arts Museum - 1964
History of the porcelain factory at
Březová

03012
Sklářské muzeum (Museum of Glass
Production)
CS-360 06 Karlovy Vary 6
Decorative Arts Museum
History of the local production of glass

Kašperské Hory

03013
Muzeum Šumavy Muzeum Šumavy,
Sušice
Náměstí Československé armády 189,
CS-341 92 Kašperské Hory
General Museum - 1925
Natural history of Šumava region; folk
glass; collections illustrating the glass
industry, paper industry, mining,
lumbering

Kelč

03014
Památník Bratří Křičků Okresní
vlastivědné muzeum, Vsetín
CS-756 43 Kelč 107
Historic Site - 1948
Memorabilia of the writer Petr Křička
(1884-1949) and his brother Jaroslav
Křička; local archeology; paleontology;
numismatics; collection of pipes

Kežmarok

03015
Múzeum
Hradna ul. 69, CS-060 01 Kežmarok
General Museum - 1928
Coll: archeology; ethnography; art
history; guild objects

Kladno

03016
Okresní muzeum
ul. Dělnického hnutí 1, zámek, CS-272
00 Kladno
General Museum - 1899
Geology; mineralogy; archeology;
ethnography; history of mining and
metallurgy; labour movement;
decorative arts

Klášterec nad Ohří

03017
Muzeum Českého Porcelánu
Uměleckoprůmyslové Muzeum, Praha
(Museum of Czech Porcelain)
CS-431 51 Klášterec nad Ohří
Decorative Arts Museum - 1953
Coll: oriental and European porcelain;
documents on the production of
Czech porcelain since 1792

Klatovy

03018
Okresní muzeum a galerie
Hostašova 1/IV, CS-339 00 Klatovy
General Museum - 1882
Local history; ethnography;
archeology; medicine and pharmacy;
cultivation of carnations; history of the
labour movement

Klenčí pod Čerchovem

03019
Muzeum Jindřicha Šimona Baara
Nám. J. Jindřicha 140, CS-345 34
Klenčí pod Čerchovem
Historic Site - 1925
Memorabilia of the writer J.Š. Baar,
composer Jindřich Jindřich and the
physician Prof. Dr. Josef Thomayer;
ethnography of the region Chodsko;
local history

Klobouky u Brna

03020
Městské muzeum
Náměstí Míru 1, zámek, CS-691 72
Klobouky u Brna
General Museum - 1906
Ethnography; local archeology;
numismatics

Kojetín

03021
Muzeum Marie Gardavské Okresní
vlastivědné muzeum Přerov
Husova 64, CS Kojetín
General Museum - 1933
Local history; archeology; ceramics;
glass

Kolín

03022
Regionálni Muzeum
Nám. obránců míru 8 / Brandlova ul
24, 27, 35, CS-280 00 Kolín
General Museum - 1895
Archeology; literature; numismatics;
memorabilia of J.G. Debureau

Komárno

03023
Oblastné Podunajské Múzeum
(Danubian Museum)
CS-945 01 Komárno
General Museum - 1887
Coll: natural history of the Danubian
area; Roman archeology; sarcophagi;
sculpture

Komárov u Hořovic

03024
Železářské muzeum (Museum of
Ironwork)
Zámek, CS-267 62 Komárov u Hořovic
Decorative Arts Museum
History of Komárov ironwork and
smithwork; cast iron

Kopidlno

03025
Místní muzeum
CS-507 32 Kopidlno
General Museum
History; archeology; numismatics

Kopřivnice

03026
Lašské muzeum
Janáčkův sad 226, CS-742 21
Kopřivnice
General Museum
Local history

03027
Technické muzeum N.P. Tatra (Tatra
Technical Motor Car Museum)
Janáčkovy sady 226, CS-742 21
Kopřivnice
Science/Tech Museum - 1947
History of automobiles and automotive
engineering, especially of the Tatra
Works; ceramic industry; local history;
ethnography; numismatics

Košice

03028
Technické múzeum
Dom hlavných kapitánov, ul. Leninova
88, CS-043 82 Košice
Science/Tech Museum - 1947
Aviation; railway; communications;
post; telecommunication; television;
textiles; cinematography; photography;
metallurgy; physics; astronomy;
mining; cartography; geodesy; motors

03029
Východoslovenská galéria (Gallery of
Eastern Slovakia)
Leninova ul. 72, CS-040 00 Košice
Fine Arts Museum - 1951
19th-20th century Slovak fine art

03030
Východoslovenské múzeum
(Museum of Eastern Slovakia)
Leninova ul. 27, CS-041 36 Košice
General Museum
Coll: history; history of art; zoology;
geology; archeology; ethnography;
religious art - library

Kostelec na Hané

03031
Památník Petra Bezruče
Bezručova 256, CS-798 41 Kostelec
na Hané
Historic Site
Memorabilia of the poet Petr Bezruč
(1867-1958); letters; original interiors

Kostelec nad Črnými Lesy

03032
**Muzeum středočeského hrnčiřstvi a
keramiky** Regionální muzeum Kolin
(Museum of Central Bohemian Pottery
and Ceramics)
Náměstí 41, CS-281 63 Kostelec nad
Črnými Lesy
Decorative Arts Museum - 1935
Pottery and ceramics

Kouřim

03033
Muzeum Kouřimska Regionální
muzeum Kolín
Náměstí 1, CS-281 61 Kouřim
General Museum - 1906
Geology; paleontology; archeology;
ethnography

03034
Muzeum vesnice (Village Museum)
CS-281 61 Kouřim
Open Air Museum
Examples of folk architecture

Kožlany

03035
Městské muzeum
CS-331 44 Kožlany
General Museum - 1946
Pottery; local history; ethnography

Králíky

03036
Městské muzeum
Náměstí Československé armády 365,
CS-561 69 Králíky
General Museum - 1907
Local history; natural history of the
region Kralický Sněžník

Králův Dvůr

03037
Muzeum
CS-267 01 Králův Dvůr
General Museum - 1936
History of the labour movement in the
region

Kravaře

03038
Muzeum Ostravské operace
Zámek, CS Kravaře
History/Public Affairs Museum
Collection illustrating the military
operation near Ostrava at the end of
World War II

Křečovice u Sedlčan

03039
Památník Josefa Suka Muzeum
české hudby, Praha
CS-257 48 Křečovice u Sedlčan 3
Historic Site - 1935
Memorabilia of the composer Josef
Suk (1874-1935) in his former home

Kremnica

03040
Múzeum minci a medaili (Museums
of Numismatics and Medals)
Nám. 1. mája 7, CS-967 01 Kremnica
General Museum
Local history; numismatics; medal
stamping

Krnov

03041
Městské muzeum Okresní
vlastivědné muzeum, Bruntál
Revoluční 20, CS-794 00 Krnov
General Museum - 1890
History of the town with special
reference to the development of the
textile industry; local natural history

Kroměřiž

03042
Okresni muzeum Kroměřižska
Sněmovní nám. 1, CS-767 00 Kroměřiž
General Museum - 1933
15th-19th century paintings and
graphics; music archives; baroque
music; numismatics; medals - library

Krupina

03043
Muzeum
CS-963 01 Krupina
General Museum
Local history

Krupka

03044
Městské muzeum Krajské muzeum,
Teplice
Husitská 21, CS-417 41 Krupka
General Museum
History of the town; mining; applied art

Kutná Hora

03045
Expozice v Kamenném Domě
Okresní muzeum
Nám. 1. máje 183, CS-284 00 Kutná
Hora
Archeology Museum
Archeology; medieval ceramics

03046
Galerie Felixe Jeneweina Okresní
muzeum
Vlašský Dvůr, CS-284 00 Kutná Hora
Fine Arts Museum
Paintings; bequest of the painter Felix
Jenewein

03047
Okresni muzeum
Barborská ul. 28, Hrádek, CS-284 00
Kutná Hora
General Museum - 1877
Archeology; geology; 14th-15th
century mining tools; medieval
ceramics; art history

03048
Památník Josefa Kajetána Tyla
Okresní muzeum
Tylova ul. 507, CS-284 00 Kutná Hora
Historic Site - 1956
Memorabilia of the dramatist Josef
Kajetán Tyl (1808-1856)

03049
Zemědělská sbirka na zámku Kačina
Československé zemědělské
muzeum, Praha (Agricultural Collection
in the Castle of Kačina)
Zámek Kačina, Kutná Hora, CS-284 00
Kutná Hora
Agriculture Museum
Coll: agriculture

Kylov

03050
Muzeum Okresní muzeum
hodonínska, Hodonín
Palackého ul. 70, CS-697 01 Kylov
General Museum - 1904
Paleontology; botany; entomology;
local archeology; ethnography

Lanškroun

03051
Městské muzeum
Zámek, CS-563 01 Lanškroun
General Museum
Paleontology; geology; local history;
applied arts; ethnography

Lázně Bělohrad

03052
Památník Karla Václava Raise
Zámek, CS-507 81 Lázně Bělohrad
Historic Site - 1959
Memorabilia of the writer Karel Václav
Rais

Ledeč nad Sázavou

03053
Městské muzeum
Horní Ledeč 701, CS-584 01 Ledeč
nad Sázavou
General Museum - 1911
History; ethnography; ceramics

Lednice na Moravě

03054
Zemědělské muzeum
Československé zemědělské
muzeum, Praha
Zámek, CS-691 44 Lednice na Moravě
Agriculture Museum - 1954
Horticulture in Czechoslovakia;
hunting

Letohrad

03055
Památník Petra Jilemnického
Zámek, CS-561 51 Letohrad
Historic Site - 1958
Memorabilia of the writer Petr
Jilemnický (1901-1949)

Levice

03056
Tekovské Múzeum
ul. Velkého októbra, poštový priečinok
69, CS-934 01 Levice
General Museum - 1927
Natural sciences; history; archeology;
numismatics; art history; ethnography

Levoča

03057
**Mestské Kulturné Stredisko-
Muzeálne Oddelenie Spišské
Múzeum**
Mierové nám. 2, CS-054 01 Levoča
General Museum
Local history; arms; guild relics;
religious art;

Libáň

03058
Mistní muzeum
CS-507 23 Libáň 96
General Museum - 1937
Local history; applied arts; arms

Liberec

03059
Galerie výtvarného uměni (Fine Arts
Gallery)
U tiskárny 1, CS-460 00 Liberec
Fine Arts Museum - 1945
17th century Duch paintings; 19th
century French, German and Austrian
paintings; 19th-20th century Czech art

03060
Severočeské Muzeum v Liberci
(Liberec North Bohemian Museum)
Leninova ul. 11, CS-460 00 Liberec
General Museum - 1873
Historical and contemporary collection
of European and Bohemian glass and
industrial arts; geology; paleontology;
botany; local history; archeology

Lidice

03061
Památník lidické tragedie
CS-273 54 Lidice
History/Public Affairs Museum
History of Lidice; photographs and
other material illustrating the
destruction of the town in the Nazi
period

Lipnik nad Bečvou

03062
Muzeum Záhoří
Bratrská ul. 353, CS-751 31 Lipník nad
Bečvou
General Museum
Local history

Liptovský Hrádok

03063
Národopisné múzeum Liptova
(Ethnographical Museum of Liptova)
CS-033 01 Liptovský Hrádok
Anthropology Museum - 1958
Costumes; agriculture; alpine farming;
wooden objects; folklore; in an 18th
century former courthouse

Liptovský Mikuláš

03064
Múzeum Janka Kráľa
Nám. Osvoboditeľov 32, CS-031 01
Liptovský Mikuláš
History/Public Affairs Museum - 1955
History of literature; books

03065
Múzeum Slovenského krasu
(Museum of Slovakian Nature)
Školská 4, CS-031 01 Liptovský
Mikuláš
Science/Tech Museum - 1904
Slovakian speleology; rock formations;
cave settlements; archeological finds
from caves; stalagmites; stalactites;
cave fauna and flora; in an 18th
century former cloister

03066
Oblastná galéria P. M. Bohúňa
(District Art Gallery)
Tranovského 3, CS-031 01 Liptovský
Mikuláš
Fine Arts Museum
Medieval, national and modern art;
applied arts

Liteň

03067
Památník Václava Beneše Třebízského a Svatopluka Čecha
U liteňského zámku, CS-267 27 Liteň
Historic Site - 1965
Memorabilia of the writers V.B. Třebízský and Svatopluk Čech (1846-1908)

Litoměřice

03068
Okresni muzeum
Mírové náměstí 1/40, CS-412 01 Litoměřice
General Museum - 1874
Local history; botany; archeology; ethnography; vine cultivation; fruit growing; ceramics

03069
Severočeská galerie výtvarného uměni (North Bohemian Gallery of Fine Arts)
Michalská 7, CS-412 01 Litoměřice
Fine Arts Museum - 1951
13th-20th century painting and sculpture; special collection of Roman, Gothic and Bohemian art ; naive painting and sculpture - library

Litomyšl

03070
Muzeum české hudby Muzeum české hudby, Praha
Zámek, CS-570 01 Litomyšl
Music Museum
Collections illustrating the development of Czech music

03071
Vlastivědné muzeum
Jiráskova ul. 6, CS-570 01 Litomyšl
General Museum - 1890
Paleontology; zoology; history; ethnography; numismatics; applied art; crafts

Litovel

03072
Muzeum Krajské vlastivědné muzeum, Olomouc
ul. Boženy Němcové 199, CS-784 01 Litovel
General Museum - 1893
Local history; pottery

Litvínov

03073
Muzeum Okresní muzeum, Most
Tř. Sovětské armády 1, CS-436 00 Litvínov
General Museum - 1896
Local geology; botany; entomology; industry; labour movement in the region of Most and Litvínov; ethnography

Lomnice nad Popelkou

03074
Městské muzeum
Náměstí 43/44, CS-512 51 Lomnice nad Popelkou
General Museum - 1891
Local history; ethnography; textile industry

Loštice

03075
Havelkovo muzeum Okresní vlastivědné muzeum, Šumperk
ul. U muzea 8, CS-789 83 Loštice
Decorative Arts Museum - 1928
Pottery; stove making from the 15th-19th century; local history

03076
Památník Adolfa Kašpara
Palackého 343, CS-789 83 Loštice
Historic Site - 1970
Memorabilia of the painter Adolf Kašpar, his paintings

Louny

03077
Galerie Benedikta Rejta
Žižkova 253, CS-440 01 Louny
Fine Arts Museum - 1966
20th century Czech art

03078
Okresni muzeum
Pivovarská 43, CS-440 01 Louny
General Museum - 1889
Local geology; archeology; medieval archeology; ethnography; local history

Luhačovice

03079
Oddeléleni oblastni muzeum Jihovýchodni Moravy (Gottwaldov)
(Branch of the Regional Museum of South-Eastern Moravia in Gottwaldov)
Villa Lipová, CS-763 26 Luhačovice
Anthropology Museum
Regional folk art

Lukavec u Pacova

03080
Památník Antonina Sovy
Zámek, CS-394 26 Lukavec u Pacova
Historic Site - 1958
Photodocuments illustrating the life and work of the poet Antonín Sova

Lysá nad Labem

03081
Muzeum starých orientálnich kultur v dile akademika Bedřicha Hrozného
Polabské muzeum, Poděbrady
(Museum of Ancient Oriental Culture)
Nám. Dr.B. Hrozného 265, CS-289 22 Lysá nad Labem
Historic Site
Archeology; oriental art; collections illustrating the work of the Czech Orientalist Dr. Bedřich Hrozný

Malacky

03082
Mestské múzeum
Družstvená 12, CS-901 01 Malacky
General Museum
Local history

Malé Svatoňovice

03083
Muzeum bratři Čapků
Náměstí, CS-542 34 Malé Svatoňovice
Historic Site - 1946
Collections illustrating the life and work of the writer Karel Čapek (1890-1938) and his brother the painter Josef Čapek (1887-1945)

Maleč

03084
Památnik Františka Palackého a Františka Ladislava Riegra
Zámek 1, CS-582 76 Maleč
Historic Site
Memorabilia of the historian and politician František Palacký (1798-1876) in the summer residence of F.L. Riegr

Manětín

03085
Muzeum Okresni muzeum, Plzeň
Zámek, CS-331 62 Manětín
General Museum
Local history; baroque art

Mariánské Lázně

03086
Městské muzeum
Gottwaldovo nám. 11, CS-353 01 Mariánské Lázně
General Museum - 1887
Mineralogy; geology; ethnography; applied arts; porcelain collection; local history of the town and the spa; memorabilia of J.W. von Goethe's, F. Chopin's and M. Gorkij's stays at Mariánské Lázně

Markušovce

03087
Nábytkové Múzeum (Furniture Museum)
CS-053 21 Markušovce
Decorative Arts Museum - 1959
Furniture; living style of Eastern Slovakia, especially of the Spiš area; portraits; painting; decorative art; porcelain; glass; wall paintings; in a 17th century Renaissance palace

Martin

03088
Matica Slovenská Literárnomúzejné oddelenie
Mudroňova 26, CS-036 01 Martin
History/Public Affairs Museum
History of Slovakian literature; book illumination

03089
Slovenské Národné Múzeum, Etnografický Ústav (Slovak National Museum, Ethnographic Institute)
CS-036 80 Martin
Anthropology Museum - 1893
Ancient archeology of Middle and Western Slovakia; Gothic cultural objects; folk art; national history; paintings by Martin Benka; ethnography; farming; fishing; hunting; forestry; agriculture; wax shaping; spinning; embroidery; lace weaving - library

03090
Turčianske múzeum Andreja Kmeťa
Engelsova 4, CS-036 01 Martin
General Museum - 1964
Natural sciences; history; memorabilia of A. Kmet, Slovakian museologist

Mělník

03091
Okresni muzeum
Zámek, CS-276 01 Mělník
General Museum - 1888
Archeology; ethnography; art; handicrafts; local wine industry; manuscripts of the politician and writer Victor Dyk

Městec Králové

03092
Mistni muzeum Polabské muzeum, Poděbrady
Náměstí 74/75, CS-289 03 Městec Králové
General Museum - 1909
Local history; archeology; ethnography; handicrafts

Michalovice

03093
Zemplínske múzeum
Nám. ČA 1, CS-071 01 Michalovice
General Museum - 1957
Fauna; flora; archeology; art; religious objects; ethnography; costumes; history of pottery; wine making

Mikulčice

03094
Národni kulturni památnik
CS Mikulčice
Archeology Museum - 1963
Archeological finds from excavations at local Slavonic sites

Mikulov na Moravě

03095
Regionální muzeum
Zámek, CS-692 01 Mikulov na Moravě
General Museum - 1913
Local history; natural history; archeology; ethnography; numismatics; applied arts

Miletin

03096
Památník Karla Jaromíra Erbena
ul. Barbory Linkové 142, CS-507 71 Miletín
Historic Site - 1911
Memorabilia of the poet Karel Jaromír Erben (1811-1870) in his former home

Milevsko

03097
Městské muzeum
Klášter 563, CS-399 01 Milevsko
General Museum - 1926
Local archeology; history; handicrafts;

Mirotice

03098
Památník Mikoláše Alše
CS-398 01 Mirotice
Historic Site - 1962
Memorabilia of the painter Mikoláš Aleš (1852-1913)

Mladá Boleslav

03099
Okresni muzeum
Hrad, CS-293 01 Mladá Boleslav
General Museum - 1885
Archeology; ceramics and glass especially from the 19th century; numismatics; ethnography - archives

Mladá Vožice

03100
Mistni muzeum
Žižkovo náměstí 190, CS-391 43 Mladá Vožice
General Museum
Ethnography; local history; memorabilia of the historian August Sedláček and Jan Jeník z Bratřic

Mnichovo Hradiště

03101
Městské muzeum
Zámek 148, cs-295 01 Mnichovo
Hradiště
General Museum - 1894
Regional archeology; history;
ethnography; anti-Fashist struggle in
World War II; memorabilia of the
politician Jan Šverma

Modra

03102
Múzeum L'udovíta Štúra
Štúrova ul. 50, CS-900 01 Modra
Historic Site
Memorabilia of the writer L'udovít Štúr
(1815-1856); literary history

Mohelnice

03103
Muzeum Okresní vlastivědné
muzeum, Šumperk
Kostelní nám. 3, CS-789 85 Mohelnice
General Museum - 1923
Local archeology; history

Moravská Třebová

03104
Městské muzeum
Třída Osvoboditelů 281, CS-571 01
Moravská Třebová
General Museum - 1872
Applied arts especially textiles;
numismatics; crafts

Moravské Budějovice

03105
Expozice řemesel Západomoravské
muzeum, Třebíč
Nám. Míru 1, CS-676 00 Moravské
Budějovice
Anthropology Museum - 1922

Moravský Krumlov

03106
Městské muzeum Jihomoravské
muzeum, Znojmo
Hlavní nám. 321, CS-672 01 Moravský
Krumlov
General Museum - 1905
Local archeology and history

Most

03107
Okresní muzeum
Švermova 3, CS-434 00 Most
General Museum - 1888
Mineralogy; geology; paleontology;
archeology; local history; mining; art;
handicrafts

Mšeno

03108
Památník Josefa Ladislava Piče
CS-277 35 Mšeno
Historic Site
Memorabilia of the historian and
archeologist Jan Ladislav Pič

Náchod

03109
Okresní galerie (Regional Gallery)
Státní zámek, CS-547 00 Náchod
Fine Arts Museum - 1966
19th-20th century Russian and Soviet
paintings and graphics; contemporary
Czech art

03110
Okresní muzeum
Zámek, CS-547 00 Náchod
General Museum - 1879
Archeology; local history;
ethnography; handicrafts;
numismatics; glass; ceramics

Napajedla

03111
**Oddělení oblastní muzeum
Jihovýchodní Moravy, Gottwaldov**
(Regional Museum of South-Eastern
Moravia in Gottwaldov, Local Branch)
CS-763 61 Napajedla
General Museum
Local history

Nelahozeves

03112
Památník Antonína Dvořáka Muzeum
české hudby, Praha
Proti nádraží 12, CS-277 51
Nelahozeves
Historic Site - 1951
Memorabilia of the composer Antonín
Dvořák (1841-1904) in his former
home

Nepomuk

03113
Místní muzeum
Přesanické náměstí 1, CS-335 00
Nepomuk
General Museum - 1957
Local and natural history,; baroque art;
memorabilia of the painter Augustin
Němejc

Netolice

03114
Místní muzeum
Náměstí 248, CS-384 11 Netolice
General Museum - 1909
Local archeology; ethnography;
history of the town

Netvořice

03115
Místní muzeum
CS-257 44 Netvořice 46
General Museum - 1931
18th-19th century ceramics; local
archeology; history

Nitra

03116
Nitrianske vlastivedné múzeum
CS-950 50 Nitra
General Museum - 1886
Local history

03117
**Slovenské poľnohospodárske
múzeum** (Slovenian Agricultural
Museum)
CS-949 01 Nitra
Agriculture Museum - 1960
Development of farming in Slovakia;
animal husbandry; vegetable growing;
farm implements; agricultural
machinery; apiculture; in a 17th
century cloister

Nová Baňa

03118
Mestské múzeum
CS-968 01 Nová Baňa
General Museum - 1952
Natural sciences; numismatics; art
history; ethnography

Nová Paka

03119
**Muzeum polodrahokamů -
'Klenotnice'** Podkrkonošske muzeum
(Museum of Semi-Precious Stones)
Gottwaldovo nám. 1, CS-509 01 Nová
Paka
Natural History Museum - 1950
Regional geology; mineralogy;
semi-precious stones (agate, jasper
etc.)

03120
Podkrkonošské muzeum
Suchardova 68, CS-509 01 Nová Paka
General Museum - 1908
History of the region; ethnography;
memorabilia of the sculptor Vojtěch
Sucharda

Nové Město na Moravě

03121
Horácké muzeum a galerie
Náměstí Dr. I. Sekaniny 114, CS-592
31 Nové Město na Moravě
General Museum - 1892/1907
Regional history; ethnography; history
of skiing in the region; collections
illustrating the life and work of the
painters Oldřich Blažíček and Karel
Němec and the sculptor Jan Štursa

Nové Mesto nad Váhom

03122
Podjavorinské Múzeum
Nám. Slobody 10, CS-915 01 Nové
Mesto nad Váhom
General Museum - 1930
Natural sciences; history;
ethnography; in an 18th century
baroque building

Nové Strašecí

03123
Městské muzeum
U školy 123, cs-271 01 Nové Strašecí
General Museum - 1895
Local archeology; ethnography; folk
art

Nové Zámky

03124
Okresné múzeum
Hurbanova 7, CS-940 01 Nové Zámky
General Museum - 1935
Archeology; art history; numismatics;
ethnography

Nový Bor

03125
Sklářské muzeum (Glass Museum)
Nám. Míru 105, CS-473 01 Nový Bor
Science/Tech Museum - 1892
History and technology of glass
production; optical glass

Nový Bydžov

03126
Městské muzeum
Mírové nám. 2, CS-504 01 Nový
Bydžov
General Museum - 1888
Local history; ethnography;
memorabilia of the writer Božena
Němcová (1820-1862) and her stay at
Nový Bydžov

Nový Jičín

03127
Kloboučnické muzeum Okresní
vlastivědné muzeum (Hat-Making
Museum)
ul. 28. října 12, CS-741 00 Nový Jičín
History/Public Affairs Museum - 1949
History of the local hat-making
industry

03128
Muzeum svítidel a chladičů Okresní
vlastivědné muzeum
ul. 28. října 12, CS-741 00 Nový Jičín
Science/Tech Museum - 1969
History of lighting and the local
production of refrigerators

03129
Okresní vlastivědné muzeum
ul. 28. října 12, CS-741 00 Nový Jičín
General Museum - 1887
Mineralogy; paleontology;
entomology; botany; zoology; local
history; ethnography; handicrafts; art

Nymburk

03130
Vlastivědné muzeum
Eliščina ul. 154/22, CS-288 00
Nymburk
General Museum - 1885
Local botany; zoology; entomology;
archeology; medieval archeology;
ethnography; local economic history

Obříství

03131
Památník Svatopluka Čecha
CS-277 42 Obříství
Historic Site - 1956
Memorabilia of the writer and poet
Svatopluk Čech (1846-1908)

Olomouc

03132
Krajské vlastivědné muzeum
Nám. Rudé armády 5/6, CS-770 00
Olomouc
General Museum - 1874
Natural science in Northern Moravia;
history; archeology; art history;
decorative arts; military art;
numismatics; agriculture; trades;
transportation; ethnography; graphics

03133
Oblastní Galerie
Wurmova 14, CS-770 00 Olomouc
Fine Arts Museum - 1952
19th-20th century Bohemian art; old
European art

Olomučany

03134
**Památník dělnického hnutí a
olomučanské keramiky**
CS-679 03 Olomučany 123
History/Public Affairs Museum - 1960
History of the local labour movement;
local ceramics

Opava

03135
Historické a hudební sbírky Slezské
muzeum (Historical and Musical
Collections of the Silesian Museum)
Tyršova 1, CS-746 00 Opava
History/Public Affairs Museum - 1897
Regional history; numismatics; history
of music of the Silesian region

03136
Národopisné sbírky Slezské muzeum
Sněmovní 1, cs-746 00 Opava
Anthropology Museum - 1883
Silesian and German medieval
sculpture and painting; applied art
(glass, porcelain, ceramics, furniture,
textiles); Italian and German
Renaissance painting; ethnography;
folk art

03137
Památník Petra Bezruče Slezské
Muzeum
Ostrožná ul. 35, CS-746 01 Opava
Historic Site
Memorabilia of the poet Petr Bezruč
(1867-1958) and other Silesian literary
figures

03138
Prehistorické sbirky Slezské muzeum
(Prehistoric Collection of the Silesian
Museum)
Komenského 8, cs-746 00 Opava
Archeology Museum - 1897
Prehistoric and medieval archeology

03139
Přirodovědecké sbirky Slezské
muzeum
Tř. Vítězného února 35, CS-746 00
Opava
Natural History Museum - 1814
Geological sciences; mineralogy;
paleontology; botany; zoology

Oravský Podzámok

03140
Oravské Múzeum
Hrad, CS-027 41 Oravský Podzámok
General Museum - 1868
Geology; botany; zoology; ancient
finds from the area; paintings;
sculpture; cultural history; furniture;
coins;

Ostrava

03141
Galerie výtvarného uměni (Fine Arts
Gallery)
Jurečkova 9, CS-700 00 Ostrava
Fine Arts Museum - 1926
European paintings and graphics;
modern Szech art

03142
**Muzeum revolučnich bojů a
budováni socialismu** (Museum of the
Revolutionary Movement and
Development of Socialism)
Dimitrova ul. 10, CS-700 00 Ostrava
History/Public Affairs Museum
History of the labour and revolutionary
movement; contemporary history

03143
**Muzeum vitkovických železáren
Klementa Gottwalda**
Výstavní 99 - zámek, CS-703 00
Ostrava 3
Science/Tech Museum - 1961
Metallurgy; technology; local labour
movement

03144
Ostravské muzeum
Nám. Lidových milici 1, CS-700 00
Ostrava
General Museum - 1872
Geology; mineralogy; paleontology;
ornithology; archeology; art history;
ethnography; folk sculpture; glass
painting

Ostředek

03145
Památník Svatopluka Čecha
Zámek, CS Ostředek
Historic Site - 1898
Memorabilia of the writer Svatopluk
Čech (1846-1908)

Ostrov nad Ohří

03146
Galerie
Zámek, CS Ostrov nad Ohří
Fine Arts Museum - 1951
20th century Czech drawings and
graphics; regional art

Pacov

03147
Městské muzeum Antonina Sovy
Hronova 274, CS-395 01 Pacov
Historic Site - 1908
Memorabilia of the poet Antonín Sova
and other local artists; local history

Pardubice

03148
Muzeum Krajské muzeum východnich
čech, Hradec Králové
Zámek 1, CS-530 00 Pardubice
General Museum - 1880
Ornithology; zoology; botany;
paleontology; petrology; mineralogy;
numismatics; archeology of Eastern
Bohemia; arms; uniforms; applied arts;
ethnography; regional literature;
history - library

03149
Východočeská galerie (East
Bohemian Gallery)
Zámek, CS-530 00 Pardubice
Fine Arts Museum - 1954
Czech modern art, especially regional
art

Paseky nad Jizerou

03150
Památník zapadlých vlastenců
Škola, CS-512 47 Paseky nad Jizerou
Historic Site
Memorabilia of the teacher Metelka
and the writer K.V. Reis

Pelhřimov

03151
Okresní muzeum
Mírové náměstí 11/12, CS-393 01
Pelhřimov
General Museum - 1901
Archeology; medieval archeology;
local history; ethnography; art
handicrafts; (embroidery; wood
carving); folk art

Pezinok

03152
**Malokarpatské vinohradnicke
múzeum** (Little Carpathian
Vine-Growing Museum)
Revolučna 4, CS-902 01 Pezinok
Agriculture Museum - 1960
Vine-growing exhibits, housed in a
16th century building

Piešťany

03153
Balneologické múzeum (Balneological
Museum)
CS-921 01 Piešťany
Science/Tech Museum - 1930
Archeological finds; numismatics;
medical equipment from the bequest
of the first bath physician Dr. F.
Scherer; ethnography; stained glass;
wood sculptures; embroidery; natural
history; balneology; history of
Slovakian bath

Plánice

03154
Památník Dr. Františka Křižika
Křižíkova 86, CS-340 34 Plánice
Historic Site - 1957
Memorabilia on the electrical engineer
Dr. František Křižík and his inventions

Plzeň

03155
Archeologické sbirky Západočeské
Muzeum (Archeological Collection of
the West Bohemian Museum in Pilsen)
Františkánská 13, CS-300 00 Plzeň
Archeology Museum
Prehistory and medieval archeology of
Western Bohemia

03156
Národopisné sbirky Západočeské
Muzeum (Ethnographical Collection of
the West Bohemian Museum in Pilsen)
Nám. Republiky 13, CS-300 00 Plzeň
Anthropology Museum - 1914
Ethnography of Western
Bohemia(19th-20th century)

03157
Památník Julia Fučika Západočeské
Muzeum
Havlíčkova ul. 32, CS-300 00 Plzeň
Historic Site - 1958
Memorabilia on the writer and
journalist Julius Fučik (1903-1943)

03158
Pivovarnické muzeum Západočeské
Muzeum (Museum of Brewing)
Veleslavínova ul. 22, CS-300 00 Plzeň
Science/Tech Museum
History of brewing; original equipment;
collection of beer labels

03159
Západočeská Galerie v Plzni
Kopeckého sady 2, CS-300 00 Plzeň
Fine Arts Museum - 1954
Czech art; painting and sculpture from
the 14th century to the present

03160
Západočeské Muzeum (West
Bohemian Museum)
Kopeckého sady 2, CS-300 00 Plzeň
General Museum - 1878
Natural history of Western Bohemia;
geology; petrography; paleontology;
mineralogy; botany; entomology;
zoology; history; applied art

Počátky

03161
Městské muzeum
Palackého nám. 27, CS-394 64
Počátky
General Museum - 1892
Local archeology; history;
ethnography; memorabilia on local
writers and artists

03162
Rodný domek Otokara Březiny
Městské muzeum
Otokara Březiny 224, CS-394 64
Počátky
Historic Site
Memorabilia on the poet Otokar
Březina

Poděbrady

03163
**Památník Krále Jiřího z Poděbrad a
Lapidarium** Oblastní Muzeum
Zámek Poděbrady, CS-290 01
Poděbrady
History/Public Affairs Museum
Lapidary

03164
Polabské muzeum (Museum of the
Elbe Region)
Palackého tř. 68/III, CS-290 01
Poděbrady
General Museum - 1902
Paleontology; zoology; herbarium; art,
especially works by the French
sculptor J.P. Dantan (1800-1869);
ethnography; numismatics; literature

Police nad Metuji

03165
Památník města
Komenského náměstí 1, CS-549 54
Police nad Metuji
General Museum - 1949
Local and regional history; folk
handicrafts

Polička

03166
Městské muzeum a galerie
Tylova ul. 112,113, CS-572 01 Polička
General Museum - 1880
Local history; ethnography; glass
making; folk art; memorabilia on local
artists; old handicrafts

03167
Památník Bohuslava Martinů
Městské muzeum a galerie
CS-572 01 Polička
Historic Site
Memorabilia on the composer
Bohuslav Martinů (1890-1959)

Poprad

03168
Podtatranské múzeum
Spišská Sobota 1103, CS-058 00
Poprad
General Museum - 1945
Natural sciences; archeology; history;
numismatics; geology; mineralogy;
paleontology; botany; zoology

Potštejn

03169
Památník Jiráskova 'Pokladu'
Muzeum Orlických Hor Rychnov nad
Kněžnou
CS-517 43 Potštejn
Historic Site
History of the linen manufacture at
Potštejn (18th century); documentation
on the novel 'Poklad' by Alois Jirásek

Prace

03170
Památník - Mohyla Miru
CS-664 58 Prace
History/Public Affairs Museum
History of the Napoleonic wars,
especially the Battle of Slavkov
(Austerlitz)

Prachatice

03171
Okresni muzeum
Gottwaldovo nám. 13, CS-383 01
Prachatice
General Museum - 1903
Local history; ethnography;
handicrafts; industry; art

Praha

03172
**Archeologické oddĕleni muzea
hlavniho mĕsta Prahy** (Archeological
Branch of the Museum of the Capital
City of Prague)
Starecká 29, CS-160 00 Praha 6
Archeology Museum - 1945
Archeology; prehistoric items

03173
**Československé zdravotnické
muzeum** (Museum of Czech Health
Sciences)
Sokolská 31, CS-120 00 Praha 2
History/Public Affairs Museum - 1934
History of the health sciences;
documents; numismatics; stamps

03174
**Entomologické oddĕlĕni
přirodovĕského muzea**
(Entomological Department of the
Museum of Natural History)
Zámek Kunratice u Prahy, CS-148 00
Praha 414
Natural History Museum
Entomology

03175
**Expozice Dĕjin Československe
Armády** Vojenske Muzeum
CS-130 00 Praha 3
History/Public Affairs Museum - 1924
Czech military history

03176
**Expozice protivzdušné obrany statu
Vojenského muzea**
Letištĕ Kbely, CS-190 00 Praha 9
History/Public Affairs Museum
History of ground-to-air defense;
development of the Czechoslovak
military and civil air force;
development of aircraft production

03177
Galerie hlavniho mĕsta Prahy
(Prague City Art Gallery)
Mickiewiczova 3, CS Praha 6
Fine Arts Museum - 1963
19th-20th century Czech art

03178
**Historická Expozice Vojenského
Muzea** (Historical Collection of the
Military Museum)
Hradčanské nám. 2,
Schwarzenbergský palác, CS-110 00
Praha 1
History/Public Affairs Museum - 1918
Development of Czech and Slovak
military history from the 10th century
onwards

03179
Historické muzeum Národní muzeum
v Praze (Historical Museum of the
National Museum in Prague)
Vítĕzného února 74, CS-110 00 Praha
1
History/Public Affairs Museum
Prehistory; numismatics; history;
archeology; theater collections;
ethnography

03180
Hrdličkovo muzeum človĕka
Universita Karlova (Hrdlička Museum
of Anthropology)
Vinična 7, CS-120 00 Praha 2
Anthropology Museum - 1930
Evolution of man; comparative
anatomy; primatology; ontogenetic
evolution; racial differences; skull
formations; postmortal cast

03181
Knihovna Národního muzea (National
Museum Library)
Václavské nám. 68, 115 79 Praha 1
History/Public Affairs Museum - 1818
Departments: Central Museum
Library; Bohemian Literature and the
Czechoslovak Book Museum at Žďar
n. S.; writings; incunabula; old prints;
enlightenment literature; recent
Bohemian literature; newspapers;
magazines

03182
Lapidarium Historického muzea
Narodní Muzeum
Park Kultury a Oddechu Julia Fučika,
CS-170 00 Praha 7
History/Public Affairs Museum
Lapidary

03183
Loretánská sbirka Muzeum Hlavního
Mĕsta Prahy (Loretto collection)
Hradčany, Loretánská námĕsti 7,
CS-110 00 Praha 1
Decorative Arts Museum
The so-called Loretto treasure (jewelry
from the 16th-19th centuries)
presented as a gift to the famous
pilgrimage convent

03184
**Muzeum Aloise Jiráska a Mikoláše
Alše** Památník národního písemnictví,
Praha
Letohrádek Hvĕzda, Liboc, CS-160 00
Praha 6
Historic Site - 1951
Memorabilia of the Czech writer Alois
Jirásek (1851-1930) and the painter
Mikoláš Aleš (1852-1913) - library

03185
Muzeum Antonina Dvořáka Muzeum
české hudby, Národní muzeum v
Praze
Ke Karlovu 20/462, 120 00 Praha 2
Music Museum - 1932
Memorabilia on the composer Antonin
Dvořák (1841-1904), his viola, piano
and other personal possesions

03186
Muzeum Bedřicha Smetany Muzeum
české hudby, Národní muzeum v
Praze
Novotného lávka 1, Staré Mĕsto,
CS-110 00 Praha
Historic Site - 1928
Memorabilia on the composer Bedřich
Smetana (1824-1884), compositions;
diaries; drawings; works of art; 19th
century Bohemian musical
development; Moravian music

03187
Muzeum hlavniho mĕsta Prahy
(Museum of the Capital City of Prague)
Švermovy sady 1554, St. Mĕsto,
Kožna 1, CS-160 00 Praha 8
History/Public Affairs Museum - 1883
History of the city; fine art;
archeology; architecture - library

03188
Muzeum hudebnich nástrojů
Muzeum české hudby, Národní
muzeum v Praze (Museum of Musical
Instruments)
Malá Strana, Velkopřevorské nám. 4,
CS-110 00 Praha 1
Music Museum - 1818
History of music; musical instruments
from the 16th to 19th century

03189
Muzeum Klementa Gottwalda
Rytířská 29, CS-110 00 Praha 1
History/Public Affairs Museum - 1954
History of the Czechoslovak
Communist Party and revolutionary
labour movement

03190
Muzeum nábytku
Umĕleckoprůmyslové muzeum, Praha
(Furniture Museum)
U Jablonného, Zámek Lemberk,
CS-110 00 Praha
Decorative Arts Museum - 1951
Furniture from the Gothic period to the
present day

03191
**Muzeum pohraniční stráže a vojsk
ministerstva vnitra** (Museum of the
Border Troops)
Horská ul. 7, CS-120 00 Praha 2
History/Public Affairs Museum - 1963
Collections illustrating the state
defence, especially defence of the
Czechoslovak frontiers; armaments;
medals; awards; militaria; art on
military history

03192
Muzeum tĕlovýchovy a sportu
Historické muzeum, Národní muzeum
v Praze (Museum of Physical Training
and Sport)
Ujezd 450, Tyršův dům, Mala Strana,
CS-110 00 Praha 1
History/Public Affairs Museum - 1924
Documents about the development of
physical training and sport; history of
physical culture

03193
Muzeum V.I. Lenina
Hybernská 7, CS-110 00 Praha 1
Historic Site - 1945
Memorabilia of V.I. Lenin (1870-1924);
history of the international labour
movement and Leninism

03194
**Náprstkovo muzeum asijských,
afrických a amerických kultur**
Národní muzeum
Betlémské nám. 1, Staré Mĕsto,
CS-110 00 Praha 1
Anthropology Museum - 1862
Ethnological and archeological
objects; Oriental art; collections from
Niss Island (Sumatra) and South
Africa; archeological collection from
Tihuanaco (Bolivia); Japanese
woodcuts; ethnography of the Berti
tribe (Sudan) - library

03195
Národní galerie v Praze (National Art
Gallery)
Hradčany, Jiřský klášter, CS-110 00
Praha 1
Fine Arts Museum - 1796
Departments: directory and collection
of Gothic and Baroque Czech art
(Praha 1, Hradčany, Jiřský klášter);
collection of old and modern European
art (Praha 1, Hradčany, Hradčanské
nám. 15); collection of Czech modern
art (Praha 1, Staré Mĕsto, Nám. Dr.
Vacka 1); collection of Czech and
European graphics (Praha 1, Staré
Mĕsto, Staromĕstské námĕstí 12);
collection of 19th century Czech
paintings and applied arts (Praha 1,
Staré Mĕsto, U milosrdných
18-Anežský klášter); collection of
19th-20th century Szech sculpture
(Zbraslav, státní zámek) - library

03196
Národní muzeum v Praze (National
Museum in Prague)
Václavské nám. 1700, CS-115 79 Praha
1
General Museum - 1818
Consists of six institutions: Museum of
Natural History; Historical Museum;
Naprstek Museum of Asian, African
and American cultures; Museum
Library; Museum of Czech Musik;
Central Office of Museology

03197
Národní technické muzeum (National
Technical Museum)
Kostelní 42, Letna, CS-170 00 Praha 7
Science/Tech Museum - 1908
Permanent exhibition of engineering,
transport, mining, metallurgy,
cinematography, photography,
broadcasting, television, astronomy,
atomic energy, - library; educational
and documentation section

03198
Národopisné oddĕleni Historické
muzeum, Národní muzeum v Praze
(Ethnographical Department of the
Historical Museum)
Petřinske sady 97-98, Letohrádek
Kinskych, CS-150 00 Praha 5
Anthropology Museum - 1891
Ethnography; development of Czech
and Slovak folk culture (textiles,
costumes, furniture, ceramics, folk art);
collection of Slavic costumes from
Bulgaria, the Ukraine, Yugoslavia etc.

03199
**Památník národního pisemnictví -
Muzeum české literatury** (Museum of
Czech Literature)
Hradčany, Strahovské nádvoří 132,
CS-110 00 Praha 1
History/Public Affairs Museum - 1950
Exhibition of the development of
Czech literature; library of the Strahov
monastery containing 900,000 vols.;
literary archives containing 4 million
objects

03200
**Památník W.A.Mozarta a manželů
Duškových - 'Bertramka'** Muzeum
české hudby, Národní muzeum v
Praze
Mozartova ul. 169, CS-150 00 Praha 5 -
Smíchov
Historic Site - 1927
Memorabilia on W.A. Mozart, his visits
in Prague (1786-1791) and his hosts
the Dušeks

03201
Pedagogické Muzeum Jana Ámose Komenského (J. A. Komenský Pedagogical Museum)
Valdštejnske nám. 4, Malá Strana, 118 00 Praha 1
History/Public Affairs Museum - 1955
Documents illustrating the development of Czechoslovak education and the life and work of Jan Amos Comenius

03202
Poštovni Muzeum (Postal Museum)
Holečkova 10, Smíchov, CS-150 00 Praha 5
Science/Tech Museum - 1918
Documents of postal history; stamp collections

03203
Přirodovědecké muzeum Národní Muzeum v Praze (Natural Sciences Museum of the National Museum in Prague)
Vítězného února 74, CS-110 00 Praha 1
Natural History Museum - 1818
Mineralogy; petrography; geology; paleontology; botany; mycology; entomology; zoology; anthropology

03204
Sbirky Husova domu
Nové Město, Jungmannova 9, CS-110 00 Praha 1
Religious Art Museum - 1895
History of the Reformation in Czechoslovakia

03205
Státni židovské muzeum (State Jewish Museum)
Jáchymova 3, CS-110 01 Praha 1
Religious Art Museum - 1950
Collection of silver liturgical objects; synagogue textiles; ancient books; archives of Bohemian and Moravian Jewish communities; works of Jewish painters; children's drawings from the concentration camp in Terezín/ Theresienstadt; Jewish cemetery of the 15th century and oldest synagogue in Gothic style of the 13th century; in 6 former synagogues (Maiselova synagóga, Dušní synagóga, Pinkasova synagóga, Klausova synagóga, Staronová synagóga; Vysoká synagóga) - library

03206
Středočeská galerie v Praze (Gallery of Central Bohemia in Prague)
Husova ul. 19, CS-150 00 Praha 1
Fine Arts Museum - 1964
Regular exhibitions; permanent exhibition of 14th to 19th century European art in Nelahozeves Manor near Kralupy n. Vltavou

03207
Uměleckoprůmyslové muzeum
ul. 17. listopadu 2, CS-110 00 Praha
Decorative Arts Museum - 1885
One of the largest collections of glass in the world; ceramics; porcelain; textiles; furniture; gold and silver works; prints - library

03208
Ústredni muzeologický kabinet
Národni Muzeum v Praze (Central Office of Museology)
U Lužického semináře 13, Malá Strana, CS-110 00 Praha 1
History/Public Affairs Museum - 1956
Museology

03209
Vojenské muzeum (Military Museum)
ul. Památníku 2, CS Praha 3
History/Public Affairs Museum - 1918
Development of the Czechoslovak army from 1917 onwards

03210
Zemědělské muzeum
Makarenkova 46, CS-120 00 Praha 2
Agriculture Museum - 1891
Exhibitions of: agriculture and the food industry located in Kačina Castle near Kutná Hora; forestry, hunting and fishery in Ohrada Castle near České Budejovice; hunting and horticulture in Lednice Castle near Břeclav - library; archive

Přelouč

03211
Městské muzeum
Nám. Rudé armády, CS-535 01 Přelouč
General Museum - 1902
Ornithology; archeology; local history; ethnography; handicrafts; numismatics

Přerov

03212
Okresni muzeum J.A.Komenského
Horni nám. 1, CS-750 00 Přerov
General Museum - 1888
Archeology; history; folklore; natural history; education

Přerov nad Labem

03213
Polabské národopisné muzeum
Polabské muzeum, Poděbrady (Ethnographic Museum of the Elbe Region)
Skanzen, CS-750 00 Přerov nad Labem
Open Air Museum - 1896
Ethnography; folk architecture; peasant furniture; household equipment

Prešov

03214
Galéria výtvarného umenia
ul. SRR 137, CS-080 01 Prešov
Fine Arts Museum
Art

03215
Múzeum Slovenskej Republiky Rád
ul. SRR 86, CS-080 01 Prešov
General Museum - 1947
Geology; botany; zoology; ecological units; marine birds; archeology; Celtic and Slavic economic history; local history; in a Renaissance house

Přibor

03216
Městské muzeum Okresni vlastivědné muzeum Nový Jičín
Piaristická 1 and 3, CS-742 58 Přibor
General Museum - 1912
History of the town and school education; collections depicting the life and work of Sigmund Freud (1856-1939)

Přibram

03217
Okresni muzeum
Zámeček I/106, CS-261 00 Přibram
General Museum - 1886
Geology; mineralogy; mining history; ethnography; handicrafts

Přibyslav

03218
Městské muzeum
Husova 300 - zamek, CS-582 22 Přibyslav
General Museum
Local history; handicrafts

Přimětice

03219
Památník Prokopa Diviše
Jihomoravské muzeum Znojmo
CS Přimětice
Historic Site
Memorabilia on the naturalist Prokop Diviš (1698-1765)

Proseč u Skutče

03220
Památník Terezy Novákové
Náměstí 61, CS-539 44 Proseč u Skutče
Historic Site
Collections illustrating the life and work of the writers Tereza Nováková and Thomas Mann

Prostějov

03221
Vlastivědné muzeum
Náměstí 9. května, CS-796 00 Prostějov
General Museum - 1894
Local history; natural history (especially botany, entomology, geology); archeology; ethnography; handicrafts; numismatics; literary archive; memorabilia on the poet Jiři Wolker

Protivín

03222
Městské muzeum
Náměstí 19, CS-398 11 Protivín
General Museum - 1932
Local history; archeology; ethnography; handicrafts

Průhonice

03223
Odděleni Botanické Přírodověckého Muzea Narodní Muzeum, Praha (Botanical Branch of the Natural Sciences Museum)
Zámek Průhonice u Prahy, CS-252 43 Průhonice
Natural History Museum
Botany

Radnice u Rokycan

03224
Městské muzeum
Dědická 84, CS Radnice u Rokycan
General Museum - 1892
Mineralogy; paleontology; botany; history; ethnography

Rakovník

03225
Okresni muzeum
Náměstí obětovaných 1/I, CS-269 00 Rakovník
General Museum - 1894
Mineralogy; paleontology; archeology; ethnography; local history; handicrafts; art

Rimavská Sobota

03226
Gemerské múzeum
Nám. ČA 24, CS-979 80 Rimavská Sobota
General Museum - 1882
Archeology; Byzantine jewelry; regional history; numismatics; ethnography

Rokycany

03227
Okresni muzeum
Urbanovo nám. 141, CS-337 01 Rokycany I
General Museum - 1905
Paleontology; history of the regional iron industry; handicrafts; library of Kašpar Šternberk

Ronov nad Doubravkou

03228
Památník Antonina Chittussiho
CS-538 42 Ronov nad Doubravkou
Historic Site
Memorabilia on the painter Antonín Chittussi

Roudnice nad Labem

03229
Galerie výtvarného uměni (Fine Art Gallery)
Očkova 5, CS-413 01 Roudnice nad Labem
Fine Arts Museum - 1910
19th-20th century Czech paintings; currant art

Rousínov u Vyškova

03230
Památník Klementa Gottwalda
CS-683 01 Rousínov u Vyškova
Historic Site - 1955
Memorabilia on the politician Klement Gottwald in the residence at Rousínov

Rožďalovice

03231
Památník Jiřiho Melantricha z Aventýna Polabské muzeum Poděbrady
CS-289 34 Rožďalovice
Historic Site - 1952
Memorial to Jiři Melantrich z Aventýna; history of letter printing

Rožmitál pod Třemšínem

03232
Městské muzeum a památnik Jakuba Jana Ryby
Náměstí, old school, CS-262 42 Rožmitál pod Třemšínem
General Museum - 1920
Local history; memorabilia on the schoolmaster and musician Jakub Jan Ryba

Rožňava

03233
Banicke muzeum (Mining Museum)
Šafárikova 31, CS-048 01 Rožňava
Science/Tech Museum - 1912/1943
Medieval mining technology; mining equipment; local history; geology; speleology

Rožnov pod Radhoštěm

03234
Valašské muzeum v přírodě
Park na Hájnici, CS-756 61 Rožnov
pod Radhoštěm
Open Air Museum - 1911/1925
17th-19th century life of the Carpathian
population; trades; folk art; agriculture;
apiculture; sheep breeding; in 42
original buildings - library

Roztoky u Prahy

03235
Středočeské muzeum
zámek 1, CS-252 63 Roztoky u Prahy
General Museum - 1957
Local natural history; archeology from
Central Bohemia; local ethnology;
history; art

Rtyně v Podkrkonoší

03236
Památník selského povstání
býv. rychta, CS-542 33 Rtyně v
Podkrkonoší
History/Public Affairs Museum - 1963
Collection depicting the peasant revolt
of 1775

Ružomberok

03237
Liptovské múzeum
Park obráncov mieru 8, CS-034 50
Ružomberok
General Museum - 1912
geology; mineralogy; botany; zoology;
history; ethnography; costumes; art;
local history

Rychnov nad Kněžnou

03238
Muzeum Orlických Hor
Zámek 1, CS-516 01 Rychnov nad
Kněžnou
General Museum - 1892
local history; ethnology; ethnography;
zoology; herpetology; handicrafts

03239
Orlická galerie
státní zámek, CS-516 01 Rychnov nad
Kněžnou
Fine Arts Museum - 1965
20th century Czech art

Sabinov

03240
Mestské múzeum
CS-083 01 Sabinov
General Museum - 1954
Natural science; archeology; history;
ethnography

Sadská

03241
Městské muzeum Polabské muzeum
Poděbrady
Palackého nám. 258, CS-289 12
Sadská
General Museum - 1909/10
Local history, archeology and
ethnography

Sázava

03242
Muzeum technického skla (Museum
of Industrial Glass)
Zámek a klášter, CS-285 06 Sázava
Science/Tech Museum - 1963
History of the production of industrial
glass; history of the glass factory
'Kavalier'

Sečovce

03243
Vlastivedné múzeum
Nám. ČA-MsNV, CS-078 01 Sečovce
General Museum - 1964
The museum has no permanent
exhibitions, occasionaly thematic
displays; in a former synagogue

Sedlčany

03244
Městské muzeum
Červený Hrádek u Sedlčan, zámek,
CS-264 01 Sedlčany
General Museum - 1894
Archeology; local history; memorabilia
on Josef Suk

Semily

03245
**Muzeum dělnického hnutí a
památník Antala Staška a Ivana
Olbrachta**
Husova 2, CS-513 01 Semily
History/Public Affairs Museum - 1960
Regional labour movement;
memorabilia on the writers Antal
Stašek and Ivan Olbracht

Sezimovo Ústí

03246
Památník archeologa Josefa Švehly
CS-391 01 Sezimovo Ústí I, č. 21
Historic Site - 1935
Archeological collections of Josef
Švehla

Skalica na Slovensku

03247
Záhorské múzeum
Nám. Slobody, CS-909 01 Skalica na
Slovensku
General Museum - 1906
Natural sciences; archeology; history;
ethnography; costumes; ceramics

Skuteč

03248
Měskské muzeum
Rybičkova 364, CS-539 73 Skuteč
General Museum - 1908
Natural history, especially local
geology and ornithology; history;
handicrafts; local cultural history

03249
Památník Vítězslava Nováka
Městské muzeum
Rybičkova 364, CS-539 73 Skuteč
Historic Site - 1955
Memorabilia on the composer
Vítězslav Novák and his musical salon

Slaný

03250
Vlastivědné muzeum
Nám. 9. května 159, CS-274 01 Slaný
General Museum - 1885
Local geography; paleontology;
entomology; ornithology; archeology;
medieval ceramics; handicrafts;
ethnography of the region; folk art; art
collection

Šlapanice

03251
Městské muzeum
Náměstí 1. máje 4, CS-664 51
Šlapanice
General Museum - 1933
Geology; local history; ethnology;
handicrafts; paintings by Alois Kalvoda

Slatiňany

03252
Hippologické muzeum
Zámek, CS-538 21 Slatiňany
Natural History Museum - 1947
Hippology

Slavkov u Brna

03253
Historické muzeum
Palackého nám. 1, zámek, CS-684 11
Slavkov u Brna
History/Public Affairs Museum - 1937
Collection from the Napoleonic wars
with a special exhibition of the battle of
Slavkov (Austerlitz); local history;
ethnography; furniture

Smiřice nad Labem

03254
Pamětní síň
CS-503 03 Smiřice nad Labem III
General Museum - 1930
Local archeology; history; handicrafts

Soběslav

03255
Muzeum Jihočeských Blat Muzeum
Husitského revolučního hnutí Tábor
(Museum of South Bohemian
Marshland)
tř. Rudé armády 152/9, CS-392 01
Soběslav
General Museum - 1896
Mineralogy; geology; botany; zoology;
entomology; ichthyology;
ethnography; local history; art history;
applied arts; numismatics;

Sobotka

03256
Dům Fráni Šrámka
Nám. 3, CS-507 43 Sobotka
Historic Site - 1958
Memorabilia on the poet František
Šrámek; original furnishings; library

03257
Literárně historický památník
Castle Humprecht, CS-507 43 Sobotka
History/Public Affairs Museum - 1912
Regional history; memorabilia on
regional writers; local ethnography;
handicrafts

Sokolov

03258
Muzeum hornického sokolovska
Zámek, CS-356 00 Sokolov
Science/Tech Museum - 1960
Mineralogy; petrology; paleontology;
local archeology; history of the local
mining industry

Spišská Béla

03259
Múzeum
CS-059 01 Spišská Belá
General Museum
Local history

03260
**Oddelenie Technické Múzeum
Košice**
J.M.Petzval dům, CS-059 01 Spišská
Béla
Historic Site
Development of optical sciences;
memorabilia on the optician and
photograph Johann Petzval
(1807-1891) in his birth house

Spišská Nová Ves

03261
**Vlastivedné Múzeum Spiša s
Galériou** (Museum and Gallery of
Local History and Domestic Life of
Spiš)
Gottwaldova 50, CS-052 80 Spišská
Nová Ves
General Museum - 1951
Archeology; local history; natural
history; art

Stará Huť u Dobříše

03262
Památník Karla Čapka
Na Strži 125, CS-262 02 Stará Huť u
Dobříše
Historic Site - 1963
Memorabilia on the writer Karel
Čapek, his brother the painter Josef
Čapek and his wife Olga
Scheinflugová; in Čapek's former
summer house

Stará Ľubovňa

03263
Okresné vlastivedné múzeum
Hrad, CS-064 01 Stará Ľubovňa
General Museum - 1956
Local history; art; ethnography; crafts;
sacral art; in a 17th castle

Šternberk na Moravě

03264
Muzeum Hodin Krajské vlastivědné
muzeum Olomouc (Horology Museum)
Bezručova 1, CS-785 01 Šternberk na
Moravě
Science/Tech Museum - 1907
History of watch-making; historical
clocks and watches; present watch-
making industry at Šternberk

Strakonice

03265
Muzeum středního Pootaví (Museum
of the Middle Otava Area)
Hrad, CS-386 00 Strakonice
General Museum - 1895
Geology; archeology; historical
documents; trades; industry; art
history; numismatics; literary history;
memorabilia of the poet František L.
Čelákovsky

Štramberk

03266
Mistni muzeum (Okresní vlastivědné muzeum Nový Jičín)
Na bráně 144, CS-742 66 Štramberk
General Museum - 1899
Local geology and paleontology; ethnography; history

Stříbro

03267
Vlastivědné muzeum
Gottwaldovo nám. 1, CS-349 01 Stříbro
General Museum - 1930
Mineralogy; paleontology; local archeology and history; local mining

Studénka

03268
Vagonářské muzeum (Museum of Carriages)
Zámek, CS-742 13 Studénka
Science/Tech Museum - 1961
History of carriages and coaches

Stupava

03269
Múzeum Ferdiša Kostku
ul. F. Kostku 25, CS-99 31 Stupava
Historic Site - 1968
Memorabilia of the artist Fertiš Kostka in his birth house; his old ceramic atelier

Šumperk

03270
Okresni vlastivědné muzeum
Sady 1.máje 1, CS-787 01 Šumperk
General Museum - 1896
Local botany, entomology and zoology; history; handicrafts; labour movement

Sušice

03271
Muzeum Šumavy
Nám. Klementa Gottwalda 2, CS-342 00 Sušice
General Museum - 1880
Local archeology and history; handicrafts; ethnography; local glass making

Svidník

03272
Duklianske múzeum
CS-089 01 Svidník
History/Public Affairs Museum - 1969
Memorial to the Battle of Dukla; commemorative lay-out of the Dukla battlefield as an open air military reservation; firing posts; headquarters; restored bunkers

03273
Múzeum ukrajinskej kultúry
Leninova 258, CS-089 01 Svidník
History/Public Affairs Museum - 1956
Historical collection: social and political struggle of the Ukrainian inhabitants of Eastern Slovakia; Ethnographical collection: folk art; costumes; crafts; Icon collection: 'The Day of Judgement' (three panel paintings); icons from Czechoslovakia

Svitavy

03274
Okresní vlastivědné muzeum
Smetanovo náměstí 1, CS-568 02 Svitavy
General Museum
Regional history; history of the labour movement

Tábor

03275
Muzeum Husitského Revolučniho Hnuti (Museum of the Revolutionary Hussite Movement)
Žiškovo nám. 1, Bechyňská brána, CS-390 00 Tábor
History/Public Affairs Museum - 1878
Ancient history; medieval archeology; Hussite movement in Southern Bohemia; local architectural history; numismatics - library

Tachov

03276
Okresni muzeum
Třída Míru 447, CS-347 01 Tachov
General Museum - 1933
Regional ethnography; natural history; handicrafts; Hussite movement

Tatranská Lomnica

03277
Múzeum správy Tatranského Národného Parku
CS-059 60 Tatranská Lomnica
Natural History Museum - 1957
Mineralogy; botany; zoology; history; mountain tourism; recreation and sport; ethnography; cartography; graphics

Telč

03278
Muzeum Muzeum Vysočiny Jihlava
Zámek, CS-588 56 Telč
Decorative Arts Museum - 1886
Gothic and Renaissance art; furniture; ceramics; arms; African sculpture by F.V Foit

Teplice

03279
Krajské muzeum
Zámecké nám. 14, CS-415 01 Teplice
General Museum - 1894
Natural sciences; archeology; ethnography; art; literature; 16th century illuminated songbooks; graphics; history - library

Teplice nad Metují

03280
Památnik románu Aloise Jiráska 'Skaly'
Zámek Skály, CS-549 57 Teplice nad Metují IV
Historic Site
Life and work of the writer Alois Jirásek, especially concerning his novel 'Skály'

Terezín

03281
Památnik
Malá pevnost, CS-411 55 Terezín
Historic Site - 1947
Documents and materials illustrating the Nazi concentration camp and Jewish ghetto at Terezín during World War II, cemetery

Tišnov

03282
Vlastivědné muzeum
Přdklášteří 2 Porta coeli, CS-666 00 Tišnov
General Museum - 1893
Local geology and mineralogy; zoology; archeology; ethnography; paleontology; numismatics

Topoľčany

03283
Vlastivedné múzeum
Gottwaldovo nám. 3, CS-955 01 Topoľčany
General Museum - 1961
Anthropology; numismatics; history

Tovačov

03284
Etnografické muzeum Okresní muzeum J.A. Komenského Přerov
Zámek, CS-751 01 Tovačov
Anthropology Museum - 1936
Local archeology; ethnography; ceramics; glass; furniture; weapons

Třebechovice pod Orebem

03285
Městské muzeum
Náměst 40, CS-503 46 Třebechovice pod Orebem
General Museum - 1901
Local and regional history; wood carving

Třebenice

03286
Muzeum českého granátu (Museum of Czech Garnet)
Na Loucké, CS-411 13 Třebenice
History/Public Affairs Museum - 1872
History of mining, processing and utilisation of garnets; mining techniques; mining ethnography

Třebič

03287
Památnik Bohuslava Šmerala
Západomoravské muzeum
Nové Dvory, Smeralova tř., CS-674 01 Třebič
Historic Site - 1960
Memorabilia on the politician Dr. Bohumil Šmeral in his former home

03288
Západomoravské múzeum
Tř. 9. kvetna, zámek, CS-674 01 Třebič
General Museum - 1898
Botany, geology, mineralogy of Western Moravia; zoology; archeology; ethnography; art; history; memorabilia on the poet Vítězslav Nezval

Třebiz

03289
Národopisné muzeum Slánska
Vlastivědné muzeum Slaný
CS-273 75 Třebiz
Open Air Museum
Rural buildings from the Slánsko region; furnishings; domestic utensils

03290
Památnik Václava Beneše Třebízského
CS-273 75 Třebíz 19
Historic Site
Memorabilia on the priest and writer V.B. Třebízský in his former home

Trenčín

03291
Trenčianske múzeum
CS-911 00 Trenčín
General Museum - 1877
Natural sciences; archeology; Roman and Slavic relics; local history; Turkish items; decorative art; crafts; Holuby and Brančik collection of insects and plants; in a 17th century baroque castle - library

Třešť'

03292
Muzeum Muzeum Vysočiny Jihlava
Zámek 234, CS-589 01 Třešť
General Museum - 1933
Local history; handicrafts; folk art

Trnava

03293
Zapadoslovenské múzeum (Museum of Western Slovakia)
Kláštorík, Sladovnicka 1, CS-917 00 Trnava
General Museum - 1954
Natural sciences; archeology; ethnography; numismatics; history; Š. C. Parrák's ceramic collection; East Asian relics; Samurai armaments; collection of the Tokyo Imperial Foundry

Trutnov

03294
Muzeum Podkrkonoši
Školní ul. 9, CS-541 00 Trutnov
General Museum - 1890
Regional botany; zoology; geology; paleontology; mineralogy; ethnography; local archeology; history

Turnov

03295
Expozice historického nábytku a oděvu 19. Stoleti
Uměleckoprůmislové Muzeum, Praha (Historical Collection of Furnishings and 19th Century Costumes)
Zámek Hrubý Rohozec, CS-511 01 Turnov
Decorative Arts Museum
Furnishings; interiors; costumes; fashion

03296
Okresni muzeum Českého Ráje
Ul. Čs. armády 71, CS-511 01 Turnov
General Museum - 1886
Mineralogy; petrography; paleontology; geology; prehistory; cultural history; numismatics; ethnography; baroque music

Týn nad Vltavou

03297
Městské muzeum
Náměstí Míru 1, CS-375 01 Týn nad Vltavou
General Museum - 1932
Local natural history; ethnography; popular musical instruments; construction of rafts and ships

Týnec nad Sázavou

03298
Muzeum týnecké keramiky
(Ceramics Museum)
Nádvoří Adama Hodějovského 48,
CS-257 41 Týnec nad Sázavou
Decorative Arts Museum - 1955
History of ceramics manufacture
(18th-19th century); history of the
spinning mill at Brodce; labour
movement

Týniště nad Orlicí

03299
Městské muzeum
CS-517 21 Týniště nad Orlicí
General Museum
Growing of tobacco and its
processing; local handicrafts; local
history

Uherské Hradiště

03300
Slovácké muzeum
Smetanovy sady 178, CS-686 01
Uherské Hradiště
General Museum - 1914
Ethnography of Moravian Slovakia;
archeology; local history; fine arts; folk
costumes

Uherský Brod

03301
Muzeum Jana Ámose Komenského
ul. Přemysla Otakary II 38, CS-688 12
Uherský Brod
General Museum - 1894
Mineralogy; ethnography; archeology;
applied arts; memorabilia of Jan Amos
Comenius (1592-1670)

Uhlířské Janovice

03302
Památník Okresní muzeum Kutná
Hora
Pečírkova 168, CS-285 04 Uhlířské
Janovice
General Museum - 1964
Local archeology; ethnography;
handicrafts; folk art

Unhošť

03303
Melicharovo městské muzeum
Jungmannova 104, CS-273 51 Unhošť
General Museum - 1913
Prehistory and medieval archeology;
local history; ethnography; handicrafts

Úpice

03304
Městské muzeum
Náměstí Míru 30, CS-542 32 Úpice
General Museum - 1895
Regional ethnography; local history;
local labour movement; memorabilia
on the brothers Karel and Josef
Čapek

Ústí nad Labem

03305
Okresní muzeum
Denisovy sady 189, CS-400 00 Ústí
nad Labem
General Museum - 1876
Archeology; local history and industry;
biology; numismatics; prints; regional
literature

Valašské Meziříčí

03306
Muzeum Okresní vlastivědné muzeum
Vsetín
Zámek, CS-757 00 Valašské Meziříčí
General Museum - 1884
Local geology; botany; paleontology;
zoology; prehistory; ceramics;
numismatics; militaria; literary history;
art handicrafts; ethnography

Valašské Klobouky

03307
Městské muzeum
Náměstí 276, CS-766 01 Valašské
Klobouky
General Museum - 1934
Local natural history; archeology;
ethnography; handicrafts; local history

Vamberk

03308
Muzeum krajky
Husovo nám. 84, CS-517 54 Vamberk
Anthropology Museum - 1924
History of folk embroidery; lace; local
history

Velká Bíteš

03309
Městské muzeum
Náměstí Rudé armády 5, CS-595 01
Velká Bíteš
General Museum - 1925
Local history

Velká nad Veličkou

03310
Památník
CS-696 74 Velká nad Veličkou
General Museum
Local ethnography; memorabilia on the
Úprka brothers

Velké Karlovice

03311
Karlovské muzeum
CS-756 06 Velké Karlovice 276
General Museum - 1971
Local history; ethnography

Velké Meziříčí

03312
Vlastivědné muzeum
Zámek, CS-594 01 Velké Meziříčí
General Museum - 1893
Regional mineralogy; zoology; history
of the town; local ethnography,
ceramics, furniture and textile

Velvary

03313
Městské muzeum
Nám. Rudé armády 10, CS-273 24
Velvary
General Museum - 1913
Local archeology; ethnography;
history; applied art

Veselí nad Lužnicí

03314
Muzeum Karla Weise Muzeum
revolučního hnutí Tábor
Náměstí 10, CS-391 81 Veselí nad
Lužnicí
General Museum - 1926
Local history; applied art; paintings;
sculpture

Veselí nad Moravou

03315
Městské muzeum Okresní muzeum
hodonínska Hodonín
Stalingradské nám. 41, CS-698 01
Veselí nad Moravou
General Museum - 1907
Archeology; paleontology;
ethnography; history

Vimperk

03316
Městské muzeum
Zámek, CS-385 01 Vimperk
General Museum - 1956
Regional natural history; history of the
town; history of glass making;
lumbering; local printing

Vodňany

03317
Městské muzeum a galerie
Družstevní 153/I, CS-389 01 Vodňany
General Museum - 1895
Local history, archeology; handicrafts;
fishery; ethnography; memorabilia on
Július Zeyer and František Herites;
art; literary history

Volyně

03318
Městské muzeum
Školní ul. 112, CS-387 01 Volyně
General Museum - 1912
Local mineralogy; archeology; history

Vrchlabí

03319
Krkonošské muzeum
Husova 213, CS-543 00 Vrchlabí
General Museum - 1883
Regional natural history; folk
handicrafts; folk art; local history

Vrutky

03320
**Múzeum revolučnej tlače Klementa
Gottwalda** (K. Gottwald Revolutionary
Museum of the Press)
CS-038 61 Vrutky
History/Public Affairs Museum - 1957
History and development of the press
of communist and Slovak workers

Všebořice

03321
Památník Zdeňka Fibicha
Všebořice, CS-257 68 Dolní Kralovice
Historic Site
Memorabilia on the composer Zdeněk
Fibich in his former house

Vsetín

03322
Okresní vlastivědné muzeum
Horní nám. 2, zámek, CS-755 01 Vsetín
General Museum - 1924
History of the region; ethnography;
resistance movement during World
War II; archeology; art

Vyškov

03323
Muzeum Vyškovska
Nám. Čsl. armády 2, CS-682 00
Vyškov
General Museum - 1922/23
Regional geology; paleontology;
zoology; botany; history; ethnography;
archeology; numismatics; art; history
of the labour movement

Vysoká u Příbrami

03324
Památník Antonína Dvořáka
Zámeček 69, CS Vysoká u Příbrami
Historic Site
Memorabilia on A. Dvořák, especially
concerning his opera 'Rusalka'

Vysoké Mýto

03325
Okresní muzeum A.V. Šembery
Šemberova 125, CS-566 01 Vysoké
Mýto
General Museum - 1884
Local archeology; ethnology; folk art;
local history; literary archive
03326
Památník Otmara Vaňorného Okresní
muzeum A.V. Šembery
Náměstí, CS-566 01 Vysoké Mýto
Historic Site - 1969
Memorabilia on the philologist Otmar
Vaňorný; correspondence; library

Vysoké nad Jizerou

03327
Vlastivědné muzeum
Náměstí 130, CS-512 11 Vysoké nad
Jizerou
General Museum - 1930
Regional and folk art; history of skiing
in the Krkonoše Mountains

Vyšší Brod

03328
Poštovní muzeum Poštovní muzeum
Praha (Post Museum)
Former convent, CS-382 73 Vyšší
Brod
Science/Tech Museum
History of postal services and
telecommunications in Czechoslovakia

Zábřeh na Moravě

03329
Muzeum Okresní vlastivědné muzeum
Šumperk
Žižkova 1, CS-789 00 Zábřeh na
Moravě
General Museum - 1930
History of the textile industry; local
ethnography

Záhlinice

03330
Památník Františka Skopalíka
CS-768 22 Záhlinice 24
Historic Site - 1935
Memorabilia on František Skopalík

Žamberk

03331
Městské muzeum
Zámek, CS-564 01 Žamberk
General Museum - 1890
Memorabilia on the naturalist Prokop
Diviš (1698-1765) and Eduard Albert
(1841-1900); local ethnography

95

Žatec

03332
Městské muzeum K.A. Polánka
Husova 678, CS-438 01 Žatec
General Museum - 1896
Regional prehistory; history of the
town; handicrafts; paleontology

Zbiroh

03333
Městské muzeum
Náměstí 41, CS-338 08 Zbiroh
General Museum - 1933
Local ethnography and history;
handicrafts

03334
Památník Josefa Václava Sládka
Náměstí 28, CS-338 08 Zbiroh
Historic Site - 1952
Memorabilia on the poet Josef Václav
Sládek (d.1912)

Zbraslav nad Vltavou

03335
Sbirka českého sochařství Národní
galerie v Praze (Museum of Czech
Sculpture)
CS-225 01 Zbraslav nad Vltavou
Fine Arts Museum
Sculpture

Ždánice

03336
Muzeum Okresní muzeum
Hodonínska Hodonín
Zámek, CS-696 32 Ždánice
General Museum - 1942
Local archeology; ceramics; folk art;
handicrafts

Žďár nad Sázavou

03337
Muzeum knihy a knižní kultury
Národní muzeum, Praha
Zamek, CS-591 00 Žďár nad Sázavou
History/Public Affairs Museum - 1955
The invention and history of book
printing; technical development of
printing presses; book illustration;
bookbinding; book art

03338
Okresní muzeum
Zámek 1, CS-591 00 Žďár nad
Sázavou
General Museum - 1934
Regional geology; mineralogy; botany;
ethnography; local history; glass
making; production of iron

Ždiar

03339
Muzeum
CS-059 55 Ždiar
Decorative Arts Museum
Ethnography; folk art

Žebrák

03340
Městské muzeum
Náměstí 89, CS-267 53 Žebrák
General Museum - 1925
Local history and archeology;
handicrafts; memorabilia on local
writers and artists

Železná Ruda

03341
Městské muzeum Muzeum Šumavy
Sušice
CS-340 04 Železná Ruda
General Museum - 1945
History and products of the local glass
industry; glass painting

Železnice

03342
**Městské muzeum a galerie T.F.
Šimona**
Muzejní nám. 94 and 181, CS-507 13
Železnice
General Museum - 1917
Local geology; mineralogy;
paleontology; archeology; folk art;
ethnography; paintings by T.F. Šimon,
F. Kaván, P. Zikmund etc.

Železný Brod

03343
**Národopisné muzeum horniho
Pojizeři** (Ethnographical Museum of
Pojizeři)
CS-468 22 Železný Brod
Anthropology Museum - 1870
Ethnography; glass products
illustrating the development of local
glass-making - library

03344
**Národopisné muzeum horniho
Pojizeři**
Velké nám. 197, CS-468 22 Železný
Brod
General Museum - 1870
Folk art and handicrafts; local glass
industry; paintings

Žilina

03345
Považské múzeum a galéria
(Museum and Gallery of the Považie
Region)
Budatínsky hrad, CS-010 00 Žilina
General Museum - 1936
Zoology; especially carnivores and
butterflies; archeology; wire crafts;
naive art; in a 14th century castle

Žirovnice

03346
Vlastivědné muzeum
Zámek, CS-394 68 Žirovnice
General Museum - 1926
Local history; applied art

Zlaté Moravce

03347
Mestské múzeum
nám. Osvoboditelov 1, CS-953 01 Zlaté
Moravce
General Museum - 1896
Natural science; archeology; history

Zlonice

03348
Památník Antonina Dvořáka
Liehmannova 20, CS-273 71 Zlonice
Historic Site - 1954
Memorabilia on the composer Antonín
Dvořak (1841-1904)

Žlutice

03349
Muzeum Husitství Karlovarské
muzeum Karlovy Vary
Nám. Rudé armády 1, CS-364 52
Žlutice
General Museum - 1900
Local archeology; local history,
especially Hussite period

Znojmo

03350
Jihomoravské muzeum (South
Moravian Museum)
ul.Přemyslovců 6, Hrad, CS-669 00
Znojmo
General Museum - 1878
Natural sciences and history;
ceramics; furniture; archeology;
handicrafts; art; in a castle with 11th
century chapel

Zvolen

03351
Vlastivedné múzeum
CS-960 00 Zvolen
General Museum - 1944
Archeology; numismatics; art history;
ethnography

Denmark

Aabenraa

03352
Aabenraa Museum
H.P. Hanssens Gade 33, DK-6200
Aabenraa
General Museum - 1887
Coll: shipping and shipbuilding; foreign
treasures brought home by sailors
from travels abroad; local handicrafts;
painted panels; furniture; silver;
pottery - library

03353
Egnsmuseet Ll. Kolstrupgaard
Toften 15A, DK-6200 Aabenraa
General Museum - 1961
Coll: furnishings; tools; peasant
furniture

Aaby

03354
Indisk-kinesisk Museum
Rosnæs gl. præstegaard, DK-5580 Aaby
Anthropology Museum
Coll: antique art objects; busts of gods
from various temples in India, Thailand,
and Nepal; Tibetan, Arabic, and Indian
traditional festive costumes; Chinese
court costumes from the Tsing
Dynasty; speers, drums, and weapons
from Africa

Aalborg

03355
Aalborg Historiske Museum
Algade 48, POB 805, DK-9100 Aalborg
General Museum - 1863
Coll: archeological findings; local
historical artifacts; applied art; silver;
glass; pottery; paneled room from
1602 - library

03356
Nordjyllands Kunstmuseum
Kong Christians Allé, DK-9000
Aalborg
Fine Arts Museum - 1972
International and Danish art from the
20th century, especially the COBRA;
graphics; sculpture; museum building
designed by Finnish architects Elissa
and Alvar Aalto - library; lecture
rooms; concert hall; film room;
amphitheater; two sculpture parks

Aalestrup

03357
Danmarks Cykelmuseum
DK-9620 Aalestrup
Science/Tech Museum
Motorcycles and motorcycle
equipment from 1865 to the present

Aarhus

03358
Aarhus Kunstmuseum
Vennelystparken, DK-8000 Aarhus C
Fine Arts Museum - 1858
Coll: Danish art from 1750 to the
present; paintings; sculpture; graphic
arts; modern international art; prints -
library

03359
**Aarhus Universitets Forhistorisk
Museum** Forhistorisk Arkaeologiske
Institut
Vester Allé, DK-8000 Aarhus
Archeology Museum
Coll: runic inscriptions; sacrificial
weapons;

03360
Købstadmuseet 'Den Gamle By'
Viborgvej, DK-8000 Aarhus C
Open Air Museum - 1914
Coll: 55 buildings from different Danish
towns together show town
development from 16th-mid 19th
centuries; shops for medieval crafts -
library; theater

03361
Naturhistorisk Museum
Universitetsparken, DK-8000 Aarhus
Natural History Museum - 1921
Coll: exhibits on geological
development of Denmark after the last
Ice Age; zoological section with
habitats of northern and African
animals; geology; biology - children's
section; mini museums

03362
Videnskabshistorisk Samling
Ny Munkegade, DK-8000 Aarhus C
Science/Tech Museum - 1968
Coll: original and reconstructed
apparatuses used to illustrate the
principles of astronomy, physics, math,
and chemistry; also paintings of the
equipment

03363
Vikingemuseet Moesgaard
Klemens Torv 6, DK-8000 Aarhus C
Archeology Museum
Coll: weapons, tools, and other
findings from Viking times;
reconstructed Viking community

Ærøskøbing

03364
Ærø Museum
Brogade 3-5, DK-5970 Ærøskøbing
General Museum
Coll: 18th century farm house; artifacts
of peasant life; traditional peasant
costumes; textiles; navigation history;
apothecary

03365
Flaskeskibssamlingen
DK-5970 Ærøskøbing
General Museum - 1943
Collection of roughly 400 ship models
in bottles

Asnæs

03366
Odsherreds Museum
Department in Høve, Høvevej 57, Høve pr.
DK-4550 Asnæs
General Museum - 1935
Coll: ecological background of the
area; natural history; culture;
prehistory

Auning

03367
Dansk Landbrugsmuseum
Gl. Estrup, DK-8963 Auning
Agriculture Museum - 1889
Farming equipment and models

03368
Gammel Estrup Jyllands
Herregaardsmuseum
Gl. Estrup, DK-8983 Auning
General Museum - 1930
Coll: manor house furnishings and
interiors; European paintings

Ballerup

03369
Egnsmuseet i Lindbjerggaard
Pederstrup, DK-2750 Ballerup
General Museum
Coll: ancient traditional tales; domestic
utensils; personal items of village life

Blaavand

03370
Blaavand Museum Varde Museum
Oxby Gl. Skole, DK-6857 Blaavand
General Museum - 1974
Coll: exhibits on fishing and navigation;
shipwrecks and lifesaving; thatched-
roofed church (1891); division of
natural history with exhibits on
ornithology, botany, and geology;
archives and photos

Brande

03371
Brande Museum
Aktivcentret, DK-7330 Brande
General Museum - 1937
Coll: items of local historical interest;
domestic utensils and tools; pottery
and faience; glass - library

Charlottenlund

03372
Ordrupgaardsamlingen
Vilvordevej 110, DK-2920
Charlottenlund
Fine Arts Museum - 1918
Coll: 19th century Danish and French
art; French impressionists

Christiansfeld

03373
Brødremenighedens Museum
Enkehuset, DK-6070 Christiansfeld
General Museum
Coll: ethnography of foreign countries,
e.g., Greenland, Tanzania, Suriname,
and Nicaragua; local historical items;
firefighting division with implements,
costumes, and history of volunteer fire
departments; paintings of Jeppe
Madsen Ohlsens

Dragør

03374
Amagermuseet
Hovedgaden 12, St. Magleby, DK-2791
Dragør
General Museum - 1901
Coll: oldest half-timbered house in
Denmark; local historical items; period
of Dutch colonization; interior and
furnishings; drawings and paintings of
local artists; peasant costumes

03375
Dragør Museum
Havnepladsen, DK-2791 Dragør
General Museum - 1930
Coll: local history; textiles; crafts;
Vikings; navigation

03376
Mølsteds Museum Dragør Museum
Blegerstræde 1, DK-2791 Dragør
Fine Arts Museum - 1971
Collection of marine paintings and
drawings of Christian Mølsted
(1862-1930) in his atelier

Dronningmølle

03377
Rudolph Tegners Museum
Museumsvej, DK-3120 Dronningmølle
Fine Arts Museum - 1938
Collection of Rudolf Tegner's
sculpture, busts, and drawings and
paintings from his travels - sculpture
park

Ebeltoft

03378
Ebeltoft Museum Det gamle Raadhus
Torvet og Juulsbakke 1, DK-8400
Ebeltoft
General Museum
Coll: historic town hall from 1576;
items from the Stone Age to medieval
times; ethnographic collection from
Thailand; agricultural tools

03379
Institutionen Fregatten 'Jylland'
DK-8400 Ebeltoft
Science/Tech Museum - 1978
Coll: ship equipment; unique 19th
century wooden naval ship

Egeskov Kraerndrup Fyn

03380
Egeskov Veteranmuseum
Slotspark, DK-5772 Egeskov
Kraerndrup Fyn
Science/Tech Museum
Coll: motorcars; motorcycles;
coaches; aeroplanes; models

Esbjerg

03381
Esbjerg Kunstforenings Samling
Kunstpavillonen
Havnegade, DK-6700 Esbjerg
Fine Arts Museum - 1962
Coll: 20th century Danish paintings
and sculptures; modern foreign
graphics

03382
Esbjerg Museum
Finsensgade 1, DK-6700 Esbjerg
General Museum - 1941
Coll: prehistory; neolithic battle-ax
culture and funnel-neck beaker
culture; Roman, Iron Age, and Viking
times; local history; early industrial
revolution; farming implements -
library

03383
Fiskeri- og Søfartsmuseet
Tarphagevej, DK-6700 Esbjerg
Natural History Museum - 1962
Historical material on development of
fisheries from Viking times to the
present - sea aquarium

03384
Den Rosendahlske Bibelsamling
Borgergade 25, DK-6700 Esbjerg
Religious Art Museum
Coll: 150 Bibles from different periods
and countries, several 500 years old;
original Gutenberg Bible

Espergærde

03385
**Museum for Tikøb-omraadet med
pædagogisk Hovedformaal**
Espergærdeskolen, Stockholmsvej,
DK-3060 Espergærde
General Museum
Coll: prehistoric items; furnishings
from peasant's and fisherman's
houses; coin treasure; history from
Middle Ages to the present; literary
history; older Danish paintings

Faaborg

03386
Faaborg Museum
Grønnegade, DK-5600 Faaborg
Fine Arts Museum - 1910
Coll: painting and sculpture

03387
Den Gamle Gaard Faaborg
Kulturhistoriske Musser
Holkegade 1, Bryggegaarden 6,
DK-5600 Faaborg
General Museum
Coll: historic farmstead; furnishings
from 1750.1850; East Indian porcelain;
Delft faience; glass; pottery; ship
models and paintings

03388
Haastrup Folkemindesamling
Haastrup Skole, Bygaden 14, DK-5600
Faaborg
General Museum - 1966
Coll: folklore; documents and records;
tools; horse-drawn fire engine

03389
Kaleko Mølle Faaborg Kulturhistoriske
Museer
Prices Havevej 38, Bryggegaarden 6,
DK-5600 Faaborg
General Museum - 1917
Coll: historic wind mill (1650); furniture;
tools; domestic utensils

Faarevejle

03390
Faarevejle Hjemstavnsmuseum
Kirkevej, DK-4540 Faarevejle
General Museum
Coll: artifacts of peasant life; domestic
utensils; textiles; tools of smithy,
carpenter, and cobbler trades;
ornamented ax from the Stone Age

Fakse

03391
**Fakse geologiske og kulturhistoriske
Museum**
Torvegade, DK-4640 Fakse
Natural History Museum
Coll: exhibits of coral and limestone;
history of local limestone quarry;
minerals; fossils

Fanø

03392
Fanø Kunstsamling
Sønderho, DK-6720 Fanø
Fine Arts Museum
Coll: paintings and watercolors
inspired by local mileau; ceramics;
maps, etchings, and lithographs of Fanø

Farsø

03393
Digterhuset
Søndergade, DK-9640 Farsø
Historic Site
Coll: birth place of the Nobel Prize
writer Johannes Vilhelm Jensens;
furnishings; paintings by his brother,
the artist Hans Deurs; books by
Jensens and his sister Thit;
photographs; excerpts from articles
on Jensens; local archives

Fjerritslev

03394
**Fjerritslev Bryggeri- og
Egnsmuseum**
Den gamle Bryggergaard, DK-9690
Fjerritslev
General Museum
Coll: rural brewery in operation from
1897 to 1968; exhibits on brewing;
brewery equipment

Flauenskjold

03395
Voergaard Slot
DK-9351 Flauenskjold
Historic Site
Coll: medieval castle; artifacts from
feudal times; sculpture; porcelain;
furnishings; paintings by Rubens,
Rafael, Goya, etc.

Fredericia

03396
Fredericia Museum
10 Jernbanegade, DK-7000 Fredericia
General Museum - 1916
Coll: furniture from the town's
churches and synagogue; war relics;
collection of lamps

Frederikshavn

03397
Bangsbomuseet
Bangsbo hovedgaard, DK-9900
Frederikshavn
General Museum - 1947
Coll: local history; military art and
science; navigation; Viking period;
Viking trade ships; collection of
historic gallion figureheads; artifacts
from the occupation period

03398
Krudttaarnsmuseet
DK-9900 Frederikshavn
General Museum
Coll: local history; Danish uniforms;
small arms and cannons from 1600 to
the present; 17th century gunpowder
tower

Frederikssund

03399
J. F. Willumsens Museum
Jenriksvej, DK-3600 Frederikssund
Fine Arts Museum
Coll: J.F. Willumsen's paintings;
drawings; sculpture; prints

Frederiksværk

03400
Frederiksværk Museum
Torvet, DK-3300 Frederiksværk
General Museum - 1800
Coll: historical items related to the
construction of canals in the 18th
century; industrial equipment; coins
and paper currency; war medals;
Stone Age finds; peasant costumes
and implements; paintings;
memorabilia of town founder, General
Classen

03401
Nordsjællands Naturmuseum
Bækkebro, DK-3300 Frederiksværk
Natural History Museum - 1962
Coll: exhibits on geology of area; fauna
and flora; European birds - auditorium;
library

Fur

03402
Fur Museum
Nederby, DK-7884 Fur
Natural History Museum - 1954
Coll: prehistory; archeology; fossilized
fish, plants, insects, turtle from lower
Eocene

Gilleleje

03403
Gilleleje Fiskerimuseum
Postgaardsvej 2, DK-3250 Gilleleje
General Museum - 1929
Coll: exhibits on fisheries, including
tools, models, panoramas; peasant
implements and furniture; items from
the Stone and Bronze Ages

Give

03404
Museet paa Give Skole
Torvegade, DK-7323 Give
Science/Tech Museum
Collection of different tools used in
wood workshop, agriculture, kitchen,
moor, etc., which visitors can use

Gjern

03405
Jysk Automobilmuseum
DK-8883 Gjern
Science/Tech Museum - 1967
Coll: 90 automobiles; 12 motorcycles;
exhibit of different technologies

Glamsbjerg

03406
Vestfyns Hjemstavnsgaard
Klaregade 23, POB 21, DK-5620
Glamsbjerg
Open Air Museum - 1750
Coll: old farm with period interiors;
wagons; tools

Gram

03407
Midtsønderjyllands Museum Gram
Slot
Slotsvej, POB 37, DK-6510 Gram
Natural History Museum - 1974
Coll: geology and paleontology of
Southern Jutland; fossils of the Upper
Miocene Gram clay from Denmark;
well-preserved baleen whale
skeletons

Grenaa

03408
Djurslands Museum
Søndergade 1A, DK-8500 Grenaa
General Museum
Coll: archeology; ethnological exhibits

Grindsted

03409
Grindsted Museum
Borgergade 25-27, DK-7200 Grindsted
General Museum - 1923
Coll: exhibits showing life of heath
dwellers from prehistoric times to the
present; runic inscriptions; coin
collection; black earthenware

03410
Zoologisk Museum
Mellemvej 16, Dal, DK-7200 Grindsted
Natural History Museum - 1965
Coll: approximately 1,100 different
birds; 250 mammals; antler collection;
snail houses; Indian elephant

Haderslev

03411
Haderslev Byhistoriske Arkiv
Bispegade 15-17, DK-6100 Haderslev
General Museum - 1947
Coll: documents and records; maps;
photographs and films; local
newspapers

03412
Haderslev Museum
Dalgade 7, DK-6100 Haderslev
Open Air Museum - 1887
Coll: local historical artifacts;
prehistoric finds of North Slesvig;
Viking history - library

Hadsund

03413
Als Hjemstavnsmuseum
Als, DK-9560 Hadsund
General Museum - 1950
Coll: reconstructed peasant home
from mid 19th century; typical
furniture, tools, and domestic utensils
of the period

Helsingør

03414
Danmarks Tekniske Museum
Ole Rømers Vej, DK-3000 Helsingør
Science/Tech Museum - 1911
Coll: industry; technology; inventions;
motorcars; navigation; fire prevention
- library

03415
**Handels- og Søfartsmuseet paa
Kronborg**
Kronborg Slot, DK-3000 Helsingør
History/Public Affairs Museum - 1914
Coll: history of the Danish merchant
marine; ship models - library

03416
Hensingør Bymuseum Marienlyst Slot
Karmeliterhuset, Hestemøllerstræde,
DK-3000 Helsingør
General Museum
Coll: 16th-18th century castle
furnished in Louis XVI style; items,
paintings, and photographs connected
with the town history; handicraft
collection; town archives

03417
Kronborg Slot
DK-3000 Helsingør
Historic Site
Coll: 16th century castle with fortress
and casemates used as setting by
Shakespear in 'Hamlet'; furnishings,
paintings, and tapestries from the
15th-16th centuries; well-preserved
castle chapel with art objects

Herning

03418
Herning Kunstmuseum
Angligarden, Birk, DK-7400 Herning
Fine Arts Museum - 1977
Coll: modern Danish and international
art and sculptures; the Gruppe Zero;
African art

03419
Herning Museum
Museumsgade 1, DK-7400 Herning
Open Air Museum - 1904
Coll: historic farm house; exhibits on
the heath; peasant life; collection of
works of the heath poet, Steen
Steensen Blicher - craft workshops

03420
**Søby Brunkulslejer og
Brunkulsmuseet**
Hansen Mindelundvej 16, DK-7400
Herning
Science/Tech Museum - 1977
Coll: photo documentation of work in
the brown coal mines (1940-1970); the
apartment of a miner in 1940

Hillerød

03421
Æbelholt Museum
Frederiksværkvejen, DK-3400 Hillerød
Archeology Museum
Coll: cloister from 1175; numerous
skeletons with signs of illnesses;
medicinal herbs

03422
**Det Nationalhistoriske Museum paa
Frederiksborg**
Frederiksborg Slot, DK-3400 Hillerød
History/Public Affairs Museum - 1878
Coll: portraits and paintings illustrating
the history of Denmark; period
furniture and appartments; the chapel
of the Renaissance castle where the
Danish kings were crowned - library

03423
Nordsjællandsk Folkemuseum
Helsingørsgade 65 a, DK-3400 Hillerød
Anthropology Museum
Coll: ethnography; folklore;
anthropology

03424
Pengehistorisk Museum
Frederiksborg Bank
Slotsgade 16, DK-3400 Hillerød
History/Public Affairs Museum
Coll: Danish currency and coins from
former times to the present;
Norwegian and Swedish coin
collections; antique Greek, Roman, and
Byzantine coins

Hjørring

03425
Hjørring Kunstmuseum
Br. Seidelingsgade 10, DK-9800 Hjørring
Fine Arts Museum - 1963
Coll: art from 1935 to present;
frescoes with local history as theme;
contemporary Danish artists; modern
graphics

03426
Vendsyssels Historiske Museum
Skolegade 8, DK-9800 Hjørring
General Museum
Coll: finds from the Iron Age and
Viking times to recent times; ceramics;
religious art; prehistoric graves -
garden with medieval curative plants
and spices

Hobro

03427
Hobro Museum Sydhimmerlands
Museum
Vestergade 21-23, DK-9500 Hobro
General Museum - 1910
Coll: archeology; silver; faience and
china; finds from the Viking fortress
Fyrkat located nearby - library

Højbjerg

03428
Forhistorisk Museum
Moesgaard, DK-8270 Højbjerg
Anthropology Museum
Coll: prehistory; findings from the
Viking times; ethnography; ethnology

Højby

03429
Stenstrup Museum
Stenstrup, DK-4573 Højby
General Museum - 1907
Coll: items of the peasant culture over
the last 200-300 years; domestic
implements; agricultural tools;
traditional peasant costumes; military
items; navigation

Holbæk

03430
Museet for Holbæk og Omegn
Klosterstræde 14-16, DK-4300 Holbæk
General Museum - 1910
Coll: folk culture; archeology; Holbæk
pottery; 19th century merchant shop -
library

Holme Olstrup

03431
Sparresholm Vognsamling
Sparresholm, DK-4684 Holme Olstrup
Science/Tech Museum
Coll: exhibits of transportation facilities
from 1750 to 1945; 100 horse-drawn
carriages, including Frederik XII's gala
carriage and everyday models; sleds;
fire engine

Holstebro

03432
Dragonmuseet
Asylgade 10, DK-7500 Holstebro
History/Public Affairs Museum - 1959
Coll: weapons; documents and books
on the resistance of 1940-1945;
concentration camps - library

03433
Hjemmeværnsmuseet
Sydbanevej 20, DK-7500 Holstebro
History/Public Affairs Museum - 1975
Coll: material from the wars of
1848-50, 1864, WW I, WW II, and the
Resistance; historical weapon
collection from 30 countries

03434
Holstebro Kunstmuseum
Sønderbrogade 2, DK-7500 Holstebro
Fine Arts Museum - 1967
Coll: modern Danish art; African art;
pre-Columbian ceramics and pottery
from Peru; Balinese art

03435
Holstebro Museum
Museumsvej 1, DK-7500 Holstebro
General Museum
Coll: local historical artifacts; crafts;
silver smithy; prehistoric tools; Viking
artifacts

03436
Jens Nielsens Museum
Nørrebrogade 1, DK-7500 Holstebro
Fine Arts Museum - 1971
Coll: works of the painter Jens
Nielsen; drawings; graphics

Holte

03437
Søllerød Kommunes Museum
Mothsgaarden, Søllerødvej 25, DK-2840
Holte
General Museum - 1930
Coll: prehistoric items from the Stone
and Bronze Ages; items illustrating
development of the district through
fishing and agriculture; local historical
paintings

Hornslet

03438
Rosenholm Slot
DK-8543 Hornslet
Historic Site
Coll: Renaissance castle from 1560; art
objects from 16th century to the
present

Horsens

03439
Glud Museum
Glud, DK-8700 Horsens
Agriculture Museum - 1912
Coll: exhibits on agriculture through
the ages; domestic utensils; farm tools
over a period of 300 years; 17th
century half-timbered house

03440
Horsens Museum
Sundvej 1 A, DK-8700 Horsens
General Museum - 1915
Div. of local history: findings from the
Bronze Age; textiles; pictures on
topographical and personal history;
Div. of art: art from 1820 to the
present, particularly after 1930;
sculpture; graphics; drawings;
painting; ceramics

Hørsholm

03441
Hørsholm Egns Museum
Sdr. Jagtvej 2, DK-2970 Hørsholm
General Museum - 1944
Coll: local history; industry; agriculture;
royal castle

03442
Jagt- og Skovbrugsmuseet
Folehavevej 15-17, DK-2970 Hørsholm
Agriculture Museum - 1942
Coll: hunting weapons; trophies; game
mammals and birds; traps; wood
samples; forestry tools and
implements; forestry industry

Humlebæk

03443
Niels W. Gades Museum
Amalievej 2, DK-3050 Humlebæk
Historic Site
Coll: effects of the composer Niels W.
Gade (1817-1890) and items of his
times; records of Gades' musical
compositions

03444
Louisiana
Gl. Strandvej 13, DK-3050 Humlebæk
Fine Arts Museum - 1958
Coll: modern Danish and international
sculptures and paintings - sculpture
garden; concert hall; theater; film
auditorium

Hundested

03445
Knud Rasmussens Hus
Knud Rasmussensvej 9, DK-3390
Hundested
Historic Site - 1933
Coll: former home of the polar
explorer and Eskimo ethnograph,
Knud Rasmussen; memorabilia;
information on his expeditions

Jægerspris

03446
Jægerspris Slot
DK-3630 Jægerspris
Historic Site - 1873
Coll: medieval castle; parks;
sculptures by J. Wiedewelt; interiors
and furnishings from 1700-1800;
memorial for King Frederik VII and
Grevinde Danners

Kalundborg

03447
Kalundborg og Omegns Museum
'Lindegaarden', Adelgade 23, DK-4400
Kalundborg
General Museum
Coll: local history; 19th century
peasant costumes; apothecary;
textiles; handicrafts; agriculture

Kastrup

03448
Kastrupgaardsamlingen
Kastrupvej 339, DK-2770 Kastrup
Fine Arts Museum
Collection of graphics of living artists

Kjellerup

03449
E. Thueninghus
Smedebakken 12, Thorning, DK-8620
Kjellerup
General Museum
Coll: 200-year old half-timbered house;
furnishings from the 18th century;
historical items from various periods,
e.g., skulls of fallen warriors of the 12th
century; effects of the writer Steen
Steensen Blicher

København

03450
Bakkehusmuseet
Rahbeks Allé 23, DK-1860 København
Historic Site - 1925
Coll: 18th century house in which the
Danish philosopher Knud Lyhne
Rahbek lived; furniture; paintings and
drawings; material on the circle of
intellectuals who frequented the
house, e.g., H.C. Andersen and Søren
Kierkegaard

03451
**Brøste's Samling Christianshavn Før
og Nu**
Overgaden oven Vandet 10, DK-1415
København K
General Museum
Coll: local history; art; war relics;
faience; furniture - library

03452
Burmeister & Wain's Museum
Strandgade 4, DK-1401 København K
Science/Tech Museum
Coll: industry; propulsion technology;
full-scale steam and diesel engines;
models of old and new ships; historical
display and developments; working
models

03453
Dansk Post- og Telegrafmuseum
Tietgensgade 37, 2., DK-1530
København V
History/Public Affairs Museum - 1907
Coll: history of the post and telegraph;
commerce and communication;
Valdemar Poulsen's generator and
telegrafon - library

03454
Det Danske Filmmuseum
Store Søndervoldstræde, DK-1419
København K
History/Public Affairs Museum - 1941
Coll: Danish film history from the silent
and sound era; collection of Asta
Nielsen's stills and films; Carl T.
Dreyer's films; literature on film and
television - library

03455
**De Danske Kongers Kronologiske
Samling paa Rosenborg** Rosenborg
Slot
Øster Voldgade 4 A, DK-1350
København K
Fine Arts Museum - 1660
Coll: history of Danish kings
(1470-1906); 18th century furnishings;
Crown Jewels; 17th-18th century
decorative arts; Rosenborg castle;
jewelry; clothing

03456
Davids Samling
Kronprinsessegade 30, DK-1306
København K
Decorative Arts Museum - 1945
Coll: 7th-17th century Islamic art;
Vincennes-Sèvres porcelain and
Meissen porcelain; 18th century
chinoiserie; 18th century English
furniture; Imperial Mughal miniatures

03457
Fyrskib Nr. XVII
ud for Nyhavn 2, DK-1051 København
K
Science/Tech Museum
Lightship built in 1895 with all signaling
and warning devices intact

03458
Geologisk Museum Københavns
Universitet
Øster Voldgade 5-7, DK-1350
København K
Natural History Museum - 1770
Coll: minerals and rocks; meteorites;
fossils; geology of Denmark and
Greenland - library

03459
Den Hirschsprungske Samling
Stockholmsgad 20, DK-2100
København Ø
Fine Arts Museum - 1911
Hirschsprung Collection of 19th and
early 20th century Danish art

03460
Jernbanemuseum The Board of DSB
Sølvgade 40, DK-1349 København K
Science/Tech Museum
Coll: models of rolling stock; railway
ferries; archives of documents;
photographs

03461
Københavns Bymuseum
Vesterbrogade 59, DK-1620 København
V
General Museum - 1901
Coll: history of city's development;
paintings; decorative art; 19th century
architecture; memorabilia of the
philosopher S. Kierkegaard;
photograph archives - library

03462
Det Kongelige Bibliotek
Christians Brygge 8, DK-1219
København K
History/Public Affairs Museum - 1673
Coll: Rare maps and prints;
manuscripts; music; rare books; book
printing art; collection of manuscripts,
drawings, and paper collages of Hans
Christian Andersen; manuscripts of
Søren Kierkegaard; Inca chronicle
(Guaman Poma de Ayala) - library

03463
Kunstindustrimuseet
Bredgade 68, DK-1260 København
Fine Arts Museum - 1894
Coll: European, Chinese, and Japan art
and applied art from medieval times
through the present - library

03464
Louis Tussaud Wax Museum
H.C. Andersens Boulevard 22,
DK-1553 København V
History/Public Affairs Museum - 1974
Coll: wax models of famous historical
and contemporary personalities;
horror chamber

03465
Medicinsk-Historisk Museum
Bredgade 62, DK-1260 København K
History/Public Affairs Museum
Coll: history of medicine; exhibits on
radiography, pharmacy, and
psychiatry; archives; surgery
amphitheater - library

03466
Mekanisk Musik Museum A/S
Vesterbrogade 150, DK-1620
København V
Music Museum - 1970
Coll: 19th century musical instruments;
automatic musical instruments,
including an automatic 12-man
orchester; mechanical piano, banjo,
and modern juke box

03467
Møntsamlingen Nationalmuseet
Frederiksholms Kanal 12, DK-1220
København K
History/Public Affairs Museum -
1780/81
Coll: ancient Greek and Roman coins;
full collection of Danish coins and
medals from 1541 to present - library

03468
**Museet for Danmarks Frihedskamp
1940-1945** Nationalmuseet
Churchillparken, DK-1263 København
History/Public Affairs Museum - 1957
Coll: archives, photos, and documents
concerning history of Denmark's fight
for freedom; military and historical
artifacts - library

03469
Museet ved Sct. Ansgar Kirke
Bredgade 64, DK-1260 København K
Religious Art Museum - 1868
Coll: history of the Catholic church
from 1654 to the present; articles used
in the mass; textiles; liturgical items;
religious paintings

03470
**Musikhistorisk Museum og Carl
Claudius' Samling**
Aabenraa 30, DK-1124 København K
Music Museum - 1898
Folk and classical music instruments
from Europe, Asia, Africa, and South
America

03471
Nationalmuseet
Prinsens Palae D, Frederiksholms
Kanal 12, DK-1220 København K
General Museum - 1807
Departments for Danish prehistory;
the middle ages; medieval weapons
and 16-17th century arms and armor;
ethnography; classical antiquities;
coins and medals; Danish Resistance
Movement; folklore; natural sciences

03472
Ny Carlsberg Glyptotek
Dantes Plads, DK-1556 København V
Fine Arts Museum - 1888
Coll: Egyptian, Greek, Etruscan, and
Roman sculpture; classical archeology;
modern 19th century art - library

03473
Orlogsmuseet
Quinti Lynette, Refshalevej, DK-1432
København K
History/Public Affairs Museum - 1957
Coll: history of the Danish Navy; ships'
models covering three centuries;
painting and photograph collection of
ships; naval artillery; mines and
torpedos; swords and firearms;
uniforms; banners - library

03474
Priors Dukketeater Museum
Købmagergade 52, II, DK-1150
København K
Performing Arts Museum
Complete collection of all Danish doll
theaters with stage decorations and
texts

03475
Statens Museum for Kunst
Sølvgade, DK-1307 København K
Fine Arts Museum - 1760
Coll: Danish painting and sculpture;
Scandinavian art; modern French art
and Old Master paintings; prints;
drawings and etchings s - library

03476
Teaterhistorisk Museum
Christiansborg Ridebane 10, DK-1218
København K
Performing Arts Museum - 1912
Coll: Danish theater history from
medieval times to present; costumes;
manuscripts; paintings in 18th century
former Royal theater; collections on
Sarah Bernhardt and Anna Pavlova -
library

03477
Thorvaldsens Museum
Porthusgade 2, DK-1213 København K
Fine Arts Museum - 1848
Coll: sculpture and drawings by the
Danish sculptor Bertel Thorvaldsen;
paintings, graphics, classical
antiquities; international art in Rome
about 1800 - library

03478
Tøjhusmuseet
Frederiksholms Kanal 29, DK-1220
København K
History/Public Affairs Museum - 1838
Coll: private and military arms of
Western civilization since 1400;
international military art and science;
uniforms; models - library

03479
Wesselstuerne
Graabrødretorv 3, DK-1154 København
K
Historic Site
Coll: home of the Danish poet Johan
Herman Wessel; original editions of
his work

03480
Zoologisk Museum
Universitetsparken 15, DK-2100
København Ø
Natural History Museum - 1770
Coll: zoology; arctic animals; whales;
Danish and South American fossils;
marine animals from the seas of the
world - library

Køge

03481
Køge Museum
Nørregade 4, DK-4600 Køge
General Museum - 1896
Coll: development of area from the
Stone Age to the medieval period;
peasant culture; half-timbered houses;
model reconstructions

Kolding

03482
**Kolding Kunstforenings
Kunstsamling**
Koldinghus, DK-6000 Kolding
Fine Arts Museum - 1903
Collection of Danish art from the
Golden Age (19th century) to modern
times

03483
Museet paa Koldinghus Slot
Koldinghus Slot, POB 91, DK-6000
Kolding
History/Public Affairs Museum - 1890
Coll: relics from the wars between
Germany and Denmark since 1848;
war and hunting weapons; Danish
uniforms; arts and crafts; porcelain;
13th century castle

Korinth

03484
Brahetrolleborg Skolemuseum
Sibyllesvej 3, DK-5783 Korinth
History/Public Affairs Museum
Coll: school from 1783; archives;
paintings; domestic utensils; local
history

Lemvig

03485
Lemvig Museum 'Vesterhus'
Vestergade 44, DK-7620 Lemvig
General Museum - 1932
Coll: exhibits on local history; items
from shipwrecks; lifesaving services;
furnishings from the ship 'Alexander
Nevsky'; painted peasant furniture;
paintings by local artists; manuscripts
and book collection

03486
Søndergaard Museet
Ferring, DK-7620 Lemvig
Fine Arts Museum - 1958
Paintings and watercolors of Jens
Søndergaard (1895-1957) in the summer
house he himself built

Lintrup

03487
Mejlby Kunsthaus
Mejlby, DK-6660 Lintrup
General Museum
Coll: geology; fossils; old agricultural
machines and tools; artifacts from the
Stone Age; art; medicine

Lundby

03488
Grundtvigs Mindestuer i Udby
Udby, DK-4750 Lundby
Historic Site - 1926
Coll: effects of N.F.S. Grundtvig,
Danish historian, theologian, and
educator; his desk, books, and Bible
with notes; photos of family and
friends; manuscripts and original
editions of his works

Lyngby

03489
Dansk Folkemuseum Nationalmuseet
Brede, DK-2800 Lyngby
General Museum - 1879
Coll: Danish guilds; faience; fisheries;
carriages - library

03490
Frilandsmuseet ved Sorgenfri
Nationalmuseet København
Kongevejen 100, DK-2800 Lyngby
Open Air Museum - 1901
Coll: rural buildings from the 18th and
19th centuries; peasant life and
handicrafts

Mariager

03491
Mariager Museum
Kirkegade, DK-9550 Mariager
General Museum - 1922
Coll: tools and ceramics from the
Stone Age; swords from the Bronze
Age; furniture from 1700 to 1800;
peasant life; domestic implements;
handicrafts

Maribo

03492
Frilandsmuseet i Maribo Lolland-
Falsters Stiftsmuseum
Meinckesvej, DK-4930 Maribo
Open Air Museum
Coll: exhibits on agriculture in the 19th
century; farmstead with six houses, a
smithy, mill, and school; medieval
curative plants and fruit trees

03493
Lolland-Falsters Kunstmuseum
Lolland-Falsters Stiftmuseum
Jernbanepladsen, DK-4930 Maribo
Fine Arts Museum - 1890
Coll: Danish paintings and sculpture
from the Golden Age (19th century) to
the present; watercolors; drawings;
graphics

03494
Lolland-Falsters Stiftsmuseum
Museumsgade 1, DK-4930 Maribo
General Museum - 1884
Coll: historic finds; ceramics; folk art;
work tools; exhibit on Polish migrant
workers; 14th century crucifixes -
library

Marstal

03495
Jens Hansen's Søfartsmuseum
Prinsensgade 2-4, DK-5960 Marstal
General Museum - 1929
Coll: 103 models of various ships;
navigation instruments and log books;
weapons; model of 19th century
shipyard; paintings on sea themes and
personalities; local collection of
costumes, furnishings, and porcelain -
library

Middelfart

03496
Middelfart Museum
Henner Frisers Hus, Brogade 8,
Knorregade 2 A, DK-5500 Middelfart
General Museum - 1919
Coll: Renaissance house; local items
dating from the Stone age to town
culture; women's hat collection from
1870-1930; history of ships; copy of
16th century bridal crown from
Middelfart

Næstved

03497
Næstved Museum
Ringstedgade 4, DK-4700 Næstved
General Museum - 1918
Coll: handicrafts and applied arts;
Holmegaard glass; Kähler ceramics;
15th century houses - library

Nivaa

03498
Nivaagaards Malerisamling
DK-2990 Nivaa
Fine Arts Museum - 1908
Coll: 19th century Danish art; 17th
century Dutch art; and 16th century
Italian art

Nørager

03499
Boldrup Museum Sydhimmerlands
Museum
Ørnbjergvej 13, Boldrup, DK-9610
Nørager
General Museum - 1965
Coll: agriculture; handicrafts; local
historical artifacts - library

Norby Fanø

03500
Fanikkerdagens Dragtudstilling
Hovedgaden, DK-6720 Norby Fanø
General Museum - 1966
Coll: traditional peasant costumes of
Fanø; items from sailors' lifes; model
ships

Nørre Søby

03501
Carl Nielsens Banrdomshjem
Nr. Lyndelse, DK-5652 Nørre Søby
Historic Site
Coll: house where the composer Carl
Nielsen was born; his writings;
furnishings

Nørresundby

03502
**Sundby-Hvorup sognehistoriske
Samling**
Lindholmsvej 136 B, DK-9400
Nørresundby
General Museum
Coll: local historical items; 18th-19th
furnishings; paintings; domestic
utensils; agricultural tools

Nuuk/Godthaab

03503
Kalaallit Nunaata Katersugaasivia
Grønlands Landsmuseum
Hans Egedesvej 8, POB 145, DK-3900
Nuuk/Godthaab
General Museum - 1965
Coll: Eskimo artifacts; European
whaling equipment; Inuit art - library

Nykøbing

03504
Falster Minder ('Czarens Hus')
Færgestræde, DK-4800 Nykøbing
General Museum
Coll: 17th century apothecary; textiles;
peasant costumes; handicrafts;
peasant culture; faience; local history;
historic house from 1700

Nykøbing Mors

03505
Morslands Historiske Museum
Dueholm Kloster, Dueholmgade,
DK-7900 Nykøbing Mors
General Museum - 1901
Coll: local history and archeology; iron
casting; fisheries; religious art; peasant
culture; Viking era; navigation; military
objects - library

Nykøbing Sjælland

03506
Anneberg-Samlingerne
Anneberg, DK Nykøbing Sjælland
Decorative Arts Museum - 1965
Coll: Greek and Roman glass,
Bohemian glass, Spanish glass;
decorated glass; sculpture;
handicrafts; paintings

03507
Odsherreds Folkemuseum
Kirkestræde 12, DK-4500 Nykøbing
Sjælland
General Museum - 1912
Coll: items from the Stone and Bronze
Ages; Barock and Empire furnishings;
local handicrafts; glass; porcelain;
dolls and toys from the last 150 years

Nysted

03508
Alholm Automobil Museum
DK-4880 Nysted
Science/Tech Museum
motor cars; model railroad system

Odder

03509
Odder Museum
Rosensgade 84, DK-8300 Odder
General Museum - 1929
Coll: excavations of medieval manor
houses; 19th century peasant
furniture; folklore; beekeeping; oldest
distillery in Scandinavia; 13th century
distillery equipment; textiles

Odense

03510
DSB Jernbanemuseum
Dannebrodsgade 24, DK 5000
Odense, Sølvgade 40, DK-1349
København K
History/Public Affairs Museum
Coll: steam locomotives; passenger
coaches; royal saloons

03511
Fyns Kunstmuseum
Jernbanegade 13, DK-5000 Odense
Fine Arts Museum
Danish art from ca. 1750 until the
present - library

03512
Fyns Stiftsmuseum
Jernbanegade 13, Odense Adelige
Jomfrukloster, Albani Torv 6, DK-5000
Odense
Archeology Museum - 1860
Coll: prehistoric findings; Viking
artifacts; items from Bronze and Iron
Ages

03513
Den Fynske Landsby
Sejerskovvej 20, DK-5260 Odense
Open Air Museum
Coll: peasant culture; farms and
peasant houses; animals

03514
H. C. Andersens Barndomshjem
Munke Møllestræde 3, DK-5000 Odense
Historic Site - 1931
Coll: house where Andersen lived as a
child (1807-19); paintings and other
materials on his life and the city of that
time

03515
H. C. Andersens Hus
Hans Jensensstræde 39-43, DK-5000
Odense
Historic Site - 1905
Coll: letters and manuscripts of
Andersen; drawings and graphics
inspired by his work; personal items;
editions of his books

03516
Landsarkivet for Fynen
Jernbaneg 36, DK-5000 Odense
History/Public Affairs Museum
Regional archives

03517
Møntergaarden Fyns Stiftsmuseum
Overgade 48-50, DK-5000 Odense G
General Museum - 1941
Coll: local history; town culture; coins
and medals; peasant costumes;
handicrafts; furniture from the
17th-18th centuries

Ølgod

03518
Hjedding Mejerimuseum Ølgod
Museum
Hjedding pr. Ølgod, DK-6870 Ølgod
Science/Tech Museum - 1948
Coll: first community dairy from 1882;
various dairy machines, centrifuge, etc.

03519
Ølgod Egnsmuseum
Vestergade 49, DK-6870 Ølgod
General Museum - 1954
Coll: peasant culture; agricultural
implements; handicrafts; pottery; local
historical artifacts; coins; exhibits on
fauna and bird life

03520
Ølgod Museum
Vestergade 7, DK-6870 Ølgod
General Museum - 1954
Items of local historical interest

Otterup

03521
Otterùp Museum
Bakkevej 3, DK-5450 Otterup, Fyn
General Museum - 1930
Local exhibits

Oxbøl

03522
Blaavandshuk Egnsmuseum Varde
Museum
Gl. Møllevej 2, DK-6840 Oxbøl
General Museum - 1972
Coll: agricultural implements; domestic
utensils; military items from the
Occupation and WW II; local archives

Padborg

03523
Bov Museum
Bovvej 2, DK-62330 Padborg
General Museum - 1979
Coll: old uniforms; pictures of the
frontier gendarmery; agricultural tools;
old fire engines; regional poetry

Præstø

03524
Thorvaldsen Samlingen
Nysø, DK-4720 Præstø
Fine Arts Museum - 1926
Coll: sculpture, reliefs, busts, and
statuettes by the Danish sculptor
Bertel Thorvaldsen, including his
self-portrait and the bust of Martin
Luther; several memorabilia of the
artist

Randers

03525
Kulturhistorisk Museum
Stemannsgade 2, DK-8900 Randers
General Museum - 1872
Coll: prehistoric and medieval
archeology; numismatics; regional
crafts, textiles, furniture, and household
utensils; woodcuts by Dürer and
etchings by Rembrandt and Ostade -
library; study room

03526
Museet
Stengaden 17, Nielstrup Skov, Voldum,
DK-8900 Randers
General Museum
Coll: traditional peasant costumes; hat
collection (1755-1896); peasant home
from the 18th-19th centuries with
furniture, domestic implements, books,
and toys; textiles

03527
Randers Kunstmuseum
Stemannsgade, DK-8900 Randers
Fine Arts Museum - 1887
Coll: Danish painting from 1770 to the
present; modern international art,
painting, graphics, and sculpture

Redsted

03528
**Finlandsmuseet ved Herregaarden
Glomstrup-Mors**
Glomstrup pr., DK-7970 Redsted
Open Air Museum - 1969
Coll: 18th century manor; interior and
furnishings; 19th century merchant's
shop; workshops; cars; clothes;
faience factory and pottery workshop

Ribe

03529
Den Antikvariske Samling
Overdammen 10, DK-6760 Ribe
General Museum
Coll: excavation finds; religious art;
Renaissance furniture; decorative arts;
porcelain and glass

03530
Museums-everten Johanne Dan
Skibbroen, DK-6760 Ribe
General Museum
Coll: local history of old shipping
mileau; 19th century ships; maritime
art; ship models; panoramas and
photos of local and Danish maritime
history

03531
Ribe Kunstmuseum
Sct. Nikolajgade 10, DK-6760 Ribe
Fine Arts Museum - 1891
Collection of Danish art with emphasis
on art from the Golden Age (19th
century)

03532
Ribe Raadhussamling
V. Støckensplads, DK-6760 Ribe
General Museum
Coll: town hall from 1528; old debtor's
prison; equipment of a medieval
executioner, e.g., thumb screws,
branding irons

Ringkøbing

03533
Ringkøbing Museum
Kongevejen 1, DK-6950 Ringkøbing
Archeology Museum - 1908
Coll: prehistory of West Jutland;
Icelandic woodcarvings from the
18th-19th centuries; ethnographic
collection from Danish expedition to
Greenland; prehistorical archeological
findings

Rønne

03534
Bornholms Museum
Sct. Mortens gade 29, POB 126,
DK-3700 Rønne
General Museum
Coll: peasant costumes; ethnography;
geology; handicrafts; art and applied
art; local historical items; navigation;
ceramics; toys and furniture from
modern times; merchant's store from
1920-1930

03535
Erichsens Gaard Bornholms Museum
Laxegade 7, DK-3700 Rønne
General Museum
Coll: 19th century farm; furnishings of
period

03536
Forsvarsmuseet paa Bornholm Rønne
Arsenal
Galløkken, Sdr. Alle, DK-3700 Rønne
History/Public Affairs Museum - 1979
Coll: military uniforms, weapons, and
equipment from the Bornholm forces;
weapons and items from the German
Occupation and the Russian forces in
1945-46 - library

Roskilde

03537
Roskilde Museum
Sankt Olsgade 18, DK-4000 Roskilde
General Museum - 1929
Coll: medieval urban artifacts; peasant
costumes; handicrafts; toys; drawings;
ceramics; furniture - library

03538
Vikingeskibshallen
Strandengen, DK-4000 Roskilde
Archeology Museum - 1969
Coll: original Viking ships of various
types; displays of Viking activities and
culture - film room

Roslev

03539
Jenle
DK-7870 Roslev
Historic Site
Coll: farm and home of the Danish
writer Jeppe Aakjær and his wife
Nanna; his books, effects, and
paintings and sculpture of his friends

Rudkøbing

03540
Langelands Museum
Jens Winhersvej 12, DK-5900
Rudkøbing
General Museum - 1900
Coll: famous Stone Age settlement
finds from late Stone Age; Viking
chieftain graves; a 16th century
fisherman's settlement; furniture from
manor houses; religious artifacts -
library

Sæby

03541
Sæby Museum
Søndergade, DK-9300 Sæby
General Museum
Coll: 18th century half-timbered house;
artifacts from the prehistorical period
to the present; early 20th century
school room with physics equipment;
a merchant's shop; photographer's
atelier; apothecary

Silkeborg

03542
Silkeborg Kunstmuseum
Hostrupsgade 41, DK-8600 Silkeborg
Fine Arts Museum - 1939
Coll: modern art; European paintings
from the late 19th-20th centuries;
graphics; ceramics

03543
Silkeborg Museum
Hovedgaarden, DK-8600 Silkeborg
General Museum - 1900
Coll: exhibits on history of area with
items from the Stone Age to the
present; 2000-year old prehistoric
corpses (The Tollund Man and the
Elling Woman); pottery and wooden
shoe workshops; glass

Skagen

03544
Drachmanns Hus
Hans Baghs Vej, DK-9990 Skagen
Historic Site
Coll: summer house of the writer
Holger Drachmanns; paintings by
Drachmanns as well as his collection
of paintings

03545
Michael og Anna Anchers Hus
Markvej 2, DK-9900 Skagen
Historic Site - 1964
Coll: house where the Anchers lived;
interior furnishings; paintings by the
artists

03546
Skagens Fortidsminder
P.K. Nielsensvej 10, DK-9990 Skagen
Fine Arts Museum - 1927
Coll: drawings and paintings of local
artists between 1830 and 1930

Skanderborg

03547
Øm Kloster Museum
Munkevej 8, DK-8660 Skanderborg
Archeology Museum
Coll: medieval cloister ruin (1172);
medieval archeological findings;
medicine collection of pathological
bones from the graveyard

03548
Skanderborg Museum
Adelgade 5, DK-8660 Skanderborg
General Museum - 1913
Coll: local historical items dating from
the Stone Age to the present; artifacts
from the Viking era; peasant culture

Skive

03549
Skive Museum
Havnevej 14, DK-7800 Skive
General Museum - 1910
Coll: prehistoric amber collection;
exhibits on local ethnography and
archeology; modern Danish paintings
and sculpture

03550
Skive Museums Kunstafdeling
Havnevej, DK-7800 Skive
Fine Arts Museum - 1964
Coll: folklore painters Dalsgaard and
Smidth; paintings and drawings of
Clausen

Skjern

03551
Skjern Museum
Anlæget, DK-6900 Skjern
General Museum
Coll: findings from the Bronze and Iron
ages; pottery; domestic utensils;
peasant furniture; fishing implements;
religious objects

Skørping

03552
Lincoln-Blokhuset
Rebild, DK-9520 Skørping
History/Public Affairs Museum - 1934
Coll: exhibits on life of the Danish
emigrants to the United States; copy
of Lincoln's birth place; collection of
historical items from pioneer times;
native costumes of Indians;
newspaper announcing assassination
of Lincoln

03553
**Spillemands-Jagt og
Skovbrugsmuseet i Rebild**
Cimbrervej 2, Rebild, DK-9520 Skørping
General Museum
Coll: forestry; hunting; local history;
folk music and instruments; folk
dancing; blacksmith shop; peasants'
furniture, pottery, and kitchen utensils

03554
Thingbæk Kalkminer
DK-9520 Skørping
Fine Arts Museum - 1969
Collection of the sculpture of Anders
Bundgaard and Carl Johan Bonnesens
exhibited in a mine

Sønderborg

03555
Flintestuen
Stjernegade 7, DK-6400 Sønderborg
Archeology Museum - 1970
Coll: 60,000 stones dating from the
Stone Age; daggers, speers, and axes;
4000-year old sacrificial ax

03556
Museet paa Sønderborg Slot
Sønderborg Castle, DK-6400
Sønderborg
General Museum - 1908
Coll: castle; history of Sleswig; local
historical items; handicrafts; paintings;
military weapons and uniforms;
medieval art - library; class room;
lecture room; auditorium

Sorø

03557
**Sorø Akademis naturhistoriske
Museum**
Akademiet, DK-4180 Sorø
Natural History Museum - 1827
Coll: exhibits of extinct animal species;
implements from the 19th century
Galathea expedition; ethnographic
collection

03558
Sorø Amts Museum
Storgade 17A, DK-4180 Sorø
General Museum - 1916
Coll: peasant costumes and culture;
development of town culture in the
18th and 19th centuries; archeological
findings from the Stone Age to the
present; furniture; glass; silver;
paintings

Stege

03559
Liselund Gamle Slot
DK-4780 Stege
Historic Site - 1938
Coll: historic castle built in 1792-95;
items and interior decorations from
period of Louis XVI; parks

03560
Møns Museum
Storegade 75, DK-4780 Stege
General Museum
Coll: religious art; local history;
archeological findings from 10,000 BC
to Bronze Age; peasant costumes;
furniture

Struer

03561
Struer Museum
Søndergade 23, DK-7600 Struer
Historic Site - 1929
Coll: home of Danish author Johannes
Buchholtz; archives of Buchholtz;
medieval religious art; local marine
collections; ethnology

Svendborg

03562
**Anne Hvides Gaard and
Viébæltegaard** Svendborg Amts
Museum
Grubbemøllevej 13, DK-5700
Svendborg
History/Public Affairs Museum
Coll: exhibits of 19th century indigents'
home and labor institute; local
historical items; navigation; wooden
ship industry

03563
Johannes Jørgensens Mindestuer
Fruestræde 15, DK-5700 Svendborg
Historic Site
Coll: the private collection of books of
the Danish writer, Johannes Jørgensen;
personal furniture brought from Assisi;
collection of letters

03564
Svendborg og Omegns Museum
Viebæltegaard, Anne Hvides Gaard,
Grubbemøllevej 13, DK-5700
Svendborg
General Museum - 1908
Coll: items from prehistory through the
Middle Ages; folklore; social history;
handicrafts; maritime history

03565
Svendborg Zoologiske Museum
Dronningemaen 30, DK-5700
Svendborg
Natural History Museum - 1935
Coll: exhibit of Denmark's fauna from
the Ice Age to the present; panoramas
of environmental habitats of each
species

03566
Taasinge Skipperhjem og
Folkemindesamling
Kirkebakken, Bregninge, DK-5700
Svendborg
General Museum - 1958
Coll: half-timbered house (1770);
agricultural implements; navigation;
articles from the Stone Age to the
present; traditional peasant costumes;
maritime paintings

Thisted

03567
Klitmøller Egnssamling
Fiskerlejet Klitmøller, DK-7700 Thisted
Science/Tech Museum - 1970
Coll: examples of different types of
fisheries; tools and implements of the
fishing trade; processing of fish;
domestic implements; photo archives;
local genealogy

03568
Museet for Thy og Vester Hanherred
Jernbanegade 4, DK-7700 Thisted
General Museum - 1903
Coll: handicrafts; local history from
Viking times to present; collection of
bronzes; memorial to the Danish poet
Jens Peter Jacobsen

Toftlund

03569
Toftlund mini Museum
Østergade 8, DK-6520 Toftlund
General Museum - 1975
Coll: domestic implements; technical
equipment; handicraft tools; machines;
cameras; objects from the past and
the present demonstrating local
history - library

Tønder

03570
Sønderjyllands Kunstmuseum
Kongevejen 55, DK-6270 Tønder
Fine Arts Museum
Danish art from the 20th century

03571
Tønder Museum
Kongevejen 55, DK-6270 Tønder
Decorative Arts Museum - 1923
Coll: 16th century tower; silver; tiles;
lace; Renaissance and Baroque
furniture; faience and porcelain; glas;
collection of Emil Nolde's works

Torrig

03572
Reventlow-Museet
Pederstrup, DK-4943 Torrig
General Museum - 1940
Coll: effects of the Danish statesman
responsible for the agricultural reform
of the 18th century, C.D.F. Reventlow;
paintings of him and family; his
collected paintings of the times;
Danish, English, German, and French
furniture; documents and books
dealing with the land reform

Vaerløse

03573
Vaerløse Museum
Mosegaarden, Skovgaards Allé 37,
DK-3500 Vaerløse
General Museum - 1968
Coll: local history; items from the
Middle Ages and Viking times;
peasant culture; furniture; tools;
textiles; rope; historical photographs;
ceramics from medieval times to the
Renaissance - library

Valby

03574
Carlsberg Museum
Valby Langgade 1, DK-2500 Valby
Science/Tech Museum - 1916
Coll: technology; industry; brewery

03575
Museumsbanen Maribo-Bandholm
Dansk Jernbane-Klub, Nakskovvej 62
A, DK-2500 Valby, Maribo St., DK-4930
Maribo
Science/Tech Museum
Coll: railroad track, Denmark's first
private railroad; 6 steam locomotives;
Europe's oldest diesel locomotive;
motor vehicles

Varde

03576
Varde Museum
Lundvej 4, DK-6800 Varde
General Museum - 1912
Coll: exhibits on town and region from
prehistoric times to the present;
furniture; weapons; applied art; Danish
paintings; Jutland pottery - library

Vejby

03577
Raageleje Bilmuseum
Hesselbjergvej 45, Raageleje, DK-3210
Vejby
Science/Tech Museum
Coll: antique automobiles from 1907;
other forms of transportation, e.g.,
motorcycles

Vejen

03578
Vejen Museum
Øster Alle, DK-6600 Vejen
Fine Arts Museum - 1923
Coll: sculptures of Niels Hansen
Jacobsen; drawings of Jens Lund;
mosaics of Einar Nielsen; paintings of
Ring, Hammershøj and others; also
modern Danish artists

Vejle

03579
Vejle Kunstmuseum
Flegborg 16, DK-7100 Vejle
Fine Arts Museum - 1900
Coll: Danish drawings from the 19th
and 20th centuries; Danish and
European graphic arts, including 500
prints from 16th century Netherlands

Vesløs

03580
Skjoldborgs Barndomshjem
Øsløs, DK-7742 Vesløs
Historic Site
Coll: birth place of the Danish writer
Johan Skjoldborg; exhibit on cobbler's
trade; personal effects of the writer

Viborg

03581
Det Danske Hedeselskabs Museum
Hjultorvet, POB 110, DK-8800 Viborg
General Museum
Exhibits on the cultivation of the heath
beginning in 1850

03582
E. Bindstouw
Lysgaard, Blichersvej 40, DK-8800
Viborg
Historic Site
Exhibits on literature up to the novelist
and poet Steen Steensen Blicher
(1782-1848) and his times

03583
Garnisonsmuseet i Viborg
Gl. Vagt, Gravene, DK-8800 Viborg
History/Public Affairs Museum - 1969
Coll: garnison 'Gamle Vagt'(1802);
uniforms, weapons, equipment from
1650 to the present

03584
Den Heibergske Fuglesamling
Viborg Centralbibliothek
Vesterbrogade 15, DK-8800 Viborg
Natural History Museum
Coll: rare and threatened bird species;
bird eggs; bat collection

03585
Skovgaard Museet i Viborg
Domkirkestræde 2-4, DK-8800 Viborg
Fine Arts Museum - 1935
Coll: paintings, drawings, graphics,
ceramics, and sculptures by the artist
family Skovgaard - library

03586
Viborg Stiftsmuseum
Hjultorvet 4, DK-8800 Viborg
General Museum - 1861
Coll: artifacts from Stone Age and
Bronze Age; finds from medieval town
excavations; costumes; toys; 18th
century Dutch star globe - library

Vinderup

03587
Frilandsmuseet paa Hjerl Hede
Jydsk Skovmuseum and Mosebrug
Museum
Hjerl Hede, DK-7833 Vinderup
Open Air Museum
Coll: reconstructions of Stone Age
sites; long houses from the Bronze
Age; ancient church; oldest farmstead
in Denmark with reconstructed
buildings

Vordingborg

03588
Sydsjællands Museum
Ruinterrænet DK, 4760 Vordingborg
General Museum - 1915
Coll: local historical artifacts from the
Stone Age to the present; medieval
religious art; traditional costumes and
textiles; ruin of medieval fort - library

Dominican Republic

Santo Domingo

03589
Galeria Nacional de Bellas Artes
Santo Domingo
Fine Arts Museum - 1943
paintings; sculptures

03590
Museo Nacional
Santo Domingo
General Museum - 1927
Archeology; Colonial and Republican
history; anthropology; Indian
ethnography; pre-Columbian period;
crafts; armaments; Spanish relics; also
modern paintings; drawings; photos;
numismatics

Ecuador

Ambato

03591
Museo Zoologico 'Colegio Bolivar'
Sucre 8 - 39, Ambato
Natural History Museum

Cuenca

03592
Museo Municipal 'Remigio Crespo
Toral'
Calle Larga 7-07 y Borrero, Cuenca
General Museum

Guayaquil

03593
Museo de la Casa de la Cultura
Ecuatoriana
Av. 9 de Octubre, Guayaquil
General Museum

03594
Museo Victor Emilio Estrada
Guayaquil
Archeology Museum

03595
Museo y Biblioteca Municipal
Av. 10 de Agosto, Guayaquil
General Museum
Art; history; archeology; ethnography;
paleontology; geology; paintings and
numismatics of colonial and modern
periods

Latacunga

03596
Museo de la Casa de la Cultura
Ecuatoriana
Latacunga
General Museum

Quito

03597
Museo Antropologico 'Antonio
Santiana' Universidad Central del
Ecuador
Casille 16b, Quito
Anthropology Museum
Archeology; ethnography;
anthropology

03598
Museo Arqueologico y Galerias de
Arte del Banco Central del Ecuador
Plaza Bolivar, Av. 10 de Agosto y
Briseño, Quito
Archeology Museum - 1959
Archeology; numismatics; Quitenian
art; Latin American modern art;
pre-Columbian gold collection from la
Tolita culture; ceramic collection (3,200
B.C.-1,500 A.D.) - library

03599
Museo de Arte 'Alberto Mena
Caamaño'
Espejo 1147, Quito
Fine Arts Museum

03600
Museo de Arte e Historia de la Ciudad
Espejo 1147, Apdo. 399, Quito
Fine Arts Museum - 1930
city history; painting; sculpture

03601
Museo de Ciencias Naturales
Quito
Natural History Museum - 1937
geology; fauna of the Galapagos
Islands; anatomy; taxidermy

03602
Museo de Etnografía
Casa de la Cultura Ecuatoriana, Av. 6
de Diciembre 332, Quito
Anthropology Museum

03603
Museo de Historia Natural Instituto
Nacional Mejía
Vargas 989, Quito
Natural History Museum

03604
**Museo de Instrumentos Musicales
'Pablo Traversari'**
Av. 6 de Diciembre 332, Apdo. 67,
Quito
History/Public Affairs Museum
musical instruments of European,
pre-Inca and colonial cultures

03605
Museo Jacinto Jijon y Caamaño
Universidad Católica del Ecuador
Av. 12 de Octubre, Quito
General Museum
History; archeology; colonial art

03606
Museo 'La Salle'
Caldas 587, Apdo 329, Quito
Natural History Museum

03607
Museo Nacional de Arte Colonial
Mejía y Cuenca esq., Apdo. 2555,
Quito, Provincia de Pichincha
Fine Arts Museum - 1941
16th-18th century art; colonial art;
Miguel de Santiago's and Caspicara's
collections

03608
**Museo Petrografico del Servicio
Nacional de Geologia y Mineria**
Carrión, Quito
Natural History Museum
Mineralogy

Egypt

Abbasieh

03609
Criminology Museum
Abbasieh
Science/Tech Museum

Al-Ghardaqa

03610
**Institute of Oceanography and
Fisheries**
Marine Biological Station, Al-Ghardaqa
Science/Tech Museum
Marine biology; Red Sea fauna;
ichthyology; fishing

Alexandria

03611
Anatomy and Pathology Museum
University of Alexandria, Alexandria
Science/Tech Museum

03612
Greek-Roman Museum
5, Al Mathaf St, Alexandria
Fine Arts Museum - 1892
Greek, Roman and Coptic collections

03613
Municipal Museum
Alexandria
General Museum

03614
**Museum of Fine Arts and Cultural
Center**
Menascha St, Alexandria
Fine Arts Museum
Painting and sculpture by traditional
and contemporary artists

03615
Museum of the Faculty of Arts
University of Alexandria, Alexandria
Fine Arts Museum

Aswan

03616
Aswan Museum
Aswan
Archeology Museum
Egyptian antiquities; mummies;
sarcophagi; monumental sculpture

Cairo

03617
Al-Gawhara Palace Museum
The Citadel, Cairo
General Museum - 1954
Oriental and French furniture, Turkish
paintings, clocks, glass, and 19th cent.
costumes housed in 19th cent.
Ottoman-style palace

03618
Arabic Museum
Midan Babel-Khalk, Cairo
Anthropology Museum
Ethnography and art collections

03619
Coptic Museum
Masr Ateeka, Cairo
Archeology Museum - 1908
Architecture; classical antiquities;
icons; ivory; pottery, glass and textiles;
papyrus manuscripts - library

03620
Cotton Museum
mail c/o Egyptian Agricultural Society,
Khediv Ismael St, POB 63, Cairo
Science/Tech Museum
Displays of Egyptian agricultural
techniques

03621
Education Museum
3 Manour St, Cairo
History/Public Affairs Museum
Materials and methods of education;
documents

03622
Egyptian Museum
Tahrir Sq, Cairo
General Museum - 1900
Exhibits from prehistoric times to 6th
cent. A.D.; Tutankhamen treasures -
library

03623
Entomological Museum
14, Milika Nazli St, Cairo
Natural History Museum
Entomology and ornithology

03624
Gayer Anderson Museum
Ibn Tolon Sq, Cairo
History/Public Affairs Museum
Oriental art objects; 18th cent.
collections

03625
Geographical Society Museum
Kasr el-Einy, Cairo
Anthropology Museum

03626
Geology Museum
Kasr el-Einy, Cairo
Natural History Museum - 1899
Geology; fossils; rocks and minerals;
gemstones; meteorites; Arsinoitherium
skulls

03627
Islamic Archaeological Museum
Cairo University, Cairo
Archeology Museum

03628
Military Museum
The Citadel, Cairo
History/Public Affairs Museum
Firearms, swords, daggers, orders,
medals, and other military artifacts

03629
Mokhtar Museum
Horrya Garden, Gezira, Cairo
Fine Arts Museum
Works of Egyptian sculptor Mahmoud
Moktar (1891-1934)

03630
Museum of Egyptian Civilizatin
18, Ismail Abu El Fetouh St, Cairo
History/Public Affairs Museum
Displays from Palaeolithic, Neolithic
and historical periods of Egyptian
civilization

03631
Museum of Islamic Art
Ahmed Maher Sq, Cairo
Fine Arts Museum - 1881
Classical antiquities; bronzes; lamps;
ceramics; carpets

03632
Museum of Modern Art
Shari Kasr el-Nil 4, Cairo
Fine Arts Museum - 1920
Painting and sculpture; copper plate
engravings

03633
Museum of the History of Medicine
Saray El Sakakini, Ghamra, Cairo
Science/Tech Museum
Medical and hygiene collections

03634
**Ornithology and Entomology
Museum**
Sharia Ramses and Av Nahdet Misv
14, Cairo
Natural History Museum

03635
Pharaonic Museum
Cairo University, Cairo
Archeology Museum
Egyptian archaeology

03636
Postal Museum
Al-Ataba Sq, Cairo
History/Public Affairs Museum - 1943
Postage stamps from Egypt and other
countries

03637
Railways Museum
Ramses Sq, Cairo
Science/Tech Museum - 1932/1933
Locomotives and other rolling stock;
railroad signal and other equipment;
bridges; documents and maps
illustrating the development of railway
transport

03638
Scientific Researches Museum
Kasr el-Eini St, Cairo
Natural History Museum
Botany; zoology; natural history

03639
Transportation Museum
Ahmed Maher Pacha, Cairo
Science/Tech Museum
Automobile collection

Dokki

03640
Agricultural Museum
Dokki
Natural History Museum - 1930
Horitculture, botany and zoology;
irrigation

El-Alamein

03641
Military Museum
El-Alamein
History/Public Affairs Museum
Military equipment; documents of the
Battle of El-Alamein (1945)

Giza

03642
Cheop's Boats Museum
The Pyramids, Giza
Archeology Museum
Classical antiquities

03643
Giza Zoological Museum Zoological
Gardens
Giza St, Giza
Natural History Museum
Egyptian birds, reptiles and
amphibians; ancient mummified
crocodile

Hurghada

03644
Marine Biological Station
Hurghada
Natural History Museum
Ichthyology; Red Sea fishes

Ismailia

03645
Ismailia Museum
Ismailia
Archeology Museum
Classical antiquities; Darius monument

Luxor

03646
Royal Tombs
Luxor
Anthropology Museum
Royal tombs with original paintings
and inscriptions

Port Said

03647
Military Museum
Port Said
History/Public Affairs Museum
History of the Suez Canal; documents
on the Battle of Port Said (1956);
military equipment and flags

Rashid

03648
Rashid Museum
Rashid
History/Public Affairs Museum
Military equipment

Sinai Peninsula

03649
Monestary of St. Catherine
Sinai Peninsula
Religious Art Museum
Codex Sinaiticus; various ancient
manuscripts; antiquities

Suez

03650
**Institute of Oceanography and
Fisheries**
Attaqa, POB 128, Suez
Natural History Museum
Marine biology; flora and fauna of the
Red Sea and Gulf of Suez

El Salvador

San Salvador

03651
Museo Nacional 'David J. Guzman'
Carretera Internacional Franklin
Delano Roosevelt
San Salvador
General Museum - 1883
archaeology; ethnography; history;
anthropology; linguistics

03652
**Parque Zoologico Nacional y Jardin
Botanico 'Finca Modelo'**
San Salvador
Natural History Museum - 1961
botany; zoology

Equatorial Guinea

Santa Isabel

03653
Museo Etnologico Misional C.M.F.
Apdo. 10, Santa Isabel
Anthropology Museum
Prehistory and ethnology; native art of
the Bubus; wooden bells; sculpture;
Druid stones

Ethiopia

Addis Ababa

03654
Musée Archéologique
Institut Ethiopien d'Archéologie, POB
1907, Addis Ababa
Archeology Museum

03655
**Museum of the Holy Trinity Church
of Ethiopia**
POB 3137, Addis Ababa
Religious Art Museum

03656
**Museum of the Institute of Ethiopian
Studies**
Addis Ababa University, Yekatit 12 Sq,
POB 1176, Addis Ababa
Fine Arts Museum
Ethnography; traditional art; liturgical
items

03657
National Museum
Sudan St, POB 1967, Addis Ababa
General Museum
Palaeontology; archaeology;
costumes; modern art

03658
Natural History Museum
Addis Ababa University, Yekatit 12 Sq,
POB 1176, Addis Ababa
Natural History Museum
Zoology; ornithology; entomology;
conchology

03659
War Museum
Ministry of Defence, Unity Sq, POB
1373, Addis Ababa
History/Public Affairs Museum
Weapons, uniforms and historical
photos

Asmara

03660
Archaeological Museum
Ministry of Culture, Asmara
Archeology Museum
Archaeology of Eritrea Province

Axum

03661
City Museum
Ministry of Culture, Axum
General Museum
Archaeology; ethnography

Gonder

03662
Castle Museum
Ministry of Culture, Gonder
History/Public Affairs Museum

Harar

03663
City Museum and Library
Ministry of Culture, Harar
General Museum

Makale

03664
City Museum
Ministry of Culture, Makale
General Museum
Ethnography; costumes

Wollamo Sodo

03665
City Museum
Municipal Council, Wollamo Sodo
General Museum
Ethnography

Yirgalem

03666
City Museum
Ministry of Culture, Yirgalem
General Museum
Ethnography

Fiji

Suva

03667
Fiji Museum
Government Bldgs., POB 2023, Suva
General Museum - 1906
Archeology; ethnology; weapons;
ornithological collections relating to
Fiji, the Solomon Islands and other
islands of the South-West Pacific;
pottery; musical instruments; masks

Finland

Anjala

03668
Anjala Kartanomuseo (Anjala Manor)
SF-46910 Anjala
Fine Arts Museum - 1955
Sculpture collection of the artist Carl
Henrik Wrede (1890-1924); 19th
century interiors; household articles;
Mathilda Wrede collection; Anjala
Manor (1800) - library

Arkkukari

03669
Saloisten Kotiseutumuseo (Saloinen
Local History Museum)
SF-92210 Arkkukari
Open Air Museum - 1966
Peasant culture; equipment for seal
hunting; public granaries, farm
buildings; fishermen's huts, boat sheds
and buildings connected with fish
salting

Asikkala

03670
Urajärven Kartanomuseo Finnish
Archaeological Society (Urajärvi
Manor)
mail c/o Suomen
muinaismuistoyhdistys, POB 913,
SF-00101 Helsinki 10, Urajärvi,
SF-17320 Asikkala
Historic Site - 1915
Coll: furnishings; household articles;
early 20th century interiors; Urajärvi
Manor (1750-1812) with English
garden

Askainen

03671
Louhisaaren Linna National Board of
Antiquities and Historical Monuments
(Louhisaari Manor)
mail c/o Suomen
muinaismuistoyhdistys, POB 913,
SF-00101 Helsinki 10, SF-21240
Askainen
Historic Site - 1967
Coll: 17th-19th century interiors,
furnishings and household articles;
portrait collection; Louhisaari castle
and wings designed by Henrik
Fleming (1655)

Dragsfjärd

03672
Söderlångvikin Museo (Söderlångvik
Manor)
SF-25870 Dragsfjärd
Historic Site - 1965
Coll: original interiors; Finnish 20th
century art collection and library of the
statesman and philanthropist Amos
Anderson

Espoo

03673
Espoon Museo Glims (Espoo City
Museum Glims)
Karvasmäentie 5, SF-02740 Espoo 74
General Museum - 1958
Coll: household articles; agricultural
equipment; carriage collection - library

03674
Gallen-Kallela Museo
Gallen-Kallelantie 27, SF-00260 Espoo
60
Fine Arts Museum - 1957
Coll: Akseli Gallen-Kallela's works:
paintings; sculpture; drawings;
graphics; studio furniture; textile
designs; illustrations to the epic, the
'Kalevala'; art, handicraft and
ethnographic collections from Africa -
library

03675
**Geologisen Tutkimuslaitoksen
Kivimuseo** Geological Research
Institute (Museum of Mineralogy)
Kivimiehentie 1, SF-02150 Espoo 15
Natural History Museum - 1956
Coll: minerals; rocks; sediments; ores;
fossils; crystals; old prospecting
equipment

Fiskars

03676
Fiskarsin Museo (Fiskars Museum)
SF-10470 Fiskars
General Museum - 1949
Fiskars' cutlery

Forssa

03677
**Forssan Luonnonhistoriallinen
Museo** (Forssa Natural History
Museum)
Kuhalankatu 19 A, POB 46, SF-30101
Forssa 10
Natural History Museum - 1951
Coll: vertebrates; insects; specimens
of plants and stones; wild life
conservation

03678
Lounais-Hämeen Museo
(Southwestern Häme Museum)
Wahreninkatu, SF-30100 Forssa
General Museum - 1923
Coll: agricultural implements;
household articles; handicrafts;
furniture; costumes; textiles;
photographs

03679
Tieteelliset Kokoelmat (Scientific
Collections)
Vapaudenkatu 5 B 20, POB 46,
SF-30101 Forssa 10
Natural History Museum
Coll: 11,000 botanical specimens;
34,000 insects and invertebrates

Halikko

03680
Halikkon Kotiseutumuseo (Halikko
Local History Museum)
SF-24800 Halikko
General Museum - 1955
Coll: ethnography; tanner, shoemaker
and carpenter workshops; 18th
century inn with furnishings

Hämeenlinna

03681
Hämeenlinnan Historiallinen Museo
(Hämeenlinna Historical Museum)
Lukiokatu 6, SF-13100 Hämeenlinna 10
General Museum - 1910
Coll: articles connected with the
history of Hämeenlinna and the
peasant culture of the province of
Häme; handicrafts; textiles; furniture;
18th and 19th century silverware from
Hämeenlinna; coins and medals;
research archives and photographs -
library

03682
Hämeenlinnan Taidemuseo
(Hämeenlinna Art Museum)
Viipurintie 2, SF-13200 Hämeenlinna 20
Fine Arts Museum - 1952
Coll: Finnish art; paintings; sculptures; graphics; drawings; designs - library

03683
Vanajan Kotiseutumuseo (Vanaja
Local History Museum)
Vanaja, SF-13100 Hämeenlinna 10
General Museum - 1958
Ethnographical and ecclesiastical objects

Hamina

03684
Haminan Kaupunginmuseo (Hamina
Town Museum)
Kadettikoulunkatu 2, SF-49400 Hamina
General Museum - 1903
Coll: the social, political and military history of the town and its surroundings; navigation and trade instruments; period interiors; costumes and textiles; numismatic collection - archives

03685
Reserviupseerikoulun Museo
(Reserve Officer School Museum)
Mannerheimintie 7 B, SF-49400
Hamina
History/Public Affairs Museum - 1975
Coll: objects connected with the traditions of the Reserve Officer School; uniforms; weapons; fighting equipment; teaching aids; guard house of the Hamina fortress (1774)

Hankasalmi

03686
Hankasalmen Kotiseutumuseo
(Hankasalmi Local History Museum)
SF-41520 Hankasalmi
General Museum - 1954
Coll: furnishings; ethnographical material

Hanko

03687
Hangon Museo
Kaupungintalo, Bulevardi 6, SF-10900
Hanko
General Museum - 1909
Handicrafts; interiors; textiles

03688
Linnoitusmuseo / Fästningsmuseet
(Fortress Museum)
Nycander St 4, SF-10900 Hanko
Historic Site - 1971

Hartola

03689
Itä-Hämeen Museo (Eastern Häme
Museum)
SF-19600 Hartola
General Museum
Coll: local ethnography and cultural history material; furniture; textiles; agricultural implements; household articles; tools of gunsmiths and tanners; Koskipää Manor and chimneyless dwelling (early 19th century)

106

Heinola

03690
Heinolan Museo (Heinola Town
Museum)
Siltakatu 20, SF-18100 Heinola
General Museum - 1962
Coll: economic and social history of the town; ecclesiastical material; manorial furniture; textiles; handicrafts; numismatic collection; photograph collection

Helsinki

03691
Amos Andersonin Taidemuseo
(Amos Anderson Art Museum)
Yrjönkatu 27, POB 14, SF-00101
Helsinki 10
Fine Arts Museum - 1965
Coll: contemporary Finnish art; 15th-19th century European art; graphics; medals - library

03692
Armfelt Museo (Armfelt Museum)
Suomenlinna, SF-00190 Helsinki 19
Historic Site - 1925
Articles connected with the Armfelt family; 18th century Finnish history; Carpelan's barracks (1805)

03693
Ateneumin Taidemuseo (Art Museum
of the Ateneum)
Kaivokatu 2-4, SF-00100 Helsinki 10
Fine Arts Museum - 1863
Coll: paintings, sculpture, drawings, graphics; especially Finnish art since the 18th century; Italian and German art since the 17th century; French art since the 18th century; Scandinavian art from various periods; modern international art; Rembrandt: 'Monk reading'; van Gogh: 'Street, Auvers-sur-Oise' - library

03694
Cygnaeuksen Galleria (Cygnaeus Art
Collection)
Kalliolinnantie 8, SF-00140 Helsinki 14
Fine Arts Museum - 1882
Fredrik Cygnaeus collection of foreign and Finnish 19th century art, especially the Düsseldorf school;

03695
Didrichsenin Taidemuseo (Didrichsen
Art Collection)
Kuusilahdenkuja 3, SF-00340 Helsinki
34
Fine Arts Museum - 1965
Coll: modern art including sculptures by Henry Moore and Jean Arp, and paintings by Kandinsky and Picasso; pre-Columbian art; old Chinese art (Shang to Tang); small collection of Persian and East-Asiatic art

03696
Ehrensvärd-Museo National Board of
Antiquities and Historical Monuments
(Ehrensvärd Museum)
Suomenlinna, SF-00190 Helsinki 19
Historic Site - 1921
Articles pertaining to the history of the Suomenlinna naval installation (1748); commandant's residence

03697
**Eläinlääketieteen Historian Museo ja
Kokoelmat** (Museum of the History of
Veterinary Medicine)
Hämeentie 57, SF-00550 Helsinki 55
Natural History Museum - 1973
Coll: instruments used by veterinarians; photographs and documents

03698
Helsingin Kaupungin Taidemuseo
Tamminiementie 6, 00250 Helsinki 25,
Annankatu 30, SF-00100 Helsinki 10
Fine Arts Museum - 1895
Modern art; Becker collection; Bäcksbacka collection; Roos-Hasselblatt collection; city collection - library

03699
Helsingin Kaupunginmuseo (Helsinki
City Museum)
Hakasalmen huvila, Karamzininkatu 2,
Dagmarinkatu 6, SF-00100 Helsinki 10
General Museum - 1911
Coll: social, economic, cultural and political history of the city; model of Helsinki in the 1870's; jewelry; porcelain; glass; home interiors; textiles; costumes; pharmaceutical collection

03700
Helsingin Teatterimuseo (Helsinki
Theater Museum)
Aleksanterinkatu 12, SF-00170
Helsinki 17
Performing Arts Museum - 1963
Coll: photographs; costumes; sets; programs; posters; archives

03701
Helsingin Yliopiston Eläinmuseo
University of Helsinki (Zoological
Museum)
P. Rautatiekatu 13, SF-00100 Helsinki
10
Natural History Museum - 1923
Coll: mammals; birds; skeletons of mammals, birds, fishes, amphibians and reptiles; insects and native invertebrates - library

03702
**Helsingin Yliopiston Kasvitieteen
Laitos** University of Helsinki (Botanical
Museum)
Unioninkatu 44, SF-00170 Helsinki 17
Natural History Museum - c. 1750
Herbarium: approximately 2.5 million specimens - library

03703
**Helsingin Yliopiston Lääetieteen
Historian Laitos ja Museo** University
of Helsinki (Department and Museum
of Medical History)
Kasarmikatu 11-13, POB 95, SF-00130
Helsinki 13
Science/Tech Museum - 1937
Coll: examination implements; instruments and furniture of the medical and nursing sciences; veterinary medicine; odontology and pharmacy - library

03704
**Helsingin Yliopiston
Maatalousmuseo** University of
Helsinki (Agricultural Museum)
Viikin Koetila, SF-00710 Helsinki 71
Agriculture Museum - 9146
Coll: peasant farm tools; old mechanized agricultural implements; dairy farming; farm vehicles; carpenter's tools; miniature statues of domestic animals

03705
Herttoniemen Museo (Herttoniemi
Museum)
Linnanrakentajantie 14, SF-00810
Helsinki 81
Historic Site
Peasant culture; carriages and charts; photograph collections; Herttoniemi manor house (18th and 19th century); Knusbacka peasant farmhouse and outbuildings

03706
Hotelli- ja Ravintolamuseo (Hotel and
Restaurant Museum)
Nuijamiestentie 10, SF-00320 Helsinki
32
History/Public Affairs Museum - 1971
Coll: hotel and restaurant history in Finland; traditional Finnish cooking; photograph collections

03707
Ilmailumuseo (Finnish Aviation
Museum)
Helsinki-Vantaan Lentoasema, POB 42,
SF-01531 Helsinki, Vantaa-Lento
Science/Tech Museum - 1972
Junkers A 50 Junior (airplane displayed at Helsinki-Vantaa Airport) - library

03708
**Kansallis-Osake-Pankin
Rahanäyttely** Kansallis-Osake-Pankki
(Exhibition of Coins and Banknotes)
Pohjoisesplanadi 29, SF-00100
Helsinki 10
History/Public Affairs Museum
Coll: currency used in Finland; complete collection of Finnish coins; 15th century Turku coins

03709
Kluuvin Galleria Helsingin Kaupungin
Taidemuseo
Unioninkatu 28 B, Annankatu 30,
SF-00100 Helsinki 10
Fine Arts Museum - 1895
Modern art

03710
Lähetysmuseo (Missionary Museum)
Tähtitorninkatu 16 A, SF-00140
Helsinki 14
Religious Art Museum - 1890
Coll: religious and ethnographical material from the Finnish missions in Africa and Asia; African folk art; Chinese textiles; articles from the estate of Martti Rautanen (pioneer of the Ovambo mission and the first person to transcribe the Ndonga language)

03711
Mannerheim Museo
Kalliolinnantie 14, SF-00100 Helsinki 10
Historic Site - 1951
Coll: memorabilia of Marshall Gustav Mannerheim, uniforms, badges of honour, personal weapons; Finnish and European furnishings; exotic collection, especially handicrafts, weapons, Asian art, textiles

03712
Meilahden Kartano (Meilahti Manor)
Meilahti 21, Tamminiementie, SF-00250
Helsinki 25
Fine Arts Museum - 1976
Bäcksbacka, Becker and Roos-Hasselblatt collections; Finnish and French 20th century art; photograph collection

03713
Museovirasto National Board of
Antiquities and Historical Monuments
Nervanderinkatu 13, POB 913,
SF-00101 Helsinki 10
History/Public Affairs Museum - 1884
Coll: maps; drawings, especially of ships; films; photographs; building plans; maritime history; documents - library

03714
Osuuskauppamuseo (Co-Operative
Museum of the KK)
Tulisuontie 3, SF-00820 Helsinki 82
History/Public Affairs Museum - 1954
Coll: 20th century shop furnishings; history of the co-operative movement; photographs and documents

03715
Posti- ja Telemuseo (Post and Telecommunications Museum)
Tehtaankatu 21 B, SF-00150 Helsinki 15
History/Public Affairs Museum - 1926
History of the Finnish postal and telegraph service; approximately 120,000 Finnish and international stamps; stamp designs

03716
Rannikkotykistömuseo (Coastal Defence Museum)
Suomenlinna, Kustaanmiekka, SF-00190 Helsinki 19
History/Public Affairs Museum
Finnish coastal defence equipment (dating back 300 years) of Kustaanmiekka in the fortress of Suomenlinna

03717
Seurasaaren Ulkomuseo National Museum of Finland (Seurasaari Open Air Museum)
Seurasaari, POB 913, SF-00250 Helsinki 25
Open Air Museum - 1909
Coll: peasant and upper class buildings from different areas of Finland; a church; sauna; cattle shelters; storehouses; mills; a smithy; 'church boats'; furnishings; tools

03718
Sinebrychoffin Taidekokoelmat (Paul and Fanny Sinebrychoff Art Collection)
Bulevardi 40 B, SF-00120 Helsinki 12
Fine Arts Museum - 1921
Coll: 18th and 19th century foreign art

03719
Sotamuseo (Military Museum)
Maurinkatu 1, POB 223, SF-00170 Helsinki 17
History/Public Affairs Museum - 1929
Coll: military items; weapons; ammunition; coast artillery museum in the Fortress of Suomenlinna; submarine Vesikko

03720
Sukellusvene Vesikko Sotamuseo
Suomenlinna, Susisaari, SF-00190 Helsinki 19
History/Public Affairs Museum - 1973
250/300 ton coastal submarine from World War II

03721
Suomen Kansallismuseo National Board of Antiquities and Historical Monuments (National Museum of Finland)
Mannerheimintie 34, POB 913, SF-00101 Helsinki 10
General Museum - 1893
Coll: Stone, Bronze and Iron Ages; 13th-19th century religious and profane art; interiors; costumes; textiles; weapons; coins and medals; hunting and fishing; folk art; furniture

03722
Suomen Rakennustaiteen Museo (Museum of Finnish Architecture)
Puistokatu 4, SF-00140 Helsinki 14
Fine Arts Museum - 1978
Coll: Finnish architecture; drawings and photographs since 1890 - library

03723
Suomen Urheilumuseo (Finnish Sport Museum)
Olympic Stadium, SF-00250 Helsinki 25
History/Public Affairs Museum - 1938
History of Finnish sports; ski collection; sports equipment; clothes; flags; prizes - library; photographic archives

03724
Suomen Valokuvataiteen Museo (Photographic Museum of Finland)
Korkeavuorenkatu 2 b F 72, SF-00140 Helsinki 14
Fine Arts Museum - 1969
Collection of photographs (about 60,000) and photographic apparatus; temporary exhibitions of photographic art

03725
Taideteollisuusmuseo (Museum of Applied Arts)
Korkeavuorenkatu 23, SF-00130 Helsinki 13
Decorative Arts Museum - 1873
Coll: objects connected with the development of industrial art; artistic handicrafts and industrial design in Finland from the second half of the 19th century to the present day; examples of industrial art and artistic handicrafts from abroad - library; lecture room with audio-visual equipment

03726
Tehniikan Museo (Museum of Technology)
Viikintie 1, SF-00560 Helsinki 57
Science/Tech Museum - 1969
Coll: the development of technology in Finland; former building of the Helsinki waterworks (1890-1940) and water mill, steam power plant - library

03727
Tullimuseo (Customs Museum)
Unionkatu 5, SF-00130 Helsinki 13
History/Public Affairs Museum - 1931
Coll: history of the Finnish customs; uniforms; flags; confiscated material; maps - photograph archives

03728
Tuomarinkylän Museo (Tuomarinkylä Museum)
Tuomarinkylän kartano, SF-00670 Helsinki 67
Historic Site - 1962
Coll: interior décor and furnishings; household utensils; firefighting equipment; agricultural implements; Tuomarinkylä manor house (1790)

03729
Yhdyspankin Museo (Museum of the Union Bank of Finland)
Aleksanterinkatu 30, SF-00100 Helsinki 10
History/Public Affairs Museum - 1936
History of the Union Bank of Finland; bank notes and coins; bank interior designed by Eliel Saarinen

Hirvihaara

03730
Sepänmäen Käsityömuseo (Sepänmäki Handicraft Museum)
SF-04680 Hirvihaara
Open Air Museum - 1969
Smithy; shoemaker's and tailor's workshops; repair shop for bicycles and cars

Hollola

03731
Hollolan Kotiseutumuseo (Hollola Local History Museum)
SF-16720 Hollola
General Museum - 1969
Coll: peasant furniture; textiles; costumes; household articles; agricultural implements; early 19th century Hentilä and Ylä-Kölli farmhouses

Hyrylä, Tuusula

03732
Ilmatorjunta Museo (Anti-Aircraft Defence Museum)
Ilmatorjuntakoulu, SF-04301 Hyrylä, Tuusula
History/Public Affairs Museum - 1968
Coll: equipment for anti-aircraft defence and fire control; weapons; photograph and drawing collection; AA-guns - library

Hyrynsalmi

03733
Kaunislehdon Talomuseo (Kaunislehto Farmhouse)
SF-89400 Hyrynsalmi
Historic Site - 1966
Coll: furnishings; tar-burning equipment; Kaunislehto farm

Hyvinkää

03734
Rautatiemuseo (Railway Museum)
Hyvinkäänkatu 9, SF-05800 Hyvinkää
Science/Tech Museum - 1898
Models of railway vehicles, networks and buildings; train of Czar Alexander III; oldest steam engine of Finland (1868); passenger coach (1873); steam engine (1903) and oldest track motor car; furnished railway station buildings (1870); railway equipment and uniforms; medal and counter collection; - library

Iittala

03735
Iittalan Lasitehtaan Museo Iittala Glassfactory's Museum
SF-14500 Iittala
Decorative Arts Museum - 1971
Coll: articles produced by the Iittala glass works since 1887; art pieces by Tapio Wirkkala, Timo Sarpaneua, and Alvar Aalto

Ilmajoki

03736
Ilmajoen Museo (Ilmajoki Museum)
SF-60800 Ilmajoki
General Museum - 1909
Coll: folk art; furniture; textiles; carriages; agricultural equipment; numismatics; church museum (housed in a reconstruction of the 1638 building); research archives and photographs

Imatra

03737
Imatran Taidemuseo (Imatra Art Gallery)
Honkaharju 7, SF-55800 Imatra 80
Fine Arts Museum - 1951
Coll: modern Finnish paintings; sculptures; medals; drawings; graphic arts

03738
Karjalainen Kotitalo (Karelian Farmhouse)
Pässiniemi, SF-55100 Imatra 10
Historic Site - 1959
Coll: peasant objects; handicrafts; textiles; farm buildings (19th century)

03739
Teollisuustyöväen Asuntomuseo (Museum of Industrial Workers' Dwellings)
Ritikanranta, SF-55400 Imatra 40
History/Public Affairs Museum - 1975
Wooden dwelling of industrial workers and outbuilding; four tenements of the building demonstrate how the workers lived at the beginning of the century, and in the 1920's, 1940's, and 1960's

Inari

03740
Saamelaismuseo (Inari Lappish Museum)
SF-99870 Inari
Open Air Museum - 1961
Coll: dwellings of non-nomadic Lapps; Lappish fishermen and Fjeld Lapps together with important outbuildings such as storehouses, drying racks for fish, fishing nets, animal shelters; Lapp's house from Petsamo; gold prospector's dwelling and washing equipment; courtroom; furnishings; household articles; textiles; hunting equipment

Isokyrö

03741
Isonkyrön Kotiseutumuseo (Isokyrö Local History Museum)
SF-61500 Isokyrö kp 5
Open Air Museum - 1947
Coll: relocated farm buildings, windmill, granaries (18th and 19th century); furnishings of buildings; textiles; handicrafts; carpenter's and shoemaker's shops

Janakkala

03742
Laurinmäen Kotiseutumuseo (Laurinmäki Local History Museum)
SF-14240 Janakkala
Open Air Museum - 1963
Croft buildings (19th and 20th centuries) and objects belonging to them

Järvenpää

03743
Ainola
SF-04400 Järvenpää
Historic Site - 1972
Home of composer Jean Sibelius, designed by Lars Sonck (1904), with furnishings

03744
Halosenniemi
SF-00440 Järvenpää
Historic Site
Studio and home of the painter Pekka Halonen (1865-1933); interiors and furnishings of the house

Joensuu

03745
Joensuun Taidemuseo (Joensuu Art Museum)
Kirkkokatu 23, SF-80100 Joensuu 10
Fine Arts Museum - 1962
Finnish art since the late 19th century; paintings, sculpture (Manzú, Marini), drawings, graphics; European, Classical, and Chinese art objects; Iris ceramics and old Finnish wall-rugs (ryjy), furniture; the Olavi Turtiainen collection; the Arla Cederberg collection; the Onni Okkonen collection - library

03746
Pohjois-Karjalan Museo (Northern
Karelia Museum)
Karjalan Talo, SF-80100 Joensuu 10
General Museum - 1901
Pre-history and history of the region;
folk art; Karjalan costumes and icons;
embroidery; numismatics; 18 icons
from the Megri Monastery (18th
century) in Ilomantsi - library

Jokioinen

03747
**Jokioisten Museorautatie ja
Kapearaidemuseo** (Jokioinen Railway
and Narrow Gauge Museum)
SF-31600 Jokioinen
Science/Tech Museum - 1976
Coll: old locomotives; small items and
pictures of Finnish narrow gauge
railways - library

03748
Jokioisten Pappilamuseo (Jokioinen
Manse)
31600 Jokioinen, POB 46, SF-30101
Forssa
Historic Site - 1959
Storehouses, smokehouse (1800);
interiors (1850) - library

Jyväskylä

03749
Alvar Aalto-Museo (Alvar Aalto
Museum)
Seminaarinkatu 7, SF-40600 Jyväskylä
60
Fine Arts Museum - 1967
Building designed by architect Alvar
Aalto (1973); Alvar Aalto collection:
sketches, drawings, designs, photostat
reproductions, furniture, experiments
with bent wood; Jyväskylä town
collection of art; Ester and Jalo
Sihtolas' Art Foundation collection of
Finnish and foreign art

03750
Jyväskylän Yliopiston Museo
(Jyväskylä University Museum)
Yliopisto, Seminaarinkatu 15, SF-40100
Jyväskylä 10
History/Public Affairs Museum
Cultural-historical section: objects
related to the history of the Jyväskylä
Teachers' Training College, College of
Education and University, including
Uno Cygnaeus' room, classrooms,
women's dormitory and teaching
implements from as early as 1863;
natural science section: zoological,
botanical and geological collections

03751
Keski-Suomen Museo (Central
Finland Museum)
Ruusupuisto, SF-40600 Jyväskylä,
Central Finland 60
General Museum
Coll: ethnographic material; native art;
rug collection - library

Kaarlela

03752
Kaarlelan Kotiseutumuseo (Kaarlela
Local History Museum)
SF-67700 Kaarlela
Open Air Museum - 1928
Furnished farmhouse, windmill,
tanner's workshop (18th century);
handicrafts

Kajaani

03753
Kainuun Museo (Kainuu District
Museum)
Asemakatu 4, SF-87100 Kajaani 10
General Museum - 1930
Coll: articles and equipment for
hunting, fishing, cultivation of charred
land, dairy farming, tar burning and
logging; articles connected with the
history of Kajaani castle; watercolors,
paintings and drawings by Louis
Sparre (1863-1964)

Käkkäräniemi, Kuopio

03754
Riuttalan Talomuseo (Riuttala Farm
Museum)
SF-71999 Käkkäräniemi, Kuopio
General Museum - 1974
Coll: 23 buildings; 2000 peasant
artifacts

Kalanti

03755
Kalannin Kotaseutumuseo (Kalanti
Local History Museum)
SF-23600 Kalanti
Open Air Museum - 1951
Coll: 18th and 19th century farm
buildings; furnishings; wooden vessel
collection

Kangasniemi

03756
Kangasniemen Museo (Kangasniemi
Museum)
SF-51200 Kangasniemi
General Museum - 1954
Coll: objects connected with peasant
culture; public granary (1908-13)

Karhula

03757
Karhulan Lasimuseo (Karhula Glass
Museum)
SF-48600 Karhula
Decorative Arts Museum - 1964
Coll: antiques; modern art; household
glassware; former glass cutter's
workshop (1900)

Karjaa

03758
Karjaan Museo (Karjaa Museum)
Kauppiaankatu 18, SF-10300 Karjaa
General Museum - 1936
Coll: cultural history; ethnography;
photographs

Kauhajoki

03759
Kauhojoen Museo
SF-61800 Kauhajoki
Open Air Museum - 1933
Coll: 19th century farmhouse and
outbuildings; public granary;
household articles; furniture; textiles;
carpenter's, tanner's and shoemaker's
tools; numismatics

Kemi

03760
Kemin Museo (Kemi Museum)
Meripuisto, SF-94100 Kemi 10
Open Air Museum - 1938
Coll: chimneyless dwelling (1796),
farmhouse (1849), storehouses and
customs hall (1873); furniture; textiles;
household articles; equipment used for
fishing in the Kemi river

03761
Kemin Taidemuseo (Kemi Art
Museum)
Pohjoisrantakatu 9-11, SF-94100 Kemi
10
Fine Arts Museum - 1947
Coll: older and modern Finnish art,
especially from Northern Finland

Kemiö

03762
Sagalundin Kotiseutumuseo
(Sagalund Local History Museum)
SF-25700 Kemiö
Open Air Museum - 1900
Coll: ethnography; cultural and school
history; Linné collection; nautical
books; teacher's quarters, courthouse
and schoolbuilding, peasant buildings,
archives building (18th and 19th
centuries)

Kerava

03763
Keravan Kotiseutumuseo (Kerava
Local History Museum)
Heikkilä, SF-04200 Kerava
General Museum - 1957
Heikkilä farmhouse and outbuildings
(18th century); domestic items and
furnishings; agricultural equipment;
handicrafts; photographs

Keuruu

03764
Keuruun Kotiseutumuseo (Keuruu
Museum)
Museotie 3, SF-42700 Keuruu
Open Air Museum - 1959
Early 19th century farm buildings;
peasant household articles

Kokemäki

03765
Kokemäen Maatalousmuseo
(Kokimäki Agricultural Museum)
SF-32800 Kokemäki
General Museum - 1925
Coll: agricultural equipment; household
articles; textiles; numismatics;
documents; old literature; public
granary (1838)

Kokimäki

03766
Kokemäen Ulkomuseo (Kokemäki
Open Air Museum)
SF-32800 Kokimäki
Open Air Museum - 1962
18 peasant buildings (17th-19th
century), smithy (17th century);
furnishings

Kokkola

03767
K. H. Renlundin Museo (K. H. Renlund
Museum)
Pitkänsillankatu 28, SF-67100 Kokkola
10
Science/Tech Museum - 1909
Coll: articles connected with
navigation, shipbuilding, trade,
handicrafts; school and military history

03768
Taidemuseo (Art Museum)
Isokatu 9, SF-67100 Kokkola 10
Fine Arts Museum
Coll: Finnish paintings, including works
from Albert Edelfelt, Pekka Halonen
and Magnus Enckell; Roos House
(1813)

Koria

03769
Pioneerimuseo (Sapper Museum)
Varuskunta, SF-45610 Koria
History/Public Affairs Museum - 1954
Coll: field equipment from fortifications
used in World War II in the Finnish
front lines; sapper equipment; military
uniforms; miniature models - library

Koski Tl

03770
Yrjö Liipolan Taidekokoelma (Yrjö
Liipola Art Collection)
SF-31500 Koski Tl
Fine Arts Museum - 1968
Sculptures and drawings by Yrjö
Liipola

Kotka

03771
Kymenlaakson Museo (Kymenlaakso
Museum)
Kotkankatu 13, SF-48100 Kotka 10
Historic Site - 1967
Coll: objects connected with the naval
battle of Ruotsinsalmi; ethnography
and cultural history; textiles; porcelain;
numismatics

03772
**Langinkosken Keisarillinen
Kalastusmaja** (Imperial Fishing Lodge)
Langinkoski, SF-48230 Kotka 23
Historic Site - 1933
Fishing lodge (1889) built for Czar
Alexander III and Czarina Maria
Feodorovna; furnishings; fishing
equipment

Kristiinankaupunki

03773
Lebellin Kauppiaantalo (Lebell
Residence)
Rantakatu 50, SF-64100
Kristiinankaupunki
Historic Site - 1940
18th century Southern Ostrobothnian
merchant's residence with furnishings

Kuopio

03774
Kuopion Museo, Kulttuurihistorian osasto ja Luonnontieteen osasto
(Kuopio Museum, Department of Cultural History and Department of Natural History)
Kauppakatu 23, SF-70100 Kuopio
General Museum - 1883/1897
Department of Cultural History: northern Savo folk culture and ecclesiastical life; history of Kuopio; art collection; numismatic collection; open-air museum demonstrating 19th century life in Kuopio; photographs, manuscripts and newspaper-clippings; Department of Natural History: Scandinavian animals; vertebrates; tropical fish; geology; plants, stones and minerals - library

03775
Ortodoksinen Kirkkomuseo
(Orthodox Church Museum)
Karjalankatu 1, SF-70300 Kuopio 30
Religious Art Museum - 1957
Coll: icons; sacred objects; liturgical textiles; all objects from Finnish monasteries and churches; manuscripts - library

Kurikka

03776
Kurikan Museo (Kurikka Local History Museum)
Kp 5, SF-61300 Kurikka
General Museum - 1939
Coll: agricultural and household articles; equipment and tools of carpenters, shoemakers, tailors, and constructors of musical instruments; objects pertaining to emigration to Canada and North America; films and photographs; farmhouse and cart maker's workshop

Kuusankoski

03777
Kettumäen Ulkomuseo ja Kotiseututalo (Kettumäki Local History Museum)
Kettumäki, SF-45700 Kuusankoski
General Museum - 1957
Local history collection; ethnographical objects; farm dwellings and school building (19th century)

Lahti

03778
Hiihtomuseo (Ski Museum)
Vuorikatu 27, SF-15110 Lahti 11
History/Public Affairs Museum - 1973
Coll: old skis; stamps; trophies - library

03779
Lahden Historiallinen Museo (Lahti Historical Museum)
Lahdenkatu 4, SF-15110 Lahti 11
General Museum - 1914
Local collections; peasant furniture; coins; modern Finnish medals; French and Italian paintings; sculpture and furniture from the Middle Ages to the 18th century - library

03780
Lahden Taidemuseo (Lahti Art Museum)
Vesijärvenkatu 11, SF-15110 Lahti 11
Fine Arts Museum - 1949
Modern Finnish paintings, graphics, drawings - library

03781
Yleisradion Museo (Broadcasting Museum)
Lahden Yleisradioasema, POB 154, SF-15101 Lahti 10
Science/Tech Museum - 1968
History of Finnish broadcasting and radio technology

Lapinlahti

03782
Lapinlahden Taidekeskus ja Eemil Halosen Museo Halosten Museosäätiö (Eemil Halonen Museum and Art Center)
SF-73100 Lapinlahti, Kuopion Lääni
Fine Arts Museum - 1973
Coll: works by the sculptor Eemil Halonen (1875-1950); Arne Paldanius collection; two dia collections; modern Finnish art; art park surrounding the art center and Eemil Halonen Museum - small library

Lappeenranta

03783
Etelä-Karjala Museo ja Taideosasto
(Southern Karelia Museum and Art Department)
Kristiinankatu 2, Linnoitus, SF-53900 Lappeenranta 90
General Museum - 1909
Coll: ethnography; local history; weapons; ecclesiastical art; Karelian folk costumes; photographs and press-clippings; two military warehouses (19th century); Art Department: mainly modern Finnish art

03784
Ratsuväkimuseo (Cavalry Museum)
Kristiinankatu 13, Linnoitus, SF-53900 Lappeenranta 90
History/Public Affairs Museum - 1973
Cavalry uniforms and equipment; photograph collection

Laukaa

03785
Museokylä Kalluntalo (Kalluntalo Museum)
SF-41300 Laukaa
Open Air Museum - 1959
Peasant dwellings; two 'church boats'; school equipment; farm buildings; windmill; public granary

Leppävirta

03786
Leppävirran Kotiseutumuseo
(Leppävirta Local History Museum)
SF-79100 Leppävirta
General Museum - 1956
Coll: ethnographical material; mining equipment and minerals connected with the Kotalahti nickel mine; samples of the art of precision forging in Sorsakoski factory; wooden public granary

Lieksa

03787
Pielisen Museo
Pappilantie 2, SF-81720 Lieksa 2
Open Air Museum - 1948
18th-20th century farm buildings; croft; water- and windmills; agriculture; forestry; ethnographic material from the district - library

Liminka

03788
Lampi-Museo (Lampi Museum)
SF-91900 Liminka
Fine Arts Museum - 1972
Finnish art; works of Vilho Lampi, Tyko Sallinen, Marcus Collin, Ellen Thesleff; modern art from Northern Finland; former school building (1868)

Loviisa

03789
Loviisan Kaupungin Museo (Loviisa Town Museum)
Komendantintalo, SF-07900 Loviisa
General Museum - 1904
Articles dealing with the history of Loviisa; military history; navigation; commerce; costumes; furniture; tin collection and workshop; stationer's shop (19th century); commandant's residence (1775)

Luopioinen

03790
Luopioisten Museo (Luopioinen Museum)
SF-36760 Luopioinen
Open Air Museum - 1952
Wooden public granary and croft museum area containing 18th-19th century buildings; windmill (1867)

Maarianhamina

03791
Ahvenanmaan Museo (Ahvenanmaa Museum)
Öhbergsvägen 1, SF-22101 Maarianhamina
History/Public Affairs Museum - 1933
Coll: prehistory; cultural history; history; art - library; film and multivision center

03792
Ahvenanmaan Taidemuseo (Ahvenanmaa Art Museum)
Öhbergsvägen, POB 60, SF-22101 Maarianhamina, Ahvenanmaa
Fine Arts Museum - 1963
Art of the Åland Islands

03793
Åland Maritime Museum
Hamngatan, SF-22100 Maarianhamina
History/Public Affairs Museum - 1936
Coll: navigation history; ships' documents; logbooks; ship paintings; figure heads, shipbells; navigation instruments; ship interiors; objects from sailing ships - library

03794
Kauppiastalo (Merchant's House)
Parkgatan, SF-22100 Maarianhamina
Historic Site - 1970
Wooden house of shopkeeper Lemberg (1885) housing tanner, shoemaker and watchmaker workshops, shoe shop and country store

Mänttä

03795
Gösta Serlachiuksen Taidemuseo
(The Gösta Serlachius' Museum of Fine Arts)
Joenniemi Manor, SF-35800 Mänttä
Fine Arts Museum - 1945
Coll: 19th and early 20th century Finnish art: works of Akseli Gallen-Kallela, Albert Edelfelt and Hannes Autere; works of Italian and Spanish Renaissance and baroque masters; collection of 17th century Dutch art; works of Tintoretto, Massys, Ribera, Zurbaran and Fragonard - library

03796
Kuoreveden Kotiseutumuseo
(Kuorevesi Local History Museum)
Joensuu, SF-35800 Mänttä
Open Air Museum - 1963
18th-19th century farm buildings; furniture; household articles; smith's, shoemaker's, and tailor's tools and equipment

Mäntyharju

03797
Mäntyharjun Museo (Mäntyharju Museum)
SF-52710 Mäntyharju
General Museum - 1970
Ethnography and cultural history; Mäntyharju mansion (1811)

Merstola

03798
Emil Cedercreutzin Museo
Museotie, SF-29210 Merstola, Satakunta
Fine Arts Museum - 1918
Coll: Emil Cedercreutz' silhouettes and sculptures; folk art; handicrafts; rugs - library

Mikkeli

03799
Kirkkomuseo (Church Museum)
Porrassalmenkatu 47, SF-50100 Mikkeli 10
Religious Art Museum
Chapel from the Middle Ages

03800
Mikkelin Taidemuseo (Mikkeli Art Museum)
Ristimäenkatu 5, SF-50100 Mikkeli 10
Fine Arts Museum - 1970
Coll: Johannes Haapasalo's sculptures; Martti Airion art collection

03801
Päämajamuseo (Headquarters Museum)
Päämajankatu 1-3, SF-50100 Mikkeli 10
Historic Site
Headquarters of Marshall C.G. Mannerheim during World War II

03802
Suur-Savon Museo (Greater Savo Museum)
Otavankatu 11, SF-50130 Mikkeli 13
General Museum - 1912
Coll: local and military history; ethnography; numismatics

Naantali

03803
Naantalin Museo (Naantali Museum)
Katinhäntä 1, SF-21100 Naantali
General Museum - 1920
Coll: town history; home furnishings;
textiles; silversmith work; carpentry;
artifacts of the 15th century nunnery at
Naantali; numismatics; three wooden
town residences with outbuildings
(18th-19th century)

Niemisjärvi

03804
Pienmäen Talomuseo (Pienmäki
Farmhouse)
SF-41490 Niemisjärvi
Open Air Museum - 1969
Farmhouse and outbuildings; 18th-19th
century interiors

Niinisalo

03805
The Niinisalo Artillery Museum
SF-38840 Niinisalo, Satakunta
History/Public Affairs Museum - 1977
Coll: traditions of the 15th Division,
which fought during World War II
(1941-1944); largest gun collection in
Scandinavia - library

Nivala

03806
Nivalan Museo (Nivala Museum)
SF-85500 Nivala
General Museum - 1936
Coll: furnishings; household objects;
precentor's house with outbuildings

Nokia

03807
**Nokian Kotiseutumuseo ja
Työläismuseo** (Nokia Local History
Museum and Museum of Workers'
Homes)
Vihnuskatu 2, SF-37100 Nokia
Open Air Museum - 1954
Coll: furnishings; household articles;
agricultural equipment; Hinttala military
residence and outbuildings; workers'
homes (early 19th century)

Nuutajärvi

03808
Prykäri Nuutajärven Lasimuseo Oy
Wärtsilä ab Nuutajärven Lasi
(Nuutajärvi Glass Museum)
SF-31160 Nuutajärvi
Science/Tech Museum - 1977
History of Nuutajärvi glass
manufacture since 1850; glassware

Orimattila

03809
Orimattilan Kotiseutumuseo
(Orimattila Local History Museum)
SF-16300 Orimattila
Open Air Museum - 1949
Coll: furnishings; agricultural
equipment; photographs; farm
buildings (18th-19th century); water
mill (18th century)

Orivesi

03810
Oriveden Paltanmäen Museo
(Paltanmäki Museum, Orivesi)
SF-35300 Orivesi
Open Air Museum - 1932
Peasant house (19th century); windmill
and water mill; furnishings; household
articles; agricultural and military
equipment; uniforms of riflemen

Oulu

03811
Oulun Taidemuseo (Oulu Art
Museum)
Asemakatu 18, SF-90100 Oulu 10
Fine Arts Museum - 1963
Modern art from Northern Finland

03812
Oulun Yliopiston Eläinmuseo
University of Oulu (Zoological
Museum)
Kasarmintie 8, SF-90100 Oulu 10
Natural History Museum - 1969
535,000 zoological specimens from
Scandinavia

03813
Pohjois-Pohjanmaan Museo
(Northern Ostrobothnia Museum)
Ainola, POB 17, SF-90101 Oulu 10
General Museum - 1896
Coll: local history; ethnology; tar
burning; shipping; trade; weapons;
coins; Lappish collection; photograph
and document archives - library

03814
Turkansaaren Ulkomuseo
(Turkansaari Open Air Museum)
Turkansaari, SF-90310 Oulu 31
Open Air Museum - 1961
Furnishings of buildings; equipment for
tar burning; Turkansaari church (1694);
Särkilahti mansion (17th-18th century);
various farm buildings (17th-18th
century)

Paattinen

03815
Paattisten Kotiseutumuseo (Paattinen
Local History Museum)
21300 Paattinen, Kalstajankatu 4,
SF-20100 Turku 10
General Museum
Agricultural objects; household
articles; handicrafts; public granary

Parainen

03816
Paraisten Kotiseutumuseo (Parainen
Local History Museum)
SF-21600 Parainen
Open Air Museum - 1928
Peasant buildings (17th-19th century)
and furnishings

Parolannummi

03817
Panssarimuseo (Parola Tank
Museum)
SF-13700 Parolannummi
History/Public Affairs Museum
Coll: tank equipment from World War I
and tank torpedo equipment used
during World War II in the Finnish
front lines

Perniö

03818
Perniön Museo
SF-25500 Perniö
General Museum - 1912
Coll: ethnography; cultural, church and
school history; weapons; tin collection;
objects from old Perniö pharmacy -
library

Pielavesi

03819
Pielaveden Kotiseutumuseo
(Pielavesi Local History Museum)
SF-72400 Pielavesi
General Museum - 1958
Coll: photographs; musical
instruments; peasant culture; fishing
and hunting; mansions, servant's
quarters and various outbuildings
(17th-20th century)

Pietarsaari

03820
Pietarsaaren Kaupunginmuseo
(Pietarsaari Town Museum)
Isokatu 2, SF-68600 Pietarsaari
General Museum - 1904
Nautical collections; ship paintings and
drawings; sea charts; trade - library

03821
Rettig-Strengbergin Tupakkamuseo
(Rettig-Strengberg Tobacco Museum)
SF-68600 Pietarsaari
Agriculture Museum - 1943
History of the Rettig-Strengberg
tobacco firm

Piikkiö

03822
Pukkilan Kartano- ja Ajokalumuseo
(Pukkila Manor and Carriage Museum)
SF-21500 Piikkiö
Historic Site
Pukkila Manor and outbuildings (1762);
18th century manor furnishings;
carriage collection

Pori

03823
Satakunnan Museo
Hallituskatu 11, SF-28100 Pori 10
General Museum
Coll: archaeology; hunting and fishing;
furniture; rugs; silver; tin; weapons;
glass; traditional Finnish paintings -
library

Porlammi

03824
Porlammin Kotiseutumuseo
(Porlammi Local History Museum)
SF-07820 Porlammi
General Museum - 1943
Peasant culture; public granary and
croft (19th century)

Porvoo

03825
Edelfelt-Vallgren Museo
Välikatu 11, SF-06100 Porvoo 10
Fine Arts Museum - 1925
Coll: paintings, sculpture, prints,
drawings; especially works by A.
Edelfelt, V. Vallgren, J. Knutson, L.
Sparre, A.W. Finch; Art Nouveau
ceramics and furniture by the Iris
Factory

03826
J. L. Runebergin Koti (J.L. Runeberg
Home)
Runeberginkatu 20, SF-06100 Porvoo
Historic Site - 1880
House of the Finnish national poet
Johan Ludvig Runeberg (1804-1877);
articles of the 1860's and 1870's

03827
Luonnentieteellinen Museo (Natural
History Museum)
Kaivokatu 40, SF-06100 Porvoo
Natural History Museum - 1957
Zoological, botanical, and mineral
collections

03828
Metsästys- ja Riistanhoitomuseo
(Hunting and Wild Animal
Conservation Museum)
Kaivokatu 40, SF-06100 Porvoo
Natural History Museum
Coll: hunting objects; trapping
equipment; stuffed animals, especially
northern beasts of prey - library;
research archives

03829
Porvoon Museo
Välikatu 11, SF-06100 Porvoo 10
General Museum - 1897
Coll: furniture; textiles; glass;
porcelain; pewter; weapons;
handicraft; photographs

03830
Walter Runebergin Veistoskokoelma
(Walter Runeberg Sculpture
Collection)
Aleksanterinkatu 5, SF-06100 Porvoo
Fine Arts Museum - 1921
Works of sculptor Walter Runeberg
(1838-1920), son of poet J.L. Runeberg

Punkalaidun

03831
Talonpoikaismuseo Yli-Kirra (Yli-Kirra
Museum)
SF-31900 Punkalaidun
Open Air Museum - 1947
Yli-Kirra farmhouse and outbuildings
(17th-19th century); cotter's dwelling
(18th century); furnishings and
household objects; hunting equipment

Pyhäjoki

03832
Pyhäjoen Kotiseutumuseo (Pyhäjoki
Local History Museum)
SF-86100 Pyhäjoki
Open Air Museum - 1957
Annala farmhouse and outbuildings,
windmill, smokehouse, smithy
(18th-19th century); furnishings

Raahe

03833
Raahen Museo (Raahe Museum)
Kauppatorinranta, SF-92100 Raahe
General Museum - 1862
Articles connected with shipping and
trade; furniture and textiles from
middle class and artisan homes;
ecclesiastical artifacts (17th century);
numismatics; customs warehouse
(1850); natural history collections:
botanical, zoological, and mineralogical
objects; photograph and research
archives

Rajamäki

03834
Rajamäen Talo (Rajamäki Farmhouse)
SF-05200 Rajamäki
Historic Site - 1955
Farmhouse and outbuildings (19th century); furnishings of the buildings

03835
Rajamäen Thedasmuseo (Rajamäki Works Museum)
SF-05200 Rajamäki
Science/Tech Museum - 1963
Alcolhol making in pre- and early manufacturing stages; building of the former yeast works (1895)

Rauma

03836
Rauman Museo
Kauppakatu 24, SF-26100 Rauma 10
General Museum - 1891
Coll: articles from sailing vessels; fishing equipment; bobbin laces; religious and peasant artifacts

03837
Rauman Taidemuseo (Rauma Art Museum)
Kuninkaankatu 37, SF-26130 Rauma 13
Fine Arts Museum - 1970
Coll: 19th and 20th century native art

Rautalampi

03838
Rautalammin Museo (Rautalampi Museum)
SF-77700 Rautalampi
General Museum - 1938
Coll: ethnography and cultural history; furniture; costumes; household articles; ecclesiastical artifacts; Finnish art collection; chimneyless dwelling, stores, church stable, 'church boat'

Riihimäki

03839
Riihimäen Kaupunginmuseo (Riihimäki City Museum)
Öllerinkatu 3, SF-11130 Riihimäki 13
General Museum - 1961
Coll: local history; home furnishings; handicrafts; trade; railway collection; history of teaching; photograph and document archives; Carelian collection (small number of artifacts from 1800 to 1940) - library

03840
Suomen Lasimuseo (Finnish Glass Museum)
Tehtaank 23, SF-11100 Riihimäki 10
Decorative Arts Museum - 1961
Tools for making Finnish glass; Finnish glass design from 1920 to the present - library

03841
Viestimuseo (Signal Museum)
Varuskunta, POB 4, SF-11311 Riihimäki 31
History/Public Affairs Museum - 1960
Objects and equipment connected with signal operations in the Finnish military forces; former officer's club (1913)

Rovaniemi

03842
Lapin Maakuntamuseo (Museum of the Province of Lapland)
Hallituskatu 11, SF-96100 Rovaniemi 10
Anthropology Museum - 1975
Exhibits on Lapps and gipsies; Lapp house designed by Alvar Aalto; Lappish paintings by Andreas Alariesto

03843
Lapin Metsamuseo (Lappish Forestry Museum)
Salmijärvi, SF-96400 Rovaniemi 40
Agriculture Museum
Logging equipment; the first steam tug (1898) and locomotive used in Lappish lumbering; photograph collection; loggers' buildings from different lumbering areas in Lapland

03844
Rovaniemen Kotiseutumuseo Pöykkölä (Pöykkölä Museum)
Pöykkölä, SF-96400 Rovaniemi 40
General Museum - 1957
Peasant life in Southern Lapland; furnishings; photograph collection; local farm buildings (18th century)

Ruokolahti

03845
Ruokolahden Kotiseutumuseo (Ruokolahti Local History Museum)
SF-56100 Ruokolahti
General Museum - 1954
Ethnographical and ecclesiastical material; objects connected with the painter Albert Edelfelt; research archives; public granary (1861) and open-air museum located in Putto village

Ruotsinpyhtää

03846
Strömforsin Teollisuusmuseo (Strömforsin Works Museum)
SF-07970 Ruotsinpyhtää
Science/Tech Museum - 1962
Coll: industry; iron work; log-floating and sylvicultural equipment; original, waterwheel-operated hammers

Ruovesi

03847
Ruoveden Kotiseutumuseo (Ruovesi Local History Museum)
SF-34600 Ruovesi, Häme
Open Air Museum - 1932
Coll: 17th-18th century farm buildings; 16th century storehouse - library

Rymättylä

03848
Rymättylän Kotiseutumuseo (Rymättylä Local History Museum)
SF-21150 Rymättylä
General Museum - 1964
Objects connected with agriculture, fishing and navigation; shoemaker's tools; household articles; farmhouse and outbuildings (17th-19th century)

Sammatti

03849
Paikkarin Torppa National Board of Antiquities and Historical Monuments (Paikkari Croft)
SF-09220 Sammatti
Historic Site - 1895
Personal accessories and home of Elias Lönroth, the collector of the Finnish national epic, the 'Kalevala'

Seinäjoki

03850
Etelä-Pohjanmaan Museo (Southern Ostrobothnia Museum)
Törnäväntie 22 C, SF-60200 Seinäjoki 20
Open Air Museum - 1962
Furnished farm buildings typical of the area (17th-19th century); agriculture; Törnävä Manor; windmill; powder laboratory; pharmacy; country stores

03851
Seinäjoen Luonto-Museo (Seinäjoki Natural History Museum)
Keskusliikenneasema, SF-60100 Seinäjoki 10
Natural History Museum
Natural history, especially concerning the marshes of Southern Ostrobothnia

Siilinjärvi

03852
Pöljän Kotiseutumuseo (Pöljä Local History Museum)
Siilinpääntie 2, SF-71800 Siilinjärvi
General Museum - 1933
Coll: stones and ceramics (3,500-1,500 B.C); farmhouse - library

Somero

03853
Someron Museo (Somero Museum)
SF-31400 Somero
Open Air Museum - 1956
Croft buildings (18th-19th century); furnishings

Taivassalo

03854
Taivassalon Museo
SF-23310 Taivassalo
General Museum - 1961
Coll: manorial furnishings; agricultural equipment; fishing equipment; handicrafts

Tammijärvi

03855
Peltolan Mäkitupalaismuseo (Peltola Cotters Museum)
SF-19910 Tammijärvi
Open Air Museum - 1959
Peltola cotters village: furnishings; displays depicting the life of the cotters

Tammisaari

03856
Tammisaaren Kaupunginmuseo (Tammisaari Town Museum)
Kustaa Vaasankatu 13, SF-10600 Tammisaari
General Museum - 1906
Coll: local history and artifacts; homes of wealthy craftsmen (early 19th century)

Tampere

03857
Hämeen Museo (Häme Museum)
Näsikallio, SF-33210 Tampere 21
General Museum
Ethnography and the cultural history of the Tampere and Häme province; folk art; rugs; ecclesiastical collection

03858
Hiekan Taidemuseo (Hieka Art Gallery)
Pirkankatu 6, SF-33210 Tampere 21
Fine Arts Museum - 1931
Coll: interiors; applied art objects; gold and silver work; 18th-20th century Finnish art; works by Albert Edelfelt, Eero Järnefelt; Akseli Gallen-Kallela, Pekka Halonen and Wäinö Aaltonen

03859
Lenin-Museo (Lenin Museum)
Hallituskatu 19, SF-33200 Tampere 20
Historic Site - 1946
Photographic material and personal mementos of Vladimir Il'ič Uljanov Lenin's life and work - library

03860
Sara Hildénin Taidemuseo (Sara Hildén Art Museum)
Särkäniemi, SF-33230 Tampere 23
Fine Arts Museum - 1979
20th century Finnish and international art, especially post-war painting, sculpture and graphics

03861
Suomen Koulumuseo (Finnish School Museum)
Tammelan Kansakoulu, SF-33500 Tampere 50
Junior Museum
Material connected with the Finnish elementary school system; classroom interiors with small scale models and teaching material

03862
Tampereen Kaupunginmuseo (Tampere Town Museum)
Hatanpään Kartano, SF-30100 Tampere
General Museum - 1970
Town history; photograph collection; Hatanpää Manor's main building designed by O.S. Gripenberg (1885) - library, archives

03863
Tampereen Luonnontieteellinen Museo (Tampere Natural History Museum)
Pirkankatu 2, SF-33210 Tampere 21
Natural History Museum
Zoological, botanical and geological specimens; conservation

03864
Tampereen Nykytaiteen Museo (Tampere Modern Art Museum)
Palomäentie, SF-33230 Tampere 23
Fine Arts Museum - 1964
Coll: paintings, sculpture, graphics, mainly Finnish art since 1916 - library

03865
Tampereen Taidemuseo (Tampere Art Museum)
Puutarhakatu 34, SF-33230 Tampere 23
Fine Arts Museum - 1931
Coll: paintings; sculptures; drawings; graphics; native art since the early 18th century; Tampere art collection - library

03866
Tampereen Teknillinen Museo
(Tampere Technical Museum)
Itsenäisyydenkatu 21, SF-33500
Tampere 50
Science/Tech Museum
Technological history; automobile and
aviation departments; former factory
building

Tankavaara

03867
Kultamuseo Tankavaara (Gold
Prospector Museum)
SF-99695 Tankavaara
General Museum - 1973
Stone and mineral collections; gold
prospecting equipment; buildings
relocated from a gold prospectors'
community in Lapland; photograph and
tape collections - library

Tarttila

03868
Emil Wikströmin Museo (Emil
Wikström Museum)
Visavuori, SF-37770 Tarttila
Historic Site - 1966
Emil Wikström's sculptures; home and
studio with outbuildings of the sculptor
(1864-1942); authentic interiors

Tokrajärvi

03869
Aaronpiha (Aaronpiha Farmhouse)
Kakonaho, SF-81350 Tokrajärvi
Historic Site - 1975
19th century farmhouse

Tornio

03870
Tornionlaakson Museo
Keskikatu 22, SF-95400 Tornio
Anthropology Museum - 1914
Coll: ethnographical material from
Tornionlaakso and Lapp territory;
furniture; costumes; handicraft; silver
work

Turku

03871
Biologinen Museo (Biological
Museum)
Neitsytpolku 1, 20810 Turku 81,
Kalastajankatu 4, SF-20100 Turku 10
Natural History Museum - 1905
Specimens of nearly all animals found
in Finland; museum building designed
by A. Nyström (1907)
03872
Luostarinmäen Käsityöläis-Museo
(Luostarinmäki Handicraft Museum)
Luostarinmäki, SF-20700 Turku 70
Decorative Arts Museum - 1940
Coll: artisan workshops and home
interiors including those of a
goldsmith, coppersmith, potter,
bookbinder, rope maker, saddler, wig
maker, glove maker, comb maker,
violin maker; printing shop, tobacco
house; in 17 wooden buildings in their
original settings (18th and 19th
centuries)
03873
Museo 'Ett Hem'
Piispankatu 14, SF-20500 Turku 50
Decorative Arts Museum - 1925
Coll: furniture; furnishing textiles;
silver; tin; porcelain; glass; traditional
Finnish art

03874
Qwensel ja Apteekkimuseo
(Qwensel and Pharmacy Museum)
Läntinen Rantakatu 13 b,
Kalastajankatu 4, SF-20100 Turku 10
Historic Site - 1956
Qwensel, middle class residence (18th
century); pharmacy; pharmacist's
home; fully equipped laboratory
03875
Sibelius-Museo
Piispankatu 17, SF-20500 Turku 50
Music Museum - 1926
Coll: manuscripts of Jean Sibelius
(1865-1957) and other Finnish
composers; native and foreign sheet
music collection; European and
non-European art and folk music
instruments - Music library of the
Turku Music Society (founded 1790)
03876
**Turku Akademin Merihistoriallinen
Museo** University of Turku (Maritime
History Museum)
Tuomiokirkkotori 3, SF-20500 Turku 50
History/Public Affairs Museum - 1936
Paintings of ships; ship models;
navigational instruments; fishing
equipment; fully equipped bark 'Sigyn';
photograph collection; logbooks;
nautical charts
03877
**Turun Kaupungin Historiallinen
Museo** (Turku City Historical Museum)
Turku castle, Kalastajankatu 4,
SF-20100 Turku 10
General Museum - 1881
Coll: cultural history since the 17th
century; ethnography; costumes and
other textiles; weapons; silver; tin;
glass; porcelain; numismatics;
restored Turku castle dating back to
1280
03878
Turun Taidemuseo (Turku Art
Museum)
Puolalanpuisto, SF-20100 Turku 10
Fine Arts Museum - 1891
International print collection; animal
sculptures by Jussi Mäntynen
(1886-1978); surrealistic art of the
Turku area
03879
Turun Yliopiston Kasvimuseo
University of Turku (Botanical
Museum)
Kasvitieteen Laitos, SF-20500 Turku 50
Natural History Museum - 1919
Herbarium Vainio; worldwide lichen
collection; 35,000 specimens; holarctic
flora of the northern hemisphere -
library
03880
Wäinö Aaltosen Museo (Wäinö
Aaltonen Museum)
Itäinen Rantakatu 38, SF-20810 Turku
81
Fine Arts Museum - 1964
Wäinö Aaltonen's (1894-1966)
sculptures, paintings and drawings;
graphics; modern Finnish art
collection; photograph collection -
library

Urjalankylä

03881
Urjalan Museo (Urjala Museum)
SF-31720 Urjalankylä
Open Air Museum - 1950
Farm buildings (18th-20th century);
furnishings

Uusikaupunki

03882
**Uudenkaupungin
Kulttuurihistoriallinen Museo**
(Uusikaupunki Cultural History
Museum)
Ylinenkatu 11, SF-23500 Uusikaupunki
General Museum - 1895
Coll: shipping; wooden vessels;
shipbuilding equipment; furniture;
ceramics; costumes; numismatics

Vaasa

03883
Bragegården (Museum Bragegården)
SF-65350 Vaasa 35
Open Air Museum - 1933
Coll: furnishings; Swedish bridal
chamber; sealing equipment; peasant
buildings from Southern Ostrobothnia

03884
Kuntsin Kokoelma (Kuntsi Art
Collection)
School of Commercial Education,
Ravikatu, SF-65140 Vaasa 14
Fine Arts Museum - 1970
Modern Finnish art

03885
**Ostrobothnia Australis, Biologinen
Museo** Ostrobothnia Australis
(Biological Museum)
Hovioikeudenpuistikko 9, SF-65100
Vaasa 10
Natural History Museum - 1924
Zoological, botanical and mineral
collections; animals and specimens
mainly from the Southern
Ostrobothnia region and Scandinavia

03886
Pohjanmaan Museo (Ostrobothnia
Museum)
Museokatu 3, SF-65100 Vaasa 10
Fine Arts Museum - 1895
Local history collection: peasant
culture, folk art, crafts; art collection:
16th-17th century Italian, Dutch,
Flemish and German art, 20th century
native art - library

Valtimo

03887
Murtovaaran Talomuseo (Murtovaara
Farmhouse)
Murtovaara, SF-75700 Valtimo
Historic Site - 1972
Murtovaara farmhouse and
outbuildings, two chimneyless
dwellings (18th-19th century);
furnishings

Vammala

03888
Tyrvään Seudun Museo (Tyrvää
Regional Museum)
Jaatsinkatu 2, SF-38210 Vammala 2
General Museum - 1932
Coll: hunting and agricultural
equipment; household objects;
handicrafts; furniture; glass; weapons;
coins - library

Vanhalinna

03889
Vanhalinnan Museo (Vanhalinna
Museum)
SF-21410 Vanhalinna
Historic Site - 1956
Coll: archaeological finds from the Iron
Age and the early Middle Ages on
Vanhalinna castle hill; ethnographical
material (1850-1940); furniture;
Vanhalinna Manor and outbuildings
(1927), crofter's cottage (1920)

Varkaus

03890
Savon Museo ja Taidemuseo
(Varkaus City Museums)
Vesitorni, Nakskovinkatu 8, SF-78200
Varkaus, Kuopio
General Museum - 1956
Coll: ethnography; household articles;
textile-making equipment;
numismatics; stamps; art gallery
containing early 20th century Finnish
works

Vasikka-aho

03891
Järviseudun Museo (Lake District
Museum)
SF-62540 Vasikka-aho
Open Air Museum - 1955
Coll: household articles; agricultural
implements; folk art and rural
handicraft; 17th-19th century buildings
from parishes in the Lake District of
Southern Ostrobothnia

Verla

03892
Verlan Tehdasmuseo (Verla Mill
Museum)
SF-47850 Verla
Science/Tech Museum - 1882
Complete paper board mill from the
beginning of the century

Vihanti

03893
Vihannin Kotiseutumuseo (Vihanti
Local History Museum)
SF-86400 Vihanti
General Museum - 1947
Peasant articles; furniture; dairy
equipment objects; blacksmith's tools;
public granary

Vöyri

03894
Vöyrin Kotiseutumuseo (Vöyri
Museum)
SF-66600 Vöyri
General Museum - 1959
Farmhouse (18th century); furnishings;
folk costumes

Yläne

03895
Yläneen Kotiseutumuseo (Yläne
Local History Museum)
SF-21900 Yläne
General Museum - 1964
Farm buildings (18th-19th century);
smithy (1883); windmill (1763);
agricultural objects; handicrafts;
furnishings

France

Abbeville

03896
Musée Boucher de Perthes
24 rue du Beffroi, F-80100 Abbeville
General Museum - 1837
Coll: prehistory of the Somme valley, especially prehistoric industrial finds; 15th-16th century wood carvings; French and Flemish paintings from the 15th-18th centuries; ceramics; 18th century furnishings; 17th century wall hangings; natural science exhibits; specimen of alca impennis - library

Agde

03897
Musée Municipal
5 rue de la Fraternité, F-34300 Agde
General Museum - 1941
Coll: local history; folklore; costumes; porcelain; glass; model ships; wine; Greek finds

Agen

03898
Musée des Beaux-Arts
Pl de l'Hôtel-de-Ville, F-47000 Agen
General Museum - 1876
Coll: Greek, Gallo-Roman, Merovingian, Celtic archeological findings; faience and ceramics; paintings; 15th-16th century Spanish tableware

Aix-en-Provence

03899
Atelier de Cézanne
av Paul Cézanne, F-13100 Aix-en-Provence
Historic Site
Coll: former studio of the artist Paul Cézanne(1839-1906); memorabilia of Cézanne

03900
Musée des Tapisseries
28 Pl des Martyrs-de-la-Resistance, F-13100 Aix-en-Provence
Decorative Arts Museum - 1910
Coll: ancient wall hangings from around the world; textiles; furnishings; 17th-18th century paintings - library; documentation center

03901
Musée du Vieil Aix
17 rue de Sagarta, F-13100 Aix-en-Provence
General Museum
Coll: local history; folklore; puppets; clay manger figures; ceramics; documents on Gabriel de Riqueti, Comte de Mirabeau (1749-1791); metalwork; crafts

03902
Musée Granet
Pl Saint-Jean-de-Malte, F-13100 Aix-en-Provence
Fine Arts Museum - 1765
Coll: European painting; sculpture beginning with Roman times; archeology of Greece, Egypt, Rome, and ancient Gaul; applied arts from medieval times to the 17th century; furnishings; wall hangings; rugs; decorative arts; ceramics; armaments; prints; numismatics

03903
Musée Paul Arbaud
2A rue r. Septembre, F-13100 Aix-en-Provence
Fine Arts Museum
Coll: painting; drawings; faience; archives on 19th-20th century Provencal writers

03904
Pavillon de Vendôme
34 rue Cellony, F-13100 Aix-en-Provence
Historic Site - 1954
Coll: 17th century historic pavillon; furnishings and paintings from the 17th-18th centuries - audiovisual room; park

Aix-les-Bains

03905
Musée Archéologique
Pl Maurice-Mollard, F-73100 Aix-les-Bains
Archeology Museum - 1872
Coll: Gallo-Roman sculpture; pottery; inscriptions; temple ruins; local prehistory

03906
Musée du Docteur Faure
bd des Côtes, F-73100 Aix-les-Bains
Fine Arts Museum - 1969
Coll: Impressionist paintings; sculpture and watercolors by Rodin; furnishings; memorabilia of the poet Alphonse de Lamartine

Ajaccio

03907
Musée National de la Maison Bonaparte
rue Saint-Charles, F-20000 Ajaccio
Historic Site
Coll: house of Napoleon's birth; historic rooms with furnishings; farming tools; memorabilia; portraits and documents of the Bonaparte family

03908
Musée-Palais Fesch
50-52 rue Cardinal Fesch, F-20000 Ajaccio
Fine Arts Museum - 1852
Coll: 14th-18th century Italian painting; 17th-18th century still life paintings; Spanish paintings - library; research and study section; documentation center

Albertville

03909
Musée de Conflans
Maison Rouge, F-73200 Albertville
General Museum - 1936
Coll: protohistory and the Gallo-Roman history; regional furniture; 16th-18th century wooden religious statuary; ethnography; reconstructed interior of peasant home; weapons

Albi

03910
Musée Toulouse-Lautrec
Pl de la Berbie, F-81000 Albi
Fine Arts Museum
Coll: paintings, drawings, lithographs, posters, and illustrated books by H. de Toulouse-Lautrec; works of his contemporaries

Alençon

03911
Musée d'Alençon formerly Musée d'Ozé and Musée de Peinture
F-61000 Alençon
General Museum - 1981
Div of Science: natural science; ethnography of Cambodia and Oceania; exhibit on the French soldier, 'Poilu'; Div of art: contemporary paintings; prints; electronic music; exhibit on types and production of the traditional lace of the area; drawings

Alès

03912
Musée Municipal
Château du Colombier, F-30100 Alès
General Museum
Coll: prehistoric and medieval archeological finds; 17th-18th century Flemish, Dutch, Italian, and Spanish painting; 17th-20th century French painting; geology and mineralogy; local paleontology

Alise-Sainte-Reine

03913
Musée Alesia Société des Sciences de Semur-en Auxois
F-21150 Les Laumes
Archeology Museum - 1906
Coll: local Gallo-Roman finds; stone and bronze statues; ceramics

Allauch

03914
Musée du Vieil Allauch
Pl Pierre-Bellot, F-13190 Allauch
History/Public Affairs Museum
Coll: pre-17th century pottery and ceramics; numismatics; glass; ornithology; geology and paleontology

Altkirch

03915
Musée Sundgovien
rue de l'Hôtel-de-Ville, F-68130 Altkirch
General Museum
Coll: pre- and ancient history; engravings; armaments; regional history and customs; works of local painters

Ambert

03916
Musée Historique du Papier
Moulin Richard de Bas, F-63600 Ambert
Science/Tech Museum - 1943
Coll: paper mill; paper production; hand-made paper fabrication; history of paper and watermarks - library

Ambierle

03917
Musée Alice Taverne
F-42820 Ambierle
General Museum
Coll: exhibits on the life of regional peasants and craftsmen; reconstructed home interiors

Amboise

03918
Le Clos-Lucé
2 rue du Clos-Lucé, F-37400 Amboise
Historic Site - 1954
Coll: memorabilia of the artist Leonardo da Vinci; the 16th century house where he died; models of his inventions (the first car, plane, parachute, etc.); furniture; tapestry

03919
Musée de la Poste
6 rue Joyeuse, F-37400 Amboise
History/Public Affairs Museum
Coll: documents from the times of the pony express; models and originals of mail coaches; equipment of mail drivers

03920
Musée Municipal
Hôtel de Ville, F-37400 Amboise
Fine Arts Museum
Coll: religious art; wood carvings; Aubusson tapestries; royal autographs

Amiens

03921
Collection Charles de l'Escalopier
Bibliothèque Municipale
50 rue de la République, F-80037 Amiens Cedex
General Museum
Coll: ancient bronze objects; goldsmith work; ivory; enamel; wood carvings; weaving; memorabilia of Monsignore Affre

03922
Musée d'Art Local et d'Histoire Régionale
36 rue Victor Hugo, F-80000 Amiens
General Museum - 1966
Coll: furnishings and interiors; memorabilia of Laclose, Gresset, Jules Verne, Voiture; 18th century French decorative arts

03923
Musée de Picardie
48 rue de la République, F-80000 Amiens
General Museum - 1854
Coll: painting; sculpture; drawings; prints; tapestry; ceramics; art objects from Ancient Egypt to Louis XII - library

Ancy-le-Franc

03924
Château d'Ancy-le-Franc
F-89160 Ancy-le-Franc
Decorative Arts Museum
Coll: in Renaissance manor; interior decorations by Primatice and Niccolo dell'Abbate; Aubusson tapestries

Andillac

03925
Musée Eugenie et Maurice de Guérin
Andillac, Château le Cayla, F-81480 Cahuzac-sur-Vère
Historic Site
Coll: original interiors, manuscripts of the poet M. de Guérin (1810-1839), housed in former home

Angers

03926
Château d'Angers
Promenade du Bout du Monde,
F-49000 Angers
Historic Site - 1954
Coll: 12th-18th century historic
monument; French and Flemish
tapestries from 14th-17th centuries;
the Apocalypse Tapestries (14th
century)

03927
**Musée des Beaux-Arts et Galerie
David**
10 rue du Musée, F-49000 Angers
Fine Arts Museum - 1797
Coll: sculpture of David d'Angers;
early Italian sculpture; 16th-17th
century Spanish, Flemish, Dutch
sculpture; 18th-19th century French
sculpture; Italian and French primitive
painting; 18th-19th century French
painting; 17th century European
painting; in 15th century house

03928
Musée Saint-Jean
4 bd Arago, F-49000 Angers
Archeology Museum - 1841
Coll: decorative arts; regional
iconography; archeology - library
laboratory

03929
Musée Turpin de Crissé
Hôtel Pincé, 32 bis rue Lenepveu,
F-49000 Angers
Fine Arts Museum - 1849-1889
Coll: Egyptian antiquities, Greek, and
Roman antiquities; Japanese
woodcuts; Oriental art; Limoges
enamels; ceramics and porcelain;
16th-20th century engravings;
17th-19th century European drawings

Angoulême

03930
**Musée de la Société Archéologique
et Historique de la Charente**
44 rue de Montmoreau, F-16000
Angoulême
Fine Arts Museum
Coll: prehistoric to early Christian
finds; bronzes; Romanesque to
Renaissance sculpture; 12th century
sculptures of the cathedral; Limoges
enamels; pottery and porcelain; folk
art; engravings

03931
Musée Municipal
1 rue Friedland, F-16000 Angoulême
General Museum
Coll: pre- and early history; African
and Oceanic anthropology; Italian,
Dutch, Flemish, and French painting;
18th century faience; decorative arts;
tapestries; cartoon art

Annecy

03932
Musée Municipal
Pl du Château, F-74000 Annecy
General Museum
Coll: prehistorical items; regional folk
art; local sculpture from medieval to
modern times; grave fragments

Annonay

03933
Musée du Vieil Annonay
Villa des Platanes, rue Sadi-Carnot,
F-07100 Annonay
General Museum
Coll: prehistory; folklore; porcelain;
18th century shipping and fishing;
memorabilia of Marc Sequin and the
Montgolfier brothers

Antibes

03934
Musée Bastion Saint-André
F-06600 Antibes
History/Public Affairs Museum
Coll: military arts and sciences

03935
**Musée Naval et Napoleonien du Cap
d'Antibes**
Batterie de Grillon, F-06600 Antibes
History/Public Affairs Museum
Coll: history of the navy; collection on
Napoleon I; history of the Imperial
epoch

03936
Musée Picasso
Château, F-06600 Antibes
Fine Arts Museum
Coll: classical Roman art; paintings,
ceramics, drawings, gouaches,
tapestry, sculpture, and lithographs by
Pablo Picasso; modern painting;
woodcuts; bronze sculptures

Anzin

03937
Musée Theophile Jouglet
av Anatole-France, F-59410 Anzin
Fine Arts Museum
Coll: drawings; lithographs; works of
local painters and sculptors; portraits;
fossils

Aoste

03938
Musée d'Antiquités Gallo-Romaines
Mairie, F-38810 Aoste
General Museum
Gallo-Roman finds; ceramics; glass;
numismatics

Apt

03939
Musée Archéologique
Chapelle Sainte-Catherine, rue
Scudéry, F-84400 Apt
General Museum
Coll: prehistoric finds; sculpture;
inscriptions; Gallo-Roman ceramics;
medals

Arbois

03940
**Musée de la Maison Paternelle de
Pasteur**
83 rue de Courcelles, F-39600 Arbois
History/Public Affairs Museum
Coll: memorabilia of the scientist Louis
Pasteur (1822-1895) in his former
home

03941
Musée Sarret-de-Grozon Musées de
Dole
9 Grande Rue, F-39600 Arbois, 85 rue
des Arènes, F-39100 Dole
Decorative Arts Museum
Coll: porcelain and faience; weapons;
silverware; art objects; furniture;
painting

Argenteuil

03942
Musée du Vieil-Argenteuil
5 rue Pierre-Guierme, F-95100
Argenteuil
General Museum
Coll: prehistory; medieval art; local
history; folklore; memorabilia of
Héloïse; history of Jansenism and
Mirabeau

Arlanc-en-Livradois

03943
Musée de la Dentelle à la Main
F-63220 Arlanc-en-Livradois
Decorative Arts Museum
Coll: old lace samples; lace production

Arles

03944
Musée Lapidaire d'Art Chrétien
rue Balze, F-13200 Arles
Archeology Museum
Coll: 4th-5th century marble
sarcophagi; Roman ceramics;
numismatics; Roman and Gothic
sculptures

03945
Musée Lapidaire d'Art Paien
Pl de la République, F-13200 Arles
Archeology Museum
Coll: Roman finds; mosaics; altars;
sarcophagi; friezes; grave sculptures;
statues from the theater

03946
Musée Réattu
rue du Grand-Prieuré, F-13200 Arles
Fine Arts Museum
Coll: 16th century Arras tapestries;
18th century local painting;
memorabilia of the painter Réattu;
sculpture; photo collection; in
16th-17th century seat of the Maltese
Order

03947
Museon Arlaten
43 rue de la République, F-13200 Arles
General Museum - 1899
Coll: 16th century house; life and
customs of the Provence

Arras

03948
Musée des Beaux-Arts
Ancienne Abbaye de Saint-Vaast, 22
rue Paul Doumer, F-62000 Arras
Fine Arts Museum - 1825
Coll: 12th-16th century wood and
stone sculptures; 17th-19th century
French paintings; Dutch and Flemish
paintings; 18th century porcelain from
Tournai and Arras; religious objects -
library

Arromanches-les-Bains

03949
Musée du Débarquement
F-14117 Arromanches-les-Bains
History/Public Affairs Museum
Coll: documents, dioramas, and films
on the Allied landing in 1944; site of
the landing

Auch

03950
Musée des Archives
F-32000 Auch
History/Public Affairs Museum
Coll: archives on the history of the
Gascogne

03951
Musée des Jacobins
Convent des Jacobins, 4 Pl Louis
Blanc, F-32000 Auch
Fine Arts Museum - 1979
Coll: paintings; sculpture; crafts;
8th-18th century pre-Columbian,
American, and colonial art of the
southern states; busts; folklore and
folk art of the Gascogne; Gallo-Roman
and medieval archeology

Aurignac

03952
Musée de Préhistoire
F-31420 Aurignac
Archeology Museum
Prehistorical finds

Aurillac

03953
Musée Hippolyte de Parieu
8 Pl de la Paix, F-15000 Aurillac
Fine Arts Museum
Coll: portraits; bust of Victor Hugo by
Rodin; modern art

03954
Musée Jean-Baptiste Rames
8 Pavillon de l'Horloge, F-15000
Aurillac
General Museum
Coll: natural history; prehistory;
regional folklore; geology;
numismatics; bronze; wrought iron;
pottery

Autun

03955
Musée Lapidaire Saint-Nicolas
10 rue Saint-Nicolas, F-71400 Autun
Archeology Museum - 1866
Coll: Gallo-Roman and medieval
structural fragments; castings of
originals

03956
Musées Municipaux
3 rue des Bancs, F-71400 Autun
General Museum - 1837
Coll: prehistorical items; Gallo-Roman
finds and Roman sculptures; Gothic
primitive paintings and statues;
16th-20th century paintings, sculptures,
furnishings

Auvillar

03957
Musée du Vieil Auvillar
Pl du Palais, F-82340 Auvillar
General Museum
Coll: prehistory; history; folklore; local
faience; 18th-19th century wrought
iron; arms; topography; painting

Auxerre

03958
Ancienne Abbaye de Saint-Germain
F-89000 Auxerre
Religious Art Museum
Coll: Carolingian crypt; medieval
sculptures

03959
Musée Lapidaire et Archéologique
rue de Paris, F-89000 Auxerre
Archeology Museum
Coll: structural fragments; chapel

03960
Musée Leblanc-Duvernoy
rue d'Egleny, F-89000 Auxerre
Decorative Arts Museum
Coll: 18th century Beauvais tapestries;
faiences of the region of Auxerre;
iconography of the Louvois family

Auxonne

03961
Musée Bonaparte
rue Lafayette, F-21130 Auxonne
General Museum
Coll: prehistoric and Gallo-Roman
finds; local history; customs;
memorabilia of Napoleon I (1769-1821);
folklore

Avallon

03962
Musée de l'Avallonais
Impasse du Collège, F-89200 Avallon
General Museum
Coll: pre- and early history; Gallo-
Roman finds; 2nd century statues of
Montmartre; sculptures; excavation
finds from Arcy-sur-Cure; religious
folk art; arms; jewels; 19th-20th
century paintings; numismatics

Avesnes-sur-Helpe

03963
Musée de la Société d'Archéologie
F-59440 Avesnes-sur-Helpe
General Museum
Coll: Gallo-Roman archeology; coins;
jewelry; pottery statuettes; 15th-17th
century sculpture; local history; book
illustrations; folk art; faience

Avignon

03964
Musée Calvet
65 rue Joseph-Vernet, F-84000
Avignon
General Museum - 1810
Coll: Egyptian, Greek, Gallo-Roman
archeology; 15th-19th century smith
work; 15th-20th century paintings -
library

03965
Musée du Petit Palais
Palais des Archevèques, Pl du Palais
des Papes, F-84000 Avignon
Fine Arts Museum - 1976
Coll: Italian paintings of the 13th-15th
centuries; local paintings from
14th-15th centuries; sculpture from
Avignon (12th-15th century); 7th-14th
century tombs - library; research and
study center of medieval art

03966
Section Lapidaire Musée Calvet
27 rue de la République, F-84000
Avignon
General Museum - 1935
Coll: 17th century chapel; Celtic
sculpture; Roman sculpture and
inscriptions; Renaissance sculpture

Avranches

03967
Musée de l'Avranchin
Place Jean-de-Saint-Avit, F-50300
Avranches
General Museum - 1963
Manuscripts of Mont Saint Michel
8th-15th centuries

Azay-le-Ferron

03968
Musée du Château
F-36290 Azay-le-Ferron
History/Public Affairs Museum

Azay-le-Rideau

03969
Musée de la Renaissance
Château, F-37190 Azay-le-Rideau
Fine Arts Museum
Coll: original furnishings; art objects;
16th century Flemish tapestries

Bagnères-de-Bigorre

03970
Musée Salies (Musée Municipal)
bd des Thermes et de l'Hyperon,
F-65200 Bagnères-de-Bigorre
General Museum - 1852
Coll: numismatics; paintings;
archeology

Bagnères-de-Luchon

03971
Musée du Pays de Luchon
18 allée d'Etigny, F-31110 Bagnères-
de-Luchon
General Museum
Coll: antiquities; anthropology;
portraits; historical monuments in the
Eastern Pyrenees; Gallo-Roman finds

Bagnols-sur-Ceze

03972
Musee Léon-Alégre
F-30200 Bagnols-sur-Ceze
General Museum - 1854
Coll: 19th century Lyon paintings;
Besson collection of paintings;
contemporary figurative paintings

Bailleul

03973
Musée Benoit-de-Puydt
24 rue du Musée, F-59270 Bailleul
Decorative Arts Museum
Coll: ceramics; lace; tapestries;
paintings; wood carvings; medals;
Chinese and Japanese porcelain

Barcelonnette

03974
Musée Chabrand
bd de la Libèration, F-04400
Barcelonnette
General Museum - 1890
Coll: archeology; zoology; ornithology

Bar-le-Duc

03975
Musée de la Meuse
Hôtel de Ville, F-55000 Bar-le-Duc
General Museum
Coll: antiquities; pre- and early history;
Gallo-Roman history; paintings;
ceramics

Barr

03976
Musée la Folie Marco
30 rue du Dr. Sultzer, F-67140 Barr
General Museum - 1963
Coll: 17th-19th century furniture; 18th
century porcelain and faience; manor
(18th century); pewter

Bastia

03977
Musée d'Ethnographie Corse
Palais des Gouverneurs, Génois-
Citadelle, F-20200 Bastia
General Museum - 1922
Coll: Greco-Roman archeology; local
historical artifacts; natural history
exhibits; ethnography; folk art;
Cardinal Fesch collection of paintings
- library

Baume-les-Messieurs

03978
**Musée des Arts et Traditions
Populaires du Jura**
F-39000 Baume-les-Messieurs
Anthropology Museum
Coll: folk art and customs

Bavay

03979
Musée Archéologique
rue de Gommeries, B.P. 47, F-59570
Bavay
Archeology Museum - 1976
Gallo-Roman bronze figures - library

Bayeux

03980
Musée de la Reine Mathilde
6 rue Léonard-Le-Forestier, F-14400
Bayeux
Decorative Arts Museum
Coll: the Bayeux Tapestry, displayed in
an 18th century residence

03981
Musée Municipal
Ancien Evêché, F-14400 Bayeux
General Museum
Coll: paintings; decorative arts;
porcelain and ceramics; tapestries

Bayonne

03982
Musée Basque de Bayonne
1 rue Marengo, F-64100 Bayonne
Anthropology Museum - 1924
Coll: history and folklore of Bayonne,
the French Basque country, the
Spanish Basque country, and the
Basques in the New World - library

03983
Musée Bonnat
5 rue Jacques-Laffitte, F-64100
Bayonne
Fine Arts Museum - 1899
Coll: Greek and Roman sculpture;
European schools of painting since the
15th century; 15th century Italian
medals; decorative arts; Italian
calligraphy; miniatures - library;
documentation center; cinema room

Beaucaire

03984
Musée Archéologique de Beaucaire
76 rue de Nîmes, F-30300 Beaucaire
Archeology Museum
Local archeological finds

Beaulieu-sur-Mer

03985
Fondation Théodore Reinach Villa
Grecque 'Kerylos'
F-06310 Beaulieu-sur-Mer
Archeology Museum - 1908
Coll: Greek art; reconstructed Greek
architecture; interiors; art objects;
bronze objects; mosaics

Beaune

03986
Collegiale Notre-Dame
Pl Maufoux, F-21200 Beaune
Decorative Arts Museum
Coll: 15th century tapestries;
decorative art

03987
Hôspice de la Charité
rue de Lorraine, F-21200 Beaune
General Museum - 1645
Coll: wrought-iron screens;
furnishings; tapestries; art objects

03988
Hôtel-Dieu de Beaune
Rue de l'Hôtel-Dieu, F-21200 Beaune
Decorative Arts Museum - 1443
Coll: 15th century hospital; original
interiors and equipment; paintings,
including Rogier van der Weyden's
'Last Judgement'; tapestries;
furnishings; statuettes; pewter;
15th-16th century ivory; wood
sculptures

03989
Musée du Vin de Bourgogne
Ancien Palais des Ducs de
Bourgogne, rue d'Enfer, F-21200
Beaune
General Museum - 1938
Coll: history of wine production;
viticulture traditions; coopery; tapestry
of Jean Lurçat

03990
Musées des Beux Arts et Marey
Hôtel de Ville, F-21200 Beaune
General Museum - 1853
Coll: 17th century convent; paintings;
Gallo-Roman findings; medieval-
Renaissance furnishings and art
objects; local historical items;
chronophotography of Etienne-Jules
Marey; technical history of the cinema

Beauvais

03991
Musée Départemental de l'Oise
Ancien Palais Épiscopal, 1 rue du
Musée, B.P. 118, F-60006 Beauvais
Cedex
General Museum - 1908
Coll: local archeological findings;
regional ceramics from the 16th-18th
centuries; faience; 12th-16th century
sculptures; 16th-19th century French
and Italian paintings; Art Deco;
furnishings

Belfort

03992
Musée des Beaux Arts
4 rue Général-Roussel, F-90000 Belfort
General Museum
Coll: fine arts; local history;
numismatics; antiquities; Merovingian
goldsmith work; Sumerian figurines;
customs

03993
Musées d'Art et d'Histoire
Château de Belfort, F-90000 Belfort
General Museum - 1899
Coll: medieval numismatics; technique
of prints from Dürer to Villon; folk art
and folklore; regional prehistoric and
medieval archeology; 19th-20th
century painting, sculpture, and
decorative arts; military arts from 1870
to 1914 - library

Bergerac

03994
Musée du Tabac
Hôtel de Ville, rue Neuve d'Argenson,
P.B. 200, F-24100 Bergerac
Anthropology Museum - 1950
Coll: pipes; snuff boxes; tobacco;
lithographs; books; a tobacco stand;
paintings with tobacco as the subject

Bergues

03995
Musée Municipal
Ancien Mont-de-Piété, F-59380
Bergues
General Museum
Coll: European paintings; drawings;
manuscripts of Lamartine; Flemish
folklore; natural science and history
collection; ornithology; butterfly
collection

Bernay

03996
Musée Municipal
Ancien Palais Abbatial, Pl Carnot,
F-27300 Bernay
Fine Arts Museum
Coll: Flemish and Spanish painting;
exhibits on Rouen ceramic works; in
17th century abbot's home

Besançon

03997
Musée Comtois
Citadelle, F-25000 Besançon
Anthropology Museum - 1960
Coll: provincial crafts; local folklore;
popular theater; traditional farming
03998
Musée des Beaux-Arts
1 Pl de la Révolution, F-25000
Besançon
Fine Arts Museum - 1843
Coll: 15th-20th century paintings;
French and foreign drawings;
ceramics; clocks and watches;
Egyptian, Greek, and Gallo-Roman
archeology
03999
Musée d'Histoire Musées de
Besançon
Palais Granvelle, 96 Grande rue,
F-25000 Besançon
General Museum
Coll: tapestries from Brugges;
documents on local history; paintings
and portraits; history of the Revolution
04000
**Musée Lapidaire de l'Abbatiale St.
Paul**
2 rue d'Alsace, F-25000 Besançon
Archeology Museum - 1956
Stones from the Gallo-Roman period
to the 18th century

Béziers

04001
Musée des Beaux-Arts
Hôtel Fabregat, Pl de la Révolution,
F-34500 Béziers
Fine Arts Museum
Coll: Greek vases; French and foreign
paintings
04002
Musée du Vieux Biterrois et du Vin
7 rue Massol, F-34500 Béziers
Archeology Museum
Coll: marine archeology; bronze and
copper finds; Greek and Roman ship
remains; amphoras; historic ships

Biarritz

04003
Musée de la Mer
Esplanade du Rocher de la Vierge, B.P.
89, F-64200 Biarritz
Natural History Museum - 1933
Coll: ethnography; local fauna; regional
marine animals and birds; exhibit on
deep sea fishing - library; aquarium

Bièvres

04004
Musée Français de la Photographie
78 rue de Paris, B.P. 3, F-91570
Bièvres
Science/Tech Museum
Coll: history, technology, and art of
photography; contemporary photos

Biot

04005
Musée National Fernand Léger
F-06410 Biot
Fine Arts Museum - 1960
Coll: works of the artist F. Léger
(1881-1955)

Blaye

04006
**Musée d'Histoire et d'Art du Pays
Blayais**
Citadelle, F-33390 Blaye
History/Public Affairs Museum
Memorabilia of the Duchess of Bérry

Blois

04007
**Musée des Beaux-Arts et
Archéologique**
Château de Blois, F-41000 Blois
Fine Arts Museum - 1850 (Musée des
Beux-Arts) and 1980 (Musée
Archéologique)
Div of art: paintings, art objects,
14th-20th century tapestries, faience,
costumes, local religious art; Div of
archeology: prehistoric findings, Gallo-
Roman antiquities - library

Bordeaux

04008
Musée d'Aquitaine
20 cours d'Albret, F-33000 Bordeaux
General Museum - 1781
Coll: prehistoric art; Gallo-Roman
fragments; Roman inscriptions; stelae;
reliefs; early Christian art; medieval
sculpture; folklore; modern and
contemporary history - library;
children's museum
04009
Musée de la Marine
Pl de la Bourse, F-3300 Bordeaux
History/Public Affairs Museum
Maritime history and shipping
04010
Musée des Arts Décoratifs
39 rue Bouffard, F-33000 Bordeaux
Decorative Arts Museum
European ceramics (12th-18th c.);
silver and furnishings; local history
04011
Musée des Beaux-Arts de Bordeaux
20 cours d'Albret, F-33000 Bordeaux
Fine Arts Museum - 1801
Coll: 17th-20th century European
paintings; sculptures; drawings from
the 16th-20th centuries - library

04012
Tresor de la Cathédrale Saint-André
Pl de la Cathédrale, F-33000 Bordeaux
Religious Art Museum
Sculpture, goldsmith work, early Italian
art

Boulogne-Billancourt

04013
**Jardins et Photothèque-
Cinémathèque Albert Kahn**
quai du 4.Septembre, F-92100
Boulogne-Billancourt
General Museum
Coll: gardens; horticulture; 72,000
photos of different countries; films
covering life in France and abroad
from 1910 to 1931; archives
04014
Musée Paul Landowsky
14 rue Max-Blondat, F-92100
Boulogne-Billancourt
Fine Arts Museum
Coll: bronze, marble sculptures,
ivories, and drawings by Paul
Landowsky, housed in sculptor's
former home

Boulogne-sur-Mer

04015
**Musée des Beaux-Arts et
d'Archéologie**
36 Grande Rue, F-62200 Boulogne-
sur-Mer
General Museum
Coll: Greek and Peruvian vases;
Alaskan masks; Egyptian art;
paintings; ceramics; geology;
prehistory; Egyptian and Gallo-Roman
archeology; local maritime history
04016
Musée Municipal
34 bis, Grande-Rue, F-62200
Boulogne-sur-Mer
General Museum
Coll: Greek and Peruvian vases;
Alaskan masks; Egyptian art;
paintings; ceramics; geology;
prehistory; Egyptian and Gallo-Roman
archeology; local maritime history

Bourbonne-les-Bains

04017
Musée Municipal
Poterne du Château, F-52400
Bourbonne-les-Bains
General Museum
Coll: prehistory; Celtic, Roman, and
Gallo-Roman finds; ancient coins

Bourg-en-Bresse

04018
Musée de l'Ain
Prieure de Brou, 65 bd de Brou,
F-01000 Bourg-en-Bresse
General Museum
Coll: local prehistoric findings; Gallo-
Roman and medieval artifacts; folklore;
16th-20th century paintings; decorative
arts; history of lighting up to the 19th
century

Bourges

04019
Musée de l'Hôtel Lallemant
6 rue Bourbonnoux, F-18014 Bourges
Fine Arts Museum
Furnishings, tapestries, objects d'art,
clocks, etc., displayed in a Renaisance
townhouse

04020
Musée du Berry
Hôtel Cujas, 4 et 6 rue des Arènes,
F-18000 Bourges
General Museum
Coll: pre- and Romanesque
archeology; ceramics; bronzes;
sculpture; provincial folklore and folk
art; household objects; costumes;
paintings; in Renaissance house

04021
Palais Jacques Coeur
rue Jacques Coeur, F-18000 Bourges
Fine Arts Museum
Gothic sculpture and tapestries
displayed in a 15th cent. palace

Bouxwiller

04022
Musée de la Ville de Bouxwiller
Hôtel de Ville, Pl du Château, F-67330
Bouxwiller
General Museum - 1934
Coll: history of Hanau-Lichtenberg and
Hessen-Darmstadt; local ethnography;
furniture; fossils

Brantôme

04023
**Musée Municipal Fernand-
Desmoulin**
Hôtel de Ville, F-24310 Brantôme
General Museum
Coll: prehistoric finds; paintings;
ceramics

Brest

04024
Musée Municipal
22 rue Traverse, F-29200 Brest
Fine Arts Museum
Coll: French and Italian paintings;
school of Pont-Aven

04025
Musée Naval de Brest
Château de Brest, F-29200 Brest
History/Public Affairs Museum
Coll: model ships; paintings; sculpture;
items documenting the maritime life of
the area

Brienne-le-Château

04026
Musée Napoléon
rue de l'Ecole Militaire, F-10500
Brienne-le-Château
History/Public Affairs Museum
Coll: memorabilia of Napoleon I
(1769-1821); Napoleonic military
history

Brignoles

04027
Musée du Pays Brignolais
Palais des Comtes de Provence,
F-83170 Brignoles
General Museum - 1945
Gallo-Roman archeology; mineralogy;
zoology; ornithology; ancient and
contemporary painting; folklore of the
Provence; 3rd-cent. sarcophagi

Brive-la-Gaillarde

04028
Musée Ernest Rupin
15 rue du Dr. Massénat, F-19100
Brive-la-Gaillarde
Fine Arts Museum
Coll: prehistory; Gallo-Roman
antiquities; sculpture; painting and
etchings; numismatics; religious art;
military arts; furniture; art objects;
folklore

Caen

04029
Musée de Normandie
Logis des Gouverneurs, F-14000 Caen
General Museum - 1946
Coll: medieval history and archeology
of Normandy; folklore; farm
implements; ceramics; costumes

04030
Musée des Beaux-Arts
Esplanade du Château, F-14000 Caen
Fine Arts Museum - 1802
Coll: Italian, French, Flemish, Dutch
paintings from the Middle Ages to the
20th century; drawings; ceramics; art
objects; engravings; prints

Cagnes-sur-Mer

04031
Château-Musée de Cagnes
F-06800 Cagnes-sur-Mer
General Museum
Coll: castle fortress (14th-17th
centuries); Renaissance interiors and
furnishings; tapestries; collection of
Suzy Solidor's portraits by Dufy,
Cocteau and others; modern
Mediterranean art

04032
Musée Renoir du Souvenir Les
Collettes
F-06800 Cagnes-sur-Mer
Historic Site - 1960
Coll: house where the French painter
Renoir spent his last 12 years; several
of his paintings; his sculpture; original
furnishings; important mural; photos;
personal effects - garden

Cahors

04033
Musée Municipal
54 rue Emile Zola, F-46000 Cahors
Fine Arts Museum
Coll: archeology; art objects; medieval
sculpture; portraits; painting;
memorabilia of the statesman L.
Gambetta (1838-1882)

Calais

04034
**Musée des Beaux-Arts et de la
Dentelle**
25 rue Richelieu, F-62000 Calais
General Museum - 1837
Coll: 15th-20th century painting and
watercolors; 18th century tapestry;
19th-20th century sculpture; 15th-18th
century Flemish and Dutch painting;
17th-20th century French and Italian
painting; 19th-20th century English
painting and watercolors; local history;
faience and porcelain; local lace
production; studies and sketches of
the monument 'The Citizens of Calais'
by Rodin

Camaret-sur-Mer

04035
Musée Naval de Camaret
Tour Vauban, F-29129 Camaret-
sur-Mer
History/Public Affairs Museum
Coll: 17th century tower; maritime
history; memorabilia of the poet Saint-
Pol-Roux

Cannes

04036
Musée de la Castre
Le Suquet, F-06400 Cannes
Archeology Museum
Art and archeology of the
Mediterranean, Near East, and
Oceania; pre-Columbian and Iranian
art and folklore

Carcassonne

04037
Cathedrale
F-11000 Carcassonne
Fine Arts Museum
Coll: 18th century paintings; textiles;
goldsmith work

04038
Depot Lapidaire
Château Comtal, F-11000
Carcassonne
Archeology Museum
Coll: sculptures from the Roman
conquest to the 16th century,
displayed in the palace of the
Vicomtes de Carcassonne

04039
Musée des Beaux-Arts Dép. de
l'Aude
1 rue de Verdun, F-11000
Carcassonne
Fine Arts Museum - 1846
Coll: 17th-18th century French
painting; Dutch painting; modern
paintings; memorabilia of the poet
André de Chéniers; faience

Carnac

04040
**Musée de Préhistoire James
Miln-Zacharie le Rouzic**
rte du Tumulus, F-56340 Carnac
Archeology Museum - 1882
Ceramics, stone tools, jewelry from
megalithic monuments of Carnac;
neolithic collection

Carpentras

04041
Musée Comtadin
234 bd Albin-Durand, F-84200
Carpentras
General Museum - 1888
Coll: folklore; works of local painters

04042
Musée d'Art Sacre
Cathédrale Saint-Siffrein, F-84200
Carpentras
Religious Art Museum
Sculpture and various religious
objects from the 14th-18th cent.

04043
Musée Duplessis
234 bd Albin-Durand, F-84200
Carpentras
Fine Arts Museum - 1888
Coll: paintings; folk art; paintings by
Duplessis and Vernet; portrait of abbot
de Rance by Rigaud; ancient bronze
pieces

04044
Musée Lapidaire
rue des Saintes-Maries, F-84200
Carpentras
Archeology Museum - 1936
Coll: Latin, Greek, and Hebrew
inscriptions; Gallo-Roman pottery and
glass; minerals

04045
Musée Sobirats
112 rue du Collège, F-84200
Carpentras
Decorative Arts Museum - 1946
Coll: Aubusson tapestries from the
17th-18th centuries; regional furniture;
faience; silver

Castéra-Verduzan

04046
Musée Lannelongue
F-32410 Castéra-Verduzan
Fine Arts Museum - 1912
Coll: works of art of all periods;
lapidary collection (exhibits from the
region)

Castres

04047
Musée Goya
Hôtel de Ville, F-81100 Castres
Fine Arts Museum
Coll: paintings by Goya (1746-1828);
early Spanish art; paintings of Spain's
Golden Age, including works by
Murillo and Velasquez; contemporary
Spanish art

04048
Musée Jaurès
Hôtel de Ville, F-81100 Castres
History/Public Affairs Museum
Coll: memorabilia of the socialist Jean
Jaurès (1859-1914); documents;
photographs; portraits

Caudebec-en-Caux

04049
Musée Biochet
rue de la Boucherie, F-76490
Caudebec-en-Caux
General Museum
Coll: architecuire; sculpture;
engravings; local history; stone work;
archives

Chalon-sur-Saône

04050
Musée Denon
Pl de l'Hôtel de Ville, F-71100 Chalon-
sur-Saône
Religious Art Museum - 16th century
Coll: wood panels; Pietà; pewter
vessels

Châlons-sur-Marne

04051
Musée Garinet
13 rue Pasteur, F-51000 Châlons-
sur-Marne
History/Public Affairs Museum - 1899
Coll: painting; furnishings; memorabilia
of the poets Friedrich Schiller
(1759-1805) and Johann Wolfgang von
Goethe (1749-1832)

04052
Musée Municipal
Pl Godart, F-51000 Châlons-sur-Marne
General Museum - 1861
Coll: Indian deities; items from the
Stone Age to Gallo-Roman times;
Romanesque and Gothic sculptures;
paintings; Rodin's bronze sculptures;
ethnography of Champagne

Chambéry

04053
Musée des Beaux-Arts
Pl du Palais-de-Justice, F-73000
Chambéry
Fine Arts Museum - 1783
Coll: Flemish and Dutch paintings
(16th-17th centuries); German painting
from the 16th to the 18th centuries;
French painting (17th-19th centuries);
Italian Renaissance painting and Italian
faience

04054
Musée des Charmettes
F-73000 Chambéry
Historic Site - 1905
Coll: former home of the philosopher
and writer Jean-Jacques Rousseau
from 1735 to 1740; furniture;
engravings; documents

04055
Musée Savoisien
sq de Lannoy-de-Bissy, F-73000
Chambéry
General Museum - 1864
Coll: classical archeology; prehistoric
objects; folklore; local history; history
of the House of Savoy; prints; medals
- library; documentation center

Chantilly

04056
Musée Condé
Château, F-60500 Chantilly
Fine Arts Museum - 1897
Coll: early French, Flemish, and Italian
paintings; drawings by Raffael,
Poussin, Watteau, Ingres, Delacroix;
miniatures by Fouquet; furniture;
manuscripts; engravings; money and
medals; objects d'art - library

Charleville-Mézières

04057
Musée de l'Ardenne Musée Rimbaud
Vieux-Moulin, F-08000 Charleville-
Mézières
General Museum - 1912
Coll: archeology; fine arts;
numismatics; regional folklore;
memorabilia of the poet Jean-Arthur
Rimbaud

Chartres

04058
Musée Municipal
29 Cloître Notre-Dame, F-28000
Chartres
Fine Arts Museum
Coll: medieval sculpture; 16th century
Italian and French painting; tapestries;
arms and armor; Greek ceramics;
enamels; faience; folklore

Château-Gontier

04059
Musée Municipal
rue de la Poste, F-53200 Château-Gontier
Fine Arts Museum
Coll: Greek and Roman archeology; wall paintings; drawings; wood sculpture; paintings

Château-Meillant

04060
Musée E. Chenon
rue de la Victoire, F-18370 Château-Meillant
General Museum - 1961
Coll: local archeology; Gallo-Roman remains; folklore

Château-Thierry

04061
Musée Jean de la Fontaine
12 rue de la Fontaine, F-02400 Château-Thierry
Historic Site
Coll: 11th century house where the fabelist and poet Jean de la Fontaine was born; exhibits on his life and work

Châteaudun

04062
Château de Châteaudun
Pl du Château, F-28200 Châteaudun
General Museum
Coll: 12th-16th century palace; 16th-17th century tapestries; 15th century sculpture

04063
Musée Municipal
3 rue Toufaire, F-28200 Châteaudun
General Museum
Coll: prehistory; Egyptology; ornithology; 18th century paintings by Restout

Châteauneuf-sur-Loire

04064
Musée de la Marine de Loire et du Vieux Châteauneuf
Pl d'Armes, F-45110 Châteauneuf-sur-Loire
General Museum - 1961
Coll: exhibits on Loire shipping; local history; objects of art; archeology; folklore - library

Châteauponsac

04065
Musée René Bauberot
Pl Saint Thyrse, F-87290 Châteauponsac
General Museum
Coll: archeology exhibits; local history; folk art and folk traditions

Châteauroux

04066
Musée Bertrand
2 rue Descente-des-Cordeliers, F-36000 Châteauroux
General Museum
Coll: 18th century home of General Bertrand; his memorabilia; history of Napoleonic times; prehistory; Celtic sculpture; Gallo-Roman stelae; folklore; 13th-20th century art objects; ceramics; Renaissance furniture; 14th-20th century painting; drawings

Châtillon-sur-Seine

04067
Musée Archéologique
7 rue du Bourg, F-21400 Châtillon-sur-Seine
Archeology Museum
Coll: excavation finds from Celtic, Greek, Gallic, and Frankian times; treasure of Vix (6th century B.C.)

Chaumont

04068
Musée de Chaumont
Pl du Palais, F-52200 Chaumont
General Museum
Coll: 13th and 16th century sections of former palace; Gallo-Roman and Merovingian finds; 15th-18th century sculpture; 17th-19th century painting

Chauny

04069
Musée National de la Coopération Franco-Americaine
Château de Blérancourt, F-02300 Chauny
History/Public Affairs Museum - 1929
Coll: memorabilia and documents on the War of Independence; weapons; items from WW I and WW II; relations between America and France - library

Chelles

04070
Musée Municipal Alfred Bonna
Hôtel de Ville de Chelles, Pl de la République, F-77500 Chelles
General Museum - 1947
Coll: local prehistoric finds; Gallo-Roman, Merovingian, and medieval artifacts; historic documents; works of local artists

Cherbourg

04071
Musée de la Guerre et de la Liberation
Fort du Roule, F-50100 Cherbourg
General Museum - 1954
Coll: local history from medieval to the modern times; local military items from WW II and the liberation

04072
Musée Thomas Henry
Hôtel de Ville, Pl de la République, F-50100 Cherbourg
Fine Arts Museum
Coll: Italian, Flemish, Spanish, Dutch, German, and French paintings

Cholet

04073
Musée des Beaux Arts
50 av Gambetta, F-49300 Cholet
Fine Arts Museum - 1979
Coll: 18th-20th century paintings, sculpture, and drawings - library

04074
Musée d'Histoire
Pl Travot, 50 av Gambetta, F-49300 Cholet
General Museum
Coll: historical items showing the development of Cholet; military artifacts

Clamecy

04075
Musée Municipal
Hôtel de la Bellegarde, F-58500 Clamecy
Fine Arts Museum
Coll: 17th century Flemish painting; 18th-19th century French painting; folklore; Nevers faience

Cleres

04076
Musée de Normandie
Pl de la Halle, F-76690 Cleres
Science/Tech Museum - 1958
Antique automobiles

Clermont-Ferrand

04077
Musée des Beaux-Arts Musée Bargoin
45 rue Ballainvilliers, F-63000 Clermont-Ferrand
Fine Arts Museum
Coll: paintings; sculpture; prehistory; Gallo-Roman antiquities

Cluny

04078
Musée deu Cellier
Ecole Nationale des Arts et Métiers, F-71250 Cluny
Fine Arts Museum
12th-18th cent. sculpture

04079
Musée du Farinier
Ecole Nationale des Arts et Métiers, F-71250 Cluny
Fine Arts Museum
Romanesque sculpture; altarpieces

04080
Musée Ochier
Palais Jean de Bourbon, rue de l'Abbatiale, F-71250 Cluny
General Museum - 1864
Coll: paintings and drawings by Prud'hon; religious objects; documents on the influence of Benedictine order in the Middle Ages; medieval sculpture; models of the town through its historical development; furnishings; faience

Cluses

04081
Salle des Collections Techniques et Pédagogiques de Cluses
Lycée Charles Poncet, Avenue Charles Poncet, F-74300 Cluses, Haute-Savoie
General Museum - 1929
Sciences and technology; horology; fine mechanics; electrical mechanics

Cognac

04082
Musée Municipal
bd Denfert-Rochereau, F-16100 Cognac
General Museum - 1892
Coll: local archeology, ethnology, and history; European art and applied art; natural history; viticulture; distillation; coopery; glass; 16th-17th century German, Flemish, and Dutch painting - library

Colmar

04083
Musée Bartholdi
30 rue des Marchands, F-68000 Colmar
General Museum - 1922
Coll: memorabilia of the sculptor Bartholdi; models of the Statue of Liberty; town history of Colmar (13th-19th centuries)

04084
Musée d'Unterlinden
1 Pl d'Unterlinden, F-68000 Colmar
Fine Arts Museum - 1849
Coll: former Dominican convent; Isenheimer Altar by Matthias Grünewald; early Alsatian painting; medieval and Renaissance paintings; local history; costumes; furniture; medieval art

Compiègne

04085
Musée Municipal Antoine Vivenel
2 rue d'Austerlitz, F-60200 Compiègne
Fine Arts Museum - 1844
European, Classican and Near Eastern archeology; Oriental and European arms; furnishings; Limoges enamels; Medieval and modern painting, drawing, sculpture

04086
Musée National de la Voiture et du Tourisme
Château de Compiège, F-60200 Compiègne
Science/Tech Museum - 1927
Coll: old carriages; sedan chairs; survey of the development of the bicycle and the automobile; vehicles

04087
Musée National du Château de Compiègne
Château de Compiège, F-60200 Compiègne
History/Public Affairs Museum - 1927
Coll: reconstructed palace rooms of 18th-19th centuries; special section of 2nd Empire furnishings

Condom

04088
Musée de l'Armagnac
Château, Pl Verte, F-32100 Condom
General Museum
Coll: regional customs; winegrowing; documents on distilling

Conflans-Sainte-Honorine

04089
Musée de la Batellerie
Château du Prieuré, F-78700 Conflans-Sainte-Honorine
General Museum - 1967
Coll: history of local navigation; shipping lore; shipping technology

Conques

04090
Abbaye de Conques
F-12320 Conques
Religious Art Museum
Coll: 8th-9th century reliquary of Pippin; gold altars; religious objects; enamels; goldsmith work; the reliquary statue of Sainte Foy (9th century); relics; tapestries

Cordes

04091
Musée Charles Portal
Grand rue, F-81170 Cordes
General Museum
Coll: prehistoric finds; Gallo-Roman
archeology; the local law codification,
'Le Livre Ferrat' from the 13th-14th
centuries; old textile mill

Coulommiers

04092
Musée de Coulommiers
Parc des Capucins, F-77120
Coulommiers
General Museum
Coll: 13th century sculpture; art
gallery; 15th century gravestones;
numismatics and bank notes;
inscriptions; documents on local
history from the Middle Ages to the
Revolution; prehistoric to medieval
archeologic findings

Coutances

04093
Musée Municipal
2 rue Quesnel-Morinière, F-50200
Coutances
Fine Arts Museum
Coll: Gallo-Roman antiquities;
18th-19th century paintings; works by
Rubens, Le Sueur, and Stella; Norman
pottery

Crépy-en-Valois

04094
Musée du Valois et de l'Archerie
F-60800 Crépy-en-Valois
General Museum
Coll: etchings; standards of guilds;
collection on archery and crossbows

Déols

04095
Musée des Trois Guerres
Château de Diors, F-36130 Déols
History/Public Affairs Museum - 1920
Coll: exhibits on the wars of 1870,
1914, and 1939 ; Indochina, Suez, and
Algeria

Die

04096
Musée Municipal
11 rue Camille-Buffardel, F-26150 Die
History/Public Affairs Museum - 1949
Coll: pre- and ancient history; Roman
inscriptions; sculpture; bronzes;
ceramics; Roman glass; early
Christian, Carolingian, and
Romanesque sculpture; documents on
local 15th-20th century history -
library

Dieppe

04097
Château Musée de Dieppe
Château Musée, rue de Chastes,
F-76200 Dieppe
General Museum - 1876
Coll: paintings inspired by local area,
especially Impressionists;
pre-Columbian pottery; memorabilia of
the composer C. Saint-Saëns; marine
collection of maps, log books,
compasses, and 18th century ship
models; 16th century ivory figurines;
modern local sculpture

Digne

04098
Musée Municipal
bd Gassendi, F-04000 Digne
General Museum
Coll: prehistory; Gallo-Roman
antiquities; 19th-20th century paintings;
local masters; regional and natural
history

Dijon

04099
Musée Archéologique
5 rue Docteur Maret, F-21000 Dijon
Archeology Museum - 1955
Coll: protohistoric and prehistoric
findings; golden bracelet of the 6th
century; Gallo-Roman and
Merovingian items; medieval art; bust
of Christ by Claus Sluter - library

04100
Musée de l'Hôpital Musée des
Beaux-Arts
2 rue de l'Hôpital, F-21000 Dijon
Religious Art Museum
Coll: 15th century chapel; 14th-15th
century sculptures; old paintings; 15th
century manuscripts (only authorized
visits)

04101
Musée des Beaux-Arts
Pl de la Sainte-Chapelle, F-2100 Dijon
Fine Arts Museum - 1787
Coll: gravestones; altar art; Egyptian
items; 15th-18th century tapestries;
early Flemish, Swiss, German, Italian,
and 16th-20th century French painting;
decorative objects of enamel, ivory,
gold; medieval sculpture; French
Renaissance furnishings; wood
carving; armaments; stained-glass
windows; 15th-16th century
Burgundian sculpture; Oriental textiles;
modern works

04102
Musée d'Histoire Naturelle
1 av Albert, F-21033 Dijon Cedex
Natural History Museum - 1836
Coll: local geology; fauna of the area;
exotic and French insects; shells of
the world; mammals of Madagascar

04103
Musée Magnin
4 rue Bons-Enfants, F-21000 Dijon
Fine Arts Museum
Coll: paintings by Poussin, Vignon,
Tiepolo, etc.; drawings; screens;
portraits; furnishings

Dinan

04104
Musée Municipal
Château de la Duchesse Anne, Donjon
de Dinan, F-22100 Dinan
General Museum
Coll: 14th century military architecture;
folklore; historical memorabilia

Dole

04105
Musée Municipal
Pavillon des Officiers, 85 rue des
Arènes, F-39100 Dole
General Museum - 1823 (painting
division) and 1901 (archeology
division)
Coll: pre- and protohistoric
archeological findings; Gallo-Roman
items; local historical painting from the
17th century

Douai

04106
Musée Municipal Ancienne
Chartreuse
rue des Chartreux, F-59500 Douai
General Museum
Coll: Flemish, Dutch, Italian, and
French painting; Gallo-Roman and
medieval antiquities

Dreux

04107
Musée d'Art et d'Histoire
7 Pl du Musée, F-28100 Dreux
Fine Arts Museum
Coll: Louis XV furniture; Romanesque
chapel; modern paintings including
Monet and Vlaminck; local history;
documents on the Orléans family

Dunkerque

04108
**Musée des Beaux-Arts de
Dunkerque**
Pl du Général de Gaulle, F-59140
Dunkerque
General Museum - 1841
Coll: local history; model ships;
French, Flemish, Dutch, and Italian
painting from the 17th-19th centuries;
natural history - library

Eauze

04109
Musée Archéologique
Mairie, F-32800 Eauze
Fine Arts Museum
Coll: antiquities; archeology; grave
sculptures; ceramics; memorabilia on
sculptor Félix Soulès

Ecouen

04110
Musée National de la Renaissance
Château d'Ecouen, F-95440 Ecouen
Fine Arts Museum - 1977
Art objects from the Renaissance

Epernay

04111
Musée Archéologique
F-51200 Epernay
Archeology Museum
Coll: prehistoric finds; Gallo-Roman
items

04112
Musée des Beaux-Arts
F-51200 Epernay
Fine Arts Museum
Coll: painting; sculpture; ceramics;
furnishings; numismatics

04113
Musée Municipal
Château-Perrier, 13 av de Champagne,
F-51200 Epernay
General Museum
Coll: wine; wine-growing in the
Champagne area; tools and
accessories; documents; customs;
trade

Epinal

04114
Musée Départemental des Vosges
Pl Lagarde, F-88000 Epinal
General Museum
Gallo-Roman medieval sculpture;
antiquities; numismatics; regional
folklore; 16th-20th century painting;
18th century drawings

Etampes

04115
Musée Municipal
Hôtel de Ville, F-91150 Etampes
General Museum
Coll: prehistoric Celtic finds; Gallo-
Roman items; paintings; sculpture;
natural history

Eu

04116
Musée Louis-Philippe
Château, F-76260 Eu
General Museum - 1973
Coll: furniture of King Louis-Philippe;
19th century wood floors; art objects
and furniture designed by Viollet-
le-Duc; glass; local folklore - library

Evreux

04117
Musée d'Evreux Ancien Eveche
6 rue Charles-Corbeau, F-27000
Evreux
Fine Arts Museum - 1833
Coll: prehistoric and Gallo-Roman
finds; bronze Jupiter statue; medieval
art and enamel; art objects; 18th
century furnishings; inlays; painting;
ceramics

Figeac

04118
Musée Champollion
Pl Vival, F-46100 Figeac
General Museum
Coll: prehistory; stonework;
numismatics; memorabilia of the
archeologist J.-Fr. Champollion, the
decipherer of the Rosetta Stone

Flers

04119
Musée du Bocage Normand
Château, B.P. 192, F-61104 Flers
General Museum - 1874
Coll: 17th-20th century painting;
regional history; folk art and local
traditions

Foix

04120
Musée de l'Ariège
F-09000 Foix
General Museum
Coll: prehistory; antiquity; exhibits on
the Middle Ages; folklore, folk art, and
customs

Fontainebleau

04121
Musée Militaire
15 rue Royale, F-77300 Fontainebleau
History/Public Affairs Museum
Military uniforms, arms, etc., from the
French Revolution to modern times

04122
Musée National du Château
F-77300 Fontainebleau
Decorative Arts Museum
Coll: 16th century palace; royal
furnishings; royal apartments;
tapestries; imperial theater; Oriental
collection

Gaillac

04123
Musée d'Histoire Naturelle Philadelphe Thomas
2 Pl Philadelphe Thomas, F-81600 Gaillac
Natural History Museum
Fossil collection - library

Gap

04124
Musée Departemental des Hautes-Alpes
6 av Maréchal Foch, F-05000 Gap
General Museum
Coll: military arts; ornithology; paintings; prehistoric and Stone Age items; coins

Gevrey-Chambertin

04125
Musée des Arts et Traditions des Hautes-Côtes
Reulle-Vergy, F-21220 Gevrey-Chambertin
General Museum - 1974
Coll: natural history exhibits; flora and fauna of the Bourgogne; prehistoric and historical items; traditions

Gien

04126
Musée Internationale de la Chasse
Château de Gien, F-45500 Gien
History/Public Affairs Museum
Coll: tapestries; paintings; armaments; screens by the animal painter Desportes; etchings and documents on hunting; trophies; horns and equipages

Gordes

04127
Musée Vasarély
B.P. 4, F-84220 Gordes
Fine Arts Museum - 1970
Coll: 16th century palace; paintings by Victor Vasarély

Granville

04128
Musée du Vieux Granville
rue Lecarpentier, F-50400 Granville
General Museum
Coll: local history; customs; regional costumes; documents on Newfoundlanders

Grasse

04129
Musée d'Art et d'Histoire de Provence
2 Passage Mirabeau, F-06130 Grasse
General Museum
Coll: 17th-19th century furnishings; household objects; costumes; ceramics; antiques; customs; paintings; etchings; works by the artist J.-H. Fragonard; 18th century palace

Grenoble

04130
Musée Dauphinois
30 rue Gignoux, F-38000 Grenoble
General Museum
Coll: archeological finds; regional history; folklore in documents; early historical finds; wood carvings; local porcelain; folk pottery; 17th century former convent

04131
Musée de Peinture et de Sculpture
Pl de Verdun, F-38000 Grenoble
Fine Arts Museum - 1798
Coll: Impressionists; Cubism; Naiveté; abstract art; 15th-16th century Italian painting; 17th-19th century European masters

04132
Musée Stendhal
Jardin de Ville, F-38000 Grenoble
Historic Site
Coll: memorabilia of the writer Stendhal; pictures; engravings; manuscripts; drawings

Grézolles

04133
Musée Historial
Mairie, F-42260 Grézolles
General Museum
Coll: local history; customs; traditional families; memorabilia of Father de la Chaise, the Father Confessor to Louis XIV

Grignan

04134
Musée Faure-Cabrol
Château, F-26230 Grignan
Decorative Arts Museum - 1942
Coll: faience; tapestry; furnishings

Hagenau

04135
Musée Municipal
9 rue du Maréchal Foch, F-67500 Hagenau
General Museum
Bronze Age finds; Roman sculpture; Alsatian numismatics; local incunabula; furnishings; armaments; tools

Hazebrouck

04136
Musée Municipal
Place Georges-Degroote, F-59190 Hazebrouck
General Museum
Coll: paintings; drawings; prints; ceramics; costumes

Héricourt

04137
Musée Minal
mail c/o Mairie Héricourt, Square Minal, F-70400 Héricourt
Fine Arts Museum
19th century painting; modern jewelry - library

Hesdin

04138
Musée de Hôtel de Ville
Pl d'Armes, F-62140 Hesdin
Decorative Arts Museum
17th century Flemish tapestries

Honfleur

04139
Musée du Vieux Honfleur
quai Saint-Etienne, F-14600 Honfleur
General Museum
Coll: Norman furnishings; costumes; history of pirates and slave traders

04140
Musée Eugène Boudin
Pl Erik Satie, F-14600 Honfleur
Fine Arts Museum - 1868
Coll: 17th-18th century painting; pre-Impressionist, Impressionist, and modern painting; costumes; engravings; drawings; ethnography collection

Illiers Combray

04141
Musée Marcel Proust
4 rue du Docteur Proust, F-28120 Illiers Combray
History/Public Affairs Museum
Memorabilia of the writer Marcel Proust (1871-1922)

Issoudun

04142
Musée de l'Ancien Hospice Saint Roch
F-36100 Issoudun
Fine Arts Museum
Coll: reliefs; stained-glass windows in the chapel

04143
Musée des Missions
38 Pl du Sacré-Coeur, F-36100 Issoudun
Anthropology Museum
Items collected by missionaries in Papua, New Guinea and Senegal

Jarville

04144
Musée de l'Histoire du Fer
av du Général de Gaulle, B.P. 15, F-54140 Jarville
Science/Tech Museum - 1966
Iron ore mining - library

Jouy-en-Josas

04145
Musée Oberkampf Musée de la Toile de Jouy
Château de Montebello, F-78350 Jouy-en-Josas
Decorative Arts Museum - 1977
18th-19th century printed textiles of French and foreign manufactures; tapestries; costumes; printing-blocks and other materials of old manufactures

Kaysersberg

04146
Musée Albert Schweitzer
F-68240 Kaysersberg
Historic Site
Coll: memorabilia of A. Schweitzer

04147
Musée de la Société Archéologique
F-68240 Kaysersberg
General Museum
Coll: items of local history; archeological finds

Kientzheim

04148
Musée du Vignoble et des Vins d'Alsace
Château de la Confrérie St Etienne, F-68240 Kientzheim
Agriculture Museum - 1980
Coll: viticulture; wine cellar materials; cooper's workshop

La Bussière

04149
Le Château des Pêcheurs
Château de la Bussière, F-45230 La Bussière
Decorative Arts Museum - 1962
Coll: art on theme of freshwater fish; 18th century English and German engravings; faience

La Charité-sur-Loire

04150
Musée Municipal
Hôtel Adam, rue Auguste Adam, F-58400 La Charité-sur-Loire
Archeology Museum - 1953
Coll: medieval archeology; local ethnography; decorative art - library

La Châtre

04151
Musée George Sand et de la Vallee Noire
71 rue Venôse, F-36400 La Châtre
General Museum - 1937
Coll: memorabilia of the writer George Sand; ethnography; local painters; collection of birds; Roman coins

La Côte Saint-André

04152
Musée Hector Berlioz
69 rue de la République, F-38260 La Côte Saint-André
Historic Site
Coll: exhibits on the life of the composer Hector Berlioz (1803-1869); in house of his birth

La Côte-Saint-André

04153
Musée Hector-Berlioz
69 rue de la République, F-38260 La Côte-Saint-André
Historic Site - 1935
Birthplace and life of composer Hector Berlioz

La Couture-Boussey

04154
Musée Jacques Hotteterre Musée Instrumental et Industriel d'Instruments à Vent
Pl de la Mairie, F-27750 La Couture-Boussey
Music Museum
Coll: antique instruments and equipment; documents and archives

La Fère

04155
Musée Jeanne d'Aboville
Pl de l'Esplanade, F-02800 La Fère
Fine Arts Museum - 1860
Coll: German, Dutch, and Flemish landscape painting; 17th-28th century French painting; general painting

La Garde

04156
Musée J. Aicard 'Les Lauriers Roses'
Vieux Chemin de Ste Marguerite, F-83130 La Garde
Fine Arts Museum - 1980
Paintings and portraits, objects d'Art, porcelain, and furnishings from 1830-1930

Langeais

04157
Château de Langeais
F-37130 Langeais
Fine Arts Museum - 1467
Coll: furniture and tapestries of the
13th-15th centuries; 15th century
architecture

Langres

04158
Musée du Breuil de Saint Germain
Conservation des Musées de Langres
2 rue Chambrûlard, F-52200 Langres
Fine Arts Museum - 1923
Coll: faience and porcelain; pewter;
locks and armor; paintings and
engravings by Claude Gillot;
memorabilia of the writer Diderot;
incunabula and book bindings;
furniture from medieval times to the
18th century; 15th-19th century
paintings

04159
Musée Saint-Didier Conservation
des Musées de Langres
2 rue Chambrûlard, F-52200 Langres
General Museum - 1846
Coll: 13th century building with 12th
century chapel; Gallo-Roman,
medieval, and classical sculpture; small
Gallo-Roman bronzes; natural history
collection; 15th-19th century paintings

Laon

04160
Musée Archéologique Municipal
32 rue Georges Ermant, F-02000 Laon
Archeology Museum - 1850
Coll: Egyptian, Greek, and Roman
antiquities; prehistory; Gallo-Roman,
Merovingian, and medieval regional
archeology; local paintings; sculpture;
faience - library

La Rochelle

04161
Musée des Beaux-Arts
28 rue Gargoulleau, F-17000 La
Rochelle
Fine Arts Museum
Coll: extensive French paintings up to
the 20th century; glass; drawings;
castings of sculptures by Charles
Depiau

04162
**Musée d'Histoire Naturelle et
d'Ethnographie**
28 rue Albert, F-17000 La Rochelle
Natural History Museum - 1782
Coll: natural science exhibits;
prehistory; primitive art from Oceania
and the Pacific - library

04163
Musée d'Orbigny Bernon
2 rue Saint-Côme, F-17000 La Rochelle
General Museum
Coll: local and regional history; 18th
century porcelain; pharmacy;
archeology; castings of French
monuments

04164
Musée Huguenot
2 rue Saint-Michel, F-17000 La
Rochelle
History/Public Affairs Museum
History of regional Protestantism

04165
Muséum Fleuriau
F-17000 La Rochelle
General Museum
Coll: prehistory; natural sciences

Lascaux

04166
Grottes de Lascaux
7 rue de la Constitution, F-24000
Perigueux
Anthropology Museum
Prehistoric cave paintings

La Seyne-sur-Mer

04167
Musée Naval de Balaguier
Fort de Balaguier, F-83500 La Seyne-
sur-Mer
History/Public Affairs Museum
Coll: ancient fortress; model ships -
garden

Laval

04168
Musée de la Perrine
F-53000 Laval
General Museum
Coll: decorative arts; paintings by
regional artists

04169
Musée des Beaux-Arts
Pl de Hercé, F-53000 Laval
Fine Arts Museum
Coll: Oriental antiquities; medieval
sculpture; tiles; paintings

04170
Musée des Sciences
F-53000 Laval
Science/Tech Museum
Coll: technology; mineralogy;
zoological exhibits

04171
Musée du Vieux-Château
Vieux-Château, Pl de la Trémoille,
F-53000 Laval
Fine Arts Museum - 1966
Coll: 11th-15th century medieval
castle; exhibition of international naive
art; medieval items

04172
Musée Henri Rousseau
F-53000 Laval
Fine Arts Museum
Coll: naive art; paintings by H.
Rousseau (1844-1910)

Lavaur

04173
Musée du Pays Vaurais
rue de la Mairie, F-81500 Lavaur
General Museum
Coll: local history; prehistory; Gallo-
Roman finds; numismatics; sundials

Le Blanc

04174
Musée des Oiseaux
Mairie, F-36300 Le Blanc
Natural History Museum - 1823
Coll: regional and exotic birds

Le Cateau

04175
Musée Henri Matisse
Hôtel de Ville, F-59360 Le Cateau
Fine Arts Museum
Coll: works of Matisse; local painters

Le Croisic

04176
Musée Naval du Croisic
Hôtel d'Aiguillon, F-44490 Le Croisic
History/Public Affairs Museum - 1956
Coll: 17th century hotel; maritime
memorabilia; canon; shipping and
sailing; marine lore

Lectoure

04177
Musée Marie Surrieu-Duler
Mairie de Lectoure, F-32700 Lectoure
Archeology Museum
Coll: 3rd-4th century sacrificial altars;
bronze; pottery; coins; grave
monuments; Celtic finds

04178
Salle du Maréchal Lannes
Hôtel de Ville, F-32700 Lectoure
Historic Site - 1975
Coll: memorabilia of Marshal Lannes;
items pertaining to the turn of the 19th
century

Le Grand-Pressigny

04179
**Musée Prehistorique du Grand-
Pressigny**
Château du Grand-Pressigny, F-37350
Le Grand-Pressigny
Archeology Museum
Coll: 15th-17th century palace;
neolithic and paleolithic finds; fossils

Le Havre

04180
Musée de l'Abbaye de Graville
rue Elisée Reclus, F-76000 Le Havre
Fine Arts Museum - 1926
Sculpture from the 12th to 18th cent;
exhibitions

04181
Musée de l'Ancien Havre
rue Jérôme Bellarmato, F-76000 Le
Havre
General Museum - 1955
Drawings and documents related to
the founding of Le Havre by François
I; pottery and glass

04182
**Musée des Beaux-Arts 'André
Malraux'**
bd J.F.-Kennedy, F-76600 Le Havre
Fine Arts Museum - 1961
Coll: 16th-19th century French, Dutch,
Flemish, and Italian painting; 18th
century modern paintings; modern art

04183
Muséum d'Histoire Naturelle
Pl du Vieux Marché, F-76600 Le Havre
Natural History Museum - 1845
Coll: local and general paleontology;
geology; mineralogy; ornithology;
general zoology; botany; prehistory;
drawings and paintings by Ch.A.
Lesueur - library; research laboratory

Le Mans

04184
Musée de la Reine Berengère
913 rue de la Reine Berengère,
F-72000 Le Mans
History/Public Affairs Museum - 1923
Coll: regional ceramics from the
Middle Ages to the 20th century;
regional history; 18th century pottery
from Ligron and Prevelles

04185
Musée de l'Automobile du Mans
Circuit des 24 Heures, F-72200 Le
Mans
Science/Tech Museum
Motocycles, automobiles, bicycles, etc.

04186
Musée de Tessé
2 av de Paderborn, F-72000 Le Mans
Fine Arts Museum - 1927
Coll: 14th-20th century paintings;
ancient and modern ceramics;
Egyptian and Mesopotamian art; glass;
sculpture; tapestry - library

Le Mas-d'Azil

04187
Centre d'Etudes de Préhistoire
F-09290 Le Mas-d'Azil
Archeology Museum
Local archeological finds

Le Mée-sur-Seine

04188
Musée Chapu
937 rue Chapu, F-77350 Le Mée-sur-
Seine
Fine Arts Museum
Originals and castings by sculptor
Henri Chapu

Le Molay-Littry

04189
Musée de la Mine
rue Philippe Guillaume Lance, F-14330
Le Molay-Littry
Science/Tech Museum
Coll: history of mining; 18th century
fire-extinguisher; fire-fighting
equipment; mining utensils; 1893 plan
of coal-pit - library

Le Petit-Couronne

04190
Musée Pierre Corneille
502 rue Pierre-Corneille, F-76650 Le
Petit-Couronne
Historic Site - 1879
Coll: home of the dramatist Pierre
Corneille; exhibits on his life and work;
17th century furniture

Le Puy

04191
Musée Crozatier
Jardin Henri-Vinay, F-43000 Le Puy
General Museum
Coll: mineralogy; paleontology;
prehistoric finds; Roman remains;
Carolingian, Romanesque, and Gothic
art; crafts and laces; goldsmith art;
paintings; sculpture

Les-Baux-de-Provence

04192
Hôtel de Manville
Impasse du Château, F-13520
Les-Baux-de-Provence
General Museum

Les Andelys

04193
Musée Municipal 'Nicolas Poussin'
rue Ste-Clotilde, F-27700 Les Andelys
General Museum - 1971
Coll: 18th century furniture; 14th-16th
century sculpture; local prehistoric
and Gallo-Roman findings;
contemporary art; memorabilia of the
painter Nicolas Poussin (1593-1665)

Les Arcs

04194
Musée Provençal et Folklorique Taradeau
F-83460 Les Arcs
General Museum
Coll: household objects; farm and craftsmen's tools; folklore; Roman finds

Les Eyzies de Tayac

04195
Musée National de Préhistoire
F-24620 Les Eyzies de Tayac
Archeology Museum - 1918
Coll: 3,000 prehistoric objects from regional excavations, including armaments, household objects, artwork, cave reliefs, sculptures, gave sites, animal and human remains; skeleton Cro-Magnon from St. Germain la Rivière; some of the oldest objects of art in the world; etchings and paintings of the Aurignac - library

Les Sables d'Olonne

04196
Musée de l'Abbaye Sainte-Croix
rue de Verdun, F-85100 Les Sables d'Olonne
General Museum
Coll: local prehistoric finds; ethnography; navigation; contemporary art

Le Vigan

04197
Musée Cevenol
1 rue des Calquières, F-30120 Le Vigan
General Museum - 1963
Coll: folk art; tools; crafts; history; silk; literature; 18th-19th century costumes

Libourne

04198
Musée Municipal
Hôtel de Ville, F-33500 Libourne
Fine Arts Museum
Coll: prehistoric and Gallo-Roman finds; 16th-19th century painting; sculpture

Lille

04199
Musée de l'Hospice Comtesse
32 rue de la Monnaie, F-59000 Lille
General Museum - 1963
Coll: 13th century former hospital; Delft tiles; Flemish furnishings; tapestries; sculpture; painting; ceramics; regional history; customs

04200
Musée des Beaux-Arts
Pl de la République, F-59000 Lille
Fine Arts Museum - 1801
Coll: Flemish, French, Dutch, Spanish, Italien, and German paintings; Italian and French drawings

04201
Musée Diocesain d'Art Religieux
68 rue Royale, F-59000 Lille
Religious Art Museum
Coll: Romanesque statues; goldsmith work; wood sculptures; paintings

Lillebonne

04202
Musée Municipal
Hôtel de Ville, F-76170 Lillebonne
General Museum
Coll: local history; Gallo-Roman finds; porcelain; decorative arts; furnishings; ornithology; folk art and customs

Limoges

04203
Musée Adrien Dubouché
pl Winston Churchill, F-87000 Limoges
Decorative Arts Museum - 1900
Ceramics

04204
Musée Municipal de Limoges
Pl de la Cathédrale, F-87000 Limoges
General Museum - 1913
Coll: 18th century palace; Egyptian and Gallo-Roman antiquities and frescoes; local enamel from the 12th century to the present; religious art objects; paintings; mineralogy and stones

Liré

04205
Musée du Bellay
Le Grand Logis, F-49530 Liré
General Museum
Coll: local history; Gallo-Roman pottery; art; customs; documents on the poet Joachim du Bellay (1522-1560)

Lisieux

04206
Château de Saint-Germain-de-Livet
B.P. 222, F-14107 Lisieux
Decorative Arts Museum - 1977
Coll: 18th century furniture; works by Henri and Léon Riesener

04207
Musée du Vieux-Lisieux-François-Cottin
38 bd Pasteur, F-14100 Lisieux
General Museum - 1834 (art division); 1968 (folk art division)
Coll: 19th century paintings; pottery; Gallo-Roman art - library

L'Isle-Adam

04208
Musée Louis Senlecq
46 Grande Rue, F-95290 L'Isle-Adam
General Museum - 1938
Coll: local history; works of artists who lived here; paintings by Vlaminck, Dupré, etc.; etchings; historical documents - library

Longwy

04209
Musée Municipal de Longwy
Porte de France, F-54400 Longwy
General Museum
Coll: historic finds; local history; ornamental cast iron plates; 19th century faience; 19th century sculpture

Lons-le-Saunier

04210
Musée Municipal
Hôtel de Ville, Pl Perraud, B.P. 492, F-39007 Lons-le-Saunier
Archeology Museum
Coll: prehistory; Gallo-Roman and Merovingian finds; 17th-18th century Flemish, Italian, and French painting

Lorient

04211
Musée Naval de Lorient
Arsenal de Lorient, F-56100 Lorient
History/Public Affairs Museum
Coll: 18th century windmill; history of the naval division for India and the Far East; ship models; naval maps; paintings

Loudun

04212
Musée Charbonneau-Lassay
24 rue du Martray, F-86200 Loudun
General Museum
Coll: Celtic, Egyptian, and Gallo-Roman antiquities; armaments; African art; local art

Lourdes

04213
Musée Pyrénéen
Château fort, F-65100 Lourdes
General Museum - 1920
Coll: costumes; ceramics; musical instruments; furniture; ethnography and local history - library

Louviers

04214
Musée Municipal
Pl Ernest-Thorel, F-27400 Louviers
General Museum
Coll: porcelain; local and regional history; antiquities; furnishings; paintings

Lovagny

04215
Collection Leon Mares Château de Montrottier
F-74330 La Balme-de-Sillingy
Fine Arts Museum - 1606
Coll: faience; ivories; weapons; rare objects from Africa and the Far East; 16th century bronze reliefs

Lunéville

04216
Musée du Château
Pl Stanislas, F-54300 Lunéville
General Museum - 1860
Coll: 18th century faiences of the area; military artifacts

Lyon

04217
Musée Africain
150 Cours Gambetta, F-69361 Lyon Cedex 2
Anthropology Museum - 1926
Coll: Western African art; crafts; masks; sculpture; copper objects; folk art from Benin and the Ivory Coast

04218
Musée de Gadagne Musée Historique de Lyon et Musée International de la Marionnette
14 rue de Gadagne, F-69005 Lyon
General Museum - 1921
Coll: local history; French and foreign puppets; ethnology

04219
Musée de la Civilisation Gallo-Romaine de Lyon
17 rue Cleberg, F-69005 Lyon
Archeology Museum - 1955
Coll: Gallo-Roman finds; paintings; mosaics; epigraphs - library

04220
Musée des Beaux-Arts
Palais Saint-Pierre, 20 Pl des Terreaux, F-69001 Lyon
Fine Arts Museum
Coll: 17th century abbey; sculpture; paintings by European masters of all periods from the 15th century to the present, including Perugino, Tintoretto, Delacroix, Picasso, Ernst; drawings; decorative arts; Oriental and Moslem art; local school of painting; medals; numismatics

04221
Musée des Hospices Civils de Lyon
Pl de l'Hôpital, F-69002 Lyon
General Museum
Coll: 17th century building; art collection; 16th-18th century furnishings; busts; tapestries; 16th-19th century apothecary jars and other memorabilia of local history of medicine

04222
Musée des Moulages d'Art Medieval et Moderne
Université Lyon II, 18 quai Claude-Bernard, F-69006 Lyon
Fine Arts Museum
Coll: castings of medieval and modern art

04223
Musée du Tresor de la Cathedrale
Pl Saint Jean, F-69005 Lyon
Religious Art Museum
Religious art

04224
Musée Guimet
28 bd des Belges, F-69009 Lyon
Fine Arts Museum
Coll: Assyrian frescoes; Greek and Roman archeological finds; Egyptian, Indian, and Oriental art

04225
Musée Historique des Tissus
34 rue de la Charité, F-69002 Lyon
Science/Tech Museum - 1864
Coll: textiles from the Mediterranean area dating from 300 BC to the 19th century; important French silk collection from the 17th-20th centuries, especially Art Deco silks; Oriental silks; Persian and Near Eastern rugs from the 16th-17th centuries - library

04226
Musée Lyonnais des Arts Decoratifs
30 rue de la Charité, F-69002 Lyon
Decorative Arts Museum - 1925
Coll: 16th-19th century French decorative art; French and Flemish tapestries from the 16th-18th centuries; 15th-17th century Italian majolicas - library

Mâcon

04227
Musée Lamartine et Musée de l'Académie
Hôtel Senecé, 41 rue Sigorgne,
F-71000 Mâcon
General Museum
Coll: furnishings; tapestries; ceramics;
painting; literature; memorabilia of the
poet Alphonse de Lamartine

04228
Musée Municipal des Ursulines
5 rue des Ursulines, F-71000 Mâcon
General Museum - 1968
Coll: 17th century convent; pre- and
early history; antiquities; medieval,
Italian, French, Dutch, Flemish painting;
European and Oriental faience;
regional costumes and hair styles;
regional ethnography

Magny-les-Hameaux

04229
Musée National des Granges de Port-Royal
F-78470 Saint-Remy-les-Chevreuse
History/Public Affairs Museum - 1952
Coll: history of Port-Royal and
Jansenism; in the house of 'Petites
Ecoles' where Racine studied

Maisons-Laffitte

04230
Musée du Château
F-78600 Maisons-Laffitte
Fine Arts Museum - 1642
Coll: paintings; sculptures; tapestries;
furniture

Marcigny

04231
Musée de la Tour du Moulin
7 rue de la Tour, F-71110 Marcigny
General Museum - 1913
Coll: folklore; faiences and ceramics;
statues; woodwork; tower from the
15th century - library

Marseille

04232
Musée Borély
Château Borély, av Clot-Bey, F-13008
Marseille
Archeology Museum - 1863
Coll: Egyptian finds, including a
sacrificial altar; Mediterranean
antiquities; terra-cotta statues; Greek
vases; glass; bronzes; Celtic-Ligurian
finds; sarcophagi; 17th-18th century
French drawings - library

04233
Musée Cantini
19 rue Grignan, F-13006 Marseille
Fine Arts Museum - 1936
Coll: 17th century palace; 17th-18th
century Provençal porcelain;
decorative arts; contemporary painting
and sculpture - library; museobus

04234
Musée d'Archéologie
Château Borély, av Clot-Bey, F-13008
Marseille
Archeology Museum - 1863
Clot-Bey's collection of Egyptian
statuary, stelae, sarcophagi, sacrificial
altars, mummies, and amulets;
ceramics from Etruscan, Greek, and
Gallo-Roman times; stained glass;
bronze statuettes; antiquity collection
from Greek to medieval times;
reconstructed pre-Roman sanctuary
(3rd c. B.C.)

04235
Musée de la Marine de Marseille
Palais de la Bourse, B.P. 826 bis,
F-13222 Marseille Cedex 1
History/Public Affairs Museum - 1933
Coll: maritime history with emphasis
on the development of the harbor of
Marseille from antiquity to the present;
etchings, paintings, drawings on naval
themes; ship models; maps;
photographs; history of Marseille, the
Provence, and former French colonies
- library

04236
Musée des Arts et Traditions Populaires du Terroir Marseillais
Château-Gombert, 5 Pl des Héros,
F-13013 Marseille
Decorative Arts Museum - 1928
Coll: costumes; pewter; ceramics;
furniture; pictures; manger figures

04237
Musée des Beaux-Arts
Palais Longchamp, pl Bernex, F-13004
Marseille
Fine Arts Museum - 1801
Coll: sculpture and castings, paintings,
drawings, watercolors by Puget;
17th-20th century Provence paintings;
Daumier's busts and lithographs;
European painting; French painting
from 15th-20th century; African art

04238
Musée des Docks Romains
28 Pl Vivaux, F-13002 Marseille
History/Public Affairs Museum - 1963
Coll: Hellenistic theater; Roman
warehouse; history of the Roman port
at Marseille; documentation on
commerce during antiquity; models
and charts; marine archeology finds

04239
Musée d'Histoire Naturelle
Palais Longchamp, F-13001 Marseille
Natural History Museum - 1869
Coll: natural history of the Provence;
paleontology; botany; zoology;
mineralogy; anthropology;
ethnography; prehistory; 19th century
frescoes

04240
Musée du Vieux-Marseille
Maison Diamantée, rue de la Prison,
F-13002 Marseille
General Museum - 1911
Coll: religious figurines and manger
scenes; playing cards; traditional
costumes from Marseille; painting,
drawings, engravings; maps; Provence
furniture; household objects -
audiovisual room

04241
Musée Grobet-Labadié
140 bd Longchamp, F-13001 Marseille
Fine Arts Museum - 1926
Coll: early Flemish, German, and Italian
paintings; French paintings and
drawings; sculpture from the medieval
times to the Renaissance; 16th-18th
century tapestries; Oriental rugs;
decorative arts; musical instruments

Martigues

04242
Musée de Martigues
bd du 14 Juillet, F-13500 Martigues
General Museum
Coll: local archeology; ethnology; 19th
century Provençal painting;
contemporary art

04243
Musée du Vieux Martigues
rue Colonel Denfert, F-13500
Martigues
General Museum
Coll: Gallo-Roman finds; history of the
Order of Penitents; shipping and
fishing; memorabilia of the founder of
the Order of the Maltese Knights;
paintings and drawings

Maubeuge

04244
Musée Henri Boez
9 rue du Chapitre, Pl Verte, F-59600
Maubeuge
General Museum
Coll: Gallo-Roman finds; local history;
folklore; 17th-19th century paintings;
porcelain

Meaux

04245
Musée Bossuet Musée Municipal
Ancien Palais Episcopal, 5 Pl C. de
Gaulle, F-77100 Meaux
General Museum - 1900
Coll: prehistory and protohistory;
medieval sculpture; decorative arts
and furniture (17th-19th centuries);
16th-19th century French painting;
18th-19th sculpture; local historical
items

Mehun-sur-Yèvre

04246
Musée du Château Charles VII
Place du Général Leclerc, F-18500
Mehun-sur-Yèvre
General Museum
Antiquities; porcelain

Melun

04247
Musée de Melun
Maison de la Vicomté, 5 rue du Franc-
Murier, F-77000 Melun
General Museum
Coll: prehistoric and Gallo-Roman
finds; medieval sculpture; decorative
arts; paintings; furnishings; works by
sculptor Henri Chapu; faience from
Rubelles

Mende

04248
Musée de la Société des Lettres, Sciences et Arts de la Lozère
av du Musée, F-48000 Mende
General Museum
Coll: prehistoric, Gallo-Roman, and
Gothic finds; ceramics; folklore;
numismatics; mineralogy; fossils

Menton

04249
Musée du Palais Carnolès
3 av de la Madone, F-06500 Menton
Fine Arts Museum - 1977
Coll: 13th-18th century European
paintings and drawings; contemporary
paintings

04250
Musée Jean Cocteau
Quai Napoléon III, F-06500 Menton
Fine Arts Museum
Coll: Jean Cocteau's drawings;
tapestries; ceramics; works of Picasso

04251
Musée Municipal
rue Lorédan-Larchey, F-06500 Menton
General Museum - 1907
Coll: prehistoric excavation finds;
fossils; bones; regional history;
folklore

Metz

04252
Musée Central
2 rue du Haut-Poirier, F-57000 Metz
General Museum
Coll: prehistory; Gallo-Roman objects;
Merovingian and Carolingian
sculpture; architectural fragments;
medieval art; French painting;
15th-16th century German painting;
Flemish, Dutch, and local paintings

Meudon

04253
Musée de l'Air et de l'Espace
8 rue des Vertugadins, F-92190
Meudon, 91 bd Péreire, F-75017 Paris
Open Air Museum - 1919
Coll: history and technology of
aviation from Montgolfière to the
present; models; 80 original planes;
motors; balloons - library; audiovisual
room

04254
Musée de Meudon
11 rue des Pierres, F-92190 Meudon
General Museum - 1941
Coll: prehistoric and Gallo-Roman
finds; paintings and engravings;
documents on local history and
famous personalities; technology; art
collection of artists who worked here;
literary collection on Ronsard,
Rabelais, Rousseau, etc.

04255
Musée Rodin
Villa des Brillants, av Auguste-Rodin,
F-92190 Meudon
Historic Site
Former dwelling of A. Rodin
(1840-1917), housing sketches,
castings, and original private collection
of the sculptor

Mézières-en-Brenne

04256
Château d'Azay-le-Ferron
F-36290 Mézières-en-Brenne
General Museum - 1952
Coll: 15th-19th century architecture;
regional painting; furnishings; tapestry;
enamel; porcelain

Mialet

04257
Musée du Désert
Mialet, Le Mas-Soubeyran, F-30140
Anduze
Religious Art Museum
Coll: documents, memorials, historical
objects relating to the period of the
'Désert' (1685-1787), a time of
persecution of Protestant churches in
France; collection of bibles - library

Millau

04258
Musée Municipal de Millau
Hôtel de Pegayrolles, Pl Foch, F-12100
Millau
Archeology Museum - 1904
Coll: prehistoric finds; Gallo-Roman
pottery from la Graufesenque; regional
paleontology

Milly-la-Forêt

04259
Chapelle Saint-Blaise-des-Simples
F-91490 Milly-la-Forêt
Historic Site
Coll: chapel decorated with drawings
by Cocteau; busts of Cocteau; the
poet's grave

Minerve

04260
Musée de Préhistoire
F-34210 Olonzac
Archeology Museum
Prehistorical items

Mirande

04261
Musée des Beaux-Arts
bd Alsace-Lorraine, F-32000 Mirande
Fine Arts Museum - 1832
Coll: 18th-19th century painting;
faience; ceramics; Gallo-Roman items

04262
Musée d'Histoire Locale
Mairie, F-32300 Mirande
General Museum
Items of local historical interest

Monsireigne

04263
**Musée de la France Protestante de
l'Ouest**
Le Bois-Tiffrais, F-85110 Monsireigne
Religious Art Museum
Coll: history of French Protestantism;
etchings, pictures, manuscripts, books;
memorabilia

Mont-de-Marsan

04264
Musée Despiau-Wlerick
6 Pl Pujolin, F-40000 Mont-de-Marsan
Fine Arts Museum - 19th century
Coll: sculpture; glass; faience

04265
Musée Dubalen
6 Pl Pujolin, F-40000 Mont-de-Marsan
General Museum - 19th century
Coll: exhibits on prehistory; natural
science; local history; ethnography

Mont-Saint-Aignan

04266
Musée de l'Education
39 rue Lacroix-Vaubois, F-76130
Mont-Saint-Aignan
History/Public Affairs Museum - 1879
Coll: school furniture; exercise books;
toys; drawings and prints of children;
photographs; autographs - library

Mont-Saint-Michel

04267
Musée Historique
F-50116 Mont-Saint-Michel
General Museum
Copper painting (15th-17th c.);
bas-reliefs; armaments; wax museum;
periscope collection

Montaigu

04268
Musée du Nord de la Vendée
Château, F-85600 Montaigu
General Museum
Coll: prehistory; Gallo-Roman,
medieval finds; painting; sculpture;
folklore

Montargis

04269
Musée Girodet
Hôtel de Ville, F-45200 Montargis
General Museum
Coll: classical art; 13th-19th century
sculpture; 16th-19th century painting;
decorative arts; folklore

Montauban

04270
**Musée d'Histoire Naturelle Victor-
Brun**
Pl Antoine-Bourdelle, F-82000
Montauban
Natural History Museum - 1854
Coll: 3,000 species of birds;
paleontology; fossils; prehistorical
skeletons and petrified items;
meteorites; mineralogy - library

04271
Musée Ingres
Palais des Evêques, 19 rue de l'Hôtel
de Ville, F-82000 Montauban
Fine Arts Museum - 1867
Coll: fine arts; archeology; ceramics;
folk art; 4,000 drawings by J.A.D.
Ingres

Montbéliard

04272
Musée du Château
Château, F-25200 Montbéliard
General Museum
Coll: natural history; archeology;
Gallo-Roman finds; fine arts; history;
science

Montbrison

04273
Musée d'Allard
bd de la Préfecture, F-42600
Montbrison
General Museum
Coll: dolls; numismatics; mineralogy;
ornithology

04274
Musée 'La Diana'
rue Florimond-Robertet, F-42600
Montbrison
Archeology Museum
Local archeology

Montfort-l'Amaury

04275
Musée Maurice Ravel
5 rue Maurice-Ravel, F-78490
Montfort-l'Amaury
Historic Site
Coll: memorabilia of the composer
Maurice Ravel; original family
furnishings

Montluçon

04276
Musée Municipal du Vieux Château
Vieux Château, F-03109 Montluçon
General Museum
Coll: local history; natural history;
folklore; history and manufacture of
string instruments; 17th-19th century
French porcelain

Montmorency

04277
Musée Jean-Jacques Rousseau
4 rue du Mont Louis, F-95160
Montmorency
History/Public Affairs Museum - 1951
Coll: etchings and manuscripts of the
writer Jean-Jacques Rousseau,
housed in his former home
(1712-1778); 10th-20th century
memorabilia of the family de
Montmorency; documents

Montpellier

04278
Musée Atger
2 rue de l'Ecole-de-Médecine, F-34000
Montpellier
Fine Arts Museum
Coll: 16th-18th century French, Italian,
Flemish drawings

04279
Musée des Moulages
Université Paul Valéry, Route de
Mende, F-34000 Montpellier
Fine Arts Museum - 1890
Coll: classical antiquities; sculpture;
medieval art

04280
Musée Fabre
13 rue Montpelliéret, F-34000
Montpellier
Fine Arts Museum - 1825
Coll: Italian, Spanish, Flemish, Dutch,
English, and French paintings;
sculpture; drawings

Montségur

04281
Musée Municipal
Hôtel de Ville, F-09300 Belesta
General Museum

Morosaglia

04282
Musée Départemental Pascal Paoli
F-20261 Morosaglia
Historic Site
Coll: memorial to the Corsican hero
Pascal Paoli in the house of his birth

Moulins

04283
Musée de Folklore et des Moulins
6 Pl de l'Ancien Palais, F-03000
Moulins
General Museum - 1934
Coll: traditional costumes; 150 flat
irons; dolls from all over the world;
objects and tools dealing with mills;
reconstructed interior of peasant
home; engravings and photographs -
library

04284
Musée Départemental et Municipal
Pl du Colonel-Laussédat, F-03000
Moulins
Fine Arts Museum
Coll: 16th century pavillon; ancient
pottery; bronzes; statuettes; early
German painting and 19th century
French painting; sculpture; tapestries;
decorative arts; porcelain; armaments

Moustiers-Sainte-Marie

04285
Musée de la Faïence
F-04360 Moustiers-Sainte-Marie
Decorative Arts Museum
Coll: local porcelain; exhibits on
porcelain production

04286
Musée Municipal
F-04360 Moustiers-Sainte-Marie
General Museum

Mulhouse

04287
Musée des Beaux-Arts
4 rue des Archives, F-68100 Mulhouse
Fine Arts Museum
Coll: paintings; drawings; collection of
lithographs

04288
Musée du Chemin de Fer
2 rue Alfred de Glehn, F-68100
Mulhouse
Science/Tech Museum
Coll: history of train transportation and
technology; models; photographs

04289
Musée du Sapeur-Pompier
2 rue Alfred de Glehn, F-68100
Mulhouse
History/Public Affairs Museum - 1978
Coll: exhibits on fire fighting;
fire-fighting technology; uniforms and
helmets; documents; fire engines

04290
Musée Historique
Hôtel de Ville, 4 rue des Archives,
F-68100 Mulhouse
General Museum
Coll: regional archeological finds;
items from the Stone Age, Hallstatt
period, and Roman times; costumes;
history of the Middle Ages - library

Nancy

04291
Eglise des Cordeliers
Grande rue, F-54000 Nancy
Religious Art Museum
Sculptures; grave monuments; grave
of Philippa de Gueldre by Ligier
Richier

04292
Musée de l'Ecole de Nancy
36-38 rue du Sergent Blandan, F-54000
Nancy
Decorative Arts Museum - 1941
Coll: glass designed by Gallé;
ceramics; wall hangings; Art Nouveau
posters; paintings; furniture

04293
Musée des Beaux-Arts
3 Pl Stanislas, F-54000 Nancy
Fine Arts Museum - 1803
Coll: European paintings including
14th-20th century Italian painting;
14th-18th century Flemish painting;
16th-17th century Dutch, German,
Alsatian painting; 16th-20th century
French painting; prints and drawings;
complete etchings and engravings of
Jacques Callot; collection of satirical
drawings of Grandville

04294
Musée Historique Lorrain
Grande rue, F-54000 Nancy
General Museum - 1849
Coll: early history; Gallo-Roman,
Merovingian objects; medieval history;
Thirty Years' War; 17th century
Lorraine masters; 18th-19th century
iron; glass; furnishings; ceramics;
Lorraine folk art; fortress fragments;
religious sculpture; works by Georges
de la Tour and Jacques Callot

Nantes

04295
**Musée des Arts Décoratifs et d'Art
Populaire**
Château des Ducs de Bretagne,
F-44000 Nantes
General Museum
Coll: folklore; furnishings; sculpture

04296
Musée des Beaux-Arts
10 rue Georges Clemenceau, F-44000
Nantes
Fine Arts Museum - 1830
Coll: Italian, Flemish, Dutch, French,
Impressionist, modern paintings;
sculpture; 19th-20th century drawings;
etchings - library

04297
Musée d'Histoire Naturelle
12 rue Voltaire, F-44000 Nantes
Natural History Museum
Coll: prehistory; zoology; mineralogy;
paleontology; botany - library

04298
Musée Dobrée
Place Jean V, F-44000 Nantes
General Museum
Coll: prehistory; Gallo-Roman,
Merovingian, Egyptian archeology;
Greek, Etruscan ceramics;
ethnography; medieval art; ivory;
enamels; book illumination; 16th-17th
century armaments; engravings;
militaria; Restoration history

Narbonne

04299
Horreum
rue Rouget de Lisle, F-11100
Narbonne
Archeology Museum - 1976
Stones from destroyed Roman
monuments; ancient ruins of Roman
warehouse

04300
**Musée d'Archéologie et de
Préhistoire**
Palais des Archevêques, F-11100
Narbonne
Archeology Museum - 1833
Coll: prehistoric and protohistoric
artifacts; Gallo-Roman artifacts and
domestic and religious utensils;
Ancient Chapel of Magdalena (1273)
with 14th century frescoes

04301
Musée d'Art et d'Histoire
Palais des Archevêques, F-11100
Narbonne
Fine Arts Museum - 1833
Coll: ceramics; European paintings;
busts; 17th century palace and
furnishings

04302
Musée des Beaux-Arts
Palais des Archevêques, F-11100
Narbonne
Fine Arts Museum
Coll: ceramics; paintings; busts;
prehistoric archeology; sepulchral
relics; Greek vases

04303
Musée Lapidaire Notre Dame de
Lamourguié
Pl Lamourguié, F-11100 Narbonne
Archeology Museum - 1850
1,300 stone remains of Roman
monuments

Neuf-Brisach

04304
Musé Vauban
F-68600 Neuf-Brisach
General Museum
Coll: local historical items; military
history; historical drawings of the local
fortress; historical models

Nevers

04305
Musée de la Nièvre
Hôtel de Vertpré, 21 rue Saint-Martin,
F-58000 Nevers
General Museum
Coll: 16th-18th century local faience

Nice

04306
Musée d'Archéologie
164 av de Arènes, F-06000 Nice
Archeology Museum - 1963
Coll: ceramics, glass, tools, sculpture,
inscriptions, jewelry from 1st-3rd
century A.D. Roman town Cemenelum;
5th-2nd century B.C. Greek ceramics;
archeological site with thermal baths

04307
Musée de Terra Amata
25 bd Carnot, F-06300 Nice
Anthropology Museum - 1976
Coll: prehistoric finds; exhibits on the
environment and way of life of the
archanthropine - library

04308
Musée des Beaux-Arts Jules Chéret
33 av des Baumettes, F-06000 Nice
Fine Arts Museum - 1928
Coll: 19th century villa; 17th-19th
European schools of painting; masters
of the French school of 19th century
painting; sculptures; collection by R.
Dufy of paintings, aquarelles, drawings,
engravings, ceramics, and tapestry;
ceramics by Picasso - library;
educational center

04309
Musée des Ponchettes
77 quai des Etats-Unis, F-06300 Nice
Fine Arts Museum

04310
Musée du Prieure du Vieux-Logis
59 av Saint-Barthélémy, F-06100 Nice
Fine Arts Museum
Coll: decorative arts; 15th-16th century
interiors; sculpture; objects of wood,
stone, and iron; window art

04311
Musée Masséna
65 rue de France, F-06000 Nice
General Museum - 1921
Coll: Empire decoration and
furnishings; local and regional history
from the 7th-19th century; Italian,
Spanish, Flemish, and French painting;
folklore; Provencal and Mediterranean
earthenware; arms and armor; popular
jewelry - library

04312
Musée Matisse
164 av des Arènes, F-06000 Nice
Fine Arts Museum - 1963
Coll: paintings, drawings, etchings,
sculpture, sketches, and gouaches by
the artist Henri Matisse (1869-1954);
furnishings and memorabilia of the
painter

04313
**Musée National Message Biblique
Marc Chagall**
av du Docteur Ménard, F-06000 Nice
Fine Arts Museum - 1973
Coll: 'Message Biblique' by Marc
Chagall, a cyclus of paintings of
scenes from the Bible; sketches;
gouaches; copper plates; mosaics;
tapestry; stained glass windows;
sculptures - library

04314
Musée Naval de Nice
Tour Bellanda, Parc du Château,
F-06000 Nice
History/Public Affairs Museum
Coll: ship models; weapons;
navigation; instruments; sea paintings;
bronze canons; historical documents

04315
Muséum d'Histoire Naturelle
60 bis bd Risso, F-06300 Nice
Natural History Museum - 1823
Exhibits on natural science

04316
Palais Lascaris
15 rue Droite, F-06300 Nice
Decorative Arts Museum
17th and 18th cent. frescoes and
furniture

Nîmes

04317
Musée Archéologique
bd Amiral Courbet, F-30000 Nîmes
Archeology Museum - 1823
Protohistoric and Gallic and Roman
archeology

04318
Musée d'Art et d'Histoire
rue de la Cathédrale, F-30000 Nîmes
Fine Arts Museum - 1823
European painting and sculpture (15th
c. to present)

04319
Musée du Vieux Nimes
Pl de la Cathédrale, F-30000 Nîmes
General Museum - 1921
Local history, folklore and popular
culture

Nissan-lez-Ensérune

04320
Tresor de l'Eglise
F-34440 Nissan-lez-Ensérune
Religious Art Museum
Coll: paintings; sculpture;
archeological finds; religious objects;
robes

Nogent-le-Rotrou

04321
Musée du Château Saint-Jean
F-28400 Nogent-le-Rotrou
General Museum - 1959
Coll: prehistory; paintings; costumes;
ceramics; sculpture

Nogent-sur-Marne

04322
Musée du Vieux Nogent
150 Grande Rue, F-94130 Nogent-
sur-Marne
General Museum - 1960
Coll: engravings by Watteau; local
history; everyday life

Nogent-sur-Seine

04323
Musée d'Art et d'Archéologie
rue Alfred Boucher, F-10400 Nogent-
sur-Seine
Fine Arts Museum - 1902
Coll: castings of sculptures by Paul
Dubois and Alfred Boucher; regional
archeology

Nohant-Vic

04324
Maison de George Sand
La Châtre, F-36100 Nohant-Vic
Historic Site - 1763
Memorabilia of George Sand and her
circle - library

Nuits-Saint-Georges

04325
Musée Municipal
Maison Rodier, 11 rue Camille Rodier,
F-21700 Nuits-Saint-Georges
Archeology Museum
Coll: Gallo-Roman and Merovingian
finds

Oltingue

04326
Musée Paysan d'Oltingue Musée
Historique de Mulhouse
F-68450 Oltingue
General Museum
Coll: items illustrating the life of the
peasantry of southern Alsatia through
the ages

Orange

04327
Musée Municipal d'Orange
Pl des Frères-Mounet, F-84100
Orange
General Museum - 1936
Coll: three Roman land registers;
remains of a Roman theater; sculpture
fragments; Roman inscriptions; local
historical items; local production of
linen; furnishings - children's atelier

Orbec-en-Auge

04328
Musée Municipal d'Orbec
Hôtel de Ville de le Vieux Manoir, rue
Grande, F-14290 Orbec-en-Auge
General Museum - 1873
Coll: local history; Renaissance art; in
Renaissance building

Orléans

04329
Musée des Beaux-Arts
1 Pl de la République, F-45000 Orléans
Fine Arts Museum - 1823
Coll: sculpture; European painting;
17th-20th century drawings; etchings;
pastels

04330
Musée des Beaux-Arts
Hôtel des Créneaux, 1 Pl de la
République, F-45000 Orleans
Fine Arts Museum - 1823
Coll: French paintings (15th-20th
centuries); French sculpture;
non-French art (16th-18th centuries) -
library

04331
**Musée des Sciences Naturelles
d'Orleans**
2 rue Marcel Proust, F-45000 Orleans
Natural History Museum - 1966
Collection of preserved ancient plants;
mammals from the Miocene period;
dioramas of mammals; preditors and
their prey - library

04332
Musée Historique
Hôtel Cabu, F-45000 Orléans
History/Public Affairs Museum - 1855
Coll: Gallo-Roman archeological finds;
bronze Gallic treasure; decorative
arts; medieval objects

04333
**Musée Historique et Archéologique
de l'Orleanais**
Sq Abbé-Desnoyers, rue
Ste.-Catherine, F-45000 Orléans
General Museum - 1855
Coll: 16th century building; Gallo-
Roman finds; bronze Gallic treasure
from Neuvy-en-Sullias; decorative
arts; medieval objects

Ornans

04334
**Musée-Maison Natale Gustave
Courbet à Ornans**
2 rue de la Froidiere, F-25290 Ornans
Historic Site - 1947
Coll: paintings and memorabilia of
Gustave Courbet - library

Paray-le-Monial

04335
Musée d'Art Sacrè 'Le Hieron'
Route de Charolles, F-71600 Paray-
le-Monial
Religious Art Museum - 1873
Coll: imprints of hosts from antiquity to
the 18th century; 12th century Roman
tympanum; goldsmith work; paintings

Paris

04336
Bibliothèque Nationale Cabinet des
Medailles
58 rue de Richelieu, F-75002 Paris
Fine Arts Museum
Coll: coins, medals, valuable art
objects, wall paintings

04337
CEDIAS Musée Social
5 rue Las-Cases, F-75007 Paris
History/Public Affairs Museum
Coll: social history - library

04338
Centre de Création Industrielle
Centre National d'Art de de Culture
Georges-Pompidou
F-75004 Paris
Decorative Arts Museum
Coll: all aspects of the design and
evolution of modern life style;
reference material

04339
Maison de Balzac
47 rue Raynouard, F-75016 Paris
Historic Site - 1908
Coll: house where Balzac lived from
1840 to 1847; portraits; caricatures;
engravings and documents dealing
with Balzac, his work, his
contemporaries, and his times -
library; audiovisual room

04340
Musée Adam Mickiewicz Polish
Library of Paris
6 quai d'Orleans, F-75004 Paris
History/Public Affairs Museum
Coll: exhibits on the life and work of
the Polish poet Adam Mickiewicz
(1798-1855); portraits, sculptures,
manuscripts, and documents on his
circle

04341
Musée Biblique Institut Catholique
21 rue d'Assas, F-75270 Paris Cédex
06
Religious Art Museum
Collection of Bibles through the ages

04342
Musée Bourdelle
16 rue Antoine-Bourdelle, F-75015
Paris
Fine Arts Museum - 1949
Coll: sculptures, paintings, drawings by
Emile-Antoine Bourdelle (1861-1929);
the artist's studio - library

04343
Musée Carnavalet
Hôtel Carnavalet, 23 rue de Sévigné,
F-75003 Paris
General Museum - 1866
Coll: history of Paris in paintings,
sculptures, drawings, sign posts, etc.;
period rooms from Parisian hotels;
literary recollections of Madame de
Sévigné

04344
Musée Cernuschi
7 av Velasquez, F-75008 Paris
Fine Arts Museum - 1896
Ancient and contemporary Chinese art

04345
Musée Clemenceau
8 rue Franklin, F-75016 Paris
Historic Site
Coll: documents on the life and work
of Georges Clemenceau; statesman's
former home

04346
Musée Cognacq-Jay
25 bd des Capucines, F-75002 Paris
Fine Arts Museum - 1929
Coll: 18th century art; paintings;
pastels; Meissen porcelain; snuff
boxes; miniatures; furniture

04347
Musée d'Art et d'Essai
Palais de Tokyo, 13 av du Président
Wilson, F-75116 Paris
Fine Arts Museum - 1978
Coll: Post-Impressionist paintings; art
exhibitions from antiquity to the
present

04348
**Musée d'Art Moderne de la Ville de
Paris**
11 av du Président Wilson, F-75116
Paris 16e
Fine Arts Museum - 1961
Div: 20th century art; animation and
research; children's section - library

04349
**Musée de la Legion d'Honneur et
des Ordres de Chevalerie**
2 rue de Bellechasse, F-75007 Paris
History/Public Affairs Museum - 1925
Coll: history of orders of all countries
since the Middle Ages; uniforms;
medals; pictures; films; memorabilia of
Napoleon I and commanders in chief
of both world wars - library;
documentation center

04350
Musée de la Marine
Palais de Chaillot, Pl du Trocadéro,
F-75116 Paris
History/Public Affairs Museum - 1827
Coll: 17th-19th century ship models;
paintings; weapons; maritime objects
from the 16th century to the present -
library

04351
Musée de la Mode et du Costume
Palais Galliera, 10 av Pierre 1er-de-
Serbie, F-75116 Paris
Decorative Arts Museum
Coll: French fashion from 1735 to the
present

04352
Musée de la Poste Maison de la
Poste et de la Philatelie
34 bd de Vaugirard, F-75731 Paris
Cédex 15
History/Public Affairs Museum - 1946
Coll: history of the post; stamps -
library

04353
Musée de la Préfecture de Police
1 bis rue des Carmes, F-75005 Paris
History/Public Affairs Museum
Coll: history of Paris police from the
16th century to the present - library

04354
Musée de l'Affiche
18 rue de Paradis, F-75010 Paris
Decorative Arts Museum - 1978
Coll: the history of the poster
throughout the world; over 60,000
posters

04355
Musée de l'Armée
Hôtel des Invalides, F-75007 Paris
History/Public Affairs Museum - 1905
Coll: artillery, armor, uniforms,
banners; history of the French Army
from its origin to present times;
photographs; prints - library

04356
**Musée de l'Ecole Nationale
Supérieure des Beaux-Arts**
17 Quai Malaquais, F-75272 Paris
Cedex 06
Fine Arts Museum - 1648
Coll: architectural drawings; drawings
by the Old Masters including Raffael
and Michelangelo; miniatures;
manuscripts - library

04357
Musée de l'Histoire de France
60 rue des Francs-Bourgeois, F-75141
Paris Cédex 03
History/Public Affairs Museum - 1867
Coll: original documents of French
history from Merovingian times to
1815; former royal chambers

04358
Musée de l'Homme
Palais de Chaillot, F-75016 Paris
Anthropology Museum
Coll: ethnography; anthropology;
prehistory - library

04359
Musée de l'Observatoire
61 av de l'Observatoire, F-75014 Paris
Science/Tech Museum - 1667
Coll: 16th-20th century scientific and
astronomical instruments; statues;
pictures of astronomers

04360
**Musée de Mineralogie de l'Ecole des
Mines de Paris**
60 bd Saint-Germain, F-75272 Paris
Cédex 06
Natural History Museum - 1794
Coll: minerals; petrography

04361
Musée de Montmartre
17 rue Saint-Vincent, F-75018 Paris
History/Public Affairs Museum
Coll: paintings; graphics; posters; 18th
century porcelains; a refurnished old
'bistro'; history of Montmartre district

04362
Musée d'Ennery
59 av Foch, F-75116 Paris
Fine Arts Museum - 1903
Coll: Chinese and Japanese art;
ceramics; furnishings; Namban chests;
wood and ivory carvings; enamel;
inlays - library

04363
**Musée des Arts Africains et
Océaniens**
293 av Daumesnil, F-75012 Paris
Fine Arts Museum - 1960
Coll: North African, African and
Oceanian art - library; tropical
aquarium

04364
Musée des Arts Decoratifs
Pavillon de Marsan, 107 rue de Rivoli,
F-75001 Paris
Decorative Arts Museum - 1863
Coll: medieval to modern decorative
arts; Oriental art; drawings; tapestries;
17th-20th century furniture; porcelain;
enamels; documents on textiles and
wallpapers - library

04365
Musée des Deux Guerres Mondiales
Bibliothèque de Documentation
Internationale Contemporaine
Hôtel National des Invalides, F-75007
Paris
History/Public Affairs Museum - 1914
Coll: 400,000 documents, paintings,
engravings, posters, cartoons dealing
with the two World Wars

04366
Musée des Plans-Reliefs
Hôtel des Invalides, 6 bd des Invalides,
F-75007 Paris
History/Public Affairs Museum - 1668
Coll: models of 63 fortified towns in
France and 23 in other countries
constructed 1668-1670; drafts of plans
constructed in the 19th century; 18th
century manuscripts of plans

04367
**Musée des Thermes et de l'Hotel de
Cluny**
6 Pl Paul-Painlevé, F-75005 Paris
Fine Arts Museum - 1844
Coll: Gallo-Roman and medieval art;
chapel in the Flamboyant style;
tapestries; art objects; sculpture;
enamel; religious art; altar from Basel;
ancient palace with 15th-16th century
furniture

04368
Musée du Cinéma
Palais de Chaillot, L du Trocadéri,
F-75116008 Paris
History/Public Affairs Museum - 1972
Coll: history of film; equipment;
collection of pre-World War II German
films

04369
Musée du Jeu de Paume
Pl de la Concorde, F-75001 Paris 1
Fine Arts Museum - 1947
Coll: paintings of the Impressionists

04370
Musée du Louvre
Pl du Carrousel, F-95001 Paris
General Museum - 19th century
Coll: Oriental antiquities; Egyptian
antiquities; Greek, Roman, Etruscan
art; Christian and Moslem archeology;
medieval and Renaissance sculpture;
decorative arts; jewelry; tapestries;
17th-18th century French furnishings;
paintings of Italian, Dutch, French,
Flemish, German, Spanish schools;
90,000 drawings, pastels, and etchings

04371
Musée du Petit Palais
1 av Dutuit, F-75008 Paris
Fine Arts Museum - 1902
Coll: Antiques of the Middle Age and
Renaissance; 17th-20th century
sculptures, porcelains, furniture,
etchings, drawings and paintings

04372
**Musée du Théâtre National de
l'Opera**
1 Pl Charles-Garnier, F-75009 Paris
Performing Arts Museum
Coll: history of lyric theater, dance,
music; memorabilia of composers;
drawings; costumes; decorations

04373
Musée Eugene Delacroix
6 Pl Furstemberg, F-75006 Paris
Historic Site
Coll: life and work of the painter E.
Delacroix (1798-1863); exhibits
displayed in artist's former home and
studio

04374
Musée Guimet
6 Pl d'Iéna, F-75116 Paris
Fine Arts Museum - 1889
Coll: art of India, Pakistan, Afghanistan,
Lamas, Khmers, Thais, Laos, Burma,
Indonesia, China, Japan, Korea,
Sin-Kiang - library

04375
Musée Gustave Moreau
14 rue de la Rochefoucauld, F-75009
Paris
Fine Arts Museum
Coll: works by the artist G. Moreau;
paintings; sketches; drawings;
watercolors

04376
Musée Hebert
Hôtel de Montmorency, 85 rue du
Cherche-Midi, F-75006 Paris

04377
Musée Henner
43 av de Villiers, F-75017 Paris
Fine Arts Museum
Paintings by the artist J.-J. Henner

04378
Musée Jacquemart-Andre
158 bd Haussman, F-75008 Paris
Fine Arts Museum - 1913
Coll: French, Italian, Flemish, and
English painting; tapestries;
furnishings; art objects; Italian and
French sculptures

04379
Musée Marmottan
2 rue Louis Boilly, F-75016 Paris
Fine Arts Museum - 1932
Coll: Primitives; Renaissance, Empire,
and Impressionists; exhibit on Monet
and his friends

04380
Musée Monetaire
Hôtel de la Monnaie, 11 quai Conti,
F-75006 Paris
History/Public Affairs Museum - 1771
Coll: coins and medals from medieval
to modern times

04381
Musée National Auguste Rodin
77 rue de Varenne, F-75007 Paris
Fine Arts Museum - 1916
Coll: the works of Rodin including
sculptures, drawings, paintings,
engravings, photographs; his personal
collection of art from antiquity, the
Middle Ages, the 19th century, and the
Orient

04382
Musée National d'Art Moderne
Centre National d'Art et de Culture
Georges-Pompidou
F-75004 Paris
Fine Arts Museum
Coll: 20th century paintings,
sculptures, prints and drawings,
photographs and art films; reference
material

04383
**Musée National des Arts et
Traditions Populaires**
6 route du Mahatma Gandhi, F-75116
Paris
Anthropology Museum - 1937
Coll: anthropology; ethnology;
ethnography; customs; folk art;
costumes - library; research
laboratory

04384
**Musée National des Monuments
Français**
Palais de Chaillot, aile de Paris, Pl du
Trocadéro, F-75116 Paris
Fine Arts Museum - 1882
Coll: castings of Romanesque, Gothic,
Renaissance, and Classic monuments;
reproductions of nearly all French
frescoes; art from the Carolingian-
Gothic periods

04385
Musée National des Techniques
292 rue Saint-Martin, B.P. 375, F-75141
Paris Cédex 03
Science/Tech Museum - 1794
Coll: old planes; first helicopter;
automobiles since 1769; bicycles; train
models; history of photography, film,
radio, and television; radar; astronomy;
industrial life

04386
Musée National d'Histoire Naturelle
57 rue Cuvier, F-75231 Paris Cedex 05
Natural History Museum - 1635
Coll: botany; zoology; paleontology;
mineralogy - library

04387
Musée Nissim de Camondo
63 rue de Monceau, F-75008 Paris
Decorative Arts Museum - 1935
Coll: Louis XVI furniture; tapestry;
wallpaper; paintings; drawings;
engravings; goldsmith work; ceramics

04388
Musée Pasteur Institut Pasteur
25 rue du Dr Roux, F-75724 Paris
Cedex 15
History/Public Affairs Museum
Coll: memorabilia, works of art, original
publications, furniture ofthe scientist
Louis Pasteur housed in his former
apartment; scientific instruments
including microscopes, sterilizers,
cultures illustrating Pasteur's scientific
research - library; scientific archives;
phototheque

04389
Musée Victor Hugo de Villequier
6 Pl des Vosges, F-75004 Paris
Historic Site - 1903
Coll: portraits and memorabilia of
Victor Hugo and his family; drawings
by Hugo; first editions of his works
and manuscripts

04390
Orangerie des Tuileries
Pl de la Concorde, F-75001 Paris
Fine Arts Museum
Coll: paintings by Claude Monet;
collection of Walter Guillaume

04391
Palais de la Découverte
Grand Palais, av Franklin-D.-Roosevelt,
B.P. 321, F-75008 Paris
Science/Tech Museum
Coll: demonstrations of experiments in
all scientific fields; photos; models -
planetarium; library; cinema room

Pau

04392
Musée Bernadotte
8 rue Tran, F-64000 Pau
Historic Site - 1952
Coll: memorabilia of Jean-Baptiste
Bernadotte, Marshal under Napoleon;
house where he was born

04393
Musée des Beaux-Arts
rue Mathieu-Lalanne, F-64000 Pau
Fine Arts Museum - 1864
Coll: Spanish, Italian, Flemish, Dutch,
English, and French painting;
sculpture; contemporary art;
numismatics

04394
Musée National du Château de Pau
2 rue du Château, F-64000 Pau
History/Public Affairs Museum
Coll: historical building, once seat of
the Kings of Navarre (15-16th
centuries); portraits and documents
relating to the 16th century; cradle of
King Henry IV who was born in castle;
16-17th century Flanders and Gobelin
tapestries - library

Périgueux

04395
Musée du Perigord
22 Cours Tourny, F-24000 Périgueux
General Museum - 1836
Coll: prehistory; Gallo-Roman and
medieval finds; local folk art and
traditions; ethnography; 17th-18th
century French, Italian, Flemish, Dutch
painting and art objects; natural
history; skeleton of 'man from
Chancelade'; painting on bones, wood,
horns

Perouges

04396
Musée du Vieux Perouges
Cité des Pérouges, Pl du Tilleul,
F-01800 Meximieux
General Museum
Coll: archeology; porcelain;
furnishings; armaments; local historical
artifacts

Perpignan

04397
Musée Hyacinthe Rigaud
16 rue de l'Ange, F-66000 Perpignan
General Museum
Coll: works by H. Rigaud; French,
Spanish, and Italian painting; 13th-18th
century porcelain; local archeological
finds - library

Pézenas

04398
Musée Vulliod Saint-Germain
3 rue A.-P.-Alliès, F-34120 Pézenas
Fine Arts Museum
Coll: 16th-19th century painting;
17th-18th century furnishings;
tapestries; memorabilia of J.-B. Molière
(1622-1673); folklore; porcelain;
customs

Pithiviers

04399
Musée des Transports
rue Carnot, F-45300 Pithiviers
Science/Tech Museum - 1966
Coll: steam locomotives; streetcars;
railcar; railway line; medals, watches,
and other objects relating to railways

04400
Musée Municipal
17 rue de la Couronne, F-45300
Pithiviers
Anthropology Museum
Coll: folk art and other objects of the
Oceanic Kanakas

Poissy

04401
Musée d'Histoire Locale
12 rue Saint Louis, F-78300 Poissy
General Museum - 1981
Coll: local historical items;
ethnography

04402
Musée du Jouet
2 enclos de l'Abbaye, F-78300 Poissy
History/Public Affairs Museum - 1976
Coll: toys and games from the
18th-early 20th century; dolls and
accessories

Poitiers

04403
Hypogée des Dunes
rue Pére-Delacroix, F-86000 Poitiers
Archeology Museum - 1974
Archeological finds from the 7th and
8th centuries

04404
Musée des Augustins
Hôtel Rupter de Chièvres, 9 rue Victor
Hugo, F-86000 Poitiers
Decorative Arts Museum - 1887
Industrial and decorative arts

04405
Musée Sainte-Croix
3 bis rue Jean Jaurès, F-86000 Poitiers
General Museum - 1974
Local history; fine arts

Pont Saint Esprit

04406
Musée Municipal
F-30130 Pont Saint Esprit
General Museum

Pont-l'Abbé

04407
Musée Bigouden
Château, F-29120 Pont-l'Abbé
General Museum
Coll: folklore

Pontarlier

04408
Musée du Château de Joux
La Cluse-et-Mijoux, F-25300 Pontarlier
General Museum
Coll: armaments; furnishings from the
First Empire, Restoration, and Second
Empire; in palace

04409
Musée Municipal
Hôtel de Ville, F-25300 Pontarlier
General Museum
Coll: local history; portraits

Pontoise

04410
Musée de Pontoise Tavet-Delacour
4 rue Lemercier, F-95300 Pontoise
Fine Arts Museum - 1892
Coll: sculpture; painting; 15th-20th
century drawings; mosaics; glass;
ancient and contemporary engravings;
documents; contemporary art; regional
history; religious sculpture - library

04411
Musée Pissarro Musée de Pontoise
17 rue du Château, F-95300 Pontoise
Fine Arts Museum - 1980
Coll: works and archives of the painter
Camille Pissarro; 19th century regional
artists

Port-Louis

04412
Musée Naval du Port-Louis
Citadelle du Port-Louis, F-56290
Port-Louis
History/Public Affairs Museum
Coll: history of the French fleet in the
Atlantic; maritime items; 16th century
citadel

Provins

04413
Musée de la Maison Romane
rue du Palais, F-77160 Provins
General Museum
Coll: prehistory; Gallo-Roman finds;
sculptures from medieval times to the
Renaissance; medieval pottery

Quimper

04414
Musée Départemental Breton
1 rue du Roi-Gradlon, F-29000
Quimper
General Museum
Coll: history; archeology; folklore;
Gallo-Roman finds; sculpture;
costumes; porcelain; tapestries

04415
Musée des Beaux-Arts
Hôtel de Ville, Pl Saint-Corentin,
F-29000 Quimper
Fine Arts Museum
Coll: paintings by masters of various
schools

Reims

04416
Musée Saint-Denis
8 rue Chanzy, F-51100 Reims
Fine Arts Museum - 1795
Coll: painting; tapestries; sculpture;
ceramics; 16th-20th century furniture

04417
Musée Saint-Remi de Reims
53 rue Simon, F-51100 Reims
Archeology Museum - 1978
Coll: prehistory; Gallic, Gallo-Roman,
and Merovingian periods; medieval
sculpture; 16th-19th century weapons;
tapestry; numismatics - library;
conference room

04418
Musée-Hôtel le Vergeur
36 Pl du Forum, F-51100 Reims
History/Public Affairs Museum - 1909
Coll: local history in portraits and
etchings; engravings by Albrecht
Dürer and Robert Nanteuil - library

Rennes

04419
Musée de Bretagne
20 quai Emile-Zola, F-35000 Rennes
General Museum - 1960
Coll: pre- and early history; Gallo-
Roman and medieval history; Breton
art; furnishings; jewelry; costumes

04420
**Musée des Beaux-Arts et
d'Archéologie**
20 quai Emile Zola, F-35100 Rennes
General Museum - 1799
Coll: 15th-20th century paintings and
drawings of all schools; sculptures;
engravings from ancient to modern
times; Egyptian, Greek, Etruscan, and
Roman archeology - library

Rethel

04421
Musée du Rethélois et du Porcien
Av J.B. Clément, F-08300 Rethel
General Museum - 1930
Coll: archeology; folklore; French
colonialism,including Indochina and the
Congo; religious art; military arts;
pottery; numismatics

Reulle-Vergy

04422
**Musée des Arts et Traditions
Populaires des Hautes-Côtes**
Pl de la Fontaine, F-21220 Gevrey
Chambertin
Anthropology Museum
Coll: regional folk art and folklore

Richelieu

04423
Musée Municipal
Hôtel de Ville, F-37120 Richelieu
History/Public Affairs Museum - 1961
Coll: 17th century objects; memorabilia
of Cardinal Richelieu (1585-1642);
tapestries; memorabilia of J.M. de
Heredia

Riom

04424
Musée Francisque Mandet
14 rue de l'Hotel-de-Ville, F-63200
Riom
Fine Arts Museum - 1866
Coll: 16th-18th century Flemish and
Dutch painting; 18th-19th century
French painting; art objects,
sculptures, and furniture from antiquity
to the 18th century

04425
**Musée Regional Folklorique
d'Auvergne**
10 bis rue Delille, F-63200 Riom
General Museum - 1969
Coll: 18th century palace; regional art;
customs and ethnography of the
Auvergne

Riquewihr

04426
Musée Archéologique et Historique
le Dolder, rue du General de Gaulle,
F-68340 Riquewihr
General Museum - 1902
Coll: Alsatian history; customs;
armaments; 13th century tower

04427
Tour des Voleurs
rue des Juifs, F-68340 Riquewihr
General Museum - 1902
Coll: medieval torture chamber with
pit, dungeons, guard rooms

Rochechouart

04428
**Musée Municipal Albert et Pierre
Masfrand**
Château, Pl du Château, F-87600
Rochechouart
General Museum
Coll: prehistory; Gallo-Roman finds;
ceramics; wall painting

Rochefort

04429
Musée des Beaux-Arts
63 rue de l'Arsenal, F-17300 Rochefort
Fine Arts Museum
Coll: Italian, Flemish, and French
painting; drawings by Rubens; Oriental
art; folk art from Oceania and New
Zealand

04430
Musée Naval de Rochefort
Hôtel de Cheusses, Pl de la
Galissonnière, F-17300 Rochefort
History/Public Affairs Museum
Coll: ship models from the times of
Louis XIV; figureheads; maritime
paintings and engravings; souvenirs of
local sailors

Rodez

04431
Musée des Beaux-Arts
Pl du Musée, F-12000 Rodez
Fine Arts Museum
Coll: 17th century Italian painting;
contemporary painting; sculpture

04432
Musée Fenaille
3 rue Saint-Just, F-12000 Rodez
Archeology Museum
Coll: prehistory; Gallo-Roman objects

Romans-sur-Isere

04433
**Musée de la Chaussure et
d'Ethnographie Regionale**
2 rue Sainte Marie, B.P. 12, F-26101
Romans-sur-Isere Cedex
General Museum
Coll: history; local customs; folklore;
4,000 years of shoemaking craft

Romorantin-Lanthenay

04434
Musée de Sologne
Hôtel de Ville, F-41200 Romorantin-
Lanthenay
Anthropology Museum
Regional folklore

Rouen

04435
**Musée Departemental des
Antiquites de la Seine-Maritime**
198 rue Beauvoisine, F-76000 Rouen
General Museum - 1831
Coll: Celtic, Gallo-Roman, Merovingian,
Viking, and medieval archeology;
Renaissance objects and art; Egyptian,
Oriental, Greek, and Etruscan art;
Italian and Moor ceramics; mosaic of
Lillebonne; tapestries

04436
**Musée des Beaux-Arts et de la
Ceramique**
26 bis rue Thiers, F-76000 Rouen
Fine Arts Museum - 1809
Coll: Dutch, Flemish, Spanish, and
French paintings from various periods;
sculpture; ceramics; local faience

04437
**Musée d'Histoire Naturelle,
Ethnographie et Prehistoire de
Rouen**
198 rue Beauvoisine, F-76000 Rouen
General Museum - 1828
Coll: ethnography; prehistory; natural
history

04438
Musée le Secq des Tournelles
F-76000 Rouen
Science/Tech Museum
Coll: wrought-iron objects; keys;
locks; tools

Rueil-Malmaison

04439
Château de Malmaison Musées
Nationaux des Châteaux de
Malmaison
av du Château, F-92500 Rueil-
Malmaison
Historic Site - 1906
Residence of Napoleon; palace
interiors; furnishings; musical
instruments; etchings; paintings;
documents on Napoleonic era;
attached: Château de Bois-Préau, 1 av
de l'Impératrice

04440
Musée National de Bois-Préau
1 av de l'Impératrice Joséphine,
F-92500 Rueil-Malmaison
History/Public Affairs Museum - 1958
Coll: Napoleonic history; court and
military clothes and weapons;
souvenirs of St. Helena, Marie-Louise
and the King of Rome

Saché

04441
Musée Balzac
Château, F-37190 Azay-le-Rideau
Historic Site
Coll: residence of the writer Honoré
de Balzac; memorabilia; portraits;
letters and manuscripts; first editions
of his works

Saint Dizier

04442
Musée Municipal
Mairie, F-52100 Saint Dizier
General Museum - 1881
Coll: mineralogy; archeology;
ornithology; a few sculptures from
ancient Carthage; 19th-20th century
local paintings - library

Saint-Amand-les-Eaux

04443
Musée Municipal
Grand' Place, F-59230 Saint-Amand-
les-Eaux
General Museum
Coll: 17th century abbey with antique
carillon; archeology and local history;
faience and porcelain

Saint-Amand-Montrond

04444
Musée Saint Vic
cours Manuel, F-18200 Saint-Amand-
Montrond
General Museum - 1922
Coll: 16th-18th century painting;
prehistoric archeology; ceramics; folk
art and customs - library

Saint-Aubin-sur-Loire

04445
Château de Saint-Aubin-sur-Loire
Saint-Aubin-sur-Loire, F-71140
Bourbon-Lancy
Decorative Arts Museum
Coll: 18th century manor; period
furniture; tapestries

Saint-Brieuc

04446
Musée Municipal
Pavillon de Bellecize, F-22000 Saint-
Brieuc
General Museum

Saint-Denis

04447
Musée d'Art et d'Histoire
4 Pl de la Légion d'Honneur, F-93200
Saint-Denis
General Museum
Coll: early history; finds of
Merovingian, Gallo-Roman, and
medieval periods; sculpture;
furnishings; collection on the poet Paul
Eluard; paintings and drawings

04448
Musée Leon Dierx
rue de Paris, B.P. 395, F-97400 Saint-
Denis
Fine Arts Museum - 1911
Coll: paintings; sculptures; French
Impressionists and
post-Impressionists; French East India
Company chinaware; Vollard
collection

Saint-Dié

04449
Musée Municipal
11 rue St-Charles, F-88107 Saint-Dié
General Museum - 1875
Coll: German and French military
items; memorabilia of the political
figure Jules Ferry; archeological finds;
local art; ornithology; folk art and
customs

Saint-Etienne

04450
Musée d'Art et d'Industrie
Palais des Arts, Pl Louis Comte,
F-42000 Saint-Etienne
General Museum - 1833
Coll: mining exhibits; armaments;
weaving; enamel; ceramics; paintings;
sculpture

04451
**Musée des Amis du Vieux Saint-
Etienne**
13 bis rue Gambetta, F-42100 Saint-
Etienne
General Museum - 1932
Coll: local historical items; paintings;
furniture; items of local production
from wood and iron; textiles; mining -
library

Saint-Flour

04452
Musée de la Haute-Auvergne
1 Pl d'Armes, F-15100 Saint-Flour
General Museum

Saint-Germain-en-Laye

04453
**Musée des Antiquités Nationales de
Saint-Germain-en-Laye**
Château, F-78100 Saint-Germain-
en-Laye
Archeology Museum - 1862
Coll: antiquities of prehistoric times,
the Bronze Age, and Celtic, Gallo-
Roman, and Merovingian periods

Saint-Gilles

04454
Maison Romane
F-30800 Saint-Gilles
General Museum - 1950
Coll: archeology; ethnography;
ornithology - library

Saint-Gilles-les-Hauts

04455
Musée Historique
F-97435 Saint-Gilles-les-Hauts
History/Public Affairs Museum - 1976
Coll: 15th-19th century weapons,
furniture, maps, and documents
housed in 18th century plantation
home

Saint-Jean-Cap Ferrat

04456
Fondation Ephrussi de Rothschild
Jardins et Musée 'Ile de France'
F-06230 Saint-Jean-Cap Ferrat
Fine Arts Museum - 1934
Coll: tapestries and rugs; 18th century
furnishings; paintings and porcelain of
the 18th century; Oriental art objects;
folk art; wrought-iron items

Saint-Jean-d'Angély

04457
Musée de la Société d'Archéologie
F-17400 Saint-Jean-d'Angély
General Museum
Coll: local history; portraits;
armaments

Saint-Lô

04458
Musée Municipal
Pl du Général de Gaulle, F-50010
Saint-Lô
Fine Arts Museum
Coll: tapestries; paintings; drawings;
miniatures; Roman sculpture

Saint-Malo

04459
Musée d'Histoire
Château de Saint-Malo, F-35400 Saint-
Malo
History/Public Affairs Museum
Coll: history of the Corsars; wax
figures

04460
Musée international du Long Cours
F-35400 Saint-Malo
History/Public Affairs Museum - 1969
Coll: history of sea voyages; sailing;
Cape Horn sailors; maps and prints

Saint-Martin-de-Re

04461
**Musée Naval et Cognacq de Saint-
Martin-de-Re**
Hôtel de Clerjotte, F-17411 Saint-
Martin-de-Re
History/Public Affairs Museum
Coll: 15th-16th century hotel;
figureheads; ancient weapons; ship
models; marine paintings illustrating
local maritime history

Saint-Omer

04462
**Musée Sandelin et Musée Henri-
Dupuis**
14 rue Carnot, F-62500 Saint-Omer
Fine Arts Museum
Coll: furnishings; Flemish, German, and
French painting; ceramics; 12th-16th
century art objects; Greek and Roman
art; Gallo-Roman medieval items

Saint-Paul

04463
Fondation Maeght
F-06570 Saint-Paul
Fine Arts Museum - 1964
Coll: architecture; mosaics; sculpture;
ceramics; 20th century paintings;
modern and contemporary art - library

Saint-Paul-de-Vence

04464
Fondation Maeght
F-06570 Saint-Paul-de-Vence
Fine Arts Museum - 1964
Modern painting and sculpture;
contemporary music - library and film
showings

Saint-Pierre-d'Oléron

04465
Musée Aliénor d'Aquitaine
25 rue Pierre Loti, F-17310 Saint-
Pierre-d'Oléron

Saint-Quentin

04466
Musée Antoine Lécuyer
28 rue Antoine Lécuyer, F-02100 Saint-
Quentin
Fine Arts Museum - mid 19th century
Coll: 18th-20th century painting;
portraits; 18th century ceramics; ivory;
porcelain; tapestry

Saint-Rémy-de-Provence

04467
Musée des Alpilles
Pl Favier, F-13210 Saint-Rémy-
de-Provence
General Museum
Portraits; sculpture; geology

Saint-Sauveur-le-Vicomte

04468
Musée Barbey d'Aurevilly
Vieux Château, F-50390 Saint-Sauveur-
le-Vicomte
Historic Site - 1925
Coll: letters and manuscripts of the
writer Barbey d'Aurevilly; house
where he was born; his bust by Rodin
- library

04469
Musée Barbey-d'Aurevilly
F-50390 Saint-Sauveur-le-Vicomte
Historic Site - 1925
Coll: memorabilia and manuscripts of
J. Barbey d'Aurevilly; iconography
related to Barbey d'Aurevilly and his
circle - library

Saint-Sever

04470
Musée Lapidaire Municipal
rue Lamarque, F-40500 Saint-Sever
Archeology Museum - 1940
Coll: Gallo-Roman capitals; ancient
stone relics

Saint-Tropez

04471
Musée de l'Annonciade
Pl Georges-Grammont, F-83990 Saint-
Tropez
Fine Arts Museum - 1955
Coll: modern paintings; sculpture;
French art (1890-1940);
Neo-Impressionists, Fauves, Nabis
artists

04472
Musée Naval de Saint-Tropez
Citadelle de Saint-Tropez, F-83990
Saint-Tropez
History/Public Affairs Museum
Coll: ship models; marine paintings;
engravings; documents; items
reflecting the history of the port from
antiquity to 1944

Sainte-Menehould

04473
Musée de l'Argonne
13 Pl du Général Leclerc, F-51800
Sainte-Menehould
General Museum - 1976
Coll: paleontology; geology; WW I in
pictures and documents; folk art and
customs

Saintes

04474
Musée Archéologique
Esplanade André Malraux, F-17100
Saintes
Archeology Museum
Coll: prehistoric items; Gallo-Roman
finds; medieval pottery - library

04475
Musées des Beaux-Arts
le Présidiel et l'Echevinage, rue V.
Hugo et Pl de l'Echevinage, F-17100
Saintes
Fine Arts Museum - 1967 (le Presidiel)
and 1977 (l'Echevinage)
Coll: 16th-20th century paintings of the
French, Italian, Dutch and Flemish
schools; wall paintings; screens;
portraits; 16th-20th century ceramics;
Sèvres porcelain

Saintes-Maries-de-la-Ville

04476
Musée Baroncelli
Ancien Hôtel de Ville, F-13460 Saintes-
Maries-de-la-Ville
General Museum - 1942
Coll: archeology; natural history;
ornithology of Camargue; folk art;
agricultural equipment

Salon-de-Provence

04477
Musée de l'Empéri
Château de l'Empéri, F-13300 Salon-
de-Provence
History/Public Affairs Museum - 1968
Coll: military history and art;
armaments; flags; uniforms and
equipment; iconography; personal
belongings of Napoleon I and
Napoleon III; paintings; drawings;
etchings - library

Samadet

04478
Musée de la Faïencerie
Château de l'Abbé de Roquepine,
F-40340 Samadet
Decorative Arts Museum
Faience

Sarrebourg

04479
Musée du Pays de Sarrebourg
13 av de France, F-57400 Sarrebourg
Archeology Museum - 1905
Coll: pre- and protohistory; Gallo-
Roman and Merovingian items;
medieval and modern sculpture -
library

Sartène

04480
**Musée Départemental de Préhistoire
Corse**
rue Crocce, F-20100 Sartène
General Museum
Regional prehistory

Saulieu

04481
Musée François Pompon
Pl de la Basilique, F-21210 Saulieu
General Museum
Coll: religious art; 12th-18th century
sculpture; crafts; archeology; regional
and local history; Gallo-Roman stelae
of the antique necropolis of Saulieu;
original works of the sculptor François
Pompon

Saumur

04482
Musée des Art Decoratifs
Château, F-49400 Saumur
Decorative Arts Museum - 1829
Coll: local prehistoric and Gallo-
Roman finds; 13th-18th century wood
sculpture; Limoges enamels; 15th-18th
century tapestries and furniture;
16th-18th century French faience and
porcelain

04483
Musée du Cheval
Château, F-49400 Saumur
Natural History Museum - 1911
Coll: History of horse and horse
breeding; horse equipment of all times
and all countries; 18th-19th century
English engravings of horses and
races - library

Sceaux

04484
Musée de l'Ile de France
Château de Sceaux, F-92330 Sceaux
Fine Arts Museum - 1935
Coll: art; history; ceramics; paintings;
drawings; etchings; tapestries -
library; documentation center; park;
auditorium; children's museum

Sedan

04485
Musée du Château
F-08200 Sedan
History/Public Affairs Museum
Interiors; historical chateau

Senlis

04486
Musée de la Vénerie
Château Royal, rue du Châtel, F-60300
Senlis
General Museum - 1935
Coll: hunting trophies; painting and
sculpture on the theme of hunting;
costumes; hunting bugles - library

04487
Musée des Beaux-Arts
Hôtel de Vermandois, Pl du Parvis
Notre-Dame, F-60300 Senlis
Fine Arts Museum - 1976
Coll: painting; drawings; art objects

04488
Musée du Haubergier
20 rue du Haubergier, F-60300 Senlis
General Museum - 1862
Coll: prehistoric, Gallic, and Gallo-
Roman archeology; medieval sculpture
and art objects; first example of Gothic
sculpture in France; local history

04489
Musée Jacquemart-André
Abbaye de Chaâlis, Fontaine Chaâlis,
F-60305 Senlis
Fine Arts Museum
Egyptian and Greco-Roman
antiquities; European art; 17th-18th
cent. furnishings; busts and
memorabilia of J.-J. Rousseau
(1712-1778)

Sérignan-du-Comtat

04490
**Musée de l'Entomologiste
Jean-Henri Fabre**
F-84100 Sérignan-du-Comtat
Historic Site
Coll: memorabilia of the French
entomologist Fabre

Sessenheim

04491
Memorial Goethe
F-67770 Sessenheim
Historic Site
Memorabilia of Goethe and his stay in
Alsace

Sète

04492
Musée Paul Valéry
Voie Communale 75, F-34200 Sète
Historic Site
Coll: memorabilia of the writer P.
Valéry; 19th-20th century works of art

Sèvres

04493
**Musée National de Ceramique,
Sèvres**
Pl de la Manufacture, F-92310 Sèvres
Decorative Arts Museum
Coll: history and production of
ceramics; ancient and modern pieces

Soissons

04494
Musée Municipal
2 rue de la Congrégation, F-02200
Soissons
General Museum - 1857
Coll: prehistory; antiquities; paintings;
medieval sculpture

Strasbourg

04495
Cabinet Numismatique
5 rue du Maréchal Joffre, F-67070
Strasbourg cedex
History/Public Affairs Museum - 1872
Coll: coins and medaillons from
Alsace-Lorraine - library

04496
Musée Archéologique
Château des Rohan, 1 Pl du Château,
F-67000 Strasbourg
Archeology Museum
Coll: prehistoric building fragments;
ceramics; sculpture; various finds

04497
Musée d'Art Moderne de Strasbourg
Ancienne Douane, 1 rue du Vieux
Marché aux Poissons, F-67000
Strasbourg
Fine Arts Museum - 1973
Coll: painting and sculpture from
Impressionism through modern times;
decorative art since 1870; church
windows from 1870 to the present -
library; children's atelier

04498
Musée de l'Oeuvre Notre-Dame
3 Pl du Château, F-67000 Strasbourg
Religious Art Museum
Coll: medieval sculpture; stained-glass
windows; statuettes; paintings; early
Alsacian and Renaissance art;
furnishings; still-life paintings; art
objects

04499
Musée des Arts Décoratifs
Château des Rohan, mail c/o Musées
Municipaux, 2 Pl du Château, F-67000
Strasbourg
Decorative Arts Museum
Coll: complete history of ceramics;
porcelain of famous European
manufacture; pewter; wrought-iron
objects; furniture

04500
Musée des Beaux-Arts
Château des Rohan, mail c/o Musées
Municipaux, 2 Pl du Château, F-67000
Strasbourg
Fine Arts Museum
Coll: 14th-19th century Italian, Spanish,
Dutch, Flemish, and French painting;
paintings of the Alsatian school

04501
Musée Historique
2 rue du Vieux-Marché-aux-Poisson,
F-67000 Strasbourg
History/Public Affairs Museum - 1920
Coll: topographical, political, economic,
and military history of Strasbourg;
16th-17th century firearms; 19th
century arms and uniforms; 19th
century collection of painted toy
soldiers; mechanical toys from
1850-1914

Suresnes

04502
Musée municipal René Sordes
Passerelle-Musée, Avenue des Cités-
Unies, F-92150 Suresnes, Hauts-
de-Seine
General Museum - 1929
Local history; viticulture; collection of
19th century political figures - library

Tanlay

04503
Château de Tanlay
F-89430 Tanlay
Historic Site - 16th-17th centuries
Coll: 17th century wood panels; period
furniture; portraits; frescoes; paintings

Tarbes

04504
Maison Natale du Marechal Foch
2 rue de la Victoire, F-65000 Tarbes
Historic Site - 1951
Coll: paintings; sstatues of Marshal
Foch; WW I memorabilia; books and
manuscripts

04505
Muse%oe Massey
Jardin Massey, F-65000 Tarbes
Fine Arts Museum - 1860
Coll: 16th-19th century painting; 2nd
century B.C. bronze mask

04506
Musée International des Hussards
Jardin Massey, F-65000 Tarbes
History/Public Affairs Museum - 1955
Coll: 15th-20th century arms; 130
complete uniforms; equipment;
iconography of hussars of 34
countries - library

Tautavel
04507
Musée de Préhistoire
F-66720 Tautavel
Archeology Museum - 1979
Coll: stone tools; fossils; paleolithic pottery; bronzes; metal tools of neolithic times

Thann
04508
Musée de la Société des Amis de Thann
Halle au Blé, 24 rue St. Thiébaut, F-68800 Thann
General Museum
Coll: 14th-18th century sculpture; Alsacian life; local history; crafts; mineralogy; World War I and II

Thiers
04509
Musée Municipal Fontenille-Mondière
10 rue de Barante, F-63300 Thiers
General Museum - 1924
Coll: international cutler's craft; cutlery; folk art; 17th-20th century paintings; toys

Thonon-les-Bains
04510
Musée Folklorique du Chablais
Château de Sonnaz, Pl de l'Hôtel de Ville, F-74200 Thonon-les-Bains
Anthropology Museum - 1863
Coll: folklore of the Chablais region; regional history; prehistory; Gallo-Roman archeology

Thorigny-sur-Oreuse
04511
Château de Fleurigny
F-89260 Thorigny-sur-Oreuse
Historic Site
Coll: 13th-16th century chapel; sculpture by Jean Cousin; wood panels; monumental Renaissance chimney

Toulon
04512
Musée d'Art
20 bd Maréchal Leclerc, F-83000 Toulon
Fine Arts Museum - 1887
Coll: Painting (16th-20th c.); contemporary art; photographs

04513
Musée Naval de la Tour Royale
le Mourillon, F-83000 Toulon
History/Public Affairs Museum
Coll: maritime history; armaments; figureheads

04514
Musée Naval de Toulon
Pl Monsenergue, F-83000 Toulon
History/Public Affairs Museum
Coll: ship models; figureheads; portraits and busts of seamen

Toulouse
04515
Musée des Augustins
21 rue de Metz, F-31000 Toulouse
Fine Arts Museum - 1795
Coll: paintings of the Netherlandish, French and Toulouse schools; Romanesque sculpture; contemporary painting; in 15th-17th century convent

04516
Musée George Labit
43 rue des Martyrs-de-la-Libération, F-31500 Toulouse
Fine Arts Museum - 1893
Coll: Oriental art; decorative arts; sculpture; Japanese prints; Egyptian archeology

04517
Musée Paul Dupuy
13 rue de la Pleau, F-31500 Toulouse
Decorative Arts Museum - 1944
Coll: crafts; regional decorative arts from the 11th century to the present; drawings; etchings; regional history - library

04518
Musée Saint-Raymond
Pl Saint-Sernin, F-31500 Toulouse
Archeology Museum - 1950
Coll: prehistoric archeology; Greek vases; bronzes; numismatics; Roman and Gallo-Roman sculpture; mosaics; epigraphs - library

Tourcoing
04519
Musée des Beaux-Arts
2 rue Paul-Doumer, F-59200 Tourcoing
Fine Arts Museum
Coll: 17th century Flemish and Dutch painting; 17th-20th century engravings; contemporary painting; ancient pottery; sculpture

Tours
04520
Musée de la Société Archjéologique de Touraine
Hôtel Gouin, rue de Commerce, F-37000 Tours
Fine Arts Museum - 1851
Coll: art from the Middle Ages to the Renaissance; crafts; regional antiquities; prehistoric finds; Gallo-Roman objects; sculpture; numismatics - library

04521
Musée des Beaux-Arts
18 Pl François Sicard, F-37000 Tours
Fine Arts Museum - 1793
Coll: 14th-20th century Italian, Dutch, and French painting; sculpture; furnishings; decorative arts; historic house - library

04522
Musée du Compagnonnage
8 rue Nationale, F-37000 Tours
Decorative Arts Museum - 1968
Coll: handicrafts from Antiquity to the present; engravings; flags; archives on military history and rites

Troyes
04523
Musée de la Bonneterie
Hôtel de Vauluisant, 4 rue de Vauluisant, F-10000 Troyes
History/Public Affairs Museum
Exhibits on the manufacture of stockings

04524
Musée des Beaux-Arts et d'Archéologie
21 rue Chrétien-de-Troyes, F-10000 Troyes
Fine Arts Museum
Coll: classical and Egyptian archeology; prehistory to Merovingian times; jewelry; 15th-20th century French and foreign painting; glass; enamel; furnishings

04525
Musée d'Histoire Naturelle
21 rue Chrestien de Troyes, F-10000 Troyes
Natural History Museum
Coll: natural history; birds; butterflies

04526
Musée Historique de Troyes et de la Champagne
4 rue de Vauluisant, F-10000 Troyes
General Museum
Coll: local 16th century art and history; paintings; sculpture; portraits; decorative arts; ceramics; crafts; bonnets; 16th century church windows of the school of Troyes

04527
Pharmacie-Musée de l'Hôtel-Dieu-le-Comte
Quai des Comtes de Champagne, F-10000 Troyes
History/Public Affairs Museum - 1979
Coll: pharmacy from the 18th century; history of hospitals during the Ancient Regime

04528
Trésor de la Cathédrale
F-10000 Troyes
Religious Art Museum - 1200
Coll: cathedral treasure; religious objects; robes; enamel; ivory; 9th-12th century codexes - library

Tulle
04529
Musée du Cloître
Pl de la Cathédrale, F-19000 Tulle
General Museum - 1928
Coll: paleontology; prehistory; Gallo-Roman antiquities; medieval architecture; numismatics; local artifacts; iconography; porcelain; armaments; regional religious art

Ussel
04530
Musée du Pays d'Ussel
Chapelle des Pénitents, 12 rue Michelet, B.P. 63, F-19200 Ussel
Religious Art Museum - 1973
Coll: 13th-18th century paintings and sculpture; religious ethnography; local crafts - library

Uzès
04531
Musée Municipal
Ancien Evêché, F-30700 Uzès
General Museum - 1907
Coll: local history; folklore; regional prehistory; Gallo-Roman finds; geology; regional botany; ceramics; snails; paintings; memorabilia of André Gide (1869-1951)

Valence
04532
Musée Municipal des Beaux-Arts
4 Pl des Ormeaux, F-26000 Valence
Fine Arts Museum
Coll: paintings of French and foreign schools; 15th and 17th century wall paintings; historic house

Valenciennes
04533
Musée des Beaux-Arts
Pl Verte, F-59300 Valenciennes
Fine Arts Museum
Coll: Flemish and French paintings; sculpture; tapestries; crafts

Vallauris
04534
Musée Municipal de Céramique et d'Art Moderne
Pl de la Mairie, F-06220 Vallauris
Fine Arts Museum
Coll: ceramics; modern art

04535
Musée National
Pl de la Libération, F-06220 Vallauris
Fine Arts Museum - 1959
Coll: wood mural by Pablo Picasso, 'La Guerre et la Paix'

Vannes
04536
Musée de la Société Polymathique du Morbihan
2 rue Noé, F-56000 Vannes
General Museum
Coll: prehistory; local history; natural sciences

Varennes-en-Argonne
04537
Musée d'Argonne
F-55270 Varennes-en-Argonne
General Museum - 1973
Coll: exhibits on Louis XVI during his arrest in 1791; World War I; art and local traditions

Vaucouleurs
04538
Musée Municipal Hôtel de Ville
rue des Annonciades, F-55140 Vaucouleurs
History/Public Affairs Museum - 1949
Memorabilia of Jeanne d'Arc; antique fireplace; sculpture of Christ (13th century); weapons - library

Vendôme
04539
Musée Municipal
Abbaye de la Trinité, F-41100 Vendôme
Fine Arts Museum - 1862
Coll: prehistoric finds; sculpture from medieval times to the Renaissance; 17th century French and Dutch painting; ceramics; regional lore

Verdun
04540
Musée de Guerre
Citadelle, Boulevard du 5' R.A.P., F-55100 Verdun
History/Public Affairs Museum - 1929
History and documents on World War I

Vernon
04541
Musée Alphonse-Georges Poulain
rue du Pont, B.P. 903, F-27200 Vernon
General Museum - 1862
Coll: paintings; sculpture; archeology; prehistory

04542
Musée Municipal
Hôtel de Ville, B.P. 903, F-27200 Vernon
General Museum

Versailles

04543
Musée des Voitures
Château-78000 Versailles
Science/Tech Museum
Coaches, carriages, and litters from
the 18th-19th centuries

04544
Musée Lambinet
5 rue Baillet-Reviron, F-78000
Versailles
Fine Arts Museum
Coll: medieval religious art; liturgical
objects; local documents; local history;
sculpture; 18th century furnishings

04545
**Musée National du Château de
Versailles et de Trianon**
Château, F-78000 Versailles
History/Public Affairs Museum - 1834
Coll: furniture, interiors, objects d'art,
sculpture, 16th-19th century painting -
library

Vervins

04546
**Musée Archéologique et d'Histoire
de la Thiérache**
3 rue du Traité-de-Paix, F-02140
Vervins
General Museum - 1873
Coll: paleontology; prehistory;
antiquities; geology; ethnography;
regional objects; archives - library

Vienne

04547
Musée d'Art Chrétien
Saint-André-le-Bas, Pl de Miremont,
F-38200 Vienne
Religious Art Museum - 1938
Coll: Merovingian, Carolingian, Gothic,
and Romanesque sculptures;
inscriptions; religious objects;
sarcophags

04548
**Musée des Beaux-Arts et
d'Archéologie**
Pl de Miremont, F-38200 Vienne
Fine Arts Museum - 1895
Coll: prehistorical finds; Gallo-Roman
archeology; decorative arts; paintings;
numismatics

04549
Musée Lapidaire Romain
Eglise Saint-Pierre, Pl Saint-Pierre, Pl
de Miremont, F-38200 Vienne
Archeology Museum - 1895
Coll: sarcophagi; busts; mosaics;
sculptures; Latin inscriptions

Villeneuve-les-Avignon

04550
Musée Municipal
14 rue de l'Hôpital, F-30400 Villeneuve-
les-Avignon
Religious Art Museum
Coll: 15th-17th century paintings of the
Provençal school

Villeneuve-sur-Lot

04551
Musée Gaston Rapin
1 bd Voltaire, F-47300 Villeneuve-
sur-Lot
General Museum
Coll: prehistoric finds; Gallo-Roman
objects; Romanesque sculpture;
painting; local folklore; religious art

Villequier

04552
Musée de Victor Hugo
Maison Vacquerie, F-76490 Villequier
History/Public Affairs Museum - 1959
Coll: memorabilia of the writer Victor
Hugo and his family; letters, drawings,
and portraits

Villers-Cotterêts

04553
Musée Alexandre Dumas
24 rue Démoustier, F-02600 Villers-
Cotterêts
Historic Site - 1905
Coll: memorabilia of Général Dumas,
A. Dumas père, and A. Dumas fils;
letters; autographs; manuscripts;
portraits

Vire

04554
Musée Municipal
Hôtel de Ville, F-14500 Vire
General Museum
Coll: paintings; furnishings; local
folklore

Vitré

04555
Musée du Château
Château, F-35500 Vitré
General Museum
Coll: 13th-15th century castle;
tapestries; porcelains; painting;
sculpture; drawings; prints;
mineralogy; history; folklore

Vougeot

04556
Château du Clos de Vougeot
F-21640 Vougeot
General Museum
Coll: 12th century wine cellar; wine
press

Wissembourg

04557
Musée Westercamp
rue du Musée, F-67160 Wissembourg
General Museum
Coll: antiquities; costumes; furnishings;
antiquities; sarcophagi; sculpture;
medieval wrought-iron items;
armaments; history of 1870-1871 war -
library

Yvetot

04558
Musée Municipal
Hôtel de Ville, F-76190 Yvetot
General Museum
Coll: carvings; decorative arts

Yzeure

04559
Musée Historique du Bourbonnais
Château de Bellevue, F-03400 Yzeure
History/Public Affairs Museum
Coll: documents; maps; etchings;
Bourbon history

French Guiana

Cayenne

04560
Musée Local
2 av du Général de Gaulle, Cayenne
General Museum
local history; art; flora and fauna

French Polynesia

Papéete

04561
Musée d'éthnologie de Tahiti
10 Rue Bréa, Papéete, Tahiti
Anthropology Museum
Ethnology; history; natural sciences

04562
Musée Paul Gauguin
POB 536, Papéete, Tahiti
Historic Site - 1965
Documents on Gauguin's (1848-1903)
life and work; 20 original works by
Gauguin (paintings, sculptures,
watercolours) - library

Gabon

Libreville

04563
**Musée des arts et traditions du
Gabon**
Av. du Général de Gaulle, POB 3115,
Libreville
General Museum
Ethnography; prehistory; musical
instruments; jewelry; masks; statues;
handicrafts; art

Germany, Democratic
Republic

Adorf

04564
Heimatmuseum
Freiberger Str.8, DDR-993 Adorf
General Museum - 1954
Coll: local history (17th - 20th century);
economic history; geology; biology

Aken

04565
Heimatmuseum
Straße der Deutsch-Sowjetischen
Freundschaft 15, DDR-4372 Aken
General Museum - 1926
Coll: pre- and early history; local
history; crafts and shipping; biology;
archives

Allstedt

04566
Thomas-Müntzer-Gedenkstätten
DDR-4702 Allstedt
Historic Site - 1975
Coll: memorabilia of the theologist
Thomas Müntzer (1489 - 1525) and
history of the Peasant Wars; local, pre-
and early history; geology (especially
slate)

Alt Schwerin

04567
Agrarhistorisches Museum
DDR-2061 Alt Schwerin
Agriculture Museum - 1962
Coll: regional agricultural history and
folklore; more than 24 buildings
including huts, old schoolhouse, black-
smith, farm-house - library

Altenberg

04568
Poch- und Zinnwäsche Bergbau-
Schauanlage
DDR-8242 Altenberg
Science/Tech Museum - 1957
Coll: stamp rock and pewter working
system with mine, washing wheel,
tools, pewter formations

Altenburg

04569
**Naturkundliches Museum
'Mauritianum'**
Schloßgarten, Park des Friedens,
DDR-74 Altenburg
Natural History Museum - 1817
Coll: comparative natural history;
ornithology; geology; memorabilia of
the Africa expedition of A.E. Brehm
(1829-1884) - library

04570
**Schloßmuseum und
Spielkartenmuseum**
Schloß Altenburg 2, DDR-74 Altenburg
General Museum - 1919
Coll: local, pre- and early history; arms
and armory; peasant life; tools;
costumes; porcelain; Div. of industrial
development and labour movement;
Div. of original and reprinted playing
cards (1475 to present time) - library

04571
Staatliches Lindenau-Museum
Ernst-Thälmann-Str.5, DDR-74
Altenburg
Fine Arts Museum - 1848
The holdings are based on a donation
by scholar Bernhard von Lindenau
(1779-1854). Panel painting (13th - 16th
century); antique vases (7th - 2nd
century b.c.); sculptures and paintings;
copper engravings; drawings, prints
and graphics; photo collection;
archives - library

Angermünde

04572
Ehm-Welk-Gedenkstätte
Puschkin-Allee 10, DDR-132
Angermünde
Historic Site - 1974
Coll: life and work of the author Ehm
Welk (1884-1966) and his revolutionary
struggle against Fascism

04573
Heimatmuseum
Brüderstr. 18, DDR-132 Angermünde
General Museum - 1912
Coll: pre- and early history; local
modern history; crafts; geology; gun
powder tower; monastery church

Anklam

04574
Heimatmuseum 'Otto Lilienthal'
Ellbogenstr.1, DDR-214 Anklam
General Museum - 1927
Coll: pre- and early history; crafts and
trades; ceramics; memorabilia of the
glider constructor Otto Lilienthal
(1848-1896)

Annaberg-Buchholz

04575
Erzgebirgsmuseum Kulturhistorische
Abteilung
Große Kirchgasse 16, DDR-93
Annaberg-Buchholz
General Museum - 1887
Coll: mining; crafts and trades;
peasant life; tools; bookart;
lace-bobbin and silk weaving; pewter
collection; history of labour movement
- library

04576
Erzgebirgsmuseum Naturkundliche
Abteilung
Kupferstr.20, DDR-93 Annaberg-
Buchholz
Natural History Museum - 1910
Coll: entomology; botany; minerals;
nature preservation - auditorium;
library

Ansprung

04577
Heimatmuseum
DDR-9341 Ansprung
General Museum - 1972
Coll: crafts and trades; minerals; stone
collection

Antonsthal

04578
**Technisches Schaudenkmal
'Silberwäsche'**
Antonsthal 156, DDR-9431 Antonsthal
Historic Site - 1970
Coll: technology of silver mining

Apolda

04579
Glockenmuseum
Bahnhofstr.41, DDR-532 Apolda
History/Public Affairs Museum - 1932
Coll: bells from the 1st century b.c.;
bell decoration (12th to 18th century);
bell foundry

Arendsee

04580
Heimatmuseum und Klosterruine
Am See 3, DDR-3552 Arendsee
General Museum - 1959
Coll: prehistoric finds; botany; fishing;
local and modern history relating to
the area and monastery Arendsee

Arneburg

04581
Heimatmuseum
Karl-Marx-Str.14, DDR-3502 Arneburg
General Museum - 1928
Coll: pre- and early history; animals
and plants; local history; crafts and
trades; shipping; ceramics

Arnstadt

04582
Bach-Gedenkstätte
Bahnhofstr.2a, DDR-521 Arnstadt
Historic Site - 1935
Coll: memorabilia to Johann Sebastian
Bach and his family

04583
Heimatmuseum
Schloßplatz 1, DDR-521 Arnstadt
General Museum - 1894
Coll: pre- and early history relating to
the area; ornithology; ceramics;
religious art (15th-17th century); photo
collection - library

04584
Schloßmuseum
Schloßplatz 1, DDR-521 Arnstadt
General Museum - 1919
Coll: historic inventory (18th century);
ceremony hall; porcelain and
ceramics; doll houses; tapestry; arts
and crafts; paintings (16th-20th
century)

Asbach

04585
Lehr- und Schaubergwerk
DDR-6081 Asbach
Historic Site - 1960
Coll: history of mining; mining
technology

Aschersleben

04586
Kreismuseum
Markt 21, DDR-432 Aschersleben
General Museum - 1908
Coll: geology; paleontology; mining;
local history; arms and armory;
numismatics; photo collection - library

Aue

04587
Traditionsstätte Erzbergbau Aue
Bergfreiheit 1, DDR-94 Aue
General Museum - 1973
Coll: local history; history of earth;
mineralogy; mining history and
technology - library

Auerbach

04588
Heimatstuben im Schloß
Schloßstr.11, DDR-97 Auerbach
General Museum - 1968
Coll: local history; excavations;
minerals; butterflies

Augustusburg

04589
**Museum für Jagdtier- und
Vogelkunde des Erzgebirges**
Schloß Augustusburg, DDR-9382
Augustusburg
Natural History Museum - 1969
Coll: hunting seat with historic interior;
birds; hunting; carriages and coaches;
local history

04590
Zweitakt-Motorrad-Museum
Schloß Augustusburg, DDR-9382
Augustusburg
Science/Tech Museum - 1961
Coll: two-stroke motorcycles; history
of racing; carriages and coaches
(18th-19th century)

Bad Saarow-Pieskow

04591
Maxim-Gorki-Gedenkstätte
Ulmenstr.20, DDR-1242 Bad Saarow-
Pieskow
Historic Site - 1972
Memorabilia of Maxim Gorki - Gorki
library; auditorium

Bad Schandau

04592
Heimatmuseum
Badallee 10-11, DDR-832 Bad
Schandau
General Museum - 1946
Coll: geology; old mines and
sandstone quarry (since 1600); nature;
local history; crafts; shipping; cultural
history; tourism; sports

Bad Sülze

04593
Heimatmuseum
Saline 8, DDR-2594 Bad Sülze
Natural History Museum - 1953
Coll: history of baths; salt source
development

Bad Blankenburg

04594
Friedrich-Fröbel-Museum
Am Goetheweg 15, DDR-6823 Bad
Blankenburg
Historic Site - 1908
Coll: life and work of Friedrich Fröbel
(1782-1852), founder of first
kindergarten in the area; letters;
documents; original library

Bad Düben

04595
**Landschaftsmuseum der Dübener
Heide**
DDR-7282 Bad Düben
General Museum - 1952
Coll: geology; ancient history; local
and castle history (10th-19th century);
crafts; mill models; documentation on
Michael Kohlhaas, 16th century
political figure

Bad Dürrenberg

04596
Borlach-Museum
Borlach Platz, DDR-4203 Bad
Dürrenberg
Science/Tech Museum - 1956
Coll: history of local salt source;
models; plans; tools; geology; local
balneology

Bad Frankenhausen

04597
Kreis-Heimatmuseum
Schloß, DDR-4732 Bad
Frankenhausen
General Museum - 1921
Coll: geology; paleontology; local
history; industrial development; flora
and fauna of the area; medieval
ceramics; numismatics; diorama of
theologist Thomas Müntzer and the
battle at Frankenhausen (1525) -
library; auditorium

Bad Freienwalde

04598
Oderland-Museum
Uchtenhagenstr.2, DDR-131 Bad
Freienwalde
General Museum - 1952
Coll: pre- and early history; local
history; peasant folk art (18th-19th
century); Oder river gap; astronomy;
aeronautics - library

Bad Kösen

04599
Museen der Stadt Bad Kösen
Heimatmuseum und Burg Saaleck
Loreleypromenade 3, DDR-4803 Bad
Kösen
History/Public Affairs Museum - 1955
Coll: architectural history of monastery
and castle; Roman tombstones;
fragments; history of baths; salt
source

Bad Köstritz

04600
Heinrich-Schütz-Gedenkstätte
Ernst-Thälmann-Str.1, DDR-6504 Bad
Köstritz
Historic Site - 1954
Coll: memorabilia on composer H.
Schütz (1585-1672) in house of his
birth; musical life (17th century) -
library

Bad Langensalza

04601
Heimatmuseum
Ernst-Thälmann-Platz 7, DDR-582 Bad
Langensalza
General Museum - 1898
Coll: monastery (restored in 18th
century); prehistoric finds; local history
and crafts

Bad Lauchstädt

04602
**Historische Kuranlagen und Goethe-
Theater**
Parkstr.18, DDR-4204 Bad Lauchstädt
History/Public Affairs Museum - 1968
Coll: Goethe theater; history of town;
balneology; history of local theater

Bad Liebenwerda

04603
Kreismuseum Bad Liebenwerda
Dresdener Str.15, DDR-795 Bad
Liebenwerda
General Museum - 1953
Coll: geology; ancient and early
history; local history; crafts; farming;
photo collection; 16th century palace -
library

Bad Muskau

04604
Museum für Stadtgeschichte
DDR-7582 Bad Muskau
General Museum - 1965
Coll: local history; history of mud bath;
park; pottery; rare books

Bad Sulza

04605
Salinemuseum
DDR-5322 Bad Sulza
History/Public Affairs Museum - 1953
Coll: history of salt mine; prehistoric
finds; memorabilia and weapons
relating to the battle by Auerstedt
(1806)

Ballenstedt

04606
Heimatmuseum
Goetheplatz 1, DDR-4303 Ballenstedt
General Museum - 1910
Coll: geology; pre- and early history;
local history (since 11th century);
crafts; costumes; farm tools; living
style; photo collection

Bauerbach

04607
Schillerhaus
DDR-6101 Bauerbach
Historic Site - 1953
Coll: memorabilia on Friedrich
Schiller's stay and his dramas written
here (1782/83)

Bautzen

04608
Museum für Sorbisches Schrifttum
Sorbenhaus am Postplatz, DDR-86
Bautzen
History/Public Affairs Museum - 1958
Coll: development of Sorbian literature
(since 16th century); documents;
engravings; paintings; sculpture;
archives - library

04609
Stadtmuseum Museum für Kunst und
Kulturgeschichte
Platz der Roten Armee 1a, DDR-86
Bautzen
History/Public Affairs Museum - 1868
Coll: paintings (16th-20th century);
sculpture; carvings; drawings;
graphics; furniture and crafts
(17th-20th century); pre- and early
history; geology; biology; porcelain;
costumes; toys; bookart; photo
collection - library

04610
**Technisches Museum 'Alte
Wasserkunst'**
Wendischer Kirchhof 7, DDR-86
Bautzen
Science/Tech Museum - 1957
Coll: old guard rooms; artificial
fountain and a significant modern
waterwork

Beeskow

04611
Biologisches Heimatmuseum
Frankfurter Str.23, DDR-123 Beeskow
General Museum - 1906
Coll: geology; regional flora and fauna;
memorabilia on Australia researcher L.
Leichhardt (1813-1848); local history;
pre- and early history of the area -
auditorium; library

Belgern

04612
Heimatmuseum
Oschatzer Str.11, DDR-7293 Belgern
History/Public Affairs Museum - 1952
Coll: prehistoric finds of the area; local
history and crafts

Belzig

04613
Museum Burg Eisenhardt
DDR-182 Belzig
General Museum - 1957
Coll: pre- and early history; local
history; tools and handicrafts (19th
century); peasant living style

Berlin

04614
Ägyptisches Museum Bode-Museum
Bodestr.1-3, DDR-102 Berlin
Archeology Museum - 1823
Coll: Egyptian art and culture; findings
from Greco-Roman period; tombs;
gold jewelry (1st century b.c.); photo
collection - library

04615
Antiken-Sammlung Pergamon-
Museum
Bodestr.1-3, DDR-102 Berlin
Archeology Museum - 1830
Coll: Greek and Roman architecture;
monuments; Greek sculpture (600
b.c.); Roman portraits; Greek
ceramics; photo collection - library

04616
**Frühchristlich-Byzantinische
Sammlung** Bode-Museum
Bodestr.1-3, DDR-102 Berlin
Archeology Museum - 1904
Coll: late antique monuments;
sarcophagi; sculpture; mosaics;
Byzantine sculpture and icons;
medieval Italian monuments; Coptic art

04617
Gemäldegalerie Bode-Museum
Bodestr.1-3, DDR-102 Berlin
Fine Arts Museum - 1830
Coll: Italian, Dutch, Flemish, French
and German paintings (13th-19th
century); miniatures; photo collection

04618
Hugenotten-Museum
Französischer Dom, DDR-102 Berlin
History/Public Affairs Museum - 1957
Coll: history of reformed church and
French Huguenots in Germany;
documents

04619
Islamisches Museum Pergamon-
Museum
Bodestr.1-3, DDR-102 Berlin
Fine Arts Museum - 1904
Coll: Muslim art and culture (8th-19th
century); oriental tapestry; Iranian and
Indian miniatures; epigraphy; arts and
crafts

04620
Johannes-R.-Becher-Haus
Majakowski-Ring 34, DDR-111 Berlin
Historic Site - 1959
Coll: memorabilia of author Johannes
R. Becher (1891-1958); house where
he lived and wrote; documents -
library

04621
**Kupferstichkabinett und Sammlung
der Zeichnungen** Bode-Museum
Bodestr.1-3, DDR-102 Berlin
Fine Arts Museum - 1830
Coll: drawings; European prints
(15th-20th century); illustrated books;
photo collection - library; auditorium

04622
Märkisches Museum
Am Köllnischen Park 5, DDR-102
Berlin
Fine Arts Museum - 1874
Coll: pre- and early history; local
history; religious sculpture;
numismatics; theatre; memorabilia of
Theodor Fontane, Gerhart Hauptmann
and Heinrich Zille; archives - library

04623
Münzkabinett Bode-Museum
Bodestr.1-3, DDR-102 Berlin
History/Public Affairs Museum - 1560
Coll: history of numismatics; minting;
forgery; 16th-19th century medals;
seals; photo collection - library

04624
Museum für Deutsche Geschichte
Unter den Linden 2, DDR-108 Berlin
History/Public Affairs Museum - 1952
Coll: history of Marxism; German
graphics (16th-20th century), especially
revolutionary graphics; decorative art
and costumes; military artifacts; photo
collection; archives - library

04625
Museum für Volkskunde Pergamon-
Museum
Bodestr.1-3, DDR-102 Berlin
Decorative Arts Museum - 1889
Coll: weaving; costumes; ceramics;
jewelry; pottery; furniture; carvings -
library

04626
Nationalgalerie
Bodestr.1-3, DDR-102 Berlin
Fine Arts Museum - 1876
Coll: 18th-20th century French and
German art; graphics; prints;
drawings; sculpture; photo collection;
archives; memorabilia of C. F.
Schinkel: drawings, sketches, furniture
- library

04627
Ostasiatische Sammlung Pergamon-
Museum
Bodestr.1-3, DDR-102 Berlin
Fine Arts Museum - 1905
Coll: prehistoric and ancient ceramics;
Chinese porcelain; paintings; enamel
and laquer work; jade carvings;
weaving

04628
Otto-Nagel-Haus
Märkisches Ufer 16-18, DDR-101
Berlin
Historic Site - 1973
Coll: house and studio of painter Otto
Nagel; memorabilia relating to his life
and work in the period

04629
Papyrus-Sammlung Bode-Museum
Bodestr.1-3, DDR-102 Berlin
Archeology Museum - 1823
Coll: hieroglyphic, hieratic, demotic,
Coptic, Greek, Latin, Aramaic, Arabic
documents and literature - library

04630
Postmuseum
Mauerstr.69-75, DDR-106 Berlin
History/Public Affairs Museum - 1898
Coll: history and development of post,
telephone and telegraph; archives;
philatelic collection - library

04631
Robert-Koch-Gedenkstätte
Clara-Zetkin-Str.96, DDR-108 Berlin
Historic Site - 1960
Coll: memorabilia of scientist Robert
Koch (1843-1910); historic building
(1874)

04632
Skulpturensammlung Bode-Museum
Bodestr.1-3, DDR-102 Berlin
Fine Arts Museum - 1904
Coll: Italian sculpture (14th-17th
century); medieval-baroque sculpture
of Germany, the Netherlands, France;
photo collection - library

04633
Staatliches Kunstgewerbe-Museum
Schloß Köpenick, DDR-117 Berlin,
Köpenick
Decorative Arts Museum - 1867
Coll: furnishings and crafts (17th-18th
century); Meisen porcelain; silver;
pewter; glass; jewelry; medieval to
19th century textiles; photo collection
- library

04634
Vorderasiatisches Museum
Pergamon-Museum
Bodestr.1-3, DDR-102 Berlin
Fine Arts Museum - 1899
Coll: art and culture of the Near East;
ceramics; mosaics; architecture;
cuneiform slabs; photo collection -
library

Bernau

04635
Heimatmuseum
Berliner Str.11, DDR-128 Bernau
History/Public Affairs Museum - 1882
Coll: battlements; historic prison cells;
history of local judiciary; dungeon;
arms and armory (15th-16th century) -
library

Bernburg

04636
Museum Schloß Bernburg
Schloßstr.24, DDR-435 Bernburg
General Museum - 1893
Coll: geology; mining; mineralogy;
entomology; ornithology; numismatics;
architectural sculpture (16th-18th
century); local history and crafts -
library

Birkenwerder

04637
Clara-Zetkin-Gedenkstätte
Summter Str.4, DDR-1403
Birkenwerder
Historic Site - 1957
Coll: memorabilia of women's rights
fighter Clara Zetkin (1857-1933);
pictures; documents; writings; historic
furnishings - library

Bitterfeld

04638
Kreismuseum
Kirchplatz 3, DDR-44 Bitterfeld
General Museum - 1893
Coll: pre- and early history; geology;
pleistocene flora and fauna;
ornithology; development of coal
industry; local history; film - library

Blankenburg

04639
Heimatmuseum 'Kleines Schloß'
Schnappelberg 6, DDR-372
Blankenburg
General Museum - 1868
Coll: local history; mining; historic
findings, especially ceramics and
religious applied arts; Baroque living
style; photo collection - library

Borna

04640
Museum der Stadt Borna
An der Mauer 2, DDR-72 Borna
General Museum - 1974
Coll: pre- and early history of the area;
local and crafts history; industrial
development; coal mining; history of
regional labour movement

Brand-Erbisdorf

04641
**Städtisches Museum für Bergbau
und Industrie**
Jahnstr.14, DDR-923 Brand-Erbisdorf
Science/Tech Museum - 1914
Coll: local history; silver and lead
mining (17th-20th century); models;
tools; ore collection of the area

Brandenburg

04642
Heimatmuseum
Hauptstr.96, DDR-18 Brandenburg
General Museum - 1887
Coll: geology; history; furnishing
(17th-19th century); European graphics
(since 16th century); ornamental
engraving collection; photo collection
- library

Burg

04643
Hermann-Matern-Gedenkstätte
Platz des Friedens 26, DDR-327 Burg,
Bez. Magdeburg
Historic Site - 1973
Coll: memorial to labour leader
Hermann Matern (1893-1971) and his
birthplace

Burgk

04644
**Staatliches Heimat- und
Schloßmuseum**
DDR-6551 Burgk
General Museum - 1952
Coll: historic furnishing; local history;
armaments; in 15th century palace

Buttstädt

04645
Heimatmuseum
Freiheitstr., DDR-5232 Buttstädt
General Museum - 1907
ancient history; local history; local
crafts; burgher and peasant household
objects; costumes; history of
firefighting

Calau

04646
Heimatmuseum der Stadt Calau
Kirchstr., DDR-754 Calau
General Museum - 1961
ancient and early history; local history;
history of crafts and guilds

Camburg

04647
Heimatmuseum
Amtshof 1-2, DDR-6903 Camburg
General Museum - 1950
geology; ancient and early history;
local history, 17th-20th century; crafts;
folk art; ceramics

Colditz

04648
Städtisches Museum
Kurt-Böhme-Str.1, DDR-7242 Colditz
General Museum - 1874
ancient history; local history; justice;
local crafts; pottery and porcelain;
numismatics; butterfly collection

Cospeda

04649
Gedenkstätte 1806
Gasthaus 'Zum Grünen Baum',
DDR-6901 Cospeda
History/Public Affairs Museum - 1956
graphics, dioramas and historic
weapons of battle of Jena-Auerstädt
1806

Coswig

04650
Heimatmuseum
Kirchstr. 6, DDR-8252 Coswig
General Museum - 1910
local, regional history; pre-historic
finds

04651
Kreismuseum
Rosa-Luxemburg-Platz 13, DDR-4522
Coswig
Science/Tech Museum - 1950
development of pottery since early
history; machines; models; technical
ceramics for chemistry and
construction

Cottbus

04652
Bezirksmuseum
Schloß Branitz, DDR-7501 Cottbus
General Museum - 1887
geological and palaeontologic finds;
coal-mining; historic furniture; local
history, 12th-19th century; local crafts;
costumes; smithwork, 16th-18th
century; tin collection, 18th-19th
century - library

Crimmitschau

04653
**Gedenkstätte 'Crimmitschauer
Textilarbeiterstreik 1903-04'**
Straße der Befreiung 1, DDR-963
Crimmitschau
History/Public Affairs Museum - 1973
natural history; history of local labour-
movement - library

Crostau

04654
Heimatstube
Forstweg 2, DDR-8601 Crostau
General Museum - 1954
local history; weaving; castle ruins

Cumlosen

04655
Heimatstube
Cumlosen 103, DDR-2901 Cumlosen
General Museum - 1945
native bird fauna; local history

Dahlen

04656
Heimatstube
Wurzener Str.1, DDR-7262 Dahlen
General Museum - 1910
local and regional history; geology of
the Dahlener Heide including samples
of boulders

Delitzsch

04657
Kreismuseum
Schloß, DDR-727 Delitzsch
General Museum - 1900
ancient and early history; documents
of nature researcher C.G. Ehrenberg;
local history (11th-17th century);
historic furniture; clock and watches;
farming and crafts equipment - library

Demmin

04658
Kreis-Heimatmuseum
Ernst-Thälmann-Str.23, DDR-203
Demmin
General Museum - 1914
ancient and early history; local history;
13th-18th century art and crafts;
smithwork and tin; porcelain; rococo
and Biedermeier furnishings; coin and
writing collection - library

Dermbach

04659
Kreis-Heimatmuseum
Bahnhofstr.16, DDR-6205 Dermbach
General Museum - 1959
geology; ancient and early history;
agriculture; crafts and industry; glass;
porcelain; carvings - library

Dessau

04660
**Museum für Naturkunde und
Vorgeschichte**
August-Bebel-Str.32, DDR-4500
Dessau
General Museum - 1927
ancient and early history; local history;
crafts; ceramics 13th-16th century;
geology; mineralogy; ornithology -
library

04661
Staatliche Galerie Dessau Schloß
Georgium und Schloß Luisium
Puschkin Allee 100, DDR-4500 Dessau
Fine Arts Museum - 1927
Old German and Dutch paintings;
paintings of the 18th century,
Classicism, Romanticism and the
period of Biedermeier; 20th century
paintings - library

04662
**Staatliches Museum Schloß
Mosigkau**
Knobelsdorff-Allee 3, DDR-4506
Dessau, Mosigkau
Fine Arts Museum - 1951
17th-18th century paitings; furniture;
decorative objects; porcelain; glass

Diesdorf

04663
Altmärkisches Freilichtmuseum
DDR-3562 Diesdorf
Open Air Museum - 1911
Low German farmhouse; bakery; loft;
storeroom; 17th-19th century historic
furniture

Dippoldiswalde

04664
Kreismuseum
Freiberger Str.18, DDR-823
Dippoldiswalde
General Museum - 1975
local history; native history; flora and
fauna

Doberlug-Kirchhain

04665
Weißgerbermuseum
Potsdamer Str.18, DDR-797 Doberlug-
Kirchhain
General Museum - 1963
development of tannery and leather
production

Dömitz

04666
Heimatmuseum
Auf der Festung, DDR-2802 Dömitz
General Museum - 1953
local history; shipping; 19th-20th
century household objects;
memorabilia on Fritz Reuter
(1810-1874) - library

Dorfchemnitz

04667
Eisenhammer Dorfchemnitz
DDR-9201 Dorfchemnitz, Brand-
Erbisdorf
General Museum
18th-19th century iron forge

04668
Museum 'Kochenstampfe'
Am Anger 1, DDR-9151 Dorfchemnitz,
Stollberg
General Museum
bone and hide stamping; folk art;
knitting in the Erzgebirge; insects;
butterflies; native birds

Dornburg

04669
Dornburger Schlösser
DDR-6904 Dornburg
History/Public Affairs Museum - 1922
historical rooms; porcelain; decorative
objects; J.W.Goethe memorabilia;
furniture

Dresden

04670
Armeemuseum der DDR
Dr.-Kurt-Fischer-Platz 3, DDR-806
Dresden
History/Public Affairs Museum - 1961
Arms, flags, uniforms, documents;
National People's Army - library

04671
**Carl-Maria-von-Weber-
Gedenkstätte**
Dresdnerstr.44, DDR-8057 Dresden
History/Public Affairs Museum - 1948
memorabilia on composer Carl Maria
von Weber (1786-1826) and the time
he served as local music master;
pictures; instruments; letters

04672
Deutsches Hygiene-Museum
Zentralinstitut für Medizinische
Aufklärung
DDR-801 Dresden
Science/Tech Museum - 1911
medicine and hygiene; health
education - library

04673
Kraszewski-Haus Institut und
Museum für Geschichte der Stadt
Dresden
Nordstr.28, DDR-806 Dresden
History/Public Affairs Museum - 1960
memorabilia on artist Josef
I.Kraszewski (1812-1887) in his former
house

04674
Landesmuseum für Vorgeschichte
Karl-Marx-Platz, DDR-806 Dresden
History/Public Affairs Museum - 1874
ancient and early history of Saxony;
castle fragments; architectural
samples

04675
Leonhardi-Museum
Grundstr.62, DDR-8057 Dresden,
Loschwitz
History/Public Affairs Museum
memorabilia on painter E.Leonhardi
(1828-1905) in his former home

04676
Marcolinipalais
Friedrichstr.41, DDR-801 Dresden
Historic Site - 1959
Memorabilia of the visit of Napoleon in
Dresden

04677
**Martin-Andersen-
Nexö-Gedenkstätte**
Collenbuschstr.4, DDR-8051 Dresden
Historic Site - 1958
Memorabilia on Danish writer M.
Andersen-Nexö (1869-1954) in his
former home

04678
**Museum für Geschichte der Stadt
Dresden**
Ernst-Thälmann-Str.2, DDR-801
Dresden
General Museum - 1866
local history; history of the labour-
movement in Dresden; paintings
18th-20th century; graphics 16th-20th
century; sculptures; furniture; arms;
numismatics - library

04679
Schillerhäuschen
Schiller Str.19, DDR-8054 Dresden
History/Public Affairs Museum - 1955
memorabilia on Friedrich Schiller
(1759-1805) in house where he
completed 'Don Carlos'

04680
**Sektion Elektrotechnik der
Technischen Universität Dresden**
Helmholtzstr.9, DDR-802 Dresden
Science/Tech Museum - 1952
Development of the typewriter since
1864, collection of historic and modern
tywriters

04681
**Staalicher Mathematisch-
Physikalischer Salon**
Zwinger, DDR-801 Dresden
Science/Tech Museum - 1728
historic instruments and apparatus for
precision engineering, clockmaking,
land surveying and cartography,
measures and weights - library

04682
**Staatliche Kunstsammlung -
Museum für Kunsthandwerk**
Wasserpalais, DDR-8057 Dresden
General Museum - 1876
Textiles and furniture; ceramics;
pewter; glass and porcelain collection;
carvings; bookbindings - library

04683
**Staatliche Kunstsammlungen -
Gemäldegalerie Alte Meister**
Semper Galerie
Zwinger, DDR-6904 Dresden
Fine Arts Museum - 1722
15th-18th century European painting -
library

04684
**Staatliche Kunstsammlungen -
Gemäldegalerie Neue Meister**
Georg-Treu-Platz 3, DDR-801 Dresden
Fine Arts Museum - 1848
19th-20th century paintings (German
Romantic, French Impressionism,
German Expressionism); sculptures -
library

04685
**Staatliche Kunstsammlungen -
Grünes Gewölbe**
Albertinum, DDR-801 Dresden
Decorative Arts Museum - 1724
15th-18th century European gold and
jewelry; 16th-18th century glass,
enamel, ivory, and amber; bronze
sculptures

04686
**Staatliche Kunstsammlungen -
Kupferstich-Kabinett**
Güntzstr.34, DDR-801 Dresden
Fine Arts Museum - 1720
500,000 sheets of European graphics,
15th-20th century; Japanese
woodcuts; photographic art - library

04687
**Staatliche Kunstsammlungen -
Münzkabinett**
Wasserpalais, DDR-8057 Dresden
History/Public Affairs Museum - 1786
History of minting and econimics,
coins and medals

04688
**Staatliche Kunstsammlungen -
Porzellansammlung**
Zwinger, DDR-801 Dresden
Decorative Arts Museum - 1717
Chinese, Japanese and Meißen
porcelain

04689
**Staatliche Kunstsammlungen -
Skulpturensammlung**
Georg-Treu-Platz 1, DDR-801 Dresden
Fine Arts Museum - 1728
antique sculptures and fine arts;
German and French sculptures,
15th-20th century - library

04690
**Staatliche Kunstsammlungen -
Zinnsammlung**
Zwinger, DDR-801 Dresden
Fine Arts Museum - 1911
European pewter, especially German
pewter 15th-19th century

04691
**Staatliches Museum für Mineralogie
und Geologie**
Auguststr.2, DDR-801 Dresden
Natural History Museum - 1857
mineralogy; geology; palaeontology;
paleobotany - library

04692
Staatliches Museum für Tierkunde
Augustusstr.2, DDR-801 Dresden
Natural History Museum - 1875
Variability, adaption and development
of fauna - library

04693
Staatliches Museum für Völkerkunde
Karl-Marx-Platz, DDR-806 Dresden
Anthropology Museum - 1875
Ethnography; anthropology of all
continents, non European skull
collection - library

04694
Staatliches Museum für Volkskunst
Köpckestr.1, DDR-806 Dresden
General Museum - 1913
Folk art from Saxony; furniture;
ceramics; smithwork; toys; costumes;
pewter figures - library

04695
Technisches Museum Dresden
Friedrich-Engels-Str.15, DDR-802
Dresden
Science/Tech Museum - 1966
History of electrical engineering and
photography

04696
Verkehrsmuseum
Augustusstr.1, DDR-801 Dresden
Science/Tech Museum - 1952
Development of railroad,
telecommunication, shipping and
motorcars - library

Ebersbach

04697
Heimatmuseum
Humboldt-Baude, DDR-8705
Ebersbach, Schlechteberg
General Museum - 1862
geology; ancient and early history;
local and settlement history; furniture;
ceramics; glass; costumes;
blueprinting

Eberswalde

04698
Stadt- und Kreismuseum
Kirchstr.8, DDR-13 Eberswalde, Finow
History/Public Affairs Museum - 1905
ancient and early historic finds; local
and regional history

Ehrenfriedersdorf

04699
Greifenstein-Museum
DDR-9373 Ehrenfriedersdorf
General Museum - 1921
local history; 16th-19th century native
pewter mining; carvings; furniture

Eibau

04700
Heimat- und Humboldt-Museum
Beckenberstr.12, DDR-8712 Eibau
General Museum - 1864
local and regional history; ceramics;
glass; peasant furniture; carvings

Eibenstock

04701
Städtische Heimatschau
DDR-9405 Eibenstock
General Museum - 1968
local and regional history; geology;
technology

Eilenburg

04702
Stadtmuseum
Mansberg, DDR-728 Eilenburg
History/Public Affairs Museum - 1900
ancient and early history; local history

Eisenach

04703
Bachhaus
Frauenplan 21, DDR-590 Eisenach
History/Public Affairs Museum - 1907
in former Bach home; historic
household objects; memorabilia on
Johann Sebastian Bach's (1685-1750)
works; 16th-19th century musical
instruments /

04704
**Gedenkstätte 'Eisenacher Parteitag
1869'**
Friedrich-Engels-Str.57, DDR-590
Eisenach
History/Public Affairs Museum - 1967
history of the German labour
movement at scene of Party Day 1869

04705
Lutherhaus
Lutherplatz 8, DDR-590 Eisenach
History/Public Affairs Museum - 1925
memorabilia on Reformation, portraits,
writings, medals, books; M.Luther
(1483-1546) rooms

04706
**Reuterhaus mit Richard-Wagner-
Sammlung**
Reuterweg 2, DDR-590 Eisenach
History/Public Affairs Museum -
1896/97
memorabilia on poet Fritz Reuter
(1810-1874); historic rooms;
memorabilia on composer Richard
Wagner (1813-1883) - library

04707
Skulpturensammlung
Am Predigerplatz 4, DDR-590
Eisenach
Archeology Museum - 1900
Merowingian gravestones; Romanic
stonework; medieval Thüringen
religious sculpture 15th century

04708
Teehaus im Karthausgarten
DDR-590 Eisenach
History/Public Affairs Museum
18th century garden house with
historic furnishings

04709
Thüringer Museum
Markt 24, DDR-590 Eisenach
History/Public Affairs Museum - 1899
local history; medieval contemporary
glass; ceramics; porcelain; costumes;
crafts; 19th century German painting -
library; auditorium

04710
Wartburg-Stiftung
DDR-590 Eisenach
History/Public Affairs Museum - 1921
historic rooms; Gothic and Baroque
furnishings; 15th-18th century crafts;
16th century paintings; Gothic
sculpture; M.Luther (1483-1546) library
- library

Eisfeld

04711
Museum 'Otto Ludwig'
Schloß Eisfeld, DDR-612 Eisfeld
General Museum - 1949
ancient and early historic finds;
geology; native flora; butterflies; local
history; crafts; 17th-19th century
peasant living style; tools and
costumes; modern applied arts;
history of porcelain industry;
memorabilia on writer Otto Ludwig
(1813-1865)

Eisleben

04712
Luthers Geburtshaus
Lutherstr.16, DDR-425 Eisleben
History/Public Affairs Museum - 1892
memorabilia on Martin Luther

04713
Luthers Sterbehaus
Andreaskirchplatz 7, DDR-425
Eisleben
History/Public Affairs Museum - 1888
memorabilia on M.Luther; natural
history

04714
Museen in der Lutherstadt Eisleben
Andreaskirchplatz 7, DDR-425
Eisleben
History/Public Affairs Museum - 1913
ancient and early history; local history;
mining of Mansfeld since 1200; labour-
movement of Mansfeld 1891-1945;
crafts; textiles; numismatic; medals;
natural history; minerals; bird and
beatle collection - library

04715
Traditionskabinett Bürgergarten
Nicolaistr.20, DDR-425 Eisleben
History/Public Affairs Museum - 1961
memorial site in the oldest meeting
room of the proletariat of Eisleben
(1905-1920) with historic furniture

Ellrich

04716
Heimatstuben
Goeckingstr.31, DDR-5503 Ellrich
History/Public Affairs Museum - 1967
local history; history of labour-
movement

Erfurt

04717
Angermuseum
Anger 18, DDR-50 Erfurt
Fine Arts Museum - 1886
14th-16th century German paintings
and sculpture; medieval glasspainting;
18th-19th century painting, German
impressionism; 20th century art;
medieval Renaissance crafts; Gothic-
Rococo furnishing; 14th-20th century
wrought iron; decorative objects -
library

04718
**Gedenkstätte 'Erfurter Parteitag
1891'**
Futterstr.15-16, DDR-50 Erfurt
History/Public Affairs Museum - 1964
history of the German labour
movement at scene of local Party Day
1891

04719
IGA-Gartenbau-Museum
DDR-50 Erfurt, Cyriaksburg
Agriculture Museum
development of horticulture; trees and
wood; apiculture; history of settlement

04720
Museum für Stadtgeschichte
Leninstr.169, DDR-50 Erfurt
History/Public Affairs Museum - 1974
ancient, early and local history; prints;
numismatics; silver - library

04721
Museum für Thüringer Volkskunde
Juri-Gagarin-Ring 140a, DDR-50 Erfurt
History/Public Affairs Museum - 1956
local antiquities; peasant folk culture of
Thüringen; machines; costumes;
crafts; decorative objects; toys; glass;
porcelain

04722
Museum Schloß Molsdorf
DDR-50 Erfurt, Molsdorf
History/Public Affairs Museum - 1966
historic rooms; furnishings

04723
Naturkundemuseum
Futterstr.13, DDR-50 Erfurt
Natural History Museum - 1919
geology; biology; astronomy - library

Erkner

04724
**Gerhart-Hauptmann-
Gedächtnisstätte**
Gerhart-Haupmann-Str.1-2, DDR-125
Erkner
History/Public Affairs Museum - 1962
memorabilia on writer Gerhart
Hauptmann (1862-1946)

Falkensee

04725
Heimatmuseum
Thälmannplatz, DDR-154 Falkensee
General Museum - 1952
local history; conservation; geology

Falkenstein

04726
Heimatmuseum
Platz der Deutsch-Sowjetischen
Freundschaft, DDR-9704 Falkenstein
General Museum - 1930
13th-19th century local history; crafts;
jurisdiction; pewter and iron mining;
costumes; wood carving

04727
**Staatliches Museum Burg
Falkenstein**
DDR-9704 Falkenstein
History/Public Affairs Museum - 1950
historic objects; Renaissance,
Baroque, Biedermeier arts;
development of hunting

Finsterbergen

04728
Heimatstuben
Lindenstr.112, DDR-5803
Finsterbergen
General Museum - 1945
local and regional history

Finsterwalde

04729
Kreismuseum
Wilhelm-Külz-Str.8, DDR-798
Finsterwalde
History/Public Affairs Museum - 1958
ancient historic finds; stones; local
history

Frankfurt/Oder

04730
Heimatmuseum
Schloß, DDR-9202 Frankfurt/Oder
History/Public Affairs Museum - 1900
castle ruins; castle and local history;
14th-15th century religious sculpture

04731
**Kleist-Gedenk- und
Forschungsstätte**
Faberstr.7, DDR-12 Frankfurt/Oder
History/Public Affairs Museum - 1969
memorabilia on poet Heinrich von
Kleist (1777-1811) and his time,
research; graphics; sculptures;
painting - library

04732
Museum Viadrina - Bezirksmuseum
Emanuel-Bach-Str.11, DDR-12
Frankfurt/Oder
History/Public Affairs Museum - 1957
prehistory, history of the city, the inner
city research (13th-18th century) -
auditorium

Freest

04733
Freester Heimatmuseum
Schule, DDR-2221 Freest
General Museum - 1961
folk art; local crafts; knotting

Freiberg

04734
Bergakademie Freiberg Sektion
Geotechnik und Bergbau
Agricolastr.1, DDR-92 Freiberg
Science/Tech Museum - 1765
mineralogy; crystallography; mineral
deposit and technological collection;
hydrology; mechanics

04735
Naturkundemuseum
Waisenhausstr.10, DDR-92 Freiberg
Natural History Museum - 1864
mineralogy; botany; zoology; atomic
physics

04736
Stadt- und Bergbaumuseum
Am Dom 1-3, DDR-92 Freiberg
History/Public Affairs Museum - 1861
history of city and crafts; labour-
movement; painting; sculpture; crafts;
furnishings; musical instruments;
16th-19th century weapons;
decorative objects; smithwork; glass

Freital

04737
Haus der Heimat
Burgker Str.61, DDR-821 Freital
General Museum - 1946
geology; mineralogy; mining and city
history

Freyburg/Unstrut

04738
Museum Schloß Neuenburg
DDR-4805 Freyburg/Unstrut
General Museum - 1934
historic furnishings; geology; ancient
and early history; local history

04739
**Turn- und Sportmuseum 'Friedrich
Ludwig Jahn'**
Schloßstr.11, DDR-4805 Freyburg/
Unstrut
History/Public Affairs Museum - 1952
memorabilia on sports promoter
Friedrich Jahn (1778-1852) in his
former home

Friedland

04740
Heimatmuseum
Neubrandenburger Stadttor,
DDR-2003 Friedland
History/Public Affairs Museum - 1928
local and regional history; history of
local labour-movement

Frohburg

04741
Museum im Schloß
Markt 20, DDR-7233 Frohburg
General Museum - 1917
local history; peasant crafts and tools

Frohnau

04742
**Technisches Museum Frohnauer
Hammer**
DDR-9301 Frohnau
Decorative Arts Museum - 1951
former forge; historic furnishing and
equipment

Gadebusch

04743
Heimatmuseum
Amtsstr.4, DDR-273 Gadebusch
General Museum - 1957
local and regional history

Gardelegen

04744
**Mahn- und Gedenkstätte
'Isenschnibben-Scheune'**
Philipp-Müller-Str.22, 357 Gardelegen
History/Public Affairs Museum - 1963
local labour-movement memorial

04745
Stadtmuseum
Phillipp-Müller-Str.22, DDR-357
Gardelegen
General Museum - 1963
local and crafts history; peasant tools
and costumes

Garz auf Rügen

04746
Ernst-Moritz-Arndt-Heimatmuseum
An den Anlagen 5, DDR-2342 Garz auf
Rügen
History/Public Affairs Museum - 1929
local, regional history; memorabilia of
the writer Ernst M.Arndt (1769-1860);
pictures; writings; first editions

Genthin

04747
Kreis-Heimatmuseum
Mützelstr.22, DDR-328 Genthin
General Museum - 1886
ancient and early history; numismatics;
peasant tools and objects - library

Georgenthal

04748
**'Kornhaus' Georgenthal-
Klosterruinen**
Neuestr.33, DDR-5805 Georgenthal
General Museum - 1966
history of local cloister; medieval
painting

Gera

04749
Kunstgalerie
Park der Opfer des Faschismus,
DDR-65 Gera
Fine Arts Museum - 1972
20th century art - library

04750
Museum für Geschichte
Straße der Republik, DDR-65 Gera
History/Public Affairs Museum - 1878
ancient, early and local history; crafts,
industry; ceramics; porcelain; glass;
furnishings; numismatics; medieval art
of East Thüringen - library

04751
Museum für Naturkunde
Am Nicolaiberg 3, DDR-65 Gera
Natural History Museum - 1953
Geology; Pleistocene zoology; history
of biology and evolution; ornithology;
shells - library

Gerstungen

04752
Heimatmuseum
Sophienstr.2, DDR-5901 Gerstungen
General Museum - 1953
ancient and early history; local history;
18th-19th century peasant living style
and tools; peasant crafts; industry

Geyer

04753
Heimatmuseum
Im Wachturm, DDR-9307 Geyer
General Museum - 1952
14th-19th century pewter mining
history; minerals; pewter collection;
local history; lace products

Gingst

04754
Historische Handwerkerstuben
DDR-2343 Gingst, Rügen
History/Public Affairs Museum - 1971
history of labour-movement; native
history; crafts

Glauchau

04755
**Städtisches Museum und
Kunstsammlung**
Schloß Hinterglauchau, DDR-961
Glauchau
General Museum - 1940
Baroque-Biedermeier furnishings and
paintings; Gothic sculpture and
drawings; ancient and early history;
geology; mineralogy; zoology; botany;
crafts; decorative objects; children's
museum

Gnandstein

04756
Kreismuseum Burg Gnandstein
DDR-7231 Gnandstein
History/Public Affairs Museum - 1937
local and castle history; crafts;
costumes; paintings; memorabilia on
poet Theodor Körner's (1791-1813)
stay here; peasant living culture;
history of labour-movement - library

Göhren

04757
Mönchguter Heimatmuseum
Strandstr., DDR-2345 Göhren
General Museum - 1960
peasant living style; fishing; crafts;
geography; geology; ancient and early
history; costumes; folk art

Goldberg

04758
Kreisheimatmuseum
Müllerweg 2, DDR-2862 Goldberg
General Museum - 1927
geology; ancient and early history;
crafts and industrial history - library

Göldenitz

04759
Landschulmuseum
DDR-2555 Göldenitz
History/Public Affairs Museum - 1976
school history during feudal-capitalist
times

Görlitz

04760
Reichenbach Turm
Deminaiplatz, DDR-89 Görlitz
History/Public Affairs Museum - 1953
14th-15th century watchtower; historic
weapons of the 18th century

04761
**Staatliches Museum für Naturkunde
(Forschungsstelle)**
Am Museum 1, DDR-89 Görlitz
Natural History Museum - 1927
geology; minerlaogy; zoology;
evolution - library

04762
**Städtische Kunstsammlung -
Kaisertrutz**
Demianiplatz 1, DDR-89 Görlitz
General Museum - 1873
local and economic history; crafts;
industry; 14th-16th century painting
and sculpture; 18th-19th century
German painting; 20th century art;
modern crafts; glass; ceramics; wood;
metals

04763
**Städtische Kunstsammlung -
Museum Haus Neißstraße**
Neißstr.30, DDR-89 Görlitz
History/Public Affairs Museum - 1873
ancient and early history of region;
local and economic history; cultural
life; crafts; drawings; numismatics -
library

Gotha

04764
Ekhof Theater
Schloß Friedenstein, DDR-58 Gotha
History/Public Affairs Museum - 1683
history of theater; music instruments

04765
**Gedenkstätte 'Gothaer Parteitag
1875'**
Straße der Pariser Kommune 10,
DDR-58 Gotha
History/Public Affairs Museum - 1955
memorial to the Party Day held here in
1875

04766
Gustav-Freytag-Gedenkstätte
Weimarer Str.145, DDR-5802 Gotha,
Siebleben
History/Public Affairs Museum - 1960
memorabilia on writer and art historian
Gustav Freytag (1816-1895) in his
former home

04767
**Museum für Regionalgeschichte und
Volkskunde**
Schloß Friedenstein, DDR-58 Gotha
History/Public Affairs Museum - 1928
history; folklore collection; costumes;
armaments - library

04768
Naturkundemuseum
Parkallee 15, DDR-58 Gotha
Natural History Museum - 1640
geology; paleontology; mineralogy;
zoology - library

04769
Schloßmuseum
Schloß Friedenstein, DDR-58 Gotha
Fine Arts Museum - 1875
historic rooms; medieval-Renaissance
painting and sculpture; engravings;
numismatics; 17th-19th century crafts;
decorative objects

Grabow

04770
Heimatmuseum
Kirchenstr.14, DDR-2804 Grabow
General Museum - 1952
ancient, early history; local history;
crafts

Greifswald

04771
**Geologische Landessammlung der
Nordbezirke** Sektion geologische
Wissenschaften der Ernst-Moritz-
Arndt-Universität
Friedrich-Ludwig-Jahn-Str.17a,
DDR-22 Greifswald
Natural History Museum - 1908
Scandinavian fossils; historic geology;
micropaleontology

04772
Museum der Stadt Greifswald
Theodor-Pyl-Str.1-2, DDR-22
Greifswald
General Museum - 1925
ancient and early history of city, region
and university; 13th-14th century local
painting; pewter; copper; silver;
Caspar-David Friedrich memorial
room; Ernst-Moritz Arndt memorial
room

Greiz

04773
Bücher- und Kupferstichsammlung
Sommerpalais, Leninpark, DDR-66
Greiz
Fine Arts Museum - 1960
history of illustrated books since 1500;
drawings; mezzotints; caricatures;
maps

04774
Heimatmuseum
Unteres Schloß, Burgplatz 12, DDR-66
Greiz
General Museum - 1920
local history; folk culture; folk art;
posters; numismatics

Greussen

04775
Heimatmuseum
Rathaus, DDR-5403 Greussen
General Museum - 1936
geology; local and regional history;
crafts

Grimma

04776
Göschenhaus
Schillerstr.25, DDR-724 Grimma
History/Public Affairs Museum - 1954
memorabilia on publisher Göschen
(1752-1805) in his former house and on
his visitors Schiller, Seume and
Körner; steel engravings; pictures;
furniture; household utensils of tin,
porcelain and glass in Empire and
Biedermeier style - library

04777
Kreismuseum
Paul-Gerhard-Str.43, DDR-724 Grimma
General Museum - 1902
geology; ancient and early historic
finds; local history; peasant crafts,
tools and living style; history of local
Hussar Regiment; toys - library

Gröbzig

04778
Heimatmuseum
Ernst-Thälmann-Str., DDR-4373
Gröbzig
General Museum - 1934
local and regional history; native birds;
ancient and early historic finds; history
of local Jewish community 18th-19th
century

Grossbeeren

04779
Gedenkstätte Grossbeeren 1813
Dorfstr., DDR-17722 Grossbeeren
History/Public Affairs Museum - 1913
memorial at the site of a local battle
1813; weapons; documents; plans;
views

Grossengottern

04780
Heimatmuseum
Langensalzaer Str., DDR-5792
Grossengottern
General Museum - 1956
ancient historic finds; local history;
peasant equipment; household
objects; costumes; nature

Grossenhain

04781
Kreismuseum
Kirchplatz, DDR-828 Grossenhain
General Museum - 1907
ancient and early history; local history;
numismatics; armaments; peasant
living style; etchings; historic toys

Grosskochberg

04782
Goethe-Gedenkstätte
Schloß, DDR-6821 Grosskochberg
History/Public Affairs Museum - 1949
memorabilia on J.W.Goethe
(1749-1832) and Charlotte von Stein
(1742-1827)

Grossröhrsdorf

04783
Heimatmuseum
Mühlstr.5, DDR-8512 Grossröhrsdorf
General Museum - 1899
local, regional history; peasant crafts
and objects; 19th century hunting
equipment; ceramics; jewelry

Grossschönau

04784
**Oberlausitzer Heimat- und
Damastmuseum**
Schenaustr., DDR-8802 Grossschönau
General Museum - 1905
historic objects; damask collection;
local crafts; religious art; native birds;
stones

Güstrow

04785
**Ernst-Barlach-Gedenkstätte der
DDR**
Gertrudenplatz 1, DDR-26 Güstrow
History/Public Affairs Museum - 1953
works of artist Ernst Barlach
(1870-1938)

04786
Museum der Stadt Güstrow
Franz-Parr-Platz 7, DDR-26 Güstrow
General Museum - 1892
ancient and early history; local history;
burgher living style; playbills since
1740 - library

Hagenow

04787
Museum der Stadt Hagenow
Fr.-Heincke-Str., DDR 282 Hagenow
General Museum - 1974
ancient and early history; local history;
crafts and guilds; maps; graphics

Hainichen

04788
Heimatmuseum
Platz der Deutsch-Sowjetischen
Freundschaft 9, DDR-926 Hainichen
History/Public Affairs Museum - 1904
memorabilia on writer C.F. Gellert
(1715-1769); memorabilia on inventor
of mechanical wood pulp, F.G. Heller
(1816-1895); local crafts; pewter
sculpture

Halberstadt

04789
Dom und Domschatz Halberstadt
Domplatz 16a, DDR-36 Halberstadt
Religious Art Museum - 1936
religious art 12th-16th century: robes,
tapestries, Gothic paintings and
sculpture, Carolingian-Gothic
manuscripts

04790
Gleimhaus
Domplatz 31, DDR-36 Halberstadt
History/Public Affairs Museum - 1863
memorabilia on poet J.W.L.Gleim
(1719-1803); 18th century intellectual
life; portraits; writings; letters; books -
library

04791
**Museum für Vogelkunde
'Heineanum'**
Domplatz 37, DDR-36 Halberstadt
Natural History Museum - 1909
ornithology; pre-historic saurianbirds -
library

04792
Städtisches Museum
Domplatz 36, DDR-36 Halberstadt
General Museum - 1905
ancient and early finds; natural science
collection; local history, Renaissance-
baroque culture; paintings; military

Haldensleben

04793
Kreismuseum
Breiter Gang, DDR-324 Haldensleben
General Museum - 1910
geology; ancient and early historic
finds; local history; industry; ceramics;
household objects and costumes;
armaments; paintings; graphics;
zoology - library

Halle

04794
**Archäologisches Museum der
Martin-Luther-Universität**
Universitätsplatz 12, DDR-402 Halle
Archeology Museum - 1891
ancient art objects; plaster casts of
ancient pictures

04795
**Geiseltal-Museum der Martin-
Luther-Universität**
Domstr.5, DDR-402 Halle
Natural History Museum - 1934
fossils; history; prehistory of Geisel
valley; copperlayer fauna and flora -
library

04796
Geschichtsmuseum
Große Märkerstr.10, DDR-402 Halle
History/Public Affairs Museum - 1945
local history and history of local
labour-movement 1865-1945 - library

04797
Händel-Haus
Große Nicolai-Str.5, DDR-402 Halle
History/Public Affairs Museum - 1948
birthplace of G.F.Händel (1685-1759)
with collection of 500 musical
instruments - library

04798
Landesmuseum für Vorgeschichte
Richard-Wagner-Str.9, DDR-402 Halle
History/Public Affairs Museum - 1884
human, evolutionary history; Stone
Age, Bronze Age, Iron Age; history of
Halle before 961; European paleolithic
- library

04799
**Museum des Wissenschaftsbereichs
Zoologie der Sektion
Biowissenschaften der Martin-
Luther Universität Halle-Wittenberg**
Domplatz 4, DDR-402 Halle
Natural History Museum - 1886
fauna; mammals; ornithology; mollusks

04800
Staatliche Galerie Moritzburg
Friedemann-Bach-Platz 5, DDR-402
Halle
Fine Arts Museum - 1885
decorative objects; textiles; rugs;
German painting; 19th-20th century
sculpture; 12th-17th century local
architectural sculpture; drawings since
15th century; numismatics

Hartenstein

04801
Burgmuseum
Stein 1, DDR-9509 Hartenstein
General Museum - 1932
castle and regime history since 12th
century; armaments; local and crafts
history; minerals; mining history

Havelberg

04802
Prignitz-Museum
Am Dom, DDR-353 Havelberg
General Museum - 1904
ancient and early historic finds;
shipping, shipbuilding, fishing;
cathedral parts

Heiligenstadt

04803
Eichsfelder Heimatmuseum
Kollegiengasse 10, DDR-563
Heiligenstadt
General Museum - 1932
geology; ancient history; local and
regional history; peasant crafts and
living style; costumes; native birds;
religious sculpture - library

Heldrungen

04804
**Gedenkstätte des Deutschen
Bauernkrieges**
Wasserburg, DDR-4733 Heldrungen
General Museum - 1955
local and regional history; the German
Peasant War 1524-25

Herrnhut

04805
**Heimatmuseum 'Alt-Herrnhuter-
Stuben'**
Löbauer Str.18, DDR-8709 Herrnhut
General Museum - 1904
18th century house with complete
Biedermeier interiors

04806
Völkerkundemuseum
Löbauer Str.18, DDR-8709 Herrnhut
Anthropology Museum - 1878
ethnology

Hiddensee

04807
**Gerhart-Hauptmann-
Gedächtnisstätte**
Kloster, DDR-2346 Hiddensee
History/Public Affairs Museum - 1956
memorabilia on poet Gerhart
Hauptmann (1862-1946) - library

04808
Museum der Insel Hiddensee
Kloster, DDR-2346 Hiddensee
General Museum - 1945
geology; natural history; culture and
history of the isle - library

Hildburghausen

04809
Stadtmuseum
Marx-Engels-Platz 25, DDR-611
Hildburghausen
General Museum - 1950
local, regional history; crafts; 19th
century living style; publisher Joseph
Meyer (1796-1856) and foundation of
Bibliographical Institute

Hinzdorf

04810
Heimatstube
DDR-2901 Hinzdorf
General Museum - 1932
historic finds; 19th century peasant
living style

Hohenleuben

04811
Museum Reichenfels
DDR-6573 Hohenleuben
General Museum - 1825
ancient and early history; stones;
minerals; fauna; crafts history; 16th
century armaments - library

Hohnstein

04812
**KZ-Gedenkstätte in der Burg
Hohnstein**
Jugendburg Ernst Thälmann,
DDR-8532 Hohnstein
History/Public Affairs Museum - 1956
memorial to concentration camp
victims

Hoyerswerda

04813
Museum Hoyerswerda
Platz des Friedens 1, DDR-77
Hoyerswerda
General Museum - 1924
geology; ancient history; zoology;
local history; pewter; costumes

Ilmenau

04814
**Goethe-Gedenkstätte Jagdhaus
Gabelbach**
Waldstr.24, DDR-63 Ilmenau
History/Public Affairs Museum - 1953
memorabilia on poet J.W.Goethe
(1749-1832) and his stay here

04815
**Goethehäuschen auf dem
Kickelhahn**
DDR-63 Ilmenau
History/Public Affairs Museum
memorabilia on J.W.Goethe
(1749-1832)

Ilsenburg

04816
Hüttenmuseum
Ernst-Thälmann-Str.9b, DDR-3705
Ilsenburg
General Museum - 1954
ancient and early history; geology; use
of granite and quartz; paintings;
drawings; watercolors

Jahnshain

04817
Lindigtmühle am Lindenvorwerk
DDR-7231 Jahnshain
General Museum
watermill built 1524

Jarmen

04818
Mühlenmuseum
DDR-2032 Jarmen
Agriculture Museum - 1957
Dutch mill; history of milling; 17th-19th
century peasant work tools

Jena

04819
Ernst-Haeckel-Haus
Berggasse 7, DDR-69 Jena
History/Public Affairs Museum - 1920
memorabilia on zoologist Ernst
Haeckel (1834-1919); bequest; letters;
manuscripts; pictures; historic
furnishings

04820
Goethe-Gedenkstätte
Goethe-Allee 26, DDR-69 Jena
History/Public Affairs Museum - 1921
memorabilia on J.W.Goethe
(1749-1832) in his former Jena home

04821
**Hilprecht-Sammlung
Vorderasiatischer Altertümer der
Friedrich-Schiller-Universität Jena**
Kahlaesche Str.1, DDR-69 Jena
Archeology Museum - 1925
3,000-300 B.C. Cuneiform writing;
Aramaic writings

04822
Karl-Liebknecht-Haus
Zwätzengasse 16, DDR-69 Jena
History/Public Affairs Museum
history of labour-movement in 19th
and 20th century; memorabilia on Karl
Liebknecht

04823
Optisches Museum
Carl-Zeiß-Platz 12, DDR-69 Jena
Science/Tech Museum - 1965
history and technology of optics;
memorabilia on Carl Zeiss (1816-1888)

04824
Phyletisches Museum
Ebertstr.1, DDR-69 Jena
Natural History Museum - 1908
phyletic systematics; genetics;
comparative anatomy and embryology;
paleontology; zoo-geography;
anatomical specimens; anthropology

04825
**Sammlung des Fachbereichs
Archäologie der Friedrich-Schiller-
Universität Jena**
Ernst-Thälmann-Ring 24a, DDR-69
Jena
Archeology Museum - 1846
ancient sculptures; coins; oriental
numismatics - library

04826
Schiller-Gedenkstätte
Schiller-Gässchen 2, DDR-69 Jena
History/Public Affairs Museum - 1924
memorabilia on Friedrich Schiller
(1759-1805) in his former Jena home;
historic furnishings

04827
Stadtmuseum
Am Planetarium 12, DDR-69 Jena
General Museum - 1901
history of city and university; crafts;
industry; sculpture; drawings; pewter;
porcelain; textiles - library

Johanngeorgenstadt

04828
Schaubergwerk 'Glöckl'
Wittigsthaler Str., DDR-9438
Johanngeorgenstadt
Science/Tech Museum - 1974
tools and equipment from the time of
mining silver ore and bismuth

Jüterbog

04829
Heimatmuseum
Planeberg 9, DDR-17 Jüterbog
General Museum - 1954
local history; crafts; costumes; ancient
and early history - library

Kahla

04830
Heimatmuseum Leuchtenburg
DDR-6906 Kahla, Seitenroda
General Museum - 1906
geology; ancient and early historic
finds; armaments; hunting history;
peasant and court living style

Kamenz

04831
Lessingmuseum
Lessingplatz, DDR-829 Kamenz
History/Public Affairs Museum - 1931
memorabilia on poet Gotthold
E.Lessing (1729-1781); theater history
- library

04832
Museum der Westlausitz
Pulsnitzer Str.16, DDR-829 Kamenz
General Museum - 1931
history of Westlausitz; zoology;
botany; culture; pewter; crafts -
auditorium

Kapellendorf

04833
**Burgmuseum der Wasserburg
Kapellendorf**
Wasserburg, DDR-5321 Kapellendorf
General Museum - 1950
geology; ancient and early history;
castle and local history; peasant
folklore; farm tools

Karl-Marx-Stadt

04834
Burg Rabenstein
Oberfrohnaer Str., DDR-90 Karl-Marx-
Stadt
General Museum - 1959
12th century castle part; Baroque
frescoes; excavation finds

04835
Fritz-Heckert-Gedenkstätte
Mühlenstr.2, DDR-90 Karl-Marx-Stadt
History/Public Affairs Museum - 1974
memorabilia on Fritz Heckert, leader of
the labour-movement - Heckert, Fritz

04836
Gedenkstätte 'Der Kämpfer'
Karl-Immermann-Str., DDR-90
Karl-Marx-Stadt
History/Public Affairs Museum - 1968
memorabilia on the newspaper 'Der
Kämpfer' as a collective propagandist,
agitator and organisator of the labour-
movement in the Erzgebirge
1918-1933; development of the
proletarian press; history of
anti-fascist resistance

04837
Museum für Naturkunde
Theaterplatz 1, DDR-90 Karl-Marx-
Stadt
Natural History Museum - 1869
zoology; geology; mineralogy;
paleontology - library

04838
Roter Turm
Wilhelm-Pieck-Str.12, DDR-90
Karl-Marx-Stadt
General Museum - 1959
13th century city tower; local historic
material

04839
Schloßbergmuseum
Schloßberg 12, DDR-90 Karl-Marx-
Stadt
General Museum - 1931
local history; development; labour-
movement; peasant crafts and culture;
13th-18th century sculpture; 18th-19th
century local painting; 13th-17th
century architecture; smithwork -
library

04840
Städtische Kunstsammlung
Theaterplatz 1, DDR-90 Karl-Marx-
Stadt
Fine Arts Museum - 1920
18th-19th century German painting;
German Impressionism and
Expressionism; 20th century art;
19th-20th century French and German
sculpture; drawings; crafts; textiles

04841
**Städtische Textil- und
Kunstgewerbe-Sammlung**
Theaterplatz 1, DDR-90 Karl-Marx-
Stadt
Decorative Arts Museum - 1898
native textiles; native arts and crafts

04842
Unterirdische Felsendome
Weg nach dem Kalkweg, DDR-90
Karl-Marx-Stadt
Natural History Museum - 1954
historic limestone quarry; processing
exhibit

Kirchdorf auf Poel

04843
Heimatstube
DDR-2404 Kirchdorf auf Poel
General Museum - 1958
history of the Poel isle; folk history

Kirschau

04844
Burgmuseum
Am Schloßberg 21, DDR-8604
Kirschau
General Museum - 1922
castle ruins; armaments; ceramics;
textiles

Kloster Vessra

04845
Agrarhistorisches Museum
DDR-6111 Kloster Vessra
Agriculture Museum - 1975
regional history of agriculture; feudal-
epoch and peasant war; alliance-
politics of workers and peasants; land
reform; development of agriculture
technologies; animal husbandry -
library

Kloster Zinna

04846
Heimatmuseum
Neue Abtei, DDR-1701 Kloster Zinna
General Museum - 1951
cloister history; weaving

Kohren-Sahlis

04847
Töpfermuseum
Ernst-Thälmann-Str. 14, DDR-7234
Kohren-Sahlis
Decorative Arts Museum - 1961
18th century potter's workshop;
workers equipment

Kölleda

04848
Heimatmuseum
Thälmannstr.10, DDR-5234 Kölleda
General Museum - 1929
geology; ancient and early history;
fauna; local history; crafts;
numismatics - library

Königstein

04849
Museum Festung Königstein
DDR-8305 Königstein
History/Public Affairs Museum - 1955
13th century fortress; Renaissance
armory; fountain; casemate - library

Köthen

04850
Heimatmuseum
Museumsstr. 4-5, DDR-437 Köthen
General Museum - 1912
ancient, early, local and crafts history;
religious art; 12th-16th century church
bells; peasant life

04851
Johann-Friedrich-Naumann-Museum
DDR-437 Köthen
History/Public Affairs Museum - 1915
memorabilia on science researcher
A.-Fr.Naumann; ornithology collection

Kriebstein

04852
Kreismuseum Burg Kriebstein
Kriebethal, DDR-9251 Kriebstein
General Museum - 1947
historic rooms; romanic chapel;
frescoes; religious sculptures
15th-17th century; painting; ceramics

Krippen

04853
**Friedrich-Gottlob-Heller-
Heimatmuseum**
Kellerstr. 54, DDR-8322 Krippen
History/Public Affairs Museum - 1972
memorabilia on Friedrich-Gottlob
Heller, inventor of mechanical pulp

Kyffhäuser

04854
**Kyffhäuser-Ruinen, Burgmuseum
und Denkmal**
DDR-473 Kyffhäuser
Archeology Museum - 1934
castle ruins, ancient and early historic
finds; geology; excavations; history of
Imperial Castle; monument; model

Lancken-Granitz

04855
Museum Jagdschloß Granitz
DDR-2331 Lancken-Granitz
General Museum - 1959
history of Rügen; cultural
development; feudal epoch

Landsberg

04856
Heimatmuseum
Bahnhofstr., DDR-4105 Landsberg
General Museum - 1954
ancient, early history; fauna; local
history, crafts, industrialization

Landwüst

04857
Vogtländisches Bauernmuseum
Landwüst 48, DDR-9931 Landwüst
General Museum - 1968
folklore; medieval - present-day
peasant culture; carved butter forms

Laucha

04858
Glockenmuseum
Glockenmuseumstr. 1, DDR-4807
Laucha
History/Public Affairs Museum - 1932
18th century bell casting; workshop;
tools; 15th-19th century bell collection

Lauscha

04859
Museum für Glaskunst
Oberlandstr. 10, DDR-6426 Lauscha
Decorative Arts Museum - 1897
glass industry of Thüringen; glass art
and technology; optical use

Lehde

04860
Freiland-Museum
Lehde 31, DDR-7543 Lehde
General Museum - 1957
farm 18th century with historic
buildings, furnishings, equipment,
costumes

Leipzig

04861
Bach-Archiv
Gohliser Schlößchen, DDR-7022
Leipzig
History/Public Affairs Museum - 1950
memorabilia on Bach family; letters;
pictures; numismatics - library

04862
**Buch- und Schriftensammlung der
Deutschen Bücherei**
Deutscher Platz, DDR-701 Leipzig
History/Public Affairs Museum - 1884
history of printing; history of book and
writing and bookbinding - library

04863
Georgi-Dimitroff-Museum
Georgi-Dimitroff-Platz 1, DDR-701
Leipzig
History/Public Affairs Museum - 1952
Demonstration of Reichstag fire trial
1933; memorabilia on Georgi Dimitrov
(1882-1949), his significance in labour-
movement - library

04864
Institut für Länderkunde
Georgi-Dimitroff-Platz 1, DDR-701
Leipzig
Science/Tech Museum - 1892
archives for explorers; exploring
expeditions; manuscript;
correspondence of German
geographers - library

04865
Iskra-Gedenkstätte
Russenstr. 48, DDR-701 Leipzig
History/Public Affairs Museum - 1956
building in which V.J. Lenin (1870-1924)
had the first issues of the Russian
Marxist paper 'Iskra' printed; historic
printing press; original and
reconstructed material; Russian
revolution material

04866
Karl-Liebknecht-Gedenkstätte
Braustr. 15, DDR-701 Leipzig
History/Public Affairs Museum - 1953
memorabilia on political figure Karl
Liebknecht (1871-1915) in house of his
birth; manuscripts

04867
Lenin-Gedenkstätte
Rosa-Luxemburg-Str. 19, DDR-701
Leipzig
History/Public Affairs Museum - 1957
memorabilia on V.J.Lenin (1870-1924)
and his stay here in former publishing
house of 'Leipziger Volkszeitung'

04868
Museum der Bildenden Künste
Georg-Dimitroff-Platz 1, DDR-701
Leipzig
Fine Arts Museum - 1848
15th-18th century Dutch, German and
Italian painting; Romanic art; German
impressionism; 18th-20th century
European painting; Baroque and
Dürer-age sculpture; 17th-18th century
prints - library

04869
**Museum des Kunsthandwerks
(Grassi-Museum)**
Johannisplatz 5-11, DDR-701 Leipzig
Decorative Arts Museum - 1874
ancient art objects; 15th-19th century
furnishing; 16th century religious
sculpture; decorative objects; medals
since 16th century; textiles; rugs;
pewter; ceramics; glass - library

04870
**Museum für Geschichte der
Leipziger Arbeiterbewegung**
Georgi-Dimitroff-Platz 1, DDR-701
Leipzig
History/Public Affairs Museum - 1054
history of Leipzig labour-movement
1830 - present - library

04871
**Museum für Geschichte der Stadt
Leipzig**
Markt 1, DDR-701 Leipzig
History/Public Affairs Museum - 1911
historical rooms; portraits; medieval
ceramics and pottery; numismatics;
13th-18th century armaments;
15th-16th century printing crafts;
Baroque furnishings; sculpture; prints;
paintings; pewter; weights and
measures; costumes - library

04872
Museum für Völkerkunde
Täubchenweg 2, DDR-701 Leipzig
Anthropology Museum - 1869
culture of Asia, America, Africa,
Australia, Oceania - library

04873
**Musikinstrumenten-Museum der
Karl-Marx-Universität Leipzig**
Täubchenweg 2c, DDR-701 Leipzig
Music Museum - 1902
Music instruments from Middle Ages
to the present; folk instruments;
mechanical instument; European and
non-European folk instruments;
archives - library

04874
Naturwissenschaftliches Museum
Lortzingstr. 3, DDR-701 Leipzig
Natural History Museum - 1906
astronomy; geology; pleistocene
zoology; regional, ancient and early
history; regional zoology; conservation
botany - library

04875
Schillerhaus
Menckestr. 42, DDR-7022 Leipzig
History/Public Affairs Museum - 1842
memorabilia on Friedrich Schiller's
(1759-1805) stay here

04876
Völkerschlacht-Denkmal
Leninstr., DDR-7027 Leipzig
History/Public Affairs Museum - 1913
architecture; sculpture; memorabilia to
the Battle of Nations 1813

Leisnig

04877
Kreismuseum Burg Mildenstein
Burglehn 6, DDR-732 Leisnig
General Museum - 1890
ancient, early and local history;
industrialization; labour-movement;
peasant culture; crafts and guild
history; 15th-16th century religious
wood sculpture; armaments;
numismatics - library

Lengenfeld

04878
Heimatstube
Otto-Nuschke-Str. 67, DDR-9802
Lengenfeld
General Museum - 1955
geology; local history; history of local
crafts; costumes

Lenzen

04879
Heimatmuseum
Burghof, DDR-2805 Lenzen
General Museum - 1954
ancient and early historic finds; stone
collection; local history and crafts

Liebstadt

04880
Museum Schloß Kuckuckstein
Am Schloßberg 1, DDR-8301 Liebstadt
General Museum - 1925
geology; botany and zoology; local
history - library

Löbau

04881
Arbeitergedenkstätte 'Hopfenblüte'
Platz der Befreiung, DDR-87 Löbau
History/Public Affairs Museum - 1971
history of labour-movement

04882
Stadtmuseum
Johannisstr. 5, DDR-87 Löbau
General Museum - 1894
ancient and early history; local history;
burgher living culture; crafts; religious
sculpture

Lommatzsch

04883
Heimatmuseum
Markt 1, DDR-826 Lommatzsch
General Museum - 1909
ancient and early history; local history;
peasant crafts and tools

04884
Robert-Volkmann-Haus
Kirchplatz 7, DDR-826 Lommatzsch
History/Public Affairs Museum - 1971
memorabilia on Robert Volkmann

Lübbenau

04885
**Spreewaldmuseum Lübbenau mit
Volkspark**
DDR-7543 Lübbenau
General Museum - 1899
ancient and early history; Sorabian
history; Luther prints; Reformation
pamphlets; crafts; costumes; 17th-19th
century painting and prints; decorative
objects; porcelain; glass; graphic

Luckau

04886
Heimatmuseum
Langestr. 71, DDR-796 Luckau
General Museum - 1912
ancient and early history; native
animals; peasant culture and tools;
crafts history; numismatics

Luckenwalde

04887
Kreis-Heimatmuseum
Platz der Jugend 11, DDR-171
Luckenwalde
General Museum - 1906
ancient and early history; local history;
development of local industry

Lugau

04888
Heimat- und Bergbaumuseum
Ernst-Thälmann-Str. 26, DDR-9159
Lugau
General Museum - 1958
history of mining; local history; history
of local labour-movement

Lützen

04889
Gustav-Adolf-Gedenkstätte
Schwedeninsel bei Lützen, DDR-4854
Lützen
History/Public Affairs Museum - 1932
monument to Swedish king Gustav-
Adolf; Swedish house with Gustav-
Adolf room; battle relief; battle-field
finds at scene of battle here 1632

04890
Heimatmuseum
Schloßstr.4, DDR-4854 Lützen
General Museum - 1928
history of Thirty Years' War; local
history

Magdeburg

04891
**Bildungsstätte 'Weltall - Erde -
Mensch'**
Weitlingerstr. 1a, DDR-301 Magdeburg
Natural History Museum - 1954
origin and evolution of universe, earth
and man - auditorium

04892
**Gedenk- und Bildungsstätte 'Erich
Weinert'**
Thiemstr. 7, DDR-3011 Magdeburg,
Buckau
History/Public Affairs Museum - 1961
memorabilia on Erich Weinert
(1890-1953) in house of his birth

04893
Kloster Unser Lieben Frauen
Regierungsstr. 4, DDR-301 Magdeburg
Fine Arts Museum - 1963
sculpture; medieval crafts - library

04894
Kulturhistorisches Museum
Otto-von-Guericke-Str. 68/73,
DDR-301 Magdeburg
Natural History Museum - 1906
mineralogy; geology; zoology; ancient
and early history; ceramics; decorative
objects; wrought iron; painting and
sculpture; technology - library

Marienberg

04895
Erzgebirgische Heimatschau
Zschopauer Str. 21, DDR-934
Marienberg
General Museum - 1966
local history; pewter and silver mining;
paintings; fauna

Markkleeberg

04896
Heimatmuseum
Raschwitzer Str. 26, DDR-7113
Markkleeberg
General Museum - 1953
local and regional history

Markneukirchen

04897
Musikinstrumenten-Museum
Bienengarten 2, DDR-9935
Markneukirchen
Music Museum - 1883
local history; musical instruments of all
cultures; mechanical instruments

Markranstädt

04898
Friedenszimmer
Schloß Altranstädt, DDR-7153
Markranstädt
History/Public Affairs Museum
historic room in which peace was
concluded between Sweden and
Saxony 1706

04899
Heimatmuseum
Platz des Friedens 5, DDR-7153
Markranstädt
General Museum - 1925
geology; mineralogy; coal mining;
historic finds; local history; crafts;
armaments

Meerane

04900
Heimatmuseum
Platz der Roten Armee 3, DDR-9612
Meerane
General Museum - 1888
geololgy; ancient and early history;
local history; history of local labour-
movement; industry and crafts -
library

Meiningen

04901
Baumbachhaus
Burggasse 22, DDR-61 Meiningen
History/Public Affairs Museum
memorabilia on poet Rudolf Baumbach
(1840-1905); memorial to writer Ludwig
Bechstein (1801-1860); 19th century
burgher living style

04902
Lehrschau für Vogelschutz
Am Bibrasberg, DDR-61 Meiningen
Natural History Museum
ornithology

04903
**Staatliche Museum, Schloß
Elisabethenburg**
DDR-61 Meiningen
General Museum - 1956
18th-19th century European painting;
religious sculpture; 20th century
furnishings, prints, paintings; 19th-20th
century theater history; 17th-19th
century musical instruments;
mineralogy; 18th century Italian
operas; paleontology; memorabilia on
Max Reger - library

Meissen

04904
Albrechtsburg
Domplatz 1, DDR-825 Meissen
Fine Arts Museum - 1900
historic rooms; 15th-16th century
religious sculpture; Meissen porcelain
production; 15th century castle

04905
**Schauhalle des VEB Staatliche
Porzellan-Manufaktur Meissen**
Leninstr. 9, DDR-825 Meissen
Decorative Arts Museum - 1916
development of industry; workshop -
library

04906
Stadt- und Kreismuseum
Rathausplatz 2, DDR-825 Meissen
History/Public Affairs Museum - 1901
ancient and early history; local
medieval history; wine production;
rooms in Baroque, Rococo, Empire,
Biedermeier styles; clocks; pottery;
18th-19th century Meissen porcelain

Merseburg

04907
Kreismuseum
Schloß, DDR-42 Merseburg
General Museum - 1965
ancient, early history; native history;
early Middle Ages-wars of liberation

Mittweida

04908
Museum der Stadt Mittweida
Kirchberg 3-5, DDR-925 Mittweida
General Museum - 1897
history; city architecture; crafts; guilds;
paintings; drawings; 15th-17th century
religious sculpture

Molchow-Stendenitz

04909
**Waldmuseum am Zermützelsee in
der Ruppiner Schweiz**
DDR-19 Molchow-Stendenitz
General Museum - 1936
local and regional history; native flora
and fauna; forestry; hunting

Molmerswende

04910
**Gottfried-August-Bürger-
Gedenkstätte**
DDR-4721 Molmerswende,
Molmerswende
History/Public Affairs Museum - 1972
memorabilia of the poet Gottfried-
August Bürger

Moritzburg

04911
Barockmuseum Schloß Moritzburg
DDR-8105 Moritzburg
History/Public Affairs Museum - 1946
historic rooms and furnishings;
17th-19th century crafts, porcelain,
glass, portraits; 18th century carriages
and coaches

04912
**Museum für Vogelkunde und
Vogelschutz**
Fasanenschlößchen, DDR-8105
Moritzburg
Natural History Museum - 1953
ornithology

Mügeln

04913
Heimatmuseum
Schulplatz 4, DDR-7263 Mügeln
General Museum - 1925
geology; ancient and early history;
local history

Mühlberg

04914
Stadtmuseum
Museumsstr. 9, DDR-7906 Mühlberg
General Museum - 1926
ancient and early history; local history;
religious sculpture; shipping and
fishing - library

Mühlhausen

04915
Heimatmuseum Mühlhausen
Leninstr. 61, DDR-57 Mühlhausen
General Museum - 1879
geology; paleontology; mineralogy;
zoology; anthropology of Africa and
South Sea; city and crafts history;
costumes; decorative objects;
numismatics - library

04916
Stadtbefestigung
Frauentor, Rabenturm und Wehrgang,
DDR-57 Mühlhausen
General Museum
seven towers with furnishing and local
history

04917
**Zentrale Gedenkstätte 'Deutscher
Bauernkrieg'**
Am Kornmarkt, DDR-57 Mühlhausen
History/Public Affairs Museum - 1976
history of German peasant war 1525;
local history; crafts history

Müllrose

04918
Heimatmuseum
Platz der Freiheit, DDR-1203 Müllrose
General Museum - 1953
ancient and early history; local crafts
and guilds; peasant folk art and culture

Mutzschen

04919
Heimatstube
Berggasse 21, DDR-7244 Mutzschen
General Museum - 1954
local and regional history; native stove
industry; ancient and early history

Mylau

04920
Kreismuseum Burg Mylau
Burg Mylau, DDR-9803 Mylau
General Museum - 1883
geology; mining history; zoology; local
history; textiles - library

Naumburg

04921
Fritz-Rentsch-Gedenkstätte
Neidschützerstr. 19, DDR-48
Naumburg
History/Public Affairs Museum - 1946
works of painter Fritz Rentsch in his
former home

04922
Heimatmuseum
Grochlitzer Str. 49, DDR-48 Naumburg
General Museum - 1904
11th-19th century local history; ancient
and early history; burgher life; crafts
history; birds; nature conservation;
labour-movement

04923
Max-Klinger-Gedenkstätte
DDR-48 Naumburg, Großjena
History/Public Affairs Museum - 1957
works and life of painter Max Klinger
(1857-1920) in his former home

Nerchau

04924
Heimatstube
Karl-Marx-Platz 3, DDR-7246 Nerchau
General Museum - 1943
ancient and early history; peasant
tools; textiles; embroideries; local
industry

Neschwitz

04925
Vogelschutzstation Neschwitz
DDR-8601 Neschwitz
Natural History Museum - 1930
ornithology

Neubrandenburg

04926
Kulturhistorisches Museum
Treptower Str. 38, DDR-20
Neubrandenburg
General Museum - 1976
ancient and early history; 13th-20th
century local history; medieval
armaments; 13th-15th century
ceramics; crafts; religious arts and
crafts; modern art; nature

Neubukow

04927
Heinrich-Schliemann-Gedenkstätte
Mühlenstr. 7, DDR-2567 Neubukow
History/Public Affairs Museum - 1974
memorabilia on archaeologist Heinrich
Schliemann, his life and expeditions

Neugersdorf

04928
Heimatmuseum
Goethestr. 2, DDR-8706 Neugersdorf
General Museum - 1932
17th-19th century local history; stones;
birds; history of labour-movement;
19th century folk culture

Neuhaus-Schierschnitz

04929
Heimatstube
Burg, DDR-6403 Neuhaus-
Schierschnitz
General Museum - 1954
18th-20th century mining history; 19th
century peasant culture; furniture;
costumes; household objects;
porcelain industry; bird types

Neukirch

04930
Neukirch
Hauptstr. 24, DDR-8505 Neukirch,
Lausitz
General Museum - 1935
ancient history; local and provincial
history, crafts; 18th-19th century
peasant living styles; costumes

Neuruppin

04931
Heimatmuseum
August-Bebel-Str. 14, DDR-195
Neuruppin
General Museum - 1865
ancient and early history; local and
regional history; nature religious art;
religious history; military history; cast
and models; tools; prints; paintings;
books; uniforms

Neusalza-Spremberg

04932
Heimatmuseum Reiterhaus
DDR-8713 Neusalza-Spremberg
General Museum - 1966
local and regional history

Nieder-Neundorf

04933
Heimatstube
Dorfstr. 45, DDR-8921 Nieder-
Neundorf
General Museum - 1951
stones; historic finds; local history;
19th century peasant household
objects

Niedercunnersdorf

04934
Heimatmuseum 'Alte Weberstube'
DDR-8714 Niedercunnersdorf
General Museum - 1930
local and regional history

Niederschmiedeberg

04935
Heimatschau
Klubheim, DDR-9341
Niederschmiedeberg
General Museum - 1969
folk art; native crafts; local carvings

Nordhausen

04936
**Mahn- und Gedenkstätte Mittelbau-
Dora**
DDR-5501 Nordhausen, Krimderode
History/Public Affairs Museum - 1950
crimes of German imperialism; the
system of concentration camps;
anti-fascist resistance

04937
Meyenburg-Museum
Alexander-Puschkin-Str. 31, DDR-55
Nordhausen
General Museum - 1876
geology; ancient and early history; city
history; furniture; porcelain;
numismatics; anthropology

Nossen

04938
Heimatmuseum
Schloß, DDR-8255 Nossen
General Museum - 1915
ancient history; stones; zoology; local
history; 18th-19th century peasant and
court living style; pewter; emergency
currency

04939
Klosterpark Altzella
DDR-8255 Nossen
General Museum - 1958
gravestones; ruins; lapidarium

Oderberg

04940
Heimatmuseum
Ernst-Thälmann-Str. 31, DDR-1305
Oderberg
General Museum - 1954
ancient history; geology; farming
history; local and crafts history;
shipping; models

Oederan

04941
Heimatmuseum
Pfarrgasse 5, DDR-9388 Oederan
General Museum - 1909
local crafts; history; folk art; history of
labour-movement

Oelsnitz

04942
Heimatmuseum Schloß Voigtsberg
Karl-Marx-Platz, DDR-9156 Oelsnitz
General Museum - 1957
local and regional history; weaving

Ohrdruf

04943
Heimatmuseum
Schloß Ehrenstein und Thüringer Hof,
DDR-5807 Ohrdruf
General Museum - 1935
geology; mining history; fauna; local
and palace history; crafts; industry;
wood toys; porcelain

Olbernau

04944
Althammer - Technisches Denkmal
Olbernauer Grünthal, DDR-933
Olbernau
Science/Tech Museum - 1959
forge of 16th century; copper mine;
workshops

04945
Haus der Heimat
Ernst-Thälmann-Platz, DDR-933
Olbernau
General Museum - 1957
geology and fauna; local and crafts
history; toys; carving; pewter

Oranienbaum

04946
Kreismuseum Gräfenhainichen
Schloß, DDR-4407 Oranienbaum
General Museum - 1969
technology; crafts; regional history

Oranienburg

04947
Kreismuseum
Breitestr. 1, DDR-14 Oranienburg
General Museum - 1932
Ancient and early history; local history
and crafts; shipping; birds;
memorabilia on chemist F.F. Runge
(1795-1867)

Oschatz

04948
Heimatmuseum
Frongasse, DDR-726 Oschatz
General Museum - 1897
ancient historic finds; local history;
peasant living style

Ossmannstedt

04949
Wieland-Gedenkstätte
DDR-5321 Ossmannstedt
History/Public Affairs Museum - 1956
memorabilia on poet Christoph
M.Wieland (1733-1813) in his former
house; memorial rooms

Osterburg

04950
Kreis-Heimatmuseum
Straße des Friedens 21, DDR-354
Osterburg
General Museum - 1954
geology; ancient and early history;
fauna; local and industrial history;
excavation finds - library

Osterwieck/Harz

04951
Heimatmuseum
Markt 11, DDR-3606 Osterwieck/Harz
General Museum - 1930
geology; ancient history; native
zoology; local history; crafts

Ostseebad Graal-Müritz

04952
Heimatstube
Ernst-Thälmann-Str. 17, DDR-2553
Ostseebad Graal-Müritz
General Museum - 1971
local and regional history

Oybin

04953
Bergmuseum Oybin
DDR-8806 Oybin
General Museum - 1972
local and regional history

Parchim

04954
Heimatmuseum
Thälmann-Platz 3, DDR-285 Parchim
General Museum - 1935
ancient, early history; local history;
18th-19th century area glass products

Pegau

04955
Historisches Lehrkabinett
Ernst-Thälmann-Str. 16, DDR-722
Pegau
General Museum - 1899
geology; ancient and early history;
local history; post and transportation

Perleberg

04956
Kreisheimatmuseum
Mönchort 7-10, DDR-291 Perleberg
General Museum - 1905
ancient and early history; local history;
crafts; trades

Pirna

04957
Stadtmuseum
Klosterhof 12, DDR-83 Pirna
General Museum - 1861
ancient, early and local history;
mineralogy; history of artificial silk
production

Plauen

04958
Vogtländisches Kreismuseum
Nobelstr. 9-13, DDR-99 Plauen
General Museum - 1923
historic rooms; geology; mining;
hydraulics; forestry - library

Pobershau

04959
Schau-Bergwerk 'Molcher Stolln'
Amtsseite 32, DDR-9344 Pobershau
Science/Tech Museum - 1959
tin and silver mining

Pockau

04960
**Museum 'Geschichte der
Arbeiterbewegung des Kreises
Marienberg'**
An der Pockau, DDR-9345 Pockau
History/Public Affairs Museum - 1976
history of regional labour-movement

04961
Schau-Ölmühle Pockau
Mühlenweg, DDR-9345 Pockau
General Museum - 1970
oil-mill used for processing flax and
rape

Posterstein

04962
Heimatmuseum Burg Posterstein
Posterstein 83, DDR-7421 Posterstein
General Museum - 1953
history of city and castle; crafts;
peasant household objects

Potsdam

04963
Armee-Museum
Neuer Garten, DDR-15 Potsdam
History/Public Affairs Museum - 1960
arms; flags; uniforms; documents;
National People's Army; models

04964
Bezirkmuseum
Tieckstr. 4, DDR-15 Potsdam
General Museum - 1909
geology; native flora and fauna; glass;
pewter; smithwork; numismatics

04965
Bildergalerie
DDR-15 Potsdam
Fine Arts Museum - 1918
Flemish; Italian and French painting;
various schools

04966
Bruno-H.-Bürgel-Gedenkstätte
Merkurstr. 10, DDR-15 Potsdam
History/Public Affairs Museum - 1954
memorabilia on nature scientist Bruno
H.Bürgel (1875-1948); scientific
instruments; archive; documents;
letters - library

04967
Chinesisches Teehaus
DDR-15 Potsdam
Fine Arts Museum - 1918
Japanese and Chinese porcelain;
architecture

04968
**Gartenanlagen außerhalb
Sanssoucis**
DDR-15 Potsdam
History/Public Affairs Museum
several palaces with interiors;
horticulture

04969
Museum für Ur- und Frühgeschichte Potsdam
Schloß Babelsberg, DDR-1502 Potsdam
Archeology Museum - 1953
Ancient and early history of the area; archaeological materials from recent excavations - library

04970
Neue Kammern
DDR-15 Potsdam
Fine Arts Museum - 1918
architecture; furnishings; paitings and sculpture; porcelain

04971
Neues Palais
DDR-15 Potsdam
Fine Arts Museum - 1918
architecture; sculpture; arts and crafts; paintings

04972
Orangerie
DDR-15 Potsdam
Fine Arts Museum
furnishings

04973
Parkbauten und Plastiken in Sanssouci
DDR-15 Potsdam
Fine Arts Museum
historic rooms; sculptures; furnishing; pheasantry; dairy-farm

04974
Römische Bäder
DDR-15 Potsdam
Fine Arts Museum - 1900
architecture; frescoes; sculpture

04975
Schloß Cecilienhof
Neuer Garten, DDR-15 Potsdam
History/Public Affairs Museum - 1955
historic conference rooms and documentation of the Potsdam Agreement

04976
Schloß Charlottenhof
Park Sanssouci, DDR-15 Potsdam
Fine Arts Museum - 1870
architecture; sculpture; furnishings and porcelain; painting; etchings

04977
Schloß Sanssouci
Park Sanssouci, DDR-15 Potsdam
Fine Arts Museum - 1870
Potsdam Rococo architecture; sculpture; art and crafts; French painting

Prenzlau

04978
Kreisheimatmuseum
Uckerwiek 813a, DDR-213 Prenzlau
General Museum - 1899/1957
historic rooms; ancient and early history; zoology; botany; farming - library

Prerow

04979
Darß-Museum
DDR-2383 Prerow
Natural History Museum - 1953
geology; botany; marine algae; forestry; fishing; shipping

Prieros

04980
Heimathaus
Am Dorfanger 1, DDR-1608 Prieros
General Museum - 1955
ancient and early history; local history

Pritzwalk

04981
Heimatmuseum des Kreises Pritzwalk
Karl-Liebknecht-Str. 10, DDR-192 Pritzwalk
General Museum - 1054
local and regional history

Pulsnitz

04982
Heimatmusuem
Platz der Befreiung, DDR-8514 Pulsnitz
General Museum - 1947
local and regional history

Quedlinburg

04983
Klopstock Museum
Schloßberg 12, DDR-43 Quedlinburg
History/Public Affairs Museum - 1946
memorabilia of Friedrich Klopstock (1724-1803) in house of his birth; memorabilia of physician Dorothea C.Erxleben (1715-1762); memorabilia of sports teacher J.C.GutsMuths (1759-1839); memorabilia of Carl Ritter (1779-1839)

04984
Museumsgalerie
Schloßberg 12, DDR-43 Quedlinburg
Fine Arts Museum
art collection

04985
Schloßmuseum
Schloßberg 1, DDR-43 Quedlinburg
History/Public Affairs Museum - 1860
Renaissance and Baroque furnishings; history; stones; minerals; crafts; guilds; costumes; painting and sculpture - library

04986
Ständerhaus
Wordgasse 3, DDR-43 Quedlinburg
History/Public Affairs Museum
architecture

Querfurt

04987
Burg- und Kreismuseum
Burg, DDR-424 Querfurt
General Museum - 1952
ancient history; castle and city history

Rabenau

04988
Heimatsammlung
Schulstr., DDR-8222 Rabenau
General Museum - 1922
local history; local chair-making industry; botany; zoology

Radeberg

04989
Heimatmuseum
Schloßstr. 6, DDR-8142 Radeberg
General Museum - 1953
geology; ancient history; city views; pewter; locks

Radebeul

04990
Heimatmuseum
Knohlweg 37, DDR Radebeul
General Museum - 1915
historic rooms; furnishings; geology; wine industry

04991
Indianer-Museum
Hölderlinstr. 15, DDR-8122 Radebeul
Anthropology Museum - 1928
tools, weapons, costumes, jewelry, trophies and cult objects of 19th century North American Indians

Radeburg

04992
Heimatmuseum
Heinrich-Zille-Str. 9, DDR-8106 Radeburg
General Museum - 1929
ancient history; local history; crafts; industry; drawings by local native artist Heinrich Zille (1858-1929)

Rammenau

04993
Museum Barockschloß Rammenau
Schloß Rammenau, DDR-8501 Rammenau
History/Public Affairs Museum - 1967
memorabilia on philosopher Johann G.Fichte (1762-1814); letters; pictures; literature

Ranis

04994
Museum Burg Ranis
DDR-6843 Ranis
General Museum - 1957
geology; ancient history; Old- and New Stone Age finds

Ravensbrück

04995
Nationale Mahn- und Gedenkstätte Ravensbrück
DDR-1432 Ravensbrück
History/Public Affairs Museum - 1959
former concentration camp

Regenstein

04996
Burgruine Regenstein
Lange Str. 34, DDR-372 Regenstein
History/Public Affairs Museum
17th century fortress; historic rooms; wall fragments

Reichenau

04997
Reichenau
Reichenau 90, DDR-8291 Reichenau
General Museum - 1955
local and regional history

Reichenbach

04998
Neuberin-Gedenkstätte
Johannisplatz 3, DDR-98 Reichenbach, Vogtland
History/Public Affairs Museum
memorabilia of actress Karoline Neuber (1697-1760) in house of her birth

Reitzengeschwenda

04999
Oberlandmuseum
DDR-6801 Reitzengeschwenda
General Museum - 1969
ancient and early history; native, local and regional history

Renthendorf

05000
Brehm-Gedenkstätte
Renthendorf Nr. 22, DDR-6541 Renthendorf
History/Public Affairs Museum - 1946
memorabilia of animal scientist A.E. Brehm (1829-1884) in his former home; manuscripts; specimen; ornithology - library

Rerik

05001
Museum der Stadt Rerik
Am Haff 2, DDR-2572 Rerik
General Museum - 1952
ancient and early history; local history; fishing equipment

Reuterstadt Stavenhagen

05002
Fritz-Reuter-Literatur-Museum
Markt 1, DDR-2044 Reuterstadt Stavenhagen
History/Public Affairs Museum - 1960
memorabilia of poet Fritz Reuter (1810-1974) in house of his birth

Ribnitz-Damgarten

05003
Bernsteinmuseum
Im Kloster, DDR-259 Ribnitz-Damgarten
General Museum - 1954
social history; city history; marine history; shipping; fishing; amber collection

Riesa

05004
Heimatmuseum
Poppitzer Platz 3, DDR-84 Riesa
General Museum - 1923
ancient and early history; local history; industry; shipping; transportation; first railroad; stones

Rittersgrün

05005
Kleinbahn-Museum
Oberrittersgrün, DDR-9444 Rittersgrün
General Museum - 1977
railroad history

Rochlitz

05006
Heimatmuseum Schloß Rochlitz
Sörnziger Weg 1, DDR-929 Rochlitz
General Museum - 1892
geology; ancient and early history; local history; flax processing; textile industry; ceramics - library

Rochsburg

05007
Museum Schloß Rochsburg
Schloßstr. 1, DDR-9291 Rochsburg
Decorative Arts Museum - 1948
historic rooms; furnishings; Baroque, Rococo and Biedermeier interiors

Rodewisch

05008
Museum Göltzsch
Schloßinsel, DDR-9706 Rodewisch
General Museum - 1951
geology; archaeology; ceramics; tools; city and industrial history; spinning and embroidery

Römhild

05009
Steinsburg-Museum
DDR-6102 Römhild
General Museum - 1929
ancient and early hsitory; local history
- library

Rosswein

05010
Heimatmuseum
Markt 4, DDR-7304 Rosswein
General Museum - 1976
early history; crafts and guilds; silver
mining; history of local labour
movement

Rostock

05011
Kulturhistorisches Museum
Im Steintor, DDR-25 Rostock
History/Public Affairs Museum - 1903
ancient and early history; history of
city and trade; shipbuilding and travel;
crafts; industry; religious sculpture;
paintings; prints; models of weapons
and ships

05012
Kunsthalle
Am Schwanenteich, DDR-25 Rostock
Fine Arts Museum - 1969
painting; sculpture; drawings of all
periods - library

05013
Schiffahrtsmuseum
August-Begel-Str. 1, DDR-25 Rostock
History/Public Affairs Museum - 1968
history of shipping; navigation history

05014
Schiffbau-Museum
Rostock-Schmare, DDR-25 Rostock
History/Public Affairs Museum - 1970
shipbuilding history; technological
equipment

Rostock-Warnemünde

05015
Heimatmuseum Warnemünde
Theodor-Körner-Str. 31, DDR-253
Rostock-Warnemünde
General Museum - 1911
historic furnishings; fishing; shipping;
models; costumes

Rothenburg

05016
**Heimatmuseum für Wild, Wald und
Naturschutz**
Karl-Marx-Platz, DDR-8923
Rothenburg
General Museum - 1931
local and regional history

Rübeland

05017
Tropfsteinhöhlen
Blankenburger Str. 34, DDR-3725
Rübeland
Natural History Museum
caves with stalactites and stalacmites;
development and history of caves and
their discovery; excavation finds; cave
bear fossils

Rudolstadt

05018
Staatliche Museen Heidecksburg
Schloßbezirk 1-3, DDR-682 Rudolstadt
General Museum - 1950
historic rooms; furnishings; paintings;
archaeology; religious art; decorative
objects; numismatics; prints; minerals;
botany; zoology; armaments; uniforms

05019
**Volkskunde-Museum 'Thüringer
Bauernhäuser'**
Große Wiese 2, DDR-682 Rudolstadt
Open Air Museum - 1914/15
2 frame houses; peasant furnishings;
household objects; work tools; crafts

Ruhla

05020
Heimatmuseum
Obere Lindenstr. 29-31, DDR-5906
Ruhla
General Museum - 1906
geology; history of mining; iron crafts;
knifesmith work; metal and clock
industry; pipe collection; costumes;
furnishings

Saalfeld

05021
Feengrotten
Feengrottenweg 2, DDR-68 Saalfeld
Natural History Museum - 1914
cave with stalactites and stalacmites

05022
**Naturkundliche Sammlungen des
Forschungsreisenden Emil Weiske**
Sonneberger Str. 44, DDR-68 Saalfeld
Natural History Museum - 1901
natural history; zoology; ethnography;
photos of America, Australia and isles
of the South Sea

05023
Thüringer Heimatmuseum
Münzplatz 5, DDR-68 Saalfeld
General Museum - 1904
religious crafts and sculpture; geology;
mineralogy; peasant culture;
costumes; tools; numismatics

Sachsenhausen

05024
Nationale Mahn- und Gedenkstätte
Straße der Nationen 22, DDR-1412
Sachsenhausen, Oranienburg
History/Public Affairs Museum - 1961
former concentration camp with
history of anti-fascist resistance of
European people; pathology with
medical instruments; persecution of
Jewish people

Salzwedel

05025
Jenny-Marx-Museum
Jenny-Marx-Str. 20, DDR-356
Salzwedel
History/Public Affairs Museum - 1969
memorabilia on Marx family in house
of Jenny Marx' birth

05026
Johann-Friedrich-Danneil-Museum
An der Marienkirche 3, DDR-356
Salzwedel
General Museum - 1836
history of the Old Mark area; history
of the shipping city; pewter;
numismatics; religious sculpture;
memorabilia on J.Fr.Danneil - library
1160; 1360

Sangerhausen

05027
Spengler-Museum
Straße der Opfer des Faschismus 33,
DDR-47 Sangerhausen
General Museum - 1912
geology; Old Pleistocene fauna;
ancient and early history; regional
history; mining; birds; butterflies and
mollusk collection - library

Scharfenberg

05028
Heimatmuseum
Scharfenberg-Kellerhaus, DDR-8251
Scharfenberg
General Museum - 1958
geology; mining

Schirgiswalde

05029
Heimatmuseum
Hentschelgasse 2, DDR-8605
Schirgiswalde
General Museum - 1924
local history; geology

Schkeuditz

05030
Schkeuditz
Mühlstr. 50, DDR-7144 Schkeuditz
General Museum - 1926
ancient and early history; city history

Schleusingen

05031
**Ausstellungszentrum Schloß
Bertholdsburg**
Bertholdsburg, DDR-6056
Schleusingen
General Museum - 1910
geology; mineralogy; city history;
glass technology and glass blowing;
papermaking; book history and art -
library

Schmalkalden

05032
Museum Schloß Wilhelmsburg
DDR-608 Schmalkalden
General Museum - 1873
historic rooms; geology; mining; iron
industry; crafts; local history;
apothecary science; stoves;
costumes; decorative objects;
furnishings; numismatics

Schmölln

05033
Heimatmuseum
Am Kulturhaus 1, DDR-8508 Schmölln
General Museum - 1958
ancient historic finds; local history;
peasant crafts; household objects;
native birds

Schneeberg

05034
**Museum für Bergmännische
Volkskunst**
Rosa-Luxemburg-Platz 1, DDR-9412
Schneeberg
General Museum - 1929
ores of minerals of area mines; history
crafts; carving pewter casting; folk art

Schönberg

05035
Heimatmuseum
An der Kirche 8-9, DDR-244
Schönberg
General Museum - 1903
ancient and early historic finds;
regional history; crafts; work tools;
pewter; costumes

Schönebeck

05036
Kreismuseum
Pfännerstr. 41, DDR-33 Schönebeck
General Museum - 1924
geology; minerals; stones; crafts and
guilds; costumes; peasant living style

Schöneck

05037
Heimatstube
Dr.-Külz-Str. 10, DDR-9655 Schöneck
General Museum - 1977
local and regional history

Schöneiche

05038
Heimatmuseum
Dorfaue 8, DDR-1254 Schöneiche
General Museum - 1935
local and regional history

Schönfels

05039
Burgmuseum Schönfels
Straße der Jugend 10, DDR-9524
Schönfels
General Museum - 1975
folklore; folk art; native crafts

Schwarzenberg

05040
Erzgebirgisches Eisen und Zinn
Obere Schloßstr. 36, DDR-943
Schwarzenberg
History/Public Affairs Museum - 1947
history of iron mining; iron processing
- library

Schwedt

05041
Stadt und Kreismuseum
Am Markt 4, DDR-133 Schwedt
General Museum - 1930
ancient and early history; history of
city; industrial history; peasant
traditions

Schwerin

05042
Historisches Museum Schwerin
Herman-Matern-Str. 28, DDR-27
Schwerin
History/Public Affairs Museum - 1962
history of peasant and labour
movement of Mecklenburg region

05043
Museum für Ur- und Frühgeschichte
Lennestr. 1, DDR-27 Schwerin
History/Public Affairs Museum - 1873
ancient and early history - library

05044
Polytechnisches Museum
Lennestr. 1, DDR-27 Schwerin
Science/Tech Museum - 1961
use of energy; technology in
agriculture and architecture

05045
Staatliches Museum Schwerin
Alter Garten 3, DDR-27 Schwerin
Fine Arts Museum - 1882
17th century Dutch painting; 18th
century European painting;
contemporary art; 18th-20th century
prints; regional folklore; peasant
furnishings; costumes; tools; jewelry;
crafts; guilds; local history; glass
decorative objects - library

Sebnitz

05046
Heimatmuseum
Bergstr., DDR-836 Sebnitz
General Museum - 1909
city history; pewter; industry

Seebach

05047
Vogelschutzwarte Seebach
DDR-5701 Seebach
Natural History Museum - 1908
ornithology

Seebad Heringsdorf

05048
Maxim-Gorki-Gedächtnisstätte
Maxim-Gorki-Str. 20, DDR-2255
Seebad Heringsdorf
History/Public Affairs Museum - 1948
memorabilia on poet Maxim Gorki
(1868-1936) in his former home

Seelow

05049
**Gedenkstätte der Befreiung auf den
Seelower Höhen**
DDR-121 Seelow
History/Public Affairs Museum - 1972
documents; weapons

Seiffen

05050
Erzgebirgisches Spielzeugmuseum
Ernst-Thälman-Str. 73, DDR-9335
Seiffen
History/Public Affairs Museum - 1953
development of toy production -
library

Seifhennersdorf

05051
Stadtmuseum
Nordstr. 21, DDR-8812
Seifhennersdorf
General Museum - 1977
geology; local history; peasant living
style

Senftenberg

05052
Kreismuseum
Schloß, DDR-784 Senftenberg
General Museum - 1907
ancient and early history; city and
castle history; mining; peasant crafts
and domestic utensils; religious art

Serrahn

05053
Biologische Station Serrahn
DDR-2081 Serrahn
Natural History Museum - 1953
ornithology; nature conservation ;
forestry; game and hunting research

Siebenlehn

05054
Heimatmuseum
Otto-Altenkirch-Str. 44, DDR-9216
Siebenlehn
General Museum - 1928
botany; zoology; local history

Sohland

05055
Heimathaus
Lessingstr. 19, DDR-8606 Sohland
General Museum - 1957
18th century weaver's house; historic
weaving shops; local history

Sondershausen

05056
**Staatliches Heimat und
Schloßmuseum**
Schloß, DDR-54 Sondershausen
General Museum - 1901
palace rooms; furnishings; Baroque-
Biedermeier paintings and applied
arts; geology; paleontology; ancient
early and local history; music history;
numismatics; decorative objects;
costumes

Sonneberg

05057
Deutsches Spielzeugmuseum
Beethovenstr. 10, DDR-64 Sonneberg
History/Public Affairs Museum - 1901
history of area and industry; crafts;
costumes; porcelain; toys - library

Sperenberg

05058
Heimatstube
Hauptstr., DDR-1631 Sperenberg
General Museum - 1965
local history; native history; folk art

Stadtilm

05059
Heimatmuseum
Straße der Einheit 1, DDR-5217
Stadtilm
General Museum - 1902
geology; early history; local crafts and
industry; 17th-19th century peasant
furnishings

Steckby

05060
Vogelschutzstation Steckby
DDR-3401 Steckby
Natural History Museum - 1943
ornithology

Stendal

05061
Altmärkisches Museum
Straße der Freundschaft 48, DDR-35
Stendal
General Museum - 1888
ancient and early history; ceramics;
porcelain; blueprints; peasant culture;
costumes; numismatics; medals

05062
Winckelmann-Museum
Winckelmannstr. 36, DDR-35 Stendal
History/Public Affairs Museum - 1954
memorabilia of archaeologist J.J.
Winckelmann (1717-1768), his African
collection; numismatics; costumes;
crafts; drawings

Sternberg

05063
Heimatmuseum
Mühlenstr. 6, DDR-272 Sternberg
General Museum - 1977
local and regional history

Stolberg

05064
Altes Stolberger Bürgerhaus
DDR-4712 Stolberg
History/Public Affairs Museum
15th century frame house; 16th-18th
century living style; furnishings

05065
Heimatmuseum
Thomas-Müntzer-Gasse 19, DDR-4712
Stolberg
General Museum - 1927
geology; mining history; city history;
industrial processing; mint workshop;
numismatics; local crafts; memorial to
theologian Thomas Münzer
(1489-1525)

Stolpen

05066
Museum Burg Stolpen
Schloßstr. 10, DDR-835 Stolpen
History/Public Affairs Museum - 1877
15th-16th century armaments;
instruments of torture; cannon models;
firefighting tools

Stralsund

05067
Kulturhistorisches Museum
Mönchstr. 25, DDR-23 Stralsund
History/Public Affairs Museum - 1858
historical finds; religious sculpture; city
history; crafts; customs; shipping;
fishing; metalwork; porcelain; playing
card collection; peasant culture; tools;
costumes; toys; numismatics;
European painting and prints;
Northeast German painting and
drawings

05068
Meeresmuseum Stralsund
Katharinenberg 14a, DDR-23 Stralsund
Natural History Museum - 1858
geology of Mecklenburg area;
hydrography of Baltic Sea; coastal
flora and fauna; ornithology;
conservation

Strausberg

05069
Heimatmuseum
August-Bebel-Str. 33, DDR-126
Strausberg
General Museum - 1976
local and regional hsitory

Stützerbach

05070
Goethehaus
Sebastian-Kneipp-Str. 18, DDR-6316
Stützerbach
History/Public Affairs Museum - 1953
memorabilia on J.W. Goethe's
(1749-1832) stay here; glass
technology

Suhl

05071
Waffenmuseum
Wilhelm-Pieck-Str. 19, DDR-60 Suhl
General Museum - 1971
ancient and early historic finds;
weapons; weapon industry; hand
weapons since 16th century - library

Tabarz

05072
Theodor-Neubauer-Gedenkstätte
Theodor-Neubauer-Str., DDR-5808
Tabarz
History/Public Affairs Museum - 1965
history of the working class;
memorabilia on anti-fascist educator
Dr. Theodor Neubauer

Tangermünde

05073
Heimatmuseum
Am Markt, DDR-3504 Tangermünde
General Museum - 1929
historic finds; local history; industrial
development; shipping; fishing;
peasant crafts and living style

Taucha

05074
Städtisches Heimatmuseum
Eilenburger Str. 8, DDR-7127 Taucha
General Museum - 1933
geology; native fauna; ancient and
early historic finds; city and crafts
history

Templin

05075
Volkskundemuseum
Prenzlauer Tor, DDR-209 Templin
General Museum - 1957
local and regional history - library

Thale

05076
Walpurgishalle Thale
Auf dem Hexenplatz über der Bode,
DDR-4308 Thale
General Museum - 1901
hall in Old-Germanic style with
ornaments, figuring in the Walpurgis
legend of Goethes 'Faust'; geology;
ancient history; botany; zoology

Tharandt

05077
**Forstliche und Jagdkundliche
Lehrschau Grillenburg**
Haupstr., DDR-8223 Tharandt
Natural History Museum - 1966
hunting trophies; game birds; hunting
equipment

05078
Tharandter Heimatstube
Siegfried-Rädel-Str. 3, DDR-8223
Tharandt
General Museum - 1971
ancient and early history; city history;
conservation; geology; mining;
development of traffic, crafts and
industry

Torgau

05079
Kreismuseum Torgau - Schloß Hartenfels
DDR-729 Torgau
History/Public Affairs Museum - 1951
ancient and early history; local history; history of palace; historic armaments; relief of battle here

Triebsees

05080
Heimatstube
Stadttor, DDR-2304 Triebsees
General Museum - 1976
local and regional history

Ummendorf

05081
Agrarmuseum der Magdeburger Börde
In der Burg, DDR-3221 Ummendorf
General Museum - 1924/1953
ancient and early history; geology; peasant living style; tools; costumes; jewelry; mushroom collection

Velten

05082
Städtisches Heimat- und Keramikmuseum
Karl-Marx-Str. 79, DDR-142 Velten
General Museum - 1905
local and regional history; local stove industry; tools; stove collection; models; tiles 17th-20th century; clay processers - library

Waldenburg

05083
Heimatmuseum und Naturalienkabinett
Geschwister-Scholl-Str. 1, DDR-9613 Waldenburg
Natural History Museum - 1840
local history; pottery; earthenware; pipe collection; zoology; paeleontoly; mineralogy; drugs and wood collection; physical instruments; herbs; birds; mammals; entomology; butterflies

Waltersdorf

05084
Volkskunde- und Mühlenmuseum
Ernst-Thälmann-Str. 24, DDR-8813 Waltersdorf
History/Public Affairs Museum - 1956
grist mill; development of miller's crafts; local history; peasant household objects

Waltershausen-Schnepfenthal

05085
GutsMuths-Gedenkstätte der Salzmannschule
Salzmann-Oberschule, DDR-5801 Waltershausen-Schnepfenthal
History/Public Affairs Museum - 1959
memorabilia on the teacher J.C.E. GutsMuths (1759-1839)

Wandlitz

05086
Museum der agraren Produktivkräfte
Breitscheidstr. 8, DDR-1292 Wandlitz
General Museum - 1955
geology; fauna; local history; peasan living style and work tools

Waren a. d. Müritz

05087
Müritz-Museum
Friedensstr. 5, DDR-206 Waren a. d. Müritz
General Museum - 1866
geology; botany; zoology; history; fishing; hunting; crafts; costumes; glass products; history of labour-movement; research on workers' and peasants' movement - library

Waschleithe

05088
Lehr- und Schaubergwerk 'Herkules-Frisch-Glück'
DDR-9431 Waschleithe
Science/Tech Museum - 1966
demonstration mine

Weesenstein

05089
Kunstmuseum Schloß Weesenstein
DDR-8301 Weesenstein
General Museum - 1933
Empire and Biedermeier rooms; hunting hall; French, Chinese and leather wall hangings; paintings; architecture

Wehlen

05090
Heimatmuseum
Lohmener Str. 17, DDR-8306 Wehlen
General Museum - 1951
local history; folklore; sand-stone industry

Weida

05091
Kreismuseum Weida
DDR-6508 Weida
General Museum - 1901
local and regional history; development of crafts and guilds; leather industry - library

Weimar

05092
Goethe- und Schiller-Gruft
Friedhof vor dem Frauentor, DDR-53 Weimar
History/Public Affairs Museum
sarcophargi of Friedrich von Schiller and Johann Wolfgang von Goethe

05093
Goethes Gartenhaus
Corona-Schröter-Str., DDR-53 Weimar
History/Public Affairs Museum - 1958
historic interiors; memorabilia of J. W. Goethe (1749-1832)

05094
Institut für Literatur
DDR-53 Weimar
History/Public Affairs Museum - 1953
history of literature in Germany - library

05095
Kassengewölbe auf dem Jakobsfriedhof
Am Rollplatz, DDR-53 Weimar
History/Public Affairs Museum
burial place of Friedrich von Schiller

05096
Kirms-Krackow-Haus
Jakobstr. 10, DDR-53 Weimar
History/Public Affairs Museum - 1916
memorabilia of J. D. Falk (1768-1826); J. G. Herder (1744-1803) and J. K. A. Musäus (1735-1787); furniture

05097
Kunsthalle am Theaterplatz
DDR-53 Weimar
Fine Arts Museum
modern arts

05098
Liszthaus
Marienstr. 17, DDR-53 Weimar
History/Public Affairs Museum - 1956
memorabilia of composer Franz Liszt in his former home; portraits; sculpture; sheet music; first edition

05099
Museum für Ur- und Frühgeschichte Thüringens
Humboldtstr. 11, DDR-52 Weimar
History/Public Affairs Museum - 1899
evolution; anthropology; ancient and early history of Thüringen - library

05100
Nationale Forschungs- und Gedenkstätte der Klassischen Deutschen Literatur in Weimar
Burgplatz 4, DDR-53 Weimar
History/Public Affairs Museum - 1914
memorabilia on J. W. Goethe (1749-1832) and F. v. Schiller (1759-1805); documents; furniture; manuscripts; history; portraits; pictures

05101
Rokokomuseum Schloß Belvedere
DDR-53 Weimar
Fine Arts Museum - 1923
18th century court art; painting; decorative objects; textiles; building plans

05102
Römisches Haus
Im Park, DDR-53 Weimar
History/Public Affairs Museum - 1962
summer home of duke Karl-August of Sachsen-Weimar (1757-1828); historic furnishings

05103
Sammlung historischer Wagen (Orangerie)
DDR-53 Weimar
History/Public Affairs Museum
orangery with historic coaches

05104
Schillerhaus
Schillerstr. 12, DDR-53 Weimar
History/Public Affairs Museum
memorabilia of F. v. Schiller (1759-1805); part of original library

05105
Schloß Tiefurt
Hauptstr. 14, DDR-53 Weimar
History/Public Affairs Museum - 1885
historic furniture and porcelain

05106
Schloßmuseum
Burgplatz 4, DDR-53 Weimar
Fine Arts Museum - 1809
historic rooms; 16th-20th century European painting; drawings; Classicist porcelain; numismatics

05107
Stadtmuseum Weimar
Karl-Liebknecht-Str. 7, DDR-53 Weimar
General Museum - 1903
city history; crafts; industrial history; peasant living style and costumes; military - library

05108
Wittumspalais
Am Palais 3, DDR-53 Weimar
History/Public Affairs Museum - 1953
18th century baroque home; scene of meetings of literary circles; historic furnishings of rococo, classic and Empire periods; memorabilia on poet Chr. M. Wieland

Weimar-Buchenwald

05109
Nationale Mahn- und Gedenkstätte Buchenwald
DDR-5301 Weimar-Buchenwald
History/Public Affairs Museum - 1958
history of concentration camp

Weissenfels

05110
Gustav-Adolf-Gedenkstätte
Große Burgstr. 22, DDR-485 Weissenfels
History/Public Affairs Museum - 1932
16th century former envoy house; autopsy room of King Gustav Adolf of Sweden II; material on Gustav Adolf and Thirty Years' War

05111
Heinrich-Schütz-Gedenkstätte
Nicolaistr. 13, DDR-485 Weissenfels
History/Public Affairs Museum - 1956
memorabilia of musician Heinrich Schütz (1585-1672)

05112
Städtisches Museum
Schloß, DDR-485 Weissenfels
History/Public Affairs Museum - 1910
geology; mineralogy; ancient and early history; local history; flora and fauna; conservation; crafts and guilds history; shoe industry; glass and ironwork

Werdau

05113
Kreis- und Stadtmuseum
Uferstr. 1, DDR-962 Werdau
General Museum - 1916
geology; mineralogy; ancient and early history; city history; peasant utensils; crafts and costumes - library

Werder

05114
Obstbaumuseum
Karl-Marx-Platz 2, DDR-1512 Werder
Natural History Museum - 1962
fruit farming; natural conditions; geology; soil types; climate; social developments in fruit growing areas to 17th century

Wermsdorf

05115
August-Bebel- und Wilhelm-Liebknecht-Gedenkstätte
Schloß Hubertusburg, DDR-7264 Wermsdorf
History/Public Affairs Museum - 1968
memorabilia of political figures August Bebel and Karl Liebknecht; history of German labour-movement; local and palace history

Wernigerode

05116
Feudalmuseum
Schloß, DDR-37 Wernigerode
History/Public Affairs Museum - 1949
historic interior; religious art;
decorative objects; glass; goldsmith
work; paintings; armaments; local and
regional history; instruments of torture
- library

05117
**Mahn- und Gedenkstätte
Wernigerode**
Veckenstedter Weg 43, DDR-37
Wernigerode
History/Public Affairs Museum - 1975
history of labour movement; socialist
documents, photos, graphics,
paintings; history of KPD

Wiederau

05118
Clara-Zetkins-Gedächtnisstätte
Wiederau Nr. 190, DDR-9291
Wiederau
History/Public Affairs Museum - 1952
memorabilia of political figure Clara
Zetkin (1857-1933) and her circle in
house of her birth

Wilhelm-Pieck-Stadt Guben

05119
Wilhelm-Pieck-Gedenkstätte
Helmut-Just-Str., DDR-756 Wilhelm-
Pieck-Stadt Guben
History/Public Affairs Museum - 1966
memorabilia of politician Wilhelm Pieck
(1876-1960); history of local labour-
movement

Wilthen

05120
Heimatstube
Bahnhofstr. 7, DDR-8609 Wilthen
General Museum - 1946
weaver's room; flax processing and
linen weaving tools

Wismar

05121
Heimatmuseum
Schweinsbrücke 8, DDR-24 Wismar
General Museum - 1932
ancient historic finds; local history;
paintings; costumes

Wittenberg-Lutherstadt

05122
Melanchthon-Haus
Collegienstr. 60, DDR-46 Wittenberg-
Lutherstadt
History/Public Affairs Museum - 1967
memorabilia of Reformation figure
Philipp Melanchthon in his former
home; medals; frescoes; armaments;
local history

05123
**Museum für Naturkunde und
Völkerkunde 'Julius Riemer'**
Schloß, DDR-46 Wittenberg-
Lutherstadt
Natural History Museum - 1949
zoological evolution; human evolution;
anthropology; historical finds from the
area - library

05124
Staatliche Lutherhalle Wittenberg
Collegienstr. 54, DDR-46 Wittenberg-
Lutherstadt
History/Public Affairs Museum - 1883
memorabilia of Martin Luther; writings;
prints; paintings; documents; history of
Reformation - library

05125
Stadtgeschichtliches Museum
Schloß, DDR-46 Wittenberg-
Lutherstadt
History/Public Affairs Museum - 1969
ancient and early history; history of
city; documents; pictures

Wittenberge

05126
Arbeiter- und Industriemuseum
Putlitzer Str. 2, DDR-29 Wittenberge
General Museum - 1971
history of industrial development;
history of social living conditions and
labour-movement

05127
Steintor
DDR-29 Wittenberge
General Museum - 1948
ancient and early history; minerals;
stones; shipping; fishing

Wittstock/Dosse

05128
Kreis-Heimatmuseum
Amtshof 5, DDR-193 Wittstock/Dosse
General Museum - 1957
ancient and early history; regional
history; city as bishops' residence;
peasant crafts; work tools; castle
fragments - library

Wöbbelin

05129
**Mahn- und Gedenkstätte - Körner
Gedenkstätte**
DDR-2801 Wöbbelin
History/Public Affairs Museum - 1937
memorabilia of poet Theodor Körner;
documents; etchings; armaments;
grave site

Woldeck

05130
Mühlenmuseum
DDR-2152 Woldeck
History/Public Affairs Museum - 1971
city history; milling history

Wolgast

05131
Heimatmuseum
Karl-Liebknecht-Platz 6, DDR-222
Wolgast
General Museum - 1955
ancient and early history; city history

Wolkenstein

05132
Heimatstube Schloß Wolkenstein
Karl-Marx-Platz 1, DDR-9372
Wolkenstein
History/Public Affairs Museum - 1957
native history; contemporary chronicle

Wolmirstedt

05133
Kreis-Heimatmuseum
Schloßdomäne, DDR-321 Wolmirstedt
History/Public Affairs Museum - 1927
ancient and early historic finds; native
birds; local history - library

Worbis

05134
Heimatmuseum
Straße der Jungpioniere 1, DDR-562
Worbis
General Museum - 1956
ancient and early history; geology;
forestry; agriculture; local history;
textile crafts

Wörlitz

05135
**Staatliche Schlösser und Gärten
Wörlitz**
DDR-4414 Wörlitz
Fine Arts Museum - 1918
historic rooms; decorative arts; Dutch,
German and Italian paintings; copper
engravings; Swiss glass painting;
china; glass

Wurzen

05136
Kreis-Heimatmuseum
Domgasse 2, DDR-725 Wurzen
General Museum - 1927
geology; ancient and early history;
local history; peasant crafts; native
birds; works and biographical material
of writer Joachim Ringelnatz

Wusterhausen

05137
Heimatmuseum Wusterhausen
Roter Platz 20, DDR-1903
Wusterhausen
General Museum - 1963
geology; ancient and early history;
folklore and folk art - library

Zechin

05138
Wilhelm-Pieck-Gedenkstätte
DDR-1211 Zechin
History/Public Affairs Museum - 1966
memorabilia on Wilhelm Pieck

Zechlinerhütte

05139
Alfred-Wegner-Gedenkstätte
Rheinsberger Str. 27, DDR-1951
Zechlinerhütte
History/Public Affairs Museum
memorabilia on geophysician and
meteorologist Prof. Alfred Wegener

Zeitz

05140
Museum Schloß Moritzburg
DDR-49 Zeitz
General Museum - 1998
geology; history of city; economic
development; mining; painting;
sculpture; devorative objects;
numismatics; costumes - library

Zella-Mehlis

05141
Heimatmuseum
Ernst-Thälmann-Str., DDR-6060 Zella-
Mehlis
General Museum - 1959
geology; folklore; industrial history

Zerbst

05142
Heimatmuseum
Weinberg 1, DDR-34 Zerbst
General Museum - 1952
geology; ancient and early history; city
history; pewter figures; numismatics;
folk art

05143
**Städtisches Kunstgewerbe und
Heimatmuseum**
Aumaische Str. 30, DDR-34 Zerbst
General Museum - 1906
city history; crafts and industry;
peasant living style; art crafts

Ziegenhals

05144
Ernst-Thälmann-Gedenkstätte
DDR-1251 Ziegenhals
History/Public Affairs Museum - 1953
memorabilia of Ernst Thälmann

Ziegenrück

05145
Wasserkraftmuseum
Lobensteiner Str. 6, DDR-6557
Ziegenrück
Science/Tech Museum - 1966
history of use of water power; water
power technology

Zingst

05146
Zingster Heimathaus
Prerower Str. 4, DDR-2385 Zingst
General Museum - 1953
historic interior; ship model; sailors'
memorabilia; local history

Zittau

05147
Dr.-Curt-Heinke-Museum
Thälmannring, DDR-88 Zittau
General Museum
geology and ancient history

05148
Museum auf dem Berg Oybin
DDR-88 Zittau
History/Public Affairs Museum - 1879
history of castle and cloister

05149
Stadtmuseum
Klosterstr. 3, DDR-88 Zittau
History/Public Affairs Museum - 1929
local history; religious sculpture;
drawings; paintings and prints;
numismatics; arms; musical
instruments; toys; glass paintings;
peasant culture

Zörbig

05150
Heimatmuseum
Am Schloß 10, DDR-4415 Zörbig
General Museum - 1923
ancient and early history; history of
castle and city; peasant and burgher
living style; crafts

Zwickau

05151
Robert-Schumann-Haus
Haupmarkt 5, DDR-95 Zwickau
History/Public Affairs Museum - 1956
memorabilia on composer Robert
Schumann; original decorations of
birthplace; manuscripts; pictures;
sheet music; first prints; program
collection

05152
Städtisches Museum
Lessingstr. 1, DDR-95 Zwickau
General Museum - 1914
mineralogy; stones; mining; local
history; pewter and porcelain;
religious sculpture; painting; portraits;
prints - library

Germany, Federal Republic

Aachen

05153
Auto-Sammlung Gut-Hand
Richterich, Handerweg 71, D-5100
Aachen
Science/Tech Museum - 1960
Coll: German motor cars from 1930;
trucks and vans; motorcycles and
scooters; minicars from the 50s -
repair workshop; archives

05154
Couven-Museum
Hühnermarkt 17, D-5100 Aachen
Decorative Arts Museum - 1928
Coll: 18th-19th century furnishings and
interiors from the Aachen-Lüttich area;
Baroque furniture; tapestry; tiles

05155
Domschatzkammer
Domhof 4a, D-5100 Aachen
Religious Art Museum - 1931
Coll: religious art from the Carolingian
and Ottonian epochs, the Gothic and
baroque periods, and the 19th century

05156
**Internationales Zeitungsmuseum der
Stadt Aachen**
Pontstr. 13, D-5100 Aachen
History/Public Affairs Museum - 1885
Coll: ca. 120,000 newspapers and
journals from throughout the world,
including in particular first, last,
anniversary, and special issues;
overview of the history of the
newspaper since the 16th century -
library

05157
Museum Burg Frankenberg
Bismarckstr. 68, D-5100 Aachen
General Museum - 1961
Coll: local history; handicrafts; in 13th
century castle

05158
Neue Galerie Sammlung Ludwig
Komphausbadstr. 19, D-5100 Aachen
Fine Arts Museum - 1970
Coll: art trends in the 70s; pop art;
photo realism; conceptual art; new
expressionism

05159
Suermondt-Ludwig-Museum
Wilhelmstr. 18, D-5100 Aachen
Fine Arts Museum - 1878
Coll: sculpture; painting; glass
windows; goldsmith work

Aalen

05160
**Geologisch-Paläontologisches
Museum**
Reichsstädterstr. 1, D-7080 Aalen 1
Natural History Museum - 1977
Coll: fossils; stones and minerals from
the Jura formations in the Schwabian
Alps; in 17th century town hall

05161
Heimat- und Schubartmuseum
Marktplatz 2, D-7080 Aalen 1
General Museum - 1907
Coll: prehistory and local early history;
industrial development; town and farm
culture; life and works of Christian
Friedrich Daniel Schubart; history of
crafts; traditional costumes

05162
Limesmuseum Württembergisches
Landesmuseum
St.-Johann-Str. 5, D-7080 Aalen 1
Archeology Museum - 1964
Coll: site of the largest Roman
castellum north of the Alps; aerial
photographs, maps, and models of the
original castellum; excavation finds
including armaments, coins, utensils,
and sculpture; gravestones and altar
stones; diorama - library

05163
**Ofenplattensammlung der
Schwäbischen Hüttenwerke**
Wilhelmstr. 67, D-7080 Aalen
General Museum - 1968
Coll: 17th-20th century stove plates;
ovens with ceramic decorations

05164
Wasseralfinger Heimatmuseum
Eichelbergstr. 5, D-7080 Aalen
General Museum - 1957
Coll: paleontology; local history;
industrial development; local ironwork
- library

Abensberg

05165
Aventinusmuseum
Karmelitenplatz 5, D-8423 Abensberg
General Museum - 1926
Coll: ethnology; pre- and early history;
local history; coins and weapons; in
former 15th century cloister

Achern

05166
Sensen- und Heimatmuseum
Berlinerstr. 31, D-7590 Achern
General Museum - 1963
Coll: scythes; tools and machines for
the production of scythes; history of
scythe production; local history -
library

Achstetten

05167
Wieland-Gedenkzimmer
Pfarrhaus, D-7959 Achstetten 2
Historic Site - 1975
Coll: birth place of the writer
Christoph Martin Wieland; documents;
busts and paintings; his literary works

Adelsheim

05168
Dorfmuseum Sennfeld
Hauptstr. 43, D-6962 Adelsheim
General Museum - 1970
Coll: local crafts; agriculture; domestic
utensils; in former 19th century
synagogue

05169
Städtische Sammlungen Bauländer
Heimatmuseum
Marktstr. 7, D-6962 Adelsheim
General Museum - 1908
Coll: agricultural implements; 19th
century town and farm furniture; local
history

Admont

05170
Kunsthistorisches Museum
Benediktinerstift Admont, D-8911
Admont
Fine Arts Museum - 1956
Coll: 11th-20th century painting,
sculpture, arts and crafts; pewter and
glass; paraments (1640-1720); coins
and medaillons - library

Ahrensburg

05171
Museum Schloß Ahrensburg
Lübecker Str. 1, D-2070 Ahrensburg
Decorative Arts Museum - 1932
18th-19th century furnishings and
interiors; porcelain (Meissen);
paintings and portraits; in 18th century
moated castle built in the late
Renaissance style - library

Albstadt

05172
Städtische Galerie Albstadt
Kirchengraben 11, D-7470 Albstadt 1
Fine Arts Museum - 1970
Coll: 20th century graphics and prints
including Expressionism and art from
1920 to 1945; paintings; drawings -
workshops

Alfeld

05173
Heimat- und Tiermuseum Alfeld
Kirchplatz 4/5, D-3220 Alfeld
General Museum - 1928
Coll: pre- and early history; geology;
local history; local economic
development; 17th century
woodcarving; zoology; conservation;
archives - library

Allendorf

05174
Heimatmuseum
D-06407 Allendorf
General Museum
Items of local interest

Allensbach

05175
Heimatmuseum
Rathausplatz, D-7753 Allensbach 1
General Museum - 1962
Coll: pre- and early history; local
history; folklore

Alsfeld

05176
Regionalmuseum Alsfeld
Rittergasse 3-5, D-6320 Alsfeld
General Museum - 1897
Coll: early history; crafts and industrial
development; local history; traditional
costumes; 16th-18th century
furnishings and interiors; religious art;
paintings of local artists; manuscripts;
in two 17th century half-timbered
buildings - library

Altena

05177
**Museum der Grafschaft Mark Burg
Altena - Deutsches Drahtmuseum -
Märkisches Schmiedemuseum**
Burg Altena, D-5990 Altena
General Museum - 1875
Coll: art and art history; geology; pre-
and early history; weapons; history of
smithwork; technology; history and
production of wire; rooms of the first
youth hostel in the world

Altenbeken

05178
Egge-Museum Altenbeken
Alter Kirchweg, D-4791 Altenbeken
General Museum - 1976
Coll: 16th-19th century stoves and
stove plates; history of local iron ore
mining and iron production; train
production; minerals and fossils

Altenhof

05179
Herrenhaus Altenhof
D-2330 Altenhof Post Eckernförde
Decorative Arts Museum - 1954
Coll: furnishings and interiors in Louis
XV and Louis XVI styles; paintings;
porcelain - library

Altenthann

05180
Sammlung Hemrich
am Kirchbuckl 3, D-8411 Altenthann
General Museum - 1960
Coll: agricultural tools; household
tools; tools for different handicrafts

Altmannstein

05181
Heimatmuseum Altmannstein
Rathaus, D-8426 Altmannstein
General Museum - ca. 1950
Coll: prehistoric and ancient items;
19th century articles from peasant
culture; documents on the 18th
century sculpturer Ignaz Günther

Altötting

05182
Schatzkammer Altötting
Kapellplatz 4, D-8262 Altötting
Religious Art Museum - 1960
Coll: votive offerings; cult articles; 16th
century sculpture

05183
**Wallfahrts- und Heimatmuseum
Altötting**
Kapellplatz 4, D-8262 Altötting
General Museum - 1912
Coll: pre- and early history; local flora
and fauna; town culture; local history;
history of pilgrimage center; graphics;
paintings; sculpture; devotional
paintings

Alzey

05184
Museum Alzey
Antoniterstr. 41, D-6508 Alzey
Archeology Museum - 1906
Coll: geology; paleontology; findings
from the Paleolithic, Neolithic, Hallstatt,
and Latène periods; Roman finds;
articles from the Merovingian period;
folklore; archives - library

Amberg

05185
Museum der Stadt Amberg
Eichenforstgasse 12, D-8450 Amberg
General Museum - 1901
Coll: prehistory; local history
(15th-19th centuries); chapel with 15th
century stained-glass windows;
religious folk art; faience; items from
the local 19th century arms factory

Amerang

05186
Ostoberbayrisches
Bauernhausmuseum Amerang
D-8201 Amerang
Open Air Museum - 1977
Coll: different types of farmsteads
including a Salzburg farmstead, a 16th
century farmstead, and a Biedermeier
quadrangular farm; smithy; bakery;
exhibits on farm life and work; folklore

05187
Schloß Amerang
D-8201 Amerang
Historic Site
Coll: 16th century Renaissance castle;
knights' hall with hunting trophies;
period furnishings and interiors;
Gothic chapel

Amorbach

05188
Fürstlich Leiningensche
Sammlungen Heimatmuseum
Kellereigasse, D-8762 Amorbach
General Museum - 1932
Coll: prehistory; local history;
handicrafts; art; folk art in particular
pottery, stove plates, and devotional
pictures

Ansbach

05189
Kreis- und Stadtmuseum
Schaitbergerstr. 10, D-8800 Ansbach
General Museum - 1830
Coll: natural history; prehistory; local
history; faience and porcelain

05190
Residenz Ansbach
Promenade 27, D-8800 Ansbach
Historic Site
Coll: 14th-18th century royal
residence; interiors with original
Baroque and Rococo furnishings;
faience and porcelain; gallery with
European Baroque paintings

Appen

05191
Luftwaffen-Museum Uetersen
Marseille Kaserne, Hauptstr. 140,
D-2081 Appen
Science/Tech Museum - 1957
Coll: airplanes (from 1891 on); engines;
weapons; aviation equipment;
documents on the history of
international military aviation beginning
with 1884; uniforms; awards - library;
repair shop

Arnsberg

05192
Deutsches Vogelbauermuseum
Cäcilienstr. 13, D-5760 Arnsberg 1
Natural History Museum - 1965
Coll: bird cages with accessories;
representation of bird cages in art
(paintings, graphics, tiles); literature on
bird keeping

05193
Leuchtenmuseum
Möhnestr. 55, D-5760 Arnsberg 1
History/Public Affairs Museum - 1965
Lamps from different epochs, in
particular from the 18th and 19th
centuries

05194
Sauerland-Museum
Alter Markt 26, D-5760 Arnsberg 2
General Museum - 1925
Coll: local cultural history; 16th-19th
century religious art; prehistory;
geology; birds; coins - library

Arolsen

05195
Kaulbachmuseum
Kaulbachstr. 3, D-3548 Arolsen
Fine Arts Museum - 1951
Coll: paintings, drawings, and sketches
by Wilhelm von Kaulbach, Friedrich
Kaulbach, Friedrich August von
Kaulbach, and Hermann Kaulbach;
memorabilia; furniture; carpenter's
workshop

05196
Rauch-Gedenkstätte
Rauchstr. 6, D-3548 Arolsen
Historic Site - 1973
Memorial to the sculptor Christian
Rauch in his birth house

Aschach

05197
Graf-Luxburg-Museum
Schloß Aschach, D-8731 Aschach
Historic Site - 1957
Coll: 16th century castle; interiors from
the 19th century; 16th-19th century
German arts and crafts; faience;
furniture; ancient Chinese ceramics
from all dynasties; antique rugs

Aschaffenburg

05198
Museum der Stadt Aschaffenburg
Schloßmuseum
Schloßplatz 4, D-8750 Aschaffenburg
General Museum - 1854
Coll: local history; pewter, silver, and
earthenware; Baroque faience;
porcelain; German glassware from late
Gothic to the Biedermeier period;
17th-19th century furniture; ceramics;
local art from 19th-20th centuries

05199
Museum der Stadt Aschaffenburg
Stiftsmuseum
Stiftsplatz 2, D-8750 Aschaffenburg
Fine Arts Museum - 1854
Coll: 12th-17th century architectural
sculpture; wood sculpture (13th-18th
centuries); religious handicrafts; 16th
century paintings; prehistory

05200
Naturwissenschaftliches Museum
Schönborner Hof, Wermbachstr. 15,
D-8750 Aschaffenburg
Natural History Museum - 1911
Coll: zoology; entomology; botany;
mineralogy

05201
Staatsgalerie im Schloß
Aschaffenburg
Schloßplatz 4, D-8750 Aschaffenburg,
Meiserstr. 10, D-8000 München 2
Fine Arts Museum - 1932
Coll: paintings of Lucas Cranach and
his circle; European Old Masters

Augsburg

05202
Deutsche Barockgalerie Städtische
Kunstsammlungen
Maximilianstr. 46, D-8900 Augsburg
Fine Arts Museum - 1970
German paintings from the Baroque
and Rococo periods; in Rococo palace
- library; workshop

05203
Graphische Sammlung Städtische
Kunstsammlungen
Schaezler-Palais, Maximilianstr. 46,
D-8900 Augsburg
Fine Arts Museum - 1828
Coll: drawings and prints, especially of
the Baroque period

05204
Maximilianmuseum Städtische
Kunstsammlungen
Philippine-Welser-Str. 24, D-8900
Augsburg
Fine Arts Museum - 1854/55
Small sculptures; Augsburg
handicrafts; goldsmith work; local
history

05205
Mozartgedenkstätte
Frauentorstr. 30, D-8900 Augsburg
Historic Site - 1937
Coll: 17th century building in which
Leopold Mozart, the father of
Wolfgang Amadeus Mozart, was born;
graphics, printed music, and other
memorabilia of the Mozarts, both
father and son

05206
Römisches Museum Städtische
Kunstsammlungen
Dominikanergasse 15, D-8900
Augsburg
Archeology Museum - 1966
Prehistoric and Roman finds in
Augsburg and Bavarian Swabia;
archives on finds - workshop

05207
Staatsgalerie am Schaezler-Palais
Maximilianstr. 46, D-8900 Augsburg
Fine Arts Museum - 1835
Swabian Old Masters from the late
Gothic

05208
Werkmuseum der M.A.N. Augsburg
Stadtbachstr. 1, D-8900 Augsburg
Science/Tech Museum - 1953
Coll: early products of M.A.N.; diesel
motors beginning in 1893; printing
machines after 1846; pictures and
documents on the development of
motors and machine construction

Autenried

05209
Ikonenmuseum
Schloß Autenried, D-8871 Autenried
Religious Art Museum - 1959
Coll: icons from Russia, Byzantium,
Crete, Greece, Rumania, and the
Balkan countries; goldsmith work;
bronzes; vestments; embroidery;
manuscripts and incunabula from the
eastern orthodox area (3rd-19th
centuries) - library

Babenhausen

05210
Fugger-Museum
Schloß, D-8943 Babenhausen
Decorative Arts Museum - 1908
Coll: decorative art from the 16th-19th
centuries including goldsmith work,
glass, porcelain, bronzes, ivory,
religious art, and miniatures; weapons;
folk art

Bad Berneck

05211
Stadtmuseum
Marktplatz 44, D-8582 Bad Berneck
Archeology Museum - 1950
Local archeological finds

Bad Brückenau

05212
Heimat- und Regionalmuseum
Rathaus, D-8788 Bad Brückenau
General Museum - 1950
Coll: local history; balneology;
geology; mineralogy; traditional
peasant furniture; handicrafts; tools for
processing flax; archives - study room

Bad Driburg

05213
Weberhaus
Weberplatz, D-3490 Bad Driburg
Historic Site - 1953
Coll: birth place of the 19th century
poet Friedrich Wilhelm Weber; original
furnishings; memorabilia; 19th century
household utensils and tools; 18th
century half-timbered house

Bad Dürrheim

05214
Narrenschopf Fasnachtsmuseum
Kurverwaltung, D-7737 Bad Dürrheim
Anthropology Museum - 1973
Swabian and Alemannic masks and
carnival costumes from the 18th
century to the present

05215
Prof.-Fritz-Behn-Museum
Kurverwaltung, D-7737 Bad Dürrheim
Fine Arts Museum - 1973
Coll: sculpture and statuettes, busts,
paintings, drawings, and sketches by
the sculptor and painter Fritz Behn

Bad Homburg v.d. Höhe

05216
Heimat- und Hutmuseum
Louisenstr. 120, D-6380 Bad Homburg
v.d. Höhe
General Museum - 1916
Coll: local history; section dedicated to
the poet Friedrich Hölderlin; local
archeological finds; 400 years' history
of the hatter's trade; hats

05217
Saalburgmuseum
Saalburg-Kastell, D-6380 Bad
Homburg v.d. Höhe 1
Open Air Museum - 1873
Coll: reconstructed Roman castellum
on the limes; Roman finds; weapons;
tools; domestic items; leather articles

Bad Honnef

05218
Stiftung Bundeskanzler-Adenauer-Haus
Konrad-Adenauer-Str. 8c, D-5340 Bad
Honnef 1
Historic Site - 1975
Coll: original house and gardens of
Konrad Adenauer; documents on
German history (1876-1955); archives;
photos and documentary films on
Adenauer Era

Bad Karlshafen

05219
Hugenottenmuseum
An der Schlagd, D-3522 Bad
Karlshafen 1
History/Public Affairs Museum - 1979
Coll: documentation on the history of
the Huguenots; Biedermeier interior;
early 20th century kitchen; lamps;
coins; in 18th century building

Bad Kreuznach

05220
Karl-Geib-Museum
Kreuzstr. 69, D-6550 Bad Kreuznach
General Museum - 1933
Coll: prehistoric and Roman finds;
geology; paleontology

Bad Krozingen

05221
**Sammlung historischer
Tasteninstrumente Fritz Neumeyer**
Am Schloßpark 7, D-7812 Bad
Krozingen
Music Museum - 1930
Coll: original keyboard instruments
from 1580 to 1860; reconstructions; in
16th century castle

Bad Mergentheim

05222
Deutschordensmuseum
Schloß 16, D-6990 Bad Mergentheim
General Museum - 1973
Coll: Baroque, Rococo, and Classical
interiors; history of the Teutonic
Order; prehistory; folk art; local
history - library

05223
Ottmar-Mergenthaler-Museum
D-6990 Bad Mergentheim
Historic Site - 1924
Coll: birth house of Ottmar
Mergenthaler, the inventor of
Linotype; exhibits on the history of
printing machines; their influence on
book and newspaper production

Bad Münstereifel

05224
Toni-Hürten-Heimatmuseum
Langenhecke, Romanisches Haus,
D-5358 Bad Münstereifel
General Museum - 1912
Finds from the Stone Age to the
Middle Ages; local history; sacred art;
bourgeois and peasant cultural
implements

Bad Nauheim

05225
Rosen- und Heimatmuseum
Altes Rathaus, Raiffeisenplatz, D-6350
Bad Nauheim
General Museum - 1974
History of local rose cultivation

05226
Salzmuseum
im Teichhausschlößchen, D-6350 Bad
Nauheim
General Museum - 1960
History of local salt mining from
prehistoric to medieval times;
municipal history

Bad Nenndorf

05227
Agnes-Miegel-Haus
Agnes-Miegel-Platz 3, D-3052 Bad
Nenndorf
Historic Site - 1974
Works and personal belongings of the
writer Agnes Miegel

Bad Neustadt a.d. Saale

05228
Heimatmuseum
Rathausgasse 2, D-8740 Bad Neustadt
a.d. Saale
General Museum - 1906
Bourgeois and peasant folk art; wood
carvings

Bad Oeynhausen

05229
**Deutsches Märchen- und
Wesersagenmuseum**
Am Kurpark 3, D-4970 Bad
Oeynhausen
Anthropology Museum - 1973
Fairy tales and legends - library

05230
Heimatmuseum
Schützenstr. 35a, D-4970 Bad
Oeynhausen
General Museum - 1969
Peasant culture (18th and 19th cent.);
domestic crafts; geology and
palaeontology

05231
**Norddeutsches Auto- und Motorrad-
Museum**
Weserstr. 225, D-4970 Bad
Oeynhausen
Science/Tech Museum - 1973
Automobiles, motorcycles and
bicycles

Bad Oldesloe

05232
Heimatmuseum Bad Oldesloe
Königstr. 32, D-2060 Bad Oldesloe
General Museum - 1931
Local history (prehistoric to present);
municipal history

Bad Orb

05233
Heimatmuseum
Rathaus, D-6482 Bad Orb
General Museum - 1916
History of the spa; municipal history;
folklore

Bad Schussenried

05234
Freilichtmuseum Kürnbach
Kürnbach, Griesweg, D-7953 Bad
Schussenried 1
Open Air Museum - 1968
Old farm buildings including thatched-
roof building from 1663-1665

Bad Segeberg

05235
Alt-Segeberger Bürgerhaus
Lübecker Str. 15, D-2360 Bad
Segeberg
General Museum - 1963/64
Furniture and furnishings, 17th to 19th
cent. and tools of local craftsmen,
housed in 16th cent. half-timber house

Bad Tölz

05236
Heimatmuseum
Schloßplatz 2, D-8170 Bad Tölz
General Museum - 1885
Local history; timber industry; furniture
and furnishings , esp. Empire and
Biedermeier; folk costumes; religious
folk art; local rocks; sculpture

Bad Wildungen

05237
Museum Schloß Friedrichstein
D-3590 Bad Wildungen
History/Public Affairs Museum - 1980
Hessian military history to 1866;
hunting weapons

Bad Wimpfen

05238
Museum im Steinhaus
Burgviertel 15, D-7107 Bad Wimpfen
General Museum - 1952
Prehistory, early history and local
history; medieval art; weapons and
coins; peasant culture

Bad Wörishofen

05239
Kneipp-Museum
Klosterhof 1, D-8939 Bad Wörishofen
Historic Site - 1855
Memorabilia of Sebastian Kneipp,
originator of the so-called 'Kneipp
cure'

Bad Zwischenahn

05240
**Freilandmuseum Ammerländer
Bauernhaus**
Auf dem Winkel 26, Postfach 1401,
D-2903 Bad Zwischenahn
Open Air Museum - 1910
Farm houses and buildings; peasant
culture

Baden-Baden

05241
Brahmshaus
Maximilianstr. 85, D-7570 Baden-Baden
Historic Site - 1968
Memorabilia of Johannes Brahms,
housed in rooms in which Brahms
vacationed; Brahms library including
scores and phonograph records

05242
**Museum für Mechanische
Musikinstrumente**
Sofienstr. 40, D-7570 Baden-Baden
Music Museum - 1975
History of mechanical music
instruments

05243
Zähringer Museum
Neues Schloß, D-7570 Baden-Baden
Decorative Arts Museum - 1960
18th and 19th cent. portraits; porcelain
collection; period rooms

05244
Zisterzienserinnen-Abtei
Hauptstr. 40, D-7570 Baden-Baden
Religious Art Museum - 1912
Sacred art; handicrafts

Balingen

05245
Museum für Waage und Gewicht
Zollernschloß, D-7460 Balingen 1
Science/Tech Museum - 1943
History of weights and scales; scales
from around the world

Bamberg

05246
E. T. A. Hoffmann-Haus
Schillerplatz 26, D-8600 Bamberg
History/Public Affairs Museum - 1930
Memorabilia from the period of
Hoffmann's residence in Bamberg;
first editions of Hoffmann's works

05247
Erzbischöfliches Diözesanmuseum
Domplatz 5, D-8600 Bamberg
Religious Art Museum - 1964
Sacred art from the 11th cent. onward;
sculpture of the Danube School;
Cathedral treasure

05248
Gärtner- und Häckermuseum
Mittelstr. 34, D-8600 Bamberg
Science/Tech Museum - 1975
Tools and implements, costumes, and
furnishings illustrating history of
gardening

05249
**Historisches Museum der Stadt
Bamberg**
Domplatz 7, D-8600 Bamberg
History/Public Affairs Museum - 1938
Handicrafts and guilds; municipal
history; clocks and astronomical
instruments; painting and sculpture

05250
Karl-May-Museum
E.T.A.-Hoffmann-Str. 2, D-0951
Bamberg
Historic Site - 1963
Memorabilia of the writer Karl May -
Archive and library of Karl-May-Verlag

05251
Naturkunde-Museum
Fleischerstr. 2, D-8600 Bamberg
Natural History Museum - i
Zoology; palaeontoloty; mineralogy
and geology - herbarium

05252
Neue Residenz
Domplatz 8, D-8600 Bamberg
Fine Arts Museum
Late Baroque, Rococo and Classicist
furnishings; paintings

05253
Staatsgalerie
Neue Residenz, Domplatz 8, D-8600
Bamberg
Fine Arts Museum - 1817
Masterworks of Cologne and
Franconian schools (late Gothic
painting)

Banz

05254
**Petrefakten- und Orientalische
Sammlung Banz**
Schloß Banz, D-8621 Banz
General Museum - 1850
Palaeontology; geology; rocks;
Egyptian antiquities

Bayreuth

05255
Eremitage Altes u. Neues Schloß
mail c/o Schloß- u. Gartenverwaltung,
Eremitage Haus Nr. 42, D-8580
Bayreuth
Decorative Arts Museum
Period rooms; grotto with late Gothic
fountain; garden architecture

05256
**Museum für Bäuerliche
Arbeitsgeräte**
Adolf-Wächter-Str. 3, D-8580 Bayreuth
Agriculture Museum - 1958
Agricultural tools and implements,
housed in 1734 barn

05257
Neues Schloß
Ludwigstr. 21, *mail c/o* Schloß- und
Gartenverwaltung, Glasenappweg 3,
D-8580 Bayreuth
Fine Arts Museum
Period rooms (Bayreuth Rococo);
Hohenzollern family portraits;
tapestries; faience; paintings

05258
**Oberfränkisches Erdgeschichtliches
Museum**
Ludwigstr. 21, D-8580 Bayreuth
Natural History Museum - 1832
Geology and palaeontology

05259
Richard-Wagner-Museum Haus
Wahnfried
Richard-Wagner-Str. 48, D-8580
Bayreuth
Historic Site - 1976
Documents from the life and works of
Richard Wagner; history of the
Bayreuth Festival - Recording studio;
archive; library

05260
Staatsgalerie
Neues Schloß, Ludwigstr. 21, D-8580
Bayreuth
Fine Arts Museum - 1925
European Baroque painting (17th and
18th cent.)

05261
Stadtmuseum Bayreuth
Ludwigstr. 21, D-8580 Bayreuth
General Museum - 1912
Local cultural history, including
specimens of peasant and bourgeois
furnishings, folk art, porcelain; works
of Bayreuth painters

Benediktbeuern

05262
Historische Fraunhofer Glashütte
Fraunhofer Str. 126, D-8174
Benediktbeuern
Historic Site - 1963
Workroom and glass manufacturing
tools of J. von Fraunhofer (1787-1926);
glass samples

Bensberg

05263
**Bergisches Museum für Bergbau,
Handwerk und Gewerbe
(Heimatmuseum Bensberg)**
Burggraben 17, Bensberg, D-5060
Bergisch Gladbach
General Museum - 1928
Mining; local history; crafts and trades

Berchtesgaden

05264
Heimatmuseum Berchtesgaden
Schroffenbergallee 6, D-8248
Berchtesgaden
General Museum - 1880
Folk art of the Berchtesgaden area,
including costumes, furniture, sculpture

05265
Museum Schloß Berchtesgaden
Schloßplatz 2, D-8240 Berchtesgaden
Decorative Arts Museum
Furniture; tapestries; porcelain and
glass; weapons

05266
Salzbergwerk mit Salzmuseum
Bergwerkstr. 83, D-8240
Berchtesgaden
History/Public Affairs Museum
Displays of ancient salt routes and salt
mining towns; history of salt trade and
industry

Berlin

05267
Ägyptisches Museum
Schloßstr. 70 (östl. Stülerbau), D-1000
Berlin 19
Fine Arts Museum - 1823
Monuments of Egyptian history, art
and culture; papyrus collection;

05268
Antikenmuseum
Schloßstr. 1 (westl. Stülerbau), D-1000
Berlin 19
Fine Arts Museum - 1830
Greek vases; Greek bronze work;
Etruscan and Roman art; antique
jewelry; Roman table silver; mummy
portraits

05269
**Bauhaus-Archiv / Museum für
Gestaltung**
Klingelhöferstr 13-14, D-1000 Berlin 30
Fine Arts Museum - 1960
Architectural sketches and models by
Gropius, van der Rohe, Muche,
Hilberseimer; drawings and paintings
by H. Beyer, Feininger, Kandinsky,
Klee; furniture, ceramics, metal work
and weaving; sculpture and
photography

05270
Berlin-Museum
Lindenstr. 14, D-1000 Berlin 61
General Museum
Documents and memorabilia of
famous Berlin families - library

05271
**Berliner Post- und
Fernmeldemuseum**
An der Urania 15, D-1000 Berlin 30
Science/Tech Museum - 1956
History of the postal service;
telecommunications; postage stamps

05272
Berlinische Galerie
Jebenstr. 2, D-1000 Berlin 12
Fine Arts Museum - 1975
Art from 1850 to the present

05273
**Botanischer Garten und Botanisches
Museum Berlin-Dahlem**
Königin-Luise-Str. 6-3, D-1000 Berlin
33
Natural History Museum - 1679/1815
History and distribution of plants;
growth forms and reproduction; finds
from Egyptian tombs; 18,000 varieties
of plants from around the world
(botanical garden)

05274
Brücke-Museum
Bussardsteig 9, D-1000 Berlin 33
Fine Arts Museum - 1964
Drawings, paintings, graphics,
sculpture of members of the Brücke
Group; bequests of Karl Schmidt-
Rottluff and Erich Heckel

05275
**Gedenk- und Bildungsstätte
Stauffenbergstrasse**
Stauffenbergstr. 14, D-1000 Berlin 30
History/Public Affairs Museum - 1968
Exhibits documenting the conspiracy
against Hitler, housed in historic
rooms

05276
Gemäldegalerie
Arnimallee 23, D-1000 Berlin 33
Fine Arts Museum - 1830
Italian painting of the 13th to the 16th
cent.; German and Netherlandish
Gothic and Renaissance painting; 18th
cent. English and German painting

05277
Georg-Kolbe-Museum
Sensburger Allee 25, D-1000 Berlin 19
Fine Arts Museum - 1950
Drawing, graphics and sculpture of
Georg Kolbe; Impressionist and
Expressionist works from the estate of
Kolbe - Kolbe archives

05278
**Historische Ausstellung 'Fragen an
die deutsche Geschichte'**
Reichstagsgebäude, Paul-Löbe-Str.,
D-1000 Berlin 21
History/Public Affairs Museum - 1971
Coll: exhibits on German history from
1800 to the present

05279
Humboldt-Museum Schloß Tegel
Gabrielenstraße, D-1000 Berlin 27
Historic Site - 1824
Coll: residence of Wilhelm and
Alexander von Humboldt; Wilhelm von
Humboldt's collection of classical art;
art of classicism; archives including
Humboldt archives - library

05280
Jagdschloß Grunewald
D-1000 Berlin 33
Historic Site - 1918
Coll: 15th-19th century German and
Dutch paintings; contemporary
furniture; hunting trophies; in
Renaissance residence

05281
Kriminalmuseum
Gothaer Str. 19, D-1000 Berlin 62
History/Public Affairs Museum - 1890
History of criminality; documatation of
actual cases

05282
**Kunstbibliothek mit Museum für
Architektur, Modebild und Graphik-
Design**
Jebensstr. 2, D-1000 Berlin 12
Fine Arts Museum - 1894
Coll: graphics on the history of
costumes; drawings; engravings;
engraving series on architecture and
European handicrafts; Grisebach
collection of 19th century illustrated
books; 19th-20th century applied
prints and posters - library

05283
Kunstgewerbemuseum
Neubau am Kemperplatz, D-1000
Berlin 30
Decorative Arts Museum - 1877
Coll: medieval goldsmith work; silver;
faience and porcelain; glass - library;
photo laboratory; workshop

05284
Kupferstichkabinett
Neubau am Kemperplatz, D-1000
Berlin 30
Fine Arts Museum - 1830
Coll: 14th-18th century drawings,
watercolors, and miniatures; prints;
15th-20th century illustrated books;
medieval book ornamentation; sketch
books from the 16th-18th centuries;
topographic collection - library;
phototheque

05285
**Museum des Blindenwesens in
Berlin**
mail c/o Johann-August-Zeune-Schule
für Blinde und Berufsfachschule Silex,
Rothenburgstr. 14, D-1000 Berlin 41
History/Public Affairs Museum
Coll: exhibits on the development of
the Braille script and Braille
typewriters; Braille educational
material (maps, atlases) - library

05286
Museum für Deutsche Volkskunde
Im Winkel 6-8, D-1000 Berlin 33
History/Public Affairs Museum - 1889
Coll: material goods of middle and
lower social levels; popular prints;
posters; traditional costumes; reading
materials; textiles; furniture; glass;
ceramics; tools; amateur paintings;
devotional items - library; workshop

05287
Museum für Indische Kunst
Takustr. 40, D-1000 Berlin 33
Fine Arts Museum - 1963
Coll: Indian art, sculpture, handicrafts,
miniatures; bronzes and paintings from
Tibet and Nepal; sculpture, bronzes,
and brick reliefs from Indonesia; art
from Central Asia; study collections;
archives - library

05288
Museum für Islamische Kunst
Takustr. 40, D-1000 Berlin 33
Fine Arts Museum - 1904
Coll: art of the Parthians, Sassanids,
and Arabs before Islam; Islamic art
and handicrafts from all epochs
including metalwork ivory, ceramics,
glass, faience, rugs, miniatures, and
Koran manuscripts; study collection -
library; workshop; phototheque

05289
Museum für Ostasiatische Kunst
Takustr. 40, D-1000 Berlin 33
Fine Arts Museum - 1906
Coll: fine arts from China, Korea, and
Japan including painting, woodcuts,
ceramics, lacquer items, statuettes,
bronze articles; study collection;
archives - library

05290
Museum für Verkehr und Technik
Trebbiner Str. 9, D-1000 Berlin 61
Science/Tech Museum - 1981
Coll: historical development of
transportation, street and rail,
navigation, aviation; exhibition of the
blockade of Berlin 1948/49;
automobile collection; typewriter and
computer collection

05291
Museum für Völkerkunde
Arnimallee 27, D-1000 Berlin 33
Anthropology Museum - 1873
Div: folk art from the South Seas;
American archeology; American Indian
tribes; West Asia; South Asia; East
Asia; non-German Europe; music
ethnology; junior and Braille museum -
library; workshop; photo laboratory;
auditorium

05292
Museum für Vor- und Frühgeschichte
Schloß Charlottenburg, D-1000 Berlin 19
Archeology Museum - 1829
Coll: late Stone Age; early Stone Age; Bronze Age; Iron Age through the early Middle Ages; Near Eastern archeology - library

05293
Museumsdorf Düppel
An der Clauertstraße, D-1000 Berlin 37
Archeology Museum - 1975
Coll: excavation of 12th century village site; demonstration of prehistoric handicrafts

05294
Musikinstrumenten-Museum des Staatlichen Instituts für Musikforschung
Bundesalle 1-12, D-1000 Berlin 15
Music Museum - 1888
Coll: European music instruments from all periods and cultures; non-European instruments; documentation on the history of music instruments; records and tapes; automatic instruments; archives - library; phototheque; workshop

05295
Nationalgalerie
Potsdamer Str. 50, D-1000 Berlin 30
Fine Arts Museum - 1861
Coll: painting; sculpture; 19th-20th century drawings - library; workshop

05296
Ofen- und Kamin-Museum
Magdeburger Platz 2, D-1000 Berlin 30
Decorative Arts Museum - 1912
Coll: stove and chimney construction; tile stoves; ceramics; smithwork

05297
Pfaueninsel, Schloß und Landschaftspark
mail c/o Verwaltung der Staatlichen Schlösser und Gärten, Luisenplatz, D-1000 Berlin 19
Historic Site - 1924
Coll: 18th century castle with other buildings from the 17th-19th centuries; historical interiors

05298
Polizeimuseum Berlin
Radelandstr. 21, D-1000 Berlin 20
History/Public Affairs Museum - 1973
Coll: history of the Berlin police; documents; pictures; uniforms; technical equipment

05299
Sammlung Bröhan
Max-Eyth-Str. 27, D-1000 Berlin 33
Fine Arts Museum - 1976
Coll: art of the turn of the century and the twenties; painting of the Berlin Secessionists; decorative art including Art Nouveau and Art Deco

05300
Schloß Charlottenburg
Luisenplatz, D-1000 Berlin 19
Fine Arts Museum - 1926
Coll: 15th-19th century painting, especially Lucas Cranach and French painting of the 18th century and German romantic painting; furniture; porcelain; archives - library; workshops

05301
Skulpturengalerie
Neubau am Kemperplatz, D-1000 Berlin 30
Fine Arts Museum - 1830
Coll: Western sculptue from late Antiquity to the 19th century, including stone sculpture, ivory, wood carving, bronzes, and icons - workshop

05302
Ständige Ausstellung Umweltschutz
Bismarckplatz 1, D-1000 Berlin 33
Natural History Museum - 1976
Coll: exhibits on the environment; information about the tasks of the environmental protection agency - library

05303
Stiftung Deutschlandhaus
Stresemannstr. 90, D-1000 Berlin 61
History/Public Affairs Museum - 1952
Coll: exhibits on prominent East Germans in Berlin; the patron figures from the Naumburg cathedral; historic seals; photographs of the Mark Brandenburg, old Berlin, and The Wall from Kreuzberg to the Reichstag - library

05304
Zucker-Museum
Amrumer Str. 32, D-1000 Berlin 65
Science/Tech Museum - 1904
Coll: history and technology of sugar production; synthetic production of sugar; by-products; model of the oldest beet-sugar factory; sugar advertisement over 100 years; sugar bowls from the 17th century on; archives - library; laboratory

Bernau

05305
Hans-Thoma-Museum
Rathaus, D-7821 Bernau
Fine Arts Museum - 1949
Coll: paintings, drawings, graphics, glass painting, carvings by Hans Thoma; furniture designed by Thoma; documents on his life and works; works of the winners of the Hans Thoma prize

05306
'Resenhof'
Bürgermeisteramt, D-7821 Bernau
General Museum - 1977
Coll: tools; exhibits on the different processes of making wooden items; domestic utensils from wood, including wooden spoons, mouse traps, wooden boxes; minerals; original interiors; in 18th century farmstead

Bertoldsheim

05307
Bildergalerie
Schloß, D-8859 Bertoldsheim
Fine Arts Museum
Coll: German and Dutch painting from the 17th and 18th centuries; furniture

Beuron

05308
Bibelmuseum
Erzabtei, D-7792 Beuron
Religious Art Museum - 1863
Coll: original biblical manuscripts; archeological finds

Bexbach

05309
Gruben- und Heimatmuseum
mail c/o Kultur- und Verkehrsamt, Rathaustr. 68, D-6652 Bexbach
Science/Tech Museum - 1934
Coll: geology; mining; metallurgy; mine safety

Biberach a.d. Riß

05310
Braith-Mali-Museum Städtische Sammlungen
Museumsstr. 6, D-7950 Biberach a.d. Riß 1
General Museum - 1910
Coll: art of the late Gothic; prehistory; local history; 17th-20th century painting; original atelier and estate of the animal painters A. Braith and Chr. Mali; works by Ernst Ludwig Kirchner; natural science; sculpture; archives - library; classroom

05311
Wieland-Archiv
Marktplatz 17, D-7950 Biberach a.d. Riß 1
Historic Site - 1907
Coll: works and manuscripts of the writer Christoph Martin Wieland; secondary literature on Wieland and the literature of the 18th century; all editions of works by Martin Walser

Biedenkopf

05312
Hinterlandmuseum im Schloß Biedenkopf
Nikolauskirchstr. 8, D-3560 Biedenkopf
General Museum - 1908
Coll: geology; ornithology; development of the iron industry in the upper Lahn valley from 500 B.C. to the 20th century; traditional costumes; embroidery; handicrafts and the guilds

Bielefeld

05313
Bauernhaus-Museum
Dornberger Str. 82, D-4800 Bielefeld
Anthropology Museum - 1917
Coll: folk art from the 16th to the 19th century; in 16th century half-timbered hall farm house; 17th-18th century mill and silo

05314
Kunsthalle Bielefeld
Artur-Ladebeck-Str. 5, D-4800 Bielefeld
Fine Arts Museum - 1928
Coll: Expressionist painting; Bauhaus art; American painting after 1945; Cubistic sculpture; graphics - library; children's atelier

05315
Naturkunde-Museum der Stadt
Kreuzstr. 38, D-4800 Bielefeld 1
Natural History Museum - 1906
Coll: mineralogy; geology; geobotany; entomology; ornithology - library; small laboratory

Bingen am Rhein

05316
Stefan-George-Gedenkstätte
Im Schulzentrum, D-6530 Bingen am Rhein
Historic Site - 1968
Coll: the painting and book collection of the poet Stefan George; secondary literature on George's work; library of his great uncle - library

Blankenheim

05317
Kreismuseum
Johannesstr. 6, D-5378 Blankenheim
General Museum - 1954
Coll: prehistory; local and regional history; ethnography; furnishings; geology; fossils; natural science; archives - library

Blaubeuren

05318
Heimatmuseum
Klosterhof, D-7902 Blaubeuren
General Museum - 1947
Coll: prehistory; geology; paleontology; zoology; ethnology; memorial to the philosopher Karl Christian Planck

05319
Urgeschichtliches Museum
Karlstr. 21, D-7902 Blaubeuren
Archeology Museum - 1965
Coll: local Ice Age finds; late Stone Age items demonstrating primitive techology and life in Africa and the American Arctic

Bocholt

05320
Galerie der Stadt Bocholt
Berliner Platz 1, D-4290 Bocholt
Fine Arts Museum - 1958
Coll: painting; watercolors; sculpture by contemporary local artists; copper and steel etchings

Bochum

05321
Deutsches Bergbau-Museum
Am Bergbaumuseum 28, D-4630 Bochum 1
Science/Tech Museum - 1930
Div: technology of mining; science of geological deposits and raw materials; economics and technology of mining; historic mining equipment and plants; mining and archeology - library; workshops; photo laboratory

05322
Eisenbahnmuseum Bochum-Dahlhausen
Dr.-C. Otto-Str. 191, D-4630 Bochum 5
Open Air Museum - 1967
Coll: steam, electric, and diesel locomotives; motor railcar; coaches - library; workshop

05323
Kunstsammlungen der Ruhr-Universität Bochum
Universitätsstr. 150, D-4630 Bochum 1
Fine Arts Museum - 1974
Coll: Greek antiquities; modern German and American painting; Greek, Roman, and medieval coins

05324
Museum Bochum
Kortumstr. 147, D-4630 Bochum 1
Fine Arts Museum - 1960
Coll: art after 1945; painting, graphics, sculpture; in 19th century Villa Marckhoff - library

Bodenwerder

05325
Baron-Münchhausen-Museum
Rathaus, D-3452 Bodenwerder
Historic Site - 1950
Coll: memorabilia of Karl Friedrich Hieronymus Freiherr von Münchhausen; literary works about him; translations

Boll

05326
Privatsammlung Willy Hohl
Gruibingerstr. 35, D-7325 Boll
Natural History Museum - 1975
Coll: finds from the Cambrium to the Quarternary periods; fossils of the Mesozoic period

Bonn

05327
Akademisches Kunstmuseum der Universität Bonn
Am Hofgarten 21, D-5300 Bonn 1
Fine Arts Museum - 1818
Coll: casts of Greek and Roman late classical sculptures; vases, bronzes, terracotta figures, and marble sculptures from the early Bronze Age to late Antiquity; coins; coptic textiles; glasses; archives - library; workshops

05328
Beethoven-Haus
Bonngasse 20, D-5300 Bonn 1
Historic Site - 1889
Coll: music instruments; autographs; prints; paintings collected by the composer; in 17th century house in which Beethoven was born - library

05329
Ernst-Moritz-Arndt-Haus
Adenauerallee 79, D-5300 Bonn 1
Historic Site - 1956
Coll: 19th century house of the writer Ernst Moritz Arndt; memorabilia of Arndt; interiors; local history (16th-19th century)

05330
Mineralogisch-Petrologisches Museum der Universität Bonn
Poppelsdorfer Schloß, D-5300 Bonn 1
Natural History Museum - 1818
Coll: systematic mineralogy; petrology; science of geological deposits; meteorites; gems; minerals and rocks from the local vulcanic region - library; workshop

05331
Rheinisches Landesmuseum Bonn
Colmantstr. 14-16, D-5300 Bonn 1
General Museum - 1820
Div: prehistory; Roman epoch; early Christianity; Franks; medieval archeology; art and handicrafts of medieval and modern times; coins; archives - library; workshops; photo laboratory

05332
Städtisches Kunstmuseum Bonn
Rathausgasse 7, D-5300 Bonn 1
Fine Arts Museum - 1882
Coll: art of the 20th century; August Macke and Rhein Expressionism after 1945; international graphics after 1945 - library

05333
Zoologisches Forschungsinstitut und Museum Alexander Koenig
Adenauerallee 150-164, D-5300 Bonn 1
Natural History Museum - 1912
Coll: ornithology; herpetology; lepidopterology; parasitic entomology; lower arthropods; dipterology - library; preparation atelier

Brackenheim

05334
Theodor-Heuss-Gedächtnisstätte
Obertorstr. 25, D-7129 Brackenheim
Historic Site - 1968
Coll: paintings, letters, documents of Theodor Heuss, the first president of the German Federal Republic

Brake

05335
Schiffahrtsmuseum der Oldenburgischen Unterweserhäfen
Unterweser, Heinrich-Schnittgerstr. 18, D-2880 Brake
Science/Tech Museum - 1960
Coll: history of navigation; wood ship building in the 19th century; development of the Oldenburg harbors; seamen's folk art; Dutch tiles with depictions of ships

Braubach

05336
Burgmuseum Marksburg
Marksburg, D-5423 Braubach
General Museum - 1900
local history; folk art and folk lore; history of the Rhein land; medieval interiors; Gimbel collection of weapons; archives; in medieval fortress on the Rhein - library

Braunfels

05337
Schloßmuseum
Schloß, D-6333 Braunfels
History/Public Affairs Museum - 1885
Coll: weapons; religious art; paintings; period rooms (Renaissance to Empire); coaches; hunting equipment; stove plates (16th-18th centuries); uniforms; costumes (17th-19th centuries)

Braunschweig

05338
Braunschweigisches Landesmuseum für Geschichte und Volkstum
Mönchstr. 1, D-3300 Braunschweig
General Museum
Local history, including prehistory; folk art and culture, including jewelry, furniture, textiles, and agricultural implements

05339
Burg Dankwarderode
Burgplatz, D-3300 Braunschweig
Fine Arts Museum
Art from local churches and monestaries

05340
Formsammlung der Stadt Braunschweig
Broitzemer Str. 230, D-3300 Braunschweig
Science/Tech Museum - 1942
Vessels and containers of various materials and from various periods illustrating the development of industrial form

05341
Herzog Anton Ulrich-Museum
Museumstr. 1, D-3300 Braunschweig
Fine Arts Museum
European painting (15th to 18th cent.)

05342
Museum für mechanische Musik
Zeigenmarkt 2, D-3300 Braunschweig
Science/Tech Museum - 1944
Music boxes and other mechanical music instruments

05343
Raabe-Gedächtnisstätte
Leonhardstr. 29a, D-3301 Braunschweig
Historic Site - 1948
Library, drawings, water colors, and manuscripts of Wilhelm Raabe, housed in the writer's last dwelling

05344
Staatliches Naturhistorisches Museum
Pockelstr. 10a, D-3300 Braunschweig
Natural History Museum - 1754
Zoology and ornithology; entomology; living reptiles and birds - library

05345
Städtisches Museum
Am Löwenwall, D-2200 Braunschweig
General Museum
Coins and money; preindustrial production methods; guilds and handicrafts; religious articles; iron work; municipal history

Breisach

05346
Breisgau-Museum für Ur- und Frühgeschichte
Münsterbergstr., D-7814 Breisach
History/Public Affairs Museum - 1972
Stone-age finds; finds from the Merdingen alemannic cemetary; Roman remains

05347
Galerie Kröner Deutsche Malerei der Gegenwart
Schloß Rimsingen, Oberrimsingen, D-7814 Breisach 3
Fine Arts Museum - 1966
Contemporary German painting

Bremen

05348
Bleikeller
Sandstr. 10-12, D-2800 Bremen
History/Public Affairs Museum - 1823
Coffins with mummified bodies; lead-working machinery; Baroque Evangelist figures

05349
Bremer Landesmuseum für Kunst- und Kulturgeschichte (Focke-Museum)
Schwachhauser Heerstr. 240, D-2800 Bremen
General Museum - 1898
Medieval collections; 18th and 19th cent. culture; folklore; prehistory; water transportatin; tobacco

05350
Gerhard Marcks-Haus
Am Wall 208, D-2800 Bremen 1
Fine Arts Museum - 1971
Drawings, graphics and sculpture of Gerhard Marcks (b. 1809), housed in classicist building

05351
Kunsthalle Bremen
Am Wall 207, D-2800 Bremen 1
Fine Arts Museum - 1823
Painting (Middle Ages to present), with emphasis on 19th and 20th cent. French and German works; 19th and 20th cent. sculpture; graphic art of all European schools and periods; illustrated manuscripts and books; 19th and 20th cent. European posters

05352
Paula-Modersohn-Becker-Haus
Böttcherstr. 8, D-2800 Bremen
Fine Arts Museum - 1927
Paintings and graphics of the artist

05353
Roselius-Haus
Böttcherstr. 6, D-2800 Bremen
General Museum - 1928
Furnishings of Bremen patrician families; art from local churches and castles; secular implements from six centuries

05354
Übersee-Museum
Bahnhofsplatz 13, D-2800 Bremen
Science/Tech Museum - 1783
Ethnology; biology; geological sciences; commerce

05355
Waffensammlung Ludwig Roselius
Böttcherstr. 8, D-2800 Bremen
History/Public Affairs Museum - 1937
Armor and weapons from the 12th to the 17th cent.

Bremerhaven

05356
Deutsches Schiffahrtsmuseum
Van-Ronzelen-Str., D-2850 Bremerhaven 1
Science/Tech Museum - 1971
German ships, shipping and seamanship from prehistoric times to present; German navy from 1848 to present; water sports in Germany

05357
Kunsthalle Bremerhaven
Karlsburg 4, D-2850 Bremerhaven
Fine Arts Museum - 1886
Art of the 20th cent.

05358
Nordseemuseum
mail c/o Institut für Meeresforschung, Am Handelshafen 12, D-2850 Bremerhaven 31
Natural History Museum - 1921
Marine flora and fauna; palaeontology; tides

Bretten

05359
Melanchthonhaus Bretten
Melanchthon-Str. 1, D-7518 Bretten
History/Public Affairs Museum - 1897
Writings of Philipp Melanchthon and documents on his life and work; works on the history of the Humanist movement and the Reformation - archive

Bruchsal

05360
Schloß Bruchsal
D-7520 Bruchsal
Fine Arts Museum - 1975
Flemish and French tapestries (17th and 18th cent.); religious articles; sculpture, ceramics and textiles; 18th cent. hunting weapons

Brüggen

05361
Jagd- und Naturkundemuseum
Burg Brüggen, D-4057 Brüggen
History/Public Affairs Museum - 1979
History of hunting

Brühl

05362
Schloß Augustusburg, Schloß Falkenlust
Schloßstr. 6, D-5040 Brühl
Fine Arts Museum
18th cent. furniture and furnishings in original settings

Bückeburg

05363
Hubschraubermuseum
Lehrsammlung für Vertikalflugtechnik
Sablé-Platz 6, Postfach 1310, D-3062 Bückeburg
Science/Tech Museum - 1971
Development of verticle takeoff aircraft; model and test helicopters

Büdelsdorf

05364
Eisenkunstguß-Museum
Glück-Auf-Allee, D-2370 Büdelsdorf
History/Public Affairs Museum - 1963
Iron stoves, fireplaces and related ornamental ironwork

Büdingen

05365
Fürstlich Ysenburg- und Büdingensches Schloßmuseum
Schloß, D-2470 Büdingen
General Museum - 1951
Romanesque and Gothic interiors; frescoes from the 14th to the 16th cent.; alchemist's and apothecary's workroom and equipment; weapons; furnishings, glass, ceramics, tapestries, iron implements, etc.

Bünde

05366
Deutsches Tabak- und Zigarrenmuseum
Fünfhausenstr. 10-12, D-4980 Bünde
Anthropology Museum - 1937
Historical pipes; history of tobacco culture and cultivation; historical furniture and cigar manufacturing equipment

Burg auf Fehmarn

05367
Peter-Wiepert-Museum
neben Nikolaikirche, D-2448 Burg auf Fehmarn
General Museum - 1897
Geology and prehistory; local history; weapons; money collection; domestic implements; crafts and folklore

Burghausen

05368
Burg zu Burghausen
mail c/o Burgverwaltung Burghausen, Burg 48, D-8263 Burghausen
Fine Arts Museum
5th and 16th cent. interiors

Staatsgalerie
05369
Hauptburg der Burg, D-8263 Burghausen
Fine Arts Museum - 1897
Austrian and Bavarian late Gothic painting

05370
Stadtmuseum
Burg 48, D-8263 Burghausen
Fine Arts Museum - 1899
Early and prehistory; municipal history; handicrafts; Baroque painting and sculpture; religious folk art; costumes; furniture; weapons; bird collection

Calw

05371
Heimatmuseum der Stadt Calw mit Hermann-Hesse-Gedenkstätte
Bischofstr. 48, D-7260 Calw
General Museum - 1950
Folk art including peasant furniture; Schöttle-bey collection of finds from the ancient Near East and documents on life and work of Hermann Hesse

Cloppenburg

05372
Museumsdorf Cloppenburg
Niedersächsisches Freilichtmuseum
Postfach 1344, D-4590 Cloppenburg
Open Air Museum - 1922
Original buildings from the 16th to 19th cent. and displays of former trades and crafts; folklore; local art history

Coburg

05373
Kunstsammlungen der Veste Coburg
Veste Coburg, D-8630 Coburg
General Museum - 1838
Weapons and carriage collection; coin collection; manuscripts; Venetian glass

05374
Naturwissenschaftliches Museum Coburg
Park 6, D-8630 Coburg
Natural History Museum - 1730
Zoology; botany; mineralogy; palaeontology; prehistory and ethnology

05375
Schloß Ehrenburg
mail c/o Coburger Landesstiftung als Staatl. Verwaltung Coburg, Schloßplatz, D-8630 Coburg
General Museum
Municipal history; 17th cent. interiors; 19th cent. furnishings; Baroque carpets and paintings; temporary exhibitions of the Coburg Landesbibliothek

Creglingen

05376
Feuerwehrmuseum Waldmannshofen
Schloß Waldmannshofen, D-6993 Creglingen
Science/Tech Museum - 1967
Fire-fighting equipment from the mid-19th cent. to the present

Creußen

05377
Creußener Krügemuseum
Am Rennsteig 36, D-8581 Creußen
Anthropology Museum - 1878
Creußen crockery from all periods

Cuxhaven

05378
Stadtmuseum Cuxhaven
Südersteinstr. 38, D-2190 Cuxhaven
General Museum - 1926
Early history of the Elbe-Weser triangle; local harbor and shipping; local culture

Dachau

05379
KZ-Gedenkstätte Dachau
Alte Römerstr. 75, D-8060 Dachau
Historic Site - 1965
History of the Dachau and other concentration camps from 1933 to 1945 - library and archives

Darmstadt

05380
Chaplin-Archiv Wilhelm Staudinger
Binger Str. 5, D-6100 Darmstadt
History/Public Affairs Museum - 1974
Films, books, articles, posters and other materials documenting the life and work of Charlie Chaplin

05381
Eisenbahnmuseum Darmstadt-Kranichstein
Steinstr. 13, D-6100 Darmstadt
Science/Tech Museum - 1976
Locomotives from 1887 to 1950; railroad equipment and techniques

05382
Großherzogliche Porzellan-Sammlung
Prinz-Georg-Palais, Im Schloßgarten 7, D-6100 Darmstadt
Fine Arts Museum - 1907
18th and 19th cent. European porcelain and faience - library

05383
Hessisches Landesmuseum
Friedensplatz 1, D-6100 Darmstadt
General Museum - 1787-1820
European painting from the Middle Ages to the present; graphic art; art nouveau crafts; archaeology, geology and mineralogy; zoology

05384
Jagdmuseum Schloß Kranichstein
Kranichsteiner Str., D-6100 Darmstadt
History/Public Affairs Museum - 1917
Hunting weapons and equipment from the 16th to the 19th cent.; 18th and 19th cent. interiors; trophies and paintings

05385
Schloßmuseum Darmstadt
Residenzschloß (Glockenbau), D-6100 Darmstadt
Fine Arts Museum - 1924
Hessian history and cultural life (17th to 20th cent.); European painting; carriages and court uniforms

05386
Stadtmuseum und Städtische Kunstsammlungen
Europaplatz 1, D-6100 Darmstadt
General Museum - 1904
Municipal history; works in Darmstadt art nouveau style; contemporary graphics

05387
Wella Museum
Berliner Allee 65, D-6100 Darmstadt
History/Public Affairs Museum - 1952
History of cosmetics and beauty care from antiquity to the present

Deidesheim

05388
Museum für Moderne Keramik
Stadtmauergasse 17, D-6705 Deidesheim
Fine Arts Museum - 1961
Roman and medieval pottery; modern ceramics from many countries

Deinste

05389
Technisches Museum, Fachgebiet Feld- und Kleinbahnen
Kleinbahnhof, D-2161 Deinste
Science/Tech Museum - 1978
Historical small-gauge trains (500 and 600 mm)

Delligsen

05390
Glasmuseum Grünenplan
Obere Hilsstr. 3 u. Kirchtalstr. 13, D-3223 Delligsen 2
Science/Tech Museum
Models of glass-manufacturing equipment; glass from various periods

Detmold

05391
Fürstliches Residenzschloß
Schloß, D-4930 Detmold
Fine Arts Museum
Period rooms (Baroque, Empire; eclectic); Amsterdam and Brussels tapestries; glass, weapons, trophies and furniture; painting

05392
Lippisches Landesmuseum Detmold
Ameide 4, D-4930 Detmold
General Museum - 1835
Div: natural science; regional and cultural history; folk art and traditions; prehistory through the Middle Ages; ethnology of pre-Columbian America, Africa, and Asia; archives - library; photo laboratory

05393
Westfälisches Freilichtmuseum Bäuerlicher Kulturdenkmale
Landesmuseum für Volkskunde
Krummes Haus, D-4930 Detmold
Open Air Museum - 1960
Coll: historical buildings and farmsteads from 16th-18th century; furnishings; domestic utensils; agricultural tools and machines; folk art; exhibit on the mechaniyation of agriculture in the 19th-20th century; photo and blueprint archives - library; workshops

Dinkelsbühl

05394
Historisches Museum Dinkelsbühl
Dr.-Martin-Luther-Str. 6, D-8804 Dinkelsbühl
General Museum - 1893
Coll: local history; handicrafts; 17th-20th century painting; traditional costumes; farm and town interiors and furnishings; ceramics; weapons; toys; agricultural tools

Dorsten

05395
Museum Schloß Lembeck
D-4270 Dorsten 12
General Museum - 1949
Baroque and Biedermeier interiors;
17th century Flemish gobelins; East
Asian porcelain; local history;
prehistoric finds; agricultural tools

Dortmund

05396
Museum am Ostwall
Ostwall 7, D-4600 Dortmund
Fine Arts Museum - 1949
Coll: German Expressionism in
paintings and graphics; modern
graphics from 1945 to the present;
modern sculpture; art of the sixties;
archives - library; children's atelier

05397
Museum für Naturkunde
Münsterstr. 271, D-4600 Dortmund 1
Natural History Museum - 1910
Coll: geological sciences including
geology, paleontology, mineralogy;
zoology; botany - children's museum;
course rooms; geological garden;
demonstration aquarium and mine

05398
Museum für Vor- und
Frühgeschichte und Stadtgeschichte
Museum für Kunst und
Kulturgeschichte der Stadt Dortmund
Rittershausstr. 34, Am Westpark,
D-4600 Dortmund 1
History/Public Affairs Museum - 1937
Coll: prehistory; early history;
provincial archeology; local history;
5000-year history of land surveying -
library; workshop

Dreieich

05399
Dreieichmuseum
Dreieichenhain, Fahrgasse 52, D-6072
Dreieich
General Museum - 1909
Coll: 9th century historical ruins;
prehistory; geology; local history;
medieval archeological finds; peasant
interiors; handicrafts; dolls; archives -
library

Duisburg

05400
Museum der Deutschen
Binnenschiffahrt
Dammstr. 11, D-4100 Duisburg 13
History/Public Affairs Museum - 1979
Coll: history of inland navigation in
central Europe; local history of
Duisburg; early 20th century
steamboat on view - library

05401
Wilhelm-Lehmbruck-Museum der
Stadt Duisburg
Düsseldorfer Str. 51, D-4100 Duisburg
1
Fine Arts Museum - 1902
Coll: complete works of the sculptor
Wilhelm Lehmbruck; 20th century
sculpture, painting, and graphics;
archives - library

Düren

05402
Leopold-Hoesch-Museum
Hoeschplatz 1, D-5160 Düren
Fine Arts Museum - 1905
Coll: modern art with emphasis on
German Expressionism; painting,
sculpture, graphics, and drawings;
local history; watermarks; archives -
library

Düsseldorf

05403
Conzen-Sammlung
Bilkerstr. 5, D-4000 Düsseldorf 1
Fine Arts Museum - 1960
Coll: engravings, paintings, and
drawings of the city Düsseldorf from
the 17th century to 1900; picture and
mirror frames from the Gothic through
Art Nouveau periods

05404
Dumont-Lindemann-Archiv
Theaterarchiv des Landeshauptstadt
Düsseldorf
Bilker Str. 12, D-4000 Düsseldorf 1
Performing Arts Museum - 1947
Coll: history of the Düsseldorf
playhouse (1905-1943); history of the
Düsseldorf theater; newspaper
archives; programs and plays; photo
archives; manuscripts; children's
paper theater; archive of sound
effects; stage designs; legal estates of
famous actors including Gustav
Gründgens; costumes; graphics;
posters - library

05405
Goethe-Museum Düsseldorf Anton-
und-Katharina-Kippenberg-Stiftung
Jägerhofstr. 1, D-4000 Düsseldorf 30
Historic Site - 1956
Coll: 18th century court gardner's
house; exhibits on the life and work
of Goethe; autographs, paintings,
busts, graphics, first editions; coins;
medallions; collection of Faust motifs;
technique and history of the silhouette;
archives - library

05406
Haus des Deutschen Ostens
Bismarckstr. 90, D-4000 Düsseldorf
History/Public Affairs Museum - 1957
Coll: customs, traditional living style,
and history of the Eastern German
settlements; charter of displaced
persons; graphics of central and East
German artists; traditional costumes;
engravings of historical events -
library; conference and lecture rooms

05407
Heinrich-Heine-Institut-Museum
Bilker Str. 14, D-4000 Düsseldorf 1
History/Public Affairs Museum - 1970
Coll: archives of the poet Heinrich
Heine; Heine and his contemporaries;
autographs and literature; art; music;
exhibit on the local region from the
16th century to the present - library

05408
Hetjens-Museum Deutsches
Keramikmuseum
Schulstr. 4, D-4000 Düsseldorf 1
Decorative Arts Museum - 1906
Coll: prehistoric ceramics; Greek and
Roman pottery; medieval and German
stoneware; lead-glazed earthenware;
ceramics from South and Central
America, the Middle East, and the Far
East; European faience and porcelain;
contemporary ceramics - library

05409
Kunstmuseum
Pempelforterstr. 50-52, D-4000
Düsseldorf 30
Fine Arts Museum - 1913
Coll: paintings from the Middle Ages
to 1900; 20th century art; graphics and
drawings; sculpture; crafts; textiles;
glass - library; workshop;
bookbinding department

05410
Kunstsammlung Nordrhein-
Westfalen
Schloß Jägerhof, Jacobistr. 2, D-4000
Düsseldorf
Fine Arts Museum - 1961
Coll: international paintings of the 20th
century from Fauvism and
Expressionism to the present - library

05411
Landesmuseum Volk und Wirtschaft
Ehrenhof 2, D-4000 Düsseldorf 30
History/Public Affairs Museum - 1926
Coll: exhibits on the principles of
economics; area and population;
mining; economics of energy; industry;
handicraft; agriculture; Nordrhein-
Westfalen; economics of water;
environmental conservation;
international economics organizations;
transportation; money and credit;
trade and wholesale - library;
workshops

05412
Löbbecke-Museum und Aquarium
Speldorferstr. 9, Postfach 1120,
D-4000 Düsseldorf
Natural History Museum - 1904
Coll: zoology; mollusks; entomology;
paleontology; geology; mineralogy;
animal sculptures - library; atelier;
specimen room

05413
Schiffahrtmuseum
Stadtgeschichtliches Museum
Bäckerstr. 7-9, D-4000 Düsseldorf 1
Science/Tech Museum - 1930
Coll: ship models; tools; paintings;
documents on European river and
coast navigation; river construction
and loading cranes; fishing ships

05414
Stiftung Ernst Schneider
Jacobistr. 2, D-4000 Düsseldorf
Decorative Arts Museum - 1954
Coll: German porcelain, especially
from Meißen; Far Eastern porcelain;
European silver; furniture; archives -
library

05415
Vester's Archiv Institut für Geschichte
der Pharmazie
Schloß Kalkum, D-4000 Düsseldorf 31
Science/Tech Museum - 1937
Coll: crude drugs; woodprints and
etchings on pharmaceutical history;
archives - library

Edewecht

05416
Dada Research Center und Archiv
Roter Steinweg 14, D-2905 Edewecht
Fine Arts Museum - 1972
Coll: conceptual art; new Dada; mail
art; correspondence art; cognition art;
stamp art; archives - multimedia
rooms

Eichstätt

05417
Diözesanmuseum Eichstätt
Residenzplatz 5, Leonrodplatz 3,
D-8078 Eichstätt
Religious Art Museum - 1899
Coll: history of the diocese; late
Gothic and Baroque sculpture;
religious folk art; archeological finds in
the cathedral - workshop

05418
Jura-Museum
Willibaldsburg, D-8078 Eichstätt
Natural History Museum - 1976
Coll: Sollnhofen limestone slabs; natural
history; mineralogy; zoology; history
of the Altmühlalb; archeology - library;
specimen workshop; aquarium

05419
Museum Bergér
Harthof, D-8078 Eichstätt
Natural History Museum - 1968
Coll: fossils from nearby Blumenberg
and twenty foreign countries; minerals;
shells; specimen sea animals -
aquarium; workshop; stone quarry

Ellingen

05420
Residenz Ellingen
Schloß, D-8836 Ellingen
General Museum - 1950
Coll: history of the German order;
furnishings from the classical French
Empire style; coins; mirrors; coats of
arms

Ellwangen

05421
Schloßmuseum
Schloß, D-7090 Ellwangen
General Museum - 1908
Coll: prehistory; local history; church
history; religious art, especially
Baroque manger scenes; faience;
metalwork; historical prints; Baroque
drawings; works of the painter Karl
Stirner

Emden

05422
Ostfriesisches Landesmuseum
Städtisches Museum
Neutorstr., Postfach 29, D-2970 Emden
General Museum - 1833
Coll: pre- and early history; local
history; paintings; arms and armor;
archives - library

Emmendingen

05423
MECF-Museumsbahn-
Unterhaltungswerkstätten
Kollmarsreuter Str., D-7830
Emmendingen
Science/Tech Museum - 1940
Coll: trains from 1900 to 1930; SWEG
steam locomotive (1927); wagons

05424
Städtisches Heimatmuseum
Emmendingen
Kirchstr. 7, D-7830 Emmendingen
General Museum - 1901
Coll: prehistory; local history;
handicrafts and the guilds; peasant life;
works of the painter and graphic artist
Fritz Boehle; memorabilia of Goethe
and his sister Cornelia Schlosser

Emmerich

05425
Rheinmuseum Emmerich
Martinikirchgang 2, D-4240 Emmerich 1
Science/Tech Museum - 1899
Coll: history of the navigation of the Rhein; models of ships and dockyards; ship equipment; maps; historical river maps; local history; archives - library

Erbach

05426
Deutsches Elfenbeinmuseum Erbach
Festhalle, D-6120 Erbach
Decorative Arts Museum - 1966
Coll: ivories from around the world; amber - library; workshop

05427
Gräfliche Sammlungen
Schloß, D-6120 Erbach
General Museum - late 18th century
Coll: hunting trophies; hunting equipment; 16th-19th century small arms; Roman sculpture; coins; prehistory; local archeological finds

Erkrath

05428
Museum Neandertal
Thekhauser Quall, D-4006 Erkrath
Anthropology Museum - 1935
Coll: history of the discovery of the Neandertal man; skeleton finds; environment, life, and geographic spread; tools and weapons; reconstructed flora and fauna (40,000 to 10,000 BC)

Erlangen

05429
Geographische und Völkerkundliche Lehrsammlung im Universitäts-Institut
Kochstr. 4, D-8520 Erlangen
Anthropology Museum - 1928
Coll: folk customs and art of East Africa; stone collection

05430
Geologische Sammlungen des Instituts für Geologie und Mineralogie
Schloßgarten 5, D-8520 Erlangen
Natural History Museum - 1896
Coll: geology; paleontology; history of geology; archives - library

05431
Graphische Sammlung der Universität Erlangen-Nürnberg
Universitätstr. 4, D-8520 Erlangen
Fine Arts Museum - 1806
Coll: drawings (14th-17th centuries); woodcuts; copper etchings (15th-18th centuries); coins and medaillons; war medals from 1870/71

05432
Platen-Häuschen
Burgbergstr. 92a, D-8520 Erlangen
Historic Site - 1977
Coll: paintings and manuscripts from the circle of the poet August Graf von Platen; in the garden house in which Platen lived; archives

05433
Städtische Sammlung
Marktplatz 1, D-8520 Erlangen
Fine Arts Museum - 1967
Coll: contemporary graphics; modern small sculpture

05434
Stadtmuseum Erlangen
Cedernstr. 1, D-8520 Erlangen
General Museum - 1885
Coll: prehistory; local history; development of handicrafts; folk art; local artists; toys; in 18th century Baroque building

05435
Ur- und Frühgeschichtliche Sammlung
Kochstr. 4, D-8520 Erlangen
Archeology Museum - 1914
Coll: central European prehistory; Roman times; early Middle Ages; finds from pre-Columbian America and the Far East - workshop; laboratory

05436
Zoologisches Museum
Universitätsstr. 19, D-8520 Erlangen
Natural History Museum - 1743
Coll: European and native birds, mammals, and insects; animals characteristic for Africa, Asia, and South America; exhibits on evolution and other biologic phenomena; phylogenetic history of man

Eschershausen

05437
Wilhelm-Raabe-Gedenkstätte
mail c/o Stadtverwaltung, Raabestr. 5, D-3456 Eschershausen
History/Public Affairs Museum - 1957
Furniture, pictures and paintings, letters and first editions of Raabe housed in the writer's birthplace

Essen

05438
Historische Sammlung Krupp
Bredeney, Hügel, D-4300 Essen 1
History/Public Affairs Museum - 1961
Documents, paintings, models and other items illustrating the history of the Krupp family

05439
Münsterschatzmuseum
Burgplatz 2, D-4300 Essen
Religious Art Museum
Sacred art from the Middle Ages to the 16th cent.

05440
Museum Folkwang Essen
Bismarckstr. 64-66, D-4300 Essen 1
Fine Arts Museum - 1922
19th cent. painting and sculpture; post-1950 American painting; 19th and 20th cent. graphics; posters; classical art of the Mediterranean area, East Asian art, African art

05441
Ruhrlandmuseum
Bismarckstr. 62, D-4300 Essen
General Museum - 1904
Local and natural history; archaeology (Orient and Mediterranean basin)

05442
Schatzkammer der Propsteikirche St. Ludgerus
Werden, Bruckstr. 77, D-4300 Essen
Fine Arts Museum - 1975
Romanesque and Baroque art and liturgical items

Esslingen

05443
Galerie der Stadt Esslingen am Neckar
Pulverwiesen 24, D-7300 Esslingen
Fine Arts Museum - 1957
Art of the 20th cent.

Ettal

05444
Schloß Linderhof
mail c/o Staatliche Verwaltung Linderhof, D-8101 Ettal
Historic Site - 1886
Ornamental residence of King Ludwig II of Bavaria (1969-1878)

Ettlingen

05445
Albgau-Museum
Schloß, D-7505 Ettlingen
General Museum - 1924
Roman finds; municipal history; clocks and music boxes; sculpture of Karl Albiker (1878-1961) and works from his circle

Eutin

05446
Carl-Maria-von-Weber-Museum
Lübecker Str. 6, D-2420 Eutin
History/Public Affairs Museum - 1976
Furnishings, letters, scores, first editions, and memorabilia illustrating life and work of C.M. von Weber, housed in rooms he frequented

05447
Schloßmuseum Eutin
Schloß, D-2420 Eutin
Fine Arts Museum
Portraits of former European sovereigns (16th-19th cent.); 19th cent. portraits, history paintings, and landscapes; 18th and 19th cent. furniture and furnishings; early 18th cent. model ships from the collection of Czar Peter III

Falkenberg

05448
Burg Falkenberg
D-8591 Falkenberg
General Museum
Antique furniture; paintings; weapons; books; glass

Feuchtwangen

05449
Heimatmuseum
Museumsstr. 19, D-8805 Feuchtwangen
General Museum - 1902
Typical work rooms of former trades; glass, tin, faience; costumes; farm implements; smithy

Finsterau

05450
Freilichtmuseum Bayerischer Wald in Finsterau
D-8391 Finsterau
Open Air Museum - 1971
Open air displays including old smithy, typical inn, grain storehouse, outdoor ovens, etc.

Fischbachtal

05451
Museum Schloß Lichtenberg
Lichtenberg, D-6101 Fischbachtal
General Museum - 1951
History and geography; agricultural implements and other artifacts illustrating social history of the farmer class; works of the Oden Forest painter J. Lippmann; 19th cent. apothecary; lead and tin soldier collections

Fladungen

05452
Rhön-Museum
Marktplatz 1, D-8741 Fladungen
General Museum - 1976
Natural history; country furniture; costumes; agricultural and domestic tools and utensils; liturgical art; pottery

Flensburg

05453
Städtisches Museum Flensburg
Lutherplatz 1, D-2390 Flensburg
General Museum - 1876
Schleswig painting, sculpture, furniture, crafts, porcelain and faience (Gothic to Art Nouveau); local history; postage stamp collection

Forchheim

05454
Pfalzmuseum Museum für die Fränkische Schweiz
Kapellenstr. 16, D-8550 Forchheim
General Museum - 1911
Prehistory; local history and culture; frescos (studio of the Parler family ca. 1370 and Jakob Ziegler, 1559); paintings by Georg Mayer-Franken (1870-1926)

Frankfurt

05455
Archiv für Filmkunde Paul Sauerlaender, Musée du Cinéma
Klarastr. 5, D-6000 Frankfurt 50
Performing Arts Museum - 1945/46
Prehistory of film (18th and 19th cent.); cameras, projectors, original photos, posters, original film copies, etc. illustrating the history of films and film music

05456
Bundespostmuseum
Schaumainkai 53, Postfach 700420, D-6000 Frankfurt 70
Science/Tech Museum - 1872
Telecommunications from antiquity to the present - library

05457
Frankfurter Goethe-Museum mit Goethehaus
Großer Hirschgraben 23-25, D-6000 Frankfurt 1
History/Public Affairs Museum - 1859
Paintings; manuscripts of German writers 1750 to 1850; period furnishings

05458
Geldmuseum der Deutschen Bundesbank
Wilhelm-Epstein-Str. 14, D-6000 Frankfurt 50
History/Public Affairs Museum
History of money from the Middle Ages to the present

05459
Heinrich-Hoffmann-Museum
Schubertstr. 20, D-6000 Frankfurt 1
History/Public Affairs Museum - 1976
Books, pictures, letters, drawings, photos, and memorabilia illustrating the life and work of H. Hoffmann, author of Struwelpeter

05460
Historisches Museum
Saalgasse 19, D-6000 Frankfurt 1
General Museum
Local history; painting and sculpture, numismatics; graphics; textiles; weapons, tools and other instruments

05461
Kindermuseum
mail c/o Historisches Museum,
Saalgasse 19, D-6000 Frankfurt 1
Junior Museum
Toys, children's clothing; books and
school articles; games - studio and
play rooms

05462
Liebieghaus Museum Alter Plastik
Schaumainkai 71, D-6000 Frankfurt 1
Fine Arts Museum - 1907
European sculpture from Egyptian
antiquity to Classicism; Oriental
sculpture

05463
Museum für Höchster Geschichte
Höchster Schloß, D-6000 Frankfurt 80
General Museum - 1976
Artifacts from prehistoric to Roman
times; faience, porcelain and ceramics
from Höchst manufacturers; furniture;
municipal history

05464
Museum für Kunst in Steatit
Hynspergstr. 4, D-6000 Frankfurt 1
Fine Arts Museum - 1980
Steatite objects from all periods and
cultures, with emphasis on China

05465
Museum für Kunsthandwerk
Schaumainkai 15, D-6000 Frankfurt 70
Decorative Arts Museum - 1877
European, Islamic; Indian, Chinese and
Japanese crafts from all periods: book
and type design tools

05466
**Museum für Technik und Musik
Heinz Panke**
Deuil-La-Barre-Str. 36, D-6000
Frankfurt 56
Science/Tech Museum - 1970
Products from the early history of
German industry, including radios,
cameras, telephones, typewriters,
calculating machines, player pianos,
phonographs, motorcycles, bicycles,
etc.

05467
Museum für Völkerkunde
Schaumainkai 29, D-6000 Frankfurt 70
Anthropology Museum - 1904
Cultural artifacts from all continents

05468
**Museum für Vor- und
Frühgeschichte**
Justinanstr. 5, D-6000 Frankfurt
.General Museum - 1937
Local prehistory and early history;
antique handicrafts und objects d'art;
Oriental artifacts

05469
**Naturmuseum und
Forschungsinstitut Senckenberg**
Senckberganlage 25, D-6000
Frankfurt
Natural History Museum - 1920
Comprehensive collections in all fields
of natural history

05470
Schopenhauer-Archiv
mail c/o Stadt- u.
Universitätsbibliothek, Bockenheimer
Landstr. 134-138, D-6000 Frankfurt 90
History/Public Affairs Museum - 1911
Manuscripts, letters, first editions,
portraits and memorabilia illustrating
the life and work of Arthur
Schopenhauer

05471
**Städelsches Kunstinstitut und
Städtische Galerie**
Dürerstr. 2, D-6000 Frankfurt 70
Fine Arts Museum - 1816
European painting (14th-20th cent.);
19th and 20th cent. sculpture; graphic
arts (16th-19th cent.)

05472
Straßenbahnmuseum
mail c/o Straßenbahndepot
Schwanheim, Rheinlandstr., D-6000
Frankfurt 71
Science/Tech Museum
Technical development of streetcars
and buses from 1872 to the present

Frauenau

05473
Glasmuseum Frauenau
Am Museumspark 1, D-8377 Frauenau
Science/Tech Museum - 1970
History of glass, with specimens from
antiquity to the present; 600 years of
glass manufacturing in the Bavarian
Forest

Frechen

05474
Keramikmuseum
Antoniterstr. 1, D-5020 Frechen
Decorative Arts Museum - 1978
Local pottery and ceramics; local
'Bartmannkrüge'; faience

Freiburg

05475
Augustinermuseum
Augustinerplatz, D-7800 Freiburg
Fine Arts Museum - 1861
Medieval and Baroque art of the
Upper Rhein; sculpture and treasure
from the Freiburg cathedral; Black
Forest folk art; 19th and 20th cent. art
from Baden

05476
Museum für Naturkunde
Gerberau 32, D-7800 Freiburg
Natural History Museum - 1895
Local and exotic animals; local rocks
and minerals; precious stones; local
varieties of wood - library

05477
Museum für Ur- und Frühgeschichte
Colombischlößchen, Postfach 5225,
D-7800 Freiburg
General Museum - 1979
Roman and early medieval finds from
Southwest Germany (Allemanic-Celtic
region)

05478
Museum für Völkerkunde
Adelshauserstr. 33, D-7800 Freiburg
Anthropology Museum - 1895
Art and cultural artifacts from Africa,
Asia, Australia and the South Seas,
with emphasis on former German
colonies

05479
Zinnfigurenklause
Schwabentor, Oberlinden, D-7800
Freiburg
Decorative Arts Museum - 1961
Diorama displays of tin figures in
typical period settings

Freising

05480
Diözesanmuseum Freising
Domberg 21, D-8050 Freising
Religious Art Museum - 1974
Altar paintings; sculpture; religious folk
arts; Upper Bavarian handicrafts

Friedrichsdorf

05481
Philipp-Reis-Gedächtnisstätte
Hauptstr. 93, D-6392 Friedrichsdorf
Science/Tech Museum
Original and model telephones, books,
pictures, and documents illustrating
the invention of the telephone by
Philipp Reis (1834-74)

Friedrichshafen

05482
**Mororrad-Museum von Fritz B.
Busch**
Ailingen, Hirschlatter Str. 14, D-7990
Friedrichshafen 5
Science/Tech Museum - 1975
Development of the modern
motorcycle

05483
Städtisches Bodensee-Museum
Kirchplatz 2, D-7990 Friedrichshafen 1
General Museum - 1869
Painting and sculpture of the Upper
Swabian region (Middle Ages to
present); prehistoric finds from Lake
Constance settlements; history of
zeppelin flight - library (literature on
zeppelins)

Friedrichsruh

05484
Bismarck-Museum
D-2055 Friedrichsruh
History/Public Affairs Museum - 1927
Manuscripts, medals and awards,
paintings (13 Lenbach originals) and
other memorabilia of Otto von
Bismarck

Fritzlar

05485
**Domschatz u. Museum des St. Petri-
Domes**
Dr.-Jestädt-Platz 11, D-2580 Fritzlar
Religious Art Museum - 1874/1912
Liturgical art including Gothic
sculpture and altar pieces,
Romanesque goldwork, medieval
crafts and precious liturgical items

Fulda

05486
Deutsches Feuerwehrmuseum
Universitätsstr. 6, D-6400 Fulda
Science/Tech Museum - 1963
Model and original fire engines from
earliest hand-pumped types to modern
systems; rescue equipment, alarms,
uniforms and fire protection devices

05487
Dom-Museum
Domplatz 2, D-6400 Fulda
Religious Art Museum
Carolingian and Romanesque
architectural fragments; reliquaries
and liturgical items; paintings and altar
pieces; cathedral treasure

05488
Vonderau-Museum u. Stadtschloß
Schloßstraße, D-6400 Fulda
General Museum - 1875
Prehistory; natural history; folklore;
numismatics; porcelain and faience;
18th cent. interiors

Fuldatal

05489
Mechanisches-Musik-Museum
Kasseler Str. 76a, D-3501 Fuldatal 2
Science/Tech Museum - 1972
Mechanical and pneumatic musical
instruments; player pianos,
phonographs, music rolls and many
other curiosities

Fürstenberg

05490
**Museum der Porzellanmanufaktur
Fürstenberg**
Schloß, D-3476 Fürstenberg
Decorative Arts Museum
Hand-painted porcelain (18th and 19th
cent.) illustrating the history of the
former Royal Braunschweig Porcelain
Manufactory

Fürth

05491
Stadtmuseum Fürth
Schloßhof 12, D-8510 Fürth
General Museum - 1937
Prehistory and early history; geology
and local natural history; folk art and
folklore; painting and graphics
(16th-19th cent.)

Furth im Wald

05492
Stadtmuseum
Schloßplatz 2, D-8492 Furth im Wald
General Museum - 1921
Arts and crafts; local history; folk art
and folklore; articles from local
manufacturers; country furniture; art
and culture of the Sudetenland

Furtwangen

05493
Uhrenmuseum Furtwangen
Gerwigstr. 11, D-7743 Furtwangen 1
Science/Tech Museum - 1852
Clocks and watches from the
Renaissance on

Füssen

05494
Heimatmuseum
Lechhalde 3, D-8958 Füssen
General Museum - 1910
Local history; instruments of local
violin makers; madonna collection; folk
art; local crafts and trades (Lech River
timber transport)

05495
Schloß Neuschwanstein
mail c/o Statl. Schloßverwaltung
Neuschwanstein, Neuschwansteiner
Str. 20, D-8959 Füssen
Historic Site
Residence built for King Ludwig II of
Bavaria, with original late romantic
(eclectic) interiors designed by Julius
Hofmann

05496
Staatsgalerie im Hohen Schloß
Magnusplatz 10, D-8958 Füssen
Fine Arts Museum - 1931
Painting and sculpture from Swabia
and the Allgäu (15th-16th cent.)

Garding

05497
Theodor-Mommsen-Gedächtnissstätte
Markt 4, D-2256 Garding
Historic Site - 1934
Documents on the life and work of
historian T. Mommsen, housed in the
scholar's birthplace

Garmisch-Partenkirchen

05498
Werdenfelser Museum
Ludwigstr. 47, D-8100 Garmisch-
Partenkirchen
General Museum - 1925
Arts and crafts of the area, including
carnival costumes and customs;
graphics and sculpture (16th-19th
cent.) - library

Geißen

05499
Stadtgeschichte- und Bürgerkultur-Sammlung Oberhessisches Museum
Georg-Schlosser-Str. 2, D-6300
Geißen
Anthropology Museum - 1879
Municipal history; urban and rural
culture; economic history - library

Gelnhausen

05500
Heimatmuseum Gelnhausen
Kirchgasse 2, D-6460 Gelnhausen
General Museum - b
Municipal history; prehistory; memorial
rooms for H.J. Chr. von
Grimmelshausen (ca. 1622-1676) and
Philipp Reis (1834-1874); East German
folklore room

Gersfeld

05501
Segelflugmuseum
Wasserkuppe, D-6412 Gersfeld
Science/Tech Museum - 1970
Glider collection illustrating the
development of glider flight

Gießen

05502
Kunst- und Kunsthandwerk-Sammlung Oberhessisches Museum
Kanzleiberg, D-6300 Gießen
Fine Arts Museum - 1879
Painting, drawing and graphics;
sculpture (ca. 1500 and Baroque);
faience (18th, 19th cent.); ceramics and
coins

05503
Liebig-Museum
Liebigstr. 12, D-6300 Gießen
Science/Tech Museum - 1920
Laboratory equipment and documents
on the life and work of Justus von
Liebig (1803-1873), housed in the
chemist's former laboratory

05504
**Sammlung Vor- und Frühgeschichte
und Völkerkunde** Oberhessisches
Museum
Alsterweg 9, D-6300 Gießen
General Museum - 1879
Local prehistory and early history;
ethnology (Ceylon, Java, East and
West Africa, New Guinea and
Australia)

Goslar

05505
Goslarer Museum
Königstr. 1, D-3380 Goslar
General Museum - 1922
Art and cultural history; natural history;
municipal and local history; history of
local mining; economic history

05506
**Kulturhistorische Sammlung zur
Deutschen und Europäischen
Geschichte** Sammlung Adam
Gemeindehof 1, D-3380 Goslar
History/Public Affairs Museum - 1936
Manuscripts, pictures, documents and
coins from the 5th to the 20th cent.
illustrating the culture of the Middle
Ages, the development of German and
Prussian literature and history, and the
history of the natural sciences

05507
**Mönchehaus-Museum für Moderne
Kunst**
Mönchstr. 3, D-3380 Goslar 1
Fine Arts Museum - 1978
Contemporary art including
international graphic collection;
collection 'art and architecture'

Göttingen

05508
**Kunstsammlung der Universität
Göttingen**
Hospitalstr. 10, Theaterplatz 15, D-3400
Göttingen
Fine Arts Museum - 1770
Netherlandish painting; late medieval
Italian painting; German Gothic
sculpture; Renaissance and Baroque
graphic arts; 19th and 20th cent. art

05509
**Sammlung des Archäologischen
Instituts der Universität**
Nicolausberger Weg 15, D-3400
Göttingen
Archeology Museum - 1767
Greek and Roman sculpture; coins,
gems, ceramics, bronzes and
teracotta; plaster copies of antique
sculpture

05510
Städtisches Museum
Ritterplan 7/8, D-3400 Göttingen
General Museum - 1889
Local history and history of the
university; medieval and Baroque art;
Jewish ceremonial instruments
(17th-19th cent.); Fürstenberg
procelain; Münden faience; Göttingen
tin and painted porcelain; model
weapons

05511
**Völkerkundliche Sammlung der
Universität**
Theaterplatz 15, D-3400 Göttingen
Anthropology Museum - 1778
Comprehensive collections from
around the world, including Cook and
Forster South Seas collection and von
Asch collection of Northern Asian and
Northwestern American cultures

Grafenau

05512
Bauernmöbelmuseum Grafenau
Postfach 7, D-8352 Grafenau
Anthropology Museum - 1977
Cabinets, chests and other typical
furniture from the Bavarian Forest;
loom and weaver's workroom

05513
Schnupftabakmuseum Grafenau
Postfach 7, D-8352 Grafenau
Anthropology Museum - 1979
Manufacture and use of snuff; snuff
boxes; liturature on snuff

Grafenhausen-Rothaus

05514
Heimatmuseum 'Hüsli'
D-7821 Grafenhausen-Rothaus
Anthropology Museum - 1966
Black Forest folk art housed in
reconstructed typical farmhouse

Greding

05515
Museum Natur und Mensch
Schloß, Marktplatz, D-8541 Greding
Natural History Museum - 1976
Geology; fossils from the Jura
mountains; local customs; hunting
weapons

Grefrath

05516
**Niederrheinisches Freilichtmuseum
Dorenburg**
D-4155 Grefrath 1
Open Air Museum - 1973
Country culture, customs, manners;
old fashioned posthouse

Greifenstein

05517
Burg- und Ortsmuseum Greifenstein
D-6349 Greifenstein
General Museum - 1972
Bells from ten centuries; development
of bell making; local history;
mineralogy and geology; peasant
culture; iron casting

Großweil

05518
**Freilichtmuseum des Bezirks
Oberbayern**
An der Glentleiten, D-8111 Großweil
Open Air Museum - 1971
Tools, handicrafts, dwellings, etc.
illustrating country culture through five
centuries - library

Güglingen

05519
Dampflok-Museum
Bahnhofstraße, D-7129 Güglingen
Science/Tech Museum - 1970
Last narrow gauge locomotive of the
Zabergäu railroad (1927);
documentation on the Royal
Württemberg State Railway

Gundelfingen

05520
Automobil-Veteranen-Salon
D-8883 Gundelfingen
Science/Tech Museum - 1972
Private collection of rare antique
automobiles, automobile motors and
parts

Gutach

05521
**Schwarzwälder Freilichtmuseum
'Vogtsbauernhof'**
D-7600 Gutach
Open Air Museum - 1964
Three furnished farmhouses with
outbuildings typical of the Black Forest
style in the 16th and 17th cent.

Hagen

05522
Karl-Ernst-Osthaus-Museum
Hochstr. 73, D-5800 Hagen
Fine Arts Museum - 1934
German Art from Expressionism to the
present; furniture, porcelain, coins and
medals, and other cultural artifacts
from the Middle Ages to the present -
library

05523
Museum Hohenlimburg
Schloß Hohenlimburg, Grünrockstr. 2,
D-5800 Hagen 5
General Museum - 1027
Regional history, including background
on the Princes of Bentheim-
Tecklenburg (17th-19th cent.); painting,
sculpture and graphic arts; weapons;
products of local industries; utensils
and implements of country culture

05524
**Westfälisches Freilichtmuseum
Technischer Kulturdenkmale**
Mäckingerbach, D-5800 Hagen 1
Open Air Museum - 1960
Approx. 40 workshops and factories
(60 planned), many in working
condition, illustrating crafts, trades and
early industrial techniques from 800 to
the Industrial Revolution - library

Hamburg

05525
Altonaer Museum in Hamburg
Norddeutsches Landesmuseum
Museumstr. 23, Postfach 500 125,
D-2000 Hamburg 50
General Museum - 1863
Cultural history; fine arts; crafts and
decorative arts; shipping and fishing;
natural history

05526
Automuseum Hillers
Kurt-Schumacher-Allee 42, D-2000
Hamburg 1
Science/Tech Museum - 1974
Documentation on the history and
development of the automobile and
motorcycle; steam engines; models

05527
Ernst-Barlach-Haus
Baron-Voght-Str. 50 (Jenischpark),
D-2000 Hamburg 52
Fine Arts Museum - 1962
Manuscripts, drawings, graphics,
ceramics and sculpture documenting
the life and work of Ernst Barlach

05528
Fahrzeugmuseum 'Oldtimer Gasse'
Hamburger Str. 195, D-2000 Hamburg
76
Science/Tech Museum - 1973
Old-timer automobiles and equipment
in historic setting

05529
Flughafen-Museum und Modellraum
Paul-Bäumer-Platz 3, Postfach 630 100,
D-2000 Hamburg 63
Science/Tech Museum - 1954
Pictures, parts and models illustrating
the history of aviation; documentary
film showings

05530
Hamburger Kunsthalle
Glockengießerwall 1, D-2000 Hamburg 1
Fine Arts Museum - 1869
Painting (14th-20th cent); 19th and 20th cent. sculpture; coins, medallions and posters; graphic arts (14th cent. to present) - library

05531
Hamburgisches Museum für Völkerkunde
Rothenbaumchaussee 64, D-2000 Hamburg 13
Anthropology Museum - 1879
Extensive collections organized in Eurasian, Indonesian and South Seas, African, South and East Asian, and American departments - library

05532
Helms-Museum Hamburgisches Museum für Vor- u. Frühgeschichte
Museumsplatz 2, D-2100 Hamburg 90
General Museum - 1898
Collections in the areas of prehistory and early history, anthropology, and municipal history - library and archive; education center

05533
Jenisch-Haus Museum Großbügerlicher Wohnkultur
D-2000 Hamburg 52
Decorative Arts Museum - 1927
Furniture and furnishings illustrating 19th cent. upper middle class taste (Classicism and Biedermeier); furniture and furnishings from the late Renaisssance to the turn of the century (Art Nouveau)

05534
Johannes-Brahms-Gedenkräume
Peterstr. 39, D-2000 Hamburg 36
Historic Site - 1970
Letters, manuscripts and autograph scores, concert programs, furniture and furnishings belonging to Johannes Brahms, in rooms he furnished

05535
Museum für Hamburgische Geschichte
Holstenwall, D-2000 Hamburg 36
General Museum - 1839
Comprehensive collections illustrating all aspects of the social, cultural, political and economic history of Hamburg - library and archive

05536
Museum für Kunst und Gewerbe
Steintorplatz 1, D-20900 Hamburg 1
Fine Arts Museum - 1877
Arts and crafts from Antiquity to the 18th cent.; modern and contemporary art; Asiatic collections; photography collection - education program; theater workshop; library

05537
Museum Rade im Naturpark Oberalster
Rader Weg, St.-Benedict-Str. 29, D-2000 Hamburg 29
Fine Arts Museum - 1964
International collection of naive art; folklore from around the world; contemporary art from Africa and Asia

05538
Museumsdorf Hamburg-Volksdorf
Im alten Dorfe 46/48, D-2000 Hamburg 67
Open Air Museum - 1962
Farmhouses from the 17th to the 19th cent.; 1831 smithy; mid-17th cent. barn; farm implements and peasant crafts

05539
Postmuseum
Stephansplatz 1, D-2000 Hamburg 36
Science/Tech Museum - 1937
Historical telegraph and telephone equipment (to 1950); TV and cable technology; postage stamps and postal marks; rubber stamp collection

05540
Sammlung Warburg im Planetarium
Hindenburgstr. O.1, D-2000 Hamburg 60
Science/Tech Museum - 1930
Pictorial exhibits illustrating the history of astronomy, space travel, and astrology

05541
Tabakhistorische Sammlung Reemtsma
Parkstr. 51, D-2000 Hamburg 52
Anthropology Museum - 1928
Pipes, paintings, cartoons, recipes, smoking utensils, etc. illustrating the history and habit of smoking

Hameln

05542
Museum Hameln
Osterstr. 9, D-3250 Hameln
General Museum - 1898
Geology; prehistory and early history; municipal history; folklore including Pied Piper collection - library; slide collection

Hamm

05543
Städtisches Gustav-Lübcke-Museum
Museumsstr. 2, D-4700 Hamm 1
General Museum - 1886
Prehistory and early history; Egyptian, Greek, and Roman art and culture; decorative arts (Gothic to Biedermeier); European domestic furnishings; Medieval miniatures and sculpture; 17th cent. Netherlandish painting

Hanau

05544
Deutsches Goldschmiedehaus
Altstädter Markt 6, D-6450 Hanau
Decorative Arts Museum - 1942
Jewelry and gold ornaments, housed in a 16th cent. half timbered house

05545
Puppenmuseum Wilhelmsbad
Parkpromenade 4, D-6450 Hanau
Anthropology Museum - 1979
European puppets from 1700 to the present; doll houses and miniature furniture and utensils; puppets from around the world

Hannover

05546
Herrenhausen-Museum
Alte Herrenhäuser Str. 14, D-3000 Hannover
Decorative Arts Museum
Period rooms and paintings from the house of Braunschweig-Lüneburg (late 17th -20th cent.)

05547
Historisches Museum am Hohen Ufer
Pferdestr. 6, D-3000 Hannover 1
General Museum - 1903
Local and municipal history; folklore

05548
Kestner-Museum
Trammplatz 3, D-3000 Hannover 1
Fine Arts Museum - 1889
Egyptian art and art of classical antiquity; European applied arts from the Middle Ages to modern times; numismatics; 20th cent. art

05549
Kunstmuseum Hannover mit Sammlung Sprengel
Kurt-Schwitters-Platz, D-3000 Hannover 1
Fine Arts Museum - 1979
20th cent. sculpture, painting and graphic art

05550
Landesgalerie Niedersächisches Landesmuseum
Am Maschpark 5, D-3000 Hannover 1
General Museum - 1852
Painting and sculpture (Middle Ages to Impressinism); graphic art from the 15th cent. to Impressionism; ethnology - library

05551
Naturkunde-Abteilung
Niedersächisches Landesmuseum
Am Maschpark 5, D-3000 Hannover 1
Natural History Museum - 1852
Biological and geological collections; terrarium and aquarium - library

05552
Postgeschichtliche Sammlung
Zeppelinstr. 8, D-32000 Hannover 1
Science/Tech Museum - 1964
Documents, pictures, uniforms and equipment illustrating the history of the postal service; model of the first German radio station - library

05553
Urgeschichte-Abteilung
Niedersächisches Landesmuseum
Am Maschpark 5, D-3000 Hannover 1
History/Public Affairs Museum - 1852
Ancient and early history of Lower Saxony - library

05554
Veterinärmedizinhistorisches Museum
Bischofsholer Damm 15, D-3000 Hannover 1
Science/Tech Museum - 1973
History of veterinary medicine in Germany; history of the Hannover Veterinary College; military veterinary medicine - library

05555
Völkerkunde-Abteilung
Niedersächisches Landesmuseum
Adelheidstr. 9, Am Maschpark 5, D-3000 Hannover 1
Anthropology Museum - 1852
Ethnographic collections from America, Asia, Euroasia, Africa and Oceania

05556
Wilhelm-Busch-Museum
Georgengarten 1, D-3000 Hannover 1
Fine Arts Museum - 1937
Paintings, drawings, original wood blocks, first editions ahd memorabilia of Wilhelm Busch; original graphics and manuscripts of Heinrich Zille - library

Hannoversch Münden

05557
Städtisches Museum
Welfenschloß, D-3510 Hannoversch Münden
General Museum - 1890
Münden faience (1732-1854); municipal history; tin foundry and other local trades; palatial furnishings; portraits from the house of Geulf

Harburg

05558
Fürstliche Oettingen-Wallerstein'sche Bibliothek und Kunstsammlung
Schloß, D-8856 Harburg
Fine Arts Museum - 1811
Illuminated manuscripts (11th-16th cent.); incunabula; gold, enamel and ivory works; tapestries (15th-16th cent.); 15th and 16th cent. wood carving - library

Haselünne

05559
Haselünner Heimathäuser
Lingener Str., D-4473 Haselünne
General Museum - 1932
Stone Age finds; farm and domestic implements; coins from the Ems region; workrooms of early craftsmen (blacksmith, barrel maker, shoemaker)

Haslach

05560
Trachtenmuseum
D-7612 Haslach
Anthropology Museum - 1976
Original peasant costumes from the Black Forest and Upper Rhein region; costume accessories

Haßmersheim

05561
Burgmuseum Burg Guttenberg
Neckarmühlbach, D-6954 Haßmersheim
General Museum - 1949
History of the fortress and environs; tin figures; weapons and armory; hunting tropies; porcelain; documents (14th-19th cent.) - library

Hausen

05562
Dorfmuseum, Hebelhaus
Bahnhofstr. 1, D-7862 Hausen
Historic Site - 1960
Documents, manuscripts, letters, contracts, original furnishings and other memorabilia of J.P. Hebel, housed in the poet's home (built 1562)

Hechingen

05563
Burg Hohenzollern
D-7450 Hechingen
History/Public Affairs Museum
Edwin v. Campe collection of engraved portraits of Friedrich the Great; Hohenzollern family portraits; stained glass windows; tombs of Prussian Kings Friedrich Wilhelm I and Friedrich II

Heidelberg

05564
Ägyptologische Sammlung der Universität Heidelberg
Marstallhof 4, D-6900 Heidelberg
Fine Arts Museum - 1914
Egyptian arts and crafts from prehistoric to Coptic period - library; slide collection

05565
Antikenmuseum und Abgußsammlung des Archäologischen Instituts der Universität Heidelberg
Marstallhof 4, D-6900 Heidelberg
Fine Arts Museum - 1848
Decorative arts from classical Greece, Italy and Cyprus (4th cent. B.C. to 3rd cent. A.D.); painted Greek vases; terracotta and bronze; casts of monumental antique sculpture - library; slide collection

05566
Deutsches Apotheken-Museum
Friedrichstr. 3, D-6900 Heidelberg
Science/Tech Museum - 1937
Documents, cabinets, instruments and equipment illustrating the history of drugs and apothecaries - library; picture archive

05567
Kurpfälzisches Museum
Hauptstr. 97, D-6900 Heidelberg
Fine Arts Museum - 1879
European painting, sculpture and graphic arts; archaeology of the Rhein-Neckar region - library

05568
Schloß Heidelberg
mail c/o Staatl. Liegenschaftsamt Heidelberg, Rohrbachstr 19, D-6900 Heidelberg
Fine Arts Museum
Furniture; tapestries; tin and ceramics (16th-18th cent.); gigantic wine barrel from 1751

05569
Völkerkundemuseum der von Portheim-Stiftung
Hauptstr. 235, D-6900 Heidelberg
Anthropology Museum - 1919
Art and culture of non-European societies

05570
Zoologisches Museum der Universität Heidelberg
Im Neuenheimer Feld 230/231, D-6900 Heidelberg
Natural History Museum - 1819
Comparative anatomy of vertebrates; Middle European birds; Australian mammals and birds; insect collection

Heidenheim

05571
Museum Schloß Hellenstein
D-7920 Heidenheim
General Museum - 1901
Local prehistory and ancient history; development of local industry and trades; folklore and country culture; Indian collection; beetle collection; Southern German and alpine sculpture (Gothic and Baroque)

Heilbronn

05572
Historisches Museum
Eichgasse 1, D-7100 Heilbronn
General Museum - 1878
Natural sciences; prehistory and ancient history; municipal history; 19th and 20th cent. art, mainly Franconian artists; history of Franconian postal service; Ludwigsburg and Nymphenburg porcelain; Neckar water transportation

Helmbrechts

05573
Heimatmuseum (Textilmuseum)
Münchberger Str. 17, D-8662 Helmbrechts
Decorative Arts Museum - 1923
Pre-WWI textiles; documentation on crafts and guilds; stone collection

Herford

05574
Städtisches Museum
Deichtorwall 2, D-05221 Herford
General Museum - 1882
Local history; crafts and trades; architectural fragments from local monuments; military history

Hersbruck

05575
Deutsches Hirtenmuseum
Eisenhüttlein 7, D-8562 Hersbruck
General Museum - 1925
Documents, implements and specimens from the history of sheep raising around the world; peasant cultural artifacts; farm implements; toys

Heubach

05576
Heimat- und Miedermuseum
Hauptstr. 53, D-7072 Heubach
General Museum - 1970/71
Undergarments documenting the history of the J.G. Weber corset factory and the local undergarment industry; local prehistory and ancient history

Hildesheim

05577
Diözesan-Museum und Domschatz
Domhof 6, Pfaffenstieg 2, D-3200 Hildesheim
Fine Arts Museum - 1978
Liturgical implements; sculpture; manuscripts, documents, and incunabula; cathedral treasure

05578
Roemer-Pelizaeus-Museum
Am Steine 1-2, D-3200 Hildesheim
General Museum - 1911
Geology, paleontology and prehistory; mineralogy, botany and zoology; ethnology; art works; Egyptian antiquities

Hirzenhain

05579
Museum für Eisenkunstguß
Buderus AG, Werk Hirzenhain, D-6476 Hirzenhain
Decorative Arts Museum - 1967
Decorative iron panels, stoves and ovens (16th-19th cent.); early 19th cent. decorative iron work

Höhr-Grenzhausen

05580
Keramikmuseum Westerwald
Deutsche Sammlung für Historische uind Zeitgenössische Keramik
Rathausstr. 131, D-5410 Höhr-Grenzhausen
Decorative Arts Museum - 1976
Historical specimens of Westerwald crockery; all media of contemporary ceramic art

Holzhausen

05581
Altes Haus Holzhausen
An der Kirche, D-6349 Holzhausen
Anthropology Museum - 1960
Original furniture, domestic tools and utensils housed in a half-timbered house; old-fashioned flax processing tools

Homburg

05582
Freilichtmuseum Römerhaus Schwarzenacker
Am Edelhaus, Am Rondell, D-6650 Homburg
Open Air Museum - 1966
Gallo-Roman finds from site excavations; domestic items from the Roman period

Homburg v.d. Höhe

05583
Museum Schloß Bad Homburg
mail c/o Schloßverwaltung, Bad Homburg Schloß, D-6380 Homburg v.d. Höhe
Historic Site
Coll: 19th century Baroque castle, summer residence of the Prussian kings; interiors; Baroque mirror-lined room; furnishings of the 19th century; 17th-18th century objects of art

Höxter

05584
Museum Höxter-Corvey
Schloß Corvey, D-3470 Höxter 1
General Museum - 1948
History of the local monastery and documentation on period of secularization; local fauna and geology; domestic utensils; peasant customs and costumes; modern graphics

Husum

05585
Freilichtmuseum Ostenfelder Bauernhaus
Nordhusumer Str. 13, D-2250 Husum
Open Air Museum - 1899
Farm implements and machinery; peasant furniture; 17th cent. buildings

05586
Hissenhaus Nordfriesisches Museum
Herzog-Adolf-Str. 25, D-2250 Husum
General Museum - 1937
Local natural history; documentation on local dikes and floods; folklore and cultural history of Husum and North Friesland; works of North Friesland artists

05587
Theodor-Storm-Haus
Wasserreihe 31, D-2250 Husum
Historic Site - 1972
Books, furniture, documents and memorabilia of writer Theodor Storm, in original setting - library

Idar-Oberstein

05588
Deutsches Edelstein-Museum
Mainzer Str. 34, D-6580 Idar-Oberstein
Decorative Arts Museum - 1973
Gemstones from around the world

05589
Heimatmuseum
Hauptstr. 436, D-6580 Idar-Oberstein
Decorative Arts Museum - 1932
Minerals and gemstones; jewelry

Illerbeuren

05590
Bauernhofmuseum
Museumstr. 4, D-8941 Illerbeuren
General Museum - 1954
Coll: peasant life; furnishings and tools from 18th and 19th centuries; equipment for processing flax; loom and weaving implements; rooms of a home brewery; traditional costumes

Ingolstadt

05591
Bayerisches Armeemuseum
Neues Schloß, Paradeplatz 4, D-8070 Ingolstadt
History/Public Affairs Museum - 1879
Coll: pre-19th century weapons and equipment; propaganda; military music; arms and equipment of the royal Bavarian army up to 1918; military equipment from 1918 to the present - library; workshops; photo laboratory

05592
Deutsches Medizinhistorisches Museum
Anatomiestr. 18/20, D-8070 Ingolstadt
Natural History Museum - 1971
Coll: medical tools, instruments, and equipment; anatomic specimens; pictures documenting the development of medicine in the early advanced civilizations in Egypt, Greece, Rome, and pre-Columbian America; the art of healing in Africa and Asia (China, Japan, and Ceylon); European medicine from the Middle Ages to the present; graphic portraits of physicians; exhibit on the history of dentistry, orthopedics, and homeopathy - garden with curative plants; workshop

05593
Städtisches Museum
Auf der Schanz 45, D-8070 Ingolstadt
General Museum - 1905
Coll: prehistory; local history from the Middle Ages to the present; history of the university at Ingolstadt; crafts

Isny

05594
Caravan Museum Isny
Schloßgraben 6, D-7972 Isny
Science/Tech Museum - 1977
Coll: the history of campers in West Germany; mobile homes from 1929 to the present

Itzehoe

05595
Germanengrab
Lornsenplatz, D-2210 Itzehoe
Archeology Museum - 1937
Coll: burial mound from the early
Bronze Age; excavation finds

Jagsthausen

05596
Schloßmuseum Jagsthausen
Rotes Schloß, D-7109 Jagsthausen
History/Public Affairs Museum - 1924
Coll: local history; Roman finds;
weapons; the iron hand of Götz von
Berlichingen

Jüchen

05597
Museum Schloß Dyck
Schloß Dyck, D-4053 Jüchen
History/Public Affairs Museum - 1960
Coll: weapons; court furnishings;
Empire style furniture; painted and silk
tapestry; 18th century Chinese
wallpaper; paintings; wall hangings -
library

Juist

05598
Küstenmuseum
Loog, D-2983 Juist
Natural History Museum - 1956
Coll: history of sea cartography;
seamarks and nautical science; marine
biology; natural gas from the North
Sea; 3,500-meter core sample; sea
rescue service; marine life ; archives -
library

Jülich

05599
Römisch-Germanisches Museum
Markt 1, D-5170 Jülich
Archeology Museum - 1957
Coll: local archeological finds from
Roman and Frankish times; archives

Kaiserslautern

05600
Pfalzgalerie Kaiserslautern
Museumsplatz 1, D-6750
Kaiserslautern
Fine Arts Museum - 1875
Coll: sculpture; glass painting; wall
hangings; ceramics and handicrafts
from the 15th-18th century; 19th-20th
century graphics; paintings and
sculpture of the 19th-20th century -
workshops; photo atelier

05601
Theodor-Zink-Museum
Steinstr. 48, D-6750 Kaiserslautern
General Museum - 1925
Coll: folk customs and art;
archeological finds; handicrafts; local
history - library

Kalkar

05602
Kunstsammlung St. Nicolai-Kirche
mail c/o Kathol. Pfarramt, St. Nicolai,
D-4192 Kalkar
Religious Art Museum - 1445
Coll: medieval altars; religious panel
paintings

Kandern

05603
Schloß Bürgeln
Sitzen Kirch, D-7842 Kandern
Historic Site - 1926
Coll: paintings; furniture; ceramics;
tiled stoves; chapel with Rococo
decoration; in reconstructed fortress
from the 12th century

Karlsruhe

05604
Alte Dorfmühle
Grötzingen, An der Pfinz, D-7500
Karlsruhe 41
Open Air Museum - 1971
Coll: the grinding and oil press
equipment of a beater mill from the
17th-18th centuries

05605
Badisches Landesmuseum Karlsruhe
Schloß, D-7500 Karlsruhe
General Museum - 1919
Div: Egyptian art; classical archeology;
provincial Roman art; local prehistory;
folk customs and art; textiles;
ceramics; arms and armor; furniture;
glass painting; numismatics;
ethnography; furniture - library;
workshops; photo laboratory

05606
Karpatendeutsches Heimatmuseum
Kaiserstr. 223, D-7500 Karlsruhe 1
Anthropology Museum - 1969
Coll: cultural items of the German
settlers in Slovakia - library

05607
Landessammlungen für Naturkunde
Museum am Friedrichsplatz
Erbprinzenstr. 13, D-7500 Karlsruhe 1
Natural History Museum - 1785
Coll: botany; geological sciences;
entomology; zoology - library; photo
laboratory; specimen workshop;
vivarium

05608
Oberrheinisches Dichtermuseum
Röntgenstr. 6, Bismarckstr. 14, D-7500
Karlsruhe
History/Public Affairs Museum - 1965
Coll: manuscripts, first editions,
reprints, paintings, illustrations,
portraits of writers of the Upper Rhein
area (from Middle Ages to the
present); archives - library

05609
Pfinzgaumuseum
Pfinztalstr. 9, D-7500 Karlsruhe 41
History/Public Affairs Museum - 1922
Coll: local history; documents on the
revolution of 1848/49 in Baden;
Durlach faience; samples of 16th
century bookprinting; paintings and
drawings of the Durlach painter Karl
Weysser; agricultural implements;
archives

05610
Staatliche Kunsthalle
Hans-Thoma-Str. 2, D-7500 Karlsruhe
Fine Arts Museum - 1837
Div: 15th-20th century paintings;
paintings of the 19th century; copper
engravings; sculpture - library;
workshops; photo laboratory

05611
**Stadtgeschichtliche Sammlungen
der Stadt**
Karlstr. 10, D-7500 Karlsruhe 1
History/Public Affairs Museum - 1885
Coll: architectural drafts of local and
regional 19th century buildings;
portraits of princes; graphic prints;
paintings of battles; caricatures; photo
documentation of WWII; coins;
medaillons

05612
Städtische Kunstsammlungen
Rathaus, D-7500 Karlsruhe 1
Fine Arts Museum
Coll: 15th-18th century European
prints; Japanese multi-colored
woodprints from the 18th and 19th
centuries; local painting; post-1945
German art

05613
Verkehrsmuseum Karlsruhe e.V.
Werderstr. 63, D-7500 Karlsruhe
Science/Tech Museum - 1969
Coll: history of transportation and
motor vehicles; coaches; sleds; four-,
three-, and two-wheeled vehicles;
automobiles from 1885 to 1960; model
trains; archives

Karolinenkoog

05614
**Sammlung alter Landmaschinen und
Hofgeräte im Karolinenhof**
Galerie Karolinenhof, D-2241
Karolinenkoog
Agriculture Museum - 1976
Coll: wooden and iron plows; iron
tools; agricultural machines; threshers;
dairy equipment - workshop

Kassel

05615
Brüder Grimm-Museum
Schöne Aussicht 2, *mail c/o*
Verwaltung und Archiv, Brüder-
Grimm-Platz 4 A, D-3500 Kassel
Historic Site - 1959
Coll: manuscripts and original
documents on the life and works of
the brothers Jacob and Wilhelm
Grimm; first editions and reprints of
their works; secondary literature;
translations; documents on their
political and scientific work - library

05616
Deutsches Tapetenmuseum
Brüder-Grimm-Platz 5, D-3500 Kassel
Decorative Arts Museum - 1923
Coll: tapestries and historical
wallpapers of all epochs and from all
countries; ancient tools used to
produce wallpaper; modern
equipment; documents on the history
of tapestries - library; workshops; film
room

05617
Landesmuseum Staatliche
Kunstsammlungen
Brüder-Grimm-Platz 5, D-3500 Kassel
General Museum - 1913
Coll: prehistorical finds; sculpture and
arts and crafts; astronomical
instruments; scientific instruments; folk
art and customs - workshops

05618
Museum Löwenburg
Park Wilhelmshöhe, D-3500 Kassel
General Museum
Coll: weapons and armor from the
16th-17th centuries; copy of a Gothic
church with altars, original medieval
panel paintings, and stained glass
windows from the 14th-16th centuries;
interiors; arts and crafts; tournament
equipment from the 17th century;
decorative rugs of the 16th century;
17th century bronzes; glass

05619
Naturkundemuseum im Ottoneum
Steinweg 2, D-3500 Kassel 1
Natural History Museum - 1568
Div: botany; geology and
paleontology; zoology; archives -
library; photo laboratory; specimen
workshop; botanical and geological
laboratory

05620
Neue Galerie Staatliche
Kunstsammlungen
Schöne Aussicht 1, D-3500 Kassel
Fine Arts Museum - 1976
Coll: German and European painting
and sculpture from 1750 to the
present; art of the sixties and
seventies - workshops

05621
Schloß Wilhelmshöhe Staatliche
Kunstsammlungen
D-3500 Kassel
Fine Arts Museum - 1779
Coll: paintings of Old Masters; antique
art from Egypt, Greece, Rome, and the
Roman provinces; copper etchings;
archives - library; workshops; photo
laboratory

Kaub

05622
Blüchermuseum
Metzgergasse, D-5425 Kaub
History/Public Affairs Museum - 1913
Coll: memorabilia of Field Marshal
Blücher; his furnishings; uniforms;
weapons; army equipment of the War
of 1812; paintings of Blücher's
crossing of the Rhein

Kaufbeuren

05623
Heimatmuseum
Kaisergäßchen 12-14, D-8950
Kaufbeuren
General Museum - 1879
Coll: prehistory; local history; town
and peasant furnishings; folk art;
paintings; sculpture; ceramics; guilds;
crucifixes; coins and medaillons;
memorial to the writer Ludwig
Ganghofer including his work room
with memorabilia and manuscripts

Kelheim

05624
Befreiungshalle
mail c/o Verwaltung der
Befreiungshalle, Befreiungshallestr. 3,
D-8420 Kelheim
History/Public Affairs Museum - 1842
Memorial to the German political union
against Napoleon in the War of 1812;
sculpture by Ludwig Schwanthaler
and his school

Kellinghusen

05625
Heimatmuseum
Am Markt 7, D-2217 Kellinghusen
General Museum - 1946
Coll: prehistory; local history; folk customs and art; traditional costumes, furniture, ceramics; handicrafts; memorabilia of the poet Detlef Freiherr von Liliencron including manuscripts and photos

Kempten

05626
Römische Sammlung Cambodunum
Allgäuer Heimatmuseum
Residenzplatz 31, D-8960 Kempten
Archeology Museum - 1961
Coll: Roman and Celtic finds excavated in the ancient city of Cambodunum; natural history

Kenzingen

05627
Oberrheinische Narrenschau
Alte Schulstr. 20, D-7832 Kenzingen
Anthropology Museum - 1976
Coll: 200 life-size carnival dolls with wooden masks; photos and writings of the carnival celebration in the upper Rhein area

Kevelaer

05628
Niederrheinisches Museum für Volkskunde und Kulturgeschichte
Hauptstr. 18, D-4178 Kevelaer 1
General Museum - 1910
prehistory; local and regional history; folk customs and art; history of economics; religious art; regional sculpture; glass; textiles; ironwork; minerals; furnishings; toys; ceramics; graphics of the 19th century; emergency currency - library; workshops

Kiedrich

05629
Sammlung handgeschriebener Choralbücher
Suttonstr. 1, D-6229 Kiedrich
Religious Art Museum - 1965
Coll: old choir books and manuscripts

Kiel

05630
Antikensammlung
Düsternbrooker Weg 1-7, D-2300 Kiel
Archeology Museum - 1843
Coll: copies of Mycenaean art; casts of Greek and Roman art, including vases, bronzes, sculpture, ceramics, and coins; Egyptian art

05631
Brandschutzmuseum
Gartenstr. 4, D-2300 Kiel
History/Public Affairs Museum - 1927
Coll: exhibits on the tasks and possibilities of fire prevention and firefighting; original items and models of causes of fires and accidents in the past and present; fire-extinguishing equipment; fires caused by children; technical causes; actual fire destruction in industry, agriculture, household, and trades; use of artificial fabrics; fire alarm and firefighting in the past; fire and light in beliefs and customs; development of lighting - library

05632
Kunsthalle zu Kiel Gemäldegalerie und Graphische Sammlung
Düsternbrooker Weg 1, D-2300 Kiel 1
Fine Arts Museum - 1855
Coll: German and Dutch masters of the 17th century; 18th century painting; 19th-20th century painting from Schleswig-Holstein; contemporary art; graphics from 16th to 20th century - library

05633
Museum für Völkerkunde der Universität Kiel
Hegewischstr. 3, D-2300 Kiel 1
Anthropology Museum - 1884
Coll: East Asian, African and South Sea weapons, clothing, shell ornaments, wood carving, masks, boat models, and Samurai armor; Japanese and Chinese sculpture and musical instruments - library

05634
Schleswig-Holsteinisches Freilichtmuseum
Molfsee, D-2300 Kiel
Open Air Museum - 1958
Coll: 57 buildings in 18 farmyard complexes characteristic of the different areas; utensils; tools; archives - library; workshops

05635
Stiftung Pommern Gemäldegalerie und Kulturgeschichtliche Sammlungen
Dänische Str. 44, D-2300 Kiel 1
Fine Arts Museum - 1966
Coll: Dutch painting of the 17th century; German and French painting of the 19th-20th centuries; graphics; drawings; watercolors (16th-20th centuries); topography and graphics of Pommern; coins and stamps; documents and autographs - library

05636
Theatergeschichtliche Sammlung und Hebbel-Sammlung
Olshausenstr. 40-60, D-2300 Kiel
Performing Arts Museum - 1924
Coll: documents on the history of the European, especially the German-language, theater; books, manuscripts, pictures, records, scenery designs, portraits of actors; memorabilia of the playwright and poet Friedrich Hebbel and his circle; theatrical history of Hebbel's dramas; archives

05637
Zoologisches Museum der Universität Kiel
Hegewischstr. 3, D-2300 Kiel 1
Natural History Museum - 18th century
Coll: invertebrate marine animals; insects; comparative collections of fauna from northern Central Europe, the North Sea, and the Baltic Sea; animals of the Ice Age from Schleswig-Holstein; extinct birds - library

Kirchberg

05638
Erzgebirgisches Heimatmuseum
Kirchstr. 17, Postfach 44, D-7184 Kirchberg
General Museum - 1976
Coll: wood carvings and toys from the Erzgebirge; lace; memorabilia on mining in the Erzgebirge; Weihnachtspyramide (wooden Christmas decorations); church models; history of the Erzgebirge; minerals; archives - library

Kirchheim unter Teck

05639
Museum der Stadt
Postfach 109, D-7312 Kirchheim unter Teck
General Museum - 1922
Coll: geology; cave finds; prehistory; Roman and Alemanni times; local history; documents on the life of Conrad Widerholt and Max Eyth; period rooms from the Baroque, Empire, and Biedermeier; handicrafts and the guilds; toys; peasant furniture; domestic utensils and tools; religious art; weapons

Kißlegg

05640
Neues Schloß
mail c/o Gästeamt, D-7964 Kißlegg
Historic Site - 1960
Coll: 18th century castle built by Johann Georg Fischer; interiors; staircase; frescoes; sculpture; furniture; painting; porcelain; Chinese paintings

Kitzingen

05641
Deutsches Fastnachtsmuseum
Postfach 11, D-8710 Kitzingen
Anthropology Museum - 1967
Coll: history of local carnival customs; masks and costumes; writings and documents

Kleve

05642
Städtisches Museum Haus Koekkoek
Kavarinerstr. 33, D-4190 Kleve 1
General Museum - 1960
Coll: painting and sculpture of the Middle Ages; Dutch Baroque painting of the 17th century; art of the 19th century; local history - library

Knittlingen

05643
Faust-Gedenkstätte
Rathaus, D-7134 Knittlingen
Historic Site - 1954
Coll: items dealing with the historical person Faust and his times; the mythological and literary figure Faust; Faust in the arts; manuscripts and books; documents

Koblenz

05644
Landesmuseum Koblenz Staatliche Sammlung technischer Kulturdenkmäler
Hohe Ostfront, Festung Ehrenbreitstein, D-5400 Koblenz
Science/Tech Museum - 1956
Coll: tools and machines of the past used in mining; winegrowing implements; whisky brewery; water supply equipment; machinery for processing tobacco; ship models; ceramics; mills - library; workshops; photo laboratory

05645
Mittelrhein-Museum
Florinsmarkt 15, D-5400 Koblenz
Fine Arts Museum - 1835
Coll: prehistory; medieval paintings and sculpture; Baroque sculpture and painting; Dutch paintings; local Romantic landscape paintings from the 19th-20th centuries; paintings of the Rococo painter Januarius Zick; 20th century art of the Rhein area; modern graphics; archives

05646
Postgeschichtliche Sammlung der Oberpostdirektion Koblenz
Friedrich-Ebert Ring 14-20, D-5400 Koblenz
History/Public Affairs Museum - 1937
Coll: exhibits on the mail and telephone service; history of transportation; beginnings of the electrical telegraph; philately; numismatics; documents; archives

05647
Rhein-Museum
Hohe Ostfront, Festung Ehrenbreitstein, D-5400 Koblenz
Science/Tech Museum - 1912
Navigation of the Rhein; ship models; construction of the current; seamarks; hydrology; fish and fisheries

Köln

05648
Besteckmuseum Bodo Glaub
Burgmauer 68, D-5000 Köln 1
Decorative Arts Museum - 1951
Coll: historical eating utensils from the Stone Age to the Modern Style; their fashions and styles

05649
Domschatzkammer
Kölner Dom, D-5000 Köln
Religious Art Museum
Coll: liturgical implements; textiles; manuscripts; illuminated books from early Christian times to the present; relics and relic receptacles; 14th-19th century monstrances; goldsmith work; goblets - library

05650
Erzbischöfliches Diözesanmuseum
Roncalliplatz 2, D-5000 Köln 1
Religious Art Museum - 1854
Coll: religious art dating from Merovingian times to the 19th century; Christian archeological finds; arts and crafts; pious folk art; grave monuments; illuminated manuscripts (9th-16th century); coins and medaillons; sculpture in the Cathedral; early Gothic sculpture; regional sculpture from 1500; crucifixes; Baroque sculpture; wall hangings and textiles; drawings; rosaries from the 15th century to the present; goldsmith work - library

05651
Herwig-Haarhaus-Lackmuseum
Vitalisstr. 198-226, D-5000 Köln
Decorative Arts Museum - 1959
History of lacquer ware from the 14th to the 19th cent. (works from the Near and Far East and from Europe)

05652
Klöckner-Humboldt-Deutz-Motorenmuseum
Deutz-Mülheimer-Str. 111, D-5000 Köln
Science/Tech Museum - 1925
History of the diesel engine; development of Deutz vehicles and technical parts

05653
Kölnisches Stadtmuseum
Zeughausstr. 1-3, D-5000 Köln
General Museum - 1888
Local history and folk art; Judaica;
textiles; graphic arts; musical
instruments

05654
Kunstgewerbemuseum
Overstolzenhaus, Rheingasse 8-12,
Eigelsteintorburg, D-5000 Köln
Decorative Arts Museum - 1888
Ceramics; glass, tin and precious
metals; furniture and textiles; sculpture

05655
Museum für Ostasiatische Kunst
Universitätsstr. 100, D-5000 Köln
Fine Arts Museum - 1909
Chinese, Korean, and Japanese art
from prehistoric period to present -
library

05656
Rautenstrauch-Joest-Museum
Museum für Völkerkunde
Ubierring 45, D-5000 Köln
Anthropology Museum - 1899
Ethnographic collections from
America, Africa and Oceania - library

05657
Römisch-Germanisches Museum
Roncalliplatz 4, D-5000 Köln 1
Archeology Museum - 1946
Prehistoric finds from the Cologne and
Rhein regions; monuments from the
local Roman period; glass, lamps,
coins, jewelry and other decorative
and applied arts - library

05658
Schnütgen-Museum
Cäcilienstr. 29, D-5000 Köln
Religious Art Museum - 1910
Religious art from the early Middle
Ages to the Baroque period, including
sculpture, ivories, enamel, bronze and
gold, illuminated manuscripts, stained
glass, tapestries - library

05659
Theatermuseum
Schloß Wahn, D-5000 Köln 90
Performing Arts Museum - 1919
Drawings, portraits, graphics,
costumes, models, programs, etc.
illustrating theater history and
techniques - library

05660
**Wallraf-Richartz-Museum, Museum
Ludwig**
An der Rechtschule, D-5000 Köln
Fine Arts Museum - 1824/1976
Painting from the Cologne school
(1550-1900); German and
Netherlandish painting to 1550;
Netherlandish painting from
1550-1800; painting from the Latin
countries; contemporary painting and
sculpture; graphic collection - library

05661
Zollmuseum
Neuköllner Str. 1, D-5000 Köln
History/Public Affairs Museum - 1964
History of German customs authority;
smuggling and crime prevention in
customs work

Königsbronn

05662
Torbogenmuseum
Bürgermeisteramt, Rathaus, D-7923
Königsbronn
General Museum - 1971
History of the local Cistercian
monestary; iron oar mining and
smelting; archaeologicl finds; domestic
and farming implements

Königsbrunn

05663
Bauernhofmuseum
Schulstr. 6, D-8901 Königsbrunn
Anthropology Museum - 1974
Tools and implements illustrating farm
life, work and culture

Konstanz

05664
Haus zur Kunkel
Münsterplatz 5, D-7750 Konstanz
Fine Arts Museum
Frescoes from ca. 1300

05665
Johannes-Hus-Haus
Hussenstr. 64, D-7750 Konstanz
Historic Site - 1965
Documents on the life and work of
Johannes Hus, Hieronymus of Prague,
and John Wycliff, housed in dwelling
used by Hus during the Council of
Constance (1414)

05666
Rosgartenmuseum
Rosgartenstr. 3-5, D-7750 Konstanz
General Museum - 1870/71
Art and cultural history of the Lake
Constance region (painting and
sculpture, 14th/15th and 17th/18th
cent.); coins, folk art, handicrafts;
chronic of the Council of Constance -
library

05667
**Städtische Wessenberg-Gemälde-
Galerie**
Wessenbergstr. 41, D-7750 Konstanz
Fine Arts Museum - 1860
Painting (16th-20th cent.); drawings
(15th-19th cent.), with emphasis on
Italian and Netherlandish masters;
graphics (15th-16th and 19th-20th
cent.)

Korbach

05668
Heimatmuseum
Kirchplatz, D-3540 Korbach
General Museum - 1924
Prehistory; mining and geology;
folklore; peasant costumes and
household utensils; weapons; minerals
and local animals; collection on
displaced persons

Kraichtal

05669
Badisches Bäckerei-Museum
Gochsheim, Hintere Gasse, D-7527
Kraichtal
Anthropology Museum - 1978
Old fashioned tools and equipment of
the bakers' trade; old recipe books;
documents and certificates illustrating
the history of the bakers' trade;
agricultural tools and machinery

Krefeld

05670
Kaiser Wilhelm Museum
Karlsplatz 35, D-4150 Krefeld
Fine Arts Museum - 1883
Decorative and fine arts from Gothic
to Art Nouveau; 19th and 20th cent.
painting, including contemporary
works by well-known artists - library

05671
Museum Haus Lange
Wilhelmshofallee 91, *mail c/o* Kaiser-
Wilhelm-Museum, Karlsplatz 35,
D-4150 Krefeld
Fine Arts Museum - 1955
Loan exhibitions of contemporary art

05672
Museumszentrum Burg Linn
D-4150 Krefeld 12
General Museum - 1926
Finds from the Krefeld-Gellep Roman-
Frankish burial grounds; culture of the
Lower Rhein region; fortress with 16th
and 17th furnishings

05673
Textilmuseum
Frankenring 20, D-4150 Krefeld
Decorative Arts Museum - 1880
Textiles from many world cultures, late
Antiquity to the present - library

Krempe

05674
Historisches Rathaus
Am Markt 1, D-2209 Krempe
General Museum
Silver from local medieval guild,
weapons, and domestic utensils,
housed in 1570 hall

Kronberg

05675
Burgmuseum Kronberg
Schloßstr. 12, D-6242 Kronberg
Decorative Arts Museum
Furniture and furnishings (17th and
18th cent.), housed in fortress dating
from 1225

Krummhörn

05676
**Ostfriesisches Freilichtmuseum
Pewsum**
D-2974 Krummhörn 1
Open Air Museum - 1968
Agricultural implements and trade
displays illustrating the history of East
Fresian culture; tombstone collection
(12th-19th cent.); folklore

Kulmbach

05677
Deutsches Zinnfigurenmuseum
Plassenburg, D-8650 Kulmbach
Decorative Arts Museum - 1929
Locally made tin figures and related
objects illustrating the history of tin
figures

05678
Landschaftsmuseum Obermain
Plassenburg, 8650 Kulmbach, *mail c/o*
Schloß- u. Gartenverwaltung Bayreuth,
Glasenappweg 3, D-8580 Bayreuth
General Museum - 1979
Natural history and paleontology; local
history; furniture, crafts, coins and
other articles representative of local
culture

05679
Staatsgalerie
Plassenburg, 8650 Kulmbach, *mail c/o*
Schloß- u. Gartenverwaltung Bayreuth,
Glasenappweg 3, D-8580 Bayreuth
Fine Arts Museum
Baroque history paintings

Kümmersbruck

05680
**Bergbau- u. Industriemuseum
Ostbayern**
Theuern, Portnerstr. 1, D-8451
Kümmersbruck 1
Science/Tech Museum - 1972
Historical industrial and technical
facilities illustrating the history of
mining and industry in Upper Bavaria

Kürnbach

05681
**Erstes Deutsches Historic-Actien-
Museum**
Sternenfelser Str. 1, D-7419 Kürnbach
History/Public Affairs Museum - 1975
Stocks and bonds from around the
world; 19th and early 20th cent.
German stocks; historic typewriter
collection

Laboe

05682
Marine-Ehrenmal
D-2304 Laboe
History/Public Affairs Museum - 1936
History of shipping and sea battles in
WWI and WWII; model commerical
and war ships; historic flags

Laichingen

05683
Museum für Höhlenkunde
Postfach, D-7903 Laichingen
Natural History Museum
Cave finds; models, plans and pictures
relating to speleology

Landshut

05684
Burg Trausnitz ob Landshut
Burg Trausnitz 168, D-8300 Landshut
Fine Arts Museum
Renaissance cultural artifacts; religious
art; tapestries

05685
Staatsgalerie in der Stadtresidenz
Altstadt 79, D-8300 Landshut
Fine Arts Museum - 1931
Wittelsbach family portraits; European
painting (17th-19th cent)

Langelsheim

05686
Bergwerks- und Hüttenschau
Wildemanner Str. 11, D-3394
Langelsheim 2
Open Air Museum - 1974
Mining and smelting technology;
mineralogy of the Upper Harz region;
multivision show

Langenargen

05687
Museum Langenargen/Bodensee
Markplatz 20, D-7994 Langenargen
Fine Arts Museum - 1976
Painting and sculpture (Romanesque
to present); collection of Hans
Purrmann paintings

Langenburg

05688
Deutsches Automuseum Schloß Langenburg
D-7183 Langenburg
Science/Tech Museum - 1970
Automobiles from 1893 to 1939; historic and contemporary sport and racing cars from various countries

05689
Schloß-Museum
D-7183 Langenburg
Decorative Arts Museum - 1960
Tapestries, weapons, armor, porcelain and other artifacts from the Renaissance to the 19th cent.

Langenenslingen

05690
Schloß Wilflingen
D-7945 Langenenslingen 1
Decorative Arts Museum
Furniture and furnishings (16th-18th cent.); family portraits - library

Langeneß

05691
Friesenstube Honkenswarf
Honkenswarf, D-2251 Langeneß
Decorative Arts Museum - 1965
Typical Friesland furniture and furnishings; family documents; manuscripts

Langerwehe

05692
Töpfereimuseum
Pastoratsweg 1, D-5163 Langerwehe
Decorative Arts Museum - 1939
Development of local pottery craft; peasant and bourgeois taste; Rococo interior

Lauenburg

05693
Elbschiffahrtsmuseum
Elbstr. 59, D-2058 Lauenburg
Science/Tech Museum - 1927
History of inland shipping; ceramics; archaeology; earth history

Leinfelden-Echterdingen

05694
Deutsches Spielkarten-Museum
Schönbuchstr. 32, D-7022 Leinfelden-Echterdingen 1
Anthropology Museum - 1923
Playing cards from all periods and cultures - library

Leitheim

05695
Schloß Leitheim
D-8851 Leitheim
Decorative Arts Museum - 1960
18th cent. furnishings; porcelain collection; cross from the possessions of Maria Stuart - library

Leverkusen

05696
Agfa-Gevaert Foto-Historama
Kaiser-Wilhelm-Allee, D-5090 Leverkusen 1
Science/Tech Museum - 1955
Cameras and photo studios illustrating the history of photography; Hugo Erfurth portrait collection

Lichtenstein

05697
Schloß Lichtenstein
D-7414 Lichtenstein
General Museum
Coll: weapons; glass painting; altar panel paintings from the 14th and 15th centuries; glass

Limburg

05698
Domschatzkammer
mail c/o Bischöfliches Ordinariat Limburg, Dezernat Bau, Roßmarkt 4, D-6250 Limburg
Religious Art Museum - 1959
Coll: religious art since the 12th century; goldsmith work from the early Middle Ages and Baroque period

Lindau

05699
Städtisches Museum 'Haus Cavazzen'
Marktplatz 6, D-8990 Lindau
General Museum - 1889
Coll: graphics and paintings from the 15th through 20th century; sculpture; handicrafts; furniture; pewter; glass; weapons; textiles; archives - library

Lohr

05700
Heimat- und Spessartmuseum
Schloßplatz 1, D-8770 Lohr 1
General Museum - 1924
Coll: rocks; ceramics; glass; mirrors; ironware; wood manufacture; wood carving; domestic utensils; painting

Lollar

05701
Zentralheizungsmuseum
Postfach, D-6304 Lollar
Science/Tech Museum - 1973
Coll: technology of central heating

Lorch

05702
Heimatmuseum Lorch
Kloster Lorch, D-7073 Lorch
General Museum - 1933
Coll: Roman finds in Lorch; local history; memorabilia of the poet Friedrich Schiller and the writer Eduard Mörike

Lörrach

05703
Museum am Burghof
Basler Str. 143, D-7850 Lörrach
General Museum - 1932
Coll: 17th-20th century painting; religious sculpture from the upper Rhein area (13th-18th centuries); prehistory; local and regional history; folk customs and art; geology; mineralogy - library

Lorsch

05704
Museum Kloster Lorsch
mail c/o Verwaltung, Nibelungenstr. 32, D-6143 Lorsch
Fine Arts Museum
Cycle of Gothic paintings; Carolingian architecture; items from the previous cloister; furniture; in remains of 8th century cloister

Loßburg

05705
Schwarzwaldmuseum Loßburg
Hauptstraße, D-7298 Loßburg 1
General Museum - 1969
Coll: peasant life; work and domestic tools; traditional costumes; copper workshop; religious art

Löwenstein

05706
Stadt- und Manfred-Kyber-Museum
Rathaus, D-7101 Löwenstein
General Museum - 1968
Coll: archeological finds; local history; estate of the writer Manfred Kyber

Lübeck

05707
Katharinenkirche Museum für Kunst und Kulturgeschichte der Hansestadt Lübeck
Königstraße, D-2400 Lübeck
Fine Arts Museum - 1920
Coll: casts of medieval works of art originating in Lübeck but now located in the Baltic Sea area

05708
Museum Behnhaus Museum für Kunst und Kulturgeschichte der Hansestadt
Königstr. 11, D-2400 Lübeck
Fine Arts Museum - 1923
Coll: 19th century German painting; 20th century paintings and sculpture; interiors from the Biedermeier times; arts and crafts

05709
Museum im Holstentor Museum für Kunst und Kulturgeschichte der Hansestadt Lübeck
Holstentorplatz, D-2400 Lübeck
General Museum - 1934
Coll: local archeological finds; town history; models; documents; paintings; medieval torture chamber; ship models; weapons

05710
Naturhistorisches Museum der Hansestadt Lübeck Museum für Natur und Naturgeschichte in Schleswig-Holstein
Mühlendamm 1-3, D-2400 Lübeck 1
Natural History Museum - 1799
Coll: paleontology; geology and mineralogy; botany and zoology of Schleswig-Holstein; environmental groups - workshop

05711
Sammlung des Amts für Vor- und Frühgeschichte
Messenring 8, D-2400 Lübeck 1
Archeology Museum - 1963
Coll: local archeological finds from the Slavic epoch, the Middle Ages, and modern times

05712
St. Annenmuseum Museum für Kunst und Kulturgeschichte der Hansestadt Lübeck
St. Annenstr. 15, D-2400 Lübeck
Fine Arts Museum - 1915
Coll: in 16th century cloister; medieval religious art; interiors, furniture, stoves, ceramics, glass, silver, and textiles from the Biedermeier period; the guilds; musical instruments; toys; German and Dutch master graphics from the 17th and 18th centuries; topography

05713
Städtische Münz- und Medaillensammlung der Hansestadt Lübeck
Mühlendamm 1-3, D-2400 Lübeck
History/Public Affairs Museum - 1789
Coins and medaillons of the city and bischopric Lübeck

05714
Völkerkunde-Sammlung Museum für Kunst und Kulturgeschichte der Hansestadt Lübeck
Dr.-Julius-Leberstr. 67, mail c/o Verwaltung, Düvekenstr. 21, D-2400 Lübeck
Anthropology Museum - 1892
Coll: folk customs and art from America, Africa, Oceania, Australia, East and Southeast Asia, and Europe

Lüdenscheid

05715
Museum der Stadt Lüdenscheid
Liebigstr. 11, D-5880 Lüdenscheid
General Museum - 1937
Coll: history of local iron industry; button production; buttons from throughout the world; orders and medaillons; town history; numismatics; fire fighting

Lüdinghausen

05716
Münsterlandmuseum Burg Vischering
Burg Vischering, D-4710 Lüdinghausen
History/Public Affairs Museum - 1972
Documentation on the ecclesiastical and secular rule of Westfalen

Ludwigsburg

05717
Höfische Kunst des Barock
Württembergisches Landesmuseum Stuttgart
Im Schloß, D-7140 Ludwigsburg
Decorative Arts Museum - 1959
Coll: local porcelain (1758-1824); 18th-19th century silver; glass (18th century); miniatures (16th-19th centuries); costumes; tapestry (17th-18th century)

05718
Schloß Ludwigsburg
Im Schloß, D-7140 Ludwigsburg
Historic Site - 1704
Coll: 18th century Baroque castle; Rococo and Classical furnishings; painting; sculpture; tapestry

05719
Städtisches Museum
Wilhelmstr. 3, D-7140 Ludwigsburg
General Museum - 1941
Coll: prehistory; town history; crafts; famous local writers; graphic collection 'Württembergica'

Ludwigshafen

05720
Schillerhaus
Schillerstr. 6, D-6700 Ludwigshafen, Oggersheim
Historic Site - 1959
Coll: house in which Schiller lived as a fugitive in 1782; documents; letters; paintings; graphics; first editions of Schiller; local history

05721
Wilhelm-Hack-Museum
Berlinerstr. 23, D-6700 Ludwigshafen
Fine Arts Museum - 1973
Coll: Frankish grave finds; medieval
altar panel paintings; sculpture;
liturgical items; painting, sculpture, and
graphics of the 20th century -
workshops; audiovisual center

Ludwigsstadt

05722
Burg Lauenstein
Ludwigsstadt 8642, *mail c/o* Staatliche
Schloßverwaltung, Domplatz 8, D-8600
Bamberg
Historic Site
Coll: in 12th century fortress;
13th-19th century furniture; paintings;
tile ovens; weapons; ironwork; musical
instruments

Lüneburg

05723
**Museum für das Fürstentum
Lüneburg**
Wandrahmstr. 10, D-2120 Lüneburg
General Museum - 1878
Coll: prehistory; local town history;
peasant life; religious art; globes and
maps; archives - library

05724
Ostpreußisches Jagdmuseum Wild,
Wald und Pferde Ostpreußens
Salzstr. 25-26, D-2120 Lüneburg
General Museum - 1958
Coll: dioramas of the fauna of East
Prussia; animal specimens; paintings
and photos; horse breeding;
ornithology; falconry; fishing;
landscape, cities, fortresses, and
buildings of East Prussia; hunting
pictures; weapons; archives; first
editions of Kant and Herder - library

Maihingen

05725
Rieser Bauernmuseum Maihingen
Maihingen, *mail c/o* Leiter, Oskar-
Mayer-Str. 51, D-8860 Nördlingen
Agriculture Museum - 1973
Coll: agricultural implements; peasant
life; handicrafts; folk art

Mainhardt-Gailsbach

05726
Pahl-Museum
D-7173 Mainhardt-Gailsbach
Fine Arts Museum - 1975
Coll: paintings and graphics by the
painter Manfred Pahl

Mainz

05727
**Bischöfliches Dom- und
Diözesanmuseum Mainz**
Domstr. 3, D-6500 Mainz 1
Religious Art Museum - 1925
Coll: religious art; paraments;
manuscripts; prints; cathedral
treasures; sculptures; archives -
library; workshop

05728
Deutsches Buchbindermuseum
Liebfrauenplatz 5, D-6500 Mainz
History/Public Affairs Museum - 1962
Coll: history of bookbinding; tools;
customs; tools used for gold
illumination; steps in production of a
hand-bound and machine-bound book

05729
Gutenberg-Museum
Liebfrauenplatz 5, D-6500 Mainz
History/Public Affairs Museum - 1900
Coll: history of book production from
the 15th to the 20th century; history of
typefaces and printing machines;
history of paper; posters and graphics;
facsimile of Gutenberg's workshop -
library; audiovisual room

05730
Kupferberg-Sammlung
Kupferberg Terrasse 29, D-6500
Mainz
History/Public Affairs Museum - 1960
Coll: history of the champagne firm,
Kupferberg; history of champagne;
advertising graphics since 1880;
engravings; historical wine
receptacles; Roman finds; archives

05731
**Mittelrheinisches Landesmuseum
Mainz**
Große Bleiche 49-51, D-6500 Mainz 1
Fine Arts Museum - 1803
Div: prehistory; Roman times; period
of folk migration; medieval paintings
and sculpture; 16th century painting;
Baroque sculpture; Dutch and German
painting of the 17th century; local 18th
century art; 19th century German
painting; Modern style; 20th century
painting and sculpture - library; photo
laboratory; workshops

05732
Naturhistorisches Museum
Reichklarastr. 1, D-6500 Mainz 1
Natural History Museum - 1910
Coll: exhibits on geological periods of
importance for region, especially the
Pleistocene and the Tertiary periods;
fauna and flora; fossils; mollusks -
library; specimen room

05733
**Römisch-Germanisches
Zentralmuseum** Forschungsinstitut für
Vor- und Frühgeschichte
Ernst-Ludwig-Platz 2, D-6500 Mainz
Archeology Museum - 1852
Div: prehistory; Roman times; early
Middle Ages; archives - library;
workshops; photo laboratory;
research laboratories

05734
Städtisches Münzkabinett Mainz
Stadtarchiv Mainz, Rheinallee 3B,
D-6500 Mainz
History/Public Affairs Museum - 1784
Coll: Roman coins; Byzantian coins;
coins and medaillons from Mainz

Mannheim

05735
Städtische Kunsthalle
Moltkestr. 9, D-6800 Mannheim 1
Fine Arts Museum - 1907
Coll: German painting of the 19th
century, German Impressionism,
French and German Expressionism,
20th century painting, painting of the
50s and 60s; 19th-20th century
sculpture; master graphics of the
19th-20th centuries - library;
workshops; photo laboratory

05736
Städtisches Reiß-Museum
Zeughaus C 5, D-6800 Mannheim 1
General Museum - 1957
Coll: art; town history; archeology;
ethnology - library; workshops; photo
laboratory

Marbach

05737
**Schiller-Nationalmuseum und
Deutsches Literaturarchiv**
Schillerhöhe 8-10, D-7142 Marbach
History/Public Affairs Museum - 1903
Coll: Swabian literature; German
literature from 1750 to the present;
manuscripts; autographs; tapes;
literary estates - library; photo
laboratory; bookbinding workshop

05738
Schillers Geburtshaus
Nikolastorstr. 31, D-7142 Marbach
Historic Site - 1859
Coll: house where the dramatist and
poet Friedrich von Schiller was born;
exhibits on his life and works

Marburg

05739
**Antiken- und Abgußsammlung des
Archäologischen Seminars**
Biegenstr. 11, D-3550 Marburg
Archeology Museum - 1875
Coll: study collection of 600 casts of
Greek and Roman sculpture; antique
objects of art; ceramics and
terracottas - library

05740
**Marburger Universitätsmuseum für
Kunst und Kulturgeschichte**
Biegenstr. 11, D-3550 Marburg
Fine Arts Museum - 1875
Coll: painting; sculpture; graphics; arts
and crafts; folk art; pre- and ancient
history - library; workshops

05741
Mineralogisches Museum
Firmaneiplatz, D-3550 Marburg
Natural History Museum - 1977
Coll: systematic sampling of minerals
and rocks including regional
specimens; ultra-violet minerals;
meteorites

05742
**Religionskundliche Sammlung der
Philipps-Universität**
Schloß 1, D-3550 Marburg
Religious Art Museum - 1927
Coll: tribal religions of Africa and the
South Sea; extinct religions;
Christianity; Judaism; Islam;
Parseeism; Hinduism; Taoism and
Confucianism; Shinto; Buddhism; new
religions; archives - library

05743
**Völkerkundliche Sammlung der
Philipps-Universität**
Kugelgasse 10, D-3550 Marburg
Anthropology Museum - 1929
Study collection of ethnographic
objects from around the world

Marktrodach

05744
Flößermuseum Unterrodach
Postfach 26, D-8641 Marktrodach
History/Public Affairs Museum - 1969
Coll: history of raft transportation;
tools; equipment; models of rafts

Marl

05745
Skulpturenmuseum
Creiler Platz, D-4370 Marl
Fine Arts Museum - 1976
Sculpture of the 20th century

Marxzell

05746
Fahrzeugmuseum Marxzell
D-7501 Marxzell
Science/Tech Museum - 1968
Coll: automobiles; motorcycles;
bicycles; motors; models; locomotives;
trollies; horse-drawn streetcars;
coaches; tractors; tools; threshing
machines; fire engines; telephones;
record players; office machines;
sewing machines; radios; cameras and
projectors; handicraft tools; musical
instruments - film room

Massing

05747
**Niederbayerisches
Bauernhofmuseum**
Schusteröderhof, D-8332 Massing
History/Public Affairs Museum - 1969
Coll: peasant life; tools; furnishings; in
two 18th century farmsteads

Maulbronn

05748
Kloster Maulbronn
Klosterhof 7, D-7133 Maulbronn
History/Public Affairs Museum - 1978
Documentation on the history of the
Cistercian order, the cloister, and the
seminar; town history; architectural
remains of the original 13th century
cloister

Mayen

05749
Eifeler Landschaftsmuseum
Eifelvereinsmuseum
Genovevaburg, Postfach 1669, D-5440
Mayen
General Museum - 1904
Coll: geology of the Eifel region;
volcanism; basalt-lava industry; pre-
and ancient history; local history;
18th-19th century furnishings and
handicraft rooms; folk customs;
regional sculpture and painting;
material on the legend of Genoveva -
workshops; laboratory

Mechernich-Kommern

05750
**Rheinisches Freilichtmuseum und
Landesmuseum für Volkskunde
Kommern**
Auf dem Kahlenbusch, Postfach 31 25,
D-5353 Mechernich-Kommern
Open Air Museum - 1953
Coll: peasant life; historic buildings;
folk art; ceramics; doll houses;
architectural archives - library; photo
laboratory; workshops

Meersburg

05751
Altes Schloß Meersburg
D-7758 Meersburg
History/Public Affairs Museum - 628
Coll: historical interiors from different
centuries; domestic utensils; weapons;
weapon smithy; memorabilia of the
poetess Annette von Droste-Hülshoff;
17th century chapel - garden

05752
Dorniermuseum
Neues Schloß, D-7758 Meersburg
Science/Tech Museum - 1970
Coll: models of seaplanes; modern
airplanes; aerospace research

05753
Droste-Museum im Fürstenhäusle
Stettener Str. 9, D-7758 Meersburg
Historic Site - 1915
Coll: house in which the poetess
Annette von Droste-Hülshoff lived;
manuscripts; furnishings; memorabilia
of the poetess and her family;
archives; first editions of her work -
library

05754
Neues Schloß
D-7758 Meersburg
History/Public Affairs Museum - 1960
Coll: 18th century Baroque residence;
stairway designed by Balthasar
Neumann; frescoes; 17th century
furnishings

05755
Weinbaumuseum Meersburg
Vorburggasse 11, D-7758 Meersburg
History/Public Affairs Museum - 1969
Coll: equipment and items from a 17th
century winery; wine press; 50,160-
liter wine container; documents on
wine growing in Meersburg

Meldorf

05756
Dithmarscher Landesmuseum
Bütjestr. 4, D-2223 Meldorf
General Museum - 1872
Coll: peasant life; handicrafts; folk art;
navigation; toys; land reclamation;
firefighting; schools; merchants'
shops; home economics in the
19th-20th centuries - library

Melle

05757
Grönegau-Museum
Museumshof 2, D-4520 Melle 1
General Museum - 1960
Coll: peasant life; historical handicrafts
including flax processing, shoemaking,
and wooden shoemaking; traditional
costumes; porcelain; silver; jewelry;
religious items and writings; archives -
library

Memmingen

05758
Städtisches Museum Memmingen
Zangmeisterstr. 8, Ulmer Str. 19,
D-8940 Memmingen
General Museum - 1880
Coll: pre- and ancient history; history
of the local guilds; local history; history
of incunabula in Memmingen; faience
from Künersberg; religious art;
Rococo interiors; in 18th century
patrician residence - library

Menden

05759
Städtisches Museum
Marktplatz 3-4, D-5750 Menden
General Museum - 1912
Coll: local history; folk customs; pre-
and ancient history of region;
weapons; geology and mineralogy;
local paleontology; native birds -
library

Mettmann

05760
Museum Neandertal
D-4020 Mettmann
Archeology Museum - 1935
Paleontology; the Neandertaler and
his environment

Michelau

05761
Deutsches Korbmuseum Michelau
Bismarckstr. 4, D-8626 Michelau
Decorative Arts Museum - 1929
Domestic and foreign basketry

Michelstadt

05762
Elfenbein-Museum
Am Kirchenplatz 5, D-6120 Michelstadt
Decorative Arts Museum - 1976
European, Asiatic and Indonesian ivory
work

05763
Odenwaldmuseum
Braunstr. 7, D-6120 Michelstadt
General Museum - 1910
Fossils; Roman finds; domestic
utensils; interiors; guildhall; seal and
coin collection; in a 15th century
frame-work house

05764
Puppenmuseum
Michelstädter Burg, D-6120
Michelstadt
Decorative Arts Museum - 1974
Coll: dolls and puppets; Jawa shadow
pantomime figures

Miltenberg

05765
Museum der Stadt Miltenberg
Amtskellerei am Marktplatz, D-8760
Miltenberg
General Museum - 1903
Roman finds; local history;
ethnography; 13th-19th century
ceramics; works by the painter and
sculpture Philipp Wirth of Miltenberg;
religious art; glass; lapidarium; textiles;
in a frame-work house built 1541

Mindelheim

05766
Heimatmuseum
Hauberstr. 2, D-8948 Mindelheim
General Museum - 1903
Prehistoric archeology; local history;
religious art; folk art; clocks; graphics;
in an 18th century baroque cloister

Minden

05767
**Ausstellungshalle des Wasser- und
Schiffahrtsamts Minden**
Am Hohen Ufer 1, D-4950 Minden
Science/Tech Museum - 1954
Boats and shipping on the Weser
River; transportation; maps; design

05768
**Mindener Museum für Geschichte,
Landes- und Volkskunde**
Ritterstr. 23-31, D-4950 Minden
History/Public Affairs Museum - 1912
Paleontology; prehistory; ethnology;
local history; coins

Mistelbach

05769
**Fränkisches Groß- und
Turmuhrenmuseum**
Zeckenmühle, D-8581 Mistelbach
Science/Tech Museum - 1980
Horology; history of watchmaking; in
an old mill granary - watchmaker's
workshop

Mittenwald

05770
Geigenbau- un Heimatmuseum
Ballenhausgasse 3, D-8102 Mittenwald
General Museum
Stringed instruments; violinmaking;
peasant life and traditions; in the
house of the violinmaker Mathias
Klotz built in 1684

Mönchengladbach

05771
Städtisches Museum Abteiberg
Abteistr. 27, D-4050 Mönchengladbach
1
General Museum - 1904
Coll: local history; arts and crafts;
textiles; graphics; 20th century art;
Etzold collection; Onnasch collection -
library; restoration workshop

05772
Städtisches Museum Schloß Rheydt
D-4050 Mönchengladbach 2
General Museum - 1953
Fine arts (Renaissance, baroque); local
history; weaving; decorative arts

Mühlacker

05773
Städtisches Heimatmuseum
Stuttgarter Str. 9, D-7130 Mühlacker
General Museum - 1935
Prehistory; peasant life; decorative
arts; history of the Waldensians

München

05774
Alte Pinakotek
Barerstr. 27, D-8000 München 2
Fine Arts Museum - 1836
Coll: various collections of 14th-18th
century European painting
(approximately 850 paintings) - library;
archives

05775
Altes Residenztheater Cuvilliés-
Theater
Residenzstr. 1, D-8000 München 2
Performing Arts Museum - 1753/1958
Theater in rococo style

05776
Anthropologische Staatssammlung
Karolinenplatz 2a, D-8000 München 2
Anthropology Museum - 1902
Coll: paleontology; evolution of man,
variability and morphology of animals;
the development of various races;
anthropology

05777
**Architektursammlung der
Technischen Universität München**
Arcisstr. 21, D-8000 München 2
History/Public Affairs Museum - 1868
Coll: Sketches and blueprints of
18th-20th century architecture -
archives

05778
**Bayerische
Staatsgemäldesammlungen**
Meiserstr. 10, D-8000 München 2
Fine Arts Museum
Coll: 19th and 20th century painting
and sculpture; Old German, Dutch and
16th-18th century German painting -
archives

05779
**Bayerische Staatssammlung für
Allgemeine und Angewandte
Geologie**
Luisenstr. 37, D-8000 München 2
Natural History Museum - 1920
Coll: geology; mineral deposits of the
world - library; laboratory

05780
**Bayerische Staatssammlung für
Paläontologie und Historische
Geologie**
Richard-Wagner-Str. 10, D-8000
München 2
Natural History Museum - 1843
Coll: micropaleontology, mainly of
fossilized mammals; paleobotany -
library; laboratories

05781
Bayerisches Nationalmuseum
Prinzregentenstr. 3, D-8000 München
22
Decorative Arts Museum - 1855
Coll: nativity scenes; clocks;
ethnology; baroque sketches; Meißen
porcelain; painting; sculpture; crafts -
library

05782
BMW-Museum
Petuelring 130, 8000 München 40
Science/Tech Museum - 1973
Coll: products of the BMW company,
including aircraft engines, motorcycles,
automobiles, racing cars

05783
Botanische Staatssammlung
Menzingerstr. 67, D-8000 München 19
Natural History Museum
Phanerogams; cryptogams

05784
Deutsches Jagdmuseum
Neuhauser Str. 53, D-8000 München 2
History/Public Affairs Museum - 1938
Coll: fossils; trophies; paintings and
graphic art with hunting themes;
hunting artifacts - library; archives

05785
Deutsches Museum
Museumsinsel 1, D-8000 München 22
Science/Tech Museum - 1903
Coll: crafts and trades; chemistry;
physics; electronics; horology;
navigation; aviation; astronomy;
industrial technology - library;
archives

05786
Deutsches Theatermuseum
Galeriestr. 4a, D-8000 München 22
Performing Arts Museum - 1910
Coll: stage sets; costumes; masks;
theatrical requisites; portraits -
archives; library

05787
**Historisches Nähmaschinen-
Museum** 'Vom Rad'l zur Nähmaschine'
Heimeranstr. 68-70, D-8000 München
2
History/Public Affairs Museum
Coll: sewing machines, ranging from
earliest models to modern versions

05788
Marstallmuseum
Schloß Nymphenburg, D-8000
München 19
History/Public Affairs Museum - 1923
Coll: housed in the building of the
royal stables in Nymphenburg Castle
(1740); carriages, sleds, riding
equipage and paintings from
1680-1918

05789
Mineralogische Staatssammlung
Theresienstr. 41, D-8000 München 2
Natural History Museum - 1797
Coll: Bavarian mineral deposits; the
symmetry, shape, growth and
magnetic and mechanical
characteristics of crystals

05790
Münchner Feuerwehrmuseum
Blumenstr. 34, D-8000 München 2
History/Public Affairs Museum - 1979
Coll: history of the Munich Fire
Department from its very beginnings
until 1904; development of special
firefighting equipment from 1904 to the
present

05791
Münchner Stadtmuseum
St.-Jakobs-Platz 1, D-8000 München 2
Decorative Arts Museum - 1854
Coll: graphic art, posters and
paintings; folk costumes; musical
instruments; puppets; photographs;
brewing techniques and equipment -
library, photographic archives

05792
**Museum für Abgüsse Klassischer
Bildwerke**
Meiserstr. 10, D-8000 München 2
Fine Arts Museum - 1869
Coll: replicas of Greek and Roman
statues and busts - library

05793
Museum Villa Stuck
Prinzregentenstr. 60, D-8000 München
80
Decorative Arts Museum - 1968
Coll: housed in the villa (1898)
belonging to painter Franz v. Stuck
(1863-1928); paintings, sculpture and
furniture; Jugendstil glass and
ceramics; porcelain - library

05794
Neue Pinakotek
Barerstr. 29, D-8000 München 40
Fine Arts Museum - 1915
Coll: 18th-20th century painting and
sculpture, especially of romantic,
French impressionist, Jugendstil and
symbolistic schools - archives, library

05795
Neue Sammlung Staatliches Museum
für angewandte Kunst
Prinzregentenstr. 3, D-8000 München
22
Decorative Arts Museum - 1925
Coll: arts and crafts; furniture; posters;
photography from 1800 to the present

05796
Prähistorische Staatssammlung
Museum für Vor- und Frühgeschichte
Lerchenfeldstr. 2, D-8000 München 22
Archeology Museum - 1885
Coll: prehistory of Bavaria, the
Mediterranean and the Near East;
archeology from former Roman
provincial sites; history of the early
Middle Ages - library, archives

05797
Residenz München
Max-Josef-Platz 3, D-8000 München 2
Decorative Arts Museum - 1920
Coll: period rooms (17th-19th century);
porcelain; silver; bronze; carpets;
majolica; paintings; furniture

05798
Ruhmeshalle und Bavaria
Theresienhöhe 16, Residenzstr. 1,
D-8000 München 2
History/Public Affairs Museum -
1853/1972
Busts of famous Bavarians

05799
**Sammlung Gleistechnik,
Oberbaumuseum**
Bahnhof München-Pasing, Hildachstr.
19, Deutsche Bundesbahn, München
Hauptbahnhof, D-8000 München
Science/Tech Museum - 1965
Railway engineering

05800
Schackgalerie
Prinzregentenstr. 9, D-8000 München
22
Fine Arts Museum - 1909
Coll: 19th century German painting

05801
**Schatzkammer der Residenz
München**
Max-Josef-Platz 3, D-8000 München 2
Decorative Arts Museum - 1958
Coll: 11th-19th century European
goldsmith work; gemstones; jewelry;
ivory carvings

05802
Schloß Nymphenburg
Schloß Nymphenburg, D-8000
München 19
History/Public Affairs Museum
Coll: historical artifacts of the castle,
built in 1664; several furnished
buildings; grotto with chapel; hunting
manor

05803
**Staatliche Antikensammlungen und
Glyptothek**
Karolinenplatz 4, D-8000 München 2
Fine Arts Museum - 1816
Div: Collection of Antiquities: Greek
and Roman terra cotta and bronze;
antique jewelry; Etruscan art.
Glyptothek: Greek and Roman
sculpture - library

05804
Staatliche Graphische Sammlung
Meiserstr. 10, D-8000 München 2
Fine Arts Museum - 1758
Coll: European graphic art and
drawings (15th-20th century); the
exhibits will be moved to the 'Neue
Pinakotek' sometime in 1981

05805
Staatliche Münzsammlung München
Residenzstr. 1, D-8000 München 2
History/Public Affairs Museum
Coll: coins, medals and monetary
notes from all over the world

05806
**Staatliche Sammlung Ägyptischer
Kunst**
Residenz, Hofgartenstr. 1, D-8000
München 2
Fine Arts Museum - 1550
Coll: Egyptian artifacts of prehistoric,
classical and Hellenistic periods; early
Christian art of the Nile Valley -
library, archives

05807
Staatliches Museum für Völkerkunde
Maximilianstr. 42, D-8000 München 22
Anthropology Museum - 1968
Coll: non-European ethnology of the
Americas, Africa, Oceania, Asia and
the Near East; textiles - archives,
library

05808
Staatsgalerie moderner Kunst
Prinzregentenstr. 1, D-8000 München
22
Fine Arts Museum - 1920
Coll: 20th century European painting
and sculpture

05809
Städtische Galerie im Lenbachhaus
Luisenstr. 33, D-8000 München 2
Fine Arts Museum - 1929
Coll: 15th-19th century painting by
Munich artists; the Lenbach
Collection; contemporary art; graphic
art; works by artists of 'Der Blaue
Reiter' group; housed in the former
villa (1887) of Franz von Lenbach

05810
Valentin-Musäum
Isartorturm, Tal 43, D-8000 München
24
History/Public Affairs Museum - 1959
Coll: memorabilia and works of Karl
Valentin (1882-1948) and Liesl
Karlstadt (1892-1960); housed in a
tower of the city gate (1337) - library,
archives

05811
**Werner-von-Siemens-Institut für
Geschichte des Hauses Siemens**
Prannerstr.10, D-8000 München 2
Science/Tech Museum - 1922
Electrical engineering

Münnerstadt

05812
Stadtmuseum Münnerstadt
Deutschordenschloß, D-8732
Münnerstadt
General Museum - 1970
Prehistory; religious art; peasant life

Münster

05813
**Archäologisches Museum der
Universität Münster**
Domplatz 20/22, D-4400 Münster
Archeology Museum - 1883
Greek and Roman art (original finds
and plaster casts)

05814
Bibelmuseum
Georgskommende 7, D-4400 Münster
Religious Art Museum - 1979
History of the bible; translation of the
bible in German and other languages;
biblical research; Greek New
Testament manuscript collection -
photographic laboratory; computers

05815
Droste-Museum
Nienberge, Am Rüschhaus 81, D-4400
Münster
Historic Site
Memorabilia of Annette von Droste-
Hülshoff; in the baroque countryseat
Rüschhaus where the poetess lived
from 1826 to 1848; original 19th
century interiors

05816
Droste-zu-Hülshoff-Museum
Burg Hülshoff, Roxel, D-4400 Münster
Historic Site - 1919
Renaissance, baroque, Biedermeier
furniture and interiors; paintings;
graphics; porcelain; glass; arms;
memorabilia of the poetess Annette
von Droste-Hülshoff in her birthplace
(castle Hülshoff built in 1200)

05817
**Geologisch-Paläontologisches
Museum**
Pferdegasse 3, D-4400 Münster
Natural History Museum - 1824
Geology; paleontology; Pleistocene
skeletons of mammals

05818
**Landesmuseum für Vor- und
Frühgeschchte Münster**
Rothenburg 30, D-4400 Münster
History/Public Affairs Museum - 1934
Pre- and early history of Westphalia

05819
**Mineralogisches Museum (Kristalle
und Gesteine)** Universität Münster
Hüfferstr. 1, D-4400 Münster
Natural History Museum - 1824
Mineralogy; precious stones; ore;
meteorites; products of metal and
mining, porcelain, glass and chemical
industries - library; archives;
restoration workshop

05820
**Westfälisches Landesmuseum für
Kunst und Kulturgeschichte**
Domplatz 10, D-4400 Münster
General Museum - 1825
20th century art; regional history;
painting; graphic arts; sculpture;
applied art; textiles; numismatics -
library; restoration workshop

05821
**Westfälisches Landesmuseum für
Naturkunde**
Himmelreichallee 50, D-4400 Münster
Natural History Museum - 1891
Coll: botany; zoology (molluscs,
insects, mammals, birds); history of
evolution - library; technical workshop

Murrhardt

05822
Carl-Schweizer-Museum
Am Stadtpark, D-7157 Murrhardt
General Museum - 1931
Natural history; history; geology

Neckarsulm

05823
Deutsches Zweirad-Museum
Urbanstr. 11, Postfach 89, D-7107
Neckarsulm
Science/Tech Museum - 1956
Historical and technical development
of the bicycle and the motorcycle

Neu-Isenburg

05824
Zeppelin-Museum
Kapitän-Lehmann-Str. 2, D-6078
Neu-Isenburg
Science/Tech Museum - 1977
History of the Zeppelin airship
(1900-1939); Zeppelin models; aviation;
uniforms; medals; photographs;
documents

Neukirchen

05825
Nolde-Museum Seebüll
D-2261 Neukirchen
Fine Arts Museum - 1957
Paintings, watercolors, drawings and
graphics of Emil Nolde (1867-1956); in
the artist's house, built in 1927 by
Seebüll

Neumünster

05826
Textilmuseum
Parkstr. 17, D-2350 Neumünster
Science/Tech Museum - 1914
History of textile manufacture; tools;
textile machines; weaving; clothing
and dress

Neuss

05827
Clemens-Sels-Museum
Am Obertor, D-4040 Neuss
General Museum - 1845
Prehistory; modern paintings; local
history; coins - library

Neustadt

05828
Trachtenpuppen-Museum
Hindenburgplatz, D-8632 Neustadt
Anthropology Museum - 1930
Folk costumes; dolls

Neuwied

05829
Kreismuseum
Raiffeisenplatz 1a, D-5450 Neuwied
General Museum - 1928
Prehistory; furniture (18th cent.); local
history - library

Nienburg

05830
Museum Nienburg
Leinstr. 4, D-3070 Nienburg
General Museum - 1908
Prehistory; local history; farm
implements - library

Nördlingen

05831
Stadtmuseum
Vordere Gerbergasse 1, D-8860
Nördlingen
General Museum - 1867
Geology; local history; art; decorative
art - library

Nürnberg

05832
Albrecht-Dürer-Haus
Stadtgeschichtliche Museen
Albrecht-Dürer-Str. 39, D-8500
Nürnberg
History/Public Affairs Museum - 1828
Coll: memorabilia on Albrecht Dürer;
Dürer medals; graphic art; located in
the house in which Dürer lived from
1509-1528

05833
Germanisches Naionalmuseum
Weinmarkt 1, D-8500 Nürnberg
General Museum - 1852
Coll: German prehistory and early
history; painting; sculpture; religious
art and architecture; copper
engravings; musical instruments;
crafts; guild relics; textiles; furniture;
toys; weapons - library; workshops

05834
Gewerbemuseum
Gewerbemuseumsplatz 2, D-8500
Nürnberg
Decorative Arts Museum - 1869
Coll: objects made of glass, ceramic
and metal; clocks; textiles; toys; ivory;
furniture

05835
Kaiserburg
mail c/o Staatliche Burgverwaltung
Nürnberg, Auf der Burg 13, D-8500
Nürnberg
History/Public Affairs Museum
Fortress built in 1050 including the
knights' and the emperor's hall, rooms
of the guards; wells; the emperor's
living room with period furnishings

05836
Kunsthalle
Lorenzer Str. 32, D-8500 Nürnberg
Fine Arts Museum - 1918
Coll: international modern art, including
constructivism, kinetic art and concept
art

05837
**Lochgefängnisse unter dem Alten
Rathaus**
Rathausplatz 2, D-8500 Nürnberg
History/Public Affairs Museum - 1925
Coll: an authentic medieval jail (14th
century) with the original prisoners'
cells; torture and execution chambers;
instruments of torture; smithy, laundry
room and kitchen

05838
Naturhistorisches Museum
Gewerbemuseumsplatz 4, D-8500
Nürnberg
Natural History Museum - 1884
Coll: geology; paleontology;
entomology; speleology; botany;
prehistory; Jordanian and Costa Rican
archeology; anthropology - library,
archives

05839
Patrizierschloß Neunhof
D-8500 Nürnberg 90
History/Public Affairs Museum - 1963
Coll: housed in a 16th century castle;
16th-18th century domestic utensils,
hunting artifacts and antiques; period
furnishings

05840
**Spielzeugmuseum der Stadt
Nürnberg**
Karlstr. 13, D-8500 Nürnberg
History/Public Affairs Museum - 1966
Coll: toys from all over the world and
made of various materials; toy
manufacture in Nuremburg; children's
books; paintings depicting toys and
games - library

05841
Städtische Graphische Sammlung
Stadtgeschichtliche Museen
Burg 2, D-8500 Nürnberg
Fine Arts Museum - 1970
Coll: graphic art, especially depicting
the cultural history of the city; portraits
- library

05842
Stadtmuseum Fembohaus
Stadtgeschichtliche Museen
Burgstr. 15, D-8500 Nürnberg
Decorative Arts Museum - 1953
Coll: Renaissance, rococo and
Biedermeier furnishings; models of the
city; coins and medals; paintings,
graphic art, works in bronze, glass and
ceramic by Nuremberg artists

05843
Tucher-Schlößchen
Stadtgeschichtliche Museen
Hirschelgasse 11, D-8500 Nürnberg
Decorative Arts Museum - 1973
Coll: completely furnished summer
residence of the Tucher family, built in
1533; painting; glass-painting;
Gobelins

05844
Verkehrsmuseum
Lessingstr. 6, D-8500 Nürnberg
History/Public Affairs Museum - 1899
coll: history of the railroad, highways,
navigation and the postal system;
models and relics of early
locomotives; philately; history of radio
and television - library; archives

Oberammergau

05845
Schloß Linderhof
D-8103 Oberammergau
History/Public Affairs Museum - 1886
One of Bavarian King Ludwig II's
castles, completed in 1878; 19th
century history and furnishings

Oberhausen

05846
**Städtische Galerie Schloß
Oberhausen**
Sterkrader Str. 46, D-4200
Oberhausen
Fine Arts Museum - 1947
International contemporary art;
classical art; glass; local history -
library

Oberkochen

05847
Optisches Museum Oberkochen
Am Ölweiher 15, Postf. 1369, D-7082
Oberkochen
Science/Tech Museum - 1971
Development of optical instruments

Oberschleißheim

05848
Altes Schloß Schleißheim
mail c/o Schloß- und
Gartenverwaltung Schleißheim,
D-8042 Oberschleißheim
History/Public Affairs Museum
Castle built from 1598 to 1623 with
furnishings from Peter Candid;
ethnology; pre-industrial implements

05849
Meißener Porzellan-Sammlung
Stiftung Ernst Schneider
Schloß Lustheim in Schloß
Schleißheim park, D-8042
Oberschleißheim
Decorative Arts Museum - 1968
Coll: one of the largest collections of
Meißener porcelain in the world; china
and ceramic animals dating from 1710
to the 2nd half of the 18th century

05850
Neues Schloß Schleißheim
mail c/o Schloß- und
Gartenverwaltung Schleißheim,
D-8042 Oberschleißheim
History/Public Affairs Museum
Coll: baroque castle completed in 1720
for Prince Elector Max Emanuel;
baroque furnishings; period rooms
with stuccowork; 18th century
gobelins

05851
Schloß Lustheim
mail c/o Schloß- und
Gartenverwaltung Schleißheim,
Schloß Lustheim in Schleißheim
Castle park, D-8042 Oberschleißheim
Decorative Arts Museum
Coll: baroque furnishings; paintings;
frescoes; the castle was built for
Prince Elector Max Emanuel in 1684

05852
**Staatsgalerie im Neuen Schloß
Schleißheim**
D-8042 Oberschleißheim
Fine Arts Museum
Coll: masterpieces of European
baroque painting, housed in the new
Schleißheim Castle

Offenbach

05853
**Deutsches Ledermuseum mit
Deutschem Schuhmuseum**
Frankfurterstr. 86, D-6050 Offenbach
Decorative Arts Museum - 1917
Coll: German Leather Museum:
leather crafts; furniture; ethnology and
folk costumes; 19th century leather
articles. German Shoe Museum:
history of footwear from all over the
world

05854
Klingspor-Museum
Herrnstr. 80, D-6050 Offenbach
Decorative Arts Museum - 1953
Coll: bookmaking arts and crafts;
bookbindings; typography; posters; ex
libris; carpets - library, archives

05855
Stadtmuseum
Parkstr. 60, D-6050 Offenbach
General Museum - 1917
Coll: prehistory; history of the town;
Senefelder collection dealing with the
invention of lithography; ivory;
fayence; paintings from local artists

Offenburg

05856
Ritterhausmuseum
Ritterstr. 10, D-7600 Offenburg
History/Public Affairs Museum - 1900
Coll: early history; regional and town
history; geology; religious art; folk art
and costumes; hunting trophies;
18th-20th century paintings by local
artists

Oldenburg

05857
**Landesmuseum für Kunst und
Kulturgeschichte**
Schloßplatz 1, D-2900 Oldenburg
Fine Arts Museum - 1919
Modern art; galerie of Old Masters;
medieval art; local folk art - library

05858
Oldenburger Stadtmuseum
Städtische Kunstsammlungen
Raiffeisenstr. 32/33, D-2900 Oldenburg
General Museum - 1914
Local art, cultural history and painting
(17th to 19th cent.); graphics; classical
vases and terra cotta; local history -
library

05859
**Staatliches Museum für Naturkunde
und Vorgeschichte**
Damm 40-44, D-2900 Oldenburg
Natural History Museum - 1836
Natural history; minerals; flora and
fauna of the region; prehistory -
library

Orsingen-Nenzingen

05860
Fastnachtmuseum Langenstein
Schwarzwalderstr. 10, D-7769
Orsingen-Nenzingen
History/Public Affairs Museum - 1969
Coll: the celebration of carnival in the
Linzgau, Bodensee, Hegau, Heuberg
and Baar regions; original costumes
and masks; the history of carnival -
archives

Osnabrück

05861
Domschatz und Diözesanmuseum
Kleine Domfreiheit 24, D-4500
Osnabrück
Religious Art Museum - 1917
Religious art and items

05862
Kulturgeschichtliches Museum Osnabrück
Heger-Tor-Wall 28, D-4500 Osnabrück
General Museum - 1879
Coll: prehistory; local history;
sculpture; painting; graphic art from
the Renaissance to the present; coins
and medals; glass; folk costumes -
library, archives

05863
Naturwissenschaftliches Museum
Heger-Tor-Wall 27, D-4500 Osnabrück
Natural History Museum - 1971
Coll: paleontology; geology; zoology;
botany - library

Ottersberg

05864
Otto-Modersohn-Museum Fischerhude
Fischerhude, In der Bredenau 88,
D-2802 Ottersberg
Historic Site - 1974
Memorabilia of the painter Otto
Modersohn (1865-1945); paintings;
drawing; diaries; letters; documents; in
a frame-work shed built 1769

Ottobeuren

05865
Kunstsammlungen der Abtei Ottobeuren
Benediktinerabtei, D-8942 Ottobeuren
Religious Art Museum - 1854
Romanic, Gothic, Renaissance,
baroque and rococo religious art;
paintings; local history; natural history
- library

Otzberg

05866
Sammlung zur Volkskunde in Hessen Museum im Alten Rathaus
Lengfeld, Bismarckstr. 2, D-6111
Otzberg
Anthropology Museum - 1974
Ethnography; folk art; costumes;
ceramics; toys

Paderborn

05867
Erzbischöfliches Diözesanmuseum und Domschatzkammer
Markt 17, D-4790 Paderborn
Religious Art Museum - 1853
9th-19th century sculpture; paintings;
textiles; folk art; icons; bells; glass art
- library; archives; restoration
workshop

Passau

05868
Oberhausmuseum
D-8390 Passau
General Museum - 1905
Local history; folk art; music
instruments; religious items; weapons;
development of firefighting (17th-20th
cent.)

Pforzheim

05869
Schmuckmuseum Pforzheim
Jahnstr. 42, D-7530 Pforzheim
Decorative Arts Museum - 1971
Ancient and modern jewelry - library;
archives

Philippsburg

05870
Festungs- und Waffengeschichtliches Museum
Senator-Burda-Haus, Schlachthausstr.
2, D-7522 Philippsburg
History/Public Affairs Museum - 1978
Development of the construction of
fortresses; coins; weapons

Pirmasens

05871
Heimatmuseum, Deutsches Schuhmuseum
Hauptstr. 26, D-6780 Pirmasens
General Museum - 1963
Pre-, ancient and early history; local
history; painting; graphics; shoe
collection; shoemakers's trade

Prien

05872
Neues Schloß Herrenchiemsee
Staatliche Verwaltung
Herrenchiemsee, Altes Schloß, D-8210
Prien
History/Public Affairs Museum -
1876/86
Historic furnishings from the time of
King Ludwig II. of Bavaria (1845-1886);
stage sets of Richard Wagner's
operas; in a castle built in 1876/86

Rastatt

05873
Erinnerungsstätte für die Freiheitsbewegungen in der deutschen Geschichte
Herrenstr., Postf. 1307, D-7550 Rastatt
History/Public Affairs Museum - 1970
Documents on the revolution of
1848/49

05874
Wehrgeschichtliches Museum
Schloß, Postf. 1443, D-7550 Rastatt
History/Public Affairs Museum - 1933
Documents on the German armed
forces from the Middle Ages to
present times - library

Ratzeburg

05875
Ernst-Barlach-Gedenkstätte
Barlachplatz 3, D-2418 Ratzeburg
Historic Site - 1956
Sculpture, drawings, lithographs by
Ernst Barlach (1870-1938); memorabilia
of the artist; letters; documents; in a
house (built 1840) where E. Barlach
lived from 1878 to 1884

Recklinghausen

05876
Ikonen-Museum Museen der Stadt
Recklinghausen
Am Kirchplatz 2, D-4350
Recklinghausen
Fine Arts Museum - 1956
13th-19th century Russian icons;
Greek icons; Coptic collection;
Romanian stained glass icons;
religious cult objects and liturgical
vestments of the Orthodox church; in
an 18th century building

05877
Städtische Kunsthalle Museen der
Stadt Recklinghausen
Franz-Große-Perdekamp-Str., D-4350
Recklinghausen
Fine Arts Museum - 1950
International contemporary art; 'junger
westen' group; kinetic art objects;
20th-century Westphalian art - library

05878
Vestisches Museum Museen der
Stadt Recklinghausen
mail c/o Städtische Kunsthalle, Franz-
Große-Perdekamp-Str. 25, D-4350
Recklinghausen
General Museum - 1925
Regional and local history; pre- and
early history; sculptures and paintings
including Flemish, Dutch and
Westphalian objects; numismatics;
geology; regional native art - library

Regensburg

05879
Domschatzmuseum
Krautermarkt 3, D-8400 Regensburg
Religious Art Museum - 1974
Church treasury of the cathedral in the
rooms of the former bishopric,
including goldsmith work, reliquaries,
vestments and religious arts and crafts
- library

05880
Fürst Thurn und Taxis Marstallmuseum
Emmeramsplatz 6, D-8400 Regensburg
History/Public Affairs Museum - ca.
1930
Coaches, carriages and vehicles
(18th-20th c.); uniforms of the prince's
servants

05881
Fürst Thurn und Taxis Schloßmuseum
Emmeramsplatz 5, D-8400 Regensburg
11
History/Public Affairs Museum
Furnishings and furniture from the
former princely residences at Brussels
and Frankfurt; 17th-century tapestries
from Brussels; paintings (18th-19th c.);
cloister with Romanic and Gothic
architectural frames - library; archives

05882
Kepler-Gedächtnishaus
Keplerstr. 5, D-8400 Regensburg
Historic Site - 1962
House of Johann Kepler,
mathematician and astronomer, who
died here in 1630; documents on
Kepler's life and work

05883
Naturkundemuseum Ostbayern
Naturwissenschaftlicher Verein
Regensburg e.V.
Am Prebrunntor 4, D-8400
Regensburg
Natural History Museum - 1846
Palaeontology; prehistory; mineralogy;
petrography; zoology; botany; natural
history from the Eastern Bavarian
region

05884
Ostdeutsche Galerie
Dr.-Johann-Maier-Str. 5, D-8400
Regensburg
Fine Arts Museum - 1967
Painting, graphics, sculpture, applied
art; topographical collection and
cultural history of Eastern Germany -
library

05885
Reichstagsmuseum
Rathausplatz 4, D-8400 Regensburg
History/Public Affairs Museum - 1910
Documentation on the history of the
'Reichstag' in Regensburg, especially
of the 'Immerwährender Reichstag'
(1663-1803), and on jurisprudence -
library; archives

Reichenau

05886
Schatzkammer des Münsters
Mittelzell, Burgstr., D-7752 Reichenau
Religious Art Museum - 1443
Crosses; reliquaries; Gothic ciborium
and late antique ivory vessel, book art;
chalices; incense vessels;
monstrances; liturgical vestments;
stained glass windows; architectural
fragments

Reinfeld

05887
Städtisches Heimatmuseum
Alter Garten 9, D-2067 Reinfeld
General Museum - 1913
Prehistory; history and monuments of
the Cistercian monastery; history of
the dukes of Plön; documents,
autographs, first editions, pictures,
letters related to Matthias Claudius
(1740-1815) - library

Remscheid

05888
Deutsches Röntgen-Museum
Lennep, Schwelmer Str. 41, D-5630
Remscheid 11
Science/Tech Museum - 1932
Memorabilia on W.C. Röntgen
(1845-1923); his bequest; x-ray cabinet
(1900); history of x-ray discovery;
technique and physics of x-rays; x-ray
diagnostics, biology and theraphy;
protective screening - restoration
laboratory; library

Remscheid-Hasten

05889
**Deutsches Werkzeugmuseum und
Heimatmuseum Remscheid**
Cleffstr. 2-6, D-5630 Remscheid-
Hasten
General Museum - 1927/1967
Deutsches Werkzeugmuseum:
development of tools from the
palaeolithic period to the present; iron
and steel production since the Middle
Ages; first electric arc furnace;
development of the seamless tire;
craft workshops; collection of
European tools; catalogues; graphics;
maps; Heimatmuseum: 18th-19th
century furnishings; tin figures; J.P.
Hasenclever (1810-53) collection of
landscape painting - library; archives

Rendsburg

05890
Schleswag-Elektro-Museum
Kieler Str. 19, D-2370 Rendsburg
Science/Tech Museum - 1972
Development of electrical appliances

Rheine

05891
Falkenhof-Museum
Tiefe Str. 22, D-4440 Rheine
General Museum - 1960
Prehistory; local history; art; weapons
- library

Rothenburg ob der Tauber

05892
Alt-Rothenburger Handwerkerhaus
Fränkisches Heimatmuseum
Alter Stadtgraben 26, D-8803
Rothenburg ob der Tauber
Anthropology Museum
Furniture and interiors; crafts; tools;
implements; in a 13th century house

05893
Historiengewölbe
Fritz-Hübscher-Str. 6, D-8803
Rothenburg ob der Tauber
History/Public Affairs Museum - 1966
History, documents, arms, maps,
pictures from the Thirty Years' War
(1618-48); in the 14th century Gothic
town hall

05894
Mittelalterliches Kriminalmuseum
Burggasse 3, D-8803 Rothenburg ob
der Tauber
History/Public Affairs Museum - 1890
13th-19th century administration of
justice; medieval torture chamber;
superstitions; in a 14th century
building - library

05895
Reichsstadtmuseum
Klosterhof 5, D-8803 Rothenburg ob
der Tauber
General Museum - 1906
Regional and local history; furnishings;
painting; sculpture; arms; crafts; farm
implements; cloister interiors; in a
13th-16th century Dominican cloister -
restoration workshop

Rottenburg

05896
Diözesanmuseum
Eugen-Bolz-Platz 1, D-7407 Rottenburg
1
Religious Art Museum - 1864
Late-gothic votive painting and
wooden sculptures; religious art;
devotional prints; in a 17th century
building

Rottweil

05897
Kunstsammlung Lorenzkapelle
Postfach 108, D-7210 Rottweil
Religious Art Museum - 1851
14th-16th century Gothic wooden and
stone sculptures; votive painting; in a
16th century chapel - restoration
workshop

Rüdesheim

05898
Rheingau- und Weinmuseum
Rheinstr. 2, D-6220 Rüdesheim
General Museum - 1948
Pre- and early history; local history;
wine growing in Rheingau; glass;
ceramics; bottles - library

05899
**Siegfrieds mechanisches
Musikkabinet**
Oberstr. 29, D-6220 Rüdesheim
History/Public Affairs Museum - 1969
18th-20th century mechanical musical
instruments; music boxes and clocks;
pianolas; barrels - restoration
workshop

Ruhpolding

05900
**Museum für bäuerliche und sakrale
Kunst**
Roman-Friesinger-Str. 1, D-8222
Ruhpolding
Religious Art Museum - 1971
Religious art; votive painting; stained
glass; 17th-19th century sculpture and
painting; folk art; costumes;
implements; ceramics

Rüsselsheim

05901
Museum der Stadt Rüsselsheim
Hauptmann-Scheuermann-Weg 4,
D-6090 Rüsselsheim
General Museum - 1910
Local history, prehistory, medieval to
industrial age history; development of
the Opel works, historical machinery;
Rüsselsheim working class movement
(1863-1945) - library

Saarbrücken

05902
**Landesmuseum für Vor- und
Frühgeschichte**
Am Ludwigsplatz 15, D-6600
Saarbrücken
History/Public Affairs Museum - 1930
Prehistory; Roman frescoes and
sculptures; early Middle Age; Celtic
burial remains - restoration lab

05903
Saarland-Museum
Bismarckstr. 11-15, D-6600
Saarbrücken
Fine Arts Museum - 1924/1952
Modern painting - library

Salem

05904
Feuerwehrmuseum
D-7777 Salem
History/Public Affairs Museum - 1976
Development of firefighting (18th-20th
cent.)

Salzgitter

05905
Städtisches Museum Salzgitter
Schloß Salder, D-3320 Salzgitter 1
General Museum - 1962
Prehistory; geology; furniture

St. Goar

05906
**Heimatkundliche Sammlung Burg
Rheinfels**
Burg Rheinfels, D-5401 St. Goar
General Museum - 1965
Excavation finds; plans and drawings;
etchings; documents; heraldry

Schleswig

05907
**Schleswig-Holsteinisches
Landesmuseum**
Schloß Gottorf, D-2380 Schleswig
General Museum - 1875
Folk art; implements and tools;
graphics; contemporary arts and
crafts; portraits - library; archives;
restoration and photo labs; research
center

05908
**Schleswig-Holsteinisches
Landesmuseum für Vor- und
Frühgeschichte** Christian-Albrechts-
Universität Kiel
Schloß Gottorf, D-2380 Schleswig
History/Public Affairs Museum - 1834
Prehistory (8000 B.C.-500 A.D.);
archaeology of settlement during the
Middle Ages; research on the Vikings;
geology of the coastal landscape and
marshes of the North Sea; Slavic
archaeology and study of fortresses -
library; archives; restoration and X-ray
labs; model construction workshop

05909
Städtisches Museum
Friedrichstr. 7-9, D-2380 Schleswig
General Museum - 1934
Local history; folk art; domestic
utensils; toys; history of printing;
documentation on excavations in
ancient Schleswig - library; picture
archives

Schöppenstedt

05910
Till-Eulenspiegel-Museum
Nordstr. 9, D-3307 Schöppenstedt
History/Public Affairs Museum - 1940
Memorabilia and literature on Till
Eulenspiegel

Schrobenhausen

05911
Lenbachmuseum
Ulrich-Peißer-Gasse 1, D-8898
Schrobenhausen
Historic Site - 1936/37
Birthplace of Franz von Lenbach
(1836-1904); memorabilia of the
painter; paintings by his friend Johann
Baptist Hofner

Schrozberg

05912
Militärmuseum Schloß Bartenstein
D-7187 Schrozberg
History/Public Affairs Museum - 1971
Local history; military history

Schwangau

05913
Schloß Hohenschwangau
D-8959 Schwangau
Fine Arts Museum - 1886
12th century castle; 19th century
interiors; frescoes pertaining to
German myths

Schweinfurt

05914
Städtisches Museum
Martin-Luther-Platz 12, D-8720
Schweinfurt
General Museum - 1890
Prehistory; local history; scientific
instruments

Schwetzingen

05915
Schloß Schwetzingen
D-6830 Schwetzingen
Fine Arts Museum - 1918
Medieval castle with moat; 18th
century Apollo temple; open-air
theater(1752); 18th-19th century
interiors and furnishings; paintings

Seesen

05916
Wilhelm-Busch-Gedenkstätte
Mechtshausen, Pastor-Nöldeke-Weg
7, D-3370 Seesen
Historic Site - 1950
Collection of paintings, graphics and
manuscripts by Wilhelm Busch;
photographies; letters; parsonage
where he lived (1898-1908)

Sehnde

05917
**Deutsches Straßenbahn-Museum
Hannover** Stiftung Deutsches
Straßenbahnmuseum Hannover e.V. -
Museum für Kommunalverkehr
Museumsanlage Hohenfels,
Wehmingen, D-3163 Sehnde
History/Public Affairs Museum - 1971
Ancient streetcars from all over the
Federal Republic of Germany

Selm

05918
**Museum für Kunst und
Kulturgeschichte der Stadt
Dortmund**
Schloß Cappenberg, D-4714 Selm 4
Fine Arts Museum - 1883
Coll: in 12th century castle; furniture
from the Gothic to Art Deco period;
tiles; wall hangings; porcelain; local
history; Westfalian folk art; painting
and sculpture up to 1900 - library;
workshops

Siegen

05919
Museum des Siegerlandes
Oberes Schloß, D-5900 Siegen 1
General Museum - 1905
Prehistory; paintings; graphics; folk art
- library

Sigmaringen

05920
Fürstlich Hohenzollernsches Museum
Schloß, D-7480 Sigmaringen
History/Public Affairs Museum - 1867
Prehistory; 15th-16th century
Alemannic art; 15th-19th century
weapons - library; archives

Soest

05921
St.Patrokli-Dom-Museum Soest
Propst-Nübel-Str. 2, D-4770 Soest
Religious Art Museum - 1968
12th-19th century liturgical utensils;
stone inscriptions; documentation on
the architectural history of the dome;
ecclesiastical art

05922
Wilhelm-Morgner-Haus
Thomästr. 2, D-4770 Soest
Historic Site - 1962
Expressionism: paintings, drawings
and prints by Wilhelm Morgner
(1891-1917); etchings by the copper
engraver Heinrich Aldegrever
(1502-1555) - cultural center

Sögel

05923
**Emslandmuseum Schloß
Clemenswerth**
D-4475 Sögel
General Museum - 1972
Prehistory; local history; hunting;
ceramics

Solingen

05924
Bergisches Museum Schloß Burg
Schloßplatz 1, D-5650 Solingen 1
History/Public Affairs Museum - 1894
13th century fortress; wall-paintings
(1900); medieval to 18th century
weapons; medieval, Renaissance and
18th-19th century local culture;
furniture; domestic utensils; ceramics;
glass; prehistory; numismatic cabinet

05925
Deutsches Klingenmuseum Solingen
Wuppertaler Str. 160, D-5650 Solingen
1
History/Public Affairs Museum - 1953
Knives; metallurgy; iron industry;
weapons; 3,000 years of smithwork;
16th-17th century local art - library

Speyer

05926
Historisches Museum der Pfalz
Große Pfaffengasse 7, D-6720 Speyer
History/Public Affairs Museum - 1869
Prehistory; medieval to modern
history; Dom- und Diözesanmuseum:
ecclesiastical art; Weinmuseum: wine
cultivation

St. Augustin

05927
Haus Völker und Kulturen
Arnold-Janssen-Str.26, D-5205 St.
Augustin
Anthropology Museum - 1973
Art objects from Africa, New Guinea
and East Asia

Stuttgart

05928
**Bibelausstellung der Deutschen
Bibelstiftung**
Hauptstätterstr. 51, D-7000 Stuttgart
51
Religious Art Museum - 1952
Coll: history of the bible; original
editions and early copies of the Luther
bible; European and non-European
editions

05929
Daimler-Benz-Museum
Mercedesstr. 137a, Untertürkheim,
D-7000 Stuttgart 60
Science/Tech Museum - 1961
Coll: originals and models of products
made by the Daimler-Benz AG from
1883 to the present - workshops,
library, archives

05930
Daimler-Gedächtnisstätte
Taubenheimstr. 13, Bad Cannstatt,
D-7000 Stuttgart 50
History/Public Affairs Museum - 1940
Coll: housed in Gottlieb Daimler's
original workshop (1882); historical
workshop material and equipment;
original engines, motorcycles and
models of automobiles

05931
Deutsches Landwirtschaftsmuseum
Garbenstr. 9 a, Hohenheim, Postfach
106, D-7000 Stuttgart 70
Agriculture Museum - 1972
Coll: one of the world's largest and
most comprehensive exhibits on
agricultural history from the early
Stone Age to the present

05932
Galerie der Stadt Stuttgart
Schloßplatz 2, D-7000 Stuttgart 1
Fine Arts Museum - 1925
Coll: 19th and 20th century painting by
local artists; realism; impressionism;
works by Hölzel and his
contemporaries; graphic arts

05933
Linden-Museum Stuttgart Staatliches
Museum für Völkerkunde
Hegelplatz 1, D-7000 Stuttgart 1
Anthropology Museum - 1889
Coll: Folklore and anthropology of the
Americas, Africa, the Orient, and
Oceania - library; workshops

05934
Porsche-Museum
Porschestr. 42, D-7000 Stuttgart 40
Science/Tech Museum - 1976
Coll: 25 Porsche automobiles and
racing cars (40-1100PS); the life and
work of Professor Porsche

05935
**Postgeschichtliche Sammlung der
Oberpostdirektion Stuttgart**
Fernmeldetechnischer Teil
Friedrichstr. 13, D-7000 Stuttgart 1
History/Public Affairs Museum - 1908
Coll: history of the development of
telecommunication; telephone and
telegraph apparatuses dating back to
1908

05936
Staatliches Museum für Naturkunde
Schloß Rosenstein, D-7000 Stuttgart 1
Natural History Museum - 1791
Coll: zoology; entomology; botany;
geology, paleontology - library;
archives; workshops

05937
Staatsgalerie Stuttgart
Konrad-Adenauer-Str. 32, D-7000
Stuttgart 1
Fine Arts Museum - 1843
Coll: 19th and 20th century German
painting; Italian and German baroque
painting; Dutch and Old German
painting; 18th-20th century graphic
arts - library, archives, workshops

05938
Städtisches Lapidarium
Mörikestr. 24/1, D-7000 Stuttgart 1
Archeology Museum - 1950
Coll: Roman artifacts; inscriptions;
sculpture; architecture

05939
**Württembergisches Landesmuseum
Stuttgart**
Altes Schloß, Schillerplatz 6, D-7000
Stuttgart 1
General Museum - 1862
Coll: archeological finds from the Iron
Age, Roman period and Middle Ages;
medieval and 19th-20th century
Swabian sculpture; crafts; clocks;
weapons; musical instruments; textiles;
coins; folklore - library, archives,
workshops

Sylt-Ost

05940
Altfriesisches Haus
Keitum, D-2280 Sylt-Ost
General Museum - 1908
Coll: 18th century farmhouse; interiors
from past life on Sylt; furniture;
domestic utensils; furnishings from the
18th and 19th centuries

Tecklenburg

05941
**Kreismuseum Tecklenburg,
Puppenmuseum**
Legge, D-4542 Tecklenburg
General Museum - 1973
17th century house; dolls from all over
the world: costumes, materials,
manufacture, dolls' houses; toys;
history of the educational aspect of
dolls and toys

Traben-Trarbach

05942
Mittelmosel-Museum
Moselstr., D-5580 Traben-Trarbach
General Museum - 1928
Prehistory; local history; weapons;
coins, history of wine cultivation -
library

Trier

05943
**Bischöfliches Dom- und
Diözesanmuseum**
Banthusstr. 6, D-5500 Trier
Religious Art Museum - 1906
Coll: early Christian archeology;
history of art; religious art; 11th-19th
century sculpture - library

05944
Domschatz
Hinter dem Dom 6, D-5500 Trier
Religious Art Museum
Coll: ivory carvings; goldsmith work;
10th century portable altar; paintings;
medieval books

05945
Karl-Marx-Haus
Brückenstr. 10, D-5500 Trier
Historic Site - 1928
Birthplace and memorabilia of Karl
Marx (1818-1883); documents
concerning social history in 19th
century Germany; history of the
international proletarian movement -
library

05946
Rheinisches Landesmuseum Trier
Ostallee 44, D-5500 Trier
History/Public Affairs Museum - 1877
Coll: prehistory; Roman and early
Christian mosaics, statues, ceramics
and tombstones; Frankish cultural
history; medieval and modern
sculpture, glass and porcelain - library,
archives, restoration workshops

05947
Städtisches Museum Simeonstift
Simeonstiftplatz, D-5500 Trier
Fine Arts Museum - 1904
Coll: 15th-19th century sculpture,
painting, folklore and handicrafts of the
Trier region; 16th and 17th century
Dutch painting; graphic arts; furniture;
ceramics

Trostberg

05948
Städtisches Heimatmuseum
Schedling 9, D-8223 Trostberg
General Museum - 1935
Local history; natural history; crafts
and guilds; furniture; folk art

Tübingen

05949
**Antikensammlung des
Archäologischen Instituts**
Numismatische Arbeitsstelle
Wilhelmstr. 9, Nauklerstr. 2, D-7400
Tübingen 1
Fine Arts Museum - 1798
Collection of Antiquities: antique
sculpture, inscriptions, bronze, terra
cotta; Greek and Italien vases;
Numismatic Collection (not open to the
public): Greek, Roman, Byzantine,
medieval and modern coins and
medals - library

05950
Hölderlin-Haus
Bursagasse 6, D-7400 Tübingen 1
Historic Site - 1922
Coll: life and work of Friedrich
Hölderlin (1770-1843); furniture;
pictures; housed in the city tower
where Hölderlin lived from 1807 on -
library

05951
**Institut und Museum für Geologie
und Paläontologie**
Sigwartstr. 10, D-7400 Tübingen
Natural History Museum - 1904
Geology; paleontology; fossils,
reptiles; ammonites - library

05952
Kunsthalle
Philosophenweg 76, D-7400 Tübingen
Fine Arts Museum - 1971
Coll: works of art by G.F. Zundel and
other Swabian impressionists and
realists; drawings; aquarelles;
gouaches

05953
Mineralogische Schausammlung
Wilhelmstr. 56, D-7400 Tübingen
Natural History Museum - 1918
Coll: mineralogy; meteorites and
craters made by meteorites

05954
**'Mittelalterliche Kunst' Kloster
Bebenhausen**
Kloster Bebenhausen, D-7401
Tübingen
Religious Art Museum - 1961
Coll: medieval sculpture, paintings,
religious objects and triptychs

05955
**Sammlung des Ägyptologischen
Instituts der Universität Tübingen**
Corrensstr. 12, D-7400 Tübingen 1
History/Public Affairs Museum - 1959
Coll: displays concerning Egypt from
prehistoric times to the beginning of
the Islamic period; the collection will
be moved to the Hohentübingen
Castle in 1985 - library, archives

05956
**Sammlungen des Instituts für
Geschichte der Medizin der
Universität Tübingen**
Denzenberghalde 12, D-7400 Tübingen
1
History/Public Affairs Museum - 1963
Coll: photographs, copper engravings
and reproductions of implements
demonstrating the history of medicine
- library

05957
Theodor-Haering-Haus Städtische
Sammlungen
Neckarhalde 31, D-7400 Tübingen 1
History/Public Affairs Museum - 1914
Coll: history of the town and the
university; prehistory; crafts and
trades; medieval art; painting; graphic
art; book printing and publishing; toys;
domestic utensils

05958
Zahnärztliches Museum
Osianderstr. 2-8, D-7400 Tübingen 1
Science/Tech Museum - 1968
Coll: instruments used in dental
surgery; history of dentistry

Überlingen

05959
Städtisches Heimatmuseum
Krummebergstr. 30, D-7770
Überlingen
History/Public Affairs Museum - 1913
Coll: prehistory; local history;
sculpture and painting, especially from
the Bodensee area; furniture; folk art;
weapons; historical doll houses dating
from the Renaissance to Jugenstil
periods

05960
Suso-Haus
Suso-Gasse 10, D-7770 Überlingen
Religious Art Museum - 1901
Birthplace of the mystic H. von Berg,
known as Suso (ca. 1295-1366);
medieval room restored in
commemoration of Suso; religious art
including votive tablets (16th-20th c.)
and sculpture (18th-19th c.)

Ulm

05961
Deutsches Brotmuseum
Fürsteneckerstr. 17, D-7900 Ulm
History/Public Affairs Museum - 1955
History of bread and baking

05962
Naturkundliche Sammlungen
Kornhausgasse 3, D-7900 Ulm
Natural History Museum - 1923
Geology; zoology; herbarium

05963
Ulmer Museum
Neue Str. 92, D-7900 Ulm
General Museum - 1923
Regional medieval art (1300-1530);
local history, crafts and guilds; graphic
arts - library

Verden

05964
Deutsches Pferdemuseum e.V.
Hippologisches Institut
Andreasstr. 7, D-2810 Verden
History/Public Affairs Museum - 1927
Equestrian history; equipment

Villingen-Schwenningen

05965
Heimatmuseum-Stadtchronik
Kronenstr.16, D-7220 Villingen-
Schwenningen
General Museum - 1931
Prehistory; local history; horology; folk
art - library

05966
Museum Altes Rathaus
Rathausgasse 1, D-7730 Villingen-
Schwenningen
General Museum - 1876
Local history; crafts and guilds;
painting (15th-20th cent.); sculptures;
decorative art - library

Wadersloh

05967
Museum Abtei Liesborn
Heimatmuseum des Kreises
Warendorf
Liesborn, Abteiring 8, Postf. 2087,
D-4724 Wadersloh
General Museum - 1966
Prehistory; history of the abbey;
peasant life; folk art

Wangen

05968
Deutsches Eichendorff-Museum
Am Atzenberg 31, D-7988 Wangen
History/Public Affairs Museum - 1936
Documents and memorabilia on the
German author Joseph Freiherr von
Eichendorff (1788-1857)

05969
Stadtmuseum Wangen im Allgäu
Postfach 54, D-7988 Wangen
General Museum - 1885
Milling; cheese making; works by the
painter Joseph Anton von Gegenbaur
(1800-1876); peasant life and traditions;
coin collection; in a 16th century
frame-work house

Wasserburg

05970
Imaginäres Museum Sammlung
Günter Dietz
Rathaus, D-8090 Wasserburg
Fine Arts Museum - 1979
'Original' reproductions by the painter
and illustrator Dietz, which can only be
distinguished from the originals with
the help of X-rays; collection includes
early altar pieces, Dutch painting
(17th-18th c.),romanticism,
impressionism, expressionism

Weil der Stadt

05971
Kepler-Museum
Keplergasse 2, D-7252 Weil der Stadt
Historic Site - 1940
House where Johann Kepler was
born; furnishings in the style of the
period; documents on the life and
work of Kepler (1571-1630) - library;
archives

Weinstadt

05972
Auto- und Motorrad-Museum
Werkstr. 4, D-7056 Weinstadt
Science/Tech Museum - 1976
Bicycles; motorcycles; aircraft
engines; automobiles

Wertheim

05973
Glasmuseum Wertheim
Mühlenstr. 24, D-6980 Wertheim
Science/Tech Museum - 1971
Technological development of the
glass industry; antique, medieval and
contemporary glasses; regional glass
industry

Wesel

05974
Städtisches Museum
Ritterstr. 14, D-4230 Wesel 1
General Museum - 1975
15th-19th century Rhine art; silver and
goldsmith work - library

Wesselburen

05975
Hebbel-Museum
Österstr. 6, Postfach 68, D-2244
Wesselburen
Historic Site - 1911
House of the poet Christian Friedrich
Hebbel (1813-1863); historic rooms,
documents, manuscripts, first printings,
photos, engravings and sculptures

Westfehmarn

05976
**Mühlen- und
Landwirtschaftsmuseum
Lemkenhafen**
D-2449 Westfehmarn
Agriculture Museum - 1961
History of mills and milling appliances;
agricultural and craftsmen's tools and
implements; customs and historic
documents of the region; local flora

Wetzlar

05977
Leitz-Museum
Postfach 2020, D-6330 Wetzlar
Science/Tech Museum - 1949
History of microscopy; history of the
Leica and other optical instruments

05978
Palais Papius
Kornblumengasse 1, D-6330 Wetzlar
Decorative Arts Museum - 1967
Furniture; clocks; tapestries; faience;
European arts and crafts (16th-18th c.)

05979
**Stadtmuseum, Lottehaus,
Zehntscheune**
Lottestr. 8-10, D-6330 Wetzlar
General Museum - 1863
Stadtmuseum: Pre- and early history;
local history; militaria; peasant life and
traditions; paintings; Lotte-Haus:
memorabilia on J.W. von Goethe's
novel 'Die Leiden des jungen Werther';
furniture; Zehntscheune: iron casting;
optical instruments - library

Wiehl

05980
**Werksmuseum Achse, Rad und
Wagen**
Postfach 1280, D-5276 Wiehl
History/Public Affairs Museum - 1952
Cars; carriages; coaches; motorcars;
smithwork; ironwork; tools and
implements

Wiesbaden

05981
Museum Wiesbaden
Friedrich-Ebert-Alee 2, D-6200
Wiesbaden
General Museum - 1825
Art collection; natural history;
antiquities of Nassau - library;
restoration workshop

Wietze

05982
Erdölmuseum
Schwarzer Weg, D-3101 Wietze
Science/Tech Museum - 1970
Geology; oil drilling and technology;
prehistory

Wilhelmshaven

05983
**Küsten-Museum der Stadt
Wilhelmshaven**
Rathausplatz 10, Postf. 1180, D-2940
Wilhelmshaven
General Museum - 1926
Local history; geology; history of
navigation

Willebadessen

05984
**Europäischer Skulpturen-Park der
Bundesrepublik Deutschland**
D-3533 Willebadessen
Open Air Museum - 1979
European sculpture

Witzenhausen

05985
Auto- und Motorradmuseum
Ziegenhausen, D-3430 Witzenhausen
4
Science/Tech Museum - 1975
Coll: 1,600 vehicles; motorcycles, cars,
old-timers; sleds; carriages; fire
engines

Wolfenbüttel

05986
Herzog-August-Bibliothek
Lessingplatz 1, Postfach 1227, D-3340
Wolfenbüttel
History/Public Affairs Museum
European book history especially of
medieval manuscripts, 15th to 18th
century printings and books depicting
20th-century painting; graphic art;
maps; portrait engravings; Lessing
house with documents on the poet
and his time - library

05987
Historische Schloßräume Stadt- und
Kreisheimatmuseum
Schloßplatz 13, D-3340 Wolfenbüttel
General Museum - 1894
Baroque castle, former residence of
the Dukes of Braunschweig-
Wolfenbüttel (1432-1754); historic
furniture and furnishings, paintings,
tapestries, porcelain, bronzes, coins,
medals and arms; local history -
library

Wolfsburg

05988
Städtische Galerie
Schloß Wolfsburg, D-3180 Wolfsburg
Fine Arts Museum - 1974
Contemporary art especially painting
and sculpture from the German-
speaking countries and international
graphic arts in a renaissance castle

05989
Volkswagenwerk-Museum
D-3180 Wolfsburg
Science/Tech Museum - 1967
Documentation on production of the
VW

Worms

05990
Museum der Stadt Worms
Weckerlingplatz, D-6520 Worms
General Museum - 1880
Pre- and early history; archeological
finds including curvilinearly ceramics,
Hallstatt, La Tène and Roman finds;
regional and local history; painting and
graphic arts - library

Worpswede

05991
Große Kunstschau
Lindenallee 3, D-2862 Worpswede
Fine Arts Museum - 1927
Works by Paula Becker-Modersohn;
paintings by the artists from the
'Worpsweder Künstlerkolonie' (Otto
Modersohn, Fritz Mackensen, Hans
am Ende, Fritz Overbeck, Heinrich
Vogeler), by Carl Vinnen and Karl
Krummacher

05992
**Heinrich-Vogeler-Sammlung und
Worpsweder Archiv** Haus im Schluh
D-2862 Worpswede
Fine Arts Museum - 1921
Vogeler collection including paintings,
drawings, graphic arts, furniture and
Jugendstil design; documents, pictures
and literature relating to local history
and the 'Worpsweder Künstlerkolonie';
manuscripts - library

Wörth

05993
Schiffahrts- und Schiffbaumuseum
Postfach 20, D-8761 Wörth
Science/Tech Museum - 1982
Inland navigation and ship building
esp. in the Main region - library in
preparation

Wunsiedel

05994
Fichtelgebirgs-Museum
Spitalhof 1-2, D-8592 Wunsiedel
History/Public Affairs Museum - 1908
Coll: local history; minerals; folklore;
crafts; folk costumes; mangers;
weapons; agricultural machinery;
ceramics - library

Wuppertal

05995
Friedrich-Engels-Haus
Engelsstr. 10, D-5600 Wuppertal 2
Historic Site - 1970
Birthplace and memorabilia of
Friedrich Engels (1820-1895); exhibits
depicting the workers's movement and
early socialism in Wuppertal

05996
Von der Heydt-Museum
Turmhof 8, D-5600 Wuppertal 1
Fine Arts Museum - 1902
Coll: 17th century Dutch painting; 19th
century German and French painting;
modern and contemporary art;
sculpture; graphic arts - library

Würzburg

05997
Festung Marienberg
Gebäude 239, Festung Marienberg,
mail c/o Schloß- und
Gartenverwaltung Würzburg,
Residenzplatz 2, D-8700 Würzburg
History/Public Affairs Museum
Historical fortress dating back to the
13th century; Renaissance furniture;
gobelins; religious artifacts

05998
Mainfränkisches Museum Würzburg
Festung Marienberg, D-8700
Würzburg
History/Public Affairs Museum - 1913
Coll: Frankish cultural history; garden
statues; tombstones; arts and crafts;
ethnology; local history - library

05999
Martin-von-Wagner-Museum
Antikensammlung
Tor A, Residenz, D-8700 Würzburg
Fine Arts Museum - 1858
Coll: antique works of art and
ceramics; Etruscan antiques; bronze -
library

06000
Martin-von-Wagner-Museum Neuere
Abteilung
Tor A, Residenz, D-8700 Würzburg
Fine Arts Museum - 1858
Coll: European painting; German
sculpture; sketches and graphic arts
of the 15th-19th centuries - library

06001
**Mineralogisches Museum der
Universität**
Am Hubland, D-8700 Würzburg
Natural History Museum - 1972
Coll: mineralogy; petrography; natural
resources

06002
**Residenz mit Hofkirche und
Hofgarten**
mail c/o Schloß- und
Gartenverwaltung Würzburg,
Residenzplatz 2, D-8700 Würzburg
Decorative Arts Museum - 1920
Coll: rooms with baroque and rococo
furnishings; frescoes by G.B. Tiepolo;
located in the former residence of the
Würzburg prince-bishops

06003
Staatsgalerie
Residenzplatz 2, D-8700 Würzburg
Fine Arts Museum - 1974
Coll: 17th and 18th century Venetian
painting

06004
Städtische Galerie
Hofstr. 3, D-8700 Würzburg
Fine Arts Museum - 1941
Coll: 19th and 20th century painting,
sculpture and graphic arts, especially
by Frankish artists - library

06005
Wirtshaus zum Riemenschneider
Franziskanergasse 1, D-8700
Würzburg
Historic Site
Former house and workshop (built in
1402) of Tilman Riemenschneider;
replicas of Riemenschneider's
woodcarvings

Wyk

06006
Dr. Haeberlin-Friesenmuseum
Rebbelstieg 34, D-2270 Wyk
General Museum - 1902
Coll: prehistory; geology; zoology;
local history; navigation; ethnology;
folk costumes and architecture;
furnished farmhouse (1617) - library

Xanten

06007
Archäologischer Park
Kartaus 2, D-4232 Xanten
Archeology Museum - 1974
Coll: excavation and reconstruction of
the antique city of Colonia Ulpia
Traiana; amphitheater; towers and city
gates

06008
Dom-Museum
Kapitel Nr. 8, Postfach 244, D-4232
Xanten
Religious Art Museum - 1951
Coll: 4th-19th century cathedral
treasure; stained glass; altars;
frescoes; religious requisites - library,
archives

06009
Regionalmuseum
Kurfürstenstr. 7-9, D-4232 Xanten
History/Public Affairs Museum - 1974
Coll: paleontology; prehistory; local
history; religious art - library

Zwiesel

06010
Waldmuseum
Stadtplatz 29, D-8372 Zwiesel
History/Public Affairs Museum - 1966
Coll: geology; biology; forestry and
lumbering; local history; crafts and
trades; glass dating back to the 15th
century

Ghana

Accra

06011
**Ghana Museum of Science and
Technology**
POB 3343, Accra
Science/Tech Museum

06012
Ghana National Museum
Barnes Rd, POB 3343, Accra
General Museum - 1957
Archeology; Ghanian painting and art;
gold and brass; ethnography - library

Cape Coast

06013
West African Historical Museum
Cape Coast Castle, POB 269, Cape
Coast
History/Public Affairs Museum - 1974
West African history; articles dealing
with the European colonialization of
West Africa; documents on the slave
trade (15th-19th c.)

Ho

06014
Volta Regional Museum
POB 340, Ho, Volta Region
General Museum - 1973
Natural history; ethnographical and
archeological materials of the Volta
Region; traditional iron-smelting and
weaving

Kumasi

06015
Ghana Military Museum
Steward Av., H.Q. Kumasi Garrison,
Private mail bag, Kumasi
History/Public Affairs Museum
War trophies; weapons; historical
photographs

06016
Prempeh II Jubilee Museum
Bantama St., POB 3085, Kumasi
General Museum
Pottery; gold, silver, leather, and
bronze work; baskets; clay sculpture

Legon

06017
**Institute of African Studies Teaching
Museum**
University of Ghana, Maintenance Rd.,
POB 73, Legon
Anthropology Museum - 1963
Ethnology and ethnography; Coptic
textiles; visual arts

06018
**Museum of the Department of
Archaeology**
University of Ghana, POB 3, Legon
Archeology Museum - 1951
Ghanaian archaeology; human
paleontology; terra-cotta figurines;
ethnographic collections - library

06019
**Museum of the Department of
Geology**
University of Ghana, POB 58, Legon
Natural History Museum - 1951
Geology; fossils; rocks

Gibraltar

Gibraltar

06020
Gibraltar Museum
18-20 Bomb House Lane, Gibraltar
General Museum - 1930
Paleolithic-Phoenician archeology;
local military and naval history; natural
history

Greece

Aegina

06021
Archeological Museum
Eynardeion, Aegina
Archeology Museum - 1926
Neolithic Greek pottery, sculpture,
architectural fragments, terra cotta;
decorative arts; early Christian and
Byzantine sculpture; inscriptions

Afandou

06022
Kandis Collection
Afandou, Rhodes
Decorative Arts Museum

Agios Andreas

06023
Agios Andreas Monastery Museum
Agios Andreas, Cephalonia
Religious Art Museum
Frescoes; icons; woodcarvings;
vestments; religious embroidery

Agios Kirikos

06024
Archeological Collection
Gymnasium, Agios Kirikos, Ikaria
Archeology Museum
Archaic Roman pottery

Agios Nikolaos

06025
Museum Ayios Nikolaos
74 Konstantinou Palaiologou St, Agios
Nikolaos, Crete
Archeology Museum - 1969
Minoan pottery, clay coffins, seals,
bronze weapons; archaic, classical,
geometric, Hellenistic and Roman
pottery, figurines, coins; finds from
Myrtos, Agios Fotia, Petsophas,
Prinias, Modi, Olous, Zakros, Agios
Nikolaos, Siteia, Krya, Myrsini, Malia

06026
Touring Club Collection
Agios Nikolaos, Crete
Decorative Arts Museum
Weaving; embroidery

Agrinion

06027
Archeological Museum of Agrinion
Agrinion, Aetolia
Archeology Museum - 1968
Prehistoric weapons; sculpture;
decorative objects; terra cotta;
bronze; inscriptions; finds from Aetolia
and Akamania

Aigion

06028
Taxiarchon Monestary
Aigion
Religious Art Museum
Vestments; post-Byzantine religious
embroidery; manuscripts, documents

Aiyani

06029
**Archeological and Folklore
Collection**
Village Hall, Aiyani, Kozani
Archeology Museum
Prehistoric pottery; weapons; Greek
and Roman decorative objects;
numismatics; post-Byzantine icons;
folk costumes

Alexandroupolis

06030
Archeological Collection
Town Hall, Alexandroupolis
Archeology Museum
Hellenistic and Roman sculpture;
fragments of prehistoric, Hellenistic
and Roman periods

06031
**Philippides' Collection of
Alexandroupolis**
33 Proussis St, Alexandroupolis
Anthropology Museum
Weaving; gold-embroidery; knitted
objects; woodcarvings; silverware of
the Nomad community

Almiros

06032
orthrys Orthrys Antiquarian Society
Collection
Almiros
Archeology Museum
Prehistoric finds; Greek and early
Christian sculptures; pottery

Ambelakia

06033
G. Schwarz Mansion
Ambelakia
Historic Site - 1797/98
Interiors; decorative arts; folk art;
woodcarvings; metalwork; documents;
in a typical Greek mansion

Amfissa

06034
**Museum of Contemporary Greek
Painters**
Town Hall, Amfissa
Fine Arts Museum
Paintings by local contemporary artists

Amphiareion

06035
Temple Museum
Amphiareion, Atica
Archeology Museum
Classical, Hellenistic and Roman
sculpture; architectural fragments and
finds from the Amphiareion Temple
excavations

Anafi

06036
Archaeological Collection
Primary School, Anafi
Archeology Museum
Roman sculptures

Ano Kardamyla

06037
**Kardamyla Cultural Center of
Michael and Stamatia Xylas**
Ano Kardamyla, (Chios)
Anthropology Museum
Icons; woodcarving; weaving

Antissa

06038
**Monastery of St. John the Divine,
Ypsilou**
Antissa, Lesbos
Religious Art Museum
Icons; religious objects; embroidery;
woodcarvings; manuscripts

Apeiranthos

06039
Archeological Collection
Apeiranthos, Naxos
Archeology Museum
Prehistoric stone and terra cotta
objects; Cycladic plaques; daggers;
Roman reliefs

Apoikia

06040
Agios Nikolaos Monastery
near Apoikia Apoikia, Andros
Religious Art Museum
Religious objects; embroidery

Argos

06041
Archeological Museum
Vass. Olgas St, Argos
Archeology Museum
Neolithic, Helladic and Mycenaean
pottery; decorative objects; Roman
sculpture; mosaic; breastplates;
weapons

Argostolion

06042
Archeological Museum
Argostolion, Kavalla
Archeology Museum
Mycenaean and sub-Mycenaean
pottery; bronze weapons; geometric
and archaic pottery; Hellenistic
sculpture and pottery; Roman bronze
head

06043
**Bassias Historical and Folklore
Museum**
Koryaleneios Library, Argostolion,
Kavalla
History/Public Affairs Museum
17th-19th century icons; liturgical
vestments; Venetian sculpture;
Byzantine and medieval art; Greek
handicraft weaving; woodcarvings;
metalwork; lithographs; maps; photos

06044
Bishop's Palace
Argostolion, Kavalla
Religious Art Museum
Post-Byzantine icons and vestments in
the collection of the Metropolitan of
Kavalla

Arta

06045
Archeological Collection
Trapeza tis Parigoritissas, Arta
Archeology Museum
Classical and Hellenistic sculpture;
decorative objects; Byzantine
sculpture; icons; art objects

Astros

06046
Archeological Collection
Astros
Archeology Museum - 1960
Ancient, Roman and Byzantine coins;
Paleolithic and Neolithic tools;
sculpture; Roman and Byzantine
inscriptions; terra cotta; pottery;
books; manuscripts

Athens

06047
Acropolis Museum
Acropolis, Athens
Archeology Museum - 1878
Archaic and classical sculpture,
pediments, friezes; statues of the
Parthenon, Temple of Niké,
Erechtheion; geometric-classical
vases; terra cotta plaques

06048
Agora Museum
Monastiraki, Athens
Archeology Museum - 1956
Neolithic, Helladic and Mycenaean
pottery; jewelry; ivory; geometric
vases and statuettes; weapons;
classical, archaic, Hellenistic and
Roman sculpture, pottery; Hellenistic-
Roman vases; bronze; terra cotta;
household objects; lamps; 4th century
mosaic floor; Byzantine pottery;
reproduction of the original building of
the 2nd century B.C.

06049
Andreadis Collection
11 Vas. Georgious II Av, Athens 138
Archeology Museum
Ancient pottery; icons

06050
Anoyanakis Collection
4 Sevastias St, Athens
Anthropology Museum
Folk instruments (18th-21th c.)

06051
Artemis Collection
42 Panayi Kyriakou St, Athens
Archeology Museum
Cycladic figurines; vases; ancient
coins

06052
Athens Numismatic Collection
1 Tositsa St, Athens
History/Public Affairs Museum
Numismatics from the 7th century B.C.
up to the present; rare Greek, Roman,
Byzantine, medieval, and modern
European coins; land seals; ancient
copper; lead tokens; ancient and
Byzantine weights; carved stone

06053
Benaki Museum
Koumbari St 1, Athens
General Museum - 1931
Ancient pottery and bronze; Byzantine
and post-Byzantine icons; vestments,
embroidery; woodcarvings; folk art;
costumes; metalwork; Oriental
armaments; memorabilia of the War of
Independence (1821); memorabilia of
the politician E. Venizelos;
manuscripts; historical archives;
18th-19th century painting; etchings,
watercolors, drawings; Coptic, Islamic
and Turkish decorative objects;
Chinese porcelain (Neolithic to the
present) - library

06054
Benakis Collection
4 Neofytou Vamba St, Athens
Archeology Museum
Classical and Hellenistic sculpture;
vases; terra cotta

06055
Byzantine Museum
Vass. Sophias 22, Athens
Archeology Museum - 1914
Early Christian, Byzantine and
Frankish sculpture; architectural
fragments; Byzantine and
post-Byzantine icons; frescoes;
manuscripts; embroidered vestments;
religious objects; woodcarvings;
pottery; mosaic floors; ivory and
bronzes; jewelry and enamels

06056
Dapergoulas Collection
Exoni, Ano Voula, Athens
Archeology Museum
Ancient pottery; post-Byzantine icons

06057
Economopoulos Collection
27 Navarchou Nikodimou St, Athens
119
Archeology Museum - 1960
Byzantine icons; pottery; seals; coins;
Greek vases

06058
Epigraphic Collection
Tositsa St 1, Athens
Archeology Museum - 1870
Inscriptions from the 6th century B.C.
to 300 A.D., including decree of
Themistocles, lists of tribute paid to the
Athenian empire, accounts of Phidias'
statue of Athena - library

06059
Evelpidis Collection
6 Vas. Sophios Av, Athens
History/Public Affairs Museum
Numismatics; coins

06060
Geroulanos Archeological Collection
Trahones, Glyphada, Athens
Archeology Museum - 1963
Finds of the area; geometric pottery;
obsidian minerals

06061
Goulandri Museum
13 Levidou St, Kifissia, Athens
Natural History Museum

06062
Goulandris Collection
4 Vas. Georgiou II Av, Athens
Archeology Museum
Cycladic figurines; vases; Greek
sculpture; pottery

06063
Hadjidimou Collection
12 Vas. Sofias Av, Athens
Archeology Museum
Vases; statuettes

06064
**I. and D. Passas Museum of
European and Oriental Art**
2 Evelpidou St, Athens
Fine Arts Museum
Paintings; Chinese art objects

06065
Iolas Collection
Paradissos, Ayia Paraskevi, Athens
Archeology Museum
Greek sculptures; pottery; bronze;
jewelry; icons; vases

06066
Kanellopoulos Collection
5 Irodou tou Attikou St, Athens
Archeology Museum
Greek sculpture; bronze vases;
statuettes; jewelry; coins; Byzantine
and post-Byzantine icons; religious
objects; decorative objects

06067
Kerameikos Museum
Ermou St, Monastiraki, Athens
Archeology Museum
Archaic-classical grave sculpture;
sub-Mycenaean-Roman pottery; burial
relics; statuettes; bronzes

06068
Konstandoglou Collection
13 Xenokratous St, Athens
Fine Arts Museum
Religious objects; decorative arts;
woodcarvings

06069
Koutlidis Collection
27 Vas. Sophias Av, Athens
Fine Arts Museum
Greek painting

06070
Kyrou Collection
29 Yperidou St, Athens
History/Public Affairs Museum
Numismatics; coins

06071
Melas Collection
36 Emm. Benaki St, Kifissia, Athens
Fine Arts Museum
Icons; woodcarvings

06072
Museum of Decorative Arts
Mosquée de Monastiraki, Athens
Decorative Arts Museum - 1916
Decorative and applied arts and crafts

06073
Museum of Greek Folk Art
17 Kydathineon, Plaka, Athens
Anthropology Museum
Ethnography; folk art

06074
Museum of Greek Folk Ceramics
1 Aeros St, Plateia, Monastiriou,
Athens
Anthropology Museum
Costumes; weaving; embroidery; lace;
jewelry; pottery; woodcarvings;
metalwork; 18th century mosque

06075
**Museum of Mineralogy and
Petrology** University of Athens
46a Akadimas St, Athens 143
Science/Tech Museum - 1875
Mineralogy; petrology; rocks

06076
Museum of Sacred Icons
21 Ayias Filotheis St, Archbishop's
Palace, Athens
Decorative Arts Museum
Post-Byzantine icons; vestments;
religious objects; ecclesiastical
documents

06077
**Museum of the Greek Folklore
Society**
12 Didotou St, Athens
Anthropology Museum
Weaving; embroidery; woodcarvings;
costumes

06078
National Archeological Museum
44 Patission St, Athens 147
Archeology Museum - 1874
Prehistoric collection; sculpture;
vases; bronzes and jewelry from
Greek and Roman periods; Egyptian
collection

06079
National Historical Museum
Historical and Ethnological Society of
Greece
Stadiou St, Athens
General Museum - 1882
History of Greek Independence Wars;
arms; local costumes; folk arts;
historical archives

06080
**National Picture Gallery (Pinakothiki)
and Alexander Soutzos Museum**
50 Vass. Konstantinou Av, Athens 516
Fine Arts Museum - 1900
Greek painting (17th-20th c.),
sculptures and prints; European
painting (14th-20th c.), including works
by El Greco, Caravaggio, Jordaens,
Poussin, Tiepolo, Delacroix, Mondrian,
Picasso; engravings; drawings -
library

06081
Papandoniou Collection
3 Plateia Victorias, Athens
Anthropology Museum
Costumes; weaving; embroidery;
jewelry

06082
Research Centre of Greek Folklore
Athens Academy
129 Leoforos Sygrou, Athens
Anthropology Museum
Weaving, embroidery and lace;
pottery; musical instruments; metal-
and woodwork

06083
Theatrical Museum Society of Greek
Theatrical Writers
19 Kavalotti St, Athens
Performing Arts Museum
Stage set models; costumes;
production pictures; memorabilia of
theatrical figures

06084
Vaos Collection
27 Polymnias St, Holargos, Athens
Archeology Museum - 1959
Neolithic objects, plowshares,
cultivation tools, axes, drills, chisels for
chipping wood, saws, knives,
spearheads, arrowheads, needles

06085
Zoological Museum University of
Athens
Panepistimiopolis, Kouponia, Athens
621
Natural History Museum - 1858
Zoology; marine ecology; pollution

Avlon

06086
Folklore Museum of Avlon
Avlon
Decorative Arts Museum
Decorative and applied arts and crafts;
embroidery; goldembroidery

Batsi

06087
**Monastery of the Zoodochos Pigi or
Agia**
Batsi, Andros
Religious Art Museum
Icons; vestments; religious objects;
codices

Canea

06088
Archeological Museum
St. Francis Monastery, Canea, Crete
Archeology Museum
Neolithic pottery; Greek and Roman
sculpture; decorative objects;
armaments; mosaics; numismatics

06089
Historical Museum
20 I. Sfakianaki St, Canea, Crete
History/Public Affairs Museum
Cretan history; memorabilia of the
literary figure E. Benizelos; folklore;
weaving; embroidery; other crafts

Chaironeia

06090
Archeological Museum
Chaironeia
Archeology Museum
Neolithic, Helladic and Mycenaean
pottery; classical and Roman vases;
sculptures; inscriptions; armaments

Chalkis

06091
Byzantine Collection
Mosque, Chalkis, Euboea
Archeology Museum
Mosaics, sculpture and pottery of
early Christian and Byzantine periods;
Venetian coats of arms; Turkish reliefs

Chios

06092
Adamantios Korais Library
Korai St, Chios
History/Public Affairs Museum
Memorabilia of Adamantios Korais and
others

06093
Archeological Museum
Mosque, Chios
Archeology Museum
Neolithic and early Helladic finds;
archaic, classical, Hellenistic and
Roman sculpture and pottery;
Byzantine sculpture and vases;
Frankish sculpture; numismatics

06094
Ethnological and Folklore Museum
Adamantios Korais Library, Korai St,
Chios
Anthropology Museum - 1937
Costumes; weaving; embroidery;
carvings

Chora

06095
Archeological Collection
Village Hall, Chora, Keos
Archeology Museum
Archaic-Hellenistic sculpture;
inscriptions

06096
Archeological Museum
Council Offices, Chora, Cerigo
Archeology Museum
Minoan vases from Kastri excavations;
Mycenaean pottery; 4th century
sculptural fragments

06097
Astipalaia Archeological Collection
Chora, Astipalaia
Archeology Museum - 1950
Hellenistic and Roman sculpture;
inscriptions; post-Byzantine icons

06098
Monastery of the Archangel Michael Panormitis
Chora, Syme
Religious Art Museum
Vestments; silver

Corfu

06099
Archeological Museum
Garitsa, Corfu
Archeology Museum
Gorgon pediment and lion from funerary mound of Menekrates; archaic terra cotta; architectural fragments; Corinthian vases; statuettes; bronzes; Roman sculpture; coins

06100
Byzantine Collection
Royal Palace, Corfu
Fine Arts Museum
11th-13th century frescoes, icons, mosaics, sculpture

06101
Ecclesiastical Museum
Church of the Pantocrator, Corfu
Religious Art Museum
Icons

06102
Historical Museum
Prefecture, Corfu
General Museum
Historic relics; folk art; 17th-19th century painting

06103
Sino-Japanese Museum
Royal Palace, Corfu
Anthropology Museum
Neolithic to 19th century Chinese and Japanese art; decorative objects; porcelain; paintings; theater; armaments

06104
Solomos Museum
Mourayio, Corfu
Historic Site
Memorabilia of the poet Dionysios Solomos (1798-1857)

Corinth

06105
Archeological Museum (Palaia Korinthos)
Corinth
Archeology Museum
Neolithic pottery; Helladic and Mycenaean objects; protogeometric, geometric, proto-Corinthian and Corinthian vases, figurines; classical, Hellenistic and Roman pottery, statuettes, lamps, gold jewelry, household articles; archaic and Roman sculpture; classical and Roman mosaics; early Christian and Byzantine sculpture; Byzantine pottery, small finds of metal, bronze and glass, coins, inscriptions; ruins of Corinth

Delos

06106
Archeological Museum
Delos
Archeology Museum
Archaic, classical, Hellenistic and Roman sculpture; architectural fragments; pottery; terra cotta; bronze figurines; jewelry; 2nd-1st century B.C. frescoes; household objects

Delphi

06107
Archeological Museum of Delphi
Delphi, Phocis
Archeology Museum - 1903
Findings from the Delphic excavations, archaic, classical, Hellenistic and Roman sculpture, inscriptions, pottery; Christian mosaic statuettes; bronze weapons, tools - library

Drama

06108
Archeological Collection
Drama
Archeology Museum
Roman and early Christian sculpture

Epidaurus

06109
Archeological Museum
Epidaurus
Archeology Museum - 1884
Architectural remains and partial reconstructions of the Tholos, the Aclepios temple, the Propylaea and the Artemis temple; original statues of the Hellenistic and Roman periods; Roman copies; surgical instruments; clay offerings and inscriptions; architectural remains of marble and clay from the temples of the sanctuary

Eresos

06110
Archeological Museum
Eresos, Lesbos
Archeology Museum
Hellenistic and Roman sculpture; pottery; statuettes from the 4th century; early Christian sculpture and mosaic floors

Eretria

06111
Archeological Museum
Eretria, Euboea
Fine Arts Museum
Prehistoric, archaic, classical and Hellenistic pottery; classical and Hellenistic sculpture; grave inscriptions

Ermoupolis

06112
Archeological Collection
Town Hall, Ermoupolis, Syros
Archeology Museum
Prehistoric marble and earthenware vases; Hellenistic and Roman sculpture and inscriptions

Falika

06113
Panachrantos Monastery
Falika, Andros
Religious Art Museum
Religious objects; liturgical vestments; wood carvings; embroidery

Farsala

06114
Archeological Collection
Farsala
Fine Arts Museum
Hellenistic and Roman architectural fragments and inscriptions

Ferai

06115
Archeological Collection
Ferai
Archeology Museum
Roman sarcophagus; Byzantine architectural fragments; 13th century Byzantine church of the Pantanassa

Filiatra

06116
Archeological Collection
Town Hall, Filiatra
Archeology Museum
Icons; early Christian sculpture

Filippi

06117
Archeological Museum
Filippi
Archeology Museum
Roman and early Christian ruins; prehistoric vases, stone tools; Roman and early Christian sculpture and architectural fragments; classical, Hellenistic and Roman finds; inscriptions; coins

Florina

06118
Archeological Museum
Railway Station Sq, Florina
Archeology Museum - 1972
Prehistoric, Hellenistic and Roman pottery; Hellenistic and Roman reliefs; post-Byzantine icons; folklore

06119
Folklore Museum of Florina
Syllogos 'Aristotelis', Florina
Anthropology Museum
Ethnography

Geraki

06120
Archeological Collection
Ralleion Bldg, Geraki
Archeology Museum
Hellenistic and Roman architectural fragments

Gythion

06121
Archeological Collection
Town Hall, Gythion
Archeology Museum
Archaic Laconian reliefs; Greek, Roman and Byzantine sculpture; inscriptions

Herakleion

06122
Archeological Museum
Xanthoudidou St 1, Herakleion, Crete
Archeology Museum - 1910
Minoan archaeological finds; frescoes, vases of stone, earthenware and alabaster; terra cotta and bronze figurines; sarcophagi, weapons, jewelry, sealstone ivory, household objects, inscriptions; archaic, classical, Hellenistic and Roman sculpture, pottery, bronzes, coins; the Disk of Phaistos; the snake Goddess - library

06123
Historical Museum of Crete
Lyssimachou Kalokerinou St, Herakleion, Crete
General Museum
Early Christian, Byzantine, Venetian and Turkish sculpture, inscriptions, Byzantine-medieval frescoes; post-Byzantine icons, woodcarvings, vestments; 17th century pottery; folklore; folk arts; weaving; embroidery; lace; local costumes; jewelry; crafts; armaments; documents; militaria; memorabilia of the poets Nikolaos Kazantzakis (1885-1957) and E. Tsouderos

06124
Kafatos Collection
21 Dedalou St, Herakleion, Crete
Archeology Museum
Cretan 'petsetes'

06125
Kastrinoyannis Collection
23 Idomenos St, Herakleion, Crete
Decorative Arts Museum
Cretan weaving; embroidery

06126
Metaxas Collection
4 Plateia Analipseos, Herakleion, Crete
Archeology Museum
Stone and earthenware vases, figurines and statuettes, bronzes and sealstones of the Minoan period; Greek and Roman vases, statuettes, bronzes and jewelry; coins from the period of Arab occupation

06127
St. George Epanosifis Monastery
Herakleion, Crete
Religious Art Museum
Religious objects; vestments; embroidery; bound gospels; illuminated manuscripts

Hierapetra

06128
Archeological Collection
Hierapetra, Crete
Archeology Museum
Mycenean pottery; painted terra cotta sarcophagi; Hellenistic statuettes; Roman sculpture and inscriptions

Ioannina

06129
Municipal Museum
Aslan Pasha Mosque, Ioannina
General Museum
Weaving; embroidery; silver; wood carvings; armaments

06130
Museum
Ano Plateia, Ioannina
Archeology Museum
Paleolithic tools and bones; neolithic and Bronze Age pottery; weapons; jewelry; geometric-Roman bronze objects from the Dodoni sanctuary; classical, Hellenistic and Roman sculpture; architectural fragments; inscriptions; coins; early Christian and Byzantine sculpture; 13th century miniatures; icons; post-Byzantine metalwork and silverware; 19th-20th century Greek painting; 20th century sculpture

Ios

06131
Archeological Collection
Primary School, Ios
Archeology Museum
Cycladic and Roman pottery; Roman
reliefs and inscriptions; Egyptian
statuettes

Istiaia

06132
Archeological Collection
Town Hall, Istiaia, Euboea
Archeology Museum
Hellenistic pottery; Roman sculpture;
architectural fragments

Kalamata

06133
Archeological Museum
Benakis Mansion, Benaki St, Kalamata
Archeology Museum
Neolithic pottery; stone tools from
Malthi; Mycenaean; protogeometric
and geometric finds from Karpophora;
archaic and Hellenistic pottery;
classical, Hellenistic and Roman
sculpture; Roman mosaic;
post-Byzantine icons; folk embroidery;
memorabilia of the 1821 revolt

06134
Historical and Folklore Museum
Kyriakou, Ayiou and Ioannon Sts,
Kalamata
General Museum
Household objects; weapons;
paintings on the 1821 revolt

06135
**Museum of the Metropolitinate of
Messina**
Frangolimnis Sq, Kalamata
Religious Art Museum
Icons; religious objects; manuscripts;
vestments

Kalavrita

06136
Agia Laora Monastery
Kalavrita
Religious Art Museum
Icons; 11th-14th century Byzantine
manuscripts; religious vestments;
ecclesiastical gold embroidery;
Venetian and Turkish documents

06137
Mega Spileon Monastery
Kalavrita
Religious Art Museum
Icons; illuminated manuscripts;
religious objects; vestments; carvings;
embroidery; silverware

Kalloni

06138
St. Ignatios Monastery
Limonos Kalloni, Lesbos
Religious Art Museum
Icons; religious objects; gold
embroidery; folk art; carvings;
manuscripts; Byzantine and Muslim art

Kalymnos

06139
Archeological Museum
Palio Tapitouryion, Kalymnos
Archeology Museum
Neolithic and classical pottery;
classical and Roman sculpture;
inscriptions; old carpet maker's
workshop

06140
Vouvalina Museum
Kalymnos
Decorative Arts Museum
Handicrafts; interiors; copies of
19th-20th century paintings

Kamena Vurla

06141
Karanassos Collection
Kamena Vurla
Archeology Museum
Archaic and classical pottery; bronze
objects; coins

Kardamlyi

06142
Archeological Collection
Mourdzinos Tower, Kardamlyi,
Messenia
Archeology Museum
Archaic and classical sculpture,
fragments; prehistoric and Hellenistic
pottery; folk art; woodcarvings; 17th
century tower

Karditsa

06143
Folklore Museum Karditsa Folklore
Society
Town Hall, Karditsa
General Museum
Local costumes; weaving; embroidery;
woodcarving; folk art

06144
Rendina Monastery
Karditsa
Religious Art Museum
Post-Byzantine icons

Karpenision

06145
Proussou Monastery
Karpenision
Religious Art Museum
Icons; vestments; silver; crosses;
bound gospels; manuscripts

06146
Tatarna Monastery
Karpenision
Religious Art Museum
Icons; 13th century mosaic icon; gold
embroidery; religious objects;
carvings; manuscripts; documents

Karystos

06147
Archaeological Museum Yiokaleion
Foundation
Karystos, (Euboea)
Archeology Museum
Hellenistic and Roman reliefs, pottery

Kastelli Kisamou

06148
Archaeological Museum
Main Sq, Kastelli Kisamou, Crete
Archeology Museum
Greek and Roman sculpture,
fragments, pottery, spears, coins; early
Christian inscriptions

Kastellorizon

06149
Archeological Museum
Mosque, Kastellorizon
Archeology Museum
Hellenistic and Roman sculpture,
pottery, inscriptions; costumes,
weaving, embroidery, Greek
handicraft

Kastoria

06150
Archaeological Collection
Girl's Orphanage, Kastoria
Archeology Museum
Prehistoric vases; Roman reliefs;
Byzantine and post-Byzantine icons;
woodcarvings; handicraft

Kavalla

06151
Archeological Museum
Kavalla
Archeology Museum
Late Neolithic and Bronze Age pottery
and figurines; architectural fragments
from the temple of the Parthonos at
Neapolis (5th century B.C.); classical,
Hellenistic and Roman sculpture,
pottery; statuettes from the archaic to
Roman periods; part of the 3rd century
B.C. tomb from Amphipolis with wall
paintings and painted stelae; gold
jewelry and wreaths; gilded and
painted terra cotta ornaments;
Hellenistic and Roman bronze utensils
and vases, coins, inscriptions, mosaic
floors

06152
Kavalla Metropolis Collection
Bishop's Palace, Kavalla
Religious Art Museum
Post-Byzantine icons

Kilkis

06153
Archaeological Museum
Kilkis
Archeology Museum
Archaic Kouros; reliefs, portraits,
inscriptions, small finds, mainly Roman

Kissos

06154
Agia Marina Collection
Kissos, Pilion
Religious Art Museum
Post-Byzantine icons; religious
objects; books

Kolymbary

06155
Gonias Monastery
Kolymbary, Crete
Religious Art Museum
Religious objects; vestments;
post-Byzantine icons; documents;
manuscripts

Komotini

06156
Archeological Museum of Komotini
Symeonidou 4, Komotini, Rhodope
Archeology Museum
Prehistoric vases and tools; sculpture
from the archaic to early Christian
periods; grave stelae; gold head of
Septimius Severus; Klazomenian type
sarcophagus - library

06157
Ecclesiastical Museum
Mitropolitou Anthimou St,
Ioakeimideion Boy's Orphanage,
Komotini, Rhodope
Religious Art Museum
Icons; gold embroidery;
woodcarvings; post-Byzantine pottery;
silver

06158
Folklore Museum of Thrace
8 Kouloglou St, Komotini, Rhodope
Decorative Arts Museum
Costumes; silver; woodcarvings;
embroidery; bronze utensils;
handicrafts

Kos

06159
Archaeological Museum
Eleutherias Sq, Kos
Archeology Museum
Prehistoric pottery and figurines;
classical, Hellenistic and Roman
sculpture and pottery; Hellenistic
mosaic floor; inscriptions

06160
Archeological Collection
Platanos Sq, Kos, Dodecanese
Archeology Museum
Classical and early Christian
sculptures; Hellenistic, Roman, early
Christian and Byzantine inscriptions

06161
**Folk Art Museum of the Metropolis
of Kos**
Bishop's Palace, Kos, Dodecanese
Decorative Arts Museum
Post-Byzantine icons; embroidery;
weaving; woodcarvings; pottery

Kosmiti

06162
Archeological Collection
Kosmiti, Xanthe
Archeology Museum
Roman sculpture

Kozani

06163
Archeological Collection
Main Sq, Public Library, Kozani
Archeology Museum
Bronze and Iron Age, Greek,
Hellenistic and Roman pottery,
armaments, reliefs, frescoe and mosaic
fragments; woodcarvings;
post-Byzantine icons; early Christian
art; handicrafts, memorabilia on Ali
Pasha; maps

Lachanas

06164
Museum
Lachanas
General Museum
Costumes; armaments; memorabilia on
the Balkan Wars

Lamia

06165
Archeological Collection
Municipal Library, Prefecture Offices,
Lamia
Archeology Museum
Mycenaean and Roman pottery; 4th
century sculptures from Echinos;
classical, Hellenistic and Roman
sculptures

06166
Kounoupis Collection
17 Myronos St, Lamia, Phthiotis
Archeology Museum
Ancient pottery, sculpture; folk art;
jewelry; armaments

06167
Platis Collection
5 Diovouniotou St, Lamia, Phthiotis
Archeology Museum
Classical pottery

Larissa

06168
Archeological Museum
2 Triakostis Protis Avgoustou St,
Larissa
Archeology Museum - 1960
Paleolithic and Neolithic finds; menhir;
archaic, classical and Hellenistic grave
stelae

06169
Folklore Museum of Larissa
Larissa
General Museum
Ethnography

06170
Gouriotis Collection
23 Kouma St, Larissa
Decorative Arts Museum - 1960
Mother-of-pearl objects;
post-Byzantine jewelry, silver, icons

06171
Katsigras Collection
Plateia Riga Fereou, Larissa
Fine Arts Museum
Greek paintings

06172
Stelios Papanikolaou Collection
Cyprou St 32, Larissa
Archeology Museum - 1958
Neolithic figurines, tools and jewels -
library

Leukas

06173
Archeological Collection
Municipal Library, Leukas, Ionian
Islands
Archeology Museum
Early Helladic finds from Nydri;
classical, Hellenistic and Roman
sculpture, vases, statuettes, relief terra
cotta plaques

06174
**Collection of Ecclesiastical Paintings
and Relics of Orthodoxy**
Municipal Library, Leukas, Ionian
Islands
Religious Art Museum
Icons; religious objects; gospels

Liknades

06175
Archeological Collection
Primary School, Liknades, Kozani
Archeology Museum
Prehistoric tools; fragments; classical,
Hellenistic and Roman pottery; coins

Limenaria

06176
Papageorgiou Collection
Papageorgiou Hotel, Limenaria, Thasos
Archeology Museum
Statuettes; vases; Greek and Roman
metalwork; coins; weaving and
embroidery

Lindos

06177
Archeological Collection
Papakonstandinou Mansion, Lindos,
Rhodes
Archeology Museum
Classical and Hellenistic sculpture;
inscriptions

06178
Georgiou Collection
Lindos, Rhodes
Decorative Arts Museum
Traditional pottery

06179
Ioannidis Collection
Lindos, Rhodes
Decorative Arts Museum
Ornamental plates

06180
Kaskines Collection
Lindos, Rhodes
Decorative Arts Museum
Traditional pottery

Lixourion

06181
Archeological Collection
Iakovateios Public Library, Lixourion,
Kefallinia
Archeology Museum
Classical and Hellenistic pottery; icons

Loutra Aidhipsou

06182
Archeological Collection
Town Hall, Loutra Aidhipsou, Euboea
Archeology Museum
Roman sculptures and inscriptions

Lykosoura

06183
Archeological Museum
Despoina sanctuary, Lykosoura
Archeology Museum
Fragments of Despoina and Demeter
statues (2nd century B.C.);
architectural fragments; inscriptions

Mandraki

06184
Archeological Collection
Town Hall and Primary School,
Mandraki, Nisyros
Archeology Museum
Hellenistic and Roman sculpture,
pottery, inscriptions; 18th-19th century
icons

Maroneia

06185
Archaeological Collection
Primary School, Maroneia
Archeology Museum
Prehistoric cave finds; neolithic and
early Helladic vases and tools;
classical, Hellenistic and Roman
sculpture and inscriptions

Mavradzei

06186
Timios Stavros Monastery
Mavradzei, Samos
Religious Art Museum
Religious objects; manuscripts; books

Mavromation

06187
Archeological Collection
Mavromation, Messenia
Archeology Museum
Finds from Messene excavations;
Hellenistic and Roman sculpture;
architectural fragments; inscriptions

Mavropigi

06188
Archeological Collection
Primary School, Mavropigi, Kozani
Archeology Museum
Hellenistic and Roman vases; coins

Megara

06189
Archeological Collection
Megara
Archeology Museum
Classical and Roman sculpture;
pottery

Mesolongion

06190
**Art Gallery of the Municipality and
Town of Mesolongion**
Town Hall, Mesolongion, Aetolia and
Acarnania
Fine Arts Museum
19th-20th century Greek and foreign
paintings; lithographs

Meteora

06191
Agion Panton Church Museum
Varlaam Monastery
Meteora, Trikkala
Religious Art Museum
Icons; manuscripts; religious objects;
embroidery; woodcarvings; frescoes -
library

06192
Agios Stephanos Monastery
Meteora
Religious Art Museum
Icons; religious objects; embroidery;
woodcarving

06193
Metamorphosis Church Museum
Meteoron Monastery
Meteora, Trikkala
Religious Art Museum - 1965
Byzantine and post-Byzantine art;
manuscripts; letters of emperors
(Chryssovula); icons; sacred
vestments; utensils and covers;
wood-carved crosses; frescoes

Metsovon

06194
Museum of Epirot Folk Art
Metsovon
Anthropology Museum
Icons; furnishings; woodcarvings;
household objects; armaments; Baron
Tositsa foundation

Mikonos

06195
Archeological Museum
Mikonos
Archeology Museum
Protogeometric, geometric, archaic,
classical pottery and statuettes;
Hellenistic and Roman sculpture;
bronze vessels; inscriptions

06196
Mikonos Folklore Museum
Mikonos
General Museum - 1958
Folkloristic and historic items of the
area of Mikonos and the sea; windmill
in operation - library

Mirina

06197
Archeological Museum
Mirina, Limnos
Archeology Museum
Prehistoric finds from Polyochni
excavations; figurines; Etruscan vases;
Roman sculpture; bronzes;
inscriptions

Mistra

06198
Museum
Metropolis, Mistra, Laconia
Archeology Museum
Fragments of frescoes and sculptures;
pottery; jewelry; metalwork; coins; late
Byzantine (Palaeologue) inscriptions

Mitilini

06199
Archeological Museum
Eftalioti and Ogdois Noemvriou Sts,
Mitilini, Lesbos
Archeology Museum - 1900
Protohelladic, helladic, archaic and
classical pottery; Aeolic capitals from
the temple of Klopedi (6th c. BC);
classical, Hellenistic and Roman
sculpture, mosaic floor, inscriptions;
Byzantine icons and pottery;
hand-carved chests

06200
Binos Colletion
2 Harilaou Trikoupi St, Mitilini, Lesbos
Decorative Arts Museum
Carved chests; embroideries

06201
National Folk Museum of Lesbos
Mitilini, Lesbos
Anthropology Museum
Pottery; embroidery and lace;
woodcarvings; metalwork; Byzantine
and post-Byzantine manuscripts and
documents

06202
Nikou Collection
19 Vyronos St, Mitilini, Lesbos
Decorative Arts Museum
Carved chests

06203
Vlachos Collection
6 Mitropoleos St, Mitilini, Lesbos
Decorative Arts Museum
Carved chests; weaving; embroidery;
metalwork

Molyvos

06204
Archeological Collection
Mayor's Residence, Molyvos, Lesbos
Archeology Museum
Hellenistic and Roman sculpture and
pottery; coins

Monemvasia

06205
Archeological Collection
Mosque, Monemvasia
Archeology Museum
Byzantine and Frankish sculptures

Nauplia

06206
Archeological Museum
Plateia Syntagmatos, Nauplia, Argolis
Archeology Museum
Prehistoric finds; Helladic pottery;
Midea menhirs; frescoe and tablet
fragments; grave stelae from
Mycenae; fragments from Atreus,
Dendra; geometric pottery; statuettes;
jewelry; small finds

06207
Folklore Museum of Nauplia
Nauplia, Argolis
Anthropology Museum
Ethnography

Navpaktos

06208
Archeological Collection
Library, Navpaktos, Aetolia and
Acarnania
Archeology Museum
Classical and Roman sculpture;
inscriptions

Naxos

06209
Archeological Museum
Naxos
Archeology Museum
Prehistoric finds; Mycenaean
weapons; decorative objects; Roman
sculpture; geometric and archaic
pottery; Byzantine icons

Nea Anchialos

06210
Archeological Collection
Nea Anchialos, Magnesia
Archeology Museum
Architectural fragments; sculptures;
early Christian pottery; Roman gold
jewelry; ruins of Thebes

Nea Moni

06211
Nea Moni Monastery
Nea Moni, Chios
Religious Art Museum
Religious objects; gold embroidery;
mosaics; 11th century monastery

Neapolis

06212
Archeological Collection
Kosti Adosidi Pasha St, Neapolis,
Crete
Archeology Museum
Prehistoric stone and earthenware
vessels, figurines and small finds;
Roman sculpture, inscriptions, coins;
Byzantine and Venetian sculpture;
Byzantine gospel manuscript

Nemea

06213
Archeological Collection
Nemea, Corinth
Archeology Museum
Sculptures, fragments and inscriptions
from Zeus' sanctuary; Roman
bathhouse

Neos Skopos

06214
Archeological Collection
Primary School, Neos Skopos, Serrai
Archeology Museum
Hellenistic and Roman vases and
statuettes

Nikopolis

06215
Archeological Collection
Nikopolis, Preveza
Open Air Museum
Ruins of the Roman and early
Christian city; Roman sculpture,
architectural fragments, inscriptions

Oinoussai

06216
Nautical Museum
Oinoussai
Fine Arts Museum
Ships; paintings, mostly by A. Glykas

Olimbos

06217
Archeological Collection
Olimbos, Karpathos, Dodecanese
Archeology Museum
Classical and early Christian sculpture;
lamps

Olympia

06218
New Archeological Museum
Olympia, Peloponnese
Archeology Museum
Finds from the Bronze Age; reliefs;
terra cota; Greek sculpture; early
classical bronze; mosaics; vases

06219
Old Archeological Museum
Olympia, Peloponnese
Archeology Museum - 1886
Mycenaean finds; geometric and
archaic bronzes; bronze votive
offerings; statues from Zeus' temple;
architectural fragments; pre-classical
terra cottas; Roman sculpture

Oreoi

06220
Archeological Collection
Village Hall, Oreoi, Euboea
Archeology Museum
Classical sculpture; classical and
Hellenistic pottery

Palaiochora

06221
**Archeological Museum of
Somothraki**
Palaiochora, Evros
Archeology Museum
Archaic, classical and Hellenistic
sculpture, architectural fragments;
reconstructed sanctuary (Bronze Age,
7th-6th c. B.C.); classical and
Hellenistic pottery; votive offerings;
decorative and household objects
relating to the worship of Cabires;
Hellenistic and Roman grave finds,
coins, inscriptions; Byzantine pottery,
bronze

Paramythia

06222
Archeological Collection
Paramythia, Preveza
Archeology Museum
Roman architectural fragments and
inscriptions; small classical and Roman
finds

Parga

06223
**Church of the Holy Apostles
Collection**
Parga, Preveza
Religious Art Museum
Local history relics; religious objects;
17th-18th century vestments; bound
gospels; manuscripts

Paros

06224
Archeological Museum
Paros, Cyclades
Archeology Museum
Neolithic and Cycladic vases and
figurines; archaic, classical and Roman
sculpture, pottery, statuettes and
inscriptions; Roman mosaic floors
from Katapoliani

06225
Byzantine Museum of Katapoliani
Paros, Cyclades
Religious Art Museum
Post-Byzantine icons, vestments and
religious objects; Byzantine sculpture

Patmos

06226
St. John the Divine Monastery
Patmos, Patmos
Religious Art Museum
Byzantine and post-Byzantine icons;
vestments; embroidery; religious
objects; Byzantine manuscripts; old
books

Patras

06227
Archeological Museum
42 Mezonos St, Patras, Peloponnese
Archeology Museum - 1936
Roman copies (gold ivory statue of
Athena Panthenos of Pheidias);
Mycenaean pottery; classical
sculptures; decorative and household
objects; weapons

Pella

06228
Archeological Museum of Pella
Pella, Macedonia
Archeology Museum - 1973
Finds from Pella excavations; classical
and Hellenistic bronze and marble
sculpture, architectural fragments,
pottery, jewelry, small finds, mosaic
floors, inscriptions

Perachora

06229
Perachora Museum
Perachora, Corinth
Archeology Museum - 1962
Corinthian pottery and bronzes from
the excavations of the Heraion
sanctuary

Petra

06230
Eleftheriadis Collection
Petra, Lesbos
Anthropology Museum
Paintings by the folk artist T.
Hadjimichail; folk art pottery;
metalwork

Piraeus

06231
Archeological Museum
38 Filellinon St, Piraeus, Attica
Archeology Museum
5th-4th century B.C. funerary and
votive reliefs; Hellenistic and Roman
sculpture; classical pottery; bronze
statuettes; small finds; coins

06232
Naval Museum of Greece
Freattys Bay, Akti Themistokleous,
Piraeus, Attica
History/Public Affairs Museum - 1949
Ship models; battle relics; Greek
maritime life; maps; documents;
memorabilia; part of the ancient murals
incorporated into the building - library;
multi screen projection system

Plaka

06233
Archeological Museum
Plaka, Milos
Archeology Museum
Cycladic vases, figurines and obsidian
blades; Greek and Roman sculpture,
pottery and inscriptions

Pogoniani

06234
Folklore Museum Society of Epirote
Studies
Pogoniani, Ioannina
Anthropology Museum
Ethnography

Polygyros

06235
Archeological Museum
Polygyros, Chalcidice
Archeology Museum
Classical and Hellenistic sculpture and
vases

06236
Lambropoulos Collection
Polygyros, Chalcidice
Archeology Museum - 1932
Athenian black- and redfigured vases,
golden ornaments, bronzes; Hellenistic
and Byzantine pottery, terra cotta

Pylos

06237
**Antonopouleion Archeological
Museum**
Pylos, Messenia
Archeology Museum
Mycenean pottery; bath made of
earthenware; gold vases and jewelry;
Hellenistic pottery and glassware form
Tsopani Rakhi and Yalova excavations;
Roman bronze statues, engravings
collected by René Pyaux

Pyrgos

06238
Kardamitsis Collection
Pyrgos, Tenos
Decorative Arts Museum
Decorative arts; crafts

06239
Kechrovuni Monastery Museum
Pyrgos, Tenos
Religious Art Museum
Post-Byzantine icons

06240
Nomikos Collection
Pyrgos, Thira
Decorative Arts Museum
19th century weavings; embroidery;
metalwork; paintings; porcelain

06241
Profitis Ilias Monastery
Pyrgos, Thira
Religious Art Museum
Post-Byzantine icons; religious
objects; carved wooden crosses;
vestments; books; firmans; bound
gospels

Pythagoreion

06242
Archeological Collection
Village Hall, Pythagoreion, Samos
Archeology Museum
Archaic and Roman sculpture;
architectural fragments; inscriptions

Rethymnon

06243
Archeological Museum
Arkadiou and Konstantinou
Paleologou Sts, Rethymnon, Crete
Archeology Museum
Sub-neolithic and Mycenean vases;
Minoan figurines, sarcophagi,
sealstones, amulets; Egyptian scarabs
and Minoan double-headed axes;
Greek and Roman sculpture;
red-figure and Hellenistic pottery;
votive plaques, bronze statuettes,
mirrors, glass vessels; Byzantine and
Venetian reliefs, coins, inscriptions

06244
Arkadi Monastery Collection
Rethymnon, Crete
Religious Art Museum
Fragments; post-Byzantine icons;
religious art objects; weapons;
woodcarvings; gold embroidery; relics
of revolts

06245
Likion Ton Ellinidon Collection
Prokymea El. Venizelou, Rethymnon,
Crete
Decorative Arts Museum
Decorative arts; crafts; embroidery;
folk art pottery

06246
Preveli Monastery
Rethymnon, Crete
Religious Art Museum - 15th century
Post-Byzantine icons; religious
objects; vestments

Rhodos

06247
Archeological Museum
Hospitals of the Knights, Rhodos
Archeology Museum - 1440
Ancient sculpture, ancient pottery from
Ialysos and Camiros from the
geometric to late classical periods;
votive and sepulchral altars;
inscriptions; small objects; weapons,
stelae, tombstones and other objects
from the medieval Period of the
Knights; Christian mosaics; classical
sepulchral relief; portrait of the comic
poet Menander - library

06248
Decorative Arts Collection
Agyrokastrou Sq, Old Town, Rhodos
Decorative Arts Museum - 1965
Handicrafts; carved chests; carvings;
embroidery; pottery; glass

06249
Palace of the Grand Masters
Kleoboulos Sq, Old Town, Rhodos
History/Public Affairs Museum - 1940
European furniture, tapestries; Roman
and early Christian mosaics from Kos,
Karpathos and Rhodes; early Christian
pieces of architecture; 14th century
palace

Salamis

06250
Archeological Museum
Salamis
Archeology Museum
Classical grave reliefs; Mycenaean
pottery, statuettes, grave sculptures,
inscriptions

Salonica

06251
Paralis Collection
Salonica
Anthropology Museum
Contemporary Greek folk pottery

Salonika

06252
Archeological Collection University
of Salonika, Faculty of Philosophy
Salonika
Archeology Museum
Pottery; statuettes

06253
Archeological Museum
Salonika
Archeology Museum
Neolithic-Iron Age pottery, weapons
and jewelry; archaic, classical,
Hellenistic and Roman sculpture,
architectural fragments, vases,
statuettes, bronzes; Roman mosaic
floors, glass; mosaic from Serrai;
Byzantine enamelled bracelets; coins

06254
City Gallery
YMCA Bldg, Salonika
Fine Arts Museum

06255
**Folklore and Ethnology Museum of
Macedonia**
Vasilissis Olgas 68, Salonika
Anthropology Museum - 1970
Folk art costumes; embroidery;
jewelry; copperware; woodcarvings;
tools; housewares - library

06256
Folklore Museum and Archives
University of Salonika, Faculty of
Philosophy
Salonika
Anthropology Museum - 1926
Woodcarvings; embroidery; weaving;
metalwork; pottery

06257
Kyriazopoulos Collection
11 Vassileos Konstantinou Av,
Salonika
Decorative Arts Museum
Decorative arts and crafts;
contemporary Greek folk pottery,
mainly by M. Arramidis

06258
Papailiakis Collection
14 Venizelou St, Salonika
Archeology Museum
Ancient sculpture

06259
Vassiliou Collection
6 Paraskevopoulou St, Salonika
Archeology Museum
Ancient pottery, bronze, coins, jewelry;
icons

Samos

06260
Archeological Museum
Samos
Archeology Museum
Finds from excavations at Heraion;
archaic, classical and Roman
sculpture; Cypriot statuettes and
vases; Egyptian and Assyrian
statuettes and utensils; geometric and
archaic bronze, ivory and wooden
figurines, utensils and pottery

06261
Byzantine Museum Metropolis of
Samos and Ikaria
Bishop's Palace, Samos
Religious Art Museum
Post-Byzantine icons; vestments;
religious objects; books

Samothraki

06262
Archeological Museum
Palaiopolis, Samothraki, Evros
Archeology Museum - 1939
Architecture, sculpture, pottery and
glass from the Sanctuary of the Great
Gods in Samothraki and from other
sites on the island

Serrai

06263
Archeological Collection
Bezesteni, Serrai
Archeology Museum
Hellenistic and Roman sculpture; in a
15th-16th century Turkish building

06264
Folklore Museum of New Petra
Serrai
General Museum
Ethnography

Siatista

06265
Archeological Collection
Gymnasium, Siatista
Archeology Museum
Pottery, stone tools, weapons, bronze
and iron ornaments from prehistoric to
Roman times

Sicyon

06266
Archeological Museum
Sicyon
Archeology Museum
Archaic, Hellenistic and Roman
sculpture, terra cotta; architectural
fragments from Artemis' temple;
pottery; statuettes; 4th century B.C.
mosaic floor; early Christian and
Byzantine sculpture; Roman
bathhouse among ancient city ruins

Sikinos

06267
Archeological Collection
Primary School, Sikinos, Cyclades
Archeology Museum
Reliefs and inscriptions

Siphnos

06268
Archeological Collection
Church of St. Antony at Kastro,
Siphnos, Cyclades
Archeology Museum
Hellenistic and Roman sculpture;
archaic statuettes and vases

Skiathos

06269
**Monastery of the Evangelismos Tis
Theotokou**
Agallianos, Mt Karafildzanakas,
Skiathos, Sporades
Religious Art Museum
Post-Byzantine icons; religious
objects; glassware; porcelain; books;
documents; bulls; firmans

Skopelos

06270
Monastery of the Evangelistria
Skopelos, Sporades
Religious Art Museum
Post-Byzantine icons; religious
objects; embroidery

Skyros

06271
Archeological Museum
Skyros, Sporades
Archeology Museum
Helladic and Mycenaean pottery;
protogeometric vases, sculpture;
Roman and Byzantine reliefs and
inscriptions, reconstructed local
interior

06272
Folklore Museum of Skyros
Skyros, Sporades
General Museum
Ethnography

Sparta

06273
Agii Saranda Monastery
Sparta, Peleponnese
Religious Art Museum
Post-Byzantine icons; religious
objects; vestments; bulls

06274
Archeological Museum
Sparta, Peloponnesus
Archeology Museum
Neolithic pottery; tools and jewelry
from caves of Alepotrypa and Pyrgos
tou Dirou; Menelaion and Mycenaean
tomb finds; archaic, classical,
Hellenistic and Roman sculpture;
geometric and archaic pottery; terra
cotta fragments; votive offerings and
archaic votive masks

06275
**Metropolis of Monemvassia and
Sparti Collection**
Bishop's Palace, Sparta, Peloponnese
Religious Art Museum
Post-Byzantine icons; carved wooden
crosses

Spetsai

06276
Museum
Hadjiyannis Mexis Mansion, Spetsai
General Museum
Maritime History; flag of the 1821
revolution; paintings on ships;
memorabilia; documents on leading
families; Roman, Christian sculpture;
post-Byzantine icons; embroidery;
costumes; folk art; pottery

Stavros

06277
Archaeological Museum
Stavros, (Ithaki)
Archeology Museum
Helladic, Mycenaean, geometric and
Corinthian pottery; bronze fragments

Steiri

06278
Monastery of Ossios Loukas
Steiri, Boothia
Religious Art Museum
11th century mosaics and frescoes;
icons; vestments; religious objects;
Byzantine monastery

Symi

06279
Archeological Collection
Symi, Dodecanese
Archeology Museum
Hellenistic and Roman sculpture and
inscriptions; Byzantine and
post-Byzantine sculpture and icons;
folk art woodcarvings; weaving;
silverware; metalwork; pottery

Tanagra

06280
Archeological Collection
Tanagra, Boothia
Archeology Museum
Archaic-Byzantine sculpture; terra
cotta; architectural fragments;
inscriptions; pottery

Tegea

06281
Archaeological Museum
Tegea, Arcadia
Archeology Museum
Prehistoric pottery from Asea,
Ayiorghitika; sculpture, mainly from
Athena temple; classical pottery;
Hellenistic statuettes and small bronze
votive offerings

Telos

06282
Archeological Collection
Village Hall, Telos
Archeology Museum
Classical and Hellenistic sculpture;
inscriptions

Tenos

06283
Archeological Museum
Tenos
Archeology Museum
Archaic and classical sculpture;
geometric pottery; inscriptions

06284
Byzantine Museum
Church of the Panagia Evangelistria,
Tenos
Religious Art Museum
Post-Byzantine icons

06285
Papadopoulos Gallery
Church of the Panagia Evangelistria,
Tenos
Fine Arts Museum
Modern Greek paintings by K.
Volanakis, K. Parthenis; copies of
Renaissance paintings

06286
Sohos Museum
Church of the Panagia Evangelistria,
Tenos
Fine Arts Museum
Sculptures by A. Sohos

Thasos

06287
Archeological Museum
Thasos
Archeology Museum
Archaic, classical, Hellenistic and
Roman sculpture; bronze and terra
cotta statuettes; archaic and classical
pottery and lamps, reliefs, jewelry,
coins, inscriptions; ancient city ruins

Thebes

06288
Archeological Museum
Threpsiadi St 1, Thebes, Boothia
Archeology Museum - 1962
Archaic sculpture from Ptoion; archaic
and classical pottery from Ritsona and
Acraiphia; Mycenaean finds from
Thebes; Anatolian cylinder seals -
library

06289
Archeological Museum
1 Threpsiadi St, Thebes
Archeology Museum
Helladic pottery, clay sarcophagi;
Mycenaean finds from Cadmeia,
vases, bronze articles, weapons, ivory
relief plaques, fragments of a throne,
gold jewelry, cylinder seals, linear
tablets; archaic, classical, Hellenistic,
Roman, early Christian and Byzantine
sculpture, stelae; geometric, archaic
and classical pottery, terra cotta and
bronze statuettes, inscriptions, mosaic
floor

Thermos

06290
Archeological Museum
Thermos, Greater Athens
Archeology Museum
Painted terra cotta metopes from the
Apollo temple; architectural fragments,
tiles; Mycenaean, archaic, Hellenistic
pottery, inscriptions

Thespiae

06291
Archeological Collection
Village Hall, Thespiae, Boothia
Archeology Museum
Archaic-Roman sculpture; architectural
fragments; inscriptions

Thira

06292
Archeological Museum
Thira, Cyclades
Archeology Museum - 1962
Prehistoric pottery; archaic, classical,
geometric, Hellenistic and Roman
sculpture and pottery; Roman glass,
lamps, inscriptions

06293
Thira Ecclesiastical Museum
Bishop's Palace, Thira, Cyclades
Religious Art Museum
Icons; carved wooden crosses

Thyrreion

06294
Archaeological Museum
Thyrreion
Archeology Museum
Classical, Hellenistic and Roman
sculpture; architectural fragments and
inscriptions; Roman mosaic floor

Traïanoupolis

06295
Archaeological Collection
Traïanoupolis, Loutros
Archeology Museum
Roman reliefs and inscriptions;
Byzantine architectural fragments;
medieval reliefs; Roman building

Trikkala

06296
Agios Vissarion Monastery
Trikkala
Religious Art Museum
Post-Byzantine icons, religious objects,
embroidery, books, documents

06297
Archeological Collection
Trikkala
Archeology Museum
Classical and Hellenistic sculpture,
stelae and statuettes; Byzantine and
post-Byzantine pottery

06298
**Ecclesiastical Museum of the
Metropolitan of Trikki and Stagoi**
Bishop's Palace, Trikkala
Religious Art Museum
16th-18th century icons, embroidery,
religious objects, woodcarvings

Vathy

06299
Archeological Museum
Vathy, Ithaca
Archeology Museum
Proto-Corinthian and Corinthian
pottery; small bronze articles from Mt.
Athos

Veroia

06300
Archeological Museum
47 Anixeos St, Veroia
Archeology Museum - 1971
Neolithic, Bronze Age and Iron Age
finds; geometric, classical, Hellenistic,
Roman and Byzantine pottery;
Hellenistic and Roman sculpture;
Greek and Roman inscriptions, coins;
Byzantine and post-Byzantine icons;
documents - library

Vitsa

06301
Folklore Museum Society of Epirote
Studies
Vitsa, Zagori
Anthropology Museum
Ethnography

Volos

06302
**Athanassakeion Archeological
Museum**
1 Athanssaki St, Volos
Archeology Museum
Paleolithic, mesolithic and neolithic
finds; neolithic and Bronze Age
pottery, figurines, bone and stone
tools; archaic, classical, Hellenistic and
Roman sculpture; 3rd-2nd century B.C.
Dimitrias stelae; geometrical and
classical pottery, grave finds, glass,
coins

06303
Bastis Collection
112 Gallias St, Volos
Archeology Museum
Neolithic figurines, tools, jewelry

06304
Makris Collection
22 Afendouli St, Volos
Anthropology Museum
Folk murals; Greek paintings, carvings,
weaving, jewelry, utensils, miniatures

06305
Municipal Art Gallery
Ogl and Orpheos Sts, Volos
Fine Arts Museum
Modern Greek art

06306
Sefel Collection
Pef Kakia, Volos
Archeology Museum
Geometric vases; bronze statuettes

Xanthe

06307
Folklore Museum
Philoproödos Enossis Xanthis, Xanthe
Anthropology Museum
Costumes; embroidery

06308
Metropolitan of Xanthe Collection
Bishop's Palace, Xanthe
Religious Art Museum
Icons; manuscripts

Ypati

06309
Agathonos Monastery Collection
Ypati
Religious Art Museum
Post-Byzantine icons; vestments;
religious objects; carved wooden
crosses; 18th-19th century religious
books

Zakinthos

06310
Byzantine Museum
Solomou Sq, Zakinthos
Fine Arts Museum
Frescoes; post-Byzantine icons;
paintings of the Heptanesian School;
woodcarvings; Hellenistic and
Byzantine sculpture; coats of arms

06311
Solomos Museum
Eleftherias Sq, Zakinthos
General Museum
Memorabilia of Th. Solomos; famous
19th cent. residents; costumes;
armaments

Guadeloupe

Pointe-à-Pitre

06312
Musée L'Herminer
27 rue Sadi-Carnet, Pointe-à-Pitre
Natural History Museum
Coll: natural history; ichthyology;
history of Guadeloupe

Guatemala

Antigua

06313
Museo Colonial
3a Av. Sur y Calle de la Universidad,
Antigua
Fine Arts Museum - 1951
period furniture; paintings; sculpture

06314
Museo de Santiago Portal Municipal
Plaza Mayor de Antigua, Antigua
General Museum - 1956
history; furniture; armaments; colonial
art

06315
Museo del Libro Antiguo Portal
Municipal
Plaza Mayor de Antigua, Antigua
General Museum - 1956
history of Guatemala

Chichicastenango

06316
Museo Regional
Plaza Central, Chichicastenango
Anthropology Museum
history; crafts of Maya-Quiché tribes

Ciudad de Guatemala

06317
**Museo Nacional de Arqueologia y
Etnologia**
Zona 13, Ciudad de Guatemala
Archeology Museum
Mayan and other archaeological finds;
ethnography

06318
**Museo Nacional de Artes e
Industrias Populares**
Av. 10 No. 10-70, Ciudad de Guatemala
Anthropology Museum
wood crafts; costumes

06319
Museo Nacional de Historia Natural
6A Calle 7-30, Zona 12, Apdo. 987,
Ciudad de Guatemala
Natural History Museum
botany; zoology; geology - library

06320
**Museo Nacional de Historia y Bellas
Artes**
Edificio No. 6 'La Aurora', Zona 13,
Ciudad de Guatemala
General Museum
art; history; furniture; numismatics

06321
**Museo Nacional y Zoologico 'La
Aurora'**
Apdo. 1120, Ciudad de Guatemala
Natural History Museum
botany; zoology

Guinea

Beyla

06322
Musée Regional de Beyla (Institut
National de Recherches et de
Documentation de la Guineé)
Beyla
General Museum
ethnology; prehistory; art

Conakry

06323
Musée Botanique Institut
polytechnique de Conakry
BP 1147, Conakry
Natural History Museum
botany

06324
Musée Géologique Institut
polytechnique de Conakry
BP 1147, Conakry
Natural History Museum
geology

06325
Musée National de Conakry
BP 561, Conakry
General Museum - 1960
prehistory; ethnology; art; fetishes;
masks of the 'Forêt Sacrée'

Kissidougou

06326
Musée Annexe de Kissidougou
(Institut National de Recherches et de
Documentation de la Guinée)
Kissidougou
General Museum
prehistory; ethnology; art; masks;
fetishes

Koundara

06327
**Musée Fédérale Annexe de
Koundara**
Koundara
Anthropology Museum
ethnology; ethnography collections of
the Coniagui and Bassare tribes

N'Zerekore

06328
Musée Annexe (Institut National de
Recherches et de Documentation de
la Guinée)
BP 114, N'Zerekore
General Museum
art; ethnography; botany; zoology;
tattoo instruments; pipes carved out of
stone

Youkounkoun

06329
Musée Annexe de Youkounkoun
(Institut National de Recherches et de
Documentation de la Guinée)
Youkounkoun, Région adm. de
Koundara
General Museum
prehistory; ethnology; art;
ethnographical collection of the
Koundara region

Guinea-Bissau

Bissau

06330
Musée da Guine Portugesa
Praca do Império, CP 37, Bissau
General Museum
Ethnographical exhibits

Guyana

Georgetown

06331
Guyana Museum
North Street, POB 1026, Georgetown
General Museum - 1853
art; history; archaeology;
anthropology; zoology; industry -
library

Haiti

Port-au-Price

06332
Musee National d'Haiti
Turgeau, Port-au-Price
General Museum - 1938
art; history; numismatics; armaments

Port-au-Prince

06333
Musee du Peuple Haitien
Cité de l'Exposition, Port-au-Prince
Anthropology Museum
folklore

06334
Port-au-Prince
Rue de la Révolution, Port-au-Prince
Fine Arts Museum
Haitian art

Honduras

Ciudad de Copán

06335
**Museo Regional de Arqueologia
Maya**
Ciudad de Copán
Archeology Museum - 1939
important relics of Mayan civilization;
ceramics; stone sculptures; jade;
obsidian; Mayan handicraft; human
bones

Comayagua

06336
**Museo Regional de Arqueologia y
Colonial**
Comayagua
General Museum - 1946
Ceramics; sculptures; jade; colonial art
and furniture; numismatics

Omoa

06337
Museo Nacional de Historia Colonial
Castillo de San Fernando de Omoa,
Omoa
History/Public Affairs Museum
colonial and historical items, in former
prison

Tegucigalpa

06338
**Museo Historico 'Miguel Paz
Baraona'** Aldea de Pinalejo
Municipio de Quimistan, Tegucigalpa
General Museum - 1953
archaeology; colonial history;
contemporary art; memorabilia of the
president Dr. Miguel Paz Baraona

Hong Kong

Hong Kong

06339
Fung Ping Shan Museum University
of Hong Kong
Fung Ping Shan Bldg, 94 Bonham Rd,
Hong Kong
Fine Arts Museum - 1953
Chinese ceramics, bronzes, sculpture
and painting

06340
Hong Kong Museum of Art
City Hall, Edinburgh Place, Hong Kong
Fine Arts Museum - 1962
Chinese ceramics; Guandong painting
and calligraphy; contemporary local
art; early Chinese bronzes and later
metal ware; Chinese textiles and
costumes; Chinese minor arts and folk
art

Kowloon

06341
The Hong Kong Museum of History
4th Fl, Star House, Salisbury Rd,
Kowloon
History/Public Affairs Museum - 1975
Local history; Fr.D. Finn archaeological
collection; Fr.R. Maglioni
archaeological collection; ethnography
and natural history

06342
Hong Kong Space Museum
Salisbury Rd, Tsim Sha Tsui, Kowloon
Science/Tech Museum - 1980
Graphics, exhibits, models, and
displays concerning astronomy and
space science; Mercury capsule;
space suit - planetarium, library

Hungary

Abony

06343
Abonyi Lajos Falumúzeum
Zalka Máté u. 17, H Abony
General Museum - 1959
Coll: local history

Aszód

06344
Petőfi Múzeum
Szontágh lépcsö 2, H-2170 Aszód
History/Public Affairs Museum - 1958
Coll: literature - library

Badacsony

06345
Egry József Emlékmúzeum (József
Egry Memorial Museum)
Egry József sétány 12, H-8261
Badacsony
Historic Site - 1973
Coll: life and work of the Balaton
landscape painter József Egry
(1883-1951)

06346
Irodalmi Emlékmúzeum
137-138 hrsz, H-8261 Badacsony
Historic Site - 1952
Coll: life and work of the poet Sándor
Kisfaludy (1772-1884); manuscripts;
works by modern poets on the Lake
Balaton area

Baja

06347
Türr István Múzeum
Deák Ferenc u. 1, POB 55, H-6501
Baja
General Museum - 1935
Coll: archeology; ethnography;
modern Hungarian painting - library

Balassagyarmat

06348
Palócmúzeum
Palóc liget 1, H-2660 Balassagyarmat
General Museum - 1891
Coll: local folk art; shepherd's art;
costumes; toys; folk musical
instruments - library

Balatonfüred

06349
Jókai Emlékmúzeum (Mór Jókai
Memorial Museum)
Honvéd u. 20, H-8230 Balatonfüred
Historic Site
Coll: bequest of the writer Mór Jókai
(1825-1904) in his former summer
residence

Balatonszárszó

06350
József Attila Emlékmúzeum (Attila
József Memorial Museum)
József Attila u. 7, H-8624
Balatonszárszó
Historic Site - 1957
Coll: life and work of the poet Attila
József (1905-1937) in his last home;
manuscripts; books; works by modern
painters

Balatonszemes

06351
Postamúzeum
Bajcsy-Zsilinszky u. 46, H-8636
Balatonszemes
History/Public Affairs Museum - 1962
Coll: research and documentation
institute and permanent exhibition of
the history of post and
telecommunications - library

Balmazujváros

06352
Helytörténeti Múzeum
Debreceni u. 1, H-4060 Balmazujváros
General Museum - 1972
Coll: local history; memorial exhibition
on life and work of Péter Veres
(1897-1970), famous Hungarian
peasant writer - library

Barcs

06353
Dráva Múzeum
Széchenyi u. 22, H-7570 Barcs
General Museum - 1979
Coll: archeology; ethnography; natural
sciences

Békés

06354
Jantyik Mátyás Múzeum
Szechenyi tér 6, H-5630 Békés
General Museum - 1938
Coll: history; ethnography - library

Békéscsaba

06355
Munkácsy Mihály Múzeum (Mihály
Mukácsy Memorial Museum)
Scéchenyi u. 9, POB 46, H-5601
Békéscsaba
Historic Site - 1899
Coll: archeology; regional
ethnography; works by the painter
Mihály Munkácsy (1844-1900), modern
Hungarian paintings and graphics;
open air Slovakian ethnographic
collection - library

Berettyóujfalu

06356
Bihari Múzeum
Kossuth u. 36, H-4100 Berettyóujfalu
General Museum - 1970
Coll: history; ethnography; literature -
library

Budapest

06357
Ady Endre Emlékmúzeum (Endre Ady
Memorial Museum)
Veres Pálné u. 4-6.I., H-1053 Budapest
Historic Site - 1977
Coll: life and work of the poet Endre
Ady (1877-1919) in his last home;
manuscripts; books; furnishings

06358
Aquincumi Múzeum Budapesti
Történeti Múzeum
Szentendrei út 139, H-1031 Budapest
Archeology Museum - 1887
Coll: remains of the Roman camp;
stone; glass; mosaics; jewelry;

06359
Arany Sas Patika
Tárnok u. 18, H-1014 Budapest
History/Public Affairs Museum - 1966
Coll: pharmacy building from the 18th
century with original furnishings

06360
Bajor Gizi Emlékmúzeum
Szinháztörténeti Múzeum (Gizi Bajor
Memorial Museum)
Stromfeld Aurél u. 16, H-1124
Budapest
Performing Arts Museum - 1952
Coll: bequests by Hungarian actors;
memorabilia; costumes; documents;
posters

06361
Batók Emlékház (Béla Batók
Memorial Museum)
Csalán u. 29, H-1025 Budapest
Historic Site
Coll: life and work of the Hungarian
composer Béla Bartók (1881-1945)

06362
Bélyegmúzeum
Hársfa u. 47, POB 86, H-1400
Budapest
History/Public Affairs Museum - 1930
Coll: ca. 9 million Hungarian and
foreign stamps; first day covers;
postmarks - library

06363
Budapesti Történeti Múzeum
(Historical Museum of Budapest)
Szt. György tér 2, H-1014 Budapest
History/Public Affairs Museum - 1887
Coll: relics of the thousand-year-old
Hungarian capital; archeology; history
of Buda Castle - library

06364
**Budavári Mátyás Templom
Egyházművészeti Gyűjteménye**
(Matthias Church History Collection)
Szentháromság tér 2, H-1014
Budapest
Religious Art Museum - 1964
Coll: applied art; documents; religious
art

06365
**Dunamelléki Református
Egyházkerület Ráday Múzeuma**
Ráday u. 28, H-1092 Budapest
Religious Art Museum - 1967
Coll: religious art collection in the
Library of Ráday - library

06366
Evangelikus Országos Múzeum
Deák tér 4, H-1052 Budapest
Religious Art Museum - 1973
Coll: religious art exhibition in a former
Evangelical school

06367
Földalatti Vasúti Múzeum A
Közlekedési Múzeum és a BKV
Kiállítóhelye (Underground Transport
Museum)
Deák téri aluljáró, H-1052 Budapest
Science/Tech Museum - 1975
Coll: urban transport collections;
underground building

06368
**Hopp Ferenc Keletázsiai Művészeti
Múzeum** Iparművészeti Múzeum
(Hopp Museum of Eastern Asiatic
Arts)
Népköztársaság utja 103, H-1062
Budapest
Fine Arts Museum - 1919
library

06369
Húsipari Múzeum
Gubacsi ut 6/b, H-1097 Budapest
Science/Tech Museum - 1972
History of the meat industry - library

06370
Iparművészeti Múzeum (Museum of
Applied Arts)
Üllői ut 33-37, POB 4, H-1450 Budapest
Decorative Arts Museum
Decorative arts and crafts; applied
arts; ivory works; bookbinding;
furnishings; textiles; metalworks;
ceramics; jewelry - library;
educational department

06371
Kassák Lajos Emlékmúzeum (Lajos
Kassák Memorial Museum)
Fő tér 1, H-1033 Budapest
Historic Site - 1976
Life and work, memorabilia of the
artist, writer and painter Lajos Kassák
(1887-1967); exhibition in the Zichy-
castle - library

06372
Kina Múzeum Iparművészeti Múzeum
(Chinese Museum)
Gorkij fasor 12, H-1086 Budapest
Fine Arts Museum - 1955
Coll: Chinese art and culture

06373
Kiscelli Múzeum
Kiscelli u. 108, H-1037 Budapest
History/Public Affairs Museum - 1887
Coll: local contemporary history; art
collection of Budapest

06374
Kispesti Helytörténeti Gyűjtemény
Ady Endre u. 57, H-1196 Budapest
History/Public Affairs Museum - 1958
Coll: local history - library

06375
Közlekedési Múzeum (Transport
Museum)
Városligeti 11, H-1146 Budapest
Science/Tech Museum - 1896
Coll: railway transportation; models;
old vehicles; nautical and aeronautical
transportation; roads and bridge
construction - library

06376
Magyar Építészeti Múzeum
(Hungarian Museum of Architecture)
Táncsics u. 1, H-1014 Budapest
History/Public Affairs Museum - 1968
Coll: history of the Hungarian
architecture; bequest of famous
Hungarian architects - library

06377
**Magyar Kereskedelmi és
Vendéglátóipari Múzeum** (Hungarian
Museum of Commerce and Tourism)
Fortuna u. 4, H-1014 Budapest
History/Public Affairs Museum - 1966
Coll: subjects of sales and services,
particulary in tourism, hotels and
hostelry; cuisine; coffee houses;
confectionary; documents; photos

06378
Magyar Mezőgazdasági Múzeum
(Hungarian Agricultural Museum)
Vajdahunyadvár, Városliget, H-1146
Budapest
Agriculture Museum - 1896
Coll: history of agriculture in Hungary;
documents; objects; models - library

06379
Magyar Munkásmozgalmi Múzeum
Budavári Palota A épület (Museum of
Hungarian Labour Movement)
Szent György tér 2, H-1014 Budapest
History/Public Affairs Museum
Coll: history of the labour movement in
Hungary since the Revolution of 1848
- library

06380
Magyar Nemzeti Múzeum (Hungarian
National Museum)
Múzeum krt. 14-16, H-1088 Budapest
General Museum - 1802
Coll: archeology; Roman finds;
medieval and contemporary history;
costumes; numismatics - library

06381
MagyarNemzeti Galéria (Hungarian
National Gallery)
Szent György tér 2, H-1014 Budapest
Fine Arts Museum
Coll: Hungarian paintings; sculptures;
medals; drawings; engravings; panel
paintings; baroque art - library

06382
Műcsarnok (Art Gallery)
Dózsa György út 36, H-1134 Budapest
Fine Arts Museum - 1896
Coll: temporary exhibition of
Hungarian and foreign art

06383
Nagytétényi Kastélymúzeum
Iparművészeti Múzeum (Castle
Museum of Nagytétény)
Csókási Pál u. 9, H-1225 Budapest
Decorative Arts Museum - 1951
15th-17th century European furniture;
18th-19th century Hungarian furniture;
stoves; Roman finds; pottery

06384
Néprajzi Múzeum (Ethnographical Museum)
Kossuth Lajos tér 12, H-1055 Budapest
Anthropology Museum - 1872
Coll: ethnography; collections and research activities cover peasant and tribal folk cultures; costumes; textiles; musical instruments; crafts - library

06385
Óbudai Helytörténeti Gyüjtemény
Fő tér 1, H-1033 Budapest
History/Public Affairs Museum - 1973
Coll: local history; ethnography; history of the labour movement

06386
Öntödei Múzeum (Foundry Museum)
Bem József u. 20, H-1027 Budapest
Science/Tech Museum - 1969
Coll: 19th century original foundry equipment; history of technological development of foundry trade; old mouldings - library

06387
Országos Hadtörténeti Múzeum (Military History Museum)
Tóth Árpád sétány 40, POB 7, H-1014 Budapest
History/Public Affairs Museum - 1919
Hungary military history; arms; documents; models; flags; uniforms; medals - library; educational department

06388
Országos Műszaki Múzeum (National Museum of Science and Technology)
Kaposvár u. 13-15, H-1112 Budapest
Science/Tech Museum - 1954
Coll: natural sciences and technology; historic exhibits from the early days of industry and its development to the present

06389
Országos Pedagógiai Múzeum és Könyvtár
Honvéd u. 15, H-1055 Budapest
History/Public Affairs Museum
Coll: history of pedagogy and education; documents; manuscripts; social sciences - library

06390
Országos Zsidó Vallási és Történeti Gyüjtemény (Museum of Jewish Religion and History)
Dohány u. 2, H-1077 Budapest
Religious Art Museum - 1916
Coll: jewish art; applied art; documents

06391
Pesterzsébeti Múzeum
Kossuth u. 39, H-1203 Budapest
History/Public Affairs Museum - 1951
Coll: local history - library

06392
Petőfi Irodalmi Múzeum (Petöfi Museum of Hungarian Literature)
Károlyi u. 16, H-1053 Budapest
History/Public Affairs Museum
Hungarian literary history; paintings; portraits; manuscripts - library; educational department

06393
Postamúzeum (Postal Museum)
Népköztársaság utja 3, H-1061 Budapest
History/Public Affairs Museum - 1954
History of post and telecommunication - library·

06394
Semmelweis Orvostörténeti Múzeum (Semmelweis Medical History Museum)
Apród u. 1-3, H-1013 Budapest
Natural History Museum - 1965
Coll: history of medicine; pharmacology - library, educational department

06395
Szépművészeti Múzeum (Museum of Fine Arts)
Dózsa György ut 41 24 POB 463, H-1134 Budapest
Fine Arts Museum - 1896
Coll: Egyptian and Greco-Roman antiquities; Hungarian and foreign old masters; sculptures; drawings; engravings; modern art - library;

06396
Szinháztörténeti Múzeum (Historical Museum of the Theatre)
Krisztina krt. 57, H-1016 Budapest
History/Public Affairs Museum - 1952
Coll: history of Hungarian theatre and stage; scenery; costumes - library

06397
Táborvárosi Múzeum
Korvin Ottó u. 63-65, H-1032 Budapest
Archeology Museum - 1953
Coll: Roman finds; Roman military camp

06398
Természettudományi Múzeum (Hungarian Natural History Museum)
Baross u. 13 24 POB 37, H-1088 Budapest
Natural History Museum - 1870
Coll: mineralogy; petrography; geology; paleontology; botany; zoology; mammals; fossils; anthropology; - library, educational department

06399
Testnevelési és Sportmúzeum (Museum of Physical Education and Sports)
Dózsa György u. 3, H-1143 Budapest
History/Public Affairs Museum - 1955
Coll: relics of sports and physical education

06400
Textilipari Múzeum (Museum of Textile Industry)
Rajk László u. 59/63, H-1133 Budapest
Science/Tech Museum - 1972
Coll: history of the textile industry in Hungary

06401
Tűzoltó Múzeum (Fire Brigade Museum)
Martinovics tér 12, H-1105 Budapest
History/Public Affairs Museum - 1955
fire-fighting equipment; pumps and hoses; universal and Hungarian history of fire protection, its means and organization - library

06402
Zenetörténeti Múzeum
Országház u. 9, H-1014 Budapest
Music Museum - 1969
Coll: music; musical instruments; life and work of Hungarian musicians; bequest of Béla Bartók (1881-1945) and Zoltán Kodály (1882-1967)

Cegléd

06403
Kossuth Múzeum
Marx u. 5, POB 32, H-2701 Cegléd
General Museum - 1917
Coll: ethnography; archeology; art; memorabilia on the revolutionary leader Lajos Kossuth (1802-1894) - library

Csongrád

06404
Csongrádi Múzeum
Iskola u. 2, H-6640 Csongrád
General Museum - 1956
archeology; local history; navigational artifacts; ethnography

Debrecen

06405
Déri Múzeum
Déri tér 1, POB 61, H-4001 Debrecen
General Museum - 1902
Coll: ethnography; archeology; local history; modern art; oriental art

06406
Református Kollégiumi és Egyházművészeti Múzeum
Kálvin tér 16, H-4000 Debrecen
Religious Art Museum - 1963
Coll: religious art; applied art; documents of the Reformed Church in Hungary and history of education

Dunaföldvár

06407
Vármúzeum
Rátkai köz 2, H-7020 Dunaföldvár
History/Public Affairs Museum
Coll: relics of medieval Dunaföldvár castle

Dunaújváros

06408
Intercisa Múzeum
Lenin tér 10, H-2400 Dunaújváros
General Museum - 1951
Coll: prehistoric, Roman and medieval archeology, modern paintings; lapidarium; ethnography - library

Eger

06409
Dobó István Vármúzeum
Vár u. 1, POB 1, H-3301 Eger
General Museum - 1872
Coll: archeology; history of Eger Castle, ethnography; relics of the Turkish invasion in Hungary; baroque art; natural history; memorabilia, life and work of the writer Géza Gárdonyi (1863-1922) - library, educational department

Esztergom

06410
Balassa Bálint Múzeum
Bajcsy-Zsilinszky ut. 28, POB 19, H-2500 Esztergom
History/Public Affairs Museum - 1894
Coll: archeology; numismatics; applied art; history - library

06411
Keresztény Múzeum (Christian Museum)
Berényi Zsigmond u. 2, H-2500 Esztergom
Religious Art Museum - 1875
Coll: Dutch, French, German, Italian medieval paintings; gold; silver; decorative arts - library

06412
Magyar Vizügyi Múzeum
Kölcsey u. 2, H-2500 Esztergom
Science/Tech Museum - 1973
Coll: history of water conservation - library

06413
Vármúzeum
Bajcsy-Zsilinszky u. 63, H-2500 Esztergom
History/Public Affairs Museum - 1967
Coll: excavated and reconstructed royal palace from the times of the Hungarian House of the Arpáds; municipal history of Esztergom, a royal seat in the Middle Ages - library

Fertőd

06414
Kastélymúzeum
Bartók Béla u. 2, H-9431 Fertőd
History/Public Affairs Museum - 1959
Coll: historical castle of the Eszterházy family; local documents; furnishings; applied art; memorabilia on Joseph Haydn (1732-1802)

Győr

06415
Xantus János Múzeum
Széchenyi tér 5, POB 93, H-9o22 Győr
General Museum - 1858
Coll: relics of the ancient town Arrabona; art; archeology; ethnography; numismatics; history of industry; modern art collection from works of Miklós Borsos (1899-), sculptor and painter - library

Gyoma

06416
Kner Nyomdaipari Múzeum
Kossuth u. 16, H-5500 Gyoma
History/Public Affairs Museum - 1970
Coll: history of printing; printing press of the Kner family

Gyöngyös

06417
Mátra Múzeum
Kossuth u. 40, H-3200 Gyöngyös
General Museum
Coll: natural science; botany and zoology of the Mátra Mountains; ethnography; history of hunting - library

Gyula

06418
Erkel Ferenc Múzeum
Kossuth Lajos u. 15, H-5700 Gyula
General Museum - 1868
Coll: archeology; etnography; local history; art; memorial site for the Hungarian composer Ferenc Erkel (1810-1893) - library

06419
Kohán Múzeum
Béke sugárút 35, H-5701 Gyula
Historic Site - 1978
Coll: memorabilia, life and work of the painter György Kohán (1910-1966)

06420
Vármúzeum
Várfürdő, H-5700 Gyula
History/Public Affairs Museum
Coll: relics of medieval castle

Hajdúböszörmény

06421
Hajdusági Múzeum
Kossuth u. 1, H-4220
Hajdúböszörmény
General Museum - 1924
Coll: archeology; ethnography; local
history ; art; primitive paintings -
library

Hajduszoboszló

06422
Bocskai István Múzeum
Vöröshadsereg u. 2, H-4200
Hajduszoboszló
History/Public Affairs Museum - 1960
Local history; ethnography - library

Herend

06423
Porcelánmúzeum
Kossuth u. 140, H-8200 Herend
Science/Tech Museum - 1964
Coll: exhibits from the famous china
factory, est. 1826; history of the
industry; applied art

Hódmezővásárhely

06424
Tornyai János Múzeum
Szántó Kovács János u. 16-18, POB 2,
H-6801 Hódmezővásárhely
General Museum - 1904
Coll: archeology; ethnography; folk
art; paintings by János Tornyai
(1869-1958); sculptures by Ferenc
Medgyessy (1881-1958); modern
Hungarian art - library

Jászberény

06425
Jász Múzeum
Táncsics Mihály u. 5, POB 30, H-5101
Jászberény
General Museum - 1873
Archeology; ethnography; local history
- library

Kalocsa

06426
Visky Károly Múzeum
I. István u. 25, H-6300 Kalocsa
General Museum
Ethnography; natural sciences; folk art
- library

Kápolnásnyék

06427
Vörösmarty Emlékmúzeum
Vörösmarty u., H-7475 Kápolnásnyék
Historic Site - 1950
Coll: 18th. century baroque building,
birthplace of the poet Mihály
Vörösmarty (1800-1855)

Kaposvár

06428
Rippl-Rónai Múzeum
Rippl-Rónai tér 1, POB 70, H-7401
Kaposvár
General Museum - 1909
Archeology; ethnography; local
history; paintings and memorabilia on
József Rippl-Rónai (1861-1927),
modern Hungarian painter - library

Kapuvár

06429
Rábaközi Múzeum
Fő tér 1, H-9330 Kapuvár
General Museum - 1960
Coll: ethnography; local history; art;
memorabilia and collection of Pál
Pátzay (1896-1979) - library

Karcag

06430
Győrffy István Nagykun Múzeum
Kálvin u. 4, POB 8, H-5301 Karcag
General Museum - 1952
Coll: ethnography; history - library

Kecskemét

06431
Katona József Múzeum
Bethlen város 75, POB 6, H-6001
Kecskemét
General Museum - 1894
Coll: archeology; ethnography;
modern Hungarian art; memorabilia on
the dramatist József Katona
(1901-1930) - library

06432
Naiv Művészek Múzeuma
Kada Elek u. 11, H-6000 Kecskemét
Fine Arts Museum - 1974
Coll: primitive art collection in an 18th
century building

Keszthely

06433
Balatoni Múzeum
Múzeum u. 2, H-8361 Keszthely
General Museum - 1898
Coll: archeology; ethnography of the
Lake Balaton area; anthropology;
archeobotany; numismatics - library

06434
Georgikon Majormúzeum
Bercsényi u. 67, H-8360 Keszthely
Agriculture Museum - 1979
Coll: history of agriculture; farm
implements in a 18th century building

06435
Helikon Kastélymúzeum
Szabadság u. 1, H-8360 Keszthely
History/Public Affairs Museum - 1979
Coll: 18th century castle of the
Festetich family

Kiskőrös

06436
Petőfi Emlékmúzeum
Petőfi tér 1, H-6200 Kiskőrös
History/Public Affairs Museum - 1951
Coll: memorabilia on the poet Sándor
Petőfi (1823-1849); ethnographical
collection of Slovakia - library

Kiskunfélegyháza

06437
Kiskun Múzeum
Vörös Hadsereg u. 9, H-6100
Kiskunfélegyháza
General Museum - 1902
Ethnography; archeology; history; life
and work of the writer Ferenc Móra -
library

Kiskunhalas

06438
Thorma János Múzeum
Köztársaság, H-6400 Kiskunhalas
General Museum - 1874
Coll: ethnography; archaeology;
applied art; lace collection; local
history - library

Kisnána

06439
Várrom és Népi Műemlék
Béke u. 22, H-3269 Kisnána
History/Public Affairs Museum - 1968
Coll: relics of the medieval castle
Kisnána; historical peasant house

Kisvárda

06440
Vármúzeum
Vár u. 30, H-4600 Kisvárda
General Museum - 1960
Coll: ethnography; local history -
library

Kőszeg

06441
Jurisich Miklós Múzeum
Jurisich tér 6, H-9730 Kőszeg
History/Public Affairs Museum - 1932
Local history; archeology;
ethnography; applied art - library

Makó

06442
Expersit Ház
Kazinczy u. 6, H-6900 Makó
General Museum
Coll: local history; Hungarian literature;
exhibition about the poet Attila József
(1905-1937)

Martonvásár

06443
Beethoven Emlékmúzeum
Székesfehérvár 14-129, H-2462
Martonvásár
History/Public Affairs Museum
18th-19th century castle of the
Brunswick family, where the famous
composer Ludwig van Beethoven
(1770-1827) lived and worked

Mátészalka

06444
Szathmári Múzeum
Hősök tere 8, H-4700 Mátészalka
History/Public Affairs Museum - 1972
Ethnography; local history - library

Mezőkövesd

06445
Matyó Múzeum
Béke tér 20, H-3400 Mezőkövesd
History/Public Affairs Museum - 1952
ethnography; folk art; local history -
library

Miskolc

06446
Borsod-Miskolci Múzeum
Department of modern history of
HOM
Kossuth u. 13, H-3501 Miskolc
History/Public Affairs Museum - 1980
Coll: contemporary history

06447
Diósgyőri Vármúzeum
Vár u. 24, H-3534 Miskolc
History/Public Affairs Museum - 1968
Coll: relics of a medieval castle

06448
Herman Ottó Múzeum
Felszabadítók útja 28, H-3501 Miskolc
General Museum - 1899
Archeology; ethnography; local
history; modern art collection;
paintings; drawing history;
numismatics - library

06449
Központi Kohászati Múzeum (Central
Foundry Museum)
Palota u. 22, H-3517 Miskolc Lillafüred
Science/Tech Museum - 1949
Archeological foundry of the 9th-10th
century; 18th century foundry - library

Mohács

06450
Kanizsai Dorotthya Múzeum
Szerb u. 2, H-7700 Mohács
General Museum - 1923
Ethnography; relics from the Turkish
invasion in Hungary; history - library

Monok

06451
Kossuth Lajos Emlékmúzeum
Magyar Nemzeti Múzeum
Kossuth u. 18, H-3905 Monok
Historic Site - 1949
Birthplace of the revolutionary leader
Lajos Kossuth (1802-1894); local
history - library

Mosonmagyaróvár

06452
Hansági Múzeum
Lenin u. 121, H-9200
Mosonmagyaróvár
General Museum - 1882
Coll: archeology; 17th-18th century
prints, 19th century paintings,
lapidarium; local history - library

Nagycenk

06453
Széchenyi Emlékmúzeum (Széchenyi
Memorial Museum)
Kiscenki u. 5, H-9485 Nagycenk
Historic Site - 1973
Coll: history of the Széchenyi family
and life of 19th century statesman
Count István Széchenyi (1790-1860) in
his family castle; development of
Hungarian transportation

Nagykanizsa

06454
Thury György Múzeum
Szabadság tér 11, H-8801
Nagykanizsa
General Museum - 1919
Coll: ethnography; archeology ; local
history - library

Nagykőrös

06455
Arany János Múzeum
Ceglédi u. 19, H-2751 Nagykőrös
General Museum - 1928
Coll: archeology; ethnography; local
history; literary documents of the poet
János Arany (1817-1882) - library

Nagyvázsony

06456
Kinizsi Vármúzeum
Kinizsi u., H-8291 Nagyvázsony
History/Public Affairs Museum - 1956
Relics of a medieval castle

Nyírbátor

06457
Báthory István Múzeum
Károlyi u. 15, POB 28, H-4301
Nyírbátor
General Museum - 1955
Coll: archeology; ethnography; local
history; art - library

Nyíregyháza

06458
Jósa András Múzeum
Benczur tér 21, POB 57, H-4401
Nyíregyháza
General Museum - 1868
Coll: archeology; ethnography; local
history; art collection by the painter
Gyula Benczur (1844-1922); literary
documents of the writer Gyula Krudy
(1878-1933) - library

06459
Sóstói Múzeumfalu
Sóstó gyógyfürdő, H-4400
Nyíregyháza
General Museum - 1970
Peasant houses of the Szabolcs-
Szathmár district

Ópusztaszer

06460
Ópusztaszeri Nemzeti Emlékpark
H-6769 Ópusztaszer
History/Public Affairs Museum - 1970
13th century church and cloister;
cyrcorama by Árpád Feszty
(1856-1914) about the Hungarian
conquest

Orosháza

06461
Szántó Kovács Múzeum
Dózsa György u. 5, H-5900 Orosháza
General Museum - 1947
Coll: ethnography; folk art;
archeology; literary documents of the
writer József Darvas (1912-1973) -
library

Ózd

06462
Kohászati Gyártörténeti Múzeum
Alkotmány u. 6, H-3600 Ózd
Science/Tech Museum - 1971
Coll: science and technology; history
of the factory in Ózd; industrial
technology

Pannonhalma

06463
**Pannonhalmi Főapátság
Gyűjteménye**
Vár u. 1, H-9090 Pannonhalma
Religious Art Museum - 1803
Archeology; applied art; religious art;
numismatics

Pápa

06464
**Dunántúli Egyháztörténeti és
Egyházművészeti Múzeum**
Fő u. 6, H-8500 Pápa
Religious Art Museum - 1931
religious art; history of art

06465
Helytörténeti Múzeum
Fő tér. 1, H-8500 Pápa
General Museum - 1960
Coll: local history, archeology;
ethnography; art collection; 18th
century castle interior - library

06466
Kékfestő Múzeum
Március 15. tér. 12, H-8500 Pápa
Science/Tech Museum - 1962
Coll: old blue-dyeing workshop;
history of blue-dyeing

Pécs

06467
Csontváry Múzeum
Janus Pannonius u. 11, H-7621 Pécs
Fine Arts Museum - 1973
Coll: art; paintings by Tivadar Kosztka
Csontváry (1853-1919)

06468
Jakováli Hasszán Dzsámi (exhibition
of JPM)
Rákóczi u. 2, H-7623 Pécs
General Museum - 1975
Turkish mosque from 16th century;
relics from the period of Turkish
invasion

06469
Janus Pannonius Múzeum Múzeumi
Igazgatóság
Kulich Gyula u. 5, POB 158, Pécs
General Museum - 1904
Coll: archeology; ethnography; local
history; Hungarian art - library;
educational department

06470
Martyn Ferenc Gyűjtemény Janus
Pannonius Múzeum
Káptalan u. 6, H-7621 Pécs
Fine Arts Museum - 1979
Coll: modern art collection by Ferenc
Martyn (born 1899) in a historical
building

06471
Modern Magyar Képtár Janus
Pannonius Múzeum
Kulich Gyula u. 4, H-7601 Pécs
Fine Arts Museum - 1957
Coll: modern art

06472
Néprajzi Kiállítás Janus Pannonius
Múzeum (Ethnographical Department
of JPM)
Rákóczi u. 15, H-7621 Pécs
Anthropology Museum - 1950
Coll: local ethnographical exhibition

06473
Régészeti Kiállítás Janus Pannonius
Múzeum (Archeological Department of
JPM)
Széchenyi tér. 12, H-7621 Pécs
Archeology Museum
Coll: prehistoric archeology

06474
Reneszánsz Kőtár
Káptalan u. 2, H-7621 Pécs
Archeology Museum - 1972
Coll: archeology; Renaissance
lapidarium

06475
Román Kori Kőtár
Dóm tér., H-7621 Pécs
Archeology Museum - 1952
Coll: Roman stonework remains

06476
Természettudományi Kiállítás Janus
Pannonius Múzeum (Natural Sciences
Department of JPM)
Rákóczi u. 64, H-7622 Pécs
Science/Tech Museum - 1951
Coll: natural history

06477
Uitz Múzeum Janus Pannonius
Múzeum
Káptalan u. 4, H-7621 Pécs
Fine Arts Museum - 1978
Coll: art collection by Béla Uitz
(1887-1972)

06478
Vasarely Múzeum Janus Pannonius
Múzeum
Káptalan u. 3, H-7621 Pécs
Fine Arts Museum
Coll: works by Vasarely (Victor
Vásárhelyi, born 1908) in a historical
building

06479
Zsolnai Kerámia Kiállítás Janus
Pannonius Múzeum
Káptalan u. 2, H-7621 Pécs
Decorative Arts Museum - 1955
Coll: applied arts; ceramics

Rudabánya

06480
Érc és Ásványbányászati Múzeum
Petőfi u. 24, H Rudabánya
Science/Tech Museum - 1956
Coll: mining; history of the industry -
library

Salgótarján

06481
Munkásmozgalmi Múzeum
Nógrádi Sándor tér. 8, POB 3, H-3101
Salgótarján
General Museum - 1959
Coll: 19-20th century history of the
revolutionary miners' movement;
underground mining - library

Sárospatak

06482
Rákóczi Múzeum
Kádár Kata u. 21, H-3950 Sárospatak
General Museum - 1950
Coll: archeology; ethnography; 17-18th
century relics of the Rákóczi family;
20th century Hungarian art collection -
library

06483
**Római Katolikus Egyházi
Gyűjtemény**
Kádár Kata u. 17, H-3950 Sárospatak
Religious Art Museum - 1969
Coll: applied art; religious art

06484
**Tiszáninneni Református
Egyházkerület Múzeuma**
Rákóczi u. 1, H-3950 Sárospatak
History/Public Affairs Museum - 1970
Coll: history of the Sárospatak college;
old school equipment; religious art;
applied art; textiles

Sárvár

06485
Nádasdi Ferenc Múzeum
Vár u. 1, POB 1, H-9601 Sárvár
History/Public Affairs Museum
Coll: late Renaissance and baroque
Hungarian milieu, reconstructed in
state rooms of a 16th century castle;
ethnography; applied art - library

Siklós

06486
Vármúzeum
Vajda János tér, H-7800 Siklós
History/Public Affairs Museum - 1952
Coll: castle museum; applied art;
lapidarium; prison museum

Simontornya

06487
Vármúzeum
Vár tér 10, HU-7081 Simontornya
History/Public Affairs Museum - 1975
Coll: relics of a medieval castle;
lapidarium

Siófok

06488
**Beszédes József Vizgazdálkodási
Múzeum** Magyar Vizügyi Múzeum
Sióu. 2, H-8600 Siófok
Science/Tech Museum - 1962
Coll: history of Hungarian science and
technology

Sopron

06489
Fabricius Ház Liszt Ferenc Múzeum
Beloiannisz tér 6, H-9400 Sopron
Archeology Museum - 1963
Coll: archeology; in an 18th century
building

06490
Középkori ó- és Új Zsinagóga
Új u. 11 és Új u.22, H-9400 Sopron
Religious Art Museum - 1976
Coll: Jewish religious art and history

06491
Központi Bányászati Múzeum
Templom u. 2, H-9400 Sopron
Science/Tech Museum - 1957
History of Hungarian coal mining since
the 13th century - library

06492
Liszt Ferenc Múzeum
Május 1.tér, POB 68, H-9401 Sopron
General Museum - 1867
Coll: archeology; ethnography; crafts;
literary documents; 18-19th century
collection of local history; memorabilia
on the composer Franz Liszt
(1811-1886); pharmacy - library

06493
Pékmúzeum
Bécsi u. 5, H-9400 Sopron
History/Public Affairs Museum - 1975
Coll: local history; ethnography; old
baker's shop; relics of bakery

06494
Várostörténeti Kiállítás
Fő tér, H-9400 Sopron
History/Public Affairs Museum - 1973
Coll: local history exhibition

Sümeg

06495
Kisfaludy Emlékmúzeum
Kisfaludy tér 3, H-8330 Sümeg
Historic Site - 1913
Coll: literary historical documents on
the brother poets Károly (1788-1830)
and Sándor (1772-1844) Kisfaludy

06496
Vármúzeum
H-8330 Sümeg
History/Public Affairs Museum - 1972
Coll: relics of a medieval castle, local
history

Szarvas

06497
Tessedik Sámuel Múzeum
Vajda Péter u. 1, H-5540 Szarvas
General Museum - 1951
Coll: local history; ethnography;
archeology; old mill; Slovakian
ethnographic collection - library

Szécsény

06498
Kubinyi Ferenc Múzeum
Ady Endre u. 7, H-3170 Szécsény
General Museum - 1973
Coll: archeology; history; numismatics
- library

Szeged

06499
Fekete-Ház
Somogyi Béla u. 15, H-6720 Szeged
History/Public Affairs Museum
Coll: contemporary local history

06500
Móra Ferenc Múzeum
Roosevelt tér 3, POB 474, H-6720
Szeged
General Museum - 1883
Coll: archeology; ethnography; local
history; natural history; literary
collection; 20th century art; lapidarium
- library; educational department

Székesfehérvár

06501
Budenz-Ház István Király Múzeum
Arany János u. 12, H-8000
Székesfehérvár
Fine Arts Museum - 1968
Coll: 19-20th century art collection;
Ervin Ybl collection; 18th century
historic building

06502
Fekete Sas Patika
Március 15. u. 5, H-8000
Székesfehérvár
Historic Site - 1974
Coll: 18th century pharmacy

06503
István Király Múzeum
Gagarin tér 3, POB 12, H-8001
Székesfehérvár
General Museum - 1873
Coll: prehistoric, Roman and medieval
collection; anthropology; ethnography;
fragments from the Basilica of King
Stephen (975-1038); 20th century art;
applied art - library; educational
department

06504
Országos Aluminiumipari Múzeum
Zombori u. 12, H-8000 Székesfehérvár
Science/Tech Museum - 1971
Coll: history of the aluminium industry
- library

Szekszárd

06505
Babits Mihály Emlékház (Mihály
Babits Memorial Museum)
Babits u. 13, H-7100 Szekszárd
Historic Site - 1967
Life and work, memorabilia on the poet
Mihály Babits (1883-1941) in his
birthplace

06506
Balogh Ádám Múzeum
Mártírok tere 26, POB 44, H-7101
Szekszárd
General Museum - 1895
Coll: archeology; ethnography; literary
documents; applied art; art;
numismatics - library

Szenna

06507
Szabadtéri Néprajzi Gyűjtemény
Rákóczi u. 2, H-7477 Szenna
Open Air Museum - 1978
Coll: Hungarian peasant houses;
furniture; textiles of the Somogy
district

Szentendre

06508
Barcsay Gyűjtemény
Dumtsa Jenő u. 10, H-2000
Szentendre
Fine Arts Museum - 1977
Coll: modern art collection by Jenő
Barcsay (born 1900)

06509
Czóbel Múzeum
Templom tér 1, H-2000 Szentendre
Fine Arts Museum - 1975
Coll: life and work, paintings by Béla
Czóbel (1883-1975)

06510
Ferenczy Károly Múzeum
Marx tér 6, H-2000 Szentendre
General Museum - 1951
Archeology; ethnology; collection of
the Szentendre Art School; bequest
by the Ferenczy family; local history -
library; educational department

06511
**Görögkeleti Szerb Egyházművészeti
Gyűjtemény**
Engels u. 5, H-2000 Szentendre
Religious Art Museum - 1964
Coll: religious art; religious items of the
Eastern Church in Hungary

06512
Kovács Margit Kerámiagyűjtemény
Wastagh György u. 1, H-2000
Szentendre
Decorative Arts Museum - 1972
Applied art (ceramics) by Margit
Kovács (1902-1977); 18th century
historic building

06513
Szabadtéri Néprajzi Múzeum
Szabadság forrás, POB 125, H-2001
Szentendre
Open Air Museum - 1971
Coll: traditional Hungarian peasant
houses; furniture; farm implements -
library ; educational department

06514
Szentendrei Képtár
Marx u. 2-5, H-2000 Szentendre
Fine Arts Museum - 1977
Coll: modern art exhibition

Szentes

06515
Koszta József Múzeum
Alsórét 187, H-6000 Szentes
General Museum - 1894
Coll: archeology; ethnography; art
collection by the painter József Koszta
(1861-1949) - library

Szerencs

06516
Zempléni Múzeum
Rákóczi u. 109/a, H-3900 Szerencs
General Museum - 1977
Coll: ethnography; local history;
medieval castle - library

Szigetvár

06517
Zrinyi Miklós Vármúzeum
Vár u. 1, H-7900 Szigetvár
History/Public Affairs Museum - 1917
Coll: history of the Zrinyi family;
history collection from the period of
the Turkish invasion in the 16th
century

Szolnok

06518
Damjanich János Múzeum
Kossuth tér 4, 128, H-5001 Szolnok
General Museum - 1934
Coll: archeology; ethnography; local
history; collection of the Szolnok Art
School - library

06519
Szabadtéri Vizügyi Múzeum
Millér, H-5000 Szolnok
Open Air Museum - 1976
Coll: science and technology; water
conservation

Szombathely

06520
**Derkovits Gyula Emlékmúzeum, Dési
Huber Emlékmúzeum**
Vorosilov u. 4, H-9700 Szombathely
Historic Site - 1967; 1976
Collections of both painters Gyula
Derkovits (1894-1934) and István Dési
Huber (1895-1944)

06521
Forradalmi Múzeum Savaria Múzeum
Alkotmáni u. 2, POB 163, H-9701
Szombathely
History/Public Affairs Museum - 1970
Coll: labour movement history - library

06522
Savaria Múzeum
Kisfaludy Sándor u. 9, H-9700
Szombathely
General Museum - 1872
Coll: natural history; minerals;
archeology; Roman finds; Iseum;
medieval stonework; ethnography -
library; educational department

06523
Schmidt Múzeum Savaria Múzeum
Hollán Ernő, H-9700 Szombathely
General Museum - 1968
Coll: archeology; costumes; furniture;
applied art - library

06524
Vasi Múzeumfalu Savaria Múzeum
Árpád u. 30, H-9700 Szombathely
Open Air Museum - 1967
Coll: traditional peasant houses from
the Vas district

Tác

06525
Gorsium Szabadtéri Múzeum
Székesfehérvár, H-8121 Tác
Open Air Museum - 1963
Coll: lapidarium; relics of the Roman
town Gorsium

Tata

06526
**Görög-Római Szobormásolatok
Múzeuma**
Rákóczi u. 8 v. Zsinagóga, H-2892 Tata
Archeology Museum
Coll: copies of Greek and Roman
sculptures (7th century B.C.-2nd
century A.D.)

06527
Kunyi Domonkos Múzeum
Öregvár, POB 224, H-2892 Tata
General Museum - 1912
Coll: archeology; Roman frescoes;
local history; medieval stonework
remains; ceramics; ethnography -
library

Tatabánya

06528
**Munkásmozgalmi és Ipartörténeti
Múzeum**
Kossuth u. 10, H-2800 Tatabánya
History/Public Affairs Museum - 1971
Coll: contemporary history; history of
industry - library

Tihany

06529
Tihanyi Múzeum
Pisky sétány 1, H-8237 Tihany
History/Public Affairs Museum - 1955
Coll: local history; history of
bookbinding; Roman and medieval
lapidarium; ethnography; pottery
workshop

Tiszafüred

06530
Kiss Pál Múzeum
Kun Béla sétány 6, H-5358 Tiszafüred
History/Public Affairs Museum - 1977
Coll: local history; ethnography -
library

Turkeve

06531
Finta Múzeum
Attila u. 1, H-5231 Turkeve
History/Public Affairs Museum - 1951
Coll: bequest of the Finta brothers,
both sculptors (20th century)

Vác

06532
Vak Bottyán Múzeum
Múzeum u. 4, H-2600 Vác
General Museum - 1895
Coll: archeology; ethnography; local
history; fine arts; applied arts; - library

Vaja

06533
Vay Ádám Múzeum
Damjanich u. 75, H-4562 Vaja
General Museum - 1963
Coll: history of the Hungarian
revolutionary movement in the 18th
century; Renaissance castle; local
history; arts - library

Várpalota

06534
Magyar Vegyészeti Múzeum
(Chemical Museum)
Hősök tere 1, H-8100 Várpalota
Science/Tech Museum - 1963
Coll: history of the Hungarian chemical industry - library

Vásárosnamény

06535
Beregi Múzeum
Rákóczi ut 13, H-4800 Vásárosnamény
General Museum - 1965
Coll: local history; archeology; ethnography

Vértesszőllős

06536
Magyar Nemzeti Múzeum
Vértesszőllősi Őstelep (Magyar Nemzeti Múzeum)
H-2837 Vértesszőllős
Archeology Museum - 1968
Coll: prehistoric tools; archeology

Veszprém

06537
Bajcsy-Zsilinszky Emlékmúzeum
(Bajcsy-Zsilinszky Memorial Museum)
Kővágóörs-Pálköve, H-8254 Veszprém
Historic Site - 1966
Coll: memorial house for Endre Bajcsy-Zsilinszky (1886-1944), progressive Hungarian politician

06538
Bakonyi Múzeum
Lenin liget 5, POB 32, H-8201 Veszprém
General Museum - 1903
Coll: archeology; historical and ethnographical exhibits from the Bakony Mountains; natural history; fine arts; applied arts - library

Visegrád

06539
Mátyás Király Múzeum
Fő u. 27-29, H-2025 Visegrád
Archeology Museum - 1950
Coll: archeology; stonework remains; Renaissance palace; 13th century tower; 14th century fountain - library

Zala

06540
Zichy Mihály Emlékmúzeum
Zichy Mihály u. 20, H-8660 Zala
Historic Site - 1951
Coll: life, work and memorabilia on the painter Mihály Zichy (1827-1906)

Zalaegerszeg

06541
Göcseji Falumúzeum
Falumúzeum u. 5, H-8900 Zalaegerszeg
Open Air Museum - 1968
Coll: traditional peasant houses; interiors; church; mill from the Göcsej district

06542
Göcseji Múzeum
Batthyányi u. 2, H-8901 Zalaegerszeg
General Museum - 1949
Coll: archeology; ethnography; folk art; local history; art; sculptures collection of Zsigmond Kisfaludy-Stróbl (1884-1975) - library

06543
Magyar Olajipari Múzeum
Falumúzeum, H-8901 Zalaegerszeg
Open Air Museum - 1969
Development of the Hungarian oil industry; technology - library

Zebegény

06544
Szőnyi István Emlékmúzeum
Bartóky u. 7, H-2627 Zebegény
Historic Site - 1967
Coll: life, work and memorabilia on the painter István Szőnyi (1894-1960)

Zirc

06545
Bakonyi Természettudományi Gyűjtemény
Rákóczi tér 1, H-8420 Zirc
General Museum - 1972
Natural history of the Bakony Mountains area - library

Iceland

Akureyri

06546
Akureyri Museum of Natural History
Harnarstræti 81, POB 580 600 Akureyri
Natural History Museum - 1951
Icelandic and European flora; worldwide shell collection; Icelandic insects - library

Neskaupstadur

06547
Museum of Natural History
Mýrargötu 37, POB 34, Neskaupstadur
Natural History Museum - 1965

Reykjavik

06548
The Asmundar Sveinsson Gallery
Silfurtún, Reykjavik
Fine Arts Museum
Sculpture

06549
The Kjarvalsstadir Gallery
Flókagata, Reykjavik
Fine Arts Museum

06550
The Labour Union Gallery
Grensásvegi 16, Reykjavik
History/Public Affairs Museum

06551
Museum of Natural History
Laugavegi 105, POB 5320, Reykjavik
Natural History Museum
Botany and zoology; geology; invertebrates; molluscs; amphibians; reptiles; mammals; minerals - library

06552
The National Einar Jónsson Gallery
Vid Eiríksgötu, POB 1051, Reykjavik
Fine Arts Museum - 1923
Sculpture and painting by Einar Jónsson - library

06553
The National Film Archives
Skipholt 31, Reykjavik
Performing Arts Museum

06554
National Gallery of Iceland
Sudurgata, POB 688, Reykjavik
Fine Arts Museum
Twentieth century art; Markús Ivarsson collection; works by Gunnlaugur Scheving - library

06555
National Museum of Iceland
Sudurgata 41, POB 1439, Reykjavik
General Museum
library

Vestmannaeyjar

06556
Museum of Natural History
Heidavegi 12, Vestmannaeyjar
Natural History Museum - 1965
Invertebrates; fossils - aquarium

India

Ahmedabad

06557
Calico Museum of Textiles
Calico Mill Premises, outside Jamalpur Gate, POB 21, Ahmedabad, Gujarat 380022
Decorative Arts Museum - 1949
Representative collections of Indian textile heritage

06558
Gandhi Smarak Sangrahalaya
Harijan Ashram, Ahmedabad, Gujarat 380013
Historic Site - 1951
Coll: manuscripts of Gandhi's correspondence; books on Gandhiana; negatives of Gandhi, Kusturba and others; Gandhi's writing desk and spinning wheel; life size oil paintings of big and small enlargements of Gandhi

06559
Gujarat Museum Gujarat Museum Society
Culture Center, Kocharle, Ahmedabad, Gujarat
General Museum - 1961
Coll: archaeology; anthropology; ethnology; costumes; paintings including N. C. Metha collection of miniatures; science

06560
Museum of Gujarat Vidya Sabha and B.J. Institute
c/o B.J. Institute of Learning and Research, R.C. Marg, Ahmedabad, Gujarat 380009
History/Public Affairs Museum - 1961
Coll: manuscripts in Sanskrit, Prakrit, Hindi, Gujarati, Arabic, and Persian; coins; sculptures; replica and photographs of ancient monuments and sculptures; paintings; stone inscriptions; old documents

06561
Tribal Museum Tribal Research and Training Institute
Gujarat Vidyapith, Ahmedabad, Gujarat 380014
Anthropology Museum - 1964
Coll: equipment for food gathering, fishing, agriculture; costumes and ornaments; material culture of religion; musical instruments; games; dioramas; maps, paintings, charts and photographs relating to different tribes; Kircho (bamboo musical instruments); Mogradev (wooden crocodile gods); Hunvlo (domestic utensils) - library

Ahmednagar

06562
History Museum Ahmednagar College
Ahmednagar, Maharashtra
History/Public Affairs Museum - 1965
Coll: specimens of sculptures; coins; pottery; icons; photographs and drawings

Ajmer

06563
Government Museum
near Naya Bazar, Ajmer, Rajastan
General Museum - 1908
Archaeological objects

06564
Rajputana Museum
Ajmer, Rajastan
General Museum - 1908
Coll: inscriptions; coins; sculpture; paintings; arms and armoury

Alampur

06565
Archaeological Site Museum
Alampur, Andhra Pradesh, Mahaboob Nagar District 509152
Archeology Museum - 1953
Sculptures of Western Chalukyan and Kakatiya periods; inscriptions on stone

Aligarh

06566
University Museum of Science and Culture Aligarh Muslim University
Kennedy House, General Education Centre, Aligarh, Uttar Pradesh
General Museum - 1964
Coll: prehistory; sculptures; terra cottas; paintings; textiles; coins

Allahabad

06567
Allahabad Museum
Motilal Nehru Park, Allahabad, Uttar Pradesh
General Museum - 1931
Coll: stone sculptures; terra cottas; miniature paintings; modern Indian paintings; seals; sealings; coins; presents from Pt. Jawaharlal Nehru; miniature objects; handicrafts; manuscripts; arms and inscriptions

06568
Archeology Museum Allahabad University
Allahabad, Uttar Pradesh
Archeology Museum - 1949
Coll: prehistory; prehistoric tools from earliest times to the end of the Pleistocene together with fossils; Mesolithic tools; human and animal skeletons; Neolithic tools and other related antiquities; proto-historic material from different sites; collection from Ghositaram, the famous Buddhist monastery

06569
G.N. Jha Kendriya Sanskrit Vidyapeetha
Motilal Nehru Park, Allahabad, Uttar Pradesh
History/Public Affairs Museum - 1943
Coll: Sanskrit, Hindi, Arabic and Persian manuscripts

06570
Hindi Sangrahalaya
Hindi Sahitya Sammelan, Allahabad,
Uttar Pradesh
Religious Art Museum
Coll: printed books; periodicals;
manuscripts; coins; letters;
photographs; memoir trophies and
personal belongings of literary
personalities

06571
Zoology Department University of
Allahabad
Allahabad, Uttar Pradesh
Natural History Museum - 1910
Coll: different phyla of the animal
kingdom - such as stuffed, preserved,
dried specimens; articulated
skeletons; fossils; models; mounted
skeleton of an elephant, camel; stone
implements of prehistoric men; rare
fossils

Alwar

06572
Government Museum
Alwar, Rajastan
General Museum - 1941
Coll: arts and handicrafts; paintings;
armoury; musical instruments

Amaravati

06573
Archaeological Museum
Amaravati, Andhra Pradesh
Archeology Museum - 1951
Coll: Stupa-slabs; railings; sculpture;
inscriptions; coins of gold, silver and
lead

Amber

06574
Archaeological Museum
Amber, Rajastan
Archeology Museum - 1938

Amreli

06575
Shri Girdharbhai Sangrahalaya
(Children's Museum)
Amreli, Gujarat
Junior Museum - 1955
Educational exhibits

Amritsar

06576
Central Sikh Museum
Clock Tower Bldg, Golden Temple,
Amritsar, Punjab
Religious Art Museum - 1958
Coll: paintings regarding Sikh history;
relics of Sikh gurus; coins; old
manuscripts about Sikh history

Annamalai Nagar

06577
Zoology Museum Annamalai
University
Annamalai Nagar, Tamil Nadu 608101
Natural History Museum - 1929
South Indian representative
invertebrates and lower vertebrates;
systematics

Aundh

06578
Shri Bhavani Museum and Library
Aundh, Maharashtra, District Satara
Fine Arts Museum - 1938
Coll: painting ; woodcarvings; ivory
carvings; arms; textiles; statues -
library

Balasore

06579
Balasore Branch Museum
Balasore, Orissa
General Museum - 1976
Stone sculptures

Banda

06580
Bundelkhand Chhatrasal Museum
Banda, Uttar Pradesh
General Museum - 1955
Coll: sculptures; terra cottas; stone
implements; beads and seals; coins;
anthropological objects; natural
science section

Bangalore

06581
**Karnataka Government Museum and
Venkatappa Art Gallery**
Kasturba Rd, Bangalore, Karnataka
560001
Fine Arts Museum - 1866
Coll: antiquities from Mohenjodaro,
Brahmagiri, Chandravalli, and T. N. Pur;
terra cottas from East Bengal;
Hoysala, Dravidian, Chola, Chalukya
and Pala sculpture; miniature paintings
from North India; traditional paintings
from Mysore; ivory and ivory inlay
articles; sandalwood caskets;
geological specimens; mammals

06582
**Visvesvaraya Industrial and
Technological Museum**
C.S.I.R. Kasturba Rd, Bangalore,
Karnataka 560001
Science/Tech Museum - 1965
Developments in science and
technology and their application to
human welfare; scientific, technological
and industrial artifacts; working
models

Bareilly

06583
Abhai Smarak Panchal Sangrahalaya
125/5 Kishore Bldgs, Kishore Bazar,
Bareilly, Uttar Pradesh
General Museum - 1974
Coll: pottery; coins; terra cotta
figurines; beads; bone implements

Baripada

06584
Baripada Museum
Baripada, Orissa, District Mayurbhanj
Archeology Museum - 1903
Coll: palaeolithic and neolithic
implements; copper axe-head;
sculpture; historical documents; gold,
silver and copper coins; seals and
beads; terra cotta; stone inscriptions;
painted palm-leaf manuscripts

Baroda

06585
Maharaja Fatehsingh Museum
Laxmi Vilas Palace Compound, Baroda,
Gujarat
Fine Arts Museum - 1961
Coll: paintings; sculptures; Graeco-
Roman sculptures; Chinese and
Japanese art; European applied art

06586
Medical College Museum M.S.
University of Baroda
Baroda, Gujarat
Natural History Museum - 1949
Coll: maps, charts, models and
specimens of different branches of
medical science

06587
The Museum and Picture Gallery
Sayaji Park, Baroda
General Museum - 1894
Coll: European oil paintings; miniature
paintings; sculptures; textiles; crafts;
woodcarvings; Islamic art; Japanese
art; Chinese art; Nepal and Tibetan art;
Egyptian art; geology section; zoology;
anthropology; ethnology; Indian and
foreign coins - children's section

06588
**Museum of Archaeology, History and
Culture** Faculty of Arts, M.S.
University of Baroda
Baroda, Gujarat
History/Public Affairs Museum
Archaeological, historical and cultural
collections; exploration and excavation
materials from the early Stone Age to
the medieval period

Barrackpur

06589
Gandhi Smarak Sangrahalaya
14 Riverside Rd, Barrackpur, West
Bengal
Historic Site - 1961
Coll: photographs portraying Gandhi's
life; photocopied letters to Gandhi ;
press clippings, bulletins and tape
recordings

Basavakalyan

06590
Government Museum
Fort, Basavakalyan, Karnataka, District
Bidar
General Museum
Coll: archaeological objects;
sculptures

Belkhandi

06591
Belkhandi Museum
Post Office Kalahandi, Belkhandi,
Orissa, District Kalahandi
Historic Site
Stone sculptures discovered at the
site

Bhagalpur

06592
Bhagalpur Museum
Tilka Manjhi Chowk, Bhagalpur, Bihar
General Museum - 1976
Coll: stone sculptures; terra cottas;
arms

Bhanpura

06593
Local Museum
Bhanpura, Madhya Pradesh
General Museum
Archaeological objects and sculpture

Bharatpur

06594
Government Museum
Bharatpur, Rajastan
General Museum - 1944
Coll: sculptures; coins; armoury;
zoological specimens; paintings and
manuscripts; arts and crafts

Bhavnagar

06595
Arts and Crafts Museum
Gandhi Smriti, Bhavnagar, Gujarat
Decorative Arts Museum - 1963
Coll: arts and crafts of Gujarat State
and well known crafts of different
States of India

06596
Barton Museum
Gandhi Smriti, Bhavnagar, Gujarat
General Museum - 1895
Coll: arts; antiquities; archaeology;
history

06597
Children's Museum
Gandhi Smriti, Bhavnagar, Gujarat
Junior Museum - 1959
Collections based on basic training
and recreation for children

06598
Gandhi Museum
Gandhi Smriti, Bhavnagar, Gujarat
Historic Site - 1955
Rare photographs of Mahatma
Gandhi; collection of documents and
personal relics; audiovisual materials;
prayer and lecture records

Bhopal

06599
Birla Museum
Vallabh Bhavan, Post Office, Bhopal,
Madhya Pradesh 462004
General Museum - 1971
Coll: stone sculptures; terra cottas;
coins; manuscripts; prehistoric tools;
photographs of monuments of
Madhya Pradesh; reproductions of
Bhimbetka rock paintings

06600
Central Museum
Bhopal, Madhya Pradesh
General Museum - 1949
Coll: paintings; coins; porcelain; toys
of metals and ivory; woodwork;
needlework; handicrafts

06601
**Madhya Pradesh Tribal Research
and Development Institute**
35 Simla Hills, Bhopal, Madhya
Pradesh
Anthropology Museum - 1954
Tribal art

Bhubaneshwar

06602
Orissa State Museum
Bhubaneshwar, Orissa
General Museum - 1932
Coll: archaeology; paintings;
costumes; ethnology; anthropology;
science; manuscripts, particularly of
palm leaf

06603
Orissa State Museum
Bhubaneshwar, Orissa
General Museum - 1932
Coll: archaeological objects;
epigraphical objects; coins; armoury;
natural history; arts and crafts;
prehistory; ethnology; musical
instruments; palm-leaf and paper
manuscripts; mining and geological
objects

Bhuj

06604
Kachchh Museum
Bhuj, Gujarat 370001
General Museum - 1877
Coll: arts, crafts and industries of
Kachchh; maritime history;
anthropology; archaeology; musical
instruments; numismatics; inscriptions
of Kshatrapa dynasty (1st and 2nd
century); Harappan relics, seals,
beads, pottery (2000 B.C.); aerospace
science; memorabilia of India's
struggle for freedom - children's
section; library

Bijapur

06605
Archaeological Museum
Bijapur, Karnataka
Archeology Museum - 1912
Coll: antiquities of the period of Adil
Shahis (1480-1680); armoury; porcelain
and china; coins; miniature paintings;
manuscripts

Bikaner

06606
Ganga Golden Jubilee Museum
Bikaner, Rajastan
General Museum - 1937
Coll: arts and crafts; fauna and culture
of Bikaner; terra cottas; paintings;
manuscripts; weapons

Bishnupur

06607
**Acharya Jogesh Chandra Purakirti
Bhavan** Bangiya Sahitya Parisat
Bishnupur Branch
POB, Bishnupur, West Bengal, District
Bankura
General Museum - 1951
Coll: art and architecture, prehistoric
to contemporary; old manuscripts; folk
art

Bodhgaya

06608
Archaeological Museum
Bodhgaya, Bihar
Archeology Museum
Archaeological objects; stone and
bronze sculptures

Bombay

06609
Dr. Bhau Daji Lad Museum
91A Dr. Babasaheb Ambedkar Rd,
Byculla, Bombay, Maharashtra 400057
Decorative Arts Museum - 1872
Coll: armour; sculpture; metalware;
pottery; stoneware; fine arts; leather
work; lacquer work; horn work; ivory;
cut glass; manuscripts; paintings;
fossils; ethnology; minerals;
photographs and maps; Old Bombay
collection - library

06610
Grant Medical College Museum
Bombay, Maharāshtra
Natural History Museum - 1845
Pathology museum: forensic medicine,
hygiene, public health; anatomy
museum: skeletons, bones

06611
**Heras Institute of Indian History and
Culture** St. Xavier's College
5 Mahapalika Marg, Bombay,
Maharashtra 400001
Fine Arts Museum - 1926
Coll: Indian archaeological finds;
Indian Christian art; icons and
miniature paintings; sculptures;
manuscripts and rare books - library

06612
Natural History Museum Bombay
Natural History Society
Hornbill House, Shahid Bhagat Singh
Rd, Bombay, Maharashtra 400023
Natural History Museum - 1883
Coll: vertebrates (mammals, birds,
reptiles, amphibians, fishes) and
insects of the Indian region

06613
**Prince of Wales Museum of Western
India**
Mahatma Gandhi Rd, Bombay,
Maharashtra 400023
Fine Arts Museum - 1922
Coll: sculpture; natural history; Indian
miniature paintings; bronzes; Nepalese
and Tibetan art; prehistoric and
protohistoric objects; decorative arts;
armour; European paintings; textiles;
Chinese and Japanese porcelain and
other antiquities; Indian metalware and
modern paintings of the Bombay
School - library

06614
Victoria and Albert Museum
Victoria Gardens, Bombay,
Maharashtra
General Museum - 1855
Coll: agriculture; ethnology; religion
and mythology; paintings; arms and
weapons; industry and industrial
products; pottery; geology; relics of
old Bombay

Bratacharigram

06615
**Gurusaday Museum of Bengal Folk
Art**
Bratacharigram, Post Office, Joka,
West Bengal, District 24 Parganas
Decorative Arts Museum - 1963
Coll: various types of precious scrolls;
paintings (Patachitra); Kalighat pat;
terra cotta plaques for temples; stone,
wood, brass, and bronze sculptures;
figurines; dolls; toys; tribal folk art;
musical instruments; manuscripts;
wooden painted manuscript covers;
archaeological specimens

Bulandshahar

06616
Government Educational Museum
Government Inter College
Bulandshahar, Uttar Pradesh
General Museum
Coll: sculptures; terra cottas; pottery

Bundi

06617
**National Heritage Preservation
Society Museum**
Bundi, Rajastan
Fine Arts Museum - 1948
Sculptures and paintings

Burdwan

06618
Museum and Art Gallery University
of Burdwan
Rajbati, Post Office, Burdwan, West
Bengal, District Burdwan
Fine Arts Museum - 1965
Coll: Indian art and antiques; folk art;
European and Indian oil paintings;
terra cotta figures and figurines;
woodcarvings; manuscripts; coins;
bronzes

Calcutta

06619
Academy of Fine Arts
Cathedral Rd, Calcutta, West Bengal
700016
Fine Arts Museum - 1933
Coll: Rabindranath's paintings,
manuscripts and personal belongings;
paintings; engravings; miniatures;
sculptures; old textiles; ancient carpets

06620
The Asiatic Society Museum
1 Park St, Calcutta, West Bengal
Fine Arts Museum - 1784
Coll: rare and illustrated manuscripts;
coins; paintings; inscriptions; sculpture

06621
Asutosh Museum of Indian Art
University of Calcutta
Centenary Bldg, Calcutta, West Bengal
700012
Fine Arts Museum - 1937
Coll: pottery; terra cotta; sculpture;
seals; coins; paintings; folk art

06622
Bangiya Sahitya Parisad Museum
243/1 Acharya Prafulla Chandra Rd,
Calcutta, West Bengal 700006
General Museum - 1906
Stone sculpture; terra cottas; old
paintings; old bronze images; copper
plates; gold, silver and bronze coins
(Indo-Greek, Indo-Scythian,
Indo-Parthian, Kusan); old wax
weapons; old banner paintings; icons;
inscriptions and images both in metal
and stone; original manuscripts of
Vidyasagar, Vivekananda,
Ramandrasundar, Kaviguru, and others
- library

06623
**Birla Academy of Art and Culture
Museum**
108-109 Southern Av, Calcutta, West
Bengal 700029
Fine Arts Museum - 1962
Coll: paintings of the medieval period;
miniature paintings; stone and bronze
sculptures; woodcarvings; terra
cottas; textiles; modern art;
archaeological specimens;
anthropology - library; Swar Sangam
art education center; auditorium

06624
**Birla Industrial and Technological
Museum**
19 A Gurusaday Rd, Calcutta, West
Bengal 700019
Science/Tech Museum - 1959
Coll: models and exhibits on various
branches of physical sciences,
industry and technology including
original objects - regional science
centre

06625
Birla Planetarium
96 Chowringhee Rd, Calcutta, West
Bengal 700016
Science/Tech Museum - 1962
Collection of exhibits pertaining to
various fields of astronomy,
astrophysics and celestial mechanics

06626
**Crafts Museum - Art in Industry
Museum**
9-12 Old Court House St, Calcutta,
West Bengal
Decorative Arts Museum - 1950
Coll: rural arts and crafts including
ivories, metal objects and textiles from
different regions of India

06627
Cultural Research Institute
N.S. Bldgs, 1st floor, Block B, 1 K.S.
Ray Rd, Calcutta, West Bengal
Anthropology Museum - 1955
Coll: different types of artifacts of the
tribal folks of West Bengal

06628
**Government Industrial and
Commercial Museum**
45 Ganesh Chandra Av, Calcutta
700013
History/Public Affairs Museum - 1939
Coll: industrial and commercial
products of West Bengal including
large, medium and small scale
industries and handicrafts and folk art

06629
Indian Museum
27 Jawaharlal Nehru Rd, Calcutta,
West Bengal 700016
General Museum - 1814
Art: miniature paintings, ivory, bead
works, textiles, woodcarvings, bronze,
jewelry, temple banners, scrolls;
anthropology: tribal and folk art
objects, artifacts, musical instruments,
dresses, costumes, masks, arms and
weapons; archaeology: Indus valley
excavated objects, sculptures, terra
cottas, bronzes, wooden sculptures,
inscriptions, seals, coins, manuscripts,
architecture; zoology: mammals,
reptiles, birds; botany: wood-yielding
plants, medicinal herbs, agricultural
products, fibres, narcotics; geology:
fossils, Siwalik objects, minerals,
precious stones, meteors, quartzite

06630
Marble Palace Art Gallery and Zoo
46 Muktaram Babu St, Calcutta, West
Bengal
Fine Arts Museum - 1842
Coll: paintings; bronzes; vases;
woodworks; terra cottas; clocks;
chandeliers; mirrors; painted tiles

06631
Municipal Museum
College Street Market, North Block,
Calcutta, West Bengal
History/Public Affairs Museum - 1932
Public and civil health and indigenous
products

06632
Nehru Children's Museum
94/1 Chowringhee Rd, Calcutta, West
Bengal 700020
Junior Museum - 1972
The Ramayana depicted in 1500
miniature models in 61 illuminated sets;
the Mahabharata depicted in 2000
miniature models in 62 multi-colour and
illuminated sets; dolls and toys;
science section

06633
Netaji Museum Netaji Research
Bureau
38/2 Lala Lajpat Raj Rd (formerly Elgin
Rd), Calcutta, West Bengal 700020
Historic Site - 1961
Coll: photographs, original letters,
manuscripts, paintings, sculptures,
films, microfilms, original documents
and photostat copies of letters,
documents concerning the life,
activities and thoughts of Netaji
Subhas Chandra Bose and Sarat
Chandra Bose

06634
Rabindra Bharati Museum
6/4 Dwarakanath Tagore Lane,
Calcutta, West Bengal 700007
Historic Site - 1961
Coll: literary artistic and organisational
activities of Rabindranath Tagore and
the Tagore family

06635
Regional Labour Institute
Lake Town, Calcutta, West Bengal
History/Public Affairs Museum - 1965
Exhibits pertaining to industrial safety,
hygiene and occupational health

06636
State Archaeological Gallery
33 Chittaranjan Av, Calcutta, West
Bengal 700013
Archeology Museum - 1962
Coll: prehistory, protohistory, medieval
and late medieval history, comprising
stone artifacts; chalcolithic material;
pottery and other antiquities;
sculptures in stone, metal, ivory, wood;
paintings including scrolls and
miniatures; coins; epigraphs;
manuscripts

06637
Victoria Memorial Hall
1 Queen's Way, Calcutta, West Bengal
700016
History/Public Affairs Museum - 1906
Coll: paintings in oil and watercolour;
Mughal and Rajput miniatures; prints
and lithographs; engravings; drawings;
busts and statues; arms and armour;
manuscripts, documents and
photographs; stamps, coins, medals
and badges; army uniforms; models
and portraits of eminent national
leaders and their personal relics;
objects relating to Indian history of the
period 1700-1900

Calicut

06638
**V.K. Krishna Menon Museum and Art
Gallery**
Malabar Collectors Bungalow, East
Hill, Calicut, Kerala
Fine Arts Museum
Coll: memorabilia of Sri. V.K. Krishna
Menon; paintings (modern, Bengal,
Rajastani, Mughal, Chinese, Japanese,
Tibetan and realistic school); works by
Renound Raja Ravi Varma; carvings in
wood, ivory and metals

Chamba

06639
Bhure Singh Museum
Chamba, Gujarat
General Museum - 1908
Coll: Pahari paintings; Chamba rumal
and other textiles; woodcarvings;
bronzes; arms; copperplates; historical
documents, declarations, coins,
manuscripts; sculptures; Rang Mahal
section

Chandigarh

06640
**Government Museum and Art
Gallery**
Sector - 10/C, Chandigarh
Fine Arts Museum - 1966
Coll: Gandhara sculptures; miniatures
of the Mughal, Basholi and Kangra
schools; geological objects, fossils,
minerals, murals on evolution of life

06641
Museum of Fine Arts Punjab
University
Chandigarh
Fine Arts Museum - 1968
Contemporary paintings and
sculptures, mostly Indian

Chhindwara

06642
**Madhya Pradesh Tribal Research
and Development Institute**
Chhindwara, Madhya Pradesh
Anthropology Museum - 1954
Tribal arts, artifacts, crafts

Chitradurga

06643
Local Antiquities Museum
Chitradurga, Karnataka
General Museum - 1951
Coll: arms; sculptures; portraits;
manuscripts; excavation material from
Chandravalli and Brahmagiri, such as
neoliths, coins, beads, pottery

Coimbatore

06644
Gass Forest Museum Southern
Forest Rangers College
R.S. Puram, POB 1031, Coimbatore,
Tamil Nadu 641002
Agriculture Museum - 1902
Collections representing forestry and
related subjects - library

06645
**Museum of the Agricultural College
and Research Institute**
Coimbatore, Tamil Nadu
Agriculture Museum - 1909
Coll: seeds and products of cereals;
fibers; minerals; rocks; fungus
diseases; models of implements and
tools; gold and silver medals; cups;
shields; stuffed birds, snakes and
poultry

Damoh

06646
**Purvattatva Sangrahalaya Madhya
Pradesh Shasan**
Civil Ward No. 1, Purana Girjaghar,
Damoh, Madhya Pradesh
General Museum - 1970
Stone sculptures

Darbhanga

06647
Chandradhari Museum
Darbhanga, Bihar
Historic Site - 1957
Coll: bronzes and terra cottas;
personal collection of Baba
Chandradhari Singh consisting of
various paintings, ivory works,
bronzes, manuscripts, textiles, coins

Darjeeling

06648
Akshaya Kumar Maitreya Museum
North Bengal University
District POB, Darjeeling, West Bengal
Fine Arts Museum - 1965
Coll: stone, bronze and wooden
sculptures; coins, mainly native states
of Eastern India; manuscripts;
Assamese-Bengali scripts; paintings;
miniatures

06649
**Museum of the Himalayan
Mountaineering Institute**
Darjeeling, West Bengal
Anthropology Museum - 1968
Coll: mountaineering equipment;
topographic models of the Sikkim-
Himalayas, showing the routes of
different Everest expeditions since
1921

06650
Natural History Museum
Darjeeling, West Bengal
Natural History Museum - 1903
Coll: butterflies; birds; birds eggs;
reptiles and amphibia; fish; insects;
invertebrates including herbarium
specimens

Dehradun

06651
Botanical Survey of India
Northern Circle, 3 Lakshmi Rd,
Dehradun, Uttar Pradesh
Natural History Museum - 1956
Coll: plants, particularly from the
Himalayas; insect-catching plants;
parasitic plants; alpine cold desert
plants; plants of economic importance,
medicinal plants, a collection of seeds,
fruits and wood samples; large
photographs and panels depicting
vegetation types of the Himalayas and
arid plains

06652
**Forest Research Institute and
College**
Dehradun, POB, New Forest, Uttar
Pradesh
Agriculture Museum - 1906
Coll: specimens of forest products,
forest diseases, insect attack, forest
management and utilisation of forest
products

06653
Zonal Museum Anthropological
Survey of India, North Western
Region
51-7 Hardwar Rd, Dehradun, Uttar
Pradesh
Anthropology Museum - 1971
Coll: physical and cultural
anthropology of North Western India,
including the Central and Western
Himalayas

06654
**Zoological Survey of India, Northern
Regional Station**
13 Subhas Rd, Dehradun, Uttar
Pradesh
Natural History Museum - 1960
Fauna of the Northern Region

Deoria

06655
**Dr. Raj Bali Pandey Puratatva
Sangrahalaya**
M.M.M. Siksha Sansthan, Bhatpar
Rani, Deoria, Uttar Pradesh
General Museum - 1970
Coll: stone sculpture; stone tools; terra
cottas; coins; microlithic stone tools;
manuscripts

06656
Government Educational Museum
Deoria, Uttar Pradesh
General Museum - 1950
Coll: plaster casts of historical
personalities; terra cottas; specimens
of Mohenjodaro and Harrapa; rocks
and minerals; stuffed birds and
animals; zoological specimens; all
kinds of charts and maps; wooden
models of irrigation industries; coins;
manuscripts; toys; clay models;
paintings; metallic images

Dhar

06657
District Archaeological Museum
12 Cotavad Darwaja, Dhar, Madhya
Pradesh
Archeology Museum - 1902
Coll: sculptures; architectural pieces;
inscriptions; coins; pottery; art objects;
ornaments; photographs; sketches;
maps and charts

Dharampur

06658
Lady Wilson Museum
POB, Dharampur, Gujarat, District
Valsad
General Museum - 1928
Coll: tribal art and culture of Gujarat,
India, and abroad; specimens of
stuffed wild animals, zoology; geology;
industrial arts from India and abroad;
musical instruments; dolls and toys
from various countries

Dharwar

06659
Kannada Research Institute
Karnataka University
Dharwar, Karnataka
Fine Arts Museum - 1939
Coll: prehistoric antiquities; terra
cottas; inscriptions; copperplates;
sculptures; metal images; wooden
figures; paintings; manuscripts

Dhulia

06660
**I.V.K. Rajwade Sanshodhan Mandal
Museum**
Dhulia, Maharashtra
Fine Arts Museum - 1932
Coll: stone sculptures; metal icons;
copperplates; coins; manuscripts with
paintings

Ernakulam

06661
Zoology and Botany Museum
Maharaja's College
Ernakulam, Karnataka
Natural History Museum - 1874
Specimens of zoology and botany

Etawah

06662
Government Educational Museum
Government Inter College Compound
Station Rd, Etawah, Uttar Pradesh
General Museum - 1957
Coll: original coins; locally collected
sculpture pieces (6th century); plaster
casts; portraits and sculptures of
national leaders; portraits of scientists
and literary figures; dioramas; fish;
printed copies of Ajanta paintings;
dome models; modern paintings and
sculptures

Faizabad

06663
Botany Museum
K.S. Saket Mahavidyalaya, Faizabad,
Uttar Pradesh
Natural History Museum
Coll: specimens of botanical interest;
algae; fungipteridophytes

06664
Geography Museum
K. S. Saket Mahavidyalaya, Faizabad,
Uttar Pradesh
Natural History Museum
Coll: specimens of rocks; minerals;
peculiar sand from Comorin

06665
Government J.T.C.
Faizabad, Uttar Pradesh
General Museum - 1952
Coll: animal skeletons; coins; horns of
different animals; wooden toys; heads
of different animals; stone toys and
idols of the past; earthen toys; foreign
recent coins

06666
Zoological Museum
K.S. Saket Mahavidyalaya, Faizabad,
Uttar Pradesh
Natural History Museum
Coll: zoological specimens and
photographs

Gauhati

06667
Anthropological Museum
Department of Anthropology, Gauhati
University
Gauhati, Assam 781014
Anthropology Museum - 1948
Coll: ethnology; all branches of
anthropology

06668
Assam Forest Museum
South Kamrup Division, Gauhati,
Assam
Agriculture Museum - 1948-49
Coll: timber, bamboos, canes and
various forest products; ivory and
lacquer works; medicinal herbs;
elephant tusks and rhino horns;
models of bridges, buildings

06669
**Assam State Archaeological
Museum Gauhati**
Gauhati, Assam 781001
Archeology Museum - 1940
Archaeological objects

06670
Commercial Museum Gauhati
University
Gauhati, Assam 781014
History/Public Affairs Museum - 1957
Coll: economic development of India;
commercial products; minerals and
rocks; forest products; handicrafts;
industrial and chemical products;
agricultural implements; office
appliances and labour saving devices;
documents; pictures and models;
coins

06671
Gauhati Medical College
Gauhati, Assam 781015
Natural History Museum
Coll: science; medicine; anatomy

Gaya

06672
Gaya Museum
Gaya, Bihar 823001
General Museum - 1952
Coll: archaeology; ethnology; geology;
natural history; decorative arts;
paintings, sketches and photographs;
numismatics; arms; manuscripts

Gorakhpur

06673
Archaeological Museum Department
of Ancient History, Archaeology and
Culture, Gorakhpur University
Gorakhpur, Uttar Pradesh
Archeology Museum - 1958
Coll: coins; sculptures; photographs

06674
Botany Museum University of
Gorakhpur
Gorakhpur, Uttar Pradesh
Natural History Museum
Coll: different plant groups;
insectivorous plants; herbarium
representing local flora and fossil
specimens

06675
**Puratatva Sangrahalaya, Rahul
Sankratayan Sansthan**
Alinagar, Gorakhpur, Uttar Pradesh
General Museum - 1967
Coll: sculptures; coins; terra cottas;
beads; manuscripts; illustrated
manuscripts; palm leaf manuscripts

06676
Zoological Museum University of
Gorakhpur
Gorakhpur, Uttar Pradesh
Natural History Museum - 1958
Coll: all the major vertebrates and
invertebrates

Gulbarga

06677
District Museum
Sedam Rd, Gulbarga, Karnataka
General Museum
Coll: archaeological objects;
sculptures; inscriptions

Guntur

06678
Archaeological Museum
Nagarjunakonda, Guntur, Andhra
Pradesh
Archeology Museum - 1947
Sculptures: limestone (early period),
granite (medieval period); terra cottas;
stuccos; gold, silver and copper coins;
pottery; beads; metallic objects;
prehistoric stone implements

06679
District Museum Regional Library
opposite A.C. College, Guntur, Andhra
Pradesh
General Museum - 1975
Coll: sculptures and inscriptions
relating to early historic and medieval
periods

Gwalior

06680
Archaeological Museum
Gujari Mahal, Gwalior, Madhya
Pradesh 474003
Archeology Museum - 1922
Coll: sculpture; stone pillars and
capitals; sati stones; metal images;
terra cotta objects; coins; excavated
objects from ancient sites such as
Pawaya (Padmavati), Besnagar
(Vidisha), Ujjain (Ujjayini) and
Maheshwar; copies of Bagh frescoes
and paintings

06681
**H.H. Maharaja Jiwaji Rao Scindia
Museum**
Museum Jai Vilas Palace, Lashkar,
Gwalior, Madhya Pradesh 474001
Historic Site - 1964
Collections of foreign articles

06682
Museum Municipal Corporation
Jamna Bagh, Moti Mahal, Gwalior,
Madhya Pradesh
General Museum - 1921
Coll: natural history; arms and
armoury; paintings; ivory works; brass
works; stone and metal sculpture; old
crockery and coins

Halebidu, via Arasikere

06683
Archaeological Museum
Halebidu, via Arasikere, Karnataka,
District Hassan 573121
Archeology Museum - 1961
Coll: sculpture; bronzes; copperplates;
inscriptions; woodcarvings

Hardwar

06684
Archaeological Museum
Gurukula Kangri, Hardwar, Uttar
Pradesh
Archeology Museum - 1945
Coll: prehistoric exhibits; sculptures;
terra cottas; coins; manuscripts;
paintings; arms

06685
Ayurvedic College Museum
Gurukul Kangri, Hardwar, Uttar
Pradesh
Natural History Museum - 1922
Coll: biology; pathology; anatomy;
pharmacy

06686
Zoological Museum Gurukul Kangri
University
Hardwar, Uttar Pradesh
Natural History Museum
Zoological specimens

Hassan

06687
District Museum
Maharaja Park, Hassan, Karnataka
General Museum - 1977
Coll: archaeological objects;
sculptures; inscriptions; arms; coins;
paintings

Hooghly

06688
Amulya Pratnassala
Hooghly, POB, Rajbalhat, West Bengal
Fine Arts Museum - 1955
Coll: wooden and stone sculptures;
coins; terra cotta; manuscripts;
collections on eminent personalities
(Rabindranath, P. C. Roy, Jagadish
Bose, Jawaharlal Nehru and others);
old books; dhokra articles; paintings
on wooden plates (Ratha fragments);
folk art

06689
Carey Museum Serampore College
Hooghly, POB, Serampore, West
Bengal
Historic Site - 1818
Coll: belongings of the founder of
Serampore mission; items connected
with the early history of the college;
rare books and manuscripts - Carey
library

06690
College of Textile Technology
12 William Carey Rd, Serampore
Hooghly, West Bengal
Science/Tech Museum - 1959
Coll: textile products

06691
Museum and Art Gallery Institute
Chanderanagar
The Residency, Chanderanagar,
Hooghly, West Bengal
History/Public Affairs Museum - 1952
Coll: relics of the French in India,
including valuable documents; relics of
local freedom fighters; bibliographical
materials; photographs; paintings;
terra cotta; other antiquities

Howrah

06692
Ananda Niketan Kirtisala (Rural
Museum on Folk Art and Archaeology)
Ananda-Niketan, Howrah, POB,
Bagnan, West Bengal
Archeology Museum - 1961
Coll: terra cotta; pottery; temple terra
cotta plaques; coins; stone sculptures;
folk arts and crafts; Bengali and
Sanskrit manuscript copies; card index
of ancient temples and mosques

06693
Central National Herbarium Botanical
Survey of India
Indian Botanical Garden, Howrah,
West Bengal
Natural History Museum - 1793
Coll: plant materials; dried plants

06694
Sarat Smriti Granthagar
Panitras, Howrah, West Bengal
Historic Site - 1956
Coll: manuscripts and articles used by
Sarat Chandra Chatterjee; terra cotta;
sculptures; coins of various countries;
folk art

Hyderabad

06695
Khajana Buildings Museum
Golkonda Fort, Golkonda, Hyderabad,
Andhra Pradesh
Historic Site - 1960
Sculptures

06696
Salar Jung Museum
Hyderabad, Andhra Pradesh 500002
Fine Arts Museum - 1951
Coll: Western paintings; Indian
miniatures; textiles; bronze; Eastern
and European porcelain; jade; carpets;
glass; ivory; clocks; bidri ware;
modern art; marble statues -
children's section

06697
State Health Museum
Public Garden, 11-6-15, Hyderabad,
Andhra Pradesh 500004
History/Public Affairs Museum - 1948
Coll: plastic human heart; 5 specimens
of poisonous and non-poisonous
snakes in India; models; objects;
photographs; dioramas; maps;
graphics - library; training center

06698
State Museum
Public Gardens, Hyderabad, Andhra
Pradesh 500004
General Museum - 1930
Arts and sciences

06699
**Tribal Cultural Research and Training
Institute**
Rd No. 1, Banjara Hills, Hyderabad,
Andhra Pradesh
Anthropology Museum - 1963
Coll: typical ornaments, dresses,
hunting artifacts, utensils, musical
instruments and other material used
by the tribals of Andhra Pradesh

06700
Yeleswasam Pavilion
Gunfoundry, Hyderabad, Andhra
Pradesh 500001
Archeology Museum - 1961
Material unearthed from the
successive excavations at
Yeleswasam

Imphal
06701
Manipur State Museum
Polo Ground, Imphal, Manipur
General Museum - 1969
Coll: art; archaeology; natural history;
geology; artifacts; textiles

Indore
06702
The Central Museum
Agra-Bombay Rd, Indore, Madhya
Pradesh 452001
General Museum - 1929
Coll: archaeological objects; fine arts;
arms; coins

Jagdishpur
06703
Kunwar Singh Memorial Museum
Jagdishpur, Bihar, District Bhojpur
Historic Site - 1973
Coll: personalia, records, photographs,
paintings related to Babu Kunwar
Singh and his times

Jaipur
06704
Government Central Museum
Ram Niwas Garden, Jaipur, Rajastan
Decorative Arts Museum - 1886
Coll: metalware; ivory and lacquer
work; jewelry; textiles; pottery; carved
wooden objects; arms and weapons;
clay models; sculptures; paintings;
educational, scientific and zoological
objects

06705
**Maharaja Sawai Man Singh II
Museum**
City Palace, Jaipur, Rajasthan 302002
Fine Arts Museum - 1959
Art; miniatures of Mughal and
Rajasthani schools; Persian and
Mughal carpets; antique arms and
weapons; textiles and costumes;
Mughal glass; decorative arts;
photographs; illuminated manuscripts
of the Razmnama and Ramayana;
astronomical manuscripts and
instruments - library

Jammu
06706
Dogra Art Gallery
Gandhi Bhawan, Dogra Hall, POB:
Kachi Chawni, Jammu, Jammu and
Kashmir 180001
Fine Arts Museum - 1954
Paintings; especially Phari miniatures,
Basholi School

Jamnagar
06707
Museum of Antiquities
Lakhoto, Jamnagar, Gujarat 361001
General Museum - 1946
Coll: sculptures; paintings;
inscriptions; coins; folk art pieces;
natural history

Jaunpur
06708
Archaeological Museum T.D. College
Jaunpur, Uttar Pradesh
Archeology Museum
Coll: sculptures; terra cottas; coins;
medals

06709
Botany Museum T.D. Post-graduate
College
Jaunpur, Uttar Pradesh
Natural History Museum - 1956
Coll: all important plant and fossil
types

06710
Zoological Museum T.D. College
Jaunpur, Uttar Pradesh
Natural History Museum
Zoological exhibits

Jeypore
06711
Jeypore Branch Museum
Jeypore, Orissa
Archeology Museum - 1976
Coll: Sculptures and other
archaeological objects

Jhajjar
06712
**Haryana Prantiya Puratatva
Sangrahalaya**
Gurukul, Jhajjar, Gujarat, District
Rohtak
Fine Arts Museum - 1961
Coll: coins; inscriptions; copperplates;
terra cotta; sculptures; beads;
manuscripts, weapons of the Indus
valley civilization; ancient and modern
art objects

Jhalawar
06713
Archaeological Museum
Jhalawar, Rajastan
Archeology Museum - 1915
Coll: sculptures; inscriptions; coins;
manuscripts; wood and ivory carvings;
old paintings; minerals

Jhansi
06714
**Rani Laxmi Bai Palace Sculpture
Collection** Archeological Survey of
India
Rani Laxmi Palace, Jhansi, Uttar
Pradesh
Archeology Museum - 1970
Hindu and Jain red sandstone images
(9th-12th c.)

Jodhpur
06715
Government Museum
Jodhpur, Rajastan
General Museum - 1915
Coll: coins; paintings; wood; lacquer
items; leather; ivory; stone; arms;
mother of pearl; minerals; glass;
textiles; metal; pottery; antiquities;
natural history; educational apparatus

06716
Sardar Museum
Jodhpur, Rajastan
General Museum - 1909
Coll: sculptures; paintings; local arts
and crafts; ivory work; metal work;
chundri and leather work of Jodhpur;
manuscripts; documents; carvings;
armour; textiles; pottery

Junagadh
06717
Darbarhall Museum
Diwan Chowk, Junagadh, Gujarat
362001
Decorative Arts Museum - 1947
Furnishings and household items;
paintings

06718
Junagadh Museum
Sakkar Bag, Junagadh, Gujarat 362001
General Museum - 1901
Coll: archaeology; coins; sculptures;
inscriptions; miniature paintings;
manuscripts; silver art; carpets;
glassware; natural history; wooden
objects; folk art; textiles

Kakinada
06719
**Andhra Sahitya Parishat
Government Museum and Research
Institute**
Ramaraopeta, Kakinada, Andhra
Pradesh, East Godavari District
Archeology Museum - 1973
Coll: art and archaeology; palm leaf
manuscripts; coins; copperplate
inscriptions, and other archaeological
antiquities

Kalpi
06720
Mahatma Gandhi Hindi Sangrahalaya
Hindi Bhawan, Kalpi, Uttar Pradesh
Historic Site - 1950
Coll: sculptures; paintings; terra cotta;
metal images; lithic inscriptions; coins;
manuscripts

Kamalapur
06721
Archaeological Museum
Hampi, POB, Kamalapur, Karnataka,
District Bellary 583221
Archeology Museum - 1954
Coll: stone sculptures and
architectural pieces of Vijaya Nagar
period; gold and copper coins; palm
leaf manuscripts and copperplates;
paintings

Kanpur
06722
Botany Museum Christ Church
College
Kanpur, Uttar Pradesh
Natural History Museum
Coll: plants of all groups, classes and
families; fossils; herberia; raw plants
and plant products

06723
Commercial and Industrial Museum
Directorate of Industries
Kanpur, Uttar Pradesh
History/Public Affairs Museum
Coll: handicrafts; handloom; cottage
industry products; marble;
woodcarving; brassware; carpets; silk;
brocades

06724
School Museum Ramakrishna
Mission, H.S. School
Ramakrishna Nagar, Kanpur, Uttar
Pradesh
General Museum - 1947
Coll: natural sciences; decorative arts

06725
Zoology Museum Christ Church
College
Kanpur, Uttar Pradesh
Natural History Museum - 1961
Coll: museum specimens preserved in
formalin; stuffed birds and animals;
models

Karim Nagar
06726
Gandhi Centenary Museum
Trunk Rd, near bus stop, Karim Nagar,
Andhra Pradesh
General Museum - 1972
Arts and sciences

Khajuraho
06727
Archeological Museum
Khajuraho, Madhya Pradesh
Archeology Museum - 1910
Sculptures, inscriptions and
architectural pieces

Khariar
06728
Khariar Branch Museum
Khariar, Orissa, District Kalahandi
General Museum - 1976
Coll: stone sculptures; art and craft
objects; prehistoric objects

Khiching
06729
Khiching Museum
Khiching, Orissa, District Mayura
Bhanj
General Museum
Coll: stone sculptures; lithic
implements; beads; pottery

Kittur

06730
Kithur Rani Channamma Memorial Museum
Kittur Fort, Kittur, Karnataka
Historic Site
Coll: archaeological objects; sculptures; inscriptions

Kodagu

06731
Government Museum
Fort, Madikedri, Kodagu, Karnataka
General Museum
Coll: sculptures; inscriptions; modern art (paintings); arms; natural history

Kohima

06732
State Museum Directorate of Art and Culture
Government of Nagaland, Kohima, Nagaland
Anthropology Museum - 1970
Anthropological specimens

Kolanupaka

06733
Kolanupaka Site Museum
Archaeological Museum
via Alair, Kolanupaka, Andhra Pradesh
Archeology Museum
Coll: inscriptions and stone sculptures of Western Chalukya, Rastrakuta, Kakatiya, Reddy and Vijaya-Nagar periods

Kolhapur

06734
Kolhapur Museum
Town Hall, Kolhapur, Maharashtra
Archeology Museum - 1946
Finds from Brahmapuri excavations; paintings, arms, sculptures and miscellaneous works of arts and stone inscriptions

Konarak

06735
Archeological Museum
Konarak, Orissa, District Puri
Archeology Museum - 1968
Coll: 13th c. sculpture from the Sun Temple complex

Kotah

06736
Museum and Saraswati Bhandar
Kotah, Rajastan
General Museum - 1944
Coll: sculptures; epigraphs; coins; manuscripts; paintings of Hadoti; Jaipur and Udaipur; arms; costumes

Krishnapuram

06737
Krishnapuram Palace Museum
Krishnapuram, Karnataka
General Museum - 1960
Coll: sculptures; coins; copies of murals

Lucknow

06738
Anthropological Museum Sri Jai Narain Degree College
Station Rd, Lucknow, Uttar Pradesh
Anthropology Museum - 1958
Coll: biological and anthropological objects; prehistoric and archaeological objects; maps, charts and models

06739
Archaeological Museum Lucknow University
Lucknow, Uttar Pradesh
Archeology Museum
Coll: plaster models of sculptures; architectural pieces and monuments

06740
Army Medical Corps Centre Museum
Lucknow, Uttar Pradesh
History/Public Affairs Museum
Coll: old uniforms, swords and equipment; photographs, albums and history of the Army, Navy and Air Force

06741
Birbal Sahani Institute of Palaeobotany Museum
53 University Rd, Lucknow, Uttar Pradesh 226007
Natural History Museum - 1946
Coll: plant fossils and specimens of palaeobotanical interest; model of Williamsonia sewardiana Sahni; geological landscape painting - library; research institute

06742
Botany and Zoology Museum I.T. College
Lucknow, Uttar Pradesh
Natural History Museum
Coll: shells; corals; fossils and other zoological specimens

06743
Botany Museum Lucknow University
Lucknow, Uttar Pradesh
Natural History Museum - 1940
Coll: important and rare botanical specimens

06744
College of Arts and Crafts Museum
Lucknow, Uttar Pradesh
Decorative Arts Museum - 1911
Ancient arts and crafts collection

06745
Gandhi Museum
Gandhi Bhawan, Mahatma Gandhi Marg, Lucknow, Uttar Pradesh
Historic Site - 1973
Coll: photographs, paintings, replica pertaining to Gandhi

06746
Geological Museum Geological Survey of India, Northern Region
Gandhi Bhawan, Lucknow, Uttar Pradesh
Natural History Museum - 1961
Coll: rocks; minerals; fossils; models; maps; charts; photographs

06747
Geological Museum Sri Jai Narain Degree College
Lucknow, Uttar Pradesh
Natural History Museum - 1964
Coll: geological specimens of rocks, minerals, ores, and fossils

06748
Geology Museum University of Lucknow
Lucknow, Uttar Pradesh
Natural History Museum - 1947
Coll: Indian rock types, minerals, fossils

06749
Jail Training School Museum
Lucknow, Uttar Pradesh
History/Public Affairs Museum - 1973
Coll: models of jails; models of the Kargha factory and flour mill; wooden model of an execution chamber (Phansi Ghar); fetters weighing 30 kg from Rampu; photos of prisons where eminent freedom fighters were kept; collections taken from prisoners; psychological apparatus

06750
Motilal Nehru Bal Sangrahalaya (Children's Museum)
Motilal Nehru Marg, Charbagh, Lucknow, Uttar Pradesh 226001
Junior Museum - 1957
Coll: paintings; sculptures; toys; dolls; scientific models; dioramas - library; audio-visual aids

06751
Museum of the Department of Anthropology Lucknow University
Lucknow, Uttar Pradesh
Anthropology Museum - 1951
Ethnographic, prehistoric, archaeological, palaeo-anthropological objects

06752
Pathology and Bacteriology Museum
K.G. Medical College
Lucknow, Uttar Pradesh
Natural History Museum
Coll: specimens of surgical, medical, gynaeological, opthalmic and other sciences

06753
State Health Institute Museum
Lucknow, Uttar Pradesh
History/Public Affairs Museum
Collection relating to health science

06754
State Museum
Banarsibag, Lucknow, Uttar Pradesh
General Museum - 1863
Coll: sculptures; terra cottas; coins; ivory; woodwork; bronzes; metalware; paintings; textiles; miniatures; crafts; natural history

06755
Zoology Museum University of Lucknow
Lucknow, Uttar Pradesh
Natural History Museum - 1921
Coll: stuffed mammals, rare mammals, skeletons of mammals

Madanapalle

06756
Madanapalle College Museum
Madanapalle, Andhra Pradesh
Fine Arts Museum - 1934
Coll: South Indian paintings and sculptures; copies of Ajanta frescoes and wall paintings from an old palace in Cochin State

Madras

06757
Anatomy Museum Madras Medical College Museums
Madras, Tamil Nadu
Science/Tech Museum - 1932
Coll: human anatomy; comparative embryology; human skeleton and skeleton parts

06758
The Anatomy Museum Stanley Medical College Museums
Madras, Tamil Nadu
Natural History Museum - 1950
Dissections of the human body, specimens of embryology, comparative anatomy

06759
Archeology Museum University of Madras
Madras, Tamil Nadu 600005
Archeology Museum - 1962
Excavated material and antiquities

06760
Central Industrial Museum
Mount Rd, Madras, Tamil Nadu
Science/Tech Museum - 1940
Exhibits on cottage and co-operative industries

06761
Fort Saint George Museum
Madras, Tamil Nadu
Historic Site - 1948
Coll: arms; uniforms; medals; porcelains; coins; manuscripts; paintings; prints; textiles

06762
Government Museum
Pantheon Rd, Egmore, Madras, Tamil Nadu 600008
Fine Arts Museum - 1851
Coll: art; archaeology; anthropology; numismatics; philately; South Indian bronzes; Buddhist sculptures; tribal and folk art; musical instruments; zoology; botany; geology - children's section; library

06763
Madras Christian College Museum
Tambaram, Madras, Tamil Nadu 600059
Natural History Museum - 1835
Zoological specimens from southern India

06764
Museum of the College of Engineering
Guindy, Madras, Tamil Nadu
Science/Tech Museum - 1920
Coll: models of bridges, dams, girders, railways, culverts, sections of soil, masonry foundations, arches over doors and windows, roof showing hip, ridge and valley, gables, trusses, variations of staircases, storeyed buildings, lime kilns, brick moulding table

Madurai

06765
Gandhi Memorial Museum
Gandhi Smarak Sangrahalaya, Madurai, Tamil Nadu 625020
Historic Site
Relics of Gandhi

06766
Sri Meenakshi Sundavesvara Temple Museum
Madurai, Tamil Nadu
Fine Arts Museum - 1937
Coll: bronzes; paintings; jewellery; musical instruments; lamps; wood carvings and other art objects

Mandapam Camp

06767
Museum of the Central Marine Fisheries Research Station
Mandapam Camp, Tamil Nadu
Natural History Museum - 1947
Coll: models of fishing gear and equipment used in different parts of India; other marine animals; plants; sea weeds; sea weed products; fish dils and fish manures

Mangalore

06768
Mahatma Gandhi Museum Canara High School
Mangalore, Karnataka
General Museum - 1939
Coll: zoology; anthropology; art; coins; manuscripts; sculptures and paintings

06769
Shreemanthi Bai Memorial Government Museum
Bejai, Mangalore, Karnataka 575004
General Museum - 1960
Coll: art; archaeology; natural history

Mathura

06770
State Museum
Museum Rd, Dampier Park, Mathura, Uttar Pradesh
General Museum - 1874
Coll: sculpture; terra cottas; Kushana and Gupta period inscriptions; coins; paintings; bronzes; folk art

06771
Vrindaban Research Institute
Loi Bazar, Vrindaban, Mathura, Uttar Pradesh
Fine Arts Museum
Coll: manuscripts in Sanskrit, Hindi, Bengali, Gujarati, Gurmukhi, Oriya, Urdu, Persian; paintings; sculpture

Meerut

06772
Zoological Museum Meerut College
Meerut, Uttar Pradesh
Natural History Museum - 1965
Zoology

Midnapore

06773
Sahitya Parishad Museum
Vidyasagar Memorial Hall, Vidyasagar Rd, Midnapore, West Bengal
Archeology Museum - 1918
Coll: stone sculptures; pottery; seals; coins; manuscripts in Bengali and Sanskrit; panja of the Mughal period; copperplates from the Maharaja Sasanka period (7th c.)

Mount Abu

06774
Government Museum
Mount Abu, Rajastan, District Sirohi
General Museum - 1965
Coll: sculptures; paintings; brass; ivory work; embroidery work; woodwork; printing

Muzaffarnagar

06775
Governmental Educational Museum
Muzaffarnagar, Uttar Pradesh
General Museum - 1959
Coll: coins; terra cottas; sculptures; plaster casts; arts and paintings; dolls; stamps; cannons

06776
Zoological Museum D.A.V. College
Muzaffarnagar, Uttar Pradesh
Natural History Museum
Coll: zoological specimens; freshwater fish of the district; fossils; skeletons

06777
Zoology Museum Sanatan Dharm College
Muzaffarnagar, Uttar Pradesh
Natural History Museum - 1970
Coll: invertebrate and vertebrate animals with a separate collection on insects

Mysore

06778
Folklore Museum University of Mysore
Manasagangotri, Mysore
General Museum
Coll: paintings; crafts; musical instruments

06779
Jagmohan Palace Chitrasala
Mysore, Karnataka
Decorative Arts Museum
Coll: paintings; crafts; musical instruments

06780
Museum of Art and Archaeology
University of Mysore
Manasagangotri, Mysore, Karnataka
Archeology Museum - 1973
Coll: archaeological specimens; sculptures; inscriptions; coins

06781
Museum of the Medical College
Mysore, Karnataka
Natural History Museum
Coll: anatomical specimens, models and charts; specimens of drugs; paintings of plants; charts and diagrams of medical-legal importance; weapons and toxicological specimens

Nagpur

06782
Central Museum
Nagpur, Maharashtra 440001
General Museum - 1864
Coll: archaeology; anthropology; natural history; art

Nalanda

06783
Archaeological Museum
Nalanda, Bihar
Archeology Museum - 1915
Coll: antiquities; sculptures, terra cotta and bronzes

Narendrapur

06784
Our India Project Museum
Ramakrishna Mission Vidyalaya
24 Parganas, POB, Narendrapur, West Bengal
General Museum - 1964
Coll: minerals; cash crops samples; models

Nasik

06785
Museum of the Sarvajanik Vachanalaya
Peshave Wade, Nasik, Maharashtra
General Museum - 1958
Coll: Marathi documents; manuscripts; coins; paintings; arms; maps; playing cards; inscribed images; terra cottas; modern oil and watercolour paintings; statues of historical personages

New Delhi

06786
Aitihasic Puratatva Sangrahalaya
Kanya Gurukul, Narela, New Delhi 110040
Archeology Museum - 1963
Coll: coins; copperplates; terra cotta; beads; weapons of the Indus valley civilization; seals and manuscripts

06787
Anthropology Museum Department of Anthropology
University of Delhi, New Delhi 110007
Anthropology Museum - 1947
Objects of physical and cultural anthropology

06788
Archaeological Museum
Red Fort, New Delhi 110006
Archeology Museum - 1918
Antiquities connected with the history of Red Fort

06789
Archaeological Museum
Purana Quila, New Delhi 110001
Archeology Museum - 1974
Excavations from Purana Quila

06790
Bharatiya Adim Jati Sevak Sangh Museum
Dr. Ambedkar Rd, New Delhi
Anthropology Museum
Coll: tribal costumes and handicrafts

06791
Crafts Museum All India Handicrafts Board
Pragati Maidan, New Delhi 110001
Decorative Arts Museum - 1952
Coll: traditional crafts including folk and tribal arts of India; dolls, toys, textiles, jewelry, stone and ivory carvings, bronzes, metalware, pottery, terra cottas, basketry, painting; open air village complex - library

06792
Gandhi Smarak Sangrahalaya
Rajghat, New Delhi 110001
Historic Site - 1950
Relics of Mahatma Gandhi, microfilms and photostats of his correspondence and journals, photographs and films, art works and objects on Mahatma Gandhi

06793
Ghalib Museum
Aiwan-E-Ghalib, Aiwan-E-Ghalib Marg, New Delhi 110002
Historic Site - 1969
Ghalib: his age and disciples; social life; Urdu poetry

06794
International Doll Museum
Nehru House, Bahadurshah Zafar Marg, New Delhi
Anthropology Museum
Dolls from all over the world

06795
National Children's Museum Bal Bhavan Society
1 Kotla Rd, New Delhi 110002
Junior Museum - 1962
Coll: children's art work and artifacts; thematic exhibitions with an educational content; dolls; photography; study kits and working models; masks based on Indian mythology; animal skins

06796
National Gallery of Modern Art
Jaipur House, Dr. Zakir Husain Rd, New Delhi 110003
Fine Arts Museum - 1954
Coll: contemporary Indian paintings, sculptures, graphics, industrial design, architecture and photography; works by Abanindranath Tagore, Rabindranath Tagore, Jamini Roy, Amrita Sher Gil and others

06797
National Museum
Janpath, New Delhi 110011
Archeology Museum - 1949
Coll: prehistory; protohistory; sculptures; bronzes; copperplates; coins; miniature paintings; arms; arts; pre-Columbian arts; anthropology; Central Asian collections

06798
National Museum of Natural History
F.I.C.C.I. Bldg, Barakhamba Rd, New Delhi 110001
Natural History Museum - 1978
Coll: natural sciences; botany; zoology; ecology; environment - objects enabling visitor to participate by touching and feeling, special facilities for children

06799
Nehru Memorial Museum and Library
Teen Murti House, New Delhi
Historic Site - 1964
Materials from the life and works of Jawaharlal Nehru; Indian struggle for freedom - library

06800
Rail Transport Museum
Chanakyapuri, New Delhi
History/Public Affairs Museum - 1976
Objects from over 100 years of railway history in India

06801
Tibet House Museum
Tibet House, 1 Institutional Area, Lodi Rd, New Delhi 110003
Anthropology Museum - 1965
Tibetan statues, ritual objects, jewelry, stamps and coins, and manuscripts - library

Nowong

06802
State Museum Dhubela
Dhubela Palace, Nowong, Madhya Pradesh, District Chhataspur
General Museum - 1955
Coll: images (Chadala and Kalchari); arms; paintings; fine art objects; inscriptions - library

Padmanabhapuram

06803
Palace and Museum of Antiquities
Padmanabhapuram, Tamil Nadu
Historic Site - 1939
Coll: images of stone; war implements; coins; inscriptions; copperplates

Panaji

06804
Institute Menezes Braganza
POB 221, Panaji, Goa
Fine Arts Museum - 1871
Coll: paintings and drawings;
sculptures; coins and stamps

Patna

06805
Gandhi Sangrahalaya
Ashok Rajpath, NW Gandhi Maidan,
Patna, Bihar 800001
Historic Site - 1968
Objects pertaining to Gandhi

06806
Patna Museum
Patna, Bihar 800001
General Museum - 1917
Coll: archeology; art; natural history;
ethnology; geology; coins; old arms;
industrial war trophies

Pilani

06807
Birla Museum
Vidya Vihar, Pilani, Rajastan
(Jhunjhunu) 333031
Science/Tech Museum - 1954
Coll: energy; metallurgy;
transportation; aerospace; mining;
textiles and agriculture; popular
science exhibits ; technological and
industrial objects; Western paintings
and sculptures; old arms and
weapons; natural history specimens -
library; school education center;
audiovisual equipment

Pillalamari

06808
District Museum
Pillalamari, Andhra Pradesh, District
Mahaboob Nagar 509002
Archeology Museum - 1975
Coll: prehistoric artifacts;
contemporary arts; miniature
paintings; manuscripts; china; coins;
bronzes; bidri ware; arms and
weapons; inscriptions on stone and
stone sculptures from Eastern
Vindhyas, Western Chalukya and
Rastrakuta periods

Pondicherry

06809
**Museum of the Government Public
Library**
Pondicherry
General Museum - 1945
Coll: Arretine ware; inscriptions in
Brahmi script on potsherds; seals;
beads; potsherds with designs

Poona

06810
Archaeological Museum Department
of Archaeology, Deccan College
Poona, Maharashtra 411006
Archeology Museum - 1940
Coll: prehistoric stone tools from all
over India; models of rock shelters;
material of the Stone Age period from
Africa, Europe, California, Australia and
Palestine; excavated material (kiln,
burial pottery, terra cotta) from
chalcolithic sites; neolithic and
megalithic potteries and stone and
copper artifacts

06811
**Bhartiya Itihasa Sanshodhak Mandal
Museum**
Poona, Maharashtra
Anthropology Museum - 1910
Coll: Marathi, Sanskrit, Persian, Hindi
and Kannad documents; paintings;
copperplates; stone inscriptions;
sculptures; arms; maps; playing cards;
dresses; antiquities and remains
excavated at Karad (north Satara)

06812
Ethnological Museum Tribal Research
and Training Institute
28 Queen's Gardens, Poona,
Maharashtra 411001
Anthropology Museum - 1962
Articles of material culture from the
tribes of Maharashtra

06813
Mahatma Phule Vastu Sangrahalaya
1203 Shivajinagar, Ghole Rd, Poona,
Maharashtra 411005
General Museum - 1875
Coll: handicrafts; industry; geology;
natural history; agriculture; forestry;
armoury

06814
Raja Dinkar Kelkar Museum
1378 Shukrawar Peth, Natu Bag,
Poona, Maharashtra
Decorative Arts Museum - 1975
Coll: archeology; art; history;
decorative arts; musical instruments

Prabhas Patan

06815
Prabhas Patan Museum
Prabhas Patan, Gujarat, District
Junagadh 362268
Archeology Museum - 1951
Coll: sculptures; coins; inscriptions in
Sanskrit and Persian; textiles;
woodcarvings; sculpture from
Somnath Temple (10th-12th c.) -
library

Pudukottai

06816
Government Museum
Big St, Thirugokarnam, Pudukottai
General Museum - 1910
Coll: geology; zoology; arts and
industries; anthropology; economic
botany; epigraphy; paintings;
numismatics; sculptures and bronzes

Purulia

06817
Zilla Samgrahasala
mail c/o Haripada Sahitya Mandir
Purulia, West Bengal
General Museum - 1960
Coll: sculpture; terra cottas; Adibasi
musical instruments; Adibasi weapons;
wood carvings; old documents and
manuscripts; coins; Dokra art, masks,
etc.; minerals

Raipur

06818
Mahant Ghasidas Memorial Museum
Raipur, Karnataka
General Museum - 1875
Coll: archaeology; anthropology;
natural history; arts; crafts; paintings

Rajamundry

06819
Government Museum
Ullithota St, Rajamundry, Andhra
Pradesh
Archeology Museum - 1967
Coll: art and archeological objects;
sculptures, coins, copper plate
inscriptions, stone epigraphs

Rajkot

06820
Watson Museum
Jubilee Garden, Rajkot, Gujarat
General Museum - 1888
Coll: sculptures and bronzes, miniature
paintings and manuscripts; Indian
textiles; silver work; copper plate
grants of Kshtrapas; science; geology;
rocks and minerals; ethnology;
embroidery work of Kutch and
Kathiawar; musical instruments;
Darbar Hall

Ranchi

06821
Anthropology Museum University of
Ranchi
Ranchi, Bihar
Anthropology Museum - 1953
Ethnographic collections of Central
Indian States and of Andaman and
Nicobar Islands

06822
**Bihar Tribal Welfare Research
Institute**
Morabadi Rd, Ranchi, Bihar
Anthropology Museum
Ethnological objects

Roorkee

06823
Geology and Geophysics Museum
University of Roorkee
Roorkee, Uttar Pradesh
Natural History Museum
Coll: minerals; rocks; fossils; models
and charts; fossilized elephant bones
and tree from Siwalik

06824
Survey Museum University of
Roorkee
Roorkee, Uttar Pradesh
Science/Tech Museum - 1950
Coll: old surveying equipment (1850);
latest surveying and mapping
equipment

Sagar

06825
Archeological Museum University of
Sagar
Sagar, Karnataka
Archeology Museum - 1951
Coll: prehistoric implements;
sculptures; terra cottas; inscriptions;
coins; beads

Sanchi

06826
Archeological Museum
Central Zone, Sanchi, Karnataka,
District Raisen
Archeology Museum - 1920
Coll: sculpture; iron objects;
archtitectural fragments ; terra cotta
objects; copper objects; coins;
inscriptions

Sangaria

06827
Sir Choturam Memorial Museum
Sangaria, Rajastan
General Museum - 1937
Coll: sculptures, terra cottas, metal
panels from Rajastan; metal images,
wooden and porcelain wares from
Chind; coins; armour

Sangli

06828
The Sangli State Museum
Sangli, Maharashtra
Decorative Arts Museum - 1914
Coll: paintings; sculptures; ivory
carvings; metalware and various other
handicrafts

Santiniketan

06829
Nandan Museum
Kala Bhavan, Visvabharati, Post Office,
Santiniketan, West Bengal, District
Birbhum
Fine Arts Museum - 1921
Coll: Rajput and Mughal miniatures;
originals by Rabindranath,
Abanindranath, Gaganendranath,
Nandalal, Binodebehari, Ramkinkar;
terra cotta of Bengal; folk bronzes;
Kalighat pata; Chinese, Japanese
scroll paintings; original tracings of
Ajanta, Bagh, Cochin Murals

06830
Rabindra-Bhavana (Tagore Memorial
Museum)
Post Office, Santiniketan, West Bengal,
District Birbhum 731235
Historic Site - 1942
Coll: memorabilia of R. Tagore - library

Satara

06831
**Shri Chhatrapati Shivaji Maharaj
Museum**
Shetkari Niwas, opposite S. T. Stand,
Satara, Maharashtra
History/Public Affairs Museum - 1966
History of the Maratha period

Satna

06832
Tulsi Sangrahalaya, Ramvan
Satna, Karnataka
General Museum - 1926
Coll: sculptures; coins; books

Shillong

06833
Central Museum
Arunachal Pradesh, Shillong,
Meghalaya
General Museum - 1956
Ethnographic and archaeological
objects

06834
Zonal Anthropological Museum
Anthropological Survey of India, North
East Region
Lachumiere, Shillong, Meghalaya
Anthropology Museum - 1954
Coll: physical anthropology including
palaeanthropology, cultural
anthropology, ethnographic specimens

Shimoga

06835
District Museum
Shimoga, Karnataka
General Museum
Coll: archaeology; sculptures;
inscriptions; paintings; arms; coins

Shirali

06836
Chitrapur Math Museum
Shirali, Karnataka, North Kanara
General Museum - 1973
Coll: sculptures; bronzes; coins;
inscriptions

Shivpuri

06837
District Museum
Shivpuri, Karnataka
General Museum - 1962
Medieval sculpture

Sibsagar

06838
**Sibsagar College Museum - Hiranya
Probha Memorial Library and
Museum**
POB Joysagar, Sibsagar, Assam
Religious Art Museum - 1950
Coll: manuscripts of old Assamese
literature; copperplates, stone images,
sculptures; cutlery and armour,
palanquin shafts; Assamese
ornaments, costumes, handicrafts of
cane or bamboo; old coins; plastercast
models; utensils of metallurgical
interest

Sikar

06839
Sikar Museum
Sikar, Rajastan
General Museum - 1945
Coll: sculptures; archaeology; arts and
crafts of Shekhawati; old arms and
weapons

Simla

06840
State Museum
Simla, Gujarat
Decorative Arts Museum - 1947
Coll: sculptures; textiles; Tibetan and
Nepalese objects; industrial arts and
crafts; musical instruments; paintings;
arms and armour; manuscripts and
jewelry

Sonagir

06841
Digambar Jain Museum
Sonagir, Karnataka, District Jhansi
Archeology Museum - 1948
Archaeological objects; sculptures

Srinagar

06842
Sri Pratap Singh Museum
Lal Mandi, Srinagar, Jammu and
Kashmir
General Museum - 1898
Coll: archaeology; miniature paintings;
decorative arts; arms; anthropology
(models); textiles; minerals;
numismatics; manuscripts; natural
history - children's section

Srirangapatna

06843
Tipu Sahib Museum
Summer Palace, Dariya-Doulat-Bagh,
Srirangapatna, Karnataka
Historic Site - 1959
Objects connected with Haidar Ali and
Tipu Sultan; paintings and prints; coins
and commemorative medals; brass
and iron cannons and personal
belongings of Tipu

Surat

06844
Sardar Vallabhbhai Patel Museum
Sonifalia, Surat, Gujarat 395003
General Museum - 1889
Coll: textiles; costumes; paintings;
wood crafts; terra cottas; manuscripts

Tamluk

06845
**Tamralipta Museum and Research
Center**
Post Office, Tamluk, West Bengal,
District Midnapore
General Museum - 1973
Coll: pottery; stone tools; bone tools;
terra cotta sculptures; figurines; stone
and bronze sculptures; manuscripts;
coins

Tanjore

06846
The Tanjore Art Gallery
Palace Buildings, Tanjore, Tamil Nadu
Fine Arts Museum - 1951
Chola stone sculptures; bronze icons

Tiruchirapalli

06847
St. Joseph's College
Tiruchirapalli, Tamil Nadu 620001
Natural History Museum - 1895
Coll: stuffed birds and animals;
butterfly, moth and beetle collections;
bottled specimens; stamp and
postcard collections; geological
specimens; skeletal mounts; coins;
gems; pith works

Tirupati

06848
Sri Venkateswara Museum
Tirupati, Andhra Pradesh
Archeology Museum - 1950
Coll: archaeological objects; stone,
wooden and metal images; pottery;
arms; Rajasthan oil paintings; marble
statues; coins; inscriptions; albums
and charts

Trichur

06849
Archeological Museum
Kollengode House, Chembukau,
Trichur, Karnataka
Archeology Museum - 1947
Coll: megalithic burial jars, pottery
wares, beads; iron implements; Stone
Age implements; stone sculptures;
wooden models of temples; Indus
valley specimens; stucco head of
Gandhara; copies of mural paintings;
coins; bronzes

06850
**State Museum and Zoological
Gardens**
Trichur, Karnataka
Natural History Museum - 1885
Coll: natural history; zoology; botany;
geology; art and industry of the area;
archaeological exhibits and old coins -
zoological garden

Trivandrum

06851
Art Museum
Trivandrum, Karnataka
Fine Arts Museum - 1855
Coll: local arts and crafts; metal
images; wood carvings; ivory works;
lamps; musical instruments;
numismatics; paintings

06852
Natural History Museum
Trivandrum, Karnataka
Natural History Museum - 1855
Coll: illustrations of local natural
history; customs; geology

06853
**Sree Moolam Shastyabdapurti
Memorial Institute**
Trivandrum, Karnataka
General Museum - 1917
Coll: Village and cottage industries
products and handicrafts

06854
Sri Chitra Art Gallery
Trivandrum, Karnataka
Fine Arts Museum - 1935
Coll: modern Indian paintings;
Indo-European paintings; works by
Raja Ravi Varmi; Mughal and Rajastan
miniatures; Persian, Chinese,
Japanese paintings; copies of mural
paintings

Udaipur

06855
Archeological Museum
Ahar, Udaipur, Rajastan
Archeology Museum - 1962
Paleoliths, microliths and relics from
excavations, especially from the Ahar
mound; medieval sculptures from the
Ahar village

06856
Rajkiya Sangrahalaya
Udaipur, Rajastan
General Museum - 1887
Coll: coins; inscriptions; sculptures;
paintings; natural history; local arts;
arms

Udupi

06857
**Mahatma Gandhi Memorial College
Museum**
Kunji Bettu, Udupi, Karnataka, South
Kanara
Fine Arts Museum - 1971
Coll: sculptures; bronzes; inscriptions;
coins

Ujjain

06858
District Archaeological Museum
Ujjain, Karnataka
Archeology Museum
Sculptures; inscriptions

06859
Vikram Kirti Mandir Museum Vikram
University
Ujjain, Karnataka 456010
Archeology Museum - 1956
Coll: images, coins, fossils, tools, arms
and antiquities from the excavation at
Kayatha, Bhimbetka and Azad Nagar,
Indore; paintings of contemporary
artists and a few miniatures

Vaisali

06860
Archaeological Museum
Vaisali, Bihar
Archeology Museum - 1971
Coll: sculptures; terra cottas; pottery;
seals; bones; metallic objects;
weapons

Vallabh Vidyanagar

06861
Museum of Art and Archaeology
Sardar Vallabh Bhai Vidyapeeth,
Vallabh Vidyanagar, Gujarat
Archeology Museum - 1949
Coll: archaeology; prehistoric,
protohistoric archaeology; art;
geology; stone sculptures; bronzes;
inscriptions; coins; wood carvings

06862
S. P. University Museum
Vallabh Vidyanagar, Gujarat
Archeology Museum - 1949
Coll: paleoliths including ancient
bricks; coins; copies and photographs
of ancient and medieval inscriptions;
bronzes; reproductions of ancient and
modern paintings; geological
specimens of Gujarat; woodworks

Varanasi

06863
Archaeological Museum
Sarnath, Varanasi, Uttar Pradesh
Archeology Museum - 1910
Coll: (3rd century B.C. to 12th century
A.D.) stone sculptures; terra cottas;
stucco; moulded bricks and pottery

06864
Archaeological Museum
Varanaseya Sanskrit Visvavidyalaya,
Varanasi, Uttar Pradesh
Archeology Museum
Coll: sculptures; paintings; coins;
archaeological objects

06865
Bharat Kala Bhavan Banaras Hindu
University
Bharat Kala Bhavan, Varanasi, Uttar
Pradesh 221005
Archeology Museum - 1920
Coll: sculpture from the Kushan and
Gupta periods; terra cottas; coins;
beads; literary materials; Gujarati and
Pala manuscripts; Rajasthani, Moghul,
Pahari miniature paintings; folk art;
contemporary paintings; decorative
arts; textiles; metal crafts; ivory;
jewelry; jades; arms and armour;
philately - library; company school

06866
Geological Museum Banaras Hindu
University
Varanasi, Uttar Pradesh
Natural History Museum - 1923
Material of geological interest

06867
Maharaja Banaras Vidya Mandir Museum
Fort Ramnagar, Varanasi, Uttar Pradesh
General Museum - 1964
Coll: arms; ivory; astronomical clock; decorative arts; paintings; manuscripts; palanquins; textiles

Vidisha
06868
District Archeological Museum
Vidisha, Karnataka
Archeology Museum - 1963
Coll: sculptures; inscriptions; earthen seals; stone pillar; terra cotta; coins

Vijayawada
06869
Victoria Jubilee Museum
Bandar Rd, Vijayawada, Andhra Pradesh, Krishna District 520002
Archeology Museum - 1963
Coll: prehistoric and historic finds; sculpture (2nd-16th c.); coins, arms and armaments; 18th and 19th century miniature painting of the Deccani school, bidri ware and celadon ware; manuscripts and modern painting

Wardha
06870
Gandhi Smarak Sangrahalaya
Sevagram, Wardha, Maharashtra
Historic Site - 1949
Memorabilia of Gandhi

06871
Magan Sangrahalaya Samiti
Maganwadi, Wardha, Maharashtra
General Museum - 1938
Village industrial products and handicrafts

Indonesia

Ambon
06872
Museum Negeri Maluku Siwa Lima
Jl. Karang Panjang, Ambon
General Museum

Banda Aceh
06873
Museum Negeri Propinsi D.I. Aceh
Jl. Yapakeh 12, Banda Aceh
General Museum

Bandung
06874
Asian-African Conference Museum
Gedung Merdeka, jalan Asia Afrika 65, Bandung, Jawa Barat
History/Public Affairs Museum
Documents, photos and artifacts relating to political history of Indonesia

06875
Kebon Binatang Taman Sari
Jl. Pattimura VI/56, Bandung
General Museum

06876
Museum Geologi
Jl. Diponegoro 57, Bandung, Java
Natural History Museum
Geology; fossils; rocks and ores

06877
Museum Mandala Wangsit Siliwangi
Jl. Mayor Lembong, Bandung
General Museum

06878
Museum Negeri Jawa Barat
Jl. Oto Iskandar Dinata, Bandung
General Museum

Bangkalan
06879
Museum Daerah Bangkalan
Jl. Letnan Abdulah 1, Bangkalan
General Museum

Banyuwangi
06880
Museum Daerah Blambangan
Jl. Sri Tanjung 1, Banyuwangi

Bengkalis
06881
Museum Istant Siak Sri Indapura
Jl Siak Sri Indapura, Bengkalis
General Museum

Bogor
06882
Museum Herbarium Bogoriensis
Jl. Ir.H. Juanda 22-24, Bogor
Natural History Museum

06883
Museum Kebun Raya Bogor
Jl. Kebun Raya, Bogor
General Museum

06884
Museum Zoologicum Bogoriense
Jl Juanda 3, POB, Bogor, Jawa Barat
Natural History Museum - 1894
Zoological exhibits from the Indo-Australian region - library

Bukit Tinggi
06885
Museum Bundo Kandung
Jl. Taman Puti Bungsu, Bukit Tinggi

06886
Museum Kebun Binatang Bukit Tinggi
Jl. Taman Puti Bungsu, Bukit Tinggi
General Museum

06887
Museum Perjuangan Eka Sapta Dharma
Jl. Panorama 22, Bukit Tinggi
General Museum

Denpasar
06888
Museum Bali
Jl. Let. Kol Wisjnu 8, Denpasar, Bali
General Museum
Archaeology; local history; anthropology and ethnography of Bali; local crafts and folk arts; masks; theatrical arts section

Jakarta
06889
Archaeological Institute of Indonesia
Jl. Kimia 12, POB 2533, Jakarta
Archeology Museum
Classical and Islamic archaeology

06890
Monument Nasional
Lapangan Merdeka, Jakarta
History/Public Affairs Museum - 1961
Memorabilia of the Proclamation of Indonesian Independence(1945)

06891
Museum ABRI 'Satriamandala'
Jl Gatot Subroto 14, Jakarta
History/Public Affairs Museum
Military aircraft, tanks, and weapons; dioaramas

06892
Museum Gedung Juang 45
Jl. Menteng Raya 31, Jakarta
General Museum

06893
Museum Indonesia
Jl. Taman Mini Indonesia Indah, Jakarta
General Museum

06894
Museum Kebun Binatang Ragunan
Jl. Ragunan, Pasar Minggu, Jakarta
General Museum

06895
Museum Komodo
Jl. Taman Mini Indonesia Indah, Jakarta
General Museum

06896
Museum Nasional
mail c/o Dept. of Education and Culture, Jl. Medan Merdeka Barat 12, Jakarta
General Museum - 1778
Archaeology; anthropology; ethnology and folklore; Chinese and South Asian ceramics; antique Indonesian bronzes

06897
Museum Sasmita Loka A. Yani
Jl. Lembang, Jakarta
General Museum

06898
Museum Sejarah Kebangkitan Nasional
Jl. Abdurachman Saleh, Jakarta
General Museum

06899
Museum Sejarah Kota Jakarta
Jl. Taman Fatahillah, Jakarta
General Museum

06900
Museum Sumpah Pemuda
Jl. Kramat Raya 106, Jakarta
General Museum

06901
Museum Taman Laut Ancol
Jl. Taman Impian Jaya Ancol, Jakarta
General Museum

06902
Museum Textil
Jl. K. Satsuit Tubun 4, Jakarta
Decorative Arts Museum

Jakarta Kota
06903
Museum Bahari
Pasar Ikan, Jakarta Kota
General Museum

06904
Museum Keramik
Jl. Taman Fatahillah, Jakarta Kota
Decorative Arts Museum

06905
Museum Seni Rupa
Jl. Fatahillah 6, Jakarta Kota
General Museum

06906
Museum Wayang
Pintu Besar Utara 27, Jakarta Kota
General Museum
History; geography; ethnography

Jepara
06907
Museum Kartini Jepara
Jl. Kartini 1, Jepara
General Museum

Kebayoran Baru Jkt.
06908
Museum Kriminil Mabak
Jl. Trunojoyo 3, Kebayoran Baru Jkt.
History/Public Affairs Museum

Loksumawe
06909
Museum Malikussaleh
Jl. Perdagangan (Komp. SMEA), Loksumawe
General Museum

Magelang
06910
Museum Diponegoro
Jl. Diponegoro, Magelang
General Museum

06911
Museum Taruna Akabri Udarat
Jl. Jendral Gatot Subroto, Magelang

Malang
06912
Museum Brawijaya
Jl. Ijen 25A, Malang

Manado
06913
Museum Wanua Paksinanta
Jl. Ki Hadjar Dewantor 72, Manado
General Museum

Medan
06914
Museum Negeri Sumatera Utara
Jl. H. Joni, Medan

06915
Museum Perjuangan Bukit Barisan
Jl. H. Zainal Arifin 8, Medan
General Museum

Mojokerto
06916
Museum Purbakala
Jl. Jend. A. Yani 18, Mojokerto
General Museum

06917
Museum Purbakala Trowulan
Raya Trowulan Km. 13, Mojokerto
General Museum

Padang
06918
Museum Negeri Sumbar Aditya Arman
Jl. Diponegoro (Lap. Tugu), Padang
General Museum

Palangkaraya
06919
Museum Balanga
Jl. Tangkiling Km. 2, Palangkaraya
General Museum

Palembang
06920
Municipal Museum
Palembang, Sumatra
General Museum

Pekalongan

06921
Museum Batik
Jl. Pasar Ratu 30, Pekalongan
Decorative Arts Museum

Pematangsiantar

06922
Museum Simalungun
Djenderal Suderman 20,
Pematangsiantar, Sumatra
General Museum
Local history; folklore

Pontianak

06923
Museum Negeri Kalimantan Barat
Jl. Jend. A. Yani, Pontianak
General Museum

Rembang

06924
Museum Kartini Rembang
Jl. Jendral Gatot Subroto 8, Rembang
General Museum

Sanur

06925
Museum Le Mayeur
Sanur, Bali
Fine Arts Museum
Works of the Belgian Painter Le
Mayeur

Semarang

06926
**Museum Kebun Binatgang
Semarang**
Jl. Sriwijaya 29, Semarang
General Museum

Sentani Abepura

06927
Museum Loka Budaya Uncen.
Jl. Universitas Cendarawasih, Sentani
Abepura, Jayapura
General Museum

Sumedang

06928
Museum Prabu Geusan Ulun
J. Kantor Kabupaten, Sumedang
General Museum

Sumenep

06929
Museum Daerah Sumenep
Jl. Kantor Kabupaten Dati II, Sumenep
General Museum

Surabaya

06930
**Museum Negeri Jawa Timur Mpu
Tantular**
Jl. Taman Mayangkara 6, Surabaya
General Museum

06931
Museum Tni A.L. Loka Jala Crana
Jl. Komp. Akabri Laut
Morokrambangan, Surabaya
General Museum

Surakarta

06932
Kebun Binatang Sriwedari
Jl. Slamet Riyadi 235, Surakarta
General Museum

06933
Museum Kraton Suaka Budaya
J. Dalam Kraton, Surakarta
General Museum

06934
Museum Pers
Jl. Gajah Mada 59, Surakarta
General Museum

06935
Museum Pura Mangkunegaran
Jl. Dalam Draton Mangkunegaran,
Surakarta
General Museum

06936
Museum Radya Pustaka
Jl. Slamet Riydi 235, Surakarta
Fine Arts Museum
Decorative arts and crafts

Tanjungpinang

06937
Museum Swasta Kandil Riau
76 Kp Melati Jalan Batu II,
Tanjungpinang, Propinsi Riau
History/Public Affairs Museum
Memorabilia of Kerajaan Lingga Riau
(Lingga Riau Kingdom); artifacts of
Riau Malay culture

Tenggarong

06938
**Museum Negeri Kalimantan Timur
Mulawarman**
Tenggarong
General Museum

Ubud

06939
Museum Puri Lukisan Ratna Wartha
Ubud, Bali
Fine Arts Museum
Modern Balinese painting and
sculpture

Yogyakarta

06940
Dewantara Kirti Griya
Jl. Taman Siswa 31, Yogyakarta
History/Public Affairs Museum - 1970
Exhibits in memory of Taman Siswa
and Ki Hadjar Dewantara

06941
Kebun Binatang Gembira Loka
Jl. Gembira Loka, Yogyakarta
General Museum

06942
Monument Pangeran Diponegoro
Jl. Tegalrejo, Yogyakarta
General Museum

06943
Museum Angkatan Darat
Jl. Bintara Wetan 3, Yogyakarta
General Museum

06944
Museum Batik
Jl. Dr. Sutomo 9B, Yogyakarta
Decorative Arts Museum

06945
Museum Biologi Ugm
Jl. Sultan Agung 22, Yogyakarta
Natural History Museum

06946
Museum Kraton Yogyakarta
Jl. Dalam Kraton, Yogyakarta
General Museum

06947
Museum Pendidikan Islam
Jl. Kapten Tendean 41, Yogyakarta
History/Public Affairs Museum

06948
Museum Perjuangan
K.H. Ahmad Dahlan 24, Yogyakarta
General Museum

06949
**Museum Pusat Tni A.U. Dirgantara
Mandala**
Jl. Komplek Akabri Udara, Yogyakarta
General Museum

06950
Museum Seni Rupa Affandi
Jl. Solo 167, Yogyakarta
General Museum

06951
Museum Sono Budoyo
Jl. Trikora 27, Yogyakarta, Java
General Museum
Archaeology; history; art; ethnology

Iran

Abādān

06952
Abādān Museum
Abādān, Khūzestān
General Museum

Bāgh Fin

06953
Kāshān National Museum
Bāgh Fin, Kāhān
General Museum

Bandar 'Abbās

06954
Mohitshenasi Museum
Bandar 'Abbās
Fine Arts Museum
Gold and silver ornaments; costumes

Haft Tappe

06955
Haft Tappe Museum
Haft Tappe, Khuzestān
General Museum

Karaj

06956
Zoological Museum
Agricultural College, Karaj
Natural History Museum - 1925
zoological collections - library

Kermān

06957
**Ethnological Museum of Hammame-
e-Ganjalixan**
Kermān
Anthropology Museum

Khorramabād

06958
**Dej Shapur Khast (Falakolaflōk)
Museum**
Khorramabād, Lorestān
General Museum

Khvoy

06959
Khvoy Museum
Khvoy
General Museum

Mashad

06960
Museum of Astān-e-Qodse Razavi
Mashad, Khorāsān
Fine Arts Museum
Decorative arts and crafts; brocades
and rugs of the Safavid period

New Dzhulfa-Esfahāhān

06961
All Saviour's Cathedral Museum
Diocese of the Armenians in Iran and
India
POB 4, New Dzhulfa-Esfahāhān
Religious Art Museum - 1905
Armenian manuscript illuminations -
library

Qazvīn

06962
Qazvīn Museum
Qazvīn
General Museum

Qom

06963
Astaneh Museum
Qom
General Museum - 1936
Archaeology; rugs and tiles of Safavid
period; valuable Korans

Rasht

06964
Rasht Museum
99 Bisotoon St, Rasht, Gīlān
General Museum - 1940
Anthropoloty; archaeology; natural
history

Sanandaj

06965
Sanandaj Museum
Sanandaj, Kordestān
General Museum

Shīrāz

06966
Takht-e-Jamshid Museum
Takht-e-Jamshid, Shīrāz
General Museum

Tabrīz

06967
Tabrīz Museum
Tabrīz, East Azerbaijan
General Museum
Archaeology; natrual history; relics of
the constitutional revolution

Teheran

06968
Azādi Museum and Monument
Azādi Square, Teheran
History/Public Affairs Museum

06969
Carpet Museum
Karegar Av, Teheran
Fine Arts Museum

06970
Contemporary Arts Museum
Karegar Av, Teheran
Fine Arts Museum
0240

06971
Crime Museum
Police Headquarters of the Islamic
Republic of Iran, Teheran
History/Public Affairs Museum
0530

06972
Golestān Palace Museum
15th of Khordād Sq, Teheran
General Museum

06973
Iran Bastan Museum
30th of Teer Av, Museum Square,
Teheran
General Museum - 1934-1937
Artifacts from earliest times to
present; Islamic arts of the region -
library

06974
Iranian Decorative Arts Museum
Karimkhāne-Zand Av, Teheran
Fine Arts Museum
Rugs; textiles; jewelery; metalwork;
costumes; calligraphy

06975
Iranian Ethnological Museum
Golestān Palace, 15th of Khordad Sq,
Teheran
Anthropology Museum

06976
Malek Museum and Library
Beinolharamein Bazar, Teheran
History/Public Affairs Museum

06977
Marbel Palace Museum
Marbel Palace, Pastor and Palestine
Avs, Teheran
History/Public Affairs Museum

06978
National Arts Museum
Bāhārestān, Ministry of Culture and
Advanced Educ. Bldg., Teheran
Fine Arts Museum
Crafts; wood carving; ivory; metal and
pottery; painting

06979
**National (Royal) Jewelry Museum of
Iran Markazi Bank**
Iran Markazi Bank, Ferdowsi Av,
Teheran
Fine Arts Museum
Jewels from various dynasties; Sea of
Light diamond; Naderi Throne and
sword; Kiani Crown

06980
Natural History Museum
mail c/o The Preservation of Living
Environment Organization, Zibā Alley,
Xeradmand Av, Teheran
Natural History Museum
1140

06981
Negārestān Museum
Imam Khomeini and Palestine Sts,
Teheran
Fine Arts Museum - 1975
Iranian and Islamic art of the 18th and
19th centuries - library

06982
**Rezā Abbassi Culture and Art
Center**
972, Seyyed Xandān Av, Teheran
Fine Arts Museum

06983
Sabā's House
92, Zahiroleslām Av, Teheran
History/Public Affairs Museum

06984
Sepah Bank Coin Museum
Central Sepah Bank, Khomeini Av,
Teheran
General Museum
0540

06985
War Equipment Museum
Army Academy of the Islamic Republic
of Iran, Khomeini Av, Teheran
History/Public Affairs Museum
1040

Urumiyeh

06986
Urumiyeh Museum
Urumiyeh, West Azerbaijan
General Museum

Iraq

Al-Basrah

06987
BAsrah Museum
Al-Basrah, As-Seef District
History/Public Affairs Museum - 1975
Middle Eastern antiquities and works
of art

Al-Mawsil

06988
Nergal Gate Museum
Al-Mawsil
History/Public Affairs Museum - 1952
Casts of the Royal Assyrian kings;
copies of ancient Assyrian sculptures

As-Sulaymānīyah

06989
Sulaymānīyah Museum
As-Sulaymānīyah
History/Public Affairs Museum - 1969
Middle Eastern antiquities, with
emphasis on Northern Iraq

Babylon

06990
Babylon Museum
Babylon
History/Public Affairs Museum - 1949
Objects from prehistoric times to the
late Assyrian period; Babylonian and
classic relics; models and maps of the
ancient city

Baghdad

06991
Costume and Ethnography Museum
mail c/o Directorate General of
Antiquities, Bab-al-Shargi, Baghdad
Anthropology Museum - 1941
Sumerian, Babylonian, Akkadian,
Assyrian, Hatrene and Islamic
costumes; personal effects of the
Royal Family; displays of local popular
culture

06992
Iraq Museum
Salihiya Quarter, Baghdad
Archeology Museum - 1963
Artifacts from prehistoric period to
19th c.

06993
**Iraq Natural History Research
Centre and Museum**
Bab Al-Muadham, Baghdad
Natural History Museum - 1946
Invertebrates; insects; fishes,
amphibians and reptiles; birds;
mammals; plants; fossils, rocks and
minerals

06994
Iraqi Military Museum
Baghdad
History/Public Affairs Museum
Ancient Arabic weapons; Othmanic
firearms; modern Iraqi weapons;
military history and historical
documents

06995
Museum of Pioneer Artists
Al-Rashid St, Baghdad
Fine Arts Museum - 1979
Painting; sculpture; ceramics; graphic
arts

06996
Museum of the July 17th Revolution
mail c/o Directorate General of
Antiquities Baghdad
History/Public Affairs Museum
Documents relating to the July 17th
Revolution, housed in dwelling of the
Ex-President of the Republic

06997
Al-Mustansiriya School
Baghdad
Historic Site
Restored building of oldest Islamic
college in the world (1227-1234 A.D.)
housing rich decorations; Arabic
calligraphy; historical cartography

06998
National Museum of Modern Art
Nafoura Sq, Kifah St, Baghdad
Fine Arts Museum - 1962
Painting; sculpture; ceramics; graphic
arts

Erbil

06999
Erbil Museum
Erbil
General Museum
Objects from Erbil and neighboring
regions depicting development from
prehistoric to Islamic period

Kirkuk

07000
Kirkuk Museum
Kirkuk
History/Public Affairs Museum
Prehistoric stone objects; history of
civilization in Iraq

Nimrud

07001
Archaeological Site Nimrud (Calah)
Nimrud
Historic Site
Ruins of Assyrian palaces of the 8th
and 9th cent. B.C.; ancient Assyrian
sculpture

Nineveh

07002
Al-Mawsil Museum
Nineveh
History/Public Affairs Museum - 1974
Prehistoric, Sumerian and Addadian
periods; Assyrian and early Arab
periods; Islamic art

Sāmarrā

07003
Sāmarrā Museum
Sāmarrā
General Museum
Local finds

Thyqar-Nāsirīyah

07004
Nāsirīyah Museum
Thyqar-Nāsirīyah
History/Public Affairs Museum
Near Eastern antiquities; Islamic art

Ireland

Bunratty

07005
Bunratty Castle and Museum
Bunratty, Co. Clare
History/Public Affairs Museum - 1960
Coll: furnishings; tapestries; pictures;
decorative art

Cork

07006
Cork Public Museum
Fitzgerald Park, Cork
General Museum - 1945
Coll: archaeology; silver; glass; lace;
books; miniatures; birds

07007
**University College Zoological
Museum**
Cork
Natural History Museum
Zoology

Dublin

07008
**Chester Beatty Library and Gallery
of Oriental Art**
20 Shrewsbury Rd, Dublin
History/Public Affairs Museum - 1954
Biblical papyri; jade books; Korans,
rhinoceros horn cups

07009
Civic Museum
58 South William St, Dublin
General Museum - 1953
History of Dublin in pictures,
tapestries, theater programs, glass,
silver decorative objects, numismatics,
newspapers

07010
The Douglas Hyde Gallery Trinity
College
Dublin 2
Fine Arts Museum - 1978
library

07011
Guinness Museum
St. James's Gate Brewery, Dublin 8
Science/Tech Museum - 1966
History of the Guiness brewing
company; brewing technological
history; brewing in Ireland; bottles;
steam engine models; locomotive;
narrow gauge railway engine; labels;
bottles; transport history - library

07012
James Joyce Museum
Sandycove, Dublin
History/Public Affairs Museum - 1965
Memorabilia on James Joyce
(1882-1941) - library

07013
Municipal Gallery of Modern Art
Parnell Square, Dublin 1
Fine Arts Museum - 1908
Modern Irish and European painting;
sculpture

07014
National Gallery of Ireland
Merrion Square, Dublin 2
Fine Arts Museum - 1864
13th-19th century paintings and
drawings by European and American
artists

07015
National Museum of Ireland
Kildare St, Dublin 2
General Museum - 1880
Antiquities; folk life; history; natural
history; fine arts; prehistoric gold
objects; early Christian metalwork;
Ardagh chalice and Tara brooch (8th
century); Cross of Con (12th century)
- library

07016
Royal College of Surgeons in Ireland
St. Stephen's Green, Dublin 2
Science/Tech Museum - 1819
Bone disease; fetal abnormalities;
head of Tasmanian Aborigine

07017
Trinity College Department of
Geology, University of Dublin
Dublin 2
Natural History Museum - 1857
Geology; fossils; minerals

07018
Trinity College Zoology Museum
University of Dublin, Dept. of Zoology,
Dublin 2
Natural History Museum
Zoology; invertebrates; mollusks;
amphibians; mammals

Galway

07019
Músaem Cathrach Na Gaillimhe
Galway City Museum
Galway
General Museum - 1972
City history

Gort

07020
Yeats Tower
Gort, Co. Galway
Historic Site - 1965
Memorabilia on William Butler Yeats
(1865-1939); in his former home

Kilkenny

07021
Rothe House Museum
Parliament St, Kilkenny, Co. Kilkenny
History/Public Affairs Museum - 1966
Coll: furnishing; antiquities; prehistoric
and ancient armaments; ornaments;
folk tools; historic books; papers -
library

Killarney

07022
MuckRoss House Folk Museum
Killarney, Co. Kerry
General Museum - 1964
Local folklore; traditional crafts; natural
history; local history

Limerick

07023
**Limerick Municipal Art Gallery and
Museum**
Pery Square, Limerick
Archeology Museum - 1906
Irish antiquities; 18th and 19th century
Irish artists; sculpture; modern art

Maynooth

07024
The College Museum St. Patrick's
College
Maynooth, Kildare
Science/Tech Museum - 1930
Original induction coil and other
apparatus of Dr. N. Callan, Inventor of
the induction coil

Monaghan

07025
Monaghan County Museum
Monaghan
General Museum - 1974
Archaeological finds form Lake
Dwellings (early historic period);
collection of Carrickmacross lace and
clones crochet; folklore; local history;
unique 14th century cross known as
the 'Cross of Clogher'

Westport

07026
Westport House
Westport, Co. Mayo
History/Public Affairs Museum - 1960
Mansion with original furnishings,
silver objects, decorative arts,
paintings, books, portraits by J.
Reynold (1723-1792) and others

Israel

Abu Gosh

07027
Crusader Church
Lazarite Monastery, Resurrection
Church, Abu Gosh
Religious Art Museum
Ceremonial artifacts; archaeological
findings

Acre

07028
Municipal Museum
Crusader Subterranean City, POB 7,
Acre
History/Public Affairs Museum
Archaeological exhibits; Arab and
Druse folklore; jewelry; weapons;
ancient Turkish bathhouse

07029
Resistance Museum
Acre Citadel, Acre
History/Public Affairs Museum
Documents depicting history of the
resistance

Alumot

07030
**Archaeological and Land Study
Collection**
Alumot
General Museum
Local history; archaeology

Ashdot Ya'aqov Kibbutz

07031
**Bet Uri and Rami Nehushtan
Museum**
Ashdot Ya'aqov Kibbutz
Fine Arts Museum
Loan exhibitions of painting by Jewish
artists from France, the U.S. and Israel

Ashkelon

07032
Archaeological Site Ashkelon
National Parks Authority, POB 7028,
Tel-Aviv
Archeology Museum
Roman finds

Avedat

07033
Archaeological Site Avedat
Avedat, National Parks Authority, POB
7028, Tel Aviv
Archeology Museum
Nabataean and Byzantine remains

Avihail Natanya

07034
Israel Defenses Forces Museum
Beth Hagdudim
Avihail Netanya, 10 Karlibah St,
Tel-Aviv
History/Public Affairs Museum - 1961
Militaria on the history of the emerging
State of Israel

Ayyelet Hashahar Kibbutz

07035
Hazor Museum
Ayyelet Hashahar Kibbutz, Upper
Galilee
General Museum
Archaeological finds from Tel Hazor
illustrating the history of Hazor from
the early Caananite to the Hellenistic
period

Bat Yam

07036
Rybak Museum
Bat Yam
Fine Arts Museum

07037
Sholem Asch House
48 Arlosoroff St, Bat Yam
History/Public Affairs Museum
Memorabilia of writer Sholem Asch

Be'er Sheva

07038
The Negev Museum
Atzma'uth St, Be'er Sheva
General Museum - 1954
Local archaeology from prehistoric to
Arab periods; Beduin ethnology;
traditional farm life

Be'eri

07039
Be'eri Archaeological Collection
Be'eri, Mobile Post, Negev 85135
Archeology Museum

Bet Alfa

07040
Synagogue
Bet Alfa, National Parks Authority,
POB 7028, Tel Aviv
Archeology Museum

Bet She'an

07041
Municipal Museum
D St 1, Bet She'an
General Museum - 1949
Artifacts from the Neolithic to the
Ottoman period; Roman and Byzantine
antiquities; antique domestic utensils

07042
Roman Theater
Bet She'an, National Parks Authority,
POB 7028, Tel Aviv
Archeology Museum
Roman ruins

Bet She'arim

07043
Ancient Synagogue and Necropolis
Bet She'arim
Archeology Museum

Dan Kibbutz

07044
Ussishkin House Institute for Natural
History of the Huleh Valley
Dan Kibbutz, Upper Galilee
Natural History Museum - 1955
Fauna and flora of the Huleh Valley
and Mt. Hermon

Deganya Alef Kibbutz

07045
Bet Gordon A.D. Gordon Agriculture,
Nature and Kinnereth Valley Study
Institute
Bet Gordon Institute, Deganya Alef
Kibbutz 15120
Natural History Museum - 1935
Birds, reptiles, insects, arthropods,
mollusks and plants of the Kinnereth
Valley; palaeolithic tools and fossil
bones from the Pleistocene site of
'Ubeidiya

Dimona

07046
Municipal Museum
Municipal Building, Dimona
Fine Arts Museum
Contemporary and modern art
including paintings of French and
Belgian schools

Elat

07047
Museum of Modern Art
Rehov Hativat Hanegev, Elat
Fine Arts Museum
Contemporary painting and graphics

07048
Red Sea Maritime Museum
POB 302, Elat
Natural History Museum
Marine fauna; marine biology

'En Harod

07049
Agriculture Museum
'En Harod
Agriculture Museum
Agricultural machinery

07050
Bet Sturman
Gilboa Regional Council, 'En Harod
Mobile Post, Gilboa
General Museum
Local archaeology; modern history of
settlement in the Jezreel Valley;
zoological collection - archive; study
rooms

07051
Mishkan Le'Omanut Museum of Art
POB 18965, 'En Harod
Fine Arts Museum
Jewish folk art; works of Israeli artists;
works of Jewish artists abroad -
library

Haifa

07052
Biological Institute Bet Pinhas
Museum of Nature
Gan Haem, Hatishbi St 124, Haifa
Natural History Museum - 1950
Bird and skeleton collection;
Mediterranean and Red Sea fishes

07053
Chagall House
mail c/o Painters and Sculptors
Association of Israel, UNO Av 24,
Haifa
Fine Arts Museum
Works of Chagall

07054
Dagon Collection Archaeological
Museum of Grain Handling in Israel
POB 407, Haifa 31000
Archeology Museum - 1955
Exhibits depicting grain production
and processing from the first Neolithic
period to the present

07055
**Ethnological Museum and Folklore
Archives**
Rehov Arlosoroff 19, Haifa
Anthropology Museum - 1955
Artifacts of Jewish ceremonial and folk
art; world-wide ethnographic
collections; loan exhibitions

07056
**Haifa Museum of Clandestine
Immigration and Naval Museum**
Rehov Allenby 24, Haifa
History/Public Affairs Museum
Models, documents and photos
depicting clandestine immigration
between 1934 and 1948; ship models;
maps, photos and documents
illustrating history of the navy

07057
Haifa Museum of Modern Art
26 Shabbetai Levy St, POB 4811, Haifa
Fine Arts Museum - 1951
Painting by contemporary Israeli
artists; works by internationally
recognized artists; poster collection -
library

07058
The Mané-Katz Museum
Rehov Panorama 89, Haifa
Fine Arts Museum
Painting, drawings and sculpture of
Mané-Katz; carpets, furniture and
Judaica of the artist

07059
**Moshe Shtekelis Museum of
Prehistory**
Rehov Hatishbi 124, Haifa 34455
Archeology Museum - 1962
Natufian figurines from Nahal Oren
site on Mt. Carmel; archaeological
finds from the Tabun Cave and sites in
the Jordan Valley

07060
Museum of Ancient Art
Rehov Shabtai Levi 26, Haifa
General Museum - 1948
Findings from excavations at
Shiqmona; archaeological exhibits
from the Mediterranean region;
Graeco-Roman sculpture; Coptic art

07061
Music Museum and Amli Library
Rehov Arlosoroff 23, Haifa
Music Museum
Musical instruments from four
continents; ancient instruments
reconstructed according to
archaeological finds; coins and
medals; pictures and sculptures
relating to music; archives of Jewish
music

07062
The National Maritime Museum
Allenby Rd 198, POB 771, Haifa
History/Public Affairs Museum - 1953
Ship models; marine archaeology,
mythology and ethnology; ancient
scientific instruments

07063
Stella Maris Museum
POB 9047, Haifa 31090
Archeology Museum - 1959
Exhibits from local excavations;
ecclesiastical vestments

07064
Tikotin Museum of Japanese Art
Sderot Hanassi 89, Mount Carmel,
Haifa
Fine Arts Museum - 1959
Japanese art and crafts from ancient
to modern times

Hanita Kibbutz

07065
Hanita Museum
Hanita Kibbutz
General Museum
Regional archaeology from the
Chalcolithic to Byzantine period;
history of Hanita since 1938

Hazor

07066
Archaeological Site Hazor
Hazor, POB 7028, Tel Aviv
Archeology Museum
Canaanite and Israelite remains

Hazorea Kibbutz

07067
**Wilfrid Israel House for Art and
Oriental Studies**
Hazorea Kibbutz 30060
Fine Arts Museum - 1951
Far Eastern art

Herzliya

07068
The Herzliya Museum
Yad Levanim, Wolfson St, Herzliya
Fine Arts Museum - 1963
Israeli arts; small collection of
European arts

Hulata

07069
Natural Sciences Museum
Hulata
Natural History Museum

Jerusalem

07070
Abraham Wix Religious Museum
Jerusalem
Anthropology Museum
Folklore; religious traditions

07071
Bezalel National Art Museum The
Israel Museum
Hakirya, POB 1299, Jerusalem
Fine Arts Museum - 1965
Jewish ceremonial art; ethnography of
the Jewish communities; European
painting and sculpture from the 15th to
20th century; art from Japan, India,
Oceania, Africa and pre-Columbian
Americas; modern sculpture

07072
**Central Archives for the History of
the Jewish People**
Hebrew University Campus, Sprintzak
Bldg, POB 1149, Jerusalem
History/Public Affairs Museum
Documents from Jewish communities
and organizations around the world

07073
Dead Sea Collection
Hebrew University, Jerusalem
Archeology Museum
Dead Sea scrolls

07074
Dominus Flevit Franciscan Custodia
di Terra Sancta
Mt. of Olives, Jerusalem
Archeology Museum
Jewish tombs; Byzantine church

07075
Ecce Homo
Via Dolorosa, Jerusalem
Archeology Museum
Roman collections

07076
Greek Orthodox Patriarchate
St. Dimitri St, Jerusalem
Religious Art Museum
Archaeology; ethnography; art

07077
**Herbert E. Clark Collection of Near
Eastern Antiquities**
YMCA Bldg., David Hamelech St,
Jerusalem
General Museum - 1933
Pottery; glass and jewelry; cylinder
seals; scarabs; terracotta and bronze
figurines

07078
The Herzl Museum
Mount Herzl, Jerusalem
History/Public Affairs Museum
Original furnishings from the Viennese
room of the father of the Zionist
movement; personal documents,
photos, books and other belongings of
Herzl; Herzl's tomb

07079
Islamic Museum Haram al Sharif
POB 19004, Jerusalem
Historic Site - 1924
Koran Manuscripts; Islamic
ceremonial items; coins; Islamic arts
and crafts (Middle Ages) - library

07080
Jerusalem City Museum
The Citadel (David's Tower), POB
14005, Jerusalem, 91140
History/Public Affairs Museum
History of the Citadel from the time of
the Judean Kings to the present; AV
presentation on the history of Israel

07081
**L. A. Mayer Memorial Institute for
Islamic Art**
Rehov Hapalmach 2, Jerusalem
Fine Arts Museum
Islamic art of various periods and
lands, including metal work, ceramics,
jewelry, carpets, miniatures, textiles;
antique European and Ottoman
watches, clocks and music boxes -
library

07082
**Musée de l'Ecole Biblique et
Archéologique Française**
6 Nablus Rd, POB 19053, Jerusalem
Archeology Museum - 1890
Finds from Tell el Fa'rah, Tell Keisan,
Umn el Biyara, Jerusalem and Abu
Gosh; ceramics; numismatics; mosaics
- library

07083
Museum Dor Vador
58 King George St, Jerusalem
Fine Arts Museum
Folklore and folk art

07084
Museum of Musical Instruments
mail c/o Rubin Academy of Music,
Rehov Smolenskin 7, Jerusalem
Anthropology Museum
Musical instruments from various
lands and periods

07085
Museum of Natural History
Rehov Mohilever 6, Jerusalem
Natural History Museum - 1961
Exhibits on biological processes,
human biology; invertebrates and
vertebrates; dioramas

07086
Museum of Taxes
32 Agron St, POB 320, Jerusalem
History/Public Affairs Museum - 1964
Artifacts and documents relating to
levy of taxes - library

07087
**Museum of the Studium Biblicum
Franciscanum**
Convent of the Flagellation, Via
Dolorosa, POB 19424, Jerusalem
Archeology Museum
Roman, Byzantine and Crusader finds;
Palestinian numismatics

07088
Old Yishuv Court Museum
6, Or Hachaim St, Jewish Quarter, Old
City, POB 68, Jerusalem
Anthropology Museum - 1976
Reconstructed house displaying life in
the Jewish community of Jerusalem in
the late 19th century

07089
Polombo Museum
Mt. Zion, POB 8110, Jerusalem
Fine Arts Museum

07090
Pontifical Biblical Institute Museum
3 Paul Emile Botta St, POB 497,
Jerusalem 9100
Archeology Museum - 1927
Chalcolithic collection; Egyptian
antiquities - library

07091
Prehistory Museum Hebrew
University, Institute of Archaeology
Hatishbi 124, Mount Scopus,
Jerusalem
Archeology Museum - 1955
Objects from prehistoric sites in Israel

07092
Rockefeller Museum The Israel
Museum
East Section, Jerusalem
Archeology Museum
Archaeology of Eretz Israel from
earliest times to the end of the Islamic
period

07093
Saint Anne
Via Dolorosa, Jerusalem
Archeology Museum
Hellenistic and Crusader collections

07094
Saint James Museum and Library
mail c/o Armenian Patriarchate
Jerusalem
History/Public Affairs Museum
Crusader and later archaeological
finds

07095
Samuel Bronfman Biblical and Archaeological Museum The Israel Museum
Hakirya, Jerusalem
Archeology Museum
Archaeological objects and ancient art from prehistoric to Crusader times

07096
Schocken Institute of Jewish Research Jewish Theological Seminary of America
6 Balfour St, Jerusalem
History/Public Affairs Museum
Photocopies of the Cairo Genizah; Mahzor Nuremberg - library

07097
Shrine of the Book The Israel Museum
Hakirya, POB 1299, Jerusalem
Archeology Museum
Dead Sea Scrolls; manuscripts from the area of Masada and Nahal Hever

07098
Sir Isaac and Lady Edith Wolfson Museum
King George St, Jerusalem
Religious Art Museum - 1959
Ceremonial objects relating to Jewish life; ethnic costumes; glass; ceramics; history of the Jewish people

07099
Yad Vashem Martyrs and Heroes Memorial
Har Hazikkaron, POB 3477, Jerusalem
History/Public Affairs Museum - 1951
Documentation on victims of the holocaust - library

07100
Youth Wing in the Israel Museum
Hakirya, Jerusalem
Junior Museum - 1066
Art and archaeological collections; doll collection; temporary exhibitions

Kefar Gil'adi Kibbutz

07101
Bet Hashomer
Kefar Gil'adi Kibbutz
General Museum
Documents, letters, maps and photos depicting the activities of 'Hashomer', an organization of guards which served during the early Jewish settlement - archives

Kefar Menahem

07102
Shephela Museum The Educational Museum
Kefar Menahem 79875
General Museum - 1949
Local antiquities; modern history of the settlement; fine arts

Kfar Giladi Kibbutz

07103
Israeli Defense Forces Museum Beth Hashomer
Kfar Giladi Kibbutz, 10 Karlibah St, Tel-Aviv
History/Public Affairs Museum - 1968
Militaria relating to history of the State of Israel

Kiriat Tivon

07104
Bet Hankin Neot Kedumim
POB 125, Kiriat Tivon
Natural History Museum
Mammals; fossils; minerals; herpetology; zoology

07105
Bet Sh'arim Museum
Kiriat Tivon
Archeology Museum

Lohame Hageta'ot Kibbutz

07106
Bet Lohame Hageta'ot Ghetto Fighters' House
P.M. Asherat 25220, Lohame Hageta'ot Kibbutz
History/Public Affairs Museum - 1949
Memorabilia of the holocaust and resistance; paintings and drawings from ghettos and camps - library

Ma'abarot Kibbutz

07107
Local Museum
Ma'abarot Kibbutz 60980
General Museum - 1968
Regional archaeology; pottery; coins and weapons of various periods - library

Ma'ayan Barukh Kibbutz

07108
Huleh Valley Regional Prehistoric Museum
Ma'ayan Barukh Kibbutz, Upper Galilee
Archeology Museum - 1952
Prehistory of the Huleh Valley from the Palaeolithic to the Chalcolithic period; Bronze Age and Roman-Byzantine objects from local excavations; collection of stone grain mills and oil presses

Midreshet Ruppin

07109
Emeq Hefer Regional Museum
Midreshet Ruppin
General Museum - 1956
Butterflies; insects

Mizpe Ramon

07110
Local Museum
Mizpe Ramon
General Museum
Technology; geology

Nahariyya

07111
Municipal Museum
Municipality Bldg , Sderot Haga'aton, POB 78, Nahariyya
General Museum - 1971
Regional archaeology, from prehistoric to Byzantine period; sea shell collection

Nazareth

07112
Museum of the Terra Sancta Convent
POB 23, Nazareth
Archeology Museum - 1920
Roman, Crusader and Byzantine remains; coins, glass and antiquities from excavations in the monastery compound

Nir David Kibbutz

07113
Museum of Mediterranean Archaeology
Nir David Kibbutz
Archeology Museum - 1963
Greek pottery and sculpture; Estrucan pottery and jewelry; Islamic pottery; archaeological finds from Beith Shean Valley - library

Palmahim Kibbutz

07114
Bet Miriam
Palmahim Kibbutz, Doar na Emek Sorek
Archeology Museum - 1958
Exhibits from local excavations

Petah Tiqwa

07115
Bet Yad Labanim
Rehov Arlosoroff 30, Petah Tiqwa
General Museum
History of Jewish settlement in the city; regional archaeology; contemporary art

07116
Museum of the Human Body
14 Anderson St, Petah Tiqwa
Science/Tech Museum
Anatomy; hygiene

Ramat Gan

07117
Bet Emmanuel Municipal Museum
Rehov Hibat Zion 18, Ramat Gan
Fine Arts Museum
Israeli and Russian painting and sculpture; Far Eastern art

Ramat HaShofet

07118
Archaeological Museum
Ramat HaShofet
Archeology Museum

Rehovot

07119
Exhibition Hall of the Weizmann Archives
mail c/o Yad Chaim Weizmann, POB 26, Rehovot
History/Public Affairs Museum
Historical documents

07120
Yad Lebanim Memorial Center
Habanim St, Rehovot
Fine Arts Museum

Revadim

07121
Archaeological Collection
Revadim
Archeology Museum

Ruhama

07122
Archaeological Collection
Ruhama
Archeology Museum

Sasa Kibbutz

07123
Local Museum
Sasa Kibbutz
General Museum
Archaeological finds

Sedot Yam Kibbutz

07124
Caesarea Museum
Sedot Yam Kibbutz
History/Public Affairs Museum
Classical antiquities

Sha'ar HaGolan Kibbutz

07125
Museum of Prehistory
Sha'ar HaGolan Kibbutz
Archeology Museum - 1950
Neolithic Yarmukian culture

Shivta

07126
Archaeological Site Shivta
mail c/o National Parks Authority, POB 7028, Shivta
Archeology Museum
Nabataean and Byzantine remains

Tabgha

07127
Church of the Bread and Fish
Tabgha, POB 52, Tiberias
Archeology Museum

Tel Adashim

07128
Sara Memorial House (Ohel Sara)
Tel Adashim
General Museum
Archaeological finds; art

Tel Aviv

07129
The Alphabet Museum Haaretz Museum
POB 17068, Tel Aviv
History/Public Affairs Museum
History of writing and the Jewish alphabet; copies of important inscriptions

07130
Beth Hatefutsoth Museum of the Jewish Diaspora
Rehov Klausner, POB 39359, Tel Aviv
History/Public Affairs Museum
Photos, models, multi-media presentations depicting Jewish life in the Diaspora

07131
Ceramics Museum Haaretz Museum
University St, POB 17068, Tel Aviv
Archeology Museum - 1966
Pre-biblical and biblical pottery; local artifacts from late Antiquity to the Middle Ages; Cypriote and Greek collections

07132
Glass Museum
Haaretz Museum, University Rd, Tel Aviv
Archeology Museum - 1959
Ancient glass vessels

07133
Israel Theater Museum
3 Melchett St, Tel Aviv
Performing Arts Museum - 1969
Exhibits on Jewish theater in Israel and abroad; original sketches from productions, 1920-1980; documents from Jewish theater in the underground and camps (WW II)

07134
Israeli Defense Forces Museum Beth
Eliahu Golomb - Beth Hagana
23 Rothschild Blvd, 10 Karlibah ST, Tel
Aviv
History/Public Affairs Museum - 1961
Militaria relating to history of State of
Israel

07135
The Jabotinsky Institute
Rehov Hamelekh George 38, Tel Aviv
History/Public Affairs Museum
Life and works of Zeev Jabotinsky,
leader of Revisionist Zionism; history
of the Revisionist Movement

07136
Kadman Numismatic Museum
Haaretz Museum, University St, POB
17068, Tel Aviv
History/Public Affairs Museum - 1962
History of money from earliest times
to the present

07137
Man and His Work Haaretz Museum
POB 17068, Tel Aviv
Science/Tech Museum
Tools and implements; reconstructed
workshops; steam power in
agriculture

07138
**Museum of Antiquities of Tel
Aviv-Yafo** Haaretz Museum
Rehov Mifratz Shelomo 10, Tel Aviv
Archeology Museum
Regional archaeology, including
monuments, jewelry, inscriptions and
coins

07139
**Museum of Ethnography and
Folklore** Haaretz Museum
POB 17068, Tel Aviv
Anthropology Museum
Jewish folk and ritual objects;
costumes of the Jewish communities -
library

07140
**Museum of Science and Technology
and the Lasky Planetarium** Haaretz
Museum
University Rd, POB 17068, Tel Aviv
Science/Tech Museum - 1964
Aeronautics and astronautics;
mathematics; energy; transportation;
astronomy

07141
**Museum of the History of Tel
Aviv-Yafo** Haaretz Museum
Rehov Bialik 27, Tel Aviv
General Museum
Photos, models and maps illustrating
the history of the city

07142
Nehusthan Pavilion Haaretz Museum
POB 17968, Tel Aviv
Archeology Museum
Finds from the ancient copper mines
at Timna in the Negev

07143
Tel Aviv Museum
Sderot Shaul Hamelekh 27-29, POB
33288, Tel Aviv
Fine Arts Museum - 1931
European and American art from the
17th century to the present, with
emphasis on modern and
contemporary art; works of Jewish
artists; loan exhibitions - library

Tel Hay

07144
Tel Hay Courtyard and Museum
Tel Hay, Upper Galilee
General Museum
Reconstructed settlement, site of
Joseph Trumpeldor's defeat by Arab
raiders in 1920; photos, documents,
models, tools and weapons relating to
early modern Jewish settlement of
Eretz-Israel

Tiberias

07145
Municipal Museum of Antiquities
Tiberias
General Museum
Objects from ancient synagogues and
tombs; 19th century views of the city

Yad Mordekhay Kibbutz

07146
Yad Mordekhay Museum
POB 79145, Yad Mordekhay Kibbutz
History/Public Affairs Museum - 1968
Documents from the holocaust;
monument to commander of the
Warsaw ghetto uprising

Yif'at Kibbutz

07147
Museum of Early Zionist Settlement
Doar Yif'at, Yif'at Kibbutz
Anthropology Museum - 1967
Agricultural tools and equipment;
domestic implements; artifacts
depicting founding of the kibbutz
movement

Zefat

07148
Glichenstein Museum
POB 1006, Zefat
Fine Arts Museum
Paintings and sculpture of Hanoch
Glichenstein; Haim Vidal Chapira
collection

07149
Museum of Printing Art
Zefat
Fine Arts Museum
Prints; photos; ancient maps; book title
pages; graphic arts by Jewish and
foreign artists

Zikhron Ya'aqov

07150
Aaronson House
Rehov Hameyasdim 40, Zikhron
Ya'aqov
History/Public Affairs Museum
original furnishings and archives of the
organizer of the 'Nili' spy network
(WW I); herbarium - library

Italy

Acireale

07151
Pinacoteca dell'Accademia Zelantea
Via San Giuliano 17, I-95024 Acireale,
Catania
Fine Arts Museum - 1848
Coll: archeology; coins; 17th and 18th
century paintings by Sicilian artists

Adrano

07152
Museo Archeologico Etneo
Castello normanno, I-95031 Adrano,
Catania
Archeology Museum
Historical exhibits in an 11th century
Norman castle

Adria

07153
Museo Archeologico Nazionale
Piazza degli Etruschi 1, I-45011 Adria,
Rovigo
Archeology Museum - 1905
Coll: Attic vases; grave and votive
stones; two-wheeled iron chariot of
the 4th century B.C.; Etruscan,
Graeco-Roman and Campanian coins

Agliè

07154
Castello Ducale
I-10011 Agliè, Torino
History/Public Affairs Museum
Former ducal residence; 17th century
decorations; archeological finds from
Tuscolo

Agrigento

07155
Antiquarium di Villa Aurea
Via dei Templi, I-92100 Agrigento
Archeology Museum
Local prehistoric culture; Graeco-
Roman objects; antiquities of the
Aurea villa

07156
Casa Natale di Pirandello
Località Caos, I-92100 Agrigento
Historic Site
Books, bibliography, manuscripts and
memorabilia of the writer Luigi
Pirandello

07157
Museo Civico
Piazza Pirandello 16, I-92100 Agrigento
General Museum
Local history; 14th to 18th century
paintings

07158
Museo Diocesano d'Arte Sacra
Annesso al Duomo, I-92100 Agrigento
Religious Art Museum
Coll: priests' vestments; 14th and 15th
century frescoes; Byzantine
reliquaries; Greek sarcophagus

07159
Museo Nazionale Archeologico
Contrada San Nicola, I-92100
Agrigento
Archeology Museum
Coll: archeological finds from
excavations of Agrigento; marble
sculpture of the Greek period; Attic
vases; terra cottas; coins

Ala

07160
Museo Civico 'Luigi Dalla Laita'
Via Battisti 2, I-38061 Ala, Trento
General Museum
Local history and archeology; fossils;
minerals; numismatics

Alagna Valsesia

07161
Museo Walser
Località Pedemonte, I-13021 Alagna
Valsesia, Vercelli
Historic Site
17th century typical house with period
furniture, artifacts and agricultural
products

Alassio

07162
**Museo di Scienze Naturali 'Don
Bosco'**
Via Don Bosco 12, I-17021 Alassio
Natural History Museum - 1950
Coll: fossils; mineralogy; petrography;
ornithology; historical-ethnographical
material

Alba

07163
**Civico Museo Archeologico e di
Scienze Naturali 'Federico Eusebio'**
Via Paruzza 1, I-12051 Alba, Cuneo
Archeology Museum - 1897
Coll: local prehistoric finds; fossils;
molluscs; Roman antiquities; ceramics;
tombs; sculpture; decorative
fragments - library

Albenga

07164
Civico Museo Ingauno
Palazzo Vecchio, I-17031 Albenga,
Savona
General Museum - 1933
Coll: archeological and medieval
exhibits; sculpture; tombstones

07165
Museo del Battistero
Piazza San Michele, I-17031 Albenga,
Savona
Religious Art Museum
Baptismal font; 5th and 6th century
mosaics

07166
Museo Navale Romano
Piazza San Michele 12, I-17031
Albenga, Savona
History/Public Affairs Museum
Coll: finds from submarine excavations
in the Ligurian Sea; photos and
documents of antique ships and naval
objects

Alessandria

07167
Museo del Cappello
Corso Cento Cannoni 23, C.P. 165,
I-15100 Alessandria
Decorative Arts Museum
Historical and modern hats; models
produced by the hatmaker Borsalino
from early to present times

07168
Museo della Battaglia
Località Marengo, I-15100 Alessandria
Historic Site
Documents and model of the battle of
Marengo in 1800

07169
Museo e Pinacoteca Civica
Via Tripoli 8, I-15100 Alessandria
General Museum - 1885
Coll: archeology; paintings;
Napoleonic and Renaissance history;
numismatics

Alfedena

07170
Museo Civico Aufidenate
I-67030 Alfedena, L'Aquila
Archeology Museum
Findings from over 12,000 tombs from
the 6th to 4th centuries B.C.

Allumiere

07171
Museo Preistorico dell'Alto Lazio
Piazza della Repubblica 29, I-00051
Allumiere, Roma
Archeology Museum
Coll: Findings from prehistoric times;
Etruscan tomb furnishings; pottery

Amalfi

07172
Museo Civico
Piazza Municipio, I-84011 Amalfi,
Salerno
General Museum
Historical costumes; nautical
instruments; paintings

Anacapri

07173
Museo San Michele
I-80071 Anacapri, Napoli
Historic Site
House of Axel Munthe; 18th century
paintings; glazed majolica floor tiles

Anagni

07174
**Mostra del Lazio Meridionale e di
Celestino V**
Plazzo Bonifaciano, I-03012 Anagni,
Frosinone
General Museum
Local history exhibits; archeology from
the area

07175
Museo del Tesoro della Cattedrale
Piazza Innocenzo III, I-03012 Anagni,
Frosinone
Religious Art Museum
Coll: cathedral treasury; religious art;
jewelry; goldsmith work; inscriptions;
antique marbles

Ancona

07176
Museo Diocesano d'Arte Sacra
Vecchio Episcopio, I-60100 Ancona
Religious Art Museum - 1960
Coll: early Christian and medieval
architecture and art from the churches
of Ancona; 4th century sarcophagus;
12th century crucifix

07177
Museo Nazionale delle Marche
Via Ferretti, I-60100 Ancona
Archeology Museum
Coll: Exhibits from the paleolithic age
to the Roman period; sculpture;
frescoes; vases

07178
**Pinacoteca Civica 'Francesco
Podesti' e Galleria Comunale d'Arte
Moderna**
Palazzo Bosdari, Via Pizzecolli 17,
I-60100 Ancona
Fine Arts Museum - 1880
14th-18th century paintings;
contemporary paintings; paintings by
Titian - library

Angera

07179
Rocca Borromeo
I-21021 Angera, Varese
Fine Arts Museum
15th century frescoes from the
Palazzo Borromeo in Milan

Anticoli Corrado

07180
Museo Civico
Piazza Santa Vittoria, I-00022 Anticoli
Corrado, Roma
General Museum
Paintings; bronzes; sculpture

Aosta

07181
**Museo dell'Accademia di
Sant'Anselmo**
Via Olivetti 3, I-11100 Aosta
History/Public Affairs Museum
Numismatics; pre-Roman, Roman and
medieval exhibits

07182
Tesoro della Cattedrale
Via de Sales 6, I-11100 Aosta
Religious Art Museum
Coll: 12th to 17th century religious art;
reliquaries; jewelry; 12th century
mosaics

07183
Tesoro della Collegiata di Sant'Orso
Via Sant'Orso, I-11100 Aosta
Religious Art Museum
14th and 15th century religious art

Aquileia

07184
Museo Archeologico Nazionale
Via Roma 1, I-33051 Aquileia, Udine
Archeology Museum - 1882
Coll: Roman architecture; mosaics;
inscriptions; sculpture - library

07185
Museo Nazionale Paleocristiano
Piazza Monastero, I-33051 Aquileia,
Udine
Archeology Museum - 1961
Coll: Christian inscriptions; remains of
Paleo-Christian architecture; mosaics

Ardea

07186
Raccolta Amici di Manzù
I-00040 Ardea, Roma
Historic Site
Sculptures, drawings, goldwork and
engravings by Giacomo Manzù

Arezzo

07187
Museo Archeologico
Via Margaritone 10, I-52100 Arezzo
Archeology Museum - 1823
Coll: bronzes; Greek and Etruscan
ceramics; goldware; sarcophagi;
mosaics

07188
Museo di Casa Vasari
Via XX Settembre 55, I-52100 Arezzo
Fine Arts Museum - 1911
Paintings and frescoes by Giogio
Vasari; Tuscan painters; memorabilia

07189
Museo Diocesano
Piazza Duomo, I-52100 Arezzo
Religious Art Museum
Coll: illuminated codices; religious art;
paintings; statues

07190
**Museo Statale di Arte Medioevale e
Moderna**
Via San Lorentino 8, I-52100 Arezzo
Fine Arts Museum - 1810
Coll: 15th to 19th century Italian
paintings; frescoes; sculpture;
majolica; medals; bronzes; ivories;
goldsmith art

Argenta

07191
Pinacoteca Comunale
Via Aleotti, I-44011 Argenta, Ferrara
Fine Arts Museum
15th to 18th century frescoes,
paintings and sculpture

Arquà Petrarca

07192
Casa di Petrarca
Via Androna 5, I-35032 Arquà Petrarca,
Padova
Historic Site - 1923
Home of scholar-poet Petrarca
(1304-1374); furniture; memorabilia

Asciano

07193
Museo d'Arte Sacra
Chiesa di Santa Croce, I-53041
Asciano, Siena
Religious Art Museum
Coll: 14th and 15th century religious
paintings; wooden statues; terra
cottas; frescoes

07194
Museo Etrusco
Corso Matteotti, I-53041 Asciano,
Siena
Archeology Museum
Finds of the Etruscan tombs in Poggio
Pinci

Ascoli Piceno

07195
Museo Archeologico Comunale
Piazza del Popolo, I-63100 Ascoli
Piceno
Archeology Museum - 1779
Coll: prehistoric finds; bronzes;
Roman sculpture; mosaics; jewelry;
ceramics

07196
Museo Diocesano
Piazza dell' Arringo, I-63100 Ascoli
Piceno
Religious Art Museum
Coll: religious paintings; ivory, silver
and stone sculptures

07197
Pinacoteca Civica
Piazza dell'Arringo, I-63100 Ascoli
Piceno
Fine Arts Museum - 1861
Coll: paintings from the Marches
region; paintings by Titian and
Tintoretto; 19th century drawings

Asolo

07198
Museo Civico
Loggia della Ragione, I-31011 Asolo,
Treviso
General Museum
Coll: archeological section with early
Venetian and Roman material;
paintings, relics and arms of the
Venetian period; room and
memorabilia on actress Eleonora Duse

Assisi

07199
Galleria d'Arte Contemporanea
Cittadella Cristiana, I-06081 Assisi,
Perugia
Fine Arts Museum
800 paintings and sculptures;
photographs; prints; children's
drawings

07200
Museo Civico e Foro Romano
Via Portica 2, I-06081 Assisi
General Museum
Coll: Etruscan and Roman urns,
pictures, sculpture, epigraphs; Roman
forum

07201
**Museo-Tesoro Basilica di S.
Francesco**
I-06082 Assisi
Religious Art Museum
12th-14th century precious relics;
goldsmith art

07202
Pinacoteca Comunale
Piazza del Comune, I-06081 Assisi
Fine Arts Museum
13th-16th century paintings and
canvas; detached frescoes

Asti

07203
Museo Alfieriano
Corso Alfieri 375, I-14100 Asti
Historic Site - 1937
Birthplace of Vittorio Alfieri;
memorabilia and rare editions of his
works - library

07204
**Museo Archeologico e
Paleontologico**
Corso Alfieri 2, I-14100 Asti
Archeology Museum - 1885
Pre-Roman and Roman archeology;
Etruscan antiquities; fossils; mummies

07205
Museo del Risorgimento
Corso Alfieri 357, I-14100 Asti
History/Public Affairs Museum - 1911
'Sala Risorgimentale' in the Pinacoteca
Civica: Paintings, arms and other
exhibits of the 'Risorgimento'

07206
Pinacoteca Civica
Corso Alfieri 357, I-14100 Asti
Fine Arts Museum - 1903
Ancient, modern and contemporary
works of art - library

Atri

07207
Museo Capitolare
Annesso Alla Cattedrale, Via Roma,
I-64032 Atri, Teramo
Religious Art Museum - 1914
Coll: wood sculpture; ceramics;
religious vestments; goldsmith work;
miniatures; old manuscripts;
incunabula; 16th-17th century
paintings; lapidarium

Avellino

07208
Museo Irpino
Corso Europa, I-83100 Avellino
Fine Arts Museum - 1934
Coll: archeological finds from Iron Age
to Roman period; numismatics;
religious art; modern section

Avola

07209
Museo Civico
Piazza Umberto 1, I-96012 Avola,
Siracusa
General Museum
Coll: prehistoric, Graeco-Roman and
medieval archeology; paintings;
pottery

Badia di Cava dei Tirreni

07210
Museo della Badia
Via Morcaldi 6, I-84010 Badia di Cava
dei Tirreni, Salerno
General Museum
Coll: Roman sarcophagi; illuminated
manuscripts; paintings; sculpture

Bagheria

07211
**Galleria d'Arte Moderna e
Contemporanea**
Strada Statale 113, I-90011 Bagheria,
Palermo
Fine Arts Museum
Paintings by contemporary artists

Baranello

07212
Museo Civico
Via Santa Maria, I-86042 Baranello,
Campobasso
General Museum
Local archeology; paintings;
decorative art; coins

Bari

07213
Gipsoteca del Castello
Piazza Federico II di Svevia, I-70122
Bari
Fine Arts Museum
Plaster sculptures of Roman
monuments in Sicily

07214
Museo Archeologico
Piazza Umberto I, I-70121 Bari
Archeology Museum
Coll: prehistoric to Roman history of
Apulia; Apulian, Greek and Corinthian
pottery; coins and medals

07215
Museo della Basilica di San Nicola
Basilica di San Nicola, I-70122 Bari
Religious Art Museum
Coll: fragments of sculptures and
silver decorations from churches of
Bari; liturgical relics

07216
Pinacoteca Provinciale
Via Spalato 19, I-70121 Bari
Fine Arts Museum - 1934
11th-19th century Apulian, Venetian
and Neapolitan paintings and sculpture

Barletta

07217
Museo Civico di Barletta
Corso Cavour 8, I-70051 Barletta, Bari
Fine Arts Museum - 1929
Coll: 17th-19th century paintings of the
Neapolitan school; Renaissance
sculpture; Italian artifacts; local
archeology - library

Bassano del Grappa

07218
Museo, Biblioteca e Archivio Museo
Civico
Via Museo 12, I-36061 Bassano del
Grappa, Vicenza
Fine Arts Museum - 1828
Coll: drawings; engravings; picture
gallery; archeology; numismatics;
manuscripts; rare book editions;
incunabula; majolica - library

Bazzano

07219
Museo Civico Archeologico
Via Contessa Matilde, I-67010
Bazzano, Bologna
Archeology Museum - 1874
Coll: prehistoric finds from local
excavations; Roman objects; bronzes;
decorated vases

Bedonia

07220
Museo del Seminario
Via s. Stefano Raffi, I-43041 Bedonia,
Parma
Archeology Museum - 1953
Prehistoric to Roman archeological
material

Belluno

07221
Museo Civico
Piazza del Duomo 16, I-32100 Belluno
General Museum - 1876
Coll: local history exhibits;
archeological section; paintings;
bronzes; Renaissance medals

Bene Vagienna

07222
Museo Civico
Via Roma, I-12041 Bene Vagienna,
Cuneo
General Museum - 1894
Coll: archeology; bronzes; glass;
ceramics; Roman architecture

Benevento

07223
Museo del Sannio
Piazza Matteotti, I-82100 Benevento
History/Public Affairs Museum - 1873
Coll: archeology; Roman sarcophagi
and vases; medieval and modern art;
regional history; numismatics - library

Bentivoglio

07224
Museo della Civiltà Contadina
Località San Marino, I-40010
Bentivoglio, Bologna
Agriculture Museum
Coll: tools; farm implements;
agricultural objects

Bergamo

07225
Civico Museo Archeologico
Piazza Cittadella 9, I-24100 Bergamo
Archeology Museum - 1561
Coll: prehistoric, Paleochristian and
Langobard findings; Roman statues,
reliefs and frescoes; epigraphs -
library

07226
**Museo Civico del Risorgimento e
della Resistenza**
Piazzale Belvedere 12, I-24100
Bergamo
History/Public Affairs Museum
History and documents on the 'Five
Days of Bergamo' in 1848 and of
Garibaldi's activity in the town

07227
**Museo Civico di Scienze Naturali
'Caffi'**
Piazza Cittadella 13, I-24100 Bergamo
Natural History Museum
Coll: ornithology; butterflies;
herbarium; fossils

07228
Museo Donizettiano
Via Arena 9, I-24100 Bergamo
Historic Site
Memorabilia on the composer
Gaetano Donizetti (1797-1848)

07229
Pinacoteca dell'Accademia 'Carrara'
Piazza Carrara 81a, I-24100 Bergamo
Fine Arts Museum - 1796
Coll: 14th to 19th century paintings;
15th century paintings of Venetian,
Lombardian and Tuscan schools by
Pisanello, Bellini, Botticelli, Mantegna,
Lotto and others

Bettona

07230
Pinacoteca e Museo Civico
Palazzetto Podestarile, I-06084
Bettona, Perugia
General Museum - 1958
Coll: paintings of the Umbrian school;
works by Perugino, Della Robbia, Di
Lorenzo; decorative arts; local history;
Etruscan archeology

Bevagna

07231
Antiquarium e Mosaico Romano
Via Porta Guelfa, I-06031 Bevagna
Archeology Museum
Mosaic pavement of the 2nd century;
antiquities; epigraphs; Roman
household objects

07232
Pinacoteca Comunale 'F. Torti'
Corso Matteotti 72, I-06031 Bevagna,
Perugia
Fine Arts Museum
Coll: paintings by Umbrian masters;
Roman coins; archeological remains

Biella

07233
**Istituto di Fotografia Alpina 'Vittorio
Sella'**
Via San Gerolamo 2, I-13051 Biella,
Vercelli
General Museum - 1948
Coll: mountain photography from 1879
to 1909; history of photography from
1839 to modern times - library

07234
Museo Civico
Via Micca 36, I-13051 Biella, Vercelli
General Museum - 1932
Coll: local archeology; Egyptian
antiquities; ancient, modern and
contemporary art; 15th and 16th
century frescoes

Bitonto

07235
Museo Civico 'E. Rogadeo'
Via Rogadeo 52, I-70032 Bitonto, Bari
General Museum
Prehistoric and Graeco-Roman
archeological remains of the area;
stone tablets; antiquities; paintings

07236
Museo Diocesano
Via del Vescovado 2, I-70032 Bitonto,
Bari
Religious Art Museum
Religious art; 15th to 19th century
paintings

Bobbio

07237
Castello Malaspina
I-29022 Bobbio, Piacenza
General Museum
Renaissance antiquities, furniture and
ornaments

07238
**Museo della Basilica di San
Colombano**
Piazza Fara, I-29022 Bobbio, Piacenza
Archeology Museum
Coll: Roman to Baroque antiquities and
architecture; sculpture

Bogliaco

07239
Museo della Villa Bettoni
Via Bogliaco, I-25080 Bogliaco, Brescia
Fine Arts Museum
Frescoes, portraits and paintings in an
18th century villa

Bologna

07240
Biblioteca e casa di Carducci
Piazza Carducci 5, I-40125 Bologna
Historic Site - 1907
Home of poet Giosuè Carducci
(1835-1907); manuscripts; his books;
personal possessions; furnishings -
library

07241
Civico Museo Bibliografico Musicale
Piazza Rossini 2, I-40126 Bologna
Music Museum
Coll: 15th to 20th century printed
music editions; 18th to 19th century
pianos; manuscripts of musical theory

07242
Collezioni Comunali d'Arte
Piazza Maggiore 6, I-40126 Bologna
Fine Arts Museum - 1936
Coll: 13th to 19th century Bolognese
and Italian paintings; furniture and
decorative arts; ivory miniatures;
embroidery; laces

07243
Donazione Putti Biblioteca Raccolta
dell'Istituto Ortopedico Rizzoli
Via Codivilla 9, I-40136 Bologna
History/Public Affairs Museum - 1925
Old books on medical subjects;
pictures, prints and autographs of
scientists' old surgical instruments;
two ivory anatomical manikins; 16th
and 18th century globes - library

07244
**Gabinetto dei Disegni e delle
Stampe**
Via Belle Arti 56, I-40126 Bologna
Fine Arts Museum
Coll: engravings; German, Flemish and
French prints; 19th century drawings

07245
Galleria Comunale d'Arte Moderna
Piazza Costituzione 3, I-40128 Bologna
Fine Arts Museum - 1975
Contemporary art mainly by Emilian
and Bolognese painters

07246
Museo Aldrovandiano Biblioteca
Universitaria
Palazzo Poggi, Via Zamboni 35,
I-40126 Bologna
Natural History Museum - 1603
Work of the Italian naturalist Ulisse
Aldrovandi; pictures; zoology; botany;
geology; mineralogy

07247
Museo Civico Archeologico
Via Archiginnasio 2, I-40124 Bologna
Archeology Museum - 1881
Coll: topographical section with
prehistoric, Etruscan, Gallic and
Roman material; Greek, Roman and
Etrusco-Italian exhibits; numismatics -
library

07248
**Museo Civico del Primo e Secondo
Risorgimento**
Via dei Musei 8, I-40124 Bologna
History/Public Affairs Museum - 1893
Memorabilia on activities and
personalities of the Risorgimento

07249
**Museo d'Arte Industriale 'Davia
Bargellini'**
Strada Maggiore 44, I-40125 Bologna
Decorative Arts Museum - 1928
Coll: 15th to 19th century locksmith's
work in iron and bronze; 18th century
Bolognese living style; furniture; 14th
to 18th century paintings

07250
Museo delle Navi
Via Zamboni 33, I-40126 Bologna
Science/Tech Museum - 1724
Antique ship models and maps

07251
Museo dell'Istituto di Zoologia
Via S. Giacomo 9, I-40126 Bologna
Natural History Museum
Coll: zoology of Mozambique; fish of
Brazil; corals; birds of Italy; various
continents

07252
Museo di Astronomia
Via Zamboni 33, C.P. 596, I-40126
Bologna
Science/Tech Museum - 1954
Coll: transit instruments from the early
18th century; miscellaneous
astronomical instruments from the
15th through the 19th centuries; early
18th century observatorium - library

07253
Museo di Mineralogia
Piazza di Porta San Donato 1, I-40127
Bologna
Natural History Museum - 1807
Mineralogy; petrography

07254
Museo di San Domenico
Piazza San Domenico 13, I-40124
Bologna
Religious Art Museum - 1956
Coll: religious painting, sculpture and
decorative art; goldsmiths' work

07255
Museo di San Giuseppe
Via Bellinzona 6, I-40135 Bologna
Fine Arts Museum - 1928
15th-20th century works by Bolognese
and Romagnese painters; miniatures;
ivories

07256
Museo di San Petronio
Piazza Maggiore, I-40124 Bologna
Religious Art Museum - 1893
History of the Basilica; designs of the
facade; 16th and 17th century religious
art

07257
Museo di Santo Stefano
Via Santo Stefano 24, I-40125 Bologna
Religious Art Museum
Coll: Roman and Byzantine epigraphs;
14th to 17th century Bolognese
paintings

07258
Museo di Veterinaria
Via Belmeloro 10, I-40124 Bologna
Natural History Museum
Veterinary sciences; anatomy;
pathology; teratology

07259
**Museo Geologico Paleontologico 'G.
Cappellini'**
Via Zamboni 63, I-40127 Bologna
Natural History Museum
Coll: geology; lithology; paleontology;
fossils and rocks mainly from Emilia,
Tuscany and Venezia

07260
Museo Marsiliano Biblioteca
Universitaria
Palazzo Poggi, Via Zamboni 35,
I-40126 Bologna
Historic Site - 1930
Coll: manuscripts, printed works and
possessions of Luigi Ferdinando
Marsili

07261
**Museo Storico dell'Università di
Bologna**
Via Zamboni 33, I-40126 Bologna
History/Public Affairs Museum - 1888
Coll: medieval to 19th century history
of Bolognese University life;
documents; antiquities

07262
**Museo Storico-Didattico della
Tappezzeria**
Via Barberia 13, I-40124 Bologna
Decorative Arts Museum
Tapestries; furnishings; antique
weaving looms; decorative art

07263
Pinacoteca Nazionale
Via Belle Arti 56, I-40126 Bologna
Fine Arts Museum - 1808
Coll: 14th to 18th century Bolognese
painting; 15th to 16th century German
engravings by Dürer and pupils; Italian
Renaissance engravings

Bolsena

07264
Antiquarium Comunale
Palazzo del Municipio, I-01023
Bolsena, Viterbo
General Museum
Local archeology and architecture;
13th and 14th century pottery

Bolzano

07265
Museo Civico
Via Cassa di Risparmo 14, I-39100
Bolzano
General Museum - 1882
Coll: archeology; ethnography;
baroque paintings from South Tyrolian
artists; 13th-16th century local
woodcarving - library

Bomarzo

07266
Parco dei Mostri
I-01020 Bomarzo, Viterbo
Fine Arts Museum
Collection of sculptures

Bordighera

07267
Museo 'Bicknell'
Via Romana 39 bis, I-18012 Bordighera,
Imperia
Natural History Museum - 1888
Coll: herbarium; entomology; copy of
prehistoric rock engravings - library

Borgosesia

07268
Istituto per la Storia della Resistenza
Via Sesone 10, I-13011 Borgosesia,
Vercelli
History/Public Affairs Museum
Documents, photographs and other
exhibits on the anti-Fascist, partisan
and peasants movements in the
province of Vercelli - library

BorgoVal di Taro

07269
Casa Natale di Toscanini
Via Tanzi 5, I-43043 BorgoVal di Taro,
Parma
Historic Site
Discs of works by Arturo Toscanini;
memorabilia on his career and life

Bormio

07270
Museo Civico
Palazzo De Simoni, I-23032 Bormio,
Sondrio
General Museum
Local history; folk art; ethnographical
section

Bovino

07271
Raccolta Comunale
Via Leggieri, I-71023 Bovino, Foggia
General Museum
Roman inscriptions; pottery; bronzes;
fossils

Bra

07272
Museo Civico 'Craveri'
Via Craveri 15, I-12042 Bra, Cuneo
Natural History Museum - 1859
Coll: geology; paleontology; zoology;
botany; herbarium; archives - library

07273
Museo di Storia Archeologia ed Arte
Palazzo Traversa, Via Parpera, I-12024
Bra, Cuneo
Archeology Museum - 1919
Roman archeological remains of
Pollenzo and surroundings

Brescello

07274
Antiquarium
Nella Sede Municipale, I-42041
Brescello, Reggio Emilia
Archeology Museum - 1960
Roman inscriptions and sculptures
from excavations in the ancient town

Brescia

07275
**Collezione d'Arte Moderna
'Cavellini'**
Via Bonomelli 16, I-25100 Brescia
Fine Arts Museum
Contemporary art collection

07276
Galleria d'Arte Moderna
Via Musei 81/1, I-25100 Brescia
Fine Arts Museum - 1964
Modern paintings and sculptures

07277
Museo Civico di Storia Naturale
Via Gualla 3/ Via Ozanam 4, I-25100
Brescia
Natural History Museum - 1949
Coll: ornithology; entomology;
geology; mineralogy; paleontology;
meteorites - library

07278
Museo Cristiano
Via Piamarta 4, I-25100 Brescia
Religious Art Museum - 1882
Religious art from the Paleochristian to
the Renaissance period; reliquaries

07279
Museo del Risorgimento
Castello, I-25100 Brescia
History/Public Affairs Museum - 1887
Coll: documents; relics; prints; arms;
local historical paintings of the
Risorgimento period

07280
Museo delle Armi 'Marzoli'
Castello, I-25100 Brescia
History/Public Affairs Museum
Armour; firearms; armes blanches

07281
Museo Romano
Via Musei 57a, I-25100 Brescia
Archeology Museum - 1830
Historic site with pre-Roman and
Roman remains; sculpture; bronzes;
numismatics

07282
Pinacoteca 'Tosio Martinengo'
Via Martinengo da Barco 1, I-25100
Brescia
Fine Arts Museum - 1832
Coll: 13th-18th century Italian and
foreign paintings; decorative and
religious art; masterpieces of Brescian
painting

Bressanone

07283
**Museo Diocesano e Collezione dei
Presepi**
Via Alboino 2, I-39042 Bressanone,
Bolzano
Religious Art Museum
13th to 18th century local woodcarving
and Cathedral treasure; religious art of
Roman and baroque eras

Brindisi

07284
**Museo Archeologico Provinciale 'F.
Ribezzo'**
Piazza Duomo, I-72100 Brindisi
Archeology Museum - 1954
Coll: regional archeological finds;
stone fragments; Greco-Roman
sculpture; inscriptions; ceramics; terra
cottas; mosaics; coins

Budrio

07285
Pinacoteca Civica 'Inzaghi'
Via Mentana 9, I-40054 Budrio,
Bologna
Fine Arts Museum - 1931
15th to 18th century Bolognese
painting, prints and drawings

Busseto

07286
Casa di Verdi
Località Roncole, I-43011 Busseto,
Parma
Historic Site - 1915
Memorabilia on Giuseppe Verdi
(1813-1901)

07287
Museo Civico
Via Provesi 41, I-43011 Busseto, Parma
General Museum - 1957
16th century historic house with
baroque annexes; 15th to 18th century
paintings; pottery; furniture

Cagliari

07288
Galleria Comunale d'Arte
Viale Regina Elena, I-09100 Cagliari
Fine Arts Museum - 1927
Coll: 17th to 20th century Sardinian
painting; Oriental decorative arts; folk
art of Sardinia

07289
Museo Archeologico Nazionale
Piazza Indipendenza 4, I-09100 Cagliari
Archeology Museum - 1802
Coll: prehistoric, Punic and Roman
archeology of Sardinia; Semitic gems;
goldsmith work; Roman glass

07290
Museo Capitolare
Via del Fossario, I-09100 Cagliari
Religious Art Museum
Coll: material concerning popes,
bishops and kings; statues; copper
and silverware

07291
**Museo Sardo di Antropologia ed
Etnografia**
Via Porcell 2, I-09100 Cagliari
Anthropology Museum - 1953
Coll: prehistory and earliest history of
Sardinia; Sardinian costumes and folk
art

Caldaro

07292
Museo Atesino del Vino
Castello Ringberg, I-39052 Caldaro,
Bolzano
Anthropology Museum
History of regional viticulture

Caltagirone

07293
Museo Civico
Via Roma 10, I-95041 Caltagirone,
Catania
General Museum
Archeological findings of the area;
18th and 19th century paintings;
contemporary pottery

Caltanissetta

07294
Museo Civico
Via Colaianni 2, I-93100 Caltanissetta
Fine Arts Museum
Archeological section; modern
sculpture

07295
Museo Folkloristico
Via Pisani 10, I-93100 Caltanissetta
Religious Art Museum
Dioramas of moments in the Passion
of Jesus

07296
Museo Mineralogico
Viale della Regione, I-93100
Caltanissetta
Natural History Museum
Minerals; fossils; Sicilian gypsum and
sulphur

Camaiore

07297
Museo d'Arte Sacra
Piazza Diaz, I-55041 Camaiore, Lucca
Religious Art Museum
Religious art; goldsmith's work;
tapestries

Camerino

07298
Museo Civico
Via Sparapani 10, I-62032 Camerino,
Macerata
General Museum
Coll: Roman and medieval inscriptions
and reliefs; coins; seals; pre-Roman
and Roman pottery; paintings by local
masters

07299
Museo di Anatomia annesso alla
Facoltà di Medicina Veterinaria
Istituto di Anatomia degli Animali
Domestici, I-62032 Camerino,
Macerata
Natural History Museum
Comparative anatomy

07300
Museo di Geologia
Via Venanzi, I-62032 Camerino,
Macerata
Natural History Museum
Geology; paleontology; petrography;
mineralogy

07301
Museo Diocesano
Palazzo Arcivescovile, I-62032
Camerino, Macerata
Religious Art Museum
Religious art from local churches
including a Madonna by Tiepolo

07302
Pinacoteca Civica
Via Sparapani 10, I-62032 Camerino,
Macerata
Fine Arts Museum
Coll: 13th and 14th century frescoes;
ceramics; 14th and 15th century
works by the Camerino school

Camogli

07303
**Museo Civico Marinaro 'Gio-Bono
Ferrari'**
Via Ferrari, I-16032 Camogli, Genova
Science/Tech Museum
Ship models; paintings of Camogli
sailing ships; relics of Garibaldi

Campobasso

07304
**Museo del Presepio in Miniatura
'Guido Colitti'**
Piazza della Vittoria 4, I-86100
Campobasso
Religious Art Museum
Manger scenes from all over the
world; manger scene postage stamps

Canosa di Puglia

07305
Museo Civico Archeologico
Via Varrone 45, I-70053 Canosa di
Puglia, Bari
Archeology Museum
5th to 3rd century B.C. archeology;
pottery; bronzes; Roman sculpture
and epigraphs

Caprera

07306
Museo Garibaldino
Località La Maddalena, I-07024
Caprera, Sassari
Historic Site
Home of Garibaldi; personal
possessions; his tomb

Caprese

07307
Museo 'Michelangelo'
Via del Castello 3, I-32033 Caprese,
Arezzo
Historic Site
Michelangelo's birthplace;
reproductions; outdoor exhibition of
works by contemporary sculptors -
library

Capua

07308
Museo Provinciale Campano
Via Roma, I-81043 Capua, Caserta
General Museum
Coll: archeological section; terra
cottas; vases; medieval sculpture;
architecture; painting; local history -
library

Carmagnola

07309
Museo Civico di Storia Naturale
Piazza Sant'Agostino 17, I-10022
Carmagnola, Torino
Natural History Museum
Coll: birds; reptiles; amphibians;
mammals; insects; minerals; fossils

Carpi

07310
Museo Civico 'Giulio Ferrari'
Piazza dei Martiri 68, I-41012 Carpi,
Modena
General Museum - 1914
Coll: 15th-20th century Emilian and
Venetian paintings; xylography; local
artifacts and craft products; local
history exhibits; archeology; historic
house - library

Carrara

07311
**Pinacoteca dell'Accademia di Belle
Arti**
Via Roma, I-54033 Carrara, Massa
Carrara
Fine Arts Museum
Coll: marble sculptures of Roman and
medieval period; plaster works;
picture gallery

Casale Monferrato

07312
Museo Civico
Via Cavour, I-15033 Casale
Monferrato, Alessandria
General Museum
Paintings; wood sculpture;
numismatics

07313
Museo d'Arte e Storia Antica Ebraica
Vicolo Salomone Olper 44, I-15033
Casale Monferrato, Alessandria
History/Public Affairs Museum - 1969
Coll: silverware; silk; bronzes;
documents of Hebrew civilization -
conference room

Casamari

07314
Museo dell'Abbazia
I-03020 Casamari, Frosinone
General Museum - 1918
Coll: archeological finds; Roman
epigraphs; coins; ceramics; sculpture
- library

Caserta

07315
Museo Vanvitelliano
Palazzo Reale, I-81100 Caserta
Historic Site
Models of works and drawings by
Luigi Vanvitelli (1700-1773)

07316
Palazzo Reale
Parco della Reggia, I-81100 Caserta
Fine Arts Museum - 1752
Coll: 18th century architecture;
neoclassic furniture; manger scenes;
19th century Italian and Dutch
paintings; decorated garden with rare
plants - library

Casole d'Elsa

07317
Sale della Prepositura
I-53031 Casole d'Elsa, Siena
Fine Arts Museum
Sculpture; paintings; silverware

Castel Sant'Elia

07318
Museo degli Arredi Sacri
Santuario Pontificio S. Maria ad Rupes,
I-01030 Castel Sant'Elia, Viterbo
Religious Art Museum - 1950
Coll: religious art; costumes;
ornaments; 12th to 15th century mitres

Castelfiorentino

07319
Pinacoteca
Chiesa di Santa Verdiana, I-50051
Castelfiorentino, Firenze
Fine Arts Museum
13th and 14th century paintings of the
Florentine school; illuminated books

Castelfranco Veneto

07320
Ca' Corner-Tiepolo
Località Sant'Andrea, I-31033
Castelfranco Veneto, Treviso
Fine Arts Museum
Greek, Roman and prehistoric works
of art; figurative components by Paolo
Veronese and other artists of the
Venetian school

Castellammare di Stabia

07321
Antiquarium Stabiano
Via Marco Mario 2, I-80053
Castellammare di Stabia, Napoli
Archeology Museum
Local archeological finds; ceramics;
pre-Roman decorative arts

Castellanza

07322
Museo d'Arte Moderna 'Pagani'
I-21053 Castellanza, Milano
Fine Arts Museum
Contemporary art

Castell'Arquato

07323
Museo della Collegiata
Chiostro dell'Abbazia, I-29014
Castell'Arquato, Piacenza
Religious Art Museum
In 14th century cloister; goldsmith's
work; paintings; sculpture

07324
Museo Geologico
Via Remondini, I-29014 Castell'Arquato,
Piacenza
Natural History Museum - 1961
Geology; paleontology; fossils

Castelli

07325
Museo della Ceramica
Palazzo Comunale, I-64041 Castelli,
Teramo
Decorative Arts Museum
16th to 18th century pottery

Castelvetrano

07326
Museo Selinuntino
Piazza Garibaldi 1, I-91022
Castelvetrano, Trapani
Archeology Museum - 1873
Coll: 6th-4th century B.C. Greek
ceramics; Corinthian pottery

Castiglion Fiorentino

07327
Pinacoteca Comunale
Piazza Municipio 12, I-52043 Castiglion
Fiorentino, Arezzo
Fine Arts Museum
Coll: Umbrian 13th century crucifix;
12th to 15th century goldwork and
sacred objects; paintings

Castiglione a Casauria

07328
Domus Clementina
Abbazia Clementina, I-65020
Castiglione a Casauria, Pescara
Fine Arts Museum
Roman archeological finds; medieval
pottery; rare books

Castiglione delle Stiviere

07329
**Museo Internazionale della Croce
Rossa**
Via Garibaldi 46, I-46043 Castiglione
delle Stiviere, Mantova
History/Public Affairs Museum
Exhibits concerning the Red Cross
from early to present times; prints and
photographs - library

07330
Museo Storico Aloisiano
Via Perati 6, I-46043 Castiglione delle
Stiviere, Mantova
Historic Site
16th to 18th century paintings,
portraits, furniture, silverware,
decorative arts and other possessions
of the Gonzaga family

Castrovillari

07331
Museo Civico
Via Porta della Catena 2, I-87012
Castrovillari, Cosenza
General Museum
Archeology from prehistoric to
medieval times

Catania

07332
Museo Belliniano
Piazza San Francesco 3, I-95124
Catania
Music Museum
Autographs and personal possessions
in the home of the composer Vincenzo
Bellini; historical documents of the
post-Risorgimento period - musical
library

07333
Museo Civico 'Castello Ursino'
Piazza Federico di Svevia, I-95121
Catania
General Museum - 1934
Coll: remains of the Roman theater of
Catania; vases; terra cottas; mosaics;
sarcophagi; frescoes; sculpture;
Byzantine bas-reliefs and epitaphs;
armaments; picture gallery; goldsmith
work; religious art; Sicilian coins;
historic house - library

07334
Museo di Geologia
Corso Italia 55, I-95129 Catania
Natural History Museum
Paleolithic geology

07335
Museo di Mineralogia e Petrografia
Corso Italia 55, I-95129 Catania
Natural History Museum
Mineralogy; petrography

07336
Museo di Vulcanologia
Corso Italia 55, I-95129 Catania
Natural History Museum
Stones of Italian vulcanoes, mainly Mt.
Aetna

07337
Museo Zoologico
Via Androne 81, I-95124 Catania
Natural History Museum
Coll: fauna from the area and other
countries; maritime fauna of the
Mediterranean Sea

Catanzaro

07338
Museo Provinciale
Villa Trieste, I-88100 Catanzaro
General Museum - 1879
Coll: prehistoric-Roman archeology;
pottery; numismatics; 16th-20th
century paintings

Cavalese

07339
Museo della Comunità di Fiemme
I-38033 Cavalese, Trento
General Museum
Folk art, life and work of the
inhabitants of the Val di Fiemme

Cefalù

07340
Museo 'Madralisca'
Via Madralisca 13, I-90015 Cefalù,
Palermo
General Museum - 1866
Coll: Sicilian coins; Greek vases;
paintings including the 'Portrait of a
Man' by Antonello da Messina

Cento

07341
**Pinacoteca Civica e Galleria d'Arte
Moderna 'A. Bonzagni'**
Via Matteotti, I-44042 Cento, Ferrara
Fine Arts Museum - 1839
Coll: paintings; drawings; modern art
gallery; especially works by Aroldo
Bonzagni and Guercino

Centuripe

07342
Antiquarium Comunale
Palazzo Comunale, I-94010 Centuripe,
Enna
General Museum
Coll: local architecture; Greek statues;
terra cottas; vases

Certaldo

07343
Casa del Boccaccio
Via Boccaccio, I-50052 Certaldo,
Firenze
Historic Site
Collection of Boccacio's works;
secondary literature

Certosa di Pavia

07344
Museo della Certosa
Palazzo Ducale, I-27012 Certosa di
Pavia, Pavia
Fine Arts Museum
Architecture; interior decoration

Cerveteri

07345
Museo Nazionale Cerite
I-00052 Cerveteri, Roma
Archeology Museum
Findings from the famous Etruscan
necropolis

Cesena

07346
**Museo della Civiltà Contadina
Romagnola 'Mario Bocchini'**
Rocca Malatestiana, I-47023 Cesena,
Forlì
Anthropology Museum
Coll: domestic utensils; kitchen;
weaving; machines; tools; ceramics;
various trades; harness

07347
Museo Storico dell'Antichità
Piazza Bufalini, I-47023 Cesena, Forlì
Archeology Museum
Prehistoric and Roman archeological
findings from the area

07348
Pinacoteca Comunale
Piazza Bufalini, I-47023 Cesena, Forlì
Fine Arts Museum
Paintings of local artists

Cherasco

07349
Museo Civico G.B. Adriani
Via Ospedale 40, I-12062 Cherasco,
Cuneo
General Museum - 1898
Coll: Roman archeology; miniatures;
paintings; engravings; relics; medals
and coins - library

Chianciano Terme

07350
Sala d'Arte Antica
Via Solferino 38, I-53042 Chianciano
Terme, Siena
Fine Arts Museum
Works of Sienese and Florentine
schools on wood and canvas

Chiari

07351
Pinacoteca 'Repossi'
Via Varisco 9, I-25032 Chiari, Brescia
Fine Arts Museum - 1854
Paintings; statues; prints of the
Venetian and Flemish schools in the
16th century

Chiavenna

07352
Museo Paradiso
Via Quadrio, I-23022 Chiavenna,
Sondrio
General Museum
Local history and natural environment
of the Chiavenna Valley

Chieri

07353
Capitolo del Duomo
Piazza Duomo, I-10023 Chieri, Torino
Religious Art Museum
Treasury of the church; 13th to 16th
century Flemish goldwork

Chieti

07354
Galleria d'Arte
Corso Marrucino, I-66100 Chieti
Fine Arts Museum
Modern and contemporary painting

07355
Museo Diocesano Teatino
Piazza Vico, I-66100 Chieti
Religious Art Museum - 1957
Religious art; sculpture; 16th to 18th
century local painting

07356
Museo Nazionale di Antichità
Villa Comunale, I-66100 Chieti
Archeology Museum - 1957
Coll: 6th to 5th century B.C. statues;
material from prehistoric Abruzzo;
sculpture; epigraphs; mosaics;
bronzes; pottery

07357
Pinacoteca 'C. Barbella'
Palazzo Martinetti, Via C. de Lollis 10,
I-66100 Chieti
Fine Arts Museum - 1976
Modern and contemporary painting
and sculpture

Chiusi

07358
Museo Nazionale Etrusco
Via Porsenna, I-53043 Chiusi, Siena
Archeology Museum - 1870
Coll: memorial stones; Etruscan urns;
Attic vases; Roman and Langobardic
relics

Ciano d'Enza

07359
Castello e Rupe di Canossa
Località Canossa, I-46026 Ciano
d'Enza, Reggio Emilia
Historic Site
Archeological material found in the
castle; medieval relics; reproductions
of documents depicting the history of
the castle

Cingoli

07360
Museo Civico
Piazza Vittorio Emanuele II 1, I-62011
Cingoli, Macerata
Archeology Museum
Roman and medieval archeology

Città di Castello

07361
Museo Capitolare
Cattedrale, I-06012 Città di Castello,
Perugia
Religious Art Museum
Coll: religious gold and silverwork;
sacred vestments; paintings; treasury

07362
Pinacoteca Comunale
Via della Cannoniera 22, I-06012 Città
di Castello, Perugia
Fine Arts Museum
Coll: paintings including works by
Signorelli and Raphael; classical,
medieval, and Renaissance sculpture;
works in terra cotta by Della Robbia;
goldsmith's art; 16th century furniture

Cividale del Friuli

07363
Museo Archeologico Nazionale
Piazza Duomo, I-33043 Cividale del
Friuli, Udine
Archeology Museum - 1820
Archeological remains from
prehistoric to medieval periods;
medieval goldwork; lapidary; coins;
armaments - library

07364
Museo Cristiano
Piazza Duomo, I-33043 Cividale del
Friuli, Udine
Religious Art Museum
Baptistery by Callisto; altar and
decorative fragments of the 18th
century; frescoes

Cividate Camuno

07365
**Museo Archeologico di
Vallecamonica**
Via Nazionale, I-25040 Cividate
Camuno, Brescia
Archeology Museum
Roman statues, epigraphs, coins and
relics of the area

Civita Castellana

07366
Rocca e Antiquarium
I-01033 Civita Castellana, Viterbo
Archeology Museum
Etruscan material, especially ceramics
from the Necropolis of ancient Falerii

Civitanova Marche

07367
Museo Polare
Via Buozzi 6, I-62012 Civitanova
Marche, Macerata
Anthropology Museum
Coll: geological samples; Arctic plants
and fishes; Eskimo carved ivories;
tools; whip for huskies; folk art of the
Lapp people; caribou skull - library

Civitavecchia

07368
Museo Civico Etrusco-Romano
Piazza Vittorio Veneto, I-00053
Civitavecchia, Roma
Archeology Museum
Etrusco-Roman archeology

Clusone

07369
Museo Sant'Andrea
Piazza Marinoni 6, I-24023 Clusone,
Bergamo
General Museum
Paintings; ancient coins; antique arms
and furniture

Coldirodi di Sanremo

07370
Pinacoteca e Biblioteca 'Rambaldi'
Piazza San Sebastiano, I-18010
Coldirodi di Sanremo, Imperia
Fine Arts Museum - 1865
Paintings; 16th and 17th century
Tuscan paintings - library

Colle di Val d'Elsa

07371
Antiquarium Etrusco
Piazza Duomo, I-53034 Colle di Val
d'Elsa, Siena
Archeology Museum
Local Etruscan remains

07372
Museo Civico
Via del Castello, I-53034 Colle di Val
d'Elsa, Siena
General Museum
Paintings; canvases; 15th to 18th
century relics

07373
Museo d'Arte Sacra
Via del Castello, I-53034 Colle di Val
d'Elsa, Siena
Religious Art Museum
14th century frescoes; 15th to 17th
century paintings

Collodi

07374
Parco Monumentale di Pinocchio
Via San Gennaro, I-51014 Collodi,
Pistoia
Fine Arts Museum
Monuments; statues; mosaics

Cologna Veneta

07375
Museo Civico Archeologico
I-37044 Cologna Veneta, Verona
General Museum - 1892
Coll: archeology; Roman-medieval
marbles; Roman and Venetian coins;
relics of the Risorgimento and World
War I

Como

07376
Civico Museo Storico 'G. Garibaldi'
Piazza Medaglie d'Oro, I-22100 Como
History/Public Affairs Museum - 1932
History and archives of the
Risorgimento and contemporary
periods

07377
**Museo Civico Archeologico 'P.
Giovio'**
Piazza Medaglie d'Oro 1, I-22100
Como
Archeology Museum - 1872
Coll: prehistoric material; Roman and
medieval stone tablets; medieval arms;
Greek vases

07378
Tempio Voltiano
Viale Marconi, I-22100 Como
Historic Site - 1927
Memorabilia and relics on the pysicist
Alessandro Volta (1745-1827);
chronological exhibition of inventions

Conegliano

07379
Museo civico del castello
Piazzale Castelvecchio, I-31015
Conegliano, Treviso
General Museum
Local history; arms; numismatics; art

Corbetta

07380
**Raccolta Archeologica 'Alberto
Pisani Dossi'**
Via F. Mussi 38, I-20011 Corbetta,
Milano
Archeology Museum - 1890
library

Corfinio

07381
Museo Corfiniese
Cattedrale di San Pelino, I-67030
Corfinio, L'Aquila
Archeology Museum - 1880
Coll: archeological findings of local
excavations; epigraphs; terra cottas;
bronzes; antique arms

Corregio

07382
Pinacoteca e Museo Comunale
Palazzo dei Principi, I-42015 Correggio,
Reggio Emilia
Fine Arts Museum - 1918
Coll: 15th-19th century paintings; 16th
century Flemish tapestries; historic
house

Corridonia

07383
Pinacoteca
Piazza Cavour 52, I-62014 Corridonia,
Macerata
Fine Arts Museum
14th to 16th century paintings

Cortina d'Ampezzo

07384
Collezione 'Rimoldi'
Corso Italia 17, I-32043 Cortina
d'Ampezzo, Belluno
Fine Arts Museum
Modern art

Cortona

07385
Museo dell'Accademia Etrusca
Piazza Signorelli, I-52044 Cortona,
Arezzo
History/Public Affairs Museum - 1948
Coll: Egyptian, Etruscan and Roman
antiquities; medieval and modern
decorative arts; coins; miniatures;
costumes

07386
Museo Diocesano
Chiesa del Gesù, Piazza del Duomo 1,
I-52044 Cortona, Arezzo
Fine Arts Museum - 1946
Religious art; paintings by Beato
Angelico, Sassetta, Signorelli and
Lorenzetti; Roman sarcophagus; 16th
century goldwork

Cosenza

07387
Museo Civico
Piazza XV Marzo, I-87100 Cosenza
General Museum
Local archeological finds; prehistoric
bronzes

Courmayeur

07388
Museo Alpino 'Duca degli Abruzzi'
Piazza Abbé Henry 2, I-11013
Courmayeur, Aosta
Natural History Museum
Flora, fauna and minerals of the area;
photographs

Crema

07389
Museo Civico
Via Dante 49, I-26013 Crema, Cremona
General Museum
Local archeology and history; pottery;
furniture

Cremona

07390
Museo Berenziano
Seminario Vescovile, I-26100 Cremona
History/Public Affairs Museum
Archeology; paintings; sculpture;
numismatics

07391
Museo Civico 'Ala Ponzone'
Via Ugolani Dati 4, I-26100 Cremona
General Museum - 1842
Coll: paintings, especially works of the
15th through 18th centuries; prints;
drawings and miniatures; archeology;
Cathedral treasury; local history of the
Risorgimento

07392
Museo Civico di Storia Naturale
Piazza Marconi 5, I-26100 Cremona
Natural History Museum - 1877
Coll: mineralogy; ornithology;
entomology

07393
Museo 'Stradivari'
Palazzo dell'Arte, I-26100 Cremona
Music Museum
Examples of the famous violin maker
Stradivari

Crotone

07394
Museo Archeologico Nazionale
Corso Risorgimento, I-88074 Crotone,
Catanzaro
Archeology Museum - 1968
Archeological finds from ancient
Crotone

Cuneo

07395
Museo Civico
Via Cacciatori delle Alpi 9, I-12100
Cuneo
General Museum
Local history; paintings; folk art;
religious art

Deruta

07396
Museo delle Maioliche
Piazza dei Consoli, I-06053 Deruta,
Perugia
Decorative Arts Museum
Original antique majolic articles and
reproductions

Desenzano del Garda

07397
Antiquarium della Villa Romana
Via Scavi Romani, I-25015 Desenzano
del Garda, Brescia
Archeology Museum
Pottery; frescoes

Diano d'Alba

07398
Museo della Battaglia di Marengo
Via Genova 7a, I-12055 Diano d'Alba,
Cuneo
History/Public Affairs Museum
Documents on the Italian campaign
and the battle of Marengo in 1800

Domodossola

07399
Museo di Palazzo San Francesco
Piazza Convenzione, I-28037
Domodossola, Novara
Natural History Museum
Mineralogy; zoology; botany;
ornithology; numismatics; documents
on the Simplon tunnel

07400
Museo di Palazzo Silva
Via del Museo, I-28037 Domodossola,
Novara
General Museum - 1860
Local history and life; domestic
utensils; 16th to 18th century furniture;
costumes; Etruscan material

Empoli

07401
Galleria della Collegiata
Piazza della Prepositura 3, I-50053
Empoli, Firenze
Fine Arts Museum - 1860
14th to 17th century Tuscan art;
frescoes; paintings; sculpture

Enna

07402
Tesoro del Duomo
Piazza Mazzini, I-94100 Enna
Religious Art Museum
Cathedral treasury; gold and
silverwork

Eraclea Minoa

07403
Antiquarium e Zona Archeologica
Eraclea Minoa, I-92016 Ribera,
Agrigento
Archeology Museum
Relics found in the excavations;
graphic illustrations and topography of
the ancient city

Erba

07404
Civico Museo Archeologico
Villa Comunale di Crevenna, Via Ugo
Foscolo, I-22036 Erba, Como
Archeology Museum - 1961
Coll: prehistory; archeology; ancient
tombs cut into granite blocks - library

Ercolano

07405
Osservatorio Vesuviano
I Ercolano, Napoli
Science/Tech Museum
Electromagnetic seismograph;
geophysical instruments; vulcanology
- library

Erice

07406
Museo Civico 'Antonio Cordici'
Piazza Municipio, I-91016 Erice,
Trapani
General Museum
Marble; deocrative arts; sculpture;
18th century paintings; wax models

Esino Lario

07407
Museo della Grigna
Via Adamello, I-22050 Esino Lario,
Como
General Museum - 1935
Gallo-Roman archeology;
paleontology; folk art

Este

07408
Museo Nazionale Atestino
Via Negri, I-35042 Este, Padova
General Museum - 1902
Coll: paleo-Venetian antiquities;
paleolithic, Iron Age and Roman
sections; paintings; mosaics;
architecture; historic house

Fabriano

07409
**Pinacoteca Civica e Museo degli
Arazzi**
Piazza Umberto di Savoia 3, I-60044
Fabriano, Ancona
Decorative Arts Museum - 1862
17th century Flemish tapestries;
paintings and frescoes of the Fabrian
school

Faenza

07410
**Museo Internazionale delle
Ceramiche**
Via Campidori 2, I-48018 Faenza,
Ravenna
Decorative Arts Museum - 1908
History and technique of ceramic
manufacture from prehistoric to
modern times; Faenza and
international pottery - library

07411
Museo Teatrale
Via Manfredi 14, I-48018 Faenza,
Ravenna
Performing Arts Museum

07412
Museo Torricelliano
Corso Garibaldi 2, I-48018 Faenza,
Ravenna
Natural History Museum - 1908
Life and work of the physicist
Evangelista Torricelli (1608-1647);
barometers; water gauges; astrolabes

07413
Pinacoteca Comunale
S. Maria dell'Angelo 2, I-48018 Faenza,
Ravenna
General Museum - 1805
Coll: Roman lapidary; mosaics;
medieval architectural decoration;
14th-20th century local paintings

07414
Pinacoteca d'Arte Moderna Sezione
della Pinacoteca Comunale
Palazzo Zauli Naldi, Corso Matteotti 2,
I Faenza, Ravenna
General Museum - 1965
Regional artists of the 19th-20th
centuries

Falerone

07415
**Museo Civico e Teatro e Serbatoio
Romano**
Palazzo Comunale, I-63022 Falerone,
Ascoli Piceno
General Museum
Roman archeology; remains of a
Roman theatre; epigraphs; urns

Fano

07416
**Museo Civico e Pinacoteca del
Palazzo Malatestiano**
Piazza XX Settembre, I-61032 Fano,
Pesaro-Urbino
General Museum - 1928
15th to 18th century paintings; local
relics; numismatics; pottery

Favara

07417
Museo Comunale 'A. Mendola'
Piazza Cavour 56, I-92026 Favara,
Agrigento
Natural History Museum
Coll: minerals; volcanic stones
(Vesuvius 1906); stuffed birds and
animals; African objects

Feltre

07418
Galleria d'Arte Moderna 'Rizzarda'
Via del Paradiso, I-32032 Feltre,
Belluno
Fine Arts Museum - 1931
Wrought-iron objects by Carlo
Rizzarda; 19th and 20th century
paintings and sculpture

07419
Museo Civico
Via Luzzo, I-32032 Feltre, Belluno
General Museum - 1903
Roman archeology; local history;
paintings of the Venetian school

Fénis

07420
Museo del Castello di Fénis
I-11020 Fénis, Aosta
General Museum - 1935
Valdostan furniture; domestic utensils;
architecture

Ferentino

07421
Museo Civico
Piazzale del Collegio, I-03013
Ferentino, Frosinone
General Museum
Local archeology and history

Fermo

07422
Civico Museo Archeologico
Piazza del Popolo 18, I-63023 Fermo,
Ascoli Piceno
General Museum - 1890
Coll: archeology; Roman bronzes;
furniture; porcelain; pottery

Ferrara

07423
Casa dell'Ariosto
Via Ariosto 67, I-44100 Ferrara
Historic Site
The house where the poet Ludovico
Ariosto (1474-1533) spent the last
years of his life - library

07424
Civico Museo di Storia Naturale
Via de Pisis, I-44100 Ferrara
Natural History Museum - 1865
Zoology; mineralogy; geology;
paleontology

07425
Galleria Civica d'Arte Moderna
Palazzo dei Diamanti, I-44100 Ferrara
Fine Arts Museum

07426
Museo Boldini
Palazzo Massari, Corso Porta Mare 9,
I-44100 Ferrara
Fine Arts Museum - 1937
Works and personal possessions of
the Ferrara painter Giovanni Boldini
(1842-1931); picture gallery

07427
Museo Civico di Schifanoia
Via Scandiana 23, I-44100 Ferrara
General Museum
14th century Ferrara frescoes;
Renaissance ceramics; bronzes;
coins; codices

07428
Museo del Duomo
Piazza Cattedrale, I-44100 Ferrara
Religious Art Museum
Illuminated hymn books; Flemish
tapestries; silver reliquaries

07429
Museo del Risorgimento e della Resistenza
Corso Ercole I d'Este 31, I-44100 Ferrara
History/Public Affairs Museum
Local documents and biographies on the history of the Risorgimento

07430
Museo Lapidario
Corso Ercole I d'Este 31, I-44100 Ferrara
Archeology Museum
Local archeological finds; antique marbles; Roman epitaphs

07431
Museo Nazionale Archeologico
Via XX Settembre 124, I-44100 Ferrara
Archeology Museum - 1932
Pottery from the ancient necropolis of the Graeco-Etruscan city of Spina

07432
Palazzina Marfisa
Corso Giovecca 170, I-44100 Ferrara
Fine Arts Museum
Original furniture, paintings and musical instruments in a 16th century aristocrat's house

07433
Pinacoteca Nazionale
Corso Ercole I d'Este 31, I-44100 Ferrara
Fine Arts Museum - 1836
14th to 20th century Ferrara painting

Fidenza

07434
Museo Storico del Risorgimento 'L. Musini'
Piazza Garibaldi 25, I-43036 Fidenza, Parma
History/Public Affairs Museum
Local documents on the Risorigmento and World War I

Fiesole

07435
Museo Archeologico
Via Portigiani 1, I-50014 Fiesole, Firenze
Archeology Museum
Etruscan and Roman finds; urns; pottery; bronzes; sculpture

07436
Museo Bandini
Via Giovanni Dupré, I-50014 Fiesole, Firenze
Fine Arts Museum - 1795
Coll: Tuscan paintings; sculpture; Della Robbia terra cotta works; 15th-17th century paintings

07437
Museo Etnologico Missionario
Convento San Francesco, I-50014 Fiesole, Firenze
Decorative Arts Museum - 1922
Egyptian, Etrusco-Roman and Chinese decorative arts

Figline di Prato

07438
Antiquarium
Pieve di San Pietro, I-50040 Figline di Prato, Firenze
General Museum
Medieval pottery; 15th and 16th century paintings; decorative arts

Finale Ligure

07439
Civico Museo del Finale
Piazza S. Caterina, I-17024 Finale Ligure, Savona
Archeology Museum - 1931
Coll: prehistoric archeology; classic history; finds from excavations in caves of Finale - library

Firenze

07440
Appartamenti Monumentali
Palazzo Pitti, I-50125 Firenze
History/Public Affairs Museum
18th and 19th century furniture and decorations in a 15th century palace; Boboli-gardens

07441
Biblioteca Medicea Laurenziana
Piazza San Lorenzo 9, I-50123 Firenze
History/Public Affairs Museum - 15th century
Coll: Greek, Latin, Arab, Hebrew, Persian, Italian, French manuscripts; incunabula; 15th-16th century miniatures; maps; architecture by Michelangelo - library

07442
Casa di Buonarroti
Via Ghibellina 70, I-50122 Firenze
Fine Arts Museum - 1858
Early bas-reliefs, sculptures and drawings by Michelangelo (1475-1564)

07443
Casa di Dante
Via Santa Margherita 1, I-50123 Firenze
Historic Site
Reproductions of documents and memorabilia of Dante's life

07444
Cenacolo del Conservatorio di Foligno
Via Faenza 48, I-50123 Firenze
Fine Arts Museum - 1850
15th to 18th century paintings; frescoes

07445
Cenacolo del Ghirlandaio
Borgognissanti 42, I-50123 Firenze
Fine Arts Museum
Collection of paintings by Domenico Ghirlandaio

07446
Cenacolo di San Salvi
Via San Salvi 16, I-50135 Firenze
Fine Arts Museum - 1820
Coll: 16th-18th century paintings; 16th century sculpture and frescos

07447
Cenacolo di Santa Apollonia
Via XXVII Aprile 1, I-50100 Firenze
Religious Art Museum
15th century frescoes and religious art; in a refectory

07448
Cenacolo di Santo Spirito e Fondazione 'Romano'
Piazza Santo Spirito, I-50125 Firenze
Religious Art Museum - 1946
Frescoes, stuccoes, marbles; 11th to 15th century sculptures in the Romano collection including works by Donatello; in a refectory

07449
Chiesa di Santa Maria Maddalena de' Pazzi
Borgo Pinti 58, I-50121 Firenze
Religious Art Museum
Detached frescoes; paintings by Perugino and his school

07450
Collezione 'Contini Bonacossi'
Palazzo Pitti, I-50125 Firenze
Fine Arts Museum
Painting; sculpture; furniture; decorative arts

07451
Erbario Tropicale di Firenze
Via la Pira 4, I-50121 Firenze
Natural History Museum - 1904
Dried plants and wood from Tropical countries; herbarium of East Africa - library

07452
Gabinetto Disegni e Stampe degli Uffizi
Via della Ninna 5, I-50122 Firenze
Fine Arts Museum
Prints and drawings

07453
Galleria 'Carnielo'
Piazza Savonarola 18, I-50132 Firenze
Fine Arts Museum
Works by the sculptor Rinaldo Carnielo (1853-1910)

07454
Galleria d'Arte Moderna
Palazzo Pitti, Piazza Pitti 1, I-50125 Firenze
Fine Arts Museum - 1924
Italian, mainly Tuscan art of the 19th to 20th century

07455
Galleria degli Uffizi
Piazzale degli Uffizi, I-50122 Firenze
Fine Arts Museum - 1581
The finest collection of Tuscan, Florentine, Venetian paintings from the 13th through 18th centuries including works by Giotto, Botticelli, Leonardo da Vinci, Masaccio, Fra Angelico, Lippi, Raphael, Titian; paintings by Flemish and German masters; classical sculpture; complete collection of artists' self-portraits

07456
Galleria dell'Accadèmia
Via Ricasoli 52, I-50122 Firenze
Fine Arts Museum - 1784
12th to 16th century paintings, mainly by Tuscan masters; 'David' and six other sculptures by Michelangelo

07457
Galleria dell'Istituto degli Innocenti
Piazza SS. Annunziata 12, I-50122 Firenze
Religious Art Museum
Religious painting; detached frescoes; enameled terra cotta

07458
Galleria Palatina
Palazzo Pitti, Piazza Pitti 1, I-50125 Firenze
Fine Arts Museum
Coll: 15th to 18th century paintings including Raphael, Titian, Tintoretto, Rubens, van Dyck, Velasquez; 18th and 19th century furniture

07459
Museo Archeologico
Via della Colonna 38, I-50121 Firenze
Archeology Museum - 1870
Egyptian, Etruscan and Greco-Roman archeology

07460
Museo 'Bardini' e Galleria 'Corsi'
Piazza dei Mozzi 1, I-50125 Firenze
Fine Arts Museum - 1922
Greek, Roman and medieval sculptures; 14th to 19th century paintings; Renaissance furniture; Oriental rugs; 16th to 18th century weapons

07461
Museo Botanico
Via la Pira 4, I-50121 Firenze
Natural History Museum - 1842
Coll: herbaria (3,800,000 specimens); historical herbaria; wax models of plants from the 19th century; xylotheca; fossils; materials from plant sources; drawings and manuscripts of famous Italian botanists - library

07462
Museo degli Argenti
Palazzo Pitti, Piazza Pitti 1, I-50125 Firenze
Decorative Arts Museum - 1860
Coll: 17th century frescoes; decorative arts; applied arts; jewelry made of precious stones, amber, ivory, gold and silver

07463
Museo del Conservatorio di Musica 'L. Cherubini'
Piazza Belle Arti 2, I-50123 Firenze
Music Museum
Musical instruments; works by the violin maker Antonio Stradivari (1644-1737)

07464
Museo della Casa Fiorentina Antica
Palazzo Davanzati, Via Portarossa 13, I-50123 Firenze
Decorative Arts Museum - 1957
Coll: furniture; ceramics; Italian, French and Flemish lace from the 16th to 19th centuries; paintings in an original 14th century patrician house

07465
Museo delle Carrozze
Palazzo Pitti, Piazza Pitti 1, I-50125 Firenze
Decorative Arts Museum
Coaches and harnesses of the early 18th century

07466
Museo delle Porcellane
Palazzo Pitti, Piazza Pitti 1, I-50125 Firenze
Decorative Arts Museum - 1896
European porcelain (Napoli, Doccia, Vincennes, Sèvres, Paris, Vienna, Meissen, Berlin, Nymphenburg, Frankenthal) of the 18th and 19th centuries

07467
Museo dell'Opera di Santa Croce
Piazza Santa Croce 16, I-50122 Firenze
Religious Art Museum
Cloisters; Chapel of the Pazzi by Brunelleschi (1376-1446); 14th century detached frescoes; Tuscan paintings

07468
Museo dell'Opera di Santa Maria del Fiore
Piazza Duomo 9, I-50122 Firenze
Religious Art Museum - 1892
Coll: Florentine sculpture; history and treasury of Cathedral

07469
Museo di Antropologia ed Etnologia
Via del Proconsolo 12, I-50122 Firenze
Anthropology Museum - 1869
Skulls of different races; ethnographic objects of Asia, Africa, America, Oceania

07470
Museo di Geologia e Paleontologia dell'Università di Firenze
Via la Pira 4, I-50121 Firenze
Natural History Museum - 1775
Coll: geology; paleontology; fossils - library

07471
Museo di Mineralogia e Litologia
Via la Pira 4, I-50121 Firenze
Natural History Museum
Coll: minerals; stones; gems;
petrography

07472
Museo di Palazzo Strozzi
Palazzo Strozzi, I-50123 Firenze
Fine Arts Museum
History of the Strozzi family and about
the construction of their house

07473
Museo di San Marco
Piazza San Marco, I-50121 Firenze
Fine Arts Museum - 1869
Beato Angelico's (1387-1455) frescoes
and paintings in the Monastery of San
Marco

07474
Museo di Storia della Scienza
Piazza dei Giudici 1, I-50122 Firenze
Natural History Museum - 1927
Coll: astronomy; medicine; physics;
anatomy; historic instruments - library

07475
Museo Horne Fondazione Horne
Via dei Benci 6, I-50122 Firenze
Decorative Arts Museum
Furniture and decorative arts of the
14th to 16th centuries; painting

07476
Museo 'La Specola'
Via Romana 17, I-50125 Firenze
Natural History Museum - 1775
Zoology; wax anatomic preparations

07477
**Museo Mediceo e Palazzo Medici
Riccardi**
Via Cavour 1, I-50129 Firenze
Fine Arts Museum
Chapel built by Michelozzo with
frescoes by Benozzo Gozzoli (1459);
frescoes by Luca Giordano (1680)

07478
Museo Nazionale del Bargello
Via Proconsolo 4, I-50122 Firenze
Fine Arts Museum - 1859
Coll: 14th to 17th century Tuscan
sculpture including works by
Michelangelo, Cellini and Donatello;
applied arts; medals; armaments

07479
Museo Preistorico
Via Sant'Egidio 21, I-50122 Firenze
Archeology Museum - 1946
Prehistoric finds from all continents

07480
Museo Stibbert
Via F. Stibbert 26, I-50134 Firenze
History/Public Affairs Museum - 1909
Coll: European and Oriental
armaments; costumes; carpets;
tapestries; furniture; porcelain - library

07481
**Museo Storico Topografico 'Firenze
Com'Era'**
Via dell'Orinolo 24, I-50122 Firenze
History/Public Affairs Museum - 1955
Topographical drawings, paintings and
prints illustrating the history of
Florence

07482
Opificio delle Pietre Dure
Via degli Alfani 78, I-50121 Firenze
Science/Tech Museum - 1952
Tools and artifacts of stone and
semi-precious stones from the 16th to
19th century

07483
Palazzo Vecchio
Piazza della Signoria, I-50122 Firenze
History/Public Affairs Museum
14th century palace; Hall of the
'Cinquecento'; frescoes by Vasari;
14th to 16th century painting and
sculpture

07484
**Raccolte d'Arte Contemporanea
'Alberto della Ragione'**
Piazza della Signoria 5, I-50122 Firenze
Fine Arts Museum - 1970
20th century painting and sculpture

Foligno

07485
Museo Archeologico
Palazzo Trinci, I-06034 Foligno, Perugia
Archeology Museum
Archeoligical remains of the
pre-Roman and Roman period;
frescoes; decorations

Fondi

07486
Antiquarium
Chiostro di San Francesco, I-04022
Fondi, Latina
General Museum - 1952
Epigraphs, local historic architecture,
sculpture collected in a cloister

Fontanellato

07487
Rocca Sanvitale
Piazza Matteotti 1, I-43012
Fontanellato, Parma
General Museum
17th and 18th century living style;
bathroom with frescoes by
Parmigianino (1503-1540)

Forli

07488
Museo Archeologico Istituti Culturali
ed Artistici
Corso della Repubblica 72, I-47100
Forlì
Archeology Museum - 1922
Prehistoric, Roman and medieval
archeological remains; lapidary;
medals; numismatics

07489
Museo del Risorgimento
Corso Garibaldi 96, I-47100 Forlì
History/Public Affairs Museum
Local history of the Risorgimento;
memorabilia on local participants

07490
Museo delle Ceramiche Istituti
Culturali ed Artistici
Corso della Repubblica 72, I-47100
Forlì
Decorative Arts Museum
Ceramics

07491
Museo Etnografico 'Pergoli' Istituti
Culturali ed Artistici
Corso della Repubblica 72, I-47100
Forlì
Anthropology Museum - 1922
Peasant and craftman living style in
Romagna; folk art

07492
Museo Romagnolo del Teatro
Corso Garibaldi 96, I-47100 Forlì
Performing Arts Museum - 1962
History of the Romagnolo Theatre,
local authors, actors and musicians

Forlimpopoli

07493
Museo Archeologico Civico
Piazza Fratti, nella Rocca Sforzesca,
I-47034 Forlimpopoli, Forlì
Archeology Museum - 1961
Prehistoric, Roman and medieval
archeology; historic house

Formia

07494
Antiquarium Nazionale
Piazza della Vittoria, I-04023 Formia,
Latina
Archeology Museum
Roman sculpture, epigraphs and
architecture

Fossombrone

07495
Museo 'A. Vernarecci'
Palazzo Ducale, I-61034 Fossombrone,
Pesaro-Urbino
General Museum - 1901
Prehistoric and medieval archeology
of the area; numismatics

Francavilla al Mare

07496
Galleria Municipale
Palazzo Comunale, I-66023 Francavilla
al Mare, Chieti
Fine Arts Museum
Paintings, mainly by painters of
Abruzzo

Frascati

07497
Museo Etiopico
Via Massaia 26, I-00044 Frascati, Roma
Anthropology Museum
Material collected by Cardinal Massaia
during his work in Ethiopia

07498
Museo Tuscolano e Rocca
Piazza Paolo III, I-00044 Frascati, Roma
General Museum - 1903
Prehistoric to Roman archeology;
sculpture and decorative arts

Gaeta

07499
Museo Diocesano
Piazza Duomo, I-04024 Gaeta, Latina
Religious Art Museum - 1956
12th to 19th century frescoes and
paintings; inscriptions; sculpture

Galeata

07500
Museo Civico 'Domenico Mambrini'
Via Zanetti 10, I-47010 Galeata, Forlì
General Museum
Local archeological finds; sculpture;
armaments

Gallarate

07501
Civica Galleria d'Arte Moderna
Viale Milano 21, I-21013 Gallarate,
Varese
Fine Arts Museum
20th century Italian painting

07502
**Museo della Società Gallaratese di
Studi Patri**
Via Borgo Antico 2, I-21013 Gallarate,
Varese
History/Public Affairs Museum
Prehistoric and Roman local finds;
local history; documents on the
Risorgimento

Gallipoli

07503
Museo Civico
Via de Pace 108, I-73014 Gallipoli,
Lecce
General Museum
Natural history; ethnography;
archeology; painting

Gandino

07504
Museo della Basilica
Piazza Emancipazione, I-24024
Gandino, Bergamo
Religious Art Museum - 1930
Religious art; Flemish tapestries;
goldsmith's work of Renaissance and
Baroque periods

Gardone Riviera

07505
Museo Dannunziano del Vittoriale
Vittoriale degli Italiani, I-25083 Gardone
Riviera, Brescia
Historic Site - 1938
Life and work of poet Gabriele
d'Annunzio (1863-1938) - library

Gavardo

07506
Museo 'Gruppo Grotte Gavardo'
Via Molino 44, I-25085 Gavardo,
Brescia
General Museum - 1956
Coll: paleontology; local prehistory;
Roman to medieval archeology; 4th
century terra cotta vases; mineralogy
- library

Gavinana

07507
Museo Ferrucciano
Piazza Ferrucci, I-51025 Gavinana,
Pistoia
History/Public Affairs Museum
History of the battle of Gavinana; arms
- library

Gela

07508
Museo Archeologico Nazionale
Corso Vittorio Emanuele 2, I-93012
Gela, Caltanissetta
Archeology Museum - 1958
Prehistoric, Graeco-Roman material
from Gela excavations; terra cotta
vases; coins

Genova

07509
Galleria d'Arte Moderna
Via Capolungo 3, I-16167 Genova
Fine Arts Museum - 1927
19th and 20th century painting, mainly
by Ligurian masters

07510
Galleria di Palazzo Bianco
Via Garibaldi 11, I-16124 Genova
Fine Arts Museum - 1892
Coll: paintings of Genoese masters
and other Italian schools; 16th and
17th century Flemish masters

07511
Galleria di Palazzo Reale
Via Balbi 10, I-16126 Genova
Fine Arts Museum - 1650
18th century royal style; mirror hall;
hall of Arras rugs; paintings; sculpture

07512
Galleria di Palazzo Rosso
Via Garibaldi 18, I-16124 Genova
Fine Arts Museum - 1874
Coll: paintings; sculpture; frescoes;
stuccoes; prints; drawings; ceramics;
numismatics - library

07513
**Galleria Nazionale di Palazzo
Spinola**
Piazza di Pellicceria, I-16123 Genova
Fine Arts Museum
Picture-gallery in a 17th-18th century
palace with paintings by the most
important Genoese and Flemish
masters

07514
Istituto ed Orto Botanico Hanbury
Corso Dogali 1c, I-16136 Genova
Natural History Museum - 1803
Coll: seeds; drugs; herbarium; flora of
Europe; living ferns - library

07515
**Istituto Policattedra di Ingegneria
Navale dell'Università di Genova**
Via Montallegro 1, I-16145 Genova
Science/Tech Museum - 1860
Coll: models of ships; sailing ships and
structural details of merchant ships;
submarines; steamer - library; ship
structural laboratory; computer center

07516
**Museo Americanistico 'Federico
Lunardi'**
Corso Solferino 25-29, I-16122
Genova
Archeology Museum - 1964
Archeological collection of
pre-Columbian civilizations;
ethnographical items; photographs;
ceramic objects of the classic Maya
period - library

07517
Museo Civico di Archeologia Ligure
Villa Durazzo Pallavicini, I-16155
Genova
Archeology Museum - 1914
Ligurian archeology; Roman and
Greek finds; historic house

07518
**Museo Civico di Storia Naturale 'G.
Doria'**
Via Brigata Liguria 9, I-16121 Genova
Natural History Museum - 1867
Coll: zoology; paleontology;
mineralogy; botany - library; didactic
center

07519
**Museo d'Arte Orientale 'Edoardo
Chiossone'**
Villetta di Negro, I-16136 Genova
Fine Arts Museum - 1905
11th to 19th century paintings;
Japanese paintings, arms, sculptures,
enamelware, pottery, porcelain,
lacquer; also material from China and
Siam

07520
**Museo degli Oggeti d'Arte e
Ceramiche degli Ospedali Civili**
Viale Benedetto XV 10, I-16132
Genova
General Museum - 1931
Ancient apothecary jars; ceramics of
Faenza; paintings by Genoese and
Flemish schools

07521
Museo del Tesoro di San Lorenzo
Cattedrale di San Lorenzo, I-16123
Genova
Religious Art Museum - 1956
Treasury of San Lorenzo including
relics, copes and goldsmiths' work

07522
**Museo dell'Accadèmia Ligustica di
Belle Arti**
Piazza de Ferrari 5, I-16121 Genova
Fine Arts Museum
Coll: drawings; frescoes; 16th-19th
century Genoese paintings

07523
Museo dell'Istituto Mazziniano
Via Lomellini 11, I-16124 Genova
History/Public Affairs Museum - 1934
Antiquities, documents, journals
pertaining to history of the
Risorgimento and Europe from the
18th and 19th century - library

07524
**Museo di Architettura e Scultura
Ligure**
Piazza R. Negri 8, I-16123 Genova
Fine Arts Museum
9th to 18th century sculpture

07525
Museo di Santa Maria di Castello
Salita Santa Maria di Castello, I-16123
Genova
Religious Art Museum
Religious art; illuminated incunabula
and hymn-books; sculpture; painting

07526
Museo Etnografico
Corso Dogali 18, I-16136 Genova
Anthropology Museum - 1932
American and pre-Columbian
ethnography and art

07527
Museo Giannettino Luxoro
Via Aurelia, I-16167 Genova
Fine Arts Museum - 1945
17th and 18th century Flemish and
Genoese paintings; furniture;
ceramics; silver ware

07528
Museo Navale
Piazza Bonavino, I-16156 Genova
History/Public Affairs Museum - 1928
Models of ships of various periods;
nautical instruments; navigation maps;
prints

07529
Raccolte di Palazzo Tursi
Via Garibaldi 9, I-16124 Genova
General Museum - 1848
Decorative arts; local antiquities;
tapestries; Paganini's violin; letters of
Columbus

Gignese

07530
Museo dell'Ombrello e del Parasole
Viale Golf Panorama, I-28040 Gignese,
Novara
History/Public Affairs Museum
History of umbrellas

Gioia del Colle

07531
Museo Archeologico
Piazza Plebiscito, I-70023 Gioia del
Colle, Bari
Archeology Museum
Finds from ancient necropoleis

Giulianova

07532
Pinacoteca Comunale 'V. Bindi'
Corso Garibaldi, I-64021 Giulianova,
Teramo
Fine Arts Museum - 1927
19th century Neapolitan paintings;
autographs

Gorizia

07533
**Museo Provinciale di Palazzo
Attems**
Piazza Edmondo de Amicis 2, I-34170
Gorizia
General Museum - 1861
Coll: paintings; stone tablets; history of
the war from 1915-1918; archives -
library

07534
Museo Provinciale di Storia e d'Arte
Borgo Castello 15, I-34170 Gorizia
General Museum - 1861
Coll: archeology; numismatics;
craftwork; items of local traditional life;
folk art

Gradara

07535
Castello e Rocca
I-61012 Gradara
General Museum
Coll: 15th-16th century furniture;
weapons; terra cotta altar by Andrea
della Robbia; in a 13th century castle

Gran San Bernardo

07536
Hospice du Grand Saint Bernard
I Gran San Bernardo, Aosta
General Museum
Roman articles; minerals; Alpine fauna
and flora; history of the Great St.
Bernard Pass

Gravina di Puglia

07537
Museo 'Ettore Pomarici Santomasi'
Via Museo 20, I-70024 Gravina di
Puglia, Bari
General Museum
Peasant life and tradition; 17th to 19th
century furnishings - library

Grosseto

07538
**Museo Archeologico e d'Arte della
Maremma**
Piazza Baccarini, I-58100 Grosseto
Archeology Museum - 1865
Prehistoric, Etruscan and Roman finds;
medieval and modern history; 13th to
18th century paintings by the Siena
and Florentine schools; archives -
library

07539
Museo Civico di Storia Naturale
Via Mazzini, I-58100 Grosseto
Natural History Museum - 1960
Coll: area minerals; fossils and local
biology - library

07540
Museo d'Arte Sacra
Piazza Duomo, I-58100 Grosseto
Religious Art Museum - 1933
13th-17th century Sienese painting;
illuminated hymnbooks; reliquaries

Grottaferrata

07541
Museo dell'Abbazia
I-00046 Grottaferrata, Roma
General Museum
Prehistoric archeology; Greek and
Roman sculpture; local finds from the
Etruscan, Greek and Roman periods;
13th century frescoes; sacred
vestments

Gualdo Tadino

07542
Pinacoteca Comunale
Piazza Martiri delle Libertà, I-06023
Gualdo Tadino, Perugia
Fine Arts Museum
Paintings; frescoes

Guardiagrele

07543
Museo Comunale
Via della Porta, I-66016 Guardiagrele,
Chieti
General Museum
Roman and Gothic remains and
sculptures

Guastalla

07544
Museo della Biblioteca Maldottiana
Corso Garibaldi 4, I-42016 Guastalla,
Reggio Emilia
General Museum - 1934
Local history; coins; medals;
autographs; paintings

Gubbio

07545
Museo e Pinacoteca Comunali
Palazzo dei Consoli, I-06024 Gubbio,
Perugia
General Museum - 1880
Coll: Finds from local excavations;
13th to 17th century paintings;
antiquities; Renaissance furniture;
ceramics

07546
Museo Francesco
Convento di S. Francesco, I-06024
Gubbio, Perugia
Religious Art Museum
Religious art and artifacts

Iglesias

07547
Museo Minerario
Via Roma, I-09016 Iglesias, Cagliari
Natural History Museum
Minerals, stones and fossils of
Sardinia

Imola

07548
**Collezioni Naturalistiche del Museo
Comunale**
Via Emilia 80, nell'ex Convento di
S.Francesco, I-40026 Imola, Bologna
Natural History Museum - 1857
Geology; botany; zoology

07549
Museo Archeologico
Via Emilia 80, I-40026 Imola, Bologna
Archeology Museum - 1857
Coll: natural history; archeology;
numismatics; ceramics; ethnography,
also of the pre-Columbian period

07550
Museo del Risorgimento
Via Emilia 80, nell'ex Convento di
S.Francesco, I-40026 Imola, Bologna
History/Public Affairs Museum - 1904
Coll: autographs; medals; portraits;
memorabilia on local history from 1796
to World War I

07551
**Museo di Armi Antiche e Maioliche
Medievali**
Rocca Sforzesca, Piazza G. dalle
Bande Nere, I-40026 Imola, Bologna
Decorative Arts Museum - 1973
13th-19th century armaments and
medieval ceramics

07552
Pinacoteca Civica Raccolta d'Arte
Comunale
Via Emilia 80, nell'ex Convento di
S.Francesco, I-40026 Imola, Bologna
Fine Arts Museum - 1938
15th-18th century paintings and
contemporary art

Imperia

07553
Pinacoteca Civica
Piazza Duomo, I-18100 Imperia
Fine Arts Museum
Antique to modern time painting

Ischia di Castro

07554
Museo Civico 'Pietro Lotti'
Via Roma 4, I-01010 Ischia di Castro
General Museum
Local archeology and history

Isernia

07555
Museo Archeologico Romano
Piazza Santa Maria 18, I-86019 Isernia
Archeology Museum - 1958
Sculpture; ruins; antiquities

Isola Bella

07556
Museo 'Borromeo'
I-28050 Isola Bella, Novara
General Museum
Painting; furniture; tapestries

Issogne

07557
Castello d'Issogne
I-11020 Issogne, Aosta
General Museum
Renaissance paintings and local
furniture

Ivrea

07558
Museo 'Garda'
Piazza di Città, I-10015 Ivrea, Torino
General Museum
Natural history; ethnography of China,
Japan

Jesi

07559
Museo e Pinacoteca Comunale
Palazzo della Signoria, I-60035 Jesi,
Ancona
General Museum - 1912
Roman and Renaissance sculpture in a
15th century Renaissance palace;
paintings by Lotto and of the local
school

L'Aquila

07560
**Museo di Speleologia 'Vincenzo
Rivera'**
Via Svolte della Misericordia 2, I-67100
L'Aquila
Science/Tech Museum - 1970
Fossils; prehistoric material from the
Grotta a Male - library

07561
Museo Diocesano
Piazza San Giuseppe, I-67100 L'Aquila
Religious Art Museum
Religious objects; sculpture; paintings
including local and Neapolitan masters

07562
**Museo Internazionale di Burattini e
Marionette**
Castello Cinquecentesco, I-67100
L'Aquila
Decorative Arts Museum
Over 2,000 marionettes and puppets
from different European countries and
periods; the collection is being
reorganized

07563
Museo Nazionale d'Abruzzo
Castello Cinquecentesco, Viale B.
Croce, I-67100 L'Aquila
Fine Arts Museum - 1950
Archeology; art from the early Middle
Ages to contemporary times;
paleontology; numismatics

07564
Museo Paleontologico
Castello Cinquecentesco, Viale B.
Croce, I-67100 L'Aquila
Natural History Museum - 1958
Paleontology; elephant fossils - library

La Spezia

07565
Museo Civico
Via Curtatone 9, I-19100 La Spezia
General Museum
Local archeology, ethnography and
natural history

07566
Museo Tecnico Navale
Piazza Chiodo, I-19100 La Spezia
Science/Tech Museum
Medieval anchors, guns and weapons;
reconstruction of a Roman galley;
navigation instruments; manuscripts
and maps

Latina

07567
Antiquarium
Corso Repubblica 134, I-04100 Latina
Archeology Museum
Prehistoric archeology; archaic
pottery; Roman remains

Laveno Mombello

07568
Civica Raccolta di Terraglia
Palazzo Perabò, I-21014 Laveno
Mombello, Varese
Decorative Arts Museum
European and local earthenware from
1880 to 1935

Lecce

07569
**Museo Provinciale 'Sigismondo
Castromediano'**
Viale Gallipoli, I-73100 Lecce
General Museum - 1868
Coll: regional archeology; Greek
vases; Roman statues; ceramics;
lamps; medieval antiquities; 15th to
20th cent. local painting; decorative
arts; numismatics - library

Lecco

07570
Manzoni Villa Musei Civici
I-22053 Lecco, Como
Historic Site
Memorabilia of the poet Alessandro
Manzoni (1785-1873) in his house

07571
Museo Storico Risorgimentale Musei
Civici
Torre Viscontea, I-22053 Lecco, Como
History/Public Affairs Museum
History of the Risorgimento and the
Resistance Movement of World War II

07572
Palazzo Belgioioso Musei Civici
I-22053 Lecco, Como
General Museum - 1900
Local archeology, natural history,
picture gallery

Legnago

07573
Museo della Fondazione Fioroni
Via Matteotti 39, I-37045 Legnago,
Verona
General Museum - 1958
Coll: weapons; pottery; Italian
Risorgimento history

Legnano

07574
Museo Civico 'G. Sutermeister'
Via Mazzini 2, I-20025 Legnano, Milano
General Museum
Regional archeology; 15th to 16th
century frescoes; vases; arms and
armor

Lentini

07575
Museo Archeologico
Via Piave, I-96016 Lentini, Siracusa
Archeology Museum
Local archeological finds

Licenza

07576
Museo Oraziano
Palazzo Baronale, I-00026 Licenza,
Roma
Archeology Museum

Lipari

07577
Museo Archeologico Eoliano
Via Castello, I-98055 Lipari, Messina
Archeology Museum - 1950
Prehistory and classical material from
the Lipari Islands; meridional
antiquities

Livorno

07578
Museo Civico Giovanni Fattori
Piazza Matteotti 19, I-57100 Livorno
Fine Arts Museum - 1896
Coll: 19th century Tuscan paintings;
Byzantine icons; numismatics;
archeology - library

07579
**Museo Progressivo d'Arte
Contemporanea 'Villa Maria'**
Via Redi 22, I-57100 Livorno
Fine Arts Museum
Contemporary art - library

07580
Museo Provinciale di Storia Naturale
Via Crispi 50, I-57100 Livorno
Natural History Museum - 1929
Ornithology; malacology; entomology;
paleontology; mineralogy; botany;
ethnology

Locri

07581
Antiquarium
Contrada Marasà, I-89044 Locri,
Reggio Calabria
Archeology Museum - 1971
Prehistorical, Greek and Roman finds;
vases; terra cottas; coins; bronzes

Lodi

07582
Collezione Gorini Raccolte
Scientifiche dell'Ospedale Maggiore
Piazza Ospedale, I-20075 Lodi, Milano
Science/Tech Museum
Preparation; Mummification; anatomy

07583
Museo Civico
Corso Umberto 63, I-20075 Lodi,
Milano
General Museum - 1868
Coll: local history and archeology;
14th-20th century paintings; ceramics;
pottery of ancient Lodi; wooden altar
by the Donati brothers

Lonato

07584
**Museo della Fondazione 'Ugo da
Como'**
Via da Como 2, I-25017 Lonato,
Brescia
General Museum - 1941
Household furnishings and articles
concerning typical life of the area;
paintings

Loreto

07585
Museo Pinacoteca Santa Casa
Palazzo Apostolico, I-60025 Loreto,
Ancona
Fine Arts Museum - 1919
Coll: tapestries; ceramics of a 16th
century pharmacy; paintings of
Lorenzo Lotto; medals; antique
furniture - library

Loreto Aprutino

07586
Galleria delle Antiche Ceramiche Abruzzesi del Barone Acerbo
Via del Baio, I-65014 Loreto Aprutino, Pescara
Decorative Arts Museum
600 pieces of Abruzzo pottery demonstrating the production from the 14th to 18th centuries

Lovere

07587
Galleria dell'Accademia di Belle Arti 'Tadini'
Via Tadini, I-24065 Lovere, Bergamo
Fine Arts Museum - 1828
From Venetian and Lombardian to 19th century painting including Bellini, Parmigianino; armaments; numismatics

Lucca

07588
Museo di Palazzo Mansi
Via Galli Tassi 43, I-55100 Lucca
General Museum - 1868
18th century furnishings and decor

07589
Museo Nazionale di Villa Guinigi
Via della Quarquonia, I-55100 Lucca
Fine Arts Museum
Coll: Roman and Etruscan archeology; pre-Romanesque, Romanesque and Renaissance sculpture and paintings; wood inlays; textiles; medieval goldsmith art

07590
Pinacoteca Nazionale
Piazza Napoleone, I-55100 Lucca
Fine Arts Museum - 1868
12th to 18th century paintings by Italian and foreign masters; Tuscan, Venetian and Bolognese schools

Lucera

07591
Museo Civico 'G. Fiorelli'
Via De Nicastri 36, I-71036 Lucera, Foggia
General Museum - 1905
Local archeology; numismatics; ceramics; picture gallery

Lucignano

07592
Museo Civico
Piazza Tribunale, I-52046 Lucignano, Arezzo
General Museum - 1930
14th century Sienese goldsmith work; 14th to 15th century local painting; decorative art

Lugagnano Val d'Arda

07593
Antiquarium e Zona Archeologica
Località Veleia, I-29018 Lugagnano Val d'Arda, Piacenza
Archeology Museum
Pre-Roman and Roman findings in Veleia

Lugo

07594
Museo 'Francesco Baracca'
La Rocca, I-48022 Lugo, Ravenna
Historic Site
Memorabilia on local hero Francesco Baracca; historic house

Macerata

07595
Museo Comunale
Piazza Vittorio Veneto 2, I-62100 Macerata
General Museum
Paintings; carriages

07596
Museo Marchigiano del Risorgimento 'G. e D. Spadoni'
Piazza Vittorio Veneto, I-62100 Macerata
History/Public Affairs Museum - 1905
Coll: manuscripts; autographs; portraits; arms; prints illustrating political and military events; local history from 1789 to 1946

07597
Museo Tipologico dei Presepi
Via Pantaleoni 4, I-62100 Macerata
Religious Art Museum
Miniature manger scenes

Maglie

07598
Museo Comunale di Paleontologia e Paletnologia
Via Umberto I, 3, I-73024 Maglie, Lecce
Archeology Museum - 1964
Coll: local prehistoric finds; paleontology; miocene fauna - library

Maiolati Spontini

07599
Museo Spontiniano
Via Gaspare Spontini 15, I-60030 Maiolati Spontini, Ancona
Historic Site - 1851
House of the musician Gaspare Spontini; manuscripts

Malcesine

07600
Museo del Castello Scaligero
Via Castello, I-37018 Malcesine, Verona
General Museum
Local history and fauna exhibits

Manduria

07601
Antiquarium Municipale
Piazza Garibaldi, I-74024 Manduria, Taranto
Archeology Museum
Messapian, Greek and Roman archeology of the area

Mantova

07602
Galleria e Museo del Palazzo Ducale
Piazza Sordello 39, I-46100 Mantova
Historic Site - 1752
Coll: paintings; frescoes; sinopias; tapestries; numismatics; 'Bridal chamber' with frescoes by Andrea Mantegna

07603
Museo del Risorgimento
Piazza Sordello 42, I-46100 Mantova
History/Public Affairs Museum
Documents and material concerning the Risorgimento up to 1945

Marsala

07604
Museo Civico
Via Cavour, I-91025 Marsala, Trapani
General Museum
Local archeology and history

07605
Museo degli Arazzi
Chiesa Madre, I-91025 Marsala, Trapani
Decorative Arts Museum
16th century Flemish tapestries

Marzabotto

07606
Museo Etrusco 'Pompeo Aria'
Via Porrettana Sud 13, I-40043 Marzabotto, Bologna
Archeology Museum - 1831
Archeological findings from the ancient Misa

Massa

07607
Castello Malaspina
I-54100 Massa
General Museum
Archeology of the North Tuscany coast; medieval pottery; furniture

Massa Lombarda

07608
Pinacoteca Civica
Piazza Matteotti 16, I-48024 Massa Lombarda, Ravenna
Fine Arts Museum
Paintings of the Sienese school; Etruscan vases and urns; ceramics

Matelica

07609
Museo 'Piersanti'
Via Umberto I 11, I-62024 Matelica, Macerata
Religious Art Museum
13th to 18th century crucifixes; tapestries; goldsmith work

Matera

07610
Museo Nazionale Domenico Ridola
Via D. Ridola 24, I-75100 Matera
Archeology Museum - 1930
Prehistoric section; Magna Grecia section; ethnology - library; didactic section

Mazara del Vallo

07611
Museo Civico
Via Carmine 21, I-91026 Mazara del Vallo, Trapani
Archeology Museum - 1931
Prehistoric findings of local interest; amphoras; coins; arms; inscriptions; pottery

Melfi

07612
Museo Nazionale del Melfese
Castello Normanno, I-85025 Melfi, Potenza
Archeology Museum
Local archeology from neolithic to medieval times

Merano

07613
Museo Civico
Via Galilei 43, I-39012 Merano, Bolzano
General Museum - 1918
Local history and folklore; paintings; archeology; local geology

07614
Museo 'Steiner'
I-39012 Merano, Bolzano
Fine Arts Museum
Paintings and sculptures

Mesagne

07615
Museo Archeologico 'U. Granafei' Mesagne
Piazza Garibaldi, I-72023 Mesagne, Brindisi
General Museum - 1975
Coll: prehistory; Roman, medieval materials; vases; bronzes; epigraphs - library

Messina

07616
Museo Nazionale
Viale Libertà 465, I-98100 Messina
General Museum - 1953
Paintings of the Messina school; sculpture; religious art; polyptych by Antonello da Messina; works by Caravaggio; 16th to 17th century decorative arts; archeology

07617
Museo Zoologico 'Cambria'
Via dei Verdi 56, I-98100 Messina
Natural History Museum
Molluscs and vertebrates mainly from Italy

Metaponto

07618
Antiquarium e Zona Archeologica
Statale Jonica 106, I-75010 Metaponto, Matera
Archeology Museum
Archeological material concerning to the Greek colony

Milano

07619
Cenacolo Vinciano
Refettorio Convento S. Maria delle Grazie, I-20123 Milano
Fine Arts Museum - 1890
'Last Supper' by Leonardo da Vinci; frescoes; paintings

07620
Cetro Nazionale di Studi Manzoniani
Via Morone 1, I-20121 Milano
Historic Site
Memorabilia and personal books of the poet Alessandro Manzoni (1785-1873)

07621
Civica Galleria d'Arte Moderna
Villa Reale, Via Palestro 16, I-20157 Milano
Fine Arts Museum - 1878
Coll: modern art; paintings; French impressionists; paintings by Marino Marini and Canavese - library

07622
Civica Raccolta dell'Arte Applicata
Castello Sforzesco, I-20121 Milano
Decorative Arts Museum
Coll: furniture; ceramics; tapestries; ivories; glassware; goldsmith work; bronzes

07623
Civica Raccolta di Stampe 'Achille Bertarelli'
Castello Sforzesco, I-20121 Milano
Fine Arts Museum - 1925
Coll: 800,000 engravings and prints from the 15th century to the present

217

07624
Civiche Raccolte Archeologiche e Numismatiche di Milano
Corso Magenta 15, I-20121 Milano
Archeology Museum - 1807
Prehistoric collection from Rome, Greece and Etruria; ceramics; tombstones; numismatic division in the Castello Sforzesco - library

07625
Civiche Raccolte di Archeologia Paletnologica ed Egizia
Castello Sforzesco, I-20121 Milano
Archeology Museum
Ethnology and archeology from the neolithic period to the Bronze and Iron Age; Ancient Egyptian exhibits

07626
Civico Museo Navale Didattico
Via San Vittore 21, I-20123 Milano
Science/Tech Museum
Relics, models, sketches and drawings concerning navigation

07627
Collezione 'Jucker'
Via Macchi 28, I-20124 Milano
Fine Arts Museum
19th century Italian painting

07628
Collezioni degli Istituti di Geologia e di Paleontologia
Piazzale Gorini 15, I-20133 Milano
Natural History Museum
Fossils; rocks

07629
Erbario dell'Istituto di Scienze Botaniche dell'Università di Milano
Istituto di Scienze Botaniche
Via G. Colombo 60, I-20133 Milano
Natural History Museum
Herbarium

07630
Galleria d'Arte Sacra dei Contemporanei
Via Terruggia 14, I-20162 Milano
Religious Art Museum
Religious art

07631
Medagliere Milanese e Museo della Moneta
Castello Sforzesco, I-20121 Milano
History/Public Affairs Museum
Coins from the 5th century to modern times

07632
Museo Civico di Storia Naturale
Corso Venezia 55, I-20121 Milano
Natural History Museum - 1838
Paleontology; mineralogy; zoology; ornithology; entomology; botany - library

07633
Museo d'Arte Antica
Castello Sforzesco, I-20121 Milano
Fine Arts Museum
Coll: sculpture from the Paleochristian period to the 17th century, including the 'Pietà' by Michelangelo; painting from the early 14th to 18th centuries, including works by Mantegna, Correggio, Tintoretto, Lippi, Bellini, Tiepolo; musical instruments; ceramics; ivories; furniture; tapestries - library

07634
Museo degli Strumenti Musicali
Castello Sforzesco, I-20121 Milano
Music Museum - 1958
641 musical instruments

07635
Museo del Cinema
Via Palestro 16, I-20121 Milano
Performing Arts Museum
History of cinematography; historical records of films

07636
Museo del Duomo
Piazza Duomo 14, I-20122 Milano
Religious Art Museum - 1953
14th century sculpture; stained glass windows; tapestries; religious art

07637
Museo del Risorgimento e Raccolte Storiche del Comune di Milano
Via Borgonuovo 23, I-20121 Milano
History/Public Affairs Museum - 1884
Documents of Italian history from 1750 to the present

07638
Museo delle Armi Antiche
Via Carducci 41, I-20125 Milano
History/Public Affairs Museum - 1948
15th to 17th century armaments

07639
Museo delle Cere
Stazione Centrale FF.SS, I Milano
History/Public Affairs Museum
Wax figures of the most celebrated personalities

07640
Museo di Arte Estremo Orientale e di Etnografia
Via Mosé Bianchi 94, I-20149 Milano
Fine Arts Museum - 1950
Coll: works from China, India, Japan, the Far East; bronzes; porcelain; paintings; numismatics; sculpture - library

07641
Museo di Milano
Via Sant'Andrea 6, I-20121 Milano
History/Public Affairs Museum - 1934
Iconography; topographical maps; prints; 17th century decorations in a historic house

07642
Museo di Storia Contemporanea
Via Sant'Andrea 6, I-20121 Milano
History/Public Affairs Museum
Documents and exhibits concerning history from 1914 to 1945

07643
Museo Nazionale della Scienza e della Tecnica Leonardo da Vinci
Via S. Vittore 21, I-20123 Milano
Science/Tech Museum - 1953
Coll: relics, models and designs with particular emphasis on Leonardo da Vinci's work; airplanes; ships; railways - library; auditorium

07644
Museo Poldi Pezzoli
Via Manzoni 12, I-20121 Milano
Fine Arts Museum - 1877
14th to 18th century painting; armaments; tapestries; rugs; jewelry; porcelain; glass; textiles; furniture; lace; clocks; sundials - library

07645
Museo Sacro di Sant'Ambrogio
Piazza Sant'Ambrogio 15, I-20123 Milano
Religious Art Museum - 1949
Coll: sculptures and decorative art; 17th century Flemish tapestries; 4th to 12th century linen and silk embroideries; fragments of early sculpture and mosaics; frescoes

07646
Museo Teatrale alla Scala
Via Filodrammatici 2, I-20121 Milano
Performing Arts Museum - 1913
History of theatrical shows from ancient times to the present days; history of the Scala of Milan - library

07647
Pinacoteca Ambrosiana
Piazza Pio XI 2, I-20123 Milano
Fine Arts Museum - 1618
Coll: prints, including many by Dürer; paintings by Titian, Raphael, Caravaggio; drawings by Leonardo da Vinci, Rubens; miniatures; enamels; ceramics

07648
Pinacoteca di Brera
Via Brera 28, I-20121 Milano
Fine Arts Museum - 1809
15th to 18th century paintings, mainly of the Lombard and Venetian school; works by Mantegna, Titian, Raphael, Tintoretto, Rembrandt, Rubens

07649
Raccolte d'Arte dell'Ospedale Maggiore di Milano
Via Francesco Sforza 28, I-20122 Milano
Fine Arts Museum
15th to 20th century drawings

07650
Siloteca Cormio
Piazza San Vittore 21, I-20123 Milano
Natural History Museum
Specimens of wood from all over the world; remains of pile dwellings; objects in wood - library

07651
Tesoro del Duomo
Piazza Duomo 16, I-20122 Milano
Religious Art Museum
5th to 20th century silver work and ivory; gold and enamelled work; tapestries; religious art

Minturno

07652
Antiquarium Nazionale
Via Appia, km. 156, I-04026 Minturno, Latina
Archeology Museum
Roman sculpture; terra cottas; coins

Mirandola

07653
Museo Civico
Via Verdi 12, I-41037 Mirandola, Modena
General Museum
Local archeology; room with illustrations of the Pico family

Modena

07654
Galleria Estense
Palazzo dei Musei, Piazza S. Agostino, I-41100 Modena
Fine Arts Museum
Paintings; statues; small bronzes; pottery; ivory; medals; coins; works by Veronese, Tintoretto, Correggio, Bernini, El Greco, Velasquez

07655
Mostra Permanente della Biblioteca Estense
Palazzo dei Musei, Piazza S. Agostino, I-41100 Modena
History/Public Affairs Museum
14th to 18th century paintings; illuminated painting by Italian and foreign schools - library

07656
Museo Civico Archeologico e Etnologico
Palazzo dei Musei, Piazza S. Agostino 337, I-41100 Modena
History/Public Affairs Museum - 1871
Prehistory; ethnographical objects from Arab, Peru, Africa, Asia, Oceania

07657
Museo Civico di Storia ed Arte Medioevale e Moderna
Palazzo dei Musei, Piazza S. Agostino, I-41100 Modena
History/Public Affairs Museum
Paintings; religious art; historical instruments; ceramics; armaments; textiles

07658
Museo del Risorgimento
Palazzo dei Musei, Piazza S. Agostino, I-41000 Modena
History/Public Affairs Museum - 1894
Local history; history of the Risorgimento (1750-1870) - library

07659
Museo dell'Istituto di Mineralogia e Petrologia
Via S. Eufemia 19, I-41100 Modena
Natural History Museum - 1927
Coll: zeolites; petrology; regional mineralogy - library

07660
Museo dell'Istituto di Zoologia
Via Università 4, I-41100 Modena
Natural History Museum - 1877
Coll: zoology from the Modena area; vertebrates of various continents

07661
Museo di Paleontologia
Via Università 4, I-41100 Modena
Natural History Museum
Paleontology; fossils; dinosaurs

07662
Museo Lapidario del Duomo
Via Lanfranco 6, I-41100 Modena
Archeology Museum
Roman and medieval sculptures and tablets

07663
Museo Lapidario Estense
Palazzo dei Musei, Piazza S. Agostino, I-41100 Modena
Archeology Museum - 1808
Roman sculpture; epigraphs; sarcophagi; tombstones

07664
Museo Muratoriano
Via Pomposa 1, I-41100 Modena
Historic Site - 1931
Memorabilia of the historian Ludovico A. Muratori; various editions of his works - library

07665
Orto Botanico ed Erbario dell'Istituto di Botanica
I-41100 Modena
Natural History Museum
Herbarium; botanical garden

Modigliani

07666
Museo 'Don Giovanni Verità'
Corso Garibaldi 32, I-47015 Modigliani, Forlì
History/Public Affairs Museum
Archeology; prehistory; documents on the Risorgimento

Molfetta

07667
Raccolta Archeologica
Viale Pio XI, I-70056 Molfetta, Bari
General Museum
Local archeology; illuminated books;
painting

Molina di Ledro

07668
Museo delle Palafitte
I Molina di Ledro, Bari
Archeology Museum
Reconstructions of the prehistoric
dwellers' pile structures on Lake
Ledro

Montalcino

07669
Museo Archeologico
Piazza Cavour 10, I-53024 Montalcino,
Siena
Archeology Museum
Prehistoric and Etruscan findings from
the area

07670
Museo Civico
Piazza Cavour 10, I-53024 Montalcino,
Siena
General Museum
14th century paintings by the Sienese
school; pottery; majolica ware

07671
Museo Diocesano
Via Ricasoli 31, I-53024 Montalcino,
Siena
Religious Art Museum
Religious art; paintings and sculptures

Montecatini Val di Nievole

07672
Museo della Prepositura
I-51010 Montecatini Val di Nievole,
Pistoia
Religious Art Museum
Silver work; vestments; 14th century
silver reliquary; frescoes

Montefalco

07673
Pinacoteca 'San Francesco'
Via Ringhiera Umbra, I-06036
Montefalco, Perugia
Fine Arts Museum
Works by Benozzo Gozzoli, Perugino;
frescoes; 13th century decorations

Montefortino

07674
Pinacoteca Comunale
Via Roma, I-63047 Montefortino, Ascoli
Piceno
Fine Arts Museum - 1842
17th century paintings; Tuscan,
Venetian and Bolognese schools

Montepulciano

07675
Museo Civico
Via Ricci 15, I-53045 Montepulciano,
Siena
Fine Arts Museum - 1905
14th to 17th century Tuscan paintings;
illuminated books; terra cottas by Della
Robbia

Monterosso Grana

07676
Museo Etnografico 'Coumboscuro'
Località Santa Lucia, I-12020
Monterosso Grana, Cuneo
Anthropology Museum
Peasant life and ethnography of the
people in the Cisalpine mountains;
weaving; transport; agriculture

Montevarchi

07677
Museo Paleontologico
Via Bracciolini 38, I-52025
Montevarchi, Arezzo
Natural History Museum
Fossils, mainly of the Valdarno
Superior area

Monza

07678
Museo Civico dell'Arengario
Piazza Roma, I-20052 Monza, Milano
General Museum
Finds and artifacts of local interest
from the Middle Ages to modern times

07679
Museo del Tesoro del Duomo
Piazza Duomo, I-20052 Monza, Milano
Religious Art Museum
5th to 9th century relics; medieval and
Renaissance sacred goldwork;
parchments; incunabula; rare books

07680
Pinacoteca Civica
Villa Reale, I-20052 Monza, Milano
Fine Arts Museum - 1935
14th-17th century paintings; modern
art

Napoli

07681
Museo Archeologico Nazionale
Piazza Museo Archeologico
Nazionale, I-80135 Napoli
Archeology Museum - 1750
Roman sculpture; painting; bronzes;
mural paintings from the excavations
of Ercolano, Pompei and Stabiae;
domestic utensils, mosaics, vases,
ivories, lamps, terra cottas from
Pompei and Ercolano; antique
technology and engineering

07682
Museo Civico Gaetano Filangieri
Piazzetta Filangieri, Via Duomo 288,
I-80138 Napoli
General Museum - 1882
Coll: painting; medieval arms; Oriental
majolica; porcelain; antique furniture;
numismatics; manuscripts - library

07683
Museo dell'Istituto Statale d'Arte
Piazza Salazar 6, I-80132 Napoli
Decorative Arts Museum
Decorative arts and crafts

07684
Museo di Mineralogia e Zoologia
Corso Umberto I, I-80138 Napoli
Natural History Museum
Minerals; zoology

07685
Museo 'Duca di Martina'
Via Cimarosa 77, I-80127 Napoli
Decorative Arts Museum - 1911
Ivories; enamels; bronzes; ceramics;
glassware of Murano and Bohemia;
porcelain

07686
Museo Nazionale di Capodimonte
Palazzo Reale di Capodimonte, I-80139
Napoli
Fine Arts Museum - 1738
Coll: paintings and sculpture;
drawings; prints; ivories; enamels;
gold and silver works; tapestry;
armaments; medals and bronzes;
porcelain - library

07687
Museo Nazionale di San Martino
Largo San Martino 5, I-80129 Napoli
General Museum - 1867
Coll: Neapolitan historical documents;
ship models; folklore and costumes;
14th to 19th century paintings and
sculpture; majolica; porcelain; glass;
miniatures; numismatics; arms - library

07688
**Museo 'Principe Diego Aragona
Pignatelli Cortes'**
Riviera di Chiaia 200, I-80121 Napoli
General Museum - 1960
18th century paintings; historic house;
carriages

07689
**Pinacoteca del Pio Monte della
Misericordia**
Piazza Riario Sforza, I-80139 Napoli
Fine Arts Museum
Paintings of the Neapolitan school

07690
Quadreria dei Girolamini
Via Duomo 142, I Napoli
Fine Arts Museum
17th century Neapolitan paintings

07691
Raccolta d'Arte Pagliara
Piazzetta Cariati, I-80132 Napoli
Fine Arts Museum
16th to 19th century drawings, prints
and ceramics

Narni

07692
Pinacoteca Comunale
Via Mazzini, I-05035 Narni, Terni
Fine Arts Museum
Marble sculptures; paintings

Nemi

07693
Museo delle Navi
I-00040 Nemi, Roma
History/Public Affairs Museum
Recovered Roman ships

Nizza Monferrato

07694
**Museo del Vino e delle Contadinerie
'Bersano'**
Piazza Dante 12, I-14049 Nizza
Monferrato, Asti
Agriculture Museum
History of viticulture; methods of
grape pressing; farm implements and
tools

Nocera Inferiore

07695
**Museo Archeologico dell'Agro
Nocentino**
Piazza Sant'Antonio, I-84014 Nocera
Inferiore, Salerno
Archeology Museum
Archeological findings of ancient
Nuceria; sarcophagi; Roman coins

Nocera Umbra

07696
Pinacoteca Comunale
Piazza Caprera, I-06025 Nocera
Umbra, Perugia
Fine Arts Museum - 1957
Archeology; paintings; frescoes -
library

Nola

07697
Antiquarium del Seminario
Via Seminario, I-80035 Nola, Napoli
Archeology Museum
Archeological findings from Cimitile

Nonantola

07698
Tesoro dell'Abbazia di San Silvestro
Piazza Caduti Partigiani 6, I-41015
Nonantola, Modena
Religious Art Museum
In church: wall paintings; Byzantine
crosses; illuminated codices

Norcia

07699
Museo 'La Castellina'
Piazza San Benedetto, I-06046 Norcia,
Perugia
General Museum
Local and religious art

Noto

07700
Museo Comunale
Corso V.Emanuele 134, I-96017 Noto,
Siracusa
Fine Arts Museum
Archeology; medieval exhibits;
modern art

Novara

07701
Museo Civico del Broletto
Via Rosselli 20, I-28100 Novara
General Museum - 1874
Paintings, sculptures and drawings of
Tuscan, Lombard and Venetian
schools; local archeology; 16th to 19th
century arms

07702
**Museo di Storia Naturale
'Faraggiana-Ferrandi'**
Via Ferrari 12, I-28100 Novara
Natural History Museum - 1937
Natural history section; zoological
collection; anthropology section;
ethnographic material on East Africa,
China and Japan

Numana

07703
Antiquarium
Via La Fenice, I-60026 Numana,
Ancona
Archeology Museum
Greek material from the necropoleis of
Sirolo and Numana

Nuoro

07704
**Museo della Vita e delle Tradizioni
Popolari Sarde**
Via Mereu 56, I-08100 Nuoro
General Museum
Folk art and peasant life of Sardinia;
costumes

Oderzo

07705
Museo Civico
Via Garibaldi 18, I-31046 Oderzo,
Treviso
Archeology Museum - 1875
Archeological finds from the area;
mosaics; medals

Offida

07706
Museo e Pinacoteca
I-63035 Offida, Ascoli Piceno
General Museum
Local archeology; paintings

Orbetello

07707
Antiquarium Comunale
Via Ricasoli 26, I-58015 Orbetello,
Grosseto
Archeology Museum
Etruscan and Roman graves, vases,
numismatics and bronzes

Oristano

07708
Antiquarium Arborense
Via Vittorio Emanuele 8, I-09025
Oristano, Cagliari
General Museum - 1938
Prehistoric, Punic and Roman
archeological findings; Sardinian art
and artifacts

Orte

07709
Museo Diocesano di Arte Sacra
Piazza Colonna, I-01028 Orte, Viterbo
Religious Art Museum
Religious art; paintings; an 8th century
mosaic of the Madonna; goldsmith
work

Ortisei

07710
Museo della Val Gardena
Località Cesa di Ladins, I Ortisei,
Bolzano
General Museum
Minerals, zoology and botany of the
Dolomites; folk arts and crafts of the
people living in the Gardena Valley

Orvieto

07711
Museo Civico e Collezione 'C. Faina'
Piazza Duomo 29, I-05018 Orvieto,
Terni
Archeology Museum - 1821
Greek, Etruscan and Roman
archeology; numismatics; documents
of civil life and communal
administration in medieval and modern
times

07712
Museo dell'Opera del Duomo
Palazzo Solimano, I-05018 Orvieto,
Terni
History/Public Affairs Museum
14th century paintings; frescoes;
sculpture; medieval art - library

Osimo

07713
Museo Sacro Diocesano
Piazza Duomo, I-60027 Osimo, Ancona
Religious Art Museum
Altar pieces; candlesticks; sacred
vestments; reliquary

Ossuccio

07714
Antiquarium 'Lucio Salvio Quintiano'
Isola Comacina, I-22010 Ossuccio,
Como
Archeology Museum
Archeological findings of the area

Ostia Antica

07715
Museo Ostiense
I-00050 Ostia Antica, Roma
Archeology Museum
Coll: Roman art and sculpture; 2nd
century sarcophagi; lead, bronzes;
terra cotta; glass; coins; mosaics

Padova

07716
Cappella degli Scrovegni
Piazza Eremitani, I-35100 Padova
Fine Arts Museum
Frescoes by Giotto

07717
Museo 'Bottacin'
Piazza del Santo 10, I-35100 Padova
History/Public Affairs Museum - 1865
Coll: Greek, Roman and medieval
Italian coins and medals; Renaissance
bronzes; seals; 18th and 19th century
paintings - library

07718
Museo Civico
Piazza del Santo 10, I-35100 Padova
Fine Arts Museum - 1825
Div: art gallery; works by Giotto;
Giorgione, Bellini - library

Padula

07719
**Museo Archeologico della Lucania
Occidentale**
Certosa San Lorenzo, I-84034 Padula,
Salerno
Archeology Museum - 1957
Archeological findings from the Diano
Valley

Paestum

07720
Museo Archeologico Nazionale
I-84063 Paestum, Salerno
Archeology Museum - 1952
Findings from the excavations of
Paestum; bronzes; sculptures, painted
slabs from the necropolis, including
the Diver's tomb

Palazzolo Acreide

07721
Casa Museo
Via Machiavelli 19, I Palazzolo Acreide,
Siracusa
Agriculture Museum
Peasant life and folk art of Sicily; farm
implements; olive mills; Sicilian
puppets; toys

Palermo

07722
**Civica Galleria d'Arte Moderna 'E.
Restivo'**
Via Turati 10, I-90139 Palermo
Fine Arts Museum - 1907
19th and 20th century art, mostly by
Sicilian artists

07723
Galleria Regionale della Sicilia
Palazzo Abatellis, Via Alloro 4, I-90133
Palermo
Fine Arts Museum - 1952
Coll: medieval and Renaissance art;
paintings by Flemish and Florentine
school; frescoes

07724
**Mostra Permanente del Tesoro della
Cattedrale**
Corso Vittorio Emanuele, I-90133
Palermo
Religious Art Museum
Silver and goldsmith work; precious
books; priest vestments; crown of
Constance of Aragon; exhibits of the
Norman Kings

07725
Museo Archeologico Regionale
Piazza Olivella, I-90133 Palermo
Archeology Museum - 1868
Coll: Greek, Punic, Roman and
Etruscan antiquities; sculpture and
metopes from temple of Selinunte;
Egyptian inscriptions - library

07726
**Museo del Risorgimento Vittorio
Emanuele Orlando**
Piazza S.Domenico 1, I-90133 Palermo
History/Public Affairs Museum
Coll: paintings, portraits, prints, medals,
sculpture and relics pertaining to the
history of the Risorgimento in Sicily

07727
**Museo di Zoologia della Università
di Palermo** Istituto di Zoologia
Via Archirafi 18, I-90123 Palermo
Natural History Museum - 1862
Coll: Mediterranean fish and molluscs;
European birds, mammalia and
reptiles; anatomy; osteology - library

07728
Museo Diocesano di Arte Sacra
Via Matteo Bonello 2, I-90134 Palermo
Religious Art Museum - 1927
Coll: 13th to 18th century paintings by
Vasari, Giordano, Novelli and
Velasquez; ceramics; gold and silver
plate; priests' vestments; mosaics;
Byzantine icons

07729
Museo Etnografico 'G. Pitré'
Via Duca degli Abruzzi, I-90146
Palermo
Anthropology Museum - 1909
Sicilian culture and folk art; Sicilian
puppets; manger scene figures

07730
**Museo Internazionale delle
Marionette**
Palazzo Fatta, Piazza Marina 19,
I-90133 Palermo
Decorative Arts Museum - 1965
Coll: Sicilian puppets and marionettes;
Oriental marionettes in amber,
parchment and wood; 19th century
manuscripts of plays from Palermo
and Naples - library

07731
Orto Botanico
Via Lincoln 2b, I-90133 Palermo
Natural History Museum - 1795
Wood samples; plants - library

07732
Palazzina Cinese
Via Duca degli Abruzzi, I-90146
Palermo
Fine Arts Museum
Chinese and English prints

Palestrina

07733
Museo Archeologico Nazionale
Palazzo Barberini, Piazza della Cortina,
I-00036 Palestrina, Roma
Archeology Museum
Coll: local excavations from the temple
of Fortuna; terracottas; mosaics

Pallanza

07734
Museo del Paesaggio Museo Storico
e Artistico del Verbano
Palazzo Viani-Dugnani, Via Ruga 44,
I-28048 Pallanza, Novara
General Museum - 1909
Coll: paintings; sculpture; archeology

Palmi

07735
Musei Comunali
Piazza Municipio, I-89015 Palmi,
Reggio Calabria
General Museum - 1955
Archeological findings from
Taurianum; peasant life and folk art of
Calabria; pottery; agricultural tools

Parma

07736
Camera di San Paolo
Via Melloni, I-43100 Parma
Fine Arts Museum
Frescoes by Corregio

07737
Casa Museo 'Toscanini'
Via Tanzi 7, I-43100 Parma
Historic Site
Memorabilia on the conductor Arturo
Toscanini (1867-1957)

07738
Galleria Nazionale
Palazzo Pilotta, Via della Pilotta 4,
I-43100 Parma
Fine Arts Museum - 1752
14th to 19th century paintings,
including works by Corregio,
Parmigianino, Van Dyck; artists of the
Parma and Bolognese school; Flemish
and French painters

07739
Museo Archeologico Nazionale
Palazzo Pilotta, Via della Pilotta 4,
I-43100 Parma
Archeology Museum - 1760
Roman insriptions, marble works,
bronzes, pottery; material from the
pre-Roman period; Egyptian, Greek
and Etruscan collections

07740
Museo Bodoniano
Palazzo della Pilotta, I-43100 Parma
History/Public Affairs Museum - 1963
Art of printing; rare editions - library

07741
Museo del Risorgimento
Barriera Bixio, I-43100 Parma
History/Public Affairs Museum
Local history of the Risorgimento

07742
Museo della Farmacia Storica
spezeria di San Giovanni
Via Borgo Pipa 1, I-43100 Parma
History/Public Affairs Museum - 1897
Furnishings and objects of an ancient
Benedictan pharmacy; 15th-17th
century pots and ceramics

07743
Museo di Arte Cinese
Via S.Martino 8, I-43100 Parma
Fine Arts Museum - 1900
Chinese bronzes, ceramics,
porcelains, paintings and coins

07744
Museo di Mineralogia e Petrografia
Via Gramsci 9, I-43100 Parma
Natural History Museum
Minerals and rocks of the area

07745
Museo Etnografico
Via S.Martino 8, I-43100 Parma
Anthropology Museum - 1900
Coll: ethnography; Chinese, Japanese
and African art; African statues in
ivory and wood

07746
Museo 'Glauco Lombardi'
Via Garibaldi 15, I-43100 Parma
General Museum
Documents and relics of the Borbonic
period; 18th century French paintings

07747
Museo Paleontologico Parmense
Via Kennedy 4, I-43100 Parma
Natural History Museum
Fossils; stones; molluscs

07748
Pinacoteca 'G. Stuard'
Via Cavestro 14, I-43100 Parma
Fine Arts Museum - 1834
Paintings, including early Tuscan
artists

Pavia

07749
Museo Civico
Castello Visconteo, I-27100 Pavia
History/Public Affairs Museum - 1838
History of Risorgimento; archeological
material; medieval, Romanesque and
Renaissance sculpture; prints

07750
Museo Civico di Storia Naturale
Strada Nuova 65, I-27100 Pavia
Natural History Museum
Mineralogy; zoology

07751
**Museo dell'Istituto di Anatomia
Comparata**
Castello Visconteo, Piazza Botta 10e,
I-27100 Pavia
Natural History Museum - 1876
Coll: comparative anatomy;
embryology; osteology

07752
**Museo dell'Istituto di Mineralogia e
Petrografia**
Via A. Bassi 4, I-27100 Pavia
Natural History Museum - 1889
Mineralogy and petrography

07753
Museo di Anatomia Patologica
Via Forlanini 16, I-27100 Pavia
History/Public Affairs Museum
Anatomic parts of pathological interest

07754
Museo di Archeologia Università di
Pavia
Strada Nuova 65, I-27100 Pavia
Archeology Museum
Numismatics; archeology; teaching
material

07755
**Museo per la Storia dell'Università
di Pavia**
Strada Nuova 65, I-27100 Pavia
History/Public Affairs Museum
History of the University of Pavia -
library

07756
Museo Zoologico
Piazza Botta, I-27100 Pavia
Natural History Museum
Birds and mammals

07757
Pinacoteca 'Malaspina' Civici Musei
Piazza Petrarca 2, C.P. 161, I-27100
Pavia
Fine Arts Museum - 1835
Medieval art collection; paintings;
numismatics; archeology - library

Perticara

07758
Museo Storico Minerario
I Perticara, Pesaro-Urbino
Natural History Museum
Minerals; mining equipment, tools and
machinery; local archeology

Perugia

07759
Galleria Nazionale dell'Umbria
Palazzo dei Priori, Corso Vannucci,
I-26100 Perugia
Fine Arts Museum - 1863
13th to 18th century paintings;
sculpture; works by Perugino,
Angelico, Giorgio; jewellery; costumes
- library

07760
**Museo Archeologico Nazionale
dell'Umbria**
Piazza Bruno 10, I-06100 Perugia
Archeology Museum - 1812
Prehistoric finds from Tuscany;
Etruscan and Roman finds from
Perugia

07761
Museo dell'Opera del Duomo
Piazza IV Novembre 23, I-06100
Perugia
Religious Art Museum - 1923
Illuminated codices; priest vestments;
miniatures and paintings; silverware

07762
Nobile Collegio del Cambio
Corso Vannucci, I-06100 Perugia
Fine Arts Museum
15th century frescoes

Pesaro

07763
Casa Natale di Rossini
Via Rossini 34, I-61100 Pesaro
Historic Site
Birthplace of the composer
Gioacchino Rossini (1792-1868);
autographs and personal possessions

07764
Museo Archeologico Oliveriano
Via Mazza 96, I-61100 Pesaro
Archeology Museum
Italic, Etruscan, Greek, Roman and
Paleochristian remains, coins, medals;
collection of ancient maps

07765
Museo Civico
Piazza Mosca 29, I-61100 Pesaro
Fine Arts Museum
Rossini's painting collection, mainly
Venetian paintings, including Bellini

07766
**Tempietto Rossiniano della
Fondazione 'Rossini'**
Piazza Olivierei 5, I-61100 Pesaro
Music Museum - 1896
Memorabilia on the composer
Gioacchino Rossini (1792-1868); music
manuscripts; autographs

Pescara

07767
Museo della 'Casa D'Annunzio'
Corso Manthonè, I-65100 Pescara
Historic Site
House of the poet Gabriele
D'Annunzio (1863-1938); possessions
and relics

Peschiera del Garda

07768
Museo Palazzina Storica
I Peschiera del Garda, Verona
History/Public Affairs Museum
Relics of the World War I

Pescia

07769
Museo Civico
Piazza Santo Stefano, I-51017 Pescia,
Pistoia
Fine Arts Museum - 1894
14th to 16th century Tuscan paintings;
14th cent. coloured wooden statues;
prints by Albrecht Dürer

Pessione

07770
**Museo 'Martini' di Storia
dell'Enologia**
I-10020 Pessione, Torino
Agriculture Museum - 1961
Coll: wine presses since the 18th
century; wine containers in silver and
crystal from the 17th through the 19th
centuries; farm carts; archeological
exhibits from Greece, Etruria and
South Italy since the 7th century B.C.

Piacenza

07771
Galleria 'Alberoni'
Via Emilia Parmense 77, I-29100
Piacenza
Fine Arts Museum - 1761
15th to 18th century paintings,
including works by da Messina,
Signorelli, Giorgione, Titian, Raphael,
Correggio; paintings by Flemish artists;
paintings from other European
countries; 16th to 18th century
tapestries

07772
Galleria d'Arte Moderna 'Ricci-Oddi'
Via San Siro 13, I-29100 Piacenza
Fine Arts Museum - 1931
19th and 20th century Italian paintings

07773
Museo del Risorgimento
Via Sopramuro 60, I-29100 Piacenza
History/Public Affairs Museum
Local history of the Risorgimento

07774
Museo del Teatro Municipale
Via Verdi 41, I-29100 Piacenza
Performing Arts Museum - 1804
History of the theatre; librettos;
manuscripts; photographs

07775
Museo di Sant'Antonino
Via Chiostro Sant'Antonino 6, I-29100
Piacenza
Religious Art Museum
Illuminated codices; miniatures;
paintings; vestments

Piedimonte D'Alife

07776
Museo Civico
Largo San Domenico, I-81016
Piedimonte D'Alife, Caserta
General Museum - 1912
Coll: archeology; sculptural relics;
vases; numismatics; ceramics

07777
Museo Internazionale 'Della Paolera'
Via Ercole d'Agnese 72, I Piedimonte
D'Alife, Caserta
Archeology Museum
Archeological material of China and
India; archives

Pienza

07778
Museo della Cattedrale
Via del Castello, I-53026 Pienza, Siena
Religious Art Museum - 1901
14th and 15th cent. paintings by the
Siena school; 15th and 16th cent.
Flemish tapestries; miniatures

Pieve di Cadore

07779
**Museo della 'Magnifica Comunità di
Cadore'**
Piazza Tiziano, I-32044 Pieve di
Cadore, Belluno
Fine Arts Museum
Works by local painters

07780
Museo Paleoveneto
Piazza Tiziano, I-32044 Pieve di
Cadore, Belluno
Archeology Museum
Local archeology from the 3rd to the
1st century B.C.

07781
Museo Risorgimentale
Piazza Tiziano, I-32044 Pieve di
Cadore, Belluno
History/Public Affairs Museum
Local history

07782
Museo Tizianesco
Piazza Tiziano, I-32044 Pieve di
Cadore, Belluno
Historic Site
Memorabilia on the painter Vecelli
Titian (1489-1576) at his birthplace

Pievebovigliana

07783
Museo della Pieve
Via Napoleone 2, I-62035
Pievebovigliana, Macerata
General Museum
Inscriptions dating back to the 3rd
century B.C.

Pinerolo

07784
Museo Civico e Pinacoteca
Piazza Vittorio Veneto, I-10064
Pinerolo, Torino
General Museum - 1905
Local history and folk art

07785
Museo d'Arte Preistorica
Viale Giolitti 1, I-10064 Pinerolo, Torino
Archeology Museum
Prehistoric art depicting the Italian
Alps, the Iberian peninsula,
Scandinavia and the French Maritime
Alps

07786
Museo Nazionale dell'Arma della Cavalleria
Via Giolitti 5, I-10064 Pinerolo, Torino
History/Public Affairs Museum - 1961
Ancient and modern arms; uniforms;
cavalry relics - library

Pisa

07787
Camposanto e Museo dell'Opera
Piazza Duomo, I-56100 Pisa
Fine Arts Museum - 1277
Detaches frescoes; sarcophagi;
sculpture

07788
Domus Galileiana
Via Santa Maria 26, I-56100 Pisa
Historic Site
Memorial house of Galileo Galilei
(1564-1642) - library

07789
Domus Mazziniana
Via Mazzini 29, I-56100 Pisa
Historic Site
Manuscripts and relics to the politician
Giuseppe Mazzini (1805-1872)

07790
Gabinetto dei Disegni e delle stampe
Via Santa Cecilia 27, I-56100 Pisa
Fine Arts Museum
Prints and drawings

07791
Museo Nazionale e Civico di San Matteo
Lungarno Mediceo, I-56100 Pisa
General Museum - 1796
Coll: archeology; Christian sarcophagi;
frescoes; sculptures from Pisa; 13th to
17th century paintings by Tuscan and
Pisan schools; Florentine Renaissance
painters; coins and medals

07792
Museo Teatrale presso il Teatro Verdi
Via Palestro, I-56100 Pisa
Performing Arts Museum
History of the theatre

Pistoia

07793
Museo Civico
Piazza del Duomo 1, I-51100 Pistoia
General Museum
13th cent. painting; sculpture;
ceramics; arms; medals

Pizzighettone

07794
Museo Civico
Torre di Francesco 1, I-26026
Pizzighettone, Cremona
General Museum
Local archeology; Etruscan ceramics;
paintings

Policoro

07795
Museo Nazionale della Siritide
Viale Colombo, I Policoro, Matera
Archeology Museum
Archeological findings from the
ancient city of Heraclea

Pompei

07796
Antiquarium
Pompei Scavi, I-80040 Pompei, Napoli
Archeology Museum
Excavation finds from the area;
domestic utensils and objects
pertaining to daily life in the Roman
period

07797
Museo Sacro
Basilica del Rosario, I-80040 Pompei,
Napoli
Religious Art Museum
Sacred goldsmith work; ancient
liturgical books; pottery; porcelain;
arms; medals

07798
Museo Vesuviano
Piazza Longo 1, I-80040 Pompei,
Napoli
Geologic material of the Vesuvius;
archeological remains of Pompei;
panoramic plan of Pompei

Ponte San Giovanni

07799
Ipogei dei Volumni
Via Assisana, I Ponte San Giovanni,
Perugia
Archeology Museum
Etruscan tomb; urns; pottery

Pontedassio

07800
Museo Storico degli Spaghetti
Via Garibaldi 96, I Pontedassio, Imperia
Agriculture Museum
History and technology of the pasta
production from the earliest times up
to the present; machines; drawings

Pordenone

07801
Museo Civico - Palazzo Ricchieri
Corso Vittorio Emanuele, I-33170
Pordenone
Fine Arts Museum - 1970
15th-20th century paintings, sculpture
and engravings

Portoferraio

07802
Museo Napoleonico di Villa San Martino
Strada Marciana, I-57037 Portoferraio,
Livorno
History/Public Affairs Museum
History of Napoleonic period

07803
Pinacoteca Comunale Foresiana
Villa San Martino, I-57037 Portoferraio,
Livorno
General Museum
Paintings and various works of art

Portogruaro

07804
Museo Nazionale Concordiese
Via Seminario 10, I-30026 Portogruaro,
Venezia
Archeology Museum - 1887
Archeological findings of the Roman
and Christian period

Possagno

07805
Gipsoteca Canoviana e Casa del Canova
Via Canova, I-31054 Possagno, Treviso
Historic Site - 1957
Memorabilia on sculptor Antonio
Canova (1757-1822) at his birthplace;
models, copies and sketches

Potenza

07806
Museo Provinciale Lucano
Via Malta, I-85100 Potenza
General Museum - 1899
Prehistoric and Roman archeology;
arms; bronzes; terra-cottas; coins;
picture gallery

Prato

07807
Galleria Comunale d'Arte
Piazza del Comune, I-50047 Prato,
Firenze
Fine Arts Museum - 1858
14th and 15th century Florentine
school; 15th to 19th century paintings
and sculptures

07808
Museo dell'Opera del Duomo
Piazza Duomo 49, I-50047 Prato,
Firenze
Religious Art Museum
Frescoes; 16th century paintings;
works by Uccello, Lippi, Toscani;
sculptures by Donatello

07809
Museo di Pittura Murale
Piazza S. Domenico 8, I-50047 Prato,
Firenze
Fine Arts Museum - 1974
Coll: detached frescoes; sgraffiti;
sinopias; didactic presentation of
mural painting technique and
restoration

07810
Quadreria Comunale
Piazza del Comune, I-50047 Prato,
Firenze
Fine Arts Museum
Portraits of historical personalities

Predazzo

07811
Museo Civico di Geologia e di Etnografia
Piazza S.S. Filippo e Giacomo, I
Predazzo, Trento
Natural History Museum - 1972
Coll: geology; paleontology;
mineralogy; petrography; ethnography

Premana

07812
Museo Etnografico
Via Roma, I Premana, Como
Science/Tech Museum
History of iron mining; products of
iron; tools; crafts; farm implements

Quarto d'Altino

07813
Museo Archeologico
Via Sant'Eliodoro 27, I Quarto d'Altino,
Venezia
Archeology Museum - 1960
Finds of the Roman necropolis of
Altino - library

Ragusa

07814
Museo Archeologico Ibleo di Ragusa
Via Natalelli 1, I-97100 Ragusa
Archeology Museum - 1960
Finds from local excavations

Ravenna

07815
Centro Dantesco
Largo Firenze 9, I-48100 Ravenna
Historic Site
All printed editions of Dante's works
(1265-1321); translations; secondary
literature; manuscripts

07816
Mausoleo di Galla Placidia
I-48100 Ravenna
Religious Art Museum
Mosaics from 450

07817
Museo Arcivescovile
Piazza Arcivescovado 1, I-48100
Ravenna
Archeology Museum
Roman and Christian sculptures and
inscriptions

07818
Museo Nazionale
Via San Vitale 17, I-48100 Ravenna
General Museum
Roman and Byzantine sculpture; ivory;
stained glass; Byzantine paintings;
furniture; bronzes

07819
Pinacoteca Comunale
Via Roma, I-48100 Ravenna
Fine Arts Museum
16th to 20th century paintings

Recanati

07820
Palazzo Leopardi
Piazza Sabato del Villagio, I-62019
Recanati, Macerata
Historic Site
Memorabilia on the poet Giacomo
Leopardi (1798-1837); manuscripts -
library

07821
Pinacoteca Comunale e Museo 'Gigli'
Piazza Leopardi, I-62019 Recanati,
Macerata
Fine Arts Museum
Paintings by local artists; works by
Lorenzo Lotto; modern art gallery;
costumes and personal possessions
of singer Benjamino Gigli (1890-1957)

Redipuglia

07822
Museo della Guerra e Sacrario della Terza Armata
I-34070 Redipuglia, Gorizia
History/Public Affairs Museum
Relics of World War I and the Italian
army

Reggio Calabria

07823
Museo Nazionale di Reggio Calabria
Piazza de Nava 26, I-89100 Reggio
Calabria
Archeology Museum - 1954
Coll: prehistoric, Greek and Roman
finds from excavations; vases and
terra cottas; coins; bronzes; paintings
from the Middle Ages to modern times
- library

Reggio Emilia

07824
**Galleria Civica 'Anna e Luigi
Parmiggiani'**
Piazza della Vittoria 5, I-42100 Reggio
Emilia
Fine Arts Museum - 1933
Coll: 13th to 18th century European
paintings, including works by
Veronese, Titian, El Greco, Velazquez;
sculpture; woodcarvings; silverware

07825
Museo Civico
Via Spallanzani 1, I-42100 Reggio
Emilia
General Museum - 1799
Local archeology; natural history;
historical relics; local art

Riese Pio X

07826
Museo 'San Pio X'
I-31039 Riese Pio X, Treviso
Historic Site
Memorabilia on Pope Pius X
(1903-1914); documents; pontifical
robes; personal possessions

Rieti

07827
Museo Civico
Palazzo Comunale, I-02100 Rieti
General Museum
15th to 18th century paintings; jewelry;
local archeology

Rimini

07828
Museo Civico
Tempio Malatestiano, I-41037 Rimini,
Forlì
General Museum - 1871
Pottery, bronzes, mosaics, statues,
paintings, frescoes from the Roman
period up to present times

07829
**Museo delle Arti Primitive 'Dinz
Rialto'**
Piazza Cavour, I-41037 Rimini, Forlì
Anthropology Museum
History and art of Africa, Oceania and
pre-Columbian America

Riva del Garda

07830
Museo Civico
La Rocca, I-38066 Riva del Garda,
Trento
General Museum
Local archeology; pile structure;
religious art; paintings; natural history;
local folk art

Roma

07831
Antiquarium Forense
Piazza S. Maria Nova 53, I-00185
Roma
Archeology Museum
Finds of the prehistoric necropolis in
the Roman Forum

07832
Antiquarium Palatino
Piazza Santa Maria Nova 53, I-00186
Roma
Archeology Museum - 1860
Sculpture, ceramics and pottery found
at the Palatine

07833
Casa di Pirandello
Via Bosio 15, Roma
Historic Site
Manuscripts and documents of the
writer Luigi Pirandello (1867-1936) -
library

07834
Casino dell'Aurora
Via XXIV Maggio 43, Roma
Fine Arts Museum
17th century paintings of hunting
scenes by the Bolognese school

07835
Castello die Giulio II
Piazza della Rocca, I Roma, Ostia
Antica
Historic Site - 1940
Archaeology

07836
Gabinetto Nazionale delle Stampe
Via della Lungara 230, I-00165 Roma
Fine Arts Museum - 1895
Italian and foreign prints and drawings
from the 14th century to present times

07837
Galleria 'Colonna'
Via Pilotta 17, I-00187 Roma
Fine Arts Museum - 1793
15th to 18th century Italian and foreign
paintings, including works by
Veronese, Tintoretto and Botticelli

07838
Galleria Comunale d'Arte Moderna
Palazzo Braschi, Piazza di San
Pantaleo 10, I-00186 Roma
Fine Arts Museum - 1925
Contemporary paintings and
sculptures, mainly by Roman artists

07839
**Galleria dell'Accademia Nazionale di
San Luca**
Piazza dell Accademia di San Luca 77,
I-00187 Roma
Fine Arts Museum
17th-20th century art gallery

07840
Galleria 'Doria Pamphilj'
Piazza del Collegio Romano 1a,
I-00186 Roma
Fine Arts Museum - 1651
Coll: Paintings by Correggio, Titian, del
Piombo, Lorrain, Filippo Lippi, Carracci,
Caravaggio

07841
**Galleria Nazionale d'Arte Antica -
Palazzo Corsini**
Via della Lungara 10, I-00165 Roma
Fine Arts Museum - 1883
Coll: Italian, Dutch and Flemish
paintings from the 17th to 18th
centuries; paintings by Ribera,
Caravaggio, Giordano, Murillo

07842
**Galleria Nazionale d'Arte Antica -
Palazzo Barberini**
Via delle Quattro Fontane 13, I-00184
Roma
Fine Arts Museum - 1895
Coll: 12th-18th century paintings;
paintings by Simone Martini, Lorenzo
Lotto, Titian, Raphael, Bellotto,
Caravaggio, Filippo Lippi; Odescalchi
collection of arms - library

07843
**Galleria Nazionale d'Arte Moderna -
Arte Contemporanea**
Viale delle Belle Arti 131, I-00197 Roma
Fine Arts Museum - 1883
Coll: 19th and 20th century Italian and
foreign paintings, sculptures and
graphic works; works by Courbet,
Monet, van Gogh, Modigliani, Braque,
de Chirico, Manzu, Mirò, Giacometti,
Duchamp - library

07844
Galleria 'Spada'
Capodiferro 13, I-00186 Roma
Fine Arts Museum - 1929
Coll: 16th to 18th century paintings;
works by Reni, Titian, Rubens,
Brueghel; Roman and 17th century
sculpture; decorative arts

07845
**Istituto di Anatomia Patologica
Policlinico Umberto I**
Viale Regina Elena 324, I-00161 Roma
History/Public Affairs Museum
Human pathology; congenital heart
diseases - library

07846
**Istituto Italiano di Paleontologia
Umana**
Piazza Mincio 2, I-00198 Roma
Anthropology Museum - 1911
Coll: prehistoric finds, mostly from
central and southern Italy; some
Neandertal human remains - library

07847
**Istituto Nazionale per la Grafica -
Calcografia**
Via della Stamperia 6, I-00187 Roma
Fine Arts Museum - 1738
Coll: copper engravings; drawings and
prints - library

07848
**Mostra Permanente della Comunità
Israelitica**
Lungotevere Cenci, I-00100 Roma
Religious Art Museum
Ritual silverware; antique sacred
furnishings; documents and
illustrations about the Israelitic
community

07849
Musei Capitolini
Piazza del Campidoglio, I-00186 Roma
Archeology Museum - 1471
Roman statues; Hellenistic replicas of
Greek originals; sarcophagi

07850
**Museo Aeronautico 'Caproni di
Taliedo'**
Via Azuni 13, I-00196 Roma
Science/Tech Museum - 1939
Models and historical documents of
aviation

07851
Museo Astronomico Copernicano
Viale Parco Mellini 84, I-00136 Roma
Science/Tech Museum - 1873
Historic astronomical and
meteorological instruments; globes;
books, pictures, medals, coins, prints
concerning to Nicolaus Copernicus
(1473-1543)

07852
Museo Barracco
Corso Vittorio Emanuele 168, I-00186
Roma
Fine Arts Museum - 1902
Evolution of sculpture from Egyptian to
Roman styles

07853
Museo 'Canonica'
Viale Canonica 2, I-00197 Roma
Fine Arts Museum - 1961
Paintings, marbles, bronzes and
plaster models by Pietro Canonica

07854
Museo Centrale del Risorgimento
Via di San Pietro in Carcere, I-00186
Roma
History/Public Affairs Museum
Documents, relics, arms and medals of
the Risorgimento

07855
Museo Civico di Zoologia
Via Aldovrandi 18, I-00197 Roma
Natural History Museum - 1932
Ornithology; malacology; entomology

07856
Museo Criminologico
Via del Gonfalone 20, I-00186 Roma
History/Public Affairs Museum
Documents and relics on the history of
criminal investigation; section on
capital executions and imprisonments

07857
Museo dei Cavalieri di Malta
Piazza dei Cavalieri di Malta 3, I-00173
Roma
History/Public Affairs Museum
Relics and documents on the Order of
the Knights of Malta

07858
Museo dei Conservatori
Piazza Campidoglio, I-00186 Roma
Fine Arts Museum
Graeco-Roman sculptures

07859
Museo del Tasso
Piazza Sant'Onofrio al Gianicolo 2,
I-00165 Roma
Historic Site
Memorabilia on the poet Torquato
Tasso (1544-1595) - library

07860
Museo della Civiltà Romana
Piazza Agnelli 15, I-00144 Roma
History/Public Affairs Museum - 1955
Reproductions, reconstructions and
documents depicting the history of
Rome

07861
**Museo della Keats-Shelley
Memorial Association**
Piazza di Spagna 26, I-00187 Roma
Historic Site
House where the poet John Keats
(1795-1821) died

07862
**Museo della Società Geografica
Italiana**
Via Navicella 12, I-00184 Roma
Anthropology Museum
Manuscripts, maps, pictures, busts of
conquerors and explorers; arms and
various objects of Africa, Asia,
America and Australia

07863
Museo dell'Alto Medioevo
Viale Lincoln 1, I-00144 Roma
Archeology Museum
Findings from the Langobard
necropolis of Nocera Umbra and
Castel Trosino; medieval pottery and
marble reliefs

07864
Museo delle Mura
Via di Porta San Sebastiano, I-00179
Roma
Archeology Museum
Models of the Aurelian Wall and
construcional details; inscriptions

07865
Museo delle Origini
Piazzale delle Scienze 5, I Roma
Anthropology Museum
Mainly Italian prehistoric material of
the Institute of Paleontology

07866
**Museo dell'Istituto di Patologia del
Libro**
Via Milano 76, I-00184 Roma
History/Public Affairs Museum - 1938
Antique writing instruments; physically,
chemically and biologically damaged
books

07867
**Museo dell'Istituto Storico e di
Cultura dell'Arma del Genio**
Lungotevere della Vittoria 31, I-00195
Roma
History/Public Affairs Museum - 1906
Uniforms; models of fortresses;
history of the Army communications
service and military architecture

07868
**Museo di Archeologia Sacra e
Profana**
Via Appia Antica 136, I-00179 Roma
Archeology Museum
Paleochristian sarcophagi

07869
Museo di Goethe
Via del Corso 18, I-00186 Roma
Historic Site - 1973
Paintings, prints, manuscripts and
photographs illustrating Goethe's
travels in Italy

07870
Museo di Mineralogia e Petrografia
Istituto di Mineralogia e Petrografia
Piazzale Aldo Moro 5, I-00185 Roma
Natural History Museum - 1804
Coll: minerals of Latium; single
crystals; meteorites

07871
Museo di Palazzo Venezia
Piazza Venezia 3, I-OO184 Roma
Decorative Arts Museum - 1926
Coll: arms; tapestries; silverware;
bronze; ceramics; Odescalchi arms
collection

07872
Museo di Paleontologia Istituto di
Geologia e Paleontologia
Città Universitaria, I-00185 Roma
Natural History Museum - 1864
Coll: quaternary mammals collected in
the Mediterranean area; invertebrate
fossils and tetrapod footprints;
molluscs - library

07873
Museo di Roma
Piazza di San Pantaleo 10, I-00186
Roma
History/Public Affairs Museum - 1930
Scenic reconstructions of Roman life;
paintings and drawings; frescoes from
the Middle Ages to present times;
festival carriages; two coaches from
the train of Pope Pius IX; pottery;
goldsmith work; all exhibits depicting
the history of Rome

07874
Museo di San Pancrazio
Piazza San Pancrazio 5d, I-00100
Roma
Religious Art Museum - 1912
Catacombs; inscriptions and
sculptures

07875
Museo di Storia della Medicina
Facoltà di Medicina e Chirurgia
Viale dell'Università 34a, I-00185 Roma
History/Public Affairs Museum - 1938
History of medicine; medical
instruments

07876
Museo Etrusco di Villa Giulia
Piazzale Villa Giulia 9, I-00196 Roma
Archeology Museum - 1889
Etruscan and Italian antiquities; bronze
sword; sarcophagus; vases; statuettes

07877
Museo Francesco
Grande raccordo anulare, km 68,800, I
Roma
Religious Art Museum
Rich collections of paintings, drawings,
sculptures, engravings, coins and
various articles concerning Franciscan
history and art

07878
Museo Galleria 'Borghese'
Piazzale Scipione Borghese 5, I-00197
Roma
Fine Arts Museum - 1613
Baroque and Neoclassical sculptures;
a group by Bernini; Canova
sculptures; paintings by Raphael,
Botticelli, Perugino, Fra Angelico, Titian,
Caravaggio, Corregio, Veronese,
Rubens, Cranach

07879
Museo Napoleonico
Piazza Ponte Umberto I, I-00186 Roma
History/Public Affairs Museum - 1927
Paintings and drawings collected by
the Bonaparte family; miniatures; coins
and medals; the marriage certificate of
Napoleon I and Marie-Louise; relics
concerning to the Bonapartes and
their relations to Rome

07880
Museo Nazionale d'Arte Orientale
Via Merulana 248, I-00185 Roma
Anthropology Museum - 1958
Sculptures, paintings, ceramics,
bronzes and wood carvings from Iran,
Afghanistan, Pakistan, India, Tibet,
Nepal, China and Japan - library

07881
**Museo Nazionale degli Strumenti
Musicali**
Piazza Santa Croce, I Roma
Music Museum
Musical instruments from ancient
times to the end of the 19th century

07882
**Museo Nazionale delle Arti e
Tradizioni Popolari**
Piazza Marconi 8, I-00144 Roma
Anthropology Museum - 1923
Italian living style; peasant life and
traditions; urban life; folk art; costumes
- library

07883
**Museo Nazionale di Castel
Sant'Angelo**
Lungotevere Castello 1, I-00193 Roma
History/Public Affairs Museum - 1925
Ancient and modern arms and armor;
Italian uniforms; decorations; frescoes;
period furniture - library

07884
**Museo Nazionale Preistorico ed
Etnografico 'Luigi Pigorini'**
Piazzale Marconi 1, I-00187 Roma
Anthropology Museum - 1875
Prehistoric findings of Latium and the
Middle East; ethnographic objects
from Africa, America, Oceania - library

07885
Museo Nazionale Romano
Piazza della Finanze, I-00185 Roma
Archeology Museum - 1889
Greek and Roman sculptures and
bronzes; pictures and mosaics;
medals and coins

07886
Museo Numismatico della Zecca
Via XX Settembre 97, I-00100 Roma
History/Public Affairs Museum - 1958
Coins from the Middle Ages to
present times; Pontifical medals from
the 15th century up to now

07887
Museo Nuovo
Piazza Campidoglio, I-00186 Roma
Archeology Museum
Greek sculptures; sarcophagi; urns
and funeral vases

07888
**Museo Sacrario delle Bandiere della
Marina Militare**
Vittoriano, I Roma
History/Public Affairs Museum
Relics concerning to the history of the
Italian navy; flags; torpedo; documents

07889
Museo Storico dei Bersaglieri
Piazzale Porta Pia, I-00198 Roma
History/Public Affairs Museum - 1887
History of Italian infantry, mainly of the
Bersaglieri; uniforms; equipment;
armaments

07890
**Museo Storico dei Granatieri di
Sardegna**
Piazza Santa Croce in Gerusalemme
7, I-00185 Roma
History/Public Affairs Museum - 1924
History of the Sardinian brigade from
17th century to present times

07891
Museo Storico della Fanteria
Piazza Santa Croce in Gerusalemme
9, I-00185 Roma
History/Public Affairs Museum - 1959
Italian uniforms; ancient and modern
arms; Alpine and parachute troops;
documents

07892
**Museo Storico della Guardia di
Finanza**
Piazza Armellini 20, I-00162 Roma
History/Public Affairs Museum - 1937
History of the customs guard and and
exhibits of current events

07893
**Museo Storico della Liberazione di
Roma**
Via Tasso 145, I-00185 Roma
History/Public Affairs Museum
Rome during the German occupation
1943-1945

07894
**Museo Storico della Motorizzazione
Militare**
Viale dell'Esercito 86, I-00143 Roma
Science/Tech Museum
Military motorization; lorries, cars,
armoured vehicles, motorcycles

07895
**Museo Storico dell'Arma dei
Carabinieri**
Piazza Risorgimento 46, I-00192 Roma
History/Public Affairs Museum - 1937
History of the Carabinieri, the Italian
police - library

07896
**Museo Storico delle Poste e
Telecomunicazioni**
Via Andreoli 11, I-00195 Roma
Science/Tech Museum - 1878
Exhibits and documents concerning to
the history of post, telegraph,
telephone, radio-television and
philately

07897
**Museo Storico Nazionale dell'Arte
Sanitaria**
Lungotevere in Sassia, I-00193 Roma
History/Public Affairs Museum - 1911
History of medical instruments

07898
Museo Torlonia
Vicolo Corsini 5, 00165 Roma
Archeology Museum - 1829
Etruscan archeology; ancient
sculptures and paintings arranged by
Winckelmann in 1765

07899
Pinacoteca Capitolina
Piazza Campidoglio, I-00186 Roma
Fine Arts Museum
14th to 17th century paintings of
various schools

07900
Pinacoteca dell'Abbazia di San Paolo
Via Ostiense 186, I-00146 Roma
Fine Arts Museum
Picture gallery

07901
**Pontificia Accademia dei Virtuosi al
Pantheon**
Piazza della Cancelleria 1, I-00186
Roma
Religious Art Museum - 1541
Crucifixes

07902
**Quadreria della Cassa Depositi e
Prestiti**
Piazza al Monte di Pietà, I-00186 Roma
Fine Arts Museum - 1857
17th century paintings

07903
Raccolta Teatrale del Burcardo
Via del Sudario 44, I-00186 Roma
Performing Arts Museum - 1931
Puppet collection; masks; pamphlets;
costumes; prints on the theatre

07904
**Raccolte dell'Istituto di Clinica delle
Malattie Tropicali e Subtropicali**
Viale Regina Elena, I-00161 Roma
History/Public Affairs Museum
Tropical and subtropical diseases; wax
preparations

07905
**Raccolte dell'Istituto di Clinica
Otorinolaringoiatrica**
Viale Policlinico, I-00161 Roma
History/Public Affairs Museum
Otolaryngology

07906
**Raccolte dell'Istituto di Clinica
Urologica**
Viale Policlinico, I-00161 Roma
History/Public Affairs Museum
Urology

07907
Raccolte dell'Istituto di Geografia
Piazzale delle Scienze, I-00185 Roma
Natural History Museum
Geography

07908
Raccolte dell'Istituto di Merceologia
Via del Castro Laurenziano 9, I-00197
Roma
History/Public Affairs Museum
Commerce; trade

07909
Raccolte dell'Istituto di Parassitologia
Piazzale delle Scienze 5, I-00185 Roma
Natural History Museum
Parasitology

07910
Raccolte dell'Istituto di Radiologia Medica
Viale Policlinico, I-00161 Roma
Science/Tech Museum
Apparatus and instruments of medical radiology from different periods

07911
Villa della Farnesina Accademia
Nazionale dei Lincei
Via della Lungara 230, I-00165 Roma
Historic Site
Renaissance building; 16th century decoration and frescoes; painted ceiling and walls by Raphael, Peruzzi, Sodoma, Sebastiano del Piombo, Giulio Romano

Rossano

07912
Museo Diocesano
Largo Duomo, I-87067 Rossano,
Cosenza
Religious Art Museum
14th century paintings; silverware; parchments

Rovereto

07913
Casa di Rosmini
Via Stoppani 3, I-38068 Rovereto,
Trento
Historic Site
Ancient house of the Rosmini family; period furniture; paintings - library

07914
Museo 'Depero'
Via della Terra 53, I-38068 Rovereto,
Trento
Fine Arts Museum
Futurist paintings by Fortunato Depero

07915
Museo Storico Italiano della Guerra
Castello Veneto, Via Castelbarco 7,
I-38068 Rovereto, Trento
History/Public Affairs Museum - 1921
Coll: World War I arms and artillery; weapons; uniforms - library

07916
Società Museo Civico
Via Calcinari 18, I-38068 Rovereto,
Trento
General Museum - 1851
Coll: prehistoric archeology; history; paleontology; numismatics; natural sciences

Rovetta

07917
Casa Museo 'Fantoni'
Via Fantoni 1, I-24020 Rovetta,
Bergamo
Fine Arts Museum - 1959
Sculptures in clay, wood and marble from the 15th to 17th centuries

Rovigo

07918
Museo Civico delle Civiltà in Polesine
Piazzale San Bartolomeo 18, I-45100
Rovigo
General Museum - 1978
Coll: prehistoric and Roman finds of the area; farm life; farm implements and equipment; local craftmanship

07919
Museo del Seminario Vescovile
Via Tre Martiri 89, I-45100 Rovigo
Archeology Museum
17th and 18th century paintings; archeological finds

07920
Museo dell'Accademia dei Concordi
Piazza Vittorio Emanuele, I-45100
Rovigo
Fine Arts Museum
Paintings of the Venetian school

Ruvo

07921
Museo Jatta
Piazza Bovio 35, I-70037 Ruvo, Bari
Archeology Museum - 1820
Finds from local tombs; antique vases (6th to 3rd centuries B.C.)

Sagrado

07922
Museo di San Michele
Piazzale Cima 3, I-34078 Sagrado,
Gorizia
History/Public Affairs Museum - 1938
Weapons used in World War I

Saint-Nicolas

07923
Museo 'Cerlogne'
I-11010 Saint-Nicolas, Aosta
History/Public Affairs Museum
Coll: literary works by Abbot Cerlogne; exhibits concerning Val d'Aosta dialects

Salerno

07924
Museo Archeologico Provinciale
Via San Benedetto, I-84100 Salerno
Archeology Museum - 1927
Archeological objects found in the Picentum district and in Lucania, dating back to earliest history

07925
Museo del Duomo
Via Monterisi, I-84100 Salerno
Religious Art Museum - 1935
Coll: 12th century ivories; manuscripts; paintings

Salò

07926
Museo Storico del Nastro Azzurro
Loggia Magnifica Patria 1, I-25087
Salò, Brescia
History/Public Affairs Museum - 1934
Historical articles ranging from the Napoleonic wars to the Resistance

Saluzzo

07927
Museo Casa 'Cavassa'
Via San Giovanni 5, I-12037 Saluzzo,
Cuneo
Fine Arts Museum
Sculpture; paintings; furnishings

San Felice Circeo

07928
Galleria Pinacoteca d'Arte 'I Templari'
Piazza Vittorio Veneto 36/37, I-04017
San Felice Circeo, Latina
Fine Arts Museum
Coll: Paintings by contemporary Italian and international artists

San Fortunato

07929
Museo e Pinacoteca del Santuario 'Madonna delle Grazie'
Via Santa Maria delle Grazie 10,
I-47040 San Fortunato, Forlì
Anthropology Museum
Ethnology; paintings

San Gimignano

07930
Museo di Arte Sacra
Piazza Pecori 1, I-53037 San
Gimignano, Siena
Religious Art Museum - 1915
Wooden statues and crucifixes; religious aricles made of silver and gold

07931
Pinacoteca Civica
Piazza Duomo, I-53037 San
Gimignano, Siena
Fine Arts Museum - 1852
Works of Florentine and Sienese schools from the 13th to 15th centuries

San Ginesio

07932
Pinacoteca Communale
Via Merelli 12, I-62026 San Ginesio,
Macerata
Fine Arts Museum
Paintings of various schools on canvas and on wood; archeological material

San Giovanni Valdarno

07933
Museo di Santa Maria delle Grazie
Piazza Masaccio, I-52027 San
Giovanni Valdarno, Arezzo
Fine Arts Museum
15th-19th century paintings of the Florentine school

San Leo

07934
Museo e Pinacoteca del Forte
I-61018 San Leo, Pesaro-Urbino
History/Public Affairs Museum
Coll: 16th-18th century paintings; prints; antique arms; 16th and 17th century furniture

San Lorenzo in Campo

07935
Antiquarium Suasanum
I-61047 San Lorenzo in Campo,
Pesaro-Urbino
Archeology Museum
Tomb requisites; bronzes; coins

07936
Museo Etnografico Africano
I San Lorenzo in Campo, Pesaro-
Urbino
Anthropology Museum
Coll: African ritual objects; sculpture and paintings; stuffed animals of Sierra Leone

San Martino della Battaglia

07937
Museo della Battaglia
I-25010 San Martino della Battaglia,
Brescia
History/Public Affairs Museum - 1939
Coll: uniforms; armaments; local history of the Risorgimento

San Mauro Pascoli

07938
Casa del Pascoli
I-47030 San Mauro Pascoli, Forlì
General Museum
Local artifacts

San Michele all'Adige

07939
Museo degli Usi e Costumi della Gente Trentina
Via Mack, I-38010 San Michele
all'Adige, Trento
Science/Tech Museum - 1968
Coll: ironworks; weaving; wood technology; grinding processing; agriculture; viticulture; alpine pasturing; traditional cooking; heating stoves; peasant life; folk art

San Miniato

07940
Museo Diocesano di Arte Sacra
I-56027 San Miniato, Pisa
Religious Art Museum
15th-17th century paintings; frescoes; parchments; liturgical items

San Nicolo' Val d'Ultimo

07941
Talmuseum
I-39010 San Nicolo' Val d'Ultimo,
Bolzano
General Museum
Indigenous animals; furnished rooms; domestic implements; paintings; watches; costumes

San Severino Marche

07942
Museo Archeologico 'G. Moretti' e Pinacoteca
Palazzo Tacchi Venturi, Via Salimbeni
39, I-62027 San Severino Marche,
Macerata
General Museum - 1972
Prehistoric section; paintings

Sansepolcro

07943
Museo Civico
Via Aggiunti 65, I-52037 Sansepolcro,
Arezzo
Fine Arts Museum - 1867
Frescoes by Piero della Francesca;
16th and 17th century paintings;
ceramics

Santa Croce Camerina

07944
Antiquarium
Casa Pace, I-97017 Santa Croce
Camerina, Ragusa
Archeology Museum
Archeological findings of the antique Siracusan colony of Camerina

225

Santa Maria Capua Vetere

07945
Santa Maria Capua Vetere
Anfiteatro Romano, I-81055 Santa
Maria Capua Vetere, Caserta
Archeology Museum
Fragments, statues and mosaics from
the Campania amphitheatre

Santa Maria degli Angeli

07946
Museo della Basilica
I-06088 Santa Maria degli Angeli,
Perugia
Religious Art Museum
14th century convent housing antique
vestments, paintings, and
ethnographical exhibits

Sant'Angelo Lodigiano

07947
Museo Cabriniano
Via Cabrini, I-20079 Sant'Angelo
Lodigiano, Milano
Religious Art Museum
Mother Cabrini's birthplace;
furnishings; religious articles

07948
Museo Morando Bolognini
Castello Visconteo, Piazza Libertà,
I-20079 Sant'Angelo Lodigiano, Milano
History/Public Affairs Museum - 1947
13th century castle interiors;
tapestries

Sant'Anna d'Alfaedo

07949
Museo di Storia Naturale
Via Roma 4, I-37020 Sant'Anna
d'Alfaedo, Verona
Natural History Museum
Prehistory; fossils

Sant'Antioco

07950
Antiquarium
I-09017 Sant'Antioco, Cagliari
Archeology Museum
Findings at the excavation site of a
Punis necropolis at Sulcis (5th to 3rd
century B.C.)

Santena

07951
Museo 'Cavour'
Castello di Cavour, I-00026 Santena,
Torino
History/Public Affairs Museum - 1955
Memorabilia on the Cavour Family and
the 'Risorgimento'

Santuario di Montevergine

07952
**Galleria e Mostra del Presepe nel
Mondo**
I Santuario di Montevergine, Avellino
Fine Arts Museum
Sculpture; gold articles; vestments;
manger figures; paintings

Sarnano

07953
Pinacoteca e Biblioteca Comunale
Piazza Perfetti 1, I-62028 Sarnano,
Macerata
Fine Arts Museum
Renaissance painting, paintings by
Crivelli, L'Alunno, Pagani and Maratta -
library

Sarsina

07954
Museo Archeologico Sarsinate
Via Cesio Sabino, I-47027 Sarsina,
Forlì
Archeology Museum - 1938
Excavations from the ancient Roman
town including sculptures and
bronzes, funerary monument and
mosaics from the baths; prehistoric
sculptures

07955
Museo Diocesano
Seminario Vescovile, I-47027 Sarsina,
Forlì
Archeology Museum
Sculptures and Roman finds; collection
of 14th century bells

Sassari

07956
Museo Giovanni Antonio Sanna
Via Roma, I-07100 Sassari
General Museum - 1932
Archeology (Central-North Sardinia);
ethnography; paintings by Vivarini;
medieval and modern art - library

07957
**Raccolta dell'Istituto di Mineralogia
e Geologia** Facoltà di Agraria
Via Encrico de Nicola, I-07100 Sassari,
Sardegna
Natural History Museum - 1963
Minerals; stones; fossils - library

Sassocorvaro

07958
Museo Civico Minore
Via Roma 2, I-61028 Sassocorvaro,
Pesaro-Urbino
General Museum - 1890
Paintings; history

Sassoferrato

07959
**Galleria Civica d'Arte Moderna e
Contemporanea**
Piazza Matteotti, I-60047 Sassoferrato,
Ancona
Fine Arts Museum
Paintings; sculpture; graphic arts

07960
Museo Civico
Piazza Matteotti, I-60047 Sassoferrato,
Ancona
General Museum
Prehistory; Roman archeology; art;
history

Savigliano

07961
Museo Civico e Gipsoteca
Piazza San Francesco 17, ex
Convento San Francesco, I-12038
Savigliano, Cuneo
Fine Arts Museum - 1904
Coll: Roman finds; paintings of local
artists; works in plaster - library

Savignano Sul Rubicone

07962
**Museo Archeologico Romano-
Gallico-Etrusco**
San Giovanni in Computo, I-47039
Savignano Sul Rubicone, Forlì
Archeology Museum
Roman antiquities

Savio

07963
**Museo degli Strumenti Musicali
Meccanici**
Strada Nazionale, Km. 163, I-48020
Savio, Ravenna
Music Museum
Organs; harmoniums; musical boxes;
pianolas; phonographs

Savona

07964
**Museo del Santuario di Nostra
Signora di Misericordia**
Piazza Santuario 6, I-17100 Savona
Religious Art Museum - 1959
Sacred vessels and vestments
(16th-19th c.)

07965
Pinacoteca Civica
Via Quarda Superiore 7, I-17100
Savona
Fine Arts Museum - 1868
Paintings of the Genoese school (17th
c.); pottery (16th-17th c.)

Sciacca

07966
Pinacoteca
Palazzo Comunale, I-92019 Sciacca,
Agrigento
Fine Arts Museum

Selinunte

07967
Antiquarium
I Selinunte, Trapani
Archeology Museum
Acropolis with tree temples

Selva di Progno

07968
Museo dei Cimbri
Località, I-37030 Selva di Progno,
Verona
History/Public Affairs Museum

Senigallia

07969
**Museo dei Centri Storici delle
Marche**
Piazza del Duca 2, I-60019 Senigallia,
Ancona
History/Public Affairs Museum
Regional history

Sermoneta

07970
Museo Archeologico
I-04010 Sermoneta, Latina
Archeology Museum

Sestino

07971
Antiquarium Sestinale
I-52038 Sestino, Arezzo
General Museum - 1930
Sculptures; coins; architecture of the
region

Sesto Calende

07972
Museo Civico
Palazzo Comunale, I-21018 Sesto
Calende, Varese
General Museum
Local finds of Roman and Gallic
period; remains of the culture of
Golasecca

Sesto Fiorentino

07973
Museo di Doccia
Via Pratese 31, I-50019 Sesto
Fiorentino, Firenze
Decorative Arts Museum
Porcelain from the local manufacture
(1737 to present); terra cotta

Sestri Levante

07974
Galleria Rizzi
Via Cappuccini 3, I-16039 Sestri
Levante, Genova
Fine Arts Museum - 1960
Paintings of the Venetian and
Genoese schools; furniture; pottery

Settignano

07975
Collezione Berenson
I-50135 Settignano, Firenze
Fine Arts Museum

Sibari

07976
Museo Archeologico della Sibaritide
Via Taranto, I-87070 Sibari, Cosenza
Archeology Museum - 1970
Greek and Roman finds; prehistoric
necropolis

Siena

07977
Museo Archeologico Etrusco
Via della Sapienza 5, I-53100 Siena
Archeology Museum - 1940
Neolithic objects; Attic and Etruscan
vases, domestic utensils, metal
ornaments and coins

07978
Museo Civico
Piazza del Campo, I-53100 Siena
Fine Arts Museum
Sculptures and monuments; frescoes;
coins

07979
Museo dell' Archivio di Stato
Via Banchi di Sotto 52, I-53100 Siena
Fine Arts Museum
'Biccherna', small paintings on wood
from the 13th through 17th centuries;
documents

07980
**Museo della Società di Esecutori di
Pie Disposizioni**
Via Roma 71, I-53100 Siena
Fine Arts Museum - 1938
Sienese paintings

07981
**Museo dell'Opera della
Metropolitana**
Piazza del Duomo, I-53100 Siena
Fine Arts Museum - 1870
Coll: Roman copy of an original of
Praxiteles; sculpture by Pisano;
frescoes; tapestry; paintings from the
12th to 16th centuries

07982
**Museo Geo-Mineralogico e
Zoologico dell'Accademia dei
Fisocratici**
Via Mattioli, I-53100 Siena
Natural History Museum - 1961
Minerals; fossils; ornithology; zoology

07983
Palazzo Piccolomini
Via Banchi di Sotto 52, I-53100 Siena
History/Public Affairs Museum
Coll: imperial diplomas; parchments;
Papal Bulls; contracts; Dante
souvenirs; manuscripts; medals; seals;
weights and measures

07984
Pinacoteca Nazionale
Via San Pietro 29, I-53100 Siena
Fine Arts Museum - 1939
13th to 17th century paintings
including Duccio, Dürer, Rubens

Siracusa

07985
Museo Archeologico Nazionale
Piazza Duomo 14, I-96100 Siracusa
Archeology Museum - 1886
Prehistory and early history; Greek,
Roman and Paleochristian remains;
numismatics

07986
Museo Nazionale di Palazzo Bellomo
Via G.M. Capodieci 14-16, I-96100
Siracusa
Fine Arts Museum - 1940
Coll: sculpture; paintings of the Sicilian
School; works by Antonello da
Messina and Antonelliani

Solferino

07987
Museo della Battaglia
I-46040 Solferino, Mantova
History/Public Affairs Museum - 1959
Documents on the war of 1859;
Gonzaga fortress

Solunto

07988
Antiquarium e Zona Archeologica
I Solunto, Palermo
Archeology Museum

Sondrio

07989
Museo Valtellinese di Storia ed Arte
Villa Quadrio, I-23100 Sondrio
General Museum
Local archeology and art; ethnography

Sorrento

07990
Museo Correale di Terranova
Via Correale 50, I-80067 Sorrento
General Museum - 1924
Greek, Roman and Byzantine marble,
inscriptions, fragments; Neapolitan
porcelain (17th-18th c.) and painting
(17th c.); manuscripts of Tasso's works

Spello

07991
Collezione Mineralogica
Via S. Severino 23, I-06038 Spello,
Perugia
Natural History Museum - 1930
Mineralogy

07992
Museo di Santa Maria Maggiore
Via Cavour, I-06038 Spello, Perugia
Fine Arts Museum
Renaissance frescoes; ciborium by
Rocca da Vicenza; majolica pavement;
wooden statues (13th-14th c.)

Sperlonga

07993
Museo Archeologico Nazionale
Via Flacca, I-04029 Sperlonga, Latina
Archeology Museum
Greek and Roman sculptures; terra
cotta; vases

Spoleto

07994
Galleria d'Arte Moderna
Via Elladio, I-06049 Spoleto, Perugia
Fine Arts Museum - 1953
Contemporary painting including
Guttuso, Leoncillo, Morlotti, Scanavino,
Ceroli

07995
Museo Civico
Piazza del Duomo, I-06049 Spoleto
General Museum - 1914
Roman inscriptions; medieval and
Renaissance sculptures

07996
Museo del Teatro
Via Elladio, I-06049 Spoleto, Perugia
Performing Arts Museum
Sketches of scenographies by
Cocteau, Moore, Manzù

07997
Pinacoteca Comunale
Piazza del Comune, I-06049 Spoleto,
Perugia
Fine Arts Museum - 1871
Painting (13th-15th c.); frescoes
(15th-16th c.); goldsmith work; seals;
coins; tapestries (16th c.)

Squinzano

07998
Museo delle Tradizioni Popolari
Località Santa Maria di Cerrate,
I-73018 Squinzano
General Museum
Agricultural and craft tools and
implements; frescoes (12th-16th c.);
pottery; abbey (12th c.)

Stresa

07999
Palazzo Borromeo
Isola Bella, I-28049 Stresa, Novara
General Museum
Lombard architecture and 17th
century paintings; 16th century
tapestries; armour; historic house -
botanical garden

Stupinigi

08000
Museo d'Arte d'Ammobigliamento
Piazza Principe Amedeo, I-10040
Stupinigi, Torino
Fine Arts Museum
Piemontese art and architecture;
baroque style building

Sulmona

08001
Museo Civico
Palazzo dell'Annunziata, I-67039
Sulmona
Fine Arts Museum - 1927
Renaissance architecture; sculptures
in wood and stone (14th-16th c.);
painting (14th-17th c.); Roman pottery;
jewelry

08002
Museo della Cattedrale
I-67039 Sulmona
Religious Art Museum - 1920
Baroque interior; cathedral
decorations and wall paintings (14th
c.); wooden crucifix; episcopal throne
(12th c.)

Susa

08003
Museo Civico
Via Palazzo di Città 38, I-10059 Susa,
Torino
General Museum - 1884
Prehistory; archeology, Roman grave,
architectural fragments; folklore

Sutri

08004
Antiquarium Comunale
Palazzo Comunale, I-01015 Sutri,
Viterbo
General Museum
Etruscan finds mainly sculptures and
inscriptions

Taggia

08005
Museo dei Domenicani
Piazza Cristoforo 6, I-18018 Taggia,
Imperia
Fine Arts Museum
Painting

Taormina

08006
Antiquarium del Teatro Greco-Romano
Via Teatro Greco, I-98039 Taormina,
Messina
Archeology Museum
Inscriptions; architectonic fragments;
marbles

Taranto

08007
Museo Archeologico Nazionale
Corso Umberto 54, I-74100 Taranto
Archeology Museum - 1899
Coll: prehistory; Greek and Roman
marble sculpture; Hellenistic finds;
ceramics; Corinthian vases; jewelry

Tarquinia

08008
Museo Nazionale Archeologico
Palazzo Vitelleschi, Piazza Cavour 1,
I-01016 Tarquinia, Viterbo
Archeology Museum - 1924
Coll: Etruscan sarcophagi and remains
with figured cemetery stones; tombs
with frescoes; Etruscan and Greek
vases; bronzes; ornaments

Teggiano

08009
Museo Civico
Piazza San Pietro, I-84039 Teggiano,
Salerno
Fine Arts Museum
Romanesque and medieval art;
sculptures; frescoes

Teramo

08010
Museo e Pinacoteca Civici
Villa Comunale, I-64100 Teramo
Fine Arts Museum - 1979
15th-20th century paintings; 17th
century ceramics; modern art picture
gallery

Terlizzi

08011
Museo de Napoli
Corso Garibaldi 9, I-70038 Terlizzi
Fine Arts Museum
Paintings and sketches by Michele De
Napoli; architectonic fragments

Termini Imerese

08012
Museo Civico
Via del Museo, I-90018 Termini
Imerese, Palermo
Archeology Museum - 1873
Prehistory; architectonic fragments of
Roman buildings; geology and
mineralogy; coins; Sicilian paintings

Termoli

08013
**Mostra Nazionale di Arte
Contemporanea**
Largo XXI Agosto, I-86039 Termoli,
Campobasso
Fine Arts Museum
Contemporary art

Terni

08014
Pinacoteca e Musei Civici
Via Manassei 6, I-05100 Terni
General Museum
Prehistory; Roman architecture;
painting of the Umbrian school

Terracina

08015
Museo Civico
Piazza Municipio, I-04019 Terracina,
Latina
General Museum
Statues, relief work and epigraphs of
the Roman period

Thiene

08016
Museo del Castello Colleoni Porto
Piazza Ferrarin, I-36016 Thiene,
Vicenza
Fine Arts Museum
Coll: 15th century frescoes; statues;
pottery; furniture

Tindari

08017
Antiquarium
I-98060 Tindari, Messina
Fine Arts Museum
Marble sculptures of the Hellenistic
period; Greek and Roman articles
made of clay

Tirano

08018
Museo Etnografico
Piazza Basilica, I Tirano, Sondrio
General Museum
Ethnography; traditional costumes,
customs, and arts of the Valtellina area

Tirolo di Merano

08019
Museo Agricolo 'Brunnenburg'
I-39019 Tirolo di Merano, Bolzano
Agriculture Museum
Exhibits on bread baking

Tivoli

08020
Museo Communale
I-00019 Tivoli, Roma
Fine Arts Museum - 1915
17th century paintings

Todi

08021
Museo Civico
Piazza Vittorio Emanuele II, I-06059
Todi, Perugia
Fine Arts Museum
Coll: goldsmith work; religious
ornaments; archeological findings of
Etruscan and Roman objects

Tolentino

08022
Museo Civico
Piazza Silveri 2, I-62029 Tolentino,
Macerata
Archeology Museum - 1882
Stone sculptures; ceramics; items
from local excavations

08023
Museo delle Ceramiche
Basilica di San Nicola, I-62029
Tolentino, Macerata
Decorative Arts Museum
Vases from Albissola, Deruta, Nove
and Castel Durante

08024
**Museo Internazionale della
Caricatura**
Palazzo Parisani-Bezzi, Via della Pace
20, C.P. 146, I-62029 Tolentino,
Macerata
Fine Arts Museum
Coll: drawings, paintings, statuettes
and puppets by the world's most
famous caricaturists; humorous
journals

Tolfa

08025
Museo Civico
Piazza Vittorio Veneto, I-00059 Tolfa,
Roma
Archeology Museum
Etruscan and Roman artifacts

Tolmezzo

08026
**Museo Carnico delle Arti e
Tradizioni Popolari 'L. e M. Gortani'**
Piazza Garibaldi 2, I-33028 Tolmezzo,
Udine
Anthropology Museum - 1920
Ethnography; local folklore

Torino

08027
Armeria reale
Piazza Castello 191, I-10122 Torino
History/Public Affairs Museum - 1837
Coll: one of the best arms and armour
collections in Europe, dating back to
the 15th century ; Oriental and exotic
armour; famous equestrian armour

08028
Centro Storico Fiat
Via Chiabrera 20, I-10126 Torino
Science/Tech Museum
Cars; airplane and ship engines;
history of the fiat Company from its
very beginning - library

08029
Civica Galleria d'Arte Moderna
Museo Civico di Torino
Via Magenta 31, I-10128 Torino
Fine Arts Museum - 1959
19th-20th century paintings, graphics
and sculptures - library

08030
**Galleria dell'Accademia Albertina di
Belle Arti**
Via Accademia Albertina 6, I-10123
Torino
Fine Arts Museum - 1833
16th-18th century paintings

08031
Galleria Sabauda
Via Accademia delle Scienze 6,
I-10123 Torino
Fine Arts Museum - 1832
Coll: Dutch and Flemish paintings;
works by the Lombard and
Piedmontese schools; sculpture;
furniture; jewelry

08032
Museo Civico Museo Civico d'Arte
Antica e Palazzo Madama
Palazzo Madama, Piazza Castello,
I-10125 Torino
Anthropology Museum - 1860
Coll: anthropolgy; tools and arms of
Africa, America, the Near East and
Oceania; adjacent museum for applied
and ancient arts: Piedmontese art from
the 12th through 19th centuries;
housed in a 15th century palace -
library

08033
**Museo dell'Automobile, Carlo
Biscaretti di Ruffia**
Corso Unità d'Italia 40, I-10126 Torino
Science/Tech Museum - 1957
Coll: automobiles; motor vehicles and
chassis; engines; tires; old posters
and prints - library

08034
Museo di Antichita
Via Accademia delle Scienze 6,
I-10123 Torino
Archeology Museum
Coll: prehistoric weapons, tools and
jewels from the Iron and Bronze Ages;
Greek pottery; Etruscan collection;
Roman sculpture, inscriptions, pottery
and necropolis

08035
Museo di Antropologia ed Etnografia
Via Accademia Albertina 17, I-10123
Torino
Anthropology Museum - 1923
Coll: skulls; skeletons; brains; fossil
casts; pictures of living primates; lithic
tools; mummies; ethnographic exhibits
of various cultures of the world -
library

08036
Museo di Geologia e Paleontologia
Palazzo Carignano, Via Accademia
delle Science 5, I-10123 Torino
Natural History Museum - 1878
Coll: geology; mineralogy; fossils;
mollusks; rocks of Frejus and Mont
Blanc tunnels

08037
**Museo di Psichiatria e Antropologia
Criminale**
Corso Galileo Galilei 22, I-10126
Torino
History/Public Affairs Museum - 1898
Forensic medicine; skulls;
anthropology

08038
Museo Egizio
Via Accademia delle Scienze 6,
I-10123 Torino
Archeology Museum - 1832
Coll: Egyptian history,; sarcophagi;
mummies; stelae; statues; papyrus;
Ptolemaic and Coptic antiquities;
reconstructed Nile temple of the 18th
dynasty

08039
Museo Nazionale del Cinema
Piazza San Giovanni 2, I-10122 Torino
Science/Tech Museum - 1941
Coll: pre-cinema exhibits; history of
photography; the silent and sound film;
8,000 cinematographic posters -
library

08040
**Museo Nazionale del Risorgimento
Italiano**
Via Accademia delle Scienze 5,
I-10123 Torino
History/Public Affairs Museum
Relics pertaining to the Resistance and
the 'Risorgimento'

08041
**Museo Nazionale della Montagna
'Duca degli Abruzzi'**
Via Giardino 37, I-10131 Torino
History/Public Affairs Museum - 1877
History of mountaineering; documents
pertaining to the Duke of Abruzzi

08042
**Museo Nazionale Storico
d'Artiglieria**
Corso Ferraris, I-10120 Torino
History/Public Affairs Museum
Coll: Small arms; shields and
defensive arms; body armour;
uniforms

08043
Museo 'Pietro Micca'
Via Guicciardini 7, I-10121 Torino
General Museum
Wooden models of the city and citadel
of Turin in various sizes

08044
Museo Zoologico
Via Giolitti 34, I-10123 Torino
Natural History Museum
Coll: insects; birds; mammals; fish;
reptiles and amphibians; several
extinct species

08045
Palazzo Reale
Piazza Castello, I-10120 Torino
Fine Arts Museum
Coll: frescoes; furniture; paintings of
the Piedmont baroque, Rocaille and
neoclassic styles

08046
Tombe Reali di Casa Savoia
Basilica di Superga, I-10132 Torino
Religious Art Museum - 1778
Crypt with royal tombs and sculptures
- library

Torre del Greco

08047
Museo del Corallo
Piazza Palomba 6, I-80059 Torre del
Greco, Napoli
Decorative Arts Museum
Sculpture; engraved coral, lava, shells,
mother-of-pearl and ivory

Torre del Lago Puccini

08048
Museo Pucciniano
I-55048 Torre del Lago Puccini, Lucca
History/Public Affairs Museum
House of Giacomo Puccini from 1900
until 1921; the musician's tomb

Torre Pellice

08049
Museo Storico Valdese
Via Roberto d'Azeglio 2, I-10066 Torre
Pellice, Torino
General Museum - 1889
Ethnographical museum of the
Waldensian valleys - library, archives

Tortona

08050
Museo Civico
Piazza Arzano 2, I-15057 Tortona,
Alessandria
Archeology Museum
Roman and medieval artifacts;
sculpture; sarcophagi; capitals

Trani

08051
Museo Diocesano
Piazza Duomo, I-70059 Trani, Bari
Religious Art Museum
Coll: 14th-17th century paintings;
religious ornaments and furnishings

Trapani

08052
Museo 'Pepoli'
Via Pepoli 196, I-91100 Trapani
Fine Arts Museum
Coll: 14th-18th century paintings;
paintings of the Tuscan school;
archeological findings; corals; pottery

Traversetolo

08053
Museo 'Renato Brozzi'
Palazzo Municipale, I-43029
Traversetolo, Parma
Fine Arts Museum
Sculptures and paintings by Renato
Brozzi

Trebisacce

08054
Museo Etnografico
I-87075 Trebisacce, Cosenza
Anthropology Museum
Ethnological objects from different
parts of the world; arms used by
African warriors; arts and crafts

Tremezzo

08055
Villa Carlotta
Via Regina, I-22019 Tremezzo, Como
Fine Arts Museum - 1927
Coll: sculptures by Canova and
Thorvaldsen; paintings by Appiani and
Hayez; gobelins

Trento

08056
Museo Diocesano Tridentino
Piazza Duomo, I-38100 Trento
Religious Art Museum - 1903
Local religious art; archeological finds

08057
Museo Nazionale
Via Clesio 5, I-38100 Trento
General Museum
Coll: archeology; ethnography; art

08058
Museo Storico Nazionale degli Alpini
Via Brescia, I-38100 Trento
History/Public Affairs Museum
History of the Alpine troops in times of war and peace

08059
Museo Trentino del Risorgimento e della Lotta per la Libertà
Castello del Buon Consiglio, I-38100 Trento
History/Public Affairs Museum - 1923
History of the Risorgimento, anti-fascism and the resistance movement

08060
Museo Tridentino di Scienze Naturali
Via Calepina 14, I-38100 Trento
Natural History Museum
Coll: prehistory; zoology; botany; minerals; petrography - alpine botanical garden, climatological observatories

Trevi

08061
Pinacoteca Comunale
Piazza Mazzini, I-06039 Trevi, Perugia
Fine Arts Museum
Paintings by artists of the Umbrian and Piedmontese schools; medieval and Renaissance sculpture

Trevignano Romano

08062
Museo Civico
Piazza Vittorio Emanuele, I-00069 Trevignano Romano, Roma
Archeology Museum
Etruscan and Roman remains

Treviso

08063
Museo Civico 'Luigi Bailo'
Borgo Cavour 22, I-31100 Treviso
General Museum - 1879
Coll: prehistory; marble statues; frescoes; paintings by Bellini, L. Lotto, Titian, Tintoretto; sculpture by Canova

08064
Museo della Casa Trevigiana
Via Canova, I-31100 Treviso
General Museum
Coll: Furniture; sculptures in wood and marble; musical instruments; pottery

08065
Museo Zoologico 'G. Scarpa'
Piazzetta Benedetto XI 2, I-31100 Treviso
Natural History Museum - 1914
Coll: 2,500 specimens of vertebrates, mainly from the Mediterranean area

08066
Raccolta Naturalistiché del Museo Civico 'L. Bailo'
Borgo Cavour 22, I-31100 Treviso
Science/Tech Museum
Astronomic and geodetic instruments

Trieste

08067
Civico Museo del Castello di San Giusto
Piazza Cattedrale 3, I-34121 Trieste
History/Public Affairs Museum - 1936
Furniture and furnishings of the castle; paintings; arms

08068
Civico Museo del Mare
Via di Campo Marzio 5, I-34123 Trieste
Science/Tech Museum - 1904
Coll: models of fishing boats of the Adriatic Sea; Adriatic harbours; nautical instruments

08069
Civico Museo del Risorgimento e Sacrario Oberdan
Via XXIV Maggio 4, I-34133 Trieste
History/Public Affairs Museum
History of the 'Risorgimento', World War I and of Oberdan

08070
Civico Museo della Risiera di San Sabba
Ratto della Pileria 1, I-34148 Trieste
History/Public Affairs Museum
Documents and photographs of World War II and especially of the Resistance movement; housed in Italy's one and only concentration camp

08071
Civico Museo di Storia ed Arte e Orte Lapidario
Via Cattedrale 15, I-34121 Trieste
General Museum - 1873
Coll: numismatics; Roman architecture; Greek gold work; prehistory - library

08072
Civico Museo di Storia Patria 'Morpurgo' e Raccolte Artistiche 'Stavropulos'
Via Imbriani 5, I-34122 Trieste
General Museum - 1952
Local history; exhibits depicting the lifestyle of the 19th century

08073
Civico Museo 'Revoltella' e Galleria d'Arte Moderna
Via Diaz 27, I-34123 Trieste
Fine Arts Museum - 1872
Coll: 19th century furnishings; 19th and 20th century European paintings, sculpture and graphics

08074
Civico Museo 'Sartorio'
Largo Papa Giovanni XXIII, 1, I-34123 Trieste
Fine Arts Museum - 1949
Furnishings; paintings; ceramics - library

08075
Civico Museo Teatrale della Fondazione 'Carlo Schmidl'
Piazza Verdi 1, I-34121 Trieste
Performing Arts Museum - 1922
Musical instruments; items related to the theatre in Triest - library

08076
Museo Civico di Storia Naturale
Piazza Attilio Hortis 4, I-34123 Trieste
Natural History Museum - 1846
Coll: zoology; botany; geology; minerals; paleontology; anthropology - library

08077
Museo della Fondazione 'Giovanni Scaramangà di Altomonte'
Via Filzi 1, I-34132 Trieste
General Museum - 1961
Paintings; prints; drawings; ceramics; local history and art - library

08078
Museo Etnografico di Servola
Via del Pane Biano 52, I-34146 Trieste
General Museum
Costumes; prints; bedroom and kitchen furnishings; bread-making equipment; tools

08079
Museo Storico del Castello di Miramare
Grignano, I-34014 Trieste
Historic Site - 1955
Furniture and decor depicting a princely residence in the middle of the 19th century - library

Troia

08080
Museo Civico
Via Regina Margherita 80, I-71029 Troia, Foggia
Archeology Museum
Epigraphic and tomb material; pre-Roman clay pottery; medieval stone tablets

Tuscania

08081
Museo Civico
Chiesa di San Pietro, I-01017 Tuscania, Viterbo
Archeology Museum
Sarcophagi (2nd and 1st cent. B.C.); pottery (12th to 17th cent.)

Udine

08082
Civici Musei e Gallerie di Storia ed Arte
Castello, I-33100 Udine
General Museum - 1906
Coll: archeology; numismatics; graphics; paintings by Carpaccio and Tiepolo; Greek and Roman excavations - library

08083
Museo Cernazai Raccolte Naturalistiche del Seminario Arcivescovile
Viale Ungheria 2, I-33100 Udine
Natural History Museum - 1881
Coll: mineralogy; zoology; botany; paleontology - library

08084
Museo Friulano delle Arti e Tradizioni Popolari
Via Viola 3, I-33100 Udine
General Museum - 1962
Ethnography and folk art of the area from the 18th century to present days

08085
Museo Friulano di Storia Naturale
Palazzo Giacomelli, Via Grazzano 1, I-33100 Udine
Natural History Museum - 1866
Coll: herbarium; local fossils; animals of North-East Italy - library; didactic center for children

08086
Raccolta Ornitologica del Comitato Provinciale della Caccia Udine
Palazzo della Provincia, Piazza Patriarcato 3, I-33100 Udine
Natural History Museum - 1960
Coll: European birds; ornithology; mammals

Ugento

08087
Museo Civico di Paleontologia e Archeologia
Via della Zecca, I-73059 Ugento, Lecce
Archeology Museum
Paleolithic, mesolithic and neolithic materials

Urbania

08088
Museo Communale
Palazzo Ducale, I-61049 Urbania, Pesaro-Urbino
General Museum
Pottery; paintings; frescoes; engravings; incunabula

Urbino

08089
Casa Natale di Raffaello
Via Sanzio 57, I-61029 Urbino, Pesaro-Urbino
Historic Site
Etchings and reproductions of works by Raphael

08090
Galleria Nazionale delle Marche
Palazzo Ducale, Piazza Duca Federico 1, I-61029 Urbino, Pesaro-Urbino
Fine Arts Museum - 1912
Coll: medieval and Renaissance works of art from town of Urbino and province of Marche; sculpture; majolica; paintings by Uccello, Piero della Francesca, Raphael, Bellini and Titian

08091
Museo Diocesano e Museo 'Albani'
Basilica, I-61029 Urbino, Pesaro-Urbino
Religious Art Museum
Frescoes; pottery; sacred objects; paintings

Valdagno

08092
Galleria Civica d'Arte Moderna
Palazzo Festari, Corso Italia, I-36078 Valdagno, Vicenza
Fine Arts Museum - 1973
Contemporary sculpture

08093
Museo di Paleontologia e di Mineralogia
Palazzo Festari, I-36078 Valdagno, Vicenza
Natural History Museum - 1974
Minerals and fossils - library

Varallo Sesia

08094
Museo 'Calderini'
Via Maio, I-13019 Varallo Sesia, Vercelli
Natural History Museum
Mineralogy; coll. of beetles

Varenna

08095
Museo Ornitologico 'Luigi Scanagatta'
Piazza San Giorgio 4, I-22050 Varenna, Como
Natural History Museum
Birds of the Lake Como area

Varese

08096
Museo Civico
Piazza Della Motta 4, I-21100 Varese
General Museum
Prehistory; archeology; 'Risorgimento';
Partisan Resistance movement; natural
sciences

08097
**Museo del Santuario e Museo
'Baroffio'**
Santa Maria del Monte, I-21100 Varese
General Museum
Paintings; goldwork; sacred vestments

08098
Museo 'Lodovico Pogliaghi'
Santa Maria del Monte, I-21100 Varese
Fine Arts Museum
Sculptures

Vasto

08099
Museo e Pinacoteca Civici
Piazza Lucio Valerio Pudente, I-66054
Vasto, Chieti
Archeology Museum - 1849
Coll: excavation objects found in the
necropolis of ancient Histonium;
1500th-1800th century and
contemporary paintings

Velletri

08100
Museo Capitolare
Cattedrale San Clemente, I-00049
Velletri, Roma
Religious Art Museum
Religious vestments; vases; paintings

08101
Museo Civico
Palazzo Comunale, I-00049 Velletri,
Roma
Archeology Museum
Archeology; Roman sarcophagus

Venezia

08102
Casa di Goldoni
San Thomà 2794, I-30125 Venezia
Performing Arts Museum
Costumes used in the Goldoni and
Venetian theatre; documents,
illustrations - library; theatre

08103
Farmacia Conventuale
Convento Cappuccini, Giudecca 194,
I-30123 Venezia
History/Public Affairs Museum
In monastery, 16th century historic
pharmacy; 17th-18th century ceramic
jars

08104
Fondazione 'Peggy Guggenheim'
701 San Gregorio, I-30123 Venezia
Fine Arts Museum - 1949
Paintings from the schools of Cubism,
Abstraction, Futurism, Surrealism,
Abstract Expressionism

08105
**Galleria della Fondazione Querini
Stampalia**
S.Maria Formosa 4778, I-30122
Venezia
General Museum - 1869
Coll: paintings of the Venetian school;
graphics; old maps; manuscripts with
miniatures; porcelains; musical
instruments - library

08106
Galleria dell'Accadémia
Campo della Carità, I-30121 Venezia
Fine Arts Museum - 1807
Venetian painting (13th-18th c.)
including works by Paolo da
Veneziano, Bellini, Carpaccio,
Giorgione, Veronese, Tintoretto,
Tiepolo and Titian

08107
**Galleria Giorgio Franchetti alla Ca'
d'Oro**
Calle Ca' d'Oro 3933, I-30173 Venezia
Fine Arts Museum - 1927
Painting of Italian and Flemish schools
(15th-18th c.) including Carpaccio,
Titian, Tiepolo, Lippi and Bellini;
sculpture and bronze (14th-17th c.)

08108
**Mostra Permanente dei Cimeli della
Biblioteca Nazionale Marciana**
Libreria Vecchia
Piazzetta San Marco 7, I-30124
Venezia
Fine Arts Museum - 1929
Ceiling and wall paintings by Titian,
Tintoretto and Veronese; precious
books; 15th century world map of Fra
Mauro - library

08109
Museo Archeologico
Piazzetta S.Marco 17, I-30124 Venezia
Archeology Museum - 1523
Greek and Roman sculpture; jewels,
gems and coins; mosaics - library

08110
Museo Civico di Storia Naturale
Santa Croce 1730, I-30125 Venezia
Natural History Museum
Coll: maritime flora and fauna; geology
from Monte Bolca - library

08111
Museo Correr
Piazza San Marco 52, I-30124 Venezia
History/Public Affairs Museum - 1830
Coll: exhibits of Venetian history and
navigation; armaments; costumes;
medals and coins; paintings of the
Venetian school; paintings by L. Lotto,
Bellini, Carpaccio - library

08112
Museo d'Arte Moderna Cà Pesaro
S.Stae, Canale Grande, I-30100
Venezia
Fine Arts Museum - 1902
Painting, drawing and sculpture
(19th-20th c.)

08113
**Museo del Risorgimento e
dell'Ottocento Veneziano**
Piazza San Marco 52, I-30124 Venezia
History/Public Affairs Museum - 1936
18th century prints and arms; history
of the Risorgimento

08114
**Museo del Settecento Veneziano di
Ca'Rezzonico**
San Barnaba, I-30123 Venezia
History/Public Affairs Museum
Venetian history and art (17th-18th c.)

08115
Museo della Basilica di San Marco
Piazza San Marco, I-30125 Venezia
Religious Art Museum
Byzantine art (10th c.); tapestries

08116
Museo della Comunità Israelitica
Cannaregio 2902, I-30121 Venezia
Religious Art Museum
Items and relics from various Jewish
schools

08117
**Museo della Congregazione
Mechitarista dei Padri Armeni**
Isola di San Lazzaro, I-30126 Venezia
Fine Arts Museum - 1717
Coll: Armenian, Egyptian, Roman and
Indian art; Armenian miniatures,
manuscripts and modern Armenian
paintings; silver works; numismatics;
ceramics; paintings of the Venetian
school - library

08118
Museo dell'Istituto Ellenico
Castello 3412, I-30122 Venezia
Fine Arts Museum
Byzantine and post-Byzantine icons

08119
Museo di Torcello
Località Torcello, I-30175 Venezia
General Museum - 1870
Medieval mosaics; painting by the
Veronese school; archeology - library;
archives

08120
Museo Orientale Ca'Pesaro
Canale Grande, I Venezia
Fine Arts Museum
Painting; sculpture; porcelain;
decorative arts from the Far East
(17th-19th c.)

08121
Museo Storico Navale
Campo S. Biagio 2148 - Riva degli
Schiavoni, I-30122 Venezia
History/Public Affairs Museum
Coll: models of historic ships, fishing
and rowing boats; models of Chinese
and Eastern junks; arms; flags;
uniforms; models of fortifications;
ship-plans; paintings

08122
Museo Vetrario
Località Murano, Fondamenta
Giustinian 8, I-30121 Venezia
Decorative Arts Museum - 1861
Coll: Murano glass from 15th through
20th centuries; Roman archeological
glass; Renaissance glass

08123
Palazzo Ducale
San Marco 1, I-30124 Venezia
History/Public Affairs Museum
Historic palace; weapons including
swords and polearms; paintings by
Tintoretto, Titian, Tiepolo and Veronese

08124
Pinacoteca Manfrediana
Dorsoduro 1, I-30123 Venezia
Fine Arts Museum - 1829
Painting; archeology including
tombstones and bas-reliefs; sculpture

08125
**Scuola Dalmata dei SS. Giorgio e
Trifone**
Calle dei Furlani, I-30122 Venezia
Fine Arts Museum - 1451
Works by Carpaccio

Venosa

08126
Museo Civico
Castello Medioevale, I-85029 Venosa,
Potenza
Archeology Museum
Prehistory

Ventimiglia

08127
Museo Archeologico 'Rossi'
Palazzo Comunale, I-18039 Ventimiglia,
Imperia
Archeology Museum - 1931
Excavations of ancient city
Albintimilium

08128
Museo e Grotte dei Balzi Rossi
Località Balzi Rossi, I-18039
Ventimiglia, Imperia
Archeology Museum
Bones of Cro-Magnon Man; tools;
weapons; fossils

Vercelli

08129
Galleria d'Arte Moderna 'L.Sereno'
Via Sereno 7, I-13100 Vercelli
Fine Arts Museum

08130
Museo Camillo Leone
Via Verdi 7, I-13100 Vercelli
Fine Arts Museum - 1907
Coll: history of Vercelli from
prehistoric period to present; Roman
inscriptions; Byzantine icon; mosaics;
pre-Columbian vases; incunabula;
coins and medals - library

08131
Museo Civico 'Borgogna'
Via Borgogna 1, I-13100 Vercelli
Fine Arts Museum
Paintings (14th to 19th century)

Verona

08132
Museo Africano Missionari
Comboniani
Vicolo Pozzo 1, I-37100 Verona
Anthropology Museum
Items collected by missionaries from
Africa; ethnology

08133
**Museo Archeologico del Teatro
Romano**
Via Rigaste Redentore, I-37100 Verona
Archeology Museum
Roman antiquities; sculptures;
mosaics; glassware; pottery; bronze

08134
Museo Civico di Storia Naturale
Lungadige Porta Vittoria 9, I-37100
Verona
Natural History Museum
Paleontology; geology; botany;
zoology

08135
Museo delle Carozze dell'Ottocento
Viale del Lavoro 8a, I-37100 Verona
Science/Tech Museum
Carriages of different types

08136
Museo di Castelvecchio
Corso Castelvecchio 2, I-37100
Verona
Fine Arts Museum
Sculptures; paintings

08137
Museo 'Miniscalchi Erizzo'
Via San Mammaso 2, I-37100 Verona
Fine Arts Museum
Excavations; sculptures; bronzes;
paintings of Venetian school

08138
**Pinacoteca della Biblioteca
Capitolare**
Piazza Duomo 13, I-37100 Verona
Fine Arts Museum
Venetian painters (15th to 19th
century)

Verucchio

08139
Galleria Comunale d'Arte Moderna
Piazza Malatesta, I-47040 Verucchio,
Forli
Fine Arts Museum

08140
Museo Preistorico e Lapidario
Via della Rocca, I-47040 Verucchio,
Forli
Archeology Museum

Vestenanuova

08141
Museo dei Fossili
I-37030 Vestenanuova, Verona
Natural History Museum
Fossils of fish, plants and molluscs

Viadana

08142
Museo Civico 'Parazzi'
Via Grossi 28, I-46019 Viadana,
Mantova
General Museum
Frescoes; coins; majolicas; paintings

Vibo Valentia

08143
Museo Archeologico Nazionale
Piazza Garibaldi, I-88018 Vibo Valentia,
Catanzaro
Archeology Museum
Western Greek and Roman finds;
vases; terracottas; coins

Vicchio

08144
Museo 'Beato Angelico'
Piazza Giotto, I-50039 Vicchio, Firenze
Religious Art Museum
Frescoes; religious items

Vicenza

08145
Museo del Risorgimento
Villa Guiccioli, I-36100 Vicenza
History/Public Affairs Museum
'Resorgimento'; World War I; Partisan
Resistance Movement

08146
Pinacoteca e Museo Civico
Piazza Matteotti, I-36100 Vicenza
General Museum
Archeology; graphics; paintings

Vigevano

08147
**Civico Museo Archeologico e
Pinacoteca**
Corso Cavour 24, I-27029 Vigevano,
Pavia
Archeology Museum
Paleontology; archeology; history;
paintings

08148
Museo della Calzatura
Corso Cavour 82, I-27029 Vigevano,
Pavia
Anthropology Museum
History of footwear

Vigna di Valle

08149
**Museo Storico dell'Aeronautica
Militare Italiana**
I-00062 Vigna di Valle, Roma
History/Public Affairs Museum - 1977
Aeroplanes; equipment; weapons

Vinci

08150
Museo Leonardino
Via della Torre 4, I-50059 Vinci, Firenze
History/Public Affairs Museum
Documents on life and work of
Leonardo da Vinci (1452-1519); models
of machines - library

Vipiteno

08151
Museo Civico
Palazzo Comunale, I-39049 Vipiteno,
Bolzano
General Museum
15th to 16th century paintings and
sculptures; triptych by Hans
Multscher

08152
Museo Hans Multscher
Piazza Mitra, I-39049 Vipiteno, Bolzano
Fine Arts Museum
Altarpieces painted by Hans
Multscher of Ulm (1458)

Viterbo

08153
Museo Civico
Piazza Crispi 2, I-01100 Viterbo
General Museum
Archeology; sarcophagi; paintings

Vittorio Veneto

08154
Museo del Cenedese
Piazza Flaminio, I-31029 Vittorio
Veneto, Udine
Fine Arts Museum
Paintings (14th to 16th century)

08155
Museo della Battaglia
Piazza Cattedrale, I-31029 Vittorio
Veneto, Udine
History/Public Affairs Museum
Documents and relics of World War I
- library

Vizzoia Ticino

08156
**Museo Aeronautico 'Caproni di
Taliedo'**
I Vizzoia Ticino, Varese
Science/Tech Museum
Aeroplanes; propellers; gliders

Volterra

08157
Museo Diocesano di Arte Sacra
Via Roma 13, I-56048 Volterra, Pisa
Religious Art Museum
Sculptures; goldwork; miniatures;
embroidery; paintings

08158
Museo Etrusco 'Guarnacci'
Via Don Minzoni 1, I-56048 Volterra,
Pisa
Archeology Museum
Urns; pottery; vases; archeology

08159
Pinacoteca Comunale
Palazzo dei Priori, I-56048 Volterra,
Pisa
Fine Arts Museum - 1905
Paintings of the Tuscan school; works
by Signorelli, Fiorentino, Ghirlandaio

Ivory Coast

Abidjan

08160
**Musée de la Côte d'Ivoire et Centre
des Sciences Humaines**
BP 1600, Abidjan
General Museum - 1945
Coll: ethnography; ethnic arts and
cultures; masks; ritual requisites;
musical instruments; scientific exhibits

Jamaica

Kingston

08161
African Museum
mail c/o Institute of Jamaica,
Half-Way-Tree, Kingston, W.I. 10
Anthropology Museum

08162
Fort Charles Maritime Museum Fort
Charles
Port Royal, Kingston, W.I. 1
Science/Tech Museum

08163
**Natural Museum of Historical
Archaeology** Old Naval Hospital
Port Royal, Kingston, W.I. 1
Archeology Museum

St. Ann

08164
The Seville Museum
St. Ann's Bay, St. Ann
General Museum

Saint Catherine

08165
The Arawak Indian Museum
White Marl, Saint Catherine
Anthropology Museum

08166
The Jamaica Folk Museum
Saint Catherine
Anthropology Museum

Spanish Town

08167
Arawak Museum Whitemall
Central Village, Spanish Town, St.
Catherines
General Museum

08168
**Jamaican People Museum Craft and
Technology** Old Kings House Cultural
Complex
Spanish Town Square, Spanish Town,
W.I.
Science/Tech Museum

08169
**Old Kings House Archaeological
Museum** Old Kings House Cultural
Complex
Spanish Town Square, Spanish Town,
W.I.
Archeology Museum

Japan

Abashiri

08170
Abashiri Municipal Art Museum
1 Nishi, Minamirokujo, Abashiri,
Hokkaido
Fine Arts Museum
Coll: 38 oil paintings by Kaichi Igushi
(1911-1955) - galleries

08171
Abashiri Municipal Museum
Katsuragaoka Park, Abashiri,
Hokkaido
General Museum - 1936
Coll: local archeology; ethnographical
material on life of Ainu, Gilyak, and
Oroko peoples; articles of historical
and geographical interest

Akita

08172
Akita City Art Museum
1-4 Senshu Koen, Akita, Akita
Fine Arts Museum
Coll: 18th century 'yoga' paintings;
local artists; calligraphy

08173
**Akita College of Economics Yukiguni
Folk Society Research Institute**
1-4-1 Barajima, Akita, Akita
Anthropology Museum
Coll: ceramics; cotton and straw
garments; wooden chests; tobacco
pipes; lamps; household utensils;
Bangaku masks; farming and fishing
tools; boats; spinning wheels and
looms

08174
Akita Prefectural Museum
52 Aza Ushiroyama, Niozaki Kana-ashi,
Akita, Akita
General Museum
Coll: history of the region in dioramas,
models, historical material; farm tools
and ethnographic material; pottery;
fossils; armor; photographs; local
natural history; handicrafts; paintings -
planetarium; lecture hall; conference
room

08175
Hirano Masakichi Art Museum
3-7 Senshu Meitoku-cho, Akita, Akita
Fine Arts Museum
Coll: paintings and drawings by
Tsuguji Fujita; Western paintings and
prints

08176
Mineral Industry Museum Mining
College, Akita University
28-2 Aza Osawa, Tegata, Akita, Akita
Natural History Museum - 1961
Coll: minerals and ores from Japan

Akiyo

08177
**Akiyoshi-dai Museum of Natural
History**
Shuho-cho, Akiyo, Yamaguchi
Natural History Museum - 1959
Coll: paleontology; archeology; fossils;
geology; earthen vessels and stone
implements; cave-dwelling animals -
library

Aomori

08178
Aomori Prefectural Museum
2-8-14 Honcho, Aomori, Aomori
General Museum
Coll: pottery vessels; exhibits on designing pottery; local historical documents and photographs; lacquer items; costumes; furniture; farm and fishing equipment; straw and wooden utensils; natural history exhibit; display on local industrial growth

08179
Munakata Shiko Memorial Museum of Art
2-1-2 Matsubara, Aomori, Aomori
Fine Arts Museum - 1974
Coll: prints, paintings, and calligraphy of Munakata

Asahikawa

08180
Asahikawa City Youth Science Center
Tokiwa Park, Asahikawa, Hokkaido
Science/Tech Museum - 1963
Coll: experimental equipment for studies in electricity, atomic energy, astronomy, and the life sciences - laboratories; lecture and meeting rooms

08181
Asahikawa Folk Museum
2-chome Hanasaki-cho, Asahikawa, Hokkaido
Anthropology Museum - 1952
Coll: cultural objects of the Ainu race; archeological items

08182
Asahikawa Municipal Local Museum
1 Ichijo, Yon-ku, Asahikawa, Hokkaido
General Museum - 1968
Coll: cultural objects of Ainu race; archeological items; garments; lacquer vessels; swords and arrows; pottery of all periods; historical items of early settlers; local teahouse; sculpture

Asakuchi

08183
Okayama Museum of Astronomy
Honjo, Kamokata-machi, Asakuchi, Okayama
Natural History Museum - 1960
Coll: models; photographs; displays on astronomy - astronomical observatory

Ashigarashimo

08184
Hakone Open-Air Museum
Ninotaira, Hakone-machi, Ashigarashimo, Kanagawa
Open Air Museum - 1969
Coll: late 19th and 20th century Western and Japanese sculpture; contemporary Japanese oil painting - sculpture garden

08185
Hakone-Jinja Treasure House
80-1 Oshiba, Motohakone, Hakone-machi, Ashigarashimo, Kanagawa
Religious Art Museum
Coll: religious sculpture; paintings; calligraphy; armor and swords; historical documents

08186
Kyusei Hakone Art Museum
1300 Gora, Hakone-machi, Ashigarashimo, Kanagawa
Decorative Arts Museum
Coll: pottery and porcelain from China, Japan, Korea, and the Near East; exhibits on ceramic techniques; tools, samples of clay, shards, and photographs; Japanese archeology - moss garden; teahouse; bamboo garden

Ashikaga

08187
Kurita Art Museum
1542 Komaba-cho, Ashikaga, Tochigi
Decorative Arts Museum
Coll: Imari and Nabeshima porcelains; raw materials; photographs of the various steps of manufacture

08188
Soun Art Museum
2-3768 Midori-cho, Ashikaga, Tochigi
Historic Site
Coll: 80 paintings by Tazaki Soun; his personal effects; furniture; house where the artist lived

Ashiya

08189
Tekisui Art Museum
60 Yama-ashiya-cho, Ashiya, Hyogo
Fine Arts Museum
Coll: Chinese bas-reliefs, ceramics, and paintings; Japanese paintings, dolls and ceramic figurines, toys and games; Kyoto ceramic wares; Korean ceramics and paintings

Atami

08190
Kyusei Atami Art Museum
26-1 Momoyama-cho, Atami, Shizuoka
Fine Arts Museum - 1957
Coll: Chinese and Japanese paintings, sculptures, and ceramics; Chinese bronzes; Japanese lacquer, metalwork, and prints; specimens of Japanese and Chinese calligraphy - library

Beppu

08191
Beppu University Ancient Culture Museum
Beppu Daigaku, 82 Kitaishigaki, Beppu, Oita
Archeology Museum
Coll: Japanese pottery vessels; stone tools from several archeological periods

Biwa-ko

08192
Chikubushima Treasure House
Hogon-ji, Chikubushima, Biwa-ko, Shiga
Religious Art Museum
Coll: sutras; paintings; documents; No masks and music instruments

Bizen

08193
Bizen Old Ceramics Art Museum
998 Imbe, Bizen, Okayama
Decorative Arts Museum
Coll: 500 pieces of Bizen ware that illustrate the development of this type of pottery

08194
Bizen Pottery, Traditional and Contemporary Art Museum
1659-6 Inbe, Bizen, Okayama
Decorative Arts Museum - 1977
Coll: contemporary Bizen ware; old Bizen ware; potters' tools - library

Chiba

08195
Chiba Prefectural Art Museum
1-10-1 Chuo Minato, Chiba, Chiba
Fine Arts Museum
Coll: 19th-20th century Japanese paintings; prints; calligraphy; sculpture

08196
Kasori Shell-Mounds Museum
163 Sakuragi-cho, Chiba, Honshu
Anthropology Museum - 1966
Coll: articles from Kasori shell mounds; earthenwares; stone tools; clay objects

Chichibu

08197
Chichibu Museum of Natural History
1417 Nagatoro, Nogami-machi, Chichibu, Saitama
Natural History Museum - 1921
Coll: natural history; zoology; mollusks; insects; fossils; minerals

Chikushi

08198
Dazaifu-tenman-gu Treasure House
Dazaifu-machi, Chikushi, Fukuoka
Religious Art Museum
Coll: art concerning Michizane Sugawara, to whom the shrine is dedicated; paintings; calligraphy; documents; sculpture; arms and armor; ceramics; lacquer items; masks; metalwork; archeological material

08199
Kanko History Hall
Dazaifu-machi, Chikushi, Fukuoka
History/Public Affairs Museum - 1977
Coll: dioramas on the life of Michizane Sugawara, a celebrated man of letters in the 10th century; scrolls

08200
Kanzeon-ji Treasure House
Kanzeon-ji, 182 Dazaifu-machi, Chikushi, Fukuoka
Religious Art Museum - 1959
Coll: Buddhist wooden sculptures; Bugaku masks; 8th century bronze bell

08201
Kyushu Historical Collection
1025 Aza Tarosakon, Oaza Dazaifu, Dazaifu-machi, Chikushi, Fukuoka
Archeology Museum - 1972
Coll: pottery vessels; gold seal; bronze swords; Kofun material including burial jars, iron swords, mirrors; reproductions of tomb paintings; photographs and maps; Buddhist relics

Chino

08202
Togari-ishi Archaeological Hall
Minami-Oshio, Toyohira, Chino, Nagano
Archeology Museum
Coll: stone and pottery items from excavation sites; small figurines; vases and jars; ornaments; swords; paleolithic stone tools; photographs and maps of excavation sites

Enzan

08203
Shingenko Treasure House
Erin-ji, 2280 Koyashiki, Enzan, Yamanashi
Religious Art Museum
Coll: material connected with the Takeda clan; armor, bows and arrows, and swords; fans; lacquer items; documents - garden

Fujinomiya

08204
Fuji Art Museum
1954 Kamijo, Fujinomiya, Shizuoka
Fine Arts Museum - 1973
Coll: Egyptian stele and Coptic textiles; prehistoric Mesopotamian pottery; 8th-13th century Persian ceramics; 17th century Turkish ceramics; 19th century European paintings, some French Impressionists and a Picasso; Chinese and Japanese ceramics; lacquer writing boxes, desks, and cabinet - library; audiovisual room

Fujiyoshida

08205
Entomological Museum of Fujikyu
Fujikyu Highland, POB 12, Fujiyoshida, Yamanashi
Natural History Museum - 1968
Largest collection of exotic Coleoptera in Japan

Fukui

08206
Fukui City Natural Science Museum
Asuwakami-cho, Fukui, Fukui
Natural History Museum
Coll: zoology; botany; mollusks; entomology; mineralogy; fossils

08207
Fukui Municipal Historical Museum
1-8-16 Asuwa, Fukui, Fukui
General Museum
Coll: local archeological material; portraits and memorabilia of local nobles; historical documents; calligraphy; farm tools; household and shop furniture

08208
Fukui Prefectural Okajima Art Memorial Hall
3-11-13 Hoei, Fukui, Fukui
Fine Arts Museum
Coll: Chinese, Tibetan, and Japanese metalwork; costumes; jewelry; coins; Japanese lacquer, tobacco pouches, and pipes; bronzes

Fukuoka

08209
Fukuoka Prefecture Cultural Hall Art Museum
5-2-1 Tenjin, Chuo-ku, Fukuoka, Fukuoka
Fine Arts Museum
Coll: Japanese oil paintings; handicrafts

Fukushima

08210
Fukushima Prefecture Art Museum
Fukushima-ken Bunka Senta, 5-54 Kasuga-machi, Fukushima, Fukushima
General Museum
Coll: Japanese paintings; sculpture; handicrafts - lecture hall

Gifu

08211
Gifu Youth Center of Science
Gifu Park, Gifu, Gifu
Science/Tech Museum - 1955
Coll: electricity; machinery; science

08212
Nawa Museum of Insects
2-18 Ohmiya-machi, Gifu, Gifu
Natural History Museum - 1912
Entomology collection

Gyoda

08213
Saitama Prefectural Sakitama Collection
4834 Sakitama, Gyoda, Saitama
General Museum
Coll: prehistoric pottery vessels;
Kofun pottery cylinders, heads, and
torsos

08214
Sakitama Archaeological Hall
5450 Sakitama, Gyoda, Saitama
Archeology Museum
Coll: prehistoric pottery; pottery
cylinders; Sue-ware vessels; armor
and swords; mirrors

Hachinohe

08215
Hachinohe Municipal History and Ethnography Hall
3-1 Aza Nakai, Oaza Korekawa,
Hachinohe, Aomori
General Museum
Coll: rare pottery vessels; lacquer
items; religious figurines; stone tools;
shells; armor; mirrors; farm tools;
ethnographic material

Hagi

08216
Kumaya Art Museum
47 Imauonotana-cho, Hagi, Yamaguchi
Fine Arts Museum
Coll: Japanese paintings; calligraphy;
pottery; lacquer items

Hakodate

08217
Hakodate Municipal Museum
17-1 Aoyagi-cho, Hakodate, Hokkaido
General Museum - 1879
Coll: archeology; ethnography of the
Ainu, Giliak, and other native tribes;
history; Japanese traditional art;
painting; coins - library

Hakone

08218
Hakone Art Museum
1300 Gora, Hakone, Kanagawa
Fine Arts Museum - 1952
Coll: Japanese and Chinese ceramics
- library

Hamamatsu

08219
Hamamatsu City Art Museum
130 Matsushiro-cho, Hamamatsu,
Shizuoka
Fine Arts Museum - 1971
Coll: Japanese, Chinese, and
European glass painting; ukiyo-e prints

08220
Hamamatsu City Museum
22-1 Shijimizuka 4 chome, Hamamatsu,
Shizuoka
General Museum - 1979
Coll: local archeological finds; history;
folklore - library

08221
Iba Site Museum Hamamatsu City
Museum
22-1 Higashi-Iba 2 chome, Hamamatsu,
Shizuoka
Archeology Museum - 1975
Archeological finds

Hanamaki

08222
Tibetan Collection at the Kotoku-ji
95 Minamikawara-machi, Hanamaki,
Iwate
Religious Art Museum
Coll: Tibetan objects, including priests'
robes, hats, prayer wheels, and ritual
objects; religious books; bronze
statuettes; paintings

Hatano

08223
Koan Collection
Kokakuen, 1-393 Tsurumaki, Hatano,
Kanagawa 257
General Museum
items of regional interest

Higashi Okitama

08224
Kikusui Handicraft Museum
2911 Naka-Komatsu, Kawanishi-machi,
Higashi Okitama, Yamagata
Decorative Arts Museum
Coll: 500 pieces Chinese, Japanese,
and Korean ceramics from the
prehistoric period to modern times

Higashimuro

08225
Kumano Nachi Taisha Treasure House
Nachi-san, Nachi-Katsuura-cho,
Higashimuro, Wakayama
Religious Art Museum
Coll: Shinto figures; swords; objects
from sutra mounds; documents; sutra
boxes; mirrors; porcelains; images of
the Buddha

Hiki

08226
Toyama Art Museum Toyama
Kinenkan Foundation
Shiroi-numa 675, Kawajima-machi, Hiki,
Saitama 350-01
Fine Arts Museum - 1970
Coll: Japanese paintings, calligraphy,
ceramics, lacquer, and textiles;
Chinese paintings and ceramics;
objects from Egypt, Italy, and the Near
East; pre-Inca arts, textiles, and
earthenware - library

Hikone

08227
Economical Document Collection of Shiga University
Nakajima-cho, Hikone, Shiga
History/Public Affairs Museum
Coll: documents concerning
economics

08228
II Art Museum
Hikone-jo, Konki-machi, Hikone, Shiga
Fine Arts Museum
Coll: Japanese paintings; calligraphy;
ceramics; lacquer items; masks;
costumes; furniture; musical
instruments; armor and swords

Hirado

08229
Hirado Castle Donjon
Iwanoue-cho, Hirado, Nagasaki
General Museum
Coll: arms and armor; costumes;
Christian relics; rebuilt castle;
ceramics

08230
Hirado Kanko Historical Hall
Okubo-cho, Hirado, Nagasaki
General Museum
Coll: swords and armor; ceramics;
paintings; calligraphy; Christian relics

08231
Matsuura Historical Museum
12 Kagamigawa-machi, Hirado,
Nagasaki
General Museum - 1941
Coll: arms and armor; household
objects; paintings and screens;
calligraphy; lacquer items; ceramics;
25,000 documents; local history
exhibits especially on early foreign
trade

08232
Saikyo-ji Treasure Hall
1206 Iwanoue-cho, Hirado, Nagasaki
Religious Art Museum - 1977
Coll: Buddhist paintings; sculpture;
sutras; ceremonial objects; wood
blocks - library

Hirata

08233
Gakuen-ji Treasure House
148 Bessho-machi, Hirata, Shimane
Religious Art Museum
Coll: Japanese paintings; calligraphy;
sculpture; metalwork; documents and
letters; sutra boxes

Hiroshima

08234
Hiroshima Castle Museum
21-1 Motomachi, Naka-ku, Hiroshima,
Hiroshima
General Museum - 1958
Coll: arms and armor; local history;
Emperor Meiji's personal belongings;
castle; photographs of the city; natural
history; ceramics

08235
Hiroshima Peace Memorial Museum
1-3 Nakajima-cho, Naka-ku, Hiroshima,
Hiroshima 733
History/Public Affairs Museum - 1955
Coll: history of the atomic bomb
dropped on Hiroshima; photo exhibit;
disaster exhibition - library

08236
Hiroshima Prefectural Museum of Art
2-22 Kaminobori-machi, Naka-ku, POB
731-01, Hiroshima, Hiroshima
Fine Arts Museum - 1968
Coll: 20th century Japanese-style
paintings; drawings; sculpture;
handicrafts; calligraphy

Hiwa

08237
Hiwa Museum for Natural History
119-1 Oaza Hiwa, Hiwa, Hiroshima
Natural History Museum - 1951
Coll: natural history exhibits;
ivertebrates; mollusks; insects;
amphibia; reptiles; mammals; fossils;
minerals

Hofu

08238
Amida-ji Treasure Storehouse
1869 Mure, Hofu, Yamaguchi
Religious Art Museum
Coll: portraits; pagodas; scrolls;
statues

08239
Hofu Tenmangu History Hall
14-1 Matsuzaki-cho, Hofu, Yamaguchi
Religious Art Museum
Coll: 14th century scrolls; portraits;
12th century gilt-bronze reliquary;
festival masks; music instruments;
mirrors

08240
Mori Museum
1-15-1 Tatara, Hofu, Yamaguchi
General Museum
Coll: paintings; calligraphy; armor;
costumes; lacquer items; documents
of the Mori family - gardens

Ibi

08241
Ogawa Eiichi Collection
Oebi Ono-machi, Ibi, Gifu
Archeology Museum
Coll: ancient ceramics excavated in
the region

Ikeda

08242
Itsuo Art Museum
7-17 Tateishi-cho, Ikeda, Osaka
Fine Arts Museum - 1957
Coll: Japanese painting; master
examples of calligraphy; lacquer items;
Chinese sculpture; Chinese, Japanese,
Korean, and Western ceramics -
garden; teahouse

Ikoma

08243
Horyu-ji Great Treasure House
Ikaruga-machi, Ikoma, Nara
Religious Art Museum
Coll: large statues and shrines; masks;
bronzes; miniature wooden pagodas;
painting

08244
Horyuji
Aza Horyuji, Ikaruga-cho, Ikoma, Nara
Religious Art Museum
Coll: Buddhist images and paintings;
temple buildings

08245
Ikoma Museum of Universal Science
2,312-1 Oaza Nabatake, Ikoma, Nara
Science/Tech Museum - 1969
Coll: instruments; models;
photographs; illustrations; slides on
astronomy; apparatuses

08246
Tomimoto Kenkichi Memorial Gallery
Higashi-Ando, Ando-mura, Ikoma, Nara
Historic Site
Coll: ceramics and designs by
Kenkichi Tomimoto

Imabari

08247
Ehime Cultural Hall
2-6-2 Kogane-cho, Imabari, Ehime
Fine Arts Museum - 1974
Coll: Chinese, Japanese, and Korean ceramics; Japanese lacquer items; swords; fragments of Japanese poems - conference room; tea-ceremony room

08248
Imabari City Kono Shin'ichi Memorial Culture Hall
1-4-8 Asahi-machi, Imabari, Ehime
General Museum
Coll: calligraphy; rare books; local archeological and ethnographic material; pottery; paper money; lacquer household utensils; furniture

Inuyama

08249
Iwata Senshinkan
26 Fujimi-cho, Inuyama, Aichi
Fine Arts Museum
Coll: paintings; calligraphy; tea-ceremony bowls and utensils

08250
Museum Meiji-Mura
1 Uchiyama, Inuyama, Aichi
Open Air Museum - 1965
Coll: fifty-three buildings demonstrating different architectural styles from the 19th and early 20th century reerected in park; also buildings in Western architectural styles - library

Ise

08251
Agricultural Museum
Kuratayama, Ise, Mie
Agriculture Museum - 1905
Coll: exhibits on agriculture, forestry, and fishing; over 40 species of sharks

08252
Jingu History Museum
Kuratayama, Ise, Mie
General Museum
Coll: calligraphy; documents; lacquer items; masks; arms and armor; ceramics; archeological material; Shinto ceremonial objects; Japanese contemporary paintings - library

08253
Kongosho-ji Treasure House
Asamadake, Ise, Mie
Religious Art Museum
Coll: mirrors; pottery and bronze sutra box covers; incense boxes; dishes; scrolls; paintings; calligraphy

Isehara

08254
Sannomiya Local Museum
1472 Sannomiya, Isehara, Kanagawa
Archeology Museum
Coll: local archeological findings; archaic jewels and rings; swords; household ware; pottery cylinders

Isesaki

08255
Aikawa Archaeological Hall
6-10 Sankocho, Isesaki, Gumma
Archeology Museum
Coll: pottery cylinders; stone memorial tablets

Ito

08256
Ikeda Museum of 20th-Century Art
614 Tottari Sekiba, Ito, Shizuoka
Fine Arts Museum
Coll: Western 20th century paintings, prints, and sculpture; contemporary Japanese paintings; in modern building designed by Bukichi Inoue

08257
Museum of Buddhist Art on Mount Kōya
Kōyasan, Kōya-cho, Ito, Wakayama
Religious Art Museum - 1926
Coll: Buddhist paintings and images; sutras; old documents

Iwakuni

08258
Iwakun Municipal Museum
7-19 2-chome Yokoyama, Iwakuni, Yamaguchi
General Museum - 1944
Coll: local paintings; photographs; maps ,records, and documents; coins; folk art; local archeological finds - library

08259
Nishimura Museum
2-10-17 Yokoyama, Iwakuni, Yamaguchi
Decorative Arts Museum
Coll: complete suits of armor; 17th-19th century swords, spears, bows and arrows; lacquer items; furniture; mirrors; music instruments; costumes including No robes and court costumes - park with ancient samurai houses

Iwata

08260
Iwata Municipal Gallery
Chuo-cho, Iwata, Shizuoka
General Museum
Coll: historical documents; items from the 19th century to the present

08261
Totomi Kokubun-ji Storehouse Iwata Shiritsu Kyodokan
Chuo-cho, Iwata, Shizuoka
Archeology Museum
Coll: archeological pieces; Yayoi and Sue ware; cylinders; tiles; Chinese bronze mirrors

Izumo

08262
Izumo Taisha Treasure House
Izumo Taisha, Taisha-machi, Izumo, Shimane
Religious Art Museum
Coll: Shinto priest garments; calligraphy; documents and letters; armor and swords; lacquer; models and map of shrine

Kagoshima

08263
Kagoshima Cultural Center
5-3 Yamashita-cho, Kagoshima, Kyushu
Natural History Museum - 1966
Coll: natural science exhibits; dinosaur fossils

08264
Kagoshima Municipal Art Museum
4-36 Shiroyama-cho, Kagoshima, Kagoshima
Fine Arts Museum
Coll: paintings by Japanese artists in the Japanese and Western styles; local ceramics; local ethnogrphic material

08265
Kagoshima Prefectural Museum
Yamashita-machi, Kagoshima, Kyushu
Natural History Museum
Exhibits on natural history

Kakogawa

08266
Kakurin-ji Treasure House
424 Kitazaike, Kakogawa-machi, Kakogawa, Hyogo
Religious Art Museum
Coll: paintings; sculpture; sutras; ceramics; bronzes; masks; lacquer items

Kamakura

08267
Kamakura National Treasure House
2-1-1 Yukinoshita, Kamakura, Kanagawa
General Museum - 1928
Coll: 12th-16th century Japanese sculpture; Japanese and Chinese paintings and ceramics; Japanese metalwork; lacquer items; furniture; prints - library

08268
Kanagawa Prefectural Museum of Modern Art
2-1-53 Yukinoshita, Kamakura, Kanagawa 248
Fine Arts Museum - 1951
Coll: Japanese and foreign art from the 19th century to the present; sculpture; paintings; handicrafts; water colors; drawings; European Old Masters' prints - library

08269
Munakata Print Gallery
1182-4 Tsuoikubo, Kamakura, Kanagawa
Fine Arts Museum
Coll: around 300 prints by Shiko Munakata; his studio

08270
Tokiwayama Collection
1993 Fueta, Kamakura, Kanagawa
Fine Arts Museum
Coll: famous examples of 10th-14th century Chinese and 8th-16th century Japanese calligraphy; Chinese and Japanese paintings; sculpture; tea-ceremony objects

08271
Tsurugaoka Hachiman-gu Treasure House
2-1-31 Yukinoshita, Kamakura, Kanagawa
Religious Art Museum
Coll: neolithic stone tools; arms and armor; costumes; Bugaku masks; sculpture; 12th century lacquer items; portrait of Yoriyoshi Minamoto, founder of the shrine; his personal possessions

Kami

08272
Ryugado Museum
1340 Sakagawa, Tosa Yamada-cho, Kami, Kochi
Natural History Museum - 1957
Coll: natural history; amphibia; reptiles; minerals; fossils

Kaminoyama

08273
Kaisendo Museum
277 Tanaka, Toka-machi, Kaminoyama, Yamagata
Decorative Arts Museum - 1951
Coll: Chinese lacquer items; Japanese armor; 8th-19th century swords and sword furniture - garden

Kamo

08274
Shimoda Marine Biological Station
Shimoda-machi, Kamo, Shizuoka
Natural History Museum
Coll: marine biology; invertebrates; mollusks; reptiles

08275
Shimoda Memorial Collection of Opening Japan to Commerce
964 Hiro'okahigashi, Shimoda-machi, Kamo, Shizuoka
History/Public Affairs Museum
Coll: exhibits on economics; history of trade

Kanazawa

08276
Edo Village
19 He, Yuwaku-machi, Kanazawa, Ishikawa
Open Air Museum
Coll: reconstructed Edo village; restored buildings, shops, gates, sections of walls; furnishings; thatched farmhouses; merchants' houses

08277
Honda Family Collection Hall
3-1 Dewa-machi, Kanazawa, Ishikawa
Decorative Arts Museum - 1973
Coll: Honda family treasures of household lacquer utensils and chests; costumes; chinaware; arms and armor - library

08278
Ishikawa Prefectural Local Museum
2-25 Hirosaka, Kanazawa, Ishikawa
General Museum - 1968
Coll: local historical materials; folklore; natural science

08279
Ishikawa Prefecture Art Museum
1-1 Kenroku-machi, Kanazawa, Ishikawa
Fine Arts Museum - 1959
Coll: paintings; ceramics; lacquer wares; dyeing and weaving; calligraphy; bronze sculptures; swords; tea-ceremony utensils; historical documents; No masks and costumes

08280
Nakamura Memorial Art Museum
3-2-30 Honda-cho, Kanazawa, Ishikawa
Fine Arts Museum
Coll: paintings; calligraphy; ceramics; lacquer items; tea-ceremony objects - tea-ceremony house; garden

08281
Seisonkaku
1-2 Kenroku-cho, Kanazawa, Ishikawa
Fine Arts Museum
Coll: paintings and portraits; examples
of calligraphy; costumes and
accessories; armor; lacquer items;
porcelain and pottery; furniture; 19th
century Japanese-style building -
garden

Kariwa

08282
Tea Cult Museum
Okano-cho, Takayanagi, Kariwa,
Niigata
Anthropology Museum
Articles connected with the cult of tea;
its history

Kasai

08283
Ichijo-ji Treasure House
Sakamoto-machi, Kasai, Hyogo
Religious Art Museum
Coll: Japanese sculpture and painting;
bronzes; wooden statues of priests;
temple masks; a copy of the 'Hannya-
ko', sutra of wisdom; paintings of
Buddhist divinities

Kashihara

08284
**Nara Prefectural Archaeological
Museum**
1 Unebi-cho, Kashihara, Nara
Archeology Museum
Coll: prehistoric vessels and shards;
bone needles; horn and stone
implements; pottery; wooden farm
tools; bronze bells; swords; mirrors;
ornaments; photographs of the
excavation sites; roof tiles of different
periods

Kashima

08285
Kashima-jingu Treasure House
2403 Kyuchu, Kashima-machi,
Kashima, Ibaraki
Religious Art Museum
Coll: religious and ceremonial items;
8th century sword and scabbard of a
god; 12th century lacquered
ornamental saddle; ceramic items;
documents; paintings

Kawachi-Nagano

08286
Amanosan Kongo-ji Treasure House
996 Amano-cho, Kawachi-Nagano,
Osaka
Religious Art Museum
Coll: sculpture; paintings; armor and
swords; metalwork; furniture; music
instruments; scrolls and documents;
mirrors; lacquer boxes - gardens

08287
Kanshin-ji Treasure House
475 Teramoto, Kawachi-Nagano,
Osaka
Religious Art Museum
Coll: 8th-12th century sculptures;
documents and scrolls; small bronze
figures

Kawasaki

08288
**Kawasaki Municipal Industrial and
Cultural Museum**
2-1-3 Fujimi, Kawasaki-ku, Kawasaki,
Kanagawa
General Museum
Coll: contemporary Japanese
paintings and pottery by Shoji
Hamada; local archeological material
including pottery and stone
implements

08289
**Kawasaki Municipal Park of
Japanese Houses**
4762 Ikuta, Tama-ku, Kawasaki,
Kanagawa
Open Air Museum
Coll: 16 rural buildings from all over
Japan

Kimitsu

08290
**Futtsu Oceanographic Museum of
Chiba Prefecture**
2280 Futtsu, Futtsu-cho, Kimitsu, Chiba
Natural History Museum
Coll: oceanography

Kisarazu

08291
Chiba Prefectural Kazusa Museum
352-3 Aza Morisaki, Oda, Kisarazu,
Chiba
General Museum
Coll: stone tools; pottery vessels;
mirrors; tiles; Buddhist sculpture; farm
tools; household utensils; material on
local literary figures

08292
**Kinreitsuka Archaeological
Collection**
361 Oda, Kisarazu, Chiba
Archeology Museum
Coll: archeological Kofun material from
large local burial mound; iron swords
and armor; dishes and jars

Kitakyushu

08293
Kitakyushu City Museum of Art
21-1 Nishisayagatani-machi, Tobataku,
Kitakyushu 804
Fine Arts Museum - 1974
Coll: prints of modern foreign artists;
sculpture; modern Japanese artists
and local artists; Chinese rubbings -
library

Kitami

08294
Kitami Municipal Museum
2-1-67 Tokiwa-cho, Kitami, Hokkaido
Natural History Museum - 1967
Coll: microliths of the arctic; botany;
butterflies of the Ohotsuku sea coast

Kobe

08295
Hakutsuru Fine Art Museum
1545 Ochiai, Sumiyoshi-cho, Higashinada-ku, Kobe, Hyogo 658
Fine Arts Museum - 1934
Coll: early Chinese bronzes; Chinese
pottery and porcelain; Japanese metal
ornaments; ritual pendants; lacquer
items - library

08296
**Hyogo Prefectural Museum of
Modern Art**
3-8-30 Harada-dori, Nada-ku, Kobe,
Hyogo
Fine Arts Museum - 1970
Coll: contemporary Japanese
paintings, prints, and sculpture; prints
of Western artists

08297
Hyogo Prefecture Ceramic Museum
5th floor, Zentan Hall, 4-43-1
Shimoyamatedori, Ikuta-ku, Kobe,
Hyogo
Decorative Arts Museum
Ceramic collection; interior of a house
from Takayama - tea-ceremony rooms

08298
Kobe Municipal Archaeological Hall
Aza Aoyama, Higashi-Suma, Suma-ku,
Kobe, Hyogo
Archeology Museum
Coll: 14 bronze bells (200 BC-250 AD);
models giving survey of Japanese
archeology; site maps and
photographs; exhibit on pottery
production

08299
**Kobe Municipal Museum of Nanban
Art**
1-chome Kumochi-cho, Fukiai-ku,
Kobe, Hyogo
Fine Arts Museum - 1951
Coll: late 16th-18th century screens,
paintings, prints, and lacquer items
depicting foreigners and foreign
objects in Japanese surroundings;
relics of Christianity

08300
Kosetsu Museum of Art
285 Ishino Gunke Mikagecho,
Higashinada-ku, Kobe 658
Fine Arts Museum - 1972
Coll: Japanese and Chinese paintings;
calligraphy; sculpture; ceramics;
metalwork; Korean pottery

Kochi

08301
Chikurin-ji Treasure House
3577 Godaizan, Kochi, Kochi
Religious Art Museum
Coll: Buddhist sculpture - garden

08302
Kochi Prefectural Cultural Hall
1-1-20 Marunouchi, Kochi, Kochi
General Museum
Coll: paintings by local artists; folk arts

08303
Museum in Kochi Park
Marunouchi, Kochi, Kochi
History/Public Affairs Museum
Coll: autographs; historical material

08304
**Yamanouchi-jinja Treasure History
Hall**
2-4-26 Takajo-machi, Kochi, Kochi
Religious Art Museum
Coll: arms and armor of the local
daimyos; No masks; tea-ceremony
objects; garments

Koganei

08305
Musashino Local Museum
Koganei Koen, Koganei, Tokyo
Anthropology Museum
Coll: dioramas illustrating local life
from prehistory to the medieval
period; pottery; reconstructed shell-
mound burial; stone implements;
charts, diagrams, and photos of
excavation sites; folk arts; sutra boxes;
scrolls of religious festivals; outdoor
section with models of houses from
the early medieval period, a burial
mound, farmhouse, watermill, and 18th
century sake shop

Kokubun-ji

08306
**Kokubun-ji Municipal
Archaeological Gallery**
1-13-16 Nishimoto-machi, Kokubun-ji,
Tokyo
Archeology Museum
Coll: local prehistorical finds;
arrowheads; pottery; sword; tile
fragments

Komagane

08307
Akaho Museum
Akaho, Komagane, Nagano
Natural History Museum
Coll: natural history; items of local
historical interest

Komatsu

08308
Komatsu Municipal Museum
Rojo Park, Marunouchikoen-machi,
Komatsu, Ishikawa
General Museum - 1958
Coll: archeological exhibits including
pottery, swords, metalwork;
ethnography; farm tools and farmers'
clothing; natural history - library;
classroom

08309
Nata-dera Treasure House
122 Yu, Nata-machi, Komatsu, Ishikawa
Religious Art Museum
Buddhist statues; portable shrine;
screen paintings; calligraphy

Kumamoto

08310
Hommyo-ji Treasure House
Hanazono-cho, Kumamoto, Kumamoto
Religious Art Museum
Coll: paintings; calligraphy; swords
and armor; ceramics; lacquer items;
documents

08311
Kumamoto Castle
1-1 Honmaru, Kumamoto, Kumamoto
History/Public Affairs Museum
Coll: objects connected with the
history of the builder of the castle,
Kiyomasa Kato, and the Hosokawa
clan; items from the Seinan War;
weapons and uniforms; prints of the
battles and burning of the castle

08312
Kumamoto International Folk Art Museum
Sannomiya Koen, Kami-Tatsuda, Tatsuda-machi, Kumamoto, Kumamoto
Decorative Arts Museum
Coll: basketry and straw objects; chests; textiles; ceramics; glass; lacquer items; toys; folk arts from Japan, Europe, Central and South America, and Southeast Asia

08313
Kumamoto Museum
3-2 Furukyo-machi, Kumamoto, Kumamoto 860
General Museum - 1952
Coll: natural history; engineering and science exhibits; archeological material; folk arts; tools of the farming and fishing communities; regional crafts - library; planetarium

08314
Kumamoto Prefectural Art Museum
2 Ninomaru, Kumamoto, Kumamoto
Fine Arts Museum - 1976
Coll: contemporary paintings and prints; handicrafts; Buddhist material; Kofun archeological material including stone slabs, stone coffin, and reproductions of painted tomb chambers - workshop for traditional crafts; children's room

Kurashiki

08315
Kojima Torajiro Gallery
Kurashiki Ivy Square, 7-2 Honmachi, Kurashiki, Okayama
Fine Arts Museum
Western-style paintings by Torajiro Kojima

08316
Kurashiki Archaeological Museum
1-3-13 Chuo, Kurashiki, Okayama
Archeology Museum
Coll: Japanese archeological material including stone tools from the neolithic period, pottery, shell and cylindrical stone ornaments; swords; mirrors; earthenware vessels; pottery sutra cases; pre-Columbian pottery; Peruvian textiles

08317
Kurashiki Art Museum
1-4-7 Chuo, Kurashiki, Okayama
Fine Arts Museum
Coll: Greek and Egyptian ceramics; Roman mosaic and sculptures; Persian wares; 19th century French and Italian marble, bronze statues, and porcelain; furnished room from a traditional Japanese house; folk art -

08318
Kurashiki Folk Art Museum
1-4-11 Chuo, Kurashiki, Okayama
Decorative Arts Museum
Coll: Japanese folk art; American Indian ceramics and baskets; European peasant ceramics and metalwork

08319
Ohara Art Gallery
1-1-15 Chuo, Kurashiki, Okayama
Fine Arts Museum - 1930
Coll: 19th-20th century Western paintings and sculpture; ceramics and sculptures from Egypt, Persia, and Turkey; Japanese paintings; arts and crafts - garden

08320
Ohara Pottery Hall, Munakata Gallery, Serizawa Gallery, Far Eastern Gallery
1-1-15 Chuo, Kurashiki, Okayama
Fine Arts Museum
Coll: contemporary pottery, prints, and textiles; Chinese archeological items

Kurayoshi

08321
Kurayoshi Municipal Museum
3445-8 Nakano-cho, Kurayoshi, Tottori
General Museum - 1972
Coll: contemporary paintings; local archeological items; photographs and drawings; building designed by Toru Kosumi - garden; lecture hall

Kurume

08322
Ishibashi Art Museum Bridgestone Museum of Art, Tokyo
1015 Nonaka-cho, Kurume, Fukuoka
Fine Arts Museum - 1956
Coll: Western-style Japanese paintings (19th-early 20th century); foreign paintings; Greek vases

Kushiro

08323
Kushiro City Center for the Study of Buried Cultures
Shunkodai, Kushiro, Hokkaido
Archeology Museum
Coll: Ainu material including clothing, lacquer utensils, libation wands, pipes, swords, jewelry, cult objects, models of houses, and photographs of Ainu life; archeological pieces including vessels and stone implements

08324
Kushiro Municipal Museum
1-10-35 Tsurugadai Park, Kushiro, Hokkaido
General Museum - 1936
Coll: archeology; Ainu folk art; earthenware; zoology; ornithology; botany; entomology; minerals

Kyoto

08325
Archaeological Collection Kyoto University Faculty of Letters
Yoshidahon-machi, Sakyo-ku, Kyoto
Archeology Museum - 1911
Coll: Chinese ceramics from neolithic times to the Tang dynasty; early Chinese bronzes and jades; Buddhist sculpture; Japanese pottery; Korean art objects - library

08326
Children's Buddhist Museum
Maruyama Park, Higashiyama-ku, Kyoto
Junior Museum
Coll: objects on Buddhism; history; geography; science; fine arts; old customs

08327
Chion-in Treasure House
400 Higashi-iru, Yamatooji, Shimbashi, Rinka-cho, Higashiyama-ku, Kyoto
Religious Art Museum
Coll: main temple of the Jodo sect of Buddhism; ancient scrolls; religious paintings; bronze relief; wooden sculpture; Chinese pictures; Buddhist embroidered screen; rare books and documents

08328
Chishaku-in Storehouse
Higashiyama-shichijo, Higashiyama-ku, Kyoto
Fine Arts Museum
Coll: decorative screens of the Momoyama period

08329
Chishakuin Treasure Hall
Higashi-Kawaramachi, Higashiyama-ku, Kyoto
Religious Art Museum
Coll: Buddhist equipment and utensils; documents; paintings; calligraphy; sutras; books

08330
Daigo-ji Treasure Hall
Daigo Higashioji-machi, Fushimi-ku, Kyoto
Religious Art Museum
Coll: religious art; historical documents relating chiefly to Buddhism; calligraphy

08331
Daihoon-ji Treasure House
Imadegawa-agaru, Shichihonmatsu-dori, Kamikyo-ku, Kyoto
Religious Art Museum
Coll: sculpture; temple furniture; temple buildings

08332
Daikaku-ji Storehouse
4 Osawa-cho, Saga, Ukyo-ku, Kyoto
Religious Art Museum
Coll: decorated room dividers; sculpture; historical documents

08333
Domoto Art Museum
Hirano, Kita-ku, 26 Kamiyanagi-cho, Kyoto
Fine Arts Museum
Coll: the works of the artist Insho Domoto including paintings, prints, and drawings; ceramics; stained glass; tapestries; and metalwork

08334
Fujii Museum
44 Enshoji-machi, Okazaki, Sakyo-ku, Kyoto
Fine Arts Museum
Coll: Chinese paintings, calligraphy, Buddhist sculpture, jades, bronzes, pottery and porcelain, lacquer items, costumes, and furniture; Gandhara sculptures; Indian bronzes; Japanese mirrors

08335
Hieizan Natural History Museum
Hieizan, Sakyo-ku, Kyoto
Natural History Museum - 1955
Coll: zoology; ornithology; botany

08336
Ikeno Taiga Art Museum
57 Matsuomangoku-cho, Nishikyo-ku, Kyoto
Fine Arts Museum
Coll: 80 paintings and examples of calligraphy by the 18th century 'buninga' painter, Taiga Ikeno

08337
Kawai Kanjiro's House
569 Kanei-cho, Gojozaka, Higashiyama-ku, Kyoto, Kyoto
Historic Site - 1973
Coll: house designed by the famous potter Kanjiro Kawai; his pottery and kiln; sculpture; his writings and samples of calligraphy - library

08338
Kitano Tenman-gu Treasure House
Kitano Tenman-gu, 41 Bakuro-cho, Kyoto
Religious Art Museum
Coll: paintings; calligraphy; sculpture; lacquer items; metalwork; a few court costumes; ancient scrolls of the legends of the Kitano Tenjin Schrine

08339
Koryu-ji Treasure Hall
36 Uzumasa Hachigaoka-cho, Ukyo-ku, Kyoto
Religious Art Museum
Coll: Japanese Buddhist sculpture; calligraphy; documents; 19th century coronation robes and other costumes; 14th century paintings

08340
Kyoto Municipal Museum of Art
Okazaki Part, Sakyo-ku, Kyoto
Fine Arts Museum - 1933
Coll: contemporary fine arts; Japanese pictures; sculptures; decorative arts exhibits

08341
Kyoto National Museum
527 Chaya-machi, Higashiyama-ku, Kyoto
General Museum - 1889
Coll: Japanese and Chinese paintings; calligraphy; group of sutras; sculptures; ceramics; tiles; bronzes; metalwork; lacquer wares; dyeing and weaving; swords and armor; Japanese Buddhist sculpture; archeological material; No robes and kimonoes - library

08342
Kyoto Prefectural Exhibition Hall
1-4 Shimogamo Hangicho Sakyo-ku, Kyoto, Kyoto
Decorative Arts Museum - 1963
Coll: industrial art works; folk arts; toys; traditional handicrafts; oriental and Japanese instruments; documents - library; lecture hall; conference room

08343
Kyoto-Arashiyama Art Museum
33-22 Tsukurimichi-cho, Tenryu-ji, Saga, Ukyo-ku, Kyoto
Decorative Arts Museum
Coll: arms and armor; lacquer furniture; hibachi; clocks: portable writing cases; music instruments; paintings

08344
National Museum of Modern Art
Enshoji-cho, Okazaki, Sakyo-ku, Kyoto, Kyoto 606
Fine Arts Museum - 1963
Coll: 20th-century art; contemporary Japanese and foreign ceramics, including exhibit of Kanjiro Kawai's works; lacquer wares; metalwork; glass; textiles; sculpture; painting and prints - library

08345
Ninna-ji Treasure House
33 Omuro Ouchi, Ukyo-ku, Kyoto
Religious Art Museum
Coll: Chinese and Japanese paintings; Japanese sculpture; documents including scrolls of Buddhist teachings; Heian medical books; iconographic drawings; lacquer items

08346
Rokuharamitsu-ji Treasure House
2 Hagashi-iru, Yamato-oji, Matsubara-dori, Higashiyama-ku, Kyoto
Religious Art Museum
Coll: sculpture; portrait statues

08347
Ryu Gei Zo
Maegawa-cho 447, Higashi-oji,
Higashiyama-ku, Kyoto 605
Religious Art Museum
Religious art and traditions; personal
effects of Hideyoshi Toyotomi

08348
Sen'oku Hakkokan
25 Shimo Miyanomae-cho,
Shikagatani, Sakyo-ku, Kyoto
Fine Arts Museum
Coll: Chinese bronzes; Chinese and
Japanese mirrors; Buddhist figures;
bells of all periods; Korean mirrors

08349
Shoren-in Treasure House
Sanjobo-machi, Awadaguchi,
Higashiyama-ku, Kyoto - 1153
Religious Art Museum
Coll: rare books; writings; paintings -
library

08350
Sumitomo Collection
25 Shimomiyanomae-cho, Shishigatani,
Sakyo-ku, Kyoto 606
Fine Arts Museum
Collection of Oriental art

08351
To-ji Treasure House
1 Kujo-cho, Minami-ku, Kyoto
Religious Art Museum
Coll: sculpture; ancient paintings,
some from the 9th century;
manuscripts, letters, and documents;
lacquer items; sutras

08352
Toyokuni-jinja Treasure Hall
Shomen Chaya-machi, Yamato-Ooji,
Higashiyama-ku, Kyoto
Religious Art Museum
Coll: treasures and possessions of
Toyotomi Hideyoshi; paintings; painted
screens; swords

08353
Yurinkan Collection
44 Okazaki-Enshoji-machi, Sakyo-ku,
Kyoto
Fine Arts Museum - 1926
Coll: rare antique Chinese fine arts
and curios; bronzes; jade; porcelain;
seals; Buddhist images; pictures;
calligraphy

Machida

08354
Machida Municipal Museum
3562 Honmachida, Machida, Tokyo
History/Public Affairs Museum
Coll: Japanese archeological material;
ethnographic items

Matsue

08355
Lafcadio Hearn Memorial Hall
322-4 Okudani-cho, Matsue, Shimane
Historic Site - 1933
Coll: personal effects of the writer
Lafcadio Hearn; books and pictures;
his manuscripts; copies of his works -
library

08356
Shimane Prefectural Museum
1 Tono-machi, Matsue, Shimane
General Museum - 1959
Coll: contemporary paintings and
prints mostly by local artists; local
pottery; Buddhist objects; small
wooden figures; Gagaku instruments

08357
**Shimane Prefectural Yakumodatsu
Fudoki No Oka History Hall**
456 Oba-machiari, Matsue, Shimane
Archeology Museum
Coll: pottery; stone tools; bone hooks;
arrowheads; Kofun Sue ware; horse
trappings; pottery cylinders; roof tiles;
photographs and drawings of
excavation sites

08358
Yaegaki-jinja Treasure Storehouse
Sakusa-cho, Matsue, Shimane
Religious Art Museum - 1965
Coll: unique Shinto wall paintings from
the Heian period

Matsumoto

08359
Japan Folklore Museum
4-1 Marunouchi, Matsumoto, Nagano
Archeology Museum
Coll: archeological objects including
pottery and swords; photos of local
excavation sites; historical documents;
natural history collection; clocks; dolls;
festival objects

08360
Matsumoto Folk Arts Museum
1312-1 Shimoganai, Matsumoto,
Nagano
Anthropology Museum - 1966
Coll: folk arts of the mountainous
regions of Japan; southeast Asian,
European, and Near Eastern folk arts;
ceramics; lacquer vessels; metalwork

08361
Matsumoto Historical Museum
2 Marunouchi, Matsumoto, Nagano
History/Public Affairs Museum
Coll: archeology; articles of geological
and historical interest; art

08362
Matsumoto Municipal Museum
3-chome, Ninomaru-machi, Matsumoto,
Nagano
General Museum
geology; history; archeology; fine art

08363
Nakayama Archaeological Museum
Toriuchi, Oaza Nakayama-ku,
Matsumoto, Nagano
Archeology Museum
Coll: pottery; small figurines; stone
implements; swords

Matsuyama

08364
Ehime Prefectural Art Museum
Horinouchi, Matsuyama, Ehime
Fine Arts Museum
Coll: local contemporary paintings;
sculpture; handicrafts

08365
Ehime Prefectural Museum
4-7-1 Niban-cho, Matsuyama, Ehime
Natural History Museum - 1958
Coll: fossils; biology; geology

08366
**Ehime Prefecture Local Handicraft
Museum**
3-3-7 Ichiban-cho, Matsuyama, Ehime
General Museum
Coll: local Japanese-style paintings;
calligraphy; lacquer items; swords with
a display about sword-making; in 20th
century Western-style building

Minami Azumi

08367
Rokuzan Art Museum
Hotaka-cho, Minami Azumi, Nagano
Fine Arts Museum - 1958
Coll: memorial to the sculptor Ogiwara
Morie; his bronzes, oil sketches, and
drawings; personal photographs; his
books and sculptor's tools

Minamikoma

08368
Minobusan Treasure House
Minobu-machi, Minamikoma,
Yamanashi
Religious Art Museum
Coll: paintings; sculpture; calligraphy;
lacquer items; masks; metalwork;
documents including the 'Book of
Rites' and biography of Saint Nichiren

Minamishidara

08369
Mt Horaiji Natural History Museum
6 Moriwaki, Kadoya, Horai-cho,
Minamishidara, Aichi
Natural History Museum - 1963
Coll: exhibits on natural history;
invertebrates; insects; amphibia;
minerals; fossils

Minamitsuru

08370
**Yamanashi Prefectural Museum of
Fiji National Park**
Kawaguchiko-machi, Minamitsuru,
Yamanashi
Natural History Museum - 1954
Coll: natural history; insects; reptiles;
mammals; fossils; minerals;
archeology; volcanic lava from Mt.
Rainier (USA); stones from the South
Pole

Misawa

08371
Ogawarako Folklore Museum
17-1 Horikiri, Ohochise, Misawa,
Aomori
Anthropology Museum - 1962
Coll: archeology; ethnology; folk arts
and folklore

Mishima

08372
Mishima Taisha Treasure House
2 Omiya-cho, Mishima, Shizuoka
Religious Art Museum
Coll: swords and armor; pottery and
stone tools; Nara tiles; mirrors;
documents; festival masks

08373
Sano Art Museum
1-43 Nakata-machi, Mishima, Shizuoka
Fine Arts Museum - 1965
Coll: Chinese bronzes, pottery, dish
ware; Japanese ukiyo-e and
contemporary paintings; swords and
sword furniture

Mitaki

08374
Archaeological Collection
International Christian University
3-10-12 Osawa, Kokusai Kirisutokyo
Daigaku, Mitaki, Tokyo 181
Archeology Museum
Coll: local archeological items;
paleolithic implements

Mito

08375
Ibaraki Prefectural Art Museum
Kenminbunka Senta, 697 Higashikubo,
Senba-cho, Mito, Ibaraki
Fine Arts Museum
Coll: paintings, sculpture, handicrafts
from the late 19th century to the
present; 3rd-5th century archeological
material

08376
Ibaraki Prefecture History Hall
2-1-15 Midore-cho, Mito, Ibaraki
General Museum
Coll: exhibit on Shinto festivals;
pottery and vessels; sculpture; sutra
boxes; paintings; calligraphy; 19th
century frame schoolhouse; thatched
farmhouse

08377
**Suifu Meitokukai Foundation
Tokugawa Museum**
1-1215 Mikawa, Mito, Ibaraki 310
General Museum - 1977
Coll: the treasure of the
Mito-Tokugawa family including armor
and swords, tea-ceremony objects,
calligraphy and manuscripts - library

08378
Tokiwa-jinja Memorial Gallery
1-3-1 Tokiwa-machi, Mito, Ibaraki
History/Public Affairs Museum
Coll: belongings of the second and
fifth daimyos; paintings; calligraphy;
pipes; pistols; swords; armor; saddles
and stirrups

Miyagi

08379
Matsushima Kanrantei Museum
56 Aza Chonai, Matsushima, Miyagi,
Miyagi
General Museum
Coll: archeological finds; local marine
shells; 17th-19th century lacquer
vessels, armor, and costumes;
calligraphy; painting

08380
Zuigan-ji Museum
91 Aza Machiuchi, Matsushima,
Matsushima-cho, Miyagi, Miyagi
Religious Art Museum
Coll: paintings and portraits; scrolls;
sculpture; No and Kyogen masks;
temple documents and calligraphy

Miyazaki

08381
Agricultural Museum Faculty of
Agriculture, Miyazaki University
3-210 Funazuka, Miyazaki 880
Agriculture Museum - 1930
Coll: natural history; insects and
mammals; animal skeletons;
agriculture; farm tools; folk crafts -
library

08382
**Historical Museum in the Miyazaki
Shrine**
360 Jingu-machi, Miyazaki, Miyazaki
History/Public Affairs Museum
Coll: objects of historical interest;
archeology

08383
Miyazaki Prefectural Institution
2-4-4 Jingu, Miyazaki, Miyazaki
General Museum - 1971
Coll: remains from the Miyazaki burial
mounds; works of art by Eikyu;
botanical specimens - library; class
room; public hall

Morioka

08384
Morioka City Local History Hall
14-1 Atago-cho, Morioka, Iwate
General Museum
Coll: archeological finds; local folk arts including baskets and pottery; farm tools; ironwork; sutra and documents; Edo-period merchant shop

08385
Morioka Hashimoto Art Museum
10 Kagano Sainokami, Morioka, Iwate
Fine Arts Museum - 1975
Coll: contemporary Japanese paintings; Barbizon school of paintings; ceramics; sculpture; folk art; reerected Japanese-style house

Mukaishima

08386
Mukaishima Marine Biological Station Faculty of Science, Hiroshima University
Mukaishima-cho, Onomichi, Mukaishima, Hiroshima
Natural History Museum - 1933
Coll: invertebrates; mollusks; marine biology - library

Munakata

08387
Munakata Taisha Treasure House
Genkai-cho, Munakata, Fukuoka
Religious Art Museum
Coll: gilt-bronze loom; stone objects; jewelry; gilt-bronze horse trappings; mirrors; swords; sculpture

Nagano

08388
Kitano Art Museum
7963 Watauchi, Wakaho, Nagano, Nagano
Fine Arts Museum
Coll: 19th century Japanese paintings to the present; guns and armor; lacquer furniture; utensils; Japanese and European ivories - gardens

08389
Kizankan
Shibasawa, Shinonoi, Nagano, Nagano
Fine Arts Museum
Coll: 80 examples of the calligraphy of Kizan Kawamura, calligrapher and scholar of the Chinese classics; his seals, brushes, inkstones, and inksticks

08390
Nagano Prefecture Shinano Art Museum
Joyama Koen, Nagano, Nagano
Fine Arts Museum
Coll: pottery; mirrors; tiles; paintings; sculpture; calligraphy

08391
Zenko-ji Jodo Sect Treasure House
500 Motoyoshi-cho, Nagano, Nagano
Religious Art Museum
Coll: paintings; documents; sculpture; lacquer items; costumes and fashion; calligraphic scrolls by different emperors

08392
Zenko-ji Tendai Sect Treasure House
Motoyoshi-cho, Nagano, Nagano
Religious Art Museum
Coll: Japanese Buddhist paintings; calligraphy; documents; sculpture; lacquer items; metalwork

Nagaoka

08393
Nagaoka City Local History Hall
80-24 Oyama-cho, Nagaoka, Niigata
General Museum
Coll: items illustrating the history and life of the region; arms and armor; costumes; lacquer items; dolls; clocks; exhibit on snow culture including clothing, boots, snowshoes, and skis

08394
Nagaoka Contemporary Art Museum
2-1-1 Sakanoue-machi, Nagaoka, Niigata
Fine Arts Museum - 1964
Coll: paintings in Japanese style; Japanese and Western artists; prints

08395
Nagaoka Municipal Science Museum
2-1 Yanagihara-cho, Nagaoka, Niigata
Natural History Museum
Coll: natural history; zoology; butterflies; local flora; literature and materials on the snow and snow fall; local archeological material

Nagasaki

08396
Nagasaki International Cultural Hall
Atomic Bomb Materials Center
7-8 Hirano-machi, Nagasaki 852
History/Public Affairs Museum
Coll: history exhibits on the atomic bomb dropped on Nagasaki in WW II

08397
Nagasaki Municipal Museum
9-22 Dejima-machi, Nagasaki, Nagasaki 850
History/Public Affairs Museum - 1941
Coll: artistic handicrafts demonstrating foreign cultural influence; rare books on the history of Nagasaki; prints - library

08398
Nagasaki Prefectural Art Museum
2 Tateyama-machi, Nagasaki, Nagasaki
Fine Arts Museum - 1965
Coll: old and contemporary paintings; wood-block prints; calligraphy; sculpture; swords; ceramics and porcelain; folk art; medieval-18th century Spanish paintings and sculpture

Nagoya

08399
Aichi Art Gallery
1-12-1 Higashisakura, Higashi-ku, Nagoya, Aichi
Fine Arts Museum - 1955
Coll: contemporary Japanese and Western paintings and prints; sculpture by Bourdelle; ceramics

08400
Atsuta-jingu Treasure House
1 Shinmiyasaka-machi, Atsuta-ku, Nagoya, Aichi
Religious Art Museum
Coll: important Shinto shrine; historical and ceremonial swords; Bugaku masks; mirrors; Sue ware; temple drums; historical scrolls; textiles and clothing; 20th century Japanese-style paintings

08401
Nagoya Castle Treasure House
Nagoya Castle, 1-1 Hon-maru, Naka-ku, Nagoya, Aichi
General Museum - 1959
Coll: frescoes; fine arts; industrial arts; history, archeology; costumes; maps

08402
Nagoya City Hosei Niko Exhibition Hall
12 Aza Chanoki, Nakamura-cho, Nakamura-ku, Nagoya, Aichi
History/Public Affairs Museum
Coll: belongings and documents connected with the 16th century military dictator of Japan, Hideyoshi Toyotomi and his aid Kiyomasa Kato; his calligraphy; his armor and arms; his clothes; portraits

08403
Nagoya City Museum
1, 27-1 Mizuho-Dori, Mizuho-ku, Nagoya, Aichi 467
General Museum - 1977
Coll: history of Nagoya from the Stone Age to the present; archeological and ethnographic materials; folk art; fine arts - library; auditoriums

08404
Nagoya Municipal Science Museum
17-22 Sakae 2-chome, Nagoya, Aichi 460
Science/Tech Museum - 1962
Coll: physics; chemistry; engineering; astronomy and space science; telecommunications; steam locomotive - planetarium; library

08405
Tokugawa Art Museum
27 Tokugawa-cho 2-chome, Higashi-ku, Nagoya, Aichi 461
Fine Arts Museum
Tokugawa collection; Japanese and Chinese paintings; calligraphy; pottery; tea and incense utensils; rare ceramic pieces; lacquer art including a 50-piece set of lacquered furniture; textiles; No masks and robes; swords - library

Naha

08406
Japan Folk Art Museum, Okinawa Branch
1-30 Kanagusuku-cho, Shuri, Naha, Okinawa
Decorative Arts Museum - 1975
Coll: Okinawan textiles; costumes; pottery; 100-year old tatami-floored building

08407
Okinawa Prefectural Museum
1-1 Onaka-machi, Shuri, Naha, Okinawa
General Museum - 1958
Coll: local archeological finds; paintings; documents; clothing; boat models; glazed mortuary urns; exhibits on agricultural and fishing communities; Okinawan pottery and lacquer items; calligraphy - library

08408
Omine Kaoru Art Museum
3-15-2 Kumoji-machi, Naha, Okinawa
Fine Arts Museum
Coll: Kaoru Omine's collection of Chinese and Japanese paintings, mirrors, lacquer items, and ceramics

Nakagami

08409
Yomitan Township History and Folk Art Hall
708-4 Aza Zakimi, Yomitan-mura, Nakagami, Okinawa
General Museum
Coll: local farming and fishing gear; household utensils; Okinawan textiles; costumes; music instruments

Naka-Kambara

08410
Northern Culture Museum
Yokogoshi-mura Soumi, Naka-Kambara, Niigata
General Museum
Coll: Chinese sculpture and ceramics; Japanese paintings, sculpture, ceramics, lacquer items, folk art, and archeology - gardens

Nakakoma

08411
Shogetsu Art Museum
726 Tokaichiba, Wakakusa-machi, Nakakoma, Yamanashi
Fine Arts Museum
Coll: Edo and Meiji paintings; bronzes; ceramics

Nakatado

08412
Kotohira Arts and Science Museum
Kotohira, Nakatado, Kagawa
General Museum
Coll: Sue ware; toys; modern calligraphy; lacquer utensils; mirrors; contemporary Japanese-style painting; science exhibits

08413
Kotohira-gü Museum
892 Kotohira-machi, Nakatado, Kagawa
Religious Art Museum
Coll: Japanese painting; calligraphy; sculpture; metalwork; arms and armor; lacquer items; masks; music instruments

Nara

08414
Kasuga Taisha Treasure House
Kasugano-cho, Nara, Nara
Religious Art Museum
Coll: masks for Bugaku dances; swords and armor; mirrors; lacquer objects; calligraphy; religious paintings; archives; ancient archeological findings - library

08415
Kofuku-ji Treasure Hall
40 Noborio-ji-cho, Nara, Nara
Religious Art Museum
Coll: Japanese sculptures; bronzes; religious paintings; 10th century scroll

08416
Museum Yamato Bunkakan
1-11-6 Gakuen-Minami, Nara, Nara
Fine Arts Museum - 1960
Coll: Far Eastern fine arts; painting; sculpture; calligraphy; lacquer items; metalwork; dyeing and weaving; jewelry; glass; ceramics - library

08417
Nara Art Museum
Isuien Park, 74 Suimon-cho, Nara, Nara
Fine Arts Museum - 1939
Coll: ancient Chinese bronze mirrors; seals; Korean pottery

08418
Nara National Museum
50 Noborioji-cho, Nara, Nara
Fine Arts Museum - 1895
Coll: Buddhist art; paintings; ritual items; 6th-14th century Buddhist statues; relics; scrolls; techniques of temple architecture; handicrafts; calligraphy; roof tiles - garden; teahouse

08419
Nara Prefectural Museum of Art
10-6 Noborioji-cho, Nara, Nara
Fine Arts Museum - 1973
Coll: ukiyo-e prints and paintings;
sculpture; 19th-20th century
handicrafts; ceramics

08420
Neiraku Art Museum
74 Suimon-cho, Nara, Nara
Fine Arts Museum
Coll: early Chinese bronzes; mirrors;
Japanese, Chinese, and Korean
ceramics

08421
Saidai-ji Shuhokan
Saidaiji-cho, Nara, Nara
Religious Art Museum
Coll: sculpture; portraits of priests

08422
Shoso-in Treasure House
129 Zoshi-cho, Nara, Nara
Religious Art Museum
Coll: repository for personal
belongings of Emperor Shomu (8th
century AD); inaugural items;
manuscripts and sutras; screens;
paintings; pottery; glass; lacquer
objects; Buddhist religious items;
textiles; mirrors; 164 masks for Gigaku
dances; items from court life

08423
Todai-ji Treasure Hall
406 Zoshi-cho, Nara, Nara
Religious Art Museum - 752
Coll: Buddhist treasures; ancient
documents; famous images of Buddha;
Shosoin Treasure House; personal
belongings of Emperor Shomu -
library

08424
Toshodai-ji New Treasure House
Gojo-cho, Nara, Nara
Religious Art Museum - 1970
Coll: early sculpture; documents;
sutras; narrative scroll

08425
Yakushi-ji Treasure House
457 Nishinokyo-machi, Nara, Nara
Religious Art Museum
Coll: paintings; religious items; rebuilt
Buddhist temple; bronze images

Narita

08426
Naritasan History Hall
Narita Koen, Narita, Chiba
General Museum - 1947
Coll: paintings; local archeological
finds; manuscripts and books;
sculpture; botanical specimens;
ethnographic items

08427
Naritasan Museum
Narita Park, Narita, Chiba
General Museum - 1947
Coll: religious art; local archeological
items; manuscripts and books;
sculptures; botanical specimens

Natori

08428
**Horsemanship Museum of Takekoma
Shrine**
Iwanuma-cho, Natori, Miyagi
Anthropology Museum
Coll: anthropology; hippology; sports

Niigata

08429
B.S.N. Niigata Art Museum
5924-10 Ichibanboridori-machi, Niigata,
Niigata
Fine Arts Museum
Coll: Japanese paintings from 19th
century to the present; Italian
paintings; Chinese and Japanese
ceramics; calligraphy

08430
Niigata Prefecture Art Museum
3-1 Ichibanbori-dori, Niigata, Niigata
Fine Arts Museum - 1967
Coll: contemporary painting; sculpture;
handicrafts by local artists

Nikko

08431
Futaarasan-jinja Treasure House
2484 Chugushi, Nikko, Tochigi
Religious Art Museum
Coll: swords and battle gear; portable
shrines; ritual items; festival bells;
lacquer items; carpenters' tools

08432
Nikko Tosho-gu Treasure House
2280 Sannai, Nikko, Tochigi
Religious Art Museum
Coll: paintings; lacquer items; masks;
music instruments; arms and armor;
costumes; temple furniture; ritual
items; model of temple

08433
Rinno-ji Jokodo Treasure House
Nikkosan, Nikko, Tochigi
Religious Art Museum
Coll: paintings; sculpture; No masks;
metalwork; historical documents and
books; swords and armor; lacquer
items

Nishi Tsugaru

08434
**Kamegaoka Archaeological
Collection**
8 Aza Kameyama, Oaza Kamegaoka,
Kizukuri-machi, Nishi Tsugaru, Aomori
Archeology Museum
Coll: finds from prehistoric site;
pottery; figurines; shards; small clubs;
hooks and pins

Nishiiwai

08435
Chuson-ji Treasure House
Hiraizumi-cho, Nishiiwai, Iwate
Religious Art Museum - 1955
Coll: sculpture; gilt-wood coffins;
reliquaries; rosaries; shrouds and
robes; sets of the entire Buddhist
canon; metalwork; furniture

08436
Hiraizumi Cultural History Hall
Sakashita, Chuson-ji, Hiraizumi,
Hiraizumi-cho, Nishiiwai, Iwate
History/Public Affairs Museum
Coll: dioramas of local historical
events; Japanese ceramics; furniture;
models of Heian temples

08437
Hiraizumi Museum
81-1 Aza Hiraizumi Shirayama,
Hiraizumi-cho, Nishiiwai, Iwate
Religious Art Museum - 1955
Coll: Chinese Buddhist painting and
sculpture; swords; Japanese Buddhist
painting; calligraphy; bronze bell

08438
Motsu-ji Storage House
48 Aza Osawa, Hiraizumi, Hiraizumi-
cho, Nishiiwai, Iwate
Religious Art Museum - 1977
Coll: Buddhist paintings and sculpture;
music instruments; masks; lacquer
utensils; swords; sutras and sutra
boxes

Nishikanbara

08439
Yahiko-jinja Treasure House
Oaza Yahiko, Yahiko-mura,
Nishikanbara, Niigata
Religious Art Museum
Coll: paintings; handicrafts; swords;
No masks; calligraphy

Nishimatsuura

08440
Arita Ceramic Museum
1356 Arita-machi, 3-ku, Nishimatsuura,
Saga 844
Decorative Arts Museum - 1954
Coll: local ceramics and documents
pertaining to their history; examples of
Imari, Kakiemon, Arita, and Nabeshima
ware - library

Nishimuro

08441
Kushimoto Okyo-Rosetsu Gallery
Muryo-ji, Kushimoto, Kushimoto-cho,
Nishimuro, Wakayama
Fine Arts Museum
Coll: decorative sliding doors; wall
scroll paintings; archeological finds
consisting of pottery and remnants of
a wooden boat

Nishinomiya

08442
Egawa Museum of Art
1-86-39 Kamikotoen, Nishinomiya,
Hyogo
Fine Arts Museum - 1973
Coll: Chinese and Japanese paintings,
calligraphy, ceramics, and lacquer
items; Korean ceramics

08443
**Nishinomiya Otani Memorial Art
Museum**
4-38 Nakahama-cho, Nishinomiya,
Hyogo
Fine Arts Museum
Coll: the Otani collection of Japanese
and Western art of the present and
recent past - garden

Noda

08444
Noda City Museum of Folklore
370 Noda, Noda, Chiba
General Museum - 1959
Coll: soi sauce manufacture;
archeology; ethnology

Nyu

08445
Fukui Prefecture Ceramic Hall
Ozowara, Miyazaki-mura, Nyu, Fukui
Decorative Arts Museum - 1941
Coll: samples of Echizen pottery
through different periods - pottery
workshop; tea-ceremony house;
garden

Ochi

08446
Oyamazumi-jinja Treasure House
Miyaura, Omishima-machi, Ochi, Ehime
Religious Art Museum
Coll: earliest known swords and armor
(10th century); paintings; shrines;
historical documents; mirrors - library

Odawara

08447
Matsunaga Memorial Gallery
517 Itabashi, Odawara, Kanagawa
Fine Arts Museum
Coll: earliest extant Japanese
paintings; examples of calligraphy by
the tea master Sen no Rikyu and
others; bronze and wooden
sculptures; ceramics; lacquer items;
Chinese art collection including
bronzes, paintings, sculpture, and
ceramics

08448
Odawara Castle Museum
6-1 Jonai, Odawara, Kanagawa
General Museum
Coll: copies of portraits of various
feudal lords of the castle; documents
of the Hojo family; calligraphy and
paintings; armor and swords;
lacquered toilet seats; maps; painted
wooden doors; local products and
household utensils

Okawa

08449
Shido-dera Treasure House
Shido-machi, Okawa, Kagawa
Religious Art Museum
Coll: paintings illustrating history of the
temple; calligraphy of literary figures
and priests; sculpture

Okaya

08450
Okaya City Silk and Art Museum
4-1-39 Honmachi, Okaya, Nagano
General Museum
Coll: archeological material;
contemporary paintings, sculpture, and
prints; history of silk-spinning and
weaving machines

Okayama

08451
Okayama Art Museum
2-7-15 Marunouchi, Okayama,
Okayama
Fine Arts Museum
Coll: Chinese and Japanese paintings,
lacquer items, and ceramics; Chinese
bronzes; Japanese swords and armor;
calligraphy; No costumes; Korean
ceramics

08452
Okayama Prefectural Museum
1-5 Korakuen, Okayama, Okayama
General Museum
Coll: archeological and ethnographic
material; paintings; calligraphy;
ceramics; sculpture; lacquer items;
swords; costumes; textiles

Omachi

08453
Omachi Alpine Museum
Omachi, Nagano
Natural History Museum - 1951
Coll: local natural history; alpine
techniques

Ome

08454
Gyokudo Art Museum
1-75 Mitake, Ome, Tokyo
Fine Arts Museum - 1961
Coll: paintings and sketches by
Gyokudo Kawai; personal effects;
photographs of the artist; reproduction
of his studio with equipment and
furniture; building designed by Isoya
Yoshida - garden

08455
**Ome Municipal Museum of
Provincial History**
1-684 Komaki-cho, Ome, Tokyo 198
General Museum - 1974
Coll: life and history of the region;
fishing gear; ceramics; armor;
documents; local paintings; folk art

Omishima

08456
Oyamazumi-jinja Kokuhokan
Oyamazumi Shrine, Omishima,
Ochigun
Religious Art Museum
Coll: ancient armor and swords; oldest
mirrors in Japan - library

Omiya

08457
Saitama Prefectural Museum
4-219 Takahana-machi, Omiya, Saitama
General Museum
Coll: local archeological finds; swords;
models of medieval castles; farm and
forestry tools; reconstructed
farmhouse interior; early Buddhist
sculpture; pottery; contemporary art -
library; reconstructred prehistoric huts

Ono

08458
Senko-ji Treasure House
Shimobo Nyukawa-mura, Ono, Gifu
Religious Art Museum - 1977
Coll: wooden sculpture by the priest
Enku; his portrait; his calligraphy;
models of temples and farmhouses;
local natural history; samples of wood
and woodcutters' tools

Osaka

08459
Fujita Art Museum
10-32 Amijima-cho, Miyakojima-ku,
Osaka
Fine Arts Museum - 1951
Coll: Chinese and Japanese painting;
calligraphy; sculpture; ceramics;
lacquer items; textiles; metalwork;
Japanese tea-ceremony objects

08460
Japan Crafts Museum
3-619 Shinkawa, Naniwa-ku, Osaka
Decorative Arts Museum
Coll: Japanese folk pottery; basketry;
paper; lacquer items; textiles

08461
Museum of Modern Transportation
3-11-10 Namiyoke, Minato-ku, Osaka
Science/Tech Museum - 1962
Coll: modern means of transportation;
models; equipment

08462
Osaka Castle Donjon
Baba-cho, Higashi-ku, Osaka
History/Public Affairs Museum
Coll: paintings, calligraphy, metalwork,
armor and swords, costumes, and
documents relating to the history of
the castle; ukiyo-e prints; puppets
from Osaka Bunraku puppet theater

08463
Osaka City Museum
1-1 Osaka-jo, Higashi-ku, Osaka
General Museum - 1960
Coll: history and culture of Osaka;
archeological material; folk art;
pottery; puppets; masks; spinning and
weaving exhibit; maps, documents and
records of city

08464
Osaka Municipal Electricity Museum
1-6 Kitadori, Nagahori, Nishi-ku, Osaka
Science/Tech Museum - 1937
Coll: apparatuses for experiments in
physics and engineering; atomic
power; electric wave and
communication exhibits - planetarium

08465
**Osaka Municipal Museum of Fine
Arts**
121 Chausuyama-cho, Tennoji-ku,
Osaka
Fine Arts Museum - 1936
Coll: over 200 Chinese paintings from
the 7th century onward; Japanese
ceramics and sculpture; Chinese
bronze; mirrors; lacquer items;
porcelain; calligraphy; Coptic
sculpture; Etruscan pottery - library

08466
Osaka Museum of Natural History
Nagai Park, Higashi-sumiyoshi-ku,
Osaka 546
Natural History Museum - 1950
Coll: fossils; local flora and plant
fossils; zoology of New Caledonia;
paleontology; entomology;
herpetology; marine invertebrates;
geology - library

08467
Shitenno-ji Treasure House
17 Moto-machi, Tennoji-ku, Osaka 543
Religious Art Museum - 1969
Coll: temple; 1,000-year old roof tiles;
statues of Buddha; Bugaku collection
of musical instruments, costumes, and
masks; 800-year old fans illustrated
with Buddhist sutras; Japanese-style
painting on silk depicting the life of
Taishi Shotoku; examples of
calligraphy

Otaru

08468
Otaru City Museum
3-7-8 Ironai-cho, Otaru, Hokkaido
General Museum - 1956
Coll: oceanography; history;
archeology; zoology; botany; minerals;
art

08469
**Otaru Youth Center of Science and
Technology**
1-9-1 Midori-cho, Otaru, Hokkaido
Science/Tech Museum - 1963
Coll: physics; machines and
apparatuses used in engineering;
scientific models; educational exhibits

Otsu

08470
Biwa-ko Bunkakan
1-1 Uchidehama, Otsu, Shiga
General Museum - 1961
Coll: Japanese archeological finds
from local excavations; Buddhist
sculptures, paintings, and ritual
objects; Japanese paintings of the Edo
period (1615-1868); zoology - library;
aquarium

08471
Omi Local Crafts Art Museum
Mii-dera, Onjo-ji, Otsu, Shiga
Fine Arts Museum
Coll: Okyo's paintings; local paintings
and ceramics - garden

Sado

08472
Aikawa Local Museum
Sakashita-machi, Aikawa-cho, Sado,
Niigata
General Museum
Coll: archeological material; folk art
including ceramics, costumes, wooden
panel; historical material; samples of
calligraphy; local gold mining exhibit

08473
Sado Museum
Yahata, Sawata-machi, Sado, Niigata
General Museum - 1956
Coll: archeological finds; maps, charts,
and photographs of the excavation
sites; natural history; Bumaku puppets,
No masks, and costumes;
contemporary Sado ceramics and
metalwork; mining exhibit; handicrafts
- garden; reconstructed prehistoric
dwelling; reerected farmhouse

08474
Toki No Sato History Hall
655 Mano-machi, Sado
General Museum
Coll: personal effects of the Emperor
Juntoku; calligraphy of the priest
Nichiren; fans; exhibit on local gold
mining with miners' lamps, clothing,
and a diorama; ceramics; metalwork;
paintings

Saeki

08475
Itsukushima-jinja Homotsukan
Miyajima-cho, Saeki
Religious Art Museum - 1895
Coll: paintings; calligraphy; sutras;
swords and other ancient weapons

Saga

08476
Saga Prefectural Museum
1-15-23 Jonai, Saga, Saga
General Museum - 1970
Coll: natural history; archeological
material; folk arts; painting; ceramics;
calligraphy - library

Saijo

08477
Saijo Municipal Local Museum
237-1 Akeyashiki, Saijo, Ehime
General Museum
Coll: archeological material; paintings;
calligraphy; armor; ceramics; natural
history; geology

Saiki

08478
Itsukushima-jinja Treasure House
Miyajima-cho, Saiki, Hiroshima
Religious Art Museum - 1895
Coll: 12th century sutras; medieval
suits of armor; No and Bugaku masks;
Buddhist items; theater and court
costumes

Saito

08479
Saitobaru Burial Mounds Museum
5670 Saitobaru-nishi, Oaza Miyake,
Saito, Miyazaki
Archeology Museum
Coll: gold-plated swords; armor;
mirrors; jewelry; horse trappings; tiles;
models of a tomb and the tomb sites;
ethnographic material including fishing,
hunting, and farming gear - park;
tombs

Sakai

08480
**Osaka Municipal Senboku
Archaeological Hall**
Ohasu Koen, 2-4 Wakamatsudai, Sakai,
Osaka
Archeology Museum
Coll: Kofun material including
Sue-ware vessels; photographs of the
excavation sites

Sakaide

08481
Kamata Local Museum
1-1-24 Sakaide Hon-machi, Sakaide,
Kagawa
General Museum - 1925
items of regional interest - library

Sakata

08482
Homma Art Museum
7-7 Onari-machi, Sakata, Yamagata
Fine Arts Museum
Coll: Japanese paintings and prints;
calligraphy; samples of Buson's
poetry; ceramics - garden

Sanbu

08483
Shibayama Haniwa Museum
298 Shibayama, Shibayama-machi,
Sanbu, Chiba
General Museum
Coll: local traditional costumes and
accessories; archeological material
from 5th century tumuli; pottery
cylinders; arms and armor;
photographs of excavation sites

Santo

08484
Ryokan Memorial Gallery
Oaza Komeda, Izumozaki-machi,
Santo, Niigata
Historic Site
Coll: calligraphy and writings of the
priest Ryokan (1757-1831); personal
effects; portraits; modern museum
building designed by Yoshiro
Taniguchi

Sapporo

08485

Historical Museum of Hokkaido
Ko-nopporo, Atsubetsu-machi,
Shiroishi-ku, Sapporo, Hokkaido
General Museum - 1971
Coll: regional geology; fossils;
ethnology of the Ainu culture;
Japanese pioneer settlement; pottery;
models and dioramas of early culture;
photographs; lacquer; industrial
development of region - library

08486

**Hokkaido Mikishi Kotaro Art
Museum**
5 Nishi Kitaichijo, Chuo-ku, Sapporo,
Hokkaido
Fine Arts Museum
Coll: 200 paintings and drawings by
Kotaro Mikishi

08487

Hokkaido Museum of Modern Art
North 1, Nishi 17 chuo-ku, Sapporo,
Hokkaido 060
Fine Arts Museum - 1977
Coll: 20th century paintings and
drawings; Japanese contemporary art;
19th-20th century European glass;
20th century Japanese glass - library;
lecture hall; audiovisual room;
auditorium

08488

**Hokkaido University Ainu Museum
in Memory of Dr. John Batchelor**
Dept of Agriculture of Hokkaido
University
Botanical Garden, 8 Nishi Kitasanjo,
Chuo-ku, Sapporo, Hokkaido
Anthropology Museum
Coll: Ainu ethnographic material
presented in honor of the American
missionary Dr. Batchelor, a scholar of
the Ainu language and culture; daily
and ceremonial clothing; ornaments;
swords; household utensils; hunting
implements; religious customs; models
of houses; photographs

08489

**Hokkaido University Natural History
Collection**
Botanical Garden, Nishi 8-chome, Kita
Sanjo, Sapporo, Hokkaido
Natural History Museum
Exhibits on natural history

Sawara

08490

Katori-jingu Treasure House
Katori, Sawara, Chiba
Religious Art Museum
Coll: Japanese mirrors; wooden
masks; documents pertaining to the
history of the shrine

Senboku

08491

Masaki Art Museum
2-9-26 Tadaokanaka, Tadaoka-cho,
Senboku, Osaka
Fine Arts Museum
Coll: ceramics; early Indian coins;
Gandhara sculpture; paintings;
calligraphy; Chinese bronzes, mirrors,
jades, tomb tiles, sculptures

Sendai

08492

Archaeological Collection Tohoku
University
2 Katahiro-cho, Sendai, Miyagi
Archeology Museum
Coll: prehistorical archeological
materials, including pottery, fetishes,
and figurines; ceramics

08493

Kawaguchi Tibetan Collection
Tohoku University Faculty of Literature
Tohoku Daigaku Bungaku-bu,
Kawauchi, Sendai, Miyagi
Fine Arts Museum
Coll: Tibetan paintings, priests' robes,
reliquaries, prayer wheels, bells,
drums; Nepalese bronzes; Indian
sculptures

08494

**Saito Ho-on Kai Museum of Natural
History**
20-2 Honcho 2-chome, Sendai, Miyagi
980
Natural History Museum - 1933
Coll: geology; petrology; mineralogy;
paleontology; zoology; botany -
library

08495

Sendai City Museum
Kawauchi Sannomaruato, Sendai,
Miyagi 980
General Museum - 1961
Coll: portraits, documents, and letters
of the family Date, the first feudal lord
of the area; family armor and clothing;
tea-ceremony objects; lacquer;
shikishi and other examples of
calligraphy; Christian religious art; 19th
century ukiyo-e prints - library

Seto

08496

Seto Ceramics Center
Kurasho-cho, Seto, Aichi
Decorative Arts Museum
Coll: traditional and contemporary
ceramics; model of old kiln

08497

**Seto City History and Folklore
Gallery**
1 Higashi Matsuyama-cho, Seto, Aichi
Decorative Arts Museum - 1978
Coll: tools and instruments used
before industry ceramics; models of
kilns; historical survey of Seto
ceramics

Shima

08498

Shima Marineland
Kashikojima, Ago-cho, Shima, Mie
517-05
Natural History Museum - 1970
Coll: subtropical coral fish, temperate
sea fish, and cold-water fish; marine
invertebrates from the Japanese
coasts; foreign freshwater fish; fossils
of aquatic life - library

Shimonoseki

08499

Akama-jingu Treasure House
Amidaji-cho, Shimonoseki, Yamaguchi
History/Public Affairs Museum
Coll:items connected with the history
of the Gempei War and Emperor
Antoku; the 20-volume edition of the
'Heike Monogatari'; paintings; screens

08500

Sumiyoshi-jinja Treasure House
1162-2 Ichinomiya-machi, Shimonoseki,
Yamaguchi
Religious Art Museum
Coll: wooden statues; calligraphy;
shikishi; lacquer items

Shingu

08501

**Kumano Hayatama Taisha Treasure
House**
1 Shingu, Shingu, Wakayama
Religious Art Museum
Coll: archeological material; small
sculptures; metalwork; ceramics;
lacquer items; 14th century
ornamented fans; portable shrines

Shiogama

08502

Shiogama-jinja Treasure House
1 Ichimoriyama, Shiogama, Miyagi
Religious Art Museum - 1965
Coll: festival floats; armor and swords;
documents; ceramics; calligraphy;
natural history; tools used in collecting
salt; fishing gear

Shiojiri

08503

**Shiojiri Municipal Hiraide Site
Archaeological Museum**
1011-3 Oaza Soga, Shiojiri, Nagano
Archeology Museum
Coll: pottery; stone implements;
Sue-ware bowls; Haji-ware dishes;
bronze bells

Shizuoka

08504

Kunozan Tosho-gu Museum
390 Nekoya, Shizuoka, Shizuoka
Religious Art Museum - 1965
Coll: personal effects of Ieyasu
Tokugawa and donations by other
members of the Tokugawa family;
exhibit on military and domestic life of
the late 16th-17th centuries

08505

**Shizuoka Municipal Toro Site
Museum**
5-10-5 Toro, Shizuoka, Shizuoka
Archeology Museum
Coll: wooden items from 200 BC to
250 AD including farming tools,
kitchen implements, stools, and
dugouts; pottery vessels; bronze bell;
stone objects; 19th century farm tools;
interior of farmhouse

08506

Sunpu Museum
15-4 Kon'ya-cho, Shizuoka, Shizuoka
Fine Arts Museum
Coll: Japanese-style paintings;
calligraphy

Soja

08507

**Okayama Prefectural Kibiji Local
Museum**
1252 Kanbayashi, Soja, Okayama
General Museum - 1976
Coll: Kofun material; photographs of
the excavation sites; reproductions of
the paintings of the 15th century
painter Sesshu who was born here

Suita

08508

National Museum of Ethnology
23-17 Yamadaogawa, Suita, Osaka
Anthropology Museum - 1977
Coll: artifacts from East Asia, Oceania,
Africa, Europe, and America

08509

Osaka Japan Folk Art Museum
41-1 Yamada Ogawa, Senri Expo Park,
Suita, Osaka
Decorative Arts Museum
Coll: chests; huge pots; straw
raincoats and baskets; textiles; pottery

Suwa

08510

Idojiri Archaeological Hall
Sakai, Fujimi-machi, Suwa, Nagano
Archeology Museum
Coll: prehistoric vessels; stone tools;
figurines; full-scale model of
prehistoric house furnished with
original vessels

08511

Ito Modern Art Museum
Takaki, Shimosuwa-machi, Suwa,
Nagano
Fine Arts Museum
Ito Mitsuru's collection of Japanese-
style paintings and sculpture

08512

Shimosuwa Local Museum
6188-8 Shimosuwa-machi, Suwa,
Nagano
General Museum
Coll: archeological items including
pottery, swords, and Sue ware;
historical fishing boats used in the
area; footwear of all kinds; lacquer
vessels; arms and armor; exhibits on
the life of commoners and samurais

08513

Suwa City Art Museum
4-1-14 Kogan-dori, Suwa, Nagano
Fine Arts Museum
Coll: archeological materials;
contemporary Japanese painting,
sculpture, and handicrafts

Tagajo

08514

Tohoku Historical Museum
133 aza Miyamae Ukishima, Tagajo,
Miyagi 985
General Museum - 1974
Coll: history and culture of the region;
prehistorical and historical items; farm
tools; lacquer utensils; clothing; folk
arts; old documents; traditional fishing
boat - library; archeological research
institute

Tajimi

08515

**Gifu Prefecture Pottery Exhibition
Hall**
135 Togen-machi, Tajimi, Gifu
Decorative Arts Museum
Coll: shards or broken pieces of
pottery; regional ware; map of all kiln
sites

Takaichi

08516
Nara National Cultural Research Center for Asuka Material
601 Okuyama, Asuka-mura, Takaichi, Nara
Archeology Museum - 1975
Coll: pottery; photographs of the excavation sites; armor and weapons; jewelry; mirrors; photos of the wall paintings of 8th century tomb; Asuka sculpture

Takamatsu

08517
Kagawa Prefecture Cultural Center
1-10-39 Bancho, Takamatsu, Kagawa
Fine Arts Museum
Coll: contemporary paintings; sculpture; handicrafts; in building designed by Hiroshi Oe - auditorium; tea-ceremony room

08518
Sanuki Folk Art Museum
1-20-16 Ritsurin-cho, Takamatsu, Kagawa
Anthropology Museum
Coll: household items; locks; ceramics; decorated oil bottles; toys; dragon masks; carpenters' tools; roof tiles

08519
Seto Naikai Historical and Folklore Hall
1412-2 Tarumi-cho, Takamatsu, Kagawa
General Museum - 1974
Coll: fishing boats and fishing gear; festivals of the fisher-folk; ship models; farm tools; archeological items including stone tools, pottery, swords, mirrors, coins

08520
Yashima-dera Treasure House
Yamaue, Yashima, Takamatsu, Kagawa
General Museum
Coll: Japanese painting; calligraphy including samples by different emperors; items of historical interest

Takaoka

08521
Takaoka Municipal Art Museum
1-5 Kojo, Takaoka, Toyama
Fine Arts Museum
Coll: contemporary paintings; sculpture; metalwork; lacquer items; textiles; ceramics

Takarazuka

08522
Tessai Art Museum
Seicho-ji Sannai, 1 Yoneya Aza Kiyoshi, Takarazuka, Hyogo
Fine Arts Museum
Coll: paintings and examples of calligraphy by the artist Tomioka Tessai; his pottery; sketchbooks

Takasaki

08523
Gumma Prefectural Museum of Modern Art
239 Iwahana-cho, Takasaki, Gumma
Fine Arts Museum
Coll: contemporary Japanese art; Chinese and Japanese paintings - gallery

Takayama

08524
Hachiga Ethnographical Art Museum
Shimosanno-machi, Takayama, Gifu
Fine Arts Museum
Coll: Hachiga family collection of ceramics, lacquer items, small figurines, relics of Christianity, and paintings

08525
Hida Folklore Village
2680 Kamiokamoto-cho, Takayama, Gifu
Open Air Museum - 1971
Coll: farmhouses and their out-buildings; priests' residences; house of a village headman; exhibits of farm tools, clothing, cooking and weaving utensils; traditional crafts

08526
Hida Takayama Shunkei Lacquer Institute
1-88 Kanda-cho, Takayama, Gifu
Decorative Arts Museum
Coll: local lacquer objects including chests, trays, food boxes, bowls; section of a tea-ceremony house; exhibits on carpentry and lacquering; tools

08527
Lion-Mask Gallery
Sakura-machi, Takayama, Gifu
Religious Art Museum
Coll: lion masks used in the lion dance in all Shinto festivals; paintings; swords and armor; lacquer utensils

08528
Takayama City Museum
75 Kami Ichino-machi, Takayama, Gifu
General Museum
Coll: local folk arts; archeological finds from nearby Japanese Alps; local records; firearms; topographic views

08529
Takayama Festival-Cart Hall
178 Sakura-machi, Takayama, Gifu
Religious Art Museum
Coll: 17th century festival carts; mannequins in old ceremonial dress; lion masks; lion-dance costumes

Takefu

08530
Takefu City Echizen Regional Gallery
Yokawa-machi, Takefu, Fukui
General Museum - 1974
Coll: Echizen ware; tiles; gongs; coins; saddles; material on the peasants' revolt of 1575

Tenri

08531
Tenri Sankokan Tenri University
1 Furu, Tenri, Nara
General Museum - 1930
Coll: Japanese and Korean pre-Buddhist antiquities; Chinese art; Near Eastern, Egyptian, and classical antiquity; ethnographic material from North and South America, India, the Near East, Oceania, and Central Africa; Japanese archeological material - library

Tokoname

08532
Tokoname Ceramic Research Center
45 Hikake, Tokoname, Aichi
Decorative Arts Museum
Coll: early-modern ceramic wares produced in Tokoname, one of the six oldest kilns in Japanese ceramic history - ceramic workshops

Tokushima

08533
Tokushima Prefecture Museum
2-20 Sinmachibashi, Tokushima, Tokushima
General Museum - 1959
Coll: Japanese archeological material; local contemporary painting and sculpture; coins; sword furniture and armor

Tokyo

08534
Aizu Memorial Exhibition Room of Oriental Arts Waseda University
Totsuka-cho, Shinjuku-ku, Tokyo
Fine Arts Museum
Oriental art

08535
Archaeological Collection
Kokugakuin University
4-10-28 Higashi, Shibuya-ku, Tokyo
Archeology Museum
Coll: Japanese archeological material from pre-ceramic to early historical times; archeological items from China, Korea, and North America; Japanese burial urns; roof tiles; small stone pagodas

08536
Archaeological Museum of Meiji University
Kanda-Surugadai, Tokyo
Archeology Museum - 1952
Coll: prehistoric items, pottery, bone implements, hand axe, etc., from different excavation sites - library

08537
Asakura Sculpture Gallery
7-18-10 Yanaka, Taito-ku, Tokyo
Fine Arts Museum
Coll: sculpture by Fumio Asakura; his ink paintings; his sculpture tools; in house designed by him - tea-ceremony room; garden

08538
Bridgestone Museum of Art
1-1 Kyobashi, Chuo-ku, Tokyo
Fine Arts Museum - 1952
Coll: Japanese modern painting in the Western style; sculpture; prints; 19th century European masters in particular the Impressionists; Roman metalwork; pottery vessels from the Mediterranean classical world and pre-Columbian Peru - library

08539
Calligraphy Museum
125 Kaminegishi, Daito-ku, Tokyo
Fine Arts Museum - 1936
Coll: multifarious objects collected by Nakamura demonstrating the history of calligraphy; ancient texts of calligraphy; pottery; jades; bronzes; mirrors; swords; rubbings; coins; inkstones and brushes; stone memorial tablets

08540
Collection of the Institute of Music
Tokyo
Music Museum
Coll: musical instruments

08541
Communications Museum
3 Fujimi-cho 2-chome, Chiyoda-ku, Tokyo
Science/Tech Museum - 1955
Coll: historical materials on radio and television broadcasting; mechanics of communications; apparatuses and models; equipment

08542
Criminal Museum of Meiji University
1 Surugadai, Kanda Chiyoda, Tokyo
History/Public Affairs Museum
Social science items

08543
Eisei Bunko Foundation
1-1-1 Mejirodai, Bunkyo-ku, Tokyo
Fine Arts Museum
Coll: paintings and screens; tea-ceremony objects; No robes and masks; Chinese belt buckles, tomb slab, Buddha, bronze mirror; letters; swords and armor

08544
Gotō Art Museum
111 Kaminoge-cho Tamagawa, Setagaya-ku, Tokyo
Fine Arts Museum - 1960
Coll: Buddhist scriptures; Japanese and Chinese paintings; calligraphy; ceramics; early Chinese jades and mirrors; Japanese tea-ceremony items; lacquer ware; archeological items; Korean ceramics

08545
The Hatakeyama Collection
20-12, 2-chome, Shiroganedai, Minato-ku, Tokyo
Fine Arts Museum
Coll: Chinese and Japanese paintings, calligraphy, sculpture, metalwork, and ceramics; Japanese lacquer, tea-ceremony objects, and costumes; Korean ceramics - tea-ceremony room

08546
Horyu-ji Treasure House Tokyo
National Museum
Ueno Koen, Taito-ku, Tokyo
Religious Art Museum
Coll: Buddhist sculpture from the 9th century onward; masks; paintings; historical documents; textiles; metalwork; ritual items

08547
Idemitsu Art Gallery
3-1-1 Marunouchi, Chiyoda-ku, Tokyo
Fine Arts Museum - 1966
Coll: Japanese and Chinese ceramics; samples of calligraphy by literary figures and monks; lacquer items; Chinese bronzes; art objects of the Middle and Near East; paintings and lithographs by Sam Francis and George Rouault

08548
Japan Calligraphy Museum
1-3-1 Tokiwadai, Itabashi-ku, Tokyo
Fine Arts Museum
Examples of 20th-century calligraphy - garden

08549
Japanese Folk Art Museum
861 Komaba, Meguro-ku, Tokyo
Decorative Arts Museum
Coll: paintings; pottery and porcelain; prints; textiles; lacquer items; masks; toys; furniture; metalwork; costumes; ethnological items; folkcraft arts from all over the world

08550
Kurita Art Museum Tokyo Branch
2-17-9 Nihonbashi-Hama-cho, Chuo-ku,
Tokyo
Decorative Arts Museum - 1974
Collection of porcelains

08551
Kuroda Seiki Memorial Hall
13-27 Ueno Koen, Taito-ku, Tokyo,
Tokyo
Fine Arts Museum - 1930
Collection of the paintings and
sketches of Seiki Kuroda, pioneer of
Western painting in Japan - library

08552
Local History Museum
16-10, 1-chome, Yutakacho,
Shinagawa-ku, Tokyo
History/Public Affairs Museum - 1924
Coll: items of local historical interest;
books; archives - library

08553
Matsuoka Museum of Art
Matsuoka Tamura-cho, 22-10,
Shinbashi 5-chome, Minato-ku, Tokyo
105
Fine Arts Museum - 1975
Coll: Chinese, Korean, and Japanese
ceramics; Japanese traditional
paintings; Egyptian, Greek, and
Mediterranean antiquities; Chinese
sculpture and bronzes; Indian
sculpture

08554
Meguro Parasitological Museum
1-1, 4 chome, Shimomeguro, Meguro-
ku, Tokyo 153
Natural History Museum
Coll: natural history exhibits; parasites
of invertebrates and vertebrates; type
specimens of helminthes described by
the well-known helminthologist, Dr.
Satyu Yamaguti - library

08555
Meiji-jingu Treasure Museum
Yoyogi, Shibuya-ku, Tokyo
History/Public Affairs Museum - 1921
Coll: treasures and possessions of
Emperor Meiji; personal effects of
Empress Shoken; memorial picture
gallery

08556
Memorial Picture Gallery Meiji
Shrine
9 Kasumigaoka, Shinjuku-ku, Tokyo
Fine Arts Museum
Paintings

08557
Museum of Scientific Study Tokyo
University
7-3-1 Hongo, Bunkyo-ku, Tokyo
Natural History Museum
Coll: paleontology; anthropology;
botany; zoology; archeology;
mineralogy; material and specimens
from Iran, Iraq, and the Andes
mountain area

08558
**Museum of the Technology of Safety
in Industry** Ministry of Labor
5-35-1 Shiba, Minato-ku, Tokyo
Science/Tech Museum - 1942
Coll: materials on industrial safety

08559
National Museum of Western Art
7-7 Ueno-koen, Taito-ku, Tokyo 110
Fine Arts Museum - 1959
Coll: European art; French
Impressionists; Old Masters' paintings;
sculpture; print collection - library

08560
National Science Museum
7-20 Ueno Park, Taito-ku, Tokyo
Science/Tech Museum - 1872
Coll: natural history; lichens; Japanese
butterflies; zoology; fossils; minerals;
geology; scientific apparatuses and
machines - library

08561
Nezu Institute of Fine Arts
6-5-36 Minami-aoyama, Minato-ku,
Tokyo 107
Fine Arts Museum - 1940
Coll: Japanese paintings; calligraphy;
sculpture; ceramics; lacquer items;
metalwork; Chinese bronzes; Buddhist
art; tea-ceremony utensils; Korean
ceramics; European clocks - library

08562
Odawara Crustacea Museum
3-11-4 Azabu-Juban, Minato-ku, Tokyo
Natural History Museum
Coll: natural sciences; specimens of
Crustacea

08563
Okura Museum
3 Aoi-cho, Akasaka, Minato-ku, Tokyo
Fine Arts Museum - 1916
Coll: Japanese paintings; sculpture;
calligraphy; poems by Koetsu;
Chinese printed books; ceramics and
porcelain; Chinese bronzes; swords;
lacquer wares; No masks and robes

08564
Paper Museum
1-8 Horifune 1 chome, Kita-ku, Tokyo
114
Science/Tech Museum - 1950
Coll: specimens of ancient hand-made
paper; various types of paper, both
hand-made and machine-made; paper-
made goods; machines and tools for
making paper; the 'Hyakumanto,' the
oldest printed matter in the world (770
A.D.) - library; audiovisual and crafts
room

08565
Riccar Art Museum
Riccar Building, 6-2-3 Ginza, Chuo-ku,
Tokyo
Fine Arts Museum
Coll: over 6,000 ukiyo-e prints; exhibits
on the technique of print-making -
library

08566
Ryushi Memorial Gallery
4-2-1 Chuo, Ota-ku, Tokyo
Historic Site
Coll: 100 works by the painter Ryushi
Kawabata; screens; his colors and
brushes; sketches; photographs of the
artist; the artist's former house

08567
Science Museum
2-1 Kitanomaru Park, Chiyodaku,
Tokyo
Science/Tech Museum - 1959
Coll: models; experimental
apparatuses; physical sciences;
industrial exhibits

08568
Seikado
2-23-1 Okamoto, Setagaya-ku, Tokyo
Fine Arts Museum - 1977
Iwasaki family collection of Chinese
paintings, Sung printed books,
Japanese painting, Buddhist paintings,
screens, ukiyo-e prints, calligraphy,
swords, and ceramics - library

08569
Sumo Museum
2-19-9 Kuramae, Asakusa Taito-ku,
Tokyo
History/Public Affairs Museum - 1954
Coll: objects related to the history and
traditions of sumo, Japanese wrestling;
pictures; printed matter and books;
photographs; sumo utensils

08570
Suntory Museum of Art
Tokyo Suntory Building, 1-2-3
Moto-akasaka, Minato-ku, Tokyo
Fine Arts Museum - 1961
Coll: lacquer objects; glassware;
costumes; genre screens; woodblock
prints; ceramics; masks; iron
teakettles; 18th-19th century ukiyo-e
prints; paintings - library; reading
room; tea-ceremony room

08571
Sword Museum
4-25-10 Yoyogi, Shibuya-ku, Tokyo
History/Public Affairs Museum
Coll: swords from all ages; suit of
armor; stirrups; sword guards; books
and photographs

08572
Takanawa Art Museum
4-10-30 Takanawa, Minato-ku, Tokyo
Fine Arts Museum
Coll: Japanese paintings of the recent
past; Buddhist sculpture; Japanese
lacquer; Chinese and Korean
ceramics

08573
Tenri Gallery
19, 1-chome, Nishiki-cho, Kanda,
Chiyoda-ku, Tokyo
Fine Arts Museum
Coll: paintings; art

08574
Tokyo Fire Department PR Center
13-20, Hatagaya 1 chome, Shibuya-ku,
Tokyo 151
History/Public Affairs Museum - 1959
Coll: uniforms of people's fire brigade
and fire coat of the feudal lord fire
brigade; wooden fire pump; fire
company standards; fire watch tower;
ladder truck - library; educational
center

08575
Tokyo Metropolitan Art Museum
8-36 Ueno Koen, Taito-ku, Tokyo
Fine Arts Museum - 1975
Coll: Japanese art over the last 50
years; paintings; prints; sculpture;
calligraphy; handicrafts - galleries; art
studios; art school

08576
Tokyo Metropolitan Art Museum
Ueno Park 8, Daito-ku, Tokyo
Fine Arts Museum - 1925
Coll: modern and contemporary art -
library

08577
Tokyo National Museum
13-9 Ueno Park, Daito-ku, Tokyo
General Museum - 1871
Coll: Japanese archeology; Buddhist
paintings; sutras and calligraphy;
narrative scrolls; prints; Buddhist
sculpture; complete range of Japanese
pottery; No and Kyogen masks and
costumes; history of arms and armor;
lacquer collection; Chinese sculptures,
paintings, ceramics, and bronzes;
Korean metalwork and ceramics

08578
**Tokyo National Museum of Modern
Art**
3 Kitanomaru Koen, Chiyoda-ku,
Tokyo 102
Fine Arts Museum - 1952
Coll: Japanese paintings; sculpture;
drawings and watercolors; prints; 20th
century Japanese crafts; modern and
contemporary art; calligraphy

08579
**Tokyo National University of Fine
Arts and Music Art Museum**
Ueno Park, Daito-ku, Tokyo
Fine Arts Museum
Coll: paintings; sculptures; industrial
art

08580
**Tokyo University of Arts Exhibition
Hall**
Taito-ku, Tokyo
Fine Arts Museum
Coll: Chinese metalwork, lacquer
items, ceramics, and paintings;
Japanese painting; 19th-20th century
handicrafts and sculpture; Japanese
Buddhist sculpture; textiles

08581
Transport Museum
25, 1-chome, Kanda-Suda-cho,
Chiyoda-ku, Tokyo
Science/Tech Museum - 1921
Coll: railway train; locomotives; motor
cars; omnibus; aeroplane; 19th century
rickshaw; models of 16th century
fighting vessels

08582
**Tsubouchi Memorial Theatre
Museum** Waseda University
1-6-1 Nishi-Waseda, Shinjuku-ku,
Tokyo
Performing Arts Museum - 1928
Coll: literary works, manuscripts, and
personal effects of Tsubouchi, 'Father
of the Japanese Theatre;' building
modeled after Elizabethan theater;
exhibits on folk dances; masks,
costumes, and pictures of dance-plays;
models of stages, masks, costumes,
musical instruments used in No and
Kyogen productions; photographs;
puppets; exhibit on Western drama
tradition; film and historical movie
equipment - library; reading room;
reference facilities

08583
Ueno Royal Museum
1-2 Ueno Koen, Taito-ku, Tokyo
Fine Arts Museum - 1971
Coll: contemporary calligraphy; print
collection

08584
Umezawa Memorial Gallery
2-9 Kanda-Surugadai, Chiyoda-ku,
Tokyo
Fine Arts Museum
Umezawa's collection of Japanese and
Chinese paintings, calligraphy, and
ceramics including Korean ceramics

08585
Yamatane Museum of Art
2-30 Kabuto-cho, Nihonbashi, Chuo-ku,
Tokyo 103
Fine Arts Museum - 1966
Coll: 700 Japanese-style paintings
from the 19th century to the present -
library; tea-ceremony room

08586
Yokoyama Taikan Memorial Gallery
1-4-24 Ikenohata, Taito-ku, Tokyo
Fine Arts Museum
Coll: paintings by Taikan Yokoyama;
his painting materials; Yokoyama's
collection of ceramics - garden

Tomioka

08587
Gumma Prefectural Museum
1353 Ichinomiya, Tomioka, Gumma
General Museum - 1957
Coll: archeological finds; ethnographic exhibition including farm tools, straw raincoats, lanterns, and puppet heads; armor and swords; ukiyo-e prints

Tottori

08588
Tottori Folk Art Museum
653 Sakae-cho, Tottori, Tottori
General Museum
Coll: Chinese, Japanese, Korean, and European ceramics; lacquer vessels; furniture; small stone Buddhist figures

08589
Tottori Prefectural Museum
2-124 Higashi-machi, Tottori, Tottori
General Museum - 1949
Coll: fine arts; archeological material; folk arts; household implements; reconstructed farmhouse interior

Toyama

08590
Toyama City Folk Art Museum
1104 Doshinzan, Anyobo, Toyama, Toyama
Anthropology Museum
Coll: textiles; ceramics; lacquer items; furniture; clothing; basketry; in reconstructed farmhouse

08591
Toyama Municipal Museum
1-62 Honmaru, Toyama, Toyama
General Museum
Coll: ukiyo-e prints on local medicine; materials illustrating manufacture of medicine; ceramics; tiles; armor; archeological material

Toyonaka

08592
Japanese Village Farmhouse Museum
1-2 Hattori Ryokuchi, Toyonaka, Osaka
Open Air Museum
Coll: farmhouses; rural buildings; thatched granaries; a rural Kabuki theater

Toyota

08593
Kosan-ji Museum
553-2 Setoda-cho, Toyota, Hiroshima
Religious Art Museum
Coll: Chinese bronze vessels, pottery vessels, figurines, and gilt-bronze Buddhist figures; Buddhist sculpture; Japanese swords and armor; miniature shrine; paintings; documents; calligraphy; ceramics

Tsu

08594
Mie Prefectural Museum
147 Komei-cho, Tsu, Mie
General Museum - 1953
Coll: fossils

Tsukubo

08595
Kibi Archaeological Collection
Yamate-mura, Jitokatayama, Tsukubo, Okayama
Archeology Museum
Coll: Jomon pottery and stone implements; ceramics; ironwork; roof tiles

Tsuruga

08596
Tsuruga Provincial Museum
Yahata Shrine, Mishima, Tsuruga, Fukui
Natural History Museum
Natural history

Tsuruoka

08597
Chido Museum
10-18 Kachu-shinmachi, Tsuruoka, Yamagata
General Museum - 1950
Coll: archeological findings with photos and illustrations of excavation sites; uniforms; Japanese and Western clothing; documents; historical photographs; rickshaws; swords and armor; calligraphy; paintings; fishing and farming gear; folk art including backpacks, dolls, lacquer items

Tsuyama

08598
Tsuyama Municipal History Hall
26 Minamishinza, Tsuyama, Okayama
General Museum
Coll: local archeological finds including pottery, swords, metal tools, and large ceramic coffins from Kofun tumuli of the region; historical documents and letters; samples of calligraphy; books - library

Ueda

08599
Ueda Municipal Museum
Ueda Koen, 3-3 Ninomaru, Ueda, Nagano
General Museum
Coll: arms and armor; chests; scrolls; ceramics; reconstructed farmhouse interior; costumes; local wares; local archeological material

08600
Yamamoto Kanae Memorial Gallery
Ueda Koen, 3-4 Ninomaru, Ueda, Nagano
Fine Arts Museum
Coll: oil paintings, watercolors, and drawings by Kanae Yamamoto; his palette and personal effects

Ueno

08601
Basho Memorial Gallery
Marunouchi, Ueno, Mie
Historic Site
Coll: 50 scrolls of calligraphy of the famous 27th century haiku poet Matsuo Basho and his pupils; statue of poet who was born here - library

08602
Iga Art and Industry Institute
6, 1-Marunouchi, Ueno, Mie
Decorative Arts Museum
Coll: art; industrial art

08603
Iga-Ryu Ninja Yashiki
Ueno Koen, Marunouchi, Ueno, Mie
General Museum
Coll: clothes, swords, ladders, climbing tools, and other equipment used by the 'ninja,' men serving as spies for the shogunate; costumed mannequins with demon masks

Uji

08604
Byodo-in Treasure House
116 Uji Renge, Uji, Nara
Religious Art Museum - 1972
Coll: painted doors; bronze phoenixes; a large bell; wooden Buddhist angels; exhibits about the painted designs on the wooden beams of the temple

Utsunomiya

08605
Tochigi Prefectural Museum of Fine Arts
4-2-7 Sakura, Utsunomiya, Tochigi
Fine Arts Museum
Coll: Japanese paintings; crafts; sculpture

Wakayama

08606
Wakayama Prefectural Modern Art Museum
1-1 Komatsubara-dori, Wakayama, Wakayama
Fine Arts Museum
Coll: contemporary paintings; sculpture; prints

08607
Wakayama Prefectural Museum
Wakayama-jo, 1 cho, Ichiban, Wakayama, Wakayama
Fine Arts Museum
Coll: painted room dividers and vertical wall scrolls; paintings; portable shrine; ceramics

Yama

08608
Dr Hideyo Noguchi Memorial Hall
Sanjogata, Inawashiro-machi, Yama, Fukushima
Historic Site - 1939
Coll: house where the bacteriologist Dr. Noguchi was born; his bust; personal effects; scientific equipment; personal library

Yamagata

08609
Geihoku Ethnographical Museum
Yashige, Chiyoda-machi, Yamagata, Hiroshima
Anthropology Museum
Coll: anthropology; ethnography; folklore

08610
Yamagata Art Museum
1-63 Ote-machi, Yamagata, Yamagata
Fine Arts Museum - 1962
Coll: paintings; sculpture; handicraft; bronzes - galleries

08611
Yamagata Prefectural Museum
Kajo Koen, 1-8 Kajo-machi, Yamagata, Yamagata
General Museum - 1970
Coll: archeological finds; ethnographic material; folk art; natural history; local wares; geology

Yamaguchi

08612
Yamaguchi Prefectural Museum
8-2 Kasuga-machi, Yamaguchi, Yamaguchi
General Museum - 1916
Coll: prehistorical and medieval archeological finds; contemporary ceramics and paintings; natural history; science exhibits

Yamato-Koriyama

08613
Nara Prefectural Ethnographic Museum
545 Yata-cho, Yamato-Koriyama, Nara
Anthropology Museum - 1974
Coll: exhibit on the agricultural life of the area before modern equipment; rice culture; tea plantations; lumbering; tools; photographs and drawings; household lacquer utensils; clothing; baskets; portable shrines

Yasugi

08614
Adachi Art Museum
320 Furukawa-cho, Yasugi, Shimane
Fine Arts Museum - 1970
Coll: 20th century Japanese paintings; ceramics; sculpture; woodprints - Japanese garden; library

Yasuki

08615
Wako Memorial Hall
881 Yasuki-machi, Yasuki, Shimane
Science/Tech Museum - 1943
Coll: iron manufacture; materials on traditional techniques; natural history

Yokohama

08616
Kanagawa Prefectural Museum
5-60 Minaminaka-dori, Naka-ku, Yokohama, Kanagawa
General Museum
Coll: exhibits on local weaving, farming, and fishing; household tools; Bunraku puppets; archeological finds with photos and models of excavation sites; late medieval sculpture and painting; models of temples and villas; history of the region

08617
Kanazawa Bunko
217 Kanazawa-machi, Kanazawa-ku, Yokohama, Kanagawa
General Museum - 1275
Coll: sculpture; painting; calligraphy; historical documents; Buddhist sutras and Zen writings - library

08618
Sankei-en
293 Sannotani, Honmoku, Naka-ku, Yokohama, Kanagawa
Open Air Museum
Coll: villas; teahouses; temple; pagoda; wealthy farmer's house; decorative sliding doors - resthouse; gallery

08619
Yokohama Museum of Oceanography
15 Yamashita-cho, Naka-ku, Yokohama, Kanagawa
Science/Tech Museum - 1961
Coll: ships; marine products; maritime transportation

Yokosuka

08620
Kannonzaki Fishery Science Museum Kannonzaki Fishery Biological Institute
Yokosuka, Kanagawa
Science/Tech Museum - 1953
Coll: fishery; fish biology; history of sea exploration; ecology of marine organisms

08621
Yokosuka City Museum Kurihama Branch
6-14-1 Kurihama, Yokosuka, Kanagawa
General Museum - 1953
Coll: archeological finds with maps and photos; ethnographic materials

Yonago

08622
San-in Historical Museum
Nishi-machi, Yonago, Tottori
History/Public Affairs Museum - 1940
Coll: exhibits and specimens of historical interest; archeology

Yonezawa

08623
Uesugi-jinga Treasure House
1-14-13 Marunouchi, Yonezawa, Yamagata
Religious Art Museum
Coll: paintings; documents; textiles; 16th century costumes; armor, swords, and spears

Yoshida

08624
Eiheiji, 'Temple of Eternal Peace'
Eiheiji, Yoshida, Fukui
Religious Art Museum - 1244
Coll: 70 buildings comprising the monastery Eiheiji for the practice of Zen; religious art and furnishings; sculpture and carvings; holy treasure house with writings of Zenji Dogen, the founder of the monastery, 14th century temple bell

Yoshino

08625
Nyoirin-ji Treasure House
1024 Yoshinoyama, Yoshino-cho, Yoshino, Nara
Religious Art Museum
Coll: paintings; calligraphy; sculpture; armor and swords; objects of historical interest

08626
Yoshimizu-jinja Collection
Yoshinoyama, Yoshino-cho, Yoshino, Nara
Religious Art Museum
Coll: paintings; calligraphy; documents; arms and armor; metalwork; lacquer items; music instruments; ceramics; in the former residence of 14th century emperor; his personal effects

Zentsu-ji

08627
Zentsu-ji Treasure House
Zentsu-ji-cho, Zentsu-ji, Kagawa
Religious Art Museum
Coll: Japanese paintings; calligraphy; sculpture; ceramics; metalwork; Chinese paintings

Jordan

Amman

08628
Centre for Manuscripts and Archives
University of Jordan, Amman
History/Public Affairs Museum - 1974
Rare manuscripts - library

08629
Folklore Museum
POB 88, Amman
Anthropology Museum

08630
Jordan archaeological Museum
POB 88, Amman
Archeology Museum - 1923
library

08631
National Gallery of Painting
Amman
Fine Arts Museum

08632
Popular Life Museum
POB 88, Amman
History/Public Affairs Museum

Irbid

08633
Archaeological Museum
Irbid, *mail c/o* Dept. of antiquities, POB 88, Amman
Archeology Museum

Kerak

08634
Archaeological Museum
Kerak, *mail c/o* Dept. of Antiquities, POB 88, Amman
Archeology Museum

Madaba

08635
Archaeological Museum
Madaba, *mail c/o* Dept. of Antiquities, POB 88, Amman
Archeology Museum

08636
Folklore Museum
Madaba, *mail c/o* Dept. of Antiquities, POB 88, Amman
Anthropology Museum

Petra

08637
Archaeological Museum
Petra, *mail c/o* Dept. of Antiquities, POB 88, Amman
Archeology Museum

Kampuchea

Battambang

08638
Musée d'Archéologie
Battambang
Archeology Museum

08639
Musée Poveal
Battambang
Religious Art Museum - 1956
Archeological fragments; sculpture

Kampong Thom

08640
Musée
Kampong Thom
Archeology Museum

Phnom Penh

08641
Exposition Permanente des Realisations du Sangkum Reastr Niyum
Phnom Penh
History/Public Affairs Museum

08642
Musée del'Armee
Phnom Penh
History/Public Affairs Museum
Militaria

08643
Musée del'Institut Bouddhique
Phnom Penh
Anthropology Museum
Customs and traditions of the Khmer

08644
Musée du Palais Royal
Phnom Penh
History/Public Affairs Museum

0806
08645
Musée National de Phnom Penh
Phnom Penh
Fine Arts Museum - 1917
Khmer art from 5th to 13th cent. including specimens from Angkor Wat, Angkor Thom and Bantea Srei; decorative arts

Siemréap

08646
Conservation des Monuments d'Angkor
Siemréap
Archeology Museum
Stelae and other inscribed monuments

Kenya

Gilgil

08647
Kariandus Prehistoric Site
POB 32, Gilgil
Archeology Museum - 1928
Stone Age finds; fossils; drawings

Hyrax Hill

08648
Hyrax Hill Field Museum
Hyrax Hill
Archeology Museum
Neolithic finds

Kitale

08649
Kitale Museum
POB 1219, Kitale, Rift Valley
General Museum - 1926
Local ethnography - library

Lamu

08650
National Museum of Lamu
POB 48, Lamu
General Museum
Ethnology and folklore; decorative arts; silver and gold work; carved wood

Meru

08651
Meru Museum
St Pauls Rd, POB 597, Meru, Eastern Province
General Museum - 1973
Material culture of the Meru tribe; tools of the prehistoric Achulean culture; entomological and ornithological collections from the Mt Kenya region

Mombasa

08652
National Museum
Nkrumah Rd, POB 82412, Mombasa
General Museum - 1962
Chinese porcelain; Islamic and local wares from archaeological sites on the coast of Kenya; Arab woodwork and ceramics

Nairobi

08653
National Museum
POB 40658, Nairobi
Natural History Museum
Natural history of Eastern Africa; palaeontology; prehistory; archaeology; ethnography; geology; zoology

Olorgesailie

08654
Olorgesailie Prehistoric Site Museum
Magadi Rd 27, Olorgesailie, POB 40658, Nairobi
Archeology Museum
Stone Age finds

Korea, Democratic People's Republic

P'yongyang

08655
Korean Revolutionary Museum
P'yongyang
History/Public Affairs Museum
Historical exhibits from 1850 to the present

08656
State Central Ethnographical Museum
P'yongyang
Anthropology Museum
Coll: anthropology; ethnography

08657
State Central Fine Arts Museum
P'yongyang
Fine Arts Museum
Korean art

08658
State Central Historical Museum
P'yongyang
History/Public Affairs Museum
Exhibits on Korean history from prehistory to the 20th century

08659
State Central Museum on the Struggle for Liberation
P'yongyang
History/Public Affairs Museum
Coll: historic material on the 19th century to the present; exhibits on the war against Japan (1930) and the Korean War

Korea, Republic

Andong

08660
Andong Teachers' College Museum
Andong, Kyongsang 660

08661
Sangji College Museum
Yulse-dong, Andong, North
Kyongsang 660

Asan

08662
Onyang Folk Museum
403 Kwongok-ni, Onyang-eup, Asan,
South Ch'ungch'ong 331
Anthropology Museum - 1978
Traditional arts of Korea; folklore -
library; audiovisual room

Cheju

08663
Cheju College Museum
Yongdam 2-dong, Cheju, Cheju 590

08664
Cheju Folklore Museum
2506-2 Samyang Sam-Dong, Cheju,
Cheju 29
Anthropology Museum - 1964
Domestic tools and utensils; cultural
artifacts - library

08665
Napeup Folklore Museum
Sokuipo-eup, Cheju, Cheju 590-40
Anthropology Museum

Ch'ongju

08666
Ch'ongju University Museum
36 Naedeok-dong, Ch'ongju, North
Ch'ungch'ong
Anthropology Museum - 1967
Coll: local customs and folklore -
library

Chonju

08667
Chonbuk University Museum
1-664-14 Dokjin-dong, Chonju, North
Cholla 520

08668
Chonju Municipal Museum
Poongnam-dong, Chonju, North Cholla
520
General Museum

08669
Chonju Teachers' College Museum
Dongsohak-dong, Chonju, North
Cholla 520

Ch'unch'on

08670
Ch'unch'on Folk Museum
Ch'unch'on, Kangwon
General Museum

Inchon

08671
Inchon Municipal Museum
1 Songhak-dong 1-ga, Inchon, Kyonggi
160
General Museum

Iri

08672
Won Kwang College Museum
344-2 Sinyong-dong, Iri, North Cholla
510-11

Jinhae

08673
Naval Academy Museum
Jinhae, South Kyongsang 602

Kamiminochi

08674
Shinshu-shinmachi Art Museum
179 Oaza Shinmachi, Shinshu-
shinmachi, Kamiminochi, Nagano
Fine Arts Museum
Coll: paintings; watercolors; sculpture;
prints; Maruyama collection of
calligraphy and paintings

Kangreung

08675
Kangreung College Museum
Kangreung, Kangwon 210

08676
Kwandong College Museum
72-1 Naegok-dong, Kangreung,
Kangwon 210

Kongju

08677
**Kongju College of Education
Museum**
9-6 Sinkwan-ri-san, Janggi-myun,
Kongju, South Ch'ungch'ong

08678
Kongju National Museum National
Museum, Seoul
Kongju, South Ch'ungch'ong
Fine Arts Museum
Coll: archeological finds; Korean art

Koryong

08679
Koryong County Museum
Yonjo-dong, Koryong-myun, Koryong,
North Kyongsang 630-30
General Museum

Kwangju

08680
Chonnam University Museum
318 Yongbong-dong, Kwangju, South
Cholla 500

08681
Kwangju Municipal Museum
21 Su-dong, Kwangju, South Cholla
General Museum

08682
Kwangju National Museum National
Museum, Seoul
Kwangju, South Cholla
Fine Arts Museum
Coll: archeological finds; Korean art

Kyongju

08683
Kyongju National Museum National
Museum, Seoul
Kyongju, North Kyongsang
Archeology Museum - 1915
Coll: cultural objects of the Silla
Dynasty; 6th-7th century funeral
offerings

Kyongsan

08684
Youngnam University Museum
214 Dae-dong, Kyongsan-eup,
Kyongsan, North Kyongsang 632

Masan

08685
Kyongnam College Museum
449 Wolyong-dong, Masan, South
Kyongsang 610

Pusan

08686
Dong-a University Museum
1 Dongdaesin-dong, 3-ga, Soh-gu,
Pusan 600

08687
Municipal Museum of Pusan
948-1 Dayeon-Dong, Nam-gu, Pusan
601-01
General Museum - 1978
Coll: earthenware of the prehistoric
and Kaya Period; ceramics; historical
materials; painting; caligraphy; arts and
crafts - library; auditorium; research
room

08688
Pusan National University Museum
31 Changjeon-dong, Jongnae-gu,
Pusan 600
Archeology Museum - 1963
Coll: archeology; cultural relics;
ethnology; art objects; historical items
from South Kyongsang

Puyo

08689
Puyo National Museum National
Museum, Seoul
Puyo, South Ch'ungch'ong
Archeology Museum - 1939
Cultural articles of the Packche
Dynasty (18 B.C.-660 A.D.)

Seoul

08690
Chang-duk Palace
Seoul
History/Public Affairs Museum
Coll: regalia and costumes; utensils;
arms; seals; manuscripts; historic
items; photographic documentation on
the Yi dynasty; furnishings

08691
Dan Kook University Museum
8-3 Hannam-dong-san, Yongsan-gu,
Seoul 140

08692
Dongguk University Museum
3-26 Pil-dong, Joong-gu, Seoul 100

08693
Duksung Women's College
114 Wunni-dong, Jongro-gu, Seoul 110
Fine Arts Museum - 1971
Folk art and crafts related to customs
and manners of women in ancient
Korea; modern painting; theatrical
masks and costumes - library

08694
Emile Museum
206 Deungchon-dong, Kangsoh-gu,
Seoul 150-01

08695
Ewha Women's University Museum
11-1 Daehyon-dong, Sodaemun-gu,
Seoul 120
Fine Arts Museum - 1935
Gold ornaments; porcelain; paintings
of Yi Dynasty; furniture; sculpture -
library

08696
Gan-Song Art Museum Center for
the Study of Korean Arts
97-1 Sung Buk-dong, Sung Buk-gu,
Seoul 132
Fine Arts Museum - 1938
Korean art

08697
Handok Medico-Pharma Museum
344 Sangbong-dong, Dongdaemun-gu,
Central POB 30, Seoul 130-01
History/Public Affairs Museum - 1964
Mortars and pots for preparation of
medicine; medicine chests; medical
instruments and equipment; old
medical books - library

08698
Hansong Women's College Museum
2-392-2 Samson-dong, Songbuk-gu,
Seoul 132

08699
Hong-ik University Museum
72-1 Sangsu-dong, Mapo-gu, Seoul
121

08700
Joongang University Museum
221 Heuksok-dong, Kwanak-gu, Seoul
151

08701
Konkuk University Museum
93 Mojin-dong, Songdong-gu, Seoul
133
Archeology Museum - 1963
Mousterian implements from the
Chungok site - library

08702
Kookmin College Museum
861-1 Jongreung-dong, Songbuk-gu,
Seoul 132

08703
Korea University Museum
5 Anam-dong, Songbuk-gu, Seoul 132
Archeology Museum
Coll: archeology; ethnology

08704
Kyong-bok Art Gallery
Kyong-bok Palace, Seoul
Fine Arts Museum
National art

08705
Kyung Hee University Museum
1 Hoeki-dong, Dongdaemun-gu, Seoul
131

08706
Military Academy Museum
Kongreung-dong, Songbuk-gu, Seoul
132

08707
Myong Ji University Museum
4-2 Namgajwa-dong, Seodaemun-gu,
Seoul 120

08708
National Folklore Museum National
Museum, Seoul
1 Se-jong Ro, Chjong-Ro Ku, Kyong-
bok Palace, Seoul 110
Anthropology Museum - 1966
Korean traditional and folk arts

08709
National Museum of Korea
1 Sejong-re, Kyongbok Palace, Seoul
110
General Museum - 1915
Coll: gold crowns and jewelry; Korean
pottery; Central Asian Buddhist
paintings; archeological material from
Korean sites; Chinese ceramics and
other items from Sung and Yuan
periods; Chinese material from burials
of a Han period Chinese settlement
(108-313 A.D.); Central Asian collection
of murals - library

08710
National Museum of Modern Art
5-1 Jong-dong, Jung-gu, Seoul 100
Fine Arts Museum - 1969
Modern and contemporary Korean art

08711
National Science Museum
2 Waryong-dong, Jongro-gu, Seoul
110
Natural History Museum - 1927
Coll: natural history; zoology; reptiles;
fossils - library; science classrooms

08712
National University Museum
Sinrim-dong, Kwanak-gu, Seoul 151
General Museum
Coll: paintings; calligraphy;
archeology; ethnology; exhibits on
rural and traditional cultures;
Shamanism

08713
Sejong College Museum
2 Kunja-dong-san, Songdong-gu, Seoul
133

08714
Sokang University Museum
1 Sinsu-dong, Mapo-gu, Seoul 121

08715
Songsin Teachers' College Museum
2-249-1 Dongson-dong, Songbuk-gu,
Seoul 132

08716
**Sookmyung Women's University
Museum**
2-52-12 Chongpa-dong, Yongsan-gu,
Seoul 140

08717
**Sung Kyun Kwan University
Museum**
3-53 Myungryun-dong, Jongro-gu,
Seoul 110

08718
Sungjon University Museum
135 Sangdo-dong, Kwanak-gu, Seoul
151

08719
Yonsei University Museum
134 Sinchon-dong, Sodaemun-gu,
Seoul 120
Anthropology Museum - 1965
Palaeolithic and Neolithic implements;
palaeontological collection; ceramics -
library

Taegu

08720
Kyemyong University Museum
Daemyong-dong, Nam-gu, Taegu,
North Kyongsang 634

08721
Kyongbuk University Museum
1370 Sangyeok-dong, Buk-gu, Taegu,
North Kyongsang 635

08722
Taegu Teachers' College Museum
Taegu, North Kyongsang 630

Taejon

08723
Chungnam University Museum
1 Munhwa-dong-san, Taejon, South
Ch'ungch'ong 300

Yongin

08724
Hoam Museum
Yongin Farm of Nature, Yongin,
Kyonggi 170-40
Agriculture Museum

Kuwait

Kuwait City

08725
Kuwait Museum
Kuwait City
Archeology Museum
Excavation findings from Failaka
Island, dating back to Babylonian times

08726
**Science and Natural History
Museum** Ministry of Education
Kuwait City
Natural History Museum - 1972
Coll: natural history; science; oil;
astronomy; health - library,
planetarium

Laos

Vientiane

08727
Ho Phakeo
mail c/o Direction de Musée National
Lao, Settathiraj Rd, BP 67, Vientiane
Historic Site - 1965
Site built in 1563 by King Setthathiraj

08728
That Luang
mail c/o Direction de Musée National
Lao, Saysettha District, BP 67,
Vientiane
Historic Site
Site built by King Saysetthathiraj in
1566

08729
Wat Sisaket
mail c/o Direction de Musée National
Lao, Lang Xang Av, BP 67, Vientiane
1828

Lebanon

Beirut

08730
Archaeology Museum American
University of Beirut
Post Hall, Bliss St, POB 236/9, Beirut
Archeology Museum - 1868
Flint implements; bronze tools;
pottery; glassware; coins; sculpture;
cylindrical seals

08731
**Musée de Préhistoire Libanaise de
l'Université Saint Joseph**
BP 293, Beirut
Natural History Museum - 1963
Natural sciences; prehistory

08732
Musée des Beaux Arts
BP 3939, Beirut
Fine Arts Museum

08733
Musée National
Rue de Damas, Beirut
Archeology Museum - 1920
Royal jewelry; arms and statues of the
Phoenician epoch; sarcophagus of
King Ahiram (13th cent. B.C.); Greek
and Hellenistic sarcophagi; Roman and
Byzantine mosaics; Arabic wooden
items and ceramics; coins

Bsharrī

08734
Musée Khalil Gibran
Bsharrī
Historic Site
Memorabilia and works of poet Khalil
Gibran

Lesotho

Maseru

08735
Lesotho National Museum
POB 1125, Maseru 100
General Museum

Morija

08736
Morija Museum
POB 4, Morija
General Museum
Ethnography of Lesotho; geological
specimens; Stone Age tools and
fossils

Liberia

Monrovia

08737
Biology Museum
University of Liberia, Monrovia
Natural History Museum

08738
National Museum of Liberia
Capitol Hill, Monrovia
General Museum
Liberian culture; ceremonial masks;
musical instruments; historical artifacts

Robertsport

08739
Tubman Centre of African Culture
Robertsport
Anthropology Museum - 1964
African sculpture; weaving; cultural
artifacts

Libya

Benghazi

08740
El-Agoria Museum
Benghazi
Archeology Museum
Classical antiquities

Cyrene

08741
Cyrene Archaeological Museum
Cyrene
Archeology Museum - 1979
Sculpture; coins; mosaics; pottery of
Greek and Roman periods

08742
Eddersia Archaeological Museum
mail c/o Dept. of Antiquities Cyrene
Archeology Museum
Greek, Roman, and Byzantine
collections

08743
**El-Gaigab Ethnographical and
Natural History Museum**
mail c/o Dept. of Antiquities Cyrene
General Museum - 1975

Marsā Sūsah

08744
Apollonia Archaeological Museum
Marsā Susāh, *mail c/o* Dept. of
Antiquities Cyrene
General Museum - 1980
Greek, Roman, Byzantine, Arabic and
Islamic collections; coins; sculpture

Sabrata

08745
Sabrata Archaeological Museum
Sabrata, *mail c/o* Directorate General
of Antiquities Tripoli
Archeology Museum
Classical antiquities

Sebha

08746
Germa Archaeological Museum
Sebha
Archeology Museum
Finds from Jerma and the Ubari Ghat
track

Tripoli

08747
Archaeological Museum
Essaraya El-Hamra, Tripoli
Archeology Museum - 1919
Phoenician, Roman and Byzantine
antiquities; Roman mosaics - library

08748
Epigraphy Museum
Essaraya El-Hamra, Tripoli
Archeology Museum - 1919
Phoenician, Roman and Byzantine
inscriptions; inscriptions of Wadi
Al-Amoud

08749
Ethnographic Museum
Essaraya El-Hamra, Tripoli
Anthropology Museum - 1952

08750
Natural History Museum
Essaraya El-Hamra, Tripoli
Natural History Museum - 1936
Geology; botany; insects; birds;
mammals; amphibians; reptiles; marine
life; embryology - library

08751
Prehistory Museum
Essaraya El-Hamra, Tripoli
Archeology Museum - 1952
Finds from the excavation at Hagfet et
Tera

Liechtenstein

Triesenberg

08752
Heimatmuseum
mail c/o Gemeinde-Vorstehung,
Hagstr. 19, FL-9497 Triesenberg
General Museum - 1961
Cultural history of the Walser region,
including interiors, weaving, farm
implements, weights and measures,
religious folk art; 17th century Walser
house

Vaduz

08753
**Liechtensteinische Staatliche
Kunstsammlung**
Städtle 37, FL-9490 Vaduz
Fine Arts Museum - 1968
Modern graphic art

08754
Liechtensteinisches Landesmuseum
Städtle 43, FL-9490 Vaduz
General Museum - 1954
Pre- and protohistory (finds from neolithic to alamannic period excavations in Liechtenstein); local history; ecclesiastical sculptures; folklore; numismatics; weapons from the prince's collection; 15th century tavern

08755
Postmuseum des Fürstentums Liechtenstein
Städtle 37, FL-9490 Vaduz
History/Public Affairs Museum - 1930
Stamp collection: philately; stamps from Liechtenstein; designs; print and colour samples; clichés and stamping machinery; exhibition awards; rare items from all over the world; literature

08756
Sammlungen des Regierenden Fürsten von Liechtenstein
Schloß Vaduz, FL-9490 Vaduz
Fine Arts Museum
15th-19th century German paintings and sculptures; Rubens collection (sketches, Decius-Mus-Zyklus); weapons; furniture; tapestry; 18th century state carriage made by Nicolas Pineau

Luxembourg

Bech-Kleinmacher

08757
Musée Folklorique et Viticole 'a Possen'
rue Sandt, 16, Bech-Kleinmacher
Anthropology Museum - 1972
Wine barrels and other wine-making equipmemt; domestic utensils; toys; all housed in a restored 17th century wine maker's house

Brandenbourg

08758
Musée Local
Brandenbourg
General Museum

Clervaux

08759
Musée Historique
Château, Clervaux
General Museum
Documents of the Battle of Ardennes; photos by Edward Steichen

Ehnen

08760
Musée du Vin
Ehnen
Agriculture Museum

Esch

08761
Musée de la Résistance
Esch
History/Public Affairs Museum

Luxembourg

08762
Galerie Municipale de Peinture de la Ville du Luxembourg
18 av de l'Arsenal, Luxembourg
Fine Arts Museum
Painting

08763
Musée de l'Etat
Marché aux Poissons, Luxembourg
General Museum
Archaeology; fine arts; folklore; decorative and applied arts; firearms; numismatics; natural history - library

08764
Museum d'Histoire Naturelle
Marché aux Poissons, Luxembourg
Natural History Museum - 1850
Zoology; botany; mineralogy and geology; invertebrates; mollusks; insects; amphibians; reptiles; mammals

Nospelt

08765
Musée de la Poterie
Nospelt
Decorative Arts Museum

Rumelange

08766
Musée des Mines
Rumelange
Science/Tech Museum

Vianden

08767
Maison Victor Hugo
Vianden
History/Public Affairs Museum

08768
Musée Folklorique
Vianden
Anthropology Museum

Weiler-la-Tour

08769
Musée Local
Weiler-la-Tour
General Museum

Wiltz

08770
Musée de la Bataille des Ardennes
Wiltz
History/Public Affairs Museum

Macao

Macao

08771
Museu Luís de Camões
Praca Luís de Camões, Macao
History/Public Affairs Museum
Historical memorabilia

Madagascar

Nosy-Bé

08772
Musée de Centre O.R.S.T.O.M.
B.P. 68, Nosy-Bé
Natural History Museum
Invertebrates; insects

Tananarive

08773
Musée d'Art et d'Archéologie
18, rue Docteur Villette, Tananarive
Fine Arts Museum
Art and archaeological collections

08774
Musée d'O.R.S.T.O.M.
B.P. 434, Tananarive
Natural History Museum - 1947
Zoology; botany; fossils; birds (aviary); herbarium; art works - library

08775
Musée Folklorique, Archéologique, Paléontologique et Faunistique
Institut de Recherches Scientifiques à Madagascar
Parc de Tsimbazaza, Tananarive
General Museum
Folklore; archaeology; paleontology; local fauna; pottery; Malagasy art

08776
Musée Historique
Palais de la Reine, Tananarive
History/Public Affairs Museum

08777
Salle des Beaux Arts
Palais de la Rein, Tananarive
Fine Arts Museum

Malawi

Chichiri Blantyre

08778
Museum of Malawi
Kamuzu Highway, POB 30360, Chichiri Blantyre, 3
General Museum - 1959
Local and national history; reconstructed trational hut with furnishings and implements; traditional weaving, iron implements and ceremonial regalia

Mangoche

08779
Lake Malawi Museum
Mangoche
General Museum
Local history and customs; artifacts related to the lake and local fishing

Namaka

08780
Mtengatenga Postal Museum
Namaka
General Museum
History of local postal services, housed in traditional carrier's rest hut - post office

Malaysia

Alor Setar

08781
Kedah State Museum
Bakar Bata, Alor Setar, Kedah
General Museum
gold and silver flowers; local weapons and ceramics - library

Ipoh

08782
Geological Survey Museum
Scrivenor Road (off Tiger Lane), POB 1015, Ipoh, Perak
Science/Tech Museum - 1955
Malaysian geological exhibits

Kinabalu

08783
Sabah Museum
Gaya Street, 1239, Kinabalu, Sabah
General Museum - 1886
Anthropology; archaeology; natural history and historic collections of Sabah

Kuala Lumpur

08784
Museum of Asian Art
University of Malaya, Kuala Lumpur
Fine Arts Museum - 1974
Southeast Asian textiles and ceramics; classical Indian, Thai, Indonesian and Cambodian sculpture; contemporary Malaysian painting; Moghul miniature painting; Malaysian applied arts and crafts; Chinese painting and sculpture; Islamic pottery

08785
National Art Gallery
109 Ampang Road, Kuala Lumpur
Fine Arts Museum - 1958
Painting, sculpture, prints, photographs and crafts

08786
National Museum
Jalan Damansara, Kuala Lumpur
General Museum - 1906
Ethnology; archaeology; natural history

08787
Police Museum
Police Training Centre, Guerney Road, Kuala Lumpur
History/Public Affairs Museum - 1961
Exhibits on crime and criminology

Kuching

08788
Police Museum
Fort Magherita, P.F.F. Brigade Headquarters, POB 1564, Kuching, Sarawak
History/Public Affairs Museum - 1971
Crime and criminology in Sarawak

08789
Sarawak Museum
Jalan Tun Haji Openg, Kuching, Sarawak
General Museum - 1891
Ethnology; archaeology; natural history; local history

Melaka

08790
Melaka Museum
7 Jalan Kota Melaka, Melaka
General Museum - 1953
Photos, prints, drawings and specimens illustrating the Portugese, Dutch and English occupations of Melaka; cultural heritage of the Malay Sultanate of Melaka

Merbok

08791
Bujang Valley Archaeological Museum
Merbok, Kedah
Archeology Museum - 1980
Remains of several Hindu, Buddhist Chandi's (temples); object of material culture from various historical sites around Bujang Valley

Pekan

08792
Sultan Abu Bakar Museum
Jalan Sultan Ahmad, Pekan, Pahang
General Museum - 1976
Cultural and historical materials of the
State of Pahang

Penang

08793
Penang Museum and Art Gallery
Farquhar Street, Penang
General Museum - 1963
Chinese culture and customs; social,
economic and educational exhibits;
fishing; natural history and weapons

Seremban

08794
Negri Sembilan State Museum
mail c/o State Secretariat Seremban,
Negri Sembilan
Anthropology Museum
Weapons; clothing; brasses; musical
instruments

Taiping

08795
Perak Museum
Taiping, Perak
General Museum - 1886
Local history; zoology; farm
implements, clothing, weapons, musical
instruments, household articles, and
other items of anthropological interest

Maldives

Malé

08796
National Museum
Malé
General Museum

Mali

Bamako

08797
Musée National du Mali
Rue du Général Leclerc, BP 159,
Bamako
General Museum
Ethnology; botany; zoology - library

08798
Musée Soudanais
Rue du Général Leclerc, Bamako

Timbuktu

08799
Centre de Documentation Arabe
Timbuktu
History/Public Affairs Museum
Historical documents

Malta

Birzebbuga

08800
Ghar Dalam Museum
Birzebbuga
Natural History Museum

Mdina

08801
Cathedral Museum
Archbishop Square, Mdina
Fine Arts Museum - 1969
Italian, French and Maltese art
(14th-18th c.); Cathedral silver; prints
by Dürer; Italian Baroque music
manuscripts; coins

Rabat

08802
Museum of Roman Antiquities
Rabat
Archeology Museum
Roman finds and ruins

Senglea

08803
**The Captain O.F. Gollcher O.B.E. Art
and Archaeological Foundation**
17 Millstone St, Senglea
Fine Arts Museum

Valletta

08804
National Museum of Malta
Kingsway, Valletta
General Museum - 1903
Prehistoric archeological remains; 17th
and 18th cent. works of art;
contemporary art; natural history

08805
Palace Armoury
Valletta
History/Public Affairs Museum
Arms and armour

08806
Saint John's Museum
mail c/o The Curator Valletta

Victoria

08807
Cathedral Museum
The Citadel, Victoria, Gozo
Archeology Museum

Xghajra

08808
Wickman Maritime Collection
La Capitana, Della Grazia Battery Rd,
Xghajra
History/Public Affairs Museum

Zabbar

08809
Museum of Our Lady of the Graces
mail c/o The Curator Zabbar
Religious Art Museum

Martinique

Fort de France

08810
**Musée Departemental de la
Martinique**
B.P. 720, Fort de France
Anthropology Museum - 1970
Pre-Columbian archeology; customs
and costumes of Martinique; Arawak
collection; history

Saint-Pierre

08811
Musée Volcanologique
Saint-Pierre
Natural History Museum

Mauritius

Mahébourg

08812
Historical Museum
Mahébourg
History/Public Affairs Museum
Naval relics; maps, prints and water
colors depicting the scenery and
customs of old Mauritius; facsimilies of
the famous 'Blue Mauritius' postage
stamps

Port Louis

08813
Natural History Museum
Port Louis
Natural History Museum
Flora and fauna of Mauritius;
meteorological exhibits; birds and
insects

Réduit

08814
The Mauritius Herbarium
Réduit
Natural History Museum - 1960 50 i
Flora of the Mascarene Islands;
herbarium

Mexico

Acapulco

08815
Museo Regional de Guerrero
Fuerte de San Diego, Acapulco
General Museum

Actopán

08816
Museo Colonial de San Augustin
Actopan Dirección de Monumentos
Coloniales
Actopán
General Museum
ethnography; crafts of Otomie Indians

Campeche

08817
**Museo Arqueológico, Etnográfico e
Histórico del Estado**
Calle 8, Campeche
General Museum
archaeology; ethnography and history
of Campeche region

08818
Museo de Armas
Calle 8, Campeche
History/Public Affairs Museum

Carmen

08819
**Museo Regional de Ciudad del
Carmen**
Carmen
General Museum

Chiapa de Corzo

08820
Museo de la Laca
Angel Albino Corzo No. 42, Chiapa de
Corzo
Anthropology Museum
folklore

Chihuahua

08821
Museo de Chihuahua
Chihuahua
General Museum

Churubusco

08822
Museo Histórico Dirección de
Monumentos Coloniales
Churubusco
History/Public Affairs Museum

Ciudad Guzmán

08823
Museo Regional de Ciudad Guzmán
Ciudad Guzmán
History/Public Affairs Museum

Colima

08824
Museo de Colima
Colima
General Museum

Cuautla

08825
Museo Casa de Morelos
Callejón del Castigo 2, Cuautla
General Museum

Durango

08826
Museo Regional de Durango Instituto
Juares, Dirección de Monumentos
Coloniales
Durango
General Museum

Guadalajara

08827
Museo de Guadalajara
Calle de Liceo 60, Guadalajara
General Museum

08828
Museo del Estado de Jalisco
Guadalajara
Anthropology Museum - 1700
early Mexican objects; folk art and
costumes; archaeological discoveries

08829
Museo 'José Clemente Orozco
Aurelio Aceves 27, Guadalajara
General Museum - 1949
memorabilia and works of painter
Orozco (1883-1949)

08830
**Museo Regional de Antropología e
Historia**
Guadalajara
General Museum - 1918
colonial art; ethnography; history

Guanajuato

08831
Museo 'Alfredo Duges' Universidad
de Guanajuato
Guanajuato
Science/Tech Museum
biology; geology; mineralogy

08832
**Museo de Historia en la Alhondiga
de Granaditas**
Mendizábal, Guanajuato
History/Public Affairs Museum - 1958
history; applied art; memorabilia of
painter Hermengildo Bustos;
pre-Columbian art; archaeology of
Chupícuaro

Hermosillo

08833
Museo de Sonora
Hermosillo
General Museum
history of Sonora region

Jalapa

08834
Museo de Antropologia de la Universidad Veracruzana
Av. Jalapa, Apdo. 191, Jalapa
General Museum - 1960
special regional collections of the Olmec, Totonac and Huastec cultures of ancient Mexico - library

Madero

08835
Museo de la Cultura Huasteca
Instituto Tecnológico de Cd. Madero
Lo. de Mayo y Sor J.I. de la Cruz,
Apartado Postal No 12, Madero,
Tamaulipas
Archeology Museum - 1960
Huastec civilization; archaeological finds

Mérida

08836
Museo Arqueológico de Yucatan
Calle 60 y 65, Mérida
Archeology Museum
finds of prehistoric, Mayan and Mayapán cultures; ceramics; copper and silver

08837
Museo Regional de Antropologia
Calle 56-A No 485 Palacio Cantón,
Paseo de Montejo, Apdo. Postal No 464, Mérida, Yucatán
Archeology Museum
Finds of prehistoric and Mayan cultures; ceramics; copper, silver, and gold

08838
Museo Regional de Mérida Palacio Cantón
Paseo de Montajo, Mérida
Archeology Museum - 1920
Mayan and Aztec finds

México City

08839
Galeria 'Nabor Carrillo' del Instituto Mexicano Norteamericano de Relaciones Culturales
Hamburgo 115, POB Z.P. 5, México City
Fine Arts Museum - 1950
modern Mexican and American paintings - library

08840
Galerias del Palacio de Bellas Artes
México City
Fine Arts Museum
19th century art; murals by Diego Rivera and other masters; paintings

08841
Galerias del Palacio de Bellas Artes
México City
Fine Arts Museum
19th century art; murals by Diego Rivery and other masters; paintings

08842
Museo de Armas
Chapultepec Heights, Mexico City
History/Public Affairs Museum
armaments

08843
Museo de Arte Moderno
Bosque de Chapultepec, México City
Fine Arts Museum
19th century paintings; murals; contemporary art; works of painter José María Velasco

08844
Museo de Arte Popular
Prolongación de Hidalgo, México City
Fine Arts Museum
decorative arts

08845
Museo de Arte Religioso
Guatemala 17, México City
Fine Arts Museum
artworks from church treasuries; gold reliquaries; paintings and sculptures from México, Europe and Asia

08846
Museo de Geologia
Cipres 176, México City
Natural History Museum

08847
Museo de Higiene
Doncleles 39, México City
Science/Tech Museum

08848
Museo de Historia Natural de la Ciudad de México
Nuevo Bosque de Chapúltepec, México City
Natural History Museum - 1964
biology; entomology; vertebrates and invertebrates; fossils; drawings; photographs - library

08849
Museo de la Ciudad de Mexico
Casa de los Condes de Santiago de Calimaya, México City
General Museum
local history

08850
Museo de las Culturas
Moneda 13, México City
Archeology Museum - 1965
Anerican and European archaeology; world-wide ethnological collection - library

08851
Museo de San Carlos
Puente de Alvarado No. 50, México City
Fine Arts Museum - 1968
18th century European art; primitive and classical paintings and sculptures; collection Olavarrieta, Mayer, Wenner-Green, Pani, Fagoaga, Cardoso

08852
Museo Etnográfico de Esculturas de Cera
Seminario No. 4 esquina con Guatemala, México City
Fine Arts Museum
wax sculptures; idols

08853
Museo 'Frida Kahlo'
Londres 127, México City
Fine Arts Museum

08854
Museo Isidro Fabela 'Casa del Risco'
Villa Obregon
Plaza de San Jacinto 15, Mexico City
General Museum
art; history

08855
Museo Nacional de Antropologia
Paséo de la Reforma, México City
Anthropology Museum - 1865
anthropology; ethnography; archaeology of Mexico and America - library

08856
Museo Nacional de Arqueologia
Publicaciones Moneda 12
México City
Archeology Museum

08857
Museo Nacional de Artes e Industrias Populares
Av. Juarez 44, Mexico City
Anthropology Museum - 1951
native pottery; textiles and laquer; applied arts of Mexico

08858
Museo Nacional de Historia
Castillo de Chapultepec, México City
History/Public Affairs Museum
history of Mexico from the Spanish conquest to 1910; ancient and modern arms; Mexican and European porcelain, ceramics, mosaics, jewelry, textiles, 19th century painting, statues, religious art and cultural history

08859
Museo Nacional de Historia Natural
Ciudad Universitaria
México City
Natural History Museum - 1810
invertebrates; fishes; reptiles; birds; vertebrates; cryptogams - library

08860
Museo Pedagógico Nacional
Presidente Masaryk 526, México City
History/Public Affairs Museum
history of education in Mexico

08861
Museo Postal Edificio de la Central de Correos
México City
Science/Tech Museum
postal communication history

08862
Museo Universitario de Ciencias y Arte
México City
General Museum

08863
Pinacoteca Virreinal de San Diego
Dr. Mora 7, México City
Fine Arts Museum
colonial paintings

08864
Recinto de Homenaje a Don Benito Juárez Palacio Nacional
México City
General Museum
life and death of Mexican revolutionary Benito Juárez (1806-1872) - library

08865
Salon de la Plástica Mexicana
Havre 7, México City
Fine Arts Museum
sculptures

Monterrey

08866
Galeria de Artes Plasticas
Aramberri 504 Pte., Monterrey
Fine Arts Museum
sculpture

08867
Museo Regional de Nuevo León
Loma de Vera, Apdo. 566, Monterrey
General Museum
paintings; history; archaeology

Morelia

08868
Casa de Morelos
Morelia
General Museum

08869
Museo Regional Michoacano
Alleute 305, Morelia
General Museum - 1886
archaeology; ethnography and prehistory of region

Nayarit

08870
Museo Regional Palacio del Gobierno
Nayarit
General Museum
history; archaeology

Oaxaca

08871
Casa de Juárez
Oaxaca
General Museum

08872
Museo Regional de Oaxaca
Independencia 33, Oaxaca
General Museum - 1933
anthropology; ethnography; archaeology; tomb treasures; jewelry

Oaxtepec

08873
Museo Colonial Dirección de Monumentos Coloniales
Oaxtepec
General Museum

Patzcuaro

08874
Museo de Artes Populares
Enseñanza y Alcantarillas s/n, Patzcuaro
Fine Arts Museum - 1935
native Indian arts

08875
Museo Regional de Patzcuaro
Dirección de Monumentos Coloniales
Patzcuaro
General Museum

Puebla

08876
Museo Colonial de Santa Mónica
Av. Poniente 103, Puebla
Fine Arts Museum - 1940

08877
Museo de Arte 'José Luis Bello y Gonzalez'
3 Poniento No. 302, Puebla
Fine Arts Museum - 1938
Mexican, Chinese and European paintings and sculptures; decorative arts in ivory, porcelain, wrought iron, pottery, also furniture, religious art, music instruments

08878
Museo de Arte Popular Poblano
Calle 3 Norte 1203, Puebla
Decorative Arts Museum - 1973
ceramic crafts; applied art; textiles

08879
Museo de los Fuertes de Guadelupe y Loreto
Puebla
History/Public Affairs Museum

08880
Museo del Estado de Puebla Casa del Alfeñique
4 Oriente No. 416, Puebla
General Museum - 1926
archaeology; history of Puebla province

Querétaro

08881
Museo Regional de Querétaro
Querétaro
History/Public Affairs Museum - 1936
History; religious art

San Luis Potosi

08882
Museo Regional Potosino
Galeana 38, San Luis Potosi
General Museum

San Miguel de Allende

08883
Centro Cultural 'Ignacio Ramirez'
Hernandez Macias 71, San Miguel de
Allende
General Museum
art; history; archaeology; folklore

Santiago Tuxtla

08884
Museo Regional de Santiago Tuxtla
Santiago Tuxtla
General Museum

Teotihuacán

08885
Museo Arqueológico de Teotihuacán
Teotihuacán
General Museum - 1922
regional archaeology; history;
ethnography

Tepexpan

08886
Museo de Prehistoria
Tepexpan
Archeology Museum

Tepic

08887
**Museo Regional de Antropologia e
Historia de Tepic**
México 91, Tepic
General Museum
history; ethnography of region

Tepotzotlán

08888
National Viceroyalty Museum
Tepotzotlán
General Museum - 1964
colocial art; painting; chinaware;
religious art; sacred restments;
goldwork; silverwork; ancient furniture
- library

Toluca

08889
Museo Charreria
Toluca
Fine Arts Museum
folk costumes

08890
Museo de Ciencias Naturales
Toluca
Natural History Museum

08891
Museo de las Bellas Artes
Santos Degollado 102, Toluca
Fine Arts Museum
modern Mexican painting; engravings;
pre-Columbian sculptures

Tuxla Gutiérrez

08892
Instituto de Historia Natural
Parque Madero, Apdo. 6, Tuxla
Gutiérrez
Natural History Museum - 1941
insects; reptiles; birds; vertebrates

08893
**Museo Regional de Antropologia e
Historia**
Tuxla Gutiérrez
General Museum - 1939
archaeology; colonial history;
anthropology

Tzintzuntzan

08894
Museo Etnográfico y Arqueológico
Tzintzuntzan
Archeology Museum - 1944
regional archaeology; ethnography

Urupan

08895
**Museo Regional de Arte
Michoacano**
Huatápera, Urupan
General Museum
history; folk art

Villa Obregon

08896
**Museo Colonial del Carmen de San
Angel**
Villa Obregon
General Museum

Villahermosa

08897
Museo de Tabasco
Villahermosa
General Museum

08898
Museo 'La Venta Parque'
Villahermosa
General Museum

Yuriria

08899
Museo Colonial Convento de
Agustinos
Yuriria
General Museum
art; religious art

Monaco

Monaco-Ville

08900
Historical Museum (Wax Museum)
Monaco-Ville
History/Public Affairs Museum

08901
**Oceanographic Museum and
Aquarium**
Monaco-Ville
Natural History Museum - 1910

08902
Palace Museum
Monaco-Ville
History/Public Affairs Museum
Napoleonic souvenirs; palace archives

Monte-Carlo

08903
Museum of Prehistoric Anthropology
bv du Jardin Exotique, Monte-Carlo
Anthropology Museum - 1902
Prehistoric human and animal remains;
prehistoric tools

08904
National Museum
Monte-Carlo
General Museum - 1772
Mechanical dolls and toys from around
the world; sculpture

Mongolia

Altanbulag

08905
Revolutionary Museum
Altanbulag
History/Public Affairs Museum - 1971
Mongolian history since 1921

Darham

08906
Friendship Museum
Darham
Science/Tech Museum
Founding and development of the
industrial city Darham; Soviet-
Mongolian co-operation

Ulan Bator

08907
**Central Museum of Revolutionary
Movement**
Ulan Bator
History/Public Affairs Museum
History and achievements of Mongolia
since 1921

08908
Fine Arts Museum
Ulan Bator
Fine Arts Museum
Paintings; sculptures

08909
Museum of Religion
Ulan Bator
Religious Art Museum
Housed in Choyjin Lamyn Hüree, a
former lamasery; Lamaistic relics

08910
Natsagdorj Museum
Ulan Bator
History/Public Affairs Museum
Life and works of the author
Dashdorjiyn Natsagdorj (1906-1937)

08911
Palace Museum
Ulan Bator
History/Public Affairs Museum
Palace of Bogd Gegeen, Head of the
Buddhist Church in Mongolia and
Head of State 1911-24; lamasery

08912
State Central Museum
Ulan Bator
General Museum
Coll: natural history; Gobi desert
dinosaur eggs and skeletons; art;
history; archeology

08913
Suhbaatar and Choybalsan Museum
Ulan Bator
History/Public Affairs Museum
Memorabilia on the two revolutionary
leaders Sühbaatar and Choybalsan

08914
Ulan Bator Museum
Ulan Bator
History/Public Affairs Museum
History of Ulan Bator and its
reconstruction

08915
V.I. Lenin Museum
Ulan Bator
History/Public Affairs Museum
Life and works of Lenin

Morocco

Fez

08916
Musée d'Armes du Bordj Nord
rue du Batha, Fez
History/Public Affairs Museum
History and ethnography

08917
Musée du Dar Batha
Pl du Batha, Fez
General Museum
Local and regional history; ethnology;
manuscripts; weapons; Moroccan art

Marrakech

08918
Musée de Dar Si Saïd
rue de la Bahia, Riad Zitoun Jdide, B.P.
16, Marrakech, Medina
General Museum
Islamic art; tapestries; jewelry; rifles;
pottery - library

Meknès

08919
Musée de Dar Jamai
Pl Hedim, Meknès
General Museum
Ethnography; folklore and folk art;
wooden sculpture; local handicrafts

Rabat

08920
Fouilles des Chellah
Rabat
Archeology Museum

08921
Musée des Antiquités
23 rue Pierre Parent, B.P. 503, Rabat
Archeology Museum - 1917
Prehistoric excavations; Phoenician
and Roman antiquities

08922
Musée des Oudâia
Kasbah des Oudâia, Rabat
General Museum - 1915
Moroccan jewelry; pottery; cermics;
Koran manuscripts (13th c.)

08923
**Musée d'Institut Scientifique
Cherifien**
av Moulay-Chérif, Rabat
Natural History Museum
Zoology; paleontology; fossils; human
skulls

Tanger

08924
**Musée Archéologique et Folklorique
de Tanger**
Pl de la Kasbah, Tanger
Archeology Museum
Prehistory; Roman antiquities;
mosaics; coins; ceramics

Tetuán

08925
Musée Archéologique
2 rue Bouhçein, Tetuán
Archeology Museum
Carthaginian, Roman and Islamic
collections

08926
Musée d'Art et Folklore
Bab El Oqla, Tetuán
Anthropology Museum
Ethnography and folk art

08927
Musée d'Art Populaire Marocain
bv Mohamed V. 30, Tetuán
Anthropology Museum
Ethnography; folklore; decorative arts

Volubilis

08928
Musée des Antiquités Ruines de
Volubilis
Volubilis
Archeology Museum
Prehistoric and Roman finds;
numismatics; marble and bronze
statues

Mozambique

Beira

08929
Museum Municipal
Town Hall, Rua Correia de Brito, C.P.
1702, Beira
General Museum
Archaeology; ethnology; mineralogy
and biology; shells; coins

Inhaca Island

08930
Museum of Marine Biology
Inhaca Island
Natural History Museum
Exhibits on sea life

Manica

08931
Museu Monstruário de Manica
Vila Manica, C.P. 80, Manica
Science/Tech Museum
Mineralogy; petrology; geology;
natural history displays

Maputo

08932
Museu de História Natural
Praça da Travessia de Zambeze, C.P.
257, Maputo
General Museum - 1915
Mainly natural history displays;
palaeontoloty; silverwork of Tete area
artisans

08933
Museu Freire de Andrade
mail c/o Direccao das Servicos de
Geológia e Minas, Avenida Infante de
Sagres 2, C.P. 217, Maputo
Natural History Museum
Precious stones; mineral and
metamorphic and sedimentary rock
displays, mostly from formations in
Mozambique; archaeology and
palaeontology

08934
Museu Histórico-Militar
Praca 7 de Marco, C.P. 2033, Maputo
History/Public Affairs Museum - 1955
Old artillery, military equipment and
arms, housed in the fortress Nossa
Senhora da Conceiçao; relics of
former missionary work; religious
paintings; furniture

Nampula

08935
Museu Ferreira de Almeida
Avenida José Cabral, C.P. 12, Nampula
General Museum
Shells and coral from the nearby
coast; silverwork, woodwork, pottery
and musical instruments; traditional
masks, hunting weapons and utensils

Namibia

Lüderitz

08936
Lüderitz Museum
Diaz St, POB 512, Lüderitz 9045
General Museum
Display of diamond mining; minerals
from various parts of S.W. Africa;
diorama of local sea birds; history of
Lüderitz; tribal arts and crafts -
aquarium

Okaukuejo

08937
Okaukuejo Museum
Okaukuejo
Natural History Museum
Displays of mammals, snakes and
predatory birds; geology of the Etosha
Pan

Swakopmund

08938
Swakopmund Museum
POB 56, Swakopmund 9180
General Museum
Flora and fauna of the Namib; fishes;
sea birds; seals; mineralogy; relics and
documents of the German colonial
administration; tribal arts and crafts

Tsumeb

08939
Fort Namutoni
Tsumeb 9260
General Museum
History of the fort, the Etosha Game
Reserve and the region in general

Windhoek

08940
Arts Association Gallery
John Meinert and Leutwein Sts, POB
994, Windhoek 9100
Fine Arts Museum
South African art; loan exhibitions

08941
State Museum
Leutwein St, POB 1203, Windhoek
General Museum
Natural history, ethnology,
archaeology displays; objects from
Nama, Bushman, Herero, Ovambo and
other cultures - library

Nepal

Bhaktapur

08942
Museum - Picture Gallery
Lal Baithak (Bhaktapur Darbar),
Bhaktapur, Bhadgaon
Fine Arts Museum - 1961
Paintings; illustrated manuscripts;
murals; stone sculptures

08943
Woodwork Museum
Palace of Fifty-Five Windows,
Bhaktapur, Bhadgaon
Fine Arts Museum - 1967
Sculptures

Kathmandu

08944
National Museum of Nepal
Museum Rd, Chhauni, Kathmandu
General Museum - 1938
Arms; historic portraits; decorative art;
paintings; sculpture; terra cotta;
ethnography; natural history;
Mahendra memorial - conservation
laboratory

08945
Natural History Museum Tribhuvan
University Institute of Science
Anandakuti, Swoyambhu, Kathmandu
Natural History Museum - 1975
Coll: botany; zoology; entomology,
with special reference to butterflies;
amphibians; reptiles; fishes;
ornithology; mammalia; geology -
library

08946
Numismatic Museum
Hanuman Dhoka Palace, Kathmandu
History/Public Affairs Museum - 1963
Numismatics

Lalitpur

08947
**Museum for Excavated
Archeological Antiquities**
Lalitpur, Patan
Archeology Museum
Archeological exhibits

Taulihawa

08948
Kapilavastu Museum
Taulihawa
Archeology Museum
Excavated material associated with the
Buddha

Netherlands

Aalten

08949
Oudheidkamer Aalten
Markt 14, NL-7121 CS Aalten
General Museum - 1928
Prehistory; geology; jewels; weaving
loom; costumes; coins

Aardenburg

08950
Gemeentemuseum
Marktstraat 18, NL-4527 ZG
Aardenburg
Archeology Museum - 1959
Prehistory; bronze; numismatics;
construction fragments; especially
12th-14th century ceramics; pottery;
regional stones; fossils

Aarle-Rixtel

08951
Heemkamer Barthold van Hessel
Gemeenschapshuis De Aar,
Boscheweg A-R, Kerkstraat 6,
NL-5735 BZ Aarle-Rixtel
General Museum
Religious standards and vestments;
photos; farm implements; paintings

Alkmaar

08952
Stedelijk Museum
Doelenstraat 3, NL-1811 KX Alkmaar
General Museum - 1875
History; archeological finds; portraits;
paintings; sculpture; old silver;
porcelain; modern art; antique toys,
dolls; tiles

Allingawier

08953
Boerderijmuseum Aldfaers ERF Farm
Museum De Izeren Kou
Kerkbuurt 19, 8758 LE Allingawier,
POB 467, NL-8901 BG Leeuwarden
History/Public Affairs Museum - 1970
Period rooms; agricultural implements;
school anno 1880; carpenter's tools;
bakery

Almelo

08954
Stichting Museum voor Heemkunde
De Waag 1, NL-7607 HP Almelo
General Museum - 1975
Tools; textiles; local history

Alphen

08955
Oudheidkundig Streekmuseum
Baarleseweg 1, NL-5131 ZL Alphen
General Museum
Archeological finds; jewels; urns

Amerongen

08956
Kasteel Amerongen
Drostestraat 20, NL-3958 BK
Amerongen
History/Public Affairs Museum
Interiors (17th c.); portraits (Emperor
Wilhelm II); silver; tin; copper

Amersfoort

08957
Historische Verzameling Cavalerie
Bernhardkazerne, Barchman
Wuytierslaan 89, Postbus 3003,
NL-3800 DA Amersfoort
History/Public Affairs Museum
History of the Dutch cavalry

08958
Museum 'Flehite'
Westsingel 50, NL-3811 BL
Amersfoort
General Museum - 1878
Coll: bones of prehistoric animals;
archeology; local history; furniture;
paintings; glass; porcelain; Gothic
sideboard and treasury; genealogical
tree of Emperor Charles V; souvenirs
of the 17th century Dutch statesman
Johan van Oldenbarnevelt - library

Ammerzoden

08959
Kasteel Ammersoyen
NL Ammerzoden
History/Public Affairs Museum - 1976
Castle (14th c.) with furniture; paintings
(16th-18th c.); archeological finds
(1400-1950); history of the castle since
the Middle Ages

Amstelveen

08960
**Gemeentelijk Expositie-Centrum
Aemstelle**
Amsterdamweg 511, NL-1182 JM
Amstelveen
General Museum - 1963
Topography; craftmen's instruments;
porcelain; modern art

Amsterdam

08961
Allard Pierson Museum
Archeologisch Museum der
Universiteit Van Amsterdam
Oude Turfmarkt 127, NL-1012 GC
Amsterdam
Archeology Museum - 1934
Egyptian, Near Eastern, Greek,
Etruscan and Roman archeology

08962
Amsterdams Historisch Museum
Kalverstraat 92, Nieuwezijds
Voorburgwal 359, NL-1021 RM
Amsterdam
History/Public Affairs Museum - 1926
History of Amsterdam, portrayed by
means of paintings (Civic guards),
maquettes, decorative arts, pottery,
glass, silver, photographs, maps;
archeology - library

08963
Anne Frank Huis
Prinsengracht 263, NL-1016 GV
Amsterdam
History/Public Affairs Museum
Documentation on the persecution of
Jews and on World War II

08964
Bilderdijk Museum
De Boelelaan 1105, POB 7161,
NL-1007 JD Amsterdam
History/Public Affairs Museum - 1908
Memorabilia on W. Bilderdijk (poet,
1756-1831), books, portraits, drawings

08965
Botanisch Museum
D'Artsenijhof, Plantage Middenlaan 2
A, NL-1018 DD Amsterdam
Natural History Museum
Botanical specimens; herbarium;
watercolours (17th-19th c.)

08966
Het Drukhuis
Herengracht 229, NL-1016 BT
Amsterdam
History/Public Affairs Museum
Typography; graphic arts

08967
**Ferdinand Domela Nieuwenhuis
Museum**
Herengracht 262-266, NL-1016 BV
Amsterdam
History/Public Affairs Museum - 1925
Library of F.D. Nieuwenhuis, especially
social and political works (Marx,
Engels, Proudhon, Kropotkin, Louise
Michel); portraits; memorabilia

08968
Frederik van Eeden Collectie
Universiteitsbibliotheek afd.
Handschriften
Singel 425, NL-1012 WP Amsterdam
History/Public Affairs Museum - 1936
Memorabilia on poet and physician
Frederik van Eeden (1860-1932)

08969
**Geologisch Museum der Universiteit
van Amsterdam**
Nieuwe Prinsengracht 130, NL-1018
VZ Amsterdam
Natural History Museum - 1934
Geology; mineralogy; ores; fossils
from Timor - library

08970
**Historische Verzameling der
Universiteit van Amsterdam**
Oude Zijs Voorbuurgwal 231, NL-1012
EZ Amsterdam
History/Public Affairs Museum
History of the university and student
life; paintings; portraits; medals;
documents

08971
**Historische Verzameling van de Vrije
Universiteit**
De Boelelaan 1105, Postbus 7161,
NL-1007 MC Amsterdam
History/Public Affairs Museum
History of the university and its
reforms

08972
Joods Historisch Museum
Nieuwmarkt 4, NL-1012 CR
Amsterdam
Religious Art Museum - 1932
Jewish ceremonial art; Sephardic
textiles; Jewish history in the
Netherlands - library

08973
Koninklijk Paleis op de Dam
NL Amsterdam
General Museum
History of Amsterdam; paintings

08974
Multatuli Museum
Korsjespoorsteeg 20, NL-1015 AR
Amsterdam
Historic Site - 1910
Works from and about Multatuli
(1820-1887); photographs;
manuscripts; medals - library

08975
Museum Amstelkring (Ons' Lieve
Heer op Solder)
Voorburgwal 40, NL-1012 GE
Amsterdam
History/Public Affairs Museum - 1888
Historic house (1661) with attic church;
religious objects; paintings; sculptures;
furniture from the period of Roman-
Catholic clandestine churches -
documentation center

08976
Museum Fodor
Keizersgracht 609, NL-1017 DS
Amsterdam
Fine Arts Museum - 1863
Modern art

08977
Museum Het Rembrandthuis
Jodenbreestraat 4-6, NL-1011 NK
Amsterdam
Fine Arts Museum - 1907
The artist's home (17th c.);
Rembrandt's etchings and some of his
drawings - library; educational
department

08978
Museum Van Loon
Keizersgracht 672, NL-1017 ET
Amsterdam
Historic Site - 1973
Furnished 17th-18th century house,
Van Loon family portraits and wedding
coins

08979
Museum Vrolik
Mauritskade 61, NL-1092 AD
Amsterdam
Natural History Museum
Anatomy and embryology of man and
vertebrate animals

08980
Museum Willet-Holthuysen
Herengracht 605, NL-1017 CE
Amsterdam
History/Public Affairs Museum
Typically furnished canal house (1687)
with objects of art and family portraits
of the Backer family; glass; porcelain;
delftware (17th-18th c.); reconstruction
of an 18th century garden - library

08981
**Natuurhistorische Verzameling van
het Amsterdamse Bos**
Koenenkade nabij Boerderij
Meerzicht, Nieuwe Kalfjeslaan,
NL-1181 CA Amstelveen
Natural History Museum - 1954
Ornithology; zoology; butterflies;
beetles; herbarium

08982
Nederlands Filmmuseum
Vondelpark 3, NL-1071 AA Amsterdam
History/Public Affairs Museum - 1946
Joris Ivens Collection; Jean Desmet
Collection; filmposters; national and
international films; old apparatuses
showing the development of
cinematography - library

08983
**Nederlands Instituut voor Nijverheid
en Techniek**
Rozengracht 224, NL-1016 SZ
Amsterdam
Science/Tech Museum - 1929
Industrial exhibits; atomic energy;
automotive technology; metals;
electrotechnology; construction;
shipping; chemistry; computer science

08984
Occo Hofje
Nieuwe Keizersgracht 94,
Keizersgracht 682, NL-1017 ET
Amsterdam
Fine Arts Museum
Paintings and family portraits
(16th-18th c.)

08985
Peter Stuyvesant Stichting
Drentsestraat 21, hoek De Boelelaan,
Postbus 7400, NL-1007 JK Amsterdam
Fine Arts Museum
Contemporary art and sculpture

08986
Roothaan-Museum
Singel 448 (Pastorie 'de Krijtberg'),
NL-1017 AV Amsterdam
Historic Site - 1957
Life and work of the Jesuit Philippus
Roothan (1785-1853)

08987
Rijksmuseum
Stadhouderskade 42, PB 50673,
NL-1007 DD Amsterdam
Fine Arts Museum - 1808
Dutch painting (15th-19th c.), including
Frans Hals, Rembrandt ('Nightwatch')
and Vermeer; prints and drawings;
sculpture and applied arts; delftware,
Dresden and Dutch porcelain; history
of the Netherlands; Asiatic art - library

08988
Rijksmuseum, Afd. Aziatische Kunst
Hobbemastraat 19, POB 50673,
NL-1071 XZ Amsterdam
Fine Arts Museum - 1928
Porcelain from China and Japan;
sculptures in stone, bronze, wood;
paintings from all Asian countries

08989
**Rijksmuseum, Afd. Beeldhouwkunst
en Kunstnijverheid**
Stadhouderskade 42, Postbus 50673,
NL-1007 DD Amsterdam
Fine Arts Museum - 1885
Coll: sculptures from the Netherlands,
France, Italy, Germany (12th-19th c.);
applied arts (12th-20th c.); furniture;
ceramics; gold and silver work; glass;
tapestries; carpets; costumes

08990
**Rijksmuseum, Afd. Nederlandse
Geschiedenis**
Stadhouderskade 42, POB 50673,
NL-1007 DD Amsterdam
History/Public Affairs Museum - 1875
Netherlands history from the 15th to
19th century

08991
**Rijksmuseum 'Nederlands
Scheepvaart Museum'**
Kattenburgerplein 1, NL-1018 KK
Amsterdam
History/Public Affairs Museum - 1916
Ship models; technical models; ships
and mechanical draughts; real ships
and ship parts; paintings, prints,
drawings; atlases, globes and charts;
nautical instruments; arms; coins and
other relics related to maritime history
of the Netherlands since the 16th
century - library

08992
Rijksmuseum Vincent Van Gogh
Paulus Potterstraat 7, NL-1071 CX
Amsterdam
Fine Arts Museum
About 300 paintings and 500 drawings
by Vincent van Gogh (1853-1890); 700
letters to his brother Theo; works by
Emile Bernard, Gauguin, Toulouse-
Lautrec, Monticelli

08993
Rijksprentenkabinet Rijksmuseum
Jan Luykenstraat 1 A, NL-1071 XZ
Amsterdam
Fine Arts Museum - 1800
Coll: Dutch graphic art (16th-19th c.);
Japanese prints; prints of different
European schools; drawings by Dutch
and foreign artists; portraits and
historical prints; prints by Master of
the Hausbuch, Seghers and
Rembrandt

08994
Schriftmuseum J.A. Dortmond
mail c/o Universiteitsbibliotheek,
Singel 425, NL-1012 WP Amsterdam
History/Public Affairs Museum - 1976
All kinds of manuscripts and
handwriting implements give a survey
of the history of the art of writing from
about 3,000 BC to the present

08995
Stedelijk Museum
Paulus Potterstraat 13, NL-1071 CX
Amsterdam
Fine Arts Museum - 1895
Modern painting and sculpture
especially by American and European
artists, including paintings by Van
Gogh, Manet, Daubigny, Monet,
Bonnard, Cézanne, Bosboom, Breitner,
Chagall, Malevich, Dubuffet, Mondrian,
Picasso, Matisse, Beckmann, Kirchner,
Pechstein, Schmidt-Rottluff, Ensor;
graphics and drawings; applied art and
industrial design - library

08996
Stichting Architectuurmuseum
Droogbak 1a, NL-1013 GE Amsterdam
Fine Arts Museum - 1912
Dutch architecture since 1850 - library

08997
Stichting Banketbakkersmuseum
mail c/o School voor Consumptieve
Beroepen, 'De Berkhoff, Wibautstraat
220, NL-1097 DN Amsterdam
History/Public Affairs Museum
Old bakery with shop, confectioner
tools, photos of menus - library

08998
**Stichting Het Nederlands
Persmuseum**
Oost-Indisch Huis, Oude Hoogstraat
24, NL-1012 CE Amsterdam
History/Public Affairs Museum - 1915
History of the Dutch press; old
newspapers; caricatures - library

08999
Theatremuseum
Herengracht 168, PB 19304, NL-1016
BP Amsterdam
Performing Arts Museum - 1925
Dutch theatre history; cabaret;
documents, photographs, graphics,
drawings, manuscripts, books, posters,
criticism, programs; miniature stage of
Baron H. van Slingelandt (1870) -
library; educational department

09000
Tropenmuseum
Linnaeusstraat 2A, NL-1092 CK
Amsterdam
Anthropology Museum - 1910
Ethnography (Asia, Africa, Oceania,
South America); artifacts, sculpture
and painting; textiles - library

09001
Veiligheidsinstituut
Hobbemastraat 22, PB 5665, NL-1007
AR Amsterdam
History/Public Affairs Museum - 1891
Prevention of accidents at work and in
the private sector - library

09002
Vondelmuseum
Universiteitsbibliotheek
Singel 425, NL-1012 WP Amsterdam
History/Public Affairs Museum - 1902
Memorabilia on poet Joos van de
Vondel (1587-1679), his works,
manuscripts, designs, portraits and
books

09003
Het Waaierkabinet
Prinsengracht 1083, NL-1017 JH
Amsterdam
Decorative Arts Museum - 1948
Collection of Chinese and Japanese
fans and fans from various centuries

09004
Werf 't Kromhout
Hoogte Kadijk 147, Dulongstraat 20,
NL-1097 RZ Amsterdam Oost -
History/Public Affairs Museum
Wharf (1750) with ships in various
stages of restoration; ship models;
ship building instruments

09005
Werkspoor Museum
Oostenburgergracht 77, NL-1018 NC
Amsterdam
History/Public Affairs Museum - 1950
History of the East-Indian Company at
Oosterburg (1663 to the beginning of
the 19th c.); local history; pictures;
photographs; models of steam
engines

09006
Het Wijnkopersgildehuys
Koestraat 10-12, NL-1012 BX
Amsterdam
History/Public Affairs Museum
Guildhall of the wine merchants (1633);
interior; paintings; glass

09007
Zoölogisch Museum Instituut voor
Taxonomische Zoölogie der
Universiteit van Amsterdam
Plantage Middenlaan 53, NL-1018 DC
Amsterdam
Natural History Museum - 1838
Zoology; ornithology; entomology;
herpetology

Anjum

09008
'De Eendracht'
Mounebuorren 18, NL-9133 MB Anjum
Science/Tech Museum - 1889
Ancient agricultural implements;
restored mill; photos

Apeldoorn

09009
Historisch Museum Marialust
Verzetstrijderspark 10, NL-7316 CM
Apeldoorn
History/Public Affairs Museum
Prehistoric finds; pottery (mainly 19th
c.); agriculture; paper industry; ancient
toys; costumes

09010
**Municipal Van Reekumgallery of
Modern Art**
2 Churchillplein, NL-7314 BZ
Apeldoorn
Fine Arts Museum - 1965
Modern art; graphics; design;
ceramics; modern jewelry - library;
educational collection

09011
Rijksmuseum Paleis Het Loo
Koninklijkpark 1, NL-7315 JA
Apeldoorn
History/Public Affairs Museum - 1970
History of the House of Orange
Nassau and its impact on the
Netherlands; portraits; paintings;
furniture; documents; prints; ceramics;
sledges; carriages and vintage cars;
ornamental cabinet, decorated by
Frans Francken the Younger
(1581-1642); silver furniture, table,
mirror and candlestands by Johann
Bartermann (1732)

Appingedam

09012
Gewestelijk Historisch Museum
Wijkstraat 17, NL-9901 AE
Appingedam
General Museum - 1953
Local history; costumes; documents;
pictures; photographs; agricultural
implements; Chinese porcelain

Arnemuiden

09013
Raadhuis
Langstraat 35, NL-4341 EC
Arnemuiden
General Museum
History of Arnemuiden and environs;
archives from 1500; topography;
silver; portraits

Arnhem

09014
Elektrum Museum
Klingelbeekseweg 45, NL-6812 DE
Arnhem
Science/Tech Museum - 1979
Electrotechnics and energy supply

09015
Gemeentemuseum Arnhem
Utrechtseweg 87, NL-6812 AA
Arnhem
Fine Arts Museum - 1856
Paintings (16th-20th c.); neorealists
(Dick Ket, Pyke Koch, Raoul Hynckes,
Carel Willink, Wim Schuhmacher);
Chinese porcelain; pottery from Delft
and Arnhem; ceramics; glasses; silver;
graphics and illustrations by regional
artists; regional finds; topography of
Gelderland

09016
**Historisch Museum Grenadiers En
Jagers**
Onder de Linden 101, NL-6822 KK
Arnhem
History/Public Affairs Museum - 1885
History of the grenadiers and hunters;
regimental collection of uniforms,
weapons, paintings of the Dutch foot
guards from 1829 to the present -
library

09017
Museum Bronbeek Museum van het
Koninklijk Tehuis voor Oud Militairen
'Bronbeek'
Velperweg 147, NL-6824 MB Arnhem
History/Public Affairs Museum - 1863
Ethnography of the former
Netherlands East Indies; history of the
former Royal Netherlands East Indian
Army, uniforms, portraits, paintings,
medals of honor, flags, arms - library

09018
**Rijksmuseum voor Volkskunde 'Het
Nederlands Openluchtmuseum'**
Schelmseweg 89, NL-6816 SJ Arnhem
Open Air Museum - 1918
70 buildings (farms, houses,
workshops, mills) from all over the
country; folk costumes, costumes of
H.M. Prinses Wilhelmina; popular art ,
'H. Wiegersma' woodcut collection;
'Maria van Hemert' needlework
collection; documentation of popular
folk art of 'Hil Bottema' - library;
educational center

Appingedam → Asselt

Asselt

09019
Folkloristisch Museum
Pastoor Pinckerstraat, t.o. de Kerk,
NL-6071 NW Asselt
General Museum - 1927
Archeological finds; domestic utensils;
earthenware; religious objects (also
Jewish)

Assen

09020
Automuseum
Rode Heklaan 3, NL-9401 SB Assen
Science/Tech Museum

09021
Provinciaal Museum van Drenthe
Brink 1 en 3, PB 134, NL-9400 AC
Assen
History/Public Affairs Museum - 1854
Regional prehistory and history;
documents about historic monuments
in the province of Drenthe;
Netherlands art around 1900;
costumes; rooms with period furniture;
coins; oldest canoe in the world (6,000
BC); wooden disk wheels (2,000 BC) -
library

Asten

09022
Nationaal Beiaardmuseum
Ostaderstraat 23, NL-5721 WC Asten
History/Public Affairs Museum - 1969
All kinds of bells from all over the
world; chimes; tower clocks;
Glockenspiel mechanisms; archeology
and ethnology in connection with bells
- library

09023
**Natuurstudiecentrum en Museum
Jan Vriends**
Ostaderstraat 23, NL Asten
Natural History Museum - 1973
Ornithology; entomology; mammals;
fish; botany

Axel

09024
Streekmuseum 'Het Land Van Axel'
Noordstraat 11-13, NL-4571 GB Axel
General Museum - 1939
19th century farmers' costumes; old
farm carts; folk costumes; jewels;
utensils; furniture from 1860 and 1900;
school books (18th-19th c.)

Barger Compascuum

09025
Veenmuseumdorp 't Aole Compas
Postweg, NL-7884 PN Barger
Compascuum
Open Air Museum
Houses of peat cutters (1850-1900);
church; school (1868); agricultural
implements; domestic utensils

Barneveld

09026
Veluws Museum 'Nairac'
Langstraat 13, NL-3771 BA Barneveld
General Museum - 1875
Prehistoric and archeological finds;
glasses; coins; furniture; old local
maps - library

Beek

09027
Heemkunde Museum
Brugstraat 4, NL-6191 KC Beek
General Museum
Craftmen's instruments and
agricultural implements ; local history;
archeology

Beers

09028
Stinzenmuseum 'De Poarte Fan Bears'
NL Beers
History/Public Affairs Museum - 1963
Heraldic figures and coats-of-arms;
items relating to swan hunting;
pictures of old gates

Bellingwolde

09029
Streekmuseum De Oude Wolden
Hoofdweg 161, Hoofdweg 53, NL-9695
AB Bellingwolde
General Museum
Prehistoric finds; fossils; tools;
costumes; crafts

Bennekom

09030
Museum 'Kijk en Luister'
Kerkstraat 1, NL-6721 VA Bennekom
General Museum - 1955
History of Bennekom and the environs

09031
Tute-Natura
Bosbeekweg 19, Gem. Ede, NL-6721
MH Bennekom
Natural History Museum - 1973
Coll: plants; birds; natural history;
prehistory

Berg En Dal

09032
Afrika Museum
Postweg 6, POB 4, NL-6570 AA Berg
En Dal
Anthropology Museum - 1954
African ethnology; African arts; Yoruba
collection; nail fetish; Edan figures;
Ogboni collection; Senufo maternity;
Angola tombstones - library;
educational center

Bergen

09033
Gemeentemuseum 't Sterkenhuis
Oude Prinsweg 21, Eeuwigelaan 61,
NL-1861 CL Bergen
General Museum - 1903
Local history; archeological finds;
historical room with porcelain,
costumes, textiles, graphics

Bergen op Zoom

09034
Gemeentemuseum Het Markiezenhof
Steenbergsestraat 6-8, NL-4611 TE
Bergen op Zoom
General Museum - 1919
Life in Bergen op Zoom and the
environs; copper; pewter; porcelain;
products of the local household
ceramics industry (1400-1900);
paintings, sculpture (15th-18th c.);
Louis XIV-XVI rooms

Bergeyk

09035
Eicha-Museum
Buurhuis 't Hof, Eerselsedijk 2A,
Postbus 65, NL-5570 AB Bergeyk
Archeology Museum
Prehistorical finds; earthenware;
Merovingian ornaments and glass

09036
Muzen Museum voor Creatief Werk
De Hof, Dennendreef 7, NL-5571 AK
Bergeyk
Fine Arts Museum
Naive painting and works by juvenile
artists; tapestries from Egypt, Italy and
the Netherlands; musical instruments

Beverwijk

09037
Kennemer Oudheidkamer
Velserweg 2, NL-1342 LD Beverwijk
General Museum - 1930
History of Beverwijk and the environs;
pictures; paintings; documents;
blazons (17th c.); pottery (14th and
20th c.)

Bolsward

09038
Oudheidskamer
Stadhuis, NL-8701 JD Bolsward
General Museum - 1949
Local history; porcelain; furniture;
missal from 1475; silver; coins; pewter;
council chamber

Borculo

09039
Boerderijmuseum 'De Lebbenbrugge'
Lebbenbruggedijk 82, NL-7271 SB
Borculo
History/Public Affairs Museum - 1926
19th century farm with interiors

09040
Brandweermuseum
Hofstraat 5, Korte Wal 9, NL Borculo
History/Public Affairs Museum - 1900
Various firefighting material from 1648
to the present; uniforms; medals; coins

09041
Stormrampmuseum
Hofstraat 7, Gemeentehuis, Kortewal
2, NL-7271 BB Borculo
History/Public Affairs Museum - 1935
Documentation on the cyclone of
August 10, 1925, which devasted
Borculo and the history of its
rebuilding

Borger

09042
Boerderij 't Flint'nhoes
Hoofdstraat 3, NL-9531 AA Borger
General Museum - 1967
Farmhouse (1619, rebuilt 1968) with
furniture and domestic utensils; folk art

Bourtange

09043
Natuur- en Oudheidsmuseum De Laatste Stuyver
Vlagtwedderstraat 9, NL-9545 TA
Bourtange
General Museum
Geology; shells; tools

Brakel

09044
Slot Loevestein
Post Woudrichem, NL Brakel
History/Public Affairs Museum
14th century castle; furniture;
paintings; prints

Breda

09045
Bisschoppelijk Museum
Grote Markt 19, NL-4811 XL Breda
Religious Art Museum - 1926
Objects relating to the Breda
bishopric; paintings; wood sculptures;
silver; bronze; vestments; devotional
prints

09046
Rijksmuseum voor Volkenkunde 'Justinus van Nassau'
Kasteelplein 13, POB 3330, NL-4800
DH Breda
Anthropology Museum - 1926
Coll: Indonesia; New Guinea; Asia;
North Africa; South Sea - library;
educational center

09047
Stedelijk Museum
Grote Markt 19, NL-4811 XL Breda
General Museum - 1903
Mainly history of the Barony of Breda;
pictures; weapons; silver; fire brigade;
costumes; folklore; coins; ceramics;
historical-topographical globe; legal
history

Breukelen

09048
Ridderhofstad Gunterstein
Zandpad 48, NL Breukelen
History/Public Affairs Museum
Manuscripts by Louis Napoleon and
statesman Johan von Oldenbarneveldt
(1547-1619); travel reports;
topography; coins; furniture; family
portraits

Broek Op Langendijk

09049
Broeker Veiling
Dorpsstraat 97, Postbus 1, NL-1720
AA Broek Op Langendijk
History/Public Affairs Museum
Oldest European vegetable auction
hall; agricultural implements

Bruinisse

09050
Oudheidkamer
Oudestraat 27, NL-4311 AL Bruinisse
General Museum - 1968
Household objects; costumes
(18th-19th c.); objects relating to the
mussel and shrimp trade

Brunssum

09051
Verzameling in het Gemeentehuis
Lindeplein, NL-6444 AT Brunssum
Decorative Arts Museum
Earthenware (1025-1450) of local
production; Roman finds; coins

Bunschoten

09052
Tentoonstelling van Poppen in Klederdracht
Jeugdgebouw achter de Noorderkerk,
Kerkstraat 18, NL-3751 AR
Bunschoten
Anthropology Museum
Dolls with historical costumes dating
back 1780

Buren

09053
Boerenwagenmuseum
Muurhuizen, Dr. Nolenslaan 27,
NL-6823 BK Arnhem
Science/Tech Museum - 1963
Country wagons of Gelderland;
coaches; wood carving; metal work -
construction workshop

09054
Museum der Koninklijke Marechaussee
Weeshuiswal 9, NL-4116 BR Buren
History/Public Affairs Museum
Paintings, prints, uniforms and
documents concerning the royal
gendarmes

Cadier en Keer

09055
Afrika-Centrum
Rijksweg 15, NL-6267 AC Cadier en
Keer
Anthropology Museum - 1893
Art objects and domestic articles from
Western Africa, Sudan and the Guinea
coast - documentation center

Castricum

09056
De Duynkant
Geversweg, Tormentil 10, NL-1902 JM
Castricum
History/Public Affairs Museum
Local history; Roman pottery;
copperplates

Culemborg

09057
Jan van Riebeeckhuis
Achterstraat 26-30, Markt 1, NL-4101
BB Culemborg
History/Public Affairs Museum
Birthplace of the explorer Jan van
Riebeeck; furniture; domestic utensils;
coins; paintings; documents on his
voyages

09058
Oudheidkamer
Elisabeth Weeshuis, Heerenstraat 27,
NL-4101 BR Culemborg
General Museum - 1928
Antiquities of Culemborg and
environs; topography; pottery; silver;
history of government and laws;
portraits of royalty (16th-18th c.);
religious paintings (16th c.)

Cuyk

09059
Amerika Museum Nederland
Molenstraat 51, NL-5431 BW Cuyk
Anthropology Museum - 1971
Coll: pre-Ccolumbian art (Mexico and
the High Andes); Canadian Indians;
the Central Eskimo culture; modern
South American Indian material

De Koog

09060
Natuurrecreatie Centrum
Ruyslaan 92, NL-1796 AZ De Koog
General Museum - 1946
Archeology; geology; natural history;
aquaria; marine animals, living seals

Delft

09061
Hofje Van Gratie
Van der Mastenstraat 26-40, NL-2611
NZ Delft
History/Public Affairs Museum - 1957
Portraits of regents' families; furniture;
earthenware

09062
**Koninklijk Nederlands Leger- en
Wapenmuseum Generaal Hoefer** Afd.
Studiecollectie en Historische
Bibliotheek
Korte Geer 1, NL Delft
History/Public Affairs Museum - 1959
Military materials (marine, coast guard,
tanks); arms from Britain, France,
Germany, Austria and the Netherlands,
America and Russia;
telecommunication equipment

09063
Mineralogisch-Geologisch Museum
Mijnbouwstraat 120, NL-2628 RX Delft
Natural History Museum
Mineralogy; paleontology

09064
Museum Paul Tétar van Elven
Koornmarkt 67, NL-2611 CG Delft
Fine Arts Museum - 1927
House of painter Paul Tétar van Elven
(1823-1896); paintings (19th c.);
furniture; porcelain; Delft pottery

09065
Oudheidskamer van het Ijkwezen
Schoemakerstraat 97, POB 654,
NL-2600 AR Delft
Science/Tech Museum - 1963
Coll: weights; measures; linear
measures; gasmeters - library

09066
**Rijksmuseum Huis Lambert van
Meerten**
Oude Delft 199, NL-2611 HD Delft
Decorative Arts Museum - 1909
Glazed eathenware (majolica); silver
from Delft; two 17th-century windows
with metalwork; furniture; paintings
(17th c.)

09067
Stedelijk Museum Het Prinsenhof
Agathaplein 1, NL-2611 HR Delft
General Museum - 1948
Paintings of local artists (Cornelius van
Vliet, Gillis de Berch, Willem van Aelst,
Daniel Vosmaer, Jan Tengnagel);
portraits (16th-18th c.); tapestries; Delft
pottery and silver; pictures and
weapons relating to Prince William's
war against Spain; W.J. Rust collection
of earthenware; European porcelain;
religious art - library

09068
Studieverzameling Elektrotechniek
University of Technology, Electrical
Engineering Dept.
Mekelweg 4, NL-2600 GA Delft
Science/Tech Museum
Machines; parts and materials relating
to electrotechnology and electronics,
radio, radar, telecommunication; valve
sets; surveying; measuring equipment
and instruments ; telephone equipment
- library

09069
Technisch Tentoonstellingscentrum
Kanaalweg 4, NL-2628 EB Delft
Science/Tech Museum - 1975
Combustion engines, steam engines

09070
Volkenkundig Museum Nusantara
(former Indonesisch Etnografisch
Museum)
St. Agathaplein 4, NL-2611 HR Delft
Anthropology Museum - 1864
Ethnology of Indonesia; arts and
handicrafts of the various islands;
Indonesian textiles; Wajang puppets
and gamelan orchestra; house and
ship models - library

Den Briel

09071
Trompmuseum
Venkelstraat 4, Catharijnehof 12,
NL-3231 XS Den Briel
History/Public Affairs Museum
Local history; earthenware; pictures;
folk costumes; furniture

Den Burg

09072
Oudheidskamer
Kogerstraat 1, NL-1791 EN Den Burg
General Museum - 1955
History and folklore of Textel; pictures;
porcelain; tiles

Denekamp

09073
Museum Natura Docet
Oldenzaalsestraat 39-41, NL-7591 GL
Denekamp
Natural History Museum - 1911
Fossils; migrant birds and mammals
from the eastern Netherlands; shells;
insects - library

09074
'Singraven'
Molendijk 37, NL-7591 PT Denekamp
Fine Arts Museum - 1968
Paintings (17th c.); French and English
pictures; 17th to 18th century furniture,
gobelins, Delft pottery

Den Ham

09075
Middendorpshuis
Grotestraat 4, NL-7683 BB Den Ham
General Museum
Local history

Den Helder

09076
Helders Marine Museum Marine
Voorlichtingsgebouw 't Torentje
Hoofdgracht, NL-1780 CA Den Helder
History/Public Affairs Museum - 1962
Naval collection; ship models; naval
uniforms, weapons, portraits, pictures;
orders of knighthood and other
decorations, flags, navigational
instruments; maps

Den Hoorn

09077
Zee- en Scheepvaartmuseum
Diek 9a, Den Hoorn (Textel), *mail c/o*
Natuurrecreatie Centrum De Koog,
Ruyslaan 92, NL-1796 AZ De Koog,
Texel
History/Public Affairs Museum
Navigation history; paintings; ship
models

Den Oever

09078
Wieringer Museum Boerderij
Hofstraat 36, NL-1779 CD Den Oever
General Museum - 1965
Old farm in West-Friesian style with
inventory; equipment; old tiles; painted
panels; modern art - theater and
cinema

De Rijp

09079
Rijper Museum 'In 't Houten Huis'
Jan Boonplein 2, NL-1483 BL De Rijp
History/Public Affairs Museum - 1937
Objects relating to whaling and herring
industry; finds (17th-18th c.)

Deurne

09080
Gemeentemuseum De Wieger
Liesselseweg 29, NL-5751 KJ Deurne
Fine Arts Museum - 1965
Former residence of artist Hendrik
Wiegersma (1891-1969); paintings,
bronzes, silver engravings by
Wiegersma, sculptures and paintings
of his contemporaries; folk art

Deventer

09081
De Drie Haringen
Brink 56, NL-7411 BV Deventer
General Museum - 1932
Toys; children's books; furniture in
miniature; costumes; building
fragments; style of living

09082
Museum De Waag
Brink 56, NL-7411 BV Deventer
General Museum - 1915
Prehistoric ceramics; numismatics;
folklore; design; graphics; paintings;
tools; construction fragments;
topography; bicycles

09083
**Museum voor Mechanisch
Speelgoed**
Noordenbergstraat 9, NL-7411 NJ
Deventer
Decorative Arts Museum - 1972
Mechanical toys

09084
**Nederlands Albert Schweitzer
Museum**
Brink 89, NL-7411 BX Deventer
History/Public Affairs Museum - 1974
Historical and biographical material
about life and work of Albert
Schweitzer, archives of newspaper
articles, photos, slides, films and
stamps - library

De Waal

09085
Wagenmuseum
Hogereind 4-6, De Waal (Texel),
Oranjestraat 2, NL-1794 BC
Oosterend
Agriculture Museum
Sleighs and coaches; tools;
agricultural implements

Diever

09086
Schultehuis
Brink 7, NL-7981 BZ Diever
Decorative Arts Museum - 1935
Furniture and porcelain dating back to
1600

Doesburg

09087
Museum 'De Roode Tooren'
Roggestraat 9-11, NL-6980 AA
Doesburg
Archeology Museum
Archeological finds; medieval relics

Doetinchem

09088
Museum 't Gevang
Nieuwstad 74-76, NL-7001 AE
Doetinchem
History/Public Affairs Museum
Jail (17th c.); cooper's workshop

Dokkum

09089
**Museum 'Master S.E. Wendelaar
Bonga'**
Keereweer 5, POB 189, NL-9100 HD
Dokkum
Natural History Museum - 1961
Birds; stones; dioramas - library

09090
**Streekmuseum 'Het
Admiraliteitshuis'**
Schoolsteeg 1, NL-9101 KZ Dokkum
General Museum - 1937
Objects about Dokkum and the
environs; silver; ceramics; toys;
costumes; topography - library

Domburg

09091
Zeeuws Biologisch Museum
Oranjerie Kasteel Westhove,
Duinvlietweg 6, Domburg, POB 2044,
NL-4462 TR Goes
Natural History Museum
Natural history; ornithology; butterflies
- library

Doorn

09092
Huis Doorn
Langbroekerweg 10, NL-3941 MT
Doorn
History/Public Affairs Museum - 1950
Furniture; paintings; porcelain; gold
and silver possessed by the German
Emperor Wilhelm II (1859-1941);
snuffboxes of Frederic the Great, King
of Prussia (1712-1786)

Doornenburg

09093
Kasteel De Doornenburg
NL Doornenburg
History/Public Affairs Museum
Castle with furniture (mainly early 16th
c.); armaments; engravings; maps

Doorwerth

09094
Museum voor Wildbeheer 'Het
Nederlands Jachtmuseum'
Kasteel Doorwerth, Fonteinallee, POB
11, NL-6865 ZG Doorwerth
History/Public Affairs Museum - 1968
Natural history; hunting, shooting and
trapping; exhibitions on hunting in the
Dutch Low Countries in the past

Dordrecht

09095
Dordrechts Museum
Museumstraat 40, NL-3311 XP
Dordrecht
Fine Arts Museum - 1842
Dutch pupils of Rembrandt (17th c.);
Ary Scheffer Collection ('Portrait of
Chopin'); Amsterdam and Hague
School; Dutch impressionists; Jan van
Goyen 'View of Dordrecht' - library;
film room

09096
Lips Slotenmuseum
Merwedestraat 48, Postbus 59,
NL-3300 AB Dordrecht
Decorative Arts Museum - 1930
Locks; safes; keys; treasuries

09097
Museum Mr. Simon Van Gijn
Nieuwe Haven 29, NL-3300 AS
Dordrecht
General Museum - 1925
Local silver; ship models;
reproductions; costumes; toys;
furniture; glass; porcelain; coins;
pewter; stamps; building fragments;
pottery; furniture; rugs (18th c.)

Drachten

09098
It Bleekerhûs
Moleneind, NL-9203 ZP Drachten
General Museum - 1936
Coins; prehistory; land and
environment; folklore; traditional and
modern art; dadaism (Theo van
Doesburg, Kurt Schwitters) - library

Drimmelen

09099
Biesbosch Museum
Klompstraat 12, Oud Drimmelen 5,
NL-4924 EJ Drimmelen
General Museum
Tools and products of the local
industry

Drouwen

09100
**Natuur -en Dierenpanorama
Drouwenerzand**
Gasselterstraat 5a, NL-9533 PC
Drouwen
Natural History Museum
Dutch landscapes; natural history;
entomology; ornithology; archeology;
geology; fossils

Drunen

09101
Lips Autotron B.V.
Museumlaan 100, POB 51 5150 AB
Drunen
Science/Tech Museum
Collection of old motorcars

Echt

09102
Carnavalsmuseum
Plats 11, NL-6101 AP Echt
Anthropology Museum
History of the carnival in the
Netherlands, Belgium and Germany;
paintings (Pieter Bruegel, Hieronymus
Bosch, James Ensor)

09103
**Oudheid- en Heemkundig Museum
Echt en Omstreken**
Gemeentehuis, Plats 1, NL-6101 AP
Echt
General Museum - 1952
Local history; geology; archeology;
domestic utensils; tools; agricultural
implements; religious objects;
entomology; zoology

Edam

09104
Edam's Museum
Damplein 6, NL Edam
General Museum - 1895
Furnished rooms, kitchen and cellar;
local and regional history

Ede

09105
Museum Oud-Ede
Museumplein 7, NL-6711 NA Ede
General Museum - 1938
Farm (1700) with inventory;
archeology (prehistoric and medieval);
craftmen's tools; domestic utensils;
costumes ; local history

09106
Museum Wegenbouw-machines
Verlengde Maanderweg 129, De
Beaufortlaan 9, NL-3971 BL Ede
Science/Tech Museum
Machines and materials used in road
construction

Ee

09107
Vlasbewerkingsmuseum
Dr. Ruinenstraat 17, NL-9131 KN Ee
Agriculture Museum
Cultivation of flax

Eernewoude

09108
Kokelhuis Fan Jan en Sjut
Fliet 16, NL Eernewoude
History/Public Affairs Museum - 1956
18th century house with living room
furnished in the original style; biblical
figures

Eersel

09109
Streekmuseum 'De Acht Zaligheden'
Kapelweg 2, NL-5521 JJ Eersel
General Museum - 1980
Old farm with interiors and farm
equipment from the beginning of the
20th century; gardens with flowers,
herbs, vegetables and trees; field with
animal food; old game called
'beugelspel' - library

Egmond aan Zee

09110
Museum Egmond Aan Zee
Zuiderstraat 7, Gemeentehuis,
Voorstraat 85, NL-1931 AJ Egmond
aan Zee
General Museum - 1951
Local history and history of fishery;
pictures; photos; paintings

Egmond-Binnen

09111
Museum van de Abdij van Egmond
Abdijlaan 26, NL-1935 BH Egmond-
Binnen
Archeology Museum
Objects found around the abbey (early
Middle Ages to the 16th c.),
earthenware, tiles, coins, textiles

Eindhoven

09112
Evoluon
Noord Brabantlaan 1a, NL-5652 LA
Eindhoven
Science/Tech Museum - 1966
Influence of science and technology
on social development

09113
Municipal Van Abbemuseum
Bilderdijklaan 10, POB 235, NL-5600
AE Eindhoven
Fine Arts Museum - 1936
Lissitzky Collection; 20th century art;
Moholy-Nagy 'Lightmachine'; Marc
Chagall 'Hommage à Appolinaire';
Joseph Beuys 'Environment' - library

09114
Museum Kempenland
Stratumseind 32, NL-5611 ET
Eindhoven
General Museum - 1920
Geology (southeastern part of the
Netherlands); costumes; pictures;
paintings; wooden shoe making; top
hats; 390 year old wooden textile
machine; Roman glass; mammoth
bones

09115
**Natuurhistorisch Onderwijsmuseum
(Vogelmuseum)**
Waagstraat 15, *mail c/o* Dienst van
Gemeentewerken afd. Plantsoenen,
Frederik van Eedenplein 1, NL-5611
KT Eindhoven
Natural History Museum
Zoology; botany; ornithology

Elburg

09116
Gemeentemuseum Elburg
Jufferenstraat 6, NL-8081 CR Elburg
General Museum
Paintings on fishery and landscape;
navigation instruments; planetarium;
silver; coins

09117
Visserijmuseum
Vischpoortstraat, Gemeentehuis
toestel 06, NL Elburg
History/Public Affairs Museum
History of fishery in the Zuidersee;
paintings

Elsloo

09118
Streekmuseum 'Schippersbeurs'
Op de Berg 4-6, NL-6181 GT Elsloo
General Museum - 1961
Prehistoric finds; Neolithic, Roman,
Gallo-Roman objects; household and
farming articles; bandceramics;
weaving; basketry; brickmaking;
beekeeping; butter and milk
production; daily life about 1880

Elst

09119
Museum Onder de N.H. Kerk
St. Maartenstraat 18, NL-6661 DA Elst
Archeology Museum
Finds from Gallo-Roman temples;
animals' skulls

Emmen

09120
Noorder Dierenpark
Hoofdstraat 18, Postbus 1010,
NL-7801 BA Emmen
Natural History Museum - 1980
Natural history and history of mankind
- connection with an ecological zoo

09121
Oudheidskamer 'De Hondsrug'
Marktplein 16, Klokkenslag 159,
NL-7811 HP Emmen
History/Public Affairs Museum - 1932
Prehistoric finds; historical costumes

Enkhuizen

09122
**Museum van Historische en
Moderne Wapens**
Zwaanstraat, Goudsbloemstraat 64,
NL-1602 XR Enkhuizen
History/Public Affairs Museum
All kinds of weapons from
prehistorical times to the present

09123
Rijksmuseum 'Zuiderzeemuseum'
Wierdijk 18, POB 42, NL-1601 LA
Enkhuizen
General Museum - 1948
Objects relating to the Zuiderzee area,
the coast and the islands; navigation;
fishing, related trades; ships and ship
models; paintings; farm tools;
costumes; open air collection of 130
houses from the Zuiderzee area -
library

09124
Stedelijk Waagmuseum
Kaasmarkt 8, NL-1600 AA Enkhuizen
Science/Tech Museum - 1910
Medical instruments, books and
manuscripts, herb books; surgeon
guild room with sweating room of
1636; weights; old tin objects; natural
history; temporary exhibitions of
modern art and history of medicine

Enschede

09125
Natuurmuseum en Vivarium
De Ruyterlaan 2, NL-7511 JH
Enschede
Natural History Museum - 1921
Zoology; botany; geology of eastern
parts of the Netherlands; fossils;
stones; amphibians; fish; insects;
molluscs; astronomical observatory
library; educational center

09126
Rijksmuseum Twenthe
Lasondersingel 129, NL-7514 BP
Enschede
General Museum - 1930
Medieval religious manuscripts,
sculptures and paintings; gobelins
(17th c.); portraits and landscapes
(16th-18th c.); French painting
(17th-19th c.); animal paintings; silver
toys; glass; gold and silver jewels;
Delft pottery (18th c.); old farm house
and tools - library

09127
Twents-Gelders Textielmuseum
Espoortstraat 182, NL-7511 CM
Enschede
Science/Tech Museum - 1959
Tools used in textile manufacturing;
spinning-wheels; handlooms;
development of the textile industry;
lace and textiles; display of decorating
techniques; natural dyes - library

Etten-Leur

09128
Grafisch Historisch Centrum
Lage Neerstraat 12, NL-4872 NB
Etten-Leur
History/Public Affairs Museum
History of printing

09129
Oudheidkundig Streekmuseum Jan Uten Houte
Markt 55-61, NL-4875 CC Etten-Leur
History/Public Affairs Museum - 1964
Reconstructed inn; interior (19th c.);
chapel (18th c.) with altar of a
clandestine church; costumes; crafts;
weights and measures; agricultural
implements

Exloo

09130
Museum Boerderij Bebinghehoes
Zuiderhoofdstraat 6, NL-7875 BX
Exloo
Agriculture Museum
Peat-cutting instruments; domestic
utensils; arts and crafts

Franeker

09131
Fries Munt -en Penningkabinet
Breedeplaats, NL-8801 LZ Franeker
History/Public Affairs Museum
Coins; balances

09132
Planetarium van Eise Eisinga
Eise Eisingastraat 3, NL-8801 KE
Franeker
Science/Tech Museum
Sundials; mirror reflex cameras;
calendarium; manuscripts by Eise
Eisinga; planetarium; astronomical
timepieces; maps

09133
Stedelijk Museum 't Dr. Coopmanshûs
Voorstraat 51, 8801 LA Franeker
General Museum - 1921
Xylotheek; memorabilia on Anna Maria
van Schurman and her family; local
academy and atheneum history,
portraits of professors; Elzinga's
mechanical works of art; botany
collection of King Louis Napoleon
(1809); miniatures; manuscripts;
ceramics - library

Frederiksoord

09134
Klokkenmuseum
Maj. van Swietenlaan 17, NL-8382 CE
Frederiksoord
Science/Tech Museum - 1973
Clocks and watches; all types of the
Frisian clock (1500-1900)

09135
Zeemuseum Miramar
Vledderweg 25, NL-8381 AB
Frederiksoord
Natural History Museum - 1966
Shells from various oceans; coral; fish
embryo fossils; starfish; marine birds;
dioramas

Geervliet

09136
Oudheidkamer Geervliet
Kaaistraat 2, NL Geervliet
General Museum
Antiquities; utensils especially from the
environs of Putten island

Geldrop

09137
Oudheidkamer
Mierloseweg 1, Gemeentehuis, NL
Geldrop
General Museum - 1964
Archeology; portraits (19th c.);
photographic material on economic,
social and cultural life of Geldrop;
tools

Genemuiden

09138
Stedelijke Oudheidkamer
Hoek 27, Nijstad 19, NL-8281 BB
Genemuiden
General Museum
Local history; furniture; tools and parts
of machinery related to the local
industry

Goes

09139
Museum voor Zuid- en Noordbeveland
Singelstraat 13, NL-4462 HZ Goes
General Museum - 1850/1865
Archeology; antiquities; costumes;
silverwork; coins; instruments of
torture; town views; paintings; toys

Goirle

09140
Heemerf De Schutsboom
Nieuwe Rielseweg 7-9, NL-5051 CB
Goirle
General Museum - 1962
Archeology; coins; cultural, social and
economic life of the Catholic
Netherlands (1853-1953); local history
and industries

Gorinchem

09141
Museum 'Dit is in Bethlehem'
Gasthuisstraat 25, Kon. Emmastraat 12,
NL-4205 BK Gorinchem
General Museum - 1912
Local history; pictures; paintings; coins

Gorredijk

09142
Streekmuseum Opsterland
Hoofdstraat 59, NL-8400 AB Gorredijk
General Museum - 1961
Geology; archeology; crafts; farm
tools; peat cutting; cable car
reproduction (1896); textiles

Gouda

09143
Pijpen- en Aardewerkmuseum De Moriaan
Westhaven, Catharinagasthuis, Achter
de Kerk 14, 2801 JX Gouda
General Museum - 1937
Inventory of a tobacco shop; pipes;
tiles; earthenware from 16th century to
present

09144
St. Janskerk (De Goudse Glazen)
Achter de Kerk 15a, NL-2801 JX
Gouda
Religious Art Museum
Stained glass windows (16th c.)

09145
Stedelijk Museum Het Catharina-Gasthuis
Achter de Kerk 14, NL-2801 JX Gouda
General Museum - 1874
French and Dutch painting (19th c.);
ancient medical instruments;
pharmacy; toys; religious art and
vestments; silver; coins; stained glass

Gramsbergen

09146
Gemeentelijke Oudheidkamer
Esch 1, NL-7783 CG Gramsbergen
General Museum - 1948
History of Gramsbergen and the
environs; prehistoric finds (found in
the field of battle 1927)

Grave

09147
Stadhuis en Museum Grave
Hoofdwagt 2, NL-5361 EW Grave
General Museum
Crafts (16th-19th c.)

Groenlo

09148
Grolsch Museum
Notenboomstraat 15, NL-7141 AB
Groenlo
General Museum
Urns, pottery and other finds;
weapons; weaving loom; fire-fighting;
religious painting

Groningen

09149
Biologisch-Archaeologisch Instituut der Rijksuniversiteit
Poststraat 6, NL-9712 ER Groningen
Natural History Museum - 1922
Prehistorical finds; diluvial mammals;
anthropology; specimens

09150
Groninger Museum voor Stad en Lande
Praediniussingel 59, NL-9711 AG
Groningen
Fine Arts Museum - 1894
Regional finds; local silver; oriental
ceramics; Dutch and Flemish drawings
and paintings including Rembrandt,
Rubens and Fabritius; contemporary
art - library

09151
Natuurmuseum Groningen
St. Walburgstraat 9, NL-9712 HX
Groningen
Natural History Museum - 1932
Coll: biology, birds, insects, wild
mammals, fresh water aquaria, shells
from the North Sea basin; geology,
Saalian erratic boulders, fossils -
library; educational center

09152
Niemeyer Nederlands Tabacologisch Museum
Brugstraat 24, NL-9711 HZ Groningen
Anthropology Museum - 1954
History of tobacco and its use in
Western Europe from 1500 until 1930;
pre-Columbian pipes

09153
Noordelijk Instituut voor Nijverheid en Techniek
Agricolastraat 33, NL-9711 TP
Groningen
Science/Tech Museum
Industrial technology and its impact on
our lives

09154
Noordelijk Scheepvaartmuseum
Brugstraat 24, NL-9711 HZ Groningen
History/Public Affairs Museum - 1932
Marine history of the Netherlands;
ship models; maps; instruments;
paintings; ship decoration

09155
Universiteitsmuseum
Broerstraat 5, POB 72, NL-9700 AB
Groningen
History/Public Affairs Museum - 1934
Documents and pictures about student
life and the history of the university;
physical and other scientific
instruments; archives and instruments
that belonged to Prof. Heymans,
psychologist (1900); minerals and
fossils - library

09156
Volkenkundig Museum Gerardus van der Leeuw
Nieuwe Kijk in 't Jatstraat 104,
NL-9712 SL Groningen
Anthropology Museum - 1968
Cultures of the so-called illiterate
peoples (especially Indonesia, the
Pacific and Africa south of the Sahara);
ethnographical objects of the Paiwan
of Taiwan

Grouw

09157
Gemeentemuseum Idaarderadeel
Stationsweg 15, NL-9001 ED Grouw
General Museum - 1956
Jewels; porcelain; costumes; utensils;
natural history of the environments

Haarlem

09158
Frans Hals Museum
Groot Heiligland 62, NL-2011 ES
Haarlem
General Museum - 1913
Paintings since the 16th century;
group portraits by Frans Hals
(1580-1666) and others; Tulip-book by
Judith Leyster; old dolls house;
collection of Haarlem silver; old
furniture; old pharmacy; copper; tin;
porcelain; glass; numismatics; pottery;
style of living; modern art

09159
Museum Enschedé
Klokhuisplein 5, Postbus 114, NL-2000
AC Haarlem
History/Public Affairs Museum - 1914
History of printing; printing art; historic
and modern printing machinery;
documents

09160
Schatkamer van de Kathedrale Basiliek St. Bavo
Leidse Vaart 146, NL Haarlem
Religious Art Museum - 1973
Treasure Chamber; gold and silver
(15th c. to present)

09161
Stadhuis
Grote Markt 2, NL-2011 RD Haarlem
General Museum
Town hall, oldest part formerly palace
of the counts of Holland; portraits of
the counts of Holland; painted ceiling;
mantelpieces; stained glass windows;
church chandeliers; tapestries

09162
Teylers Museum
Spaarne 16, NL-2011 CH Haarlem
General Museum - 1778
Paintings (19th-20th c.); drawings of
Dutch, Italian, and French schools
(16th-19th c.); historical scientific
instruments; electricity machine by van
Marum; fossils; minerals; coins;
medals - library

Haarzuilens

09163
Kasteel De Haar
Kasteelaan 1, NL-3455 RR Haarzuilens
Fine Arts Museum - 1925
Family portraits; furniture from the
Netherlands, England, France and
Italy; Persian rugs; Flemish gobelins
(14th-15th c.); paintings (14th-19th c.)

Haastrecht

09164
Ambachtsmuseum Verborg
Hoogstraat 164, Postbus 12, NL-2850
AA Haastrecht
History/Public Affairs Museum
Historical craftmen's tools; pictures
and scripts related to the crafts

09165
Museum Bisdom Van Vliet
Hoogstraat 166, NL-2851 BE
Haastrecht
History/Public Affairs Museum - 1923
Family house (19th c.) with complete
original furniture

Hardenberg

09166
Oudheidkamer
Voorstraat 34, NL-7772 AD
Hardenberg
General Museum
Saxon farm kitchen; agricultural
implements; crafts; fossils; coins;
Saxon costumes

Harderwijk

09167
Veluws Museum
Donkerstraat 4, POB 61, NL-3841 CC
Harderwijk
General Museum - 1952
Coins of Gelderland made in
Harderwijk; academical dissertations
of the University of Gelderland in
Harderwijk; archeological finds of the
North and West Veluwe; seal of
Harderwijk with so-called 'kogge-ship'
(14th c.)

Harlingen

09168
Hannemahuis
Voorstraat 50, NL-8861 BM Harlingen
General Museum - 1957
Harlinger history; silver; paintings
(17th-19th c.); tiles; ship models;
steamers in Harlingen town history

Hasselt

09169
Stadhuis
Markt 1, 8061 GG Hasselt, Postbus 23,
NL-8061 AA Hasselt
General Museum
Town hall (15th-16th c.); history of
Hasselt; paintings (17th c.); weapons

Hattem

09170
Bakkerijmuseum
Kerkhofstraat 13, NL-8051 GG Hattem
History/Public Affairs Museum
Municipal bakery (15th-16th c.) with
interior and shop; pottery; utensils and
models

09171
Streekmuseum Hattem
Achterstraat 48, Veldweg 15, NL-8051
NL Hattem
General Museum - 1949
Local history; agricultural tools;
costumes; archeology (prehistoric and
medieval)

Hazerswoude

09172
Gemeentemuseum
Dorpsstraat 66, Rubenslaan 6, NL-2391
HG Hazerswoude
History/Public Affairs Museum
Local history

Heemse

09173
Museum Hardenberg
Voorstraat 34, NL Heemse
General Museum
Prehistoric finds; fossils; coins; farm
implements; old Saxon kitchen; smithy

Heerenveen

09174
Batavus Museum
Industrieweg 2, POB 515, NL-8440 AM
Heerenveen 9300
Science/Tech Museum - 1963
History of the bicycle and motorized
two-wheelers, motorcycles,
accessories, posters; curiosity items

09175
Oudheidkamer Heerenveen
Vleesmarkt 9, NL-8441 EW
Heerenveen
General Museum
Prehistoric finds; old furniture;
agricultural tools; living room (18th c.);
porcelain; gold- and silverwork; coins;
medieval kitchen utensils; turf cutting
equipment

Heerlen

09176
Museum Geologisch Bureau
Akerstraat 86-88, 6411 HC Heerlen,
POB 126, NL-6400 AC Heerlen
Natural History Museum
Geology and paleontology from the
Netherlands and other countries;
carboniferous flora of the Netherlands
- library

09177
Thermenmuseum
Coriovallumstraat 9, NL-6411 CA
Heerlen
Archeology Museum - 1877
Roman provincial archeology; ruins of
a Roman bath (2nd-4th c.) under the
roof of a modern building - library

Heille

09178
**Streeklandbouwmuseum West
Zeeuws-Vlaanderen**
Zuiderbruggeweg 25, NL-4524 KH
Heille
Agriculture Museum - 1973
Agricultural history of the Zeeuws-
Vlaanderen area; old barn (1740); plow
used only in this area ('Wale Ploeg',
1610-1900)

Heinenoord

09179
Streekmuseum Hoeksche Waard
Hofweg 13, NL-3274 BK Heinenoord
General Museum - 1968
Local history; jewels; costumes;
agricultural instruments in their original
workshops; topography; crafts tools

Heino

09180
Hannema-De Stuers Fundatie
Kasteel het Nyenhuis, NL Heino
Fine Arts Museum - 1948
Paintings (17th c., Dutch, French and
Italian painters); designs; sculptures;
Chinese ceramics; furniture (18th-20th
c.)

Hellendoorn

09181
Oudheidkamer
Reggeweg 1, NL Hellendoorn
General Museum - 1966
Objects relating to old trades; clog
making; spinning; weaving; tanning;
churning; wood turning; turf cutting;
dyeing; workshop of an old Saksian
farm

Hellevoetsluis

09182
Nationaal Brandweermuseum
Gallasplein 5, NL-3221 AB
Hellevoetsluis
History/Public Affairs Museum - 1927
Firefighting material, vehicles and
engines since 1550

Helmond

09183
Gemeentemuseum
Kasteelplein 1, NL-5701 PP Helmond
General Museum - 1923
History of the 19th century

Heusden

09184
Streekmuseum Heusden
Gemeentehuis, NL Heusden
General Museum - 1968
Archeology; clog making; local relics

Hilvarenbeek

09185
De Doornboom
Doelenstraat 51, *mail c/o* Stichting
Geschied en Oudheidkundig Museum
Hilvarenbeek en Diessen, Joh. van
Brabantlaan 23, NL-5081 SC
Hilvarenbeek
Science/Tech Museum
Windmill; old tools

09186
Museum Het Oude Ambacht
Doelenstraat 53, NL-5081 CK
Hilvarenbeek
History/Public Affairs Museum
Crafts; agricultural implements

09187
De Schorsmolen
Vrijthof 28, *mail c/o* Stichting
Geschied en Oudheidkundig Museum
Hilvarenbeek en Diessen, Joh. van
Brabantlaan 23, NL-5081 SC
Hilvarenbeek
History/Public Affairs Museum
Prehistory; architecture; ceramics;
topography; genealogy; - library

Hilversum

09188
**Gemeentelijke Dienst voor Cultuur
'De Vaart'**
Vaartweg 163, NL-1217 SP Hilversum
General Museum - 1969
Porcelain objects relating to
Loosdrecht and Amstel; regional
archeology and geology of Gooi;
antiquities of Gooi; topographic atlas
of Gooi

Hindeloopen

09189
Hidde Nijland Museum
Dijkweg 1, NL-8713 KD Hindeloopen
General Museum - 1919
Local interiors (18th c.); painted
furniture; local costumes; history of
the town and navigation

Hoensbroek

09190
Kasteel Hoensbroek
Schutterijmuseum voor de beide
Limburgen
Klinkerstraat 118, NL-6433 PB
Hoensbroek
History/Public Affairs Museum
History of the regional militias;
uniforms; weapons; documents

Hollum

09191
Sorgdragershuis Ouwe Pôlle
Oosterlaan, NL Hollum, Ameland
Historic Site
Captain's house of 1751 with interior;
folk art

Holten

09192
Natuurhistorisch Museum Piet Bos
Holterbergweg 5, NL-7451 KB Holten
Natural History Museum - 1929
Mounted birds and mammals;
dioramas

Hoogeveen

09193
Hoogeveens Museum Venendal
Hoofdstraat 9, NL-7902 EA
Hoogeveen
General Museum - 1971
Old furniture; objects of art; old
costumes; tools used in agriculture
and peat cutting; decorated antique
tiles; old weapons

Hoorn

09194
Westfries Museum
Rode Steen 1, Kerkstraat 10, NL-1621
CW Hoorn
General Museum - 1879
History of Hoorn, West-Friesland and
navigation; archeological finds;
paintings (17th-19th c.); drawings;
maps; coins; furniture; interiors
(18th-19th c); tin; glass; pottery; tiles
(17-18th c.); costumes (18th-19th c.);
contemporary Westfrisian naive
painting; painted map of Batavia (1627)

Horst

09195
Oudheidkamer
Lambertusplein 3a, NL-5961 EW Horst
History/Public Affairs Museum
Archeological finds; agricultural
implements; local history

Hulst

09196
Streekmuseum 'De Vier Ambachten'
Steenstraat 28, Moersluisstraat 2,
NL-4561 HE Hulst
General Museum - 1929
Archeological finds; old maps; pictures
and objects relating to the geology,
geography (land reclamation),
government and the fortifications and
fortified cities in East Zealand-
Flanders, particularly the medieval
fortified city of Hulst; history of the
bow and arrow marksmen corps;
agricultural implements; old trades;
folk costumes; explanation about the
medieval animal epic 'Van den Vos
Reynaerde', which takes place in the
region between Ghent and Hulst

Huijbergen

09197
Wilhelmietenklooster
Instituut Ste Marie, Staartsestraat 8,
NL-4635 BB Huijbergen
History/Public Affairs Museum
Religious art and history; documents
(14th-19th c.)

Janum

09198
Kerkmuseum
NL Janum
Religious Art Museum - 1947
Church (1200); sarcophagi; sculptures;
paintings; baptismal font

Joure

09199
Johannes Hessel-huis
Geelgietersstraat 1, NL-8500 AB Joure
General Museum
Tobacco, coffee, tea; bell casting

Kampen

09200
Frans Walkate Archief
mail c/o Spaarbank, Burgwal 41,
NL-8261 EP Kampen
General Museum
Works of local painters; topography

09201
Oude Raadhuis
Oudestraat, NL-8261 CK Kampen
History/Public Affairs Museum
Town hall (14th c.) with original
furniture

09202
Stedelijk Museum Broederpoort
2e Ebbingestraat 50, 8261 JW Kampen
History/Public Affairs Museum - 1947
Coins; paintings; local silver collection;
a horn with silver decorations either
from the skippers of 'St.Anne' or the
'Rhineskippersguild' (1369) - library

Katwijk an Zee

09203
Gebouw Genootschap 'Oud Katwijk'
Voorstraat 81, NL-2225 EM Katwijk an
Zee
General Museum - 1966
Local art and history; folklore;
costumes; lace - library

Kerkrade

09204
Mining Museum
Abbay Rolduc, Heyendahllaan 82,
NL-6464 EP Kerkrade
Science/Tech Museum - 1974
Coll: mining lamp; fossils; minerals;
wooden water pump (18th c.) - library

Ketelhaven

09205
Museum voor Scheepsarcheologie
Vossemeerdijk 21, NL-8251 PM
Ketelhaven
History/Public Affairs Museum - 1969
Parts of shipwrecks from prehistory to
present; excavated shipwrecks (180
BC, 17th c.); complete ships'
household inventories; shipbuilding
and shipping

Koog an de Zaan

09206
Oliemolen Het Pink
Pinkstraat 12, Koog an de Zaan, 't
Weefhuis, Lagedijk 39, NL-1544 BB
Zaandijk
History/Public Affairs Museum - 1940
Mill from 1620 with original inventory;
models; weaving tools; work benches;
mill panorama

09207
Zaansch Molenmuseum
Museumslaan 18, Koog an de Zaan, 't
Weefhuis, Lagedijk 39, NL-1544 BB
Zaandijk
History/Public Affairs Museum - 1940
Old mill; paintings; fragments; models;
work instruments relating to industry
and watermills

Krimpen aan den IJssel

09208
Streekmuseum 'Crimpenerhof'
IJsseldijk 312, 2922 BM Krimpen aan
den IJssel, *mail c/o* A.A.
Murk-Veerkamp, Oostzoom 10, NL
Krimpen an den Lek
History/Public Affairs Museum - 1964
Farm from about 1730 with farm
implements and interiors; ship building;
stone bakery; pottery

Laren

09209
Geologisch Museum Hofland
Zevenend 8a, IJsbaanweg 25, NL-1251
VT Laren
Natural History Museum
Geology; fossils; minerals

09210
Singer Museum Stichting Singer
Memorial Foundation
Oude Drift 1, NL-1251 BS Laren
Fine Arts Museum - 1956
International collection of paintings
from the schools of Amsterdam, Den
Haag and Laren; collection of the
American painter William H. Singer

Lauwersoog

09211
Expo-Zee
Strandweg 1, NL-9976 VS
Lauwersoog
Science/Tech Museum
Land reclamation and dike
construction

Leek

09212
Nationaal Rijtuigmuseum 'Nienoord'
Castle Nienoord, NL-9351 AC Leek
Science/Tech Museum - 1958
Carriages; sleighs; cars (18th-20th c.);
paintings; graphics; travel accessories
- library

Leens

09213
Ommelander Museum
Borg Verhildersum, Wierde 40,
NL-9965 TB Leens
General Museum - 1966
Castle (1398-1400, rebuilt 16th c.);
interiors and style of living (18th-19th
c.); portraits; agricultural implements;
local history and art

Leerdam

09214
Hofje Van Aerden
Kerkstraat 67a, Leerdam, Kralingse
Plaslaan 200, NL-3061 DJ Rotterdam
Fine Arts Museum
Paintings (17th c.), Frans Hals
'Lachende Jongens', Dubbels, Pieter
Claesz, Gerard Terboch; family
portraits

09215
Museum 't Poorthuis
Kerkstraat 91, NL-4140 AA Leerdam
General Museum - 1965
History of Leerdam; crafts
instruments; wheel making

09216
Nationaal Glasmuseum
Lingedijk 28, NL-4142 LD Leerdam
Decorative Arts Museum - 1953
Old and modern glass from the
Netherlands and other countries;
single pieces made by artists in the
Leerdam glassworks 1925-1980 -
library

Leeuwarden

09217
Fries Museum
Turfmarkt 24, NL-8911 KT Leeuwarden
General Museum - 1881
Regional antiquities; archeology;
Middle Ages; paintings; portraits;
silver (16th-19th c.); ceramics; Chinese
and Japanese porcelain; pottery; folk
arts; numismatics; topographic atlas of
Friesland; copper engravings

09218
Fries Natuurhistorisch Museum
Herestraat 13, NL-8911 LC
Leeuwarden
Natural History Museum - 1923
Geology; flora and fauna of Friesland
and the environs; birds; eggs; insects;
shells; herbarium - library

09219
**Frysk Letterkundich Museum en
Dokumintaesjesintrum**
Grote Kerkstraat 28, POB 884,
NL-8901 BR Leeuwarden
History/Public Affairs Museum - 1959
Objects about literature of Friesland
including manuscripts, letters, portraits,
paintings, posters, programs;
collection about Pieter Jelles Troelstra
(Frisian poet and politician), his wife
Nynke van Hichtum (authoress of
children's books) and other members
of the Troelstra family; Mata Hari lived
in this house from 1883-1890 - library

09220
**Fryske Kultuerried/Culturele Raad
van Friesland**
Grote Kerkstraat 41, NL-8901 BP
Leeuwarden
Fine Arts Museum
Contemporary art; costumes
(18th-19th c.)

09221
**Gemeentelijk Museum Het
Princessehof** Algemeen Ceramisch
Studiecentrum
Grote Kerkstraat 9-15, NL-8911 DZ
Leeuwarden
Decorative Arts Museum - 1917
Ceramics from Asia and Europe; tiles
from Europe and the Middle East;
modern studio ceramics from Europe;
archeological sherd collections; other
applied arts; fine arts from the
Netherlands (20th c.); ceramic
workshop - library; educational center
for ceramic study in the Netherlands

09222
Pier Pander Museum
Prinsentuin, *mail c/o* Gemeentelijk
Museum 'het Princessehof', NL-8911
DE Leeuwarden
Fine Arts Museum - 1924
Sculptures by Pier Pander and
monument to the artist (1864-1919)

Leiden

09223
Academisch Historisch Museum
Rapenburg 73, NL-2311 GJ Leiden
History/Public Affairs Museum - 1930
University history, portraits,
documentation - library

09224
Koninklijk Nederlands Leger- en Wapenmuseum Generaal Hoefer
Pesthuislaan 7, NL-2333 BA Leiden
History/Public Affairs Museum - 1913
Military history of the Netherlands;
weapons from prehistory to present;
uniforms; flags; paintings - library

09225
Meermansbrug Hofje
Oude Vest 159, Bank, Breestraat 81,
NL-2311 CV Leiden
History/Public Affairs Museum
Manor house (1681) with family
portraits (17th-19th c.)

09226
Molenmuseum De Valk
2e Binnenvestgracht 1, De Lakenhal,
Oude Singel 28-32, NL-2312 RA
Leiden
Science/Tech Museum - 1966
Mill (1743) with original machinery,
tools and implements; mill models;
documentation

09227
Munt- en Penningkabinet der Rijksuniversiteit
Rapenburg 65, NL-2311 EZ Leiden
History/Public Affairs Museum - 1835
Coins and decorations, especially from
Portugal and Brazil; French
commemorative medals

09228
Museum Boerhaave National
Museum of the History of Science and
Medicine
Steenstraat 1 A, NL-2312 BS Leiden
Natural History Museum - 1928
History of science and medicine;
microscopes; telescopes; medical
instruments; electric machines;
physical demonstration models (18th
c., van 's-Gravesande and
Musschenbroek collection); Ehrenfest-
Archives; quadrant of Snellius;
microscope of Antoni van
Leeuwenhoek; lenses by Chr.
Huygens; heliumliquefactor of
Kamerlingh Onnes - library

09229
Pilgrim Fathers Documentatie Centrum
Boisotkade 2A, NL-2311 PZ Leiden
History/Public Affairs Museum - 1958
Photocopies of documents about the
Pilgrim Fathers (1609-1620 in Leiden);
historic prints of Leiden; model of 17th
century printing press; model of the
'Mayflower' (scale 1:36)

09230
Prentenkabinet der Rijksuniversiteit
Rapenburg 65, NL-2311 SK Leiden
Fine Arts Museum - 1815
Flemish and Dutch schools; history of
photography; iconography; book
illustrations - library

09231
Rijksherbarium
Schelpenkade 6, NL-2313 ZT Leiden
Natural History Museum - 1829
Coll: dried plants, especially from the
Netherlands and Malaysia; wood
specimens; botanic iconography -
library

09232
Rijksmuseum Van Natuurlijke Historie
Raamsteg 2, POB, NL-2300 RA Leiden
Natural History Museum - 1820
Coll: recent animals; pleistocene
fossils from former Dutch East Indies;
mammals; birds; fish; molluscs; shells;
pithecantropus erectus - library

09233
Rijksmuseum van Oudheden
Rapenburg 28, NL-2311 EW Leiden
Archeology Museum - 1818
Egyptian sculptures and decorative
arts, Nubian Temple rebuilt in special
hall; collections from Palestine,
Mesopotamia, Persia; Greek, Roman,
Cypriot and Etruscan antiquities;
prehistory and early history of the
Netherlands - library

09234
Rijksmuseum voor Geologie en Mineralogie
Hooglandse Kerkgracht 17, NL-2312
HS Leiden
Natural History Museum - 1878
Regional geology; fossils of mammals;
paleontology; mineralogy;
petrography; geology; precious stones

09235
Rijksmuseum voor Volkenkunde
Steenstraat 1, Postbus 212, NL-2300
AE Leiden
Anthropology Museum - 1837
Ethnology (China, Japan, India,
Southeast Asia, South Pacific, North-,
Central- and South America, Africa
and Middle East); archeology from
Java (Hindu-Javanese art); Japanese
art (prints and drawings);
pre-Columbian art; bronze from Benin
and other African art; Buddhist art; the
'Leyden Plate' (oldest
contemporaneously dated inscription
from the Maya civilisation) - library

09236
Stedelijk Museum De Lakenhal
Oude Singel 28-32, NL-2312 Leiden
Fine Arts Museum - 1869
Coll: paintings including Lucas van
Leyden (1489-1533), Rembrandt, Jan
Steen, Van Goyen; sculptures; glass;
silver; period rooms (17th-19th c.);
local archeological finds - library

Leidschendam

09237
Het Nationaal Automobielmuseum
Veursestraatweg 280, NL-2265
Leidschendam
Science/Tech Museum - 1968
Historical automobiles; motorcycles;
bicycles; sleds; tractors; pictures and
posters

Leleystad

09238
Informatiecentre 'Nieuw Land'
Oostvaardersdyk 1-13, NL-8242 PA
Leleystad
Science/Tech Museum - 1976
Land reclamation in Lake Yissel -
library; slide shows; films

Lemmer

09239
Oudheidkamer Lemster Fiifgea
Gemeentehuis Lemmer, NL-8531 EK
Lemmer
General Museum
Local history; fishing; peat cutting

Lievelde

09240
Openluchtmuseum Erve Kots
Eimersweg 4, Post Groenlo, NL-7137
HG Lievelde
General Museum - 1936
Prehistoric finds; household objects;
tools

Limmen

09241
Museum voor de Bloembollenteelt
Dusseldorperweg 64, Gemeentehuis,
Middenweg 3a, NL-1960 AP Limmen
Agriculture Museum - 1934
Tools and machinery used in the
culture of bulbs

Loosdrecht

09242
Kasteel Sypesteyn
Nieuw-Loosdrechtsedijk 150, NL-1231
LC Loosdrecht
Fine Arts Museum - 1927
Art (16th-18th c.); paintings; family
portraits; furniture; weapons; clocks;
porcelain; glasses; silver; pottery

Luyksgestel

09243
Bakkerijmuseum De Grenswachter
Kapelweg, NL-5575 BG Luyksgestel
History/Public Affairs Museum

Maassluis

09244
Gemeentemuseum
Zuiddijk 16, NL-3143 AS Maassluis
Fine Arts Museum - 1933
Modern art after 1900; local history -
library

Maastricht

09245
Bonnefantenmuseum
Dominikanerplein 5, NL-6211 DZ
Maastricht
Archeology Museum - 1865/1968
Archeological finds from the province
of Limburg (prehistorical to medieval
periods); sculptures and paintings by
masters from the southern
Netherlands (14th-17th c.); silver from
Maastricht and other local historical
objects; contemporary art - library

09246
Glas- en Keramiekmuseum
Pand Victor de Stuers, Brusselsestraat
77, Batterijstraat 47, Postbus 1985,
NL-6201 BZ Maastricht
General Museum - 1980
18th and 19th century glass and
crystal from Western Europe; 20th
century glass and cristal produced by
the Kristal Unie at Maastricht;
machinery and different stages of
glassproduction

09247
Museum De Helpoort
St. Bernardusstraat, Postbus 216,
NL-6200 AE Maastricht
General Museum
Archeology; geology

09248
Natuurhistorisch Museum
De Bosquetplein 6-7, NL-6211 KJ
Maastricht
Natural History Museum - 1912
Fossils; local flora and fauna; geology;
paleontology; fish and reptiles - library

09249
Schatkamer van de Basiliek van Onze Lieve Vrouwe
O.L. Vrouweplein 8, NL Maastricht
Religious Art Museum
Religious art and objects

09250
Schatkamer van de Sint Servaaskerk
Keizer Karelplein 6, NL-6211 TC
Maastricht
Religious Art Museum
Religious art; vestments; paintings

09251
Spaans Gouvernement
Vrijthof 18, NL-6211 LD Maastricht
History/Public Affairs Museum
Residence of dukes of Brabant;
Wagner-De Wit collection of antique
furniture, clocks, sculptures, paintings,
earthenware

Makkum

09252
Fries Aardewerkmuseum 'De Waag'
Waaggebouw, Waagsteeg 1, POB 11,
NL-8754 ZN Makkum
Decorative Arts Museum - 1960
Tin glazed earthenware and tiles;
delftware

Marssum

09253
Heringa State
Slotlaan 1, NL-9034 HM Marssum
History/Public Affairs Museum
16th century nobleman's seat; furniture
and paintings (17th c.); silver (1880);
bedsteads (16th c.)

Medemblik

09254
Oudtheytkamer tot Medenblick
p/a Weeshuis, Torenstraat 5, NL
Medemblik
General Museum - 1964
Local history

Meersen

09255
Natuurhistorisch Museum en Heemkunde Centrum
Markt 31, Prinses Beatrixweg 33,
NL-6231 GH Meersen
General Museum
Natural history; ornithology; shells;
entomology; botany; geology; minerals

Middelburg

09256
Zeeuws Museum
Abdij 4, POB 378, NL-4330 AJ
Middelburg
General Museum - 1769
Porcelain; archeological finds;
paintings; furniture; tapestries (16th c.)
and costumes

Middelstum

09257
Museum Bakkerij Mendels
Kerkstraat 3, NL-9991 BL Middelstum
History/Public Affairs Museum
Historical bakery (16th-17th c.) with
interior (1829) and equipment

Midden-Beemster

09258
Huize Betje Wolff
Middenweg 178, Middenweg 170,
NL-1462 HL Midden-Beemster
General Museum
Furnished living room (18th-19th c.);
objects relating to dairy economy and
cattle breeding

Moddergat

09259
't Fiskershûske
Fiskerspaed 4-8, NL-9142 VN
Moddergat
General Museum
Three fishermen's houses with 19th
century interiors; fishing equipment;
costumes; folk art; history of the
Frisian rescue work; lifeboat models;
rescue articles; medals; pictures

Muiden

09260
Rijksmuseum Muiderslot
Herengracht 1, NL-1398 AA Muiden
History/Public Affairs Museum - 1878
13th century castle; interiors with
furniture (17th c.); carpets; copper
crowns; tin; earthenware; weapons;
paintings; household objects; books
by Pieter Cornelisz Hooft, who lived in
Munderslot from 1609 until his death
in1647

Naaldwijk

09261
Westlands Streekmuseum
Heilige Geest Hofje 7, NL-2671 GW
Naaldwijk
General Museum - 1908
Finds dating back to the late Stone
Age; Roman finds; finds from the
earliest Middle Ages; paintings,
portraits of the lords of Naaldwijk;
maps; reproductions; objects from
Naaldwijk and from other villages in
Westland; ruins of Honselaarsdijk
castle

Naarden

09262
Comenius Museum
Turfpoortstraat 27, NL-1411 ED
Naarden
History/Public Affairs Museum - 1892
Writings of Jan Amos Comenius
(1592-670) and objects relating to the
philosopher, pedagogue and
theologian

09263
Historisch Vestingmuseum
Westwalstraat, Stadhuis,
Raadhuisstraat 1, NL-1411 EC
Naarden
General Museum - 1955
History of fortress Turfpoort and its
casemates (17th-19th c.);
watercolours; pictures; maps; historic
dioramas; canons; uniforms; history of
Red Cross in the Netherlands

Nieuw-Vossemeer

09264
A.M. de Jonghuis
Voorstraat 29, NL-4681 AC Nieuw-
Vossemeer
History/Public Affairs Museum - 1968
Drawings, letters, photos and books of
writer A.M. de Jong (1888-1943)

09265
Molenmuseum Assumburg
Veerweg 1, Gemeentehuis, NL Nieuw-
Vossemeer
History/Public Affairs Museum
Ancient mill with intact interior;
different models of mill types used in
the Netherlands; drawings and photos

Noordwijk Aan Zee

09266
Museumboerderij Oud Noordwijk
Jan Kroonsplein 4, NL-2202 SP
Noordwijk Aan Zee
General Museum - 1961
18th century farm with complete
interior (19th c.); costumes; models of
fishing boats; collection of shells found
in the North Sea; photographs

Nuenen

09267
Van Gogh Documentatiecentrum
Papenvoorts 15, Gemeentehuis,
NL-5671 CP Nuenen
Fine Arts Museum
Photos and reproductions of Van
Gogh's works; documents on his stay
at Nuenen 1883-1885

Nunspeet

09268
Veluws Diorama
Marktstraat 17-19, NL-8071 GV
Nunspeet
Natural History Museum - 1957
Mounted birds; mammals; botany

Nijbeets

09269
Veenderijmuseum Damshus
Domela Nieuwenhuisweg, NL Nijbeets
General Museum - 1960
Room of a peat cutter (1870); tools

Nijmegen

09270
**Bijbels Openluchtmuseum Heilig
Land Stichting**
Heilig Land Stichting 14, Groesbeek,
NL-6564 BV Nijmegen
Open Air Museum - 1911
Reconstructions of houses and daily
life in the Palestine up to the Roman
period; objects relating to biblical
countries and their cultures

09271
Nijmeegs Museum 'Commanderie
Van St. Jan'
Franseplaats 3, NL-6511 VS Nijmegen
Fine Arts Museum - 1974
Modern art; local history - library

09272
Rijksmuseum G.M. Kam
Museum Kamstr. 45, NL-6522 GB
Nijmegen
Archeology Museum - 1922
Regional prehistoric finds; local and
regional Roman finds; relics from a
graveyard and fortress; early medieval
finds; Roman silver cup; bronze head
of Trajan - library

Oirschot

09273
Museum De Vier Quartieren
Sint-Odulphusstraat 11, NL-5688 BA
Oirschot
General Museum
Folk art of Brabant (18th-19th c.);
religious art; tools and implements
used in the van Den Bosch dairy

Oldenzaal

09274
Historisch Museum Het Palthe-Huis
Marktstraat 13, NL-7571 ED Oldenzaal
General Museum - 1907
Archeology; prehistory; fossils;
heraldic figures; pipes; old library;
farm kitchen; mirrors; sundial

09275
**Schatkamer van de St.
Plechelmusbasiliek**
St. Plechelmusplein, NL-7571 EG
Oldenzaal
Religious Art Museum - 1810
Religious objects; memorabilia of St.
Plechelmus; vestments

Olst

09276
Letterkundig Museum Dépendance
Diepenveenseweg 1, NL-8121 DV Olst
History/Public Affairs Museum
Documents on literary history of the
Netherlands and Flanders

Ommen

09277
Stichting Oudheidkamer Ommen
Den Oordt 7, Gemeentehuis, NL-7731
CM Ommen
General Museum
Local costumes; vessels; jewels;
geology; prehistory; tools; parts of
restored wood and corn mills

Oosterbeek

09278
Airborne Museum 'Hartenstein'
Utrechtsweg, NL-6862 AZ Oosterbeek
History/Public Affairs Museum - 1949
Objects relating to the battle of
Arnhem in September 1944

Oostkapelle

09279
Fossilien-Museum
Molenweg 36, NL-4356 AB
Oostkapelle
Archeology Museum - 1977

Ospel-Nederweert

09280
Bezoekerscentrum Mijn Op Zeven
Moostdijk 8, NL-6035 RB Ospel-
Nederweert
History/Public Affairs Museum - 1966
Local flora and fauna; history of peat
cutting

09281
Peelmuseum
Cassaweg 1a, NL-6035 PP Ospel-
Nederweert
General Museum
Peat cutting; local flora and fauna ·
craftmen's and agricultural implements;
costumes

Oss

09282
Jan Cunen Museum
Molenstraat 65, NL-5341 GC Oss
General Museum - 1935
Local and regional history; prehistory;
geology; sculptures; topography;
paintings and sketches (19th c.); Dutch
paintings of the romantic period;
impressionism - library

Ost-Vlieland

09283
Natuurhistorisch Museum
Dorpstraat 152, NL Ost-Vlieland
Natural History Museum - 1958
Birds; butterflies; shells; plants

09284
Tromp's Huys
Dorpstraat 99, NL-8899 AD
Ost-Vlieland
General Museum
Folklore of Norway; paintings of Belzy
R. Akersloot, H.W. Mesdag, Max
Liebermann - library

Otterlo

09285
Rijksmuseum Kröller-Müller
Houtkampweg 6, NL-6730 AA Otterlo
Fine Arts Museum - 1937
Coll: Van Gogh ('Draw-bridge at Arles',
'Potato-eaters', 'Night-café');
contemporary sculptures (group of
Lipchitz sculptures); realism;
impressionism; cubism; abstract art;
ceramics - library

09286
Tegelmuseum 'It Noflik Ste'
Eikenzoom 10, NL-6731 BH Otterlo
Decorative Arts Museum - 1961

Oudemirdum

09287
Natuurhistorisch Streekmuseum Klif
En Gaast
Brink 4, NL-8567 JD Oudemirdum
Natural History Museum - 1958
Fauna and flora of the environs

Oudenbosch

09288
Natuurhistorisch en Vogelmuseum
Instituut St.Louis, Markt 34, NL-4731
HP Oudenbosch
Natural History Museum
Ornithology; ethnography (Indonesia,
Africa, China)

09289
Nederlands Zouavenmuseum
Markt 31, NL-4731 HM Oudenbosch
History/Public Affairs Museum
Religious history

Oudewater

09290
De Heksenwaag
Leeuweringerstraat 2, NL-3421 AC
Oudewater
General Museum - 1943
Topography; paintings; old customs;
coins; weights

Petten

09291
De Dijk Te Kijk
Tentoonstellingsgebouw
Zuiderhazedwarsdijk, Petten, mail c/o
p/a Hoogheemraadschap
Noordhollands Noorderkwartier,
Kennemerstraatweg 13, Postbus 22,
NL-1800 AA Alkmaar
Science/Tech Museum
Information about dikes

Piaam

09292
't Fûgelhûs' Natuurhistorisches
Museum
Buren 6, NL-8756 JP Piaam
Natural History Museum - 1972
Photos of poultry; slides

Purmerend

09293
Purmerend's Museum
Stadhuis, Kaasmarkt, NL-1441 BG
Purmerend
General Museum
Local history; handicrafts; firebrigade
material; religious objects

Raamsdonksveer

09294
Het Nationaal Automobielmuseum
Raamsdonksveer
Science/Tech Museum - 1968
Passenger cars; commercial vehicles;
cycles; motorcycles; carriages; toys;
posters

Rhenen

09295
Ouwehands Dierenpark
Grebbeweg 109, POB 9, NL-3910 AA
Rhenen
Natural History Museum - 1932
Dolphinarium and Aquarium and Zoo;
Breeding of endangered species -
Educational room; plans to create an
educational centre for flora, fauna,
history and geology of the region

09296
Streekmuseum
'de Brakken', Molenstraat 25, NL-3911
KK Rhenen
History/Public Affairs Museum - 1910
Historical collection of Rhenen;
summer residence of Frederic V and
Mary Stuart; archeology; jewels;
porcelain; tiles; guild silver; sketches;
graphics; modern art

Roden

09297
Museum Kinderwereld
Brink 31, NL-9301 JK Roden
Anthropology Museum
Antique toys

Roermond

09298
**Gemeentelijk Museum Hendrik
Luyten-Dr. Cuypers**
Andersonweg 8, NL-6041 JE
Roermond
General Museum - 1931
Local history; archeological finds
(Roman and medieval); coins; painting
(since 16th c.); medieval manuscripts;
furniture and interiors; antiquities from
Egypt; sculpture

Roosendaal

09299
Museum De Ghulden Roos
Molenstraat 2, NL-4701 JS
Roosendaal
General Museum - 1932
Folklore; stoneware (15th-18th c.);
glass; Delft pottery; porcelain from
Asia; toys

Rotterdam

09300
De Dubbelde Palmboom
Voorhaven 12 Delfshaven, NL-3024
RM Rotterdam
History/Public Affairs Museum
Ancient crafts and social life; silver
(18th-19th c.)

09301
Maritiem Museum Prins Hendrik
Scheepmakers-Haven 48, NL-3011 VC
Rotterdam
History/Public Affairs Museum - 1873
Ship models (15th-20th c.);
construction designs; globes, atlases;
maps; navigation instruments;
paintings; ship decorations;
documents relating to the history of
navigation and maritime constructions;
fishing boat models - library

09302
Museum Boymans-Van Beuningen
Mathenesserlaan 18-20, POB 2277,
NL-3000 CG Rotterdam
Fine Arts Museum - 1847
Div: applied art; Renaissance and
baroque; paintings from the
Netherlands (15th-17th c.), Italy
(14th-16th c.), France; modern art,
expressionists and surrealists,
impressionists, realists, sculpture, pop
art and photorealism

09303
Museum Hendrik Chabot
Berglustlaan 12, NL-3054 BG
Rotterdam
Fine Arts Museum - 1962
Paintings by Hendrik Chabot
(1894-1949), war cycle 1940-1945,
sculptures 1923-1939; Dutch
expressionism - educational center

09304
Museum voor Land- en Volkenkunde
Willemskade 25, NL-3016 DM
Rotterdam
Anthropology Museum - 1883
Ethnological and archeological
collections from Indonesia, Oceania,
the realm of Islam, Asia, Africa, the
Americas; nusmismatics; sculpture of
'Travelling European, borne by two
men in a hammock' (Sundi sub-style
from lower Congo); 'Avalokiteshvara-
Chenresi' with 11 heads and 8 arms
(gold-coloured bronze, 18th century
from Tibet) - library

09305
Natuurhistorisch Museum
Van Aerssenlaan 49, NL-3000 LA
Rotterdam
Natural History Museum - 1927
Plio-Pleistocene, Miocene, Oligocene
and Eocene; mollusca, marine and land
mollusca from Europe and the
Indo-Australian region; Pleistocene
mammalia from the Netherlands;
European hymenoptera aculeata and
lepidoptera; European birds and
mammals; geology; botany; European
marine invertebrates - library

09306
**Nederlands Economisch
Penningkabinet**
Erasmusuniversiteit, Burg. Oudlaan 50,
NL-3062 PA Rotterdam
History/Public Affairs Museum - 1961
Medals relating to the economic life of
Rotterdam and to public works

09307
**The Professor van der Poel Museum
of Taxation**
Parklaan 14-16, NL-3016 BB
Rotterdam
History/Public Affairs Museum - 1936
History of taxes from ancient times to
the present, paintings, prints, furniture,
ceramics, pewter, coins, medals, fiscal
seals and stamps, instruments, tools,
measures and weights, assessment
materials, playing cards, round games,
uniforms, weapons, means of
smuggling - library

09308
Stichting Atlas van Stolk
Aelbrechtskolk 12, NL-3024 RE
Rotterdam
History/Public Affairs Museum - 1835
Drawings, engravings, photos
concerning the history of the
Netherlands, pictures of daily life,
historical events and persons
(including illustrated books, maps,
allegorical prints and caricatures) -
room for slideshows

09309
Zakkendragershuisje
Voorstraat 13-15, NL-3012 LB
Rotterdam
History/Public Affairs Museum - 1966
Pewterer's workshop; bronze casting
moulds (esp. 17th c.); stamps

Rozendaal

09310
**Museum van het Internationaal
Kastelen Instituut**
Kasteel Rosendael, NL-6891 DA
Rozendaal
History/Public Affairs Museum
Sketches; weapons; photographs of
castles from all over the world

Ruinerwold

09311
Museumboerderij Ruinerwold
Dr. Larijweg 21, NL-7960 AA
Ruinerwold
History/Public Affairs Museum - 1954
Farm (18th c.) with complete inventory

Rijnsburg

09312
Het Spinozahuis
Spinozalaan 29, NL-2231 SG Rijnsburg
History/Public Affairs Museum - 1899
Reconstruction of the library of the
philosopher B. de Spinoza (1632-1677),
editions of his works, works relating to
him; portraits; old instruments for
grinding lenses

Rijssen

09313
Oudheidkamer Riessen
Stadhuis, Schild 1, NL-7461 AS Rijssen
General Museum - 1948
Town views; photographs; agricultural
implements and tools for clog making;
dolls with costumes; coins

Rijswijk

09314
Museum Rijswijk, Tollenshuis
Herenstraat 67, NL-2282 BR Rijswijk
General Museum - 1940
Archeological finds; paintings;
furniture; local history; contemporary
art

Santpoort

09315
Ruïne Van Brederode
Velserenderlaan 2, NL-2082 LA
Santpoort
Archeology Museum
Archeological objects found in the
environs of the ruin; earthenware;
weights and measures; glass

Schaarsbergen

09316
Museum Korps Rijdende Artillerie
Oranje Kazerne, Deelenseweg 20,
NL-6816 TS Schaarsbergen
History/Public Affairs Museum - 1890
Uniforms and equipment of the Dutch
Horse Artillery

Schaesberg

09317
Documentatiecentrum Aad de Haas
Heerlenseweg 162, NL-6371 HX
Schaesberg
Fine Arts Museum
Works of the painter Aaad de Haas

Schagen

09318
Kaasmuseum Staverman
Hoep 8-10, Postbus 30, NL-1740 AA
Schagen
Agriculture Museum
Machinery and instruments for cheese
production (1800-1940)

09319
Museum Schagen
Loet 14, Plantsoen 10, NL-1741 EM
Schagen
General Museum
Local history

Schermerhorn

09320
Stichting Museummolen
Noordervaart 2, NL-1636 VL
Schermerhorn
Science/Tech Museum
17th century mill with original interior

Scheveningen

09321
Schevenings Museum
Neptunusstraat 92, NL-2586 GT
Scheveningen
General Museum - 1952
History of fishing and related trades;
models of ships; instruments;
costumes; paintings; ornaments:
jewels

09322
Zeebiologisch Museum
Dr. Lelykade 39, NL-2583 CL
Scheveningen
Natural History Museum - 1966
Atlantic, Mediterranean and tropical
sea collections; shells; 20,000 species
of molluscs - information and advice
center

Schiedam

09323
Stedelijk Museum
Hoogstraat 112, NL-3111 HL
Schiedam
General Museum
Archeological finds (prehistorical and medieval); history of the destillation of spirits; post-1945 painting and graphics, American pop art; contemporary sculpture and ceramics

Schinveld

09324
Oudheidkundige Verzameling der Gemeente
Wilhelminaplein 21, NL-6451 CK
Schinveld
Archeology Museum
Medieval pottery

Schiphol

09325
Aviodome National Aerospace Museum
Schiphol-Airport, Haarlemmermeer, NL-1118 AA Schiphol
Science/Tech Museum - 1971
Evolution of aviation and astronautics in the past, present and future

Schokland

09326
Museum Schokland
Mideelbuurt, NL Schokland
General Museum - 1947
Archeology, geology, finds from the IJsselmeer-polders; history of the population of the former island

Schoonhoven

09327
Nederlands Goud-, Zilver- en Klokkenmuseum
Oude Haven 7, NL-2871 DG
Schoonhoven
Decorative Arts Museum - 1902
Gold and silver objects; clocks; watches; tools; books; documents - library

09328
Oudheidkundige Verzameling
Haven 41, NL Schoonhoven
General Museum - 1929
Topography; furniture; tools; paintings; engravings; portraits of members of the house of Orange; coins

Schoonoord

09329
Openlucht Museum De Zeven Marken
Tramstraat 73, NL-7848 BJ
Schoonoord
Open Air Museum - 1954
Saksian farm; social life around 1900; geology

's-Gravenhage

09330
Esso Museum
Zuid-Hollandlaan 7, Postbus 110, NL-2500 DA 's-Gravenhage
Science/Tech Museum
Photos, models, documents and instruments related to the oil industry

09331
Haags Gemeentemuseum
Stadhouderslaan 41, NL-2517 HV
's-Gravenhage
General Museum - 1862/1935
Div: modern art (19th-20th c., including Mondrian drawings and paintings); applied art; musical instruments, prints, library and archives of composers; history of The Hague - library; education department

09332
Koninklijk Huisachief
Noordeinde 74, NL-2514 GL
's-Gravenhage
History/Public Affairs Museum - 1825
History of the House of Orange-Nassau and court departments; archives; miniatures; coins; pictures; plates; paintings - library

09333
Koninklijk Kabinet Van Munten, Penningen En Gesneden Stenen
Koninklijk Penningkabinet
Zeestraat 71 B, NL-2518 AA
's-Gravenhage
History/Public Affairs Museum - 1816
Coins of the Netherlands and all the other countries of the world; Greek and Roman coins; medals dating back to the 15th century; seals; engraved gems - library

09334
Koninklijk Kabinet Van Schilderijen
(Mauritiushuis)
Plein 29, NL-2582 MC 's-Gravenhage
Fine Arts Museum - 1820
Flemish painting (15th-17th c.); Dutch painting (16th-18th c.); portrait miniatures (16th-18th c., esp. from England); sculpture

09335
Museum Bredius
Prinsegracht 6, NL-2512 GA
's-Gravenhage
Fine Arts Museum - 1923
Dutch art (17th c.), including paintings and drawings by Rembrandt, van Ruysdael, Jan Steen, van Dyck; applied arts

09336
Museum 's-Gravenhage
Buitenhof 33, NL-2513 AH
's-Gravenhage
History/Public Affairs Museum - 1882
Prison with torture instruments; documentation on former judicial practices; memorabilia on some former prisoners especially the Cornelis brothers and the statesman Jan de Witt (1625-1672)

09337
Museum van de Kanselarij der Nederlandse Orden
Javastraat 50, NL-2585 AR
's-Gravenhage
History/Public Affairs Museum - 1954
Medals of honour and recompense awarded by the Netherlands provinces; Dutch and foreign orders and decorations; swords of honour; portraits and objects relating to orders and decorations; colonial costumes of the civil service; court costumes and costumes of the regional nobility

09338
Museum voor het Onderwijs
Hemsterhuisstraat 2e and 154, NL-2513 RD 's-Gravenhage
General Museum - 1904
Biology; ethnology; science and technology; prehistory; history; geology; reconstruction of the Dodo; Eskimo collection - library

09339
Museum voor het Poppenspel
Nassau Dillenburgstraat 8, NL-2596
AD 's-Gravenhage
Performing Arts Museum - 1971
Puppets; graphic and books on puppetry - library

09340
Nederlands Circus-, Clowns- en Kermis-Museum
Zieken 175, NL-2515 SC
's-Gravenhage
Performing Arts Museum
Photos and materials related to theatre, kermis and variety theatre exhibited in a mobile circus wagon

09341
Het Nederlands Kostuummuseum
Dienst voor Schone Kunsten
Lange Vijverberg 14-15, NL-2513 AC
's-Gravenhage
History/Public Affairs Museum - 1952
Fashionable costumes and accessories from 18th century to present - library

09342
Nederlands Letterkundig Museum en Dokumentatie-Centrum
Juffrouw Idastraat 11, NL-2501 CB
's-Gravenhage
History/Public Affairs Museum - 1956
Manuscripts, letters, galley proofs and other documents relating to Netherlands authors, newspapers, reviews, periodicals, articles

09343
Het Nederlandse Post Museum
Zeestraat 82, NL-2518 AD
's-Gravenhage
History/Public Affairs Museum - 1924
Stamps from all over the world; sketches, models and machines relating to technical post office equipment; transportation and telecommunication - library

09344
Panorama Mesdag
Zeestraat 65 b, NL-2518 AA
's-Gravenhage
Fine Arts Museum - 1881
Panorama of Scheveningen (1880) painted by Hendrik W. Mesdag (1831-1915), his wife, Th. de Bock and Breitner; paintings; watercolours and studies by Mesdag and his wife

09345
Rijksmuseum Hendrik Willem Mesdag
Laan van Meerdervoort 7 f, NL-2582
MC 's-Gravenhage
Fine Arts Museum - 1903
Paintings of Barbizon school and The Hague school (19th c.); Italian, Hungarian paintings; paintings from the Netherlands

09346
Rijksmuseum Meermannowestreenianum Museum van het Boek
Prinsessegracht 30, NL-2514 AP
's-Gravenhage
History/Public Affairs Museum - 1849
Books; manuscripts; incunabula; modern typography; antiquities from Egypt, Greece and Rome; Bible of Charles V of France by Jean Bondol (1371); 'Rijmbijbel' of Jacob van Maerlant (1332)

09347
Schilderijenzaal Prins Willem V
Buitenhof 35, NL-2513 AH
's-Gravenhage
History/Public Affairs Museum
Paintings including works by Jan Brueghel the younger, Potter, N. Berchem, Jan Steen

09348
Visserijmuseum
Neptunusstraat 92, Scheveningen, Van Beverningkstraat 108, NL-2582 VK
's-Gravenhage
Science/Tech Museum
Costumes; ship models; fishing equipment and implements for related crafts; furniture; paintings and prints; flags

's-Heerenberg

09349
Gouden Handen
Emmerikseweg 13, POB 75, NL-7040
AB 's-Heerenberg
Anthropology Museum - 1975
Native art; icons; sculptured candles; evolution of mankind, including model of cave men in authentic settings

09350
Huis Bergh
Hof van Bergh 18, NL-7041 AL
's-Heerenberg
General Museum - 1946
Castle (15th-17th c.) with furniture; sculptures; carvings; book bindings; manuscripts; weapons; coins; regional topography and cartography; geology; paintings of Dutch, German and Italian masters (14th-18th c.)

's-Hertogenbosch

09351
Illustre Lieve Vrouwe Broederschap
Zwanenbroedershuis, Hinthamerstraat 94, NL-5211 MS 's-Hertogenbosch
History/Public Affairs Museum
Religious art; tin; coins

09352
Museum Slager
Choorstraat 16, NL-5211 KZ
's-Hertogenbosch
Fine Arts Museum - 1970
Works by members of the Slager family (1841 to present); a painting in commemoration of the battle of Waterloo (P.M. Slager 1875), representing the old warriors of 's-Hertogenbosch who fought against Napoleon - library

09353
Noordbrabants Museum
Bethaniëstraat 4, NL-4211 LJ
's-Hertogenbosch
General Museum - 1837
Finds of pre- and ancient history; drawings; paintings; religious art; coins; silver

Sint Annaland

09354
Streekmuseum Tholen en Sint Philipsland
Bierenstraat 6, Sint Annaland, Markt 10, NL-4724 BK Wouw
General Museum
Farm interior; costumes; agricultural implements; topographical and religious prints; toys; pottery

Sint Michielsgestel

09355
Oudheidkundig Museum
Theerestraat 42, NL-5271 GD Sint
Michielsgestel
Archeology Museum - 1962
Roman antiquities; pottery; coins;
bronze; glass; reconstructions of a
Roman grave, well and kiln; collection
of Roman mortaria stamps - library

Sint Odiliënberg

09356
Streekmuseum Roerstreek
Kerkplein 10, NL-6077 AA Sint
Odiliënberg
General Museum
Local history; archeology (prehistoric,
Roman and medieval); geology,
zoology; ornithology; entomology;
coins; crafts

Sittard

09357
Streekmuseum Den Tempel
Gruizenstraat 27, *mail c/o*
Stadskantoor, Baenjenstraat 1,
NL-6131 JK Sittard
General Museum
Local history; geology; archeology
(prehistoric, Roman , medieval); Jewish
religious traditions

Sliedrecht

09358
Nationaal Baggermuseum
Molendijk 204, NL-3361 ER Sliedrecht
Science/Tech Museum - 1973
National dredging industry

09359
Sliedrechts Museum
Kerkbuurt 99, NL-3361 BD Sliedrecht
General Museum - 1964
Local history; instruments for water
construction, hoop and rope works

Slochteren

09360
Fraeylemaborg
Hoofdweg 82, NL-9621 AL Slochteren
History/Public Affairs Museum
Small restored castle (15th-18th c.);
prints particularly concerning the
Royal Dutch family

Sloten

09361
Toverlantaarnmuseum
Heerenwal 48, NL-8556 XW Sloten
General Museum - 1979
Cinematografisch material;
topography; paintings; weapons; laws;
flags; work instruments

Sluis

09362
**Oudheidkundige Verzameling Van
De Gemeente**
Grote Markt 1, NL-4524 CD Sluis
General Museum - 1877
Town hall (14th c.); paintings (16th-17th
c.); tapestries (17th c.); grave
fragments

Sneek

09363
Fries Scheepvaart Museum
Kleinzand 12-14, NL-8601 BH Sneek
General Museum - 1938
History of navigation in Friesland; ship
models; navigation instruments; maps;
coins; paintings; archeology;
topography; silver

09364
Schutterskamer
Stadhuis, Marktstraat 11, NL-8600 HA
Sneek
History/Public Affairs Museum
Historic house (1550) used by the
militia (18th-19th c.)

Soesterberg

09365
Luchthavenmuseum
Vliegbasis, Van Weerden
Poelmanweg, NL-3768 MN
Soesterberg
Science/Tech Museum
Planes; photos; paintings; history of
military aviation

Sommelsdijk

09366
**Streekmuseum Goeree en
Overflakkee**
Kerkstraat, NL Sommelsdijk
General Museum - 1956
Roman finds; objects relating to
fishery, navigation and militia; folk
costumes; living style

Stadskanaal

09367
Streekhistorisch Centrum
Ceresstraat 2, NL-9502 EA
Stadskanaal
General Museum
Documents on navigation; potatoe
industry; crafts

Staphorst

09368
Staphorster Boerderij
Muldersweg 4, NL-7951 DG Staphorst
General Museum - 1938
Farm (18th c.) with interior and
costumes

Stein

09369
Archeologisch Reservaat
Schepersgats 6, NL-6171 VM Stein
Archeology Museum - 1967
Galery-tomb of the Seine-Oise-Marne-
culture (dated from about 2850 BC);
prehistoric finds from Stein and the
environs

Stellendam

09370
Delta Expo
Haringvlietsluizen, NL-3251 LD
Stellendam
Science/Tech Museum - 1972
Exposition of the Delta-works -
educational center; library

Steyl

09371
Missiemuseum Steyl
St. Michaëlstraat 7, NL-5935 BL Steyl
Anthropology Museum - 1882
Objects relating to the missionary
countries; ethnography; exotic animals,
butterflies, beetles

Tegelen

09372
Pottenbakkersmuseum
Raadhuislaan 11, Gemeentehuis,
NL-5931 NR Tegelen
General Museum
Earthenware (19th c.); tobacco-boxes;
sculptures; decorated dishes

Ter Apel

09373
Museum 'Klooster Ter Apel'
Boslaan 3, NL-9561 LH Ter Apel
Religious Art Museum
15th century cloister; inventory;
construction fragments; stained glass;
tower clock (17th c.)

Terneuzen

09374
**Stichting Terneuzens Museum en
Oudheidkamer**
Burg. Geilstraat 2a, Oostelijk Bolwerk
4, NL-4531 GS Terneuzen
History/Public Affairs Museum - 1973
Legaat Van Sprang collection; gold
and silver peasants' decorations;
navigation (in preparation)

Thorn

09375
Museum in de Stiftkerk
p/a Hoogstraat 17, NL-6017 AP Thorn
Religious Art Museum - 1931
Liturgical objects; portraits; silver

Tiel

09376
Streekmuseum De Groote Sociëteit
Plein 48, Tielseweg 18, NL-4012 BK
Tiel
General Museum
Interiors; topography; coins; tin;
copper; porcelain

Tilburg

09377
Natuurhistorisch Museum
Kloosterstraat 26, NL-5038 VP Tilburg
Natural History Museum - 1933
Coll: birds; mammals; insects; fossils;
plants; wood; fishing; mining;
agriculture - library; department of
education

09378
Nederlands Textielmuseum
Gasthuisring 23, NL-5041 DP Tilburg
Science/Tech Museum - 1958
Textiles, instruments, antique textile
products - library

09379
Schrift- en Schrijfmachinemuseum
Gasthuisring 54, NL-5041 DT Tilburg
History/Public Affairs Museum - 1949
Various writing and typing
apparatuses; calculating machines;
pens, inkwells and related materials

09380
Volkenkundig Museum
Kloosterstraat 24, NL-5038 VP Tilburg
Anthropology Museum - 1932
Coll: Mexico; Peru; Bolivia; Black
Africa; Southeast Asia; New-Guinea;
ancestral figure from the Philippines;
ancestral altar from Tanembar eil,
Indonesia - library

Uden

09381
Museum voor Religieuze Kunst
Vorstenburg 1, NL-5401 AZ Uden
Religious Art Museum
Religious objects and art; paintings;
manuscripts (15th-16th c.)

Uithuizen

09382
Menkemaborg
Menkemaweg 2, NL-9981 CV
Uithuizen
History/Public Affairs Museum
Castle (17th-19th c.) with complete
inventory, portraits, carved
mantelpieces (about 1700), furniture,
glass, silver; formal garden with maze
and kitchen gardens

Urk

09383
**Visserijtentoonstelling Hulp en
Steun**
Westhavenkade, Heerenkamp 15,
NL-8321 BW Urk
General Museum
History of fishery at Urk; local
costumes and folk art; fossils

Utrecht

09384
Archeologisch Instituut
Domplein 24, NL Utrecht
Archeology Museum - 1913
Egyptian, Greek, Etruscan, Roman
finds

09385
Centraal Museum
Agnietenstraat 1, NL-3500 GC Utrecht
General Museum - 1838
Paintings; sculptures; designs;
graphics (mainly artists of Utrecht
15th-19th c.); furniture; doll's house
(1680); ceramics; porcelain; silver;
numismatics; costumes (18th-19th c.);
lace; textiles; art objects relating to the
history of Utrecht; archeology; ship
(800); architectural fragments

09386
Hedendaagse Kunst
Achter de Dom 14, NL-3512 JP
Utrecht
Fine Arts Museum - 1970
Coll: new figuration; American
photorealists; political and social
engaged art - library; educational
center

09387
Historisch Kostuum Centrum
Loeff Berchmakerstraat 50, NL-3512
TE Utrecht
History/Public Affairs Museum
Antique stylish costumes from
European countries

09388
**Munt- en Penningkabinet van 's
Rijks Munt**
Leidseweg 90, Postbus 2407, NL-3500
GK Utrecht
History/Public Affairs Museum
Coins and medals especially from the
Netherlands (600 to present); weights
and measures - library

09389
**Nationaal Museum 'Van Speeldoos
Tot Pierement'**
Achter de Dom 12, NL-3512 JP
Utrecht
History/Public Affairs Museum - 1958
Automatic musical instruments

09390
Nederlands Spoorwegmuseum
Johan van Oldenbarneveltlaan 6,
NL-3581 XZ Utrecht
Science/Tech Museum - 1927
History of the railway and tramway,
especially in the Netherlands;
sketches; originals; models;
instruments; graphics; drawings;
photographs; numismatics; prints;
locomotives; electric tram engines;
horse and buggy steam trams; signals

09391
Palaeobotanisch Museum Laboratory
of Palaeobotany and Palynology
Heidelberglaan 2, NL-3508 TC Utrecht
Natural History Museum - 1977
library

09392
**Pijpenkamer en Koffie- en
Theekabinet** (Douwe Egberts B.V.)
Keulsekade 143, NL-3532 Utrecht
History/Public Affairs Museum - 1942
History of the use of tobacco, tea,
coffee

09393
Rijksmuseum Het Catharijneconvent
Nieuwe Gracht 63, NL-3512 LG
Utrecht
History/Public Affairs Museum - 1976
Cultural history of Christianity in the
Netherlands; paintings; sculptures;
manuscripts; textiles; minor arts;
Carolingian ivory chalice, Aachen;
ivory icon with the Hodogetria,
Constantinopel (beginning of the 9th
c.); Rembrandt van Rijn 'The baptism of
the eunuch' - library; educational
center

09394
Universiteitsmuseum
Trans 8, NL-3512 JK Utrecht
Science/Tech Museum - 1938
Coll: microscopes, Van Leeuwenhoek
microscope, Huygens lenses including
the lens which Huygens used when he
found Titan, a moon of Saturnus;
scientific instruments; weights and
measures; astrolabia and clocks;
zoological specimens; portraits;
medals; music; books

09395
Universiteitsmuseum Afd.
Diergeneeskunde
Yalelaan 1, POB 80159, NL-3508 TD
Utrecht
History/Public Affairs Museum - 1954
History of education in veterinary
sciences in the Netherlands;
veterinary instruments

09396
**Universiteitsmuseum, Afd.
Tandheelkunde**
Sorbonnelaan 16, POB 80080, NL-3508
TB Utrecht
Science/Tech Museum - 1954
Evolution of dental surgery since the
16th century; documents and
photographs; old dental books;
Kalman Klein collection - library

09397
**Zoölogisch Museum der
Rijksuniversiteit**
Plompetorengracht 9, 3512 CA
Utrecht
Natural History Museum
Zoological specimens

Vaassen

09398
Kasteel De Cannenburgh
Vaassen, Kasteel Zijpendael,
Zijpendaalseweg 44, NL-6814 CL
Arnhem
History/Public Affairs Museum
Castle (14th c.); interior; family
portraits of Gelderland (16th-19th c.);
ceramics

Valkenburg

09399
Museum der Katakombenstichting
Plenkerstraat 55, NL-6301 GL
Valkenburg
History/Public Affairs Museum - 1910
Religious objects from ancient Rome;
reconstructed Roman catacombs

09400
Steenkolenmijn Valkenburg
Daelhemerweg 31, NL-6301 BJ
Valkenburg
History/Public Affairs Museum
Reconstructed coal mine with original
tools and machines; fossils

09401
**Streekmuseum 'Het Land van
Valkenburg'**
Grote Straat 31, NL-6301 CW
Valkenburg
General Museum - 1951
Timber-frame building; geology;
history of the local castle; devotionalia;
regional architecture - educational
center in progress

Veendam

09402
Het Veenkoloniaal Museum
Kerkstraat 18, NL-9641 AR Veendam
General Museum - 1939
Local history, documents,
reproductions, books; library Winkler
Prins and Geert Teis; English and
Russian ceramics (18th c.); photos of
the local surroundings; old maps, ship
models and many objects regarding
shipping and sea history of the marsh
colonies - library

Veenkloster

09403
Fogelsangh State
Veenkloster, Turfmarkt 24, NL-8911 KT
Leeuwarden
General Museum - 1963
Old glass; porcelain; family portraits;
furniture; old kitchen; coppersmith's
shop with workshop; toys; carriage
house with carriages; hunting room

Veere

09404
'De Schotse Huizen'
Kaai 27, NL-4351 AA Veere
General Museum - 1947
Topography of Veere; crafts;
costumes of Zeeland; Chinese and
Japanese ceramics; jewelry; porcelain;
fishery; pictures; furniture

09405
Vierschaar
Stadhuis, Markt 5, NL-4351 AG Veere
General Museum - 1881
Hall with Gobelin tapestries and
paintings; guild pieces; laws; historical
objects

Velp

09406
**Historische Kruidenierswinkel Fa.
Wijlhuizen**
Emmastraat 10, NL-6881 ST Velp
History/Public Affairs Museum
Historical grocer's shop with coffee
and peanut roaster

Velsen

09407
Beeckestijn
Rijksweg 136, NL-1981 LD Velsen
Decorative Arts Museum
Interiors (18-19th c.); paintings
(17th-19th c.)

Venlo

09408
Goltziusmuseum Museum van
Geschiedenis en Kunst
Goltziusstraat 21, NL-5911 AS Venlo
General Museum - 1967
Archeology; local history; weapons;
numismatics; topography; silver;
varied antique porcelain; glasses; tin;
paintings; pottery; style of living

09409
Museum Limburgse Jagers
Goltziusstraat 21, NL Venlo
History/Public Affairs Museum - 1967
Uniforms, battle materials, paintings,
pictures, military documents, mainly
relating to the Regiment of Limburg
Hunters

09410
Museum Van Bommel-Van Dam
Deken van Oppensingel 8, NL-5911
CE Venlo
Fine Arts Museum - 1971

Venray

09411
**Geschied- en Oudheidkunkundige
Verzameling**
Grote Marktstraat 1, Gemeentehuis,
NL-5801 BL Venray
Archeology Museum
Archeology (Stone Age, Roman and
Merovingian times); coins (15th-17th
c.)

Vianen

09412
Museumzaal
Stadhuis, Voorstraat 30, NL-4132 AS
Vianen
General Museum
Archeological finds, tin, bronze, silver;
furniture; paintings; porcelain; Delft
pottery

Vlaardingen

09413
Stadhuis
Markt 11, NL-3131 CR Vlaardingen
History/Public Affairs Museum
Medieval banners of various cities in
the Netherlands

09414
Streekmuseum Jan Anderson
Kethelweg 50, NL-3135 GM
Vlaardingen
General Museum
Local-history; folk art; toys

09415
Visserijmuseum Instituut voor de
Nederlandse Zeevisserij
Westhavenkade 53-54, NL-3131 AG
Vlaardingen
Science/Tech Museum - 1962
Fishery; ship models; fishing gear and
techniques; fish detection and
navigation; interiors; costumes; folk art

Vledder

09416
Bijenteelt Museum
De Hoek 5, NL-8381 BK Vledder
Agriculture Museum
Beekeeping

Vlissingen

09417
Stedelijk Museum
Bellamypark 19, NL-4381 CG
Vlissingen
General Museum - 1890
History of Vlissingen; paintings;
sculptured objects in wood; local
silver; facade stones; numismatics;
metal objects; ship models; 18th
century room; tiles

Volendam

09418
Volendams Museum
Kloosterbuurt 5, Jupiterlaan 26,
NL-1131 VE Volendam
General Museum
Local history; furniture; costumes;
coins

Voorburg

09419
Hofwijck
Westeinde 2, Postbus 533, NL-2270
AM Voorburg
History/Public Affairs Museum - 1928
Family portraits, sculptures and
documents concerning the Huygen
family

09420
Museum Swaensteyn
Heerenstraat 101, NL-2271 CC
Voorburg
General Museum - 1961
Roman finds; topography of Voorburg;
period rooms (19th c.)

Voorschoten

09421
Kasteel Duivenvoorde
NL Voorschoten
History/Public Affairs Museum - 1964
Castle (17th c.) with interior (17th-19th
c.); family portraits; porcelain

Vries

09422
Kerkmuseum 'De Klokkengieterij
Brink 3, NL-9481 BE Vries
General Museum
Church (11th c.) with Gothic choir
(1425); model of regional bell foundry
(1577); sarcophagi

Vriezenveen

09423
Oudheidkamer Vriezenveen
Westeinde 65, Boerhaavelaan 3,
NL-7671 HA Vriezenveen
General Museum - 1953
Prehistoric finds; fossils; agricultural
implements; craftmen's tools; pottery
(16th-18th c.); farm kitchen with
antique furniture; memorabilia on
relations to Czarist Russia

Vught

09424
Oudheidkamer
Taalstraat 88, NL-5261 BH Vught
General Museum
Local history; crafts; toys

Vijfhuizen

09425
De Cruquius (Poldergemaal)
Cruquiusdijk 27 en 32, NL-2141 EW
Vijfhuizen
General Museum - 1934
Regional agriculture; steam engine and
tools; sketch of the Netherlands as
Polderland; dike construction; windmill
modells; maps

Waalwijk

09426
**Nederlands Museum van Schoenen
Leder en Lederwaren**
Grotestraat 148, NL-5141 HC Waalwijk
History/Public Affairs Museum - 1954
Historic and exotic shoes of all
cultures; modern shoes; old work
instruments; other leather wares; old
shoemaker's living room and
workshop of Brabant; paintings; silver
of the old shomakers' corps

Wageningen

09427
**Internationaal Bodemkundig
Museum**
Duivendaal 9, Postbus 353, NL-6700
AJ Wageningen
Natural History Museum - 1966
Soil profiles from many parts of the
world - library

Warffum

09428
Museum 'Het Hogeland'
Schoolstraat 2, NL-9989 AG Warffum
Open Air Museum - 1959
Coll: folk art; style of living; history of
fashion, textiles, historic clothes
(costumes and underclothing); school
curiosities; Dutch inn; history of the
isle of Rottum; agriculture; antiquities
library

Weert

09429
Gemeentemuseum 'De Tiendschuur'
Recollectenstraat 5, NL-6001 AJ
Weert
General Museum - 1936
Natural history, mounted birds;
antiquities relating to Weert and
environs; prehistory; pictures;
numismatics; old town views; rifle and
trade organizations; folklore

09430
Nederlands Tram Museum
Kruisstraat 6, NL-6006 ZL Weert
Science/Tech Museum - 1950
Trams in the Netherlands, vehicles,
cars, lamps, clocks, photographs

Weesp

09431
Gemeentemuseum
Nieuwstraat 41, NL-1382 BB Weesp
General Museum - 1911
Local history; porcelain (1759-1768);
paintings; topography; weapons

Westerbork

09432
Nederlands Museum van Knipkunst
Gualtherie van Weezelplein 15,
NL-9430 AA Westerbork
Decorative Arts Museum - 1965
Paper cutouts from various countries
in the past and present

West-Terschelling

09433
**Gemeentelijk Natuurhistorisch
Streekmuseum**
Burg. Redekerstraat 11, NL-8880 AA
West-Terschelling
Natural History Museum - 1954
Regional flora, fauna, aviflora and
environment - sea aquarium; youth
field center for education in nature

09434
**Gemeentemuseum 't Behouden
Huys'**
Commandeurstraat 30-32, NL-8880 AA
West-Terschelling
General Museum - 1952
Living style; folk costumes; folklore;
tools of old trades; ship models

Winterwijk

09435
Het Museum Freriks
Groenloseweg 86, NL-7101 AK
Winterwijk
General Museum - 1976
Geology; natural history; local history;
folklore - library

Woerden

09436
Gemeentemuseum
Kerkplein 6, NL-3441 BJ Woerden
General Museum
Pictures and relics from the reformed
Church in the Netherlands (15th-16th
c.); sculptures; weapons; archeology;
facade stones; topography; paintings
and works of artists born in Woerden
(Leo Gestel, C.Vreedenburgh, Jan
Kriege, H.van Kempen)

Wolvega

09437
Oudheidkamer Weststelling-Werf
Molen de Windlust, Hoofdstraat, NL
Wolvega
General Museum - 1955
Mill (1888); local history; photographs;
portraits; tools; topography

Workum

09438
Oudheidkamer 'Warkums Erfskip'
Merk 4, NL Workum
General Museum - 1966
Pottery; tiles; silver; old tools and
instruments; historic engravings; scale
models of mills

Woudrichem

09439
Visserijmuseum
Kerkstraat, Arsenaal, NL Woudrichem
Science/Tech Museum
Fishing instruments; ship models; two
original trawlers

Wijchen

09440
**Oudheidkundig Museum 'Frans
Bloemen'**
Kastellaan, Wijchen, Boksdoornstraat
84, NL-6543 SH Nijmegen
Archeology Museum
Archeological finds from Stone Age to
early Middle Ages

Wijk bij Duurstede

09441
**Kantonaal en Stedelijk Museum Wij
bij Duurstede**
Volderstraat 15-17, NL-3916 BA Wijk
bij Duurstede
General Museum - 1926/1973
Local and regional antiquities;
prehistory; topography; coins; sketch
of the castle of Duurstede

IJmuiden

09442
Pieter Vermeulen Museum
Moerbergplantsoen 20, NL-1972 XG
IJmuiden
General Museum - 1951
Natural history; shells; birds; algae of
the coast; food web of the North Sea;
fishery; port sketch; ship model -
library

IJzendijke

09443
**Streekmuseum 'West Zeeuwsch-
Vlaandren presenteert'**
Markt 28, IJzendijke, Raadhuisplein 1,
NL-4501 BG Oostburg
General Museum
Ancient agricultural implements;
costumes; archeological finds

Zaandam

09444
Czaar Peterhuisje
Krimp 23, Hogendijk 62-64, NL-1506
AJ Zaandam
History/Public Affairs Museum
Objects relating to Czar Peter (who
stayed here in 1697) and his family;
paintings; furniture; memories of
important persons who have visited
the house

09445
De Zaanse Schans
NL Zaandam
History/Public Affairs Museum
Several historic houses and mills
reconstructed at this site: bakery,
grocer's shop; house with Dutch
clocks

Zaandijk

09446
Zaanlandse Oudheidkamer
Lagedijk 80, NL-1544 BJ Zaandijk
General Museum - 1899
Coll: environments of Zaandijk; trades;
living style; topography; ship models;
folklore; costumes; toys - library

Zaltbommel

09447
Maarten van Rossum Museum
Nonnenstraat 5, NL-5301 BE
Zaltbommel
General Museum - 1905
Local and regional antiquities;
paintings; sketches; plates; pastels;
photographs; manuscripts; copper; tin;
weapons; coins; facade stones;
construction fragments; old furniture;
porcelain; glass; pottery; relics; books
- library

Zeelst

09448
Gemeentelijk Museum 't Oude Slot
Hemelrijken 14, Kruisstraat 69,
NL-5502 JC Zeelst
Archeology Museum - 1967
Local archeological finds (prehistory to
Middle Ages)

Zeist

09449
Van de Poll-Stichting
Zinzendorflaan 1, NL-3703 CE Zeist
General Museum
Topographic atlas; local historical
documents

09450
Het Zeister Slot
Zinzendorflaan 1, NL-3703 CE Zeist
Historic Site
Castle (17th c.) with interiors

Zevenaar

09451
Peter Stuyvesant Stichting
Kerkstraat, Postbus 12, NL-6900 AA
Zevenaar
Fine Arts Museum
Contemporary painting and sculpture

Zevenbergen

09452
Oudheidkamer Willem van Strijen
Zuidhaven 17, *mail c/o* J. van Oers,
Kreitenborg 10, NL-4761 BM
Zevenbergen
General Museum
Clothes; work instruments; farm tools;
porcelain; pottery; crystal; silver;
maps; room with interior; kitchen

Zierikzee

09453
Burger Weeshuis
Poststraat 45, NL-4301 AB Zierikzee
History/Public Affairs Museum - 1860
16th century orphanage; regents'
room; walls in Louis XV covering; gold
leather (1725); tin; paintings

09454
Maritiem Museum
Noordhavenpoort 1, NL-4301 EC
Zierikzee
History/Public Affairs Museum - 1971
Paintings; ship models; old sea charts;
musselfishing and oysterfishing
attributes; prehistorical bones

09455
Stadhuismuseum
Meelstraat 8, NL-4301 EC Zierikzee
General Museum - 1930
History of Zierikzee and its trades;
commerce; agriculture; fishing;
pictures; local silver; crystal; porcelain;
pottery; ship models

Zoetermeer

09456
Oudheidkamer Zoetermeer
Julianalaan 21, NL-2712 CB
Zoetermeer
General Museum - 1976

Zuilen

09457
Slot Zuylen
Tournooiveld 1, Oud-Zuilen,
Huygenslaan 6, NL-3818 WC
Amersfoort
History/Public Affairs Museum - 1952
Medieval inventory; gobelins; history;
art

Zutphen

09458
Librije der St. Walburgskerk
Kerkhof 3, NL-7201 DM Zutphen
History/Public Affairs Museum
16th century church library;
manuscripts, theological works;
history; literature; law; incunabula

09459
Museum Henriette Polak
Zaadmarkt 88, p/a Rozengracht 3,
NL-7201 JL Zutphen
Fine Arts Museum - 1975
Modern Dutch figurative art - library

09460
Stedelijk Museum
Rozengracht 3, NL-7201 JL Zutphen
General Museum - 1866
Archeology; construction fragments;
maps; topography; silver; glass;
numismatics; tiles; pharmacy; kitchen;
living style (19th c.); toys; costumes;
Gothic hall - library

Zwartsluis

09461
**Natuurhistorisch Museum
Schoonewelle**
Museumslaan 2, NL-8064 XN
Zwartsluis
Natural History Museum - 1958
Birds; mammals; butterflies; eggs

Zwolle

09462
Provinciaal Overijssels Museum
Melkmarkt 41, NL-8011 MB Zwolle
General Museum - 1884
Prehistory; paintings and drawings;
silver; furniture; porcelain; glass;
interiors from Gothic to Jugendstil;
coins; objects concerning the history
of Zwolle and Overijssel - library

Netherlands Antilles

Curaçao

09463
Curaçao Museum
Curaçao
General Museum
Local history; paintings

New Zealand

Alexandra

09464
**Alexandra District Historical
Association Museum**
Walton St, Alexandra, Otago
General Museum
Gold mining ; pioneers' life;
photographs

Arrowtown

09465
Lakes District Centennial Museum
Buckingham St, Arrowtown, Otago
General Museum - 1948
Gold; minerals; gold-miners' tools and
implements; relics of Chinese miners;
domestic utensils; photographs, books
and documents; vehicles

Ashburton

09466
Ashburton Museum
118 Cameron St, Ashburton,
Canterbury
General Museum - 1958
Victoriana; irrigation scheme

Auckland

09467
Auckland City Art Gallery
POB 5449, Auckland 1
Fine Arts Museum - 1888
Old master paintings, drawings, prints;
Mackelvie collection; European
paintings, prints, sculpture (19th-20th
c.); British drawings; drawings by
Thomas Rowlandson; New Zealand
paintings, drawings, prints, sculpture
(19th-20th c.); Frances Hodgkins
collection; drawings by Henry Fuseli;
contemporary American drawings;
Japanese prints (20th c.)

09468
Auckland War Memorial Museum
The Domain, Private Bag, Auckland 1
General Museum - 1852
Maori and Pacific archeology and
ethnology; natural history; applied arts
(especially Asian); military history;
Maori war canoe and meeting house;
Nukuoro goddess figure - library

09469
Entomology Division Dept. of
Scientific and Industrial Research
120 Mount Albert Rd, Private Bag,
Auckland 3
Natural History Museum - 1921
Systematical research collection of
New Zealand and overseas
arthropoda

09470
**Museum of Transport and
Technology**
Great North Rd, Western Springs,
Auckland 2
Science/Tech Museum - 1964
Aspects of transport, industrial and
domestic technology; engineering;
physical science; history of New
Zealand since European settlement;
printing and graphic arts; business and
office equipment; colonial village -
library

09471
**New Zealand Dental Association
Museum**
NZ Dental Headquarters, Remuera Rd,
POB 28084, Auckland 5
Natural History Museum - 1968
Dental exhibits

09472
Plant Diseases Division Dept. of
Scientific and Industrial Research
120 Mt Albert Rd, Private Bag,
Auckland 3
Natural History Museum - 1938
Herbarium specialising in pathogenic
plant fungi, New Zealand rusts, smuts,
gasteromycetes, polyporaceae,
thelephoraceae, hypocreales and
hypohomycetes; about 700 type
specimens - library

Avarna

09473
**Cook Islands Library and Museum
Society**
Takamoa Rd, POB 7, Avarna,
Rarotonga, Cook Islands, South Pacific
General Museum - 1963
Ethnology; artifacts; natural history;
shells; historical printing machinery;
stamps

Balclutha

09474
**South Otago Historical Society
Museum**
POB 67, Balclutha
History/Public Affairs Museum

Christchurch

09475
Canterbury Museum
Rollestone Av, Christchurch 1
General Museum - 1870
Geology; zoology; ethnology;
archeology; Wairau Bar Moa hunter
material; Maori and Polynesian
ethnology and archeology; Melanesian
ethnology; furniture; archives and
documents of early Canterbury; local
shipping and whaling exhibits;
firearms; stamps; coins

09476
**Canterbury Society of Arts CSA
Gallery**
66 Gloucester St, POB 772,
Christchurch
Fine Arts Museum - 1880
Contemporary New Zealand art

09477
Ferrymead Historic Park
269 Bridle Path Rd, Christchurch 2
Science/Tech Museum - 1965
Fire display; Dinni collection of
mechanical musical instruments

09478
Robert McDougall Art Gallery
Botanic Gardens, Rolleston Av, POB
237, Christchurch
Fine Arts Museum - 1932
Coll: European paintings (17th-20th c.);
British paintings and watercolours
(18th-20th c.); New Zealand paintings,
watercolours, sculpture and pottery
(19th-20th c.) - education department

Clyde

09479
**Vincent County and Dunstan
Goldfields Historical Museum**
Dunston Court House, Blythe St,
Clyde, Otago
General Museum - 1878
Mining; gold nuggets, gold sand, gold
coins and jewelry; minerals; dock
leg-irons, goal door; pioneer
household goods; clothing; books;
crystal chandelier; horse-drawn
vehicles; farm implements; fully-
equipped manual herb processing
factory

Coromandel

09480
**Coromandel School of Mines
Museum**
Rings Rd, Coromandel
Natural History Museum - 1887
Geological specimens; mining;
photographs and mining books, plans
newspapers

Cromwell

09481
Cromwell Borough Museum
Athenaeum, Sligo St, POB 2, Cromwell,
Otago
General Museum

Dargaville

09482
**Northern Wairoa Maori, Maritime
and Pioneer Museum**
POB 166, Dargaville, Auckland
History/Public Affairs Museum - 1960
Maori artifacts; kauri gum; local
historical photographs; pioneer and
early shipping relics

Dunedin

09483
Dunedin Public Art Gallery
Logan Park, POB 566, Dunedin
Fine Arts Museum - 1884
British portraits (late 17th to early 19th
c.); British landscapes (18th-20th c.);
Smythe Collection of British
watercolours (18th-19th c.); British
Victorian genre painting; British
contemporary painting; European
masters, chiefly Italian, French and
Flemish (late Middle Ages to 18th c.);
contemporary New Zealand painting
and sculpture; contemporary
Australian painting; antique furniture,
silver, glass, porcelain and oriental
rugs - conservation laboratory and
school

09484
Geology Museum of the University of Otago
Dunedin
Natural History Museum

09485
Hocken Library University of Otago
Castle St, POB 56, Dunedin
Natural History Museum - 1907
History and ethnology of New Zealand and the Pacific Islands; archives and manuscripts; original paintings, prints and drawings

09486
Otago Early Settlers' Association (INC) Museum
220 Cumberland St, Dunedin
General Museum - 1898
Portrait collection of pre-1869 settlers; whaling; pioneer cottage; early horse-drawn vehicles; early printing-press; locomotives; gold-mining display - library

09487
Otago Military Museum
Dunedin
History/Public Affairs Museum

09488
Otago Museum
Great King St, Dunedin, Otago
General Museum - 1865
Zoology; geology; botany; physical anthropology; archeology; ethnology; technology; furniture; numismatics; Maori war canoe; Hawaiian royal feather cape; Japanese and Korean ceramics; Egyptian, classical and West-European antiquities

09489
Otakou Memorial Church Museum
Tamatea Rd, Otakou, mail c/o Ms C. Wesley, Pipikaretu Rd, No 2 RD, Dunedin, Otago
General Museum
Local history

09490
The Theomin Gallery
42 Royal Terrace, Dunedin
History/Public Affairs Museum - 1967
Jacobean style home; antique furniture; pictures; silverware; porcelain; carved ivory; Japanese artifacts, weapons, inro, embroidery

Geraldine

09491
Geraldine Farm Machinery Museum
mail c/o D. Robinson, Four Peaks, Geraldine
Agriculture Museum

Gisborne

09492
Gisborne Museum and Arts Centre
18-22 Stout Street and at A.P.Showgrounds Makaraka, POB 716, Gisborne
General Museum - 1954
Maori artifacts; local bygones; photographs; documents; New Zealand paintings; geology; natural history; transport and technological items; examples of East Coast Maori carving - library; studios (artists, potters, photographers); area for concerts

Gore

09493
Gore District Museum
POB 305, Gore
General Museum

Greymouth

09494
Greymouth RSA War Museum
187 Tainui St, Greymouth, Westland
History/Public Affairs Museum - 1966
Weapons; uniforms; medals; badges; photographs; war relics

Greytown

09495
Cobblestones Museum
Main St, Greytown
General Museum

Hamilton

09496
Clydesdale Agricultural Museum
Private Bag, Hamilton
Agriculture Museum

09497
Waikato Society of Arts Studio Gallery
83 Anglesea St, POB 1018, Hamilton, Waikato
General Museum - 1948
New Zealand archeology and history; Pacific ethnology and traditional arts; New Zealand, Australian and English painting, prints, drawings and sculpture; Te Winika-Maori war canoe; Bewick tailpieces - library

Havelock

09498
Havelock Historical Museum
mail c/o Lions Club of Havelock, Union St, POB 35, Havelock, Marlborough
General Museum - 1968
Saw milling equipment; old steam and conbustion engines; bottle collection; minerals

Hawarden

09499
Waipara County Historical Society Museum
Hawarden, North Canterbury
History/Public Affairs Museum

Helensville Borough

09500
Helensville and District Pioneer Museum
Helensville Borough
Open Air Museum

Hokianga

09501
Kohukohu Regional Museum
mail c/o Hokianga County Council
Hokianga
General Museum

Hokitika

09502
West Coast Historical Museum
Public Library Bldg, Tancred St, Hokitika, Westland
General Museum - 1960
History of the region; gold mining methods; Maori crafts in working with nephrite; photos, maps and manuscripts - library

Holdens Bay

09503
Te Amorangi Museum
35 Robinson Av, Holdens Bay, Auckland
General Museum - 1952
Maori artifacts; armed constabulary; pioneer materials; whaling relics and ship logs

Howick

09504
Howick Colonial Village
Bells Road, Pakuranga, POB 38-105, Howick, Auckland
Historic Site - 1962
Buildings of the early colonial period 1840-1880, restored authentically; some of the buildings of the early Royal New Zealand fencibles who arrived in New Zealand in 1847 to protect the village of Howick from attacks of the Maoris

Invercargill

09505
Anderson Park Art Gallery
Victoria Av, Invercargill, Otago
Fine Arts Museum - 1951
New Zealand contemporary paintings; watercolours of Invercargill (19th-20th c.); European paintings

09506
Southland Museum and Art Gallery
Victoria Av, POB 1012, Invercargill, Southland
General Museum - 1871
Maori artifacts; geology; live tuataras; sub-fossil moa bones

Kaikoura

09507
Kaikoura Historical Society Museum
mail c/o Mrs. J. Fowlie, 51 Deal St, Kaikoura, Marlborough
General Museum - 1968
Maori collection; early colonial items; archives

Kaitaia

09508
Far North Regional Museum
6 South Rd, POB 94, Kaitaia
General Museum - 1969
Colonial room of local furniture; Maori culture room with Moa hunter and Maori carvings, artifacts and implements; photographic collection; local mounted birds, shells and fossils; kauri gum collection; de Surville anchor with associated display material; early missionary, colonial and Dalmation settlemet

Karamea

09509
Karamea Museum
Karamea, mail c/o Secretary Arapito R.D.3. Westport
General Museum

Kerikeri

09510
Society for Preservation of the Stone Area
POB 77, Kerikeri
Natural History Museum

Lawrence

09511
Lawrence and District Museum
mail c/o Secretary Mr K. Rahey, Brooklands No 1 R.D., Lawrence
General Museum

Lower Hutt

09512
DSIR Ecology Division
66 Bloomfield Terrace, Private Bag, Lower Hutt
Natural History Museum - 1948
Ecology and behaviour of the wild populations of rabbits and hares; horticulture; agriculture; migrations of red deer; vegetation; mammals' and birds' skins; skeletal material

09513
New Zealand Geological Survey
State Insurance, Andrews Av, POB 30368, Lower Hutt
Natural History Museum - 1865
New Zealand rock types, samples from Antarctica, sub-Antarctic Islands, Pacific; marine fossil invertebrates, molluscs; fossil plant collection - library

Lumsden

09514
Lumsden and District Museum
Lions Club Hall, Lumsden
General Museum

Lyttelton

09515
Lyttelton Historical Museum Society
Gladstone Quay, POB 91, Lyttelton, Canterbury
History/Public Affairs Museum - 1965
Maritime display; antarctic display; local history

Masterton

09516
Wairarapa Arts Centre
POB 90, Masterton, Wellington
Fine Arts Museum - 1969
Contemporary New Zealand prints, paintings and sculptures

Matakohe

09517
Otamatea Kauri and Pioneer Musem
State Hwy 12, between Maungaturoto and Dargaville, Matakohe, Auckland
General Museum - 1962
Regional history; kauri gum; kauri, rimu and other native timbers; artifacts of the kauri timber industry; rooms furnished with kauri period furniture

Matamata

09518
Firth Tower Historical Trust Museum
mail c/o Town Clerk, Matamata County and Borough Council, Matamata
History/Public Affairs Museum

Milton

09519
Tokomairiro Historical Society Museum
Union St, Milton
History/Public Affairs Museum

Napier

09520
Hawke's Bay Art Gallery and Museum
Herschel St, POB 429, Napier, Hawke's Bay
General Museum - 1936
Maori and Polynesian artifacts; early New Zealand home and farm equipment; antique furniture, porcelain and silver; New Zealand painting, sculpture and pottery; relics of the earthquake in Hawke's Bay (1931)

Naseby

09521
Maniototo Early Settlers Museum
Leven St, Naseby, Otago
General Museum
Gold specimen; implements for gold collecting and weighing; household articles of gold-mining days

Nelson

09522
Bishop Suter Art Gallery
Bridge St, Nelson
Fine Arts Museum - 1898
Watercolours by John Gully (1819-1888), J.C. Richmond (1827-1898); contemporary English and European works

New Plymouth

09523
Govett Brewster Art Gallery
Queen St, New Plymouth, Taranaki
Fine Arts Museum - 1969
Art objects from New Zealand, Australia, Japan, USA, Mexico and other countries - library

09524
Taranaki Museum
War Memorial Building, Brougham St, POB 315, New Plymouth, Taranaki
General Museum - 1919
Maori wood carvings of Te Atiawa and Taranaki dating from pre 1830; household relics; weapons; tools; items of early settlement; natural history - library

Norsewood

09525
Norsewood Pioneer Museum
POB 52, Norsewood, Hawke's Bay
Historic Site - 1965
Early settlers' household, farming and milling equipment; history of the Scandinavian settlement

Oamaru

09526
North Otago Museum
60 Thames St, POB 347, Oamaru, North Otago
General Museum - 1882
George Meek collection of pioneer and early settlers' domestic and industrial articles; historical photographs and archives; Thomas Forrester section; Oamaru limestone display

Okains Bay

09527
Okains Bay Maori and Colonial Museum
Okains Bay, Banks Peninsula
General Museum - 1961
Maori collection (archeological and ethnological) including a meeting house and a stone house; colonial collection of cottages, farming implements, transport vehicles

Onehunga

09528
Fencible and Historical Society
Jellicoe Park, Onehunga
History/Public Affairs Museum

Ongaonga

09529
Ongaonga Old School Museum
mail c/o Secretary Ongaonga, Hawke's Bay
General Museum - 1966
Furnished classroom (1975-1886); local history; firearms from Maori wars; kitchen utensils; sewing machines; historic sword; New Zealand newspapers from 1879; phonograph; photographs

Oturehua

09530
Oturehua District Historical Society Bank and Gold Office Museum
Main St, Oturehua
History/Public Affairs Museum

Outram

09531
Taieri Historical Society
Old court house and jail, Outram, Otago, *mail c/o* Ms Vera Crozier, Gladstone Rd, Mosgiel, Otago
General Museum - 1970
Local history

Owaka

09532
Owaka Museum
Main St, Owaka
General Museum

Oxford

09533
Oxford Historical Records Museum
mail c/o Mr R. Meyer, Harewood Rd, Oxford
History/Public Affairs Museum

Palmerston North

09534
Manawatu Art Gallery
398 Main St, POB 565, Palmerston North, Wellington
Fine Arts Museum - 1959
Paintings, watercolours, prints, ceramics and sculptures by New Zealand artists

Paraparaumu Beach

09535
Kapiti Coast Historical Museum
Paraparaumu Beach
History/Public Affairs Museum

Patea

09536
South Taranaki Regional Museum
(Former Patea District Museum)
Egmont St, POB 2, Patea, Taranaki
General Museum - 1974
Documents relating to local military settlement; Maori carvings depicting the arrival of the Aotea canoe and history of the Ruanui and Ngarauru tribes; vehicles; machinery; farm implements - library and archives

Petone

09537
Petone Settlers Museum
Centennial Memorial Building, Esplanade, POB 38001, Petone, Wellington
General Museum - 1977
Photographs of early Petone; dolls; china; silver; clothes

Picton

09538
Smith Memorial Museum
POB 45, Picton, Marlborough
General Museum - 1959
Maori artifacts; whaling industry relics; household utensils; maps; old photographs

Pleasant Point

09539
Pleasant Point Railway and Historical Society Museum
Main Rd, Pleasant Point
History/Public Affairs Museum

Rangiora

09540
Rangiora and District Early Records Society Museum
mail c/o The Secretary, 60 Ayers St, Rangiora, Canterbury
History/Public Affairs Museum
Local history

Reefton

09541
Black's Point Museum
20 Davis St, Reefton, Nelson
General Museum
Wesley Church; gold mining equipment; early Reefton papers

Renwick

09542
Renwick Library and Museum
High St, Renwick
General Museum

Riverton

09543
Wallace Early Settlers Museum
Main St, Riverton
History/Public Affairs Museum

Rotorua

09544
Rotorua Art Gallery
Tudor Towers, Government Gardens, *mail c/o* Rotorua District Council, Private Bag, Rotorua
Fine Arts Museum - 1977
New Zealand arts and crafts, historical and contemporary; different collections showing the development of painting and print-making in New Zealand; collection of images of the Maori in paintings, drawings, photographs and prints

09545
Rotorua Museum
Tudor Towers, Government Gardens, Private Bag, Rotorua
General Museum - 1969
Carvings of the Arawa people; photographic history of the Volcanic Plateau; Kumara goddess - library

Roxburgh

09546
Teviot District Museum
off Main St, Roxburgh
General Museum

Russell

09547
Captain Cook Memorial Museum
York St, POB 85, Russell, Bay of Islands
General Museum - 1954
Memorial to Captain Cook; Maori artifacts; whaling; pioneer and colonist items

Shantytown

09548
West Coast Historical and Mechanical Society Museum
Post Office, Shantytown, Via Greymouth, Westland
Historic Site - 1971
Historic building of a gold mining town; steam trains (1897 and 1913); horse-drawn vehicles - library

Silverdale

09549
Wainui Historical Society Pioneer Village
mail c/o Mrs R. Aickin, 14 Elliston Cres., Stanmore Bay, Whangaparoa, Silverdale
Open Air Museum

Stoke

09550
Nelson Provincial Museum
Isel Park, POB 2069, Stoke, Nelson
General Museum - 1841
Prehistory; history; natural history; Isel House with early furniture and china is affiliated; contains stock of former Cawthron Institute - library; archives

Taihape

09551
Taihape and Districts Historical and Museum Society
Huia St, Old Methodist Church, R.D.5, Taihape, Rangitikei
Decorative Arts Museum - 1970
China Collection depicting early Taihape street scenes

Tauranga

09552
Tauranga District Museum
17th Av West, POB 597, Tauranga,
Auckland
Anthropology Museum - 1977
Historic Maori village township;
restored vintage tractors; goldmining
exhibits

Te Awamutu

09553
Te Awamutu and District Museum
Civic Centre, Roche St, POB 526, Te
Awamutu, Auckland
General Museum - 1935
Maori and local history; Uenuku Tainui
tribal god - library; archives

Te Kauwhata

09554
Waikare Historical Society
Homestead rise, Aparangi, *mail c/o*
Mr. R.P. Moorfield, R.D. 2, Te Kauwhata
History/Public Affairs Museum - 1974

Thames

09555
Thames Art Gallery
mail c/o Town Clerk, Thames Borough
Council, Thames
Fine Arts Museum

09556
Thames Mineralogical Museum
Cnr Cochrane and Brown Sts, POB
79, Thames
Science/Tech Museum - 1886
Ores; minerals; metals; rocks; fossils;
semiprecious stones; carved kauri
gum; models of mining machinery;
tools; photographs of mining days

Timaru

09557
Aigantighe Art Gallery
Waiiti Rd, Timaru, Canterbury
Fine Arts Museum - 1956
New Zealand paintings (1910 to
present); prints; drawings; sculpture;
china and New Zealand pottery

09558
**South Canterbury Centennial
Museum**
4 Perth St, Timaru, Canterbury
General Museum - 1966
Period furniture; costumes; china;
paintings; Maori artifacts; maps;
photographs; documents; books;
records of the development of the
port of Timaru

Tokanui

09559
Waikawa District Museum
mail c/o Secretary, No 1 R.D., Tokanui,
Southland
General Museum - 1975
Maori artifacts; early colonial shipping
and whaling articles and various
colonial items; photos of early settlers

Tokomaru

09560
Tokomaru Steam Engine Museum
Main Rd, POB 46, Tokomaru,
Manawatu
Science/Tech Museum - 1970
Steam engines; working scale models
- library

Tuatapere

09561
Tuatapere Museum
Main St, Tuatapere
General Museum

Turangi

09562
Turangi Museum
mail c/o Ministry of Works and
Development Turangi
General Museum

Waihi

09563
Waihi Arts Centre and Museum
Kenny St, POB 149, Waihi, Thames
Valley
General Museum - 1962
Local gold mining history; Ohinemuri
district history; geological specimens;
maps; photographs; paintings

Waikouaiti

09564
Waikouaiti Museum
Main Rd and Kildare St, Waikouaiti,
Otago
General Museum - 1966
Greenstone; moa bones; trypot
whaleboat oars

Waimate

09565
Waimate Historical Museum
Harris St, POB 13, Waimate, South
Canterbury
General Museum - 1954
Pioneer household and farm
implements; machinery; farm vehicles;
relics from gold-digging times; old
firearms; relics of World War I; Maori
artifacts; historical records;
photographs

Waiouru

09566
**Queen Elizabeth II Army Memorial
Museum**
mail c/o Army Training Group, State
Hwy No 1, Waiouru
History/Public Affairs Museum - 1978
Small arms; medals; badges; General
Sir Alexander Godley's orders,
decorations, medals, sword and
uniform

Waipu

09567
Pioneers' Memorial Museum
Main Hwy 1, Waipu, Northland
General Museum - 1953
Local pioneering relics; Maori
artifacts; kauri gum, polished and
unpolished; war relics; genealogies of
original clans who settled in Waipu;
documents and photographs

Wairoa

09568
Wairoa Museum
POB 54, Wairoa
General Museum

Waiuku

09569
Waiuku Museum
13 King St, Waiuku, South Auckland
Anthropology Museum - 1966
Farm implements; clothing; local
hand-crafted furniture; Maori carving;
local photographs

Wanganui

09570
Sarjeant Gallery
Queen's Park, POB 637, Wanganui,
Wellington
Fine Arts Museum - 1919
Drawings by Bernadino Poccetti
('Passion of our Lord Jesus Christ'
1548-1612); early New Zealand and
contemporary paintings; World War I
cartoons and posters; British and
European oils, watercolours and prints
(19th-20th c.)

09571
Wanganui Regional Museum
Maria Place, POB 352, Wanganui
General Museum - 1892
Maori and Polynesian artifacts; war
canoe; New Zealand birds; whale
skeletons, fish, shells; minerals;
entomology; firearms; medals and
coins; early colonial relics; local
history; Maori ornaments and
weapons and pigment pot - library

Wellington

09572
National Art Gallery
Buckle St, Wellington
Fine Arts Museum - 1936
19th century New Zealand painting
and drawing; 18th and 19th century
English watercolours and graphic art;
20th century English painting - library

09573
National Museum
Buckle St, Wellington
General Museum - 1865
Mammals, especially marine mammals;
birds; reptiles; fishes; mollusca;
crustacea; echinoderms; insects;
plants; ethnology of New Zealand and
the Pacific; colonial history; fine arts -
library

09574
**New Zealand Oceanographic
Institute**
Greta Point, Evans Bay, POB 12-346,
Wellington North
Natural History Museum - 1954
Marine benthos and plankton of the
New Zealand region, Southwest
Pacific, Antarctic; geological sediments
and cores

09575
**Wellington Harbour Board Maritime
Museum**
Head Office, Queens Wharf, POB 893,
Wellington
History/Public Affairs Museum - 1972
Watercolour paintings of New Zealand
ships as well as of ships that visited
New Zealand ports in the 1930's; early
shipping records; model of Wellington
harbour; restored captain's cabin of
the steam ship 'Te Anau' (1879) -
library; visual and sound records

09576
**The Zillah and Ronald Castle Music
Museum**
27 Colombo St, Wellington
Music Museum
Early keyboards including Kirkman
harpsichord (1781), clavicord, virginals,
forte pianos (Clementi, Broadwood,
Clough); medieval instruments, tromba
marina, liras, T. Stanesby tenor
recorder (1690); baroque wind and
stringed instruments; folk instruments
from many parts of the world - library

Wellsford

09577
**Albertland Centennial Memorial
Museum**
Port Albert Domain, Wellsford,
Auckland
General Museum
Domestic utensils; firearms; farm
implements; tools; Maori artifacts;
printing press; photographs from the
pioneer period

Whakatane

09578
Whakatane and District Museum
Boon St, POB 203, Whakatane,
Auckland
General Museum - 1967
Maori artifacts; pioneer relics; Ellis
collection of New Zealand books

Whangarei

09579
Clapham's Clock Museum
Rose Gardens, Water St, Private Bag,
Whangarei
Science/Tech Museum - 1900
Clocks and watches; Dan Rey clock
(1650); Grand Sonnerie clock (1800);
Viennese hand-painted clock on a
French rose onyx base (1840)

09580
Northland Regional Museum
mail c/o Treasurer, POB 1359,
Whangarei
General Museum

Whitianga

09581
Mercury Bay District Museum
6 Buffalo Beach Rd, Whitianga
General Museum

Nicaragua

Chontales

09582
Museo 'Gregorio Aguilar Barea'
Juigalpa, Chontales
General Museum

Managua

09583
Museo Nacional de Nicaragua
4a Avenida No. 606, Managua
General Museum - 1896
archaeology; history; natural history

Masaya

09584
Museo 'Tenderi'
Masaya
General Museum

Niguinohoma

09585
Museo de Sandini
Niguinohoma
General Museum

Niger

Niamey

09586
National Museum of Niger
POB 248, Niamey
General Museum - 1959
Prehistory; archaeology; costumes;
crafts; tribal houses; history

Nigeria

Argungu

09587
Kanta Museum Argungu
Gidan Yakubu Nabame Argungu,
Argungu, Northern Region
General Museum
Weapons; ancient metal pots

Benin City

09588
Benin Museum
Benin City, Western Region
General Museum
Local antiquities, bronzes

Ibadan

09589
**Museum of the Institute of African
Studies**
University of Ibadan, Ibadan, Western
Region
Anthropology Museum
Ethnographic and archaeological
exhibits

09590
West African Museum
Ibadan, Western Region
General Museum

09591
Zoology Museum University of
Ibadan
Ibadan, Oyo
Natural History Museum
Vertebrate and invertebrate
specimens, particularly of tropical
species

Ife

09592
Museum of Ife Antiquities
Enuwa Square, Ife, Oyo, Western
Region
General Museum
Archaeology of ancient Ife; bronze
and terra-cotta sculpture; history of
Western Nigeria

Ilorin

09593
Esie Museum
Esie via Ora, Ilorin, Northern Region
General Museum

Jos

09594
Jos Museum
Jos, Plateau State, Northern Region
General Museum - 1952
Archaeology; ethnography; terra-cotta
Nok figurines; Benin-Ife-Yoruba
works; traditional architecture - library

09595
**Museum of the Institute of African
Studies**
University of Ife, Jos, Plateau State,
Northern Region
General Museum - 1965
Archaeology; ethnology; terra cotta;
masks and Yoruba cult objects

Kano

09596
Gidan Makama Museum
Kano, Northern Region
General Museum - 1959
Ethnography; folklore; local art

Lagos

09597
National Museum
Awolowo Rd, Onikan, POB 12556,
Lagos
General Museum - 1957
Ethnology; archaeology; Nok and Ife
terra cottas; Ife, Igbo Ukwu and Benin
bronzes - libray

Oron

09598
Oron Museum
Oron, Calabar, Eastern Region
General Museum - 1959
Traditional carvings from the Oron
area

Oshogbo

09599
**Museum of the Institute of African
Studies**
25 Aiyetoro Rd., Ikirun Byepass,
Oshogbo, Western Region
Anthropology Museum - 1966
Wood and metal sculpture; bead work
and embroidery; leather applique and
brass work; drums; ritual objects and
Afikpo Ibo masks

Osogbo

09600
Museum of Antiquities
24 Ayetoro St, Osogbo, Oyo
Anthropology Museum
Local ceremonial artifacts; costumes

Norway

A i Afjord

09601
Afjord Bygdetun
N-8393 Å i Åfjord, Sør-Trøndelag
General Museum
Old cottage and local history items

Aga

09602
Agatunet
N-5775 Aga, Hordaland and Bergen
Open Air Museum - 1938
Group of 31 buildings in their original
settings; including the medieval
'Lagmannstova', a smokehouse;
furnishings and equipment resembling
a hamlet from about 1850

Ål

09603
Ål Bygdemuseum
Leksvold, 2 km from Hwy 7, N-3570 Ål,
Buskerud
General Museum - 1924
Old farm-yard with two 18th century
cottages; 15 buildings, including old
school house, grinding mill, cottage
(17th century); 'rose-painting' collection

Ålen

09604
Alen Bygdetun
near Hwy 30, N-7480 Ålen,
Sør-Tro%ondelag
General Museum
Local history; utensils and implements;
old cottage

Ålesund

09605
Alesunds Museet
Rasmus Rønnebergsgt 16, N-6000
Ålesund, Møre and Romsdal
General Museum - 1903
Local history; natural history; social
history; archaeology section;
seafaring, fishing and arctic hunting -
library

Alvdal

09606
Nordre Husan
Østerdal valley north of Alvdal village
on Hwy 30, N-2560 Alvdal, Hedmark
Open Air Museum
Mountain village farmyard consisting
of sixteen houses (many from the 17th
century) on their original sites

Åndalsnes

09607
Ner Hole Museum
close to the E 69, Nedre Hole, N-6300
Åndalsnes, Møre and Romsdal
Open Air Museum - 1950
Stonebuilt farmhouse (1814) and other
buildings

Andenes

09608
Polarmuseet
old Doctor's House, *mail c/o*
Kommunekontoret, N-9480 Andenes,
Nordland
History/Public Affairs Museum
Exhibits related to Svalbard; Polar
expeditions section; sealing and
trapping in the Arctic

Aremark

09609
Aremark Bygdetun
Hwy 21, N-1770 Aremark, Østfold
Open Air Museum - 1964
Grain mill (1885)

Arendal

09610
Aust-Agder-Museet
Langsæ Gård, Parkveien 16, N-4800
Arendal, Aust-Agder
General Museum - 1832
Maritime section; prehistory;
ethnography; geology; coins and
medals; furniture; arts and crafts

09611
Merdøgård Aust-Agder-Museet
Merdøy Island, Parkveien 16, N-4800
Arendal, Aust-Agder
Open Air Museum - 1930
18th century captain's or 'skipper's'
house, demonstrating the close
connection between domestic life and
house furnishing in Southern Norway,
Holland and England in the days of the
sailing vessels

Årnes

09612
Gamle Hvam
on Hwy 173, Akershus
Landbruksskole, N-2150 Årnes,
Akershus
General Museum - 1915
17th century farmyard with 12 old
buildings; furnishings and equipment;
collection of old agricultural machinery

Åsestranda

09613
Sunmøre Museum
Borgundgavlen, N-6017 Åsestranda,
Møre and Romsdal
General Museum - 1931
Boats and fishing implements; regional
prehistory; agriculture; handicrafts;
copies of 3 prehistoric ships (600 A.D.)
in full scale; about 30 old houses
grouped in farmyards - library

Åsgårdstrand

09614
Munch-Huset
N-3155 Åsgårdstrand, Vestfold
Historic Site
House of Edvard Munch where he
created one of his best known
paintings 'Girls on the Bridge'

Askim

09615
Askim Bygdemuseum
E 18, outskirts, N-1800 Askim, Østfold
Open Air Museum - 1939
Courtyard with 7 old farm houses,
equipped with furniture and utensils

Aurland

09616
Aurland Bygdetun
Onstadstova, N-5745 Aurland, Sogn
and Fjordane
Historic Site
Sheriff's home with a collection of
mementoes from Per Sivle
(Norwegian poet 1857-1904)

Bagn

09617
Bagn Bygdesamling
E 68, Islandmoen Farm, N-2930 Bagn,
Oppland
Open Air Museum - 1914
Nine old farm houses; local history
artifacts

Ballangen

09618
Ballangen Bygdemuseum
near the E 6, N-8540 Ballangen,
Nordland
General Museum - 1962
Local history

Bergen

09619
Bergenhus Festning
POB 25, N-5014 Bergen, Hordaland
and Bergen
Historic Site
Håkonshallen (Royal Ceremonial Hall,
1248-61) in Gothic style;
Rosenkrantztårnet (Tower, 1562-67)
built around a medieval core; several
18th century buildings

09620
Bergens Billedgalleri
Rasmus Meyers Allé, N-5000 Bergen,
Hordaland and Bergen
Fine Arts Museum - 1825
Norwegian paintings and sculptures
from the 19th and 20th centuries;
European art - library

09621
Bergens Sjøfartsmuseum
Møhlenprisbakken 3, POB 2736, N-5010
Bergen, Hordaland and Bergen
History/Public Affairs Museum - 1921
History of shipping; models including
Norwegian smallcrafts; plans,
drawings, pictures, banners from
shipyards - library

09622
Botanisk Museum Universitetet i
Bergen
Olaf Ryesvei 7, N-5014 Bergen,
Hordaland and Bergen
Natural History Museum - 1825/1948
Exhibits of Norwegian flora

09623
Bryggens Museum University of
Bergen, Erling Dekke Næss' Institutt for
Middelalderarkeologi
Dreggen, N-5000 Bergen, Hordaland
and Bergen
Archeology Museum - 1976
Medieval archaeology; cultural and
economic history of Bergen
throughout the Middle Ages -
information center

09624
Fiskerimuseet i Bergen
Permanenten, Nordahl Brunsgt 9,
N-5000 Bergen, Hordaland and
Bergen
Science/Tech Museum - 1880
Fishery in Norway; models illustrating
various fishing methods; old gear; boat
models

09625
Geologisk Museum Universitetet i
Bergen, Geologisk Institutt
Muséplassen 3, N-5014 Bergen,
Hordaland and Bergen
Natural History Museum - 1825/1948
Extensive exhibitions showing
different aspects of the geology of
Norway as well as geological
processes; comprehensive collections
of minerals and rocks

09626
Det Hanseatiske Museum
Finnegård, Bryggen, N-5000 Bergen,
Hordaland and Bergen
Historic Site - 1872
Oldest and best preserved house of
the old Hanseatic town, furnished and
equipped to show what life on the
Quay was like about 1700;
meetinghouses and clubs of the
merchants on the Quay, used until
about 1840

09627
Historisk Museum Universitetet i
Bergen
POB 25, N-5014 Bergen, Hordaland
and Bergen
History/Public Affairs Museum -
1825/1948
Pre- and proto-history; medieval
archaeology and architecture;
antiquities; history of art; Norwegian
folk art; cultural anthropology;
post-medieval social history;
ecclesiastical art; ethnography

09628
Lepramuseet St. Jorgens Hospital
Kong Oscarsgt, N-5000 Bergen,
Hordaland and Bergen
History/Public Affairs Museum
Medieval leprosy hospital, rebuilt after
the great fire in 1702; collection
dealing with Norway's part in the fight
against leprosy, especially on the
Bergen doctor G. Armauer Hansen

09629
Museum 'Gamle Bergen' ('Old
Bergen' Museum)
Elsero, N-5000 Bergen, Hordaland and
Bergen
General Museum - 1949
18th and 19th century buildings;
furnishings

09630
Rasmus Meyers Samlinger Bergen
Billedgalleri
Rasmus Meyers Allé 7, N-5000
Bergen, Hordaland and Bergen
Fine Arts Museum - 1916
Period furniture; art gallery including
32 paintings and 105 prints by Edvard
Munch

09631
Stiftelsen Stenersens Samling
Bergen Billedgalleri
Rasmus Meyers Allé 3, N-5000
Bergen, Hordaland and Bergen
Fine Arts Museum - 1976
Modern art including works by Paul
Klee (36), Edvard Munch (10), Pablo
Picasso (15), Max Ernst, Lionel
Feininger, Jorn, Wassilij Kandinsky,
Miró, Nesch, Poliakoff, de Staël,
Tamayo, Tobey, Vasarely, Vieira da
Silva, Wols, and others

09632
**Vestlandske Kunstindustrimuseum
'Permanenten'** (West Norway
Museum of Applied Art)
Permanenten, Nordahl Brunsgt 9,
N-5000 Bergen, Hordaland and
Bergen
Decorative Arts Museum - 1887
Applied and decorative arts;
Norwegian and European furnishings,
goldsmith work, costumes, textiles,
ceramics, glass, porcelain, silver
(Renaissance period to the present);
antiquities; photographs; J.W.N.
Munthe's Chinese collection - library

09633
Zoologisk Museum Universitetet i
Bergen
Muséplassen 3, N-5014 Bergen,
Hordaland and Bergen
Natural History Museum - 1825/1948
Norwegian and non-Norwegian fauna
exhibitions; unique specimens such as
the extinct Lofoten horse; skeletons of
large whales

Billingstad

09634
Norges Birøkterlags Museum
Bergerveien 15, N-1362 Billingstad,
Akershus
Agriculture Museum - 1884
Development of beekeeping in
Norway

Bjerka

09635
Hemnes Bygdetun
Lillebjerka on the E 6, N-8643 Bjerka,
Nordland
Open Air Museum - 1967
Nine buildings including an
open-hearth cottage (1830) illustrating
19th century peasant life

Bleikvasslia

09636
Malla Bleikvasslis Samlinger
near Hwy 806, N-8647 Bleikvasslia,
Nordland
General Museum
Local history; domestic utensils;
harness items and carts; implements
and tools

Bodø

09637
Det Gamle Handelssted Nordland
Fylkesmuseum
Kjerringøy on Hwy 81, Prinsensgt 116,
N-8000 Bodø, Nordland
Open Air Museum
Old trading post (ca. 1800) with many
furnished buildings forming a
courtyard

09638
Nordland Fylkesmuseum
Prinsensgt 116, N-8000 Bodø, Nordland
General Museum - 1888
Fisheries; traditional boats; local
history; weapons; life in Nordland
County; departments of social history,
natural history, and archaeology -
library; open air museum; 'dry'
aquarium

Borge

09639
Roald Amundsens Minne
Hwy 111, west of Sarpsborg, Borge,
Tomta, N-1700 Sarpsborg, Østfold
Historic Site - 1972
Birthplace and childhood home of
arctic explorer Roald Amundsen

Borkenes

09640
Kvæford Bygdetun
at Rå near Hwy 849, N-9410 Borkenes,
Troms
General Museum - 1955
Four old farm buildings, two water-
powered grinding mills (1861/1880)

Bøverbru

09641
Toten Museum
between Hwys 4 and 33 at Stenberg
farm, N-2846 Bøverbru, Oppland
Open Air Museum - 1931
Stenberg farm (1790) with a ring of
farm buildings around the courtyard;
local antiquities, church art; old crafts;
weapons; coins; costumes;
implements; carriages

Brevik

09642
Brevik Bymuseum
Brevik Rådhus, Kirkegaten 4, POB 103,
N-3951 Brevik, Telemark
General Museum - 1975
Collection representing the resistance
movement and everyday life during
World War II; exhibition illustrating old
maritime traditions; original rococo
wall-paintings (building from 1761);
grocer's shop (1900)

Bryne

09643
Garborgheimen - Knudaheio
near Hwy 505 south of Bryne, N-4340
Bryne, Rogaland
Historic Site
Two small houses commemorating the
poet Arne Garborg; Garborgheimen,
19th century Jæren house, is his
birthplace; Knudaheio, a few
kilometers to the east, was built by the
poet

Bygland

09644
Bygland Bygdetun
on Hwy 12, N-4684 Bygland,
Aust-Agder
Open Air Museum - 1937
Open-hearth cottage (1650); 5 other
timbered buildings

Bykle

09645
Huldreheimen
north of Hwy 12, N-4694 Bykle,
Aust-Agder
Open Air Museum
Open-hearth cottage, two store-
houses, grinding mill and 'seter' house,
all furnished

Dagali

09646
Dagali Museum
Halland near Hwy 8, N-3588 Dagali,
Buskerud
Open Air Museum
Various buildings; grinding mill (1774);
barn (ca. 1740); stable, kiln, cowshed
with implements (18th century); school
and church cottage (1850-70);
furniture; arms - exhibition hall

Dalen i Telemark

09647
Anne Grimdalens Minne
Grimdalen farm near Hwy 45, N-3880
Dalen i Telemark
Fine Arts Museum
300 of Anne Grimdalen's sculptures

09648
Lårdal Bygdemuseum
near Hwy 45 north of Dalen, N-3880
Dalen i Telemark
Open Air Museum - 1950
Nine houses including the Vindlaus
farm; Eidsborg stave church

Dokka

09649
Lands Museum
near Hwy 35, N-2870 Dokka, Oppland
Open Air Museum - 1927
Fourteen old farmhouses and local
history artifacts

Drammen

09650
Drammens Kunstforening
Bragernes Torg 13, POB 214, N-3001
Drammen, Buskerud
Fine Arts Museum - 1867
Art collection; loan exhibitions

09651
Drammens Museum, Fylkemuseum
for Buskerud
Konnerudgaten 7, N-3000 Drammen,
Buskerud
General Museum - 1908
Coll: ethnology; civil and peasant
culture, folk art; ecclesiastical art;
maritime section; agriculture; textiles;
manor (1770) furnished with period
interiors; arms, flags, and uniforms -
library; open-air museum

Drangedal

09652
Drangedal Bygdetun
N-3750 Drangedal, Telemark
Open Air Museum - 1962
Ten old buildings

Drøbak

09653
Follo Museum
Seiersten, N-1440 Drøbak, Akershus
Open Air Museum - 1948
Old buildings; artifacts

Egersund

09654
Dalane Folkemuseum
Slettebø, POB 338, N-4371 Egersund,
Rogaland
Open Air Museum - 1910
Old houses (1850); interiors; old
workshops; tools; agricultural
implements; local history - library

Eggedal

09655
Hagan
N-3359 Eggedal, Buskerud
Historic Site
Home of the painter Christian
Skredsvig with his studio and some of
his paintings

09656
Tveitens Samlinger
N-3359 Eggedal, Buskerud
Open Air Museum - 1964
Implements pertaining to local history;
three old houses; Eggedal mill

Eidsvoll

09657
Eidsvoll Bygdemuseum
Hammerstad, E6 Hwy, N-2080 Eidsvoll,
Akershus
General Museum
Local curiosities such as distillery
utensils from the past; washing
machine (1900); pram (1870); old
buildings; Oppsal manor house (1800)

Eidsvoll Verk

09658
Eidsvollsminnet - Eidsvoll
Bygningens Nasjonalhistoriske
Samlinger
E 6 hwy, N-2074 Eidsvoll Verk,
Akershus
Historic Site
Building presented to the Norwegian
Storting (1851), memorial of May 17th,
1814 (Constitution Day); originally
furnished Assembly Hall (Rikssalen);
portrait gallery; historical collections;
documents

Elverum

09659
Glomdalmuseet
west banks of the Glomma river,
N-2400 Elverum, Hedmark
Open Air Museum - 1911
Eighty old farmhouses arranged in
courtyards; fireproof building with
systematic collections; Tynset farm,
Rendalen farm, Åmot farm, and Solør
farm; Stemsrud building

09660
Norsk Skogbruksmuseum -
Skogbruk, Jakt og Fiske (Norwegian
Forestry Museum - Forestry, Hunting
and Fishing)
POB 117, N-2400 Elverum, Hedmark
Agriculture Museum - 1954
Norwegian forestry; logging and
timber transport; history of Norwegian
hunting and trapping; Norwegian
fauna; stuffed animals and birds;
weapons; freshwater fishing, fishing
traps, sport fishing, flies for trout and
salmon - library; lecture hall; aquarium;
open-air museum

Enebakk

09661
Enebakk Museum
Hwy 120, southeast of Oslo, N-1835
Enebakk, Akershus
Open Air Museum - 1931
Farmhouse, storehouse, kiln, barn,
cowshed and stable

Erfjord

09662
Erfjord Bygdemuseum
near Hwy 13, N-4140 Erfjord, Rogaland
Open Air Museum
Old houses; boats

09663
Håland
farm near Hwy 13 in the Erfjord area,
N-4140 Erfjord, Rogaland
Open Air Museum - 1936
Old cottage, 'rose-painted' guesthouse

Etne

09664
Sæbøtunet Sunnhordland Folkemuseum
near the E 76, N-5590 Etne, Hordaland
and Bergen
Open Air Museum
Farmyard with a smokehousee, a
'glass-window' cottage, storehouse,
cowshed, cookhouse; all equipped
with furniture, household utensils and
implements

Fagernes

09665
Valdres Folkemuseum
N-2900 Fagernes, Oppland
Open Air Museum - 1901
70 old houses; exhibitions illustrating
life in the mountains, hunting and
fishing; medieval tapestries and
chests, old silver and textiles; folk
music instruments; weapons;
ethnography - library

Fannrem

09666
Orkdal Bygdemuseum
Torshus Folkehøgskole on Hwy 65,
N-7320 Fannrem, Sør-Trøndelag
Open Air Museum - 1929
Three old houses with furniture and
utensils

Farsund

09667
Farsund Museum
N-4550 Farsund, Vest-Agder
Open Air Museum - 1946
Small sea-captain's house, containing
furnishings and utensils

Fjørde

09668
Sunnfjord Folkemuseum
Mo, near Hwy 14, N-6800 Fjørde, Sogn
and Fjordane
General Museum - 1910
Old farmyard, cottage (1500), and
other farm buildings with utensils and
implements; exhibition hall with
collections of woodcarving, textiles
and costumes, bridal crowns

Fjøsanger

09669
Gamlehaugen
N-5042 Fjøsanger, Hordaland and
Bergen
Historic Site
Home of Christian Michelsen,
Norway's Prime Minister in 1905, now
a royal residence, with old interiors
and memorabilia of the year 1905,
when the union with Sweden was
disbanded

Flekkefjord

09670
Flekkefjord Bymuseum
N-4400 Flekkefjord, Vest-Agder
General Museum - 1924
18th century house in the Dutch
Quarter; furniture; porcelain; textiles;
silver

Foldereid

09671
Leirvika Bygdesamling
near Hwy 770, N-7975 Foldereid,
Nord-Trøndelag
General Museum - 1906
Two old buildings furnished with
utensils, implements and books

Follebu

09672
Aulestad
N-2620 Follebu, Oppland
Historic Site - 1934
Home of Karoline and Bjørnstjerne
Bjørnson; memorabilia of the poet and
Nobel Prize winner (1903) and his
family (1875-1910); authentic interior;
Norwegian ethnology; freshwater
fishing

Frederikstad

09673
Frederikstad Museum
Det Gamle Slaveri, Tollbodgaten 107,
POB 1144, N-1601 Frederikstad,
Østfold
General Museum - 1903
Local history exhibits; military objects;
Tordenskiold collection - arts and
crafts center

Frosta

09674
Frosta Bygdemuseum
near Hwy 753, N-7633 Frosta,
Nord-Trøndelag
General Museum - 1909
Local history items; two old buildings

Fygle

09675
Vestvågøy Museum
N-8374 Fygle, Nordland
General Museum - 1962
Local history; fishing gear; rural
artifacts; school items, fishermen's
shed ('rorbu'); Nordland boat

Fyresdal

09676
Fyresdal Bygdemuseum
near Hwy 355, N-3870 Fyresdal,
Telemark
Open Air Museum
Old cottages, loft, grinding mill, sauna,
court room; local artifacts

Gausvik

09677
Sandtorg Bygdetun
N-9430 Gausvik, Troms
General Museum - 1960
Two old buildings; local history
artifacts

Gladstad

09678
Vega Bygdemuseum
POB 23, N-8980 Gladstad
General Museum - 1976
Local history

Gol

09679
Gol Bygdemuseum
1 km north of Hwy 7, Hallingdal Folk
High School, N-3550 Gol, Buskerud
Open Air Museum
Skaga farm, consisting of seven old
houses and three rebuilt houses

Granvin

09680
Granvin Bygdemuseum
N-5736 Granvin, Hordaland and
Bergen
Open Air Museum - 1920
Brynjulfstova cottage; items of local
interest; Kapteinsgården (18th century)

Gratangsbotn

09681
Gratangen Bygdemuseum
N-9470 Gratangsbotn, Troms
General Museum - 1955
O.M. Eilivsen-Thranings collections of
old boats and fishing gear

Grimstad

09682
Ibsenhuset og Grimstad Bymuseum
N-4890 Grimstad, Aust-Agder
General Museum - 1916
Apothecary's shop (1839) with original
furnishings, where Henrik Ibsen
worked and where his first play
'Catilina' was written; local history;
maritime section

Grøa på Nordmøre

09683
Sunndal Bygdemuseum
Løken near Hwy 16, N-7420 Grøa på
Nordmøre, Møre and Romsdal
General Museum - 1935
Old Sunndal farm, chapel; local history
artifacts; exhibition about English
salmon fishing in Western Norway
during the 19th century

Grovane

09684
Setesdalsbanen
Hwy 405 north of Kristiansand, N
Grovane, Vest-Agder
Open Air Museum - 1962
Grovane station on the Sørland
Railway; narrow-gauge Setesdal
Railway remains, some engines, 5 km
long track, bridges and tunnels

Grue-Finnskog

09685
Finnetunet
Svulrya on Hwy 205, N-2256
Grue-Finnskog, Hedmark
Open Air Museum - 1942
Collections depicting the life of the
Finnish emigrants during the famine
years who settled in the vast forests
around 1600; eight buildings forming
an old courtyard including a cottage
(1750), storehouse (ca. 1780), a barn
and a flour mill

Halden

09686
Haldens Minder - Idd Bygdemuseum
Freriksten, Rød Herregård, N-1750
Halden, Østfold
History/Public Affairs Museum - 1896
Military items including 270 year old
citizens' banners, uniforms, weapons;
paintings; women's and men's clothing
from the 1700's; Fredriksten (latter half
of the 17th century)

09687
**Rød Herregård - De Ankerske
Samlinger**
outskirts, Rød Herregård, N-1750 Halden,
Østfold
Historic Site - 1961
Old manor with park and garden (late
17th century); furniture; weapons

Halsnøy Kloster

09688
Klostertunet
island of Halsnøy, east of Leirvik
(Stord), N-4555 Halsnøy Kloster,
Hordaland and Bergen
Open Air Museum - 1958
Ruins of the Halsnøy Monastery (1164);
fishery department with boats and
gear (belonging to the Sunnhordland
Folkemuseum)

Haltdalen

09689
Haltdalen Bygdetun
Heksem farm, N-7487 Haltdalen,
Sør-Trøndelag
Open Air Museum
Old farmhouse, cowshed and
storehouse

Hamar

09690
Hedmarksmuseet - Domkirkeodden
Lake Mjøsa banks, N-2301 Hamar,
Hedmark
Open Air Museum - 1902
Ruins of the medieval cathedral and
the bishop's residence; about thirty old
farm buildings containing local history
and domestic life exhibitions

09691
Jernbanemuseet
Strandveien 132, N-2301 Hamar
Open Air Museum - 1896
Collections illustrating the
development of Norway's railways; old
locomotives and carriages; 300-meter
railway track with old stations and
signal arrangements

Haugesund

09692
Haugesund Billedgalleri
Erling Skjalgssonsgt 4, N-5501
Haugesund, Rogaland
Fine Arts Museum - 1973
Art from the Western part of Norway
- library

09693
Museet for Haugesund og Bygdene
Rådhusgt 66, N-5500 Haugesund,
Rogaland
General Museum - 1925
Ethnographical objects; town
department; maritime section;
agricultural collection; prehistory and
social history of the area

Haugfoss

09694
**Modums Blaafarveværk -
Bygdemuseet Modum**
near Hwy 287, 5 km north of Åmot,
N-3353 Haugfoss, Buskerud
History/Public Affairs Museum
19th century workers's houses at the
Modum cobalt mines and Haugfoss
works, smalt production; local history
section

Haus i Hordaland

09695
Havråtunet
south of Gjerstad, on the road
between Haus and Bruvik, N-5248
Haus i Hordaland, Hordaland and
Bergen
Open Air Museum
Havråtunet farmyard with a group of old
houses

Hemnes i Høland

09696
Aurskog - Høland Bygdetun
Bråte school near Hwy 125, southeast
of Oslo, N-1970 Hemnes i Høland,
Akershus
Open Air Museum
Seven old farmhouses; items
illustrating life in these forest districts
in earlier times

Hemsedal

09697
Hemsedal Bygdetun
Øvre Løken, N-3560 Hemsedal,
Buskerud
Open Air Museum - 1956
Old farmhouses

Hjelmeland

09698
Hjelmeland Bygdetun Rogaland
Folkemuseum
Vikatunet near Hwy 13, N-4130
Hjelmeland, Rogaland
Open Air Museum - 1912
200-year-old farmyard, grinding mill,
kiln, boathouse; implements and
utensils, demonstrating domestic life
back to 1660

Hol

09699
Hol Bygdemuseum
near Hwy 7 at Hagafoss, N-3576 Hol,
Buskerud
Open Air Museum - 1914
Hol farmyard with 15 old houses, the
Nestegard and Raunsgard cottages
with remarkable 'rose painting'

Holmestrand

09700
Holmestrand Museum
Nils Kjærsgt 4, N-3080 Holmestrand,
Vestfold
General Museum - 1929
Local history; maritime history; fine
arts; Holst House (1756)

Holmsbu

09701
Holmsbu Billedgalleri
N-3484 Holmsbu, Buskerud
Fine Arts Museum - 1973
Paintings from most periods in Henrik
Sørensen's life; works by his Holmsbu
friends, Oluf Wold Torne and Thorvald
Erichsen

Homborsund

09702
Nørholm
near E 18 and 6 km west of Grimstad,
N-4897 Homborsund, Aust-Agder
Historic Site
Nobel Prize winner Knut Hamson's
farm (1918), now a memorial museum
with his books, paintings and other
belongings

Hommelstø

09703
Velfjord Bygdemuseum
at Strøm near Hwy 803, N-8960
Hommelstø, Nordland
Open Air Museum - 1944
Six old houses; systematic collection
including Lapp section

Hønefoss

09704
Ringerikes Museum
Norderhov church on E 68 south of
Hønefoss, POB 23, N-3501 Hønefoss,
Buskerud
General Museum - 1923
Items connected with P.Chr.
Asbjørnsen and Jørgen Moe, the earliest
collectors of Norwegian folk tales;
section dealing with the resistance
movement during World War II; old
rectory office; Riddergården House
including eight buildings

Hop

09705
Troldhaugen
on the edge of Lake Nordåsvatnet,
N-5043 Hop, Hordaland and Bergen
Historic Site
Victorian home of Edvard and Nina
Grieg, urn containing the composer's
burial remains

Hornindal

09706
Anders Svors Museum
on Hwy 60, Grodås, N-6790 Hornindal,
Sogn and Fjordane
Fine Arts Museum
Approximately 400 works by the
sculptor Anders Svor (1864-1929)

Horten

09707
Marinemuseet
Karljohansveien, N-3191 Horten,
Vestfold
History/Public Affairs Museum - 1854
History of the Norwegian Navy; ship
models; weapons; curiosities; the
world's first torpedo boat, 'RAP' (1873)

Høvikodden

09708
Sonja Henies og Niels Onstads Stiftelser
Kunstsentret, N-1311 Høvikodden, Akershus
Fine Arts Museum
20th century painting; theater, dance, and cinema exhibitions; outdoor sculptures

Høydalsmo

09709
Trovatn Museum
near the county road between Rauland and Høydalsmo, N-3860 Høydalsmo, Telemark
General Museum - 1920
Local culture; domestic utensils; farm implements; folk art

Hurdal

09710
Hurdal Bygdetun
Garjøgrenda, north of Lake Hurdal, N-2090 Hurdal, Akershus
Open Air Museum
Local history; 17th century inn and post office

Hvalstad

09711
Asker Museum - Valstads Samlinger
Kirkeveien 6b, N-1364 Hvalstad, Akershus
General Museum
Old buildings and furniture; paintings; local antiquities

Jaren

09712
Hadeland Folkemuseum
near Hwy 4 at Brandbu, N-2770 Jaren, Oppland
Open Air Museum - 1913
Romanesque Tingelstad church (ca. 1100) with Renaissance interior; open-air section with 26 old houses representative of the area; systematic collection ranging from Stone Age finds to modern Hadeland glass

Jessheim

09713
Ullensaker Bygdetun
Ullensaker Rådhus, N-2050 Jessheim, Akershus
General Museum
Local history

Kabelvåg

09714
Lofotmuseum - Kabelvåg Fiskerimuseum
N-8310 Kabelvåg, Nordland
Anthropology Museum - 1936
Exhibits illustrating the life and work of the Lofoten fishermen - aquarium

Karasjok

09715
De Samiske Samlinger
near Hwy 96, N-9730 Karasjok, Finnmark
Anthropology Museum - 1939
Exhibits illustrating the life and work of the Lapps on the Finnmark plateau and outside of Finnmark; open-air museum including farms typical of the various Lapp livelihoods, such as fishing and the herding of reindeer

Kaupanger

09716
De Heibergske Samlinger - Sogn Folkemuseum
700 yds from the ferry quay, N-5880 Kaupanger, Sogn and Fjordane
Open Air Museum - 1909
Nineteen old houses, including the Geithus house (1596), the Rå storehouse (1589), a cookhouse from Vadheim, the Veta hut from Vetanosi, an old inn from Glavær and an 18th century rectory from Vik; collection of various tools and implements; large boat gallery

Kirkenær

09717
Gruetunet
1 km from Kirkenær village on Hwy 3, N-2260 Kirkenær, Hedmark
Open Air Museum - 1942
Fourteen buildings; local history

Kirkenes

09718
Sør-Varanger Museum
mail c/o Captain Knut G. Svestøl, N-9901 Kirkenes, Finnmark
History/Public Affairs Museum - 1967
Greek-Orthodox chapel (1565) in Neiden on Hwy 6 45 km west of Kirkenes; King Oscar II's chapel (1869) at Grense Jakobselv on the Soviet border 63 km east of Kirkenes; Bjørklund farm near Svanvik 40 km south of Kirkenes

Klepp Station

09719
Klepp Bygdemuseum
Kleppekrossen near Hwy 44, N-4062 Klepp Station, Rogaland
General Museum - 1954
Old building; local history artifacts

Kollungtveit

09720
Grindheim Bygdemuseum
Sveindal, off Hwy 9, N-4545 Kollungtveit, Vest-Agder
Open Air Museum - 1926
Old timbered building, fully furnished

Kongsberg

09721
Bergverksmuseet
Hyttegt 3, N-3600 Kongsberg, Buskerud
Science/Tech Museum - 1945
History of the silver mines from the 17th century to 1957; silver collection and Royal mint exhibition; technical objects from Kongsberg silver mines; silver specimens

09722
Lågdalsmuseet
east of the Lågen river, Tillischbakken 8, N-3600 Kongsberg, Buskerud
Open Air Museum - 1924
23 old lofts and cottages from Uvdal, Nore, Flesberg, Rollag and Sandsvær

09723
Våpenfabrikkens Museum
mail c/o Kongsberg Våpenfabrikk, N-3600 Kongsberg, Buskerud
Science/Tech Museum
Weapons and equipment produced by Norway's largest armament factory since 1814

Kragerø

09724
Berg-Kragerø Museum
N-3770 Kragerø, Telemark
Decorative Arts Museum - 1927
Manor with furniture; paintings

Kristiansand S

09725
Christianssands Billedgalleri
Rådhusgt 7/9, POB 163, N-4601 Kristiansand S, Vest-Agder
Fine Arts Museum - 1902
Paintings; drawings; graphic art; sculptures

09726
Kristiansands Museum
Gyldenløvesgt 14, N-4600 Kristiansand S, Vest-Agder
General Museum - 1828
Local history; natural history

09727
Vest-Agder Fylkesmuseum
Øvre Kongsgård, POB 4048, N-4601 Kristiansand S
Open Air Museum - 1903
Old farmyards and houses including old workshops; maritime section; cultural history; ethnography; folklore - library

Kristiansund

09728
Nordmøre Museum
Knudtzondalen, N-6500 Kristiansund, Møre and Romsdal
General Museum - 1894
Local history; archaeology; ethnography; folklore; fishery department; old farmhouses

Kvernaland

09729
Time Bygdemuseum
N-4344 Kvernaland, Rogaland
General Museum - 1962
Agricultural implements and utensils; tools; items from the old school; local curiosities; Kverneland smithy (1879); Kvernelands Factory Museum: tools and 19th century products

Kvernes

09730
Kvernes Bygdemuseum
Averøy island, N-6540 Kvernes, Møre and Romsdal
Open Air Museum - 1941
Ten old buildings, including cottages, a storehouse (17th century); fishery section

Kvisvik

09731
Straumsnes Museum
at Grimstad church on Hwy 16, N-6677 Kvisvik, Møre and Romsdal
General Museum - 1922
Items of local interest

Larvik

09732
Fritzøe Værks Museum
N-3250 Larvik, Vestfold
Science/Tech Museum - 1939
Stoves, stove plates, casting moulds from the iron works (1640-1868)

09733
Larvik Kunstforening
N-3250 Larvik, Vestfold
Fine Arts Museum - 1916
Art collection; old Customs House

09734
Larvik Museum
N-3250 Larvik, Vestfold
Historic Site - 1916
Period furnishings of an aristocratic, 17th century Scandinavian home; former residence of the Danish governor Ulrich Frederik Gyldenløve (1673)

09735
Larvik Sjøfartsmuseum
Tolderodden, N-3250 Larvik, Vestfold
History/Public Affairs Museum - 1926
Maritime history of the area, featuring the boat builder Colin Archer, Magnus Andersen, who sailed in 1893 with a copy of the Gokstad Viking ship across the North Atlantic, and Thor Heyerdahl's Kon-Tiki and RA expeditions

Leirvik

09736
Sunnhordland Folkemuseum
township of Leirvik on the island of Stord, POB 51, N-5401 Stord
Open Air Museum - 1913
Ådlandstova cottage (Middle Ages), Kvinnherad storehouse, Huglo sheriff's house; sculptures by Torleiv Agdestein; watermill on the Vikabekken stream

Leka

09737
Leka Bygdemuseum
N-7994 Leka, Nord-Trøndelag
Open Air Museum - 1962
Two old buildings; fishery section with 5 different types of boats and fishing gear; Herlaugshaugen burial mound from the Viking period, the second largest of its kind in Norway

Leksvik

09738
Leksvik Bygdesamling
2 km from the village, N-7120 Leksvik, Nord-Trøndelag
General Museum - 1949
Two old buildings; local history artifacts

Lillehammer

09739
By's Malerisamling
Kirkegata 69, N-2600 Lillehammer,
Oppland
Fine Arts Museum - 1921
19th and 20th century Norwegian
paintings, drawings, graphic arts,
sculpture; works of the 'Lillehammer
colony' including Thorvald Erichsen
and Einar Sandberg

09740
De Sandvigske Samlinger
Maihaugen, N-2600 Lillehammer,
Oppland
General Museum - 1887
Textiles; church art; ethnology;
weapons; 17th century swords;
Norwegian firearms; gunmaker's
workshop; medieval helmets and
crossbows; uniforms; open air
museum with old farms and Garmo
stave church (about 1200)

Lillesand

09741
Carl-Knudsen-Gården
N-4790 Lillesand, Aust-Agder
General Museum - 1967
Local culture; patrician house (ca.
1830) with furnishings and decoration

Lom

09742
**Lom Bygdemuseum - Lom
Heimbygdlag**
near Hwy 15 and 55, N-2628 Lom,
Oppland
Open Air Museum - 1925
St. Olav's cottage (1021); Glømsdal
cottage (1761); eleven other buildings;
poet Olav Aukrust's collection

Lonevåg

09743
Osterøy Museum
Gjerstad on the island of Osterøy,
N-5250 Lonevåg, Hordaland and
Bergen
Open Air Museum - 1920
Six old houses from the island,
including a smokehouse from Solbjør,
two farm buildings from Kleiveland; old
rural crafts and traditions of the area,
such as fitting, tanning and
woodworking

Lørenskog

09744
Lørenskog Bygdetun
Kjenn School, Hasselveien, N-1470
Lørenskog, Akershus
General Museum
Local history

Lundenes

09745
Grytøya Bygdetun
on the Grytøy island, N-9420 Lundenes,
Troms
Open Air Museum - 1965
Large dwelling, storehouse, boathouse
containing boats and fishing gear; local
history exhibits

Mandal

09746
Mandal Bymuseum
Andorsengården, N-4500 Mandal,
Vest-Agder
General Museum - 1954
Art gallery: paintings by Adolph
Tidemand and Amaldus Nielsen; local
maritime museum; Andorsengården
(1801)

09747
Mandal og Opplands Folkemuseum
Øyslebø, near Hwy 455, N-4500 Mandal,
Vest-Agder
Open Air Museum - 1912
Old buildings, old farmhouse from
Åseral

09748
Olav Holmegaards Samlinger Mandal
Bymuseum
Andorsengården, N-4500 Mandal,
Vest-Agder
Decorative Arts Museum
Furniture; textiles; domestic utensils
and implements

Melbu

09749
Vesterålen Bygdemuseum
near Hwy 19, N-8490 Melbu, Nordland
General Museum - 1923
Old buildings; exhibits illustrating arts
and crafts, social history

Meldal

09750
Meldal Bygdemuseum Bergslia
Hwy 700, N-7390 Meldal, Sør-Trøndelag
General Museum - 1930
Old buildings; local history; folklore

Meråker

09751
Meråker Bygdemuseum
near Meråker station, 1 km from the E
75, N-7530 Meråker, Nord-Trøndelag
Open Air Museum - 1951
Two old buildings, a smithy, a 'seter'
cottage; local history and domestic
artifacts

Mo i Rana

09752
Friluftmuseet Steinneset
on Hwy 805, N-8600 Mo i Rana,
Nordland
Open Air Museum
Old rectory; small farmyard

09753
Rana Museum
N-8600 Mo i Rana, Nordland
General Museum - 1910
Local history; folklore; old buildings -
library

Moen i Målselv

09754
Målselv Bygdetun
Fossmo: 4 km east of Bardufoss and
the E 6; Kongsli: Øverbygd east of
Hwy 87 and north of Lake Lille
Rostavatn, N-9220 Moen i Målselv,
Troms
Open Air Museum - 1947
Fossmo: farmhouse (1824), smithy,
storehouse, tools and rural utensils;
Kongsli: Konglistua cottage (1840),
domestic utensils

Molde

09755
Fiskerimuseet Pa Hjertøy
Romsdalmuseet
POB 70, N-6400 Molde, Møre and
Romsdal
Open Air Museum
Small fishing village with shore
houses, boathouses, cod-liver oil
refinery

09756
Romsdalsmuseet
Museumsveien 9, N-6400 Molde, Møre
and Romsdal
Open Air Museum - 1912
Old buildings, including farmyards,
open-hearth cottage, open-stove
cottage, storehouses, barns and
stables, chapel; ethnography and
folklore

Morgedal

09757
Olav Bjålandmuseet
close to the E 76, N-3848 Morgedal,
Telemark
Historic Site - 1966
Collections of Olav Bjåland, a member
of Roald Amundsen's South Pole
expedition; tradition of skiing in
Morgedal

09758
Sondre Nordheimstova
in the hills 1,5 km off E 76, N-3848
Morgedal, Telemark
Historic Site
Birthplace of the pioneer of modern
skiing, Sondre Nordheim (1825-97)

Mosjøen

09759
Vefsn Bygdesamling
N-8650 Mosjøen, Nordland
Open Air Museum - 1909
Old church (1734); old buildings,
including Persjordstua containing local
history collections

Moss

09760
Rabekk - Moss Museum
Rabekk Manor, N-1500 Moss, Østfold
General Museum - 1928
Local history; artifacts

Mosterøy

09761
Rennesøy Bygdemuseum
island of Rennesøy, N-4156 Mosterøy,
Rogaland
General Museum - 1966
One building and local artifacts

Mosvik

09762
Mosvik - Sæteråsgården
near Hwy 755, N-7690 Mosvik,
Nord-Trøndelag
General Museum - 1960
Farmhouse; artifacts

Mysen

09763
Folkenborg Museum Eidsberg og
Mysen Historielag
Folkenborg, N-1850 Mysen, O%østfold
Open Air Museum - 1936
Local history; farmhouse (1720);
cottage, storehouse, smithy, implement
house (ca. 1780)

Namsos

09764
Namsdalsmuseet
N-7800 Namsos, Nord-Trøndelag
Open Air Museum - 1925
Five old buildings forming a courtyard;
Lapp culture section; old tools and
implements illustrating rural life in the
district; Namdal fembøring (big open
fishing boat)

Narvik

09765
Røde Rors Krigsmuseum
N-8500 Narvik, Nordland
History/Public Affairs Museum - 1964
Red Cross war museum showing
weapons and uniforms from World
War II; three-dimensional map of the
Narvik front (1940); illegal newspapers
and items pertaining to the resistance
movement

Nesbyen

09766
Hallingdal Folkemuseum
N-3540 Nesbyen, Buskerud
Open Air Museum - 1899
Old timber buildings, including the
medieval loft from Stave, Trøymstua,
and the 18th century Villandsstua;
textiles; weapons; rose painting; folk
costumes; ethnography and folklore

Nesna

09767
Nesna Bygdemuseum
N-8700 Nesna, Nordland
General Museum - 1957
Antiquities; fishing gear; domestic
utensils; farm implements

Nesttun

09768
Vestlandske Setermuseum
Fanafjell, 20 km south of Bergen, mail
c/o Eilif Åsbo, Midtunveien 26, N-5050
Nesttun, Hordaland and Bergen
Open Air Museum
Old summer farms from West Norway,
the eldest 'seter' house (1685); all
buildings are equipped with dairy and
domestic utensils

Nordli

09769
Gamstuggu Nordli
at Hwy 74, N-7882 Nordli,
Nord-Trøndelag
Open Air Museum
Two old houses; local history artifacts

Norheimsund

09770
Mons-Breidvik-Museet
Vikøy church, close to Hwy 551, N-5600
Norheimsund, Hordaland and Bergen
Fine Arts Museum
Works by the painter and graphic
artist Mons Breidvik (1881-1950)

Notodden

09771
**Heddal and Notodden
Bygdemuseum**
Rute 10, N-3670 Notodden, Telemark
Open Air Museum - 1954
Nine old houses arranged as a
courtyard; Heddal stave church

Oppdal

09772
Oppdal Bygdemuseum
N-7400 Oppdal, Sør-Trøndelag
Open Air Museum
Sixteen old buildings, including
storehouses, a smithy, a steam bath, a
grinding mill, a threshing barn (1656);
woodcarvings; utensils and
implements

Opphaug

09773
Austråt Slott
Ørlandet, 4 km from Hwy 719, N-7140
Opphaug, Sør-Trøndelag
Historic Site
Castle (mid 17th century), said to be
the most original work of the
Norwegian Renaissance period;
church from about 1200

Ørsta

09774
Brudavoll Bygdetun
near Hwy 655, Høgebru, N-6150 Ørsta,
Møre and Romsdal
Open Air Museum - 1959
Five old buildings in their original
settings

09775
Ivar-Aasen-Museet
close to Hwy 14, N-6150 Ørsta, Møre
and Romsdal
Historic Site - 1897
Cottage and fireproof house where
the books and other belongings of the
author and linguist Ivar Aasen
(1813-1896) are preserved

Oslo

09776
Amaldus Nielsens Malerisamling
mail c/o Oslo Kommunes
Kunstsamlinger, Tøyengt 53, N Oslo 5
Fine Arts Museum - 1933
Paintings (landscapes, townscapes,
seascapes) from the 1850s up to 1933

09777
Bogstad Stiftelse
Sørkedalen, mail c/o Norsk
Folkemuseum, Museumsveien 10, N
Oslo 2
Historic Site - 1955
18th century manor with the original
18th and 19th century interiors

09778
Botanisk Museum Universitetet i Oslo
Botanisk Hage, Trondheimsveien 23 B,
N Oslo 5
Natural History Museum
Extensive herbarium of Norwegian
flora

09779
Forsvarsmuseet (Norwegian Defence
Museum)
Akershus, N Oslo 1
History/Public Affairs Museum - 1860
Weapons; uniforms; military
equipment; military history;
documentation about World Wars I
and II - library

09780
Kon-Tiki Museet
Bygdøynes, N Oslo 2
Historic Site - 1949
Archaeology; arts and crafts; the balsa
raft Kon-Tiki (1947); the papyrus boat
Ra II (1970); the vessel Tigris; stone
sculptures from the secret caves of
the Easter Island; replica of an Easter
Island statue (9.2 meters); boat models;
'dry' aquarium - library

09781
Kunstindustrimuseet i Oslo
St. Olavsgt 1, N Oslo 1
Decorative Arts Museum - 1876
Goldsmith's and silversmith's work;
woven tapestry (Baldishol tapestry, ca.
1180); glass and faience; iron stoves
and specimens of furniture from
different periods, starting with
Southern European Renaissance;
costumes and textiles; posters and
books - library

09782
Kunstnernes Hus
Wergelandsveien 17, N Oslo
Fine Arts Museum - 1930
Changing exhibitions of modern
Norwegian and foreign art

09783
Minneparken i Gamlebyen
Oslogate, N Oslo
Open Air Museum
Ruins of St. Hallvard's Church, the
Cross Church, and the Olav
Monastery (Middle Ages); Ladegården
(1725, built on the ruins of the bishop's
palace); Bishop Nikolas Chapel (ca.
1200); rooms preserved from the Olav
Monastery; medieval masonry and
stones

09784
Munch-Museet Oslo Kommunes
Kunstsamlinger
Tøyengata 53, N Oslo 5
Fine Arts Museum - 1963
Paintings, drawings, watercolors,
prints, and a few sculptures by Edvard
Munch - library

09785
Nasjonalgalleriet
Universitetsgata 13, N Oslo
Fine Arts Museum - 1836
Norwegian art, especially 19th and
20th century painting and sculpture;
works from other Scandinavian
countries; French art since Delacroix;
some old masters; Russian icons;
Greek-Roman sculptures; casts of
antique, medieval, and Renaissance
sculpture; prints and drawings -
library

09786
Norges Hjemmefrontmuseum
(Norwegian Resistance Museum)
Akershus Festning og Slott, N Oslo 1
Historic Site - 1966
Coll: authentic documents, photos,
models, weapons and equipment
pertaining to the Resistance during the
Occupation years 1940-45; fortress
and castle which were rebuilt by
Christian IV (1630); royal tombs -
library

09787
Norsk Filminstitutt
Aslaksveien 14, POB 5, N Oslo 7
Performing Arts Museum - 1955
Comprehensive collection of
Norwegian and foreign films

09788
Norsk Folkemuseum
Museumsveien 10, Bygdøy, N Oslo 2
History/Public Affairs Museum - 1894
Life of the people of Norway from the
Reformation (16th century) to the
present; open-air section: old
buildings, rural and urban, Gol stave
church (ca. 1200), Raulandstua; indoor
section: furniture, household items,
'rose-painting' and wood carving,
clothing, tapestries, farming
implements, logging gear, trappings,
conveyances; music section;
ecclesiastical section; Lappish section:
fishing, hunting, reindeer herding,
Lappish art and handicrafts; study of
the dramatist Henrik Ibsen - library;
education department

09789
Norsk Sjøfartsmuseum
Bygdøynesveien 37, N Oslo 2
Science/Tech Museum - 1914
Ship models, ship portraits;
navigational instruments; underwater
finds; a first class accomodation from
a passenger steamer; a deckhouse
from a sailing ship; Norwegian coastal
crafts; the polar ship 'Gjøa'; archives of
logbooks, manuscripts, photographs -
library

09790
Norsk Teknisk Museum
Fyrstikkalleen 1, N Oslo 6
Science/Tech Museum - 1914
Technology; handicrafts; industry;
communications; Norwegian
inventions; working models; model
railway; vintage cars - library

09791
Norsk Tollmuseum
Customs House, Schweigaardsgt 15,
Oslo dep., N Oslo
History/Public Affairs Museum - 1915
Development of the Norwegian
Customs Service

09792
Oscarshall
Bygdøy, Oscarshallveien, N Oslo 2
Fine Arts Museum
Neo-Gothic summer residence (1850)
with a beautiful garden; portrait
gallery; paintings from the Norwegian
romantic period

09793
Oslo Bymuseum
Frognerveien 67, N Oslo 2
History/Public Affairs Museum - 1905
Pictures; photos; models of old
buildings relating to the history of Oslo
as city and capital of Norway - library

09794
Oslo Kommunes Modellsamling
mail c/o Oslo Byplankontor,
Trondheimsveien 5, N Oslo 1
History/Public Affairs Museum
Municipal collection of town plans and
models

09795
Paleontologisk Museum Universitetet
i Oslo
Botanisk Hage, Sarsgt 1, N Oslo 5
Natural History Museum - 1916
Prehistoric animal and plant life; fossils
from Cambro-Silurian beds of Norway
and from Precambrian-Tertiary beds of
Svalbard; Pleistocene fossils; sea
scorpion, collections of trilobites,
agnathes, primitive fishes

09796
Pharmacological Museum
Museumsveien 10; Bygdøy, N Oslo 5
Science/Tech Museum - 1963
History of pharmacy in Norway,
starting with Svaneapotek in Bergen
(1595); development of the
pharmaceutical industry

09797
Polarskipet Fram
Bygdøynes, N Oslo 2
Historic Site - 1933
3-masted schooner 'Fram' (built by
Colin Archer in 1892), the ship used by
Fridtjof Nansen, Roald Amundsen, and
Otto Sverdrup on their expeditions;
arctic and antarctic equipment
displayed on board; 40-ton vessel
'Gjøa', with which Roald Amundsen
forced his way through the North-
West passage (belonging to Norsk
Sjøfartsmuseum)

09798
Postmuseet
Post Office Building, Dronningensgt
15, POB 1181 Sentrum, N Oslo 1
History/Public Affairs Museum - 1947
Complete collection of Norwegian
stamps

09799
Riksantikvaren Central Office of
Historic Monuments
Akershus Festning, Bygning 18, N
Oslo 1
Fine Arts Museum - 1912
Surveys and original drawings of
ancient Norwegian architecture; about
500,000 photographs of listed houses
and churches; surveys of 30 stave
churches - library

09800
Riksarkivet
Folke Bernadottes vei 21, N Oslo 8
History/Public Affairs Museum - 1814
Private archives; historical map
collection - library

09801
Skimuseet
Holmenkollen ski jump, N Oslo 3
Anthropology Museum
History of skiing in Norway; skis,
bindings, and poles from the earliest
days; equipment used by Nansen and
Amundsen in their polar expeditions;
photos, prizes, and medals

09802
Teatermuseet
N Slottsgt 1, N Oslo 1
Performing Arts Museum - 1939
Material associated with theatrical life
in Oslo

09803
Universitetets Etnografiske Museum
Frederiksgate 2, N Oslo 1
Anthropology Museum - 1857
Modern ethnographical collection;
African art; Indian art; Arctic and
Indonesian ethnography - library

09804
**Universitetets Mineralogisk-
Geologiske Museum**
Botanisk Hage, Sarsgate 1, N Oslo 5
Natural History Museum - 1920
Geological history of Norway and
Svalbard; mining and stone-cutting
industries; petrology; geochemistry;
mineralogy; geology - library with
Paleontology Museum

09805
Universitetets Myntkabinett
Frederiksgt 2, N Oslo 1
History/Public Affairs Museum - 1817
Numismatics; collection of coins,
medals, orders and decorations -
library

09806
Universitetets Oldsaksamling
Frederiksgt 2, N Oslo 1
Archeology Museum - 1829
Exhibits from prehistoric times, Stone
Age, Bronze Age, Iron Age, and Viking
times; medieval painted objects;
12th-13th century Gothic art;
sculptures; altar, furnishings and
equipment, stave church porches;
arms - library

09807
Veterinærmuseet Veterinary College of
Norway
Ullevålsveien 72, POB 8146 Dep., N
Oslo 1
Natural History Museum - 1967
Veterinary sciences - library

09808
Vigeland-Museet
Nobelsgt 32, N Oslo 2
Fine Arts Museum - 1947
Works by the sculptor Gustav
Vigeland, bronzes, plaster models for
monumental sculptures, models in clay,
drawings and woodcuts

09809
Vigeland-Parken
Kirkeveien, N Oslo 8
Open Air Museum - 1947
Sculpture park created by Gustav
Vigeland (1869-1943)

09810
Vikingskipene Universitetets
Oldsaksamling (The Viking Ship
Museum)
Huk Aveny 35, N Oslo 2
Archeology Museum
Three Viking ships excavated at
Oseberg, Gokstad and Tune; finds
from the Oseberg mound including
sledges, a ceremonial carriage, carved
dragon heads, household utensils and
other sepulchral relics connected with
the 'Oseberg Queen'

09811
Vinmonopolets Museum Norwegian
Wine and Spirits Monopoly
Haslevangen 16, N Oslo 5
History/Public Affairs Museum
History of wine making and distillation
of spirits

09812
Zoologisk Museum Universitetet i
Oslo (Institute of Systematics and
Zoogeography)
Botanisk Hage, Sarsgate 1, N Oslo 5
Natural History Museum - 1813
Zoology - library

Øvre Rendal

09813
Jacob Breda Bullmuseet
N-2530 Øvre Rendal, Hedmark
Historic Site
Birthplace and residence of Jacob
Breda from 1853 to 1869

Øystese

09814
Kvam Bygdemuseum
near the E 68, N-5610 Øystese,
Hordaland and Bergen
Open Air Museum - 1925
Torstein house (1861), a boathouse, a
churchboat from Fiske; nearby the old
Vavollen farm with storehouse (18th
century) and 'open-hearth' cottage with
original interior 'kroting' decorations
(geometrical festive decor applied to
sooted logs with a mixture of chalk
and water)

Porsgrunn

09815
Porsgrunn Bymuseum
Storgaten 59, N-3900 Porsgrunn,
Telemark
Decorative Arts Museum - 1930
Porsgrunn Porcelain Factory, fine
china produced in the last 100 years;
customs house (1661)

Prestfoss

09816
Sigdal-Eggedal Bygdemuseum
Hwy 287, 20 km north of Åmot, N-3350
Prestfoss, Buskerud
Open Air Museum - 1940
Nine old buildings including 'rose-
painted' cottage (1799); implements

Råde

09817
Råde Bygdetun
N-1640 Råde
General Museum - 1949
Textile collection from home-produced
flax; three old farm houses

Rakkestad

09818
Rakkestad Bygdetun
near Hwy 22, N-1890 Rakkestad,
Østfold
Open Air Museum - 1950
Five old houses illustrating farming life
and work in the past

Rælingen

09819
Rælingen Bygdetun
Rælingen Church on Hwy 120, N-2009
Rælingen, Akershus
General Museum
Local history; main building with
period furnishings and storehouse (ca.
1800)

Rasvåg

09820
Fedrenes Minne
4438 Rasvåg, N-4432 Hidrasund,
Vest-Agder
General Museum - 1944
Local curiosities and antiquities -
library

Rauland

09821
Myllargut-Heimen
near Lake Totak and Hwy 362,
Arabygdi, N-3864 Rauland, Telemark
Historic Site - 1951
Cottage where Thorgeir Øygarden
Augundson (1801-72), the best-known
Norwegian fiddler, spent his last years

Rennebu

09822
Rennebu Bygdetun
near Hwy 700, N-7393 Rennebu,
Sør-Trøndelag
Open Air Museum - 1953
Old farmyard with 6 buildings on the
original site; local history items

Rindalsskogen

09823
Rindal Bygdemuseum
near Hwy 65, N-7383 Rindalsskogen,
Møre and Romsdal
Open Air Museum - 1950
Old farmhouses; local artifacts

Risøyhamn

09824
Andøymuseet
N-9490 Risøyhamn, Nordland
Open Air Museum - 1933
Three old buildings

Rissa

09825
Rissa Bygdemuseum
on Hwy 717, Reinskloster, N-7100
Rissa, Sør-Trøndelag
Open Air Museum
Old cottage (ca. 1720); ruins of the
Reinskloster monastery (ca.1250); old
dairy, Norway's first dairy museum

Rjukan

09826
Rjukan og Tinn Museum
N-3660 Rjukan, Telemark
Open Air Museum - 1928
Øverland East and Øverland West
courtyards; implements; folk art;
textiles; weapons; cabin used by the
heavywater plant saboteurs from
Hardangervidda (1943) including
weapons, maps and equipment;
Øverland school house

Roan

09827
Roan Bygdetun
N-7180 Roan, Sør-Trøndelag
General Museum
Brandsøy cottage (ca. 1770), containing
some interesting items

Rollag

09828
Rollag Bygdetun
N-3626 Rollag, Buskerud
Open Air Museum - 1946
Six timber buildings; old rectory (17th
century) with a bishop's cottage and a
storehouse (18th century)

Rolvsøy

09829
Hans Nielsens Hauges Minne
near Hwy 109, Rolvsøy, N-1700
Sarpsborg, Østfold
Historic Site
Birthplace of the evangelist Hans
Nielsen Hauge; memorabilia and
personal items, books and leaflets

Røros

09830
Røros Kobberverks Samlinger
Hyttstuggu, N-7460 Røros, Sør-Trøndelag
Science/Tech Museum
Tools and implements from mines and
smelters giving a vivid impression of
conditions in the old mines; great bell
which was used to summon the
miners to work

09831
Rørosmuseet
near Hwy 30, Doktorjønna, N-7460
Røros, Sør-Trøndelag
General Museum - 1930
Old buildings and local history artifacts
portraying the life of miners, mountain
farmers, and 'reindeer Lapps' - artists'
studios

Rørvik

09832
Woksengs Samlinger
POB 177, N-7900 Rørvik, Nord-Trøndelag
General Museum - 1974
Local history; exhibits about the coast

Rosendal

09833
Baroniet Rosendal University of Oslo
Hwy 13, on the Hardanger fjord,
N-5470 Rosendal, Hordaland and
Bergen
Historic Site
Rosendal chateau (17th century) with a
beautiful park and garden

Rugldalen

09834
Ratvollen
N-7483 Rugldalen, Sør-Trøndelag
Historic Site
Home of the famous Norwegian
author Johan Falkberget (1897-1967)

Sakshaug

09835
Inderøy Bygdemuseum
close to Hwy 755, N-7670 Sakshaug,
Nord-Trøndelag
Open Air Museum - 1924
Four old buildings illustrating life on
the Inderøy peninsula in former times

Salangsdalen

09836
Bardu Bygdetun
Lundamo on the E 6, N-9270
Salangsdalen, Troms
Open Air Museum - 1965
Old farmyard (1860) with 5 original
buildings

Sandane

09837
Nordfjord Folkemuseum
N-6860 Sandane, Sogn and Fjordane
General Museum - 1920
Folk arts and folklore; agricultural
implements; old buildings

Sandefjord

09838
Kommandør Chr. Christensen's Hvalfangst Museum
Rådhusgata 4, Rådhusgaten 2 A, N-3200 Sandefjord, Vestfold
Historic Site - 1917
Development of whaling from primitive methods to pelagic whaling and whale factory ships in the Antarctic

09839
Sandefjord Bymuseum
Pukkestad, Rådhusgaten 2 A, N-3200 Sandefjord, Vestfold
General Museum - 1898
Local history; arts and crafts collections; Pukkestad vicarage (1792)

09840
Sandefjord Sjøfartsmuseum
Prinsensgate 18, Rådhusgaten 2 A, N-3200 Sandefjord, Vestfold
Science/Tech Museum - 1957
Pictures and paintings; models of windjammers, Roald Amundsen collection; maritime history; horology; navigation

Sandnes

09841
Høyland Bygdemuseum
Austrått farm 200 yds off E 18 south of Sandnes center, N-4300 Sandnes, Rogaland
General Museum - 1934
Farm implements; furniture; utensils; carts and carriages

Sarpsborg

09842
Borgarsyssel Museum
St. Olavs Vold, Borregaardsveien 10, N-1700 Sarpsborg, Østfold
General Museum - 1921
Ruins of St. Nicholas church (ca. 1100); old buildings (1660-1825); complete farm (Middle Ages); prehistoric archaeological exhibition; baptismal fonts; high seat panels; Østfold Gallery: silver, stoneware (Herrebø), rose painting - library

Selbu

09843
Selbu Bygdemuseum
Mebonden near Hwy 705, N-7580 Selbu, Sør-Trøndelag
General Museum - 1925
Furniture, implements; mineral collection; open-air section at Kalvåa 10 km from Mebonden

Singsås

09844
Singsås Bygdemuseum
N-7494 Singsås, Sør-Trøndelag
General Museum - 1935
Local history; implements and utensils; old schoolhouse

Skarnes

09845
Odalstunet
Hwy 2, N-2100 Skarnes, Hedmark
Open Air Museum
Courtyard consisting of several old farmhouses

Skaun

09846
Skaun Bygdemuseum
N-7360 Skaun, Sør-Trøndelag
Open Air Museum
Two old houses; medieval church

Skedsmokorset

09847
Skedsmo Bygdetun
Hwy 120 near E6, N-2020 Skedsmokorset, Akershus
Open Air Museum
Huseby farm with main building, cottage and storehouse; dwellings of government officials (19th century)

Skien

09848
Fylkesmuseet for Telemark og Grenland
Brekkeparken, Øvregt 41, N-3700 Skien, Telemark
Decorative Arts Museum
Folk art; agriculture; horticulture; forestry; handicrafts; navigation; communications; church art; local history; Ibsen section; open-air museum with several log houses (medieval to 19th century), including Borgestua (1584) and Rambergstua, decorated with 'rose-painting' (1788); Brekkeparken (planned by Pries, completed in 1816); Søndre Brekke (1780) with furnishings from the 17th, 18th, and 19th centuries; section for the presentation of 'rose-painting', woodcarving, folk costumes, weaving, embroidery and siversmith's work

09849
Ibsens Venstøp
just outside Skien, N-3700 Skien, Telemark
Historic Site
Place where the Ibsen family lived from 1835 to 1843; marionette theater Henrik Ibsen used to show his dramatic abilities for the first time

Skiptvet

09850
Skiptvet Bygdemuseum
N-1886 Skiptvet, Østfold
Open Air Museum - 1939
Farmyard with farmhouse, barn, storehouse, kiln and smithy; furniture; domestic utensils

Skjønhaug

09851
Trøgstad Bygdemuseum
Skjønhaug village on Hwy 22, N-1860 Trøgstad, Østfold
General Museum - 1928
Local history; folklore; 18th century farmhouses

Skogn

09852
Skogn Bygdetun
near the E 6, N-7620 Skogn, Nord-Trøndelag
Open Air Museum - 1918
Ammestua house (ca. 1600), where mothers used to breastfeed their children before baptism; large burial mound from the Viking period

Skotselv

09853
Bakke Bygdeminnelag
N-3330 Skotselv, Buskerud
General Museum
Stoves and other items made by the Hassel iron works; furniture and household utensils from the parish of Øvre Eiker; Düvelgården House

Skulestadmo

09854
Voss Folkesmuseum
Nesheimtunet farmyard, on the east side of Lake Lønavatn, north of Voss, N-5710 Skulestadmo, Hordaland and Bergen
Open Air Museum - 1972
Thirteen old buildings (1688-1835)

Snåsa

09855
Sørsamiske Samlinger
Vinje school near Hwy 763, N-7760 Snåsa, Nord-Trøndelag
Anthropology Museum
Collection of arts and crafts illustrating Lapp culture

Snertingdal

09856
Eiktunet Vardal-Snertingdal Museumslag
4 km from the centre of Gjøvik, N-2828 Snertingdal, Oppland
Open Air Museum - 1954
Bekkemellom mill (ca. 1850); some twenty old farmhouses

Søgne

09857
Søgne Bygdemuseum
mail c/o Kulturadm., Rådhuset, N-4630 Søgne, Vest-Agder
General Museum - 1909
Coll: 16th - 19th century articles of farmers and countrymen used in this rural district

Soknedal

09858
Soknedal Museumslag
near the E 6, N-7450 Soknedal, Sør-Trøndelag
Open Air Museum
Old buildings; local history artifacts

Sørli

09859
Sørli Museum
near Hwy 765, N-7884 Sørli, Nord-Trøndelag
Open Air Museum
Farmhouse, storehouse; local history

Sørumsand

09860
Aurskog - Hølandsbanen
Hwy 171, north of Oslo, Sørumsand, Vinderen, POB 14, N Oslo, Akershus
History/Public Affairs Museum - 1960
Old-fashioned, narrow-gauge railway line (0.75 m)

Spydeberg

09861
Galtebosamlingen
rd to Lake Lysern north of the village, N-1820 Spydeberg, Østfold
History/Public Affairs Museum
Weapons

09862
Spydeberg Bygdetun
Hov north of Spydeberg and the E 18, N-1820 Spydeberg
Open Air Museum - 1938
Farmyard with five old buildings; Iron Age burial mounds

Stangvik

09863
Stangvik Bygdemuseum
north-west of Hwy 620, N-6642 Stangvik, Møre and Romsdal
Open Air Museum
Open-hearth cottage with furniture

Stavanger

09864
Arkeologisk Museum i Stavanger
Storgt 27, N-4000 Stavanger, Rogaland
Archeology Museum - 1975
Archeology; reconstructed Iron Age farm at Ullandhaug - library

09865
Stavanger Faste Galleri
Madlav 33, N-4000 Stavanger, Rogaland
Fine Arts Museum
Collection of Norwegian painting, sculpture and graphics; works by the great Stavanger painter Lars Hertervig

09866
Stavanger Museum
Muségata 16, N-4000 Stavanger, Rogaland
General Museum - 1877
Coll: cultural history; archaeology; ethnography; numismatics; the Viste find (oldest-known human skeleton in Norway); Bronze Age collection; zoology; fossils; Cannary Museum; Ledaal Mansion (1800) with furnishings in the styles of 1800 to 1865; Breidablikk Mansion (1880); Maritime Museum (est. 1926): ship models and pictures, ship drawings, models of shipyards, shipbuilding tools, navigation instruments, figure heads, marine archaeological finds, curiosities - library

09867
Vestlandske Skulemuseum
Storgate 27, Nymannsveien 194, N-4000 Stavanger, Rogaland
Junior Museum - 1925
Old and new school equipment; means of instruction; pedagogical books

Steinkjer

09868
Steinkjer Museum
Flathaugen, N-7700 Steinkjer, Nord-Trøndelag
Open Air Museum - 1933
Seven old buildings, including a farmhouse (1760), a storehouse (1670), a steambath, a smithy, a grinding mill, a drying house for grain, and a bathhouse; domestic utensils, farm implements, folk art; a cotter's farm in Sør-Beistad with rockcarvings nearby at Hammer and the Bardal rock-carving field with about 500 carvings from different periods

Stend

09869
Hordaland Folkemuseum
N-5047 Stend, Hordaland and Bergen
Agriculture Museum - 1945
Exhibits illustrating the ecological
cultural pattern which has developed
on the west coast of Scandinavia
throughout the centuries, especially
the interplay between agriculture and
fishing; open-air museum and
Hordaland Landbruksmuseum at
Stend Agricultural School; Bogatun
farmyard in Manger

Stjørdal

09870
Stjørdal Bygdemuseum
at Værnes medieval church, N-7500
Stjørdal, Nord-Trøndelag
General Museum - 1956
Arts and crafts; minerals; tools; village
home (1910) including shed and
storehouse; smithy and open-hearth
'seter' hut

Suldalsosen

09871
Kolbeinstveit Rogaland Folkemuseum
Hwy 36, N-4240 Suldalsosen,
Rogaland
Open Air Museum
Guggedals 'loft' (13th century); Røsseli
cottage; watermills, kiln, sauna
(1850-70)

09872
Røynevarden Rogaland Folkemuseum
road along Lake Suldalsvatnet, N-4240
Suldalsosen, Rogaland
Open Air Museum
Cotter's farm (19th century); consisting
of: open-hearth cottage, barn,
cookhouse, two sheepsheds

Sulitjelma

09873
Sulitjelma Gruvemuseum
N-8230 Sulitjelma, Nordland
History/Public Affairs Museum - 1970
Life and work in the mines

Sund i Lofoten

09874
Fiskerimuseet i Sund
N-8384 Sund i Lofoten, Nordland
General Museum - 1966
Old boats; fishing gear; engine (1908)
still in operation; curiosities

Svartskog

09875
**Roald Amundsens Hjem,
Uranienborg**
Roald Amundsensveien 192, N-1420
Svartskog, Akershus
Historic Site - 1934
Memorabilia of Roald Amundsen

Svelvik

09876
Svelvik Museum
N-3060 Svelvik, Vestfold
Historic Site - 1937
Collection commemorating the
windjammer days, and the national
celebrity, author and businessman
Elias Kræmmer

Tingvatn

09877
**Hægebostad Bygdemuseum og Eiken
Bygdemuseum**
near Hwy 43 in the Lyngdal valley,
N-4595 Tingvatn, Vest-Agder
Open Air Museum - 1965
Old moot-place with burial mounds
and stone monuments from the Iron
Age

Tingvoll

09878
Tingvoll Bygdemuseum
1,5 km from Hwy 16, N-6630 Tingvoll,
Møre and Romsdal
Open Air Museum - 1937
Old farmhouse, storehouse, barn,
stable, gate-saw, grinding mill;
furniture, utensils and implements

Tønsberg

09879
Vestfold Fylkesmuseum
Farmannsveien 30, N-3100 Tønsberg,
Vestfold
Open Air Museum - 1939
Medieval to 18th century farm
buildings with an agricultural section;
whaling department; maritime
department; local history and
ethnography section; prehistoric
section; the Viking ship from Klåstad -
library

Tresfjord

09880
Tresfjord Museum
near E 69, N-6380 Tresfjord, Møre and
Romsdal
Open Air Museum - 1943
Five old houses with furnishings;
open-hearth cottage (1650)

Tromsø

09881
Polarmuseet
Søndrtollbugt 9, N-9000 Tromsø, Troms
Historic Site - 1978
Collections pertaining to hunting in the
Arctic; exhibits on scientific
expeditions; Helmer Hansen's skis;
finds from Wilhelm Barent's winter
camp at Novaja Zemlja; a few items
from the arctic explorers Roald
Amundsen and Fritjof Nansen

09882
Troms Folkemuseum
Folkeparken, N-9000 Tromsø, Troms
Open Air Museum - 1952
Seven houses; local history exhibitions

09883
Tromsø Museum Universitetet i Tromsø,
Institutt for Museumsvirksomhet
Folkeparken, N-9000 Tromsø, Troms
General Museum - 1872
Cultural history; archaeology; Lapp
ethnography; botany; zoology; marine
biology; geology; folk music;
ecclesiastical art - library

Trondheim

09884
Erkebispegården (Archbishop's
Palace)
N-7000 Trondheim, Sør-Trøndelag
History/Public Affairs Museum
Oldest secular building still standing in
Scandinavia (ca. 1160); Nidaros
cathedral sculpture and stone
collection; Armoury: military museum
containing a Hall of Fame with banners
and memorabilia of the men and
women who died in World War II,
weapons and equipment ranging from
the 16th to the 20th century;
Nordenfjeldske Resistance Museum
containing weapons, equipment, illegal
newspapers from the period of the
German occupation (1940-45)

09885
**Det Kongelige Norske Videnskabers
Selskab (DKNVS) Museet**
Universitetet i Trondheim (The
Museum of the Royal Norwegian
Scientific Society)
Erling Skakkesgt 47, N-7000
Trondheim, Sør-Trøndelag
General Museum - 1760
Prehistory; medieval archaeology;
numismatics; natural history; zoology;
botany; marine biology; mineralogy;
Høyland tapestry ; Foslie's calcareous
algae; Trondheim Biologiske Stasjon -
library

09886
Kriminalmuseet Trondheim police
station
Kongensgt 7, N-7000 Trondheim,
Sør-Trøndelag
History/Public Affairs Museum - 1918
Items and curiosities connected with
the history of the Trondheim police
force

09887
Nordafjelske Skolemuseum (The
Mid-Norway School Museum)
Bispegt 9 c, N-7000 Trondheim,
Sør-Trøndelag
History/Public Affairs Museum - 1923
Psychology; education; school and
local history; religion; social sciences

09888
**Nordenfjeldske
Kunstindustrimuseum**
Munkegt 5, N-7000 Trondheim,
Sør-Trøndelag
Decorative Arts Museum - 1893
Coll: design and arts and crafts from
the early 1600s up to the present;
Norwegian and foreign applied art;
furniture, silver, glass, ceramics,
textiles and metalwork; 20th century
art-nouveau movement; works of Van
de Velde; tapestry by Hannah Ryggen

09889
Ringve Musikhistorisk Museum
Ringve, N-7000 Trondheim,
Sør-Trøndelag
Music Museum - 1952
Valuable instruments from all over the
world in their contemporary settings,
based on the collection of Mrs.
Victoria Bachke; Mozart room,
Beethoven room, Chopin room,
Tchaikovsky room; Ringve manor
(1860) with period interiors - concert
hall

09890
Stiftsgården
Munkegt 23, N-7000 Trondheim,
Sør-Trøndelag
Historic Site
Rococo house from the 1770's, the
second largest wooden building in
Scandinavia, with wrought iron work
on stairways, painted wall hangings,
beautiful old furniture, and the manor
garden with lime trees

09891
Tordenskioldmuseet
Ringve, N-7000 Trondheim,
Sør-Trøndelag
Historic Site - 1950
Memorabilia on the naval hero Petter
Wessel Tordenskiold (1690-1720)

09892
Trøndelag Folkemuseum
POB 1107, N-7001 Trondheim,
Sør-Trøndelag
Open Air Museum - 1913
55 old buildings; Meldal and Oppdal
farmyards; Aspås farm; Haltdalen stave
church; 'Hans Nissen-gården', a
merchant's house; crofters' cottages;
fishermen's sheds (rorbuer); Lapp
section; ski collection; folk art; wood
carving, painting, textiles and everyday
utensils

09893
Trondhjems Sjøfartsmuseum
Gamle Slaveriet, Fordgaten 6a, N-7000
Trondheim, Sør-Trøndelag
General Museum - 1920
Development of shipping in Trøndelag
from the 1500s to modern times;
sailing vessels, steam ship photos,
paintings and models; naval
equipment; logs; documents - library

Trondhjem

09894
Trøndelag Kunstgalleri Trondhjems
Kunstforening
Bispegt 7b, N-7000 Trondhjem,
Sør-Trøndelag
Fine Arts Museum - 1845
Norwegian painting, especially from
the 19th and 20th centuries; Edvard
Munch room (25 graphic works);
European painting

Trysil

09895
Trysil Bygdemuseum
Innbygda, close to Hwy 26, N-2420
Trysil, Hedmark
Open Air Museum - 1901
Ten buildings including several
cottages, a sawmill, flour mill, sauna,
barn

Tuddal

09896
Tuddal Bygdetun
N-3697 Tuddal, Telemark
Open Air Museum
Old buildings

Tune

09897
Tune Bygdemuseum - Gamle Grålum
E 6 west of Sarpsborg, N-1712
Valaskjold, Østfold
General Museum - 1921
Local antiquities

Tydal

09898
Tydal Bygdetun
beside Hwy 705, N-7590 Tydal,
Sør-Trøndelag
Historic Site - 1929
Storaunstuggu cottage (1666); items
connected with the fateful retreat of
the Swedish army from the Trøndelag
district in 1718

Tynset

09899
Tynset Bygdemuseum
N-2500 Tynset, Hedmark
General Museum - 1923
Furnished old cottages illustrating life
and work of a mountain community;
antiquities; skis; weapons; books and
newspapers

Utne

09900
Hardanger Folkemuseum
Neset, N-5797 Utne, Hordaland and
Bergen
General Museum - 1911
Thirteen old buildings, including
'smoke-oven' houses from Trones and
Tveisme, a storehouse from Utne, a
seashed, a boathouse and a smithy;
furniture; weapons; crockery; local
costumes; books; implements; works
by the sculptor Lars Utne (1862-1923)

Utstein Kloster

09901
Utstein Kloster
island of Mosterøy, N-4157 Utstein
Kloster, Rogaland
Religious Art Museum - 1965
Augustinian monastery (13th century)

Uvdal i Numedal

09902
Uvdal Bygdetun
N-3632 Uvdal i Numedal, Buskerud
1960
Local history; parson's cottage and a
loft

Vadsø

09903
Vadsø Museum
N Vadsø, Finnmark
Historic Site
Tuomainen house (1809); exhibition
portraying the life of the Finnish
immigrants in the 18th and 19th
centuries - library

Vågåmo

09904
Bygdetunet Jutulheimen Vågå
Historielag
near the village on Hwy 15, N-2680
Vågåmo, Oppland
Open Air Museum
Several old Vågå farmhouses with
furniture and implements

09905
Håkenstad Gardsmuseum
2 km north of the village, N-2680
Vågåmo, Oppland
Open Air Museum
Ten preserved buildings (mostly 18th
century); room furnishings; utensils
illustrating life at this estate during
different periods

Valle

09906
Setesdalmuseet
Ryngestad farm 2 km off Hwy 12,
N-4690 Valle, Aust-Agder
Open Air Museum - 1938
Medieval Ryngestad 'loft' (ca. 1580);
eleven old buildings; medieval
open-hearth cottage; 3-storied 'loft'

Vanse

09907
Lista Museum
Midthasselhuset, POB 61, N-4561
Vanse, Vest-Agder
Open Air Museum - 1921
Cultural and historical collections;
works by the sculptor Mathias
Skeibrok - rescue station

Vardø

09908
Vardøhus Museum
Vardøhus fortress, N-9950 Vardø,
Finnmark
General Museum
Vardøhus fortress (1737); cultural,
military and natural history collections;
curiosities

Varhaug

09909
Grødaland Bygdetun Rogaland
Folkemuseum
N-4360 Varhaug, Rogaland
Open Air Museum - 1936
Early 18th century farm, stave-built
barns

Varteig

09910
Varteig Bygdemuseum
near Hwy 111 north of Sarpsborg,
N-1735 Varteig, Østfold
General Museum - 1933
Cultural-historical collections from
Varteig parish

Vassenden i Jølster

09911
Astrupheimen
12 km from Vassenden on Hwy 14,
N-6840 Vassenden i Jølster, Sogn and
Fjordane
Open Air Museum - 1965
Old houses collected by the painter
Nikolai Astrup (1880-1928)

Vennesla

09912
Vennesla Bygdemuseum
near Hwy 405, N-4700 Vennesla,
Vest-Agder
Open Air Museum - 1952
Two old buildings and local artifacts

Verdal

09913
Verdal Museum
N-7650 Verdal, Nord-Trøndelag
Open Air Museum - 1926
Stiklestad medieval church, where St.
Olav fell in battle in 1030; group of
farm buildings including large, partly
furnished dwelling (1793), grinding mill,
cotter's farm

Vigrestad

09914
Hå Bygdemuseum
Kommunehuset at Varhaug station,
mail c/o Ingebret Særheim, N-4362
Vigrestad
General Museum - 1954
Local history artifacts

Vinjesvingen

09915
Vinjestova
E 76, N-3893 Vinjesvingen, Telemark
Historic Site - 1904
Cottage (1824) where the poet Å.O.
Vinje (1818-70) grew up

Volda

09916
Sivert Aarflotmuseet
Hwy 14 north of Volda village, N-6100
Volda, Møre and Romsdal
History/Public Affairs Museum - 1935
Printing press set up by Sivert Aarflot
in 1808; memorabilia on the Aarflot
family

09917
Volda Bygdetun
Haueleitet, N-6100 Volda, Møre and
Romsdal
General Museum - 1911
Old farmhouses and a storehouse;
items of local interest

Voss

09918
Voss Folkemuseum
Mølstertunet in the hills above the
station town Voss, N-5700 Voss,
Hordaland and Bergen
Open Air Museum - 1917
Mølster farm, including 20 houses, most
of them from the 18th century, barn
(1680), two medieval 'lofts'; artifacts
illustrating life and work at Voss
through the ages

Vrådal

09919
Kviteseid Bygdetun
near Hwy 39, N-3853 Vrådal, Telemark
Open Air Museum
Farmhouse (1739); lofts (17th and 18th
centuries); barn, cowshed, sauna,
smithy, and grinding mill (18th century);
domestic utensils; farm implements;
medieval church with painted ceiling
and Rococo decoration

Oman

Qurm

09920
Oman Museum
mail c/o Ministry of Information and
Culture, POB 600, Qurm
General Museum - 1974
Archeology; ethnology

Pakistan

Bahawalpur

09921
Bahawalpur Museum
Bahawalpur
General Museum - 1971
Archeology; ethnology

09922
Natural History Museum
Bahawalpur
General Museum - 1945
Natural history; applied arts

Banbhore

09923
Archaeological Museum
Banbhore
Archeology Museum - 1967
Cultural remains from the Scytho-
Parthian, Hindu-Buddhist and early
Islamic periods; Kufic inscriptions;
coins of the Umyyad period; glass
objects; glazed Mesopotamian type
pottery and white-paste pottery of
Syrian origin; Chinese porcelain

Bhitshah

09924
Bhitshah Cultural Museum
Bhitshah
Decorative Arts Museum - 1962
Arts and crafts

Chakdara

09925
Dir Museum
Chakdara, N.W.F.P.
Archeology Museum - 1970
Archeology; terra cotta - library

Dokri

09926
**Museum of Archaeological Site
Moenjodaro**
Dokri
Archeology Museum - 1924
Excavations from Moenjodaro
including a statuary, seals, household
objects, personal ornaments, ivory,
bone and shell objects, painted and
plain pottery (2500-1500 B.C.); fresco
paintings

Faisalabad

09927
Agricultural Museum Agricultural
University
Faisalabad
Agriculture Museum - 1907

Guddu

09928
Guddu Barrage Museum
Guddu
History/Public Affairs Museum

Harappa

09929
Archaeological Museum
Harappa
Archeology Museum - 1927
Indus Valley objects including a human
skeleton; pottery

Hyderabad

09930
Education Museum Sind University
Hyderabad
History/Public Affairs Museum - 1959
Education

09931
Hyderabad Museum
Hyderabad
General Museum - 1971
Arts; crafts; archeology; anthropology

09932
Talpur House Museum
Tando Nur Muhammad Khan,
Hyderabad
History/Public Affairs Museum

Islamabad

09933
Folk Heritage Museum
Islamabad
General Museum - 1973
Folk arts and crafts

09934
National Museum of Natural History
Islamabad
Natural History Museum
Natural History

Karachi

09935
Archaeological Museum Karachi
University
Karachi
Archeology Museum - 1955

09936
National Museum of Pakistan
Burns Garden, Victoria Rd and Bonus
Rd, Karachi
General Museum - 1950
Archeology from the Stone Age to the
Mughal period (16th-19th c. A.D.);
Indus Valley material (3000-1500 B.C.);
Gandhara sculptures (1st-4th c. A.D.)
depicting the life of Buddha;
calligraphy; ceramics and glassware;
coins; ethnography

09937
Natural History Museum Karachi
University
Karachi
Natural History Museum - 1950's
Natural History

09938
Quaid-i-Azam Birthplace Wazir
Mansions
Karachi
Historic Site - 1953
Birthplace of Quaid-i-Azam
Mohammad Ali Jinnah, the founder of
Pakistan (born 1876); furniture and law
books - library

Lahore

09939
Faqir Khana Museum
Lahore
General Museum - 1937
Arts; applied arts; crafts; history

09940
Folk Arts of the Punjab Museum
Lahore
Anthropology Museum - 1976

09941
Industrial and Commercial Museum
Dept. of Industries
Bank Square, Lahore
Science/Tech Museum - 1950
National resources and their utilisation
in the field of industry and commerce;
arts and crafts - library

09942
Iqbal Museum Javed Manzil
Lahore
Historic Site - 1977
Home of the poet and philosopher
Allama Sheikh Muhammad Iqbal;
original manuscripts and personal
belongings

09943
Lahore Fort Museum
Lahore
History/Public Affairs Museum - 1928
Coll: Sikh arms and armour, drums,
banners, quilts, chakras; Princess
Bamba collection of oil paintings,
watercolors, photographs and metallic
objects; portraits of Sikh princes; the
fort is a monument of the Mughal
period

09944
Lahore Museum
Shahrah-e-Quaid-e-Azam, Lahore
General Museum - 1864
History; art; Buddhist, Bramanical and
Jain sculptures; pottery; metalware;
carpets; rugs; calligraphy; coins;
Napalese and Tibetan objects
including a copper and brass statuary,
banners and ornaments; Mughal and
Pabari miniatures; Muslim coins and
costumes; folk arts; models of some
monuments

09945
**National Museum of Science and
Technology**
Lahore 31
Science/Tech Museum - 1965
Engines; fluid mechanics; light and
sound; magnetism and electricity;
mechanics; behavioral psychology;
meteorology; astronomy and time;
human anatomy - library

09946
Natural History Museum
Government College
Lahore
Natural History Museum - 1909

09947
Shakir Ali's Residence Museum
Lahore
Fine Arts Museum - 1975

Mangla

09948
Dam Site Museum
Mangla
Natural History Museum - 1967
Natural history; geology; archeology

Peshawar

09949
Archaeological Museum Peshawar
University
Peshawar
Archeology Museum - 1964

09950
Islamia College Museum
Peshawar
Natural History Museum - 1934
Zoology

09951
Pakistan Air Force Museum
Peshawar
Science/Tech Museum
Aircraft and history of the Air Force

09952
Pakistan Forest Museum
Abbottabad, Peshawar
Agriculture Museum - 1952/1966
Forest products

09953
Peshawar Museum
Peshawar
General Museum - 1907
Excavations from various sites in the
ancient Gandhara region; stone
inscriptions in Kharoshti, Sarda, Kufic
and Persian characters; specimens of
Kashmir papier-mâché; needlework;
Persian manuscripts; ethnography;
wooden effigies from Kafiristan

Quetta

09954
Archaeological Museum
Quetta
Archeology Museum - 1972

09955
Geological Museum
Quetta
Natural History Museum
Geology

Rawalpindi

09956
Botanical Museum Gordon College
Rawalpindi
Natural History Museum - 1930
Botany

09957
Pakistan Army Museum
Eftikhar Khan Rd, Rawalpindi
History/Public Affairs Museum - 1962
Old weapons; colors and standards;
uniforms and medals; paintings

Saidu Sharif

09958
Swat Museum
Saidu Sharif
General Museum - 1959
Archeology; ethnology

Swat

09959
Archaeological Museum
Swat
Archeology Museum - 1963
Excavations from Butkara I, Panr and
Udegram including Buddhist objects
and specimens of Gandhara
sculptures (1st c. B.C.-7th c. A.D.);
pre-Buddhist material; ethnology

Taxila

09960
Archaeological Museum
Taxila
Archeology Museum - 1928
Ghandara sculptures in stone, stucco
and terra cotta; pottery, household
vessels, toilet articles and personal
ornaments from an early historical
period; beads and gems, gold and
silvel jewelry; coins; inscriptions; tools
and implements; weapons - library

Umerkot

09961
Archeological Museum
Umerkot
Historic Site - 1968
Birthplace of the Mughal Emperor
Akbar; manuscripts, paintings, Imperial
documents, coins and armory relating
to the Mughal period and to Akbar's
reign

Panama

Ancon

09962
**Panama Canal Commission Library-
Museum**
Ancon, APO 34011, Miami, FL
History/Public Affairs Museum - 1914
Documents; history and memorabilia
of canal construction; 19th century
paintings; historic boats; medals -
library

Ciudad de Panamá

09963
Museo Afro Antillano
Calle 24 y Avenida Justo Arosemena,
Ciudad de Panamá
General Museum

09964
Museo de Arte Religioso Colonial
Catedral, Casco Viejo
Calle 3a, Ciudad de Panama
General Museum

09965
Museo de Ciencias Naturales
Ave. Cuba y Calle 30, Ciudad de
Panamá
Natural History Museum

09966
Museo de Historia de Panamá
Palacio Municipal
Plaza de la Catedral, Ciudad de
Panamá
History/Public Affairs Museum

09967
Museo del Hombre Panameño
Plaza 5 de Mayo, Ciudad de Panamá
Anthropology Museum

09968
Museo Nacional de Panamá
Esquina Av. Cuba y Calle 30, Ciudad
de Panamá
General Museum - 1925
Natural history; archaeology;
ethnography; history; decorative arts;
ceramic and stone objects discovered
in native tombs

Guarraré

09969
Casa Manuel F. Zárate
Guarraré
General Museum

Las Tablas

09970
Museo Belisario Porras
Las Tablas
General Museum

Los Santos

09971
Museo de la Nacionalidad
Los Santos
General Museum

Natá

09972
Parque Arqueológico El Caño
Natá
General Museum

Panama City

09973
Museum of Natural History
29 y 30 St no. 2939, POB 662, zona 1,
Panama City
Natural History Museum - 1975
Birds, mollusks and fossils

Parita

09974
Museo de Arte Religioso Iglesia de
Santo Domingo
Parita, Herrera
Fine Arts Museum

Papua New Guinea

Boroko

09975
Papua New Guinea National Museum and Art Gallery
POB 5560, Boroko
General Museum - 1954
Cultural anthropology; ethnology; natural history - library

Paraguay

Asunción

09976
Coleccion Carlos Alberto Pusineri Scala
Hernandarias 1313, Asunción
History/Public Affairs Museum - 1950
colonial and military history; archaeology; numismatics; anthropology

09977
Colección Numismática Juan Bautista Gill Aguinaga
O'Leary 285, Asunción
History/Public Affairs Museum
numismatics; history; armaments

09978
Museo de Arte Moderno de Asunción
España 229, Asunción
Fine Arts Museum
Modern art, especially from Paraguay and the River Plate Area (Argentina and Uruguay) - library

09979
Museo de Cerámica y Bellas Artes 'Julián de la Herreria'
Estados Unidos 1120, Asunción
Fine Arts Museum - 1938
ceramics; fine arts; folk art - library

09980
Museo de Ciencias Naturales
Colegio Internacional, Rio de Janeiro
Asunción
Natural History Museum

09981
Museo de Historia Natural del Paraguay Jardín Botánico
Santisima Trinidad, Asunción
Natural History Museum - 1921
natural history; archaeology

09982
Museo de la Casa de la Independencia
14 de Mayo y Presidente Franco, Asunción
History/Public Affairs Museum - 1965
colonial history

09983
Museo Etnográfico 'Andrés Barbero'
España, Asunción
Anthropology Museum - 1929
ethnography; archaeology; mineralogy; Guarani urns and earthenware of Indian tribes

09984
Museo Histórico Militar
Av. Mariscal Lopez 140, Asunción
History/Public Affairs Museum
military artifacts

09985
Museo 'Mons. Juan Sinforiano Bogarin'
Av. Kubitschek y Cerro Corá, Asunción
History/Public Affairs Museum

09986
Museo Nacional de Bellas Artes y Antigüedades
Presidente Franco esq. a Juan E. O'Leary, Asunción
Fine Arts Museum
paintings and sculptures

Trinidad

09987
Museo Botánico y Zoológico
Jardín Botánico y Zoológico, Trinidad
Natural History Museum - 1914

Yaguarón

09988
Museo Doctor Francia
Yaguarón
General Museum - 1968

Peru

Ancash

09989
Museo Arqueológico Regional de Ancash
Av. Pedro García Villon 725, Ancash
Archeology Museum - 1936
finds from Huarás; stone carvings; megalithic statues

Arequipa

09990
Museo de Arqueologia e Historia de la Universidad Nacional San Augustin de Arequipa Ciudad Universitaria
Av. La Salle, Arequipa
General Museum
archaeology; history

09991
Museo de Cayma
Arequipa
General Museum
archaeology; history; ethnology

Ayacucho

09992
Museo Histórico Regional de Ayacucho
Jirón 28 de Julio No. 106, Ayacucho
General Museum - 1046
history; archaeology; crafts; anthropology; religious art; colonial art; pre-Columbian ceramics; folk art; numismatics - library

Callao

09993
Museo Histórico Militar del Perú
Castillo del Real Felipe, Callao
History/Public Affairs Museum - 1946
military history of Perú since 1730

Cuzco

09994
Museo de la Universidad
Cuzco
Archeology Museum

09995
Museo Histórico Regional del Cuzco
Calle Heladeros, Cuzco
General Museum - 1946
history; native art; Peruvian colonial art

Huancayo

09996
Museo Arqueológico 'Frederico Galvez Durand' de la Gran Unidad 'Santa Isabel'
Huancas 251, Apdo. 189, Huancayo
Archeology Museum
archaeological finds form Nazca and other Peruvian cultures; weaving; gold and bronze ornaments; fossils

Huánuco

09997
Museo y Biblioteca 'Leoncio Prado'
2 de Mayo de Tarapacá, Huánuco
Anthropology Museum - 1945
ethnology

Ica

09998
Museo Regional de Ica
Ica
General Museum - 1946
archaeology; history

Lambayeque

09999
Museo Arqueológico 'Bruning'
Calle 2 de Mayo 48, Lambayeque
Archeology Museum - 1924
gold and silver objects, textiles, ceramics, wood and stone; two blue and black granite mortars in Chavin style

Lima

10000
Centro de Arte Miraflores
Ricardo Palma 246, Lima
Fine Arts Museum

10001
Museo Amano Miraflores
Retiro 131, Lima
Archeology Museum
textiles; decorative art; weaving

10002
Museo Arqueológico 'Rafael Larco Herrera' Pueblo Libre
Av. Bolívar 1515, Lima
Archeology Museum - 1926
gold and silver objects, copper, ceramics, textiles - library

10003
Museo de Arqueologia y Etnologia
Azangaro 931, Lima
Archeology Museum - 1919
Chavin, Moche, Chimu collection; pre-Columbian items; musical instruments

10004
Museo de Arte
Paseo Colón 125, Lima
Fine Arts Museum - 1961
pre-Columbian native arts; colonial furniture; paintings; sculptures; religious art; 19th - 20th century paintings and furniture

10005
Museo de Arte Italiano
Paseo República, Lima
Fine Arts Museum - 1921
Italian paintings and sculpture

10006
Museo de Historia Natural 'Javier Prado' Universidad Mayor de San Marco
Av. Arenales 1256, Apdo. 1109, Lima
Natural History Museum - 1918
botany; zoology - library

10007
Museo del Virreinato
Quinta Presa, Lima
History/Public Affairs Museum - 1935
Perú in the period of Spanish Viceroy rule

10008
Museo Geológico de la Universidad Nacional de Ingeniería del Perú
Camino Ancón, Lima
Natural History Museum - 1891
geology; mineralogy

10009
Museo Incaico Universidad Nacional Mayor de San Marcos
Lima
General Museum

10010
Museo Nacional de Antropologia y Arqueologia Pueblo Libre
Plaza Principal, Lima
Archeology Museum - 1938
pre-Inca and Inca finds

10011
Museo Nacional de Hìstoria
Plaza Bolívar, s/n, Pueblo Libre, Lima
History/Public Affairs Museum - 1921
paintings; arms; pictures from Colonial to Republican times

10012
Museo Nacional de la Cultura Peruana
Av. Alfonso Ugarte 650, Apdo. 3048, Lima 100
Anthropology Museum - 1946
anthropology; folklore; ceramics; textiles; folk costumes; folk wood-carvings; paintings and drawings - library

10013
Museo 'Oro del Perú' y 'Armas Antiguas'
Belen 1058, Apdo. 988, Huerta de San Antonio, Lima
Archeology Museum - 1924
pre-Columbian gold objects; pre-Columbian, European and Oriental weapons

10014
Museo Postal y Filatelico de Correos del Perú Correos del Perú-Lima
Lima
History/Public Affairs Museum - 1931
postal history; postage stamps; numismatics

10015
Pinacoteca Municipal 'Ignacio Merino'
Paseo Colón, Lima
Fine Arts Museum

Pisco

10016
Museo Arqueológico
Pisco
Archeology Museum

Trujillo

10017
Museo Arqueológico de la Universidad de Trujillo
Bolívar 446, Apdo. 299, Trujillo
Archeology Museum - 1939
ceramics; metals; wood; stone; textiles - library

Philippines

Badoc

10018
Juan Luna Shrine
Badoc, Ilocos Norte, POB 3398, Manila
History/Public Affairs Museum - 1976
Reproductions of Juan Luna's paintings; artifacts and relics related to the history of the town

Baguio

10019
Baguio-Mt.Provinces Museum Foundation Inc.
Ministry of Tourism Compond, Gov. Park Rd, Baguio City 0201
History/Public Affairs Museum

10020
Bibak Museum Benguet, Ifugao, Bontoc, Apayao and Kalinga Museum of Culture
University of Baguio, Baguio City 0210
History/Public Affairs Museum

10021
Saint Louis University Museum
Baguio City 0201
General Museum
Coll: ethnology; natural history

Batac

10022
Marcos Museum
Batac, Ilocos Norte
General Museum

Batan

10023
Kalantiaw Shrine
Batan, Aklan, POB 3398, Manila
History/Public Affairs Museum - 1957
Memorial to Datu Benhadara Kalantiaw, first Filipino lawgiver

Bolinao

10024
Bolinao Museum
Bolinao, Pangasinan 0716
General Museum

Bongao

10025
Tawi-Tawi Ethnological Museum
MSU-Sulu College of Technology and Oceanography
Bongao, Tawi-Tawi 7602
Anthropology Museum

Butuan

10026
Butuan Regional Museum
Butuan City
General Museum

Cagayan de Oro

10027
Xavier Folklife Museum Xavier University
Corrales Av, Cagayan de Oro City 8401
Anthropology Museum - 1967
Altar paraphenalia in silver, gold and bronze; religious figurines; paintings of religious scenes and local natural events

Calamba

10028
Rizal Shrine
Rizal St, Calamba, Laguna, POB 3398, Manila
History/Public Affairs Museum - 1948
Originals and replicas of relics and memorabilia related to Dr. Jose Rizal, national hero of the Philippines - library

Cebu

10029
St. Theresa's College Museum
Elizabeth Pond St, Cebu City 6401
General Museum
Coll: ethnography; folklore; literature

10030
University Museum University of San Carlos
P. del Rosario St, Cebu City 6401
General Museum - 1967
Magsuhot collection of terra cotta burial and funerary vessels - library

Dapitan

10031
Rizal Shrine
Dapitan, Zamboanga del Norte, POB 3398, Manila
History/Public Affairs Museum - 1945
Replicas of relics and memorabilia related to Dr. Jose Rizal, national hero of the Philippines

Dumaguete

10032
Anthropology Museum Silliman University
Dumaguete City 6501
Anthropology Museum - 1970
Metal Age pottery; metal implements; late Neolithic and early Iron Age carved limestone - library

Iloilo

10033
Iloilo Museum
Iloilo City 5901
General Museum
Artifacts from Pasnay Island; elephant fossils from Iloilo; gold-leaf masks; porcelain; stoneware; colonial sculpture

Jolo

10034
Sulu Ethnological Museum
Notre Dame Jolo College, Jolo, Sulu 7901
Anthropology Museum

Kabacan

10035
Cultural Museum State University Museum
Mindanao Institute of Technology, Kabacan, North Cotabato 9321
Science/Tech Museum

Kabayan

10036
Kabayan Mummy Caves Site Museum
Kabayan, Benguet 0206
Natural History Museum

Kawit

10037
Aguinaldo Shrine
General Tirona St, Kawit, Cavite, POB 3398, Manila
History/Public Affairs Museum - 1964
Relics and memorabilia related to the Philippine revolution

Lipa

10038
Teodoro M. Kalaw Memorial Museum
T.M. Kalaw St, Lipa City 4216
General Museum - 1973
Furniture and household objects from the Spanish period to the early American period; archeology, excavated gold and porcelain artifacts; liturgical objects; memorabilia and library of Teodoro M. Kalaw

Magsinal

10039
Magsinal Regional Museum
Magsinal, Ilocos Sur
General Museum

Makati

10040
Ayala Museum
Makati Av, POB 259, Makati, Manila
History/Public Affairs Museum - 1967
Social and cultural history of the Philippines - lLibrary

Malacañang

10041
Presidential Museum
Malacañang, Manila
History/Public Affairs Museum
President Ferdinand E. Marcos collection; local history; natural history; folklore

Malate

10042
Carfel Seashell Museum
Carfel, 1786 A. Mabini St, Malate, Manila
Natural History Museum - 1973
Shells and fossils

Malolos

10043
Barasoain Historical Landmark
Malolos, Bulacan, POB 3398, Manila
History/Public Affairs Museum - 1973
Religious relics; exhibit on important events in Philippine history

10044
Hiyas NG Bulakan Provincial Museum
Malolos, Bulacan 2601
General Museum

Mandaluyong

10045
Munting Museo NG Namayan
Barangay Museum
Namayan, Mandaluyong, Manila 3119
General Museum

10046
Vargas Museum and Art Gallery
Jorge V. Vargas Filipiniana Foundation
211 Shaw Bd, Mandaluyong, Manila 3119
General Museum

Manila

10047
Animal Museum
Sining Kayumanggi Gardens, Arroceros St, Manila
Natural History Museum
Stuffed wild animals from Nairobi and Kenya displayed in conditions simulating their natural habitat

10048
Anthropology Research Room
National Museum of the Philippines
Ministry of Tourism Bldg, 2nd and 3rd floors, T.M. Kalaw St, Manila
Anthropology Museum
Archeology; ethnology

10049
Ateneo Art Gallery
Ateneo de Manila University, Manila
Fine Arts Museum

10050
Bayanihan Folks Arts Center Private University Museum
Taft Av, Manila 2801
Decorative Arts Museum
Artifacts, wares, instruments and costumes from Mindanao and Igorot tribes; Maria Clara costumes and prints

10051
Carlos P. Garcia Memorabilia
mail c/o National Library Filipiniana Div., T.M. Kalaw St, Manila 2801
History/Public Affairs Museum
Personal memorabilia of President Carlos P. Garcia

10052
Central Bank Money Museum
Roxas Bd, Manila 2801
History/Public Affairs Museum
History of money from pre-Christian times to the present; numismatics collection

10053
Centro Escolar University Museum and Archives Private University Museum
Mendiola St, Manila
History/Public Affairs Museum
Personal belongings of university members including togas, albums, certificates of awards and publications

10054
Cultural Center of the Philippines Art Gallery
Roxas Bd, Manila 2801
Fine Arts Museum

10055
Kamaynilaan Museum of the City of Manila
Arroceros St, Manila
General Museum
Local history

10056
Mabini Shrine
Malacañang Compound, Pandacan, POB 3398, Manila
History/Public Affairs Museum - 1968
Relics and memorabilia related to Apolinario Mabini ('brains of the Philippine revolution')

10057
Metropolitan Museum of Manila
Central Bank Compound, Manila 2801
General Museum

10058
Metropolitan Police Museum
United States Av, Manila 2801
History/Public Affairs Museum

10059
Museum of Arts and Sciences
University of Santo Tomás
Calle España, Manila 2806
General Museum - 1848
Anthropology; natural sciences;
specimens; mineralogy; petrology;
ethnological material; coins; medals;
philately; religious paintings and
sculptures; portraits; costumes;
furniture; architectural fragments
(18th-19th c.)

10060
Museum of Philippine Art
Roxas Bd, T.M. Kalaw St, Manila 2801
Fine Arts Museum

10061
Museum of Philippine Costumes
Mercury Bldg, T.M. Kalaw St, Manila
Decorative Arts Museum
Tribal costumes; Philippine
embroidery, beadwork and appliqué

10062
National Museum of the Philippines
P. Burgos St, Rizal Park, POB 2659,
Manila
General Museum
Fine arts; historical, ethnographical,
botanical, and zoological exhibits -
planetarium

10063
**Philippine National Railway
Historical Museum** State Museum
Tutuban Railway Terminal, Divisoria,
Manila 2807
History/Public Affairs Museum
History of the Philippine railway
system

10064
Ramon Magsaysay Memorabilia
RM Center, Roxas Bd, Manila 2801
History/Public Affairs Museum

10065
Resurreccion Memorial Museum
Ilocos Museum of Music and Fine Arts
21 Calle Real, Luna La Union, POB
3016, Manila
Fine Arts Museum

10066
Rizal Shrine
Fort Santiago, Intramuros, POB 3398,
Manila 2801
History/Public Affairs Museum - 1951
Relics and memorabilia related to Dr.
Jose Rizal, national hero of the
Philippines

10067
San Agustin Museum
Intramuros, Manila 2801
Religious Art Museum
Religious artifacts; history of
Christianity

10068
Santa Ana Site Museum
Plaza Felipe Calderon, Manila 2802
Archeology Museum
Excavated pre-Spanish 13th century
graveyard; polychrome religious
images from churches of the 17th and
18th centuries

Marawi

10069
Aga Khan Museum Mindanao State
University
Marawi 9001
Anthropology Museum - 1962
Artifacts relating to socio-cultural life
of Philippine Muslims

Muñoz

10070
**Central Luzon State University
Museum** Central Luzon State
University
Muñoz, Nueva Ecija 2311
History/Public Affairs Museum

Naga

10071
University Museum University of
Nueva Caceres
Naga 4701
General Museum
Archeology; crafts; decorative arts

Paranaque

10072
Museo Ng Buhay Pilipino
784 Quirino Av, Paranaque, Manila
3128
Anthropology Museum
Furniture and furnishings; farm tools
and implements; costumes; carriages;
folk arts and native crafts

Pasay

10073
**A.S.A. (Aurelio Sevilla Alvero)
Library and Museum**
111 P. Manahan St, Pasay City 3129
General Museum
Art; local history; classical antiquities;
ethnology; natural history; folklore -
library

10074
Kailokuan Historical Ilocano Museum
Vigan House, Nayong Pilipino, Pasay
City 3129
General Museum
Art, culture and industry of the Ilocano
people; antiquities

10075
Lopez Memorial Museum and Library
10 Lancaster Av, Pasay City 3129
Fine Arts Museum - 1960
Coll: Filippiana; Spanish era in
Philippine history and art; letters of Dr.
Jose Rizal; manuscripts; books;
artifacts; paintings - library

10076
Panamin Museum
Muslim Region, Nayong Pilipino, Pasay
City 3129
General Museum
Traditional Philippine cultures

10077
Philippine Air Force Museum State
Museum
Nichols Air Base, Pasay City 3129
Science/Tech Museum

10078
Philippine Lepeidoptera
Bohol House, Nayong Pilipino, Pasay
City 3129
Natural History Museum
Butterflies

10079
**Philippine Marine and Terrestrial
Fauna**
Badjao House, Nayong Pilipino, Pasay
City 3129
Natural History Museum

10080
**Philippine Marine Life and Philippine
Shells**
Samal House, Nayong Pilipino, Pasay
City 3129
Natural History Museum

Pila

10081
Pila Museum
Pila, Laguna 3722
General Museum
Local history; archeology

Quezon

10082
Ateneo Art Museum Ateneo
University
Rizal Library Building, POB 154,
Quezon City 2800
Fine Arts Museum - 1960
Post World War II Philippine painting

10083
Philippine Constabulary Museum
Camp Crame, Quezon City 3129
History/Public Affairs Museum

10084
Quezon Memorial Shrine
Diliman, Quezon City, POB 3398,
Manila
History/Public Affairs Museum - 1945
Relics and memorabilia of the late
president Manuel L. Quezon, a Filipino
patriot, revolutionist, statesman and
first president of the Commonwealth
of the Philippines

10085
Tabon Cave Site Museum
Quezon, Palawan 2920
Archeology Museum

10086
University Museum of Anthropology
University of the Philippines
Diliman, Quezon City 3004
Anthropology Museum
Archeology; ethnology

Sampaloc

10087
The Beyer Collection
1610 Laurel St, Sampaloc, Manila
Archeology Museum
Art; archeology

10088
Museums of Filipinana and Rizaliana
Arallano University, Sampaloc, Manila
History/Public Affairs Museum
History; ethnography

San Miguel

10089
Marcos Foundation Museum
Ang Maharlika, 838 Gen. Solano St,
San Miguel, Manila 2804
General Museum

San Pablo

10090
Escudero Private Museum
Villa Escudero, San Pablo City 3723
General Museum
Art; local history; archeology; religious
art - library

Santo Tomas

10091
Malvar Historical Landmark
Santo Tomas, Batangas, POB 3398,
Manila
History/Public Affairs Museum - 1974
Photographic exhibit on the Filipino-
American War (1899-1901)

Sarrat

10092
Sarrat Museum
Sarrat, Ilocos Norte
General Museum

Taal

10093
Apacible Historical Landmark
Marcela M. Agoncillo St, Taal,
Batangas, POB 3398, Manila
History/Public Affairs Museum - 1976
Relics and memorabilia related to the
late Galicano and Leon Apacible (local
heroes)

10094
**Marcela M. Agoncillo Historical
Landmark**
Taal, Batangas, POB 3398, Manila
History/Public Affairs Museum - 1980
Relics and memorabilia related to
Doña Marcela M. Agoncillo, who
created the first Filipino flag

Tacloban City

10095
Divine Word University Museum
Divine Word University, Tacloban City
7101
History/Public Affairs Museum

10096
Leyte-Samar Museum Divine Word
University
Romualdez Hall, Tacloban City 7101
General Museum - 1966
Local excavation findings from
Paleolithic and Neolithic ages; World
War II ammunition of Filipino guerrilla
groups

Tanauan

10097
**Jose P. Laurel Memorial Museum
and Library**
Tanauan, Batangas
History/Public Affairs Museum
Documents and personal possessions
of Dr. J.P. Laurel (1890-1960)

10098
Mabini Shrine
Talaga, Tanauan, Batangas, POB 3398,
Manila
History/Public Affairs Museum - 1958
Relics and memorabilia related to
Apolinario Mabini ('brains of the
Philippine revolution')

Tuguegarao

10099
Cagayan Museum Provincial Museum
Tuguegarao, Cagayan 1101
General Museum

Vigan

10100
Ayala Museum
Vigan, Ilocos Sur
History/Public Affairs Museum
Materials relating to important
Ilocanos and Ilocano writers

10101
Laoag Museum
Vigan, Ilocos Sur 0405
General Museum

10102
**University of Northern Philippinies
Museum**
Vigan, Ilocos Sur
General Museum

10103
Vigan Museum
Padre Burgos Residence, Vigan, Ilocos
Sur
General Museum
Art; history

Vinzons

10104
Vinzons Historical Landmark
Vinzons Av, Vinzons, Camarines
Norte, POB 3398, Manila
History/Public Affairs Museum - 1974
Relics and memorabilia of the late
Wenceslao Q. Vinzons (World War II
hero)

Poland

Andrychów

10105
Muzeum Tkactwa
PL Andrychów, woj. Kraków
History/Public Affairs Museum
Coll: old weaving tools; 18th-19th
century weavers' guild books; registry
books;

Antonin

10106
Izba Pamiatek (Memorial Room)
PL Antonin, woj. Poznań
Historic Site
Coll: room in pałac Radziwiłłów, where
the composer Chopin (1810-1849)
lived in 1829; sheet music; furniture

Augustów

10107
Muzeum
ul.1. Maja 60, PL Augustów, woj.
Białystok
General Museum - 1968
Coll: ethnography; fishing; farming;
stockbreeding; apiculture; hunting

Babimost

10108
Izba Pamiætek Regionalnych (Room of
Regional Mementoes)
PL Babimost, woj. Zielona Góra
General Museum - 1963
Coll: agricultural equipment; folk
costumes; folk musical instruments;
documents on the struggle against
Germanization

Baranów Sandomierski

10109
Muzeum Zamkowe (Castle Museum)
PL Baranów Sandomierski, woj.
Rzeszów
History/Public Affairs Museum
Coll: geology; archeology; 17th-18th
century Renaissance palace

Barczewo

10110
Feliksa Nowowiejskiego-Muzeum
(The Feliks Nowowiejski Museum)
ul. Mickiewicza 13, PL Barczewo, woj.
Olsztyn
Historic Site - 1961
Coll: memorabilia on the composer
Feliks Nowowiejski (1877-1946) in his
birthplace; local history

Bartne

10111
**Oddział Muzeum Regionalnego w
Bieczu** (Branch of the Regional
Museum in Biecz)
PL Bartne, woj. Rzeszów
General Museum
Coll: 19th century wooden Orthodox
church; stonecutting

Bendomin

10112
Muzeum Biograficzne (Józef Wybicki
Memorial Room)
PL Bendomin, woj. Gdańsk
Historic Site
Coll: birthplace of Józef Wybicki
(1747-1822), political leader, author of
the Polish national anthem

Białowieża

10113
**Muzeum Przyrodniczo-Leśne
Białowieskiego Parku Narodowego**
(Natural History and Forestry Museum
of the Białowieża National Park)
PL Białowieża, woj. Białystok
Science/Tech Museum - 1920
Coll: geography; botany; zoology;
ornithology; enthomology - library

Biały Dunajec

10114
Muzeum Lenina Muzeum Lenina w
Krakowie (Lenin Museum)
ul.Lenina 6, PL Biały Dunajec, woj.
Kraków
History/Public Affairs Museum - 1949
Memorabilia on V.I. Lenin in the house
where he and his wife lived (1913/14);
original interiors

Białystok

10115
Muzeum Okręgowe (District
Museum)
Rynek Kościuszki - Ratusz, PL
Białystok
General Museum - 1949
Coll: archeology; 18th-20th century
historical documents; Polish paintings;
ethnography
10116
Muzeum Ruchu Rewolucyjnego
Muzeum Okręgowe (Museum of the
Revolutionary Movement)
ul. Kilińskiego 6, PL Białystok
History/Public Affairs Museum - 1962
Coll: history of the revolutionary
movement in Białystok; banners; arms
10117
Muzeum Tkactwa Muzeum
Okręgowego
PL Białystok
History/Public Affairs Museum
origin and development of the textile
industry; old weaving mill

Biecz

10118
Muzeum Regionalne (Regional
Museum)
ul. Kromera 2, PL Biecz, woj.Rzeszów
General Museum - 1953
Coll: archeology; history; art; old
prints; coins; 500 year-old potter's kiln;
guild documents; 15th century Gothic
Madonna; life and work of the
historian Marcin Kromer (1512-1589);
late Renaissance house

Bieliny

10119
Punkt Etnograficzny Muzeum
Świętokrzyskiego w Kielcach
(Peasant House)
PL Bieliny, woj. Kielce
Anthropology Museum
Coll: ethnography; larchwood peasant
house from 1789; domestic utensils

Bielsk-Podlaski

10120
Muzeum Martyrologii (Museum of
Martyrdom)
ul: Hołowieska 18, PL Bielsk-Podlaski,
woj. Białystok
History/Public Affairs Museum
Coll: struggle and martyrdom of the
inhabitants of Bielsk county during the
Nazi occupation

Bielsko-Biała

10121
Muzeum
zamek, ul. Kosmonautów 16a, PL
Bielsko-Biała, woj. Katowice
General Museum - 1948
Coll: applied weaving art; ethnology;
arts; paintings and scetches by Julian
Fałat (1853-1929)

Bierutowice

10122
Muzeum
PL Bierutowice, woj. Wrocław
Open Air Museum
Early 13th century wooden church
with carvings, moved to the present
location from Vang, Province of
Valdres, Norway

Biłgoraj

10123
Muzeum Regionalne (Regional
Museum)
PL Biłgoraj, woj. Lublin
General Museum - 1967
Coll: local history; costumes; sieve-
making industry; resistance movement
during World War II

Biskupin

10124
Muzeum Oddział Państwowego
Muzeum Archeologicznego w
Warszawie
PL Biskupin, woj. Bydgoszcz
Archeology Museum - 1958
Coll: finds from settlements of the
Danubian culture of about 3,500 B.C.;
fortifications; smokehouses; tar works

Blizne

10125
Wiejska Izba Pamiætek
PL Blizne, woj. Rzeszów
General Museum - 1966
Coll: folk art; local history

Błonie

10126
Muzeum Stała Wystawa
Państwowego Muzeum
Archeologicznego w Warszawie
(Permanent Exhibition of the State
Archeological Museum in Warsaw)
PL Błonie, woj. Warszawa
Archeology Museum
Coll: archeology

Bóbrka

10127
**Muzeum-Skansen Przemysłu
Naftowego** (Oil Prospecting Open Air
Museum)
PL Bóbrka
Open Air Museum
Coll: history of the earliest known oil
prospectings (1854); models and
life-size reconstruction of devices
used in oil exploration in the past

Bochnia

10128
Muzeum
Rynek 20, PL Bochnia, woj. Kraków
General Museum - 1959
Div: Gallery of paintings and sculpture;
Ethnographic Collection: folk graphics,
paintings by peasant women from
Zalipie, works by the naive painter
Nikifor, folk ceramics; Exotic
Collection: Chinese, Indonesian,
African art; Historical Mementoes

Bolesławiec

10129
Muzeum Ceramiki
ul. Mickiewicza 13, PL Bolesławiec,
woj. Wrocław
Decorative Arts Museum - 1909
Coll: local ceramics

Bolków

10130
Muzeum-Zamek Oddział Muzeum
Narodowego we Wrocławiu (Castle
Museum)
Zamek, PL Bolków, woj. Wrocław
History/Public Affairs Museum - 1900
Coll: local history; hunting in Lower
Silesia; 14th century castle

Brzeg

10131
Muzeum Piastów Śląskich (Museum of
the Silesian Piasts)
zamek, pl. Zamkowi 1, PL Brzeg, woj.
Opole
History/Public Affairs Museum
Coll: history of the Piast dynasty in the
Silesian area; historical relics;
numismatics; 17th century sarcophagi;
parchment documents; medieval
paintings; sculptures; crafts

Bydgoszcz

10132
Izba Pamiætek (Memorial Room)
PL Bydgoszcz
Historic Site
Coll: mementoes of Adam Grzymała-
Siedlecki (1876-1967), literary critic
and dramatist; theatrical exhibits;
letters of the writer Przybyszewski
(1868-1927) and T.Boy-Zeleński
(1874-1941); books by authors of the
'Young Poland' period
10133
**Muzeum im. Leona
Wyczółkowskiego** (The Leon
Wyczółkowski Museum)
al. 1 Maja 4, PL Bydgoszcz
General Museum - 1923
Coll: archeology; history; numismatics;
collection of the painter Leon
Wyczółkowski (1852-1936),containing
paintings, drawings, prints; works by
the painter M.A. Piotrkowski
(1813-1875); 19th-20th century Polish
paintings

Bystrzyca Kłodzka

10134
Muzeum Filumenistyczne
Mały Rynek 1, PL Bystrzyca Kłodzka,
woj. Wrocław
History/Public Affairs Museum - 1964
Coll: history of fire; medieval lighters;
flints; mining lamps; matches; match-
box labels; local history;

Bytom

10135
Muzeum Górnoślæskie (The Upper
Silesian Museum)
pl.E.Thälmann 2, PL Bytom
General Museum - 1927
Div. of Natural History: geology;
zoology; botany; Div. of Archeology:
exhibits from the Bronze Age;
Hallstatt; Roman period; Middle Ages;
Div. of Ethnography: folk costumes;
laces; tools; Div. of History; Div. of Art:
Polish painting; foreign painting;
graphic art; guild art; applied arts

Bytów

10136
**Muzeum Zachodniej
Kaszubszczyzny** (Museum of
Western Kashubia)
Zamek, PL Bytów, woj. Koszalin
General Museum
Coll: ethnography; local history; old
castle

Cedynia

10137
Muzeum Regionalne (Regional
Museum)
pl. Wolności 8, PL Cedynia, woj.
Szeczin
Archeology Museum - 1966
Coll: exhibits from the excavations of
the castle in Cedynia

Chełm

10138
Muzeum
ul. Lubelska 55, PL Chełm, woj. Lublin
General Museum - 1892
Div. of Archeology: relics of the Stone
Age; Div. of History: 18th-19th century
collection; Div. of Ethnography:
farming; fishing; weaving implements;
Div. of Art: paintings; applied art; Div.
of War, Occupation and Liberation:
covering the period of World War II;
Div. of Natural History: geology;
mineralogy; zoology; botany;
anthropology

Chlewiska

10139
Zabytkowa Huta Muzeum Techniki w
Warszawie (Ancient Foundry)
Chlewiska
Science/Tech Museum
Coll: foundry equipment; old
mouldings

Chmielno

10140
Punkt Muzealny
PL Chmielno, woj. Gdańsk
General Museum
Coll: local history; fisherman's house

Chojnice

10141
**Kolekcja Hystoryczno-Regionalna
Makowskich** (Regional Historical
Collection)
ul. Drzymały, PL Chojnice, woj.
Bydgoszcz
History/Public Affairs Museum
Coll: archeological finds; history of the
area during the period of Nazi
occupation; lodged in the home of
Albin Makowski, former prisoner of
the concentration camp at Stutthof -
library

10142
Muzeum Regionalne (Regional
Museum)
Brama Człnchowska, ul. 31 Stycznia,
PL Chojnice, woj. Bydgoszcz
General Museum - 1932
Coll: archeology; history of the town
and country; ethnography from
Southern Kashubia; sports, including a
wooden bicycle from 1860

Chojnów

10143
Muzeum Miejskie (Municipal
Museum)
Zamek Piastowski, pl. Zamkowy 1, PL
Chojnów, woj. Wrocław
General Museum - 1905
Coll: burial remains from 2,000 B.C.;
urns; regional industry and crafts;
smithery; furniture; flax processing
tools; stained glass

Chorzów

10144
Muzeum
ul. Powstańców 25, PL Chorzów, woj.
Katowice
General Museum - 1925
Coll: Silesian folk costumes; chests;
carvings; interiors; farm implements;
local history; numismatics; art

Chrzanów

10145
Muzeum
ul. Mickiewicza 13, PL Chrzanów, woj.
Kraków
General Museum - 1960
Coll: archeology; ethnography;
history; geology; photographs;
graphics

Ciechanowiec

10146
**Muzeum Rolnictwa im. Jana
Krzysztofa Kluka** (Jan Krzysztof
Museum of Agriculture)
ul. Pałacowa 5, PL Ciechanowiec, woj.
Białystok
Agriculture Museum
Local history; farm implements;
domestic utensils; weaving;
memorabilia on the scientist J.K. Kluk
(1739-1796)

Cieplice Ślæskie Zdrój

10147
Muzeum Przyrodnicze (Natural
History Museum)
Pawilon Norweski, Park Norweski, PL
Cieplice Ślæskie Zdrój, woj. Wrocław
Science/Tech Museum - 1920
Coll: natural history; mammals; birds;
insects; invertebrates; fungi; minerals;
established by the owner of Cieplice,
Count Schaffgotsch

Cieszyn

10148
Muzeum
ul. Regera 6, PL Cieszyn
General Museum - 1808
Coll: archeology; geography;
ethnography; folk art

Czarnolas

10149
Muzeum Jana Kochanowskiego (Jan
Kochanowski Museum)
PL Czarnolas, woj. Kielce
Historic Site
Coll: works of Poland's greatest
Renaissance poet Jan Kochanowski
(1530-1584); 19th century country
house of the Jabłonowski family

Częstochowa

10150
Muzeum
Ratusz, budynek B. pl.im.dra
W.Biegańskiego, PL Częstochowa,
woj. Katowice
General Museum
Div. of Natural History: insects; fossils;
minerals; ornithology; Div. of
Archeology: Lusatian culture; arms;
Roman finds; burial remains; Div.of
Ethnography: farm implements;
costumes; Div.of History: resistance
movement; documents of political
leaders; Div. of Art: contemporary
Polish paintings

10151
Muzeum Górnictwa Rud Żelaza
(Museum of Iron Ore Mining, Branch
of the Museum in Częstochowa)
park im. S. Staszica, PL Częstochowa,
woj. Katowice
Science/Tech Museum
Coll: history of iron ore mining

10152
**Rezerwat Archeologiczny
Cmentarzyska Kultury Łużyckiej**
(Archeological Reserve of Burial
Remains of the Lusatian Culture,
Branch of the Museum in
Częstochowa)
al. Pokoju, PL Częstochowa, woj.
Katowice Raków
Archeology Museum
Coll: archeology of the Lusatian
culture

10153
Skarbiec na Jasnej Górze (Jasna
Góra Treasury)
Klasztor Paulinów, ul. Kordeckiego, PL
Częstochowa, woj. Katowice
Religious Art Museum
Coll: religious art; liturgical vestments
and vessels; votive shields; jewelery;
orders, coins and medals; bequest by
Sigismund I and Sigismund Augustus,
Queen Bona, Sigismund III

Człuchów

10154
Wystawa Muzealna (Museum
Exhibition)
PL Człuchów, woj.Koszalin
General Museum
Coll: regional history; archeology; art;
Gothic castle

Dæbrowa Górnicza

10155
**Muzeum Historii Ruchów
Robotniczych im. Aleksandra
Zawadskiego** Muzeum Górnoślæskie,
Bytom (Aleksander Zawadski Museum
of History of the Revolutionary
Movement)
pl. Wolnosci, PL Dæbrowa Górnicza,
woj. Katowice
Historic Site
Coll: memorabilia on the politician A.
Zawadzki (1899-1964); objects from
Poland and abroad; 20 year history of
Upper Silesia and the Dæbrowa Basin

10156
**Regionalne Muzeum Geologiczne im.
Zygmunta Glogera** (Zygmunt Gloger
Regional Geological Museum)
PL Dæbrowa Górnicza, woj. Katowice
Science/Tech Museum - 1912
Coll: history of coal mining in Silesia;
history of mining schools; geology

Darłowo

10157
Muzeum
Zamek Książæt Pomorskiech, ul.
Zamkowa 4, PL Darłowo, woj. Koszalin
General Museum - 1923
Coll: geology; natural history;
archeology; ethnography; history;
applied art; fine art; 12th century castle

Dębica

10158
**Muzeum Regionalne Towarzystwa
Społeczno-Kulturalnego**
PL Dębica, woj. Rzeszów
General Museum
Coll: local history; memorabilia on
World War II

Dębno

10159
Muzeum
PL Dębno, woj. Kraków
General Museum
Coll: local history; 15th century Gothic
castle

Dobczyce

10160
**Muzeum Regionalne Polskiego
Towarzystwa Turystyczno-
Krajoznawczego** (Regional Museum
of the Polish Tourist Association)
Rynek 15, PL Dobczyce, woj. Kraków
General Museum - 1964
Coll: archeological finds; ceramics;
tools; arms; domestic utensils; coins;
old books; costumes

Dobra

10161
Muzeum Parafialne Muzeum
Diecezjalne, Tarnów (Parish Museum)
PL Dobra, woj. Kraków
Religious Art Museum - 1955
Coll: sacral art; folk art; local archival
material

Dobra Szlachecka

10162
Punkt Muzealny Muzeum Budownictwa Ludowego (Museum in a 15th century Orthodox Church Belfry) PL Dobra Szlachecka, woj. Rzeszów Fine Arts Museum Rare example of folk architecture, a unique specimen of a fortified church

Dubiecko

10163
Muzeum Ignacego Krasickiego (Ignacy Krasicki Museum) PL Dubiecko, woj. Rzeszów History/Public Affairs Museum Coll: works of the poet Ignacy Krasicki (1735-1801)

Dukla

10164
Muzeum Braterstwa Broni (Museum of the Brotherhood in Arms) ul. 1.Maja 9a, PL Dukla, woj. Rzeszów History/Public Affairs Museum Coll: history of the battle of Dukla in 1944; lodged in a 17th century palace, rebuilt in Rococo style by the Mniczech family in 1764

Duszniki Zdrój

10165
Muzeum Papiernicze (Museum of the Paper Industry) ul. Kłdzka 48, PL Duszniki Zdrój, woj. Wrocław Science/Tech Museum Coll: history of the paper industry in Poland and around the world; old paper mill; tools and watermarks; manifacture of hand-made paper

Dynów

10166
Izba Pamiætek PL Dynów, woj. Rzeszów General Museum - 1967 Coll: local ethnography; local history

Elblæg

10167
Muzeum ul. Wybrzeżna 11/12, PL Elblæg, woj. Gdańsk General Museum - 1954 Coll: archeological finds, including 13th century baptismal font; medieval sword crafts; art; iconography; local history;

Frombork

10168
Muzeum Mikołaja Kopernika (Nicolaus Copernicus Museum) ul. Katedralna 12, PL Frombork, woj. Olsztyn History/Public Affairs Museum - 1948 Coll: life, scientific work and activities of N. Copernicus; paintings; sculptures; prints; numismatics; medals; observation instruments - library

Gdańsk

10169
Centralne Muzeum Morskie (Central Maritime Museum) ul. Szeroka 67/68, PL-80835 Gdańsk Science/Tech Museum - 1960 Coll: history of shipbuilding; history of maritime shipping; ship models; marine fine arts; history of yachting; underwater archeology - library

10170
Muzeum Archeologiczne (Archeological Museum) ul. Mariacka 25/26, PL Gdańsk Archeology Museum - 1953 Coll: prehistoric collection: ceramics from the later Stone Age; metal and ceramic exhibits of the Lusatian Culture; amber articles; early history collection: boat building trade; four early medieval stave boats - educational department

10171
Muzeum Historii Miasta Gdańska (Museum of History of the City of Gdańsk) Ratusz Głównego Miasta, ul. Długa 47, PL Gdańsk History/Public Affairs Museum - 1970 Coll: cultural history of Gdańsk with special reference to current town activities; coins; medals from the Gdańsk mint

10172
Muzeum Narodowe (National Museum) ul. Toruńska 1, PL Gdańsk General Museum Div. of Polish Art: medieval art; modern art; currant art; Div. of Foreign Art: 17th century Flemish and Dutch painting; Italian painting; French painting; contemporary art; Div. of Decorative Art: textiles; furniture; ceramics; goldsmithery etc. exhibits from the Middle Ages, Renaissance, Baroque, Rococo, Neo-Classicism; Div. of Prints: containes ca 6000 items; Kabrun collection and Giełdziński collection including foreign and Polish art - library

Gdynia

10173
Muzeum Marynarki Wojennej Bulwar Szwedzki, PL Gdynia History/Public Affairs Museum - 1953 Coll: model of the Gdańsk ship 'Mars' (built 1697); the Navy in the period between the two World Wars; the World War II period; naval warfare; heavy arms and guns

Giecz

10174
Rezerwat Archeologiczny (Muzeum Archeologiczne, Gdańsk) (Archeological Reserve) PL Giecz, woj. Poznań PL Archeology Museum history of the castle; exhibits from the early Middle Ages

Gliwice

10175
Muzeum ul. Dolnych Wałów 8a, PL Gliwice, woj. Katowice General Museum - 1906 Div. of Archeology: earliest history of the Gliwice region; Div. of History: 13th-20th century history; exhibits depicting the period of the Plebiscite and the Silesian uprisings; Div. of Ethnography: folk art from Upper Silesia and Little Poland; folk sculptures; Div. of Art: applied art; ceramics; prints; sculptures

Głógow

10176
Muzeum Hutnictwa i Odlewnictwa Metali Kolorowich (Museum of Non-Ferrous Metallurgy) PL Głógow, woj. Zielona Góra Science/Tech Museum - 1967 Local history; metallurgy; non-ferrous metal casting; Piast castle from the 13th-17th centuries

Głucha Puszcza

10177
Muzeum PL Głucha Puszcza, woj. Bydgoszcz General Museum - 1964 Natural history; geology; hunting; forestry; archeology; ethnography; history; numismatics; in a forester's cottage - library

Gołotczyzna

10178
Punkt Muzealny PL Gołotczyzna, woj. Warszawa Historic Site Life and work of the writer-publicist Aleksander Świętochowski (1849-1938) in his former home

Golub-Dobrzyń

10179
Muzeum Regionalne Ziemi Dobrzyńskiej (Museum of the Dobrzyń Region) PL Golub-Dobrzyń, woj. Bydgoszcz General Museum - 1967 Archeology; history; numismatics; in a 14th century Gothic castle

Gołuchów

10180
Muzeum Muzeum Narodowego w Poznaniu PL Gołuchów, woj. Poznań Fine Arts Museum - 1962 Coll: European and Oriental art; applied art; furniture; arms; weaving art; Polish painting; painting by an artist of Raphael's School; in a 16th century castle of the Leszczyński family

10181
Muzeum Regionalne PL Gołuchów, woj. Poznań General Museum Coll: local history; ethnography

Gorlice

10182
Muzeum Regionalne Polskiego Towarzystwa Turystyczno-Krajoznawczego (Regional Museum of the Polish Tourist Association) ul. Wæska 11, PL Gorlice, woj. Rzeszów General Museum Coll: local history; Pogórzanie ethnography

Gorzén Górny

10183
Muzeum Emila Zegadłowicza PL Gorzén Górny, woj. Kraków Historic Site Coll: memorabilia on the writer E. Zegadłowicz (1888-1941) in his former home

Gorzów Wielkopolski

10184
Muzeum ul. Warszawska 35, PL Gorzów Wielkopolski, woj. Zielona Góra General Museum - 1945 Coll: natural history; general history; regional geography and history; tomb from the later Stone Age

Gostyń

10185
Muzeum Regionalne ul. Marchlewskiego 257, PL Gostyń, woj. Poznań General Museum Coll: local history

Granica

10186
Muzeum Kampinoskiego Parku Narodowego (Museum of the Kampinos National Park) Nadleśnictwo Kampinos, PL Granica, woj. Warszawa Science/Tech Museum - 1965 Coll: protected flora and fauna; birds; history of the forest; documents; photographs; weapons

Grodzisk Mazowiecki

10187
Muzeum Polskiego Towarzystwa Turystyczno-Krajoznawczego (Museum of the Polish Tourist Association) ul. Parkowa 1, PL Grodzisk Mazowiecki, woj.Warszawa General Museum - 1961 Coll: local history in an 18th century farmstead

Grudziædz

10188
Muzeum ul. Wodna 3/5, PL Grudziædz, woj. Bydgoszcz General Museum - 1884 Coll: local history; 19th-20th century Polish painting; contemporary Pomeranian painting; numismatics; natural history; in 17th-18th century cloister;

Gubin

10189
Muzeum Wilhelma Piecka (Wilhelm Pieck Museum)
ul. W. Piecka 5, PL Gubin, woj. Zielona Góra
Historic Site
Memorabilia of the former president of the German Democratic Republic, Wilhelm Pieck (1876-1960) in his birthplace

Haczów

10190
Punkt Muzealny Muzeum Budownictwa Ludowego w Sanoku
PL Haczów
Religious Art Museum
Coll: 15th century wooden church; baroque interior; two Gothic sculptures

Hel

10191
Muzeum Rybackie (Fishing Museum)
ul. Portowa, PL Hel, woj. Gdańsk
Anthropology Museum
Coll: natural history; fishing equipment; history of navigation; in a 15th century Gothic church

Hrubieszów

10192
Muzeum Regionalne
ul. Dzierzyńskiego 7a, PL Hrubieszów, woj. Lublin
General Museum
Coll: local history; archeology; ethnography; memorabilia on the poet and political leader Stanisław Staszic (1755-1826); in a baroque-classicistic mansion from the end of the 18th century

Igołomia

10193
Rezerwat Archeologiczny
(Archeological Reserve)
PL Igołomia, woj. Kraków
Archeology Museum
Coll: archeological finds from the excavations of a Roman settlement (3rd-4th centuries A.D.)

Inowrocław

10194
Muzeum im. Jana Kasprowicza
pl. Obrońców, PL Inowrocław, woj. Bydgoszcz
General Museum - 1931
Div. of History: history of Inowrocław and the West Kuyavy region; Lusatian culture; tomb from Opoki; Div. of Art: modern art; Biographical and Memorial Div.: devoted to Stanisław Przybyszewski; Jan Kasprowicz (1860-1926) etc.; Div. of Natural History: salt mining

Istebna

10195
Beskidzka Izba Twórcza (Open Air Museum of Creative Folk Art)
PL Istebna, woj. Katowice
Anthropology Museum - 1962
Coll: peasant life and tradition; folk art; folk musical instruments

Istebna na Kubalonce

10196
Muzeum Sztuki Sakralnej Muzeum, Cieszyn (Museum of Sacral Art)
PL Istebna na Kubalonce, woj. Katowice
Religious Art Museum - 1965
Coll: religious art; in a wooden church, moved from Pszynowice

Jagniætkow

10197
Dom Gerharta Hauptmanna (Gerhart Hauptmann's House)
PL Jagniætkow, woj. Wrocław
Historic Site
House, where the Nobel Prize winner Gerhart Hauptmann lived and worked until his death in 1946

Jarocin

10198
Muzeum Regionalne
PL Jarocin, woj. Poznań
General Museum - 1960
Coll: ethnography; farm implements; archeology of the Lusatian culture; history; numismatics

Jarosław

10199
Muzeum
ul. Rynek 4, PL Jarosław, woj. Rzeszów
General Museum - 1925
Coll: 17th-18th century costumes; furniture; domestic utensils

Jasło

10200
Muzeum Regionalne
PL Jasło, woj. Rzeszów
General Museum
Coll: local history; crafts and guilds; icons; Gothic and baroque sculptures; documents from the Nazi period

Jawór

10201
Muzeum Regionalne
PL Jawór, woj. Kielce
General Museum - 1929
Coll: local history; archeology; militaria; applied art; ethnography of the Sub-Sudeten region and Lower Silesia

Jaworzynka

10202
Muzeum Regionalne
PL Jaworzynka, woj. Katowice
General Museum - 1968
Coll: material culture and art of the Beskid highlanders; exhibits from the 18th and 19th centuries

Jelenia Góra

10203
Muzeum Regionalne
ul. Matejki 28, PL Jelenia Góra, woj. Wrocław
General Museum - 1889
Coll: glassmaking and glasspainting; weaving; ethnography; folk furniture

Kalisz

10204
Muzeum Ziemi Kaliskiej (Museum of the Kalisz Region)
ul. Kościuszki 12, PL Kalisz, woj. Poznań
General Museum - 1906
Div. of Archeology: Roman finds; early medieval period; ceramics; tombstone; coins from the 11th-12th centuries; Div. of History: local history; crafts; documents from the Nazi period; Div. of Natural History: regional flora and fauna; Central European and exotic butterflies; Div.of Ethnography: farm implements; folk costumes; lace making - library

Kamień Pomorski

10205
Muzeum
PL Kamień Pomorski, woj. Szczecin
General Museum
Coll: archeology; natural history; monuments; religious art; old prints; in a former cathedral treasury

10206
Muzeum Regionalne Ziemi Kamieńskiej (Regional Museum of the Kamień Region)
ul. Solskiego, PL Kamień Pomorski, woj. Szczecin
General Museum

Kamienna Góra

10207
Muzeum Tkactwa Dolnoślæskiego (Museum of Lower Silesian Weaving)
pl. Wolności 24, PL Kamienna Góra, woj. Wrocław
General Museum - 1947
Coll: local and regional history; crafts; weaving; carving; wooden sculptures; silver coins; house dating back to 1650

Kartuzy

10208
Muzeum Kaszubskie (Kashubian Museum)
ul. Ludowego Wojska Polskiego 1, PL Kartuzy, woj. Gdańsk
Anthropology Museum - 1932
Coll: ethnography; fishing; farming; furniture; ceramics; masks; musical instruments; rare Kashubian painting on glass

Katowice-Janów Ślæski

10209
Muzeum im. Józefa Wieczorka
ul. Szopienicka 1, PL Katowice-Janów Slæski
History/Public Affairs Museum
Collection, devoted to Józef Wieczorek, a distinguished leader of the Polish Communist Party of Silesia; notes; letters; personal mementoes

Kazimierz Dolny

10210
Muzeum Regionalne
ul. Senatorska 11, PL Kazimierz Dolny, woj. Lublin
General Museum - 1963
Coll: iconography; local and regional history; ethnography; painting; drawing; graphics; in a 16th century Renaissance house

Kępno

10211
Muzeum Regionalne
PL Kępno, woj.Poznań
General Museum - 1936
Coll: archeology; ethnography; history; art culture

Kętrzyn

10212
Muzeum
ul. Struga 1, PL Kętrzyn, woj. Olsztyn
General Museum - 1945
Coll: Neolithic archeology; 15th-17th century sculptures; painting; numismatics; furniture; Meissen porcelain; natural history; geology; lodged in a 14th century Gothic castle

Kielce

10213
Muzeum Lat Szkolnych Stefana Żeromskiego (Museum of Stefan Żeromski's School Years)
ul. Święrczewskiego 25, PL Kielce
Historic Site - 1965
Coll: memorabilia on the poet Stefan Żeromski (1864-1924); manuscripts of his works

10214
Muzeum Świętokrzyskie
pl. Partyzantów 3-5, PL Kielce
General Museum - 1846
Gallery of Polish Painting: paintings from the 18th-20th centuries; Polish Sarmatian portraits; works by Misiowski, A; Orłowski,L; Grassi, G.; Lampi, G.B.; etc.; Interiors: exhibits from the 17th-18th centuries; Ethnographic Exhibition: folk culture from Kielce county, the Łsogory region; agriculture; weaving; crafts; Div. of Recent History of the Region of Kielce; Div. of Archeology; Div. of Natural History

Kłdzko

10215
Muzeum Ziemi Kłodzkiej (Museum of the Kłodzko Region)
pl. Bolesława Chrobrego 22, PL Kłdzko, woj. Wrocław
General Museum - 1963
Coll: archeology; history; ethnography; contemporary painting; glass painting; sacral art; seal presses of the town Kłodzko; collection of travelling escritoires

Kluczbork

10216
Muzeum i. Jana Dzierżonia (Jan Dzierżoń Museum)
ul. 15 Grudnia 12, PL Kluczbork, woj. Opole
History/Public Affairs Museum - 1957
Coll: primitive beehive from the 1st century B.C.; local history; archeology; apiculture

Kluki

10217
Zagroda Słowińska Muzeum Pomorza Środkowego, Słupsk (Slovintzian Homestead)
PL Kluki, woj. Koszalin
Open Air Museum - 1963
Coll: households in three buildings; folk culture of the Slovintzi, a small Slavonic group of Pomerania

Kolbuszowa

10218
Muzeum Regionalne Lasowiaków
(Oddział Muzeum Okręgowego w
Rzeszowie) (Lasowiak Regional
Museum)
ul. Pijarska 19, Kolbuszowa, woj.
Rzeszów
General Museum - 1958
Coll: archeology; relics from the
paleolithic, mesolithic and neolithic
periods; ethnography; farm
implements of the Lasowiaks;
costumes; furniture in the historic
building of the former Synagogue;

Kołobrzeg

10219
Muzeum Oręża Polskiego (Polish
Arms Museum)
ul. Emilii Gierczak 5, PL Kołobrzeg,
woj. Koszalin
General Museum - 1963
Military history; local history

Koniaków

10220
Muzeum Koronek (Lace Museum)
PL Koniaków, woj. Katowice
Decorative Arts Museum
Coll: decorative arts and crafts; history
of lacemaking

Koniecpol

10221
Muzeum Regionalne
PL Koniecpol, woj. Kielce
General Museum
Coll: archeological relics; guild
memorials; archival materials

Konin

10222
Muzeum Zagłębia Konińskiego
(Museum of the Konin Basin)
ul. Słwackiego 8, PL Konin, woj.
Poznań
General Museum - 1956
Coll: geology; mineralogy;
paleontology; archeology (Mesolithic
and Neolithic period); local history;
militaria; numismatics; ethnography;

Kórnik

10223
**Biblioteka Kórnicka Polskiej
Akademii Nauk - Dział Muzealny**
(Kórnik Library of the Polish Academy
of Sciences)
Zamek, PL Kórnik, woj. Poznań
History/Public Affairs Museum
17th century Danzig, Dutch, Bretonian
cupboards; furniture; 16th-19th
century Polish, Dutch, German
painting; militaria; arms; 18th century
porcelain; miniatures; 19th century
engravings and drawings; Australian
and Polynesian ethnography; in a 15th
century castle - library

Koryznówka

10224
Muzeum Jana Matejki (Jan Matejko
Museum)
PL Koryznówka, woj. Kraków
Historic Site
Coll: memorabila on the painter Jan
Matejko (1838-1893); in the house of
the Serafiński family, where the artist
used to spend the summer

Koszalin

10225
Muzeum Pomorza Środkowego
(Museum of Central Pomerania)
ul. Armii Czerwonej 53, PL Koszalin
General Museum - 1924
Archeology; ethnography; applied arts

Kraków

10226
Biblioteka Jagiellońska (Jagiellonian
Library)
ul. Mickiewicza 22, PL Kraków
Fine Arts Museum - 1919
Collection of prints: Dutch and Italian
engravings from the 16th century;
engravings by J. Callot (17th century),
G.B. Piranesi (18th century); Polish
graphics (18th-20th century); Polish
exlibris from the 16th century; works
by Polish and foreign poets and
writers, illustrated by original graphic
works; collection of Italian miniatures
of the 13th-15th centuries

10227
**Biblioteka Polskiej Akademii Nauk w
Krakowie, Dział Zbiorów Graficznych**
(Library of the Polish Academy of
Sciences in Cracow, Department of
Print Collections)
ul. Sławkowska 17, PL Kraków
Fine Arts Museum - 1935
Coll: development of graphic art from
the 15th to the 19th centuries; Italian,
French, Dutch, German School

10228
Dom Jana Matejki Muzeum
Narodowe w Krakowie
ul. Floriańska 41, PL Kraków
Historic Site
Cottage where the painter Jan
Matejko (1833-1893) lived

10229
Kamienica Scołayskich Muzeum
Narodowe w Krakowie (Szołayski
House)
pl. Szczepański 9, PL Kraków
Fine Arts Museum
Gallery of Polish painting and
sculpture; the collection from the
15th-16th centuries ranks among the
most valuable in Poland

10230
Kossakówka
ul. J. Kossaka, PL Kraków
Historic Site
Collection in the villa 'Wygoda', a family
house of three generations of painters
of the Kossak family (Juliusz, Wojciech
and Jerzy); furniture; armor; paintings

10231
**Muzeum Akademii Górniczo-
Hutniczej** (Museum of the Academy
of Mining and Metallurgy)
al.Mickiewicza 30, PL Kraków
Science/Tech Museum - 1959
Coll: mathematics; physics; chemistry;
geology; mining; electrotechnology;
metallurgy; ceramics - library

10232
**Muzeum Antropologiczne
Uniwersytetu Jagiellońskiego**
(Anthropological Museum of the
Jagiellonian University)
ul. Krupnicza 50, PL Kraków
Anthropology Museum - 1880
Coll: anthropology; series of skulls of
various ethnic groups

10233
Muzeum Archeologiczne
ul. Senacka 3, ul. Poselska 3, PL
Kraków
Archeology Museum - 1850
Coll: Paleolithic and Mesolithic Age;
Neolithic and early-Bronze Age;
Lusatian Culture; La Têne and Roman
Periods; early Middle Ages; Middle
Ages; Mediterranean and
Non-European Archeology - scientific
and educational section; workroom for
research in metallography; library

10234
Muzeum Etnograficzne
(Ethnographical Museum)
pl. Wolnica 1, PL Kraków
Anthropology Museum - 1904
Coll: rural economy; customs and
observances; folk art; non-European
ethnography (collections from
Cameroon, Siberia and Indonesia) -
library; conservation workshop

10235
**Muzeum Farmacji Akademii
Medicznej** (Pharmaceutical Museum
of the Medical Academy)
ul.Basztowa 3, PL Kraków
Science/Tech Museum - 1946
Coll: history and development of the
pharmacy; pharmacy cellar and
laboratory from the 17th century;
herbarium and drying room; drug
trade; receptacles - library

10236
Muzeum Historyczne m. Krakowa
(History Museum of the City of
Cracow)
Rynek Główny 35, PL Kraków
History/Public Affairs Museum - 1899
Coll: history, culture and art of the city
of Cracow; relics of the old Cracow
guilds; numismatics; iconography;
arms; history of the theatre

10237
Muzeum Lenina
ul.Topolowa 5, PL Kraków
Historic Site - 1950
Coll: life and work of V.I. Lenin,
especialy in the period from 1912-1914

10238
Muzeum Lotnictwa i Astronautyki
(Museum of Aviation and Astronautics)
PL Kraków
Science/Tech Museum - 1967
Coll: historical aircraft exhibitions at
the former Rakowice-Czyżyny airport;
air force uniforms; photographs -
library

10239
Muzeum Narodowe w Krakowie
(National Museum in Cracow)
ul. Manifestu Lipcowego 12, PL-30-960
Kraków
General Museum - 1879
The Museum consists of the following
departments: Kamienica Szołayskich (
Szołayski House); Sukiennice (The
Cloth Hall); Nowy Gmach (The New
Building); Zbiory Czartoryskich
(Czartoryski Collections); Dom Jana
Matejki (Jan Matejko House); Oddział
im. Emeryka Hutten-Czapskiego
(Emeryk Hutten-Czapski Branch)

10240
**Muzeum Przyrodnicze przy
Zakładzie Zoologii Systematycznej i
Doświadczalnej PAN** (Natural
Science Museum of the Zoological
Institute of the Polish Academy of
Sciences)
ul. Sławkowska 17, PL Kraków
Science/Tech Museum - 1863
Entomology; mammals; reptiles;
amphibians from the Pliocene and
Pleistocene

10241
**Muzeum Przyrodnicze Uniwersytetu
Jagiellońskiego** (Natural Science
Museum of the Jagiellonian University)
ul. Krupnicza 50, PL Kraków
Natural History Museum - 1969
Coll: natural history; zoology; Nowicki
Collection of diptera and fishes

10242
**Muzeum Uniwersytetu
Jagiellońskiego** (Jagiellonian
University Museum)
ul. Św. Anny 8, PL Kraków
General Museum
Coll: portrait gallery; sculptures; prints;
numismatics; goldsmithery; textiles;
ancient art; instruments; globes

10243
Nowy Gmach Muzeum Narodowe w
Krakowie (The New Building)
al. Trzeciego Maja 1, PL Kraków
Fine Arts Museum
Coll: 20th century Polish painting and
sculpture; art of the 'Young Poland'
period (1890-1914); Art Nouveau style;
Symbolism; Abstractionism;
Surrealism; Polish art of the present
day

10244
**Oddział im. Emeryka Hutten-
Czapskiego** Muzeum Narodowe w
Krakowie (Emeryk Hutten-Czapski
Branch)
ul. Manifestu Lipcowego 10, PL
Kraków
History/Public Affairs Museum
Cabinet of Numismatics; Section of
Prints, Drawings and Watercolours;
Section of Old Books and
Manuscripts - library

10245
Państwowe Zbiory Sztuki na Wawelu
(Wawel State Art Collection)
Wawel 5, PL-31-001 Kraków
Fine Arts Museum
The Collection in the Royal Castle at
Wawel is divided in five departments:
The Furnishings of the Royal
Chambers: Renaissance and Baroque
interiors; King Sigismund August's
16th century collection of Flemish
tapestries; Italian and Dutch painting;
Polish carpets; The Crown Treasury:
crown jewels; historical relics;
banners; The Armoury: Polish and
West European weapons; Oriental
Items: Persian and Turkish weaponry
and tents; oriental rugs; Chinese and
Japanese pottery; The Waweliana
Collection: archeology; history of
Wawel Hill; lapidarium; maps and
charts; archives; The Cathedral
Church and Treasury - library

10246
Placówka Muzealna KTG (Museum of
the Committee of Mountainclimbing)
ul. Westerplatte 15/16, PL Kraków
History/Public Affairs Museum
History of tourism in Poland;
Kazimierz Sosnowski Collection ;
tourist equipment

10247
Pracownia i Muzeum Geologii Młodych Struktur ZNG PAN
(Laboratory and Museum of Geology of Younger Structures of the Polish Academy of Sciences)
ul. Senacka 3, PL Kraków
Science/Tech Museum
Coll: exhibits from Poland with special emphasis on Southern Poland

10248
Sukiennice (Muzeum Narodowe w Krakowie) (The Cloth Hall)
Rynek Głowny, PL Kraków
Fine Arts Museum - 1879
Coll: Polish painting and sculpture from 1764 to the end of the 19th century

10249
Zbiory Czartoryskich Muzeum Narodove w Krakowie (Czartoryski Collection)
ul. Św. Jana 19, PL Kraków
Fine Arts Museum - 1801
Department of Antique Art: excavations from Mesopotamia; Ancient Egypt; Greek art; Roman art; Permanent Exhibition of the Czartoryski Collection: consists of three sections: Decorative Art; Venetian glassware; 16th-18th century Czech,Silesian, Polish and German glassware; Italian and Spanish majolica; Viennese, Meissen, Polish and French porcelain; Persian rugs; furniture; Painting Gallery: 550 paintings; miniatures and sculptures; The Armoury; Prints Cabinet: about 35,000 prints, drawings, watercolours by Polish and foreign artists; Czartoryski Library: has over 150,000 vol., including 30,000 old books; The Czartoryski Archives and Manuscript Collection

Krasnystaw

10250
Muzeum
ul. Nocznickiego 3, PL Krasnystaw, woj. Lublin
General Museum - 1958
Coll: history; archeology; ethnography; numismatics; natural history; in a former Jesuit monastery

Krościenko

10251
Muzeum Pienińskiego Parku Narodowego (Museum of the Pieniny Natural Park)
PL Krościenko, woj. Kraków
Natural History Museum - 1935
Coll: geology; botany; zoology

Krośniewice

10252
Zbiory Jerzego Dunin-Borkowskiego (Collection of Jerzy Dunin-Borkowski)
pl. Wolności 1, PL Krośniewice, woj. Łódź
History/Public Affairs Museum
Coll: archives; numismatics; painting; arms; applied art - library

Krosno

10253
Muzeum
ul. Marcelego Nowotki 16, PL Krosno, woj. Rzeszów
General Museum - 1954
Coll: archeology; history of lighting; history of oil exploration; local history; art; lodged in a 17th century building

Krosno Odrzańskie

10254
Punkt Muzealny Muzeum Ziemi Lubuskiej (Museum of the Lubusk Region)
PL Krosno Odrzańskie, woj. Zielona Góra
General Museum
Castle from the 13th-16th centuries; archeology; history

Krotoszyn

10255
Muzeum Ziemi Krotoszyńskiej (Museum of the Krotoszyn Region)
pl. 1. Maja 1, PL Krotoszyn, woj. Poznań
General Museum - 1957
Ethnography; history; archeology

Krynica

10256
Muzeum Przyrodnicze (Natural History Museum)
ul. Świerczewskiego 11, PL Krynica, woj. Kraków
Science/Tech Museum
Coll: natural sciences; ornithology; Mrs. Kmietowicz collection

Krzemionki Opatowskie

10257
Rezerwat Archeologiczny
Państwowe Muzeum Archeologiczne w Warszawie (Archeological Reserve)
PL Krzemionki Opatowskie
Archeology Museum
Coll: exhibition depicting flint mining and processing in the later Stone Age (c. 2000 B.C.)

Kwidzyn

10258
Muzeum-Zamek (Castle Museum)
ul. Parkowa 1, PL Kwidzyn, woj. Gdańsk
General Museum - 1950
Coll: archeology; history; applied arts; ethnography; natural history

Łambinowice

10259
Muzeum Martyrologii Jeńców Wojennych (Museum of Martyrdom of Prisoners of War)
ul. Muzealna 1, PL-49-140 Łambinowice, woj. Opole
History/Public Affairs Museum - 1964
Coll: remains the of prisoners of war camp; cemetery where 60,000 prisoners of war from various countries are buried

Łańcut

10260
Muzeum
Zamek, ul. Zamkowa 2, PL Łańcut, woj. Rzeszow
History/Public Affairs Museum - 1944
Coll: interiors from the 17th-20th centuries (Zodiac Hall; Ceiling Hall; Rococo Salon; Boucher drawing room; Chinese room; Ballroom); Art Collection: Polish and foreign art; majolica; porcelain; carriages - library

10261
Muzeum Regionalne
Tkacka 5, PL Łańcut, woj. Rzeszów
General Museum
Coll: local history

Lębork

10262
Muzeum
ul. Młynarska 14/15, PL Lębork, woj. Gdańsk
General Museum - 1952
Coll: archeology; furniture; arms; minerals

Łęcna

10263
Muzeum Regionalne
ul. Bóżnicza 17, PL Łęcna, woj. Lublin
General Museum - 1966
Coll: local history; ethnography; archeology; history of art; military history; in a 17th century synagogue

Łęczyca

10264
Muzeum
Zamek, PL Łęczyca, woj. Łódź
General Museum - 1949
Coll: history; ethnography; natural history; in a 14th century castle

Legnica

10265
Muzeum Miedzi (Copper Museum)
ul. Partyzantów 1, PL Legnica, woj. Wrocław
General Museum - 1897
Coll. archeology; local history; 19th-20th century Polish painting; technology of copper production; in a baroque palace from the 18th century

Legnickie Pole

10266
Muzeum Bitwy Legnickiej (Museum of the Battle of Legnica)
PL Legnickie Pole, woj. Wrocław
History/Public Affairs Museum - 1961
Coll: history of the battle with the Tatars in 1241; in a former 13th-14th century sacral edifice

Leśnica

10267
Muzeum Czynu Powstańczego
Oddział Muzeum Ślæska Opolskiego w Opolu
ul. Powstańców Ślæskich 1, PL Leśnica, woj. Opole
History/Public Affairs Museum - 1964
History of the revolutionary movement against the Germans in the Nazi period

Leszno

10268
Muzeum
pl. dra Metziga 17, PL Leszno, woj. Poznań
General Museum
History Section: local history; history of the Leszczyński family in the 16th-17th centuries and Sułkowski family in the 18th century; Ethnographic Section: folk costumes; furniture; farm implements; weaving implements

Leżajsk

10269
Muzeum
Rynek 15, PL Leżajsk, woj. Rzeszów
General Museum - 1960
Coll: archeology; history; ethnography; in an 18th century house

Lidzbark Warmiński

10270
Muzeum Muzeum Mazurskie, Olsztyn
PL Lidzbark Warmiński, woj. Olsztyn
General Museum - 1967
Coll: castle interior; ceramics; glass; in a castle, built 1350-1375

Liw

10271
Muzeum Zbrojownia (Museum-Armoury)
ul. S. Batorego 2, PL Liw, woj. Warszawa
History/Public Affairs Museum - 1963
Coll: arms and weapons from the 16th-19th centuries; ethnography; in a 15th century Gothic castle

Łobżenica

10272
Izba Muzealna
PL Łobżenica, woj. Bydgoszcz
General Museum - 1967
Coll: folk art; old prints; documents; numismatics; archeology

Łódź

10273
Muzeum Archeologiczne i Ethnograficzne
pl. Wolności 14, PL Łódź
Archeology Museum - 1929
Coll: archeology: Paleolithic Age; Neolithic Age; Bronze Age; early Iron Age; late La Tène and Roman periods; period of the Great Migration and Middle Ages; numismatics; ethnography - library; radiocarbon workshop; conservation section

10274
Muzeum Historii Ruchu Rewolucyjnego (Museum of History of the Revolutionary Movement)
ul. Gdańska 13, PL Łódź
History/Public Affairs Museum - 1960
Activities of the revolutionary movement in the city and region of Łódź in the years 1820-1945; development of industry; organized labor movement up to 1917; lodged in a former prison

10275
Muzeum Historii Włókiennictwa
(Museum of the History of Textile
Industry)
ul. Piotrkowska 282, PL Łódź
Science/Tech Museum - 1960
Coll: history of textiles; folk weaving;
history of textile technology; history of
textile industry - library

10276
Muzeum Sztuki (Museum of Art)
ul. dra Stanisława Więckowskiego 36,
PL Łódź
Fine Arts Museum - 1930
Coll: Gothic art; 15th-19th century
Italian, French, German and Dutch art;
Polish painting of the 17th-20th
century; international modern art

10277
**Muzeum Zakładu Ewolucjonizmu i
Antropologii Uniwersytetu
Łodzkiego** (Museum of the Institute of
Evolutionism and Anthropology of the
Łódź University)
Park Sienkiewicza, PL Łódź
Natural History Museum - 1930
Coll: paleontology; zoology;
entomology; anthropology

Łomża

10278
Muzeum Regionalne
ul. Sadowa 10, PL Łomża, woj.
Białystok
General Museum - 1912
Coll: archeology (Neolithic handmill
and ceramics, exhibits from the
excavation of the castle at Old Łomża);
history; ethnography; natural history

Łopuszna

10279
Muzeum Historii Taternictwa
PL Łopuszna, woj. Kraków
History/Public Affairs Museum
Coll: memorial to the writers K.
Tetmajer (1805-1840); B. Zaleski
(1802-1886) and S. Goszczyński
(1801-1876)

Łowicz

10280
Muzeum (Muzeum Narodowe w
Warszawie)
Rynek Kościuszki 4, PL Łowicz, woj.
Łódź
General Museum - 1959
Coll: prehistoric and early-historic
archeology; history; ethnography;
open-air centre of folk architecture;
natural history

10281
Muzeum Baroku Polskiego
PL Łowicz, woj. Łódź
Fine Arts Museum
Coll: 17th-18th century Polish Baroque
art; applied arts; furniture; ceramics;
goldsmithery; textiles; in a former
chapel

Lubaczów

10282
Muzeum Regionalne PTTK
ul. Mickiewicza 13, PL Lubaczów, woj.
Rzeszów
General Museum
Coll: archeology; history; numismatics;
ceramics; ethnography

Lubartów

10283
Muzeum
ul. Kościuszki 28, PL Lubartów, woj.
Lublin
General Museum - 1970;
Coll: ethnography; numismatics;
history; archeology; 19th century
ceramic manifactury

Lublin

10284
Muzeum Józefa Czechowicza
(Muzeum Okręgowe, Lublin) (Józef
Czechowicz Museum)
ul. Narutowicza 10, PL Lublin
Historic Site - 1968
Coll: memorabilia on the poet Jozef
Czechowicz (1903-1939); in a 17th
century cloister

10285
Muzeum Okręgowe (District
Museum)
Zamek, ul. Zamkowa 9, PL Lublin
General Museum - 1906
Coll: archeology; ethnography; Polish
and foreign painting, graphics and
applied art; numismatics; iconographic
collection; history - library

10286
Muzeum Zoologiczne
ul. Królewska 6, PL Lublin
Natural History Museum - 1946
Coll: zoology; vertebrates and
invertebrates

Łuków

10287
Muzeum Regionalne
ul. Świerczewskiego 23, PL Łuków,
woj. Lublin
General Museum - 1964
Coll: folk art; weaving; local history;
documents from the years of Nazi
occupation

Majdanek

10288
Państwowe Muzeum na Majdanku
(State Museum at Majdanek)
PL Majdanek, woj. Lublin
History/Public Affairs Museum - 1944
Former concentration camp; gas
chambers; crematorium; prisoners'
barracks; history of the Nazi policy of
extermination; resistance movement;
archives; documents; photographs -
library

Malbork

10289
Muzeum Zamkowe (Castle Museum)
PL Malbork, woj. Gdańsk
History/Public Affairs Museum - 1961
Coll: arms; medals; history of the
castle; amber collection; archeology;
medieval sculptures; numismatics; in a
13th-14th century castle, built by the
Teutonic Knights

Markow Szczawiny

10290
Muzeum Turystyki Górskiej
Markow Szczawiny, PL Markow
Szczawiny, woj. Kraków
History/Public Affairs Museum - 1966
Coll: history of mountain tourism

Miechów

10291
**Muzeum Regionalne Ziemi
Miechowskiej** (Museum of Miechów
Region)
ul. Racławicka 2, PL Miechów, woj.
Kraków
General Museum - 1912
Coll: natural history; geology;
prehistoric archeology; local history;
numismatics

Międzyrzecz Wielkopolski

10292
Muzeum
ul. Podzamcze 1/3, PL Międzyrzecz
Wielkopolski, woj. Zielona Góra
General Museum - 1946
Coll: archeology; ethnography; history
of art; applied arts; in a 17th-18th
century building

Międzyzdroje

10293
**Muzeum Przyrodnicze Wolińskiego
Parku Narodowego im. Adama
Wodziczki** (Adam Wodziczko Natural
History Museum of Wolin Natural
Park)
ul. Niepodległości 3, PL Międzyzdroje,
woj. Szczecin
Natural History Museum - 1962
Flora and fauna of Wolin island;
geology; dendrology; entomology;
ornithology; nature of the Baltic Coast

Mława

10294
Muzeum Ziemi Zawkrzańskiej
(Museum of the Zawkrzańska Region)
ul. Obrońców Stalingradu 5, PL Mława,
woj. Warszawa
General Museum - 1963
Coll: archeology; ethnography;
history; art; paintings by W.
Piechowski

Młynary

10295
**Zbiory Prywatne Tadeusza
Balickiego** (Private Collection of
Tadeusz Balicki)
ul. Szopena, PL Młynary, woj. Olsztyn
History/Public Affairs Museum - 1946
Coll: archeology; ceramics; crafts;
weaving; carving; numismatics; old
prints

Moræg

10296
Muzeum Johanna Gottfrieda Herdera
(Johann Gottfried Herder Museum)
Ratusz, PL Moræg, woj. Olsztyn
History/Public Affairs Museum - 1960
Furniture; coins; applied art; first
editions of works by the German
philosopher and poet Johann G.
Herder (1744-1803); local history; in a
15th century town hall

Muszyna

10297
Muzeum Regionalne PTTK
ul. Kity 26, PL Muszyna, woj. Kraków
General Museum - 1958
Coll: folklore; folk art; local history; in a
15th century building

Myślenice

10298
Muzeum Regionalne PTTK
ul. Trzeciego Maja 1a, PL Myślenice,
woj. Kraków
General Museum - 1953
Coll: ethnology; folk art; costumes;
local history; archeology; natural
history

Nakło

10299
Muzeum Ziemi Krajeńskiej
Dom Kultury, PL Nakło, woj.
Bydgoszcz
General Museum - 1964
Coll: archeology; local history

Nałęczów

10300
Muzeum Bolesława Prusa (Bolesław
Prus Museum)
Pałac Małachowskich, PL Nałęczów,
woj. Lublin
Historic Site - 1961
Life and literary work of the Polish
positivist, B. Prus (1847-1912);
manuscripts; photographs; books;
periodicals; foreign language editions

10301
**Muzeum Ruchu Spółdzielczego w
Polsce** (Museum of the Cooperative
Movement in Poland)
Chmielewskiego 4, PL Nałęczów, woj.
Lublin
History/Public Affairs Museum - 1968
Coll: history of the Polish cooperative
movement - library

10302
Muzeum Stefana Żeromskiego
(Stefan Żeromski Museum)
ul. Stefana Żeromskiego 2, PL
Nałęczów, woj. Lublin
Historic Site - 1928
Coll: memorabilia on the poet Stefan
Żeromski (1864-1925) in his summer
house

Nieborów i Arkadia

10303
Muzeum w Nieborówie i Arkadia
Muzeum Narodowe w Warszawie
PL Nieborów i Arkadia, woj. Łódź
General Museum
Coll: The Palace of Nieborów:
18th-19th century interiors; Greek and
Roman sculptures; lapidarium; Polish
and foreign painting; decorative art;
Helena Radziwill collection; in a 17th
century palace; pseudo-antique and
romantic edifices - library

Niedzica

10304
**Muzeum Wnętrz, Historii Regionu i
Etnografii Spisza** (Museum of
Interiors, Local History and
Ethnography of the Spisz Region)
PL Niedzica, woj. Kraków
History/Public Affairs Museum
Coll: old furniture; 17th-19th century
portrait gallery; in a 14th-15th century
Gothic castle

Nowa Sól

10305
Muzeum
ul. Świerczewskiego 20, PL Nowa Sól,
woj. Zielona Góra
General Museum - 1947
Coll: natural history; archeology;
militaria; numismatics; ethnology; in a
19th century palace

Nowe Miasto

10306
Muzeum Regionalne
PL Nowe Miasto, woj. Łódź
General Museum - 1961
Coll:local history

Nowe Miasto Lubawskie

10307
Muzeum Regionalne
PL Nowe Miasto Lubawskie, woj.
Olsztyn
General Museum - 1959
Coll: ethnography; domestic utensils;
ceramics; archeology; history; in a
14th century Gothic building

Nowogród Łomżyński

10308
Muzeum Kurpiowskie Muzeum
Regionalne, Łomz05a (The Kurpie
Museum)
PL Nowogród Łomżyński, woj.
Byałystok
Agriculture Museum
Coll: apiculture; beehives; apiarian
equipment; farm implements;
handmills; domestic utensils

Nowy Jasieniec

10309
Muzeum Rolniczo-Pryrodnicze
PL Nowy Jasieniec, woj. Bydgoszcz
Natural History Museum
Agricultural and natural sciences

Nowy Sæcz

10310
Muzeum
ul. Lwowska 3, PL Nowy Sæcz, woj.
Kraków
General Museum - 1938
Coll: natural history; archeology;
history; art; sacral painting and
sculptures; 400 paintings by Nikifor
(also known as Matejko)

Nowy Targ

10311
Muzeum Ziemi Nowotarskiej
ul. Szaflarska 1, PL Nowy Targ, woj.
Kraków
General Museum - 1962
Coll: history; ethnography; interiors

Nysa

10312
Muzeum
ul. Marcinkowskiego 1, PL Nysa, woj.
Opole
General Museum - 1897
Coll: archeology: relics from the
13th-14th centuries; ethnography:
glass painting collection; history: guild
documents; art: old furniture (16th-19th
centuries); Italian Manneristic painting;
Dutch painting; paintings from the
workshop of Lucas Cranach the Elder

Oblęgorek

10313
Muzeum Henryka Sienkiewicza
(Henryk Sienkiewicz Museum)
PL Oblęgorek, woj. Kielce
Historic Site - 1958
Coll: memorial to the writer Henryk
Sienkiewicz (1846-1916); interiors;
photographs; letters; portraits;
translations

Odolanów

10314
Muzeum Regionalne
PL Odolanów, woj. Poznań
General Museum - 1963
Coll: costumes; rural musical
instruments; straw articles; carvings;

Ojców

10315
Muzeum
PL Ojców, woj. Kraków
General Museum - 1951
Coll: local history; natural history

Olesno

10316
**Muzeum Regionalne im. Jana
Nikodema Jaronia** (Nikodem Jaroń
Regional Museum)
ul. Pieloka 18, PL Olesno, woj. Opole
General Museum - 1960
Coll: ethnography; farmhouse interior;
history of the struggle for national
liberation in the 19th-20th centuries

Oliwa

10317
**Filia Muzeum Narodowego w
Gdańsku** (Branch of the National
Museum in Gdańsk)
ul. Cystersów 15, PL Oliwa, woj.
Gdańsk
General Museum - 1965
Ethnographical Department: folk art;
domestic utensils; Gallery of
Contemporary Gdańsk Art; in a
historical baroque palace

Olkusz

10318
Muzeum PTTK
pl. 15 Grudnia, PL Olkusz, woj. Kraków
General Museum
Coll: prehistory and history of Olkusz;
silver mining

Olsztyn

10319
Muzeum Mazurskie (Mazurian
Museum)
ul. Zamkowa 2, PL Olsztyn
General Museum - 1945
Coll: archeology; ethnography;
medieval and modern art;
contemporary art; decorative and
applied arts; natural history; in a 14th
century castle - library

Olsztynek

10320
Muzeum Budownictwa Ludowego
Muzeum Mazurskie (Museum of Folk
Architecture)
PL Olsztynek, woj. Olsztyn
Anthropology Museum - 1926
18 examples of regional wooden
architecture; wooden Masurian
church; inn; two windmills; interiors

Opinogóra

10321
Muzeum Romantyzmu (Museum of
Romanticism)
PL Opinogóra, woj. Warszawa
History/Public Affairs Museum - 1961
Coll: history of the period of
Romanticism; mementoes connected
with Zygmunt Krasiński (1812-1859),
one of the leading poets of Polish
Romanticism; in a small 19th century
Neo-Gothic castle

Opoczno

10322
Muzeum Regionalne
PL Opoczno, woj. Kielce
General Museum
Coll: local history; folk art;
ethnography; in a Gothic castle

Opole

10323
Muzeum Ślæska Opolskiego (Museum
of Opole Silesia)
Mały Rynek 7, PL Opole
General Museum - 1900
Coll: Div. of Archeology: Paleolithic;
Neolithic, Bronze Age; Hallstatt, La
Tène, Roman, Early Medieval Period;
Div. of History: history of the city and
region of Opole, especially the Silesian
Plebiscit period and Silesian Uprising;
Div. of Art: medieval and modern
sculptures; Polish painting of the
19th-20th centuries; Div. of Natural
History; in a 17th century building

Opole-Bierkowice

10324
Muzeum Wsi Opolskiej (Museum of
the Opole Countryside)
PL Opole-Bierkowice
Open Air Museum - 1961
Coll: wooden architecture; interiors

Oporów

10325
Muzeum
PL Oporów, woj. Łódź
General Museum - 1949
Coll: furniture; 15th century Gothic
table; 16th century Renaissance
cupboard; in a 15th century Gothic
castle

Ostrów Lednicki

10326
Muzeum
PL Ostrów Lednicki, woj. Poznań
Open Air Museum
Coll: 8th-9th century settlement; ruins
of a temple; 10th-11th century
palatium; folk architecture

Ostrowiec Świętokrzyski

10327
Muzeum Regionalne
ul. Parkowa 2, PL Ostrowiec
Świętokrzyski, woj. Kielce
General Museum - 1966
Coll: local history; history of regional
metallurgy; porcelain and faience
production; in a 19th century palace of
the Wielopolski family

Ostrzyce

10328
Punkt Muzealny
PL Ostrzyce, woj. Gdańsk
General Museum
Coll: Kashubian farm cottage with
complete interior

Oświęcim

10329
**Państwowe Muzeum Oświęcim-
Brzezinka** (State Museum of
Oświęcim-Brzezinka (Auschwitz-
Birkenau))
PL Oświęcim, woj. Kraków
History/Public Affairs Museum - 1947
Memorial of the Martyrdom of the
Polish Nation on the grounds of the
former concentration camp Auschwitz-
Birkenau, established in 1940. About
four million people of various
nationalities were murdered in the
camp; history of extermination;
photographs; documents; camp
prison; torture cells; instrumens of
torture; gas chambers; crematoria;
library

Pabianice

10330
Muzeum Regionalne
pl. Obrońców Stalingradu 1, PL
Pabianice, woj. Łódź
General Museum - 1907
Coll: archeology and history;
ethnography (collection of Central
Africa and Asia); folk art of the region;
natural history; in a 16th century estate

Pasym

10331
Muzeum Regionalne
PL Pasym, woj. Olsztyn
General Museum - 1966
Coll: local history; ethnography

Pelpin

10332
Muzeum Diecezjalne (Diocesan
Museum)
PL Pelpin, woj. Gdańsk
Religious Art Museum - 1928
Coll: medieval painting and sculpture
from Pomerania; in an episcopal
palace

Pieskowa Skała

10333
Muzeum Zamkowe Państwowe
Zbiory Sztuki na Wawelu, Kraków
(Castle Museum)
PL Pieskowa Skała, woj. Krako%ow
Fine Arts Museum
Coll: European art from the Middle
Ages to the 19th century in a 14th
century castle; history of the castle -
library

Piła

10334
Muzeum Stanisława Staszica
ul. Browarna 18, PL Piła, woj. Poznań
Historic Site - 1951
Coll: memorial to the poet Stanisław
Staszic (1755-1826) in his birthplace;
letters; first editions of his
publications; natural history; drawings;
Staszic's geological maps; history of
the town and region of Piła

Piotrków Trybunalski

10335
Muzeum Pańswowe
pl. Zamkowy 4, PL Piotrków
Trybunalski, woj. Łódź
General Museum - 1908
Coll: archeology; history; art;
numismatics; ethnography

Płock

10336
Muzeum Diecezjalne (Diocesan
Museum)
ul. Tumska 3A, PL Płock, woj.
Warszawa
Religious Art Museum - 1903
Coll: sculpture; Italian, Dutch, French,
Spanish and Polish painting;
woodcuting; goldsmithery; textiles;
liturgical garments; glassware and
ceramics; history

Płosk

10337
Muzeum Mazowieckie (Mazovian
Museum)
ul. Tumska 2, PL Płosk, woj. Warszawa
General Museum - 1820
Coll: Polish painting; applied art;
contemporary art; art Nouveau; folk
sculpture; history of the region;
petrochemical industry; archeology;
ethnography

Poddębice

10338
Muzeum Regionalne
PL Poddębice, woj. Łódź
General Museum - 1961
Coll: local history; in a historical
late-Renaissance palace

Podegrodzie

10339
Muzeum Regionalne
PL Podegrodzie, woj. Kraków
General Museum - 1961
Coll: folk art and culture; crafts; farm
implements

Police

10340
Izba Pamiætek Obozowych
PL Police, woj. Szczecin
History/Public Affairs Museum - 1965
Coll: local collection; in a former SS
prisoners' camp, where thousands of
prisoners were murdered

Polichno

10341
Muzeum Czynu Partyzanckiego
Muzeum, Piotrków Trybunalski
(Museum of Partisan Struggle)
PL Polichno, woj. Piotrków
History/Public Affairs Museum
Coll: history of the partisan struggle;
maps; uniforms; mementoes

Poręba Wielka

10342
**'Orkanówka', dom Władysława
Orkana**
PL Poręba Wielka, woj. Kraków
Historic Site
Coll: memorabilia of the poet
Władysław Orkan (1875-1930); family
belongings

Poronin

10343
Muzeum Lenina (Muzeum Lenina w
Krakowie)
PL Poronin, woj. Kraków
History/Public Affairs Museum - 1947
Coll: memorabilia of V.I. Lenin and his
stay in Poland 1912-1914 - library

Poznan

10344
Muzeum Archeologiczne
Pałac Gorków, ul. Wodna 27, PL
Poznań
Archeology Museum
Coll: archeological relics from the
Stone Age, early Bronze Age, middle
and late Bronze Age, early Iron Age
(Lusatian Culture), La Tène Period,
early Medieval Period - library

10345
Muzeum Archidiecezjalne
(Archdiocesan Museum)
ul. Lubrańskiego 1, PL Poznań
Religious Art Museum - 1893
Coll: sacral painting and sculptures;
applied art; textiles; numismatics -
library

10346
**Muzeum Fabryczne przy Zakładach
Hipolita Cegielskiego**
PL Poznań
Science/Tech Museum - 1966
Coll: machinery; development of
industrial technology; history of the
labour movement

10347
Muzeum Historii Miasta Poznania
Muzeum Narodowe w Poznaniu
Stary Ratusz, PL Poznań
History/Public Affairs Museum - 1954
Coll: history of the town from the 13th
century to the present day; in
13th-14th century city hall

10348
**Muzeum Historii Ruchu
Robotniczego im. Marcina Kasprzaka**
(M. Kasprzak Museum of the History
of the Labour Movement)
PL Poznań
History/Public Affairs Museum
Coll: history of the labour movement,
especially in the Great Poland region;
documents; photographs; memorials
of revolutionary leaders; art; lodged in
an 18th century neo-classical building

10349
Muzeum Instrumentów Muzycznych
Muzeum Narodowe w Poznaniu
Stary Rynek 45, PL Poznań
Science/Tech Museum - 1945
Collection of over 750 musical
instruments; 16th-20th century Polish
stringed instruments; memorials of
Frédéric Chopin; folk instruments;
musical instruments from
archeological excavations

10350
Muzeum Kultury i Sztuki Ludowej
Muzeum Narodowe w Poznaniu
(Museum of Folk Culture and Art)
ul. Grobla 25, PL Poznań
Anthropology Museum - 1911
Coll: carved roadside posts from
Great Poland; folk painting and
sculpture; costumes; ceramics;
exhibits from New Guinea, Africa,
Asia; pre-Columbian Central American
ceramics

10351
Muzeum Martyrologii (Museum of
Martyrdom)
ul. Polska, PL Poznań
History/Public Affairs Museum
Coll: mementoes and documents,
relating to the time of World War II
and Nazi occupation

10352
Muzeum Narodowe w Poznaniu
(National Museum)
al. Marcinkowskiego 9, PL Poznań
General Museum - 1857
Div. of Medieval Art; Gallery of Polish
Painting; Gallery of Contemporary
Polish Art; Gallery of Foreign Painting;
Cabinet of Prints - library

10353
Muzeum Przyrodnicze
ul. Świerczewskiego 19, PL Poznan
Natural History Museum - 1924
Coll: domestic fauna; history of the
earth

10354
Muzeum Rzemiosł Artystycznych
(Museum of Decorative Arts and
Crafts)
Góra Przemysława 1, PL Poznań
Decorative Arts Museum - 1965
Coll: Chinese Sung bowls; 14th
century Korean ceramics; Italian
majolicas; Dutch faience; old Venetian
glassware; 16th-19th century clocks;
arms; tin and silver tableware;
furniture; tapestries; Roman portrait
sculptures; numismatics; in a 13th
century castle

10355
Muzeum Wyzwolenia Muzeum
Historii Ruchu Robotniczego (Museum
of the Liberation)
na Cytadeli, PL Poznań
History/Public Affairs Museum
History of growth of the Prussian
fortress Poznań; history of the Citadel;
struggle for liberation of Great Poland
and Poznań in World War II; heavy
arms

10356
Wielkopolskie Muzeum Wojskowe
Muzeum Narodowe w Poznaniu (The
Great Poland Military Museum)
Stary Rynek, PL Poznań
History/Public Affairs Museum - 1963
Coll: Polish and foreign weapons and
armaments; liberation struggles in
Great Poland (1848; 1918; 1945);
uniforms; banners

Pranie

10357
**Muzeum Konstantego I.
Gałczyńskiego**
PL Pranie, woj. Olsztyn
Historic Site
Coll: memorabilia of the poet-satirist K.
I. Gałczyński (1905-1953); in a forest
cottage

Prudnik

10358
Muzeum Muzeum Ślæska Opolskiego
w Opolu
PL Prudnik, woj. Opole
General Museum - 1959
Coll: local history

Przemysł

10359
Muzeum Diecezjalne (Diocesan
Museum)
pl. Czackiego 10, PL Przemysł, woj.
Rzeszów
Religious Art Museum - 1902
Coll: painting; sculpture; applied arts;
liturgical garments; in a 17th century
church

Przeworsk

10360
Muzeum
Ratusz, PL Przeworsk, woj. Rzeszów
General Museum - 1958
Coll: archeology; local history; applied
arts; costumes; in a 15th century city
hall

Pszczyna

10361
Muzeum
PL Pszczyna, woj. Katowice
General Museum - 1946
Coll: interiors; paintings; sculptures;
graphics; tapestries; textiles; ceramics;
glass; goldsmithery; arms;
numismatics; archeology;
ethnography; in a 18th century palace

Puck

10362
Muzeum Rybackie (Fishing Museum)
ul. Morska, PL Puck, woj. Gdańsk
Anthropology Museum
Coll: fishing history; models of boats
and cutters

Puławy

10363
Muzeum Regionalne
PL Puławy, woj. Lublin
General Museum - 1949
Coll: archeology; ethnography;
graphics; paintings; furniture

Pułkowo Wielkie

10364
Muzeum Ziemi Dobrzynskiej
PL Pułkowo Wielkie, woj. Bydgoszcz
General Museum
Coll: folk architecture; folk art and
material culture; in 17th-18th century
farmhouse

Puszczykowo

10365
**Muzeum Wielkopolskiego Parku
Narodowego** (Museum of the Great
Poland National Park)
PL Puszczykowo, woj. Poznań
Natural History Museum - 1952
Coll: natural history; environmental
sciences

Pyzdry

10366
**Muzeum Regionalne Ziemi
Pyzderskiej** (Museum of the Region of
Pyzdry)
pl. Wolności 17, PL Pyzdry, woj.
Poznań
General Museum - 1957
Coll: arms; guild books; documents;
costumes; numismatics; local history

Rabka Zdrój

10367
Muzeum im. Władysława Orkana
ul. Sædecka 13, PL Rabka Zdrój, woj.
Kraków
General Museum - 1936
Coll: fishing; hunting; sheepherding;
crafts; costumes; folk culture; folk art

Racibórz

10368
Muzeum
ul. Chopina 12, PL Racibórz, woj.
Opole
General Museum - 1927
Coll: archeology; ethnography; art;
history; Egyptian section

Radom

10369
Muzeum
ul. Nowotki 12, PL Radom, woj. Kielce
General Museum - 1923
Coll: 19th-20th century Polish painting;
ethnography; archeology; history

Radzyn Chełmiński

10370
Muzeum Regionalne Muzeum Ziemi
Bydgorskiej im. L. Wyczółkowskiego
PL Radzyn Chełmiński, woj.
Bydgoszcz
General Museum
Coll: local history in the 13th-14th
century castle of the Teutonic Knights

Rawa Mazowiecka

10371
Muzeum Ziemi Rawskie
pl. Świerczewskiego 9, PL Rawa
Mazowiecka, woj. Łódź
History/Public Affairs Museum - 1963
Coll: archeology; numismatics;
ethnography

Rawicz

10372
Muzeum Ziemi Rawickiej
Rynek 1, Ratusz, Rawicz, woj. Poznań
General Museum - 1972
Coll: archeology; history;
ethnography;

Rogalin

10373
Muzeum Muzeum Narodowe w
Poznaniu
PL Rogalin, woj. Poznań
Fine Arts Museum - 1949
Coll: Italian and Dutch baroque
furniture; tapestry; Meissen porcelain;
Polish painting and sculpture; French
and German painting from the
Romantic period; French
impressionists

Romanów

10374
**Muzeum Józefa Ignacego
Kraszewskiego** (Józef Kraszewski
Museum)
mail c/o Post Office: Sosnówka, PL
Romanów, woj. Lublin
Historic Site - 1962
Coll: memorial to the writer J.I.
Kraszewski (1812-1887); manuscripts;
paintings; drawings; photos; various
editions of his works

Ropczyce

10375
Muzeum Miejskie (Municipal
Museum)
ul. J. Kochanowskiego 15, PL
Ropczyce, woj. Rzeszów
General Museum - 1962
Coll: archeology; folk art; history;
crafts

Rozewie

10376
**Muzeum Latarnictwa w Latarni
Morskiej** Muzeum Morskiego w
Gdańsku (The Lighthouse Museum)
PL Rozewie, woj. Gdańsk
History/Public Affairs Museum - 1963
Coll: Polish coast lighthouse;
navigation instruments; mementoes to
the writer S. Żeromski, connected with
his stay at Rozewie; lodged in a
lighthouse

Rybnik

10377
Muzeum
Rynek 18, PL Rybnik, woj. Katowice
General Museum - 1958
Coll: ethnography; archeology; history
and culture of the region; coal mining

Rzeszów

10378
Muzeum Okręgowe (District
Museum)
ul. Trzeciego Maja 19, PL Rzeszów
General Museum - 1935
Coll: archeology; ethnography; art;
applied art; history; mementoes -
library

Samsonów

10379
Zabytkowy Wielki Piec Muzeum
Techniki w Warszawie (Historic Blast
Furnace)
PL Samsonów, woj. Kielce
Science/Tech Museum
Coll: old blast furnace

Sandomierz

10380
Muzeum
Rynek 10, PL Sandomierz, woj. Kielce
General Museum - 1956
Coll: archeology; ethnography;
numismatics

10381
Muzeum Diecezjalne (Diocesan
Museum)
ul. Długosza 9, PL Sandomierz, woj.
Kielce
Religious Art Museum - 1905
Coll: archeology; 18th-19th century
glass painting; ceramics; old Polish
noblemen's national dress ; furniture;
15th-19th century religious painting of
the Cracow school; tapestry; textiles

Sanok

10382
Muzeum Budownictwa Ludowego
(Museum of Folk Architecture)
ul. Traugutta 3, PL Sanok, woj.
Rzeszow
General Museum - 1958
The Museum represents the ethnic
group of Dolinianie, Pogórzanie,
Łemkowie and Bojkowie; folk
architecture; churches; cottages;
water-mill and windmill; beehives;
Russian icons - library

10383
Muzeum Historyczne w Sanoku
ul. Zamkowa 2, PL Sanok, woj.
Rzeszów
History/Public Affairs Museum - 1934
Coll: archeology; numismatics;
orthodox church art (Poland's largest
collection of icons, dating from the
14th to the 19th century); painting
gallery; ethnography; weapons and
arms - library

Siedlice

10384
Muzeum Ziemi Podlaskiej (Museum
of the Region of Podlasie)
PL Siedlice, woj. Warszawa
General Museum
Coll: history; folk art; in an 18th
century baroque city hall

Siekierki

10385
Punkt Muzealny
PL Siekierki, woj. Szczecin
History/Public Affairs Museum
Coll: memorial to the soldiers of Polish
Army; arms; uniforms; archeology

Sielpia Wielka

10386
Muzeum Zagłębia Staropolskiego
Muzeum Techniki w Warszewie
(Museum of the Old Poland Basin)
PL Sielpia Wielka, woj. Kielce
Science/Tech Museum
Coll: industrial technology; old foundry

Sieradz

10387
Muzeum
ul. Dominikańska 2, PL Sieradz, woj.
Łódź
General Museum - 1953
Div. of Archeology: relics from the
Stone, Bronze and Iron Age, period of
the Great Migration, Middle Ages; Div.
of Ethnography: folk art; lace;
ceramics; musical instruments; crafts;
farm implements; Div. of Art: Polish
painting; sculpture; applied art; Div. of
Natural History: paleontology - library

Sierpc

10388
Muzeum Etnograficne
pl. Jedności Robotniczej, ratusz, PL
Sierpc, woj. Warszawa
Anthropology Museum
Coll: folk sculptures; ethnography;
local history

Siołkowice

10389
Izba Jakuba Kania (The Room of
Jakub Kania)
PL Siołkowice, woj. Opole
Historic Site - 1964
Coll: memorial to the Silesian poet
Jakub Kania (1872-1957) in the house
where the poet lived and worked

Skoczów

10390
Muzeum Gustawa Morcinka
Muzeum, Cieszyn (Gustaw Morcinek
Museum)
PL Skoczów, woj. Katowice
Historic Site - 1965
Coll: memorial to the Silesian poet
Gustav Morcinek (1891-1963); in his
former villa; original interior; books;
manuscripts; documents from the
concentration camp where the poet
was imprisoned - library

Słupia Nowa

10391
Muzeum Starożytnego Hutnictwa
Muzeum Techniki w Warszawie
(Museum of Ancient Metallurgy)
PL Słupia Nowa, woj. Kielce
Science/Tech Museum
Coll: history of metallurgy in the region
of the Świętokrzyskie Mountains;
furnaces; documents and mementoes
connected with the struggle for
independence and World War II

Służewo

10392
Izba Pamiætek po Fryderyku Chopinie
(Frédéric Chopin Memorial Room)
PL Służewo, woj. Bydgoszcz PL
Historic Site - 1968
Coll: memorabilia of the composer
Frédéric Chopin (1810-1849)

Śmiełów

10393
**Muzeum Regionalne Powiatu
Jarocinskiego** (Regional Museum of
Jarocin County)
PL Śmiełów, woj. Poznań
History/Public Affairs Museum
Coll: memorial to the poets Adam
Mickiewicz and Henryk Sienkiewicz;
in a palace dated 1797

Sobieszów

10394
**Muzeum Przyrodnicze
Karkonoskiego Parku** (Natural
History Museum of the Karkonosze
National Park)
ul. Chałubińskiego 23, PL Sobieszów,
woj. Wroclaw
Natural History Museum
Coll: geology; flora and fauna of the
Park; environmental sciences

Sobótka

10395
Muzeum Ślęży Muzeum
Archeologiczne, Wrocław
ul. Armii Czerwonej 9, PL Sobótka,
woj. Wrocław
General Museum - 1962
Coll: archeology; art; natural history;
local history; lapidarium; in a 16th
century building

Sosnowiec

10396
Związkowe Muzeum Górnicze (Mining Trade-Union Museum)
Dom Kultury 'Gornik' ul. Tomasza Bando 10, PL Sosnowiec, woj. Katowice
Science/Tech Museum - 1947
Coll: mining; material culture; geology; technical drawings; photographs

Środa Śląska

10397
Muzeum Miasta Środy Śląskiej (Municipal Museum)
Ratusz, PL Środa Śląska, woj. Wrocław
General Museum - 1964
Coll: 16th-17th century furniture; local history

Stara Kuźnica

10398
Kuźnia Wodna Muzeum Techniki w Warszawie (Water Forge)
PL Stara Kuźnica, woj. Kielce
Science/Tech Museum
Old forge driven by water; 18th century equipment

Stara Święta

10399
Zagroda Krajeńska (Muzeum Ziemi Złotowskiej) (Krajna Homestead)
PL Stara Święta, woj. Koszalin
Open Air Museum
Coll: folk architecture; peasant life; interiors

Stare Drawsko

10400
Rezerwat Archeologiczny (Archeological Reserve)
PL Stare Drawsko, woj. Koszalin
Archeology Museum
Coll: finds from a 7th-12th century medieval settlement; in an early Gothic castle

Stargard Szczeciński

10401
Muzeum Regionalne
Rynek Staromiejski 2-3, PL Stargard Szczeciński, woj. Szczecin
General Museum - 1960
Coll: archeology; history; art; militaria

Stary Sacz

10402
Muzeum Towarzystwa Miłośnikow Starego Sącza (Museum of the Society of Frends of Stary Sącz)
Rynek 6, PL Stary Sacz, woj. Kraków
General Museum - 1947
Coll: folk sculptures from the 18th-19th century; crafts; ceramics; local history

Stębark

10403
Muzeum Grunwaldzkie (Grunwald Museum)
Pole Bitwy 28, PL Stębark, woj. Olsztyn
History/Public Affairs Museum - 1960
Coll: militaria; archeological finds from the Battle of Grunwald in the 15th century

Strzeżów

10404
Zbiory Prywatne Juliana Piwowarskiego (Privat Collection of Julian Piwowarski)
PL Strzeżów, woj. Kraków
History/Public Affairs Museum
Coll: numismatics; Roman coins; 12th century Polish silver dinars

Strzyżów

10405
Muzeum Społeczne
ul. Mickiewicza 10, PL Strzyżów, woj. Rzeszów
General Museum
Coll: local history

Sulejów

10406
Izba Regionalna Polskiego Towarzystwa Turystyczno-Krajoznawczego (Regional Room of the PTTK)
PL Sulejów, woj. Łódź
General Museum
Coll: finds from the former Cistercian abbey; stone heraldry; local ceramics; wooden sculptures; paintings; numismatics; ethnography; memorials of the writer Lucjan Rudnicki

Sulmierzyce

10407
Muzeum Ziemi Sulmierzyckiej im. S.F.Klonowica (S.F.Klonowic Museum of the Sulmierzyce Region)
Stary Ratusz, PL Sulmierzyce, woj. Poznań
General Museum - 1957
Coll: Stone and Bronze Age finds; costumes; crafts; guilds; local history; in a wooden Town Hall dated 1743

Suraż

10408
Punkt Muzealny (Museum Centre)
PL Suraż, woj. Byałystok
General Museum
Coll: archeological finds from an 11th century medieval castle

Suwałki

10409
Muzeum Ziemi Suwalskiej (Museum of the Suwałki Region)
ul. Kościuszki 81, PL Suwałki, woj. Białystok
General Museum
Coll: geology; mineralogy; archeology; ethnography; history; art

Świdnica

10410
Muzeum Kupiectwa (Museum of Old Silesian Trade)
PL Świdnica, woj. Wrocław
History/Public Affairs Museum - 1967
Coll: crafts; weights and measures; local history

Świerzawa

10411
Punkt Muzealny
PL Świerzawa, woj. Wrocław
General Museum
Local history; in a 15th century Gothic church

Święty Krzyż

10412
Muzeum Świtokrzyskiego Parku Narodowego
PL Święty Krzyż, woj. Kielce
Natural History Museum - 1954
Coll: geomorphology; synecology; geology; climatology; water; soil science; flora; vegetation; forestry

Szafarnia

10413
Ośrodek Kultu Fryderyka Chopina
PL Szafarnia, woj. Bydgoszcz
History/Public Affairs Museum - 1960;
Coll: memorial to the composer F. Chopin (1810-1849)

Szamotuły

10414
Muzeum Ziemi Szamotulskiej (Museum of the Szamotulski Region)
Zamek Górków, PL Szamotuły, woj. Poznań
General Museum - 1957
Coll: archeology; ceramics of the Lusatian Culture; ethnography; history; applied art; numismatics; in a 16th century Gothic tower

Szczecin

10415
Muzeum Narodowe (National Museum)
ul. Staromłynska 27; Wały Chrobrego 3, PL Szczecin
General Museum - 1945
Div. of Art: 13th-15th century sculptures; painting; applied art; folk carving; religious art; prints; Div. of Applied Arts: crafts; Pomeranian goldsmithery; jewels; Maritime Exhibition: models of sailing vessels from the 13th to the 19th century; present-day shipping; Div. of Ethnography: Pomeranian folk art; West African collection; ceramics; musical instruments; Div. of Archeology: Neolithic and Bronze Age exhibits; Roman finds; 9th century Slav boat; Div. of History; Div. of Numismatics

Szczecinek

10416
Muzeum
ul. Księżnej Elżbiety 6, PL Szczecinek, woj. Koszalin
General Museum - 1958
Coll: archeology; local history; in a 16th century tower

Szczekociny

10417
Muzeum Ziemi Włoszczowskiej
PL Szczekociny, woj. Kielce
General Museum
Coll: tools; weapons; ceramics; seals; documents;

Szczyrzyc

10418
Muzeum Muzeum Diecezjalne w Tanowie
PL Szczyrzyc, woj. Kraków
Religious Art Museum
Coll: religious art; painting; sculptures; liturgical vestments; prints; arms; applied arts; in an old 16th-19th century Cistercian monastery

Szczytno

10419
Muzeum
ul. Sienkiewicza 1, PL Szczytno, woj. Olsztyn
General Museum
Coll: ethnography; archeology; history; natural science

Szreniawa

10420
Muzeum Rolnictwa
PL Szreniawa, woj. Poznań
Agriculture Museum - 1964
Coll: agricultural history and economics; farming; soil science

Sztum

10421
Muzeum
PL Sztum, woj. Gdańsk
General Museum - 1968
Coll: crafts; folk culture; local history; in a Gothic castle

Sztutowo

10422
Muzeum Stutthof
PL Sztutowo, woj. Gdańsk
Open Air Museum
Former concentration camp Stutthof; gas chambers; women's barracks; barbed-wire fences; watch tower; crematorium

Szydłów

10423
Muzeum
PL Szydłów, woj. Kielce
General Museum - 1961
Coll: archeology; militaria; geology; in a Treasury, built 1528

Szydłowiec

10424
Muzeum Ludowych Instrumentów Muzycznych Muzeum Świętokrzyskie, Kielce
Zamek, PL Szydłowiec, woj. Kielce
Music Museum - 1972
Coll: folk musical instruments representing all ethnographic regions, displayed in a 16th century castle

Tarnów

10425
Muzeum Diecezjalne (Diocesan Museum)
pl. Katedralny 5, PL Tarnów, woj. Kraków
Religious Art Museum - 1888
Coll: Gothic art (painting, sculptures); applied arts; crafts; folk art

10426
Muzeum Miejskie (Municipal Museum)
ul. Kniewskiego 24, PL Tarnów, woj. Kraków
General Museum - 1927
Coll: 17th-18th century Polish portraits; 17th-19th century Italian, Dutch, French and German painting; 17th-19th century glassware; 16th-19th century European and Oriental ceramics; tapestry; ethnography - library

Tarnowskie Góry

10427
Muzeum Rud Metali Nieżelaznych
(Museum of Non-Ferrous Metal Ores)
Rynek 1, PL Tarnowskie Góry
Science/Tech Museum
Coll: iron mining; old 17th century
mine

Tomaszów Lubelski

10428
**Muzeum Regionalne im. Janusza
Petera**
ul. Grunwaldzka, PL Tomaszów
Lubelski, woj. Lublin
General Museum - 1902
Coll: archeology; ethnography; history

Tomaszów Mazowiecki

10429
Muzeum
ul. Armii Ludowej, PL Tomaszów
Mazowiecki, woj. Łódź
General Museum - 1927
Coll: ethnography; history; natural
science; archeology

Toruń

10430
Muzeum Etnograficzne
Wały Gen. Sikorskiego 13, PL Toruń,
woj. Bydgoszcz
Anthropology Museum
Coll: fishing implements; hunting;
domestic utensils; folk art; furniture;
ceramics; spoken folklore (fables,
legends, proverbs, folk dances);
costumes; homestead from the
Kuyavia region

10431
Muzeum Okregowe
Rynek Staromiejski 1, PL Toruń, woj.
Bydgoszcz
General Museum
Coll: medieval art; modern painting
and sculpture; graphics; in an old
Town Hall, dated 1393

10432
Oddział Archeologii Muzeum
Okręgowe (Archeological Branch of
the Regional Museum in Toruń)
ul. Ciasnej 6-8, PL Toruń, woj.
Bydgoszcz
Archeology Museum - 1968
Coll: archeological finds from the
Neolithic Age; militaria and
adornments from the Bronze Age;
Roman relics

10433
**Oddział Historii i Kultury Miasta oraz
Regionu** Muzeum Okręgowe
(Departments of the History and
Culture of the Town and Region)
ul. Przedzamcze 4, PL Toruń, woj.
Bydgorszcz
History/Public Affairs Museum
Studies of the town and region; recent
history; in a Baroque building

10434
Oddział Mikolaja Kopernika Muzeum
Okręgowe
ul. Kopernika 15/17, PL Toruń, woj.
Bydgoszcz
Historic Site - 1960
The Museum is located in two burgher
houses from the 14th and 15th
centuries. House at ul. Kopernika 15:
furniture; applied art; medieval
architectonic decoration. House at ul.
Kopernika 17: birth house of N.
Copernicus; old books; astronomical
instruments; portraits; prints;
documents

10435
Sztuka Dalekiego Wschodu Muzeum
Okręgowe (Far Eastern Art Museum)
PL Toruń, woj. Bydgoszcz
Fine Arts Museum
Coll: decorative arts and crafts;
applied arts; art of China, Japan, India,
Siam, Tibet, and Vietnam; precious and
semi-precious stones; painting;
graphics; fabrics and furniture

10436
Zamek Krzyżacki (Castle of the
Teutonic Knights)
ul. Przedzamcze 3, PL Toruń, woj.
Bydgoszcz
Archeology Museum
Coll: Lusatian culture (10th-4th century
B.C.); finds from the pre Teutonic
settlement; early-medieval ceramics;
medieval architectonic details; militaria;
banners

Toszek

10437
Muzeum Ziemi Toszeckiej (Muzeum
w Gliwicach)
Zamek, PL Toszek, woj. Katowice
General Museum - 1963
Coll: local history; militaria; guild relics;
documents; furniture; in a 15th century
castle

Trzcianka Lubuska

10438
Muzeum im. Wiktora Stachowiaka
ul. Żeromskiego 36a, PL Trzcianka
Lubuska, woj. Poznań
General Museum - 1971
Coll: archeology; history

Ulucz

10439
**Oddział Muzeum Budownictwa
Ludowego w Sanoku**
PL Ulucz, woj. Rzeszów
Religious Art Museum
Larchwood Orthodox church from
1510; valuable iconostasis from 1682
painted by Stefan Dzengałowicz

Wałbrzych

10440
Muzeum
ul. 1.Maja 9, PL Wałbrzych, woj.
Wrocław
General Museum - 1908
Coll: natural history; mining; geology;
local history; porcelain

Warka-Winary

10441
Muzeum im. Kazimierza Pułaskiego
PL Warka-Winary, woj. Warszawa
Historic Site - 1967
Coll: memorial to General Kazimir
Pulaskî, hero of Polish and American
history, his role in the War of
Independence; memorials to 19th
century political émigrés

Warszawa

10442
**Biblioteka, Muzeum i Archiwum
Warszawskiego Towarzystwa
Muzycznego im. Stanisława
Moniuszki** (Library, Museum and
Archives of the Stanisław Moniuszko
Warsaw Musical Society)
ul. Zakroczymska 2, PL Warszawa
Music Museum
Coll: mementoes of Polish composers:
Moniuszko, S.; Kamieński, M.; Stefani,
J.; Karłowicz, J.; Noskowski, M.;
Elsner, J.; Dobrzyński, I.F.; letters;
musical editions - library

10443
**Gabinet Numizmatyczny Mennicy
Państwowej**
Numismatic Cabinet of the State Mint,
PL Warszawa
History/Public Affairs Museum
Collection of speciments of the
Warsaw mint from the 18th century to
the present day; coins; medals;
medallions; stamps; plaques; insignia

10444
**Gabinet Rycin Biblioteki
Uniwersyteckiej**
ul. Krakowskie Przedmieście 32, PL
Warszawa
Fine Arts Museum
Coll: engravings of the Royal
collection from the 17th-18th
centuries; Polish portraits;
architectonic and decorative drawings;
Stanisław Potocki Collection;
19th-20th century lithographs;
contemporary graphics;

10445
**Instytut Zoologiczny Polskiej
Akademii Nauk** (Zoological Institute of
the Polish Academy of Sciences)
ul. Świętokrzyska, Pałac Kultury, PL
Warszawa
Natural History Museum - 1818
Coll: domestic fauna; world fauna
(European, Asian and South
American); insects, molluscs,
arachnids and crustaceans collections
- library

10446
Mauzoleum Walki i Męczeństwa
Muzeum Historii Polskiego Ruchu
Rewolucyjnego (Mausoleum of
Struggle and Martyrdom)
al. I.Armii Wojska Polskiego 25, PL
Warszawa
History/Public Affairs Museum
Coll: documents; instruments of
torture; in a former Gestapo building

10447
**Muzeum Geologiczne Instytutu
Geologicznego** (Geological Museum
of the Institute of Geology)
ul. Rakowiecka 4, PL Warszawa
Science/Tech Museum - 1919
Coll: Exhibition of Poland's minerals;
stratigraphy of Poland; paleontology;
geology; mineral resources; energy
resources; non-ferrous metals; metallic
ores - archival section

10448
**Muzeum Historii Polskiego Ruchu
Rewolucyjnego** (Museum of the
History of the Polish Revolutionary
Movement)
pl. F. Dzierżyńskiego 1, PL-00 139
Warszawa
History/Public Affairs Museum - 1957
Coll: Polish revolutionary movement
from 1794 to the present day

10449
**Muzeum Historyczne m. st.
Warszawy** (Historical Museum of the
City of Warsaw)
Rynek Starego Miasta 28-42, PL
Warszawa
History/Public Affairs Museum - 1936
Coll: history of Warsaw from the 10th
century to the present day; Ludwik
Gocel Collection - library

10450
**Muzeum im. Xawerego
Dunikowskiego w Królikarni** Muzeum
Narodowe w Warszawie (Xavery
Dunikowski Museum at Królikarnia)
ul. Puławska 113, PL Warszawa
Historic Site - 1965
Coll: memorial to the artist Xawer
Dunikowski (1875-1964); paintings;
sculptures; in an 18th century palace

10451
**Muzeum Kultury Fizycznej i
Turystyki** (Museum of Physical
Culture and Tourism)
ul. Wawelska 5, PL Warszawa
History/Public Affairs Museum - 1952
Coll: sports and tourism equipment;
documents and mementes; medals
and prizes in the field of sports and
tourism; fine arts, music, literature
devoted to sports and tourism

10452
Muzeum Lekarskie
ul. Chocimska 22, PL Warszawa
Science/Tech Museum
Coll: manuscripts, documents and
mementoes of Polish physicians;
medical instruments

10453
Muzeum Lenina (Lenin Museum)
al. Gen. K. Swierczewskiego 62, PL-00
240 Warszawa
Historic Site
Coll: life and work of V.I. Lenin
especially his stay in Poland
1912-1914; the Polish and international
revolutionary movement; paintings;
graphics

10454
**Muzeum Literatury im. Adama
Mickiewicza** (Museum of Literature)
Rynek Starego Miasta 18/20, PL
Warszawa
History/Public Affairs Museum - 1951
Coll: permanent biographical exhibition
on Adam Mickiewicz (1798-1855);
mementoes of Julian Tuwim; Maria
Dæbrowska Room; manuscripts by
Polish autors of the 18th-20th
centuries; portraits; art and historical
relics - library

10455
Muzeum Łowieckie
ul. Nowy Świat 35, PL Warszawa
Anthropology Museum - 1954
Coll: hunting trophies; hunting
equipment and arms; mammals and
birds of Poland

10456
Muzeum Marii Skłodowskiej-Curie
(Marie Curie Museum)
ul. Freta 16, PL Warszawa
Historic Site - 1968
Coll: memorial to the scientist Marie
Curie (1867-1934) in her birthplace

10457

Muzeum Narodowe w Warszawie
(National Museum)
al. Jerozolimskie 3, PL-00-495
Warszawa
Fine Arts Museum - 1862
Gallery of Ancient Art, sections:
Egyptian, Greek, Etruscan, Byzantine;
Gallery of Foreign Art: North
European School, Italian School,
Russian Painting; Medieval Art
Gallery; Modern Polish Art Gallery;
Cabinet of Miniatures; Collection of
Decorative Art; Cabinet of Drawings
and Prints; Cabinet of Coins and
Medals; Gallery of Modern Art;
Documentary Department

10458

Muzeum Plakatu
w Wilanowie, PL Warszawa
Decorative Arts Museum - 1968
Coll: 13,000 speciments of Polish and
foreign posters; applied graphic art;
sculptures

10459

Muzeum Teatralne (Theatrical
Museum)
ul. Moliera 3/5, PL Warszawa
Performing Arts Museum - 1957
Coll: history of Polish theatre since the
18th century; mementoes of Polish
actors; posters; photographs;
manuscripts; stage costumes

10460

Muzeum Techniki N O T (Museum of
Technology)
Pałac Kultury i Nauki, PL Warszawa
Science/Tech Museum - 1955
Coll: history of technology;
technological progress; popularization
of technology; mining; metallurgy;
transportation; astronautics; forestry;
timber industry; agriculture; food
industry; physics; telecommunication;
energetics; geodesy; chemistry -
library

10461

**Muzeum Towarzystwa im. Frederyka
Chopina** (Museum of the Frédéric
Chopin Society)
ul. Okólnik 1, PL Warszawa
Music Museum - 1953
Coll: works of Chopin; first editions;
letters; autographs; portraits; works
by various composers - library

10462

Muzeum w Łazienkach Muzeum
Narodowe w Warszawie (Museum at
Łazienki)
ul. Agrykola 1, PL Warszawa
Fine Arts Museum
Coll: includes the Palace on the Isle
(18th century); White Cottage (18th
century); Old Orangery with the old
theatre (18th century); Stanysław
Augustus Collection of gems; Gallery
of Polish Sculpture; Officer-Cadet
School (1788); interiors; sculptures;
painting; furniture

10463

Muzeum w Wilanowie Muzeum
Narodowe w Warszawie
PL Warszawa
History/Public Affairs Museum
17th century palace; 18th-19th century
interiors; 16th-19th century porcelain;
enamels; textiles; goldsmithery;
Gallery of Polish Portraits

10464

Muzeum Wiezienia 'Pawiak' Muzeum
Historii Polskiego Ruchu
Rewolucyjnego (Pawiak Prison
Museum)
PL Warszawa
History/Public Affairs Museum
History of the prison 'Pawiak' in the
Tsarist times; martyrdom of political
prisoners in the years of the Nazi
occupation

10465

Muzeum Władysława Broniewskiego
Muzeum Adama Mieckiewicza
(Władysław Broniewski Museum)
ul. J. Dæbiowskiego 51, PL Warszawa
Historic Site - 1963
Coll: memorial to the contemporary
poet W. Broniewski; manuscripts;
letters; first editions - library

10466

Muzeum Wodociægów (Museum of
Waterworks)
PL Warszawa
Science/Tech Museum
Coll: history of Warsaw waterworks
from 1880 to the present day

10467

Muzeum Wojska Polskiego (Polish
Army Museum)
Al. Jerozolimskie 3, PL-00-950
Warszawa
History/Public Affairs Museum - 1919
Coll: weapons; uniforms; banners;
decorations; militaria; collection of
modern paintings, sculptures and
graphics - conservation workshop;
library;

10468

**Muzeum X. Pawilonu Cytadeli
Warszawskiej** (Muzeum Historii
Polskiego Ruchu Rewolucyjnego)
(Museum of the 10th Pavilion of the
Warsaw Citadel)
ul. Skazańców 25, PL Warszawa
History/Public Affairs Museum
History collection in a citadel,
established by the Tsarist government
in 1835-39 after the November
Uprising

10469

**Muzeum Żydowskiego Institutu
Historycznego w Polsce** (Museum of
the Jewish Historical Institute in
Poland)
al. Gen. Karola Świerczewskiego 79,
PL Warszawa
History/Public Affairs Museum
Coll: history and culture of the Polish
Jews; art by Jewish artists;
ethnography; relics and documentary
photographs from the years of Nazi
occupation; manuscripts; old books -
library

10470

**Muzeum Zegarów i Rzemiosł
Artystycznych i Precyzyjnych**
(Museum of Clocks and Handicrafts)
ul. Piekarska 20, PL Warszawa
Science/Tech Museum - 1966
Coll: crafts and guilds; old clocks;
jewellry; optics; engraving;
goldsmithery

10471

Muzeum Ziemi P A N (Museum of
Earth Science of the Polish Academy
of Sciences)
al. Na Skarpie 20-26, PL Warszawa
Science/Tech Museum - 1946
Coll: geological sciences; mineralogy;
petrography; amber; paleobotany;
paleozoology; zoology; history of
geology - library

10472

Państwowe Muzeum Archeologiczne
ul. Długa 52, PL Warszawa
Archeology Museum - 1923
Coll: Paleolithic and Mesolithic
periods; Neolithic period and early
Bronze Age; Bronze and early Iron
Age; late La Tène and Roman periods;
early Medieval period; middle Ages
and later times

10473

Państwowe Muzeum Ethnograficzne
(State Ethnographic Museum)
ul. Kredytowa 1, PL Warszawa
Anthropology Museum - 1875/1946
Basic economy and handicrafts;
weaving; costumes, embroidery and
lace; folklore; painting; graphic art and
cut-out art; sculpture; non-European
cultures - library

10474

**Zbiory Graficzne Biblioteki
Narodowej** (Graphical Collection of
the National Library)
pl. Krasińskich 5, PL Warszawa
Fine Arts Museum
Coll: drawings; engravings; prints;
lithographs; photos; Czetwertyński,
Potocki and Krasiński Collections;
Wilanów albums - library

10475

**Zbiory Metrologiczne Polskiego
Komitetu Normalizacji i Miar**
(Metrological Collection of the Central
Bureau of Standards)
ul. Elektoralna 2, PL Warszawa
Science/Tech Museum - 1952
Coll: history of metrology; weights and
measures

Wdzydze Kiszewskie

10476

Muzeum
PL Wdzydze Kiszewskie, woj. Gdańsk
Open Air Museum
Coll: two Kashubian huts;
ethnography; interiors

Wejherowo

10477

**Muzeum Piśmiennictwa i Muzyki
Kaszubsko-Pomorskiej** (Museum of
Kashubian and Pomeranian Literature
and Music)
PL Wejherowo, woj. Gdańsk
History/Public Affairs Museum - 1969

Wieliczka

10478

**Muzeum Żup Krakowskich-
Wieliczka** (Museum of the Cracow
Salt Mines-Wieliczka)
Park Kingi, PL Wieliczka, woj. Kraków
Science/Tech Museum
Underground museum ; historical part
of the medieval salt mine; 17th-19th
century mining excavation; Chapel of
St. Kinga carved in salt; historical
exhibits relating to geology, natural
history, history of mining - library

Wieluń

10479

Muzeum Ziemi Wieluńskiej (Museum
of the Wieluń Region)
ul. Narutowicza 15, PL Wieluń, woj.
Łódź
General Museum - 1969
Coll: archeology; history;
ethnography; numismatics; in a former
monastery

Wierzchosławice

10480

**Muzeum Państwowego
Gospodarstwa Rolnego**
PL Wierzchosławice, woj. Bydgoszcz
Agriculture Museum
Coll: development of agriculture;
farming; folklore; costumes; crafts

Wieza Ratuszowa

10481

Muzeum Historyczne
Rynek, PL Wieza Ratuszowa, woj.
Pułtusk
History/Public Affairs Museum - 1964
Coll: archeology; numismatics; folk art;
crafts; literature; maps; Polish portraits
from the 18th century; in a 16th
century city hall tower

Wisla Zdrój

10482

Muzeum Beskidzkie Muzeum w
Cieszynie (Museum of the Beskid
Mountains)
PL Wisla Zdrój, woj. Katowice
Anthropology Museum - 1965
Coll: folk culture of the Beskid
highlanders; costumes; folk art; farm
implements; domestic utensils

Wiślica

10483

Muzeum Regionalne
PL Wiślica, woj. Kielce
General Museum
Coll: archeology; local history

Włocławek

10484

Muzeum Kujawskie (Museum of the
Kuyavian Region)
ul. Słowackiego 1a, PL Włocławek,
woj. Bydgoszcz
General Museum - 1909
Coll: archeology; history;
ethnography; art (works by Stanisław
Noakowski)

10485

Muzeum Miar Józefa Arentowicza
(Museum of Weights and Measures)
ul. Świerczewskiego 29, PL
Włocławek, woj. Bydgoszcz
Science/Tech Museum
library

Wodzisław Ślæski

10486

Muzeum
ul. Dworcowa 2, PL Wodzisław Ślæski,
woj. Katowice
General Museum
Coll: archeology; history of industry
and culture; numismatics

Wola Okrzejska

10487

Muzeum Henryka Sienkiewicza
PL Wola Okrzejska, woj. Lublin
Historic Site - 1966
Coll: memorial to the poet H.
Sienkiewicz (1846-1916); in a historical
farmstead where he was born

Wolin

10488
Muzeum Regionalne
ul. Bohaterów Stalingradu 24, PL
Wolin, woj. Szczecin
General Museum - 1966
Coll: archeology; local history of Wolin
from the 9th to the 12th century

Wolsztyn

10489
Muzeum im. Roberta Kocha
PL Wolsztyn, woj. Poznań
Historic Site - 1958
Coll: life and work of the scientist
Robert Koch (1843-1910)

10490
**Muzeum Regionalne Ziemi
Wolsztyńskiej im. Marcina Rożka**
ul. 5 Stycznia 34, PL Wolsztyn, woj.
Poznań
General Museum - 1968
Coll: memorial to the artist Marcin
Rożek, murdered by the Nazis in 1944;
sculptures; paintings; photographs

Wrocław

10491
**Dział Numizmatyczno-Sfragistyczny
Biblioteki Zakładu Narodowego im.
Ossolińskich P A N** (Cabinet of
Numismatics and Sphragistics of the
Ossoliński National Foundation, Polish
Academy of Sciences)
ul. Szewska 37, PL Wrocław
History/Public Affairs Museum - 1955
Coll: numismatics; medalography;
sphragistics; heraldry

10492
**Gabinet Grafiki Biblioteki Zakładu
Narodowego im. Ossolińskich P A N**
(Cabinet of Prints of the Ossoliński
National Foundation, Polish Academy
of Sciences)
ul. Szewska 37, PL Wrocław
Fine Arts Museum - 1817
Coll: 16th-20th century Polish and
foreign graphics; 17th-18th century
English, French, Dutch, Italian and
German graphics; 18th-19th century
Polish drawings; 16th-19th century
drawings by foreign artists (20
drawings by Rembrandt); collection of
Polish and foreign exlibrises;
photographs; miniatures - library

10493
Muzeum Archeologiczne
ul. Kazimierza Wielkiego 34, PL
Wrocław
Archeology Museum - 1945
The museum has following divisions:
Stone Age and Early Bronze Age;
Bronze Age (Lusatian Culture); Iron
Age; Early Medieval and Medieval
Age; Mediterranean Archeology; -
library

10494
Muzeum Archidiecezjalne
(Archdiocesan Museum)
ul. Kanonia 12, PL Wrocław
Religious Art Museum
Coll: Gothic sculpture and painting;
liturgical garments; goldsmithery;
Gothic altarpieces - library

10495
Muzeum Architektury
ul. Bernardyńska 5, PL Wrocław
Fine Arts Museum - 1965
Coll: architecture (ancient, medieval,
modern); town planning; drawings;
models; photographs; in a 15th-16th
century Bernardine monastery -
library

10496
Muzeum Etnograficzne (Muzeum
Narodowe, Wrocław)
ul. Kazimierza Wielkiego 33, PL
Wrocław
Anthropology Museum - 1953
Coll: farming; animal husbandry;
hunting and fishing; weaving; smithery;
pottery; folk art; Lower-Silesian culture

10497
Muzeum Narodowe
pl. Powstańców Warszawy 5, PL
Wrocław
General Museum - 1947
Divisions: Medieval Silesian Art;
Painting; Sculpture; Applied Art;
Graphic Art; Contemporary Art; Polish
Photography; Arms and National
Liberation Struggle; History of
Material Culture; Numismatics and
Sphragistics; Documents of Polish
Culture in Silesia; Documentation and
Conservation of Movable Art Objects
- library

10498
Muzeum Poczty i Telekomunikacji
(Post and Telecommunication
Museum)
ul. Krasińskiego 1, PL Wrocław
Science/Tech Museum - 1921
Coll: paintings; prints; plans of postal
and telecommunication connections;
uniforms; philatelic collection; 18th
century post office; 16th century mail
coffer; stagecoaches

10499
Muzeum Sztuki Medalierskiej
(Museum of Medallic Art)
Stary Ratusz, Rynek, PL Wrocław
Decorative Arts Museum - 1965
Coll: Polish and foreign medals,
medallions, decorations, insignia,
stamps; drawings and sketches for
medals - library

10500
**Muzeum Zoologiczne Uniwersytetu
Wrocławskiego** (Zoological Museum
of Wrocław University)
ul. Sienkiewicza 21, PL Wrocław
Natural History Museum
Coll: zoology; insects; corals; birds

10501
Stary Ratusz Muzeum Narodowe,
Wrocław (Old Town Hall)
Rynek, PL Wrocław
History/Public Affairs Museum
Coll: history of Wrocław; in a historic
building of the Old Town Hall dating
back to the 13th century; rich Gothic
and early Renaissance sculptural
decorations

10502
**Zbiory Prac Studyjnych Państwowej
Wyższej Szkoły Sztuk Plastycznych**
(Collections of Studio Works of the
State Higher School of Fine Arts)
ul. Traugutta 19/20, PL Wrocław
Fine Arts Museum - 1954
Coll: painting; sculpture; graphics;
industrial, decorative and building
ceramics; glassware; furniture

Września

10503
**Muzeum Regionalne im. Dzieci
Wrzesińskich** (Children of Września
Regional Museum)
ul. Dzieci Wrzesińskich 13, PL
Września, woj. Poznań
General Museum - 1961
Coll: local history, especially from the
period of the revolution of 1848

Wschowa

10504
Muzeum Ziemi Wschowskiej
(Museum of Wschowa Region)
pl. Jedności Robotniczej 2, PL
Wschowa, woj. Zielona Góra
General Museum
Coll: local history; numismatics;
furniture; portraits; old books; first
editions of works by Elżbieta
Drużbacka; in a 17th century baroque
house

Żagań

10505
**Muzeum Martyrologii Alianckich
Jeńców Wojennych** (Museum of the
Martyrdom of Allied Prisoners of War)
PL Żagań, woj. Zielona Góra
History/Public Affairs Museum
Documents and mementoes illustrating
the martyrdom of prisoners of war
during World War II; in a former Stalag
VIIIc camp

Żarnowiec

10506
Muzeum Marii Konopnickiej
PL Żarnowiec, woj. Rzeszów
Historic Site - 1960
Memorial to the poetess and novelist
Maria Konopnicka (1842-1910); in a
18th century house - library

Żelazowa Wola

10507
Muzeum Oddział Muzeum
Towarzystwa im. Fryderyka Chopina
w Warszawie (Frédéric Chopin House,
a Branch of the Museum of the F.
Chopin Society in Warsaw)
PL Żelazowa Wola, woj. Warszawa
Historic Site - 1932
Memorial to the composer F. Chopin
in his birthplace; documents; furniture

Żórawina

10508
Muzeum Manieryzmu Oddział
Muzeum Narodowego we Wrocławiu
(Museum of Mannerist Art)
PL Żórawina, woj. Wrocław
Fine Arts Museum
Mannerist art; in a 16th century church

Żywiec

10509
Muzeum
ul. Kościuszki 5, PL Żywiec, woj.
Kraków
General Museum - 1927
Coll: local history; guild art;
ethnography; natural history

Zabrze

10510
Muzeum
pl. Krakowski 9, PL Zabrze, woj.
Katowice
General Museum - 1935
Coll: archeology; history of Upper
Silesia; ethnography; art; mining;
metallurgy; chemical coal processing

10511
Muzeum Kopalni 'Zabrze' (Museum
of the 'Zabrze' Mine)
PL Zabrze, woj. Katowice
Science/Tech Museum - 1965
Underground museum; history of coal
mining

Zachełmie

10512
**Punkt Muzealny z pamiątkami po
kompozytorze Ludomirze Różyckim**
(L. Różycki Memorial Room)
Pan Twardowski willa, PL Zachełmie,
woj. Wrocław
Historic Site - 1958
Coll: memorabilia of the composer
Ludomir Różycki (1884-1953); his
piano; photographs; editions of his
works; libretto scripts; printed music;
portraits

Zagórze Śląskie

10513
Muzeum Regionalne
PL Zagórze Śląskie, woj. Wrocław
General Museum
Coll: arms; local history; in a 14th
century castle

Zakopane

10514
Chata 'Tea' Muzeum Tatrańskie
ul. Słowackiego 39, PL Zakopane, woj.
Kraków
Anthropology Museum
Ethnography in a mountaineer's 19th
century hut

10515
Muzeum im. Jana Kaspowicza
PL Zakopane, woj. Kraków
Historic Site - 1950
Memorial to the poet Jan Kaspowicz
(1860-1950), representative of the
'Young Poland' Movement

10516
**Muzeum Tatrańskie im. Tytusa
Chałubińskiego** (Tytus Chałubiński
Tatra Museum)
ul. Krupówski 10, PL Zakopane, woj.
Kraków
General Museum - 1888
Ethnography and natural history from
the Tatra Mountains region

10517
Punkt Muzealny
ul. Tetmajera 15, PL Zakopane, woj.
Kraków
Historic Site
Memorial to the writer Kornel
Makuszynski (1884-1953) in his former
home

Zamość

10518
Muzeum
ul. Ormiańska 26, PL Zamość, woj.
Lublin
General Museum - 1925
Coll: weapons; furniture; numismatics;
costumes; ceramics; carvings; in a
17th century building

Zawoja

10519
**Muzeum Przyrodnicze
Babiogórskiego Parku Narowego**
(Natural History Museum of Babia
Góra National Park)
Dolina Barańcowa, PL Zawoja, woj.
Kraków
Natural History Museum - 1958
Protection of nature in Babia Góra;
plants and animals under protection;
geology; hydrology; ethnography of
the Western Carpathians - library

Zbæszyń

10520
Muzeum Regionalne Ziemi Zbæszyńskiej (Regional Museum of the Zbæszyń Region)
PL Zbæszyń
General Museum - 1965
Folk art; musical instruments; in a 13th century castle

Ziębice

10521
Museum Regionalne
ul. Przemysłowa 10, PL Ziębice, woj. Wrocław
General Museum - 1931
Coll: applied art; ethnography

Zielona Góra

10522
Muzeum Ziemi Lubuskiej (Museum of the Lubusz Region)
al. Niepodległości 15, PL Zielona Góra
General Museum - 1946
Coll: archeology; ethnography; art; wine-making; natural history

Złotów

10523
Muzeum Ziemi Złotowskiej
al. Wojska Polskiego 2a, PL Złotów, woj. Koszalin
General Museum
Local history; archeology; ethnography
10524
Park Etnograficzny
PL Złotów, woj. Koszalin
Anthropology Museum
Ethnography; wooden architecture; contemporary folk art

Złoty Stok

10525
Punkt Muzealny
PL Złoty Stok, woj. Wrocław
Science/Tech Museum
Gold mining in the 15th-16th century

Znin

10526
Muzeum Regionalne PTTK
pl. Wolności, PL Znin, woj. Bydgoszcz
General Museum - 1963
Coll: local history; archeology; applied art; ethnography; mementoes of the Renaissance poet Klemens Janicki (1516-1543); the author and educator Erazm Gliczner (1535-1608); the scientist Jan Śniadecki (1756-1820) and Jędrzej Śniadecki (1768-1838)

Zofopole

10527
Rezerwat Archeologiczny (Archeological Reserve)
PL Zofopole, woj. Kraków
Archeology Museum
Pottery-producing settlement from the Roman period

Zubrzyca Górna

10528
Orawski Park Etnograficzny
PL Zubrzyca Górna, woj. Kraków
Anthropology Museum - 1955
Original old manor of the Moniak family; 18th century peasant cottage from Jabłonka; old inn; furnishing

Zyrardów

10529
Muzeum Historii Ruchu Robotniczego (Museum of the History of the Labour Movement)
ul. Malinowskiego 1, PL Zyrardów, woj. Warszawa
History/Public Affairs Museum - 1961
History of workers' movement; local history; development of the linen industry; lodged in a 19th century palace

Portugal

Aeouca

10530
Museu Regional de Arte Sacra
Mosteiro de Aeouca, Aeouca
Religious Art Museum
Painting and sculpture; religious articles

Alenquer

10531
Museu 'Hipólito Cabaço'
Cámara Municipal, Alenquer
General Museum - 1945
Archeology; history and ethnography

Alpiarça

10532
Museu Casa de Patudos
Alpiarça
Fine Arts Museum
Spanish, Italian, English, and Dutch painting

Alverca

10533
Museu do Ar
2615 Alverca
Science/Tech Museum - 1969
600 aircraft models, aeroplanes, engines, scale models, medals, stamps, photos - library

Amarante

10534
Biblioteca-Museu de Albano Sardoeira
Convento Gonçalo, Amarante
Fine Arts Museum
Art of the Amarante school; 20th cent. painting and sculpture

Angra do Heroismo

10535
Angra do Heroismo
Convento de S. Francisco, Angra do Heroismo
General Museum
Painting, sculpture, drawing and prints; furniture and decorative arts; military equipment; maps

Avanca

10536
Casa-Museu de Egas Moniz
Casa do Marinheiro, Avanca
Decorative Arts Museum
Furniture and applied arts

Aveiro

10537
Museu Regional de Aveiro
Aveiro
General Museum - 1911
Sculpture and painting (14th-17th c.); modern regional art; religious objects; fishing equipment; ceramics

Azambuja

10538
Museu Municipal
Azambuja
Decorative Arts Museum
Handicrafts and art works from Portugal and former colonies

Barcelos

10539
Museu Regional de Cerâmica
Barcelos
General Museum
ceramics mainly local

Bargança

10540
Museu do Abade de Baçal
Rua Serpa, Bargança
General Museum
Roman archeological finds; painting; furnishings; religious objects; folklore and decorative arts

Beja

10541
Museu da Rainha D. Leonor
Convento Nossa Senhora da Conceição, Beja
General Museum
Manuelinic finds; 14th-16th cent. painting; armaments, uniforms and costumes; handicrafts

Braga

10542
Museu de Arte Sacra
Sé Primaz, Braga
Religious Art Museum
Sculpture, religious artifacts, etc.
10543
Museu de Etnografia História e Arte Regional
Braga
General Museum
ethnography; history; art regional

Caldas da Rainha

10544
Museu de José Malhoa
Parque D. Carlos I, Caldas da Rainha, Estremadura
Fine Arts Museum - 1933
modern Portuguese art, paintings, sculpture

Caramulo

10545
Museu do Caramulo
Caramulo
General Museum - a
Portugese and European fine arts, decorative arts; automobile collection (1902 models onward)

Cascais

10546
Cascais
Museu Biblioteca dos 'Conde de Castro Guimarães', Cascais
General Museum
Prehistoric ceramics; furnishings and decorative objects; visual arts
10547
Museu do Mar
2750 Cascais
Natural History Museum
Marine mammals; roman amphores - library

Castelo Branco

10548
Museu de 'Francisco Tavares Proença Junior'
Castelo Branco
General Museum - 1910
archaeology; ethnography; numismatics; art gallery; tapestries; objects found in tombs at Beira Baixa; Bronze Age weapons and ornaments from a complete workshop found at Castelo Novo; rupestral art 0060; 0040; 1160

Chaves

10549
Museu Municipal de Chaves
C.M. de Chaves, Chaves
General Museum
Archeology, numismatics, ceramics, arts

Coimbra

10550
Museu Bairro Sousa Pinto
Cidada Universitária, Coimbra
Anthropology Museum
anthropology
10551
Museu de Arte Sacra da Universidade de Coimbra
Capela da Universidade, Coimbra
Religious Art Museum
Liturgical objects, icons, etc.
10552
Museu do Laboratório de Fisica
Faculdade de Ciências, Coimbra
Science/Tech Museum
Scientific instruments
10553
Museu e Laboratório Antropológico
Colégio de S. Bento Bairro Sousa Pinto, Coimbra
Anthropology Museum - 1885
anthropology of Angola and Brasil - library
10554
Museu e Laboratório Mineralógico e Geológico
Faculdade de Ciências, Coimbra
Natural History Museum
10555
Museu e Laboratório Zoológico
Cidade Universitária
Largo do Marquês de Pombal, Coimbra
Natural History Museum - 1772
Portugese, European, and overseas zoological collections - library

10556
Museu Nacional de 'Machado de Castro'
Largo da Feira, Coimbra
Fine Arts Museum - 1911
Carpets; wood carving (13th-16th c.);
religious art; medieval and
Renaissance sculpture; 16th cent.
painting; faience and textiles

Conímbriga
10557
Museu Monográfico de Conímbriga
Conímbriga
Archeology Museum
Roman archeology; local archeological
finds

Evora
10558
Museu de Évora
Largo Conde Vila Flor, 7000 Evora,
Alto Alentejo
Fine Arts Museum - 1915
Roman sculptures; art of the Middle
Ages; Renaissance art; furniture;
Flemish, Portuguese, Dutch paintings;
ceramics

Faro
10559
Colecção Ferreira d'Almeida
Praça Afonso, 3, 8000 Faro, Algarve
Fine Arts Museum - 1944
Paintings; sculpture; china; porcelain

10560
Colecção Marítima do Comandante Ramalho Ortigão
Capitania do Porto de Faro, Faro
History/Public Affairs Museum - 1931
Model ships; fishing gear; marine
paintings

10561
Museu Antonino
Ermida de Santo António do Alto, Faro
Religious Art Museum
Liturgical objects

Farso
10562
Museu Arqueológico e Lapidar do Infante D. Henrique
Praça Afonso, 3, 8000 Farso, Algarve
Archeology Museum - 1894
history archaeology; ethnography;
paintings; Roman and Arabian pottery;
fossils; Roman mosaic pavement

Figueira da Foz
10563
Museu Municipal do 'Dr. Santos Rocha'
Rua Fernandes Tomás, Figueira da Foz
General Museum - 1894
Archeology, ethnology, anthropology

Funchal
10564
Museu Muinicipal do Funchal e Aquario
Rua da Mouraria 29-31, Funchal
Natural History Museum
Fishes and crustaceans of Madeira -
library

Guimarães
10565
Museu de Alberto Sampaio
Rua Afredo Guimarães, 4800
Guimarães
Fine Arts Museum - 1928
14th-16th century sculptures, chests,
armaments, sarcophargi, altars;
15th-18th century religious paintings;
Portuguese and Delft porcelain;
decorative objects - library

10566
Museu de Alberto Sampaio
Largo da Oliveira, Guimaræes
Fine Arts Museum
Portugese painting; sculpture and
frescoes; furniture

10567
Museu de Martins Sarmento
Rua de Paio Galvão, Guimarães
Archeology Museum
Prehistoric finds

10568
Paço dos Duques de Bragança
Guimarães
Decorative Arts Museum
Furnishings, interiors and artworks
from the 15th to the 18th cent.

Lamego
10569
Museu de Lamego
Lamego
Fine Arts Museum
Painting, sculpture, tapestries, and
religious decorative objects

Lisboa
10570
Museu Agrícola do Ultramar
Calçada do Galvão, 1400 Lisboa
Science/Tech Museum - 1906
agriculture in overseas zones - library

10571
Museu Arqueológico
Largo do Carmo, Lisboa
Archeology Museum - 1866
Prehistoric finds; Spanish, Portuguese
and Dutch ceramic tiles; armaments;
sarcophagi; numismatics

10572
Museu Calouste Gulbenkian
av. de Berna, Lisboa
Fine Arts Museum - 1960
Islamic and Far Eastern art; European
art (12th-20th c.); decorative arts

10573
Museu da Cidade
Palácio Pimenta, Campo Grande,
Lisboa
General Museum - 1941
Archeology; painting and engravings;
ceramics

10574
Museu da Liga dos Combatentes da Grande Guerra
Rua de João Pereira da Rosa 18,
Lisboa
History/Public Affairs Museum
Memorabilia from the First World War;
African art

10575
Museu de Arte Popular
Av. de Brasilia, Lisboa
Archeology Museum
Ceramics, dolls, textiles, costumes, etc.

10576
Museu de Arte Sacra da Misericórdia
Rua da Misericórdia, Lisboa
Religous painting; liturgical objects;
musical instruments; furnishings;
Baroque goldwork

10577
Museu de Marinha
Praçca do Imperio, 1400 Lisboa
Science/Tech Museum - 1863
ships, nautical instruments, sea maps,
cannons, uniforms, flags, paintings,
models - library

10578
Museu de Rafael Bordalo Pinheiro
Campo Grande, 382, Lisboa
History/Public Affairs Museum - 1916
Caricatures and satirical documents;
painting and ceramics - library

10579
Museu de São Roque
Largo Rindade Coelho, 1400 Lisboa
Religious Art Museum - 1905
religious paintings, objects; 18th
century robes and vessels;
Portuguese painting from 16th
century; Portuguese silver

10580
Museu dos CTT/TLP
R.D. Estefânia, 172-175, 1000 Lisboa
Science/Tech Museum - 1878
Postage stamps and postmarks;
models of postal vehicles and
buildings; telecommunications
equipment

10581
Museu Etnográfico da Sociedade de Geografia de Lisboa
Rua das Portas de Santo Antão,
Lisboa
Anthropology Museum - 1875
Musical instruments from former
overseas provinces; armaments and
costumes; fine arts

10582
Museu Etnológico do Ultramar
Dormitorio Jerónimus-Cloister, Belém,
Lisboa
Archeology Museum - 1893
Roman mosaics; jewelry; inscribed
stones; stone tools; etc.

10583
Museu Instrumental
R. Ocidental do Campo Grande, 83,
1799 Lisboa
Music Museum - 1977
several rare wind instruments; Asiatic
and Portuguese folk instruments; two
unique Portuguese made harpsichords
and Portuguese clavichords

10584
Museu Militar
Largo do Museu de Artilharia, Lisboa
History/Public Affairs Museum - 1851
Firearms and cannons from the 14th
cent. to WW I; armour

10585
Museu Mineralógico e Geológico
Faculdade de Ciências, Universidade
Rua da Escola Politécnica, Lisboa
Natural History Museum - 1781

10586
Museu Nacional de Arte Antiga
Rua das Janelas Verdes, Lisboa
Fine Arts Museum - 1884
paintings (Portuguese and European);
Oriental sculpture collection and
decorative art - library

10587
Museu Nacional de Arte Contemporânea
Rua Serpa Pinto 6, Lisboa
Fine Arts Museum - 1911
19th cent. Portugese art;
contemporary painting and sculpture

10588
Museu Nacional de História Natural
Faculdade de Ciências, Universidade
Lisboa
Natural History Museum - 1859
Mineralogy and geology; botany,
zoology, and anthropology - library

10589
Museu Nacional dos Coches
Praça Afonso de Albuquerque, 1300
Lisboa, Estremadura
History/Public Affairs Museum
royal coaches, carriages, sedan chairs,
litters; 17th-20th century arts; harness;
portraits of the Royal Family; paintings;
engravings - library

10590
Museu Numismático Português
Av. Dr. A.J. de Almeida, Lisboa
History/Public Affairs Museum - 1934
Portugese, Roman, Visigoth, and
Iberian coin collections; coins from
former colonies

10591
Museu Tauromáquico
Praça de Touros do Campo Pequeno,
Lisboa
Anthropology Museum
History of bullfighting; documents on
famous natinal and international
bullfighters

10592
Museu-Escola de Artes Decorativas da Fundação R. Espirito Sante
Largo das Portas do Sol 2, Lisboa
Decorative Arts Museum - 1953
Furnishings, silver, porcelain and rugs;
painting

10593
Palácio Nacional da Ajuda
Lisboa
Decorative Arts Museum
Furnishings and interiors (18th-19th c.);
sculpture and painting

Mafra
10594
Museu de Escultura Comparada
Convento de Mafra, Mafra
Fine Arts Museum
Portuguese, French and Italian
sculpture (12th-14th c.); casts of
contemporary sculpture

10595
Palácio Nacional de Mafra
Mafra
Decorative Arts Museum
Furnishings and interiors (18th c.);
painting and sculpture (18th-19th c.)

Minde
10596
Museu de Roque Gameiro
Minde
Fine Arts Museum
Works of Roque Gameiro and his
family; ethnographic collections

Nazaré

10597
**Museu Etnográfico e Arqueológico
do Dr. Joaquim Manso**
R. D. Fuas Roupinho, 2450 Nazaré,
Estremadura
Natural History Museum - 1976
ethnography and archaeology

Óbidos

10598
Museu Municipal de Óbidos
Praça de Santa Maria, 2510 Óbidos,
Estremadura
Fine Arts Museum - 1970
paintings of Josepha d'Obidos 18th
century; archaeology; religious art;
arms of the war between Portugal and
France

Odrinhas

10599
**Museu Arqueológico do Prof. Dr.
Joaquim Fontes**
S. Miguel de Odrinhas, Odrinhas
Archeology Museum
Roman archeology

Ovar

10600
Museu de Ovar
Rua de Heliodoro Salgado, Ovar
General Museum
Contemporary painting and ceramics;
ethnography

Pinhel

10601
Museu Municipal
Pinhel
General Museum
Archeology; applied arts; numismatics

Ponta Delgada

10602
Museu de Carlos Machado
Ponta Delgada
General Museum
Fine arts; ethnography; science and
technology

Porto

10603
Casa de Vitorino Ribeiro
Travessa das Cavadas, 148, Porto
General Museum
Applied arts; ethnography
10604
Casa-Museu de Guerra Junqueiro
Rua de D. Hugo, 32, Porto
Decorative Arts Museum
Applied arts; belongings of the poet
Guerra Junqueiro
10605
**Casa-Museu Teixeira Lopes e
Galerias Diego de Macedo**
Rua Teixeira Lopes, 32, 4400 Porto,
Vila Nova de Gaia
Fine Arts Museum - 1933
sculpture 19th century; paintings
19th-20th century; African art - library
10606
Casa-Oficina de António Carneiro
Rua de António Carneiro, 363, Porto
History/Public Affairs Museum
Works of the writer António Carneiro
and his circle

10607
Fundação Eng. António de Almeida
Rua Tenente Valadim, 257, 4100 Porto
General Museum - 1069
CoLL: Numismatic collections
composed of Greek, Roman,
Byzantine, French and Portuguese
gold coins; Saxon porcelains
10608
**Museu de Etnografia e História da
Junta Distrital de Porto**
Largo de S. João Novo, 11, Porto
General Museum
Local ethnography and history
10609
**Museu do Instituto de Zoologia Dr.
Augusto Nobre**
Campo dos Martires da Pátria, 4,000
Porto, Douro Litoral
Natural History Museum - 1916
zoology; invertebrates; mollusks;
insects; fishes; amphibia; reptiles;
birds and mammals - library
10610
Museu Nacional de Soares dos Reis
Rua D. Manuel II, Porto
Fine Arts Museum - 1836
medieval sculpture, sarcophargi,
fresoes, decorative objects; Flemish,
Italian, French, Portuguese paintings,
portraits; carved furnishings;
archaeological finds

Queluz

10611
Palácio Nacional de Queluz
Queluz
Decorative Arts Museum
Furnishings and interiors (18th-19th c.)

Santarém

10612
Museu Arqueológico
São João d'Alporão, Santarém
Archeology Museum
Medieval sculpture; archeological
fragments

Santo Tirso

10613
Museu do Abade Pedrosa
Santo Tirso
Archeology Museum
Prehistoric and medieval archeology

São Miguel de Ceide

10614
Casa de Camilo Castelo Branco
São Miguel de Ceide
Historic Site
Furnishings, documents and personal
belongings of the writer Camilo C.
Branco

Setúbal

10615
Museu de Setúbal
Largo de Jesus, Setúbal
Fine Arts Museum
Painting (important 15th cent.
Portugese works), sacred and applied
arts; archeology
10616
Museu Oceanográfico e de Pesca
Avenida de Luísa Todi, 181, rés-do-
chão, Setúbal
Natural History Museum
Fish and fishing

Sintra

10617
Museu Municipal Palácio Valenças
Rua do Visconde de Monserrate,
Sintra
Fine Arts Museum
Painting and graphic arts
10618
Palácio Nacional da Pena
Sintra
Decorative Arts Museum
Furnishings and interiors in 9th cent.
electic style; decorative arts and
ceramics
10619
Palácio Nacional de Sintra
Sintra
Decorative Arts Museum
Furnishings and interiors (17th-18th c.)

Tomar

10620
**Museu Luso-Hebraico de Abraão
Zacuto**
Rua da Judiaria, 85, Tomar
Religious Art Museum
Funerary sculpture from the ancient
synagogue of Tomar
10621
**Museu Municipal de João de
Castilho**
Av. de Cândido Madureira, Tomar
Fine Arts Museum
Contemporary painting and sculpture

Torres Novas

10622
Museu Carlos Reis
Largo do Salva, 2350 Torres Novas
General Museum - 1937
fine arts; religious art; archaeology;
history; ethnography; numismatics

Viana do Castelo

10623
**Museu Municipal de Viana do
Castelo**
Largo de S. Domingos, 4900 Viana do
Castelo, Alto-Minho
Fine Arts Museum - 1888
paintings; drawings; furnishings;
earthenware

Vila do Conde

10624
Museu Etnográfico
Praça da República, Vila do Conde
General Museum
Ethnography and folklore; archeology;
natural history

Viseu

10625
Casa-Museu de Almeida Moreira
Viseu
Fine Arts Museum
paintings; ceramics; furniture; arms
and armour
10626
Museu de 'Grão Vasco'
Paço dos Tres Escalões, Viseu
General Museum - 1913
Flemish and Portugese painting;
14th-17th cent. sculpture; furnishings
and decorative objects; Roman finds

Puerto Rico

Barranquitas

10627
**Luis Munoz Rivera, Library and
Museum**
Barranquitas
General Museum - 1959
history; literature; memorabilia of Luis
Muñoz Rivera - library
10628
Luis Munoz Rivera, Mausoleum
Calle Padre Berrios, Barranquitas
General Museum - 1916
memorabilia of patriot Luis Munõz
Rivera; documents; photographs and
pictures

Mayaguez

10629
Marine Station Museum Dep. of
Marine Sciences, University of Puerto
Rico
PR Mayaguez 00708
Natural History Museum - 1954
marine invertebrates; marine fishes

Ponce

10630
Museo de Arte
POB 1492, PR Ponce, Puerto Rico
00731
Fine Arts Museum - 1956
European and American paintings and
sculptures - library

Puerto de Tierra

10631
**Museo de Historia Natural del
Departamento de Agricultura y
Comercio**
Parque Luis Muñoz Rivera, Puerto de
Tierra PR 00906
Natural History Museum

Rio Piedras

10632
**Museum of Archaeology, History and
Art** University of Puerto Rico
Rio Piedras
Anthropology Museum - 1940
archaeology; history

San German

10633
Museo de Arte Religioso
Hermita Porta Coeli, San German
Fine Arts Museum
religious art

San Juan

10634
Ateneo Puertorriqueño
Ponce de León, Stop 1, San Juan PR
00902
Fine Arts Museum - 1876
sculpture; graphics; paintings; plastic
art; physical sciences; political
sciences; history
10635
La Casa del Libro
Calle del Cristo 255, POB 2265, PR
San Juan 00903
History/Public Affairs Museum
calligraphy; typography; papermaking;
bookbinding; book illustrations;
bibliography; Spanish incunabula -
library

10636
Museo de Arquitectura Colonial
Fortaleza 319, San Juan
Fine Arts Museum
architecture

10637
Museo de Arte Popular
Calle Cristo, San Juan
Fine Arts Museum

10638
Museo de Bellas Artes
Calle del Santo Cristo de la Salud 253,
San Juan
Fine Arts Museum - 1967
graphics; paintings; sculpture;
archaeology

10639
**Museo de la Familia Puertorriqueña
S. XIX**
Fortaleza 319, San Juan
History/Public Affairs Museum

10640
**Museum of Military and Naval
History**
Fort San Jerónimo beside Caribe
Hilton Hotel, San Juan
History/Public Affairs Museum - 1962
military and naval artifacts

Utuado

10641
Museo y Parque Arqueológico
Centro Ceremonial de Caguana,
Utuado
General Museum

Qatar

Doha

10642
National Museum
Doha
General Museum - 1975
Ethnography; archeology; ecology;
history; maritime history

Réunion

Saint-Denis

10643
Musée des Beaux-Arts Léon Dierx
rue Sainte Marie et rue de Paris, BP
395 97400 Saint-Denis
Fine Arts Museum - 1912
Paintings; sculptures; French
impressionists - library

10644
Musée d'Histoire Naturelle
rue Poivre, 97400 Saint-Denis
Natural History Museum - 1854
Natural history; zoology; ornithology;
mineralogy - library

Romania

Adamclisi

10645
Muzeul de arheologie Adamclisi
Adamclisi
Archeology Museum - 1977
Archaeology; lapidarium

Agnita

10646
Muzeul 'Valea Hîrtibaciului'
Str. 23 August 29, Agnita
General Museum - 1957
Archaeology; numismatics; art;
ethnography

Aiud

10647
Muzeul de istorie Aiud
Piaţa Republicii 24, Aiud
History/Public Affairs Museum - 1796
Archaeology; numismatics; history;
ethnography; housed in a 16th century
building

10648
Muzeul de ştiinţele naturii Aiud
Str. 11 iunie 1, Aiud
Natural History Museum - 1796
Mineralogy; palaeontology; zoology;
herbarium

Alba Iulia

10649
Muzeul Unirii
Str. Mihai Viteazul 12-14, Alba Iulia
General Museum - 1887
Archaeology; numismatics; national
union of 1918; ethnography; art

Albeşti

10650
Muzeul memorial 'Petöfi Sándor'
Albeşti
Historic Site
Life and work of the Hungarian poet
Petöfi (1823-1849)

Alexandria

10651
**Muzeul judeţean de istorie
Alexandria**
Str. Dunării 188, Alexandria
General Museum - 1951
Archaeology; numismatics; history;
ethnography

Arad

10652
Muzeul judeţean Arad
Piaţa Enescu 1, Arad
General Museum - 1862
Archaeology; history; Romanian and
European art; ethnography

Aurel Vlaicu

10653
Muzeul Aurel Vlaicu
Aurel Vlaicu
Historic Site
Documents and objects related to the
life and accomplishments of Arel
Vlaicu (1882-1913)

Avram Iancu

10654
Muzeul Avram Iancu
Avram Iancu
Historic Site - 1924
Letters, documents and weapons
dedicated to the revolutionary fighter
Avram Iancu (1824-1872), in his
birthplace

Babadag

10655
Muzeul Babadag
Babadag
Fine Arts Museum - 1972
Medieval art; contemporary Romanian
art

Bacău

10656
Muzeul Bacău
Str. Karl Marx 23, Bacău
General Museum - 1957
Archaeology; history; paintings

10657
Muzeul de stiinţele naturii Bacău
Str. Karl Marx 2, Bacău
Natural History Museum - 1959
Evolution; flora and fauna

Baia Mare

10658
Muzeul judeţean Maramureş
Str. 1 Mai 8, Baia Mare
General Museum - 1905
Archaeology; local and Transylvanian
history; mining; ethnography; natural
science; classical and contemporary
painting

Beiuş

10659
Muzeul etnografic Beiuş
Str. 23 August 1, Beiuş
General Museum - 1958
Ethnography; folk art

Bicaz

10660
Muzeul de istorie Bicaz
Str. Barajului 1, Bicaz
History/Public Affairs Museum - 1960
Archaeology; documents and models
of the Bicaz hydropower station;
ethnography; local art

Birlad

10661
Muzeul 'Vasile Pîrvan'
Str. Sterian Dumbravă 1, Bîrlad
History/Public Affairs Museum - 1914
Archaeology; numismatics; local
history; natural science; art

Bistriţa

10662
Muzeul judeţean Bistriţa
Str. Dornei 5, Bistriţa
General Museum - 1950
Archaeology; numismatics; regional
history; ethnography; natural sciences

Blaj

10663
Muzeul de istorie Blaj
Str. Armata Rosie 2, Blaj
History/Public Affairs Museum - 1850
Archaeology; history; housed in a 17th
century building

Botoşani

10664
Muzeul judeţean Botoşani
Str. Unirii 13, Botoşani
General Museum - 1953
Archaeology; numismatics; local
history; ethnography; natural science;
art

Brăila

10665
Muzeul Brăilei
Piaţa Lenin 3, Brăila
General Museum - 1955
Archaeology; local history; documents
related to the revolutionary Bulgarian
poet Christo Botev (1849-1876);
ethnography; natural science; art

Bran

10666
Muzeul 'Cetatea Bran'
Str. Principală 460, Bran
General Museum - 1957
Medieval history; weapons; tools;
furniture; local history; ethnography;
medieval art; open air ethnography
park

Braşov

10667
**Muzeul culturii româneşti in Scheii
Braşovului**
Piaţa Libertăţii 2, Braşov
History/Public Affairs Museum - 1964
Ancient books; documents;
manuscripts; medieval art; housed in
the building of the first Romanian
school (15th century)

10668
Muzeul de artă Braşov
Bd. Gheorghe Gheorghiu Dej, Braşov
Fine Arts Museum - 1950
Romanian and foreign art

10669
Muzeul judeţean Braşov
Str. 23 August 30, Braşov
General Museum - 1908
Archaeological finds; numismatics;
history; ethnography; housed in the
medieval city hall (15th c.)

Bucureşti

10670
Muzeul Arhivelor Statului
Str. Arhivelor 2, Bucureşti
History/Public Affairs Museum - 1957
Ancient books, documents,
manuscripts, engravings regarding
Romanian history

10671
Muzeul Cecilia şi Frederic Storck
Str. Vasile Alecsandri 16, Bucureşti
Fine Arts Museum - 1951
Exhibits in connection with the
sculptor Karl Storck (1820-1877), his
sons Carl (1854-1926) and Frederic
(1872-1924) and his wife Cecilia
Storck; history of fine arts in Romania

10672
Muzeul colecţiilor de artă
Calea Victoriei 113, Bucureşti
Fine Arts Museum - 1978
The museum includes collections from
the following people: Prof. George
Oprescu, Elisabeta and Moise
Weinberg, Krikor Zambaccian, Elena
and Dr. Iosif Dona, Beatrice and
Hrandt Avakian, Alexandra and Barbu
Slătineanu, Serafima and Gheorge
Răut, Iosif Iser, Marcu Beza, Hortensia
and Vasile George Beza, Victor
Eftimiu, Alexandru Phoebus, Garabet
Avakian, Elena and Anastasie Simu,
Ion Pas

10673
Muzeul 'Cornel Medrea'
Str. General Budişteanu 16, Bucureşti
Fine Arts Museum - 1956
Works by sculptor Cornel Medrea
(1888-1964)

10674
Muzeul 'Curtea Veche'
Str. 30 Decembrie 25-31, Bucureşti
Archeology Museum - 1972
Archaeology; housed in a 15th century
palace

10675
**Muzeul de artă al Republicii
Socialiste România**
Str. Stirbei Vodă 1, Bucureşti
Fine Arts Museum - 1948
Woodcarving; embroidery; jewelry;
ceramics; tapestries; prints; ancient
books; porcelain; furniture; Romanian
and international art

10676
**Muzeul de artă Brîncovenească
Mogoşoaia**
Str. Donca Simo 18, Bucureşti
Fine Arts Museum - 1057
Silversmith work; woodcarvings;
embroidery; documents; rare prints;
ancient books

10677
**Muzeul de istorie a municipiului
Bucureşti**
Bd. 1848 2, Bucureşti
History/Public Affairs Museum - 1921
Archaeological finds; numismatics;
history of the city; documents; maps

10678
**Muzeul de istorie a Partidului
Comunist Român, a mişcării
revoluţionare şi democratice din
România**
Soseaua Kiseleff 3, Bucureşti
History/Public Affairs Museum - 1948
History of the revolutionary-
democratic movement and of the
Romanian Communist Party;
documents; articles; books;
pamphlets; photos

10679
**Muzeul de istorie al Republicii
Socialiste România**
Calea Victoriei 12, Bucureşti
History/Public Affairs Museum - 1968
Archaeology; Stone and Bronze Age
finds; Daco-Getic, Greek and Roman
objects; numismatics; medieval tools
and weapons; icons; inscriptions;
lapidarium; documents; other exhibits
on modern and contemporary history;
the army; the revolutionary and
working-class movement

10680
**Muzeul de istorie naturală 'Grigore
Antipa'**
Soseaua Kiseleff 1, Bucureşti
Natural History Museum - 1831/1908
Fauna and flora of all continents;
butterflies; fossils; skeletons; minerals;
insects; birds

10681
Muzeul literaturii române
Str. Fundaţiei 4, Bucureşti
History/Public Affairs Museum - 1957
History of literature in Romania;
documents; manuscripts; rare editions

10682
Muzeul militar central
Str. Izvor 137, Bucureşti
History/Public Affairs Museum - 1923
Archaeology; weapons; trophies;
flags; documents; photos; military
costumes; military history

10683
Muzeul pompierilor
Bd. Dimitrov 33, Bucureşti
History/Public Affairs Museum - 1963
Development of fire fighting in
Romania

10684
Muzeul satului şi de artă populară
Soseaua Kiseleff 20, Bucureşti
Open Air Museum - 1874/1936
Handicrafts; pottery; costumes; village
reconstructed with original houses,
workshops and churches

10685
Muzeul Teatrului National
Bd. Nicolae Bălcescu 1, Bucureşti
Performing Arts Museum - 1942
History of the Romanian theater;
documents on actors; stage sets;
costumes; programmes, Romanian
playwrights

10686
Muzeul tehnic 'Prof. Ing. D. Leonida'
Str. Candiano Popescu 2, Bucureşti
Science/Tech Museum - 1909
Old tools; modern equipment;
documents; Romanian inventions

10687
Muzeul 'Teodor Aman'
Str. C.A. Rosetti 8, Bucureşti
Fine Arts Museum - 1908
Paintings; drawings; original
furnishings; house of painter Teodor
Aman (1831-1891)

Buzău

10688
Muzeul judeţean de istorie Buzău
Str. Unirii 178, Buzău
General Museum - 1952
Archaeology; numismatics; medieval
and modern history of the region;
ethnography; folk art; contemporary
Romanian art

Călăraşi

10689
Muzeul de istorie Călăraşi
Str. Progresului 90, Călăraşi
History/Public Affairs Museum - 1951
Archaeology; numismatics; medieval
history of the area

Caracal

10690
Museul de istorie Caracal
Str. Negru Vodă 1, Caracal
History/Public Affairs Museum - 1949
Archaeology; ethnography; art

Caransebes

10691
**Muzeul judeţean de etnografie şi
istorie locală Caransebes**
Str. Bistrei 2, Caransebes
General Museum - 1962
Archaeology; history of the area;
ethnography

Carei

10692
Muzeul orăşenesc Carei
Str. Armata Rosie 1, Carei
General Museum - 1958
Archaeology; natural science

Cîmpina

10693
Muzeul memorial 'B.P. Hasdeu'
Str. 23 August 199, Cîmpina
Historic Site - 1965
Documents on the life and activity of
the scientist, professor, writer and
historian B.P. Hasdeu (1838-1907);
exhibits related to his daughter Iulia
(1869-1888)

10694
**Muzeul memorial 'Nicolae
Grigorescu'**
Str. 23 August 170, Cîmpina
Fine Arts Museum - 1955
Documents on painter Nicolae
Grigorescu (1838-1907); paintings,
letters

Cîmpulung Moldovenesc

10695
**Muzeul 'Arta lemnului' Cîmpulung
Moldovenesc**
Str. Pictor Grigorescu 1, Cîmpulung
Moldovenesc
General Museum - 1936
Ethnography; woodcarving; folk art;
local history

Cîmpulung Muscel

10696
**Muzeul orăşenesc Cîmpulung
Muscel**
Str. Negru Vodă 127, Cîmpulung
Muscel
General Museum - 1951
Archaeology; lapidarium; ethnography;
folk art; modern Romanian art; natural
science

Cluj-Napoca

10697
Muzeul de artă Cluj-Napoca
Piaţa Libertăţii 30, Cluj-Napoca
Fine Arts Museum - 1951
Romanian and European art of
medieval, modern and contemporary
times; housed in an 18th century
palace

10698
**Muzeul de istorie a farmaciei
Cluj-Napoca**
Piaţa Libertăţii 28, Cluj-Napoca
Natural History Museum
Pharmaceutical equipment and
documents

10699
**Muzeul de istorie al Transilvaniei
Cluj-Napoca**
Str. Emil Isac 2, Cluj-Napoca
History/Public Affairs Museum - 1859
Archaeology; numismatics; lapidarium;
weapons; jewelry; maps; rare books;
history of Transylvania

10700
**Muzeul etnografic al Transilvaniei
Cluj-Napoca**
Str. 30 Decembrie, Cluj-Napoca
Anthropology Museum - 1922
Handicrafts; pottery; woodcarving;
costumes; folk art; open air
ethnography museum (Hoia)

10701
Muzeul memorial 'Emil Isac'
Str. 1 Mai, Cluj-Napoca
Historic Site - 1955
Manuscripts, documents, letters,
photos and books dedicated to the
poet Emil Isac (1886-1954)

Constanta

10702
**Complexul muzeal de stiinţe ale
naturii Constanta**
Bd. 16 Februarie 1, Constanta
Natural History Museum - 1958
Aquarium; Black Sea fauna; zoology;
ichthyology

10703
Muzeul de artă Constanta
Str. Muzeelor 12, Constanta
Fine Arts Museum - 1961
Modern Romanian art

10704
**Muzeul de istorie natională şi
arheologie Constanta**
Piaţa Independenţei 1, Constanta
General Museum - 1879
Archaeology; numismatics; lapidarium;
mosaics; jewelry of the Greek-Roman
period in Dobruja; local history;
medieval and modern history

10705
Muzeul Marinei Române
Str. Traian 53, Constanta
History/Public Affairs Museum - 1969
Navy history; maps; documents;
uniforms; archaeological finds

Corabia

10706
Muzeul orăşenesc Corabia
Str. Cuza Vodă 65, Corabia
General Museum - 1951
Archaeological finds; coins;
ethnography; folk art

Coşbuc

10707
Muzeul memorial 'George Coşbuc'
Coşbuc, Hordou
Historic Site - 1949
Books, manuscripts, photos and
documents on life and work of the
poet George Coşbuc (1866-1919)

Craiova

10708
Muzeul de artă Craiova
Str. Calea Unirii 15, Craiova
Fine Arts Museum - 1908
Romanian and European art;
sculptures by Constantin Brâncuşi

10709
Muzeul Olteniei
Str. Maxim Gorki 44, Craiova
General Museum - 1915
Archaeological finds; numismatics;
history of the area; ethnography; folk
art

Cristuru Secuiesc

10710
Muzeul orăşenesc Cristuru Secuiesc
Str. Libertăţii 45, Cristuru Secuiesc
General Museum - 1946
Archaeology; numismatics;
ethnography; folk art; natural science

Curtea de Argeş

10711
Muzeul orăşenesc Curtea de Argeş
Str. Negru Vodă 1, Curtea de Argeş
General Museum - 1958
Local history; archaeology;
ethnography; folk art

Deva

10712
Muzeul judeţean Hunedoara
Str. Dr Petru Groza 39, Deva
General Museum - 1882
Archaeology; finds of the Dacian and
Roman periods; lapidarium; medieval
and modern history; ethnography; folk
art; geology; mineralogy; natural
science; housed in a 16th century
building

Doftana

10713
Muzeul Doftana
Doftana
History/Public Affairs Museum - 1952
History of the revolutionary
movement; photos, documents,
personal belongings of political
prisoners; housed in former prison

Dorohoi

10714
Muzeul de stiințe naturale Dorohoi
Str. Al. I. Cuza 43, Dorohoi
Natural History Museum - 1953
Mineralogy; geology; local fauna

10715
Muzeul memorial 'George Enescu'
Str. Republicii 81, Dorohoi
Historic Site - 1957
Documents, letters and photos on the
life and work of the Romanian
musician George Enescu (1881-1955)

Drobeta-Turnu Severin

10716
Muzeul Regiunii Porților de Fier
Str. Independenței 2, Drobeta-Turnu
Severin
General Museum - 1912
Archaeology; lapidarium; history;
ethnography, folk art; Romanian art;
aquarium; flora and fauna of the area

Făgăraş

10717
Muzeul 'Cetatea Făgăraş'
Str. Mihai Viteazul 1, Făgăraş
General Museum - 1954
Archaeology; medieval testimonies;
ethnography; folk art; housed in a 14th
century fortress

Fălticeni

10718
Muzeul Fălticenilor
Str. Republicii 296, Fălticeni
General Museum - 1914
Cultural history; literature;
ethnography; folk art; regional flora
and fauna

Focsani

10719
Muzeul de stiințele naturii
Str. Republicii 79, Focsani
Natural History Museum - 1949
Natural history; herbarium

10720
**Muzeul județean de istorie şi
etnografie**
Bd. Karl Marx 1, Focsani
General Museum - 1951
Archaeology; numismatics;
ethnography and folk art

Galați

10721
**Muzeul de artă contemporană
românească**
Str. Republicii 141, Galați
Fine Arts Museum - 1966
Modern and contemporary Romanian
art

10722
Muzeul de stiințele naturii Galați
Str. Stiinței 115, Galați
Natural History Museum - 1956
Regional fauna

10723
Muzeul județean Galatîi
Str. Cuza Vodă 80, Galați
General Museum - 1939
Archaeology; numismatics;
ethnography; folk art

Giurgiu

10724
**Muzeul luptei pentru independență a
poporului român**
Str. Dorobanți 16, Giurgiu
History/Public Affairs Museum - 1950
Archaeology; weapons; flags;
documents; the revolutionary
movement

Golesti

10725
Complexul muzeal Golesti
Golesti-Stefăneşti
History/Public Affairs Museum -
1942/1971
Documents; personal objects of the
Golescu family; ethnography; folk art;
open air ethnography museum

Humulesti

10726
**Muzeul etnografic din Gura
Humorului**
Calea principală 18, Humulesti, Gura
Humorului
Anthropology Museum - 1958
Folk art of the area

Hunedoara

10727
Muzeul 'Castelul Corvineştilor'
Str. Curtea Corvineştilor 1-3,
Hunedoara
History/Public Affairs Museum - 1956
Archaeological finds; inscriptions;
sculptures; medieval history; weapons;
housed in a 14th century castle

Iaşi

10728
Complexul muzeistic Iaşi
Str. Palat 1, Iaşi
General Museum

10729
Muzeul de artă
Str. Palat 1, Iaşi
Fine Arts Museum - 1860
Modern and contemporary Romanian
and European art

10730
Muzeul de istorie al Moldovei
Str. Palat 1, Iaşi
History/Public Affairs Museum - 1916
Archaeology; medieval, modern and
contemporary history of Moldavia

10731
Muzeul de istorie naturală Iaşi
Str. G. Dimitrov 72, Iaşi
Natural History Museum - 835
Mineralogy; fossils; botany; zoology

10732
Muzeul de literatură al Moldovei
Str. I.C. Frimu 4, Iaşi
History/Public Affairs Museum - 1971
History of literature in Moldavia;
ancient prints; books; documents;
photos

10733
Muzeul etnografic al Moldovei
Str. Palat 1, Iaşi
Anthropology Museum - 1943
Handicrafts; traditions; costumes;
musical instruments; folk art

10734
**Muzeul memorial 'Bojdeuca Ion
Creangă'**
Str. Simion Bărnuţiu, Iaşi
Historic Site - 1918
Documents, photos, books, personal
objects of writer Ion Creangă
(1837-1889)

10735
Muzeul politehnic
Str. Palat 1, Iaşi
Science/Tech Museum - 1955
Models of machinery and equipment

10736
Muzeul teatrului
Str. Vasile Alecsandri 3, Iaşi
Performing Arts Museum - 1976
History of theater; documents; photos

10737
Muzeul Unirii
Str. Alexandru Lăpuşneanu 14, Iaşi
History/Public Affairs Museum - 1955
Medieval and modern historical
documents; paintings; sculptures;
maps; documents referring to the
Union of 1859

Ipoteşti

10738
Muzeul memorial 'Mihai Eminescu'
Ipoteşti
Historic Site - 1950
Documents, books, photos, personal
objects of poet Mihai Eminescu
(1850-1889)

Limanu

10739
Muzeul de artă Limanu
Limanu
Fine Arts Museum - 1961
Contemporary art

Lipova

10740
Muzeul orăşenesc Lipova
Str. Nicolae Bălcescu 21, Lipova
General Museum - 1952
Archaeological finds; history;
ethnography; folk art

Lugoj

10741
Muzeul de istorie şi etnografie Lugoj
Str. Nicolae Bălcescu 2, Lugoj
General Museum - 1905
Archaeology; history; cultural history;
ethnography

Lupşa

10742
Muzeul etnografic Lupşa
Lupşa
General Museum - 1939
Handicrafts; costumes; woodcarvings

Mangalia

10743
Muzeul de arheologie Mangalia
Str. Mangalia, Calea Constanței,
Mangalia
Archeology Museum - 1925
Numismatics; history of the ancient
city of Callatis

Medgidia

10744
Muzeul de artă
Aleea trandafirilor 2, Medgidia
Fine Arts Museum - 1964
Contemporary Romanian art

Mediaş

10745
Muzeul municipal Mediaş
Str. Viitorului 46, Mediaş
General Museum - 1950
Archaeology; history of the area;
ethnography; art; natural science

Miercurea Ciuc

10746
Muzeul județean Miercurea Ciuc
Str. Gheorghe Doja 2, Miercurea Ciuc
General Museum - 1949
Archaeology; history; ethnography;
folk art; natural science; housed in a
17th century building

Mirceşti

10747
Muzeul memorial 'Vasile Alecsandri'
Mirceşti
Historic Site - 1957
Books, manuscripts, photos, personal
objects of the poet Vasile Alecsandri
(1821-1890); in his country house

Năsăud

10748
Muzeul năsăudean
Bd. Republicii 19, Năsăud
General Museum - 1931
Archaeology; history; ethnography;
natural science; housed in an 18th
century building

Negresti

10749
Muzeul Tării Oasului
Str. Victorie 96, Negresti
General Museum - 1972
Ethnography; folk art

Odorhei

10750
Muzeul din Odorheiul Secuiesc
Bd. 1 Mai 29, Odorhei
General Museum - 1772/1949
Archaeological finds; history of the
area; ethnography

Oltenița

10751
Muzeul de istorie Oltenița
Str. Arges 101, Oltenița
General Museum - 1957
Archaeology; history

Orăştie

10752
Muzeul de artă populară Orăştie
Piata Aurel Vlaicu 1, Orăştie
General Museum - 1952
History; ethnography; folk art

Oradea

10753
Muzeul memorial 'Ady Endre'
Parcul Traian 10, Oradea
Historic Site - 1955
Documents, photos, books, personal
objects of the revolutionary Hungarian
poet Ady Endre (1877-1919)

10754
Muzeul memorial 'Iosif Vulcan'
Str. Iosif Vulcanuli 16, Oradea
Historic Site - 1965
Memorabilia of writer Iosif Vulcan
(1841-1907)

10755
Muzeul Tării Crişurilor
Str. Stadionuli 2, Oradea
General Museum - 1872
Archaeology; history; ethnography;
folk art; housed in an 18th century
palace

Piatra Neamţ

10756
Muzeul de stiinţele naturii
Str. V.I. Lenin 26, Piatra Neamţ
Science/Tech Museum - 1965
Fossils; minerals; geology; flora and
fauna of the Carpathians

10757
Muzeul judeţean de istorie
Piaţa Libertăţii 1, Piatra Neamţ
History/Public Affairs Museum - 1938
Archaeological finds; history;
ethnography; Romanian art

Piteşti

10758
Muzeul judeţean Argeş
Str. Horia, Cloşca şi Crişan 44, Piteşti
General Museum - 1928
Archaeology; numismatics; history;
ethnography; art; natural science;
housed in an 18th century building

Ploieşti

10759
Muzeul de artă Ploieşti
Bd. Gheorghe Gheorghiu-Dej 1,
Ploieşti
Fine Arts Museum - 1929
Classical and contemporary Romanian
art

10760
Muzeul de ştiinţele naturii Ploieşti
Str. 6 Martie 1, Ploieşti
Natural History Museum - 1956
Natural resources; regional flora and
fauna

10761
Muzeul judeţean de istorie Prahova
Str. Teatrului 10, Ploieşti
General Museum - 1955
Archaeology; numismatics; history;
ethnography

10762
Muzeul republican al petrolului
Str. Dr Bagdasar 8, Ploieşti
Science/Tech Museum - 1960
History of the use of oil ; oil drilling;
modern technology; geology;
documents; photos

Poiana Sibiului

10763
Muzeul etnografic Poiana Sibiului
Poiana Sibiului
General Museum - 1935
Ethnography; folk art

Prislop

10764
Muzeul memorial 'Liviu Rebreanu'
Prislop
Fine Arts Museum - 1957
Photos, books, personal objects of the
writer Liviu Rebreanu (1885-1944)

Rădăuţi

10765
**Muzeul 'Tehnicii populare
bucovinene'**
Piaţa Republicii 65, Rădăuţi
Anthropology Museum - 1920
Woodcarvings; costumes; handicrafts

Reghin

10766
Muzeul etnografic Reghin
Str. Vînătorilor 51, Reghin
Anthropology Museum - 1959
Folk art; open air ethnography park

Rîmnicu Sărat

10767
Muzeul orăşenesc Rîmnicu Sărat
Str. Suvorov 132, Rîmnicu Sărat
General Museum - 1960
History; ethnography; local art

Rîmnicu Vîlcea

10768
Muzeul judeţean
Str. Arges 35, Rîmnicu Vîlcea
General Museum - 1955
Archaeology; history; ethnography;
art; open air ethnography museum

Roman

10769
Muzeul de istorie şi artă Roman
Str. Cuza Vodă, Roman
History/Public Affairs Museum - 1957
Archaeology; history; art

10770
Muzeul de stiinţele naturii
Str. Proletariatului 4, Roman
Natural History Museum - 1965
Flora and fauna of the area

Roşiori

10771
Muzeul orăşenesc Roşiori
Str. Dunării, Roşiori
General Museum - 1965
Archaeology; history; ethnography; art

Sarmizegetusa

10772
**Muzeul de artă Sarmizegetusa-Ulpia
Traiana**
Sarmizegetusa 218
Archeology Museum - 1924
Lapidarium; inscriptions; coins; ancient
art; at the site of a former Roman city

Satu Mare

10773
Muzeul judeţean Satu Mare
Piaţa Libertăţii 21, Satu Mare
General Museum - 1890
Archaeology; history; ethnography;
folk art; Romanian painting

Sebes

10774
Muzeul municipal Sebes
Parcul 8 Mai 4, Sebes
General Museum - 1951
History; ethnography; natural science;
housed in a 15th century building

Sfintu Gheorghe

10775
Muzeul judeţean Covasna
Str. 16 Februarie 10, Sfintu Gheorghe
General Museum - 1879
Archaeology; history; ethnography;
modern Romanian and Hungarian art

Sibiu

10776
Muzeul Brukenthal
Bd. Republicii 4-5, Sibiu
General Museum - 1817
Archaeology; numismatics; rare prints;
folk art; modern and contemporary
Romanian art; European art; lapidarium

10777
Muzeul de istorie naturală Sibiu
Str. Cetăţii 1, Sibiu
Natural History Museum - 1849
Zoology; botany; paleontology;
mineralogy; flora and fauna; open air
ethnography section

Sighetu Marmaţiei

10778
**Muzeul maramureşan Sighetu
Marmaţiei**
Str. V.I.Lenin 2, Sighetu Marmaţiei
Anthropology Museum - 1954
Folk art; costumes; icons; handicrafts;
woodcarvings of the Maramures area;
open air museum

Sighişoara

10779
Muzeul municipal Sighişoara
Piaţa Muzeului 1, Sighişoara
General Museum - 1899
Archaeological finds; coins; history of
guilds; tools; weapons; documents

Sinaia

10780
Muzeul Peleş
Str. Peleşului 2, Sinaia
Fine Arts Museum - 1947
Art; paintings; sculptures; weapons;
tapestries; porcelain; furniture; carpets

Slatina

10781
Muzeul judeţean Olt
Str. Ionaşcu 73, Slatina
General Museum - 1952
Archaeology; history; ethnography;
folk art

Slobozia

10782
Muzeul judeţean Slobozia
Str. Matei Basarab 31, Slobozia
General Museum - 1971
Ethnography; folk art

Suceava

10783
Muzeul judeţean Suceava
Str. Stefan cel Mare 33, Suceava
General Museum - 1900
Archaeology; numismatics; history;
ethnography; art; natural science;
documents on composer Ciprian
Porumbescu (1853-1883)

Tecuci

10784
Muzeul mixt Tecuci
Str. 23 August 37, Tecuci
General Museum - 1934
Archaeology; history; natural science

Timişoara

10785
Muzeul Banatului
Piaţa Huniade 1, str. Popa Sapcă 4,
Timişoara
General Museum - 1872
Archaeology; numismatics; lapidarium;
history; ethnography, folk art;
Romanian and foreign art; natural
science; open air ethnography section;
housed in a 14th century castle

Tîrgovişte

10786
**Complexul monumental 'Curtea
Veche'**
Str. Nicolae Bălcescu 221, Tîrgovişte
General Museum - 1967
Archaeology; documents referring to
the city; housed in a 14th century
building

10787
Muzeul judeţean Dimbovita
Str. Justiţiei 3, Tîrgovişte
General Museum - 1944
Archaeology; numismatics, history;
ethnography; literature; art

10788
**Muzeul tiparului şi al cărţii vechi
româneşti**
Str. Justiţiei 5, Tîrgovişte
History/Public Affairs Museum - 1967
Cultural history; history of printing; old
Romanian books

Tîrgu Jiu

10789
Muzeul judeţean Gorj
Str. Griviţei 8, Tîrgu Jiu
General Museum - 1894
Archaeology; history; ethnography;
natural science; open air ethnography
section

Tîrgu Mureş

10790
Muzeul de artă Tîrgu Mureş
Piaţa Eroilor Sovietici 1, Tîrgu Mureş
Fine Arts Museum - 1912
Classical and contemporary Romanian
art; Hungarian paintings

10791
Muzeul judeţean Mureş
Str. Horov 24, Tîrgu Mureş
General Museum - 1893
Archaeological finds; coins; history;
ethnography; folk art; natural science

Topalu

10792
Muzeul de artă 'Dinu şi Sevasta Vintilă'
Topalu
Fine Arts Museum - 1960
Paintings; sculptures by Romanian artists

Tulcea

10793
Muzeul Deltei Dunării
Str. 9 Mai 4, Tulcea
General Museum - 1949
Archaeological finds; lapidarium; numismatics; medieval history; ethnography; flora and fauna of the region

Turda

10794
Muzeul de istorie Turda
Str. B.P.Hasdeu 2, Turda
History/Public Affairs Museum - 1951
Archaeology; history; ethnography; housed in a 15th century palace

Urlaţi

10795
Muzeul etnografic Urlaţi
Str. Orzoaia de Sus 12, Urlaţi
Anthropology Museum - 1955
Ethnography; folk art

Vălenii de Munte

10796
Muzeul memorial 'Nicolae Iorga'
Str. George Enescu 3, Vălenii de Munte
Historic Site - 1965
Documents, photos, furniture of the historian Nicolae Iorga (1871-1940); in his country house

Vaslui

10797
Muzeul judeţean Vaslui
Str. I.C.Frimu 1, Vaslui
General Museum - 1974
Archaeology; history; ethnography

Vatra Dornei

10798
Muzeul de stiinţele naturii Vatra Dornei
Str. 7 Noiembrie 17, Vatra Dornei
Natural History Museum - 1957
Geology; flora and fauna of the area

Zalău

10799
Muzeul judeţean de istorie şi artă Zalău
Str. Pieţii 9, Zalău
General Museum - 1951
Archaeology; numismatics; lapidarium; history; ethnography; folk art; contemporary Romanian art

308

Rwanda

Butare

10800
Musée National
B.P. 218, Butare
General Museum - 1953
Ethnology; archaeology; geology; botany; basket-works; carvings; handicrafts

Kabgayi

10801
Musée de Kabgayi
Evêché de Kabgayi, Kabgayi, Gitarama
General Museum - 1943
Ethnography; lances; pottery; basketry; mineralogy; geology; art

Kigali

10802
Musée de Géologique du Rwanda
mail c/o Ministère des Ressources Naturelles, des Mines et des Carrières, B.P. 413, Kigali
Natural History Museum - 1977
Rocks; minerals; photographs

San Marino

San Marino

10803
Museo delle Armi da Fuoco
San Marino
History/Public Affairs Museum
Firearms

10804
Museo delle Cere
San Marino
History/Public Affairs Museum - 1966
History of the Risorgimento

10805
Museo e Pinacoteca Governativi
Via Carducci 141, San Marino
General Museum
Furniture; pottery; numismatics; archaeology; paintings

10806
Museo e Pinacoteca 'San Francesco'
Via Orafo, San Marino
Fine Arts Museum
Ancient and modern works; incunabula

10807
Museo Postale, Filatelico-Numismatico
Borgo Maggiore, San Marino
History/Public Affairs Museum - 1972
Stamps; coins

São Tomé and Principe

São Tomé

10808
Museu Nacional
Praça de Juventude, CP 188, São Tomé
Fine Arts Museum - 1975
African art; religious art

Saudi Arabia

Riyadh

10809
Dept. of Antiquities and Museums
POB 3734, Riyadh
Archeology Museum
Several museums near the major archeological sites are about to be established

10810
Geological Museum University of Riyadh
Almilaz, Riyadh
Natural History Museum
Geology

10811
Museum of Archaeology and Ethnography
Riyadh
General Museum - 1978
Coll: Stone Age; 'Age of Trade'; 'After the Revelation' (development of Islam)

Senegal

Dakar

10812
Musée d'Art Africain de Dakar
Institut Fondamental d'Afrique Noire
Place Tacher, B.P. 206, Dakar
Fine Arts Museum - 1936
African art; ethnology

10813
Musée de la Mer Institut Fondamental d'Afrique Noire
Place du Gouvernement à l'Ile de Gorée, Dakar
Natural History Museum - 1959
Oceanography; marine biology

10814
Musée Géologique Africain
Route de l'Université, B.P. 1238, Dakar
Natural History Museum - 1963
Geology; rocks - library

10815
Musée Historique Institut Fondamental d'Afrique Noire
Rue Malavois, Gorée, Dakar
Archeology Museum
Archaeology of West Africa

Saint-Louis

10816
Centre de Recherches et de Documentation du Sénégal
Rue Neuville, Pointe-Sud, B.P. 382, Saint-Louis
Natural History Museum - 1943
Zoology; botany; geology; anthropology; history; art

Seychelles

Mahé

10817
Seychelles National Museum
Independence Avenue, Victoria, Mahé
Natural History Museum - 1964
History; natural history; Stone of Possession

Sierra Leone

Freetown

10818
Sierra Leone National Museum
Junction of Wilberforce and Pademba Rd, POB 908, Freetown
General Museum
Archaeology; ethnology; chieftain crowns; ceremonial carvings; documents

Singapore

Singapore

10819
Fort Siloso
mail c/o Mr. Lim Kim Foong, Curator, Sentosa Development Corporation, Jetty Rd, Sentosa, Singapore 0208
History/Public Affairs Museum

10820
The Lee Kong Chian Museum of Asian Culture Nanyang University
mail c/o Mdm. Wan Suet Yee, Curator, Upper Jurong Rd, Singapore 2263
Anthropology Museum

10821
The Maritime Museum
Port of Singapore Authority, Maritime Square, Singapore 0409
History/Public Affairs Museum - 1975
Paintings; ship models; fishing artifacts; local watercraft; charts; photographs; coins and medals - library

10822
Museum
National Development Building, mail c/o Mr. Philip Chua, Secretary, Preservation of Monuments Board, Maxwell Rd, Singapore 0106

10823
National Museum of Singapore
Stamford Rd, Singapore 0617
General Museum - 1849
University of Singapore art collection; Haw Par jade collection; portrait of Sir Frank Swettenham by John Singer Sargent; prehistory of Southeast Asia; history of Singapore with a collection of historical paintings, photographs, prints and maps; Singapore Chinese furniture; ancient Chinese bronzes; West Malaysian aborigines' artifacts - library

10824
Sentosa Coralarium
Sentosa, mail c/o Mr. Lim Eng Leong, Curator, Sentosa Development Corporation Singapore 0208

10825
Singapore Science Centre
mail c/o Dr. R.S. Bhathal, Director, Science Centre Rd, off Jurong Town Hall Rd, Singapore 2260
Natural History Museum

10826
William Willetts Art Museum
University of Singapore
Bukit Timah Rd, Singapore
Decorative Arts Museum
Fine and applied arts of China, India, and South East Asia

Solomon Islands

Honiara

10827
National Museum and Cultural Centre
313, Honiara
General Museum - 1969
Prehistory; language and oral tradition; music; dance; architecture

Somalia

Mogadishu

10828
National Museum of Somalia
Corso Republica, Mogadishu
General Museum
Coll: ethnology; traditional Somali objects; Arab metal work; weapons; jewelry; documents and old Arab books; numismatics; philately; natural history; fossils; minerals

South Africa

Adelaide

10829
Our Heritage Museum
Queen St, Adelaide 5760
General Museum - 1967
Victorian, Jacobean and Voortrekker furniture; silver, glass and china; farm implements; wagons and carts

Alice

10830
F.S. Malan Ethnological Museum
mail c/o University of Transkei, POB 314, Alice 5700
Anthropology Museum
Artifacts from Cape Nguni, Zulu and Sotho tribes; implements and ornaments; works by contemporary African artists

Barberton

10831
Barberton Museum
Pilgrim St, POB 33, Barberton 1300
General Museum
Relics of the Lowveld goldrush during the 1880s; mining and geology

Barkley East

10832
Barkley East Museum
Barkley East 5580
General Museum
Local history and geology; early transportation

Beaufort West

10833
Beaufort West Museum
mail c/o Old Mission Church, Donkin St 89, POB 370, Beaufort West 6970
General Museum
Local history; ethnology; 19th century firearms; domestic implements; furnishings

Bethlehem

10834
Bethlehem Museum
7 Muller St East, POB 551, Bethlehem 9700
General Museum
Items of local historic import; farm implements; objects from early railway transport

Bethulie

10835
Pellissier House
1 Voortrekker St, POB 7, Bethulie 9992
General Museum
Clothing; domestic utensils; relics pertaining to the history of the ara; photographs

Bloemfontein

10836
A.C. White Gallery
Municipal Theatre, Charles and Markgraaf Sts, POB 288, Bloemfontein 9300
Fine Arts Museum
Works of contemporary South African artists

10837
First Raadsaal Museum 2
95 St. Georges St, *mail c/o* National Museum, POB 266, Bloemfontein 9300
Historic Site - 1877

10838
National Museum
36 Aliwal St, POB 266, Bloemfontein 9300
General Museum - 1877
Anthropology; natural history; local history; Florisbad skull; Pachygenelus fossil; Homoiceras horn cores; Hottentot skulls; Achilleoceras fossil; Malvern meteorite - library

10839
National Museum for Afrikaans Literature
Old Government Bldg, Pres Brand St, POB 517, Bloemfontein 9300
History/Public Affairs Museum - 1973
Manuscripts, books; letters and photos illustrating history of Afrikaans language; exhibits on individual literary figures, Afrikaans theater and musical life

10840
War Museum of the Boer Republics
National Women's Monument Grounds, POB 704, Bloemfontein 9300
History/Public Affairs Museum - 1931
Oils and drawings of Boer generals, leaders and war scenes; arms, uniforms, flags and maps; photographs

Bredasdorp

10841
Bredasdorp Museum
6 Independent St, Bredasdorp 7280
General Museum
Local history exhibits housed in an old church

Burgersdorp

10842
Burgersdorp Museum
49 Piet Retief St, POB 156, Burgersdorp 5520
General Museum - 1970
History of the northeastern Cape border farmers; reconstructed buildings

Caledon

10843
Caledon Museum
11 Krige St, Caledon 7230
General Museum - 1973
Local period furnishings; Victorian costume, porcelain, firearms; glass; Cape silver

Calvinia

10844
Calvinia Museum
44 Church St, POB 93, Calvinia 8190
General Museum - 1968
Local history exhibits housed in a former synagogue

Cape Town

10845
Castle of Good Hope William Fehr Collection
POB 1, Cape Town 8000
Fine Arts Museum - 1964
Painting; furniture and furnishings; china, silver and copper - library

10846
Clock Tower Maritime Museum
Victoria Basin, Table Bay Harbour, POB 4379, Cape Town 8000
General Museum - 1978
Nautical exhibits; photo display of early local shipping; clock mechanism and tide guage

10847
Groot Constantia Manor House
Constantia, Private Bag, Constantia 7848, Cape Town 7800
General Museum
17th and 18th century Dutch painting; Cape funiture; Oriental ceramics; wine history collection

10848
Irma Stern Museum
mail c/o The Firs, Cecil Road, Rosebank, Cape Town 7700
Fine Arts Museum - 1972
African art and paintings of Irma Stern housed in former home of the artist; furnishings and objects d'art

10849
Jewish Museum
mail c/o Old Synagogue, 84 Hatfield St, Gardens, Cape Town 8001
Religious Art Museum
Jewish ceremonial art and Judaica housed in first synagogue built in South Africa - archives

10850
Koopmans De Wet House
35 Strand St, POB 645, Cape Town 8000
Fine Arts Museum - 1917
18th century Cape furniture and furnishings; Chinese porelain; Japanese Imri ware; silver glass and porcelain

10851
Michaelis Collection
Old Town House, Greenmarket Sq, Cape Town 8001
Fine Arts Museum - 1916
17th century Dutch and Flemish painting; 16th-17th century graphic art

10852
Military Museum
The Castle, Grand Parade, POB 1, Cape Town 8000
History/Public Affairs Museum - 1966
Militaria

10853
Rust en Vreugd Museum William Fehr Collection
78 Buitenkant St, Cape Town 8000
Fine Arts Museum - 1940
Africana painting, water colors and drawings housed in 18th century house

10854
South African Cultural History Museum
49 Adderley St, POB 645, Cape Town 8000
Fine Arts Museum - 1855
Egyptian, Roman and Greek antiquities; Chinese and Japanese maritime arms and armour; South African coinage; Cape, Malay, Indonesian and European furniture and furnishings

10855
South African Museum
Government Av, POB 61, Cape Town 8000
Natural History Museum - 1855
Paleontology; entomology; ethnology; archaeology; marine biology; zoology

10856
South African National Gallery
Government Av, POB 2420, Cape Town 8000
Fine Arts Museum - 1871
Traditional African sculpture; Sir Abe Bailey collection of sporting and hunting pictures; African metal sculpture; Dutch, French and English painting (17th to 20th century); South African 19th and 20th century art

Colenso

10857
R.E. Stevenson Museum
mail c/o Town Clerk, Old Toll House, POB 22, Colenso 3360
General Museum - 1974
Weapons, badges, medals; personal relics; historical photographs

Colesberg

10858
Kemper Museum
Campbell St, Colesberg 5980
General Museum - 1924
History of the Boer War, history of South African settlers

Constantia

10859
Nova Constantia
Spaanschemat River Road, Constantia 7800
General Museum
18th cent. furniture and furnishings in original setting; original Cape and English antiques

Cradock

10860
Great Fish River Museum
87 High St, Cradock 5880
General Museum - 1979
English and Afrikaans furniture; furnishings; 19th century domestic and farming implements and equipment

Dundee

10861
Dundee and District Museum
Municipal Civic Centre, POB 76,
Dundee
General Museum - 1930
Local history; geology; archaeology;
ethnology; metallurgy; anthropology;
fossils

Durban

10862
Campbell Collections
220 Marriott Rd, Durban 4001
General Museum
Cape Dutch furniture; cultural relics;
Africana pictures

10863
Centenary Aquarium
2 West St, POB 736, Durban 4000
Natural History Museum - 1959
Whales, sharks, seals, dolphins

10864
Durban Museum and Art Gallery
City Hall, Smith St, Durban, Natal 4001
General Museum - 1887
South African flora and fauna;
geology; ethnography; archaeology;
European and South African painting,
sculpture and graphic art;
contemporary pottery; porcelain,
bronze and glass; laces; ivory

10865
Geological Museum University of
Natal
King George V Av, Durban 4001
Natural History Museum
Geological exhibits; Karroo reptiles;
homonoid skulls and artifacts

10866
Local History Museum
Old Court House, Aliwal St, Durban,
Natal 4001
General Museum - 1966
Material relating to the settlement of
Natal from 1497; history of the Zulu
and Boer wars; relics of the wreck of
the Grosvenor (1784); art works

10867
**Mahatma Gandhi Library and
Museum**
Inanda Rd, Phoenix, Private Bag 4104,
Durban 4000
History/Public Affairs Museum - 1970
Exhibits depicting the life and
teachings of Gandhi on premises on
which he lived and taught from 1893 to
1914 - library

10868
Natal Herbarium
mail c/o Botanical Research Unit,
Botanic Gardens Road, Durban 4001
Natural History Museum
Foreign and local specimens with
special emphasis on flora and fauna of
Natal and Zululand

10869
Old House Museum
31 St Andrew's St, Durban 4001
General Museum - 1954
Furniture and domestic utensils; local
works of art; period furnishings

East London

10870
Ann Bryant Art Gallery
9 St. Marks Road 2, East London 5201
Fine Arts Museum - 1947
South African painting

10871
East London Museum
Upper Oxford St, East London 5201
General Museum - 1931
Archaeology; cultural history; shells;
birds; specimens of coelacanth and
Karroo fossils

10872
Gately House
Park Gates Road, East London 5201
Fine Arts Museum
Original period furnishings and objects
d'art housed in former home of John
Gates, 'father' of East London

Eshowe

10873
Zululand Historical Museum
mail c/o Town Clerk, 37, Eshowe,
Zululand 3815
General Museum - 1960
Zulu handicrafts; local historical
artifacts

Estcourt

10874
Bushman Museum
Main Caves, Giant's Castle Nature
Reserve, Estcourt 3310
Natural History Museum - 1969
Prehistoric rock paintings; displays
showing skills and crafts of Bushmen

Fort Beaufort

10875
Fort Beaufort Historical Museum
44 Durban St, Fort Beaufort 5720
General Museum - 1938
Firearms; spears and arrows;
costumes; old photographs;
documents

Franschhoek

10876
Huguenot Memorial Museum
Lambrechts St, POB 37, Franschhoek
7690
History/Public Affairs Museum - 1967
Huguenot history and genealogy

Genadendal

10877
Genadendal Museum
mail c/o Church Office, Church
Square, Genadendal 7234
Historic Site
Documents of early missionary work
housed on site of first South African
missionary activity

George

10878
George Museum
mail c/o The Old Drostdy, Courtenay
St, POB 564, George 6530
General Museum - 1969
Antique gramophones and music
boxes; antique cameras, telephones,
typewriters; domestic items;
documents

Graaff-Reinet

10879
Graaff-Reinet Museum
Reinet House, Parsonage St, POB 104,
Graaff-Reinet 6280
General Museum - 1956
Eastern Cape furniture; wooden
agricultural implements; Cape silver;
largest vine stem in the world

10880
Hester Rupert Art Museum
Graaff-Reinet 6280
Fine Arts Museum - 1965
Contemporary South African art

Grabouw

10881
Elgin Apple Museum
Grabouw, POB 27, Elgin 7180
General Museum
History of Grabouw and local apple-
growing industry

Grahamstown

10882
Albany Museum
Somerset St, Grahamstown 6140
Natural History Museum - 1882/1900
Fresh water ichthyology; mammalogy;
entomology; arachnology; ornithology;
archaeology

10883
**Rhodes Museum of Classical
Antiquities**
Rhodes University, Dept. of Classics,
POB 94, Grahamstown 6140
Fine Arts Museum
Greek and Roman vases; coins;
various artifacts

10884
Settlers' Memorial Museum
Somerset St, Grahamstown 6140
General Museum - 1965
Household utensils; agricultural
implements; costumes; painting and
sculpture

10885
Temlett House
53 Beaufort St, Grahamstown 6140
General Museum
Victorian furnishings housed in early
19th cent. dwelling; 19th cent. cottage
(Scott's Farm Cottage) located in
surrounding gardens

Great Brak River

10886
Great Brak River Museum
Amy Searle St, POB 15, Great Brak
River 6525
General Museum
Local history; period furnishings and
domestic utensils housed in typical
late 19th cent. worker's cottage

Greytown

10887
Greytown Museum
68 Scott St, Greytown 3500
General Museum - 1961
Relics of pioneer families and the 1906
rebellion; stone implements; Zulu
artifacts

Griquatown

10888
Mary Moffat Museum
Main St, Griquatown
General Museum
Local history

Harrismith

10889
Burns-Thompson Memorial Museum
Town Hall, Warden St, Harrismith
General Museum - 1910
Birds; war relics; minerals;
ethnological specimens; fossils;
firearms

Hartenbos

10890
Hartenbos Museum
Majuba Av, Hartenbos 6520
General Museum - 1976
Displays depicting daily life of early
Voortrekkers; authentic early
equipment and utensils

Heidelberg

10891
Heidelberg Transport Museum
Old Railway Station, POB 320,
Heidelberg 2400
Science/Tech Museum - 1974
Early bicycles, tricycles and
motorcycles; antique motor vehicles;
ancient transportation vehicles;
railway cars and locomotives

Hermanus

10892
Old Harbour Museum
POB 118, Hermanus 7200
General Museum - 1973
Open-air, on-site collection of early
harbour structures and boats

Himeville

10893
Settlers Museum
Loteni Nature Reserve, Himeville 4584
General Museum
Victoriana; early farming machinery

Howick

10894
Howick Museum
24 Morling St, POB 5, Howick 3290
General Museum
Local cultural and agricultural history

Isandlwana

10895
Saint Vincent Church Museum
mail c/o Saint Vincent's Rectory
Isandlwana
General Museum
Local history; Battle of Isandlwana
memorial

Johannesburg

10896
Africana Museum
Public Library, Market Square,
Johannesburg 2001
General Museum - 1935
Ethnology; pictorial Africana; Cape
silver and furniture; numismatics and
philately; costumes; musical
instruments

10897
Archaeological Research Unit
University of Witwatersrand
Jan Smuts Av, Johannesburg 2000
Anthropology Museum - 1935

10898
Bensusan Museum of Photography
17 Empire Rd, Parktown,
Johannesburg 2 2001
Science/Tech Museum - 1960
W.H. Fox Talbot collection; callotpye
photographs - library

10899
Bernard Price Institute for Paleontological Research
University of Witwatersrand, Johannesburg 2001
Natural History Museum - 1948
Paleontoloty; micro paleontology; paleoanthropology; Karroo vertebrates; mammalian fossils; bone artifacts

10900
Bernberg Museum of Costume
Duncombe Rd and Jan Smuts Av, Johannesburg 2001
History/Public Affairs Museum
South African dress from ca. 1790 to 1929

10901
Bleloch Museum University of Witwatersrand, Dept. of Geology
1 Jan Smuts Av, POB 1176, Johannesburg 2000
Natural History Museum - 1922
Rocks, minerals and ores

10902
Ethnological Museum University of Witwatersrand
Jan Smuts Av, Johannesburg 2000
Anthropology Museum
Bushman, Owamba, Pedix, Venda, Tsanga, Bemba, Sotho, Zulu, and Luba carvings and masks

10903
Geological Museum
Public Library, Market Square, Johannesburg 2001
Natural History Museum - 1904
Geology; archaeology; minerals; gold

10904
Gertrud Posel Gallery University of Witwatersrand
Senate House, 1 Jan Smuts Av, Johannesburg 2001
Fine Arts Museum
Permanent collection of modern South African art; loan exhibitions of modern South African art

10905
Harry and Friedel Abt Jewish Museum
4th Floor, Sheffield House, Main and Kruis Sts, POB 1180, Johannesburg 2000
Religious Art Museum - 1957
Jewish ceremonial art; Jewish Africana; silver and jewelry

10906
Hunterian Museum
Old Medical School, Johannesburg 2001
Anthropology Museum
African masks; human skeletons; South African fossil hominids

10907
James Hall Museum of Transport
Pioneer's Park, Rosettenville Rd, Johannesburg 2001
Science/Tech Museum - 1964
Transportation; fire engines

10908
Johannesburg Art Gallery
Joubert Park, 23561, Johannesburg 2044
Fine Arts Museum - 1915
Dutch, French and English collections (17th to 20th century); South African collectin; modern international collection; print collection (15th century to present)

10909
Medical Ecology Centre Collections
mail c/o Dept. of Health, S.A. Institute of Medical Research, Hospital St, POB 1038, Johannesburg 2000
Natural History Museum
Mammal skins

10910
Museum of Science
78 The Valley Rd, Johannesburg 2000
Science/Tech Museum
Agriculture; mining and manufacture; commerce and transport; architecture; power generation; astronomy; space engineering

10911
Museum of South African Rock Art
Zoological Gardens, Johannesburg 2000
Anthropology Museum
Petroglyphs; rock engravings

10912
Museum of the History of Medicine
University of Witwatersrand, Hospital St, POB 1038, Johannesburg 2000
Science/Tech Museum - 1962
History of medicine; witchcraft; tribal medicine

10913
Museum of the Institute for the Study of Man in Africa
mail c/o Medical School, Hospital St, Johannesburg 2000
Anthropology Museum
Archaeology; prehistory; paleoanthropology; ethnography; folklore

10914
Reza Shah Museum
41 Young Av, Mountain View, POB 7461, Johannesburg 2000
History/Public Affairs Museum - 1972 5
Ancient and modern Persian art - library

10915
South African Railway Museum
De Villiers St, POB 1111, Johannesburg
Science/Tech Museum - 1920
Early model locomotives used in South Africa

Kimberley

10916
Duggan-Cronin Bantu Gallery
Egerton Rd, POB 316, Kimberley 8300
Anthropology Museum - 1937
Photographic collection covering Southern African tribes

10917
Kimberley Mine Museum
mail c/o De Beers Consolidated Mines Ltd, Tucker St, Kimberley 8301
General Museum
Diamond display; shops and dwellings of early Kimberley mining period; Kimberley 'Big Hole' open mine

10918
McGregor Museum
Chapel St and Egerton Rd, POB 316, Kimberley 8301
Natural History Museum - 1907
Local history; anthropology; archaeology; botany; zoology; fossils

10919
Magersfontein Battlefield Museum
Off National Road to Cape Town via Modder River, POB 316, Kimberley 8300
Historic Site
Original defenses and memorials marking the Battle of 11 Dec. 1899; displays of uniforms, equipment and weapons; relics and photographs taken during the battle

10920
William Humphreay Art Gallery
Civic Centre, POB 885, Kimberley 8300
Fine Arts Museum - 1952
Old master painting; South African painting; 17th cent. European art

King William's Town

10921
Kaffrarian Museum
3 Lower Albert Rd, King William's Town 5600
General Museum
History of early German settlers; militaria; mammals; birds; lower vertebrates; insects; shells

10922
South African Missionary Museum
27 Berkeley St, King William's Town 5600
General Museum - 1973
Photographs; documents and records relating to missionaries and missions stations

Klerksdorp

10923
Klerksdorp Museum
Lombard and Magrietha Sts, POB 99, Klerksdorp 2570
General Museum
Prehistory and history of Klerksdorp and Western Transvaal; geological and archaeological displays

Knysna

10924
Millwood House
Queen St, POB 12, Knysna 6570
General Museum
Photos and relics related to Millwood goldrush of 1887; original furniture

Ladysmith

10925
Ladysmith Museum
POB 380, Ladysmith 3370
General Museum
Local history exhibits with emphasis on the period of the South African War

Mafeking

10926
Mafeking Museum
Town Hall, POB 526, Mafeking 8670
General Museum
Antique guns; local history exhibits; diamond and gold mining

Mariannhill

10927
Africana Museum
Monastery, Mariannhill 3601
Anthropology Museum
Bantu ethnology; old African beadwork; musical instruments; domestic utensils; weapons; Bushmen paintings

Matjiesfontein

10928
Marie Rawdon Museum
mail c/o Hotel Lord Milner
Matjiesfontein 6901
General Museum
Victorian and Edwardian furnishings and domestic utensils housed in typical 19th cent. village cottage; period costumes and dresses

Messina

10929
Messina Museum
National Rd, Private Bag X611, Messina 0900
Science/Tech Museum - 1971
Voortrecker firearms; mining equipment; copper ore; tribal weapons

Middelburg Cape

10930
P.W. Vorster Museum
mail c/o Grootfontein Agricultural College Middelburg Cape 5900
General Museum
Local history displays housed in 1827 homestead; farm implements

Molteno

10931
Molteno Museum
Smith St, Molteno 5500
General Museum
Fossils; stone implements; arrowheads; pottery; beadwork

Montagu

10932
Montagu Museum
Long St, Montagu 6720
General Museum
Photos and documents housed in 19th cent. dwelling; 18th cent. furniture

Mossel Bay

10933
Mossel Bay Museum
Market St, POB 371, Mossel Bay 6500
General Museum - 1961
Maps; photographs; maritime history of Mossel Bay; shells

Muizenberg

10934
Rhodes Cottage
246 Main Road, Muizenberg 7945
Historic Site
Memorabilia of Cecil Rhodes housed in traditional-style cottage in which Rhodes died (1903)

New Germany

10935
New Germany Museum
Public Library, Shepstone, New Germany 3600
General Museum
Personal items, photos, domestic utensils, etc. donated by descendants of German settlers

Newlands

10936
Rugby Museum
Newlands Rugby Grounds, Boundary Road, Newlands 7700
General Museum
History of rugby in South Africa; Rugby equipment - library

Onderstepoort

10937
Onderstepoort Pathology Museum
mail c/o Veterinary Research Institute Onderstepoort 0110
History/Public Affairs Museum - 1939
Veterinary pathology; wax models of toxic plants common to South Africa; pathology of infectious diseases of indigenous animals

Oudtshoorn

10938
Arbeidsgenot
217 Jan van Riebeeck Rd, Oudtshoorn 6620
Historic Site
Former home of C.J. Langenhoven

10939
Cango Caves Museum
POB 453, Oudtshoorn 6620
General Museum - 1967
Bushmen rock paintings; fossils; minerals

10940
C.P. Nel Museum
Voortrekker Rd, POB 453, Oudtshoorn 6620
General Museum - 1953
Photographs; furniture; porcelain; Bushmen paintings; musical instruments; firearms; household utensils; natural history exhibits

Paarl

10941
Afrikaans Language Museum
Gideon Malherbe House, Parsonage Lane, POB 498, Paarl 7620
History/Public Affairs Museum - 1875
Exhibits related to development of Afrikaans as a written, national language; first editions of early Afrikaans publications; period furnishings

10942
Old Parsonage Museum
Main Road, Paarl 7647
General Museum - 1939
18th cent. Dutch furniture; Cape and English silver; Chinese, English and Dutch porcelain; glass, copper and brass kitchen utensils; coach house; farming implements; French Hugenot exhibits - library

Pietermaritzburg

10943
Macrorie House Museum
11 Loop St, POB 42, Pietermaritzburg 3200
General Museum - 1975
Restored Victorian mansion of the 1970s; furniture and furnishings

10944
Mines Department Museum
mail c/o Department of Mines Pietermaritzburg 3200
Science/Tech Museum
0735; 1080

10945
Natal Museum
237 Loop St, Pietermaritzburg 3201
General Museum - 1904
Natural and cultural history exhibits; archaeology and ethnology of Southern Africa; local history; ungulate mammals of Africa - library

10946
Tatham Art Gallery
City Hall, Pietermaritzburg 3201
Fine Arts Museum - 1903
18th-19th cent. English and French painting; graphic arts (19th cent. to present); objects d'art; oriental carptes

10947
Voortrekker Museum
Church St, POB 998, Pietermaritzburg 3200
General Museum
Voortrekker history; homemade furniture; firearms; household utensils; costumes; wagons

Pietersburg

10948
Northern Transvaal Regional Art Gallery
mail c/o Civic Center, Maré St, POB 111, Pietersburg 0700
Fine Arts Museum - 1972

Pilgrim's Rest

10949
Pilgrim's Rest Museum
Private Bag X519, Pilgrim's Rest 1290
General Museum - 1974
Mining reduction works with original equipment; furnished miner's and mine manager's houses; robey steam engine

Port Elizabeth

10950
King George VI Art Gallery
1 Park Drive, Port Elizabeth 6001
Fine Arts Museum - 1957
English painting; South African art; Indian miniatures; Japanese woodcuts; graphics

10951
Port Elizabeth Museum
Beach Rd, Humewood, 13147, Port Elizabeth 6001
General Museum - 1856
Oceanarium; snake park; tropical house; marine biology; vehicles; archaeological and natural history exhibits; skulls

Potchefstroom

10952
Ethnological Museum
University of Potchefstroom, Potchefstroom 2520
Anthropology Museum
Charles More collection of Phalaborwa culture; items of material culture of most South African Bantu peoples; exhibits from other world cultures

10953
Potcefstroom Museum
Gouws and Potgieter Sts, POB 113, Potchefstroom 2520
General Museum - 1960
Household utensils; furniture; clothing; weapons transport; Bantu and Bushmen housing; Voortrekker oxwagon - library

10954
University Art Gallery
University of Potchefstroom, Ferdinand Postma Library Bldg, Potchefstroom 2520
Fine Arts Museum
Contemporary South African aft

Potgietersrus

10955
Arend Dieperink Museum
Voortrekker Road, POB, Potgietersrus 0600
General Museum - 1968
Relics of Voortrekker leader Piet Potgieter; farming implements and wagons; old music instruments; furniture and furnishings; photos and documents

Pretoria

10956
Anthropological Museum
mail c/o Dept. of Anthropology and Bantu and Native Law, University of South Africa, Library Bldg, Skinner and v.d.Walt Sts, Pretoria 0001
Anthropology Museum
Ethnography; folklore; archaeology

10957
Anton van Wouw House
299 Clark St, Pretoria 0002
Fine Arts Museum
Works of Anton van Wouw

10958
Engelbrecht Museum
224 Jacob Mare St, POB 2368, Pretoria 0001
General Museum
Artifacts relating to the history of the Dutch Reformed Church of Africa; coins and commemorative medals; painting; incunabula; cultural antiquities

10959
Engelenburg House Art Collection
Hamilton and Edmund Sts, POB 538, Pretoria 0001
Fine Arts Museum - 1942
Oriental and Cape ceramics; Cape, English and Dutch furniture; tapestries; painting; carpets

10960
Jansen Collection National Cultural History Museum
214 Struben St, POB 3300, Pretoria 0001
General Museum - 1964
18th and 19th century South African and imported furniture; Chinese and Japanese porcelain; ceramics and paintings by famous South African artists

10961
Kruger House Museum Natural Cultural History Museum
60 Church St West, Boom St, POB 3300, Pretoria 0001
General Museum - 1925
Memorabilia of President Paul Kruger (1825-1904); local history

10962
Maritime Museum
The Castle, POB 414, Pretoria 0001
History/Public Affairs Museum - 1971
Model ships; maritime history

10963
Martello Tower Naval Museum
POB 414, Pretoria 0001
History/Public Affairs Museum - 1973
Navel history of South Africa from 1625 to present

10964
Melrose House
275 Jacob Maré St, Pretoria 0002
General Museum - 1971
Late Victorial interior; dining room in which peace treaty ending Anglo-Boer War was signed

10965
Military Museum Fort Klapperkop
Private Bag x175, Pretoria 0001
History/Public Affairs Museum - 1966
Military history of Transvaal, 1852-1910; relics of the Boer War; militaria

10966
Museum of Science and Industry
Scutter St, POB 1758, Pretoria 0001
General Museum - 1960
Natural history; art; education; history; biography; travel

10967
Museum of the Geological Survey
223 Visagie St, Private Bag X112, Pretoria 0002
Natural History Museum - 1903
Rocks and minerals; Karroo reptiles; Gibeon meteorites; Alexander Bay marine diamonds; fossils; economic ores of South Africa

10968
National Cultural History Museum
Boom St, POB 3300, Pretoria 0001
Anthropology Museum
South African history, cultural history archaeology and ethnology; personal objects of Generals Louis Botha, J.B.M Hertzog and J.C. Smuts

10969
National Herbarium
2 Cussonia Av, Private Bag X101, Botanical Garden, Pretoria 0001
Natural History Museum
Flora of the African continent

10970
Pathology Museum
mail c/o University of Pretoria, Institute of Pathology, Beatrix St, POB 2034, Pretoria 0001
History/Public Affairs Museum
Pathology exhibits

10971
Post Office Museum
Church Square, POB 1522, Pretoria 0001
Science/Tech Museum - 1970
Postal equipment; telephones and telecommunications equipment; postage stamps - library

10972
Pretoria Art Museum
Arcadia Park, Schoeman St, Pretoria 0083
Fine Arts Museum - 1964
South African art from the 19th century to the present; graphic arts

10973
South African Mint Museum
Visagie St, POB 464, Pretoria
History/Public Affairs Museum - 1923
Coins, tokens and medals; plaques
and badges; history of the mint -
library

10974
**South African National Sports
Museum**
Munitoria Bldg, Van der Walt and
Vermeulen Sts, Pretoria 0002
History/Public Affairs Museum
History of sports and games in South
Africa

10975
South African Police Museum
Kompol Bldg, Pretorius St and
Volkstem Lane, Private Bag X94,
Pretoria 0001
History/Public Affairs Museum
Uniforms, insignia, arms, and other
artifacts showing the history of the
police force in South Africa; crime
detection and prevention

10976
Transvaal Education Museum
185 Gerhard Moerdykstraat,
Sunnyside, Private Bag X434, Pretoria
History/Public Affairs Museum - 1972
Old school desks and other furniture;
writing materials; old text books; early
types of certificates; reports and
documents; photographs

10977
Transvaal Museum
Paul Kruger St, POB 413, Pretoria
0001
Natural History Museum - 1893
South African fossil ape-men;
mammals; birds; lower vertebrates;
insects

10978
Voortrekker Monument Museum
Monument Kop, POB 998, Pretoria
0001
General Museum - 1957
Pioneer cottage furniture; tapestries
depicting pioneer history; items of
local history

Queenstown

10979
Queenstown and Frontier Museum
13 Shepstone St, POB 296,
Queenstown 5320
Natural History Museum - 1933
Lepidoptera

Rayton

10980
**Willem Prinsloo Agricultural
Museum** National Cultural History
Museum
near Rayton, Boom St, POB 3300,
Pretoria 0001
General Museum
Late 19th century farm house and
outbuildings; collection of antique farm
implements

Richmond

10981
Richmond Museum
19 Main St, Richmond 7010
General Museum
Cape Dutch and Victorian furnishings
in former (1863) school house;
displays devoted to the American
saddle horse

Riversdale

10982
Julius Gordon Africana Centre
Versveld House, Long St, Riversdale
6770
Fine Arts Museum - 1966
South African painting and antiques;
furniture; domestic utensils; clocks

Rondebosch

10983
Bolus Herbarium
mail c/o University of Cape Town
Rondebosch 7700
Natural History Museum - 1865
Fungi, lichens, algae; Bryophytes,
Pteridophytes and Phanerogams;
special collections of
Mesembryanthemaceae, Ericaceae,
Orchidaceae, Pelargonium and
Stapeliae

Roodepoort

10984
Roodepoort Municipal Museum
18 Dieperink St, POB 217, Roodepoort
1725
General Museum
Domestic and farming implements;
hand-made Transvaal pioneer
furniture; relics from Witwatersand
gold fields

Saxonwold

10985
**South African National Museum of
Military History**
Erlswold Way, POB 52090, Saxonwold
2196
History/Public Affairs Museum - 1947
Military items; South African war art
and photographs; aircraft and armored
vehicles - library

Silverton

10986
Pioneer House National Cultural
History Museum
Pretoria Road, Silverton, POB 3300,
Pretoria 0001
History/Public Affairs Museum
1846 house furnished in pioneer style;
old watermill, orchard, stables and
other outbuildings

Simon's Town

10987
Martello Tower Naval Museum
Simon's Town, POB 1, Cape Town
8000
History/Public Affairs Museum - 1970
History of Simon's Town as a naval
base; historic tower

10988
Simon's Town Museum
St George's St, POB 31, Simon's Town
7995
History/Public Affairs Museum - 1977
Militaria and naval relics; Winifred and
Llew Gay collection of cultural
material; Willis collection of archival
material; Flack collection of ship
models; photographic glass plate
negative collection

Skukuza

10989
**Stevenson-Hamilton Memorial
Information Centre**
Kruger National Park, POB 50,
Skukuza 1350
Natural History Museum - 1964
Early, middle and late Stone Age
artifacts; local cultural history; Africana
collection; photographic and archival
material

Somerset East

10990
Somerset East Museum
Beaufort and McKay Sts, POB 151,
Somerset East 5850
General Museum
Period furnishings in original setting;
outbuildings and grounds

Somerset West

10991
Hotentots-Holland Museum
Town Hall, POB 19, Somerset West
7130
General Museum - 1977
History of the Hottentot-Holland area

Stellenbosch

10992
D.F. Malan Museum University of
Stellenbosch
mail c/o University Library, Van
Ryneveld St, Private Bag 5036,
Stellenbosch 7600
History/Public Affairs Museum - 1967
Memorabilia of Dr. D. F. Malan
(1874-1959); documents; photo
collection - library

10993
Ethnology Museum University of
Stellenbosch
C.L. Marais Library, Crozier St,
Stellenbosch 7600
Anthropology Museum
Exhibits depicting Bantu, Khoisan,
Nguni, and Wambo cultures; musical
instruments; beadwork collection

10994
Geology Museum University of
Stellenbosch
Chamber of Mines Building,
Stellenbosch 7600
Science/Tech Museum - 1911
Geology; mineralogy; gemmology;
palaeontology

10995
Grosvenor House Stellenbosch
Museum
Drostdy St, Van der Bijlhuis, 37 Market
St, POB X5048, Stellenbosch 7600
Fine Arts Museum - 1966
Period furniture and furnishings;
gardens

10996
John R. Ellerman Museum of Zoology
University of Stellenbosch
Merriman Av, Stellenbosch 7600
Natural History Museum
Small mammals; items of
palaeontological and embryological
interest

10997
Missionary Museum of the N.G. Kerk
University of Stellenbosch
D.R. Seminary, Dorp St, Stellenbosch
7600
History/Public Affairs Museum
Relics of early missionaries; photos
and maps showing spread of
missionary activity in Africa; artifacts
related to Islam, Hinduism, Judaism

10998
Oude Meester Brandy Museum
Old Strand Road, Private Bag 5001,
Stellenbosch 7600
History/Public Affairs Museum - 1977
Brandy distilling equipment and related
cultural artifacts

10999
Rembrandt van Rijn Art Gallery
31 Dorp St, POB 456, Stellenbosch
7600
Fine Arts Museum - 1979
Sculpture of Anton van Wouw; works
of Käthe Kollwitz; panorama of Cape
Town by Josephus Jones; changing
exhibitions of works owned by the
Rembrandt van Rijn Art Foundation

11000
Schreuder House Stellenbosch
Museum
10 Van Ryneveld St, Van der Bijlhuis,
37 Market St, POB X5048,
Stellenbosch 7600
Fine Arts Museum - 1975
Period furniture and furnishings;
kitchen utensils

11001
University Art Gallery University of
Stellenbosch, Dept. of Creative Arts
Bird and Dorp Sts, Stellenbosch POB
7600
Fine Arts Museum
Temporary exhibitions of works by
university students and South African
and overseas artists

11002
V.O.C. Kruithuis Stellenbosch
Museum
Die Braak, Van der Bijlhuis, 37 Market
St, POB X5048, Stellenbosch 7600
Historic Site
Weapons and ammunition

Sterkstroom

11003
Sterkstroom Museum
34 Van Zyl St, POB 100, Sterkstroom
5425
General Museum
Local historical relics; agricultural
implements; general store items

Swellendam

11004
Drostdy Museum
Swellengrebel St, Swellendam 6740
General Museum - 1939
Cape furniture; period buildings; crafts
equipment; agricultural equipment

Tulbagh

11005
De Oude Drostdy
Drostdy Village, Tulbagh 6822
General Museum - 1974
Cape furniture; contemporary South
African ceramics; display on
production of sherry

11006
Oude Kewrk Volksmuseum
4 Church St, Tulbagh 6820
General Museum - 1925
Furniture and furnishings; dolls;
kitchen utensils; weapons; books

Uitenhage

11007
Africana Museum
Town Hall, Market St, POB 45,
Uitenhage 6230
General Museum - 1960
Clothing; furniture and household
utensils; personal relics of Gen. J.G.
Cuyler (Landdrost 1806-1828) and
Adriaan van Kervel (Cape governor
1737); 'De Mist Bible'

11008
Cuyler Manor
Uitenhage 6230
General Museum
manor house and old water mill on
grounds of farm founded in 1814 by
American-born British officer Jacob
Glen Cuyler

11009
Old Railway Station
Market St, POB 225, Uitenhage 6230
General Museum - 1974
Railroad equipment from 1870 on

Vereeniging

11010
Vereeniging Museum
mail c/o Library Bldg, Leslie St, POB
136, Vereeniging
General Museum - 1966
Photos relating to the Anglo-Boer
War; local history; local fossils

Verulam

11011
**Mahatma Gandhi Library and
Museum**
mail c/o Phoenix Settlement, Inanda
Rd, POB 331, Verulam 4340
History/Public Affairs Museum - 1969
Personal possessions of Mahatma
Gandhi - library

Verwoerdburg

11012
General Smuts Museum
Verwoerdburg Irene 1675
General Museum
Original furnishings of General J.C.
Smuts, Prime Minister of the Union of
South Africa 1918-1924

Victoria West

11013
Victoria West Museum
Church St, Victoria West 7070
General Museum - 1970
Relics, photos and documents relating
to history of the town; local pre-history

Vryburg

11014
Vryburg Museum
POB 49, Vryburg 8600
General Museum
Historic relics of the town

Vryheid

11015
Nieuwe Republiek Museum
119 Landdrost St, POB 57, Vryheid
3100
General Museum - 1938
Articles from the period of the Nieuwe
Republiek (1884-1888) and the Zuid
Afrikaanse Republiek (1888-1900)

Weenen

11016
Weenen Museum
POB 13, Weenen 3325
General Museum
Costumes; firearms; relics from the
Voortrekker period; period kitchen

Windhoek

11017
Alte Feste State Museum
Leutwein St, POB 1023, Windhoek
History/Public Affairs Museum
Relics and documents of the German
colonial administration, housed in 1890
fortress; local and national history

Worcester

11018
Worcester Museum
23 Traub St, POB 557, Worcester 6850
General Museum - 1941
19th cent. Cape furniture; domestic
utensils; works by Worcester artist
Hugo Naudé; documents and
photographs; local history; farm
outbuildings

Spain

Agreda

11019
**Museo 'Sor Maria de Jesús de
Agreda'**
Convento de la Concepción, Agreda,
Soria
Religious Art Museum - 1965
Religious art; memorabilia on María
Coronel y de Arana (1602-1665), her
books, correspondence and personal
objects

Albacete

11020
Museo de Albacete
Parque de Abelardo Sánchez s/n,
Albacete
Fine Arts Museum - 1926
Archaeology: ceramics; sculptures;
inscriptions; numismatics; fine arts:
117 works of Benjamin Palecia;
contemporary art - library

Albarracín

11021
Museo Catedralicio
Calle de la Catedral, Albarracín, Teruel
Religious Art Museum - 1961
Tapestry; goldsmith work; painting;
sculpture; 13th century cathedral

Albocácer

11022
Colección Parroquial
Plaza de la Iglesia, Albocácer,
Castellón de la Plana
Religious Art Museum - 1968
Ecclesiastical art; painting; sculpture;
goldsmith work

Alcalá de Henares

11023
Casa Natal de Cervantes
Calle Mayor, 48, Alcalá de Henares,
Madrid
Historic Site - 1955
Memorial to and birthplace of the poet
Miguel de Cervantes Saavedra
(1547-1616) - library

11024
**Museo Histórico de la
Administración Española**
Antigua Universidad, Alcalá de
Henares, Madrid
History/Public Affairs Museum - 1962
History of the Spanish administration

Alcantarilla

11025
**Museo Municipal Etnológico de la
Huerta de Murcia**
desvio carretera núm. 340 Murcia-
Granada, Acequia Barreras,
Alcantarilla, Murcia
General Museum - 1963
Local ethnography; interiors, furniture,
ceramics, glass, metalwork, textiles;
Murciana - library

Alcazar de San Juan

11026
**Museo Arqueológico 'Fray Juan
Cobo'**
Capilla del Palacio, Calle Don Quijote,
16, Alcazar de San Juan, Ciudad Real
General Museum - 1952
Roman mosaics; regional ethnography

Alcoy

11027
**Museo Arqueológico Municipal
'Camilo Visedo Moltó'**
Calle San Miguel, 29, Alcoy, Alicante
Archeology Museum - 1945
Prehistoric, Iberian, Roman finds;
ceramics, terra cotta, painting,
numismatics; local history; natural
history

Alcudia

11028
Museo Arqueológico Municipal
Calle Goded, 7, Alcudia, Mallorca,
Baleares
Archeology Museum - 1948
Roman finds from local excavations

Alicante

11029
Museo Arqueológico Provincial
General Mola, 6, Alicante
General Museum - 1949
Prehistory; archaeology; regional and
local history; medieval pottery; Islamic
bronzes from Egypt found at Benia
(11th century) - library

Almeria

11030
**Museo Arqueológico Provincial 'Luis
Siret'**
Calle Javier Sanz, 15, Almería
Archeology Museum - 1933
Prehistory; archaeology; Greek,
Roman and Iberian finds

11031
Museo Catedralicio
Catedral, Almería
Religious Art Museum - 1965
Religious art; paintings; liturgical
vestments

Alquezar

11032
Museo Parroquial
Antigua Colegiata, Alquezar, Huesca
Religious Art Museum - 1931
Ecclesiastical art; painting; sculpture;
goldsmith work; liturgical vestments

Altamira

11033
Museo de las Cuevas de Altamira
Altamira, Santander
Archeology Museum
Prehistorical finds in the caves of
Altamira

Ambrona

11034
**Museo de las Excavaciones de
Torralba**
Ambrona, Soria
Archeology Museum - 1909
Local prehistory; fossils

Amposta

11035
Museo Municipal
Ayuntamiento, Plaza de España,
Amposta, Tarragona
General Museum - 1967
Prehistory; local archaeology; zoology
from the Ebro delta

Ampudia

11036
Colección 'Fontaneda'
Castillo de Ampudia, Ampudia,
Palencia
History/Public Affairs Museum - 1965
Prehistoric and ancient cultures;
medieval art

Ampurias

11037
**Museo Monográfico de las
Excavaciones**
Ampurias, La Escala, Gerona
Archeology Museum - 1961
Archaeological finds from Ampurias;
Greek, Roman and Iberian
archaeological objects

Antequera

11038
Museo Municipal
Palacio de Nájera, Plaza Guerrero
Muñoz, Antequera, Málaga
General Museum - 1966
Archaeology, especially Roman;
16th-18th century painting, sculpture
and goldsmith work; history; local
ethnography

Aranjuez

11039
Casa de Marinos
Aranjuez, Madrid
History/Public Affairs Museum
Royal harbor launches

11040
Palacio Real
Jardín de la Isla, Aranjuez, Madrid
Fine Arts Museum
Former royal palace; 18th century art;
decorative arts

11041
Real Casa del Labrador
Calle de la Reina, Jardín del Príncipe,
Aranjuez, Madrid
Religious Art Museum - 1967
Ecclesiastical art

Arcos de la Frontera

11042
Museo-Tesoro Parroquial
Plaza de España, Arcos de la Frontera,
Cádiz
Religious Art Museum - 1962
Ecclesiastical art; painting; sculpture;
goldsmith work; liturgical vestments;
choral books

Arenas de San Pedro

11043
Museo de la Real Capilla
Convento de San Pedro de Alcántara,
Arenas de San Pedro, Avila
Religious Art Museum
Religious art; tomb of San Pedro de
Alcántara

Arenys de Mar

11044
Museo-Archivo Municipal 'Fidel Fita'
Plaza de la Villa, 2, Arenys de Mar,
Barcelona
General Museum - 1918
Local archaeology; folk art; maritime
history

Aroche

11045
Colección del Santo Rosario
Calle Alférez Lobo, 7, Aroche, Huelva
Historic Site - 1960
Memorabilia on Santo Rosario

11046
Museo Municipal
Ayuntamiento (archaeology) and
Grupo Escolar Municipal (natural
sciences), Ayuntamiento, Aroche,
Huelva
General Museum - 1958
Prehistory; Roman and Arab
archaeology; mineralogy; zoology

Artá

11047
Museo Regional
Calle Rafael Blanes, 8, Artá, Mallorca,
Baleares
General Museum - 1927
Natural history; prehistory; Roman
archaeology; folklore

Astorga

11048
Museo de los Caminos
Calle Santa Marta, Astorga, León
General Museum - 1963
Art and history pertaining to the
pilgrimage routes to Santiago de
Compostela; Roman and medieval
archaeology; regional ethnography

11049
Museo Diocesano-Catedralicio
Catedral, Avenida del Dr. Mérida,
Astorga, León
Religious Art Museum - 1945
14th-16th century sculpture, painting;
10th-16th century goldsmith work and
ceramics; 16th century liturgical
vestments; Romanic cathedral

Avila

11050
Basilica de San Vincente
Calle de San Vincente, Avila
Religious Art Museum
Religious art; sculptures and paintings

11051
Museo Catedralicio
Catedral, Avila
Religious Art Museum - 1947
12th-17th century paintings; 12th-17th
century goldsmith art; 15th-18th
century choral books; medieval
documents; 14th-17th century wood
sculptures

11052
Museo de Arte Oriental
Apartado, 10, Avila
Fine Arts Museum - 1964
Art and crafts from China, Japan, the
Philippines and Vietnam

11053
Museo Provincial
Casa de los Deanes, Plaza Nalvillos, 3,
Avila
General Museum - 1915
Archaeology; paintings; ceramics; folk
arts and crafts

11054
Museo 'Virgen de la Porteria'
Convento de San Antonio, Paseo de
San Antonio, 5, Avila
Religious Art Museum - 1943
Religious art; paintings, embroidery
and lace

Avilés

11055
Museo de Ciencias Naturales
Calle Dr. Graiño, 25, Avilés, Oviedo
Natural History Museum - 1944
Mineralogy; botany

Ayllón

11056
Museo Municipal
Edificio de Ayuntamiento, Calle Mayor,
29, Ayllón, Segovia
Fine Arts Museum - 1965
Art and history; painting, sculpture

Azpeitia

11057
Caserio de Errecarte (Casa natal del
Hermano Francisco Gárate)
about 80 m from the birthplace of San
Ignacio de Loyola Azpeitia, Guipúzcoa
Historic Site - 1929
Memorabilia of the blessed Hermano
Francisco Gárate

Azpeitia (Véase Loyola)

11058
Casa Natal de 'San Ignacio'
Avenida de Loyola, Azpeitia (Véase
Loyola), Guipúzcoa
Historic Site - 1954
Memorabilia of Iñigo López de Loyola
(1491-1556), the founder of the Jesuit
order and later (1622) sanctified 'San
Ignacio'

Badajoz

11059
Museo Arqueológico
La Galera, Plazoleta del Reloj, Badajoz
Archeology Museum - 1938
Roman and Iberian antiquities; 6th-7th
century Visigothic art; Gothic
inscription (1512); Islam art

11060
Museo Catedralicio
Badajoz
Religious Art Museum
16th-18th century religious paintings;
religious sculptures and documents

11061
Museo Diocesano-Catedralicio
Catedral, Badajoz
Religious Art Museum
16th-18th century religious paintings;
religious sculptures and documents;
goldsmith work

11062
Museo Provincial de Bellas Artes
Calle Meléndes Valdés, 32, Badajoz
Fine Arts Museum - 1919
19th-20th century regional painting and
sculpture and graphic arts, especially
from Estremadura; works by
Francísco de Zurbarán and Juan de
Avalos - library

Badalona

11063
Museo Municipal
Plaza del Obispo Irurita, Badalona,
Barcelona
General Museum - 1966
Roman archaeology; folk art; local
history - observatory 'Baetulo' and
meteorological service

Balsareny

11064
**Colección de Pintura y Recuerdos
Históricos**
1,5 km fuera de la ciudad, Castillo,
Balsareny, Barcelona
History/Public Affairs Museum
Art and history; painting, furniture,
books, heraldry

Bañolas

11065
Museo Arqueológico Comarcal
Bañolas, Gerona
Archeology Museum - 1943
Prehistory; Roman and Iberian finds;
medieval architecture; folklore;
numismatics; 14th-18th century
ceramics

11066
**Museu Municipal Darder d'Història
Natural**
Plaça dels Estudis, 2, Bañolas, Gerona
Natural History Museum - 1910
Mineralogy; paleontology; micology;
herpetology; ichthyology; conchology;
ornithology; mammalogy;
anthropology - library

Baños de Cerrato

11067
Basilica de San Juan Bautista
Baños de Cerrato, Palencia
Religious Art Museum - 1897
Art; architecture; sculpture

Barbastro

11068
Museo Diocesano-Catedralicio
Catedral, Palacio Episcopal, Barbastro,
Huesca
Religious Art Museum - 1965/68
Ecclesiastical art; gothic cathedral

Barcelona

11069
**Biblioteca i Museo de l'Institut del
Teatre**
c/ Nou de la Ramlia, 3-5, Barcelona 1
Performing Arts Museum - 1912
Theater; cinema; opera; dance;
puppets; special collections of
scenography and puppetry - library

11070
Casa Museo 'Gaudí'
Parque Güell, Barcelona
Decorative Arts Museum - 1963
Furniture and architectural projects
designed by A. Gaudí and his
collaborators

11071
Colección Cambó
Ramblas, 99, POB 2, Barcelona,
Barcelona
Fine Arts Museum - 1955
European painting

11072
Gabinete Numismático de Cataluña
Palacio del Museo de Arte Moderno,
Parque de la Ciudadela, Barcelona
History/Public Affairs Museum - 1945
Numismatics, medals and coins

11073
Instituto 'Amatller' de Arte Hispánico
Paseo de Gracia, 41, Barcelona
Fine Arts Museum - 1963
Art; medieval painting; 16th-18th
century Roman and Hispanic glass
manufacture - library; photo archive

11074
Instituto Botánico
Parque de Montjuich, Avenida de
Muntañans, Barcelona
Natural History Museum - 1917
Botanical collections - library;
botanical garden

11075
**Monasterio de Santa Maria de
Pedralbes**
Plaza del Monasterio, Barcelona
Religious Art Museum - 1931
Ecclesiastical art

11076
Museo Arqueológico
Parque de Montjuich, Barcelona
Archeology Museum - 1932
Prehistoric art from Catalunya and
Baleares; Greek antiquities, especially
from Ampurias; Roman antiquities;
sculptures, mosaics, inscriptions;
Iberian and Visigothic art; 7th century
Byzantine bust - library

11077
Museo Catedralicio
mail c/o Claustro de la Catedral, Calle
Obispo Irurita, Barcelona
Religious Art Museum - 1952
Ecclesiastical art; painting, liturgical
vestments, goldsmith work

11078
Museo 'Clara'
Tres Torres, Calle Calatrava, 27-29,
Barcelona
Fine Arts Museum - 1969
Sculpture, painting, drawing,
watercolor painting

11079
Museo de Arte Moderno
Parque de la Ciudadela, Barcelona
Fine Arts Museum - 1946
Modern art; Spanish works by Nonell,
Picasso, Gargallo and Junyer, some
other European paintings, drawings,
sculptures (19th-20th century) - library

11080
Museo de Artes Decorativas
Ramblas 99, Barcelona, Barcelona
Fine Arts Museum - 1932
ceramics; glass; furniture

11081
Museo de Cerámica
Palacio Nacional, Parque de Montjuich,
Barcelona
Decorative Arts Museum - 1966
Medieval to modern Spanish ceramics

11082
Museo de Geología
Seminario Conciliar, Calle Diputación,
231, Barcelona 7
Natural History Museum - 1874
Fossils especially from Spanish
territories and Cataluña; geology;
paleontology - library

11083
Museo de Geología
Parque de la Ciudadela, Barcelona
Natural History Museum - 1882
Geology; petrology; mineralogy;
paleontology; sedimentology

11084
Museo de Historia de la Ciudad
Plaza del Rey, Barcelona 2
History/Public Affairs Museum - 1943
Prehistory; Roman antiquities; Islamic,
Visigothic and Jewish art; medieval
art; royal church (14th century); 7th
century local maps; 15th-20th century
history and cultural history of
Barcelona; Roman and West Gothic
ruins - library; educational center

11085
Museo de la Técnica
Escuela de Ingenieros Industriales,
Avenida Generalísimo Franco, 999,
Barcelona
Science/Tech Museum - 1966
Industrial mechanical engineering

11086
Museo de Zoología
Parque de la Ciudadela, Barcelona
Natural History Museum - 1882
Zoology, particularily European and
African specimens

11087
Museo del Delito Instituto de
Criminología
Facultad de Derecho, Avenida
Generalísimo Franco, Barcelona
History/Public Affairs Museum - 1960
Instruments of torture; means for
execution; criminal history

11088
Museo Diocesano
Seminario Conciliar, Calle de la
Diputación, Barcelona
Religious Art Museum - 1916
12th-15th century painting; 12th-16th
century sculpture; religious art;
goldsmith work

11089
Museo Etnológico
Parque de Montjuich, Barcelona
Anthropology Museum - 1948
Archaeological and ethnological finds
from Africa, America, Asia and
Oceania; graphic art; religious art -
library

11090
Museo 'Federico Marés'
Calle Condes de Barcelona, 8,
Barcelona
Fine Arts Museum - 1946
12th-17th century religious sculptures;
17th-19th century cultural history;
Roman and Hellenistic terra cotta;
medieval wood sculptures; decorative
arts; ethnograpy

11091
Museo Marítimo
Puerto de la Paz, Barcelona
History/Public Affairs Museum - 1941
Marine archaeology; maritime history;
cartography; ship models;
figureheads; quay facilities; folk art;
fishing; numismatics; ceramics -
library

11092
**Museo Militar del Castillo de
Montjuich**
Barcelona 4
History/Public Affairs Museum - 1963
Arms and weapons; military history

11093
Museo Municipal de Música
Calle Bruch, 110, Barcelona
Music Museum - 1945
Music history; antique, popular and
exotic musical instruments

11094
Museo 'Picasso'
Calle Montcada, 15-17, Barcelona 3
Fine Arts Museum - 1963
paintings, sculptures, drawings and
engravings by Pablo Picasso
(1890-1973) - library

11095
Museo Postal
Palacio de la Virreina, Ramblas de las
Flores, 99, Barcelona 2
History/Public Affairs Museum
Postage stamps; letters; history of mail
services

11096
Museo Taurino
Plaza de Toros Monumental,
Barcelona
History/Public Affairs Museum - 1969
Bullfighting costumes and arms;
photographs and documents

11097
Museo 'Verdaguer'
Villa Joana, Vallvidrera, Barcelona
History/Public Affairs Museum - 1902
Memorabilia of the poet Jacinto
Verdaguer

11098
Museu d'Art de Catalunya
Palau Nacional, Parc de Montjuic,
Barcelona 4
Fine Arts Museum - 1934
11th-13th century Romanesque wall
painting from Catalan churches;
11th-13th century painting; Spanish
and Gothic art; sculpture; 14th-15th
century painting; Spanish works by
Zurbarán, El Greco, Ribera, Velazquez;
16th-18th century Italian, Dutch
painting; 18th century drawings;
enamels

11099
**Museu d'Indumentária 'Manuel
Rocamora'**
Palau del Marquès de Llió, Carrer de
Montcada, 12, POB 3, Barcelona
Decorative Arts Museum - 1969
Textiles, 16th-20th century costumes
and accessories - library

11100
Museu Textil
Palau Nadal, Montcada, 14, POB 3,
Barcelona
Decorative Arts Museum - 1961
Textiles: Coptic, Hispanic-Moorish,
Oriental, Japanese, pre-Columbian,
European (Renaissance to the 20th
century); tapestry and carpets;
embroidery; folk costumes

11101
Palacio de Pedralbes
Avenida Generalísimo Franco,
Barcelona
History/Public Affairs Museum
19th century royal residence; art,
furniture, decorative arts, 18th-20th
century carriages and coaches

11102
Sala-Museo 'Miguel Soldevila'
Escuela Massana, Calle Hospital, 156,
Barcelona
Fine Arts Museum - 1964
Memorabilia of and enamel works by
Miguel Soldevila Valls (1886-1956)

11103
**Salmer, Archivo Fotográfico
Internacional**
Rambla de Cataluña, 54, Barcelona 7
History/Public Affairs Museum - 1962
Photographs of art works from every
museum in Spain; color slides on
geography and monuments from all
countries

Barco de Avila

11104
Museo Parroquial
Iglesia de Ntra. Sra. de la Asunción,
Plaza de la Iglesia, Barco de Avila,
Avila
Religious Art Museum - 1960
Religious art; painting, sculpture, 15th
century goldsmith work

Béjar

11105
Museo Municipal
Palacio Ducal, Plaza Mayor, 29, Béjar,
Salamanca
Fine Arts Museum - 1966
Spanish, Flemish and Dutch painting;
sculpture; decorative arts; Oriental art

Belmonte

11106
Colección Parroquial
Colegiata-Parroquia de San Bartolomé,
Belmonte, Cuenca
Religious Art Museum - 1931
Ecclesiastical art; painting, sculpture,
goldsmith work,liturgical vestments;
books and documents

Benalmádena

11107
Museo Arqueológico Municipal
Avenida de Juan Luis Peralta,
Benalmádena, Málaga
Archeology Museum - 1970
Local and Mexican archaeology

Berga

11108
Museo Municipal
Ajuntament, Carrer dels Angels, 7,
Berga, Barcelona
General Museum - 1955
Archaeology; natural history;
palaeontology; local history; goldsmith
work

Besalú

11109
Colección Arqueológica Municipal
Plaza de San Pedro, 11, Besalú,
Gerona
General Museum - 1962
Archaeology; painting

Bilbao

11110
Museo de Bellas Artes
Parque de dona Casilda Iturriza, 3,
Bilbao
Fine Arts Museum - 1914
13th-19th century Spanish painting;
15th-17th century Flemish painting;
15th-20th century European painting;
19th-20th modern sculpture; ceramics

11111
**Museo de Reproducciones
Artisticas**
Calle Conde de Mirasol, 2, Bilbao,
Vizcaya
Fine Arts Museum - 1930
Casts of sculptures and architectural
fragments

11112
Museo Histórico de Vizcaya
Calle Cruz, 4, Bilbao
General Museum - 1920
Prehistory; archaeology; Celtiberian,
Roman antiquities; Romanic art;
architecture; 12th-17th century
religious painting; 17th-18th century
European ceramics; coins; ethnology;
folklore; local history

Blanes

11113
**Estación Internacional de Biología
Mediterránea 'Carlos Faust'**
Jardín Botánico 'Mar y Murtra', Blanes,
Gerona
Natural History Museum - 1951
Mediterranean and exotic plants;
especially cacti

Bocairente

11114
Museo Parroquial
Calle Abadía, Bocairente, Valencia
General Museum - 1966
Ecclesiastical art; goldsmith work;
painting; sculpture; ornamentation

Bueu

11115
Museo Marinero 'Massó'
Bueu, Pontevedra
History/Public Affairs Museum - 1928
Maritime history; historical nautical
books

Burgo de Osma

11116
Museo Catedralicio
Plaza de la Catedral, Burgo de Osma,
Soria
History/Public Affairs Museum - 1928
Historical documents, miniature books,
codices; 11th-13th century miniatures;
15th century painting; sculpture;
goldsmith work; liturgical vestments;
14th century crafts

Burgos

11117
Museo Arqueológico Provincial
Casa Miranda, Calles Calera, 25 y
Miranda, 13, Burgos
Archeology Museum - 1871
Prehistory; Roman antiquities,
especially from the Roman town
Clunia; Iberian antiquities; 6th-7th
century Visigothic and Mozarabian art;
Romanic and Gothic architecture;
15th-16th century tombs; 10th-11th
century Islamic ivory; 12th century
crafts; 13th-16th century sculpture;
14th-19th century Spanish and Italian
painting; enamels; coins and medals

11118
Museo del Seminario Metropolitano
Calle Fernán González, Burgos
Natural History Museum - 1966
Natural sciences

11119
Museo Diocesano-Catedralicio
Catedral, Plaza Rey San Fernando y
Santa María, Burgos
Religious Art Museum - 1930
13th-16th century religious painting;
Romanesque architecture; 16th-17th
century tapestry; 15th-18th century
documents and codes;liturgical
vestments, ivories, tombs, goldsmith
work

11120
Museo 'Marceliano Santa Maria'
Claustro Antiguo Monasterio de San
Juan, Burgos
Fine Arts Museum - 1969
Art; 16th and 17th century painting and
sculpture; furniture

11121
Palacio de la Isla
Paseo de la Isla, Burgos
History/Public Affairs Museum - 1939
History

11122
Real Cartuja de Miraflores
Carretera Burgos-Cardeña, km 3,
Burgos
History/Public Affairs Museum
15th century building; art and history;
Gothic architecture; sculpture;
painting; glass painting

11123
Real Monasterio de las Huelgas
Museo de Telas y Preseas
Prolongación de la Castellana, Burgos
Religious Art Museum - 1949
Art and history; medieval textiles;
jewelry; religious art; Panteón de los
Reyes de Castilla y León; monastery
founded by Alfonso VII in the 9th
century

Burriana

11124
Museo Histórico Municipal
Ayuntamiento, Plaza de España, 7,
Burriana, Castellón
General Museum - 1967
Archaeology; ethnology

Cáceres

11125
Casa del Mono
Cuesta de Aldana, 5, Cáceres
Fine Arts Museum - 1971
Painting and sculpture

11126
Museo Provincial
Plaza Veletas, 1, Cáceres
General Museum - 1917
Prehistory; archaeology; Roman,
Iberian, Visigothic and Islamic
antiquities; painting; Spanish pottery;
religious art; numismatics; folklore and
ethnology

Cádiz

11127
Museo Catedralicio
Calle Arquitecto Acero, Cádiz
Religious Art Museum - 1931
Ecclesiastical art; painting, sculpture,
goldsmith work, liturgical vestments

11128
Museo de Cadiz
Plaza de Mina, Cádiz
General Museum - 1849/1887
Museo Provincial de Bellas Artes:
15th-20th century Spanish, French,
Italian and Flemish painting; 19th
century sculpture; drawings; tapestry;
jewelry; Museo Arqueológico: fossils;
pre-Columbian ethnography; Greek,
Roman, Punic antiquities; early
Christian archaeology; Visigothic and
Islamic art; archaeological numismatics

11129
Museo Histórico Municipal
Calle Santa Inés, Cádiz
History/Public Affairs Museum - 1909
Historical documents and letters;
maps; 19th century paintings

Calahorra

11130
Colección 'Gutiérrez Achutegui'
Biblioteca Pública Municipal,
Calahorra, Logroño
Archeology Museum - 1924
Prehistory and archaeology

11131
**Museo-Tesoro Catedralicio y
Diocesano**
Anejo a la Catedral, Calahorra,
Logroño
Religious Art Museum - 1958
Painting; liturgical vestments;
goldsmith work; 12th century
miniature codices; documentation on
the 11th-12th centuries

Calatayud

11132
Museo Bilbilitano
Casa de la Cultura, Calatayud,
Zaragoza
History/Public Affairs Museum
Local art and history

Caldas de Montbuy

11133
**Museo Arqueológico y Termas
Romanas**
Calle José Antonio, 98, Caldas de
Montbuy, Barcelona
Archeology Museum - 1949
Archaeology and local history; Roman
hot springs

Canduela

11134
**Museo Etnográfico de los Valles de
Campoo**
La Torrona, Canduela, Palencia
General Museum
Local ethnography

Capdepera

11135
Torre de Canyamel
Capdepera, Mallorca, Baleares
General Museum - 1965
Insular ethnography

Capellades

11136
**Molino-Museo Papelero y Colección
'Amador Romani'**
Molí de la Vila, Calle Inmaculada,
Concepción, Capellades, Barcelona
History/Public Affairs Museum - 1961
History of paper fabrication; Amador
Romaní collection of prehistoric
archaeology; local history; 16th
century paper mill

Cardedeu

11137
Museu-Arxiu Tomas Balvey
Josep Daurella, 1, Cardedeu,
Barcelona
General Museum - 1965
Archaeology; Roman antiquities; 19th
century weapons; numismatics;
antique pharmacy including pharmacy
pottery (18th century); folk art and
costumes; 11th-19th century local
history; 11th-19th century parchments

Carmona

11138
**Museo Arqueológico y Necrópolis
Romana de Carmona**
Avenida Jorge Bonsor, 5, Carmona,
Sevilla
Archeology Museum - 1881
Roman finds from Carmona

11139
Museo Municipal
Plaza de San Fernando, Carmona,
Sevilla
General Museum
Local prehistory and archaeology

Cartagena

11140
Museo Arqueológico Municipal
Calle Baños del Carmen, Cartagena,
Murcia
Archeology Museum - 1943
Prehistory; Roman, Classical and
submarine archaeology; Iberian and
Islamic finds; architecture; sculpture;
inscriptions; mining; 19th century
crafts; 14th-18th century document
collection

Castelló de Ampurias

11141
Colección Parroquial
Plaza Jacinto Verdaguer, Castelló de
Ampurias, Gerona
Religious Art Museum - 1967
Ecclesiastical art; goldsmith work,
liturgical vestments, painting, sculpture

Castellón de la Plana

11142
Museo de Bellas Artes
Diputación, Plaza de las Aulas, 5,
Castellón de la Plana
Fine Arts Museum - 1845
15th-19th century painting; Roman
antiquities; textiles; 15th century coat
of arms

Celanova

11143
Museo Parroquial
Monasterio de San Salvador,
Celanova, Orense
Religious Art Museum - 1931
Ecclesiastical art

Cervera

11144
Museo Comarcal 'Durán y Sanpere'
Centro Comarcal de Cultura, Calle
Mayor, 15, Cervera, Lérida
General Museum - 1914
Iberian and Roman finds; Gothic
painting and sculpture

11145
Museo del Blat y de la Pagesia
Antiguo Universidad, Calle Vidal de
Montpalau, 45, Cervera, Lérida
General Museum - 1964
Ethnography

Chillon

11146
Museo Parroquial
Plaza del Caudillo, Chillon, Ciudad Real
Religious Art Museum - 1956
Ecclesiastical art; goldsmith work,
sculpture, wall painting and painting;
books and documents

Chipiona

11147
**Museo Misional de Nuestra Señora
de Regla** Colegio de Misioneros
Franziscanos
Chipiona, Cádiz
Archeology Museum - 1939
Early Roman Christian relics; ancient
Egyptian and other North African
objects; antique coins

Ciudad Real

11148
Colección de Arqueologia
Casa de la Cultura, Calle Prado, 7,
Ciudad Real
Archeology Museum - 1962
Local archaeology

11149
**Colección de Arte y Ciencias
Naturales**
Palacio de la Diputación, Toledo, 27,
Ciudad Real
General Museum
Local art; painting; sculpture; natural
history; coleoptera

11150
Museo Catedralicio
Paseo del Prado, Ciudad Real
Religious Art Museum - 1966
Ecclesiastical art and history; liturgical
vestments; memorabilia on Concilio
Vaticano II

Ciudadela

11151
Museo Arqueológico Diocesano
Calle Obispo Villa, 9, Ciudadela,
Menorca, Baleares
Fine Arts Museum - 1880
Art; local archaeology

Clunia

11152
**Museo Monográfico de las
Excavaciones**
Peñalba de Castro Clunia, Burgos
Archeology Museum - 1931
Archaeology; excavations of the
Roman colony Clunia Sulpicia

Colmenar de Oreja

11153
Museo Municipal 'Checa'
Calle Costanilla de los Silleros, 1,
Colmenar de Oreja, Madrid
General Museum - 1960
Local historical documents;
memorabilia of the painter Ulpiano
Checa (1860-1916)

Colmenar Viejo

11154
Colección Parroquial
Parroquia de la Asunción, Calle del
Cura, Colmenar Viejo, Madrid
Religious Art Museum - 1954
Ecclesiastical art; goldsmith work;
liturgical vestments; choral books

Combarro

11155
**Museo de Artes y Costumbres
Populares**
Combarro, Pontevedra
General Museum - 1969
Local ethnology

Comillas

11156
Museo Cantábrico
Comillas, Santander
General Museum
Prehistory; Roman archaeology;
medieval paintings; ceramics;
numismatics

Consuegra

11157
Museo Municipal
Plaza de España, 1, Consuegra, Toledo
Archeology Museum - 1964
Local archaeology

Córdoba

11158
Alcázar de los Reyes Cristianos
Campo Santo de los Mártires,
Córdoba
History/Public Affairs Museum - 1960
Roman archaeology; 14th century
residence of the Catholic kings

11159
Colección de la Mezquita
Calle de Velázquez Bosco, Córdoba
Fine Arts Museum
History and archaeology of the
Mezquita

11160
Museo Arqueológico Provincial
Plaza Jerónimo Páez, 7, Córdoba
Archeology Museum - 1868
Prehistoric collection; Roman
archaeology; Iberian, Visigothic,
Islamic, Mozarabian and Mudejar art;
Gothic and Renaissance art; goldsmith
work, ivory, ceramics and sculpture -
library

11161
Museo de Bellas Artes
Plaza del Potro, 2, Córdoba
Fine Arts Museum - 1844
15th-20th century local and Spanish
painting; 19th century local sculpture;
16th-17th century Flemish and Italian
painting; paintings of Flemish and
Italian schools; Spanish drawings and
etchings

11162
**Museo de las Excavaciones de
Medina Az-Zahara**
unos kilómetros fuera de la ciudad
Córdoba
Archeology Museum - 1910/67
Arabian architectural remains;
excavations of the palace built by Abd
al-Rahman III in 936 and destroyed in
1010

11163
Museo Histórico de la Ciudad
Torre de la Calahorra, Puente Romano,
Córdoba
Archeology Museum - 1955
Local history; antique Arabian
fortification

11164
Museo 'Julio Romero de Torres'
Plaza del Potro, 2, Córdoba
Historic Site - 1931
Memorabilia of the painter Julio
Romero de Torres

11165
**Museo Municipal de Artes
Cordobesas y Taurino**
Plaza Maimónides, 5, Córdoba
Anthropology Museum - 1954
Local crafts; jewelry, modern
leatherwork, antique weights and
measures; Portuguese sculptures;
documents on famous bullfighters

11166
Museo-Tesoro Catedralicio
Catedral, Córdoba
Religious Art Museum - 1882
Ecclesiastical art; goldsmith work,
tapestry, liturgical vestments; painting;
sculpture; miniature books

11167
Palacio de los Marqueses de Viana
Reja de Don Gome, 2, Córdoba
History/Public Affairs Museum
Art; painting; furniture; tapestry;
leatherwork; special library on hunting

Covadonga

11168
Museo-Tesoro de la Santina
Calle Santuario, Covadonga, Cangas
de Onís
Religious Art Museum - 1965
Religious art and history

11169
Museo-Tesoro de la Santina
Calle Santuario, Covadonga, Cangas
de Onís, Oviedo
Religious Art Museum - 1965
Ecclesiastical art; goldsmith work,
liturgical vestments; history; royal
tombs

Covarrubias

11170
Museo Parroquial
Iglesia de San Cosme y San Damián,
Covarrubias, Burgos
History/Public Affairs Museum - 1929
Art and history; medieval documents,
treasures, costumes; 13th century
tombs of the first Condes de Castilla e
Infantas de Covarrubias; 14th-16th
century religious sculpture and
painting; 15th-18th century liturgical
vestments; goldsmith work

Crevillente

11171
Museo Municipal 'Mariano Benlliure'
Calle de San Cayetano, Crevillente,
Alicante
Fine Arts Museum - 1967
Drawings and models of sculptures by
Mariano Benlliure

Cuenca

11172
Casas Colgadas Museo Colleccíon
de Arte Abstracto Español
Cuenca
Fine Arts Museum - 1963
Contemporary art; abstract painting
and sculpture

11173
Museo Diocesano-Catedralicio
Palacio Episcopal y Catedral, Cuenca
Religious Art Museum - 1902
Art; goldsmith work, painting,
sculpture, liturgical vestments; 12th
century cathedral

11174
Museo Provincial
Calle Pósito, 2, Cuenca
General Museum - 1963
Art; Iberian, Roman and Visigothic
archaeology; especially plastic from
Segóbriga and Valeria

Daroca

11175
Museo del Santísimo Misterio
Daroca, Zaragoza
Religious Art Museum - 1929
Liturgical vestments; 15th century
sculptures; 13th-17th century religious
crafts; paintings

11176
Museo del Santísimo Misterio
Colegiata de Santa María, Plaza de
España, Daroca, Zaragoza
Religious Art Museum - 1929
Ecclesiastical art; painting, sculpture,
goldsmith work, liturgical vestments

Denia

11177
**Museo Arqueológico Municipal de la
Ciudad**
Calle Castillo, Denia, Alicante
Archeology Museum - 1957
Local archaeology

Deya

11178
Museo Arqueológico
Calle Torrente, Deya, Mallorca,
Baleares
Archeology Museum - 1963
Local archaeology

11179
Son Marroig
Deya, Mallorca, Baleares
Decorative Arts Museum - 1925
Ceramics; furniture; paintings

Ecija

11180
Museo Parroquial
Plaza de Santa María, Ecija, Sevilla
General Museum - 1947
Local art; Roman and Islamic
archaeology

Elche

11181
Museo Arqueológico de Elche
Parque Municipal, Elche, Alicante
Archeology Museum - 1945
Archaeology; Greek, Roman and
Iberian finds

El Escorial

11182
Salas Capitulares del Monasterio
Monasterio de San Lorenzo, El
Escorial, Madrid
Fine Arts Museum
15th-17th century painting; 16th
century sculpture; liturgical vestments;
religious crafts and treasures; ivory

El Pardo

11183
Casa del Principe
Paseo del Pardo, El Pardo, Madrid
Decorative Arts Museum - 1961
Furniture and lamps of La Granja; 18th
century manor

El Toboso

11184
Casa 'Dulcinea'
Calle José Antonio, El Toboso, *mail
c/o* Museo de Santa Cruz, Calle
Cervantes, 1, Toledo
History/Public Affairs Museum - 1967
Artifacts pertaining to the era of Don
Quixote - library

Epila

11185
Colección de la Casa de Alba
Palacio de los Condes de Aranda,
Epila, Zaragoza
History/Public Affairs Museum - 1808
Royal costumes; history

Espluga de Francolí

11186
Museo de la Villa
Espluga de Francolí, Tarragona
General Museum - 1963
History and archaeology; local arts
and crafts

Estella

11187
Museo 'Gustavo de Maeztu'
Palacio de los Reyes de Navarra, San
Nicolás, 2, Estella, Navarra
Historic Site - 1949
Memorabilia on the painter Gustavo
de Maeztu (1887-1947); 12th century
palace

Falset

11188
Museo-Archivo de Falset y Comarca
Calle Calvo Sotelo, 1, Falset,
Tarragona
General Museum - 1965
History; art; local crafts and
archaeology; wine growing

Figueras

11189
Museo Dali
Plaza del Teatro, Figueras, Gerona
Fine Arts Museum - 1904
Wall painting by Salvadore Dalí; town
theater (1850)

11190
Museo del Ampurdán
Rambla, 2, Figueras, Gerona
General Museum - 1946
Local art and history; painting,
watercolors

Fromista

11191
San Martin
Plaza San Martín, Fromista, Palencia
Religious Art Museum - 1904
Art; architecture; sculpture

Fuendetodos

11192
Casa Natal de Goya
Plaza Goya-Zuloaga, Fuendetodos,
Zaragoza
Historic Site - 1928
Memorial to Francisco de Goya in his
birthplace

Gandesa

11193
Colección Arciprestal
Plaza de la Iglesia, Gandesa,
Tarragona
General Museum - 1938
Archaeology; goldsmith work;
numismatics

Gandía

11194
Museo Municipal de Prehistoria
Plaza del Rey, Gandía, Valencia
General Museum
Local art and history

11195
Palacio del Santo Duque
Plaza San Francisco de Borja, Gandía,
Valencia
Historic Site - 1893
Palace of the Jesuit duke Francisco de
Borja y Aragón (1510-1572); 15th
century portal

Gascueña

11196
Colección Parroquial
Gascueña, Cuenca
Religious Art Museum
Ecclesiastical art

Gerena

11197
Colección Taurina
Calle Millán Astray, 19, Gerena, Sevilla
History/Public Affairs Museum - 1970
Posters and artifacts pertaining to
bullfighting

Gerona

11198
Museo Arqueológico Provincial
San Pedro de Galligans, Subida Santa
Lucía, Gerona
Archeology Museum - 1855
Prehistoric collections; archaeological
finds from Ampurias; Greek, Roman,
Iberian, Punic finds; 13th-14th century
Christian tombs; 13th century
sculpture; 13th century Romanesque
architecture; 16th-19th century
painting; 16th century ceramics, arms,
tapestry; numismatics; inscriptions;
applied and folk art

11199
Museo Diocesano
Plaza de España, 2, Gerona
Fine Arts Museum - 1943
17th century Visigothic inscriptions;
12th-13th century Islamic art,
Romanesque art and codes; 14th-17th
century religious painting; 15th-18th
century textiles; 12th-17th century
church treasures; jewelry and
goldsmith work, miniature codices;
16th-17th century sculpture; Greek
ceramics from Ampurias; glass;
numismatics; drawings by Francisco
de Goya (1746-1828) - library

11200
Museo Histórico de la Ciudad
Calle Forsa, 13, Gerona
General Museum - 1960
Local history and art

11201
Museo Parroquial de San Félix
Subida de San Félix, Gerona
Religious Art Museum - 1962
Ecclesiastical art; painting, sculpture,
jewelry and goldsmith work

11202
Museo-Tesoro Catedralicio
Catedral, Gerona
Religious Art Museum - 1952
Art; tapestry, jewelry and goldsmith
work, painting, sculpture, applied art,
miniature books

Gijón

11203
Museo Internacional de la Gaita
Antiguo Instituto de Jovellanos, Plaza
Generalísimo, 8, Gijón, Oviedo
Music Museum - 1966
Antique and modern bagpipes from
Europe, Orient and Occident, and from
Spain

11204
**Museo 'Jovellanos' (Pinacoteca
Municipal)**
Plaza de Jovellanos, Gijon
General Museum - 1971
Paintings by and memorabilia on
Gaspar Melchor de Jovellanos
(1833-1874)

Granada

11205
La Alhambra
Colina de la Alhambra, Granada
Fine Arts Museum - 1870
Art and history; decorative arts; partial
architectural remnants of the Alhambra

11206
Basilica de San Juan de Dios
Calle de San Juan de Dios, 23,
Granada
Religious Art Museum
Church (737/59); painting and
ecclesiastical art

11207
Cartuja de la Asunción
Paseo de la Cartuja, Granada
Religious Art Museum - 1931
Art; painting and sculpture; ceramics

11208
Casa de los Tiros
Calle Pavaneras, 19, Granada
General Museum - 1928
Painting; decorative arts; crafts;
documents; folklore; local history

11209
Casa-Museo Manuel de Falla
Calle Antequeruela Alta, 11, Granada
Historic Site - 1965
Memorabilia of Manuel de Falla y
Matheu (1876-1946)

11210
Colección de Arte
Carmen Rodríguez Acosta, Torre
Bermeja, Granada
Fine Arts Museum - 1934
Art; contemporary Spanish painting
and Oriental art

11211
Colección Municipal
Ayuntamiento, Plaza del Carmen,
Granada
General Museum - 1939
15th-17th century crafts and
documents

11212
Museo Arqueológico Provincial
Carrera del Darro, 43, Granada
Archeology Museum - 1876
Prehistoric art; Greek, Roman, Iberian,
Punic, Celtic, Gothic and Visigothic
antiquities; Islamic art and architecture;
archaeological and Islamic ceramic
collections; Mozarabian art; 15th
century art and architecture;
inscriptions; numismatics; textiles;
glass

11213
Museo Catedralicio
Plaza de Alonso Cano, Granada
Religious Art Museum - 1929
Treasures; 16th century tapestry;
15th-17th century religious painting;
16th-18th century religious sculpture;
liturgical vestments; miniature choral
books; crafts

11214
Museo de Bellas Artes
Palacio de Carlos V, Alhambra,
Granada
Fine Arts Museum - 1839
15th-20th century art mainly of the
Granada school; 15th-19th century
painting, 16th century sculpture, 16th
century enamels and painted glass;
works by Sanchez Cotán, Alonso
Cano and José de Mora - library

11215
Museo de los Reyes Católicos
Capilla Real, Calle de Oficios, Granada
Fine Arts Museum - 1945
14th-15th century Flemish painting and
painting of Flemish schools; 15th
century Spanish, German, Italian
painting; 15th century crafts; sculpture;
goldsmith work; liturgical vestments;
miniature books; flags and banners;
tombs of the Catholic Kings and of
Donna Juana and Don Felipe el
Hermoso

11216
Museo del Sacromonte
3 km from Granada, Abadía del
Sacromonte, Camino del Sacromonte,
Granada
Fine Arts Museum - 1925
Sculpture; painting; goldsmith work;
liturgical vestments; tapestry; Arabian
codices

11217
**Museo Nacional de Arte Hispano-
Musulmán**
Casa Real de la Alhambra, Patio del
Palacio de Carlos I, Granada
Fine Arts Museum - 1870
Hispanic-Islamic ceramics,
architectonical fragments, glass, and
inscriptions from the Alhambra;
archaeology and ethnology

Granollers

11218
Museo Municipal
Granollers, Barcelona
General Museum - 1953
Archaeology; painting; medieval
pottery; natural sciences -
meteorological service

Guadelupe

11219
**Monasterio de Nuestra Señora de
Guadelupe**
Plaza Generalísimo Franco,
Guadelupe, Cáceres
Religious Art Museum - 1964
Art; painting; goldsmith work; choral
books

Guadix

11220
Museo Catedralicio
Catedral, Guadix, Granada
Religious Art Museum - 1063
Ecclesiastical art; 15th century
cathedral

Guarnizo

11221
Museo del Real Astillero
Guarnizo, Santander
History/Public Affairs Museum - 1948
Maritime history

Guernica y Luno

11222
Museo Documental
Casa de Juntas de Guernica, Calle
Allendesalazar, Guernica y Luno,
Vizcaya
History/Public Affairs Museum
History of the dominion in Vizcaya

Guisona

11223
**Museo Municipal 'Eduardo Camps
Cava'**
Calle Eduardo Camps, 1, Guisona,
Lérida
General Museum - 1952
Local history and archaeology

Gumiel de Hizán

11224
Museo de Gomellano
Iglesia de Nostra Señora de la
Asunción, Plaza Mayor, Gumiel de
Hizán, Burgos
Religious Art Museum - 1962
Art; Romanesque architectural
remains; painting

Huelva

11225
Museo Provincial
Alameda Sundheim, 8, Huelva
Archeology Museum - 1968
Prehistoric collections; Roman,
Christian archaeological and Islamic
antiquities; painting (Instituto de
Enseñanza Media 'La Rábida')

Huesca

11226
Museo Arqueológico Provincial
Universidad Sertoriana
Plaza de la Universidad s/n, Huesca
Archeology Museum - 1873
Prehistory; Iberian, Roman and
Christian archaeology; 12th century
architecture; sculptures; 15th-19th
century painting; 17th century painting
of French, Italian and Spanish schools;
Spanish ceramics; decorative arts -
library
11227
**Museo Episcopal y Capitular de
Arqueologia Sagrada**
Sala Capitular, Plaza de la Catedral,
Huesca
Fine Arts Museum - 1950
14th-15th century Gothic wall painting,
sculpture; 17th century painting;
12th-14th century crafts; goldsmith
work; 11th century documents,
medieval codices and miniature books

Ibiza

11228
Museo Arqueológico
Plaza Catedral, Ibiza, Baleares
Archeology Museum - 1907
Prehistory; Ibiza, Roman, Punic,
Egyptian, Greek archaeological
antiquities; Islamic art; 13th century
sculpture; Gothic ceramics; 14th-16th
century historical documents;
ethnography and local crafts - library
11229
Museo Catedralicio
Catedral, Ibiza, Baleares
Religious Art Museum - 1964
Religious art; goldsmith work,
14th-17th century paintings
11230
**Museo Monográfico y Necrópolis
Púnica de Puig des Moulins**
Via Romana, 31, Ibiza, Baleares
Archeology Museum - 1907
Carthagian and Roman relics from
excavations; burial remains; necropolis
- library

Igualada

11231
Museo de la Ciudad y Comarca
Carretera de Manresa, Igualada,
Barcelona
General Museum - 1949
Religious and popular art; textiles; local
history; fossils - library

11232
Museo de la Piel Museo de la Ciudad
y Comarca
Carretera de Manresa, Igualada,
Barcelona
Decorative Arts Museum - 1954
Leather and leather processing

Illescas

11233
**Hospital-Santuario de Nuestra
Señora de la Caridad**
Calle Cardenal Cisneros, 2, Illescas,
Toledo
Religious Art Museum - 1966
Ecclesiastical art; painting, goldsmith
work, liturgical vestments

Isla Plana o Nueva Tabarca

11234
**Colección Arqueológica 'Soledad
Alvarez Estrada'**
Bajada al Puerto Viejo, Isla Plana o
Nueva Tabarca, Alicante
General Museum - 1968
Local archaeology; cultural artifacts of
the Roman and of later periods

Jaca

11235
Museo Diocesano
Jaca, Huesca
Fine Arts Museum
11th-12th century Romanesque art and
architecture

Jaén

11236
Museo Catedralicio
Catedral, Plaza Santa María, Jaén
Religious Art Museum - 1962
Ecclesiastical art; painting; sculpture;
goldsmith work; choralbooks;
manuscripts; liturgical vestments
11237
Museo Provincial
Avenida del Generalísimo, 27, Jaén
General Museum - 1901
Prehistory; archaeology; Roman,
Iberian, Islamic finds; Renaissance to
20th century art; painting and
sculpture

Jerez de la Frontera

11238
Museo Arqueológico Municipal
Jerez de la Frontera, Cádiz
Archeology Museum - 1931
Prehistory; Roman, Greek, Punic,
Visigothic, Islamic Iberian antiquities
11239
Museo del Flamenco
Jerez de la Frontera, Cádiz
Performing Arts Museum - 1967
Documentary and bibliographical
archives; musical instruments;
records; folk art and costumes

Jérica

11240
Museo Municipal
Ayuntamiento, Jérica, Castellón
General Museum - 1946
Roman archaeology; art and local
history

Jumilla

11241
Museo Municipal
Plaza del Claudillo, 3, Jumilla, Murcia
Archeology Museum - 1958
Local archaeology; Bronze Age,
Iberian, Roman and Hispano-Arabian
finds

Junquera de Ambia

11242
Museo Parroquial
Antigua Colegiata, Junquera de Ambia,
Orense
Religious Art Museum - 1931
Ecclesiastical art

La Coruña

11243
Museo de Bellas Artes
Plaza Pintor Sotomayor, La Coruna
Fine Arts Museum - 1864
Archaeology; Roman finds; 14th
century Romanesque architecture;
16th-20th century regional and
Spanish paintings; 17th century
Flemish and Italian paintings; 13th-18th
century Spanish sculptures; drawings
and etchings; musical compositions;
numismatics; furnishings; porcelain;
clocks
11244
Museo de Relojes
Palacio Municipal, Plaza de María Pita,
1, La Coruña
Decorative Arts Museum - 1970
Horology; 17th-20th century English,
French, German, Dutch and Spanish
clocks
11245
Museo Histórico Arqueológico
Castillo de San Antón, La Coruña
History/Public Affairs Museum - 1964
Archaeology and history; heraldry;
Celtic treasure from Elviña;
memorabilia of the explorer Sir Francis
Drake

Laguardia

11246
Museo de la Citania de Santa Tecla
Cumbre del Monte de Santa Tecla, La
Guardia, Pontevedra
Archeology Museum - 1914
Finds from the prehistoric town Santa
Tecla
11247
**Museo de la Sociedad 'Amigos de
Laguardia'**
Laguardia, Alava
General Museum - 1964
Local history; archaeology;
ethnography; numismatics; ceramics;
war items (Guerras Carlistas)

La Rábida

11248
Monasterio de Santa Maria
Palos de la Frontera, La Rábida,
Huelva
History/Public Affairs Museum - 1856
Memorabilia of the explorer
Christopher Columbus (Colón), room
where he held conferences (1484/85);
collection of flags and boxes with soil
from all American countries; frescoes
by the painter Daniel Vázquez Díaz

La Riba

11249
Biblioteca-Museo 'José Serra Farré'
Ayuntamiento, La Riba, Tarragona
History/Public Affairs Museum
18th-19th century arms; tiles;
documents - library

Las Palmas

11250
Casa-Museo 'Colón'
Calle Colón, 1, Las Palmas, Gran
Canaria
History/Public Affairs Museum - 1951
History pertaining to Cristóbal Colón;
16th-20 century Spanish and Italian
painting
11251
Casa-Museo 'Pérez Galdós'
Calle Cano, 33, Las Palmas, Gran
Canaria
Historic Site
Memorabilia of the author Benito
Pérez Galdós (1843-1920) - library
11252
El Museo Canario
Calle Doctor Chil, 33, Las Palmas,
Gran Canaria
General Museum - 1880
Anthropology; fossils; mineralogy;
natural history; regional prehistory and
archaeology - library
11253
Museo de Bellas Artes Cabildo
Insular
Plaza Pilar Nuevo, 1, Las Palmas, Gran
Canaria
Fine Arts Museum - 1949
17th-20th century Spanish painting;
18th-20th century painting and
sculpture of the Canary Islands
11254
Museo Diocesano de Arte Sacro
Calle Doctor Chil, 31, Las Palmas,
Gran Canaria
Religious Art Museum - 1971
Painting; sculpture; goldsmith work;
furniture; tapestry; ornamentation;
incunabula and rare books

León

11255
Museo Arqueológico Provincial
Plaza de San Marcos, Léon
Archeology Museum - 1869
Regional prehistory; Roman,
Celtiberian, medieval architectural
elements; 11th-13th century art and
sculpture; 14th-16th century painting
and sculpture; 15th century Flemish
paintings; 13th-17th century ivory,
goldsmith work and liturgical
vestments; 10th century Mozarabian
art; 14th century ceramics; 12th-13th
century textiles
11256
Museo Catedralicio
Calle Cardenal Landazuri, 2, León
Religious Art Museum - 1932
Romanesque Cathedral; 13th-17th
century sculpture; medieval crafts;
carvings; goldsmith work; liturgical
vestments; 16th-17th century painting;
10th century Mozarabian Bible;
medieval documents and missals
11257
Museo Diocesano de Arte Sacro
Seminario Mayor, León
Religious Art Museum - 1948
10th-18th century ecclesiastical art

11258
Real Colegiata de San Isidoro
(Panteón, Biblioteca, Tesoro)
Plaza de San Isidoro, León
History/Public Affairs Museum - 1910
Art and history; Romanesque wall
painting; liturgical objects; goldsmith
work; textiles; miniature codices;
choral books; royal tombs

Lérida
11259
**Museo Arqueológico del Instituto de
Estudios Ilerdenses**
Avenida Blondel, 62, Lérida
Archeology Museum
archaeology

11260
Museo Catedralicio
Plaza de la Catedral, Lérida
Religious Art Museum - 1963
Tapestry; painting; liturgical vestments;
goldsmith work; documents and
miniature codices - archives; library

11261
**Museo de Arte Moderno 'Jaime
Morera'**
Antiguo Hospital de Santa María,
Avenida Blondel, 62, Lérida
Fine Arts Museum - 1917
19th-20th century painting, drawings
and prints; 20th century sculpture

11262
Museo de la Paheria
Plaza de la Paheria, Lérida
General Museum - 1961
Local history; heraldry, seals of
documents; prints - archives

11263
Museo del Libro Leridano
Plaza de la Catedral, Avenida Blondel,
62, Lérida
History/Public Affairs Museum
Book art; rare books

11264
Museo Diocesano
Seminario, Rambla de Aragón, 37,
Lérida
History/Public Affairs Museum - 1893
13th-15th century Spanish painting
and sculpture; local prehistoric
archaeological finds; crafts, textiles,
tapestry; numismatics, medals;
incunabula and manuscripts

Linares
11265
Museo Arqueológico
Calle Pontón, Linares, Jaén
Archeology Museum - 1957
Local history and archaeology,
especially from the Iberic-Roman town
of Cástulo

Llinars del Vallés
11266
**Museo Monográfico del Castell Vell
de Llinars**
Carretera de Mataró s/n, Llinars del
Vallés, Barcelona
Archeology Museum - 1978
14th-15th century archaeology

Llivia
11267
Museo de Farmacia
Ayuntamiento, Plaza Mayor, Llivia,
Gerona
General Museum - 1930
15th-19th century history of pharmacy;
apothecary's shop (1415) with interiors

Lluch
11268
Museo-Tesoro de Lluch
Santuario de Lluch, Lluch, Escorca,
Mallorca, Baleares
General Museum - 1950
Prehistory; archaeology; Romanesque
and Gothic art; 16th-18th century
liturgical vestments; furnishings;
numismatics; historical books, letters
and documents; silverwork (1616);
tapestry; ceramics

Loarre
11269
Castillo
forestry rd 5,5 km from Loarre Loarre,
Huesca
History/Public Affairs Museum - 1906
Art and history; 11th century
Romanesque fort

Logroño
11270
Museo Arqueológico Provincial
Palacio de Espartero, Calle San
Agustín, Logroño
General Museum - 1964
Architecture; sculpture; painting; local
archaeology; casts of Classical and
Renaissance sculptures

Los Barrios de Salas
11271
Museo 'Yebra'
Villa de Barrios, Calle Herrería, 17, Los
Barrios de Salas, León
Historic Site
Numismatics; philately; arms; codices;
painting; sculpture; popular and
decorative arts; ceramics from
Sargadelos - library

Luanco
11272
Museo Marítimo de Asturias
Calle del Conde del Real Agrado,
Luanco, Oviedo
History/Public Affairs Museum
Maritime history; marine cartography,
maps and drawings; nautical
instruments; ship models

Lugo
11273
Museo Diocesano
Seminario, Calle Angel López Pérez, 2,
Lugo
Religious Art Museum - 1918
Ecclesiastical art

11274
Museo Provincial
Plaza de la Soledad, 6, Lugo
General Museum - 1932
Prehistory; Roman and Iberian finds;
Mozarabian and Visigothic art;
Romanesque architecture; 10th-15th
century tombs; sculptures; paintings;
crafts; furniture; folklore; marine
history; numismatic and ceramic
collection

11275
Museo-Tesoro Catedralicio
Catedral, Plaza de Santa María, Lugo
Religious Art Museum - 1931
11th century cathedral with Gothic,
Renaissance, Baroque and
neo-Classical annexes and interiors,
religious art

Madrid
11276
Calcografía Nacional
Calle Alcalá, 13, Madrid
Fine Arts Museum - 1790
Copper engraving; 18th-20th century
copperplates and copper engravings;
copperplate engravers' studios

11277
Capilla del Obispo
mail c/o Parroquia de San Andrés,
Plaza del Marqués de Comillas s/n,
Madrid
Fine Arts Museum - 1898
Architecture; sculpture; painting; 16th
century Gothic chapel

11278
Casa de 'Lope de Vega'
Calle Cervantes, 11, Madrid
Historic Site - 1935
Memorial to Lope de Vega
(1562-1635), house where he had lived
(1610-1635) - research center

11279
Colección de Anatomia Facultad de
Medicina
Ciudad Universitaria, Madrid
Natural History Museum - 1834
Anatomical objects; human
embryology; skeleton evolution;
osteology

11280
**Colección de Arqueología y
Etnografía Americana** Facultad de
Filosofia y Letras
Departamento de Antropología de
America, Ciudad Universitaria, Madrid
3
Anthropology Museum - 1966
Archaeology; ethnology from Tukuna
and Cayapa - library

11281
Colección de Iconografia
Plaza Sta. Catalina de los Donados, 2,
Madrid
Fine Arts Museum
Oriental religious art; Byzantine,
Greek, Russian and Oriental Christian
icons; 10th-20th century art; painting;
copper engravings; enamels;
Byzantine crosses; embroidery;
medals; miniatures

11282
Colección de la Biblioteca Musical
Calle Imperial, 8, Madrid
Music Museum - 1919
Musical instruments; musical scores,
especially about Don Quixote;
autographs and photographs; musical
history - library

11283
Colección de la Casa de Alba
Palacio de Liria, Princesa, 20, Madrid
Fine Arts Museum - 1956
Roman and Greek sculpture; Italo-
Greek pottery; 16th-19th century
Spanish painting; 15th-17th century
Italian painting; 17th century Dutch
painting; 19th century paintings by
Ingres; 19th century sculpture and
furnishings; collections of miniatures
and tapestry; porcelain; arms; codices
and documents; history and paintings
of the family of the Duke of Alba

11284
**Colección de la Facultad de Filosofia
y Letras**
Ciudad Universitaria, Madrid
Fine Arts Museum
Spanish painting; works by Sorolla,
Beruete, Inza and Sala; Phoenician and
Roman archaeological objects

11285
Colección de Pintura
Fernando El Santo, 14, Madrid
Fine Arts Museum - 1907
17th-19th century Spanish painting

11286
Colección del Banco de España
Alcalá, 50, Madrid
Fine Arts Museum - 1856
19th century Spanish painting;
tapestry and furniture

11287
Colección del Banco Exterior
Carrera de San Jerónimo, 36, Madrid
Fine Arts Museum - 1929
Painting; sculpture

11288
Colección del Banco Urquijo
Casa de las Siete Chimeneas, Plaza
del Rey, Madrid
Fine Arts Museum - 1871
Painting; furniture

11289
**Colección del Observatorio
Astronómico Nacional**
Alfonso XII, 3, Madrid
Science/Tech Museum - 1796
Scientific apparatuses; telescopes,
chronographs, signal recording
apparatuses, clocks, oscilloscopes,
photometers, spectrographs

11290
Colección Municipal
Ayuntamiento, Casa de Cisneros,
Plaza de la Villa, Madrid
General Museum
Local art and history; goldsmith work,
painting, tapestry, antique maps of
Madrid

11291
Gabinete de Antigüedades
mail c/o Real Academia de la Historia,
Calle del Léon, 21, Madrid
History/Public Affairs Museum - 1738
Art and history; prehistory; classical
and paleo-Christian archaeology;
Iberian and Visigothic finds; Islamic
art; Mozarabian crafts; 4th century
'Silver dish of Theodosius'; 4th century
tombs; 15th-19th century painting;
textiles; numismatics; 11th century
documents

11292
**Gliptoteca y Museo Nacional de
Reproducciones Artisticas**
Plaza de Ruiz Gimenez s/n, Edificio
del Museo de América, Ciudad
Universitaria, Madrid 3
Fine Arts Museum - 1878
Ancient to modern copies of
sculptures; copies of ancient jewelry;
casts of architectural elements;
Egyptian, Oriental, Greek, Visigothic,
Roman, Gothic, Renaissance and
modern art; numismatics; glass;
photographical reproductions - library

11293
Instituto de Valencia de Don Juan
Calle de Fortuny, 43, Madrid
Fine Arts Museum - 1916
Medieval crafts and sculptures;
14th-17th century textiles and
costumes; Islamic inscriptions, ivory
and other arts; 15th-18th century
Islamic and Spanish ceramics; 15th
century tapestry; 15th-16th century
furnishings; porcelain; Celtic and
Iberian jewelry; 15th, 17th, 19th
century painting; 16th century
miniatures; 14th century Koran;
documents; Spanish numismatic
collections; 15th-16th century arms;
prehistoric archaeology and Visigothic
finds; arms and armor - library;
archive

11294
Monasterio de la Encarnación
Plaza de la Encarnación, 1, Madrid
Religious Art Museum - 1965
Monastic life in the 16th and 17th
century; ecclesiastical art; painting,
sculpture, furniture, reliquaries

11295
Monasterio de las Descalzas Reales
Plaza de las Descalzas, 3, Madrid
Religious Art Museum - 1960
Monastic life in the 16th and 17th
centuries; ecclesiastical art; painting;
sculpture; tapestry; goldsmith work

11296
Museo Arqueológico Nacional
Calle Serrano, 13, Madrid
Archeology Museum - 1867
Prehistoric collections; Roman, Greek,
Etruscan, Punic, Celtic, Iberian
antiquities; archaeological finds from
Balearic Islands' cultures; early
Christian and Visigothic archaeology;
Islamic art; 12th-15th century Mudejar
art; medieval tombs and 11th-17th
century sculpture; 13th-18th century
Spanish painting; 16th century Flemish
painting; 13th-19th century crafts;
10th-18th century ceramics; 15th-19th
century Spanish glass; European
porcelain, enamels, 16th-17th century
jewelry; 14th-15th century French
ivory; 16th-19th century arms;
tapestry; numismatics; miniatures;
Oriental antiquities - library;
photographical archives

11297
Museo 'Cajal'
Calle Velázquez, 144, Madrid
Historic Site - 1957
Memorial to the histologist Santiago
Ramón y Cajal (1825-1934); objects
pertaining to his life and work

11298
Museo Cerralbo
Calle Ventura Rodríguez, 17, Madrid
Fine Arts Museum - 1922
Paintings, drawings, engravings and
sculptures (15th-19th century);
tapestry; furniture; ceramics;
porcelain; numismatics - library

11299
**Museo de Aeronáutica y
Astronáutica**
mail c/o Ministerio del Aire y Hangar
de Cuatro Vientos Madrid
Science/Tech Museum - 1966
History of Spanish aviation; projects
and models

11300
Museo de Africa
Paseo de la Castellana, 5, Madrid
Anthropology Museum - 1961
Prehistory and ethnology from
Marruecos, Sahara, Fernando Poo and
Río Muni

11301
Museo de América
Avenida Reyes Católicos, Ciudad
Universitaria, Madrid 3
Anthropology Museum - 1941
Archaeology; anthropology; art from
former Spanish colonies;
pre-Columbian goldwork; colonial
painting; Ibero-American history

11302
Museo de Carruajes
Palacio Nacional, Campo del Moro,
Ribera del Manzanares, Madrid
History/Public Affairs Museum - 1967
Carriages and coaches; saddles;
litters (16th-20th centuries)

11303
Museo de Doctor Olavide
Hospital de San Juan de Dios, Calle
Doctor Esquerdo, 46, Madrid
Natural History Museum - 1903
Wax reproductions of lesions and
diseased parts of the body for
dermatological research

11304
Museo de la Bibliografia Española
Biblioteca Nacional
Paseo de Recoletos, 20, Madrid
History/Public Affairs Museum - 1901
Bibliographical, documentary, artistic
and musical collections; incunabula;
rare books; book art; manuscripts and
illuminations

11305
Museo de la Escuela de Minas
Calle Ríos Rosas, 21, Madrid
Natural History Museum - 1777
Mineralogy; fossils

11306
**Museo de la Escuela General de
Policia**
Calle Miguel Angel, 5, Madrid
History/Public Affairs Museum - 1943
History of the Spanish police; photo
gallery; anthropometry; criminal
weapons and utensils

11307
**Museo de la Fábrica Nacional de
Moneda y Timbre**
Calle Dr. Esquerdo, 38, Madrid
History/Public Affairs Museum - 1964
History of money and medals; Spanish
numismatic collection, including
European and Ibero-American issues
of money related to Spain's political
expansion; medals; etchings; stamps
and machinery for coining; graphic
arts

11308
Museo de la Farmacia Hispana
Facultad de Farmacia
Ciudad Universitaria, Madrid
Natural History Museum - 1951
Various pharmacies and reproductions
(17th-18th century); reproduction of a
Yatroquímico laboratory; 14th-19th
century pharmaceutical ceramics;
scales, weights and measures,
apparatuses for the production of
medicaments, microscopes, mortars,
medicine-chests, paintings and
drawings

11309
**Museo de la Real Academia de
Bellas Artes de San Fernando**
Calle Alcalá, 13, Madrid
Fine Arts Museum - 1774
15th-19th century painting; 19th-20th
century sculpture; 15th-19th century
Spanish, Italian, French, Flemish, Dutch
drawing; musical section

11310
Museo de Mesonero Romanos
Plaza de la Villa, 3, Madrid
Historic Site - 9142
Memorial to the writer Ramón
Mesonero Romanos (1803-1882); 15th
century building

11311
Museo del Ejército
Calle Méndez Núñez, 1, Madrid
History/Public Affairs Museum - 1803
Military history and models of military
equipment; uniforms and insignia of
different branches of the service;
exotical collections from Africa,
America, Asia and Oceania

11312
Museo del Ferrocarril Español
Calle de San Cosme y San Damián,
Madrid
History/Public Affairs Museum - 1848
Railroad history and antique railroad
material

11313
**Museo del Instituto Arqueológico
Municipal de Madrid**
Quinta del Berro, Calle Enrique
D'Almonte, 1, Madrid 28
Archeology Museum - 1953
Prehistory, archaeology and
paleontology of Madrid and the
environs; Iranian ceramics; ancient
and medieval coins - library

11314
Museo del Pueblo Español
Plaza de la Marina Española, 9, Madrid
Anthropology Museum - 1940
Spanish crafts, costumes, folklore,
embroidery, weaving, textiles, laces,
ceramics, goldsmith work, furniture;
transportation; agriculture; cattle-
breeding; music; folk literature -
library

11315
Museo del Teatro
Calle Beneficencia, 16, Madrid
Performing Arts Museum - 1920
Theater history; scenographical
material and art

11316
**Museo Español de Arte
Contemporáneo**
Avenida Calvo Sotelo, 20, Madrid
Fine Arts Museum - 1898
19th-20th century Spanish painting,
sculpture, drawing and graphic arts -
library

11317
Museo 'Lázaro Galdiano'
Calle Serrano, 122, Madrid
Fine Arts Museum - 1951
Coll: 13th-19th century painting;
15th-16th century early Flemish,
German, Spanish painting; 17th
century Flemish, Dutch painting;
18th-19th century English painting;
12th-16th century sculpture; ivory;
enamels; 12th-14th century religious
Romanesque art; crafts; Spanish
ceramics; Roman, Byzantine, Greek,
Punic, Visigothic, Renaissance jewels;
Roman antiquities; arms; Italian
bronces; English miniatures and
drawings; enamels; ivory; textiles;
furniture; fans; goldsmith work; medals
- library

11318
Museo Municipal
Calle Fuencarral, 78, Madrid
General Museum - 1927
History (16th-20th century) and art
from Madrid; prehistoric finds;
17th-19th century painting and
sculpture; crafts and folk art;
porcelain; ceramics; arms;
numismatics and medals pertaining to
the local mint; insignia; Madrid church
history; 17th-19th century maps;
Madrid drawings and reproductions;
photos; engravings; historical
documents; military history; theater
history; Madrid bullfights

11319
Museo Nacional de Arquitectura
mail c/o Escuela Superior de
Arquitectura, Ciudad Universitaria,
Madrid
Fine Arts Museum - 1943
Designs; models; drawings and prints;
architectional fragments

11320
**Museo Nacional de Artes
Decorativas**
Calle Montalbán, 12, Madrid
Decorative Arts Museum - 1912
15th-19th century Spanish ceramics;
15th-19th century furniture; folk art;
crafts; tapestry; 16th century
paintings; porcelain; glass collections
from prehistoric, Visigothic and
medieval times to the 20th century;
Oriental arts and crafts; leatherwork

11321
**Museo Nacional de Ciencias
Naturales**
Paseo de la Castellana, 84, Madrid
Natural History Museum - 1776
Malacological objects from the
Americas sent by the viceroys;
geology; palaeontology; zoology -
library

11322
Museo Nacional de Etnologia
Alfonso XII, 68, Madrid
Anthropology Museum - 1910
Prehistory; arts and crafts from the
Philippines, Australia, Brazil, South
Africa, South America, Cuba, Malaysia,
Spanish Guinea, Formosa, Morocco,
Teneriffa, Mexico, Puerto Rico;
mummies from the Andes; groups
from the Amazonas, Patagonia;
physical anthropology; Spanish
ethnography - library

11323
Museo Nacional de Geología
mail c/o Instituto Geológico y Minero
de España, Calle Ríos Rosas, 23,
Madrid
Natural History Museum - 1927
Mineralogy; palaeontology; section of
vertebrates and invertebrates;
petrology; metallography

11324
**Museo Nacional del Grabado
Contemporáneo y Sistemas de
Estampación**
Teatro Real, Felipe V, Madrid
Fine Arts Museum - 1967
20th century history and graphic arts

11325
Museo Nacional del Prado
Paseo del Prado, Madrid
Fine Arts Museum - 1818
12th-19th century painting of the
Spanish school; 14th-18th century
Italian painting; 15th-16th century
German painting; 15th-17th century
Flemish and Dutch painting; 17th-18th
century French and English painting;
18th-19th century drawing and graphic
arts; Spanish Romanesque wall
painting; Greek and Roman sculpture;
Iberian sculpture 'Dama de Elche';
jewelry 'Tesoro de Delfin'; tapestry,
furnishings, clocks, numismatics -
library

11326
Museo Naval
Calle de Montalbán, 2, Madrid 14
History/Public Affairs Museum - 1843
Nautical sciences and Spanish marine
history (16th-20th century); 16th-17th
century maritime paintings; models of
ships; historical maritime maps and
documents; historical nautical
instruments and books - library;
photographic archive; microfilm and
research center

11327
Museo Penitenciario
mail c/o Escuela de Estudios
Penitenciarios, Avenida de los
Poblados, Madrid
History/Public Affairs Museum - 1945
Penal institution; documents and
curiosities connected with crime and
punishment

11328
Museo Romántico
Calle San Mateo, 13, Madrid
Fine Arts Museum - 1924
Painting, sculpture, drawing,
miniatures, tapestry, furnishings,
domestic utensils, engravings of the
Spanish Romantic period (1820-1868);
books and graphic arts

11329
Museo 'Sorolla'
Calle Martínez Campos, 37, Madrid 10
Historic Site - 1932
Memorabilia of the painter Joaquín
Sorolla y Bastida (1863-1923); furniture
and decorative arts; ceramics;
sculptures; archaeological objects;
paintings and drawings by the artist

11330
Museo Taurino
Plaza Monumental de las Ventas, Patio
de Caballos, Madrid
Anthropology Museum - 1952
History and art of bullfighting

11331
Palacio de la Moncloa
Ciudad Universitaria, Madrid
Fine Arts Museum - 1866
Painting; furniture; tapestry; lamps;
clocks

11332
Palacio de Oriente Palacio Real
Calle Bailén, Madrid
Fine Arts Museum - 1950
Painting; 16th-18th century tapestry;
sculpture; furniture; porcelain; crystal;
clocks; miniatures; lamps; coaches;
arms, - library

11333
Palacio Real de Madrid
Madrid
History/Public Affairs Museum
16th-18th century tapestry; clocks;
paintings; porcelain; armoury;
coaches; archives and incunabula -
library

11334
Panteón de Goya
San Antonio de la Florida, Paseo de la
Florida, Madrid
Fine Arts Museum - 1905
Memorabilia on the royal painter
Francisco José de Goya y Lucientes
(1746-1828); frescoes; tomb of the
artist

11335
Panteón de Hombres Ilustres
Julián Gayarre, 3, Madrid
Historic Site - 1901
Art and history; memorial to famous
19th and 20th century politicians and
artists (Benlliure, Casanovas, Dato,
Mendizábal, Prim, Querol, Sagasta,
Zuloaga, etc.)

11336
Real Armería
Palacio de Oriente, Calle Bailén,
Madrid
History/Public Affairs Museum - 1893
Collections of 13th-19th century royal
arms and armour; historical jewelry

11337
**Real Basílica de San Francisco el
Grande**
Plaza de San Francisco el Grande,
Madrid
Religious Art Museum - 1926
18th and 19th century painting

11338
Real Biblioteca
Palacio de Oriente, Calle Bailén,
Madrid
History/Public Affairs Museum - 1950
Incunabula; manuscripts; 15th century
books of hours; 16th-20th century rare
books; prints; documents; musical
partitures; bourbon medals

11339
Real Fábrica de Tapices
Calle Fuenterrabía, 2, Madrid
Decorative Arts Museum - 1889
Tapestry; 18th century drawings and
carpets

11340
Real Oficina de Farmacia
Palacio de Oriente, Calle Bailén,
Madrid
History/Public Affairs Museum - 1799
History; royal pharmacies (16th-20th
century)

11341
San Antonio Abad
mail c/o Colegio de San Antón,
Hortaleza, 63, Madrid
Fine Arts Museum - 1962
Painting, including two pieces by Goya

Madrid 310 SP

11342
Colección Farmacéutica
Hospital Provincial, Santa Isabel, 52,
Madrid 310 SP
Science/Tech Museum - 18th century
pharmacy; pharmaceutical ceramics;
rostrum and laboratory of don
Santiago Ramón y Cajal

Madrigal de las Altas Torres

11343
Casa Natal de Isabel la Católica
Palacio de Juan II, Plaza del Cristo,
Madrigal de las Altas Torres, Avila
Fine Arts Museum - 1942
15th-17th century art; paintings,
sculptures and tapestry

Mahon

11344
Museo de Bellas Artes
Plaza de la Conquista, Mahon,
Menorca, Baleares
Fine Arts Museum - 1889
Prehistory; archaeology; local
ethnology; Aztec artifacts;
numismatics; ceramics

Málaga

11345
Museo Arqueológico Provincial
Alcazaba, Málaga
Archeology Museum - 1949
Prehistory; Roman, paleo-Christian
and Arabian archaeology; Hispano-
Arabian ceramics; finds from the
excavations of Alcazaba

11346
Museo Catedralicio
Plaza de la Catedral, Málaga
Religious Art Museum - 1946
Ecclesiastical art; painting; textiles;
manuscripts

11347
Museo de Bellas Artes
Calle San Agustín, 6, Málaga
Fine Arts Museum - 1961
16th-20th century painting; sculpture;
Roman archaeology - library

11348
**Museo-Tesoro de la Cofradía de la
Expiración**
Plaza de San Pedro, Málaga
Religious Art Museum - 1968
Ecclesiastical art; goldsmith work;
liturgical vestments

Manacor

11349
Museo Arqueológico Municipal
Plaza del Rector Rubí s/n, Manacor,
Baleares
Archeology Museum - 1925
Regional prehistory and archaeology;
Roman finds; ceramics

Manises

11350
**Museo Municipal 'Casanova Dalfo-
Sanchis Causa'**
Calle Sagrario, 22, Manises, Valencia
General Museum - 1967
Local art and history; ceramics

Manresa

11351
Museo de Manresa
Calle Villadordis, 1, Manresa,
Barcelona
General Museum - 1942
Art; prehistory; archaeology; painting;
popular and applied arts

11352
Museo Histórico de la Seo
Basílica de Santa María del Alba,
Bajada de la Seo, Manresa, Barcelona
Religious Art Museum - 1934
Ecclesiastical art; painting, sculpture,
textiles, goldsmith work; historical
artifacts

Manzanares El Real

11353
Museo de los Castillos Españoles
Manzanares El Real, Madrid
History/Public Affairs Museum - 1931
Art and history

Marchena

11354
Museo Parroquial
Iglesia de San Juan Bautista, Calle
Cristóbal de Morales, Marchena,
Sevilla
Religious Art Museum - 1965
15th century Mudejar church; Gothic
to 16th century paintings; goldsmith
work; liturgical vestments; choral and
miniature books

Marratxi

11355
Colección 'Veri'
Son Veri, La Cabaneta, Marratxi,
Mallorca, Baleares
Fine Arts Museum
Mudejár paintings and wainscots

*Martín Muñoz de las
Posadas*

11356
Museo 'Cardenal Espinosa'
Martín Muñoz de las Posadas,
Segovia
General Museum - 1931
Local ethnography

Martorell

11357
Museo Municipal 'Vicente Ros'
Calle Capuchinos, Martorell, Barcelona
General Museum - 1956
Art; local archaeology; painting;
14th-18th century ceramics

11358
Museo Provincial 'L'Enrejolada'
Calle Francisco Santacana, 15,
Martorell, Barcelona
Fine Arts Museum - 1850
Architectural elements of decaying
buildings; 15th century convent;
painting, ceramics, especially Catalan
and Valencian

Masnou

11359
Museo Municipal
Calle Anselmo Clavé, Masnou,
Barcelona
General Museum - 1957
Maritime history; archaeology; local
history

11360
**Museo Retrospectivo de Farmacia y
Medicina**
Laboratorios del Norte de España
(Cusí), Carretera a Francia, km 639,
Masnou, Barcelona
Natural History Museum - 1925
History of medicine and pharmacy,
especially of Spain; rare books, 17th
century apothecary's shop, including
furnishings and laboratory - library

Mataro

11361
Museo Municipal
Calle Enrique Granados, 17, Mataro,
Barcelona
History/Public Affairs Museum - 1894
Art and history; archaeology, applied
arts, modern painting

11362
**Museu-Arxiu de Santa Maria de
Mataró**
Sant Francesc d'Assis, 25, Mataró,
Barcelona
General Museum - 1946
Ecclesiastical art and local history;
18th century art work in Baroque style
by Antoni Viladomat; 13th century
documents; canonical files - library

Medina de Pomar

11363
Museo Conventual
Calle Santa Clara, 6, Medina de Pomar,
Burgos
Religious Art Museum
Ecclesiastical art

Medina de Ríoseco

11364
Museo-Tesoro Interparroquial
Santa María de Mediavilla, Calle de
Santa María, Medina de Ríoseco,
Valladolid
Religious Art Museum - 1959
Ecclesiastical art; goldsmith work

Medinaceli

11365
Museo de la Colegiata
Plaza de la Colegiata, Medinaceli,
Soria
Religious Art Museum - 1968
Ecclesiastical art; painting; sculpture;
goldsmith work; liturgical vestments;
choral books

Melilla

11366
Museo Municipal
Baluarte de la Concepción, Calle
Concepción Alta, Melilla
General Museum - 1953
Local art and history

Mendoza

11367
Castillo
11 km from Vitoria Mendoza, Alava
History/Public Affairs Museum
14th century castle; heraldry of Alava

Mérida

11368
Museo Arqueológico
Plaza de Santa Clara, 5, Mérida,
Badajoz
Archeology Museum - 1838
Archaeology; Roman and Visigothic
art

Moguer

11369
Casa-Museo 'Zenobia–Juan Ramón'
Calle Juan Ramón Jiménez, 10,
Moguer, Huelva
Historic Site - 1958
Memorabilia of the poet Juan Ramón
Jiménez (1881-1958); partial library
containing books and reviews

Molins de Rey

11370
Museu Municipal
Calle Pintor Fortuny, 55, Molins de
Rey, Barcelona
Fine Arts Museum - 1953
popular arts and crafts; ex libris;
Iberian and Roman amphoras - library

Monforte de Lemos

11371
Convento de Santa Clara
Monasterio de Clarisas, Monforte de
Lemos, Lugo
Religious Art Museum
Religious art; goldsmith work, painting,
16th century sculpture, alabaster
carving by Gregorio Fernández

Monóvar

11372
Casa-Museo 'Azorín'
Calle Calvo Sotelo, 6, Monóvar,
Alicante
Historic Site - 1969
Memorabilia of the poet José Martínez
Ruiz 'Azorín' (1874-1967) and on other
authors of his era

Montblanch

11373
**Museo-Archivo de Montblanch y
Comarca**
Calle Josa, 6, Montblanch, Tarragona
General Museum - 1958
History and arts of the region;
prehistory, archaeology, painting,
sculpture, palaeontology, documents

Montserrat (Monistrol)

11374
Museum
Abadía de Montserrat, Montserrat
(Monistrol), Barcelona
Fine Arts Museum - 1913
Art; biblical archaeology; Italian,
French and Spanish painting since the
15th century

Morella

11375
Museo Arciprestal
Basílica de Santa María la Mayor,
Plaza de la Arciprestal-Basílica, n. 1,
Morella, Castellón
Religious Art Museum - 1951
Ecclesiastical art; goldsmith work;
liturgical vestments; painting; archives
including medieval documents,
incunabula and choralbooks

11376
**Museo Etnológico de Morella y el
Maestrazgo**
Real Convento de San Francisco,
Plaza de San Francisco, Morella,
Castellón
Anthropology Museum - 1962
Ethnography; 15th-19th century textile
handicraft; folk and applied arts; farm
implements; graphic and documentary
material; archaeology; local art:
painting, sculpture and goldsmith work

Moyá

11377
Museo Comarcal
Calle Casanovas, Moyá, Barcelona
General Museum - 1935
Art and history; local archaeology

Murcia

11378
Museo Catedralicio
Catedral, Calle Salzillo, 2, Murcia
Religious Art Museum - 1956
Roman archaeology; sculpture;
painting; goldsmith work; liturgical
vestments; historical documents;
choralbooks

11379
Museo de la Muralla Arabe
Plaza de Santa Eulalia, Murcia
History/Public Affairs Museum - 1966
Ibero-Moorish excavations; ceramics

11380
Museo de Murcia Sección de Bellas
Artes
Calle Obispo Frutos, 12, Murcia
Fine Arts Museum - 1864
17th-20th century painting; prints and
drawings; sculpture - library

11381
Museo de Murcia Sección de
Arqueología
Calle Alfonso X el Sabio, Murcia
General Museum - 1910
Prehistory; Bronze Age, Iberian,
Roman, Arabian, Christian and
Medieval archaeological finds;
architecture; inscriptions; numismatics;
16th-18th century heraldry; medieval
and modern crafts - library

11382
Museo 'Salzillo'
Calle San Andrés, 1, Murcia
Historic Site - 1960
Sculptures and designs by Francisco
Salzillo (1707-1783); memorabilia of the
artist

Muriedas

11383
Museo Etnográfico de Cantabria
Casa de Velarde, Muriedas, Camargo,
Santander
Anthropology Museum - 1966
Regional ethnology; memorial to Pedro
Velarde (1779-1808) - library

Nájera

11384
Monasterio de Santa María la Real
Calle del Rey Don García, Nájera,
Logroño
Religious Art Museum - 1889
11th century monastery with 15th-16th
century annexes; art; history

Nerja

11385
Museo Arqueológico
Cueva, Anejo de Maro, Nerja, Maro,
Málaga
General Museum - 1960
Local archaeology

Olot

11386
Museo Arqueológico
Calle Hospicio, 4, Olot, Gerona
General Museum - 1893
Archaeology; popular and applied arts;
numismatics; arms

11387
Museo de Arte Moderno
Parque de la Ciudad, Olot, Gerona
Fine Arts Museum - 1943
Contemporary art; painting, sculpture,
prints and drawings

11388
Museo-Tesoro Parroquial
Iglesia de San Esteban, Olot, Gerona
Religious Art Museum
Art; painting; carvings; goldsmith
work; liturgical vestments

Oncala

11389
Museo de Tapices
Iglesia de San Millán, Oncala, Soria
Decorative Arts Museum
17th century Flemish tapestry and 18th
century liturgical vestments

Onda

11390
Museo de Ciencias Naturales
Carretera de Tales, Onda, Castellón
Natural History Museum - 1955
botany; mineralogy; fossils;
entomology - library

11391
Museo Histórico Municipal
Calle Cervantes, 4, Onda, Castellón
General Museum - 1968
Local history and art; ceramics

Orense

11392
Museo Arqueológico Provincial
Calle Obispo Carrascosa, 1, POB 145,
Orense
Archeology Museum - 1845
Prehistory; Roman and Iberian finds;
Visigothic art (7th century);
Mozarabian art (10th century);
Romanesque architecture; Gothic art;
sculptures; paintings (16th century);
contemporary art; crafts; history

11393
Museo Diocesano-Catedralicio
Catedral, Orense
Religious Art Museum - 1957
Ecclesiastical art; goldsmith work,
painting, sculpture, liturgical vestments
- library

Orihuela

11394
Museo Arqueológico Comarcal
Calle Alfonso XIII, 1, Orihuela
General Museum - 1970
Archaeology; art; local history

11395
Museo Diocesano de Arte Sacro
Catedral, Orihuela
Religious Art Museum - 1944
Religious art; paintings; sculptures;
goldsmith work; codices

11396
**Museo-Tesoro Parroquial de
Santiago**
Plaza de Santiago, 3, Orihuela
Religious Art Museum - 1933
Religious art; sculptures from Salzillo;
religious goldsmith work

Osuna

11397
Monasterio de la Encarnación
Descalzas, Osuna, Sevilla
Religious Art Museum - 1969
Baroque church; painting; sculpture;
goldsmith work; ceramics

11398
Museo Arqueológico
Torre del Agua, Osuna, Sevilla
General Museum - 1971
Local archaeology; Roman and Iberian
finds

11399
Museo de Arte Sacro
Iglesia Colegial, Osuna, Sevilla
Religious Art Museum - 1968
Ecclesiastical art; painting, sculpture,
15th-19th century goldsmith work,
choralbooks, liturgical objects;
documents; ducal pantheon

Oviedo

11400
Camara Santa
Catedral, Oviedo
Religious Art Museum - 1931
Liturgical goldsmith work; archives

11401
Museo Provincial
Calle San Vicente, 3, Oviedo
General Museum - 1845
Prehistory; archaeology; pre-Romanic,
Romanesque and Gothic art;
inscriptions; numismatics

Padrón

11402
Casa-Museo 'Rosalia de Castro'
Lugar de 'La Matanza', Iria Flavia,
Padrón, La Coruña
Historic Site - 1971
Memorabilia of the poet Rosalía de
Castro (1837-85) and of the poet and
historian Manuel Martínez Murguía
(1833-1923) - library

11403
Museo de Arte Sacro de Padrón
Casa Rectoral, Calle Santa María,
Padrón, La Coruña
Religious Art Museum - 1947
Ecclesiastical art; 15th-18th century
goldsmith work and liturgical
vestments

Palamós

11404
Museo 'Cau de la Costa Brava'
Plaza del Horno, 4, Palamós, Gerona
General Museum - 1920
Local prehistory and archaeology;
numismatics; exlibris; 20th century
painting

Palencia

11405
Museo Arqueológico Provincial
Palacio de la Diputación, Calle Burgos,
1, Palencia
Archeology Museum - 1845
Prehistory; archaeology; medieval
wood carving; 14th century paintings;
numismatics

11406
Museo Catedralicio
Catedral, Plaza de la Inmaculada,
Palencia
Religious Art Museum - 1965
Ecclesiastical art; painting, sculpture,
goldsmith work, tapestry, liturgical
vestments

Palma de Mallorca

11407
Colección 'Krekovic'
Son Fusteret, Camino Viejo de Buñola,
Palma de Mallorca, Baleares
Fine Arts Museum
Paintings

11408
Colección 'Vivot'
Calle Zavellá, 2, Palma de Mallorca,
Baleares
Fine Arts Museum
18th century building; furniture;
paintings and sculptures - library

11409
Museo 'Castillo de Bellver'
2,5 km from the capital, Castillo de
Bellver, Palma de Mallorca, Baleares
General Museum - 1932
Local history; prehistory; archaeology;
copies of 16th century Roman statues;
Celda de Jovellanos

11410
Museo Catedralicio
Catedral, Palma de Mallorca, Baleares
Religious Art Museum - 1932
Religious art; paintings; goldsmith
work, tapestry, liturgical vestments;
documents and antique books

11411
Museo de Arte 'Saridakis'
Calle de Calvo Sotelo, Porto Pi, Palma
de Mallorca, Baleares
Decorative Arts Museum
19th-20th century decorative arts

11412
Museo de la Iglesia de Mallorca
Palacio Episcopal, Plaza Mirador,
Palma de Mallorca, Baleares
Religious Art Museum - 1916
Mallorca prehistory and archaeology;
14th-18th century painting and
sculpture; ceramics; numismatics;
liturgical vestments; hymnals

11413
Museo de Mallorca
Sección de Arqueología: Casa de
Cultura; Sección de Bellas Artes,
Antigua Lonja: Paseo Sagrera;
Sección de Etnología: Calle Mayor, 15,
mail c/o Oficinas, Calle Lulio, 5, Palma
de Mallorca, Baleares
General Museum - 1961
Archaeological, fine arts and
ethnographical section; Roman finds
from excavations on Mallorca; Gothic
paintings; ethnography; folk art;
applied arts; old pharmacy

11414
Museo Maritimo Balear
Consulado del Mar, Paseo Sagrera,
Palma de Mallorca, Baleares
History/Public Affairs Museum - 1951
Maritime History; ethnography

11415
Palacio 'Morell'
San Cayetano, 22, Palma de Mallorca,
Baleares
Fine Arts Museum
Paintings; furniture

11416
Palacio-Residencia de la Almudaina
Plaza Almoina, Palma de Mallorca
History/Public Affairs Museum
History of the city; local art

Pamplona

11417
Museo de Navarra
Calle Santo Domingo, Pamplona,
Navarra
Fine Arts Museum - 1910
Prehistory; archaeology; Gothic
frescoes and paintings; architectural
remains; Romanesque capitals;
16th-18th century painting

11418
Museo de Recuerdos Históricos
Calle Mercado, 11, Pamplona, Navarra
History/Public Affairs Museum - 1940
Regional and local history; folklore; art
and history pertaining to the Carlistic
era

11419
Museo Diocesano
Catedral, Calle Dormitalería, Pamplona,
Navarra
Religious Art Museum - 1960
Ecclesiastical art; Gothic painting;
goldsmith work; liturgical vestments;
embroidery

11420
Museo Etnológico de Navarra
Calle de Santo Domingo, Pamplona,
Navarra
Anthropology Museum
Popular costumes and folk art

11421
Museo 'Sarasate'
Conservatorio de Música, Calle Aoiz,
Pamplona, Navarra
Historic Site - 1908
Memorabilia on the violinist and
composer Pablo Martín Sarasate de
Navascués (1844-1908)

Paradas

11422
Museo Parroquial
Parroquia de San Eutropio, Calle
Padre Barea, 33, Paradas, Sevilla
Religious Art Museum - 1968
Painting; ornamentation; goldsmith
work; 'La Magdalena' by El Greco

Paredes de Nava

11423
Museo Parroquial de Santa Eulalia
Plaza de España, Paredes de Nava,
Palencia
Religious Art Museum - 1964
Ecclesiastical art; painting, sculpture,
goldsmith work,liturgical vestments,
furniture

Pastrana

11424
Museo Parroquial
Iglesia de Nostra Señora de la
Asunción, Plaza de los Caidos,
Pastrana, Guadalajara
Religious Art Museum - 1927
15th century tapestry; goldsmith work;
wood and ivory carvings; 8th century
crucifix; ornaments; parchments; 16th
century tombs

Peñaranda de Duero

11425
Museo de Farmacia
Calle José Grijalba, 13, Peñaranda de
Duero, Burgos
Natural History Museum - 1964
18th century pharmacy and laboratory;
medicaments; utensils and
instruments; medical library; garden
with medical plants

Peñíscola

11426
Castillo 'El Macho'
Final de la calle del Castillo, Peñíscola,
Castellón
History/Public Affairs Museum - 1931
Art and history; medieval fort

Perelada

11427
**Colección 'Mateu' Museo del Castillo-
Palacio de Perelada**
Convento del Carmen, Calle del
Castillo, Perelada, Gerona
Fine Arts Museum - 1923
Painting, sculpture, numismatics,
ceramics, antique windows, glass;
incunabula; Spanish history; 14th-15th
century architectural elements -
library

Piedrafita de El Cebrero

11428
**Museo de Artes y Costumbres
Populares**
Pallozas, Piedrafita de El Cebrero,
Lugo
Anthropology Museum - 1969
Ethnology from the Galician
mountains: interiors, domestic crafts,
weaving, fowl breeding, painting,
implements and utensils; architecture;
ecclesiastical goldsmith work:
chalices, reliquaries

Plasencia

11429
Museo-Tesoro Catedralicio
Plazuela de la Catedral, Plasencia,
Cáceres
Religious Art Museum - 1948
Ecclesiastical art; goldsmith work;
painting; ornaments; antique hymnals

Poblet

11430
Real Monasterio de Santa Maria
Poblet, Tarragona
General Museum - 1960
12th century monastery; 14th century
palace of Martín el Humano; local art
and prehistory

Pontevedra

11431
Colección de Historia Natural
Instituto, Calle Montero Ríos,
Pontevedra
Natural History Museum - 1890
Mineralogy; zoology

11432
Museo de Pontevedra
Plaza de la Leña, Calle de Pasantería y
Ruinas de Santo Domingo, Pontevedra
General Museum - 1895
Local archaeology and prehistory;
sculpture; painting; prehistoric and
medieval goldsmith work; jewelry; folk
arts and crafts - library

Puerto Pollensa

11433
Anglada Camarasa
Paseo Anglada Camarasa 87, Puerto
Pollensa, Mallorca-Baleares
General Museum - 1967
Chinese furniture; porcelain;
costumes; paintings; drawings

11434
Museo del Colegio ' Costa y Llobera'
Calle Guillermo Cifre, 13, Puerto
Pollensa, Mallorca, Baleares
Natural History Museum - 1949
Natural history; fossils and regional
zoology

Puerto Real

11435
Museo Municipal
Calle Marqués de Comillas, Puerto
Real, Cádiz
General Museum
Local archaeology

Quejana

11436
Monasterio de Dominicas
Quejana, Ayala, Alava
Religious Art Museum - 1957
Religious art; paintings; goldsmith
works; tomb of the chancelor of Ayala

Quesada

11437
Museo 'Zabaleta'
Plaza Coronación, 10, Quesada, Jaén
Historic Site - 1960
Memorabilia of the painter Rafael
Zabaleta (1907-60); his heritage
consisting of oilpaintings, watercolors
and drawings

Requena

11438
Museo Histórico de Requena y su Comarca
Calle del Castillo, Requena, Valencia
General Museum - 1968
Local art and history; archaeology; ethnology; historical books and documents

Reus

11439
Museo Municipal
Avenida Mártires, 13, Reus, Tarragona
General Museum - 1961
Art and history of the region; prehistory, archaeology, painting, sculpture, heraldry, decorative and folk art

11440
Museo 'Prim-Rull'
Calle San Juan, 27, Reus, Tarragona
General Museum - 1920
Art and history

Ribadavia

11441
Museo de Artes y Costumbres Populares
Ribadavia, Orense
General Museum - 1969
Local ethnography

Riofrió

11442
Museo Nacional de Caza
Palacio Real, Riofrió, Segovia
History/Public Affairs Museum - 1970
History of hunting in Spain; dioramas; arms, porcelain, tapestry, furniture, painting, sculpture, drawings, trophies

Ripoll

11443
Archivo-Museo Folklórico Parroquial
Antigua Iglesia de San Pedro, Plaza del Abad Oliba, Ripoll, Gerona
General Museum - 1929
Ethnography; local arms and smithwork; numismatics; folk costumes; antique religious parchments and documents

11444
Monasterio de Santa María
Plaza del Abad Oliba, Ripoll, Gerona
General Museum - 1883
Art and history

Roda de Isábena

11445
Museo Parroquial
Sala Capitular de la antigua catedral, Roda de Isábena, Huesca
Religious Art Museum - 1944
Art; furniture; 15th-16th century painting; sculpture; liturgical objects; liturgical vestments; medieval textiles

Roncesvalles

11446
Museo Artístico de Roncesvalles
Real Colegiata, Roncesvalles, Navarra
General Museum - 1925
Art and history; painting, goldsmith work, ornaments; royal pantheon of Sancho el Fuerte and Clemencia de Toulouse

Rubí

11447
Museo de Rubí
Biblioteca Municipal, Calle Doctor Maximi Fornés, 5, Rubí, Barcelona
General Museum - 1924
Art; archaeology; local history - library

Sabadell

11448
Instituto-Museo Provincial de Paleontologia
Calle Escuela Industrial, 23, Sabadell, Barcelona
Natural History Museum - 1969
Paleontology, especially mammals from the Tertiary and Quaternary in Spain; palaeontological philately

11449
Museo de Bellas Artes
Calle Dr. Puig 16, Sabadell, Barcelona
Fine Arts Museum
art

11450
Museo de Historia
Calle San Antonio, 13, Sabadell, Barcelona
General Museum - 1931
Prehistory; Iberian and Roman antiquities; local history (13th-17th century); local paintings, maps, textiles, pottery, furniture, coins, folklore

Sagunto

11451
Museo Arqueológico
Calle Castillo, Sagunto, Valencia
General Museum - 1943
Local excavations

Sahagún

11452
Monasterio de la Santa Cruz
Calle Alfonso VI, Sahagún, León
Religious Art Museum - 1962
Art and history; sculpture; painting; goldsmith work; textiles

Salamanca

11453
Casa-Museo de Unamuno
Antigua rectoral, Libreros, 7, Salamanca
Historic Site - 1952
Memorabilio on the author Miguel de Unamuno y Jugo (1864-1936)

11454
Museo de Salamanca
Patio Escuelas, 2, Salamanca
Fine Arts Museum - 1848
Palaeolithic, Bronze Age and Roman finds, 15th-19th century painting; 15th-18th century stone and wood sculpture; folk art; ceramics; glass - library

11455
Museo del Convento de Santa Ursula
Calle de las Ursulas, 2, Salamanca
Fine Arts Museum - 1968
14th-16th century painting; sculpture; 16th century hymnal

11456
Museo Diocesano
Catedral Vieja, Salamanca
Religious Art Museum - 1953
15th-16th century painting; 14th-18th century sculpture; goldsmith work; textiles; historical documents

San Cugat del Valles

11457
Monasterio de San Cugat
Plaza Octaviano, San Cugat del Valles
History/Public Affairs Museum - 1931
Art and History; architecture, painting, ecclesiastical artifacts

San Feliu de Guixols

11458
Museo Municipal
Porta Ferrada, Plaza Monasterio, San Feliu de Guixols, Gerona
General Museum - 1904
Archaeological copies of different origins; 18th-19th century Catalan and Valencian ceramics; 15th-18th century choral books

San Gines de Vilasar

11459
Museo Arqueológico Municipal
Plaza del Caudillo, 7, San Gines de Vilasar
General Museum - 1961
Local art and history; prehistory and archaeology

San Ildefonso o La Granja

11460
Palacio Real
San Ildefonso o La Granja, Segovia
Religious Art Museum - 1931
Ecclesiastical art and history; lamps, furniture, tapestry; gardens with fountains

San Juan de la Peña

11461
Real Monasterio de San Juan de la Peña
San Juan de la Peña, Botaya, Huesca
Historic Site - 1889
Art and history; architectural fragments from different periods

San Juan de las Abadesas

11462
Archivo-Museo del Monasterio
Antiguo Monasterio, San Juan de las Abadesas, Gerona
Religious Art Museum - 18th century
Ecclesiastical art; liturgical vestments, hymnals, sculpture; archives

San Juan de Vilasar

11463
Gliptoteca 'Monjó'
Camino Real, 36, San Juan de Vilasar, Barcelona
Fine Arts Museum - 1964
Sculptures; in a 18th century building

San Lorenzo de El Escorial

11464
Monasterio de San Lorenzo
San Lorenzo de El Escorial, Madrid
Decorative Arts Museum - 1963
Painting; tapestry; furniture; lamps; goldsmith work; liturgical vestments; architectural elements - library

11465
Santa Cruz del Valle de los Caidos
Valle de Cuelgamuros, San Lorenzo de El Escorial, Madrid
General Museum - 1940
Art and history; national monument, memorial to the dead of the civil war (1936-39) - library

San Lorenzo de Morunys

11466
Museo del Patronato de Vall de Lord
Nuestra Señora dels Colls, 1, San Lorenzo de Morunys, Lérida
General Museum - 1946
Archaeology; painting; numismatics; folk arts and crafts; geology

San Mateo

11467
Colección Parroquial
Iglesia de San Mateo, Plaza Generalísimo, San Mateo, Castellón
Religious Art Museum
Art; liturgical goldsmith work; antique Gothic altar fragments; artifacts

San Millán de la Cogolla

11468
Monasterio de San Millán de Yuso
San Millán de la Cogolla, Logroño
Religious Art Museum - 1931
Art and history; painting, sculpture, 11th century ivory, smithwork - archives; library

San Millán de Suso

11469
Monasterio de San Millán de Suso
1,3 km from the village, carretera forestral, San Millán de Suso, Logroño
Religious Art Museum - 1931
Art and history; architecture, sculpture, tombs

San Pedro de Cardeña

11470
Monasterio de San Pedro
Carretera Local de la Cartuja de Miraflores, San Pedro de Cardeña, Castrillo del Val, Burgos
History/Public Affairs Museum - 1931
Art and history

San Pedro de Roda

11471
Monasterio de San Pedro de Roda
San Pedro de Roda, Gerona
General Museum - 1930
12th century church; architecture

San Roque

11472
Museo Histórico del Campo de Gibraltar
Palacio de los Gobernadores, San Roque, Cádiz
General Museum - 1969
Art and history

San Sebastián

11473
Acuario
Palacio del Mar, San Sebastián, Guipúzcoa
Natural History Museum - 1928
Marine zoology; natural history; navigation - library

11474
Casa de Oquendo
Barrio de Gros. Junto al Matadero, San Sebastián, Guipúzcoa
Fine Arts Museum - 1950
16th-17th century painting and furniture

11475
Museo Histórico Militar
Monte Urgull, San Sebastián,
Guipúzcoa
History/Public Affairs Museum - 1964
Arms and military history

11476
Museo Municipal de San Telmo
Plaza Ignacio Zuloaga, San Sebastián,
Guipúzcoa
General Museum - 1899
15th-20th century painting; Basque
ethnography; furniture; prehistory;
tomb stelae

Santa Coloma de Queralt

11477
**Museo de la Asociación
Arqueológica de la Villa**
Santa Coloma de Queralt, Tarragona
General Museum - 1947
Local archaeology and history;
archives

Santa Cruz

11478
Museo de Bellas Artes
Calle Pérez de Brito, 25, Santa Cruz,
Isla de la Palma, Santa Cruz de
Tenerife
Fine Arts Museum - 1971
19th century Spanish painting

11479
**Museo Etnográfico y de Historia
Natural**
Wandevalle, Santa Cruz, Isla de la
Palma, Santa Cruz de Tenerife
General Museum - 1883
Local ethnography; natural history

Santa Cruz de Tenerife

11480
Museo Arqueológico
Calle Bravo Murillo, Apartado 133,
Santa Cruz de Tenerife
Archeology Museum - 1958
Archaeology; neolithic ceramics; local
anthropology

11481
Museo Municipal
Antiguo Convento de San Francisco,
Calle J. Murphy, 6, Santa Cruz de
Tenerife
General Museum - 1900
Painting; sculpture; arms; ethnology

Santa Eulalia del Río

11482
Museo 'Barrau'
Iglesia del Puig de Missa, Santa Eulalia
del Río, Ibiza, Baleares
Historic Site - 1963
Memorabilia on the Barcelona
impressionist Laureano Barrau y Buñol

Santa Gadea del Cid

11483
Museo Parroquial
Iglesia de San Pedro Apóstol, Plaza de
la Fuente, Santa Gadea del Cid,
Burgos
Religious Art Museum - 1932
Ecclesiastical art; goldsmith work,
liturgical vestments, sculpture, prayer
books, medieval documents

Santa María de Huerta

11484
Monasterio de Santa María
Plaza del Monasterio, Santa María de
Huerta, Soria
Religious Art Museum - 1882
Art and history; 12th century
monastery

Santa María del Campo

11485
Museo Parroquial
Parroquia de la Asunción, Plaza
Mayor, Santa María del Campo,
Burgos
Religious Art Museum - 1931
Ecclesiastical art; painting, goldsmith
work, tapestry from Bruxelles; 15th
century church

Santa María del Puig

11486
**Real Monasterio de Santa María del
Puig**
Santa María del Puig, Valencia
Fine Arts Museum - 1969
Painting; liturgical vestments;
goldsmith work; ceramics; metalwork;
numismatics

Santander

11487
Casa-Museo 'Menéndez Pelayo'
Calle Gravina, 4, Santander
Historic Site
Memorial to Marcelino Menéndez y
Pelayo (1856-1912)

11488
Museo Maritimo del Cantabrico
San Martín de Abajo s/n, Santander
Natural History Museum - 1980
Maritime history of the Cantabrico
Sea; fishing ethnography; Cetacea
skeletons; skeleton of balaenoptery
phisalus (24 m.) - library; aquarium

11489
Museo Municipal de Bellas Artes
Biblioteca Menéndez Pelayo, Calle
Rubio, 6, Santander
Fine Arts Museum - 1948
Regional painting and sculpture

11490
**Museo Provincial de Prehistoria y
Arqueologia**
Diputación Provincial, Calle de Juan de
la Cosa, 1, Santander
Archeology Museum - 1926
Prehistory; archaeology

Santes Creus

11491
Monasterio de Santes Creus
Plaza San Bernardo, Santes Creus,
Aiguamurcia, Tarragona
Religious Art Museum - 1835
Architectural elements of the antique
monastery; royal tombs

Santiago de Compostela

11492
Museo Catedralicio
Platerías, Santiago de Compostela, La
Coruña
Religious Art Museum - 1943
Art: sculpture, tapestry, goldsmith
work, ornaments; Roman archaeology
and remnants of the original Roman
cathedral; archives, miniature codices

11493
Museo de Historia 'Luis Iglesias'
Facultad de Ciencias
Avenida de las Ciencias, 1, Santiago
de Compostela, La Coruña
Natural History Museum - 1900
Zoology; especially specimens
representing the region

11494
Museo de las Peregrinaciones
Calle San Miguel, 4, Santiago de
Compostela, La Coruña
Religious Art Museum - 1951
Painting, sculpture, goldsmith work,
drawings and popular art pertaining to
Jacobinism and pilgrimage

11495
Museo Municipal
Convento de Santo Domingo,
Santiago de Compostela, La Coruña
General Museum - 1895
Art; archaeology; local history

Santillana del Mar

11496
Museo de Altamira
Santillana del Mar, Santander
Archeology Museum - 1979
Implements and remains from the
palaeolithic caves of Cantabrian Spain
(Altamira, Juyo, Salitre, Rascaño);
paleolithic burial remains of the
Aurignacian period (30.000 years ago)
found in Morin Cave

11497
**Museo de la Colegiata de Santa
Juliana**
Claustro Románico, Santillana del Mar,
Santander
Fine Arts Museum - 1889
Romanesque architecture; art; archive
containing antique documents

11498
Museo Diocesano
Monasterio de Regina Coeli, Santillana
del Mar, Santander
Fine Arts Museum - 1968
Religious folk art; furniture;
photographs of regional Romanic
architecture

Santiponce

11499
Museo Arqueológico de Itálica
8 km fuera de Sevilla Santiponce,
Sevilla
Archeology Museum - 1970
Finds from excavations of the Roman
colony Aelia Augusta Itálica (founded
by Publio Cornelio Escipión 'El
Africano' 206 B.C.)

Santo Domingo de la Calzada

11500
Museo Catedralicio
Santo Domingo de la Calzada,
Logroño
Religious Art Museum - 1931
Art: sculpture, painting, baroque
goldsmith work, 16th-17th century
vestments; archives: bulls, codices,
incunabula, hymnals

Santo Domingo de Silos

11501
**Museo Arqueológico y de Historia
Natural**
Monasterio de Santo Domingo, Santo
Domingo de Silos, Burgos
Archeology Museum - 1905
17th century pharmacy; archaeological
ceramics; goldsmith work;
numismatics; manuscripts; Roman art;
geology; local natural history

Segorbe

11502
Museo Diocesano-Catedralicio
Calle de Santa María, Segorbe,
Castellón
Religious Art Museum - 1949
Ecclesiastical art; painting; goldsmith
work; liturgical vestments; historical
documents

Segovia

11503
Alcázar
Plaza del Alcázar, Segovia
History/Public Affairs Museum - 1951
Arms; furniture; painting

11504
Casa-Museo 'Antonio Machado'
Calle de los Desamparados, 11,
Segovia
Historic Site
Memorabilia of the poet Antonio
Machado y Ruiz (1875-1936)

11505
Convento de San Antonio el Real
Calle de San Antonio el Real, 4,
Segovia
Religious Art Museum - 1960
Painting; alto relievos; 15th century
stucco; furnishing; liturgical vestments;
carpets; hymnals

11506
Museo Arqueológico
San Agustín, 8, Segovia
Archeology Museum - 1950
Local archaeology and numismatics

11507
Museo Catedralicio
Plaza Mayor, Segovia
Religious Art Museum - 1924
Ecclesiastical art; painting; sculpture;
goldsmith work; tapestry;
ornamentation; miniature codices

11508
Museo de Bellas Artes
Casa del Hidalgo, San Agustín, 8,
Segovia
Fine Arts Museum - 1917
Painting; sculpture; decorative arts;
ceramics, crystal of La Granja,
smithwork

11509
Museo 'Zuloaga'
Iglesia de San Juan de los Caballeros,
Segovia
Decorative Arts Museum - 1947
Painting; ceramics by Daniel Zuloaga

11510
La Vera-Cruz
Barrio de San Marcos, Segovia
History/Public Affairs Museum - 1919
Art and history; frescoes;
Romanesque church

Seo de Urgel

11511
Museum Diocesá d'Urgell
Plaça del Cardenal Casañes, 3, Seo de Urgel, Lérida, Catalunya
Fine Arts Museum - 1957
Ecclesiastical and folk art; Romanesque wallpaintings, sculpture; late Romanesque architectural elements; goldsmith work, ornaments, 13th century Oriental textiles; codices and miniature hymnbooks; Beato de Liébana (11th century) - library

Sevilla

11512
Alcázar
Plaza del Triunfo, Sevilla
Religious Art Museum - 1965
Ecclesiastical art; tapestry, painting, mosaics

11513
Casa de las Dueñas
Calle de las Dueñas, Sevilla
Religious Art Museum - 1931
Ecclesiastical art

11514
Casa de Pilatos
Plaza de Pilatos, Sevilla
Fine Arts Museum - 1931
Painting; ceramics; 16th century palace

11515
Colección 'Osuna'
Calle Alfonso XII, 48, Sevilla
Fine Arts Museum - 1967
Painting; furniture; tapestry; porcelain; fans

11516
Hospital de la Santa Caridad
Iglesia de San Jorge, Calle Temprado, 3, Sevilla
Fine Arts Museum - 1679
Painting and sculpture

11517
Museo Arqueológico Provincial
Plaza de América, Sevilla
Archeology Museum - 1880
Prehistory, Roman, Iberian and medieval archaeology; finds from Roman town Italica; sculpture; culture; treasury of 'El Carambolo' - library

11518
Museo Catedralicio
Avenida Queipo de Llano, Sevilla
Religious Art Museum - 1931
Painting; sculpture; goldsmith work; liturgical vestments; 15th-20th century historical objects

11519
Museo de Arte Contemporáneo
Antigua Iglesia de San Hermenegildo, Sevilla
Fine Arts Museum - 1971
20th century art

11520
Museo de Bellas Artes
Plaza del Museo, 9, Sevilla 1
Fine Arts Museum - 1841
12th-20th century painting and sculpture; drawings, enamels; glass; ceramics; engravings; furniture; arms - library

11521
Museo de la Semana Santa
Hospicio de Venerables Sacerdotes, Plaza Venerables, 8, Sevilla
Religious Art Museum - 1965
Religious art of the lay brotherhood; goldsmith work; embroidery; gold and silver laces

11522
Museo de la Torre del Oro
Paseo de Cristóbal Colón, Sevilla
History/Public Affairs Museum - 1943
Antique nautical material; maritime history

11523
Museo-Templo de la Anunciación
Calle Laraña, Sevilla
History/Public Affairs Museum - 1971
Art and history

11524
Museo-Tesoro de la Basilica de la Macarena
Calle Bécquer, 1, Sevilla
Religious Art Museum - 1949
Ecclesiastical art; 19th and 20th century lace; goldsmith work; liturgical vestments; cloister

11525
Museo-Tesoro del Templo del Gran Poder
Plaza de San Lorenzo, Sevilla
Religious Art Museum
Ecclesiastical art; goldsmith work and ornamentation

11526
Palacio de Lebrija
Calle Cuna, 18, Sevilla
Archeology Museum - 1969
Roman; Islamic and Mudejar archaeology

Sierra de Yeguas

11527
Museo del Campo
Calle de la Cruz, 2, Sierra de Yeguas, Málaga
General Museum - 1965
Ethnography; local prehistory

Sigüenza

11528
Museo Catedralicio
Catedral, Sigüenza, Guadalajara
Religious Art Museum - 1949
Sculpture, painting, tapestry; books and documents

11529
Museo Diocesano de Arte Antiguo
Antigua Casa de los Barrenas, Plaza del Obispo D. Bernardo, Sigüenza, Guadalajara
Religious Art Museum - 1967
Local archaeology and ecclesiastical art; painting, sculpture, goldsmith work, liturgical vestments; 12th-18th century architectural fragments

Sitges

11530
Museo del Cau Ferrat y Sección Maricel
Casa Rusiñol, Calle Fonollar, 25, Sitges, Barcelona
Fine Arts Museum - 1933
Arms; painting; sculpture; furniture; ceramics; glass

11531
Museo Maricel de Mar
Calle Fenollar, Sitges, Barcelona
Fine Arts Museum - 1969
Art; painting, sculpture, furniture, ceramics, smithwork

11532
Museo Romántic
Can Llopis, Sant Gaudenci, 1, Sitges, Barcelona
Decorative Arts Museum - 1949
18th-19th century furniture and decorative arts; lamps, porcelain, clocks, crystal, musical instruments; Lola Anglada collection of 17th-19th century dolls; folklore and ethnology - library; garden

Solsona

11533
Museo Diocesano
Palacio Episcopal, Solsona, Lérida
Religious Art Museum - 1896
Regional prehistory and archaeology; 10th-15th century painting; Gothic and Renaissance sculpture

11534
Museo Etnográfico Comarcal
Calle Castillo, 20, Solsona, Lérida
Anthropology Museum - 1969
Ethnology; art; history

Soria

11535
Museo Numantino
Propio, Paseo del Espolón, 8, Soria
Archeology Museum - 1919
Finds from the excavations of Numantia; ceramics; Museo Celtibérico: local prehistory and archaeology; Museo Epigráfico de San Juan: Roman art, mosaics and inscriptions, 13th century architectural elements; Ruinas de Numancia (12 km from Soria): pre-Roman, Iberian and Hispano-Roman finds from Numantia

Talavera de la Reina

11536
Museo de Cerámica 'Ruiz de Luna'
Museo de Santa Cruz, Toledo
Plaza General Primo de Rivera, 5, Talavera de la Reina, Toledo
General Museum - 1963
local ceramics

Tarragona

11537
Colección 'Molas'
Llano de la Catedral, 6, Tarragona
Fine Arts Museum
arts of several eras; numismatics

11538
Museo Arqueológico Provincial
Plaza del Rey, 1, Tarragona
General Museum - 1960
Roman archaeology; 14th-16th century painting; 15th century ceramics

11539
Museo de Arte Moderno
Casa Montoliú, Calle Caballeros s/n, Tarragona
Fine Arts Museum - 1969
Contemporary art

11540
Museo de Arte y Costumbres Populares
Plaza Pallol, 1, Tarragona
General Museum - 1959
Inscriptions; heraldry; Iberian and Roman ceramics; glass; coins; drawings and history of the town

11541
Museo Diocesano
Claustro Catedral, Tarragona
Fine Arts Museum - 1915
14th-18th century painting; folk paintings; 14th-18th century sculpture; tapestry; ornamentation; goldsmith work; decorative arts; 18th-19th century medals and coins; inscriptions; local archaeology and prehistorical finds from Escornalbou

11542
Museo Paleocristiano
Carretera de Alcolea, Tarragona
Archeology Museum - 1928
Roman-Christian necropolis (3rd century); 4th-6th century sarcophagi; mosaics; burial grounds

11543
Museo Romántico
Palacio Castellarnau, Calle Caballeros, Tarragona
Decorative Arts Museum
Local history; 18th-19th century decorative arts; wall painting

Tarrasa

11544
Iglesias de 'Egara'
Plaza del rector Horns, Tarrasa, Barcelona
Fine Arts Museum - 1931
Art; architecture and painting

11545
Museo Municipal de Arte
Castillo-Cartuja Vallparadis, Calle General Sanjurjo, 24, Tarrasa, Barcelona
Fine Arts Museum - 1959
Art; archaeology; decorative arts; painting; sculpture; architectural elements; numismatics

11546
Museo Provincial Textil
Parc de Vallparadis, Tarrasa, Barcelona
Decorative Arts Museum - 1946
Egyptian and Coptic textiles; 10th-13th century secular and religious clothing ; 7th century Islamic textiles; Mozarabian, Mudejar, Moroccan and Byzantine fabrics; American textiles (pre-Columbian and of the viceroy era); Gothic to Renaissance European, 17th-18th century Spanish textiles; 19th century French, Portuguese and Valencian silks; old Persian, Turkish, Chinese, Indian fabrics; 18th-19th century French and Spanish prints and embroidery; religious and folk costumes - library

Tárrega

11547
Museo Municipal
Calle las Picas, 1, Tárrega, Lérida
General Museum - 1963
Prehistory; archaeology; palaeontology; art; local numismatics and ethnology - archives, library

Telde

11548
Casa-Museo 'León y Castillo'
Biblioteca Pública Municipal, Telde, Las Palmas, Gran Canaria
Historic Site - 1965
Memorabilia of the politician Fernando de León y Castillo - library

Teruel

11549
Museo Arqueológico Provincial
Plaza de Pérez Prado, Teruel
General Museum - 1959
Local archaeology; ceramics (13th
century to modern); furniture and
ordinary utensils

11550
Museo Diocesano de Arte Sacro
Palacio Episcopal, Plaza del Venerable
Francés de Aranda, Teruel
Religious Art Museum
Ecclesiastical art

Toledo

11551
Casa y Museo del 'Greco'
Alamillos del Tránsito y Calle Samuel
Leví, Toledo
Fine Arts Museum - 1910
Furnishings and objects from the time
of 'El Greco' Domenicos
Theotocopoulos (1541-1614); paintings
by the artist; 15th-17th century
painting and sculpture

11552
Casa-Museo 'Benlliure'
Calle Blanquerias, 23, Toledo
Fine Arts Museum - 1968
Paintings by José Benlliure Gil
(1855-1937); memorabilia on the artist

11553
Casa-Museo 'Victorio Macho'
Roca Tarpeya, Calle Santa Ana, 1,
Toledo
Historic Site - 1967
Memorabilia of Victorio Macho
(1887-1966); sculptures and drawings

11554
**Monasterio de San Juan de los
Reyes**
San Juan de los Reyes, Toledo
Fine Arts Museum - 1929
Art; architecture; painting; late Gothic
monastery - library

11555
**Museo de la Fundación 'Duque de
Lerma'**
Hospital Tavera (Vega), Toledo
Fine Arts Museum - 1940
Painting; furniture; ecclesiastical art;
antique pharmacy - library

11556
Museo de 'La Santa Hermandad'
Calle Hermandad, 4, Toledo
History/Public Affairs Museum - 1958
15th century building; history

11557
**Museo de los Concilios y de la
Cultura Visigoda** Museo de Santa
Cruz
Iglesia de San Roman, Calle San
Clemente, Toledo
Archeology Museum - 1969
Visigothic archaeology and art

11558
Museo de Santa Cruz
Calle Cervantes, 1, Toledo
Fine Arts Museum - 1961
Archaeology; painting; sculpture;
tapestry; textiles; goldsmith work;
furniture; documents

11559
Museo del Asedio
Alcázar, Calle General Moscardó, 4,
Toledo
History/Public Affairs Museum - 1936
History, especially this of the state of
siege; Romanesque, Gothic and
Islamic fortification

11560
Museo Parroquial de Santo Tomé
Calle de Santo Tomé, Toledo
Fine Arts Museum
Painting

11561
Museo Sefardí
Sinagoga de Samuel-Ha-Leví, Alamillos
del Tránsito, Toledo
Religious Art Museum - 1964
Hebrew art and history; liturgical
lamps, documents; 14th century
architecture

11562
Museo Taller del Moro Museo de
Santa Cruz
Calle del Taller del Moro, 4, Toledo
Archeology Museum - 1963
Mudejar archaeology and art

11563
Museo-Palacio de Fuensalida Museo
de Santa Cruz
Palacio de Fuensalida, Plaza del
Conde, Toledo
History/Public Affairs Museum - 1969
Art and history pertaining to the 'siglo
de Oro' of Spanish culture

11564
Museo-Tesoro Catedralicio
Catedral, Plaza Generalísimo, Toledo
Religious Art Museum - 1900
Ecclesiastical art; painting; goldsmith
work; liturgical vestments; miniature
books

11565
Santa Maria la Blanca
Calle Reyes Católicos, 2, Toledo
History/Public Affairs Museum - 1931
Art and history

Tomelloso

11566
Museo del Carro y la Labranza
Carretera a Pedro Muñoz, Tomelloso,
Ciudad Real
General Museum - 1967
Ethnography

Tordesillas

11567
Real Monasterio de Santa Clara
Tordesillas, Valladolid
Religious Art Museum - 1963
Architecture; painting; sculpture;
textiles; furniture; hymnals

Tortosa

11568
Museo Catedralicio
Catedral, Plaza de la Olivera, Tortosa,
Tarragona
Religious Art Museum - 1931
Ecclesiastical art; tapestry, goldsmith
work, enamels; manuscripts

11569
Museo-Archivo Municipal
Calle Santo Domingo, Tortosa,
Tarragona
General Museum - 1900
Local art and history; documents;
Roman stone inscriptions and busts

Tossa

11570
Museo Municipal
Vila Vella, Tossa, Gerona
General Museum - 1930
Archaeological objects from
excavations of a Roman Villa;
contemporary painting and sculpture,
especially Catalan

Traiguera

11571
Colección Parroquial
Parroquia de la Asunción, Plaza de la
Iglesia, 10, Traiguera, Castellón
Religious Art Museum - 1964
Ecclesiastical art; 15th-17th century
liturgical goldsmith work

Tudela

11572
Museo Diocesano
Catedral, Plaza de Santa María, Tudela,
Navarra
Religious Art Museum - 1884
Art and history; painting, sculpture,
archaeology, ornaments, books and
documents

Tuy

11573
Museo Catedralicio
Tuy, Pontevedra
Fine Arts Museum - 1976
Ecclesiastical art; archaeology; stone
inscriptions; codices; 17th-18th
century silver and goldsmith work

Ullastret

11574
**Museo Monográfico de las
Excavaciones**
Yacimiento Arqueológico, Ullastret,
Gerona
Archeology Museum - 1961
Archaeological material of Greek-
Iberian excavations (7th-2nd century
B.C.)

Valdepeñas

11575
Molino-Museo 'Gregorio Prieto'
Calle Gregorio Prieto, Valdepeñas,
Ciudad Real
General Museum - 1954
Mill

Valencia

11576
Biblioteca de la Universidad
Universidad, Calle de la Nave, 2,
Valencia
History/Public Affairs Museum - 1837
Incunabula; first book printed in Spain;
manuscripts; miniature codices; gems;
coins; paintings

11577
Colección de la Caja de Ahorros
Caja de Ahorros, General Tovar, 3,
Valencia
Fine Arts Museum
Painting; sculpture

11578
Museo de Bellas Artes
Calle San Pío V, 9, Valencia
Fine Arts Museum - 1768
Painting; sculpture; archaeology;
drawings; graphic arts; decorative
arts; architectural elements

11579
Museo de Prehistoria
Palacio de la Bailía, Plaza de Manises,
2, Valencia
Archeology Museum - 1927
Prehistory; Greek, Roman and Iberian
finds - library

11580
Museo del Patriarca
Colegio Corpus Christi, Calle de la
Nave, 1, Valencia
Fine Arts Museum - 1954
Painting; goldsmith work; tapestry;
furniture

11581
Museo del Tejido Sedero Valenciano
Calle Hospital, 7, Valencia
Decorative Arts Museum
Textile and silk manufacture - library

11582
Museo Diocesano-Catedralicio
Plaza Almoyna, Valencia
Religious Art Museum - 1954
Archaeology; painting; sculpture;
goldsmith work; enamels; liturgical
vestments; codices and rare books

11583
Museo Histórico de la Ciudad
Ayuntamiento, Plaza Claudillo, 1,
Valencia
General Museum - 1928
History of Valencia

11584
**Museo Nacional de Cerámica y de
las Artes Santuarias**
Rinconada García Sanchiz, Valencia
Decorative Arts Museum - 1954
Prehistoric, Greek, Roman, medieval
and modern ceramics from Aragón,
Cataluña, Valencia, Sevilla, Talavera,
Toledo and Italy; silk; 18th century
fans; arms; glass - library

11585
Museo Paleontológico Municipal
Calle del Almudín, Valencia
Natural History Museum - 1906
South American zoology and
anthropology; Rodrigo Botet
collection; paleontology

11586
Museo Taurino
Plaza de Toros, Pasaje Dr. Serra,
Valencia
Anthropology Museum - 1930
History and art of bullfighting

Valladolid

11587
Casa de Cervantes
Calle del Rastro, Valladolid
Historic Site - 1948
Memorial to Don Miguel de Cervantes
Saavedra; Biblioteca Cervantina;
house where the poet lived in 1603 -
library

11588
Casa de Zorrilla
Calle Fray Luis de Granada, 1,
Valladolid
Historic Site - 1918
Memorabilia on the writer José de
Zorrilla (1817-1893); documents and
furniture

11589
Casa-Museo de Colón
Calle Colón, Valladolid
History/Public Affairs Museum - 1965
Memorial to Cristóbal Colón; history
of the American colonization

11590
Museo Arqueológico Provincial
Palacio de Fabio Nelli, Plaza de Fabio
Nelli, Valladolid
General Museum - 1875
Prehistory; Roman, Iberian, Visigothic
finds; Islamic and Mozarabian art;
numismatic collection; 13th-16th
century sculpture and painting; crafts;
folklore; prehistory to Renaissance
Spanish ceramics; religious art;
Etruscan mirror - library

11591
**Museo del Monasterio de San
Joaquin y Santa Ana**
Plaza de Santa Ana, 4, Valladolid,
Valladolid
Fine Arts Museum - 1978
paintings; sculpture; frescoes

11592
Museo Diocesano-Catedralicio
Catedral, Calle Arribas, 1, Valladolid
Religious Art Museum - 1965
Ecclesiastical art; painting, sculpture,
goldsmith work, liturgical vestments;
Mudejar and Gothic architecture

11593
Museo Misional (Filipinas, China y
América del Sur)
Paseo de Filipinos, 7, Valladolid
Anthropology Museum - 1908
National archaeology; Oriental
painting, porcelain, and bronzes;
artifacts and costumes from Peru and
Colombia; numismatics

11594
Museo Nacional de Escultura
Calle Cadenas de San Gregorio, 1,
Valladolid, Valladolid
Fine Arts Museum - 1933
Spanish sculpture (13th-18th century);
painting (15th-18th century)

11595
Sección de Pintura Museo Nacional
de Escultura
Iglesia de la Pasión, Calle de la Pasión
s/n, Valladolid
Fine Arts Museum - 1968
14th-18th century painting

Valldemosa

11596
Real Cartuja
Plaza Cartuja, Valldemosa, Mallorca,
Baleares
Fine Arts Museum - 1924
Antique pharmacy (17th century);
Chopin and George Sand Cabinet;
wood engraving and prints from
Mallorca; memorabilia of the Archduke
Luis Salvador; Pinacoteca Municipal:
painting, sculpture, archaeology;
Palacio del Rey Sancho; local art and
history

Valls

11597
Museo de la Ciudad
Casa Municipal de Cultura, Paseo de
los Capuchinos, 24, Valls, Tarragona
General Museum - 1956
Local history and art; contemporary
painting and sculptures

Vélez Málaga

11598
Museo Municipal
Casa Cervantes, Teniente Coronel
Baturone, 20, Vélez Málaga, Málaga
General Museum - 1967
Art; history; ethnology

Vendrell

11599
Museo Municipal
Calle Calvo Sotelo, 14, Vendrell,
Tarragona
General Museum - 1966
Prehistory; archaeology; modern art;
ethnography

Verdú

11600
Casa Santuario de San Pedro Claver
Calle San Pedro Claver, 30, Verdú,
Lérida
Religious Art Museum - 1888
Memorabilia of the Jesuit priest Pedro
Claver (1580-1654)

11601
Museo-Tesoro Parroquial
Iglesia de Santa María, Plaza Obispo
Comella, 6, Verdú, Lérida
Religious Art Museum - 1942
Ecclesiastical art, especially goldsmith
work - archive

Veruela

11602
Monasterio de Santa María
Veruela, Vera de Moncayo, Zaragoza
General Museum - 1917
Local history and Iberian archaeology

Vich

11603
Museo 'Balmes'
Casa de la Cultura, Plaza de Don
Miguel de Clariana, Vich, Barcelona
Historic Site - 1968
Memorabilia of the philosopher Jaime
Balmes (1810-48)

11604
**Museu Arqueológico Artistic
Episcopal**
Plaza Bispe Oliba, Vich, Barcelona
Fine Arts Museum - 1891
Medieval art; sculpture; 11th-15th
century religious paintings and
objects; Romanesque and Gothic art;
archaeology; numismatics; coins and
medals; decorative and applied arts

Vigo

11605
**Pazo-Museo Municipal 'Quiñones de
León'**
Parque de Quiñones de León, Vigo,
Pontevedra
Fine Arts Museum - 1924
Painting; sculpture; miniatures

Vilafranca del Panades

11606
Museo de Vilafranca
Palacio de los Reyes de Aragón, Plaza
de Jaime I, Vilafranca del Panades,
Barcelona
General Museum - 1958
Coll: archaeology; geology;
winegrowing implements; tombstones;
tomb inscriptions; regional
ornithology; local history; archives:
bibliographical material, 15th-19th
century history of the records of the
Comunidad de Presbíteros de la
Basílica de Santa María, photographs

Vilajuiga

11607
Colección de Geología
Calle San Sebastián, Vilajuiga, Gerona
Natural History Museum - 1902
Mineralogy; applied and folk arts;
arms

Vileña de Bureba

11608
**Museo del Monasterio de Santa
María la Real**
Calle Alta, Vileña de Bureba, Burgos
Religious Art Museum - 1943
Art; 13th-14th century sarcophagi;
medieval sculpture; liturgical objects;
documents

Villagarcía de Campos

11609
Museo de la Colegiata
Avenida Generalísimo, Villagarcía de
Campos, Valladolid
General Museum - 1959
Art and history; painting, sculpture,
goldsmith work, liturgical vestments;
local historical archives

Villanueva de Lorenzana

11610
Museo de Arte Sacro Antiguo
Iglesia de Santa María de Valdeflores,
Plaza del Conde Santo, Villanueva de
Lorenzana, Lugo
Religious Art Museum
Goldsmith work, sculpture, painting;
5th century sarcophagus; 9th century
altar

Villanueva y Geltrú

11611
Museo 'Victor Balaguer'
Plaza Estación, Castillo de La Geltrú,
Calle de la Torre, Villanueva y Geltrú,
Barcelona
History/Public Affairs Museum - 1900
Prehistory; archaeology; 12th-17th
century sculpture; 16th-20th century
painting; decorative and applied arts;
former residence of the poet and
politician Victor Balaguer y Cirera
(1826-1901) - library

11612
Museu Romántic
Can Papiol, Major, 32, Villanueva y
Geltrú, Barcelona
Religious Art Museum - 1961
18th-19th century furnishings and
interiors; decorative arts; coaches;
archives

Villasobroso

11613
Castillo de Sobroso
Villasobroso, Pontevedra
History/Public Affairs Museum - 1923
Art and history

Villena

11614
**Museo Arqueológico Municipal
'José Maria Soler'**
Edificio de Ayuntamiento, Plaza de
Santiago, 2, Villena, Alicante
General Museum - 1957
Prehistory; archaeology; pre-Roman
goldsmith work (Tesoro de Villena,
Tesorillo del Cabezo Redondo);
medieval ceramics

Viso del Marqués

11615
**Archivo-Museo 'Don Alvaro de
Bazan'**
Antiguo Palacio de Don Alvaro de
Bazán, Viso del Marqués, Ciudad Real
Historic Site - 1948
Memorabilia of captain general Don
Alvaro de Bazán; documentation on
the Spanish navy during his era

Vitoria

11616
Casa del Cordón
Calle Cuchillería, 24, Vitoria, Alava
History/Public Affairs Museum
History; 15th century house and 13th
century Gothic tower

11617
Museo de la Batalla de Vitoria
El Portalón, Calle Correría, Vitoria,
Alava
History/Public Affairs Museum - 1963
Memorabilia of the battle for
independence (1813); 16th century
early Renaissance building with Gothic
and Mudejar elements

11618
Museo de Naipes
Calle Heraclio Fournier, 19, POB 94,
Vitoria, Alava
Anthropology Museum
playing cards from Spain, Italy and
Germany (15th-16th century) - library

11619
Museo Provincial de Alava
Paseo Fray Francisco, 8, Vitoria, Alava
General Museum - 1942
Prehistory; archaeology; 15th-20th
century paintings and sculptures;
weapons

11620
Museo Taurino
'El Portalón', Calle Correría, 151,
Vitoria, Alava
Anthropology Museum
Art and history of bullfighting

Xátiva

11621
Museo Municipal
Calle José Carchano s/n, Xátiva,
Valencia
General Museum - 1918
Islamic art; Gothic architecture and
sculpture; Roman inscriptions;
16th-20th century painting

11622
Museo Municipal
Almodi, Calle José Carchano, Xátiva,
Valencia
General Museum - 1917
Islamic art; Gothic architecture and
sculpture; Roman inscriptions;
16th-20th century painting

Yecla

11623
Museo Arqueológico Municipal
Casa Municipal de la Cultura, San
Antonio, 5, Yecla, Murcia
Archeology Museum - 1980
Archaeology; Iberic sculptures from
'Cerro de los Santos'

11624
**Museo de Reproducciones de El
Greco**
San Jose, 8, Yecla, Murcia
Fine Arts Museum - 1980
73 replicas of famous pictures by El
Greco

Yuste

11625
Museo-Palacio del Emperador Carlos V Museo Histórico-Artístico
Monasterio de San Jerónimo de Yuste, Yuste, Cuacos, Cáceres
Historic Site - 1958
Art and history; palace of Carlos V when he retired to the monastery

Zafra

11626
Convento de Santa Clara
Calle Sevilla, Zafra, Badajoz
Religious Art Museum - 1965
Religious art; paintings, sculptures, goldsmith work, 16th-18th century ornaments

Zamora

11627
Museo Catedralicio
Catedral, Plaza de Pío XII, Zamora
Religious Art Museum - 1926
14th-16th century Flemish and French tapestry; sculpture; painting; goldsmith work; documents

11628
Museo de Bellas Artes
Iglesia de la Gota de Sangre, Calle Santa Clara, 17, Zamora
Fine Arts Museum - 1914
Painting; sculpture; prehistory; archaeology; numismatics; drawings; graphic arts; heraldry; reproductions

11629
Museo de la Semana Santa
Plaza Santa María la Nueva, Zamora
Religious Art Museum - 1963
Religious pictures; cloister

Zaragoza

11630
Basilica de Nuestra Señora del Pilar
Plaza del Pilar, 19, Zaragoza
Religious Art Museum - 1904
Painting; sculpture; goldsmith work

11631
Museo Catedralicio de la Seo
Catedral, Plaza de la Seo, Zaragoza
Religious Art Museum - 1940
Tapestry; ecclesiastical painting and goldsmith work

11632
Museo de Bellas Artes
Plaza de José Antonio, 6, Zaragoza
Fine Arts Museum - 1844
French and Spanish prehistory; Hallstatt culture finds; Iberian ceramics and bronzes; Roman and Iberian archaeology; Islamic art; Romanesque, Gothic, Mudejar art; 13th-16th century sculpture; 14th-20th century Spanish painting; Spanish crafts and ceramics, drawings and engravings; collection of Italian drawings; paintings of German and Flemish schools; ethnography collections; folklore - library

11633
Museo Etnológico y de Ciencias Naturales de Aragón
Parque Primo de Rivera, Zaragoza
General Museum - 1956
Folk costumes; zoology; botany; ethnology

Zumárraga

11634
Casa Natal de Legazpi
Avenida Padre Urdaneta, Zumárraga, Guipúzcoa
Historic Site - 1945
Memorabilia of Miguel López de Legazpi, the conquistador of the Philippines, who died in Manila in 1572

Sri Lanka

Colombo

11635
National Museums of Sri Lanka
Marcus Fernando Mawatha, POB 845, Colombo 7
General Museum - 1877
Art and antiquities of Sri Lanca; local pleistocene fossils; local birds and insects; sculpture; ivories and bronzes - library

Ratnapura

11636
Museum of Ethnology and Folk Art
mail c/o Ratnapura Gem Bureau and Laboratory Ratnapura, Sabaragamuwa
Anthropology Museum - 1980
Folk art; paintings; ancient palm leaf manuscripts; ritual objects; Sri Lanka handicrafts, gems, and minerals; gold jewelry

Sudan

El-Obeid

11637
Shiekan Museum
El-Obeid, POB 178, Khartoum
General Museum
Archaeology; ethnography; Shiekan battle weapons

Khartoum

11638
Ethnographic Museum
mail c/o Sudan National Museum, POB 178, Khartoum
Anthropology Museum

11639
Geological Survey Museum
Sharia Abu Sin, POB 410, Khartoum
Natural History Museum
Rocks and minerals; fossils; meteorites

11640
Sudan Archaeological Museum
Nile Av, POB 178, Khartoum
Archeology Museum - 1905
Fossil skulls; statues of ancient kings; seals; golden ornaments and utensils

11641
Sudan National Museum
POB 178, Khartoum
General Museum

11642
Sudan Natural History Museum
POB 321, Khartoum
Natural History Museum - 1920
Birds and wild game of Sudan

Medani

11643
Natural History Museum
Medani
Natural History Museum

Merowe

11644
Merowe Museum
Place Merowe, Merowe
General Museum
Monumental granite statues of Napatan Kings; archaeological and ethnographic collections

Omdurman

11645
Khalifa's House Museum
Omdurman
Historic Site

Port Sudan

11646
Natural History Museum
Port Sudan
Natural History Museum

Wadi Halfa

11647
Halfa Museum
Wadi Halfa
Anthropology Museum
Archaeology; ethnography and folklore

Suriname

Nieuw Amsterdam

11648
Openluchtmuseum
POB 2306, Nieuw Amsterdam
Open Air Museum - 1747
Coll: 18th century fort with barracks, smithy, powder house, wind-powered flour mill

Paramaribo

11649
Stichting Joden Savanna
mail c/o Mrs. I. da Costa, Albergastraat 28, Paramaribo
Historic Site
Coll: early Jewish settlement

11650
Stichting Surinaams Museum
POB 2306, Paramaribo Zorg en Hoop
Natural History Museum - 1968
Coll: archaeology; natural history exhibits - library; workshops

11651
Stichting Surinaams Museum
Fort Zeelandia, POB 2306, Paramaribo
General Museum - 1972
Coll: history of the Fort and the City of Paramaribo; pre- and post-Columbian artifacts; exhibitions about slaves; weapons

Swaziland

Lobamba

11652
Swaziland National Centre
Behind Parliament, POB 100, Lobamba
Anthropology Museum
Displays illustrating material culture of Swaziland

Sweden

Alingsås

11653
Alingsås Museum
Lilla Torget, Box 2, S-441 01 Alingsås
Archeology Museum
Prehistory, textiles

Älvdalen

11654
Hembygdsgården Rots Skans
Holen, Rot, Box 26, S-796 02 Älvdalen
Open Air Museum - 1911
Ethnography; 20 different houses

Åmål

11655
Åmål Konsthall
Kungsgatan 20, Box 18, S-662 00 Åmål
Fine Arts Museum - 1968

11656
Åmåls Museum
Örnäsparken, S-662 00 Åmål
General Museum
Local history

Arboga

11657
Arboga Museum
Nygatan 41, S-732 00 Arboga
General Museum
Local history, archaeology

Arjeplog

11658
Silvermuseet
Torgatan, S-930 90 Arjeplog
Anthropology Museum - 1965
Lapp culture, silver, ethnography

Arvika

11659
Arvika Museum
Sågudden, S-671 00 Arvika
Archeology Museum
Archaeological finds, ethnography; open air museum

Askersund

11660
Stjernsunds Slott
S-696 00 Askersund
Historic Site - 1951
Interiors

Bålsta

11661
Skoklosters Slott
S-198 00 Bålsta
Fine Arts Museum - 1709
17th-18th century interiors, furniture, tapestry, silver, glass, ceramics, ivory, fine handicrafts, bookbinder's art, textiles; Swedish and Dutch paintings, armoury; in 17th century castle - library

Bengtfors

11662
Gammelgården
S-666 00 Bengtfors
General Museum
Local history

Borås

11663
Borås Museum
Ramnaparken, S-502 65 Borås
General Museum
Archaeology, ethnography, local
history; open air museum

11664
Museet Kulturhuset Borås
Box 55015, S-500 05 Borås
Fine Arts Museum

11665
Teko-Museum
Skaraborgsvägen 7, S-502 65 Borås
Science/Tech Museum
Weaving, textile manufacturing

Borgholm

11666
Ölands Forngård
Badhusgatan, S-380 70 Borgholm
General Museum
Archaeology, local history

Borgsjöbyn

11667
Hembygdsgården
Erikslund, S-910 53 Borgsjöbyn
General Museum
Local history

Borlänge

11668
Tunabygdens Gammelgård
Domnarsvsvägen, S-781 52 Borlänge
General Museum
Local history

Broby

11669
Göinge Hembygdsmuseum
Göinge Hembygdspark, S-280 60
Broby
General Museum
Local history

Dalarö

11670
Tullmuseet
Dalarö Tullhus, S-130 54 Dalarö
History/Public Affairs Museum
Commerce, communication, customs

Delsbo

11671
Delsbo Forngård, Hillgrenmuseet
Hembygdsgård i Åsby, S-820 60 Delsbo
General Museum
Local history, ethnography

Drottningholm

11672
Drottningholms Slott
S-170 11 Drottningholm
History/Public Affairs Museum
Baroque rooms, interiors in rococo
style, royal portraits, tapestries,
furniture (18th cent.), sculptures

11673
Kina Slott
S-170 11 Drottningholm
Historic Site
Rococo interiors, 18th century
chinoiserie

Ed

11674
**Edstraktens Fornminnes- och
Hembygdförenings Museum**
Dals-Ed, S-660 01 Ed
General Museum
Archaeology, local history

Edsbyn

11675
Ovanåkers Hembygdsgård
Box 28, S-828 00 Edsbyn
General Museum
Ethnography

Eksjö

11676
**Eksjö Museum med Albert
Engströms Samlingarna**
Österlånggatan 31, S-575 00 Eksjö
Fine Arts Museum - 1969
Works by Albert Engström and
contemporary art exhibitions - library

11677
Fornminnesgården
Arent Byggmästaregatan 24, S-575 00
Eksjö
General Museum - 1923
Local history, domestic products,
machines, motorcycles, bicycles

Eldersberga

11678
Oppenheimers Konsthall
Tönnersjö, S-310 31 Eldersberga
Fine Arts Museum
17th century still-life paintings

Enköping

11679
**Sydvästra Upplands Kultur-
Historiska Museum**
S-199 00 Enköping
General Museum
Local cultural history, ethnography

Eskilstuna

11680
**Djurgårdsmuseet med
Sörmlandsgården**
Djurgårdsvägen-Carlavägen, mail c/o
Eskilstuna Museer,
Kulturförvaltningen, S-631 86
Eskilstuna
General Museum - 1924/1932
Archaeology, ethnology, cultural
history; archaeological objects from
Södermanland, furniture, arts, crafts;
Sörmlandian homestead from the
preindustrial period

11681
Eskilstuna Konstmuseum
Kyrkogatan 9, mail c/o Eskilstuna
Museer, Kulturförvaltningen, S-631 86
Eskilstuna
Fine Arts Museum - 1937
Sculpture, painting, drawing (mainly
Swedish or Scandinavian)

11682
**Faktorimuseet med Vapenteknisk
Avdelning**
Faktoriholmarna, mail c/o Eskilstuna
Museer, Kulturförvaltningen, S-631 86
Eskilstuna
Science/Tech Museum - 1979
Industrial history, weapon technology;
steam engines, still in operation;
reconstruction of a Remington
workshop ca.1869; weapons from the
17th-20th century - lecture room

11683
Rademachersmedjorna
Rademachergatan 50, mail c/o
Eskilstuna Museer,
Kulturförvaltningen, S-631 86
Eskilstuna
Science/Tech Museum - 1906
Preserved forges and dwellings from
the 17th century; items produced at
the Rademacher forges during three
centuries; metal handicrafts

Eslöv

11684
**Eslövs Stads- och
Hembygdsmuseum**
S-241 00 Eslöv
General Museum
Local history

Falkenberg

11685
Falkenbergs Museum
St Lars Kyrkogatan 8, S-311 00
Falkenberg
General Museum - 1937
Archaeology; ethnography; local
history; salmon smoking; barrel-
making handicraft (17th century);
furniture (18th-19th century) - library

Falköping

11686
Falbygdens Museum
St.Olofsgatan 23, S-521 00 Falköping
General Museum
Archaeology, ethnography

Falsterbo

11687
Falsterbo Museum
Sjövägen, S-230 11 Falsterbo
General Museum
Archaeology, ethnography, maritime
collection

Falun

11688
Bergslagets Museum
S-791 00 Falun
Science/Tech Museum
History of mining, Falun copper mine,
minerals, copper coins, documents,
oldest company charter in the world
(1347)

11689
Dalarnas Museum
Box 21, S-791 01 Falun
General Museum
Archaeology, art, ethnography,
peasant paintings, peasant furniture

11690
Stora Kopparbergs Museum
S-792 00 Falun
History/Public Affairs Museum
Art; technology

Farösund

11691
Kulturhistoriska Museet i Bunge
Bunge, S-620 35 Farösund
Open Air Museum - 1907
4 stone paintings (8th cent.); 2
farmsteads (17th-18th cent.) fully
furnished; sawmills, smithies, limekilns,
sheds for half-wild horses and sheep,
fishermen's cottages and boats

Filipstad

11692
**Filipstads Bergslags
Hembygdsmuseum**
Hembygdsgården på Munkeberg, S-682
00 Filipstad
General Museum
Local history

Funäsdalen

11693
Fornminnesparken
S-820 95 Funäsdalen
General Museum
Archaeology

Gammelstad

11694
Friluftsmuseet Norrbottens Museum
S-954 00 Gammelstad
Open Air Museum
Ethnography, peasant furniture, 10
peasant buildings

Gävle

11695
Järnvägsmuseum
Rälsgatan 1, Box 571, S-801 08 Gävle
Science/Tech Museum - 1915
Original locomotives and carriages
dating back to 1854; collection of
models (scale 1:10) - library

11696
Länsmuseet i Gävleborgs Län
S. Strandgatan 20, S-802 22 Gävle
General Museum - 1940
Archaeology, ethnography, art,
handicrafts, furnishings, maritime
collection

11697
Silvanum
Kungsbäcksvägen 32, S-802 28 Gävle
Science/Tech Museum
forestry; forest industry

11698
Soldat-Museet
Kungsbäcksvägen, Box 614, S-801 26
Gävle
History/Public Affairs Museum - 1957
Old Uniforms, weapons, photographs

Göteborg

11699
Göteborgs Arkeologiska Museum
Ostindiska huset, Norra Hamngatan
12, Norra Hamngatan 14, S-411 14
Göteborg
Archeology Museum - 1861
Archaeological finds from the western
part of Sweden and the Gothenburg
area - library

11700
Göteborgs Etnografiska Museum
Norra Hamngatan 12, S-411 14
Göteborg
Anthropology Museum
Ethnography, archaeology, collections
from Central and South America, Lapp
collection, archaeological textiles from
South America - library

11701
Göteborgs Historiska Museum
Norra Hamngatan 12, S-411 14
Göteborg
History/Public Affairs Museum - 1861
History and social life of Göteborg;
history of the East India Company of
Sweden; folk life of Western Sweden;
handicrafts; interior decoration;
dresses; medals and coins - library

11702
Göteborgs Konstmuseum
Götaplatsen, S-412 56 Göteborg
Fine Arts Museum - 1861
European painting since 1500,
sculpture, drawings, graphic art;
French impressionists, Scandinavian
art - library

11703
Göteborgs Naturhistoriska Museum
Slottsskogen, Box 11049, S-400 30
Göteborg
Natural History Museum - 1833
Natural history, marine fauna from the
west coast of Southern Sweden,
Southern Swedish terrestrial
invertebrate fauna, mammals, birds,
osteological collection, vertebrates,
molluscs, insects, invertebrates,
geological and mineralogical
collections - library

11704
Industrimuseet
Götaplatsen, S-412 56 Göteborg
Science/Tech Museum - 1957
Industrial and technological history,
veteran cars and motorcycles, early
textile machinery, John Ericsson
engine, first Volvo motor car - library

11705
Militärmuseet Skansen Kronan
Risåsgatan, S-413 04 Göteborg
History/Public Affairs Museum - 1897
Military history

11706
Röhsska Konstslöjdmuseet
Vasagatan 37-39, S-441 37 Göteborg
Decorative Arts Museum - 1916
Furniture, ceramics, textiles,
bookbinding, glass, metalwork,
decorative arts from Greece, China,
Japan and the Near East - library

11707
Sjöfartsmuseet och Akvariet
Karl Johansgatan 1-3, S-414 59
Göteborg
Open Air Museum
Scandinavian shipping, shipbuilding,
fishing fleets, models; paintings with
maritime themes, portraits, nautical
instruments, maps - library

11708
Teaterhistoriska Museet
Berzeliigatan, Lorensberg-Parken,
S-412 53 Göteborg
Performing Arts Museum - 1954
Theater history

11709
Utlandssvenska Museet
Teatergatan 4, S-411 35 Göteborg
History/Public Affairs Museum - 1923
Documents and prints concerning
Swedes and Swedish activity abroad
- library

Gränna

11710
Andréemuseet
Brahegatan 62, S-560 30 Gränna
History/Public Affairs Museum
Memorial collection of polar explorer
and balloonist Salomon Andrée
(1854-1897); finds from White Island

11711
Vättermuseet
Brahegatan 62, S-560 30 Gränna
General Museum
Local history, ethnography

Halmstad

11712
Hallands Skolmuseum
Galgberget, Box 2073, S-300 02
Halmstad
History/Public Affairs Museum
School history; the museum is part of
'Hallandsgården'

11713
Hallandsgården
Galgberget, S-305 90 Halmstad
Open Air Museum
Ethnography

11714
Stiftelsen Hallands Länsmuseer
Museet i Halmstad
Tollsgatan, Box 2073, S-300 02
Halmstad
General Museum - 1886
Archaeology; maritime collections;
furniture from rural and urban homes;
wooden religious objects; peasant
tapestry paintings; figureheads from
old sailing vessels; ceramic model of
old Halmstad - library

Hammarby

11715
Linneanska Stiftelsen
S-690 43 Hammarby
Historic Site
Memorabilia on scientist and botanist
Carl von Linné (1707-1778) in his
former country house; original
furnishings

Härnösand

11716
Länsmuseet Murberget
Box 2007, S-871 00 Härnösand
Open Air Museum - 1880
Archaeology, cultural history,
ethnography, handicrafts, religious art,
medieval sculpture, textiles; old town
hall, school, farmhouses, fishing sheds

Hässleholm

11717
Västra Göinge Hembygdsmuseum
Hembygdsparken, S-281 00
Hässleholm
General Museum
Archaeology; ethnography

Helsingborg

11718
Helsingborgs Museum
Stadsmuseum, Vikingbergs
Konstmuseum, Fredriksdals
Friluftmuseum
S. Storgatan 31, S-252 23 Helsingborg
General Museum - 1909
Local history, archaeology, applied
arts, crafts, art collection; open air
museum with different types of
buildings - library; botanical garden;
open air theater

Hudiksvall

11719
Hälsinglands Museum
Storgatan 31, S-824 00 Hudiksvall
General Museum - 1859
Archaeology, art, cultural history, 16th -
18th century tapestries, furniture, folk
art, fishing, religious art, pewter, silver,
paintings - library

Huskvarna

11720
Huskvarna Stadsmuseum
Grännavägen, S-561 00 Huskvarna
General Museum
Archaeology, ethnography, history,
technology

11721
Svenska Transportmuseet
Gisebo, S-561 90 Huskvarna
Science/Tech Museum
Technology, motorcars

Jokkmokk

11722
Jokkmokks Museum
Kyrkogatan, S-960 40 Jokkmokk
Anthropology Museum - 1965
Lapp culture

Jönköping

11723
Jönköping Läns Museum
Box 2133, S-550 02 Jönköping
General Museum - 1901
Cultural history of Småland, ironwork,
naive art, modern art, John Bauer
Collection, ceramics

11724
Tändsticksmuseet
Storgatan 18, S-552 55 Jönköping
Science/Tech Museum
History of matchmaking

Jukkasjärvi

11725
Jukkasjärvi Museum
S-980 21 Jukkasjärvi
Anthropology Museum
Lapp culture

Julita

11726
Julita Museum och Skans
S-640 25 Julita
History/Public Affairs Museum
Furnishings, decorative arts; open air
museum with an ethnographic
collection

Kalix

11727
Kalix Museum
S-952 01 Kalix
General Museum - 1967
Local history

Kalmar

11728
Kalmar Konstmuseum
Slottsvägen 1, S-392 33 Kalmar
Fine Arts Museum - 1942
Swedish art (19th-20th century), crafts

11729
Kalmar Läns Museum
Skansen, S-381 00 Kalmar
History/Public Affairs Museum
Archaeology, Bronze and Iron Ages
finds, gold treasure, weapons of the
medieval and later periods,
ethnography, local history, maritime
and military history, applied and fine
arts; in a 16th century castle

11730
Krusenstjernska Gården Kalmar Läns
Museum
Stora Dammgatan 11, S-392 46 Kalmar
Decorative Arts Museum - 1940
18th-19th century interiors, Chinese
porcelain, Swedish household utensils
(18th cent.), furniture, clothes

Karlshamn

11731
Karlshamn Museum
Drottninggatan 85, S-292 00
Karlshamn
General Museum
Local history, ethnography, maritime
history

Karlskrona

11732
Blekinge Museum
Fisktorget 2, Box 111, S-371 01
Karlskrona
General Museum
Local history, archaeology, prehistory,
ethnography, fishing, boatbuilding

11733
Marinmuseum
Amiralitetstätten, S-371 30 Karlskrona
History/Public Affairs Museum - 1752
Swedish marine development,
shipbuilding and machinery (18th-20th
century); figureheads from the 18th
century - library

Karlstad

11734
Värmlands Museum
Box 335, S-651 05 Karlstad
General Museum - 1839
Archaeology, local history, art,
handicrafts, 19th century revival
collection - library

Kiruna

11735
Jukkasjärvi Hembygdsgård
S-981 00 Kiruna
General Museum
Ethnography, Lapp collection

Köping

11736
Köpings Museum
Järnvägsgatan, S-731 00 Köping
General Museum
Local history, crafts, fire safety; old
farmhouse

Kristianstad

11737
Kristianstads Länsmuseum
Nya Boulevarden 9, S-291 32
Kristianstad
General Museum - 1915 (1877)
Archaeology, art, ethnography, local
peasant culture, military history -
library

Kristinehamn

11738
**Kristinehamns Stadsmuseum och
Hembygdsgård**
Trädgårdsgatan 9, S-681 00
Kristinehamn
General Museum - 1925
Local history; archaeology; photo
collection (70,000 pieces) - library

Kungsbacka

11739
Nordhallands Hembygdsförening
S-434 00 Kungsbacka
General Museum
Local history

Kungsör

11740
Kungsör Museum
S-736 00 Kungsör
General Museum
Local history

Laholm

11741
Södra Hallands Hembygdsmuseum
S-312 00 Laholm
General Museum
Archaeology, local history,
ethnography, art

Landskrona

11742
Landskrona Museum
Slottsgatan, S-261 31 Landskrona
General Museum - 1911
Archaeology; technology, aircraft
collection; art, glass paintings;
ethnography; interiors; workshops -
library

Laxå

11743
Laxå Bruks- och Hembygdsmuseum
S-695 00 Laxå
General Museum
Local history

Lidingö

11744
Millesgården
Carl Millesväg 2, S-181 34 Lidingö
Fine Arts Museum
Work and memorabilia of Swedish
sculptor Carl Milles (1875-1955) in his
former residence; medieval sculpture,
European painting, Chinese statuettes,
Greco-Roman antiquities

Linköping

11745
**Östergötlands och Linköpings Stads
Museum**
Vasavägen 16, Box 232, S-581 02
Linköping
General Museum - 1884
Local history, archaeology,
ethnography; international and
Swedish art (13th-20th cent.); textiles -
library

Ljungby

11746
Ljungby Hembygdsmuseum
S-341 00 Ljungby
General Museum
Local history

Lödöse

11747
Lödöse Museum
S-460 10 Lödöse
History/Public Affairs Museum - 1965
Finds from medieval the town Lödöse
(11th-17th cent.); history

Ludvika

11748
**Ludvika Gammelgård och
Gruvmuseum**
Box 342, S-771 03 Ludvika
Open Air Museum - 1920
Ethnography; mining; electricity;
wooden water wheel (1770) - library

Luleå

11749
Norrbottens Museum
Storgatan 2, Box 266, S-951 24 Luleå
General Museum - 1886
Archaeology, ethnography, Lapp
culture, handicrafts, costumes - library

Lund

11750
Antikmuseet
Sölvegatan 2, S-223 62 Lund
Archeology Museum
Greek archaeology, Italian antiquities

11751
Arkiv för Dekorativ Konst
Finngatan 2, S-223 62 Lund
Fine Arts Museum - 1934
Sketches, outlines and models of
monuments in Europe, Mexico, Africa;
Scandinavian, French, Mexican, and
African collections of art - library

11752
Kulturhistoriska Museet
Adelgatan 1 A, Box 1095, S-221 04
Lund
Open Air Museum - 1882
History of Southern Sweden; town
and country houses representing
different classes; applied arts
(ceramics, textiles, silver, glass);
archaeological finds from medieval
Lund; at Östarp, old Scanian farm with
inn (30 km from Lund) - library

11753
**Lunds Universitets Historiska
Museum**
Kraftstorg 1, S-223 50 Lund
History/Public Affairs Museum
Prehistory, medieval archaeology,
religious art, liturgical objects, wooden
sculpture, coins and medals, bronze,
early medieval crafts

11754
Lunds Universitets Konstmuseum
Universitetshuset, Fack, S-221 04 Lund
Fine Arts Museum

11755
Zoologiska Museet
Helgonavägen 3, S-223 62 Lund
Natural History Museum - 1735
Zoology, entomology; 19th century
collections of insects; fossils;
Scandinavian insects, vertebrates,
invertebrates; scientific expedition
collections from South Africa, Azores,
Ceylon, Chile, Canada, Iceland,
Afghanistan

Malmö

11756
Malmö Museum
Malmöhusvägen, S-211 20 Malmö
General Museum - 1841
Art, applied art, handicrafts, textiles,
history, arms, uniforms, natural history,
minerals, anthropology, anatomy,
technology, maritime items - library

11757
Malmö Sjöfartsmuseum
Malmöhusvägen 7, S-211 20 Malmö
History/Public Affairs Museum - 1890
Ship history, South Sweden shipping,
lighting and pilotage service,
shipbuilding, navigation, fishing,
yachting and boat sport; paintings,
drawings - library

11758
Tekniska Museet
Malmöhusvägen 7, S-211 20 Malmö
Science/Tech Museum - 1960
Energy, air transport, rail transport,
South Sweden industry, tannery,
telecommunications, physics,
chemistry, astronomy - library

11759
Vagnmuseet
Drottningtorget, S-211 25 Malmö
Science/Tech Museum - 1963
Transportation on land, carriages, cars,
motorcycles, cycles

Malung

11760
Malungs Gammelgård
S-782 00 Malung
General Museum
Local history

Mariefred

11761
Mariefreds Bygdens Museum
Callanderska Gården, Klostergatan 5,
S-150 30 Mariefred
General Museum
Local history

11762
Svenska Statens Porträttsamling
Gripsholm Slott, S-150 30 Mariefred
Fine Arts Museum
Royal portraits; in 16th century castle

Mariestad

11763
**Vadsbo Hembygds- och
Fornminnesmuseum**
S-542 00 Mariestad
General Museum
Local history, archaeology,
ethnography

Markaryd

11764
Markarydsortens Hembygdsmuseum
Kungsgatan 48, S-285 00 Markaryd
General Museum
Local history

Mölndal

11765
Gunnebo
S-431 36 Mölndal
Historic Site
Interior decoration, furniture, wall
panels, tiled stoves, drawings and
plans; in an 18th century manor house

Mönsterås

11766
Stranda Härads Hembygdsförening
S-383 00 Mönsterås
General Museum
Local history

Mora

11767
Zornsamlingarna
S-792 00 Mora
Fine Arts Museum
Paintings, sculptures and prints by
Anders Zorn (1860-1920) and others,
peasant paintings, applied arts, crafts,
silver, textiles

Motala

11768
Motala Museum
Kungsgatan 4, S-591 00 Motala
General Museum
Local history, natural history

Nårunga

11769
**Nårungabygdens Missionshistoriska
Museum**
Ljurhalla, S-440 23 Nårunga
History/Public Affairs Museum
Missionary history, religious objects

Nässjö

11770
Hembygdaparken
S-571 00 Nässjö
General Museum
Local history

11771
Klockargarden
Box 23, S-571 00 Nässjö
History/Public Affairs Museum
Bells

Norberg

11772
Norbergs Hembygdsmuseum
S-778 00 Norberg
Open Air Museum
Ethnography

Norrköping

11773
Färgargården Department of
Norrköpings Stadsmuseum
S:t Persgatan 3, S-602 33 Norrköping
Science/Tech Museum - 1932
Dye-house with dying instruments and
equipment - library

11774
Löfstad Slott Östergötlands Museum
Löfstad, S-605 90 Norrköping
Historic Site - 1940
Manor from 17th century preserved
as historical monument - library

11775
Norrköpings Konstmuseum
Kristinaplatsen, S-602 34 Norrköping
Fine Arts Museum - 1913
17th - 20th century Swedish art;
international graphic art - library

11776
Norrköpings Stadsmuseum
Västgötegatan 21, S-602 21
Norrköping
Science/Tech Museum - 1946
Textile industry; crafts; local
archaeology and history - library

Nybro

11777
Nybro Hembygdsgård
S-382 00 Nybro
General Museum
Local history

Nyköping

11778
Södermanlands Museum
Nyköpinghus, Box 11, S-611 22
Nyköping
General Museum
Scandinavian art (17th-19th cent.),
painting, cultural history, interiors,
furniture, costumes, archaeology,
military history; in 16th cent. tower

Ödeshög

11779
Ellen Keys Strand
S-599 00 Ödeshög
Historic Site - 1910
Swedish paintings, jugendstil furniture;
memorabilia on Swedish teacher and
writer Ellen Key (1849-1926) in her
former home - library

Örebro

11780
Örebro Läns Museum
Engelbrektsgatan 3, S-702 12 Örebro
General Museum - 1856
Art, history, archaeology, religious art,
ethnography, crafts and industries,
coins, medals; Collection of art
handicrafts from China

Örnsköldsvik

11781
Örnsköldsviks Museum
Läroverksgatan 1, S-891 00
Örnsköldsvik
General Museum
Local art, history and ethnography;
peasant handicraft and art
archaeology - library

Oskarshamn

11782
Dödarhultar Museet
Hantverksgatan 18-20, S-572 00
Oskarshamn
General Museum
Crafts; decorative arts

11783
Frederiksberg
Frederiksberg gård, S-572 00
Oskarshamn
General Museum
Local history

11784
Sjöfartmuseum
Varvsgatan 5, S-572 00 Oskarshamn
History/Public Affairs Museum
Maritime Collection

Östersund

11785
Jämtlands Läns Museum
Museiplan, Box 650, S-831 27
Östersund
General Museum - 1912
Archaeology, ethnography, textiles,
woodcarvings, art, decorative arts

11786
Jamtli Jämtlands läns museum
Box 631, S-831 27 Östersund
Open Air Museum - 1912
Ethnography; 15th century pilgrim's
hut, 18th century farm

11787
**Stadsmuseet och Olof
Ahlbergshallen**
Rådhusgatan 42, S-831 34 Östersund
General Museum
Local history; art collection

Sala

11788
Gruvmuseet
Sala Silvergruva, S-733 00 Sala
Science/Tech Museum
Silver mining

11789
**Salabygdens Fornminnesförinings
Museum**
Väsby Kungsgård, S-733 00 Sala
General Museum
Local history

Säter

11790
Säters Hembygdsmuseum
Åsgårdana, S-783 00 Säter
General Museum
Ethnography, history; open air
museum

Sigtuna

11791
Sigtuna Museer
Storagatan 55, S-193 00 Sigtuna
General Museum - 1916
Local history, crafts, medieval
archaeology

Simrishamn

11792
Österlens Museum
Storgatan 24, Box 58, S-272 01
Simrishamn
General Museum
Archaeology, ethnography, peasant
furniture, history of fishing, agriculture,
maritime commerce; in an old granary

Skara

11793
Skaraborgs Länsmuseum
Stadsträdgården, Box 195, S-532 00
Skara
General Museum - 1919 (1750)
Archaeology, local history, art,
medieval sculpture in wood and stone,
textiles, metalwork; open air museum

Skellefteå

11794
Gamla Bilsalongen
S-931 00 Skellefteå
Science/Tech Museum
Motorcars, cameras, music boxes,
typewriters

11795
Skellefteå Museum
Nordanå, S-931 33 Skellefteå
General Museum
Archaeology, religious art, cultural
history, ethnography, fishing, hunting,
handicrafts, costumes, textiles; also
open-air-museum

Skokloster

11796
Motormuseum
S-190 64 Skokloster
Science/Tech Museum
Motorcars

Skövde

11797
Skövde Museum
Hertig Johans Torg, Box 86, S-541 33
Skövde
General Museum - 1946
Archaeology, ethnography, local
history

Skurup

11798
Svaneholms Slott
S-274 00 Skurup
General Museum - 1936
Livingrooms (18th-19th century);
regional folklore; archaeology; textiles

Söderhamn

11799
Söderhamns Museum
Oxtorsgatan, S-826 00 Söderhamn
General Museum
Technology

Södertälje

11800
Torekällbergets Museum
Torekällbergsparken, S-151 46
Södertälje
General Museum
Local history

Sollefteå

11801
Sollefteåortens Hembygdsgård
Hembygdsgården, Ådelsbyn, S-818 00
Sollefteå
General Museum
Local history

Solna

11802
Gustav III.s Paviljong
Haga, S-171 64 Solna
Historic Site
Interior decoration and furniture in an
18th century building

Sölvesborg

11803
Gammelgården
Västra Storgatan, S-294 00
Sölvesborg
General Museum
Archaeology, local history

Stockholm

11804
Arkitekturmuseet
Skeppsholmen, S-111 49 Stockholm
Fine Arts Museum - 1962
Photos and drawings of 19th and 20th
century architecture; archives

11805
Biologiska Museet Stiftelsen
Skansen
Djurgården, S-100 90 Stockholm
Natural History Museum
Biology

11806
Bryggerimuseet
Äögatan 113-119, S-116 24 Stockholm
Science/Tech Museum
Brewery equipment

11807
Carl Eldhs Studio Museum
Lögebodavägen 10, S-113 47
Stockholm
Fine Arts Museum - 1963
Sculpture, paintings, antiques,
furniture; paintings and artifacts from
Carl Eldhs' years in Paris (1897-1904)

11808
Dansmuseet
Filmhuset, Borgvägen 8, S-115 26
Stockholm
Performing Arts Museum
History of dance and ballet; theater
and dancing in Asia, collections from
India, Ceylon, Indonesia, Siam, China
and Japan; costumes, masks, musical
instruments, shadow plays, puppet
theater; films, photos, recordings;
decor and costume design

11809
Drottningholms Teatermuseum
Borgvägen 1-5, Box 27050, S-102 51
Stockholm
Performing Arts Museum - 1922
History of stage scenery; stage
machinery; costumes; drawings,
engravings, paintings; housed in the
18th century Royal Court Theater;
records of the Royal Theater of
Stockholm - library

11810
Etnografiska Museet
Djurgårdsbrunnsvägen 34, S-115 27
Stockholm
Anthropology Museum - 1880
145,000 objects from all parts of the
world except Europe; collections from
Cook's voyages; old ethnographical
objects from North America, Central
Asia, Japan, lower Congo; mask
collection from Sri Lanka; the Akamba
collection from Kenya; archaeological
collections from Mexico and Costa
Rica - library

11811
**Geologiska Undersökningens
Museum**
Frescati, S-10405 Stockholm, *mail c/o*
Geological Survey of
Sweden,Museum Dept., Box 670,
S-751 28 Uppsala
Natural History Museum - 1858
Swedish rocks, minerals and fossils;
collections of ores and ore minerals
from Sweden - library

11812
Gustav III.s Antikmuseum
Kungl. Slottet, S-111 30 Stockholm
Fine Arts Museum - 1792
Antiquities, mostly classical sculpture

11813
Gymnastik- och Idrottsmuseet
Lidingövägen 1, S-114 33 Stockholm
History/Public Affairs Museum
Sports

11814
Hallwylska Museet
Hamngatan 4, S-111 47 Stockholm
Historic Site
Patrician residence with collections of
furniture, Dutch paintings, silver,
European and Oriental ceramics, arms

11815
Järnvägsmuseum
Torsgatan 19, S-113 21 Stockholm
Science/Tech Museum
Railway history, railway carriages and
wagons, ferry boats, steamships;
models of engines and locomotives

11816
Kungl. Akademien för de Fria Konsterna
Fredsgatan 12, Box 16317, S-103 26 Stockholm
Fine Arts Museum
Collection of Swedish paintings (17th-20th century); collection of Swedish and international drawings and graphics (17th-20th century) - library

11817
Kungl. Armémuseum
Riddargatan 13, Box 14095, S-104 41 Stockholm
History/Public Affairs Museum - 1879
15th-20th century military history, weapons, vehicles, engineering and signalling material, standards, uniforms, surgery and veterinary material, musical instruments, badges for merit, reproductions and models of forts, collections of trophies - library

11818
Kungl. Myntkabinettet (National Museum of Monetary History)
Narvavägen 13-17, Storgatan 41, Box 5405, S-114 84 Stockholm
History/Public Affairs Museum - 1975
Almost complete Swedish coin collection; Swedish medals, bonds, shares, tokens; medals and coins from the entire world and from all periods - library

11819
Kungliga Slottet (The Royal Palace)
S-111 30 Stockholm
Historic Site
Baroque interiors, rococo decorations, art collection, tapestries, furniture, Meissen and Sèvres porcelain, Swedish silver

11820
Liljevalchs Konsthall
Djurgårdsvägen 60, S-115 21 Stockholm
Fine Arts Museum - 1916

11821
Livrustkammaren
Kungl. Slottet, Slottsbacken 3, S-111 30 Stockholm
History/Public Affairs Museum - 1628
Royal collection of arms and armours; costumes; coaches - library

11822
Medelhavsmuseet
Narvavägen 17 and Järntorget 84, Storgatan 41, Box 5405, S-114 84 Stockholm
Archeology Museum - 1954
Greek, Roman, and Egyptian archaeology; antiquities from mediterranean area - library

11823
Medicinhistoriska Museet
Åsögatan 146, S-116 32 Stockholm
History/Public Affairs Museum - 1955
Instruments, objects, books, documents; Dutch paintings with medical-historical motives; prototype of sedimentation reaction apparatus - library

11824
Moderna Museet
Skeppsholmen, Box 16382, S-103 27 Stockholm
Fine Arts Museum - 1958
Modern art including Picasso, Matisse, Léger, Gris, Kandinsky; paintings, sculptures and photographs (about 200,000 prints and negatives from 1845 to the present day), American art from the 50s and 60s, 'The New York Collection' - library; workshop for children and adults; room for creative activity

11825
Museum Memoria Musica
Riddargatan 35-37, S-114 57 Stockholm
Music Museum

11826
Musikmuseet
Sibyllegatan 2, S-114 51 Stockholm
Music Museum - 1899
Musical instruments, including those of India, Africa and the Far East; Swedish folk music; folk music instruments; art

11827
Nationalmuseum
S. Blasieholmshamnen, Box 16176, S-103 24 Stockholm
Fine Arts Museum - 1792
17th century Dutch and Flemish paintings; 18th - 19th century French paintings; 17th - 19th century Swedish art - paintings, drawings, prints, decorative arts - library

11828
Naturhistoriska Riksmuseet
Roslagsvägen 120, Box 50007, S-104 05 Stockholm
Natural History Museum - 1819
Natural history, entomology, botany, paleobotany, mineralogy, fossils, vertebrates, reptiles, mammals

11829
Nordiska Museet
Djurgården, S-115 21 Stockholm
Anthropology Museum - 1873
Cultural history, ethnography, folk art, Lapp collection, crafts, trades, guilds, industrial arts, glass, textiles, folk costumes, fashion dresses 1600-1940, furniture, household objects, archives - library

11830
Östasiatiska Museet
Skeppsholmen, Box 16381, S-103 27 Stockholm
Archeology Museum - 1959
Far Eastern antiquities, Chinese Stone Age ceramics, jade objects

11831
Polis- och Kriminalmuseet
Bergsgatan 48, S-112 31 Stockholm
History/Public Affairs Museum
Police, criminology

11832
Postmuseum
Lilla Nygatan 6, Gamla Stan, Box 2002, S-103 11 Stockholm
History/Public Affairs Museum - 1906
Permanent exhibition of Swedish and foreign stamps and postal history subjects; 1847 Mauritius stamps - library

11833
Prins Eugens Waldemarsudde
Djurgården, S-115 21 Stockholm
Fine Arts Museum - 1948
Art, mainly of Swedish origin (19th cent.)

11834
Skattkammaren (The Treasury)
Kungl. Slottet, S-111 30 Stockholm
Historic Site
Swedish Crown Jewels; 12 royal and princely crowns and other treasures

11835
Slottsmuseum
Kungl. Slottet, S-111 30 Stockholm
History/Public Affairs Museum - 1959
Archaeology, history, art

11836
Sparvägsmuseet
Tulegatan 8, S-113 53 Stockholm
Science/Tech Museum
Tramway vehicles, fare-collecting methods, signalling, uniforms, equipment

11837
Statens Historiska Museum
(Museum of National Antiquities)
Narvavägen 17, Storgatan 41, Box 5405, S-114 84 Stockholm
History/Public Affairs Museum - 1630
Prehistory, late iron age, Vikings, medieval archaeology and art; gold treasures of the Migration period; the Vendel Finds; Viking age hoards; medieval wooden sculptures; church textiles - library

11838
Statens Sjöhistoriska Museum
Djurgårdsvägen 24, S-115 27 Stockholm
History/Public Affairs Museum - 1938
Swedish shipbuilding, 17th-18th century models, uniforms, weapons, guns, paintings, drawings, original stern of the schooner 'Amphion' and her two sloops 'Galten' and 'Delfinen' (owned by King Gustav III) - library

11839
Stiftelsen Skansen
Djurgården, S-115 21 Stockholm
Open Air Museum - 1891
125 fully furnished and equipped buildings, farmsteads and craftmen's workshops; folklore; natural history, zoology

11840
Stockholms Stadsmuseum
Peder Myndes backe 6, S-116 46 Stockholm
General Museum - 1932
History of the Stockholm area, archaeological finds, town models, paintings, engravings, photographs, remains of a 15th cent. armed vessel, silver treasure, coins, memorabilia on poet and musician Carl Michael Bellmann (1740-1795)

11841
Strindbergsmuseet
Drottningatan 85, S-111 60 Stockholm
Historic Site - 1960
Memorial to dramatist August Strindberg (1849-1912), his study with all details and the completely furnished flat of his last residence - library; theater

11842
Svenska Pressmuseet
Teknologatan 11, S-100 90 Stockholm
History/Public Affairs Museum
History of the Swedish press

11843
Tekniska Museet
Museivägen 7, S-115 27 Stockholm
Science/Tech Museum - 1924
Steam engines, water turbines, internal combustion engines, automobiles, motorcycles, aeroplanes; mining, metallurgy, electricity, telecommunication, nuclear physics, atomic energy

11844
Telemuseum
Karlaplan 2, S-114 60 Stockholm
Science/Tech Museum
Telecommunication techniques, telegraph constructions, telephon sets, radio equipment, drawings, photographs

11845
Thielska Galleriet
Djurgården, S-115 25 Stockholm
Fine Arts Museum - 1905
19th and 20th century Scandinavian and French art

11846
Tobaksmuseet
Skansen, S-115 21 Stockholm
Anthropology Museum - 1938
History of tobacco in Sweden; packages, pipes, snuffboxes, manufacture of cigarettes

11847
Vin- och Sprithistoriska Museet
St Eriksgatan 121, Box 6061, S-102 31 Stockholm
Anthropology Museum - 1967
History of the wine and liquor industry; Swedish legislation concerning alcoholic beverages since the Middle Ages; wine and liquor labels, old price lists, archives of distilleries and wine companies, photos

11848
Wasavarvet Statens Sjöhistoriska Museum
Djurgårdsbrunnsvägen 24, S-115 27 Stockholm
History/Public Affairs Museum - 1962
Warship 'Wasa' which capsized in 1628 and was raised in 1961

Storvik

11849
Ovensjö Sockens - Gammelgård
Backvägen, Box 18, S-812 00 Storvik
General Museum
Local history, national costumes

Strängenäs

11850
Roggenmuseet
Roggenborgen, S-152 00 Strängenäs
General Museum
Local history, religious art

Sundborn

11851
Carl Larsson-Garden
S-790 15 Sundborn
Historic Site
Home of the artist Carl Larsson and his family; original furnishings, paintings, watercolours and memorabilia of Carl Larsson (1853-1919), painter of family life and the Swedish countryside

Sundsvall

11852
Medelpads Fornhem
S-852 50 Sundsvall
General Museum
Ethnography, history; open air
museum

11853
Sundsvalls Hantverksmuseum
S-852 50 Sundsvall
Decorative Arts Museum

Sundvall

11854
Sundvalls Museum
Storgatan 29, S-852 30 Sundvall
General Museum
Archaeology, 6th century grave finds,
technology, forest industry,
handicrafts, art, photography

Sunne

11855
Mårbacka Manor
Mårbacka, S-686 00 Sunne
Historic Site
Memorabilia on Selma Lagerlöf
(1858-1940), in her former home; local
history

11856
Sunne Hembygdsförening
S-686 00 Sunne
General Museum
Local history

Surahammar

11857
Surahammars Bruksmuseum
S-735 00 Surahammar
Decorative Arts Museum
Applied arts

Trelleborg

11858
**Trelleborgs Museum och Axel Ebbes
Konsthall**
Östergatan 52, S-231 00 Trelleborg
General Museum - 1908
History, archaeology, ethnography; art
gallery

Trollhättan

11859
Forngården
S-461 00 Trollhättan
Archeology Museum

Tyresö

11860
Tyresö Slott
S-135 00 Tyresö
Historic Site
18th and 19th century interiors; in a
17th century castle

Uddevalla

11861
Bohusläns Museum
Kungsgatan 30-32, Box 34, S-453 00
Uddevalla
General Museum - 1862
Archaeology, local history, 19th
century Swedish art, fishing gear -
library

Ugglarp-Slöinge

11862
Svendinos Bilmuseum
S-310 50 Ugglarp-Slöinge
Science/Tech Museum
Vehicles

Umeå

11863
**Västerbottens Museum med
Svenska Skidmuseet**
Gammlia, S-902 34 Umeå
General Museum - 1943
Local history, archaeology,
ethnography, open air museum,
Swedish Skimuseum - library

Uppsala

11864
Antiksamlingen Museet för Klassiska
Fornsaker
Gustavianum, S-752 20 Uppsala
Archeology Museum - 1912
Classical antiquities, pottery

11865
Disagården
S-750 00 Uppsala
Open Air Museum
Ethnography

11866
Geografiska Institutionen
Kabovägen 2-4, S-752 36 Uppsala
Anthropology Museum
Geography, ethnography

11867
Linnemuseet
Svartbäcksgatan 27, S-753 32 Uppsala
History/Public Affairs Museum - 1937

11868
Museum för Nordiska Fornsaker
Gustavianum, S-752 33 Uppsala
Archeology Museum
National antiquities, grave artifacts
from Valsgärde

11869
Upplandsmuseet
S:t Erikstorg 10, S:t Eriksgränd 6, Box
2076, S-750 02 Uppsala
General Museum - 1959
Local history; ethnography; peasant
art; handicrafts - library

11870
Uppsala Universitets Konstsamling
Domkyrkoplan 7, S-752 20 Uppsala
Fine Arts Museum
Art, religious art

11871
**Uppsala Universitets Zoologiska
Museum**
Villavägen 9, Box 561, S-751 22
Uppsala
Natural History Museum - 1916
(Linnaean Museum Academicum:
1743)
2,500 zoological specimens,
invertebrates, amphibians, reptiles,
mammals; Linnaean Collection -
library

11872
**Victoriamuseet för Egyptiska
Fornsaker**
Gustavianum, S-752 00 Uppsala
Archeology Museum
Egyptian antiquities

Väddö

11873
Roslagens Sjöfartsmuseum
Kaplansbacken, Box 56, S-760 40
Väddö
History/Public Affairs Museum - 1938
Maritime collection

Vänersborg

11874
Vänersborgs Museum
Östra Plantaget, Box 206, S-462 01
Vänersborg
General Museum - 1891
Local history, archaeology,
ethnography, art, natural history;
collection of birds from Botswana and
Namibia; Egyptian antiquities;
prehistorical finds from Vänersborg
and the vicinity

Varberg

11875
Hallands Länsmuseer Museet i
Varberg
Fästningen, S-432 000 Varberg
General Museum - 1916
Ethnography; local history; crafts; the
Bocksten find (complete medieval
dress about 1360); in a 17th century
castle - library; video set

Västerås

11876
Västerås Konstmuseum
S-721 87 Västerås
Fine Arts Museum - 1972
Paintings, sculpture, graphics,
drawings

11877
Västmanlands Läns Museum
Slottet, S-722 11 Västerås
General Museum
Archaeology, regional history,
ethnography, crafts, religious art

Västervik

11878
**Tjustbygdens Kulturhistoriska
Museum**
Kulbacken, S-593 00 Västervik
General Museum
Local history, maritime collection

Vaxholm

11879
Vaxholms Fästnings Museum
Vaxholms kastell, S-185 00 Vaxholm
History/Public Affairs Museum - 1947
Military history, models of fortresses,
pictures - library

Växjö

11880
Smålands Museum
Södra Järnvägsgatan 2, Box 66, S-351
03 Växjö
General Museum - 1867
History of glass making, religious art,
weapons, ethnology, archaeology,
coins, local history, forest industry -
library

Ventlinge

11881
Ottenby Fågelmuseum
Ödlands Södra Udde, Box 37, S-380
66 Ventlinge
Natural History Museum
Ornithology, migration research

Vetlanda

11882
**Forngården-Hembygds- och
Fornminnesföreningen Njudung**
Forngården, S-574 00 Vetlanda
General Museum
Ethnography, local history; open air
museum

Vimmerby

11883
**Sevedebygdens Fornminnes- och
Hembygdsmuseum**
Gästgivarehagen, S-598 00 Vimmerby
General Museum
Local history

Visby

11884
Gotlands Fornsal
Strandgatan 12-14, Mellangatan 19,
Box 83, S-621 01 Visby
History/Public Affairs Museum - 1875
Archaeology, 5th-11th century stone
paintings, Viking treasures, religious
art, medieval sculpture, stained glass,
weapons and armour, coins, regional
history and ethnography, collections
illustrating peasant and urban life -
library

Ystad

11885
Charlotte Berlins Museum Ystads
Konstmuseum
S-271 00 Ystad
History/Public Affairs Museum
Furnished 19th century burgher
house; decorative arts

11886
Dragonmuseet Ystads Konstmuseum
St. Knuts Torg, S-271 00 Ystad
History/Public Affairs Museum
Military history; Hedberg Arms
Collection

11887
Klostermuseet
Dammgatan 23, S-271 00 Ystad
General Museum
Archaeology, ethnography, local
history

11888
Ystads Konstmuseum
St Knuts torg, S-271 00 Ystad
Fine Arts Museum - 1936
Swedish and Danish art; special
collections of art from Skåne

Switzerland

Aarau

11889
Aargauer Kunsthaus
Rathausplatz, CH-5000 Aarau
Fine Arts Museum - 1860
Swiss paintings, graphics and
sculptures (18th-20th century)
including works by C. Wolf, A. Stäbli,
C. Amiet, R. Auberjonois, G.
Giacometti, F. Hodler, O. Meyer-
Amden, L. Soutter, Varlin; regional folk
art; French masters; Theodor Bally
donation - library

11890
**Museum für Natur- und
Heimatkunde**
Bahnhofsplatz, CH-5000 Aarau
General Museum - 1922
Zoology; geology; mineralogy;
agricultural industries; prehistory;
hunting; environmental protection;
herbarium pertaining to local botany;
butterfly collection; geology of the
Swiss Jura mountains

11891
Stadtmuseum Alt-Aarau
Schloßplatz 12, CH-5000 Aarau
General Museum - 1919
Local history; tools and implements; tin
figures; weapons; castle (11th century)

Aarburg

11892
Heimatmuseum Aarburg
CH-4663 Aarburg
General Museum - 1930
Local history; weapons; uniforms;
paintings; domestic utensils; tools;
furniture; piano

Adligenswil

11893
Feuerwehrmuseum
CH-6043 Adligenswil
History/Public Affairs Museum - 1976
History of firefighting, implements and
tools

Aesch

11894
Heimatmuseum
CH-4147 Aesch
General Museum - 1975
Local history; farm implements;
memorabilia on the poet Traugott
Meyer

Agno

11895.
Museo Plebano
Rivolgersi alla parrocchia, CH-6982
Agno
General Museum - 1955
Local history

Aigle

11896
Musée suisse du sel
Château, CH-1860 Aigle
History/Public Affairs Museum - 1973
History of the local salt industry;
implements and tools for salt mining;
cultural artifacts connected with salt -
library

11897
Musée vaudois de la vigne et du vin
Château, CH-1860 Aigle
Agriculture Museum - 1971
History of wine cultivation and trade;
tools and implements used in
viticulture; bottles and glasses

Albisrieden

11898
Ortsmuseum
Triemlistr. 2, CH-8047 Albisrieden,
Zürich
General Museum - 1950
Local history; farm implements and
tools; ecclesiastical objects; old house
(16th century)

Allschwil

11899
Heimatmuseum Allschwil
Baslerstr. 48, CH-4123 Allschwil
General Museum - 1966
Furniture and furnishings (17th-19th
century); farm implements and tools;
palaeolithic to early medieval artifacts;
ceramics; Tschan collection of
weapons

Altdorf

11900
Historisches Museum
Gotthardstr., CH-6460 Altdorf
General Museum - 1892
Cultural history of the canton Uri;
ecclesiastical art; archaeological finds;
weapons and banners; textiles and
costumes; furnishings

Altishofen

11901
Schreinermuseum
Schloß, CH-6246 Altishofen
Decorative Arts Museum - 1978
Joiner's tools; 16th century castle

Altstätten

11902
Historisches Museum
Rabengasse, CH-9450 Altstätten
General Museum - 1895
Local history; ecclesiastical and
profane art; furniture; coats of arms;
documents; weapons; utensils

Altstetten

11903
Ortsmuseum Altstetten
Altstetten, Dachslernstr. 20, CH-8048
Zürich
General Museum - 1954
Local history; furnishings; crafts and
guilds; agriculture; archeological finds;
15th century house

Amriswil

11904
Kutschensammlung
St. Gallerstr. 12, CH-8580 Amriswil
History/Public Affairs Museum - 1974
18th-19th century carriages, coaches
and sledges; harness

Appenzell

11905
Heimatmuseum
Rathaus, CH-9050 Appenzell
General Museum - 1879
Prehistorical finds; antiquities;
furnishings; folk art; ecclesiastical art;
16th century house

11906
Retonios Musik- und Zaubermuseum
Galerie Bleiche, CH-9050 Appenzell
Performing Arts Museum - 1977
Mechanical musical instruments;
magic items

11907
Retonios Raritätenkabinett
Retonio-Center, CH-9050 Appenzell
Performing Arts Museum - 1978
Gambling automatons; juke-boxes

Arbon

11908
Historisches Museum
Schloß, CH-9320 Arbon
History/Public Affairs Museum - 1912
Local pre- and protohistory;
furnishings; crafts and guilds; pictures
and documents on contemporary
history; history of local trades and
industries; textiles; automobiles; arms
and armor; weapons; 16th century
castle

Arenenberg

11909
Napoleon-Museum
Schloß, CH-8268 Arenenberg
History/Public Affairs Museum - 1905
Napoleonic interiors; memorabilia of
the Bonaparte family

Arosa

11910
Heimatmuseum Schanfigg
CH-7050 Arosa
General Museum - 1949
Furnishings; agriculture and crafts;
weaving; ornithology; wood and stone
collection; mining; weapons; hunting;
sports

Ascona

11911
Museo Marianne Werefkin
Casa Don Pietro Pancaldi, Via Borgo,
CH-6621 Ascona
Historic Site - 1967
Memorabilia of Marianne Werefkin
(1860-1938); works by the painter

Attiswil

11912
Heimatmuseum
Dorfstr. 5, CH-4536 Attiswil
General Museum - 1961
Local history; farm implements; craft
tools; antiquities

Au

11913
Weinbaumuseum am Zürichsee
Vordere Au, CH-8804 Au
Agriculture Museum - 1968
Presentation of wine cultivation and
the wine grower's tasks; tools and
implements; wine storage and
subsequent treatment

Aubonne

11914
Musée du Bois
CH-1170 Aubonne
Agriculture Museum - 1977
Wood processing; implements and
tools; domestic utensils and farm
implements

Augst

11915
Römermuseum Augst
Giebenacherstr. 17, CH-4302 Augst
Archeology Museum - 1955/57
Finds and architectural remains from
the Roman town Augusta Raurica and
from the late Roman fortification;
reconstructed Roman house and
interiors - archives; restoration
laboratory

Avenches

11916
Musée romain
CH-1580 Avenches
Archeology Museum - 1824
Finds from the Roman site Aventicum;
Roman amphitheater; medieval
defence tower - library; laboratory

Baden

11917
**Historisches Museum der Stadt
Baden**
Landvogteischloß, CH-5400 Baden
History/Public Affairs Museum - 1876
Finds from the Roman colony Aquae
Helveticae; pre- and protohistory;
Roman archaeology; history of the
town; period interiors; weapons;
ironwork; glass painting; Dutch tiles;
ecclesiastical art; photograph
collection; cliché collection; stone
collection

11918
Kirchenschatz-Museum
Kirchplatz 4, CH-5400 Baden
Religious Art Museum - 1969
Church treasure; crosses (14th-17th
century); monstrance; reliquary;
chandeliers; chalices; ecclesiastical
artifacts and vestments (15th-18th
century)

11919
Kleines technisches Museum
Kraftwerk Kapplerhof, CH-5401 Baden
Science/Tech Museum - 1977
Electrotechnical instruments,
switchkeys, motors; generator

Balgach

11920
Heimatmuseum
Steigstr., CH-9436 Balgach
General Museum - 1969
Local history; farm implements and
tools; wine growing; 16th century
bulkhead painting; 14th century
farmhouse

Balsthal

11921
Heimatmuseum Alt-Falkenstein
Burg, CH-4710 Balsthal
General Museum - 1919
Ceramics from local manufactures;
peasant furniture and utensils; coins;
weapons; 11th century castle

Basel

11922
Anatomische Sammlung
Pestalozzistr. 20, CH-4056 Basel
Natural History Museum - 1689
Systematical and topographical
anatomy; embryology; prepared
skeletons by Vesalius and Plattner
(16th century); original models of
embryos by Wilhelm His

11923
Antikenmuseum
St. Albangraben 5, CH-4051 Basel
Fine Arts Museum - 1961
Greek, Italian, Etruscan, Roman art;
sculptures; ceramics; terra cottas;
gold jewelry; bronzes - restoration
workshops; photo laboratory

11924
Basler Papiermühle Museum für
Papier, Schrift und Druck
St.-Alban-Tal 35, CH-4052 Basel
History/Public Affairs Museum - 1949
Paper manufacturing in various
techniques and during diverse
periods; other writing materials;
history of the different kinds of types,
type foundry, typography, printing,
book binding; Gallician paper mill
(1180/1453); Dr. W.Fr. Tschudin
donation; collection of the Haas' type
foundry; botanical section of 'paper-
manufacturing plants' - library

11925
Gewerbemuseum
Spalenvorstadt 2, CH-4003 Basel
Decorative Arts Museum - 1893
Decorative and applied arts; glass;
metalwork; ceramics; textiles; book
art; graphics; placards and posters;
chairs; exhibits of professions, trades
and industries - library

11926
Historisches Museum
Barfüßerplatz, CH-4051 Basel
History/Public Affairs Museum - 1856
Cultural history; Gallic, Roman and
Alemanic finds; ecclesiastical and
profane art; Romanic and late Gothic
stone and wood sculptures; big altar
by Yvo Striegel; religious goldsmith
work, chalices, crosses and
monstrances (14th-15th century);
tapestry (15th century); furniture;
Renaissance and Baroque decorative
arts; interiors (16th-17th century);
goldsmith work from Basel (16th-18th
century); glass paintings including
works by Hans Holbein the Younger;
memorabilia on Erasmus von
Rotterdam (1465-1536); small
sculptures; coins; weapons; banners
and uniforms (15th-19th century); old
musical instruments; 18th-19th century
furnishings; Barfüßer Church (14th
century) - library

11927
Jüdisches Museum der Schweiz
Kornhausgasse 8, CH-4051 Basel
Religious Art Museum - 1966
Jewish life and dogma; Jewish year;
documents pertaining to the history of
Jews in Switzerland; tombstones from
the Jewish cemetary in Basel;
ceramics from scriptural times

11928
Kirschgarten
Elisabethenstr. 27, CH-4051 Basel
Decorative Arts Museum - 1951
18th-19th century interiors, arts and
crafts; 17th-19th century costumes;
16th-19th century timepieces;
ceramics and porcelain; ironwork;
17th-19th century children's toys

11929
Museum der Basler Mission
Missionsstr. 21, CH-4003 Basel
Religious Art Museum - 1860
Ethnographica from Cameroon,
Ghana, India, Borneo and China -
library

11930
Museum für Gegenwartskunst
St.-Alban-Tal 2, Ch-4010 Basel
Fine Arts Museum - 1980
Emanuel Hoffmann donation including
works by Delaunay, Alan Davie,
Mathieu, Segui, Viera da Silva, Louis
Cane, Robert Ryman, Bruce Naumann,
Richard Long; contemporary art
including works by Beuys, Twombly,
Long, Tinguely; sculptures and
drawings of the Sixties and Seventies;
loans from the collection of Graf
Guiseppe Panza di Biumo

11931
**Museum für Völkerkunde und
Schweizer Museum für Volkskunde**
Augustinergasse 2, CH-4001 Basel
Anthropology Museum - 1849
Anthropology and ethnology: Oceania;
Southeast Asia, Indonesia, musical
ethnology; East Asia, textiles; South
and Central Asia, non-European
prehistory; America, textiles; Africa,
textiles; European prehistory; Swiss
ethnography - library; archives;
restoration workshop; photo
laboratory

11932
Naturhistorisches Museum
Augustinergasse 2, CH-4001 Basel
Natural History Museum - 1821
Anthropology; entomology: ants and
coleoptera; geology and stratigraphy;
mineralogy; osteology: fossils and
extinct mammals; zoology: mammals,
ornithology, acarology, herpetology -
library; bookbindery; photo and
preparation laboratories

11933
Öffentliche Kunstsammlung
Kunstmuseum
St.-Alban-Graben 16, CH-4010 Basel
Fine Arts Museum - 1662
B. Amerbach collection (16th century);
Faeschisches Museum (1823);
Birmann collection (1847); Dienast
collection (1860); Bachofen-Burckhardt
donation (1920); Emanuel Hoffmann
donation (1952); gifts from artists and
maecenas; art work from the 15th
century to the present; works by
Konrad Witz and Hans Holbein d.J.;
local paintings (15th-16th century);
Dutch paintings (16th-17th century);
German and Swiss paintings
(18th-19th century); Classicism,
Romanticism, Biedermeier, French
naturalism and impressionism, cubism,
abstract art and modern European art;
modern American painting; sculptures;
copper engraving section containing
15th century to contemporary
drawings, graphics and books with
original graphics

11934
Rheinschiffahrts-Ausstellung 'Unser
Weg zum Meer'
Rheinhafen Basel-Kleinhüningen,
CH-4019 Basel
History/Public Affairs Museum - 1954
Models of vessels navigating the
Rhine (19th-20th century); model of the
docks of Basel; exhibits pertaining to
origin and distribution of transported
goods; history of the town as a traffic
center

11935
Sammlung alter Musikinstrumente
Historisches Museum Basel
Leonhardstr. 8, CH-4051 Basel
Music Museum - 1872
European art and folk musical
instruments

11936
**Schweizerisches Feuerwehrmuseum
Basel**
Kornhausgasse 18, CH-4003 Basel
History/Public Affairs Museum - 1957
History and technical development of
fire fighting from the 13th century to
the present; Lützelhof (12th century
monastery) - library

11937
**Schweizerisches Pharmazie-
Historisches Museum**
(Apotekenmuseum)
Totengässlein 3, CH-4051 Basel
History/Public Affairs Museum - 1924
Obsolete medicaments from Europe,
Asia and Africa; 16th-19th century
laboratories; microscopes; healing-
amulets; 18th century apothecary's
interiors; receptacles; graphics -
historic library

11938
Schweizerisches Sportmuseum
Missionsstr. 28, CH-4055 Basel
History/Public Affairs Museum - 1945
Development of all kinds of sports
from all over the world; rare sports
equipment; posters and pictorial
documents - library

11939
Skulpturhalle
Mittlere Str. 17, CH-4056 Basel
Fine Arts Museum - 1849
Casts of Greek and Roman
sculptures; special exhibition of copies
from all intact sculptures and
fragments of the Parthenon -
workshops

11940
Stadt- und Münstermuseum
Unterer Rheinweg 2, CH-4058 Basel
General Museum - 1939
Original sculptures and copies from
the Münster in Basel; plan views and
models of the town; medieval
monastery Klingental (13th/14th
century)

Bellinzona

11941
Museo civico
Castello di Montebello, CH-6500
Bellinzona
General Museum - 1914
Archaeology, especially Roman finds;
local history; 13th century citadel

Bennwil

11942
Dorfmuseum
Gemeindehaus, CH-4431 Bennwil
General Museum - 1971
Local history; paintings; tools;
implements for textile manufacture;
memorabilia of the poet Carl Spitteler;
minerals from the region

Beringen

11943
Heimatmuseum
CH-8222 Beringen
General Museum - 1950
Local history; farm implements;
domestic utensils; hemp and flax
manufacture

Berlingen

11944
Adolf-Dietrich-Haus
Seestr. 26, CH-8267 Berlingen
Historic Site - 1957
Memorabilia of the painter Adolf
Dietrich (1877-1957); original paintings
and reproductions; originally furnished
rooms

Bern

11945
Bernische Abguß-Sammlung
Mattenenge 10, CH-3011 Bern
Fine Arts Museum - 1806
Plaster casts of Classical sculptures

11946
Bernisches Historisches Museum
Helvetiaplatz 5, CH-3000 Bern 6
History/Public Affairs Museum - 1881
History and applied arts: textiles,
national costumes, military items,
ceramics, fayence, paintings, graphics,
sculptures, glass painting, folklore;
treasures from the Lausanne cathedral
and from the monastery Königsfelden;
Dr. Albert Kocher porcelain collection;
numismatics: Greek, Roman, Oriental
and Swiss coins and medals;
prehistory of the region, classical
archaeology; ethnography: Near and
Middle East, Johann Wäber Oceania
and Alaska collection, America, Africa,
Far East, Henri Moser-Charlottenfels
collection of Islamic art and decorative
arts - library; restoration and photo
laboratory

11947
Einstein-Haus
Kramgasse 49, CH-3004 Bern
Historic Site - 1979
Memorabilia of the physicist Albert
Einstein, photos and documents

11948
Kantonales Gewerbemuseum
Zeughausgasse 2, CH-3011 Bern
Decorative Arts Museum - 1869
Decorative and applied arts;
smithwork; embroideries; 18th century
building - library

11949
Kunstmuseum Bern
Hodlerstr. 12, CH-3011 Bern
Fine Arts Museum - 1809
Paintings and sculptures; graphics;
Gottfried Keller, Paul Klee, Hermann
and Margrit Rupf, Max Muggler, and
Adolf Wölfli bequests - library;
restoration laboratory

11950
Naturhistorisches Museum Bern
Bernastr. 14, CH-3005 Bern
Natural History Museum - 1800
Geology; mineralogy; palaeontology;
vertebrates and invertebrates; largest
diorama show in Europe - library;
preparatory; laboratory

11951
Schweizerische Theatersammlung
Schanzenstr. 15, CH-3008 Bern
Performing Arts Museum - 1943
Documentation of theatrical history in
Switzerland; designs of stage pictures
and costumes; masks, marionettes and
costumes; memorabilia of famous
persons - library

11952
Schweizerisches Alpines Museum
Helvetiaplatz 4, CH-3005 Bern
General Museum - 1905
Development of equipment for
mountaineering; history of
mountaineering; map collection and
history of cartography; relief
collection; folklore of the Alps - library

11953
Schweizerisches Gutenbergmuseum
Zeughausgasse 2, POB 3289, CH-3000
Bern
Science/Tech Museum - 1900
Exhibits about the development of
printing, including instruments and
books - library

11954
**Schweizerisches Post-, Telegrafen-
und Telefon-Museum**
Helvetiaplatz 4, CH-3030 Bern
History/Public Affairs Museum - 1907
History of transportation and post,
telecommunication technique; stamps
and philately

11955
Schweizerisches Schützenmuseum
Bernastr. 5, CH-3005 Bern
History/Public Affairs Museum - 1885
Weapons; ammunition; trophies;
documentation about the Swiss rifle-
associations

Berneck

11956
Färberhaus
CH-9442 Berneck
General Museum - 1978
Local history; tools and implements for
wine- and fruit-growing; tools for
cooperage

Beromünster

11957
**Dr.med. et h.c. Edmund-Müller-
Stiftung**
Schloß Heidegg, CH-6215
Beromünster
Historic Site - 1969
Art and decorative arts; ethnography;
ecclesiastical and profane folk art;
furniture; domestic utensils; jewelry -
library

11958
Schloß-Museum
CH-6215 Beromünster
History/Public Affairs Museum - 1928
Reconstructed printing room of Helias
Helye (1470); prehistorical finds;
furnished period rooms; stained glass;
ecclesiastical folk art; jewelry; old card
games and toys; craftmen's tools and
farm implements; music room and
poet's room including memorabilia on
poets from Münster; 12th century
tower

11959
Stiftsschatz
Stiftskirche, CH-6215 Beromünster
Religious Art Museum - 1981
Medieval ecclesiastical art; 7th-15th
century goldsmith work; early and late
medieval textiles; baroque goldsmith
work; Baroque embroidery and silks

Bex

11960
Musée du Mandement du Bex
Rue du Signal, CH-1880 Bex
General Museum - 1975
Local history; documents; tools;
costumes; paintings - library

Biel

11961
Museum Schwab
Seevorstadt, CH-2502 Biel
Archeology Museum - 1865
Neolithic, Bronze Age, Iron Age and
Roman (especially Petinesca) finds
from the environ of the Bieler See;
Oberst Friedrich Schwab
lake-dwelling collection - library

Bischofszell

11962
Kirchenschatz
Kirchgasse 16, CH-9220 Bischofszell
Religious Art Museum - 1968
Church treasure, including chalices,
chandeliers, monstrances, late
Renaissance, baroque and rococo
reliquaries from Germany and
Switzerland; St. Pelagius Church (14th
century)

11963
Ortsmuseum
Marktgasse 4, CH-9220 Bischofszell
General Museum - 1930
Local history; Bronze Age, Roman and
early medieval finds; documents;
coins; seals; pictures; glass painting;
8th-18th century ecclesiastical art;
weapons; documents pertaining to the
Reformation period; Gothic to 20th
century interiors; crafts and guilds;
children's toys; 15th-20th century
maps and plans - library

Bissone

11964
Casa Tencalla
Via Tencalla, CH-6816 Bissone
Historic Site - 1942
16th century patrician house; 17th-19th
century interiors

Blonay

11965
**Musée-dépôt du Chemin de fer
touristique Blonay-Chamby**
CH-1807 Blonay
Science/Tech Museum - 1976
Steam engines; electric locomotives;
railroad cars; maintenance carriages;
wagons

Bosco-Gurin

11966
Walserhaus Gurin
CH-6671 Bosco-Gurin
General Museum - 1936
16th century wooden house; local
history artifacts; furnishings; textiles;
folk costumes; tools

Bottmingen

11967
Dorfmuseum
Therwilerstr. 14/18, CH-4103
Bottmingen
General Museum - 1978
Local history; farm implements; tools;
carriages; workshops; domestic
utensils; documents and pictures;
wine-vault and distillery

Boudry

11968
Musée de la vigne et du vin
Château, CH-2017 Boudry
Agriculture Museum - 1957
Winegrowing and viticulture; tools and
implements used in wine production;
documents pertaining to wine culture;
18th century wine cellar; 13th century
castle

11969
Musée de l'Areuse
18, avenue du Collège, BP 185,
CH-2017 Boudry
General Museum - 1866
Local history; ethnography; prehistoric
finds; mammals and birds of the
region; documents

Bremgarten

11970
Kirchenschatz
Pfarrgasse 4, CH-5620 Bremgarten
Religious Art Museum - 1970
Monstrances; chalices; vessels;
chandeliers; crosses; statues and
wood sculptures; reliquaries and
reliquary statues; missals; pictures and
paintings

Brienz

11971
**Ausstellung der Kantonalen
Schnitzerschule**
CH-3855 Brienz
Fine Arts Museum - 1884
Wood carvings

11972
**Ausstellung der Schweizerischen
Geigenbauschule**
CH-3855 Brienz
Music Museum - 1944
String instruments and the
manufacture of violins; tools;
documents; Swiss musical instruments
(18th-20th centuries); Prof. Dr. H.
Hanselmann donation of violins

11973
**Schweizerisches Freilichtmuseum
für ländliche Bau- und Wohnkultur
Ballenberg**
CH-3855 Brienz
Open Air Museum - 1978
Peasant architecture and interiors of
dwelling houses and outhouses;
building materials; construction types;
furnishings; tools and implements;
ornaments; inscriptions; paintings -
library

Brig

11974
Museum im Stockalperschloß
CH-3900 Brig
General Museum - 1970
Local history documents; silver;
minerals; works of art; ethnography;
17th century castle - library

Brissago

11975
Museo etnografico africano
CH-6614 Brissago
Anthropology Museum - 1968
African ethnology, artifacts; weapons
from Egypt, the Sudan and the Congo
- botanical garden

Brugg

11976
Adolf-Stäbli-Stübli
Hofstatt, CH-5200 Brugg
General Museum - 1911
Old weapons, farm implements and
domestic utensils; toys; paintings,
especially works by Adolf Stäbli
(1842-1901)

11977
Heimatmuseum
Untere Hofstatt 23, CH-5200 Brugg
General Museum - 1963
Local history; weapons; domestic
utensils; pewter items; weights; fire
engines; paintings; 17th century house

11978
Vindonissa-Museum
Museumsstr. 1, CH-5200 Brugg
Archeology Museum - 1912
Roman finds; archaeological finds from
the camp Vindonissa; weapons, tools,
coins, ceramics; documentation about
the excavations - library

Bubikon

11979
Johannitermuseum
Ritterhaus, CH-8608 Bubikon
Religious Art Museum - 1936
History of ecclesiastical orders of
knighthood, especially Johanniter;
12th-18th century weapons; 12th-16th
century architecture and interiors -
library

Buchegg

11980
Heimatmuseum Schloß Buchegg
CH-4571 Buchegg
General Museum - 1956
Farm implements; peasant interiors;
tools; archaeological finds from the
area; 17th century prison tower

Bulle

11981
Musée Gruérien
19, rue de la Condémine, CH-1630
Bulle
General Museum - 1917
History of Gruyère and neighbouring
areas; folk art; ecclesiastical art;
ethnography; exhibition about cheese
production; Swiss and French
paintings; numismatics; memorabilia of
the poet Victor Tissot - library

Büren an der Aare

11982
Heimatmuseum 'Spittel'
Spittelgasse 36, CH-3294 Büren an
der Aare
General Museum - 1975
Local history; archaeological finds,
coins, coats of arms, weights;
domestic utensils, chandeliers;
carpenter's and weaver's implements
and tools; 15th century circular wall
building - library

Burgdorf

11983
Historische Sammlungen Schloß Burgdorf
CH-3400 Burgdorf
History/Public Affairs Museum - 1886
Historical collections from Emmental: prehistory; ethnography; militaria; crafts; agriculture; cheese dairy; potter's workshop; picture collection; memorial room to Heinrich Pestalozzi (1746-1827); coins and seals; medieval castle - library

11984
Sammlung für Völkerkunde
Kirchbühl, CH-3400 Burgdorf
Anthropology Museum - 1909
Ethnography from nearly everywhere outside Europe

Bürglen

11985
Tell-Museum Uri
Tellenturm, CH-6463 Bürglen
Historic Site - 1957
Documentation on Wilhelm Tell and the Tell games

Castagnola

11986
Sammlung Thyssen-Bornemisza
Villa Favorita, CH-6976 Castagnola
Fine Arts Museum - 1928
13th-18th century European painting, sculpture and decorative arts

Cevio

11987
Museo di Vallemaggia
Antica Casa Franzoni, CH-6675 Cevio
General Museum - 1963
Farm implements; folk art and folk costumes; local history; works by the painter Giovanni A. Vanoni (1810-86)

Château d'Oex

11988
Musée du Vieux-Pays d'Enhaut
CH-1837 Château d'Oex
General Museum - 1922
16th-19th century folk art and interiors; cheese-dairy, smithy, tools; paintings, decorative arts

Chur

11989
Bündner Kunstmuseum
Postplatz, CH-7000 Chur
Fine Arts Museum - 1900
18th-20th century paintings and sculptures from Bünden; collection of graphics; Swiss 19th-20th century art

11990
Bündner Natur-Museum
Masanerstr. 31, CH-7000 Chur
Natural History Museum - 1929
Zoology; botany; geology; mineralogy; geography of the canton Graubünden

11991
Dommuseum
Hof 18, CH-7000 Chur
Religious Art Museum - 1943
Medieval dome treasure including 14th-18th century ecclesiastical art; late classical and early medieval ivory, textiles, sculptures

11992
Rätisches Museum
Hofstr. 1, CH-7000 Chur
General Museum - 1872
Archaeology, including finds from the canton Graubünden; numismatics; cultural history; ethnography - restoration and carpenter's workshops; photo laboratory

Clarens

11993
Maison Kruger
17, Villa Dubochet, CH-1815 Clarens
Historic Site - 1904
Memorabilia on the South African president of Transvaal Paul Kruger (1825-1904); villa where he spent his last years during exile (1900-1904)

Coffrane

11994
Musée agricole
CH-2207 Coffrane
Agriculture Museum - 1956
Local history; farm implements and agricultural machinery; peasant artifacts; tools for hemp production

Cologny

11995
Fondation Martin Bodmer
19-21, route du Guignard, CH-1223 Cologny
Fine Arts Museum - 1972
Significant writings and editions of world literature; oriental writings and palm leaf manuscripts; incunabula and first editions; decorative arts; classical reliefs; sculptures; vases; coins; tapestries; drawings

Colombier

11996
Musée des indiennes
Château, CH-2013 Colombier
Decorative Arts Museum - 1953
Printed cotton cloths; wooden models; designs; memorabilia of the founder of the Boudry textile factory Claude Bovet

11997
Musée militaire
Château, CH-2013 Colombier
History/Public Affairs Museum - 1952
Military art and science; arms and armor; uniforms; armours; flags and banners; memorabilia of the Meuron regiment; 15th century castle

Coppet

11998
Château de Coppet
CH-1296 Coppet
Historic Site - 1948
18th century castle; memorabilia of the Geneva banker Jacques Necker and of his daughter Madame de Staël; 18th-19th century princelike furnishings; porcelain, tapestry, portraits and busts

11999
Musée régional du Vieux-Coppet
Maison Michel, Grand Rue, CH-1296 Coppet
General Museum - 1935
16th century mansion; local history; late 19th century bourgeois interiors; decorative and applied arts; historical documents

Davos Platz

12000
Bergbaumuseum Schmelzboden
Gasthaus Schmelzboden, CH-7270 Davos Platz
History/Public Affairs Museum - 1979
History of mining; tools and implements

Delémont

12001
Musée jurassien
52, rue du 23 juin, CH-2800 Delémont
History/Public Affairs Museum - 1909
Prehistoric and Roman finds; Merowingian items; history of the old bishopric Basel and of the Jura; ecclesiastical art; coins and medals; peasant interiors; weapons - library

Diessenhofen

12002
Ortsmuseum Diessenhofen
Im oberen Amtshaus, CH-8253 Diessenhofen
General Museum - 1961
Dye plants; cloth-printing and cloth-printing techniques in Thurgau during the 19th century; works by the local artist Carl Roesch; 16th century building - library

Dietikon

12003
Ortsmuseum Dietikon
Schöneggstr. 20, CH-8953 Dietikon
General Museum - 1931
Roman finds from Dietikon; finds from the medieval castles Schönenwerd and Glanzenberg; collection of stove tiles; local history artifacts - archives

Donzhausen

12004
Heimatmuseum
CH-8583 Donzhausen
General Museum - 1968
Local history; farm implements; domestic utensils; interiors; weapons; glass; ceramics; fire engines; toys

Dornach

12005
Heimatmuseum Schwarzbubenland
Mauritiuskirche Oberdornach, CH-4143 Dornach
General Museum - 1949
Local history; archaeological finds; ecclesiastical art; farm implements; documents on the battle of Dornach (1499); memorabilia of the geologist A. Gressly

Dübendorf

12006
Museum der schweizerischen Fliegertruppen
POB, CH-8600 Dübendorf
History/Public Affairs Museum - 1978
Military aviation in Switzerland; documentation on the development of military aviation; aircraft engines, power units, propellers; aircraft (1910-70); special devices and constructions; aircraft cameras, navigation, wireless sets; uniforms

Ebikon

12007
Tierweltpanorama
Luzernerstr. 63, CH-6030 Ebikon
Natural History Museum - 1950
Dioramas of Middle European and exotic animal kingdom; collection of birds of paradise; insects, especially chrysididae; animal paintings; drawings by Walter Linsenmaier

Ebnat-Kappel

12008
Heimatmuseum der Albert-Edelmann-Stiftung
Ackerhusweg 16, CH-9642 Ebnat-Kappel
General Museum - 1963
Historical musical instruments; peasant furniture; folk costumes; domestic utensils; paintings by Hans Brühlmann, Karl Hofer and Albert Edelmann; 18th century house

Ederswiler

12009
Museum Löwenburg
Hofgut Löwenburg, CH-2801 Ederswiler
General Museum - 1970
Local history; archaeological finds; fossils; medieval to modern history; agriculture

Eglisau

12010
Ortsmuseum Eglisau im Weierbach-Huus
CH-8193 Eglisau
General Museum - 1958
Architectural history of Eglisau; fishing in the upper Rhine; domestic utensils

Ernen

12011
Kirchenmuseum
CH-3981 Ernen
Religious Art Museum - 1975
Church treasure; monstrances; crosses; paraments; reliquaries; chalices and other sacramental artifacts (15th-18th century); pictures; documents

Eschikon

12012
Pflugsammlung
mail c/o Institut für Pflanzenbau der ETH, CH-8307 Eschikon
Agriculture Museum - 1977
Plows

Estavayer-le-Lac

12013
Museum
Rue du Musée, CH-1470 Estavayer-le-Lac
General Museum - 1925
Local history; prehistoric finds; Roman coins; weapons; craftmen's tools; domestic utensils and 17th century kitchen; interiors; old railway lanterns

Frauenfeld

12014
Historische Sammlung und Urgeschichtliche Sammlung Museum des Kantons Thurgau
CH-8500 Frauenfeld
History/Public Affairs Museum - 1859
Pre- and protohistoric finds since the Neolithic Age; ecclesiastical art; bourgeois and peasant interiors; glass paintings; clocks; numismatics; weapons; ceramics; graphics of different parts of the canton; state antiquities - library; restoration workshop

12015
Kunstsammlung des Kantons Thurgau
Ringstr. 16, CH-8500 Frauenfeld
Fine Arts Museum - 1974
Contemporary art from Thurgau

12016
Naturwissenschaftliche Sammlung
Museum des Kantons Thurgau
CH-8500 Frauenfeld
Natural History Museum - 1859
Geology; botany; zoology; palaeontology; entomology; erratic blocks from the Rhine glacier; herbarium of the canton Thurgau

Frauenkirch

12017
Kirchner-Haus
Wildboden, CH-7275 Frauenkirch, Davos
Historic Site - 1964
Memorabilia of the painter Ernst Ludwig Kirchner (1880-1938); watercolors, drawings and graphics by the artist

Fribourg

12018
Anatomisches Museum
1, rue Albert Gockel, CH-1700 Fribourg
Natural History Museum - 1938
Human anatomy and embryology; models, preparations, and moulages - library; archives; restoration workshops

12019
Ethnographische Sammlung
mail c/o Ethnographisches Seminar, Universität, CH-1700 Fribourg
Anthropology Museum - 1941
Objects from New Guinea, Northern Africa, North and South America and India

12020
Musée d'art et d'histoire
227, rue Pierre-Aeby, CH-1700 Fribourg
History/Public Affairs Museum - 1920
Archaeology; art and history of the canton Fribourg; prehistoric, Roman and medieval finds; 10th-18th century sculpture and painting including works by Hans Fries, H. Gieng, J. Sautter, G. Locher; 15th-19th century interiors; pewter, porcelain, tapestry; 15th-18th century glasscases; 18th-19th century drawings and watercolors including works by J.-E. Curty, Ph. de Fégeli, P. Lacaze, F. Bonnet, Marcello; coins and medals - library

12021
Naturhistorisches Museum
Pérolles, CH-1700 Fribourg
Natural History Museum - 1832
Mineralogy; geography; geology and palaeontology; local animal life; zoology; collection of minerals of the Binnental

Gelfingen

12022
Schloß Heidegg
CH-6284 Gelfingen
Religious Art Museum - 1951
17th-18th century interiors; stoves; paintings; 11th-12th century castle - rose garden

Genève

12023
Cabinet des estampes Musée d'art et d'histoire
5, promenade du Pin, CH-1204 Genève
Fine Arts Museum
Graphic prints from Italy, Germany, the Netherlands, France, England and Spain; contemporary graphic prints

12024
Collection de la Fondation in memoriam Comtesse Tatiana Zoubov
2, rue des Granges, CH-1204 Genève
Religious Art Museum - 1973
Interiors; furnishings: Régence, Louis XV, Louis XVI, Chippendale; paintings; portraits; 18th century decorative arts; porcelain; busts; vases; tapestry; art objects from China; Hôtel de Sellon (18th century)

12025
Collections Baur
8, rue Munier-Romilly, CH-1206 Genève
Fine Arts Museum - 1964
Chinese and Japanese art since 1807 collected by Alfred Baur (1865-1951)

12026
Institut et Musée Voltaire
25, rue des Délices, CH-1203 Genève
Historic Site - 1952
Voltaire (1694-1778) and the 18th century; prints, manuscripts and iconographic collections - library

12027
Musé d'instruments anciens de musique Musée d'art et d'histoire
23, rue François Lefort, CH-1206 Genève
Music Museum - 1960
Historical musical instruments from Europe, Asia, Oceania and Africa; Fritz Ernst collection - auditorium

12028
Musée Ariana Musée d'art et d'histoire
10, avenue de la Paix, CH-1202 Genève
Religious Art Museum - 1884/1934
18th and 19th century porcelain and fine pottery from Europe, China, Japan and the Islamic sphere; modern ceramics; Neobaroque villa Ariana (1877-84)

12029
Musée Barbier-Muller
4, rue de l'École-de-Chimie, CH-1205 Genève
Fine Arts Museum - 1977
Ethnology; native art from Africa, America, Melanesia and Oceania

12030
Musée d'art et d'histoire
2, rue Charles-Galland, CH-1211 Genève 3
Fine Arts Museum - 1910
Archaeology: prehistoric, Egyptian Greek and Roman archaeology. Fine arts: 15th-20th century Swiss paintings; works by J.E. Liotard, A.W. Toepffer, J.L. Agasse, A. Calame, F. Diday, R. Gardelle, R.-L. De la Rive, B. Menn, F. Hodler and others; early Italian paintings; German and Flemish paintings; 18th-20th century French paintings including works by M.-Q. de la Tour, C. Corot and impressionists; sculpture including works by J. Arp, M. Bill, César, A. Giacometti, B. Luginbühl, H. Laurens, H. Moore, J. Tinguely. Applied arts department: weapons, uniforms, furniture, carpets, glass, jewelry, numismatics. Estates of Jean-Jacques Rigaud, Walter Fol, Gustave Revillico, Favre, Baszanger and others - auditorium with audio-visual equipment; library; photo and restoration laboratories

12031
Musée de l'Institut Henry Dunant
114, rue de Lausanne, CH-1202 Genève
Historic Site - 1974
Memorabilia of Henry Dunant (1828-1910) and presentation of the Red Cross; personal items of H. Dunant, documents, scripts, pictures; development of the Red Cross; posters; memorabilia of Frédéric Ferrière, a Red Cross pioneer; military medicinal instruments - library; archives; documentation center

12032
Musée d'ethnographie
65-67 boulevard Carl-Vogt, CH-1205 Genève
Anthropology Museum - 1901
Ethnography from five continents; musical instruments; ceramics and pottery - library

12033
Musée d'histoire des sciences
Musée d'art et d'histoire
Villa Bartolini, 128, rue de Lausanne, CH-1202 Genève
Science/Tech Museum - 1964
History of science in Bern: astronomical instruments (1772-1836), physics (apparatuses by H.B. de Saussure and J.D. Colladon); barometers; microscopes; medicine; geology

12034
Musée d'horlogerie et de l'émaillerie Musée d'art et d'histoire
15, route de Malagnou, CH-1208 Genève
Religious Art Museum - 1972
Development of horology in Geneva and Europe since the 16th century; 17th-19th century enamel paintings

12035
Musée Jean-Jacques Rousseau
mail c/o Bibliothèque publique et universitaire, Promenade des Bastions, CH-1211 Genève 4
Historic Site - 1916
Work and life of Jean-Jacques Rousseau (1712-78), especially manuscripts, first editions, statues, paintings, etchings

12036
Muséum d'histoire naturelle
1, route de Malagnou, CH-1211 Genève
Natural History Museum - 1820
Natural history; geology and mineralogy: sediments, precious stones, fluorescent minerals; palaeontology: fossils of vertebrates and invertebrates, especially finds from the Argentinian Pampas; zoology: mammalogy; ornithology; entomology; herpetology; ichthyology - library

12037
Petit Palais - Musée d'art moderne
2, terrasse Saint-Victor, CH-1206 Genève
Fine Arts Museum - 1968
French paintings 1880-1930: impressionism, neo-impressionism, Fauves, Montmartre painters, school of Paris, naive painting

12038
Philatelistisches Museum der Postverwaltung der Vereinten Nationen
Palais des Nations, CH-1211 Genève
History/Public Affairs Museum - 1962
Stamps, envelopes, postcards and documents - audio-visual equipment

12039
Salle Ami Lullin
mail c/o Bibliothèque publique et universitaire, Promenade des Bastions, CH-1205 Genève
Historic Site - 1905
Portraits from well-known Geneva personalities; history ofthe Reformation; manuscripts, precious books and paintings; autographs; palm leaf manuscripts; iconographic collection; Ami Lullin (1695-1765) bequest - restoration workshop

Giornico

12040
Museo di Leventina
Casa Stanga, CH-6745 Giornico
General Museum - 1966
Local history; folklore; weights and measures; coins; 16th century building

Glarus

12041
Kunsthaus
CH-8750 Glarus
Fine Arts Museum - 1870
19th-20th century paintings and sculptures by Swiss artists; international graphics; iconography of the canton Glarus; autographs of famous musicians

12042
Naturwissenschaftliche Sammlungen des Kantons Glarus
Museumsstr., CH-8750 Glarus
Natural History Museum - 1839
Natural history; animal life of the canton Glarus, mammals, vertebrates and invertebrates, birds; butterflies; fish fossils; geology

Goldau

12043
Bergsturz-Museum
CH-6410 Goldau
Historic Site - 1956
Cultural history pertaining to the avalanche of Goldau in 1806; pictures, literature, excavated artifacts; local history; avalanche landscape

Gontenschwil

12044
Dorfmuseum
CH-5728 Gontenschwil
General Museum - 1972
Local history; peasant interiors;
carpenter's and cooper's tools;
memorabilia on the poet Jakob Frey;
pewter, porcelain, glass, brass,
tobacco pipes, furniture, weapons;
15th century parsonage

Gossau

12045
Burgenmuseum
Schloß, CH-9202 Gossau
History/Public Affairs Museum - 1972
15th century castle; castles in Eastern
Switzerland; photos, models; torture-
chamber containing instruments of
torture

12046
Motorrad-Museum
Kirchstr., CH-9202 Gossau
Science/Tech Museum - 1974
Motorcycles; racing bikes (1896-1968);
carburetors, lighting and other
accessories

Grandson

12047
Château de Grandson
CH-1422 Grandson
History/Public Affairs Museum - 1961
13th-16th century interiors and
furniture; family history of the
Grandson barons; 15th century arms;
torture chamber; models of castles;
motocar museum; documentation on
the battle of Grandson (1476); Swiss
Institute of Arms; international center
for restoration, conservation and
research

Grandvaux

12048
Maison Buttin-de Loës
Place du village, CH-1603 Grandvaux
General Museum - 1941
Local history; 17th-19th century
interiors and utensils; M. and Mme.
Louis Buttin-de Loës private collection

Gränichen

12049
Dorfmuseum
Kirchenbündten 4, Oberdorf, CH-5722
Gränichen
General Museum - 1976
Local history; farm implements; dairy
industry; craft trades; domestic
utensils; weapons; handicrafts;
distilling utensils; archaeological finds

Grenchen

12050
Museum Grenchen
mail c/o Stadtarchiv, Schulhaus I,
CH-2540 Grenchen
General Museum - 1974
Town history; history of the clock
industry in Solothurn

Grindelwald

12051
Heimatmuseum
Talhaus, CH-3818 Grindelwald
General Museum - 1963
Local history; tools; furniture; alpine
economy, winter sports and
mountaineering

Grüningen

12052
Museum
Schloß, CH-8627 Grüningen
General Museum - 1947
Local history; historical artifacts from
the bailliff Grüningen; documents,
graphics, models; tools and
implements; 13th century castle

Gruyères

12053
Château
CH-1663 Gruyères
Fine Arts Museum - 1938
13th/15th century castle; interiors,
furniture, glasscases, tapestry,
weapons; bailliff hall; paintings by C.
Corot, H.-C.-A. Baron, F. Furet, B.
Menn; works by the sculptor A. Bovy,
paintings by A. Baud-Bovy and André
Valetin, memorabilia of the artists

Güllen

12054
Ortsmuseum
CH-8911 Güllen
General Museum - 1956
Local history; shoemaker's tools; folk
costumes; memorabilia of local
personages; C. Zachanassian private
collection

Gurbrü

12055
Bauernmuseum Althus
CH-3249 Gurbrü
Agriculture Museum - 1970
Local history; peasant interiors; tools
and implements for cattle breeding
and tillage; craftsmen's tools

Guttannen

12056
Kristallmuseum
Wirzen, CH-3861 Guttannen
Natural History Museum - 1975
Local minerals; quartz, fluorites,
amethysts, iron pyrites

Güttingen

12057
Puppenmuseum Jeannine
Haus zum Adler, Hauptstr., CH-8594
Güttingen
Decorative Arts Museum - 1975
Dolls from Germany and France (19th
century); toys; mechanical dolls;
theater dolls; children's books

Hallau

12058
Heimatmuseum
Kirchschulhaus, CH-8215 Hallau
General Museum - 1858
Local history; archaeological finds;
documents; coins; jewelry; weapons;
peasant and bourgeois domestic
utensils

Hallwil

12059
Schloß
CH-5705 Hallwil
General Museum - 1925
12th century castle with moat; local
history; documents on the castle and
its inhabitants; 17th-18th century
interiors; archaeological finds; neolithic
workshop; craft trades and local
peasant culture and traditions

Halten

12060
**Heimatmuseum Wasseramt - Turm in
Halten**
CH-4566 Halten
General Museum - 1965
13th century tower; 16th-18th century
attics; peasant interiors; craft trades;
weights and measures, scales and
weights; the development of lighting;
farm implements; bricks and tiles;
weaving chamber; folk costumes;
furnished house with oven

Heiden

12061
Heimatmuseum
Postgebäude, CH-9410 Heiden
General Museum - 1878
Local history; peasant interiors,
domestic utensils; pictures,
documents; weapons, uniforms;
domestic musical instruments;
minerals from the Alps; local animal
life; artifacts from Indonesia

12062
Henri-Dunant-Museum
CH-9410 Heiden
Historic Site - 1969
Documents on the founder of the Red
Cross, Henri Dunant; house where he
died

Herisau

12063
Heimatmuseum
CH-9100 Herisau
General Museum - 1946
Weapons; ethnology; painted peasant
furniture; embroidery and weaving

Herzogenbuchsee

12064
Ortsmuseum Herzogenbuchsee
Bernisches Historisches Museum
Restaurant 'Kreuz', CH-3360
Herzogenbuchsee
General Museum - 1947
18th century baroque mansion;
excavated lake dwellings from the
Lake of Burgäschi; plans and
illustrations of a Roman farmyard

Hilterfingen

12065
Jugendstilmuseum Schloß Hünegg
CH-3652 Hilterfingen
Decorative Arts Museum - 1966
Historical furnishings; historical
painting; Jugendstil interiors; artifacts
pertaining to student societies in
Swiss Universities

12066
Martin-Lauterburg-Stiftung
Schloß Hünegg, CH-3652 Hilterfingen
Fine Arts Museum - 1973
Paintings and drawings by Martin
Lauterburg (1891-1960)

Hinwil

12067
Ortsmuseum Hinwil
Oberdorfstr. 11, CH-8340 Hinwil
General Museum - 1925
18th century peasant interiors;
craftsmen's tools; farm implements;
uniforms and weapons; local history;
18th century farm building - library

Hitzkirch

12068
Baldegger-Museum
Kantonales Lehrerseminar, CH-6285
Hitzkirch
Archeology Museum - 1939
Neolithic and Bronze Age excavation
finds from the settlements on the
banks of Lake Baldegger

12069
Schatzkammer
Deutschordenskirche, CH-6285
Hitzkirch
Religious Art Museum - 1978
Church treasure; monstrances;
crosses; chalices; candles; statues;
18th century wooden sculptures

Höngg

12070
Ortsmuseum Höngg
Vogtsrain 2, CH-8049 Höngg
General Museum - 1926
16th century wine growers' feudal
tenure; viticulture; peasant interiors;
craft trades - library; wood workshop

Horgen

12071
Ortsmuseum Horgen
Sust, Bahnhofstr. 27, CH-8810 Horgen
General Museum - 1954
Alte Sust, 16th century building;
prehistoric finds; local history;
collection of 18th-20th century
weapons - library

Huttwil

12072
Heimatmuseum
Schulhaus Nyffel, Wiesenstr. 12,
CH-4950 Huttwil
General Museum - 1959
Local history; documents; weapons,
uniforms; folk costumes; craftmen's
tools and implements

Immensee

12073
Ausstellung im Missionshaus
CH-6405 Immensee
Anthropology Museum - 1971
Ethnography; documentation on
missionary work in the Far East, South
America, Africa; pictures; jewelry;
everyday utensils

Isérables

12074
Musée
CH-1914 Isérables
General Museum - 1967
Local history; crystals from Valais;
craftsmen's and farmers' tools and
implements

Jegenstorf

12075
Schloß
CH-3303 Jegenstorf
Historic Site - 1936
Interiors; Renaissance to 19th century
furnishings; documents; memorabilia
of the writer Rudolf von Tavel
(1866-1934); medieval castle

Kaltbrunn

12076
Ortsmuseum
Uznacherstr., CH-8722 Kaltbrunn
General Museum - 1976
Local history; domestic utensils and
farm implements; crafts; manufacture
of hemp and flax; ecclesiastical items;
finds from the historical ruin Bibiton;
coal mining

Kiesen

12077
Milchwirtschaftliches Museum
Bernstr., CH-3117 Kiesen
Agriculture Museum - 1965
Interiors of an old cheese dairy;
pictures, artifacts; audiovisual
presentation of cheese production

Kilchberg

12078
Ortsgeschichtliche Sammlung
Alte Landstr. 170, CH-8802 Kilchberg
General Museum - 1941
Porcelain, fine pottery and ceramics
from the Zurich factory at 'Schooren'
near Kilchberg and nearby factories;
objects and documentation about
fishing and shipping on the Lake of
Zurich; local winegrowing; study of the
poet Conrad Ferdinand Meyer
(1825-98); 18th century building

Klosters

12079
Heimatmuseum Nutlihüsli
CH-7252 Klosters
General Museum - 1918
16th century farmhouse; cultural
history of Prättigau; furniture, domestic
utensils; farm implements;
wood-working tools; ceramics

Kölliken

12080
Ikonenmuseum
Haus Klostermatt 474, CH-5742
Kölliken
Fine Arts Museum - 1971
Icons; related fields; Amberg-Herzog
collection

Kreuzlingen

12081
Feuerwehrmuseum
Konstanzerstr. 39, CH-8280
Kreuzlingen
History/Public Affairs Museum - 1956
Firefighting; several 19th-20th century
fire engines and manual apparatuses;
tools and implements; pictures and
documents

Küblis

12082
Heimatmuseum Prättigau
Haus Pajola, CH-7240 Küblis
General Museum - 1969
Local history; archaeological finds;
agricultural and crafts implements and
tools; domestic utensils

Küssnacht am Rigi

12083
Heimatmuseum
CH-6403 Küssnacht am Rigi
General Museum - 1951
Local history; prehistory;
documentation on the Tell tale;
customs and traditions; ecclesiastical
art

Kyburg

12084
Schloß Kyburg
CH-8311 Kyburg
Decorative Arts Museum - 1917
12th-13th and 16th century castle; 15th
and 17th century wall paintings; 18th
century interiors; 16th-18th century
glass paintings; arms and armour

La Chaux-de-Fonds

12085
Musé d'histoire naturelle
63, avenue Léopold-Robert, CH-2300
La Chaux-de-Fonds
Natural History Museum - 1850
Zoology, mammalogy, ornithology,
herpetology, entomology; dioramas;
marine biology; Angolan zoology -
laboratory; auditorium

12086
Musée des beaux arts
33, rue des Musées, CH-2300 La
Chaux-de-Fonds
Fine Arts Museum - 1864
19th-20th century paintings and
sculpture; Le Corbusier room;
Léopold Robert room (1794-1835);
ethnography

12087
Musée historique et medailler
11, rue de la Loge, CH-2300 La Chaux-
de-Fonds
General Museum - 1876
Local history; 17th-18th century
interiors; 19th century weapons; coins,
medals, pictures, glass, furniture

12088
Musée international d'horlogerie
29, rue des Musées, CH-2300 La
Chaux-de-Fonds
Science/Tech Museum - 1902
History of timekeeping; collection of
clocks and automatons, musical clocks
and chronometers since the 16th
century - library; workshop

La Neuveville

12089
Musée historique
Ruelle de l'Hôtel-de-Ville, CH-2520 La
Neuveville
History/Public Affairs Museum - 1876
Local history; Neolithic finds; 15th
century cannons; firearms (16th-17th
c.); portraits of historical personalities;
pictures and documents

Langnau im Emmental

12090
Heimatmuseum Langnau
Bärenplatz 2a, CH-3550 Langnau im
Emmental
General Museum - 1930
Local pottery and glass; implements
used in the production of cheese or in
the linen industry

La Sarraz

12091
Château
CH-1315 La Sarraz
General Museum - 1949
Interiors (16th-19th c.); painting (19th
c.); porcelain

L'Auberson

12092
Musée Baud
23, Grand-Rue, CH-1451 L'Auberson
Science/Tech Museum - 1955
Mechanical apparatuses; musical
instruments and automatons; hand
organs; phonographs

Laufen

12093
Museum Laufental
Am Helye-Platz, CH-4242 Laufen
General Museum - 1945
Geology; documents on regional
history; crafts and industries; religious
art; Roman farmhouse 'Müschlag';
memorabilia of the book printer
Helyas Helye; works of the local
painter August Cueni (1883-1966) -
library

Lausanne

12094
Cabinet des médailles
Place de la Riponne, CH-1005
Lausanne
History/Public Affairs Museum - 19th
c.
Coins and medals from Switzerland
and neighbouring countries; Gallo-
Roman and Greek coins - library

12095
Collection de l'art brut
11, av des Bergières, CH-1004
Lausanne
Fine Arts Museum - 1976
Contemporary art

12096
**Musée cantonal d'archéologie et
d'histoire**
Palais de Rumine, CH-1005 Lausanne
General Museum - 1845
Prehistoric finds; Greek vases; history
- library; phototheque

12097
Musée cantonal des beaux-arts
Place de la Riponne, CH-1005
Lausanne
Fine Arts Museum - 1841
Regional painting, drawing, wood
carving and scuplture (18th c. to
present); Swiss painting (school of
Geneva); Dutch painting (17th-18th c.);
French painting (19th c.); Gothic and
Egyptian sculpture; Far-Eastern art;
contemporary painting and sculpture -
library; phototheque

12098
Musée de la Cathédrale
2, Place de la Cathédrale, CH-1005
Lausanne
Religious Art Museum - 1976
Archeology; sculpture; church
windows and furniture; religious
objects

12099
**Musée de la pipe et des objects du
tabac**
7, rue de l'Academie, CH-1005
Lausanne
History/Public Affairs Museum - 1979
Historical pipes and related utensils;
pipes from Africa and Asia; wooden
sculpture; ceramics; porcelain

12100
Musée des arts décoratifs
4, av Villamont, CH-1005 Lausanne
Decorative Arts Museum - 1862
Arts and crafts

12101
Musée géologique
Palais de Rumine, CH-1005 Lausanne
Natural History Museum - 1818
Regional geology; paleontology;
mineralogy

12102
**Musée historique de l'Ancien-
Evêché**
2, Place de la Cathédrale, CH-1005
Lausanne
General Museum - 1898
Local history; archeological finds from
the Roman period and the Middle
Ages; history of the bishopric;
interiors (17th-19th c.); tin; silver;
furniture; wood carving; paintings and
drawings; plans relating to town
development - library

12103
Musée zoologique cantonal
Place de la Riponne, CH-1005
Lausanne
Natural History Museum - 1933
Zoology; extinct birds; local fauna;
Swiss vertebrates; entomology

Lauterbrunnen

12104
Alpines Freiballonmuseum
Internationale Spelterini-Gesellschaft
Altes Schulhaus, CH-3822
Lauterbrunnen
Science/Tech Museum - 1976
Balloons and balloon baskets; pictures,
reports, medals and documents
relating to ballooning sports

Le Grand-Saint-Bernard

12105
Musée de l'Hospice
CH-1931 Le Grand-Saint-Bernard
General Museum - 1900
Local history; Roman finds, statues,
votive tablets, inscriptions; Gallic and
Roman coins; ecclesiastical gold
jewelry; pewter; pictorial documents;
local minerals and insects

Le Landeron

12106
Musée
Hôtel de Ville, CH-2525 Le Landeron
General Museum
Local history; Roman archeological
finds; pictures and photos; goldsmith
art (15th-18th c.); interiors; birds;
uniforms; arms

Le Locle

12107
Musée des beaux-arts
6, rue Marie-Anne-Calame, CH-2400
Le Locle
Fine Arts Museum - 1880
Collection of art from Neuchâtel and
Switzerland; printing press (19th c.)

12108
Musée d'histoire
Château des Monts, 65 Monts,
CH-2400 Le Locle
History/Public Affairs Museum - 1849
Local history; documents - library

12109
Musée d'horlogerie
Château des Monts, 65, Monts,
CH-2400 Le Locle
Science/Tech Museum - 1959
Chronometry from its early beginnings
to the present; M. and E.M. Sandoz
collection - library

Lenzburg

12110
Historisches Museum
Schloß Lenzburg, CH-5600 Lenzburg
General Museum - 1877
Cultural history of the region; furniture;
painting; sculpture; glass painting;
arms; pewter; ceramics and tiles;
domestic utensils - library; Frank
Wedekind archives; restoration
workshop

12111
Stadt- und Seetalmuseum
Aavorstadt 20, CH-5600 Lenzburg
General Museum - 1938
Pre- and early history; town history;
crafts and industries; rural culture

Les Éplatures

12112
Musée paysan et artisanal
CH-2304 Les Éplatures
General Museum - 1971
Local history; farm and crafts;
interiors; bakehouse; furnished rooms;
smithy including tools and implements;
watchmaker's shop - library

Lichtensteig

12113
Toggenburger Museum Lichtensteig
Ch-9620 Lichtensteig
General Museum - 1896
History and cultural history of the
region, esp. arts and crafts; painted
furniture; Alpine folk art; early cotton
industry

Liestal

12114
Dichtermuseum Liestal
Rathaus, CH-4410 Liestal
History/Public Affairs Museum - 1946
Memorabilia of Georg Herwegh, Carl
Spitteler, Josef Viktor Widmann, Hugo
Marti; Theodor Opitz' collection of
autographs - Herwegh archives

12115
Kantonsmuseum Baselland
Altes Zeughaus, CH-4410 Liestal
General Museum - 1837
Coll: archeology (pre- and early
history, Middle Ages), numismatics,
arms, folklore, graphic arts; natural
history, zoology, geology,
paleontology, mineralogy,
anthropology, entomology,
petrography, shells - library; archives;
phototheque

Ligerz

12116
Rebbaumuseum am Bielersee
Hof, CH-2514 Ligerz
Agriculture Museum - 1963
Viticulture - library; index of archives
about viticulture

Ligornetto

12117
Museo Vela
CH-6853 Ligornetto
Fine Arts Museum - 1898
Works by the sculptor Vincenzo Vela
(1820-1891) and documents on his life;
contemporary Italian painting and
sculpture

Locarno

12118
Museo civico
Castello, CH-6600 Locarno
General Museum - 1875
Archeology; paleontology; mineralogy;
zoology; regional history

12119
Museo d'arte contemporanea
Castello, CH-6600 Locarno
Fine Arts Museum - 1965
20th century painting and graphic arts
(Arp, Jacometti)

Loco

12120
Museo onsernonese
CH-6611 Loco
General Museum - 1966
Regional history; furniture; costumes;
industries; religious art; works of the
painter Carlo Meletta

Lottigna

12121
Museo di Blenio
Casa dei landfogti, CH-6711 Lottigna
General Museum - 1950
Regional history; agriculture;
viticulture; forestry; folklore; arms
(15th c. to present)

Lucens

12122
Fondation Conan Doyle
Château de Lucens, CH-1522 Lucens
Historic Site - 1966
Memorabilia of Arthur Conan Doyle
and his son, reconstruction of the
'working room of the detective
Sherlock Holmes'

Lugano

12123
Museo cantonale di storia naturale
Viale Cattaneo 4, CH-6900 Lugano
Natural History Museum - 1854
Minerals; geology; fossils; regional
flora and fauna - library

12124
Museo civico di belle arti
Villa Ciani, CH-6900 Lugano
Fine Arts Museum - 1903
Regional painting and sculpture
(17th-20th c.); European painting
(16th-20th c.); graphic arts

12125
Museo di Santa Maria degli Angioli
Chiesa Santa Maria degli Angioli,
CH-6900 Lugano
Religious Art Museum - 1974
Religious art

Lutry

12126
Salle Gustave Doret
Château, CH-1095 Lutry
Historic Site - 1972
Memorabilia of the composer Gustave
Doret (1866-1943), his furniture and
piano, portraits, manuscripts -
archives

Lützelflüh

12127
Gotthelfstube
CH-3432 Lützelflüh
Historic Site - 1954
Memorabilia of Jeremias Gotthelf
(1797-1854), pictures and documents
concerning the poet; furniture and
peasants' implements - archives

Luzern

12128
Gletschergartenmuseum
Denkmalstr. 4, CH-6000 Luzern
Natural History Museum - 1873
Glacier mill from the Ice Age; models
of Swiss and other mountain ranges;
town views; finds from the cave
'Steiglfadbalm'; minerals; fossils;
personal possessions of the founder
of the museum Amrein-Troller - library

12129
Handharmonikamuseum Utenberg
Landhaus Utenberg, CH-6000 Luzern
Music Museum - 1975
European accordions

12130
Historisches Museum
Rathaus, CH-6000 Luzern
History/Public Affairs Museum - 1875
Pre- and early history; costumes and
textiles; glass painting (15th-17th c.);
coins and arms

12131
Kunstmuseum Luzern
Robert Zünd-Str. 1, CH-6005 Luzern
Fine Arts Museum - 1933
Swiss art (15th-20th c.); European art
(20th c.), German expressionists; some
pieces of current international art -
library

12132
Natur-Museum Luzern
Kasernenplatz 6, CH-6003 Luzern
Natural History Museum - 1825
Geology; paleontology; mineralogy;
botany; zoology; prehistorical regional
finds; marine-limnological collection
'Documenta Maritima Heberlein' -
library; phototheque

12133
Picasso-Sammlung
Am Rhyn-Haus, Furrengasse, CH-6004
Luzern
Fine Arts Museum - 1978
Works by Pablo Picasso (1881-1973),
paintings, drawings, graphic art;
sculpture 'Femme au chapeau' (1963)

12134
Richard Wagner-Museum Städtische
Sammlung alter Musikinstrumente
Tribschen, CH-6000 Luzern
Music Museum - 1933
Memorabilia of the composer Richard
Wagner (1813-1883); European and
non-European musical instruments

12135
**Schweizerisches Trachten- und
Heimatmuseum**
Utenberg, CH-6006 Luzern
General Museum - 1950
Costumes; room of the Swiss
Yodelers' Associatcion; seals; antique
peasant furniture; connected with the
European accordion museum

12136
Verkehrshaus der Schweiz Hans
Erni-Museum
Lidostr. 5, CH-6006 Luzern
Science/Tech Museum - 1959
Aviation and space technology;
modern railway; navigation; post and
telecommunications; tourism; Hans
Erni-Haus - library; restoration
workshop; planetarium

Marthalen

12137
Orts- und Wohnmuseum
Hirschenplatz, CH-8460 Marthalen
Agriculture Museum - 1978
Peasant tools and implements;
domestic utensils and furnished farm
house; viticulture; village blacksmith;
firefighting instruments

Martigny

12138
Musée gallo-romain d'Octodure
rue du Forum, CH-1920 Martigny
Archeology Museum - 1978
Roman finds; finds from Octodorus
Forum Claudii Vallensium; coins;
historical development of Martigny as
a Roman point of support on the
Great-Saint-Bernhard road; furnishing
and interiors

Matzendorf

12139
Keramiksammlung
CH-4713 Matzendorf
Decorative Arts Museum - 1968
Ceramics from Matzendorf and
Ädermannsdorf; ceramics by Urs
Studer (1787-1846)

Maur

12140
Herrlibergersammlung
Burgstr. 8, CH-8124 Maur
General Museum - 1974
Works of engraver and publisher
David Herrliberger (1697-1777); local
history; religious objects; stove
ceramics

Meilen

12141
Ortsmuseum
Kirchgasse 14, CH-8706 Meilen
General Museum - 1927
Regional history; prehistory; farm
implements; cellarman's shop;
interiors; graphic arts

Mellingen

12142
Sammlung Alt-Mellingen im Zeitturm
CH-5507 Mellingen
General Museum - 1954
Regional history; lamps - archives

Meride

12143
Museo dei fossili
CH-6866 Meride
Natural History Museum - 1973
Fossils; Triassic original finds,
reproductions and pictures of
saurians, fishes and molluscs - library

Monthey

12144
Musée du Vieux-Monthey
Nouveau Château, CH-1870 Monthey
General Museum - 1939
Local history; interiors; pictures and
documents on village history; crafts
and industries

Montreux

12145
Musée du Vieux- Montreux
40, rue de la Gare, CH-1820 Montreux
General Museum - 1873
Local history; domestic utensils;
viticulture and dairy; crafts; military
objects and items of the local
riflemen's association

Morges

12146
Musée Alexis Forel
54, Grand-Rue, CH-1110 Morges
Decorative Arts Museum - 1948
Applied art; wood carving (16th-19th
c.); complete works of the engraver
Alexis Forel (1852-1922), engravings
by Dürer and Rembrandt; interiors
(15th-19th c.); glass; porcelain; toys

12147
Musée militaire Vaudois
Le Château, CH-1110 Morges
History/Public Affairs Museum - 1932
Arms (15th-20th c.); uniforms; banners;
documents; tin solders

Môtiers

12148
Musée Jean-Jacques Rousseau
CH-2112 Môtiers
Historic Site - 1969
Works and life of Jean-Jacques
Rousseau (1712-1778); iconographic
documents; rooms where Rousseau
lived during his exile 1762-1765

12149
**Musée régional d'Histoire et
d'Artisanat du Val-de-Travers**
Grand-Rue, CH-2112 Môtiers
General Museum - 1859
Local history; arts and crafts;
documents - library

Moudon

12150
Musée du Vieux-Moudon
Château de Rochefort, CH-1510
Moudon
General Museum - 1910
Regional history; pre- and early
history; interiors (16th-19th c.); arms
and military documents; tools and
implements from ancient handicrafts;
farm implements; wooden models for
hand-printed textiles

12151
Musée Eugène Burnand
Au Bourg, CH-1510 Moudon
General Museum - 1960
Works by Eugène Burnand
(1850-1921); ethnology; ceramics;
decorations; arms; painting, drawing
and engravings by local artists

Moutier

12152
Musée jurassien des Beaux-Arts
9, rue de l'Hôtel-de-Ville, CH-2740
Moutier
Fine Arts Museum - 1958
Painting by Swiss and foreign artists

Muhen

12153
Strohhaus
Hardstraße, CH-5037 Muhen
Agriculture Museum - 1963
Interior of an Aargau farm house with
thatched roof; peasant life and
agricultural implements; dairy; forestry;
rural industries

Münster

12154
Museum
Pfarrhaus, CH-3985 Münster
Religious Art Museum - 1969
Treasury of the church; sculptures;
painting (12th-19th c.); historical
documents on the parish and on
popular religious beliefs

Muri

12155
Klostermuseum
Klosterkirche, CH-5630 Muri
Religious Art Museum - 1972
Church treasury (17th-19th c.); glass
painting (16th c.)

Murten

12156
Historisches Museum Murten
CH-3280 Murten
General Museum - 1978
Prehistory; folk art; iconography;
numismatics; arms; coats of arms;
documents on the Burgundian wars

Müstair

12157
Klostermuseum
CH-7531 Müstair
Religious Art Museum - 1938
Carolingian marble fragments;
reproductions of Carolingian frescoes;
sculptures; furnishings (16th-17th c.)

Muttenz

12158
Ortsmuseum
Schulstraße, CH-4132 Muttenz
General Museum - 1972
Estate of the painter Karl Jauslin
(1842-1904), his oil paintings, drawings,
graphic art, manuscripts; pre- and
early history; archeological finds;
geology; local history; tools and
implements ; agriculture; crafts -
library

Näfels

12159
Museum des Landes Glarus
Freulerpalast, CH-8752 Näfels
General Museum - 1946
Cultural history of canton Glarus;
archeological finds; uniforms and
arms; banners; documents on colonel
Caspar Freuler (17th c.) and on local
personalities in arts and science;
antiquities; pictures; textile printing
industry (18th-20th c.)

Neftenbach

12160
Orts- und Weinbaumuseum
Stadt- und Dorftrotte, CH-8413
Neftenbach
General Museum - 1971
Local history; interiors; domestic
utensils; agricultural tools and
implements; vestments; viticulture and
wine press; firefighting instruments

Neuchâtel

12161
Musée cantonal d'Archéologie
7, av Du Peyrou, CH-2000 Neuchâtel
Archeology Museum - 1952
Prehistoric finds; classical, Gallo-
Roman and Merovingian archeology;
finds from Mycene (1814); Neolithic
collection

12162
Musée d'Art et d'Histoire
Quai Léopold-Robert, CH-2001
Neuchâtel
General Museum - 1835
Art and history of canton Neuchâtel;
clock making and automats by Jaquet-
Droz; coins; ceramics; porcelain;
glass; gold ornaments; arms from the
Napoleonic period; documents and
pictures concerning regional history;
painting, drawing, engravings and
sculpture by Swiss artists; French
impressionist painting - library

12163
Musée d'Histoire naturelle
14, Terraux-Nord, CH-2000 Neuchâtel
Natural History Museum - 1835
Zoology; mammals; birds; geology;
minerals

Nürensdorf

12164
Ortsmuseum
Post, CH-8303 Nürensdorf
General Museum - 1976
Local history; agricultural implements;
antiquities; pictures; relics from the
former brewery at Nürensdorf

Nyon

12165
Maison du Léman
8, quai Louis Bonnard, CH-1260 Nyon
General Museum - 1954
Documents on lake Léman; navigation
and fishing; archeology; local flora and
fauna

12166
Musée historique et des Porcelaines
Château, CH-1260 Nyon
General Museum - 1869
Regional history; prehistory; furnishing
and interiors (17th-18th c.); porcelain
and faience manufactored in Nyon
(1781-1831)

12167
Musée romain
rue Maupertuis, CH-1260 Nyon
Archeology Museum - 1979
Roman finds; finds from Colonia Julia
Equestris; architecture; painting;
ceramics; mosaic pictures;
inscriptions; glass; coins; iron and
bronze; relics of 1st century basilica

Oberhofen am Thunersee

12168
Schloßmuseum
CH-3653 Oberhofen am Thunersee
Decorative Arts Museum - 1954
Interiors from the Middle Ages to the
19th century

Oberriet

12169
Gemeindemuseum Rothus
Eichenwies, CH-9463 Oberriet
General Museum - 1975
Local history; agricultural implements;
crafts; interiors; religious folk art;
blacksmith's shop and models of
buildings - library ; phototheque

Oberweningen

12170
Heimatmuseum
Speicher, CH-8165 Oberweningen
General Museum - 1936
Regional history; costumes from
Wehntal; peasant furnishings; religious
antiquities; tools and implements for
viticulture, agriculture and forestry;
crafts; weights and measures

Olivone

12171
Museo di San Martino
Piazzale della Chiesa, CH-6718
Olivone
General Museum - 1965
Regional history; furniture; folklore;
religious art

Olten

12172
Historisches Museum Olten
Konradstr. 7, CH-4600 Olten
History/Public Affairs Museum - 1901
Pre- and early history; ceramics; arms
and uniforms; glass painting; tin;
clocks; local industries; documents on
town history

12173
Kunstmuseum
Kirchgasse 8, CH-4600 Olten
Fine Arts Museum - 1846
Works by Martin Disteli (1802-1844)
and his pupils; documents on Disteli's
life; Swiss painting (19th-20th c.);
sculpture; graphic art esp. from
Solothurn, works by Altert Welti -
library

12174
Naturhistorisches Museum Olten
Kirchgasse 10, CH-4600 Olten
Natural History Museum - 1872
Swiss fauna; mineralogy; geology;
paleontology

Orbe

12175
Pro Urba Musée du Vieil Orbe et
Mosaïques romaines d'Urba
CH-1350 Orbe
General Museum - 1921
Regional history; furnishings and
interiors; local fauna

Oron-le-Châtel

12176
Château d'Oron
CH-1699 Oron-le-Châtel
History/Public Affairs Museum
Medieval castle with furnishings
(17th-18th c.); vessels; paintings and
graphic art; arms - library

Payerne

12177
Musée
Place du Tribunal, CH-1530 Payerne
General Museum - 1869
Religious art; archeological finds;
glasses; coins; capitals; paintings by
Aimée Rapin (1868-1956); memorabilia
of the general A.-H. Jomini (1779-1869)

Pfäffikon

12178
Ortsmuseum
Kehrstraße, CH-8330 Pfäffikon
General Museum - 1876
Local history; archeological finds;
agricultural implements - library

Porrentruy

12179
**Exposition de la Bibliothèque de
l'Ecole cantonale**
10, rue des Annonciades, CH-2900
Porrentruy
History/Public Affairs Museum
Exhibition of the library's most
beautiful books (9th-18th c.)

12180
Musée
5, Grand-Rue, CH-2900 Porrentruy
General Museum - 1949
Local history; pharmaceutics; posters;
books and journals; manuscripts;
engravings; works by local writers -
library

Pregny

12181
Musée des Suisses à l'étranger
Château de Penthes, 18, Chemin de
l'Imperatrice, CH-1292 Pregny
History/Public Affairs Museum - 1961
Swiss military and political history in
foreign countries; memorabilia esp.
from France (15th-19th c.); documents;
medals; silver decorations;
engravings; portraits; furniture;
uniforms; arms; banners

Pully

12182
Musée
2, chemin Davel, CH-1009 Pully
General Museum - 1946
Contemporary painting; memorabilia of
local artists, writers and philosophers ;
local history and town views

Rafz

12183
Ortsmuseum
Dorfstr. 412, CH-8197 Rafz
General Museum - 1966
Local history; agricultural implements;
interiors; cooper's shop, wine press
and distillery

Rancate

12184
Pinacoteca cantonale Giovanni Züst
CH-6862 Rancate
Fine Arts Museum - 1967
Painting; graphic arts; Tessin artists
(19th-20th c.)

Rapperswil

12185
Heimatmuseum Rapperswil
Am Herrenberg, CH-8640 Rapperswil
General Museum - 1942
Early history (pile worker, Roman,
Allemannic); arts and crafts; religious
art; paintings and portraits; arms;
interiors; Gothic hall with mural
paintings

12186
Polenmuseum Rapperswil
Schloß Rapperswil, Postfach 270,
CH-8640 Rapperswil
History/Public Affairs Museum -
1870/1935
History and cultural history of Poland;
folklore; Wincenty Lesseur collection
of miniatures - library

Regensdorf

12187
Gemeindemuseum
Mühlestr. 20, CH-8105 Regensdorf
General Museum - 1977
Regional history; peasant life; village
history

Reigoldswil

12188
Historische Ortssammlung
Stückben 27, CH-4418 Reigoldswil
History/Public Affairs Museum - 1926
Pre- and early history; local and
regional history

Reinach

12189
Heimat-Museum Reinach
CH-4153 Reinach
General Museum - 1961
Pre- and early history; local and
regional history; porcelain and
earthenware; religious traditions;
handicrafts; agriculture; hunting and
forestry; arms

Rheinfelden

12190
Fricktaler Museum
Haus zur Sonne, Marktgasse 12,
CH-4310 Rheinfelden
General Museum - 1934
Pre- and early history; town history;
crafts; industries; navigation; fishing;
religious art; furniture; works of the
painter Jakob Strasser - library;
phototheque

12191
Oldtimer Museum
Baslerstr. 17, CH-4310 Rheinfelden
Science/Tech Museum - 1978
European and American cars and
racing cars; bicycles and motorcycles

Richterswil

12192
Heimatkundliche Sammlung
Langacher 39, CH-8805 Richterswil
History/Public Affairs Museum - 1939
Local history

Rickenbach

12193
Hannseli Spycher
Alte Dorfstraße, CH-8545 Rickenbach
General Museum - 1967
Local and regional history; agricultural
implements; handicrafts; peasants'
furniture (17th-19th c.)

Riehen

12194
Rebkeller
Wettsteinhaus, Baselstr. 34, CH-4125
Riehen
Agriculture Museum - 1972
Viticulture

12195
Spielzeug- und Dorfmuseum
Baselstr. 34, CH-4125 Riehen
General Museum
Toys from various contries (mainly
European); arts and crafts; peasants'
life

Riggisberg

12196
Abegg-Stiftung Bern
CH-3132 Riggisberg
Decorative Arts Museum - 1961
Applied art (8th c. B.C.-8th c. A.D.);
textiles - library; restoration workshop

Roggwil

12197
Ortsmuseum
Sekundarschulstraße, CH-4914
Roggwil
General Museum - 1970
Local history; agricultural implements

Rorschach

12198
Heimatmuseum
Kornhaus am Hafen, Postfach,
CH-9400 Rorschach
General Museum - 1925
Early history; reconstructed cottages
from Neolithic and Bronze Ages with
inventories; interiors (15th-18th c.);
history of embroidery since 1830;
geography; natural history

Rothrist

12199
Heimatmuseum
Lässerhaus, CH-4852 Rothrist
General Museum - 1967
Local history; fossils; furniture;
agricultural and craftmen's tools

Rougemont

12200
Collection minéralogique
Collège, CH-1838 Rougemont
Natural History Museum - 1975
Minerals and fossils from Switzerland
and France

Rüeggisberg

12201
Klostermuseum Rüeggisberg
Pfarramt Rüeggisberg, CH-3088
Rüeggisberg
Fine Arts Museum - 1947
Romanic sculpture (12th c.)

Rüschlikon

12202
Ortsmuseum Rüschlikon
mail c/o Kommission Ortsmuseum,
Gemeindeverwaltung, CH-8803
Rüschlikon
General Museum
(Temporarily closed for restoration)

Sachseln

12203
Ausstellung Heinrich Federer
Museum Bruder Klaus, CH-6072
Sachseln
History/Public Affairs Museum - 1978
Memorabilia of the writer Heinrich
Federer (1866-1928)

12204
Museum Bruder Klaus
CH-6072 Sachseln
Religious Art Museum - 1976
Documents on the hermit Nikolaus
von der Flüe (1417-1487)

Sainte-Croix

12205
Musée industriel
10, av des Alpes, CH-1450 Sainte-
Croix
Science/Tech Museum - 1872
Local industries from the 18th century
to the present; mineralogy;
paleontology; paintings

Saint-Maurice

12206
Musée militaire du Valais
Château, CH-1890 Saint-Maurice
History/Public Affairs Museum - 1974
Uniforms; arms; various military items

12207
Trésor de l'Abbaye
CH-1890 Saint-Maurice
Religious Art Museum
Religious gold- and silversmith art
from the Merovingian period to the
present

Samedan

12208
Plantahaus/Chesa Planta
CH-7503 Samedan
Historic Site - 1946
Patrician house (16th c.) with Engadin
interior; memorabilia of the Planta
family; costumes; arms

San Vittore

12209
Museo Moesano
Palazzo Viscardi, CH-6534 San Vittore
General Museum - 1949
Local history; peasants' implements;
religious art

St. Gallen

12210
Historisches Museum
Museumstr. 50, CH-9000 St. Gallen
History/Public Affairs Museum - 1877
Prehistory; history; ethnology - library
12211
Industrie- und Gewerbemuseum
Vadianstr. 2, CH-9000 St. Gallen
Decorative Arts Museum - 1878
History of lace industry since the
Renaissance; popular and religious
embroidery; textiles
12212
Kunstmuseum St. Gallen
Museumstr. 50, CH-9000 St. Gallen
Fine Arts Museum
Painting (19th-20th c.); graphic art
(16th-20thc.); sculpture
12213
Völkerkundliche Sammlung
Museumstr. 50, CH-9000 St. Gallen
Anthropology Museum - 1877
Ethnography of non-European
countries

St. Moritz

12214
Engadiner Museum
Badstraße, CH-7500 St. Moritz
General Museum - 1905
Pre- and early history; Engadin
interiors (16th-19th c.); domestic
utensils; costumes; natural history;
flora of the Alps
12215
Segantini-Museum
CH-7500 St. Moritz
Fine Arts Museum - 1908
Oil paintings, sketches and drawings
by S. Segantini (1858-1899)

Sargans

12216
Historicum
Zürcherstr. 5, CH-7320 Sargans
Science/Tech Museum - 1940
Motorcars from 1910-1930; bicycles
and motorcycles
12217
Schloß Sargans
CH-7320 Sargans
General Museum - 1966
Local ans regional history; arms;
hunting; furniture; paintings; history of
mining

Saxon

12218
Musée du Vieux-Saxon
Rue du Collège, CH-1907 Saxon
General Museum - 1963
Local history; peasants' furniture;
handicrafts; arms; local fauna

Schaffhausen

12219
Museum Stemmler
Sporrengasse 7, CH-8200
Schaffhausen
Natural History Museum - 1962
Ornithology; mammals
12220
Museum zu Allerheiligen
CH-8200 Schaffhausen
General Museum - 1921
Pre- and early history; history from the
Roman period to the 19th century; art
(15th-20th c.)
12221
Waffenkammer im Munot-Turm
Postfach 22, CH-8203 Schaffhausen
History/Public Affairs Museum - 1906
Arms and weapons from the 15th to
17th century

Schleitheim

12222
Gipsmuseum Oberwiesen
Ch-8226 Schleitheim
History/Public Affairs Museum - 1937
Plaster production and manufacturing;
pictures and documents; plaster mill
(18th c.)

Schönenwerd

12223
Museumsstiftung Bally-Prior
Oltnerstr. 80, CH-5012 Schönenwerd
General Museum - 1910
Minerals and meteorites; pre- and
early history; paleontology; zoology;
precious stones
12224
Schuhmuseum
Gösgerstr. 15, Haus zum Felsgarten,
CH-5012 Schönenwerd
History/Public Affairs Museum - 1895
Shoes from various countries and
cultures; shoemaking

Schötz

12225
Museum zur Ronmühle
Ronmühle, Postfach, CH-6247 Schötz
General Museum - 1950
Peasant furnishings and implements;
folklore; arms and uniforms; furnished
classroom (19th c.)
12226
Sammlung Bossardt
Burghalde, CH-6247 Schötz
Archeology Museum - 1959
Finds from the Stone Age
12227
Wiggertaler Museum
CH-6247 Schötz
General Museum - 1937
Prehistoric and Roman finds; arms
(1780-1911); folklore - workshop

Schwyz

12228
Bundesbriefarchiv
CH-6430 Schwyz
History/Public Affairs Museum - 1936
Documents of the ancient
confederacies; banners
12229
Turm-Museum Schwyz
Archivgasse, CH-6430 Schwyz
General Museum - 1948
Geology; early history; local history;
folklore; religious art

Scuol

12230
Unterengadiner Museum
Plaz 66, CH-7550 Scuol
General Museum - 1954
Furnishings and domestic utensils;
agricultural implements; folklore;
prehistory; local history; local flora and
fauna

Semione

12231
Collezione di minerali e fossili
Casa San Carlo, CH-6714 Semione
Natural History Museum - 1972
Minerals and fossils from the region

Sempach

12232
Rathausmuseum
Rathaus, CH-6204 Sempach
General Museum - 1971
Pre- and early history; regional history;
agricultural and craftmen's implements

Siebnen

12233
March-Museum Rempen
Ringstr. 3, CH-8854 Siebnen
General Museum - 1977
Pre- and early history; regional history;
religious art; domestic and agricultural
implements; furniture; masks and
carnival utensils - library; archives

Sierre

12234
Rilkezimmer
Hôtel CHâteau-Bellevue, CH-3960
Sierre
Historic Site - 1967
Letters and manuscripts by Rainer
Maria Rilke (1875-1926)
12235
Zinnsammlung
Hôtel Château-Bellevue, CH-3960
Sierre
Decorative Arts Museum - 1971
Tin collection (17th-19th c.)

Sion

12236
Musée archéologique du Valais
12, place de la Majorie, CH-1950 Sion
Archeology Museum - 1976
Archeological finds from Wallis;
sculptures, glass and ceramics from
the Mediterranean area
12237
Musée cantonal de Valère
CH-1950 Sion
General Museum - 1829
Pre- and early history; religious art;
furniture; goldsmith art; arms and
uniforms; folklore - library

12238
Musée cantonal des Beaux-Arts
19, place de la Majorie, CH-1950 Sion
Fine Arts Museum - 1947
Painting and graphic arts - library
12239
Musée cantonal d'Histoire Naturelle
40, av de la Gare, CH-1950 Sion
Natural History Museum - 1830
Geology; mineralogy; zoology; botany

Solothurn

12240
Altes Zeughaus Waffen- und
Uniformenmuseum
Zeughausplatz 1, CH-4500 Solothurn
History/Public Affairs Museum - 19th
century
Arms and armor; uniforms; cannons
12241
Domschatz
St.-Ursen-Kathedrale, CH-4500
Solothurn
Religious Art Museum - 1932
Religious arts and crafts; textiles
(15th-19th c.); Papal coins and medals
12242
Kościuszko-Museum
Gurzelngasse 12, CH-5400 Solothurn
Historic Site - 1936
Memorial to the general Tadeusz
Kościuszko (1746-1817)
12243
Kunstmuseum
Werkhofstr. 30, CH-3400 Solothurn
Fine Arts Museum
Art objects by Holbein the younger,
Amiet, Hodler; Swiss painting (20th c.)
12244
Lapidarium
Hauptgasse 60, CH-4500 Solothurn
Archeology Museum - 1954
Roman stone inscriptions
12245
Museum Schloß Blumenstein
Historisches Museum
Blumensteinweg 12, CH-4500
Solothurn
History/Public Affairs Museum - 1952
Little castle in Renaissance style with
18th century interiors; pre- and early
history; local history
12246
Naturmuseum Solothurn
Klosterplatz 2, CH-4500 Solothurn
Natural History Museum - 1902
Regional animals, minerals and fossils;
mammals and insects from around the
world

Spiez

12247
Schloß
Schloßstr, CH-3700 Spiez
History/Public Affairs Museum - 1929
History of the castle since the 15th
century; furnishings and interiors
(13th-18th c.)

Stadel

12248
Schloß Mörsburg
CH-8543 Stadel
History/Public Affairs Museum - 1902
Cultural history of Winterthur and the
environs

Stampa

12249
Ciäsa Granda
CH-7649 Stampa
General Museum - 1953
Archeology; mineralogy; regional
history; domestic utensils; agricultural
implements

12250
Palazzo Castelmur
CH-7649 Stampa
History/Public Affairs Museum
Completely furnished patrician house
(1723); interior in the style of Louis
Philippe's and Napoléon III's times;
local furniture and crafts

Stans

12251
Historisches Museum
Stansstader Straße, CH-6370 Stans
History/Public Affairs Museum - 1872
Pre- and early history; arms and
uniforms; costumes; local history;
religious art and art history;
ethnography

12252
**Naturwissenschaftliche Sammlung
des Kollegiums St. Fidelis**
Kollegium St. Fidelis, CH-6370 Stans
Natural History Museum
Fauna; minerals

Steckborn

12253
Bernina Nähmaschinen-Museum
Fritz Gegauf AG, Bernina
Nähmaschinen
CH-8266 Steckborn
Science/Tech Museum - 1961
Historic sewing machines (1800-
present)

12254
Heimatmuseum
Im Turmhof, CH-8266 Steckborn
General Museum - 1934
Prehistory; Alemanic grave finds;
Steckborn crafts esp. stove
construction and tin vessels; religious
objects; works of local artists

Stein am Rhein

12255
Klostermuseum St. Georgen
CH-8260 Stein am Rhein
Religious Art Museum
Benedictine monastery (11th c.) with
interior (15th-16th c.); wooden
sculpture

12256
Rathaussammlung
Rathaus, CH-8260 Stein am Rhein
General Museum - 1894
Arms; stained glass windows (16th c.);
vessels; silver; porcelain; carved
wooden chests; historic banners

Sursee

12257
Kapuzinerkloster
CH-6210 Sursee
Religious Art Museum - 1960
Sacral arts and crafts (15th-19th c.);
history of Capuchin and Franciscan
friar orders; documents on St. Francis
of Assisi

12258
Kirchenschatz Pfarrkirche St. Georg
Sursee
mail c/o Katholische
Kirchengemeinde, CH-6210 Sursee
Religious Art Museum
Ecclesiastical implements (17th-18th
c.); sacral objects esp. with motifs of
St. George

12259
Stadtmuseum Sursee
St. Urbanhof, CH-6210 Sursee
General Museum
Prehistory; other divisions temporarily
closed

Tarasp

12260
Schloß Tarasp
CH-7553 Tarasp
History/Public Affairs Museum
Furnishings and glass painting (esp.
16th-17th c.); sculpture; Swiss arms

Thun

12261
Historisches Museum
Schloß, CH-3600 Thun
General Museum - 1888
Tapestries (14th-15th c.); rural
ceramics from canton Bern; Swiss
military arms and uniforms; toys;
folklore

12262
Kunstsammlung der Stadt Thun
Thunerhof, CH-3600 Thun
Fine Arts Museum - 1948
Swiss and international 20th century
art; ancient graphic arts

Travers

12263
Musée Banderette
CH-2105 Travers
Natural History Museum - 1960
Natural history; local flora; birds and
insects; prehistoric finds; fossils;
minerals; local history

Trun

12264
Museum Sursilvan
CH-7166 Trun
General Museum - 1934
History; folklore; furnishings

Twann

12265
Pfahlbausammlung
Hauptstr. 120, CH-2513 Twann
Archeology Museum - 1976
Finds from pile-work settlements

Unterstammheim

12266
Heimatmuseum Stammertal
Gemeindehaus, CH-8476
Unterstammheim
General Museum - 1961
Rural furnishings and domestic
utensils; local handicrafts; agriculture;
viticulture; firefighting; toys - library

Unterwasser

12267
Sennerei-Museum
Dorfstraße, CH-9657 Unterwasser
Agriculture Museum - 1978
Alpine dairy

Urnäsch

12268
Museum für Appenzeller Brauchtum
Dorfplatz, CH-9107 Urnäsch
General Museum - 1972
Alpine dairy; folklore; crafts;
furnishings; local history - library;
archive; phototeque

Utzenstorf

12269
Kornhausmuseum
Schloß Landshut, CH-3427 Utzenstorf
General Museum - 1967
Local history; agricultural tools and
implements; domestic utensils;
peasant room with paintings (18th c.);
weaving and spinning

12270
Schloß Landshut
CH-3427 Utzenstorf
Historic Site - 1958
Furnishings and interiors (17th c.)

12271
**Schweizerisches Museum für Jagd
und Wildschutz Schloß Landshut**
Naturhistorisches Museum Bern
CH-3427 Utzenstorf
History/Public Affairs Museum
History of hunting; natural history

Valangin

12272
Château et Musée de Valangin
CH-2042 Valangin
General Museum - 1894
Historic furniture; arms; vessels; arts
and crafts

Vevey

12273
Collection d'Histoire Naturelle
2, av de la Gare, CH-1800 Vevey
Natural History Museum
Mineralogy; paleontology; zoology

12274
Musée d'appareils photographiques
5, Grande Place, CH-1800 Vevey
Science/Tech Museum - 1979
Photograhic apparatuses and
instruments

12275
**Musée de la Contrérie des
vignerons**
Château, 43, rue d'Italie, CH-1800
Vevey
Agriculture Museum
Viticulture since 1897; wine growers'
festivals

12276
Musée du Vieux-Vevey
Château, 43, rue d'Italy, CH-1800
Vevey
General Museum - 1897
Pre- and early history; local history;
furniture; arts and crafts; arms

12277
Musée Jenisch
2, av de la Gare, CH-1800 Vevey
Fine Arts Museum - 1897
Swiss painting and sculpture
(19th-20th c.); graphic arts (16th-20th
c.); painting by Gustave Courbet

Veytaux-Chillon

12278
Château de Chillon
CH-1820 Veytaux-Chillon
Historic Site
Decorated halls, vaults, coffered
ceilings

Wädenswil

12279
Ortsmuseum zur Hohlen Eich
Schönenbergstr. 22, CH-8820
Wädenswil
General Museum - 1941
Local history; peasant furnishings
(18th-19th c.); agricultural tools and
implements; dairy; natural history -
library; restoration workshop

Werdenberg

12280
Schloß Werdenberg
CH-9470 Werdenberg
Historic Site - 1957
13th century castle with furniture
(17th-18th c.); painting; graphic art;
arms

Wettingen

12281
Kloster Wettingen
CH-5430 Wettingen
Religious Art Museum
Cistercian monastery; glass painting
(13th-17th c.); Renaissance and
baroque interior in church;
late-Renaissance choir chancels with
engravings

Wetzikon

12282
Ortsmuseum Wetzikon
Farbstr. 1, CH-8620 Wetzikon
General Museum - 1887
Finds from pile-work settlement
Robenhausen; peasant furniture;
agricultural implements; assets of the
composer H.G. Nägeli - library

Wiesendangen

12283
Ortsmuseum Wiesendangen
CH-8542 Wiesendangen
General Museum - 1968
Local history; furniture (18th c.);
kitchen utensils; flax cultivation and
treatment, including all phases of
processing; tools and implements
used in agriculture and crafts

Wil

12284
Stadtmuseum Wil
CH-9500 Wil
General Museum - 1909
Local history; furniture; religious art;
tin; porcelain; seals; coins; arms;
stoves; oil paintings

Wildegg

12285
Schloß Wildegg Stiftung von Effinger
Wildegg
CH-5103 Wildegg
Historic Site
13th century castle with historic
interior (15th-19th c.); stoves; kitchen;
oil paintings and graphic art; arms -
library

Wildhaus

12286
Zwinglihaus
CH-9658 Wildhaus
Historic Site - 1901
Zwingli's birthplace; memorabilia of the
reformer Huldrych Zwingli (1484-1531)

Willisau

12287
Landwirtschaftsmuseum Burgrain
CH-6130 Willisau
Agriculture Museum - 1974
Architecture and interiors of rural
buildings; agricultural tools,
implements, machinery and vehicles;
peasant art of Switzerland

Winterthur

12288
Gewerbemuseum
Kirchplatz 14, CH-8400 Winterthur
Decorative Arts Museum - 1874
Art metalwork from five centuries;
ceramics; stoves; tiles; textiles

12289
Kleinmeistersammlung Jakob Briner
Marktgasse 20, CH-8400 Winterthur
Fine Arts Museum - 1970
European painters (16th-19th c.) esp.
Dutch Little Masters; European
portrait miniatures (17th-19th c.)

12290
Kunstmuseum
Museumstr. 52, CH-8400 Winterthur
Fine Arts Museum - 1848
Swiss art (16th-20th c.); European art
(since 1870); European sculpture
(18th-20th c.); graphic art - library;
phototheque

12291
Mensch und Arbeit
Arbeitsschutzausstellung der
Eidgenössischen Arbeitsinspektion
Ackerstr. 17, CH-8400 Winterthur
Science/Tech Museum - 1883
Factory construction; prevention of
accidents and occupational diseases;
firefighting

12292
Münzkabinett der Stadt
Museumstr. 52, CH-8400 Winterthur
Decorative Arts Museum
Swiss and antique coins and medals

12293
Museum Lindengut
Römerstr. 8, CH-8400 Winterthur
Decorative Arts Museum - 1874
Local arts and crafts; interiors (18th c.);
clock making; tin; ceramics; glass
painting

12294
**Naturwissenschaftliche Sammlungen
der Stadt Winterthur**
Museumstr. 52, CH-8400 Winterthur
Natural History Museum - 1660
Paleontology; mineralogy;
petrography; geology; botany;
zoology; ethnography - library;
workshop

12295
**Sammlung Oskar Reinhart 'Am
Römerholz'**
Haldenstr. 95, CH-8400 Winterthur
Fine Arts Museum - 1970
European Old Master painting and
drawing; works by French 19th
century painters and sculptors -
library

12296
Stiftung Oskar Reinhart
Steinhausstr. 6, CH-8400 Winterthur
Fine Arts Museum - 1951
German, Swiss and Austrian art esp.
German romanticism, realism, idealism
and contemporary Swiss art; graphic
arts - library

12297
Technorama Schweiz
Technoramastr. 1-3, CH-8400
Winterthur
Science/Tech Museum - 1981
Energy and energy technology;
materials and processing; textile
technology; musical instruments;
photography; chemistry; cybernetics;
construction engineering - library;
Amman-Archiv; Prof. Karolus-Archiv;
restoration workshops

12298
Uhrensammlung K. Kellenberger
Rathaus, Marktgasse 20, CH-8400
Winterthur
Science/Tech Museum - 1970

12299
**Völkerkundliche Sammlung der
Stadt**
Museumstr. 52, CH-8400 Winterthur
Anthropology Museum - 19th century
Ethnology

Wittenbach

12300
Ortsmuseum Wittenbach
CH-9303 Wittenbach
General Museum - 1964
Peasant musical instruments, furniture
and implements; folklore; documents;
tree-root carving by Wilhelm Lehmann

Wohlen

12301
Historische Gesellschaft Freiamt
CH-5610 Wohlen
Archeology Museum - 1929
Pre- and early history

Wohlenschwil

12302
Bauernmuseum
Alte Kirche, CH-5512 Wohlenschwil
Decorative Arts Museum - 1957
Peasant arts and crafts; models of
Swiss farmhouse types

Yverdon

12303
Collection d'ethnographie
Château, CH-1400 Yverdon
Anthropology Museum
0680

12304
Maison d'Ailleurs
5, rue du Four, CH-1400 Yverdon
Science/Tech Museum - 1976
Books, documents, pictures relating to
extraterrestrial journeys and science
fiction

12305
Musée d'Yverdon
Château, CH-1400 Yverdon
General Museum - 1763
Pre- and early history; regional history;
folklore; arms; natural history;
memorabilia of Johann H. Pestalozzi
(1746-1827)

Zeihen

12306
Dorfmuseum
Gemeindehaus, CH-5256 Zeihen
General Museum - 1975
Local history; geology; fossils

Zermatt

12307
Alpines Museum
CH-3920 Zermatt
General Museum - 1958
Minerals and stones; relics from the
Matterhorn catastrophe in 1865 and
history of the first ascent; interior (19th
c.) from canton Wallis - library

Zimmerwald

12308
Blasmusik-Museum
CH-3086 Zimmerwald
Music Museum - 1970
Wind instruments

Zofingen

12309
Museum
General-Guisan-Str. 18, CH-4800
Zofingen
General Museum - 1901
Pre- and early history; geology and
mineralogy; zoology; arms; coins; tin

Zollikon

12310
**Ortsgeschichtliche Sammlung
Zollikon**
Zolliker Str. 91, CH-8702 Zollikon
General Museum - 1961
Topography; pre- and early history;
regional history; viticulture; coins -
library

Zug

12311
Fischereimuseum Zug
Unteraltstadt 16, CH-6300 Zug
History/Public Affairs Museum - 1870
History of fishing and fishing
implements

12312
**Kantonales Museum für
Urgeschichte**
Aegeristr. 56, CH-6300 Zug
Archeology Museum - 1928
Regional finds

12313
Museum in der Burg Zug
Burg Zug, Hofstr. 22, CH-6300 Zug
General Museum - 1879/1982
Prehistory; painting; sculpture; graphic
arts; furniture; goldsmith work; tin;
clocks; textiles; costumes; arms;
uniforms; seals; coins - restoration
workshop

Zürich

12314
**Archäologische Sammlung der
Universität Zürich**
Rämistr. 73, CH-8006 Zürich
Archeology Museum - 1854
Egyptian, Assyrian, Greek, Etruscan
and Roman art objects; plaster casts
of antique Roman, Egyptian and Greek
originals - restoration workshop

12315
Atelier Hermann Haller
Zollikerstr. 21, CH-8000 Zürich
Fine Arts Museum - 1954
Works of sculptor Hermann Haller
(1880-1950)

12316
**Geologisch-Mineralogische
Sammlungen der Eidgenössischen
Technischen Hochschule Zürich**
Sonneggstr. 5, CH-8006 Zürich
Natural History Museum - 1855
Mineralogy; crystallography; geology;
precious stones; paleontology

12317
Graphische Sammlung
Zentralbibliothek Zürich
Zähringersplatz 6, CH-8025 Zürich
History/Public Affairs Museum - 1854
Graphic arts (15th-20th c.);
topographic sights; portraits; artistical
remains of Gottfried Keller and
Johann Rudolf Rahn; paintings and
sculpture; Erich Steinthal collection of
20th century books - library

12318
**Graphische Sammlung der
Eidgenössischen Technischen
Hochschule Zürich**
Rämistr. 101, CH-8092 Zürich
Fine Arts Museum - 1867
European graphic arts (15th-20th c.);
Greek vases (6th-5th c. BC)

12319
Indianer-Museum der Stadt
Feldstr. 89, CH-8004 Zürich
Anthropology Museum - 1962
Ethnography of North-American Indian
cultures

12320
**Keramische Sammlung des
Landesmuseums**
Zunfthaus zur Meisen, Münsterhof 20,
CH-8000 Zürich
Decorative Arts Museum - 1956
Faience and porcelain (18th c.) esp. of
Swiss manufacture

12321
Kulturama
Zentralstr. 153, CH-8003 Zürich
Natural History Museum - 1978
Development of life on earth; anatomy

12322
**Kunstgewerbemuseum der Stadt
Zürich**
Ausstellungsstr. 60, Postfach, Ch-8031
Zürich
Decorative Arts Museum - 1875
Graphic arts (16th-20th c.); illustrated
books; posters - library

12323
Kunsthaus Zürich
Heimplatz 1, CH-8001 Zürich
Fine Arts Museum - 1910
Div: painting and sculpture (antiquity to
present); graphic arts (17th-20th c.) -
library

12324
Kunstkammer zum Strauhof
Augustinergasse 9, CH-8001 Zürich
Fine Arts Museum - 1952
Contemporary Swiss art

12325
**Medizinhistorische Sammlung der
Universität Zürich**
Im Turm der Universität, Rämistr. 71,
CH-8006 Zürich
Natural History Museum - 1932
Medical instruments and documents of
two millennia, esp. relating to
ophthalmology, surgery, orthopedics,
and medicine in Switzerland - library

12326
Museum Bellerive
Höschgasse 3, CH-8008 Zürich
Decorative Arts Museum - 1968
Ancient and modern textiles from
various countries; tapestries; ceramics
and glass (Jugendstil to present);
furniture; musical instruments; puppets
(1916-1960); folk art

12327
Museum der Zeitmessung Beyer
Bahnhofstr. 31, CH-8001 Zürich
Science/Tech Museum - 1965
Chronometers since the pre-Christian
period such as non-mechanical clocks,
iron clocks, Swiss wooden wheel
clocks (1550-1750), French clocks
(17th-19th c.), pendulum clocks from
Neuenburg (1700-1850), clocks from
the Far East; navigation instruments

12328
Museum Rietberg
Gablerstr. 15, CH-8002 Zürich
Fine Arts Museum - 1952
Art and ethnographical objects from
the ancient advanced civilisations of
the Near East and America; sculpture
from South and East Asia; bBronze,
painting and ceramics from the Far
East; African and Oceanian sculpture;
Swiss masks; tapestries and carpets

12329
**Paläontologisches Museum der
Universität Zürich**
Künstlergasse 16, CH-8006 Zürich
Natural History Museum - 1956
Triassic fossils; vertebrates and
mammals from the Tertiary and Ice
Age

12330
Pestalozzimuseum
Beckenhofstr. 31-37, CH-8055 Zürich
Historic Site - 1875
Memorial for the pedagogue Heinrich
Pestalozzi (1746-1827) with pictures,
letters and manuscripts - library

12331
Puppenmuseum Sasha Morgenthaler
Bärengasse 22, CH-8001 Zürich
Decorative Arts Museum - 1977
Dolls by Sasha Morgenthaler
(1893-1975)

12332
Schweizerisches Landesmuseum
Museumstr. 2, CH-8023 Zürich
General Museum - 1890
Military science; archeology; early
Middle Ages and Roman period;
painting and sculpture; ceramics and
glass; textiles and costumes; painted
glass; toys; precious metals; clocks;
scientific instruments; folklore; coins
and medals - library; restoration
workshop

12333
Spielzeugmuseum
Bahnhofstr. 62, CH-8001 Zürich
Decorative Arts Museum - 1956
Toys from the 18th century to the
present

12334
Stiftung Sammlung E.G. Bührle
Zollikerstr. 172, CH-8008 Zürich
Fine Arts Museum - 1961
Painting (19th-20th c.) esp.
impressionism; Old Masters; medieval
sculpture

12335
**Thomas-Mann-Archiv der
Eidgenössischen Technischen
Hochschule**
Schönberggasse 15, CH-8001 Zürich
Historic Site - 1956
Literary bequest of Thomas Mann;
documents on his life and work;
interior of his working room at
Kilchberg

12336
Völkerkundemuseum der Universität
Pelikanstr. 40, CH-8039 Zürich
Anthropology Museum - 1888
Ethnography of America, Africa, Asia
and polar regions - library; archives

12337
Wohnmuseum Bärengasse
Bärengasse 20-22, CH-8001 Zürich
Decorative Arts Museum - 1976
Interiors from ancient Zurich

12338
**Zoologisches Museum der
Universität Zürich**
Künstlergasse 16, CH-8006 Zürich
Natural History Museum - 1914
Vertebrates and invertebrates from
Switzerland; birds and mammals from
around the world; skeletons of extinct
animals; molluscs

Zurzach

12339
August Deusser-Museum
Schloß, CH-8437 Zurzach
Fine Arts Museum - 1972
Works of the painter August Deusser
(1870-1942)

12340
Messe- und Bezirksmuseum
Im Höfli, Hauptstr. 77, CH-8437
Zurzach
General Museum - 1948
Pre- and early history; religious
traditions; agricultural implements;
handicraft products

Syria

Damascus

12341
National Museum of Damascus
Bd de l'Université, Damascus
Fine Arts Museum
Ancient Oriental art; Greek, Roman
and Byzantine art; prehistoric and
modern art

Homs

12342
Homs Museum
Cultural Center, Tripoli St, Homs
Archeology Museum - 1978
Prehistoric exhibits

Tanzania

Arusha

12343
Arusha Declaration Museum
Kaloleni Rd, POB 7423, Arusha
History/Public Affairs Museum - 1977
Uhuru independence torch;
photographs of furniture and utensils
used at the Arusha Declaration
Meeting (Jan. 1967)

12344
The Azimio la Arusha Museum
POB 7423, Arusha
General Museum

12345
Ngurdoto Gate Museum
mail c/o Arusha National Park, POB
3134, Arusha
Natural History Museum - 1960
Coll: elephant teeth; rhinoceros horn
and skulls; mounted mammals and
birds; lepidopteran exhibits - library

Bagamoyo

12346
Bagamoyo Historical Museum
mail c/o Bagamoyo Catholic Mission,
POB Bagamoyo, Bagamoyo
General Museum - 1963
Coll: natural history; history of slavery
and of the German colonial period

12347
Mission Museum
Bagamoyo Catholic Church, POB 16,
Bagamoyo
History/Public Affairs Museum
Relics and documents of the slave
trade

Dar es Salaam

12348
National Museum of Tanzania
Shaban Robert St, POB 511, Dar es
Salaam
Archeology Museum - 1937
Coll: anthropology; ethnography;
history; Zinjanthropus Boisei skull and
paleo-faunal material from Olduvai and
other early Stone Age sites - library

12349
Village Museum
mail c/o Ethnographic Department of
the National Museum of Tanzania,
Bagamoyo Rd/Makaburi St, POB 511,
Dar es Salaam
Open Air Museum - 1967
Coll: ethnography; folklore; traditional
Tanzanian architecture; settlement and
community layout; canoe

Dodoma

12350
**Mineral Resources Divisional
Museum**
Kikuya Av, Dodoma
Natural History Museum
Geology; rocks and minerals; fossils

Manyara

12351
Manyara Museum
Manyara National Park, Entry Gate,
Manyara, POB 3134, Arusha
Natural History Museum
Wildlife and natural history

Marangu

12352
Kibo Art Gallery
Kilimanjaro, Marangu, POB 98, Moshi
Fine Arts Museum - 1961
Coll: paintings by Elimo Njau;
sculptures by Kiasi Nikwitikie and
Samwel Wanjau; stitch and dye
pictures; African arts; anthropological
exhibits from non-African cultures

Mikumi

12353
Mikumi Museum
Mikumi National Park, Entry Gate,
Mikumi, POB 642, Morogoro
Natural History Museum
Wildlife and natural history

Mwanza

12354
The Sukuma Museum
POB 76, Mwanza

Serengeti

12355
Serengeti Museum
Headquarters of Serengeti National
Park, Seronera, Serengeti, POB 3134,
Arusha
Natural History Museum
Coll: wildlife; ornithology; illustrations
of the migration of large mammals

Tabora

12356
Livingstone and Stanley Memorial
Tabora-Kwihara, POB 247, Tabora
History/Public Affairs Museum - 1957
Slavery chains; Nyamezi spears;
Arabic weapons; memorabilia on
David Livingstone

Zanzibar

12357
Zanzibar Government Museum
Mnazi Mmoja, POB 116, Zanzibar
General Museum
Local history; items relating to
exploration in East Africa; ceramics;
Arab silverware and ornaments;
stamps; coins - library

Thailand

Bangkok

12358
**Armed Forces Survey Department
Museum**
Kalyanmaitri Rd, Bangkok
History/Public Affairs Museum

12359
Bangkok Planetarium
928 Sukhumvit Rd, Amphoe
Phrakhanong, Bangkok
Natural History Museum

12360
Benchamabophit National Museum
Amphoe Dusit, Bangkok

12361
The Bhirasri Institute of Modern Art
Soi Attakarn Prasit, South Sathorn Rd,
Bangkok
Fine Arts Museum

12362
Chumbhot-Punthip Museum
Suan Phakkad Palace, 352 Sri
Ayutthaya Rd, Phya Thai, Bangkok

12363
Congdom Anatomical Museum
Anatomical Science Department
Siriraj Hospital, Mahidol University,
Bangkok
Natural History Museum

12364
Fishery Museum
Kasetsat University, Lad Yao, Amphoe
Bangkhen, Bangkok
Natural History Museum

12365
Forensic Medicine Museum
Forensic Medicine Building, Siriraj
Hospital, Bangkok
Natural History Museum

12366
Forest Entomology Museum
Lad Yao, Amphoe Bangkhen, Bangkok
Natural History Museum

12367
Forestry Museum
Forensic Medicine Building, Siriraj
Hospital, Bangkok
Natural History Museum

12368
Fungus Herbarium The Royal
Forestry Department
Phaholyothin Road, Bangkhen,
Bangkok
Natural History Museum

12369
The Hill Tribes Museum
Commissioner's Office of the Border
Patrol Police
Phaholyothin Rd, Bangkok

12370
Kamthieng House
Skhumvit 21, Bangkapi, Bangkok

12371
Mineralogy Museum
Rama VI Rd, Amphoe Phya Thai,
Bangkok
Natural History Museum

12372
Museum of Medical Equipment
315 Rajvithi Rd, Amphoe Phya Thai,
Bangkok
Natural History Museum

12373
Museum of the Royal Thai Air Force
Phaholyothin Rd, Bangkok
Science/Tech Museum

12374
The National Museum
Na Phra Thart Rd, Amphoe Phra
Nakhon, Bangkok
General Museum - 1926
Archaeology; textiles; weapons;
ceramics; theatrical masks; books;
musical instruments

12375
Parasite Museum
Pathology Building, Siriraj Hospital,
Bangkok
Natural History Museum

12376
**Phra Chetuponwimonmangkhalaram
National Museum**
Amphoe Phra Nakhon, Bangkok

12377
Royal Barges National Museum
Amphoe Bangkoknoi, Bangkok

12378
**Sood Sangvichien Prehistoric
Museum and Laboratory**
Fakulty of Medicine, Mahidol
University, Bangkok
Archeology Museum

Battani

12379
Thrai Kao
Amphoe Khok Pho, Battani

Chiang Mai

12380
Chiang Mai National Museum
Tambon Khuangsing, Amphoe Muang,
Chiang Mai
Archeology Museum - 1971

12381
Ob Luang
Amphoe Hod, Chiang Mai

Chiang Rai

12382
Chiang Saen National Museum
Tambon Wiang, Amphoe Chiang Saen,
Chiang Rai

Chieng-Saen

12383
National Museum
Chieng-Saen, Chiengrai
Archeology Museum - 1957
Thai art and antiquities

Kamphaeng Phet

12384
Kamphaeng Phet National Museum
Tambon Nai Muang, Amphoe Muang,
Kamphaeng Phet
Archeology Museum - 1971

Kanchanaburi

12385
Ban Kao Prehistoric Museum
Tambon Ban Kao, Amphoe Muang,
Kanchanaburi
Archeology Museum

Khon Kaen

12386
Khon Kaen National Museum
Tambon Sala, Amphoe Muang, Khon
Kaen
Archeology Museum - 1967

Lampang

12387
Lanna Museum
Amphoe Muang, Lampang

12388
Phathai Cave
Amphoe Ngao, Lampang

12389
**Wat Phra Thart Lampang Luang
Museum**
Luang Amphoe Muang, Lampang

Loei

12390
Phukradung
Amphoe Phukradung, Loei

Lop Buri

12391
Somdet Phra Narai National Museum
Tambon Tahin, Amphoe Muang, Lop
Buri

Nakhon Pathom

12392
**Phra Pathom Chedi National
Museum**
Amphoe Muang, Nakhon Pathom
Archeology Museum - 1971

Nakhon Ratchasima

12393
Maha Wirawong National Museum
Wat Sutthichinda, Amphoe Muang,
Nakhon Ratchasima

Nakhon Si Thammarat

12394
Kao Luang
Amphoe Muang, Nakhon Si
Thammarat

12395
**Nakhon Si Thammarat National
Museum**
Ratdamnern Rd, Tambon Sala Michai,
Amphoe Muang, Nakhon Si
Thammarat

12396
Phra Borommathat National Museum
Ratdemnern Rd, Tambon Nai Muang,
Amphoe Muang, Nakhon Si
Thammarat

Nonthaburi

12397
**Nonthaburi Natural History Museum
and Public Library**
Tambon Suan Yai, Nonthaburi
Natural History Museum

Petchabun

12398
Nam Nao
Amphoe Lomkao, Petchabun

Petchaburi

12399
Wachiraprasat Museum
Tambon Tarab, Amphoe Muang,
Petchaburi

12400
Wat Ko Museum
Tambon Tarab, Amphoe Muang,
Petchaburi

Phachuab Khiri Khan

12401
Army Museum of Infantry Center
Amphoe Pranburi, Phachuab Khiri
Khan
History/Public Affairs Museum

12402
Sam Roi Yod
Amphoe Pranburi, Phachuab Khiri
Khan

Phitsanulok

12403
**Phra Phuttachinnarat National
Museum**
Wat Phra Sri Ratana Mahathat,
Amphoe Muang, Phitsanulok

12404
Tung Salaeng Luang
Amphoe Wang Theng, Phitsanulok

Phra Nakhon Si Ayutthaya

12405
Chantharakhasem National Museum
U-Thong Rd, Tambon Huaro, Phra
Nakhon Si Ayutthaya

12406
Chao Sam Phraya National Museum
Rochana Rd, Tambon Pratuchai, Phra
Nakhon Si Ayutthaya

Phuket

12407
Ton Trai
Amphoe Thalang, Phuket

Rayong

12408
Phe
Amphoe Klaeng, Rayong

Sakon Nakhon

12409
Phupan
Amphoe Muang, Sakon Nakhon

Samut Prakan

12410
Ancient City
Sukhumvit Rd, Bang Pu, Samut Prakan

12411
Royal Thai Navy Museum
126/1 Sukhumvit Rd, Tambon
Bangmuang, Samut Prakan
History/Public Affairs Museum

Saraburi

12412
Kao Yai
Amphoe Muak Lek, Saraburi

Sing Buri

12413
In Buri National Museum
Wat Bot, Amphoe In Buri, Sing Buri

Songkhla

12414
Matchimawas National Museum
Wat Matchimawas, Tambon Boyang,
Songkhla

Sukhothai

12415
Kao Ta Phet
Amphoe Muang, Sukhothai

12416
Ramkhamhaeng National Museum
Tambon Muang Kao, Amphoe Muang,
Sukhothai

12417
Sawanworanayok National Museum
Tambon Wang Pin Pat, Amphoe
Sawankhalok, Sukhothai

Suphan Buri

12418
U-Thong National Museum
Malaimaen, Amphoe U-Thong, Suphan
Buri

Surat Thani

12419
Chaiya National Museum
Tambon Wiang, Amphoe Chaiya, Surat
Thani

Tak

12420
Lan Sang
Amphoe Muang, Tak

Trang

12421
Kao Chong
Tambon Kachong, Trang

Uttaradit

12422
Ton Sak Yai
Amphoe Nam Pat, Uttaradit

Togo

Lomé

12423
Musée National du Togo
BP 3146, Lomé
Anthropology Museum - 1975
Ethnography; art exhibits

Trinidad and Tobago

Port-of-Spain

12424
National Museum and Art Gallery
117 Frederick St, Port-of-Spain
General Museum

12425
Royal Victoria Institute Museum
117 Frederick St, Port-of-Spain
Natural History Museum - 1892
Coll: archeology; local history; natural
history; oil refinery objects; ambard
butterflies; bats; marine life; earth's
crust; geological structure of Trinidad;
wildlife; snakes, birds and eggs; bones
and shell artifacts; aboriginal pottery;
moon dust sample

Tunisia

Carthage

12426
Musée de Carthage
2016 Carthage
Archeology Museum - 1975
Punic, Phoenician and Greek finds;
Roman antiquities; Islamic items; near
by: Tophet de Salambo, Parc
Archéologique des Thermes d'Antonin,
Parc Archéologique des Villas
Romaines de l'Odéon

El-Jem

12427
Musée Archéologique d'El-Jem
5160 El-Jem
Archeology Museum

Enfida

12428
Musée d'Enfida
4030 Enfida
General Museum
Archaeology; early Christian mosaics
and inscriptions

Ksar Hellal

12429
Musée Dar Ayed
5070 Ksar Hellal
History/Public Affairs Museum

Le Bardo

12430
Musée National du Bardo
2000 Le Bardo
Archeology Museum - 1888
Relics of Punic, Greek and Roman art;
ancient and modern Islamic art; largest
collection of Roman mosaics in the
world

Le Kef

12431
**Musée des Arts et Traditions
Populaires du Kef**
7100 Le Kef
Anthropology Museum
Ethnography; history; art

Mahdia

12432
**Musée des Arts et Traditions
Populaires de Mahdia**
5100 Mahdia
Anthropology Museum
Ethnography; history; art

Maktar

12433
Musée de Maktar
6140 Maktar
Archeology Museum
Punic and Roman antiquities;
sepulchral relics; pillars

Moknine

12434
**Musée des Arts et Traditions
Populaires de Moknine**
5050 Moknine
Anthropology Museum
Ethnography; history; art -

Monastir

12435
Musée du Ribat de Monastir
5000 Monastir
Fine Arts Museum
Middle Ages history; Islamic art

Salambô

12436
**Musée Océanographique de
Salambô**
Av du 2 Mars 1934, 2025 Salambô
Natural History Museum - 1924
Zoology; marine biology; aquarium -
library

Sfax

12437
Musée Dar Jellouli
3001 Sfax
Anthropology Museum
Ethnography; history; art

12438
Musée de Sfax
3001 Sfax
Archeology Museum
Archaeology; mosaics

Sousse

12439
Musée Archéologique de Sousse
4000 Sousse
Archeology Museum
Roman and Punic mosaics; sculptures;
ceramics

Téboursouk

12440
Musée du 18 Novembre 1939
9040 Téboursouk
History/Public Affairs Museum

Tunis

12441
Centre d'Art Vivant
1002 Tunis, Belvédère
Fine Arts Museum

12442
Musée Dar Ben Abdallah
1000 Tunis
Anthropology Museum
Ethnography; history; art

12443
Musée Dar Bourguiba
Place du Leader, 1008 Tunis, Bab
Menara
History/Public Affairs Museum

12444
**Musée des Arts et Traditions
Populaires**
1000 Tunis
Anthropology Museum
Ethnography; history; art

12445
Musée des P.T.T.
29 bis, Rue Gamel Abdel Nasser, 1000
Tunis
History/Public Affairs Museum

12446
Musée du 9 Avril 1938
La Kasbah, Tunis
History/Public Affairs Museum

12447
Musée du Mouvement National
Boulevard du 9 Avril 1939, 1006 Tunis,
Bab-Souika
History/Public Affairs Museum

Utique

12448
Musée d'Utique
7060 Utique
Archeology Museum
Punic and Roman antiquities

Turkey

Adana

12449
Regional Museum
TR Adana
General Museum - 1924
Archeology; ethnography - library;
laboratory; conference hall

Afyon

12450
Archeological Museum
TR Afyon
Archeology Museum - 1933
Finds from the Neolithic, Hitite,
Phrygian, Hellenistic, Roman and
Byzantine periods - library;
conference hall; laboratory

12451
Ethnographic Museum
Gedik Ahmed Pasha Medrese, TR
Afyon
Anthropology Museum
Weapons; embroidery; tapestries;
guilded books; copper dishes; in a
15th century medrese (Islamic
university)

Ahlat

12452
Open Air Museum
TR Ahlat, Bitlis province
Open Air Museum - 1971
Architectural works of the Seljuk
period; tombs; stone masonery;
ethnography

Akşehir

12453
Ataturk and Ethnographic Museum
TR Akşehir
Anthropology Museum - 1966
Memorabilia of the Turkish politician
Ataturk (1880-1938); ethnography

12454
Museum of Stone Masonery
Sahir-Ata Medrese, TR Akşehir
Decorative Arts Museum - 1961
Inscriptions, tombstones and building
blocks from the Roman, Byzantine,
Seljuk and Ottoman periods; in a 13th
century medrese (Islamic university)

Alacahoyuk

12455
Museum
TR Alacahoyuk, Alaca, Çorum province
Archeology Museum - 1935
Findings from the Chalcolithic, Copper
and Old Bronze Ages; Hitite, Phrygian
and Late Phrygian periods

Alagoz

12456
Ataturk's Headquarters
TR 31 Alagoz, Polatli district
Historic Site - 1968
Memorial to the Turkish politician
Ataturk (1880-1938)

Alanya

12457
Museum
TR Alanya
General Museum - 1967
Archeology; ethnography

Amasra

12458
Zonguldak-Amasra Museum
TR Amasra, Zonguldak province
General Museum - 1945
Archeology; ethnography

Amasya

12459
Museum
Gök Medrese, TR Amasya
General Museum - 1926
Archeology; weapons; ethnographic
objects from the Seljuk and Ottoman
periods; mummies

Ankara

12460
Ataturk's Mausoleum and Museum
TR Ankara
Historic Site
Memorial to the great Turkish
politician Ataturk (1880-1938) - library

12461
Ethnographic Museum
TR Ankara
Anthropology Museum - 1930
Clothing Room; Embroidery Room;
Tapestry Room; Hall of Crafts; Ankara
House; Hall of Objects from Tekkes;
Hall of Besim Atalay; Hall of Written
Works; Hall of Woodcarving - library;
archives

12462
**First Turkish Grand National
Assembly Museum**
Ulus Sq., TR Ankara
History/Public Affairs Museum - 1961
Documents and photographs
concerning the First Assembly

12463
Museum of Anatolian Civilisations
Mahmud Pasha Bazaar, TR Ankara
Archeology Museum
Exhibits from the Paleolithic, Neolithic,
Calcolithic, Old Bronze, Hitite,
Phrygian, Urartu and Assyrian Trade
Colonies periods; numismatics -
laboratory; workshop; library

12464
Old Residence (Cankaya Ataturk
Museum)
TR Ankara
Historic Site - 1950
Memorial to the great Turkish
politician Ataturk (1880-1938) - library

12465
Turkish Natural History Museum
TR Ankara
Natural History Museum - 1968
Paleontology; mineralogy; petrology;

Antakya
12466
Hatay Archeological Museum
TR Antakya, Hatay province
Archeology Museum - 1938
Mosaics from the 2nd to 5th centuries
AD; column capitals, frescoes and
statues from the Hitite to Roman
periods; grave stelae; statue
sarcophagi from the province of Hatay
- conference hall; laboratory

Antalya
12467
Art Gallery
Mevlevi dervish tekke, Yivli Minare
Mosque, TR Antalya
Fine Arts Museum - 1973
Paintings and sculpture of Turkish
artists

12468
Ethnographic Museum
Yivli Minare Mosque, TR Antalya
Anthropology Museum - 1974
Clothing; domestic utensils;
embroidery; tapestries; kilims;
ornaments

12469
Regional Museum
TR Antalya
General Museum - 1923
Natural history; archeology; history;
ethnography - conference hall

Aydin
12470
Museum
TR Aydin
General Museum - 1973
Archeology; ethnography; ruins from
the ancient city of Tralles

Balat
12471
Miletus Museum
TR Balat, Aydin province, Söke
sub-province
Archeology Museum - 1973
Finds from the excavations at Miletus;
ceramics; statues; capitals; stelae;
inscriptions

Ballihisar
12472
Pessinus Museum
TR Ballihisar, Eskisehir province
Open Air Museum
Remains of Pessinus, a Phrygian city;
ruins of the Cybele Temple

Bergama
12473
Museum
TR Bergama
Archeology Museum - 1936
Examples of architecture from the
Hellenistic, Roman, Byzantine and
Ottoman periods; findings from the
Bergama Acropolis and Aesclepion

Bodrum
12474
Museum
Bodrum Castle, TR Bodrum, Mugla
province
Archeology Museum - 1964
Exhibits from the Mycenaean
civilisation (1500-1000 B.C.);
underwater finds from the 6th century
to the 1st century B.C.; in a 15th
century castle - library; workshop

Boğazkale
12475
Bogazkoy Museum
TR Boğazkale, Sungurlu, Çorum
province
General Museum - 1966
Findings of the excavations in the
Buyukkale and Yazikaya temples in
Hattusas from the Hitite period (2000
BC); ethnography

Burdur
12476
Museum
Burgurlu Medrese, TR Burdur
General Museum - 1963
Finds from the Neolithic, Chalcolithic
Ages, Phrygian, Hellenistic, Roman and
Byzantine periods; in a medrese
(Islamic university) from the Ottoman
period

Bursa
12477
Archeological Museum
Cekirge Culture Park, TR Bursa
Archeology Museum - 1972
Coins and works of prehistoric times;
works in stone and metal; ceramics;
glass; art gallery - laboratory; library

12478
Art Gallery
Republic Sq., TR Bursa
Fine Arts Museum
Works of Turkish artists and sculptors

12479
Ataturk Museum
Cekirge, TR Bursa
Historic Site - 1973
Memorabilia of the great Turkish
politician Ataturk (1880-1938);
furnishing; photographs; documents

12480
Museum of Turkish and Islamic Art
Yesil Medrese, TR Bursa
Fine Arts Museum - 1974
Works from the 14th century to the
late Ottoman period

12481
Ottoman House
Murad House, Muradiye, TR Bursa
Anthropology Museum
Typical Ottoman house; furniture;
wooden ceiling and cupboards

Camyayla
12482
Ataturk Museum
TR Camyayla, Eceabat, Çanakkale
province
Historic Site - 1973
Memorabilia of the great Turkish
politician Ataturk (1880-1938); original
furniture; documents; photographs

Çanakkale
12483
**Çanakkale Martyrs Monument and
War Museum**
TR Çanakkale
History/Public Affairs Museum - 1972
Memorial to the Turkish soldiers who
fell in the Çanakkale War of
1914-1915; documents; photographs

12484
Museum
TR Çanakkale
General Museum - 1961
Archeological finds from the
excavations of Bozcaada Necropolis
and Dardanos Tumulus; exhibits from
the Phoenician, Greec, Roman,
Byzantine and Ottoman periods;
Calverton collection; ethnography;
Turkish art works

Cifteler
12485
Yazilikaya Museum
TR Cifteler, Eskisehir province
Open Air Museum
Remains of Midas, a Phrygian city

Çorum
12486
Museum
TR Çorum
General Museum - 1968
Archeological finds from the
prehistoric, Hitite, Phrygian, Byzantine,
classical and Islamic periods;
ethnography

Denizli
12487
Museum
TR Denizli
Archeology Museum
Finds from the excavations at
Hierapolis; Roman bath; column
capitals; grave stelae; inscriptions;
sarcophagi

Derinkuyu
12488
Underground City Museum
TR Derinkuyu, Nevsehir province
History/Public Affairs Museum - 1965
Underground Christian dwellings from
the Byzantine period (7th. century
A.D.)

Diyarbakir
12489
**Archeological and Ethnographic
Museum**
Sincariye Medrese, TR Diyarbakir
General Museum
Exhibits from the Assyrian, Hitite,
Roman, Byzantine, Artuk and Ottoman
periods; ethnography; in a 12th
century medrese (Islamic university) -
library

12490
Ataturk House
Semanoglu House, TR Diyarbakir
Historic Site
Memorabilia of the Turkish politician
Ataturk (1880-1938) in the house in
which he lived from 1916-1917

12491
Cahit Sitki Taranci Culture Museum
TR Diyarbakir
Historic Site - 1973
Memorabilia of the poet Cahit Sitki
Taranci (d. 1956) in his birthplace;
books; manuscripts; photographs

12492
Ziya Gökalp Museum
TR Diyarbakir
Historic Site - 1962
Memorabilia of the Turkish
philosopher Ziya Gökalp (d. 1924) in
his birthplace; books; manuscripts;
photographs

Edirne
12493
**Archeological and Ethnographic
Museum**
TR Edirne
General Museum - 1971
Carpets and kilims; ethnographic
works; archeological examples from
the civilisations of Anatolia and Thrace

12494
Museum of Turkish and Islamic Art
Selimiye Mosque, TR Edirne
Fine Arts Museum - 1971
Stone inscriptions from the Ottoman
period; embroidery; weapons; glass
objects; carved wooden doors and
cupboards

Elâziğ
12495
**Archeological and Ethnographic
Museum**
TR Elâziğ
General Museum - 1965
Archeological findings from prehistoric
times to the Byzantine period;
ethnographic works including
embroidery, kilims and tapestries,
domestic utensils, costumes

Erdemli
12496
Museum
TR Erdemli, Icel province
General Museum - 1968
Ethnographic and archeological works
from the area

Ereğli

12497
Archeological and Ethnographic Museum of Ereğli
Bd. Caddesi 16, TR Ereğli, Konya province
General Museum
Archeological works from the Roman, Byzantine and Islamic periods; rock relief at Ivriz from the Neo-Hitite period (8th century B.C.); manuscripts; etnographical objects; Enata collection; Canhasan collection

Erzurum

12498
Archeological Museum
TR Erzurum
Archeology Museum
Findings from prehistoric times to the Byzantine period; ethnographic works; guilded books

12499
Cifte Minareli Medrese Museum
TR Erzurum
Anthropology Museum
Seljuk and Ottoman gravestones; in an 18th century medrese (Islamic university) from the Seljuk period

12500
Erzurum Cogress Museum
TR Erzurum
History/Public Affairs Museum
Documents, declarations and telegraphs concerning the Erzurum Congress 1919; paintings

Eskisehir

12501
Archeological Museum
TR Eskisehir
Archeology Museum
Archeological finds from the Chalcolithic, Hitite, Byzantine, Roman and Islamic periods - laboratory; workshop

12502
Ataturk and Culture Museum
TR Eskisehir
Historic Site - 1970
Memorabilia of the Turkish politician Ataturk (1880-1938); ethnography

12503
Ethnographic Museum (Ottoman House)
Yesil Efendi House, Dede district, TR Eskisehir
Anthropology Museum
Etnographic works from the region of Eskisehir; woodcarving;

12504
Picture and Sculpture Gallery
Kursunlu Mosque, TR Eskisehir
Fine Arts Museum
Paintings and sculpture of Turkish artists; in a mosque of the Ottoman period

Fethiye

12505
Museum
TR Fethiye, Mugla province
Archeology Museum - 1965
Exhibits from the Lycia, Roman and Byzantine periods; coins

Gaziantep

12506
Museum
TR Gaziantep
General Museum - 1969
Archeological objects from the Neolithic, Chalcolithic, Bronze, Hitite, Mitanni, Hurrian and Babylonian periods; finds from excavations of Timen and Gedikli barrows; ethnography - conference hall; laboratory

Geyre

12507
Aphrodisias Museum
TR Geyre, Aydin province
Archeology Museum
Finds from the archeological excavations of the ancient city of Aphrodisias; theatre; bath; sculpture; temples

Hacibektas

12508
Museum
Haci Bektas Dergah, TR Hacibektas, Nevsehir province
History/Public Affairs Museum
Exhibits from the Ottoman period, mescid (small mosque), tombs

Harput

12509
Harput Museum
Alaca Mosque, TR Harput, Elâziğ province
Archeology Museum - 1960
Inscriptions from the Urartu Monarchy and Roman period; Islamic grave stones

Istanbul

12510
Arasta Mosaic Museum
Sultan Ahmet Mosque, TR Istanbul
Archeology Museum
Mosaics from the 4th and 5th centuries AD

12511
Archeological Museum
TR Istanbul
Archeology Museum - 1874
Includes the Classical, Ancient Orient and Mosaic museums; exhibits from the Sumerian, Akkadian, Hittite, Assyrian, Egyptian, Urartu, Greek, Roman and Byzantine periods - library

12512
Ayasofya Museum (Saint Sophia Museum)
Sultan Ahmet, TR Istanbul
Archeology Museum - 1934
Byzantine and Turkish antiquities; housed in the Byzantine basilica, built by Justinian in the 6th century AD

12513
Dolmabahçe Palace
TR Istanbul
History/Public Affairs Museum
19th century palace, built in a mixture of Renaissance and baroque styles; original furnishings; historical documents; room where the Turkish politician Ataturk (1880-1938) died

12514
Galata Mevlevihane Museum (Museum of Divan Literature)
Galata Mevlevihane, TR Istanbul
History/Public Affairs Museum - 1973
Works of the school of Mevlana; graves of famous scholars of the order of Mevlana - library

12515
Istanbul City Museum
Gazanferaga Medrese, Sarachane, TR Istanbul
General Museum - 1946
Local history; applied art; ethnography

12516
Kariye Mosaics Museum
Kariye Mosque, TR Istanbul
Archeology Museum
Byzantine period mosaics; in a 12th century church

12517
Military Museum
TR Istanbul
History/Public Affairs Museum - 1959
Weapons; military equipment; documents; uniforms; exhibits from the Liberation War and the Republic

12518
Museum of Picture and Sculpture
Dolmabahçe Palace, TR Istanbul
Fine Arts Museum - 1937
Works of Turkish artists and sculptors; folk art; ceramic

12519
Museum of Turkish and Islamic Art
Süleymaniye Kulliye, TR Istanbul, Süleymaniy
Decorative Arts Museum - 1914
Collection of Turkish and Islamic rugs; illuminated manuscripts; sculpture in stone and stucco; woodcarvings; metalwork; ceramics; miniatures; in a 16th century building

12520
Museum of Turkish Construction and Interior Decoration
Amcazade Huseyin Pasha Medrese, TR Istanbul
Decorative Arts Museum
Examples of stone masonery and plaster moulding; brick and stone inscriptions; architectural techniques of the past; building equipment

12521
Museum of Turkish Written Art
Vatan Boulevard, Sultan Selim Medrese, TR Istanbul
Decorative Arts Museum
Examples of writing in Arab script; calligraphy; hand-written Korans; inscriptions

12522
Naval Museum
Beşiktaş, TR Istanbul
History/Public Affairs Museum - 1897
Turkish naval history; models of Turkish ships; pictures; maps; documents; collection of historical caiques - library; archives

12523
Reformation Museum
Cadir House, Yildiz Park, TR Istanbul
History/Public Affairs Museum
Objects and documents from the Ottoman Reformation period of 1839

12524
Rumeli Fortress Museum
TR Istanbul
History/Public Affairs Museum - 1958
15th century fortress on the Bosphorus; local history - open air theatre

12525
Şişli-Ataturk Museum (Museum of Revolution)
Halaskar Gazi Bd., TR Istanbul, Şişli
Historic Site - 1943
Memorial to the Turkish politician Ataturk (1880-1938); documents; cloths; photographs;

12526
Tevfik Fikret House Museum
Rumeli Fortress, TR Istanbul
Historic Site
Memorabilia of Tevfik Fikret (d. 1915), a poet of the Serveti Funun school of literature; documents; photographs; pictures

12527
Topkapi Palace Museum
TR Istanbul
General Museum
Coll: Turkish armour; cloth; embroidery; tiles; glass and porcelain; copper- and silverware; treasury objects; paintings; miniatures; illuminated manuscripts; royal coaches; Sèvres and Bohemian crystal and porcelain; selection of Islamic relics; clocks; Chinese and Japanese porcelain; Revan House; Baghdad House; Mecidiye House; Harem; in a 15th century palace - library; archives

12528
Vakiflar Carpet Museum
Sultanahmet Hünkar Kasri, TR Istanbul
Decorative Arts Museum - 1979
14th-15th century carpets; Pious Foundation Collections

12529
Yedikule Fortress Museum
TR Istanbul
History/Public Affairs Museum
Seven towers fortress; local history

12530
Yenicami Imperial Pavillion Museum
Eminonu, TR Istanbul
Decorative Arts Museum
The building is a masterpiece of Turkish architecture and decorative art from the 17th century; inscribed friezes; tiled stoves; carved wooden ceilings

12531
Yerebatan Cistern Museum
Byzantine Cistern
Sultan Ahmet Square, TR Istanbul
Archeology Museum
Water cistern, built in the 6th century AD by the Byzantine emperor Justinian

Izmir

12532
Art and Sculpture Museum
TR Izmir
Fine Arts Museum - 1973
Turkish art and sculpture

12533
Ataturk Museum
Gundoglu, Ataturk Bd., TR Izmir
Historic Site
Memorabilia of the Turkish politician Ataturk (1880-1938); paintings; photographs

12534
Izmir Culture Park Archeological Museum
TR Izmir
Archeology Museum
Works from the Chalcolithic Age to the Byzantine period from the regions Izmir, Bergama, Sart and Ephesus

Izmit

12535
Museum
Hunting Lodge, TR Izmit
General Museum - 1967
Archeology; works from the Ottoman
period

Iznik

12536
Iznik Museum
Nilufer Hatun Soup Kitchen, TR Iznik,
Bursa province
General Museum - 1060
Archeological and ethnographical
works of the Hellenistic, Roman,
Byzantine, Seljuk and Ottoman
periods; marble sarcophagus; in a 14th
century house, one of the earliest
examples of Ottoman architecture -
library

Kadirli

12537
Karatepe Open Air Museum
TR Kadirli, Adana province
Open Air Museum
Finds from the excavations of a Late
Hitite city dated 700-730 BC

Kahraman Maraş

12538
Maraş Museum
Station St. 35, TR Kahraman Maraş
General Museum - 1947
Neo-Hittite reliefs; statues from the
Roman and Byzantine periods;
gravestones and masonery; ceramics;
ethnography; coins - library

Karain Cave

12539
Museum
TR Karain Cave, Antalya province
Archeology Museum
Finds from the Paleolithic to
Chalcolithic Ages; skeletons; stone
tools;

Karaman

12540
Museum
Hastahane Caddesi, TR Karaman,
Konya province
General Museum - 1962
Can Hasan excavation founds from
the Chalcolithic period (5000-3000
B.C.); archeological finds from the
Roman, Byzantine, Karamanogullari
and Ottoman periods; ethnography -
library

Kars

12541
Museum
Kumbet Mosque, TR Kars
Archeology Museum - 1963
Archeology

Kastamonu

12542
Museum
TR Kastamonu
General Museum - 1943
Weapons; local history; archeology;
ethnography - library

Kaymakli

12543
Underground City Museum
TR Kaymakli, Nevsehir province
History/Public Affairs Museum - 1965
Underground Christian dwellings from
the Byzantine period (7th century A.D.)

Kayseri

12544
Archeological Museum
Gultepe, TR Kayseri
Archeology Museum - 1969
Finds from the Kultepe excavations;
Hitite works; ceramics from the
Phrygian, Roman and Byzantine
periods

12545
Museum of Turkish and Islamic Art
Hudavend Hatun Medrese, TR Kayseri
Decorative Arts Museum - 1969
Tiles; wooden and metal objects;
manuscripts; carpets; kilims; jewelry;
embroidery; ethnographic works from
the Seljuk, Beylikler and Ottoman
periods

Konya

12546
Archeological Museum
Sahipata Kulliye, TR Konya
Archeology Museum - 1963
Gravestones; sarcophagi; inscriptions;
exhibits from the Classic period

12547
Ataturk House-Culture Museum
Station Bd., TR Konya
Historic Site - 1964
Memorabilia of the Turkish politician
Ataturk (1880-1938)

12548
Grave Museum
Sircali Medrese, TR Konya
Decorative Arts Museum - 1960
Gravestones of historical and artistic
value from the Seljuk, Beylik and
Ottoman periods; in a 13th century
medrese (Islamic university)

12549
Koyunoglu Museum
TR Konya
Anthropology Museum - 1975
Koyunoglu Collection including
ethnographical objects, carpets, cloths,
embroidery, guilded books, oil
paintings

12550
Mevlana Museum
TR Konya
Anthropology Museum - 1927
Oriental art; manuscripts; crafts from
the Seljuk period; tomb of the great
Turkish philosopher Mevlana
Celaleddin; mescid (small mosque);
dervish cells; Mevlevi kitchen - library

12551
Museum
Karatay Medrese, TR Konya
Decorative Arts Museum
Wall tiles and porcelain dishes from
the Seljuc, Beylik and Ottoman
periods; in a 13th century medrese
(Islamic university)

12552
**Museum of Seljuk Period Stone- and
Woodcarving** (Inseminare Museum)
Inseminare Dar'ül Hadis, TR Konya
Decorative Arts Museum - 1956
Examples of gravestones, inscriptions
and building stones from the Seljuk
and Karamangullari periods;
figurative stone decorations from
Konya castle; in a 13th century
inseminare

12553
Regional Ethnographic Museum
Sahip-Ata Bd., TR Konya
Anthropology Museum - 1974
Costumes; handicrafts; jewelry;
domestic utensils; weapons; coins

Kultepe

12554
Museum
TR Kultepe, Kayseri province
Archeology Museum - 1969
Finds from the Kultepe excavations
from the Assyrian, Roman, Phrygian
and Hitite periods

Kutahya

12555
Museum
Vacidiye Medrese, TR Kutahya
General Museum - 1965
Archeological findings from prehistoric
times, the Hitite, Phrygian, Hellenistic,
Roman and Byzantine periods;
ethnographical collection from the
region of Kutahya; in a 14th century
medrese (Islamic university)

Malatya

12556
Museum
TR Malatya
Archeology Museum - 1969
Exhibits from the Chalcolithic, Early
Bronze, Assyrian, Hitite Ages,
Hellenistic, Roman, Byzantine, Seljuk
and Ottoman periods

Manisa

12557
Museum
Muradiye Kulliye, TR Manisa
General Museum - 1935
Archeology; ethnography; Turkish art

Mardin

12558
Museum
TR Mardin
General Museum - 1945
Collection of Islamic and pre-Islamic
works, coins etc.

Milas

12559
Museum
TR Milas
Archeology Museum - 1959
Archeology

Misis

12560
Mosaic Museum
TR Misis, Adana province
Archeology Museum - 1959
Late Roman period mosaics from the
3rd century AD

Mudanya

12561
Armistice Museum
TR Mudanya, Bursa province
History/Public Affairs Museum - 1960
Historical house, where the Mudanya
Armistice was signed; original
furniture; bedrooms of Ismet Inonu
and General Asim

Narlikuyu

12562
Mosaic Museum
Silifke- Anamur Road, Narlikuyu köyü,
TR Narlikuyu, Içel province
Archeology Museum - 1967
Roman period mosaics

Nevsehir

12563
**Archeological and Ethnographic
Museum**
Imaret building, TR Nevsehir
General Museum
Archeological works from the Hitite,
Phrygian, Byzantine periods;
ethnography; in an 18th century
building

12564
Goreme Museum
TR Nevsehir
Open Air Museum
Byzantine period (7th-12th century)
stone churches decorated with
frescoes

Nigde

12565
Museum
Akmedrese, TR Nigde
General Museum - 1936
Archeology from the Roman,
Byzantine, Hellenistic, Seljuk and
Ottoman periods; ethnography

Samsun

12566
Ataturk Museum
Samsun Fair, TR Samsun
Historic Site - 1968
Memorabilia of the Turkish politician
Ataturk (1880-1938)

12567
May 19 Museum
Mintika palace, Gazi Bd., TR Samsun
History/Public Affairs Museum - 1930
History; archeology - library

Selçuk

12568
Ephesus Archeological Museum
TR Selçuk
Archeology Museum - 1964
Objects from the excavations of
Ephesus since 1897; finds from the
Greek, Roman, Mycean, Byzantine
periods

Selimiye

12569
Side Museum
TR Selimiye, Köyü Manavgat, Antalya
Archeology Museum - 1961
Roman period sculptures, reliefs,
sarcophagi; lodged in an ancient
Roman bath

Seyitgazi

12570
Museum
Seyit Battalgazi Külliye, TR Seyitgazi,
Eskisehir province
General Museum - 1970
Archeology; ethnography; in a house
built in the Seljuk period

Silifke

12571
Museum
Taşucu Caddesi 175, TR Silifke, İçel
province
General Museum - 1940
Archeological finds from the Greek,
Roman, Byzantine, Seljuk and Ottoman
periods; Hellenistic ceramics;
ethnography; numismatics; Ptolemy's
golden coin collection - conservation
laboratory; library

Sinop

12572
Museum
TR Sinop
General Museum - 1941
Archeology; ethnography; carpets;
sarcophagi; inscriptions

Sivas

12573
Museum of Antiquities
Buruciye Medrese, TR Sivas
General Museum - 1934
Coll: silverware; ceramics; archeology;
ethnography; sarcophagi; in a 13th
century medrese (Islamic university)
from the Seljuk period

12574
September 4 Ataturk Museum
Tasli Street, TR Sivas
History/Public Affairs Museum
Historical hall where the Sivas
Congress was held in 1919; Ataturk
room; furniture; documents

Tarsus

12575
Museum
TR Tarsus, Icel province
General Museum - 1972
Archeology; ethnography

Tekirdag

12576
Museum
TR Tekirdag
General Museum - 1967
Natural history; archeology;
ethnography

Tire

12577
Museum
Imaret Mosque, TR Tire
General Museum - 1935
Roman period statues; clay
sarcophagus; Roman, Byzantine and
Islamic coins; embroidery; domestic
utensils; hand-written Korans;
Ottoman period glass objects; arms

Tokat

12578
Museum
Gokmedrese, TR Tokat
General Museum - 1926
Archeology; ethnography; in a 13th
century medrese (Islamic university) -
archives

Trabzon

12579
Ataturk House
Soğuksu, TR Trabzon
Historic Site
Memorabilia of the Turkish politician
Ataturk (1880-1938)

12580
Saint Sophia Museum
TR Trabzon
History/Public Affairs Museum - 1963
Exhibits from the Roman, Byzantine
and Ottoman periods; in a 13th
century Byzantine church, decorated
with frescoes

Troy

12581
Museum
TR Troy, Çanakkale province
Archeology Museum
Finds from the excavations of the
ancient city of Troy, carried out by
Schlieman in 1868

Urfa

12582
Museum
TR Urfa
General Museum - 1948
Exhibits from prehistoric times, the
Greek, Roman and Byzantine periods;
mosaics from Urfa Necropolis; Seljuk
and Ottoman period inscriptions;
ethnography

Ürgüp

12583
Museum
TR Ürgüp, Nevsehir province
General Museum - 1971
Archeology from the Hitite, Phrygian,
Roman and Byzantine periods;
ethnography

Usak

12584
Museum
TR Usak
General Museum - 1970
Archeology; ethnography

Van

12585
Museum
TR Van
General Museum - 1972
Archeology; Urartu inscriptions;
ethnography

Yalvac

12586
Museum
TR Yalvac, Isparta province
General Museum - 1965
Coll: archeology from 2500 BC to the
4th century AD; works from the ruins
of the ancient city of Antioch;
ethnography; paintings by Turkish
artists; Ottoman period manuscripts
and inscriptions;

Yarimca

12587
Museum
TR Yarimca, Kocaeli (Izmit) province
General Museum - 1974
Archeology; ethnography; modern
pictures and sculpture

Yassihoyuk

12588
Museum
TR Yassihoyuk, Polatli district
Archeology Museum - 1965
Archeological finds from the Gordion
excavation; objects from the Old
Bronze, Hitite and Phrygian Ages

Yenisehir

12589
Semaki House
TR Yenisehir, Bursa province
Anthropology Museum
The 18th century house is a valuable
example of Turkish civil architecture;
wooden ceiling and cupboards

Yunus Emre

12590
Yunus Emre Museum
TR Yunus Emre, Mihaliççik, Eskisehir
province
Historic Site - 1971
Memorabilia of the Turkish poet Yunus
Emre

Uganda

Entebbe

12591
**Game and Fisheries Museum, Zoo,
Aquarium and Library**
POB 4, Entebbe
Natural History Museum
Coll: heads of game animals; bird
skins; reptiles; fish; butterflies; hunting
and fishing implements; weapons -
library, aquarium, zoo

12592
**Geological Survey Museum and
Library**
POB 9, Entebbe
Natural History Museum
Geology; rocks and minerals;
meteorites - library

Kampala

12593
Department of Geology Museum
Makarere University
Kampala
Natural History Museum
Geology

12594
Department of Zoology Museum
Makarere University
POB 262, Kampala
Natural History Museum - 1963
Coll: invertebrates; mollusks; insects;
reptiles; mammals; fossils; ecology of
the hippopotamus; clan animals of
Bugunda

12595
**Forest Department Utilisation
Division and Museum**
POB 1752, Kampala
Agriculture Museum - 1952
Uganda timber; preservation,
seasoning and woodworking tests;
logging and milling; entomology -
library

12596
Makerere Art Gallery
mail c/o Makerere School of Fine Art,
POB 7062, Kampala
Fine Arts Museum - 1968
Coll: paintings; sculpture; ceramics;
graphics; works of East African artists

12597
Nommo Gallery
52 Kampala Rd, POB 16132, Kampala
Fine Arts Museum
National collection of art

12598
Uganda Museum
5-7 Kira Rd, POB 365, Kampala
General Museum - 1908
Coll: natural history; paleontology;
anthropology; ethnography; African
musical instruments; science and
industry - library, aquarium

Lake Katwe

12599
**Queen Elisabeth National Park
Museum**
POB 22, Lake Katwe, Abdonio Odur
Natural History Museum - 1952
Coll: reptiles; mammals; hippopotamus
skull; snakes; birds; fossils

Mbarara

12600
Folk Museum
Mbarara
General Museum
Ethnography

Murchison Falls

12601
Murchison Falls National Park
Murchison falls via Majindi Murchison
Falls
Natural History Museum - 1952
Amphibia; reptiles; mammals

Soroti

12602
Folk Museum
Kennedy Square, POB 58, Soroti
General Museum
Ethnography; charms and bangles

United Arab Emirates

Abu Dhabi

12603
Archeological Museum
Sites at Buraimi and Umm Al Nar
Island, Al Ain, Abu Dhabi
Archeology Museum
Archeological excavations

United Kingdom

Aberdeen

12604
Aberdeen Art Gallery and Museums Department
Schoolhill, Aberdeen AB9 1FQ
Fine Arts Museum - 1885
contemporary painting and sculpture;
Scottish school 17th and 20th century;
French Impressionist school - library

12605
Anthropological Museum University of Aberdeen
Aberdeen AB9 1AS
Anthropology Museum - 1907
ethnography; Egyptian scarabs;
classical vases; Chinese bronzes;
ceramics; jades - library

12606
Gordon Highlanders' Regimental Museum
Viewfield Rd, Aberdeen AB1 7HX
History/Public Affairs Museum - 1937
history of Gordon Highlanders
regiment; uniforms; medals; pictures;
trophies

12607
Natural History Museum Department of Zoology, University of Aberdeen
Tillydrone Av., Aberdeen AB9 2TN
Natural History Museum
ornithology; entomology

12608
Provost Skene's House
Guestrow, Aberdeen AB9
General Museum - 1953
Scottish furniture; industrial and
agricultural archaeology; painted
chapel ceiling (17th century)

Aberford

12609
Lotherton Hall
Aberford, Nr. Leeds, Yorks
General Museum - 1968
English and Continental paintings
(17th-19th century), furniture, silver,
ceramics

Abergavenny

12610
Monmuth District Museum Service and Abergavenny Castle Museum
Castle St., Abergavenny, Gwent NP7 5EE
General Museum - 1958
history and industries of the town and
district; kitchen; mural craft; tools;
Roman relics from Gobannium site

Aberlady

12611
Myreton Motor Museum
Aberlady, East Lothian
Science/Tech Museum
W.P. Dale collection

Aberystwyth

12612
Aberystwyth Art Centre University College of Wales
Penglais, Aberystwyth, Cardigans
Fine Arts Museum - 1970
mainly contemporary art; paintings;
glass; pottery; porcelain

Abingdon

12613
Abingdon County Hall Museum and Guildhall Art Gallery
Market Place, Abingdon, Berks
General Museum - 1925
local history, archaeological finds;
pottery; armaments and objects from
Anglo Saxon cemetery

12614
Abingdon Museum
Abingdon, Oxfords
General Museum - 1928
grave artifacts from local Saxon
cemeteries; Roman and Iron Age
finds; pewter; measures

Accrington

12615
Haworth Art Gallery
Haworth Park, Manchester Rd,
Accrington, Lancs BB5 2JS
Fine Arts Museum - 1921
19th-20th century paintings;
watercolors; Tiffany glass

Alcester

12616
Ragley Hall
Alcester, Warwicks B49 5NJ
History/Public Affairs Museum - 1680
Palladian house by Robert Hooke with
finest baroque plaster work; French
furniture, porcelain and paintings -
library

Aldbrough

12617
Roman Town and Museum
Department of Environment
Aldbrough, N Yorks
General Museum
Roman archaeological finds; ruins of
the former Roman town

Alderney

12618
Alderney Museum
Alderney, CI
General Museum - 1966
local history; arts and crafts; history of
the German occupation 1940-1945;
Iron Age pottery finds

Aldershot

12619
Airborne Forces Museum Browning
Barracks
Aldershot GU11 2DS
History/Public Affairs Museum - 1969
World War II operational briefing
models; aircraft models; equipment;
vehicles; guns

12620
Queen Alexandra's Royal Army Nursing Corps Museum Qaranc
Training Centre
Farnborough Rd, Aldershot, Hants
GU11 1PZ
History/Public Affairs Museum - 1957
history of Army Nursing Service since
Florence Nightingale's services in
Crimean War (1854); Nightingale
(1820-1910) relics; memorabilia;
costumes and medals of Qaranc

12621
Royal Army Medical Corps Historical Museum Keogh Barracks
Ash Vale, Aldershot, Hants
History/Public Affairs Museum
history of Army Medical Service since
pre-Tudor times; Crimean relics;
memorabilia on Napoleon I (1769-1821)
and Wellington (1769-1852)

12622
Royal Army Service Corps - Royal Corps of Transport Museum Buller
Barracks
Aldershot, Hants
History/Public Affairs Museum
military uniforms and vehicles

Alloway

12623
Burns' Cottage
Alloway, Ayr
History/Public Affairs Museum - 1880
cottage where poet Robert Burns
(1759-1796) was born; memorabilia;
manuscripts

Alnwick Castle

12624
Alnwick Castle
Alnwick Castle, Northumberland
History/Public Affairs Museum
interiors in the classical style of the
Italian Renaissance; furniture;
decorative arts; pictures; 11th century
fortress

Alton

12625
Curtis Museum Hampshire County
Museum Service
High St, Alton, Hants
General Museum - 1855
folklore; archaeology; decorative arts

Altrincham

12626
Altrincham Museum and Art Gallery
Talbot Rd, Altrincham, Ches
General Museum - 1892
local history; paintings; watercolors;
prints

Annan

12627
Annan Burgh Museum
Bruce St, Annan, Dumfriesshire
General Museum
ethnography; local history; relics;
contemporary art; biographical essays

Anstruther

12628
Scottish Fisheries Museum
St. Ayles, Anstruther
History/Public Affairs Museum - 1969
history of Scotland's fishing industry
and related trades; fishing gear; ship
models and gear; fishermen's
ethnography; whaling; aquarium;
paintings and photographs with marine
themes

Arbroath

12629
Arbroath Abbey Museum Scottish
Development Dept. Edinburgh
Arbroath, Angus
History/Public Affairs Museum
archaeology; folklore

12630
Arbroath Art Gallery
Hill Terrace, Arbroath, Angus
Fine Arts Museum - 1898
local artists' works; 2 paintings by
Breughel

12631
St. Vigeans Museum
Arbroath, Angus
History/Public Affairs Museum - 1960
Early Christian stone church

Armagh

12632
Armagh County Museum
The Mall East, Armagh, N Ireland BT61
9BE
General Museum - 1935
Irish art; history and natural history of
Armagh County since prehistoric
times; local folklore; applied art -
library

12633
Royal Irish Fusiliers Regimental Museum
The Mall, Armagh, N Ireland BT61 9BE
History/Public Affairs Museum
history of the regiment; uniforms;
photographs

Arundel

12634
Totems Museum
High St, Arundel, Sussex
Archeology Museum
the Hooper collection of primitive art

Ashburton

12635
Ashburton Museum Newton Abbot
No 1 West St, Ashburton, S Devon
General Museum - 1954
local history; American Indian
antiques; costumes; rifles; arrows;
tools

Ashford

12636
Intelligence Corps Museum Templer
Barracks
Ashford, Kent
History/Public Affairs Museum
history of Intelligence Corps

Ashton Munslow

12637
The White House Country Life Museum
Ashton Munslow, Shrops
Anthropology Museum - 1966
medieval settlement; carts; cider mill
and equipment; farming tools and
machinery; horse-drawn implements;
kitchen and domestic utensils

Ashton-Under-Line

12638
Museum of the Manchester Regiment Ladysmith Barracks
Ashton-Under-Line, Lancs
History/Public Affairs Museum
military history

Ashwell

12639
Ashwell Village Museum
Swan St, Ashwell, Herts SG7 5NY
General Museum - 1930
rural village life from the Stone Age to
the present; a Tudor building; ancient
monument; snuff and tinder boxes;
eyeglasses; straw-plaiting tools;
lace-making tools; objects formerly
used in farming and everyday life;
leather eyeglasses

Avebury

12640
Alexander Keiller Museum
Department of Environment
Avebury, Wilts
General Museum - 1938
prehistory; pottery; stone paths of the
Avebury sanctuary; stone axes; animal
skeletons

Axbridge

12641
**Axbridge Archaeological Society
Museum**
The Square, Axbridge, Som
Archeology Museum
archaeology

Aylesbury

12642
Buckinghamshire County Museum
Church St, Aylesbury, Bucks HP20
2QP
General Museum - 1862
geology; natural history; archaeology
and cultural history of
Buckinghamshire county; paintings;
prints; finds from Hambleden; Roman
Villa

12643
Waddesdon Manor National Trust
Aylesbury, Bucks
Fine Arts Museum - 1959
18th century French decorative arts;
18th century English portraits; 17th
century Dutch and Flemish paiting;
majolica; glass; 16th century
Renaissance jewelry; 16th-17th
century European arms; 14th-16th
century French, Italian and Flemish
illuminated manuscripts; 18th century
French books and bindings

Aylsham

12644
Blickling Hall
Aylsham, Norfolk
History/Public Affairs Museum
family manor with furnishings,
paintings, tapestries

Ayot St. Lawrence

12645
Shaw's Corner National Trust
Property
Ayot St, Ayot St. Lawrence, Herts
History/Public Affairs Museum
former home of George Bernard
Shaw (1856-1950) from 1906 until his
death; memorabilia including Nobel
Prize related literature of 1925 and
objects concerning the Oscar-winning
work 'Pygmalion'

Ayr

12646
**Kyle and Carrick District Library,
Museum Service**
12 Main St, Ayr KA8 8ED
General Museum - 1934
local history; rotating art collections

Bacup

12647
**Natural History Society and Folk
Museum**
24 Yorkshire St, Bacup, Lancs
General Museum - 1900
geology; Neolothic objects; local
nature; household objects

Bagshot

12648
**Royal Army Chaplains' Department
Museum**
Bagshot Park, Bagshot, Surrey GU19
5PL
History/Public Affairs Museum - 1967
history of chaplain services in British
and Royal Armies; archives; medals;
Communion plate; field service;
religious objects; Churche's influence
on the soldiers' lives - library

Bamburgh

12649
Grace Darling Museum Royal
National Lifeboat Institution
1 Radcliff Rd, Bamburgh,
Northumberland
History/Public Affairs Museum - 1938
relics on Grace Darling, who rescued
survivors of wrecked ship SS
Forfarshire Sept. 7, 1838

Banbury

12650
Banbury Museum
Marlborough Rd, Banbury OX16 8DF
General Museum - 1969
material relating to life in Banbury;
local history

12651
Banbury Museum
8 Horsefair, Banbury, Oxfords
General Museum - 1884
Banbury municipal collection
containing weights and measures,
banners; objects illustrating the
material culture of Banbury and
surrounding villages - classrooms;
lecture room

Banff

12652
Banff Museum School Service
Museum
High St, Banff AB4 1BY
General Museum - 1930
local history; educational material

Bangor/Northern Ireland

12653
Bangor Borough Museum
Town Hall, Bangor/Northern Ireland
General Museum
local history

Bangor/Wales

12654
Bangor Art Gallery
Old Canonry, Bangor/Wales
Fine Arts Museum - 1963
Art

12655
Museum of Welsh Antiquities
University College of North Wales
Bangor/Wales
Anthropology Museum
old farm tools; Welsh antiquities;
crafts; furniture; early Christian
inscribed stones; 500-600 A.D. grave
slabs; medieval woodcarvings

12656
Penrhyn Castle
Bangor/Wales
General Museum
19th century furnished castle,
neo-Norman architecture; industrial
railway; dolls; natural history

12657
Penrhyn Castle Museum
Bangor/Wales
History/Public Affairs Museum
castle with interiors; locomotive
collection; dolls; mounted birds and
animals

12658
Zoology Department Museum
University College of North Wales
Bangor/Wales
Natural History Museum
zoology

Barlaston

12659
Wedgwood Museum
Barlaston, Staffs
Fine Arts Museum - 1906
historical pottery; comprehensive
collection of the works of Wedgwood
- library

Barnard Castle

12660
Bowes Museum
Barnard Castle, Durham
Fine Arts Museum - 1892
European painting; works by El Greco,
Goya, Tiepolo, Boudin, Fragonard;
pottery and porcelain, especially
French; textiles; sculpture; furniture;
other decorative arts

Barnet

12661
Barnet Museum
31 Wood St, Barnet, Herts
General Museum - 1935
Barnet district history; bags and
purses - library

Barnsley

12662
**Cannon Hall Museum and Art
Gallery**
Cannon Hall, Barnsley, S Yorks
General Museum - 1957
country house with interios; paintings;
glass; history

12663
Cooper Gallery
Church Street, Barnsley, S Yorks S70
2AH
Fine Arts Museum - 1980
Coll: 17th, 18th and 19th century
European paintings and English
drawings and watercolours

Barnstaple

12664
North Devon Athenaeum
The Square, Barnstaple, Devon
General Museum - 1888
local antiques; North Devon pottery;
geology; fossils; Roman pottery and
coins from Martinhoe and old Barrow;
natural history including butterflies;
bird eggs; coins

12665
St. Anne's Chapel Museum
High St, Parish Churchyard,
Barnstaple, Devon
Fine Arts Museum
church objects; works of art

Barrow-in-Furness

12666
The Furness Museum
Ramsden Square, Barrow-in-Furness,
Cumbria LA14 1LL
General Museum - 1882
ship models; local birds; prehistoric
finds and local history relics

Basingstoke

12667
The Vyne
Sherborne St, Basingstoke, Hants
History/Public Affairs Museum - 1958
Tudor house with renovations
(1650-1760); Flemish glass; majolica
tiles; panelling; furniture of Charles II;
Queen Anne and Chippendale
periods; rococo decoration

12668
Willis Museum and Art Gallery
Hampshire County Museum Service
New St, Basingstoke, Hants
General Museum - 1930
Local history; works of art;
archaeology

Bath

12669
American Museum in Britain
Claverton Manor, Bath BA2 7BD
Anthropology Museum - 1961
17th-19th century American decorative
art and social history; furnished period
rooms; maritime history; replica of
Captain's cabin; Indian section; 18th
century tavern; folk art gallery - library

12670
Holburne of Menstrie Museum
University of Bath
Great Pulteney St, Bath BA2 4DB
Fine Arts Museum
decorative art; furniture; silver;
miniatures; porcelain; majolica;
bronzes; netsukes; paintings by
Stubbs, Gainsborough, Guardi -
library

12671
Museum of Costume
Bennet St, Bath BA1 2QH
History/Public Affairs Museum - 1963
Pre-18th century costumes; 17th
century baby clothing; special
garments worn by Lord Byron, Lady
Byron, Lawrence of Arabia, Queen
Victoria, Alexandra, Mary, Queen
Mother; haute couture pieces

12672
Roman Baths Museum
Stall St, Bath, Avon
Archeology Museum - 1895
archaeological history of Bath in
prehistoric, Roman, Saxon, medieval
and later times

12673
Victoria Art Gallery
Bridge St, Bath BA2 4AT
General Museum - 1900
miniatures; watches; English ceramics
and glass; Bohemian glass coins; local
topographical prints and drawings;
geology collection; fine arts; applied
arts

Batley

12674
Bagshaw Art Gallery
Market Place, Batley, Yorks WF17
5DA
Fine Arts Museum - 1948
local arts and crafts; children's art;
19th-20th century art; works by
Francis Bacon and Max Ernst

12675
Bagshaw Museum
Wilton Park, Batley, Yorks
Anthropology Museum - 1911
archaeology; antiquities of Britain and
other areas; relics; ethnography; local
history; and industries; natural history;
geology; textile industry; Oriental
ceramics and finds; marine bird
diorama

12676
Oakwell Hall
Nova Lane, Batley, Yorks
History/Public Affairs Museum - 1929
period house dating from 1583 with
interiors; 16th-19th century furniture;
English pottery gardens

Battle

12677
**Battle and District Historical Society
Museum**
Abbey Green, Battle, Sussex TN33
0AQ
General Museum - 1956
Local history; Romano-British
ironwork; gunpowder industry; battle
artifacts; diorama of the Battle of
Hastings and reproductions of the
Bayeux Tapestry

Beaconsfield

12678
**Royal Army Educational Corps
Museum** Army School of Education
Wilton Park, Beaconsfield, Bucks
History/Public Affairs Museum
History of the Army School

Beamish

12679
North of England Open Air Museum
Beamish Hall, Beamish, Durham
Open Air Museum - 1971
Various buildings and objects relating
to local history, industries and
technology

Beaulieu

12680
Beaulieu Abbey Museum
Brockenhurst, Beaulieu, Hants
Fine Arts Museum
religious art

12681
Buckler's Hard Maritime Museum
Buckler's Hard, Beaulieu, Hants
Science/Tech Museum - 1963
shipping; 18th century naval vessels;
model of Hard in 1803; memorabilia on
Nelson; Sir Francis Chichester

12682
National Motor Museum
Beaulieu, Hants
Science/Tech Museum
cars; motorcycles; history of road
transportation

Bedford

12683
Bedford Museum The Embankment
Bedford MK40 3NY
General Museum - 1860/1959
local archaeological finds; history;
natural history; farming relics;
industrial archaeology; bronze; Celtic
mirror

12684
**Bedfordshire and Hertfordshire
Regimental Museum**
Bedford
History/Public Affairs Museum
History of the Bedfordshire and
Hertfordshire regiments

12685
Bunyan Collection
Harpur St, Bedford
History/Public Affairs Museum - 1860
memorabilia on writer John Bunyan
(1628-1688), editions of his works
including 'Pilgrim's Progress' in 150
languages

12686
Cecil Higgins Art Gallery
Bedford MK40 3NY
Fine Arts Museum - 1949
fine and decorative arts; English
watercolors; English and continental
porcelain; glass; furniture; silver;
sculptures; lace; costume; Handley-
Read collection of Victorian and
Edwardian decorative arts

12687
Elstow Moot Hall
Elstow, Bedford
History/Public Affairs Museum - 1951
17th century cultural history;
memorabilia of John Bunyan
(1628-1688)

Belfast

12688
**Museum of the Royal Ulster Rifles
RHQ** The Royal Irish Rangers
5 Waring St, Belfast BT1 2EW
History/Public Affairs Museum - 1935
Uniforms; medals; history of the
regiment

12689
Natural History Museum
Department of Zoology, Queen
University, Belfast BT7 1NN
Natural History Museum
educational zoology collection

12690
Ulster Museum National Museum of
Northern Ireland, Botanic Gardens
Belfast BT9 5AB
General Museum - 1892
international art; Irish painting;
contemporary Irish art; silver;
Williamite glass; Irish and European
antiquities; treasure from Spanish
Armada galleass Girona; Irish botany,
zoology, geology, wildlife art, industrial
technology and history; numismatics

Bembridge

12691
Bembridge Windmill
Bembridge, Isle of Wight
Science/Tech Museum
windmill dating from 1700 with original
wood machinery last used 1913

12692
Ruskin Gallery Bembridge School
Bembridge, Isle of Wight
History/Public Affairs Museum - 1929
memorabilia of writer John Ruskin;
paintings; drawings by artists
associated with him; photographs;
letters - library

Berwick-upon-Tweed

12693
**Berwick-upon-Tweed Museum and
Art Gallery**
Marygate, Berwick-upon-Tweed,
Northumberland TD15 1DG
General Museum - 1920/1949
Local history; decorative objects in
ceramics, silver, bronze and brass;
paintings

12694
**Kings's Own Scottish Borderers
Regimental Museum**
The Barracks, Berwick-upon-Tweed,
Northumberland TD15 1DG
History/Public Affairs Museum - 1947
Uniforms; medals; trophies; history of
the regiment

Beverley

12695
Art Gallery and Museum
Champrey Rd, Beverley, North
Humberside HU17 9BQ
General Museum - 1906/1910
local relics; porcelain; Victorian
objects; paintings and prints; local art;
maps

12696
**The East Yorkshire Regimental
Museum**
11 Butcher Row, Beverley, North
Humberside HU17 0AA
History/Public Affairs Museum - 1920
Militaria; medals - library

Bexhill-on-Sea

12697
Bexhill Museum
Egerton Rd, Bexhill-on-Sea, Sussex
TN40 2AP
General Museum - 1920
regional history; geology; antiquities

Bexley

12698
**Bexley Library and Museums
Department**
Bourne Rd, Bexley, Kent
General Museum - 1934
local geology; archaeology; fauna and
flora; minerals; Roman finds; local
history and industries

Bibury

12699
Arlington Mill
Bibury, Cirencester
General Museum - 1966
corn mill; farm tools; Victorian-
Edwardian furniture; costumes;
Staffordshire porcelain

Bideford

12700
Bideford Museum Municipal Building
Bideford, Devon
General Museum - 1906
local pottery; tools

12701
Burton Art Gallery
Kingsley Rd, Bideford, Devon
Decorative Arts Museum - 1951
decorative objects in silver, pewter,
porcelain; paintings; visiting card
cases from England, France and the
Orient; pottery

Biggar

12702
Gladstone Court Museum
Biggar, Lancashire
General Museum - 1968
reconstructed street with various
shops and trades; 17th century
furniture

Biggleswade

12703
Shuttleworth Collection Old Warden
Aerodrome
Biggleswade, Beds
Science/Tech Museum - 1946
historic veteran aircraft; demonstration
cars; fire engines; carriages; bicycles

Bignor

12704
Roman Villa Museum
Bignor, Sussex RH20 1PH
Archeology Museum - 1960
Samian pottery; tiles; finds from 1811
excavations; mosaics

Billericay

12705
The Cater Museum
74 High St, Billericay, Essex
General Museum - 1960
Local and regional history; prehistory;
kitchen with implements dating from
the 19th century to 1914; fire fighting;
saddlery and harness trade;
agricultural and crafts equipment;
exhibits on the Zeppelin airship L32
which was destroyed near Billericay in
1916

Binns

12706
House of the Binns National Trust for
Scotland
Binns, West Lothian, Scotland
History/Public Affairs Museum
historic home of the Dalyells; 17th
century moulded plaster ceilings

Birchington

12707
Powell-Cotton Museum
Quex Park, Birchington, East Kent
Anthropology Museum - 1896
African and Asian natural history and
ethnography; Pacific ethnography;
primates; bovidae; dioramas of African
and Asian animals; archaeology;
firearms - library

Birchover

12708
Heathcote Museum
Birchover, Derbys
General Museum
local history; local Bronze Age
excavations

Birkenhead

12709
Williamson Art Gallery and Museum
Slatey Rd, Birkenhead, Merseyside
L43 4UE
Fine Arts Museum
paintings; sculpture; etchings; pottery;
porcelain; glass; silver; furniture; local
history; geology; numismatics;
porcelain; shipping history

Birmingham

12710
Aston Hall City of Birmingham
Museums
Trinity Rd, Birmingham B66 JD
History/Public Affairs Museum - 1864
Jacobean house dating from
1616-1635, period furniture and rooms

12711
Barber Institute of Fine Arts
University of Birmingham
Edgbaston Rd, Birmingham B15 2TS
Fine Arts Museum - 1932
European art up to the 20th century;
works by Bellini, Veronese, Rubens,
Rembrandt, Franz Hals, Gainsborough,
Reynolds, Degas, Gauguin

12712
Birmingham Nature Center
Pershore Rd, Birmingham B5 7RL
Natural History Museum
birdwatching; apiary culture; fishing;
house pets; bird dioramas; African
bush reconstruction

12713
Blakesley Hall
Blakesley Rd, Birmingham B25 8RN
History/Public Affairs Museum - 1935
historic and archaeological objects;
period rooms in Tudor house

12714
**City of Birmingham Museum and Art
Gallery**
Congreve St, Birmingham B3 3DH
General Museum - 1867
17th century Italian paintings;
sculpture; ceramics; silver; jewelry;
costumes; archaeology; Oriental finds;
numismatics; zoology; botany;
geology; fossils; mineralogy

12715
Geological Department Museum
University of Birmingham
POB 363, Birmingham B15 2TT
Natural History Museum
rocks; mineralogy; fossils; coal from
South Staffordshire

12716
Medical School Museum Department
of Anatomy, University
Birmingham B15 2TJ
History/Public Affairs Museum
history of medical education

12717
Museum of Science and Industry
Newhall St, Birmingham B3 1RZ
Science/Tech Museum - 1950
Machine tools, small arms, aircraft,
locomotives, motorcars, motorcycles;
bicycles; mechanical musical
instruments; clocks and watches;
ornamental turning lathes; process
machinery; computers; replica
jeweller's, gun maker's, nail-maker's
workshops; pens and writing
instruments; model steam road vehicle
made by William Murdock in 1784;
Woolrich's electro-plating generator of
1844; cartridge-loading carbine with
self-priming lock by Acqua Fresca
1694, 650 ton extrusion press by
George Alexander Dick - library

12718
Sarehole Mill City of Birmingham
Museums
Colebank Rd, Birmingham B13 0BD
History/Public Affairs Museum - 1969
Restored water mill (1760); history of
rural life, corn production

12719
Weoley Castle Archaeological Site
150 Alwold Rd, Birmingham B29 5RX
Archeology Museum
12th century castle ruins with moat;
excavation finds

Bishop's Stortford

12720
**Rhodes Memorial Museum and
Commonwealth Centre**
South Rd, Bishop's Stortford, Herts
CM23 3JG
History/Public Affairs Museum - 1936
Life and work of statesman Cecil John
Rhodes in the house of his birth,
memorabilia, photos; documents

Blackburn

12721
East Lancashire Regiment Museum
Library St, Blackburn, Lancs
History/Public Affairs Museum
Uniforms; medals; history of the
Regiment; militaria

12722
Lewis Museum of Textile Machinery
Exchange St, Blackburn, Lancs
History/Public Affairs Museum - 1938
18th and 19th century cotton
machinery; art gallery; history of textile
production; period furnishings

12723
Museum and Art Gallery
Library St, Blackburn, Lancs
General Museum - 1974
natural history; geology; ethnography;
applied and fine arts; Hart collection of
coins; philatelics; medieval illuminated
manuscripts; books; local history;
Lewis collection of Japanese prints;
ornithology

Blackheath

12724
Ranger's House
Chesterfield Walk, Blackheath, London
SE10 8QX
History/Public Affairs Museum - 1688
The Suffolk Collection

Blackpool

12725
Grundy Art Gallery
Queen St, Blackpool
Fine Arts Museum - 1911
contemporary paintings; watercolors;
ivory; porcelain

Blair Atholl

12726
Blair Castle and Atholl Museum
Blair Atholl, Perth PH18 5TH
History/Public Affairs Museum
general history

Blandford

12727
Royal Signals Museum
Blandford Camp, Blandford, Dorset
History/Public Affairs Museum - 1935
History of the Signal Corps, old
communication equipment; uniforms;
prints and photos relating to the Corps

Blantyre

12728
**Scottish National Memorial to David
Livingstone**
Station Rd, Blantyre, Lancs G72 9BT
History/Public Affairs Museum - 1926
Memorabilia on explorer David
Livingstone in the house of his birth

Bodiam

12729
Castle Museum
Bodiam, E Sussex
History/Public Affairs Museum - 1922
relics connected with Bodiam castle

Bodmin

12730
**Duke of Cornwall's Light Infantry
Regimental Museum**
The Barracks, Bodmin, Cornwall
History/Public Affairs Museum
Armaments; uniforms; military history
of the regiment

Bolton

12731
Hall-I'Th'-Wood Museum Bolton
Museums and Art Gallery
Off Crompton Way, Bolton, Lancs
History/Public Affairs Museum - 1902
Manor dating from 1483-1648;
furnishings; memorabilia of inventor
Samuel Crompton

12732
Museums and Art Gallery Civic
Centre
Bolton, Lancs
General Museum - 1893
Natural history; British bird skins;
geology; fossils; archaeology;
Egyptian collection; early English
watercolors; British sculpture with
works by Epstein, Moore, Hepworth;
costumes; papers of inventor Samuel
Crompton

12733
Smithills Hall Museum Bolton
Museums and Art Gallery
Off Smithills Dean Rd, Bolton, Lancs
History/Public Affairs Museum - 1962
16th-19th century timbered manor;
funishings

12734
Textile Machinery Museum Bolton
Museums and Art Gallery
Tonge Moor Rd, Bolton, Lancs
Science/Tech Museum - 1947
old cotton-processing machinery

Bootle

12735
Art Gallery and Museum
Central Library, Stanley Rd, Bootle L20
6AG
General Museum
pottery; ceramics; rotating exhibits;
English porcelain

Boston

12736
Guildhall Museum
South St, Boston, Lincs PE21 8QR
General Museum - 1926
15th century building with medieval
kitchen, cells used by Pilgrim Fathers
pending trial, local Roman and
medieval pottery finds

Bournemouth

12737
**Bournemouth Natural Science
Society Museum**
39 Christchurch Rd, Bournemouth,
Dorset BH1 3NS
Natural History Museum - 1903
local natural history; archaeology;
fossils

12738
Rothesay Museum
8 Bath Rd, Bournemouth, Dorset BH1
2ER
General Museum - 1963
maritime history; armaments;
ethnography of Africa, Oceania,
Australia and New Zealand; natural
history; 17th century furniture;
majolicas; early Italian painting;
Victorian relics; maritime art

12739
**Russel-Cotes Art Gallery and
Museum**
East Cliff, Bournemouth, Hants
General Museum - 1894
Theater history; Victorian house and
interiors; Oriental art; numismatics;
18th-19th century watercolors;
paintings and sculptures - aquarium

Bradford

12740
Bolling Hall Museum
Bolling Hall Rd, Bradford BD4 7LP
General Museum - 1915
house with historic furniture; 17th
century plaster ceilings; Regency
furniture; watercolors; costumes; local
history

12741
Bradford Industrial Museum
Bradford BD2 3HP
General Museum
history of local industry; industrial
archaeology; wool; textiles

12742
Cartwright Art Gallery and Museum
Lister Park, Bradford BD9 4NZ
Fine Arts Museum - 1902
Italian Old Masters; old and modern
British painting; drawings;
watercolors; modern prints;
archaeology

12743
Cliffe Castle
Keighley, Bradford
General Museum
.natural history; regional history

12744
Manor House
Ilkley, Bradford
General Museum
in Elizabethan Manor house; Roman
artifacts; Roman fort wall

Brading

12745
Osborn-Smith's Wax Museum
High St, Brading, Isle of Wight PO3
6DQ
History/Public Affairs Museum - 1965
with wax demonstration of Isle of
Wight history since Tudor period, in
the oldest house on the Island dated
1228 AD; instruments of torture from
the Royal Castle of Nuremberg;
Chinese antique furniture

12746
Roman Villa
Brading, Isle of Wight PO36 OAB
Archeology Museum - 1903
Roman finds; villa ruins; mosaics

Bramber

12747
House of Pipes Museum
Bramber, Sussex
History/Public Affairs Museum - 1973
Articles related to smoking, pipes,
matches, containers - library

Breamore

12748
Breamore Carriage Museum
Breamore, Hants
General Museum - 1972
coaches, carriages

12749
Breamore Carriage Museum
Nr Fodingbridge, Breamore, Hants
History/Public Affairs Museum - 1972
Mail phaeton (1830) used mostly in the
country for exercising coach horses
and for mail delivery; Malvern dog cart
(1880); fire equipment; four-wheeled
buggy; private drag used for driving to
race meetings; vehicle (1845) for
transporting a larger number of
people; saddle room

12750
Breamore Countryside Museum
Breamore, Hants
General Museum - 1972
hand tools; tractors; steam engines;
blacksmith's and wheel-wright's shops;
brewery; dairy

12751
Breamore House
Breamore, Hants
History/Public Affairs Museum - 1951
Elizabethan manor house; paintings of
the Dutch school 17th-18th century;
tapestries; English and Oriental
porcelain; furniture

12752
Breamore House
Nr Frodingbridge, Breamore, Hants
SP6 2DE
History/Public Affairs Museum - 1953
Coll: 17th and 18th century furniture
and paintings (mainly Dutch);
tapestries; porcelain; 14 paintings of
the intermingling of Indian Races by
the son of Murillo (late 17th century);
development of agricultural machinery;
farm implements

Brechin

12753
Brechin Museum Mechanics Institute
St. Ninian's Square, Brechin
General Museum
local history; antiquities

Brecon

12754
Brecknock Museum
Captains Walk, Brecon, Wales
General Museum - 1928
natural history; archaeology; folklore;
pottery; porcelain; costumes;
numismatics; armaments; county
history; early Christian monuments -
library

12755
**South Wales Borderers and
Monmouthshire Regiment Museum**
The Barracks, Brecon, Wales
History/Public Affairs Museum - 1934
regimental history; medals; armaments

Brentford

12756
British Piano and Musical Museum
368 Hight St, Brentford, Middx TW8
OBD
Music Museum - 1963
automatic musical instruments in
working order; pianos; music rolls;
Welte Philharmonic Reproducing Pipe
Organ Model; Wurlitzer Theater
Organ; Double Mills Violano Virtuoso;
Hupfeld Phonoliszt Violina; Hupfeld
Animatic Clavitist Sinfonie-Jazz and
orchestra; Edison Phonograph;
Hupfeld Piano; Street Barrel Pianos
and Organs; Broadwood Grand Piano

12757
Syon House
Brentford TW8 8JG
History/Public Affairs Museum - 1415
Robert Adam furniture and decoration;
famous picture collection; home of the
Dukes of Northumberland

Brentwood

12758
Essex Regiment Museum
Eagle Way, Brentwood, Essex
History/Public Affairs Museum
regimental history

Bridgewater

12759
Admiral Blake Museum
Blake St, Bridgewater, Soms
General Museum - 1926
local history; archaeology; life and
work of Admiral Blake (1599-1657) in
the supposed place of his birth; relics
on the Battle of Sedgemoor

Bridlington

12760
Bayle Museum
Baylegate, Bridlington, Yorks
General Museum
local history

12761
Bridlington Art Gallery and Museum
Sewerby Hall, Bridlington, Yorks
General Museum - 1953
paintings; archaeology; local history;
fishing; memorabilia on air-woman
Amy Johnson

Bridport

12762
Museum and Art Gallery
South St, Bridport, Dorset DT6 3NR
General Museum - 1932
local history; archaeology; natural
history; geology; trades; costumes;
Victorian relics; net weaving

Brierley Hill

12763
Brierley Hill Glass Museum
Moor St, Brierley Hill, Staffs
Fine Arts Museum - 1923
local and foreign glass work; cameo
glass by George Woodall

Brighouse

12764
Smith Art Gallery Victoria Art Gallery
Halifax Rd, Brighouse, W Yorks
Fine Arts Museum - 1907
Paintings; English watercolors; 19th
century woodcarvings

Brighton

12765
Booth Museum of Natural History
194 Dyke Rd, Brighton, Sussex BN1
5AA
Natural History Museum - 1874
British birds; dioramas; butterflies

12766
Preston Manor Thomas-Stanford
Museum
Preston Park, Brighton, Sussex BN1
6SD
History/Public Affairs Museum - 1933
Macquoid bequest English and
Continental period furniture; silver;
pictures; panels of stained glass;
16th-19th century original 16th century
leather wall-hangings

12767
Royal Pavilion Art Gallery and
Museum
Church St, Brighton, Sussex BN1 1UE
General Museum - 1851
Old master paintings; the Willet
collection of pottery and porcelain;
20th century European decorative art
and furniture; Surrealist paintings;
ethnography; archaeology; musical
instruments

Bristol

12768
Blaise Castle House Museum City
Museum
Henbury, Bristol BS10 7QS
General Museum - 1947
regional social history; agricultural
history; domestic life; costumes; toys;
dairy

12769
Chatterton House Museum City
Museum
Redcliffe Way, Bristol
History/Public Affairs Museum
local history

12770
City Museum and Art Gallery
Queen's Rd, Bristol BS8 1RL
General Museum
Archaeology; geology; natural history;
transportation and technology of the
area; ethnography; Classical and
Egyptian finds; numismatics; local
history

12771
Georgian House
7 Great George St, Bristol BS1 5RR
History/Public Affairs Museum - 1937
period furnishings

12772
Red Lodge
Park Row, Bristol BS1
History/Public Affairs Museum
Elizabethan house, modified 18th
century; furnishings

Brixham

12773
Brixham Museum
Bolton Cross, Brixham, Devon
General Museum - 1958
fishing; shipping; maritime and local
history; archaeology; coins

Broadstairs

12774
Bleak House
Broadstairs, Kent
History/Public Affairs Museum
Memorabilia on writer Charles
Dickens (1811-1870) in the house
where he wrote 'David Copperfield'
and 'Bleak House'

12775
Bleak House
Fort Road, Broadstairs, Kent
History/Public Affairs Museum - 1890
original Dickens manuscripts, personal
belongings

Broadway

12776
Snowshill Manor The National Trust
Broadway, Hereford and Worcs
Anthropology Museum - 1951
the Wade Collection; Chinese and
Japanese objects; nautical
instruments; Japanese Samurai
armour; musical instruments;
costumes; toys; spinning and weaving
tools; bicycles; farm wagon models

Brodick

12777
Brodick Castle and Gardens
Bute, Brodick, Island of Arran,
Scotland
History/Public Affairs Museum
Silver, porcelain, paintings, sport
photos and trophies

Brokerswood

12778
The Phillips Countryside Museum
The Woodland Park, Brokerswood,
Wilts
Natural History Museum - 1971
Natural history and forestry; botany;
ornithology

Bromsgrove

12779
Avoncroft Museum of Buildings Ltd.
Redditch Rd, Stoke Heath,
Bromsgrove, Worcs B60 4JR
Open Air Museum - 1969
16th century inn being reconstructed;
19th century post mill; granary and
barn; 15th century merchant's house;
hand-made nail and chain workshops;
medieval roof; Iron Age
reconstructions; medieval guest hall
roof

Budleigh Salterton

12780
Fairlynch Museum
27 Fore St, Budleigh Salterton, Devon
General Museum
art; local history

Burford

12781
Tolsey Museum
Burford, Oxon
General Museum
local governmental history; folklore;
crafts

Burnley

12782
Gawthorpe Hall
Burnley, Lancs
History/Public Affairs Museum
manor house with interiors; collection
of embroidery and needlework

12783
**Towneley Hall Art Gallery and
Museum**
Burnley, Lancs
General Museum - 1902
paintings; water colors; furnishings;
period house

Burton-upon-Trent

12784
Museum and Art Gallery
Guild St, Burton-upon-Trent, Staffs
General Museum - 1913
Natural history; ornithology; local
history; works of art

Burwash

12785
Bateman's Kipling's House National
Trust Porperty
Burwash, Sussex
History/Public Affairs Museum - 1939
work and living rooms of writer
Rudyard Kipling (1865-1936) in his
former home, built 1634; manuscripts -
library

Bury

12786
Art Gallery and Museum
Moss St, Bury, Lancs
General Museum - 1901
British paintings and drawings; local
history; natural history; ornithology;
archaeology; Wedgwood and local
pottery; Bronze Age finds

12787
**Lancashire Fusiliers Regimental
Museum**
Wellington Barracks, Bury, Greater
Manchester
History/Public Affairs Museum
History of the regiment since 1688;
uniforms; medals; militaria; Napoleonic
relics

Bury St. Edmunds

12788
Ickworth House
Bury St. Edmunds
History/Public Affairs Museum
manor dating from 1794-1830 with
Regency 18th century French
furniture; silver; paintings

12789
**John Gershom-Parkington
Collection of Timekeeping
Instruments**
8 Angel Corner, Bury St. Edmunds,
Suffolk
Science/Tech Museum - 1953
technological history of timekeeping
instruments

12790
Moyses Hall Museum
Cornhill, Bury St. Edmunds, Suffolk
General Museum
prehistoric-medieval finds; regional
natural history; local history; 12th
century Norman building

12791
Suffolk Regiment Museum
Bury St. Edmunds, Suffolk
History/Public Affairs Museum - 1935
regimental history

Buscot

12792
Buscot House
Buscot, Berks
Fine Arts Museum - 1780
manor with Italian, Dutch, Flemish,
Spanish and English paintings

Buxton

12793
Buxton Museum
Terrace Rd, Buxton, Derbyshire SK17
6DU
General Museum - 1928
local history; prehistoric cave finds;
geology; mineralogy; arts and crafts

Caerleon

12794
Legionary Museum
Caerleon, Gwent
Archeology Museum
Finds from excavations at the fortress
of the Second Augustan Legion

Caernarvon

12795
**Royal Welch Fusiliers Regimental
Museum**
Caernarvon Castle, Caernarvon,
Wales
History/Public Affairs Museum - 1960
History of the regiment since 1689;
documents; portraits; dioramas

12796
Segontium Museum
Caernarvon
Archeology Museum
Finds from excavations at the former
Roman fort Segontium; inscriptions;
medals; urns; tools; armaments;
pottery; household objects

Calstock

12797
Cotehele House
Calstock, Cornwall
History/Public Affairs Museum
house dating from 1485-1627 with
furniture; tapestry; needlework; armor

Camberley

12798
Camberley Museum
Knoll Rd, Camberley, Surrey GU15
3SY
General Museum - 1951
local history; archaeology; natural
history; Victorian relics

12799
National Army Museum Detachment
Royal Military Academy
Camberley, Surrey
History/Public Affairs Museum
Indian Army Memorial Room; colonial
section; Irish regiments

12800
**Royal Army Ordnance Corps
Museum** Blackdown Barracks
Deepcut, Camberley, Surrey
History/Public Affairs Museum - 1950
Items of historical interest relating to
the Royal Army Ordnance Corps;
medals; archives

Cambo

12801
Wallington Hall
Cambo, Morpeth, Northumberland
History/Public Affairs Museum
House built in 1688 with 18th century
furnishings; rococo plaster
decorations; porcelain; needlework;
19th century hall decorated by W.
Scott, Ruskin and others; Scott's
pre-Raphaelite paintings

Camborne

12802
**Camborne School of Mines
Geological Museum** Camborne
School of Mines
Camborne TR14 8LF
Natural History Museum
mineralogy; geology; Cornish minerals

12803
Public Library and Museum
Cross St, Camborne, Cornwall
History/Public Affairs Museum - B
Stone Age finds; Iron and Bronze Age
pottery; Roman Villa excavation finds;
Mexican and Egytian antiquities; old
china and silver; numismatics;
geology; mineralogy; local history;
mining

Cambridge

12804
Botany School
Downing St, Cambridge CB2
Natural History Museum - 1761
botany; herbarium; Charles Darwin
and John Lindley collections;
specimens from all over the world;
particularly Australia - library

12805
**Cambridge and County Folk
Museum**
Castle St, Cambridge CB3 OAQ
General Museum - 1936
History of Cambridge and
Cambridgeshire county since the 17th
century; photos; views of the old
town; 19th century seal replicas;
historic relics

12806
Cambridge University Archives
University Library
West Rd, Cambridge CB3 9DR
History/Public Affairs Museum
archival collections; records of the
University and its departments;
13th-20th century; records of
Cambridge University Press

12807
Collection of Aerial Photography
Cambridge University
11 West Rd, Cambridge CB2 3RF
Science/Tech Museum
development and technology of aerial
photographic techniques

12808
Fitzwilliam Museum
Trumpington ST, Cambridge CB2 1RB
General Museum - 1816
Egyptian, Greek and Roman
antiquities; numismatics; medieval
manuscripts; paintings; drawings;
pottery; porcelain; textiles; armaments;
medieval Renaissance art objects;
autographs; English ceramics;
Chinese jade and bronze objects;
samplers

12809
Kettle's Ward University of
Cambridge
Northampton St, Cambridge, Cambs
CB3 OPZ
Fine Arts Museum - 1966
collection of Gaudier-books; English
20th century art including Ben
Nicholson, Henry Moore, Christopher
Wood

12810
Museum of Classical Archaeology
Little St, Cambridge CB2 1RR
Archeology Museum - 1882
Greek, Roman sculpture copies; small
original finds

12811
Scott Polar Research Institute
Lensfield Rd, Cambridge CB2 1ER
Anthropology Museum - 1920
polar exploration and research;
material from Antarctic expeditions of
Captain Scott and from other historical
British polar expeditions; relics;
manuscripts; paintings; photographs;
Eskimo art; ethnological collections -
library

12812
Sedgwick Museum of Geology
Downing St, Cambridge CB2 3EQ
Natural History Museum - 1904
local, British, foreign rocks; fossils;
memorabilia of scientist Adam
Sedgwick

12813
**University Museum of Archaeology
and Ethnology**
Downing St, Cambridge CB2 3DZ
Archeology Museum - 1884
Archaeology of the Cambridge region
from the Palaeolithic period to the 17th
century; Stones Age finds from the
Old World; ethnological collections
from Africa, America, Australia,
Oceania and Asia; Cook collection of
Polynesia; Fijian collection; Thomas
collection from West Africa

12814
University Museum of Mineralogy and Petrology
Downing St, Cambridge
Natural History Museum
educational collections of mineralogy, petrography

12815
University Museum of Zoology
Downing St, Cambridge CB2 3ET
Natural History Museum
zoology; entomology; invertebrates

12816
Whipple Museum of the History of Science
Free School Lane, Cambridge CB2 3RH
History/Public Affairs Museum - 1951
Old scientific instruments; 16th-20th century books

Canterbury

12817
Buffs Regimental Museum
Stour St, Canterbury, Kent
History/Public Affairs Museum - 1961
Uniforms; medals; memorabilia on regimental history; prints; watercolors

12818
Coleridge Museum St. Augustines's
Abbey Museum
Canterbury
Fine Arts Museum
religious art

12819
Roman Pavement
Butchery Lane, Canterbury, Kent
Archeology Museum - 1961
ruins of Roman house; finds; mosaic; pottery; coins

12820
Royal Museum
Hight St, Canterbury, Kent
General Museum - 1899
local archaeology, especially finds from Roman, Saxon and medieval periods; natural history; geology; decorative china and glass objects; Roman silver, Anglo-Saxon glass; jewelry finds

12821
Westgate Museum
St. Peters St, Canterbury, Kent
History/Public Affairs Museum - 1906
British and foreign armaments; relics in 14th century medieval gate

Cardiff
12822
Museum of the Welch Regiment
Cardiff Castle, Cardiff, S Wales
History/Public Affairs Museum
regimental military history

12823
National Museum of Wales
Amgueddfa Genedlaethol Cymru
Cathays Park, Cardiff CF1 3NP
General Museum - 1907
Geology; mineralogy; fossils; botany; plant ecology; Welsh zoology; mollusks; entomology; Welsh archaeology up to the 16th century; numismatics; industrial history; European painting; sculpture; applied art; decorative objects; French art

12824
Welsh Folk Museum Amgueddfa
Werin Cymru
St. Fagan's Castle, Cardiff DF5 6BX
Anthropology Museum - 1947
branch of National Museum of Wales with Welsh folk music, reconstructed buildings, folklore

12825
Welsh Industrial and Maritime Museum
Bure Street, Cardiff, S Glam CF1 6AN
Science/Tech Museum - 1977
power; machines; industrial progress; pumping, winding and driving engines, powered by steam, compressed air, gas oil and electricity; steel works; cement works, gas and electricity generation plants

Carlisle
12826
The Border Regiment & King's Own Royal Border Regiment Museum
Queen Mary's Tower, Carlisle, Cumberland CA3 8UR
History/Public Affairs Museum - 1932
uniforms; badges; medals; pictures; silver; arms; dioramas; documents; trophies; militaria

12827
Museum and Art Gallery
Tullie House, Castle St, Carlisle CA3 8TP
General Museum - 1892
regional antiquities; natural history; Lake District specimens; pre-Raphaelite; 19th century painting; modern paintings; English porcelain; Roman finds; ornithology

Carmarthen
12828
Carmarthen Museum
Abergwili, Carmarthen, Dyfed
General Museum - 1905
library

12829
County Museum
5 Quay St, Carmarthen, Wales
General Museum - 1920
Folklore; archaeology of the county

Carnforth
12830
Leighton Hall
Carnforth, Lancs
History/Public Affairs Museum
Manor house dating from the 13th century with old and modern painting; antique furniture; Gillow family portraits

Castle Ashby
12831
Castle Ashby
Castle Ashby, Northampton NN7 1LJ
History/Public Affairs Museum
house with interiors

Castle Howard
12832
Castle Howard Costume Galleries
Castle Howard, Yorks YO6 7DA
History/Public Affairs Museum - 1965
social history; 17th-20th century costumes in period settings; collection of Diaghilev ballet costumes

Castleford
12833
Castleford Museum Area Library and Museum
Carlton St, Castleford, Yorks
General Museum - 1935
Finds from the old Roman town Legiolium; local pottery and glass

Castletown
12834
Nautical Museum
Castletown, Isle of Man, British Isles
General Museum - 1951
Maritime life of the Isle of Man; a late 18th century schooner-rigged, clinker-built yacht; small coastal craft of the period

Cawthorne
12835
Victoria Jubilee Museum
Taylor Hill, Cawthorne, Barnsley S75 4HQ
History/Public Affairs Museum - 1889
local history; example of Cruck formation timbered building

Chalfont St. Giles
12836
Milton's Cottage
Deanway, Chalfont St. Giles, Bucks HP8 4JH
History/Public Affairs Museum - 1887
life and times of writer John Milton (1608-1674); editions of Milton's work, portraits and engravings of Milton; memorabilia

Chatham
12837
Royal Engineers Museum
Brompton Barracks, Chatham, Kent ME4 4UG
History/Public Affairs Museum - 1912
History of engineers' work; military engineering science; memorabilia on Maj. General C.G. Gordon, Lord Kitchener

Chawton
12838
Jane Austen Memorial Trust
Main ST, Chawton, Hants
History/Public Affairs Museum
memorabilia of writer Jane Austen (1775-1817)

Cheddar
12839
Cheddar Veteran and Vintage Car Museum
Cliff St, Cheddar, Soms
Science/Tech Museum - 1964
veteran and vintage cars; motorcycles; steam engines

12840
Gough's Cave Museum
The Gorge, Cheddar, Soms
Archeology Museum - 1934
archaeology and zoology of Cheddar Gorge area; paleolithic pleistocene finds

Cheddleton
12841
Cheddleton Flint Mill
Leek Road; Cheddleton, *mail c/o*
Industrial Heritage Trust, Tittensor, Stoke-on-Trent, Staffs ST12 9HH
Science/Tech Museum - 1967
Coll: 'prime movers' for the grinding of raw materials for the pottery industry; steam engines; transportation; grinding equipment

Chelmsford
12842
Chelmsford and Essex Museum
Oaklands Park, Moulsham St, Chelmsford CM2 9QO
General Museum - 1835
natural history; ornithology; archaeology; Victorian history and furniture; trades and industry; geology; shells; numismatics; paintings; prints; costumes; crafts; militaria on Essex Regiment

Cheltenham
12843
Chedworth Roman Villa Museum The Roman Villa
Cheltenham GL54 3LT
Archeology Museum - 1865
ruins of Roman villa; finds

12844
Cheltenham Art Gallery and Museum Service
Clarence St, Cheltenham GL50 3JT
Fine Arts Museum - 1899
Dutch and other paintings; watercolors and local prints; English pottery and porcelain; geology; natural history; Cotswold area history; Regency room; Chinenese porcelain; memorabilia on Edward Wilson

12845
Cheltenham college Museum
Bath Rd, Cheltenham, Glos
General Museum - 1860
numismatics; ornithology; butterflies; eggs; finds of Greek, roman and Egyptian periods

Chepstow
12846
Chepstow Museum
Board School, Bridge ST, Chepstow, Gwent NP6 5EY
General Museum - 1949
local material

Chertsey
12847
Chertsey Museum The Cedars
33 Windsor St, Chertsey, Surrey KT16 8AT
General Museum
Olive Matthews collection of English costumes and accessories from the 18th century; furniture; porcelain; local history

Chester
12848
Cheshire Military Museum The Castle
Chester, Cheshire
History/Public Affairs Museum - 1924
Militaria on the 22nd Regiment; Battle of Miani 1843; memorabilia of Sir Charles Napier

12849
Grosvenor Museum
27 Grosvenor St, Chester CH1 2DD
General Museum - 1886
Archaeological finds since prehistory from the North Wales area; local history; furnished rooms; costumes; 18th century recorders; coins; natural history; geology; topography; Chester in Roman, Civil War and medieval times

Chesterfield

12850
Revolution House
Hight St, Chesterfield, Derbys
History/Public Affairs Museum - 1938
Restored 17th century building with
17th century furnishings; history of the
Revolution of 1688; manuscripts; local
glass

Chesters

12851
Roman Fort and Museum
Hadrian's Wall, Chesters,
Northumberland
Archeology Museum - 1903
Inscriptions; sculptures; small finds;
armaments

Chichester

12852
Chichester District Museum
29 Little London, Chichester, W
Sussex PO19 1PB
General Museum - 1964
Local history; militaria on the Royal
Sussex Regiment

12853
**Corps of Royal Military Police
Museum** Roussillon Barracks
Broyle Rd, Chichester, Sussex
History/Public Affairs Museum - 1946
military police; uniforms; medals;
history; books; pictures; arms;
archives

12854
Goodwood House
Goodwood, Chichester, W Sussex
PO18 OPX
General Museum
Coll: family portraits; Sèvres porcelain;
French furniture; 4 Gobelin tapestries

12855
Guildhall Museum
Priory Park, Chichester, W Sussex
History/Public Affairs Museum - 1968
History of the city and of Franciscan
Friars

12856
Roman Palace and Museum
Salthill Rd, Chichester, W Sussex
Archeology Museum
Roman ruins and finds

12857
Royal Sussex Regiment Museum
29 Little London, Chichester, W
Sussex PO19 1PB
History/Public Affairs Museum - 1930
militaria on regimental history

Chiddingstone

12858
Chiddingstone Castle
Chiddingstone, Kent
Fine Arts Museum - 1956
Stuart royal letters and memorabilia;
Jacobite collection; portraits;
manuscripts; medals; Japanese inro;
boxes; swords; lacquer; armaments;
netsuke and metal objects; Buddhistic
art; Egyptian objects 4000 BC - Roman
times

Chippenham

12859
Corsham Court
Chippenham, Wilts SN13 OB2
General Museum
Coll: paintings by various old masters
including Filippo Lippi, Rubens, van
Dyck, Reynolds, Guido Reni; furniture

Chirk

12860
Chirk Castle
Chirk, Clwyd
General Museum
Coll: paintings; decorative art; history;
16th, 17th, 18th and early 19th century
decorations

Chorley

12861
Astley Hall Museum and Art Gallery
Astley Park, Chorley, Lancs PR7 1NP
Fine Arts Museum - 1577
Jacobean furniture; paintings and
etchings; Flemish tapestries; Leeds
pottery; 18th century English glass;
magnificent plaster ceilings

Christchurch

12862
**Red House Museum, Art Gallery and
Gardens**
Quay Rd, Christchurch, Dorset BH23
1BU
General Museum - 1951
Paleolithic to medieval local
archaeology; local history; geology
and natural history; costumes; toys;
dolls; domestic equipment; agricultural
equipment; fashion plates; Victoriana;
paintings; drawings; prints and
photographs of local interest - library

Church Stretton

12863
Acton Scott Working Farm Museum
Church Stretton, Shrops SY6 6QN
Agriculture Museum - 1975
Stock, crops and machinery
(1870-1920) - library

Cirencester

12864
Corinium Museum
Park St, Cirencester, Glos
Archeology Museum - 1856
Romano-British antiquities from the
site of Corinium Dobunnorum, second
largest town of Roman Britain; mosaic
floors; Roman sculpture; regional
museum for Cotswolds

Clandon

12865
Clandon Park
Clandon, Surrey
History/Public Affairs Museum
18th century country house in the
Palladian manner; with collection of
pictures, furniture, textiles

Clayton-le-Moors

12866
Mercer Museum and Art Gallery
Mercer Park, Clayton-le-Moors, Lancs
General Museum
local history; art

Clitheroe

12867
Castle Museum The Castle
Clitheroe, Lancs BB7 1BA
General Museum
local history; fossils

Clun

12868
Town Trust Museum
Clun, Salop
General Museum
local history; geology

Cockermouth

12869
Wordsworth House
Main Street, Cockermouth, Cumbria
History/Public Affairs Museum - 1937
Coll: first edition of William
Wordsworth's work, personal
possesions; original paintings and
watercolours by Turner, Morellese and
Edward Oayes

Colchester

12870
Colchester and Essex Museum The
Castle
Colchester, Essex CO1 1TJ
Archeology Museum - 1860
material from Iron Age and Roman
Colchester; Roman military
tombstones; Roman pottery; bronze
figure of Mercury - library

12871
The Hollytrees Colchester and Essex
Museum
High St, Colchester, Essex CO1 1TJ
Anthropology Museum - 1928
costumes; social history; post-Roman
antiquities - library

12872
The Minories Gallery
74 High St, Colchester CO1 1UE
Fine Arts Museum - 1956
drawings and paintings by John
Constable

Colne

12873
British in India Museum
Sun Street, Colne, Lancs
History/Public Affairs Museum - 1972
Coll: model soldiers; photograhs;
documents; paintings; postage
stamps; letters; military uniforms;
model of the Kalka-Simla Railway -
library

Compton

12874
Watts Gallery
Compton, Surrey GU3 1DQ
Fine Arts Museum - 1903
paitings and sculptures by artist G.F.
Watts

Congleton

12875
Little Moreton Hall National Trust
Property
Congleton, Cheshire
History/Public Affairs Museum
Elizabethan house with woodwork;
plaster decorations; oak furniture;
pewter objects

Coniston

12876
Ruskin Museum Coniston Institute
Yewdale Rd, Coniston, Cumbria
History/Public Affairs Museum - 1900
memorabilia of John Ruskin
(1819-1900)

Conway

12877
Royal Cambrian Academy of Art
High St, Conway, Wales
Fine Arts Museum - 1881
paintings; sculpture

Conwy

12878
Aberconwy House
Conwy, Gwynedd
General Museum
medieval house that dates from the
14th century, now houses the Conwy
Exhibition, depicting the life of the
borough from Roman times to the
present day

Cookham-on-Thames

12879
Stanley Spencer Gallery King's Hall
High St, Cookham-on-Thames, Berks
Fine Arts Museum - 1959
paintings and drawings by Stanley
Spencer, reference works

Corbridge

12880
Corstopitum Roman Site Museum
Corbridge, Northumberland
Archeology Museum - 1920
Roman inscriptions and other finds
from the Roman town Corstopitum

Coventry

12881
Herbert Art Gallery and Museum
Coventry CV1 5PQ
General Museum - 1960
Sutherland sketches used in making a
Cathedral tapestry; local art;
topography; local natural history;
transportation

12882
Lunt Roman Fort Reconstruction
Baginton, Coventry, Warwicks
Archeology Museum
reconstructed Roman fort

12883
**Whitefriars Museum of Coventry
History** Whitefriars
Coventry, Warwicks
Archeology Museum - 1970
Anglo-Saxon and medieval
archaeology

Craigievar Castle

12884
Craigievar Castle
Craigievar Castle, Aberdeenshire
History/Public Affairs Museum
plaster ceilings; baronial architecture

Crathes Castle

12885
Crathes Castle and Gardens National
Trust for Scotland
Crathes Castle, Kincardineshire,
Scotland
History/Public Affairs Museum
furnishings and decoration; painted
ceiling from the end of the 16th
century

Creetown

12886
Creetown Gem Rock Museum
Chain Rd, Creetown, Newton Stewart,
Galloway DG8 7HJ
Natural History Museum - 1969
Gem rocks; valuable minerals

Cregneash

12887
The Folk Museum
Cregneash, Isle of Man, British Isles
Open Air Museum - 1938
historic buildings, workshops,
cottages; history of the way of life of
the Manxs crofting community

12888
Manx Village Folk Museum
Cregneash, Isle of Man
General Museum - 1938
ethnography; history; thatched crofter-
fisherman's cottage; thatched
farmstead; other historical buildings

Cromarty

12889
Hugh Miller's Cottage
Church St, Cromarty, Ross
History/Public Affairs Museum - 1900
birthplace of Scottish geologist Hugh
Miller with memorabilia; equipment;
letters

Culloden

12890
Old Leanach Farmhouse
Culloden, Ivernesshire, Scotland
History/Public Affairs Museum
military items

Culross

12891
Erskine of Torrie Institute Dunimarle
Castle
Culross, Fife KY12 8JN
History/Public Affairs Museum
Palace (1597-1611) with
wood-panelling; tempera ceiling

Culzean Castle

12892
Culzean Castle and Country Park
Culzean Castle KA19 8JX
History/Public Affairs Museum
interiors; fittings designed by Robert
Adam; staircase; plaster ceilings; 18th
century castle built by Robert Adam

Dagenham

12893
Valence House Museum
Becontree Ave, Dagenham RM8 3HT
General Museum
local history

Darlington

12894
Darlington Museum
Tubnell Row, Darlington DL1 1PD
General Museum
Local and natural history; items from
the Stockton and Darlington Railway
and North Eastern Railway Companies

12895
**Edward Pease Public Library and Art
Gallery**
Crown St, Darlington, Durham
Fine Arts Museum - 1933
Art in general

12896
Raby Castle
Staindrop, Darlington, Durham
Fine Arts Museum
Dutch and Flemish paintings

Dartford

12897
Dartford Borough Museum
Central Park, Dartford, Kent DA1 1HS
Archeology Museum - 1916
natural history; geology; prehistoric
finds; Roman, Saxon and medieval
finds; Saxon finds from Horton Kirby
site

Dartmouth

12898
Borough Museum
6 The Butterwalk, Dartmouth, Devon
TQ6 9PZ
General Museum
Local and maritime history; ship
models; 17th century panelling

Dawlish

12899
Dawlish Museum
The Knowle, Barton Terrace, Dawlish
EX7 9QJ
General Museum
local history

Deal

12900
Museum
Town Hall, High St, Deal, Kent
General Museum
local history

Derby

12901
Derby Museum and Art Gallery
The Strand, Derby DE1 1BS
General Museum - 1879
paintings of Joseph Wright; history;
geology; porcelain; contemporary
paintings; drawings; engravings;
numismatics; railway history;
costumes

12902
Royal Crown Derby Museum
Osmaston Rd, Derby DE3 8JZ
General Museum
History of ceramics production in
Derby; Indian style vases made in the
1880s

Devizes

12903
**Museum of the Wiltshire
Archaeological and Natural History
Society**
41 Long St, Devizes, Wilts SN10 1NS
General Museum - 1853
Stone, Bronze and Iron Age finds;
Stourhead Stone and Bronze Age
collection; geological fossils - library

12904
Wiltshire Regiment Museum
Le Marchant Barracks, Devizes, Wilts
History/Public Affairs Museum - 1933
Militaria on 62nd and 99th Regiment of
Foot, Wiltshire Regiment and Militaria

Dewsbury

12905
Museum and Art Gallery The
Mansion
Crow Nest Park, Temple St,
Dewsbury, Yorks
General Museum - 1898
local history; natural history; Egyptian
collection

Disley

12906
Lyme Hall
Lyme Park, Disley, Cheshire
History/Public Affairs Museum - 1946
Elizabethan house with Palladian
architecture; Mortlake tapestries;
Pearwood carvings; Heraldic glass

Diss

12907
Bressingham Steam Museum
Diss, Norfolk
Science/Tech Museum - 1964
Several standard gauge railway
locomotives; stationary and
transportable steam engines;
mechanical organs

Dolwyddelan

12908
Ty Mawr Wybrnant
Dolwyddelan, Gwynedd
General Museum
Birthplace of Bishop William Morgan
who translated the Bible into Welsh -
this translation became the foundation
of modern Welsh literature

Doncaster

12909
Cusworth Hall Museum
Doncaster, Yorks
History/Public Affairs Museum - 1967
industrial history illustrating the
development of industrial, commercial
and social life in South Yorkshire;
archives - library

12910
Doncaster Museum and Art Gallery
Chequer Rd, Doncaster, Yorks
General Museum - 1899
regional history; archaeology; natural
history; costumes; applied art

Dorchester

12911
Athelhampton
Dorchester
History/Public Affairs Museum
house with 15th-16th century furniture

12912
Dorset County Museum
High West St, Dorchester, Dorset
General Museum - 1846
county archaeology; geology; local
and regional history; memorabilia

12913
Dorset Military Museum The Keep
Bridport Rd, Dorchester, Dorset
History/Public Affairs Museum - 1927
Exhibits of the Dorset Regiment
(1702-1758); local militaria and
volunteers; Queen's Own Dorset
Yeomanry; Devonshire & Dorset
Regiment; uniforms; weapons; silver -
library

Dorking

12914
Polesden Lacey National Trust
Property
Dorking, Surrey
Fine Arts Museum
pictures; furniture; tapestries; art
objects

Douglas

12915
The Manx Museum
Douglas, Isle of Man, British Isles
History/Public Affairs Museum - 1886
Coll: archaeological finds of the period
of the Norse kingship; pagan grave
artifacts; carved grave markers of the
Christian period; coin hoards;
metalwork; watercolours - library

12916
Nautical Museum
Douglas, CI
Science/Tech Museum
Local maritime history; ship models;
18th century yacht

Dover

12917
Dover Museum Ladywell
Dover
General Museum - 1836
local history; ceramics; geology;
transportation; pipes; embroidery;
cameras; natural history; silver

Downe

12918
Darwin Museum Royal College of
Surgeons, London
Downe, Kent
History/Public Affairs Museum - 1927
memorabilia of biologist Charles
Darwin, his study, other rooms;
portraits; mural depicting evolution

Driffield

12919
Burton Agnes Hall
Driffield, Yorks
Fine Arts Museum - 1946
Elizabethan house with ceilings,
overmantels, paintings by Reynolds,
Gainsborough, Cotes, Marlow,
Reinagle, also modern French
paintings

Dudley

12920
Museum and Art Gallery
St. James's Rd, Dudley, Worcs
General Museum
artworks; geology; reconstructed
Black Country forge; glass

Dumfries

12921
Burn's Granary
Ellisland, Dumfries
Archeology Museum
rural life; folk crafts

12922
Dumfries Museum The Observatory
Corberry Hill, Dumfries
General Museum - 1835/1934
geology; paleontology; mineralogy;
botany; zoology; ethnography;
costumes; photos

12923
Old Bridge House The Observatory
Corbell Hill, Dumfries
History/Public Affairs Museum -
1959/1960
period furnishings; interiors; various
rooms; ceramics; costumes; toys;
books

Dunblane

12924
Dunblane Cathedral Museum
Cathedral Square, Dunblane,
Perthshire
Religious Art Museum
paintings; prints; medieval carvings;
letters of Bishop Robert Leighton

Dundee

12925
Barrack Street Museum Corporation
of the City of Dundee Art Galleries
and Museums Dept.
Barrack St, Ward Rd, Dundee
Science/Tech Museum - 1910
local shipping; industrial and
technological development; ship and
technological models

12926
Broughty Castle Museum
Corporation of the city of Dundee Art
Galleries and Museum Dept.
Broughty Ferry, Dundee
History/Public Affairs Museum - 1969
castle and town history; whaling;
armaments; furniture; militaria; ecology

12927
City Museum and Art Gallery
Corporation of the City of Dundee Art
Galleries and Museums Dept.
Albert Square, Dundee
General Museum - 1873
Works of art; archaeology; natural
history; numismatics; ethnography;
furnishings

12928
James Guthrie Orchard Art Gallery
31 Beach Crescent, Dundee
Fine Arts Museum
Victorian paintings; sculpture; Whistler
original etchings; watercolors

12929
St. Mary's Tower Corporation of the
City of Dundee Art Galleries and
Museum Dept.
Kirk Stile, Nethergate, Dundee
Religious Art Museum - 1971
history of St. Mary's pre-reformation
church, and of post-reformation
churches; stained glass

12930
Spalding Golf Museum Corporation
of the City of Dundee Art Galleries
and Museums Dept.
Camperdown House, Camperdown
Park, Dundee
History/Public Affairs Museum
history of golf; equipment; famous
golfers

Dunfermline

12931
Andrew Carnegie Birthplace
Memorial
Moodie St, Dunfermline
History/Public Affairs Museum
birthplace of industrialist-philanthropist
Andrew Carnegie with memorabilia,
costumes, decorative arts

12932
Dunfermline Museum
Viefiled Terrace, Dunfermline
General Museum - 1961
local history; natural history

12933
Pittencrieff House Museum
Piettencrieff Park, Dunfermline
History/Public Affairs Museum - 1961
costumes since 1800; paintings
relating to costumes

Durham

12934
Dean and Chapter Library, Monk's
Dormitory Museum The College
Durham
Religious Art Museum
in monastery dating 1398-1404,
manuscripts and books from original
library; religious objects relating to St.
Cuthbert; medieval numismatics;
jewelry

12935
Durham Light Infantry Museum and
Art Centre
Aykley Heads, Durham
History/Public Affairs Museum - 1969
medals, uniforms, weapons,
documents

12936
Gulbenkian Museum of Oriental Art
School of Oriental Studies, The
University
Elvet Hill, Durham
Fine Arts Museum - 1960
Eastern and Islamic art and
archaeology; ceramics; Tibetan art;
Chinese and Japanese paintings and
ceramics; jade; Egyptian funerary art;
Chinese metal wares; Indian paintings
and sculptures

Dursley

12937
R.A. Lister Museum
Long Street, Dursley, Gloucestershire
GL11 4HS
Agriculture Museum
agricultural machinery; diesel engines;
generating sets for industrial and
marine duties

Eardisland

12938
Burton Court
Eardisland, Herefords
Science/Tech Museum - 1967
Coll: Oriental and European costumes
dating from the 16th century; natural
history; model ships

East Budleigh

12939
James Countryside Museum
East Budleigh, Devon EX9 7DP
General Museum - 1967

East Cowes

12940
Osborne House and Swiss Cottage
Museum
East Cowes, CI
General Museum

Eastbourne

12941
Museum of the Royal National
Life-Boat Institution
Grand Parade, Eastbourne, E Sussex
History/Public Affairs Museum
history of lifeboat rescues

12942
Tower 73 The Wish Tower
King Edward's Parade, Eastbourne, E
Sussex
History/Public Affairs Museum - 1970
Displays showing the building,
manning and armament of Martello
towers to defend the community
against invasion during the Napoleonic
Wars, coastal defense

12943
Towner Art Gallery
Borough Lane, Eastbourne, E Sussex
Fine Arts Museum - 1923
19th and 20th century British painting;
prints; Georgian caricatures; book
illustrations; topographical collection of
watercolors and drawings of Old
Eastbourne

Eastney

12944
Eastney Pumping Station - Gas
Engine House
Henderson Rd, Eastney, Hants
Science/Tech Museum - 1972
Industrial transportation; pair of
Boulton & Watt Reciprocal Steam
Pumps (1887), Crossley Gas Engines
and Tanoye Pumps

Ecclefechan

12945
Carlyles's Birthplace
Ecclefechan, Dumfries
History/Public Affairs Museum
Birthplace of writer Thomas Carlyle,
collection of his belongings and misc.
letters

Eccles

12946
Monks Hall Museum
42 Wellington Rd, Eccles M30 ONP
General Museum - 1961
rotating exhibits of art, science,
technology, local history, also Nasmyth
machinery, apiculture

Edgehill

12947
Upton House National Trust Property
Edgehill, Warwicks
Fine Arts Museum
Brussels tapestries, porcelain from
Sèvres, Chelsea figurines, furniture,
paintings

Edinburgh

12948
Bute House National Trust for
Scotland
5 Charlotte Square, Edinburgh
History/Public Affairs Museum - 1966
Georgian house built by the architect
Robert Adam, official residence

12949
Canongate Tolbooth
Canongate, Edinburgh EH8 8BN
General Museum - 1954
History of the Canongate district,
tartans, Highland costumes, paintings
of the 19th century

12950
Gallery of the Royal Scottish
Academy
The Mound and Princes St, Edinburgh
EH2 2EL
Fine Arts Museum

12951
Hunty House
Canongate, Edinburgh
Fine Arts Museum
local history, Scottish pottery, local
glass and silver, paintings, prints

12952
John Knox's House
45 High Street, The Royal Mile,
Edinburgh, Lothian EH1 1SR
History/Public Affairs Museum - 1849
Coll: memorabilia on John Knox

12953
Lady Stair's House
Lady Stair's Close, Lawnmarket,
Edinburgh EH1 2PA
History/Public Affairs Museum - 1907
memorabilia of poets Robert Burns, Sir
Walter Scott, Robert Louis Stevenson

12954
Lamb's House National Trust for
Scotland
Leith, Edinburgh
History/Public Affairs Museum - 1958
16th or 17th century residence and
warehouse of merchant

12955
Lauriston Castle
2A Cramond Rd. South, Edinburgh
History/Public Affairs Museum - 1926
'Blue John' Derbyshire Spare, wool
mosaics, castle with period
furnishings, tapestries, decorative arts

12956
Museum of Childhood
38 High St, Edinburgh
History/Public Affairs Museum - 1955
social history of childhood, children's
pastimes and hobbies, education, toys,
dolls, model soldiers, trains and
vehicles

12957
National Gallery of Scotland
The Mound, Edinburgh
Fine Arts Museum - 1850
14th-19th century Western painting,
drawings, prints, sculpture, 17th-19th
century Scottish painting, old painting
by Titian, Raphael, Rembrandt, Poussin
and others

12958
National Museum of Antiquities of
Scotland
Queen St, Edinburgh
General Museum - 1781
ancient and modern Scottish
archaeology; history; domestic life;
applied art; numismatics; agriculture

12959
Royal College of Surgeons of
Edinburgh
18 Nicholson St, Edinburgh
Science/Tech Museum - 1807
Surgery, pathology and medicine

12960
The Royal Scots Regimental
Museum
The Castle, Edinburgh
History/Public Affairs Museum - 1951
History; uniforms; medals; weapons;
trophies of the regiment; militaria

12961
Royal Scottish Museum
Chambers St, Edinburgh
General Museum - 1855
archaeology; natural history; geology;
technology; Oriental arts; ethnography
of Plains Indians; Eastern Island and
Maori cultures; Baule figures;
minerals; fossils; mining and
metallurgy; power industries; shipping;
aeronautics; radiation; primitive arts;
British birds - library

12962
Scottish Arts Council Gallery
19 Charlotte Square, Edinburgh
Fine Arts Museum

12963
**Scottish National Gallery of Modern
Art** Inverleith House and Royal
Botanic Garden
Edinburgh
Fine Arts Museum - 1960
20th century paintings, sculptures,
drawings, prints

12964
Scottish National Portrait Gallery
1 Queen St, Edinburgh
Fine Arts Museum - 1882
portraits in various media illustrating
the history of Scotland from the 16th
century up to the present day

12965
Scottish United Services Museum
The Castle, Crown Square, Edinburgh
History/Public Affairs Museum - 1931
history; uniforms; armaments of all
armed forces in Britain, military
contemporary prints

12966
University Departmental Museums
Old College, South Bridge, Edinburgh
Science/Tech Museum
anatomy, chemistry, fine art, forensic
medicine, geology, music, prehistoric
archaeology, forestry, mining,
agricultural zoology, forest zoology,
botany, natural history

Egham

12967
**Royal Holloway College Picture
Gallery** Royal Holloway College
(University of London)
Egham Hill, Egham
Fine Arts Museum - 1887
paintings by Turner, Gainsborough,
Frith, Constable, Millais and others

Elgin

12968
Elgin Museum
1 High St, Elgin, Morayshire
General Museum
Local antiquities, fish fossils, Triassic
and Permian reptile fossils, birds and
eggs, butterflies

Enfield

12969
Forty Hall
Forty Hill, Enfield, Middx
General Museum - 1955
furniture, paintings, decorative arts,
17th-18th century English metalwork
and needlework, local history,
antiquities, maps, prints, Delft pottery,
finds from excavations at Elsynge

Enniskillen

12970
**County Fermanagh and Royal
Inniskilling Fusiliers Regimental
Museum**
The Castle, Enniskillen, Fermanagh
History/Public Affairs Museum - 1931
History of the regiments, militaria,
historical records - library

Epsom

12971
Bourne Hall Museum Bourne Hall
Spring St, Epsom, Surrey
General Museum - 1970
local history; early photography; 20th
century costumes - library

Exeter

12972
Devonshire Regiment Museum
Wyvern Barracks, Exeter, Devon
History/Public Affairs Museum - 1931
History of the regiments (1685-1967),
uniforms, medals, Boer War

12973
Rougemont House Museum
Castle St, Exeter, Devon
General Museum - 1911
archaeology of Devon and Exeter,
local history, militaria

12974
Royal Albert Memorial Museum
Queen St, Exeter, Devon
General Museum - 1868
natural history; butterflies; birds; local
geology; fine art; local artists; applied
arts; Exeter silver; Devon pottery;
18th-20th century costumes; Devon
lace; ethnography; Polynesian, N.
American Indian material; Yoruba
sculptures; 18th and early 19th century
Eskimo and N.W. Coast material;
Benin head and staff mount; 18th
century Tahitian morning dress; flute
glass 'Exeter flute' c 1660; harpsichord
by Vincentius Sodi; technology

12975
St. Nicholas Priory The Mint
Fore St, Exeter, Devon
History/Public Affairs Museum - 1916
Monastery with 11th century cellar,
13th century entry, 15th century
kitchen and guest hall, 17th century
furnishings, 17th-19th century kitchen
objects

12976
Topsham Museum
25 The Strand, Exeter
Science/Tech Museum - 1967
shipping, fishing

Falkland

12977
**Royal Palace of Falkland and
Gardens** National Trust for Scotland
Falkland, Scotland
History/Public Affairs Museum
Royal apartments

Falmouth

12978
Falmouth Art Gallery
The Moor, Falmouth, Cornwall
Fine Arts Museum - 1978
Call: late 19th and early 20th century
paintings (mainly British) donated by
Alfred de Pass

Farleigh-Hungerford

12979
Farleigh Castle Museum
Farleigh-Hungerford, Soms
General Museum

Farnham

12980
Farnham Museum Willmer House
38 West St, Farnham
General Museum - 1960
House (1718) with English decorative
arts, local history, archaeology,
ethnography, 18th century furniture,
costumes, numismatics

Filkins

12981
**Filkins and Broughton Poggs
Museum**
Filkins, Glos
General Museum
ethnography, household and farm
tools, forging and stone-carving tools,
stone craft

Folkestone

12982
Museum and Art Gallery
Grace Hill, Folkestone, Kent
General Museum - 1857
local, regional history, archaeology,
natural history

Forfar

12983
Museum and Art Gallery Meffan
Institute
20 West High St, Forfar
General Museum - 1898
local history

Forres

12984
Falconer Museum
Tolbooth St, Forres, Moray IV36 0PH
General Museum - 1871
specializied herbaria; local history;
natural history - library

Fort George

12985
**Museum of Seaforth Cameron
Highlanders and Queen's Own
Highlanders**
Fort George, Inverness-shire,
Scotland
History/Public Affairs Museum - 1967
uniforms, medals, silver, arms

Gainsborough

12986
Gainsborough Old Hall
Parnell St, Gainsborough
History/Public Affairs Museum
In building dating from 1420; Victoriana
and period furniture, portraits,
costumes, dolls, china, toys

Gateshead

12987
Shipley Art Gallery
Prince Consort Rd, Gateshead
Fine Arts Museum - 1917
17th-20th century British painting, also
French, Flemish, German, Dutch and
Italian painting; Schäufelein altar,
Canaletto work, Roubilias bust; local
glass; natural history

Georgetown

12988
Fort Hayes Museum
Georgetown, Ascension Island
General Museum - 1966
Navy relics; natural history; geology;
biology; communication equipment;
1873 fire wagon; photographs and
other memorabilia from 1880 to
present day

Glamis

12989
Angus Folk Museum National Trust
for Scotland
Kirkwynd Cottages, Glamis, Tayside
Anthropology Museum
local 17th century stone-roofed
cottages

Glandford

12990
Shell Museum
Glandford, Norfolk
Fine Arts Museum - 1915
Jodrell shell collection; jewelry,
pottery, agate

Glasgow

12991
Burrell Collection, Camphill Museum
Queen's Park, Glasgow
Fine Arts Museum - 1896
Paintings, watercolors by Glasgow
artists, ceramics, pottery

12992
Collins Exhibition Hall University of
Strathclyde
22 Richmond St, Glasgow G1 1XQ
Science/Tech Museum - 1973
Anderson collection of scientific
instruments

12993
Glasgow Art Gallery and Museum
Kelvingrove Park, Glasgow
Fine Arts Museum - 1902
British and European paintings
including pictures by Rembrandt and
Giorgione, 19th century French
Impressionists, Scottish painting,
sculpture, costume, silver, pottery and
porcelain, arms and armour, wildlife
and story of man in Scotland, ship
models, Burrell collection

12994
**Heatherbank Museum of Social
Work**
Mugdock Rd 163, Glasgow,
Strathclyde G62 6BR
History/Public Affairs Museum - 1974
Coll: photographic collection of
historic pictures; some archive
material and ephemera - library

12995
**Hunterian Museum and University
Art Collections** University of Glasgow
Glasgow
General Museum - 1807
Numismatics; archaeology;
Mediterranean collection; history;
Roman finds; geography; zoology;
geology; anatomy; fine arts

12996
Museum of Costumes Aikenhead
Museum
Aikenhead House, Glasgow
History/Public Affairs Museum
costumes

12997
Museum of Transport Glasgow
Museums and Art Galleries 230
Albert Drive Glasgow
Science/Tech Museum - 1864
railroad locomotives, bicycles,
motorcycles, streetcars, automobiles,
models, fire engines, baby carriages,
steam road vehicles, horse-drawn
carriages

12998
Old Glasgow Museum Glasgow
Museum and Art Galleries
People's Palace, Glasgow
General Museum - 1898
Archeology; history; weapons;
memorabilia; costumes, maps,
decorative objects, paintings; theater
history; pipes; pottery

12999
Pollok House Glasgow Museums and
Art Galleries
2060 Pollikshaws Rd, Glasgow
Fine Arts Museum
Stirling Maxwell collection of the
Spanish school of painting including El
Greco, Goya, Murillo; decorative arts;
furniture; pottery; porcelain

13000
Provan Hall National Trust for
Scotland
Auchinlea Rd, Glasgow
History/Public Affairs Museum - 1935
pre-Reformation mansion house

13001
**Royal Highland Fusiliers Regimental
Museum**
518 Sauchiehall St, Glasgow
History/Public Affairs Museum - 1969
History of the regiment since 1678

13002
Tolcross Museum
Tolcross Park, Glasgow
General Museum - 1905
Dolls, costumes, landscapes, models,
woodcarvings

Glastonbury

13003
Lake Village Museum (Glastonbury
Antiquarian Society)
High St, Glastonbury, Soms
History/Public Affairs Museum
local history

Glenesk

13004
Glenesk Trust Museum
The Retreat, Glenesk, Angus
General Museum - 1955
local rural life, period rooms

Gloucester

13005
Bishop Hooper's Lodging Folk life
and Regimental Museum
99-103 Westgate St, Gloucester
General Museum - 1935
History of Gloucester since 1500, old
crafts, trades; historic militaria of the
Gloucestershire Regiment since 1694,
uniforms, medals

13006
City Museum and Art Gallery
Brunswick Rd, Gloucester
General Museum - 1850
archaeology; geology; botany; natural
history; English pottery, glass and
silver objects; numismatics; art

Glynde

13007
Glynde Place
Glynde, Sussex
History/Public Affairs Museum
Historical documents; portraits;
bronzes; needlework; Rubens original
cartoon for the ceiling of the
Banqueting Hall in White Hall, a house
built in 1569 in London

Godalming

13008
Charterhouse School Museum
Godalming, Surrey
General Museum

13009
Godalming Museum Old Town Hall
High St, Godalming
General Museum
local history; Romano-British pottery;
wool

Goldsithney, Penzance

13010
**West Cornwall Museum of
Mechanical Music**
Goldsithney, Penzance, Cornwall TR20
9LD
History/Public Affairs Museum - 1972
Pier amusement machines; Worlitzer
roll-playing cinema organ;-pianola;
magic lanterns; music boxes;
gramophones

Goodwood

13011
Goodwood House
Goodwood, Sussex
History/Public Affairs Museum
furniture; flintworks; paintings;
porcelains; tapestries

Goole

13012
**Garside Collection of Local History,
Goole Museum**
Carlisle St, Goole
General Museum - 1964
local history; shipping; paintings

Gosport

13013
Gosport Museum and Art Gallery
Walpole Rd, Gosport, Hants PO12
1NS
General Museum - 1974
geology; local crafts and industries -
library

13014
**Royal Navy Submarine Museum and
HMS 'Alliance'**
HMS 'Dolphin', Gosport, Hants PO12
2AB
History/Public Affairs Museum - 1963
Models of all British submarines from
1879 to the present day; H.M.
Submarine Alliance - library

Grantham

13015
Grantham Museum
St. Peter's Hill, Grantham, Lincs
General Museum
Local history from prehistoric to
modern times

Grasmere

13016
**Dove Cottage and the Wordsworth
Museum**
Grasmere, Cumbria
History/Public Affairs Museum -
1890/1935
former home of William Wordsworth
(1770-1850) with memorabilia of the
poet

Grays

13017
Thurrock Local History Museum
Central Library
Orsett Rd, Grays, Thurrock
General Museum
local history

Great Yarmouth

13018
Elizabethan House Museum Ministry
of Works
4 South Quay, Great Yarmouth,
Norfolk NR30 2QH
History/Public Affairs Museum
house with plaster ceilings dated 1603

13019
The Exhibition Galleries
Tollhouse St, Great Yarmouth, Norfolk
History/Public Affairs Museum - 1951
16th-17th century domestic life; 16th
century panelling; Lowestoft china and
glass

13020
Maritime Museum for East Anglia
25 Marine Parade, Great Yarmouth,
Norfolk
General Museum
Maritime history of the city, fishing,
historic racing lateener (1829)

Greenock

13021
McLean Museum and Art Gallery
9 Union St, Greenock, Renfrewshire
PA16 9JH
General Museum - 1876
Caird and McKellar collection of
pictures; shipping; objects of J. Watt

Gressenhall, Dereham

13022
Norfolk Rural Life Museum
Gressenhall, Dereham, Norfolk NR20
4DR
General Museum - 1976
Agricultural history of Norfolk county

Grimsby

13023
Doughty Museum
Town Hall Square, Grimsby, South
Humberside DN31 1HX
General Museum - 1958
ship models; porcelain; local history

Guernsey

13024
**National Trust of Guernsey Folk
Museum**
Saumarez Park, Guernsey, Guernsey,
British Isles
Agriculture Museum - 1968
Coll: agricultural tools of the island

Guildford

13025
Guildford House Gallery
155 High Street, Guildford, Surrey
GU1 3AJ
Fine Arts Museum - 1969
local paintings of topographical
interest; architecture; iron window;
carved staircase; plaster ceilings -
library

13026
Guildford Museum
Castle Arch, Guildford, Surrey GU1
3SX
General Museum - 1898
county archaeology; history;
needlework; ethnography; Saxon
cemetery finds from Guildtown

13027
Losely House
Guildford, Surrey
History/Public Affairs Museum
House (1562) with Elizabethan
architecture; works of art; furniture;
paintings; ceilings

13028
**Regimental Museum of the Women's
Royal Army Corps** WRAC Centre
Queen Elizabeth Park, Guildford,
Surrey GU2 6QH
History/Public Affairs Museum - 1950
History of the women's corps since
1917

Halesworth

13029
Heveningham Hall
Halesworth, Suffolk
History/Public Affairs Museum - 1967
1780 built house with original furniture

Halifax

13030
**Duke of Wellington's Regimental
Museum** Bankfield Museum
Ackroyd Park, Haley Hill, Halifax,
Yorks HX3 6HG
History/Public Affairs Museum - 1959
History of the regiment; memorabilia
on the first Duke of Wellington
(1769-1852)

13031
Folk Museum of West Yorkshire
Shibden Hall, Halifax, Yorks HX3 6XG
General Museum - 1937
15th century house with 17th-18th
century furnishings; other old
buildings, workshops, farm tools,
vehicles

Hamilton

13032
Hamilton District Museum
129 Muir St, Hamilton, Lanarkshire
ML3 6BJ
General Museum - 1967
Transportation; costumes; weaving;
natural history; industrial history;
period kitchen; local history; mining;
engineering; in 17th century building

13033
**Regimental Museum, the
Cameronians (Scottish Rifles)**
129 Muir St, Hamilton, Lanarkshire
ML3 6BJ
History/Public Affairs Museum - 1968
Militaria, regimental history

Hampton Court

13034
Hampton Court Palace
Hampton Court, Middx
Fine Arts Museum - 1514
Coll: Italian, Flemish, German, Dutch, French, Spanish paintings; in royal palace

Harlow

13035
Harlow Museum
Third Avenue, Harlow, Essex CM18 6YL
General Museum - 1973
Coll: Roman post-medieval pottery - library

Harlyn Bay

13036
Harlyn Bay Museum
Harlyn Bay, Cornwall
Archeology Museum - 1902
Prehistoric finds from burial grounds, burial remains

Harrogate

13037
Harrogate Art Gallery
Public Library, Victoria Av, Harrogate, Yorks
Fine Arts Museum - 1931
Paintings, watercolors, lithographs, drawings, prints, reproductions

13038
Nidderdale Museum
King Street, Pateley Bridge, Harrogate, Yorks HG3 5LE
General Museum
7 rooms featuring Dale's life in the past including several historic shops and rooms, photographs and agricultural implements

13039
Royal Pump Room Museum
Royal Parade, Crescent Rd, Harrogate, Yorks
General Museum - 1953
History of sulphur and mineral wells; costumes, pottery, archaeology, local social life

Harrow

13040
Kodak Museum
Headstone Drive, Harrow, Middx
Science/Tech Museum - 1927
History of photography, camera design, cinematography, magic lanterns, stereoscopy, radiography

Hartlebury

13041
Hereford and Worcester County Museum
Hartlebury Castle, Hartlebury, Worcs DY11 7XZ
General Museum - 1964
Horse-drawn vehicles including gypsy caravans; glass, crafts, toys, costumes - library

Hartlepool

13042
Gray Art Gallery and Museum
Clarence Rd, Hartlepool, Cleveland TS26 8BT
General Museum - 1920
Local history since Roman, Saxon and medieval times; natural history, paintings, oriental art objects

13043
Hartlepool Maritime Museum
Northgate, Hartlepool, Cleveland TS24 0LP
Science/Tech Museum - 1971
Ship models, model engines, fishing equipment, navigation instruments, craftsmen's tools, marine paintings, replica of 19th century fisherman's cottage with contemporary furnishings, ship's wheelhouse with simulated radar display, lighthouse lamp and lens system (1847)

Haslemere

13044
Educational Museum
High St, Haslemere, Surrey
Natural History Museum - 1888
Natural history, geology, ornithology, botany, prehistory, local history, peasant art

Hastings

13045
Museum and Art Gallery
John's Place, Cambridge RD, Hastings, Sussex TN34 1FT
General Museum - 1890
Paintings, Oriental art, Pacific and American Indian ethnography, geology, zoology, archaeology, history, folklore, topography; Durbar Hall, Hawaiian feather cloak, majolica dish of 1594, Sussex pottery - library, archives

13046
Museum of Local History
Old Town Hall, High St, Hastings, Sussex TN34 1ET
General Museum - 1890
Local archaeology and history, topography

Hatfield

13047
The Old Mill House Museum
Mill Green, Hatfield, Hertfords
General Museum - 1973
Belgic and Roman pottery from Welwyn; medieval and post medieval pottery from Hatfield - library

Havant

13048
Havant Museum and Art Gallery
East Street, Havant, Hants PO9 1BS
General Museum - 1977
Vokes Collection of sporting firearms; Havant local industries

Haverfordwest

13049
Graham and Kathleen Sutherland Foundation
Haverfordwest, Dyfed
Fine Arts Museum - 1976
Coll: paintings; lithographs; works in various medias

13050
Pembrokeshire County Museum
Amugueddfeydd Sir Benfro
The Castle, Haverfordwest, Pembrokeshire
General Museum

Hawick

13051
Hawick Museum and Art Gallery
Wilton Lodge, Hawick, Roxburgshire TD9 7JL
General Museum - 1856
Scottish history, natural history, militaria, coins, knitwear industry

Haworth

13052
Brontë Parsonage Museum
The Old Parsonage, Haworth, W Yorks BD22 8DR
Historic Site
Memorabilia on the Brontë sisters

13053
Keighley & Worth Valley Light Railway
Mill Hey, Haworth, W Yorks BD22 8NJ
History/Public Affairs Museum - 1968
Coll: World War II steam locomotive built for the Allied forces, obtained from Poland, Sweden and the USA; British Rail and British industrial railway systems; 35 steam and 7 diesel locomotives and two German railbusses; steam engines dated between 1874 and 1957 from Britain, Sweden, Poland and the USA

Hayes

13054
Hayes and Harlington Museum
Hayes Library, Golden Crescent, Hayes, Middx
General Museum - 1955
Local history

Helston

13055
Cornwall Aero Park
Glodgey Lane, Helston, Cornwall
History/Public Affairs Museum - 1976
Coll: The Ford Collection containing motorcars from 1911-1956; flying machines; Goonhilly Earther Satellite Tracking Station; several aircrafts; fire engines; motorcars and vehicles; historic streets, shops, houses, coaches, dresses

13056
Town Museum
Old Butter Market, Church St, Helston, Cornwall TR13 8ST
General Museum
Local history

Hemel Hempstead

13057
Piccots End Medieval Wall Paintings
Piccots End, Hemel Hempstead, Herts
Religious Art Museum - 1952
15th century religious wall paintings, Elizabethan painted room

Hereford

13058
Churchill Gardens Museum
3 Venn's Lane, Hereford HR4 9AU
General Museum - 1966
Costumes 1750-1940, furniture, early English watercolors, local art, glass, toys

13059
Hereford City Museum
Broad St, Hereford HR4 9AU
General Museum - 1874
Roman remains, agricultural implements, natural history, paintings and prints, glass and china, militaria, coins

13060
Museum of Cider The Cider Mills
Ryeland Street, Hereford, Hereford and Worcs HR4 0LW
General Museum - 1981
Farm cider making; the evolution of the modern cider factory

13061
The Old House
High Town, Hereford HR4 9AU
History/Public Affairs Museum - 1928
17th century furniture, memorabilia on local personalities, model of the city (1640)

Herne Bay

13062
Public Library and Museum
High St, Herne Bay, Kent
General Museum
Local history, natural history, Roman finds from Reculver

Hertford

13063
Hertford Museum
18 Bull Plain, Hertford, Herts SG14 1DT
General Museum - 1902
Geology, natural history, archaeology, history, ethnography of East Hertfordshire, militaria, Saxon coins

High Wycombe

13064
Hughenden Manor
High Wycombe, Bucks HP14 4LA
Historic Site - 1947
Home of Prime Minister Benjamin Disraeli (1804-1881), containing much of his furniture, pictures, books, correspondence

13065
Wycombe Chair and Local History Museum
Castle Hill House, Priory Av, High Wycombe, Bucks HP13 6PX
General Museum - 1932
Local chair making industry, lace, local history

Higher Bockhampton

13066
Hardy's Cottage
Higher Bockhampton, Dorset
Historic Site
Memorabilia of writer Thomas Hardy (1840-1928)

Hill of Tarvit
13067
Hill of Tarvit
Hill of Tarvit, Fife, Scotland
History/Public Affairs Museum
Furniture, tapestries, porcelain,
paintings; mansion house built 1696

Hindley, Nr. Wigan
13068
Hindley Museum
Market Street, Hindley, Nr. Wigan,
Greater Manchester WN2 3AN
General Museum - 1977

Hitchin
13069
Hitchin Museum and Art Gallery
Paynes Park, Hitchin, Herts SG5 1EQ
General Museum
Local history, archaeology, militaria,
costumes, natural history; paintings of
Samuel Lucas

Hockley Heath
13070
Packwood House
Hockley Heath, Warwicks
Fine Arts Museum - 1941
Country house with tapestries,
needlework, English antique furniture;
topiary

Hoddesdon
13071
Hoddesdon Museum
Lowewood, High St, Hoddesdon,
Herts EN11 8BH
General Museum - 1948

Holywood
13072
Ulster Folk and Transport Museum
Cultra Manor, Holywood, Co. Down, N.
Ireland BT18 0EU
General Museum - 1958
History and social life of Northern
Ireland; various restored buildings,
homes and shops, paintings, domestic
and rural life, agriculture, fishing, crafts,
transportation

Honiton
13073
Honiton and Allhallows Museum
High St, Honiton, Devon
General Museum - 1945
Lace, antiquities, fossils, Devon
kitchen, old armaments, coins

Horsham
13074
Horsham Museum
Causeway House, Horsham, W
Sussex
General Museum - 1893
Costumes, toys, old bicycles, local
crafts and industries, reconstructed
shops; in 16th century house

Housesteads
13075
**Housesteads Roman Fort and
Museum**
Haydon Bridge, Housesteads,
Northumberland
Archeology Museum

Hove
13076
Hove Museum of Art
19 New Church Rd, Hove, Sussex
BN3 4AB
Fine Arts Museum - 1927
18th and 19th century English art,
English ceramics, dolls

Huddersfield
13077
Art Gallery
Princess Alexandra Walk,
Huddersfield, Yorks HD1 2SU
Fine Arts Museum - 1898
British paintings, drawings, prints and
sculpture since 1850
13078
Tolson Memorial Hall
Ravensknowle Park, Huddersfield,
Yorks HD1 2SU
General Museum - 1920
Local history, natural history;
mineralogy, geology, botany, zoology;
local life in Stone Age, Bronze Age,
Iron Age, Roman and medieval
periods; dolls, English glass, woolens,
old vehicles, money scales

Huntingdon
13079
Cromwell Museum
Grammar School Walk, Huntingdon,
Cambs
History/Public Affairs Museum - 1962
Documents on Cromwell's time;
portraits; memorabilia on Oliver
Cromwell (1599-1658)

Hutton-le-Hole
13080
Ryedale Folk Museum
Hutton-le-Hole, Yorks Y06 6UD
General Museum - 1966
Tools, spinning, weaving;
reconstructions of a 15th century
Cruck house, 16th century manor
house, 18th century cottage, 16th
century glass furnace

Hythe
13081
**Hythe Local History Room and
Archives**
Oaklands, Stade St, Hythe, Kent CT21
6BG
General Museum
Local history (pre-WW II), bronze
objects, Roman finds

Ilchester
13082
Fleet Air Arm Museum
RN Air Station Yeovilton, Ilchester,
Somerset
Science/Tech Museum - 1964
Display of historic aircraft engines,
armaments, aircraft carrier models,
photographs and documents, naval
aircraft - library

Ilfracombe
13083
Ilfracombe Museum
Wilder Rd, Ilfracombe, Devon EX34
8AF
General Museum
Local history, archaeology, natural
history, fauna, Victorian relics,
shipping, armaments, militaria

Ilkley
13084
**Manor House Museum and Art
Gallery**
Castle Yard, Ilkley, Yorks LS29 9DT
General Museum - 1961
Local history, Roman finds, works of
art; in Tudor building

Ingatestone
13085
Ingatestone Hall
Ingatestone, Essex
General Museum - 1953
Essex history, furniture, china

Innerleithen
13086
Traquair House
Innerleithen, Peebleshire
General Museum
16th-17th century embroidery,
Jacobite glass, silver, manuscripts,
books, household objects, furniture,
musical instruments, memorabilia of
Mary, Queen of Scotland; 18th century
Brew House

Inverness
13087
Inverness Museum and Art Gallery
Castle Wynd, Inverness, Scotland IV2
3ED
General Museum - 1825
Local history, archaeology,
paleontology, geology, bagpipes, local
prints and paintings, old kitchen, silver,
uniforms, costumes, weapons

Inverurie
13088
Inverurie Carnegie Museum
The Square, Inverurie, Aberdeenshire,
Scotland
General Museum - 1884
Local archaeology, geology,
paleontology of Northern Scotland
and England; coins, shells, natural
history; North American Eskimo
anthropological collection

Ipswich
13089
Christchurch Mansion
Ipswich, Suffolk IP1 3QH
Fine Arts Museum - 1798
English pottery, porcelain, glass,
paintings, prints, sculptures, furniture;
in 16th century house
13090
Ipswich Museums and Art Galleries
High St, Ipswich, Suffolk IP1 3QH
General Museum - 1798
Archaeology, geology, natural history,
ethnology

Jersey
13091
Elizabeth Castle
Jersey, C.I.
General Museum
Regional history, historical tableaux,
paintings by Jersey artists, German
militaria
13092
Jersey Militia Museum
Fort Regent, Jersey, C.I.
History/Public Affairs Museum - 1971
Militaria relating to Royal Jersey Militia

13093
The Jersey Museum La Hougue Bie
mail c/o La Société Jersiaise, 9 Pier
Rd, Grouville, Jersey, C.I.
General Museum - 1873/1924
Archaeology, coins, silver, archives,
Bronze Age gold torque and
Armorican coin hoards, local artists;
German occupation; prehistoric
passage dating from 3000 B.C.
13094
Mont Orgueil Castle
Gorey, Jersey, C.I.
General Museum
Regional history, historical tableaux,
artifacts discovered on the grounds of
the castle

Johnstown Castle
13095
The Irish Agriculture Museum
Johnstown Castle, Wexford
Agriculture Museum - 1976
agriculture and rural life; machinery;
tools - library

Keighley
13096
Cliffe Castle
Spring Gardens Lane, Keighley BD20
6LH
General Museum - 1899
Paintings, sculpture, applied arts,
household and farm tools, natural
history, geology, archaeology,
reconstructed craft shops, militaria,
sports, toys, costumes

Kendal
13097
Abbot Hall Art Gallery
Kendal, Cumbria LA9 5AL
Fine Arts Museum - 1962
18th century furnished rooms,
paintings, sculpture, pottery, portraits
by Kendal painters
13098
Kendal Museum
Station Rd, Kendal, Cumbria LA9 5AL
General Museum - 1835
Local history, geology, natural history,
British birds
13099
**Museum of Lakeland Life and
Industry**
Abbot Hall, Kendal, Cumbria LA9 5AL
General Museum - 1970
Local cultural history of the Lake
District area, industry, period rooms,
costumes, trades, farming, printing
presses, weaving equipment

Kent
13100
Eyhorne Manor Laundry Museum
Hollingbourne, POB ME 17 100, Kent,
Kent
Science/Tech Museum - 1971
Laundry

Keswick
13101
Fitz Park Museum and Art Gallery
Fitz Park, Keswick, Cumbria CA12
4NF
General Museum - 1897
Manuscripts of Robert Southey and
Hugh Walpole; geology; art gallery

371

Kettering

13102
Alfred East Art Gallery
Shep St, Kettering, Nothants
Fine Arts Museum - 1931
English paintings, watercolors,
drawings and prints since 1800

13103
Westfield Museum
West St, Kettering, Nothants
General Museum - 1960
Local history, archaeology, geology,
industry, shoe industry

Kidderminster

13104
**Kidderminster Art Gallery and
Museum**
Market St, Kidderminster, Worcs
DY10 1AB
General Museum - 1927
Etchings of Frank Brangwyn, local
history, archaeology

Kilbarchan

13105
Weaver's Cottage
The Cross, Kilbarchan, Renfrewshire
History/Public Affairs Museum - 1954
18th century cottage, handloom
weaver, looms, weaving equipment,
domestic utensils

Kilmarnock

13106
Burns' Monument and Museum
Kay Park, Burgh Parks, Kilmarnock,
Ayrshire KA1 3BU
Historic Site
Life and work of poet Robert Burns
(1759-1796), manuscripts

13107
Museum and Art Gallery
Dick Institute, Elmbank Av,
Kilmarnock, Ayrshire KA1 3BU
General Museum - 1893
Geology, ethnography, archaeology,
conchology, armaments, numismatics,
church and trade relics, paintings,
etchings, sculptures; old bibles,
incunabula

King's Lynn

13108
The Lynn Museum
Old Market St, King's Lynn, Norfolk
PE30 1NL
General Museum - 1904
Local history, pilgrims' badges, glass,
ceramics, textiles

Kingsbridge

13109
Cookworthy Museum
108 Fore Street, Kingsbridge, S Devon
General Museum - 1941
Coll: Cookworthy's porcelain and
work as a chemist; costumes; craft
tools; photos - library

Kingston upon Hull

13110
Town Docks Museum
Queen Victoria Square, Kingston upon
Hull, Humber
General Museum - 1975
whaling; maritime history; shipping
archives; paintings - library

13111
Transport & Archaeology Museum
36 High St, Kingston upon Hull,
Humber
Archeology Museum - 1906
Transport: horse-drawn vehicles,
English Daimler, motor vehicles
(1890-1910); Archaeology: Roman
mosaics, Iron Age burial relics,
Horlestow mosaic - library

13112
Wilberforce & Georgian Houses
25 High St, Kingston upon Hull,
Humber
General Museum - 1906
Coll: silver; costumes; dolls; slavery;
items relating to William Wilberforce,
born here in 1759 - library

Kingston-upon-Hull

13113
City Museum and Art Galleries
mail c/o c/o Town Docks Museum,
Queen Victoria Square, Kingston-
upon-Hull HU1 3RA
General Museum
European old Masters, sculpture,
science and technology, archaeology,
transportation, numismatics,
armaments, pottery, costumes, silver,
furniture, whaling and fishing
industries; house of M.P. William
Wilberforce

Kingussie

13114
Highland Folk Museum
Duke St, Kingussie, Inverness,
Scotland PH21 1JG
History/Public Affairs Museum

Kinsale

13115
Kinsale Regional Museum
Kinsale, Co. Cork
General Museum - 1940
Maritime crafts - library

Kirkcaldy

13116
**Industrial and Social History
Museum**
Forth House, Abbotshall Rd, Kirkcaldy,
Fife KY1 1YG
History/Public Affairs Museum - 1971
Industrial and social history, displays
relating to Fife industries including
linoleum and coal; horse-drawn
vehicles

13117
Museum and Art Gallery
War Memorial Grounds, Kirkcaldy,
Fife KY1 1YG
General Museum - 1926
Archaeology, history, natural sciences,
decorative art, Scottish and English
paintings (19th-20th century), works of
Peploe and McTaggart, Adam Smith
items

Kirkcudbright

13118
The Stewartry Museum
6 St. Mary St, Kirkcudbright, Scotland
General Museum - 1881
Items concerning the Stewartry of
Kirkcudbright

Kirkintilloch

13119
Auld Kirk Museum
Cowgate, Kirkintilloch, Glasgow G66
1PW
General Museum
Local history

Kirkoswald

13120
Souter Johnnie's House
Kirkoswald, Strathclyde
Historic Site
Home of John Daidson, village cobbler
and original Souter

Kirkwall

13121
Antiquarian Museum
Broad St, Kirkwall, Orkney
General Museum

Kirriemuir

13122
Barrie's Birthplace
11 Brechin Rd, Kirriemuir, Tayside
Historic Site - 1963
Life and work of writer Sir James M.
Barrie (1860-1937), memorabilia,
manuscripts

Lacock

13123
Lackham Agricultural Museum
Chippenham, Lacock, Wilts SN15 2NY
History/Public Affairs Museum - 1960
Agricultural tools, machinery

Lancaster

13124
Lancaster Museum and Art Gallery
Old Town Hall, Market Square,
Lancaster LA1 1HT
General Museum - 1923
Local history, decorative arts, maritime
history, Roman finds, weights and
measures, ship models, Gillow
furniture, drawings, local paintings

Leamington Spa

13125
Leamington Spa Art Gallery
Avenue Rd, Leamington Spa,
Warwicks CV31 3PP
Fine Arts Museum - 1928
British, Dutch, Flemish paintings
(16th-20th century); ceramics from
Delft, Wedgewood-Whieldon,
Worcester; 18th century drinking
glasses, costumes, household utensils,
tools, dolls

Ledbury

13126
Eastnor Castle
Ledbury, Herefords
General Museum - 1850
Coll: armour; Italian furniture; pictures;
tapestries - library

Leeds

13127
Abbey House Museum
Kirkstall, Leeds LS5 3EH
History/Public Affairs Museum - 1931
Part of an ancient Cistercian
monastery, history of Yorkshire, 19th
century restored pub, other restored
buildings

13128
City Art Gallery
Municipal Buildings, Leeds LS1 3AA
Fine Arts Museum - 1888
16th century Italian paintings, modern
English paintings, English pottery,
sculpture, decorative arts

13129
City Museum
Municipal Buildings, Leeds LS1 3AA
General Museum - 1921
Natural history, prehistoric dioramas,
ethnography and archaeology of
Northern England, Roman pavement

13130
Department of Semitic Studies
University of Leeds, Leeds LS2 9JT
History/Public Affairs Museum - 1960
Biblical history, Palestina archaeology,
Near Eastern ethnology, manuscripts

13131
Museum of Industry and Science
Canal Rd, Armley, Leeds, Yorks
Science/Tech Museum
History of science and industry,
discoveries and inventions made in
Northern England during the last 200
years

13132
Temple Newsam House
Leeds LS15 0AE
Fine Arts Museum - 1922
English and Continental paintings
(16th-19th century), furniture, silver,
ceramics; country house from 1490

13133
**University Museum of the History of
Education**
University, Leeds LS2 9JT
History/Public Affairs Museum - 1951
History of education in England, old
school books, samplers, equipment,
portraits, foundation charters, local
school history

Leek

13134
Art Gallery
Nicholson Institute, Stockwell St, Leek,
Staffs ST13 6DW
Fine Arts Museum - 1884

Leicester

13135
Belgrave Hall
Church Rd, Belgrave, 96 New Walk,
Leicester LE1 6TD
History/Public Affairs Museum
Queen Anne House with 18th-19th
century furniture; coach and carriage
collections; agriculture

13136
Guildhall
Guildhall Lane, 96 New Walk,
Leicester LE1 6TD
History/Public Affairs Museum
Medieval timber construction

13137
Jewry Wall Museum
St. Nicholas Circle, 96 New Walk,
Leicester LE1 6TD
Archeology Museum
Roman wall dating from the 2nd
century; local archaeology; Roman
milestone and mosaic; 16th century
painted glass

13138
Leicester Museum and Art Gallery
96 New Walk, Leicester LE1 6TD
General Museum - 1849
Geology; natural history; mammalogy;
ornithology; ichthyology; biology;
English painting; German
expressionists, French painting
(19th-20th century); old masters;
English ceramics; silver - library

13139
Museum of Technology
Corporation Rd, 96 New Walk,
Leicester LE1 6TD
Science/Tech Museum
Horse drawn vehicles; bicycles;
motorcycles; motor vehicles; 1891
Beam pumping engines

13140
**Museum of the Royal Leicestershire
Regiment**
Oxford St, 96 New Walk, Leicester
LE1 6TD
History/Public Affairs Museum
History of the Regiment; in building
from 1400

13141
Newarke Houses Museum
The Newarke, 96 New Walk, Leicester
LE1 6TD
General Museum
Hosiery industry, costumes, clock
making, prints, drawings, photos,
mechanical music demonstrations;
reconstructed 19th century street,
reconstructed workshop of 18th
century clockmaker Samuel Deacon

13142
Railway Museum
London Rd, Stoneygate, Leicester
History/Public Affairs Museum - 1968
History of railway transportation,
locomotives, maps, illustrations

13143
**Wygston's House Museum of
Costume**
St. Nicholas Circle, 96 New Walk,
Leicester LE1 6TD
History/Public Affairs Museum - 1974
Costumes from 1769-1924;
reconstructions of draperie, millinerie
and shoe shops of the 1920's

Leighton Buzzard

13144
Ascott
Leighton Buzzard, Beds
Decorative Arts Museum
French and Chippendale furniture,
original needlework, paintings by
Rubens, Hogarth, Gainsborough,
Hobbema; Oriental porcelain; former
possession of Anthony de Rothschild

Letchworth

13145
Museum and Art Gallery
Broadway, Letchworth, Herts SG6
3PD
General Museum - 1914
Archaeology, natural history, local
history, cinematography

Lewes

13146
Museum of Local History
Southover High St, Lewes, Sussex
BN7 1JA
General Museum - 1930
Folk art; ironwork

13147
Museum of Sussex Archaeology
Barbican House, High St, Lewes,
Sussex BN7 1YE
Archeology Museum - 1908
Prehistoric, Roman and Saxon
archaeology; watercolors

Lichfield

13148
Art Gallery
Bird St, Lichfield, Staffs WS13 6PN
Fine Arts Museum - 1859

13149
Johnson Birthplace Museum
Breadmarket St, Lichfield, Staffs WS13
6LG
Historic Site - 1901
Memorabilia of Dr. Samuel Johnson
(1709-1784); paintings, association
books, documents, letters of Johnson,
Boswell, Anna Seward, Josiah
Wedgewood - library

13150
Letocetum Wall Roman Site and
Museum
Lichfield, Staffs
Archeology Museum - 1912
Roman finds, pottery, coins, tools,
glass

13151
Staffordshire Regiment Museum
Whittington Barracks, Lichfield, Staffs
History/Public Affairs Museum - 1963
History of the regiment; medals,
armaments, diorama of the Battle of
Ulundi

Linby

13152
Newstead Abbey
Linby, Notts NG15 8GE
General Museum - 1931
Coll: Roe-Byron Collection: Poet's
possessions and furniture,
manuscripts, letters and first editions;
18th and 19th century furniture -
library

Lincoln

13153
City and County Museum
Broadgate, Lincoln LN2 1EZ
General Museum - 1906
History of the city and county;
armaments; natural history

13154
**Royal Lincolnshire Regiment
Museum**
Burton Rd, Lincoln, Lincs LN1 3PY
History/Public Affairs Museum - 1958
History of the regiment, uniforms,
medals, war trophies, armaments

13155
Usher Gallery
Lindum Rd, Lincoln, Lincs LN2 1NN
Fine Arts Museum - 1927
Paintings, watercolors, watches,
miniatures, silver, porcelain;
manuscripts and memorabilia of Alfred
Lord Tennyson (1809-1892)

Lindisfarne

13156
Lindisfarne Priory
Holy Island, Lindisfarne,
Northumberland
Religious Art Museum

Littlehampton

13157
Littlehampton Museum
12a River Rd, Littlehampton, Sussex
General Museum - 1928
Nautical and maritime exhibits

Liverpool

13158
Merseyside County Museums
William Brown St, Liverpool,
Merseyside L3 8EN
General Museum - 1851
Archaeology, astronomy, botany,
ethnology, geology, ceramics,
decorative arts, zoology, shipping,
musical instruments, regimental
collections

13159
**Museum of the School of Dental
Surgery**
Pembroke Place, Liverpool,
Merseyside
Science/Tech Museum
History of dentistry, dentistal
education

13160
Museum of the School of Hygiene
126 Mt. Pleasant, Liverpool,
Merseyside L3 4SU
History/Public Affairs Museum
History of hygienic education

13161
Speke Hall
The Walk, Liverpool, Merseyside L24
1XD
History/Public Affairs Museum - 1970
Decorative art, social history, interior
design (16th-19th century), furniture
(17th-19th century)

13162
Sudley Art Gallery and Museum
Mossley Hill Rd, Liverpool,
Merseyside L18 8BX
Fine Arts Museum - 1948
British paintings

13163
Walker Art Gallery
William Brown St, Liverpool,
Merseyside L3 8EL
Fine Arts Museum - 1873
European painting, sculpture,
drawings, watercolors and prints since
1300; Italian, Dutch and Flemish
paintings (13th-17th century); British
paintings (17th-19th century); 19th
century Liverpool art; contemporary
painting

Llandrindod Wells

13164
Llandrindod Wells Museum
Temple St, Llandrindod Wells, Powys
LD1 5DL
General Museum
Castell Collen Roman Fort,
archaeology, local history, dolls

13165
**Tom Norton's Collection of old
Cycles and Tricycles** The Automobile
Palace
Temple St, Llandrindod Wells, Powys
History/Public Affairs Museum - 1920
Coll: cycles and tricycles

Llandudno

13166
**Rapallo House Museum and Art
Gallery**
Fferm Bach Rd, Llandudno, Wales
LL30 1UA
General Museum

Llanelli

13167
**Parc Howard Museum and Art
Gallery**
Llanelli, Dyfed
General Museum

Llanfairpwll

13168
Plas Newydd
Llanfairpwll, Gwynedd
General Museum
Coll: wall paintings; relics of the 1st
Marquess of Anglesey and the Battle
of Waterloo; and the Ryan collection of
military uniforms and headdresses

Llanidloes

13169
**Museum of Local History and
Industry**
Old Market Hall, Llanidloes, Powys
General Museum - 1933

London

13170
**The Armouries, H. M. Tower of
London**
London EC3 4AB
History/Public Affairs Museum - 1547
Armaments, 14th-17th century armor,
Oriental armaments, 16th-19th century
national arsenal, British military
armaments, Greenwich school armour
- library

13171
Army Museums Ogilby Trust
85 Whitehall, London SW1 2NP
History/Public Affairs Museum - 1954
British Army Regiments; Spenser
Wilkinson Papers - library

13172
Baden-Powell-Story
Baden-Powell-House, Queensgate,
London SW7 5JS
Historic Site - 1961
Life and work of Lord Robert Baden-
Powell (1857-1941), founder of the Boy
Scouts

13173
**Bethnal Green Museum of
Childhood**
Cambridge Heath Rd, London E2 9PA
History/Public Affairs Museum - 1872
Costumes, dolls, toys, 19th century
decorative arts

13174
British Dental Association Museum
64 Wimpole St, London W1M 8AL
Science/Tech Museum - 1934
History of dental surgery

13175
British Museum
Great Russell St, London WC1B 3DG
General Museum - 1753
Prehistoric, Romano-British, Greek,
Roman, Egyptian, medieval, Western
Asiatic, Oriental antiquities; coins and
medals; prints and drawings;
sculptures from the Parthenon;
Rosetta stone; Portland vase; Royal
Gold Cup; Sutton Hoo burial ship;
Sumerian treasures from Ur; Chinese
porcelain; Benin bronzes

13176
**British Museum - Museum of
Mankind**
6 Burlington Gardens, London W1X
2EX
Anthropology Museum
African ethnography

13177

British Museum - Natural History
Cromwell Rd, London SW7 5BD
Natural History Museum - 1881
Botany, entomology, mineralogy,
palaeontology, zoology, ornithology

13178

Broomfield House
Broomfield Park, Palmers Green,
London N13 4HE
General Museum - 1910
Local history, staircase, murals, art

13179

Bruce Castle Museum
Lordship Lane, London N17 8NU
History/Public Affairs Museum - 1906
Local history, British postal history,
Middlesex Regimental history - library

13180

Carlyle's House
24 Cheyne Row, Chelsea, London
SW3
Historic Site - 1936
Home of Thomas and Jane Carlyle
with furniture, books, letters, personal
effects and portraits - library

13181

**Chartered Insurance Institute's
Museum**
The Hall, 20 Aldermanbury, London
EC2V 7HY
History/Public Affairs Museum - 1934
History of insurance, insurance
company fire brigades, fire masks,
early firefighting equipment - library

13182

Church Farm House Museum
Church End, Hendon, London NW4
4JR
General Museum - 1955
Period furniture, local history

13183

Clipper Ship 'Cutty Sark'
King William Walk, Greenwich, London
SE10
Historic Site - 1957
Restored ship, launched 1859, with
figureheads; ship history

13184

Clockmakers' Company Museum
Guildhall, Aldermanbury, London EC2
2EJ
History/Public Affairs Museum - 1873
Old timepieces, marine chronometers,
watch keys

13185

Commonwealth Institute
Kensington High St, London W8 6NQ
General Museum - 1958
Exhibitions of all commonwealth
countries; art gallery - library;
educational facilities; theater

13186

Courtauld Institute Galleries
Woburn Square, London WC1E 7HU
Fine Arts Museum - 1958
French impressionists, European old
masters (14th-15th century), Italian
paintings and sculptures (14th-15th
century); decorative objects, English
and French art (1910-1930),
post-impressionist watercolors,
drawings and engravings; old master
drawings, English landscape
watercolors

13187

Cricket Memorial Gallery
Lord's Cricket Ground, St. John's
Wood, London NW8 8QN
History/Public Affairs Museum - 1953
History of cricket; pictures, relics,
trophies, art objects - library

13188

Cuming Museum
Walworth Rd, London SE17 1RS
General Museum - 1902
Roman and medieval remains from
archaeological excavations; collection
of London superstitions

13189

Dickens' House
48 Doughty St, London WC1N 2LF
Historic Site - 1925
Former home of the writer Charles
Dickens (1812-1870); memorabilia,
manuscripts, letters, first editions,
furniture - library

13190

Dulwich College Picture Gallery
College Rd, Dulwich, London SE21
7BG
Fine Arts Museum
Paintings

13191

**Epping Forest Museum at Queen
Elizabeth's Hunting Lodge**
Rangers Rd, Chingford, London E4
7QH
Natural History Museum - 1895
Local history, archaeology, forestry,
zoology, botany

13192

Geffrye Museum
Kingsland Rd, London E2 8EA
General Museum - 1914
Period rooms from 17th to 20th
century; 18th century street with
shops

13193

Geological Museum
Exhibition Rd, South Kensington,
London SW7 2DE
Natural History Museum - 1837
Fossils and rocks of Great Britain,
minerals, gemstones in their parent
rock associations, in their natural
crystal form and in their final cut state;
national collections of photographs of
British scenery and geology - library

13194

Goldsmith's Hall
Foster Lane, London EC2V 6BN
Decorative Arts Museum
English silver, modern jewelry since
1960

13195

Gordon Museum
Guy's Hospital Medical School, St.
Thomas St, London SE1
Science/Tech Museum
Specimens of human disease, wax
models of anatomical dissection and
skin diseases

13196

Guildhall Art Gallery
King St, London EC2P 2ET
Fine Arts Museum - 1886
London paintings, 19th century
landscapes, portraits, sculpture

13197

Gunnersbury Park Museum
Gunnersbury Park, London W3 8LQ
General Museum - 1929
Local archaeology, Sadler collection of
flints, Middlesex maps and
topography, costumes, toys and dolls,
transportation, local crafts and
industries - library

13198

Hirsch Collection Branch of British
Museum
Great Russell St, London WC1
Fine Arts Museum

13199

Hogarth's House
Hogarth Lane, Chiswick, London W4
Fine Arts Museum - 1904
Prints, engravings

13200

Horniman Museum
London Rd, Forest Hill, London SE23
3PQ
Anthropology Museum - 1890
Ethnography; ancient Mexican pottery,
Egyptian tomb model, Maori tattooing,
Javanese puppets, Congolese masks,
Indian shell trumpets, Ethiopian lyres,
Canadian Indian rattles, Tibetan skull
cap drums, small Italian lutes, English
serpents; musical instruments; natural
history; British fossils - library

13201

Imperial War Museum
Lambeth Rd, London SE1 6HZ
History/Public Affairs Museum - 1917
Wars since 1914; armaments,
documents, books, films, records,
photographs, drawings, paintings,
sculpture

13202

**Independent Broadcasting Authority,
Broadcasting Gallery**
70 Brompton Rd, London SW3 1EY
Science/Tech Museum - 1968
Development of television

13203

Jewish Museum
Woburn House, Upper Woburn Place,
London WC1 0EP
Anthropology Museum
Cultural history of the Jewish people

13204

Dr.Johnson's House
17 Gough Square, London EC4A 3DE
Historic Site - 1914
Memorabilia on Samuel Johnson
(1709-1784)

13205

Keats' House
Wentworth Place, Hampsted, London
NW3 2RR
Historic Site - 1925
Life and work of the poet John Keats
(1795-1821); manuscripts, relics,
furniture - library

13206

Kenwood, The Iveagh Bequest
Hampstead Lane, London NW3 7JR
Fine Arts Museum - 1927
The Iveagh collection of European
paintings (Rembrandt, Vermeer, Hals,
Gainsborough, Reynolds, Romney);
the Lady Maufe collection of shoe
buckles; English 18th century furniture

13207

**Leighton House Art Gallery and
Museum**
12 Holland Park Rd, London W14 8LZ
General Museum

13208

Livesey Museum
682 Old Kent Rd, London SE15 1JF
History/Public Affairs Museum - 1974

13209

**London Hospital Medical College
Museum**
Turner St, Whitechapel, London E1
2AD
Science/Tech Museum - 1897
Medical science history

13210

Madame Tussaud's
Marylebone Rd, London NW1
History/Public Affairs Museum
Wax figures, mannequins

13211

Martin Ware Pottery Collection
Southhall, London, Middlesex VB2 4BL
Decorative Arts Museum - 1935
Pottery, vases, tiles

13212

Middlesex Regimental Museum
Bruce Castle, Tottenham, London N17
History/Public Affairs Museum
Uniforms, medals, armaments, history
of the regiment

13213

Museum of British Transport
British Railways Board, High St,
Clapham, London SW 4
Science/Tech Museum
Development of public transport by
rail and by road

13214

Museum of London
London Wall, London EC2Y 5HN
Anthropology Museum - 1912
Prehistoric, Roman and medieval
antiquities; costumes; decorative art
objects; topography; history and social
life of London, royal relics, Parliament
and legal history, Cromwellian period
relics, objects relating to the Great
Fire of London; toys, fire engines,
glass; suffragettes

13215

**Museum of the Institute of
Ophthalmology**
University of London, Judd St, London
WC1H 9QS
Science/Tech Museum
History of ophthalmological science

13216

Museum of the Order of St. John
St. John's Gate, Clerkenwell, London
EC1M 4DA
History/Public Affairs Museum - 1915
Silver, coins, armaments, medals,
furniture; documents on the order of
St. John; manuscripts - library

13217

**Museum of the Pharmaceutical
Society of Great Britain**
1 Lambeth High St, London SE1 7JN
Science/Tech Museum - 1841
History of pharmacy, 17th-18th
century drugs, English Delft drug jars,
mortars, equipment

13218

National Army Museum
Royal Hospital Rd, Chelsea, London
SW3 4HT
History/Public Affairs Museum - 1959
History of the British Army 1572-1914,
Indian Army until 1947, colonial forces,
uniforms, British military painting, early
photographs - library

13219

National Gallery
Trafalgar Square, London WC2N 5DN
Fine Arts Museum - 1824
Western European paintings
1250-1900; British painters from
Hogarth to Turner; 19th century
French painting

13220

National Maritime Museum
Romney Rd, Greenwich, London SE10
9NF
Science/Tech Museum - 1934
Maritime history of Britain; Navy,
Merchant Service, Fishing Fleet,
yachting; ship models and plans
1700-1950; oil paintings; Nelson
memorabilia; astronomical instruments
(17th-20th century), globes since 1530

13221
National Portrait Gallery
2 St. Martin's Place, London WC2H
0HE
Fine Arts Museum - 1856
National collection of portraits
(15th-20th c.), including paintings,
sculptures, miniatures, engravings and
photographs

13222
National Postal Museum
King Edward St, London EC1A 1LP
History/Public Affairs Museum - 1965
Philatelics, British stamps since 1840,
world collection since 1878; archives,
special display on the creation of the
One Penny Black 1840

13223
Nelson Collection
Lime St, London EC3M 7HA
History/Public Affairs Museum
Silver, documents, letters, objects of
art associated with Admiral Lord
Nelson and his contemporaries

13224
Passmore Edwards Museum
Romford Rd, Stratford, London E15
4LZ
General Museum - 1898
Archaeology, ethnography, geology,
local history, natural history of Essex
area, porcelain

13225
**Percival David Foundation of
Chinese Art**
53 Gordon Square, London WC1H
OPD
Fine Arts Museum - 1951
Chinese ceramics (3rd-18th century);
Lung-ch'uan celadon, Ju ware, early
blue and white, 18th century
monochromes, the 'David' vases, blue
and white temple vases dated 1351

13226
**Petrie Museum of Egyptian
Archaeology**
University College London, Gower St,
London WC1
Archeology Museum
Archaeology, hieroglyphic texts

13227
Plumstead Museum
232 Plumstead High St, London SE18
1JL
General Museum - 1919
Local history, natural history

13228
Pollock's Toy Museum
1 Scala St, London W1
Anthropology Museum
Old toys and games

13229
Public Record Office Museum
Chancery Lane, London WC2A 1LR
History/Public Affairs Museum
Historical documents

13230
The Queen's Gallery
Buckingham Palace, London SW1
Fine Arts Museum - 1962
Paintings, drawings, artworks from
Royal collection, furniture, clocks,
porcelain, silver, scientific instruments,
books, miniatures, gems

13231
Royal Academy of Arts
Burlington House Picadilly, London
W1V 0DS
Fine Arts Museum - 1768
Painting, sculpture, architecture,
engravings

13232
Royal Air Force Museum
Aerodrome Rd, London NW9 5LL
History/Public Affairs Museum
History of air force, uniforms, medals,
artworks

13233
Royal Artillery Museum Royal
Military Academy
London SE18 4JJ
History/Public Affairs Museum
Military items

13234
**Royal College of Music Museum of
Instruments**
Prince Consort Rd, London SW7 2BS
Music Museum - 1883
Old stringed, wind and keyboard
instruments; printed music; portraits

13235
**Royal College of Surgeons'
Hunterian Museum**
Loncoln's Inn Fields, London WC2A
3PN
Science/Tech Museum - 1813
Anatomy; physiology and pathology
from the collection of John Hunter
(1728-1793) historical surgical
instruments

13236
Royal Fusiliers Regimental Museum
HM Tower of London
London EC3 4AB
History/Public Affairs Museum
History of regiment 1685-1968, silver,
documents, armaments, uniforms

13237
Royal Hospital
Chelsea, London SW 4SL
History/Public Affairs Museum
History of the hospital; medals dating
back to the Battle of Waterloo

13238
**St. Bartholomew's Hospital
Pathological Museum**
West Smithfield, London EC1A 7BE
Science/Tech Museum

13239
St. Bride's Crypt Museum St. Bride's
Church
Fleet St, London EC4
Archeology Museum - 1957
History of Fleet Street; Roman ruins;
former church ruins

13240
Science Museum
Exhibition Rd, London SW7 5NH
Science/Tech Museum - 1857
History of science and industry;
agriculture; astronomy; air, sea and
land transport; civil, electrical, marine
and mechanical engineering; jet
engines; geophysics;
telecommunications; domestic
appliances

13241
Sir John Soane's Museum
13 Lincoln's Inn Fields, London WC2A
3BP
Fine Arts Museum - 1833
Soane's private art and antiquities
collection, paintings

13242
South London Art Gallery
Peckham Rd, London SE5 8UH
Fine Arts Museum - 1891
Victorian paintings and drawings; small
collection of contemporary British art;
collection of 20th century original
prints; topographical paintings and
drawings

13243
Tate Gallery
Millbank, London SW1P 4RG
Fine Arts Museum - 1897
National art collection of British
painting from 16th century to the
present; modern foreign painting from
the Impressionists, modern British and
foreign sculpture - library

13244
**Thomas Coram Foundation for
Children**
40 Brunswick Square, London WC1N
1AZ
History/Public Affairs Museum - 1739
Foundling hospital mementos; tokens
found with the children (1741-1760); art
collection (120 paintings)

13245
Tudor Barn Art Gallery
Well Hall Pleasaunce, Eltham, London
SE9
Fine Arts Museum - 1935
Art; topography

13246
Victoria and Albert Museum
South Kensington, London SW7 2RL
General Museum - 1852
European and early medieval art;
Gothic art and tapestries; Italian
Renaissance art; Raphael cartoons;
continental art from 1500-1800; British
art (1500-1900) and watercolors; Far
Eastern and Islamic art; Indian art;
applied arts, jewellery, costumes,
musical instruments, textiles,
embroidery, metalwork, armour,
stained glass, pottery and porcelain,
Limoges enamels, earthenware,
alabasters, casts, furniture, bookart,
miniatures - library

13247
Wallace Collection
Hertford House, Manchester Square,
London W1M 6BN
Fine Arts Museum - 1900
Paintings of all European schools; 17th
century Dutch painting, 18th century
French art; sculpture, goldsmith art,
porcelain, majolica, European and
Oriental armaments

13248
**Wellcome Museum of Medical
Science**
183-193 Euston Rd, London NW1 2BP
Science/Tech Museum - 1914
Tropical medicine, molecular biology,
contagious diseases

13249
Wellington Museum
Hyde Park Corner, 149 Picadilly,
London W1V 9RA
History/Public Affairs Museum - 1952
Memorabilia on Duke of Wellington;
art collection, decorative objects

13250
Wesley's House and Museum
47 City Rd, London EC1Y 1AU
Religious Art Museum

13251
Whitechapel Art Gallery
Whitechapel High St, London E1 7QX
Fine Arts Museum - 1900
Modern art

13252
**William Morris Gallery and
Brangwyn Gift**
Lloyd Park, Forest Rd, Walthamstow,
London E17 4PP
Decorative Arts Museum - 1950
19th century English arts and crafts,
silver since 16th century, modern
jewelry since 1960, decorative arts,
books; life and work of poet William
Morris (1834-1896) - library

13253
Wimbledon Museum
Church Rd, London SW19 5AE
History/Public Affairs Museum
Prints, photos, pictures on Wimbledon

East Looe

13254
The Cornish Museum
Lower St, East Looe PL13 1DA
General Museum - 1959
Life and culture of Cornwall, arts and
crafts, local history, folklore, fishing,
early travel, lighting, games, mining,
collection of relics dealing with
witchcraft, charms and superstitions

Lower Broadleaf

13255
Elgar Birthplace Museum
East Crown Lane, Lower Broadleaf,
Worcs
Historic Site - 1938
Memorabilia of composer Edward
Elgar (1857-1934); manuscripts,
clippings, photos

Lowestoft

13256
**Lowestoft and East Suffolk Maritime
Museum**
Fisherman's Cottage, Sparrows Nest
Park, Lowestoft, Suffolk
General Museum

Lullingstone

13257
Roman Villa and Museum
Lullingstone Park, Lullingstone, Kent
Archeology Museum
Roman ruins and finds

Luton

13258
Museum and Art Gallery
Wardown Park, Luton LU2 7HA
General Museum - 1928
Regional social history, archaeology,
industrial history, local art, lace, textiles,
costumes, toys, rural trades, crafts,
porcelain, glass, furniture, household
objects

Lutterworth

13259
**Stanford Hall Motor Cycle and Car
Museum**
Lutterworth, Leics LE17 6DH
Science/Tech Museum - 1962
old motor vehicles; motor cycles;
machines; flying machines

Lyme Regis

13260
Philpot Museum
Bridge St, Lyme Regis, Dorset DT7
3QA
General Museum

Macclesfield

13261
West Park Museum and Art Gallery
Prestbury Rd, Macclesfield, Cheshire
General Museum - 1898
art; Egyptian antiquities; local
collection

Maidenhead

13262
Henry Reitlinger Bequest
Oldfield, Riverside, Maidenhead SL6
8DN
Fine Arts Museum - 1951
Painting and sculpture; porcelain;
prints and drawings; glass

Maidstone

13263
Museum and Art Gallery
St. Faith's St, Maidstone, Kent ME14
1LH
General Museum - 1858
Period furnishings in Elizabethan
setting; costumes; musical
instruments; military collection; 17th c.
Dutch and Italian paintings; water
colors

13264
**Queen's Own Royal West Kent
Regiment Museum**
St. Faith's St, Maidstone, Kent ME14
1LH
History/Public Affairs Museum
History of the unit

13265
Tyrwhitt-Drake Museum of Carriages
Mill St, Maidstone, Kent
History/Public Affairs Museum - 1946
Horse-drawn vehicles from the 18th
and 19th centuries

Malton

13266
Malton Museum
Milton Rooms, Yorkersgate, Malton,
Yorks
Archeology Museum
Roman finds; coins; Samian ceramics;
iron, bronze and stone objects

Manchester

13267
Athenaeum Manchester Art Gallery
Princess St, Manchester M1 4HR
Fine Arts Museum - 1837
Decorative arts; English pottery from
the Thomas Greg collection; oriental
art including jade; English and
continental glass from late 17th to
early 19th c.; enamels

13268
Fletcher Moss Museum City Art
Galleries
Old Parsonage, Wilmslow Rd,
Didsbury, Manchester, M20 8AY
Fine Arts Museum
English water colors

13269
The Gallery of English Costume
Platt Fields, Rusholme, Manchester,
M14 5LL
History/Public Affairs Museum - 1947
History of costumes since 1700;
housed in a 19th c. building - library

13270
Heaton Hall City Art Galleries
Heaton Park, Prestwich, Manchester,
M25 5SW
Fine Arts Museum
Paintings; 18th c. furnishings in original
setting

13271
Manchester Museum
The University, Oxford Rd,
Manchester, M13 9PL
General Museum
Egyptian collections; geology;
zoology; entomology; botany;
ethnology; numismatics; archaeology

13272
**North Western Museum of Science
and Technology**
97 Grosvenor St, Manchester, M1
7HF
Science/Tech Museum - 1969
Collections in all areas of science and
technology - library

13273
Quen's Park Art Gallery City Art
Galleries
Queen's Park, Harpurhey, Manchester,
M9 1SH
General Museum
Victorian painting; Oriental armaments;
militaria

13274
Whitworth Art Gallery
Whitworth Park, Manchester M25 6ER
Fine Arts Museum - 2889
British water colors and drawings; Old
Master prints and drawings; Japanese
prints; textiles; contemporary British
art; wallpapers - library

13275
Wythenshawe Hall City Art Galleries
Wythenshawe Park, Northenden,
Manchester M23 0AB
History/Public Affairs Museum
17th c. furniture and pictures housed in
country manor

Mansfield

13276
Hardwick Hall
Mansfield, Notts.
History/Public Affairs Museum
Furniture, tapestry, needlework, and
portraits of the Cavendish family;
housed in a late 16th c. house

13277
Museum and Art Gallery
Leeming St, Mansfield, Notts.
General Museum - 1905
Natural history; local history; art
works; ceramics; archaeology; Buxton
watercolors; Wedgewood and
Rockingham china

Margate

13278
Margate Museum
Victoria Rd, Margate, Kent
General Museum - 1923
Local history; archaeology; art works;
books, manuscripts and prints

Maryport

13279
Maryport Maritime Museum
1 Senhouse St, Maryport, Cumbria
CA15 6AB
Natural History Museum - 1976
Maryport local history; maritime
history

Matlock

13280
Tramway Museum
Cliff Quarry, Matlock
Science/Tech Museum
history of streetcar operation in
Britain, streetcars from Britain

Matlock Bath

13281
Peak Districts Mining Museum
Matlock Bath, Derbys
Science/Tech Museum - 1978
Coll: artifacts relating to the history of
lead mining from the Roman period to
present day; mining tools; water
pressure engine built in 1819

Mauchline

13282
Burns House Museum
Castle Street, Mauchline, Ayr
History/Public Affairs Museum - 1969
memorabilia on Poet Robert Burns

Maybole

13283
Culzean Castle
Maybole, Ayrshire KA19 8LE
General Museum - 1945
armoury containing collection of 18th
century pistols and swords; interiors
including neo-classical plaster ceilings
and furniture

Meigle

13284
Meigle Museum
Meigle, Perthshire
General Museum
early Christian stone objects

Melrose

13285
Abbotsford
Melrose, Roxburghshire
History/Public Affairs Museum
relics of Sir Walter Scott - library

13286
Melrose Abbey Museum
Melrose, Roxburghshire
History/Public Affairs Museum
Abbey pottery, floor, tiles, stone
sculpture

Melton Mowbray

13287
Melton Carnegie Museum
Thorpe End, Melton Mowbray, 96 New
Walk, Leicester LE1 6TD
General Museum
Local history; hunting pictures

13288
**National Trust Collection of
Staffordshire Portrait Figures**
Melton Mowbray, Leics LE14 2SF
General Museum
Coll: Staffordshire Portrait Figures

Menstrie

13289
Menstrie Castle
Menstrie, Clackmannanshire
History/Public Affairs Museum
Furnished commemorative rooms

Merthyr Tydfil

13290
**Cyfarthfa Castle Art Gallery and
Museum**
Cyfarthfa Park, Merthyr Tydfil, Glam
General Museum - 1910
paintings; ceramics; silver; glass;
natural history; geology; ethnology;
local history

Middle Claydon

13291
Florence Nightingale Museum
Claydon House, Middle Claydon,
Bucks
History/Public Affairs Museum
In an 18th century house; exhibits on
Florence Nightingale (1820-1910)

Middlesborough

13292
Dorman Museum
Linthorpe Rd, Middlesborough,
Cleveland
General Museum - 1901
natural history; industrial and social
history; pottery; conchology

13293
Middlesborough Art Gallery
Linthorpe Rd, Middlesborough,
Cleveland
Fine Arts Museum - 1958
modern painting

Millport

13294
Robertson Museum and Aquarium
University Marine Biological Station,
Millport, Isle of Cumbrae KA28 0EG
Natural History Museum - 1900
Local marine life

Milngavie

13295
Lillie Art Gallery
Station Rd, Milngavie, Dunbartonshire
Fine Arts Museum - 1962
paintings, water colors and etchings
by Robert Lillie; sculptures

Milton Regis

13296
Court Hall Museum of Local History
and Archaeology
Milton Regis, Kent
History/Public Affairs Museum
Hall built 1450; corn measure; weights;
local history; photographs

Monmouth

13297
Monmouth Museum
Priory St, Monmouth, Gwent
History/Public Affairs Museum
local history; documents and material
concerning Nelson

Montacute

13298
Montacute House
Montacute, Soms
History/Public Affairs Museum
furniture; tapestries; wood panelling;
amorial glass

Montrose

13299
Angus District Museum
Panmure Place, Montrose, Angus
General Museum - 1837
Social history; ethnography; natural
science; fossils; watercolours;
sculpture and etchings; geology;
molluscs; 2 paintings done by Peter
Breughel (1618)

Moreton-in-Marsh

13300
Chasleton House
Moreton-in-Marsh, Glous
History/Public Affairs Museum
furniture; tapestries; panelling;
embroidery

Morpeth

13301
Wallington Hall
Morpeth, Northumberland NE61 4AR
History/Public Affairs Museum - 1688
needlework; paintings; porcelain;
furniture

Nether Alderley

13302
Nether Alderley Mill
Nether Alderley
Science/Tech Museum - 1851
Corn mill in operation; corn
production; history of the water mill

Nether Stowey

13303
Coleridge's Cottage
Lime St, Nether Stowey, Soms
History/Public Affairs Museum
relics on poet Sam T. Coleridge
(1772-1834)

New Barnet

13304
Abbey Art Centre and Museum
89 Park Rd, New Barnet, Herts
Anthropology Museum

Newark-on-Trent

13305
Newark Museum and Art Gallery
Appleton Gate, Newark-on-Trent,
Notts
General Museum - 1908
archaeology; topography; illustrations

Newbury

13306
Newbury District Museum
Wharf St, Newbury, Berks
General Museum - 1904
archaeology; medieval history; natural
history; Bronze Age objects; local
pottery

Newcastle-upon-Tyne

13307
The Greek Museum The University
Newcastle-upon-Tyne NE1 7RU
History/Public Affairs Museum - 1956
Classical art and archaeology;
Corinthian bronze helmet, Apulian
helmet; 6th century Laconian handles;
Greek bronze hand mirrors; 7th
century B.C. Etruscan bucchero;
Pelike by Pan Painter; Ilatic late
archaic carved amber; Tarnatine and
Sicilian terra cotta antefixes,
Hellenistic moulded glass

13308
Hancock Museum
Barras Bridge, Newcastle-upon-Tyne
General Museum - 1829
Natural history; mounted birds; Hutton
fossilized plants; ethnography;
drawings and etchings

13309
Hatton Gallery University
Newcastle-upon-Tyne
Fine Arts Museum - 1926
14th-18th century European paintings;
16th-18th century Italian art;
contemporary English drawings -
library

13310
John George Joicey Museum
1 City Rd, Newcastle-upon-Tyne
General Museum - 1971
In a former 17th century hospital; local
history

13311
Keep and Black Gate Museums
Society of Antiquaries
16 Market St, Newcastle-upon-Tyne
General Museum
local history

13312
Laing Art Gallery
Higham Place, Newcastle-upon-Tyne
Fine Arts Museum - 1904
modern British paintings and water
colors; Egyptian, Greek and Roman
finds; pottery; porcelain; silver; glass;
pewter; armaments; costumes; textiles

13313
**Museum of Antiquities of the
University and the Society of
Antiquaries of Newcastle on upon
Tyne** Dept of Archaeology
The University, Newcastle-upon-Tyne,
Tyne and Wear NE1 7RU
Archeology Museum - 1813
Coll: Roman inscriptions, sculptures,
small finds - library

13314
Museum of Science and Engineering
Exhibition Park, Great North Rd,
Newcastle-upon-Tyne
Science/Tech Museum
engineering; shipbuilding; mining;
transportation; electronics; models

13315
Plummer Tower Museum
Croft St, Newcastle-upon-Tyne
History/Public Affairs Museum

Newlyn

13316
Passmore Edwards Art Gallery
Main Rd, Newlyn
Fine Arts Museum - 1895
painting; sculpture; pottery

Newport

13317
Arreton Manor
Newport, CI
History/Public Affairs Museum - 1961
manor from period of Henry VIII to
Charles I, Jacobean and Elizabethan
furniture, dolls, toys, relics

13318
Carisbrooke Castle Museum
Newport, CI
General Museum - 1898
Isle of Wight history; archaeology;
relics of Charles I, Bronze Age
weapons

13319
Shide Roman Villa
Avondale Rd, Newport, CI
Archeology Museum
Roman remains

Newtown

13320
Newton Textile Museum
5-7 Commercial Street, Newtown,
Powys
Decorative Arts Museum - 1964
crafts

13321
Robert Owen Memorial Museum
Broad St, Newtown
History/Public Affairs Museum
life of socialist Robert Owen
(1774-1888)

Northampton

13322
Abington Park Museum
Abington Park, Northampton
General Museum

13323
Central Museum and Art Gallery
Guidhall Rd, Northampton
General Museum - 1865
Northampton archaeology; geology;
natural history; ethnography; Italian
and modern English paintings;
decorative arts; footwear

13324
**Museum of the Northampton
Regiment**
Gibraltar Barracks, Barracks Rd,
Northampton
History/Public Affairs Museum - 1933
history of regiment since 1741

13325
Museum of the Royal Pioneer Corps
Simpson Barracks, Northampton
History/Public Affairs Museum - 1962
history of Corps, armaments

Norwich

13326
**Bridewell Museum of Local
Industries** City of Norwich Museum
Bridewell Alley, Norwich
General Museum - 1925
local and Norfolk crafts; textiles;
16th-20th century shoes; construction
materials; timepieces

13327
Castle Museum City of Norwich
Museums
Norwich
General Museum - 1894
fine and applied arts; archaeology;
geology; natural history; social history;
Norwich paintings; porcelain; silver;
coins

13328
**Museum of the Royal Norfolk
Regiment**
Britannia Barracks, Norwich
History/Public Affairs Museum - 1933
history of regiment; medals; uniforms;
armaments; history of British Army

13329
St. Peter Hungate Church Museum
City of Norwich Museum
Princess St, Norwich
Fine Arts Museum - 1936
In 15th century church; religious and
illuminated objects; church musical
instruments

13330
**Strangers' Hall Museum of Domestic
Life** City of Norwich Museum
Charing Cross, Norwich
Anthropology Museum - 1922
house with parts dating from 14th
century; period rooms; costumes;
toys; transportation; tapestries

Nottingham

13331
The Castle Museum and Art Gallery
Nottingham
General Museum - 1878
fine and applied arts; archaeology;
militaria; medieval alabaster; English
glass and silver; ceramics;
embroidery; costumes

13332
Natural History Museum
Wollaton Hall, Nottingham
Natural History Museum - 1872
mounted Britsh and foreign birds;
birds eggs; herbaria; European
deptera, lepidoptera; British aculeates;
British beetles; mounted African big
game heads; paleontology; fossils -
library

13333
Nottingham University Museum
University Park, Nottingham
Archeology Museum
prehistoric, Roman and medieval
pottery from Eastern England

13334
**Regimental Museum of the
Sherwood Foresters**
The Castle, Nottingham
History/Public Affairs Museum - 1964
history of Nottinghamshire and
Derbyshire Infantry Regiments since
1741; armaments; medals; uniforms

13335
University Art Gallery Department of
Fine Arts
Portland Bldg, University Park,
Nottingham
Fine Arts Museum - 1956
loan exhibits

13336
Victoria Street Art Gallery
14 Victoria St, Nottingham
Fine Arts Museum

Nuneaton

13337
Cadeby Light Railway
Nuneaton, Warwicks
Science/Tech Museum - 1962
Coll: railway relics; trains; locomotives;
steam traction engine; steam rollers -
library

13338
Museum and Art Gallery
Riversley Park, Nuneaton, Warwicks
General Museum - 1916
Roman to late-medieval archaeology;
ethnography; George Eliot Collection;
Baffin Land Eskimo material;
miniatures; oil painting and
watercolours

Oakham

13339
Rutland County Museum
Catmos St, Oakham, 96 New Walk,
Leicester LE1 6TD
General Museum - 1967
Local history and archaeology; Anglo-
Saxon and other finds; farm tools

Oldham

13340
Art Gallery and Museum
Union St, Oldham, Greater
Manchester OL1 1DN
Fine Arts Museum - 1883
19th-20th century British paintings and
sculpture, English watercolors, glass,
Oriental art objects

Olney

13341
Cowper and Newton Museum
Orchardside, Market Place, Olney,
Bucks
General Museum - 1900
Memorabilia of writer William Cowper
(1731-1800); lace industry

Omagh

13342
Ulster-American Folk Park
2 Mellon Rd, Omagh, Co. Tyrone BT78
5QY
Open Air Museum - 1976
Series of buildings representing life in
Ulster and North America in the 18th
and 19th centuries - library

Oxford

13343
**Ashmolean Museum of Art and
Archaeology**
Beaumont St, Oxford OX1 2PH
General Museum - 1683
Archaeology of Britain, Europe, the
Mediterranean, Egypt, the Near East;
Italian, French, Dutch, Flemish and
English paintings; Old Master
drawings, modern drawings,
watercolors, prints, miniatures;
European ceramics, sculpture, bronze
and silver, engraved portraits,
numismatics; Oriental art, Indian and
Islamic arts and crafts

13344
Christ Church Picture Gallery
Canterbury Quadrangle, Oxford OX1
1DP
Fine Arts Museum - 1968
Old Master paintings and drawings
1300-1750

13345
Museum of Modern Art
30 Pembroke St, Oxford OX1 1BP
Fine Arts Museum - 1966
Contemporary painting, sculpture,
photographs, architecture

13346
Museum of Oxford
St. Aldates, Oxford, Oxfords OX1 1DZ
General Museum - 1975
objects relating to the history of the
city and university of Oxford - lecture
rooms; classrooms

13347
Museum of the History of Science
Broad St, Oxford OX1 3AZ
Natural History Museum - 1925
Historic scientific instruments;
astronomical, optical, horological
equipment

13348
Pitt Rivers Museum
Parks Rd, Oxford OX1 3PP
Anthropology Museum - 1851
Ethnology, prehistoric archaeology,
musical instruments, history of Captain
Cook's voyages 1773-1774

13349
**The Rotunda Museum of Antique
Dolls' Houses**
44 Iffley Turn, Oxford, Oxfords
History/Public Affairs Museum - 1963
antique doll houses and their contents
(glass, china, silver) showing social
history 1700-1900

13350
University Museum
Parks Rd, Oxford
Natural History Museum - 1860
Entomology, geology, mineralogy,
zoology

Padiham

13351
Gawthorpe Hall
Padiham, *mail c/o* Principal Nelson &
Colne College, Scotland Rd, Nelson,
Lancs BB9 7YT
Fine Arts Museum - 1970

Paisley

13352
Museum and Art Galleries
High St, Paisley PA1 2BA
General Museum - 1870
Art, local history, natural history, local
weaving art; Paisley Shawl Collection
- library

Peebles

13353
Tweeddale Museum
High Street, Peebles, Borders
General Museum - 1857
Coll: geology collection and local
prehistoric material

Pembroke Dock

13354
Pembrokeshire Motor Museum
Old Royal Dockyard, Pembroke Dock,
Dyfed SA72 6YH
Science/Tech Museum
Coll: motors; motorcycles; cycles

Penarth

13355
Turner House
Plymouth Rd, Penarth, Glam
Fine Arts Museum
Fine and applied arts

Penzance

13356
**Museum of the Royal Geological
Society of Cornwall**
Alverton, Penzance, Cornwall
Natural History Museum - 1914
Mineralogy, petrography,
paleontology, Cornwall geology

13357
**Natural History and Antiquarian
Museum**
Penlee House, Penzance, Cornwall
General Museum - 1839
Archaeology, local history, natural
history, Bronze age pottery

Perth

13358
Art Gallery and Museum
George St, Perth, Scotland
General Museum - 1935
Scottish and other paintings, regional
natural history, ethnography,
archaeology, geology, antiquities

13359
**The Regimental Museum of the
Black Watch**
Balhousie Castle, Perth, Scotland PH1
5HR
History/Public Affairs Museum - 1924
History of Black Watch, related
regiments, paintings, royal relics,
uniforms, trophies from 1740 to the
present

13360
Scone Palace
Perth, Tayside PH2 6BD
History/Public Affairs Museum - 1600
Coll: finest French furniture; china;
clocks; ivories; neddlework; vases;
several historic rooms, halls and
galleries

Peterborough

13361
City Museum and Art Gallery
Priestgate, Peterborough, Nothants
PE1 1LF
General Museum - 1880
Archaeology, history, geology, natural
history, ceramics, glass, portraits,
paintings, finds from Castor

Peterhead

13362
Arbuthnot Museum and Art Gallery
St. Peter St, Peterhead, Aberdeen AB4
6QD
General Museum
Local history, fishing, coins

Pickering

13363
Beck Isle Museum of Rural Life
Beck Isle, Pickering, N Yorks YO18
8DU
General Museum - 1967
reconstructed rooms and shops

Plymouth

13364
Buckland Abbey
Nr. Yelverton, Plymouth, Devon
Fine Arts Museum

13365
City Museum and Art Gallery
Drake Circus, Plymouth PL4 8AJ
Fine Arts Museum - 1897
Cookworth's Plymouth and Bristol
porcelain; Cottonian Collection of
paintings, drawings, prints and early
printed books; Clarendon Collection
of 17th century portraits; collection of
American birds in ceramic by Dorothy
Doughty; personalia of Sir Francis
Drake - library

13366
Elizabethan House
32 New St, Plymouth, Devon PL1 2NA
History/Public Affairs Museum - 1931
16th century house with furniture

Pontefract

13367
**King's Own Yorkshire Light Infantry
Regimental Museum**
Wakefield Rd, Pontefract, Yorks WF8
4ES
History/Public Affairs Museum - 1950
History of King's Own Yorkshire Light
Infantry; medals, armaments

Poole

13368
Old Town House
High St, Poole, Dorset
General Museum - 1961
Local history, archaeology, prehistoric
dugout canoe, industrial archaeology,
pottery; in a 15th century building

13369
Poole Guildhall Museum
Market St, Poole, Dorset BH15 1NP
General Museum - 1972
Local history, archaeology, 18th
century ceramics and glassware, fauna
and flora

Port Sunlight

13370
Lady Lever Art Gallery
Port Sunlight, Merseyside L62 5EQ
Fine Arts Museum - 1922
British and other paintings,
watercolors, sculpture, porcelain,
furniture

Portmadoc

13371
Festiniog Railway Museum
Portmadoc, Wales
Science/Tech Museum - 1955
History of Festiniog and allied railway
systems

Portsmouth

13372
Charles Dickens Birthplace Museum
393 Commercial Rd, Portsmouth,
Hants
Historic Site - 1970
Birthplace of writer Charles Dickens
(1812-1870); furniture, memorabilia,
prints

13373
City Museum and Art Gallery
Museum Rd, Old Portsmouth, Hants
PO1 2LJ
General Museum - 1972
Local archaeology, ceramics,
sculpture, paintings, wood engravings,
prints, furniture, glass, metalwork -
library

13374
Portsmouth Royal Naval Museum
Naval Base, Portsmouth, Hants PO1
3LR
History/Public Affairs Museum - 1953
Figureheads, ship models, ship
furniture, memorabilia of Lord Nelson;
panorama of the Battle of Trafalgar -
library

13375
Round Tower
Broad St, Point Battery, Portsmouth,
Hants
Archeology Museum - 1961
Old fortification tower

13376
Royal Marines Museum
Eastney, Southsea, Portsmouth, Hants
PO4 9PX
History/Public Affairs Museum - 1958
History of marines since 1664,
uniforms, photos, medals

13377
Southsea Castle
Clarence Esplanade, Portsmouth,
Hants
History/Public Affairs Museum - 1967
History of Portsmouth fortress,
blockmaking machines, maritime items,
history of artillery

Preston

13378
Harris Museum and Art Gallery
Market Square, Preston, Lancs PR1
2PP
Fine Arts Museum - 1893
Fine art; Devis Collection of 18th
century paintings; Newsham Bequest
of 19th century British paintings,
Haslam Bequest of 19th century
watercolors; decorative art, costumes,
ceramics, porcelain, social history,
archaeology, skeleton of Mesolithic
elk

13379
The Queen's Lancashire Regiment
Fulwood Barracks, Watling St. Rd,
Preston, Lancs PR2 4AA
History/Public Affairs Museum - 1926
Regimental history; uniforms, silver,
trophies, weapons - library

13380
**The Ribchester Museum of Roman
Antiquities**
Riverside, Ribchester, Preston PR3
3XS
Archeology Museum - 1914
Roman finds from old Roman fort;
models; finds from Iron age Hill Fort

Pulborough

13381
Parkham Park
Pulborough, W Sussex RH20 4HS
History/Public Affairs Museum - 1577
historical portraits; needlework;
Equestrian portrait of Henry Frederick,
Prince of Wales; Madam Kirke by van
Dyck

Radcliffe

13382
Radcliffe Local History Museum
Stand Lane, Radcliffe, Lancs M26 9WR
General Museum - 1907
Local history

Ramsey

13383
The Grove
Ramsey, Isle of Man, British Isles
History/Public Affairs Museum - 1978
this museum complements the folk
museum at Cregneash, centre is 'The
Grove', a large Victorian house with a
collection of agricultural implements
and vehicles used on larger farms

Ramsgate

13384
Ramsgate Museum
Guildford Lawn, Ramsgate, Kent
General Museum - 1948

Ravenglass

13385
The Railway Museum
mail c/o c/o The Ravenglass and
Eskdale Railway Co Ltd Ravenglass,
Cumbria CA18 1SW
History/Public Affairs Museum - 1978
Coll: history of the Ravenglass and
Eskdale Railway since 1875 and its
effect on the area

Reading

13386
Cole Museum of Zoology
University of Reading, London Rd,
Reading, Berks RG6 2AJ
Natural History Museum

13387
Institute of Agricultural History
University of Reading, Whiteknights,
Reading, Berks RG6 2AG
Agriculture Museum - 1951
Farming development; history of local
rural life - library

13388
Reading Museum and Art Gallery
Town Hall, POB 17, Reading, Berks
RG1 1QN
General Museum - 1883
Natural history; archaeology; Roman
finds from Silchester; prehistoric and
medieval metalwork

13389
Ure Museum of Greek Archaeology
University of Reading, Whiteknights,
Reading, Berks RG6 2AA
Archeology Museum - 1922
Greek, Egyptian antiquities; Boetian
and South Italian vases

Redcar

13390
The Zetland Museum
King St, Redcar, Cleveland
General Museum - 1969
Shipping and fishing; industrial
development; sea rescue; oldest
lifeboat; ship models; marine paintings;
scientific instruments

Redruth

13391
**Camborne School of Mines
Geological Museum**
Trenvenson, Pool, Redruth, Cornwall
TR15 3SE
Archeology Museum - 1880
Coll: Robert Hunt Collection of
minerals; flurorescent minerals;
radioactive minerals; fossils;
worldwide collection of rocks and
minerals - library

13392
Tolgos Tin
Redruth, Cornwall
Science/Tech Museum - 1921
Tin-streaming machinery in operation;
Holmans Museum of aviation
equipment - library

Repton

13393
Repton School Museum
Repton School, Repton, Derby
History/Public Affairs Museum
History of school and village, medieval
documents

Richborough

13394
Richborough Castle
Richborough, Kent
Historic Site

Richmond

13395
The Green Howards Museum
Trinity Church Square, Richmond,
Yorks
History/Public Affairs Museum - 1061
History of the regiment since 1688;
uniforms, medals

Ripley

13396
Ripley Castle
Ripley, N Yorks
History/Public Affairs Museum - 1418
Civil War armour; Elizabethan paneling
- library

Rochdale

13397
Rochdale Museum and Art Gallery
Esplanade, Rochdale, Lancs
General Museum - 1903
English paintings and watercolors,
contemporary paintings; local history,
archaeology, textiles, glass

13398
**Rockdale Pioneers Memorial
Museum**
31 Toad Lane, Rochdale, Lancs
History/Public Affairs Museum - 1931
Coll: relics and documents relating to
the formation of the Rochdale
Equirable Pioneers Society, which
marked the beginning of the world-
wide co-operative movement;
documents relating to the formation of
the co-operative wholesale society;
mementoes relating to the 1944
centenary celebrations; documents
relating to international social reformer
and co-operator Robert Owen

Rochester

13399
Eastgate House Museum
High St, Rochester, Kent
General Museum - 1903
Local history, archaeology, Victorian
furniture, arms and armour, ship
models, geology, mineralogy, natural
history; memorabilia of Charles
Dickens

Rossendale

13400
Rossendale Museum
Whitaker Park, Rawtenstall,
Rossendale BB4 6RE
General Museum - 1902
Fine arts, history, 19th century
paintings

Rotherham

13401
Clifton Park Museum
Clifton Lane, Rotherham, S Yorks
General Museum - 1893
Coll: pottery; natural history; social
history; archaeology

13402
**Rotherham Municipal Museum and
Art Gallery**
Clifton Park, Rotherham, Yorks S65
2AA
General Museum - 1893
Natural history, ceramics, antiquities,
fine art

Rothesay

13403
Bute Museum
Stuart St, Rothesay, Isle of Bute
General Museum - 1905
Local archaeology, geology,
mineralogy, natural history, social
history

Rottingdean

13404
**Rottingdean Grange Art Gallery and
National Toy Museum**
Rottingdean Grange, Rottingdean,
Sussex BN2 7HA
General Museum - 1955
Coll: toys; Kipling letters and books;
memorabilia on painter Sir William
Nicholson who lived here 1912-1914

Rufford

13405
Rufford Old Hall
Rufford, Lancs L4O 1SG
General Museum - 1936
Antique furniture, tapestries,
armaments, costumes, English coins

Rugby

13406
Museum and Art Gallery
St. Matthew's St, Rugby, Warwicks
CV21 3BZ
General Museum - 1891
Local agricultural relics; contemporary
paintings

Runbridge Wells

13407
**Tunbridge Wells Municipal Museum
& Art Gallery**
Mount Pleasant, Runbridge Wells,
Kent
General Museum - 1918
Coll: Victorian paintings; local history;
natural history; prints; dolls; toys

Runcorn

13408
Norton Priory Museum
Near Astmoor, Runcorn, Ches
Agriculture Museum - 1975
medieval decorated floor tiles;
medieval carved stonework; remains
of medieval priory; medieval mosaic
tile floor (70 sq.m.); statue of St.
Christopher - auditorium

Ryope

13409
Ryhope Engines Museum
Rhyope Pumping Station, Ryope,
Sunderland SR2 0ND
Science/Tech Museum - 1973
Mechanical engineering design and
construction; beam engines and
pumps; machinery and exhibits
illustrating the history of water supply;
pair of beam engines (1868) complete
with boilers, chimneys etc

Saffron Walden

13410
Saffron Walden Museum
Museum St, Saffron Walden
General Museum - 1832
local archaeology; hilt of a 6th century
ring sword; necklace; social and
natural history; geology; ethnology;
ceramics; glass; costumes; furniture;
dolls; arms; musical instruments

St. Albans

13411
**City Museum (The Verulamium
Museum)**
Hatfield Rd, St. Albans, Herts
General Museum - 1955
local history; natural history;
ethnography; tools; crafts;
reproductions of various shops;
costumes; porcelain; vehicles

St. Andrews

13412
St. Andrews Cathedral Museum
St. Andrews, Scotland
Fine Arts Museum - 1950
early Christian crosses; medieval
cathedral relics; pre-Reformation tomb
stones; 9th-10th century sarcophargus

St. Helens

13413
Pilkington Glass Museum
Prescot Rd, St. Helens, Merseyside
WA10 3TT
Science/Tech Museum - 1964
Coll: antique vessel glass, historical
development of glassmaking; the use
of glass; Posset pot (c.1677) and
ceremonial glass goblet with cover
(c.1675) attributed to George
Ravenscroft; oinochoe from an
Etruscan site near Rome, 4th century
B.C. - library

13414
St. Helens Museum and Art Gallery
College Street, St. Helens, Merseyside
WA10 1TW
General Museum - 1892
Coll: Guy and Margery Pilkington
English watercolour bequest;
Egyptology from Thebes and Abydos;
Doulton art; local clay pipes - library

St. Ives, Cornwall

13415
Barnes Museum of Cinematography
44 Fore Street, St. Ives, Cornwall
History/Public Affairs Museum - 1963
Coll: puppets used in the ancient
Chinese and Japanese shadowplays;
peepshows; thaumatrope;
phenakisticope; zoetrope;
praxinoscope; examples of the camera
obscura; early photographic
techniques including the
daguerreotype and abrotype; 3-D
photography; stereoscopes; early film
cameras and projectors; history of the
magic lantern slides

13416
Penwith Galleries
Back Rd, St. Ives, Cornwall
Fine Arts Museum - 1949
Coll: paintings; sculpture; pottery

13417
St. Ives Museum
Wheal Dream, St. Ives, Cornwall
General Museum - 1951
local industries; arts; crafts; fishing;
mining; paintings; folklore

St. Ives, Huntingdon

13418
Norris Museum & Library
41 The Broadway, St. Ives,
Huntingdon, Cambs PE17 4BX
General Museum - 1931
Coll: archaeology of all periods;
French prisoner-of-war material from
Norman Cross; ice-skates; 18th
century fire engine; local prints;
paintings; newspapers; paleolithic
finds; lace production - library

St. Mary's

13419
Isles of Scilly
Church Streets, St. Mary's, Isle of
Scilly, Cornwall
General Museum - 1967
Coll: archaeology; some brooch
designs found for the first time in this
area

St. Peter

13420
**St. Peter's Bunker German
Occupation Museum**
St. Peter, Jersey, British Isles
General Museum - 1965
Coll: military items of the German
army in World War II; seven rooms in
an original underground bunker;
German 'Enigma' decoding machine

St. Peter Port

13421
**Castle Cornet Military and Maritime
Museum**
St. Peter Port, CI
History/Public Affairs Museum

13422
Hauteville House Maison de Victor
Hugo
38 Hauteville, St. Peter Port, CI
Fine Arts Museum - 1927
Coll: tapestries; porcelain; carvings;
drawings; pen & ink washes done by
Victor Hugo and Madame Hugo; exil
home of Victor Hugo - library

13423
Island Museum
Candie Gardens, St. Peter Port,
Guernsey; Channel Islands
General Museum - 1882
Coll: natural history; local watercolors

13424
Lukis Island Museum
Cornet St, St. Peter Port, CI
General Museum

St. Petter's Village

13425
Jersey Motor Museum
St. Petter's Village, Jersey
History/Public Affairs Museum - 1973
Coll: Veteran and Vintage cars, motorcycles, Allied and German military
vehicles of World War II, aero engines,
railway carriage, early motor car
lamps; early car radios and
accessories

Salcombe

13426
Sharpitor Museum
Salcombe, Devon
General Museum

Salford

13427
Ordsall Hall Museum
Taylorson Street, Salford, Greater
Manchester M5 3EX
Anthropology Museum - 1972
Folk life; leather figures; sword made
in Solingen

13428
Salford Art Gallery and Museum
The Crescent Peel Park, Salford,
Manchester M5 4WU
General Museum - 1858
Coll: fine and applied arts; folk life and
paintings by L.S. Lowry; social history

13429
The Salford Museum of Mining Blue
Hill Park
Eccles Old Road, Salford, Greater
Manchester M6 8GL
Science/Tech Museum - 1906
mining items

Salisbury

13430
**Salisbury and South Wiltshire
Museum**
65 The Close, Salisbury, Wilts
General Museum - 1860
Coll: natural history; ceramics; pottery;
English china; glass; 5th century
Wilton hanging bowl - library

Saltcoats

13431
Noth Ayrshire Museum
Kirksgate, Saltcoats
General Museum - 1957
local history; stone carvings; old
kitchen

13432
Old Custom House Museum
The Harbour, Saltcoats, Ayrshire
General Museum - 1970
maritime history

Samlesbury

13433
Samlesbury Old Hall
Samlesbury, Lancs
History/Public Affairs Museum
medieval manor house

Sandown

13434
Museum of Isle of Wight Geology
Public Library
High St, Sandown, CI
General Museum - 1913
fossils; geology; mineralogy

Sandwich

13435
Richborough Castle Museum
Sandwich
Archeology Museum - 1930
Roman finds, pottery, tools, coins,
ornaments

Scarborough

13436
Museum of Natural History
Wood End, The Crescent,
Scarborough, Yorks
Natural History Museum - 1951
regional fauna, flora and geology

13437
Rotunda Museum
Vernon Rd, Scarborough, Yorks
Archeology Museum - 1829
Coll: Mesolithic, Bronze Age, Iron Age,
Roman , Medieval regional finds;
pottery

13438
St. Thomas' Museum
East Sandgate, Sandside,
Scarborough
General Museum - 1970
local relics; Victorian relics; period
rooms; transport

13439
Scarborough Art Gallery
The Crescent, Scarborough, Yorks
Fine Arts Museum - 1967
Coll: local paintings; water colors;
modern prints

Scunthorpe

13440
Normanby Hall
Normanby, Scunthorpe, S Humber
History/Public Affairs Museum
Coll: period furniture; decorations

13441
Scunthorpe Museum & Art Gallery
Oswald Road, Scunthorpe, S Humber
DN15 7BD
General Museum
Coll: geology; history and natural
history; archaeology; agriculture; art;
furniture - library

Selborne, Nr. Alton

13442
**Oates Memorial Library and Museum
and the Gilbert White Museum**
The Wakes, Selborne, Nr. Alton, Hants
GU34 3JH
General Museum - 1955
Coll: natural history of Selborne;
Antarctic birds; travels of Frank Oates
in Africa; Gilbert White's Great Parlour
and study - library

Sevenoaks

13443
Knole House
Sevenoaks, Kent
History/Public Affairs Museum
state rooms; paintings; furniture;
tapestries; silver

Shaftesbury

13444
Abbey Ruins
Park Walk, Shaftesbury, Dorset
Archeology Museum - 1951
tiles; stone finds; Saxon relics;
reconstruction of old church

13445
Historical Society Museum
Gold Hill, Shaftesbury, Dorset
General Museum
local history

Sheffield

13446
Abbeydale Industrial Hamlet
Abbeydale Rd, Sheffield
History/Public Affairs Museum - 1970
Local industrial history; 18th century
scythe

13447
Bishops' House Museum
Norton Lees Lane, Sheffield, S Yorks
S8 9BE
General Museum - 1976
Coll: 16th and 17th century oak
furniture - library

13448
Sheffield City Art Galleries (Graves
Art Gallery and Mappin Art Gallery)
Surrey St, Sheffield
Fine Arts Museum - 1887
British portraiture; modern art; English
watercolours; graphic art; 19th century
French painting and drawing; 17th
century Dutch and Italian painting;
works by Murillo, Sargent, Cezanne;
Islamic, Chinese and Indian art

13449
Sheffield City Museum
Weston Park, Sheffield
General Museum - 1875
archaeology; antiquities; armaments;
applied arts; natural history; relics;
conchology; ethnography; geology;
glass; entomology; numismatics;
porcelain

13450
Sheffield Industrial Museum
Sheffield, S Yorks S3 8RY
Science/Tech Museum - 1969
Coll: approximately 400 miners' safety
lamps; material relating to the
manufacturing industries of Sheffield
including tools, equipment and
products; 3-cylinder steam engine
12,000 H.P. used to power an armour
plate rolling mill - library; lecture room

13451
Shepherd Wheel
Whitley Wood, Sheffield
General Museum
old water-driven cutlery-grinding shop

13452
**The York and Lancaster Regimental
Museum** Regimental Headquaters,
Endcliff hall, Endcliff Vale Rd
Sheffield
History/Public Affairs Museum
History of the regiment; uniforms;
medals

Shepton Mallet

13453
Shepton Mallet Museum Council
Offices
Shepton Mallet, Soms
General Museum - 1900
Geology; fossils; Roman kiln and
jewelry

Sherborne

13454
Sherborne Castle
Sherborne, Dorset DT9 3PY
General Museum - 1594
Coll: Oriental porcelain; painting
'Procession of Elizabeth I' attributed to
Peake the Elder - library

13455
Sherborne Museum Abbey Gate
House
Church Lane, Sherborne, Dorset
General Museum - 1972
local history; prehistoric finds;
geology; Roman and medieval relics;
silk production; 20th century
fiberglass; local architecture

Shifnal

13456
Weston Park
Weston Park, Shifnal, Shropshire
History/Public Affairs Museum
house built 1671 with English, Flemish
and Italian paintings, furniture, books,
tapestries, art objects

Shoreham-by-Sea

13457
Marlipins Museum
36 High St, Shoreham-by-Sea
General Museum - 1922/1928
Local history; paintings of ships; ship
models; in a 12th-14th century building

Shrewsbury

13458
Clive House Museum
College Hill, Shrewsbury
General Museum - 1968
Industrial artifacts; ceramics; porcelain,
geology; militaria on Dragoon Guards;
Georgian furniture

13459
The King's Shropshire Light Infantry
Sir John Moore Barracks, Shrewsbury
History/Public Affairs Museum - 1924
history of regiment, medals, uniforms

13460
Rowley's House Museum
Barker St, Shrewsbury
Archeology Museum - 1929
Roman and prehistoric finds,
inscriptions, silver mirror from
Viroconium

13461
Shrewsbury Borough Art Gallery
Castle Gate, Shrewsbury
Fine Arts Museum - 1885
paintings, water colors

Shugborough

13462
Museum of Staffordshire County
Staffordshire County Council
Shugborough
General Museum - 1966
in 18th century house, French
furniture; architecture by James Stuart
and Samuel Wyatt; ethnography;
transportation; 18th century brewery

Sidmouth

13463
Sidmouth Museum
Hope Cottage, Church St, Sidmouth,
Devon
General Museum
local history

Silchester

13464
Calleva Museum
The Rectory, Silchester, Berks
General Museum - 1951
Roman period

Singleton

13465
**Weald and Downland Open Air
Museum**
Singleton, W Sussex
Open Air Museum - 1967
Buildings of historic interest
re-erected on 40 acre parkland site;
plumbing, carpentry, wheelwrighting,
blacksmithing and shepherding
equipment

Sittingbourne

13466
Court Hall
High St, Sittingbourne, Kent
General Museum - 1963
Insignias of the Office for Feudal
Courts; weights and measures; corn
measure dated 1560; town crier's
bells; typical 'open frame' building of
the 15th century

Skipton

13467
Craven Museum
13 High St, Skipton, Yorks
General Museum - 1928
ethnography; prehistoric, Roman and
other finds

South Molton

13468
South Molton Museum
The Guildhall, The Square, South
Molton, Devon
General Museum - 1951
local history; farming and mining;
pewter; fire engines; cider presses;
local painting; pottery

South Queensferry

13469
Hopetoun House
South Queensferry, West Lothian
History/Public Affairs Museum - 1700
paintings; mid-18th century furniture;
sculpture; manuscripts; costumes;
tapestries; architecture

South Shields

13470
Roman Fort and Museum
Baring St, South Shields, Durham
Archeology Museum - 1953
Roman and Samian finds; enamels;
tiles; bronze jewelry

13471
South Shields Museum
Ocean Rd, South Shields, Durham
General Museum - 1876
glass; natural history; local history

Southampton

13472
Bargate Guildhall Museum
(Southampton City Museums and Art
Gallery)
High St, Southampton
General Museum - 1951
temporary exhibitions of museums and
art gallery material on themes of local
interest

13473
God's House Tower Museum
Southampton City Museums and Art
Gallery
Southampton
Archeology Museum - 1960
local archaeology (prehistory to
modern) medieval and post-medieval
ceramics from excavations in
Southampton; in early 15th century
tower

13474
Southampton Art Gallery
(Southampton City Museums and Art
Gallery)
Commercial Rd, Civic Centre,
Southampton
Fine Arts Museum - 1939
18th-20th century English paintings;
Continental Old Masters 14th-18th
century; modern French paintings,
including the Impressionist, also
sculpture and ceramics; paintings and
drawings of the Camden Town Group

13475
Tudor House Southampton City
Museums and Art Gallery
Bugle St, Southampton
History/Public Affairs Museum - 1912
Furniture and musical instruments;
paintings and drawings of
Southampton; costumes and
decorative arts; in a late medieval
town house

13476
**Wool House Museum (Maritime
Museum)** (Southampton City
Museums and Art Gallery)
The Wool House, Bugle St,
Southampton
History/Public Affairs Museum - 1962
ship models; paintings; in 14th century
warehouse with a magnificent
chestnut roof

Southend-on-Sea

13477
Beecroft Art Gallery
Station Rd, Southend-on-Sea
Fine Arts Museum - 1953
17th-18th century paitings; early
English watercolours; contemporary
British art; drawings; prints

13478
Prittlewell Priory Museum
Priory Park, Victoria Av, Southend-
on-Sea
General Museum - 1922
archaeology; history and natural
history of Southeastern Essex;
prehistoric finds; microliths

13479
Southchurch Hall Museum
Southchurch Hall Close, Southend-
on-Sea
History/Public Affairs Museum - 1974
Medieval manor house with 17th
century furnishings; built in 1340

Southport

13480
Atkinson Art Gallery
Lord St, Southport, Lancs
Fine Arts Museum - 1878
paintings; drawings; watercolours;
prints; sculptures

13481
Botanic Gardens Museum
Botanic Gardens, Southport,
Merseyside PR9 7NB
General Museum - 1938
Coll: dolls; Liverpool porcelain; natural
sciences; natural history

Southwold

13482
Southwold Museum
St. Bartholomew's Green, Southwold,
Suffolk
General Museum - 1933
local history; Southwold railway relics

Spalding

13483
Bird Museum
Churchgate, Aysconghfee Hall,
Spalding, Lincs
Natural History Museum

13484
**Museum of the Spalding
Gentlemen's Society**
Broad St, Spalding, Lincs
General Museum - 1710
local history

Stafford

13485
Izaak Walton Cottage
Stafford
General Museum
local history; fishing; material on Izaak
Walton (1593-1683)

13486
Stafford Museum and Art Gallery
The Green, Stafford
General Museum

Stalybridge

13487
Astley Cheetham Art Gallery
Trinity St, Stalybridge
General Museum - 1932

Stamford

13488
Stamford Museum
Broad St, Stamford, Lincs
General Museum - 1961
archaeology; mounted birds; Saxon
and medieval pottery

Stanraer

13489
Wigtown County Museum
London Rd, Stanraer
General Museum - 1950
local history; archaeology; farming

Stevenage

13490
Stevenage Museum
George's Way, Stevenage, Herts
General Museum - 1954
local history; archaeology; natural
history; geology

Sticklepath

13491
**Finch Foundry Trust and Sticklepath
Museum of Rural Industry**
Oakhampton, Sticklepath, Devon
Agriculture Museum
agriculture

Stirling

13492
**The Argyll and Sutherland
Highlanders Regimental Museum**
The Castle, Stirling, Scotland
History/Public Affairs Museum - 1961
history of regiment; medals; pictures;
silver; armours

13493
Smith Art Gallery and Museum
Albert Place, Stirling, Scotland
General Museum - 1874
local history; archaeology; ethnology;
geology; paintings; watercolors;
pistols

Stockport

13494
Stockport Art Gallery
Wellington Rd, Stockport, Cheshire
Fine Arts Museum - 1924
paintings; sculptures; bronze of Yehudi
Menuhin by Epstein

13495
Stockport Municipal Museum
Vernon Park, Tuncroft Lane, Stockport
General Museum - 1860
local history; natural history; applied
arts; example of a window made from
'Blue John' fluorspar;

Stockton-on-Tees

13496
Preston Hall Museum
Yarm Rd, Preston Park, Stockton-
on-Tees, Cleveland
History/Public Affairs Museum - 1968
armaments; Victorian period rooms;
toys; transport

13497
**Stockton and Darlington Railway
Museum**
Bridge Rd, Stockton-on-Tees,
Cleveland
History/Public Affairs Museum
railway history; old ticket office

Stoke Bruerne

13498
Waterways Museum
Stoke Bruerne, Northants
General Museum - 1963
19th and 20th century canal history;
exhibits relating to canal boats and
family boating

Stoke-on-Trent

13499
Arnold Bennett Museum
205 Waterloo Rd, Stoke-on-Trent,
Staffs
History/Public Affairs Museum - 1960
former home of writer Arnold Bennett
(1867-1931), memorabilia

13500
City Museum and Art Gallery
Broad St, Stoke-on-Trent
General Museum - 1956
Staffordshire pottery and porcelain;
Continental and Oriental pottery,
sculpture; natural history; local history;
18th century watercolors; English
paintings

13501
Ford Green Hall Folk Museum
Ford Green Rd, Stoke-on-Trent
History/Public Affairs Museum - 1952
in 16th century framed house; period
furniture; household objects

13502
Spode Museum Spode Ltd
Church St, Stoke-on-Trent
Decorative Arts Museum - 1938
Spode porcelain since 1780; porcelain
production

13503
Wedgwood Museum (Josiah
Wedgwood and Sons Ltd., Barlaston)
Stoke-on-Trent, Staffs
Decorative Arts Museum - 1906
Wedgwood family history; porcelain

Stourton

13504
Stourhead House
Stourton, Wilts
Fine Arts Museum
furniture; paintings; porcelain; furniture
designed by Thomas Chippendale, the
younger

Stowmarket

13505
**Abbot's Hall Museum of Rural Life of
East Anglia**
Stowmarket, Suffolk
Anthropology Museum - 1965
rural life in East Anglia; household
equipment; farm and craft tools;
re-erected watermill

Stratford-upon-Avon

13506
Anne Hathaway's Cottage
(Shakespeare Birthplace Trust)
Shottery, Stratford-upon-Avon,
Warwicks
History/Public Affairs Museum
Tudor house; former home of Anne
Hathaway; period furniture since 16th
century

13507
Hall's Croft (Shakespeare Birthplace
Trust)
Old Town, Stratford-upon-Avon,
Warwicks
History/Public Affairs Museum
home of Shakespeare's daughter;
Tudor-Jacobean furniture; 16th
century doctor's dispensary; history of
Stratford festivals

13508
Mary Arden's House (Shakespeare
Birthplace Trust)
Wilmcote, Stratford-upon-Avon,
Warwicks
Historic Site
in Tudor farmhouse; home of
Shakespeare's mother; period
furnishings; old Warwickshire rural life

13509
New Place (Shakespeare Birthplace
Trust)
Chapel St, Stratford-upon-Avon,
Warwicks
Historic Site
reconstruction of Shakespeare's last
home; Thomas Nash house; Tudor
furnishings; local history

13510
**Royal Shakespeare Theatre Picture
Gallery and Museum**
Waterside, Stratford-upon-Avon,
Warwicks
Performing Arts Museum - 1881
relics of famous actors and actresses;
portraits of actors; paintings of scenes
from Shakespeare's plays; scenery
and costume designs

13511
Shakespeare's Birthplace
(Shakespeare Birthplace Trust)
Stratford-upon-Avon, Warwicks
Historic Site
16th century timbered house;
Shakespeare's birthplace;
memorabilia; ceramics; books;
documents; pictures

Stretford

13512
Longford Hall Art Gallery
Longford Park, Edge Lane, Stretford,
Lancs
Fine Arts Museum
paintings

Stromness

13513
Stromness Museum
52 Alfred St, Stromness, Orkney
General Museum - 1837
Orkney county and local history;
natural history; birds and fossils;
Stone Age finds; ship models; Eskimo
carvings

Stroud

13514
Stroud Museum
Landsdown, Stroud
General Museum - 1899
geology and archaeology of
Gloucester, architecture, local
industries, ethnography; Neolithic and
Bronze Age pottery; Roman finds;
fossils; glass

Sudbury

13515
Gainsborough's House
Gainsborough St, Sudbury, Suffolk
Fine Arts Museum - 1958
early Gainsborough portraits; plaster
horse from original by Gainsborough

Sulgrave

13516
Sulgrave Manor
Sulgrave, Northants
History/Public Affairs Museum

Sunderland

13517
Grindon Close Museum
Grindon Lane, Sunderland, Tyne and
Wear SR4 8HW
History/Public Affairs Museum - 1955
Coll: Edwardian period room and shop
interiors

13518
Monkwearmouth Station Museum
North Bridge Street, Sunderland, Tyne
and Wear SR5 1AP
Science/Tech Museum - 1973
Coll: Land transport in North East
England; rail exhibits and other land
transport items

13519
Sunderland Museum and Art Gallery
Borough Road, Sunderland, Tyne and
Wear SR1 1PP
General Museum - 1846
Coll: pottery and glass; Wearside
paintings, prints and photographs;
Wearside maritime history; British
silver; zoology; botany; geology;
industries; archaeology; etchings

Swaledale

13520
Swaledale Folk Museum
Reeth, Swaledale, N Yorks DL11 6RT
General Museum - 1975
Folk exhibits

Swansea

13521
Glynn Vivian Art Gallery
Alexandra Rd, Swansea, Glamorgan
Fine Arts Museum - 1911
Local pottery, porcelain and glass; Old
Masters; 20th century British art

13522
Swansea Museum University College
of Swansea and Royal Institution of
South Wales
Victoria Rd, Swansea, Wales SA1 1SN
General Museum - 1835
Coll: archaeology; ceramics; natural
history; Welsh ethnography;
numismatic; maps - library

Swindon

13523
Great Western Railway Museum
Faringdon Rd, Swindon, Wilts
History/Public Affairs Museum - 1962
Coll: history of railway; historic
locomotives; models; illustrations

13524
Lydiard House
Lydiard Tregoze, Swindon SN5 9PA
History/Public Affairs Museum - 1946
history

13525
Richard Jefferies Museum
Marlborough Rd, Swindon, Wilts
History/Public Affairs Museum - 1962
memorabilia on Richard Jefferies,
manuscripts; memorabilia on local poet
Alfred Williams

13526
Swindon Museum and Art Gallery
Bath Rd, Swindon, Wilt
General Museum - 1919
Coll: numismatics; natural history;
ethnography; 20th century British
paintings; pot lids and ware; bygones

Tamworth

13527
Tamworth Castle Museum
Tamworth, Staffs B79 7LR
General Museum - 1898
Coll: local history; archaeology; Saxon
and Norman coins; costumes;
heraldry; arms

Tarbolton

13528
Bachelor's Club National Trust for
Scotland
7 Croft St, Tarbolton, Ayr; Scotland
History/Public Affairs Museum - 1938
Coll: memorabilia of Robert Burns and
his friends; period furnishings

Taunton

13529
Somerset County Museum
Castle Green, Taunton, Somerset
General Museum - 1878
Archaeology; history; ethnography;
ceramics; natural history; Roman
mosaic

13530
The Somerset Military Museum
The Castle, Taunton, Somerset
History/Public Affairs Museum - 1921
Militaria

Tavistock

13531
Morwellham Quay Open Air Museum
Morwellham, Tavistock, Devon PL18
8TL
Archeology Museum - 1970
George and Charlotte Copper Mine;
industry; archaeology; local history

Tenby

13532
Tenby Museum
Castle Hill, Tenby, Pembroke
General Museum

Ternterden

13533
Ellen Terry Memorial Museum
Smallhythe Place, Ternterden, Kent
TN30 7NG
History/Public Affairs Museum - 1929
Coll: memorabilia on actress Dame
Ellen Terry; costumes

Thetford

13534
Ancient House Museum
White Hart St, Thetford, Norfolk IP24
1AA
General Museum - 1922

Thursford

13535
The Thursford Collection
Thursford, Nr Fakenham, Norfolk
Science/Tech Museum - 1947
Coll: steam and locomotives including
showman's traction and ploughing
engines; steam wagons; mechanical
musical organs; Wurlitzer theater
organ; concert organ; German organ
Karl Frei

Thurso

13536
Thurso Museum
High St, Thurso, Caithness
General Museum

Tiverton

13537
Tiverton Museum
St. Andrew St, Tiverton, Devon
General Museum - 1960
Coll: wagons; agricultural implements;
railway; clocks; maritime history;
industries - library

Torquay

13538
Torquay Natural History Museum
Babbacombe Road 529, Torquay,
Devon TA1 1HG
Natural History Museum - 1844
Coll: geology; entomology; botany;
folk life - library

13539
Torre Abbey Art Gallery
Kings Dr, Torquay, Devon
Fine Arts Museum - 1933
Coll: paintings; furniture; glass

Totnes

13540
Elizabethan House
70 Fore Street, Totnes, Devon TQ9
5RU
General Museum - 1961
Coll: period furniture; costumes; farm
and household objects; archaeology;
toys; computers - library

Towyn

13541
Narrow Gauge Railway Museum
Wharf Station, Towyn, Merionethshire
Science/Tech Museum - 1951
Locomotives; rolling stock; narrow-
gauge railway history

Truro

13542
County Museum and Art Gallery
River St, Truro, Cornwall
General Museum - 1818
History of Cornwall; mineralogy; fine
arts

Turriff

13543
Delgatie Castle
Turriff, Aberdeen AB5 7TD
History/Public Affairs Museum
Coll: art; arms and armour; paintings;
furniture; history

Twickenham

13544
Royal Military School of Music
Kneller Hall, Twickenham, Middx
Music Museum - 1935
Coll: old music instruments

Upper Dicker

13545
Michelham Priory Sussex
Archaeological Society
Upper Dicker, Nr Hailsham, E Sussex
BN27 3QS
History/Public Affairs Museum - 1960
Medieval and Tudor-Jacobean
furniture; 17th century tapestries;
16th-17th century ironwork; glass;
18th century paintings; 18th-20th
century musical instruments;
agricultural and wheelwright tools and
equipment

Wakefield

13546
Wakefield City Art Gallery
Wentworth Terrace, Wakefield, Yorks
Fine Arts Museum - 1934
20th century British and other
paintings; sculpture

13547
Wakefield City Museum
Wood St, Wakefield, Yorks
General Museum
Local history; natural history;
costumes; period rooms

Walsall

13548
Museum of Leathercraft
Lichfield St, Walsall, Staffs
History/Public Affairs Museum
articles of leather throughout the ages;
guilds; products

13549
Walsall Museum and Art Gallery
Lichfield St, Walsall
General Museum - 1965
local history; leathercraft; lorinery; fine
art; Garman-Ryan collection

Wantage

13550
Wantage Museum
Portway, Wantage, Oxfords
General Museum - 1958
Roman and Iron Age excavations;
tramway relics - library

Wareham

13551
**Royal Armoured Corps Tank
Museum and Royal Tank Regiment
Museum**
Bovington Camp, Wareham, Dorset
History/Public Affairs Museum
history of tank units

Warley

13552
Avery Historical Museum
Foundry Lane, Warley
History/Public Affairs Museum - 1928
Collection of scales, weights and
records relating to the history of
weighing

Warminster

13553
Longleat House
Warminster, Wilts BA12 7NN
Historic Site - 1949
Lord Bath's private collection of
Churchilliana and Hitleriana; Italian
ceilings designed by Grace in the 19th
century - library

Warrington

13554
**South Lancashire Regiment,
Regimental Museum**
Peninsula Barracks, Warrington
History/Public Affairs Museum - 1924
history of regiment, medals, uniforms,
militaria

13555
Warrington Museum and Art Gallery
Bold St, Warrington
General Museum - 1857
local history; Romano-British finds
from Wilderspool; prehistory;
ethnology; natural history; local
industries; early English watercolours;
ceramics

Warwick

13556
The Queens's Own Hussars Regimental Museum The Lord Leycester Hospital
High St, Warwick, Sutherland
History/Public Affairs Museum - 1966
Coll: history of regiment; uniforms; medals; silver goblets - library

13557
Warwick Doll Museum Oken's House
Castle St, Warwick, Warwicks
History/Public Affairs Museum - 1955
old dolls and toys

13558
Warwickshire Museum
Market Place, Warwick, Warwicks
General Museum
Coll: archaeology; geology; costumes; natural history; musical instruments; tapestry map

Watford

13559
Watford Museum
194 High Street, Watford, Herts WD1 3EU
General Museum - 1874
Coll: material on the gravure industry in Watford; works from the local art collections of Sir Hubert von Herkomer and Dr. Monro's Academy; Bronze Age finds; art

Wednesbury

13560
Wednesbury Art Gallery and Museum
Holyhead Rd, Wednesbury, W Midlands
Fine Arts Museum - 1891
Coll: English 19th century oil paintings and watercolours; ethnography; local history

Wells

13561
Wells Museum
8 Cathedral Gren, Wells, Soms
General Museum - 1893
archaeology; natural history; geology; ethnology

13562
Wookey Hole Caves Museum
Wookey Hole, Wells, Som
Agriculture Museum - 1980
Coll: archaeological finds; cave exploration; geology; cave diving; myth and legends

Welshpool

13563
Powis Castle
Welshpool, Poweys
General Museum
Coll: plasterwork and panelling; paintings; tapestries; early Georgian furniture and relics of Clive of India

Welwyn

13564
Welwyn Roman Bath House
Welwyn By-Pass, Welwyn, Hertfords
Historic Site
archaeology

Wendron

13565
Poldark Mine
Wendron, Helston, Cornwall
History/Public Affairs Museum - 1971
18th century tin mine; domestic antiques; mining artifacts - library

West Bromwich

13566
The Oak House
Oak Road, West Bromwich, W Midlands
General Museum - 1898
Coll: fine collection of oak furniture of 16th and 17th centuries

Weston-super-Mare

13567
Museum and Art Gallery
Boulevard, Weston-super-Mare, Soms
General Museum
archaeology

13568
Somerset Railway Museum Bleadon and Uphill Railway Station
Toll Rd, Weston-super-Mare, Soms
Science/Tech Museum - 1968
railway; train parts

Weybridge

13569
Weybridge Museum
Church Street, Weybridge, Surrey KT13 8DE
General Museum - 1909
local history; archaeology; excavated material from Oatlands palace; costume; natural history - library

Weymouth

13570
Museum of Local History
Westham Rd, Weymouth, Dorset DT4 8NF
General Museum - 1971
Coll: extensive collection of local illustrations; 'Royal' bathing machine; Chesil Beach lerret

Whitby

13571
Whitby Museum
Pannett Park, Whitby, N Yorks YO21 1RE
General Museum - 1823
Coll: local history; archaeology; geology; natural history; shipping; fossils; paintings

Whitehaven

13572
Whitehaven Museum and Art Gallery
Market Place, Whitehaven, Cumbria CA28 7JG
General Museum - 1975
Coll: maritime history; coal mining; pottery - library

Wick

13573
Museum
Carnegie Public Library, Wick, Caithness
General Museum

Wigan

13574
Powell Museum
Station Rd, Wigan, Greater Manchester WN1 1YQ
General Museum - 1948
Coll: local history; musical instruments

13575
Wigan Museum and Art Gallery
Station Rd, Wigan, Lancs
General Museum - 1884
local history; archaeology; numismatics; local art; industries

Willenhall

13576
Willenhall Lock Museum
Walsall St, Willenhall, Staffs
Decorative Arts Museum - 1961
17th-20th century locks and keys

Wilmington

13577
Wilmington Priory
Polegate, Wilmington, Sussex
Agriculture Museum
old agricultural implements

Wimborne

13578
Priest's House Museum
High St, Wimborne, Dorset
General Museum - 1962
local history; archaeology; crafts; Bronze Age and Romano-British finds

Winchelsea

13579
Court Hall Museum
The Court Hall, Winchelsea, Sussex
General Museum - 1945
local history and customs of the Cinque Ports

Winchester

13580
City Museum
The Square, Winchester, Hants
General Museum - 1898
local history; old weights and measures; in medieval building

13581
Royal Green Jacketts Museum
Peninsula Barracks, Winchester, Hants
History/Public Affairs Museum - 1966
regimental history; pictures; silver; medals

13582
The Royal Hampshire Regiment Museum
Southgate St, Winchester
History/Public Affairs Museum
history of the regiment

13583
Westgate Museum
High St, Winchester, Hants
General Museum - 1847
local history; geology; archaeology; Roman, Saxon and medieval finds

13584
Winchester College Museum The College
Kingsgate St, Winchester, Hants
History/Public Affairs Museum
college history

Windsor

13585
Household Cavalry Museum
Combermere Barracks, Windsor, Berks
History/Public Affairs Museum - 1952
regimental history; uniforms; armaments; pictures

13586
Myers Museum Eton College
Wick Rd, Windsor, Berks
Archeology Museum - 1899
Egyptology; Greek pottery; historic finds - library

Wisbech

13587
Wisbech and Fenland Museum
5 Museum Square, Wisbech, Cambs
General Museum - 1835
pottery and porcelain; figures; local photographs; manuscripts, including a manuscript by Dickens and Lewis

Withorn

13588
Withorn Priory Museum (Ministry of Public Buildings and Works, Edinburgh)
Withorn, Wigtownshire
Archeology Museum - 1918
early Christian medieval stonework

Woburn

13589
Woburn Abbey Art Gallery
Woburn, Beds
Fine Arts Museum - 1969
contemporary paintings; sculptures; art objects

Wolverhampton

13590
Bantock House
Bantock Park, Merridale Rd, Wolverhampton, Staffs
Decorative Arts Museum
decorative arts; local history; costumes; archaeology; English enamels and porcelain

13591
Wolverhampton Art Gallery and Museum
Lichfield St, Wolverhampton
Fine Arts Museum - 1894
English paintings, watercolors, prints, applied art; also Indian, Japanese armaments and applied art

Worcester

13592
The Commandery
Sidbury, Worcester, Hereford and Worcs
General Museum - 1977
local history; English Civil War; trades and industry; 15th century wall paintings

13593
Dyson Perrins Museum Royal Porcelain Co.Ltd.
Severn St, Worcester
Decorative Arts Museum - 1951
Worcester porcelain since 1751

13594
Tudor House Museum
Friar St, Worcester
General Museum - 1971
local social history

13595
Worcester City Museums and Gallery
Foregate St, Worcester
General Museum - 1833
area history; geology; natural history; archaeology; glass; ceramics; local prints; watercolors

13596
The Worcestershire Regimental Museum (Worcester City Museums and Art Gallery)
Foregate St, Worcester
History/Public Affairs Museum - 1929
history of regiment; medals, uniforms, decorations, documents and prints

Worksop

13597
Worksop Museum
Memorial Av, Worksop, Notts
General Museum
local history; archaeology; natural history; Stone Age finds

Worsbrough

13598
Worsbrough Mill Museum
Worsbrough, Barnsley, S Yorks S70 5LJ
General Museum - 1976
working 17th century water powered corn mill; working 19th century oil engine powered corn mill

Worthing

13599
Worthing Museum and Art Gallery
Chapel Rd, Worthing, Sussex
General Museum - 1908
archaeology; geology; history; costumes; paintings; decorative arts; toys

Wrexham

13600
Erddig
Wrexham, Clwyd
General Museum
Furniture; several domestic outbuildings; agriculture

13601
Erddig Agricultural Museum
Felin Puleston, Wrexham, Clwyd
General Museum
Coll: local farm machinery mainly from the second half of the 19th century

Wroxeter

13602
Viroconium Museum
Wroxeter
General Museum

Wye

13603
Wye College Agricultural Museum
Wye College
Wye, Kent
Agriculture Museum
old farm tools in medieval buildings

Yanworth

13604
Chedworth Roman Villa Museum
The Roman Villa, Yanworth, Cheltenham, Glos GL54 3LJ
Historic Site - 1865
Roman walls; mosaic floors; bath suites; wooden buildings; heating in Roman houses; Roman gardens; religion in Roman times; archaeology; classical history - classroom; lecture room

13605
Museum of Roman Antiquities
(National Trust Property)
Chedworth Villa, Yanworth, Cheltenham
Archeology Museum
Archaeological finds from an old Roman site

Yeovil

13606
Yeovil Borough Museum Hendford Manor Hall
Yeovil, Soms
General Museum - 1928
archaeology; industries; household and farm tools; topography; armaments; glass; costumes

York

13607
Castle Museum York
Tower St, York
History/Public Affairs Museum
Yorkshire ethnology; period rooms; household and farm tools; militaria; costumes; crafts

13608
National Railway Museum
Leeman Rd, York, Yorks YO2 4XJ
Science/Tech Museum

13609
York City Art Gallery
Exhibiton Square, York
Fine Arts Museum - 1879
European painting 1350-1930; topographical prints and drawings; Italian paintings; English stoneware pottery - library

13610
Yorkshire Museum
Museum Gardens, York
General Museum - 1822
archaeology; decorative art; pottery; biology; mammals; entomology; herbarium; geology; fossils; minerals; numismatics; figures - library

Zennor

13611
Wayside Museum
Old Mill House, Zennor, Cornwall
General Museum - 1936
mining; household objects; milling; fishing; archaeology

United States

Abercrombie ND

13612
Fort Abercrombie Historic Site
Abercrombie, ND 58001
Historic Site - 1961
Coll: Red River ox cart; relics from pioneer days; Blockhouses and Guard House

Aberdeen MD

13613
US Army Ordnance Museum US Army Ordnance Center and School Aberdeen Proving Ground, Aberdeen, MD 21040
History/Public Affairs Museum - 1926
Coll: ordnance equipment from many countries and wars; foreign military equipment; small arms from 16th century to present; artillery tanks; tank destroyers; ammunition explosives; war history - library

Aberdeen SD

13614
Dacotah Prairie Museum
21 S. Main St, POB 395, Aberdeen, SD 57401
General Museum - 1964
Coll: pioneer artifacts; tools, furniture; Indian artifacts and craft work; photographs; natural history; history; archives; art gallery - library

Abilene KS

13615
Dickinson County Historical Society
412 S Campbell St, POB 506, Abilene, KS 67410
History/Public Affairs Museum - 1928
Coll: agriculture; cattle drive memorabilia; toys; medicine; carnivals; local art; early settling of the West

13616
Dwight D. Eisenhower Library
Abilene, KS 67410
History/Public Affairs Museum - 1046
Coll: archives; paintings; sculpture; graphics; military; political history - library

13617
Greyhound Hall of Fame
407 S Buckey, Abilene, KS 67410
History/Public Affairs Museum - 1963
Coll: historic items relating to the sport of greyhound racing and the greyhound animal - theater; library

13618
Museum of Independent Telephony
412 S Campbell, Abilene, KS 67410
Science/Tech Museum - 1973
Coll: early artifacts of communications; telephones from the primative to the modern - library

13619
Western Museum
201 SE 6th, Abilene, KS 67410
General Museum
Coll: items from the early West; Historic houses of the 18th century

Abilene TX

13620
Abilene Fine Arts Museum
Oscar Rose Park, POB 1858, Abilene, TX 79604
Fine Arts Museum - 1927
Coll: paintings and prints - classrooms

Abington MA

13621
Dyer Memorial Library
Centre Ave, Abington, MA 02351
History/Public Affairs Museum - 1932
Coll: agriculture; apothecary; law office; glass - library; reading room

Abiquiu NM

13622
Ghost Ranch Museum Visitor Center
Hwy 84, Abiquiu, NM 87510
Natural History Museum - 1959
Living animals; native botanical specimens; miniature national forest; paleontological and geological objects; art objects; fossils of American beaver - library; botanical garden; zoological park; nature/conservation center; aquarium; reading room; classrooms

Academia PA

13623
Tuscarora Academy
Academia PA 17059, Rd No. 2, Port Royal, PA 17082
Historic Site - 1962
Coll: early boarding school; education

Accokeek MD

13624
National Colonial Farm
Rte 1, POB 697, Accokeek, MD 20607
Agriculture Museum - 1958
Coll: sample crops; Indian corn and tobacco seed; botany; folklore; marine; technology - library

Adrian MI

13625
Lenawee County Historical Museum
104 E Church St, POB 511, Adrian, MI 49221
General Museum - 1972
Coll: furniture; paintings; carriages and cars; street art; weapons; clothing and textiles; farm equipment - library

Aiken SC

13626
Aiken County Historical Museum
226 Chesterfield, Aiken, SC 29801
General Museum - 1970
Coll: South Carolina artifacts; war collection; Indian artifacts; historic building - library; auditorium

Ainsworth NE

13627
Sellor's Memorial Museum
Court House Park, Junction of Hwy 20 and Hwy 7, Ainsworth, NE 69210
General Museum - 1934
Coll: Indian artifacts; guns; copper kettle; hand tools; birds; furniture

Akron CO

13628
Washington County Museum
Henry Route, POB 24, Akron, CO 80720
General Museum - 1958
Coll: antiques and memorabilia of local area - library

Akron OH

13629
Akron Art Institute
69 E Market St, Akron, OH 44308
Fine Arts Museum - 1920
Coll: American and European painting, sculpture, photographs and prints from 1850 to the present - library; reading room; auditorium; classrooms; sculpture garden; children's zoo

13630
Stan Hywet Hall
714 N Portage Bath, Akron, OH 44303
Decorative Arts Museum - 1957
Coll: antique silver; Tudor and Stuart
furniture; fine linens; pewter; 16th and
17th century Flemish tapestries; 18th
century English portraits; Gothic
sculpture; rare oriental rugs; Revival
Tudor home (1911-1915) - library;
auditoria; greenhouses

13631
Summit County Historical Society
550 Copley Rd, Akron, OH 44320
General Museum - 1925
Coll: early Americana; transportation;
pottery; costumes; glass; John Brown
House (1830); Bronson Church (1839);
old stone school (1840); Simon
Perkins Mansion (1837) - library;
reading room

Alamo TX
13632
Live Steam Museum, Inc.
Route 1, POB 11A, Alamo, TX 78516
Science/Tech Museum - 1965
Coll: aeronautics; industry; steam
engines - library

Alamogordo NM
13633
**Tularosa Basin Historical Society
Museum**
POB 518, Alamogordo, NM 88310
History/Public Affairs Museum - 1971
Coll: Indian artifacts; fossils; displays
dating from early man to the atomic
age

13634
White Sands National Monument
POB 458, Alamogordo, NM 88310
Open Air Museum - 1933
Coll: insects; herbs; birds; mammals;
reptiles; amphibians; cultural artifacts;
selenite crystals - library; native plant
display area

Alamosa CO
13635
Adams State College Museums
ES Building, Alamosa, CO 81102
Archeology Museum - 1968
Coll: Paleo-Indian Folsom points;
Pueblo Indian cultural artifacts; Navajo
weaving; Spanish cultural artifacts;
local historical items - library;
planetarium; auditorium; classrooms

Albans VT
13636
Franklin County Museum
Albans, VT 05478
General Museum - 1971
Coll: items of local historical interest;
china and glass

Albany GA
13637
**Thronateeska Heritage Foundation,
Inc.**
100 Roosevelt Av, Albany, GA 31701
General Museum - 1959
Coll: costumes; pioneer tools; rocks
and minerals; historic artifacts; historic
buildings; Indian artifacts

Albany NY
13638
**Albany County Historical
Association**
9 Ten Broeck Place, Albany, NY 12210
General Museum - 1942
Coll: period furniture; herb garden;
decorative arts; wine cellar (19th
century); home of General Ten Broeck
(1798) - nature trail

13639
Albany Institute of History and Art
125 Washington Av, Albany, NY 12210
Fine Arts Museum - 1791
fine arts; decorative arts - library;
reading room; arts and crafts center;
auditorium; paper conservation
laboratory

13640
Historic Cherry Hill
523 1/2 S. Pearl St, Albany, NY 12202
General Museum - 1964
Coll: furnishings; fabrics; ceramics;
paintings; silver and personal
belongings of the Van Rensselaer-
Rankin family; Georgian Mansion
House (1787) - library

13641
New York State Museum Cultural
Education Center
Empire State Plaza, Albany, NY 12224
General Museum - 1870
Coll: entomology; geology;
mineralogy; archaeology; NY Indian
ethnology; zoology; NY historical
artifacts; architecture; costumes;
decorative art; fire engines; militaria;
musical instruments; Shakeriana; toys;
transportation; agricultural, industrial
and domestic technology; art works
by NY artists; botany - library; field
research station

13642
**Schuyler Mansion State Historic
Site**
27 Clinton St, Albany, NY 12202
Historic Site - 1911
Coll: 18th century furnishings and
decorative arts; books; glass; silver -
interpretation center

13643
University Art Gallery State
University of New York at Albany
1400 Washington Av, Albany, NY
12222
Fine Arts Museum - 1967
Coll: small study collection of 20th
century graphics

Albemarle NC
13644
Morrow Mountain State Park
Rte 2, POB 204, Albemarle, NC 28001
Open Air Museum - 1962
Coll: geological history; Indian
civilization; artifacts of Morrow
Mountain area; display of reversion to
a climax forest area; local plant
species - library

13645
Stanly Historical Kitchen Museum
813 W. Main St, Albemarle, NC 28001
General Museum - 1965
Coll: early kitchen and lighting
devices; history of Stanly County

Albion IN
13646
Old Jail Museum
N Orange, Albion, IN 46701
Historic Site - 1968
Furnishings - library

Albion MI
13647
**Albion College Department of Visual
Arts**
Albion, MI 49224
Fine Arts Museum - 1835
graphic arts from the 15th century to
the present; folk arts of the world;
decorative arts, glass; paintings;
sculpture; archaeology - library

13648
Gardner House Museum
509 S Superior St, Albion, MI 49224
History/Public Affairs Museum - 1968
Coll: furniture; domestic and
commercial artifacts; manuscripts -
library

Albuquerque NM
13649
Albuquerque Museum
2000 Mountain Rd, NW, POB 1293,
Albuquerque, NM 87103
Fine Arts Museum - 1967
Coll: general; decorative arts; fine arts
and crafts; costumes; photography -
library

13650
Art Museum The University of New
Mexico
Fine Arts Center, Albuquerque, NM
87131
Fine Arts Museum - 1963
Graphics; paintings; photography;
sculpture; decorative arts

13651
Jonson Gallery
mail c/o The University of New
Mexico, 1909 Las Lomas Rd, NE,
Albuquerque, NM 87106
Fine Arts Museum - 1948
Jonson retrospective collection; other
artists - library

13652
Maxwell Museum of Anthropology
Roma & University, NE, Albuquerque,
NM 87131
Anthropology Museum - 1932
archaeology; ethnology; specialized
Southwestern collections; Navajo and
other Southwestern weaving; silver;
Mimbres and Pueblo pottery;
American Indian basketry; musical
instruments; Pakistani textiles and
jewelry - library; laboratory of
physical anthropology; ethno-botanical
garden; reading room

13653
Meteorite Museum University of New
Mexico, Institute of Meteoritics
Albuquerque, NM 87131
Natural History Museum - 1946
Coll: meteorites; tektite; impact
glasses

13654
National Atomic Museum
Kirtland Air Force Base East,
Albuquerque, NM 87115
Science/Tech Museum - 1969
Coll: nuclear weapon cases and
related materials; exhibits concerning
current energy programs - library;
theater

13655
Telephone Pioneer Museum
201 Third, NW, POB 1355,
Albuquerque, NM 87103
Science/Tech Museum - 1961
Coll: telephones; switchboards;
insulators; directories; hand tools;
photographs - reading room

13656
**University of New Mexico Biology
Department**
Albuquerque, NM 87131
Natural History Museum - 1890
Coll: plants; mammals; birds; reptiles;
amphibians; fish

Alden NY
13657
Alden Historical Society, Inc.
13213 Broadway, Alden, NY 14004
General Museum - 1965
Coll: farm tools; kitchen utensils; early
American bedroom; historic house
(1859)

Alexandria LA
13658
Alexandria Museum Visual Art Center
933 Main St, Alexandria, LA 71301
Fine Arts Museum
Coll: contemporary works in sculpture,
painting, ceramics, weaving, drawings,
photography, batiks

Alexandria VA
13659
Carlyle House Historic Park
121 N Fairfax St, Alexandria, VA 22314
Historic Site - 1976
Coll: 18th century furniture and
decorative arts; local history

13660
Fort Ward Museum and Park
4301 W Braddock Rd, Alexandria, VA
22304
Historic Site - 1964
Coll: Civil War artifacts - library;
outdoor amphitheater

13661
**George Washington Masonic
National Memorial**
Alexandria, VA 22301
Historic Site - 1910
Coll: replica lodge room; items
pertaining to George Washington;
portraits

13662
Robert E. Lee Boyhood Home
607 Oronco St, Alexandria, VA 22314
Historic Site
decorative arts and furnishings;
history 1795-1825

Allen NE
13663
Dixon County Historical Society
Allen, NE 68710
General Museum - 1964
Coll: medical; military; textiles

Allentown PA
13664
Allentown Art Museum
Fifth and Court Sts, POB 117,
Allentown, PA 18105
Fine Arts Museum - 1959
Kress memorial collection of
Renaissance and Baroque paintings of
Italy, Holland and Germany; 19th and
20th century American paintings and
prints - library; auditorium

13665
Lehigh County Historical Society
Old Court House, Hamilton at Fifth St,
Allentown, PA 18101
General Museum - 1904
Coll: local archives and artifacts;
historic buildings - library

Allison IA

13666
Butler County Historical Society
303 - 6th St, Allison, IA 50602
General Museum - 1956
Coll: agriculture; history; music;
preservation project - library

Allison Park PA

13667
Depreciation Lands Museum
4743 S Pioneer Rd, Allison Park, PA
15101
Historic Site - 1974
Coll: Covenanter Church (1852);
history - nature/conservation center;
library

Alma CO

13668
Alma Firehouse Museum
POB 27, Alma, CO 80420
General Museum - 1976
Coll: gold mining implements;
fire-fighting equipment; pictures and
other local articles

Alma KS

13669
**Mill Creek Museum and Camp
Ground**
R.R. 1, Alma, KS 66401
General Museum
Coll: early farm machinery; household
articles of 1856 period

13670
**Wabaunsee County Historical
Museum**
Corner of Missouri and Third St, POB
127, Alma, KS 66401
General Museum - 1968
Coll: Gen. Lewis Walt's display; Indian
artifacts; old time school room display;
guns; buggies; cloths; costumes;
marines - theater; library

Almond NY

13671
Almond Historical Society, Inc.
114 S Main St, Almond, NY 14804
General Museum - 1970
Coll: costumes; photographs;
furniture; glass; pottery and china -
library

Alpena MI

13672
Jesse Besser Museum
491 Johnson St, Alpena, MI 49707
General Museum
19th and 20th century furnishings and
decorative arts; Great Lakes copper
culture artifacts; agricultural exhibits;
early vehicles; 19th century shop
interiors

Alpine TX

13673
Museum of the Big Bend
Sul Ross State University, Alpine, TX
79830
History/Public Affairs Museum - 1969
Coll: historical materials (19th-20th
century); archaeological artifacts from
paleo-man to modern ethnology;
regional art - library

Altenburg MO

13674
**Perry County Lutheran Historical
Society**
Altenburg, MO 63732
Religious Art Museum - 1912
Coll: religious books; bibles; sermon
books - library

Altus OK

13675
Museum of the Western Prairie
1100 N Hightower, POB 574, Altus, OK
73521
General Museum - 1970
Coll: fossils; Indian artifacts; historic
items; memorabilia and genealogical
items; early agricultural tools; cattle
country items - reading room

Alva OK

13676
Cherokee Strip Museum
14th and U.S. Hwy, 725 N Sunset, Alva,
OK 73717
General Museum - 1961
Coll: costumes; history; flags of
Oklahoma; dolls; dishes; furniture; war
uniforms - library

13677
**Northwestern State College
Museum** Northwestern Oklahoma
State University
Jesse Dunn Hall, Alva, OK 73717
Natural History Museum - 1902
Coll: mounted bird and mammal
species; study skins of birds and
mammals; pleistocene fossils; Indian
artifacts; natural science;
paleontology; zoology; mineralogy;
geology; botany; anthropology;
archaeology; entomology - library;
laboratory

Amagansett NY

13678
East Hampton Town Marine Museum
Bluff Rd, Amagansett, NY 11930
General Museum - 1966
Coll: marine; natural history; whaling
and commercial fishing; folklore;
archaeology - library; photography
collections

Amarillo TX

13679
Amarillo Art Center
S. Van Buren, Amarillo, TX 79109
Fine Arts Museum - 1966
Coll: areas of conservation; art history;
native American ceramic technology -
library; classrooms; theater; auditorium

13680
Don Harrington Discovery Center
Amarillo Foundation for Health and
Science Education, Inc.
1200 Streit Drive, Amarillo, TX 79106
History/Public Affairs Museum - 1968
Coll: medical, dental science -
planetarium; solar telescope

Ambridge PA

13681
Harmonie Associates, Inc.
Old Economy, 14th and Church Sts,
Ambridge, PA 15003
Historic Site - 1956
Coll: furnishings; handcrafted items
relating to Harmony Society

13682
Old Economy Village
14th and Church Sts, Ambridge, PA
17120
General Museum - US
Coll: history; communitarian society;
textiles; technology; industry;
decorative arts; archives; historic
houses - library; reading room;
classrooms; outdoor museum

American Falls ID

13683
Massacre Rocks State Park
American Falls, ID 83211
General Museum - 1967
Coll: Indian artifacts; fossils; natural
history; pioneer and Oregon Trail
history - information center

Americus GA

13684
**Georgia Southwestern College Art
Department**
Americus, GA 31709
Fine Arts Museum - 1971
Coll: contemporary prints; Indian art of
the southeast

Amherst MA

13685
Mead Art Museum Amherst College
Amherst, MA 01002
Fine Arts Museum - 1821
Coll: graphic work; paintings;
sculpture - library; reading room;
classrooms; auditorium

13686
The Pratt Museum of Natural History
Amherst College
Amherst, MA 01002
Natural History Museum - 1821
Coll: rocks; minerals; fossils;
archaeological materials

Amherst VA

13687
Amherst County Historical Museum
POB 741, Amherst, VA 24521
General Museum - 1973
Coll: local history exhibits; maps and
books - library

Amsterdam NY

13688
Walter Elwood Museum
300 Guy Park Av, Amsterdam, NY
12010
General Museum - 1940
Coll: early-American and Indian
material; history; natural history;
ethnology; costumes; prints and
paintings; artifacts; antiques - library;
classrooms; children's museum; junior
museum

Anacortes WA

13689
**Anacortes Museum of History and
Art**
1305 8th, Anacortes, WA 98221
General Museum - 1957
Coll: clothing; furnishings; tools;
medical and dental instruments; local
history - library

Anadarko OK

13690
Anadarko Philomathic Museum
311 E Main St, Anadarko, OK 73005
General Museum - 1936
Coll: pioneer exhibits; Indian artifacts;
military and railroad items; early day
physician's office; general store

13691
Indian City U.S.A.
two miles Southeast of Anadarko,
POB 695, Anadarko, OK 73005
Anthropology Museum - 1955
Coll: Indian artifacts; pottery; dance
costumes; cradles; bags; moccasins;
leggens; rags; Indian dolls; paintings;
arrowheads; Indian dressed
mannequins; early American Indian
articles

13692
**National Hall of Fame for Famous
American Indians**
POB 808, Anadarko, OK 73005
History/Public Affairs Museum - 1952
Coll: bronze portrait busts of great
American Indians in landscaped area;
sculpture; famous Indians in American
history - visitor's information center;
outdoor museum

13693
**Southern Plains Indian Museum and
Crafts Center**
Hwy 62 E, POB 749, Anadarko, OK
73005
Fine Arts Museum - 1947
Coll: historic and contemporary arts of
the Southern Plains Indian Peoples

Anchorage AK

13694
**Anchorage Historical and Fine Arts
Museum**
121 W. Seventh Ave, Anchorage, AK
99501
General Museum - 1968
Coll: Alaskan art and artifacts of all
periods; archeology; ethnology;
history - library; auditorium

Anchorage KS

13695
Louisville School of Art
100 Park Rd, Anchorage, KS 40223
Fine Arts Museum - 1909
paintings; prints; graphics - library

Anderson IN

13696
**Alford House-Anderson Fine Arts
Center**
226 W Historical 8th St, Anderson, IN
46016
Fine Arts Museum - 1966
Coll: paintings, drawings, and prints of
midwestern and Indiana artists;
paintings, drawings, prints, and
sculpture by American and European
artists - reading room; classrooms;
theater

13697
**Anderson College Museum of Bible
and Near Eastern Studies** School of
Theology
1123 E Third St, Sanderson College,
Anderson, IN 46011
Archeology Museum - 1963
Archeological objects related to
Biblical and Near Eastern studies

Anderson SC

13698
Anderson County Arts Center
405 N Main St, Anderson, SC 29621
Fine Arts Museum - 1972
Coll: paintings; environmental arts;
photography - dark room;
classrooms; reading room

Andover IL

13699
Andover Historical Society
Locust St, POB 100, Andover, IL 61233
Historic Site - 1967
Coll: furniture; implements; dishes;
utensils; clothing

Andover MA

13700
**Robert S. Peabody Foundation for
Archaeology**
Corner of Phillips and Main Sts,
Andover, MA 01810
Archeology Museum - 1901
Coll: archaeology of New England,
Labrador, Quebec; collections from
Etowah, Mexico, Pecos; ethnology -
library

Angola IN

13701
Tri-State University General Lewis B.
Hershey Museum
Angola, IN 46703
History/Public Affairs Museum - 1970
Coll: memorabilia of General Lewis B.
Hershey; selective service
memorabilia since the Civil War -
library; reading room; auditorium;
theater; classrooms

Ann Arbor MI

13702
**Kelsey Museum of Ancient and
Mediaeval Archaeology**
434 S State St, Ann Arbor, MI 48109
Archeology Museum - 1929
Coll: classical and Near Eastern
archaeology; Coptic and Islamic
textiles; Roman sculpture - library

13703
**Stearns Collection of Musical
Instruments** University of Michigan
Stearns Bldg, 2005 Baits Dr, Ann
Arbor, MI 48109
Anthropology Museum - 1899
Coll: Western and non-Western
musical instruments

13704
**The University of Michigan Exhibit
Museum**
1109 Geddes, Ann Arbor, MI 48109
Natural History Museum - 1928
Coll: anthropology; astronomy; botany;
geology; herpetology; North American
Indian artifacts; mineralogy;
paleontology; zoology

13705
**University of Michigan Museum of
Anthropology**
Ann Arbor, MI 48109
Anthropology Museum - 1922
Coll: archaeology; ethnology;
ethnobotany; zoo-archaeology; human
osteology; geology

13706
**The University of Michigan Museum
of Art**
Corner of S State and S University
Sts, Alumni Memorial Hall, Ann Arbor,
MI 48109
Fine Arts Museum - 1946
Coll: Western art from the 6th century
to modern times; Asian art from
ancient to modern times; African and
Oceanic art; Islamic art objects

Annandale VA

13707
Fairfax County Park Authority
4030 Hummer Rd, POB 236,
Annandale, VA 22003
Historic Site - 1972
Coll: period furniture; decorative arts;
agricultural machinery

Annapolis MD

13708
**United States Naval Academy
Museum**
Annapolis, MD 21402
General Museum - 1845
Coll: sculpture; ship models;
navigational instruments; naval
weapons; flags; anthropology;
numismatics - library

Anniston AL

13709
Anniston Museum of Natural History
The John B. Lagarde Environmental
Interpretive Center
McClellan Blvd, POB 1587, Anniston,
AL 36201
Natural History Museum - 1930
Coll: zoology; anthropology;
archeology; botany; Regar-Werner
ornithology collection; Egyptian
mummies; William H. Werner natural
habitat groups; John B. Lagarde
International Mammal Collection -
library; multi-media auditorium; theater;
classrooms; laboratories; nature trails
& lecture-demonstration areas;
wildflower botanical gardens

Ansted WV

13710
**Fayette County Historical Society,
Inc.**
Ansted WV 25812 Hico, WV 25854
General Museum - 1926
3 unit complex with restored one room
schoolhouse, Antebellum house and
museum; Indian relics; costumes;
antique furnishings; utensils and
implements of pioneer mountain
families - library

Antigo WI

13711
**Langlade County Historical Society
Museum**
404 Superior St, Antigo, WI 54409
General Museum - 1929
Coll: pioneer farm and logging tools;
domestic implements and furnishings;
historic houses

Antwerp OH

13712
**Otto E. Ehrhart - Paulding County
Historical Society**
City Hall, N Main St, Antwerp, OH
45813
Natural History Museum - 1963
Coll: archaeoloy; ethnology; geology;
philatelic; mounted birds and animals;
insects; historical artifacts - library;
nature center

Apalachicola FL

13713
John Gorrie State Museum
Apalachicola, FL 32320
General Museum - 1055
Coll: replica of the first ice-making
machine invented by John Gorrie;
early scenes of Apalachicola; artifacts
of the time

Appleton WI

13714
Dard Hunter Paper Museum
1043 E South River St, Appleton, WI
54911
Science/Tech Museum - 1939
Coll: hand paper mills; papermaking
hand moulds; old and decorated
papers; watermarks - library

Appomattox VA

13715
**Appomattox Court House National
Historical Park**
POB 218, Appomattox, VA 24522
Historic Site - 1940
Coll: furnishings; Civil War objects;
historic village buildings - library

Arabi LA

13716
Chalmette National Historical Park
POB 429, Arabi, LA 70032
History/Public Affairs Museum - 1939
Coll: history of the Battle of New
Orleans; weapons and ammunition;
history of Beauregard House - library;
auditorium

Arcadia CA

13717
**Los Angeles State and County
Arboretum**
301 N. Baldwin Ave, Arcadia, CA
91006
Natural History Museum - 1948
Coll: plants of Australia, South Africa,
South America, Asia, North America;
plants related to Southern California
history; historic buildings - library;
reading room; nature center; botanical
gardens; auditorium; classrooms

Archbold OH

13718
**Sauder Museum Farm and Craft
Village**
POB 332, Archbold, OH 43502
General Museum - 1971
Coll: farm equipment; woodworking
tools

Ardmore OK

13719
Eliza Cruce Hall Doll Museum
Grand at E Northwest, Ardmore, OK
73401
Decorative Arts Museum - 1971
Threehundred 18th century dolls;
three original dolls belonging to Marie
Antoinette; porcelain and bisque dolls;
Lenci dolls; miniature tea services -
library

13720
Tucker Tower Museum
POB 1649, Ardmore, OK 73401
General Museum - 1952
fossils; minerals; meteorite; Indian and
Western artifacts - nature center

Argonia KS

13721
Salter House Museum
South Main St, Argonia, KS 67004
History/Public Affairs Museum - 1961
Coll: 19th century home furnishing

Arkadelphia AR

13722
Henderson State University Museum
Henderson St, Arkadelphia, AR 71923
General Museum - 1953
Coll: local prehistoric artifacts; natural
history specimens; fossils; military
hardware; antique guns; local historic
items; antique lighting devices - library

Arkansas KS

13723
Cherokee Strip Living Museum
S Summit St Rd, 230, Arkansas, KS
67005
History/Public Affairs Museum - 1965
Coll: items relating to the Cherokee
Strip Run; historical objects and
houses of the 18th and 19th centuries
- library

Arlington TX

13724
University Art Gallery The University
of Texas at Arlington
Fine Arts Bldg., Arlington, TX 76019
Fine Arts Museum - 1976
Coll: prints; paintings; sculpture

Arlington VA

13725
Arlington Historical Museum
POB 402, Arlington, VA 22210
General Museum - 1956
Coll: late 1800's schoolroom and
parlor; clothing; farm machinery and
tools; medical instruments - library;
auditorium

13726
Arlington House The Robert E. Lee
Memorial
Arlington National Cemetery, Arlington
VA 22211, Turkey Run Park, McLean,
VA 22101
Historic Site - 1925
Coll: decorative arts and furnishing in
the home of General Robert E. Lee -
library

Armour SD

13727
Douglas County Museum
Armour, SD 57313
General Museum - 1958
Coll: historical items from people of the area; Indian artifacts; photos; rock collection; records of early organizations

Artesia NM

13728
Artesia Historical Museum and Art Center
505 Richardson Av, Artesia, NM 88210
General Museum - 1970
Coll: agriculture; archaeology; folklore; geology; pictures and objects of early-day residents; Indian artifacts - reading room

Ashburnham MA

13729
Ashburnham Historical Society
77 Main St, Ashburnham, MA 01430
History/Public Affairs Museum - 1958
Coll: textiles; transportation; paintings; industry; maps - library; reading room

Asheboro NC

13730
Randolph County Historical Society
Asheboro Public Library
201 Worth St, Asheboro, NC 27203
General Museum - 1911
Coll: local history and genealogy; Asheboro Female Academy (1839) - library

Asheville NC

13731
Asheville Art Museum
Asheville Civic Center, Asheville, NC 28801
Fine Arts Museum - 1948
Coll: contemporary Southeastern American and Appalachian paintings; prints; sculpture; crafts - classroom

13732
Colburn Memorial Mineral Museum
Civic Center Complex, Asheville, NC 28801
Natural History Museum - 1960
Coll: gems; minerals - library

13733
Thomas Wolfe Memorial
48 Spruce St, Asheville, NC 28801
Historic Site - 1949
Coll: boarding house furnishings (1920); memorabilia of Thomas Wolfe

Ashford WA

13734
Mt. Rainier National Park
Tahoma Woods, Star Rte, Ashford, WA 98304
Science/Tech Museum - 1899
Coll: zoology; geology; botany; historic houses - library

Ashland KS

13735
Pioneer Museum
Highway 160, Ashland, KS 67831
General Museum - 1968
Coll: dishes, glassware and other kitchen equipment; toys; furniture; handcrafts; military memorabilia; pioneer pictures; church furniture; barbed wire collection; farm machinery; collection of pioneer era saddles and tack; fossils from the area; Indian artifacts; display of aerobatic airplanes and trophies - reading room; library

Ashland MA

13736
Ashland Historical Society
POB 321, Ashland, MA 01721
History/Public Affairs Museum - 1905
Coll: genealogy; furniture; glassware; china; old books - reading room

Ashland OR

13737
Southern Oregon State College Museum of Vertebrate Natural History
Siskiyou Blvd, Ashland, OR 97520
Natural History Museum - 1969
Coll: vertebrate specimens; bird skins; mammal skins; reptiles; amphibians; fish

Ashland PA

13738
Ashland Anthracite Museum
Pennsylvania Anthracite Museum Complex, Pine and 17th Sts, Ashland, PA 17921
Science/Tech Museum - 1970
Coll: geology; mining technology

Askov MN

13739
Pine County Historical Society
Askov, MN 55704
History/Public Affairs Museum - 1948
Coll: agriculture; archives; folklore; historic buildings - library

Aspen CO

13740
Aspen Historical Society Museum
620 W. Bleeker, POB 1323, Aspen, CO 81611
General Museum - 1963
Coll: general collection of items demonstrating all phases of Aspen history and life styles from 1879-1977; fire-fighting equipment; mining; historic buildings - library; reading room

Astoria OR

13741
Columbia River Maritime Museum
16th and Exchange Sts, Astoria, OR 97103
Science/Tech Museum - 1962
Coll: shipmodels; navigation instruments; shipbuilding and rigging gear; fish models; small craft; marine artifacts; books; prints; paintings; photographs - library

13742
Fort Clatsop National Memorial
Rte 3, POB 604 FC, Astoria, OR 97103
Historic Site - 1958
Coll: interpretive exhibits of Lewis and Clark Expedition (1805-1806) - library

Atascadero CA

13743
Treasure of El Camino Real
6500 Palma Ave, POB 1047, Atascadero, CA 93422
General Museum - 1965
Coll: E. G. Lewis material; Hooper collection including elephants, WW I artifacts, miscellaneous household items; historical photographs; doll collection - library

Atchison KS

13744
Benedictine College Museum Dept. of Biology
North Campus, Atchison, KS 66002
Natural History Museum - 1927
Coll: geology; natural history; archaeology; ethnology; paleontology

13745
The Muchnic Gallery
704 N 4th, Atchison, KS 66002
Fine Arts Museum - 1970
Coll: paintings and lithographs of John Falters, John S. Curry, Thomas Hart Benton, Robert Sudlow, Jack O'Hara; furniture and pictures of the Muchnic family

Athens GA

13746
Georgia Museum of Art The University of Georgia
Jackson St, North Campus, Athens, GA 30602
Fine Arts Museum - 1945
Coll: Eva Underhill Holbrook Memorial collection of American art; graphics; paintings; sculpture; Kress study collection - library

13747
University of Georgia Museum of Natural History University of Georgia
Biological Science Bldg, Athens, GA 30602
Natural History Museum - 1977
Coll: anthropology; botany; entomology; geology; mycology; zoology - laboratories; classrooms

Athens PA

13748
Tioga Point Museum
724 Main St, Athens, PA 18810
General Museum - 1895
Coll: Indian lore; local and natural history; fine arts; early canals, railroads; Stephen C. Foster; Revolutionary War; Civil War - library; reading room

Atlanta GA

13749
Atlanta Historical Society
3099 Andrews Drive, NW, POB 12423, Atlanta, GA 30305
General Museum - 1926
Coll: manuscripts; photograph collection; maps; books; memorabilia of Margaret Mitchell; 19th century furniture and tools; Civil War artifacts; historic houses - garden

13750
Atlanta Museum
537-39 Peachtree St, NE, Atlanta, GA 30308
General Museum - 1938
Coll: confederate money; archives on famous men, such as George Washington, Thomas Jefferson, Jefferson Davis, Napoleon, F.D. Roosevelt, etc; Georgian and Confederate items; early Chinese items; household utensils; original Eli Whitney cotton gin; Eli Whitney gun collection; decorative arts

13751
Emory University Museum Emory University
Sociology Bldg, Kilgo Circle, Atlanta, GA 30322
Natural History Museum - 1836
Coll: archeology; entomology; ethnology; geology; natural history - library

13752
Fernbank Science Center
156 Heaton Park Dr, NE, Atlanta, GA 30307
Natural History Museum - 1967
Coll: skins and hides; entomology; ornithology; herbarium; geology; mammals - library; planetarium; classrooms; forest observatory

13753
Georgia State Museum of Science and Industry
Georgia State Capitol, Rm 431, Atlanta, GA 30334
Science/Tech Museum - 1895
Coll: rocks and minerals; dioramas of industry; reptiles; Indian artifacts; mounted birds, animals, and fish

13754
The High Museum of Art
1280 Peachtree St, NE, Atlanta, GA 30309
Fine Arts Museum - 1905
Coll: Western art from early Renaissance to present; decorative arts; graphics; sculpture; 19th and 20th century photography - library; auditorium; classrooms; play environment

Atlantic City

13755
Historic Gardner's Basin
N New Hampshire Ave & the Bay, Atlantic City NJ
History/Public Affairs Museum - 1976
Coll: 25 vessels, some of which are the oldest or the last of their kind in the nation or the world; maritime artifacts; whaling artifacts and other seafaring memorabilia - aquarium; laboratory; amphitheater; classrooms

Attleboro MA

13756
Bronson Museum
8 N Main St, Attleboro, MA 02703
Archeology Museum - 1946
Coll: archaeological specimens dealing with the Stone Age in New England - library; reading room; auditorium; classrooms

Atwood KS

13757
Rawlins County Historical Society
208 State St, 700 Vine, Atwood, KS
67730
History/Public Affairs Museum - 1961
Coll: Indian artifacts; mineralogy;
natural history; furnished rooms;
pictorial mural of the history of Rawlins
County by artist Rudolph Wendelin -
library

Auburn CA

13758
Placer County Museum
1273 High Street, Auburn, CA 95603
General Museum - 1948
Coll: mining equipment; California
Indian artifacts; Chinese artifacts;
rooms of early days; collection of
winery and agriculture equipment;
farm tools; local minerals - library

Auburn IN

13759
Auburn-Cord-Duesenberg Museum
1600 S Wayne St, POB 148, Auburn,
IN 46706
History/Public Affairs Museum - 1973
Coll: antique and classic cars; historic
radios; photographs; literature and
memorabilia on cars manufactured in
Auburn - library

Auburn NY

13760
Cayuga College Art Gallery
Franklin St, Auburn, NY 13021
Fine Arts Museum - 1978
Coll: paintings; graphics; sculpture -
library

13761
Cayuga County Agricultural Museum
Silver S Rd, POB 309, Auburn, NY
13021
Agriculture Museum - 1975
agriculture machinery and implements;
country kitchen; blacksmith shop;
wheelwright shop; country store;
photos of rural Cayuga County; dairy
processing equipment; sleighs;
buggies; milking equipment; cooper's
bench

13762
Cayuga Museum of History and Art
203 Genesee St, Auburn, NY 13021
History/Public Affairs Museum - 1936
Coll: theater; textiles; Indian artifacts;
archaeology; medical items;
mineralogy; log cabin, Fillmore
Memorial (1791); Sherwood Library
and Museum (1840) - library

13763
Owasco Stockaded Indian Village
Emerson Park, Auburn, NY 13021
Anthropology Museum - 1961
Coll: Indian artifacts; history - Indian
library

13764
Seward House
33 South St, Auburn, NY 13021
Historic Site - 1951
Coll: original furnishings; Civil War
material; Lincoln letters; paintings;
uniform; cane; rifle; china; articles of
the career of William H. Seward (1816)
- library

Auburn WA

13765
**White River Valley Historical Society
Museum**
918 H St SE, Auburn, WA 98002
General Museum - 1957
Coll: Indian artifacts; histories of
pioneers; photographs - library

Augusta GA

13766
Augusta Richmond County Museum
540 Telfair St, Augusta, GA 30901
General Museum - 1927
Coll: military science; art; natural
science; archeology; local history;
Civil War artifacts; archives; sculpture

13767
Ezekiel Harris House
1822 Broad St, Augusta, GA 30904
General Museum - 1956
Coll: furnishings; Revolutionary and
Indian relics; historic house (1760)

13768
**Gertrude Herbert Memorial Institute
of Art**
506 Telfair St, Augusta, GA 30901
Fine Arts Museum - 1937
Coll: paintings; sculpture; graphics;
European Renaissance and modern
paintings; sculpture; historic house -
library

Augusta ME

13769
Blaine House
State St, Augusta, ME 04330
History/Public Affairs Museum
Coll: silver from battleship Maine
(1895-98, 1905-22)

13770
Maine State Museum
State House, Augusta, ME 04333
General Museum - 1965
Coll: anthropology; ethnology;
mineralogy; technology; marine -
library; classrooms; auditorium

Auriesville NY

13771
Kateri Museum The National Shrine
of the North American Martyrs
Auriesville, NY 12016
Historic Site - 1950
Coll: local Indian artifacts; paintings
and charts; geology; anthropology -
library; auditorium

Aurora IL

13772
Aurora Historical Museum
304 Oak Av, Aurora, IL 60506
General Museum - 1906
Coll: Indian artifacts; costumes; clocks
and watches; musical instruments;
vehicles; carriage house; pioneer
cabin (1840)

Aurora OH

13773
Aurora Historical Society, Inc.
115 Aurora Rd, Aurora, OH 44202
General Museum - 1968
Coll: church and business records;
cheese-making equipment; farm
implements; home furnishings

Austin TX

13774
**Daughters of the Republic of Texas
Museum**
112 E. Eleventh St, Austin, TX 78701
General Museum - 1919
Coll: Indian artifacts; numismatics;
philately; archives; early Texas;
paintings; sculpture

13775
Elisabet Ney Museum
304 E. 44th St, Austin, TX 78751
Fine Arts Museum - 1909
Coll: Elisabet Ney's works in marble,
bronze and plaster; letters; documents

13776
Laguna Gloria Art Museum
3809 W. 35th St, POB 5568, Austin, TX
78763
Fine Arts Museum - 1961
Coll: paintings; sculpture; decorative
arts; photographs; graphics - library;
arboretum

13777
**Lyndon Baines Johnson Library and
Museum**
2313 Red River St, Austin, TX 78705
History/Public Affairs Museum - 1971
Coll: manuscripts and records; tapes;
head of state gifts; political cartoons;
documents and objects relating to
President Lyndon Baines Johnson -
library; theater

13778
O. Henry Museum
409 E. 5th St, Austin, TX 78701
History/Public Affairs Museum - 1934
Coll: furnishings; memorabilia

13779
**Outdoor Nature Programs, City of
Austin Parks and Recreation Dept.**
401 Deep Eddy Av, Austin, TX 78703
Natural History Museum - 1960
Div. of Natural Science: native Texas
mammals; fish; birds; reptiles; insects;
Div. of Jourdan-Bachman Pioneer
Farm: typical animals; tools and
paraphernalia of an 1870's farm; Div. of
Mayfield Park: resident flock of
peacocks; old palms; hand-laid stone
patios and ponds - nature trails

13780
Texas Confederate Museum
112 E. 11th, Austin, TX 78701
History/Public Affairs Museum - 1903
Coll: relics of Confederate period;
Southern history; military records -
library

13781
Texas Memorial Museum
2400 Trinity, Austin, TX 78705
Natural History Museum - 1936
Coll: archaeology; anthropology;
ethnology; zoology; paleontology -
laboratories; archives; library

13782
Texas State Library
1201 Brazos St, Austin, TX 78711
History/Public Affairs Museum - 1839
Coll: documents; artifacts; firearms;
archives - library

13783
University Art Museum
23rd and San Jacinto Sts, Austin, TX
78705
Fine Arts Museum - 1963
Coll: Michener collection; The Barbara
Duncan collection; C. R. Smith
collection; paintings; drawings;
graphics; etchings; woodcuts;
sculpture - auditorium

Avalon CA

13784
Catalina Island Museum Society, Inc.
POB 366, Avalon, CA 90704
General Museum - 1953
Coll: Indian artifacts; historical
photographs; ship models; pottery;
natural history of Santa Catalina Island
- library

Aztec NM

13785
Aztec Museum Association
125 N Main, Aztec, NM 87410
General Museum - 1963
Lobato Collection of Rocks and
Minerals; pioneer items

13786
Aztec Ruins National Monument
POB U, Aztec, NM 87410
Archeology Museum - 1923
Coll: Indian artifacts - library

Bailey NC

13787
The Country Doctor Museum
POB 34, Bailey, NC 27807
Historic Site - 1967
Coll: 18th and 19th century medical
and pharmacy instruments, furnishings,
and supplies; Dr. Freeman office
(1857); Dr. Brantley office (1887) -
library; medicinal herb garden

Baker NE

13788
Lehman Caves National Monuments
Lehman Caves Toll Sta 1, Baker, NE
89311
General Museum - 1923
Coll: geology; botany; zoology -
library

Bakersfield CA

13789
Cunningham Memorial Art Gallery
1930 R St, Bakersfield, CA 93301
Fine Arts Museum - 1955
paintings; sculpture; graphics;
decorative arts - library

13790
Kern County Museum
3801 Chester Ave, Bakersfield, CA
93309
General Museum - 1945
Coll: pioneer village; firearms; Indian
artifacts; ornithology; mineralogy;
antique vehicles; photographic image
collection - library

Baldwin KS

13791
William A. Quayle Bible Collection
Baker University
Spencer-Quayle Wing, 8th St, Baldwin,
KS 66006
Decorative Arts Museum - 1925
Coll: 600 rare Bibles or portions,
including illuminated manuscripts and
incunabula - reading room; library

Ballston Spa NY

13792
Brookside Museum
Brookside, Charlton St & Fairground Av, Ballston Spa, NY 12020
General Museum - 1970
Coll: county history; folk art; costumes; toys and sports; agriculture; lumbering; resort life; manuscript collection; photographic collection - library

Balsam Lake WI

13793
Polk County Museum
14 Polk County Center Bldg, Balsam Lake, WI 54810
General Museum - 1960
Coll: county history; art and craft exhibits; historic house - library

Baltimore MD

13794
The Baltimore Museum of Art
Art Museum Drive, Baltimore, MD 21218
Fine Arts Museum - 1914
Coll: graphics; decorative arts; 2nd-6th century mosaics from Antioch - library; auditorium; classrooms

13795
Baltimore Seaport The Baltimore Maritime Museum
Pier 4, Pratt St, Baltimore, MD 21202
History/Public Affairs Museum
Coll: historic ships; the last American submarine to sink Japanese shipping and warships; navigational instruments; scrimshaw - library

13796
Carroll Mansion
800 E Lombard, Baltimore, MD 21202
Fine Arts Museum - 1967
Coll: paintings; decorative arts; general; glass; textiles

13797
Cylburn Museum Cylburn Mansion
4916 Greenspring Ave, Baltimore, MD 21209
Natural History Museum - 1954
Coll: birds; mammals; insects; plants; local material; rocks; minerals - auditorium; classrooms

13798
The Decker Gallery of the Maryland Institute College of Art
1300 W Mt. Royal Ave, Baltimore, MD 21217
Fine Arts Museum - 1826
Coll: George A. Lucas Collection of 19th century paintings, sculpture, drawings and prints - library; auditorium; classrooms

13799
Edgar Allan Poe House and Museum
203 N Amity St, City Hall, Room 601, Baltimore, MD 21202
Historic Site
Coll: candlesticks; lamps; lighting devices

13800
Evergreen House
4545 N Charles St, Baltimore, MD 21210
Fine Arts Museum
Coll: French Impressionist and post-Impressionist paintings; furnishings, paintings

13801
Fort McHenry National Monument and Historic Shrine
Baltimore, MD 21230
Historic Site - 1935
Coll: archives; military artifacts; E. Bowie-Berkley Gun Collection - library; auditorium

13802
Gallery of Art Morgan State University, Carl Murphy Fine Arts Center
Coldspring Lane and Hillen Rd, Baltimore, MD 21239
Fine Arts Museum - 1955
19th and 20th century American and European sculpture; graphics; paintings; African and New Guinea Sculptures

13803
LaCrosse Foundation Inc Newton H. White Athletic Center
Baltimore, MD 21218
History/Public Affairs Museum - 1959
Coll: various LaCrosse memorabilia; trophies; plaques of inductees; prints

13804
Maryland Academy of Sciences
601 Light St, Baltimore, MD 21230
Science/Tech Museum - 1797
geological exhibits; local history and resources; space science; energy; life sciences - planetarium; theater; classrooms; laboratories

13805
Mount Clare Museum
Carroll Park, Baltimore, MD 221230
Historic Site - 1917
Coll: 18th century silver; furniture; china; glassware; portraits by Charles Wilson Peale - library

13806
Mount Vernon Museum of Incandescent Lighting
717 Washington Place, Baltimore, MD 21201
History/Public Affairs Museum - 1963
Coll: history of the electric light bulb, beginning with electric bulbs from Edison's first installations

13807
Museum and Library of Maryland History Maryland Historical Society
201 W Monument St, Baltimore, MD 21201
History/Public Affairs Museum - 1893
Coll: Maryland portraits; period furnishings; Chesapeake Bay maritime collection; manuscripts including original draft of 'Star Spangled Banner' - library

13808
Museum of the Baltimore College of Dental Surgery Dental School, University of Maryland at Baltimore
666 W Baltimore St, Rm G-F-11, Baltimore, MD 21201
Science/Tech Museum - 1840
Coll: early dental instruments and equipment; replicas

13809
Peale Museum
225 Holliday St, Baltimore, MD 21202
Fine Arts Museum - 1931
history of Baltimore; memorabilia of Rembrandt and Rubens Peale; paintings by Peale family - library

13810
Star-Spangled Banner Flag House
844 E Pratt St, Baltimore, MD 21010
History/Public Affairs Museum - 1927
Coll: new and old flags of historic importance; fire arms; uniforms; War of 1812 artifacts; furnishings

13811
Walters Art Gallery
Charles and Centre Sts, Baltimore, MD 21201
Fine Arts Museum - 1931
Coll: arts from antiquity through 19th century; decorative arts - library; auditorium

Bancroft ME

13812
John G. Neilhardt Center
Bancroft, ME 68004
General Museum - 1968
Coll: Memorabilia of John G. Neilhardt, poet laureate of Nebraska; author of Black Elk Speaks & A Cycle of the West

Banning CA

13813
Malki Museum
Morongo Indian Reservation, 11-759 Fields Rd, Banning, CA 92220
Anthropology Museum - 1964
Coll: Cahuilla and other Southern California Indian tribe artifacts; anthropology; archeology; history; archives; ethnology; music; natural history - library; ethno-botanical garden

Baraboo WI

13814
Circus World Museum
426 Water St, Baraboo, WI 53913
Performing Arts Museum - 1959
Coll: circus artifacts; circus wagons; railroad cars; programs; litographs; housed in the original winter quarters of Ringling Bros. Circus - library

13815
Sauk County Historical Museum
531 4th Av, 133 11th St, Baraboo, WI 53913
General Museum - 19o5
Coll: artifacts and photos from pioneer days to present; Indian artifacts; circus mementoes and displays; archeology; geology - library

Bardstown KY

13816
Barton Museum of Whiskey History
Barton Rd, Bardstown, KY 4004
History/Public Affairs Museum - 1957
Coll: history of the American whiskey industry - library

Barnesville OH 43713

13817
Gay 90'S Mansion Museum
532 N Chestnut St, POB 434, Barnesville, OH 43713
General Museum - 1966
Coll: glass; china; utensils; furniture; clothing; Indian artifacts; quilts; Richardsonian mansion (1890) - library; reading room

Barrington IL

13818
Barrington Historical Society, Inc.
111 W Station St, Barrington, IL 60010
History/Public Affairs Museum - 1969
Coll: early farm tools and equipment; blacksmith and harness-making tool collections; clothing and furniture; local artifacts

Barron WI

13819
Barron County Historical Society Museum
1 1/2 mile west of Cameron on Museum Rd, 426 S 5th St, Barron, WI 54812
General Museum - 1960
Coll: agricultural, logging and household items; books and manuscripts; dental, medical and veterinary tools; historic houses

Bartlesville OK

13820
Frank Phillips Home
1107 S Cherokee, Bartlesville, OK 74003
Historic Site - 1973
1930's period furniture; Frank Phillips Home (1909) - library

13821
History Room of the Bartlesville Public Library
6th and Johnstone, Bartlesville, OK 74003
General Museum - 1964
Coll: local artifacts; documents; photographs; manuscripts; Delaware Indian materials - library; reading room

13822
Woolaroc Museum
State Hwy 123, Bartlesville, OK 74003
General Museum - 1929
Coll: Indian artifacts; paintings; sculpture; ethnology; archaeology; anthropology; Colt Patterson gun collection - library; nature/conservation center

Batavia NY

13823
The Holland Land Office Museum
131 W Main St, Batavia, NY 14020
General Museum - 1894
Coll: medical collection; military collection; glass and china; furniture; musical instruments; guns; toys; costumes; early hand tools and fireplace tools; cooking utensils; woodenware; Indian artifacts - work room; library

Bath ME

13824
Maine Maritime Museum
963 Washington St, Bath, ME 04530
History/Public Affairs Museum - 1963
Coll: maritime history; models; trade goods; seamen's possessions; boats; historic properties - library

Bath OH

13825
Hale Farm and Western Reserve Village
2686 Oak Hill Rd, POB 256, Bath, OH 44210
Historic Site - 1957
Coll: agriculture; crafts; log schoolhouse (1816); Hale house (1825); Wade law office (1825); salt box house (1830); Greek revival house (1844); church (1851); Franklin glassworks (1825); steam saw mill

Baton Rouge IA

13826
Museum for Natural Science
Louisiana State University
Baton Rouge, IA 70893
Natural History Museum - 1936
Coll: ornithology; mammalogy;
ichthyology; herpetology - classrooms

Baton Rouge LA

13827
Anglo-American Art Museum
Louisiana State University
Memorial Tower, Baton Rouge, LA
70803
Fine Arts Museum - 1960
Coll: English culture; decorative arts;
paintings; graphics; sculpture - library

13828
Louisiana Arts and Science Center
100 S River Rd, POB 3373, Baton
Rouge, LA 70801
Fine Arts Museum - 1960
Coll: Tibetan religious art; Eskimo
soapstone carvings, artifacts and
lithographs; Egyptology collection;
pottery and weavings - planetarium;
auditorium

13829
Museum of Geoscience Louisiana
State University
Baton Rouge, LA 70803
Natural History Museum - 1954
Coll: paleontology; anthropology;
archaeology; geology; macro-fauna
and micro-fauna types

Battle Creek MI

13830
Battle Creek Civic Art Center
265 E Emmett St, Battle Creek, MI
49017
Fine Arts Museum - 1948
Coll: contemporary fine arts - library

13831
Kimball House Museum
196 Capital Av, NE, Battle Creek, MI
49017
Historic Site - 1966
Coll: household items; phonographs;
cameras; typewriters; medical
instruments relating to Battle Creek in
the 1880's

13832
Kingman Museum of Natural History
W Michigan Av at 20th St, Battle
Creek, MI 49017
Natural History Museum - 1869
Coll: birds of North and South
America; minerals and fossils; Amazon
Valley Indian artifacts; American Indian
artifacts; Rueben Rector Human
Embryo collection - library

Battle Ground IN

13833
Battle Ground Historical Corp.
POB 225, Battle Ground, IN 47920
Historic Site - 1972
Coll: material pertaining to the Battle of
Tippecanoe and the election of 1840;
historic house - library

Bay City MI

13834
Museum of the Great Lakes
1700 Center Av, Bay City, MI 48706
General Museum - 1919
Coll: artifacts relating to the history of
Bay County, Michigan and the Great
Lakes area - library

Bay Village OH

13835
**Lake Erie Nature and Science
Center**
28728 Wolf Rd, Bay Village, OH 44140
Natural History Museum - 1945
Coll: astronomy; botany; geology;
physical science; zoology; Indian
anthropology - library; classrooms;
wildflower garden and herbarium

13836
Rose Hill Museum
27715 Lake Rd, Bay Village, OH 44140
General Museum - 1960
Coll: furniture of the first settlers;
Empire and Victorian furniture;
summer kitchen; food storeroom;
Western Reserve farmhouse (1818) -
library

Bayfield CO

13837
The Gem Village Museum
Bayfield, CO 81122
Natural History Museum - 1946
Coll: anthropology; geology; Indian
artifacts; mineralogy - library; reading
room

Bayfield WI

13838
Apostle Islands National Lakeshore
Old Courthouse Bldg, POB 729,
Bayfield, WI 54814
Science/Tech Museum - 1970
Coll: lighthouse artifacts and objects;
buildings and docks from small family
commercial fishing operations; insects,
furs and study skins - library;
auditorium

Bear Mountain NY

13839
Bear Mountain Trailside Museums
Bear Mountain State Park, Bear
Mountain, NY 10911
Natural History Museum - 1927
Coll: local collections of animals,
plants, minerals and rocks; Indian
artifacts; history - zoological park;
botanical garden; aquarium; library

Beatrice NE

13840
Gage County Historical Museum
2nd & Court, POB 793, Beatrice, NE
68310
History/Public Affairs Museum - 1975
Coll: medical and dental equipment;
quilts; hand woven, spun bed spreads,
table cloths & shawls; 100 year old
organs - library

Beaufort NC

13841
Beaufort Historical Association
POB 1709, Beaufort, NC 28516
Historic Site - 1962
Coll: 19th century furniture; Victorian
furnishings; Joseph Bell House (1767);
Josiah Bell House (1825); Carteret
County Courthouse (1796);
Apothecary Shop (1859); J. Pigott
House (1830); Carteret County Jail
(1829); Old Burying Grounds (1731)

13842
Hampton Mariners Museum
120 Turner St, Beaufort, NC 28516
Science/Tech Museum - 1975
Coll: mounted marine specimens;
seashells; aquariums; ship models;
marine artifacts; traditional small craft
collection - library

Beaufort SC

13843
Beaufort Museum
Craven St, Beaufort, SC 29902
General Museum
Coll: Indian artifacts; Civil War
artifacts; natural history; local history

Beaumont TX

13844
Beaumont Art Museum
1111 Ninth St, Beaumont, TX 77702
Fine Arts Museum - 1950
Coll: Texas and American painting;
sculpture; graphics; photography;
archaeology - library

13845
Spindletop Museum
Lamar University, POB 10082,
Beaumont, TX 77710
Science/Tech Museum - 1971
Coll: History of the Petroleum
Industry; Southeast Texas History;
Industrial Technology - library

Beaver Falls NY

13846
American Maple Museum
POB 47, Beaver Falls, NY 13305
Agriculture Museum - 1977
Coll: historic and modern materials
from the maple products industry -
library; auditorium

Bedford OH

13847
Bedford Historical Society
30 S Park St, POB 282, Bedford, OH
44146
General Museum - 1955
Coll: Americana; archaeology;
archives; glass; Indian artifacts; Jacka
1876 Centennial Collection;
numismatic; Bedford Township Hall
(1874)

Bedford PA

13848
Fort Bedford Park and Museum
Fort Dr, Bedford, PA 15522
General Museum - 1958
Coll: Indian artifacts; antique vehicles;
antiques

Bedford VA

13849
Peaks of Otter Visitor Center
Blue Ridge Pkwy, POB 86, Bedford,
VA 24523
Science/Tech Museum - 1960
Coll: minerals; mining

Belchertown MA

13850
Belchertown Historical Association
Maple St, Belchertown, MA 01007
History/Public Affairs Museum - 1914
Coll: jewelry; pewter; musical
instruments; old vehicles; shaker -
library

Bellefontaine OH

13851
Logan County Historical Museum
W Chillocothe Av at Seymour,
Bellefontaine, OH 43311
General Museum - 1945
Coll: household appliances; tools;
clothing; cameras; communications;
music; firearms; uniforms and other
insignia; replicas of railroad trains;
threshing equipment; autos; military
and pioneer costumes; geology;
Ebenezer Zane Log House (1885) -
library; auditorium; reading room

Bellefonte PA

13852
**Centre County Library and Historical
Museum**
203 N Allegheny St, Bellefonte, PA
16823
General Museum - 1939
Coll: furniture; china; county artifacts;
Miles-Humes House (1814-16) -
library

Bellevue NE

13853
Strategie Aerospace Museum
2510 Clay St, Bellevue, NE 68005
History/Public Affairs Museum - 1959
Coll: 27 aircraft and seven large
missiles; artifacts - theater

Bellevue WA

13854
Bellevue Art Museum
10310 NE 4th, Bellevue, WA 98004
Fine Arts Museum - 1975
20th century American art - library

Bellingham WA

13855
Whatcom Museum of History and Art
121 Prospect St, Bellingham, WA
98225
History/Public Affairs Museum - 1940
Coll: regional art; history;
ethnography; photography - library;
photo archives

Bellows Falls VT

13856
**Steamtown Foundation for
Preservation of Steam and Railroad
Americana**
POB 71, Bellows Falls, VT 05101
History/Public Affairs Museum - 1963
Coll: steam locomotives; passenger
coaches; dining cars

Bellport, L.I. NY

13857
**Bellport-Brookhaven Historical
Society Museum**
Bellport Lane, Bellport, L.I., NY 11713
General Museum - 1963
Coll: wild fowl and shore bird decoys;
dolls; toys; guns; wild fowl hunting
boats; batteries; scooters; tinware;
stencils; barn museum; blacksmith
shop; milk house; Underhill Studio of
Decorative Art

Beloit WI

13858
Bartlett Memorial Historical Museum
2149 St, Lawrence Av, Beloit, WI
53511
History/Public Affairs Museum - 1910
Coll: Norwegian artifacts; farm
implements; archives of local history;
decorative arts; dolls; fans - library

13859
Logan Museum of Anthropology
Beloit College, Beloit, WI 53511
Anthropology Museum - 1850
Coll: Indian and North American
archeology and ethnology; European
and North African paleolithic exhibits;
North African ethnology - laboratories

13860
Theodore Lyman Wright Art Center
Beloit College
Beloit College, Beloit, WI 53511
Fine Arts Museum - 1892
Coll: paintings; graphics; decorative
arts

Belvidere NE

13861
Thayer County Museum
Belvidere, NE 68315
General Museum - 1969
Coll: crafts; religious items; industry;
several historic rooms - library

Bement IL

13862
Bryant Cottage
146 E Wilson Ave, Bement, IL 61813
Historic Site - 1925
Coll: period furnishings

Bennettsville SC

13863
Marlboro County Historical Museum
119 S Marlboro St, Bennettsville, SC
29512
General Museum - 1970
Coll: antiques; local history; historic
houses

Bennington VT

13864
Bennington Museum
W Main St, Bennington, VT 05201
General Museum - 1876
regional historical materials;
genealogy; flags; costumes; porcelain
and pottery; paintings - library

13865
**Southern Vermont College Art
Gallery**
Monument Av, Bennington, VT 05201
Fine Arts Museum - 1979
Arts

Berea KY

13866
Berea College Museums
Berea, KY 40404
Natural History Museum - 1855
Coll: folk culture of the Southern
Appalachian Highlands; biology;
geology; prints; paintings;
photographs - library; theater

Berkeley CA

13867
**The Bade Institute of Biblical
Archeology**
1798 Scenic Ave, Berkeley, CA 94709
Archeology Museum - 1930
Coll: biblical archeology; major
collection from Tell en-Nasbeh, Israel;
artifacts from Egypt, Syria, Cyprus,
Greece, and Rome

13868
Entomology Museum University of
California
313 Wellman Hall, University of
California, Berkeley, CA 94720
Natural History Museum - 1939
Coll: 3 million terrestrial arthropods -
library

13869
Judah L. Magnes Memorial Museum
2911 Russell St, Berkeley, CA 94705
Religious Art Museum - 1962
Coll: Jewish ceremonial art; fine arts;
rare books and manuscripts;
collections from Jews of India and
North Africa; Holocaust collection;
Magnes Archives - library

13870
Lawrence Hall of Science University
of California
Centennial Drive, Berkeley, CA 94720
Science/Tech Museum - 1960
Coll: science education and curriculum
materials; collection of birds and
mammals of the San Francisco Bay
area - library; auditorium;
amphitheater; planetarium; nature
center; biology laboratory; classrooms
and labs

13871
Museum of Paleontology
Earth Sciences Building, University of
California, Berkeley, CA 94720
Natural History Museum - 1921
Coll: fossil vertebrates, invertebrates,
plants; recent molluscan shells,
foraminifera, vertebrate skeletal
elements; central California marine
sediments - library; classrooms

13872
Museum of Vertebrate Zoology
University of California
2593 Life Sciences Bldg, Berkeley, CA
94720
Natural History Museum - 1908
Coll: amphibians; reptiles; birds;
mammals; natural history - library;
field research station

13873
**Robert H. Lowie Museum of
Anthropology**
103 Kroeber Hall, University of
California, Berkeley, CA 94720
Anthropology Museum - 1901
Coll: archeological and ethnological
specimens from the Americas,
Oceania, Europe, Asia, and Africa;
entries of human skeletal material;
photographic negatives and prints -
library

13874
University Art Museum
Bancroft Way, Berkeley, CA 94720
Fine Arts Museum - 1965
Coll: 20th century American and
European paintings; sculpture garden;
drawings, prints; Hans Hofman
paintings and archives; Japanese,
American avant garde, and animated
films; photography; Oriental paintings;
pre-20th century works - library;
theater

13875
University Herbarium University of
California
Berkeley, CA 94720
Natural History Museum - 1872
Coll: world-wide plant kingdom -
library

Berlin WI

13876
Clark School Museum
Riverside Park - Water St, Berlin, WI
54923
History/Public Affairs Museum - 1962
Artifacts pertaining to a rural school;
local history; historic schoolhouse -
library

Berryville AR

13877
Saunders Memorial Museum
113-15 Madison St, Berryville, AR
72616
Decorative Arts Museum - 1956
Coll: Colonel C. Burton Saunders' gun
collection; silver; china; arts and crafts

Bessemer AL

13878
Bessemer Hall of History
1830-4th Ave North, Bessemer, AL
35020
General Museum - 1970
Coll: local historical items; Tom Gloor
collection of newspapers on microfilm,
1888-1919; 1916 Southern Railway
Depot - library

Bethel AK

13879
Yugtarvik-Regional Museum
POB 388, Bethel, AK 99559
General Museum - 1967
Coll: Eskimo artifacts of Southwestern
Alaska, Kuskokwim delta, and Yukon
delta; Indian artifacts

Bethel ME

13880
**Steam Era Railroadiana Exhibit and
Museum**
POB 75, Bethel, ME 04217
Science/Tech Museum - 1972
Coll: locomotive and train models of
the steam era; pictures of steam era
railroading; papers; artifacts - library

Bethlehem PA

13881
Annie S. Kemerer Museum
427 N New St, Bethlehem, PA 18018
General Museum - 1954
Coll: 18th and 19th century American
furniture, glass and china; 19th century
oil landscapes; oldest fire engine in
country - library

13882
Historic Bethlehem Inc.
516 Main St, Bethlehem, PA 18018
General Museum - 1957
Coll: historic artifacts (1700-1850);
archives; historic buildings - library;
reading room

13883
**Lehigh University Exhibitions and
Collections**
Bethlehem, PA 18015
Fine Arts Museum - 1864
Coll: 18th and 19th century American,
English and French paintings; prints
and photography; 20th century
American, The Eight; 17th - 19th
century Chinese porcelain etchings;
Etruscan bronzes, engravings and
lithographs; 20th century prints and
photographs; architecture;
archaeology; music; natural history -
nature center; library

13884
Moravian Museum of Bethlehem
66 W Church St, Bethlehem, PA 18018
Religious Art Museum - 1938
Coll: religious and secular objects
reflecting the life of early Moravian
settlers; furniture; clocks; silver;
musical instruments; art and
needlework of Moravian Seminary;
kitchen ware; tools - library

Bethune SC

13885
Lynches River Historical Society
Bethune, SC 29009
General Museum - 1965
Coll: agriculture; costumes; folklore;
glass; Indian artifacts; Blue Willow
china; archives

Beverly MA

13886
**Beverly Historical Society and
Museum**
117 Cabot St, Beverly, MA 01915
History/Public Affairs Museum - 1891
Coll: guns; transportation; furnishings;
ship papers; genealogy - library

Beverly Hills CA

13887
**The Francis E. Fowler, Jr. Foundation
Museum**
9215 Wilshire Blvd, Beverly Hills, CA
90210
Decorative Arts Museum - 1953
Coll: European and Asiatic decorative
arts; 15-19th century English, Early
American, and Continental European
silver; Russian silver and other
decorative arts; European and Far
Eastern porcelain; Oriental and
European carved ivories; antique
glassware; antique firearms

Big Horn WY

13888
Bradford Brinton Memorial Museum
POB 23, Big Horn, WY 82833
Fine Arts Museum - 1960
Coll: western paintings and sculpture;
Indian arts and crafts; American Indian
ethnology; historic house - library

Big Rapids MI

13889
Mecosta County Historical Museum
Elm and Stewart, Big Rapids, MI 49307
General Museum - 1957
Coll: Agriculture; numismatic;
pharmacy; folklore

Big Stone Gap VA

13890
Southwest Virginia Museum Historical State Park
10 W 1st St, Big Stone Gap, VA 24219
Historic Site - 1943
Coll: items associated with early history and pioneer period of Southwest Virginia; Indian artifacts - library

Billings MT

13891
Yellowstone Art Center
401 N 27th St, Billings, MT 59101
Fine Arts Museum - 1964
Coll: Mary Malloy Carmichal Collection of original contemporary graphics; Malcom McKay Collection of Olaf Wieghorst; Poindexter collection of abstract expressionists - library; reading room; auditorium; classrooms

13892
Yellowstone County Museum
Logan Field, POB 959, Billings, MT 59103
General Museum - 1953
Coll: dinosaur bones; jewelry; vehicles; clothing; paintings; saddles; brands

Binghamton NY

13893
Boome County Historical Society
30 Front St, Binghamton, NY 13905
General Museum - 1919
Historic 1910 artifacts; paintings; prints; drawings; decorative art; manuscript collections - library

13894
Robertson Center for the Arts and Sciences
30 Front St, Binghamton, NY 13905
Fine Arts Museum - 1954
Coll: Indian artifacts; archaeology; sculptures; furnishings of 1904; Royal Worcester Doughty Birds; Meissen figurines; local history; fans; paintings and prints - library; theater; classrooms; planetarium; observatory

13895
University Art Gallery
State University of New York at Binghamton, Binghamton, NY 13901
Fine Arts Museum - 1967
Coll: paintings; sculpture; graphics; decorative arts; archaeology; Mario Romano coin collection; Wedgwood collection; ancient Egyptian, pre-Columbian collections; Rodney A. Horne collection of Chinese art; modern graphics collection (Cobra group) - library

Birdsboro PA

13896
Daniel Boone Homestead
Daniel Boone Rd, No 2 POB 162, Birdsboro, PA 19508
Historic Site - 1937
Historic houses; Delaware Indians - demonstration pioneer farm; ecology study area

Birmingham AL

13897
Birmingham Museum of Art
2000 8th Ave N., Birmingham, AL 35203
Fine Arts Museum - 1951
Coll: European and American paintings; classical and oriental antiques; silver, porcelain, and glass; graphics; pre-Columbian and old western art - library; classrooms; auditorium

Bisbee AZ

13898
Bisbee Civic Center and Mining and Historical Museum
POB 451, Bisbee, AZ 85603
General Museum - 1972
Coll: photo archive, articles and artifacts of local history; historic house(1905) - library; reading room; auditorium

Biship Hill IL

13899
Bishop Hill State Memorial
POB 51, Biship Hill, IL 61419
Historic Site - 1946
paintings by Olaf Krans pertaining to Bishop Hill Colony; artifacts and furniture from Bishop Hill Colony, 1846-1862; 1850 Bjorklund Hotel

Bishop Hill IL

13900
Bishop Hill Heritage Association
POB 1853, Bishop Hill, IL 61419
History/Public Affairs Museum - 1962
Coll: artifacts and historic buildings belonging to Bishop Hill Colony, Swedish communal settlement founded in 1846

Bismarck ND

13901
State Historical Society of North Dakota
Liberty Memorial Bldg, Bismarck, ND 58505
General Museum - 1895
Coll: archaeoloy; ethnology; general history; firearms; clothing; household items; natural history; agriculture; military - library; reading room

Black River Falls WI

13902
Jackson County Historical Society
223 N 4th St, Black River Falls, WI 54615
General Museum - 1934
Coll: costumes; tools; photographs; glass plates; furniture

Blacksburg SC

13903
Kings Mountain National Military Park
Blacksburg SC 29702 Kings Mountain, SC 28086
History/Public Affairs Museum - 1931
Military artifacts - library

Blacksburg VA

13904
Museum of the Geological Sciences
Virginia Polytechnic Institute and State University, Blacksburg, VA 24061
Science/Tech Museum - 1969
Coll: minerals and crystallography - library; laboratory; classrooms

Blakely GA

13905
Kolomoki Mounds Museum
Rte 1, Blakely, GA 31723
Historic Site - 1951
Coll: archeology; Indian artifacts; rebuilt 13th century Indian burial mound and village site

Blanding UT

13906
Edge of the Cedars State Historical Monument
POB 48, Blanding, UT 84511
Historic Site
Coll: artifacts of the pre-historic Anasazi Indian culture, of the Navajo, Ute and Piute Indians - library; auditorium

13907
Natural Bridges National Monument
Star Rte, Blanding, UT 84511
Science/Tech Museum - 1966
Coll: geology; archaeology - library

Bloomfield Hills MI

13908
Cranbrook Institute of Science
500 Lone Pine Rd, Bloomfield Hills, MI 48013
Natural History Museum - 1930
Coll: anthropology; zoology; botany - library; auditorium; classrooms; herbarium

Bloomfield NM

13909
Chaco Canyon National Monument
Star Rte No. 4, POB 6500, Bloomfield, NM 87413
Archeology Museum - 1907
Coll: archaeology; ethnology; herpetology; geology; herbarium; natural history collection; zoology; prehistoric and historic sites - library

Bloomington IL

13910
Clover Lawn, The David Davis Mansion
Davis Av at Monroe Dr, Bloomington, IL 61701
Historic Site
Coll: furnishings; formal garden

13911
McLean County Art Association
McLean County Arts Center
210 E Washington St, Bloomington, IL 61701
Fine Arts Museum - 1922
Permanent collection of McLean County Art Assn.

Bloomington IN

13912
Indiana University Art Museum
Fine Arts Building, Rm 007, Bloomington, IN 47405
Fine Arts Museum - 1962
Coll: ancient Egyptian, Greek, Roman sculpture; vases; coins and glass; 14th-20th century European and American paintings; decorative arts; African, Oceanic, pre-Columbian, Japanese, Chinese, SE Asian paintings

13913
Indiana University Museum Indiana University
Student Building 107, Bloomington, IN 47401
Anthropology Museum - 1963
Coll: archeology; ethnology; historical collections from North America, Latin America, and West Africa - library; classrooms

Bloomsburg PA

13914
Columbia County Historical Society
303 E Main St, Bloomsburg, PA 17815
General Museum - 1914
Coll: Indian artifacts; agricultural implements; household items; local history - library; reading room

Bloomsfield Hills MI

13915
Cranbrook Academy of Art/Museum
500 Lone Pine Rd, POB 806, Bloomsfield Hills, MI 48013
Fine Arts Museum - 1927
Coll: sculpture; nineteenth century prints; study collection of textiles - auditorium

Blue Hill ME

13916
Parson Fisher House
Blue Hill, ME 04614
History/Public Affairs Museum - 1945
Coll: paintings; woodcuts; other art work and furniture made by Jonathan Fisher

Blue Mounds WI

13917
Little Norway
Rte 1, Blue Mounds, WI 53517
Historic Site - 1926
Furnishings and artifacts; an original log farmstead built by a Norwegian immigrant in 1856 - library

Blue Mountain Lake NY

13918
Adirondack Museum
Blue Mountain Lake, NY 12812
Agriculture Museum - 1952
Coll: work and recreation in Adirondack region; wood industries; transportation; outdoor recreation; paintings - exhibits in 20 buildings; large research library

Blue Springs MO

13919
Missouri Town 1855
Jackson County Parks and Recreation, Rte 1, POB 124, Blue Springs, MO 64015
General Museum - 1973
Coll: archaeology; folklore; technology; textiles; agriculture

Bluffton IN

13920
Wells County Historical Museum
420 W Market St, Bluffton, IN 46714
General Museum - 1937
Items pertaining to Wells County
history, culture, and industry - library;
reading room

Blunt SD

13921
Mentor Graham Museum
Blunt, SD 57522
General Museum - 1950
Coll: original furnishings; home of
Mentor Graham (1880), Abraham
Lincoln's tutor

Boalsburg PA

13922
**Christopher Columbus Family
Chapel, Boal Mansion and Museum**
Boalsburg, PA 16827
Historic Site - 1952
Coll: history; art; weapons from
Colonial period through World War I;
Boal Mansion (1789); Christopher
Columbus Chapel interior (16th
century), brought from Spain in 1919 -
library

13923
**Pennsylvania Military Museum, 28th
Division Shrine**
POB 148, Boalsburg, PA 16827
History/Public Affairs Museum - 1969
Coll: military; history; uniforms;
medicine; navy; aeronautics - library

Boise ID

13924
Boise Gallery of Art
Julia Davis Park, POB 1505, Boise, ID
83701
Fine Arts Museum - 1931
Coll: Idaho art; crafts; international
prints; Oriental art; Japanese netsuke
- library; reading room

13925
Idaho State Historical Museum
610 N Julia Davis Dr, Boise, ID 83706
History/Public Affairs Museum - 1881
Coll: Indian and Chinese artifacts;
objects pertaining to mining, farming,
household, transportation; manuscripts
and archives; maps and photographs;
history of Idaho and Pacific
Northwest; historic buildings - library;
reading room; auditorium; classrooms;
children's museum

Bonner Springs KS

13926
**Agricultural Hall of Fame & National
Center**
630 N 126th, Bonner Springs, KS
66012
Agriculture Museum - 1959
Coll: harvesting and planting
equipment; steam traction engines;
rural-living items - library

13927
Wyandotte County Museum
631 N 126th St, Bonner Springs, KS
66012
Anthropology Museum - 1955
Coll: Plains Indian textiles and crafts;
photographs; costumes; decorative
arts - library; auditorium

Boothbay Harbour ME

13928
Boothbay Region Historical Society
Boothbay Harbour, ME 04538
History/Public Affairs Museum - 1968
Coll: shipbuilding; fishing; marine;
history; archaeology

Boothbay ME

13929
Boothbay Railway Museum
Route 27, Boothbay, ME 04537
Science/Tech Museum - 1962
Coll: antique auto display; railroad
memorabilia; transportation

13930
The Boothbay Theater Museum
Corey Lane, Boothbay, ME 04537
Performing Arts Museum - 1957
Coll: theater memorabilia from the 18th
century to the present; actress glass;
stage furniture; costumes; jewelry;
autographs; photographs - library;
theater

13931
Grand Banks Schooner Museum
POB 123, Boothbay, ME 04537
History/Public Affairs Museum - 1968
Coll: fishing industry; cod fishing

Boston MA

13932
Boston Public Library
Copley Square, Boston, MA 02117
Fine Arts Museum - 1852
Coll: Albert H. Wiggin print collection;
Dicken's London; murals by Edwin
Austin Abbey; John Singer Sargent;
Pierre Cecile Puvis de Chavannes;
sculpture - library; reading room

13933
Children's Museum
300 Congress St, Boston, MA 02210
Junior Museum - 1913
Coll: Native American, Americana,
Japaneese and other cultures; insects;
birds; shells; dolls

13934
Isabella Stewart Gardner Museum
2 Palace Rd, boston, MA 02115
Fine Arts Museum - 1900
Coll: paintings; sculpture; tapestries;
stained glass; prints; decorative arts;
music; archives - library

13935
Massachusetts Historical Society
1154 Boylston St, Boston, MA 02215
History/Public Affairs Museum - 1791
Coll: archives; paintings; sculpture;
American and New England history -
library; reading room

13936
Museum of Afro American History
Smith Court, Boston, MA 02114
Anthropology Museum - 1967
coll: Artifacts and archival material
relating to the history of Afro
Americans in New England - library;
auditorium

13937
Museum of Fine Arts
Huntington Ave, Boston, MA 02115
Fine Arts Museum - 1870
Coll: Asiatic, Egyptian, Greek, Roman
and Near-Eastern art; Old Master
European paintigs; French
Impressionist and post-Impressionist
painting; American portraits; French
and Flemish tapestries; Peruvian and
Coptic weavings; lace, printed fabrics;
costumes; silver; musical instruments;
porcelain - library

**Museum of the National Center of
Afro-American Artists**
300 Walnut Ave, Boston, MA 02119
Fine Arts Museum - 1969
Coll: paintings; prints and graphics by
Afro-American artists

13939
Museum of Transportation Museum
Wharf
300 Congress St, Boston, MA 02210
Science/Tech Museum - 1949
Coll: masstranportation; gas, electric
and steam cars; bicycles; carriages;
motorcycles - library

13940
New England Aquarium Corporation
Central Wharf, Boston, MA 02110
Natural History Museum - 1957
Coll: maritime history; oceanography;
fishing industry - library; laboratory;
auditorium

Boulder City NV

13941
**Lake Mead National Recreation Area
Museum**
601 Nevada Hwy, Boulder City, NV
89005
General Museum
Coll: archaeology; mining; geology;
entomology - library; auditorium ;
theater

Boulder CO

13942
Leanin' Tree Museum of Western Art
6055 Longbow Dr, POB 9500, Boulder,
CO 80301
Fine Arts Museum - 1974
Coll: Western cowboy and Indian art;
60 major Western bronze sculptures;
250 paintings by major contemporary
American artists

13943
Pioneer Museum
1655 Broadway at Arapahoe, Boulder,
CO 80302
General Museum - 1959
Coll: alcoves representing pioneer life
from Boulder and surrounding
territory; mining relics; musical
instruments; costumes; historic house
- library

13944
University of Colorado Museum
Broadway, between 15th and 16th St,
Boulder, CO 80309
Science/Tech Museum - 1902
Coll: Indian artifacts and Kachina doll
collection; butterflies and mammals;
fossils; mineral specimens; clothing
and jewelry; art objects - library

Boulder UT

13945
**Anasazi Indian Village State
Historical Monument**
POB 393, Boulder, UT 84716
Historic Site - 1970
Coll: artifacts of the Kayente Anasazi
culture

Bowling Green KY

13946
Hardin Planetarium Western
Kentucky University
Bowling Green, KY 42101
Natural History Museum - 1967
Coll: meteorite; astronomy
photographs - library; auditorium

13947
Kentucky Museum Western
Kentucky Univeristy
Bowling Green, KY 42101
General Museum - 1930
Coll: American and European art;
anthropology; ornithology; musical
instruments; decorative art - library

Bowling Green VA

13948
Caroline Historical Society
POB 324, Bowling Green, VA 22427
General Museum - 1968
Coll: history; natural history; geology;
preservation objects - library

Boyertown PA

13949
**Boyertown Museum of Historic
Vehicles**
Warwick St, Boyertown, PA 19512
Science/Tech Museum - 1968
Coll: transportation

Boys Town NE

13950
Philamatic Center
Boys Town, NE 68010
History/Public Affairs Museum - 1951
Coll: displays of paper money;
containing over 10,000 notes; 7,000 US
and foreign coins, tokens and medals;
70,000 stamps of early US and foreign
origin - library

Bozeman MT

13951
Museum of the Rockies Montana
State University
Bozeman, MT 59717
General Museum - 1956
Coll: paleontology; archaeology;
history; geology - library

Bradenton FL

13952
Conquistador Historical Foundation
809 14th St, W, Bradenton, FL 33505
History/Public Affairs Museum - 1965
Spanish artifacts - library

13953
**South Florida Museum and Bishop
Planetarium**
201 10th St, W, Bradenton, FL 33505
Science/Tech Museum - 1946
Coll: archeology; astronomy; natural
history and science; costumes;
numismatics - aquarium; classrooms

Bradford VT

13954
Bradford Historical Society
Brook Rd, Bradford, VT 05033
General Museum - 1972
Coll: Civil War artifacts; 19th century
costumes; genealogy - library

Brainerd MN

13955
**Crow Wing County Historical
Society**
Court House, Brainerd, MN 56401
History/Public Affairs Museum - 1927
Coll: Indian artifacts; industrial;
archaeology; paintings; customs -
library

Branchville SC

13956
Branchville Railroad Shrine and Museum
109 W Edward St, Branchville, SC 29432
Science/Tech Museum - 1969
Coll: railroad artifacts; model trains; Branchville Southern Railroad Depot (1877); first railroad junction of the world

Brattleboro VT

13957
Brattleboro Museum and Art Center
Old Railroad Station, POB 800, Brattleboro, VT 05301
Fine Arts Museum - 1972
Coll: art; local history - classrooms

Brazosport TX

13958
Brazosport Museum of Natural Science
400 College Dr, Brazosport, TX 77566
Natural History Museum - 1962
Coll: botany; geology; marine; malacology; paleontology - library; aquarium; classrooms

Breckenridge TX

13959
Swenson Memorial Museum of Stephens County
116 W. Walker, POB 350, Breckenridge, TX 76024
History/Public Affairs Museum - 1970
Coll: farming; furniture; oil equipment; photographs and memorabilia of oil boom times in county - library

Bremerton WA

13960
Naval Shipyard Museum
Washington State Ferry Terminal Bldg, Bremerton, WA 98310
History/Public Affairs Museum - 1954
Coll: naval history; articles and photos pertaining to history of Puget Sound and Naval Shipyard - library

Brenham TX

13961
Texas Baptist Historical Center Museum
Rte 5, POB 150, Brenham, TX 77833
General Museum - 1965
Coll: artifacts of Sam Houston and family; items from Baylor University; furniture; church artifacts - library

Brewerton NY

13962
Fort Brewerton Historical Association
Rte 11 North, Brewerton, NY 13029
General Museum - 1964
Coll: history; military; archaeology; Indian artifacts; transportation; archives; costumes; glass - library

Brewster MA

13963
Cape Cod Museum of Natural History
Rte 6A, Brewster, MA 02631
Natural History Museum - 1954
Coll: flora and fauna of cape Cod; marine aquaria and displays; herbarium - library; reading room; auditorium; classrooms

13964
New England Fire and History Museum
Rte 6a, Brewster, MA 02631
History/Public Affairs Museum - 1972
Coll: antique fire equipment and memorabilia; reproduction of Benjamin Franklin's first fire house - library; reading room; auditorium

Brewster NY

13965
Southeast Museum Association, Inc.
Main St, Brewster, NY 10509
General Museum - 1962
McLane railroad exhibit of the history of the Harlem line; Trainer collection of minerals; Borden condensed milk factory collection; costume and quilt collection; manuscripts, books and photographs illustrating economic and social history from the 18th century to the present

Brewster WA

13966
Fort Okanogan Interpretive Center
Bridgeport State Park, POB 846, Brewster, WA 98812
History/Public Affairs Museum
Indian and pioneer items; fur trade and Indian History Interpretive Center

Bridgeport AL

13967
Russell Cave National Monument
Rte 1, POB 175, Bridgeport, AL 35740
Archeology Museum - 1961
Coll: archeology; geology; Southeastern archaic material; woodlands Indians - library; interpretive station in excavation; nature and hiking trail

Bridgeport CT

13968
Housatonic Museum of Art
510 Barnum Av, Bridgeport, CT 06680
Fine Arts Museum - 1967
Coll: ethnographic artifacts; African artifacts

13969
Museum of Art, Science and Industry, Inc.
4450 Park Ave, Bridgeport, CT 06604
Science/Tech Museum - 1958
Coll: painting; antique furniture; circus memorabilia; Indian artifacts; products of 19th century Bridgeport manufacturers - planetarium; auditorium; classrooms; tactile gallery for visually impaired

13970
P. T. Barnum Museum
820 Main St, Bridgeport, CT 06604
History/Public Affairs Museum - 1893
Coll: P. T. Barnum memorabilia; Tom Thumb and Jenny Lind memorabilia; Colonial, Civil War, and early Bridgeport historical items; original century-old Swiss village

Bridgewater VA

13971
Reuel B. Pritchett Museum
Bridgewater College
East College St, Bridgewater, VA 22812
General Museum - 1954
Coll: rare books and bibles; coins and currency; bottles and jugs; weaving looms and spinning wheels - library; laboratory

Brigham City UT

13972
Brigham City Museum-Gallery
24 North 3rd West, POB 583, Brigham City, UT 84302
General Museum - 1970
Coll: paintings; pottery; crystal - library

Bristol CT

13973
American Clock and Watch Museum, Inc.
100 Maple St, Bristol, CT 06010
Science/Tech Museum - 1952
Coll: clocks, watches and other horological items - library

Bristol IN

13974
Elkhart County Historical Society, Inc., Museum Rush Memorial Center
Vistula St, POB 434, Bristol, IN 46507
General Museum - 1896
Coll: local historical artifacts; agriculture - library; children's museum

Bristol RI

13975
Bristol Historical and Preservation Society
48 Court St, Bristol, RI 02809
General Museum - 1938
Coll: costumes; Indian artifacts; war relics; 18th century furnishings - children's museum; library

13976
Coggeshall Farm Museum
Colt State Park, POB 562, Bristol, RI 02809
Agriculture Museum - 1958
Coll: furniture; blacksmithing items - working farm; vegetable gardens; orchards; hayfields

13977
Haffenreffer Museum of Anthropology
Mt. Hope Grant, Bristol, RI 02809
Anthropology Museum - 1956
Coll: American Indian, Central and South American, Arctic, Asian, Pacific and African collections; anthropology; archaeology; ethnology - library

Broken Bow NE

13978
Custer County Museum and Library
225 S 10th Ave, Broken Bow, NE 68822
General Museum - 1962
Coll: guns; clocks; musical instruments; sea shells; coins; archives; archaeology - library

Broken Bow OK

13979
Forest Heritage Center
POB 157, Broken Bow, OK 74728
Agriculture Museum - 1976
Coll: old logging tools; wood working tools; displays showing the past, present and future evolvement of trees and their use by man - library; auditorium; classrooms; nature trail

13980
Memorial Indian Museum
Second and Allen Sts, POB 483, Broken Bow, OK 74728
Anthropology Museum - 1961
Coll: pre-historic Indian artifacts; modern textiles and basketry; early bead work; pre-historic Indian skeletal remains; original paintings and prints; early American glass; fossils - library; laboratory

Bronx NY

13981
The Bronx County Historical Society
3266 Bainbridge Av, Bronx, NY 10467
General Museum - 1955
Coll: Indian artifacts; military and natural history artifacts; paintings; prints; manuscripts, books and photographs tracing the history of the Bronx; Valentine-Varian House (1758); Edgar Allan Poe Cottage (1812)

13982
The Bronx Museum of the Arts
851 Grand Concourse, Bronx, NY 10451
Fine Arts Museum - 1971
Artist's file on Bronx artists - community gallery; arts exchange in public spaces

13983
Museum of Migrating People
750 Baychester Av, Bronx, NY 10475
History/Public Affairs Museum - 1974
Coll: artifacts; documents; photographs; memorabilia depicting the immigration and in-migration experiences of Americans - library; classrooms

Brook IN

13984
George Ade Memorial Assn., Inc.
Brook, IN 47922
Historic Site - 1961
Coll: home of George Ade, humorist, author and playwright; objects of art and personal effects of George Ade; furniture

Brookfield VT

13985
Museum of the Americas
Brookfield, VT 05036
Decorative Arts Museum - 1971
Coll: Anglo-American paintings and prints; Hispanic-American decorative arts - library; classrooms

Brookings SD

13986
Agriculture Heritage Museum
South Dakota State University, Brookings, SD 57007
Agriculture Museum - 1967
Coll: agriculture; archaeology; botany; geology; military; ethnography; farm machinery; claim shanty (1882)

13987
South Dakota Memorial Art Center
Medary Av at Harvey Dunn St,
Brookings, SD 57007
Fine Arts Museum - 1969
Coll: paintings; sculpture; graphic arts;
decorative arts - library; auditorium;
classrooms

Brookline MA

13988
John F. Kennedy National Historic Site
83 Beals St, Brookline, MA 02146
Historic Site - 1969
Coll: furnishings as it appeared May
29, 1917, the date of John F. Kennedy's
birth

13989
Mary Baker Eddy Museum
120 Seaver St, Brookline, MA 02146
Religious Art Museum - 1926
Coll: manuscripts; letters; paintings
pertaining to Mary Baker Eddy, her
early students and the early history of
Christian science - library

Brooklyn NY

13990
The Brooklyn Children's Museum
145 Brooklyn Av, Brooklyn, NY 11213
Junior Museum - 1899
Coll: 50,000 objects, primarily in
ethnology, natural history and
technology - auditorium; children's
library and take-home collection;
outdoor theater; indoor greenhouse;
windmill; steam engine; arts and
humanities workshop spaces

13991
The Brooklyn Museum
188 Eastern Pkwy, Brooklyn, NY
11238
Fine Arts Museum - 1823
Coll: ancient Egyptian art, pre-dynastic
through Coptic, Greek and Roman art;
Islamic and pre-Islamic Middle Eastern
art; Oriental art; pre-Columbian
Central and South American
collections; American Indian
collections; art of Africa and of
Oceania; European and American
prints and drawings; 27 American
period rooms (1675-1930); American
and European decorative arts;
costumes and textiles; American
paintings and sculpture (colonial to
contemporary); European paintings
and sculpture (medieval to 20th
century); outdoor sculpture garden -
Wilbour Library of Egyptology

13992
Harbor Defense Museum of New York City
Fort Hamilton, Brooklyn, NY 11252
History/Public Affairs Museum - 1966
Coll: U.S. military (17th century to
present); coast defense (1800-1950)

13993
The Long Island Historical Society
128 Pierrepont St, Brooklyn, NY 11201
General Museum - 1863
Coll: genealogies, paintings, graphics,
costumes and history of the four
countys which comprise Long Island -
library

13994
Museum of the Arnold & Marie Schwartz College of Pharmacy and Health Sciences
75 DeKalb Av, Brooklyn, NY 11201
Science/Tech Museum - 1967
Coll: drugs; pharmaceutical equipment;
archives; glass; medical items - library

Brooks Air Force Base TX

13995
Hangar 9 Museum of Flight Medicine
Hq 6570th Air Base Group, Brooks Air
Force Base, TX 78235
Science/Tech Museum - 1966
Coll: aviation medical training devices
and artifacts; flight nursing artifacts
and memorabilia; space material
dealing with the development of
manned space flight

Brookville IN

13996
Franklin County Seminary and Museum
Fifth and Mill St, RR 3, POB 87,
Brookville, IN 47012
General Museum - 1969
Coll: local records and artifacts;
historic houses

Brown Valley MN

13997
Sam Brown Log House
Brown Valley, MN 56219
History/Public Affairs Museum - 1932
Coll: guns; furniture; archaeology;
clothing; Indian artifacts

Browning MT

13998
Museum of the Plains Indian and Crafts Center
US Hwy 89, POB 400, Browning, MT
59417
Anthropology Museum - 1038
Coll: historic and contemporary arts of
the Plains Indians; costumes; tipis

13999
Scriver Museum of Montana Wildlife
POB 172, Browning, MT 59417
Natural History Museum - 1953
Coll: mammals; birds; reptiles; fish;
foliage; insects

Brownington VT

14000
The Old Stone House
Brownington, VT 05860
General Museum - 1916
Coll: antique furniture; local history;
household and military items - library

Brownsville TX

14001
Brownsville Art League
Neale Drive, POB 3404, Brownsville,
TX 78520
Fine Arts Museum - 1935
Coll: fine arts; paintings; acrylics;
collages; sculpture - library;
classrooms

Brownville NE

14002
Brownville Historical Society Museum
Main St, Brownville, NE 68321
History/Public Affairs Museum - 1956
Coll: glass; agriculture; Indian artifacts;
tools; costumes

Brunswick GA

14003
Hofwyl-Broadfields Plantation
Rte 2, POB 83, Brunswick, GA 31520
General Museum - 1974
Coll: dairy equipment; rice tools;
period furnishings; plantation (1854)

Brunswick ME

14004
Bowdoin College Museum of Art
Walker Art Bldg, Brunswick, ME 04011
Fine Arts Museum - 1811
Coll: ancient Mesopotamian sculpture;
Greek and Roman antiquities; Oriental
ceramics; European and American
silver; European old master drawings;
Warren Collection; Winslow Homer
Collection; Kress Collection of
Renaissance; Molinari Collection of
Renaissance and Baroque medaillons
and plaquettes

Bryan TX

14005
Brazos Valley Museum of Natural Science
204 W. Villa Maria, Bryan, TX 77801
Natural History Museum - 1961
Coll: shells; mammals; amphibians;
reptiles; fossils; minerals; Indian
artifacts - classrooms

Bryce Canyon UT

14006
Bryce Canyon Visitor Center
Bryce Canyon National Park, Bryce
Canyon, UT 84717
Science/Tech Museum - 1959
Coll: geology; herbarium - library

Bucksport ME

14007
Bucksport Historical Society
Main St, Bucksport, ME 04416
History/Public Affairs Museum - 1964
Coll: marine; military; naval;
transportation - library; reading room

Buena Park CA

14008
Buena Park Historical Society
7842 Whitaker St, Buena Park, CA
90621
General Museum - 1967
Coll: period furnishings; First Lady
Doll Collection; historic building

Buffalo NY

14009
Albright-Knox Art Gallery The Buffalo
Fine Arts Academy
1285 Elmwood Av, Buffalo, NY 14222
Fine Arts Museum - Robert T. Buck
Coll: paintings: 18th century English;
19th century French and American;
contemporary American and
European; sculpture from 3000 B.C. to
the present; graphics - library;
auditorium; classrooms

14010
Buffalo and Erie County Historical Society
25 Nottingham Ct, Buffalo, NY 14216
General Museum - 1862
Coll: archaeology; ethnology;
costumes; crafts; industry; military;
stamps; coins; transportation;
agriculture; marine; medical items;
ephemera - library; auditorium;
television news film collection

14011
Buffalo Museum of Science
Humboldt Parkway, Buffalo, NY 14211
Natural History Museum - 1861
Coll: anthropology; botany; Clinton
herbarium; invertebrate and vertebrate
zoology; geology; paleontology;
mineralogy; mycology - Kellog
observatory; solar observatory; field
research station; library

14012
Theodore Roosevelt Inaugural National Historic Site
641 Delaware Av, Buffalo, NY 14202
Historic Site - 1971
Coll: artifacts relating to the period and
Theodore Roosevelt's inauguration

Buffalo WY

14013
Jim Gatchell Memorial Museum
10 Fort St, Buffalo, WY 82834
General Museum - 1956
Coll: military; pioneer items; indian
history and artifacts; archeology;
archives; mineralogy; numismatic;
paintings; old vehicles

Bunnell FL

14014
Bulow Plantation Ruins State Historic Site
POB 655, Bunnell, FL 32010
Historic Site - 1967
Coll: plantation; sugar kettle and mill;
small tools - nature trail

Burlingame KS

14015
Railroad Museum
Santa Fe Depot, 26 Townsite Apts,
Burlingame, KS 66413
Science/Tech Museum - 1963
Coll: Railroad items; telegraph items -
library

Burlington NJ

14016
Burlington County Historical Society
457 High St, Burlington, NJ 08016
History/Public Affairs Museum - 1915
Coll: lighting equipment dating from
2,000 B.C. to 1920; tools; costumes;
furniture

Burlington VT

14017
Robert Hull Fleming Museum
Colchester Av, Burlington, VT 05401
Fine Arts Museum - 1931
Coll: Oriental, primitive, pre-Columbian,
ancient, medieval, Renaissance,
modern and American art; decorative
art - library

Burlington WI

14018
Burlington Historical Society
232 N Perkins Blvd, Burlington, WI
53105
General Museum - 1928
Coll: dolls and children's toys;
costumes; local history; historic
houses - library

Burns OR

14019
Harney County Museum
18 W D St, Burns, OR 97720
General Museum - 1960
Coll: archaeology; history; natural
history; pioneer and Indian artifacts;
geology; zoology; historic buildings -
club room

Burwell NE

14020
Fort Hartsuff State Historical Park
Burwell, NE 68823
History/Public Affairs Museum - 1874
Coll: uniforms; tools; firearms;
furniture - library

Butte MT

14021
Copper King Mansion
219 W Granite, Butte, MT 59701
Fine Arts Museum - 1966
Coll: crystal; cutglass; silver;
porcelains; art - library; ballroom

14022
Mineral Museum
West Park St, Butte, MT 59701
Natural History Museum - 1900
Coll: 14,000 mineral specimens from
throughout the world; fossils; relief
map of Montana

14023
World Museum of Mining
End of West Park and Granite Sts,
POB 3333, Butte, MT 59701
Science/Tech Museum - 1964
Coll: mining artifacts and equipment;
underground fire fighting equipment;
ore wagon and other transportation
equipment; art of mining subjects;
turn-of-the-century mining camp; 'Hell
Roaring Gulch' including an old mine

Buxton NC NC

14024
Museum of the Sea
Buxton, NC 27920, Cape Hatteras
National Seashore, Rte 1, POB 675,
Manteo, NC 27954
Open Air Museum - 1953
Coll: history; natural history; Cape
Hatteras Lighthouse and Lighthouse
Keeper's dwellings (1870)

Cahokia IL

14025
Cahokia Courthouse
214 W First St, Cahokia, IL 62206
History/Public Affairs Museum - 1940
Coll: furniture; local artifacts; historic
buildings

Cairo IL

14026
Magnolia Manor
2700 Washington Av, Cairo, IL 62914
Historic Site - 1952
Coll: 19th century furnishings; local
and Civil War artifacts

Caldwell ID

14027
Van Sylke Museum
Caldwell Memorial Park, POB 925,
Caldwell, ID 83605
Agriculture Museum - 1958
Coll: farm implements; agriculture;
history; historic houses

Caldwell TX

14028
Burleson County Historical Museum
Burleson County Courthouse,
Caldwell, TX 77836
General Museum - 1968
Coll: Fort Tenoxtitlan artifacts; early
settler's artifacts; toys; furniture;
Victorian bedroom and farm kitchen

Caledonia NY

14029
Big Springs Museum
Main St, Caledonia, NY 14423
General Museum - 1936
Coll: early farm implements; Indian
collection; Civil War; World War I and
II collections; household objects; toys;
games; dolls; costumes; weaving
equipment; school room articles;
china; glass; medical items

Calhoun GA

14030
New Echota
Rte 3, Calhoun, GA 30701
Historic Site - 1956
Coll: capital town of Cherokee nation;
historic buildings

Calumet MI

14031
Coppertown U.S.A.
101 Red Jacket Rd, Calumet, MI 49913
History/Public Affairs Museum
Coll: recreated miner's village;
industrial technology and artifacts
reflecting the mining of copper; the life
of the deep-shaft miner - library

Cambridge City IN

14032
Huddleston Farmhouse Inn Museum
R.R. 1, POB 555, Cambridge City, IN
47327
Historic Site - 1960
Coll: three-story farm house (1840);
graphic exhibits; decorative art -
library; reading room; auditorium;
meeting rooms

Cambridge MA

14033
**Botanical Museum of Harvard
University**
Oxford St, Cambridge, MA 02138
Natural History Museum - 1858
Coll: narcotic plants; pre-Columbian
Peruvian ethnobotany; economic
botany; paleobotany; fossil woods -
library

14034
Busch-Reisinger Museum
29 Kirkland St, Cambridge, MA 02138
Fine Arts Museum - 1901
Coll: Germanic culture; Scandinavian,
German, Austrian and Swiss art from
the early Middle Ages to the present

14035
Fogg Art Museum Harvard University
32 Quincy St, cambridge, MA 02138
Fine Arts Museum - 1895
Coll: Egyptian antiquities; sculpture
from Persepolis; Greek and Roman
sculpture and vases; Chinese
sculpture, bronzes, jades, crystals,
prints and paintings; Cambodian
sculpture; Early Italian, Flemish,
Spanish paintings; American paintings
- library; reading room; classrooms

14036
**Francis Russel Hart Nautical
Museum**
77 Massachusetts Av, Cambridge, MA
02139
Science/Tech Museum - 1922
Coll: rigged and half models, plans,
prints and photographs of merchant
vessels; naval vessels; yachts - library

14037
Museum of Comparative Zoology
Oxford St, Cambridge, MA 02138
Natural History Museum - 1859
Coll: herpetology; paleontology;
ichthyology; arachnology; ornithology;
malacology - library

14038
**Peabody Mueum of Archaeology and
Ethnology**
11 Devinity Ave, Cambridge, MA
02138
Anthropology Museum - 1866
Coll: archaeology; ethnology; human
osteology - library; classrooms

Cambridge OH

14039
Guernsey County Museum
POB 741, Cambridge, OH 43725
General Museum - 1963
Coll: glass; military; china; pottery;
McFarland Home (1837)

Camden ME

14040
Camden-Rockport Historical Society
Camden, ME 04843
General Museum - 1962
Coll: archives; paintings; books;
photographs; costumes; folklore;
marine - library; reading room

Camden NJ

14041
Camden County Historical Society
Park Blvd & Euclid Ave, Camden, NJ
08103
History/Public Affairs Museum - 1899
Coll: crafts; fire fighting; glass; lighting
devices - library

Camden SC

14042
**Blue Ridge Numismatic Association
Museum**
POB 721, Camden, SC 29020
History/Public Affairs Museum - 1974
Coll: coins; currency; stamps; art and
historical documents related to
southern fiscal history - library;
reading room

14043
**Camden District Heritage
Foundation, Historic Camden**
POB 710, Camden, SC 29020
Historic Site - 1970
Coll: Revolutionary period artifacts;
weapons; dioramas; archaeology;
Indian artifacts; maps; archives;
historic houses (1798-1812) - library

Camp Hill PA

14044
Historic Peace Church
St. John's and Trindle Rds, Camp Hill,
PA 17011
Historic Site - 1968
Coll: pewter communion service; doll
organ made with wooden and pewter
pipes (1807); stone church in the
Gregorian style (18th century)

Camp Verde AZ

14045
Fort Verde State Park Museum
POB 397, Camp Verde, AZ 86322
General Museum - 1956
Coll: military hardware; historic
photographs; Indian artifacts; historic
buildings; furniture, clothing, toys -
library

14046
**Montezuma Castle National
Monument**
POB 219, Camp Verde, AZ 86322
General Museum - 1906
Coll: archeology; natural history;
Indian artifacts; ethnology - library

Canal Fulton OH

14047
Canal Fulton Heritage Society
POB 607, Canal Fulton, OH 44614
General Museum - 1968
Coll: furnishings; canal artifacts;
photographs; maps; Oberlin House
(1847); Heritage House (1870)

Canandaigua NY

14048
**The Granger Homestead Society,
Inc.**
295 N Main St, Canandaigua, NY
14424
Historic Site - 1946
Coll: decorative arts; furniture; silver;
china; glass and textiles; horse-drawn
vehicle collection (1820-1930); historic
outbuildings (1820-1904) - library

14049
Ontario County Historical Society
55 N Main St, Canandaigua, NY 14424
General Museum - 1902
Coll: objects and manuscripts relating
to the history of Ontario County -
library

Canon City CO

14050
Canon City Municipal Museum
612 Royal Gorge Blvd, Canon City,
CO 81212
History/Public Affairs Museum - 1928
Coll: Dall De Weese big game
collection; George Boll mounted bird
collection; Vinnie Hoover doll
collection; holotype fossils; dinosaur
habitat group in diorama; Indian
artifacts; mineral collections; Robert
Wesley Amick Colorado paintings;
historic houses - library

Canterbury CT

14051
Prudence Crandall Museum
Canterbury Green, Canterbury, CT
06331
History/Public Affairs Museum - 1969
Coll: Afro-American photos, artifacts
and manuscripts - library

Canton MA

14052
Canton Historical Society
1400 Washington St, POB 540, Canton, MA 02021
History/Public Affairs Museum - 1893
Coll: Indian relics; manuscripts; genealogies; musical instruments - library

Canton NY

14053
Research / History Center of St. Lawrence County
3 1/2 E Main St, POB 43, Canton, NY 13617
General Museum - 1944
Coll: folklore; geology; archives; crafts; records; microfilms; genealogical collections - library

14054
Richard F. Brush Art Gallery of St. Lawrence University
Romoda Dr, Canton, NY 13617
Fine Arts Museum - 1967
Coll: 19th and 20th century American and European paintings, prints, and sculpture; photographs; Frederic Remington collection; Dorothy Feigin collection of modern art; Annie Lenney collection; Andre Niteki and Nathaniel Burwash collections of African art; Roman coins; pre-Columbian pottery - library; reading room; auditorium; classrooms

Canton OH

14055
The Canton Art Institute
1001 Market Av N, Canton, OH 44702
Fine Arts Museum - 1935
Coll: American, Italian and Spanish paintings; 18th and 19th century English and American portraiture; 20th century National and regional art; graphics; sculpture; decorative arts; costumes; art objects - library; reading room; classrooms; sculpture courtyard

14056
Pro Football Hall of Fame
2121 Harrison Av NW, Canton, OH 44798
History/Public Affairs Museum - 1960
Coll: mementoes from the games and players including equipment, photos, films; material pertinent to the development of the pro football in the U.S.; printed game accounts; files on players, games, and circumstances contributing to football's growth; artists' illustrations, photos and paintings - library; theater

14057
The Stark County Historical Society
749 Hazlett, NW, POB 483, Canton, OH 44701
General Museum - 1946
Coll: health; archives; astronomy; glass; canal boat replica; McKinley Museum; dolls; toys; Dueber-Hampden watches - library; planetarium; children's museum; auditorium; classrooms

Canton OK

14058
Cheyenne and Arapaho Museum and Archives
B. Star Rte, POB 19, Canton, OK 73772
General Museum - 1977
Coll: history; tribal history; former headquarters of 23rd Infantry - library; reading room

Canyon City OR

14059
Herman and Eliza Oliver Historical Museum
101 S Canyon City Blvd, Hwy 395, Canyon City, OR 97820
General Museum - 1953
Coll: pioneer antiques and relics; native rock display; Indian artifacts; gold mining; historic buildings; archives

Canyon TX

14060
Panhandle-Plains Historical Museum
2401 Fourth Av, Canyon, TX 79015
History/Public Affairs Museum - 1921
Coll: geology; paleontology; transportation; anthropology; agriculture - library; archive

Cape May NJ

14061
Cape May County Historical Museum
Rte 9-R.D., Cape May, NJ 08210
History/Public Affairs Museum - 1927
Coll: Indian artifacts; period rooms; Colonial kitchen; china; whaling; glass - library

14062
Physick House, Victorian Museum
1048 Washington St, POB 164, Cape May, NJ 08204
General Museum
Coll: toys; tools; furniture; costumes; books - library

Capulin NM

14063
Capulin Mountain National Monument
Capulin, NM 88414
Natural History Museum - 1916
Coll: herbarium; geological and zoological specimens; entomology collection; lepidopteran collection - library

Carbondale IL

14064
University Museum and Art Galleries Southern Ullinois University
Faner 2469, Carbondale, IL 62901
General Museum - 1869
Coll: European and American art from 13th to 20th century with emphasis on 19th and 20th centuries; photography; 20th century sculpture; extensive Oceanic collection; natural history; decorative arts; Southern Illinois history

Carlisle PA

14065
Cumberland County Historical Society and the Hamilton Library
21 N Pitt St, Carlisle, PA 17013
General Museum - 1874
Coll: documents; county lore and crafts; photo collection of identified Indians; woodcarvings; furniture; publications of the Carlisle Indian School - library

14066
United States Army Military History Institute
Carlisle Barracks, Carlisle, PA 17013
History/Public Affairs Museum - 1967
Hessian Powder Magazine Museum and Omar N. Bradley Museum - U.S. Army Research Library

Carlsbad CA

14067
San Luis Rey Historical Society
Carlsbad By The Sea
2855 Carlsbad Blvd, Carlsbad, CA 92008
General Museum - 1932
Coll: archeology; anthropology; archives; ethnology; Indian artifacts; paleontology - library

Carlsbad NM

14068
Carlsbad Caverns Museum
3225 National Parks Hwy, Carlsbad, NM 88220
Natural History Museum - 1923
Coll: history of the caverns; cavern paintings; botany; entomology; geology; paleontology; archaeology; herpetology - library

14069
Carlsbad Municipal and Fine Arts Museum
Halagueno Park, 101 S Halagueno St, Carlsbad, NM 88220
General Museum - 1931
Coll: archaeology; history; potash; astrobelems; New Mexico Art

Carpinteria CA

14070
Carpinteria Valley Historical Society and Museum of History
956 Maple Ave, Carpinteria, CA 93013
General Museum - 1959
Coll: artifacts of Chumash Indians and early pioneers of the Valley

Carrollton MS

14071
Old Jail Museum
Carrollton, MS 38917
History/Public Affairs Museum - 1964
Coll: agriculture; archaeology; folklore

Carrollton OH

14072
Carroll County Historical Society
POB 174, Carrollton, OH 44615
General Museum - 1963
Coll: history; military; antique medical instruments; McCook house (1837)

Carson City NV

14073
Nevada State Museum
Carson City, NV 89710
Natural History Museum - 1939
Coll: biology; geology; anthropology - library; conference rooms; auditorium

Cartersville GA

14074
Etowah Mounds Archaeological Area
Rte 1, Cartersville, GA 30120
Archeology Museum - 1953
Archeological excavations of prehistoric Indian center

Casa Grande AZ

14075
Casa Grande Valley Historical Society
110 W. Florence Blvd, Casa Grande, AZ 85222
General Museum - 1964
local artifacts of historic interest - library; auditorium

Cascade CO

14076
Ute Pass Historical Society
POB 2, Cascade, CO 80809
General Museum - 1967
Coll: Ute Indian art and artifacts; pioneer items; railroad, lumber, and ranch equipment - library

Cashmere WA

14077
Willis Carey Historical Museum
E Sunset Hwy, Cashmere, WA 98815
General Museum - 1956
Coll: history of Central Washington from earliest inhabitants to present ; Indian artifacts; natural history; historic houses - library

Casper WY

14078
Fort Caspar Museum and Historic Site
14 Fort Caspar Rd, Casper, WY 82601
History/Public Affairs Museum - 1936
Coll: Civil War; Indian wars; Indian and pioneer artifacts; guns

14079
Nicolaysen Art Museum
104 Rancho Rd, Casper, WY 82601
Fine Arts Museum - 1967
European watercolors and prints; Matisse lithographs; South American crafts; pre-Columbian clay sculpture

Caspian MI

14080
Iron County Museum
Museum Rd, Caspian MI 49915, Rte 2, Bernhardt Rd, Iron River, MI 49935
Science/Tech Museum - 1962
Coll: lumbering and mining tools; hand-carved miniature lumbering display of 2,000 pieces - library

Cassville WI

14081
Stonefield
Nelson Dewey State Park, Cassville, WI 53806
Agriculture Museum - 1953
Coll: agricultural machinery; carriages; dairying exhibits; historic farmstead

Castile NY

14082
Castile Historical Society
17 E Park Rd, Castile, NY 14427
General Museum - 1953
Coll: Seneca Indian relics; farm
implements; war relics; maps,
historical books, deeds, genealogical
files - library; reading room

Castine ME

14083
Wilson Museum
Perkins St, Castine, ME 04421
Anthropology Museum - 1921
Coll: Paleolithic; Neolithic; Bronze and
Iron Age material from Europe;
geology; anthropology - library

Cathedral City CA

14084
Museum of Antiquities and Art
Glenn, Plumley and Grove, Cathedral
City, CA 92234
General Museum - 1960
Coll: anthropology; archeology;
paintings; sculpture; geology;
numismatics; paleontology; science -
library; reading room

Cazenovia NY

14085
Lorenzo State Historic Site
Ledyard Av, R.D. 2, Cazenovia, NY
13035
Decorative Arts Museum - 1968
Coll: decorative and fine arts;
carriages; furniture; Carriage House
(1892); toolbuilding, garage, playhouse,
smokehouse - library

Cedar City UT

14086
Braithwaite Fine Arts Gallery
Southern Utah State College, Cedar
City, UT 84720
Fine Arts Museum - 1976
Coll: 19th and 20th century American
art - classrooms

Cedar Falls IA

14087
Cedar Falls Historical Society
303 Clay St, Cedar Falls, IA 50613
General Museum - 1963
Coll: tape-recorded interviews with old
settlers; ice-cutting, harvesting, storing
and selling tools; agricultural artifacts
and household items - reading room

14088
Gallery of Art University of Northern
Iowa
27th St and Hudson Rd, Cedar Falls,
IA 50613
Fine Arts Museum - 1978
Coll: sculpture and graphics; 20th
century American and European
painting

14089
University of Northern Iowa Museum
31st and Hudson Rd, Cedar Falls, IA
50613
General Museum - 1890
Coll: minerals; rocks; fossils;
mammals; birds; reptiles; fish; marine
invertebrates; North, Central, South
American Indians; Africa, Asia, Pacific
Islands; pioneer items; military history;
antique and modern china - library

Cedar Key FL

14090
Cedar Key State Museum
POB 538, Cedar Key, FL 32625
General Museum - 1960
Coll: local historical artifacts; shell
collection; natural history

Cedar Rapids IA

14091
Cedar Rapids Art Center
324 3rd St SE, Cedar Rapids, IA 52301
Fine Arts Museum - 1906
Coll: 20th century modern and
regionalist paintings; works by Grant
Wood and Marvin Cone; decorative
arts; crafts; prints; photographs -
library

Cedarburg WI

14092
Ozaukee County Historical Society
W 61 N 619 Meguon St, POB 206,
Cedarburg, WI 53012
Open Air Museum - 1960
A historic pioneer village; agricultural
and household equipment; folklore -
library

14093
Wisconsin Fine Arts Association Inc.
Ozaukee Art Center
W 63 N 645 Washington Av,
Cedarburg, WI 53012
Fine Arts Museum - 1971
Coll: paintings; sculpture; prints;
ceramics

Celina OH

14094
Mercer County Historical Museum
130 E Market, Celina, OH 45883
General Museum - 1959
Coll: archives; agriculture; carpenter's
and blacksmith's tools; period
furniture; school display; costumes;
glassware; guns; Indian artifacts;
medical, health and dental display; art;
The Riley Home (1896) - library

Centennial WY

14095
Centennial Valley Historical Assn.
Second St, Centennial, WY 82055
General Museum - 1976
Coll: local history; gold mining;
lumbering; ranching and railroading -
library

Centerport NY

14096
**Vanderbilt Museum Commission of
Suffolk County**
Little Neck Rd, Box F, Centerport, NY
11721
General Museum - 1950
Coll: marine biology and wildlife;
antique and classic automobiles;
Aeolian player organ; European and
Oriental fine and decorative arts;
South Pacific, Asian, and African
ethnology and anthropology - library;
planetarium; seaplane hanger

Central City CO

14097
Gilpin County Historical Museum
POB 244, Central City, CO 80427
General Museum - 1971
Coll: authentic items from the lives of
early pioneers; replica of Victorian
home, including furnishings; mementos
from Central City opera presentations;
dioramas of early mill and mining town

Chadds Ford PA

14098
Brandywine Battlefield
U.S. Rte 1, POB 202, Chadds Ford, PA
19317
Historic Site - 1947
Coll: history; costumes; period
furnishings; paintings; prints;
agricultural tools; historic houses

14099
Brandywine River Museum
U.S. Rte 1, POB 141, Chadds Ford, PA
19317
General Museum - 1971
Coll: art works related to the region;
American illustration; Hoffmann's Mill
(1864) - library; auditorium; nature/
conservation center

14100
The Christian C. Sanderson Museum
Rte 100 North, Chadds Ford, PA 19317
General Museum - 1967
Coll: personal and family items;
historical artifacts; early Andrew
Wyeth items

Chadron NE

14101
Chadron State College Museum
Main St, Chadron, NE 69337
Natural History Museum - 1939
Coll: paleontology; archaeology;
mineralogy; anthropology; geology

14102
Museum of the Fur Trade
Rte 2, POB 18, Chadron, NE 69337
History/Public Affairs Museum - 1949
Coll: North American fur trade with
emphasis on objects; mountain man
material - library

Chagrin Falls OH

14103
Chagrin Falls Historical Society
250 N Main St, Chagrin Falls, OH
44022
General Museum - 1965
Coll: costumes; household articles;
china; Ohio pottery; glassware -
library

Champaign IL

14104
**Champaign County Historical
Museum**
709 W University Av, Champaign, IL
61820
History/Public Affairs Museum - 1972
Coll: period furnishings and furniture;
clothing; 1860 Greek Revival cottage

14105
Krannert Art Museum University of
Illinois
500 Peabody Dr, Champaign, IL 61820
Fine Arts Museum - 1961
Coll: Trees and Krannert collection of
old master paintings; European and
American 20th century painting,
sculpture, prints, drawings and crafts;
Ewing collection of Malayan textiles;
Moore collection of decorative art

Chandler AZ

14106
Chandler Historical Society
897 N. Oregon, POB 926, Chandler,
AZ 85224
General Museum - 1969
historical records and pictures; Indian
artifacts; local artifacts

Chandler OK

14107
**Lincoln County Historical Society
Museum of Pioneer History**
717 Manvel Av, Chandler, OK 74834
General Museum - 1952
Coll: artifacts, relics and history of
pioneer families of Lincoln County;
memorabilia of Sheriff Bill Tilghman
and Benny Kent - library; auditorium

Chanute KS

14108
**Martin and Osa Johnson Safari
Museum**
16 S Grant St, Chanute, KS 66720
Fine Arts Museum - 1961
Coll: films, photographs, manuscripts
and artifacts of Martin and Osa
Johnson; Western African art
collection - library

Chapel Hill NC

14109
Morehead Planetarium University of
North Carolina
East Franklin St, Chapel Hill, NC 27514
Science/Tech Museum - 1947
Coll: Carl Zeiss Model VI; Copernican
orrery; giant sundial; Genevieve
Morehead art collection; astronomy;
science - library

14110
William Hayes Ackland Art Museum
University of North Carolina
Columbia and Franklin Sts, Chapel Hill,
NC 27514
Fine Arts Museum - 1958
Coll: Renaissance and Baroque
painting, sculpture and drawings; 19th
and 20th century paintings, sculpture
and drawings; 15th - 20th century
prints; Greek and Roman antiques -
library; auditorium; classrooms

Chappaqua NY

14111
**Chappaqua Historical Society
Museum**
New Castle Town Hall, 200 S. Greely
Av, Chappaqua, NY 10514
General Museum - 1971
Coll: Quaker relics - library

Chappel Hill TX

14112
Chappel Hill Historical Society Museum
Chappel Hill, TX 77426
General Museum - 1967
Coll: Confederate, early Texan and Victorian rooms; archives; blacksmith shop; quilts and needlework of other eras; toys

Charles City IA

14113
Floyd County Historical Society
107 N Main St, Charles City, IA 50616
General Museum - 1961
Coll: archaeology; zoology; pharmacology; agriculture; industry; Mutchlar Cabin (1850); Drugstore Museum 1873 - reading room

Charles City VA

14114
Sherwood Forest Plantation
POB 8, Charles City, VA 23020
Historic Site - 1730
Home of President John Tyler; original furniture, silver and china; paintings - library

Charleston IL

14115
Paul Sargent Gallery
LIncoln at Seventh, Charleston, IL 61920
Fine Arts Museum - 1948
Coll: prints and paintings; temporary and traveling exhibitions

Charleston MO

14116
Mississippi County Historical Society
403 N Main, Charleston, MO 63834
General Museum - 1967
Coll: archaeology; archives; costumes; military

Charleston SC

14117
Charles Towne Landing
1500 Old Town Rd, Charleston, SC 29407
Historic Site - 1970
Pre-history to 1775; native animals; crafts - botanical garden; zoological park; auditorium; theater

14118
Charleston Museum
Rutledge Av, Charleston, SC 29401
General Museum - 1773
Coll: anthropology; natural history; history and decorative arts; silver and furniture; period rooms; Civil War naval history; historic houses - bird sanctuary; herbarium; library; auditorium; classrooms

14119
Citadel Archives and Museum
The Citadel, Charleston, SC 29409
History/Public Affairs Museum - 1960
Collections of Generals Mark W. Clark, Hugh P. Harris, Charles Summerall; Admiral Arleigh Burke; Vice Admiral Friedrich Ruge; L. Mendel Rivers; Wm. C. Westmoreland; Lt. General George M. Seignious - library; reading room; classrooms

14120
Gibbes Art Gallery
135 Meeting St, Charleston, SC 29401
Fine Arts Museum - 1858
Coll: American portraits; prints; miniatures; contemporary art; European and Oriental art objects; sculpture; Japanese prints - library; book bindery; art school

14121
Historic Charleston Foundation
51 Meeting St, Charleston, SC 29401
General Museum - 1947
Coll: period furniture and furnishings; silver; porcelain; brass; fabrics; wallpaper; needlework

14122
Macaulay Museum of Dental History
Medical University of South Carolina
171 Ashley Av, Charleston, SC 29403
Science/Tech Museum - 1975
Antique dental collection of antique dental chairs, foot powered drills, wooden dental cabinets, dental lathe, old dental x-ray units, itinerant dentists' medicine cases, cases of molds for crowns, dental turn keys - library

14123
Patriots Point Naval and Maritime Museum
Patriots Point, Charleston SC 29464, POB 986, Mt. Pleasant, SC 29464
Science/Tech Museum - 1976
Coll: navy and marine corps aircraft; naval and maritime artifacts - theater

14124
Post-Courier Museum of Newspaper History
134 Columbus St, Charleston, SC 29402
History/Public Affairs Museum - 1972
Coll: historic editions of newspapers; printing equipment; Pulitzer prize entry - library

14125
Powder Magazine
79 Cumberland St, Charleston, SC 29401
History/Public Affairs Museum - 1703
Coll: costumes; military artifacts; powder magazine (1703)

14126
The Provost
East End of Broad St, POB 39, Charleston, SC 29402
History/Public Affairs Museum - 1965
Coll: artifacts from sea wall excavation under the floor of the dungeon; figures depicting British prisoners

14127
The Thomas Elfe Workshop
54 Queen St, Charleston, SC 29401
General Museum - 1971
Coll: reproductions of accessories and furnishings of 18th century; tools; ceramics

14128
Waring Historical Library Medical University of South Carolina
171 Ashley Ave, Charleston, SC 29403
History/Public Affairs Museum - 1966
Coll: antique medical instruments and equipment - library

14129
WCSC Broadcast Museum
80 Alexander St, Charleston, SC 29402
History/Public Affairs Museum - 1976
Coll: broadcasting and communications equipment - library

Charleston SC SC

14130
The Old Slave Mart Museum
6 Calmers St, Charleston SC 29401, POB 446, Sullivan's Island, SC 29482
Anthropology Museum - 1937
Coll: exhibits on cultural history of the Black; documents, photographs on history of slavery; handicrafts made by slaves; African and art artifacts; archives; folklore; textiles; African ethnology; paintings - Black Heritage Research Center; library

Charleston WV

14131
Sunrise Foundation, Inc.
746 Myrtle Rd, Charleston, WV 25314
Fine Arts Museum - 1960
Coll: American painting, sculpture, graphics, decorative arts; native American, African and Oceanic artifacts; natural history specimens in geology, mineralogy, botany - children's museun; 2 libraries; classrooms; planetarium

14132
West Virginia State Museum
Archives and History Division
Capitol Complex, Charleston, WV 25305
History/Public Affairs Museum - 1905
Coll: life and history of West Virginia; prehistoric and historic artifacts; historic documents; stuffed animals and birds; Civil War regimental flags; evolution of lighting from pioneer days to present - library

Charlotte NC

14133
Charlotte Nature Museum, Inc.
1658 Sterling Rd, Charlotte, NC 28209
Natural History Museum - 1977
Coll: entomology; archaeology; herpetology; geology; ethnology - planetarium; auditoria; library; aviary; aquarium

14134
The Mint Museum of Art
501 Hempstead Pl, POB 6011, Charlotte, NC 28207
Fine Arts Museum - 1933
Coll: European and American art from Renaissance to contemporary; painting, decorative arts, and prints; exhibition of minting operations and gold coins; survey collections of pre-Columbian and African materials; American ceramics; Hezekiah Alexander Homesite and Springhouse (1774); first branch building of the U.S. Mint (1835) - library; auditorium; theater; puppet theater; reading room

Charlottesville VA

14135
Ash Lawn
Rte 6, POB 36, Charlottesville, VA 22901
Historic Site - 1930
Coll: furnishings of the period 1790-1825

14136
Monticello Home of Thomas Jefferson
POB 316, Charlottesville, VA 22902
Historic Site - 1923
Coll: Jeffersonian furniture and memorabilia; books and manuscripts

14137
University of Virginia Art Museum
Rugby Rd, Thomas H. Bayly Memorial Bldg, Charlottesville, VA 22903
Fine Arts Museum - 1935
Coll: 19th century American paintings; 17th-18th century European paintings; contemporary American art

Chattanooga TN

14138
Chattanooga Nature Center
Garden Rd, Chattanooga, TN 37409
Natural History Museum
Coll: specimens of Tennessee wildlife (mounted), including mammals, reptiles, birds and insects; rocks and minerals - library; botanical garden; nature and conservation center; auditorium; classrooms

14139
Harris Swift Museum of Religious and Ceremonial Arts and Library of Rare Books
526 Vine St, Chattanooga, TN 37403
Religious Art Museum - 1950
Coll: religious and ceremonial arts; objects pertaining to all religions; rare books - library

14140
Houston Antique Museum
High St, Chattanooga, TN 37403
Decorative Arts Museum - 1949
Coll: early American, French and English glass; Tiffany glass; 19th Century decorative arts; furniture; pewter, steins; porcelains; dolls; pitcher collection - library

14141
Hunter Museum of Art
Bluff View, Chattanooga, TN 37403
Fine Arts Museum - 1951
Coll: American painting, drawing and sculpture of 18th, 19th and 20th centuries; oriental decorative objects - library; auditorium; classrooms

14142
Tennessee Valley Railroad and Museum Inc.
POB 9173, Chattanooga, TN 37412
Science/Tech Museum - 1961
Coll: railway cars; rare and original drawings from the Pullman Company; telegraph keys and sounders; artifacts indicative of daily train operations

Chehalis WA

14143
Lewis County Historical Museum
841 Front St, Chehalis WA, 98532, 78 NE Washington Av, Chehalis, WA 98532
General Museum - 1965
Coll: general county historical artifacts; photographs; Indian artifacts; historic houses - library

Cherokee IA

14144
Joseph A. Tallmann Museum Mental Health Institute
1200 W Cedar, Cherokee, IA 51012
History/Public Affairs Museum - 1961
Coll: pharmacy; three-room replica of first Superintendent's apartment; business offices; examining room - library

14145
Sanford Museum and Planetarium
117 E Willow St, Cherokee, IA 51012
General Museum - 1941
Coll: archaeology; history; geology;
paleontology, zoology; ethnology;
archives - reading room; library

Cherokee NC

14146
Museum of the Cherokee Indians
US 441, Cherokee, NC 28719
Anthropology Museum - 1948
Coll: Indian artifacts; relics; archives;
rare documents - library

Cherry Valley CA

14147
**Edward-Dean Museum of Decorative
Arts** Riverside County Art and Cultural
Center
9401 Oak Glen Rd, Cherry Valley, CA
92223
Decorative Arts Museum - 1958
Coll: furniture; paintings; statuary;
chinaware; antiques - library; botanical
garden; classrooms

Chesapeake VA

14148
Chesapeake Planetarium
300 Cedar Rd, Chesapeake, VA 23320
Science/Tech Museum - 1963
Coll: astronomy; space science

Chester MT

14149
Liberty County Museum
Chester, MT 59522
General Museum - 1969
Coll: agriculture; archaeology;
costumes; Indian artifacts; old
machinery

Cheyenne OK

14150
Black Kettle Museum
Cheyenne, OK 73628
General Museum - 1958
Coll: Indian arts and crafts (1860-1880);
relics and equipment of U.S. Cavalry
and the Battle of Washita; pioneer
items - library; reading room

Cheyenne WY

14151
Warren Military Museum
Francis E. Warren Air Force Base,
Bldg 210, POB 9625, Cheyenne, WY
82001
History/Public Affairs Museum - 1967
Coll: military uniforms; military
equipment from 1840 to the present;
model airplanes; missiles;
photographs; maps

14152
Wyoming State Art Gallery
Barrett Bldg, 22nd St, Cheyenne, WY
82002
Fine Arts Museum - 1969
Paintings; sculpture - library

14153
Wyoming State Museum
Barrett Bldg, 22nd and Central Av,
Cheyenne, WY 82002
History/Public Affairs Museum - 1895
Coll: historic and prehistoric Indian
exhibits; historical items; military and
pioneer relics; costumes;
transportation; ethnology;
anthropology; archeology - library

Chicago IL

14154
The Adler Planetarium
1300 S Lake Shore Drive, Chicago, IL
60605
Science/Tech Museum - 1930
Coll: antique astronomical instruments;
navigation; engineering - planetarium;
library; observatory; auditorium

14155
The Art Institute of Chicago
Michigan Av and Adams St, Chicago,
IL 60603
Fine Arts Museum - 1870
All periods of European and American
art; Oriental art; African, Oceanic and
pre-Hispanic art - library; 4
auditoriums

14156
**Balzekas Museum of Lithuanian
Culture**
4021 S Archer Ave, Chicago, IL 60632
Anthropology Museum - 1966
Coll: Lithuanian memorabilia;
Lithuanian art and folklore; armor and
antique weapons - library; Center for
the Study of U.S. Presidents

14157
Chicago Historical Society
Clark St at North Av, Chicago, IL
60614
History/Public Affairs Museum - 1856
library

14158
**Chicago Public Library G.A.R.
Memorial Hall**
78 E Washington St, Chicago, IL 60602
General Museum - 1898
Coll: weapons and memorabilia
relating to the Civil War and the Grand
Army of the Republic Veterans'
Association

14159
**The David and Alfred Smart Gallery
of the University of Chicago**
5550 S Greenwood Ave, Chicago, IL
60637
Fine Arts Museum - 1974
Coll: Western painting, sculpture,
decorative arts, photography from
ancient to modern times; Oriental art

14160
Douglas Tomb State Historic Site
636 E 35th St, Chicago, IL 60616
Historic Site - 1865
1866-1881 Stephen A. Douglas Tomb
designed by Leonard W. Volk

14161
**Dusable Museum of African
American History, Inc.**
740 E 56th Place, Chicago, IL 60637
History/Public Affairs Museum - 1961
Coll: Afro-American art - library

14162
Field Museum of Natural History
Roosevelt Rd at Lake Shore Dr,
Chicago, IL 60605
Natural History Museum - 1893
Coll: natural history exhibits; Indian
artifacts; textiles; costumes - library;
theater; classrooms; restaurant

14163
George F. Harding Museum
86 E Randolf St, Chicago, IL 60601
History/Public Affairs Museum - 1930
Coll: armor and weapons; ship models
and figureheads; marine collection;
American art

14164
Glessner House
1800 S Prairie Av, Chicago, IL 60616
Fine Arts Museum - 1966
Coll: drawings; Frank Lloyd Wright
furniture; Issac Scott original furniture;

14165
**International Museum of Surgical
Sciences and Hall of Fame**
1524 N Lake Shore Dr, Chicago, IL
60610
Science/Tech Museum - 1956
Coll: exhibits showing the growth and
perfection of various branches of
surgery - hall of fame

14166
Lorado Taft Midway Studios
6016 So Ingleside Av, Chicago, IL
60627
Fine Arts Museum - 1906
Coll: exhibitions of painting, sculpture,
graphics, and ceramics by students of
the University of Chicato Dept. of Art

14167
Martin D'Arcy Gallery of Art Loyola
University
6525 N Sheridan Rd, Chicago, IL
60626
Fine Arts Museum - 1969
Coll: Western art from the 12th to the
18th century; enamels; textiles;
metalwork; jewels - library

14168
Maurice Spertus Museum of Judaica
618 S Michigan Ave, Chicago, IL
60605
Anthropology Museum - 1968
Coll: archaeology; decorative arts;
Jewish ceremonial arts; folklore -
slide library; library

14169
Museum of Contemporary Art
237 E Ontario St, Chicago, IL 60611
Fine Arts Museum - 1967
Coll: 20th century art - library;
education department

14170
Museum of Ecology Chicago
Academy of Sciences
2001 N Clark St, Chicago, IL 60614
Natural History Museum - 1857
Coll: birds; mammals; herpetology;
geology; paleontology; malacology;
botany; entomology - library;
auditorium

14171
Museum of Science and Industry
57th St and Lake Shore Dr, Chicago,
IL 60637
Science/Tech Museum
Coll: visitor-participation exhibits
depicting scientific principles,
technological applications and social
implications in all fields of science and
industry - library

14172
Oriental Institute University of
Chicago
1155 E 58th St, Chicago, IL 60637
Fine Arts Museum - 1919
Coll: art and archaeology of the
ancient Near East, Egypt - auditorium;
classrooms

14173
Polish Museum of America
984 Milwaukee Av, Chicago, IL 60622
History/Public Affairs Museum - 1937
Coll: art; costumes; religious artifacts;
Polish military memorabilia;
memorabilia of T. Kosciuszko;
memorabilia of Paderewski - library

14174
**Swedish American Museum
Association of Chicago**
5248 N Clark St, Chicago, IL 60640
History/Public Affairs Museum - 1976
Coll: paintings, tools and artifacts
describing the emigration of the
Swedish people to the U.S.

14175
Telephony Museum
225 Randolph St, Lobby 1C, Chicago,
IL 60606
History/Public Affairs Museum - 1967
Coll: antique telephone equipment;
telephone systems of the future -
library

Childress TX

14176
Childress County Heritage Museum
POB 672, Childress, TX 79201
History/Public Affairs Museum - 1976
Coll: history of Paleo-man, Archaic and
Neo-Indian: Spanish occupation; Texas
local history; pioneering; rocks;
minerals - library

Chillicothe OH

14177
**Mound City Group National
Monument**
16062 State Rte 104, Chillicothe, OH
45601
Archeology Museum - 1923
Coll: archaeological artifacts from
Hopewell period; prehistoric Indian
mounds, necropolis site of ceremonial
burials of Hopewell Indian culture;
World War I era items from Camp
Sherman - library; environmental
study area

14178
Ross County Historical Society, Inc.
45 W 5th St, Chillicothe, OH 45601
General Museum - 1896
Coll: pre-historic artifacts; pioneer
tools; household furnishings; 19th and
20th century toys and costumes; naval
painting of Admiral Henry W. Walke;
Ohio's Constitution Table from
1800-1816; pioneer crafts; early state
history; William T. and Elizabeth A.
McClintick Home (1838); McKell
Library (1838); Marianne Scott
Franklin Home (1901) - library

Chincoteague VA

14179
Oyster Museum of Chinco
Beach Rd, POB 14, Chincoteague, VA
23336
Science/Tech Museum - 1966
Coll: fossils; seashells; shellfish
farming implements - library; aquarium

Chinook WA

14180
Fort Columbia State Park Museum
POB 172, Chinook, WA 98614
History/Public Affairs Museum
Coll: Indian and pioneer artifacts;
shipwreck materials housed in
restored artillery barracks, former
coastal fortification

Church Rock NM

14181
Museum of Indian Art
Red Rock State Park, POB 328,
Church Rock, NM 87311
Archeology Museum - 1950
crafts and artifacts of the pre-historic
Zuni, Navajo, Hopi Anaszi, Rio Grande
Pueblos, Apache and Plains Indians -
auditorium; archaeology laboratory;
office

Cimarron NM

14182
Kit Carson Museum
Philmount Scout Ranch and Explorer
Base, Cimarron, NM 87114
Historic Site - 1967
Kit Carson home (1849) - library

Cincinnati OH

14183
Alfred K. Nippert Nature Museum
10245 Winton Rd, Cincinnati, OH
45231
Natural History Museum - 1931
Coll: natural history; flora and fauna;
archaeological artifacts; exhibits of
burials; anthropology; entomology;
geology; herpetology; mineralogy;
paleonotolgy - nature/conservation
center; aquarium; field research
station; auditorium; classrooms;
children's museum

14184
Cincinnati Art Museum
Eden Park, Cincinnati, OH 45202
Fine Arts Museum - 1881
Coll: ancient art; sculpture, painting,
ceramics of Egypt, Greece, Rome;
Near and Middle Eastern art:
sculpture, ceramics, textiles, 15th-20th
century European and American art:
sculpture, paintings, prints, drawings,
photographs, ceramics, decorative
arts, costumes, architectural elements;
primitive art of the South Pacific,
Africa, North and South American
Indians; 2nd-20th century musical
instruments from all countries; playing
cards - library

14185
Cincinnati Historical Society
Eden Park, Cincinnati, OH 45202
General Museum - 1831
Coll: history; botany; manuscripts -
library

14186
**Cincinnati Museum of Natural
History**
1720 Gilbert Av, Cincinnati, OH 45202
Natural History Museum - 1835
Coll: anthropology; archaeology;
conchology; entomology; ethnology;
geology; mineralogy; paleontology;
arachnology; ornithology; herpetology
- library; film library; auditorium;
planetarium; nature preserve

14187
Contemporary Arts Center
115 E 5th St, Cincinnati, OH 45220
Fine Arts Museum - 1939
Coll: contemporary art - auditorium;
library

14188
Geology Museum University of
Cincinnati
Cincinnati, OH 45221
Natural History Museum - 1819
Coll: geology; science; natural history;
petrology; mineralogy; paleontology -
outdoor museum; library

14189
**The Hebrew Union College of Art
and Artifacts**
3101 Clifton Av, Cincinnati, OH 45202
Fine Arts Museum - 1913
Coll: ceremonial objects relating to
Jewish customs, rituals and life cycle
events; biblical archaeology

14190
Miami Purchase Association
812 Dayton St, Cincinnati, OH 45214
General Museum - 1964
Coll: 19th century decorative arts;
furnishings housed in John Hauck
House (1870); Sharon Woods Village,
historical museum of restored
buildings - library

14191
Ohio Covered Bridge Committee
18 Elm Av, Cincinnati, OH 45215
Historic Site - 1940
Coll: transportation - library

14192
The Taft Museum
316 Pike St, Cincinnati, OH 45202
Fine Arts Museum - 1932
Coll: Dutch, English, Spanish and
French paintings; K'ang Hsi, Yung
Cheng, Ch'ien Lung Chinese
porcelains; French 16th century
Limoges enamels; Italian 16th century
maiolica and engraved rock crystals;
European and English 17th and 18th
century watches; decorative arts -
library

14193
Trailside Nature Center and Museum
Burnet Woods, POB 20027, Cincinnati,
OH 45220
Natural History Museum - 1930
Coll: exhibits of live and stuffed birds;
animals; tree and plant specimens;
rocks and stones; seeds - auditorium;
classrooms; planetarium; nature library

Claksdale MS

14194
Delta Blues Museum
1109 State St, Claksdale, MS 38614
Music Museum - 1979
Coll: books and periodicals on blues
music, artists and Afro-American;
recordings of blues artists - library;
reading room

Claremont CA

14195
Galleries of the Claremont Colleges
Pomona College, Claremont, CA
91711
Fine Arts Museum
Lang Gallery (Scripps College): Young
collection of American paintings;
Johnson collection of Japanese prints;
Routh collection of cloisonne; Marer
collection of contemporary American
and Japanese ceramics; Montgomery
Gallery (Pomona College): Kress
collection of Renaissance paintings;
prints, drawings, and photographs -
library

Claremore OK

14196
J. M. Davis Gun Museum
Fifth and Hwy 66, 333 N. Lynn Riggs
Blvd, Claremore, OK 74017
General Museum - 1965
Coll: guns; history; Indian artifacts;
music; archaeology; 'John Roger's
Sanctuary' collections; steins; saddles;
animal horns and trophy heads;
swords and knives - library;
auditorium

14197
Will Rogers Memorial
POB 157, Claremore, OK 74017
General Museum - 1938
Coll: statue of Will Rogers by Jo
Davidson; personal items; documents;
saddles; dioramas; archives; sculpture;
history - library

Clarion PA

14198
**The Clarion County Historical
Society**
18 Grant St, Clarion, PA 16214
General Museum - 1955
Coll: household items and tools of
early settlers; local historical artifacts
and documents - library

Clarkston WA

14199
Valley Art Center
842 6th St, Clarkston, WA 99403
Decorative Arts Museum - 1968
Coll: historical and Indian art; graphic
art; sculpture

Clarksville VA

14200
**Roanoke River Museum, Prestwould
Foundation**
POB 872, Clarksville, VA 23927
General Museum - 1959
Coll: costumes; archaeology - library;
archives

Claymont DE

14201
Robinson House
Naaman's Corner & U.S. 13, Claymont,
DE
Historic Site
Coll: furniture; decorative arts; historic
inn (1723)

Clayton ID

14202
Custer Museum
Yankee Fork Ranger District, Clayton,
ID 83227
Historic Site - 1961
Coll: Gold Rush mining equipment
found on site of 1870 Gold Rush;
household artifacts; Chinese personal
itmes pertaining to mining;
photographs; historic houses - library

Clayton NY

14203
1000 Islands Museum
Old Town Hall, 401 Riverside Dr,
Clayton, NY 13624
General Museum - 1964
Coll: boats and boat building; village
buildings and shops; railroad station;
Berta Frey, Emily Belding, Elizabeth
Terlouw, textile collections; Muskie
Hall of Fame; pictorial history of 1000
Islands Bridge - library; classrooms

Cle Elum WA

14204
Cle Elum Historical Museum
221 E 1st, Cle Elum, WA 98922
History/Public Affairs Museum - 1967
Coll: old and new phones; history of
the phone; housed in a former Bell
Telephone Building

Clearfield PA

14205
Clearfield County Historical Society
104 E Pine St, Clearfield, PA 16830
General Museum - 1960
Coll: Indian flints; built-in mine mouth;
lumbering display; Pennsylvania
natives - library

Clearwater FL

14206
Florida Gulf Coast Art Center
222 Ponce de Leon Blvd, Clearwater,
FL 33516
Fine Arts Museum - 1945
Coll: 19th and 20th century American
paintings; artifacts - library; reading
room; classrooms

Cleburne TX

14207
Layland Museum
201 N. Caddo, Cleburne, TX 76031
General Museum - 1864
Coll: local history; Southwest Indian;
Civil War

Clemson SC

14208
Fort Hill Clemson University
Clemson, SC 29631
History/Public Affairs Museum - 1803
Coll: original furnishings; Flemish and
family portraits

14209
Hanover House Clemson University
Clemson, SC 29631
Historic Site - 1716
Coll: antique furnishings; historic
building (1716)

14210
Rudolph E. Lee Gallery College of
Architecture, Clemson University
Lee Hall, Clemson, SC 29631
Fine Arts Museum - 1956
Coll: paintings; graphics

Cleveland GA

14211
White County Historical Society
POB 281, Cleveland, GA 30528
General Museum - 1965
Coll: old newspapers; Civil War
documents; diaries and letters; historic
building

Cleveland OH

14212
Cleveland Health Education Museum
8911 Euclid Av, Cleveland, OH 44106
History/Public Affairs Museum - 1939
Robert L. Dickinson collectionon
human reproduction; anatomy and
physiology; environmental health -
library

14213
Cleveland Museum of Art
11150 East Blvd, Cleveland, OH 44106
Fine Arts Museum - 1913
Coll: art from all cultures and periods;
paintings; sculpture; graphics;
decorative arts; music; numismatic;
textiles; photography - library;
auditorium; seat halls

14214
Cleveland Museum of Natural History
Wade Oval, University Circle, Cleveland, OH 44106
Natural History Museum - 1920
Coll: Haplocanthosaurus; Simplexosaurus; Johnstown mastodon; Dunkleosteus, armored fish of the Devonian period; pre-historic Ohio and North American Indian cultures; formation and 4 1/2 billion year history of the earth; birds and insects of Ohio; paleontology; entomology; geology; mineralogy; zoology; ethnology; archaeology; anthropology; astronomy; botany; medicine; herpetology; fossil man - library; auditorium; classrooms; planetarium; zoological park; botanical garden; nature center; field research station; preservation project

14215
Dunham Tavern Museum
6709 Euclid Av, Cleveland OH 44103, Northampton Rd, Cleveland Heights, OH 44121
Historic Site - 1824
Coll: folklore; glass; textiles; mocha ware; pewter; lustre ware; Shaker period rooms; Ohio room; early American antiques; herb garden; Dunham Tavern (1824) - library

14216
Frederick C. Crawford Auto-Aviation Museum of the Western Reserve Historical Society
10825 East Blvd, Cleveland, OH 44106
Science/Tech Museum - 1937
Coll: 200 vehicles of transportation; carriages and bicycles; early automobiles; 19th century shops including Alexander Winton's horseless carriage shop; Hechler Pharmacy; Crawford's Saloon; Ellyn's Apparel - library; reading room

14217
Greater Cleveland Ethnographic Museum
137 The Arcade, Cleveland, OH 44114
History/Public Affairs Museum - 1975
Coll: oral history of immigrant people, tapes and transcriptions; immigrant possessions and documents; items relating to cultural traditions of the people who settled in the Cleveland area

14218
The Gund Collection of Western Art
One Erieview Plaza, Cleveland, OH 44114
Fine Arts Museum - 1966
Coll: 19th and 20th century American Western Art

14219
Howard Dittrick Museum of Historical Medicine
11000 Euclid Av, Cleveland, OH 44106
History/Public Affairs Museum - 1926
Coll: historical objects relating to medicine; dentistry; pharmacy; 1880 doctor's office; surgical instruments from ancient Rome; history of medicine in Western Reserve; history of common diagnostic instruments; pharmaceutical apparatus; 18th and 19th century microscopes; nursing; archives; numismatic - library; auditorium

14220
St. Mary's Ethnic Museum
3256 Warren Rd, Cleveland, OH 44111
Anthropology Museum - 1960
Coll: Romanian folk art and culture - library; reading room; classrooms

14221
Salvador Dali Museum
24050 Commerce Park Rd (Beachwood), Cleveland, OH 44122
Fine Arts Museum - 1954
Coll: Salvador Dali oils, drawings, watercolors, graphics and sculpture - library

14222
Shaker Lakes Regional Nature Center
2600 S Park Blvd, Cleveland, OH 44120
Open Air Museum - 1966
Coll: natural history; environmental education - library; auditorium; classrooms; nature center

14223
The Temple Museum of Jewish Religious Art and Music
University Circle and Silver Park, Cleveland, OH 44106
Religious Art Museum - 1950
Coll: religious objects; ritual silver; paintings; sculpture; graphics; decorative arts; archaeology - library

14224
Ukrainian Museum and Archives, Inc.
1202 Kenilworth Av, Cleveland, OH 44113
Anthropology Museum - 1952
Coll: artifacts; documents; books; pictures and other items pertaining to Ukrainian culture and history; particularly in the United States - library; reading room

14225
Western Reserve Historical Society
10825 East Blvd, Cleveland, OH 44106
General Museum - 1867
Coll: antique furniture; pioneer objects; glassware; china; costumes; ship models; Washingtoniana, Lincolniana, Shaker items; archaeology of Ohio; early aircraft engines, miniature aircraft models, planes; archives; paintings; costume gallery; Ohio City center portraying Cleveland's West Side; sculpture; graphics; decorative arts; historic buildings (1812-1815) - library; reading room

Clinton CT

14226
Stanton House
63 E Main St, Clinton, CT 06413
Historic Site - 1916
Coll: antique furniture; china; glass

Clinton IL

14227
Fine Arts Center of Clinton
119 W Macon St, Clinton, IL 61727
Fine Arts Museum - 1960
Coll: contemporary painting and graphics

14228
The Homestead Museum
219 E Woodlawn St, Clinton, IL 61727
General Museum - 1967
Coll: clothing; dolls; furnishings; agriculture; railroad artifacts; guns

Clinton MS

14229
Mississippi Baptist Historical Commission
POB 51, Clinton, MS 39056
History/Public Affairs Museum - 1887
Coll: Baptist history - reading room; library

Clinton NH

14230
Clinton Historical Museum Village
56 Main St, POB 5005, Clinton, NH 08809
Open Air Museum - 1960
Coll: 18th, 19th and early 20th century rural American life; industry; agriculture; domestic utensils; technology

Clinton OK

14231
Western Trails Museum
2229 Gary Freeway, Clinton, OK 73601
General Museum - 1967
Coll: anthropology; archaeology; Indian artifacts - library

Clintonville WI

14232
Four Wheel Drive Foundation
105 E 12th St, Clintonville, WI 54929
Science/Tech Museum - 1948
Coll: racing and passenger cars; trucks; fire engines

Cocoa FL

14233
Brevard Museum, Inc.
2201 Michigan Av, Cocoa, FL 32922
Science/Tech Museum - 1969
Coll: natural science exhibits; historical and prehistoric artifacts; historical photos; marine fish and mollusks - auditorium; nature/conservation center

Cody WY

14234
Buffalo Bill Historical Center
POB 1020, Cody, WY 82414
Historic Site - 1917
Coll: firearms; Winchester guns; Wild West Show items; furniture; portraits; paintings; Buffalo Bill's boyhood home; attached: Plains Indian Museum containing ethnological and archeological materials - library

Coeur d'Alene ID

14235
Museum of North Idaho, Inc.
POB 812, Coeur d'Alene, ID 83814
General Museum - 1968
Logging and lumber manufacturing artifacts

Cohasset MA

14236
Cohasset Maritime Museum
Elm St, Cohasset, MA 02025
General Museum - 1928
Coll: folklore; marine; naval; military; mineralogy; archives; music - library

Colby KS

14237
Sod Town Pioneer Homestead Museum
US Highway 24 E, POB 393, Colby, KS 67701
General Museum - 1955
Coll: reproductions of sod buildings during the settlement of the treeless prairie regions, Indian artifacts; live prairie animals and plants; pioneer clothing, furniture and household items - library

14238
Thomas County Historical Society and Museum
1525 W 4th St, Colby, KS 67701
History/Public Affairs Museum - 1959
Coll: articles relating to the area's history from the beginning of the homesteaders living in sod homes to the period of World War II; the Kuska Collection, containing 2,000 dolls, signed Tiffany and Sevres, Capo De Monte, Royal Vienna, Satsuma, Ridgway, Wedgewood, Lomoge and Meissen; cut glass including redford, Steigel, Stuben, Galle and Cameo; furniture; textiles; silver; books; other memorabilia - library; reading room

Cold Spring Harbor NY

14239
Whaling Museum Society, Inc.
Main St, POB 25, Cold Spring Harbor, NY 11724
History/Public Affairs Museum - 1936
Coll: displays of sailors' knots; scrimshaw; ship models; seashells; whalebone; by-products of the whaling industry; whaleboat; harpoons - library; film library

Cold Spring NY

14240
Putnam County Historical Society
63 Chestnut St, Cold Spring, NY 10516
General Museum - 1906
Coll: 19th century paintings; manufactured articles from the West Point Foundry; photos, documents, records, manuscripts - library; reading room

College Park MD

14241
Art Gallery University of Maryland Sociology Building, College Park, MD 20742
Fine Arts Museum - 1966
Coll: 20th century American paintings; sculpture; prints; contemporary Japanese prints; African sculpture

Collegeville PA

14242
Museum of the Historical Society of Trappe
Main St, Trappe, Collegeville, PA 19426
General Museum - 1964
Coll: archives; history; historical markers - library

Coloma CA

14243
Marshall Gold Discovery State Historic Park
POB 265, Coloma, CA 95613
History/Public Affairs Museum - 1927
Historic buildings - library; lecture room

Colorado Springs CO

14244
Carriage House Museum
Broadmoor, Colorado Springs, CO 80906
History/Public Affairs Museum - 1941
Coll: antique carriages; covered wagons; stage coaches

14245
Colorado Springs Fine Arts Center
30 W. Dale St, Colorado Springs, CO
80903
Fine Arts Museum - 1936
Coll: Southwestern Spanish Colonial
and Native American art; ethnographic
collections; American paintings,
sculpture, graphics, and drawings;
survey collection of world art - library;
theater; classrooms; reading room

14246
May Natural History Museum
8 miles SW of Colorado Springs on
State Hwy 115, Lytle Star Rte, POB
101, Colorado Springs, CO 80906
Natural History Museum - 1947
Coll: exotic entomological specimens;
primitive artifacts; geological exhibits -
library; nature center

14247
**Museum of the American
Numismatic Association**
818 N Cascade, POB 2366, Colorado
Springs, CO 80901
History/Public Affairs Museum - 1891
Coll: coins; currency; tokens; medals
- library; classrooms; reading room

14248
Pioneers' Museum
215 S. Tejon, Colorado Springs, CO
80903
General Museum - 1908
Coll: Pike's Peak regional history of
pioneers; furniture; tools; costumes;
smoking pipes; Indian materials -
library; reading room; courtroom

14249
**Western Museum of Mining &
Industry**
1025 Northgate Rd, Colorado Springs,
CO 80908
Science/Tech Museum - 1971
Coll: metal mining and milling
machinery; steam, water, and
electrically powered prime movers;
electrical equipment; machine tools -
library; blacksmith machine shop; 19th
century farm house

Columbia MO

14250
Geology Museum University of
Missouri
Columbia, MO 65201
Natural History Museum - 1830
Coll: mineralogy; paleontology;
geology

14251
Museum of Anthropology University
of Missouri
100 Swallow Hall, Columbia, MO
65201
Anthropology Museum - 1900
Coll: ethnographic: Plains and
Southwest Indians; contemporary
material from most ares in the US;
Eskimo and Mexican materials;
archaeology; ethnography

14252
Museum of Art and Archaeology
University of Missouri
1 Pickard Hall, Columbia, MO 65201
Archeology Museum - 1957
Coll: archaeology of Near East, Egypt,
Mediterranean; Chinese and Japanese
art - library; lecture hall

14253
State Historical Society of Missouri
Elmer Ellis Library Building
Corner Hitt and Lowry Sts, Columbia,
MO 65201
Fine Arts Museum - 1898
Coll: paintings; drawings; prints -
library; reading room

Columbia PA

14254
**Museum of the National Association
of Watch and Clock Collectors, Inc.**
514 Poplar St, POB 33, Columbia, PA
17512
Science/Tech Museum - 1971
Coll: American and Foreign clocks,
watches, horological tools;
timekeeping from the sundial to the
atomic clock; Beeler escapement
collection - library

Columbia SC

14255
**Columbia Museum of Art and
Science**
1112 Bull St, Columbia, SC 29201
General Museum - 1950
Coll: Spanish Colonial coll.; graphics;
English furniture; dolls; European and
American paintings and decorative
arts - library; botanical garden;
auditorium

14256
Historic Columbia Foundation, Inc.
1616 Blanding St, Columbia, SC 29201
General Museum - 1961
Coll: period furnishings; china; silver;
other accessories - botanical garden

14257
**South Carolina Confederate Relic
Room and Museum**
920 Sumter St, Columbia, SC 29201
History/Public Affairs Museum - 1896
Coll: costumes; military; relics from all
periods of South Carolina history -
library

14258
**The University of South Carolina
Mckissick Museums**
Mckissick Library Bldg., Columbia, SC
29208
Decorative Arts Museum - 1976
Coll: Baruch silver; Howard
gemstones; Kohn dolls; Mandell Art
Nouveau - library

Columbia TN

14259
Ancestral Home of James Knox Polk
301 W. 7th St, Columbia, TN 38401
General Museum - 1924
Coll: historic house (1816)
possessions of Polk family; law books;
furniture; china - library

Columbus GA

14260
**Columbus Museum of Arts and
Sciences, Inc.**
1251 Wynnton Rd, Columbus, GA
31906
General Museum - 1952
Coll: paintings; sculpture; graphics;
archeology general natural history;
southern history; costumes; ethnology
- library; greenhouse; garden for the
blind; nature trail

14261
Confederate Naval Museum
202 4th St, POB 1022, Columbus, GA
31902
History/Public Affairs Museum - 1962
Coll: Confederate naval gun boats;
CSS Muscogee and CSS
Chattahoochee on display; other
exhibits pertaining to the Confederate
Navy and Marine Corps

Columbus IN

14262
**Bartholomew County Historical
Society**
524 Third St, Columbus, IN 47201
General Museum - 1921
Coll: archives; local historical artifacts;
restored parlor from the 1880s;
historic house - library

Columbus MS

14263
**The Columbus and Lowndes County
Historical Society Museum**
316 7th St N, Columbus, MS 39701
History/Public Affairs Museum - 1059
Coll: glass; documents; silver; books -
library

Columbus OH

14264
**Center of Science and Industry of
the Franklin County Historical
Society**
280 E Broad St, Columbus, OH 43215
Science/Tech Museum - 1948
Coll: industry; marine; medicine;
science; history - planetarium; library

14265
Columbus Cultural Arts Center
139 W Main St, Columbus, OH 43215
Fine Arts Museum - 1978
Coll: visual arts including painting,
sculpture, fabric arts, jewelry and
printing

14266
Columbus Museum of Art
480 E Broad St, Columbus, OH 43215
Fine Arts Museum - 1878
Frederick Schumacher collection;
Derby collection; Ferdinand Howald
collection of French and American
modern art; George Bellows oils and
lithographs; outdoor sculpture park
featuring 15th and 16th century Italian
and 19th and 20th century European
and American masters; South Pacific
primitive pieces; decorative arts;
Indian artifacts - lecture room;
auditorium

14267
Ohio Historical Center
Interstate 71 and 17th Av, Columbus,
OH 43211
General Museum - 1885
Coll: historical objects; paintings;
decorative arts, drawings, prints; craft
tools and products; textiles, costumes;
glass of Ohio and Midwest;
pre-Columbian Indian artifacts and art
objects; prehistoric archaeology of
Midwest; natural history;
invertebrates, insects, fish, reptiles,
birds, mammals, minerals; industry;
military - library; nature center;
reading room; auditorium; classrooms

14268
Orton Museum
155 S Oval Dr, Columbus, OH 43210
Natural History Museum - 1892
Coll: paleontology; mineralogy

Columbus TX

14269
Koliba Home Museum Complex
1124 Front, Columbus, TX 78934
General Museum - 1961
Coll: smoothing irons; political
memorabilia; blacksmith shop; Texas
court history

Concord MA

14270
Concord Antiquarian Society
200 Lexington Rd, Concord, MA 01742
Decorative Arts Museum - 1895
Coll: furniture; glass; ceramics;
pewter; Ralph Waldo Emerson's study;
Henry David Thoreau memorabilia -
library

14271
**Ralph Waldo Emerson Memorial
Association**
28 Cambridge Turnpike-at S.R. 2A,
POB 333, Concord, MA 01742
Historic Site - 1930
Coll: preservation project of
Emerson's personal objects

14272
The Thoreau Lyceum
156 Belknap St, Concord, MA 01742
History/Public Affairs Museum - 1966
Coll: early editions of works by
Thoreau; 19th century photographs;
old maps including original Thoreau
survey maps - reading room; library

Concord NH

14273
New Hampshire Historical Society
30 Park St, Concord, NH 03301
Fine Arts Museum - 1823
Coll: decorative and fine arts related to
New Hamshire furniture; silver;
paintings; ceramics - library;
auditorium

14274
The Pierce Manse
14 Penacook St, Concord, NH 03301
History/Public Affairs Museum - 1966
Coll: furniture; memorabilia of Pres.
Pierce and his family - library;
auditorium

Concordia KS

14275
Cloud County Historical Museum
Seventh & Broadway, Concordia, KS
66901
General Museum - 1959
Coll: Prisoner of war camp, military;
casket flags; clothing; farm equipment

Conneaut OH

14276
Conneaut Railroad Museum
POB 643, Conneaut, OH 44030
Science/Tech Museum - 1962
Coll: engines; hopper car; wood
caboose; stock certificate of Red River
Line, N.Y.C. (1866); relics of Ashtabula
disaster (1876); scale models of
locomotives and equipment; lanterns;
photos; timeables; watches; passes;
steam era display - library

Connersville IN

14277
Henry H. Blommel Historic Automotive Data Collection
Rte 5, Connersville, IN 47331
History/Public Affairs Museum - 1928
Coll: automotive archives; history of automotive industry; automotive transportation - library

Conrad MT

14278
Banka's Shell Museum
403 S Delaware St, Conrad, MT 59425
Natural History Museum
Coll: 100,000 sea shells; marine atifacts; whale bone and teeth; human skeletons; arrowheads; turtleshells; poison spears

Constantine MI

14279
Governor Barry Historical Society
280 N. Washington, Constantine, MI 49042
History/Public Affairs Museum - 1945
Coll: needlework; lamps; clothing; musical instruments

Cookson OK

14280
Fort Chickamauga
Fort Chickamauga, Cookson, OK 74427
History/Public Affairs Museum - 1972
Coll: furnishings; horse equipment; weapons; uniforms; Red Lantern (1841); Commanding Officer's Building (1881); Farrier's Building (1881); Etta Building (1882); Elm Springs Mission (1850) - library; classrooms

Coolidge AZ

14281
Casa Grande Ruins National Monument
POB 518, Coolidge, AZ 85228
General Museum - 1892
Coll: archeology; ethnology; pre-Columbian Indian artifacts; archives; prehistoric villages; natural history - library

Cooperstown NY

14282
National Baseball Hall of Fame and Museum, Inc.
Main St, Cooperstown, NY 13326
History/Public Affairs Museum - 1936
Coll: plaques of members; autographed baseballs; bats; trophies; books; pictures; paintings; cigarette and gum cards; uniforms; cartoons - library; reading room

14283
New York State Historical Association
Lake Rd, Cooperstown, NY 13326
Fine Arts Museum - 1899
Coll: academic and folk paintings; sculpture; decorative arts; graphics; costumes; history; life masks of famous Americans; Fenimore House - galleries; lecture hall; library

Coos Bay OR

14284
Coos Art Museum
515 Market St, Coos Bay, OR 97420
Fine Arts Museum - 1965
Coll: paintings; sculpture; graphics; junior art from area high schools; contemporary American artists - library; reading room; classrooms

Coral Gables FL

14285
Lowe Art Museum
1301 Miller Dr, Coral Gables, FL 33146
Fine Arts Museum - 1951
Kress collection of Renaissance, Baroque, and Rococo painting and sculpture; Barton collection of Southwestern American Indian textiles and pottery; Lothrop collection of Guatemalan textiles; pre-Columbian artifacts; Oriental paintings; Spanish-American art - library; classroom

14286
Metropolitan Museum and Art Centers, Inc.
1212 Anastasia, Coral Gables, FL 33134
Fine Arts Museum - 1960
Coll: 20th century sculpture; contemporary Latin American painting; contemporary American painting; oriental sculpture and ceramics; African and pre-Columbian art; graphics and decorative arts - library; studio workshops; children's museum; conservation laboratory

Cordele GA

14287
Georgia Veterans Memorial Museum
Cordele, GA 31015
History/Public Affairs Museum
Coll: historic aircraft; fighting vehicles; uniforms; weapons

Corning NY

14288
The Benjamin Patterson Inn
59 W Pulteney St, Corning, NY 14830
General Museum - 1976
Coll: furnishings and artifacts (1800-1850); costume collection - library

14289
The Corning Museum of Glass
Corning Glass Center
Corning, NY 14830
Decorative Arts Museum - 1951
Coll: glass vessels; objects; archaeological remains; tools from every period and area of glass history - library

14290
The Rockwell-Corning Museum
Baron Steuben Place, Market at Centerway, Corning, NY 14830
Decorative Arts Museum - 1976
Collection on loan from Robert F. Rockwell; Western American art by Frederic Remington, C. M. Russell, W. R. Leigh, Edward Borein, Henry Farny, George Catlin, Alfred Jacob Miller, Albert Bierstadt; bronzes by Frederic Remington, James Earl Frazier, Carl Rungius, Shrady; pistols and rifles; collection of saddles and spurs; Navajo rugs

Cornish NH

14291
Saint-Gaudens National Historic Site
Saint-Gaudens Road, Cornish, NH 03746
Fine Arts Museum - 1926
Coll: works of Saint Gaudens from 1848-1907 in bronze, plaster casts, models, sketches, molds and furnishings - library

Cornwall PA

14292
Cornwall Iron Furnace
POB V, Cornwall, PA 17016
Science/Tech Museum - 1931
Coll: charcoal process; ironmaking exhibits; geological exhibits; furnace and charcoal pile

Cornwall-on-Hudson NY

14293
Museum of the Hudson Highlands
The Boulevard, Cornwall-on-Hudson, NY 12520
Natural History Museum - 1962
Coll: natural history; ichthyology; herpetology; entomolgy; botany - library; hiking trails

Corpus Christi TX

14294
Art Museum of South Texas
1902 N. Shoreline, Corpus Christi, TX 78402
Fine Arts Museum - 1960
Coll: paintings; drawings; sculpture; graphics; photographs - library; auditorium; classrooms

14295
Corpus Christi Museum
1919 N. Water, Corpus Christi, TX 78401
General Museum - 1957
Coll: anthropology; history; marine science; earth sience; natural history - library; auditorium; classrooms

14296
Japanese Art Museum
426 S. Staples St, Corpus Christi, TX 78401
Fine Arts Museum - 1973
Coll: decorative and applied arts; historical and cultural dioramas; architectural models; illustrations and paintings of Buddhism and Hinduism; oriental fan collection - library; auditorium; classrooms

Corry PA

14297
Corry Area Historical Society
Mead Av, POB 107, Corry, PA 16407
General Museum - 1965
Coll: industry; transportation; costumes; agriculture; music - library

Corsicana TX

14298
Navarro County Historical Society, Pioneer Village
912 W. Park Av, Corsicana, TX 75110
General Museum - 1956
Coll: period furnishings; agriculture; archaeology; archives; ethnology

Cortez CO

14299
Four Corners Museum
802 E. Montezuma, Cortez, CO 81321
General Museum - 1956
Coll: historical items; Indian artifacts; inaugural ball gowns of the presidents' wives

Cortland NY

14300
Cortland County Historical Society, Inc.
25 Homer Av, Cortland, NY 13045
General Museum - 1925
Coll: textiles; industries; lighting devices; hair wreaths; jewelry - library

14301
Science Museum
State University Campus, Science Bldg, Bowers Hall, Cortland, NY 13045
Natural History Museum - 1964
Coll: anatomy; botany; human biology; ecology; ethnology; geology; physics - nature/conservation center; aquarium; field research station; planetarium; auditorium; nature trail; teaching units; reading room; classrooms; laboratory

Corvallis OR

14302
Oregon State University Memorial Union Building Oregon State University
Corvallis, OR 97331
Fine Arts Museum - 1927
Coll: paintings; sculpture

14303
Oregon State University Museum of Natural History Zoology Dept.
Corvallis, OR 97331
Natural History Museum - 1948
Coll: birds; mammals; amphibians; reptiles - library; reading room

Corydon IA

14304
Wayne County Historical Society
Corydon, IA 50060
General Museum - 1942
Coll: agriculture; paintings; Indian artifacts; natural history - library

Corydon IN

14305
Corydon Capital State Memorial
Corydon, IN 47112
Historic Site
Period furnishings

Coshocton OH

14306
Johnson-Humrickhouse Museum
Roscoe Village, Coshocton, OH 43812
Decorative Arts Museum - 1931
Coll: Indians of the Americas Gallery;
The Jay Sadler and Cornelia Flood
Shaw Gallery; The Adolph Golden
Gallery; The Edward E. & Frances B.
Montgomery Gallery; The Joe R. Engle
Gallery; paleo to modern North
American Indian and Eskimo arts,
crafts, basketry and beadwork;
Chinese and Japanese porcelains,
pottery, lacquers, cloisonne, jade,
amber, ivory, wood carvings, bronze,
brass, copper and pewter ware, prints,
arms and armor; costumes and
textiles; European prints, pottery,
porcelain and pewter; collections of
documents, implements and
furnishings from local pioneer families

Cottonwood ID

14307
St. Gertrude's Museum College of St.
Gertrude
Cottonwood, ID 83522
General Museum - 1931
Coll: philately; mineralogy; zoology;
Indian artifacts; archives; entomology;
botany; natural history - library

Coudersport PA

14308
Potter County Historical Society
308 N Main St, Coudersport, PA 16915
General Museum - 1919
Coll: pioneer artifacts; Bliss Indian
collection; documents - library;
reading room

Coulee Dam WA

14309
Fort Spokane Museum
POB 37, Coulee Dam, WA 99116
History/Public Affairs Museum - 1965
Coll: originals and machine copies of
historic documents and photographs;
historic houses - library; auditorium

Coupeville WA

14310
**Island County Historical Society
Museum**
between Coveland and Front St on
Alexander St, POB 305, Coupeville,
WA 98239
General Museum - 1958
Local and county history; Indian
artifacts - library

Coxsackie NY

14311
Bronck House Museum
Route 9 W, Coxsackie, NY 12051
General Museum - 1929
Coll: art; silver; weaving paraphernalia
- library

Cranbury NJ

14312
**Cranbury Historical and
Preservation Society**
4 Park Place, Cranbury, NJ 08512
History/Public Affairs Museum - 1967
Coll: genealogy; vital statistic; census,
cemetery and church records - library

Crawford NE

14313
Fort Robinson Museum
POB 304, Crawford, NE 69339
History/Public Affairs Museum - 1956
Coll: military items; anthropology;
ethnology; archaeology; old military
rooms, stables and shops - library;
reading room

Crawfordville GA

14314
Confederate Museum
Alexander H. Stephens State Park,
Crawfordville, GA 30631
History/Public Affairs Museum - 1952
Coll: arms and memorabilia of the Civil
War; historic house (home of
Alexander H. Stephens, vice-president
of the Confederacy); furnishings; slave
quarters

Crazy Horse SD

14315
Indian Museum of North America
Av of the Chiefs, Black Hills, Crazy
Horse, SD 57730
Anthropology Museum - 1972
Coll: Indian art; artifacts - library;
theater

Crescent City CA

14316
Del Norte County Historical Society
577 H St, Crescent City, CA 95531
General Museum - 1951
Coll: archeology; historical artifacts;
lumber industry; marine history;
mining; agriculture; genealogy; historic
houses - reading room; library

Cresson PA

14317
**Allegheny Portage Railroad National
Historic Site**
POB 247, Cresson, PA 16630
Science/Tech Museum - 1964
Coll: transportation - library;
auditorium; theater

Crested Butte CO

14318
Rock School Museum
POB 428, Crested Butte, CO 81224
General Museum - 1967
Coll: items of Croatian heritage; old
mining tools; samples of minerals;
antiques; old firewagon

Creswell NC

14319
Somerset Place State Historic Site
POB 215, Creswell, NC 27928
Historic Site - 1965
Coll: agriculture; dairy; ice house;
smoke house; kitchen storehouse;
kitchen-laundry; plantation; Colony
House (1820); Collins Mansion House
(1830)

Cripple Creek CO

14320
Cripple Creek District Museum, Inc.
E. Bennett Av, POB 475, Cripple
Creek, CO 80813
General Museum - 1953
Coll: pioneer artifacts; mining and
geological displays; Victorian furniture;
working assay office; photographic
history gallery - library; assay office

Crookston MN

14321
Polk County Historical Society
Hwy 2, POB 214, Crookston, MN
56716
General Museum - 1930
Coll: anthropology; transportation;
folklore; archaeology; graphics -
auditorium

Cross River NY

14322
Trailside Nature Museum
Ward Pound Ridge Reservation, Cross
River, NY 10518
Natural History Museum - 1937
Coll: birds of prey; songbirds;
mammals; insects; geology; Coastal
Algonkin Indians; Delaware Indians -
library

Crystal River FL

14323
**Crystal River State Archaeological
Site**
Rte 3, POB 457-H, Crystal River, FL
32629
Archeology Museum - 1965
Coll: archeology; Indian artifacts

Cullman AL

14324
Cullman County Museum
211 Second Avenue N.E., Cullman, AL
35055
General Museum
Coll: local historic items

Currie NC

14325
Moores Creek National Military Park
POB 69, Currie, NC 28435
History/Public Affairs Museum - 1926
Coll: weapons; diorama - library

Cushing OK

14326
Cimarron Valley Railroad Museum
South Kings Hwy, Cushing, OK 74023
History/Public Affairs Museum - 1970
Coll: railroad lanterns, timetables,
maps, passes, tools, signal equipment,
telegraph and depot equipment; dining
car; china and silver; uniforms;
standard gauge railroad track beside
station exhibits; wooden box car
(1902); tank car (1917); wooden Frisco
caboose (1900) - library

Dade City FL

14327
Pioneer Florida Museum
N Hwy 301, POB 335, Dade City, FL
33525
General Museum - 1961
Coll: articles depicting pioneer family
life in the state; local historical items

Dagsboro DE

14328
Prince George's Chapel
Route 26, Dagsboro, DE 19939
Religious Art Museum
Coll: ecclesiastical furniture;
decorative arts; chapel (1755)

Dallas NC

14329
**Gaston County Art and History
Museum**
131 N Gaston St, POB 429, Dallas, NC
28034
General Museum - 1975
Coll: contemporary art; regional
history; textile history; Old Gaston
County Courthouse (1848) - library;
reading room; classrooms

Dallas TX

14330
'Age of Steam' Railroad Museum
Fairground-State Fair of Texas, Dallas
TX 75201, 7226 Wentwood Dr, Dallas,
TX 75225
Science/Tech Museum - 1963
Coll: passenger and freight, steam, gas
and electric locomotives; trolley car;
small rail vehicles; equipment typical of
the 'Golden Age'era (1920-1950)

14331
Dallas Health and Science Museum
Fair Park, First and Forest Av, Dallas,
TX 75226
General Museum - 1946
Coll: medical artifacts; exhibition
anatomy; physical science; astronomy;
communications; veterinary medicine
- library; planetarium; auditorium;
classrooms

14332
Dallas Historical Society
Hall of State, Fair Park, POB 26038,
Dallas, TX 75226
History/Public Affairs Museum - 1922
Coll: artifacts; books; archive materials
relating to Texas history - library;
archives; auditorium

14333
Dallas Museum of Fine Arts
Fair Park, Dallas, TX 75226
Fine Arts Museum - 1909
Coll: European and American painting
and sculpture; ancient Mediterranean,
pre-Columbian, African, Oceanic and
Japanese art; decorative arts;
drawings; prints - library; auditorium

14334
Dallas Museum of Natural History
Fair Park Station, POB 26193, Dallas,
TX 75226
Natural History Museum - 1935
Coll: zoology; paleontology; mammals;
dioramas of Texas principal animals;
Boehm and Doughty bird collections -
library; auditorium

14335
McCord Theatre Collection
Southern Methodist University, POB
413, Dallas, TX 75275
Performing Arts Museum - 1933
Coll: Texas theatre history; all material
relative to the performing arts theater;
photographs; clipping files; artifacts -
library

14336
**Meadows Museum and Sculpture
Court** Southern Methodist University
Owen Fine Arts Center, Dallas, TX
75275
Fine Arts Museum - 1965
Coll: Spanish paintings, prints and
drawings from 1500 to Picasso;
modern sculpture from Rodin to Claes
Oldenburg - library

14337
Old City Park Dallas County Heritage
Society
1717 Gano, Dallas, TX 75215
General Museum - 1966
Coll: 22 historic structures from the
period 1840-1910; furnishings;
decorative arts; paintings; emphasis
on Texas materials - library

14338
**SIL (Summer Institute of Linguistics)
Museum of Anthropology, Inc.**
7500 W. Camp Wisdom Rd, Dallas, TX
75236
Anthropology Museum - 1974
Coll: ethnographic collections from
South America, West Africa, Central
America, Papua, New Guinea - library

Dalton MA

14339
Crane Museum
Housatonic St, Dalton, MA 01226
Science/Tech Museum - 1930
Coll: history of Crane & Co. in the fine
papermaking field since 1801 - library

Dana IN

14340
Ernie Pyle State Memorial
North of U.S. 36, Dana, IN 47847
Historic Site
Coll: house where Ernie Pyle was
born; period furniture; photographs;
Pyle's memorabilia

Danbury CT

14341
**Danbury Scott-Fanton Museum and
Historical Society, Inc.**
43 Main St, Danbury, CT 06810
History/Public Affairs Museum - 1942
Coll: 18th century furnishings including
working kitchen; Charles Ives parlor
and memorabilia; textiles; costumes;
toys; Indian artifacts; Charles Ives
homestead

Danville IL

14342
Vermilion County Museum Society
116 N Gilbert St, Danville, IL 61832
History/Public Affairs Museum - 1964
Coll: costumes; painting; sculpture;
graphics; decorative arts

Danville VA

14343
**Danville Museum of Fine Arts and
History**
975 Main St, Danville, VA 24541
History/Public Affairs Museum - 1974
Coll: paintings; memorabilia of area
and citizens; furnishings - classrooms

14344
**National Tobacco and Textile
Museum**
614 Lynn St, POB 541, Danville, VA
24541
Science/Tech Museum - 1971
Coll: historical data, artifacts, scientific
data and demonstrations pertaining to
the tobacco and textile industries past
and present - library

Darien GA

14345
Fort King George
POB 711, Darien, GA 31305
General Museum - 1961
Coll: aboriginal and Spanish artifacts;
reproductions of uniforms, weapons,
and accoutrements of the British
garrison

Darlington SC

14346
Joe Weatherly Stock Car Museum
Hwy. 34, POB 500, Darlington, SC
29532
History/Public Affairs Museum - 1965
Coll: stock cars; photos; trophies;
engines and parts; Hall of Fame of
stock car racers

Dartmouth MA

14347
**Children's Museum and Museum
Outdoors**
POB 98, Dartmouth, MA 02714
Junior Museum - 1971
Coll: natural history; dolls; shoes;
artifacts from countries - library;
classrooms

Davenport IA

14348
Davenport Municipal Art Gallery
1737 Twelfth St, Davenport, IA 52804
Fine Arts Museum - 1925
Coll: 19th and early 20th century
American paintings; Spanish Colonial;
Grant Wood Collection; Haitian
painting and sculpture; John Steuart
Curry Lithographs Suite - classrooms;
library

14349
Putnam Museum
1717 W 12th St, Davenport, IA 52804
General Museum - 1867
Coll: natural history; ethnology;
archaeology; botany; paleontology;
anthropology; arts of Asia; Near and
Middle East; Africa; Oceanic;
American Indian; pre-Columbian -
aquarium; reading room; auditorium;
classrooms; library

Davenport WA

14350
Lincoln County Historical Museum
POB 585, Davenport, WA 99122
General Museum - 1972
Coll: county and early agricultural
tools; costumes; furniture; guns -
library

Davis CA

14351
Entomology Museum University of
California
Davis, CA 95616
Natural History Museum - 1946
Coll: over three million arthropod
specimens - library

Daviston AL

14352
**Horseshoe Bend National Military
Park**
Rte 1, POB 103, Daviston, AL 37256
History/Public Affairs Museum - 1959
Coll: Indian artifacts; military gear and
historic documents of the 1814 period
- library; nature trail; tour road through
battlefield

Dayton OH

14353
Aullwood Audubon Center and Farm
1000 Aullwood Rd, Dayton, OH 45414
Open Air Museum - 1957
Coll: herbarium; natural history;
working farm including buildings,
housings, livestock and machinery;
pastures - library; nature center

14354
Dayton Art Institute
Forest and Riverview Avs, Dayton, OH
45401
Fine Arts Museum - 1919
Coll: European and American paintings
and sculpture; Classical, Oriental,
pre-Columbian primitive objects;
prints, ceramics and decorative arts;
archaeology - library; reading room;
auditorium; lecture hall; classrooms

14355
Dayton Museum of Natural History
2629 Ridge Av, Dayton, OH 45414
Natural History Museum - 1893
Coll: entomology; paleontology;
geology; archaeology; ethnology;
birds, mammals, insects, invertebrates,
herpetology; astronomy - library;
planetarium; Apollo observatory;
auditorium

14356
**Dayton Power and Light Company
Museum**
Courthouse Plaza SW, Dayton, OH
45401
Science/Tech Museum - 1942
Coll: historic artifacts pertaining to gas
and electricity utility industry

14357
Deeds Carillon and Celestron
2001 S Patterson Blvd, Dayton, OH
45409
Science/Tech Museum - 1974
Wright Brothers airplane (1905);
replica of Wright cycle shop; Concord
coach; B & O No.1 Grasshopper
locomotive; Barney & Smith railroad
coach (1903); covered bridge;
Stoddard Dayton auto (1908); Cadillac
auto (1912); blacksmith shop; open
streetcar; Conestoga wagon; original
lock of Miami and Erie canal; Newcom
Tavern (1798); pioneer home (1815)

14358
**Fine Arts Gallery at Wright State
University, Inc.**
Colonel Glenn Hwy, Dayton, OH
45431
Fine Arts Museum - 1974
Coll: contemporary works of art on
paper; contemporary 'in Situ' sculpture

14359
**The Montgomery County Historical
Society**
7 N Main St, Dayton, OH 45402
General Museum - 1897
Coll: Miami Valley history; decorative
arts; textiles; tools - library; lecture
hall; reading room

14360
Patterson Homestead
1815 Brown St, Dayton, OH 45409
Historic Site - 1953
Coll: antique and period furniture,
including pioneer, Victorian Eastlake,
Chippendale, Hepplewhite, Sheraton
and American Empire styles; portraits;
Patterson Homestead (1816) -
auditorium

Daytona Beach FL

14361
Halifax Historical Museum
128 Orange Av, POB 5051, Daytona
Beach, FL 32018
General Museum - 1949
Coll: early photographs; portraits;
documents and letters; Indian artifacts;
Civil War memorabilia; Florida folk
arts; antique dolls - library

14362
Museum of Arts and Sciences
1040 Museum Blvd, Daytona Beach,
FL 32014
Fine Arts Museum - 1971
Coll: contemporary collection of
paintings, prints, and photos by Florida
artists; 19th century American and
European fine and decorative arts;
18th-20th century Cuban paintings
from the collection of F. Batista;
Caribbean and Central American fine
and decorative arts - library; science
wing; planetarium

Deadwood SD

14363
Adams Memorial Hall Museum
54 Sherman, Deadwood, SD 57732
General Museum - 1930
Coll: costumes; geology; Indian
artifacts; mineralogy; military;
paleontology; pioneer room; authentic
pictures of Wild Bill and Calamity Jane;
gun collection; homestake engine
(1879); steam locomotive; Potato
Creek Johnny, largest nugget in the
world

14364
Deadwood Gulch Art Gallery
665 1/2 Main St, Deadwood, SD
57732
Fine Arts Museum - 1967
Coll: paintings; Chinese artifacts

Deansboro NY

14365
Musical Museum
Deansboro, NY 13328
Music Museum - 1948
Coll: Civil War melodeons;
nicklodeons (1900-1920); early pipe
organs; Swiss and American music
boxes; street organs (1880);
woodwinds; brass; strings; early
phonographs; early lighting; 1,000
early radios and related equipment -
library

Dearborn MI

14366
Dearborn Historical Museum
915 Brady St, Dearborn, Mi 48124
General Museum - 1950
Coll: textiles; decorative arts;
transportation; industry - library;
reading room

14367
Greenfield Village and Henry Ford Museum
Oakwood Blvd, Dearborn, MI 48121
History/Public Affairs Museum - 1929
Coll: 17th-20th century American decorative arts; 18th-20th century American mechanical and industrial art; Ford archives consisting of 14,000,000 manuscripts and documents, 450,000 historic photographs - library; reading room; theater; classrooms

Death Valley CA

14368
Death Valley Museum
Death Valley National Monument, Death Valley, CA 92328
Science/Tech Museum - 1933
Coll: archeology; history; anthropology; geology; herbarium; natural history; historic buildings - library

Decatur AL

14369
The Art Gallery John C. Calhoun State Community College
Room 237, Fine Arts Building, POB 2216, Decatur, AL 35601
Fine Arts Museum

Decatur IL

14370
Kirkland Fine Arts Center
Millikin University, Decatur, IL 62522
Fine Arts Museum - 1924
Coll: 19th and 20th century art - auditorium

•

Decorah IA

14371
Frankville Museum
Decorah, IA 52101
History/Public Affairs Museum - 1963
Coll: agriculture; archives; costumes; Indian artifacts; music

14372
Vesterheim, Norwegian-American Museum
502 W Water St, Decorah, IA 52101
Anthropology Museum - 1877
Coll: Norwegian immigrant items; comparative Norwegian material; wooden ware; textiles; furniture; silver; china; glass; tools; implements; architecture; painting; sculpture; Egge log house (1851); Haugen log house (1865); log schoolhouse (1880); drying house (1860); waterpower grain mill (1860); grist mill (1851), stone church (1863); Norwegian house (1860); immigrant farmstead (1850 - 1929) - reading room; classrooms; library

Deerfield MA

14373
Historic Deerfiels Inc
The Street, Deerfield, MA 01342
History/Public Affairs Museum - 1952
Coll: decorative arts; furniture; ceramics; silver; metalwork; houses of the 17th and 18th century - library; reading room

14374
Memorial Hall Museum Pocumtuck Valley Memorail ASSN
Memorial St, Deerfield, MA 01342
History/Public Affairs Museum - 1870
Coll: ceramics; pewter; musical instruments; architectural fragments; tin and woodenware - library

Defiance OH

14375
Au Glaize Village
POB 801, Defiance, OH 43512
General Museum - 1966
Coll: farm utensils; household items; clothing; local history; Mark Center Post Office (1875); St. John Luthern Church (1875)

DeKalb IL

14376
Ellwood House Museum
509 N First St, DeKalb, IL 60115
General Museum - 1965
Coll: barbed wire; costumes; Victorian furniture; buggies - library

De Land FL

14377
Deland Museum
449 E New York Av, POB 941, De Land, FL 32720
General Museum - 1951
Coll: natural history; Florida birds; dolls; fine arts; artifacts of local history; Indian baskets - library; ceramic studio

14378
Gillespie Museum of Minerals
Stetson University
De Land, FL 32720
Science/Tech Museum - 1958
Minerals

Delaware City DE

14379
Fort Delaware
Pea Patch Island in Delaware River, Delaware City DE 19706, 22 Boulder Brook Drive, Wilmington, DE 19803
History/Public Affairs Museum - 1950
Coll: materials and artifacts relating to Delaware's role in the Civil War; military items; marine; archeology; local historical items

Delray Beach FL

14380
The Morikami Museum of Japanese Culture
4000 Morikami Park Rd, Delray Beach, FL 33446
Anthropology Museum - 1977
Coll: historical materials related to the Yamato Colony of Japanese farmers; Japanese folk art; Edward N. Potter memorial Bonsai collection - library; botanical garden; reading room; nature trail

Del Rio TX

14381
Whitehead Memorial Museum
1308 S. Main St, Del Rio, TX 78840
General Museum - 1962
Coll: Roy Bean relics and date; Border War items; archives; Black Seminole Army Scouts; Indian relics - library

Delta CO

14382
Delta County Historical Society
POB 125, Delta, CO 81416
General Museum - 1964
Coll: North and South American butterflies; county newspapers and photographs; agricultural items; Indian artifacts; transportation and industrial exhibits - library

Deming NM

14383
Deming Luna Mimbres Museum
301 S Silver, Deming, NM 88030
General Museum - 1957
Louise Southerland Toys and Dolls Collection; Harry Cheney Minerals Collection; Bessie C. May Cdllection of Clothing from 1880-1950

Demopolis AL

14384
Marengo County Historical Society, Inc.
North Commissioners Ave, Demopolis, AL 36732
General Museum - 1961
Coll: costumes; archives

Denison TX

14385
Eisenhower Birthplace State Historic Site
208 E. Day, Denison, TX 75020
Historic Site - 1946
Coll: historic house (1881), where Dwight D. Eisenhower was born; furniture

Denton TX

14386
DAR Museum First Ladies of Texas Historic Costumes Collection
Texas Woman's University, TWU Station, POB 23975, Denton, TX 76204
Decorative Arts Museum - 1940
Coll: Inaugural ball gowns of Texas First Ladies; gowns worn by the wives of Vice President John Nance Garner, President Dwight D. Eisenhower and President Lyndon B. Johnson - library; auditorium

14387
North Texas State University Historical Collection
West Mulberry and Av A, Denton, TX 76203
General Museum - 1930
Coll: ethnography; military; antique weapons; Texas pioneer artifacts; regional archaeology

14388
Texas Woman's University Art Galleries
1 Circle Dr, Denton, TX 76204
Fine Arts Museum - 1901
Coll: paintings; sculpture; graphics

Denver CO

14389
Children's Museum of Denver, Inc.
931 Bannock St, Denver, CO 80204
Junior Museum - 1973
Coll: exhibits dealing with crafts, cultures, theater, cycle of life, handicaps, and career

14390
Colorado Heritage Center
1300 Broadway, Denver, CO 80203
History/Public Affairs Museum - 1879
Coll: historical artifacts of Colorado from prehistoric to present times; Mesa Verde archeology; costumes; late Victorian furnishings; Ute Indian materials; minerals - library; auditorium; classrooms; reading room

14391
Colorado Historical Society
1300 Broadway, Denver, CO 80203
History/Public Affairs Museum - 1879
Coll: anthropology; archeology; paintings; ethnology; historical and Indian items; numismatics; textiles - library; auditorium; classrooms; reading room

14392
The Denver Art Museum
100 W. 14th Av Pkwy, Denver, CO 80204
Fine Arts Museum - 1894
Coll: South Seas, African, British Columbian, American Indian, pre-Columbian, Southwestern and New England colonial, Peruvian folk art; 19th and 20th century American art; Mediterranean and European art; Oriental art; photography; Kress, Guggenheim, Hendrie, and Hanley collections - library

14393
Denver Museum of Natural History
City Park, Denver, CO 80205
Science/Tech Museum - 1900
Coll: ecological exhibits; specimen displays of archeology, minerals, gems, vertebrate and invertebrate paleontology, paleobotany, anthropology, insects, amphibians, reptiles, birds, and mammals - library

14394
Forney Transportation Museum
1416 Platte St, Denver, CO 80202
History/Public Affairs Museum - 1961
Coll: antique and historic cars, carriages, cycles, costumes, railroad locomotives, and coaches - reading room; theater

14395
Historic Denver, Inc.
770 Pennsylvania St, Denver, CO 80203
General Museum - 1970
Coll: furnishings; fashions; historic house - library

14396
The Molly Brown House
1340 Pennsylvania St, Denver, CO 80203
General Museum - 1970
Coll: memorabilia of Brown family; furnishings; historic house - library

14397
Museum of the Central City Opera House Association
910 Sixteenth St Nr 636, Denver, CO 80202
Performing Arts Museum - 1932
Coll: set designs and miniature sets; costume designs; restored parlors and rooms from the Victorian era; historic buildings - opera house; theater

14398
The Turner Museum
773 Downing, Denver, CO 80218
Fine Arts Museum - 1973
Coll: works of J.M.W. Turner, engravings, etchings, reprints, watercolors, prints, and drawings; paintings of Thomas Moran - library

14399
Veteran Car Museum
2030 S Cherokee, Denver, CO 80223
History/Public Affairs Museum - 1963
Coll: motoring clothes of the period; antique costume jewelry; old photographs and prints; antique, classic, and thoroughbred motor cars

Des Moines IA

14400
Des Moines Art Center
Greenwood Park, Des Moines, IA 50312
Fine Arts Museum - 1933
Coll: 19th and 20th century American and European paintings and sculptures - auditorium; classrooms; library

14401
Des Moines Center of Science and Industry
Grand Ave, Greenwood Park, Des Moines, IA 50312
Science/Tech Museum - 1965
Coll: rocks, minerals and fossils of Iowa - auditorium; library; planetarium; classrooms

14402
Iowa State Historical Department Division of Historical Museum and Archives
E 12th and Grand Ave, Des Moines, IA 50319
General Museum - 1892
Coll: geology; fossils; minerals; North American Indian archaeology; beadwork; pottery; lithies; two airplanes; firearms; glassware; china; household primitives; farm equipment; toys; mounted wildlife; money; transportation, cars, covered wagons, bicycles; Civil War - library

14403
Polk County Historical Society
317 S.W. 42nd St, Des Moines, IA 50312
General Museum - 1938
Coll: Historic Log Cabin (1843 - 1846) - library

14404
Salisbury House
4025 Tonawanda Dr, Des Moines, IA 50312
History/Public Affairs Museum - 1954
Coll: 15th-17th century furnishings and tapestries; paintings - library

Des Plaines IL

14405
Historical Society of Des Plaines
789 Pearson, Des Plaines, IL 60017
General Museum - 1969
Coll: furnishings; items of local history

Desert Hot Springs CA

14406
Cabot's Old Pueblo Museum
67-616 E. Desert View Ave, Desert Hot Springs, CA 92240
General Museum - 1969
Coll: Indian costumes and pottery; paintings; mineral specimens; Indian artifacts; Eskimo artifacts; historic house - library; classrooms; art gallery

Detroit Mi

14407
Children's Museum
67 East Kirby, Detroit, MI 48202
Junior Museum - 1917
Coll: ethnology; folk arts; musical instruments; costumes; textiles - library; planetarium; classrooms

14408
Detroit Historical Museum
5401 Woodward Ave, Detroit, MI 48202
History/Public Affairs Museum - 1945
Coll: maritime history; tools; furniture - library; classrooms

14409
The Detroit Institute of Arts
5200 Woodward Ave, Detroit, Mi 48202
Fine Arts Museum - 1885
coll: European, Modern and Ancient Art; Oriental art; French-Canadian art; African art - library; auditorium

14410
Dossin Great Lakes Museum
Belle Isle, Detroit, Mi 48207
History/Public Affairs Museum - 1948
Coll: ship models; paintings; antique and modern nauticalia - library

14411
Money Museum National Bank of Detroit
200 Renaissance Ctr, Detroit, MI 48243
History/Public Affairs Museum - 1059
Coll: coins; currency; medals; tokens; old coins - library

14412
State of Michigan Sports Hall of Fame Inc Cobo Hall
One Wahington Blvd; Detroit; MI; 48226, 1959 E. Jefferson, Detroit, Mi 48207
Anthropology Museum - 1955
Coll: bronze wall plaques and photos of each honoree

14413
Wayne State University Museum of Anthropology
Merrick and anthony Wayne Dr, Detroit, Mi 48202
Anthropology Museum - 1958
Coll: archaeology; history; West Indian artifacts; ethnology; glass - library

14414
Wayne State University Museum of Natural History
Crass & Warren, Detroit, MI 48202
Natural History Museum - 1972
Coll: birds; mammals; insects; vertebrates and invertebrates; plants

14415
Your Heritage House
110 East Ferry, Detroit, Mi 48202
Anthropology Museum - 1969
Coll: children's artifacts, including dolls, toys and games of the world from the 19th century to the present; paintings; graphics; photos - library

Dewey OK

14416
Dewey Hotel
8th and Delaware Sts, Dewey, POB 255, Bartlesville, OK 74003
Historic Site - 1967
furnishings of 1900; Delaware Indian artifacts

Dillon CO

14417
The Summit Historical Society
403 E. LaBonte St, POB 747, Dillon, CO 80435
General Museum - 1972
Coll: local historical furnishings; blacksmith shop with original tools; historic building - library

Dixon IL

14418
John Deere Historic Site
RR 3, Dixon, IL 61021
Historic Site - 1964
1836 Deere House

Dodge City KS

14419
Boot Hill Museum
500 W Wyatt Earp, Dodge City, KS 67801
History/Public Affairs Museum
Coll: artifacts and momentos of the era including furnishings, tools, guns, and other cowboy equipment; historic buildings of the 18th century - theater; library

Dorris CA

14420
Herman's House of Guns
204 S. Oregon St, Dorris, CA 96023
History/Public Affairs Museum
Coll: shoulder and hand guns; cannon and related items; Indian artifacts; household items; farm implements; Edison phonographs

Douglas WY

14421
Fort Fetterman State Museum
Douglas WY 82366, *mail c/o* Wyoming State Museum, Barrett Bldg, Cheyenne, WY 82002
History/Public Affairs Museum - 1963
Coll: military; artifacts; archeology

Douglass KS

14422
Douglass Museum
314-316 S Forest, Douglass, KS 67039
General Museum - 1949
Coll: Indian artifacts; tools; costumes; historic room

Douglaston NY

14423
Alley Pond Environmental Center
228-06 Northern Blvd, Douglaston, NY 11363
Open Air Museum - 1976
Coll: herbarium; archaeological artifacts; archives, maps and displays - library; nature conservation center; reading room; classrooms; recycling center; multi-purpose garden; interpretive trails

Dover DE

14424
Delaware State Museum
316 S. Governors Av, Dover, DE 19901
General Museum
Coll: work of American silversmiths; ceramics; furnishings; agricultural and tradesmen's tools; maritime and space exhibits; Indian artifacts; fire-fighting equipment; phonographs

14425
John Dickinson Mansion
Kitts Hummock Rd, Dover, DE 19901
Historic Site
Dickinson family furnishings

14426
Octagonal School
Cowgill's Corner, Rte 9, Dover, DE 19901
General Museum
historic building (1863); early educational artifacts

14427
Old State House
The Green, Dover, DE 19901
Historic Site
Coll: legislative, judicial, and government furniture; decorative arts; historic building (1792)

Dover NH

14428
Annie E. Woodman Institute
182-192 Central Ave, Dover, NH 03820
General Museum - 1916
Coll: mineralogy; insects; geology; herpetology; fire-fighting equipment; guns; whaling - library

Dover OH

14429
Dover Historical Society
325 E Iron Av, Dover, OH 44622
General Museum - 1958
Coll: historical maps; agriculture; archaeology; archives; paintings; costumes; geology; glass; music; mineralogy; period furniture; vehicles; communications; cameras

Dover TN

14430
Fort Donelson National Military Park
Hwy 79, Dover, TN 37058
History/Public Affairs Museum - 1928
Coll: Civil War memorabilia; historic house (1853) - library

Downey CA

14431
Downey Museum of Art
10419 S. Rives Ave, Downey, CA 90241
Fine Arts Museum - 1957
Coll: paintings; sculpture; graphics; photographs - galleries; community services room

Downieville CA

14432
Sierra County Museum
POB 224, Downieville, CA 95936
General Museum - 1932
Coll: replica of gold stamp mill; horse snowshoes; pictures; Indian and Chinese artifacts; historical items - library

Doylestown PA

14433
Mercer Museum of the Bucks County Historical Society
Pine and Ashland Sts, Doylestown, PA 18901
General Museum - 1916
Fonthill Museum; home of Henry Chapman Mercer, containing Mercer memorabilia, personal library, prints and engravings; and Mercer Tiles; artifacts; Henry Chapman Mercer collection of pre-industrial era tools and products; ceramics; Pennsylvania German items; folk art; crafts; paintings of Edward Hicks; artifacts - library

Dragoon AZ

14434
The Amerind Foundation, Inc.
POB 248, Dragoon, AZ 85609
General Museum - 1937
Coll: archeological specimens; ethnological material; ivory and scrimshaw; oil paintings and sculpture - library; reading room; separate laboratory operation

Drummond Island Mi

14435
Drummond Island Historical Museum
Drummond Island, Mi 49726
General Museum - 1961
Coll: archives; geology; Indian artifacts

Drumright OK

14436
Drumright Oilfield Museum
E Broadway on Hwys 99 and 33, Santa Fe Depot, Drumright, OK 74030
Science/Tech Museum - 1965
Coll: oilfield history; Old Santa Fe depot (1915)

Dubois WY

14437
Dubois Museum
POB 896, Dubois, WY 82513
Science/Tech Museum - 1976
Coll: logging and lumbering; Indian artifacts; timbering relics; wild life trophies; old ranch equipment; rocks; historical documents; photographs - library

Dubuque IA

14438
Mathias Ham Museum
2241 Lincoln Ave, POB 305, Dubuque, IA 52001
General Museum - 1964
Coll: local and natural history; Indians; explorers; lead mining; riverboating; woodworking; Civil War; Victorian Mansion (1839 - 1857); log cabin (1828); one-room school house (1883); wooden caboose (1907); CBQ caboose; log cabin

Duluth MN

14439
A. M. Chisholm Museum
506 W Michigan St, Duluth, MN 55802
General Museum - 1930
Coll: anthropology; natural history - library

14440
The St. Louis County Historical Society
506 W Michigan St, Duluth, MN 55802
History/Public Affairs Museum - 1922
Coll: paintings; books; shipping; mining; photographs

14441
Tweed Museum of Art University of Minnesota
2400 Oakland Ave, Duluth, MN 55812
Fine Arts Museum - 1950
Coll: graphics; sculpture; decorative arts; archaeology - library; reading room

Duncan OK

14442
Stephens County Historical Museum
Hwy 81 and Beach, POB 1294, Duncan, OK 73533
General Museum - 1971
Coll: anthropology; archaeology; paintings; sculpture; graphics; decorative art; costumes; ethnology; geology; Indian artifacts; mineralogy; numismatics; oil industry depicting exploration, drilling, completion and refining of oil; dioramas; philately; technology; transportation; gems and lapidary - library

Dunedin FL

14443
Dunedin Historical Society
94 Diane Dr, Dunedin, FL 33528
General Museum - 1969
Coll: local history; railroad history; historic house - library

Durham NC

14444
Duke Homestead State Historic Site
2828 Duke Homestead Rd, Durham, NC 27705
Historic Site - 1974
Coll: furnished house (1870); tobacco barn; well house; packhouse; third factory (1870); first factory (reconstructed); tobacco history

14445
Duke University Museum of Art
College Station, POB 6877, Durham, NC 27708
Fine Arts Museum - 1968
Coll: medieval sculpture and decorative art; classical pottery, glass, sculpture; Chinese jade and porcelain; African sculpture; pre-Columbian art; Peruvian textiles; Navajo rugs

14446
Museum of Art North Carolina Central University
POB 19555, Durham, NC 27707
Fine Arts Museum - 1971
Coll: contemporary painting, sculpture, and original prints, especially works from American minority artists; traditional African sculpture and artifacts

14447
North Carolina Museum of Life and Science
433 Murray Av, Durham, NC 27704
Science/Tech Museum - 1946
Coll: geology; paleontology; primatology; aerospace; primates; reptiles; prehistoric reconstructions of dinosaurs, reptiles, early man and saurs; bears; aircrafts; barnyard - nature trails; miniature railway; wildlife sanctuary

14448
Trent Collection in the History of Medicine Duke University Medical Center Library
Durham, NC 27710
Science/Tech Museum - 1956
Coll: history of medicine - library; reading room

Duxbury MA

14449
Duxbury Rural and Historical Society
Snug Harbor Station, POB 176, Duxbury, MA 02332
History/Public Affairs Museum - 1883
Coll: Pilgrim relics and histories; furniture; glass; silver - library

Duxbury MS

14450
Art Complex Inc
189 Alden St, POB 1411, Duxbury, MS 02332
Fine Arts Museum - 1967
Coll: Oriental, European and American paintings; modern and old prints - library

E Granby CT

14451
Old New-Gate Prison and Copper Mine
Newgate Rd, E Granby, CT 06016
History/Public Affairs Museum - 1969
Coll: mining and prison memorabilia housed in first U.S. state prison

Eagle AK

14452
Eagle Historical Society
Eagle, AK 99738
History/Public Affairs Museum - 1960
Coll: old photos; maps; court room; old machinery; vehicles; furniture

Eagle WI

14453
Old World Wisconsin
Eagle, WI 53119
Open Air Museum - 1976
Historic immigrant village; artifacts; furnishings; folklore

East Bloomfield NY

14454
Antique Wireless Association Museum
East Bloomfield, Main St, Holcomb, NY 14469
Science/Tech Museum - 1953
Coll: radio and communications; electricity and electronics - library; photographic library; magnetic tape library; motion picture collection

East Durham NY

14455
Durham Center Museum, Inc.
East Durham, NY 12423
General Museum - 1960
Coll: Indian and Pioneer tools and weapons; natural history; marine; little red schoolhouse (1850) - reading room

East Greenwich RI

14456
James Mitchell Varnum House and Museum
57 Peirce St, 36 Bayview Av, East Greenwich, RI 02818
General Museum - 1938
Coll: 18th century furnished rooms; historic house (1773)

14457
New England Wireless and Steam Museum, Inc.
Frenchtown Rd, East Greenwich, RI 02818
Science/Tech Museum - 1964
Coll: electrical communication equipment; stationary steam engines - library; auditorium; theater

East Hampton NY

14458
Guild Hall
158 Main St, East Hampton, NY 11937
Fine Arts Museum - 1931
Coll: works by regional artists; paintings and sculpture by Jackson Pollock, Balbomb Greene, James Brooks, Alexander Brook, Perle Fine, Lee Krasner Pollock, Childe Hassam, Thomas Moran

14459
'Home Sweet Home' Museum
14 James Lane, East Hampton, NY 11937
Decorative Arts Museum - 1928
Coll: Staffordshire and other English china; English lustre; American furniture of 17th, 18th, and 19th centuries; G. H. Buek collection of furniture; The Hook Mill; Pantigo Mill

East Haven CT CT

14460
Branford Trolley Museum
17 River St 27, East Haven CT, POB 457, Short Beach, CT 06405
Science/Tech Museum - 1945
Coll: electric street railway, interurban and rapid transit railway cars and equipment; models

East Lansing MI

14461
Kresge Art Center Gallery Michigan State University
East Lansing, MI 48823
Fine Arts Museum - 1959
Coll: 15th century European sculpture; 16th century prints and drawings; 17th century paintings - library

East Leansing MI

14462
The Museum Michigan State University
West Circle Drive, East Leansing, MI 48824
History/Public Affairs Museum - 1857
Coll: archaeology; paleontology; agriculture; vertebrates - auditorium

East Liverpool OH

14463
East Liverpool Museum of Ceramics
400 E 5th St, East Liverpool, OH 43920
Decorative Arts Museum - 1907
Coll: ceramics

East Prairie MO

14464
Towosahgy, State Archaeological Site
East Prairie MO 63845, *mail c/o* Hunter Dawson House, Dawson Rd, New Madrid, MO 63869
Archeology Museum - 1967
archaeology; anthropology

East Troy WI

14465
The East Troy Trolley Museum
POB 726, East Troy, WI 53120
Science/Tech Museum - 1972
Coll: antique streetcars from Wisconsin electric railways; technical data; early buses and trolley buses - library

East Windsor CT

14466
Connecticut Electric Railway Museum
58 North Rd, East Windsor CT, POB 436, Warehouse Point, CT 06088
Science/Tech Museum - 1940
Coll: electric transportation equipment from 1880 to 1947; specialized steam locomotives

Eastchester NY

14467
Eastchester Historical Society
POB 37, Eastchester, NY 10709
General Museum - 1959
toys; 19th century costumes; archives; photographs; Marble School House (1835) - library

Easton MD

14468
Academy of the Arts
Harrison and South Sts, Easton, MD 216601
Fine Arts Museum - 1958
Coll: painting; sculpture; prints; photography

Easton PA

14469
Northampton County Historical Society
101 S 4th St, Easton, PA 18042
General Museum - 1906
Coll: Moon portraits; Indian artifacts; antique dolls; costumes, uniforms, and military equipment; craft and trade implements - library

Eau Claire WI

14470
Chippewa Valley Museum, Inc.
Carson Park, POB 1204, Eau Claire, WI 54701
General Museum - 1964
Historical artifacts of the area; manuscripts; historic houses - library

Ebensburg PA

14471
Cambria County Historical Society
521 West High St, Ebensburg, PA 15931
General Museum - 1925
Coll: 19th century items; history; agriculture; industry; archives; numismatics; Indian artifacts - library; reading room

Edenton NC

14472
Historic Edenton, Inc.
S Broad St, POB 474, Edenton, NC 27932
General Museum - 1969
Coll: Cupola House (1725); Chowan County Courthouse (1767); Barker House (1782); James Iredell House (1759); St. Paul's Episcopal Church (1736) - North Carolina Department of Archives and History publications

Edgartown MA

14473
Dukes County Historical Society
Cooke & School Sts, POB 827, Edgartown, MA 02539
History/Public Affairs Museum - 1922
Coll: archaeology; herbarium; whaling collection; glass; china; scrimshaw; domestic tools - library; reading room

Edgefield SC

14474
Oakley Park, UDC Shrine
Columbia Road, Edgefield, SC 29824
General Museum - 1944
memorabilia of the Civil War; furniture and furnishings of the period

14475
Pottersville Museum
Route 2, POB 4, Edgefield, SC 29824
Decorative Arts Museum - 1970
Coll: stoneware made in Edgefield District from 1810 to 1870

Edgerton WI

14476
Albion Academy Historical Museum
1 Hwy A 1129, Edgerton, WI 53534
History/Public Affairs Museum - 1959
Original furniture; books of the Academy; school equipment - library; auditorium

Edinburg TX

14477
Hidalgo County Historical Museum
POB 482, Edinburg, TX 78539
General Museum - 1967
Coll: items pertaining to the history and culture of the Rio Grande Valley; citrus memorabilia; books; pictures; furniture - library

Edwardsville IL

14478
Madison County Historical Museum
715 N Main St, Edwardsville, IL 62025
General Museum - 1924
Coll: Indian artifacts; furniture; clothing; tools - library

Eglin Air Force Base FL

14479
Air Force Armaments Museum
3201/AFAM, Eglin Air Force Base, FL 32542
History/Public Affairs Museum - 1974
Coll: air force armament; aircraft - library; gun room; theater

Ekalaka MT

14480
Carter County Museum
Ekalaka, MT 59324
Natural History Museum - 1937
Coll: mounted dinosaur skeletons: Anatosaurus, Tricerytops skull, Pachycephalosaurus skull, Ichthyosaur skeleton; Flourescent minerals - library; reading room

El Dorado AR

14481
South Arkansas Arts Center
110 E. Fifth St, El Dorado, AR 71730
Fine Arts Museum - 1962
Coll: paintings; Oriental woodblock prints; Children's Oriental Collection - library; reading room; auditorium; theater; conference rooms; classrooms

El Dorado KS

14482
The Butler County Historical Society
POB 11, El Dorado, KS 67042
History/Public Affairs Museum - 1956
Coll: historical collections emphasizing local history; Indian artifacts - library

Elgin ND

14483
Grant County Museum
119 Main St, POB 100, Elgin, ND 58533
General Museum - 1970
Coll: railroad equipment; bedroom display and kitchen; pioneer items; old school desks; printing equipment; post office display

Elizabeth City NC

14484
Museum of the Albemarle
Rte 6, POB 132, Elizabeth City, NC 27909
General Museum - 1963
Coll: Indian artifacts; farm exhibits; old fire engines; lumbering items; duck carvings and decoys - library; theater

Elizabethtown NY

14485
Adirondack Center Museum
Court St, Elizabethtown, NY 12932
General Museum - 1954
Coll: dolls and toys; agricultural implements and household items; horse drawn vehicles; transportation; Colonial Gardens; Maple Sugar House - library; auditorium

Elk City OK

14486
Elk City Old Town and Museum
Pioneer Rd and Hwy 66, POB 542, Elk City, OK 73644
General Museum - 1967
Coll: music; costumes; glass; medicine; Rock Bluff School; Wagon yard; Western Rodeo - library

Elkhart IN

14487
Midwest Museum of American Art
429 S Main St, POB 1812, Elkhart, IN 46515
Fine Arts Museum - 1978
American paintings, prints, drawings, sculpture, and photography

Elkhorn WI

14488
Webster House Museum
Southwest Corner Rockwell and Washington, Elkhorn, WI 53121
General Museum - 1955
Coll: costumes; music; history; Indian artifacts; agriculture; historic houses - library; children's museum

Ellensburg WA

14489
Museum of Man Central Washington University, Dept. of Anthropology
Ellensburg, WA 98926
Anthropology Museum - 1890
Coll: ethnographic materials from New Guinea, Northwest Coast, Mexico, Western Plateau, Africa; archeology; ethnology - classrooms

Ellenton FL

14490
The Judah P. Benjamin Confederate Memorial at Gamble Plantation State Historic Site
Ellenton, FL 33532
Historic Site - 1926
Coll: historic mansion; antebellum furnishings

Ellis Grove IL

14491
Pierre Menard Home State Historic Site
POB 58, Ellis Grove, IL 62241
Historic Site - 1927
Coll: original furniture and artifacts of the early 19th century

Ellsworth KS

14492
Hodgen House Museum
104 W Main St, Ellsworth, KS 67439
General Museum - 1961
Coll: folklore; Indian; agriculture; archaeology; costumes - library

Elmhurst IL

14493
Lizzadro Museum of Lapidary Art
220 Cottage Hill Av, Elmhurst, IL 60126
Natural History Museum - 1962
Coll: precious and semi-precious gems; mineral specimens; crystals; geology - library; auditorium

Elmira NY

14494
Arnot Art Museum
235 Lake St, Elmira, NY 14901
Fine Arts Museum - 1913
14th, 17th, 18th, and 19th century European paintings; 19th-20th century American paintings; graphics; sculpture; decorative arts - pottery; printmaking; photography studios; classrooms

14495
Chemung County Historical Society, Inc.
304 Williams St, Elmira, NY 14901
General Museum - 1923
Coll: Civil War and Indian items; Mark Twain collection; industry; transportation; archaeology - library

14496
National Soaring Museum
Harris Hill Rd 1, Elmira, NY 14903
Science/Tech Museum - 1972
Coll: motorless aircraft; relevant
artifacts; archives of Soaring Society
of America; displays relating to
aerodynamics and motorless flights -
film library; library; reading room;
theater

El Monte CA

14497
El Monte Historical Museum
3150 N. Tyler Ave, El Monte, CA 91731
General Museum - 1958
Coll: art; household furnishings;
historical items and archives; farm
implements; natural history; historic
buildings - library; reading room;
theater

El Paso TX

14498
El Paso Centennial Museum
University of Texas at El Paso
University Av at Wiggins Rd, El Paso,
TX 79968
Natural History Museum - 1936
Coll: natural and human history;
archaeology; geology; paleontology;
mineralogy; Josephine Clardy Fox
collection of art objects - library

14499
El Paso Museum of Art
1211 Montana Av, El Paso, TX 79902
Fine Arts Museum - 1960
Coll: Kress collection of European art
(14th-17th century); American art;
pre-Columbian art; post-Columbian
decorative art; US and Mexican art -
library; auditorium; theater; classrooms

El Reno OK

14500
Canadian County Historical Society
Museum
600 W. Wade, El Reno, OK 73036
General Museum - 1968
Coll: railway exhibits; Indian artifacts;
pioneer furniture; barbed wire; tools;
vehicles; farm machinery; mounted
wildlife; - library

Elsah IL

14501
School of Nations Museum Principia
College
Elsah, IL 62028
Decorative Arts Museum - 1930
Coll: American Indian crafts;
decorative arts; textiles; costumes;
dolls; pottery; Oriental objects of art

Elverson PA

14502
Hopewell Village National Historic
Site
R.D. 1, POB 345, Elverson, PA 19520
General Museum - 1938
Coll: historic buildings and equipment;
furniture - library; auditorium

Elyria OH

14503
Lorain County Historical Society
Museum
509 Washington Av, Elyria, OH 44035
General Museum - 1889
Coll: genealogy; costumes; agriculture;
railroad; Indian artifacts; historic
buildings (1837-1909) - library

Emporia KS

14504
Richard H. Schmidt Museum of
Natural History Emporia State
University
1200 Commercial St, Emporia, KS
66801
Natural History Museum - 1959
Coll: skins and mounted specimens of
birds, fishes, reptiles, mammals;
ornithology; mammalogy; ichthyology;
herpetology

Encampment WY

14505
Grand Encampment Museum, Inc.
Encampment, WY 82325
Science/Tech Museum - 1965
Coll: costumes; glass; Indian artifacts;
mining; transportation - library

Enid OK

14506
Grace Phillips Johnson Art Gallery
Phillips University
University Station, Enid, OK 73701
Fine Arts Museum - 1966
Coll: paintings; sculpture; graphics;
decorative arts; early documents and
photographs pertaining to the
university

Ephrata PA

14507
Ephrata Cloister
632 W Main St, Ephrata, PA 17522
Historic Site - 1732
Coll: rare books; furniture; buildings of
medieval Germanic architectural style
(18th century) - library; auditorium;
theater

Ephrata WA

14508
Grant County Museum
742 Basin St NW, POB 1141, Ephrata,
WA 98823
General Museum - 1951
Coll: furnishings; early cattleman's
equipment; early history of county

Epping ND

14509
Buffalo Trails Museum
Epping, ND 58843
Natural History Museum - 1966
Coll: geology; mineralogy;
archaeology; natural history; regional
history and historic buildings (1906)

Erie PA

14510
Erie Art Center
338 W 6th St, Erie, PA 16507
Fine Arts Museum - 1898
Coll: paintings; sculpture; graphics;
decorative arts; photography

14511
Erie County Historical Society
417 State St, Erie, PA 16501
General Museum - 1903
Coll: local history; Cashier's House
(1839) - library

14512
Erie Public Museum and Planetarium
356 W Sixth St, Erie, PA 16507
General Museum - 1899
Coll: Moses Billings paintings; Eugene
Iverd paintings; pioneer artifacts;
costumes; Indian crafts; science; local
history - library; planetarium

Escanaba MI

14513
Delta County Historical Society
Ludington Park, POB 1776, Escanaba,
MI 49829
General Museum - 1947
Coll: aeronautics; anthropology;
archives; Indian artifacts

Essex Jct. VT

14514
Discovery Museum
51 Park St, Essex Jct., VT 05452
Junior Museum - 1974
Physical and natural science; art
gallery

Esterville IA

14515
Emmet County Historical Society,
Inc.
POB 101, Esterville, IA 51334
History/Public Affairs Museum - 1964
Coll: general collection pertaining to
Emmet County and country school -
library

Estes Park CO

14516
Estes Park Area Historical Museum
Hwy 36, Estes Park, CO 80517
General Museum - 1962
Coll: pictures and drawings of the
park; artifacts; implements; tools; early
pioneer articles

Eugene OR

14517
Butler Museum of American Indian
Art
1155 W 1st, Eugene, OR 97402
Anthropology Museum - 1974
Coll: baskets, pottery, weavings,
jewelry, clothing, masks and carvings,
dating from 18th century to present
and representing Southwest,
California, Northwest Coast,
Athapascan, Plateau, Great Basin,
Plains, Woodlands and Southeast
Indians - library; reading room

14518
Lane County Museum
740 W 13th Av, Eugene, OR 97402
General Museum - 1935
Coll: horse-drawn vehicles; clothing;
tools; utensils; household furnishings;
historic buildings - library

14519
Museum of Art University of Oregon
Eugene, OR 97403
Fine Arts Museum - 1930
Coll: Oriental and contemporary
Northwest art; contemporary
European art; works of painter Morris
Graves; American print collection;
paintings; sculpture; decorative arts;
Ghandaran and Indian sculpture;
Chinese funerary jade; Persian
miniatures; Syrian glass; West African
collection - library; reading room;
classrooms; garden and sculpture
court

Eureka CA

14520
Clarke Memorial Museum, Inc.
240 E. St, Eureka, CA 95501
General Museum - 1960
Coll: anthropology; archeology;
paintings; decorative arts; historical
items; Victorian collection; natural
history - library

Eureka Springs AR

14521
The Castle
Route 2, POB 375, Eureka Springs, AR
72632
Anthropology Museum - 1974
Coll: furniture of the early 1900's; early
tools, implements, and devices; radios,
cameras, projectors; talking machines
and phonographs; early appliances;
early medical and dental equipment

14522
Geuther Doll Museum
off Rte 23, North on Rte 187, POB 741,
Eureka Springs, AR 72632
Decorative Arts Museum - 1973
Coll: over 2,000 dolls, both modern
and antique, from all over the world -
library

14523
Miles Musical Museum
Hwy 62 West, Eureka Springs, AR
72632
Music Museum - 1960
Coll: nickelodeons; cylinder and disc
music boxes with bells; musical
singing bird boxes; mechanical musical
machines; early Edisons; Indian
artifacts; paintings; wood-carvings

Eureka UT

14524
Tintic Mining Museum
POB 218, Eureka, UT 84628
General Museum - 1974
Coll: history of the mines - library

Evanston IL

14525
Levere Memorial Foundation
1856 Sheridan Rd, Evanston, IL 60204
History/Public Affairs Museum - 1929
Coll: antique jewelry; exhibits
pertaining to early fraternity life and
customs; original Tiffany stained glass
windows - inter-fraternity hall of fame;
library

14526
Willard House WCTU Museum
1730 Chicago Av, Evanston, IL 60201
Historic Site - 1865
Coll: antique furniture; costumes;
pictures; items gathered from around
the world by Miss Frances Willard

Evansville IN

14527
Angel Mounds State Memorial
8215 Pollack Av, Evansville, IN 47715
Archeology Museum
Coll: Indian skeletons; Indian artifacts
of Middle Mississippi; photos of
excavations - auditorium; restored
village

14528
**Evansville Museum of Arts and
Science**
411 SE Riverside Dr, Evansville, IN
47713
General Museum - 1926
Coll: painting; sculpture; prints and
drawings; decorative arts;
transportation; arms and armor; steam
locomotive and cars; natural history -
library; planetarium; classrooms; town
hall

Eveleth MN

14529
United States Hockey Hall of Fame
Hat Trick Ave, POB 657, Eveleth, MN
55734
History/Public Affairs Museum - 1969
Coll: Cleve Bennewith skate collection
1850-1921 - library; theater

Evergreen CO

14530
Hiwan Homestead Museum
4208 S. Timbervale Dr, Evergreen, CO
80439
General Museum - 1974
Coll: Indian artifacts; historical items;
religious objects; period furnishings;
historic log house (1886) - library;
classrooms

Exira IA

14531
Audubon County Historical Society
Exira, IA 50076
History/Public Affairs Museum - 1960
Coll: Indian history - library

Exton PA

14532
**Thomas Newcomen Library and
Museum**
412 Newcomer Rd, Exton PA 19341,
POB 113, Downingtown, PA 19335
Science/Tech Museum - 1923
Coll: history of steam and steam
technology; working models of
Newcomen and other engines -
library

Fabius NY

14533
Pioneer's Museum
Highland Forest, Fabius, NY 13063
General Museum - 1959
Coll: settler's relics; agriculture;
archaeology; Indian artifacts; glass;
guns and military - children's museum;
library

Fairbanks AK

14534
University of Alaska Museum
University of Alaska, Fairbanks, AK
99701
Natural History Museum - 1929
Coll: ethnography; archeology;
geology; paleontology; herbarium;
botany; mammals

Fairfax VT

14535
Fairfax Historical Society
RFD 2, Fairfax, VT 05454
History/Public Affairs Museum - 1963
Coll: tools; photographs; historic
houses - library

Fairfield CT

14536
**Audubon Society of the State of
Connecticut**
2325 Burr St, Fairfield, CT 06430
Natural History Museum - 1898
Coll: mounted birds of Connecticut;
Shang Wheeler Decoy Collection -
library; auditorium; classrooms; animal
care facility; nature store; teacher
resource center

14537
Fairfield Historical Society
636 Old Post Rd, Fairfield, CT 06430
History/Public Affairs Museum - 1902
Coll: exhibits of local tools; kitchen
equipment; painting; early Fairfield
furniture; dolls; toys; cxlocks; textiles;
costumes; tableware; maritime
artifacts; Indian artifacts

Fairfield IA

14538
Fairfield Public Library Museum
Court and Washington Sts, Fairfield, IA
52556
General Museum - 1853
Coll: Indian artifacts; mounted birds;
rocks; Iowa pioneer items; mammals;
antiques - library

Fairfield VT

14539
**President Chester A. Arthur
Birthplace**
Fairfield, VT 05455
Historic Site
Coll: memorabilia; original furnishings

Fairhope AL

14540
Percy H. Whiting Art Center
401 Oak St, Fairhope, AL 36532
Fine Arts Museum - 1952
Coll: paintings by American artists -
three galleries

Fairlee VT

14541
Walker Museum
Fairlee, VT 05045
Decorative Arts Museum - 1959
Coll: regional American 18th and 19th
century fabrics, looms; furniture, farm
tools and wagons; East Asian art;
paintings - library

Fairplay CO

14542
South Park City Museum
POB 460, Fairplay, CO 80440
History/Public Affairs Museum - 1957
30 historic buildings from late 19th
century; furnishings

14543
South Park City Museum
POB 460, Fairplay, CO 80440
General Museum - 1957
Coll: 30 historic buildings from the
19th century; furnishings

Fairport Harbor OH

14544
Fairport Marine Museum
129 Second St, Fairport Harbor, OH
44077
Science/Tech Museum - 1945
Coll: naviagation instruments; marine
charts; pictures and paintings of ships;
lanterns; lighthouse lens; ship
carpenter's tools; models and half hulls
of ships; iron ore; Indian relics -
library; observation tower

Fairview UT

14545
Fairview Museum of History and Art
85 N 100 E, Fairview, UT 84629
General Museum - 1966
Coll: pioneer relics; historic farm
machines; geology

Fall River MA

14546
Battleship Massachusetts
Battleship cove, Fall River, MA 02721
Historic Site - 1965
Coll: equipment and memorabilia
connected with the operation of the
USS Massachusetts; USS Lionfish,
USS Joseph P. Kennedy during World
War II - library

14547
Fall River Historical Society
452 Rock St, Fall River, MA 02720
History/Public Affairs Museum - 1921
Coll: glass; china; costumes; guns;
marine - library; reading room

Fall River Mills CA

14548
Fort Crook Historical Museum
Fort Crook Ave & Hwy 299, Fall River
Mills, CA 96028
General Museum - 1963
Coll: agriculture; Indian artifacts;
industry; transportation; pioneer
homemaking; historical archives -
reading room

Fallon NV

14549
Churchill County Museum
1050 S Maine St, Fallon, NV 89406
General Museum - 1967
Coll: archives; mineralogy; music;
geology; glass; Indian artifacts

Farmington CT

14550
Farmington Museum
37 High St, Farmington, CT 06032
History/Public Affairs Museum - 1935
Coll: early American furniture; glass;
china; musical instruments; silver;
pewter

14551
Hill-Stead Museum
671 Farmington Av, Farmington, CT
06032
Fine Arts Museum - 1946
Coll: impressionist paintings; prints;
sculpture; antique furniture; Chinese
porcelain - library

Farmington ME

14552
Nordica Homestead
Holley Rd, Farmington, ME 04938
History/Public Affairs Museum - 1927
Coll: items relating to the life of Lillian
Nordica, opera singer - library

Farmington NM

14553
**San Juan County Archaeological
Research Center and Library at
Salmon Ruins**
Rte 3, POB 169, Farmington, NM
87401
Archeology Museum - 1973
Coll: historical; archaeological;
anthropological; root cellar, corral and
barn carriage house and adobe house
(1903) - library; audio-visual meeting
rooms; research center; restoration
laboratory

Farmington PA

14554
Fort Necessity National Battlefield
The National Pike, Farmington, PA
15437
Historic Site - 1931
Coll: history; historic buildings -
library

Farmington UT

14555
Pioneer Village
POB N, Farmington, UT 84025
General Museum - 1954
Coll: carriages; guns - library

Fayetteville AR

14556
University of Arkansas Museum
University of Arkansas, Fayetteville,
AR 72701
General Museum - 1873
Coll: prehistoric Arkansas Indian
artifacts; geology; ethnological
collections from Oceania, Africa, and
America; early American pressed
glass; Americana - library

Fayetteville NC

14557
Fayetteville Museum of Art
POB 35134, Fayetteville, NC 28303
Fine Arts Museum
Coll: contemporary North Carolinian
art; pottery - classrooms; garden

Fergus Falls MN

14558
Otter Tail County Historical Society
110 Lincoln Ave W, Fergus Falls, MN
56537
History/Public Affairs Museum - 1927
Coll: 10,000 artifacts dealing with
American Indians; norwegian and
scandinavian arts; photographs; maps
- library

Ferrisburgh VT

14559
Rokeby Ancestral Estate of Rowland
Evans Robinson
US Rte 7, Ferrisburgh, VT 05456
Historic Site - 1962
Coll: 18th and 19th century Vermont
furnishings; local history; writings of
Rowland Robinson - library

Ferrum VA

14560
Blue Ridge Institute
Ferrum, VA 24088
General Museum
Historical items from the area; farm tools and implements; folklife - library

Fessenden ND

14561
Wells County Museum
POB 345, Fessenden, ND 58438
General Museum - 1972
Coll: ethnology; pioneer tools and utensils; stoves; early hymnaries; hats; wearing apparel; photos; Hurd Round House (1902) - library; auditorium

Fiddletown CA

14562
Chinese Museum
POB 12, Fiddletown, CA 95629
General Museum - 1968
Coll: Chinese and early California artifacts; historic building

Fifield WI

14563
Price County Historical Society
Flambeau Av, Fifield, WI 54524
Science/Tech Museum - 1977
Artifacts of the logging era - library; auditorium; theater

Filer ID

14564
Twin Falls County Historical Society, Inc.
Rte 2, Filer, ID 83328
General Museum - 1957
Coll: period clothing; phonographs and musical instruments; Indian artifcts; massacre site collection; pioneer artifacts; historic buildings

Fillmore UT

14565
Territorial Statehouse
50 W Capitol Av, POB 57, Fillmore, UT 84631
Historic Site - 1930
Coll: pioneer furniture, tools, handicrafts; Indian artifacts - library

Fishers NY

14566
Valentown Museum
Valentown Sq, Fishers, NY 14453
General Museum - 1940
Coll: stores and shops furnished with original material; scientific exhibition (1830); archaeological Indian artifacts; Civil War materials

Fishkill NY

14567
Van Wyck Homestad Museum
Rte 9, Fishkill, NY 12524
General Museum - 1971
Coll: early Dutch settler artifacts; Revolutionary War items; archaeology; agriculture; technology - library; reading room

Fitchburg MA

14568
Fitchburg Historical Society
50 Grove St, POB 953, Fitchburg, MA 01420
General Museum - 1892
Coll: war relics; industries; invention; maps; musicla instrument; minerals - library; auditorium

Flagstaff AZ

14569
Museum of Northern Arizona
Fort Valley Road, Route 4, POB 720, Flagstaff, AZ 86001
General Museum - 1928
Coll: artifacts; Indian arts and crafts; geological and paleontological material; herbarium; historic house - library; reading room; field research station; laboratory

14570
Northern Arizona Pioneers' Museum
Fort Valley Rd, POB 1968, Flagstaff, AZ 86001
General Museum - 1953
Coll: photos, materials, and artifacts; local history; military items; Rough Riders' memorabilia; historic buildings - library

14571
Northern Arizone University Art Gallery
POB 6021, Flagstaff, AZ 86011
Fine Arts Museum - 1961
Coll: graphics; paintings; sculpture; ceramics

14572
Walnut Canyon National Monument
Rte 1, POB 25, Flagstaff, AZ 86001
General Museum - 1915
prehistoric Indian ruins of the Sinagua Indians - library; self-guided trails

14573
Wupatki National Monument
Tuba Star Rte, Flagstaff, AZ 86001
General Museum - 1924
Coll: pre-Columbian Indian artifacts of the Sinagua and Anasazi Indians - library

Flandreau SD

14574
Moody County Museum
East Pipestone Av, Flandreau, SD 57028
General Museum - 1964
Coll: antique autos and carriages; early dental office; pioneer utensils; Indian artifacts; all county newspapers

Flat River MO

14575
Lead Belt Mineral Museum
Forest and Taylor Aves, POB 81, Flat River, MO 63501
Natural History Museum - 1964
Coll: rocks and minerals

Flemmington NJ

14576
Raggedy Ann Antique and Toy Museum
171 Main St, Flemmington, NJ 08822
History/Public Affairs Museum - 1964
Coll: antique dolls; American dolls; antique toys; antique music boxes; cast iron; tin; baby carriages

Flint MI

14577
Flint Institute of Arts in the DeWaters Art Center
1120 E. Kearsley St, Flint, MI 48503
Fine Arts Museum - 1928
Coll: Renaissance and Baroque decorative arts; Chinese painting; jades; African sculpture - library; classrooms; auditorium

Flora MS

14578
Mississippi Petrified Forest
Petrified Forest Rd, POB 98, Flora, MS 39071
Natural History Museum - 1063
Coll: petrified wood of all types from around the US and the world; mineral collections; vertebrate and invertebrate fossil collection

Florence AL

14579
W.C. Handy Restored Birthplace and Museum
620 W. College St, Florence, AL 35630
Historic Site
Coll: artifacts and memorabilia related to the life of W. C. Handy

14580
Wesleyan Archives and Museum
University of North Alabama
POB 5206, Florence, AL 35630
General Museum - 1854
Coll: local archives; business machines

Florence AZ

14581
Pinal County Historical Society and Museum
2201 S. Main St, POB 851, Florence, AZ 85232
General Museum - 1959
agriculture, ranching, and mining of the local area; Indian, Spanish, Mexican and Anglo artifacts - library

Florence CO

14582
Florence Pioneer Museum and Historical Society
Pikes Peak Ave and Front St, Florence, CO 81226
General Museum - 1964
Coll: Indian artifacts; minerals; industrial artifacts; folklore; first city jail (1875) - library

Florence SC

14583
Florence Air and Missile Museum
US Hwy. 301, North Airport Entrance, Florence, SC 29503
Science/Tech Museum - 1963
Coll: 38 types of missiles, rockets and aircraft; artifacts - library

14584
Florence Museum
558 Spruce St, Florence, SC 29501
General Museum - 1936
Art of the Western World; paintings; primitive art; Amerindian ceramics; SC history rooms; Oriental ceramics and textiles; African sculpture

Florissant CO

14585
Florissant Fossil Beds National Monument
POB 185, Florissant, CO 80816
Natural History Museum - 1969
Coll: fossil insects, leaves, fish, and several other categories of fossils of the Oligocene period; archeological specimens; furnishings from 1870-1910 - library

Flushing NY

14586
Hall of Science of the City of York, Inc.
POB 1032, Flushing, NY 11352
Science/Tech Museum - 1964
Coll: technology; science; aeronautics; communications; energy; space science; environment; metrics; sound; light; engineering - planetarium; reading room; auditorium; classrooms; amateur radio station; weather station

14587
Queens College Art Collection
Paul Klapper Library, Flushing, NY 11367
Fine Arts Museum - 1957
Coll: ancient Oriental; Western and Contemporary art; graphics; paintings; glass; sculpture; prints - library

14588
The Queens Museum
City Bldg, Flushing-Meadow Corona Park, Flushing, NY 11368
Fine Arts Museum - 1972
Coll: paintings; sculpture; prints; photographs; panorama of the city of New York - theater; classrooms; workshop areas

Fond du Lac WI

14589
Galloway House and Village
336 Old Pioneer Rd, Fond du Lac, WI 54935
General Museum - 1955
Coll: Victorian household items and furniture; clothing; artifacts; historic houses - library

Fonda NY

14590
Mohawk-Caughnawaga Museum
Fonda Memorial Shrine of Catherine Takakwitha, R.D. 1, POB 6, Fonda, NY 12086
Archeology Museum - 1949
Coll: archaeology; North, South, and Central American Indian artifacts; Caughnawaga, excavated Iroquois village - library; nature trail; chapel

Forest Grove OR

14591
Pacific University Museum Pacific University
Forest Grove, OR 97116
Historic Site - 1949
Coll: Indian artifacts; Pacific University and Forest Grove artifacts; Oriental art objects; manuscripts; Old College Hall (1850)

Fort Atkinson WI

14592
Hoard Historical Museum
409 Merchant Av, Fort Atkinson, WI
53538
General Museum - 1933
Coll: local history; artifacts; agriculture;
local Indian culture - library

Fort Belvoir VA

14593
**United States Army Engineer
Museum**
16th and Belvoir Rd, Fort Belvoir, VA
22060
Science/Tech Museum - 1953
Coll: military engineering; uniforms;
photographs; paintings - library

Fort Benning GA

14594
National Infantry Museum U.S. Army
Infantry Center
Fort Benning, GA 31905
History/Public Affairs Museum - 1959
Coll: weapons; military art; local Indian
and early military archeological
materials; photographic archives;
collection of firearms - library

Fort Bliss TX

14595
Fort Bliss Replica Museum
Pleasonton and Sheridan Rds, Fort
Bliss, TX 79916
History/Public Affairs Museum - 1954
Coll: military hardware and uniforms;
military and civilian firearms; early
Southwest domestic items; Indian craft
- library

Fort Bragg CA

14596
Ft. Bragg Redwood Museum
90 W. Redwood Ave, Fort Bragg, CA
95437
General Museum - 1950
old logging and lumber mill artifacts;
photos

Fort Bragg NC

14597
**82nd Airborne Division War
Memorial Museum**
Ardennes St, Fort Bragg, NC 28307
History/Public Affairs Museum - 1957
Coll: history of World Wars I and II,
Dominican Republic and Vietnam;
trophies, documents, books,
photographs, mementos, relating to
the history of the 82nd Airborne
Division; U.S. and foreign materials,
weapons, uniforms, equipment, flags,
vehicles, aircraft, art - library; reading
room

Ft. Bridger WY

14598
Fort Bridger State Museum
Ft. Bridger, WY 82933
General Museum - 1928
Coll: history; Indian, military and
pioneer exhibits; industry;
anthropology; ethnology; archeology;
textiles; transportation; historic houses

Fort Calhoun NE

14599
**Washington County Historical
Museum**
14th and Monroe Sts, Fort Calhoun,
NE 68023
General Museum - 1938
Coll: Indian artifacts; furniture; glass;
toys; musical instruments - library;
reading room

Fort Campbell KY

14600
Don F. Pratt Memorial Museum
Wickam Hall
Fort Campbell, KY 42223
History/Public Affairs Museum - 1956
library

Fort Carson CO

14601
**Fort Carson Museum of the Army in
the West**
849 Oconnel Blvd, Fort Carson, CO
80913
History/Public Affairs Museum - 1957
Coll: uniforms; accoutrements and
firearms of the US foreign military
forces from the Revolutionary War
through the Vietnam War era - library;
theater; classrooms

Fort Collins CO

14602
Fort Collins Museum
200 Mathews, Fort Collins, CO 80524
General Museum - 1940
Coll: Folsom points and artifacts;
Indian artifacts; mineralogy; early
pioneer history of area

Fort Davis TX

14603
Fort Davis National Historic Site
POB 1456, Fort Davis, TX 79734
History/Public Affairs Museum - 1963
Coll: history; period weapons;
photographs; regimental records;
Indian artifacts - library; laboratory;
auditorium

Fort De Russy HI

14604
U.S. Army Museum, Hawaii Battery
Randolph
Kalia Rd, Fort De Russy, HI 96815
History/Public Affairs Museum - 1976
Military materials, domestic and
foreign, associated with the history of
the US Army in the Pacific - library

Fort Dodge IA

14605
Blanden Memorial Art Gallery
920 Third Ave S, Fort Dodge, IA
Fine Arts Museum - 1931
Coll: American and European paintings
and sculpture; 19th and 20th century
graphic art; drawings; Oriental
decorative arts; photography - studio-
art classroom; library

14606
Fort Dodge Historical Museum
Museum Rd, Fort Dodge, IA 50501
History/Public Affairs Museum - 1962
Coll: local Indian artifacts; items of
FortDodge history; costumes; country
schoolhouse (1855); blacksmith shop;
jailhouse

Fort Douglas UT

14607
Fort Douglas Museum
Building 32, Fort Douglas, UT 84113
Historic Site - 1975
Coll: military uniforms; documents;
military transportation - library

Fort Duchesne UT

14608
Ute Tribal Museum
Hwy 40, Bottle Hollow Resort, Fort
Duchesne, UT 84026
Historic Site - 1976
Coll: Indian and Early Western
American history; artifacts ; Ute
history - library

Fort Edward NY

14609
Fort Edward Historical Association
POB 106, Fort Edward, NY 12828
General Museum - 1927
Coll: archaeology; glass; Colonial-
Victorian period furniture; Indian and
Colonial War artifacts; broom-making
machine; Toll House

Fort Eustis VA

14610
US Army Transportation Museum
US Army Transportation Center, Fort
Eustis, VA 23604
Science/Tech Museum - 1959
Coll: transportation; military - archives

Fort Garland CO

14611
Old Fort Garland
POB 208, Fort Garland, CO 81133
History/Public Affairs Museum - 1858
Coll: military, pioneer, and Indian
artifacts; dioramas pertaining to period
from 1880

Fort Hood TX

14612
Second Armored Division Museum
Fort Hood, TX 76546
History/Public Affairs Museum - 1975
Coll: history relating to the 2nd
Armored Division; tank destroyer
units; weapons; German Nazi
memorabilia collection; flags; outdoor
static armored vehicle park - library;
TV room

Fort Huachuca AZ

14613
Fort Huachuca Historical Museum
POB 766, Fort Huachuca, AZ 85613
History/Public Affairs Museum - 1960
Coll: military history of the Indian
Wars; military and western artifacts -
library

Fort Jackson SC

14614
Fort Jackson Museum
Bldg. 4442, Fort Jackson, SC 29207
History/Public Affairs Museum
Coll: US military history - library

Fort Johnson NY

14615
**Montgomery County Historical
Society**
N.Y. Rte 5, Fort Johnson, NY 12070
General Museum - 1904
18th and 19th century furnishings,
textiles, and costumes; Mohawk Valley
Indian artifacts; Civil War and
Montgomery County artifacts - library

Fort Laramie WY

14616
Fort Laramie National Historic Site
Fort Laramie, WY 82212
Historic Site - 1938
Army; textiles; glass; historic houses
(refurnished)

Fort Lauderdale FL

14617
**Broward County Historical
Commission**
Rm 800, Courthouse, 201 SE 6th St,
Fort Lauderdale, FL 33301
General Museum - 1973
Coll: books, artifacts, documents, and
photographs; maps - library; reading
room

14618
**Fort Lauderdale Historical Society
Museum**
219 SW 2nd Av, Fort Lauderdale, FL
33301
General Museum - 1962
Coll: local archives; historical artifacts
- library; reading room; auditorium

14619
Fort Lauderdale Museum of the Arts
426 E Las Olas Blvd, Fort Lauderdale,
FL 33301
Fine Arts Museum - 1958
Coll: American and European
graphics; paintings and sculpture from
late 19th century to present; American
Indian artifacts; African tribal
sculpture; pre-Columbian ceramics;
Golda and Meyer Marks' COBRA
collection; Mai-Kai Oceanic collection
- library; reading room; classrooms

14620
International Swimming Hall of Fame
One Hall of Fame Dr, Fort Lauderdale,
FL 33316
History/Public Affairs Museum - 1965
Coll: Axel Nordquist sports stamp
collection; dioramas, murals, photos,
films, books, sculpture devoted
primarily to aquatic lore; memorabilia;
Olympic medals - library; auditorium

Fort Leavenworth KS

14621
Fort Leavenworth Museum
Reynolds & Gibbon Aves, Fort
Leavenworth, KS 66027
History/Public Affairs Museum - 1938
Coll: horse-drawn vehicles; wagons of
various types; military uniforms,
accoutrements and equipment from
1827 to present; general collections of
historic artifacts relating to missions -
library

Fort Lee VA

14622
**The United States Army
Quartermaster Corps Museum**
A Av at 22nd St, Fort Lee, VA 23801
History/Public Affairs Museum - 1957
Coll: uniforms; flags; insignia;
weapons; equestrian equipment

Fort Lewis WA

14623
Fort Lewis Military Museum
Bldg T4320, Fort Lewis, WA 98433
History/Public Affairs Museum - 1970
Coll: uniforms, equipment, weapons,
photographs related to the military
history of the Northwest - library

Fort Lyon CO

14624
Kit Carson Memorial Chapel
Veterans Administration Hospital, Fort
Lyon, CO 81038
Historic Site - 1957
Historical pictures of Kit Carson and
early history of entire area

Fort Madison IA

14625
North Lee County Historical Society
POB 385, Fort Madison, IA 52627
General Museum - 1962
Coll: collection of old school books;
diplomas; merit certificates

Fort McClellan AL

14626
Military Police Corps Museum
Bldg 3182, Fort McClellan, AL 36205
History/Public Affairs Museum
Coll: items pertaining to the history of
the military police corps

14627
Women's Army Corps Museum
US AMPS/TC & Fort McClellan, Fort
McClellan, AL 36205
History/Public Affairs Museum - 1955
Coll: military uniforms; war art;
costumes; music; archives pertaining
to the WAAC/WAC - library

Fort Meade MD

14628
**Fort George G. Meade Army
Museum**
4674 Griffin Av, Fort Meade, MD
20755
History/Public Affairs Museum - 1966
Coll: uniforms; weapons and
equipment of the U.S. Army from the
Revolution to the present; flags;
photographs; World War I and II
research collections; captured
German War art

Fort Mitchell KY

14629
Vent Haven Museum
33 W Maple, Fort Mitchell, KY 41011
Performing Arts Museum - 1973
Coll: 520 ventriloquial figures - library;
reading room

Fort Monmouth NJ

14630
**US Army Communications and
Electronics Museum** Myer Hall
Avenue of Memories, Fort Monmouth,
NJ 07703
Science/Tech Museum - 1942
Coll: evolution and development of
American military communications for
the Armed Forces; communications
equipment from foreign armies -
library

Fort Monroe VA

14631
Fort Monroe Casemate Museum
POB 341, Fort Monroe, VA 23651
History/Public Affairs Museum - 1950
Coll: models; dioramas; documents on
the history of Fort Monroe and Civil
War and Coast Artillery - library

Fort Morgan CO

14632
Fort Morgan Heritage Foundation
POB 184, Fort Morgan, CO 80701
General Museum - 1969
Coll: prehistoric Indian relics;
agricultural implements; photographs;
textiles and quilts

Fort Myers FL

14633
Edison Home Museum
2350 McGregor Blvd, Fort Myers, FL
33901
General Museum - 1947
Coll: historic house; Edison's
inventions - library; botanical garden

Fort Oglethorpe GA

14634
**Chickamauga-Chattanooga National
Military Park**
Fort Oglethorpe, GA 30741
History/Public Affairs Museum - 1890
Coll: Civil War relics; Fuller gun
collection of American military
shoulder arms; historic houses -
library; auditorium

Fort Pierce FL

14635
St. Lucie County Historical Museum
414 Seaway Dr, Fort Pierce, FL 33450
General Museum - 1965
Coll: Seminole Indian artifacts; fossils;
glass; shells; foreign and American
money; cattle brands, farm tools, and
equipment; firefighting equipment -
library; reading room

Fort Pierre SD

14636
Verendreye Museum
Fort Pierre, SD 57532
General Museum - 1966
Coll: ranching and homestead items -
library

Fort Riley KS

14637
**United States Cavalry Museum at
Fort Riley** United States Cavalry
Museum
Fort Riley, KS 66442
History/Public Affairs Museum - 1957
Coll: historical artifacts of the US
Cavalry and Fort Riley - reading room;
library

Fort Rucker AL

14638
U.S. Army Aviation Museum
Bldg 6007, Fort Rucker, AL 36362
History/Public Affairs Museum - 1962
Coll: aircraft; army aviation
memorabilia - an outside display yard;
library

Fort Scott KS

14639
Fort Scott National Historic Site Old
Fort Blvd
Fort Scott, KS 66701
Historic Site - 1965
Coll: Historic Buildings - library

14640
**Historic Preservation Association of
Bourbon County**
502 National Ave, Fort Scott, KS 66701
History/Public Affairs Museum - 1973
Coll: religious items; historic artifacts;
furnishings; documents - Library

Fort Sill OK

14641
**US Army Field Artillery and Fort Sill
Museum**
Fort Sill, OK 73503
History/Public Affairs Museum - 1934
Coll: U.S. Army field artillery for all
periods; U.S. Cavalry, Infantry and
Indian items for Western frontier
period; military ordnance, uniforms,
equipment, horse furnishings, vehicles,
paintings, prints - library; reading
room

Fort Smith AR

14642
Fort Smith Art Center
423 N. 6th St, Fort Smith, AR 72901
Fine Arts Museum - 1948
Coll: contemporary American
paintings; graphics; sculpture;
decorative arts - classrooms

14643
Fort Smith National Historic Site
POB 1406, Fort Smith, AR 72902
History/Public Affairs Museum - 1961
Coll: historic buildings - library

Fort Walton Beach FL

14644
Temple Mound Museum
139 Miraclestrip Parkway, SE, Fort
Walton Beach, FL 32548
Anthropology Museum - 1962
Coll: lithic and ceramic artifacts of
local aboriginal origin - library; reading
room

Fort Wayne IN

14645
**Allen County-Fort Wayne Historical
Society Museum**
302 E Berry St, Fort Wayne, IN 46802
General Museum - 1926
Coll: manuscripts and archives
pertaining to local history; 19th and
20th century costumes; paintings;
toys; china and glass; Indian artifacts;
industrial products and equipment -
library

14646
Fort Wayne Museum of Art
1202 W Wayne St, Fort Wayne, IN
46804
Fine Arts Museum - 1922
Coll: 19th and 20th century prints and
paintings; pioneer painters of Indiana;
Japanese woodcuts; West African
sculpture; medieval and ancient
sculpture; Weatherhead and
Tannenbaum contemporary art;
Fairbanks print collection; 19th and
20th century Theime and Hamilton
collections of prints and paintings

14647
Historic Fort Wayne, Inc.
107 S Clinton St, Fort Wayne, IN
46802
History/Public Affairs Museum - 1971
Coll: reconstructed fort; local history
from the Ice Age to 1819

14648
**Louis A. Warren Lincoln Library and
Museum**
1300 S Clinton St, Fort Wayne, IN
46801
History/Public Affairs Museum - 1928
Coll: books and pamphlets exclusively
on Lincoln; periodicals and clippings;
paintings; original photographs;
manuscript collections - library

Fort Worth TX

14649
**Amon Carter Museum of Western
Art**
3501 Camp Bowie Blvd, POB 2365,
Fort Worth, TX 76113
Fine Arts Museum - 1961
Coll: American painting; photographs;
Carter collection of Remington and
Russell works; Sid W. Richardson
collection of paintings of the Western
frontier; Jo and Fred Mazulla
photographic collection - library;
theatre; microfilm archive

14650
Fort Worth Art Museum
1309 Montgomery St, Fort Worth, TX
76107
Fine Arts Museum - 1910
Coll: paintings (20th century);
sculpture; drawings; photographs;
video tapes; prints - library

14651
**Fort Worth Museum of Science and
History**
1501 Montgomery St, Fort Worth, TX
76107
Natural History Museum - 1939
Coll: acarology; archeology; botany;
entomology; malacology; herpetology
- library; laboratory; planetarium;
auditorium; classrooms

14652
Kimbell Art Museum
Will Rogers Rd, POB 9440, Fort Worth,
TX 76107
Fine Arts Museum - 1972
Coll: European paintings, sculpture,
drawings and prints from prehistoric
to early 20th century; pre-Columbian
objects; Asian and African sculpture -
library; auditorium

14653
**Log Cabin Village Historical
Complex**
2100 Log Cabin Village Lane, Fort
Worth, TX 76107
Open Air Museum - 1963
Coll: log cabins furnished with
authentic artifacts of the 19th century

14654
Museum of Aviation Group
300 North Spur 341, Fort Worth, TX
76108
Science/Tech Museum - 1972
Coll: aircraft; associated equipment
and documents; pictures; plaques;
certificates; publications - library

14655
Pate Museum of Transportation
Hwy 377, POB 711, Fort Worth, TX
76101
Science/Tech Museum - 1969
Coll: antique and classic autos;
aircraft; railroad artifacts - library

Fort Yukon AK

14656
Dinjii Zhuu Enjit Museum
POB 42, Fort Yukon, AK 99740
General Museum - 1976
Coll: history of the Athapascan Indians
of the Yukon Flats region; artifacts;
photographs - library; reading room

Fountain City IN

14657
Levi Coffin House
U.S. 27, POB 77, Fountain City, IN
47341
Historic Site
Coll: furnishings of the period; historic
house which served as a stop for
fleeing slaves on the Underground
Railroad

Frankfort KY

14658
Kentucky Military History Museum
East Main St, POB H, Frankfort, KY
40602
History/Public Affairs Museum - 1974
rifles; flags; uniforms; weapons;
accoutrements - library

Frankfort SD

14659
Fisher Grove Country School
RR 1, POB 130, Frankfort, SD 57440
General Museum
Coll: Deiter School (1884); articles
from schoolhouse

Franklin Center PA

14660
The Franklin Mint Museum of Art
c/o Franklin Mint, Franklin Center, PA
19091
Fine Arts Museum - 1973
Franklin Mint collectables: medals,
ingots, plates, philatelic-numismatic
combinations, coin of the Realm;
objects in porcelain and crystal; limited
edition lithographs and etchings;
pewter figures; bronze sculpture and
leatherbound books; artifacts of Great
Americans - audio-visual facilities

Franklin IN

14661
Johnson County Historical Museum
150 W Madison St, RFD 2, POB 57,
Franklin, IN 46131
General Museum - 1023
Coll: a century of fashions; Indian
artifacts; medical itmes; World War I
and II guns and equipment; farm tools
and items; historic building - library

Franklin OH

14662
Harding Museum
302 Park Av, Franklin, OH 45005
General Museum - 1972
Coll: war memorials and personal
effects of Major-General E. Forrest
Harding; local history - library; reading
room

Franklin TN

14663
Carter House
1140 Columbia Av, Franklin, TN 37064
General Museum - 1951
Coll: artifacts of Ante-Bellum era; Civil
War relics; clothing; house furnishings;
historic house (1830) - library

Franklin WI

14664
EAA Air Museum Foundation, Inc.
11311 W Forest Home Av, Franklin, WI
53132
Science/Tech Museum - 1963
Coll: aeronautics; aircraft: pre-1900,
military, rotor craft, gliders, engines;
photos - library; auditorium

Frederica DE

14665
Barratt's Chapel and Museum
R.D. 1, POB 25, Frederica, DE 19946
Religious Art Museum - 1964
Coll: church records; artifacts; chapel
(1780) - library

14666
**Bowers Beach Maritime Museum
Inc.**
Cooper Av, N. Bowers Beach,
Frederica, DE 19946
General Museum - 1976
Coll: paintings and water colors by
local Delaware artists; artifacts from
old 2-masted schooners; artifacts from
shores of Delaware Bay; passenger
and freight boats

Fredericksburg TX

14667
The Admiral Nimitz Center
340 E. Main St, Fredericksburg, TX
78624
History/Public Affairs Museum - 1967
Coll: World War II relics; aircraft;
tanks; guns; landing craft; items and
photographs relating to the career of
Admiral Nimitz and the war in the
Pacific; Japanese style garden;
Garden of Peace - library; auditorium

Fredericksburg VA

14668
Belmont The Gari Melchers Memorial
Gallery
224 Washington St, Fredericksburg,
VA 22401
Fine Arts Museum - 1975
Coll: paintings and sketches by Gari
Melchers; European antiquities; china
and furnishings

14669
**Fredericksburg National Military
Park**
1301 Lafayette Blvd, Fredericksburg,
VA 22401
Open Air Museum - 1927
Coll: military artifacts; Civil War
military history - library; auditorium

14670
**Historic Fredericksburg Foundation
Museum**
623 Caroline St, POB 162,
Fredericksburg, VA 22401
General Museum - 1965
Coll: ladies costumes; Civil War
exhibits; transportation

14671
Hugh Mercer Apothecary Shop
1020 Caroline St, Fredericksburg, VA
22401
Historic Site - 1761
Coll: pharmaceutical and medical
implements

14672
**James Monroe Museum and
Memorial Library**
908 Charles St, Fredericksburg, VA
22401
History/Public Affairs Museum - 1928
Coll: Louis XVI furniture; costumes;
jewelery; possessions of President
James Monroe - library

14673
Kenmore
1201 Washington Av, Fredericksburg,
VA 22401
Decorative Arts Museum - 1922
Coll: 18th century decorative and fine
arts

Fredonia KS

14674
**Wilson County Historical Society
Museum**
416 N 7th, POB 477, Fredonia, KS
66736
History/Public Affairs Museum - 1962
Coll: pioneer relics related to farming,
industry, schools, churches,
household; Indian artifacts; costumes;
toys, books and clothing; photographs;
archives; glass - library

Fredonia NY

14675
**Historical Museum of the D.R. Barker
Library**
20 E Main St, Fredonia, NY 14036
General Museum - 1884
Coll: portraits and photographs; period
costumes and accessories; military
uniforms and records; documents and
records; tools and equipment - library

14676
**Michael C. Rockefeller Arts Center
Gallery**
State University College, Fredonia, NY
14063
Fine Arts Museum - 1826
contemporary sculpture, paintings and
drawings

Freehold NJ

14677
**Monmouth County Historical
Association**
70 Court St, Freehold, NJ 07728
History/Public Affairs Museum - 1898
Coll: paintings; 17th-19th century
furnishing and decorations; ceramics -
library

Freeman SD

14678
**Heritage Hall Museum and Historical
Library**
Freeman, SD 57029
General Museum - 1940
Coll: natural history and archives; old
church and schoolhouse; local cultural
artifacts; Indian artifacts - library

Freeport IL

14679
The Freeport Art Museum
511 S Liberty, Freeport, IL 61032
Fine Arts Museum - 1975
Coll: W.T. Rawleigh art collection;
American Indian art; textiles; primitive
and Oriental art; cross-cultural
ceramics; Islamic art; 19th century
European painting; bronzes; marbles

Fremont OH

14680
**The Rutherford B. Hayes Library and
Museum**
1337 Hayes Av, Fremont, OH 43420
History/Public Affairs Museum - 1911
Coll: Hayes family memorabilia; the
President's carriage; Civil War relics;
Abraham Lincoln's White House desk,
side table; Indian relics; weapons;
Hayes residence (1859); Dillon House
(1873); White House gates - library;
reading room; auditorium

Fresno CA

14681
The Discovery Center
1944 N. Winery Ave, Fresno, CA
93703
Science/Tech Museum - 1953
Coll: local habitat diaramas; Indian
artifacts; Yokuts baskets - science
center; cactus garden

14682
Fresno Arts Center
3033 E. Yale Ave, Fresno, CA 93703
Fine Arts Museum - 1949
Coll: Oriental, pre-Columbian, Mexican,
contemporary local and California
works of art; graphics - library;
classrooms; galleries

14683
**Fresno City and County Historical
Society**
7160 W. Kearney Blvd, Fresno, CA
93706
General Museum - 1919
Coll: clothing; furniture; household and
farm items; archives; photos - library

Friday Harbor WA

14684
San Juan Historical Society
POB 441, Friday Harbor, WA 98250
General Museum - 1961
Coll: artifacts, furniture, tools,
machinery, photographs relating to
history and citizens of San Juan Island
- library

14685
**San Juan Island National Historical
Park**
300 Cattle Point Rd, Friday Harbor,
WA 98250
General Museum - 1966
Artifacts associated with the Pig War,
the US Army and British Royal
Marines; historic houses - library

Front Royal VA

14686
Warren Rifles Confederate Museum
95 Chester St, Front Royal, VA 22630
History/Public Affairs Museum - 1959
Coll: relics of the War between the
States, including guns, uniforms, flags,
bayonets - library

Fullerton CA

14687
Museum of North Orange County
301 N. Pomona Ave, Fullerton, CA
92632
General Museum - 1973
Coll: paleontology; North Orange
County area local history - auditorium

Fulton Mo

14688
**Winston Churchill Memorial and
Library in the United States**
7th and Westminster Aves, Fulton, Mo
65251
Historic Site - 1962
Coll: Churchill memorabilia; Wren
architecture; rare historical map
collection - library

Gadsden AL

14689
Gadsden Museum of Fine Arts, Inc.
856 Chestnut St, Gadsden, AL 35902
Fine Arts Museum - 1965
Coll: paintings; antique dishware;
antiques

Gaffney SC

14690
Limestone College
Limestone College, POB 29, Gaffney,
SC 29340
History/Public Affairs Museum - 1976
Coll: college memorabilia; local history;
South Carolina history - library

Gainesville FL

14691
Florida State Museum University of
Florida
Gainesville, FL 32611
Natural History Museum - 1917
Coll: Southeastern US and Caribbean
area mammals; birds and bird eggs;
fish; reptiles; zooarcheology;
ichthyology; natural history -
classrooms

14692
University Gallery University of
Florida
Gainesville, FL 32611
Fine Arts Museum - 1965
Coll: Florida archives of photography;
Indian sculptures and painting; African
sculpture; pre-Columbian artifacts;
graphics; decorative arts - library

Galena IL

14693
**Old Market House State Historic
Site**
Market Square, Galena, IL 61036
Historic Site - 1947
Coll: 1845 Greek Revival house; local
history

14694
**Uslyssus S. Grant Home State
Historic Site**
61036, Bouthillier St, Galena, IL
Historic Site - 1932
Coll: U.S. Grant memorabilia; Victorian
furnishings; historic buildings - library

Galesburg IL

14695
Carl Sandburg Birthplace, Inc.
331 E Third St, Galesburg, IL 61401
Historic Site - 1945
antique furniture; belongings of the
Sandburg family; Sandburg burial site

Galeton PA

14696
Pennsylvania Lumber Museum
POB K, Galeton, PA 16922
Agriculture Museum - 1970
Coll: logging tools and equipment;
sawmill; furnishings; natural history -
library; outdoor museum; auditorium

Gallatin TN

14697
**Cragfont Project Summer County
Association for Preservation of
Tennessee Antiquities**
Highway 25, Gallatin, TN 37066, Rte. 1,
POB 42, Castalian Springs, TN 37031
General Museum - 1958
Coll: historic house (1798); American
Federal furnishings; stenciled walls in
parlor; antique farming tools; archives
- library

Galliopolis OH

14698
French Art Colony
530 First Av, POB 472, Galliopolis, OH
45631
Fine Arts Museum - 1971
Coll: contemporary art - library;
classrooms

Galveston TX

14699
Galveston County Museum
2219 Market St, Galveston, TX 77553
History/Public Affairs Museum - 1971
Coll: artifacts of coastal Indian origin
(1500-1950); Texas navy artifacts;
archives - library; auditorium

14700
Rosenberg Library
2310 Sealy Av, Galveston, TX 77550
General Museum - 1900
Coll: archives; Indian artifacts; folklore;
maritime and Gulf of Mexico history;
paintings; sculpture; graphics;
archaeology; decorative arts - library

Ganado AZ

14701
**Hubbell Trading Post National
Historic Site**
POB 150, Ganado, AZ 86505
General Museum - 1876
Coll: Indian arts and crafts;
furnishings; archives; military items;
archeological and ethnological items;
historic buildings - library

Garden City KS

14702
**Finney County Kansas Historical
Society**
Finnup Park S 4, Garden City, KS
67846 POB 59
History/Public Affairs Museum - 1958
Coll: old newspaper clippings; antique
cars; dental office equipment; antique
musical instruments - library

Gardner KS

14703
Lanesfield Historical Society
R.R. 1, POB 156, Gardner, KS 66030
History/Public Affairs Museum - 1965
Coll: school room furniture;
schoolhouse; wood tools; clocks; pots
and pans; church articles

Garnavillo IA

14704
Garnavillo Historical Museum
Garnavillo, IA 52049
General Museum - 1965
Coll: archives; archaeology;
anthropology; general history; Indian
artifacts; restored furnished Log
Cabin; Log Hall (1860) - library

Garnett KS

14705
Anderson County Historical Museum
Court House
Garnett, KS 66032
General Museum - 1968
Coll: guns; history of early settlers;
Indian artifacts

Garrett IN

14706
Garrett Historical Museum
Rte 1, POB 19, Garrett, IN 46738
General Museum - 1971
Coll: railroad memorabilia; local history

Gastonia NC

14707
**Schiele Museum of Natural History
and Planetarium**
1500 E Garrison Blvd, POB 953,
Gastonia, NC 28052
Natural History Museum - 1960
Coll: eggs; birds; reptiles; amphibians;
mammals; fish; minerals; fossils; shells;
habitat exhibits of North America's
mammals; insects; archaeology;
wildflowers; trees and shrubs of the
Carolinas; pioneer site (1754); North
Carolinan hall of Natural History; The
Goodliest Land - library; planetarium;
nature trail; learning center; auditorium

Gates Mills OH

14708
Gates Mills Historical Society
Old Mill Rd, Gates Mills, OH 44040
General Museum - 1946
Coll: interior furnishings; kitchen
utensils; local memorabilia - library

Gatlinburg TN

14709
Cades Cove Open-Air Museum
Great Smoky Mountains National
Park, Gatlinburg, TN 37738
Open Air Museum - 1951
Coll: water powered grist mill

14710
Sugarlands Visitor Center
Great Smoky Mountains National
Park, Gatlinburg, TN 37738
Natural History Museum - 1961
Coll: herbarium; insect specimens -
library; auditorium

Geneso NY

14711
Fine Arts Gallery State University
College of Arts and Science
Fine Arts Building, Geneso, NY 14454
Fine Arts Museum - 1967
Coll: paintings; graphics; sculpture;
ceramics; furniture - library

14712
Livingston County Historical Society
30 Center St, Geneso, NY 14454
General Museum - 1876
Coll: agriculture; transportation;
military; archaeology; Concord Coach;
Shaker prayer stone; china; education;
silver; antique fire apparatus

Geneva NY

14713
**Geneva Historical Society and
Museum**
543 S Main St, Geneva, NY 14456
General Museum - 1884
Coll: Federal, Empire, and Victorian
furnishings; archival material; industrial
items; Prouty-Chew House (1825);
Rose Hill Mansion (1839) - library;
reading room; auditorium

Geneva OH

14714
Shandy Hall
6333 S Ridge W, Geneva, OH 44041
Historic Site - 1935
Coll: furnishings; clothes; books; toys;
Shandy Hall (1815)

Georgetown CO

14715
Georgetown Society Inc.
POB 657, Georgetown, CO 80444
General Museum - 1971
Coll: original furnishings and
woodwork; mining memorabilia;
historic houses from late 19th century

14716
Hotel de Paris
Georgetown, CO 80444
Historic Site - 1875
Coll: original furniture, dishes, utensils
pertaining to a 19th century hotel;
building (1875)

Georgetown SC

14717
Hopsewee Plantation
Route 2, POB 197-B, Georgetown, SC
29440
General Museum - 1970
Coll: eighteenth and nineteenth
century furniture and furnishings

14718
The Rice Museum
Lafayette Park, Front and Screven Sts,
Georgetown, SC 29440
General Museum - 1968
Coll: rice culture in South Carolina low
country; Clock and Bell Tower (1842)
- auditorium

Gering NE

14719
Oregon Trail Museum
POB 427, Gering, NE 69341
General Museum - 1935
Coll: paintings relating to theme of
'Overland Migrations' along the
Oregon, Califorina, and Mormon Trials;
paleontology; archaeology - library

Gettysburg PA

14720
Adams County Historical Society
Lutheran Seminary Campus,
Gettysburg, PA 17325
General Museum - 1934
Coll: archives; Indian artifacts - library

14721
Gettysburg National Military Park
Gettysburg, PA 17325
History/Public Affairs Museum - 1895
Coll: 14,000 item Rosensteel Civil War
Collection; 30 Civil War period farms;
Paul Philippoteaux's Gettysburg
Cyclorama - library; Gettysburg
National Cemetery

Giddings TX

14722
Lee County Museum
190 E. Industry, Giddings, TX 78942
General Museum - 1966
Coll: ethnology; household artifacts;
agriculture tools; archives

Gillette WY

14723
Rockpile Museum
Hwy 14-16 West Gillette, POB 922,
Gillette, WY 82716
General Museum - 1974
Coll: Indian artifacts; guns; cowboy
equipment; pioneer and homestead
items; local historical newspapers

Glen Ellen CA

14724
Jack London State Historic Park
End of London Ranch Rd, Glen Ellen,
CA 95442, POB 167, Sonoma, CA
95476
Historic Site - 1959
Coll: historical items; paintings;
sculpture; ruins of London's Wolf
House mansion and other houses

Glen Rose TX

14725
Somervell County Museum
Elm and Vernon Sts, Glen Rose, TX
76043
General Museum - 1966
Coll: agriculture; archaeology;
archives; geology; Indian artifacts

Glencoe MO

14726
**Wabash, Frisco and Pacific
Association**
Glencoe MO 63042, 42 Greendale Dr,
St Louis, MO 63121
History/Public Affairs Museum - 1939
Coll: locomotives; flat cars; tanks;
hoppers; gondolas

Glendale CA

14727
Forest Lawn Museum
1712 S. Glendale Ave, Glendale, CA
91205
History/Public Affairs Museum - 1951
Coll: American history from 1770;
American bronze statuary;
pre-Christian and Christian era coins;
gems; autographs - theater

Glens Falls NY

14728
The Chapman Historical Museum
348 Glen St, Glens Falls, NY 12801
General Museum - 1964
Coll: social and industrial history of the
area; Stoddard collection of the
photographs, paintings, published
works and memorabilia; Glen Falls
YMCA and Insurance Company
collections - library; photographic
library

14729
The Hyde Collection
Warren St, Glens Falls, NY 12801
Fine Arts Museum - 1952
Coll: 2,000 first editions and other rare
books; 14th-20th century paintings,
drawings and sculpture of Europe and
America emphasizing Italian
Renaissance; European and American
decorative arts - library; galleries;
educational building

Glenwood IA

14730
**Mills County Historical Society and
Museum**
211 N Chestnut St, Glenwood, IA
51534
General Museum
Coll: machinery hall; dolls; guns;
household furniture; glass and china;
Indian artifacts; antiques

Glenwood MN

14731
**Pope County Historical Society
Museum**
South Hwy 104, Glenwood, MN 56334
General Museum - 1931
Coll: costumes; dolls; decorative arts;
Indian artifacts

Glenwood OR

14732
**Oregon Electric Railway Historical
Society, Inc.**
Star Rte, Glenwood, OR 97120
Science/Tech Museum - 1957
Coll: light electric streetcars of
1894-1948; interurban cars; operating
tramway with all related equipment
and facilities to 1910; wooden engine
house of Gales Creek and Wilson
River Railroad - library

Gloversville NY

14733
Fulton County Museum
N Kingsboro Av, Gloversville, NY
12078
General Museum - 1972
Coll: glove and leather industry; 18th
and 19th century weavings; Kingsboro
School (1891) - library; auditorium;
reading room

Glucester MA

14734
The Hammond Museum Inc
80 Hesperus Av, Glucester, MA 01930
Historic Site - 1931
Coll: furniture; tapestries; stained
glass; icons; pipe organ containig over
8,200 pipes

Golden CO

14735
Buffalo Bill Memorial Museum
Rte 5, POB 950, Golden, CO 80401
Historic Site - 1921
Items connected with the life of
William F. Cody (Buffalo Bill); Indian
artifacts; paintings - library

14736
Colorado Railroad Museum
17155 West 44th Av, Golden, CO
80401
History/Public Affairs Museum - 1958
Coll: rolling stock and traction lines of
Colorado railroads; interior exhibits of
railroad items, documents; photos;
memorabilia - library

14737
Geology Museum
Colorado School of Mines, Golden,
CO 80401
Natural History Museum - 1940
Coll: minerals; paleontological exhibits;
mining

Goldendale WA

14738
Maryhill Museum of Fine Arts
Goldendale, WA 98620
Fine Arts Museum - 1922
Coll: European and American art;
Rodin drawings and sculptures;
paintings; ceramics

Goliad TX

14739
Presidio La Bahia
Refugio Hwy, 1 mile south of Goliad,
POB 57, Goliad, TX 77963
Historic Site
Coll: artifacts showing 9 levels of
civilization, going back to the Indians
who camped here before the
Spaniards arrived; including
pre-colonial and Republic era

Goodwell OK

14740
No Man's Land Historical Museum
Sewel St, Goodwell, OK 73939
General Museum - 1932
Hal Clark and William B. Baker
collection of Indian artifacts;
anthropology; archaeology; geology;
mineralogy; paleontology; entomology;
archives; zoology; agriculture;
costumes; art - library; reading room

Gorham ME

14741
Art Gallery University of Southern
Maine
Gorham Campus, Gorham, ME 04038
Fine Arts Museum - 1967
Coll: paintings; sculpture; graphics

Goshen CT

14742
Goshen Historical Society
Old Middle Rd, Goshen, CT 06756
General Museum - 1955
Coll: pewter; rocks and shells; Indian
artifacts; natural history; textiles; dolls;
farm tools; historic flags - library

Goshen NY

14743
**Orange County Community of
Museums and Galleries**
101 Main St, POB 527, Goshen, NY
10924
General Museum - 1961
Coll: maps; manuscripts; canal
artifacts; Staffordshire; early clothing -
library

Gothenburg NE

14744
Old Bron House Doll Museum
1421 Ave F, Gothenburg, NE 69138
Decorative Arts Museum - 1976
Coll: Dolls from many countries, dating
back to the late 1800's; apple head
dolls

Gouverneur NY

14745
Gouverneur Museum
Rte 2, Leadmine Rd, Gouverneur, NY
13642
General Museum - 1974
Coll: furnishings; military; rock and
minerals collection; farm tools; fire
fighting wagon - library; classrooms

Grafton MA

14746
Willard House and Clock Shop
Willard St, Grafton, MA 01519
Decorative Arts Museum - 1718
Coll: original Willard Clocks by
Benjmin, Simon, Ephraim and Aaron
Willard

Grafton VT

14747
Grafton Historical Society
Grafton, VT 05146
General Museum - 1962
Coll: artifacts; local history; genealogy
- library

Granby CT

14748
**Salmon Brook Historical Society,
Inc.**
208 Salmon Brook St, Granby, CT
06035
General Museum - 1959
Coll: household and farm furniture;
historical items; local genealogy -
library

Grand Forks ND

14749
Myra Museum and Campbell House
1904 Belmont Rd, Grand Forks, ND
58201
General Museum - 1977
Coll: curios, artifacts, relics of the area;
Tom Campbell Farm - reading room

14750
University Art Galleries University of
North Dakota
University Station, POB 8136, Grand
Forks, ND 58202
Fine Arts Museum - 1970
Coll: Contemporary art - mobile
gallery unit

14751
Zoology Museum University of North Dakota
Grand Forks, ND 58201
Natural History Museum - 1883
Coll: birds; fishes; mammals; insects; reptiles and amphibians; parasites of Aquatic Invertebrates - library; field research station; laboratories; classrooms

Grand Haven MI

14752
Tri-Cities Historical Society Museum
1N. North Water St, Grand Haven, MI 49417
History/Public Affairs Museum - 1959
Coll: medical; costumes; textiles; lumbering - library; reading room

Grand Island NE

14753
Stuhr Museum of the Prairie Pioneer
3133 W Hwy 34, Grand Island, NE 68801
General Museum - 1961
Coll: machinery; antique autos; Indian artifacts - auditorium

Grand Junction CO

14754
Museum of Western Colorado
4th and Ute Sts, Grand Junction, CO 81501
General Museum - 1965
Coll: small arms; costumes; archeology; paleontology; minerals and geology; archives - library

Grand Lake CO

14755
Grand Lake Area Historical Society
POB 656, Grand Lake, CO 80447
General Museum - 1973
Coll: furniture and furnishings; historical artifacts; historical building (1870)

Grand Marais MN

14756
Cook County Museum
Grand Marais, MN 55604
General Museum - 1966
Coll: sports, medical; commercial fishing; folklore; military

Grand Rapids MI

14757
Calvin College Center Art Gallery
1801 East Beltline S.E., Grand Rapids, MI 49506
Fine Arts Museum - 1974
Coll: 17th century Dutch paintings; 19th century Dutch drawings; 20th century prints - library; auditorium; theater; classrooms

14758
Grand Rapids Art Museum
230 East Fulton, Grand Rapids, Mi 49503
Fine Arts Museum - 1911
Coll: Renaissance paintings; French 19th century painings; German Expressionism paintings; master prints of all eras - library

14759
Grand Rapids Public Museum
54 Jefferson, Grand Rapids, MI 49503
General Museum - 1854
Coll: ethnology; archaeology; paleontology; history; natural history - library; planetarium; auditorium; classrooms

Grandview WA

14760
Ray E. Powell Museum
313 Division, Grandview, WA 98930
Decorative Arts Museum - 1969
Coll: china; glass; silver; archeology; antiques; costumes; furniture; lapidary; money

Granite CO

14761
Clear Creek Canyon Historical Society of Chaffee County
POB 2181, Granite, CO 81228
General Museum - 1971
Coll: artifacts of the mining era; historic buildings from the 19th century

Granite Falls MN

14762
Yellow Medicine County Historical Museum
POB 160, Granite Falls, MN 56241
History/Public Affairs Museum - 1952
Coll: geology; archaeology; Indian artifacts; pioneer artifacts - library; reading room

Granville OH

14763
Denison University Gallery
Burke Hall of Music and Art, Granville, OH 43023
Fine Arts Museum - 1946
Coll: Eastern, Western and primitive art and artifacts; Asian textiles; lacquerware; sculpture; rubbings; European and American 19th and 20th century prints; cartoons; baroque drawings; Cuna Indian art

14764
Granville Historical Museum
Broadway, Granville, OH 43023
General Museum - 1885
Coll: village records; artifacts; carpenter tools; industry; agriculture; archaeology; decorative arts; geology; military

Great Falls MT

14765
C. M. Russell Museum
1201 Fourth Ave N, Great Falls, MT 59401
Fine Arts Museum - 1953
Coll: paintings; bronzes; pottery; contemporary art - library; theater; classrooms

Greeley CO

14766
Centennial Village
14th Av & B St, Greeley, CO 80631
Open Air Museum - 1976
12 architectural structures showing development of period from the Frontier era through the Victorian period

14767
Greeley Municipal Museum
919 7th St, Greeley, CO 80631
General Museum - 1968
Coll: local historic items; Indian artifcts; farm items; costumes; historic building - library

Green Bay WI

14768
Green Bay Packer Hall of Fame
1901 S Oneida, POB 3776, Green Bay, WI 54303
History/Public Affairs Museum - 1969
Sports memorabilia of Green Bay Packers - theater

14769
Heritage Hill State Park
2640 S Webster Av, Green Bay, WI 54301
Open Air Museum - 1976
Historic buildings and their furnishings from 1776 to 1840

14770
National Railroad Museum
POB 3251, Green Bay, WI 54303
Science/Tech Museum - 1957
Coll: railroads; English locomotives; steam locomotives; rolling stock dating to 1890 - library

14771
Neville Public Museum
129 S Jefferson, Green Bay, WI 54301
General Museum - 1915
Coll: history; natural history; underwater archeology; geology; anthropology - library

Green Lane PA

14772
Goschenhoppen Folklife Library and Museum
POB 476, Green Lane, PA 18054
General Museum - 1965
Coll: folklore and folkculture; agriculture; archives; archaeology; costumes; decorative arts; history; textiles - library; auditorium; herbarium

Green River WY

14773
Sweetwater County Museum
50 W Flaming Gorge Way, POB 25, Green River, WY 82935
General Museum - 1967
Coll: Indian and pioneer artifacts; industry, ranching and Chinese mementos; guns; photographs - library; auditorium

Greenboro NC

14774
Guilford Courthouse National Military Park
New Garden Rd and Old Battleground Rd, POB 9334, Greenboro, NC 27408
History/Public Affairs Museum - 1917
Coll: Revolutionary War weapons; soldier mannequins - library

14775
The Natural Science Center of Greenboro, Inc.
4301 Lawndale Dr, Greenboro, NC 27408
Natural History Museum - 1957
Coll: geology; ornithology; entomology; mammals; reptiles; Edisonia - zoo; marine aquarium; nature trails; aviary; health theater; Spitz automated 512 hyosphere planetarium; science mobile; auditorium; botanical courtyard

Greenbush WI

14776
Jung Carriage Museum
Greenbush, WI 53026
Science/Tech Museum - 1967
Coll: horse and hand-drawn vehicles of late 19th and early 20th centuries

Greendale WI

14777
National Bowling Hall of Fame and Museum
5301 S 76th St, Greendale, WI 53129
History/Public Affairs Museum
Sports artifacts and relics; general history of the sport of bowling - library

Greeneville TN

14778
Andrew Johnson National Historic Site
Depot St, Greeneville, TN 37743
General Museum - 1942
Coll: artifacts of the Johnson period; historic houses (1830) - library

Greenfield IN

14779
James Whitcomb Riley Birthplace
250 W Main St, Greenfield, IN 46140
Historic Site - 1937
Coll: furniture; relics; manuscripts; paintings; china; crafts; historic house, the birthplace of James Whitcomb Riley - library

14780
Old Log Jail Museum
Rte 40 & North A Sts, 203 N Wood, Greenfield, IN 46140
General Museum - 1966
Coll: Tom Indian arrowhead collection; coverlets from the mid 1800s; log jail; photos of local families, business, and agriculture of 1870-1917 - library

Greenfield WI

14781
Greenfield Historical Society
11313 W Coldspring Rd, Greenfield, WI 53228
General Museum - 1965
Tools; housewares; clothing; furnishings; local history

Greensboro NC

14782
Greensboro Historical Museum, Inc.
130 Summit Av, Greensboro, NC 27401
General Museum - 1924
Coll: transportation; military; county and industrial history; Dolley Madison Collection; O. Henry Collection; decorative arts; period rooms; late 19th century village exhibit; Francis McNairy House (1762); Christian Isley House (1780); Hockett Blacksmith Shop (1830) - library; auditorium

14783
Heritage Center N.C.A. & T. State University
Greensboro, NC 27411
Anthropology Museum - 1968
Coll: arts and crafts from over 31 African nations, New Guinea and Haiti - library; reading room; classrooms

14784
Weatherspoon Art Gallery University of North Carolina
Greensboro, NC 27412
Fine Arts Museum - 1942
Coll: modern and contemporary paintings; sculpture; graphic arts; Oriental and primitive arts

Greensburg PA

14785
The Westmoreland County Museum of Art
221 N Main St, Greensburg, PA 15601
Fine Arts Museum - 1949
Coll: American paintings, sculpture, drawings, prints, decorative arts; English 18th century pine-pannelled rooms; furniture; paintings; silver; Victorian period rooms; 19th and early 20th century toy collection - library; auditorium; classrooms

Greentown IN

14786
Greentown Glass Museum, Inc.
112 N Meridian, Greentown IN 46936, 508 E Main St, Greentown, IN 46936
Decorative Arts Museum - 1969
Coll: glassware manufactured from 1894 to 1903; chocolate glass; tools and materials used in the production of glassware - library

Greenville DE

14787
Delaware Museum of Natural History
Kennett Pike, Route 52, POB 3937, Greenville, DE
Natural History Museum - 1957
Coll: birds and bird eggs; molluscs; mammals - library; auditorium

Greenville NC

14788
Greenville Art Center
802 Evans St, Greenville, NC 27834
Fine Arts Museum - 1956
Coll: paintings; sculpture; graphic arts; ceramics - library

Greenville OH

14789
Garst Museum
205 N Broadway, Greenville, OH 45331
General Museum - 1903
Coll: historical artifacts from Anthony Wayne army; items relating to the history of Darke County - library; reading room

Greenville SC

14790
Bob Jones University Collection of Sacred Art
Bob Jones University, Greenville, SC 29614
Fine Arts Museum - 1951
Coll: 13th-19th century religious art; archaeological and illustrative material relating to Bible lands; paintings; decorative arts; sculpture; graphics

14791
Greenville County Museum of Art
420 College St, Greenville, SC 29601
Fine Arts Museum - 1959
Coll: North American painting; Sculpture; graphics and crafts including the Magill Collection of Works by Andrew Wyeth - theatre; multi-media audio visual center with color television production studios

Greenwich CT

14792
The Bruce Museum
Museum Drive, Greenwich, CT 06830
General Museum - 1909
Coll: mounted mammals and birds; wildlife dioramas; minerals and fossils; North American Indian cultures; American, European, and Oriental decorative arts; 19th and 20th century European and American paintings - library; lecture room

Greenwood AR

14793
Old Jail Historical Museum
725, Greenwood, AR 72936
General Museum - 1963
Coll: artifacts; farm equipment; coal mine equipment

Greenwood MS

14794
Cottonlandia Museum
Highway 49-82 Bypass, POB 1635, Greenwood, MS
General Museum - 1069
Coll: polychrome ceramics from Humber-McWilliams; contemorary arts and crafts; bone, bead, lithic and ceramic analysis of pre-and proto-historic Indian relics

14795
Florewood River Plantation
Hwy 82 West, Greenwood, MS 38930
History/Public Affairs Museum - 1976
Coll: 1800-1865 furniture; lighting devices; food preparations utensils - library; auditorium

Greenwood SC

14796
The Museum
Phoenix St, Greenwood, SC 29646
General Museum - 1968
Coll: natural science and technology; Indian artifacts; Thomas A. Edison display, showing replica first phono made; full scale replica of Cinderella coach; oriental collection of Frank Delono; ancient tapestry from Egypt; Indian, African and other cultures; miscellaneous other displays

Groton CT

14797
Submarine Force Library & Museum
Naval Submarine Base, POB 700, Groton, CT 06340
Science/Tech Museum - 1964
Coll: submarine models; pictures; battle flags; submarine parts; medals and personal memorabilia from submarines - library

Guilford CT

14798
Henry Whitfield Museum
Whitfield St, Guilford, CT 06437
Historic Site - 1903
Coll: 17th and 28th century American furniture; textiles; firearms; stone house (1639) - library; herb garden

Gulf Shores AL

14799
Fort Morgan Museum
Star Rte, POB 2780, Gulf Shores, AL 36542
General Museum
Coll: weapons; flags; memorabilia of the Civil War and the War of 1812; Indian artifacts

Gunnison CO

14800
Gunnison County Pioneer and Historical Society
South Adams St off Hwy 50 East, Gunnison, CO 81230
General Museum - 1930
Coll: geology; costumes; mineralogy; transportation; agriculture; historic houses - library

Guthrie OK

14801
Oklahoma Territorial Museum
402 - 406 E Oklahoma Av, Guthrie, OK 73044
General Museum - 1970
Coll: artifacts dating before statehood 1907; documents and photos of the territorial era - library

Haddam CT

14802
Youthmobile Museum Inc.
Old Ponsett Rd, Haddam, CT 06438
Junior Museum - 1973
Coll: natural science; ethnology; historical items - library; outdoor classrooms; minitrails

Hagerstown IN

14803
Wilbur Wright State Memorial
R.R. 2, POB 258A, Hagerstown, IN 47346
Historic Site
Coll: recreated birthplace of Wilbur Wright; period furniture; F-84 jet fighter plane

Hagerstown MD

14804
Hager House Museum
19 Key St, Hagerstown, MD 217640
Historic Site - 1962
Coll: 18th century furnishings; china; 18th century coins

14805
Washington County Historical Society
135 W Washington St, Hagerstown, MD 21740
History/Public Affairs Museum - 1910
Coll: clocks; Bell pottery; dolls

14806
Washington County Museum of Fine Arts
City Park, POB 423, Hagerstown, MD 21730
Fine Arts Museum - 1929
Coll: American art; 16th, 17th, and 18th century old masters; Oriental art

Hailey ID

14807
Blaine County Historical Museum
N Main St, Hailey, ID 83333
General Museum - 1964
Coll: 5,000 political buttons; Indian arrowheads

Haines AK

14808
Alaska Indian Arts, Inc.
Port Chilkoot, Haines, AK 99827
Anthropology Museum - 1957
Coll: Tlingit Indian costumes; ethnology; Fort William H. Seward (1904) - library

14809
Sheldon Museum and Cultural Center
POB 236, Haines, AK 99827
General Museum - 1911
Coll: Indian arts; Eskimo carvings; pioneer mementos and pictures - library

Haines OR

14810
Eastern Oregon Museum
Rte 1, POB 109, Haines, OR 97833
General Museum - 1958
Coll: farm implements; blacksmith shop; buggies; cutters; hacks and a surrey; musical instruments; bells; replica kitchen; old newspapers; uniforms; guns; arrowheads; railroad depot (1880) - library

Halifax NC

14811
Historic Halifax State Historic Site
POB 406, Halifax, NC 27839
Historic Site - 1955
Coll: Owens House (1760); Constitution-Burgess House (1810); clerk's office (1833); jail (1838); Taproom (1770); Eagle Tavern (1790); Sally-Billy House (1808) - Visitor Center with audio-visual show

Halstead KS

14812
Kansas Health Museum
309 Main St, Halstead, KS 67056
Science/Tech Museum - 1965
Coll: medical instruments; research papers; research movies; functions of the human body - auditorium; library

Hamilton NY

14813
The Picker Art Gallery Charles A. Dana Creative Arts Center, Colgate University
Hamilton, NY 13346
Fine Arts Museum
Luis de Hayos collection of pre-Columbian art; paintings; sculptures; prints; Herbert Mayer collection; Gary M. Hoffer '74 Memorial Photography collection

Hammondsport NY

14814
Glenn Curtiss Museum of Local History
Lake and Main Sts, Hammondsport, NY 14840
Science/Tech Museum - 1961
Coll: history of Glenn Curtiss aircraft; OX5 engines and Jenny plane; aviation - library

14815
The Greyton H. Taylor Wine Museum
R.D. 2, Hammondsport, NY 14840
History/Public Affairs Museum - 1967
Coll: old winemaking equipment; cooperage; wine bottles and labels; presidential glass - library; reading room

Hammonton NJ

14816
Batsto Historic Site
Batsto R.D. 1, Hammonton, NJ 08037
General Museum - 1956
Coll: archives; archaeology; herbarium; industry - library

Hampton VA

14817
The College Museum
Hampton Institute, Hampton, VA 23668
Fine Arts Museum - 1909
Coll: ethnology; traditional African, Oceanic and American Indian art; contemporary art - library

14818
Hampton Center for the Arts and Humanities
22 Wine St, Hampton, VA 23369
Fine Arts Museum - 1966
Coll: archaeology; photography - library

14819
Syms-Eaton Museum
418 W Mercury Blvd, Hampton, VA 23666
General Museum - 1952
Coll: local history exhibits; archives - library

Hana HI

14820
Hana Cultural Center
Hana, HI 96713
General Museum - 1970
Coll: artifacts; utensils; antiques - library

Hanalei Kauai HI

14821
Hanalei Museum
POB 81, Hanalei Kauai, HI 96714
General Museum - 1966
Coll: local artifacts; agricultural implements; photographs; furniture; historic building - aquarium

14822
Waioli Mission House Museum
Hanalei Kauai HI 96766, POB 1631, Lihue, HI 96766
Historic Site - 1952
Coll: historic house furnishings; traditional Hawaiian horticulture

Hanford CA

14823
Fort Roosevelt
870 W. Davis, POB G 1067, Hanford, CA 93230
Junior Museum - 1976
Coll: whole mounts and head mounts of exotic and North American game animals; gems and minerals; native birds and mammals; herbarium - library; botanical gardens; zoological park

Hannibal MO

14824
Mark Twain Home and Museum
208 Hill St, Hannibal, MO 63401
Historic Site - 1936
Coll: Mark Twain memorabilia - library

Hanover NH

14825
Dartmouth College Museum and Galleries Dartmouth College
Hanover, NH 03755
Fine Arts Museum - 1769
Coll: American and European paintings, sculpture, drawings and prints; posters; decorative arts; far and near Eastern Art; coins; scientific instruments

14826
Montshire Museum of Science, Inc
45 Lyme Rd, Hanover, NH 03755
Science/Tech Museum - 1975
Coll: anthropology; geology; biology - classrooms

Harbor Springs MI

14827
Chief Andrew J. Blackbird Museum
349 E. Main St, Harbor Springs, MI 49740
Anthropology Museum - 1952
Coll: arts and crafts; tools; clothing of early American Indians

Hardy VA

14828
Booker T. Washington National Monument
Rte 1, POB 195, Hardy, VA 24101
Historic Site - 1956
Coll: plantation equipment and furniture; blacksmith tools - library

Harlingen TX

14829
Confederate Air Force
Rebel Field, Harlingen, TX 78550
History/Public Affairs Museum - 1957
Coll: US and foreign combat aircrafts of World War II; weapons; uniforms; photographs; memorabilia of the era 1939-1945

Harper KS

14830
Harper City Historical Society
804 E 12th St, POB 275, Harper, KS
History/Public Affairs Museum
Coll: furniture; antiques; early kitchen; tools, broom factory; cider press; bibles; clothing - library

Harpers Ferry WV

14831
Harpers Ferry National Historical Park
Shenandoah St, POB 65, Harpers Ferry, WV 25425
Historic Site - 1944
Artifacts of life style of historic period; John Brown memorabilia; historic houses - library

Harpursville NY

14832
St. Luke's Episcopal Church and Museum
Harpursville NY 13787 Tunnel, NY 13848
Historic Site - 1970
Coll: Indian artifacts; early Americana; sanctuary

Harrisburg PA

14833
The Historical Society of Dauphin County
219 S Front St, Harrisburg, PA 17104
General Museum - 1869
Coll: Indian relics; furniture; china and glass

14834
William Penn Memorial Museum
3rd and North Sts, POB 1026, Harrisburg, PA 17120
General Museum - 1905
Pennsylvania Collection of fine arts; Indian and historic archaeology; natural science; science and technology; decorative arts and crafts items - library; reading room; planetarium; auditorium; classrooms

Harrison AR

14835
Robinson Heritage Center
POB 728, Harrison, AR 72601
General Museum - 1967
Coll: Ozarkia materials from the 19th century; historic buildings; furnishings; farm machinery; farm tools

Harrisonburg VA

14836
D. Ralph Hostetter Museum of Natural History
Harrisonburg, VA 22801
Science/Tech Museum - 1968
Coll: geology; mineralogy; botany; zoology

Harrodsburg KY

14837
Shakertown at Pleasant Hill
Kentucky
Rte 4, Harrodsburg, KY 40330
General Museum - 1961
Coll: decorative arts; 27 historic buildings; Shaker and Utopian social history of the 19th century - library

Harrogate TN

14838
University Museum Lincoln Memorial University
Harrogate, TN 37752
History/Public Affairs Museum - 1897
Coll: Abraham Lincoln and Civil War materials; 250,000 artifacts, books, manuscripts, pictures, statuary

Hartford CT

14839
Austin Arts Center Trinity College
Summit St, Hartford, CT 06106
Fine Arts Museum - 1964
Samuel H. Kress collection; George F. McMurray collection of American 19th century art

14840
Connecticut Historical Society
1 Elizabeth St, Hartford, CT 06105
General Museum - 1825
Coll: furniture; portraits and prints; glass, silver, and china; Indian relics; manuscripts - library; reading room; gallery rooms

14841
Mark Twain Memorial
351 Farmington Av, Hartford, CT 06105
Historic Site - 1929
Coll: memorabilia, photographs, furniture of Mark Twain; 19th century American paintings, prints, and drawings; decorative arts; Louis C.Tiffany collection of furniture and art glass; Candace Wheeler collection of fabrics and memorabilia - library

14842
Museum of Connecticut History
Connecticut State Library
231 Capitol Av, Hartford, CT 06115
History/Public Affairs Museum - 1910
Coll: exhibits on Connecticut; governors' portraits; royal charter; Colt firearms; numismatics; war relics - library

14843
Stowe-Day Foundation
77 Forest St, Hartford, CT 06105
Historic Site - 1941
Coll: furniture, memorabilia, and paintings of Harriet Beecher Stowe; study samples of 19th century wallpaper; archives; decorative arts; historic houses - library

14844
Wadsworth Atheneum
600 Main St, Hartford, CT 06103
Fine Arts Museum - 1842
J.P. Morgan collection of antique bronzes, European ceramics, and silver; Wallace Nutting collection of early American furniture; European and American paintings from 1400 to present; sculptures, prints, and drawings; art of the Middle Ages and Renaissance; Lifar collection of ballet costumes - library; auditorium; classrooms

Harvard MA

14845
Fruitland Museum
Prospect Hill, Harvard, MA 01451
General Museum - 1914
Coll: paintings; ethnology; folklore; Memorabilia of Ralph Waldo Emerson and Henry David Thoreau - library

Hastings MI

14846
Charlton Park Village and Museum
2545 S Charlton Park Rd, Hastings, MI 49058
History/Public Affairs Museum - 1936
Coll: folklore; transportation; weapons; military; costumes - library

Hastings NE

14847
Hastings Museum
1330 N Burlington, Hastings, NE 68901
History/Public Affairs Museum - 1926
Coll: George W. Cole Smith and
Wesson guns; Richards Coin
collection; Richard T. Conroy big game
trophies; automobiles; china; clocks;
rocks - library; planetarium

Hattiesburg MS

14848
**John Martin Frazier Museum of
Natural Science**
POB 5087, Southern Sta, Hattiesburg,
MS 59401
Natural History Museum - 1936
Coll: geology; paleontology;
ethnology; archaeology - classrooms

14849
Turner House
500 Bay, Hattiesburg, MS 39401
History/Public Affairs Museum - 1970
Coll: 18th century French, English and
some American furniture; crystal
chandelier; post Impressionist English,
American and French periods - library

Hatton ND

14850
Hatton-Eielson Museum
607 6th St, Hatton, ND 58240
Historic Site - 1973
Coll: pioneer furniture; Andrew O.
Ness House (1907) - library

Haven KS

14851
Reno County Historical Society
108 W Main, Haven, KS 67543
General Museum - 1960
Coll: historical newspapers; farm and
home artifacts; clothing, dishes; books;
pictures - library

Haverford PA

14852
**Haverford Township Historical
Society**
Karakung Dr, Powder Mill Park, POB
825, Haverford, PA 19083
General Museum - 1939
Coll: period furnishings; costumes;
glass photographic plates of
Philadelphia and Westchester Traction
Co. (1913-1915); railroads; engines -
library

Haverhill MA

14853
Haverhill Historical Society
240 Water St, Haverhill, MA 01830
General Museum - 1893
Coll: glassware; archaeology; naval
history; portraits; military artifacts

Havre MT

14854
**Northern Montana College
Collections** Northern Monatana
College
Havre, MT 59501
Natural History Museum - 1952
Coll: mammals; botany; geology;
fossils

Hawaii National Park HI

14855
Wahaulu Visitor Center
Hawaii National Park, HI 96718
General Museum - 1916
Coll: Hawaiian artifacts; natural history;
paintings; photographs - library;
nature and conservation center;
auditorium

Hawthorne FL

14856
**Marjorie Kinnan Rawlings State
Historic Site**
Rte 3, POB 92, Hawthorne, FL 32640
Historic Site - 1970
Coll: home of Marjorie Kinnan
Rawlings; original furnishings

Hays KS

14857
Sternberg Memorial Museum Fort
Hays State University
Hays, KS 67601
Natural History Museum - 1902
Coll: mineralogy; geology;
archaeology; paleontology; natural
history; historical materials - library

Hayward WI

14858
**National Fresh Water Fishing Hall of
Fame**
Hall of Fame Dr, Hayward, WI 54843
Natural History Museum - 1960
Coll: antique and classic outboard
motors; 200 mounted fishes; reels;
rods - library; aquarium

Heavener OK

14859
**Clem Hamilton Heavener Runestone
State Park**
Heavener, OK 74937
Historic Site
Runestone inscription dating to
November 11, 1012

Helena AR

14860
Phillips County Museum
623 Pecan St, Helena, AR 72342
General Museum - 1929
Coll: memorabilia of the Civil War,
Spanish-American War, Phillippine
Insurrection, and World Wars I and II;
Edison collection of inventions;
costumes; local historic items

Helena MT

14861
Montana Historical Society
225 N Roberts, Helena, MT 59601
General Museum - 1865
Coll: archaeology; aeronautics;
ethnology - library

Hellertown PA

14862
Gilman Museum
at the Cave, Hellertown, PA 18055
General Museum - 1955
Coll: guns; natural history; gem
stones; minerals; fossils; colonial items
- botanical garden

Hempstead NY

14863
Emily Lowe Gallery
Hofstra University, Hempstead, NY
11550
Fine Arts Museum - 1963
Coll: European and American painting
and sculpture; prints and drawings;
African, Oceanic and pre-Columbian
sculpture - library

Henderson KY

14864
John James Audubon Museum
Audubon State Park, Henderson, KY
42420
Fine Arts Museum - 1938
Coll: works, prints and personal
memorabilia of John James Audubon;
botany; natural history; paintings;
archives

Henderson NV

14865
Southern Nevada Museum
240 Water ST, Henderson, NV
History/Public Affairs Museum
Coll: pre-historic; mineralogy; miners;
ranchers; Indians; pioneers

Hereford AZ

14866
Coronado National Memorial
Rural Rt 1, POB 126, Hereford, AZ
85615
History/Public Affairs Museum - 1952
Coll: historical books; mid-16th
century Spanish costumes,
documents, and weapons; natural
history

Hereford TX

14867
Deaf Smith County Museum
POB 1007, Hereford, TX 79045
General Museum - 1966
Coll: domestic utensils; early farm
machinery; Santa Fe Caboose; old
windmill; fashions; historic chapel -
library

Hermann MO

14868
Historic Hermann Museum
4th and Schiller Sts, POB 88,
Hermann, MO 65041
General Museum - 1956
Coll: textiles; marine; Indian artifacts -
library

Hermitage MO

14869
Hickory County Historical Society
Hermitage, MO
General Museum - 1950
Coll: archaeology; genealogy;
costumes

Hermitage TN

14870
Ladies Hermitage Association
Rte. 4, Hermitage, TN 37076
History/Public Affairs Museum - 1889
Coll: agriculture; arboretum; archives;
costumes; history; outdoor museum;
preservation project; relics of Jackson
family; furniture; documents; historic
houses (1823, 1836) - botanical
garden; library

Hershey PA

14871
Hershey Museum of American Life
One Chocolate Av, Hershey, PA 17033
Decorative Arts Museum - 1937
Coll: American decorative arts; North
American Indian ethnographic
materials - library

Hickory Corners MI

14872
Gilmore Car Museum
5272 Sheffield Rd, Hickory Corners,
MI 49060
Science/Tech Museum - 1964
Coll: antique and classical cars

Hickory NC

14873
Catawba Science Center
406 3rd Av, N.W., Hickory, NC 28601
Science/Tech Museum - 1972
Coll: shells; marine life; rocks;
minerals; birds; insects; animal
skeletons; fossils

14874
The Hickory Museum of Art
3rd St and First Av, N.W., Hickory, NC
28601
Fine Arts Museum - 1944
Coll: American art; European art;
sculpture and decorative art; history;
relics - library; classrooms

Hicksville NY

14875
The Gregory Museum Long Island
Earth Science Center
Heitz Place, Hicksville, NY 11801
General Museum - 1963
Coll: Indian artifacts; nature artifacts;
local historical artifacts - library;
lecture hall; field research station

High Falls NY

14876
**Delaware and Hudson Canal
Historical Society Museum**
Mohonk Rd, High Falls, NY 12440
General Museum - 1966
Coll: canals in the 19th century

High Point NC

14877
High Point Historical Society, Inc.
1805 E. Lexington Av, High Point, NC
27262
General Museum - 1966
Coll: 18th and 19th century tools,
ceramics, textiles, furniture; industrial,
social, civic, military exhibits pertaining
to local area history; historic houses
(1786-1824) - library; meeting room

14878
**Springfield Museum of Old Domestic
Arts**
514 Hayworth Circle, High Point, NC
27262
General Museum - 1935
Coll: items used by early settlers;
guns; cooking utensils; woodworking
tools; shoe making items, old plank
road material, looms; Indian artifacts -
nature center

Highlands NJ

14879
Sandy Hock Museum
Gateway National Recreation Area,
POB 437, Highlands, NJ 07732
History/Public Affairs Museum - 1968
Coll: uniforms; weapons; shells; maps;
dishes; herbarium - library

Hillsboro KS

14880
Pioneer Adobe House and Museum
Ash and D Streets, Hillsboro, KS
67063
History/Public Affairs Museum - 1958
Coll: agriculture; folklore

Hillsboro ND

14881
Trail County Museum
Hillsboro, ND 58045
General Museum - 1965
Coll: household furnishings of the 18th
century; Red River fur trader's cart;
Indian artifacts; farm implements

Hillsboro OH

14882
Fort Hill Museum
136314 Fort Hill Rd, Hillsboro, OH
45133
General Museum
Coll: Hopewell culture; natural
sciences

Hillsboro WV

14883
Pearl S. Buck Birthplace
US Hwy 219, POB 126, Hillsboro, WV
24946
Historic Site - 1966
Books and memorabilia of Pearl S.
Buck; original furnishings

Hillsborough NC

14884
Orange County Historical Museum
King St, Hillsborough, NC 27278
General Museum - 1957
Coll: crafts of early settlers; 20-piece
set of King standard weights and
measures; china; silver; loom, spinning
wheels and home spun bed spreads
and costumes; guns; pump organ

Hilo HI

14885
Lyman House Memorial Museum
276 Haili St, Hilo, HI 96720
General Museum - 1932 50: B
Coll: Hawaiiana and missionary items
of the period; ethnology; local volcanic
displays; Oriental collections;
geological and mineralogical exhibits;
natural history; historic house - library

Hinsdale IL

14886
Graue Mill and Museum
York Rd, Hinsdale, IL 60521
General Museum - 1950
Coll: Civil War relics; farm implements
and vehicles; dolls; period furnishings

Hobart IN

14887
Hobart Historical Society Museum
706 E Fourth St, Hobart, IN 46342
General Museum - 1968
Coll: exhibits of historical development
of area; wheelright and woodworking
tools; replica of blacksmith shop;
agricultural implements - library

Hodgenville KY

14888
**Abraham Lincoln Birthplace National
Historic Site**
Rte 1, Hodgenville, KY 42748
History/Public Affairs Museum - 1916
Coll: early life of Lincoln and the
environment of his birth - library;
auditorium

Hohenwald TN

14889
Meriwether Lewis Museum
Rte. 3, POB 147, Hohenwald, TN 38462
History/Public Affairs Museum - 1936
Coll: death and burial site of
Meriwether Lewis (1809); memorabilia

Holdrege NE

14890
Phelps County Historical Society
Hwy 183, Holdrege, NE 68949
General Museum - 1966
Coll: agriculture; antiques; religious art;
anthropolog; ethnology

Holland MI

14891
Netherlands Museum
8 E 12th St, Holland, MI 49423
History/Public Affairs Museum - 1937
Coll: early Dutch settlers and their
heritage; Dutch replicas; crafts from
Indonesia, Netherland; Antilles and
Surinam - library

14892
Poll Museum
31 New Holland St, Holland, MI 49423
Science/Tech Museum - 1953
Coll: antique and classic cars; early
fire equipments; model trains; model
ships

Hollywood FL

14893
Art and Culture Center of Hollywood
1301 S Ocean Dr, Hollywood, FL
33019
Fine Arts Museum - 1976
Contemporary paintings and sculpture
- library; reading room; auditorium

Holyoke CO

14894
Phillips County Museum
109 S. Campbell, Holyoke, CO 80734
General Museum - 1967
Coll: agricultural tools; pioneer
household items; doll collection;
photographs - library

Holyoke MA

14895
Holyoke Museum Wistariahurst
238 Cabot St, Holyoke, MA 01040
General Museum - 1959
Coll: glass; porcelain; silver; 18th, 19th
and 20th century paintings - library;
auditorium

Homer AK

14896
Pratt Museum
POB 682, Homer, AK 99603
Natural History Museum - 1968
Coll: Alaskan anthropology,
archeology, and history; biology;
marine aquarium and botanical garden
- library; visitor information center;
Senior Citizen Center; two galleries;
multi-purpose meeting room

Honaunau HI

14897
**Pu'uhonua O Honaunau National
Historical Park**
POB 128, Honaunau, HI 96726
History/Public Affairs Museum - 1961
Coll: Hawaiian artifacts; burial remains;
historic building - library; auditorium

Honesdale PA

14898
Wayne County Historical Society
810 Main, POB 446, Honesdale, PA
18431
General Museum - 1917
Coll: archives; paintings; costumes;
glass; history; Indian artifacts;
numismatics; historic buildings -
library

Honolulu HI

14899
Bernice Pauahi Bishop Museum
1355 Kalihi St, POB 19000-A, Honolulu,
HI 96819
Natural History Museum - 1889
Coll: anthropology and ethnology;
archives; archeology; natural history;
philately; maritime artifacts - library;
reading room; planetarium; theater;
classrooms; museum ship

14900
Contemporary Arts Center of Hawaii
605 Kapiolani Blvd, Honolulu, HI 96813
Fine Arts Museum - 1961
Contemporary art by artists of Hawaii

14901
The Hawaii Bottle Museum, Inc.
POB 25153, Honolulu, HI 96825
History/Public Affairs Museum - 1976
Antique bottles from 1776-1900,
showing the history of the Hawaiian
Islands - library

14902
Honolulu Academy of Arts
900 S Beretania St, Honolulu, HI 96814
Fine Arts Museum - 1922
Coll: Asian painting, sculpture,
ceramics, bronzes, lacquer, and
furniture; ancient Mediterranean and
medieval Christian art; European and
American painting, prints, sculpture,
and decorative arts; Kress collection
of Italian Renaissance painting; James
A. Michener collection of Japanese
prints; textiles; traditional arts of
Oceania, the Americas, and Africa -
library; reading room; auditorium;
classrooms

14903
Iolani Palace
POB 2259, Honolulu, HI 96804
Historic Site
Coll: artifacts of the period 1882-1893;
original artifacts of Iolani Palace

14904
Mission Houses Museum
553 S King St, Honolulu, HI 96813
General Museum - 1852
Coll: 19th century clothing and toys;
furniture and effects used by
American Protestant missionaries;
printing press; artifacts; historic
houses - library

14905
Queen Emma Summer Palace
2913 Pali Hwy, Honolulu, HI 96817
Historic Site - 1915
Coll: household furnishings and
personal effects of Queen Emma and
her family; feather work; portraits;
Hawaiian artifacts; tapa cloth

Hoosick Falls NY NY

14906
**Bennington Battlefield State Historic
Site**
State Route 67, Hoosick Falls NY
12090, Capital District State Parks and
Recreation Commission, Saratoga
Springs, NY 12866
Historic Site - 1913
Coll: military artifacts; archaeological
artifacts; battle site (1777)

Hopewell NJ

14907
Hopewell Museum
28 E Broad St, Hopewell, NJ 08525
General Museum - 1924
Coll: weapons; agricultural
implements; Indian artifacts; natural
history - library

Hot Springs SD

14908
Fall River County Historical Museum
POB 529, Hot Springs, SD 57747
General Museum - 1961
Coll: artifacts; furniture; tools, dishes,
books and other items showing how
pioneers lived; photos

14909
Wind Cave National Park
Hot Springs, SD 57747
Natural History Museum - 1903
Coll: geology; Indian artifacts;
archaeology - library

Houghton MI

14910
A.E. Seaman Mineralogical Museum
Michigan Technological University
Houghton, MI 49931
Natural History Museum - 1890
Coll: minerals; native copper; silver;
iron - library

Houston TX

14911
The Bayou Bend Collection
1 Westcott, POB 13157, Houston, TX
77019
Decorative Arts Museum - 1956
Coll: American decorative arts
(1670-1870); American paintings -
library

14912
Harris County Heritage Society
1100 Bagby, Houston, TX 77002
General Museum - 1954
Coll: decorative arts; historical material
building; craft displays; archives;
folklore; herbarium - library;
auditorium

14913
Houston Museum of Natural Science
5800 Caroline St, Houston, TX 77030
Natural History Museum - 1909
Coll: zoology general; Indian artifacts;
archives; paleontology; anthropology;
herbarium - library; auditorium;
classrooms

14914
Institute for the Arts Rice University
Houston, TX 77001
Fine Arts Museum - 1969
Coll: sculpture; paintings; graphics -
library

14915
**Museum of American Architecture
and Decorative Arts** Houston Baptist
University
7502 Fondren Rd, Houston, TX 77036
Decorative Arts Museum - 1964
Coll: decorative arts; history; archives;
folklore; architecture - library;
children's museum

14916
The Museum of Fine Arts, Houston
1001 Bissonnet, POB 6826, Houston,
TX 77005
Fine Arts Museum - 1900
Coll: European and American
paintings; decorative arts; sculpture;
graphics; pre-Columbian archaeology;
photography; Indian art; African and
Oceanic primitive art; Oriental art -
library; auditorium

14917
Museum of Medical Science
Caroline St in Hermann Park, Houston,
TX 77004
History/Public Affairs Museum - 1964
Coll: historical collection of anatomy
studies; transparent digestive system;
medical and dental science general -
theater

14918
**NASA Lyndon B. Johnson Space
Center** Office of Public Affairs
Johnson Space Center, Houston, TX
77058
Science/Tech Museum - 1964
Coll: artifacts and exhibits pertaining to
America's manned space program -
mission simulating and training facility;
space shuttle crew station simulators;
laboratory; auditorium; theater

14919
Sarah Campbell Blaffer Gallery
4800 Calhoun, Houston, TX 77004
Fine Arts Museum - 1973
Coll: contemporary Mexican graphics;
contemporary print study collection;
pre-Columbian artifacts - library

Hudson NY

14920
American Museum of Fire Fighting
Fireman's Home, Harry Howard Ave,
Hudson, NY 12534
History/Public Affairs Museum - 1925
Coll: antique fire-fighting equipment

14921
Olana State Historic Site
State Rte 9-G, R.D. 2, Hudson, NY
12534
General Museum
Coll: paintings of F.E. Church; Church
family possessions - library

Hudson WI

14922
The Octagon House
1004 Third St, Hudson, WI 54016
General Museum - 1948
Coll: furniture; books; dolls; tools;
clothing; local history; genealogy;
historic houses - library

Hugoton KS

14923
**Stevens County Gas and Historical
Museum**
905 Adams, Hugoton, KS 67951
History/Public Affairs Museum - 1961
Coll: antiques; old equipment used in
gas industry; 2 model drilling rigs

Humboldt IA

14924
**Humboldt County Historical
Association**
Humboldt, IA 50548
General Museum - 1962
Coll: Indian artifacts; Mill farmhouse
(1879) - library

Hungtington NY

14925
Hungtington Historical Society
POB 506, Hungtington, NY 11743
General Museum - 1903
Coll: furniture; glass; china; pottery;
costumes; textiles; paintings - library

Huntingdon PA

14926
Swigart Museum
POB 214, Huntingdon, PA 16652
Science/Tech Museum - 1927
exhibition of American automobiles
including Scripps-Booth (1916),
Studebaker Electric (1908), and Carroll
(1920); license plates; name plates;
automobiliana; toys; photographs;
paintings - library

Huntington NY

14927
Heckscher Museum
Prime Av, Huntington, NY 11743
Fine Arts Museum
Coll: 16th-20th century painting and
sculpture, emphasis on American
artists - library

14928
**Suffolk County Indian and
Archaeological Museum**
Harbor Arts Center, Brown's Rd,
Huntington NY, POB 126, Northport,
NY 11768
Anthropology Museum - 1971
Coll: Indian artifacts - library; field
research station; laboratory; nature
center; classrooms

Huntington Station NY

14929
**Walt Whitman Homestead State
Historic Site**
246 Walt Whitman Rd, Huntington
Station, NY 11702
Historic Site
furnishings; literary materials

Huntington WV

14930
Geology Museum Marshall University
3rd Av, Morrow Library, Huntington,
WV 25701
Natural History Museum - 1837
Geology

14931
The Huntington Galleries, Inc.
2033 McCoy Rd, Huntington, WV
25701
Fine Arts Museum - 1947
Coll: 19th and 20th century American
paintings, glass and sculpture;
Georgian silver; 19th century English
and French paintings; American and
European graphics; pre-Columbian
ceramics; American decorative arts;
regional collection - library; arboretum
and bird sanctuary; auditorium;
observatory

Huntsville AL

14932
Alabama Space and Rocket Center
Tranquility Base, Huntsville, AL 35807
Science/Tech Museum - 1968
Coll: missiles; rockets; related space
hardware, ranging from early space
history to space shuttle & other future
programs; documents on Wernher
von Braun - library, auditorium; theater

14933
Huntsville Museum of Art
700 Monroe St,S.W., Huntsville, AL
35801
Fine Arts Museum - 1970
Coll: 19th and 20th century paintings
and prints - four galleries; workshop

Huntsville TX

14934
Sam Houston Memorial Museum
Sam Houston Av, Huntsville, TX 77340
Fine Arts Museum - 1927
Coll: personal possessions of Sam
Houston; relics of Texas revolution;
historic houses - library

Hurley WI

14935
**Old Iron County Courthouse
Museum**
Iron St, Hurley, WI 54534
Science/Tech Museum - 1976
Coll: mining; lumbering; household
items - library; auditorium

Hurleyville NY

14936
**Sullivan County Historical Society,
Inc.**
POB 247, Hurleyville, NY 12747
General Museum - 1960
Coll: Civil War artifacts; Anti-Rent War
artifacts; ledgers - library

Huron SD

14937
**South Dakota State Fair Pioneer
Museum**
State Fair Grounds, Huron, SD 57350
General Museum - 1960
Coll: pioneer exhibits; Indian artifacts;
history; stuffed birds

Hutchinson KS

14938
Hutchinson Planetarium
1300 N Plum, Hutchinson, KS 67501
Science/Tech Museum - 1962
Coll: geology; space artifacts;
astronomy; paleontology -
planetarium; theater

Hyde Park NY

14939
**Franklin D. Roosevelt Library and
Museum**
Albany Post Rd, Hyde Park, NY 12538
Historic Site - 1939
materials relating to the lives and
careers of Franklin D. and Eleanor
Roosevelt - library; auditorium

14940
**Franklin D. Roosevelt National
Historic Site**
Hyde Park, NY 12538
Historic Site - 1946
Ancestral portraits; naval prints;
memorabilia

14941
**Vanderbilt Mansion National Historic
Site**
Hyde Park, NY 12538
Historic Site - 1940
furniture; tapestries; rugs; porcelains

Idaho City ID

14942
Boise Basin Museum
POB 4065, Idaho City, ID 83631
General Museum - 1958
Coll: local historical items; glass;
costumes

Idaho Falls ID

14943
**Intermountain Science Experience
Center**
1776 Science Center Dr, Idaho Falls,
ID 83401
Science/Tech Museum - 1976
Coll: archeology; items pertaining to
dentistry; mining; agriculture; energy;
forestry - auditorium; classrooms;
nature and conservation center

Idaho Springs CO

14944
**Clear Creek Historic Mining and
Milling Museum**
23rd Av & Riverside Dr, POB 1498,
Idaho Springs, CO 80452
Science/Tech Museum - 1977
Coll: original mill equipment;
photographic displays, journals,
ledgers; historic mining items -
prospectors' gold mine

14945
Underhill Museum
1416 Miner St, 120 Montane Dr, POB
568, Idaho Springs, CO 80452
History/Public Affairs Museum - 1964
Coll: mining equipment; historical
photographs

Ilion NY

14946
Remington Gun Museum
Hoefler Av, Ilion, NY 13357
History/Public Affairs Museum - 1959
Remington firearms and artifacts from
the 1840's to the present

Ilwaco WA

14947
Lewis and Clark Interpretive Center
Fort Canby State Park, POB 488,
Ilwaco, WA 98624
History/Public Affairs Museum - 1976
Coll: Lewis and Clark related items;
coast artillery items; Coast Guard and
lighthouse artifacts

Independence CA

14948
Eastern California Museum
155 Grant St, POB 206, Independence,
CA 93526
General Museum - 1928
Coll: Paiute and Shoshone Indian
baskets; pioneer artifacts and
memorabilia; costumes; minerals;
steam locomotive; historic buildings -
library; historic equipment yard

Independence KS

14949
Independence Museum
123 N 8th St, Independence, KS 67301
General Museum - 1882
Coll: coinglass from the Fred Hudiburg
Collection; early samplers; Jessamine
Cobb Worley Collection of Christmas
plates; blue glass; tankard and bible
owned by George Washington;
standing bronze Buddha from
Alexander Griswold's Breezewood
Collection; 1698 Mandarin skirt and a
Persian Nobleman's robe; paintings
including a Bierstadt; historic rooms

Independence MO

14950
Harry S. Truman Library and Museum
US 24 and Delaware Sts,
Independence, MO 64050
History/Public Affairs Museum - 1957
Coll: career and administration of
Harry S. Truman; numismatics;
philately - library; auditorium

14951
**Harry S. Truman Office and
Courtroom** Jackson County Park
Dept
Main and Lexington Sts,
Independence MO 64050, mail c/o
Jackson County Parks and Recreation
Dept, Rte 1, POB 124, Blue Springs,
MO 64015
Historic Site - 1933
Coll: Judge Truman's office and
courtroom; memorabilia of Truman era

Indian Springs GA

14952
Indian Museum
Indian Springs State Park, Indian
Springs, GA 30231
General Museum - 1950
Indian artifacts

Indiana PA

14953
**Historical and Genealogical Society
of Indiana County**
S 6th and Wayne Av, Indiana, PA
15701
General Museum - 1938
Coll: archives and artifacts relating to
local history - library

Indianapolis IN

14954
**Archives and Company Museum-Eli
Lilly and Company** Lilly Center
893 S Delaware, Indianapolis, IN 46206
Science/Tech Museum - 1956
Coll: materials relating to the company
and the pharmaceutical industry; early
medicine; archives; replica of original
Lilly laboratory

14955
The Children's Museum
3000 N Meridian St, POB 88126,
Indianapolis, IN 46208
Junior Museum - 1925
Coll: archeology and ethnology;
natural history; transportation;
railroading; prehistory; toys and dolls
- library; resource center; theater;
library; classroom; craft rooms

14956
**Historic Landmarks Foundation of
Indiana**
3402 Blvd Pl, Indianapolis, IN 46208
General Museum - 1960
Coll: period furnishings; paintings by
Indiana artists - library; reading room

14957
Hoosier (Art) Salon
143 N Meridian, 415, Indianapolis, IN
46204
Fine Arts Museum - 1924
Coll: paintings; sculpture; prints

14958
Indiana State Museum
202 N Albama St, Indianapolis, IN
46204
General Museum - 1869
Coll: state natural history; archeology;
botany; geology; decorative arts; art
and art history of Indiana - library;
auditorium

14959
Indianapolis Museum of Art
1200 W 38th St, Indianapolis, IN 46208
Fine Arts Museum - 1883
Coll: European and American
paintings; contemporary art; Oriental
art; ethnographic art; Clowes Fund
collection; J.M.W. Turner collection;
Holiday collection - library;
conservation laboratory; auditorium;
theater

14960
**Lockerbie Street Home of James
Whitcomb Riley**
528 Lockerbie St, Indianapolis, IN
46202
Historic Site
Coll: art works; books; furnishings;
historic house - library

14961
**Morris-Butler Museum of the
High-Victorian Decorative Arts**
1204 N Park Av, Indianapolis, IN 46202
Decorative Arts Museum - 1960
Coll: parlor furniture; twenty-one
rooms furnished in period furniture;
paintings by local artists

14962
Museum of Indian Heritage
6040 DeLong Rd, Indianapolis, IN
46254
History/Public Affairs Museum - 1967
Coll: archeology; ethnology; historic
and contemporary items dealing with
the American Indian - library

14963
**President Benjamin Harrison
Memorial Home**
1230 N Delaware St, Indianapolis, IN
46202
Historic Site - 1936
Coll: furniture; books; election
campaign items; inaugural Bible and
other memorabilia - library

Iola KS

14964
Allen County Historical Society
207 N Jefferson, Iola, KS 66749
History/Public Affairs Museum
Coll: Allen County memorabilia; A. E.
Gibson collection of negatives and
photos

Iowa City IA

14965
Museum of Natural History
University of Iowa
Iowa City, IA 52240
Natural History Museum - 1858
Laysan Island cyclorama; sandhill
crane fall migration; beaver and
antelope habitat groups; major phyla
of animal kingdom series; North
American birds; mammals; marine
invertebrates; archaeology; geology of
Iowa - library

14966
Old Capitol University of Iowa
Clinton St and Iowa Ave, Iowa City, IA
52242
Historic Site
furniture and furnishing of the period -
library

14967
Robert Lucas Plum Grove Home
Carroll St at Kirkwood Ave, Iowa City,
IA 52240
History/Public Affairs Museum - 1844
period furnishings

14968
University of Iowa Museum of Art
Riverside Drive, Iowa City, IA 52242
Fine Arts Museum - 1967
Coll: paintings; prints and drawings;
African sculpture; pre-Columbian art;
silver and jade; photography;
sculpture - print study room

Ipswich SD

14969
Edmunds County Museum
Ipswich, SD 57451
General Museum - 1931
Coll: clocks; local history; pioneer
small farmtools; household items;
animal trophies; Indian relics

Iraan TX

14970
Iraan Museum
Alley Oop Park at West City Limits Off
Hwy. 190, Iraan, TX 79744
History/Public Affairs Museum - 1965
Coll: stone tools and weapons;
historical objects of Spanish period;
relics from military forts and stage
coach stations; oil well artifacts

Irvine CA

14971
Museum of Systematic Biology
University of California, Irvine, CA
92717
Science/Tech Museum - 1965
Coll: herbarium; entomology;
conchology; herpetology; ichthyology
- library; reading room

Ishpeming MI

14972
National Ski Hall of Fame
Mather Ave, POB 191, Ishpeming, MI
49849
History/Public Affairs Museum - 1054
Coll: ski-related exhibits - library

Ithaca NY

14973
**DeWitt Historical Society of
Tompkins County**
116 N. Cayuga St, Ithaca, NY 14850
General Museum - 1863
Indian artifacts; pioneer household
items; iron domestic machines -
library; auditorium

14974
Herbert F. Johnson Museum of Art
Cornell University, Ithaca, NY 14853
Fine Arts Museum - 1973
graphics; Asian art; European and
American painting; sculpture; primitive
art; Ecuadorian art - library; auditorium

14975
Hinckley Foundation Museum
410 E Seneca St, Ithaca, NY 14850
General Museum - 1972
Coll: furnishings; toys; costumes;
tools; ceramics

Jackson MS

14976
Dizzy Dean Museum
Lakeland Dr, Jackson, MS 39216
History/Public Affairs Museum - 1977
Coll: baseball; trophies, uniforms,
possessions and mementoes of the
late Dizzy Dean

14977
Mississippi Museum of Art
Pascagoula at Lamar, POB 1330,
Jackson, MS 39205
Fine Arts Museum - 1911
Coll: 19th and 20th century American
and Mississippi artists; mid-18th to
early 19th English paintings; Lovanov-
Rostovsky collection of Russia;
Lovanov-Rostovskyn costumes and
stage design - library

14978
**Mississippi Museum of Natural
Science**
111 N Jefferson St, Jackson, MS
39202
Natural History Museum - 1934
Coll: ichthyology; mammalogy;
ornithology; herpetology - library

14979
Mississippi State Historical Museum
North State and Capitol Sts, Jackson,
MS 93205
History/Public Affairs Museum - 1902
Coll: artifacts of social and political
history of Mississippi; archaeology -
library; auditorium

Jackson TN

14980
Casey Jones Home and Railroad Museum
Casey Jones Village, 514 Airways Blvd, Jackson, TN 38301
Science/Tech Museum - 1956
Coll: items pertaining to the steam era and the home of Casey Jones - library

Jackson WY

14981
Jackson Hole Historical Museum
101 N Glenwood, Jackson, WY 83001
General Museum - 1958
Coll: archeology; Indian artifacts; mineralogy; geology; fur trade; numismatics

Jacksonport AR

14982
Jacksonport Courthouse Museum
Jacksonport State Part, Jacksonport, AR 72075
History/Public Affairs Museum - 1965
Coll: furnishings; military uniforms; archives; transportation; costumes; medical instruments

Jacksonville al

14983
Dr. Francis Medical and Apothecary Museum
100 Gayle St, Jacksonville, al 36265
History/Public Affairs Museum
Coll: antebellum doctor's office and apothecary

Jacksonville FL

14984
Cummer Gallery of Art
829 Riverside Av, Jacksonville, FL 32204
Fine Arts Museum - 1958
Coll: European and American paintings; sculpture; prints; tapestries; furniture; formal gardens; graphics; Oriental art; Meissen porcelain - library

14985
Fort Caroline National Memorial
12713 Fort Caroline Rd, Jacksonville, FL 32225
General Museum - 1953
Coll: Indian relics; drawings by Le Moyne; armor; spinet; jewelry - library

14986
Jacksonville Art Museum, Inc.
4160 Boulevard Center Dr, Jacksonville, FL 32207
Fine Arts Museum - 1948
Coll: 20th century graphics; painting; sculpture; pre-Columbian artifacts; Koger collection of Oriental ceramics; African sculpture - library; reading room; auditorium; classroom

14987
Jacksonville Museum of Arts & Sciences
1025 Gulf Life Dr, Jacksonville, FL 32207
General Museum - 1941
Coll: 19th and 20th century antique and ethnic dolls; folk art; Florida wildlife mounts, fossils, and shells; historical artifacts and building - classrooms; planetarium; observatory; touch aquarium; library

Jacksonville IL

14988
David Strawn Art Gallery
331 W College Av, Jacksonville, IL 62650
Fine Arts Museum - 1879
Coll: pre-Coliumbian pottery

Jacksonville OR

14989
Jacksonville Museum
206 N 5th St, POB 480, Jacksonville, OR 97530
General Museum - 1948
Coll: Studio photographs, and paintings of pioneer photographer Peter Britt; gold mining, rocks and minerals; Indian artifacts; costumes; china, glassware, silver; fire-fighting equipment; furniture; historic houses (1863-1875) - library

Jamaica NY

14990
King Manor
150-03 Jamaica Av, 147-4984 Rd, Jamaica, NY 11435
Historic Site - 1900
antiques from the 1700's to the Victorian period

14991
The Store Front Museum and Paul Robeson Theatre
162-02 Liberty Av, Jamaica, NY 11433
Fine Arts Museum - 1970
Works by Black artists in U.S. and abroad; African art

Jamestown ND

14992
Fort Seward Historical Society, Inc.
321 3rd Av, SE, POB 1002, Jamestown, ND 58401
General Museum - 1964
Coll: agriculture; costumes; dolls; dishes; music; medical; military; Indian artifacts - library; reading room

Jamestown NY

14993
Fenton Historical Society
68 S Main St, Jamestown, NY 14701
General Museum - 1964
Coll: military; industrial; Victorian Era artifacts; Swedish and Italian cultural artifacts

14994
James Prendergast Library Association, Art Gallery
509 Cherry St, Jamestown, NY 14701
Fine Arts Museum - 1880
Coll: 19th century American painting

Jamestown RI

14995
Jamestown Museum
131 Narragansett Av, Jamestown, RI 02835
General Museum - 1972
Coll: items relating to the history of Jamestown; items relating to the old ferry system - library

Jamestown VA

14996
Jamestown Museum
Jamestown VA, 23081, Colonial National Park, POB 210, Yorktown, VA 23690
General Museum - 1930
Coll: 17th century artifacts; glass

Janesville WI

14997
Rock County Historical Society
440 N Jackson St, POB 896, Janesville, WI 53545
General Museum - 1948
Coll: local history; 19th century decorative arts and furnishings; historic houses - library

Jeannette PA

14998
Bushy Run Battlefield
Bushy Run Rd, Jeannette, PA 15644
Historic Site - 1933
18th century military equipment; documentation - amphitheater

Jefferson City MO

14999
Missouri State Museum State Capitol
Jefferson City, MO 65101
General Museum - 1919
Coll: paintings; artifacts; documents

Jefferson GA

15000
Crawford W. Long Medical Museum
U.S. Highway 129, Jefferson, GA 30549
History/Public Affairs Museum - 1957
History of the discovery of anaesthetics

Jefferson MO

15001
Cole County Historical Museum
109 Madison, Jefferson, MO 65101
History/Public Affairs Museum - 1941
Coll: archives; glasses; furniture - library

Jefferson OH

15002
Ashtabula County Historical Society
POB 193, Jefferson, OH 44047
General Museum - 1847
Coll: period furnishings (1800-1978); Jennie Munger Gregory Memorial Museum (1823); Joshua R. Giddings law office (1821) - library

Jefferson TX

15003
Jefferson Historical Society and Museum
223 Austin, Jefferson, TX 75657
General Museum - 1948
Coll: Civil War artifacts; doll collections; glass; paintings; Republic of Texas documents and money - library

Jefferson WI

15004
Aztalan Museum
R.R. 2, Jefferson, WI 53549
General Museum - 1941
Coll: Indian artifacts; history; archeology; historic houses - library

Jeffersonville IN

15005
Clark County Historical Society Howard Steamboat Museum Inc.
1101 E Market St, POB 606, Jeffersonville, IN 47130
General Museum - 1958
Coll: furnishings; steamboat artifacts

Jekyll Island GA

15006
Jekyll Club Village
375 Riverview Dr, Jekyll Island, GA 31520
Historic Site - 1954
Coll: furnishings; portraits; documents; photographs; clothing and memorabilia; historic houses

Jennings LA

15007
The Zigler Museum
411 Clara St, Jennings, LA 70546
Fine Arts Museum - 1963
Coll: art collection including works by Camille Pissaro, Joshua Reynolds, John James Audubon, Peter Hurd, Charles Sprague Pearce, Knute Heldner

Jerome AZ

15008
Jerome State Historic Park
POB D, Jerome, AZ 86331
General Museum - 1962
Coll: mining industry, mineralogy

15009
Verde Valley Art Association, Inc.
Main St, POB 985, Jerome, AZ 86331
Fine Arts Museum - 1977
Coll: paintings and graphic collection

Jersey City NJ

15010
Jersey City Museum
472 Jersey Ave, Jersey City, NJ 07302
Fine Arts Museum - 1901
Coll: August Will Collection of Paintings and Drawings; John D. McGill Collection of coins; 20th century American Painting; posters; flags; weapons

Johnson City TN

15011
Carroll Reece Museum
East Tennessee State University, Johnson City, TN 37601
General Museum - 1964
Coll: paintings; graphics; history; music; textiles; Tennessee crafts; costumes; folklore

15012
Tipton-Haynes Living Historical Farm
Erwin Hwy 19 W., Johnson City, TN 37601
Open Air Museum - 1965
Coll: agriculture; history; folklore; historic buildings (1784-1850) - library

Johnson City TX

15013
Lyndon B. Johnson National Historic Site
P.O. Box 329, Johnson City, TX 78636
Historic Site - 1969
Coll: Lyndon B. Johnson's boyhood home, Johnson Family Cemetery

Johnstown PA

15014
Johnstown Flood Museum
304 Washington St, Johnstown, PA
15901
General Museum - 1971
Coll: photographs and items pertaining
to everyday life in the 1890's; Cambria
Public Library Building (1891), built by
Andrew Carnegie - library;
mini-theater

Jonesboro AR

15015
Arkansas State University Museum
Learning Resources Center,
Jonesboro, AR 72401
General Museum - 1936
Coll: archeology; ethnology;
costumes; natural history;
paleontology - library; reading room;
classrooms

Julesburg CO

15016
Fort Sedgwick Depot Museum
202 W. 1st St, Julesburg, CO 80737
General Museum - 1940
Coll: agriculture; archeology; archives;
folklore; historical items

Juliette GA

15017
Jarrell Plantation Historic Site
Juliette Rd, Juliette, GA 31046
Historic Site
Coll: tools; furnishings; clothing; grist
mill; cotton gin; boiler and steam
engines

Junction City OR

15018
Junction City Historical Society
655 Holly, POB 317, Junction City, OR
97448
General Museum - 1971
Coll: furnishings,dental and medical
tools; Indian artifacts, including the war
bonnet of Chief Red Cloud

Juneau AK

15019
Alaska State Museum
Subport, Pouch F.M., Juneau, AK
99811
General Museum - 1900
Coll: Alaskan history, art, natural
history, and ethnography; early
industry; habitat groups - gallery;
audio-visual studio; conservation lab;
library; workshop

15020
**Last Chance Mining Museum &
Historical Park**
End of Basin Rd, 490 S. Franklin St,
Juneau, AK 99801
General Museum - 1976
Coll: mining tools and equipment
related to gold mining activities in the
Juneau Gold Belt; Air Compressor
Building (1912); Tram Equipment
Repair Facility (1912) - auditorium

Kailua-Kona HI

15021
Hulihee Palace
Alii Drive, POB 1838, Kailua-Kona, HI
96740
General Museum - 1926
Coll: furniture and effects of the royal
families; ancient artifacts; fishing
implements; feather work and tapa

Kalamazoo Mi

15022
**Genevieve and Donald Gilmore Art
Center** Kalamazoo Institute of Art
314 S. Park St, Kalamazoo, MI 49007
Fine Arts Museum - 1024
Coll: 20th century American art;
watercolors; graphics; sculpture;
ceramics - library

15023
Kalamazoo Nature Center Inc
7000 N. Westnedge Ave, Kalamazoo,
MI 49007
Natural History Museum - 1960
Coll: ornithology; ecology; human
environment - library; auditorium;
classrooms

15024
**Western Michigan University Art
Department**
Sangren Hall, Kalamazoo, Mi 49008
Fine Arts Museum - 1975
Coll: prints; reliefs; litho - classrooms

Kalispell MT

15025
Hockaday Center for the Art
Second Ave E and Third St, Kalispell,
MT 59901
Fine Arts Museum - 1968
Coll: paintings; prints; sculpture and
pottery - library; darkroom

Kankakee IL

15026
**Kankakee County Historical Society
Museum**
8th Av and Water St, Kankakee, IL
60901
General Museum - 1906
Coll: Indian artifacts; furnishings and
domestic items; local relics

Kansas City Mo

15027
**Kansas City Museum of History and
Science**
3218 Gladstone Blvd, Kansas City, Mo
64123
Natural History Museum - 1939
Coll: natural history; geology;
paleontology; archives - library;
planetarium; classrooms

15028
The Liberty Memorial Museum
100 West 26th St, Kansas City, MO
64108
History/Public Affairs Museum - 1919
Coll: Art and sculpture dealing with
World War I, including the 'Pantheon
de la Guerre', a 69-ft wide mural
conceived by two French artists and
painted by 130 artists over a period of
four years; wartime maps; artifacts

15029
**Thomas Hart Benton Home State
Historic Site**
3616 Belleview, Kansas City, MO
64111
Historic Site - 1978
Coll: period furnishing; books and
photographs relating to the life of
Thomas Hart Benton

15030
**William Rockhill Nelson Gallery and
Atkins Museum of Fine Art**
4525 Oak St, Kansas City, Mo 64111
Fine Arts Museum - 1926
library; reading room; auditorium;
classrooms

Katonah NY

15031
**John Jay Homestead State Historic
Site**
Jay St, POB AH, Katonah, NY 10563
Historic Site - 1958
Coll: portraits; period furnishings; Jay
family possessions - library

15032
The Katonah Gallery
28 Bedford Rd, Katonah, NY 10536
Fine Arts Museum - 1953
Coll: loan exhibitions

Kaukauna WI

15033
Grignon Home
Augustine St, *mail c/o* Recreation
Dept, 201 W Second St, Kaukauna, WI
54130
General Museum - 1836
Coll: Indian artifacts; books 1840-1900;
decorative arts; paintings

Kearney NE

15034
Fort Kearney Museum
311 S Central Ave, Kearney, NE 68847
General Museum - 1950
Coll: European and Oriental material;
Egyptian and African objects;
anthropology; numismatic; mineralogy;
music; glass; costumes

Keene NH

15035
The Colony House Museum
104 West St, Keene, NH 03431
General Museum - 1973
Coll: Keene and Stoddard-made early
19th century glass; Hampshire
Pottery; Staffordshire historical ware;
cast iron toys

Kelso WA

15036
Cowlitz County Historical Museum
5th and Allen St, Kelso, WA 98626
General Museum - 1953
Coll: log cabin; Indian artifacts; dolls;
historic houses - library

Kenai AK

15037
Kenai Historical Society & Museum
POB 1348, Kenai, AK 99611
General Museum - 1967
Coll: mounted wildlife trophies;
pioneer; Russian, Indian, Eskimo
inhabitants

Kennebunkport ME

15038
Kennebunkport Historical Society
North St, Kennebunkport, ME 04046
History/Public Affairs Museum - 1952
Coll: shipbuilding; genealogy;
maritime; local craft

15039
Seashore Trolley Museum
Log Cabin Rd, POB 220,
Kennebunkport, ME 04046
Science/Tech Museum - 1939
Coll: old trolley cars; transportation;
tracks - library

Kennesaw GA

15040
Big Shanty Museum
2829 Cherokee St, Kennesaw, GA
30144
Science/Tech Museum - 1972
Coll: Civil War locomotive;
memorabilia of local historical value;
site of the Great Locomotive Chase -
theater

Kennett MO

15041
Dunklin County Museum Inc
122 college, Kennett, MO 63857
General Museum - 1976
Coll: coin collection; 40 model engines
showing power from wind, water, gas,
steam to electricity; furnishing

Kenosha WI

15042
Kenosha County Historical Museum
6300 3rd Av, Kenosha, WI 53140
General Museum - 1878
Coll: Indian artifacts; Chinese snuff
bottles; antiques; guns; toys and dolls;
apothecary; local and state history -
library

15043
Kenosha Public Museum
5608 10th Av, Kenosha, WI 53140
Science/Tech Museum
Coll: Oriental art and artifacts; carved
ivory; ethnology; birds; mammals -
library; auditorium

Kent CT

15044
**Sloane-Stanley Museum and Kent
Furnace**
Rte 7, Kent, CT 06757
History/Public Affairs Museum - 1969
Coll: early American tools; diorama of
early iron industry at Kent Furnace;
paintings by Eric Sloane

Kent OH

15045
Kent State University Art Galleries
Kent State University, Kent, OH 44242
Fine Arts Museum - 1950
Coll: paintings, sculpture, prints;
decorative arts; Hazel Janicki and
William Schock collection; James A.
Michener collection; James A.
Michener and Milton Adams collection

Kenton OH

15046
Hardin County Relic Room
Hardin County Courthouse, Kenton,
OH 43326
General Museum - 1915
Coll: pionieer and Indian artifacts;
genealolgy - library

Keokuk IA

15047
Keokuk River Museum
Foot of Johnson St, Keokuk, IA 52632
General Museum - 1962
Coll: river transportation; marine

Keosauqua IA

15048
Van Buren County Historical Society
Keosauqua, IA 52565
History/Public Affairs Museum - 1960
Historical Buildings of the 18th century

Kerby OR

15049
**Josephine County Kerbyville
Museum**
24195 Redwood Hwy, POB 34, Kerby,
OR 97531
General Museum - 1959
Coll: military items of World War I and
II; Indian artifacts; rocks, minerals, and
mining; farming and logging
equipment; drugs and medicines;
bottles, glassware, and dishes; picture
gallery, dolls, and musical instruments;
historic buildings

Ketchikan AK

15050
Ketchikan Indian Museum
318 Mission St, POB 5454, Ketchikan,
AK 99901
Anthropology Museum - 1976
Coll: Indian & Eskimo baskets,
woodcarvings, tools, ivory carvings,
and other artifacts

15051
Tongass Historical Society Museum
629 Dock St, Ketchikan, AK 99901
History/Public Affairs Museum - 1961
Coll: pioneer life; Indian artifacts;
anthropology; ethnology; archives -
library

15052
Totem Heritage Center
601 Deermount, 629 Dock St,
Ketchikan, AK 99901
Anthropology Museum - 1976
Coll: totem poles and fragments from
local Indian villages - library;
workshops

Kewaunee WI

15053
Kewaunee County Jail Museum
Court House Square, Kewaunee, WI
54216
General Museum - 1970
Coll: furnished rooms; sheriff office;
Indian and early settlers artifacts;
rocks and shells; silver; coins - library

Key West FL

15054
Audubon House and Gardens
Whitehead & Greene Sts, Key West,
FL 33040
Historic Site - 1960
Coll: original period furniture; original
Audubon Double Elephant Folio 'Birds
of America'; historic house where
Audubon sketched and painted birds
of the Florida Keys - botanical garden

15055
East Martello Gallery and Museum
S Roosevelt Blvd, Key West, FL 33040
General Museum - 1951
Coll: local historic artifacts;
Holzscheiter collection of clocks,
watches, and arms; costumes WPA
paintings

15056
The Hemingway Home and Museum
907 Whitehead, Key West, FL 33040
Historic Site - 1964
Coll: furniture; mementos from other
parts of the world; Hemingway's home
(1931-1961) - gardens

15057
Lighthouse Military Museum
938 Whitehead at Truman, Key West,
FL 33040
History/Public Affairs Museum - 1966
Coll: military items from the Civil War
to Vietnam; naval exhibits; Japanese
submarine; steam-driven torpedos;
pictorial exhibit of growth of Key West
Naval Station; weapons

15058
Old Key West Historic Center
512 Greene St, Key West, FL 33040
General Museum - 1967
Coll: rocks and minerals; shells, fish,
coral, sponge house; historic buildings;
railroad artifacts; tropical gardens; bird
and insect collections - library

Keystone SD

15059
Big Thunder Gold Mine
POB 706, Keystone, SD 57751
General Museum - 1958
Coll: mining equipment; photographs -
theater

15060
Mount Rushmore National Memorial
Keystone, SD 57751
Open Air Museum - 1925
Coll: 1,500 assorted tools utilized in
the construction and carving of Mount
Rushmore - library; amphitheater

15061
Parade of Presidents Wax Museum
Highway 16-A, POB 237, Keystone,
SD 57751
History/Public Affairs Museum - 1970
Coll: 100 lifesize wax figures, including
all of the US presidents and other
famous Americans

Keytesville MO

15062
General Sterling Price Museum
303 Bridge St, Keytesville, MO 65261
General Museum - 1964
Coll: glass; silver; geology; insects;
furniture - library

Kinderhook NY

15063
**Columbia County Historical Society,
Inc.**
16 Broad St, Kinderhook, NY 12106
General Museum - 1916
Coll: New York Dutch and Federal
furnishings; decorative and fine arts;
county documents and historical
artifacts - library

15064
**Martin van Buren National Historic
Site**
POB 545, Kinderhook, NY 12106
Historic Site - 1974
furnishings; effects of President
Martin van Buren

King WI

15065
Wisconsin Veterans Museum
Veterans Home, King, WI 54946
History/Public Affairs Museum - 1935
Coll: World War I and II artifacts;
displays; uniforms; arms; equipment

Kingfisher OK

15066
Chisholm Trail Museum
605 Zellers Av, Kingfisher, OK 73750
General Museum - 1970
Coll: agriculture; archaeology; Indian
artifacts; Gov. Seay Mansion (1892)

Kingman AZ

15067
Mohave Museum of History and Arts
400 W. Beale, Kingman, AZ 86401
General Museum - 1961
Coll: Indian artifacts; archeological and
anthropological items; military items -
library; reading room

Kingman KS

15068
Kingman County Historical Museum
242 Ave A, POB 126, Kingman, KS
67068
History/Public Affairs Museum
Coll: uniforms; salt mine; tools;
dresses; hospital surgical instruments
- library; auditorium

Kingsport TN

15069
Netherland Inn Association
POB 293, Kingsport, TN 37660
General Museum - 1966
Coll: costumes; documents;
furnishings; historic building under
restoration (Preston Farm, 1845)

Kingston NY

15070
Senate House State Historic Site
312 Fair St, Kingston, NY 12401
Historic Site - 1887
Revolutionary Period furnishings; 19th
century American painting - library

Kingston RI

15071
Pettaquamscutt Historical Society
1848 Kingstown Rd, Kingston, RI
02881
General Museum - 1958
Coll: Civil War items; period furniture;
historic houses and historic artifacts;
archives - library

Kingsville TX

15072
John E. Conner Museum
Texas A&I University Kingsville, TX
78363
General Museum - 1925
Coll: Pre-Columbian artifacts, Indian
and Mexican-American cultures, south
Texas archaeology - library, photo
archive

Kinston NC

15073
Caswell-Neuse State Historic Site
POB 3043, Kinston, NC 28501
Historic Site - 1955
Coll: artifacts from the ram Neuse;
sunken Confederate iron clad gun
boat (1862-1865); items depicting life of
Governor Caswell

Klamath Falls OR

15074
Collier State Park Logging Museum
POB 428, Klamath Falls, OR 97601
Science/Tech Museum - 1946
Coll: pioneer surveying instruments;
Dolbeer Donkey Engine; large logs;
Giant Sumner Sash Gang Saw;
locomotives, track layer, trout
spawning beds; Giant Carliss twin
steam engine; photographs - library

15075
**Favell Museum of Western Art and
Indian Artifacts**
125 W Main St, Klamath Falls, OR
97601
Fine Arts Museum - 1972
Coll: Indian artifacts, including 60,000
arrowheads, stonework, bonework,
pottery, beadwork, and quillwork;
contemporary Western art; paintings,
bronzes, dioramas, woodcarvings;
miniature firearms; guns; rocks and
minerals - auditorium

15076
Klamath County Museum
1451 Main St, Klamath Falls, OR 97601
Natural History Museum - 1953
Coll: anthropology; archaeology;
botany; herbarium; history; natural
history - library

Knoxville TN

15077
**Confederate Memorial Hall 'Bleak
House'**
3148 Kingston Pike, Knoxville, TN
37919
General Museum - 1959
Coll: Confederate history; furniture
and relics of Civil War period;
archives; botany; costumes - library

15078
**'Crescend Bend' Armstrong-Lockett
House**
2728 Kingston Pike, Knoxville, TN
37919
Decorative Arts Museum
Coll: American and English furniture
(1750 - 1820); paintings; mirrors;
collection of English silver (1680 -
1820) - library

15079
Dulin Gallery of Art
3100 Kingston Pike, Knoxville, TN
37919
Fine Arts Museum - 1962
Coll: paintings; sculpture; graphics;
Thorne Miniature rooms - library

15080
Frank H. McClung Museum
University of Tennessee, Knoxville, TN
37916
General Museum - 1961
Coll: Lewis-Kneberg collection of
Tennessee archaeology; Eleanor
Deane Audigier art collection;
historical and natural science materials
- library; auditorium

15081
'Marble Springs' Farm Home of
Governor John Sevier
Neubert Springs Rd, Rte. 10, Knoxville,
TN 37920
General Museum - 1941
Coll: agriculture; costumes; pioneer
furniture and artifacts; historic houses
(1783-1815)

15082
Students' Museum, Inc.
516 Beaman, Chilhowee Park,
Knoxville, TN 37914
Natural History Museum - 1960
Coll: fossils of local area; rocks and
minerals; insects; shells; stuffed birds;
fish of Tennessee; sponges; sea life;
Indian points; dolls; stamps; coins -
library; planetarium; classrooms

Kodiak AK

15083
Kodiak Historical Society , Baranof
Museum
Erskine House, 101 Marine Way, POB
61, Kodiak, AK 99615
General Museum - 1954
Coll: archeology; ethnology; folklore;
geology; Indian artifacts; marine and
natural history - reading room

Kokomo IN

15084
Elwood Haynes Museum
1915 S Webster St, Kokomo, IN 46901
Science/Tech Museum - 1967
Coll: automobile; stainless steel and
stellite invented by Elwood Haynes;
industrial products - auditorium

Kotzebue AK

15085
Kotzebue Museum, Inc.
POB 73, POB 46, Kotzebue, AK 99752
General Museum - 1967
Coll: Eskimo artifacts; arts and crafts;
costumes; Indian artifacts;
anthropology; archeology

Kure Beach NC

15086
Fort Fisher State Historic Site
POB 68, Kure Beach, NC 28449
Historic Site - 1961
Coll: underwater archaeology; military;
archaeology; history; Civil War
artifacts; artifacts from sunken
blockade runners

La Jolla CA

15087
T. Wayland Vaughan Aquarium-
Museum Scripps Institution of
Oceanography
8602 La Jolla Shores Dr, La Jolla, CA
92093
Natural History Museum - 1905
Coll: living marine organisms -
aquarium

La Conner WA

15088
Skagit County Historical Museum
POB 32, La Conner, WA 98257
General Museum - 1959
Coll: sewing and farm equipment;
household items; tools; furniture;
musical instruments - library

La Crosse KS

15089
Post Rock Museum
La Crosse, KS 67548
Natural History Museum
Coll: history of post rock; post rock
products; tools

La Crosse WI

15090
Swarthout Memorial Museum
800 Main St, La Crosse, WI 54601
General Museum - 1898
Coll: 19th century lifestyle; brewing
industry; lumbering; river lore - library

15091
Viterbo College Museum
815 S 9th St, La Crosse, WI 54601
History/Public Affairs Museum - 1890
Coll: antiques; carved furniture;
buttons; ceramics; dolls; fossils; birds;
mammals; mollusks; glassware;
philatelics

La Fargeville NY

15092
Agricultural Museum Northern New
York Agricultural Historical Society
Rte 180, La Fargeville, NY 13656
Agriculture Museum - 1968
Coll: farm and home implements;
historic buildings

Lafayette CO

15093
Lafayette Miners Museum
108 E. Simpson St, Lafayette, CO
80026
General Museum - 1976
Coll: mining artifacts; furniture and
furnishings; pictures; newspapers

Lafayette IN

15094
Lafayette Art Center
101 S Ninth St, Lafayette, IN 47901
Fine Arts Museum - 1909
19th and 20th century paintings and
prints of midwestern artists - library

15095
Tippecanoe County Historical
Museum
909 South St, Lafayette, IN 47901
General Museum - 1925
Coll: relics from the Battle of
Tippecanoe; porcelains; glass and
metals; decorative arts; Indian
artifacts; medicine; military - library;
reading room

Lafayette LA

15096
Lafayette Museum
Lafayette St, Lafayette, LA 70501
General Museum - 1954
Coll: portraits; archives; historical
documents; costumes; picture
photographs

15097
Lafayette Natural History Museum
and Planetarium
637 Girard Park Dr, Lafayette, LA
70503
History/Public Affairs Museum - 1069
Coll: Indian and Acadian artifacts; floral
and faunal specimens - planetarium;
auditorium

La Grange IN

15098
La Grange County Museum
Rte 1, La Grange, IN 46761
General Museum - 1966
Coll: historical papers; local historical
artifacts

Laguna Beach CA

15099
Laguna Beach Museum of Art
307 Cliff Dr, Laguna Beach, CA 92651
Fine Arts Museum - 1918
Coll: paintings by early California
artists; contemporary works of art
including McLaughlin, Francis, Natkin;
photo collection by Hurrell and
Outerbridge

Lahaina Maui HI

15100
Lahaina Restoration Foundation
Dickenson & Front Sts, Lahaina Maui
HI 96761, POB 338, Lahaina Maui, HI
96761
History/Public Affairs Museum - 1962
Coll: marine items; archives; period
furniture; artifacts; historic ship -
library; reading room; botanical garden

Laie HI

15101
Polynesian Cultural Center
Laie, HI 96762
General Museum - 1963
Coll: botany; costumes; music;
anthropology; paintings; graphics;
decorative arts

La Jolla CA

15102
La Jolla Museum of Contemporary
Art
700 Prospect St, La Jolla, CA 92037
Fine Arts Museum - 1941
Coll: contemporary art including
paintings, sculptures, drawings, and
prints; photography; ethnic art -
library; auditorium; classrooms;
sculpture garden

La Junta CO

15103
Koshare Indian Museum, Inc.
18th and Santa Fe, La Junta, CO 81050
Anthropology Museum - 1949
Coll: paintings; archeology;
anthropology; Indian artifacts - library

Lake Charles LA

15104
Imperial Calcasieu Museum Inc
204 W Sallier St, Lake Charles, LA
70601
General Museum - 1963
glass; crystal; china; sulphur; rice,
timber and oil industries - library

Lake City SD

15105
Fort Sisseton State Park Visitors
Center
Lake City, SD 57247
General Museum - 1972
Coll: Indian artifacts; Civil War
weapons and military uniforms; John
Brown family collection; Fort Sisseton
archives - audio-visual room

Lake George NY

15106
Fort William Henry Museum
Canada St, Lake George, NY 12845
Historic Site - 1952
Coll: Colonial artifacts and documents;
weapons - library; auditorium; theater

15107
Lake George Institute of History, Art
and Science
Canada St, Lake George, NY 12845
General Museum - 1946
Coll: painting; natural history; local
crafts - auditorium

Lake of the Woods MN

15108
Fort St. Charles
Magnussen Island, Lake of the Woods
MN 55407, 5867 139th St W, Apple
Valley, MN 55124
History/Public Affairs Museum - 1951
Coll: gravemakers; crosses; skulls and
bones; burial places

Lake Placid NY

15109
John Brown Farm State Historic Site
John Brown Rd, Lake Placid, NY
12946
Historic Site - 1896
Coll: period furnishings; personal
possessions of John Brown and family

15110
Lake Placid/North Elba Historical
Society
Averyville Rd, Lake Placid, NY 12946
Historic Site - 1961
Coll: general store replica; local
memorabilia; taxidermy exhibits

Lakeland FL

15111
Polk Public Museum
800 E Palmetto, Lakeland, FL 33801
Fine Arts Museum - 1966
Coll: decorative art objects; original
oils and watercolors; local historical
artifacts - library; classrooms;
galleries

Lakeport CA

15112
Lake County Museum
175 Third St, Lakeport, CA 95453
General Museum - 1936
Coll: Indian artifacts; geological
collection; historic exhibits of pioneer
life

Lakeview OR

15113
Schminck Memorial Museum
128 S 'E' St, Lakeview, OR 97630
General Museum - 1936
Coll: glass; graphics; costumes; Indian
artifacts; history; dolls; quilts; barbed
wire; saddles; guns - library

Lakewood CO

15114
Belmar Museum of the City of Lakewood
797 S. Wadsworth Blvd, Lakewood, CO 80226
General Museum - 1976
Coll: agricultural exhibits; archeological artifacts from the region - library; nature/conservation center; auditorium

Lakewood OH

15115
Lakewood Historical Society
14710 Lake Av, 1200 Andrews Av, Lakewood, OH 44107
Historic Site - 1952
Coll: local landmark houses and early settlers artifacts; Old Stone House (1838) - library; botanical gardens

Lancaster OH

15116
The Georgian
105 E Wheeling St, Lancaster, OH 43130
General Museum - 1976
Coll: furniture; silver; costumes; tools; glass; Fairfield County historical items; The Georgian (1830-1833) - library

Lancaster PA

15117
James Buchanan Foundation for the Preservation of Wheatland
1120 Marietta Av, Lancaster, PA 17603
Historic Site - 1936
Coll: mid-19th century decorative arts collection most of which belonged to James Buchanan and his first Lady, Harriet Lane; period rooms

15118
Lancaster County Historical Society
230 N President Av, Lancaster, PA 17603
General Museum - 1886
Coll: items relating to local history; glass; pewter; costumes; books; Judge Yeates Law library; county archives - meeting room; reading room

15119
North Museum Franklin and Marshall College
College and Buchanan Avs, Lancaster, PA 17604
General Museum - 1901
Coll: anthropology; ethnology; Indian artifacts; archaeology; glass; numismatics; decorative arts; botany; entomology; geology; mineralogy; natural history; paleontology; zoology - library; planetarium; herbarium

15120
Pennsylvania Farm Museum of Landis Valley
2451 Kissel Hill Rd, Lancaster, PA 17120
Agriculture Museum - 1925
Coll: agriculture; decorative arts; folk culture; textiles; transportation; historic houses (1750-1880) - library

Lancaster VA

15121
Mary Ball Washington Museum and Library
POB 97, Lancaster, VA 22503
General Museum - 1958
Colonial history; local genealogy; archeology - library

Lansing MI

15122
Carl G. Fenner Arboretum
2020 E. Mt. Hope Rd, Lansing, MI 1959
Natural History Museum - 1959
Coll: herpetology; artifacts; geology - library; reading room; auditorium; classrooms

15123
Michigan Historical Museum
Michigan History Div., Michigan Dept. of State
108 N. Capitol Ave, Lansing, MI 48918
History/Public Affairs Museum - 1879
Coll: Prehistoric and aboriginal history; technology; transportation

Laona WI

15124
'Lumberjack Special' and 'Camp Five' Museum
Laona and Northern Railway, Laona WI, 54541, *mail c/o* Connor Forest Industries, POB 847, Wausau, WI 54401
Science/Tech Museum - 1969
Coll: forestry and ecology complex; railroad depot; rolling stock; steam engine; logging equipment; historic houses - conservation and nature center

Laramie WY

15125
Laramie Plains Museum
603 Ivinson, Laramie, WY 82070
General Museum - 1966
Coll: early pioneers domestic utensils; furniture; tools; Indian artifacts; pictures and maps of area - library

15126
Rocky Mountain Herbarium
University of Wyoming, Laramie, WY 82071
Natural History Museum - 1893
Herbarium; 330.000 plant specimens

15127
University of Wyoming Anthropological Museum
Anthropology Bldg, Laramie, WY 82071
Anthropology Museum - 1966
Ethnology; anthropology; archeology; Indian artifacts

15128
University of Wyoming Art Museum
Fine Arts Bldg, N 19th St, POB 3138, Laramie, WY 82071
Fine Arts Museum - 1960
Paintings; graphics; sculpture

15129
University of Wyoming Geological Museum Geology Dept., University of Wyoming
Laramie, WY 82070
Natural History Museum - 1905
Coll: vertebrate and invertebrate paleontology; rocks; minerals; fossils; anthropology; geology - library

Laredo TX

15130
Nuevo Santander Museum Complex
Laredo Jr. College Campus
West Washington St, Laredo, TX 78040
General Museum - 1976
regional history; arts - laboratory

Largo FL

15131
Pinellas County Historical Museum-Heritage Park
11909-125 St, N, Largo, FL 33540
General Museum - 1961
Coll: 5,000 photographs showing growth of local area; archives; pioneer furnishings; archeological material; historic buildings - library; reading room

Larned KS

15132
Fort Larned National Historic Site
Rte 3, Larned, KS 67550
History/Public Affairs Museum
Coll: historic houses; military items; weapons - library

15133
Santa Fe Trail Center
Rte 2, Larned, KS 67550
History/Public Affairs Museum
Coll: prehistoric and historic artifacts - library

Las Cruces NM

15134
New Mexico State University Museum
POB 3BV, Las Cruces, NM 88003
General Museum - 1959
Coll: anthropology; archaeology; ethnology; history; agriculture; industry; science - University archives

15135
The Playhouse Museum of Old Dolls and Toys
1201 N Second St, Las Cruces, NM 88001
History/Public Affairs Museum - 1974
Coll: Dolls mainly from 1930-35; carriages; doll furniture, dishes, houses; hobby horses; children's toys

15136
University Art Gallery New Mexico State University
POB 3572, Las Cruces, NM 88003
Fine Arts Museum - 1973
Coll: 19th century Mexican retablos; prints; photographs

Las Animas CO

15137
Kit Carson Museum
125 9th St, Las Animas, CO 81054
General Museum - 1959
Coll: Indian artifacts; cattle industry items; railroad and agriculture exhibits; historic buildings

Las Vegas NM

15138
Rough Riders Memorial and City Museum
Municipal Building, POB 179, Las Vegas, NM 87701
General Museum - 1960
Coll: Teddy Roosevelt Rough Riders collection; pioneer artifacts; Indian and local artifacts

Las Vegas NV

15139
Las Vegas Art Museum
3333 W Washington, Las Vegas, NV 89107
General Museum - 1950
Coll: contemporary fine art; early Las Vegas area collection - classrooms

15140
Museum of Natural History
University of Nevada
Las Vegas, NV 89154
Natural History Museum - 1967
Coll: paleontology including invertebrate and vertebrate fossils; archaeology; geology

Laurel MS

15141
Lauren Rogers Library and Museum of Art
5th Ave at 7th St, POB 1108, Laurel, MS 39440
Fine Arts Museum - 1923
Coll: 19th and 20th century American and European paintings; Oriental artifacts; furniture; graphics; archaeology - library; reading room

Laurens SC

15142
The Dunklin House
544 W. Main St, Laurens, SC 29360
General Museum - 1972
furniture, some locally, mainly southern; historic house (1812)

Laurinburg NC

15143
Indian Museum of the Carolinas, Inc.
Turnpike Rd, Laurinburg, NC 28352
Anthropology Museum - 1969
Coll: Indian artifacts - library; botanical garden

La Veta CO

15144
Fort Francisco Museum
POB 3, La Veta, CO 81055
General Museum - 1947
Coll: antiques; Indian artifacts; natural history; art; historic houses - library

Lawrence KS

15145
Helen Foresman Spencer Museum of Art University of Kansas
Lawrence, KS 66045
Fine Arts Museum
Coll: European painting and sculpture; American art; ancient and medieval art; Oriental art; decorative art

15146
Museum of Anthropology University of Kansas
Lawrence, KS 66044
Anthropology Museum
Coll: anthropology; ethnology; archaeology

15147
Systematics Museums University of Kansas
Dyche Hall, Lawrence, KS 66044
Natural History Museum
Coll: mammalogy; ichthyology; ornithology; anthropology; paleontology; herpetology; entomology - library; auditorium; classrooms

Lawson MO

15148
Watkins Woolen Mill State Historic Site
R.R. 2, POB 270, Lawson, MO 64062
Science/Tech Museum - 1964
Coll: textile weaving machine; several historic buildings - library

Lawton OK

15149
Museum of the Great Plains
601 Ferris Av, POB 68, Lawton, OK
73502
General Museum - 1961
Coll: Primary documents pertaining to
immediate region; photographs of
Plains Indians and white settlement;
artifacts representing the material
culture of man from pre-historic times
to the present - library; auditorium;
laboratories

Leadville CO

15150
House with the Eye Museum
127 W. Fourth St, POB 911, Leadville,
CO 80461
General Museum - 1964
Coll: carriages; mining tools; musical
instruments and sheet music; historical
house; furniture - theater

15151
**Lake County Civic Center
Association**
100-102 E. Ninth St at Harrison St,
POB 962, Leadville, CO 80461
General Museum - 1971
Coll: mining artifacts; diorama display
of mining history; local historical
artifacts; historic buildings - library;
botanical park; auditorium

15152
Tabor Opera House Museum
306-310 Harrison Ave, 815 Harrison
Ave, Leadville, CO 80461
Performing Arts Museum - 1955
Coll: paintings; costumes; theatrical
momentos; historical items

Lebanon Mo

15153
Nature Interpretive Center
Bennett Spring State Park, Lebanon,
Mo 65536
Natural History Museum - 1969
Coll: botany; zoology; geology -
classrooms; amphitheater

Lebanon OH

15154
**Warren County Historical Society
Museum**
105 S Broadway, POB 223, Lebanon,
OH 45036
General Museum - 1940
Coll: paleontology; Shaker collection
of furniture and household articles -
library; reading room

Leesburg VA

15155
Loudoun Museum
16 W Loudoun St, Leesburg, VA 22075
General Museum - 1967
Coll: local history items; furnishings

15156
Oatlands
Rte 2, POB 352, Leesburg, VA 22075
General Museum - 1965
Coll: 19th-20th century French, English
and American furniture; sporting prints
- library

15157
**Westmoreland Davis Memorial
Foundation**
Rte 2, POB 50, Leesburg, VA 22075
Natural History Museum - 1955
Coll: botany; agriculture; preservation
project; folklore; arboretum;
herbarium; costumes; 16th century
tapestries from Flanders - library

Lehi UT

15158
**John Hutchings Museum of Natural
History**
685 N Center, Lehi, UT 84043
General Museum - 1955
Coll: pioneer relics; undersea life from
Puerto Rico and Pacific; archaeology -
library

Leland MI

15159
Leelanau Historical Museum
POB 246, Leland, MI 49654
History/Public Affairs Museum - 1957
Coll: glass; silver; agriculture - library

Lemmon SD

15160
Petrified Wood Park Museum
500 Main Av, Lemmon, SD 57638
History/Public Affairs Museum - 1961
Coll: petrified wood and stone native
to the area; tools, implements,
household furnishings and costumes
(1900-1920); photographs; business
and range scenes; historic building
(1907)

Lenhartsville PA

15161
**Pennsylvania Dutch Folk Culture
Society, Inc.**
Lenhartsville, PA 19534
General Museum - 1965
folk art; agriculture; costumes

Lerna IL

15162
**Lincoln Log Cabin State Historic
Site**
RR1, Lerna, IL 62440
History/Public Affairs Museum - 1929
Coll: period furnishings; reconstructed
cabin and farm of Thomas and Sara
Lincoln

Le Roy NY

15163
Le Roy House
23 E Main St, Le Roy, NY 14482
General Museum - 1940
Coll: archives; decorative arts;
agriculture; Indian artifacts - library;
children's museum

Lewes DE

15164
Lewes Historical Society
Lewes, DE 19958
General Museum - 1962
Coll: furniture; Indian artifacts;
Swedish log cabin furnished as early
settlers lived; early physician's office;
historic houses from 19th century;
historic ship - children's museum

15165
Zwaanendael Museum
Kings Hwy & Savannah Rd, Lewes, DE
19958
General Museum
Coll: Indian artifacts; colonial items;
china; glass; silver

Lewisburg PA

15166
Packwood House Museum
10 Market St, Lewisburg, PA 17837
Historic Site - 1972
American decorative arts; 18th - 20th
century furniture, glassware,
stoneware, chinaware, quilts,
coverlets; primitive farm accessories;
Oriental rugs and other objects; Mrs.
Fetherston's painting and costume
collection - botanical garden; reading
room

Lewiston ID

15167
H. L. Talkington Collection Lewis-
Clark State College
8th Av & 6th St, Lewiston, ID 83501
General Museum - 1943
Coll: Gold Rush days and historic
events in the area; materials on
missions; Talkington collection

15168
Luna House Museum
3010 Third & C Sts, Lewiston, ID 83501
General Museum - 1963
Pioneer artifacts - sternwheel
showboat

Lewiston ME

15169
Treat Gallery Bates College
College St, Lewiston, ME 04240
Fine Arts Museum - 1959
Chinese art; drawings; paintings;
poems; sculptures

Lewiston PA

15170
Mifflin County Historical Society, Inc.
17 N Main St, Lewiston, PA 17044
General Museum - 1921
Coll: historic artifacts, pictures,
documents pertaining to area and
state history; Frank R. McCoy
memorial collection; McCoy House -
library; reading room

Lewistown IL

15171
Dickson Mounds Museum
Lewistown, IL 61542
Archeology Museum - 1927
Coll: exhibits on prehistoric man;
Paleo-Indian to Mississippian cultures

Lexington KY

15172
The Headley-Whitney Museum Inc.
Old Frankfort Pike, Lexington, KY
40511
Fine Arts Museum - 1968
Coll: minerals; oriental porcelains;
European and American paintings;
dolls; bibelots - library; reading room

15173
International Museum of the Horse
Iron Works Rd, POB 11892, Lexington,
KY 40578
General Museum - 1978
Coll: equine history and the horse in
sport - library; reading room

15174
Mary Todd Lincoln House
511 W Short St, Lexington, KY 40507
History/Public Affairs Museum
Coll: Lincoln book collection; rare
leather bound books; julep cups;
posters concerning Lincoln

15175
Museum of Anthropology University
of Kentucky
Lafferty Hall, Lexington, KY 40506
Anthropology Museum - 1936
archaeological materials and human
skeletal remains; ethnographic
materials

15176
Transylvania Museum
300 N Broadway, Lexington, KY 40508
Science/Tech Museum - 1882
Coll: scientific instruments; scientific
apparatus; implements used in
teaching 19th century medicine

15177
University of Kentucky Art Museum
Kinkead Hall, University of Kentucky
Room 213, Lexington, KY 40506
Fine Arts Museum - 1975
Coll: 14th to 20th century painting,
sculpture, works of art on paper;
pre-Columbian, African and Oriental
art

Lexington NE

15178
Dawson County Historical Society
805 N Taft St, Lexington, NE 68850
General Museum - 1958
Coll: china; glass; silver; textiles; local
history - auditorium

Lexington OH

15179
Richland County Museum
51 Church St, Lexington, OH 44904
General Museum - 1966
Coll: history; agriculture; art; Indian
artifacts; medical items - children's
museum

Lexington SC

15180
Lexington County Museum
230 Fox St, POB 637, Lexington, SC
29072
General Museum - 1970
Coll: Indian artifacts; rare antique dolls;
furniture (18th century); textile
collection; looms; spinning wheels;
farm implements; Historic Houses
(18th century)

Lexington VA

15181
**George C. Marshall Research
Foundation**
POB 920, Lexington, VA 24450
Historic Site - 1953
Coll: 20th century American military
history and diplomatic history of War I
and II - library; archive

15182
Lee Chapel
Washington and Lee University,
Lexington, VA 24450
Historic Site - 1867
Coll: Custis-Washington-Lee art
collection; Lee archives; Lee's original
office; china and porcelain -
auditorium

433

15183
Rockbridge County Historical Society
101 E Washington St, Lexington, VA 24450
General Museum - 1939
Coll: books and documents; photographs; tools; furniture; local architecture - library

15184
VMI Museum Virginia Military Institute
Jackson Memorial Hall, Lexington, VA 24450
General Museum - 1908
Coll: artifacts, paintings and photographs relating to the history of VMI; military uniforms and equipment - library

Liberty MO

15185
Historic Liberty Jail Visitors Center and Museum
Mississippi and Main Sts, Liberty, MO 64068
Religious Art Museum
Coll: religious history

15186
Jesse James Bank Museum
104 E Franklin St, Liberty, MO 64068
History/Public Affairs Museum - 1966
Coll: Civil War banking; pictures and documents pertaining to the Jesse James Gang bank robbery, Feb. 13, 1866 - library

Ligonier PA

15187
Fort Ligonier Memorial Foundation
S Market St, Ligonier, PA 15658
General Museum - 1946
Coll: archaeological artifacts; decorative arts; military arms; accoutrements of French and Indian War period; Indian relics; restored fort - library; research room

Lihue HI

15188
Kauai Museum
4428 Rice St, POB 248, Lihue, HI 96766
General Museum - 1960
Coll: Hawaiiana with particular emphasis on items dealing with the island of Kauai; art exhibits; ethnic and heritage displays - library

Lima OH

15189
Allen County Historical Society
620 W Market St, Lima, OH 45801
General Museum - 1908
Coll: Indian relics; minerals; fossils; documents; photographs; drawings pertaining to steam and electric railroads; pioneer rooms; tools; furniture; 19th century fire fighting equipment - library

Lincoln MA

15190
Drumlin Farm Education Center
Lincoln Rd, Lincoln, MA 01773
Agriculture Museum - 1954
Coll: agriculture; aviary; botany; entomology; geology; herpetology - library

Lincoln NE

15191
Elder Art Gallery Nebraska Wesleyan University
50th and Baldwin Sts, Lincoln, NE 68504
Fine Arts Museum - 1965
Coll: graphics; paintings; sculpture; ethnic and contemporary crafts

15192
Nebraska Conference United Methodist Historical Center Lucas Bldg, Nebraska Wesleyan University
50th and St. Paul Sts, Lincoln, NE 68504
Religious Art Museum - 1889
Coll: artifacts related to the United Methodist Church and its predecessor denominations in Nebraska; archives; documents; Bibles; hymnals; memorabilia from the United Methodist Church - library; reading room

15193
Nebraska State Historical Society
1500 'R' St, Lincoln, NE 68508
General Museum - 1878
Coll: anthropology; archaeology; ethnology; archives; costumes - library; reading room

15194
University of Nebraska Art Galleries
12th and R Sts, Lincoln, NE 68588
Fine Arts Museum - 1963
Coll: American art of the 20th century; paintings; F. M. Hall collection; sculpture; graphics; photographs - reading room; auditorium

15195
University of Nebraska State Museum 212 Morrill Hall
14th and U Sts, Lincoln, NE 68588
Natural History Museum - 1871
Coll: numismatics; philately; paleontology; zoology; health science; mineralogy; entomology - library; planetarium; auditorium; classrooms

Lincoln NM

15196
Old Lincoln County Courthouse Museum
Lincoln State Monument, Lincoln, NM 88338
General Museum - 1937
Coll: Indian artifacts; papers; furniture; clothing; tools; guns; art objects; local history - reading room

Lincoln RI

15197
Blackstone Valley Historical Society
N Gate Louisquisset Pike, Lincoln, RI 02863
General Museum - 1957
Coll: area memorabilia; antiquities - library

Lincolnton GA

15198
Elijah Clark State Park Museum
Rte 4, Lincolnton, GA 30817
General Museum - 1961
Coll: archives; uniforms; historical artifacts from the 1770s

Lindenhurst NY

15199
Old Village Hall Museum
215 S Wellwood Av, POB 296, Lindenhurst, NY 11757
General Museum - 1958
Coll: miscellaneous; restored railroad depot (1901) and freight house

Lindsborg KS

15200
Birger Sandzen Memorial Gallery
401 N 1st St, Lindsborg, KS 67456
Fine Arts Museum
oils, watercolors and prints; Japanese bronzes; graphics

15201
McPherson County Old Mill Museum and Park
120 Mill St, Lindsborg, KS 67456
General Museum
industrial; folklore; geology; archives; agriculture - library

Litchfield CT

15202
Litchfield Historical Society and Museum
On-the-Green, POB 385, Litchfield, CT 06759
General Museum - 1856
Coll: documents and manuscripts relating to Litchfield history; costumes and textiiles; pewter; decorative arts; historic houses - library

15203
White Memorial Conservation Center, Inc.
South of Rte 202, Litchfield, CT 06759
Science/Tech Museum - 1964
Coll: native fauna and flora; butterflies and moths; rocks and minerals; birds' eggs - library; nature/conservation center; auditorium

Lithopolis OH

15204
The Wagnalls Memorial
150 E Columbus St, Lithopolis, OH 43136
General Museum - 1924
Coll: paintings of John Ward Dunsmore; poems of Edwin Markham; books and personal items of Mabel Wagnalls Jones - library; reading room; auditorium

Little Compton RI

15205
Little Compton Historical Society
W Rd, Little Compton, RI 02837
General Museum - 1937
Coll: 17th and 18th century furniture; accessories; agricultural items; historic houses - library; meeting place

Little Falls NY

15206
Herkimer House State Historic Site
Rte 169, RD 2, Little Falls, NY 13365
Historic Site - 1913
Coll: period furnishings; personal belongins of American Revolutionary leader Nicholas Herkimer

15207
Little Falls Historical Museum
S Ann St, Little Falls, NY 13365
General Museum - 1962
Coll: books; scrapbooks; geneological records; pictures

Little Rock AR

15208
Arkansas Arts Center
MacArthur Park, Little Rock, AR 72203
Fine Arts Museum - 1960
Coll: paintings; sculpture; graphics; decorative arts; costumes; music - library; reading room; classrooms; theater

15209
Arkansas' Old State House
300 W. Markham St, Little Rock, AR 72201
General Museum
Coll: history collection; Arkansas flags; costumes and decorative arts of the 19th century - library

15210
Museum of Science and History
MacArthur Park, Little Rock, AR 72202
General Museum - 1924
Coll: patterned glass; birds; mammals; reptiles; pottery; historic and pioneer items; South American and African anthropology - library; planetarium; classrooms

Littleton CO

15211
Arapahoe Community College Museum of Anthropology
5900 S. Santa Fe Dr, Littleton, CO 80120
History/Public Affairs Museum - 1974
Coll: human fossil material; prehistoric pottery; reproductions and displays of ethnographic material

15212
Littleton Historical Museum
6028 S. Gallup, Littleton, CO 80120
General Museum - 1969
Coll: agricultures; archives; costumes; transportation; historic buildings - library

Liverpool NY

15213
Sainte Marie deGannentaha
Onondaga Lake Park, POB 146, Liverpool, NY 13088
Historic Site - 1933
artifacts and documents relating to French settlement in North America - craft and garden areas

15214
Salt Museum
POB 146, Liverpool, NY 13088
General Museum - 1934
Coll: painting; photographs; tools; vehicles; reconstructed salt boiling block

Livingston TX

15215
Polk County Memorial Museum
601 W Church, PO Drawer 511, Livingston, TX 77351
General Museum - 1963
Coll: agriculture, archaeology, Indian artifacts, military - archives

Loachapoka AL

15216
Lee County Historical Society
POB 206, Loachapoka, AL 36865
General Museum - 1968
Coll: tools, artifacts, documents, furnishings belonging to early settlers - library

Lockport NY

15217
The Niagara County Historical Center
215 Niagara St, Lockport, NY 14094
General Museum - 1947
artifacts relating to Niagara area and local Indian cultures - library; auditorium

Lodi CA

15218
San Joaquin County Historical Museum
11793 N. Micke Grove Rd, POB 21, Lodi, CA 95240
General Museum - 1961
Coll: tool collection; Indian artifacts; anthropology; agricultural tools and implements; transportation; history of wine industry - library; botanical garden; garden for the blind

Logan KS

15219
Dane G. Hansen Memorial Museum
Logan, KS
Fine Arts Museum - 1973
Coll: Oriental art; gun and coin collection

Logan UT

15220
Alliance for the Varied Arts
290 North 400 E, Logan, UT 84321
Fine Arts Museum - 1969
Fine arts - auditorium; theater

15221
Intermountain Herbarium Utah State University
Logan, UT 84321
Science/Tech Museum - 1931
Coll: plants of the Intermountain Region; herbarium - library

15222
Man and Bread Museum Utah State University
Logan, UT 84321
Agriculture Museum - 1959
Coll: farm implements; tractors

Logansport IN

15223
Cass County Historical Society
1004 E Market St, Logansport, IN 46947
General Museum - 1907
Coll: flags; lustre ware; glass; natural history; numismatics; regional art - library; reading room

Lompoc CA

15224
La Purisima Mission State Historic Park
POB R.F.D. 102, Lompoc, CA 93436
General Museum - 1935
Coll: mission period artifacts; archives; historic building - library; botanical garden; laboratory

15225
Lompoc Museum
200 South H St, Lompoc, CA 93436
General Museum - 1969
Coll: Chumash Indian artifacts; natural history and wildlife exhibits; mining; historical articles related to the area - library; slide collection

Long Beach CA

15226
Long Beach Museum of Art
2300 E. Ocean Blvd, Long Beach, CA 90803
Fine Arts Museum - 1951
Coll: paintings, prints, drawings, photographs by 19th and early 20th century Southern California artists, contemporary American and West Coast artists - library; video tape archive

15227
Rancho Los Cerritos
4600 Virginia Rd, Long Beach, CA 90807
Historic Site - 1969
Coll: historic house; furniture and tools; costumes; archeology; Indian artifacts - library; reading room; gardens

Longmeadow MA

15228
Longmeadow Historical Society
697 Longmeadow St, Longmeadow, MA 01106
History/Public Affairs Museum - 1899
Coll: genealogy; folklore; history; documents; 1600-1800 early American and English furniture - library

Longmont CO

15229
Longmont Pioneer Museum
375 Kimbark, Longmont, CO 80501
General Museum - 1940
Coll: pioneer artifacts; dolls; photographs and documents pertaining to local area; Noland R. Fry Indian artifact collection; pottery - library

Longview TX

15230
Longview Museum and Arts Center
102 W College, Longview, TX 75603
Fine Arts Museum - 1970
Coll: paintings, sculpture, graphics - library, studios

Loretto PA

15231
Southern Alleghenies Museum of Art
Saint Francis College Mall, POB 8, Loretto, PA 15940
Fine Arts Museum - 1975
paintings, sculptures, drawings, prints, stressing American art - library; auditorium; painting studios; photographic studio; community arts center

Lorton VA

15232
Gunston Hall Plantation
Lorton, VA 22079
Historic Site - 1932
Coll: portraits; furniture; rare books - library

Los Alamos NM

15233
Bandelier National Monument
Los Alamos, NM 87544
Open Air Museum - 1916
Coll: archaeological and ethnological items of Pueblo Indians of the Parajito Plateau - library

15234
Los Alamos County Historical Museum
Fuller Lodge Cultural Center, Central Av, Los Alamos, NM 87544
General Museum - 1968
Coll: outdoor museum; archaeoloy; geology; paleontology; wartime atomic bomb memorabilia; pre-historic Pueblo Indian artifacts; guest cottage of Los Alamos Ranch (1920); photographs by T. Harmon Parkhurst and Laura Gilpin - library; reading room

Los Altos Hills CA

15235
Space Science Center
12345 El Monte Rd, Los Altos Hills, CA 94022
Science/Tech Museum - 1966
Coll: electronic material from 1890 to the present - 2 planetariums; observatory; classrooms

Los Angeles CA

15236
American Society of Military History
Patriotic Hall
1816 S. Figueroa St, Los Angeles, CA 90015
History/Public Affairs Museum - 1948
Coll: American and foreign military equipment - nature conservation center; library; reading room; auditorium; theater; classrooms

15237
California Museum of Science and Industry
700 State Dr, Los Angeles, CA 90037
Science/Tech Museum - 1880
Coll: natural resources; technology; science; industrial, medical instruments; transportation; mineralogy; aeronautics and space; health and dentistry

15238
Craft and Folk Art Museum
5814 Wilshire Blvd, Los Angeles, CA 90036
Decorative Arts Museum - 1976
Japanese folk art; East Indian quilts; folk paintings; contemporary ceramics

15239
El Pueblo de Los Angeles State Historic Park
420 North Main St, Los Angeles, CA 90012
Historic Site - 1953
Coll: historic buildings

15240
The Frederick S. Wight Art Gallery of the University of California at Los Angeles
405 Hilgard Ave, Los Angeles, CA 90024
Fine Arts Museum - 1952
Coll: paintings; 19th and 20th century European and American prints and drawings; sculptures from the 19th-20th centuries - library

15241
Grunwald Center for the Graphic Arts University of California at Los Angeles
405 Hilgard Ave, Los Angeles, CA 90024
Fine Arts Museum - 1954
Coll: prints and drawings from the 15th century to the present - gallery; study room

15242
Hebrew Union College Skirball Museum
3077 University Mall, Los Angeles, CA 90007
General Museum - 1913
Coll: Kirschstein collection of Jewish ceremonial art; Dr. Nelson Glueck memorial collection of archeological artifacts; Joseph Hamburger numismatic collection; I. Solomon and L. Grossman collections of engravings and photo prints; manuscripts, paintings, sculpture, prints, and drawings by artists of Jewish origin; textiles; decorative arts; Israel archeology; graphics - galleries

15243
History Center California Historical Society
6300 Wilshire Blvd, Los Angeles, CA 90048
History/Public Affairs Museum - 1871
Coll: art collection; historical photographs; archives - library; galleries

15244
Junior Arts Center
4814 Hollywood Blvd, Los Angeles, CA 90027
Fine Arts Museum - 1966
Coll: art works by young contemporary artists and outstanding students; children's art from foreign countries - library

15245
Library of Los Angeles County Medical Assn.
634 S Westlake Av, Los Angeles, CA 90057
History/Public Affairs Museum - 1891
Coll: old medical and surgical instruments; rare books on medicine and surgery - library

15246
Los Angeles Art Association and Galleries
825 N La Cienega Blvd, Los Angeles, CA 90069
Fine Arts Museum - 1925
Coll: archives and histories of Southern California artists - auditorium

15247
Los Angeles County Museum of Art
5905 Wilshire Blvd, Los Angeles, CA 90036
Fine Arts Museum - 1910
Coll: Egyptian and Greco-Roman sculptures and antiquities; Chinese and Japanese paintings, sculptures, and ceramics; European painting, sculpture, prints, drawings, and decorative arts; American art; English silver; Italian mosaics; 20th century painting; textiles and costumes - library; conservation center; auditorium; theater

15248
Museum of Cultural History
Haines Hall, University of California, Los Angeles, CA 90024
General Museum - 1963
Coll: ancient and primitive art; archeology; ethnology - library

15249
Natural History Museum of Los Angeles County
900 Exposition Blvd, Los Angeles, CA 90007
Science/Tech Museum - 1910
Coll: anthropology; paleontology; industry and technology; entomology; mineralogy - library; laboratory; auditorium; classrooms; reading room

15250
Southwest Museum
234 Museum Dr, Los Angeles, CA
90065
General Museum - 1907
Coll: culture of American Indians,
prehistoric and historic; Spanish
Colonial and Mexican Provincial
artifacts and decorative arts; historic
house - library; auditorium

15251
University Galleries University of
Southern California
823 Exposition Blvd, Los Angeles, CA
90007
Fine Arts Museum - 1939
Coll: European and American
paintings; sculpture; graphics; Armand
Hammer and Elizabeth Holmes Fisher
collection of 15th to 20th century
paintings; prints and drawings

Los Banos CA

15252
Ralph Leroy Milliken Museum
US Hwy 152, Los Banos, CA 93635
General Museum - 1954
Coll: agriculture; archeology;
archives;costumes; paleontology -
library

Louisa County VA

15253
North Anna Visitor's Center
Rte 700, POB 402, Louisa County, VA
23117
Science/Tech Museum - 1973
Coll: exhibits describing how
electricity is generated by nuclear fuel
- library; auditorium

Louisville KY

15254
Allen R. Hite Art Institute University
of Louisville
Third St, Belknap Campus, Louisville,
KY 40208
Fine Arts Museum
Coll: 15th-20th century European and
American prints; drawings and
paintings - library

15255
**American Saddle Horse Museum
Association Inc**
730 W Main St, Louisville, KY 40202
General Museum - 1962
Coll: horse paintings by George Ford
Morris; skeletal structures depicting
the evolution of the horse; carriage
collection; gallery of world champion
saddle horses since 1916 - library

15256
Eisenberg Museum Southern Baptist
Theological Seminary
2825 Lexington Rd, Louisville, KY
40205
Archeology Museum - 1963
excavation materials from Caesarea;
Machaerus; numismatics; sculpture;
archaeology - library; reading room

15257
The Filson Club
118 W Breckinridge St, Louisville, KY
40203
History/Public Affairs Museum - 1884
coll: portraits; pre-historian Indian
artifacts; guns and rifles; steamboats;
prints - library

15258
J. B. Speed Art Museum
2035 S Third St, Louisville, KY 40208
Fine Arts Museum - 1925
Coll: European and American
decorative arts; paintings; sculpture;
Oriental arts; antiquities; primitive arts
- library; auditorium

15259
Junior Art Gallery Inc
301 W. York St, Louisville, KY 40203
Junior Museum - 1949
Coll: arts of interest to children -
classrooms

15260
Kentucky Derby Museum
Central Ave, Louisville, KY 40208
History/Public Affairs Museum - 1962
Coll: murals; racing memorabilia;
saddles; bridles; trophy

15261
Kentucky Railway Museum Inc
Ormsby Station Site, POB 295,
Louisville, KY 40201
History/Public Affairs Museum - 1954
Coll: railroad engines; model train
collection; passenger and freight cars

15262
**Museum of Natural History and
Science**
727 W Main St, Louisville, KY 40202
Natural History Museum - 1872
Coll: archeology; geology; history;
mineralogy; technology - library;
classrooms; auditorium

15263
**Photographic Archives, University of
Louisville Libraries** University of
Louisville
Louisville, KY 40208
History/Public Affairs Museum - 1967
history of photography; documentary
photography; photography as a fine
art - library, reading room

Loveland CO

15264
Loveland Museum
503 Lincoln, Loveland, CO 80537
History/Public Affairs Museum - 1929
Coll: pioneer and natural history
exhibits; archeology; mineralogy -
library; dioramas; art gallery

Lubbock TX

15265
**The Museum of Texas Tech
University**
POB 4499, Lubbock, TX 79409
General Museum - 1929
Coll: physical, biological and social
heritages of the semi-arid and arid
regions - laboratory, planetarium

Lucas OH

15266
The Louis Bromfield Malabar Farm
Rte 1, Lucas, OH 44843
Agriculture Museum - 1939
Coll: ecology; natural history;
agriculture; antiques and furnishings -
library; nature center

Ludington MI

15267
Rose Hawley Museum
305 E. Filer St, Ludington, MI 49431
General Museum - 1037
Coll: laces; silver; shells; textiles;
glass; china - library

Ludlow VT

15268
Black River Academy Museum
POB 16, Ludlow, VT 05149
General Museum - 1972
Coll: paintings, photographs and
artifacts depicting the economic,
cultural and political history of the area
- library

Lufkin TX

15269
**Lufkin Historical and Creative Arts
Center**
2nd and Paul St, POB 771, Lufkin, TX
75901
Fine Arts Museum - 1975
Coll: East Texas art - meeting
auditorium

15270
Texas Forestry Museum
1903 Atkinson Dr, POB 1488, Lufkin,
TX 75901
Agriculture Museum - 1976
Coll: logging equipment, tools, wood
identification

Lumpkin GA

15271
Providence Canyon State Park
Rte 2, POB 33, Lumpkin, GA 31815
Natural History Museum - 1970
Coll: natural history exhibits; displays
on erosion - nature trails

Lutherville MD

15272
Fire Museum of Maryland, Inc.
1301 York Rd, Lutherville, MD 21093
History/Public Affairs Museum - 1971
Coll: antique fire fighting apparatus,
1753-1950; photographs; operational
fire alarm telegraph system

Lynchburg VA

15273
Lynchburg Fine Arts Center
1815 Thomson Dr, Lynchburg, VA
24501
Performing Arts Museum - 1958
Coll: music; costumes - theater;
studios

15274
Lynchburg Museum System
POB 60, Lynchburg, VA 24505
History/Public Affairs Museum - 1976
Coll: furniture; costumes; photographs

Lynn MA

15275
Lynn Historical Society Inc
125 Green St, Lynn, MA 01902
General Museum - 1897
Coll: antiques; paintings; glass; china;
shoe industry; costumes - library;
reading room; auditorium

Lyons Falls NY

15276
**Lewis County Historical Society
Museum** Gould-Hough Cultural &
Educational Center
High St, POB 306, Lyons Falls, NY
13368
General Museum - 1930
Coll: archaeology; ethnology;
costumes; geology; military;
technology; photographs, documents,
local history - library

Lyons KS

15277
Rice County Historical Museum
221 E Ave S, Lyons, KS 67554
History/Public Affairs Museum - 1959
Coll: Coronado and Quiviran Indian
artifacts; Choronado chain mail;
Papapo Indian baskets; anthropology;
archaeology

Lyons NY

15278
**Wayne County Historical Society,
Inc.**
21 Butternut St, Lyons, NY 14489
General Museum - 1946
Coll: local history artifacts; early
criminology; agriculture; sheriff's
residence (1854); county jail (1854); St.
Peter exhibit - library; nature center

McAllen TX

15279
McAllen International Museum
1900 Nolana, McAllen, TX 78501
General Museum - 1969
Coll: art, science, local history -
library; meeting rooms

McConnells SC

15280
Brattonsville Historic District
Rte. 1, McConnells, SC 29726
General Museum - 1976
Coll: Preservationed Historic Houses
(1776 - 1843)

McCook NE

15281
High Plains Museum
423 Norris Ave, McCook, NE 69001
History/Public Affairs Museum - 1969
Coll: German bibles; fashion from
1779-present; musical instruments;
dolls; railroad memorabilia; uniforms
from Spanish-American War and
Vietnam War - library

McGregor IA

15282
Effigy Mounds National Monument
POB K, McGregor, IA 52157
Archeology Museum - 1949
Coll: Indian artifacts; ethnology;
archaeological collections of mound
excavation - auditorium; library

Mackinac Island MI

15283
**Mackinac Island State Park
Commission**
POB 370, Mackinac Island, MI 49757
History/Public Affairs Museum - 1895
Coll: historic buildings; archaeological
artifacts; maritime materials - library

McKinney TX

15284
**Heard Natural Science Museum and
Wildlife Sanctuary**
Rte 7, POB 171, McKinney, TX 75069
Science/Tech Museum - 1964
Coll: malachology; insects;
herpetology; ornithology - classrooms

Macomb IL

15285
Western Illinois University Art Gallery
Garwood Hall, Macomb, IL 61455
Fine Arts Museum - 1899
Coll: contemporary graphics, painting, sculpture, glass, jewelry; American Indian pottery; WPA graphics and painting

Macon GA

15286
Middle Georgia Historical Society, Inc.
935 High St, Macon, GA 31201
History/Public Affairs Museum - 1964
Coll: documents and photographs; archives of Middle Georgia; birthplace of poet Sidney Lanier; historic houses

15287
Museum of Arts and Sciences
4182 Forsyth Rd, Macon, GA 31210
General Museum - 1956
Coll: archeological artifacts; exotic moths and butterflies; local wildlife specimens; toys; paintings and drawings by American and European artists - library; arboretum; nature trails; observatory; nature center; planetarium; classrooms

15288
Ocmulgee National Monument
1207 Emery Hwy, Macon, GA 31201
Archeology Museum - 1936
Coll: Indian artifacts; archeology representing six culture levels covering 10,000 years; anthropology; history; ethnology - library; nature trails

McPherson KS

15289
McPherson Museum
1130 E Euclid, McPherson, KS 67460
General Museum - 1890
Coll: Oriental items; snuff bottles from China; bells; clocks - library, auditorium

Madison CT

15290
Madison Historical Society
853 Boston Post Rd, Madison, CT 06443
General Museum - 1917
Coll: costumes; dolls; tools and equipment for farming; carpentry; spinning and weaving - library

Madison IN

15291
Historic Madison, Inc.
301 W 1st St, Madison, IN 47250
General Museum - 1960
Coll: house furnishings; office and hospital furnishings of early 19th century

Madison SD

15292
Prairie Village
POB 256, Madison, SD 57042
General Museum - 1966
Coll: 40 restored buildings; furniture; steam equipment; threshing machines; rock collection - library; auditorium; classrooms

15293
Smith-Zimmermann Historical Museum
Dakota State College, Madison, SD 57042
General Museum - 1953
Coll: early history of the area and the state; Indian artifacts; coins; silver; farm and home articles

Madison WI

15294
Elvehjem Museum of Art
800 University Av, Madison, WI 53706
Fine Arts Museum - 1962
Coll: paintings; graphics; sculpture; archeology; decorative arts - library; classrooms; auditorium

15295
Grand Army of the Republic Memorial Hall Museum
State Capitol 419 N, Madison, WI 53702
History/Public Affairs Museum - 1901
Coll: Spanish-American and Civil War arms; uniforms; flags; military equipment; photos

15296
Madison Art Center, Inc.
720 E Gorham St, Madison, WI 53703
Fine Arts Museum - 1901
Coll: Japanese, Mexican and American paintings, sculpture, prints; Randolph E. Langer collection of graphics; 17th century Flemish tapestries - reading and print study rooms; auditorium; classrooms

15297
State Historical Society of Wisconsin
816 State St, Madison, WI 53706
History/Public Affairs Museum - 1846
Coll: Wisconsin history exhibits; firearms; dolls; Civil War items; coins; stamps; anthropology; ethnology; decorative arts - library; auditorium

15298
University of Wisconsin Arboretum
1207 Seminole Hwy, Madison, WI 53711
Natural History Museum - 1934
Coll: botany; natural history; plants and animals in ecological communities; zoology; geology

15299
University of Wisconsin Zoological Museum
Lowell Noland Building, Madison, WI 53706
Natural History Museum - 1875
Coll: zoology; ornithology; mammalogy; ichthyology; herpetology; osteology; paleontology; malacology - library

15300
The Wisconsin Union
800 Langdon St, Madison, WI 53706
Fine Arts Museum - 1928
Coll: paintings, prints, photographs, mostly of American University of Wisconsin students - theater; reading room

Mahomet IL

15301
Early American Museum and Botanical Garden
POB 336, Mahomet, IL 61853
History/Public Affairs Museum - 1967
Coll: tools, implements and furniture; lighting devices and household items dating between 1700 and 1900 - library

Mainfield ME

15302
Willowbrook at Newfield
Main St, Mainfield, ME 04056
General Museum - 1970
Coll: washing machines; shoe and harness making; bicycles; gasoline engines; wheelrights; musical instruments

Makawao HI

15303
Hakeakala National Park
POB 537, Makawao, HI 96768
Natural History Museum - 1916
Coll: geology; zoology; botany - library; nature trail

Makoti ND

15304
Makoti Threshers Museum
Makoti, ND 58756
Agriculture Museum - 1961
250 stationary engines; 150 antique farm tractors and implements

Malibu CA

15305
J. Paul Getty Museum
17985 Pacific Coast Hwy, Malibu, CA 90265
Fine Arts Museum - 1953
Coll: Greek and Roman antiquities; 18th century French decorative arts; Western European paintings from the 13th to 20th centuries - library; conservation laboratories; auditorium

Malone NY

15306
Franklin House of History
51 Milwaukee St, Malone, NY 12953
General Museum - 1903
Coll: history; agriculture; period rooms; headquarter papers of the 16th Civil War Regiment of New York State volunteers - library

Manassas VA

15307
Manassas Museum
9406 Main St, Manassas, VA 22018
General Museum - 1974
Coll: architectural history of area - library

15308
Manassas National Battlefield Park
POB 1830, Manassas, VA 22110
General Museum - 1940
Coll: Battles of Manassas artifacts; medical items; history - library

Manchester CT

15309
Lutz Junior Museum
126 Cedar St, Manchester, CT 06040
Junior Museum - 1953
Coll: live animals; antiques; natural history; ethnology - nature center; classrooms

Manchester NH

15310
The Currier Gallery of Art
192 Orange St, Manchester, NH 03104
Fine Arts Museum - 1929
Coll: European and American painting and sculpture; American 17th, 18th and early 19th century furniture, silver, glass, pewter and textiles; graphics; 15th century Tournai tapestry - library; auditorium; classrooms

15311
Manchester Historic Association
129 Amherst St, Manchester, NH 03104
General Museum - 1896
Coll: decorative arts; fire-fighting equipment; costumes; architectural illustrations and fragments; photographs; prints - library; auditorium

Manchester VT

15312
The Museum of American Fly Fishing
Manchester, VT 05254
History/Public Affairs Museum - 1968
Coll: reels; fly rods; flies - library

15313
Southern Vermont Art Center
Manchester, VT 05254
Fine Arts Museum - 1929
Coll: paintings; sculptures; graphics - library

Mandan ND

15314
Fort Abraham Lincoln State Historical Park
Rte 2, POB 139, Mandan, ND 58554
Historic Site - 1936
Coll: Mandan Indian artifacts; military (1870); memorabilia of 7th Cavalry and General Custer

15315
Great Plains Museum
St. Anthony Rd, POB 3, Mandan, ND 58554
General Museum - 1936
Coll: autos; farm machinery; musical instruments; firearms; antique bottles; costumes; Seagrave fire truck (1926); barbed wire; barber shop; gas engines; Mathew O'Brien Home (1877); Nancy Christenson Homestead Claim Shack (1915)

Manhasset NY

15316
Historical Society of the Town of North Hempstead
220 Plandome Rd, Manhasset, NY 11030
General Museum - 1963
Coll: agriculture; history; botany; transportation; Indian artifacts - arboretum; aviary; herbarium

Manhattan KS

15317
Riley County Historical Museum
2309 Claflin Rd, Manhattan, KS 66502
History/Public Affairs Museum - 1914
Coll: furniture; tools; glass; china; dolls; transportation - library

Manistique MI

15318
Imogene Herbert Historical Museum
Deer St, Pioneer Park, POB 284,
Manistique, MI 49845
General Museum - 1963
Coll: geology; Indian artifacts

Manitou Springs CO

15319
Cameron's Doll and Carriage Museum
218 Beckers Lane, Manitou Springs,
CO 80829
Anthropology Museum - 1963
Dolls and baby carriages of every
category and size - library

15320
Miramont Castle Museum
9 Capitol Hill Ave, Manitou Springs,
CO 80829
General Museum - 1976
Coll: Victorian period furniture and
furnishings; archives of area; historic
castle (1895) - children's museum

Manitowoc WI

15321
Manitowoc Maritime Museum
809 S 8th St, Manitowoc, WI 54220
Science/Tech Museum - 1969
Coll: submarine artifacts; ship tools;
ship models; salvage artifacts; life
boat; photos; documents - library

15322
Rahr West Museum
Park St at N 8th, Manitowoc, WI 54220
Fine Arts Museum - 1950
Coll: American paintings; Chinese
ivories; 19th century American
decorative arts and furnishings; dolls;
Indian anthropology - library;
classrooms

Mankato KS

15323
Jewell County Historical Museum
Mankato, KS 66956
History/Public Affairs Museum - 1961
Coll: historic rooms; geology - library

Mankato MN

15324
Blue Earth County Historical Society Museum
606 S Broad St, Mankato, MN 56001
History/Public Affairs Museum - 1916
Coll: documents; archives;
transportation; Indian and pioneer
artifacts - library

Mansfield OH

15325
The Mansfield Art Center
700 Marrion Av, Mansfield, OH 44903
Fine Arts Museum - 1946
Coll: contemporary art - library

Manteo NC

15326
Bodie Island Visitor Center Cape
Hatteras National Seashore
Rte 1, POB 675, Manteo, NC 27954
Open Air Museum - 1956
Coll: natural history; panels; shells;
Bodie Island Light Station (1872) -
auditorium

15327
Roanoak Indian Village
POB 906, Manteo, NC 27954
Historic Site - 1971
Coll: tools and methods of ancient
inhabitants; relics and reconstructed
items - library

15328
Wright Brothers National Memorial
Cape Hatteras National Seashore
Rte 1, POB 675, Manteo, NC 27954
Historic Site - 1928
Coll: replicas of flyer (1903) and glider
(1902); wind tunnel and tools used by
the Wright Brothers

Mantorville MN

15329
Dodge County Old Settlers and Historical Society
Mantorville, MN 55955
General Museum - 1949
Coll: military; agriculture; paintings -
library

Maquoketa IA

15330
Jackson County Historical Museum
Fairgrounds, POB 1245, Maquoketa, IA
52060
General Museum - 1964
Coll: dolls; country store; farm kitchen;
country school; Maude Brooks exhibit;
farm machinery

Marietta GA

15331
Cobb County Youth Museum
649 Cheatham Hill Dr, Marietta, GA
30064
Junior Museum - 1970
Coll: farm wagon; jet trainer; a
caboose; street car stop; history
exhibits

15332
Kennesaw Mountain National Battlefield Park
Jct Stilesboro Rd and Old Hwy 41,
POB 1167, Marietta, GA 30061
History/Public Affairs Museum - 1899
Coll: dress and weapons of Civil War
soldiers; historic house; site of Civil
War battle field - library; auditorium

Marietta OH

15333
Campus Martius Museum
601 2nd St, Marietta, OH 45750
General Museum - 1919
Coll: objects, manuscripts pertaining to
local history; steamboat photographs;
Ohio Company Land Office (1788);
Rufus Putnam House (1789) - library

15334
Ohio River Museum
Muskingum River, at St. Clair near
Front St, *mail c/o* Campus Martius
Museum, 601 2nd St, Marietta, OH
45750
History/Public Affairs Museum - 1941
Coll: history of the 19th century
steamboat era; stern-wheel Steamer
W. P. Snyder, Jr. (1918) - auditorium

Marinette WI

15335
Marinette County Logging Museum
US Hwy 41, POB 262, Marinette, WI
54143
Science/Tech Museum - 1962
Logging and historical artifacts;
logging camp replica - library

Marlinton WV

15336
Pocahontas County Museum
Seneca Trail, Marlinton, WV 24954
General Museum - 1962
Coll: historic photographs; archives;
local history items - library

Marquette MI

15337
Bishop Baraga Association
239 Baraga Ave, Marquette, MI 49855
History/Public Affairs Museum - 1930
Coll: archives - library

15338
Marquette County Historical Society
213 N. Front St, Marquette, MI 49855
General Museum - 1918
Coll: minerals; ethnology; technology;
geology; folklore; glass; silver; toys -
library

Marshall MI

15339
Honolulu House Museum
POB 15, Marshall, MI 49068
History/Public Affairs Museum - 1917
Coll: decorative arts; folklore; maps -
library

Marshall Mn

15340
Lyon County Historical Society Old
Courtroom
Lyon County Courthouse, Marshall,
Mn 56258
General Museum - 1950
Coll: geology; natural history; clocks;
Indian artifacts

Marshall TX

15341
Harrison County Historical Museum
Old Courthouse, Peter Whetstone
Square, Marshall, TX 75670
General Museum - 1965
paintings; porcelains; costumes; radios
- library

Marshfield WI

15342
North Wood County Historical Society Museum
212 W 3rd St, Marshfield, WI 54449
General Museum - 1972
Pioneer artifacts; household goods;
furnishings; clothing; toys - library

Marysville KS

15343
Original Pony Express Home Station
809 North St, Marysville, KS 66508
History/Public Affairs Museum - 1967
agriculture; threshing machine; Pony
Express mementos; steam tractor;
Indian artifacts

Maryville TN

15344
Sam Houston Memorial Association
Rte. 8, Sam Houston Schoolhouse Rd,
Maryville, TN 37801
General Museum - 1965
Coll: early school and pioneer
artifacts; genealogy of Houston family;
historic building (1794)

Mason City IA

15345
Charles H. McNider Museum
303 2nd St SE, Mason City, IA 50401
Fine Arts Museum - 1964
Coll: American and Iowa art including
paintings, prints, drawings and pottery
- classroom; library; reading room

15346
Kinney Pioneer Museum and Historical Society of North Iowa
Highway 18 West, POB 421, Mason
City, IA 50401
History/Public Affairs Museum - 1964
Coll: hand-drawn fire engine; milk
wagon; Indian artifacts; furniture and
furnishing; fossil collection, hand-made
implements; old dolls and toys; other
items of local history

Massillon OH

15347
The Massillon Museum
212 Lincoln Way E, Massillon, OH
44646
General Museum - 1933
Coll: American folk art; glass; china;
pottery; metal; American and
European fine and decorative arts;
ivories; costumes; graphics; Indian
artifacts; war items; tools and utensils;
photographs; quilts and coverlets -
library; classrooms

Mattapoisett MA

15348
Mattapoisett Museum and Carriage House
5 Church St, Mattapoisett, MA 02739
General Museum - 1959
coll: glass; guns; china; canes;
maritime and whaling items; cobblers;
farm equipment - library

Mauston WI

15349
The Old Manse
215 Oak St, Mauston, WI 53948
General Museum - 1963
Local history; artifacts - library

Maxwell IA

15350
Community Historical Museum
Maxwell, IA 50161
General Museum - 1964
Coll: agriculture; costumes; history;
Indian artifacts; children's museum;
archives; transportation; numismatics;
textiles - reading room; library

Mayville WI

15351
Mayville Historical Society, Inc.
Corner Bridge and German Sts,
Mayville, WI 53050
General Museum - 1968
Coll: local history items; wagons;
agricultural materials; glassware;
clothing; religious articles; pictures
and manuscripts; historic houses -
library

Meade KS

15352
**Meade County Historical Society
Museum**
200 E Carthage, Meade, KS 67864
History/Public Affairs Museum - 1969
Coll: historic rooms; Indian artifacts -
library

Meadville PA

15353
Baldwin-Reynolds House Museum
639 Terrace St, 848 N Main St,
Meadville, PA 16335
General Museum - 1963
Coll: agriculture; Indian artifacts;
paintings; costumes; history; glass;
medicine; mineralogy; natural history;
numismatics; historic house - library

Medford OK

15354
Grant County Museum
Main and Cherokee Sts, Medford, OK
73759
General Museum - 1968
Coll: general artifacts; sod plow;
wheel; wheat cradle; churns; pictures;
old fashioned kitchen

Medora ND

15355
De Mores Historic Site
Medora, ND 58645
Historic Site - 1936
home of Marquis de Mores (1883) with
original furnishings

15356
**Theodore Roosevelt National Park
Visitor Center**
Medora, ND 58645
General Museum - 1959
Coll: partial collection of Theodore
Roosevelt's ranching effects;
anthropology; archaeology; botany;
geology; industry; natural history;
Indian artifacts; Maltese Cross cabin
(1883) - library; park museum;
herbarium

Meeker CO

15357
The White River Museum
565 Park St, Meeker, CO 81641
General Museum - 1956
Coll: rocks; furniture; Indian artifacts;
pioneer artifacts

Memphis TN

15358
Brooks Memorial Art Gallery
Overton Park, Memphis, TN 38112
Fine Arts Museum - 1913
Coll: Kress collection of Italian
Renaissance paintings and sculpture;
North European paintings and
sculpture (16th-19th century); English
portraits and landscapes (17th, 18th
century); International collection of
paintings and sculpture (20th century);
AAA 1930-1961 prints; porcelain;
glass; textiles - library; auditorium

15359
C. H. Nash Museum-Chucalissa
1987 Indian Village Dr., Memphis, TN
38109
Archeology Museum - 1955
Coll: archaeological research
collection from sites in Western
Tennessee and adjacent areas; Chert
reference collection from various
geological formations in the Midsouth
- library; laboratory; auditorium

15360
The Dixon Gallery and Gardens
4339 Park Av, Memphis, TN 38117
Fine Arts Museum - 1976
Coll: paintings, prints and sculptures
(18th and 19th century) with emphasis
on French and American
Impressionists; fine European
porcelain and furniture - library

15361
E. H. Little Gallery
Memphis State University Campus,
Memphis, TN 38152
General Museum - 1969
Coll: paintings; graphics; archaeology;
costumes - library

15362
Memphis Academy of Arts
Overton Park, Memphis, TN 38112
Fine Arts Museum - 1936
Coll: Jacob Marks Memorial
Collection; works of college graduates
- library; auditorium; classrooms

15363
Memphis Pink Palace Museum
3050 Central Av, Memphis, TN 38111
General Museum - 1928
Coll: artifacts; specimens and
documents relating to the cultural and
natural history of Memphis and the
mid-southern region; historic house
(1835) - library, classrooms,
planetarium; auditorium

15364
PT Boats Inc.
POB 109, Memphis, TN 38101
History/Public Affairs Museum - 1967
Coll: WW II PT Boats; one-man
Japanese suicide Submarine; books;
diaries; insignias; memorabilia of 43
operating squadrons of WW II PT
boats; films; photographs; plans -
library

Mendenhall PA

15365
Hillendale Museum
Hillendale and Hickory Hill Rds, POB
129, Mendenhall, PA 19357
History/Public Affairs Museum - 1961
geography; North American
exploration

Menomonie WI

15366
Art Center Gallery University of
Wisconsin - Stout
Fourth St, Menomonie, WI 54751
Fine Arts Museum - 1964
Coll: prints, paintings, sculpture of 20th
century America; graphics; decorative
arts; ceramics

Mentor OH

15367
Lake County Historical Society
8095 Mentor Av, Mentor, OH 44060
General Museum - 1936
Coll: decorative arts; costumes;
archival material - library

Mequon WI

15368
Crafts Museum
11458 N Laguna Dr, 21 W, Mequon,
WI 53092
Science/Tech Museum - 1972
Tools of traveling craftsmen for ice,
wood and leather; photos - library

Meriden CT

15369
Meriden Historical Society, Inc.
424 W. Main St, Meriden, CT 06450
General Museum - 1893
Coll: costumes; glass and china;
historical items; industry; dolls;
furniture; manuscripts - junior
museum

Meridian MS

15370
Jimmie Rodgers Museum
POB 1928, Meridian, MS 39301
History/Public Affairs Museum - 1976
Coll: items belonging to the late
Jimmie Rodgers, father of country
music

15371
Meridian Museum of Art
15th Ave and 7th St, Meridian, MS
30301
Fine Arts Museum - 1969
Coll: Caroline Durieux prints; works
by Salvador Dali, Will Barnet, Eduardo
Paolozi, Marie Hull, Andrew Bucci and
Helen Garardia - library; reading
room; classrooms

Merion PA

15372
Buten Museum of Wedgwood
246 N Bowman Av, Merion, PA 19066
Decorative Arts Museum - 1957
comprehensive collection of 10,000
pieces of Wedgwood of 1759 to the
present - library

Mesa Verde CO

15373
Mesa Verde National Park Museum
Mesa Verde National Park, Mesa
Verde, CO 81330
Archeology Museum - 1917
Coll: archeological remains;
southwestern US ethnography -
library

Mesilla NM

15374
American Cowboy Museum
State Hwy 28 at Boutz Rd, Mesilla NM
88046, 644 West Court, Las Cruces,
NM 88001
Agriculture Museum - 1975
Coll: items relating to cowboys and
cattle raising in America; Billy the Kid
historama

15375
American Desert Museum
Old Mesilla Rd & Hwy 28, POB 357,
Mesilla, NM 88046
Natural History Museum - 1970
Coll: botany - library

15376
**United States Postal History
Museum, Inc.**
Old Mesilla Rd at State Rd 28, POB
357, Mesilla, NM 88046
History/Public Affairs Museum
Coll: U.S. Postal Service history;
Aerophilately and Lindberghiana (1926
through the present)

Metamora IN

15377
Whitewater Canal State Memorial
POB 88, Metamora, IN 47030
General Museum
Coll: milling machinery; early
transportation and industrial
development; early tools

Metlakatla AK

15378
Duncan Cottage Museum
Duncan St, POB 282, Metlakatla, AK
99926
Historic Site
Coll: antique items from 19th century;
Indian artifacts - library

Mexico City MO

15379
Audrain County Historical Society
501 S Muldrow, Mexico City, MO
65265
General Museum - 1939
Coll: paintings; dolls; Saddle Horse
Museum traces the history of the
Saddle horse; piano; glass - library

Miami FL

15380
**The American Foundation for the
Arts**
3841 NE 2nd Av, Miami, FL 33137
Fine Arts Museum - 1974
Coll: contemporary paintings;
photography; architecture

15381
Bass Museum of Art
2100 Collins Av, Miami, FL 33139
Fine Arts Museum - 1964
Coll: sculpture; vestments; tapestries;
John and Johanna Bass collection of
paintings

15382
**Historical Museum of Southern
Florida**
3280 S Miami Av, Bldg B, Miami, FL
33129
History/Public Affairs Museum - 1962
Coll: archives; archeology;
anthropology; historical artifacts -
library; classroom

15383
Marine Laboratory Marine Museum
4600 Rickenbacker Causeway, Miami,
FL 33149
Natural History Museum - 1945
Coll: research collections of 40,000
catalogued entries of marine animals
and plants from the Tropical Atlantic
and the Panamaic region of the
eastern Pacific from marine
environments to the deep sea

15384
Museum of Science
3280 S Miami Av, Miami, FL 33129
Science/Tech Museum - 1949
Coll: anthropology; archeology;
astronomy; entomology; geology;
Indian artifacts ; marine artifacts; live
biome; live native and tropical animals
and reptiles; Mayan artifacts - library;
environmental information center;
nature center; planetarium; auditorium;
theater; classrooms; observatory

15385
Villa Vizcaya Museum and Gardens
3251 S Miami Av, Miami, FL 33129
Historic Site - 1952
Coll: European interiors of the
16th-19th centuries; art objects of
marble, bronze, wood, textile, ceramic,
and ivory; Italian Renaissance palace
(1916) - library; formal gardens

Miami MO

15386
**Lyman Archaeological Research
Center Museum**
Rte 1, Miami, MO 65344
Archeology Museum - 1959
Coll: archaeology; history; Indian
cultures - library

Michigan City IN

15387
Old Lighthouse Museum
At the Bend of the Harbor, POB 512,
Michigan City, IN 46360
History/Public Affairs Museum - 1973
Coll: lighthouse (1858); lighthouse
service artifacts; boat builder's tools;
shipwreck artifacts; local Indian
artifacts; early farm tools - library

Middleborough MA

15388
**Middleborough Historical
Association Inc**
Jackson St, Middleborough, MA 02346
General Museum - 1960
Coll: G.A.R collection including rifles;
history; folklore; archaeology; glass -
library

Middleburg PA

15389
**The Snyder County Historical
Society, Inc.** Dr. Geo. F. Dunkleberger
Memorial Library
30 E Market St, POB 276, Middleburg,
PA 17842
General Museum - 1898
Coll: archives; geology; Indian
artifacts; Civil War relics

Middlebury VT

15390
**Johnson Gallery of Middlebury
College**
Middlebury, VT 05753
Fine Arts Museum - 1968
Historic art of all cultures and media

15391
**The Sheldon Art Museum,
Archaeological and Historical
Society**
1 Park St, Middlebury, VT 05753
History/Public Affairs Museum - 1882
Coll: 19th century home furnishings;
pianos; clocks - library

Middletown CT

15392
Davison Art Center Wesleyan
University
301 High St, Middletown, CT 06457
Fine Arts Museum - 1952
Coll: prints from early 15th century to
the present; period furnishings;
antebellum mansion - library

15393
Middlesex County Historical Society
151 Main St, Middletown, CT 06457
General Museum - 1901
Coll: decorative arts; antique
furnishings; genealogical materials -
library

Middletown NJ

15394
Marlpit Hall
137 Kings Hwy, Middletown, NJ 07748
General Museum
Coll: 17th and 18th century period
furnishings; woodpaneling and
carving; porcelain; paintings

Middletown NY

15395
**Historical Society of Middletown and
the Wallkill Precinct, Inc.**
25 East Av, Middletown, NY 10940
General Museum - 1923
Coll: Indian artifacts; photographs;
clothing; china; historic buildings -
library; reading room

Midland MI

15396
Chippewa Nature Center
400 S Badour Rd, Rte 9, Midland, MI
48640
Historic Site - 1966
Coll: birds; mammals; insects; Indian
artifacts - library; auditorium

15397
Midland County Historical Society
1801 W. Andrews Dr, MIdland, MI
48640
History/Public Affairs Museum - 1952
Coll: silver; glass; textiles; music;
photography - library; auditorium;
classrooms

Midland TX

15398
Midland County Historical Museum
301 W Missouri, Midland, TX 79701
General Museum - 1930
Coll: archaeology; Indian artifacts;
geology

15399
Museum of the Southwest
1705 W Missouri St, Midland, TX
79701
General Museum - 1965
Coll: American art; 17th and 18th
century European fan; Southwestern
US archaeology - library; auditorium;
planetarium

15400
**Permian Basin Petroleum Museum,
Library and Hall of Fame**
1500 Interstate 20 W, Midland, TX
79701
Science/Tech Museum - 1967
technology relating to petroleum; oil
industry antique machinery and
subjects - library; auditorium

Midway GA

15401
Midway Museum
U.S. Hwy 17, Midway, GA 31320
General Museum - 1957
Colonial furnishings

Milan OH

15402
Milan Historical Museum
10 Edison Dr, Milan, OH 44846
General Museum - 1929
Coll: glass; folklore; dolls; textiles;
agriculture; history; decorative arts;
ethnology; marine; mineralogy; natural
history; numismatics; transportation -
junior and children's museum

Milford CT

15403
Eells-Stow House Milford Historical
Society
34 High St, POB 337, Milford, CT
06460
General Museum - 1930
Coll: antiques of local interest; Claude
C. Coffin Indian collection; furniture;
historic house (1785) - library

Milford NJ

15404
Velendam Windmill Museum, Inc
R.D. 1, POB 242, Milford, NJ 08848
History/Public Affairs Museum - 1965
Coll: 1700-1800 milling implements;
antique mill machinery; tools

Milford PA

15405
Pike County Historical Society
Harford St, Milford, PA 18337
General Museum - 1930
Coll: antique farm and household
implements; Lincoln assassination
tableau; Indian relics; old photos; early
school house and school house
memorabilia - library

Millersburg OH

15406
Holmes County Historical Society
233 N Washington St, Millersburg, OH
44654
General Museum - 1965
Coll: period furniture; furnishings and
artifacts; early medical furnishings;
early law office - library

Millville NJ

15407
Wheaton Historical Association
Wheaton Village, Millville, NJ 08332
History/Public Affairs Museum - 1968
Coll: southern New Jersey and United
States glass; operating reproduction
of a 19th century glass factory and
other craft shops - library

Millwood VA

15408
Burwell-Morgan Mill
Millwood, VA 22620
Historic Site - 1964
Coll: wooden water wheel and
equipment; mill construction and
operation

Milton Ma

15409
**Museum of the American China
Trade**
215 Adams St, Milton, Ma 02186
Decorative Arts Museum - 1964
Coll: Asian export art 1500-1900;
export porcelain; lacquerware; carved
and other decorative wares; China
trade memorabilia - library; reading
room

Milton MS

15410
Blue Hills Trailside Museum
1904 Canton Av, Milton, MS 02186
Natural History Museum - 1959
Coll: herpetology; zoology; geology;
aquatic; avian; archaeology - library;
aquarium

Milton WI

15411
Milton House Museum
Hwy 26&59, POB 245, Milton, WI
53563
General Museum - 1954
Coll: early pioneer items; Civil War
artifacts; costumes; clocks; tools;
historic houses - library

Milwaukee

15412
Greene Memorial Museum University
of Wisconsin
3367 N Downer Av, Milwaukee 53201
Natural History Museum - 1913
Coll: fossils; geology; paleontology;
mineralogy; conchology - library

Milwaukee WI

15413
Art History Galleries University of
Wisconsin
Milwaukee, WI 53201
Fine Arts Museum - 1964
Coll: Greek and Russian icons;
liturgical objects; paintings; graphics

15414
Charles Allis Art Library
1630 E Royall Place, Milwaukee, WI
532o2
Fine Arts Museum - 1947
Coll: Chinese porcelains; 19th century
French paintings; 19th century
American landscape paintings; antique
Greek and Roman art; French
antiques; decorative arts - reading
room; theater

15415
Fine Arts Galleries University of
Wisconsin
3200 Downer Av, Milwaukee, WI
53201
Fine Arts Museum - 1963
Coll: 20th century paintings; sculpture;
prints; drawings; photography;
Oriental art

15416
Milwaukee Art Center
750 N Lincoln Memorial Dr,
Milwaukee, WI 53202
Fine Arts Museum - 1888
Coll: primarily American and European
20th century painting, sculpture,
graphics, decorative arts - library;
learning center for children with multi-
media theater

15417
**Milwaukee County Historical
Society**
910 N Third St, Milwaukee, WI 53203
General Museum - 1935
Coll: county history; fire equipment;
brewery materials; transportation
items; paintings; early settlers
materials; aeronautics; decorative arts;
military; technology - library; archives

15418
Milwaukee Public Museum
800 W Wells St, Milwaukee, WI 53233
Natural History Museum - 1882
Coll: anthropology; botany; geology;
natural history; invertebrate and
vertebrate zoology - library;
conservation lab; photography studio;
classrooms

Minden NE

15419
Pioneer Village
Minden, NE 68959
General Museum - 1953
Coll: aeronautics; agriculture; music;
philatelic; graphics

Mineral Point WI

15420
Mineral Point Historical Society
311 High St, Mineral Point, WI 53565
General Museum - 1939
Coll: folklore; geology; mineralogy;
costumes; historic house - archives

Minneapolis MN

15421
American Swedish Institute
2600 Park Ave, Minneapolis, MN
55407
History/Public Affairs Museum - 1929
Coll: Swedish and Swedish-American
art; glass; textiles; silver; furniture;
folklore; archives - library; reading
room

15422
Bakken Museum of Electricity in Life
3537 Zenith Ave S, Minneapolis, MN
55416
Science/Tech Museum - 1975
Coll: Apparatus dating back to 1740;
illustrating the use of electricity in
medicine and biology; electric fish and
other exhibits illustrating
electrophysiology; rare book
collection on electromedicine,
electrophysiology and magnetism -
library

15423
**Hennepin County Historical Society
Museum**
2303 3rd Ave, Minneapolis, MN 55404
History/Public Affairs Museum - 1938
Coll: clocks; lighting; telephones;
pioneer furnishings - library;
auditorium

15424
**James Ford Bell Museum of Natural
History**
10 Church St SE, Minneapolis, MN
55455
Natural History Museum - 1872
Coll: ornithology; ichtyology;
herpetology; ecology; ethology -
library; reading room; auditorium;
classrooms

15425
The Minneapolis Institute of Arts
2400 Third Ave S, Minneapolis, MN
55404
Fine Arts Museum - 1012
Coll: Oriental art; Pre-Columbian art;
Islamic art; African and Oceanic art -
library; reading room; auditorium;
theater; classrooms

15426
**Minneapolis Public Library Science
Museum and Planetarium**
300 Nicollet Mall, Minneapolis, MN
55401
Science/Tech Museum - 1872
Coll: fossils; Egyptian mummies;
minerals; ecology; geology - library;
auditorium

15427
University Gallery University of
Minnesota
110 Northrop Memorial Auditorium, 84
Church St SE, Minneapolis, MN 55455
Fine Arts Museum - 1934
Coll: 20th American painting; 18th
century Italian and Austrian paintings;
ancient vases; decorative arts

15428
Walker Art Center
Vineland Place, Minneapolis, MN
55403
Fine Arts Museum - 1879
Coll: contemporary art; paintings;
sculptures; drawings; prints - library

Mishawaka IN

15429
Hannah Lindahl Children's Museum
410 Lincoln Way East, Mishawaka, IN
46544
Junior Museum - 1946
Coll: sculpture; Indian artifacts;
costumes; archeology; archives;
military; natural history - aquarium;
arboretum

*Mississippi State University
MS*

15430
Dunn-Seiler Museum
POB G6, Mississippi State University,
MS 39762
Natural History Museum - 1947
Coll: Mesozioc and Cenozoic
paleontology; upper cretaceous
lepadomorph barnacles; mineralogy;
geology

Mitchell GA

15431
Hamburg State Park Museum
Mitchell, GA 30820
Science/Tech Museum
Coll: farm tools; ginning equipment;
milling machinery

Mitchell IN

15432
**Spring Mill State Park Pioneer
Village**
POB 376, Mitchell, IN 47446
History/Public Affairs Museum - 1927
Pioneer artifacts (more than 7,000) -
garden; nature center

15433
Virgil I. Grissom State Memorial
Spring Mill State Park, POB 376,
Mitchell, IN 47446
General Museum - 1971
Mementos of the life of Virgil I.
Grissom, second astronaut in space

Mitchell SD

15434
**Friends of the Middle Border
Pioneer Museum**
1311 S. Duff St, Mitchell, SD 57301
History/Public Affairs Museum - 1939
Coll: items pertaining to the Middle
Border homestead era; Indian
artifacts; military; transportation;
historic buildings (1885-1900)

15435
Mitchell Car Museum
1130 S. Burr St, Mitchell, SD 57301
Science/Tech Museum - 1976
Coll: antique, classic and special
interest cars and trucks

15436
Oscar Howe Art Center
119 W. Third, Mitchell, SD 57301
General Museum - 1972
Coll: original paintings and lithographs
by Sioux artist Oscar Howe -
auditorium

Moab UT

15437
Arches National Park
Moab, UT 84532
Science/Tech Museum
Coll: herbarium; geology; botany -
library

15438
Moab Museum
118 E Center, Moab, UT 84532
History/Public Affairs Museum - 1958
Coll: archaeology; mineralogy

Mobile 28 AL

15439
Museums of the City of Mobile
355 Government St, Mobile 28 AL
36602
History/Public Affairs Museum - 1962
Coll: French, British, and Spanish
Colonial history; Indian and
Confederate artifacts; costumes;
documents; transportation; Phoenix
Museum fire-fighting equipment

Mobile AL

15440
**The Fine Arts Museum of the South
at Mobile**
Langan Park, Mobile, AL 36608
Fine Arts Museum - 1964
19th and 20th century American and
European paintings, sculpture, prints
and decorative arts; contemporary
American handicrafts; African,
Oriental, and Pre-Columbian art;
Southern Folk art; photography;
Wellington collection of wood
engravings - library

15441
Historic Mobile Preservation Society
Landmark Hall, 1005 Government St,
Mobile, AL 36604
General Museum - 1935
Coll: archives; period silver, china,
furniture, and paintings; local history;
Civil War artifacts; costumes

15442
**USS Alabama Battleship
Commission Museum**
POB 65, Mobile, AL 36601
History/Public Affairs Museum - 1963
Coll: 1942 Battleship USS Alabama;
1941 Submarine USS Drum; army and
marine weapons and field equipment

Mobridge SD

15443
Klein Museum
Highway 12, Mobridge, SD 57601
General Museum - 1976
Coll: pioneer artifacts; Indian artifacts;
building of antique machinery and
automobiles

Moccasin AZ

15444
Pipe Spring National Monument
Arizona Hwy 389, Moccasin, AZ 86022
Religious Art Museum - 1923
Coll: artifacts of Mormon Pioneers;
three historic buildings

Moline IL

15445
**Rock Island County Historical
Society**
822 11th Av, Moline, IL
Historic Site - 61265
Coll: folklore; costumes; Indian
artifacts; agricultural implements -
library

Monkton MD

15446
Breezewood Foundation
3722 Hess Rs, Monkton, MD 2111
Fine Arts Museum - 1955
Coll: Buddhist art; Southeast Asian art
and history; stone; bronze;
archaeology

Monroe CT

15447
Monroe Historical Society
Monroe Center, POB 212, Monroe, CT
06468
General Museum - 1959
Coll: costumes; folklore; agriculture;
archives; historical items; mineralogy;
historic buildings - library

Monroe MI

15448
Monroe County Historical Museum
126 S. Monroe St, Monroe, MI 48161
History/Public Affairs Museum - 1939
Coll: musical instruments; medical and
dental equipment - library

Monroe NY

15449
Museum Village in Orange County
Monroe, NY 10950
Open Air Museum - 1950
technology of 19th century Northeast
America - library; auditorium

Monroeville AL

15450
Monroe County Museum and Historical Society
POB 765, Monroeville, AL 36460
General Museum - 1965
Coll: local historic artifacts

Montague MI

15451
Montague Museum and Historical Society
Church and Meade Sts, Montague, MI 49437
General Museum - 1964
Coll: clocks; religious; manikins; toys; dolls; rocks; musical - library

Montclair NJ

15452
Montclair Art Museum
3 S Mountain Ave, Montclair, NJ 07042
Fine Arts Museum - 1912
Coll: American art; prints; drawings; Indian art; Chinese snuff bottles - library

Monterey CA

15453
Allen Knight Maritime Museum
550 Calle Principal, POB 805, Monterey, CA 93940
History/Public Affairs Museum - 1971
Coll: marine artifacts; ship models; paintings; photographs - library; reading room

15454
Colton Hall Civic Center
Pacific St, Monterey, CA 93940
General Museum - 1939
Coll: research files of information on delegates to the Constitutional Convention; local history; genealogical data; photographs of historical interest - library

15455
Monterey History and Art Association
POB 805, Monterey, CA 93940
General Museum - 1931
Coll: paintings; costumes; historic buildings - library

15456
Monterey Peninsula Museum of Art
559 Pacific St, Monterey, CA 93940
Fine Arts Museum - 1959
Coll: historical and contemporary art; international folk art; American photography; graphics - library

15457
Presidio of Monterey Museum
Monterey, CA 93940
General Museum
Coll: artifacts from the Rumsen Indian, Spanish, and Mexican periods; miniatures of calvary uniforms; war artifacts

15458
Robert Louis Stevenson House
530 Houston St, Monterey, CA 93940
Historic Site - 1941
Coll: costumes; decorative arts - library

Montgomery AL

15459
First White House of the Confederacy
644 Washington St, Montgomery, AL 36130
Historic Site - 1900
Coll: furniture and personal property of President Jefferson Davis; war relics; local items from the Civil War period - library

15460
Montgomery Museum of Fine Arts
440 S. McDonough St, Montgomery, AL 36104
Fine Arts Museum - 1930
Coll: 19th and 20th century American paintings; prints; drawings; 19th century French paintings; decorative arts - library

15461
Museum of the Alabama Department of Archives and History
624 Washington Ave, Montgomery, AL 36130
General Museum - 1901
Coll: family life of French and Colonial settlers; anthropology; archives; paintings; Indian artifacts; military relics - library; reading room

15462
Tumbling Waters Museum of Flags
131 S. Perry St, Montgomery, AL 36104
History/Public Affairs Museum - 1974
Coll: historical and contemporary flags, banners, and flag or symbolic-related materials; U.S. and international flags from all eras; John J. Dave collection of religious flags; the Annin & Company collection; the General Deichelmann collection; the National Commemorative collection - library; auditorium; Learning & Study Center; multi-media library; textile examination laboratory; galleries

Montgomery NY

15463
Brick House
Rte 17K, Montgomery, NY 11549
Historic Site - 1979
furnishings representing seven generations of a Hudson Valley family; brick dwelling (1768)

Monticello IL

15464
Illinois Pioneer Heritage Center
315 W Main, Monticello, IL 61856
General Museum - 1965
Coll: costumes; Indian artifacts; horse-drawn vehicles; Civil War relics

Montour Falls NY

15465
Schuyler County Historical Society, Inc.
Montour Falls, NY 14865
General Museum - 1960
Coll: local history; agriculture; artifacts; antiques; costumes; archives; old Bible collection - library; reading room

Montpelier OH

15466
Williams County Historical Museum
E Main St, Williams County Fairgrounds, Montpelier, OH 43543
General Museum - 1968
Coll: agricultural items; anthropology; archaeology; archives; Indian artifacts; railroads; Hopewell Indian mounds - library; Farm and Craft Museum

Montpelier VT

15467
Vermont Museum
Pavilion Bldg, Montpelier, VT 05602
History/Public Affairs Museum - 1838
Coll: Indian artifacts; pewter; tools; genealogy - library

Montreat NC

15468
The Historical Foundation of the Presbyterian and Reformed Churches, Inc.
POB 847, Montreat, NC 28757
Religious Art Museum - 1927
Coll: 16,000 communion tokens; costumes; paintings; sculpture; graphics; music; furniture; photographs; materials from mission fields; household items; items relating to the Presbyterian and Reformed churches of the world - library; research room; classrooms

Montrose CO

15469
Montrose County Historical Society
Main and Rio Grande, POB 1882, Montrose, CO 81401
History/Public Affairs Museum - 1974
Coll: farm machinery; railroad memorabilia; tools; country store

15470
Ute Indian Museum
17253 Chipeta Dr., Montrose, POB 1736, Montrose, CO 81401
History/Public Affairs Museum - 1956
ethnology of the Ute Indians; Indian artifacts

Montrose PA

15471
Susquehanna County Historical Society and Free Library Association
Monument Square, Montrose, PA 18801
General Museum - 1890
Cope collection; Audobon and Gould bird prints; James D. Smilie print collection; African collection; folk art collection; items related to the area - library

Montville NJ

15472
Montville Township Historical Museum
84 Main Rd, Montville, NJ 07045
General Museum - 1963
Coll: agriculture; geology; Indian artifacts

Moorhead MN

15473
Plains Art Museum
521 Main ave, POB 37, Moorhead, MN 56560
Fine Arts Museum - 1965
Coll: African, Oceanic, pre-Columbian and North American Indian art; Persian glass and ceramics - classrooms

Moose WY

15474
Colter Bay Indian Art Museum
Grand Teton National Park, POB 67, Moose, WY 83012
General Museum - 1929
Coll: fur trade history; fire history of park; historic houses - library

Moraga CA

15475
Hearst Art Gallery St. Mary's College
POB AE, Moraga, CA 94575
Fine Arts Museum - 1977
Coll: Eastern European icons; medieval statuary; William Keith paintings; European paintings from the 16th century to the 29th century; 19th century American paintings

Moravia NY

15476
Cayuga Owasco Lakes Historical Society
15 S Main St, POB 241, Moravia, NY 13118
General Museum - 1966
Coll: records, files; local artifacts; Millard Fillmore collection - library; auditorium; reading room

Morgantown WV

15477
Creative Arts Center
West Virginia University, Morgantown, WV 26506
Fine Arts Museum - 1867
Coll: paintings; costumes; music; theater - library

Morrilton AR

15478
The Museum of Automobiles
Rte 3, Petit Jean Mountain, Morrilton, AR 72110
Science/Tech Museum - 1964
Coll: antique and classic automobiles

Morris IL

15479
Illinois Valley Museum
RR 4, 835 Southmore Rd, Morris, IL 60450
General Museum - 1966
Coll: Norwegian collection; paintings; costumes; dolls and toys; agricultural implements; Civil War and Lincoln artifacts

Morristown NJ

15480
Morris Museum of Art and Sciences
Normandy Heights & Columbia Rds, Morristown, NJ 07961
History/Public Affairs Museum - 1913
Coll: dolls; toys; decorative arts; natural history; costumes - library; reading room; auditorium; theater; classrooms

15481
Morristown National Historical Park
Old Court House Museum
Morristown, NJ 07960
History/Public Affairs Museum - 1933
Coll: furnishings; fine arts; weapons;
manuscripts - library

15482
The Speedwell Village
333 Speedwell Ave, Morristown, NJ
07960
General Museum - 1966
Coll: telegraph instruments; furniture;
historic buildings; genealogy;
transportation; communication

15483
Yesteryear Museum
POB 1890M, Morristown, NJ 07960
History/Public Affairs Museum - 1970
Coll: communication; mechanical and
automotive music; antiques;
entertainment; transportation - library

Morrisville PA

15484
Pennsbury Manor
R.R. 9, Morrisville, PA 19067
Historic Site - 1939
17th century English furniture and
accessories; Pennsbury Manor (1683),
residence of William Penn - library;
auditorium; farm; period gardens

Morro Bay CA

15485
**Morro Bay State Park Museum of
Natural History**
State Park Rd, Morro Bay, CA 93442
Science/Tech Museum - 1962
Coll: Chumash Indian collection;
marine algae; migratory birds; history
of the central California coast marine
life; archeology - library; auditorium

Moscow ID

15486
The Appaloosa Museum
POB 8403, Moscow, ID 83843
General Museum - 1973
Coll: art work; photographs; history of
the Appaloosa horse and the Nez
Perce Indians who bred it

15487
Latah County Historical Society
110 S Adams, Moscow, ID 83843
General Museum - 1968
Coll: archives; photos; artifacts; local
historical objects - library

15488
University of Idaho Museum
Moscow, ID 83843
General Museum - 1963
Coll: West African masks and
figurines; objects from North Africa,
the Near East, and Philippines; North
American ethnography; local history

Moses Lake WA

15489
Adam East Museum
5th and Balsam, Civic Center, Moses
Lake, WA 98837
General Museum - 1957

Moundsville WV

15490
**Delf Norona Museum and Cultural
Center**
801 Jefferson Av, Moundsville, WV
26041
General Museum - 1978
Archeology of West Virginia; archives

Mount Gilead NC

15491
**Town Creek Indian Mound State
Historic Site**
Rte 3, POB 306, Mount Gilead, NC
27306
Historic Site - 1936
Coll: anthropology; archaeology;
Indian artifacts

Mount Holly NJ

15492
**Historic Burlington County Prison
Museum**
128 High St, Mount Holly, NJ 08060
General Museum - 1966
Coll: paintings; sculpture; graphics;
military; glass; Indian artifacts - library

Mount Pleasant IA

15493
Harlan-Lincoln Home
mail c/o Iowa Wesleyan College, 101
W Broad St, Mount Pleasant, IA 52641
Historic Site - 1959
Coll: original furnishings and
memorabilia of the Harlan and Lincoln
families; objects of the same period

15494
**Midwest Old Settler and Threshers
Association Inc.**
R.R.1, Mount Pleasant, IA 52641
Agriculture Museum - 1950
Coll: steam traction engines; stationary
steam; folk theater; historic buildings;
transportation - theater; library

Mount Pleasant MI

15495
**Center for Cultural and Natural
History**
Bellows St, Rowe Hall, Mount
Pleasant, MI 48858
Natural History Museum - 1970
Coll: anthropological materials;
paleontological materials; zoological
collection; mammalogy; herpetololgy

Mount Pleasant OH

15496
Mount Pleasant Historical Society
Union and Concord Sts, Mount
Pleasant, OH 43939
General Museum - 1948
Coll: books; documents; tools;
clothing; dolls; old bottles and jars;
Quaker history - library; reading room

Mount Pulaski IL

15497
Mount Pulaski Court House
POB 134, Mount Pulaski, IL 63548
Historic Site - 1917
1847 Greek Revival court house in 8th
judicial circuit in which Loncoln
practiced law

Mount Vernon VA

15498
Mount Vernon
Mount Vernon, VA 22121
Historic Site - 1853
Coll: artifacts, horticulture and
household furnishings of the period of
George Washington's ownership;
memorabilia, manuscripts - library

15499
Pope-Leighey House
Mount Vernon, VA 22121
Historic Site
Coll: Frank Lloyd Wright furniture and
design

Mountainair NM

15500
Gran Quivira National Monument
Rte 1, Mountainair, NM 87036
General Museum - 1909
Coll: archaeological artifacts from
historic and prehistoric ruins;
photograph collection of 5,000 prints,
negatives and slides; natural science
collection of 1,000 specimens of plants
and insects; prehistoric pithouses (c.
A.D. 800); prehistoric Indian ruins (c.
A.D. 1100-1670); San Isidro Mission
(1627); San Buenaventure Mission
(1659); Pueblo de Las Humanas
(1300-1670) - library

Mountainside NJ

15501
Trailside Nature and Science Center
Coles Ave & New Providence Rd,
Mountainside, NJ 07092
Natural History Museum - 1941
Coll: fossils; shells; Indian artifacts;
fish; snakes; minerals - planetarium;
auditorium

Mountainville NY

15502
Storm King Art Center
Old Pleasant Hill Rd, Mountainville, NY
10953
Fine Arts Museum - 9159
painting; drawings; graphics; outdoor
sculpture by European and American
artists, 1955 to present - library

Mumford NY

15503
Genesee Country Museum
Mumford NY 14511, POB 1819,
Rochester, NY 14603
General Museum
18th and 19th century buildings;
painting; sculpture; graphics; carriage
museum - library

Muncie IN

15504
Ball State University Art Gallery
2000 University Av, Muncie, IN 47306
Fine Arts Museum - 1936
Coll: Italian Renaissance art and
furniture; 19th and 20th century
American paintings, prints, and
drawings; Ball-Kraft collection of
Roman glass; graphics

15505
Muncie Children's Museum
519 S Walnut St, Muncie, IN 47305
Junior Museum - 1977
Touch exhibits designed to deal with
specific concepts - auditorium;
classrooms

Muncy PA

15506
**Muncy Historical Society and
Museum**
N Main St, Muncy, PA 17756
General Museum - 1936
archaeology; history; archives -
library; reading room; formal gardens

Murdo SD

15507
Pioneer Auto Museum
Murdo, SD 57559
Science/Tech Museum - 1953
Coll: antique and classic cars; antique
motorcycles; farm equipment; buggies
and other horse drawn vehicles;
musical instruments; costumes; toys
and dolls; furniture; collectibles

Murfreesboro NC

15508
Murfreesboro Museum
POB 3, Murfreesboro, NC 27855
General Museum - 1967
Coll: agriculture; general history;
Indian artifacts; early educational
materials; manuscript and photograph
collection; Richard J. Gatling Room
with artifacts and memorabilia

Murphy ID

15509
Owyhee County Historical Museum
Murphy, ID 83650
General Museum - 1960
Coll: school house; Owyhee County
historical items; agriculture; Indian
artifacts; geology; archives

Murray KY

15510
**Clara M. Eagle Gallery-Murray State
University**
University Station, Murray, KY 42071
Fine Arts Museum - 1971
Coll: Asian art and artifacts; prints of
Harry L. Jackson

Muskegon MI

15511
Hackley Art Museum
296 W. Webster, Muskegon, MI 49440
Fine Arts Museum - 1911
Coll: American and European paintings
& sculptures - auditorium; classrooms

15512
Muskegon County Museum
30 W. Muskegon, Muskegon, MI
49440
General Museum - 1937
Coll: Indian artifacts; archaeology;
geology

Muskogee OK

15513
Antiques, Inc., Car Museum
2215 W Shawnee, Muskogee, OK
74401
History/Public Affairs Museum - 1970
Coll: rare antique and vintage
automobiles; airplanes; motorcycles -
library

15514
Bacone College Museum
Muskogee, OK 74401
General Museum - 1880
Coll: Indian artifacts; Ataloa Lodge
(1932)

15515
Five Civilized Tribes Museum
Agency Hill on Honor Heights Dr,
Muskogee, OK 74401
Anthropology Museum - 1966
Coll: paintings in traditional Indian style
and sculpture by the Cherokee,
Choctaw, Chickasaw, Creek and
Seminole tribes on tribal subjects;
artifacts; photographs; books;
documents; manuscripts; maps -
library

Mystic CT

15516
Mystic Seaport Museum, Inc.
Greenmanville Av, Mystic, CT 06355
History/Public Affairs Museum - 1929
Coll: items demonstrating the 19th
century skills and trades of the sea;
technology; maritime treasures;
historic buildings and ships; American
art collections of the sea; philately -
library; reading room; planetarium;
classrooms

Nacogdoches TX

15517
Stone Fort Museum
Stephen F. Austin University, POB
6075, Nacogdoches, TX 75962
History/Public Affairs Museum - 1936
Coll: Indian artifacts; pioneer farming
equipment, historic buildings and
furniture

Naknek AK

15518
Bristol Bay Historical Society
POB 136, Naknek, AK 99663
History/Public Affairs Museum - 1969
Erickson
Coll: items from the salmon canning
and fishing industry; taxidermy;
ethnographic items; fossil wood; ivory
& bone; furs - library

Nampa ID

15519
Cleo's Ferry Museum
311 14th Av, S, Nampa, ID 83651
General Museum - 1965
Coll: medical items; old toys; stuffed
birds; music - nature trail; children's
museum

Nantucket MA

15520
Nantucket Historical Association Old
Town Building
Union St, POB 1016, Nantucket, MA
02554
General Museum - 1894
Coll: fire fighting; prints; dishes; tools;
geneology - library; reading room

Naperville IL

15521
Caroline Martin-Mitchell Museum
Rt 65, Aurora Av, 201 W Porter,
Naperville, IL 60540
General Museum - 1939
Coll: dolls; costumes; furnishings;
military artifacts

Narrowsburg NY

15522
Fort Delaware
Narrowsburg, NY 12764
Historic Site - 1957
Artifacts of fort life; 18th century
household furnishings; early
gravestones; farm tools

Nashua IA

15523
**Chickasaw County Historical
Society Museum**
East on Highway 346, Nashua, IA
50658
General Museum - 1955
Coll: pioneer articles of farm
machinery; Indian artifacts; arts and
crafts; clothing; Victorian cottage and
furniture; railroad tracks, objects of
peasant's life

Nashville IN

15524
**Brown County Art Gallery
Association, Inc.**
Nr. 1 Artist Dr, POB 443, Nashville, IN
47448
Fine Arts Museum - 1926
Paintings by contemporary artists; oil
paintings and pastels by Glen Cooper
Henshaw

15525
Brown County Historical Society
Gould St, POB 668, Nashville, IN
47448
General Museum - 1959
Coll: furnishings; doctor's office;
weaving and spinning collections;
pioneer artifacts - library

15526
T.C. Steele State Memorial
R.R. Nr. 1, Nashville, IN 47448
Historic Site
Coll: Steele paintings; period
furnishings; books

Nashville TN

15527
**Baptist Museum of Dargan-Carver
Library**
127 9th Av, N., Nashville, TN 37234
Religious Art Museum - 1951
Coll: artifacts and archival materials
related to Baptist history - library

15528
**Carl Van Vechten Gallery of Fine
Arts** Fisk University
18th Av and Jackson St, N., Nashville,
TN 37203
Fine Arts Museum - 1949
Coll: European and American
collections; Afro-American paintings
and graphics; African sculpture;
photography - library

15529
Cohen Memorial Museum of Art Art
Faculty
George Peabody College for
Teachers, POB 513, Nashville, TN
37203
Fine Arts Museum - 1909
Coll: European painting, sculpture
(18th, 19th century); English china,
silver; contemporary American
painting, sculpture; lace tapestries and
antique furniture; Sullivan collection;
Kress collection of Renaissance
paintings - library

15530
**Country Music Hall of Fame and
Museum**
4 Music Square, East, Nashville, TN
37203
Music Museum - 1961
Coll: costumes; musical instruments
and memorabilia associated with the
development of country music; sight
and sound exhibits; dioramas - library;
theater; classrooms

15531
**Cumberland Museum and Science
Center**
Ridley Av, Nashville, TN 37203
Natural History Museum - 1944
Coll: natural history; anthropology;
archaeology; geology; transportation;
general science; technology; live
animals; dolls; American Indian items -
library; planetarium; classrooms;
laboratory; theater; live animal room

15532
Disciples of Christ Historical Society
1101 19th Av, S., Nashville, TN 37212
Religious Art Museum - 1941
Coll: historical artifacts and art objects
pertaining to the religious heritage,
backgrounds, origins, development
and general history of the Disciples of
Christ, Christian Churches, Churches
of Christ and related groups - library

15533
Nashville Parthenon
Centennial Park, Nashville, TN 37203
Fine Arts Museum - 1931
Coll: James M. Cowan collection of
paintings; exact copies of Elgin
marbles

15534
**Tennessee Botanical Gardens and
Fine Arts Center**
Cheekwood, Cheek Rd, Nashville, TN
37205
Fine Arts Museum - 1957
Coll: Chinese snuff bottles and
porcelain; Japanese woodblock prints;
European glass (17th-19th century);
American and European art; graphics;
sculpture - library; botanical garden;
auditorium; classrooms

15535
Tennessee State Museum
War Memorial Building, Nashville, TN
37219
General Museum - 1937
Coll: military memorabilia from 1780 to
present; historic paintings of
prominent Tennesseans; fine arts
collections of contemporary artists;
historic materials reflecting the history
and culture of the state

15536
Traveller's Rest Museum House
Farrell Pkwy, Nashville, TN 37220
General Museum - 1955
Coll: Indian artifacts; furniture;
decorative arts and books; Civil War
Reconstruction period; documents;
weaving equipment; old Sheffield
silver; toys - library

15537
**Upper Room Chapel Devotional
Library and Museum**
1908 Grand Av, Nashville, TN 37207
Religious Art Museum - 1957
Coll: art objects having religious
significance - library

15538
Vanderbilt University Gallery
23rd at West End Av, Station B, POB
1801, Nashville, TN 37235
Fine Arts Museum - 1873
Coll: Vanderbilt Art Collection of
paintings; Contini-Volterra
photographic archives; sculpture;
graphics - slide library

15539
Watkins Institute
Sixth and Church, Nashville, TN 37219
Fine Arts Museum - 1885
Coll: Tennessee All-State Artists
Purchase Award Collection of
paintings, drawings, sculpture;
paintings by Elihu Vedder; pictures -
auditorium; classrooms

Natchez MS

15540
Grand Village of the Natchez Indian
400 Jefferson Davis Blvd, Natchez,
MS 39120
History/Public Affairs Museum - 1076
Coll: French trade items of the early
eighteenth century, such as Faience
ceramics, beads, clay pipes, iron tools
- library; auditorium

National City CA

15541
Museum of American Treasures
1315 E. 4th, National City, CA 92050
Decorative Arts Museum - 1954
Coll: desert glass; marble and bronze
busts; Indian artifacts; archives; wood
and ivory carvings; bells; artillery shell
art

Nauvoo IL

15542
Joseph Smith Historic Center
Main and Water Sts, Nauvoo, IL 62354
Historic Site - 1918
Joseph Smith homestead and mansion

Nazareth PA

15543
Moravian Historical Society
214 E Center St, Nazareth, PA 18064
Religious Art Museum - 1857
Coll: art and artifacts concerning the
history of the Moravian Church; 18th
century paintings by John Valentine
Haidt; early musical instruments;
hand-wrought and cast bells

Nederland CO

15544
Nederland Historical Society
POB 427, Nederland, CO 80466
General Museum - 1974
Coll: mining equipment and furnishings
of a typical house at the turn of the
century

Neenah WI

15545
**John Nelson Bergstrom Art Center
and Museum**
165 N Park Av, Neenah, WI 54956
Fine Arts Museum - 1954
Coll: antique and modern glass
paperweights; Germanic glass;
American paintings, sculpture and
graphics; Tiffany glass; antique glass
bottles; lustreware; decorative arts -
library; classrooms

Neptune NJ

15546
Neptune Historical Museum
25 Neptune Blvd, Neptune, NJ 07753
History/Public Affairs Museum - 1971
Coll: police and business; toys and
dolls; maps; books; Indian artifacts -
library

Nevada City CA

15547
**Nevada County Historical Society,
Inc.**
POB 1300, Nevada City, CA 95959
History/Public Affairs Museum
Coll: cultural artifacts; native American
artifacts; railroad; communications;
archives; furnishings - library

New Almaden CA

15548
New Almaden Museum
21570 Almaden Rd, POB 1, New
Almaden, CA 95042
General Museum - 1949
Coll: mineralogy; archives; children's
museum; numismatics; archeology -
library

New Bedford MA

15549
New Bedford Whaling Museum
18 Jonny Cake Hill, New Bedford, MA
02740
History/Public Affairs Museum - 1903
Coll: gear and tools associated with
the whaling industry; a whaleship of
the 1840's ship carvings, scrimshaw
and pictorial depictions of the
American whaling industry - library;
auditorium; reading room

New Bern NC

15550
New Bern Firemen's Museum
420 Broad St, POB 1249, New Bern,
NC 28560
History/Public Affairs Museum - 1955
firefighting display; Civil War display;
world record horse-drawn steamer;
horse-drawn hose wagon and
handreel

15551
Tyron Palace Restoration Complex
610 Pollock St, New Bern, NC 28560
Historic Site - 1945
Coll: English and American antiques;
Stevenson House (1805); Stanly
House (1780) - library; auditorium

New Braunfels TX

15552
Sophienburg Museum
401 W Coll St, New Braunfels, TX
78130
History/Public Affairs Museum - 1932
historical materials typical of period of
German colony - library

New Brighton PA

15553
The Merrick Art Gallery
Fifth Av and Eleventh St, New
Brighton, PA 15066
Fine Arts Museum
Coll: French, English, German and
American 18th and 19th century
paintings; works by Franz
Winterhalter, Courbet, Thomas Sully,
Thomas Hill, A. B. Durand - library;
classrooms

New Britain CT

15554
**Museum of Central Connecticut
State College**
New Britain, CT 06050
General Museum - 1965
Coll: anthropology; paintings;
sculpture; graphics; decorative arts;
archeology and folklore; industrial
technology - library

15555
**The New Britain Museum of
American Art**
56 Lexington St, New Britain, CT
06052
Fine Arts Museum - 1903
Coll: American art from colonial times
to contemporary period; paintings;
sculpture; graphics - library; reading
room

15556
New Britain's Youth Museum
30 High St, POB 111, New Britain, CT
06051
Junior Museum - 1957
Coll: natural history; live animals;
Kachina and general Indian artifacts;
circus; antique dolls and doll houses;
ethnology - library; circus; nature
trails

New Brunswick NJ

15557
Buccleuch Mansion
Buccleuch Park, George St, New
Brunswick NJ 08901, Franklin Park,
POB 12, New Brunswick, NJ 08823
History/Public Affairs Museum
Coll: wallpapers; crafts; toys; furniture

15558
Rutgers University Art Gallery
Voorhees Hall-Hamilton St, New
Brunswick, NJ 08903
Fine Arts Museum - 1966
Coll: 19th century French graphics;
19th and 20th century American
graphics; paintings - library

15559
Serological Museum Rutgers
University
University Heights, New Brunswick,
NJ 08903
Natural History Museum - 1948
Coll: animal bloods and sera; blood
testing and systematic serology; seed
extracts; reactions of lectins

New Canaan CT

15560
New Canaan Historical Society
13 Oenoke Ridge, New Canaan, CT
06840
History/Public Affairs Museum - 1889
Coll: historical items; costumes;
sculpture; archives; antique tool
museum; old printing press; historic
buildings - library

15561
New Canaan Nature Center
144 Oenoke Ridge, New Canaan, CT
06840
Science/Tech Museum - 1960
Coll: live native cold-blooded
vertebrates; mineral specimens -
library; auditorium; classrooms;
arboretum; herb gardens

15562
Silvermine Guild of Artists, Inc.
1037 Silvermine Rd, New Canaan, CT
06840
Fine Arts Museum - 1922
Coll: graphics; prints - library;
auditorium; theater; classrooms

New Castle DE

15563
New Castle Court House
New Castle, DE 19720
Historic Site
Coll: portraits of famous Delawareans;
archeological artifacts; furniture; maps;
historic building

15564
New Castle Historical Society
2 E. 4th St, New Castle, DE 19720
General Museum - 1929
Coll: early Dutch furnishings; 18th
century furnishings; historic houses
from 18th century

New Castle IN

15565
Henry County Historical Society
606 S 14th St, New Castle, IN 47362
General Museum - 1886
Coll: archives; furniture; tools; china,
glass, and silver; natural history; Indian
relics; dolls - library; reading room

New City NY

15566
**Historical Society of Rockland
County**
20 Zukor Rd, New City, NY 10956
General Museum - 1965
Coll: furniture; glass; china paintings;
dolls; folk art; guns; farm equipment -
library

New Fairfield CT

15567
Hidden Valley Nature Center
Gillotti Rd, New Fairfield, CT 06810
Natural History Museum - 1960
Coll: entomology; geology; Indian
artifacts; live exhibits; mineralogy -
trails; observation tower; amphitheater

New Glarus WI

15568
Chalet of the Golden Fleece
618 2nd St, New Glarus, WI 53574
History/Public Affairs Museum - 1955
Coll: antique Swiss and early
American furniture, glass and china;
weapons; jewelry; Swiss carvings;
ancient parchments; Swiss doll
collection

15569
Swiss Historical Village
6th Av and 7th St, New Glarus, WI
53574
Historic Site - 1938
Period tools and artifacts; historic
village built by Swiss immigrants

New Harmony IN

15570
Historic New Harmony Inc.
506 Main St, POB 248, New Harmony,
IN 47631
History/Public Affairs Museum - 1973
Coll: geological and natural science
collections; early theater collection;
historic buildings - library; auditorium;
theater

15571
**The New Harmony Gallery of
Contemporary Art**
New Harmony, IN 47631
Fine Arts Museum - 1975
Contemporary art

New Haven CT

15572
**New Haven Colony Historical
Society**
114 Whitney Av, New Haven, CT
06510
History/Public Affairs Museum - 1862
Coll: fine, decorative, inventive arts;
historic photographs of New Haven;
historic houses - library; auditorium

15573
Peabody Museum of Natural History
170 Whitney Av, New Haven, CT
06520
Natural History Museum - 1867
Coll: anthropology; paleontology;
botany; ichthyology; herpetology;
meteorites; scientific instruments -
library; field research station;
auditorium; scanning electron
microscope

15574
Yale Center for British Art
Yale Station, POB 2120, New Haven,
CT 06520
Fine Arts Museum - 1977
Coll: British art including paintings,
drawings, prints, and rare books from
the 16th to 19th centuries - library;
reading room; auditorium; classrooms

15575
Yale University Art Gallery
1111 Chapel St, New Haven, CT 06520
Fine Arts Museum - 1831
Coll: European and American painting
and sculpture; Mabel Brady Garvan
collection of 17th, 18th, and 19th
century paintings and decorative arts;
Jarves and Griggs collections of Italian
Renaissance paintings; Hobart and
Edward Small Moore collection of
Near and Far Eastern art; 20th century
paintings and sculpture; Olsen
collection of pre-Columbian art; Linton
collection of African sculpture -
library; auditorium

15576
**Yale University Collection of Musical
Instruments**
15 Hillhouse Av, New Haven, CT
06520
Music Museum - 1900
Coll: keyboard instruments from the
16th, 17th, and 18th centuries; stringed
instruments from 17th-20th centuries;
extensive collection of bells - library

New Holstein WI

15577
Pioneer Corner Museum
Main St, New Holstein, WI 53061
General Museum
Coll: artifacts; old manuscripts; letters;
dolls; farm machinery; household
goods; furnishings

New London CT

15578
Lyman Allyn Museum
625 Williams St, New London, CT 06320
Fine Arts Museum - 1930
Coll: American and European drawings and paintings; American and English furniture and silver; 19th and 20th century costumes, dolls and toys; early Chinese and American ceramics; Mediterranean antiquities; historic house - library; laboratory; reading room; class rooms; auditorium

15579
New London County Historical Society
11 Blinman St, New London, CT 06320
General Museum - 1870
Coll: furniture and manuscripts; Indian relics; newspapers; whaling collection - library

15580
The Tale of the Whale Museum
3 Whale Oil Row, New London, CT 06320
History/Public Affairs Museum - 1975
Coll: whale boat; whale jaw bones; pictures; photos; whaling instruments - library

15581
Thames Science Center, Inc.
Gallows Lane, New London, CT 06320
Natural History Museum - 1949
Coll: shells; minerals; stuffed birds; native live wild animals; bee hives; dommestic solar hot water system - marine touch tank; trails; arboretum

15582
US Coast Guard Museum
New London, CT 06320
Science/Tech Museum - 1967
Coll: ship and airplane models, paintings, and artifacts relating to the U.S. Coast Guard and its predecessors - library

New London NH

15583
New London Historical Society
Little Sunapee Rd, New London, NH 03257
General Museum - 1954
Coll: folklore; agriculture; archives; costumes; military

New London WI

15584
New London Public Museum
412 S Pearl St, New London, WI 54961
General Museum - 1932
Coll: mounted birds; bird skins; Indian and African artifacts; minerals; rocks; fossils - library

New Market VA

15585
New Market Battlefield Park
POB 1864, New Market, VA 22844
General Museum - 1967
Coll: Civil War artifacts - library

New Orleans LA

15586
Confederate Museum
929 Camp St, New Orleans, LA 70130
History/Public Affairs Museum - 1891
Coll: weapons; silver; uniforms; flags

15587
The Historic New Orleans Collection
533 Royal St, New Orleans, LA 70130
History/Public Affairs Museum - 1966
Coll: ephemera; maps; documents; manuscripts; books; pamphlets - library; reading room

15588
Louisiana State Museum
751 Chartres St, New Orleans, LA 70116
Decorative Arts Museum - 1906
Coll: fine, decorative, folk, costume, textil, photographic and inventive arts of Louisiana; Chennault Collection of Asian Art; historic houses - library

15589
New Orleans Museum of Art
Lelong Ave, City Park, POB 19123, New Orleans, LA 70179
Fine Arts Museum - 1910
Coll: old master paintings of various schools; Kress Collection of Italian Renaissance and Baroque painting; Chapman H. Hyams Collection of Barbizon and Salon paintings; pre-Columbian masterpieces from Mexico, Central and South America; Latin colonial painting and sculpture; works of Edgar Degas; 20th century European art, featuring Surrealism and the School of Paris; Japanese Edo period painting; African art; Melvin P. Billups Glass Collection; Latter-Schlesinger Collection of African, Oceanic, Northwest Coast, American Indian - library; classrooms; auditorium

15590
Tulane University Art Collection
Tulane University Library
7001 Freret St, New Orleans, LA 70118
Fine Arts Museum - 1889
Coll: 19th and 20th century European and American paintings and prints; Japanese block prints; architectural drawings; jewelry

New Paltz NY

15591
College Art Gallery State University College
New Paltz, NY 12562
Fine Arts Museum
Coll: 19th and 20th century American art; Japanese and Chinese prints; German Expressionist prints and watercolors; pre-Columbian artifacts

15592
Huguenot Historical Society
6 Broadhead Av, New Paltz, NY 12561
Historic Site - 1894
historic houses on oldest street in the U.S.; 17th-18th century French and Dutch documents - library; auditorium

New Rochelle NY

15593
Wildcliff Museum
Wildcliff Rd, New Rochelle, NY 10805
Natural History Museum - 1965
Coll: animals; natural sciences items; horticulture; crafts - green houses; craft centers

New Sweden ME

15594
New Sweden Historical Society
Rte 161, New Sweden, ME 04762
History/Public Affairs Museum - 1925
Coll: history of early colonists of Maine's Swedish Colony in New Sweden

New York NY

15595
Abigail Adams Smith Museum
Colonial Dames of America
421 E 61st St, New York, NY 10021
Decorative Arts Museum - 1939
Coll: American decorative arts; Adams family letters and belongings - auditorium

15596
The African-American Institute
833 United Nations Plaza, New York, NY 10017
History/Public Affairs Museum - 1953
Loan exhibitions of traditional or modern African arts and crafts - library

15597
American Academy and Institute of Arts and Letters
633 W 155th St, New York, NY 10032
Fine Arts Museum - 1898
Coll: works by Childe Hassam and Eugene Speicher; painting; sculpture; graphics; music - library

15598
American Bible Society Museum
1865 Broadway, New York, NY 10023
Religious Art Museum - 1816
Coll: historic and unusual scriptures in 1,567 languages, dating from before the invention of printing to the most recent editions - library; reading room

15599
American Craft Museum
44 W 53rd St, New York, NY 10019
Decorative Arts Museum - 1956
Coll: American crafts since 1900 - library

15600
American Museum of Immigration
Statue of Liberty National Monument
Liberty Island, New York, NY 10004
Historic Site - 1972
Folk art; materials pertaining to history of the Statue of Liberty; immigrant oral histories with transcripts

15601
The American Museum of Natural History
79th St and Central Park West, New York, NY 10024
Natural History Museum - 1869
Coll: anthropological exhibits; insects; reptiles; fishes; fossils; mammals; rocks, minerals and gems; birds; shells - library; auditorium; planetarium; environmental and nature science center

15602
American Museum - Hayden Planetarium
81st St and Central Park West, New York, NY 10024
Science/Tech Museum - 1935
Astronomical exhibits - library; sky theater; Guggenheim Space Theater; Hall of the Sun; classrooms

15603
The American Numismatic Society
Broadway and 155th St, New York, NY 10032
History/Public Affairs Museum - 1858
coins; historical and archaeological artifacts - library

15604
Archives of American Art, Smithsonian Institution
41 E 65th St, New York, NY 10021
Fine Arts Museum - 1954
Coll: manuscripts and photographs relating to arts in America from 1620 to the present - library; reading room

15605
Asia House Gallery
112 E 64th St, New York, NY 10021
Fine Arts Museum - 1956
Coll: loan exhibitions of paintings; sculpture; graphics; decorative arts; archaeology - library

15606
Aunt Len's Doll and Toy House, Inc.
6 Hamilton Terrace, New York, NY 10031
History/Public Affairs Museum - 1970
Coll: antique and rare dolls; baby carriages; doll houses - plan and learn room

15607
Bartow-Pell Mansion Museum and Garden
Pelham Bay Park, New York, NY 10464
Historic Site - 1914
Coll: Greek Revival period furnishings; paintings; sunken gardens - library

15608
Castle Clinton National Monument
Battery Park, New York NY 10004, 26 Wall Street, New York, NY 10005
History/Public Affairs Museum - 1950
Coll: restored rooms dating to the War of 1812; exhibits on the building's history

15609
Center for Inter-American Relations Art Gallery
680 Park Av, New York, NY 10021
Fine Arts Museum - 1967
contemporary Latin American art

15610
China House Gallery
125 E 65th St, New York, NY 10021
Fine Arts Museum - 1966
Coll: loan exhibitions of Chinese art

15611
Cloisters Metropolitan Museum of Art
Fort Tryon Park, New York, NY 10040
Fine Arts Museum - 1938
Medieval art - library

15612
Cooper-Hewitt Museum The Smithsonian Institution's National Museum of Design
2 E 91st St, New York, NY 10028
Decorative Arts Museum - 1897
Design and decorative arts of all periods and countries

15613
Dyckman House and Museum
204th St and Broadway, New York, NY 10053
Historic Site - 1915
Dutch farmhouse with furnishings (1783)

15614
Federal Hall National Memorial
26 Wall St, New York, NY 10005
Historic Site - 1939
Artifacts relating to George
Washington, first President of the U.S.,
and other figures and events in
American history; historical
development of New York City, 1626
to present

15615
Fraunces Tavern Museum
54 Pearl St, New York, NY 10004
Historic Site - 1876
Coll: 18th and 19th century American
decorative arts; Revolutionary War
memorabilia; George Washington
memorabilia - library; American
history audiovisual center

15616
The Frick Collection
1 E 70th St, New York, NY 10021
Fine Arts Museum - 1920
Paintings; sculpture; furniture;
decorative arts; prints and drawings -
library

15617
Gallery of Prehistoric Art
20 E 12th St, New York, NY 10003
Fine Arts Museum - 1975
Prehistoric paintings from French,
Spanish, Saharan, and North American
sites - library

15618
General Grant National Memorial
Riverside Dr and W 122nd St, New
York, NY 10031
Historic Site - 1897
Memorabilia of Ulysses S. Grant;
military artifacts

15619
**The Grey Art Gallery and Study
Center** New York University Art
Collection
33 Washington Place, New York, NY
10003
Fine Arts Museum - 1958
Coll: 20th century painting, sculpture
and graphics; Ben and Abby Grey
Foundation Collection of
contemporary art - library

15620
**The Hall of Fame for Great
Americans**
University Av and 181 St, Bronx, NY
10012, *mail c/o* New York University
Affairs Office, 21 Washington Place,
New York, NY 10003
History/Public Affairs Museum - 1900
Coll: 97 original bronzes of notable
Americans in the arts, sciences,
humanities, government, business, and
labor, elected by a College of Electors
- outdoor columned arcade for display
of sculptures; visitor information and
orientation building

15621
Hispanic Society of America
155th St and Broadway, New York, NY
10032
Fine Arts Museum - 1904
Coll: culture of Iberian peninsula from
prehistoric times to present - library

15622
The Interchurch Center
475 Riverside Dr, New York, NY 10027
Religious Art Museum - 1959
Coll: Russian Orthodox Church
materials; revised standard version of
the Bible exhibit; temporary exhibits of
contemporary art - library; auditorium

15623
International Center of Photography
1130 Fifth Av, New York, NY 10028
Fine Arts Museum - 1974
Coll: works of over 100 20th century
photographers - library; auditorium;
classrooms; black/white and color
photo labs

15624
Japan House Gallery
333 E 47th St, New York, NY 10017
Fine Arts Museum - 1907
Coll: Japanese art loan exhibitions -
library; auditorium; classrooms

15625
The Jewish Museum
1109 5th Av, New York, NY 10028
Religious Art Museum - 1904
Judaica collection; loan exhibitions of
contemporary art - library; auditorium,
multi-medium teaching environment

15626
**Junior Museum of the Metropolitan
Museum of Art**
5th Av at 82nd St, New York, NY
10028
Junior Museum - 1941
Exhibitions from collections of the
Metropolitan Museum of Art - library;
auditorium

15627
**Marine Museum of the City of New
York**
Fifth Av at 103rd St, New York, NY
10029
General Museum - 1928
Coll: marine paintings; prints; ship
models; figureheads; memorabilia -
auditorium

15628
The Metropolitan Museum of Art
5th Av at 82 St, New York, NY 10028
Fine Arts Museum - 1870
Art works in all genres and from all
cultures covering a period of 5,000
years - library; auditorium; classrooms

15629
Morris-Jumel Mansion
160th St and Edgecombe Av, New
York, NY 10032
Historic Site - 1903
Coll: furnishings from the Colonial,
Federal and Empire periods

15630
El Museo del Barrio
1230 Fifth Av, New York, NY 10029
Fine Arts Museum - 1969
Graphics; paintings; photographs;
limited Pre-Columbian collection -
library

15631
Museum of American Folk Art
49 W 53rd St, New York, NY 10019
Fine Arts Museum - 1961
Coll: American 18th and 19th century
folk sculpture and painting; decorative
arts

15632
The Museum of Broadcasting
1 E 53rd St, New York, NY 10022
Science/Tech Museum - 1975
Coll: radio and TV tapes from the
1920s to the present; original radio
scripts

15633
Museum of Holography
11 Mercer St, New York, NY 10013
Fine Arts Museum - 1976
Contemporary holographic art; first
laser hologram; exhibits tracing the
development of holography since 1948
- library; auditorium

15634
The Museum of Modern Art
11 W 53rd St, New York, NY 10019
Fine Arts Museum - 1929
Coll: all genres of 20th century art;
crafts and industrial design;
photography; decorative arts - library;
auditorium

15635
Museum of the American Indian
Heye Foundation
Broadway at 155th St, New York, NY
10032
Anthropology Museum - 1916
Coll: American Indian archaeology and
ethnology from North, Central, South
America and the Caribbean; Eskimo
culture

15636
Museum of the City of New York
Fifth Av at 103 St, New York, NY
10029
History/Public Affairs Museum - 1923
Exhibits relating to all aspects of the
social, economic and political history
of New York - auditorium

15637
Museum of the Printed Word
mail c/o The New York Times, 229 W
43rd St, New York, NY 10036
History/Public Affairs Museum - 1936
Coll: history of printing, especially
newspapers

15638
National Academy of Design
1083 Fifth Av and 89th St, New York,
NY 10028
Fine Arts Museum - 1825
Coll: American painting, sculpture,
graphic arts; architectural drawings
and photographs from 1825 to present
- art school; auditorium

15639
The New Museum
65 Fifth Av, New York, NY 10003
Fine Arts Museum - 1977
Coll: contemporary art - library

15640
**New York City Police Academy
Museum**
235 E 2o0th St, New York, NY 10003
History/Public Affairs Museum - 1929
Coll: world's largest collection of
police memorabilia; uniforms; unusual
weapons - library

15641
New York Fire Department Museum
104 Duane St, New York, NY 10007
History/Public Affairs Museum - 1932
Antique fire fighting equipment;
memorabilia

15642
The New York Historical Society
170 Central Park West, New York, NY
10024
Decorative Arts Museum - 1804
Original Audubon watercolors; glass;
ceramics; furniture; toys; paintings;
decorative arts - library; auditorium

15643
Nicholas Roerich Museum
319 W 107th St, New York, NY 10025
Fine Arts Museum - 1956
paintings of Tibet, India, Himalayas and
monuments of ancient Russia by
Nicholas Roerich - library

15644
The Parish of Trinity Church Museum
74 Trinity Place, New York, NY 10006
Religious Art Museum - 1966
Coll: artifacts and religious objects;
paintings; archives including
photographs, documents, prints
(1644-1979); St. Paul's Chapel (1766) -
library

15645
Pen and Brush, Inc.
16 E 10th St, New York, NY 10003
Fine Arts Museum - 1893
Coll: paintings; sculpture - library; arts
center

15646
The Pierpont Morgan Library
29 E 36th St, New York, NY 10016
Fine Arts Museum - 1924
Coll: 62,000 Medieval and
Renaissance manuscripts and rare
books; autograph and musical
manuscripts; old master drawings;
letters, documents, and reference
works; bookbindings - library; reading
room

15647
Scalamandre Museum of Textiles
950 Third Av, New York, NY 10022
Decorative Arts Museum - 1946
Coll: textiles

15648
**The Solomon R. Guggenheim
Museum**
1071 Fifth Av, New York, NY 10028
Fine Arts Museum - 1937
Coll: paintings; sculpture; graphic arts
including works of Picasso, Delaunay,
Chagall, Modigliani, Brancusi,
Mondrian, Leger, Marc, Klee,
Kandinsky; post-war sculpture and
painting - library; auditorium

15649
The South Street Seaport Museum
203 Front St, New York, NY 10038
History/Public Affairs Museum - 1967
Historic ship models; printing museum

15650
**Synagogue Architectural & Art
Library**
838 Fifth Av, New York, NY 10021
Religious Art Museum - 1957
Coll: Synagogue architecture and
Synagogue art; ceremonial objects;
works of Jewish artists - library

15651
The Ukrainian Museum
203 Second Av, New York, NY 10003
Anthropology Museum - 1976
Coll: folk art, fine arts, history of
Ukraine; history of Ukrainian
immigration in the United States -
library; auditorium

15652
**Walter Hampden - Edwin Booth
Theatre Collection and Library at the
Players**
16 Gramercy Pk, New York, NY 10003
Performing Arts Museum - 1888
Coll: pertaining to the American and
English stage - library; reading room

15653
Whitney Museum of American Art
Madison Av, New York, NY 10021
Fine Arts Museum - 1930
Coll: paintings; sculpture; graphic arts
- library; auditorium

15654
Yeshiva University Museum
2520 Amsterdam Av, New York, NY
10033
Religious Art Museum - 1973
Coll: Jewish ceremonial objects of
metals; ceremonial costumes; rare
scrolls and books, manuscripts,
archival materials, slides, photographs
- library; theater

Newark NJ

15655
The Newark Museum
49 Washington St, Newark, NJ 07101
Fine Arts Museum - 1909
Coll: paintings; Oriental art, esp.
Tibetan glass; coins ; physical
sciences; ethnology; horology;
archaeology - planetarium; auditorium

Newark OH

15656
The Dawes Arboretum
7770 Jacksontown Rd SE, Newark,
OH 43055
Natural History Museum - 1929
Coll: shells; fossils; minerals; natural
history - library; auditorium; botanical
garden; nature center; classrooms

15657
Licking County Art Gallery
391 Hudson Av, Newark, OH 43055
Fine Arts Museum - 1959
Coll: 19th and 20th century prints and
paintings - studio; classrooms

15658
Licking County Historical Society
6th St Park, POB 535, Newark, OH
43055
General Museum - 1947
Coll: Federal and early Victorian
furnishings; historical costumes; toys;
antique books; glass; prehistoric
Moundbuilder Indian artifacts;
Buckingham House (1835) - library

Newburgh NY

15659
**Washington's headquarters State
Historic Site**
84 Liberty St, Newburgh, NY 12550
Historic Site - 1850
Coll: documents and military artifacts
of the American Revolution; statuary;
Centennial Monument (1887); Tower of
Victory; Jonathan Hasbrouck House
(1725) - audio-visual gallery

Newburyport MA

15660
**The Custom House Maritime
Museum of Newburyport**
25 Water St, Newburyport, MA 01950
History/Public Affairs Museum - 1969
Coll: objects brought back from the
Orient; Europe and the South Seas in
the 1800's; artifacts relating to the
maritime history of Merrimac Valley -
library

Newcastle TX

15661
Fort Belknap Museum and Archives
POB 68, Newcastle, TX 76372
General Museum - 1851
Coll: military, Indian artifacts - library

Newcastle WY

15662
Anna Miller Museum
POB 698, Newcastle, WY 82701
General Museum - 1959
Coll: local history; Indian artifacts;
natural history; mineralogy;
paleontology; folk art; archives;
historic house - library

Newhall CA

15663
William S. Hart County Park
24151 N. Newhall Ave, Newhall, CA
91321
Fine Arts Museum - 1958
Coll: paintings by Russell, De Yong,
Remington; sculpture; ivory and
woodcarvings; farm animals; period
furniture - library

Newington CT

15664
Museum of Amateur Radio American
Radio Relay League
255 N Main St, Newington, CT 06111
Science/Tech Museum - 1914
Coll: antique radio transmitters;
receivers - library

Newport Beach CA

15665
Newport Harbor Art Museum
San Clemente Dr, Newport Beach, CA
92660
Fine Arts Museum - 1961
Coll: 20th century art with emphasis
on American and Californian art -
library; workshops; galleries; sculpture
garden

Newport News VA

15666
The Mariners Museum
Museum Dr, Newport News, VA
23606
Science/Tech Museum - 1930
Coll: navigational instruments; ship,
whaling and fishing equipment; naval
armament - library; archive;
auditorium

15667
**Peninsula Nature and Science
Center**
524 J. Clyde Morris Blvd, Newport
News, VA 23601.W1
Science/Tech Museum - 1964
Coll: bird eggs and nests; rocks;
minerals; fossils - aquarium;
planetarium; observatory

15668
**The War Memorial Museum of
Virginia**
9285 Warwick Blvd, Huntington Park,
Newport News, VA 23607
General Museum - 1923
Coll: US war posters; uniforms;
weapons - library

Newport OR

15669
Burrows House
545 SW Ninth, Newport, OR 97365
General Museum - 1895
Coll: Indian dance skirts; strings of
trade beads; dentallium; horn; bone;
wood; dugout canoe; obsidian; agate
and stone points; clothing and pioneer
items; logging and carpenter tools;
shells and marine artifacts - library;
reading room

15670
**Oregon State University Marine
Science Center**
Marine Science Dr, Newport, OR
97365
Natural History Museum - 1965
Coll: marine; history - junior museum;
aquarium

Newport RI

15671
The Art Association of Newport
76 Bellevue Av, Newport, RI 02840
Fine Arts Museum - 1912
Coll: works by Howard Gardiner
Cushing in Cushing gallery; historic
building - library

15672
**International Tennis Hall of Fame and
Tennis Museum**
194 Bellevue Av, Newport, RI 02840
History/Public Affairs Museum - 1954
Coll: tennis rackets; balls; trophies;
photographs; prints; paintings;
statuary; women's tennis fashions;
tennis surfaces - library; reading
room; auditorium

15673
Newport Historical Society
82 Touro St, Newport, RI 02840
General Museum - 1854
Coll: local history and records;
paintings; marine; furniture;
numismatics; glass; silver; pewter;
historic houses - library

15674
Redwood Library and Athenaeum
50 Bellevue Av, Newport, RI 02840
Fine Arts Museum - 1747
Coll: paintings by Gilbert Stuart and
Charles Bird King; sculpture; historic
buildings by architect Peter Harrison -
library

Newton KS

15675
Kauffman Museum
E 27th St, Newton, KS 67117
Natural History Museum - 1940
Coll: anthropology; mineralogy

Newton NC

15676
Catawba County Historical Museum
1716 S College Dr, Hwy 321, Newton,
NC 28658
General Museum - 1949
Coll: household utensils; agricultural
implements; folk art; manufacturing;
historic buildings (1760-1870) - library;
reading room; botanical garden

Newton NJ

15677
Sussex County Historical Society
82 Main St, Newton, NJ 07860
History/Public Affairs Museum - 1906
Coll: Indian artifacts; archaeology -
library

Niagara Falls NY

15678
Schoellkopf Geological Museum
Prospect Park, Niagara Falls, NY
14303
Natural History Museum - 1971
Coll: marine invertebrates from middle
Silurian and Devonian periods;
minerals of local varieties - library;
theater; classrooms; nature trails

Niles IL

15679
The Bradford Museum
9333 Milwaukee Av, Niles, IL 60648
Fine Arts Museum - 1978
Coll: limited editions of collectors'
plates by well-known porcelain
manufacturers - library; theater

Niles MI

15680
Fernwood Inc
1720 Rangeline Rd, Niles, MI 49120
Natural History Museum - 1964
Coll: botany; geology; herbarium -
library; reading room

Niles OH

15681
**National McKinley Birthplace
Memorial Association Museum**
40 N Main St, Niles, OH 44446
Historic Site - 1911
Coll: McKinleyana; furniture; archives;
costumes; glass; military; music -
auditorium; reading room

Noank CT

15682
Noank HistoricalSociety, Inc.
17 Sylvan St, Noank, CT 06340
General Museum - 1966
Coll: Indian artifacts; marine items;
naval and local history artifacts

Noblesville IN

15683
Conner Prairie Pioneer Settlement
13400 Allisonville Rd, Noblesville, IN
46060
General Museum - 1964
Coll: historic buildings of rural
settlement from early 19th century;
furnishings - library

15684
**Indiana Museum of Transport and
Communication, Inc.**
POB 83, Noblesville, IN 46060
Science/Tech Museum - 1960
Coll: early 20th century railway and
trolley equipment; automobiles, trucks,
horse-drawn vehicles; related tools
and machinery; communication and
printing apparatus - library

Nogales AZ

15685
Primeria Alta Historical Society
Grand Ave, POB 2281, Nogales, AZ
85621
General Museum - 1948
Coll: archeology; geology; mineralogy;
costumes; art; medical items - library

Nome AK

15686
Carrie McLain Museum
POB 53, Nome, AK 99762
General Museum - 1967
Traditional and modern art;
ethnography; archeology; cross-
cultural aviation; gold mining; historic
photographs and newsprints

Norfolk CT

15687
Norfolk Historical Society, Inc.
Village Green, Norfolk, CT 06058
General Museum - 1960
Coll: decorative arts; costumes; folklore; maps and manuscripts; farm tools - library

Norfolk VA

15688
Chrysler Museum at Norfolk
Olney Rd and Mowbray Arch, Norfolk, VA 23510
Fine Arts Museum - 1933
Coll: arts from Egypt, Greece, Rome, Near East, Far East, Africa, Orient, pre-Columbian America; European paintings and sculptures; glass - library

15689
General Douglas MacArthur Memorial
MacArthur Square, Norfolk, VA 23510
General Museum - 1961
Coll: history; personal papers and mementos - library

15690
Hermitage Foundation Museum
7637 North Shore Rd, Norfolk, VA 23505
Decorative Arts Museum - 1937
Coll: paintings, sculptures and decorative arts from Western and Oriental cultures - library

15691
Naval Amphibious Museum
NAB Little Creek, Norfolk, VA 23521
History/Public Affairs Museum - 1970
Naval history; marine history; ship models; military equipment

Normal IL

15692
Center for the Visual Arts Gallery
College of Fine Arts, Illinois State University, Normal, IL 61761
Fine Arts Museum - 1973
Coll: contemporary art

Norman OK

15693
Museum of Art University of Oklahoma
410 W Broadway St, Norman, OK 73019
Fine Arts Museum - 1936
Coll: American, European and Oriental contemporary art - library

15694
Stovall Museum of Science and History University of Oklahoma
1335 Asp St, Norman, OK 73069
General Museum - 1899
Coll: mammals; birds; fish; amphibians; reptiles; insects; invertebrates; botany; anthropology; ethnology; archaeology; history; classical art; paleontology; paleobotany; minerals; textiles - research laboratories; auditorium

Norris TN

15695
Museum of Appalachia
POB 359, Norris, TN 37828
General Museum - 1968
Coll: Over 35,000 early-American and pioneer items

North Andover Ma

15696
Merrimack Valley Textile Museum
800 Massachusetts Ave, North Andover, Ma 01845
History/Public Affairs Museum - 1960
Coll: textiles; swatches; samplebooks; trade catalogues and books; machines

North Bend OR

15697
Coos-Curry Museum
Simpson Park, North Bend, OR 97459
General Museum - 1891
Coll: household utensils and implements - library

North Bend WA

15698
Snoqualmie Valley Historical Museum
222 North Bend Blvd, POB 179, North Bend, WA 98045
General Museum - 1960
Coll: local logging; early carpentry tools; Indian artifacts

North Bennington VT

15699
The Park-McCullough House Association
POB 95, North Bennington, VT 05257
General Museum - 1968
Coll: furniture; carriages; documents; Victorian artifacts and clothes - library

North East PA

15700
Lake Shore Railway Historical Society, Inc.
POB 571, North East, PA 16428
History/Public Affairs Museum - 1956
George M. Pullman collection of historical railroad passenger train cars and equipment built and operated by the Pullman Company; historical locomotives and other cars; historic station (1899) - library

North Freedom WI

15701
Mid-Continent Railway Museum
North Freedom, WI 53951
Science/Tech Museum - 1959
Railway equipment and artifacts; historic house - library

North Kingstown RI

15702
South County Museum, Inc.
Scrabbletown Rd, POB 182, North Kingstown, RI 02852
General Museum - 1933
Coll: rural early America; agriculture; technology; transportation; household items - nature trail

North Miami Beach FL

15703
Monastery Cloister of Saint Bernard
16711 W Dixie Hwy, North Miami Beach, FL 33160
Fine Arts Museum - 1963
Coll: paintings; sculpture; original monastery built in 1141 in Segovia, Spain

North Newton KS

15704
Mennonite Library and Archives
North Newton, KS 67117
Religious Art Museum - 1938
Anabaptist and Mennonite manuscripts, prints, paintings, lithographs; archives - library

North Platte NE

15705
Buffalo Bill's Ranch
R.R 1, North Platte, NE 69101
History/Public Affairs Museum - 1964
Coll: personal property and correspondence of Buffalo Bill; showbills; photo collection; film clips - theater

15706
Sioux Lookout D.A.R. Log Cabin Museum
Memorial Park, North Platte, NE 69101
General Museum - 1923
Coll: folklore; history; glass; Indian artifacts; costumes; music - library

North Salem NY

15707
Hammond Museum
Deveau Rd, off Rte 124, North Salem, NY 10560
Fine Arts Museum - 1957
Coll: painting, sculpture, graphics; decorative arts; folk art; archaeology; Museum of the Humanities - botanical garden

Northampton MA

15708
Calvin Coolidge Memorail Room
Forbes Library
20 West St, Northampton, MA 01060
Historic Site - 1920
Coll: manuscripts; books; scrapbooks; portraits - library; reading room

15709
Smith College Museum of Art
Elm St at Bedford Terrace, Northampton, MA 01060
Fine Arts Museum - 1920
Coll: 18th and 20th century European and American paintings; sculpture; graphics; decorative arts - library

Northborough MA

15710
Northborough Historical Society Inc
52 Main St, Northborough, MA 01532
General Museum - 1906
Coll: lighting; apothecary supplies; china; buttons and combs; genealogy; toys; books - library; archives; auditorium

Northfield VT

15711
Norwich University Museum
on Rte 12(Main St) 1/4 mile north of Jct 12&12A, Northfield, VT 05663
General Museum - 1819
Coll: history of Norwich exhibits; uniforms; flags; weapons

Northfiled MN

15712
Norwegian-American Historical Association
Northfiled, MN 55057
History/Public Affairs Museum - 1925
Coll: Norwegian-American history - library

Northport NY

15713
Northport Historical Society, Inc.
215 Main St, POB 545, Northport, NY 11768
General Museum - 1962
Coll: artifacts; shipbuilding tools; photographs

Norwalk OH

15714
Firelands Museum
4 Chase Av, Norwalk, OH 44957
General Museum - 1857
Coll: archaeology; archives; primitive paintings; costumes; decorative arts; folklore; geology; glass; Indian artifacts; numismatics; paleontology; transportation; weapons; guns - library; reading room

Norwich CT

15715
The Leffingwell Inn
348 Washington St, Norwich, CT 06360
General Museum - 1901
Coll: antique dolls; Norwich silver; Indian artifacts; local genealogical and historical material; early colonial silver and pewter; antiques - library

15716
The Slater Memorial Museum
108 Crescent St, Norwich, CT 06360
Fine Arts Museum - 1888
Coll: American paintings, sculpture, graphics, and furnishings; Oriental art; African and South Sea Islands folk art; costumes; Indian artifacts; gun collection

Norwich NY

15717
Chenango County Historical Society Museum
Rexford St, Norwich, NY 13815
General Museum - 1938
Coll: costumes; folklore; agriculture; archaeology; Indian artifacts - library

Norwood NY

15718
Norwood Historical Association and Museum
39 Main St, Norwood, NY 13668
General Museum - 1968
Coll: railroad articles; folklore; history; industrial technology - library

Notre Dame IN

15719
Herbaria
Dept of Biology, University of Notre Dame, Notre Dame, IN 46556
Natural History Museum - 1876
Greene collection of Western and Middle Atlantic state plants; Nieuwland collection of Midwestern plants

15720
The Suite Museum of Art University of Notre Dame
O'Shaughnessy Hall, Notre Dame, IN 46556
Fine Arts Museum - 1842
Coll: Italian Renaissance paintings and sculpture; Kress study collection of paintings; pre-Columbian sculptures and textiles; 17th and 18th century European paintings; 20th century paintings and sculpture; prints and drawings; tapestries; archeology - library

Novato CA

15721
Marin Miwok Museum
2200 Novato Blvd, POB 864, Novato, CA 94947
Archeology Museum - 1967
Coll: archeological, ethnographic, and archival materials ranging from Alaska to Peru; photographic materials pertaining to California; original Edward S. Curtis photogravures - library; gallery; classroom; lab; nature trails; reading room

Nowata OK

15722
Nowata County Historical Society Museum
121 Pine St, POB 646, Nowata, OK 74078
General Museum - 1969
Coll: cowboy artifacts; tools; old dentist tools; furniture; Indian wood carvings - library

Oak Part IL

15723
Frank Lloyd Wright Home and Studio
Chicago and Forest Avs, Oak Part, IL 60302
Historic Site - 1974
original Prairie Style constructions built by Frank Lloyd Wright between 1889 and 1898

Oak Ridge TN

15724
American Museum of Science and Energy
Tulane Av, POB 117, Oak Ridge, TN 37830
Science/Tech Museum - 1949
Exhibits on energy production and conservation - auditorium; library; classrooms

Oakland CA

15725
Merritt College Anthropology Museum
12500 Campus Dr, Oakland, CA 94619
History/Public Affairs Museum - 1973
Coll: ethnological material from North and South America, Africa, the Pacific, and Asia; prehistoric collection - library; classrooms

15726
Mills College Art Gallery
Seminary & MacArthur Blvd, Oakland, CA 94613
Fine Arts Museum - 1925
Coll: international graphics; textiles; Indian artifacts; ceramics

15727
The Oakland Museum
1000 Oak St, Oakland, CA 94607
General Museum - 1969
Coll: paintings; oceanography; zoology; decorative arts; geology - library; aquarium; auditorium; theater; classroom; multi-media center

15728
Rotary Natural Science Center
1520 Lakeside Dr, Oakland, CA 94612
Science/Tech Museum - 1953
Coll: mounted birds; mammals; reptiles; study skins - library; reading room; nature center; wildlife refuge; auditorium

Oakley ID

15729
Oakley Pioneer Museum
Oakley, ID 83346
General Museum - 1967
Coll: antique furniture; photos; clothing; rock and arrowhead collections

Oberlin OH

15730
Allen Memorial Art Museum
Oberlin, OH 44074
Fine Arts Museum - 1917
Coll: paintings; sculpture; graphics; decorative arts; archaeology - library

Oconto WI

15731
Beyer Home Oconto County Historical Society Museum
917 Park Av, Oconto, WI 54153
General Museum - 1940
Coll: Indian artifacts; antique furnishings; fur trade; copper culture people artifacts; lumbering - library

Odessa DE

15732
Wilson-Warner House
Main St, Odessa, DE 19730
Decorative Arts Museum - 1923
Coll: 18th and 19th century American, English, and European furniture; decorative arts; local archeological finds

Odessa TX

15733
The Presidential Museum
622 N Lee, Odessa, TX 79760
Historic Site - 1965
Presidential history, numismatics, philatelics - library

Ogden UT

15734
Weber State College Museum of Natural History
3750 Harrison Blvd, Ogden, UT 84408
Science/Tech Museum - 1969
Coll: mineralogy; skeletons of dinosaurs

Ogdensburg NY

15735
Remington Art Museum
303 Washington St, Ogdensburg, NY 13669
Fine Arts Museum - 1923
Coll: Frederic Remington's paintings, sculpture, drawings, manuscripts; archives; decorative arts; glass; Rosseel paintings; Parish Collection of Belter furniture; Haskell Collection of 19th century American and European paintings; Addie Priest Newell galleries - library

Okemah OK

15736
Territory Town
Rte 2, POB 297-A, Okemah, OK 74859
General Museum - 1967
Coll: guns; Indian relics; Civil War relics; documents; early pictures

Oklahoma City OK

15737
National Cowboy Hall of Fame and Western Heritage Center
1700 NE 63rd St, Oklahoma City, OK 73111
Historic Site - 1955
Western Art collection; James Earle and Laura G. Fraser studio collection; Albert K. Mitchell Russell-Remington collection; Taos collection; Fechin collection; Schreyvogel collection; End of the Trail and Buffalo Bill statues - library; botanical garden

15738
Oklahoma Art Center
3113 Pershing Blvd, Oklahoma City, OK 73107
Fine Arts Museum - 1946
Coll: American paintings; sculpture; prints; early American glass; graphics; drawings; decorative arts - library

15739
Oklahoma Firefighters Museum
2716 NE 50, POB 11507, Oklahoma City, OK 73136
History/Public Affairs Museum - 1970
Coll: fire-fighting apparatus and appliances; Fire Station (1869)

15740
Oklahoma Historical Society
Historical Building, Oklahoma City, OK 73105
General Museum - 1893
Coll: material pertaining to state history; pioneer relics; Indian artifacts; military; archaeology; paintings; 20th century Western culture items - library

15741
Oklahoma Museum of Art
7316 Nichols Rd, Oklahoma City, OK 73120
Fine Arts Museum - 1958
Coll: 13th to 20th century European and American painting, drawings, graphics, furniture, tapestries, porcelain, decorative art, sculpture - library; lecture hall; landscaped park; classrooms

15742
Omniplex
2100 NE St, Oklahoma City, OK 73111
Science/Tech Museum - 1958
Coll: Apollo type space capsule (AS 202); Foucault pendulum; Gravitram 2; weather station; science exhibits; trading post; holograms; 1st atomic pile; link trainer; nature area with bee hives, snakes, egg incubators - planetarium; classrooms; laboratories; facilities for the handicapped

Okmulgee OK

15743
Creek Indian Museum
Creek Council House, Okmulgee, OK 74447
Anthropology Museum - 1923
Coll: Indian history; archives; archaeology; paintings of the Creek chiefs; Okmulgee pioneer history - library

Old Chatham NY

15744
The Shaker Museum
Shaker Museum Rd, Old Chatham, NY 12136
Decorative Arts Museum - 1950
Coll: Shaker arts; crafts; industries; textiles; costumes; shops; room settings; furniture; books; manuscripts; photographs; maps; vehicles; tools; Herb House (1860) - library; reading room; auditorium; education center; nature trails; herb garden

Old Fort NC

15745
Carson House Restoration, Inc.
R.D. POB 179, Old Fort, NC 28762
Historic Site - 1964
Coll: pioneer artifacts; hand-woven quilts and towels; clocks; period furniture; grand piano; organ; musical instruments - library; reading room

Old Lyme CT

15746
Lyme Historical Society, Inc.
Lyme St, Old Lyme, CT 06371
History/Public Affairs Museum - 1953
Coll: American Impressionist paintings; decorative arts; archives; toys; furniture; historic houses

Olivet MI

15747
Armstrong Museum of Art and Archaeology Olivet College
Olivet, MI 49076
Fine Arts Museum
Coll: 20th century prints; sculptures from Thailand; primitive art from Melanesia and Africa; artifacts from Sumeria, Lebenon, the Phillipines - classrooms; library

Olustee FL

15748
Olustee Battlefield State Historic Site
U.S. 90, 2 miles east, POB 2, Olustee, FL 32072
Historic Site
Military artifacts

Olympia WA

15749
State Capitol Museum
211 W 21st Av, Olympia, WA 98501
General Museum - 1941
Coll: Indian artifacts; decorative arts; pioneer life; local and state history - library

Omaha NE

15750
Joslyn Art Museum
2200 Dodge St, Omaha, NE 68102
Fine Arts Museum - 1931
Coll: ancient and modern art; Renaissance paintings; graphics; paintings; decorative art; archaeology; sculpture - library

15751
Union Pacific Historical Museum
1416 Dodge St, Omaha, NE 68179
History/Public Affairs Museum - 1929
Coll: Shoshone Indian headdress; tomahawks; bows; arrows; Indian clothing; locomotive pictures; guns; rifles; documents

15752
Western Heritage Museum
801 S 10th St, Omaha, NE 68108
History/Public Affairs Museum - 1970
Coll: railroad memorabilia; early Midwest advertising art; Northwestern Bell Telephone Co. collection; Dr. Lee DeForest radio equipment; Edward May Antique Radio Collection - library; auditorium; classrooms

Onchiota NY

15753
Six Nations Indian Museum
Onchiota, NY 12968
Anthropology Museum - 1955
Coll: Six Nations Indian artifacts; ancient and modern Iroquois utensils, clothing, belts, art work and dwellings; Iroquois culture and history

Oneida NY

15754
Madison County Historical Society
435 Main and Grove, Oneida, NY 13421
General Museum - 1898
Coll: furniture; glassware; ceramics; textiles; tools; woodworking; blacksmithing and tinsmithing; Cottage Lawn (1849) - library

Oneonta AL

15755
Blount County Memorial Museum
308 5th Ave, Oneonta, AL 35121
General Museum - 1970
Coll: genealogical materials; family histories; Edison Collection for State of Alabama - auditorium

Oneonta NY

15756
The Museums at Hartwick College
Hartwick College, Oneonta, NY 13820
Fine Arts Museum - 1928
Yager Museum: collection of upper Susquehanna Indian artifacts; Furman collection of Mexican, Central American and South American artifacts; Sandell collection of Ecuadorian and Peruvian artifacts. The Gallery, Fine Arts Center: collection of paintings, sculpture, prints; Van Ess collection of Renaissance and Baroque works; Hoysradt herbarium. Archives: newspaper collection; photographs; historic manuscripts - library; auditorium; classrooms

Ontario NY

15757
Town of Ontario Historical and Landmark Preservation Society, Inc.
107 Ridge Rd, Ontario, NY 14519
General Museum - 1969
Coll: iron ore mining; antiques; agriculture; education - auditorium

Ontonagon MI

15758
Ontonagon County Historical Society Museum
Greenland Rd, POB 7, Ontonagon, MI 49953
History/Public Affairs Museum
Coll: crafts and tools; copper

Orange CA

15759
Museum of Dentistry
295 S Flower St, Orange, CA 92668
History/Public Affairs Museum - 1968
Coll: old dental equipment and artifacts dating from 1700 - library

15760
Tucker Wildlife Sanctuary
Star Rte, POB 858, Orange, CA 92667
Natural History Museum - 1938
Coll: entomology; botany; geology - library; botanical garden; nature center; research station

Orange TX

15761
Stark Museum of Art
712 Green Av, POB 1897, Orange, TX 77630
Fine Arts Museum - 1974
Coll: Western American art including Paul Kane collection; American Indian art - library

Orange VA

15762
The James Madison Museum
129 Caroline St, Orange, VA 22960
Historic Site - 1976
Agricultural artifacts demonstrating the progress in agriculture

Orchard Lake MI

15763
Galeria The Orchard Lake Schools
Orchard Lake, MI 48033
Fine Arts Museum
Coll: Polish and Polish American art

Orchard Park NY

15764
Orchard Park Historical Society
5800 Armor Rd, Orchard Park, NY 14127
General Museum - 1951
Coll: artifacts; agricultural items; dishes; loom - library

Orient NY

15765
Oysterponds Historical Society
Village Lane, Orient, NY 11957
General Museum - 1944
Coll: Indian artifacts; marine paintings; whaling and fishing mementos; ship models and navigating instruments; spinning and weaving - library

Orlando FL

15766
The John Young Museum and Planetarium Lock Haven Park
810 E Rollins Av, Orlando, FL 32803
Science/Tech Museum - 1948
Coll: anthropology; geology; shells - planetarium; observatory; meeting rooms; auditorium Laboratory

15767
Loch Haven Art Center, Inc.
2416 North Mills Av, Orlando, FL 32803
Fine Arts Museum - 1926
Coll: pre-Columbian art; 20th century American paintings; African graphics - library; auditorium; galleries; classrooms

15768
Orange County Historical Commission
812 E Rollins St, Orlando, FL 32803
General Museum - 1957
Coll: historical exhibits; furniture collections; Indian artifacts; historical buildings or replicas - library

15769
Pine Castle Center of the Arts Inc.
5903 Randolph St, Orlando, FL 23809
Fine Arts Museum - 1976
Coll: local antique tools; clothing; historic farm and buildings; oral history tapes of local pioneers

Orleans MA

15770
French Cable Station Museum in Orleans
Corner of Cove Rd & Route 28, Orleans, MA 02653
Science/Tech Museum - 1971
Coll: all the equipment necessary to send and receive submarine cable messages from the United States to Deolen, France

Ormond Beach FL

15771
Tomoka Museum Tomoka State Park
POB 695, Ormond Beach, FL 32074
General Museum - 1967
Coll: paintings and sculpture by Fred Dana Marsh; geology; wildlife; Indian artifacts; local history

Orofino ID

15772
Clearwater Historical Society Museum
315 College Av, POB 1454, Orofino, ID 83544
General Museum - 1960
Coll: Nez Perce Indian artifacts; pictures and photographs; pioneer articles; Lewis and Clark histories; pioneer folklore; manuscript collections - library; reading room

Orono ME

15773
Anthropology Museum University of Maine
Orono, ME 04473
Anthropology Museum - 1966
Coll: ethnology from Oceania, Africa, North and South America, the Arctic, Greenland, Northeastern Asia

15774
University of Maine at Orono Art Galleries
Carnegie Hall, Orono, ME 04469
Fine Arts Museum - 1865
Coll: contemporary American art; American and European graphics - reading room; classrooms

Oroville CA

15775
Oroville Chinese Temple
1500 Broderick St, Oroville, CA 95965
Religious Art Museum - 1863
Coll: preserved and restored Chinese temple, including religious figures, tapestries, writings, screens, altars - library

Osage IA

15776
Mitchell County Historical Museum
North 6th, Rte 4, Osage, IA 50461
General Museum - 1965
Coll: dolls; clothing; guns; tools; household items; wagons; musical instruments; historic houses - reading room; library

Oshkosh WI

15777
Oshkosh Public Museum
Algoma Blvd, Oshkosh, WI 54901
General Museum - 1911
Coll: paintings; sculpture; glassware; china; decorative arts; local history; natural history; Indian archeology and ethnography; meteorites - library; auditorium; photography studio; classrooms

15778
Paine Art Center and Arboretum
1410 Algoma Blvd, POB 1097, Oshkosh, WI 54901
Fine Arts Museum - 1947
Coll: 19th century English and French paintings; Russian and Greek icons; decorative arts; American glass; Chinese porcelains, jades, bronzes, sculpture; Oriental carpets; period rooms; arboretum - library; auditorium; classrooms

Oskaloosa IA

15779
Nelson Pioneer Farm and Crafts Museum
Rte 1, POB 24, Oskaloosa, IA 52577
Agriculture Museum - 1942
Coll: agriculture; Indian artifacts;
archaeology; Historic Houses - library

Ossineke MI

15780
Dinosaur Gardens Inc
11160 U.S. 23 South, Ossineke, MI
49766
Natural History Museum - 1934
prehistoric animals and birds

Ossining NY

15781
Ossining Historical Society Museum
196 Croton Av, Ossining, NY 10562
General Museum - 1938
Coll: costumes; paintings; Indian
artifacts; war relics; doll collection;
band box collection; photographs; oral
history collection - reading room

Oswego NY

15782
Fort Ontario State Historic Site
East 7th St, Oswego, NY 13126
History/Public Affairs Museum - 1949
Coll: military furnishings, firearms,
equipment, uniforms, prints, paintings
and other items pertaining to
fortifications, development and military
activities - library; classrooms;
auditorium

15783
Oswego County Historical Society
135 E 3rd St, Oswego, NY 13126
General Museum - 1896
Coll: Indian artifacts; Oswego County
materials; furniture and decorative
arts; personal and medical possesions
of Dr. Mary Walker - library

15784
**Tioga County Historical Society
Museum**
110 Front St, Oswego, NY 13827
General Museum - 1914
Coll: Indian artifacts; military and
firemen's displays; pioneer crafts;
pewter; numismatics - library; reading
room; auditorium

15785
Tyler Art Gallery State University of
New York College of Arts and
Science
Oswego, NY 13126
Fine Arts Museum
Coll: European and American
drawings; prints; paintings; sculptures

Ottawa KS

15786
Franklin County Historical Society
POB 145, Ottawa, KS 66067
General Museum - 1962
Coll: Russian posters and personal
correspondence of World War II;
Chautauqua artifacts; autographed
picture collection; the Wallen
collection of original cartoons - library

Ottumwa IA

15787
Wapello County Historical Museum
402 Chester Ave, Ottumwa, IA 52501
History/Public Affairs Museum - 1966
Coll: records of early industries; old
blacksmith; tools; early furniture;
costumes - library

Owensboro KY

15788
Owensboro Area Museum
2829 S Griffith Ave, Owensboro, KY
42301
General Museum - 1966
Coll: astronomy; botany; herpetology;
planetarium; numismatics;
paleontology; zoology - library

15789
Owensboro Museum of Fine Art
901 Frederica St, Owensboro, KY
42301
Fine Arts Museum - 1977
Coll: Contemporary American Art;
19th century paintings and graphics;
18th century English painting and
decorative arts; 18th century Chinese
porcelain - library; classrooms

Oxford OH

15790
**William Holmes McGuffey House
and Museum**
Spring and Oaks Sts, Oxford, OH
45056
Historic Site - 1960
Coll: McGuffey readers and other 19th
century textbooks; children's books;
McGuffey manuscripts, letters,
memorabilia; 19th century furniture
and other decorative arts - library

Oyster Bay NY

15791
Sagamore Hill National Historic Site
Cove Neck Rd, POB 304, Oyster Bay,
NY 11771
Historic Site - 1963
Coll: personal and household effects
of Theodore Roosevelt and his family;
books; printings; prints and
photographs - library; exhibit space

Pacific Grove CA

15792
**Pacific Grove Museum of Natural
History**
165 Forest Ave, Pacific Grove, CA
93950
Science/Tech Museum - 1881
Coll: amphibians; marine life; insects of
Monterey County; ethnology; zoology
- library; botanical garden

Pacific Palisades CA

15793
Will Rogers State Historic Park
14253 Sunset Blvd, POB 845, Pacific
Palisades, CA 90272
Historic Site - 1044
Coll: personal items of Will Rogers;
Western art; Indian artifacts; cowboy
souvenirs

Paducah KY

15794
**William Clark Market House
Museum**
2nd & Broadway, POB 12, Paducah,
KY 42001
History/Public Affairs Museum - 1968
Coll: rare musical instruments; tools;
old steamboats - library; theater

Page AZ

15795
**Glen Canyon National Recreation
Area**
POB 1507, Page, AZ 86040
General Museum - 1968
Coll: natural history; history; geology;
Indian artifacts; industry;
anthropology; archeology; botany;
ethnology

15796
**John Wesley Powell Memorial
Museum**
6 North Seventh Ave, Page, AZ 86040
Junior Museum - 1969
Coll: archives; anthropology;
archeology; ethnology; paleontology;
coins; stamps; - library; reading room;
film room; auditorium

Paicines CA

15797
Pinnacles National Monument
Paicines, CA 95043
Science/Tech Museum - 1908
Coll: herbarium; herpetology;
entomology; geology; zoology -
library

Palm Beach FL

15798
The Henry Morrison Flagler Museum
Whitehall Way, POB 969, Palm Beach,
FL 33480
General Museum - 1959
Coll: paintings; sculpture; furnishings;
mansion (1901); costumes - library;
auditorium

15799
**Historical Society of Palm Beach
County** Henry Morrison Flagler
Museum
1 Whitehall Way, POB 1492, Palm
Beach, FL 33480
General Museum - 1937
Coll: furniture; Indian artifacts; sheet
music; historic house - library; reading
room

15800
The Society of the Four Arts
Four Arts Plaza, Palm Beach, FL 33480
Fine Arts Museum - 1936
Coll: paintings; sculpture; shells -
library; reading room; botanical
garden; auditorium

Palm Desert CA

15801
Living Desert Reserve
47-900 Portola Rd, Palm Desert, CA
92260
Science/Tech Museum - 1970
Coll: live animal collection of native
wildlife; bird eggs of Southwest US;
desert herbarium - library; botanical
garden; nature center; reading room;
auditorium

Palm Springs CA

15802
Palm Springs Desert Museum, Inc.
101 Museum Dr, POB 2288, Palm
Springs, CA 92262
General Museum - 1938
Coll: paintings; sculpture; graphics;
ethnology; natural science; geology;
archeology - library; nature center;
reading room; auditorium; classrooms

Palmer AK

15803
**Transportation Museum of Alaska,
Inc.**
State Fairgrounds, POB SR Box S-875,
Palmer, AK 99645
Science/Tech Museum - 1976
Coll: antique airplanes; tractors and
wagons; locomotives and railroad
cars; kayaks; memorabilia and
archives - library; reading room

Palmer Lake CO

15804
Palmer Lake Historical Society
POB 601, Palmer Lake, CO 80133
History/Public Affairs Museum - 1956
Coll: local relics and photographs

Palmyra NY

15805
Alling Coverlet Museum
122 William St, Palmyra, NY 14522
Decorative Arts Museum - 1976
Coll: woven coverlets (1800)

Palo Alto CA

15806
Palo Alto Junior Museum
1451 Middlefield Road, Palo Alto, CA
94301
Junior Museum - 1934
Coll: natural history; anthropology -
classrooms; zoo and aquarium; nature
interpretive center

Pampa TX

15807
White Deer Land Museum
116 S Cuyler, Pampa, TX 79065
General Museum - 1970
local history, arrowheads, carriages -
library

Panama City FL

15808
Good Life Showboat
6057 W Hwy 98, Panama City, FL
32401
History/Public Affairs Museum - 1973
Coll: maritime artifacts from 1600 to
present; 'The Willow', one of the last
remaining sidewheel riverboats -
library

15809
The Junior Museum of Bay County
1731 Jinks Av, POB 977, Panama City,
FL 32401
Junior Museum - 1969
Coll: pioneer exhibit, including
traditional buildings; mounted African
animal trophies; natural science
collection - auditorium; puppet
theater; nature trail

Panhandle TX

15810
Carson County Square House Museum
5th and Elsie Sts, POB 276, Panhandle, TX 79068
General Museum - 1965
Coll: local history; Indian artifacts; Pueblo Indian culture (800-1300) - library; auditorium

Paoli PA

15811
Wharton Esherick Museum
POB 595, Paoli, PA 19301
Fine Arts Museum - 1972
200 pieces of Wharton Esherick's work including oil and watercolor paintings, woodcuts and prints, sculpture in wood, stone and ceramic, furniture, utensils and furnishings - library

Paramus NJ

15812
Bergen Community Museum
Ridgewood Ave, Paramus, NJ 07652
General Museum - 1956
Coll: minerals; shells; jewelry; paintings

Park Rapids MN

15813
North County Museum of Arts
Third St W and Court Ave, POB 328, Park Rapids, MN 56470
Fine Arts Museum - 1977
Coll: 15th to 19th century European paintings

Park Ridge IL

15814
Wood Library-Museum of Anesthesiology
515 Busse Hwy, Park Ridge, IL 60068
Science/Tech Museum - 1950
Coll: history of anesthesiology; anesthesiology equipment - library

Park Ridge NJ

15815
Pascack Historical Society
19 Ridge Ave, Park Ridge, NJ 07656
General Museum - 1942
Coll: archives; costumes; glass paperweights; wampum; drilling machine

Parker AZ

15816
Colorado River Indian Tribes Museum
Route 1, POB 23-B, Parker, AZ 85344
Anthropology Museum - 1958
Coll: historic site; anthropology; archeology; historic house; archives - library

Pasadena CA

15817
Norton Simon Museum
Colorado and Orange Grove Blvds, Pasadena, CA 91105
Fine Arts Museum - 1924
Coll: European painting from early Renaissance to mid-twentieth century; 19th and 20th century sculpture; stone and bronze sculpture from India and Southeast Asia; 20th century European and American art; Galka E. Scheyer Blue Four collection - library

15818
Pacific Asia Museum
46 N. Los Robles Ave, Pasadena, CA 91101
Fine Arts Museum - 1971
Coll: Chinese and Japanese textiles, scrolls, screens, toys, and ceramics - library; reading room; auditorium; theater; classrooms

15819
Pasadena Historical Society Museum
470 W. Walnut St, Pasadena, CA 91103
General Museum - 1924
Coll: photos of early Pasadena; costumes; Finnish folk art collection; antique furnishings - library

Pascagoula MS

15820
Old Spanish Fort and Museum
4602 Fort St, Pascagoula, MS 39567
History/Public Affairs Museum - 1949
Coll: mineralogy; paleontology; lithography

Pasco WA

15821
Sacajawea Interpretive Center
Sacajawea State Park, Rd 40 East, Pasco, WA 99301
Anthropology Museum
Interpretive Center honoring Sacajawea of the Lewis and Clark Expedition

Patagonia AZ

15822
Stradling Museum of the Horse, Inc.
POB 413, Patagonia, AZ 85624
General Museum - 1960
Coll: horse accoutrements; Indian artifacts; paintings; sculpture - library

Patchogue NY

15823
Fire Island National Seashore
120 Laurel St, Patchogue, NY 17772
Natural History Museum - 1964
Coll: natural history; preservation project; recreation - library

Paterson NJ

15824
Passaic County Historical Society
Valley Rd, Paterson, NJ 07503
Fine Arts Museum - 1926
Coll: decorative arts; paintings; furniture; sculpture; textiles; Indian artifacts - library

Pawhuska OK

15825
Osage County Historical Museum
700 Lynn Av, POB 267, Pawhuska, OK 74056
General Museum - 1964
Coll: pioneer artifacts; oil industry; military; Indian artifacts; Santa Fe Depot Building (1923)

Pawling NY

15826
Museum of Natural History
Quaker Hill, Pawling, NY 12564
Natural History Museum - 1960
Coll: Gunnison Collection of rocks, minerals, native birds and flora; agriculture; anatomy; entomology; geology; mineralogy - library

Pawtucket RI

15827
Slater Mill Historic Site
Roosevelt Av, POB 727, Pawtucket, RI 02862
Historic Site - 1921
Coll: furnished historic house; textile weaving exhibits; 19th century machine shop; machine tools; historic buildings - library

Pea Ridge AR

15828
Pea Ridge National Military Park
Pea Ridge, AR 72751
General Museum - 1960
Coll: Civil War artifacts; military items

Peace Dale RI

15829
Museum of Primitive Culture
604 Kingstown Rd, Peace Dale, RI 02883
Anthropology Museum - 1904
Artifacts from New England, North America and other continents

Peacham VT

15830
Peacham Historical Association
POB 25, Peacham, VT 05862
General Museum - 1927
Coll: old carpentry tools; local history - library

Pearl Harbor HI

15831
Pacific Submarine Museum
Naval Submarine Base, Pearl Harbor, HI 96860
History/Public Affairs Museum - 1970
Coll: original equipment from submarines; models; historical flags and plaques; photo collection and documents; personal mementos - library; reading room; theater

Peebles OH

15832
Serpent Mound Museum
State Rte 73, Peebles, OH 45660
Anthropology Museum - 1900
Coll: Adena Indian culture

Pella IA

15833
Pella Historical Village
505 Franklin, Pella, IA 50219
History/Public Affairs Museum - 1965
Coll: archives; ethnology; authentic Dutch costumes; complete set of newspapers printed in Pella; Wyatt Earp boyhood home (1851) and other historic buildings

Pembina ND

15834
Pembina State Museum
176 S Cavalier St, Pembina, ND 58271
General Museum - 1962
Barry collection

Penasco NM

15835
Picuris Pueblo Museum
POB 228, Penasco, NM 87553
Historic Site - 1969
Coll: anthropology; archaeology; Indian artifacts

Pendleton SC

15836
Foundation for Historic Restoration in Pendleton Area
POB 444, Pendleton, SC 29670
General Museum - 1960
Coll: historic houses; home furnishings

15837
Pendleton District Historical and Recreational Commission
125 E. Queen St, Pendleton, SC 29670
General Museum - 1966
Coll: artifacts; farm tools; glass; family genealogies; historic buildings - library; agricultural museum

Penn Yan NY

15838
Yates County Genealogical and Historical Society, Inc.
200 Main St, Penn Yan, NY 14527
General Museum - 1860
Coll: home furnishings; antique china; games; toys; dolls; costumes and clothes - library; classrooms

Pennsburg PA

15839
Schwenkfelder Museum
Seminary St, Pennsburg, PA 18073
General Museum - 1913
Coll: early Americana illustrating the economic and social life of the region; Indian artifacts; Pennsylvania Dutch household and farm implements; agriculture; costumes; decorative arts; military

Pensacola FL

15840
Historic Pensacola Preservation Board
200 E Zaragoza St, Pensacola, FL 32501
General Museum - 1967
Coll: transportation vehicles; marine artifacts; regional historical and archeological collections; historic houses - library

15841
Naval Aviation Museum
U.S. Naval Air Station, Pensacola, FL
32508
Science/Tech Museum - 1963
Coll: history of naval aviation depicted
by photographs, charts, diagrams,
artifacts, scale models; full-size aircraft
covering early aviation through the
space age - library

15842
Pensacola Historical Museum
405 S Adams St, Pensacola, FL 32501
General Museum
Coll: clothing; household utensils;
Indian artifacts; Viola A. Blount fine art
glass collection; the Carpenter glass
negative collection; local historical
items; historic house - library

15843
**Pensacola Historical Preservation
Society**
204 S Alcaniz St, Pensacola, FL 32501
General Museum - 1960
Coll: period furniture; historical houses

15844
Pensacola Museum of Art
407 S Jefferson St, Pensacola, FL
32501
Fine Arts Museum - 1954
Coll: paintings; graphics; watercolors;
historical building - library; auditorium;
classrooms

15845
T. T. Wentworth, Jr. Museum
POB 806, Pensacola, FL 32549
General Museum - 1957
Coll: local items; stamps; aeronautics;
agriculture; anthropology; archives;
paintings; Indian artifacts; natural
history - library

15846
Visual Arts Gallery
1000 College Blvd, Pensacola, FL
32504
Fine Arts Museum
Coll: contemporary drawings; prints;
paintings; crafts

Peoria IL

15847
**Lakeview Museum of Art and
Sciences**
1125 West Lake Av, Peoria, IL 61614
General Museum - 1965
Coll: archaeology; decorative and fine
arts; ethnology; natural and physical
sciences

15848
Peoria Historical Society
942 NE Glen Oak Av, Peoria, IL 61603
General Museum - 1934
Coll: furniture, furnishings and
domestic utensils; tools; costumes
from pre-Civil-War period to present -
library

Perkinsville VT

15849
**Reverend Dan Foster House,
Museum of the Weathersfield
Historical Society**
Perkinsville, VT 05151
General Museum - 1951
Coll: costumes; furniture; Civil War
items; local history - library

Perris CA

15850
Orange Empire Railway Museum
2201 S A St, Perris, CA 92370
Science/Tech Museum - 1956
Coll: steam locomotives; electric
railway vehicles; motor buses and
motor trucks; historic building

Perry OK

15851
**Cherokee Strip Historical Museum
and Henry S. Johnston Library**
Rte 2, 1/4 mile east of Fir St exit from
Interstate No. 35, POB 81-A, Perry, OK
73077
General Museum - 1965
Coll: agriculture; history; medical;
Indian artifacts; costumes; glass;
County School House (1896) - library

Perth Amboy NJ

15852
Kearny Cottage Historical Society
Catalpa Av, Perth Amboy, NJ 08861
General Museum - 1938
Coll: furniture; works by local artists;
documents

Peru IN

15853
Miami County Historical Museum
Court House
Junction, U.S. 24 and Business U.S. 31,
Peru, IN 46970
General Museum - 1916
Coll: historical exhibits; Indian artifacts;
natural history; circus; archives -
library

15854
Puterbaugh Museum
11 N Huntington St, Peru, IN 46970
General Museum - 1932
Coll: pioneer history; Indian artifacts;
military; natural history; circus relics

Petersburg AK

15855
Clausen Memorial Museum
POB 708, Petersburg, AK 99833
General Museum - 1967
old newspapers; history of local first
families; music boxes and pianos;
pictures

Petersburg IL

15856
Lincoln's New Salem Village
Petersburg, IL 62675
Open Air Museum - 1917
Coll: reconstructed timber houses,
shops, stores, and other buildings and
artifacts of New Salem Village in the
1830's where Lincoln lived as a young
man

Petersburg VA

15857
Farmers Bank
mail c/o Fort Henry Branch, APVA, 19
Bollingbrook St, POB 501, Petersburg,
VA 23803
History/Public Affairs Museum
Coll: pre-Civil War banking; bank
furnishings; notes

15858
Petersburg National Battlefield
POB 549, Petersburg, VA 23803
History/Public Affairs Museum - 1926
Coll: artillery; maps; military history of
campaign for Petersburg - library

Pharr TX

15859
Old Clock Museum
929 E Preston St, Pharr, TX 78577
Science/Tech Museum - 1968
Coll: clocks - library

Philadelphia PA

15860
**Academy of Natural Sciences of
Philadelphia**
19th and Parkway, Philadelphia, PA
19103
Natural History Museum - 1812
Coll: plants; mammals; birds; reptiles;
amphibia; fish; insects; molluscs; lower
invertebrates; fossils; minerals -
library; Benedict Laboratories, for
studies in estuarine and offshore
marine biology; Stroud Laboratories,
for freshwater stream studies;
research wing; children's museum;
auditorium; classrooms

15861
**Afro-American Historical and
Cultural Museum**
7th and Arch Sts, Philadelphia, PA
19106
History/Public Affairs Museum - 1976
Coll: African sculpture and artifacts;
paintings, prints and sculpture by
Black artists; Afro-Americana; artifacts
relating to Slave Trade, American
Revolution, Black Church, Civil War,
Reconstruction Period, Westward
Movement, Harlem Renaissance, Civil
Rights Movement, Black scientists and
investors - auditorium

15862
The Athenaeum of Philadelphia
219 S 6th St, East Washinton Sq,
Philadelphia, PA 19106
Fine Arts Museum - 1814
research collections relating to 19th
century social and cultural history; fine
and decorative arts of the Empire style
period (1820-1840) - library

15863
Atwater Kent Museum
15 S 7th St, Philadelphia, PA 19143
General Museum
Coll: artifacts relating to the history fo
the Delaware Valley; prints and
drawings - botanical garden

15864
Cliveden
6401 Germantown Av, Philadelphia, PA
19144
General Museum - 1972
Philadelphia Chippendale furniture;
silver; porcelain; paintings - library;
conference center

15865
Cyclorama of Life
Lankenau Hospital, City Line and
Lancaster Avs, Philadelphia, PA 19151
Science/Tech Museum - 1954
medical history; human growth and
development

15866
Drexel Museum Collection Drexel
University
32nd and Chestnut Sts, Philadelphia,
PA 19104
Fine Arts Museum - 1892
Coll: porcelains; ceramics; 19th
century paintings; American furniture;
European textiles (14th c.-present) ;
Oriental, East Indian and American
graphics and costumes; American
textiles; decorative arts

15867
**Franklin Institute, Science Museum
and Planetarium**
20th and Benjamin Franklin Pkwy,
Philadelphia, PA 19103
Science/Tech Museum - 1824
Coll: science; history; industry;
technology; transportation; marine;
naval; aeronautics; astronomy; space
exploration; energy; mathematics;
stamp and coin collection; Benjamin
Franklin National Memorial - library;
reading room; auditorium; theater;
children's museum; classrooms;
planetarium

15868
Germantown Historical Society
5214 Germantown Av, Philadelphia, PA
19144
General Museum - 1900
Coll: 18th and 19th century artifacts
relating to early Germantown;
furniture; crystal; china; needlework;
coverlets; toys; hardware; crafts -
library

15869
Historical Dental Museum Temple
University School of Dentistry
3223 N Broad St, Philadelphia, PA
19140
History/Public Affairs Museum - 1938
Coll: dental equipment, furniture,
instruments, paintings and documents
(1750-1930) - library

15870
Ina Corporation Museum
1600 Arch St, Philadelphia PA 19103,
POB 7728, Philadelphia, PA 19101
General Museum - 1792
Coll: products manufactured in
Philadelphia; paintings, prints;
apparatus, equipment; manuscripts -
reading and research room; library

15871
Independance National Park
313 Walnut St, Philadelphia, PA 19106
History/Public Affairs Museum - 1948
Coll: decorative arts; history;
archaeology; American portraits from
1770-1830 by Peale, Sharples, West,
Sully, Pine; 18th century American
period furnishings; objects and
documents relating to Independence
Hall, Congress Hall; personal
memorabilia relating to Revolution and
early Federal period; archives; military;
graphics; historic sites (1732-1834) -
library

15872
**Institute of Contemporary Art of the
University of Pennsylvania**
34th and Walnut St, Philadelphia, PA
19104
Fine Arts Museum - 1963
contemporary art; archives of
statements and notes by Agnes Martin

15873
La Salle College Art Gallery
20th and Olney Av, Philadelphia, PA
19141
Fine Arts Museum - 1969
Coll: oils; prints; drawings;
watercolors; rare books; 15th-20th
cent. sculpture

15874
Lemon Hill Mansion
E River and Sedgely Dr, Philadelphia,
PA 19130
Historic Site - 1800
Decorative arts and furnishings from
the period 1800-1836

15875
Library Company of Philadelphia
1314 Locust St, Philadelphia, PA 19107
History/Public Affairs Museum - 1731
Coll: rare books dealing with American
history from colonial times to the
centennial; 18th century Anglo-
American and Franco-American
culture; manuscripts; paintings;
graphics; furniture - library; reading
room

15876
'Man Full of Trouble' Tavern
127-129 Spruce St, Philadelphia, PA
19106
Historic Site - 1961
Decorative arts; 18th century
furnishings; American pewter; English
delftware; glass

15877
Moore College of Art Gallery
20th and Race St, Philadelphia, PA
19103
Fine Arts Museum - 1844
Coll: paintings; sculpture; graphics;
decorative arts; textiles - library

15878
Museum of American Jewish History
55 N 5th St, Independence Mall East,
Philadelphia, PA 19106
Religious Art Museum - 1976
Coll: Judaica Americana including
documents and artifacts from the
colonial period to the present;
synagogue archives; ceremonial
objects; memorabilia - library;
auditoria; classrooms

15879
**Museum of the Philadelphia Civic
Center**
Civic Center Blvd at 34th St,
Philadelphia, PA 19104
General Museum - 1894
ethnology; folklore; decorative arts

15880
Mutter Museum College of
Physicians of Philadelphia
19 S 22nd St, Philadelphia, PA 19103
History/Public Affairs Museum - 1849
Coll: human and comparative anatomy
and pathology; medical history and
biography; development of medical
instrumentation; development of fetus
and anomalies; folklore; quackery;
military medicine; nursing and
apothecary artifacts; memorabilia of
physicians and dentists; medical
antiques; oil portraits; prints;
photographs; sculpture - herb garden;
meeting rooms; audio-visual
equipment; library

15881
**Naomi Wood Collection at Woodford
Mansion**
33rd and Dauphin St, Philadelphia, PA
19132
Historic Site - 1926
Coll: decorative arts; English
Delftware; Federal, Victorian and
French Empire furnishings; modern
and contemporary furnishings; colonial
furnishings

15882
**La Napoule Art Foundation - Henry
Clews Memorial**
133 Bennett Hall, University of
Pennsylvania, Philadelphia, PA 19104
Historic Site - 1950
Sculptures and paintings of Henry
Clews, Jr.; Chateau de la Napoule (9th
and 11th century), Alpes Maritimes,
France, a medieval fortress

15883
**New Year's Shooters and Mummers
Museum, Inc.**
Two St at Washington Av, Philadelphia,
PA 19147
History/Public Affairs Museum - 1976
Coll: memorabilia of Philadelphia
Mummers including comic, fancy and
string band divisions; mummer suits of
present and past years, photographs,
badges - library; reading room;
theater

15884
**Pennsylvania Academy of the Fine
Arts**
Broad and Cherry Sts, Philadelphia,
PA 19102
Fine Arts Museum - 1805
Coll: 18th and 19th century American
painting and sculpture, including works
of Charles W. Peale, James Peale and
family, Benjamin West, Stuart, Sully,
Neagle, Eakins, Homer, Cassatt,
Chase, Anshutz, Sargent; major
holdings of American Impressionists
and the Eight; 19th century American
landscape and genre - library;
auditorium; classrooms

15885
Perelman Antique Toy Museum
270 S 2nd St, Philadelphia, PA 19106
Anthropology Museum - 1962
Antique toys; mechanical banks; toy
pistols; automatic toys - library

15886
The Philadelphia Art Alliance
251 S 18th St, Philadelphia, PA 19103
Fine Arts Museum - 1962
Changing exhibitions of crafts, prints,
paintings, sculpture, jewelry,
photography, architecture

15887
Philadelphia Gas Light Museum
2714 E Ontario, Philadelphia, PA 19134
Science/Tech Museum - 1969
Exhibitions portraying the history of
light

15888
Philadelphia Maritime Museum
321 Chestnut St, Philadelphia, PA
19106
History/Public Affairs Museum - 1961
Coll: ship models; figureheads;
paintings; prints; drawings; weapons;
memorabilia and artifacts related to
ships and the sea - library; reading
room; auditorium

15889
Philadelphia Museum of Art
26th St and Benjamin Franklin Pkwy,
POB 7646, Philadelphia, PA 19101
Fine Arts Museum - 1876
Coll: Far and Near Eastern art; Indian
art; Far Eastern, Indian, European and
American period rooms; Johnson
collection of Italian, Dutch, Flemish,
French and English 19th century
master paintings; Kress collection of
Barberini tapestries; American
paintings; Titus C. Geesey collection of
Pennsylvania Dutch folk art; American
furniture, silver, ceramics, glass,
costumes, textiles; European paintings
including Gallatin and Arensberg;
collections of Cubist and post-Cubist
masters with works by Brancusi and
Duchamp; sculpture; prints; drawings;
historic houses - library; auditorium;
classrooms

15890
Presbyterian Historical Society
425 Lombard St, Philadelphia, PA
19147
Religious Art Museum - 1852
Coll: oil portraits, communion tokens,
silver, pewter; pictures, maps,
manuscripts, early European imprints
before 1800; early Bibles; archives;
numismatics - library; reading room

15891
Print Club
1614 Latimer St, Philadelphia, PA
19103
Fine Arts Museum - 1915
Print collection - library

15892
**Robert W. Ryerss Library and
Museum**
Burholme Park, Cottman and Central
Avs, Philadelphia, PA 19111
Decorative Arts Museum - 1910
18th and 19th century decorative arts;
Chinese and Oriental collections;
Victorian and other period furnishings
- library; reading room

15893
Rodin Museum
Benjamin Franklin Pkwy at 22nd St,
Philadelphia, PA 19101
Fine Arts Museum - 1926
Sculpture and drawings of Auguste
Rodin

15894
The Rosenbach Museum and Library
2010 Delaney Place, Philadelphia, PA
19103
Fine Arts Museum - 1954
Coll: English and American literature
and antique furnishings; incunabula;
Judaica; Marianne Moore archive;
Maurice Sendak archive - library

15895
**St. George's United Methodist
Church**
235 N Fourth St, Philadelphia, PA
19106
Religious Art Museum - 1767
Coll: original John Wesley Chalice
Cup; Francis Asbury's personal Bible;
Asbury watch - library; reading room

15896
The Stephen Girard Collection
Corinthian and Girard Avs,
Philadelphia, PA 19121
Historic Site - 1831
Coll: antique furniture owned by
Stephen Girard, including furniture by
Trotter, Connelly, Haines; American,
French and English silver; China Trade
items

15897
The University Museum University of
Pensylvania
33rd and Spruce Sts, Philadelphia, PA
19174
Archeology Museum - 1889
Coll: Near Eastern, Syro-Palestinian,
South and Southeast Asian, Egyptian,
Mediterranean, North, Middle and
South American, African, Oceanic,
Chinese and Australian archaeology,
anthropology and ethnology - library;
reading room; auditorium; classrooms

15898
Wagner Free Institute of Science
17th St and Montgomery Av,
Philadelphia, PA 19121
Natural History Museum - 1855
Coll: mineralogy; paleontology; fossils;
shells; animals; birds; reptiles - library;
reading room; auditorium

15899
**War Library and Museum of the
Military Order of the Loyal Legion of
the United States**
1805 Pine St, Philadelphia, PA 19103
History/Public Affairs Museum - 1886
Coll: uniforms; arms; accoutrements;
personal memorabilia; standards;
insignias; Lincoln items - library;
reading room

Phillips ME

15900
Phillips Historical Society
Pleasant St, Phillips, ME 04966
General Museum - 1959
Coll: railroad relics; glass; maps;
documents; archives; farm
implements; furniture

Phoenix AZ

15901
Arizona Capitol Museum
3rd Floor Capitol, 1700 W. Washington,
Phoenix, AZ 85007
History/Public Affairs Museum - 1978
Coll: Arizona history

15902
Arizona Mineral Museum
State Fairgrounds, Phoenix, AZ 85007
Natural History Museum - 1953
Coll: lapidary; petrology; paleontology;
geology; minerals

15903
The Arizona Museum
1002 W. Van Buren St, Phoenix, AZ
85007
General Museum - 1923
Coll: pioneer relics and costumes;
paintings; steam locomotives; first
motorcycle engine; historic house

15904
Hall of Fame
6101 E. Van Buren, Phoenix, AZ 85008
History/Public Affairs Museum - 1961
Coll: antique fire engines; objects
relating to the history of fire fighting -
library

15905
Heard Museum
22 E. Monte Vista Rd, Phoenix, AZ
85004
Anthropology Museum - 1029
Coll: American Indians' works;
primitive arts from the cultures of
Africa, Asia, and Oceania; archeology,
ethnology; paintings; sculpture;
anthropology - library

15906
Judaica Museum of Temple Beth Israel
3310 No. 10th Ave, Phoenix, AZ 85013
Religious Art Museum - 1966
Coll: Jewish arts and ceremonials from 1600 to present; archeology of Israel; Israeli philatelic collection - library; reading room

15907
Phoenix Art Museum
1625 N. Central Ave, Phoenix, AZ 85004
Fine Arts Museum - 1925
Coll: general painting; American painting; Oriental painting; sculpture; graphics; decorative arts; Thorne miniature rooms - library; auditorium; junior museum; satellite museum

15908
Phoenix Museum of History
1242 N. Central, Phoenix, AZ 85004
General Museum - 1973
Coll: textiles and costumes; decorative arts; photographs; ranching, mining, and transportation; Mexican and ethnic culture - library

15909
Pioneer Arizona
I-17 & Pioneer Rd, POB 11242, Phoenix, AZ 85061
History/Public Affairs Museum - 1956
Coll: 26 late 19th cent. homes and shops; pioneer life; agricultural items; historical items - library; nature center; outdoor museum

Pickens SC

15910
Pickens County Historical Museum
POB 506, Pickens, SC 29671
General Museum - 1958
Coll: artifacts pertaining to the history of Pickens County; Indian relics; old items from early homes

Pierre SD

15911
Robinson Museum
Memorial Building, Pierre, SD 57501
History/Public Affairs Museum - 1901
Coll: archaeology; Plains Indian collection; historical material of white settlement and industry; military collection; political Americana - library

Pima AZ

15912
Eastern Arizona Museum and Historical Society, Inc. of Graham County
2 N Main St, Pima, AZ 85543
General Museum - 1963
Coll: pioneer and Indian artifacts; authentic reproduction of a pioneer home

Pine Bluff AR

15913
Southeast Arkansas Arts and Science Center
Civic Center, Pine Bluff, AR 71601
Fine Arts Museum - 1968
Coll: 19th century European paintings; 20th century American paintings and prints - library; theater; classrooms

Pinehurst NC

15914
World Golf Hall of Fame
Gerald R. Ford Blvd, Pinehurst, NC 28374
History/Public Affairs Museum - 1974
Coll: Lew Worsham's wedge; irons used in tournaments by Arnold Palmer; Jack Nicklaus's putter; Dwight D. Eisenhower's cart; Bobby Jones clubs; ball and scorecard used by Al Gleiberger; portraits; placques - library; theater

Pineville PA

15915
Wilmar Lapidary Museum
Rte 232 and Pineville Rd, Pineville, PA 18946
Natural History Museum - 1967
Coll: carved stones; specimens of gemology; art; nature history; mineralogy - library

Piney Flats TN

15916
Rocky Mount
Piney Flats, TN 37686
General Museum - 1961
Coll: furniture and furnishings of a log house including kitchen, servant's quarters, barn; textile collection - library

Pipestone MN

15917
Pipestone National Monument
POB 727, Pipestone, MN 56164
General Museum - 1937
Coll: Indian ceremonial pipes; Indian culture - library

Piqua OH

15918
Piqua Historical Area
9845 N Hardin Rd, Piqua, OH 45356
Historic Site - 1972
Coll: 18th century furnishings; tools; historic Indian tools; weapons, costumes, art; canoes; Indian trade items; graphic art

Pittsburg KS

15919
Crawford County Museum
69 Bypass to 20th St, 610 W 2nd St, Pittsburg, KS 66762
General Museum
Coll: art; decorative arts; industry; transportation; education; biology - library

15920
Natural History Museum Pittsburg State University
Pittsburg, KS 66762
Natural History Museum - 1903
Coll: study specimens of skin and skulls; ichthyology; entomology - auditorium, theater, classrooms

15921
Old Fort Bissell
Pittsburg, KS 67661
History/Public Affairs Museum - 1961
Coll: guns; dolls; historic houses

Pittsburgh PA

15922
Buhl Planetarium and Institute of Popular Science
Allegheny Sq, Pittsburgh, PA 15212
Science/Tech Museum - 1939
Coll: science; technology; space artifacts - library; planetarium; auditorium; classrooms

15923
Carnegie Museum of Natural History
Carnegie Institute
4400 Forbes Av, Pittsburgh, PA 15213
Natural History Museum - 1896
Coll: geology; mineralogy; invertebrate and vertebrate paleontology; anthropology; plants; insects; spiders; amphibians; reptiles; birds; mammals - library; nature/conservation center; field research station

15924
Fisher Collection
711 Forbes Av, Pittsburgh, PA 15219
Fine Arts Museum - 1924
17th and 18th Dutch and Flemish oil paintings; genre pieces with emphasis on alchemy

15925
The Fort Pitt Blockhouse and Museum
Point State Park, Pittsburgh, PA 15219
Historic Site - 1894
Indian artifacts; paleontology; archaeology; local history - library

15926
Foster Hall Collection University of Pittsburgh
Forbes Av, Pittsburgh, PA 15260
Music Museum - 1937
Material relating to the life and works of Pittsburgh composer Stephen Collins Foster (1826-1864) - library; reading rooms; auditorium; theater; classrooms

15927
The Frick Art Museum
7227 Reynolds St, Pittsburgh, PA 15208
Fine Arts Museum - 1970
Coll: Italian Renaissance paintings; Franco-Flemish paintings; tapestries; French 18th century period room; decorative arts; sculpture - auditorium

15928
Gallery of the Associated Artists of Pittsburgh
6300 5th Av, Pittsburgh, PA 15232
Fine Arts Museum - 1910
paintings; sculpture; arts and crafts

15929
Historical Society of Western Pennsylvania
4338 Bigelow Blvd, Pittsburgh, PA 15213
General Museum - 1843
Coll: dioramas; glass; paintings; furniture; artifacts and memorabilia of local history - library; reading room; auditorium

15930
Museum of Art Carnegie Institute
4400 Forbes Av, Pittsburgh, PA 15213
Fine Arts Museum - 1896
Coll: European and American paintings and sculptures; Impressionist and post-Impressionist collection; contemporary art collection; antiquities; oriental and decorative arts; watercolor, drawing and print collections; Japanese Woodblock collection; photographs and films; Sarah Scaife gallery; Heinz galleries; Ailsa Mellon Bruce galleries

15931
The Old Post Office Pittsburgh History and Landmarks Museum
One Landmarks Sq, Pittsburgh, PA 15212
General Museum - 1972
Coll: antique toys; architectural artifacts; fashions; furniture; prints and engravins - library; auditorium; artifact garden court

Pittsfield MA

15932
The Berkshire Museum
29 South St, Pittsfield, MA 01201
General Museum - 1903
Coll: Chinese art; silver; biology; paleontology; minerals; animals - library; theater; auditorium; classrooms

15933
Hancock Shaker Village Shaker Community
Rte 20, POB 898, Pittsfield, MA 01201
History/Public Affairs Museum - 1960
Coll: furniture and artifacts of Shaker communities; agricultural tools; paintings; folklore; crafts - library

Plainfield NJ

15934
The Drake House Museum
602 W Front St, Plainfield, NJ 07060
Historic Site - 1921
Coll: Americana; antique furnishings in period room settings

Plainview TX

15935
Llano Estacado Museum
Wayland College, Plainview, TX 79072
General Museum - 1976
Coll: geological and archaeological development of the Llano Estacado region - auditorium

Platteville CO

15936
Fort Vasquez Visitor Center
13412 US Highway 85, Platteville, CO 80651
History/Public Affairs Museum - 1958
Coll: items related to Rocky Mountain fur trade era; historic buildings

Platteville WI

15937
Platteville Mining Museum
385 East Main, Platteville, WI 53818
Science/Tech Museum - 1965
Mining; geology - library

Plattsburgh NY

15938
Myers Fine Arts and Rockwell Kent Galleries
Myers Fine Arts Bldg, State University of New York, Plattsburgh, NY 12901
Fine Arts Museum - 1978
Coll: paintings, drawings, print, and sculpture; Rockwell Kent Collection of paintings, prints, drawings, sketches, proofs and designs, illustrations, books, commercial illustration proofs

Plattsmouth NE

15939
Cass County Historical Society Museum
644 Main St, Plattsmouth, NE 68048
General Museum - 1935
Coll: rocks and fossils; paleontology; geology; furnishing; tools - library; reading room

Pleasant Hill CA

15940
Diablo Valley College Museum
Golf Club Rd, Pleasant Hill, CA 94523
Science/Tech Museum - 1957
Coll: anthropology; zoology; mineralogy; scientific instruments - library; botanical garden; planetarium

Pleasant Hill OH

15941
Miami County Archaeological Museum
Indian Hills 4-H Camp, Lauver Rd, Pleasant Hill OH 45359, 7385 N Troy-Sidney Rd, Piqua, OH 45356
Archeology Museum - 1961
Coll: archaeology

Pleasanton KS

15942
Linn County Historical Society Museum
POB 137, Pleasanton, KS 66075
History/Public Affairs Museum
Coll: pictures; maps; documents - library

Plymouth IN

15943
Marshall County Historical Museum, Inc.
317 W Monroe, Plymouth, IN 46563
General Museum - 1957
Coll: local historical artifacts; tools; furniture; household itmes; local genealogy; photos; Indian artifacts; clothing - library

Plymouth MA

15944
The Pilgrim Society
75 Court St, Plymouth, MA 02360
History/Public Affairs Museum - 1820
Coll: fine and decorative arts; manuscripts; books; Pilgrim history

15945
Plymoth Plantation Inc
Warren Ave, POB 1620, Plymouth, MA 02360
History/Public Affairs Museum - 1947
Coll: archaeology; arms and armor; replicas of the Mayflower ship; English and American artifacts - library; theater

15946
Plymouth Antiquarian Society Inc
Spooner House
27 North St, Plymouth, MA 02360
History/Public Affairs Museum - 1919
Coll: 17th and 18th centruy antique furnishings; fashions; Chinese export porcelain; dolls - classrooms

Plymouth VT

15947
Plymouth Historic Site
Plymouth, VT 05056
Historic Site
Coll: furnishings; Calvin Coolidge birthplace and homestead

Pocatello ID

15948
Idaho Museum of Natural History
Idaho State University, Pocatello, ID 83209
Natural History Museum - 1934
Coll: Northwest Coast, Plateau, and Great Basin collections in archeology, ethnology, and linguistics; Anatolian and Polish textiles; Crabtree flint-working collection; manuscripts and photographs of North Rocky Mountains region; vertebrate fossils - library; exhibits trailer

Point Lookout MO

15949
The Ralph Foster Museum
School of the Ozarks, Point Lookout, MO 65726
General Museum - 1930
Coll: prehistoirc Ozarks Indian cultures; arts; history; sciences; archaeology - library; auditorium

Poland Spring ME

15950
The Shaker Museum
Sabbathday Lake, Poland Spring, ME 04274
History/Public Affairs Museum - 1931
Coll: folk art; pharmaceutical implements; woodenware; tin

Pomeroy OH

15951
Meigs County Museum
144 Butternut Av, POB 145, Pomeroy, OH 45796
General Museum - 1960
Coll: Ohio history; river history - library; theater; meeting room

Ponca City OK

15952
Ponca City Cultural Center Museum
1000 E Grand, Ponca City, OK 74601
Anthropology Museum - 1939
Coll: ethnology and archaeology of Ponca City's five neighbouring tribes: Ponca, Kaw, Otoe, Osage and Tonkawa; pre-Columbian material; sculptures - library; Bryant Baker studio

Port Angeles WA

15953
Port Angeles Visitor Center
2800 Hurricane Ridge Rd, Port Angeles, WA 98362
Science/Tech Museum - 1957
Coll: anthropology; herbarium; zoology; botany - library

Port Chester NY

15954
Museum of Cartoon Art
Colmy Av, Town of Rye, Port Chester, NY 10573
Fine Arts Museum
Coll: comics; film and videotape screenings; Cartoon Hall of Fame - library; theater; classrooms

Port Clinton OH

15955
Ottawa County Historical Museum
City Hall, Adams and 2nd Sts, Port Clinton, OH 43452
General Museum - 1932
Coll: Indian relics; early household items; hand machine equipment; clothing; toys; china; land grants

Port Gamble WA

15956
Port Gamble Historical Museum
POB 84, Port Gamble, WA 98364
Historic Site - 1976
Coll: maritime artifacts; historic houses - library

Port Hueneme CA

15957
Seabee Museum Civil Engineer Corps
Naval Construction Battalion Center, Code 2232, Port Hueneme, CA 93043
Science/Tech Museum - 1947
Coll: weapons and uniforms; crude handmade native tools from all over the world; archives; unit plaques and flags; nuclear power plant model and displays from Antarctic and Alaska - library; auditorium

Port Huron MI

15958
Museum of Arts and History
11156 Sixth St, Port Huron, MI 48060
History/Public Affairs Museum - 1968
Coll: marine; natural history; Indian artifacts; ship models - library

Port Jefferson NY

15959
Historical Society of Greater Port Jefferson
115 Prospect St, Port Jefferson, NY 11777
General Museum - 1967
Coll: tin; maps; books; half hulls; paintings; sailmaker's and ship builder's tools; looms - library

Port Sanilac MI

15960
Sanilac Historical Museum
228 S. Ridge St, Port Sanilac, MI 48469
General Museum
Coll: marine; medical; military; agriculture; farming

Port Townsend WA

15961
Jefferson County Historical Society
City Hall, Port Townsend, WA 98368
General Museum - 1879
Coll: military archives; uniforms; guns; memorabilia; early pioneer exhibits; Indian artifacts

15962
Rothschild House
mail c/o Old Fort Townsend State Park, Rte 1, Port Townsend, WA 98368
Historic Site
Artifacts and furnishings from the Rothschild familiy

Port Washington WI

15963
Sunken Treasures Maritime Museum
POB 64, Port Washington, WI 53074
Science/Tech Museum - 1976
Coll: ships and shipping; underwater scenes of sunken ships in dioramas - library

Portage WI

15964
Fort Winnebago Surgeons Quarters
R.R. 1, Portage, WI 53901
History/Public Affairs Museum - 1938
Coll: relics and furniture of fort period; surgical instruments; Indian artifacts; military; historic building - library

15965
The Old Indian Agency House
Hwy 33, Portage WI 53901, 3110 E Hampshire St, Milwaukee, WI 53211
General Museum
Decorative arts of the American Empire period; local history

Portales NM

15966
Blackwater Draw Museum Eastern New Mexico University
7 miles north of campus on Hwy 70, Portales, NM 88130
Archeology Museum - 1969
Coll: paleo-Indian archaeology and geology; paleontology; anthropology

15967
Miles Museum Eastern New Mexico University
Portales, NM 88130
Natural History Museum - 1969
Coll: geology, mineralogy; archaeology and ethnology collections; paleontology

15968
Natural History Museum Eastern New Mexico University
POB 2289, Portales, NM 88130
Natural History Museum - 1968
Coll: 6,500 specimens of mammals; 3,900 specimens of reptiles and amphibians; 600 specimens of birds; 10,000 specimens of fish

15969
Paleo-Indian Institute and Museum
Eastern New Mexico University
POB 2154, Portales, NM 88130
General Museum - 1963
Coll: archaeology; anthropology; paleontology - library

15970
Roosevelt County Museum Eastern New Mexico University
Portales, NM 88130
General Museum - 1934
Coll: technology; early settlers; ethnology; folklore; archives; costumes; numismatics

Portland ME

15971
Maine Historical Society
485 Congress St, Portland, ME 04101
General Museum - 1822
Coll: firearms; glass; pottery; textiles; prints - library; reading room

15972
Morse-Libby House
109 Danforth St, Portland, ME 04101
Decorative Arts Museum - 1943
Coll: china; glass; furnishing - library

15973
Portland Museum of Art
111 High St, Portland, ME 04101
Fine Arts Museum - 1882
Coll: American paintings; sculptures;
Japanese prints and sword fittings -
library

15974
Portland Veteran Fireman Association
157 Spring St, Portland, ME 04101
History/Public Affairs Museum - 1891
Coll: old fire-fighting memorabilia; fire
helmets; hand hoses and a fire truck

Portland OR

15975
Contemporary Crafts Association
3934 SW Corbett Av, Portland, OR
97201
Decorative Arts Museum - 1936
Coll: Northwest craftsmen; ceramics;
sculpture; pottery; textiles; jewelry -
library

15976
The Old Church Society, Inc.
1422 SW 11th Av, Portland, OR 97201
Historic Site - 1968
Coll: Lannie Hurst Parlor with
Victorian furnishings; Hook & Hastings
tracker action pipe organ (1883) -
auditorium

15977
Oregon Historical Society
1230 SW Park Av, Portland, OR 97205
General Museum - 1873
Coll: anthropology; ethnography;
maritime collection; paintings;
drawings; prints; Collins miniature
wagon collection; photographs;
historic buildings - library; photo
laboratory; auditorium; audivisual
facilities

15978
Oregon Museum of Science and Industry
4015 SW Canyon Rd, Portland, OR
97221
Science/Tech Museum - 1943
Coll: mineralogy; paleontology;
ethnology; zoology; natural history;
industry; electricity - botanical garden;
nature center; field research station;
laboratory; planetarium; auditorium;
classrooms

15979
Portland Art Museum
1219 SW Park Av, Portland, OR 97205
Fine Arts Museum - 1892
Coll: European and American paintings
and sculpture from the 16th-20th
century; Asian and pre-Columbian art;
Gebauer collection of Cameroon West
African art; Rasmussen collection of
Northwest Indian Art; Ethiopian
crosses; Kress collection of
Renaissance art; Lewis collection of
classical antiquities; Nunn and Cabell
collection of English silver - museum
art school; conservation laboratory;
film study center; library; auditorium;
classrooms

15980
Portland Children's Museum
2027 SW 2nd Av, Portland, OR 97201
Junior Museum - 1949
Coll: natural history; paleontology;
cultural history; transportation; color
and light; children's art - playroom;
auditorium; classrooms

15981
Western Forestry Center
4033 SW Canyon Rd, Portland, OR
97221
Agriculture Museum - 1971
Jesup Wood collection of North
American trees; Langdon Plate
collection of 600 plates made from
woods from around the world; logging
equipment - nature center

Portsmouth NH

15982
Portsmouth Athenaeum
9 Market Square, Portsmouth NH
03801
General Museum - 1817
Coll: genealogy; paintings; rare old
books pertainign to history of New
England and Canada - library

15983
Strawbery Banke, Inc.
Hancock & Marcy Sts, Portsmouth,
NH 03801
Open Air Museum - 1958
Coll: historic shops and houses (18th
c.) in village setting - library

Portsmouth OH

15984
Southern Ohio Museum and Cultural Center
825 Galia St, POB 990, Portsmouth,
OH 45662
Fine Arts Museum - 1977
Coll: American art; contemporary art -
theater; reading room; classrooms

Portsmouth RI

15985
Portsmouth Historical Society
E Main Rd and Union St, Portsmouth,
RI 02871
General Museum - 1938
Coll: farm and home tools; furniture;
clothing; hymnals; old toys; historic
buildings - library

Portsmouth VA

15986
Portsmouth Naval Museum
2 High St, POB 248, Portsmouth, VA
23705
General Museum - 1949
Coll: history of the Naval Shipyard;
ship models; uniforms; flags - library

Poteau OK

15987
Kerr Museum
POB 588, Poteau, OK 74953
General Museum - 1968
Coll: Spiro Mounds artifacts; farm and
house implements; geology of East
Oklahoma; barbed wire; pioneer
material; Norse runestones

Potsdam NY

15988
Brainerd Art Gallery State University
College at Potsdam
Potsdam, NY 13676
Fine Arts Museum - 1968
Coll: contemporary American
sculpture, decorative arts, graphics,
drawings and paintings; the Roland
Gibson Collection of 20th century
contemporary art - library

15989
Potsdam Public Museum
Civic Center, Potsdam, NY 13676
General Museum - 1940
Coll: decorative arts; glass; Burnap
Collection of English pottery;
American china; costumes; local
historical artifacts and furniture;
archives - library; classrooms

Pottsville PA

15990
Historical Society of Schuylkill County
14 N 3rd St, Pottsville, PA 17901
General Museum - 1903
Coll: photographs; anthracite coal
fields; old railroads; archives and
artifacts - library; reading room

Poughkeepsie NY

15991
Dutchess County Historical Society
Clinton House, 5219 Main St,
Poughkeepsie NY 12601, POB 88,
Poughkeepsie, NY 12602
General Museum - 1914
Coll: manuscripts; local artifacts -
library

15992
Vassar College Art Gallery
Raymond Av, Poughkeepsie, NY
12601
Fine Arts Museum - 1865
Coll: Renaissance, Baroque and
modern painting; Hudson River School
painting; Oriental jades and ceramics;
Rembrandt and Dürer Prints;
sculpture; decorative arts;
archaeology - library

Poultney VT

15993
East Poultney Museum
The Green, Poultney, VT 05764
General Museum - 1954
Coll: costumes; farm and home
implements; local history items

Poynette WI

15994
MacKenzie Environmental Education Center
Rte 1, Poynette, WI 53955
Natural History Museum - 1961
Coll: arboretum; native wildlife
exhibits; herbarium specimens;
lumbering; tools; log cabin - library;
classrooms; auditorium

Prairie du Chien WI

15995
Museum of Medical Progress Stovall
Hall of Health
717 S Beaumont Rd, Prairie du Chien
WI 53821, POB 1109, Madison, WI
53701
History/Public Affairs Museum - 1960
Coll: medical artifacts; doctor's and
dentist's office and pharmacy of the
1890's; medical history

Prairie du Rocher IL

15996
Fort DeChartres Historic Site Museum
Fort DeChartres Historic Site, Prairie
du Rocher, IL 62277
Historic Site - 1917
Coll: historical texts; archaeology;
military artifacts; tools and utensils;
reconstructed period buildings -
library

Prescott AZ

15997
Sharlot Hall Museum Sharlot Hall
Historical Society, Prescott Historical
Society
415 West Gurley St, Prescott, AZ
86301
History/Public Affairs Museum - 1929
Coll: archives; costumes; vehicles;
Indian artifacts; mineralogy; historic
buildings

Price UT

15998
Prehistoric Museum of the College of Eastern Utah
Price, UT 84501
Science/Tech Museum - 1961
Coll: anthropology; ethnology;
dinosaurs; fossils; Indian artifacts -
auditorium

Princeton NJ

15999
The Art Museum Princeton University
Princeton, NJ 08544
Fine Arts Museum - 1882
Coll: classical art; contemporary art;
Oriental art; European art;
pre-Columbian art; African art;
paintings, drawings, sculptures, prints,
photographs

16000
Historical Society of Princeton
158 Nassau St, Princeton, NJ 08540
General Museum - 1938
Arts; artifacts; documents;
photographs; glass-plate negatives;
historical archives; architectural
research materials

16001
Princeton University Museum of Natural History
Guyot Hall Princeton, NJ 08544
Natural History Museum - 1805
Coll: invertebrate paleontology;
vertebrate paleontology; paleobotany;
geology; mineralogy; ornithology;
ethnology; archaeology - library; 500
seat auditorium

16002
Seventh Day Baptist Historical Society
510 Watchung Av, POB 868, Princeton, NJ 08544
Religious Art Museum - 1916
Coll: German Pietistic movement; Sabbatarian Baptists in England; manuscript collections - library

Providence RI

16003
Annmary Brown Memorial
21 Brown St, Providence, RI 02912
Fine Arts Museum - 1905
Coll: 15th century printed books (incunabula); 17th-19th century American manuscripts; old and later master paintings; Brown family heirlooms and correspondence - library; reading rooms; seminar room

16004
Museum of Art Rhode Island School of Design
224 Benefit St, Providence, RI 02903
Fine Arts Museum - 1877
Coll: Classical art; numismatics; Medieval art; 15th-20th century painting, sculpture and decorative arts; Albert Pilavin collection of 20th century American art; Nancy Sayles Day collection of modern Latin American art; American furniture, silver, china and decorative arts of the 18th-19th centuries (Pendleton House collection); costume center; Oriental textiles and art; Lucy Truman Aldrich collection of 18th century European porcelain; Abby Aldrich Rockefeller collection of Japanese prints; ethnographic art - library; reading room; auditorium

16005
Rhode Island Historical Society
52 Power St, Providence, RI 02906
General Museum - 1822
Coll: furniture; art; history; Chinese porcelain and furniture; dolls and glassware; textiles and clothing; wallpaper; military artifacts; Indian artifacts; musical instruments - library; auditorium; reading room; classrooms

16006
Rhode Island State Archives
Room 43, State House, Smith St, Providence, RI 02903
History/Public Affairs Museum - 1760
archives; history; legislature; military; Indian artifacts - library; reading room

16007
Roger Williams Park Museum
Roger Williams Park, Providence, RI 02905
Natural History Museum - 1896
Hall of the Pacific; Indian and Eskimo Hall; Hall of Wildlife; Hall of Mammals; Hall of Rocks and Minerals; Narragansett Bay exhibit - planetarium; reading room; auditorium; classrooms

Provo UT

16008
Brigham Young University Fine Arts Collection
F-303 Harris Fine Arts Center, Provo, UT 84602
Fine Arts Museum - 1965
Coll: paintings; Mormon art

16009
Brigham Young University Museum of Archaeology and Ethnology
Provo, UT 84602
Archeology Museum - 1946
Coll: Mesoamerica; Southwest archaeology - library; laboratory

16010
Monte L. Bean Life Science Museum
Brigham Young University
290 MBLM Bldg, Provo, UT 84602
Science/Tech Museum - 1964
Coll: herbarium; entomology; herpetology - library

Pueblo CO

16011
Pueblo Metropolitan Museum
419 W 14th St, Pueblo, CO 81003
General Museum - 1967
Coll: 1891 furnishings; exhibits from cultures around the world - library

16012
El Pueblo Museum
905 S Prairie Ave, Pueblo, CO 81005
History/Public Affairs Museum - 1959
Coll: prehistoric and historic Indian artifacts; artifacts related to cattle industry; railroad memorabilia; artifacts of early Colorado home and social life; historic fort

Pueblo of Acoma NM

16013
Acoma Museum
POB 309, Pueblo of Acoma, NM 87034
Anthropology Museum
Coll: Acoma Culture - library; archives

Pullman WA

16014
Museum of Anthropology Dept. of Anthropology, Washington State University
Pullman, WA 99164
Anthropology Museum - 1966
Archeological collections from Alaska and Washington; basketry from Western U.S.

16015
Museum of Art
Washington State University, Pullman, WA 99164
Fine Arts Museum - 1974
Coll: late 19th century to present day American art; Northwest regional art scene - classrooms; library

16016
Washington State University Herbarium
Pullman, WA 99164
Natural History Museum - 1900
Coll: botany; vascular plants; herbarium specimens - library

Purchase NY

16017
Neuberger Museum State University of New York
Purchase, NY 10577
Fine Arts Museum - 1968
Coll: 20th century painting, sculpture, drawing, prints, and photographs from the Marie and Roy R. Neuberger Collection; Edith and George Rickey; Hans Richter Bequest; Aimee Hirshberg Collection of African Art

Putney VT

16018
Putney Historical Society
R.D. 2, POB 53, Putney, VT 05346
General Museum - 1959
Coll: local geology; artifacts; genealogy - library

Puyallup WA

16019
Ezra Meeker Museum
POB 103, Puyallup, WA 98371
Historic Site - 1970
Furnishings of the period; the books and writings of Ezra Meeker - library

16020
Paul H. Karshner Memorial Museum
426 4th St NE, Puyallup, WA 98371
Junior Museum - 1930
Coll: Indian artifacts; geology; paleontology; entomology; natural science; American pioneer - library

Quakertown PA

16021
Quakertown Historical Society
26 N Main St, Quakertown, PA 18951
General Museum - 1965
Coll: costumes; glass; household items; dolls; antique furniture - meeting room

Quantico VA

16022
United States Marine Corps Aviation Museum
Brown Field, Marine Corps Base, Quantico, VA 22134
History/Public Affairs Museum - 1940
Coll: aircrafts; tanks; artillery

Quincy CA

16023
Plumas County Museum
500 Jackson St, POB 776, Quincy, CA 95971
General Museum - 1968
Coll: Indian artifacts; geology; costumes - library

Quincy IL

16024
Historical Society of Quincy and Adams County
425 S 12th St, Quincy, IL 62301
General Museum - 1896
Coll: paintings; items connected with the assassination of Lincoln; historic Mormon settlement - library

16025
Quincy Art Center
1515 Jersey St, Quincy, IL 62301
Fine Arts Museum - 1923
Coll: painting; sculpture; graphics; crafts - library; classrooms

16026
Quincy Indian Museum
Quinsippi Island, 1008 Maine St, Quincy, IL 62301
Anthropology Museum - 1966
Coll: bannerstones; pipes; axes; artifacts from several ancient Mexican cultures; Tlingit baskets; Navajo rugs; Plains Indian material - library

Quincy MA

16027
Adams National Historic Site
135 Adams St, POB 531, Quincy, MA 02269
History/Public Affairs Museum - 1927
Coll: paintings; sculpture; graphics; decorative arts; glass; numismatic - library

16028
Quincy Historical Society
Adams Academy Bldg, 8 Adams St, Quincy, MA 02169
History/Public Affairs Museum - 1893
Coll: John Quincy Adams birthplace; local artifacts - library

Racine WI

16029
Racine Art Association Wustum Museum of Fine Arts
2519 Northwestern Av, Racine, WI 53404
Fine Arts Museum - 1940
Coll: contemporary American paintings; graphics and sculpture - library

16030
Racine County Historical Museum, Inc.
701 S Main St, Racine, WI 53403
History/Public Affairs Museum - 1962
Coll: local history; natural history; Philo R. Hoy collection of natural history; fine arts; glass; genealogy - library

Radium Springs NM

16031
Fort Selden State Monument
POB 58, Radium Springs, NM 88054
History/Public Affairs Museum - 1972
Coll: Indian artifacts; military artifacts, including uniforms, saddles, and an 1864 Springfield rifle; home of Douglas MacArthur (1884-1886) - library; botanical garden

Raleigh NC

16032
North Carolina Museum of Art
107 E Morgan St, Raleigh, NC 27611
Fine Arts Museum - 1956
Coll: European and American painting, sculpture and decorative arts; ethnic art; Kress collection; Phifer collection; Mary Duke Biddle gallery for the blind - library

16033
North Carolina Museum of History
109 E Jones St, Raleigh, NC 27611
General Museum - 1903
Coll: decorative arts; furnishings; costumes and uniforms; photography; industry; archaeology; folklore; numismatics; weapons; textiles; anthropology; paintings; graphics; military; medicine; transportation - library; reading room; auditorium; classrooms

16034
North Carolina State Museum
102 N Salisbury St, Raleigh, NC 27611
Natural History Museum - 1877
Coll: zoology; geology; paleontology; archaeology - library; aquarium; auditorium

Ramah NM

16035
El Morro National Monument
Ramah, NM 87321
Historic Site - 1906
Coll: archaeological finds, pots, implements, handcrafts, weapons, religious items (18th to 19th centuries); Inscription Rock (1605-1906) - library

Randolph VT

16036
Randolph Historical Society
Village Bldg, Salisbury St, Randolph, VT 05060
General Museum - 1960
Early medicine and pharmacy exhibits

Randsburg CA

16037
Desert Museum
Butte St, Randsburg, CA 93554
Science/Tech Museum - 1948
Coll: mineralogy; mining equipment; Indian artifacts

Rapid City SD

16038
Horseless Carriage Museum
POB 2933, Rapid City, SD 57708
Science/Tech Museum - 1953
Coll: antique cars and vehicles; pioneer items; antique music boxes; costumes - library

16039
Minnilusa Pioneer Museum
West Blvd between Main St and St. Joe, Rapid City, SD 57701
General Museum - 1952
Coll: Black Hills and Western South Dakota items; pioneer artifacts; natural history of the area

16040
Museum of Geology, South Dakota School of Mines and Technology
Rapid City, SD 57701
Natural History Museum
Coll: rocks; minerals; fossil vertebrates; invertebrates; plants - library

16041
Sioux Indian Museum and Crafts Center
POB 1504, Rapid City, SD 57701
Anthropology Museum - 1939
Coll: historic and contemporary arts of the Sioux

Raton NM

16042
Raton Museum
South First St, Raton, NM 87740
General Museum
Coll: railroading; mining; ranching; history of the region and its early settlers - 50 seat auditorium

Ravenna OH

16043
Portage County Historical Society
6549 State Rte 44, Ravenna, OH 44266
General Museum - 1951
Coll: history; archives; archaeology; glass; historic house (1829) - library; reading room

Reading PA

16044
Historical Society of Berks County
940 Centre Av, Reading, PA 19601
General Museum - 1869
Coll: agriculture; archives; decorative arts; history; Indian artifacts - library; auditorium

16045
Reading Public Museum and Art Gallery
500 Museum Rd, Reading, PA 19611
General Museum - 1904
Coll: anthropology; archaeology; paintings; sculpture; graphics; decorative arts; Pennsylvania folk art; Indian artifacts; natural history; mineralogy; paleontology; entomology - arboretum; library; park museum; auditorium; classrooms

16046
Reading School District Planetarium
1211 Parkside Dr S, Reading, PA 19611
Science/Tech Museum - 1967
astronomical artifacts; meteorites; serigraphs - library; satellite weather station; spacesphere; planetarium; observatory

Reading VT

16047
Reading Historical Society
Reading, VT 05062
General Museum - 1953
Coll: local history; military; medical - library

Red Cloud NE

16048
Webster County Historical Museum
721 W 4th Ave, Red Cloud, NE 68970
General Museum - 1964
Coll: antiques; natural history; medical; military; history - library; reading room

16049
Willa Cather Pioneer Memorial and Educational Foundation
326 N Webster, Red Cloud, NE 68970
History/Public Affairs Museum - 1955
Coll: library with 200 Willa Cather letters; 100 first editions; Willa Cather memorabilia; historic houses

Red Wings MN

16050
Goodhue County Historical Society
1166 Oak St, Red Wings, MN 55066
General Museum - 1869
Coll: folklore; sports; musical history; theatrical events; transportation; mineralogy - library; reading room

Redding CA

16051
Redding Museum and Art Center
POB 427, Redding, CA 96001
General Museum - 1963
Coll: Indian basketry and artifacts; historical artifacts; Indian ethnology - gallery

16052
Shasta College Museum and Research Center
1065 N. Old Oregon Trail, Redding, CA 96001
General Museum - 1970
Coll: artifacts; archives; farming equipment; mining tools; costumes

Redlands CA

16053
Lincoln Memorial Shrine
Fourth and Eureka, POB 751, Redlands, CA 92373
History/Public Affairs Museum - 1932
Coll: rare manuscripts and documents of Lincoln and leading Civil War figures; artifacts of Lincoln's and the Civil War period; paintings; murals - library

16054
San Bernadino County Museum
2024 Orange Tree Lane, Redlands, CA 92373
General Museum - 1959
Coll: archeology; art; natural history; history; geology; paleontology - library; botanical garden; research station; auditoriums; classrooms

Redmond WA

16055
Marymoor Museum
6046 Lake Sammamish Pkwy NE, POB 162, Redmond, WA 98052
General Museum - 1965
Coll: artifacts and archival material of local history; Indian artifacts; lumbering; costumes; furnishings - library

Reedsburg WI

16056
Reedsburg Area Historical Society Inc.
POB 405, Reedsburg, WI 53959
General Museum
Coll: local antiques; apothecary shop; furnished rooms; Indian artifacts; tools - library

Regent ND

16057
Hettinger County Historical Society
POB 176, Regent, ND 58650
General Museum - 1962
Pioneer Street, with blacksmith shop, harness shop, bar, bank, insurance co., general merchandise store, post office, hotel, jail, meat market, and pioneer machinery; original furnishings; doctor's equipment and tools; clothing; farm tools; artifacts; pictures - library

Reidsville NC

16058
Chinqua-Penn Plantation House
Rte 3, Reidsville, NC 27320
Decorative Arts Museum - 1965
Coll: European furniture; art objects; Oriental art - flower and shrub garden

Reno NV

16059
Harrah's Automobile Collection
POB 10, Reno, NV 89504
History/Public Affairs Museum - 1948
Coll: 1,000 antique, vintage, classic and special inteest vehicles; motorcycles; boats; aircrafts & western memorabilia - library

Rensselaer IN

16060
Jasper County Historical Society
624 Clark St, Rensselaer, IN 47978
General Museum - 1966
Coll: Civil War mementos; books; pictures; clothing; furniture; historic buildings

Rexburg ID

16061
Upper Snake River Valley Historical Society
Rte 2, POB 244, Rexburg, ID 83440
General Museum - 1965
Coll: Idaho and local historical items; guns; agriculture; antiques - library; reading room

Rhinelander WI

16062
Rhinelander Logging Museum
Pioneer Park-Martin Lynch Dr, POB 64, Rhinelander, WI 54501
Science/Tech Museum - 1932
Logging; history

Richey MT

16063
Richey Historical Museum
POB 218, Richey, MT 59259
General Museum - 1973
Coll: farm tools; ranch items; kitchen utensils; clothing; machinery - library

Richland WA

16064
Hanford Science Center
POB 800, Richland, WA 99352
Science/Tech Museum - 1963
Nuclear and alternate energy displays - library; auditorium

Richmond CA

16065
Richmond Art Center
25th & Barrett Aves, Richmond, CA 94804
Fine Arts Museum - 1936
Coll: contemporary paintings, prints, and crafts by Bay Area artists - galleries; sculptor court

Richmond Hill GA

16066
Fort McAllister
POB 198, Richmond Hill, GA 31324
Historic Site - 1958
Coll: restored earthworks of Confederate Fort; military artifacts

Richmond IN

16067
Art Association of Richmond
McGuire Memorial Hall
Whitewater Blvd, Richmond, IN 47374
Fine Arts Museum - 1897
Coll: paintings; sculpture; graphics; decorative arts - library; reading room; auditorium

16068
Hayes Regional Arboretum
801 Elks Rd, Richmond, IN 47374
Natural History Museum - 1959
Specimens of each species of plant indigenous to the Whitewater Drainage Basin of Indiana and Ohio - library; nature/conservation center; reading room; auditorium; classrooms

16069
Joseph Moore Museum
Earlham College, Richmond, IN 47374
Natural History Museum - 1887
Coll: skins of birds and mammals;
insects; reptiles; vertebrate and
invertebrate fossils; Indian artifacts -
library; planetarium

16070
Wayne County Historical Museum
1150 North A St, Richmond, IN 47374
General Museum - 1929
Coll: china and glass; silver; textiles;
anthropology; agriculture; firefighting
equipment; numismatics; toys and
dolls; historic house - library;
children's museum

Richmond KY

16071
Fort Boonesborough Museum
Fort Boonesborough State Park, Rte 5,
Richmond, KY 40475
History/Public Affairs Museum
Coll: the story of Daniel Boone's life;
rifles; documents - theater

Richmond TX

16072
Fort Bend County Museum
500 Houston, Richmond, TX 77469
General Museum - 1967
Coll: agricultural, crafts, industry -
auditorium; library

Richmond VA

16073
The Agecroft Association
4305 Sulgrave Rd, Richmond, VA
23221
Historic Site - 1968
15th and 16th century English country
life and related pursuits exhibited in a
reconstructed English country manor
house - library

16074
The Archeological Society of Virginia
562 Rossmore Rd, Richmond, VA
23225
Archeology Museum - 1940
Archeology; Indian artifacts - library

16075
**Association for the Preservation of
Virginia Antiquities**
2705 Park Av, Richmond, VA 23220
Decorative Arts Museum - 1889
Coll: 17th-19th century furniture;
decorative arts; textiles - library;
laboratory

16076
Division of State Parks
1201 State Office Building, Capitol
Square, Richmond, VA 23219
Science/Tech Museum - 1926
Coll: botany; entomology; geology;
herbarium; herpetology - library

16077
Edgar Allan Poe Museum
1914 E Main St, Richmond, VA 23223
Historic Site - 1921
Coll: Poe books; manuscripts;
memorabilia - library

16078
Maymont Foundation
1700 Hampton St, Richmond, VA
23220
General Museum - 1925
Coll: turn of the century furniture and
decorative arts; 19th century carriages

16079
Museum of the Confederacy
1201 E Clay St, Richmond, VA 23219
History/Public Affairs Museum - 1890
Artifacts and documents pertaining to
the Confederate States of America -
library

16080
Richmond National Battlefield Park
3215 E Broad St, Richmond, VA 23223
General Museum - 1944
Coll: military artifacts; Civil War and
Richmond history - library

16081
Science Museum of Virginia
2500 W Broad St, Richmond, VA 23220
Science/Tech Museum - 1970
Coll: rocks and minerals; space and
aeronautical exhibits - aquarium;
planetarium

16082
Valentine Museum
1015 E Clay St, Richmond, VA 23219
History/Public Affairs Museum - 1892
Coll: costumes from 1600-1979;
textiles; quilts; embroidery; decorative
arts; toys; paintings - library

16083
**Virginia Historic Landmarks
Commission**
221 Governor St, Richmond, VA 23219
General Museum - 1966
History and Architecture of Virginia -
library

16084
Virginia Historical Society
428 North Blvd, Richmond, VA 23221
General Museum - 1831
Coll: books, maps, manuscripts on
Virginia history; portraits and paintings
- library

16085
Virginia Museum of Fine Arts
Boulevard and Grove St, Richmond,
VA 23221
Fine Arts Museum - 1934
Coll: from 15 world cultures - theater;
sculpture garden; library; auditorium;
classrooms

Ridgecrest CA

16086
**Maturango Museum of Indian Wells
Valley**
POB 1776, Ridgecrest, CA 93555
Science/Tech Museum - 1962
Coll: minerals and geology; mining
tools and equipment; flora and fauna of
the upper Mojave desert;
paleontology; archeology - library;
auditorium

Ridgewood NJ

16087
**Paramus Historical and Preservation
Society, Inc.**
650 E Glen Av, Ridgewood, NJ 07450
General Museum - 1949
Coll: farming and domestic utensils,
tools, and implements; local Indian
artifacts; Bergen County and New
Jersey heirlooms from the 17th, 18th,
and 19th centuries

Ringoes NJ

16088
Religious Americana Museum
Van Lieu's Rd, R.D. 1, POB 313,
Ringoes, NJ 08551
Religious Art Museum - 1971
Coll: original antiques (1680-1899)
including printed matter, ceramics,
bottles, chalkware, cloth, costumes,
pottery, metals, quilts; prints,
woodcuts, engravings, lithographs

Ringwood NJ

16089
Ringwood Manor House Museum
Sloatsburg Rd, POB 1304, Ringwood,
NJ 07465
General Museum - 1935
Coll: furniture; archives; paintings;
graphics; decorative arts

Ripon WI

16090
Ripon Historical Society
508 Watson St, Ripon, WI 54971
General Museum - 1899
Local history; archives; costumes -
library

River Edge NJ

16091
Bergen County Historical Society
River Edge, NJ 07661
General Museum - 1902
Coll: prints, maps, books and
manuscripts of Bergen County;
furniture; art objects; industrial
exhibits; Indian artifacts - library

16092
Von Steuben House
River Edge, NJ 07661
Historic Site
Coll: colonial furniture; china;
glassware

River Falls WI

16093
Area Research Center Chalmer
Davee Library
University of Wisconsin, River Falls,
WI 54022
History/Public Affairs Museum - 1934
Coll: local history and artifacts; Civil
War relics; Ku Klux Klan relics -
library

Riverhead NY

16094
**Suffolk County Historical Society
Museum**
300 W. Main St, Riverhead, NY 11901
General Museum - 1886
Coll: Long Island Indian artifacts;
Revolutionary and Civil War firearms;
Farm tools and crafts; vehicles and
boat models; dioramas; dolls, toys, and
games; china and glass; whaling
artifacts; spinning and weaving;
decoys; history of transportation -
library

Riverside CA

16095
Book of Life Building and Museum
8432 Magnolia Ave, Riverside, CA
92504
Religious Art Museum - 1950
Coll: exhibits demonstrating the
influence of the Bible on varied
aspects of everyday life - library;
conference rooms

16096
Jurupa Mountains Cultural Center
7621 Highway 60, Riverside, CA 92509
Science/Tech Museum - 1964
Coll: mineralogy; paleontology;
herbarium; Indian artifacts on
aboriginal Indian campsite;
entomology - botanical garden;
children's zoo; classrooms

16097
Riverside Art Center and Museum
3425 Seventh St, Riverside, CA 92501
Fine Arts Museum - 1931
Coll: paintings; sculpture; porcelains;
graphics - library

16098
Riverside Municipal Museum
3720 Orange St, Riverside, CA 92501
Science/Tech Museum - 1925
Coll: fossils; ethnology; archeology;
archives; entomology; historic house -
library

16099
**UCR Entomological Teaching and
Research Collection** Department of
Entomology, University of California
Riverside, CA 92502
Natural History Museum - 1962
Coll: insects and related non-insect
arthropods - library; laboratory;
classrooms

Riverton CT

16100
The Hitchcock Museum
Riverton, CT 06065
Decorative Arts Museum - 1972
Painted and decorated furniture of the
early and mid 19th century - library

Riverton WY

16101
Riverton Museum
700 E Park, Riverton, WY 82501
General Museum - 1968
Coll: guns; clocks; farm machinery;
dishes; furniture; clothing; logging;
trappers material; typewriters; musical
instruments - library

Roanoke VA

16102
Roanoke Fine Arts Center
301-23rd St SW, Roanoke, VA 24014
Fine Arts Museum - 1951
Coll: Mediterranean archeology;
contemporary prints and paintings;
19th-20th century American paintings
- library

16103
Roanoke Transportation Museum
14 Kirk Av, Roanoke, VA 24011
Science/Tech Museum - 1964
Coll: transportation equipment;
railroading exhibits; model train layout
- outdoor museum

16104
Roanoke Valley Historical Society
10 Franklin Rd, POB 1904, Roanoke,
VA 24008
General Museum - 1957
Historical articles and implements -
library

16105
Roanoke Valley Science Museum
2323 Overlook Rd NE, Roanoke, VA
24012
Science/Tech Museum - 1970
Coll: exhibits on aeronautics and
space; mineralogy; natural history -
auditorium; conservation center

Rochester IN

16106
**Fulton County Historical Society
Museum**
7th and Pontiac Sts, Rochester, IN
46975
General Museum - 1963
Coll: furniture; farm equipment; photos
and first Tarzan films and posters;
artifacts; tools - library

Rochester MI

16107
Meadow Brook Art Gallery Oakland
University
Rochester, MI 48063
Fine Arts Museum - 1959
Coll: African, Oceania, pre-Columbian
art - theater

Rochester MN

16108
Mayo Medical Museum Mayo Clinic
200 1st St SW, Rochester, Mn 55901
Science/Tech Museum - 1936
Coll: biology of man; medical and
surgical problems and care and
treatment - theater

16109
Olmsted County Historical Society
Historical Center and Museum
Salem Rd and Co. 122 SW, POB 6411,
Rochester, MN 55901
History/Public Affairs Museum - 1926
Coll: general Norwegian history -
library; reading room; auditorium;
classrooms

Rochester NY

16110
American Baptist Historical Society
1106 S. Goodman St, Rochester, NY
14620
Religious Art Museum - 1853
Coll: communion sets; paintings; silver;
books; records - library

16111
Dar-Hervey Ely House
11 Livingston Park, Rochester, NY
14608
Historic Site - 1894
Coll: furniture of 1800; china, glass,
and silver; Washington's drummer
boy's drum; antiques - library; reading
room

16112
**International Museum of
Photography at George Eastman
House**
900 East Av, Rochester, NY 14607
Performing Arts Museum - 1949
Coll: photographic apparatus; photo
archives; motion picture archive -
library; auditorium; theater

16113
**The Landmark Society of Western
New York**
130 Spring St, Rochester, NY 14608
Decorative Arts Museum - 1937
Coll: furnishings and decorative arts of
the 1830's and the 19th century;
country-style architecture; Campbell-
Whittlesey House (1835/36); Stone-
Tolan House (1792); Brewster-Burke
House (1849) - library

16114
**Memorial Art Gallery of the
University of Rochester**
490 University Av, Rochester, NY
14607
Fine Arts Museum - 1913
Coll: ancient, classical, medieval,
Renaissance, baroque, 18th-20th
century American, 19th and 20th
century French, American folk,
pre-Columbian, African, Oriental art -
library; reading room; auditorium;
classrooms

16115
Monroe County Parks Herbarium
374 Westfall Rd, Rochester, NY 14620
Natural History Museum - 1927
Coll: 15,000 herbarium specimens;
plant collections; botany; Monroe
County Parks Arboretum (1888);
Highland Castle (1854) - library;
botanical garden; conservatory

16116
**New York State Archaeological
Association**
Rochester Museum and Science
Center, 657 East Av, Rochester NY
14607, POB 1480, Rochester, NY
14603
Archeology Museum - 1916
Coll: archaeology; anthropology;
ethnology; Indian artifacts;
preservation project - library

16117
**Rochester Museum and Science
Center**
657 East Av, Rochester, NY 14603
General Museum - 1912
Coll: natural history; history;
technology; costumes; ethnology;
military; geology; glass; anatomy;
mineralogy; medical industry; music;
paleontology; theater; entomology;
transportation - library; planetarium;
reading room; auditoria; classrooms

16118
The Strong Museum
700 Allen Creek Rd, Rochester, NY
14618
General Museum - 1968
Coll: social and cultural history of
Northeastern America in the 1820s -
library

16119
Temple B'rith Kodesh Museum
2131 Elmwood Av, Rochester, NY
14618
Religious Art Museum - 1954
Coll: archaeology; archives;
ethnology; folklore; numismatics;
philatelics - library

Rock Hill SC

16120
Museum of York County
Rte. 4, POB 211, Rock Hill, SC 29730
General Museum - 1950
Coll: herpetology; history; Indian
artifacts; world's largest collection
African hooved mammals; hall of
yesteryear; age of earth hall; hall of the
Carolinas; industry; marine;
mineralogy; textiles - Planetarium;
nature trail; petting zoo; outdoor
museum

Rock Island IL

16121
Fryxell Geology Museum
New Science Bldg, Augustana
College, Rock Island, IL 61201
Natural History Museum - 1929
Coll: paleontology; fossils; minerals;
geology - library; preparation lab

16122
**John M. Browning Memorial
Museum**
Rock Island Arsenal, Rock Island, IL
61299
History/Public Affairs Museum - 1905
Weapons and equipment

Rock Springs WY

16123
Community Fine Arts Center
400 C St, Rock Springs, WY 82901
Fine Arts Museum - 1938
Coll: paintings; sculpture; drawings;
graphics - workshop rooms

Rockford IL

16124
**Burpee Art Museum/Rockford Art
Association**
737 N Main St, Rockford, IL 61103
Fine Arts Museum - 1936
Coll: 19th and 20th century American
paintings; sculpture; graphics; and
decorative arts - library; classrooms;
auditorium

16125
Burpee Museum of Natural History
813 N Main St, Rockford, IL 61103
Natural History Museum - 1942
Coll: natural history; zoology;
archeology; anthropology; American
Indian artifacts - library; herbarium

16126
The Time Museum
7801 E State St, POB 5285, Rockford,
IL 61108
Science/Tech Museum - 1970
Display of the development of
timekeeping devices including 1,500
pieces dating from 1240 B.C. to the
present - library; auditorium; theater

16127
Tinker Swiss Cottage, Inc.
411 Kent St, Rockford, IL 61102
General Museum - 1944
Coll: original household furnishings;
fabrics; hand-crafted pieces from
around the world; historic house -
library

Rockhill Furnace PA

16128
Railways to Yesterday, Inc.
adjacent to East Broad Top Railroad,
Rockhill Furnace PA 17249, POB 1601,
Allentown, PA 18105
Science/Tech Museum - 1960
Coll: passenger trolley cars; electric
snow sweepers; road maintenance
trolley; Mack locomotive; trolley bus;
artifacts and other railcars - library

Rockingham VT

16129
**Vermont Country Stores and
Museum**
Vermont Rte 103, Rockingham, VT
05101
General Museum - 1945
Coll: artifacts; farm kitchen and
country store exhibits

Rockland ME

16130
**William A. Farnsworth Library and
Art Museum**
19 Elm St, Rockland, ME 04841
Fine Arts Museum - 1935
Coll: 18th, 19th and 20th century
works of American, Continental art
and decorative arts - library; reading
room; auditorium

Rockport MA

16131
**Sandy Bay Historical Society and
Museum Inc**
40 King St, Rockport, MA 01966
History/Public Affairs Museum - 1925
Coll: glass; minerals; dolls; marine;
industrial; archaeology; furniture -
library

Rockville MD

16132
Judaic Museum
6125 Montrose Rd, Rockville, MD
20852
Anthropology Museum - 1926
Coll: archaeology; folklore

Rockwell City IA

16133
Calhoun County Historical Society
626-8 St, Rockwell City, IA 50579
General Museum - 1956
Coll: Farm exhibit hall; antique farm
machinery - library

Rocky Ford CO

16134
Rocky Ford Public Museum
City Hall, Rocky Ford, CO 81067
General Museum - 1940
Coll: minerals; fossils; first fire engine;
military and other artifacts

Rocky Hill CT

16135
**Academy Hall Museum of the Rocky
Hill Historical Society, Inc.**
785 Old Main St, POB 185, Rocky Hill,
CT 06067
General Museum - 1962
Coll: Indian relics; domestic
implements; clothes; farming
equipment; furniture - library

Rocky Hill NJ

16136
Rockingham
Route 518, Rocky Hill, NJ 08553
Historic Site
Coll: authentic period furnishings

Rocky Mount NC

16137
Rocky Mount Children's Museum, Inc.
1610 Gay St, Rocky Mount, NC 27801
Junior Museum - 1952
Coll: natural and physical sciences; Thomas Alva Edison material; Americana; Bishop collection of model horsedrawn vehicles - planetarium; library; botanical garden

Roebuck SC

16138
Walnut Grove Plantation
Rte. 1, Roebuck, SC 29376
General Museum - 1957
Coll: furnishings (1760-1830); The Manor House and kitchen; doctor's office; outbuildings - Rocky Springs academy

Rogers AR

16139
Daisy International Air Gun Museum
U.S. Hwy 71 South, Rogers, AR 72756
Science/Tech Museum - 1966
Coll: non-powder guns

16140
Rogers Historical Museum
114 S First St, Rogers, AR 72756
General Museum - 1974
documents and artifacts illustrating Rogers' growth - library

Rolla Mo

16141
Ed Clark Museum of Missouri Geology
Buehler Park, POB 250, Rolla, MO 65401
Natural History Museum - 1963
Coll: geology; mineralogy; paleontology

16142
University of Missouri-Rolla Geology Museum
Rolla, Mo 65401
Natural History Museum - 1870
Coll: mineralogy; paleontology; geology

Rome City IN

16143
Gene Stratton Porter State Memorial
R.R. No. 1, Rome City, IN 46784
Historic Site
Coll: period furnishings; historic house; photographs and memorabilia of Gene Stratton Porter - gardens

Rome NY

16144
Fort Stanwix Museum
207 N. James St, Rome, NY 13440
General Museum - 1936
Coll: archaeology; tools; clothing; furniture; newspaper files and documents; Tomb of the Unknown Soldiers of the American Revolution; French and Indian war site (1755) - library

16145
Fort Stanwix National Monument
112 E. Park St, Rome, NY 13440
Historic Site - 1935
Coll: arms and accoutrements; clothing; hardware; utensils

Roseburg OR

16146
Douglas County Museum
County Fairgrounds, POB 1550, Roseburg, OR 97470
General Museum - 1968
Coll: Indian artifacts; pioneer tools; guns; utensils; agricultural equipment; marine relics; vehicles; machinery; photographs - library; reading room

Roswell NM

16147
Chaves County Historical Museum
200 N Lea Av, Roswell, NM 88201
General Museum - 1976
Coll: period rooms with furnishings; agricultural exhibits - library

16148
Roswell Museum and Art Center
100 West 11th, Roswell, NM 88201
Fine Arts Museum - 1937
Coll: 20th Century American paintings and sculpture; European and American prints; Southwestern painting; paintings and prints by Peter Hurd and Henriette Wyeth; Witter Bynner collection of Chinese paintings and jade; ethnological and archaeological collection of Southwestern Indian art; Robert H. Goddard rocket collection - library; planetarium; auditorium; classrooms; exhibition galleries; offices; workshop; photo lab; storage vault

Round Rock TX

16149
'El Milagro' Washington Anderson-Irvin Home Museum
POB 188, Round Rock, TX 78664
Historic Site - 1950
Coll: Texas-made furniture; American antiques - library

Round Top TX

16150
Winedale Historical Center
University of Texas at Austin
POB 11, Round Top, TX 78954
History/Public Affairs Museum - 1967
Coll: decorative arts; folk art; furniture, tools and agricultural implements pertaining to German settlement of Texas - auditorium

Royalton VT

16151
Royalton Historical Society
Royalton, VT 05068
General Museum - 1967
Coll: exhibits of local history; furniture; clothing - library

Rugby ND

16152
Geographical Center Historical Society Museum
Rugby, ND 58368
General Museum - 1960
Coll: agricultural tools; antiques; log cabin; church; one-room rural school; livery stable; old autos, farm tractors and implements; railroad caboose and depot

Russell Springs KS

16153
Butterfield Trail Historical Museum
Russell Springs, KS 67755
History/Public Affairs Museum - 1964
Coll: furniture; fossils; Indian relics; dishware; agricultural implements - reading room; library

Rutherford NJ

16154
Rutherford Museum
Crane Av, Rutherford, NJ 07070
General Museum - 1961
Coll: local and fluorescent rocks; minerals; shells; fossils; Indian artifacts; tools; crafts; domestic artifacts; toys; clothing; furniture; permanent kitchen exhibits (1900-1913); turn-of-century general store and post office - library

Sabetha KS

16155
Albany Historical Society
211 S Washington, Sabetha, KS 66534
History/Public Affairs Museum - 1965
Coll: vehicles; train equipment; military; historic houses; agricultural machinery - library

Sackets Harbor NY

16156
Sackets Harbor Battlefield State Historic Site
Sackets Harbor, NY 13685
History/Public Affairs Museum - 1933
Coll: weapons (War of 1812); uniforms and accoutrements; 19th century furniture; archaeology; historic buildings (19th century) - library; theater

Saco ME 30 04072

16157
York Institute Museum
375 Main St, Saco, ME 30 04072
General Museum - 1867
Coll: sculpture; mineralogy; archives; paintings - reading room

Sacramento CA

16158
California State Indian Museum
2618 K St, Sacramento CA 95816, 2527 Port St, W. Sacramento, CA 95691
History/Public Affairs Museum - 1940
Coll: California Indian artifacts; limited North American Indian artifacts

16159
Central Pacific Passenger Depot
Front and J Sts, Old Sacramento CA 95814, 2572 Port St, W. Sacramento, CA 95691
Science/Tech Museum - 1976
Coll: locomotives and other rolling stock from 1863-1912; railroad memorabilia; historic building

16160
Crocker Art Museum
216 O St, Sacramento, CA 95814
Fine Arts Museum - 1885
Coll: paintings from early Renaissance to 20th century; 15th to 20th century master drawings; Oriental arts; sculpture; pottery and glass - library

16161
Sacramento History Center
1931 K St, Sacramento, CA 95814
History/Public Affairs Museum - 1967
Coll: local photographs; railroad materials; archives; horse-drawn equipment; 19th century artifacts - library

16162
Sacramento Museum and History Commission
1931 K St, Sacramento, CA 95814
General Museum - 1953
Coll: transportation; history; city and county records; photographs; archives - library

16163
Sacramento Science Center and Junior Museum
3615 Auburn Blvd, Sacramento, CA 95821
Science/Tech Museum - 1951
Coll: mounted specimens; insects; fossils; rocks and minerals; live animals - classroom; nature areas

Safety Harbor FL

16164
Safety Harbor Museum of History & Fine Arts, Inc. & Peninsular Archaeological Society, Inc.
115 Main St, 329 S Bayshore Blvd, Safety Harbor, FL 33572
Archeology Museum - 1977
Coll: pre- and Indian history; 15th century artifacts; historical items; marine science; archeology; natural history - library; reading room; auditorium; theater; classrooms

Safford AZ

16165
Graham County Historical Society
808 8th Ave, Safford, AZ 85546
General Museum - 1962
Coll: western memorabilia; pioneer and Indian artifacts; archeology - library

Sag Harbor NY

16166
Suffolk County Whaling Museum of Sag Harbor, Long Island
Main St, Sag Harbor, NY 11963
General Museum - 1936
Coll: whaling tools; books; models; antiques; guns; toys - whaleboat; children's museum

Saginaw MI

16167
Saginaw Art Museum
1126 N Michigan Ave, Saginaw, MI
48602
Fine Arts Museum - 1947
Coll: Oriental paintings; English silver
and porcelain; Japanese prints; textiles
- library; reading room

St. Augustine FL

16168
**Historic St. Augustine Preservation
Board**
POB 1987, St. Augustine, FL 32084
General Museum - 1959
Coll: Spanish and Spanish-Colonial
artifacts; decorative arts; historical
archeology; restored or reconstructed
colonial buildings from the 18th and
19th centuries - library; auditorium

16169
St. Augustine Historical Society
271 Charlotte St, St. Augustine, FL
32084
General Museum - 1883
Coll: local historical items; historic
houses from the 18th century - library

St. Bonaventure NY

16170
St. Bonaventure Art Collection St.
Bonaventure University
St. Bonaventure, NY 14778
Fine Arts Museum - 1856
Coll: manuscripts; rare books;
incunabula; literary manuscripts of Jim
Bishop and Thomas Merton; archives;
paintings; history; Indian artifacts;
numismatics; philatelics; porcelain -
library; reading room

St Clair MO

16171
**Phoebe Apperson Hearst Historical
Society**
850 Walton St, St Clair, MO 63077
History/Public Affairs Museum - 1961
Coll: life of Phoebe Apperson Hearst -
library

St. Francis SD

16172
Buechel Memorial Lakota Museum
St. Francis Indian Mission, St. Francis,
SD 57572
Anthropology Museum - 1915
Coll: ethnographic materials of the
early reservation period of the
Rosebud and Pine Ridge Sioux -
library

Saint George UT

16173
Brigham Young's Winter Home
67 West 2nd North, Saint George UT
84770, LDS Church 50 E North
Temple, Salt Lake City, UT 84150
Historic Site - 1975
Coll: household furnishings; Mormon
history

St. Helena CA

16174
The Silverado Museum
1490 Library Lane, POB 409, St.
Helena, CA 94574
Historic Site - 1969
Coll: first editions, manuscripts, letters,
memorabilia of Robert Louis
Stevenson; books, periodicals,
paintings, photographs, sculptures
relating to Stevenson - library

St. Ignace MI

16175
Fort De Buade Museum Inc
334 N State St, St. Ignace, MI 49781
Anthropology Museum - 1975
Coll: guns; Indian artifacts; lithographs
and oils of woodland Indians

St. James MI

16176
Beaver Island Historical Society
St. James, MI 49782
History/Public Affairs Museum - 1957
Coll: maps of island; Irish fishing and
lumbering artifacts; antiques

St James MO

16177
Maramec Museum The James
Foundation
Maramac Spring Park, 320 S
Bourbeuse St, St James, MO 65559
History/Public Affairs Museum
Coll: iron works; grist mill; iron ore
bank; sinkholes; archaeology related
to Maramec and Indian culture;
transportation

St. Johnsbury VT

16178
Fairbanks Museum and Planetarium
Main and Prospect Sts, St. Johnsbury,
VT 05819
General Museum - 1889
Coll: operating exhibits of magnetism,
astronomy, machines and electricity;
zoology; anthropology; geology; native
arts; ethnology; energy technology -
library; planetarium; weather station;
classrooms

16179
St. Johnsbury Athenaeum
30 Main St, St. Johnsbury, VT 05819
Fine Arts Museum - 1873
Primarily 19th century American art -
library

St Joseph MN

16180
Benedicta Arts Center College of St.
Benedict
St Joseph, MN 56374
Fine Arts Museum - 1963
Coll: New Guinea artifacts;
anthropological artifacts; ceramics -
lecture hall; classrooms; auditorium

St. Joseph MO

16181
Albrecht Art Museum
2818 Frederick Blvd, St Joseph, MO
64506
Fine Arts Museum - 1014
Coll: late 19th century American
paintings; contemporary American
paintings; American drawing and
engraving collections; other print
collections - reading room;
classrooms; library

16182
Jesse James House Museum
12th and Mitchell Sts, St Joseph, MO
64502
History/Public Affairs Museum - 1882
House in which Jesse James was shot
and killed April 3, 1882

16183
Patee House Museum
1202 Penn St, POB 1022, St Joseph,
MO 64502
General Museum - 1964
Coll: railroad mail car; cars; trucks;
buggies; wagons; fire trucks - library

16184
Pony Express Stables Museum
914 Penn St, St Joseph, MO 64501
History/Public Affairs Museum - 1950
Coll: exhibits relating to the Pony
Express - library; rading room

16185
St. Joseph Museum
11th and Charles, St. Joseph, MO
64501
Natural History Museum - 1926
Coll: ethnology; geology;
anthropology; vertebrate animals;
invertebrates, - library; classrooms;
reading room

St Louis MO

16186
Concordia Historical Institute
801 DeMun Ave, St Louis, MO 63105
Religious Art Museum - 1847
Coll: Reformation and Lutheran medals
and coins; costumes and crafts; works
by Lutheran artists; materials
pertaining to the Lutheran Church;
archives; Saxon Lutheran Memorial
Frohna - library

16187
**Jefferson National Expansion
Memorial**
11 N 4th St, St Louis, MO 63102
History/Public Affairs Museum - 1935
Coll: 19th century Western America
artifacts; horse-drawn transportation;
Indian artifacts; archives - library;
theater

16188
McDonnell Planetarium
5100 Clayton Rd, St Louis, MO 63110
Science/Tech Museum - 1955
Coll: space science and astronomy
exhibits; Gemini VI and VIII
spacecrafts; seismograph - library;
planetarium; reading room; theater;
classrooms

16189
Missouri Historical Society
Lindell and De Baliviere, St Louis, MO
63112
History/Public Affairs Museum - 1866
Coll: costumes from 1773 to present;
ethnography - library

16190
**Museum of Science and Natural
History**
Oak Knoll Park, St Louis, MO 63105
Science/Tech Museum - 1959
Coll: pre-Columbian North American
Indian artifacts; space and
aeronautics; communications; lighting
equipment; sea shells; industry -
library; reading room; classrooms

16191
National Museum of Transport
3015 Barrett Station Rd, St Louis, MO
63122
Science/Tech Museum - 1944
Coll: railway cars; automobils;
streetcars; buses; trucks - library

16192
The St Louis Art Museum
Forest Park, St Louis, MO 63110
Fine Arts Museum - 1907
Coll: decorative arts from early Egypt
and China; art of Japan, India, Near
East; classical, medieval, Renaissance,
18th and 19th century art;
contemporary art; painting, sculpture -
library; reading room; auditorium;
classrooms

16193
St Louis Artists Guild
227 E Lockwood, St Louis, MO 63119
Fine Arts Museum - 1886
Coll: paintings; graphics; decorative
arts; sculpture

16194
**St Louis Medical Museum and
National Museum of Medical
Quackery**
3839 Lindell Blvd, St Louis, MO 63108
Science/Tech Museum - 1964
Coll: instruments; apparatus and
pictures of physicians, dentist,
pharmacists and medical school
educators dating back to 1800 -
library; reading room; auditorium

16195
Soldiers' Memorial
1315 Chestnut St, St Louis, MO 63103
History/Public Affairs Museum - 1938
Coll: pistols; medals; maps; uniforms;
helmets; papers

16196
**Washington University Gallery of
Art, Steinberg Hall**
Forsyth and Skinker Campus, St
Louis, MO 63130
Fine Arts Museum - 1879
Coll: European paintings and sculpture
of 16th-20th centuries; 19th-20th
century American painting and
sculpture; decorative arts;
numismatics - library; auditorium

St. Marks FL

16197
**San Marcos de Apache State
Historic Site**
POB 27, St. Marks, FL 32355
General Museum - 1964
Coll: archeology; military artifacts;
Indian artifacts; fort ruins

St. Martinsville LA

16198
Acadian House Museum
POB 497, St. Martinsville, LA 70582
History/Public Affairs Museum - 1926
Coll: basketry; palmetto artistry;
weaving

St. Mary's City MD

16199
St. Mary's City Commission
POB 38, St. Mary's City, MD 20686
History/Public Affairs Museum - 1966
Coll: archaeology; architecture;
anthropology

St. Marys PA

16200
Historical Society of St. Marys and Benzinger Township
Municipal Bldg, Room 13, Erie Av, St. Marys, PA 15857
General Museum - 1960
photographs and artifacts of early history of the area - library; reading room

St. Michael PA

16201
Johnston Flood National Memorial
Pennsylvania Rte 869, St. Michael PA 15951, POB 247, Cresson, PA 16630
Historic Site - 1964
books, articles, photos, artifacts relating to the Johnstown Flood in 1889; 300 item collection

St Michaels MD

16202
Chesapeake Bay Maritime Museum
POB 636, St Michaels, MD 21663
General Museum - 1065
Coll: aquarium; art; indigenous vessels; small craft, decoys, waterfowling - library; aquarium

St. Paul MN

16203
Catholic Historical Society of St. Paul John Ireland Memorial Library of the St. Paul Seminary
2260 Summit Ave, St. Paul, MN 55105
Religious Art Museum - 1912
Coll: The John Ireland Papers; The James Reardon Papers; church artifacts; priest portraits; 19th and 20th century Catholicism

16204
Hamline University Galleries
Department of Art
Snelling and Hewitt, St. Paul, MN 55104
Fine Arts Museum - 1850
Coll: paintings; graphics; sculpture

16205
Minnesota Historical Society
690 Cedar St, St. Paul, MN 55101
History/Public Affairs Museum - 1849
Coll: maps and atlases; art and graphics; genealogy; Indian artifacts - library; reading room

16206
Minnesota Museum of Art Permanent Collection Gallery
305 St. Peter St, St. Paul, MN 55102
Fine Arts Museum - 1927
Coll: contemporary crafts; 20th century drawings; Asian art - library; auditorium; classrooms

16207
Ramsey County Historical Society
75 W Fifth St, St. Paul, MN 55102
Agriculture Museum - 1949
Coll: implements and tools used by pioneer farmers - library

16208
The Science Museum of Minnesota
30 E 10th St, St. Paul, MN 55101
Natural History Museum - 1907
Coll: ethnology; paleontology; zoology; archaeology; geology - library

St. Petersburg FL

16209
Haas Museum and Grace S. Turner House and Village
3511 2nd Av, S, St. Petersburg, FL 33711
General Museum - 1962
Coll: antiques; shell collection; mineral exhibit; historic buildings

16210
Museum of Fine Arts of St. Petersburg, Florida, Inc.
255 Beach Dr, N, St. Petersburg, FL 33701
Fine Arts Museum - 1961
Coll: American and European paintings, drawings, prints, and photographs; sculpture; decorative arts; pre-Columbian art - library

16211
St. Petersburg Historical Museum
335 2nd Av, NE, St. Petersburg, FL 33701
General Museum - 1920
Coll: local historical items; pioneer life; uniforms; guns; flags; archeology; natural history; numismatics - library; children's museum

16212
The Science Center of Pinellas County
7701 22nd Av, N, St. Petersburg, FL 33710
Science/Tech Museum - 1959
Coll: anatomy; anthropology; astronomy; botany; medicine; natural history - library; laboratory; botanical garden; aquarium; planetarium; reading room; auditorium

St. Simons Island GA

16213
Fort Frederica National Monument
Rte 4, POB 286-C, St. Simons Island, GA 31552
Historic Site - 1945
Coll: ruins of 18th century English barracks, fort, and house foundations; military and local artifacts - library; auditorium

16214
Museum of Coastal History
beside the lighthouse, POB 1151, St. Simons Island, GA 31552
General Museum - 1971
Coll: local archeological material; folk culture collection; furnished Victorian parlor; historic building - library; reading room

Ste. Genevieve MO MO

16215
Bolduc House
S Main St, Ste. Genevieve MO 63670, 7 Sunningdale Dr, St. Louis, MO 63124
History/Public Affairs Museum
Coll: archaeology; furniture; history

Salado TX

16216
Central Texas Area Museum
Main and Front Sts, Salado, TX 76571
General Museum - 1958
Coll: genealogy; Central Texas artifacts - library

Salamanca NY

16217
Seneca-Iroquois National Museum
Broad St Extension, POB 442, Salamanca, NY 14779
Anthropology Museum - 1977
Coll: prehistoric, historic and contemporary materials dealing with the Iroquois people; archaeology and history - library; laboratory

Salem IN

16218
Washington County Historical Society, Inc.
307 E Market St, Salem, IN 47167
Historic Site - 1897
Coll: historic house where John Hay was born; antiques; furniture; farm tools; dentistry and medicine; pioneer life; Indian artifacts; textiles - library; reading room; auditorium

Salem MA

16219
Peabody Museum of Salem
161 Essex St, Salem, MA 01970
History/Public Affairs Museum - 1799
Coll: maritime history; ethnology of non-European peoples; natural history; prints; ship models; charts - library; reading room; classrooms

16220
Ropes Mansion
318 Essex St, Salem, MA 01970
History/Public Affairs Museum - 1912
Coll: Chinese Export porcelain; 1817 Irish table glass; early 18th-late 19th century original furnishings

Salem MO

16221
The Wildwood Art Gallery
205 Rolla St, Salem, MO 65560
Fine Arts Museum - 1944
Coll: paintings of Indians; European art; folklore

Salem NJ

16222
Salem County Historical Society
79-83 Market St, Salem, NJ 08079
General Museum - 1884
Coll: agriculture; archaeology; archives; costumes; glass; Indian artifacts; military; Headquarters, Grant Building (1721); brick law office (1735) - children's museum; library

Salem OR

16223
Bush House and Bush Barn Art Center Salem Art Association
600 Mission St SE, Salem, OR 97301
Decorative Arts Museum - 1919
Coll: costumes; decorative arts - classrooms

Salida CO

16224
Salida Museum
Salida Museum Bldg, US 50 at I St, Salida, CO 881201
General Museum - 1954
Coll: local historic artifacts; Indian artifacts; mineralogy; mining; homesteading; textiles

Salisbury NC

16225
Catawba Museum of Anthropology
Heath Hill Forest, Salisbury, NC 28144
Anthropology Museum - 1959
Coll: prehistoric and historic culture of American Indians, primarily from the Mid-Atlantic and South East Plains - field research station; library; student and museum laboratories

16226
Salisbury Supplementary Educational Center
1636 Parkview Circle, Salisbury, NC 28144
General Museum - 1967
Coll: art; natural science; astronomy; biology; historic buildings - library; nature center; planetarium; classrooms

Salisbury NH

16227
Salisbury Historical Society
Salisbury, NH 03268
General Museum - 1966
Coll: clothing; tools; silver; furniture; genealogy - library; reading room; auditorium

Salmon ID

16228
Lemhi County Historical Museum
Salmon, ID 83467
General Museum - 1963
Coll: Historical items; Indian artifacts; Oriental collection

Salt Lake City UT

16229
Daughters of Utah Pioneers
300 N Main St, Salt Lake City, UT 84103
History/Public Affairs Museum - 1901
Coll: Utah Pioneer history; pioneer vehicles - library

16230
Hansen Planetarium
15 S State St, Salt Lake City, UT 84111
Natural History Museum - 1965
Coll: meteorites; technology; history of mythology - library; planetarium; theater

16231
Salt Lake Art Center
20 SW Temple, Salt Lake City, UT 84101
Decorative Arts Museum - 1931
Coll: regional painting and crafts - reference library; auditorium

16232
Utah Museum of Fine Arts
104 AAC, University of Utah, Salt Lake City, UT 84112
Fine Arts Museum - 1951
Coll: 19th century American and French landscape painting; 18th century French furnishings and tapestries; 17th-18th century English furniture and pictures; contemporary graphic works - library; auditorium

16233

Utah Museum of Natural History
University of Utah, Salt Lake City, UT
84112
Science/Tech Museum - 1963
Coll: Utah geology-Jurassic Dinosaur
group; Great Basin archaeology; Utah
plant and animal dioramas; minerals

16234

Utah State Historical Society
307 W Second So, Salt Lake City, UT
84101
General Museum - 1897
Coll: Utah, Western and Mormon
history; furnishing; prints; paintings -
library

16235

Wheeler Historic Farm
6351 South 900 East, Salt Lake City,
UT 84121
Historic Site - 1976
Coll: agricultural, dairy and ice industry
- classrooms

San Andreas CA

16236

**Calaveras County Museum and
Archives**
30 N. Main St, POB 1281, San
Andreas, CA 95249
General Museum - 1967
Coll: county archives and
newspapers; Indian artifacts; mining
and pioneer artifacts; historic buildings
- library

San Angelo TX

16237

**Fort Concho Preservation and
Museum**
213 East Ave D, San Angelo, TX 76903
History/Public Affairs Museum - 1928
Coll: military; preservation projects;
costumes - library

San Antonio TX

16238

Hall of Texas History Wax Museum
Hemis Fair Plaza, POB 2060, San
Antonio, TX 78297
General Museum - 1968
Coll: Texas history

16239

Hertzberg Circus Collection
210 W Market St, San Antonio, TX
78205
Performing Arts Museum - 1941
Coll: circus history and artifacts -
library

16240

History and Traditions Museum
Military Training Center / LGH
Lackland Air Force Base, San Antonio,
TX 78236
Science/Tech Museum - 1956
Coll: rare aeronautical equipment;
aircrafts; aerospace history - library

16241

Institute of Texan Cultures The
University of Texas at San Antonio
801 S. Bowie at Durango Blvd, San
Antonio, TX 78205
History/Public Affairs Museum - 1965
humanities; ethnic history; history -
library; field research station

16242

Marion Koogler McNay Art Institute
6000 N New Braunfels, San Antonio,
TX 78209
Fine Arts Museum - 1950
Coll: 19th and 20th century French and
American painting and sculpture; print
collection; Gothic and Medieval
collection - library; cooperative
programs with University of Texas at
San Antonio

16243

O. Henry House
600 Lone Star Blvd, San Antonio, TX
78297
Historic Site - 1962
O. Henry's first editions

16244

Pioneer Hall
3805 Broadway, San Antonio, TX
78209
History/Public Affairs Museum - 1936
Coll: mementos, photographs, furniture
of pioneers

16245

San Jose Mission
6539 San Jose Dr, San Antonio, TX
78214
Historic Site - 1720
Coll: archaeology; Indian artifacts;
Spanish Colonial collection - library;
outdoor amphitheater

16246

Spanish Governor's Palace
105 Military Plaza, San Antonio, TX
78205
Historic Site - 1929
Coll: Spanish culture; decorative arts;
agriculture - botanical garden

16247

Steves Homestead
509 King William St, San Antonio, TX
78204
Historic Site - 1952
Period furnishing

16248

**Witte Memorial Museum and San
Antonio Museum of Transportation**
San Antonio Museum Association
3801 Broadway, San Antonio, TX
78209
General Museum - Witte Memorial
Museum: 1926; San Antonio Museum
of Transportation: 1969
Coll: American and Texas paintings,
decorative arts and furniture; antique
and classic autos; carriages - library;
auditorium

San Diego CA

16249

**Maritime Museum Association of
San Diego**
1306 N Harbor Dr, San Diego, CA
92101
History/Public Affairs Museum - 1948
Coll: maritime artifacts; maritime art;
photo collection; antiques - library

16250

Natural History Museum
POB 1390, San Diego, CA 92112
Science/Tech Museum - 1874
Coll: shells; insects; mammals; birds;
invertebrates; reptiles; botany -
library; auditorium; nature center;
classrooms

16251

San Diego Aero-Space Museum, Inc.
Balboa Park, 2001 Pan American
Plaza, San Diego, CA 92101
Science/Tech Museum - 1961
Coll: aircraft, engines, and related
exhibits; archives; photographs -
library

16252

San Diego Hall of Champions
Balboa Park, 1439 El Prado, San
Diego, CA 92101
History/Public Affairs Museum - 1961
Coll: items pertaining to sports -
library

16253

San Diego Historical Society
2727 Presidio Dr, San Diego , CA
92103, POB 81925, Presidio Park, San
Diego, CA 92138
General Museum - 1928
Coll: artifacts; archival materials on
history of the area - library; field
research station; reading room

16254

San Diego Museum of Art
POB 2107, San Diego, CA 92112
Fine Arts Museum - 1925
Coll: European paintings; American
paintings and decorative arts;
Japanese, Chinese, and other oriental
arts, including Indian and Persian
miniatures; contemporary sculpture -
library; auditorium

16255

San Diego Museum of Man
1350 El Prado, Balboa Park, San
Diego, CA 92101
History/Public Affairs Museum - 1915
Coll: ethnological and archeological
collections pertaining to peoples of the
Americas; physical anthropology
primarily from California, the
Southwest, and Peru; historical
building - library

San Francisco CA

16256

Asian Art Museum of San Francisco
The Avery Brundage Collection
Golden Gate Park, San Francisco, CA
94118
Fine Arts Museum - 1969
Coll: nearly 10,000 objects of Asian art,
including the Avery Brundage
collection and the Roy C. Leventritt
collection - library; conservation
laboratory; photography laboratory;
auditorium

16257

California Academy of Sciences
Golden Gate Park, San Francisco, CA
94118
Science/Tech Museum - 1853
Coll: ichthyology; invertebrate
zoology; ornithology; mammalogy;
natural history; artifacts - library;
aquarium; planetarium; auditorium;
classrooms

16258

**California Division of Mines &
Geology**
Ferry Building, San Francisco, CA
94111
Science/Tech Museum - 1880
Coll: paleontology; gold and gold
facsimiles exhibits; minerals; geologic
maps; mine models; gems - library;
reading room

16259

California Historical Society
2090 Jackson St, San Francisco, CA
94109
Fine Arts Museum - 1871
Coll: paintings; drawings; watercolors;
sculpture; decorative arts - library;
meeting rooms

16260

**California Palace of the Legion of
Honor**
San Francisco, CA 94121
Fine Arts Museum - 1924
Painting, sculpture and decorative arts
from Europe and America; Achenbach
Foundation for the Graphic Arts

16261

Chinese Culture Center Gallery
750 Kearny St, San Francisco, CA
94108
Fine Arts Museum - 1965
Coll: photographs of Chinese-
Americans; Chinese art; Chinese folk
arts and crafts - library; auditorium;
classrooms

16262

**Fort Point and Army Museum
Association**
Funston Av at Lincoln Blvd, San
Francisco, CA 94129
History/Public Affairs Museum - 1959
Coll: artifacts dating from the Mexican
era to Vietnam

16263

Josephine D. Randall Junior Museum
199 Museum Way, San Francisco, CA
94114
Junior Museum - 1947
Coll: live animals; natural history;
children's art; geology; Indian artifacts;
rocks and minerals - library; reading
room; nature center

16264

M. H. de Young Museum
Golden Gate Park, San Francisco, CA
94118
Fine Arts Museum - 1895
Coll: paintings, sculpture, and
decorative arts from Europe and
America; arts of ancient Egypt,
Greece, and Rome; traditional arts of
Africa, Oceania, and the Americas -
library; auditorium; theater;
conservation laboratories; classrooms

16265

Museum of Russian Culture
2450 Sutter St, San Francisco, CA
94115
History/Public Affairs Museum - 1948
Coll: archives; history; military
artifacts; ethnology; numismatics

16266

National Maritime Museum
Golden Gate National Recreation
Area, San Francisco, CA 94123
History/Public Affairs Museum - 1951
Coll: photographs of ships and
shipping ports; ship models; artifacts
from historic vessels; historic ships

16267

Presidio Army Museum
Bldg 2, Presidio of San Francisco, San
Francisco, CA 94129
General Museum - 1974
Coll: uniforms, insignia, and weapons;
furniture, art, and related artifacts;
photograph collection related to
California and the Pacific - library

16268

San Francisco Art Institute Galleries
800 Chestnut St, San Francisco, CA
94133
Fine Arts Museum - 1871
Coll: contemporary West Coast
painting, sculpture, and graphics; 19th
and 20th century European and
American painting, sculpture, and
prints

16269
San Francisco Fire Department Pioneer Memorial Museum
Presidio Av & Bush St, San Francisco, CA 94115
History/Public Affairs Museum - 1964
Coll: artifacts, memorabilia, and apparatus relating to the firefighting history of San Francisco

16270
San Francisco Museum of Modern Art
McAllister & Van Ness Ave, San Francisco, CA 94102
Fine Arts Museum - 1921
Coll: European and American paintings, sculpture, graphics, photography, and ceramics from the early 20th century to the present - library; painting conservation laboratory; auditorium; classrooms

16271
Wells Fargo Bank History Room
420 Montgomery St, San Francisco, CA 94104
History/Public Affairs Museum - 1929
Coll: stagecoach; gold ore; historical implements and documents; San Francisco photographs; Pony Express, and mining; guns - library

16272
The Wine Museum of San Francisco
633 Beach St, San Francisco, CA 94109
History/Public Affairs Museum - 1974
Coll: wine related art works: glasses; sculptures; graphics; wine books - library

San Jacinto CA

16273
San Jacinto Museum
181 E. Main St, 605 San Marcos Pl, San Jacinto, CA 92383
General Museum - 1940
Coll: Indian archeology; minerals and geology; paleontology; antiques; local history

San Jose CA

16274
Gallery I San Jose State University Art Dept, San Jose, CA 95192
Fine Arts Museum
Coll: 20th century painting, sculpture, and graphics

16275
Rosicrucian Egyptian Museum and Art Gallery
Rosicrucian Park, San Jose, CA 95191
Archeology Museum - 1929
Coll: Assyrian, Babylonian, and Egyptian antiquities; paintings; sculpture; archeology

16276
Rosicrucian Planetarium and Science Museum
Rosicrucian Park, San Jose, CA 95191
Science/Tech Museum - 1035
Coll: meteorites; geophysics; Foucalt pendulum; seismograph; astronomy - planetarium

16277
San Jose Historical Museum
635 Phelan Ave, San Jose, CA 95112
General Museum - 1971
Coll: animal-drawn farm vehicles; motorcycles; motor vehicles; dolls; mining artifacts; historic house - library

16278
San Jose Museum of Art
110 S. Market St, San Jose, CA 95113
Fine Arts Museum - 1969
Coll: Dorothy Liebes textile collection; paintings by regional artists; prints - galleries

16279
Youth Science Institute
16260 Alum Rock Ave, San Jose, CA 95127
Science/Tech Museum - 1953
Coll: insects; mammals; reptiles; rocks and minerals - library; nature and conservation center

San Luis Obispo CA

16280
San Luis Obispo County Historical Museum
696 Monterey St, San Luis Obispo, CA 93401
General Museum - 1956
Coll: archeology; archives; costumes; decorative arts; folklore; historic houses - library; children's museum

San Marcos TX

16281
General Edward Burleson Museum
Aquarena Springs, POB 2330, San Marcos, TX 78666
Historic Site
Coll: furnishings

San Marino CA

16282
Huntington Library, Art Gallery, and Botanical Gardens
1151 Oxford Rd, San Marino, CA 91108
Fine Arts Museum - 1919
Coll: 18th century British art; paintings, drawings, watercolors, sculpture, silver, miniatures, furniture, porcelain; French 18th century decorative arts; 18th century French sculpture; Renaissance paintings and bronzes; 18th century European paintings - library; botanical garden

16283
El Molino Viejo Museum
1120 Old Mill Rd, San Marino, CA 91108
General Museum - 1871
Coll: art; history of California

San Mateo CA

16284
The Coyote Point Museum
Coyote Point Drive, Coyote Point, San Mateo, CA 94401
Science/Tech Museum - 1953
Coll: birds; mammals; insects; plants; shells; reptiles and amphibians - library; nature/conservation center; classrooms

16285
San Mateo County Historical Association
1700 W. Hillsdale Blvd, San Mateo, CA 94402
General Museum - 1935
Coll: archives of local history; decorative arts; archeology; agriculture; transportation - library

San Pedro CA

16286
Cabrillo Beach Marine Museum
3720 Stephen White Dr, San Pedro, CA 90731
General Museum - 1934
Coll: shore birds; marine fossils; sea shells; tropical and subtropical fish; historical ship models; nautical instruments - library; nature center; classroom; laboratories; auditorium

Sandpoint ID

16287
Bonner County Historical Museum
W Ontario & Ella Av, POB 1063, Sandpoint, ID 83864
General Museum - 1950
Coll: local historical items; early Americana; geology; Indian artifacts; aboriginal sites; forest history and logging - library; children's discovery room

Sandusky OH

16288
Follett House Museum
404 Wayne St, mail c/o Sandusky Library Association, West Adams and Columbus Av, Sandusky, OH 44870
General Museum - 1902
Coll: household objects and furniture; toys; artifacts of Sandusky; Erie County and Johnson's Island Civil War Prison - library

Sandwich MA

16289
Thornton W. Burgess Museum
4 Water St, POB 972, Sandwich, MA 02563
History/Public Affairs Museum - 1976
Coll: published writings of Thornton W. Burgess including many first editions; autographs; related items; original illustrations by Harrison Cady - library

16290
Yesteryears Museum
Main and River Sts, Sandwich, MA 02563
Anthropology Museum - 1961
Coll: old and rare dolls, both Occidental and Oriental; miniature and toy colleciton - library

Sandwich MS

16291
Heritage Plantation of Sandwich
Grove St, Sandwich, MS 02563
History/Public Affairs Museum - 1969
Coll: antique cars; military miniatures; weapons - library; theater

Santa Ana CA

16292
Charles W. Bowers Memorial Museum
2002 N. Main St, Santa Ana, CA 92706
General Museum - 1927
Coll: artifacts from American Indian cultures, Asia, Africa, and Oceania; 19th and 20th century American art and transportation; natural history and natural science exhibits; 19th and 20th century Oriental costumes; decorative arts - library

Santa Barbara CA

16293
The Santa Barbara Historical Society
136 E. De la Guerra St, POB 578, Santa Barbara, CA 93102
General Museum - 1932
Coll: archives; genealogical material; newspapers; old photographs; historic houses - library

16294
The Santa Barbara Museum of Art
1130 State St, Santa Barbara, CA 93101
Fine Arts Museum - 1941
Coll: Greek, Roman, and Egyptian antiquities; Oriental sculpture, painting, porcelain, musical instruments; American paintings from colonial period to present; European and American watercolors; European painting and sculpture; Schott antique doll collection - auditorium

16295
Santa Barbara Museum of Natural History
2559 Puesta del Sol Rd, Santa Barbara, CA 93105
Science/Tech Museum - 1916
Coll: natural history and prehistoric life of Pacific Coast; zoology; archeology; mineralogy; botany - library; planetarium; auditoriums; laboratory; classrooms

16296
University Art Museum
University of California, Santa Barbara, CA 93106
Fine Arts Museum - 1960
Coll: Sedgwick collection of Italian, Flemish, Dutch, and German paintings; Morgenroth collection of Renaissance medals and plaquettes; Dreyfus collection of Luristan bronzes, near Eastern ceramics, and pre-Columbian art; American paintings; archeology

Santa Clara CA

16297
De Saisset Art Gallery and Museum
University of Santa Clara, Santa Clara, CA 95053
Fine Arts Museum - 1955
Coll: D'Berger collection of 28th century French Boulle furniture and ivories; 17th century tapestries Sevre; porcelain; Kolb collection of 17th and 18th century graphics; Oriental art; 19th and 20th century sculpture; photographs and videotapes - library; auditorium

16298
Triton Museum of Art
1505 Warburton Ave, Santa Clara, CA 95050
Fine Arts Museum - 1965
Coll: paintings by Californian artist Theodore Wores; other American artists; Vivan Woodward Elmer majolica collection; historic house - library

Santa Cruz CA

16299
Santa Cruz County Historical Museum
118 Cooper St, Santa Cruz, CA 95060
General Museum - 1972
Coll: regional memorabilia

16300
Santa Cruz Museum
1305 E. Cliff Dr, Santa Cruz, CA 95062
General Museum - 1904
Coll: California Indian artifacts; local historical artifacts; local natural history specimens; anthropology; local historical art collection - library; laboratory; classroom

Santa Fe NM

16301
Institute of American Indian Arts Museum
Cerillos Rd, Santa Fe, NM 87501
Decorative Arts Museum - 1962
Coll: Indian artifacts; contemporary Indian arts and crafts - library; classrooms; BIA Bicentennial Videotape Archives

16302
Museum of International Folk Art
706 Camino Lejo, POB 2087, Santa Fe, NM 87501
Decorative Arts Museum - 1953
Coll: costumes; religious art; ceramics; textiles; jewelry; silverwork; metalwork; dolls; folk art - library; reading room

16303
Museum of New Mexico
POB 2087, Santa Fe, NM 87501
Anthropology Museum - 1909
Coll: anthropology; archaeology and ethnology of the Southwest; fine arts; international folk art; Spanish Colonial history; history of New Mexico - library; auditorium

16304
Old Cienega Village Museum
Rte 2, POB 214, Santa Fe, NM 87501
Historic Site - 1970
Coll: Leger Gristmill (1880); Talpa Water Mill; Padilla Water Mill; Barela Water Mill; Apodaca Blacksmith Shop; Casias Wheelwright shop; Gallegos Winery; Sile Syrup Mill; Las Trampas country store (1850-1900); hacienda-type dwellings of various periods and styles; Morada and Oratorio Chapels - lecture and film hall; dormitory

16305
Santuario de nuestra Senora de Guadalupe
100 Guadalupe St, Santa Fe, NM 87532
Religious Art Museum - 1975
Coll: paintings and murals in the Hispanic tradition - botanical garden

16306
The Wheelwright Museum
704 Camino Lejo, POB 5153, Santa Fe, NM 87501
Anthropology Museum - 1937
Coll: Native American artifacts and art works; musical recordings of Navajo ceremonies; ceremonial objects; Navajo sandpainting reproductions; archives; manuscripts - library

Santa Maria CA

16307
Santa Maria Valley Historical Society, Inc.
616 S Broadway, POB 584, Santa Maria, CA 93454
General Museum - 1955
Coll: Indian artifacts; historical memorabilia; room displays; historic house - library; reading room; auditorium

Santa Paula CA

16308
California Oil Museum
1003 Main St, Santa Paula, CA 93060
Science/Tech Museum - 1950
Coll: old drilling rigs; papers and pictures relating to the era

Santa Rosa CA

16309
Codding Museum
557 Summerfield Rd, Santa Rosa, CA 95401
Science/Tech Museum - 1961
Coll: natural history; dioramas of wildlife groups and pioneer life

16310
Jesse Peter Memorial Museum
Santa Rosa Junior College
1501 Mendocino Ave, Santa Rosa, CA 95401
History/Public Affairs Museum - 1932
Coll: native American artifacts

Santa Ynez CA

16311
Santa Ynez Valley Historical Society
POB 181, Santa Ynez, CA 93460
General Museum - 1961
Coll: Parks/Janeway carriage house; stage coaches; wagons; buggies - library; reading room

Sarasota FL

16312
John and Mable Ringling Museum of Art
POB 1838, Sarasota, FL 33578
Performing Arts Museum - 1930
Coll: Art Museum: European paintings of the 16th, 17th, 18th centuries; 20th century American paintings; decorative arts; archeology of Cyprus; theater history; Circus Museum: circus vehicles; graphic arts illustrating history of circus from 16th century to present; Theater Museum: 18th century Italian theater - library; theater; classrooms

16313
Sarasota Art Association Civic Center
POB 2077, Sarasota, FL 33578
Fine Arts Museum - 1926
Coll: paintings; sculpture; graphics; photography - library

Saratoga CA

16314
Montalvo Center for the Arts
end of Montalvo Rd, POB 158, Saratoga, CA 95070
Fine Arts Museum - 1930
Coll: paintings; sculpture; decorative arts; graphics; historic houses - arboretum

Saratoga Springs NY

16315
Art Gallery Skidmore College
Skidmore Campus, N. Broadway, Saratoga Springs, NY 12866
Fine Arts Museum - 1926
Coll: paintings; graphics

16316
National Museum of Racing, Inc.
Union Av, Saratoga Springs, NY 12866
History/Public Affairs Museum - 1950
Coll: equine paintings; sporting art; thoroughbred racing trophies; racing colors; sculpture - auditorium; theater

16317
Walworth Memorial Museum
Historical Society of Saratoga Springs
The Casino, Congress Park, POB 216, Saratoga Springs, NY 12866
General Museum - 1883
Coll: furnishings of Chancellor Reuben Hyde Walworth; local history; manuscripts of the writer Frank Sullivan - library

Saratoga TX

16318
Big Thicket Museum
POB 198, Saratoga, TX 77585
General Museum - 1970
Coll: early oil field equipment; early implements; furnishing - library

Saugus MA

16319
Saugus Iron Works National Historic Site
233 Central St, Saugus, MA 01906
Science/Tech Museum - 1054
Coll: archaeological remains of original ironworks; historic furnishings; 17th century ironmaking technology - library

Sauk Center MN

16320
Sinclair Lewis Museum and Inerpretive Center
194 and US 71, Sauk Center, MN 56378
History/Public Affairs Museum - 1960
Coll: books written by Sinclair Lewis - library

Savannah GA

16321
Cunningham Historic Center
Bethesda Home for Boys, POB 13039, Savannah, GA 31406
General Museum - 1970
Coll: memorabilia and photographs; ship models and artifacts; local historical documents and artifacts - library

16322
Davenport House Museum
324 E State St, POB 1733, Savannah, GA 31402
General Museum - 1955
Coll: Chippendale, Hepplewhite, and Sheraton furniture; Davenport China

16323
Georgia Historical Society
501 Whitaker St, Savannah, GA 31404
General Museum - 1839
Coll: books, manuscripts, maps, photographs, newspapers, and portraits relating to local history; historical artifacts - library; reading room; auditorium

16324
Georgia Salzburger Society Museum
9375 Whitfield Av, Savannah, GA 31406
General Museum - 1956
Coll: tools; furniture; letters; books and Bibles; deeds and maps; records of early settlers

16325
Historic Savannah Foundation, Inc.
Scarbrough House
41 W Broad St, Savannah GA 31401, POB 1733, Savannah, GA 31402
General Museum
historic houses

16326
Historical Museum First African Baptist Church
23 Montgomery St, Savannah, GA 31401
Religious Art Museum
Coll: photographs, documents, books, papers; antique communion pieces; furniture and artifacts relating to the church and its membership - classrooms

16327
Juliette Gordon Low Girl Scout National Center
142 Bull St, Savannah, GA 31401
General Museum - 1956
Memorabilia, art, and furniture of Juliette Gordon Low, the founder of the Girl Scouts of America; historic house - garden

16328
Kiah Museum-A Museum for the Masses
505 W 36 St, Savannah, GA 31401
General Museum - 1959
Coll: Howard J. Morrison, Jr. zoology exhibit; Harmon Foundation collection of African art; 18th and 19th century furniture, china, silver, and glass; contemporary art; photography; Indian and Civil War artifacts

16329
Museum of Antique Dolls
505 President St, E, Savannah, GA 31401
History/Public Affairs Museum
Coll: dolls; doll houses; doll furniture; toys; banks; Victorian clothing; children's books; other artifacts related to childhood - library

16330
Old Fort Jackson
POB 782, Savannah, GA 31402
General Museum
local historical and military items - library

16331
Owens-Thomas House
124 Abercorn, Savannah GA 31401, POB 8424, Savannah, GA 31402
General Museum - 1951
Coll: period rooms housing 18th and 19th century decorative arts; European and Chinese porcelains; American silver; English and American furniture - library

16332
Savannah Science Museum, Inc.
4405 Paulsen St, Savannah, GA 31405
Natural History Museum - 1954
Reptiles and amphibians of Southern Georgia - planetarium; laboratory; nature preserve

16333
Ships of the Sea Maritime Museum
503 E River St, Savannah, GA 31401
History/Public Affairs Museum - 1966
Coll: ship models; ships in bottles; figureheads; 19th century English tavern signs; macrame creations; historical artifacts - library

16334
Telfair Academy of Arts and Sciences, Inc.
121 Barnard St, Savannah GA 31412, POB 10081, Savannah, GA 31402
Fine Arts Museum - 1874
Coll: 18th, 19th, and early 20th century American and European paintings; sculpture; prints and drawings; decorative arts; 19th century mansion - library

16335
William Scarbrough House Museum
41 West Broad St, POB 1733,
Savannah, GA 31402
General Museum - 1955
Coll: local historical artifacts;
decorative arts; architecture

16336
Wormsloe Historic Site
POB 13852, Savannah, GA 31406
Historic Site - 1974
Coll: ruins of fortified house (1736);
archeological artifacts from period
1733-1850

Sayville NY

16337
Sayville Historical Society
Sayville, NY 11782
General Museum - 1945
Coll: costumes and textiles; folklore;
marine; agriculture; Indian artifacts;
glass; early lamps; country store -
library; children's museum

Scarsdale NY

16338
Weinberg Nature Center
455 Mamaroneck Rd, Scarsdale, NY
10583
Natural History Museum - 1958
Coll: rocks; shells; leaves; pictures of
birds and wild flowers; live exhibits -
library; nature trails

Schaefferstown PA

16339
Historic Schaefferstown, Inc.
N Market St, Schaefferstown, PA
17088
General Museum - 1966
exhibits portraying 19th century
Pennsylvania German life and culture;
tools and implements; furniture; quilts;
Indian artifacts; historic buildings -
library; reading room

Schenectady NY

16340
**Schenectady County Historical
Society**
Washington Av, Schenectady, NY
12305
General Museum - 1906
Coll: paintings; guns; toys and dolls;
early General Electric equipment;
decorative arts; archives - library;
reading room; auditorium

16341
The Schenectady Museum
Nott Terrace Heights, Schenectady,
NY 12308
General Museum - 1934
Coll: 19th and 20th century costumes,
textiles; minerals and fossils; birds and
molluscs; Native American, African,
Australian, New Guinea Highlands
collections; decorative and fine arts;
technology and industry - library;
planetarium; auditorium; studios;
amateur radio station; nature preserve

Schoharie NY

16342
**Old Stone Fort Museum and William
W. Badgley Historical Museum**
N. Main St, Schoharie, NY 12157
General Museum - 1889
Coll: Indian artifacts; tools; vehicles;
firearms; arts and crafts - library;
reading room

Scio OH

16343
Scio Pottery Museum
R.D. No. 1, Scio, OH 43988
General Museum - 1941
Coll: motor vehicles including antique
classic motorcycles and racing cars;
wood carvings; mounted animals

Scituate MA

16344
Scituate Historical Society
121 Maple St, Scituate, MA 02066
General Museum - 1916
Coll: textiles; costumes; books and
documents; sail lofts; sail making tools
- library; reading room

Scotia CA

16345
The Pacific Lumber Co.
US Hwy 101, POB 37, Scotia, CA
95565
Agriculture Museum - 1959
Coll: displays of old logging
equipment; pictorial history of the
Pacific Lumber Co.; historic building

Scottsdale PA

16346
**Westmoreland-Fayette Historical
Society**
Scottsdale, PA 15683
General Museum - 1928
Coll: pre-historic artifacts; historic
archaeological collections; Colonial
and Civil War; coal mining; ceramics;
glassware; clothing; natural history;
documents; historic buildings

Scranton PA

16347
**Everhart Museum of Natural History,
Science and Art**
Nay Aug Park, Scranton, PA 18510
General Museum - 1908
Coll: American Indian, Oriental, African
and Oceanic art; American and
European paintings, sculpture and
graphics; American folk art; birds,
shells, butterflies, insects, fish and
reptiles, small animals; rocks and
minerals; coal fossils; natural history;
zoology; archaeology; ethnology -
library; planetarium; auditorium;
classrooms; theater

Searcy AR

16348
White County Pioneer Museum
Rte 1, Searcy, AR 72143
History/Public Affairs Museum - 1966
Coll: early farm implements; historic
buildings

Searsport ME

16349
Penobscot Marine Museum
Church Std, Searsport, ME 04974
Science/Tech Museum - 1936
Coll: ship models; shipbuilding tools;
navigational instruments; American
and Oriental furnishings - library

Seattle WA

16350
Charles and Emma Frye Art Museum
704 Terry Av, Seattle, WA 98104
Fine Arts Museum - 1952
19th century European and American
paintings - library

16351
Costume and Textile Study Center
School of Nutritional Science and
Textiles
University of Washington, Seattle, WA
98195
Decorative Arts Museum - 1958
Coll: costumes and textiles; cultures
and techniques from the Egyptian
dynasties to present day; 16th-19th
century Italian velvets, brocades and
damasks; embroideries; fabrics -
library

16352
Henry Art Gallery
University of Washington, Seattle, WA
98195
Fine Arts Museum - 1925
Coll: 19th and 20th century American
and European paintings, photographs
and prints; contemporary American
ceramic pottery and sculpture

16353
Museum of History and Industry
2161 E Hamlin St, Seattle, WA 98112
General Museum - 1914
Coll: china; glass; silver; textiles;
history; maritime; aeronautics; natural
history; communications; costumes;
industrial; mining; musical instruments;
logging and lumber; toys and dolls -
library; auditorium; classrooms

16354
Pacific Museum of Flight Pacific
Northwest Aviation Historical
Foundation
400 Broad St, Seattle, WA 98109
Science/Tech Museum - 1965
Coll: powered aircraft; sailplanes;
vintage engines; aircraft and aviation
artifacts; aviation and space industry
history in the Pacific Northwest -
library; theater

16355
Pacific Science Center
200 2nd Av N, Seattle, WA 98109
Science/Tech Museum - 1962
Coll: exhibits in astronomy; space
science; anthropology; biological,
geological, historical models -
laboratories; classrooms; theater;
spacearium theater; library; starlab
planetarium; computer lab

16356
Puget Sound Railroad Museum
POB 3801, Seattle, WA 98124
Science/Tech Museum - 1957
Coll: steam locomotives; passenger
coaches; rotary snowplow cranes and
work equipment; refurbished 19th
century railroad station

16357
Seattle Art Museum
Volunteer Park, Seattle, WA 98112
Fine Arts Museum - 1917
Coll: archeology; decorative arts;
ethnology; Far and Near Eastern,
pre-Columbian art; Egyptian, Greek,
Roman, Gothic, Renaissance and
Baroque painting and sculpture;
numismatics - library; auditorium

16358
**Thomas Burke Memorial Washington
State Museum**
University of Washington, Seattle, WA
98195
Natural History Museum - 1885
Coll: Northwest Coast Indians;
ethnology of the Pacific Rim and
islands; paleontology; mineralogy;
geology - classrooms

16359
**University of Washington School of
Medicine**
Seattle, WA 98195
History/Public Affairs Museum - 1964
Medicine - library

16360
**Washington State Fire Service
Historical Museum, Inc.**
Bldg So, Seattle Center, POB 9521,
Seattle, WA 98109
History/Public Affairs Museum - 1964
Coll: fire-fighting exhibits; fire
apparatus and memorabilia; working
models of fireboats; badges and
uniforms - library

16361
Wing Luke Memorial House
414 Eighth Av So, Seattle, WA 98104
General Museum - 1966
library

Sedalia MO

16362
Pettis County Historical Society
Sedalia Public Library
Third and Kentucky Sts, Sedalia, MO
65301
General Museum - 1943
Coll: military; agiculture; costumes;
farm life; war; Indian artifacts - library

Sedan KS

16363
Emmett Kelly Historical Museum
Sedan, KS 67361
History/Public Affairs Museum - 1967
Coll: clowns; circus

Seguin TX

16364
Fiedler Memorial Museum
Texas Lutheran College, Seguin, TX
78155
Science/Tech Museum - 1973
Coll: geology; Texas pioneer items

Selkirk NY

16365
**Town of Bethlehem Historical
Association**
Clapper Rd and Rte 144, Selkirk, NY
12158
General Museum - 1965
Coll: ice-harvesting; railroading; fruit-
growing; farm and household items;
education - library

Selma AL

16366
Sturdivant Hall
713 Mabry St, Selma, AL 36701
General Museum - 1957
Coll: furnishings of the pre-Civil War
period

Seneca Falls NY

16367
Seneca Falls Historical Society
55 Cayuga St, Seneca Falls, NY 13148
General Museum - 1904
Coll: memorabilia of the first Women's Rights Convention (1848); apparels; paintings of Carlos Bellows; folklore; industry; Silsby Steam Fire engine - children's room; library; reading room

Setauket NY

16368
Society for the Preservation of Long Island Antiquities
POB 206, Setauket, NY 11733
Decorative Arts Museum - 1948
Coll: antique furnishings of the houses; Lloyd Manor (1722); Thompson House (1700); Sherwood-Jayne House (1730); Rock Hall (1767); Custom House (1790); Barn Complex (1750) - library

Sewanee TN

16369
Fine Arts Gallery of the University of the South
Sewanee, TN 37375
Fine Arts Museum - 1965
Coll: paintings; graphics; period pieces; furniture; sculpture; photography

Seward NE

16370
Koenig Art Gallery Concordia Teachers College
800 No Columbia St, Seward, NE 68434
Fine Arts Museum - 1951
Coll: contemporary art; international original prints; ceramics; glass

Shaftsbury VT

16371
Shaftsbury Historical Society
Rte 1, POB 101, Shaftsbury, VT 05262
General Museum - 1966
Coll: tools and furnishing; historical documents; crafts; industries - library; auditorium

Sharon CT

16372
Sharon Audubon Center
Rte 4, Sharon, CT 06069
Natural History Museum - 1961
Coll: bird skins; wildlife; cold-blooded animals; mammal skins - library; nature center; classrooms

Sharon MA

16373
Kendale Whaling Museum
Everett St, Sharon, MA 02067
History/Public Affairs Museum - 1956
Coll: marine; graphics; technique of whaling; manuscripts - library

Shawano WI

16374
Shawano County Historical Society, Inc.
524 N Franklin St, 1003 S Main St, Shawano, WI 54166
General Museum - 1940
Coll: furniture; lamps; houshold goods; children's nursery; clothing; glassware and dishes - library

Sheboygan WI

16375
John Michael Kohler Arts Center
608 New York Av, Sheboygan, WI 53081
Fine Arts Museum - 1967
Coll: Kuehne collection of pre-historic Wisconsin Indian artifacts; American furniture; contemporary glass and ceramics; grass-root art - library; theater; classrooms

16376
Sheboygan County Historical Museum
3110 Erie Av, Sheboygan, WI 53081
General Museum - 1954
Coll: artifacts of local history; farm implements; household articles; medical aids; genealogy; historic house - library

Sheffield Lake OH

16377
103rd Ohio Volunteer Infantry Memorial Foundation
5501 E Lake Rd, Sheffield Lake, OH 44054
History/Public Affairs Museum - 1972
Coll: historic Civil War relics - library

Shelburne VT

16378
Shelburne Museum
US Rte 7, Shelburne, VT 05482
General Museum - 1947
Coll: American fine, folk and decorative art; architecture; steam train and private car; carriages; tools; weapons; hunting trophies; Indian artifacts - library

Shelby

16379
Marias Museum of History and Art
Corner of 1st S and 12th Ave, 59474, Shelby
General Museum - 1963
Coll: Indian artifacts; sewing machines; costumes; historic rooms; geology - library

Sherburne NY

16380
Rogers Environmental Education Center
New York State Rte 80 West, Sherburne, NY 13460
Natural History Museum - 1966
Coll: botany; arboretum; herbarium; geology; zoology; ornithology - libary; outdoor museum; nature center

Shiloh TN

16381
Shiloh National Military Park and Cemetery
Shiloh, TN 38376
History/Public Affairs Museum - 1894
Coll: history; military; Indian artifacts - library

Shiner TX

16382
Edwin Wolters Memorial Museum and Library
609 E Av I, Shiner, TX 77984
General Museum - 1963
Coll: local history; costumes; Indian artifacts - library

Shippensburg PA

16383
Shippensburg Historical Society Museum
W King St, Library Bldg, Shippensburg, PA 17257
General Museum - 1960
material pertaining to local events and history; Indian artifacts; costumes - arts center; library

Shrevenport LA

16384
Grindstone Bluff Museum and Environmental Education Center
501 Jenkins Rd, POB 7965, Shreveport, LA 71107
History/Public Affairs Museum - 1976
Coll: anthropology; ethnology; mythology; biology; sociology; geography; history - library; theater; reading room

Shreveport LA

16385
Louisiana State Exhibit Museum
3015 Greenwood Rd, Shreveport, LA 71109
General Museum - 1939
Coll: murals; money from various countries; paper; glass; china; industry; agriculture - auditorium

16386
Meadows Museum of Art of Centenary College
Centenary Blvd, Shreveport, LA 71104
Fine Arts Museum - 1975
Coll: 360 paintings and drawings by Jean Despujols; 18th-20th century prints

16387
The R. W. Norton Art Gallery
4747 Creswell Ave, Shreveport, LA 71106
Fine Arts Museum - 1946
Coll: works by Charles M. Russell, Frederic Remington; Wedgewood Collection; John Gould ornithology works; rare books; atlases - library

Sidney MT

16388
J. K. Ralston Museum & Art Center
221 Fifth SW, Sidney, MT 59270
General Museum - 1971
Coll: guns; glass; bottles; historic rooms; Indian hammers; historical artifacts - library

Silver City NM

16389
Gila Visitor Center
Gila Cliff Dwelling National Monument, Rte 11, POB 100, Silver City, NM 88061
General Museum - 1968
Coll: archaeology; botany; ethnology; history - library

16390
Silver City Museum
312 W Broadway, Silver City, NM 88061
General Museum - 1967
Coll: frontier Victorian antiques and artifacts; Eisley Indian artifacts; items from model mining town of Tyrone; photographs and documents

16391
Western New Mexico University Museum
POB 43, Silver City, NM 88061
History/Public Affairs Museum - 1974
Coll: anthropological, archaeological, historical, and cultural areas; Eisele collection of Indian artifacts (Mimbres Pottery, bone, lithic material and botanical specimens); The McMillen collection (ranching equipment); The Hunter collection (mining implements); Hinman photograph collection; Harlan photograph collection; Alvan N. White memorial collection (legislature papers, memorabilia)

Silver Plume CO

16392
Miners' Ridge Museum
POB 481, Silver Plume, CO 80476
History/Public Affairs Museum - 1974
Coll: mining records; mining tools; early firearms; municipal records - library

Silverdale WA

16393
Kitsap County Historical Society Museum
3343 NW Byron St, Silverdale, WA 98383
General Museum - 1949
Coll: memorabilia pertaining to Kitsap County; books; photographs; handcarved furniture; local Indian artifacts - library

Silverton CO

16394
San Juan County Historical Society Museum
POB 154, Silverton, CO 81433
General Museum - 1964
Coll: mining equipment; railroad cars; hardware; home furnishings

Simsbury CT

16395
Massacoh Plantation Simsbury Historic Center
800 Hopmeadow St, Simsbury, CT 06070
General Museum - 1911
Coll: domestic tools and utensils; sleighs and carriages; historic houses - library

Sioux City IA

16396
Sioux City Art Center
513 Nebreska St, Sioux City, IA 51101
Fine Arts Museum - 1914
Coll: works by regional, contemporary national and international artists - classrooms

16397
Sioux City Public Museum
2901 Jackson St, Sioux City, IA 51104
History/Public Affairs Museum - 1858
Coll: Indian artifacts; national, state and local history; archives; archaeology; mineralogy; paleontology; military costumes - auditorium; library; classrooms

Sioux Falls SD

16398
The Center for Western Studies
Augustana College 29th, and S.
Summit, Sioux Falls, SD 57102
General Museum - 1964
Coll: Native American art work and
artifacts; Herbert Fisher water colors;
Alfred Ziegler bronzes; local western
art

16399
Civic Fine Arts Association
235 W Tenth St, Sioux Falls, SD 57102
Fine Arts Museum - 1961
Coll: contemporary paintings; graphics

16400
Sioux Empire Medical Museum
1100 S Euclid Av, Sioux Falls, SD
57105
History/Public Affairs Museum - 1975
Coll: patient's room (1930);
orthopaedics; pediatrics; surgery;
nursery; x-ray; two dental units;
uniformed dolls; photographs of
medical staff members - library

16401
Siouxland Heritage Museum
W. 6th St, Sioux Falls, SD 57102
General Museum - 1926
Coll: mineral specimens; Indian
artifacts; pioneer artifacts; local history
- library

Sitka AK

16402
Sheldon Jackson Museum
POB 479, Sitka, AK 99835
Anthropology Museum - 1888
Coll: Haida slate carvings; Eskimo
implements, ivory carvings;
Athapascan canoes and implements;
Tlingit relics, totems and totem poles,
shaman charms; Russian Orthodox
and Finnish Lutheran religious objects
and other historic items

16403
Sitka National Historical Park
POB 738, Sitka, AK 99835
General Museum - 1910
Coll: baskets; totem poles; Indian and
Russian artifacts - library; auditorium
exhibit hall; 1-mile totem walk

Smyrna DE

16404
Allee House
Dutch Neck Rd at Route 9, Smyrna,
DE 19977
General Museum
Coll: furniture; decorative arts; historic
house (1753)

16405
The Lindens
Route 65, Smyrna, DE 19977
General Museum
Coll: furniture; decorative arts; historic
mill (1705)

Snohomish WA

16406
Blackman Museum
118 Av B, Snohomish, WA 98290
General Museum - 1969
Coll: local logging; late furniture and
furnishings; historic house - library

Snyder TX

16407
Diamond M Foundation Museum
Diamond M Building, 909 25th St, POB
1149, Snyder, TX 79549
Fine Arts Museum - 1950
Coll: paintings; original Currier and
Ives lithographs; bronzes

16408
Scurry County Museum
Western Texas College, POB 696,
Snyder, TX 79549
History/Public Affairs Museum - 1970
Coll: local history; artifacts; geology -
library; auditorium

Solomons MD

16409
Calvert Marine Museum
Solomons, MD 20688
General Museum - 1969
Coll: maritime history; small craft;
estuarine biological specimens; naval
paintings

Somers NY

16410
Somers Historical Society
Elephant Hotel, Somers, NY 10589
General Museum - 1956
Coll: furniture, artifacts and
manuscripts relating to local history;
couriers, posters, lithographs,
manuscripts, route books and other
memorabilia of a pioneer circus;
Mount Zion Methodist Church and
cemetary (1794) - library

Somers Point NJ

16411
Atlantic County Historical Society
907 Shore Rd, Somers Point, NJ 08244
General Museum - 1914
Indian artifacts; ship models; seafaring
equipment; Victorian furniture, clothing
and artifacts; Somers Mansion
(1720-1730); manuscript collections -
Victorian museum; lecture hall

16412
Somers Mansion
Mays Landing Rd at Somers Point,
Somers Point, NJ 08244
Historic Site - Dorothy Wertley
furnishings

Somerset PA

16413
**Historical and Genealogical Society
of Somerset County**
POB 533, Somerset, PA 15501
General Museum - 1959
Coll: agriculture; archaeology;
genealogy; archives; historic buildings
- library; reading room

16414
Somerset Historical Center
R.D. 2, Somerset, PA 15501
General Museum - 1969
Coll: agriculture; decorative arts;
history; Indian artifacts; historic
buildings - library

Somerville NJ

16415
Old Dutch Parsonage
38 Washington Place, Somerville, NJ
08876
Historic Site
Dutch furnishings

16416
Wallace House
38 Washington Place, Somerville, NJ
08876
Historic Site
Coll: original architectural features;
kitchen and slave quarters;
Revolutionary War relics; furnishings;
glass

South Bend IN

16417
The Art Center
120 S St. Joseph St, South Bend, IN
46601
Fine Arts Museum - 1947
Coll: paintings; prints; ceramics -
library; reading room; classrooms;
photography lab

16418
Discovery Hall Museum
Century Center, 120 S St and Joseph
St, South Bend, IN 46601
General Museum - 1977
Coll: historic vehicle collection of
carriages, wagons, and automobiles;
manufactured products of area

16419
**The Northern Indiana Historical
Society**
112 S Lafayette Blvd, South Bend, IN
46601
General Museum - 1900
Coll: pioneer items; tools; china;
pottery; glass; local historical artifacts;
military artifacts; photo collection -
library; reading room

South Bend WA

16420
Pacific County Historical Society
POB P, South Bend, WA 98586
General Museum - 1970
Coll: Indian artifacts and relics;
records; documents; photographs;
relics of pioneers - library

South Bowers DE

16421
Island Field Museum
South Bowers, DE
Archeology Museum
Coll: archeological remains;
prehistoric Indian artifacts; site of
prehistoric Indian cemetery

South Carver MA

16422
Edaville Railroad Museum
Rochester Rd, POB 7, South Carver,
MA 02366
History/Public Affairs Museum - 1946
Coll: transportation; railroad gear; fire
engines; antique guns; industry

South Carver MA MA

16423
The National Fire Museum
Edaville R.R., South Carver MA 02366,
21 Endicott St, Newton Highlands, MA
02161
History/Public Affairs Museum - 1955
Coll: fire helmets; safety;
transportation; fire department badges

South Effingham NH

16424
Effingham Historical Society
POB 33, South Effingham, NH 03882
General Museum - 1951
Coll: tools; tinware; hand weaving
rools including full size loom - library

South Hadley MA

16425
Mount Holyoke College Art Museum
South Hadley, MA 01075
Fine Arts Museum - 1875
Coll: medieval art; Renaissance, Asian
and American art; prints; drawings -
library

South Orange NJ

16426
Seton Hall University Museum
S Orange Av, South Orange, NJ 07079
General Museum - 1960
Coll: archaeology; graphics; Eastern
Woodland Indian artifacts - library

South St. Paul MN

16427
Dakota County Historical Museum
130 3rd Ave N, South St. Paul, MN
55075
General Museum - 1957
Coll: trades and industry items;
railroading - library; reading room

Southampton NY

16428
The Parrish Art Museum
25 Job's Lane, Southampton, NY 11968
Fine Arts Museum - 1898
Coll: Italian Renaissance and 19th and
early 20th century American Paintings;
William Merritt Chase Collection and
Archive; graphics; sculpture; Japanese
stencils and woodblock prints;
Chinese ceramics; D. Doughty
porcelains; personal library of Aline B.
Saarinen - library; auditorium;
arboretum

16429
Southampton Historical Museum
Meeting House Lane, Southampton,
NY 11968
General Museum - 1898
Coll: costumes; whaling exhibit;
country store, one-room schoolhouse,
carpenter shop; arts and crafts, china,
silver, glass; Halsey Homestead
(1648); Capt. Rogers Homestead
(1840) - library

Southern Pines NC

16430
**Weymouth Woods-Sandhills Nature
Preserve Museum**
1386 Southern Pines, Southern Pines,
NC 28387
Natural History Museum - 1968
Coll: Indian artifacts; turpentine
industry artifacts; herbarium; wildlife
refuge and bird sanctuary; study
specimens - library; nature center;
field search station; auditorium

Southold NY

16431
Southold Historical Society and Museum
Main Rd and Maple Lane, Southold, NY 11971
General Museum - 1960
Coll: decorative arts; agriculture; paintings; costumes; glass; Hallock Currie-Bell House (1899); Pine Neck barn (1750); Thomas Moore House (1790); Irving Downs Carriage House (1845); Henry Cleveland blacksmith shop (1845); Horton's Point Lighthouse (1857) and Marine Museum - library

Southport NC

16432
Brunswick Town State Historic Site
POB 356, Southport, NC 28461
Historic Site - 1958
Coll: 18th century English and Civil War artifacts; excavated foundations of port town (1726-1776) - nature trail

Spalding ID

16433
Nez Perce National Historical Park
POB 93, Spalding, ID 83551
Historic Site - 1965
Coll: Nez Perce ethnological items; prehistoric lithics; Western Americana; rural early 20th century general store products; local pioneer and historical documents and memorabilia; photos of Nez Perce Indians and local region - library; reading room

Spartanburg SC

16434
Spartanburg County Regional Museum
501 Otis Blvd, Spartanburg, SC 29302
General Museum - 1961
Coll: Indian artifacts; dolls; quilts; General Daniel Morgan's rifle; historic house (1765)

Spencer IA

16435
Clay County Museum and Parker Historical Society of Clay County
300 E 3rd St, Spencer, IA 51301
General Museum - 1960
Coll: furniture; agriculture; decorative arts

Spilville IA

16436
Bily Clock Exhibit
Spilville, IA 52168
Decorative Arts Museum - 1965
Coll: hand carved clocks; historic house, former home of composer Antonín Dvořák (1865)

Spokane WA

16437
Eastern Washington State Historical Society, Cheney Cowles Memorial Museum
2316 First Av, Spokane, WA 99204
General Museum - 1916
Coll: Indian and pioneer artifacts; frontier firearms; mineralogy; natural history; costumes; ancient coins; historic house - library; archives; auditorium

16438
Fort Wright College Historical Museum
4000 Randolph Rd, Spokane, WA 99204
General Museum - 1964
Coll: furnishings from 1899-1958; military artifacts; glass; clothing; dolls; historic house

16439
Spokane Valley Pioneer Museum, Inc.
E 10303 Sprague, Spokane, WA 99206
General Museum - 1965
Coll: pioneer relics; photographs of Spokane Valley and surrounding areas; local history - library

Spotsylvania County VA

16440
Spotsylvania Historical Association, Inc.
POB 64, Spotsylvania County, VA 22553
History/Public Affairs Museum - 1962
Coll: Indian relics; Early Colonial artifacts; china; tools; pottery; genealogy - library

Spring Place GA

16441
Vann House
U.S. Highway 76, Spring Place, GA 30705
General Museum - 1952
Coll: furniture; personal items

Springdale UT

16442
Zion National Park Museum
Park Headquaters, Springdale, UT 84767
Science/Tech Museum - 1919
Coll: herbarium; zoology; entomology; geology - library

Springfield IL

16443
Illinois State Museum
Corner Spring and Edwards Sts, Springfield, IL 62706
General Museum - 1877
Coll: natural history; anthropology; archeology; glass collection; art and art history in Illinois - library; studies center

16444
Springfield Art Association
Edwards Place, 700 N Fourth St, Springfield, IL 62702
Decorative Arts Museum - 1913
Coll: 19th-20th century paintings; Oriental ceramics, bronzes, and jewelry; eight rooms of 17th-18th century and early American furniture - classrooms

16445
Vachel Lindsay Association
603 S Fifth St, Springfield, IL 62704
Historic Site - 1946
Coll: historic house, home of the poet Vachel Lindsay; drawings; letters and manuscripts; recordings of the poet - library

Springfield MA

16446
George Walter Vincent Smith Art Museum
222 State St, Springfield, MA 01103
Decorative Arts Museum - 1889
Coll: Asiatic decorative arts; Islamic rugs; American and European 19th century paintings and sculpture - library; classrooms

16447
Museum of Fine Arts
49 Chestnut St, Springfield, MA 01103
Fine Arts Museum - 1933
Coll: Oriental art; European and American graphics; painting; sculpture; decorative art - library; auditorium

16448
Springfield Science Museum
236 State St, Springfield, MA 01103
Science/Tech Museum - 1859
Coll: anthropology; archaeology; astronomy; botany; entomology; enthnology; herpetology; ichthyology; lithology; malacology; mammalogy; mineralogy; ornithology; paleontology

Springfield MO

16449
Springfield Art Museum
1111 E Brookside Dr, Springfield, MO 65807
Fine Arts Museum - 1946
Coll: American and European painting, sculpture, drawing, photography, prints and decorative art of 18th, 19th and 20th centuries - library; reading room; auditorium; classrooms

Springfield NJ

16450
Springfield Historical Society
126 Morris Av, Springfield, NJ 07081
General Museum - 1954
Coll: local history items; drawings; prints; decorative arts; costumes; textiles; coins; The Cannon Ball House (1741) - library

Springfield OH

16451
Clark County Historical Society
300 W Main St, Springfield, OH 45504
General Museum - 1897
Coll: newspaper files and documents; antique china, pewter and furniture; pioneer utensils; early tools and farm equipment - library; reading room

Springfield VT

16452
Springfield Art and Historical Society
Elm Hill, Springfield, VT 05156
Fine Arts Museum - 1956
Coll: Richard Lee pewter; pottery; paintings; dolls; toys; marble - library; classrooms

Springs PA

16453
Springs Historical Society
Springs, PA 15562
General Museum - 1957
Coll: fossils; flaming rocks; pioneer tools; furniture - library; reading room

Springville NY

16454
Concord Historical Society, Warner Museum
98 E. Main St, 13153 Mortons Corners Rd, Springville, NY 14141
General Museum - 1953
carpenter tools; pictures; 'Pop' Warner's Indian artifact collection; archives - reading room

Springville UT

16455
Springville Museum of Art
126 E 400 S, Springville, UT 84663
Fine Arts Museum - 1903
Coll: works of early 20th century American art

Spruce Pine NC

16456
Museum of North Carolina Minerals
Blue Ridge Parkway, Rt. 1 POB 798, Spruce Pine NC 28777, Blue Ridge Parkway, POB 9098, Ashville, NC 28805
Natural History Museum - 1955
geology; minerals; industry

Saint. Augustine FL

16457
Lightner Museum
City Hall-Museum Complex King St, Saint. Augustine, FL 32084
History/Public Affairs Museum - 1948
Coll: 19th century decorative arts; Tiffany glass; dolls and toys; 19th century mechanical musical instruments; Indian artifacts; shells and fossils

16458
Oldest House and Tovar House
14 St. Francis St, Saint. Augustine, FL 32084
General Museum - 1883
Coll: archeology; archives; historical items - library

St. Helens OR

16459
Columbia County Historical Museum
Old Court House Museum, St. Helens, OR 97051
General Museum - 1972
Coll: furniture; archives; artifacts - library; reading room

St. Matthews SC

16460
Calhoun County Museum
303 Butler St, St. Matthews, SC 29135
General Museum - 1954
Coll: archives; costumes; agriculture; archaeology; history; medical; preservation project - library

St. Paul OR

16461
Champoeg State Park Visitor Center
7679 Champoeg Rd NE, St. Paul, OR 97137
General Museum - 1901
Coll: tools; furniture; implements; transportation; Indian and pioneer artifacts; natural history

Stamford CT

16462
Stamford Historical Society, Inc.
713 Bedford St, Stamford, CT 06901
General Museum - 1901
Coll: 17th and 18th century Americana;
farm implements; needlework and
quilts; dolls; household equipment;
early pottery and craft tools; archives
- library

16463
**Stamford Museum and Nature
Center**
39 Scofieldtown Rd, Stamford, CT
06903
Science/Tech Museum - 1936
Coll: agriculture; paintings; sculpture;
astronomy; natural history; Indian
artifacts - auditorium; trails;
classrooms; studio; planetarium;
observatory

Stanfield NC

16464
Reed Gold Mine
Reed Mine Rd, Rte 2, Stanfield, NC
28163
Historic Site - 1971
Coll: underground workings; tools;
first authenticated discovery of gold in
the United States (1799) - trails

Stanford CA

16465
**Stanford University Museum and Art
Gallery**
Museum Way, Stanford, CA 94305
Fine Arts Museum - 1891
Coll: paintings; sculpture (Rodin);
graphics; decorative arts; archeology

Stanford MT

16466
Judith Basin Museum
Stanford, MT 59479
General Museum - 1966
Coll: Indian artifacts; antiques; 2,500
salt & pepper shakers; 50,000 buttons

Stanton DE

16467
Hale-Byrnes House
Route 7 at Route 4, Stanton, DE 19804
Historic Site
Coll: furnishings; decorative arts;
historic building where General
Washington and Lafayette met for war
council (1750)

Stanton TX

16468
Martin County Historical Museum
Convent and Broadway Sts, POB 612,
Stanton, TX 79782
History/Public Affairs Museum - 1969
Coll: local history; early farming and
ranching - library

State University AR

16469
**Arkansas State University Art
Gallery**
POB 846, State University, AR 72467
Fine Arts Museum - 1967
Coll: contemporary and historical
prints, drawings, paintings and
sculpture - auditorium; classrooms

Staten Island NY

16470
Conference House Association, Inc.
Conference House Park, Staten Island,
NY 10307
Historic Site - 1927
18th century furnishings; Conference
House, or Billopp House (1680)

16471
**Jacques Marchais Center of Tibetan
Arts**
338 Lighthouse Av, Staten Island, NY
10306
Fine Arts Museum - 1946
Coll: Tibetan and Buddhist art - library;
reading room; gardens

16472
**Museum of Archaeology at Staten
Island**
631 Howard Av, Staten Island, NY
10301
Archeology Museum - 1975
Coll: New World, pre-Columbian,
Roman, African, Egyptian, Ancient
Near Eastern, Greek and Far Eastern
antiquities - library

16473
Staten Island Children's Museum
15 Beach St, Staten Island, NY 10304
Junior Museum - 1974
Coll: arts and sciences

16474
Staten Island Historical Society
441 Clarke Av, Staten Island, NY
10306
General Museum - 1856
Coll: furniture; china; glass; costumes;
military; tools; archives; Decker Farm
(1810); Billou-Stillwell-Perine House
(1662) - library; auditorium

16475
**Staten Islands Institute of Arts and
Sciences**
75 Stuyvesant Place, Staten Island, NY
10301
General Museum - 1881
Coll: science and ecology exhibits;
plants, animals, insects typical of
Staten Island; herpetology; geology;
archaeology; herbarium; paintings;
graphics; decorative arts; arts; marine
exhibits - library; nature center;
auditorium; classrooms

Staunton VA

16476
**Woodrow Wilson Birthplace
Foundation, Inc.**
20 N Coalter St, Staunton, VA 24401
Historic Site - 1938
Former Presbyterian Manse and
birthplace of Woodrow Wilson, with
original furnishings, musical
instruments and manuscripts - library;
film theater

Steamboat Springs CO

16477
Tread of Pioneers
505 Oak St, Steamboat Springs, CO
80477
General Museum - 1959
Coll: Indian artifacts; mining; skiing

Steilacoom WA

16478
**Steilacoom Historical Museum
Association**
POB 16, Steilacoom, WA 98388
General Museum - 1970
Pioneer memorabilia associated with
the town of Steilacoom, the first
incorporated town in the State of
Washington; Indian artifacts - library

Stephenville TX

16479
**Stephenville Historical House
Museum**
525 E Washington, Stephenville, TX
76401
General Museum
Coll: pressed glass; rocks; Indian
arrowheads; local history -
classrooms

Sterling CO

16480
Overland Trail Museum
Junction I-76 and Hwy 6 East, Sterling
CO, Centenial Sq, Sterling, CO 80751
General Museum - 1936
Coll: Indian artifacts; local natural
history; mammal and marine fossils;
frontier rifles and shot guns; cattle
branding irons; tools; ranch and farm
equipment and furnishings; musical
instruments; dolls

Stevens Point WI

16481
The Museum of Natural History
University of Wisconsin
Stevens Point, WI 54481
Natural History Museum - 1966
Coll: marine and fresh water fish;
mammals; birds; Schoenebeck egg
collection; reptiles and amphibians;
Indian relics; fossils; insects and
invertebrates; herbarium

Stillwater MN

16482
**Washington County Historical
Museum**
602 N Main St, Stillwater, MN 55083
General Museum - 1941
Coll: costumes; Indian artifacts;
military - library

Stillwater NY

16483
Saratoga National Historical Park
POB 113-C, Stillwater, NY 12170
General Museum - 1938
Coll: items related to military history
and the Burgoyne Campaign - library;
auditorium; theater

Stillwater OK

16484
Gardiner Art Gallery Oklahoma State
University
Stillwater, OK 74074
Fine Arts Museum - 1970
Coll: graphics

16485
**Oklahoma State University Museum
of Natural and Cultural History**
Oklahoma State University, Stillwater,
OK 74074
Natural History Museum - 1966
Coll: mammals; birds; amphibians;
reptiles; fish; insects; plants; rocks and
minerals; Western pioneer artifacts;
period clothing; Kodachrome
collections: African art, flora, fauna -
laboratory; conference room

Stockbridge MA

16486
Chesterwood
POB 24, Stockbridge, MA 01262
Fine Arts Museum - 1955
Coll: works of Daniel Chester French;
18th and 19th century American
furniture and furnishings - library;
auditorium

Stockton CA

16487
**Holt-Atherton Pacific Center for
Western Studies** University of the
Pacific
Stockton, CA 95204
History/Public Affairs Museum - 1947
Coll: John Muir papers; mission and
Gold Rush country photographs;
maps; local history periodical
collection; Merner collection of 3,000
Southwestern Indian artifacts;
McLeod collection of 13,000 West
Coast Indian artifacts - library

16488
**Pioneer Museum and Haggin
Galleries**
1201 N Pershing Av, Stockton, CA
95203
History/Public Affairs Museum - 1928
Coll: 19th century French and
American paintings; American,
European, and Oriental decorative
arts; folk art; historical artifacts -
library; auditorium

Stone Mountain GA

16489
Stone Mountain Park
POB 778, Stone Mountain, GA 30086
General Museum - 1958
Coll: Indian artifacts; Civil War items;
early automobiles; musical
instruments; furniture; historic houses
- garden; nature trails; arboretum

Stonington CT

16490
Stonington Historical Society
POB 103, Stonington, CT 06378
General Museum - 1927
Coll: historical items; paintings;
archives; furniture; silver and pewter;
domestic utensils - library; reading
room

Stony Brook NY

16491
**Museum of Long Island Natural
Sciences** State University of New
York at Stony Brook
Earth & Space Sciences Bldg, Stony
Brook, NY 11794
Science/Tech Museum - 1973
Coll: modern and fossil marine
invertebrates, especially Mollusca;
Brachiopoda; insects and their host
plants; general herbarium; minerals
and fossils - classrooms

16492
The Museums at Stony Brook
Stony Brook, NY 11790
General Museum - 1935
Coll: 19th century American Art including the William Sidney Mount Collection of paintings, drawings, memorabilia; carriages and carriage accoutrements; costumes and accessories; dolls; toys; wildfowling decoys; decorative arts; miniature rooms; early photographs; local archives; Story Brook Grist Mill, barn, Schoolhouse (18th and 19th centuries) - library; nature walk; craft school; classrooms

Stony Point NY

16493
Stony Point Battlefield State Historic Site
U.S. 9W, POB 182, Stony Point, NY 10980
Historic Site - 1897
Revolutionary War equipment and artifacts; archaeological materials

Storrs CT

16494
Mansfield Historical Society Museum
Rte 32 and S. Eagleville Rd, POB 145, Storrs, CT 06268
General Museum - 1961
Coll: furniture; household equipment; tools; farm equipment; industrial exhibits; textiles; archives; costumes - library

16495
The William Benton Museum of Art
University of Connecticut
Storrs, CT 06268
Fine Arts Museum - 1966
Coll: paintings; the Louise Crombie Beach collection; the Walter Landauer collection of prints and drawings by Kaethe Kollwitz

Strasburg PA

16496
Eagle Americana Shop and Gun Museum
R.D. 1, Strasburg, PA 17579
General Museum - 1965
Coll: rifles history; military; Indian artifacts; archaeology; medical; glass; costumes; archives - library; children's museum

16497
Railroad Museum of Pennsylvania
POB 15, Strasburg, PA 17579
Science/Tech Museum - 1964
Coll: transportation; railroad history; locomotives; railroad cars; railroad models; tools; lamps - library

16498
Toy Train Museum of the Train Collector's Association
Paradise Lane, POB 248, Strasburg, PA 17579
History/Public Affairs Museum - 1954
Coll: toy trains, primarily 'Tin Plate' dating back to the 1840's; model trains and related paraphernalia and accessories - library

Stratford CT

16499
Stratford Historical Society
967 Academy Hill, Stratford, CT 06497
General Museum - 1925
Coll: archives; decorative arts; costumes; glass, china, and silver; antique furniture; toys; textiles - library

Stratford VA

16500
Stratford Hall, Robert E. Lee Memorial Association, Inc.
Stratford, VA 22558
General Museum - 1929
Coll: 18th century furnishings; glass and china; textiles - library

Stroudsburg PA

16501
Monroe City County Historical Society
9th and Main Sts, Stroudsburg, PA 18360
General Museum - 1921
Coll: local history; furniture; costumes; Indian artifacts; Bell Schoolhouse (1871) - library; reading room

Strubridge MA

16502
Strubridge Auto Museum
Rte 20, Strubridge, MA 01566
Science/Tech Museum - 1960
Coll: antique automobiles including steam, gas and electric models - library

Stuart FL

16503
Elliott Museum State Historic Memorial
825 NE Ocean Blvd, Stuart, FL 33494
General Museum - 1961
Coll: paintings; sculpture; graphics; circus; costumes; natural history; transportation

16504
Gilbert's Bar House of Refuge
301 SE McArthur Blvd, Stuart, FL 33494
General Museum - 1956
Coll: archives; marine artifacts; historic house

Sturbridge MA

16505
Old Sturbridge Village
Sturbridge, MA 01566
Open Air Museum - 1938
Coll: farm and domestic tools and utensils; scientific and medical equipment; furniture and furnishings; vehicles - library; classrooms

Sturgeon Bay WI

16506
Door County Maritime Museum Inc.
6427 Green Bay Rd, Sturgeon Bay, WI 54235
Science/Tech Museum - 1969
Coll: ships; ship building pictures; marine artifacts and books

Sturgis SD

16507
Old Fort Meade Museum and Historic Research Association
1113 Poisley Terrace, Sturgis, SD 57785 .
History/Public Affairs Museum - 1964
Coll: chronological story of Old Fort Meade's 66 years as a military installation (1878-1964)

Stuttgart AR

16508
Arkansas County Agricultural Museum
921 E. Fourth St, Stuttgart, AR 72160
Agriculture Museum - 1972
Coll: farming equipment used in the development of the hay and rice industries; furnishings in the replica of a prairie home; wildlife of the swamp, prairie, and wooded areas - library

Suisun City CA

16509
California Railway Museum
Hwy 12, Star Route 283, POB 150, Suisun City, CA 94585
Science/Tech Museum - 1961
Coll: vintage railway equipment; freight and work cars; Pullman cars; steam locomotives; cable car - library

Sullivan's Island SC

16510
Fort Sumter National Monument
Middle St, POB R., Sullivan's Island, SC 29482
History/Public Affairs Museum - 1948
Coll: artifacts and manuscripts, connected with Fort Sumter and Fort Moultrie; military uniforms; military equipment - library; auditorium

Sulphur OK

16511
Travertine Nature Center, Chicksaw National Recreation Area
POB 201, Sulphur, OK 73086
Natural History Museum - 1969
Coll: ecology; local history; live snakes, turtles, frogs, insects, fish, plants - library; reading room; auditorium

Sumter SC

16512
Museum-Archives of the Sumter County Historical Society, Inc.
122 N. Washington St, Sumter, SC 29150
General Museum - 1950
Coll: complete South Carolina Census Rolls; paintings; furniture; dolls; toys; farm and household equipment; historic house (1845) - library

16513
Sumter Gallery of Art
421 N. Main St, Sumter, SC 29150
Fine Arts Museum - 1970
Coll: historic house (pre-1850); small collection of works by Elizabeth White - classrooms

Sunbury PA

16514
Fort Augusta
1150 N Front St, Sunbury, PA 17801
Historic Site - 1920
military and Indina artifacts; Frontier outpost (1756-57); Hunter Mansion (1852)

Sunnyvale CA

16515
Sunnyvale Historical Museum
POB 61301, Sunnyvale, CA 94088
General Museum - 1973
Coll: personal items of first city clerk; photographs; old newspapers, oral history tapes, furnishings - library

Sunset TX

16516
Sunset Trading Post - Old West Museum
Rte 1, Sunset, TX 76270
General Museum - 1956
Indian artifacts; agriculture; anthropology - library

Superior AZ

16517
Boyce Thompson Southwestern Arboretum
U.S. Hwy 60, POB AB, Superior, AZ 85273
Natural History Museum - 1924
Coll: xerophytes; botany; geology; zoology; historic house - library; botanical garden; research station

Superior WI

16518
Douglas County Historical Museum
906 E 2nd St, Superior, WI 54880
General Museum - 1931
Coll: marine exhibits; Indian ethnology; dolls; toys; David F. Barry collection of Sioux Indian portraits; Thomas Catlin lithographs of Plaines Indians; logging; musical instruments; furniture; china; glass; silver - library

Susanville CA

16519
Lassen County Historical Society Museum
N. Weatherlow Sts, POB 321, Susanville, CA 96130
General Museum - 1959
Coll: historical items related to Lassen County - stamp mill

Sussex NJ

16520
Space Farms Zoological Park and Museum
Beemerville Rd, Sussex, NJ 07461
General Museum - 1927
Coll: early American tools; household equipment; clocks; phonographs; dolls; guns; autos; wagons; sleighs; farm machinery; Indian artifacts; antiques; mounted wildlife specimens; musical instruments - Zoo

Swampscott MA

16521
Atlantic 1
Burrill St, POB 224, Swampscott, MA 01907
History/Public Affairs Museum - 1956
Coll: antique fire engine and cannon

Sweetwater TX

16522
City County Pioneer Museum
610 E Third, Sweetwater, TX 79556
General Museum - 1968
Coll: furniture; artifacts; ranch and
farm equipment

Syosset NY

16523
Nassau County Museum
Muttontown Rd, Syosset, NY 11791
General Museum - 1956
Coll: general historical collections of
American material before 1870;
archaeological, geological and natural
history specimens of local area; Old
Bethpage Village, farm community of
pre-Civil War era - library; reading
room; nature center; auditorium

Syracuse NY

16524
Canal Museum
Weighclock Bldg, Erie Blvd, E.,
Syracuse, NY 13202
Science/Tech Museum - 1962
Coll: models, artifacts, pictures,
manuscripts, maps, engineering
records, account volumes, finance
records, operational records, prints,
photos and paintings of the canal era -
library; towpath trail; orientation center

16525
**Daniel Parrish Witter Agricultural
Museum**
New York State Fair Grounds,
Syracuse, NY 13209
Agriculture Museum - 1924
Coll: tools; artifacts; prints and
photographs; books and magazines;
fabrics; furniture; log cabin (1809);
print shop (1880); blacksmith shop
(1888) - library; classrooms

16526
**Everson Museum of Art of Syracuse
and Onondaga County**
401 Harrison St, Syracuse, NY 13202
Fine Arts Museum - 1896
Coll: 18th - 20th century American and
English paintings; Oriental Art;
sculpture, drawing and graphics; 20th
century ceramics; English pottery and
porcelains; pre-Columbian, American
Indian and African Collections;
Wampler Collection; Benjamin Lake
Collection - library; auditorium;
classrooms

16527
Joe & Emily Lowe Art Gallery
Syracuse University
Sims Hall, Syracuse, NY 13210
Fine Arts Museum - 1840
Coll: 19th and 20th century American
painting; prints including Rembrandt,
Dürer, Florsheim, Castellon;
decorative arts; glass; Indian and
African sculpture and textiles - library

16528
Onondaga Historical Association
311 Montgomery St, Syracuse, NY
13202
General Museum - 1862
Coll: objects and reference material
relating to local history; Iroquois Indian
artifacts; New York State canal
history; works by local artists;
archaeology; ethnology; graphics;
transportation - library

Table Rock NE

16529
**Table Rock Historical Society and
Museums**
Table Rock, NE 68447
General Museum - 1965
Coll: furnishings; antiques; paintings;
tools; automobiles

Tacoma WA

16530
**Puget Sound Museum of Natural
History**
University of Puget Sound, Tacoma,
WA 98416
Natural History Museum - 1926
Coll: Northwest flora and fauna;
mammal skins and skulls; bird skins
and sets of bird eggs; reptiles and
amphibians; plants on herbarium
sheets - library

16531
Tacoma Art Museum
12th and Pacific Av, Tacoma, WA
98402
Fine Arts Museum - 1890
Coll: Japanese woodcuts; major
works of Morris Graves, Mark Tobey,
Andrew Wyeth, Motherwell,
Rauschenberg, Lichtenstein;
contemporary American glass and
ceramics - library; auditorium

16532
Washington State Historical Society
315 N Stadium Way, Tacoma, WA
98403
General Museum - 1891
Coll: Pacific Northwest history;
artifacts; rare books, manuscripts and
maps; pioneer and Indian exhibits;
historic house - library; auditorium

Tahlequa OK

16533
**Cherokee National Historical
Society, Inc.**
POB 515, Tahlequa, OK 74464
General Museum - 1963
Coll: 17th century Indian Village;
Cherokee history, culture, heritage,
library, and archives; Cherokee Hall of
Fame - library; outdoor theater

16534
Murrell Home
Rte 5, POB 212, Rte 2, POB 45,
Tahlequa, OK 74464
Historic Site - 1948
Coll: history; Indian artifacts; archives;
costumes; Murrell Home (1844) -
library; nature trail; art gallery

Talkeetna AK

16535
**Talkeetna Historical Society &
Museum**
POB 76, Talkeetna, AK 99676
General Museum - 1972
Coll: old trading post materials and
equipment; mining equipment; papers
and photographs; Alaskan art -
library; auditorium; reading room

Tallahassee FL

16536
Florida State University Art Gallery
Fine Arts Building, Tallahassee, FL
32306
Fine Arts Museum - 1950
Coll: Dutch paintings; Cypriote
sculpture and vases; graphics -
lecture room; sculpture garden

16537
Lemoyne Art Foundation, Inc.
125 N Gadsden, Tallahassee, FL 32301
Fine Arts Museum - 1964
Coll: contemporary art; sculpture -
classrooms; sculpture garden

16538
Museum of Florida History
R.A. Gray Bldg, Tallahassee, FL 32301
History/Public Affairs Museum - 1967
Coll: archeological, historical, and
contemporary material on settlement
of Florida; Spanish New World
numismatics; Spanish trade and
maritime cultural materials

16539
Tallahassee Junior Museum
3945 Museum Dr, Tallahassee, FL
32304
Junior Museum - 1962
Coll: reproduction of pre-Columbian
Indian artifacts; costumes; agricultural
implements; native animals and
reptiles; historic houses - library;
nature/conservation center;
classrooms

Tampa FL

16540
Henry B. Plant Museum of Tampa
401 W Kennedy Blvd, Tampa, FL
33606
Decorative Arts Museum - 1933
Coll: furnishings; prints; paintings;
porcelains; bronzes; early Chinese
earthenware

16541
**Hillsborough County Historical
Commission Museum**
County Court House, Tampa, FL 33602
General Museum - 1949
Coll: local memorabilia; artifacts from
Spanish-American War; southern state
histories - library; reading room

16542
**Museum of Science and Industry of
Tampa/Hillsborough County**
4801 E Fowler Av, Tampa FL 33617,
POB 8311, Tampa, FL 33674
Science/Tech Museum - 1962
Coll: science; natural history; industry;
history of man - library; reading room;
auditorium; classroom

16543
Tampa Museum
600 Doyle Carlton Dr, Tampa, FL
33602
Fine Arts Museum - 1923
Coll: 20th century paintings and prints;
C. Paul Jennewein collection of
sculpture; pre-Columbian art - library;
reading room

16544
University Galleries
4202 E Fowler Av, Tampa, FL 33620
Fine Arts Museum - 1968
Coll: contemporary graphics;
paintings; photography; folk and ethnic
arts; sculpture; decorative arts;
archeology - library

Taos NM

16545
The Gaspard House
Ratone Hwy, POB 2625, Taos, NM
87571
Fine Arts Museum - 1978
Coll: paintings of Leon Gaspard;
copper, brass, textiles, furniture and
Oriental costumes; fine art and folk art
- library

16546
Governor Bent Museum
Bent St, Taos, NM 87571
Historic Site - Otto T. Noeding
Coll: Indian artifacts; Bent family
possessions; American antiques;
Eskimo collection; guns; spinning
wheels; paintings; photographs;
anthropology; mineralogy;
archaeology; graphics

16547
**The Harwood Foundation of the
University of New Mexico**
25 Le Doux St, Taos, NM 87571
Fine Arts Museum - 1923
Coll: Taos artists in all media from
1898 to the present; Santos, tin works,
furniture of Hispanic culture; Pueblo
and Rio Grande rugs; Native American
artifacts; Persian miniature - library;
auditorium

16548
Kit Carson Memorial Foundation, Inc.
Old Kit Carson Rd, Taos, NM 87571
General Museum - 1949
Coll: pre-historic Indian culture ;
Spanish colonial culture; fur-trading;
furnishings; archives; photographs;
Penitente Chapel; Historic Houses
(1800-1860); Simeon Turley Trade
Post; Mill and Distillery Site (1830) -
library

16549
**Millicent A. Rogers Memorial
Museum**
POB A, Taos, NM 87571
Fine Arts Museum - 1956
Coll: pre-historic and historic
American Indian arts; Spanish Colonial
art; Penitente religious artifacts -
library

16550
**Stables Gallery of the Taos Art
Association**
POB 198, Taos, NM 87571
Fine Arts Museum - 1952
Coll: works of local artists; Manby-
Thorne House (1898)

Tappan NY

16551
Tappantown Historical Society
POB 71, Tappan, NY 10983
General Museum - 1965
Coll: American architecture,
architectural heritage, preservation
project; maps, plans, photographs;
early painting of Major Andre; Tappan
Memorial Park - library

Tarrytown NY

16552
**The Historical Society of the
Tarrytowns, Inc.**
1 Grove St, Tarrytown, NY 10591
History/Public Affairs Museum - 1889
Coll: Indian artifacts; early Dutch
history of the region; local
memorabilia; material on American
Revolution, capture of Major John
Andre at Tarrytown, Washington Irving
and other; material from World War I
and II; paintings; costumes;
manuscripts; art collection of Ezra
Aimes, John Mare, Emily N. Hatch,
DeWitt C. Hay, Edgar Mayhew Bacon;
stones and minerals; firearms; jewelry;
toys - library; reading room

16553
Lyndhurst
635 S. Broadway, Tarrytown, NY
10591
Historic Site - 1964
Coll: Gothic revival residence and
furniture designed by A.J. Davis ; 19th
century paintings; sculpture; silver;
glass; textiles; 19th and 20th century
furnishings; period vehicles - coach
house; National Trust Restoration
Workshop; parkgrounds

Taunton MA

16554
Old Colony Historical Society
66 Church Green, Taunton, MA 02780
History/Public Affairs Museum - 1853
Coll: weapons; domestic tools,
utensils, and furnishings from the
1800's - library

Taylorsville MS

16555
Watkins Museum
POB 68, Taylorsville, MS 39168
History/Public Affairs Museum - 1968
Coll: 1837 hand printing press;
typewriter; early medical and farm
equipment - library

Teague TX

16556
**Burlington-Rock Island Railroad
Museum**
108 S 9th Av, Teague, TX 75860
History/Public Affairs Museum - 1969
Coll: railroad memorabilia; local
history; dishes and cooking utensils

Tecumseh NE

16557
**Johnson County Historical Society
Inc.**
Third and Lincoln Sts, Tecumseh, NE
68450
History/Public Affairs Museum - 1962
Coll: Indian artifacts; 2,000 wooden
household articles; linens; silver;
china; glass; toys; genealogy - library

Tekamah NE

16558
Burt County Museum
Tekamah, NE 68061
General Museum - 1967
Coll: agriculture; clothing; furniture

Telluride CO

16559
San Miguel Historical Society
Telluride, CO 81435
General Museum - 1964
Coll: anthropology; costumes;
geology; glass; Indian artifacts;
mineralogy; mining; old miners'
hospital building

Tempe AZ

16560
Center for Meteorite Studies
Arizona State University, Tempe, AZ
85281
Natural History Museum - 1961
Coll: representatives of individual
meteorite falls and finds - library;
laboratory

16561
University Art Collections Arizona
State University
Mathews Center, Tempe, AZ 85281
Fine Arts Museum - 1950
Coll: Oliver B. James collection of
American art 18th-20th centuries;
collection of European 16th-20th
century painting and sculpture;
American and European print
collection, 15th century to present;
crafts: Joseph & Astrid Thomas
collection of 19th century American
crockery; Lenore & Lewis Ruskin
collection of European painting;
contemporary ceramics; Latin
American art - library; reading room;
seminar rooms

Temple TX

16562
Railroad and Pioneer Museum
710 Jack Baskin St, POB 5126,
Temple, TX 76501
History/Public Affairs Museum - 1966
Coll: Railroad and pioneer items; local
history; genealogy - library; archives

16563
**Slavonic Benevolent Order of the
State of Texas**
520 N Main, POB 100, Temple, TX
76501
History/Public Affairs Museum - 1971
Coll: artifacts and articles of early
Texas settlers; folk history - library

Terra Alta WV

16564
Americana Museum
401 Aurora Av, Terra Alta, WV 26764
General Museum - 1968
Coll: artifacts; furniture; horse-drawn
vehicles; antique cars; historic houses

Terre Haute IN

16565
Eugene V. Debs Foundation
451 N Eighth St, POB 843, Terre
Haute, IN 47808
Historic Site
Coll: historic house, the home of
Eugene V. Debs; furnishings;
mementos of Debs' campaigns for the
Presidency - library

16566
**Historical Museum of the Wabash
Valley**
1411 S 6th St, Terre Haute, IN 47802
General Museum - 1958
Coll: textiles; archeology; costumes;
Indian artifacts; military; historic
building - library; meeting room

16567
Paul Dresser Memorial Birthplace
First & Farrington Sts, 1411 S Sixth St,
Terre Haute, IN 47802
Historic Site - 1967
Coll: birthplace of Paul Dresser;
furniture; household items; historical
artifacts of the period

16568
Sheldon Swope Art Gallery
25 S 7th St, Terre Haute, IN 47807
Fine Arts Museum - 1942
Coll: American paintings, prints,
drawings, and sculpture of the 19th
and 20th centuries; European art of
14th-20th centuries; ancient Far
Eastern and primitive art; decorative
arts; glass - library

16569
Turman Gallery Indiana State
University
Terre Haute, IN 47809
Fine Arts Museum - 1870
Coll: paintings; sculpture

The Dalles OR

16570
Fort Dalles Museum
16th St and Garrison St, The Dalles,
OR 97058
Historic Site - 1928
Coll: history; military; Fort Dalles
Surgeon quarters (1856)

16571
The Nichols Museum
601 Union St, The Dalles, OR 97058
Natural History Museum - 1966
Coll: minerals; crystals; geological
formations and fossils; Indian artifacts
- library; auditorium

Thetford VT

16572
**Thetford Historical Society Library
and Museum**
Thetford, VT 05074
Agriculture Museum - 1948
Coll: agricultural implements; tools;
portraits - library

Thousand Oaks CA

16573
Stagecoach Inn Museum
POB 1692, Thousand Oaks, CA 91360
General Museum - 1967
Coll: artifacts illustrating three eras of
local history: Chumash Indian,
Spanish-Mexican, Anglo-American
eras - library

Ticonderoga NY

16574
Fort Mt. Hope
Burgoyne Rd, Ticonderoga, NY 12883
Historic Site - 1947
Coll: guns; artifacts; cannon; relics;
restored blockhouse, guardhouse;
trading post; maple sugar camp -
library

16575
Fort Ticonderoga
POB 390, Ticonderoga, NY 12883
History/Public Affairs Museum - 1909
Coll: paintings, manuscripts, guns,
cannon, swords, personal memorabilia
of American prominents in the early
history; Barracks (1755) - library

Tiffin OH

16576
**Jones Collection of Minerals and
Biology Museum** Heidelberg College
Greenfield St, Tiffin, OH 44883
Natural History Museum - 1920
Coll: minerals; fluorescent exhibit;
fossils; shells; bird skulls; Indian
points; natural history - library

16577
Seneca County Museum
28 Clay St, Tiffin, OH 44883
General Museum - 1942
Coll: aviary; costumes; glass; Tiffin
glassware; philately; history; weapons;
folk craft pieces; Rezin W. Shawhan
residence and carriage house (1853) -
library; educational center

Tifton GA

16578
Georgia Agrirama
8th St at Interstate 75, Tifton, GA
31794
Agriculture Museum - 1971
Coll: agricultural equipment; printing
and typesetting equipment; furniture
and furnishings of the period; historic
buildings - library

Tillamook OR

16579
Tillamook County Pioneer Museum
2106 Second St, Tillamook, OR 97141
General Museum - 1935
Coll: pioneer artifacts; archaeology;
natural history; wildlife dioramas;
implements - library

Tishomingo OK

16580
Chickasaw Council House Museum
Rte 1, POB 14, Tishomingo, OK 73460
Anthropology Museum - 1971
Coll: pictures and articles by the
Chickasaws; furniture; jewelry; tools;
art objects; fire-arms; saddles; bridles
and saddle bags; documents and
photographs - library

Titusville NJ

16581
Ferry Museum
Washington Crossing State Park, POB
337, Letter A Rd 1, Titusville, NJ 08560
Historic Site
Coll: antiques; Colonial furniture

Titusville PA

16582
Drake Well Museum
R.D. 3, Titusville, PA 16354
Historic Site - 1934
Coll: early lighting devices; oil well
drilling and production tools and
equipment; collodion wet plate
negatives of development of the
Pennsylvania oil industry; replica of
Drake's derrick and engine house -
library; auditorium; theater

Tobias NE

16583
Tobias Community Historical Society
Tobias, NE 68453
General Museum - 1968
Coll: numismatic; philatelic; medical
kitchen wares; old bottles; military

Toccoa GA

16584
Historic Traveler's Rest
Rte 3, Toccoa, GA 30577
Historic Site - 1955
Coll: historic stagecoach inn (1825);
furnishings; Indian artifacts

Toledo IA

16585
Tama County Historical Society
POB 64, Toledo, IA 52342
General Museum - 1942
pioneer and Indian artifacts;
Mesquakie Indian clothing and tools -
library

Toledo OH

16586
Blair Museum of Lithophanes and Wax Carvings
2032 Robinwood Av, Toledo, OH 43620
Decorative Arts Museum - 1966
Coll: wax molds; plaster of paris molds and lithophanes; wax carvings from 300 B.C. to 20th century

16587
The Toledo Museum of Art
2445 Monroe St, Toledo OH 43697, POB 1013, Toledo, OH 44120
Fine Arts Museum - 1901
Coll: European and American painting and decorative arts; ancient, European and American glass; ancient and medieval art; books and manuscripts; prints; sculpture; graphics; archaeology - library; reading room; auditorium; lecture hall; glass study room; print study room; classrooms; concert hall

16588
Toledo Museum of Health and Natural History University of Toledo
2700 Broadway, Toledo, OH 43609
Natural History Museum - 1938
Coll: anthropology; aquarium; entomology; herpetology; archaeology; geology; paleontology; mineralogy - library; auditorium; classrooms; botanical garden; zoological park

Tombstone AZ

16589
Tombstone Courthouse State Historic Park
219 Toughnut St, POB 216, Tombstone, AZ 85638
General Museum - 1959
Coll: historical artifacts; glass; china; silver; anthropology; archeology; mineralogy; medical items; natural history; guns; furniture; dolls; domestic utensils; archives

Toms River NJ

16590
Ocean County Historical Society
26 Hadley Av, Toms River, NJ 08742
General Museum - 1950
Coll: Indian artifacts; history of the dirigible and Naval Air Station at Lakehurst; Revolutionary War salt works

Tonanwanda NY

16591
Historical Society of the Tonawandas, Inc.
113 Main St, Tonanwanda, NY 14150
General Museum - 1961
Coll: industry and transportation; military history; Indian artifacts; circus memorabilia; costumes; archives - library; reading room

Tonkawa OK

16592
The A. D. Buck Museum of Natural History and Sciences
1220 E Grand, Tonkawa, OK 74653
Natural History Museum - 1901
Coll: Indian culture; mineralogy; archaeology; geology; zoology

Topeka KS

16593
Gallery of Fine Arts Topeka Public Library
1515 W 10th, Topeka, KS 66604
Fine Arts Museum - 1870
Coll: glass; pottery; paintings; prints; antique fans; lace

16594
Kansas State Historical Society Museum
120 W 10th St, Topeka, KS 66612
History/Public Affairs Museum - 1875
Coll: ethnology; archaeology; transportation; interiors; costumes

16595
Mulvane Art Center
17th and Jewell, Topeka, KS 66621
Fine Arts Museum - 1925
Coll: modern and contemporary Midwestern painting; prints; sculpture; ceramics - library

16596
Museum & Archives The Menninger Foundation
5600 W. 6th Ave, Topeka, KS 66601
History/Public Affairs Museum - 1925
Coll: letters of Freud, Benjamin Rush, Dorothea Dix, Clifford Beers; rocks; shells; history of psychiatry and parent institutions - library, auditorium

Toppenish WA

16597
Toppenish Museum
1 South Elm, Toppenish, WA 98948
General Museum - 1975
Coll: antique artifacts; Indian baskets; regional contemporary arts and crafts - library

Torrington CT

16598
Torrington Historical Society, Inc.
POB 353, Torrington, CT 06790
General Museum - 1944
Coll: local historical items; industrial exhibits; farming; glass, china, and silver; costumes; household utensils - library

Towanda PA

16599
French Azilum
R.D. 2, POB 266, Towanda, PA 18848
Historic Site
Coll: emigree heirlooms; antique farm tools; blacksmith tools; carpenter's tools; spinning and weaving implements; historic houses (1793-1836)

Traverse City MI

16600
Con Foster Museum
Grandview Parkway, Traverse City, MI 49684
General Museum - 1934
Coll: agriculture; natural history; transportation; Indian artifacts

16601
Great Lakes Area Paleontological Museum
9121 S Long Lake, Traverse City, MI 49684
Natural History Museum - 1971
Coll: over 15,000 specimens, including many phyla of fossils; fossil fish ranging in size from 4 inches to 40 feet; invertebrates, vertebrates and paleobotanical specimens such as corals, brachiopods, gastropods and cephalopods - library; reading room; classrooms

16602
Indian Drum Lodge Museum Camp Greilick
6419 W Bay Shore Rd, Traverse City, MI 49684
Decorative Arts Museum - 1966
Coll: ceremonial artifacts; basketry; Indian garments; animal products; Indian-made wood crafts

Trenton NJ

16603
New Jersey State Museum
205 W State St, Trenton, NJ 08625
General Museum - 1890
Coll: fine arts; decorative arts; cultural history; archaeology and ethnology; natural history - staff library; planetarium; solar observatory; auditorium

16604
Old Barracks Association
S Willow St, Trenton, NJ 08608
Decorative Arts Museum
Coll: American furniture, ceramics; American silver, firearms and accoutrements; portraits; books and manuscripts (18th and 19th centuries); barracks (1758) - auditorium; dioramas of battles of Trenton and Princeton

16605
Trenton City Museum
Ellarslie, Cadwalader Park, Trenton, NJ 08618
General Museum - 1971
Furniture and furnishings; Tuscan Villa (1850)

16606
The W2Z1 Historical Wireless Museum
19 Blackwood Dr, Trenton, NJ 08628
Science/Tech Museum - 1945
Coll: apparatus and instruments from the 1899 period; early radios - library

16607
William Trent House
15 Market St, Trenton, NJ 08611
Historic Site - 1939
Coll: William and Mary and Queen Anne furniture (18th century)

Troy AL

16608
Pike Pioneer Museum
U.S. 231 North, Troy, AL 36081
Agriculture Museum
Coll: artifacts related to the social and agricultural history of tenant farming in Alabama and history of Pike County - 10-acre complex including original tenant house, log house, old general store, caretaker's house

Troy NY

16609
Rensselaer County Junior Museum
282 Fifth Av, Troy, NY 12182
General Museum - 1954
early toys; dolls; shells; geology; live snakes; science and natural history items; Colonial artifacts and tools - planetarium

Troy OH

16610
Overfield Tavern
201 E Water St, Troy, OH 45373
Historic Site - 1966
Coll: 18th and 19th century antiques - library

Tuckahoe NY

16611
Westchester County Historical Society
43 Read Av, Tuckahoe, NY 10707
General Museum - 1874
Coll: furnishings from 1760 Civil War period; tools and farm implements; weapons and accoutrements of the Revolution and Civil War - library

Tucson AZ

16612
The Aquary Museum
1011 E. Lee St, Tucson, AZ 85719
General Museum - 1976
Coll: artifacts relating to marine and fresh water; historic and current problems; naval history; water resources; conservation; pollution; recreational usages; safety - library; laboratory; reading room

16613
Arabian Horse Museum
4101 N. Bear Canyon Rd, Tucson, AZ 85715
Natural History Museum - 1957
Coll: exhibits; history; paintings; sculpture; saddles; trophies - library; reading room; auditorium

16614
Arizona Historical Society
949 E. 2nd St, Tucson, AZ 85719
History/Public Affairs Museum - 1884
Coll: Spanish Colonial and Mexican culture; American military weapons; transportation, ranching equipment, mining equipment; household effects; historic houses - library

16615
Arizona State Museum University of Arizona
Tucson, AZ 85721
Anthropology Museum - 1893
Coll: Southwestern archeology; ethnohistory; ethnology; osteology; natural history - library; reading room

16616
Arizona-Sonora Desert Museum
Route 9, POB 900, Tucson, AZ 85704
Natural History Museum - 1952
Coll: amphibians; insects; reptiles; birds; mammals; mineralogy; herpetology; natural history - library; botanical garden; zoological park; aquarium; classrooms

16617
Kitt Peak National Observatory
POB 26732, Tucson, AZ 85726
Natural History Museum - 1958
Coll: introduction to astronomy;
descriptions of various instruments -
library; field research station;
laboratory; reading room; auditorium;
theater

16618
Tucson Museum of Art
235 W. Alameda St, Tucson, AZ 85701
Fine Arts Museum - 1924
Coll: pre-Hispanic, Spanish Colonial,
19th and 20th century American and
European paintings, sculpture,
graphics; contemporary American arts
and crafts of the Southwest; Latin
American art - library; slide library;
craft gallery

16619
University of Arizona Mineralogical
Museum
University of Arizona, Tucson, AZ
85721
Natural History Museum - 1885
Coll: over 10,000 mineral specimens
from around the world; fossils

16620
University of Arizona Museum of Art
Olive and Speedway, Tucson, AZ
85721
Fine Arts Museum - 1955
Coll: Samuel H. Kress collection of
Italian art; Gallagher Memorial
collection of contemporary American
and European painting and sculpture;
C. Leonard Pfeiffer collection of
American painting; graphics; Jacques
Lipchitz plaster models

16621
Western Archeological Center
1415 N. Sixth Ave, Tucson, AZ 85717
Archeology Museum
Coll: Southwestern culture and
artifacts - library; field research
station; laboratory

Tucumcari NM

16622
Tucumcari Historical Museum
416 S Adams, Tucumcari, NM 88401
General Museum - 1958
Coll: agriculture; anthropology;
archaeology; archives; botany;
costumes; folklore; geology; glass;
herbarium; Indian artifacts; mineralogy;
military; music; natural history;
paleontology; firetruck - library; junior
museum; preservation project; park
museum

Tulia TX

16623
Swisher County Archives and
Museum Association
POB 145, Tulia, TX 79088
History/Public Affairs Museum - 1965
Coll: local history; furniture; clothing -
library

Tulsa OK

16624
Philbrook Art Center
2727 Rockford Rd, Tulsa Ok 74114,
POB 52510, Tulsa, OK 74152
Fine Arts Museum - 1938
Coll: Kress collection of Italian
Renaissance painting and sculpture;
Laura A. Clubb collection of American
and European painting; Clark Field
collection of American Indian baskets
and pottery; Roberta Campbell
Lawson collection of American Indian
costumes and artifacts, and Indian
library; Philbrook collection of
American Indian paintings; George H.
Taber collection of Oriental art; John
W. Starr collection of miniatures;
Gussman collection of African
sculpture; Shinenkan collection of
Japanese screens and dolls; Ancient
Heritage collection of ancient and
classical artifacts; Standard Oil of New
Jersey collection of oil industry
paintings; Gillert collection of
Southeast Asian ceramics; other
collections including American glass,
antique toys, and sculpture - library;
junior gallery; classrooms

16625
Thomas Gilcrease Institute of
American History and Art
1400 N 25 W Av, Tulsa, OK 74127
History/Public Affairs Museum - 1942
Coll: American sculpture and painting;
cultures of five civilized tribes; Plains
and Central American people's
artifacts; the westward movement in
U.S.; documents; anthropology;
archaeology; graphics - library;
reading room; auditorium

16626
Tulsa County Historical Society
Museum
631 S Gary Place, Tulsa, OK 74104
General Museum - 1974
Coll: pictures; costumes; artifacts

16627
Tulsa Zoological Park
5701 E 36th St N, Tulsa, OK 74115
Natural History Museum - 1927
Coll: live animals and plants; North
American fossils, geological
specimens; Indian artifacts - zoo;
library; North American Living
Museum

16628
World Museum Art Center
1400 E Skelly Dr, POB 7572, Tulsa, OK
74105
Fine Arts Museum - 1972
Coll: marble, bronze and wood
statuary; classic car collection;
buggies; over 500 oil paintings;
16th-8th century masters; primitive
carvings; Chinese and Oriental
collection; antiques; shrunken heads;
rare pianos; porcelain and ceramic
collection; original clay sculptures;
African art collection, including
witchcraft gods; Asian musical
instruments; gongs; Asian Buddhas,
temples and imagery; modern metal
art; period treasures - auditorium;
chapel; meditation area

Tumacacori AZ

16629
Tumacacori National Monument
POB 67, Tumacacori, AZ 85640
General Museum - 1938
Coll: Indian and Spanish Colonial
artifacts - library

Tupelo MS

16630
Natchez Trace Parkway
R.R. 1, NT143, Tupelo, MS 38801
History/Public Affairs Museum - 1938
Coll: herbarium; ethnology; geology;
archaeology - library

Tuscaloosa AL

16631
The Old Tavern
Capitol Park, POB 1665, Tuscaloosa,
AL 35401
General Museum - 1965
Coll: 19th century furnishings; exhibits
of old artifacts; folklore

Tuscumbia AL

16632
Ivy Green Birthplace of Helen Keller
300 W. North Commons, Tuscumbia,
AL 35674
Historic Site - 1952
Coll: books; gifts; objects connected
with Helen Keller's life; period furniture

16633
Tennessee Valley Art Center
511 N. Water St, POB 474, Tuscumbia,
AL 35674
Fine Arts Museum - 1973
research material and poster
collection of Sheldon Cheney -
workrooms; classrooms

Tuskegee AL

16634
George Washington Carver Museum
Tuskegee Institute, Tuskegee, AL
36088
General Museum - 1941
Coll: natural history collections;
paintings; needleworks; personal
memorabilia and awards of Dr. George
W. Carver; furnishings in the Oaks
home of the Booker T. Washington
family - library

Twentynine Palms CA

16635
Twentynine Palms Oasis Visitor
Center Joshua Tree National
Monument
74485 National Monument Dr,
Twentynine Palms, CA 92277
Science/Tech Museum - 1936
Coll: archeology; geology; zoology;
botany - library

Twin Falls ID

16636
The Norman Herrett Museum
College of Southern Idaho, POB 1238,
Twin Falls, ID 83301
Natural History Museum - 1952
American archeology - library;
classrooms

Two Harbors MN

16637
Lake County Historical Society and
Railroad Museum Deport Bldg
Two Harbors, MN 55616
History/Public Affairs Museum - 1026
Coll: minerals; shipping and
shipwrecks - library

Tybee GA

16638
Fort Pulaski National Monument
POB 98, Tybee, GA 31328
General Museum - 1924
Coll: Civil War cannon and projectiles;
uniform accessories; personal effects
of soldiers; bottle collection; antique
and replica room furnishings - library

Tybee Island GA

16639
Tybee Museum
Tybee Island, GA 31328
General Museum
Coll: guns and pistols; antique dolls;
old Spanish-American War coastal
defense battery

Tyler TX

16640
Goodman Museum
624 N Broadway, Tyler, TX 75702
Historic Site
Coll: house furnishing; pioneer tools

16641
Tyler Museum of Art
1300 S Mahon Av, Tyler, TX 75701
Fine Arts Museum - 1969
Coll: paintings; sculptures - library

Ukiah CA

16642
Held-Poage Memorial Home and
Research Library
603 W. Perkins St, Ukiah, CA 95482
General Museum - 1970
Coll: historical items; Indian artifacts;
children's toys - library; reading room

Uncasville CT

16643
Tantaquidgeon Indian Museum
Rte 32 Norwich-New London Rd,
Uncasville, CT 06382
Anthropology Museum - 1931
Coll: crafts made by Mohegan and
other New England craftsmen of past
and present; archeology;
reproductions of a wigwam and
longhouse typical of early Eastern
woodland tribes

Union IL

16644
Illinois Railway Museum
Olson Rd, Union, IL 60180
History/Public Affairs Museum - 1953
Coll: 150 historic railway cars;
locomotives; streetcars; trolley
coaches - library

16645
McHenry County Historical Society
McHenry County Historical Museum
6422 Main St, POB 434, Union, IL
60180
General Museum - 1964
Coll: local historical artifacts; papers
and records of early settlers; historic
house (1847) - library

Union NJ

16646
Kean College of New Jersey
Morris Av, Union, NJ 07083
Fine Arts Museum - 1971
Alumni, faculty, and undergraduate art;
works of well-known artists - 1,000
seat auditorium

Union OR

16647
Union County Museum
311 Main St, Union, OR 97883
General Museum - 1969
Coll: material relating to the settlement and development of the area; artifacts; archives - library; reading room; auditorium

Union SC

16648
Union County Historical Museum
Drawer 220, Union, SC 29379
General Museum
Coll: Confederate War collection; guns; tools; dolls; china and crystal; bottles; pottery; artifacts currency; furniture; newspapers; books from early Union Library; family genealogy material; historic buildings (1791-1823) - library; auditorium

University AL

16649
University of Alabama Art Gallery
Garland Hall, POB F, University, AL 35486
Fine Arts Museum - 1831
Coll: primitive art; paintings; drawings; prints; photos; sculpture; crafts

16650
University of Alabama Museum of Natural History
POB 5897, University, AL 35486
Natural History Museum - 1848
Coll: anthropology; archeology; conchology; ichthyology; mineralogy; herpetology

University MS

16651
University Museum The University of Mississippi
University, MS 38677
Decorative Arts Museum - 1916
Coll: Greek and Roman pottery; coins; Sumerian clay tablets; Roman glass; Egyptian antiquities; scientific instruments - library; classrooms

University Park PA

16652
College of Earth and Mineral Sciences Museum Pennsylvania State University
University Park, PA 16802
Natural History Museum - 1925
Coll: paintings; geology; natural history; mineralogy; paleontology; science and technology

16653
The Frost Entomological Museum The Pennsylvania State University
Patterson Bldg, Department of Entomology, University Park, PA 16802
Natural History Museum - 1968
entomology; zoology - library; laboratory

16654
Museum of Art The Pennsylvania State University
University Park, PA 16802
Fine Arts Museum - 1963
Coll: American and European paintings, drawings, graphics and sculpture with emphasis on Pennsylvania artists; Oriental ceramics, paintings and prints; limited material in Ancient, African and Near Eastern areas; the Kehl and Nena Markley collection of Ancient Peruvian ceramics; the Ralph C. Marcove collection of Oriental art

Upland CA

16655
Chaffey Communities Cultural Center
825 W. 18th St, POB 772, Upland, CA 91786
General Museum - 1965
Coll: Indian artifacts; agricultural implements; dolls; Civil War artifacts

Upland PA

16656
The Friends of the Caleb Pusey House, Inc.
15 Race St, Upland, PA 19015
General Museum - 1960
Coll: furniture; archichecture; archaeology; farm equipment; linens; historic houses - herbarium

Upper Sandusky OH

16657
Wyandot County Historical Society
130 S 7th St, Upper Sandusky, OH 43351
General Museum - 1924
Coll: agriculture; archives; paintings; costumes; glass; history; Indian artifacts; marine; medical; musical instruments; McCutchenville Overland Inn (1852) - library; children's museum; arboretum

Urbana IL

16658
Museum of Natural History
University of Illinois
Matthew & Green Sts, Urbana, IL 61801
Natural History Museum - 1870
Coll: natural history; archeology; zoology; historical items of Gregor Mendel

16659
World Heritage Museum University of Illinois at Urbana-Champaign
484 Lincoln Hall, Urbana, IL 61801
General Museum - 1912
Coll: archeology; art; history; numismatics; glass; anthropology - library

Urbana OH

16660
Champaign County Historical Museum
809 E Lawn Av, Urbana OH 43078, 8155 E Rte 29, Mechanicsburg, OH 43044
General Museum - 1934
Coll: Indian artifacts; Civil War history; local history - library

USAF Academy CO

16661
U. S. Air Force Academy Visitor Center
USAF Academy, CO 80840
History/Public Affairs Museum - 1955
Coll: pictorial exhibits explaining the history and current programs of the U.S. Air Force Academy

Utica IL

16662
LaSalle County Historical Museum
POB 577, Utica, IL 61373
General Museum - 1968
Coll: Indian artifacts; furnishings of early pioneers; clothing; farm tools; pioneer implements - library; reading room

Utica NY

16663
Children's Museum of History, Natural History and Science at Utica, New York
620 Memorial Pkwy, Utica, NY 13501
Junior Museum - 1965
Coll: dolls; Indian artifacts; rocks and minerals; birds and animals; armor - nature trail; classrooms

16664
Munson-Williams-Proctor Institute
310 Genesee St, Utica, NY 13502
Fine Arts Museum - 1919
Coll: 18th and 19th century American paintings; 20th century European and American paintings and sculpture; European, Japanese, American prints; American decorative arts; pre-Columbian, Greek and Persian art; archives of central New York architecture; Fountain Elms, designed by William L. Woolett, Jr. (1850) - library; music library; school of art; meetinghouse; auditorium

16665
Oneida Historical Society
318 Genesee St, Utica, NY 13502
General Museum - 1876
Coll: local history books, pamphlets, photographs, maps, manuscripts and artifacts pertaining to the history of the Upper Mohawk Valley and Oneida County - reading room

Vail CO

16666
Colorado Ski Museum - Ski Hall of Fame
15 Vail Rd, POB 1565, Vail, CO 81657
History/Public Affairs Museum - 1976
Coll: artifacts, photographs and books pertaining to the history of skiing in Colorado

Vails Gate NY

16667
New Windsor Cantonment State Historic Site
Temple Hill Rd, POB 207, Vails Gate, NY 12584
General Museum - 1967
Coll: material relating to the Revolutionary War and period; military equipment and artifacts; archaeological materials; wooden officer's hut (1782) - library; auditorium

Valdez AK

16668
Valdez Historical Society, Inc.
Keystone Mall, POB 6, Valdez, AK 99686
History/Public Affairs Museum - 1959
Coll: historical and ethnological items of Alaska - library; reading room

Valentinne NE

16669
Cherry County Historical Society
Main St and Highway 20, Valentinne, NE 69201
General Museum - 1959
Coll: buttons; furnishings; musical instruments; clothing - library

Valley City ND

16670
Barnes County Historical Museum
County Courthouse, Valley City, ND 58072
General Museum - 1930
Coll: historical exhibits; military items; costumes; tools; glassware; dolls; Far Eastern artifacts

Valley Forge PA

16671
The Valley Forge Historical Society
Valley Forge, PA 19481
General Museum - 1918
Coll: Washington memorabilia; Revolutionary firearms; historic Staffordshire; Dutch and Presidential china; antique furniture; colonial lighting - library

16672
Valley Forge National Historic Park
Valley Forge, PA 19481
Historic Site - 1976
Coll: period furnishings (1770-1778); original headquarters of General Washington and other generals; reconstructed huts of the Continental soldiers; archaeological collection of artifacts from encampment - library; visitor center; bicycle, hiking and bridle trails

Valparaiso FL

16673
Historical Society Museum
115 Westview Av, Valparaiso, FL 32580
General Museum - 1970
Coll: documents; genealogical material; farm and industrial tools; household utensils; furnishings; photographs - library; classrooms

Valparaiso IN

16674
Historical Society of Porter County Museum Old Jail Building
153 Franklin St, Valparaiso, IN 46383
General Museum - 1916
Coll: mastodon bones found in the county; pioneer artifacts - library

16675
University Art Galleries and Collections Valparaiso University
Valparaiso, IN 46383
Fine Arts Museum - 1979
Coll: paintings by Junius R. Sloan; 19th-20th century American paintings; ancient Palestinian ceramics

Vancouver WA

16676
Clark County Historical Museum
1511 Main St, Vancouver, WA 98660
General Museum - 1964
Northwest history including Indian
exhibits - library

16677
**Fort Vancouver National Historic
Site**
Vancouver, WA 98661
General Museum - 1954
Coll: archeology; military; fur trade;
manufacturing; Hudson's Bay
Company in the Pacific Northwest -
library

Ventura CA

16678
San Buenaventura Mission Museum
225 E. Main St, Ventura, CA 93001
History/Public Affairs Museum - 1782
Coll: paintings; statues; Indian
artifacts; religious artifacts and
vestments; historic structures - library

16679
Ventura County Historical Museum
100 E. Main St, Ventura, CA 93001
General Museum - 1913
Coll: local historical items; artifacts of
native American, Hispanic, and early
settler periods; geology; marine life;
archives - library

Vermilion OH

16680
**Great Lakes Historical Society
Museum**
480 Main St, Vermilion, OH 44089
Science/Tech Museum - 1944
Coll: Great Lakes ship models;
paintings; photographs; marine
artifacts and relics; marine engines;
yachting and racing artifacts - library;
reading room

Vermillion SD

16681
The Shrine to Music Museum
The University of South Dakota, USD
Box 194, Vermillion, SD 57069
Music Museum - 1973
Coll: more than 3,000 American,
European and non-Western musical
instruments; supporting library of
music; books; photographs;
recordings; memorabilia - library

16682
W. H. Over Museum
University of South Dakota, Vermillion,
SD 57069
History/Public Affairs Museum - 1913
Coll: archeology; geology; natural
history; regional history; Plains Indian
ethnology; photographs; Stanley J.
Morrow Collection; David and
Elizabeth Clark Memorial Collection;
contemporary Sioux paintings -
library; classroom

Vernal UT

16683
**Dinosaur Natural History State
Museum**
235 E Main St, POB 396, Vernal, UT
84078
Science/Tech Museum - 1946
Coll: geology; fossils; plants and
animals; prehistoric replicas - library

Vernon TX

16684
Red River Valley Museum
POB 2004, Vernon, TX 76384
History/Public Affairs Museum - 1963
Indian artifacts; local history

Vernon VT

16685
Vernon Historians
Maple Glen Farm, Vernon, VT 05354
General Museum - 1968
Coll: books, Bibles and diaries of early
pioneers; school-related material; early
kitchen utensils - library

Versailles IN

16686
**Ripley County Historical Society
Museum**
POB 224, Versailles, IN 47042
General Museum - 1930
Coll: Civil War relics; Indian artifacts;
books - library

Vevay IN

16687
**Switzerland County Historical
Society Museum**
Main & Market Sts, Vevay, IN 47043
General Museum - 1925
Coll: archeology; costumes; pioneer
artifacts; history; Indian artifacts;
historic building - library

Vinalhaven ME

16688
Vinalhaven Historical Society
POB 387, Vinalhaven, ME 04863
History/Public Affairs Museum - 1963
Coll: granite industry; lobstering;
fishing; folklore - library

Vincennes IN

16689
**George Rogers Clark National
Historical Park**
401 S Second St, Vincennes, IN 47591
General Museum - 1967
Coll: British and American frontier
weapons and uniforms; French
Canadian household items; maps and
diagrams; oil murals; bronze statue of
George Rogers Clark - library;
auditorium

16690
Indiana Territory State Memorial
First & Harrison Sts, Vincennes, IN
47591
General Museum
Coll: period furnishings; printing
equipment; historic building (1801)

16691
William H. Harrison Museum
Grouseland
3 W Scott St, Vincennes, IN 47591
General Museum - 1911
Coll: Indian artifacts; furniture and
furnishings; historic mansion where
Harrison resided; contemporary
pieces - library; reading room

Virginia Beach VA

16692
Seashore State Park Natural Area
2500 Shore Dr, Virginia Beach, VA
23451
Science/Tech Museum - 1936
Seashells - library

Viroqua WI

16693
Vernon County Historical Museum
West Broadway, Viroqua, WI 54665
General Museum - 1942
Coll: early kitchen furniture and
artifacts; carpenter and household
materials; Indian artifacts

Visalia CA

16694
Tulare County Museum
27000 Mooney Blvd, Visalia, CA 93277
General Museum - 1948
Coll: sculptures by James Earle Frazer
and Salon Borglum; Indian relics;
agricultural implements; transportation;
historical buildings

Volga SD

16695
**Brookings County Historical Society
Museum**
Volga, SD 57071
General Museum - 1968
Coll: artifacts connected with
settlement of county; historic buildings
(1872, 1880) - library

Vonore TN

16696
Fort Loudoun Association
Rte. 1, Vonore, TN 37885
General Museum - 1933
Coll: archaeology; agriculture; botany;
Cherokee Indian artifacts - library

Vulcan MI

16697
Iron Mountain Iron Mine
US Hwy 2, Vulcan, MI 49892
Science/Tech Museum - 1956
Coll: mining machinery; diamond drills;
stoper drills; water liner drills;
underground locomotives

Wabasso FL

16698
McLarty Museum Sebastian Inlet
State Recreation Area
POB 728, Wabasso, FL 32970
Historic Site - 1970
Coll: treasures and artifacts of the
Spanish Fleet ship wreck of 1715

Waco TX

16699
Armstrong Browning Library
Baylor University, Eighth and Speight
Sts, Waco, TX 76706
Historic Site - 1918
Coll: anything pertaining to Robert and
Elizabeth Barrett Browning and the
Victorian Age - library; classrooms

16700
The Art Center
POB 5396, Waco, TX 76708
Fine Arts Museum - 1972
Coll: contemporary art - library

16701
Historic Waco Foundation
3217 Robin Rd, Waco, TX 76708
Historic Site - 1960
Coll: period furnishings and costumes
of Old Waco

16702
Strecker Museum
Baylor University, Waco, TX 76703
Science/Tech Museum - 1856
Coll: natural history; zoology;
herpetology - library; classrooms

16703
**Texas Ranger-Homer Garrison
Memorial Museum**
Fort Fisher Park, Interstate 35 and the
Brazos River, Waco, TX 76703
History/Public Affairs Museum - 1975
Coll: Western history; Texas Ranger
items - library

16704
Youth Cultural Center
815 Columbus Av, Waco, TX 76702
Junior Museum - 1963
Coll: Indian artifacts; natural history;
geology - library

Wadesboro NC

16705
Anson County Historical Society
210 E Wade St, Wadesboro, NC 28170
General Museum - 1962
Coll: period furniture; agriculture;
paintings; colonial garden; historic
houses (19th century) - auditorium

Wahaula HI

16706
Thomas A. Jaggar Memorial Museum
Hawaii Volcanoes National Park,
Wahaula, HI 96718
Natural History Museum - 1953
Coll: Hawaiian artifacts; geological
specimens; birds; archeology;
anthropology; ethnology - auditorium

Wahpeton ND

16707
**Richland County Laura Hughes
Memorial Museum**
2nd St and 7th Av N., Wahpeton, ND
58075
General Museum - 1948
Coll: archives; Indian artifacts - library;
reading room

Wailuku HI

16708
Hale Hoikeike
POB 1018, Wailuku, HI 96793
General Museum - 1957
Coll: pre-white man Hawaiian artifacts
of stone, wood, shell, feathers;
furniture and clothing of missionary
era - library

Waimea HI

16709
Kamuela Museum
Kawaihae-Kohala Junction, Rte 19 &
250, POB 507, Waimea, HI 96796
General Museum - 1968
Coll: ancient and royal artifacts from
ancient Hawaii; historical objects;
military items; rare royal items from
the Iolani Palace; European and
Oriental art-objects

Waitsfield VT

16710
Bundy Art Gallery
Waitsfield, VT 05673
Fine Arts Museum - 1962
Coll: contemporary painting and
sculpture - library

Walker MN

16711
Walker Museums
Minnesota Ave, Walker, MN 56484
Natural History Museum - 1037
Coll: anthropology; butterflies; mineralogy; history; geology

Walla Walla WA

16712
Whitman Mission National Historic Site
Rte 2, Walla Walla, WA 99362
Historic Site - 1936
Various exhibits dealing with history of Whitman and missionary era in Pacific Northwest - library; A-V auditorium

Wallace ID

16713
Coeur d'Alene District Mining Museum
507 Bank St, Wallace, ID 83873
Science/Tech Museum - 1964
Mining exhibits - library

Walnut Creek CA

16714
Alexander Lindsay Junior Museum
1901 1st Ave, Walnut Creek, CA 94596
Science/Tech Museum - 1955
Coll: local flora and fauna; geological specimens; Indian artifacts; aviary; herpetology; astronomy - zoo; aquarium; classrooms

Walterboro SC

16715
Colleton County Cultural Complex
POB 173, Walterboro, SC 29488
General Museum - 1977
Coll: arts and crafts; theater; history - auditorium; classrooms

Waltham MA

16716
American Jewish Historical Society
2 Thornton Rd, Waltham, MA 02154
History/Public Affairs Museum - 1892
Coll: portraits and memorabilia of 18th century American Jewish families; posters and programs of the Yiddish theaters of the early 1900's; Yiddish motion pictures - library

16717
Rose Art Museum Brandeis University
415 South St, Waltham, MA 02254
Fine Arts Museum - 1961
Coll: American and European 19th and 20th century painting and sculpture

16718
The Waltham Museum
194 Charles St, 15 Noonan St, Waltham, MA 02154
General Museum - 1971
Coll: clocks and watches; automobiles; bottles; stoves; radios; tools; lanterns - library

Warehouse Point CT

16719
Scantic Academy Museum East Windsor Historical Society, Inc.
Scantic Rd, Rte 191, Warehouse Point, CT 06088
General Museum - 1965
Coll: industry; agriculture; paintings; transportation - library

Warm Springs GA

16720
Franklin D. Roosevelt Warm Springs Memorial Site
Warm Springs, GA 31830
Historic Site - 1946
Coll: historic buildings; personal items and gifts of F.D.R. - library

Warner OK

16721
Connors State College
Warner, OK 74469
General Museum - 1908
Coll: geology; history; Indian artifacts

Warren PA

16722
Warren County Historical Society
710 Pennsylvania Av W, POB 427, Warren, PA 16365
General Museum - 1900
Coll: photographs; paintings; documents; manuscripts; letters; diaries; county records; genealogical records; tools and implements; utensils; Victorian furniture - library; reading room

Warrensburg MO

16723
Central Missouri State University Museum Central Missouri State University
Warrensburg, MO 64093
General Museum - 1968
Coll: archaeology; ethnology; history; biology - library

Warsaw NY

16724
Warsaw Historical Museum
15 Perry Av, Warsaw, NY 14569
General Museum - 1938
Coll: period furniture; local history; military items; clothing; dishes; farm and carpental tools - library

Warwick NY

16725
Warwich Historical Society
POB 353, Warwick, NY 10990
General Museum - 1906
Coll: furniture from Queen Anne through Duncan Phyfe periods; examples of work done by local cabinet makers of 1810-30; hunting and trapping equipment used by the writer Frank Forester; old carriages, sleighs, ploughs, ice-cutting equipment, farm tools; Lehigh & Hudson River Railways four-wheeled caboose (1890); costumes; archaeology; historic houses (1764 - 1825) - library; herb garden

Washington AR

16726
Old Washington Historic State Park
Washington, AR 71862
General Museum - 1958
Coll: archeology; weapons; 19th century furnishings; documents; historic buildings - library

Washington Crossing PA

16727
Washington Crossing Historic Park
Washington Crossing, PA 18977
Open Air Museum - 1917
exhibits of artifacts and paintings; botanical exhibits; historic buildings - library; reading room

Washington CT

16728
American Indian Archeological Institute
Curtis Rd, POB 260, Washington, CT 06793
Archeology Museum - 1975
Coll: prehistoric artifacts primarily from Connecticut and Northeastern US; ethnographic items - library; Indian habitat trail; reconstructed Indian farm; classrooms

16729
Historical Museum of the Gunn Memorial Library
Wykeham Rd, Washington, CT 06793
General Museum - 1908
Coll: Revolutionary, Civil War, and World War I items; newspapers; letters of George Washington and Thomas Jefferson; Indian collection; archives; textiles; glass; dolls; costumes - library

Washington DC

16730
Anderson House Headquarters and Museum of the Society of the Cincinnati
2118 Massachusetts Av, NW, Washington, DC 10008
Fine Arts Museum - 1783
Coll: paintings; sculpture; furniture; decorative arts of Asia and Europe; artifacts; archives relating to the American Revolution - library; reading room

16731
Archives of American Art
FA-PG Bldg, 8th & F Sts, NW, Washington, DC 20560
History/Public Affairs Museum - 1954
Coll: personal and professional records of American artists, dealers, critics, curators, and collectors; records of galleries, museums, and art societies; oral historical material

16732
Armed Forces Medical Museum
Walter Reed Army Medical Center
6825 16th St, NW, Washington, DC 20306
Natural History Museum - 1862
Coll: gross pathology collection of 11,000 specimens; specimens from deaths of Presidents Lincoln and Garfield; Yakovlev collection of normal and pathologic brain sections; Billings microscope collection; medical equipment - library; auditorium

16733
Arts and Industries Building The Smithsonian Institution
900 Jefferson Dr, S.W., Washington, DC 20560
Science/Tech Museum
Coll: 19th century historic building; working steam engines; 19th century locomotive; 51-foot model of naval sloop-of-war; Victorian Americana including furniture, glass, silver, tools, clothing

16734
B'nai B'rith Museum
1640 Rhode Island Av, Washington, DC 20036
Religious Art Museum - 1957
Coll: pre-20th century Jewish ceremonial and folk art; Israelite archeology; Jewish historical documents

16735
Bureau of Alcohol, Tobacco, and Firearms Museum
1200 Pennsylvania Av, NW, Washington, DC 20226
History/Public Affairs Museum - 1976
Artifacts pertaining to history of the bureau from 1776 to present - library; reading room; theater

16736
Columbia Historical Society
1307 New Hampshire Av, NW, Washington, DC 20036
General Museum - 1894
Coll: Victorian furniture; archives; photographs and maps of the history of the federal city; historic house - library

16737
Corcoran Gallery of Art
17th & New York Av, NW, Washington, DC 20006
Fine Arts Museum - 1869
Coll: American painting and sculpture from 18th-20th century; European paintings, sculpture, and decorative arts; American and European drawings, prints, and photographs - library

16738
Daughters of the American Revolution Museum
1776 D St, NW, Washington, DC 20006
Decorative Arts Museum - 1890
Coll: American arts to 1830; period rooms of china, glass, furniture, musical instruments, toys, dolls, textiles; guns; silver; costumes; pewter - library; auditorium

16739
Dimock Gallery George Washington University
Lower Lisner Auditorium, Washington, DC 20006
Fine Arts Museum - 1964
Coll: paintings; sculpture; graphic arts; W. Lloyd Wright collection of Washingtoniana; works pertaining to George Washington; U. S. Grant collection of photographs, documents, prints, and newspaper clippings; Joseph Pennell collection of prints - reading room

16740
Dumbarton Oaks Research Library and Collection
1703 32nd St, NW, Washington, DC 20007
Fine Arts Museum - 1940
Coll: Byzantine artifacts; pre-Columbian items; some European and American paintings, sculpture, and decorative arts - library; gardens

16741
Explorer's Hall National Geographic Society
17 & M Sts, NW, Washington, DC 20036
Science/Tech Museum - 1964
Coll: archeology; natural history; technology; items relating to exploration; astronomy; anthropology - library; reading room; auditorium

16742
Ford's Theatre Lincoln Museum
511 10th St, NW, Washington, DC
20004
History/Public Affairs Museum - 1932
Coll: theater archives; Ford's Theatre
study collection; military artifacts;
philately; numismatics; building in
which Lincoln was assassinated

16743
**Franciscan Monastery (Holy Land of
America)**
14th and Quincy St, NE, Washington,
DC 20017
Religious Art Museum - 1898
Coll: monastery; architectural
reproductions; replicas of chapels and
shrines of the Holy Land; decorative
arts; frescos of early Christian art

16744
Freer Gallery of Art
12th and Jefferson Dr, SW,
Washington, DC 20560
Fine Arts Museum - 1906
Coll: Far Eastern, Indian, Indo-Chinese,
and Near Eastern bronze, jade,
sculpture, painting, lacquer, pottery,
porcelain, manuscripts, metalwork, and
glass; Whistler's works - library;
auditorium

16745
Georgetown University Collection
Georgetown University, POB 1595
Hoya Station, Washington, DC 20057
Fine Arts Museum - 1789
Coll: historical objects; works by Van
Dyck and Gilbert Stuart; paintings;
sculpture; graphics; American portraits

16746
**Hirshhorn Museum and Sculpture
Garden**
Independence Av at Eighth St, S.W.,
Washington, DC 20560
Fine Arts Museum - 1966
Coll: modern art; sculpture of all
periods, particularly 19th and 20th
centuries - library; auditorium;
photography studio; study;
conservation laboratory

16747
Howard University Gallery of Art
2455 6th St, NW, Washington, DC
20059
Fine Arts Museum - 1928
Coll: Afro-American and American
painting, sculpture, graphic art; Alain
LeRoy Locke African collection;
Samuel H. Kress collection of Italian
paintings and sculpture; Irving Gumbel
print collection

16748
Howard University Museum
Moorland Spingarn Research Center
500 Howard Place, NW, Washington,
DC 20059
History/Public Affairs Museum - 1914
Coll: African artifacts; historic
materials relative to the Black
experience - research center

16749
Indian Arts and Crafts Board U.S.
Department of the Interior
18th & C Sts, NW Rm 4004,
Washington, DC 20006
Fine Arts Museum - 1935
Contemporary native American arts of
the US

16750
Museum of African Art
316-318 A St, NE, Washington, DC
20002
Fine Arts Museum - 1964
Coll: African sculpture, textiles, crafts,
and musical instruments; paintings and
sculpture by Afro-American artists;
historic house - library; auditorium;
reading room

16751
**Museum of Modern Art of Latin
America**
Washington, DC 20006
Fine Arts Museum - 1976
Latin American contemporary art
paintings; sculpture; graphics - library

16752
National Air and Space Museum
Seventh St and Independence Av,
SW, Washington, DC 20560
Science/Tech Museum - 1946
Coll: aeronautical and astronautical
items; air and space craft; instruments;
art; uniforms; personal memorabilia -
library; planetarium; theater; reading
room

16753
The National Archives
Pennsylvania Av and 8th St, NW,
Washington, DC 20408
History/Public Affairs Museum - 1934
Coll: federal records of the US
government from 1774 to present; the
original Declaration of Independence;
the Constitution; the Bill of Rights -
library; laboratory; auditorium; theater;
classrooms

16754
National Collection of Fine Arts
8th & G Sts, NW, Washington, DC
20560
Fine Arts Museum
Coll: graphics; paintings; decorative
arts; sculpture; historic buildings -
library; conservation laboratories;
lecture hall

16755
National Gallery of Art
14th St & Constitution Av, NW,
Washington, DC 20565
Fine Arts Museum - 1937
Coll: European and American painting,
sculpture, decorative arts and graphic
arts from 12th-20th century; European
Old Master paintings; sculpture from
Late Middle Ages to present;
Renaissance bronzes; Chinese
porcelains - library; conservation
laboratories

16756
**National Museum of History and
Technology**
14th St and Constitution Av, NW,
Washington, DC 20560
Science/Tech Museum - 1846
Coll: agriculture; archeology; philately;
technology; science; archives -
library; laboratory; auditorium

16757
National Museum of Natural History
10th St and Constitution Av, NW,
Washington, DC 20560
Natural History Museum - 1846
Coll: anthropology; gems; meteorites;
zoology; entomology - library;
ecology theater; auditorium

16758
National Portrait Gallery
F St at 8th, NW, Washington, DC
20560
Fine Arts Museum - 1962
Portraits of men and women who have
made notable contributions to the
history and development of the United
States - library; research station;
reading room; auditorium; classrooms

16759
**National Rifle Association Firearms
Museum**
1600 Rhode Island Av, NW,
Washington, DC 20036
Anthropology Museum - 1871
Coll: more than 1,500 firearms
including antique and modern
shotguns, rifles, and hand guns; big
game trophies

16760
**National Society of Children of
American Revolution Museum**
1776 D St, NW, Washington, DC
20006
Junior Museum - 1895
Decorative and applied arts

16761
**National Trust for Historic
Preservation**
740-48 Jackson Pl, NW, Washington,
DC 20006
History/Public Affairs Museum - 1949
Coll: decorative arts; history;
furnishings of historic houses - library

16762
The Octagon
1799 New York Av, NW, Washington,
DC 20006
Historic Site
Coll: furnishings of the period
1800-1828; exhibits on architecture
and the allied arts; historic house

16763
The Phillips Collection
1600-12 21st St, NW, Washington, DC
20009
Fine Arts Museum - 1918
Coll: primarily 19th and 20th century
European and American paintings and
sculpture; historic building - library

16764
Renwick Gallery The Smithsonian
Institution
Pennsylvania Av at 17th St, N.W.,
Washington, DC 20560
Decorative Arts Museum - 1972
Coll: American crafts; designs;
decorative arts; 19th century court
building

16765
Rock Creek Nature Center
5200 Glover Rd, NW, Washington, DC
20015
Junior Museum - 1960
Coll: botany; entomology; geology;
zoology - library; aquariums;
auditorium; planetarium

16766
Smith-Mason Gallery-Museum
1207 Rhode Island Av, NW,
Washington, DC 20005
Fine Arts Museum - 1967
Coll: paintings; graphics; ethnology;
sculpture; textiles; decorative arts -
library; reading room; arts center

16767
**The Supreme Court of the United
States**
U.S. Supreme Court Building,
Washington, DC 20543
History/Public Affairs Museum - 1973
Coll: portraits of the Justices
throughout history; historic images,
such as photos, etchings, and
drawings, of the Justices and the
architecture of the building;
memorabilia; antiques; clippings -
library; reading room

16768
The Textile Museum
2320 S St, NW, Washington, DC 20008
Decorative Arts Museum - 1925
Coll: 9,000 textiles from the Old World
and New World; 800 rugs - library;
classrooms; conservation laboratory

16769
Truxtun-Decatur Naval Museum
1610 H St, NW, Washington, DC
20006
History/Public Affairs Museum - 1950
Coll: papers and memorabilia relating
to naval personalities; nautical
paintings, prints, photographs; ship
models - library

16770
United States Capitol
Washington, DC 20510
Fine Arts Museum - 1793
Coll: 19th and 20th century paintings,
sculpture, and decorative arts;
restored historic chambers;
architectural drawings; photographs;
archives - library

16771
United States Department of Justice
J. Edgar Hoover FBI Bldg, E St
between 9th and 10th Sts., NW,
Washington, DC 20535
History/Public Affairs Museum - 1908
Coll: exhibits of interesting cases;
displays explaining FBI jurisdiction and
work performed in FBI laboratory

16772
**United States Department of the
Interior Museum**
18th and C Sts, NW, Washington, DC
20240
General Museum - 1938
Coll: American Indian, Eskimo,
Micronesia, Virgin Island and Guam
handicrafts and artifacts; rocks and
fossils; meteoritic material; paintings;
mining equipment; models and
dioramas

16773
**United States Marine Corps
Museum**
Marine Corps Historical Center, Navy
Yard, Washington, DC 20374
History/Public Affairs Museum - 1940
Coll: military weapons; equipment and
uniforms; insignia and flags;
photographs; numismatics; philately;
historic buildings - library

16774
United States National Arboretum
24th & R St, NE, Washington, DC
20002
Natural History Museum - 1927
Coll: horticulture; ornamental trees
and shrubs; herbarium; National
Bonsai collection; National Herb
Garden - library

16775
United States Navy Memorial Museum
Bldg 76, Washington Navy Yard, Washington, DC 20374
History/Public Affairs Museum - 1962
Coll: documents; paintings; weapons; photographs; medals; ship models; flags; scientific instruments - dioramas

16776
United States Senate Commission on Art & Antiquities
Rm S-411, U.S. Capitol Bldg, Washington, DC 20510
Fine Arts Museum - 1968
Coll: paintings; sculpture; documents; furnishings - library

16777
Watkins Gallery
Massachusetts & Nebraska Avs, NW, Washington, DC 20016
Fine Arts Museum - 1944
Coll: American paintings from 1900-1960; prints and drawings; European paintings, prints, and drawings

16778
The White House
1600 Pennsylvania Av, NW, Washington, DC 20500
Historic Site - 1792
Coll: American period furniture and decorative arts from the late 18th and 19th centuries; collections of Presidential porcelain and glassware; portraits of the Presidents, First Ladies, and other national notables; late 18th, 19th, and 20th century paintings and prints; archival materials on the White House - library

16779
Woodrow Wilson House
2340 S St, NW, Washington, DC 20008
Historic Site - 1963
Coll: original furnishings; memorabilia of World War I; gifts from various heads of state; historic house - garden

Washington GA

16780
Robert Toombs House
216 E Robert Toombs Av, Washington, GA 30673
General Museum - 1974
Furniture and furnishings from the period 1840-1890

16781
Washington-Wilkes Historical Museum
308 E Robert Toombs Av, Washington, GA 30673
General Museum - 1959
Confederate history

Washington PA

16782
Arden Trolley Museum
N Main St, Washington PA 15301, POB 832, Pittsburg, PA 15230
Science/Tech Museum - 1949
Coll: city and interurban trolley cars, steam, diesel and electric locomotives; railroad cars - library

16783
Washington County Historical Society
Le Moyne House, 49 E Maiden St, Washington, PA 15301
Historic Site - 1901
Coll: archives; history; Washington County artifacts and memorabilia; display of Duncan Miller glass

Washington RI

16784
Western Rhode Island Civic Historical Society
1 Station St, Washington, RI 02816
General Museum - 1945
Coll: costumes; tools and utensils; period furnishings; Paine House (1745) - library

Washington TX

16785
Star of the Republic Museum
POB 317, Washington, TX 77880
History/Public Affairs Museum - 1970
Coll: documents of the history of the Republic of Texas; manuscripts; maps - library; theatre

Washington's Birthplace VA

16786
George Washington Birthplace National Monument
Washington's Birthplace, VA 22575
Historic Site - 1932
Coll: colonial furnishings; costumes; folklore - colonial garden

Wasilla AK

16787
Wasilla Museum
POB 874, Wasilla, AK 99687
General Museum - 1966
Historical photos, tools, household items and equipment; historic building (1908) - historical park

Water Mill NY

16788
Old Water Mill Museum
Old Mill Rd, Water Mill, NY 11976
Historic Site - 1969
Coll: early tools of the cooper, carpenter, joiner, weaver and spinner, leatherworker, miller, farmer, housewife, and ice harvester; Grist Mill (1644) - crafts classrooms

Waterbury CT

16789
The Mattatuck Museum of the Mattatuck Historical Society
119 W. Main St, Waterbury, CT 06702
Fine Arts Museum - 1877
Coll: Connecticut artists; decorative arts; local historical material; Indian artifacts; industrial items - library; junior museum

Waterford PA

16790
Fort LeBoef Museum
123 S High St, Waterford, PA 16441
Historic Site - 1929
Coll: period furniture; artifacts from French occupation; archives; history; historic houses - library

Waterloo IA

16791
Grout Museum of History and Science
503 South St, Waterloo, IA 50701
History/Public Affairs Museum - 1933
Coll: early American arts and crafts; spinning, weaving, wood working, textiles; early man; astronomy; anthropology; paleontology; geology - auditorium; library

Waterloo NY

16792
Waterloo Library and Historical Society
31 E. Williams St, Waterloo, NY 13165
General Museum - 1875
Coll: local history and genealogy; antique autos; industry; agriculture; Memorial Day material and Civil War items - library; reading room; auditorium

Watertown CT

16793
Watertown Historical Society
22 DeForest St, Watertown, CT 06795
General Museum - 1947
Coll: articles, utensils, and tools; furniture - library; auditorium; classroom

Watertown MA

16794
Museum on the History of Blindness
Perkins School for the Blind
175 N Beacon St, Watertown, MA 02172
History/Public Affairs Museum - 1829
Coll: Nella Braddy Henney Collection including letters and memorabilia of Helen Keller; writing devices and educational aids from the early 19th century to the present

Watertown NY

16795
Jefferson County Historical Society
228 Washington St, Watertown, NY 13601
General Museum - 1886
Coll: 19th century Americana; agricultural and woodworking tools; early machinery; clothing; portraits; archives and photographs; northern New York Indian artifacts; Tyler coverlets (1834-58); collection of water turbines - library; classrooms

Watertown WI

16796
Watertown Historical Society
919 Charles St, Watertown, WI 53094
General Museum - 1933
Coll: folk art; Civil War materials; decorative arts; local memorabilia and history; first kindergarten in U.S. - library; children's museum

Waterville ME

16797
Colby College Museum of Art
Mayflower Hill, Waterville, ME 04901
Fine Arts Museum - 1959
Coll: painting; folk art; oriental art; painters of the Impressionist Period; Jette Collection; Winslow Homer Watercolors; A. A. D'Amico Print Collection

16798
Redington Museum
64 Silver St, Waterville, ME 04901
History/Public Affairs Museum - 1927
Coll: furnishings; tools and utensils of the early 19th century; maps; charts; manuscripts - library

Watford City ND

16799
Pioneer Museum
408 E Third, Watford City, ND 58854
General Museum - 1968
Coll: pioneer furnishings; Grassy Butte Post Office (1914)

Watkins Glen NY

16800
American Life Foundations and Study Institute
Old Irelandville, Watkins Glen, NY 14891
Decorative Arts Museum - 1958
Coll: decorative arts and art library; children's doll and toy museum; folklore; music; preservation project; paintings; costumes; Manor House (1833) - library

Watonga OK

16801
T. B. Ferguson Home
519 N Weigel, Watonga, OK 73772
Historic Site - 1972
Coll: early-day items of pioneers of area from 1890 to 1924; historic buildings (1870-1901)

Watrous NM

16802
Fort Union National Monument
Watrous, NM 87753
History/Public Affairs Museum - 1956
Coll: history of the three Fort Unions (1851-1891); development of Santa Fe trade, Civil War and settling of the West; Fort Union (1860) - library

Watseka IL

16803
Iroquois County Historical Society Museum Old Courthouse
2nd & Cherry, Watseka, IL 60970
History/Public Affairs Museum - 1967
Coll: art; military; archeology; medical history; agriculture; natural history; numismatics; industry; toys - library; reading room; auditorium

Watsonville CA

16804
Pajaro Valley Historical Association
261 E. Beach St, Watsonville, CA 95076
General Museum - 1940
Coll: photographs; vignettes; slides of buildings and houses in Watsonville - library

Wauconda IL

16805
Lake County Museum
Lakewood Forest Preserve, Wauconda, IL 60084
General Museum - 1957
Coll: vehicles; military arms and equipment; Indian artifacts; local historical objects - research center

Waukegan IL

16806
Waukegan Historical Society
1917 N Sheridan Rd, Waukegan, IL
60085
General Museum - 1968
Coll: local artifacts; Lincoln room; Civil
War artifacts and furnishings; clothing;
photos of historic landmarks; Indian
artifacts - library; reading room

Waukesha WI

16807
**Waukesha County Historical
Museum**
101 W Main St, Waukesha, WI 53186
General Museum - 1914
Coll: pioneer and Indian artifacts;
military; toys; Victorian furniture and
costumes; natural history; local
history; genealogy

Waurika OK

16808
Chisholm Trail Historical Museum
Intersection U.S. 81 and State 70,
Waurika, OK 73573
General Museum - 1965
Coll: anthropology; Chisholm Trail
history and pioneer collections

Wausau WI

16809
Leigh Yawkey Woodson Art Museum
700 N 12th St, Wausau, WI 54401
Decorative Arts Museum - 1973
Coll: decorative arts; porcelain; glass;
ornithological paintings and
woodcarvings - library

16810
Marathon County Historical Society
403 McIndoe St, Wausau, WI 54401
General Museum - 1952
Coll: local history; lumbering; antiques;
pioneer artifacts; Indian artifacts;
photographs

Waxahachie TX

16811
Ellis County Museum
201 S College, POB 706, Waxahachie,
TX 75165
History/Public Affairs Museum - 1967
Coll: manuscripts; antiques; genealogy

Waycross GA

16812
Okefenokee Heritage Center
Rte 5, POB 406 A, Waycross, GA
31501
General Museum - 1975
Coll: history of Okefenokee Swamp
and area; renovated 1912 train and
cars; historic buildings - classrooms;
conference room

Wayne NJ

16813
Dey Mansion,
199 Totowa Rd, Wayne, NJ 07470
Historic Site - 1934
Period furniture restored and
furnished in 18th century style;
antiques; barnyard; gardens; Dey
Mansion (1780)

16814
Van Riper-Hopper House Wayne
Museum
533 Berdan Av, Wayne, NJ 07470
General Museum - 1964
Coll: furnishings from Colonial Period
to 1860; Indian artifacts; antiques;
tinsel painting exhibits; clothing; china;
crystal; dolls; bird exhibit; artifact
display; Van Duyne House (1706) -
library; archaeological lab; nature
center

Wayne PA

16815
Radnor Historical Society
113 W Beech Tree Lane, Wayne, PA
19087
General Museum - 1948
Coll: early vehicles; early local
photographs; maps; manuscripts;
decorative arts - library

Waynesboro PA

16816
Renfrew Museum and Park
1010 E Main St, Waynesboro, PA
17268
Decorative Arts Museum - 1975
Coll: the Nicodemus collection of
American decorative arts, including
furniture and furnishings of the
American Federal period; Windsor
chairs; John Bell pottery collection;
spatterware; quilts - library; reading
room; park, nature and conservation
center

Waynesburg PA

16817
Greene County Historical Society
R.D. 2, Waynesburg, PA 15370
General Museum - 1925
Coll: Victorian rooms; archives;
archaeology; Indian artifacts - library;
reading room

Weatherly PA

16818
Eckley Miner's Village Pennsylvania
Anthracite Museum Complex
R.D. 2, Weatherly, PA 18255
General Museum - 1970
Coll: town life, tools, equipment, house,
shops and church furniture pertaining
to miners - visitors center

Weaverville CA

16819
J. J. Jackson Memorial Museum
POB 333, Weaverville, CA 96093
General Museum - 1953
Coll: mining; Chinese and Indian
artifacts; local historical items

16820
Weaverville Joss House
State Historic Park, POB W,
Weaverville, CA 96093
Religious Art Museum - 1956
Coll: articles relating to the function of
a Taoist temple of worship; Chinese
artifacts from Gold Rush period; Taoist
temple

Weeping Water NE

16821
Heritage House Museum
Weeping Water, NE 68463
History/Public Affairs Museum - 1969
Coll: prehistoric Indian artifacts;
fossils; medical books of 1800's;
medical instruments and drugs -
library

Weiser ID

16822
**Washington County Museum and
Fiddler's Hall of Fame**
46 W Commercial St, Weiser, ID 83672
General Museum - 1962
Coll: music; costumes; folklore; glass;
geology; historic houses - library;
children's museum; auditorium

Wellesley MA

16823
**Cardinal Spellmann Philatelic
Museum**
Regis College, 235 Wellesley St,
Wellesley, MA 02193
History/Public Affairs Museum - 1960
Coll: postage stamps of the world and
related material - library; meeting
rooms

16824
The Wellesley College Museum
Jewett Arts Center, Wellesley College,
Wellesley, MA 02181
Fine Arts Museum - 1883
Coll: European, American and Oriental
paintings, drawings, sculpture

Wellington KS

16825
Chisholm Trail Museum
502 N Washington, Wellington, KS
67152
History/Public Affairs Museum - 1964
china; glass; silver; folk art; historic
rooms - library

Wellington OH

16826
Spirit of '76 Museum
202 Main St, POB 76, Wellington, OH
44090
General Museum - 1970
Coll: items associated with Archibald
M. Willard's painting, 'The Spirit of '76';
artifacts associated with the history of
Southern Lorain County - reading
room; auditorium

Wells ME

16827
Wells Auto Museum
Rte 1, Wells, ME 04090
History/Public Affairs Museum - 1954
Coll: antique cars; motorcycles;
bicycles; nickelodeons

Wenatchee WA

16828
North Central Washington Museum
127 S Mission, Wenatchee, WA 98801
General Museum - 1939
Coll: North Central Washington
pioneer exhibits and history; farm
equipment; sewing machines;
Pangborn transpacific flight; Indian
artifacts

16829
Rocky Reach Dam
POB 1231, Wenatchee, WA 98801
Science/Tech Museum - 1963
Coll: paintings; graphics; electrical
antiques; Thomas Edison artifacts;
interpretive local geology -
observatory, theater

Wenham MA

16830
**Wenham Historical Association and
Museum, Inc.**
132 Main St, Wenham, MA 01984
History/Public Affairs Museum - 1921
Coll: dolls and doll houses; toys;
costumes and textiles; embroidery and
needlework; quilts; early domestic and
kitchen utensils; historic houses;
Wenham Lake Ice Industry Exhibit -
library

West Allis WI

16831
West Allis Historical Society
8405 W National Av, West Allis, WI
53227
General Museum - 1966
Coll: toys; model steam engine;
motors; early dental office, post office
and grocery; clothing - library;
classrooms

West Bend WI

16832
**Washington County Historical
Library and Museum**
340 Fifth Av, 815 S 7th Av, West Bend,
WI 53095
General Museum - 1937
Coll: artifacts; pictures; maps;
genealogies - library

West Boothbay Harbor ME

16833
**State of Maine Marine Resources
Laboratory**
McKown Point, West Boothbay
Harbor, ME 04575
Natural History Museum - 1905
Coll: marine; aquarium; natural history
- library

West Branch IA

16834
Herbert Hoover Presidential Library
234 S Downey, West Branch, IA 52358
History/Public Affairs Museum - 1962
Coll: personal papers, books,
memorabilia of Herber Hoover and
materials related to his life and times -
auditorium; library

West Chester PA

16835
Chester County Historical Society
225 N High St, West Chester, PA
19380
General Museum - 1893
Coll: agriculture; archives; paintings;
sculpture; graphics; decorative arts;
archaeology; costumes; history;
artifacts; medicine; mineralogy;
numismatics; philately; textiles; dolls;
Tucker china - library; children's
museum; reading room; auditorium

16836
West Chester State College Museum
West Chester, PA 19380
Natural History Museum - 1871
Coll: botany; geology; archaeology; ornithology; history ; Darlington herbarium (1810-1860) - library

West Fargo ND
16837
Cass County Historical Society
POB 719, West Fargo, ND 58078
General Museum - 1962
Coll: Indian artifacts; pioneer home equipment; crafts; textiles; minerals; farm machinery; replica of pioneer village

West Fulton NY
16838
Archaeological Field Museum New York Institute of Anthropology
West Fulton Rd, West Fulton, NY 12194
Anthropology Museum - 1971
Coll: prehistoric art and archaeological specimens; colonial and early American artifacts; historical manuscripts and documents; European and American Art; American Indian and Foreign folk art - library; field research station; reading room

West Hartford CT
16839
Children's Museum of Hartford
950 Trout Brook Dr, West Hartford, CT 06119
Junior Museum - 1927
Coll: American Indian articles; fossils; birds; heart exhibit; natural history - planetarium; nature center; aquarium; touch tank; live animal center

West Haven CT
16840
National Art Museum of Sport, Inc.
University of New Haven
300 Orange Av, West Haven, CT 06516
Fine Arts Museum - 1959
Paintings, sculpture, and graphics on sporting subjects

West Henrietta NY
16841
New York Museum of Transportation
POB 136, West Henrietta, NY 14586
Science/Tech Museum - 1974
Coll: street cars; interurbans; railroad equipment; autos; trucks; fire equipment; photos, maps, printed matter (1880-1955); Rochester and Eastern Rapid Railway Station (1904) - library; demonstrational railway

West Liberty OH
16842
Piatt Castles
R.R. 2, West Liberty, OH 43357
Historic Site - 1913
Coll: early American and French period antiques; rare art and furnishings (200-800 years old); Castle Piatt Mac-A-Cheek (1864); Castle Mac-O-Chee (1871)

West Orange NJ
16843
Edison National Historic Site
Main St at Lakeside Av, West Orange, NJ 07052
Historic Site - 1956
Coll: papers; photographs; historical objects; mineralogy; history; industrial technology

West Palm Beach FL
16844
Norton Gallery and School of Art
1451 S Olive Av, West Palm Beach, FL 33401
Fine Arts Museum - 1940
Coll: 19th and 20th century American and French paintings and sculpture; Chinese jades, bronzes, ceramics, and Buddhist sculpture; European painting from the Renaissance through the 18th century - library; auditorium; theater; classrooms

16845
Science Museum and Planetarium of Palm Beach County, Inc.
4801 Dreher Trail North, West Palm Beach, FL 33405
Science/Tech Museum - 1959
Coll: Central American pottery; African tribal carvings; natural history; astronomy; ethnology - planetarium; discovery room; observatories; auditorium; lapidary workroom

16846
Science Museum and Planetarium of Palm Beach County, Inc.
4801 Dreher Trail North, West Palm Beach, FL 33405
Science/Tech Museum - 1959
Coll: Central American pottery; African tribal carvings; natural history; astronomy; ethnology - planetarium; discovery room; observatories; auditorium; lapidary workroom

West Point NY
16847
Constitution Island Association
POB 41, West Point, NY 10996
Historic Site - 1916
Coll: Warner House Collection of furnishings, furniture, art, china, glass, kitchen and gardening utensils, memorabilia; Victorian house (1800) - library; Anna B. Warner Memorial Garden

16848
West Point Museum United States Military Academy
West Point, NY 10996
History/Public Affairs Museum - 1854
Coll: international military history, civil history, fine arts and culture; American and foreign military ordnance, dress, accoutrements, portraiture, paintings, prints, posters - library

West Salem WI
16849
Hamlin Garland Homestead
357 W Garland St, West Salem, WI 54669
General Museum - 1976
Coll: local historical and musical items; fans; historic house - library

West Sayville NY
16850
Suffolk Marine Museum
Montauk Hwy, West Sayville, NY 11796
Science/Tech Museum - 1969
Coll: marine; history; naval - library

West Union IA
16851
Fayette County Historical Center
100 N Walnut St, West Union, IA 52175
History/Public Affairs Museum - 1975
Coll: history of Fayette County; genealogical materials and records - reading room; library

Westerly RI
16852
Westerly Public Library
Broad St, Westerly, RI 02891
General Museum - 1894
Coll: Indian artifacts; Civil War artifacts; paintings; zooology; minerals; toys, dolls and doll furniture; furniture; local history - library; auditorium; Wilcox Park

Westfield NY
16853
History Center and Museum
Main and Portage Sts, Center of Village Park, POB 173, Westfield, NY 14787
General Museum - 1883
Coll: agriculture; archaeology; history; military; Indian artifacts; archives; costumes; genealogy of Chautauqua County; historic house (1818) - library; children's museum

Weston CT
16854
Barn-Museum of the Weston Historical Society
Weston Rd, POB 1092, Weston, CT 06883
Agriculture Museum - 1961
Coll: early handicrafts; furnishings; old farm tools; old barn (1835) - library

Weston VT
16855
Farrar-Mansur House
On the Common, Weston, VT 05161
General Museum - 1933
Coll: local antiques; murals; dolls - library

Westport CT
16856
Nature Center for Environmental Activities, Inc.
10 Woodside Lane, POB 165, Westport, CT 06880
Natural History Museum - 1958
Coll: geology; entomology; ornithology; mineralogy - library; nature center; field research station; auditorium; classrooms

Wethersfield CT
16857
The Webb-Deane-Stevens Museum
211 Main St, Wethersfield, CT 06109
Decorative Arts Museum - 1919
Coll: American furniture; decorative arts; ceramics; silver; needlework; toys - library

16858
The Wethersfield Historical Society
150 Main St, Wethersfield, CT 06109
History/Public Affairs Museum - 1932
Coll: local history; maritime; documents; genealogy; tools and crafts; furniture; decorative arts - reading room; reception center

Wewoka OK
16859
Seminole Nation Museum
524 S Wewoka Av, Wewoka, OK 74884
Anthropology Museum - 1974
Coll: Seminole Indian artifacts - reading room

Wheaton IL
16860
Catigny
1 S 151 Winfield Rd, Wheaton, IL 60187
History/Public Affairs Museum
Coll: push-button exhibits telling the story of World Wars I and II and Vietnam War; historic house - library; theater; gardens

16861
Dupage County Historical Museum
102 E Wesley St, Wheaton, IL 60187
General Museum - 1967
Coll: furniture; pressed glass; flags; farm implements; guns; photographs; dolls and toys; antiques - library

Wheeling WV
16862
Oglebay Institute-Mansion Museum
Oglebay Park, Wheeling, WV 26003
History/Public Affairs Museum - 1930
Coll: glass; china; ceramics; decorative arts; pottery; history - library; auditorium

White Plains NY
16863
County of Westchester, Department of Parks, Recreation and Conservation
County Office Bldg, Room 618, White Plains, NY 10601
General Museum - 1951
Coll: history; farm animals; historic house (1732)

White Springs FL
16864
Stephen Foster State Folk Culture Center
Suwannee River at White Springs, POB 8, White Springs, FL 32096
General Museum - 1939
Coll: paintings; bells; musical instruments; dolls; Minstrel Show material; manuscripts; Foster's famous folk songs; historic houses - auditorium; theater

White Swan WA
16865
Fort Simcoe Interpretive Center
Rte 1, POB 39, White Swan, WA 98952
History/Public Affairs Museum
Interpretive Center and restored buildings of 1856-1859 military outpost; materials related to life at the fort

Whitewater WI

16866
Whitewater Historical Museum
Whitewater, WI 53190
General Museum - 1974
Coll: china; glass; furniture; clothing;
tools; early industries

Wichita Falls TX

16867
Wichita Falls Museum and Art Center
2 Eureka Circle, POB Z, Wichita Falls,
TX 76308
General Museum - 1965
Coll: American art; graphics - library;
auditorium; planetarium;

Wichita KS

16868
Edwin A. Ulrich Museum of Art
Wichita State University
POB 46, Wichita, KS 67208
Fine Arts Museum - 1974
Coll: nineteenth and twentieth Century
American Art; European Art; Primitive
Art of the Americas; American and
European prints - classrooms

16869
The Indian Museum Mid-America
All-Indian Center
650 N Seneca, Wichita, KS 67203
Anthropology Museum - 1975
Coll: Native American art and artifacts
- library

16870
Wichita Art Association
9112 E Central, Wichita, KS 67206
Fine Arts Museum - 1920
Coll: enamels; Oriental art; Twentieth
century decorative arts; porcelains;
fine prints - library; classrooms;
auditorium

16871
Wichita Art Museum
619 Stackman Dr., Wichita, KS 67203
Fine Arts Museum - 1935
Coll: Roland P. Murdock Collection of
American Art; L.S. and Ida L. Naftzger
Collection of American and European
Prints and Drawings; M.C. Naftzger
Collection of Charles M. Russell
Drawings and Sculpture; Gwendolyn
Houston Naftzger Porcelain
Collection; Kurdian Collection of
Pre-Columbian Mexican artifacts;
European porcelain and faience -
library

Wickliffe KY

16872
Ancient Buried City
POB 155, Wickliffe, KY 42087
Natural History Museum - 1932
fossils; minerals; 1,000 year-old
botanical remains

Wilber NE

16873
Wilber Czech Museum
POB 253, Wilber, NE 68465
General Museum - 1962
Coll: agriculture; costumes; decorative
arts; medical equipment; guns;
antiques

Wild Rose WI

16874
Pioneer Museum
Main St, Wild Rose, WI 54984
General Museum - 1964
Coll: agriculture; costumes; medical;
textiles; historic houses - children's
museum

Wilkes-Barre Pa

16875
Wyoming Historical and Geological Society
69 S Franklin St, 49 S Franklin St,
Wilkes-Barre, Pa 18701
General Museum - 1858
Coll: archaeology; archives; costumes;
geology; Indian artifacts; industry;
military; mineralogy; textiles; historic
houses - library; reading room

Williams CA

16876
Sacramento Valley Museum Association, Inc.
1491 E Street, Williams, CA 95987
General Museum - 1963
Coll: historic buildings; minerals; toys;
costumes; documents; farm machinery
- library; reading room

Williamsburg VA

16877
Abby Aldrich Rockefeller Folk Art Center
307 S England St, POB C,
Williamsburg, VA 23185
Decorative Arts Museum - 1939
Coll: American folk art: paintings,
sculpture, decoys, needlework -
library

16878
Colonial Williamsburg
Goodwin Building, Williamsburg, VA
23185
History/Public Affairs Museum - 1926
Coll: archeology; decorative arts;
costumes; military; music; folk art;
historic houses - library; archival
materials; auditorium; theater;
classrooms

16879
Jamestown Festival Park The
Jamestown-Yorktown Foundation
PO Drawer JF, Williamsburg, VA
23185
General Museum - 1957
Coll: English arts and history of the
17th century; early Virginia house
furnishings; Virginia Indian objects of
the 17th century - library

Williamsport PA

16880
Lycoming County Historical Society and Museum
858 W 4th St, Williamsport, PA 17701
General Museum - 1895
Coll: Indian artifacts; archives;
lumbering; Civil War items; industry
and industry trades; military; textiles;
farm and home utensils; agriculture;
costumes; transportation; music;
natural history; science; historic
buildings

Williamstown MA

16881
Sterling and Francine Clark Art Institute
225 South St, POB 8, Williamstown,
MA 01267
Fine Arts Museum - 1950
European painting from the 14th-18th
centuries; French 19th century
painting; works of Homer and
Sargent; 19th century sculpture;
porcelain; antique silver - library;
auditorium

16882
Williams College Museum of Art
Main St, Williamstown, MA 01267
Fine Arts Museum - 1926
Coll: American antique furniture; 18th
and 19th century British and American
portraits; 15th-18th century Spanish
painting and furniture; 19th and 20th
century American painting and
sculpture; pre-Columbian, African, and
Oriental sculpture; Italian Renaissance
art; non-Western sculpture

Williston ND

16883
Fort Buford Historic Site
Buford Rt, Williston, ND 58801
Historic Site - 1962
Powder magazine; officers quarters of
Fort Buford (1871); site of Sitting Bull's
surrender July 19, 1881

16884
Fort Union Trading Post National Historic Site
Buford Rt, Williston, ND 58801
General Museum - 1966
Coll: archaeological specimens; fur
trade related material; American Fur
Trading Company fort at the
confluence of the Missouri and
Yellowstone Rivers - library;
auditorium

16885
Frontier Museum
Williston, ND 58801
General Museum - 1958
Coll: history; paintings; sculpture;
graphics; decorative arts;
archaeology; military; numismatics;
philately; textiles; transportation; log
cabin (1890); old judge's home;
country church; Grocery Store; Great
Northern Caboose (1906); country
school; old time doctor's and dentist's
office (1914) - library

Willits CA

16886
Mendocino County Museum
400 E. Commercial St, Willits, CA
95490
General Museum - 1972
Coll: Indian artifacts; historical items;
period rooms; stagecoaches; early
20th century hat collection; local art
collection - amphitheater; art galleries;
botanical garden

Willmar MN

16887
Kandiyohi County Historical Society
610 Hwy 71 NE, Willmar, MN 56201
General Museum - 1898
Coll: transportation; Indian artifacts -
library

Wilmette IL

16888
Wilmette Historical Museum
565 Hunter Rd, Wilmette, IL 60091
General Museum - 1947
Coll: local history archives; art;
costumes; history - library

Wilmington DE

16889
Delaware Art Museum
2301 Kentmere Pkwy, Wilmington, DE
19806
Fine Arts Museum - 1912
Coll: general American paintings;
English pre-Raphaelite paintings;
Howard Pyle, John Sloan, Wyeth
family collections; graphics;
photography; sculpture - library;
classrooms

16890
The Hagley Museum
POB 3630 Greenville, Wilmington, DE
19807
Science/Tech Museum - 1952
Coll: archeology; agriculture;
technology; patent models; industry;
textiles; ceramics; historic houses

16891
Historical Society of Delaware
505 Market St, Wilmington, DE 19801
General Museum - 1864
Coll: documents and artifacts related
to Delaware history; silver; decorative
arts; costumes; historic houses -
library; garden

16892
Rockwood Museum
610 Shipley Rd, Wilmington, DE 19809
Decorative Arts Museum - 1976
Coll: original family furnishings
covering five generations; decorative
arts of the 17th century through
Victorian age - reading room;
conference center

Wilmington NC

16893
New Hanover County Museum
814 Market St, Wilmington, NC 28401
General Museum - 1898
Coll: Civil War and other military
material; Dudley Chinese collection;
Belgium Congo African material;
costumes; photographs; Victorian
furniture; human physiology exhibit

16894
St. John's Art Gallery
114 Orange St, Wilmington, NC 28401
Fine Arts Museum - 1962
Coll: scent bottles; pottery; paintings;
St. John's Masonic Lodge (1804) - art
studio; gardens

16895
USS North Carolina Battleship Memorial
Cape Fear River on Eagles Island,
Wilmington NC 28401, POB 417,
Wilmington, NC 28402
History/Public Affairs Museum - 1961
Coll: World War II and U.S. Navy
paintings; Kingfisher float plane

Wilson AR

16896
Hampson Museum State Park
Lake Dr at Hwy 61, Wilson, AR 72395
Archeology Museum - 1937
Coll: Late Mississippian culture;
archeological collections; Ozark Bluff
Dwellers' textiles

Wilson NY

16897
Wilson Historical Society
4559 Chestnut Rd, Wilson, NY 14172
General Museum - 1972
Coll: woodworking tools; dresses;
quilts; railroad artifacts; books - library

Wilton CT

16898
Craft Center Museum, Inc.
78 Danbury Rd, Wilton, CT 06897
Decorative Arts Museum - 1931
Coll: armor; tools and finished
products in areas of metal spinning;
burnishing; blacksmithing; leadwork;
woodwork; leatherwork; brass casting
- library

16899
Wilton Heritage Museum
249 Danbury Rd, Wilton, CT 06897
General Museum - 1938
Coll: 18th and 19th century
furnishings; tools; dolls; costumes;
manuscripts and map collection;
historic house (1732) - library;
classrooms

Wimberley TX

16900
Pioneer Town
7A Ranch Resort, Route 1, POB 259,
Wimberley, TX 78676
Historic Site - 1956
Coll: artifacts of the Old West;
authentic reproduction of an Old West
town

Winchester IN

16901
Randolph County Historical Museum
412 E North St, Winchester, IN 47394
General Museum - 1959
Coll: furniture and furnishings of the
19th century; historic house - library

Winchester VA

16902
**Winchester-Frederick County
Historical Society, Inc.**
POB 58, Winchester, VA 22601
General Museum - 1930
Coll: furniture; artifacts; Civil War
relics; historic houses

Windom MN

16903
**Cottonwood County Historical
Society**
812 Fourth Ave, Windom, MN 56101
General Museum - 1901
Coll: clothings; music case displays;
historic rooms - library

Window Rock AZ

16904
Navajo Tribal Museum
POB 308, Window Rock, AZ 86515
General Museum - 1961
Coll: Southwest archeology; Navajo
history and ethnology; herbarium;
archives; paleontology; geology; arts
and crafts

Windsor Locks CT

16905
**Bradley Air Museum of the
Connecticut Aeronautical Historical
Association, Inc.**
Bradley International Airport, Windsor
Locks, CT 06096
Science/Tech Museum - 1959
Coll: aircraft; propulsion systems;
aeronautics - library

Windsor NC

16906
Historic Hope Foundation
Windsor, NC 27983
Historic Site - 1965
Coll: antique period furniture;
Georgian Mansion (1800)

Windsor NY

16907
Old Stone House Museum
10 Chestnut St, POB 306, Windsor, NY
13865
General Museum - 1970
Coll: Civil War artifacts, weapons,
accoutrements; local historical items;
business and industries; Indian relics;
lamps; bottles; whips - library

Windsor VT

16908
American Precision Museum
Windsor, VT 05089
Science/Tech Museum - 1966
Coll: machine tools; gun-making
machines - library; archives

16909
Old Constitution House
North Main St, Windsor, VT 05089
Historic Site - 1777
Coll: items from Colonial and Civil War
periods; pottery; furniture

Winona MN

16910
Steamer 'Julius C. Wilkie'
Levee Park, Winona, MN 55987
Science/Tech Museum - 1956
Coll: underwater archaeology; naval
steamboats; technology;
transportation - library

16911
Winona County Historical Society
160 Johnson St, Winona, MN 55987
General Museum - 1935
coll: horse drawn vehicles; fire fighting
equipment; Indian artifacts

Winslow AZ

16912
Museum of Astrogeology Great
Meteor Crater
U.S. 66, East of Flagstaff, POB AC,
Winslow, AZ 86001
Natural History Museum - 1962
Coll: space capsule; NASA space suit;
meteorite oxide; minerals and rocks;
photos; moon maps - library

Winston-Salem NC

16913
Historic Bethabara
2147 Bethabara Rd, Winston-Salem,
NC 27106
Historic Site - 1970
Coll: excavated fragments of 18th
century Moravian pottery; furniture;
tools; Bethabara Brewer's House
(1803); Potter's House (1782);
Bethabara Church and Gemeinhaus
(1788) - library; nature trails

16914
**Museum of Early Southern
Decorative Arts**
924 Main St, Winston-Salem, NC
27101
Decorative Arts Museum - 1960
Coll: architecture; furniture; paintings;
ceramics; textiles; prints; metalwares -
research center

16915
Museum of Man Wake Forest
University
106 Reynolda Village, Winston-Salem,
NC 27106
Anthropology Museum - 1962
Coll: anthropology; archaeology;
Indian artifacts; ethnology; African Art;
Oceanic Art

16916
Nature Science Center
Museum Dr, Winston-Salem, NC
27105
Natural History Museum - 1964
Coll: animals; plants; rocks; minerals;
archaeological and anthropological
materials; anthropological specimens
and artifacts - library; wildflower trails;
theater

16917
Old Salem, Inc.
Drawer F, Salem Station, Winston-
Salem, NC 27108
Historic Site - 1950
Coll: 18th and 19th century Moravian
artifacts; furnishings; tools; music;
decorative arts; Moravian
Congregation Town (1766) - outdoor
museum; library; reading room;
auditoria

16918
Reynolda House, Inc.
Reynolda Rd, POB 11765, Winston-
Salem, NC 27106
Fine Arts Museum - 1964
Coll: doughty birds; American
paintings; costumes; Reynolda House
(1915-1917) - library; botanical
gardens

16919
**The Southeastern Center for
Contemporary Art**
750 Marguerite Dr, Winston-Salem,
NC 27106
Fine Arts Museum - 1956
Coll: annual exhibitions - library;
reading room; nature center; children's
creative center

Winter Park FL

16920
Beal-Maltbie Shell Museum Rollins
College
Holt Av, POB 1037, Winter Park, FL
32789
Natural History Museum - 1940
Coll: two million shells - library

16921
**The George D. and Harriet W.
Cornell Fine Arts Center Museum**
Rollins College
Winter Park, FL 32789
Fine Arts Museum - 1932
Coll: 19th and 20th century American
paintings; European paintings of the
Renaissance through the 19th century;
bronzes; sculptures; prints; Smith
watch key collection

16922
The Morse Gallery of Art
133 E Welbourne Av, 151 E
Welbourne Av, Winter Park, FL 32789
Fine Arts Museum - 1942
Coll: windows; lamps; blown glass;
pottery; paintings; furniture

Winterthur DE

16923
**Henry Francis Du Pont Winterthur
Museum**
Winterthur, DE 19735
Decorative Arts Museum - 1930
Coll: American decorative arts from
the 17th century to 1840; interior
architecture; metalwork; ceramics,
glass, and textiles; paintings; lighting
fixtures - library; auditorium;
classrooms; botanical gardens

Winterville GA

16924
**Carter-Coile Country Doctors
Museum**
POB 306, Winterville, GA 30683
History/Public Affairs Museum - 1971
Coll: medical equipment; furnishings;
books; specimens from 1800s and
1900s

Wiscasset ME

16925
Musical Museum Musical Wonder
House
18 High St, Wiscasset, ME 04578
Music Museum - 1962
Coll: music boxes; player and crank
pianos; crank organs; talking
machines - library

Woodbury CT

16926
Glebe House
Hollow Rd, Woodbury, CT 06798
General Museum - 1900
Coll: original paneling; early American
furnishings; historical documents
relating to Samuel Seabury; historic
house (1690) - library

Woodbury NJ

16927
**Gloucester County Historical
Society**
58 N Broad St, POB 409, Woodbury,
NJ 08096
General Museum - 1903
Coll: military; Indian artifacts; antique
furnishings; Colonial and Victorian
furniture; farm implements; archives;
history; costumes; glass; Hunter-
Lawrence house (1765); Moravian
Church (1786) - library; children's
museum

Woodstock CT

16928
Woodstock Historical Society, Inc.
POB 65, Woodstock, CT 06281
General Museum - 1967
Coll: agriculture; local historical items;
historic building (1851)

Woodstock VA

16929
**Woodstock Museum of Shenandoah
County, Inc.**
147 N Main St, Woodstock, VA 22664
General Museum - 1969
Local history

Woodstock VT

16930
Woodstock Historical Society
26 Elm St, Woodstock, VT 05091
General Museum - 1942
Coll: furniture; silver and glass;
costumes; early photographs - library;
auditorium

Woodville TX

16931
Allan Shivers Museum and Library
302 N Charlton, Woodville, TX 75979
Historic Site - 1963
Coll: period furnishings and costumes
- library

Woodward OK

16932
**Plains Indians and Pioneer Historical
Foundation Pioneer Museum**
2009 Williams Av, POB 1167,
Woodward, OK 73801
General Museum - 1956
Coll: pioneer life and Indian artifacts

Wooster OH

16933
College of Wooster Art Museum
E University St, Wooster, OH 44691
Fine Arts Museum - 1930
Coll: John Taylor Arms collection of
European and American prints; 16th -
20th century Persian decorative arts;
Chinese paintings and bronzes;
African sculpture; pottery of ancient
Middle East - library; reading room
16934
Wayne County Historical Society
546 E Bowman St, Wooster, OH 44691
General Museum - 1954
Coll: lusterware; mounted birds and
small animals; minerals; military
equipment; portraits of early Wooster
citizens; Indian artifacts; tools and
furniture; Civil War Log House (1880);
Little Red Schoolhouse; Kister building
- library

Worcester MA

16935
John Woodman Higgins Armory, Inc
Barber Av, Worcester, MA 01505
History/Public Affairs Museum - 1928
Ancient, Medieval and Renaissance
arms and armor; stained glass -
library; auditorium
16936
Worcester Art Museum
55 Salisbury St, Worcester, MA 01508
Fine Arts Museum - 1896
European, Oriental and American arts
from all periods - library; auditorium;
classrooms

Worthington MN

16937
Nobles County Historical Society
416-12th St, Worthington, MN 56187
General Museum - 1933
Coll: books; harnesses; medical
equipment; tools; toys - library

Worthington OH

16938
Ohio Railway Museum
990 Proprietors Rd, POB 171,
Worthington, OH 43085
Science/Tech Museum - 1945
Coll: historic steam, gas and electric
railway equipment
16939
Orange Johnson House
POB 355, Worthington, OH 43085
Historic Site - 1955
Coll: doll collection; early community
memorabilia; Orange Johnson House
(1816); The Old Rectory (1830);
Worthington Indian Mound - library

Wrangell AK

16940
Tribal House of the Bear
Wrangell, AK 99929
General Museum - 1850
Coll: decorative arts; archeology;
costumes; history; Indian totem poles
and houses; wood carvings; pictures -
outdoor museum

Wright-Patterson AFB OH

16941
United States Air Force Museum
Wright-Patterson AFB, OH 45433
Science/Tech Museum - 1923
Coll: 150 aircraft and major missiles;
uniforms; personal military related
memorabilia; aviation guns and
instruments; aircraft squadron insignia;
military badges; space hardware and
foods; model collections - library;
auditorium

Wyandotte MI

16942
Wyandotte Historical Commission
2610 Biddle Ave, Wyandotte, MI 48192
History/Public Affairs Museum
Coll: genealogy; shipbuilding; chemical
industry collection - library

Wyoming NY

16943
**Middlebury Historical Society
Museum**
32 S. Academy St, Wyoming, NY
14591
General Museum - 1941
Coll: military equipment; musical
instruments; farm tools; photographs;
women's costumes and accessories;
Middlebury Academy (1817) - library

Xenia OH

16944
Greene County Historical Society
74 W Church St, Xenia, OH 45385
General Museum - 1931
Coll: Indian artifacts; military; antique
furniture; paintings; agricultural
implements; dolls; Galloway Cabin
(1798); Treben-Flynn Victorian style
home - library

Yadkinville NC

16945
Yadkin County Historical Society
Yadkinville, NC 27055
General Museum - 1965
Coll: artifacts; history - library; reading
room

Yakima WA

16946
**Yakima Valley Museum and
Historical Association**
2105 Tieton Dr, Yakima, WA 98902
General Museum - 1952
Coll: minerals; vehicles; Indian
artifacts; period costumes; weapons;
household furnishings; blacksmith
shop; early day post office - archives

Yonkers NY

16947
The Hudson River Museum
511 Warburton Av, Trevor Park-on-
Hudson, Yonkers, NY 10701
General Museum - 1924
Coll: historic American painting,
sculpture, photography, decorative
arts and documents; contemporary art
and architecture; Trevor House (1877)
and Andrus Space Planetarium -
library; reading room
16948
Philipse Manor State Historic Site
Warburton Av and Dock St, POB 496,
Yonkers, NY 10702
Historic Site - 1908
Coll: Windsor chairs, furniture and
furnishings of the period; Cochran
Collection of portraits of famous
Americans; Philipse Manor Hall
(1700-50) - auditorium

York ME

16949
Old Gaol Museum Committee
Lindsay Rd and York St, York, ME
03909
General Museum - 1900
Coll: local history; ceramics;
furnishings; prison manuscripts and
implements - library

York PA

16950
**The Historical Society of York
County**
250 E Market St, York, PA 17403
General Museum - 1895
Coll: Lewis Miller drawings; local
history; musical instruments;
Tannenberg organ (1804); period
rooms; folklore; circus; historic houses
- library; reading room; auditorium

Yorktown Heights NY

16951
Town of Yorktown Museum
1974 Commerce St, Yorktown
Heights, NY 10598
General Museum - 1966
Coll: agricultural tools and equipment;
costumes and textiles; dollhouses,
toys and dolls; spinning and weaving
equipment; Indian artifacts; archives,
genealogical books, photographs;
Sylvia Newton Thorne marionettes;
Old Put Line of New York Central R. R.
- library

Yorktown VA

16952
Colonial National Historical Park
POB 210, Yorktown, VA 23690
General Museum - 1930
Coll: 17th and 18th century arms and
artifacts; 18th century historic houses
- library
16953
Yorktown Visitor Center
Colonial National Historical Park, POB
210, Yorktown, VA 23690
History/Public Affairs Museum - 1930
Coll: paintings and relics relating to the
American Revolution, especially the
siege and battle of Yorktown - library

Youngstown NY

16954
Old Fort Niagara Associations, Inc.
Old Fort Niagara, POB 169,
Youngstown, NY 14174
Historic Site - 1926
Coll: military; history - library

Youngstown OH

16955
The Arms Museum
648 Wick Av, Youngstown, OH 44502
General Museum - 1961
Coll: Arms family possessions; 19th
and 20th century memorabilia and
furnishings; local history; household
and farm articles; antique toys; Indian
relics; period gowns - library
16956
The Butler Institute of American Art
524 Wick Av, Youngstown, OH 44502
Fine Arts Museum - 1919
Coll: American art from colonial to
present times; miniature paintings of
U.S. presidents; paintings and
drawings of the American Indians;
paintings, prints and scale models of
clipper ships; antique glass bells;
ceramics and sculpture - library

Yreka CA

16957
Siskiyou County Museum
910 S. Main St, Yreka, CA 96097
General Museum - 1951
Coll: local historical items; household
items; replicas of historical buildings;
archeology; archives; mineralogy -
library; outdoor museum

Yuba City CA

16958
**Community Memorial Museum of
Sutter County**
1333 Butte House Rd, POB 1555, Yuba
City, CA 95991
General Museum - 1975
Coll: Maidu Indian artifacts; historical
items and documents; photo
collection; pioneer relics; agricultural
items - library

Yucaipa CA

16959
Mousley Museum of Natural History
11555 Bryant St, Yucaipa, CA 92399
Science/Tech Museum - 1970
Coll: minerals; fossils; shells; primitive
artifacts - nature/conservation center;
auditorium; wildlife sanctuary

Yucca Valley CA

16960
Hi-Desert Nature Museum
5711729 Palms Hwy, Yucca Valley, CA
92284
Science/Tech Museum - 1964
Coll: butterflies from local and foreign
areas; fossils; rocks, gems, and
minerals; Indian artifacts; historical
items; zoology - nature trails

Yuma AZ

16961
Yuma Fine Arts Association, Inc.
281 Gila St, POB 1471, Yuma, AZ
85364
Fine Arts Museum - 1962
Coll: contemporary Arizona paintings;
ceramics; sculpture; graphics -
classrooms; studios

Zanesville OH

16962
Zanesville Art Center
620 Military Rd, Zanesville, OH 43701
Fine Arts Museum - 1936
Coll: paintings; drawings; prints;
photography; ceramics; glass;
Oriental, New Zealand, Australian,
South Seas, Mexican, African,
European and American art; Zanesville
area ceramics; Zanesville and
Midwestern glass - library; reading
room; auditorium; classrooms

Zion IL

16963
Zion Historical Society
1300 Shiloh Blvd, POB 333, Zion, IL
60099
Religious Art Museum - 1967
Coll: original furnishings; antiques;
religious artifacts - library

Zoar OH

16964
Zoar State Memorial
Zoar, OH 44697
Historic Site
Coll: folk Germanic-American arts and
crafts; tools; restored buildings of
German religious sect village (1817)

Zolfo Springs FL

16965
Pioneer Park Museum
Hwy & State Rd 64, Zolfo Springs, FL
33873
General Museum - 1966
Coll: aeronautics; agriculture;
anthropology; archeology; decorative
arts; archives; industry; natural history;
transportation

Upper Volta

Ouagadougou

16966
Musée National de Haute-Volta
Av Oubritenga, BP 6, mail c/o
Direction des Musées, des Sites et
Monuments, BP 55, Ouagadougou
General Museum
Ethnology; ethnography

Uruguay

Mercedes

16967
Museo de Mercedes
Mercedes
General Museum

Montevideo

16968
Museo de Armas
Fortaleza del Cerro de Montevideo,
Montevideo
History/Public Affairs Museum
military; armaments

16969
Museo de Arte Industrial
San Salvador 1674, Montevideo
Decorative Arts Museum
applied arts; crafts

16970
**Museo del Banco de la Republica
Oriental del Uruguay**
Montevideo
General Museum

16971
**Museo del Instituto Geologico del
Uruguay**
Montevideo
Natural History Museum
geology

16972
Museo 'Ernesto Laroche'
Gregorio Suarez 2716, Punta Carretas,
Montevideo
General Museum

16973
Museo Historico Nacional Casa
Rivera
Rincón 437, Montevideo
General Museum - 1900
prehistoric and colonial Indian cultural
history; Uruguay political history;
military; armaments; music

16974
Museo Juan Zorilla de San Martin
Ellauri 96, Montevideo
History/Public Affairs Museum

16975
Museo Municipal de Bellas Artes
Av. Millan 4015, Montevideo
Fine Arts Museum - 1928
paintings; graphic arts; sculpture;
woodcarvings

16976
Museo Nacional de Artes Plasticas
Tomás Giribaldi 2283, Apdo. 271,
Parque Rodó, Montevideo
Fine Arts Museum
paintings; sculptures; graphic arts of
Uruguay and America; works by
Joaquín Torres Carcía - library

16977
Museo Nacional de Historia Natural
Buenos Aires 652, POB 399,
Montevideo, Montevideo
Natural History Museum - 1837
botany; zoology; anthropology;
geology; paleontology - library

16978
Museo Pedagogico
Plaza Cagancha 1175, Montevideo
General Museum - 1888
educational history

16979
**Museo y Archivo Historico
Municipal**
Juan Carlos Gómez 1362, Montevideo
General Museum - 1915
paintings; jewelry; icons; furniture;
documents; maps

16980
Museo y Biblioteca Blanco Acevedo
Zabala 1469, Montevideo
General Museum

16981
**Museo y Jardin Botanico de
Montevideo**
Av. 19 de Abril 1179, Montevideo
Natural History Museum - 1940
botany

16982
**Museo Zoológico 'Dámaso A.
Larrañaga'**
Rambla Rep. de Chile 4215,
Montevideo
Natural History Museum - 1956
zoology - library

Salto

16983
Museo Historico Municipal
Amorin 55, Salto
History/Public Affairs Museum

San José de Mayo

16984
Museo Departamental de San Jose
Dr. Julián B. de Bengoa 493, San José
de Mayo
Fine Arts Museum
paintings; sculptures; graphic art;
ceramics

Tacuarembó

16985
Museo del Indio
Calle 25 de Mayo 315, Tacuarembó
Anthropology Museum
Indian and Gaucho arts and crafts;
armaments; implements

USSR

Abramcevo

16986
Muzej-usad'ba 'Abramcevo'
Abramcevo, platforma Moskovskaja
obl.
Fine Arts Museum
Russian and Soviet fine art; art history;
literature; theatre

Aginskoe

16987
**Aginskij okružnyj kraevedčeskij
muzej**
Aginskoe, Čitinskaja obl.
General Museum - 1961
Natural history; local history;
economics; culture - library

Alma-Ata

16988
**Central'nyj gosudarstvennyj muzej
Kazachskoj SSR** (Central State
Museum of the Kasach SSR)
Park im. 28 Panfilovcev, Alma-Ata
General Museum
History; geology; meteorology of the
Kasach region

16989
**Kazachskaja gosudarstvennaja
chudožestvennaja galerija im. T. G.
Ševčenko** (Kazach State Art Gallery)
ul. Sovjetskaja 22, Alma-Ata 2
Fine Arts Museum
Modern Kazach, Soviet and foreign
works of art - library

Alupka

16990
Muzej-dvorec (Alupka Palace
Museum)
Alupka, Krymskaja obl.
Decorative Arts Museum
Interiors; art works

Alušta

16991
**Aluštinskij literaturno-memorial'nyj
muzej S.N. Sergeeva-Censkogo**
(Alušta S.N. Sergeev-Censkij Literary
Museum)
ul. Sergeeva-Censkogo, 15, Alušta
Historic Site - 1962
Memorabilia of the writer Sergej
Nikolaevič Sergeev-Censkij
(1875-1958) in his former home -
library

Archangel'sk

16992
**Archangel'skij oblastnoj
kraevedčeskij muzej**
ul. P. Vinogradova, 100, Archangel'sk
61
General Museum - 1940
History of the Northern Coast area of
the USSR; art; ethnography - library

16993
**Archangel'skij oblastnoj muzej
izobraziteľnych iskusstv** (Regional
Museum of Fine Art)
nab. im. Lenina, 79, Archangel'sk 61
Fine Arts Museum - 1960
Fine art; contemporary art - library

Archangel'skoe

16994
Muzej i usad'ba 'Archangel'skoe'
(Country Estate Museum
'Archangel'skoe')
Archangel'skoe, Moskovskaja obl.
143420
History/Public Affairs Museum - 1919
History; ancient history; military
history; archeology - library

Ašchabad

16995
**Central'nyj gosudarstvennyj muzej
Turkmenskoj SSR** (Central State
Museum of the Turkmen SSR)
ul. Engel'sa 90, Ašchabad
General Museum
History of the Turkmen people;
archeology; ethnography

16996
**Turkmenskij gosudarstvennyj muzej
izobraziteľnych iskusstv** (Turkmen
State Museum of Fine Arts)
Prosp. Svobody, 84, Ašchabad
Fine Arts Museum
Soviet and West-European art; rugs
from the Turkmenian region

Astrachan'

16997
**Astrachanskij oblastnoj
kraevedčeskij muzej**
Sovetskaja, 15, Astrachan'
General Museum - 1836
Natural history; local history;
economics; culture - library

Baku

16998
Azerbajdžanskij gosudarstvennyj teatral'nyj muzej im. D. Džabarly
(State Theatrical Museum of Azerbajdžan)
Baku
Performing Arts Museum
library

16999
Central'nyj muzej V.I. Lenina
Bakinskij filial (Baku Branch of the Central Lenin Museum)
prosp. Neftjanikov, 123a, Baku
History/Public Affairs Museum - 1951
Memorial to V.I. Lenin (1870-1924);
documents; photographs - library

17000
Gosudarstvennyj muzej azerbajdžanskoj literatury (State Museum of Azerbajdžan Literature)
ul. Kommunističeskaja 33, Baku
History/Public Affairs Museum - 1940
Literature; literary history - library

17001
Gosudarstvennyj muzej iskusstv im. R. Mustafaeva (R. Mustafaev State Art Museum)
Čkalova, 9, Baku 1
Fine Arts Museum - 1936
Art; contemporary art - library

17002
Muzej istorii Azerbajdžana AN AzSSR (Museum of Azerbajdžans' History of the Academy of Sciences of AzSSR)
ul. Malygina, 4, Baku
History/Public Affairs Museum - 1920
Regional history; archeology; ethnography; numismatics - library

17003
Pedagogičeskij muzej (Museum of Education)
ul. Čkalova, 11, Baku
History/Public Affairs Museum
Pedagogics; history of education - library

Barnaul

17004
Altajskij kraevedčeskij muzej
Barnaul 43
General Museum - 1823
Natural history; history; economics; culture - library

Batumi

17005
Gosudarstvennyj muzej Adžarskoj ASSR (State Museum of Adjar ASSR)
ul. Džinčaradze, 4, Batumi
General Museum - 1910
Natural history; history; economics; culture - library

Belgorod

17006
Belgorodskij oblastnoj kraevedčeskij muzej
ul. Popova, 11, Belgorod
General Museum - 1946
Natural history; local history; economics; culture - library

Belgorod-Dnestrovskij

17007
Belgorod-Dnestrovskij kraevedčeskij muzej
ul. Timirjazeva, 19, Belgorod-Dnestrovskij, Odesskaja obl.
General Museum - 1945
Natural history; history; economics; culture - library

Belinskij

17008
Gosudarstvennyj muzej V.G. Belinskogo (V.G. Belinskij State Memorial Museum)
ul. Belinskogo 11, Belinskij, Penzenskaja obl.
Historic Site - 1938
Life and work of the literary critic Vissarion Grigor'evič Belinskij (1811-1848)

Belovežskaja pušča

17009
Muzej-zapovednik 'Belovežskaja pušča'
Belovežskaja pušča, Brestskaja obl.
Natural History Museum
Natural history; preservation of the bison and other rare species

Bijsk

17010
Bijskij kraevedčeskij muzej im. B.V. Bianki
Sovetskaja, 42, Bijsk, Altajskij kraj
General Museum - 1920
Natural history; local history; economics; culture - library

Blagoveščensk

17011
Amurskij oblastnoj muzej kraevedenija
Internacional'nyj per., 6, Blagoveščensk
General Museum - 1896
Natural history; history; economics; culture - library

Borodino

17012
Gosudarstvennyj Borodinskij voenno-istoričeskij muzej-zapovednik (Borodino State Museum of Military History)
Borodino, Moskovskaja obl.
History/Public Affairs Museum - 1903
Research on the campaign of 1812, the Battle of Borodino and the World War II; documents - library

Brjansk

17013
Brjanskij oblastnoj kraevedčeskij muzej
ul. Kalinina, 42, Brjansk
General Museum - 1945
Natural history; history; economics; culture - library

Cchinvali

17014
Gosudarstvennyj muzej Jugo-Osetinskoj avtonomnoj oblasti
(State Museum of the South-Ossetian Autonomous District)
ul. 13 kommunarov, 7, Cchinvali
General Museum - 1941
Natural history; history; economics; culture - library

Čeboksary

17015
Čuvašskaja gosudarstvennaja chudožestvennaja galerija
ul. R. Ljuksemburg, 13, Čeboksary
Fine Arts Museum - 1952
Fine art - library

Čeljabinsk

17016
Čeljabinskij oblastnoj kraevedčeskij muzej
ul. Kirova, 60a, Čeljabinsk
General Museum - 1924
Natural history; history; economics; culture - library

Čerkassy

17017
Čerkasskij oblastnoj kraevedčeskij muzej
ul. Gogolja, 265, Čerkassy
General Museum - 1918
Natural history; history; economics; culture - library

Černigov

17018
Černigovskij istoričeskij muzej
ul. Ševčenko, 54, Černigov 7
History/Public Affairs Museum - 1925
History; art history; local history - library

17019
Černigovskij literaturno-memorial'nyj muzej M.M. Kocjubinskogo (Literary Museum)
ul. Kocjubinskogo, 3, Černigov 1
Historic Site - 1935
Life and work of the Ukrainian writer M.M. Kocjubinskij (1864-1913) - library

Černovcy

17020
Černovickij kraevedčeskij muzej
Kobyljanskoj, 28, Černovcy
General Museum - 1944
Natural history; economics; culture - library

17021
Memorial'nyj muzej Ju. Feďkoviča (Ju. Feďkovič Memorial Museum)
ul. Puškina, 17, Černovcy
Historic Site
Memorial to the Ukrainian writer Jurij Feďkovič (1834-1888); portraits; photographs; book illustrations; books

Chabarovsk

17022
Dal'nevostočnyj chudožestvennyj muzej (Far Eastern Art Museum)
ul. Frunze, 45, Chabarovsk
Fine Arts Museum - 1931
Art - library

Chanty-Mansijsk

17023
Chanty-Mansijskij okružnoj kraevedčeskij muzej
Komsomol'skaja, 9, Chanty-Mansijsk, Tjumenskaja obl.
General Museum - 1936
Natural history; history; economics; culture - library

Char'kov

17024
Char'kovskij chudožestvennyj muzej (Charkov Art Museum)
ul. Sovnarkomovskaja, 11, Char'kov
Fine Arts Museum
Ukrainian and Russian art; painting - library

17025
Char'kovskij istoričeskij muzej (Charkov Historical Museum)
ul. Universitetskaja, 10, Char'kov 3
History/Public Affairs Museum
History of the Revolution; labour movement - library

Cherson

17026
Chersonskij kraevedčeskij muzej
prosp. Ušakova, 16, Cherson 25
General Museum - 1890
Natural history; history; economics; culture - library

Chmel'nickij

17027
Chmel'nickij oblastnoj kraevedčeskij muzej
ul. K. Libknechta, 38, Chmel'nickij
General Museum - 1925
Natural history; history; economics; culture - library

Dneprodzeržinsk

17028
Dneprodzeržinskij istoričeskij muzej
Dneprodzeržinsk
History/Public Affairs Museum
Ukrainian history; archeology; town history

Dnepropetrovsk

17029
Dnepropetrovskij gosudarstvennyj chudožestvennyj muzej
(Dnepropetrovsk State Art Museum)
Ševčenko, 21, Dnepropetrovsk 44
Fine Arts Museum - 1914
Russian and foreign art; history of art; applied art; folk art - library

17030
Dnepropetrovskij istoričeskij muzej im. akad. D.I. Javornickogo
ul. K. Marksa, 16, Dnepropetrovsk
History/Public Affairs Museum - 1905
History, economy and culture of the Ukrainian people; labour movement - library

Doneck

17031
Doneckij oblastnoj kraevedčeskij muzej
ul. Artema, 84, Doneck 55
General Museum - 1924
Natural history; history; economics; culture - library

Dušanbe

17032
Tadžikskij istoričeskij muzej
ul. Ajni, 31, Dušanbe
History/Public Affairs Museum
History; cultural history and art - library

Ėlista

17033
Kalmyckij respublikanskij kraevedčeskij muzej im. prof. N.N. Pal'mova
Teatral'nyj per., 2, Ėlista
General Museum - 1961
Natural history; history; economics; culture - library

Erevan

17034
Armjanskaja gosudarstvennaja kartinnaja galerija (Armenian State Art Gallery)
ul. Spandarjana, 2, Erevan
Fine Arts Museum
Painting; sculpture

17035
Dom-muzej Ovanesa Tumanjana (House Museum of O. Tumanjan)
Moskovskaja, 40, Erevan 9
Historic Site - 1953
Memorabilia of the poet Ovanes Tumanjan (1869-1923); cultural and literary history of Armenia

17036
Gosudarstvennyj istoričeskij muzej ArmSSR (State Historical Museum of the Armenian SSR)
pl. Lenina, Erevan centr
History/Public Affairs Museum - 1921
Armenian ancient and modern history - library

17037
Muzej literatury i iskusstva im. Egiše Čarenca (Museum of Literature and Art)
ul. Spandarjana, 2, Erevan
History/Public Affairs Museum - 1954
History of Armenian 14th-19th century literature ; art - library

Frunze

17038
Gosudarstvennyj istoričeskij muzej Kirgizskoj SSR (State Historical Museum of the Kirgiz SSR)
Krasnooktjabr'skaja ul., 236, Frunze
History/Public Affairs Museum
History of the Kirgiz region from ancient times to the present

17039
Kirgizskij gosudarstvennyj muzej izobraziteľnych iskusstv (Kirgiz State Museum of Fine Arts)
ul. Pervomajskaja, 90, Frunze 40
Fine Arts Museum
Contemporary art - library

Gagarin

17040
Memorial'nyj muzej Ju. Gagarina (Ju. Gagarin Memorial Museum)
ul. Gagarina, Gagarin
Historic Site - 1970
Life and work of the cosmonaut Jurij Gagarin (1934-1968)

Gori

17041
Muzej Stalina (Stalin Museum)
Gori
Historic Site - 1965
Life and work of Josif Vissarionovič Stalin (1879-1953); role of Georgia in the Revolution of 1917

Gor'kij

17042
Gor'kovskij gosudarstvennyj chudožestvennyj muzej (Gor'kij State Art Museum)
nab. im. Ždanova, 5, Gor'kij D-5
Fine Arts Museum - 1896
Fine art - library

17043
Gor'kovskij istoriko-architekturnyj zapovednik
nab. im. Ždanova, 7, Gor'kij
History/Public Affairs Museum - 1896
Archeology; history of the Central Volga area dating back to ancient times - library

17044
Gosudarstvennyj muzej A.M. Gor'kogo (State A.M. Gor'kij Memorial Museum)
ul. Minina, 26, Gor'kij 24
Historic Site - 1928
Memorabilia of the writer Maksim Gor'kij (1868-1936); literary history; original furnishings - library

Gorno-Altajsk

17045
Gorno-Altajskij oblastnoj kraevedčeskij muzej
Socialističeskaja, 35, Gorno-Altajsk
General Museum - 1920
Natural history; economics; culture; local history - library

Grodno

17046
Grodnenskij gosudarstvennyj istoriko-archeologičeskij muzej (Grodno State Historical and Archeological Museum)
ul. Zamkovaja, 22, Grodno
History/Public Affairs Museum
History; economy; natural history; archeology; ethnography - library

Groznyj

17047
Čečeno-Ingušskij respublikanskij kraevedčeskij muzej
Proletarskaja, 54, Groznyj 21
General Museum - 1925
Natural history; history; economics; culture - library

Irkutsk

17048
Irkutskij oblastnoj kraevedčeskij muzej
ul. Karla Marksa, 2, Irkutsk 3
General Museum
Natural history; history; economics; culture - library

Ivano-Frankovsk

17049
Ivano-Frankovskij kraevedčeskij muzej
Galickaja, 4, Ivano-Frankovsk
General Museum - 1939
Natural history; history; economics; culture - library

Ivanovo

17050
Ivanovskij oblastnoj chudožestvennyj muzej (Regional Art Museum)
prosp. Lenina, 33, Ivanovo
Fine Arts Museum - 1959
Art - library

17051
Ivanovskij oblastnoj kraevedčeskij muzej
ul. Baturina, 6/40, Ivanovo
General Museum - 1915
Natural history; history; economics; culture - library

Iževsk

17052
Udmurskij respublikanskij kraevedčeskij muzej
ul. V. Sivkova, 180, Iževsk
General Museum - 1930
Natural history; history; economics; culture - library

Jakutsk

17053
Jakutskij muzej izobraziteľnych iskusstv (Jakutsk Museum of Fine Arts)
ul. Maksima Ammosova, 14, Jakutsk
Fine Arts Museum
17th-20th century Western European, Russian and Soviet art; folk art

17054
Jakutskij respublikanskij kraevedčeskij muzej im. Emeľjana Jaroslavskogo
Muzejnyj per., 2, Jakutsk 20
General Museum - 1956
Natural history; history; economics; culture - library

Jaroslavľ

17055
Jaroslavskij istoriko-architekturnyj muzej-zapovednik (Jaroslavl State Historical Museum)
pl. Podbelskogo, 25, Jaroslavľ
History/Public Affairs Museum - 1920
Local history; manuscripts; documents - library

Jasnaja Poljana

17056
Muzej-usaďba L.N. Tolstogo 'Jasnaja Poljana' (Museum of the L.N. Tolstoj Estate 'Jasnaja Poljana')
Jasnaja Poljana, Tulskaja obl.
Historic Site - 1921
Memorabilia of the writer Lev Nikolaevič Tolstoj (1828-1910) in his former house and estate - library

Kalinin

17057
Kalininskaja oblastnaja kartinnaja galerija (Regional Art Gallery)
Sovetskaja, 3, Kalinin
Fine Arts Museum
Fine art; contemporary art - library

17058
Kalininskij oblastnoj kraevedčeskij muzej
pl. Revoljucii, 3, Kalinin
General Museum - 1866
Natural history; local history; economics; culture - library

Kaliningrad

17059
Kaliningradskij oblastnoj kraevedčeskij muzej
ul. B. Chmeľnickogo, 61b, Kaliningrad
General Museum - 1947
Natural history; history; economics; culture - library

Kaluga

17060
Gosudarstvennyj muzej istorii kosmonavtiki im. K.E. Ciolkovskogo (State Museum of the History of Cosmonautics)
ul. Koroleva, 2, Kaluga
Science/Tech Museum - 1964
Aviation; aeronautics; cosmonautics; manned spaceships; works of the astronautical scientist Konstantin Ėduardovič Ciolkovskij (1857-1935) - library

17061
Kalužskij oblastnoj chudožestvennyj muzej (Regional Art Museum)
ul. Lenina, 104, Kaluga
Fine Arts Museum - 1935
Art - library

17062
Kalužskij oblastnoj kraevedčeskij muzej
ul. Puškina, 14, Kaluga
General Museum - 1917
Natural history; economics; local history; culture - library

Kamenec-Podoľskij

17063
Gosudarstvennyj istoričeskij muzej-zapovednik
ul. K.Marksa, 20, Kamenec-Podoľskij
Chmeľnickaja obl.
History/Public Affairs Museum
Ukrainian revolutionary history

Kamenka

17064
Kamenskij literaturno-memoriaľnyj muzej A.S. Puškina i P.I. Čajkovskogo (Literary Memorial Museum of A.S. Puškin and P.I. Čajkovskij)
ul. Lenina, 44, Kamenka, Čerkasskaja obl.
Historic Site - 1937
History of music; literary history; rare books; memorial to A.S. Puškin and P.I. Čajkovskij - library

Kanev

17065
Kanevskij muzej-zapovednik 'Mogila T.G. Ševčenko' (Memorial Museum 'The Grave of T.G. Ševčenko')
Kanev, Čerkasskaja obl.
Historic Site - 1939
Memorial to the Ukrainian writer Taras Grigor'evič Ševčenko (1814-1861); literary history; grave of the poet - library

Kaunas

17066
Gosudarstvennyj chudožestvennyj muzej im. M.K. Cjurlenis (Kaunas State Art Museum)
ul. S. Neris 45, Kaunas
Fine Arts Museum - 1925
Lithuanian, Russian, French and Italian art - library

17067
Kaunasskij istoričeskij muzej
ul. K. Donelajčio, 64, Kaunas
History/Public Affairs Museum - 1921
Archeology; military history 1918-1945; weapons; numismatics - library

17068
Muzej Literatury (Museum of Literature)
pl. Rotušes, 13, Kaunas
History/Public Affairs Museum - 1936
Literary history - library

17069
Respublikanskij pedagogičeskij muzej (Museum of Pedagogics)
Lajsves alleja, 24, Kaunas
History/Public Affairs Museum - 1958
Pedagogics; history of education; documents; photographs - library

Kazan'

17070
Gosudarstvennyj muzej Tatarskoj ASSR (State Museum of the Tatar ASSR)
ul. Lenina, 2, Kazan' 84
General Museum - 1894
Art; natural history; cultural history of the Tatar region - library

17071
Kazan'skij muzej A.M. Gor'kogo (Gor'kij Memorial Museum)
ul. Gor'kogo, 10, Kazan'
Historic Site - 1950
Memorabilia of the writer Maksim Gor'kij (1868-1936); literary history - library

17072
Tatarskij gosudarstvennyj muzej izobraziteľnych iskusstv (Tatar State Muzeum of Fine Arts)
ul. K.Marksa, 64, Kazan'
Fine Arts Museum
Fine art; contemporary art

Kemerovo

17073
Kemerovskij oblastnoj kraevedčeskij muzej
Sovetskij prosp., 89, Kemerovo 99
General Museum - 1957
Natural history; history; economics; culture - library

Kerč

17074
Gosudarstvennyj istoriko-archeologičeskij muzej (State Historical and Archeological Museum)
ul. Sverdlova, 16, Kerč, Krymskaja obl.
Archeology Museum
Archeology; Kurgan finds; regional history

Kiev

17075
Gosudarstvennyj istoričeskij muzej USSR (State Historical Museum)
ul. Vladimirskaja, 2, Kiev 25
History/Public Affairs Museum - 1906
Exhibits tracing the history, economy and culture of the Ukrainian people from earliest times - library

17076
Gosudarstvennyj muzej teatraľnogo, muzykaľnogo i kinoiskusstva USSR (State Museum of Theatrical, Musical and Cinematographical Art)
Janvarskogo vosstanija, 21, Kiev 15
Performing Arts Museum - 1926
History of the performing arts in the Ukraine

17077
Gosudarstvennyj muzej T.G. Ševčenko (Kiev T.G. Ševčenko State Museum)
bul. Ševčenko, 12, Kiev 4
Historic Site - 1929
Life and work of the Ukrainian poet and revolutionary democrat Taras Grigor'evič Ševčenko (1814-1861) - library

17078
Gosudarstvennyj muzej ukrainskogo narodnogo dekorativnogo iskusstva (State Museum of Ukrainian Decorative Folk Art)
ul. Janvarskogo vosstanija, 21, Lavra, Kiev
Decorative Arts Museum - 1954
Crafts; decorative arts in wood; folk art; embroidery; weaving; ceramics; glass; porcelain; costumes - library

17079
Kievskij filial Central'nogo muzeja Lenina v Moskve (Kiev Branch of the Central Lenin Museum in Moscow)
ul. Vladimirskaja, 57, Kiev
History/Public Affairs Museum
Memorial to Vladimir Il'ič Lenin ; documents

17080
Kievskij gosudarstvennyj muzej ukrainskogo isskustva (Kiev State Museum of Ukrainian Art)
ul. Kirova 6, Kiev 1
Fine Arts Museum - 1899
Icons; medieval and modern painting; portraits; wood carvings; fine art; archeology; art history - library

17081
Kievskij muzej russkogo iskusstva (Kiev State Museum of Russian Art)
ul. Repina 9, Kiev 4
Fine Arts Museum - 1922
Russian painting; sculpture; drawings; applied art - library

17082
Kievskij muzej zapadnogo i vostočnogo iskusstva (Kiev Museum of Western and Oriental Art)
ul. Repina, 15, Kiev 4
Fine Arts Museum - 1919
Paintings; sculptures; history of Russian and European art; archeology - library

Kirov

17083
Kirovskij oblastnoj chudožestvennyj muzej im. A.M. Gor'kogo (Kirov Regional Art museum)
ul. Karla Marksa, 70, Kirov
Fine Arts Museum - 1910
Art - library

17084
Kirovskij oblastnoj kraevedčeskij muzej
ul. Lenina, 82, Kirov
General Museum - 1918
Contemporary literature of the Urals and Siberia; local history; natural history - library

Kirovograd

17085
Kirovogradskij oblastnoj kraevedčeskij muzej
ul. Lenina, 40, Kirovograd
General Museum - 1945
Natural history; history; economics; culture - library

Kišinev

17086
Gosudarstvennyj chudožestvennyj muzej MSSR (Moldavian State Art Museum)
ul. Lenina 115, Kišinev
Fine Arts Museum
Fine art; applied art - library

Kislovodsk

17087
Kislovodskij chudožestvennyj muzej N. A. Jarošenko (Kislovodsk Art Museum)
ul. Jarošenko, 3, Kislovodsk
Fine Arts Museum - 1960
Fine art - library

Kiži

17088
Gosudarstvennyj istoričeskij muzej (State Historical Museum)
Kiži, Medvežegorskij r-n
Open Air Museum
Architectural wooden ensemble of churches and Russian houses of the 16th and 17th centuries; folk art

Klin

17089
Gosudarstvennyj dom-muzej P.I. Čajkovskogo (P.I. Čajkovskij Memorial House)
Klin, 141600 Moskovskaja obl.
Historic Site
Memorabilia of P.I. Čajkovskij (1840-1893); documents; records; books; sheet music - library

Kobrin

17090
Kobrinskij voenno-istoričeskij muzej im. A.V. Suvorova
ul. Suvorova, 18, Kobrin, Brestskaja obl.
History/Public Affairs Museum
Military history; memorial to Aleksandr Vasil'evič Suvorov - library

Kolomja

17091
Gosudarstvennyj muzej narodnogo iskusstva (State Museum of Folk Art)
Teatraľnaja ul., 25, Kolomja, Ivano-Frankovska obl.,
Decorative Arts Museum
Folk art; applied art

Komsomoľsk-na-Amure

17092
Muzej izobraziteľnych iskusstv (Museum of Fine Arts)
prosp. Truda, 50, Komsomoľsk-na-Amure
Fine Arts Museum
Fine arts; Soviet art

Končanskoe-Suvorovskoe

17093
Muzej-zapovednik A.V. Suvorova
Končanskoe-Suvorovskoe, Novgorovskaja obl.
History/Public Affairs Museum - 1942
Memorabilia of the commander-in-chief Aleksandr Vasil'evič Suvorov; military history - library

Kostroma

17094
Kostromskij istoriko-architekturnyj muzej-zapovednik (Kostroma Historical and Architectural Museum)
Prosveščenija, 1, Kostroma 4
History/Public Affairs Museum - 1885
History; ethnography; architecture; archeology; art - library

17095
Kostromskij muzej izobraziteľnych iskusstv (Kostroma Museum of Fine Arts)
prosp. Mira, 1, Kostroma
Fine Arts Museum
Fine arts

Krasnodar

17096
Krasnodarskij kraevoj chudožestvennyj muzej im. A.V. Lunačarskogo
Krasnaja, 13, Krasnodar 23
Fine Arts Museum - 1907
Art - library

Krasnojarsk

17097
Krasnojarskaja chudožestvennaja galerija (Krasnojarsk Art Gallery)
prosp. Krasnojarskij rabočij, 68, Krasnojarsk 37
Fine Arts Museum - 1958
Fine art; decorative and applied art - library

17098
Krasnojarskij kraevoj muzej
ul. Dubrovinskogo, 84, Krasnojarsk 49
General Museum - 1889
Natural history; history; economics; culture - library

Krivoj Rog

17099
Krivorožskij istoriko-kraevedčeskij muzej
1.j per. Lenina, 16, Krivoj Rog
General Museum - 1960
Natural history; history; economics; culture - library

Kudymkar

17100
Komi-Permjackij okružnyj muzej
Sovetskaja, 31, Kudymkar, Permskaja obl.
General Museum - 1920
Natural history; history; economics; culture - library

Kujbyšev

17101
Kujbyševskij chudožestvennyj muzej
(Kujbyšev Art Museum)
pl. Kujbyševa, dvorec Kultury,
Kujbyšev
Fine Arts Museum - 1937
Art - library

17102
Kujbyševskij literaturno-
memoriaľnyj muzej A.M. Gor'kogo
(Literary-Memorial Museum)
ul. St. Razina, 126, Kujbyšev
Historic Site - 1946
Life and work of Maksim Go'kij
(1868-1936) and other literary figures;
original furniture; literary history -
library

17103
Kujbyševskij oblastnoj muzej
kraevedenija
Frunze, 157, Kujbyšev 10
General Museum
Natural history; economics; local
history; culture - library

Kurgan

17104
Kurganskij oblastnoj kraevedčeskij
muzej
ul. Volodarskogo, 42, Kurgan
General Museum - 1950
Natural history; local history;
economics; culture - library

Kursk

17105
Kurskaja oblastnaja kartinnaja
galerija (Kursk Regional Art Gallery)
Sovetskaja, 3, Kursk
Fine Arts Museum - 1935
Fine art - library

17106
Kurskij oblastnoj kraevedčeskij
muzej
ul. Lunačarskogo, 6, Kursk
General Museum - 1903
Natural history; history; economics;
culture - library

Kutaisi

17107
Kutaisskij gosudarstvennyj muzej
istorii i ètnografii (Kutaisi State
Museum of History and Ethnography)
ul.Tbilisi, 1, Kutaisi
History/Public Affairs Museum
Archeology; ethnography; history;
climatology

Kyzyl

17108
Tuvinskij respublikanskij
kraevedčeskij muzej im. '60
bogatyrej'
ul. Lenina, 7, Kyzyl
General Museum - 1930
Natural history; history; economics;
culture - library

Leningrad

17109
Centraľnyj geologorązvedočnyj
muzej im. akad. F.N. Černyševa
(Central Geological and Prospecting
Museum)
Vasiľevskij ostrov, Srednyj pr., 72-b,
Leningrad
Natural History Museum - 1923
Geological sciences; paleontology;
petrology; geological education

17110
Centraľnyj muzej svjazi im. A.S.
Popova (Central Museum of
Communication)
per. Podbeľskogo, 4, Leningrad
Science/Tech Museum - 1877
History of communication technology;
stage postage stamp collection

17111
Domik-muzej Petra I (Peter the
Great's Home-Museum)
Petrovskaja nab., 2, Leningrad
Historic Site - 1930
Little wooden home (built 1703) where
Peter the Great stayed during the
construction of the Peter and Paul
Fortress; 18th century furniture

17112
Gornyj muzej (Mining Museum)
Vasiľevskij ostrov, 21-ja linija, 2,
Leningrad
Science/Tech Museum - 1773
19th-20th century mining history; earth
sciences; mineralogy; paleontology;
geology; crystallograph; cosmogony

17113
Gosudarstvennyj Ėrmitaž (State
Hermitage Museum)
Dvorcovaja nab., 36, Leningrad
Fine Arts Museum - 1764
Richest collection in the Soviet Union
of the art of prehistoric, ancient,
Greek, Roman and medieval times;
drawings; engravings; Italian, Dutch,
Spanish, French and German paintings
including works by Leonardo da Vinci,
Raphael, Titian, Rubens, Rembrandt;
applied arts; numismatics; arms

17114
Gosudarstvennyj muzej A.V.
Suvorova (State A.V. Suvorova)
ul. Saltykova-ŠČedrina, 41-b,
Leningrad
History/Public Affairs Museum - 1904
Russian military history; exposition on
the great Russian commander-in-chief
Aleksandr Vasiľevič Suvorov; military
painting; documents

17115
Gosudarstvennyj muzej ètnografii
narodov SSSR (State Ethnographical
Museum of the Peoples of the USSR)
Inženernaja ul., 4/1, Leningrad
Anthropology Museum - 1901
19th-20th century ethnographical
exhibits; crafts; contemporary folk art
of the peoples of the USSR

17116
Gosudarstvennyj muzej gorodskoj
skuľptury (State Museum of
Sculpture)
pl. Aleksandra Nevskogo, 1, Leningrad
Fine Arts Museum
Largest collection of Russian sculpture
in the Soviet Union, documents on
architecture and town planning;
architectural drawings

17117
Gosudarstvennyj muzej istorii
Leningrada (State Museum of the
History of Leningrad)
Nab. Krasnogo Flota, 44, Leningrad
History/Public Affairs Museum - 1907
History and development of local city
planning and construction;
architectural and cultural history of
Leningrad; rare book with 500
drawings of buildings of St.
Petersburg up to 1836

17118
Gosudarstvennyj muzej istorii religii
i ateizma (Museum of the History of
Religion and Atheism)
Kazanskaja pl., 2, Leningrad
Religious Art Museum - 1932
Origin of Christianity; history of the
struggle against religion; objects
relating to various sects and
denominations; documents; books;
religious art; in a 19th century church

17119
Gosudarstvennyj muzej Velikoj
Oktjabr'skoj socialističeskoj
revoljucii (State Museum of the Great
October Socialist Revolution)
ul. Kujbyševa, 4, Leningrad
History/Public Affairs Museum - 1919
History of the 1917 Revolution,
Russian Civil War and World War II,
development of socialism in the USSR
- library

17120
Gosudarstvennyj Russkij muzej
(State Russian Museum)
ul. Inženernaja, 4, Leningrad
Fine Arts Museum - 1898
11th-20th century Russian art; Soviet
art; painting; drawings and sculpture;
applied and folk arts; coins; medals

17121
Gosudarstvennyj teatraľnyj muzej
(State Theatrical Museum)
pl. Ostrovskogo, 6, Leningrad
Performing Arts Museum - 1918
History of the theatre in Russia, the
USSR and other countries;
documents; records

17122
Kvartira-muzej A.S. Puškina
Vsesojuznyj muzej A.S. Puškina
Nab. Mojki, 12, Leningrad
Historic Site
Life and work of the poet A.S. Puškin
(1799-1837) in the flat where the poet
died; original interiors; documents;
manuscripts

17123
Kvartira-muzej I.I. Brodskogo (I.I.
Brodskij House-Museum)
pl. Iskusstv, 3, Leningrad
Historic Site - 1949
Memorabilia of the painter Isaak
Izraiľevič Brodskij (1883-1939);
drawings; paintings; documents; the
artist's oridinal studio

17124
Kvartira-muzej N.A. Nekrasova (N.A.
Nekrasov House-Museum)
Litejnyj pr., 36, Leningrad
Historic Site - 1946
Life and work of the poet Nikolaj· A.
Nekrasov (1821-1878) in his former
home

17125
Leningradskij filial Centraľnogo
muzeja V.I. Lenina v Moskve
(Leningrad Branch of the Central
Lenin Museum in Moscow)
Chalturina, 5, Leningrad
History/Public Affairs Museum - 1937
Documents on the life and work of V.I.
Lenin (1870-1924)

17126
Letnyj dvorec Petra I v Letnem sadu
(Summer Garden and Museum Palace
of Peter the Great)
Leningrad
Fine Arts Museum - 1934
18th century architecture and
sculpture; original interiors; decorative
and applied art

17127
Literaturnyj muzej Instituta russkoj
literatury AN SSSR (Literary Museum
of the Institute of Russian Literature of
the USSR Academy of Sciences)
Nab. Makarova, 4, Leningrad
History/Public Affairs Museum - 1899
Literary history of Russia and the
USSR; objects relating to Radiščev,
Lermontov, Gogoľ, Dostoevskij,
Turgenev and other Russian writers -
library

17128
Muzej antropologii i ètnografii im.
Petra Velikogo (Peter the Great
Museum of Anthropology and
Ethnography)
Universitetskaja nab., 3, Leningrad
B-164
Anthropology Museum - 1836
Ethnography; archeology;
anthropology of North and South
America, Australia, Oceania, the Near
East, Central and Eastern Asia;
Miklucho-Maklaj collection

17129
Muzej Arktiki i Antarktiki (Museum
of the Arctic and Antarctic)
ul. Marata 24a, Leningrad
Natural History Museum - 1937
History of the Soviet expeditions to
the Arctic and Antarctic; documents;
original equipment; polar aviation;
natural history; in a 19th century
church

17130
Muzej A.S. Popova
ul. prof. Popova, 5, Leningrad
Historic Site - 1948
Memorabilia of the scientist Aleksandr
Stepanovič Popov (1859-1905);
documents; manuscripts

17131
Muzej D.I. Mendeleeva (D.I.
Mendeleev House-Museum)
Universitetskaja nab., 7-9,
Leningradskij Universitet, Leningrad
Historic Site - 1911
Memorabilia of Dmitrij Ivanovič
Mendeleev (1834-1907); scientific
archives; in the house where the
scientist lived from 1866 to 1890

17132
Muzej Gosudarstvennogo
akademičeskogo teatra opery i
baleta im. S.M. Kirova (Museum of the
Kirov Academic Theater of Opera and
Ballet)
Teatraľnaja pl., Leningrad
Performing Arts Museum
Dramatic art; history of the performing
arts; historic objects - library

17133
Muzej Kirovskogo zavoda (Museum
of the Kirov Works)
pr. Staček, 72, dvorec kuľtury im. I.I.
Gaza, Leningrad
History/Public Affairs Museum - 1962
Labour movement; documents on the
1917 Revolution and World War II;
rare photographs; contemporary
history

17134
Muzej krajsera 'Avrora' Centraľnyj
Voenno-morskoj muzej (Battleship
Museum 'Avrora')
Petrogradskaja nab., bliz mosta
Svobody, Leningrad
History/Public Affairs Museum - 1956
History of the 1917 October
Revolution and the historical role of
the battleship 'Avrora'

17135
Muzej M.V. Lomonosova (M.V.
Lomonosov Memorial Museum)
Universitetskaja nab., 3 , Kunstkamera,
Leningrad
Historic Site
Memorabilia of the great Russian
scientist Michail Vasiľevič Lomonosov
(1711-1765); development of Russian
astronomy in the 18th century; in an
18th century building

17136
Muzej S.M. Kirova
Kirovskij pr., 26-28, Leningrad
Historic Site - 1938
Memorabilia of the Soviet politician
Sergej Mironovič Kirov (1886-1934);
documents; photographs; paintings;
sculpture

17137
Muzej zdravoochranenija (Museum of
Public Health)
ul. Rakova, 25, Leningrad
History/Public Affairs Museum - 1918
Anatomy; physiology; preventive
medicine; hygiene

17138
Muzej železnodorožnogo transporta
(Leningrad Museum of Railway
Transport)
Sadovaja ul., 50, Leningrad
Science/Tech Museum - 1813
History of railway transportation in
Russia; miniature models of engines
and carriages

17139
Muzej-pamjatnik Isaakievskij sobor
Gosudarstvennyj muzej istorii
Leningrada (St. Isaac's Cathedral)
Isaakievskaja pl., Leningrad
Fine Arts Museum
The Cathedral is an example of
Russian architecture of the 19th
century; religious art; decorative art;
painting; sculpture; mosaics

17140
**Muzej-zapovednik Petropavlovskaja
kreposť** (Peter and Paul Fortress)
pl. Revoljucii, Leningrad
History/Public Affairs Museum
Military history; 18th century church;
various buildings showing the history
and architectural history of St.
Petersburg

17141
**Voenno-istoričeskij muzej artillerii,
inženernych vojsk i vojsk svjazi**
(Museum of Artillery, the Signal Corps
and Corps of Engineers)
park im. V.I. Lenina, 7, Leningrad
History/Public Affairs Museum - 1756
History of Russian and Soviet artillery;
exhibits from the War of 1812; military
techniques; weapons; flags; uniforms

17142
Voenno-medicinskij muzej (Military
Medical Museum)
Lazaretnyj per., 2, Leningrad F-180
History/Public Affairs Museum - 1942
History of Russian and Soviet military
medicine since the 14th century;
documents; relics; manuscripts;
instruments; pictures; sculptures;
photographs

17143
Zoologičeskij muzej (Museum of
Zoology)
Vasiľevskij ostrov, Universitetskaja
nab., 1, Leningrad
Natural History Museum - 1901
Natural sciences; zoology; evolution of
fauna

Lermontovo

17144
**Muzej-zapovednik M. Ju.
Lermontova 'Tachrany'** (M. Ju.
Lermontov Estate)
Lermontovo, Penzenskaja obl.
Historic Site - 1939
Life and work of the poet Michail
Jur'evič Lermontov (1814-1841)

Lipeck

17145
**Lipeckij oblastnoj kraevedčeskij
muzej**
pl. Lenina, 4, Lipeck
General Museum - 1966
Natural history; local history;
economics; culture - library

Lomonosov

17146
Dvorec-muzej Petra III (Palace
Museum of Peter the III)
Verchnyj park, Lomonosov
Decorative Arts Museum
Palace, built by A. Rinaldi 1758-1762;
original interiors; porcelain; furniture;
wood carvings; embroidery; enamels

17147
Kitajskij dvorec-muzej (The China
Palace Museum)
Verchnyj park, Lomonosov
Fine Arts Museum
China palace, built by A. Rinaldi
1762-1768; original interiors; fine arts;
Oriental art

17148
Muzejnyj pavil'on 'Kataľnaja gorka'
Verchnyj park, Lomonosov
Decorative Arts Museum
Decorative art; wood carvings;
mosaics; porcelain; hunting

Luck

17149
Volynskij kraevedčeskij muzej
ul. Sopena, 7, Luck, Volynskaja obl.
General Museum - 1940
Natural history; history; economics;
culture - library

L'vov

17150
**Gosudarstvennyj muzej ėtnografii,
iskusstva i remesla Akademii Nauk
Ukrainskoj SSR** (State Museum of
Ethnography, Arts and Crafts of the
Ukrainian Academy of Sciences)
Prosp. Lenina, 15, L'vov
Anthropology Museum - 1873
Folklore; costumes; applied arts; crafts

17151
L'vovskaja kartinnaja galerija (Lvov
Picture Gallery)
ul. Stefanika 3, L'vov
Fine Arts Museum - 1907
Russian and foreign painting - library

17152
**L'vovskij filial Centraľnogo muzeja
Lenina v Moskve** (L'vov Branch of the
Central Lenin Museum in Moscow)
prosp. im. Lenina 20, L'vov
History/Public Affairs Museum
Memorial to Vladimir Iľič Lenin;
documents; photographs

17153
**L'vovskij gosudarstvennyj
prirodovedčeskij muzej** (Lvov State
Museum of Natural History)
Teatraľnaja, 18, L'vov 6
Natural History Museum
Natural history; biology - library

17154
L'vovskij istoričeskij muzej (Lvov
Historical Museum)
pl. Rynok, 6, L'vov 6
History/Public Affairs Museum
History of the western Ukraine from
the earliest periods to the present -
library

17155
**L'vovskij literaturno-memoriaľnyj
muzej Ivana Franko** (Literary
Memorial Museum of Ivan Franko)
ul. Ivana Franko, 152, L'vov 26
Historic Site - 1940
Memorabilia of the writer Ivan Franko
(1856-1916); literary history - library

17156
**L'vovskij muzej ukrainskogo
iskusstva** (L'vov Museum of Ukrainian
Art)
ul. Dragomanova, 42, L'vov
Fine Arts Museum - 1905
Ukrainian fine and decorative arts; folk
art; art history

Malojaroslavec

17157
**Malojaroslavskij muzej voennoj
istorii 1812 goda** (Museum of Military
History of the War of 1812)
Moskovskaja ul., 13, Malojaroslavec,
Kalužskaja obl.
History/Public Affairs Museum
History; military history; archives;
documents

Melichovo

17158
Memoriaľnyj muzej A.P. Čechova
Melichovo, Čechovskij r-n
Historic Site
Memorabilia of the writer Anton
Pavlovič Čechov (1860-1904)

Miass

17159
**Iľmenskij gosudarstvennyj
zapovednik-muzej im. V.I. Lenina**
(Ilmen Mineral Preserve Museum)
Miass 1
Science/Tech Museum - 1920
Mineralogy; geology - library

Michajlovskoe

17160
**Puškinskij gosudarstvennyj
zapovednik** (National Puškin Estate)
Puškinskie gory, Michajlovskoe,
Pskovskaja obl.
Historic Site - 1922
Memorabilia of the poet Aleksandr
Sergeevič Puškin (1799-1837) in his
former estate; literary history; history
of the revolutionary Decembrist
movement - library

Minsk

17161
**Belorusskij gosudarstvennyj muzej
istorii Velikoj Otečestvennoj vojny**
(Belorussian State Museum of the
History of World War II)
prosp. Lenina, 25a, Minsk
History/Public Affairs Museum
Military history; local history - library

17162
**Gosudarstvennyj chudožestvennyj
muzej BSSR** (Belorussian State Art
Museum)
ul. Lenina 20, Minsk
Fine Arts Museum
Russian, Belorussian, Soviet and
foreign art - library

17163
**Gosudarstvennyj muzej Belorusskoj
SSR** (State Museum of the
Belorussian SSR)
ul. K. Marksa, 12, Minsk
General Museum
History of Belorussia - library

17164
Literaturnyj muzej Janki Kupaly
(Literary Museum)
ul. Ja. Kupaly, 4, Minsk
History/Public Affairs Museum - 1947
Literary history; collection of
manuscripts and works of the poet
Janka Kupala (1882-1942)

Minusinsk

17165
**Minusinskij muzej im. N.M.
Marť janova**
ul. Lenina, 60, Minusinsk, Krasnojarskij
kraj
General Museum - 1878
Natural history; local history;
economics; culture - library

Moskva

17166
Archangeľskij sobor
Gosudarstvennyje muzei
Moskovskogo Kremlja (Archangel
Cathedral)
Sobornaja ploščaď, Moskva
Religious Art Museum
Religious art; tombs of Ivan Kalita and
other Russian Grand Dukes and Czars

17167
Blagoveščenskij sobor
Gosudarstvennyje muzei
Moskovskogo Kremlja (Cathedral of
the Annunciation)
Sobornaja ploščaď, Moskva
Religious Art Museum
Icons; iconostasis by leading artists of
the 15th century; in a cathedral built
1489

17168
Centraľnyj muzej revoljucii SSSR
(Central Museum of the Revolution)
ul. Gor'kogo, 21, Moskva 103050
History/Public Affairs Museum - 1924
History of the revolution in Russia;
history of the contemporary Soviet
society - library

17169
Centraľnyj muzej V.I. Lenina (Central
Lenin Museum)
pl. Revoljucii, 2, Moskva 103012
History/Public Affairs Museum - 1936
Contains ca. 12,500 items including
documents, photographs, works of art
and other exhibits relating to the life
and work of Lenin (1870-1924) -
library

17170
Central'nyj muzej Vooružennych Sil SSSR (Central Museum of the Soviet Army)
Sovetskoj Armii, 2, Moskva 127157
History/Public Affairs Museum
History of the Soviet Army from its foundation the present day - library

17171
Cerkov' Rispoloženija
Gosudarstvennye muzei Moskovskogo Kremlja (Rispolozhensky Cathedral)
Sobornaja ploščad', Moskva
Religious Art Museum
Icons; collection of wooden sculptures; religious art; in a cathedral built in 1485

17172
Darvinskij muzej (State Darwin Museum)
Malaja Pirogovskaja ul., 1, Moskva
Natural History Museum
History and development of the Darwinian theory; evolution of life

17173
Dom-muzej aviacii i kosmonavtiki im. M.V. Frunze (Frunze Aviation and Cosmonautics Museum)
Krasnoarmejskaja, 4, Moskva
Science/Tech Museum
Development of aeronautics and astronautics; original aircrafts; spacecraft; space exploration vehicles; instruments

17174
Dom-muzej K.S. Stanislavskogo
Muzej chudožestvennogo teatra im. A.M. Gor'kogo
Moskva
Historic Site - 1940
Memorabilia of the theatrical artist Konstantin Stanislavskij (1863-1938)

17175
Farmacevtičeskij muzej Ministerstva zdravoochranenija SSSR
(Pharmaceutical Museum of the Ministry of Health)
Krasikova, 34, Moskva
Natural History Museum
History of pharmacy

17176
Gossudarstvennyj muzej iskusstva narodov Vostoka (State Museum of Oriental Art)
ul. Obucha 16, Moskva
Fine Arts Museum - 1918
Large collection of Middle and Far Eastern art; art of the Soviet Central Asian Republics and Zakavkazie; carpets; fabrics; ceramics - library

17177
Gosudarstvennaja Tretjakovskaja Galerija (State Tretjakov Gallery)
Lavrušenskji per., 10, Moskva
Fine Arts Museum - 1856
Rich collection of 40,000 Russian icons and works of Russian and Soviet painters, sculptors graphic artists from the 11th century to modern times - library

17178
Gosudarstvennyj biologičeskij muzej im. K.A. Timirjazeva (State Museum of Biology)
Malaja Gruzinskaja, 15, Moskva 123376
Natural History Museum
Natural science; biology; evolution of life

17179
Gosudarstvennyj central'nyj muzej muzykal'noj kul'tury im. M.I. Glinki
(M.I. Glinka State Central Museum of Musical Culture)
Georgievskij per., 4, Moskva 103009
Music Museum - 1943
Archives, manuscripts, memorabilia of musicians; musical instruments; records; sheet music - library

17180
Gosudarstvennyj central'nyj teatral'nyj muzej im. Bachrušina
(Central A.A. Bachrušin State Theatrical Museum)
ul. Bachrušina, 31/12, Moskva 113054
Performing Arts Museum - 1894
Materials on the history and theory of theatre; manuscripts of Ostrovskij, Lenskij, Stanislavskij - library

17181
Gosudarstvennyj istoričeskij muzej
(State Historical Museum)
Krasnaja pl., 1/2, Moskva 103012
History/Public Affairs Museum
Exhibits covering Russian history from prehistory to the present - library

17182
Gosudarstvennyj literaturnyj muzej
(State Literature Museum)
Roždestvenskij bul'var, 16, Moskva 103045
History/Public Affairs Museum - 1934
History of Russian and Soviet literature - library

17183
Gosudarstvennyj muzej A.S. Puškina
ul. Kropotkinskaja, 12, Moskva 119034
Historic Site - 1957
Memorabilia of the poet A.S. Puškin (1799-1837); books; manuscripts; permanent exhibitions on his life and work - library; cinema and lecture hall

17184
Gosudarstvennyj muzej izobraziteľnych iskusstv im. A.S. Puškina (State Puškin Museum of Fine Arts)
ul. Volchonka, 12, Moskva 121019
Fine Arts Museum - 1912
Ancient Eastern, Greek, Roman, Byzantine, European and American art; numismatics; sculpture; graphics - library

17185
Gosudarstvennyj muzej keramiki i 'Usad'by Kuskovo XVIII veka' (State Museum of Ceramics, country-seat Kuskovo)
3-ja Muzejnaja ul., 43, Moskva 111402
Decorative Arts Museum
Collection of Russian art; carpets; fabrics; ceramics

17186
Gosudarstvennyj muzej L.N. Tolstogo
(State L.N. Tolstoj Museum)
ul. Kropotkinskaja, 11, Moskva 119034
History/Public Affairs Museum - 1911
Original works of the writer Lev Tolstoj (1828-1910); manuscripts; archival material on Tolstoj and his circle; paintings; sculptures; photographs - library

17187
Gosudarstvennyj muzej M.I. Kalinina
(M.I. Kalinin State Museum)
prosp. Marksa, 21, Moskva 121019
History/Public Affairs Museum - 1950
Life and work of the Soviet politician Michail Kalinin (1875-1946) - library

17188
Gosudarstvennyj muzej V.V. Majakovskogo (State V.V. Majakovskij Museum)
pr. Serova 3/5, Moskva 101000
Historic Site - 1937
Memorabilia of V.V. Majakovskij (1893-1930) in the house where the poet lived from 1919 to 1930; manuscripts; documentary material; notebooks - library

17189
Gosudarstvennyj naučno-issledovateľskij muzej architektury im. A.V. Ščuseva (A.V. Ščusev State Research and Scientific Museum of Architecture)
prosp. Kalinina, 5, Moskva 101000
Science/Tech Museum - 1934
History of architecture; outstanding contemporary work; monumental sculpture and painting; collection and care of documents on architecture and town planning; architectural drawings; photography; - library

17190
Gosudarstvennyj politechničeskij muzej (Polytechnical Museum)
Novaja pl. 3, Moskva
Science/Tech Museum - 1872
History and development of science and technology

17191
Istoriko-revoljucionnyj muzej 1905 goda 'Krasnaja Presnja' Centraľnnyj muzej revoljucii SSSR
Boľševistkaja, 4, Moskva
History/Public Affairs Museum
History of the 1905 Revolution; labour movement

17192
Memoriaľnyj muzej K.A. Timirjazeva
ul. Granovskogo 2, Moskva 103009
Historic Site - 1942
Memorabilia of the scientist Kliment Arkaďevič Timirjazev (1843-1920); natural history; evolutionary theory; physiology - library

17193
Memoriaľnyj muzej kosmonavtiki
(Memorial Museum of Cosmonautics)
p-t. Mira, alleja Kosmonavtov, Moskva
Science/Tech Museum
Cosmonautics; objects of technical, historical and biographical interest

17194
Mineralogičeskij muzej im. A.E. Fersmana AN SSSR (A.E. Fersman Mineralogical Museum of the Academy of Sciences of the USSR)
Leninskij prosp., 18, Moskva 117071
Natural History Museum
Natural sciences; mineralogy; geology - library

17195
Musej usad'ba L.N. Toľstogo (L.N. Tolstoj House-Museum)
ul. Toľstogo 21, Moskva
Historic Site
Memorabilia of the writer Lev N. Toľstoj (1828-1910) in his former home; original interiors

17196
Muzej A.N. Skrjabina Muzej istorii i rekonstrukcii g. Moskvy
ul. Vachtangova, 11, Moskva
Historic Site - 1919
Memorabilia of the composer Aleksandr N. Skrjabin (1872-1915); letters; Skrjabin's personal library; tape archives of his compositions performed by Skrjabin himself and other famous artists; in the house where the composer lived and died - library

17197
Muzej Boľšogo Akademičeskogo teatra (USSR State Academic Bolšoj Theatre Museum)
pl. Sverdlova, 7/2, Moskva
Performing Arts Museum - 1920
History of the Bolšoj theatre; documents; objects

17198
Muzej drevnerusskogo isskustva im. Andreja Rubleva (Andrej Rublev Museum of Ancient Russian Art)
ul. Prjamikova, 10, Moskva
Fine Arts Museum
Icons; in an ancient monastery

17199
Muzej Gosudarstvennogo akademičeskogo Malogo teatra SSSR (Museum of the State Academic Maly Theatre)
pl. Sverdlova, 1/6, Moskva 10309
Performing Arts Museum - 1932
History of the theatre; documents - library

17200
Muzej Gosudarstvennogo central'nogo teatra kukol pod rukovodstvom narodnogo artista SSSR S.V. Obrazcova (Obrazcov's Central State Puppet Theater Museum)
Sadovo Samotečnaja ul., 3, Moskva
Performing Arts Museum - 1937
History of the puppet theater in the USSR and other countries - library

17201
Muzej im. A.M. Gor'kogo pri institute mirovoj literatury AN SSSR (A.M. Gor'kij Museum, Institute of World Literature of the Academy of Sciences of USSR)
ul. Vorovskogo, 25a, Moskva
Historic Site - 1937
Memorabilia of the writer Maksim Gor'kij (1868-1936) - library

17202
Muzej istorii i rekonstrukcii Moskvy
Novaja pl., 12, Moskva 103012
History/Public Affairs Museum - 1896
History of Moscow; economics; urban planning; architecture - library

17203
Muzej Marksa i Ėngeľsa
ul. Marksa i Ėngeľsa, 5, Moskva
History/Public Affairs Museum - 1962
Memorial on Karl Marx (1818-1883) and Friedrich Engels (1820-1895)

17204
Muzej Moskovskogo chudožestvennogo akademičeskogo teatra SSSR im. M. Gor'kogo (MCHAT) (Moscow Arts Theatre Museum)
pr. Chudožestvennogo teatra 3a, Moskva 103009
Performing Arts Museum - 1922
History of the theatre - library

17205
Muzej N.A. Ostrovskogo
ul. Gor'kovo, 14, Moskva
Historic Site - 1940
Memorabilia of the writer N.A. Ostrovskij (1904-1936) in his former home

17206
Muzej narodnogo iskusstva (Folk Art Museum)
ul. Stanislavskogo, 7, Moskva
Decorative Arts Museum - 1885
Folk art; ancient and modern applied art; decorative art

17207
Muzej zemlevedenija Moskovskogo Gosudarstvenogo Universiteta
(Museum of Earth Science of the Moskow State Lomonosov University)
Leninskie gory, Universitet, Moskva
Natural History Museum - 1955
Earth science; climatology; water resources; soil science; fauna; flora; zoology

17208
Muzej-kvartira A.P. Čechova Muzej literatury
ul. Sadovaja Kudrinskaja, 6, Moskva
Historic Site - 1954
Memorabilia of the writer Anton Pavlovič Čechov (1860-1904) in his former home

17209
Muzej-kvartira F.M. Dostoevskogo
ul. Dostoevskogo, 2, Moskva
Historic Site - 1928
Memorabilia of the writer F.M. Dostoevskij (1821-1881) in his former home

17210
Muzej-kvartira Lunačarskogo
ul. Vesnina 9/5, Moskva
Historic Site
Flat where the writer and first minister of public education and art lived from 1918 to 1920

17211
Muzej-kvartira M. Gor'kogo
ul. Kačalova, 4/2, Moskva
Historic Site - 1965
Memorabilia of the writer Maksim Gor'kij (1868-1936), his private library

17212
Muzej-kvartira V.I. Nemiroviča-Dančenko Muzej chudožestvennogo teatra im. A.M. Gor'kogo
ul. Nemiroviča-Dančenko, 5/7, Moskva
Historic Site - 1944
Memorabilia of the theatre founder Vladimir Nemirovič-Dančenko (1858-1943)

17213
Naučno-issledovateľskij institut i muzej antropologii Moskovskogo gosudarstvennogo universiteta im. M.V. Lomonosova (Anthropological Institute and Museum of the Moscow Lomonosov University)
prosp. Marksa, 18, Moskva 103099
Anthropology Museum - 1879
Anthropology; archeology; collections from Africa; Mesolithic burial remains from the Dniepr region; ethnography - library

17214
Naučno-memoriaľnyj muzej N.E. Žukovskogo
ul. Radio, 17, Moskva
Historic Site
Memorabilia of the scientist Nikolaj Egorovič Žukovskij (1847-1921); history of aeronautics and astronautics in USSR

17215
Novodevičij monastyr'
Gosudarstvennyj istoričeskij muzej
Novodevičij pr., 1, Moskva
Religious Art Museum
16th-17th century fine and applied arts; religious art; in the 16th century cathedral of a former monastery

17216
Oružejnaja palata Gosudarstvennye muzei Moskovskogo Kremlja (Kremlin Armoury)
Kreml', Moskva
Decorative Arts Museum - 1851
Russian and foreign applied art; arms and armour; jewelry; textiles; garments; embroidery; insignia; enamels; religious art; harnesses; sattles; couches; rare books

17217
Ostankinskij dvorec-muzej tvorčestva krepostnych (Ostankino Palace Museum of the Serfs' Art)
1-ja Ostankinskaja, Moskva 129515
Fine Arts Museum - 1927
Fine art; applied art; ethnography; folk art; archeology - library

17218
Paleontologičeskij muzej AN SSSR (Paleontological Museum of the Academy of Sciences of the USSR)
Leninskij prosp. 16, Moskva
Natural History Museum - 1936
Paleontology; fossil specimens of fish, amphibians, reptiles and mammals

17219
Pokrovskij sobor-chram Vasilija Blažennogo Gosudarstvennyj istoričeskij muzej (St. Basil Cathedral)
Krasnaja pl., Moskva
Religious Art Museum
Religious art; architecture

17220
Uspenskij sobor Gosudarstvennyje muzei Moskovskogo Kremlja (Cathedral of the Assumption)
Sobornaja ploščaď, Moskva
Religious Art Museum
Icons of the 14th-17th centuries; mosaics; throne of Ivan the Terrible ; in a cathedral built 1479

17221
Zoologičeskij muzej Moskovskogo gosudarstvennogo universiteta M.V. Lomonosova (Moscow State University Museum of Zoology)
ul. Gercena, 6, Moskva 103009
Natural History Museum
Systematics; speciation; zoogeography; faunistic investigations - library

Murmansk

17222
Murmanskij oblastnoj kraevedčeskij muzej
prosp. Lenina, 54, Murmansk 12
General Museum - 1927
Natural history; local history; economics; culture - library

Naľčik

17223
Kabardino-Balkarskij kraevedčeskij muzej
ul. M. Gor'kogo, 76, Naľčik
General Museum - 1921
Natural history; local history; economics; culture - library

Nikolaev obl.

17224
Nikolaevskij kraevedčeskij muzej
ul. Dekabristov, 32, Nikolaev obl.
General Museum - 1950
Natural history; history; economics; culture - library

Nižnij Tagil

17225
Nižnetagiľskij gosudarstvennyj muzej izobraziteľnych iskusstv (State Museum of Fine Arts)
Ulaľskaja, 7, Nižnij Tagil
Fine Arts Museum - 1945
Fine art; contemporary art - library

17226
Nižnetagiľskij kraevedčeskij muzej
prosp. Lenina, 1, Nižnij Tagil 3
General Museum - 1853
Natural history; history; economics; culture - library

Novgorod

17227
Novgorodskij istoriko-chudožestvennyj i architekturnyj muzej (Novgorod Museum of Art History and Architecture)
Kreml', 11, Novgorod
History/Public Affairs Museum - 1865
History; manuscripts; art history; rare books - library

Novočerkassk

17228
Novočerkasskij muzej istorii donskich kozakov (Novočerkassk Museum of the History of the Don Cossacks)
ul. Sovetskaja, 38, Novočerkassk
History/Public Affairs Museum
History of the Don Cossacks; exhibition on Stepan Timofeevič Razin, the 17th century leader of the peasant liberation movement

Novokuzneck

17229
Kemerovskij oblastnoj muzej sovetskogo izobraziteľnogo iskusstva v g. Novokuznecke (Regional Museum of Soviet Fine Art)
prosp. Metallurgov, 3, Novokuzneck, Kemerovskaja obl.
Fine Arts Museum - 1963
Fine art; Soviet art - library

Novorossijsk

17230
Novorossijskij istoriko-kraevedčeskij muzej
ul. Sovetov, 58, Novorossijsk, Krasnojarskij kraj
History/Public Affairs Museum - 1944
Natural history; history; economics; culture - library

Novosibirsk

17231
Novosibirskaja oblastnaja kartinnaja galerija (Regional Art Gallery)
ul. Sverdlova, 37, Novosibirsk 7
Fine Arts Museum - 1958
Painting; sculpture - library

17232
Novosibirskij oblastnoj kraevedčeskij muzej
krasnyj prosp., 9, Novosibirsk 11
General Museum - 1927
Natural history; history; culture; economics - library

Nukus

17233
Karakalpakskij istoričeskij muzej
ul. Rachmatova, 3, Nukus
History/Public Affairs Museum
Uzbek history; military history

Odessa

17234
Odesskij archeologičeskij muzej
ul. Lastočkina 4, Odessa
Archeology Museum - 1825
Archeology; history; numismatics - library

17235
Odesskij chudožestvennyj muzej (Odessa Art Museum)
ul. Korolenko 5a, Odessa 57
Fine Arts Museum - 1899
Fine art

17236
Odesskij gosudarstvennyj muzej zapadnogo i vostočnogo iskusstva (Odessa State Museum of European and Oriental Art)
ul. Puškinskaja, 9, Odessa
Fine Arts Museum - 1920
Art; contemporary art

17237
Odesskij istoriko-kraevedčeskij muzej
ul. Chalturina, 4, Odessa
History/Public Affairs Museum
Natural history; economics; culture; history - library

Omsk

17238
Omskij muzej izobraziteľnych iskusstva (Omsk Fine Art Museum)
ul. Lenina, 23, Omsk 46
Fine Arts Museum - 1941
Fine art - library

17239
Omskij oblastnoj kraevedčeskij muzej
ul. Lenina, 23, Omsk 46
History/Public Affairs Museum - 1864
Natural history; history; economics; culture - library

Ordžonikidze

17240
Respublikanskij muzej kraevedenija Severo-Osetinskoj ASSR
prosp. Mira, 11, Ordžonikidze
General Museum - 1961
Natural history; history; economics; culture - library

17241
Severoossetinskij memoriaľnyj muzej K.L. Chetagurova (North-Ossetian K.L. Chetagurov Memorial Museum)
prosp. Mira, 12, Ordžonikidze
Historic Site
Caucasian poetry and literature; memorabilia of the poet Konstantin Levanovič Chetagurov (1859-1906)

Orel

17242
Gosudarstvennyj muzej I.S.
Turgeneva (State Museum of I.S.
Turgenev)
ul. Turgeneva, 11, Orel
Historic Site - 1918
Life and work of the writer Ivan
Sergeevič Turgenev (1818-1883);
photos; art works; personal
memorabilia; original furniture from his
home in Spasskoe Lutovino - library

17243
Muzej pisatelej-orlovcev
Gosudarstvennyj muzej I.S. Turgeneva
(Orel Literary Museum)
ul. 7-ogo Nojabrja, 24, Orel
History/Public Affairs Museum - 1918
Life and work of the writers Andreev,
Apuchtin, Bunin, Leskov, Pisarev,
Prišvin, Tjutčev, Fet, Kireevskij and
Jakušin; contemporary literature -
library

17244
Orlovskaja kartinnaja galerija (Orel
Picture Gallery)
ul. Saltykova-Ščedrina, Orel
Fine Arts Museum
Fine art; painting

17245
Orlovskij oblastnoj kraevedčeskij
muzej
Moskovskaja, 1/3, Orel 1
General Museum - 1897
Natural history; history; economics;
culture - library

Orenburg

17246
Orenburgskij muzej izobraziteľnych
iskusstv (Orenburg Museum of Fine
Arts)
ul. Pravdy, 6, Orenburg
Fine Arts Museum
Fine art; contemporary art

17247
Orenburgskij oblastnoj
kraevedčeskij muzej
Sovetskaja, 28, Orenburg
General Museum - 1887
Natural history; history; economics;
culture - library

Pavlovsk

17248
Muzej chudožestvennogo ubranstva
russkich dvorov konca XVIII-načala
XIX v. (Museum of Late 18th Century
Palatial Design)
ul. Revoljucii, 20, Pavlovsk
Fine Arts Museum
18th century Pavlovsk palace; Russian
architecture and garden architecture;
interiors; ancient sculpture; picture
gallery; tapestry; applied art

Penza

17249
Penzenskij oblastnoj kraevedčeskij
muzej
Krasnaja, 73, Penza 26
General Museum - 1905
Natural history; history; economics;
culture - library

Perm'

17250
Permskaja gosudarstvennaja
chudožestvennaja galerija (Perm
State Art Gallery)
Komsomoľskij prosp., 4, Perm'
Fine Arts Museum - 1937
Painting; sculpture - library

17251
Permskij oblastnoj kraevedčeskij
muzej
Komsomoľskij prosp., 6, Perm'
GSP-291
General Museum - 1890
Natural history; history; economics;
culture - library

Petrodvorec

17252
Dvorcy-muzei v parkach goroda
Petrodvorca (Museum Palaces and
Parks in Petrodvorec)
Petrodvorec, Leningradskaja obl.
History/Public Affairs Museum - 1918
18th-19th century architecture and
landscape gardening - library

Petrokrepost'

17253
Muzej-pamjatnik Šlisseľburgskaja
krepost' Gosudarstvennyj muzej istorii
Ļeningrada (Fortress Museum
Slisseľburg)
Petrokrepost'
History/Public Affairs Museum - 1918
Historical fortress built 1323; military
history; former political prison

Petrozavodsk

17254
Kareľskij gosudarstvennyj
kraevedčeskij muzej
Zavodskaja pl., 1, Petrozavodsk
General Museum - 1928
Cultural and economic history; natural
history of the region; local history -
library

17255
Muzej izobraziteľnych iskusstv
Kareľskoj ASSR (Karelian Museum of
Fine Art)
prosp. K. Marksa, 8, Petrozavodsk
Fine Arts Museum - 1960
Art - library

Pjatigorsk

17256
Gosudarstvennyj literaturno-
memoriaľnyj muzej M.Ju.
Lermontova (State Lermontov Literary
Memorial Museum)
Lermontovskaja ul., 4, Pjatigorsk
Historic Site - 1912
Memorabilia of the poet Michail
Jur'evič Lermontov (1814-1841) -
library

17257
Pjatigorskij kraevedčeskij muzej
ul. Sakko i Vancetti, 2, Pjatigorsk
General Museum - 1906
Natural history; history; economics;
culture - library

Poltava

17258
Poltavskij chudožestvennyj muzej
(Poltava Art Museum)
ul. Dzerdžinskogo, 11, Poltava
Fine Arts Museum

17259
Poltavskij kraevedčeskij muzej
(Poltava Regional Museum)
pl. Lenina 2, Poltava
General Museum - 1891
Life and work of the writers P. Mirny,
I.P. Kotljarevskij, V.G. Korolenko, N.V.
Gogoľ; local history - library

Pskov

17260
Pskovskij istoričeskij muzej (Pskov
Historical Museum)
ul. Nekrasova, 7, Pskov
History/Public Affairs Museum
History and ethnography of Russia

Puškin

17261
Muzej Licej Vsesojuznyj muzej A.S.
Puškina (Lyceum Museum)
Komsomolskaja ul., 1, Puškin
Historic Site
Memorial to the poet Aleksandr
Sergeevič Puškin (1799-1837)

17262
Muzej-dača A. S. Puškina
Vsesojuznyj muzej A.S. Puškina
(Country House Museum)
Puškinskaja ul., 2, Puškin
Historic Site - 1958
Memorial to the poet Aleksandr
Sergeevič Puškin (1799-1837); original
interiors

17263
Vsesojuznyj muzej A.S. Puškina
Ekaterininskij dvorec, Puškin
History/Public Affairs Museum - 1949
Exhibits, illustrating the life and work of
the poet Aleksandr Sergeevič Puškin
(1799-1837) and his epoch; portraits;
rare books; manuscripts and drawings
by the poet; in a lyceum where the
poet studied from 1811 to 1817 -
library

Repino

17264
Muzej-usaď ba I.E. Repina 'Penaty'
(Country House Museum of I.E. Repin)
Repino, Leningradskaja obl.
Historic Site - 1940
Memorabilia of Iľja Efimovič Repin
(1844-1930) in the country house
where the painter lived from 1900 to
1930; original interiors; park; artist's
grave

Riga

17265
Gosudarstvennyj musej latvijskogo i
russkogo iskusstva (State Museum of
Latvian and Russian Art)
ul. Gor'kogo, 10, Riga
Fine Arts Museum
Art

17266
Gosudarstvennyj muzej istorii
literatury i iskusstva im. Ja. Rajnisa
(Ja. Rajnis Museum of the History of
Literature and Art)
pl. Pionerov 3, Riga
History/Public Affairs Museum - 1949
Literature; theatre; music; performing
arts; film history of Latvia; literary
history - library

17267
Gosudarstvennyj muzej istorii Rigi
(State Museum of the History of Riga)
Palasta, 4, Riga
History/Public Affairs Museum - 1773
Archeology; local history; maritime
history and navigation

17268
Istoriko-medicinskij muzej im. P.
Stradina (P. Stradin Museum of
Medical History)
Riga
History/Public Affairs Museum - 1957
History of medicine from ancient times
to the present; public health; drawings;
photographs; 16th-20th century rare
medical books - library

17269
Latvijskij etnografičeskij muzej-
zapovednik (Latvian Open Air
Ethnographical Museum)
Riga
Open Air Museum
Wooden folk architecture of Latvia;
ethnography; art;

17270
Muzej revoljucii LatvSSR (Latvian
SSR Revolution Museum)
Smilšu, 20, Riga 47
History/Public Affairs Museum - 1948
Role of Latvia in the Revolution of
1917, the Russian Civil War and World
War II; militaria - library

17271
Muzej zarubežnogo iskusstva
(Museum of Foreign Art)
pl. Pionerov, 3, Riga
Fine Arts Museum - 1946
Foreign art - library

Rjazan'

17272
Rjazanskij kraevedčeskij muzej
Kremľ-15, Rjazan'
General Museum - 1918
Natural history; history; economics;
culture - library

17273
Rjazan'skij oblastnoj
chudožestvennyj muzej (Rjazan
Regional Art Museum)
Kremľ, 11, Rjazan'
Fine Arts Museum - 1913
Art - library

Roslavľ

17274
Roslavskij istoričeskij muzej
ul. Proletarskaja, 63, Roslavľ
History/Public Affairs Museum
History, economy and culture of the
Russian people from earliest times

Rostov-na-Donu

17275
Rostovskij oblastnoj muzej
izobraziteľnych iskusstv (Regional
Museum of Fine Arts)
Puškinskaja, 115, Rostov-na-Donu
Fine Arts Museum - 1938
Fine arts - library

17276
Rostovskij oblastnoj muzej
kraevedenija
ul. Ėngeľsa, 79, Rostov-na-Donu
General Museum - 1957
Natural history; history; economics;
culture - library

Rovno

17277
Rovenskij kraevedčeskij muzej
Krasnoarmejskaja, 33, Rovno
General Museum - 1940
Natural history; economics; culture
history - library

Salechard

17278
Okružnyj kraevedčeskij muzej
Jamalo-Neneckogo nacional'nogo
okruga
ul. Sverdlova, 14, Salechard,
Tjumenskaja obl.
General Museum - 1902
Natural history; history; economics;
culture - library

Samarkand

17279
**Gosudarstvennyj muzej istorii
kul'tury i iskusstva UzSSR** (Museum
of Culture and Art History of the
Uzbek SSR)
Sovetskaja, 51, Samarkand
General Museum - 1874
Cultural history, art, folklore of
Uzbekistan - library

Saransk

17280
Mordovskaja kartinnaja galerija
(Mordovian Painting Gallery)
ul. Sovetskaja, 29, Saransk
Fine Arts Museum
Painting; sculpture; contemporary art

17281
**Respublikanskij kraevedčeskij
muzej Mordovskoj ASSR**
Moskovskaja, 48, Saransk
General Museum - 1918
Natural history; history; economics;
culture - library

Saratov

17282
**Gosudarstvennyj memorial'nyj muzej
A.N. Radiščeva**
ul. Radiščeva, 39, Saratov
Historic Site
Memorabilia of the writer Aleksandr
Nikolaevič Radiščev (1749-1802)

17283
Memorial'nyj muzej Černyševskogo
ul. Černyševskogo, 142, Saratov
Historic Site
Memorabilia of the writer Nikolaj
Gavrilovič Černyševskij (1828-1889);
documents

17284
**Saratovskij gosudarstvennyj
chudožestvennyj muzej im. A.I.
Radiščeva** (Saratov State Art
Museum)
ul. Radiščeva, 39, Saratov
Fine Arts Museum - 1885
Fine art; contemporary art - library

17285
**Saratovskij oblastnoj muzej
kraevedenija**
ul. Lermontova, 34, Saratov 2
General Museum - 1930
Natural history; history; economics;
culture - library

17286
**Saratovskij oblastnoj muzej
kraevedenija**
ul. Lermontova, 34, Saratov 2
General Museum - 1930
Natural history; history; economics;
culture - library

Šauljaj

17287
**Šauljajskij istoriko-étnografičeskij
muzej** (Historical and Ethnographical
Museum of Šauljaj)
ul. Vitauto, 89, Šauljaj
History/Public Affairs Museum - 1923
History; ethnography; archeology -
library

Semipalatinsk

17288
**Respublikanskij literaturno-
memorial'nyj muzej Abaja** (Abaj
Literary Memorial Museum)
ul. Lenina, 50, Semipalatinsk
History/Public Affairs Museum - 1940
Kazakh literary history; memorabilia of
the poet Ibrahim Abaj Kunanbaev
(1845-1904) - library

Šepetovka

17289
**Šepetovskij literaturno-memorial'nyj
muzej N.A. Ostrovskogo** (Literary
Memorial Museum of N.A. Ostrovskij)
ul. Karla Marksa, 82, Šepetovka,
Chmel'nickaja obl.
Historic Site - 1947
Memorabilia of the writer Nokolaj
Alekseevič Ostrovskij (1904-1936);
Russian and Soviet literature - library

Sevastopol'

17290
**Chersonskij muzej istorii i
archeologii** (Chersones Museum of
History and Archeology)
Sevastopol'
Archeology Museum - 1860
Finds from the excavation of the site of
Chersones, an ancient Greek colony

Simferopol'

17291
**Krymskij kraevedčeskij muzej
'Tavrika'**
ul. Puškina, 18, Simferopol'
General Museum - 1973
Natural history; history; economics;
culture - library

Smolensk

17292
**Smolenskij oblastnoj kraevedčeskij
muzej**
Sobornyj dvor, 7, Smolensk
General Museum - 1888
Natural history; history; economics;
culture - library

Spasskoe-Lutovinovo

17293
Dom-muzej I.S. Turgeneva
Gosudarstvennyj muzej I.S.
Turgeneva, Orel
Spasskoe-Lutovinovo, Orlovskaja obl.
Historic Site
Memorabilia of the writer Ivan
Sergeevič Turgenev (1818-1883) in his
country estate; literary history

Staročerkassk

17294
Staročerkasskij muzej
Novočerkasskij muzej istorii donskich
kozakov
Staročerkassk
History/Public Affairs Museum
History of the Don Cossacks;
exhibition on Stepan Timofeevič Razin,
17th century leader of the peasant
liberation movement

Stavropol'

17295
Stavropol'skij kraevedčeskij muzej
ul. Dzerdžinskogo, 135, Stavropol'
General Museum - 1904
Natural history; history; economics;
culture - library

17296
**Stavropol'skij muzej izobraziteľnych
iskusstv** (Stavropol Museum of Fine
Art)
ul. Dzerdžinskogo, 115, Stavropol'
Fine Arts Museum
Fine art

Stepanakert

17297
**Stepanakertskij istoričeskij muzej
Nogorno-Karabachskoj avtonomnoj
oblasti** (Stepanakert Museum of the
History of the Nagorno-Karabach
Autonomous District)
ul. Gor'kogo, 4, Stepanakert
History/Public Affairs Museum
Archeology, ethnography, history of
Azerbajdžan SSR

Strachovo

17298
**Gosudarstvennyj muzej-usad'ba V.D.
Polenova** (V.D. Polenov Museum
Estate)
Strachovo, Tul'skaja obl.
Historic Site - 1892
Memorabilia of the painter Vasilij
Dmitrievič Polenov (1844-1927) and his
family; paintings; original interiors -
library

Suchumi

17299
Abchazskij gosudarstvennyj muzej
(State Museum of the Abchasian SSR)
ul. Lenina 22, Suchumi
General Museum - 1922
Regional history; economics; natural
history - library

Sumy

17300
**Sumskij oblastnoj kraevedčeskij
muzej**
ul. Lenina, 45, Sumy
General Museum - 1952
Natural history; history; economics;
culture - library

Sverdlovsk

17301
Sverdlovskaja kartinnaja galerija
(Sverdlovsk Painting Gallery)
ul. Vajnera, 11, Sverdlovsk L-14
Fine Arts Museum - 1936
Painting; metal objects; Western
European, Russian and Soviet art -
library

17302
**Sverdlovskij oblastnoj kraevedčeskij
muzej**
Zelenaja rošča, Sverdlovsk 1
General Museum - 1871
Natural history; history; economics;
culture - library

Syktyvkar

17303
Chudožestvennyj muzej Komi ASSR
(Komi Art Museum)
ul. Kommunističeskaja, 6, Syktyvkar
Fine Arts Museum
Art; contemporary art of the Komi
SSR

17304
**Respublikanskij kraevedčeskij
muzej Komi ASSR**
ul. Ordzonikidze, 2, Syktyvkar
General Museum - 1911
Natural history; local history;
economics; culture - library

Tallin

17305
**Gosudarstvennyj istoričeskij muzej
Éstonskoj SSR** (State Historical
Museum of the Estonian SSR)
Pikk ul. 17, Tallin
History/Public Affairs Museum - 1864
Estonian history from ancient times to
the present

17306
Muzej teatra i muzyky ÉSSR
(Museum of Theatre and Music of the
Estonian SSR)
ul. Mjujrivache, 12, Tallin
Performing Arts Museum - 1924
Theatrical art and music in Estonia;
musical instruments - library

17307
Tallinskij gorodskij muzej (Tallin City
Museum)
ul. Vene,17, Tallin
History/Public Affairs Museum - 1937
Local history; fine art - Library

17308
**Tallinskij gosudarstvennyj
chudožestvennyj muzej** (Tallin State
Art Museum)
Vejcenbergi, 31, Tallin 10
Fine Arts Museum
Estonian and foreign paintings -
library

Tambov

17309
Tambovskaja kartinnaja galerija
(Tambov Picture Gallery)
ul. Sovetskaja, 56, Tambov
Fine Arts Museum
Painting; contemporary art

17310
**Tambovskij oblastnoj kraevedčeskij
muzej**
Oktjabr'skaja pl., 4, Tambov
General Museum - 1918
Natural history; history; economics;
culture - library

Tartu

17311
**Gosudarstvennyj étnografičeskij
muzej Éstonskoj SSR** (State
Ethnographical Museum of the
Estonian SSR)
ul. N. Burdenko, 32, Tartu
Anthropology Museum
Ethnography; peasant life of the
Estonian people; folk art

17312
**Literaturnyj muzej im. Fr.R.
Krejcvaľda AN ĖSSR** (Literary
Museum of the Estonian Academy of
Sciences)
ul. Vanemuize, 42, Tartu
History/Public Affairs Museum - 1909
Literary history of Estonia - library

17313
**Muzej klassičeskoj archeologii
Tartuskogo universiteta** (Museum of
Classical Archeology of the Tartu
University)
Ülikooli, 18, Tartu
Archeology Museum - 1803
Archeological finds; 15th-19th century
European graphics; gems; coins -
library

17314
**Tartuskji gosudarstvennyj
chudožestvennyj muzej** (Tartu Art
Museum)
ul. Valikraavi, 14, Tartu
Fine Arts Museum - 1940
Western European, Estonian and
Russian paintings; sculpture; applied
art

Taškent

17315
**Gosudarstvennyj muzej iskusstv
Uzbekistana**
Kujbyševa, 4, Taškent 47
Fine Arts Museum - 1918
Art; architecture; sculpture; fine arts;
graphics; music; theatre; ethnography
- library

17316
**Muzej istorii narodov Uzbekistana
im. T. Ajbeka** (Uzbekistan T. Ajbek
Historical Museum)
ul. Kujbyševa 15, Taškent
History/Public Affairs Museum - 1922
History of the Central Asian area;
exhibits on the life of Central Asiatic
life ranging from primitive communal
societies to the present time - library

17317
**Taškentskij filial Central'nogo muzeja
Lenina v Moskve** (Taškent Branch of
the Central Lenin Museum in
Moscow)
bul. Lenina, Taškent
History/Public Affairs Museum
Memorabilia of Vladimir Il'ič Lenin
(1870-1924)

Tbilisi

17318
Dom-muzej Il'i Čavčavadze
ul. Ordžonikidze, 22, Tbilisi
Historic Site - 1957
Memorabilia of the writer Ilja
Čavčavadze; literary history - library

17319
Gosudarstvennaja kartinnaja galerija
(Georgian State Painting Gallery)
prosp. Rustaveli, 3, Tbilisi
Fine Arts Museum
Paintings; contemporary art

17320
**Gosudarstvennyj istoriko-
ėtnografičeskij muzej goroda Tbilisi**
(Tbilisi Museum of History and
Ethnography)
Komsomol'skaja alleja, 11, Tbilisi 7
History/Public Affairs Museum
Archeology; history; ethnography

17321
**Gosudarstvennyj literaturnyj muzej
Gruzii** (State Literary Museum of
Georgia)
Džordžiašvili, 8, Tbilisi 4
History/Public Affairs Museum - 1928
Georgian literary history since the
19th century - library

17322
**Gosudarstvennyj muzej Gruzii im. S.
N. Džanašia AN GSSR** (State
Museum of Georgia)
ul. Kecchoveli, 10, Tbilisi
General Museum - 1852
Archeology; Georgian history and
ethnography from ancient times to the
present - library

17323
**Gosudarstvennyj muzej iskusstv
GSSR** (Georgian State Art Museum)
ul. Kecchoveli, 1, Tbilisi
Fine Arts Museum
Art - library

17324
**Gosudarstvennyj muzej narodnogo
obrazovanija GSSR** (State Museum of
the Public Education of the Georgian
SSR)
ul. Čičinadze, 1, Tbilisi
History/Public Affairs Museum - 1938
Public education; linguistics; literary
history - library

17325
**Gosudarstvennyj teatral'nyj muzej
GSSR** (State Theatrical Museum of
GSSR)
ul. Kecchoveli, 1, Tbilisi 7
Performing Arts Museum - 1927
Performing arts; documents;
photographs - library

17326
**Tbiliskij filial Central'nogo muzeja
Lenina v Moskve** (Tbilisi Branch of the
Central Lenin Museum in Moscow)
prosp. Rustaveli 29, Tbilisi
History/Public Affairs Museum
Memorabilia of Vladimir Il'ič Lenin
(1870-1924)

Ternopol'

17327
Ternopol'skij kraevedčeskij muzej
Muzejnaja, 11, Ternopol'
General Museum - 1907
Natural history; history; economics;
culture - library

Tichvin

17328
**Gosudarstvennyj dom-muzej N.A.
Rimskogo-Korsakova** (Rimskij-
Korsakov Memorial House)
ul. Rimskogo-Korsakova, 13, Tichvin,
Leningradskaja obl.
Historic Site - 1944
Life and work of the composer Nikolaj
Andreevič Rimskij-Korsakov
(1844-1908) in his birthplace - library

Tjumen'

17329
Tjumenskaja kartinnaja galerija
(Tjumen Painting Gallery)
ul. Republic 29, Tjumen'
Fine Arts Museum
Fine art; contemporary art

Tobol'sk

17330
Tobol'skaja kartinnaja galerija
(Tobolsk Picture Gallery)
pl. Krasnaja, 2, Tobol'sk
Fine Arts Museum
Painting

17331
**Tobol'skij gosudarstvennyj istoriko-
architekturnyj muzej-zapovednik**
(Tobolsk State Historical Museum)
Krasnaja pl., 2, Tobol'sk, Tjumenskaja
obl.
History/Public Affairs Museum - 1870
History of Siberia - library

Tomsk

17332
**Tomskij oblastnoj kraevedčeskij
muzej**
prosp. Lenina, 75, Tomsk
General Museum - 1922
Natural history; history; economics;
culture - library

Tula

17333
**Tul'skij oblastnoj chudožestvennyj
muzej** (Tula Art Museum)
ul. Ėngel'sa, 144, Tula 8
Fine Arts Museum - 1939
Fine art; contemporary art - library

17334
**Tul'skij oblastnoj kraevedčeskij
muzej**
Sovetskaja, 68, Tula
General Museum - 1930
Local history; materials on the 1917
October Revolution - library

Ufa

17335
**Baškirskij gosudarstvennyj
chudožestvennyj muzej im. M.V.
Nesterova** (Baškirian State Art
Museum)
ul. Gogolja, 27, Ufa
Fine Arts Museum - 1919
Art; manuscripts - library

17336
**Respublikanskij kraevedčeskij
muzej Baškirskoj ASSR**
ul.Oktjabr'skoj revoljucii, 10, Ufa 25
General Museum - 1864
Natural history; history; economics;
culture - library

Uglič

17337
Istoričeskij muzej
Kreml', Uglič
History/Public Affairs Museum
Russian history

Ulan-Udé

17338
**Respublikanskij kraevedčeskij
muzej im. M.I. Changalova Burjatskoj
ASSR**
Profsojuznaja, 29, Ulan-Udé
General Museum - 1923
Natural history; history; economics;
culture - library

Uljanovsk

17339
**Uľjanovskij filial Central'nogo
muzeja V.I. Lenina** (Uljanovsk Branch
of the Central Lenin Museum)
ul. Lenina, 58, Uľjanovsk
Historic Site - 1941
Memorabilia of V.I. Lenin; history -
library

17340
**Uľjanovskij oblastnoj kraevedčeskij
muzej im. I.A. Gončarova**
bul. Novyj Venec, 3/4, Uljanovsk
General Museum - 1895
Natural history; history; economics;
culture - library

Užgorod

17341
Zakarpatskij kraevedčeskij muzej
Kremlevskaja, 33, Užgorod
General Museum - 1947
Natural history; economics; culture -
library

Velikie Soročincy

17342
**Velikosoročinskij literaturno-
memorial'nyj muzej N.V. Gogolja**
(Literary Memorial Museum of N.V.
Gogol')
ul. Gogolja, 32, Velikie Soročincy,
Poltavskaja obl.
Historic Site - 1951
Memorabilia of the writer Nikolaj
Vasil'evič Gogol' (1809-1852); literary
history - library

Vil'njus

17343
Chudožestvennyj muzej LitSSR
(Lithuanian State Art Museum)
ul. Gor'kogo 55, Vil'njus
Fine Arts Museum - 1941
Lithuanian art; 16th-19th century
French, German and English art -
library

17344
Istoriko - Ėtnografičeskij muzej
ul. Rublevskogo, 1, Vil'njus
General Museum - 1856
Archeology; ethnography; history;
numismatics - library

17345
Muzej ateizma LitSSR (Museum of
Atheism)
M. Gor'kogo, 74, Vil'njus
History/Public Affairs Museum - 1962
Religious history; atheism

17346
Muzej revoljucii LitSSR (Museum of
the Revolution of the Lithuanian SSR)
ul. Požolos, 32/1, Vil'njus
History/Public Affairs Museum - 1948
History of the revolutionary movement
in Lithuania (19th-20th century) -
library

Vinnica

17347
Vinnickij kraevedčeskij muzej
ul. Lenina, 13a, Vinnica
General Museum - 1919
Natural history; history; economics;
culture - library

Vladimir

17348
Vladimiro-Suzdaľskij istoriko-chudožestvennyj i architekturnyj muzej-zapovednik (Vladimir-Suzdal Museum of Art History and Architecture)
ul. III Internacionala, 58, Vladimir
History/Public Affairs Museum - 1862
History; archeology; art; architecture - library

Vladivostok

17349
Muzej Tichookeanskogo naučno-issledovateľskogo instituta rybnogo chozjajstva i okeanografii (Museum of the Pacific Scientific Research Institute of Fisheries and Oceanography)
ul. Leninskaja, 20, Vladivostok centr
Natural History Museum - 1925
Marine biology; ichthyology; molocology; biology of sea mammals; flora and fauna of the Pacific Ocean

17350
Primorskij kraevedčeskij muzej im. V.K. Arsen'eva
ul. 1 Maja, 6, Vladivostok
General Museum - 1936
Natural history; history; economics; culture - library

Volgograd

17351
Gosudarstvennyj muzej zaščity Volgograda (State Museum of the Defense of Volgograd)
ul. Gogolja, 10, Volgograd
History/Public Affairs Museum
60,000 items feature the defence of the city during the Civil War (1918-1920) and the Battle of Stalingrad (1942-1943)

17352
Volgogradskij oblastnoj kraevedčeskij muzej
prosp. V.I. Lenina, 39, Volgograd 5
General Museum - 1924
Natural history; local history; economics; culture - library

Vologda

17353
Vologodskaja kartinnaja galerija (Vologda Art Gallery)
Kremlevskaja pl., 2, Vologda
Fine Arts Museum - 1953
Fine art; contemporary art - library

17354
Vologodskij kraevedčeskij muzej
ul. Majakovskogo, 15, Vologda
General Museum - 1923
Natural history; local history; economics; culture - library

Voronež

17355
Voronežskij oblastnoj kraevedčeskij muzej
ul. Plechanovskaja, 29, Voronež 18
General Museum - 1894
Natural history; history; economics; culture

17356
Voronežskij oblastnoj muzej izobraziteľnych iskusstv (Voronež Fine Art Museum)
prosp. Revoljucii, 18, Voronež
Fine Arts Museum - 1947
library

Vorošilovgrad

17357
Vorošilovgradskij chudožestvennyj muzej im. Artema (Museum of Fine Art)
Počtovaja, 3, Vorošilovgrad
Fine Arts Museum - 1955
Fine arts - library

17358
Vorošilovgradskij kraevedčeskij muzej
K. Marksa, 30, Vorošilovgrad
General Museum - 1931
Natural history; history; economics; culture - library

Vyra

17359
Muzej 'Stancionnyj smotriteľ' (Postmaster Museum)
Vyra, Leningradskaja oblasť
History/Public Affairs Museum - 1980
Museum connected with Puškin's short story 'Stancionnyj smotriteľ' ('Postmaster'); in a former post house, described by the poet in his story; original interiors; samovar; travel document of A.S. Puškin dated 5.5.1829; harnessry

Zagorsk

17360
Zagorskij muzej istorii i iskusstva (Zagorsk Museum of History and Art)
Zagorsk, Moskovskaja obl.
History/Public Affairs Museum - 1920
The museum consists of most of the buildings of the Trojce-Sergieva Larva monastery; Russian art from the 17th century to the present

Zaporoz'e

17361
Zaporožskij kraevedčeskij muzej
prosp. Lenina, 59, Zaporoz'e
General Museum - 1948
Natural history; history; economics; culture - library

Žitomir

17362
Žitomirskij oblastnoj kraevedčeskij muzej
ul. Komarova, 8a, Žitomir
General Museum - 1900
Natural history; history; economics; culture - library

Vatican

Città del Vaticano

17363
Cappelle, Sale e Gallerie Affrescate Musei Vaticani
Viale Vaticano, V-00120 Città del Vaticano, Roma
Fine Arts Museum
Chapel of Beato Angelico; Sistine Chapel with frescoes by Michelangelo; Borgia Appartment: decorated by Pinturicchio; Chapel of Urbano VIII; rooms and loggias decorated by Raphael; Gallery of Maps

17364
Collezione d'Arte Religiosa Moderna Musei Vaticani
Viale Vaticano, V-00120 Città del Vaticano, Roma
Religious Art Museum - 1973
Coll: paintings, sculptures and drawings offered to the Pope by artists and donors

17365
Museo Chiaramonti e Braccio Nuovo Musei Vaticani
Viale Vaticano, V-00120 Città del Vaticano, Roma
Archeology Museum
Findings excavated in the beginning of the 19th century including the statues of the Nile, of Demosthenes and of the Augustus of 'Primaporta'

17366
Museo Gregoriano Egizio Musei Vaticani
Viale Vaticano, V-00120 Città del Vaticano, Roma
Fine Arts Museum - 1839
Coll: Egyptian papyri; mummies; sarcophagi; statues including statue of Queen Tuia

17367
Museo Gregoriano Etrusco Musei Vaticani
Viale Vaticano, V-00120 Città del Vaticano, Roma
Fine Arts Museum - 1837
Objects from the Tomba Regolini Galassi of Cerveteri; the Mars of Todi; bronzes; terra cottas and jewelry; Greek vases from Etruscan tombs

17368
Museo Gregoriano Profano Musei Vaticani
Viale Vaticano, V-00120 Città del Vaticano, Roma
Fine Arts Museum - 1844
Coll: Roman sculpture from the Pontifical States; portrait-statue of Sophocles; the Marsyas of the Myronian group of Athena and Marsyas; the Flavian reliefs from the Palace of the Apostolic Chancery

17369
Museo Missionario Etnologico Musei Vaticani
Viale Vaticano, V-00120 Città del Vaticano, Roma
Anthropology Museum - 1926
Ethnographical collection from all over the world

17370
Museo Pio Clementino Musei Vaticani
Viale Vaticano, V-00120 Città del Vaticano, Roma
Fine Arts Museum - 1770
Coll: sculptures including the Apollo of Belvedere; the Apoxyomenos by Lysippus; the Laocoon Group; the Apollo Sauroktonous by Praxiteles

17371
Museo Pio Cristiano Musei Vaticani
Viale Vaticano, V-00120 Città del Vaticano, Roma
Fine Arts Museum - 1854
Coll: sarcophagi; Latin and Greek inscriptions from Christian cemeteries and basilicas

17372
Museo Profano Musei Vaticani
Viale Vaticano, V-00120 Città del Vaticano, Roma
Fine Arts Museum - 1767
Bronze sculptures and art of the classical era

17373
Museo Sacro Musei Vaticani
Viale Vaticano, V-00120 Città del Vaticano, Roma
History/Public Affairs Museum - 1756
Coll: objects of liturgical art; historical relics and curios from the Lateran; paleolithic, medieval and Renaissance art; paintings of the Roman era

17374
Pinacoteca Vaticana Musei Vaticani
Viale Vaticano, V-00120 Città del Vaticano, Roma
Fine Arts Museum - 1932
Coll: paintings by Fra Angelico, Raphael, Leonardo da Vinci, Titian and Caravaggio; Raphael Tapestries

17375
Tesoro di San Pietro Musei Vaticani
V-00120 Città del Vaticano, Roma
Religious Art Museum
Sacred vestments; silver and goldsmith work

Venezuela

Aragua

17376
Museo Ornitológico
Vía Ocumare de la Costa, Parque Nacional 'Rancho Grande', Aragua, Estado Aragua
Natural History Museum
ornithology

Barcelona

17377
Museo de la Tradición
Calle Juncal 3-45, Barcelona, Estado Anzoátegui
General Museum - 1969
Coll: 17th, 18th, and 19th century painting and sculpture; authentic 19th century weapons; 19th century documents and furniture - library

Caracas

17378
Castillete 'Armando Reveron'
Macuto, Caracas
General Museum

17379
Colección Ornitológica W.H. Phelps
Apdo. 2009, Caracas 1010A
Natural History Museum
ornithology; bird skins - library

17380
Escuela Naval de Venezuela Meseta de Mamo
Catia La Mar, Caracas
History/Public Affairs Museum - 1965
history; ethnography; technology

17381
Galeria de Arte Nacional
Plaza Morelos, Los Caobos, Caracas
Fine Arts Museum
paintings

17382
Museo Arturo Michelena
Esquina de Urapal 82, Caracas 101
Fine Arts Museum

17383
Museo Audiovisual Academia Nacional de Ciencias y Artes del Cine y la Televisión
Parque Central, Edif. Catuche, Nivel Bolívar, Abdo. 17030, Caracas
Science/Tech Museum
Exhibition of technical audioviusal instruments and apparatus used in T.V., radio, and theatre - library, archives

17384
Museo Bolivariano
San Jacinto a Trapazos, Caracas 101
History/Public Affairs Museum - 1911
personal memorabilia of revolutionary
hero Simón Bolívar (1783-1830);
portraits; historical paintings of Bolívar
contemporaries

17385
Museo Criollo 'Raul Santana' Esquina
de las Monjas
Caracas 101
Anthropology Museum - 1970
anthropology

17386
Museo 'Cuadra de Bolivar'
Piedras a Bárcenas, Caracas 101
General Museum

17387
Museo de Arte Colonial
Quinta de Anauco, Avenida Panteón
San Bernardino, Caracas 1011
Fine Arts Museum - 1942
Paintings, sculpture, furniture, china of
the Venezuelan Colonial period -
library

17388
**Museo de Arte Contemporáneo de
Caracas**
Zona Cultural, Parque Central, POB
17093, Caracas
Fine Arts Museum - 1973
Coll: Venezuelan and international
works of art; sculpture; painting; arts
and crafts; Calder's tapestries; works
by Soto and Vasarely - library

17389
Museo de Bellas Artes de Caracas
Los Caobos, Caracas 105
Fine Arts Museum - 1938
Venezuelan paintings from the end of
the 19th century to the present; inter-
American collection of paintings and
sculptures; European paintings;
European porcelain; collection of
prints and drawings; contemporary
sculpture; Chinese porcelain; Egyptian
art - library

17390
Museo de Ciencias Naturales
Apdo. 8011, Caracas
Natural History Museum - 1940
geology; zoology; ethnology;
archaeology; paleontology; gold
'guaca' funeral treasure of the Tairona
culture; artificially deformed
prehistoric crania

17391
Museo del Folklore
Avda. Avila, Qta. Silueta, Los Chorros,
Caracas 106
Anthropology Museum
anthropology

17392
Museo del Transporte
Parque del Este, Caracas
Science/Tech Museum - 1970
transportation

17393
Museo 'Emilio Boggio'
Esquina de las Monjas, Caracas 101
Fine Arts Museum
paintings

17394
Museo Fundación 'John Boulton'
Bolívar 180, La Guaira, Caracas
History/Public Affairs Museum - 1970

17395
Museo Ornitológico
Parque El Calvario, Caracas
Natural History Museum
ornithology

17396
**Museo Pedagógico de Historia del
Arte** Instituto del Arte, Facultad de
Humanidades y Educación
Ciudad Universitaria, Caracas
Fine Arts Museum
paintings; Latin American art

17397
Panteón Nacional
Caracas 101
History/Public Affairs Museum

17398
**Sociedad de Ciencias Naturales de
Salle** Ed. Fundación La Salle
Av. Bogotá, Caracas 101
Natural History Museum
natural history; anthropology;
archaeology

Ciudad Bolívar

17399
**Museo de Arte Moderno 'Jesus
Soto'**
Av. Germania y Mario Briceno
Iragorry, Ciudad Bolívar
Fine Arts Museum - 1971

17400
Museo de Ciudad Bolivar
Casa del Correo del Orinoco, Ciudad
Bolívar, Estado Bolívar
General Museum

17401
Museo 'Talavera'
Calle Bolívar, Ciudad Bolívar
General Museum - 1940
pre-Columbian finds; Colonial periods;
natural history; numismatics; religious
art

Ciudad del Tocuyo

17402
Museo Colonial
Ciudad del Tocuyo
General Museum - 1945

Colonia Tovar

17403
**Museo de Historia y Artesania de la
Colonial Tovar**
Calle del Museo, Colonia Tovar
Natural History Museum - 1970
art; history; natural history;
anthropology; ethnography;
archaeology; geology

Coro

17404
**Museo Diocesano 'Monseñor Lucas
Guillermo Castillo'**
Zamora, Coro
General Museum - 1947
art and history

La Asunción

17405
Museo 'Nueva Cadiz'
Independencia, La Asunción
General Museum
history; ethnography; natural history;
archaeology

Los Teques

17406
**Museo de Antropologia del Instituto
Venezolano de Investigaciones
Científicas - I.V.I.C**
Carretera Panamericana, Los Teques,
Estado Miranda
General Museum

Maracaibo

17407
**Museo Histórico 'General Rafael
Urdaneta'**
Calle 91A No. 7A-70, Maracaibo
History/Public Affairs Museum - 1936
military history

Maracay

17408
Museo de Antropologia e Historia
Fundación 'Lisandro Alvarado'
Calle 99-A Oueste. La Alcaldia,
Apartado de Correos 4518, Maracay,
Estado Aragua 2101A
General Museum - 1964
Coll: Pre-Columbian archeology;
Venezuelan ethnology, anthropology,
and history; vertebrate paleontology;
religious art - library

17409
**Museo de las Fuerzas Aéreas
Venezolana**
Av. Las Delicias y Av. 19 de Abril,
Maracay
Science/Tech Museum - 1964
aeronautical history

Mérida

17410
Museo de Arte Colonial
Avda. 3, entre calles 18 y 19, Mérida,
Estado Mérida
Fine Arts Museum

17411
Museo de Arte Moderno
Calle Flamboyán, Santa Maria (frente a
la Plaza Beethoven), Mérida, Estado
Mérida
Fine Arts Museum - 1969

17412
Museo del Estado de Mérida
Universidad de Mérida
Merida
General Museum

17413
Museo Estatal de Historia
Av. 2 No. 35-64, Mérida
General Museum - 1954

Trujillo

17414
Museo 'Christobal Menoza'
Trujillo
General Museum

Valencia

17415
Museo de la Historia y Antropologia
Casa de los Celis
Avda. Soublette, Valencia, Estado
Carabobo
Anthropology Museum
history; anthropology

Viet Nam

Da-Nang

17416
National Museum of Cham Sculpture
Da-Nang
Archeology Museum - 1919
Cham sculpture and architectural
fragments from various periods and
places

Dien-Bien-Phu

17417
Dien-Bien-Phu Museum
Dien-Bien-Phu
General Museum
Local history

Haiphong

17418
Haiphong Museum
Haiphong
General Museum
Local history

Hanoi

17419
Army Museum
Hanoi
History/Public Affairs Museum
Military history

17420
Historical Museum
Hanoi
History/Public Affairs Museum - 1958

17421
**Revolutionary and Armed Resistance
Museum**
Hanoi
History/Public Affairs Museum

17422
Vietnam Museum of Fine Arts
66 Nguyen Thai Hoc, Hanoi
Fine Arts Museum - 1966
Folk drawings; modern paintings and
sculptures; lacquers and silks;
bronzes and stones; ancient ceramics
- library

Ho Chi Minh City

17423
Geological Museum
31 Han Thuyan St, Ho Chi Minh City
Natural History Museum
Mineralogy; fossils

17424
Museum of Ho Chi Minh City
65 Ly Tu Trong, Ho Chi Minh City
General Museum - 1978
History; revolutionary movement and
War of Liberation - library

Hong-Gay

17425
Hong Quang Museum
Hong-Gay
General Museum
Local history

Hue

17426
Museum of Hue
Hue
Archeology Museum
Cham sculptures (10th-11th century)

Hung-Yen

17427
Hung-Yen Museum
Hung-Yen
General Museum
Local history

Nhatrang

17428
Oceanographic Museum
Nhatrang
Science/Tech Museum

Thai-Nguyen

17429
Viet Bac Museum
Thai-Nguyen
General Museum
Local history

Vinh

17430
Soviet Nghe-Tinh Museum
Vinh
History/Public Affairs Museum

Yemen Arab Republic

San'a

17431
Yemen National Museum
San'a
History/Public Affairs Museum
South Arabian antiques of the
pre-Islamic and Islamic periods;
folklore

Ta'izz

17432
Ta'izz Museum
Ta'izz
History/Public Affairs Museum
Housed in a former Imam's palace;
items pertaining to the 1962 Revolution
and the events that led up to it

Zafar

17433
Zafar Museum
Zafar
General Museum
Antiques found in Zafar and the
vicinity dating back to pre-Islamic
times

Yemen, People's Democratic Republic

Aden

17434
Crater Folk Museum
Tawila, Aden
General Museum
Architecture; handicrafts; traditional
costumes; musical instruments

17435
Crater Military Museum
Aden
History/Public Affairs Museum
Historic weapons

17436
National Museum of Antiquities
Tawahi, Aden
History/Public Affairs Museum
South Arabian antiques dating back to
pre-Islamic times

Al-Mukalla

17437
Al-Mukalla Museum
Al-Mukalla
General Museum
Folk costumes; traditional handicrafts

Seiyun in Wadi Hadhramaut

17438
Seiyun in Wadi Hadhramaut Museum
Seiyun in Wadi Hadhramaut
General Museum
Housed in a former Imam's palace;
handicrafts; folkore items; antiques
found in the region

Wadi Baihan

17439
Baihan al-Qasab Museum
Wadi Baihan
History/Public Affairs Museum
Antiques found in the Qataban region
dating back to pre-Islamic times

Yugoslavia

Aleksinac

17440
Zavičajni Muzej
Ul.Mome Popovića 20, YU-18220
Aleksinac
General Museum
Ethnography

Arandelovac

17441
Muzej NOB
YU-34300 Arandelovac
History/Public Affairs Museum
History of revolution

Bački Petrovac

17442
Narodni Muzej
Ul.Maršala Tita 10, YU-21470 Bački
Petrovac
General Museum
Ethnography, local contemporary
painting

Bakar

17443
Gradski Muzej
Ul. Kogule 212, YU-51222 Bakar
General Museum
Local history

Banja Luka

17444
Muzej Bosanske Krajne
YU-78000 Banja Luka
General Museum - 1930
Archaeology, history, ethnography and
natural history of north-west Bosnia;
national revolutionary history

17445
Umjetnička Galerija
YU-78000 Banja Luka
Fine Arts Museum

Bar

17446
**Memorijalna Galerija Veliša
Lekovića**
YU-81350 Bar
Fine Arts Museum
Paintings; memorabilia on painter V.
Leković

17447
Zavičajni Muzej
Topolica, YU-81350 Bar
General Museum
Natural history, archaeology,
ethnography, history, technology

Baška

17448
Muzejska Zbirka
YU-51523 Baška, otok Krk
History/Public Affairs Museum
Navigation history

Begunje

17449
Spominski Muzej Talcev (Memorial
Museum of Hostages)
Castle, YU-64275 Begunje, *mail c/o*
Muzeji Radovljiške Občine, Linhartov
trg 1, YU-64240 Radovljica
History/Public Affairs Museum - 1960
Exhibits on Gorenjsko hostages in
WW II

Bela Crkva

17450
Muzejska Zbirka
YU-26340 Bela Crkva
General Museum
Archaeology, ethnography,
numismatics

Belišče

17451
Društvo Prijatelja Starina Belišče
Valkaja 15, YU Belišče
General Museum - 1971
Local history, traffic

Beograd

17452
Etnografski Muzej
Studentski Trg 13, YU-11000 Beograd
Anthropology Museum - 1901
Ethnology, architecture, Serbian
mythology, crafts, ceramics, folk
costumes, jewelry, hunting and fishing,
weapons, religious items, music
instruments, textiles, weaving,
paintings, medicine, economic and
social history documents - library

17453
Galerija Fresaka
Ul. Cara Uroša 20, YU-11000 Beograd
Fine Arts Museum
Medieval frescoes, casts, medieval art
and architecture, sculpture

17454
**Galerija Srpske Akademije Nauka i
Umetnosti (SANU)**
Knez Mihailova 35, YU-11000 Beograd
Fine Arts Museum - 1968
19th to 20th century paintings,
drawings, and sculptures of member-
artists of the Serbian Academy of
Sciences and Arts

17455
Istorijska Muzej Srbije
Ul. Nemanjina 24, YU-11000 Beograd
History/Public Affairs Museum
Archaeology, ethnography,
manuscripts, cards, posters, seals,
medals, weapons, numismatics,
18th-20th century art, archives

17456
Jevrejski Istorijski Muzej
Ul.'7. juli'71a, P.P. 841, YU-11000
Beograd
Religious Art Museum
History of Yugoslav Jewry, Jewish
culture, religious art, archaeology,
archives

17457
**Jugoslavenska Galerija
Reprodukcija i Umetničkih Dela**
Ul. Dositejeva 1, YU-11000 Beograd
Fine Arts Museum

17458
Jugoslavenska Kinoteka
Ul. Kneza Mihaila 19, YU-11000
Beograd
History/Public Affairs Museum
History of Yugoslavian
cinematography, photography, films,
posters

17459
Muzej Afričke Umetnosti Zbirka
Vede i Dr Zdravka Pečara
Andre Nikolića 14, YU-11000 Beograd
Anthropology Museum - 1977
Articles used for cult, magical,
decorative and everyday purposes;
masks, ancestor carvings and other
cult objects, musical instruments,
textiles, weapons, household utensils
and miniature weights; Collection of
Dogon art, bronze weights for
weighing gold from Ghana, Nomoli
stone sculptures from Guinea and
Bassari ceramic jugs from Senegal -
library; educational department

17460
Muzej Grada Beograda
Zmaj Jovina 1, P.P.87, YU-11000
Beograd
General Museum - 1938
History of Beograd, archaeology,
prehistory, 19th-2oth century art,
cultural and political history,
architecture, antiquities, ceramics,
metalwork

17461
Muzej Nicole Tesle
Proleterskih brigada 51, YU-11000
Beograd
Natural History Museum - 1952
Memorabilia on physicist Nicola Tesla
(1856-1943)

17462
Muzej Pozorišne Umetnosti
Gospodar Jevremova 19, YU-11000
Beograd
Performing Arts Museum - 1950
Serbian theater history, programs,
stage scenery, photos, posters,
archives

17463
Muzej Pravoslavne Crkve
Ul. 7.Juli 5, Yu-11000 Beograd
Religious Art Museum - 1936
History of Serbian Orthodox Church,
icons, sacramental items, portraits,
vestments, manuscripts, engravings,
seals

17464
Muzej Primenjene Umetnosti
Ul. Vuka Karadžića 18, YU-11000
Beograd
Decorative Arts Museum - 1950
Furniture, ceramics, porcelain, glass,
textiles, costumes, bookbinding, wood
carving, metalwork, contemporary
applied arts - library

17465
Muzej Rečnog Brodarstva
Ul. Kneza Miloša 82, YU-11000
Beograd
Science/Tech Museum
History of shipbuilding, archives

17466
**Muzej Revolucije Naroda i
Narodnosti Jugoslavije**
Mihaila Avramovića 12, P.P. 582,
YU-11000 Beograd
History/Public Affairs Museum - 1960
History of revolution, armaments,
manuscripts, documents, printing
material, photographs - library

17467
Muzej Savremene Umetnosti
Ušče Save b.b., YU-11000 Beograd
Fine Arts Museum
Yugoslavian paintings, sculptures,
graphics, tapestry, drawings - library

17468
Muzej Šumarstva i Lova
Kalemagdan, YU-11000 Beograd
Natural History Museum
Forestry, zoology, hunting weapons
and trophies

17469
Narodni Muzej
Trg Republike 1, YU-11000 Beograd
General Museum - 1844
National history; prehistorical,
classical, and medieval archaeology;
Turkish period; epigraphs; medieval
frescoes; icons; manuscripts;
Yugoslavian art; Dutch, Italian, French
painting; numismatics; 16th-20th
century Yugoslavian and foreign
graphic art; Oriental art - library

17470
Pedagoški Muzej
Uzum Mirkova 14, YU-11000 Beograd
History/Public Affairs Museum
History of education, archives

17471
Prirodnjački Muzej
Ul. Njegoševa 51, P.P.401, YU-11000
Beograd
Natural History Museum - 1895
Botany, zoology, ornithology,
entomology, herpetology, geology,
mineralogy, paleontology, petrography
 - library

17472
**Vojni Muzej Jugoslovenske Narodne
Armije**
Kalemagdan 69, YU-11000 Beograd
History/Public Affairs Museum - 1878
Oriental and European arms, flags,
uniforms, medals, military equipment;
World War I, Balcan Wars, Turkish
period, National Liberation War
(1941-1945); gravures, war paintings,
hunting arms - library

17473
**Vukov i Dositejev Muzej - Narodni
Muzej**
Ul. G. Jevremova 21, YU-11000
Beograd
History/Public Affairs Museum
Memorabilia; Yugoslavian literature

17474
Železnički Muzej
Ul. Nemanjina 6, YU-11000 Beograd
Science/Tech Museum
History of national railway system,
paintings, archives - library

Beran

17475
Spomen-Kuća Vladimira Gortana
YU-52300 Beran
Historic Site
Memorabilia of Vladimir Gortan

Bihać

17476
Muzej Prvog Zasjedanja AVNOJ-a
Ul. AVNOJ-a 2, YU-77000 Bihać
History/Public Affairs Museum
Yugoslavian history, medieval finds,
local history

17477
Regionalni Muzej
Ul. AVNOJ-a 2, YU-77000 Bihać
General Museum
Archaeology, ethnography, national
revolutionary history

Bileća

17478
Zavičajni Muzej
YU-79320 Bileća
General Museum
Local history

Biograd

17479
Zavičajni Muzej
Maršala Tita 22, YU-57210 Biograd, na
Moru
General Museum - 1969
Archaeology, ethnology - library

Bitola

17480
Lapidarij Islamskih Spomenika
Ajdar, Kadi džmija, YU-97000 Bitola
Archeology Museum
Islamic art, sculptures

17481
Naroden Muzej
Ul. Maršala Tita 91, YU-97000 Bitola
General Museum
Prehistory, ethnography, antiquities,
numismatics, history of the revolution

Bjelovar

17482
Gradski Muzej
Trg Jedinstva 1, YU-43000 Bjelovar
General Museum
Cultural history, ethnography,
numismatics, natural history, history of
the revolution

Bled

17483
Muzejska Zbirka
YU-64260 Bled
General Museum
11th-19th century local history,
weapons

Bor

17484
Muzej Rudarstva i Metalurgije
Trg oslobodjenja, P.P. 45, YU-19210
Bor
General Museum - 1961
Archaeology, ethnography, history,
geology, mining - library

17485
Narodni Muzej
YU-12210 Bor
General Museum
Archaeology, ethnography

Bosansko Grahova

17486
**Memorijalni Muzej Gavrila Principa u
Obljaju**
YU-77270 Bosansko Grahova
History/Public Affairs Museum
Birthplace of Gavrilo Princip,
memorabilia

Brežice

17487
Posavski Muzej
Cesta Prvih Borcev, P.P. 5, YU-68250
Brežice
General Museum - 1949
Coll.: archaeology, ethnography,
history, baroque art; relics onthe
peasant revolt 1573 and National
Liberation War (1941-1945) - library

Brioni

17488
Muzejska Zbirka
YU-52214 Brioni
Archeology Museum

Brseč

17489
**Memorijalna Zbirka Eugena
Kumičića**
YU-51418 Brseč
Historic Site
Memorabilia of Eugen Kumičić

Budva

17490
Arheološka Zbirka
Crkva sv. Marije, YU-81310 Budva
Archeology Museum

Buzet

17491
Zavičajna Muzejska Zbirka
YU-52310 Buzet
General Museum
Local history

Čačak

17492
Muzej Revolucionarne Omladine
Bate Jankovića 68, YU-32000 Čačak
History/Public Affairs Museum
History of the revolutionary youth
movement

17493
Narodni Muzej
Ul. Cara Dušana 1, YU-32000 Čačak
General Museum
Archaeology, history, art, ethnography

17494
**Umetnička Galerija Nadežde
Petrović**
Cara Dus%/oana 4, YU-32000 Čačak
Fine Arts Museum
Yugoslavian contemporary art

Čajetina

17495
**Muzejska Zbirka pri Narodnoj
Biblioteci 'Dimitrije Tucović'**
Ul. Maršala Tita 8, P.P.56, YU-31310
Čajetina
General Museum
Natural history, archaeology,
ethnology, memorabilia of Dmitrij
Tucović

Čakavec

17496
Muzej Medžimurja
Trg Republike 5, YU-42300 Čakavec
General Museum
Archaeology, ethnography, cultural
history, history of the revolution, art

Cavtat

17497
Knežev Dvor
YU-50210 Cavtat
General Museum
Cultural history, graphics,
ethnography, numismatics

Čazma

17498
Muzejska Zbirka
Trg Pobjede 7, YU-43240 Čažma
General Museum
Ethnography, history of the revolution

17499
Zavičajni Muzej
Trg Pobjede 10, YU-43240 Čazma
General Museum - 1958
Coll.: ethnography, history of
revolution, archaeology - library

Čelarevo

17500
**Stalna Izložba Stilskog Namještaja
18.-19. st.**
Dvorac u Čelarevu, YU-21413
Čelarevo
Decorative Arts Museum
18th-19th century furnishings

Celje

17501
Muzej Revolucije
Trg V. Kongresa 3, YU-63000 Celje
History/Public Affairs Museum
Labour movement, history of the
revolution

17502
Pokrajinski Muzej
Muzejski Trg 1, YU-63000 Celje
General Museum - 1882
Prehistory, antiquities, numismatics,
ethnography, cultural history,
European and Japanese graphics -
library

Cetinje

17503
Etnografski Muzej Crne Gore
YU-81250 Cetinje
Anthropology Museum

17504
Istorijski Muzej Crne Gore
Trg Revolucije, YU-81250 Cetinje
History/Public Affairs Museum
History of the region

17505
Manastirski Muzej
Manastir cetinjski, YU-81250 Cetinje
Religious Art Museum
Art, religious items

17506
Umetnička Galerija Crne Gore
Trg Revolucije 14, YU-81250 Cetinje
Fine Arts Museum
Yugoslavian art, icons, copies of
frescoes

Cres

17507
Creski Muzej Arheološka Zbirka
Osor
Palača Arsan, YU-51557 Cres
Archeology Museum

Danilovgrad

17508
Zavičajni Muzej
Yu-81410 Danilovgrad
General Museum
Local history

Dečane

17509
Manastirska Riznica
YU-38322 Dečane
Religious Art Museum

503

Doboj

17510
Zavičajni Muzej
Ul. V. Nazora 4, YU-74000 Doboj
General Museum
Natural history, archaeology,
ethnography, national revolutionary
history

Drvar

17511
Spomen Muzej '25. Maja 1944'
Ul. Prvoborca J. Marića, YU-77260
Drvar
General Museum
History, memorabilia

Dubrovnik

17512
Dubrovački Muzej
Knežev Dvor, YU-50000 Dubrovnik
General Museum
Cultural history, ethnography,
archaeology, history

17513
Memorijalna Zbirka Antuna Masle
Ul. N. Božidarevića 11, YU-50000
Dubrovnik
Fine Arts Museum
Memorabilia

17514
**Muzejska Zbirka Dominikanskog
Samostana**
Ploča 5, YU-50000 Dubrovnik
Religious Art Museum
Religious items, paintings, manuscripts

17515
Muzejska Zbirka i Stara Apoteka
Samostan Male Braće, Placa 2, P.P. 53,
YU-50000 Dubrovnik
Religious Art Museum - 1950
Religious items; old pharmacy,
founded 1317

17516
Pomorski Muzej
Tvrdžava sv. Ivana, YU-50000
Dubrovnik
History/Public Affairs Museum - 1872
Navigation history, archaeology,
submarine archaeology - library

17517
Prirodoslovni Muzej
Biološki institut JAZU, Lokrum,
YU-50000 Dubrovnik
Natural History Museum
Natural history

17518
Umjetnička Galerija
Put F. Supila 45, YU-50000 Dubrovnik
Fine Arts Museum
Icons, 19th-20th cent. paintings, park
sculptures

17519
Zbirka Ikona i Portreta
Srpske pravoslavne crkve, Ul. od Puća
2, YU-50000 Dubrovnik
Religious Art Museum - 1953
Icons from Serbia, Crete, Corfu,
Venice, Russia, Greece, Dubrovnik,
Boka-Kotorska; collection of portraits
- library

Džakovica

17520
Gradski Muzej
YU-38320 Džakovica
General Museum
Local history

Džakovo

17521
Dijecezanski Muzej
Trg Štrosmajerov 6, YU-54400
Džakovo
Religious Art Museum

17522
Muzej Džkovštine
P. Preradovića, YU-54400 Džakovo
General Museum
Ethnography

Ečka kod Zrenjanina

17523
**Savremena Galerija Umetničke
Kolonije Ečka**
YU-23203 Ečka kod Zrenjanina
Fine Arts Museum
Paintings

Foča

17524
Muzej Jugoistočne Bosne
Ul. Maršala Tita 11, YU-71480 Foča
General Museum
History of south-east Bosnia

Fojnica

17525
Franjevački Samostan Fojnica
Rupnovac 4, YU-71270 Fojnica
Religious Art Museum
Coll.: numismatics, religious items, art,
ethnography - library

Gospič

17526
Muzej Like
Ul. Maršala Tita 27, YU-48000 Gospič
General Museum
Archaeology, ethnography, art, history
of revolution

Gračanica

17527
Manastirska Riznica
YU-38205 Gračanica
Religious Art Museum

Hercegnovi

17528
Memorijalna Soba 'Lučev Lenković'
Ul. Njegoševa 55, YU-81340
Hercegnovi
Historic Site
Memorabilia of Lučev Lenković

17529
Umjetnička Galerija
Ul. M. Vojnovića 11, YU-81340
Hercegnovi
Fine Arts Museum

17530
Zavičajni Muzej
Ul. Topla 23, YU-81340 Hercegnovi
General Museum
Archaeology, ethnography, cultural
history, National Liberation War;
lapidarium

Hlebina

17531
Galerija Naivnih Umjetnika
YU-43323 Hlebina
Fine Arts Museum
Naive art

Humač

17532
Humačka Arheološka Zbirka
Franjevački Samostan, YU-79450
Humač, kod Ljubuškog
Archeology Museum

Hvar

17533
Centar za Zaštitu Kulturne Baštine
Villa Lukić, YU-58450 Hvar
Archeology Museum - 1950
Ethnology; archaeology; archives;
prehistoric cave of Gračeva Špilja -
library

17534
Katedralna Zbirka
Biskupi dvor, YU-58450 Hvar
Religious Art Museum

17535
**Lapidarij i Arheološka Zbirka sv.
Marka**
YU-58450 Hvar
Archeology Museum
Christian archaeology; sculptures

17536
**Zbirka Umjetnina Franjevačkog
Samostana**
YU-58450 Hvar
Religious Art Museum
Paintings, numismatics, vestments,
Glagolitic books

Idrija

17537
Galerija Idrija
Trg Svobode, YU-65280 Idrija
Fine Arts Museum

17538
Mestni Muzej Idrija
Ul. Prelovčeva 9, YU-65280 Idrija
Science/Tech Museum
Geology, mineralogy, metallurgy,
ethnography, history

Ilok

17539
Muzej Grada Iloka
Šetalište Braće Jaksić, YU-56236 Ilok
General Museum
Medieval archaeology, Turkish period,
history of revolution; art gallery

Imotski

17540
**Muzejska Zbirka Franjevačkog
Samostana**
YU-58260 Imotski
Religious Art Museum

Ivangrad

17541
Polimski Muzej
YU-84300 Ivangrad
General Museum
Natural history, archaeology,
ethnography, history, numismatics,
paleography, heraldry, art,
photography; archives

Jajce

17542
Muzej II. Zasjedanja AVNOJ-a
Ul. 29.Novembra 8, YU-78240 Jajce
History/Public Affairs Museum
National revolutionary history,
memorabilia, books

17543
**Muzejska Zbirka Franjevačkog
Samostana**
N. oslobodenja 20, YU-78240 Jajce
Religious Art Museum
Archaeology, ethnography, religious
items

Jaša Tomić

17544
Mestni Muzej
YU-23230 Jaša Tomić
General Museum
Local history

Jasenovac

17545
Spomen Područje Jasenovac
YU-41324 Jasenovac
History/Public Affairs Museum
Local history

Jasenovo

17546
Etnolos%oka Muzejska Zbirka
YU-26346 Jasenovo
Anthropology Museum

Jastrebarsko

17547
Muzejska Zbirka Jastrebarsko
Dvorac Erdödi, YU-41420
Jastrebarsko
General Museum
Local history, ethnography

Jesenice

17548
Tehnički Muzej Železarne Jesenice
c. Železarjev 8, YU-64270 Jesenice
Science/Tech Museum
History of mining and railroads, labour
movement, history

Kalinovac

17549
Zavičajni Muzej Kalinovac
YU-43361 Kalinovac
General Museum
Local history, ethnography

Kamnik

17550
Kamniški Muzej
Ul. Zaprice 12, YU-61240 Kamnik
General Museum
Archaeology, ethnography, furniture,
history

Karlobag

17551
**Muzejska Zbirka Kapucinskog
Samostana**
YU-51288 Karlobag
Religious Art Museum

Karlovac

17552
Galerija Slika 'Vjekoslav Karas'
YU-47000 Karlovac
Fine Arts Museum
Paintings

17553
Gradski Muzej Karlovac
Štrossmayerov Trg 7, YU-47000
Karlovac
General Museum
Cultural history, art, ethnography,
biology, botany

Kikinda
17554
Narodni Muzej
Trg palih heroja 3, YU-23300 Kikinda
General Museum
Archaeology, ethnography, labour
movement, history

Knić
17555
Muzejska Zbirka
YU-34240 Knić
General Museum
Prehistory, local history

Knin
17556
Muzej Kninske Krajine
YU-59300 Knin
General Museum
Local history

Kočevje
17557
Pokrajinski Muzej
Ul. Prešernova 11, YU-61330 Kočevje
General Museum - 1960
Dept. of ethnography, archaeology,
movement and history of revolution,
art - library

Komiža
17558
Memorijalna Galerija 'Djure Tiljka'
YU-58485 Komiža
Fine Arts Museum

Koper
17559
Galerija 'Loža'
Trg Titov 1, YU-66000 Koper
Fine Arts Museum
17560
Pokrajinski Muzej Koper
Ul. Kidričeva 19, YU-66000 Koper
General Museum
Ethnography, navigation, art, labour
movement, history, lapidarium

Koprivnica
17561
Muzej Grada Koprivnice
Trg L. Brozovića 1, YU-43300
Koprivnica
General Museum
Archaeology, cultural history,
ethnography, naive art, history

Koprivnički Bregi
17562
Etnografska Zbirka
Župni dvor, YU-43324 Koprivnički
Bregi
General Museum
Ethnography, local history

Korčula
17563
Galerija Maksimilijana Vanke (JAZU)
YU-50260 Korčula
Fine Arts Museum
17564
Gradski Muzej Korčula
YU-50260 Korčula
General Museum
Archaeology, ethnography,
shipbuilding, history
17565
Opatska Riznica sv. Marka
YU-50260 Korčula
Religious Art Museum
Numismatics, art, religious items,
decorative art
17566
Zbirka Bratovštine Gospe od Utjehe
YU-50260 Korčula
Religious Art Museum
Religious art, decorative art,
numismatics
17567
Zbirka Bratovštine sv. Roka
YU-50260 Korčula
Religious Art Museum
Religious art, decorative art
17568
Zbirka Ikona Bratovštine Svih Svetih
YU-50260 Korčula
Religious Art Museum
Religious art, decorative art

Kosovska Mitrovica
17569
Gradski Muzej
YU-38330 Kosovska Mitrovica
General Museum
Archaeology, ethnography

Kotor
17570
Pomorski Muzej
Trg Bokeljske Mornarice 391,
YU-81330 Kotor
History/Public Affairs Museum
Navigation, cultural history, history,
books, archives
17571
Zbirka Katedrale sv. Trifuna
Katedrale sv. Trifuna, YU-81330 Kotor
Religious Art Museum
Archaeological finds, paintings,
frescoes, religious books, art, religious
items

Kragujevac
17572
Muzej Zavoda 'Crvena Zastava'
Ul. Spanskih boraca 2, YU-34000
Kragujevac
Science/Tech Museum
Old armaments, automobiles
17573
Narodni Muzej
Ul. Vuka Karadžića 1, YU-34000
Kragujevac
General Museum - 1949
Prehistoric, Roman, and medieval
archaeology; ethnography; art history;
Byzantine art; Serbian painting
(18th-20th cent.); local history - library

Kraljevo
17574
Narodni Muzej
Ul. Karadžorđeva 3, YU-36000 Kraljevo
General Museum
Ethnology, history, numismatics, art,
copies of 13th cent. frescoes

Kranj
17575
Galerija v Mestni Hiši
Trg Titov 4, YU-64001 Kranj
Fine Arts Museum
17576
Galerija v Prešernovi Hiši
Ul. Prešernova 7, YU-64001 Kranj
Fine Arts Museum
17577
Gorenjski Muzej Kranj
Tavčarjeva 43, YU-97317 Kranj
History/Public Affairs Museum - 1963
Gallery of works of the sculptor Alojz
Dolinar; memorabilia of the national
poet Dr. France Prešeren; National
Liberation War 1941-1945 in
Gorenjsko; Slovene women's part in
the revolution
17578
Prešernov Spominski Muzej
Ul. Prešernova 7, YU-64001 Kranj
History/Public Affairs Museum
Literary and art history

Krapina
17579
Gajev Muzej
Ul. Gajev 14, YU-41230 Krapina
General Museum
Local history
17580
Muzejska Zbirka 'Krapina i Okolica'
Stari Grad, Perivoj Matije Gupca 1,
YU-41230 Krapina
General Museum
Ethnography, cultural history

Križevci
17581
Gradski Muzej
Ul. Sekmardijeva 1, YU-43260 Križevci
General Museum
Local history

Kropa
17582
Kovaški Muzej
YU-64245 Kropa, *mail c/o* Muzeji
Radovljiške Občine, Linhartov trg 1,
YU-64240 Radovljica
Science/Tech Museum - 1952
Iron-forging items, artistic smiths of
Kropa

Kruševac
17583
Narodni Muzej - Kruševac
Ul. Branka Cekića 1, YU-37000
Kruševac
General Museum - 1951
Prehistory; antiquities; medieval
history and art; Turkish slavery;
ethnography; old history and history of
revolution; Kosovo battle as theme in
contemporary art; modern art; coins
and medals

Kruševo
17584
Istoriski Muzej
Ul. Taka Berber 44, YU-92520 Kruševo
History/Public Affairs Museum

Kutina
17585
Muzej Moslavine
Trg N. Božića Juga 13, YU-41320
Kutina
General Museum
Archaeology, ethnography, history

Labin
17586
Narodni Muzej
Ul. 1. maja 6, P.P. 44, YU-52220 Labin
General Museum - 1960
Coll: archaeology, ethnography,
mining, art, labor movement;
memorabilia of Giuseppina Martinuzzi
and Mathias Flacius Illyricus - library

Laško
17587
Muzejska Zbirka Laško
YU-63270 Laško
General Museum
Ethnography, history of the city

Lesak kod Tetova
17588
**Spomen-Muzej Prosvetitelja i Pisca
Kirila Pejčinovića**
YU-91220 Lesak kod Tetova
History/Public Affairs Museum

Leskovac
17589
Narodni Muzej
Ul. Učitelja Josifa 10, YU-16000
Leskovac
General Museum
History, archaeology, ethnology,
numismatics, art

Liboje
17590
Zbirka Keramike
Keramnička industrija, YU Liboje
Decorative Arts Museum
Crafts, ceramics

Ljubljana
17591
Arkade - Rastavni Salon
Trg Revolucije 18, YU-61000 Ljubljana
Fine Arts Museum
17592
Mestni Muzej
Ul. Gosposka 15, YU-61000 Ljubljana
General Museum - 1935
Furniture, arts and crafts, local
topography, militaria, archaeology,
finds from Celtic-Illyrian and Roman
periods
17593
Moderna Galerija
Tomšičeva 14, P.P. 265, YU-61000
Ljubljana
Fine Arts Museum - 1948
20th century art, especially Slovene
and Yugoslavian - library
17594
Muzej Ljudske Revolucije Slovenije
C. Celoveška 23, YU-61000 Ljubljana
History/Public Affairs Museum - 1944
Arms, uniforms and medals of
partisans and occupying armies,
history of resistance movement
1941-45, documents

17595
Narodna Galerija
Ul. Cankarjeva 20, P.P. 432, YU-61000
Ljubljana
Fine Arts Museum - 1918
Paintings and sculpture (13th to 19th
century), medieval frescoes, Slovenian
impressionist art (18th to 20th century),
Slovenian graphics, photographies,
documents - library

17596
Narodni Muzej
Prešerova 20, P.P. 529-X, YU-61000
Ljubljana
General Museum - 1821
Prehistoric archaeological finds;
applied art; history; numismatics;
graphic arts; early Slavic material;
relief of the Battle of Sisak against the
Turks; Balkan coins - library

17597
Prirodoslovni Muzej Slovenije
Prešerova 20, P.P. 290, YU-61000
Ljubljana
Natural History Museum - 1821
botany, entomology, herpetology;
collections of minerals, insects,
herbaria - library

17598
Slovenski Etnografski Muzej
Trg Herojev 1, YU-61000 Ljubljana
Anthropology Museum - 1923
Slovenian and non-european
ethnography, cultural history, crafts

17599
Slovenski Gledališki Muzej
Ul. Cankarjeva 11, YU-61000 Ljubljana
Performing Arts Museum
Theater, textbooks, manuscripts,
programs, costumes, scenery

17600
Slovenski Školski Muzej
Poljanska c. 28, YU-61000 Ljubljana
History/Public Affairs Museum - 1938
School and educational history since
12th century - library

17601
Tehnički Muzej Slovenije
Parmova 33, YU-61000 Ljubljana
Science/Tech Museum
Forestry and wood technology,
hunting, smithwork, textiles,
transportation, electrotechnology

17602
Zemljopisni Muzej Slovenije
Trg Francoske Revolucije 7, YU-61000
Ljubljana
Natural History Museum - 1946
Maps, geography of Slovenia

Majdanpek
17603
Zbirka Rudnika 'Majdanpek'
YU-19250 Majdanpek
Natural History Museum
Mineralogy, petrography

Makarska
17604
**Malakološki Muzej Franjevačkog
Samostana**
Žrtava Fašizma 1, YU-58300 Makarska
Natural History Museum
Paleontology, botany, paintings

17605
Muzej NOB-a Biokovskog Područja
Titova Obala 17, YU-58300 Makarska
History/Public Affairs Museum
History of revolution

Mali Lošinj
17606
Općinski Muzej
Ul. Brdina 13, YU-51550 Mali Lošinj
General Museum
Local history

Maribor
17607
Muzej Narodne Osvoboditve
(Museum of the People's Liberation)
Ul. Heroja Tomšiča 5, YU-62000
Maribor
History/Public Affairs Museum - 1958
National Liberation War (1941-1945),
documents, archives, photographs,
publications of the Partizan Movement,
history of Maribor

17608
Pokrajinski Muzej
Ul. Grajska 2, YU-62000 Maribor
General Museum - 1903
Coll: local history, archaeology,
ethnography, topography, cultural
history, art, uniforms, costumes,
goldsmith art - library

17609
Rastavni Salon Rotovž
Trg Rotovški 1, YU-62000 Maribor
Fine Arts Museum

17610
Umetnostna Galerija
Ul. Strossmayerjeva 6, YU-62000
Maribor
Fine Arts Museum - 1954
Coll.: paintings and sculptures
(19th-20th century)

Metković
17611
**Ornitološka Zbirka Lovačkog
Društva**
Trg Žrtava Fašizma 1, YU-58350
Metković
Natural History Museum
Ornithology

Metlika
17612
Belokranjski Muzej
Trg svobode 4, YU-68330 Metlika
General Museum - 1951
Coll: archaeology, ethnography,
cultural history, art, history of
revolution

17613
Slovenski Gasilski Muzej
Trg svobode 4, YU-68330 Metlika
History/Public Affairs Museum - 1969
Development of fire fighting in
Slovenija

17614
**Spominska Hiša Alojža in Engelberta
Gangla**
Mestni trg 17, YU-68330 Metlika
History/Public Affairs Museum
Memorabilia; sculptures; literature

Mostar
17615
Muzej Hercegovine
Ul. Maršala Tita 160, YU-79000 Mostar
General Museum
Archaeology, ethnography, labour
movement, National Liberation War

17616
Umjetnička Galerija
Dom Kulture-Rondo, YU-79000 Mostar
Fine Arts Museum

Motovun
17617
Galerija Slika
YU-52273 Motovun
Fine Arts Museum
Yugoslavian painting

Murska Sobota
17618
Pokrajinski Muzej
Trubarjev drevored b.b., YU-69000
Murska Sobota
History/Public Affairs Museum
National Liberation War

Nazarje
17619
Galerija Jaki
YU-63331 Nazarje
Fine Arts Museum

Negotin
17620
Narodni Muzej Krajine
Ul. S. Radosavljević 1, YU-19300
Negotin
General Museum
Archaeology, ethnography, icons

Nerezine
17621
Arheološka Zbirka Osor
YU-51554 Nerezine, Osor
Archeology Museum

Nikšić
17622
Nikšićki Muzej
Ul. Moše Pijade 19, YU-81400 Nikšić
General Museum
Natural history, archaeology,
ethnography, numismatics, history,
weapons, art

Nin
17623
Arheološka Zbirka
YU-57232 Nin
Archeology Museum

Niš
17624
Koncentracioni Logor '12. Februar'
YU-18000 Niš
History/Public Affairs Museum

17625
Narodni Muzej
Ul. V. Kongresa 59, YU-18000 Niš
General Museum
History, prehistory, archaeology,
numismatics, medieval-modern
Yugoslavian art, ethnography, labour
movement, National Liberation War

Nova Gorica
17626
Galerija Meblo
Ul. Leninova 4, YU-65000 Nova Gorica
Fine Arts Museum
Paintings

17627
Goriški Muzej grad Kromberk
YU-65000 Nova Gorica
General Museum
Local history, ethnography, art, history

Novi Dojran
17628
Ribarsko-Biološka Zbirka
YU-91485 Novi Dojran
Natural History Museum
Ichthyology, marine biology, fishing

Novi Sad
17629
Galerija Matice Srpske
Trg Proleterskih brigada 8, YU-21000
Novi Sad
Fine Arts Museum - 1847
18th-19th century Serbian art, graphics

17630
**Galerija Savremene Likovne
Umetnosti**
Ul. JNA 45, YU-21000 Novi Sad
Fine Arts Museum

17631
Muzej Grada Novog Sada
Petrovaradin-Tvrdžava, YU-21000 Novi
Sad
General Museum
Archaeology, ethnography, cultural
history, contemporary art, crafts,
applied art, weapons, numismatics

17632
**Muzej Radničkog Pokreta i Narodne
Revolucije**
Ul. Dunavska 37, YU-21000 Novi Sad
History/Public Affairs Museum
History of revolution, labour
movement, archives

17633
Spomen-Zbirka Pavla Beljanskog
Trg Proleterskih Brigada 2, YU-21000
Novi Sad
Fine Arts Museum
20th century Yugoslavian art

17634
Vojvodjanski Muzej
Petrovaradin-Tvrdžava, YU-21000 Novi
Sad
General Museum - 1947
Archaeology, ethnography, culural
history, decorative arts, theater -
library

17635
Zavičajna Galerija
Petrovaradin-Tvrdžava, YU-21000 Novi
Sad
Fine Arts Museum
Contemporary art

17636
Zbirka Poduzeća 'Naftagas'
YU-21000 Novi Sad
Natural History Museum
Geology

17637
Zbirka Strane Umetnosti
Ul. Dunavska 29, YU-21000 Novi Sad
Fine Arts Museum

Novi Vinodolski
17638
Narodni Muzej N. Vinodolski
Stari Grad 39, YU-51250 Novi
Vinodolski
General Museum
Natural history, archaeology,
ethnography, cultural history,
numismatics, art, history

Novi Pazar
17639
Zavičajni Muzej
P.P. 58, YU-36300 Novi Pazar
General Museum
Coll.: archaeology, history,
ethnography - library

Novo Mesto

17640
Dolenjski Muzej
Ul. Muzejska 7, YU-68000 Novo Mesto
General Museum
Archaeology, history, cultural history,
art gallery

Odžaci

17641
Školska Zbirka Odžaci
Osnovna Škola 'Boris Kidrić',
YU-25250 Odžaci
Archeology Museum
Prehistorical archaeology

Ogulin

17642
Zavičajni Muzej
Frankopana kula, YU-47300 Ogulin
General Museum
Archaeology, ethnography, history

Ohrid

17643
Naroden Muzej
Ul. Cara Samuila 62, YU-97300 Ohrid
General Museum
Archaeology, ethnography, history, art

Oplenac kod Topole

17644
Crkva-Muzej na Oplencu
YU-34360 Oplenac kod Topole
Religious Art Museum

Orebić

17645
Pomorski Muzej
YU-50250 Orebić
Science/Tech Museum

Osijek

17646
Galerija Likovnih Umjetnosti
Bulevar JNA 9, YU-54000 Osijek
Fine Arts Museum - 1954
Slovene portrait painting (18th-19th
cent.), landscape painting (19th cent.),
contemporary art - library
17647
Muzej Slavonije
Trg Partizanski 6, YU-54000 Osijek
General Museum
Archaeology, paleontology,
prehistorical and early medieval
antiquities, numismatics, medals,
posters, decorative art; history of the
revolution

Otočac

17648
Zavičajni Muzej
Narodno sveučilište, YU-48220 Otočac
General Museum
Archaeology, history

Pančevo

17649
Narodni Muzej
Trg B. Kidriča 7, YU-26000 Pančevo
General Museum
Natural history, archaeology,
ethnography, local history, art

Pazin

17650
Etnografski Muzej Istre
Trg Olge Ban 1, YU-52300 Pazin
Anthropology Museum

Peć

17651
Muzej Revolucije 'Miladin Popović'
Ul. Miladina Popovića 56, YU-38300
Peć
History/Public Affairs Museum
History of the revolution, memorabilia
17652
Riznica Pećke Patrijaršije
YU-38300 Peć
Religious Art Museum

Perast

17653
Muzej Grada Perasta
YU-81338 Perast
General Museum
Archaeology, ethnography, history of
navigation
17654
Zbirka Crkve Gospe od Skrpjela
YU-81336 Perast
Religious Art Museum
Archaeology, religious items, paintings
17655
Zbirka Crkve sv. Nikole
YU-81336 Perast
Religious Art Museum
Vestments, paintings, icons

Piran

17656
Mestna Galerija
Trg Tartinijev, YU-6630 Piran
Fine Arts Museum
17657
Pomorski Muzej 'Sergej Mašera'
Cankarjevo nabr. 3, YU-66330 Piran
History/Public Affairs Museum
History of Slovenia, folklore,
archaeology

Pirot

17658
Etnografski Muzej Pomišavlja
Ul. Prizrenska 11, YU-18300 Pirot
Anthropology Museum

Pivnice

17659
Etnološka Zbirka
YU-21469 Pivnice
Anthropology Museum
Ethnology

Pljevlja

17660
Zavičajni Muzej
Trg 13.Jula 12, YU-84210 Pljevlja
General Museum
Local history, archaeology,
ethnography

Poreč

17661
Zavičajni Muzej Poreštine
Ul. Dekumanska 9, YU-51440 Poreč
General Museum - 1884
Local history; archaeology; National
Liberation War - library

Postojna

17662
**Kraška Muzejska Zbirka Inštituta za
Raziskovanje Krasa SAZU**
Titov trg 2, P.P. 59, YU-66230 Postojna
General Museum - 1974
Coll.: karstology, speleology,
archaeology, cultural history, local
history - library

Požarevac

17663
Galerija 'Milene Pavlović-Barili'
Ul. Voja Dulića 8, YU-12000 Požarevac
Fine Arts Museum
17664
Muzej Kulturne Istorije
Ul. Nemanjina 9, YU-12000 Požarevac
History/Public Affairs Museum
Cultural history
17665
Narodni Muzej
Ul. Voje Dulića 2, YU-12000 Požarevac
General Museum
Archaeology, ethnography, prehistory,
medieval history, art, antiquities,
numismatics

Prčanj

17666
Privatna Zbirka Marija Lukovića
broj 153, YU-81335 Prčanj
History/Public Affairs Museum
Paintings, numismatics, stamps,
furniture, old documents, weapons,
navigation items
17667
Zbirka Župne Crkve
YU-81335 Prčanj
Religious Art Museum
Religious art, old and contemporary
Yugoslavian painting, sculpture

Predjamski Grad kraj Postojne

17668
**Muzejska Zbirka v Predjamskom
Gradu**
YU-66230 Predjamski Grad kraj
Postojne
General Museum
Archaeology, cultural history, history
of the revolution

Predjamski Grad pri Postojni

17669
**Muzejska Zbirka v Predjamskem
Gradu (Kraška muzejska zbirka IZRK
SAZU)**
YU-66230 Predjamski Grad pri
Postojni
General Museum
Coll.: archaeology, cultural history,
history of revolution

Prijedor

17670
Muzej Kozare
Ul. Partizanska 23, YU-78300 Prijedor
General Museum
Archaeology, ethnography, history

Prilep

17671
Naroden Muzej
Ul. Moše Pijade 138, P.P.93, YU-97000
Prilep
General Museum
Archaeology, prehistory, medieval
history, numismatics

Priština

17672
**Kriminalistička Zbirka na Pravom
Fakultetu**
Ul.Remiza Sadika 56, YU-38000
Priština
History/Public Affairs Museum
Criminology
17673
Muzej Kosova i Metohije
Ul. Valjevska 2, YU-38000 Priština
General Museum - 1951
Prehistory, antiquities, Middle Ages,
ethnology; natural history, history,
numismatics

Prizren

17674
Muzej Orijentalnih Rukopisa
Sinan Pašina Džamija, YU-38400
Prizren
History/Public Affairs Museum
Oriental manuscripts
17675
Muzej Prizrenske Lige
YU-38400 Prizren
General Museum
Local history

Prokuplje

17676
Narodni Muzej Toplice
YU-18400 Prokuplje
General Museum
Natural history, archaeology,
ethnography, numismatics, labour
movement, history

Ptuj

17677
Pokrajinski Muzej
Trg Muzejski 1, YU-62250 Ptuj
General Museum - 1945
Archaeology, art, local history, cultural
history, ethnography, viticulture; three
temples of Mithras
17678
Razstavni Paviljon Dušana Kvedra
YU-62250 Ptuj
Fine Arts Museum

Pula

17679
Arheološki Muzej Istre
Ul. M.Balote 3, YU-52000 Pula
Archeology Museum
17680
Muzej Narodne Revolucije Istre
Uspon Muzeju revolucije 14, YU-52000
Pula
General Museum
National Liberation War

Punat

17681
**Muzej Franjevačkog Samostana
Košljun (otok Krk)**
Košljun, YU-51521 Punat
General Museum - 1926
Coll: archaeology, ethnography,
natural history, art; archives - library

Radovljica

17682
Čebelarski Muzej
Linhartov trg 1, YU-64240 Radovljica
Anthropology Museum - 1959
Illustrated front-boards of beehives;
beekeeping tools; unique items of
Slovene folk art - library

Raška

17683
Riznica Manastira Studenica
YU-36350 Raška
Religious Art Museum

Ravne na Koreškem

17684
Delavski Muzej Ravne na Koreškem
Na Gradu 1, YU-62390 Ravne na
Koreškem
Science/Tech Museum
Ethnography, mining, railroads,
forestry

Ribnica na Dolenjskem

17685
Ribniški Muzej
YU-61310 Ribnica na Dolenjskem
General Museum
Local history

Rijeka

17686
Moderna Galerija
Ul. Dolac 1/II, P.P. 26, YU-51000 Rijeka
Fine Arts Museum - 1948
Paintings from Rijeka (19th cent.);
paintings, sculptures, graphics, and
designs by Yugoslav artists (20th
cent.); contemporary art from abroad;
posters - library

17687
Muzej Narodne Revolucije
Ul.P.Zrinskog 12, YU-51000 Rijeka
History/Public Affairs Museum
History of the revolution; archives

17688
**Pomorski i Povijesni Muzej
Hrvatskog Primorja**
Ul. Žrtava Fašizma 18, YU-51000 Rijeka
History/Public Affairs Museum
Maritime history, navigation,
archaeology, antiquities, history,
ethnology

17689
Prirodoslovni Muzej
Šetalište V.Nazora 3, YU-51000 Rijeka
Science/Tech Museum - 1946
Natural history, geology, paleontology,
entomology, biology

Rogoška Slatina

17690
Muzejska Zbirka
Zdravilišče, YU-63250 Rogoška Slatina
Fine Arts Museum
Paintings, graphics, cultural history

Rovinj

17691
Muzejska Zbirka
YU-52210 Rovinj
Fine Arts Museum
Paintings, old masters and modern art,
ethnology, cultural history

Ruma

17692
Zavičajna Muzejska Zbirka
Ul. Maršala Tita 182, YU-22400 Ruma
General Museum
Archaeology, ethnography, local
history, art

Šabac

17693
Narodni Muzej
Ul. Masarikova 13, YU-15000 Šabac
General Museum
Natural history, archaeology,
ethnography, numismatics, cultural
history, paintings

Samobor

17694
Samoborski Muzej
Ul. Perkovčeva 7, YU-41430 Samobor
General Museum
Local history

Sarajevo

17695
Kuća Danila Ilića
Ul. Danila Ilića 3, YU-71000 Sarajevo
Historic Site
Memorial to Danilo Ilić, in his former
home

17696
Muzej Grada Sarajeva
Ul.sv.Markovića 54, YU-71000
Sarajevo
General Museum
Archaeology, ethnology, Oriental art,
National Liberation War

17697
Muzej Jevreja Bosne i Hercegovine
Ul. Maršala Tita 98, YU-71000 Sarajevo
History/Public Affairs Museum
Jewish history in Bosnia and
Hercegovina

17698
Muzej Književnosti
Ul. S. Milutinovića 5, YU-71000
Sarajevo
History/Public Affairs Museum
History of Yugoslavian literature

17699
Muzej 'Mlada Bosna'
Obala Vojvode Stepe 35, YU-71000
Sarajevo
History/Public Affairs Museum
History of Bosnia; memorabilia on
Gavrilo Princip

17700
**Muzej Revolucije Bosne i
Hercegovine**
Vojvode Putnika 9, YU-71000 Sarajevo
History/Public Affairs Museum
Labour movement 1878-1918, National
Liberation War 1941-1945,
development of socialism since 1945

17701
**Muzej-Riznica Stare Srpske
Pravoslavne Crkve**
Ul. Maršala Tita 87, YU-71000 Sarajevo
Religious Art Museum
Art, religious items

17702
Svrzina Kuća
Ul. Dr. Jovana Kršića 5, YU-71000
Sarajevo
Historic Site
Feudal Turkish house, local history

17703
**Umjetnička Galerija Bosne i
Hercegovine**
Ul. JNA 38, YU-71000 Sarajevo
Fine Arts Museum
Modern art, paintings, sculptures,
icons, graphic arts; memorial to painter
Smiljan Popović

17704
Zemaljski Muzej
Vojvode Putnika 7, YU-71000 Sarajevo
General Museum - 1888
Prehistoric, Roman, Greek and
medieval archaeology, ethnography,
natural history, geology, anthropology,
folklore, economics, transportation,
jewelry, customs, mineralogy,
petrography - library

Šarengrad

17705
**Muzejska Zbirka Franjevačkog
Samostana**
YU-56234 Šarengrad
General Museum
Archaeology, ethnography, cultural
history

Senj

17706
**Dijecezanski Muzej i Arhiv-
Biblioteka**
YU-51270 Senj
Religious Art Museum
Religious items, documents - library

17707
Gradski Muzej
Ul. M. Ogrizovića 7, YU-51270 Senj
General Museum
Archaeology, ethnography, glagolitic
literature, history of the revolution;
maritime trade - library

Senta

17708
Senćanski Muzej
Trg Maršala Tita 5-7, YU-24400 Senta
General Museum
Coll: biology, archaeology, ethnology,
numismatics, regional history

17709
Slikarska Kolonija Senćanski Muzej
Ul. Nemanjina 16, YU-24400 Senta
Fine Arts Museum

Šibenik

17710
Muzej Grada
Gradska Vrata 3, YU-59000 Šibenik
General Museum
Archaeology, cultural history, local
history

17711
Zbirka Crkvene Umjetnosti
pri Biskupskom Ordinarijatu, YU-59000
Šibenik
Religious Art Museum

17712
Zbirka Ikona
u Crkvi Uznesenja, YU-59000 Šibenik
Religious Art Museum

Šid

17713
Galerija Save Šumanovića
Ul. Lenjinova 7, YU-22240 Šid
Fine Arts Museum

17714
Muzej Naivne Umetnoste 'Ilijanum'
Ul. Lenjinova 5, YU-22240 Šid
Fine Arts Museum
Naive art

Sinj

17715
**Arheološka Zbirka i Lapidarij
Franjevačkog Samostana**
Ul. A. Jonića 1, YU-58238 Sinj
Archeology Museum
Prehistory, Roman and Christian
archaeology; numismatics

17716
Muzej Cetinjske Krajine
Ul. Duše Čikare 5, YU-58238 Sinj
General Museum
Archaeology, ethnography

Sisak

17717
Muzej Siska
Trg Slobode 8, YU-44000 Sisak
General Museum
Archaeology, ethnography, cultural
history; labour movement; art gallery

Škofja Loka

17718
Loški Muzej
Loški Grad, YU-64220 Škofja Loka
General Museum - 1937
Ethnography, topography, natural
history, medieval guilds, art gallery,
history; open air museum

Skopje

17719
Arheološki Muzej
Kuršumli an, YU-91000 Skopje
Archeology Museum - 1924
Prehistory, antiquities, numismatics

17720
Etnološki Muzej na Makedonija
Ul. Maršala Tita 18, YU-91000 Skopje
Anthropology Museum - 1949

17721
Istoriki Muzej na Makedoija
Ul. Mito Hadživasilev, P.P.74, YU-91000
Skopje
History/Public Affairs Museum
National history, Middle Ages, 19th
century Macedonian history, National
Liberation War, socialist period in
Macedonia

17722
Muzej na Grad Skopje
Ul. Mito Hadživasilev, P.P.93, YU-91000
Skopje
General Museum
Local archaeology, prehistory, Middle
Ages, 7th-20th century history; art
history; anthropology

17723
Muzejot no Sovremenata Umetnost
Ul. Maršala Tita, P.P.482, YU-91000
Skopje
Fine Arts Museum
International contemporary art

17724
**Prirodonaučen Muzej na
Makedonija-Skopje**
Bulevar Ilinden b.b., P.P. 431, YU-91000
Skopje
Natural History Museum - 1926
Coll: natural history, entomology,
palaeontology, hydrobiology, botany,
ichthyology - library

17725
Ribarski Muzej i Akvarium
Zavod za Ribarstvo SRM, YU-91000
Skopje
Natural History Museum
Ichthyology, marine biology, fishing

17726
Umetnička Galerija
Daut Pašin Amam, Kruševska 1, P.P.
278, YU-91000 Skopje
Fine Arts Museum - 1948
Medieval Yugoslavian paintings; icons;
Macedonian and Yugoslavian
contemporary art - library

Slavonska Požega
17727
Muzej Požeške Kotline
Ul. Nikole Demonje 1, YU-55300
Slavonska Požega
General Museum - 1924
Coll: palaeontology, archaeology,
cultural history, ethnography, history of
revolution; memorabilia of Miroslav
Kraljević - library

Slavonski Brod
17728
Muzej Brodskog Posavlja
Ul. Starčevićeva 40, YU-55000
Slavonski Brod
General Museum
Natural history, archaeology,
ethnography, cultural history
17729
**Muzej Radničkog Pokreta i NOB za
Slavoniju i Baranju**
Ul. Starcevićeva 8, YU-55000
Slavonski Brod
General Museum
Labour Movement
17730
**Muzej Radničkog Pokreta i NOB za
Slavoniju i Baranju**
Ul. Starceviceva 8, YU-55000
Slavonski Brod
General Museum
Labour movement; National Liberation
War

Slovenj Gradec
17731
**Muzej Ljudske Revolucije Slovenj
Gradec**
YU-62380 Slovenj Gradec
History/Public Affairs Museum
History of the revolution
17732
Umetnostni Paviljon
YU-62380 Slovenj Gradec
Fine Arts Museum

Smederevo
17733
Muzej u Smederevu
YU-11300 Smederevo
General Museum
Local history

Sombor
17734
Gradski Muzej Sombor
Trg Republike 4, YU-25000 Sombor
General Museum - 1883
Coll: archaeology, local history, crafts,
decorative arts, ethnography,
numismatics - library

Šoštanj
17735
Napotnikova Galerija
Osnovna Škola Biba Röck, YU-63325
Šoštanj
Fine Arts Museum
Contemporary painting

Split
17736
Arheološki Muzej
Zrinsko-Frankopanska 25, YU-58000
Split
Archeology Museum - 1820
Finds from Greek, Roman and
Christian sites, 9th-10th century
Croatian monuments, numismatics -
library
17737
Etnografski Muzej u Splitu
Iza Lože 1, P.P.268, YU-58000 Split
Anthropology Museum - 1910
Dalmatian costumes, jewelry,
weapons, ceramics - library
17738
Galerija Meštrović
Šetalište Moše Pijade 46, YU-58000
Split
Fine Arts Museum - 1952
Works of sculptor Ivan Meštrović
(1883-1962) - library
17739
Galerija Umjetnina
Ul. Lovretska 11, YU-58000 Split
Fine Arts Museum - 1931
Ancient and modern paintings and
sculptures - library
17740
Muzej Grada Splita
Ul. Papalićeva 1, YU-58000 Split
General Museum - 1946
Political and cultural history from
medieval times on up to the 20th
century - library
17741
**Muzej Hrvatskih Arheoloških
Spomenika**
Obala JNA 7, YU-58000 Split
Archeology Museum
17742
Muzej Narodne Revolucije
Šetalište 1.Maja 10, YU-58000 Split
History/Public Affairs Museum
History of the revolution
17743
Prirodoslovni Muzej - Zoološki Vrt
Vrh Marjana 2, P.P. 213, YU-58000 Split
Natural History Museum - 1924
Coll: mineralogy, palaeontology,
zoology, botany - library
17744
Riznica Katedrale Split
Ul. Kraj sv. Duje 5, YU-58000 Split
Religious Art Museum
Treasury, religious items
17745
**Vojno Pomorski Muzej Ratne
Mornarice**
Klaićeva Poljana 4, YU-58000 Split
History/Public Affairs Museum
Maritime history, Yugoslavian Navy
history

Sremska Kamenica
17746
Muzej Jovana Jovanovića-Zmaja
Ul. Zmaj Jovina 1, YU-21208 Sremska
Kamenica
General Museum

Sremska Mitrovica
17747
Muzej Srema
Trg Narodnih Heroja 4, YU-22000
Sremska Mitrovica
General Museum
Natural history, archaeology,
ethnography, numismatics, local
history, art

Sremski Karlovci
17748
Gradski Muzej
Ul. Maršala Tita 10, YU-21205 Sremski
Karlovci
General Museum
Local history
17749
Zbirka Barona Josifa Rajačića 'Ilion'
Dvorac 'Ilion', YU-21205 Sremski
Karlovci
Historic Site
Palace with interiors

Srpska Crnja
17750
**Spomen Muzej Pesnika i Slikara
Džure Jakšića**
Ul. B. Kidriča 68, YU-23220 Srpska
Crnja
History/Public Affairs Museum
Memorial to writer and painter Džuro
Jakšić

Stari Grad na Hvaru
17751
**Arheološka Zbirka Dominikanskog
Samostana**
YU-58460 Stari Grad na Hvaru
Archeology Museum - 1948

Stari Trg
17752
Mineraloška Zbirka Rudnika Trepča
YU-38226 Stari Trg
Science/Tech Museum
Mining, mineralogy

Štip
17753
Naroden Muzej na Štipskiot Kraj
Ul. Tošo Aros 10, YU-92000 Štip
General Museum
Archaeology, ethnography, art

Stolac
17754
Muzej Branka Šotre
YU-79430 Stolac
Fine Arts Museum

Štrigova
17755
Muzejska Zbirka
YU-42312 Štrigova
General Museum
Local history

Struga
17756
**Naroden Muzej 'Dr.Nikola
Nezlobinski'**
Kej 8-mi Novembri 69, YU-97330
Struga
General Museum - 1938
Archaeology, history, zoology, botany
- library

Strumica
17757
Pokrajinski Muzej
Ul. Nenineva 23, YU-92400 Strumica
General Museum
Local history, ethnography

Subotica
17758
Gradski Muzej
Trg Slobode 1, YU-24000 Subotica
General Museum - 1892
Biology, archaeology, ethnography,
history, art, coins - library

Svetozarevo
17759
Zavičajni Muzej Svetozareva
Ul. Maršala Tita 80, YU-35000
Svetozarevo
General Museum
15th-20th century history, archaeology,
ethnography

Tetovo
17760
Muzej na Tetovskiot Kraj
Derviška Tekija 'Arabati Sersem-Ali
baba', YU-91220 Tetovo
Archeology Museum
Archaeology, ethnography

Titograd
17761
Arheološka Zbirka Crne Gore
Ul. Vuka Karadžića 4, YU-81000
Titograd
Archeology Museum
17762
Galerija Akad. Kipara Rista Stijevića
YU-81000 Titograd
Fine Arts Museum
Modern art, sculptures
17763
Moderna Galerija
Ul. Miljana Vukovar 27, YU-81000
Titograd
Fine Arts Museum
Modern art
17764
Muzej Grada Titograda
Ul. Vuka Karadžića 4, YU-81000
Titograd
General Museum
Ethnography, cultural history, National
Liberation War

Titov Veles
17765
Naroden Muzej
Ul. Maršala Tita 22, P.P.96, YU-91400
Titov Veles
General Museum
Archaeology, ethnography, labour
movement 1918-1941, National
Liberation War

Titovo Užice
17766
Narodni Muzej
Ul. Maršala Tita 18, YU-31000 Titovo
Užice
General Museum
Archaeology, prehistory, antiquities,
ethnography, archives

Tolmin
17767
Tolminska Muzejska Zbirka
Trg Maršala Tita 3, YU-65220 Tolmin
General Museum
Local history, archaeology,
ethnography

Topola-Oplenac

17768
Istorijski Muzej
Karadordev Konak, YU-34310 Topola-
Oplenac
History/Public Affairs Museum
Serbian history 1804-1817

Topusko

17769
Muzejska Zbirka
YU-47215 Topusko
General Museum
Local history

Trakoščan

17770
Dvor Trakoščan
YU-42254 Trakoščan
History/Public Affairs Museum
15th-19th century furniture, weapons,
paintings, crafts

Travnik

17771
Zavičajni Muzej
Ul. Lončarica 25, YU-72270 Travnik
General Museum
Mineralogy, petrography, natural
history, archaeology, ethnography,
numismatics, National Liberation war

Trebinje

17772
Zavičajni Muzej
Ul. Alekse Šantića 1, YU-79300
Trebinje
General Museum
Local history

Trogir

17773
**Lapidarij - Klaustar Samostana sv.
Domenika**
YU-58220 Trogir
General Museum

17774
Muzej Grada Trogira
Gradska vrata 4, YU-58220 Trogir
General Museum
Local history

17775
Riznica Katedrale
YU-58220 Trogir
Religious Art Museum
Treasury, religious items, art

17776
**Zbirka Umjetnina u Opatiji sv. Ivana
Krstitelja**
YU-59220 Trogir
Religious Art Museum
Religious items, art

Tržič

17777
Delavska Univerza - Enota Muzej
Ul. Heroja Grajzarja 11, YU-64290
Tržič
General Museum
Crafts, shoemaking, leather, textiles

17778
Kurnikova Hiša
YU-64290 Tržič
Anthropology Museum
Ethnography

Tuzla

17779
Muzej Istične Bosne
Ul. Moše Pijade 24, YU-75000 Tuzla
General Museum
Natural history, archaeology,
ethnography, art, National Liberation
War

17780
Umjetnička Galerija
YU-75000 Tuzla
Fine Arts Museum

Ulcinj

17781
Zavičajni Muzej
YU-81360 Ulcinj
General Museum
Local history, cultural history

Urh

17782
Muzejska Zbirka NOB
YU-61000 Urh, pri Ljubljani
History/Public Affairs Museum
National Liberation War

Valjevo

17783
Narodni Museum
YU-14000 Valjevo
General Museum
Local history

Valpovo

17784
Muzej Valpovštine
YU-54560 Valpovo
General Museum
Local history

Varaždin

17785
Gradski Muzej
Štrossmayerovo Šetalište 7, YU-42000
Varaždin
General Museum
Local history

Varaždinske Toplice

17786
Zavičajni Muzej
Trg Slobode 16, YU-42223
Varaždinske Toplice
General Museum
Coll.: archaeology, balneology, cultural
history, ethnography

Velenje

17787
Muzej Slovenskih Premogovnikov
Ul. Ljubljanska 54, YU-63320 Velenje
Science/Tech Museum
Mining

Velika Gorica

17788
Muzej Turopolja
YU-41410 Velika Gorica
General Museum
Local history, ethnography

Vid

17789
Arheološka Zbirka
YU-58350 Vid, kod Metkovića
Archeology Museum

Vinica

17790
**Rojstna Hiša Pesnika Otona
Župančiča**
YU-68344 Vinica, pri Črnomlju
History/Public Affairs Museum
Memorabilia on poet Oton Župančič

Vinkovci

17791
Galerija Umjetnosti Vinkovci
Ul. JNA 3, YU-56000 Vinkovci
Fine Arts Museum

17792
Gradski Muzej Vinkovci
Trg Republike 8, YU-56000 Vinkovci
General Museum
Natural history, archaeology,
ethnography, local history,
numismatics; National Liberation War

Virovitica

17793
Gradski Muzej
Dvorac, YU-43400 Virovitica
General Museum
Archaeology, ethnology, cultural
history, labour movement, National
Liberation War

Visoko

17794
**Etnografska Zbirka i Lapidarij
Franjevačke Gimnazije**
Nazorova 4, YU-71300 Visoko
Archeology Museum - 1932
Prehistory, ethnography, Bosnian
history - library

17795
Zavičajni Muzej
Ul. Ognjena Price 32, YU-71300 Visoko
General Museum
Local history

Vranje

17796
Narodni Muzej
Ul. Pionirska 2, YU-18500 Vranje
General Museum
Archaeology, ethnography

Vrhnika

17797
**Spominska Zbirka Pisatelja Ivana
Cankarja**
Cankarjev Klanac 1, YU-61360 Vrhnika
History/Public Affairs Museum
Literature; memorabilia of Ivan Cankar

Vršac

17798
Narodni Muzej
Ul. Andje Ranković 19, YU-26300
Vršac
General Museum
Natural history, geology, archaeology,
ethnography, regional history, art,
folklore

17799
Zbirka Eparhije Banatski
Eparhija Banatska, YU-26300 Vršac
Religious Art Museum
Portraits, religious items

Vrsno

17800
Rojstna Hiša Simona Gregorčiča
YU-65222 Vrsno, kod Kobarida
General Museum
Local history, ethnography

Vukovar

17801
Gradski Muzej
Ul. Ive Lole Ribara 2, YU-56230
Vukovar
General Museum
Local history, archaeology,
ethnography, numismatics, armaments,
labour movement, National Liberation
War

17802
Zbirka Bauer i Galerija Umjetnina
Maršala Tita 19, YU-56230 Vukovar
Fine Arts Museum

Zadar

17803
Arheološki Muzej
Obala Maršala Tita 2, YU-57000 Zadar
Archeology Museum - 1830
Roman architecture, Roman epigraphy
and archaeology, medieval
archaeology

17804
Narodni Muzej
Ul. Poljana V. Gortana, YU-57000
Zadar
General Museum
History, folk art, folklore,
contemporary arts, 15th-17th century
glass and ceramics, natural history,
crafts

17805
Pinakoteka sv. Franje
Trg Vranjanina 1, YU-57000 Zadar
Religious Art Museum
Paintings

17806
Pomorski Muzej Institute JAZU
Put Mornarice 8, YU-57000 Zadar
History/Public Affairs Museum
Prehistory, antiquities, sailing and
navigation

17807
**Stalna Izložba Crkvene Umjetnosti
Zadar**
Stomorica bb, YU-57000 Zadar
Religious Art Museum - 1967
Religious items; polyptych by Vittore
Carpaccio; Paolo Veneziano:
Madonna and Child

Zagorje

17808
Muzejska Zbirka NOB
YU-61410 Zagorje, ob Savi
History/Public Affairs Museum
History of the National Liberation War

Zagreb

17809
Arheološki Muzej
Trg N. Zrinskog 19, P.P. 542, YU-41000
Zagreb
Archeology Museum - 1846
Prehistory; Egyptian Coll.; Greco-
Roman Coll.: stone monuments,
painted Greek vases; the longest
written text in the Etruscan language
on a linen cloth (Liber linteus
Zagrebiensis); Medieval Coll.;
numismatics - library

17810
Atelier Ivan Meštrović
Mletačka 8, YU-41000 Zagreb
Fine Arts Museum
Studio of the sculptor Ivan Meštrović
(1883-1962)

17811
Dijecezanski Muzej Zagrebačke Nadbiskupije
Kaptol 28, YU-41000 Zagreb
Religious Art Museum
Religious items, art

17812
Etnografski Muzej
Mažuranićev trg 14, YU-41000 Zagreb
Anthropology Museum - 1919
National costumes of the three ethnographic regions of Croatia: Pannonic, Dinaric, Adriatic; collections of pottery, carpets, kerchiefs, laces, musical instruments of Croatia; collections of non-European cultures - library

17813
Galerija 'Benko Horvat'
Habdelićeva 2, P.P. 233, YU-41000 Zagreb
Fine Arts Museum - 1947
Coll: drawings, paintings, graphics

17814
Galerija Grada Zagreba
Katarinski Trg 2, YU-41000 Zagreb
Fine Arts Museum - 1954

17815
Galerija Primitivne Umjetnosti
Ćirilo Metodska 3, YU-41000 Zagreb
Fine Arts Museum - 1952
Contemporary art, Yugoslavian naive painting

17816
Galerija Suvremene Umjetnosti
Katarinski Trg 2, YU-41000 Zagreb
Fine Arts Museum
Contemporary art

17817
Geološko-paleontološki Muzej
Ul. Demetrova 1, YU-41000 Zagreb
Natural History Museum - 1846
Coll: geology, palaeontology, fossils; neogene malacological fauna of the Pannonian region (ca. 20000 specimens), the Krapina Neandertal remains (680 specimens) - library

17818
Gliptoteka JAZU
UL. Medvedgradska 2, YU-41000 Zagreb
Fine Arts Museum - 1937
Archaeology; ancient, medieval and modern frescos; castings; 19th-20th century sculptures

17819
Grafička Zbirka Nacionalne i Sveučilišne Biblioteke
Trg Marulićev 21, YU-41000 Zagreb
Fine Arts Museum
Graphics, documents

17820
Hrvatski Narodni Zoološki Muzej
Demetrova 1, YU-41000 Zagreb
Natural History Museum - 1846
Zoology; malacology; entomology - library

17821
Hrvatski Školski Muzej
Trg Maršala Tita 4, YU-41000 Zagreb
History/Public Affairs Museum - 1901
History of education in Croatia - library

17822
Kabinet Grafike JAZU
Ul. Braće Kavurića 1, YU-41000 Zagreb
Fine Arts Museum - 1951
Prints, drawings and posters

17823
Lovački Muzej
Ul. V. Nazora 63, YU-41000 Zagreb
Anthropology Museum

17824
Mineraloško-Petrografski Muzej
Ul. Demetrova 1, YU-41000 Zagreb
Natural History Museum - 1846
Mineralogy, petrography

17825
Moderna Galerija
Ul. Braće Kavurića, YU-41000 Zagreb
Fine Arts Museum - 1934
19th-20th century Croatian art

17826
Muzej Grada Zagreba
Opatička 20, YU-41000 Zagreb
General Museum - 1907
Sculpture (14th-18th cent.), paintings and drawings of Zagreb, portraits of Zagreb personalities (18th-19th cent), guild articles, furniture, applied arts, plans and old photos of the city, stone sculpture from the Cathedral (14th-17th cent.) - library

17827
Muzej Hrvatske Književnosti i Kazališne Umjetnosti Instituta za književnost i teatrologiju
Ul. Opatčka 18, YU-41000 Zagreb
Performing Arts Museum
History of Croatian literature and theater

17828
Muzej Revolucije Naroda Hrvatske
Trg Žrtava Fašizma, YU-41000 Zagreb
History/Public Affairs Museum - 1945
History of the National Liberation War - library

17829
Muzej za Umjetnost i Obrt
Trg Maršala Tita 10, YU-41000 Zagreb
Decorative Arts Museum - 1880
14th-20th century decorative arts in furniture, tapestries, textiles, ceramics, gold, silver; paintings, sculpture, costumes, miniatures, industrial art - library

17830
Muzejska Zbirka 'Anka Gvozdanović'
Zgb Visoka 8, YU-41000 Zagreb
Decorative Arts Museum
Applied arts

17831
Poštansko-Telegrafsko-Telefonski Muzej
Ul. Jurišećeva 13, YU-41000 Zagreb
History/Public Affairs Museum
Postal history, philately, archives

17832
Povijesni Muzej Hrvatske
Ul. Matoševa 9, YU-41000 Zagreb
History/Public Affairs Museum - 1846
Croatian history - library

17833
Riznica Zagrebačke Katedrale
Kaptol 31, YU-41000 Zagreb
Religious Art Museum
Treasury, religious items, art

17834
Štrossmayerova Galerija Starih Majstora
Zrinski Trg 11, YU-41000 Zagreb
Fine Arts Museum - 1884
13th-19th century art

17835
Tehnički Muzej
C. Savska 18, YU-41000 Zagreb
Science/Tech Museum - 1954
Astronomy, mineralogy, petrography, firefighting

17836
Tiflološki Muzej Jugoslavije
Ul. Draškovićeva 80, YU-41000 Zagreb
Science/Tech Museum - 1953
Exhibits relating to the blind; tactile gallery - library

17837
Umjetnički Paviljon
Tomislavob trg 22, YU-41000 Zagreb
Fine Arts Museum

Zaječar

17838
Narodni Muzej Zaječar
Ul. Moše Pijade 2, P.P. 58, YU-19000 Zaječar
General Museum - 1951
Coll.: archaeology, ethnography, local history, paintings - library

Zaostrog

17839
Etnografska Zbirka Franjevačkog Samostana
YU-58334 Zaostrog
Anthropology Museum
Ethnography, religious art, paintings, archives

Zemun

17840
Zavičajni Muzej Zemuna
ul.Maršala Tita, 9, P.P. 72, YU-11081 Zemun
General Museum - 1954
Local history; portraits of inhabitants of Zemun

Zenica

17841
Muzej Grada Zenice
Ul. F. Spanca 1, YU-72000 Zenica
General Museum
Archaeology, ethnography, local history, art

Zrenjanin

17842
Mala Galerija
Trg Slobode 7, YU-23000 Zrenjanin
Fine Arts Museum

17843
Narodni Muzej
Ul. Subotićeva 1, YU-23000 Zrenjanin
General Museum
Archaeology, ethnography, art history, folklore; labour movement

Županja

17844
Muzej Županje
UL. Savska 3, YU-56270 Županja
General Museum
Paleontology, archaeology, ethnography

Zaire

Jadotville

17845
Musée Geologique Sengier-Cousin
mail c/o Générale Congolaise des Minerals Jadotville
Natural History Museum
Geology; minerals

Kanaga

17846
Musée National de Kananga
BP 612, Kanaga
General Museum

Kinshasa

17847
Academie des Beaux-Arts
Av des Victimes de la Rébellion, BP 8249, Kinshasa
Fine Arts Museum
Modern sculptures

17848
Musée d'Anthropologie
mail c/o Université Lovanium, BP 139, Kinshasa
Anthropology Museum
Coll: anthropological handicrafts, pottery, and woodcarvings; musical instruments; traditional agricultural, fishing, and hunting methods; sculptures; coins

17849
Musée Préhistorique
mail c/o Université Lovanium
Kinshasa 6
Archeology Museum
Prehistory exhibits

Kisangani

17850
Musée Regional
Kisangani
General Museum
Ethnography

Lubumbashi

17851
Musée National de Lubumbashi
BP 2375, Lubumbashi, Katanga
Anthropology Museum
Ethnology; ethnography; archeology

Luluabourg

17852
Musée Regional
Luluabourg
General Museum
Ethnography

Mbandaka

17853
Musée National de Mbandaka
Av du Commerce 16, BP 344, Mbandaka
General Museum
Ethnography; archeology; antiquities

Mushenge

17854
Musée du Roi de Cuba
mail c/o Ecole d'Art de Mushenge
Mushenge, Western Kasai
General Museum
Ethnography of Kasai; statues; goblets

Zambia

Livingstone

17855
Eastern Cataract Field Museum
POB 124, Livingstone
General Museum
Displays illustrating formation of the
Victoria Falls; Stone Age implements

17856
National Museum of Zambia The
Livingstone Museum
Mosi-oa-Tunya Rd, POB 60498,
Livingstone
General Museum - 1934
Natural history exhibits; general
history; fine arts; relics of Dr.
Livingston - library

Lusaka

17857
The Art Centre
74 Independence Av, POB 1986,
Lusaka
Fine Arts Museum
Works of contemporary art in the
Zambian national art collection

17858
**Military and Police Museum of
Zambia**
mail c/o Commissioner of Police,
Independence Av, Lusaka
History/Public Affairs Museum
Objects connected with police and
army of Zambia; relics from German
campaign in WWI

17859
National Archives of Zambia
POB 10, Ridgeway, Lusaka
History/Public Affairs Museum
Stamps and coins; local history

Ndola

17860
Copperbelt Museum
POB 661, Ndola
Science/Tech Museum
Displays on the copper mining
industry; nature and ecology

Zimbabwe

Bulawayo

17861
Bulawayo Art Gallery
Grey St and Selborne Av, POB 1993,
Bulawayo
Fine Arts Museum
Works of contemporary English and
South African artists; loan exhibitions

17862
Khami Ruins Site Museum
Bulawayo
Historic Site
Ruins of one of Mambo dynasty
capitals (15th to early 19th cent.);
archaeological finds from the area

17863
**Matopos National Park Site
Museums**
Bulawayo
General Museum
Prehistoric rock paintings; Stone Age
tools; grave of Cecil Rhodes

17864
National Museum of Natural History
Centenary Park, Selborne Av, POB
240, Bulawayo
Natural History Museum - 1901
Zoology collections covering Ethiopian
region and Southern Africa - library

17865
**National Railways of Zimbabwe
Museum**
Prospect Av and 1st St, Raylton, POB
596, Bulawayo
Science/Tech Museum
Former Rhodesian Railways steam
locomotives, coaches, and freight cars

Fort Victoria

17866
National Museum Great Zimbabwe
Ruins
Private Bag 9158, Fort Victoria
General Museum

Gwelo

17867
National Military Museum
Lobengula Av, POB 1300, Gwelo
History/Public Affairs Museum - 1974
Weapons; military vehicles, uniforms,
and equipment; aircraft and aviation
uniforms and equipment

Inyanga

17868
Nyahokwe Ruins Site Museum
Inyanga
History/Public Affairs Museum
Relics of Iron Age; locally found relics
of Ziwa culture

Marandellas

17869
Children's Museum
Children's Libray, The Green,
Marandellas
Junior Museum
Objects illustrating man and his
implements from the early Stone Age
to pioneering days; rocks and
minerals; local birds

Salisbury

17870
Macgregor Museum
Maufe Bldg, 4th St and Selous Av,
POB 8039 Causeway, Salisbury
Natural History Museum - 1940
Economic minerals; displays dealing
with the Deweras and Umkondo
groups

17871
National Archives
Gun Hill, Borrowdale Rd, Private Bag
7729, Causeway, Salisbury
History/Public Affairs Museum - 1935
Historical manuscripts; paintings,
printillustrations, and maps - library

17872
National Gallery of Zimbabwe
20 Kings Crescent, POB 8155
Causeway, Salisbury
Fine Arts Museum - 1957
Traditional African art; Zimbabwean
stone sculpture ('shona sculpture') -
library

17873
Queen Victoria Museum
Civic Centre; Rotten Row, POB 8006,
Causeway, Salisbury
Anthropology Museum - 1902
National collection of Iron and Stone
Age artifacts; rock paintings;
ethnographic collections - library

Umtali

17874
Umtali Museum
Victory Av, Umtali
General Museum - 1957
Local flora and fauna; national
antiquities collection; national land
transport collection; national firearms
collection - library

National and International Museum Associations

International

Commonwealth Association of Museums, c/o R.J. Varney, Commonwealth Institute, Kensington High Street, London W8 6NQ, United Kingdom

International Association of Agricultural Museums (IAMA), c/o Prof. Dr. W. Jacobeit, Museum für Volkskunde, Bodestr. 1-3, 102 Berlin, Federal Republic of Germany

International Association of Agricultural Museums (IAMA), c/o Dr. Klaus Schreiner, Agrarhistorisches Freilichtmuseum, 2061 Alt-Schwerin/Waren, German Democratic Republic

International Association of Arms and Military History Museums (IAMAM), c/o Dr. Z. Zygulski, Muzeum Narodowe w Krakovie, Ul. Pijarska 6, Krakow, Poland

International Association of Arms and Military History Museums (IAMAM), c/o Mr. William Reid, National Army Museum, Royal Hospital Road, London SW3, United Kingdom

International Association of Transport Museums (IATM), c/o Dr. Przemyslaw Smolarek, Centralne Muzeum Morskie, Ul. Szeroska 67-68, 80-835 Gdansk, Poland

International Association of Transport Museums (IATM), c/o Mr. Wolf-Dieter Hoheisel, Deutsches Schiffahrtsmuseum, Van-Ronzelen-Str., 2850 Bremerhaven, Federal Republic of Germany

International Center for the Study of the Preservation and the Restoration of Cultural Property (Rome Center), 256 Via Cavour, Roma, Italy

International Committee of Architecture and Museum Techniques (ICAMT), c/o Mr. Per Kåks, Riksutställningar, Sandhamnsgatan 63, 115 28 Stockholm, Sweden

International Committee of Architecture and Museum Techniques (ICAMT), c/o Mlle Germaine Pélegrin, Musée du Louvre, 75041 Paris Cedex 01, France

International Committee of Museums of Archaeology and History (ICMAH), c/o Dr. Ferenc Fülep, Magyar Nemzeti Muzeum, Muzeum Körut 14-16, 1370 Budapest 8, Hungary

International Committee of Museums of Archaeology and History (ICMAH), c/o Mr. Louis Valensi, Cité Administrative, St. Sever, 76037 Rouen, France

International Committee of Museums of Ethnography (ICME), c/o Dr. H. Ganslmayr, Übersee-Museum, Bahnhofsplatz 13, 2800 Bremen, Federal Republic of Germany

International Committee of Museums of Ethnography (ICME), c/o Mr. Tibor Sekelj, Ul. Borisa Kidriča 15, 24000 Subotica, Yugoslavia

International Committee of Museums of Modern Art (CIMAM), c/o Mr. Pontus Hulten, Musée d'art moderne, CNAC, G. Pompidou, 35 Bd. de Sébastopol, 75004 Paris, France

International Committee of Museums of Modern Art (CIMAM), c/o Mlle Suzanne Pagé, Musée d'Art moderne de la Ville de Paris, 9 rue Gaston de St. Paul, 75116 Paris, France

International Committee of Museums of Musical Instruments (CIMCIM), c/o Mr. Friedmann Hellwig, Germanisches Nationalmuseum, Postfach 9580, 8500 Nürnberg, Federal Republic of Germany

International Committee of Museums of Musical Instruments (CIMCIM), c/o Mr. Peter A. Kjellberg, Ringve Museum, 7000 Trondheim, Norway

International Committee of Museums of Science and Technology (CIMUSET), c/o Mr. Theo Stilger, Deutsches Museum, Museumsinsel, 8000 München 26, Federal Republic of Germany

International Committee of Museums of Science and Technology (CIMUSET), c/o Mr. Günther Gottmann, Deutsches Museum, Museumsinsel, 8000 München 26, Federal Republic of Germany

International Committee of Museum Security (ICMS), c/o Mr. R.G. Tillotson, National Museum of History and Technology, Smithsonian Institution, Washington DC 20560, USA

International Committee of Museum Security (ICMS), c/o Dr. Philip Lundeberg, National Museum of History and Technology, Smithsonian Institution, Washington DC 20560, USA

International Council of Monuments and Sites (ICOMOS), Hotel Saint-Aignan, 75 rue du Temple, 75003 Paris, France

International Council of Museums (ICOM), Maison de l'UNESCO, 1 rue Miollis, 75015 Paris, France

Museums Association of Tropical Africa, c/o Dr. Ekpo O. Eyo, Department of Antiquities, Lagos, Nigeria

Organization of Museums, Monuments and Sites of Africa, c/o Mr. K.A. Myles, Museums and Monuments Board, Accra, Ghana

Argentina

Instituto Argentino de Museologia, Marcelo T. de Alvear 2084, 1122 Buenos Aires

Australia

Art Galleries Association of Australia, c/o The Art Gallery of South Australia, North Terrace, Adelaide SA 5000

Museums Association of Australia, c/o The Australian Museum, 6-8 College St, Sydney NSW 2000

Austria

Arbeitsgemeinschaft der Museumsbeamten und Denkmalpfleger Österreichs, c/o Dr. Gerhard Lücker, Wien 1, Neue Burg

Belgium

Association des Musées de Belgique/ Belgische Museumvereniging, c/o Etnografisch Museum, Kloosterstraat 11-13, 2000 Antwerpen

Brazil

Associação de Membros do ICOM - Brasil, c/o Ms. Fernanda de Camargo Almeida Moro, C.P.38016 ZC-19, Rio de Janeiro 2000

Canada

Canadian Museums Association, 331 rue Cooper Street, Suite 400, Ottawa, Ontario K2P 0G5

Colombia

Asociación Colombiana de Museos, Institutos y Casas de Cultura, ACOM, c/o Museo del Oro, Calle 16 No 5-41, Bogota

Comité Nacional del Consejo Internacional de Museos, ICOM, y de la Asociación Latinoamericana de Museos, ALAM, c/o División de Museos y Restauración, Calle 24 No 5-60, oficina 211, Bogota

Czechoslovakia

Muzeologicky kabinet pri Národním muzeu v Praze, u Luzickeho seminäre 13, Praha 1

Ústredná správa múzeí a galérií, Lodná 2, 89129 Bratislava

Danmark

Dansk Kulturhistorisk Museums Forening, Postbox 26, 4000 Roskilde

Danske Museers Fællesraad, c/o Thorvaldsens Museum, 1213 København K

Foreningen af Danske Museumsmaend, Nationalmuseet, København K

Skandinavisk Museumsforbund, Danske Afdeling, c/o Tojhusmuseet, 1220 København K

Ecuador

Asociacion Ecuatoriana de Museos, Casilla 175 b, Quito

Finland

Suomen Museoliitto-Finlands Museiförbund, Museokatu 5 a, Helsinki 10

Skandinavisk Museumsforbund, Finnish Section, c/o Turun Kaupungin Historiallinen Museo, Turku

France

Association générale des Conservateurs des Collections publiques de France, 107 rue de Rivoli, 75001 Paris

Federal Republic of Germany

Deutscher Museumsbund DMB, Senckenberganlage 25, 6000 Frankfurt 1

ICOM-Deutsches Nationalkomitee, c/o Deutsches Museum, 8000 München 26

German Democratic Republic

Institut für Museumswesen, Müggelseedamm 200, 1162 Berlin

Ghana

Ghana Museums and Monuments Board, Barnes Rd, POB 3343, Accra

Great Britain

The Museums Association of Great Britain, 87 Charlotte St., London W1P 2BX

Hungary

Muzeumi Restaurator - es Modszertani Központ, Könyves Kalman krt. 40, Budapest

India

Indian Association for the Study of Conservation of Cultural Property, c/o National Archives of India, Janpath, New Delhi

The Museums Association of India, c/o National Museum, Janpath, New Delhi 110011

Indonesia

ICOM-National Committee, c/o Directorate of Museums, Directorate-General of Culture, Jalan Merdeka Barat 12, Jakarta

Israel

Museums Association of Israel, c/o M.
Broshi, POB 1299, Jerusalem

Italy

Associazione Nazionale dei Musei
Italiani, Piazza S. Marco 49,
00186 Roma

Japan

Nihon Hakubutsukan Kyokai, c/o
Tokyo Kokuritsu Hakubutsukan,
Ueno Park 7-20, Daito-ku, Tokyo 110

Mexico

Sociedad Mexicana de Antropologia,
Cordoba 45, Mexico D.F.

Netherlands

Nederlandse Museumsvereniging,
Wierdijk 18, 1601 LA Enkhuizen

New Zealand

Art Galleries and Museums
Association of New Zealand,
POB 57016, Owairaka, Auckland

Norway

Norske Kunst-og Kulturhistoriske
Museer, Pilestredet 15, Oslo 1

Norske Naturhistoriske Museers
Landsforbund, c/o Zoologisk
Museum, Sarsgate 1, Oslo 5

Skandinavisk Museumsforbund,
Norwegian Section, c/o
Ethnographical Museum, Oslo
University, Oslo

Pakistan

Museums Association of Pakistan,
Victoria Memorial Hall, Peshawar

Poland

Zarzæd Muzeów i Ochrony Zabytków,
Krakowskie Przedmieście 15/17,
Warszawa

South Africa

Southern African Museums
Association, POB 61, Cape
Town 8000

Sweden

Skandinaviska Museiförbundet,
Swedish Section, Länsmuseet,
80128 Gävle

Svenska Museiföreningen, Nordiska
museet, Djurgarden,
11521 Stockholm

Switzerland

ICOM - Comité National Suisse,
Helvetiaplatz 5, 3000 Bern 6

Verband der Museen der Schweiz,
Association des Musées Suisses,
Museumstr. 2, Postfach 2760,
8023 Zürich

Taiwan

Museum Association of China,
49 Nanhai Road, Taipei

United States of America

American Association of Museums,
1055 Thomas Jefferson St, N.W.,
Washington D.C.20007

Yugoslavia

Savez muzejskih društva Jugoslavije,
Vuka Karadžića 18, Beograd

Savez muzejskih društva Hrvatske,
Tehnički muzej, Savska cesta 18,
Zagreb

Name Index (Persons, Places, Collections)

Jovkov, Jordan   01713
Joyce, James   07012
József, Attila   06350
Judaism   15906
Junqueiro, Guerra   10604
Kableškov, Todor   01596
Kabrun Collection   10172
Kalaw, Teodoro M.   10038
Kalinin, Michail   17187
Kane, Paul, Collection   15761
Kania, Jakub   10389
Karavelov, Ljuben   01595
Kashubia   10136, 10142, 10328
Kašpar, Adolf   03076
Kasprowicz, Jan   10194
Kassák, Lajos   06371
Kateri Tekakwitha   01856
Kato, Kiyomasa   08311, 08402
Katona, József   06431
Kaulbach, Wilhelm von   05195
Kaw Indians   15952
Kawabata, Ryushi   08566
Kawai, Gyokudo   08454
Kawai, Kanjiro   08337, 08344
Kawamura, Kizan   08389
Kazantzakis, Nikolaos   06123
Keats, John   07861, 13205
Keene, Charles S.   02211
Keith, William   15475
Keller, Gottfried, Bequest   11949
Keller, Helen   16632, 16794
Kelly, Emmett   16363
Kennedy, John F.   13988
Kent, Benny   14107
Kent, Rockwell, Collection   15938
Kepler, Johann   05882, 05971
Kernstock, Ottokar   00639
Kervel, Adriaan van   11007
Key, Ellen   11779
Kiam, Victor, Collection   15589
Kierkegaard, Søren   03450, 03461, 03462
Kießling, Franz   00643
King, William Lyon MacKenzie   02072, 02228
Kipling, Rudyard   12785
Kirchner, Ernst Ludwig   12017
Kirkov, Georgi   01656
Kirov, Sergej Mironovič   17136
Kirschstein Collection   15242
Kisfaludy, Károly   06495
Kisfaludy, Sándor   06346, 06495
Kisfaludy-Stróbl, Zsigmond   06542
Klee, Paul, Bequest   11949
Klein, Kalman, Collection   09396
Kleist, Heinrich von   04731
Klíč, Karel   02974
Klicpera, Václav Kliment   02911
Kloepfer, Hans   00646
Klopstock, Friedrich   04983
Kluk, Jan Krzysztof   10146
Kneipp, Sebastian   05239
Knox, John   12952
Koch, Robert   04631, 10489
Kochanowski, Jan   10149
Kocher, Dr. Albert, Collection   11946
Kocjubinskij, Michail Michajlovič   17019
Kodaly, Zoltán   06402
Koger Collection   14986
Kohán, György   06419
Kohlhaas, Michael   04595
Kohn, Erin, Collection   14255
Kojima, Torajiro   08315
Kolarov, Vasil   01662, 01683
Kolb Collection   16297
Kolbe, Georg   05277
Kollwitz, Kaethe   16495
Konopnicka, Maria   10506
Konstantinov, Aleko   01686
Korais, Adamantios   06092
Körner, Theodor   05129
Kościuszko, Tadeusz   12242
Kossak, Jerzy   10230
Kossak, Juliusz   10230

Kossak, Wojciech   10230
Kossuth, Lajos   01682, 06403, 06451
Kostka, Fertiš   03269
Kosumi, Toru   08321
Kovács, Margit   06512
Koyunoglu, A. Izzet, Collection   12549
Kraljević, Miroslav   17727
Kræmmer, Elias   09876
Krasicki, Ignacy   10163
Krasiński Collection   10474
Krasiński, Zygmunt   10321
Kraszewski, József   10374
Krekovic, Kristian, Collection   11407
Kress Collection   13664, 13746, 13897, 14004, 14255, 14285, 14499, 14839, 14902, 15358, 15529, 15589, 15720, 15889, 15979, 16032, 16620, 16624, 16747
Křička, Jaroslav   03014
Křička, Petr   03014
Křižík, František   03154
Kromer, Marcin   10118
Kruger, Paul   10961, 11993
Kuba, Ludvík   02872
Kubin, Alfred   00730
Kumičić, Eugen   17489
Kunwar, Babu Singh   06703
Kupala, Janka   17164
Kuroda, Seiki   08551
Kuska Collection   14238
Kutenai   01967
Kvapil, Jaroslav   02919
Kyber, Manfred   05706
Labia, Natale, Collection   10856
Laclose, Pierre   03922
Lafayette, Marie Joseph de Motier   16467
Lagarde, John B., Collection   13709
Lagerlöf, Selma   11855
Lake, Benjamin, Collection   16526
Lamartine, Alphonse de   01624, 03906, 03995, 04227
Lamprecht, J.E.   00796
Landauer, Walter, Collection   16495
Lane, Harriet   15117
Langdon Collection   15981
Langenhoven, C. J.   10938
Langer, Randolph E., Collection   15296
Lanier, Sidney   15286
Lannes, Jean   04178
Lapps   03842, 09703, 09715, 09764, 09788, 09831, 09855, 09883, 09892
Larreta, Enrique   00134
Larsson, Carl   11851
Latin America   16561, 16618, 16751
Latter-Schlesinger Collection   15589
Laumann, Carlos Alberto   00407
Laurel, J. P.   10097
Laurier, Wilfrid   02228
Lauterburg, Martin, Bequest   12066
Lawson, Roberta Campbell, Collection   16624
Leacock, Stephen   02215
Lee, Robert E.   13662, 13726, 15182
Legazpi, Miguel López de   11634
Léger, Fernand   04005
Lehár, Franz   00621, 00623
Lehmann, Wilhelm   12300
Lehmbruck, Wilhelm   05401
Leichhardt, L.   04611
Leković, V.   17446
Lemonnier, Camille   01007
Lenin, Vladimir Iľič   02867, 03193, 03859, 04867, 10114, 10237, 10343, 10453, 16999, 17079, 17125, 17152, 17169, 17317, 17326, 17339
Lenković, Lučev   17528
Lenney, Annie, Collection   14054
León y Castillo, Fernando   11548
Leopardi, Giacomo   07820
Lermontov, Michail Jur'evič   17144, 17256
Lesseur, Wincenty, Collection   12186
Lessing, Gotthold Ephraim   05986

Leszczyński Family   10180
Leventritt, Roy C., Collection   16256
Levski, Vasil   01585, 01602
Lewis, E. G., Collection   13743
Lewis-Kneberg Collection   15080
Lewis, Meriwether   13742, 14947
Lewis, Sinclair   16320
Liebes, Dorothy, Collection   16278
Liebig, Justus von   05503
Liebknecht, Karl   04822, 04866, 05115
Lifar Collection   14844
Liliencron, Detlef Freiherr von   05625
Lilienthal, Otto   04574
Lincoln, Abraham   03552, 13764, 13921, 14648, 14838, 14888, 15174, 16024, 16053, 16732, 16742, 16806
Lindenau, Bernhard von   04571
Lindsay, Norman, Collection   00553
Lindsay, Vachel   16445
Liniers, Virrey   00058
Linnaean Collection   11871
Linné, Carl von   11715
Linné Collection   03762
Linton Collection   15575
Lippmann, J.   05451
Lissitzky Collection   09113
Liszt, Franz   00761, 05098, 06492
Livingstone, David   12728
Lobato Collection   13785
Locke, Alair LeRoy, Collection   16747
Lomonosov, Michail Vasiľevič   17135
London, Jack   14724
Lönroth, Elias   03849
Loon, Van   08978
Lothrop Collection   14285
Lovanov-Rostovsky Collection   14977
Low, Juliette Gordon   16327
Loyola, San Ignacio de   11058
Lu Xun   02628
Lucas, George A., Collection   13798
Lucas, Robert   14967
Lucich Collection   00541
Ludwig Collection   05159
Ludwig, Otto   04711
Lugones, Leopoldo   00426
Lullin, Ami   12039
Lunačarskij, Anatolij Vasiľevič   17210
Luther, Martin   04705, 04710, 04712, 04713, 05124
Mabini, Apolinario   10056
MacArthur, Douglas   15689, 16031
McCoy, Frank R., Collection   15170
MacDonald, John a.   02061
Macgregor Collection   00494
McGuffey, William Holmes   15790
Mácha, Karel Hynek   02928
Machado y Ruiz, Antonio   11504
Macho, Victorio   11553
McKay, Malcom, Collection   13891
McKellar Collection   13021
Mackelvie Collection   09467
MacKenzie, William   02453
McKinley, William   15681
McLane Exhibit   13965
Macleay, William, Collection   00582
McLeod Collection   16487
Macleod, Thomas   00494
McMillan, Angus   00535
McMillen Collection   16391
McMurray, George F., Collection   14839
MacNab, Allan Napier   02023
Madison, Dolley, Collection   14782
Madison, James   15762
Maeterlinck, Maurice   01083
Maeztu, Gustavo de   11187
Magill Collection   14791
Maglioni, Fr. R., Collection   06341
Magsaysay, Ramon, Collection   10064
Magsuhot Collection   10030
Mahen, Jiří   02891
Mai-Kai   14619
Maidu Indians   16958

Majakovskij, Vladimir Vladimirovič   17188
Makariopolski, Ilarion   01573
Makuszynski, Kornel   10517
Malan, D. F.   10992
Malloy Carmichal, Mary, Collection   13891
Mandan Indians   15314
Mandell Collection   14258
Mánes, Josef   02893
Mann, Thomas   03220
Mannerheim, C. G.   03801
Mannerheim, Gustav   03711
Manzoni, Alessandro   07570, 07620
Manzù, Giacomo   07186
Mao Zedong   02627, 02674
Maori   09468
Marchais, Jacques   16471
Marcks, Gerhard   05350
Marconi, Guglielmo   16606
Marcos, Ferdinand E. Collection   10041
Marcove, Ralph C., Collection   16654
Marer, Fred and Mary, Collection   14195
Markley, Kehl and Nena, Collection   16654
Marks, Golda and Meyer, Collection   14619
Marks, Jacob, Collection   15362
Marsh, Fred Dana   15771
Marshall-Hall, G. W .L.   00552
Marsili, Luigi Ferdinando   07260
Martí, José   02815
Martin, Agnes   15872
Martin, Alexandre-Louis   01036
Martin, Bohuslav   03167
Martínez Ruiz, José   11372
Martinuzzi, Giuseppina   17586
Martyn, Ferenc   06470
Maruyama Collection   08674
Marx, Jenny   05025
Marx, Karl   03010, 05945, 17203
Matejko, Jan   10224, 10228
Matern, Hermann   04643
Mathias Flacius Illyricus   17586
Matisse, Henri   04175, 04312
Matsukata, Kojiro, Collection   08559
Matsuoka, Seijiro, Collection   08553
Maufe Lady Collection   13206
May, Edward, Collection   15752
Mayer, Herbert, Collection   14813
Mazulla, Jo and Fred, Collection   14649
Mazzini, Giuseppe   07789
McCulloch, Thomas   02257
McDougall, G.   01929
McKenzie, R. Tait   01847
McRae, John   02008
Medgyessy, Ferenc   06424
Meek, George, Collection   09526
Meeker, Ezra   16019
Meiji   08555
Meiji, Emperor   08234
Melanchthon, Philipp   05359
Melantrich z Aventýna, Jiří   03231
Melba, Dame Nellie, Collection   00531
Melchers, Gari   14668
Memling, Hans   00993
Mendel, Gregor J.   16658
Mendel, Gregor Johann   02881, 02984
Mendeleev, Dmitrij Ivanovič   17131
Menéndez y Pelayo, Marcelino   11487
Menon, V. K. Krishna   06638
Mercer, Henry Chapman   14433
Merner Collection   16487
Merton, Thomas   16170
Mesonero Romanos, Ramón   11310
Mesquakie Indians   16585
Meštrović, Ivan   17738, 17810
Metha, N. C., Collection   06559
Meunier, Constantin   01010

Rocha, Dardo 00244
Rockefeller, Abby Aldrich, Collection 16004
Rockefeller, Michael C. 14676
Rockwell, Robert F., Collection 14290
Rodgers, Jimmie 15370
Rodin, Auguste 04255, 04381, 14738, 15893, 16465
Roerich, Nicholas 15643
Rogers, Will 14197, 15793
Rojas, Ricardo 00084
Romaní, Amador, Collection 11136
Romania 14220
Romano, Mario, Collection 13895
Röntgen, W. C. 05888
Roos-Hasselblatt Collection 03698, 03712
Roosevelt, Franklin D. 14939, 14940, 16720
Roosevelt, Teddy, Collection 15138
Roosevelt, Theodore 14012, 15356, 15791
Roothan, Philippus 08986
Rops, Felicien 01207
Rose, Edward, S., Collection 16717
Rosebud and Pine Ridge Sioux 16172
Rosegger, Peter 00605, 00606, 00716
Rosensteel Collection 14721
Rosmini-Serbati, Antonio 07913
Rosseel 15735
Rossini, Gioacchino 07763, 07766
Rossini, Gioacchino, Collection 07765
Rothschild, D. C. H. 15962
Rousseau, Henri 04172
Rousseau, Jean-Jacques 04489, 12035, 12148
Routh, Dorothy Adler, Collection 14195
Rožek, Marcin 10490
Różycki, Ludomir 10512
Rubens, Peter Paul 00949
Rudnicki, Lucjan 10406
Runciman, Walter, Viscount of Doxford 02895
Runeberg, Johan Ludvig 03826
Runeberg, Walter 03830
Runge, F. F. 04947
Rupf, Hermann and Margrit, Bequest 11949
Rush, Benjamin 16596
Ruskin, John 12692, 12876
Rust, W. J., Collection 09067
Rutherford, A. C. 01936
Ryan Collection 13168
Ryggen, Hannah 09888
Saar, Friedrich von 00830
Saarinen, Aline B. 16428
Saarinen, Eliel 03729
Sacajawea Indians 15821
Sadler Collection 13197
Saint-Saëns, Charles Camille 04097
Salter, Susanna M. 13721
Salvador, Luis 11596
Salzillo, Francisco 11382
San Martín, José de 00114
Sand, George 04151, 04324, 11596
Sandell Collection 15756
Sanderson, Christian C. 14100
Sandoz, M. and E. M., Collection 12109
Sandzen, Birger 15200
Sarasate de Navascués, Pablo Martín 11421
Sarmiento, Domingo Faustino 00127
Saunders, C. Burton, Collection 13877
Saussure, H. B. de 12033
Schaffer, Charles A., Collection 14363
Scheffer, Ary, Collection 09095
Scheyer, Galka E., Collection 15817

Schiller, Friedrich von 04051, 04679, 04826, 04875, 05092, 05095, 05100, 05104, 05720, 05738
Schinkel, C. F. 04626
Schliemann, Heinrich 04927, 12581
Schlosser, Cornelia 05424
Schmidt-Rottluff, Karl 05274
Schoenebeck Collection 16481
Schopenhauer, Arthur 05470
Schott Collection 16294
Schott, Philippe, Collection 01030
Schöttle-bey Collection 05371
Schreyvogel Collection 15737
Schubert, Christian F.D. 05161
Schubert, Franz 00858, 00894, 00895
Schumacher, Frederick, Collection 14266
Schumann, Robert 05151
Schurmann, Anna Maria van, Collection 09133
Schütz, Heinrich 04600, 05111
Schwab, Friedrich, Collection 11961
Schwartz, Arnold & Marie 13994
Schweitzer, Albert 04146, 09084
Scotese Collection 14255
Scott, Issac 14164
Scott, Sir Walter 13285
Scott, Sir Walter 12953
Seabury, Samuel 16926
Sedgwick, Adam 12812
Sedgwick Collection 16296
Seibels Collection 14255
Selby Collection 00582
Seminole Indians 14635, 15515, 16625, 16859
Sendak, Maurice 15894
Seneca Indians 14082
Seneca-Iroquois Indians 16217
Sergeev-Censkij, Sergej Nikolaevič 16991
Serizawa, Keisuke 08320
Şerra, Fray Junipero 16678
Ševčenko, Taras Grigor'evič 17065, 17077
Sévigné, Madame de 04343
Seward, William H. 13764
Shakespeare, William 13509, 13511
Shaw, George Bernard 12645
Shen Zong, Emperor 02620
Shinenkan Collection 16624
Shivers, Allan 16931
Shomu, Emperor 08422, 08423
Shoshone Indians 14948, 15751
Shotoku, Taishi 08467
Sienkiewicz, Henryk 10313, 10393, 10487
Sihtolas, Ester and Jalo, Collection 03749
Sikhs 06576
Simu, Elena and Anastasie, Collection 10672
Sinagua Indians 14572, 14573
Sinebrychoff, Paul and Fanny, Collection 03718
Singer, William H., Collection 09210
Sioux Indians 02563, 16041
Sitting Bull 16883
Sivle, Per 09616
Şkjoldborg, Johan 03580
Skopalík, František 03330
Skredsvig, Christian 09655
Skrjabin, Aleksandr Nikolaevič 17196
Sládek, Josef Václav 03334
Slătineanu, Alexandra and Barbu, Collection 10672
Slavejkov, Penčo 01661
Sloan, John, Collection 16889
Sloane, Eric 15044
Slovakia 06436, 06497
Šmeral, Bohumil 03287
Smetana, Bedřich 02849, 02987, 03186
Smilie, James D., Collection 15471
Smirnenski, Christo 01654

Smith Collection 16921
Smith, C.R., Collection 13783
Smits, Jakob 01188
Smythe Collection 09483
Soldevila, Miguel Valls 11102
Solidor, Suzy 04031
Solomos, Dionysios 06104
Solomos, Th. 06311
Somer, Richard 16412
Søndergaard, Jens 03486
Sorolla, Joaquín 11329
Sosnowski, Kazimierz, Collection 10246
Soulès, Félix 04109
Soun, Tazaki 08188
South America 15210
Southern Plains Indians 13693
Şova, Antonín 03080, 03147
Spaniel, Otakar 02990
Spencer, Stanley 12879
Spinoza, Baruch de 09312
Spitteler, Carl 11942
Spontini, Gaspare 07599
Şprang, Legaat van, Collection 09374
Srámek, František 03256
Stäbli, Adolf 11976
Staël, Madame de 11998
Štáfl, Otakar 02955
Stalin, Josif Vissarionovič 17041
Stambolijski, Aleksandăr 01653
Standard Oil of New Jersey Collection 16624
Stanislavskij, Konstantin Sergeevič 17174
Starr, John W., Collection 16624
Staszic, Stanisław 10192, 10334
Stein, Charlotte von 04782
Stendhal (Beyle, Marie Henri) 04132
Stephen, King of Hungary 06503
Stephens, Alexander H. 14314
Steuart Curry, John 14348
Stevenson, Robert Louis 12953, 15458, 16174
Stifter, Adalbert 00729, 02969
Stoddard Collection 14728
Storie, José 00991
Storm, Theodor 05587
Stowe, Harriet Beecher 14843
Stradivari, Antonio 07393
Streeter Aldrich, Bess, Collection 14087
Streuvel, Stijn 01121
Striegel, Yvo 11926
Strindberg, August 11841
Ştuck, Franz v. 05793
Štúr, L'udovit 03102
Sturt, Charles 00499
Stuyvaert, Victor 01083
Suermondt, Barthold, Collection 05159
Sugawara, Michizane 08198, 08199
Suk, Josef 03039
Sullivan, Frank 16317
Şullivan Macy, Anne 16794
Šumava Region 03013
Suso (H. von Berg) 05960
Susquehanna Indians 15756
Suvorov, Aleksandr Vasil'evič 17090, 17093, 17114
Švehla, Josef 03246
Sverdrup, Otto 09797
Světlá, Karolina 02905
Sweden 15421
Swiętochowski, Aleksander 10178
Switzerland 15568, 15569
Széchenyi, István 06453
Szentendre Art School 06510
Szőnyi, István 06544
Taber, George H., Collection 16624
Tagore, Rabindranath 06634, 06830
Tait Collection 00531
Talich, Václav 02850
Talkington Collection 15167
Tasso, Torquato 07859
Tate, Henry 00552

Tatra Mountains 10516
Tavel, Rudolf von 12075
Tegner, Rudolph 03377
Tell, Wilhelm 11985, 12083
Tennyson, Alfred Lord 13155
Terry, Dame Ellen 13533
Terry, Jose Antonia 00413
Tesla, Nicola 17461
Tessai, Tomioka 08522
Tetmajer, K. 10279
Thai 00433
Theime and Hamilton Collections 14646
Thiery, Michel 01090
Thoma, Hans 05305
Thomas, Joseph and Astrid, Collection 16561
Thoreau, Henry David 14270, 14272, 14845
Thornton, William 16762
Thorvaldsen, Bertel 03524
Tibet 06801, 13828, 16471
Tiffany, Louis C., Collection 14841
Tilghman, Bill 14107
Tilley, Leonard 01975
Timirjazev, Kliment Arkad'evič 17192
Timmermans, Felix 01167
Tissot, Victor 11981
Titian, Vecelli 07782
Tlingit Indians 13694, 15051, 15052, 16026, 16402, 16403
Todorov, Petko J. 01573
Tokagawa, Ieyasu 08504
Tokugawa Collection 08405
Tolstoj, Lev Nikolaevič 17056, 17186, 17195
Tom Collection 14780
Tomimoto, Kenkichi 08246
Tonkawa Indians 15952
Tordenskiold Collection 09673
Tordenskiold, Petter Wessel 09891
Tornyai, János 06424
Torres, Julio Romero de 11164
Torricelli, Evangelista 07412
Toscanini, Arturo 07269, 07737
Toulouse-Lautrec, Henri de 03910
Toyotomi, Hideyoshi 08347, 08402
Trainer Collection 13965
Trakl, Georg 00781
Třebízský, Václav Beneš 03067
Třebízský, V.B. 03290
Trent Collection 14448
Troelstra Collection 09219
Truman, Harry S. 14950, 14951
Trumpeldor, Joseph 07144
Tschan Collection 11899
Tschudin, Dr. W. Fr., Bequest 11924
Tsimshian Indians 15051, 15378
Tsouderos, E. 06123
Tsubouchi, Sohyo 08582
Tucović, Dimitrij 17495
Tukuna 11280
Tumanjan, Ovanes 17035
Turgenev, Ivan Sergeevič 17242, 17293
Turner, J. M. W. 14398, 14959
Turtiainen, Olavi, Collection 03745
Tuwim, Julian 10454
Twain, Mark 14824, 14841, 14843
Tyl, Josef Kajetán 03048
Tyler, John 14114
Uilenspiegel, Tijl 01047
Uitz, Béla 06477
Ukraine 01767, 01933, 01937, 01938, 01999, 02182, 02462, 02485, 02545, 02555, 02556, 14224, 15651
Umezawa, Hikotaro, Collection 08584
Unamuno y Jugo, Miguel de 11453
Uniacke, Richard John 02180
Ute Indians 13906, 14076, 14390, 14608
Václavek, Bedřich 02892
Valencia, Guillermo 02766
Valéry, Paul 04492

Valetin, André   12053
Van Buren, Martin   15064
Van Dyck, Albert, Collection   01230
Van Heurck, H., Collections   00933
Van Humbeeck, Pierre   01147
Vanderbilt Collection   15538
Van de Velde, Henry   01000
VanDoren, Emiel   01075
VanEss Collection   15756
Vaňorný, Otmar   03326
Vanvitelli, Luigi   07315
Vapcarov, Nikola Jonkov   01550
Vasarely, Victor   04127, 06478
Vasari, Giorgio   07188
Vazov, Ivan   01555, 01657, 01676
Vega Carpio, Lope Felix   11278
Vela, Vincenzo   12117
Velarde, Pedro   11383
Verdaguer, Jacinto   11097
Verdi, Giuseppe   07286
Veres, Péter   06352
Verhaeren, Emile   01240, 01254
Verne, Jules   03922
Vesalius, Andreas   11922
Vigeland, Gustav   09809
Viking   02340
Vinje, Å. O.   09915
Vlaicu, Aurel   10653
Voiture, Vincent   03922
Vokes Collection   13048
Volkmann, Robert   04884
Volta, Alessandro   07378
Vondel, Joos van de, Collection
   09002
VonImhoff, Berthold   02348
Vörösmarty, Mihály   06427
Vrchlický, Jaroslav   02934
Vulcan, Iosif   10754
Wäber, Johann, Collection   11946
Wagner-De Wit Collection   09251
Wágner, Josef   02990
Wagner, Richard   04706, 05259
Walker, Dr. Mary   15783
Wallen Collection   15786
Wallenstein, Albrecht von, Herzog von
   Friedland   02908
Walser, Martin   05311
Walter, John   01930
Walton, Izaak   13485
Wampler Collection   16526
Warner, Anna and Susan   16847
Warren Collection   14004
Washington, Booker T.   14828, 16634
Washington, George   13661, 15498,
   15614, 15615, 15659, 16467, 16671,
   16672, 16729, 16739, 16786
Watts, G. F.   12874
Wayne, Anthony   14789
Weatherhead and Tannenbaum
   Collection   14646
Weatherly, Joe   14346
Weber, Carl Maria von   05446
Weber, Friedrich Wilhelm   05213
Wedekind, Frank   12110
Wedgewood Collection   16387
Wegener, Alfred   05139
Weinberg, Elisabeta and Moise,
   Collection   10672
Weissenkircher, Hans Adam   00671
Welk, Ehm   04572
Wellington, Arthur, Duke of   12621,
   13030
Wellington, Arthur Wellesley   01305
Wellington Collection   15440
Welti, Altert   12173
Wentworth, William Charles   00590
Werner, William H., Collection   13709
Wessel, Johan Herman   03479
West Africa   13913
Wheeler, Candace, Collection   14841
Wheeler, Shang, Decoy Collection
   14536
White, Alvan N., Collection   16391
Whitman, Marcus   16712
Whitman, Walt   14929

Whitney, Eli   13750
Whitney, Eli, Collection   13750
Wieczorek, Józef   10209
Wiegersma, H., Collection   09018
Wiegersma, Hendrik   09080
Wieland, Christoph M.   04949, 05108,
   05311
Wielopolski Family   10327
Wiertz, Antoine   01031
Wiggin, Albert H., Collection   13932
Wijnants, Ernest   01180
Wikström, Emil   03868
Wilberforce, William   13112
Wilbour Library   13991
Willard, Archibald M.   16826
Willard, Frances E.   14526
Willet Collection   12767
Williams, Alfred   13525
Williamson, J. C., Collection   00531
Willis Collection   10988
Wilson, Woodrow   16476, 16779
Winchester, James   14697
Winckelmann, J. J.   05062
Wittgenstein, Ludwig   00706
Wolf, Hugo   00752
Wolfe, Thomas   13733
Wölfli, Adolf, Bequest   11949
Wood, Grant, Collection   14348
Woodlands Indians   13967
Woolett, William L., Jr.   16664
Wordsworth, William   12869, 13016
Wores, Theodore   16298
Wrede, Carl Henrik   03668
Wrede, Mathilda, Collection   03668
Wright Brothers   15328
Wright, Frank Lloyd   14164, 15499
Wright, W. Lloyd, Collection   16739
Wright, Wilbur   14803
Wybicki, Józef   10112
Wycliff, John   05665
Wyczółkowski, Leon   10133
Wyeth, Andrew   14100, 14791
Wyeth Collection   16889
Yakovlev Collection   16732
Yamaguchi Collection   08189
Yamaguti, Satyu   08554
Yamamoto, Kanae   08600
Ybl, Ervin   06501
Yeats, William Butler   07020
Yokoyama, Taikan   08586
Yokuts Indians   14681
Yoruba Collection   09032
Yoshida, Isoya   08454
Young, Brigham   16173
Young, Gen. Edward, Collection
   14195
Yrurtia, Rogelio   00085
Zabotinsky, Zeev   07135
Zachanassian, C., Collection   12054
Zaimov, Stojan   01618
Zaimov, Vladimir   01618
Zaleski, B.   10279
Zambaccian, Krikor, Collection
   10672
Zawadzki, Aleksander   10155
Zegadłowicz, Emil   10183
Zeiß, Carl   04823
Zeppelin, Ferdinand Graf von   05824
Żeromski, Stefan   10213, 10302,
   10376
Zetkin, Clara   04637, 05118
Zhou Enlai   02627
Zichy, Mihály   06540
Ziegler, Alfred, Collection   16398
Zille, Heinrich   04622, 04992, 05556
Zirkenbach, K., Collection   01020
Ziya Gökalp, Mehmed   12492
Zorn, Anders   11767
Zorrilla, José de   11588
Zrinyi family   06517
Žukovskij, Nikolaj Egorovič   17214
Zuni Indians   14181
Županчič, Oton   17790
Zwingli, Huldrych   12286

Subject Index

Aeronautics
Argentina
  Buenos Aires 00137
  Ensenada 00209
  Mendoza 00274
Australia
  Alice Springs 00441
  Beverley 00457
  Brisbane 00461
  Bullcreek 00466
  Melbourne 00532
  Mundingburra 00539
Brazil
  São Paulo 01510
Canada
  Calgary 01828
  Edmonton 01925
  Gander 01977
  Harbour Grace 02029
  Moose Jaw 02174
  Ottawa 02229, 02233
  Richmond 02305
  Sioux Lookout 02393
  Wetaskiwin 02526
  Winnipeg 02558
Denmark
  Egeskov Kraerndrup Fyn 03380
Finland
  Helsinki 03707
  Tampere 03866
France
  Meudon 04253
Germany, Federal Republic
  Appen 05191
  Berlin 05290
  Bückeburg 05363
  Friedrichshafen 05483
  Gersfeld 05501
  Hamburg 05529, 05540
  Meersburg 05752
  München 05785
  Neu-Isenburg 05824
Israel
  Tel Aviv 07140
Italy
  Roma 07850
  Torino 08028
  Vigna di Valle 08149
  Vizzoia Ticino 08156
Japan
  Nagoya 08404
Netherlands
  Schiphol 09325
  Soesterberg 09365
Pakistan
  Peshawar 09951
Philippines
  Pasay 10077
Poland
  Kraków 10238
Portugal
  Alverca 10533
Spain
  Madrid 11299
Switzerland
  Dübendorf 12006
  Lauterbrunnen 12104
  Luzern 12136
Thailand
  Bangkok 12373
United Kingdom
  Aldershot 12619
  Biggleswade 12703

  Bridlington 12761
  Edinburgh 12961
  Helston 13055
  Ilchester 13082
United States
  Alamo TX 13632
  Bellevue NE 13853
  Brooks Air Force Base TX
  13995
  Cheyenne WY 14151
  Cleveland OH 14225
  Cordele GA 14287
  Dayton OH 14357
  Dover DE 14424
  Durham NC 14447
  Eglin Air Force Base FL 14479
  Elmira NY 14496
  Escanaba MI 14513
  Florence SC 14583
  Fort Rucker AL 14638
  Fort Worth TX 14654, 14655
  Franklin WI 14664
  Hagerstown IN 14803
  Hammondsport NY 14814
  Harlingen TX 14829
  Helena MT 14861
  Houston TX 14918
  Huntsville AL 14932
  Los Angeles CA 15237
  Manteo NC 15328
  Mesilla NM 15376
  Minden NE 15419
  Mitchell IN 15433
  Muskogee OK 15513
  New London CT 15582
  Nome AK 15686
  Pensacola FL 15841
  Pittsburgh PA 15922
  Quantico VA 16022
  St Louis MO 16188, 16190
  San Antonio TX 16240
  San Diego CA 16251
  Scituate MA 16344
  Seattle WA 16354
  Toms River NJ 16590
  Washington DC 16752
  Windsor Locks CT 16905
  Winslow AZ 16912
  Wright-Patterson AFB OH
  16941
USSR
  Gagarin 17040
  Kaluga 17060
  Moskva 17173, 17193, 17214
Venezuela
  Maracay 17409
Zimbabwe
  Gwelo 17867
Agricultural machinery
Algeria
  Alger 00022
  Oran 00037
  Tazoult 00042
Australia
  Colac 00478
  Cunderdin 00483
  Franklin 00495
  Kadina 00508
  Spalding 00573
  Swan Hill 00575
Belgium
  Jehay-Bodegnée 01126
  Mortroux 01199

  Neufchâteau 01210
  Schelle 01250
  Wommelgem 01315
  Xhoris 01316
Canada
  Bonshaw 01802
  Chilliwack 01870
  Cottonwood 01887
  Eddystone 01922
  Elkhorn 01944
  Fort Langley 01959
  Frobisher 01974
  Grandview 01998
  Hamiota 02026
  Innisfail 02043
  Maple Creek 02119
  North Battleford 02206
  Readlyn 02291
  St. Catherines 02328
  Stratford 02411
Czechoslovakia
  Kačina 03004
Denmark
  Auning 03367
  Lintrup 03487
Finland
  Helsinki 03704
  Kerava 03763
  Kokemäki 03765
France
  Saintes-Maries-de-la-Ville 04476
Germany, Democratic Republic
  Alt Schwerin 04567
Germany, Federal Republic
  Bayreuth 05256
  Husum 05585
  Karolinenkoog 05614
  Kraichtal 05669
  Stuttgart 05931
Israel
  Haifa 07060
  Hanita Kibbutz 07065
  Jerusalem 07093
  Nazareth 07112
Italy
  Sutri 08004
Malta
  Rabat 08802
Netherlands
  Allingawier 08953
  Broek Op Langendijk 09049
  Heille 09178
  Heinenoord 09179
New Zealand
  Geraldine 09491
Norway
  Egersund 09654
South Africa
  Grahamstown 10883
Switzerland
  Coffrane 11994
  Eschikon 12012
  Kiesen 12077
United Kingdom
  Church Stretton 12863
  Lacock 13123
  Reading 13387
  Wilmington 13577
  Wrexham 13601
United States
  Annandale VA 13707
  Archbold OH 13718
  Auburn NY 13761

  Carrollton MS 14071
  Cassville WI 14081
  Klamath Falls OR 15074
  Logan UT 15222
  Madison SD 15292
  Makoti ND 15304
  Mandan ND 15315
  Murdo SD 15507
  Portland OR 15981
  Roseburg OR 16146
  Rugby ND 16152
  Russell Springs KS 16153
  Sabetha KS 16155
  Selkirk NY 16365
  Stuttgart AR 16508
  Tifton GA 16578
  West Fargo ND 16837
Agriculture *(see also* Horticulture;
Farms and farming)
Angola
  Luanda 00051
Argentina
  Pergamino 00298
Austria
  Bad Wimsbach-Neydharting
  00629
  Maria Saal 00733
  Stübing bei Graz 00817
  Wien 00900, 00901
Belgium
  Beveren 00966
  Boekhoute 00970
  Brecht 00981
  Essen 01069
  Lahamaide 01139
  Lembeke 01143
  Massemen 01179
  Poperinge 01234
Canada
  Austin 01771
  Baddeck 01774
  Barrie 01784
  Beausejour 01791
  Blind River 01799
  Cartwright 01851
  Cheticamp 01867
  Comber 01882
  Girouxville 01981
  Gore Bay 01987
  Guelph 02009
  High River 02034
  Kirkland Lake 02070
  La Pocatière 02083
  Madoc 02111
  Merrickville 02130
  Milton 02137
  Minesing 02139
  New Ross 02195
  Peace River 02245
  Port Rowan 02270
  Red Deer 02292
  Revelstoke 02303
  Richmond 02305
  Roblin 02310
  Saanichton 02319
  Trois-Rivières 02467
  Williams Lake 02534
Chile
  Linares 02587
Cuba
  La Habana 02801
Czechoslovakia
  Horažďovice 02966

Kačina   03004
Kutná Hora   03049
Nitra   03117
Pezinok   03152
Praha   03210
Denmark
Auning   03367
Horsens   03439
Hørsholm   03441
Maribo   03492
Nørager   03499
Odense   03513
Viborg   03581
Egypt
Cairo   03620
Dokki   03640
Finland
Helsinki   03704
Kerava   03763
Lieksa   03787
Paattinen   03815
Rymättylä   03848
Yläne   03895
Germany, Democratic Republic
Alt Schwerin   04567
Dermbach   04659
Kloster Vessra   04845
Worbis   05134
Germany, Federal Republic
Adelsheim   05168
Bad Nauheim   05225
Bamberg   05248
Hersbruck   05575
Rüdesheim   05898
Westfehmarn   05976
Hungary
Budapest   06378
Keszthely   06434
India
Bombay   06614
Poona   06813
Israel
Haifa   07054
Italy
Alagna Valsesia   07161
Bentivoglio   07224
Tirolo di Merano   08019
Japan
Ise   08251
Miyazaki   08381
Yamato-Koriyama   08613
Luxembourg
Ehnen   08760
Netherlands
Apeldoorn   09009
Barger Compascuum   09025
Borculo   09039
Borger   09042
Broek Op Langendijk   09049
De Waal   09085
Ee   09107
Hattem   09171
Heille   09178
Hilvarenbeek   09186
Horst   09195
Leens   09213
Limmen   09241
Midden-Beemster   09258
Nijbeets   09269
Ospel-Nederweert   09280, 09281
Ruinerwold   09311
Schoonoord   09329
Stadskanaal   09367
Staphorst   09368
Tilburg   09377
Vriezenveen   09423
Vijfhuizen   09425
Warffum   09428
Zierikzee   09455
New Zealand
Hamilton   09496
Norway
Stend   09869

Pakistan
Faisalabad   09927
Poland
Nowy Jasieniec   10309
Szreniawa   10420
Wierzchosławice   10480
Portugal
Lisboa   10570
South Africa
Howick   10894
Johannesburg   10910
Switzerland
Aarau   11890
Altstetten   11903
Au   11913
Gurbrü   12055
Kiesen   12077
Ligerz   12116
Lottigna   12121
Marthalen   12137
Montreux   12145
Muttenz   12158
Neftenbach   12160
Oberweningen   12170
Rafz   12183
Reinach   12189
Riehen   12194
Unterstammheim   12266
Unterwasser   12267
Urnäsch   12268
Vevey   12275
Wädenswil   12279
Wiesendangen   12283
Willisau   12287
Zollikon   12310
United Kingdom
Edinburgh   12958
Gressenhall, Dereham   13022
Holywood   13072
Johnstown Castle   13095
Leicester   13135, 13136
Rugby   13406
Scunthorpe   13441
Sticklepath   13491
Wrexham   13600
United States
Abington MA   13621
Allison IA   13666
Alpena MI   13672
Askov MN   13739
Ballston Spa NY   13792
Big Rapids MI   13889
Bristol IN   13974
Bristol RI   13976
Brookings SD   13986
Brownville NE   14002
Caldwell ID   14027
Canyon TX   14060
Cassville WI   14081
Cedar Falls IA   14087
Chester MT   14149
Clinton NH   14230
Corsicana TX   14298
Dayton OH   14353
East Leansing MI   14462
Edinburg TX   14477
Ellsworth KS   14492
Fabius NY   14533
Fall River Mills CA   14548
Florence AZ   14581
Fort Atkinson WI   14592
Glen Rose TX   14725
Greenwood AR   14793
Gunnison CO   14800
Hermitage TN   14870
Hillsboro KS   14880
Holdrege NE   14890
Hopewell NJ   14907
Idaho Falls ID   14943
Jamestown ND   14992
Johnson City TN   15012
Kingfisher OK   15066
Knoxville TN   15081
Lakewood CO   15114
Lancaster PA   15120

Las Animas CO   15137
Las Vegas NV   15140
Leesburg VA   15157
Lexington OH   15179
Lincoln MA   15190
Lindsborg KS   15201
Littleton CO   15212
Livingston TX   15215
Logan UT   15222
Los Banos CA   15252
Lucas OH   15266
Lyons NY   15278
Manhasset NY   15316
Marysville KS   15343
Moline IL   15445
Monroe CT   15447
Montpelier OH   15466
Montville NJ   15472
Moscow ID   15488
New London NH   15583
Ontario NY   15757
Orange VA   15762
Oskaloosa IA   15779
Pensacola FL   15845
Perry OK   15851
Phoenix AZ   15909
Rexburg ID   16061
Richmond IN   16070
Richmond TX   16072
Salem NJ   16222
Salt Lake City UT   16235
San Antonio TX   16246
San Mateo CA   16285
St. Matthews SC   16460
Sedalia MO   16362
Somerset PA   16413, 16414
Spencer IA   16435
Sunset TX   16516
Tekamah NE   16558
Thetford VT   16572
Tifton GA   16578
Traverse City MI   16600
Troy AL   16608
Upper Sandusky OH   16657
Vonore TN   16696
Warehouse Point CT   16719
Washington DC   16756
Waterloo NY   16792
Wilber NE   16873
Wild Rose WI   16874
Wilmington DE   16890
Woodstock CT   16928
Zolfo Springs FL   16965
Zaire
Kinshasa   17848

Alabaster
Israel
Jerusalem   07081
Japan
Mito   08375
Korea, Republic
Pusan   08688
Puyo   08689
Poland
Torún   10435
Portugal
Viana do Castelo   10623
Viseu   10625
Spain
Monforte de Lemos   11371
Amber
Germany, Democratic Republic
Ribnitz-Damgarten   05003
Germany, Federal Republic
Erbach   05426
Poland
Malbork   10289
Amusements
Argentina
Buenos Aires   00101, 00116, 00142
Córdoba   00188
Mendoza   00276
Rosario   00326

Australia
Melbourne   00531
Norwood   00550
Austria
Bad Ischl   00621
Graz   00672
St. Pölten   00794
Wien   00873, 00881
Belgium
Antwerpen   00928, 00941, 00951
Bruxelles   01026
Brazil
Rio de Janeiro   01462, 01478
Canada
Sherbrooke   02385
Verdun   02491
Czechoslovakia
Chlumec nad Cidlinou   02911
Denmark
Aarhus   03360
København   03474, 03476
Finland
Helsinki   03700
France
Besançon   03997
Paris   04372
Germany, Democratic Republic
Bad Lauchstädt   04602
Gotha   04764
Reichenbach   04998
Germany, Federal Republic
Darmstadt   05380
Düsseldorf   05404
Kiel   05636
Köln   05659
München   05786, 05810
Greece
Athens   06083
Hungary
Budapest   06360, 06396
Ireland
Dublin   07009
Israel
Tel Aviv   07133
Italy
Faenza   07411
Forlì   07492
Milano   07646
Piacenza   07774
Pisa   07792
Roma   07903
Spoleto   07996
Trieste   08075
Venezia   08102
Japan
Nagoya   08405
Sado   08473
Tokyo   08543, 08563, 08582
Toyonaka   08592
Korea, Republic
Seoul   08693
Netherlands
Amsterdam   08999
's-Gravenhage   09340
Norway
Høvikodden   09708
Oslo   09802
Poland
Bydgoszcz   10132
Warszawa   10459
Romania
Bucureşti   10685
Iaşi   10736
South Africa
Bloemfontein   10839
Spain
Barcelona   11069
Jerez de la Frontera   11239
Madrid   11315
Sweden
Göteborg   11708
Stockholm   11808, 11809, 11841
Switzerland
Appenzell   11906
Bern   11951

Thailand
  Bangkok   12374
United Kingdom
  London   13185
  Stratford-upon-Avon   13510
  Ternterden   13533
United States
  Baraboo WI   13814, 13815
  Boothbay ME   13930
  Dallas TX   14335
  Denver CO   14389, 14397
  Farmington ME   14552
  Fort Mitchell KY   14629
  Golden CO   '14735
  Leadville CO   15152
  Morgantown WV   15477
  New Harmony IN   15570
  New York NY   15636, 15652
  Red Wings MN   16050
  San Antonio TX   16239
  Sarasota FL   16312
  Sedan KS   16363
  Somers NY   16410
  Stuart FL   16503
  Tonanwanda NY   16591
  Walterboro SC   16715
  Waltham MA   16716
  White Springs FL   16864
  Zolfo Springs FL   16965
USSR
  Abramcevo   16986
  Baku   16998
  Kiev   17076
  Leningrad   17121, 17132
  Moskva   17174, 17180, 17197, 17199, 17200, 17204, 17212
  Riga   17266
  Tallin   17306
  Tbilisi   17325
Yugoslavia
  Beograd   17462
  Ljubljana   17599
  Zagreb   17827

Anthropology (see also Folklore; Totems and totemism)
Angola
  Luanda   00053
Argentina
  Bahía Blanca   00067
  Bernasconi   00071
  Buenos Aires   00118
  Carmen de Patagonés   00167
  Córdoba   00194
  El Cadillal   00206
  Goya   00220
  Ingeniero   00228
  La Plata   00238
  La Rioja   00249
  Lomas de Zamora   00255
  Mar del Plata   00267
  Mendoza   00270, 00275
  Paraná   00293, 00295
  Pedro Luro   00297
  Posadas   00303
  Resistencia   00316
  Río Gallegos   00320
  San Jorge   00350
  San Juan   00357
  San Miguel de Tucumán   00364
  San Salvador de Jujuy   00381
  Tres Arroyos   00418
  Villa Rivera Indarte   00429
Australia
  Adelaide   00433, 00436
  Albany   00439
  Brisbane   00462
  Castlemaine   00473
  Coober Pedy   00479
  Fortitude Valley   00494
  Hahndorf   00501
  Hervey Bay   00502
  Hobart   00505
  Latrobe   00516
  Launceston   00518
  Melbourne   00529

  Nedlands   00541
  New Norcia   00544
  Parkville   00553
  Perth   00558
  Sydney   00577, 00578, 00580-00582
Austria
  Bad Deutsch-Altenburg   00615
  Bad Wimsbach-Neydharting   00628
  Graz   00674
  Hallstatt   00684
  Linz   00731
  Rosenau   00770
  Schladming   00798
  Wien   00837, 00861, 00868
Belgium
  Antwerpen   00929
  Gent   01079
  Lasne   01140
  Liège   01159
  Mons   01193
  Tervuren   01270
  Visé   01298
Bolivia
  La Paz   01341
Brazil
  Belém   01351
  Curitiba   01371, 01372
  Florianópolis   01375
  Fortaleza   01377
  Goiânia   01382
  Guaíra   01385
  João Pessoa   01389
  Juazeiro do Norte   01390
  Natal   01402, 01405
  Rio de Janeiro   01465, 01472
  Salvador   01499
  São Paulo   01511, 01521, 01530, 01531
  Sobral   01533
Bulgaria
  Plovdiv   01626
Canada
  Baie Comeau   01775
  Banff   01778
  Barkerville   01782
  Barrie   01784
  Brantford   01812
  Bridgewater   01814
  Brooks   01817
  Burnaby   01822, 01823
  Calgary   01830
  Churchill   01871
  Edmonton   01924, 01933, 01934
  Fort Smith   01966
  Gaspé   01978
  Grand Falls   01992
  Grondines   02007
  Halifax   02013, 02017
  Hazelton   02032
  Kingston   02060
  Lancaster Park   02080
  Lethbridge   02090
  Minesing   02139
  Mission City   02142
  Montréal   02158
  Moosehorn   02175
  Nakusp   02184
  Oakville   02212
  Ottawa   02231
  Red Deer   02292
  St. John's   02337
  Ste.-Foy   02351
  Sangudo   02358
  Saskatoon   02365, 02369
  Sherbrooke   02387
  Skidegate   02394
  Sudbury   02414
  Tatla Lake   02425
  Vancouver   02480, 02487
  Victoria   02499, 02506
  Winnipeg   02544, 02554, 02557
Chile
  Arica   02580

  La Serena   02586
  Linares   02587
  Osorno   02588
  Santiago   02592, 02596, 02601
China, People's Republic
  Beijing   02611, 02618
  Harbin   02633
China, Republic
  Taipei   02688
Colombia
  Bogotá   02694, 02695, 02700, 02713, 02718, 02720
  Bucaramanga   02723
  Cali   02725
  Cartagena   02730
  Cartago   02733
  Ibagué   02741
  Manizales   02744, 02745
  Medellín   02749, 02753, 02758
  Pamplona   02760
  Sogamoso   02778
  Sonsón   02779
Costa Rica
  San José   02797
Cuba
  La Habana   02802, 02810, 02812
Czechoslovakia
  Brno   02882
  Humpolec   02982
  Praha   03180, 03194
  Topoľčany   03283
Denmark
  Aaby   03354
  Grenaa   03408
  Hillerød   03423
  Højbjerg   03428
  København   03471
  Køge   03481
  Skive   03549
Dominican Republic
  Santo Domingo   03590
Ecuador
  Quito   03597
Egypt
  Cairo   03622, 03630
El Salvador
  San Salvador   03651
Fiji
  Suva   03667
Finland
  Mikkeli   03802
  Oulu   03813
  Rovaniemi   03842
France
  Angoulême   03931
  Bagnères-de-Luchon   03971
  Bayonne   03982
  Issoudun   04143
  Lascaux   04166
  Lyon   04217, 04218
  Marseille   04239
  Martigues   04242
  Nice   04307
  Paris   04358, 04383
French Polynesia
  Papéete   04561
Germany, Democratic Republic
  Dresden   04693
  Herrnhut   04806
  Jena   04824
  Leipzig   04872
  Magdeburg   04891
  Nordhausen   04937
  Saalfeld   05022
  Weimar   05099
  Wittenberg-Lutherstadt   05123
  Zella-Mehlis   05141
Germany, Federal Republic
  Abensberg   05165
  Berlin   05291
  Blaubeuren   05318
  Detmold   05392
  Erkrath   05428
  Erlangen   05429
  Frankfurt   05467

  Freiburg   05478
  Hamburg   05531, 05532
  Hannover   05555
  Heidelberg   05569
  Hildesheim   05578
  Köln   05656
  Lübeck   05714
  Mannheim   05736
  Marburg   05743
  München   05776, 05807
  Nürnberg   05838
  Oberschleißheim   05848
  Offenbach   05853
  Stuttgart   05933
  Tübingen   05955
  Würzburg   05998
Ghana
  Accra   06012
  Legon   06017
Guinea
  Beyla   06322
  Conakry   06325
  Kissidougou   06326
  Koundara   06327
  Youkounkoun   06329
Guinea-Bissau
  Bissau   06330
Guyana
  Georgetown   06331
Hungary
  Keszthely   06433
  Székesfehérvár   06503
Iceland
  Reykjavik   06555
India
  Ahmedabad   06559, 06561
  Baroda   06587
  Bhubaneshwar   06602
  Dehradun   06653
  Gauhati   06667
  Hyderabad   06699
  Kohima   06732
  Lucknow   06738, 06751
  Madras   06762
  Mangalore   06768
  New Delhi   06787
  Patna   06806
  Poona   06812
  Rajkot   06820
  Ranchi   06821, 06822
  Shillong   06833, 06834
Indonesia
  Tanjungpinang   06937
  Yogyakarta   06940
Iran
  Rasht   06964
Israel
  Be'er Sheva   07038
Italy
  Cagliari   07291
  Civitanova Marche   07367
  Firenze   07469
  Frascati   07497
  Milano   07625
  Novara   07702
  Parma   07745
  Roma   07846, 07865, 07880, 07882
  San Fortunato   07929
  Torino   08032, 08035
  Trebisacce   08054
  Verona   08132
Ivory Coast
  Abidjan   08160
Japan
  Abashiri   08171
  Akita   08173
  Asahikawa   08181, 08182
  Chiba   08196
  Kushiro   08323
  Misawa   08371
  Natori   08428
  Noda   08444
  Sapporo   08485, 08488
  Shizuoka   08505

Suita 08508
Tenri 08531
Yamagata 08609
Kampuchea
Phnom Penh 08643
Kenya
Meru 08651
Korea, Democratic People's
Republic
P'yongyang 08656
Korea, Republic
Pusan 08688
Seoul 08703, 08712
Libya
Tripoli 08749
Malaysia
Kinabalu 08783
Kuala Lumpur 08786
Kuching 08789
Melaka 08790
Penang 08793
Taiping 08795
Mali
Bamako 08797
Mexico
Chiapa de Corzo 08820
Guadalajara 08828
Jalapa 08834
México City 08850, 08855,
08857
Oaxaca 08872
Tuxla Gutiérrez 08893
Monaco
Monte-Carlo 08903
Morocco
Fez 08916, 08917
Meknès 08919
Tetuán 08926, 08927
Mozambique
Nampula 08935
Namibia
Windhoek 08941
Nepal
Kathmandu 08944
Netherlands
Amsterdam 08979, 09000
Berg En Dal 09032
Breda 09046
Cadier en Keer 09055
Cuyk 09059
Delft 09070
Emmen 09120
Groningen 09149, 09156
Leiden 09232, 09235
Rotterdam 09304
's-Gravenhage 09338
's-Heerenberg 09349
Tilburg 09380
New Zealand
Auckland 09468
Avarna 09473
Christchurch 09475, 09476
Dargaville 09482
Dunedin 09485, 09488
Hamilton 09497
Hokitika 09502
Invercargill 09505
Kaikoura 09507
Kaitaia 09508
Napier 09520
Okains Bay 09527
Ongaonga 09529
Patea 09536
Rotorua 09545
Russell 09547
Te Awamutu 09553
Timaru 09558
Tokanui 09559
Waipu 09567
Wanganui 09571
Wellington 09573
Niger
Niamey 09586
Nigeria
Argungu 09587

Benin City 09588
Ibadan 09589
Jos 09594, 09595
Osogbo 09600
Norway
Bergen 09627
Haugesund 09693
Karasjok 09715
Lillehammer 09740
Oslo 09803
Oman
Qurm 09920
Pakistan
Bahawalpur 09921
Hyderabad 09931
Saidu Sharif 09958
Swat 09959
Taxila 09960
Papua New Guinea
Boroko 09975
Paraguay
Asunción 09976
Peru
Arequipa 09991
Huánuco 09997
Lima 10012
Philippines
Baguio 10021
Bongao 10025
Cagayan de Oro 10027
Dumaguete 10032
Jolo 10034
Makati 10040
Manila 10059, 10062
Marawi 10069
Pasay 10073
Quezon 10086
Sampaloc 10088
Poland
Blizne 10125
Kraków 10232, 10234
Łódź 10277
Portugal
Braga 10543
Coimbra 10550, 10553
Lisboa 10588
Minde 10596
Nazaré 10597
Ponta Delgada 10602
Puerto Rico
Rio Piedras 10632
Rwanda
Butare 10800
Senegal
Saint-Louis 10816
Singapore
Singapore 10820, 10823
Solomon Islands
Honiara 10827
Somalia
Mogadishu 10828
South Africa
Beaufort West 10833
Dundee 10861
Estcourt 10874
Johannesburg 10897, 10913
Kimberley 10916
Pietermaritzburg 10945
Potchefstroom 10952
Pretoria 10956, 10960, 10968,
10977
Skukuza 10989
Stellenbosch 10993
Victoria West 11013
Spain
Barcelona 11089
Burriana 11124
Combarro 11155
Granada 11217
Las Palmas 11252
Madrid 11280, 11300, 11322,
11330
Mahon 11344
Muriedas 11383
Palma de Mallorca 11413

Requena 11438
Santa Cruz de Tenerife 11480,
11481
Solsona 11534
Valladolid 11593
Vélez Málaga 11598
Zaragoza 11633
Swaziland
Lobamba 11652
Sweden
Eskilstuna 11680
Switzerland
Basel 11931
Bern 11946
Brissago 11975
Burgdorf 11984
Fribourg 12019
Genève 12029, 12032
Immensee 12073
Moudon 12151
St. Gallen 12210, 12213
Winterthur 12299
Zürich 12319, 12336
Uganda
Kampala 12598
United Kingdom
Aberdeen 12605
Annan 12627
Arundel 12634
Batley 12675
Birchington 12707
Brighton 12767
Cambridge 12811, 12813
Colchester 12871
Farnham 12980
Hastings 13045
London 13176, 13185, 13200
Merthyr Tydfil 13290
Montrose 13299
New Barnet 13304
Oxford 13348
Salford 13427
Swindon 13526
Wednesbury 13560
United States
Alamogordo NM 13633
Albuquerque NM 13652
Andover MA 13700
Ann Arbor MI 13705
Anniston AL 13709
Arkansas KS 13723
Atchison KS 13744
Athens GA 13747
Augusta ME 13770
Auriesville NY 13771
Banning CA 13813
Baton Rouge LA 13829
Bayfield CO 13837
Beloit WI 13859
Berkeley CA 13873
Big Horn WY 13888
Bloomfield Hills MI 13908
Bloomfield NM 13909
Bloomington IN 13913
Boston MA 13936
Boulder CO 13944
Bridgeport CT 13968
Bristol RI 13977
Brooklyn NY 13990
Cambridge MA 14033, 14038
Camp Verde AZ 14046
Carlsbad CA 14067
Carson City NV 14073
Cathedral City CA 14084
Charleston SC 14118
Charlotte NC 14133
Cherokee IA 14145
Cheyenne WY 14153
Cimarron NM 14182
Cleveland OH 14212, 14214
Clinton OK 14231
Cody WY 14234
Columbia MO 14251
Coolidge AZ 14281
Corpus Christi TX 14295

Corsicana TX 14298
Crawford NE 14313
Crested Butte CO 14318
Crookston MN 14321
Dallas TX 14338
Davenport IA 14349
Denver CO 14389, 14391
Detroit MI 14407
Dragoon AZ 14434
Duluth MN 14439
Duncan OK 14442
East Prairie MO 14464
Ellensburg WA 14489
Escanaba MI 14513
Eureka CA 14520
Exira IA 14531
Fayetteville AR 14556
Fort Walton Beach FL 14644
Gainesville FL 14691
Garnavillo IA 14704
Giddings TX 14722
Goodwell OK 14740
Grand Rapids MI 14759
Greenwich CT 14792
Haddam CT 14802
Haines AK 14808
Hanover NH 14826
Harvard MA 14845
Hattiesburg MS 14848
Helena MT 14861
Hilo HI 14885
Holdrege NE 14890
Holyoke MA 14895
Homer AK 14896
Honolulu HI 14899
Houston TX 14913
Huntington NY 14928
Indianapolis IN 14955, 14962
Juneau AK 15019
Kearney NE 15034
Ketchikan AK 15050, 15052
Kotzebue AK 15085
Laie HI 15101
La Junta CO 15103
Lancaster PA 15119
Laramie WY 15127
Las Cruces NM 15134
Lawrence KS 15146
Lihue HI 15188
Lincoln NE 15193
Little Rock AR 15210
Littleton CO 15211
Los Alamos NM 15233
Los Angeles CA 15248, 15249
Lubbock TX 15265
Lyons KS 15277
McGregor IA 15282
Macon GA 15288
Madison WI 15297
Manchester CT 15309
Marquette MI 15338
Mesa Verde CO 15373
Miami FL 15382
Montpelier OH 15466
Mount Pleasant MI 15495
Nashville TN 15531
New Britain CT 15554
New York NY 15601
Newton KS 15675
Nome AK 15686
Novato CA 15721
Oakland CA 15725
Orlando FL 15766
Orono ME 15773
Page AZ 15795, 15796
Palm Springs CA 15802
Palo Alto CA 15806
Peace Dale RI 15829
Pella IA 15833
Peoria IL 15847
Philadelphia PA 15897
Phoenix AZ 15905
Pleasant Hill CA 15940
Pocatello ID 15948
Ponca City OK 15952

527

Port Angeles WA 15953
Portales NM 15966, 15969
Portland OR 15977, 15978
Price UT 15998
Princeton NJ 16001
Provo UT 16009
Pullman WA 16014
Reading PA 16045
Redding CA 16051
Richmond IN 16070
Riverside CA 16098
Rochester NY 16116
Rockford IL 16125
Rockville MD 16132
St. Ignace MI 16175
St. Johnsbury VT 16178
St Joseph MN 16180
St. Joseph MO 16185
St. Mary's City MD 16199
St. Paul MN 16208
St. Petersburg FL 16212
Salamanca NY 16217
Salem MA 16219
San Antonio TX 16241
San Diego CA 16255
San Francisco CA 16265
Santa Ana CA 16292
Santa Barbara CA 16295
Santa Fe NM 16303, 16306
Scranton PA 16347
Seattle WA 16355, 16358
Shrevenport LA 16384
Silver City NM 16391
Spalding ID 16433
Superior WI 16518
Telluride CO 16559
Toledo OH 16588
Topeka KS 16594
Trenton NJ 16603
Tucson AZ 16615
Tupelo MS 16630
Uncasville CT 16643
University AL 16650
Urbana IL 16659
Valdez AK 16668
Wahaula HI 16706
Walker MN 16711
Warrensburg MO 16723
Washington CT 16728
Washington DC 16757
Waurika OK 16808
Winston-Salem NC 16915, 16916
Upper Volta
Ouagadougou 16966
Uruguay
Montevideo 16977
USSR
Leningrad 17115, 17128
Moskva 17213
Vatican
Città del Vaticano 17369
Venezuela
Caracas 17385, 17390, 17391, 17398
Colonia Tovar 17403
Maracay 17408
Valencia 17415
Yugoslavia
Skopje 17720, 17722
Slavonski Brod 17728
Sremska Mitrovica 17747
Štip 17753
Strumica 17757
Subotica 17758
Tolmin 17767
Tržič 17778
Velika Gorica 17788
Vinkovci 17792
Virovitica 17793
Vranje 17796
Zaire
Kinshasa 17848
Lubumbashi 17851

Zimbabwe
Bulawayo 17863
Inyanga 17868
Marandellas 17869
Apiculture see Bees
Applied art see Decorative and applied art
Archeology (see also Archeology, Far Eastern; Archeology, Ibero-American; Archeology, Near and Middle Eastern; Christian antiquities; Classical antiquities; Historical ruins; Man, Prehistoric; Marine archeology)
Albania
Durrës 00010
Tirana 00017
Algeria
Béjaia 00029
Souk-Ahras 00041
Tipasa 00045
Argentina
Bahía Blanca 00067
Belén 00069
Buenos Aires 00118, 00141
Carlos Tejedor 00166
Chilecito 00173
Comodoro Rivadavia 00179
Córdoba 00182
Corrientes 00199
Goya 00220
Ingeniero 00228
La Rioja 00248
Lobería 00254
Longchamps 00257
Mendoza 00275
Mercedes 00279
Paraná 00295
Posadas 00303
Resistencia 00316
Salta 00336, 00339
San Antonio de Areco 00340
San Jorge 00350
San Juan 00353
San Miguel de Tucumán 00364
Santa Fé 00388
Sarmiento 00401
Tres Arroyos 00418
Zapala 00432
Australia
Beachport 00449
Melbourne 00526
Sydney 00583
Austria
Bad Mitterndorf 00624
Bregenz 00637
Eisenstadt 00649
Klagenfurt 00711
Leibnitz 00723
Lendorf 00725
Petronell 00755
Salzburg 00779
Warmbad-Villach 00822
Wien 00885, 00886
Wiener Neustadt 00904
Wieselburg 00905
Belgium
Aalst 00924
Antwerpen 00940
Arlon 00954
Aubechies 00957
Blicquy 00969
Brugge 00988
Bruxelles 01032
Buzenol 01035
Cerfontaine 01037
Charleroi 01039
Deinze 01050
Dendermonde 01052
Durbuy 01064
Elouges 01067
Flobeçq 01071
Gent 01078
Grobbendonk 01097
Hamme 01102

Han-sur-Lesse 01103
Hastière-par-delà 01105
Hoegaarden 01110
Hoeilaart 01111
Izenberge 01124
Jette-Saint-Pierre 01127
Knokke-Heist 01130
Koksijde 01131
Lommel 01171
Melle 01184
Merksem 01186
Mons 01190, 01191, 01196
Namur 01201
Nevele 01212
Nivelles 01217
Oedelem 01218
Orp-le-Grand 01229
Oudenburg 01232
Roly 01241
Ronse 01242
Temse 01268
Tournai 01279
Turnhout 01288
Velzeke 01290
Verviers 01291
Virton 01296
Vlijtingen 01300
Wavre 01306
Bolivia
Cochabamba 01337
La Paz 01338, 01339, 01341
Potosí 01343
Sucre 01344
Brazil
Fortaleza 01377
Goiânia 01382
Guaíra 01385
Macapá 01395
Recife 01431
Rio de Janeiro 01449, 01476
Salvador 01498
Brunei
Kota Batu 01546
Bulgaria
Asenovgrad 01547
Balčik 01549
Blagoevgrad 01557
Botevgrad 01558
Burgas 01562
Chaskovo 01565
Chisarja 01566
Etropole 01575
Gabrovo 01578
Jambol 01580
Kărdžali 01582
Karlovo 01584
Karnobat 01586
Kazanlăk 01587
Kjustendil 01590
Lom 01601
Loveč 01603
Madara 01605
Melnik 01606
Nesebăr 01608
Nova Zagora 01609
Orjachovo 01610
Pazardžik 01614
Pernik 01616
Pleven 01620
Pliska 01623
Plovdiv 01625
Preslav 01633
Razgrad 01634
Ruse 01639
Samokov 01642
Sandanski 01643
Silistra 01645
Sliven 01649
Smoljan 01651
Sofija 01663, 01664
Stara Zagora 01680
Šumen 01684
Targovište 01687
Tolbuchin 01689
Varna 01699

Veliko Tărnovo 01703
Vidin 01707
Vraca 01710
Cameroon
Foumban 01742
Canada
Baie Comeau 01775
Brandon 01808
Dauphin 01899
Elk Point 01943
Fort Saskatchewan 01965
Gaspé 01978
Gore Bay 01987
Grondines 02007
Invermere 02045
Morpeth 02178
Neepawa 02189
Ottawa 02231
Port Moody 02269
Shaunavon 02381
Sherbrooke 02387
Skidegate 02394
Toronto 02459
Vancouver 02480
Winnipeg 02547, 02554
Central African Republic
Bangassou 02572
Chad
Fort Archambault 02577
N'Djamena 02578
Chile
Calama 02581
Valparaíso 02605
China, Republic
Taipei 02685
Cuba
La Habana 02810
Czechoslovakia
1884 02838
Banská Bystrica 02843
Bardejov 02845
Benátky nad Jizerou 02849
Beroun 02850
Bílovec 02853
Blansko 02854
Blovice 02855
Bojkovice 02856
Boskovice 02858
Bratislava 02866, 02869
Březnice 02872
Brno 02880
Bučovice 02886
Budyně nad Ohří 02887
Čáslav 02891
Čelákovice 02894
Česká Lípa 02899
České Budějovice 02902
Český Brod 02904
Cheb 02908
Choceň 02913
Chomutov 02914
Chrudim 02918
Dačice 02920
Gottwaldov 02947
Hořice v Pokrkonoši 02967
Hořovice 02971
Horšovský Týn 02972
Hradec Králove 02976
Hranice na Moravě 02978
Ivančice 02986
Jesenice u Rakovníka 02992
Jeseník 02993
Jičín 02995
Jihlava 02996
Jílové u Prahy 02999
Jur pri Bratislave 03002
Kelč 03014
Kežmarok 03015
Kladno 03016
Klobouky u Brna 03020
Kojetín 03021
Kolín 03022
Komárno 03023
Kopidlno 03025
Košice 03030

Kutná Hora   03045, 03047
Kylov   03050
Levice   03056
Louny   03078
Martin   03089
Mělník   03091
Městec Králové   03092
Michalovice   03093
Mikulčice   03094
Mikulov na Moravě   03095
Milevsko   03097
Mladá Boleslav   03099
Mnichovo Hradiště   03101
Mohelnice   03103
Moravský Krumlov   03106
Most   03107
Mšeno   03108
Náchod   03110
Netolice   03114
Netvořice   03115
Nové Strašecí   03123
Nové Zámky   03124
Nymburk   03130
Olomouc   03132
Ostrava   03144
Pardubice   03148
Pelhřimov   03151
Piešťany   03153
Plzeň   03155, 03160
Počátky   03161
Poprad   03168
Praha   03172, 03179, 03196
Přelouč   03211
Přerov   03212
Prešov   03215
Prostějov   03221
Protivín   03222
Rakovník   03225
Rimavská Sobota   03226
Roztoky u Prahy   03235
Ružomberok   03237
Sabinov   03240
Sadská   03241
Sezimovo Ústí   03246
Skalica na Slovensku   03247
Slaný   03250
Smiřice nad Labem   03254
Spišská Nová Ves   03261
Strakonice   03265
Sušice   03271
Teplice   03279
Třebíč   03288
Trenčín   03291
Trutnov   03294
Uherské Hradiště   03300
Uhlířské Janovice   03302
Ústí nad Labem   03305
Valašské Meziříčí   03306
Valašské Klobouky   03307
Velvary   03313
Veselí nad Moravou   03315
Volyně   03318
Vsetín   03322
Vysoké Mýto   03325
Ždánice   03336
Žebrák   03340
Zlaté Moravce   03347
Zvolen   03351
Denmark
    Aalborg   03355
    Grenaa   03408
    Hobro   03427
    Holbæk   03430
Ecuador
    Quito   03597, 03605
Equatorial guinea
    Santa Isabel   03653
Ethiopia
    Addis Ababa   03654
Fiji
    Suva   03667
Finland
    Helsinki   03721
France
    Agde   03897

Aix-en-Provence   03902
Alès   03912
Angers   03928
Auxerre   03959
Bagnères-de-Bigorre   03970
Barcelonnette   03974
Bavay   03979
Beaucaire   03984
Beauvais   03991
Besançon   03998, 04000
Bourges   04020
Cahors   04033
Charleville-Mézières   04057
Château-Meillant   04060
Châteauneuf-sur-Loire   04064
Cháteauponsac   04065
Cognac   04082
Eauze   04109
Etampes   04115
Figeac   04118
Gevrey-Chambertin   04125
Grenoble   04130
Kaysersberg   04147
La Rochelle   04163
Martigues   04242
Mende   04248
Montbéliard   04272
Montbrison   04274
Nantes   04298
Nîmes   04317
Nissan-lez-Ensérune   04320
Nogent-sur-Seine   04323
Paris   04370
Perouges   04396
Perpignan   04397
Poitiers   04403
Quimper   04414
Saint-Dié   04449
Saint-Denis   04447
Saint-Gilles   04454
Saulieu   04481
Troyes   04524
Vienne   04548
Gabon
    Libreville   04563
Germany, Democratic Republic
    Potsdam   04969
    Schwerin   05043
    Stendal   05062
Germany, Federal Republic
    Alzey   05184
    Bad Homburg v.d. Höhe   05216
    Essen   05441
    Frankfurt   05463
    Freiburg   05477
    Homburg   05582
    Mannheim   05736
    St. Goar   05906
    Schleswig   05908
    Stuttgart   05939
    Worms   05990
Ghana
    Accra   06012
    Legon   06018
Greece
    Athens   06084
    Eretria   06111
    Larissa   06168
    Olympia   06218
    Patras   06227
Guatemala
    Ciudad de Guatemala   06319
Guinea
    Conakry   06324
Guyana
    Georgetown   06331
Honduras
    Tegucigalpa   06338
Hong Kong
    Kowloon   06341
Hungary
    Baja   06347
    Barcs   06353
    Budapest   06363, 06380, 06397
    Cegléd   06403

Csongrád   06404
Debrecen   06405
Eger   06409
Esztergom   06410
Győr   06415
Gyula   06418
Hajdúböszörmény   06421
Hódmezővásárhely   06424
Jászberény   06425
Kaposvár   06428
Kecskemét   06431
Keszthely   06433
Kiskunfélegyháza   06437
Kiskunhalas   06438
Kőszeg   06441
Miskolc   06448
Mosonmagyaróvár   06452
Nagykanizsa   06454
Nagyvázsony   06456
Nyírbátor   06457
Pápa   06465
Pécs   06468, 06469, 06474
Sárospatak   06482
Sopron   06489, 06494
Szarvas   06497
Szécsény   06498
Székesfehérvár   06503
Szekszárd   06506
Szentendre   06510
Szentes   06515
Szolnok   06518
Szombathely   06522, 06523
Tata   06527
Vác   06532
Vásárosnamény   06535
Veszprém   06538
Visegrád   06539
Zalaegerszeg   06542
Iceland
    Reykjavik   06555
India
    Gauhati   06669
    Madras   06762
Iran
    Rasht   06964
    Tabrīz   06967
Ireland
    Limerick   07023
Israel
    Abu Gosh   07027
    Alumot   07030
    Ayyelet Hashahar Kibbutz
    07035
    Bet Alfa   07040
    Bet She'an   07041
    Bet She'arim   07043
    'En Harod   07050
    Hazor   07066
    Jerusalem   07092, 07095, 07100
    Kiriat Tivon   07105
    Ma'abarot Kibbutz   07107
    Ma'ayan Barukh Kibbutz   07108
    Nahariyya   07111
    Petah Tiqwa   07115
    Ramat HaShofet   07118
    Ruhama   07122
    Sasa Kibbutz   07123
    Shivta   07126
    Tabgha   07127
    Tel Aviv   07138
Italy
    Ala   07160
    Asciano   07194
    Asti   07204
    Avellino   07208
    Avola   07209
    Baranello   07212
    Bedonia   07220
    Biella   07234
    Bobbio   07238
    Caltanissetta   07294
    Capua   07308
    Castrovillari   07331
    Cerveteri   07345
    Chiusi   07358

Cividale del Friuli   07363
Civita Castellana   07366
Civitavecchia   07368
Colle di Val d'Elsa   07371
Cologna Veneta   07375
Corfinio   07381
Cortona   07385
Cosenza   07387
Crema   07389
Cremona   07390
Crotone   07394
Eraclea Minoa   07403
Ferrara   07431
Fossombrone   07495
Galeata   07500
Gallarate   07502
Gela   07508
Genova   07517
Gioia del Colle   07531
Grosseto   07538
Grottaferrata   07541
Isernia   07555
Lecco   07572
Lentini   07575
Lipari   07577
Locri   07581
Lucera   07591
Marsala   07604
Marzabotto   07606
Massa   07607
Melfi   07612
Mirandola   07653
Modigliani   07666
Oristano   07708
Padula   07719
Pavia   07754
Pesaro   07764
Piedimonte D'Alife   07776
Pieve di Cadore   07780
Pizzighettone   07794
Potenza   07806
Reggio Emilia   07825
Roma   07835, 07876
Solunto   07988
Varese   08096
Japan
    Akiyo   08177
    Hamamatsu   08220, 08221
    Komatsu   08308
    Mitaki   08374
Jordan
    Amman   08630
    Irbid   08633
    Madaba   08635
Kampuchea
    Battambang   08639
Libya
    Cyrene   08742
Madagascar
    Tananarive   08773
Malaysia
    Kinabalu   08783
    Kuala Lumpur   08786
    Kuching   08789
Mexico
    Campeche   08817
    Guanajuato   08831
    México City   08850
Morocco
    Rabat   08920
    Volubilis   08928
Mozambique
    Beira   08929
Namibia
    Windhoek   08941
Netherlands
    Aardenburg   08950
    Alkmaar   08952
    Alphen   08955
    Amsterdam   08961
    Asselt   09019
    Beek   09027
    De Koog   09060
    Doesburg   09087
    Doetinchem   09088

Drouwen 09100
Echt 09103
Ede 09105
Geldrop 09137
Goes 09139
Goirle 09140
Gorredijk 09142
Groningen 09149, 09150
Hattem 09171
Heemse 09173
Heusden 09184
Hilversum 09188
Horst 09195
Hulst 09196
Leeuwarden 09217
Leiden 09233
Maastricht 09245, 09247
Middelburg 09256
Naaldwijk 09261
Oldenžaal 09274
Rhenen 09296
Roermond 09298
Santpoort 09315
Schiedam 09323
Schokland 09326
Sint Michielsgestel 09355
Sint Odiliënberg 09356
Sittard 09357
Sneek 09363
Stein 09369
Utrecht 09384
Valkenburg 09399
Venlo 09408
Venray 09411
Vianen 09412
Wijchen 09440
Wijk bij Duurstede 09441
Uzendijke 09443
Zeelst 09448
Zoetermeer 09456
Zutphen 09460
New Zealand
Okains Bay 09527
Nicaragua
Managua 09583
Nigeria
Ibadan 09589
Ife 09592
Jos 09595
Norway
Oslo 09780, 09810
Stavanger 09864, 09866
Paraguay
Asunción 09983
Peru
Ancash 09989
Huancayo 09996
Philippines
Cebu 10030
Manila 10048
Naga 10071
Pila 10081
Quezon 10085, 10086
Sampaloc 10087
San Pablo 10090
Poland
Białystok 10115
Biecz 10118
Biskupin 10124
Błonie 10126
Bytom 10135
Chełm 10138
Chojnice 10141, 10142
Chrzanów 10145
Cieszyn 10148
Częstochowa 10150
Człuchów 10154
Darłowo 10157
Dobczyce 10160
Elblæg 10167
Gdańsk 10170
Gliwice 10175
Głucha Puszcza 10177
Golub-Dobrzyń 10179
Hrubieszów 10192

Jarocin 10198
Kalisz 10204
Kamień Pomorski 10205
Kępno 10211
Kielce 10214
Kłdzko 10215
Kluczbork 10216
Kolbuszowa 10218
Koniecpol 10221
Konin 10222
Koszalin 10225
Kraków 10233, 10239
Krasnystaw 10250
Krosno 10253
Krosno Odrzańskie 10254
Kwidzyn 10258
Lębork 10262
Łęcna 10263
Legnica 10265
Leżajsk 10269
Łódź 10273
Łomża 10278
Lubaczów 10282
Międzyrzecz Wielkopolski 10292
Mława 10294
Młynary 10295
Nakło 10299
Nowa Sól 10305
Nowy Sæcz 10310
Odolanów 10314
Olsztyn 10319
Opole 10323
Pabianice 10330
Piotrków Trybunalski 10335
Poznań 10344
Przeworsk 10360
Puławy 10363
Racibórz 10368
Radom 10369
Rawa Mazowiecka 10371
Rawicz 10372
Ropczyce 10375
Rzeszów 10378
Sandomierz 10380
Siekierki 10385
Sieradz 10387
Sobótka 10395
Stargard Szczeciński 10401
Suwałki 10409
Szczecin 10415
Szczecinek 10416
Szczytno 10419
Szydłów 10423
Tarnów 10426
Tomaszów Lubelski 10428
Tomaszów Mazowiecki 10429
Toruń 10436
Trzcianka Lubuska 10438
Warszawa 10472
Wieluń 10479
Wieza Ratuszowa 10481
Wiślica 10483
Włocławek 10484
Wodzisław Ślæski 10486
Wolin 10488
Wrocław 10493
Zabrze 10510
Zielona Góra 10522
Zlotów 10523
Znin 10526
Portugal
Alenquer 10531
Chaves 10549
Figueira da Foz 10563
Lisboa 10573
Nazaré 10597
Santo Tirso 10613
Torres Novas 10622
Viseu 10626
Puerto Rico
Rio Piedras 10632
Romania
Adamclisi 10645
Agnita 10646

Aiud 10647
Alba Iulia 10649
Alexandria 10651
Arad 10652
Bacău 10656
Baia Mare 10658
Bicaz 10660
Bîrlad 10661
Bistriţa 10662
Blaj 10663
Botoşani 10664
Brăila 10665
Braşov 10669
Bucureşti 10674, 10677, 10679, 10682
Buzău 10688
Călăraşi 10689
Caracal 10690
Caransebes 10691
Carei 10692
Cîmpulung Muscel 10696
Cluj-Napoca 10699
Constanta 10704, 10705
Corabia 10706
Craiova 10709
Cristuru Secuiesc 10710
Curtea de Argeş 10711
Deva 10712
Drobeta-Turnu Severin 10716
Focsani 10720
Galaţi 10723
Hunedoara 10727
Iaşi 10730
Lipova 10740
Lugoj 10741
Mangalia 10743
Mediaş 10745
Miercurea Ciuc 10746
Năsăud 10748
Odorhei 10750
Olteniţa 10751
Oradea 10755
Piatra Neamţ 10757
Piteşti 10758
Ploieşti 10761
Rîmnicu Vîlcea 10768
Roman 10769
Roşiori 10771
Satu Mare 10773
Sfintu Gheorghe 10775
Sibiu 10776
Sighişoara 10779
Slatina 10781
Suceava 10783
Tecuci 10784
Timişoara 10785
Tîrgovişte 10786, 10787
Tîrgu Jiu 10789
Tîrgu Mureş 10791
Tulcea 10793
Turda 10794
Vaslui 10797
Zalău 10799
Rwanda
Butare 10800
Senegal
Dakar 10815
Sierra Leone
Freetown 10818
South Africa
Pretoria 10956
Spain
Barcelona 11089
Burriana 11124
Cádiz 11128
Llinars del Vallés 11266
Madrid 11296
Manacor 11349
Palma de Mallorca 11413
San Feliu de Guixols 11458
Sudan
Khartoum 11640
Suriname
Paramaribo 11650

Sweden
Arboga 11657
Arvika 11659
Borås 11663
Borgholm 11666
Ed 11674
Eskilstuna 11680
Falkenberg 11685
Falköping 11686
Falsterbo 11687
Falun 11689
Funäsdalen 11693
Göteborg 11699, 11700
Halmstad 11714
Härnösand 11716
Hässleholm 11717
Helsingborg 11718
Huskvarna 11720
Kalmar 11729
Karlskrona 11732
Karlstad 11734
Kristianstad 11737
Kristinehamn 11738
Laholm 11741
Landskrona 11742
Mariestad 11763
Simrishamn 11792
Skara 11793
Skellefteå 11795
Skövde 11797
Skurup 11798
Sölvesborg 11803
Stockholm 11835, 11840
Sundvall 11854
Trelleborg 11858
Trollhättan 11859
Uddevalla 11861
Uppsala 11868
Vänersborg 11874
Västerås 11877
Ystad 11887
Switzerland
Basel 11926
Buchegg 11980
Chur 11992
Estavayer-le-Lac 12013
Fribourg 12020
Genève 12030
Lausanne 12098, 12102
Liestal 12115
Locarno 12118
Luzern 12130, 12132
Muttenz 12158
Neuchâtel 12161
Nyon 12165, 12167
Payerne 12177
Pfäffikon 12178
Reigoldswil 12188
Reinach 12189
Rorschach 12198
Schötz 12227
Sion 12236, 12237
Stampa 12249
Twann 12265
Wetzikon 12282
Zug 12312
Thailand
Bangkok 12374
Trinidad and Tobago
Port-of-Spain 12425
Turkey
Adana 12449
Afyon 12450
Alacahoyuk 12455
Alanya 12457
Amasra 12458
Amasya 12459
Ankara 12463
Antakya 12466
Antalya 12469
Aydin 12470
Bergama 12473
Bodrum 12474
Bursa 12477
Çanakkale 12484

Ruma   17692
Šabac   17693
Šarajevo   17704
Šarengrad   17705
Senj   17707
Šenta   17708
Šibenik   17710
Sinj   17716
Slavonski Brod   17728
Sombor   17734
Split   17741
Štari Grad na Hvaru   17751
Štip   17753
Struga   17756
Subotica   17758
Svetozarevo   17759
Tetovo   17760
Titograd   17761
Titov Veles   17765
Titovo Užice   17766
Tolmin   17767
Tuzla   17779
Varaždinske Toplice   17786
Vid   17789
Vinkovci   17792
Virovitica   17793
Vranje   17796
Vukovar   17801
Zagreb   17818, 17834
Zaječar   17838
Zenica   17841
Zrenjanin   17843
Županja   17844
Zaire
Kinshasa   17849
Mbandaka   17853
Zimbabwe
Bulawayo   17862
Inyanga   17868

Archeology, Far Eastern
Bangladesh
Dacca   00918, 00919
Mainamati   00921
Belgium
Morlanwelz-Mariemont   01198
Burma
Banbhore   01714
Myohaung   01722
Pagan   01723
Rangoon   01729
Shrikshetra   01732
China, People's Republic
Anyang   02609
Baoji   02610
Beijing   02613, 02615
Changping   02620
Fufeng   02626
Guangzhou   02629, 02630
Jinan   02635
Jiuquan   02637
Kunming   02638
Lanzhou   02639
Lintong   02641
Liquan Xian   02642
Luoyang   02644
Nanjing   02648
Nanning   02651
Qian Xian   02652
Suzhou   02662
Urumqi   02666
Wuhan   02667
Wuxi   02669
Xian   02670, 02671
Xianyang   02672
Xinhui   02673
Zhengzhou   02676
China, Republic
Taipei   02682
Cuba
La Habana   02809
Czechoslovakia
Lysá nad Labem   03081
France
Laval   04169

Greece
Corfu   06103
Indonesia
Denpasar   06888
Jakarta Kota   06906
Italy
Piedimonte D'Alife   07777
Japan
Abashiri   08171
Aomori   08178
Asahikawa   08181, 08182
Ashigarashimo   08186
Beppu   08191
Chiba   08196
Chikushi   08201
Chino   08202
Fukui   08207
Gyoda   08213, 08214
Hachinohe   08215
Hakodate   08217
Imabari   08248
Isehara   08254
Isesaki   08255
Kashihara   08284
Kawasaki   08288
Kisarazu   08291, 08292
Kobe   08298
Koganei   08305
Kokubun-ji   08306
Kumamoto   08313, 08314
Kurashiki   08316, 08320
Kushiro   08323, 08324
Kyoto   08341
Machida   08354
Matsue   08357
Matsumoto   08359, 08361-08363
Misawa   08371
Mito   08375
Miyagi   08379
Miyazaki   08382, 08383
Morioka   08384
Munakata   08387
Nagaoka   08395
Nagoya   08401, 08403
Naha   08407
Naka-Kambara   08410
Narita   08426, 08427
Nishi Tsugaru   08434
Noda   08444
Okayama   08452
Omiya   08457
Osaka   08463
Otaru   08468
Otsu   08470
Sado   08472, 08473
Saga   08476
Sakai   08480
Sanbu   08483
Sendai   08492
Shingu   08501
Shiojiri   08503
Shizuoka   08505
Soja   08507
Suwa   08510, 08512, 08513
Tagajo   08514
Takaichi   08516
Takamatsu   08519
Takayama   08528
Tenri   08531
Tokushima   08533
Tokyo   08535, 08536, 08577
Tomioka   08587
Tottori   08589
Toyama   08591
Tsukubo   08595
Tsuruoka   08597
Tsuyama   08598
Ueda   08599
Yamagata   08611
Yamaguchi   08612
Yokohama   08616
Yokosuka   08621
Yonago   08622
Kampuchea
Battambang   08638

Kampong Thom   08640
Phnom Penh   08645
Siemréap   08646
Korea, Republic
Kongju   08678
Kwangju   08682
Kyongju   08683
Pusan   08688
Puyo   08689
Seoul   08703, 08709, 08712
Malaysia
Merbok   08791
Mongolia
Ulan Bator   08912
Sweden
Stockholm   11830
Thailand
Chiang Mai   12380
Khon Kaen   12386
Nakhon Pathom   12392
United Kingdom
Durham   12936
Viet Nam
Da-Nang   17416
Hue   17426
Archeology, Ibero-American
(see also Art, Pre-Columbian)
Argentina
Andalgalá   00060
Bolívar   00072
Buenos Aires   00081
Cachi   00162
Carhué   00165
Catamarca   00168
Chascomús   00172
El Cadillal   00206
General Pico   00216
Martínez   00268
Olavarría   00289
Paraná   00292
Río Segundo   00322
Salliqueló   00333
Salta   00334
San Carlos de Bariloche   00342
San Miguel de Tucumán   00371
San Salvador de Jujuy   00383, 00384
Santa María   00394
Tilcara   00410, 00411
Vichigasta   00422
Villa Dolores   00427
Brazil
Natal   01402
São Paulo   01509
Canada
London   02103
Midland   02134
Pointe-Bleue   02261
St.-Jean   02353
Sept-Iles   02378
Yellowknife   02569
Chile
Chiu Chiu - Comuna de Calama   02582
Concepción   02584
La Serena   02586
San Pedro de Atamaca   02590
Colombia
Armenia   02689
Bogotá   02695, 02696
Meléndez-Cali   02759
Ecuador
Quito   03598
Italy
Genova   07516, 07526
Japan
Tenri   08531
Tokyo   08535
Martinique
Fort de France   08810
Mexico
Madero   08835
Mérida   08837, 08838
México City   08855
Monterrey   08867

Morelia   08869
Nayarit   08870
Puebla   08880
San Miguel de Allende   08883
Teotihuacán   08885
Tuxla Gutiérrez   08893
Tzintzuntzan   08894
Peru
Arequipa   09990, 09991
Ayacucho   09992
Ica   09998
Lambayeque   09999
Lima   10001, 10002, 10010, 10013
Trujillo   10017
Spain
Benalmádena   11107
Madrid   11280, 11301
Santiago de Compostela   11492
Tudela   11572
United States
Blakely GA   13905
Bloomfield NM   13909
Bloomington IN   13913
Bridgeport AL   13967
Carlsbad NM   14068
Coolidge AZ   14281
Crystal River FL   14323
Death Valley CA   14368
Delaware City DE   14379
Denver CO   14390, 14391
Des Moines IA   14402
Dragoon AZ   14434
Evansville IN   14527
Fonda NY   14590
Fort Benning GA   14594
Homer AK   14896
Huntington NY   14928
Indianapolis IN   14962
Julesburg CO   15016
Kingman AZ   15067
La Junta CO   15103
Lakewood CO   15114
Ligonier PA   15187
Long Beach CA   15227
Los Alamos NM   15233
Los Angeles CA   15250
Macon GA   15287, 15288
Mesa Verde CO   15373
Midland TX   15399
Mishawaka IN   15429
Morro Bay CA   15485
Mountainair NM   15500
Novato CA   15721
Odessa DE   15732
Panhandle TX   15810
Parker AZ   15816
Penasco NM   15835
Pensacola FL   15840
Phoenix AZ   15905
Ponca City OK   15952
Ramah NM   16035
Redlands CA   16054
Riverside CA   16096
Rockford IL   16125
Safford AZ   16165
St. Augustine FL   16168
St. Marks FL   16197
St. Simons Island GA   16214
Salisbury NC   16225
San Diego CA   16255
Saint. Augustine FL   16458
Santa Fe NM   16303
Savannah GA   16336
South Bowers DE   16421
Syosset NY   16523
Tallahassee FL   16538
Tucson AZ   16615, 16621
Twin Falls ID   16636
Uncasville CT   16643
Washington AR   16726
Wilson AR   16896
Window Rock AZ   16904
Wrangell AK   16940
Yreka CA   16957

Spain
  Barcelona   11092
  La Riba   11249
  Madrid   11332, 11336
  Olot   11386
  San Sebastián   11475
  Santa Cruz de Tenerife   11481
  Segovia   11503
  Sitges   11530
  Vilajuiga   11607
Sweden
  Stockholm   11821
Switzerland
  Aarau   11891
  Colombier   11997
  Kyburg   12084
  La Neuveville   12089
  Morges   12147
  Murten   12156
  Saint-Maurice   12206
  Samedan   12208
  Sargans   12217
  Saxon   12218
  Schaffhausen   12221
  Schötz   12227
  Solothurn   12240
  Stein am Rhein   12256
  Tarasp   12260
  Valangin   12272
  Werdenberg   12280
  Wildegg   12285
  Yverdon   12305
Turkey
  Amasya   12459
United Kingdom
  Abingdon   12613
  Bodmin   12730
  Canterbury   12821
  Eastbourne   12942
  Edinburgh   12965
  Honiton   13073
  Ilfracombe   13083
  Ledbury   13126
  Lincoln   13153
  London   13170, 13216, 13247
  Manchester   13273
  Maybole   13283
  Nottingham   13334
  Ripley   13396
  Tamworth   13527
  Turriff   13543
  Wolverhampton   13591
United States
  Aberdeen MD   13613
  Ainsworth NE   13627
  Alexandria VA   13660
  Alma KS   13670
  Auburn NY   13764
  Austin TX   13782
  Baltimore MD   13801
  Beverly MA   13886
  Brown Valley MN   13997
  Burwell NE   14020
  Cheyenne OK   14150
  Chicago IL   14156, 14163
  Claremore OK   14196
  Cody WY   14234
  Corning NY   14290
  Crawfordville GA   14314
  Darien GA   14345
  Dodge City KS   14419
  Eglin Air Force Base FL   14479
  Farmington UT   14555
  Frankfort KY   14658
  Front Royal VA   14686
  Garnett KS   14705
  Gillette WY   14723
  Green River WY   14773
  Hastings NE   14847
  Iraan TX   14970
  Jacksonville FL   14985
  Ligonier PA   15187
  Logan KS   15219
  Louisville KY   15257
  Madison WI   15295, 15297

Marietta GA   15332
Middleborough MA   15388
New Market VA   15585
Omaha NE   15751
Osage IA   15776
Oswego NY   15782
Pittsburg KS   15921
Plymouth MA   15945
Portland ME   15971
Radium Springs NM   16031
Riverhead NY   16094
Rome NY   16145
Sackets Harbor NY   16156
St Louis MO   16195
Sidney MT   16388
South Carver MA   16422
Spokane WA   16437
Toms River NJ   16590
Washington DC   16773
West Point NY   16848
Wilton CT   16898
Windsor NY   16907
Worcester MA   16935
Yorktown VA   16952
Uruguay
  Montevideo   16968, 16973
  Tacuarembó   16985
USSR
  Moskva   17216
Yugoslavia
  Beograd   17466

Art (see other Art headings; also
Decorative and applied art;
Drawing; Graphic arts; Folk art;
Painting; Religious art and
symbolism; Sculpture)
Algeria
  Béjaia   00029
  Tebessa   00043
Argentina
  Buenos Aires   00084, 00085,
  00100, 00110, 00122, 00125,
  00135, 00153
  Chilecito   00173
  Cipolletti   00176
  Colón   00178
  Córdoba   00189
  Hernando   00225
  La Plata   00242, 00244
  Los Toldos   00260
  Luján   00261
  Mercedes   00279, 00280
  Moreno   00283
  Morón   00286
  Olavarría   00290
  Río Grande   00321
  Rosario   00330
  Salta   00335
  San Antonio de Areco   00341
  San Fernando del Valle de
  Catamarca   00343
  San Isidro   00348
  San Lorenzo   00360
  San Luis   00361
  San Martín de los Andes   00363
  San Miguel de Tucumán   00365,
  00369
  San Nicolás de los Arroyos
  00377
  San Salvador de Jujuy   00383
  Santiago del Estero   00399
  Tilcara   00411
  Totoral   00415
  Valentín Alsina   00419
  Zapala   00431
Australia
  Adelaide   00433
  Burnie   00467
  Carlton   00472
  Castlemaine   00473
  Geelong   00497
  Hobart   00503
  Melbourne   00528
  Mildura   00534
  Perth   00556

Sydney   00577, 00584
Austria
  Bad Ischl   00622
  Horn   00691
  Imst   00692
  Innsbruck   00696, 00699
  Jedenspeigen   00703
  Salzburg   00779
  Wien   00848, 00871
  Wiener Neustadt   00904
Bangladesh
  Dacca   00918, 00919
Belgium
  Antwerpen   00932, 00937
  Brugge   00984, 00987
  Bruxelles   01003, 01016, 01030
  Charleroi   01038
  Ecaussinnes-Lalaing   01065
  Liège   01153
  Lier   01167
  Namur   01203
  Nivelles   01217
Brazil
  Campinas   01361
  Campos do Jordão   01366
  Cataguases   01368
  Fortaleza   01377
  Natal   01403
  Nova Era   01408
  Porto Alegre   01420
  Salvador   01486, 01491, 01493,
  01497
  Santana do Ipanema   01503
Bulgaria
  Balčik   01549
  Berkovica   01554
  Jambol   01581
  Kjustendil   01591
  Nova Zagora   01609
  Pazardžik   01615
  Pleven   01621
  Plovdiv   01628
  Razgrad   01635
  Rilski Manastir   01637
  Ruse   01640
  Samokov   01642
  Sliven   01650
  Sofija   01652, 01674
  Stara Zagora   01681
  Varna   01695
  Veliko Tărnovo   01704
Burma
  Mandalay   01718, 01719
  Moulmein   01720
Cameroon
  Douala   01737
  Fort Fourreau   01740
  Foumban   01741
  Maroua   01743
  Yaoundé   01746
Canada
  Banff   01779, 01780
  Burnaby   01821
  Calgary   01826, 01835, 01838
  Charlottetown   01863
  Churchill   01871
  Cobourg   01878
  Czar   01896
  Dawson Creek   01901
  Edmonton   01924, 01927, 01934
  Fredericton   01970
  Gaspé   01978
  Grande Prairie   01997
  Guelph   02010
  Halifax   02012, 02016
  Hamilton   02021
  Imperial   02042
  Kleinburg   02074
  Leamington   02088
  Lethbridge   02091
  London   02099
  Mistassini   02144
  Moncton   02145
  Montréal   02156, 02162, 02168,
  02170

Nelson   02191
North Battleford   02205
Ottawa   02227
Penticton   02248
Québec   02283
Regina   02294
Saint John   02334
St. John's   02336
Salmon Arm   02356
Sarnia   02359
Saskatoon   02360, 02364, 02367
Sherbrooke   02386
Stony Plain   02408
Toronto   02444, 02459
Vaudreuil   02490
Victoria   02496, 02503
Ville Saint-Laurent   02509
Wesleyville   02524
Windsor   02536
Winnipeg   02556, 02559
Yellowknife   02569
Colombia
  Bogotá   02716
Cyprus
  Nicosia   02831
Czechoslovakia
  Aš   02840
  Budyně nad Ohří   02887
  Chotěboř   02915
  Dačice   02920
  Děčin   02922
  Hlinsko v Čechách   02957
  Hořice v Pokrkonoši   02967
  Karlovy Vary   03009
  Klatovy   03018
  Kutná Hora   03047
  Litoměřice   03069
  Manětín   03085
  Nepomuk   03113
  Nové Město na Moravě   03121
  Nové Zámky   03124
  Ostrava   03141
  Pardubice   03149
  Polička   03166
  Praha   03177, 03187, 03195,
  03206
  Stará L'ubovňa   03263
  Veselí nad Lužnicí   03314
Denmark
  Hornslet   03438
  Lintrup   03487
Ecuador
  Quito   03607
Egypt
  Alexandria   03614, 03615
  Cairo   03618
Ethiopia
  Addis Ababa   03656
Finland
  Helsinki   03693, 03718
  Kemi   03761
  Maarianhamina   03791
  Tampere   03858, 03865
France
  Azay-le-Rideau   03969
  Castéra-Verduzan   04046
  Châteauroux   04066
  Lyon   04221, 04222
  Mont-Saint-Michel   04267
  Montauban   04271
  Montbéliard   04272
  Nancy   04294
  Nantes   04298
  Orleans   04330
  Paris   04347, 04370
  Poitiers   04405
  Saint-Dié   04449
  Sceaux   04484
Germany, Democratic Republic
  Dresden   04673
  Quedlinburg   04984
Germany, Federal Republic
  Bamberg   05249
  Bremen   05351, 05353
  Bruchsal   05360

Flensburg 05453
Freiburg 05475
Friedrichshafen 05483
Furth im Wald 05492
Goslar 05505
Göttingen 05510
Hamburg 05525, 05530, 05536, 05537
Husum 05586
Konstanz 05666
Mannheim 05736
Osnabrück 05862
Regensburg 05884
Rheine 05891
Wiesbaden 05981
Worms 05990
Ghana
Legon 06017
Greece
Athens 06053
Salonika 06254
Guinea
Beyla 06322
Hungary
Budapest 06381, 06382, 06395
Cegléd 06403
Debrecen 06405
Kecskemét 06432
Nyirbátor 06457
Pápa 06464
Székesfehérvár 06501
Szentendre 06510
Szolnok 06518
Vác 06532
Vaja 06533
Veszprém 06538
Iceland
Reykjavik 06549
India
Madras 06762
New Delhi 06797
Indonesia
Yogyakarta 06951
Iran
Teheran 06973
Iraq
Baghdad 06997
Israel
Bat Yam 07036
Herzliya 07068
Jerusalem 07071, 07089, 07100
Kefar Menahem 07102
Ramat Gan 07117
Rehovot 07120
Italy
Conegliano 07379
Napoli 07686
Roma 07839
Trento 08057
Korea, Republic
Seoul 08708
Lebanon
Beirut 08732
Luxembourg
Luxembourg 08763
Madagascar
Tananarive 08773-08775
Malaysia
Kuala Lumpur 08785
Mongolia
Ulan Bator 08912
Morocco
Fez 08917
Namibia
Windhoek 08940
Netherlands
Alkmaar 08952
Amsterdam 08989, 08993, 08995
Apeldoorn 09011
Arnhem 09015
Assen 09021
Delft 09067
Drachten 09098
Gouda 09145
Heino 09180

Laren 09210
Leeuwarden 09222
Leiden 09230, 09235
Loosdrecht 09242
Oss 09282
Rotterdam 09302
Netherlands Antilles
Curaçao 09463
New Zealand
Hamilton 09497
New Plymouth 09523
Rotorua 09544
Thames 09555
Timaru 09557
Norway
Drammen 09650
Larvik 09733
Pakistan
Lahore 09939
Philippines
Mandaluyong 10046
Manila 10049, 10054, 10060, 10062, 10065
Pasay 10073, 10074
Sampaloc 10087
San Pablo 10090
Vigan 10103
Poland
Biecz 10118
Bytom 10135
Człuchów 10154
Darłowo 10157
Frombork 10168
Gdańsk 10172
Gołuchów 10180
Inowrocław 10194
Kazimierz Dolny 10210
Kępno 10211
Kętrzyn 10212
Kraków 10236, 10239, 10242, 10249
Łańcut 10260
Łęcna 10263
Łódź 10276
Łowicz 10281
Nowy Sæcz 10310
Olsztyn 10319
Płosk 10337
Poznań 10352
Pszczyna 10361
Sieradz 10387
Sobótka 10395
Szczecin 10415
Warszawa 10457, 10462
Wolsztyn 10490
Wrocław 10497, 10502
Portugal
Angra do Heroísmo 10535
Aveiro 10537
Azambuja 10538
Caramulo 10545
Guimarães 10568
Lisboa 10581
Minde 10596
Ponta Delgada 10602
Torres Novas 10622
Romania
Alba Iulia 10649
Bacău 10656
Baia Mare 10658
Bucureşti 10672, 10675, 10687
Caracal 10690
Cîmpina 10694
Mediaş 10745
Sinaia 10780
Timişoara 10785
San Marino
San Marino 10806
Singapore
Singapore 10823
South Africa
Alice 10830
Bloemfontein 10840
Durban 10862, 10866
Pietersburg 10948

Pretoria 10966, 10972
Spain
Ayllón 11056
Balsareny 11064
Barcelona 11089, 11101
Cádiz 11128
Ciudad Real 11149
Córdoba 11166, 11167
Cuenca 11174
Gerona 11202
Granada 11205
Los Barrios de Salas 11271
Madrid 11281, 11283, 11290-11292, 11296, 11318
Martorell 11358
Mataró 11362
Montblanch 11373
Montserrat (Monistrol) 11374
Nájera 11384
Palma de Mallorca 11408, 11412, 11413, 11416
Peñíscola 11426
Ripoll 11444
Roncesvalles 11446
Sabadell 11449
San Cugat del Valles 11457
San Juan de la Peña 11461
San Lorenzo de El Escorial 11464
San Pedro de Cardeña 11470
San Roque 11472
Santa Cruz de Tenerife 11481
Santiago de Compostela 11492
Segovia 11508
Sevilla 11523
Sitges 11530, 11531
Tarragona 11537, 11541
Tarrasa 11544, 11545
Toledo 11558, 11563, 11565
Valencia 11578
Valldemosa 11596
Villanueva y Geltrú 11611
Villasobroso 11613
Zamora 11628
Zaragoza 11632
Sweden
Åmål 11655
Borås 11664
Eksjö 11676
Falun 11690
Helsingborg 11718
Kalmar 11728
Lund 11751
Malmö 11756
Mora 11767
Örebro 11780
Östersund 11787
Stockholm 11820, 11835, 11845
Trelleborg 11858
Uddevalla 11861
Ystad 11888
Switzerland
Basel 11933
Genève 12024, 12030
Le Locle 12107
Lenzburg 12110
Luzern 12131
St. Gallen 12212
Schaffhausen 12220
Zug 12313
Zürich 12314, 12332
Togo
Lomé 12423
United Kingdom
Ayr 12646
Bangor/Wales 12654
Darlington 12895
Edinburgh 12950, 12957, 12962
Hereford 13059
Ilkley 13084
Keswick 13101
Kidderminster 13104
Lichfield 13148
London 13245, 13246, 13249
Manchester 13268

Mansfield 13277
Margate 13278
Nottingham 13336
Penarth 13355
Southport 13480
United States
Albany NY 13639
Albuquerque NM 13649
Austin TX 13776
Baltimore MD 13811
Bennington VT 13865
Binghamton NY 13895
Boalsburg PA 13922
Brattleboro VT 13957
Bronx NY 13982
Brooklyn NY 13991
Brownsville TX 14001
Carbondale IL 14064
Carlsbad NM 14069
Centerport NY 14096
Chicago IL 14155, 14159, 14161, 14167
Cincinnati OH 14184
Cleveland OH 14213, 14225
Colorado Springs CO 14245
Corpus Christi TX 14294
Danville IL 14342
Davenport IA 14349
Decatur IL 14370
Duncan OK 14442
Easton MD 14468
Enid OK 14506
Erie PA 14510
Florence SC 14584
Franklin Center PA 14660
Freeport IL 14679
Gadsden AL 14689
Geneso NY 14711
Glens Falls NY 14729
Greenville NC 14788
Harrisburg PA 14834
Hickory NC 14874
Indianapolis IN 14960
Jamaica NY 14991
Katonah NY 15032
Kent OH 15045
La Veta CO 15144
Lexington OH 15179
Logan UT 15220
Loretto PA 15231
Los Angeles CA 15243
Lufkin TX 15269
McAllen TX 15279
Madison WI 15294, 15296
Manchester VT 15313
Middlebury VT 15390
Morgantown WV 15477
Nashville TN 15534
New Haven CT 15572
New York NY 15616, 15626, 15628, 15630
Newport RI 15671
Nogales AZ 15685
Nome AK 15686
North Salem NY 15707
Oberlin OH 15730
Ogdensburg NY 15735
Oneonta NY 15756
Oswego NY 15785
Peoria IL 15847
Philadelphia PA 15866, 15875, 15877, 15880, 15886, 15889
Pineville PA 15915
Portland OR 15977, 15979
Princeton NJ 15999
Providence RI 16004, 16005
Reading PA 16045
Redlands CA 16054
Richmond VA 16085
Salisbury NC 16226
Salt Lake City UT 16231
San Antonio TX 16248
San Marino CA 16283
Santa Fe NM 16303
Scranton PA 16347

Germany, Federal Republic
Darmstadt 05383, 05385, 05386
Detmold 05391
Eutin 05447
Forchheim 05454
Frankfurt 05460
Fulda 05488
Fürth 05491
Göttingen 05508
Hagen 05523
Homburg v.d. Höhe 05583
Mönchengladbach 05772
München 05778
Recklinghausen 05878
Wesel 05974
Israel
Tel Aviv 07143
Italy
Sassari 07956
Stupinigi 08000
Venezia 08112, 08114, 08115
Japan
Nishinomiya 08443
Norway
Bergen 09620
Haugesund 09692
Poland
Kielce 10214
Pieskowa Skała 10333
Tarnów 10425
Portugal
Lisboa 10572
Romania
Arad 10652
Braşov 10668
Cluj-Napoca 10697
Craiova 10708
Iaşi 10729
South Africa
Port Elizabeth 10950
Spain
Albarracín 11021
Antequera 11038
Ciudadela 11151
Jaén 11237
Madrid 11325
Sevilla 11520
Toledo 11557
Vitoria 11619
Sweden
Linköping 11745
Norrköping 11775
Stockholm 11827, 11833
Switzerland
Basel 11926
Castagnola 11986
Fribourg 12020
Genève 12023
La Chaux-de-Fonds 12086
Luzern 12131
Moudon 12151
Rancate 12184
Solothurn 12243
United Kingdom
Birmingham 12711
Glasgow 12999
Hove 13076
Huddersfield 13077
London 13246, 13247
Manchester 13275
Melton Mowbray 13288
Watford 13559
United States
Akron OH 13629
Ann Arbor MI 13706
Atlanta GA 13754
Baton Rouge LA 13827
Bowling Green KY 13947
Canton NY 14054
Champaign IL 14105
Charlotte NC 14134
Dayton OH 14354
East Lansing MI 14461
Fort Worth TX 14652
Goldendale WA 14738

Granville OH 14763
Houston TX 14916
Louisville KY 15254
Mobile AL 15440
New York NY 15651
Oklahoma City OK 15741
Raleigh NC 16032
Salem MO 16221
Springfield MA 16446, 16447
Storrs CT 16495
Terre Haute IN 16568
Wellesley MA 16824
West Fulton NY 16838
Wichita KS 16868
Williamstown MA 16881
USSR
Kiev 17081, 17082
Odessa 17236
Yugoslavia
Novi Sad 17629
Art, Greek and Roman (see also
Classical antiquities)
Austria
Bad Deutsch-Altenburg 00616
Enns 00652
Pischeldorf 00758
Denmark
København 03471, 03477
Finland
Joensuu 03745
France
Angers 03929
Antibes 03936
Bar-le-Duc 03975
Béziers 04001
Brive-la-Gaillarde 04028
Douai 04106
Ecouen 04110
Hagenau 04135
Lisieux 04207
Loudun 04212
Marseille 04232
Montargis 04269
Montpellier 04279
Paris 04367
Senlis 04489
Tours 04520
Germany, Democratic Republic
Halle 04794
Germany, Federal Republic
Berlin 05279
Bochum 05323
Bonn 05327
Essen 05440
Hamm 05543
Hannover 05548
Kassel 05621
Marburg 05739
München 05806
Münster 05813
Oberhausen 05846
Greece
Aiyani 06029
Alexandroupolis 06030
Anafi 06036
Argostolion 06043
Athens 06066
Canea 06088
Corinth 06105
Epidaurus 06109
Eretria 06111
Ioannina 06130
Istiaia 06132
Karystos 06147
Kastellorizon 06149
Kavalla 06151
Kos 06159
Kosmiti 06162
Lamia 06167
Limenaria 06176
Mandraki 06184
Mavropigi 06188
Mikonos 06195
Molyvos 06204
Navpaktos 06208

Neos Skopos 06214
Olimbos 06217
Olympia 06218, 06219
Oreoi 06220
Paros 06224
Pella 06228
Polygyros 06236
Pylos 06237
Salonika 06258, 06259
Samos 06260
Serrai 06263
Skyros 06271
Tegea 06281
Thasos 06287
Thira 06292
Volos 06302, 06306
Zakinthos 06310
Hungary
Budapest 06395
India
Baroda 06585
Italy
Agliè 07154
Agrigento 07155
Alba 07163
Assisi 07200
Bazzano 07219
Bene Vagienna 07222
Benevento 07223
Canosa di Puglia 07305
Castelfranco Veneto 07320
Castellammare di Stabia 07321
Catania 07333
Centuripe 07342
Guardiagrele 07543
Napoli 07681
Ostia Antica 07715
Palermo 07725
Ravenna 07818
Roma 07849, 07885
Terracina 08015
Tindari 08017
Venezia 08117
Vercelli 08130
Japan
Tokyo 08553
Libya
Marsā Sūsah 08744
Morocco
Rabat 08921
Tanger 08924
Volubilis 08928
Norway
Oslo 09785
Romania
Ploieşti 10759
Sarmizegetusa 10772
Sibiu 10776
Tîrgu Mureş 10790
Spain
Barcelona 11090
Lugo 11274
Madrid 11317
Valladolid 11590
Switzerland
Basel 11923
Bern 11945
Nyon 12167
Zürich 12314, 12318
Syria
Damascus 12341
United Kingdom
Manchester 13274
Yanworth 13604
United States
Ann Arbor MI 13706
Boston MA 13937
cambridge MA 14035
Chapel Hill NC 14110
Dayton OH 14354
Durham NC 14445
Los Angeles CA 15247, 15248
Malibu CA 15305
Norfolk VA 15688
Norman OK 15694

Rochester NY 16114
St Louis MO 16192
San Francisco CA 16264
Seattle WA 16357
USSR
Moskva 17184
Vatican
Città del Vaticano 17365, 17367,
17368, 17370, 17372
Art, Medieval (see also Icons)
Austria
Altenburg 00608
Friedberg 00656
Graz 00665
Herzogenburg 00689
Salzburg 00772
Sankt Paul i. Lav. 00792
St. Pölten 00794
Belgium
Brugge 00994, 00998
Namur 01205
Bulgaria
Preslav 01633
Varna 01693
Canada
Joliette 02048
Czechoslovakia
Liptovský Mikuláš 03066
Denmark
København 03463
Sønderborg 03556
Struer 03561
Finland
Mikkeli 03799
France
Bordeaux 04008
Cluny 04080
Douai 04106
Evreux 04117
Montpellier 04279
Narbonne 04300
Paris 04367, 04371
Tours 04520
Germany, Democratic Republic
Berlin 04632
Gotha 04769
Germany, Federal Republic
Bad Wimpfen 05238
Biberach a.d. Riß 05310
Essen 05442
Kleve 05642
Lübeck 05707
Mainz 05731
Oldenburg 05857
Stuttgart 05939
Tübingen 05954, 05957
Greece
Karditsa 06144
Monemvasia 06205
Zakinthos 06310
India
Calcutta 06623
Jhansi 06714
Shivpuri 06837
Italy
Benevento 07223
Palermo 07723
Pavia 07757
Teggiano 08009
Trevi 08061
Urbino 08090
Netherlands
Enschede 09126
Maastricht 09245
Norway
Oslo 09806
Poland
Tarnów 10426
Toruń 10431
Portugal
Evora 10558
Romania
Babadag 10655
Bran 10666
Braşov 10667

Spain
  Alquezar 11032
  Ampudia 11036
  Aranjuez 11040
  Barcelona 11073, 11081, 11088
  Barco de Avila 11104
  Burgo de Osma 11116
  Burgos 11117, 11119, 11122
  Cervera 11144
  Comillas 11156
  Córdoba 11160
  Daroca 11175
  El Escorial 11182
  Gerona 11198, 11199
  Granada 11214-11216
  Huesca 11227
  Jaca 11235
  Léon 11255, 11258
  Lérida 11264
  Lluch 11268
  Loarre 11269
  Madrid 11293, 11325
  Madrigal de las Altas Torres
    11343
  Orense 11392
  Oviedo 11401
  Palencia 11405
  Pastrana 11424
  Riofrío 11442
  Roda de Isábena 11445
  Santa María del Campo 11485
  Santillana del Mar 11497
  Seo de Urgel 11511
  Vileña de Bureba 11608
  Villena 11614
  Xátiva 11622
Switzerland
  Bischofszell 11962
  Chur 11991
  Lausanne 12097
United States
  Burlington VT 14017
  Cambridge MA 14034
  Chapel Hill NC 14110
  Durham NC 14445
  Honolulu HI 14902
  New York NY 15611
  Rochester NY 16114
  St Louis MO 16192
  San Antonio TX 16242
  South Hadley MA 16425
USSR
  Moskva 17198
Vatican
  Città del Vaticano 17373
Yugoslavia
  Beograd 17453, 17469
  Zagreb 17834

Art, Modern and Contemporary
Algeria
  Alger 00027
  Oran 00037
  Skikda 00040
Argentina
  Buenos Aires 00090, 00092,
    00140
  Humahuaca 00226
  La Rioja 00246, 00250
  Lincoln 00253
  Luján 00262
  Mendoza 00276
Australia
  Geelong 00497
  Mornington 00536
  Shepparton 00570
Austria
  Eisenstadt 00651
  Krems 00714
  Wien 00862, 00869, 00871,
    00890
Belgium
  Antwerpen 00944
  Bruxelles 01012
  Gent 01085, 01086
  Ieper 01119

Lièege 01150
Liège 01162
Oostende 01225
Veurne 01293
Brazil
  Belo Horizonte 01353
  Campinas 01362
  Feira de Santana 01374
  Rio de Janeiro 01438, 01460
  Salvador 01492
  São Paulo 01515, 01519
  Vitória 01540
Bulgaria
  Burgas 01563
  Jambol 01581
  Pleven 01621
  Plovdiv 01628
  Sliven 01650
  Sofija 01674
  Ştara Zagora 01681
  Šumen 01685
  Varna 01695
  Veliko Tărnovo 01704
  Vidin 01708
  Vraca 01711
Canada
  Brantford 01811
  Calgary 01830
  Downsview 01907
  Dundas 01917
  Grimsby 02005
  Grondines 02007
  Hamilton 02021
  Montréal 02160
  Ottawa 02230, 02238
  Owen Sound 02240
  Québec 02283
  St. Catherines 02327
  Saskatoon 02367
  Stratford 02410
  Sudbury 02414 .
  Toronto 02436, 02437, 02443,
    02448, 02457
  Vancouver 02486
  Waterloo 02513
  Weyburn 02527
  Winnipeg 02543
Chile
  Santiago 02595, 02600
Colombia
  Bogotá 02698, 02699, 02717
  Cartagena 02729
  Cúcuta 02734
  Ibagué 02740
  Medellín 02751
Czechoslovakia
  Banská Bystrica 02842
  Bratislava 02863
  Cheb 02909
  Dolný Kubín 02933
  Gottwaldov 02946
  Hluboká nad Vltavou 02959
  Hodonín 02961
  Horný Smokovec 02970
  Hradec Králové 02975
  Jičín 02994
  Jihlava 02997
  Karlovy Vary 03008
  Košice 03029
  Liberec 03059
  Liptovský Mikuláš 03066
  Louny 03077
  Náchod 03109
  Olomouc 03133
  Ostrava 03141
  Plzeň 03159
  Praha 03177, 03195, 03206
  Prešov 03214
  Roudnice nad Labem 03229
  Rychnov nad Kněžnou 03239
Denmark
  Aalborg 03356
  Esbjerg 03381
  Herning 03418
  Hjørring 03425

Holstebro 03434, 03436
Horsens 03440
Humlebæk 03444
København 03463
Randers 03527
Skive 03549
Tønder 03570
Ecuador
  Quito 03598
Egypt
  Cairo 03629, 03632
Ethiopia
  Addis Ababa 03657
Finland
  Dragsfjärd 03672
  Espoo 03674
  Helsinki 03691, 03693, 03695,
    03698, 03709, 03712, 03725
  Jyväskylä 03749
  Kemi 03761
  Lahti 03780
  Lapinlahti 03782
  Lappeenranta 03783
  Liminka 03788
  Oulu 03811
  Porvoo 03825
  Rauma 03837
  Tampere 03864
  Turku 03878, 03880
  Vaasa 03884
  Varkaus 03890
France
  Antibes 03936
  Aurillac 03953
  Belfort 03993
  Cagnes-sur-Mer 04031
  Cholet 04073
  Le Havre 04182
  Les Andelys 04193
  Les Sables d'Olonne 04196
  Marseille 04233
  Nice 04312
  Paris 04348, 04382
  Pau 04393
  Pontoise 04410
  Saint-Paul 04463
  Saint-Paul-de-Vence 04464
  Sète 04492
  Toulon 04512
  Vallauris 04534, 04535
Germany, Democratic Republic
  Erfurt 04717
  Gera 04749
  Görlitz 04762
  Weimar 05097
Germany, Federal Republic
  Aachen 05158
  Albstadt 05172
  Berlin 05269, 05272, 05274,
    05277
  Bochum 05324
  Bonn 05332
  Breisach 05347
  Bremen 05350, 05352
  Bremerhaven 05357
  Dortmund 05396
  Duisburg 05401
  Düren 05402
  Düsseldorf 05409, 05410
  Edewecht 05416
  Essen 05440
  Esslingen 05443
  Ettlingen 05445
  Hagen 05522
  Hannover 05548
  Heilbronn 05572
  Karlsruhe 05612
  Köln 05660
  Krefeld 05670, 05671
  Langenargen 05687
  Ludwigshafen 05721
  Mainz 05731
  Mannheim 05735
  Mönchengladbach 05771
  München 05778, 05808, 05809

Münster 05820
Nürnberg 05836
Oberhausen 05846
Oldenburg 05857
Recklinghausen 05877
Soest 05922
Stuttgart 05932
Tübingen 05952
Wolfsburg 05988
Worpswede 05991, 05992
Greece
  Ioannina 06130
  Salonica 06251
  Tenos 06286
  Volos 06305
Hungary
  Budapest 06373
  Győr 06415
  Gyula 06419
  Hódmezővásárhely 06424
  Kaposvár 06428
  Kapuvár 06429
  Kecskemét 06431
  Miskolc 06448
  Pécs 06470, 06471, 06477,
    06478
  Sárospatak 06482
  Szeged 06500
  Szentendre 06508, 06509, 06514
Iceland
  Reykjavik 06552, 06554
India
  Calcutta 06623
  New Delhi 06795, 06796
  Pillalamari 06808
  Ujjain 06859
Indonesia
  Ubud 06939
Ireland
  Limerick 07023
Israel
  Ashdot Ya'aqov Kibbutz 07031
  Dimona 07046
  Elat 07047
  'En Harod 07051
  Haifa 07053, 07058
  Petah Tiqwa 07115
  Tel Aviv 07143
  Zefat 07148
Italy
  Ardea 07186
  Assisi 07199
  Asti 07206
  Bologna 07245
  Brescia 07275
  Castellanza 07322
  Cento 07341
  Chieti 07357
  Cortina d'Ampezzo 07384
  Faenza 07414
  Firenze 07484
  Imola 07552
  L'Aquila 07563
  Livorno 07579
  Milano 07621
  Monza 07680
  Palermo 07722
  Roma 07838, 07839, 07843
  Rovereto 07914
  San Felice Circeo 07928
  Settignano 07975
  Termoli 08013
  Torino 08029
  Trieste 08073
  Vercelli 08129
  Verucchio 08139
Japan
  Ito 08256
  Nagaoka 08394
  Nagoya 08399
  Niigata 08430
  Sapporo 08487
  Takasaki 08523
  Tokyo 08576, 08578
  Yasugi 08614

Korea, Republic
  Seoul 08710
Liechtenstein
  Vaduz 08753
Netherlands
  Amstelveen 08960
  Amsterdam 08976, 08985
  Apeldoorn 09010
  Arnhem 09015
  Eindhoven 09113
  Leeuwarden 09220
  Maassluis 09244
  Nijmegen 09271
  Rhenen 09296
  Schaesberg 09317
  Schiedam 09323
  's-Gravenhage 09331
  Utrecht 09386
  Venlo 09410
  Zutphen 09459
New Zealand
  Christchurch 09476
  Masterton 09516
  Palmerston North 09534
  Rotorua 09544
  Wellington 09572
Norway
  Åsgårdstrand 09614
  Bergen 09631
  Høvikodden 09708
  Oslo 09782, 09784, 09785
  Trondheim 09888
Paraguay
  Asunción 09978
Poland
  Kraków 10243
  Żórawina 10508
Portugal
  Amarante 10534
  Caldas da Rainha 10544
  Lisboa 10587
  Ovar 10600
  Tomar 10621
Romania
  Babadag 10655
  Cîmpulung Muscel 10696
  Constanta 10703
  Galaţi 10721
  Limanu 10739
  Medgidia 10744
  Ploieşti 10759
  Sfîntu Gheorghe 10775
  Tîrgu Mureş 10790
South Africa
  Bloemfontein 10836
  Durban 10869
  Graaff-Reinet 10880
  Johannesburg 10904
  Potchefstroom 10954
  Stellenbosch 10999, 11001
Spain
  Cuenca 11172
  Granada 11210
  Lérida 11261
  Madrid 11316, 11324
  Mataro 11361
  Olot 11387
  Sevilla 11519
  Tarragona 11539
  Tossa 11570
  Valls 11597
Sweden
  Eksjö 11676
  Jönköping 11723
  Stockholm 11824
Switzerland
  Aarau 11889
  Basel 11930
  Frauenfeld 12015
  Frauenkirch 12017
  Genève 12023, 12037
  La Chaux-de-Fonds 12086
  Lausanne 12095
  Luzern 12131, 12133
  Rancate 12184

  Steckborn 12254
  Thun 12262
  Zürich 12324
Syria
  Damascus 12341
Thailand
  Bangkok 12361
Tunisia
  Tunis 12441
Turkey
  Antalya 12467
  Bursa 12478
  Eskisehir 12504
  Istanbul 12518
  Izmir 12532
  Yarimca 12587
United Kingdom
  Aberystwyth 12612
  Annan 12627
  Batley 12674
  Cambridge 12809
  London 13251
  Manchester 13274
  Southend-on-Sea 13477
United States
  Albuquerque NM 13651
  Alexandria LA 13658
  Alpine TX 13673
  Anadarko OK 13693
  Arlington TX 13724
  Auburn NY 13760
  Austin TX 13783
  Battle Creek MI 13830
  Beaumont TX 13844
  Bellevue WA 13854
  Bloomington IL 13911
  Brookings SD 13987
  Brunswick ME 14004
  Burlington VT 14017
  Canton NY 14054
  Champaign IL 14105
  Chapel Hill NC 14110
  Charleston IL 14115
  Charleston SC 14120
  Chicago IL 14166, 14169
  Cincinnati OH 14187
  Cleveland OH 14221
  Clinton IL 14227
  College Park MD 14241
  Columbia SC 14258
  Coos Bay OR 14284
  Coral Gables FL 14286
  Dallas NC 14329
  Dayton OH 14358
  Detroit Mi 14409
  Durham NC 14446
  Eugene OR 14519
  Fayetteville NC 14557
  Flushing NY 14587
  Fort Wayne IN 14646
  Fredonia NY 14676
  Fresno CA 14682
  Galliopolis OH 14698
  Grand Forks ND 14750
  Great Falls MT 14765
  Greensboro NC 14784
  Greenville SC 14791
  Hampton VA 14817
  Honolulu HI 14900
  Kalamazoo MI 15022
  Klamath Falls OR 15075
  Knoxville TN 15080
  La Jolla CA 15102
  Las Vegas NV 15139
  Lincoln NE 15194
  Los Angeles CA 15240, 15244, 15246
  Louisville KY 15254
  Macomb IL 15285
  Madison WI 15300
  Mansfield OH 15325
  Mason City IA 15345
  Memphis TN 15362
  Menomonie WI 15366
  Miami FL 15380

  Milwaukee WI 15416
  Minneapolis MN 15428
  Monterey CA 15456
  Muskogee OK 15515
  Nashville TN 15529, 15533, 15535
  New Harmony IN 15571
  New York NY 15597, 15609, 15619, 15625, 15633, 15634, 15639
  Normal IL 15692
  Norman OK 15693
  Notre Dame IN 15720
  Orono ME 15774
  Owensboro KY 15789
  Philadelphia PA 15872
  Pittsburgh PA 15930
  Plattsburgh NY 15938
  Portsmouth OH 15984
  Potsdam NY 15988
  Purchase NY 16017
  Racine WI 16029
  Rapid City SD 16041
  Rochester NY 16114
  Rockland ME 16130
  Roswell NM 16148
  San Antonio TX 16242
  San Francisco CA 16270
  Seward NE 16370
  Sioux City IA 16396
  Sioux Falls SD 16398, 16399
  Sumter SC 16513
  Tallahassee FL 16537
  Taos NM 16545, 16547, 16550
  Topeka KS 16595
  Toppenish WA 16597
  Tucson AZ 16620
  Union NJ 16646
  Waco TX 16700
  Waitsfield VT 16710
  Washington DC 16746, 16747, 16749, 16751
  Wellesley MA 16824
  Wichita KS 16870
USSR
  Alma-Ata 16989
  Archangel'sk 16993
  Chabarovsk 17022
  Char'kov 17024
  Dnepropetrovsk 17029
  Frunze 17039
  Gor'kij 17042
  Ivanovo 17050
  Kalinin 17057
  Kaluga 17061
  Kaunas 17066
  Kiev 17080, 17081
  Kislovodsk 17087
  Krasnodar 17096
  Kujbyšev 17101
  Kursk 17105
  L'vov 17151
  Minsk 17162
  Moskva 17177, 17184
  Nižnij Tagil 17225
  Novokuzneck 17229
  Odessa 17235
  Omsk 17238
  Perm' 17250
  Petrozavodsk 17255
  Rjazan' 17273
  Saratov 17284
  Sverdlovsk 17301
  Tbilisi 17323
  Tula 17333
  Ufa 17335
  Vil'njus 17343
  Vologda 17353
  Voronež 17356
  Vorošilovgrad 17357
Venezuela
  Caracas 17388
Yugoslavia
  Beograd 17454, 17460
  Čačak 17494
  Hlebina 17531

  Koprivnica 17561
  Kruševac 17583
  Ljubljana 17593
  Novi Sad 17631, 17633
  Rijeka 17686
  Sarajevo 17703
  Šid 17714
  Skopje 17723, 17726
  Šoštanj 17735
  Titograd 17762, 17763
  Zadar 17804
  Zagreb 17815, 17816, 17825
Zambia
  Lusaka 17857
Zimbabwe
  Bulawayo 17861
Art, Pre-Columbian (see also
  Archeology, Ibero-American)
Argentina
  Rosario 00328
  San Ignacio 00346
Denmark
  Holstebro 03434
Finland
  Helsinki 03695
France
  Cannes 04036
  Dieppe 04097
India
  New Delhi 06797
Israel
  Jerusalem 07071
Italy
  Corbetta 07380
  Genova 07516, 07526
  Rimini 07829
Japan
  Hiki 08226
  Tokyo 08538
Norway
  Oslo 09803
Peru
  Cuzco 09995
  Lima 10003, 10004
Spain
  Madrid 11280, 11301
  Mahon 11344
  Valladolid 11593
Switzerland
  Genève 12029
  Zürich 12328
United States
  Anadarko OK 13693
  Birmingham AL 13897
  Burlington VT 14017
  Canton NY 14054
  Casper WY 14079
  Champaign IL 14105
  Chicago IL 14155
  Columbus OH 14266, 14267
  Coral Gables FL 14285, 14286
  Dallas TX 14333
  Dayton OH 14354
  Durham NC 14445
  Farmington NM 14553
  Fort Worth TX 14652
  Fresno CA 14682
  Hamilton NY 14813
  Iowa City IA 14968
  Jacksonville FL 14986
  Jacksonville IL 14988
  Kansas City Mo 15030
  Kingsville TX 15072
  Minneapolis MN 15425
  Mobile AL 15440
  Moorhead MN 15473
  Muskogee OK 15515
  New Haven CT 15575
  New Orleans LA 15589
  New Paltz NY 15591
  Norfolk VA 15688
  Notre Dame IN 15720
  Orlando FL 15767
  Rochester MI 16107
  St. Petersburg FL 16210

New Zealand
  Auckland   09471
Poland
  Tarnów   10426
  Wolsztyn   10489
Romania
  Bacău   10657
  Piatra Neamţ   10756
  Ploieşti   10760
  Roman   10770
Suriname
  Paramaribo   11650
Sweden
  Stockholm   11805
Switzerland
  Chur   11990
  Frauenfeld   12016
United States
  Albuquerque NM   13656
  Alva OK   13677
  Bay Village OH   13835
  Berea KY   13866
  Bryce Canyon UT   14006
  Carson City NV   14073
  Cincinnati OH   14183
  Cleveland OH   14214
  Dayton OH   14355
  Hanover NH   14826
  Hickory NC   14873
  Homer AK   14896
  Little Rock AR   15210
  Logan UT   15221
  Madison WI   15298
  Norman OK   15694
  Philadelphia PA   15860
  Pittsburg KS   15919
  Pittsfield MA   15932
  Poynette WI   15994
  Rochester Mn   16108
  Salisbury NC   16226
  San Diego CA   16250
  Shrevenport LA   16384
  Tulsa OK   16627
  Vernal UT   16683
  Warrensburg MO   16723
  Winston-Salem NC   16916
USSR
  Moskva   17172, 17178
Yugoslavia
  Karlovac   17553
  Rijeka   17688, 17689
  Senta   17708
  Subotica   17758

Birds
Australia
  Melbourne   00529
Austria
  Kufstein   00717
  Linz   00731
Belgium
  Booischot   00972
  Borsbeek   00976
  Lavaux-Sainte-Anne   01142
  Mol   01189
  Nieuwpoort   01213
  Turnhout   01285
  Weert   01307
Bermuda
  Hamilton   01329
Brazil
  Goiânia   01380
  Porto Alegre   01418
Canada
  Calgary   01827, 01832
  Forest   01955
  Grand Manan   01994
  Milton   02136
  Saskatoon   02361
  Waterloo   02514
Colombia
  Medellín   02748
  Popayán   02768
Cuba
  La Habana   02809, 02810

Czechoslovakia
  Boskovice   02858
  Choceň   02913
Denmark
  Frederiksværk   03401
  Viborg   03584
Egypt
  Cairo   03623, 03634
Ethiopia
  Addis Ababa   03658
Fiji
  Suva   03667
France
  Barcelonnette   03974
  Châteaudun   04063
  Le Blanc   04174
  Montauban   04270
  Montbrison   04273
  Saint-Dié   04449
  Saint Dizier   04442
  Saint-Gilles   04454
  Saintes-Maries-de-la-Ville   04476
  Troyes   04525
Germany, Democratic Republic
  Altenburg   04569
  Arnstadt   04583
  Cumlosen   04655
  Halberstadt   04791
  Halle   04799
  Köthen   04851
  Meiningen   04902
  Moritzburg   04912
  Neschwitz   04925
  Neugersdorf   04928
  Renthendorf   05000
  Seebach   05047
  Seifhennersdorf   05051
  Serrahn   05053
  Steckby   05060
  Stralsund   05068
Germany, Federal Republic
  Arnsberg   05192, 05194
  Burghausen   05370
  Erlangen   05436
  Heidelberg   05570
  Kiel   05637
Italy
  Bergamo   07227
  Bologna   07251
  Brescia   07277
  Cremona   07392
  Udine   08086
  Varenna   08095
Japan
  Kyoto   08335
Kenya
  Meru   08651
Madagascar
  Tananarive   08774
Namibia
  Okaukuejo   08937
Netherlands
  Amsterdam   08981, 09007
  Asten   09023
  Bennekom   09031
  Denekamp   09073
  Dokkum   09089
  Drouwen   09100
  Eindhoven   09115
  Frederiksoord   09135
  Leeuwarden   09218
  Meersen   09255
  Nunspeet   09268
  Oudenbosch   09288
  Umuiden   09442
  Zwartsluis   09461
New Zealand
  Waikouaiti   09564
  Wellington   09573
Panama
  Panama City   09973
Peru
  Ayacucho   09992
Poland
  Cieplice Ślæskie Zdrój   10147

Krynica   10256
South Africa
  East London   10871
  Grahamstown   10882
  Harrismith   10889
  Pretoria   10977
Spain
  Amposta   11035
  Bañolas   11066
Sweden
  Ventlinge   11881
Switzerland
  Le Landeron   12106
  Neuchâtel   12163
  Schaffhausen   12219
  Travers   12263
Tanzania
  Arusha   12345
  Serengeti   12355
Uganda
  Entebbe   12591
United Kingdom
  Aberdeen   12607
  Brighton   12765
  Brokerswood   12778
  Burton-upon-Trent   12784
  Bury   12786
  Carlisle   12827
  Chelmsford   12842
  Cheltenham   12845
United States
  Atlanta GA   13752
  Baton Rouge IA   13826
  Battle Creek MI   13832
  Bowling Green KY   13947
  Chattanooga TN   14138
  Chicago IL   14170
  Dallas TX   14334
  Detroit MI   14414
  Emporia KS   14504
  Fairfield CT   14536
  Greenville DE   14787
  Huron SD   14937
  Iowa City IA   14965
  Jackson MS   14978
  Kalamazoo MI   15023
  Key West FL   15054
  McKinney TX   15284
  Madison WI   15299
  Miami FL   15384
  Midland MI   15396
  Minneapolis MN   15424
  Morro Bay CA   15485
  Oakland CA   15728
  Sharon CT   16372
  Shreveport LA   16387
  Springfield MA   16448
  Tacoma WA   16530
  Wahaula HI   16706
  West Chester PA   16836
  Westport CT   16856
Venezuela
  Aragua   17376
  Caracas   17379, 17395
Yugoslavia
  Metković   17611
Boats and shipping (see also
Transportation)
Argentina
  Bernal   00070
  Buenos Aires   00075, 00144,
  00145
  Tigre   00409
Australia
  Brisbane   00463
  Busselton   00468
  Port Victoria   00564
  Redcliffe   00565
  Renmark   00566
  Swan Hill   00575
  Wanneroo   00591
  Williamstown   00598, 00599
Austria
  Baden   00631
  Grein a.d.Donau   00678

Spitz   00810
  Stadl-Paura   00811
Bahamas
  Hope Town   00910
Belgium
  Antwerpen   00943
  Damme   01048
  Rupelmonde   01245
Brazil
  Rio de Janeiro   01450, 01477
Bulgaria
  Tutrakan   01692
  Varna   01701
Canada
  Carleton   01846
  Centreville   01858
  Collingwood   01881
  Grand Bank   01990
  Gravenhurst   02001
  Havre-Aubert   02031
  Kingston   02067, 02068
  La Have Island   02079
  L'Islet-sur-mer   02094
  Mattawa   02126
  Midland   02133
  Milford   02135
  Minden   02138
  Montréal   02167
  Peace River   02245
  Port Hill   02268
  St. Catherines   02328
  St.-Joseph de Sorel   02354
  Salvage   02357
  Sault Sainte Marie   02374
  Selkirk   02377
  Thunder Bay   02431
  Toronto   02450, 02454
  Trinity   02464
  Vancouver   02488
  Victoria   02504
  Wasaga Beach   02511
  Welland   02519
China, People's Republic
  Quanzhou   02653
Colombia
  Bogotá   02711
Denmark
  Aabenraa   03352
  Ærøskøbing   03365
  Blaavand   03370
  Dragør   03375
  Ebeltoft   03379
  Esbjerg   03383
  Faaborg   03387
  Frederikshavn   03397
  Helsingør   03415
  Højby   03429
  København   03452, 03457, 03473
  Lemvig   03485
  Marstal   03495
  Norby Fanø   03500
  Nykøbing Mors   03505
  Ribe   03530
  Roskilde   03538
  Svendborg   03562, 03566
Finland
  Helsinki   03713, 03720
  Kokkola   03767
  Maarianhamina   03793
  Pietarsaari   03820
  Turku   03876
  Uusikaupunki   03882
France
  Antibes   03935
  Bordeaux   04009
  Boulogne-sur-Mer   04015
  Brest   04025
  Camaret-sur-Mer   04035
  Châteauneuf-sur-Loire   04064
  Conflans-Sainte-Honorine
  04089
  Dieppe   04097
  Dunkerque   04108
  La Seyne-sur-Mer   04167
  Le Croisic   04176

Netherlands
  Amsterdam 08982
  Sloten 09361
Norway
  Oslo 09787
United Kingdom
  Harrow 13040
  Letchworth 13145
  St. Ives, Cornwall 13415
United States
  Berkeley CA 13874
  New York NY 15652
  Rochester NY 16112
USSR
  Kiev 17076
Yugoslavia
  Beograd 17458
Circus *see* Amusements
Classical antiquities *(see also* Art,
Greek and Roman)
Algeria
  Annaba 00028
  Cherchell 00031
  Djemila 00033
  Sétif 00039
  Skikda 00040
  Timgad 00044
  Tizi-Ouzou 00046
  Tlemcen 00047
Argentina
  Buenos Aires 00081
Australia
  Hobart 00504
Austria
  Bad Deutsch-Altenburg 00616
  Baden 00631
  Dölsach 00641
  Enns 00652
  Gleisdorf 00659
  Pischeldorf 00758
  St. Pölten 00793
  Wien 00833
  Zwentendorf 00908
Belgium
  Arlon 00954
  Ath 00956
  Aubechies 00957
  Berneau 00965
  Charleroi 01039
  Jehay-Bodegnée 01126
  Kortrijk 01136
  Liège 01154
  Morlanwelz-Mariemont 01198
  Rumes 01244
  Tienen 01272
Brazil
  Curitiba 01370
  São Paulo 01514
  Vitória 01539
Bulgaria
  Chisarja 01566
  Plovdiv 01625
  Sandanski 01643
  Sofija 01664
  Varna 01693
Colombia
  Ipiales 02742
  Benecito-Medellín 02753
  Pasto 02762
  Popayán 02764
  Socorro 02777
  Tunja 02781
  Valledupar 02786
Czechoslovakia
  Komárno 03023
Denmark
  København 03472
Egypt
  Alexandria 03612
  Cairo 03619
France
  Agen 03898
  Aix-les-Bains 03905
  Alise-Sainte-Reine 03913
  Aoste 03938

Apt 03939
Arles 03944, 03945
Avallon 03962
Avesnes-sur-Helpe 03963
Avignon 03964
Bagnères-de-Luchon 03971
Bastia 03977
Bayonne 03983
Beaune 03990
Béziers 04002
Blois 04007
Bordeaux 04008
Boulogne-sur-Mer 04015
Bourbonne-les-Bains 04017
Bourg-en-Bresse 04018
Brignoles 04027
Cannes 04036
Châlons-sur-Marne 04052
Château-Gontier 04059
Château-Meillant 04060
Chaumont 04068
Cordes 04091
Coutances 04093
Digne 04098
Dijon 04099
Dole 04105
Evreux 04117
Laon 04160
Lavaur 04173
Lectoure 04177
Le Mas-d'Azil 04187
Limoges 04204
Lyon 04219, 04224
Marseille 04238
Martigues 04243
Maubeuge 04244
Melun 04247
Metz 04252
Millau 04258
Narbonne 04299, 04300, 04303
Nice 04306
Nuits-Saint-Georges 04325
Orange 04327
Orléans 04332, 04333
Paray-le-Monial 04335
Provins 04413
Rennes 04420
Rochechouart 04428
Rodez 04432
Saint-Germain-en-Laye 04453
Saint-Sever 04470
Saintes 04474
Sarrebourg 04479
Senlis 04488
Soissons 04494
Thonon-les-Bains 04510
Toulouse 04518
Germany, Democratic Republic
  Berlin 04615
  Jena 04825
  Neubukow 04927
Germany, Federal Republic
  Aalen 05162
  Augsburg 05206
  Bad Berneck 05211
  Bad Homburg v.d. Höhe 05217
  Bad Kreuznach 05220
  Berlin 05268
  Bonn 05331
  Erlangen 05435
  Frankfurt 05468
  Göttingen 05509
  Heidelberg 05565
  Jagsthausen 05596
  Jülich 05599
  Karlsruhe 05605
  Kempten 05626
  Kiel 05630
  Lorch 05702
  Mainz 05730, 05731, 05733
  Marburg 05739
  Miltenberg 05765
  München 05806
  Xanten 06007

Greece
  Aegina 06021
  Agios Kirikos 06024
  Agios Nikolaos 06025
  Agrinion 06027
  Alexandroupolis 06030
  Anafi 06036
  Arta 06045
  Athens 06047, 06048, 06051,
  06054, 06057, 06058, 06062,
  06065-06067, 06078
  Chaironeia 06090
  Chora 06095-06097
  Corfu 06099
  Corinth 06105
  Delphi 06107
  Drama 06108
  Eresos 06110
  Farsala 06114
  Geraki 06120
  Gythion 06121
  Herakleion 06122, 06126
  Hierapetra 06128
  Kalymnos 06139
  Kardamlyi 06142
  Karystos 06147
  Kastelli Kisamou 06148
  Kastoria 06150
  Kilkis 06153
  Komotini 06156
  Kosmiti 06162
  Lamia 06167
  Larissa 06168
  Lixourion 06181
  Loutra Aidhipsou 06182
  Lykosoura 06183
  Maroneia 06185
  Mavromation 06187
  Megara 06189
  Mikonos 06195
  Molyvos 06204
  Nauplia 06206
  Naxos 06209
  Neapolis 06212
  Nemea 06213
  Neos Skopos 06214
  Nikopolis 06215
  Olympia 06218, 06219
  Oreoi 06220
  Palaiochora 06221
  Paramythia 06222
  Paros 06224
  Pella 06228
  Perachora 06229
  Piraeus 06231
  Plaka 06233
  Polygyros 06235, 06236
  Pylos 06237
  Pythagoreion 06242
  Rhodos 06247
  Salamis 06250
  Salonika 06252, 06253, 06258,
  06259
  Samos 06260
  Samothraki 06262
  Serrai 06263
  Siatista 06265
  Sicyon 06266
  Sikinos 06267
  Siphnos 06268
  Skyros 06271
  Sparta 06274
  Stavros 06277
  Symi 06279
  Tegea 06281
  Telos 06282
  Tenos 06283
  Thasos 06287
  Thebes 06288, 06289
  Thermos 06290
  Thespiae 06291
  Thira 06292
  Thyrreion 06294
  Traïanoupolis 06295
  Trikkala 06297

Vathy 06299
Veroia 06300
Volos 06302
Hungary
  Budapest 06358, 06383, 06397
  Dunaújváros 06408
  Pécs 06475
  Szombathely 06522
  Tác 06525
  Tata 06526
  Tihany 06529
Indonesia
  Jakarta 06889
Israel
  Ashkelon 07032
  Bet She'an 07042
  Jerusalem 07075
  Sedot Yam Kibbutz 07124
Italy
  Adria 07153
  Agrigento 07159
  Alfedena 07170
  Ancona 07177
  Aquileia 07184
  Arezzo 07187
  Ascoli Piceno 07195
  Asolo 07198
  Assisi 07200
  Asti 07204
  Badia di Cava dei Tirreni 07210
  Belluno 07221
  Bergamo 07225
  Bevagna 07231, 07232
  Bitonto 07235
  Bologna 07247
  Brescello 07274
  Brescia 07281
  Brindisi 07284
  Cagliari 07289
  Canosa di Puglia 07305
  Casamari 07314
  Castelvetrano 07326
  Castiglione a Casauria 07328
  Catanzaro 07338
  Cesena 07347
  Cherasco 07349
  Cingoli 07360
  Cividate Camuno 07365
  Como 07377
  Corbetta 07380
  Este 07408
  Falerone 07415
  Feltre 07419
  Fermo 07422
  Ferrara 07430
  Fiesole 07435
  Finale Ligure 07439
  Firenze 07459
  Foligno 07485
  Forlì 07488
  Forlimpopoli 07493
  Formia 07494
  Frascati 07498
  Grosseto 07538
  Grottaferrata 07541
  Imola 07549
  Jesi 07559
  Lecce 07569
  Locri 07581
  Lucca 07589
  Lugagnano Val d'Arda 07593
  Manduria 07601
  Matera 07610
  Mesagne 07615
  Metaponto 07618
  Milano 07624
  Minturno 07652
  Modena 07662, 07663
  Napoli 07681
  Nocera Inferiore 07695
  Nola 07697
  Numana 07703
  Oderzo 07705
  Orbetello 07707
  Orvieto 07711

Nykøbing Sjælland   03507
France
  Aix-en-Provence   03901
  Lyon   04218
  Montbrison   04273
  Moulins   04283
  Poissy   04402
Germany, Democratic Republic
  Arnstadt   04584
Germany, Federal Republic
  Hanau   05545
  Mechernich-Kommern   05750
  Michelstadt   05764
  München   05791
  Neustadt   05828
  Tecklenburg   05941
  Überlingen   05959
India
  Muzaffarnagar   06775
  New Delhi   06794
Italy
  Palermo   07729, 07730
Japan
  Osaka   08462, 08463
Monaco
  Monte-Carlo   08904
Netherlands
  Bunschoten   09052
  Delft   09070
  's-Gravenhage   09339
New Zealand
  Petone   09537
Portugal
  Lisboa   10575
Spain
  Barcelona   11069
  Sitges   11532
Switzerland
  Güttingen   12057
  Zürich   12326, 12331
United Kingdom
  Bangor/Wales   12656, 12657
  Edinburgh   12956
  Hove   13076
  London   13173
  Newport   13317
  Oxford   13349
  Runbridge Wells   13407
  Southport   13481
  Warwick   13557
United States
  Ardmore OK   13719
  Atascadero CA   13743
  Beatrice NE   13840
  Beloit WI   13858
  Boston MA   13933
  Buena Park CA   14008
  Clinton IL   14228
  Colby KS   14238
  Columbia SC   14255, 14258
  Daytona Beach FL   14361
  Detroit Mi   14415
  Eureka Springs AR   14522
  Fairfield CT   14537
  Flandreau SD   14574
  Flemmington NJ   14576
  Fort Wayne IN   14645
  Glenwood IA   14730
  Glenwood MN   14731
  Gothenburg NE   14744
  Hagerstown MD   14805
  Hinsdale IL   14886
  Holyoke CO   14894
  Jacksonville FL   14987
  Jefferson TX   15003
  Las Cruces NM   15135
  Lexington SC   15180
  McCook NE   15281
  Madison CT   15290
  Manhattan KS   15317
  Manitou Springs CO   15319
  Maquoketa IA   15330
  Mason City IA   15346
  Morris IL   15479
  Morristown NJ   15480

Naperville IL   15521
Neptune NJ   15546
New Britain CT   15556
New York NY   15606
Norwich CT   15715
Ossining NY   15781
Penn Yan NY   15838
Pittsburg KS   15921
San Jose CA   16277
Sandwich MA   16290
Savannah GA   16329
Spartanburg SC   16434
Springfield VT   16452
Sterling CO   16480
Trenton NJ   16604
Tybee Island GA   16639
Upland CA   16655
Watkins Glen NY   16800
Wenham MA   16830
Weston VT   16855
Wilton CT   16899
Worthington OH   16939
Xenia OH   16944
Yorktown Heights NY   16951

Domestic utensils
Albania
  Tirana   00017
Argentina
  Buenos Aires   00086
Australia
  Euroa   00492
  Hahndorf   00500
  Kadina   00508
  Landsborough   00514
  Norseman   00548
  Strathalbyn   00574
Austria
  Graz   00674
  Längenfeld   00719
  Straßburg   00816
  Wildschönau-Oberau   00906
Belgium
  Antwerpen   00945
  Beveren   00966
  Borgerhout   00975
  Brugge   00999
  Geel   01074
  Martelange   01178
  Neufchâteau   01210
  Tielt   01271
  Tongeren   01273
  Wommelgem   01315
  Xhoris   01316
Brazil
  Natal   01403
  Recife   01426
  São Paulo   01511
Canada
  Austin   01771
  Baddeck   01774
  Beaverlodge   01793
  Boissevain   01800
  Camrose   01840
  Carleton   01846
  Carman   01849
  Cartwright   01851
  Cheticamp   01867
  Eaton   01921
  Emerson   01946
  Foam Lake   01954
  Frobisher   01974
  Grand Falls   01991
  Grandview   01998
  Hope   02036
  Horsefly   02038
  Hudson's Hope   02039
  Lac-à-la-Croix   02077
  Lachine   02078
  Manor   02117
  Mississauga   02143
  New Denmark   02192
  New Glasgow   02193
  North Battleford   02206
  Oshawa   02220
  Pembroke   02246

St. Catherines   02328
St. Mary's   02344
St. Viktor   02347
Sombra   02395
Summerland   02415
Tatamagouche   02424
Weyburn   02528
Wynyard   02566
Czechoslovakia
  Třebíz   03289
Denmark
  Ballerup   03369
  Brande   03371
  Give   03404
  Horsens   03439
  Korinth   03484
  Nørresundby   03502
  Skjern   03551
  Toftlund   03569
Finland
  Anjala   03668
  Espoo   03673
  Forssa   03678
  Kauhajoki   03759
  Kemi   03760
  Mänttä   03796
  Nivala   03806
  Nokia   03807
  Orivesi   03810
  Paattinen   03815
  Punkalaidun   03831
  Pyhäjoki   03832
  Rymättylä   03848
  Tokrajärvi   03869
  Vammala   03888
  Varkaus   03890
France
  Les Arcs   04194
Germany, Democratic Republic
  Buttstädt   04645
  Eisenach   04703
  Jena   04827
Germany, Federal Republic
  Bad Driburg   05213
  Bad Münstereifel   05224
  Bad Wimpfen   05238
  Bernau   05306
  Bremen   05353
  Fladungen   05452
  Großweil   05518
  Hannover   05547
  Haselünne   05559
  Holzhausen   05581
  Homburg   05582
  Höxter   05584
  Köln   05648
  Königsbronn   05662
  Königsbrunn   05663
  Krefeld   05672
  Krempe   05674
  Meersburg   05751
  Michelstadt   05763
  Nürnberg   05839
Greece
  Kalamata   06134
  Metsovon   06194
Hungary
  Budapest   06391
Israel
  Bet She'an   07041
  Yif'at Kibbutz   07147
Italy
  Cesena   07346
  Fénis   07420
  Pompei   07796
  San Nicolo' Val d'Ultimo   07941
Japan
  Hirado   08231
  Nagano   08388
  Nakagami   08409
  Takamatsu   08518
  Takayama   08526
  Tottori   08589
Korea, Republic
  Cheju   08664

Netherlands
  Borger   09042
  Bruinisse   09050
  Den Oever   09078
  Echt   09103
  Ede   09105
  Eernewoude   09108
  Eersel   09109
  Heemse   09173
  Lievelde   09240
  Nijmegen   09270
  Oldenzaal   09274
  Ruinerwold   09311
  Sint Annaland   09354
  Staphorst   09368
New Zealand
  Arrowtown   09465
  Naseby   09521
  Norsewood   09525
  Picton   09538
  Waimate   09565
  Wellsford   09577
Nigeria
  Argungu   09587
Norway
  Arendal   09611
  Bleikvasslia   09636
  Eidsvoll   09657
  Etne   09664
  Fannrem   09666
  Fjørde   09668
  Hamar   09690
  Høydalsmo   09709
  Mandal   09748
  Meråker   09751
  Moen i Målselv   09754
  Nesna   09767
  Nesttun   09768
  Prestfoss   09816
  Skiptvet   09850
  Skotselv   09853
  Tingvoll   09878
  Vågåmo   09904
  Vrådal   09919
Poland
  Bieliny   10119
  Chmielno   10140
  Ciechanowiec   10146
  Jarosław   10199
  Nowogród Łomżyński   10308
South Africa
  Beaufort West   10833
  Bethulie   10835
  Caledon   10843
  Cradock   10860
  George   10878
  Grahamstown   10884
  Great Brak River   10886
  Hartenbos   10890
  Mariannhill   10927
  Matjiesfontein   10928
  New Germany   10935
  Oudtshoorn   10940
  Paarl   10942
  Pietermaritzburg   10947
  Potchefstroom   10953
  Stellenbosch   11000
  Tulbagh   11006
  Uitenhage   11007
  Weenen   11016
  Worcester   11018
Spain
  Teruel   11549
Switzerland
  Aarburg   11892
  Aubonne   11914
  Beringen   11943
  Eglisau   12010
  Gränichen   12049
  Hallau   12058
  Neftenbach   12160
  Unterstammheim   12266
  Wildegg   12285
United Kingdom
  Ashton Munslow   12637

Kent 13100
Redruth 13392
Stowmarket 13505
Wendron 13565
United States
Ainsworth NE 13627
Albion MI 13648
Alden NY 13657
Alma KS 13669
Almond NY 13671
Andover IL 13699
Antigo WI 13711
Armour SD 13727
Atascadero CA 13743
Austin TX 13778
Batavia NY 13823
Battle Creek MI 13831
Bishop Hill IL 13900
Bloomsburg PA 13914
Bonner Springs KS 13926
Boulder CO 13943
Brownington VT 14000
Caledonia NY 14029
Chappel Hill TX 14112
Clinton NH 14230
Columbia TN 14259
Columbus TX 14269
Dallas TX 14337
Decorah IA 14372
Defiance OH 14375
Des Moines IA 14402
Edgartown MA 14473
Estes Park CO 14516
Eugene OR 14518
Fairfield CT 14537
Fond du Lac WI 14589
Fort Bliss TX 14595
Fort Pierre SD 14636
Franklin TN 14663
Gardner KS 14703
Gates Mills OH 14708
Georgetown CO 14716
Giddings TX 14722
Greeneville TN 14778
Greenwood MS 14795
Haven KS 14851
Hereford TX 14867
Kankakee IL 15026
Lake Placid NY 15110
Lancaster OH 15116
Laramie WY 15125
Lebanon OH 15154
Lerna IL 15162
Lewisburg PA 15166
Mainfield ME 15302
Marshfield WI 15342
Milford PA 15405
Monroe NY 15449
Morris IL 15479
North Bend OR 15697
North Kingstown RI 15702
Pennsburg PA 15839
Pensacola FL 15842
Peoria IL 15848
Petersburg IL 15856
Pickens SC 15910
Port Clinton OH 15955
Portsmouth RI 15985
Poteau OK 15987
Quakertown PA 16021
Richey MT 16063
Rocky Hill CT 16135
Sandusky OH 16288
Scottsdale PA 16346
Shawano WI 16374
Spartanburg SC 16434
Stamford CT 16462
Stanford MT 16466
Sturbridge MA 16505
Sumter SC 16512
Taunton MA 16554
Teague TX 16556
Tecumseh NE 16557
Torrington CT 16598
Tucson AZ 16614

Vernon VT 16685
Vincennes IN 16689
Viroqua WI 16693
Volga SD 16695
Waltham MA 16718
Watertown CT 16793
Wenham MA 16830
Williamsport PA 16880
Youngstown OH 16955
Drawing *(see also* Graphic arts;
Calligraphy)
Argentina
Avellaneda 00063
Buenos Aires 00129
Chivilcoy 00175
Coronel Pringles 00197
Godoy Cruz 00218
La Plata 00240
Mar del Plata 00266
Rauch 00312
San Juan 00356
San Miguel de Tucumán 00373
Santa Fé 00392
Austria
Bleiburg 00635
Wien 00842
Belgium
Lier 01167
Uccle 01289
Brazil
Curitiba 01369
Canada
Oshawa 02221
Regina 02294, 02295
Saskatoon 02364
Whitby 02529
Chile
Santiago 02600
Colombia
Cali 02724
Cúcuta 02734
Denmark
Dragør 03376
København 03475
Vejen 03578
Vejle 03579
Viborg 03585
Finland
Helsinki 03722
Kajaani 03753
Koski Tl 03770
Lahti 03780
France
Albi 03910
Angers 03929
Anzin 03937
Besançon 03998
Bordeaux 04011
Chantilly 04056
Château-Gontier 04059
Dijon 04103
Grenoble 04132
Lille 04200
Menton 04249, 04250
Milly-la-Forêt 04259
Montauban 04271
Montpellier 04278, 04280
Mulhouse 04287
Nancy 04293
Nantes 04296
Neuf-Brisach 04304
Nice 04308, 04312, 04313
Orléans 04329
Paris 04342, 04356, 04372, 04375
Pontoise 04410
Rochefort 04429
Senlis 04487
Toulouse 04517
Germany, Democratic Republic
Berlin 04621
Görlitz 04763
Halle 04800
Radeburg 04992

Germany, Federal Republic
Albstadt 05172
Augsburg 05203
Berlin 05282, 05284, 05295
Düsseldorf 05403
Erlangen 05431
India
Ahmednagar 06562
Dhar 06657
Gaya 06672
Italy
Ascoli Piceno 07197
Bologna 07244
Firenze 07452
Milano 07647, 07649
Napoli 07691
Pisa 07790
Roma 07836, 07847
Tolentino 08024
Japan
Hikone 08227
Minami Azumi 08367
Ueda 08600
Netherlands
Amsterdam 08977
Rozendaal 09310
New Zealand
Auckland 09467
Wanganui 09570
Norway
Oslo 09808
Poland
Wrocław 10492
Portugal
Viana do Castelo 10623
Spain
Barcelona 11078, 11094
Las Palmas 11251
Madrid 11309, 11339
Quesada 11437
Toledo 11553
Switzerland
Frauenkirch 12017
Hilterfingen 12066
United Kingdom
Bembridge 12692
Colchester 12872
Cookham-on-Thames 12879
London 13175
Maidenhead 13262
Newcastle-upon-Tyne 13308
United States
Alexandria LA 13658
Chadds Ford PA 14099
Columbia MO 14253
Cornish NH 14291
Fort Worth TX 14649
Lewiston ME 15169
Minneapolis MN 15428
Montclair NJ 15452
Mountainville NY 15502
Nashville TN 15539
New Orleans LA 15590
Pensacola FL 15846
Philadelphia PA 15873, 15893
Plattsburgh NY 15938
Port Chester NY 15954
Sacramento CA 16160
State University AR 16469
Washington DC 16777
York PA 16950
Viet Nam
Hanoi 17422
Earthenware *see* Porcelain and
ceramics
Ecology
Austria
Salzburg 00773
Belgium
Bon-Secours 00971
Canada
Brighton 01815
Woodbridge 02564
Czechoslovakia
Soběslav 03255

Denmark
Viborg 03581
Finland
Tampere 03863
India
New Delhi 06798
New Zealand
Wellington 09574
Uganda
Kampala 12594
United Kingdom
Dundee 12926
Zambia
Ndola 17860
Economics
Austria
Wien 00876, 00877
Belgium
Leuven 01148
Germany, Democratic Republic
Adorf 04564
Germany, Federal Republic
Düsseldorf 05411
Geißen 05499
Goslar 05505
India
Calcutta 06635
Gauhati 06670
Japan
Kamo 08275
Netherlands
Amsterdam 09005
Rotterdam 09307
New Zealand
Lower Hutt 09512
Poland
Nałęczów 10301
Szreniawa 10420
Education
Argentina
Avellaneda 00064
General Belgrano 00214
Rosario 00327
Austria
Vöcklamarkt 00820
Wien 00863
Bulgaria
Gabrovo 01577
Canada
Ottawa 02224
Pictou 02257
Toronto 02447
China, Republic
Taipei 02686
Czechoslovakia
Praha 03201
Rožmitál pod Třemšínem 03232
Denmark
Korinth 03484
Maribo 03492
Sæby 03541
Egypt
Cairo 03621
Finland
Hamina 03685
Jyväskylä 03750
Perniö 03818
Tampere 03861
France
Mont-Saint-Aignan 04266
Paris 04348
Germany, Democratic Republic
Göldenitz 04759
Germany, Federal Republic
Berlin 05285, 05291
Hungary
Budapest 06389
Sárospatak 06484
India
Amreli 06575
Bhavnagar 06597
Calcutta 06632
Etawah 06662
Jaipur 06704
Jodhpur 06715

Lucknow 06750
New Delhi 06795
Israel
Revadim 07121
Japan
Kyoto 08326
Otaru 08469
Netherlands
Naarden 09262
Norway
Stavanger 09867
Trondheim 09887
Pakistan
Hyderabad 09930
South Africa
Pretoria 10976
Sweden
Farösund 11691
Halmstad 11712
Switzerland
Zürich 12330
United Kingdom
Leeds 13133
Repton 13393
United States
Academia PA 13623
Berlin WI 13876
Charleston WV 14131
Dover DE 14426
Essex Jct. VT 14514
Louisville KY 15259
Marietta GA 15331
Muncie IN 15505
New York NY 15626
Pittsburg KS 15919
Portland OR 15980
Puyallup WA 16020
Rocky Mount NC 16137
Staten Island NY 16473
Tallahassee FL 16539
Utica NY 16663
Watertown WI 16796
USSR
Baku 17003
Kaunas 17069
Tbilisi 17324
Yugoslavia
Beograd 17470
Ljubljana 17600
Zagreb 17821, 17836

Electricity (see also Energy)
Austria
Wien 00832
Canada
Cape Spear 01841
Fredericton 01971
France
Cluses 04081
Germany, Federal Republic
München 05811
Rendsburg 05890
Netherlands
Amsterdam 08983
Arnhem 09014
Delft 09068
Pakistan
Lahore 09945
Poland
Bystrzyca Kłodzka 10134
Sweden
Ludvika 11748
Stockholm 11843
Switzerland
Baden 11919
United Kingdom
Cardiff 12825
United States
Dayton OH 14356
East Greenwich RI 14457
Kennett MO 15041
Los Altos Hills CA 15235
Louisa County VA 15253
Minneapolis MN 15422
Oneonta AL 15755
Philadelphia PA 15887

Portland OR 15978
St. Johnsbury VT 16178
Schenectady NY 16340
Embroidery see Needlework
Energy (see also Electricity)
Belgium
Bruxelles 01001
Canada
Ottawa 02236
France
Paris 04391
Israel
Tel Aviv 07137, 07140
Kuwait
Kuwait City 08726
Switzerland
Winterthur 12297
United States
Dayton OH 14356
Flushing NY 14586
Idaho Falls ID 14943
Louisa County VA 15253
New York NY 15633
Richland WA 16064
St. Johnsbury VT 16178
Watertown NY 16795
Engraving see Graphic arts
Entomology see Insects
Epitaphs see Inscriptions and epitaphs
Ethnology see Anthropology
Expeditions see Scientific expeditions
Explosives
Australia
Beechworth 00452
Eyeglasses see Optics
Faience see Porcelain and ceramics
Farms and farming (see also Agricultural machinery; Agriculture; Peasant life and traditions)
Argentina
La Paz 00233
Australia
Cleveland 00477
Colac 00478
Cunderdin 00483
Euroa 00492
Maylands 00525
Pinjarra 00560
Snug 00571
Strathalbyn 00574
Wauchope 00593
Wongan Hills 00601
Austria
Asparn a.d.Zaya 00613
Bad Goisern 00617
Längenfeld 00719
Mittersill 00738
Mondsee 00741
Mürzzuschlag 00744
Straßburg 00816
Zwettl 00909
Brazil
Recife 01426
Canada
Bear River 01790
Beaverlodge 01793
Boissevain 01800
Camrose 01840
Carillon 01845
Cooks Creek 01883
Eaton 01921
Flesherton 01953
Fort Frances 01958
Grand Falls 01991
Grand Pré 01995
Horsefly 02038
Jordan 02051
Kamloops 02053
Kelowna 02055, 02056
Lang 02082
Lillooet 02092
Milton 02137
Mission City 02142
Moncton 02146

New Denmark 02192
New Glasgow 02193
Norwich 02210
Orwell Corner 02218
Oyen 02242
Pickering 02255
Port Rowan 02270
Rock Island 02312
Saanichton 02319
St. Joseph 02341
St. Martins 02343
Sangudo 02358
Saskatoon 02371
Stanbridge East 02402
Stoney Creek 02407
Summerland 02415
Tatamagouche 02424
Teeterville 02426
Tofield 02434
Vernon 02493
Vernon 02495
Wellington 02520
Whitemouth 02533
Windsor 02538
Wynyard 02566
China, People's Republic
Beijing 02618
Czechoslovakia
Brno 02875
Nitra 03117
Denmark
Auning 03367
Esbjerg 03382
Give 03404
Horsens 03439
Ølgod 03518
Oxbøl 03522
Padborg 03523
Svendborg 03566
Finland
Espoo 03673
Forssa 03678
Helsinki 03704
Nokia 03807
Orimattila 03809
Siilinjärvi 03852
Taivassalo 03854
Tokrajärvi 03869
France
Caen 04029
Germany, Democratic Republic
Frohburg 04741
Gardelegen 04745
Genthin 04747
Wittstock/Dosse 05128
Germany, Federal Republic
Achern 05166
Adelsheim 05169
Bad Zwischenahn 05240
Bayreuth 05256
Braunschweig 05338
Detmold 05393
Feuchtwangen 05449
Hamburg 05538
Haselünne 05559
Husum 05585
Karolinenkoog 05614
Königsbronn 05662
Königsbrunn 05663
Krummhörn 05676
Maihingen 05725
Massing 05747
Nienburg 05830
Stuttgart 05931
Wunsiedel 05994
Hungary
Keszthely 06434
Israel
'En Harod 07049
Yif'at Kibbutz 07147
Italy
Bentivoglio 07224
Nizza Monferrato 07694
Palazzolo Acreide 07721
Premana 07812

Japan
Miyazaki 08381
Nakagami 08409
Shizuoka 08505
Takamatsu 08519
Netherlands
Aarle-Rixtel 08951
Anjum 09008
Axel 09024
Beek 09027
Eersel 09109
Enkhuizen 09123
Exloo 09130
Hardenberg 09166
Heemse 09173
Hellendoorn 09181
Krimpen aan den IJssel 09208
Ruinerwold 09311
Sint Annaland 09354
Uzendijke 09443
Zevenbergen 09452
New Zealand
Clyde 09479
Geraldine 09491
Okains Bay 09527
Patea 09536
Waimate 09565
Waiuku 09569
Wellsford 09577
Norway
Bøverbru 09641
Etne 09664
Fjørde 09668
Høydalsmo 09709
Kvernaland 09729
Moen i Målselv 09754
Nesna 09767
Nesttun 09768
Prestfoss 09816
Sandane 09837
Sandnes 09841
Tingvoll 09878
Vågåmo 09904
Vrådal 09919
Philippines
Paranaque 10072
Poland
Augustów 10107
Babimost 10108
Ciechanowiec 10146
Nowogród Łomżyński 10308
Ostrzyce 10328
Rabka Zdrój 10367
Szreniawa 10420
Wierzchosławice 10480
South Africa
Bethlehem 10834
Cradock 10860
Graaff-Reinet 10879
Grahamstown 10884
Hartenbos 10890
Himeville 10893
Middelburg Cape 10930
Paarl 10942
Potgietersrus 10955
Rayton 10980
Roodepoort 10984
Sterkstroom 11003
Swellendam 11004
Switzerland
Aesch 11894
Albisrieden 11898
Attiswil 11912
Balgach 11920
Beringen 11943
Berneck 11956
Bottmingen 11967
Buchegg 11980
Cevio 11987
Coffrane 11994
Gränichen 12049
Gurbrü 12055
Hinwil 12067
Marthalen 12137
Meilen 12141

Muhen 12153
Nürensdorf 12164
Oberriet 12169
Pfäffikon 12178
Rickenbach 12193
Roggwil 12197
Scuol 12230
Sempach 12232
Zurzach 12340
United Kingdom
Ashton Munslow 12637
Bedford 12683
Bibury 12699
Breamore 12752
Guernsey 13024
Harrogate 13038
Hereford 13059
Reading 13387
Stanraer 13489
Wrexham 13601
Wye 13603
Yeovil 13606
United States
Alma KS 13669
Altus OK 13675
Archbold OH 13718
Arlington VA 13725
Armour SD 13727
Auburn CA 13758
Auburn NY 13761
Aurora OH 13773
Austin TX 13779
Barrington IL 13818
Barron WI 13819
Beloit WI 13858
Bloomsburg PA 13914
Blue Mounds WI 13917
Bonner Springs KS 13926
Brunswick GA 14003
Bunnell FL 14014
Caldwell ID 14027
Chadds Ford PA 14098
Concordia KS 14275
Davenport WA 14350
Des Moines IA 14402
Dorris CA 14420
Dubois WY 14437
Elizabeth City NC 14484
El Monte CA 14497
Fairview UT 14545
Ferrum VA 14560
Fort Morgan CO 14632
Fort Pierre SD 14636
Fresno CA 14683
Gallatin TN 14697
Giddings TX 14722
Goshen CT 14742
Gouverneur NY 14745
Greeley CO 14767
Haines OR 14810
Hanalei Kauai HI 14821
Hardy VA 14828
Hereford TX 14867
Hillsboro ND 14881
Hinsdale IL 14886
Holyoke CO 14894
Ipswich SD 14969
Juliette GA 15017
Kingsville TX 15072
Lewisburg PA 15166
Little Compton RI 15205
Lodi CA 15218
Logan UT 15222
Madison CT 15290
Madison SD 15293
Maquoketa IA 15330
Marysville KS 15343
Mattapoisett MA 15348
Medford OK 15354
Michigan City IN 15387
Milford PA 15405
Mitchell GA 15431
Monroe NY 15449
Montrose CO 15469
Nacogdoches TX 15517

Narrowsburg NY 15522
New Braunfels TX 15552
New Holstein WI 15577
Newton NC 15676
Norfolk CT 15687
Pendleton SC 15837
Portsmouth RI 15985
Poultney VT 15993
Reading PA 16044
Redding CA 16052
Richey MT 16063
Ridgewood NJ 16087
Riverton WY 16101
Rochester IN 16106
Rockwell City IA 16133
Rocky Hill CT 16135
Round Top TX 16150
St. Paul MN 16207
Salem IN 16218
Salt Lake City UT 16235
Saratoga TX 16318
Searcy AR 16348
Sheboygan WI 16376
Stanton TX 16468
Storrs CT 16494
Stuttgart AR 16508
Sumter SC 16512
Sweetwater TX 16522
Syracuse NY 16525
Tallahassee FL 16539
Torrington CT 16598
Tuckahoe NY 16611
Upland PA 16656
Visalia CA 16694
Warwick NY 16725
Watertown NY 16795
Wenatchee WA 16828
Wheaton IL 16861
Williams CA 16876
Williamsport PA 16880
Xenia OH 16944
Yorktown Heights NY 16951
Youngstown OH 16955
Fashion *see* Clothing and dress
Festivals
Belgium
Binche 00967
Germany, Federal Republic
Bad Dürrheim 05214
Kenzingen 05627
Kitzingen 05641
Orsingen-Nenzingen 05860
Netherlands
Echt 09102
United States
Abilene KS 13615
Fire fighting and rescue work
Australia
Bli Bli 00458
Austria
Wien 00835
Belgium
Antwerpen 00947
Canada
Niagara-on-the-Lake 02202
Yarmouth 02567
Denmark
Christiansfeld 03373
Finland
Helsinki 03728
Hyrylä, Tuusula 03732
France
Le Molay-Littry 04189
Mulhouse 04289
Germany, Federal Republic
Creglingen 05376
Fulda 05486
Kiel 05631
München 05790
Passau 05868
Salem 05904
Hungary
Budapest 06401
Japan
Tokyo 08558, 08574

Netherlands
Amsterdam 09001
Borculo 09040
Breda 09047
Hellevoetsluis 09182
Purmerend 09293
New Zealand
Christchurch 09477
Poland
Bystrzyca Kłodzka 10134
Romania
Bucureşti 10683
South Africa
Johannesburg 10907
Sweden
Köping 11736
Switzerland
Adligenswil 11893
Basel 11936
Brugg 11977
Donzhausen 12004
Kreuzlingen 12081
Neftenbach 12160
Unterstammheim 12266
Winterthur 12291
United Kingdom
Billericay 12705
Kingston upon Hull 13110
London 13181
United States
Alma CO 13668
Aspen CO 13740
Brewster MA 13964
Brooklyn NY 13992
Butte MT 14023
Camden NJ 14041
Hudson NY 14920
Lutherville MD 15272
Manchester NH 15311
Milwaukee WI 15417
Mobile 28 AL 15439
Moose WY 15474
Nantucket MA 15520
New Bern NC 15550
New York NY 15641
Oklahoma City OK 15739
Phoenix AZ 15904
Portland ME 15974
Richmond IN 16070
Rocky Ford CO 16134
San Francisco CA 16269
Seattle WA 16360
South Carver MA MA 16423
Swampscott MA 16521
West Point NY 16848
Winona MN 16911
Yugoslavia
Metlika 17613
Zagreb 17835
Firearms *see* Arms and armor
Fishing and fisheries
Australia
Albany 00439
Austria
Orth 00751
Petronell 00754
Seeboden 00803
Belgium
Boekhoute 00970
Knokke-Heist 01130
Oostduinkerke 01223
Brazil
Manaus 01399
São Paulo 01523
Bulgaria
Tutrakan 01692
Canada
Alert Bay 01752
Basin Head 01786
Bear River 01790
Calgary 01837
Centreville 01858
Durrell 01919
Lunenburg 02109
Musgrave Harbour 02183

North East Margaree 02207
Richmond 02305
St. John's 02335, 02337
Salvage 02357
Selkirk 02377
Trinity 02464
Vancouver 02488
Czechoslovakia
Hluboká nad Vltavou 02960
Denmark
Blaavand 03370
Esbjerg 03383
Gilleleje 03403
Lyngby 03489
Nuuk/Godthaab 03503
Nykøbing Mors 03505
Thisted 03567
Egypt
Al-Ghardaqa 03610
Finland
Inari 03740
Kemi 03760
Kotka 03772
Rauma 03836
Taivassalo 03854
France
La Bussière 04149
Germany, Democratic Republic
Havelberg 04802
Mühlberg 04914
Prerow 04979
Rerik 05001
Ribnitz-Damgarten 05003
Rostock-Warnemünde 05015
Stralsund 05067
Tangermünde 05073
Waren a. d. Müritz 05087
Wittenberge 05127
Germany, Federal Republic
Düsseldorf 05413
Hamburg 05525
Koblenz 05647
India
Mandapam Camp 06767
Italy
Trieste 08068
Japan
Ise 08251
Ome 08455
Suwa 08512
Takamatsu 08519
Yokosuka 08620
Malaysia
Penang 08793
Netherlands
Bruinisse 09050
De Rijp 09079
Egmond aan Zee 09110
Elburg 09117
Enkhuizen 09123
Lemmer 09239
Moddergat 09259
Scheveningen 09321
's-Gravenhage 09348
Sommelsdijk 09366
Tilburg 09377
Urk 09383
Veere 09404
Vlaardingen 09415
Woudrichem 09439
Zierikzee 09455
New Zealand
Holdens Bay 09503
Picton 09538
Tokanui 09559
Waikouaiti 09564
Norway
Åsestranda 09613
Bergen 09624
Bodø 09638
Elverum 09660
Fygle 09675
Gratangsbotn 09681
Grøa på Nordmøre 09683
Halsnøy Kloster 09688

Boom 00973
Borgerhout 00974, 00975
Bouillon 00977
Braine-le-Comte 00980
Brugge 00986, 00999
Bruxelles 01002, 01019
Cerfontaine 01037
Comblain-au-Pont 01042
Cul-des-Sarts 01044
Damme 01046-01048
Dendermonde 01052
Durbuy 01064
Eeklo 01066
Elouges 01067
Essen 01068
Genk 01076, 01077
Gent 01084, 01091
Heist-op-den-Berg 01106
Herstal 01109
Hoegaarden 01110
Hoeilaart 01111
Huy 01114
Keerbergen 01129
Knokke-Heist 01130
Kontich 01134
Kortrijk 01136
Latour 01141
Lembeke 01143
Liège 01159
Lokeren 01170
Maaseik 01173
Massemen 01179
Mechelen 01182
Melle 01184
Merksem 01185
Mesen 01187
Mons 01191, 01195
Mouscron 01200
Nieuwpoort 01214
Nismes 01215
Oedelem 01218
Oostduinkerke 01222
Oostende 01224
Opheylissem 01228
Overmere 01233
Rochefort 01237
Roeselare 01239
Roly 01241
Ronse 01242
Rupelmonde 01245
Saint-Vith 01249
's-Gravenwezel 01253
Sint-Niklaas 01256
Temse 01268
Tielt 01271
Tournai 01277
Tubize 01284
Turnhout 01288
Verviers 01291
Visé 01298
Vresse-sur-Semois 01301
Wachtebeke 01303
Wetteren 01309
Woluwe-Saint-Lambert 01314
Zichem 01318
Benin
Cotonou 01325
Parakou 01327
Porto-Novo 01328
Bolivia
La Paz 01338, 01339, 01342
Potosí 01343
Sucre 01344, 01345
Botswana
Kanye 01348
Mochudi 01350
Brazil
Belém 01351
Campo Grande 01365
Itú 01388
Macapá 01395
Pœrto Alegre 01422
Rio de Janeiro 01437, 01466, 01472
Salvador 01486, 01498

Santana do Ipanema 01503
São Leopoldo 01508
São Paulo 01521, 01522, 01527
Vitória 01539, 01542
Bulgaria
Asenovgrad 01547
Belogradčik 01552
Berkovica 01553
Blagoevgrad 01557
Botevgrad 01558
Boženci 01559
Burgas 01561, 01562
Chaskovo 01565
Elchovo 01572
Etăra 01574
Etropole 01575
Gabrovo 01578
Ichtiman 01579
Jambol 01580
Kărdžali 01582
Karlovo 01584
Karnobat 01586
Kazanlăk 01587
Kjustendil 01590
Koprivštica 01593
Kotel 01598
Lom 01601
Loveč 01603
Melnik 01606
Nesebăr 01608
Orjachovo 01610
Pazardžik 01614
Pernik 01616
Pleven 01620
Plovdiv 01626
Razgrad 01634
Ruse 01639
Samokov 01642
Sevlievo 01644
Silistra 01645
Sliven 01649
Smoljan 01651
Sofija 01663, 01666
Stara Zagora 01680
Šumen 01684
Targovište 01687
Varna 01694, 01699
Veliko Tărnovo 01702
Vidin 01707
Vraca 01710, 01712
Burma
Mandalay 01719
Rangoon 01729
Cameroon
Douala 01737
Foumban 01741, 01742
Canada
Abbotsford 01748
Adolphustown 01749
Alberton 01751
Alert Bay 01752
Alexandria 01753
Alliston 01757
Arkona 01763
Ashville 01767
Atikokan 01768
Battleford 01789
Biggar 01797
Bridgewater 01814
Bulyea 01819
Burnaby 01823
Calgary 01831
Campbell River 01839
Caraquet 01842
Cardston 01844
Castlegar 01852
Castor 01855
Cereal 01859
Chilliwack 01870
Colinton 01879
Cornwall 01884
Dauphin 01899
Drumheller 01910
Dryden 01912
Edmonton 01937

Elbow 01941
Esterhazy 01948
Evansburg 01950
Fenelon Falls 01951
Foam Lake 01954
Fort Langley 01961
Fort Steele 01967
Gananoque 01976
Gibsons 01980
Golden Lake 01986
Grand Forks 01993
Grande Prairie 01996
Grandview 01999
Grenfell 02004
Halifax 02013
Hanna 02028
Havelock 02030
Huntsville 02040
Innisfail 02043
Innisville 02044
Kinistino 02069
Kitchener 02071
Knowlton 02075
La Prairie 02076
Lancer 02081
La Pocatière 02083
Lindsay 02093
Lloydminster 02096
London 02098
McCord 02110
Madoc 02111
Magnetawan 02112
Manitowaning 02116
Manor 02117
Maplewood 02121
Masset 02124
Medicine Hat 02127
Midland 02133
Minden 02138
Minesing 02139
Mississauga 02143
Morden 02177
Muenster 02181
Mundare 02182
Nanaimo 02185
Napanee 02188
Niagara Falls 02198
Norwich 02210
Ottawa 02231
Owen Sound 02239
Oxbow 02241
Oyen 02242
Pembroke 02246
Penetanguishene 02247
Peribonka 02251
Pictou 02256
Plamondon 02259
Porcupine Plain 02264
Port Carling 02266
Port Colborne 02267
Port Moody 02269
Pouce Coupe 02273
Powell River 02274
Prince William 02279
Regina 02293
Richibucto 02304
Rimbey 02308
Rocanville 02311
Rock Island 02312
Rockton 02313
St. Ann's 02324
St. Basile 02325
Saint John 02332
St. Peters 02345
Saskatoon 02371
Selkirk 02376
Shandro 02379
Shaunavon 02381
Sheguiandah 02383
Sherbrooke 02388
Shoal Lake 02390
Sioux Lookout 02393
Spy Hill 02400
Stettler 02405
Strasbourg 02409

Sutton 02419
Swift Current 02420, 02421
Teeterville 02426
Thunder Bay 02431
Toronto 02462
Truro 02470
Uxbridge 02473
Vancouver 02485
Veregin 02492
Vernon 02495
Weekes 02518
Welland 02519
Weyburn 02528
Whitehorse 02531
Winnipeg 02544
Wolfville 02561
Yarmouth 02568
Yorkton 02570
Central African Republic
Bangassou 02572
Bangui 02573
Bouar 02574
Chad
Fort Archambault 02577
N'Djamena 02578
Chile
La Serena 02586
Punta Arenas 02589
Santiago 02592, 02596
Temuco 02604
Colombia
Barranquilla 02690
Bogotá 02713, 02718
Cartagena 02727, 02730, 02731
Cartago 02732
Duitama 02735
Ipiales 02742
Manizales 02744, 02745
Benecito-Medellín 02753-02755
Pamplona 02760
Pasto 02762, 02763
Popayán 02764
Socorro 02777
Sogamoso 02778
Sonsón 02779
Valledupar 02786
Congo
Brazzaville 02789
Cuba
La Habana 02802, 02807
Cyprus
Nicosia 02834
Yeroskipou 02837
Czechoslovakia
Banská Štiavnica 02844
Bardejov 02845
Bardejovské Kúpele 02846
Bělá pod Bezdězem 02848
Benátky nad Jizerou 02849
Beroun 02850
Bílovec 02853
Blovice 02855
Bojkovice 02856
Brandýs nad Labem -
Stará Boleslav 02860
Bratislava 02866
Březnice 02872
Brezno 02873
Brno 02875
Broumov 02884
Bučovice 02886
Bystřice nad Pernštejnem 02888
Čáslav 02891
Červený Kláštor-Kúpele 02897
Česká Lípa 02899
České Budějovice 02902
Český Brod 02904
Český Dub 02905
Český Krumlov 02906
Český Těšín 02907
Cheb 02908
Choceň 02913
Chrudim 02918
Dolní Domaslovice 02931

Csongrád 06404
Debrecen 06405
Gyöngyös 06417
Györ 06415
Gyula 06418
Hajdúböszörmény 06421
Hajduszoboszló 06422
Hódmezővásárhely 06424
Jászberény 06425
Kalocsa 06426
Kaposvár 06428
Kapuvár 06429
Karcag 06430
Kecskemét 06431
Keszthely 06433
Kiskörös 06436
Kiskunfélegyháza 06437
Kiskunhalas 06438
Kisvárda 06440
Kőszeg 06441
Mátészalka 06444
Mezőkövesd 06445
Miskolc 06448
Mohács 06450
Nagykanizsa 06454
Nagykőrös 06455
Nyirbátor 06457
Nyiregyháza 06458, 06459
Orosháza 06461
Pápa 06465
Pécs 06469, 06472
Sárospatak 06482
Sárvár 06485
Sopron 06492, 06493
Szarvas 06497
Szeged 06500
Szekszárd 06506
Szentendre 06510
Szentes 06515
Szerencs 06516
Szolnok 06518
Szombathely 06522, 06524
Tiszafüred 06530
Vác 06532
Vásárosnamény 06535
Veszprém 06538
Zalaegerszeg 06541
India
Hyderabad 06699
Ranchi 06821
Shillong 06834
Indonesia
Denpasar 06888
Jakarta Kota 06906
Pematangsiantar 06922
Yogyakarta 06951
Iraq
Baghdad 06991
Israel
Haifa 07055
Jerusalem 07070, 07098
Tel Aviv 07139
Italy
Bolzano 07265
Bormio 07270
Cagliari 07291
Civitanova Marche 07367
Firenze 07469
Forli 07491
La Spezia 07565
Milano 07640
Modena 07656
Monterosso Grana 07676
Napoli 07687
Palmi 07735
Parma 07745
Roma 07880, 07884
San Lorenzo in Campo 07936
Santa Maria degli Angeli 07946
Sassari 07956
Sondrio 07989
Susa 08003
Tirano 08018
Tolmezzo 08026
Torino 08035

Trento 08057
Udine 08084
Japan
Akita 08173
Aomori 08178
Hachinohe 08215
Hakodate 08217
Hamamatsu 08220
Imabari 08248
Kagoshima 08264
Kanazawa 08278
Kisarazu 08291
Komatsu 08308
Machida 08354
Matsumoto 08359
Misawa 08371
Mito 08376
Morioka 08384
Nagoya 08403
Narita 08426
Okayama 08452
Sapporo 08488
Takayama 08525
Tokyo 08545
Tomioka 08587
Yamagata 08609, 08611
Yamato-Koriyama 08613
Yokosuka 08621
Jordan
Amman 08629
Madaba 08636
Kenya
Kitale 08649
Lamu 08650
Nairobi 08653
Korea, Democratic People's
Republic
P'yongyang 08656
Korea, Republic
Asan 08662
Cheju 08664, 08665
Ch'ongju 08666
Seoul 08693
Lesotho
Morija 08736
Liechtenstein
Triesenberg 08752
Luxembourg
Bech-Kleinmacher 08757
Vianden 08768
Malawi
Chichiri Blantyre 08778
Mangoche 08779
Martinique
Fort de France 08810
Mexico
Actopán 08816
Campeche 08817
Chiapa de Corzo 08820
Guadalajara 08830
México City 08855
Morelia 08869
San Miguel de Allende 08883
Teotihuacán 08885
Tepic 08887
Tzintzuntzan 08894
Morocco
Tetuán 08927
Netherlands
Amsterdam 09000
Appingedam 09012
Arnhem 09018
Den Briel 09071
Den Burg 09072
Den Ham 09075
Deventer 09082
Drachten 09098
Drimmelen 09099
Egmond aan Zee 09110
Elsloo 09118
Etten-Leur 09129
Geervliet 09136
Geldrop 09137
Gorinchem 09141
Hardenberg 09166

Hazerswoude 09172
Leens 09213
Medemblik 09254
Oudenbosch 09288
Oudewater 09290
Rotterdam 09300, 09308
Rijssen 09313
Rijswijk 09314
Schagen 09319
Schoonoord 09329
Sommelsdijk 09366
Veenkloster 09403
Velp 09406
Vlaardingen 09414
Warffum 09428
West-Terschelling 09434
Winterwijk 09435
Zaandijk 09446
Zutphen 09460
New Zealand
Alexandra 09464
Auckland 09470
Cromwell 09481
Dunedin 09486
Gore 09493
Greytown 09495
Helensville Borough 09500
Hokianga 09501
Howick 09504
Karamea 09509
Lawrence 09511
Lumsden 09514
Oamaru 09526
Ongaonga 09529
Outram 09531
Petone 09537
Rangiora 09540
Reefton 09541
Renwick 09542
Riverton 09543
Roxburgh 09546
Russell 09547
Silverdale 09549
Taihape 09551
Tauranga 09552
Te Kauwhata 09554
Tokanui 09559
Tuatapere 09561
Turangi 09562
Waipu 09567
Wairoa 09568
Wellsford 09577
Whangarei 09580
Nigeria
Kano 09596
Lagos 09597
Norway
Arendal 09610
Bergen 09627
Follebu 09672
Hommelstø 09703
Kabelvåg 09714
Karasjok 09715
Kristiansand S 09727
Kristiansund 09728
Meldal 09750
Mo i Rana 09753
Molde 09756
Namsos 09764
Nesbyen 09766
Oslo 09788
Røros 09831
Sandane 09837
Skjønhaug 09851
Vadsø 09903
Pakistan
Lahore 09940
Peshawar 09953
Panama
Ciudad de Panamá 09968
Paraguay
Asunción 09983
Peru
Lima 10012

Philippines
Baguio 10020
Cebu 10029
Malacañang 10041
Pasay 10074-10076
Poland
Augustów 10107
Bieliny 10119
Bielsko-Biała 10121
Biłgoraj 10123
Bytów 10136
Chełm 10138
Chojnice 10142
Chrzanów 10145
Cieszyn 10148
Częstochowa 10150
Dynów 10166
Gliwice 10175
Głucha Puszcza 10177
Gołuchów 10181
Gorlice 10182
Hrubieszów 10192
Jarocin 10198
Jawór 10201
Jaworzynka 10202
Kalisz 10204
Kępno 10211
Kielce 10214
Kluki 10217
Kolbuszowa 10218
Kórnik 10223
Koszalin 10225
Kraków 10234
Krasnystaw 10250
Kwidzyn 10258
Łęcna 10263
Łęczyca 10264
Leszno 10268
Leżajsk 10269
Liw 10271
Łobżenica 10272
Łódź 10273
Łomża 10278
Łowicz 10280
Lubaczów 10282
Międzyrzecz Wielkopolski
10292
Mława 10294
Niedzica 10304
Nowa Sól 10305
Nowe Miasto Lubawskie 10307
Nowy Targ 10311
Nysa 10312
Odolanów 10314
Olesno 10316
Oliwa 10317
Opoczno 10322
Ostrzyce 10328
Pabianice 10330
Pasym 10331
Piotrków Trybunalski 10335
Płosk 10337
Podegrodzie 10339
Poznań 10350
Puławy 10363
Radom 10369
Rawa Mazowiecka 10371
Rawicz 10372
Ropczyce 10375
Rzeszów 10378
Sandomierz 10380
Sanok 10383
Sieradz 10387
Sierpc 10388
Suwałki 10409
Szamotuły 10414
Szczytno 10419
Sztum 10421
Tomaszów Lubelski 10428
Tomaszów Mazowiecki 10429
Toruń 10430
Warszawa 10473
Wdzydze Kiszewskie 10476
Wieluń 10479
Włocławek 10484

Oshkosh WI   15777
Peace Dale RI   15829
Peebles OH   15832
Pennsburg PA   15839
Philadelphia PA   15879
Piqua OH   15918
Pittsfield MA   15933
Portales NM   15970
Rochester NY   16119
Salem MO   16221
San Antonio TX   16241
San Luis Obispo CA   16280
Schenectady NY   16341
Seattle WA   16361
Taos NM   16546, 16548
Tulsa OK   16625
Tuscaloosa AL   16631
Urbana OH   16660
Vinalhaven ME   16688
Weiser ID   16822
Wewoka OK   16859
Worthington OH   16939
Xenia OH   16944
York PA   16950
USSR
Archangel'sk   16992
Ašchabad   16995
Kiev   17078
Kutaisi   17107
Leningrad   17115, 17128
L'vov   17150
Moskva   17206, 17213
Pskov   17260
Riga   17269
Šamarkand   17279
Šauljaj   17287
Stepanakert   17297
Tartu   17311
Tbilisi   17320, 17322
Tula   17334
Vil'njus   17344
Vatican
Città del Vaticano   17369
Venezuela
Caracas   17380
La Asunción   17405
Yemen Arab Republic
San'a   17431
Yemen, People's Democratic
Republic
Seiyun in Wadi Hadhramaut
17438
Yugoslavia
Aleksinac   17440
Bački Petrovac   17442
Bar   17447
Bela Crkva   17450
Beograd   17452, 17455
Bihać   17477
Biograd   17479
Bitola   17481
Bjelovar   17482
Bor   17484, 17485
Čačak   17493
Čakavec   17496
Cavtat   17497
Cažma   17498, 17499
Cetinje   17503
Doboj   17510
Dubrovnik   17512
Džakovo   17522
Gospič   17526
Hercegnovi   17530
Idrija   17538
Jasenovo   17546
Jastrebarsko   17547
Kalinovac   17549
Kočevje   17557
Koper   17560
Koprivnički Bregi   17562
Korčula   17564
Kosovska Mitrovica   17569
Kragujevac   17573
Kraljevo   17574
Krapina   17580

Kutina   17585
Laško   17587
Ljubljana   17598
Maribor   17608
Metlika   17612
Mostar   17615
Nikšić   17622
Nova Gorica   17627
Novi Pazar   17639
Ohrid   17643
Pazin   17650
Piran   17657
Pirot   17658
Pivnice   17659
Pljevlja   17660
Prokuplje   17676
Rovinj   17691
Ruma   17692
Šabac   17693
Sarajevo   17696, 17704
Šarengrad   17705
Senta   17708
Sinj   17716
Sisak   17717
Slavonska Požega   17727
Varaždinske Toplice   17786
Visoko   17794
Vršac   17798
Vrsno   17800
Zagreb   17812
Zaječar   17838
Zaostrog   17839
Zenica   17841
Zrenjanin   17843
Županja   17844
Zaire
Kisangani   17850
Luluabourg   17852
Mbandaka   17853
Mushenge   17854

Food *(see also* Baking and cookery;
Beverage technology; Sugar)
Argentina
Necochea   00287
Australia
Franklin   00495
Belgium
Battice   00960
Denmark
Ølgod   03518
Finland
Helsinki   03706
Germany, Federal Republic
Wangen   05969
Hungary
Budapest   06369, 06377
Sopron   06493
Italy
Pontedassio   07800
Tirolo di Merano   08019
Trieste   08078
Japan
Noda   08444
Luxembourg
Bech-Kleinmacher   08757
Netherlands
Schagen   09318
Norway
Rissa   09825
Switzerland
Kiesen   12077
Langnau im Emmental   12090
United States
Creswell NC   14319
Hammondsport NY   14815
Naknek AK   15518

Forest products
Argentina
Buenos Aires   00094
Mendoza   00272
Australia
Cannington   00471
Chinchilla   00475
Manjimup   00524

Austria
Bad Wimsbach-Neydharting
00627
Großreifling   00679
Belgium
Maredret   01176
Brazil
São Paulo   01526
Burma
Rangoon   01730
Taungdwingyi   01733
Canada
Blind River   01799
Duncan   01915
Fort Frances   01958
Gravenhurst   02001
Hinton   02035
KIngston   02066
Manicougan   02115
Massey   02125
Mooretown   02172
Nipawin   02204
Pembroke   02246
Thunder Bay   02429
Victoria   02497
Czechoslovakia
Antol   02839
Hluboká nad Vltavou   02960
Denmark
Hørsholm   03442
Skørping   03553
Finland
Rovaniemi   03843
Ruotsinpyhtää   03846
Germany, Democratic Republic
Krippen   04853
Plauen   04958
Serrahn   05053
Worbis   05134
Germany, Federal Republic
Bernau   05306
Füssen   05494
Hungary
Szentendre   06513
India
Coimbatore   06644
Dehradun   06652
Gauhati   06668
Italy
Firenze   07451, 07461
Genova   07514
Milano   07650
Palermo   07731
Japan
Ise   08251
Yamato-Koriyama   08613
Netherlands
Franeker   09133
New Zealand
Matakohe   09517
Norway
Elverum   09660
Pakistan
Peshawar   09952
Sweden
Gävle   11697
Sundvall   11854
Växjö   11880
Switzerland
Altishofen   11901
Aubonne   11914
Lottigna   12121
Thailand
Bangkok   12366, 12367
Uganda
Kampala   12595
United Kingdom
London   13191
United States
Archbold OH   13718
Blue Mountain Lake NY   13918
Broken Bow OK   13979
Coeur d'Alene ID   14235
Crescent City CA   14316
Dubois WY   14437

Dubuque IA   14438
Elizabeth City NC   14484
Fifield WI   14563
Fort Bragg CA   14596
Galeton PA   14696
Hobart IN   14887
Klamath Falls OR   15074
La Crosse WI   15090
Laona WI   15124
Leesburg VA   15157
Lufkin TX   15270
Madison WI   15298
Marinette WI   15335
Portland OR   15981
Poynette WI   15994
Rhinelander WI   16062
Riverton WY   16101
Sandpoint ID   16287
Scotia CA   16345
Snohomish WA   16406
Waterloo IA   16791
Wausau WI   16810
Yugoslavia
Beograd   17468
Ljubljana   17601
Ravne na Koreškem   17684

Fossils
Argentina
Córdoba   00186
Corrientes   00201
Mercedes   00279
San Miguel de Tucumán   00374
Australia
Esk   00491
Melbourne   00527
South Nanango   00572
Austria
Admont   00603
Altaussee   00607
Villach   00819
Belgium
Bruxelles   01006
Genk   01076
Gesves   01094
Kanne   01128
Brazil
Rio de Janeiro   01449
Canada
Arkona   01763
Bracken   01807
Courtenay   01888
Dalhousie   01897
Denare Beach   01905
Drumheller   01910
Eastend   01920
Forest   01955
Grande Prairie   01996
High River   02034
Morden   02177
Riverhurst   02309
Saskatoon   02361
Simcoe   02392
Waterloo   02514
Winnipeg   02560
Chile
Valparaíso   02605
China, People's Republic
Beijing   02612
Colombia
Bogotá   02714
Denmark
Fakse   03391
Fur   03402
Gram   03407
København   03458, 03480
Lintrup   03487
Egypt
Cairo   03626
Finland
Espoo   03675
France
Bouxwiller   04022
Gaillac   04123
Le Grand-Pressigny   04179
Menton   04251

Germany, Democratic Republic
  Bitterfeld 04638
  Greifswald 04771
  Halle 04795
  Rübeland 05017
Germany, Federal Republic
  Blankenheim 05317
  Boll 05326
  Eichstätt 05419
  Mainz 05732
  Michelstadt 05763
  München 05780, 05784
  Münster 05817
  Tübingen 05951
Ghana
  Legon 06019
Iceland
  Reykjavik 06551
India
  Allahabad 06568, 06571
  Bombay 06609
  Gorakhpur 06674
  Jaunpur 06709
  Kanpur 06722
  Lucknow 06741, 06742, 06747, 06748
  Muzaffarnagar 06776
  Roorkee 06823
Indonesia
  Bandung 06876
Ireland
  Dublin 07017
Israel
  Sha'ar HaGolan Kibbutz 07125
Italy
  Alassio 07162
  Alba 07163
  Bologna 07259
  Firenze 07461
  L'Aquila 07560, 07564
  Roma 07872
  Sant'Anna d'Alfaedo 07949
  Udine 08085
  Valdagno 08093
  Vestenanuova 08141
Japan
  Akita 08174
  Akiyo 08177
  Chichibu 08197
  Kagoshima 08263
  Kami 08272
  Matsuyama 08365
  Minamishidara 08369
  Minamitsuru 08370
  Osaka 08466
  Shima 08498
  Tokyo 08560
  Tsu 08594
Kenya
  Gilgil 08647
Korea, Republic
  Seoul 08711
Lesotho
  Morija 08736
Morocco
  Rabat 08923
Netherlands
  Amsterdam 08969
  Bellingwolde 09029
  Denekamp 09073
  Hardenberg 09166
  Laren 09209
  Leiden 09232
  Maastricht 09248
  Oostkapelle 09279
  Valkenburg 09400
New Zealand
  Invercargill 09506
  Lower Hutt 09513
Norway
  Oslo 09795
Panama
  Panama City 09973
Peru
  Huancayo 09996

Philippines
  Iloilo 10033
  Malate 10042
Romania
  Bucureşti 10680
  Iaşi 10731
  Piatra Neamţ 10756
South Africa
  Bloemfontein 10838
  Dundee 10861
  East London 10871
  Kimberley 10918
  Molteno 10931
  Oudtshoorn 10939
  Pretoria 10977
  Vereeniging 11010
Spain
  Ambrona 11034
  Barcelona 11082
  Igualada 11231
  Madrid 11305
  Onda 11390
  Puerto Pollensa 11434
Sweden
  Stockholm 11811, 11828
Switzerland
  Ederswiler 12009
  Glarus 12042
  Meride 12143
  Rothrist 12199
  Rougemont 12200
  Semione 12231
  Zeihen 12306
Tanzania
  Dodoma 12350
Uganda
  Kampala 12594
  Lake Katwe 12599
United Kingdom
  Barnstaple 12664
  Birmingham 12714, 12715
  Bolton 12732
  Bournemouth 12737
  Cambridge 12812
  Clitheroe 12867
  Devizes 12903
  Elgin 12968
  Honiton 13073
  London 13193
  Newcastle-upon-Tyne 13308
  Nottingham 13332
  Redruth 13391
  Sandown 13434
  Stromness 13513
  Whitby 13571
United States
  Altus OK 13675
  American Falls ID 13683
  Amherst MA 13686
  Ashland KS 13735
  Battle Creek MI 13832
  Berkeley CA 13871
  Bryan TX 14005
  Cambridge MA 14033
  Cedar Falls IA 14089
  Flora MS 14578
  Florissant CO 14585
  Fort Pierce FL 14635
  Havre MT 14854
  Hellertown PA 14862
  Knoxville TN 15082
  Las Vegas NV 15140
  Lemmon SD 15160
  Lima OH 15189
  Littleton CO 15211
  McKinney TX 15284
  Mason City IA 15346
  Milwaukee 15412
  Minneapolis MN 15426
  Mountainside NJ 15501
  Pocatello ID 15948
  Price UT 15998
  Rapid City SD 16040
  Richmond IN 16069
  Riverside CA 16098

  Rock Island IL 16121
  Rocky Ford CO 16134
  Russell Springs KS 16153
  Sacramento CA 16163
  San Pedro CA 16286
  Solomons MD 16409
  Springs PA 16453
  Stony Brook NY 16491
  The Dalles OR 16571
  Tiffin OH 16576
  Traverse City MI 16601
  Tucson AZ 16619
  Washington DC 16772
  Weeping Water NE 16821
  West Hartford CT 16839
  Wickliffe KY 16872
  Yucaipa CA 16959
Viet Nam
  Ho Chi Minh City 17423
Yugoslavia
  Zagreb 17817
Fresco painting *see* Mural painting and decoration
Funeral rites and ceremonies
Austria
  Wien 00852, 00866
Belgium
  Andenne 00926
  Arlon 00953
China, People's Republic
  Changping 02620
  Changsha 02621
  Kunming 02638
  Wuhan 02667
  Zhengzhou 02676
Germany, Federal Republic
  Saarbrücken 05902
India
  Udaipur 06855
Japan
  Nishiiwai 08435
  Saito 08479
  Tsuyama 08598
Norway
  Leka 09737
  Oslo 09810
  Skogn 09852
  Spydeberg 09862
  Tingvatn 09877
Poland
  Chojnów 10143
Spain
  Ibiza 11230
  Santillana del Mar 11496
  Tarragona 11542
United States
  Hohenwald TN 14889
  Honaunau HI 14897
Fur *see* Hides and skins
Furniture and interiors
Argentina
  Buenos Aires 00085, 00125, 00135, 00138
  Corrientes 00199
  La Plata 00239
  Posadas 00304
  Rosario 00329
  San Isidro 00347
  San Juan 00359
  San Lorenzo 00360
  San Miguel de Tucumán 00365, 00366, 00372
  San Nicolás de los Arroyos 00378
  Santa Fé 00389
  Yatasto 00430
Australia
  Ballarat 00448
  Bendigo 00455
  Deloraine 00485
  Dowerin 00488
  Elsternwick 00490
  Hobart 00506
  Launceston 00517
  Mahogany Creek 00522

  Manjimup 00524
  Maylands 00525
  Nile 00546
  Pinjarra 00560
  Tea Tree Gully 00588
  Vaucluse 00590
  Wauchope 00593
  Westbury 00595
Austria
  Alpl 00606
  Altenburg 00608
  Bad Ischl 00622, 00623
  Bernstein 00634
  Döllach 00640
  Eisenstadt 00651
  Frohnleiten 00657
  Gobelsburg 00663
  Göttweig-Furth 00664
  Graz 00667, 00671, 00674
  Innsbruck 00695, 00696
  Kufstein 00717
  Maria Saal 00733
  Reidling 00763
  Riegersburg 00766
  Rohrau 00768
  Salzburg 00782
  Sankt Florian 00785
  St. Johann i.S. 00788
  Schallaburg 00795
  Schlaining 00799
  Schlierbach 00800
  Seckau 00802
  Stainz 00812
  Steyr 00815
  Wien 00831, 00840, 00848, 00854, 00857, 00878, 00893
Belgium
  Antwerpen 00935, 00945, 00949
  Awirs 00958
  Beloeil 00964
  Brugge 00991
  Bruxelles 01016, 01017, 01027, 01030
  Damme 01045
  Ecaussinnes-Lalaing 01065
  Gaasbeek 01073
  Gent 01087, 01088
  Geraardsbergen 01093
  Ieper 01117
  Ingooigem 01121
  Keerbergen 01129
  Laarne 01138
  Lessines 01144
  Liège 01153, 01155, 01164
  Lier 01166, 01167
  Maaseik 01173
  Martelange 01178
  Namur 01203
  Olsene 01221
  Rekem 01236
  Saint-Hubert 01248
  Schelle 01250
  Turnhout 01288
  Verviers 01291
  Vieux-Genappe 01294
  Virton 01296
Bermuda
  Hamilton 01331
  St. George's 01333-01335
Brazil
  Caeté 01358
  Natal 01404
  Ouro Preto 01410
  Pœrto Alegre 01422
  Recife 01430
  Recôncavo 01433
  Rio de Janeiro 01436, 01456, 01469, 01473
  Salvador 01485, 01487, 01491
  São Cristóvão 01505
  Teresina 01534
  Vitória 01538
Canada
  Arthabasca 01765
  Batiscan 01787

Meersburg 05751, 05753, 05754
München 05793, 05795, 05797
Münster 05816
Neuwied 05829
Nürnberg 05835, 05839, 05842
Oberammergau 05845
Oberschleißheim 05848, 05850, 05851
Prien 05872
Regensburg 05881
Rothenburg ob der Tauber 05892
Salzgitter 05905
Schwetzingen 05915
Selm 05918
Sylt-Ost 05940
Trostberg 05948
Wetzlar 05978
Wolfenbüttel 05987
Würzburg 05997, 06002
Greece
  Kalymnos 06140
  Mitilini 06200, 06202
  Rhodos 06249
  Skyros 06271
Guatemala
  Antigua 06313, 06314
  Ciudad de Guatemala 06320
Hungary
  Budapest 06359, 06370, 06383
  Fertőd 06414
  Keszthely 06435
  Pápa 06465
  Sárvár 06485
  Szenna 06507
  Zalaegerszeg 06541
India
  New Delhi 06800
Ireland
  Bunratty 07005
  Kilkenny 07021
  Westport 07026
Italy
  Anacapri 07173
  Bobbio 07237
  Bologna 07249
  Busseto 07287
  Caserta 07316
  Castiglione delle Stiviere 07330
  Città di Castello 07362
  Clusone 07369
  Crema 07389
  Ferrara 07432
  Firenze 07440, 07460, 07464, 07475
  Fontanellato 07487
  Genova 07527
  Gradara 07535
  Gubbio 07545
  Isola Bella 07556
  Issogne 07557
  Lucca 07588
  Milano 07622
  Napoli 07682
  Rovereto 07913
  San Leo 07934
  San Nicolo' Val d'Ultimo 07941
  Sant'Angelo Lodigiano 07948
  Sestri Levante 07974
  Thiene 08016
  Torino 08045
  Treviso 08064
  Trieste 08067, 08074, 08079
Japan
  Ashikaga 08188
  Fukui 08207
  Iwakuni 08259
  Kamakura 08267
  Kanazawa 08276
  Kawachi-Nagano 08286
  Kobe 08297
  Kurashiki 08317
  Takayama 08526
  Tokyo 08549
  Tottori 08588

Korea, Republic
  Seoul 08695
Mexico
  Tepotzotlán 08888
Netherlands
  Amerongen 08956
  Amersfoort 08958
  Ammerzoden 08959
  Amsterdam 08975, 08978, 08980, 08989
  Axel 09024
  Barneveld 09026
  Bergen op Zoom 09034
  Bolsward 09038
  Borculo 09039
  Brakel 09044
  Breukelen 09048
  Delft 09064, 09066
  Den Oever 09078
  Deventer 09081
  Diever 09086
  Doorn 09092
  Doornenburg 09093
  Dordrecht 09097
  Edam 09104
  Genemuiden 09138
  Haarlem 09158
  Haarzuilens 09163
  Haastrecht 09165
  Heerenveen 09175
  Hindeloopen 09189
  Hollum 09191
  Hoogeveen 09193
  Hoorn 09194
  Kampen 09201
  Leens 09213
  Leiden 09236
  Loosdrecht 09242
  Maastricht 09251
  Marssum 09253
  Midden-Beemster 09258
  Muiden 09260
  Noordwijk Aan Zee 09266
  Roermond 09298
  Rijswijk 09314
  Schoonhoven 09328
  's-Gravenhage 09348
  's-Heerenberg 09350
  Tiel 09376
  Uithuizen 09382
  Vaassen 09398
  Velsen 09407
  Volendam 09418
  Voorburg 09420
  Voorschoten 09421
  Zaandam 09444
  Zaltbommel 09447
  Zeist 09450
  Zierikzee 09453
  Zuilen 09457
  Zwolle 09462
New Zealand
  Dunedin 09490
  Kaitaia 09508
  Matakohe 09517
  Napier 09525
  Norsewood 09525
  Timaru 09558
  Waiuku 09569
Norway
  Arendal 09611
  Bergen 09629, 09630
  Dagali 09646
  Fannrem 09666
  Fjøsanger 09669
  Halden 09687
  Hvalstad 09711
  Kragerø 09724
  Larvik 09734
  Mandal 09748
  Oslo 09777
  Sandnes 09841
  Selbu 09843
  Skiptvet 09850
  Skotselv 09853

Trondheim 09889, 09890
Vågåmo 09905
Peru
  Lima 10004
Poland
  Antonin 10106
  Biały Dunajec 10114
  Chojnów 10143
  Chorzów 10144
  Jarosław 10199
  Kraków 10230, 10245
  Łańcut 10260
  Lidzbark Warmiński 10270
  Młynary 10295
  Niedzica 10304
  Olsztynek 10320
  Opole-Bierkowice 10324
  Oporów 10325
  Ostrzyce 10328
  Pszczyna 10361
  Rogalin 10373
  Środa Śląska 10397
  Toruń 10434
  Warszawa 10463
Portugal
  Avanca 10536
  Guimarães 10568
  Mafra 10595
  Queluz 10611
  Sintra 10619
Romania
  Sinaia 10780
San Marino
  San Marino 10805
South Africa
  Adelaide 10829
  Caledon 10843
  Cape Town 10845, 10847, 10850, 10854
  Constantia 10859
  Cradock 10860
  Durban 10862, 10869
  East London 10872
  Graaff-Reinet 10879
  Grahamstown 10885
  Great Brak River 10886
  Himeville 10893
  Johannesburg 10896
  Knysna 10924
  Matjiesfontein 10928
  Montagu 10932
  Oudtshoorn 10940
  Paarl 10941
  Pietermaritzburg 10943, 10947
  Potchefstroom 10953
  Pretoria 10960, 10964, 10978
  Richmond 10981
  Riversdale 10982
  Roodepoort 10984
  Silverton 10986
  Somerset East 10990
  Stellenbosch 10995, 11000
  Tulbagh 11005, 11006
  Verwoerdburg 11012
  Worcester 11018
Spain
  Barcelona 11070, 11080
  Burgos 11120
  Deya 11179
  El Pardo 11183
  Madrid 11288
  Palma de Mallorca 11408, 11415
  Paredes de Nava 11423
  Puerto Pollensa 11433
  San Sebastián 11474
  Santillana del Mar 11498
  Segovia 11503
  Sitges 11532
  Teruel 11549
  Toledo 11555
  Valencia 11580
  Villanueva y Geltrú 11612
Sweden
  Askersund 11660
  Bålsta 11661

Drottningholm 11672, 11673
Göteborg 11706
Halmstad 11714
Julita 11726
Kalmar 11730
Landskrona 11742
Lund 11752
Mölndal 11765
Norrköping 11774
Nyköping 11778
Skurup 11798
Solna 11802
Stockholm 11807, 11814, 11819
Sundborn 11851
Tyresö 11860
Ystad 11885
Switzerland
  Aarburg 11892
  Allschwil 11899
  Altstetten 11903
  Arenenberg 11909
  Bischofszell 11963
  Bissone 11964
  Brienz 11973
  Coppet 11998, 11999
  Estavayer-le-Lac 12013
  Gelfingen 12022
  Genève 12024
  Grandson 12047
  Grandvaux 12048
  Gruyères 12053
  Hallwil 12059
  Herisau 12063
  Hilterfingen 12065
  Höngg 12070
  Jegenstorf 12075
  Kyburg 12084
  La Chaux-de-Fonds 12087
  La Sarraz 12091
  Lausanne 12102
  Lenzburg 12110
  Martigny 12138
  Monthey 12144
  Müstair 12157
  Nyon 12166
  Oberhofen am Thunersee 12168
  Olivone 12171
  Orbe 12175
  Oron-le-Châtel 12176
  Rorschach 12198
  Rothrist 12199
  Samedan 12208
  St. Moritz 12214
  Sargans 12217
  Saxon 12218
  Schötz 12225
  Scuol 12230
  Solothurn 12245
  Stampa 12250
  Tarasp 12260
  Trun 12264
  Utzenstorf 12270
  Valangin 12272
  Vevey 12276
  Veytaux-Chillon 12278
  Werdenberg 12280
  Wiesendangen 12283
  Wil 12284
  Wildegg 12285
  Winterthur 12293
  Zermatt 12307
  Zürich 12337
United Kingdom
  Aberdeen 12608
  Aberford 12609
  Alcester 12616
  Alnwick Castle 12624
  Aylsham 12644
  Bangor/Wales 12655
  Barnard Castle 12660
  Barnsley 12662
  Basingstoke 12667
  Bath 12669, 12670
  Batley 12676

Beveren 00966
Blankenberge 00968
Brecht 00981
Bree 00982
Brugge 00992
Cul-des-Sarts 01044
Deinze 01050
Deurne 01058
Essen 01068
Flobecq 01071
Gent 01088
Hoegaarden 01110
Izegem 01123
Izenberge 01124
Kortrijk 01137
Mechelen 01183
Mouscron 01200
Neufchâteau 01210
Nevele 01212
Oelegem 01219
Oevel 01220
Oostduinkerke 01222
Opheylissem 01228
Ronse 01242
Saint-Hubert 01248
Saint-Vith 01249
Sint-Niklaas 01256
Stavelot 01265
Tongeren 01273, 01276
Tournai 01277
Visé 01299
Weert 01307
Wommelgem 01315
Xhoris 01316
Brazil
Paranaguá 01413
Salvador 01490, 01493
Bulgaria
Etãra 01574
Cameroon
Foumban 01742
Canada
Arichat 01762
Barkerville 01781
Biggar 01797
Dorval 01906
Georgetown 01979
Goderich 01984
Hampton 02027
Iroquois 02046
Kitchener 02071
London 02100
Manitowaning 02116
Miscouche 02141
Mooretown 02172
Oakville 02212
Revelstoke 02303
Rockton 02313
St. Boniface 02326
St. John's 02337
Sombra 02395
South Rawdon 02398
Thunder Bay 02430
Toronto 02456
China, People's Republic
Shanghai 02659
Shenyang 02660
Cuba
La Habana 02806
Czechoslovakia
Bouzov 02859
Česká Třebová 02901
Jemnice 02991
Jesenice u Rakovníka 02992
Jilemnice 02998
Krupka 03044
Nový Jičín 03127, 03129
Přibyslav 03218
Protivín 03222
Rychnov nad Kněžňou 03238
Skuteč 03248
Smiřice nad Labem 03254
Tachov 03276
Týniště nad Orlicí 03299
Žatec 03332

Zbiroh 03333
Ždánice 03336
Žebrák 03340
Žilina 03345
Denmark
Aabenraa 03352
Aarhus 03360
Dragør 03375
Helsingør 03416
Lyngby 03489, 03490
Nørager 03499
Nykøbing Sjælland 03506, 03507
Rønne 03534
Roskilde 03537
Silkeborg 03543
Sønderborg 03556
Svendborg 03564
Thisted 03568
Finland
Halikko 03680
Hämeenlinna 03681
Hanko 03687
Helsinki 03725
Hirvihaara 03730
Imatra 03738
Isokyrö 03741
Kaarlela 03752
Kajaani 03753
Kerava 03763
Kokkola 03767
Kurikka 03776
Maarianhamina 03794
Mänttä 03796
Naantali 03803
Paattinen 03815
Porvoo 03829
Riihimäki 03839
Taivassalo 03854
Turku 03872
Yläne 03895
France
Crépy-en-Valois 04094
Le Puy 04191
Le Vigan 04197
Tours 04522
Ussel 04530
Germany, Democratic Republic
Aken 04565
Bad Liebenwerda 04603
Ballenstedt 04606
Berlin 04619
Borna 04640
Buttstädt 04645
Calau 04646
Colditz 04648
Dessau 04660
Dömitz 04666
Erfurt 04721
Gingst 04754
Gnandstein 04756
Goldberg 04758
Görlitz 04762, 04763
Greussen 04775
Grimma 04777
Grossschönau 04784
Hagenow 04787
Hainichen 04788
Halberstadt 04792
Hildburghausen 04809
Jüterbog 04829
Karl-Marx-Stadt 04839
Landsberg 04856
Lenzen 04879
Naumburg 04922
Oderberg 04940
Oederan 04941
Oelsnitz 04942
Olbernau 04945
Oranienbaum 04946
Oranienburg 04947
Osterwieck/Harz 04951
Perleberg 04956
Plauen 04958
Posterstein 04962
Riesa 05004

Rosswein 05010
Rostock 05011
Schmalkalden 05032
Schönfels 05039
Schwerin 05045
Sonneberg 05057
Stadtilm 05059
Stolberg 05065
Stralsund 05067
Taucha 05074
Weida 05091
Weissenfels 05112
Werdau 05113
Zerbst 05143
Zörbig 05150
Germany, Federal Republic
Aachen 05157
Aalen 05161
Adelsheim 05168
Admont 05170
Alsfeld 05176
Amorbach 05188
Aschach 05197
Aschaffenburg 05199
Augsburg 05204
Baden-Baden 05244
Bensberg 05263
Biedenkopf 05312
Braunschweig 05345
Dinkelsbühl 05394
Erlangen 05434
Feuchtwangen 05449
Frankfurt 05465
Hagen 05524
Hamburg 05536
Haselünne 05559
Helmbrechts 05573
Herford 05574
Kassel 05617
Krempe 05674
Lindau 05699
Melle 05757
Memmingen 05758
Nürnberg 05833
Rothenburg ob der Tauber 05892
Stuttgart' 05939
Trostberg 05948
Tübingen 05957
Ulm 05963
Villingen-Schwenningen 05966
Würzburg 05998
Zwiesel 06010
Greece
Kalymnos 06140
Kastellorizon 06149
Komotini 06158
Pyrgos 06238
Rethymnon 06245
Rhodos 06248
Salonika 06255
Guatemala
Chichicastenango 06316
Ciudad de Guatemala 06318
India
Allahabad 06567
Alwar 06572
Bharatpur 06594
Bhavnagar 06595
Bhopal 06600
Bhuj 06604
Bikaner 06606
Calcutta 06626, 06628
Chhindwara 06642
Gauhati 06670
Jodhpur 06715, 06716
Kanpur 06723
Lucknow 06744, 06754
Mysore 06778, 06779
New Delhi 06790, 06791
Poona 06813
Pudukottai 06816
Sangli 06828
Trivandrum 06851, 06853
Udaipur 06856

Wardha 06871
Indonesia
Surakarta 06936
Iran
Teheran 06978
Italy
Gorizia 07534
Napoli 07683
Premana 07812
Rovigo 07918
Japan
Akita 08174
Fukuoka 08209
Fukushima 08210
Hiroshima 08236
Kumamoto 08314
Kyoto 08342
Matsuyama 08364
Mito 08377
Nagasaki 08397
Nara 08419
Nishikanbara 08439
Suwa 08513
Takamatsu 08517
Tokyo 08575, 08578
Utsunomiya 08605
Yamagata 08610
Mexico
Puebla 08878
Namibia
Lüderitz 08936
Netherlands
Amstelveen 08960
Amsterdam 09006
Barger Compascuum 09025
Beek 09027
Doetinchem 09088
Ede 09105
Eindhoven 09114
Elsloo 09118
Exloo 09130
Goirle 09140
Gorredijk 09142
Grave 09147
Haastrecht 09164
Hellendoorn 09181
Heusden 09184
Hilvarenbeek 09186
Hulst 09196
Leerdam 09215
Ospel-Nederweert 09281
Purmerend 09293
Rotterdam 09300, 09309
Schoonhoven 09327
's-Gravenhage 09348
Stadskanaal 09367
Tilburg 09378
Vriezenveen 09423
Vught 09424
Niger
Niamey 09586
Norway
Lonevåg 09743
Melbu 09749
Sandefjord 09839
Skien 09848
Snåsa 09855
Stjørdal 09870
Philippines
Naga 10071
Poland
Jasło 10200
Kamienna Góra 10207
Koniecpol 10221
Kraków 10236
Poznań 10354
Rabka Zdrój 10367
Sulmierzyce 10407
Sztum 10421
Toszek 10437
Żywiec 10509
Portugal
Azambuja 10538
Beja 10541

Romania
 Bucureşti 10684
 Lupşa 10742
 Rădăuţi 10765
 Sighişoara 10779
South Africa
 Eshowe 10873
Spain
 Avila 11052, 11053
 Espluga de Francolí 11186
 Falset 11188
 Granada 11208, 11211, 11213
 Madrid 11314
 Molins de Rey 11370
 Murcia 11381
 Olot 11386
 Valencia 11584
 Vilajuiga 11607
Sri Lanka
 Ratnapura 11636
Sweden
 Göteborg 11706
 Helsingborg 11718
 Köping 11736
 Örebro 11780
 Oskarshamn 11782
 Stockholm 11829
 Sundsvall 11853
Switzerland
 Altishofen 11901
 Altstetten 11903
 Attiswil 11912
 Baden 11917
 Basel 11925
 Bern 11948
 Coppet 11999
 Hallwil 12059
 Höngg 12070
 Kaltbrunn 12076
 Lenzburg 12111
 Les Éplatures 12112
 Monthey 12144
 Montreux 12145
 Môtiers 12149
 Rapperswil 12185
 Rheinfelden 12190
 Rickenbach 12193
 Riehen 12195
 Urnäsch 12268
 Wohlenschwil 12302
United Kingdom
 Abergavenny 12610
 Alderney 12618
 Bangor/Wales 12655
 Batley 12674
 Dumfries 12921
 Filkins 12981
 Gloucester 13005
 Gosport 13013
 Horsham 13074
 Kettering 13103
 Kingsbridge 13109
 Kinsale 13115
 Newtown 13320
 Sheffield 13446, 13451
 Singleton 13465
United States
 Belvidere NE 13861
 Camden NJ 14041
 Cedar Rapids IA 14091
 Charleston SC 14117
 Denver CO 14389
 Elsah IL 14501
 Erie PA 14512
 Flagstaff AZ 14569
 Ganado AZ 14701
 Greenfield IN 14780
 Greensboro NC 14783
 Greenville SC 14791
 High Point NC 14878
 Holland MI 14891
 Kotzebue AK 15085
 Lake George NY 15107
 Mequon WI 15368
 Nashua IA 15523

 New Brunswick NJ 15557
 New Rochelle NY 15593
 New York NY 15596, 15599, 15634
 Newton NC 15676
 Old Chatham NY 15744
 Pensacola FL 15846
 Pittsburgh PA 15928
 Pittsfield MA 15933
 Portland OR 15975
 Richmond CA 16065
 Richmond TX 16072
 Roebuck SC 16138
 Rutherford NJ 16154
 San Francisco CA 16261
 Schoharie NY 16342
 Walterboro SC 16715
 Washington DC 16764
 Water Mill NY 16788
 West Fargo ND 16837
 Zoar OH 16964
Uruguay
 Montevideo 16969
 Tacuarembó 16985
USSR
 Kolomja 17091
 L'vov 17150
Yemen, People's Democratic Republic
 Aden 17434
 Al-Mukalla 17437
 Seiyun in Wadi Hadhramaut 17438
Yugoslavia
 Beograd 17452
Heraldry see Geneology
Hides and skins
Australia
 Loxton 00521
Germany, Democratic Republic
 Doberlug-Kirchhain 04665
Germany, Federal Republic
 Offenbach 05853
Ghana
 Kumasi 06016
Netherlands
 Waalwijk 09426
Spain
 Igualada 11232
 Madrid 11320
United Kingdom
 Walsall 13548, 13549
United States
 Gloversville NY 14733
 Mainfield ME 15302
Yugoslavia
 Tržič 17777
Historical ruins
Austria
 Dölsach 00641
Belgium
 Arlon 00953
 Comblain-au-Pont 01042
 Gent 01092
 Sint-Truiden 01258
 Villers-devant-Orval 01295
Canada
 Côteau-du-lac 01886
Denmark
 Skanderborg 03547
 Vordingborg 03588
France
 Narbonne 04299
Germany, Democratic Republic
 Regenstein 04996
Germany, Federal Republic
 Dreieich 05399
 Reichenau 05886
 Schleswig 05909
Greece
 Amphiareion 06035
 Epidaurus 06109
 Istiaia 06132
 Kavalla 06151
 Lykosoura 06183

 Mavromation 06187
 Mistra 06198
 Nea Anchialos 06210
 Nemea 06213
 Nikopolis 06215
 Olympia 06219
 Paramythia 06222
 Pella 06228
 Pythagoreion 06242
 Sicyon 06266
 Tanagra 06280
 Thasos 06287
 Thermos 06290
 Thyrreion 06294
 Traïanoupolis 06295
Hungary
 Budapest 06358, 06363
India
 Lucknow 06739
Norway
 Halsnøy Kloster 09688
 Hamar 09690
 Oslo 09783
 Rissa 09825
 Sarpsborg 09842
 Tingvatn 09877
 Trondheim 09884
Spain
 Ampurias 11037
 Barcelona 11084
 Clunia 11152
 Córdoba 11162
 La Guardia 11246
 Linares 11265
 Martorell 11358
 Pamplona 11417
 San Juan de la Peña 11461
 Santes Creus 11491
 Santiponce 11499
 Sigüenza 11529
 Tarrasa 11545
 Tossa 11570
Suriname
 Paramaribo 11649
Switzerland
 Augst 11915
 Avenches 11916
 Biel 11961
 Brugg 11978
 Goldau 12043
 Kaltbrunn 12076
Turkey
 Ballihisar 12472
 Cifteler 12485
United States
 Chillicothe OH 14177
 Heavener OK 14859
 Kure Beach NC 15086
 Mount Gilead NC 15491
 Poteau OK 15987
 St. Marks FL 16197
 St. Simons Island GA 16213
 Savannah GA 16336
 Southport NC 16432
History, Medieval
Argentina
 Buenos Aires 00102, 00114, 00120, 00124
Belgium
 Bouillon 00977
 Gent 01080
 Latour 01141
 Sint-Truiden 01257
 Turnhout 01287
Denmark
 Sønderborg 03556
France
 Angoulême 03931
 Bayeux 03980
 Caen 04029
 Cherbourg 04071
 Cholet 04074
 Colmar 04083
 Martigues 04243
 Paris 04357

 Rennes 04419
 Riquewihr 04426
Germany, Democratic Republic
 Allstedt 04566
 Anklam 04574
 Bad Frankenhausen 04597
 Bad Kösen 04599
 Bad Köstritz 04600
 Bad Muskau 04604
 Bernau 04635
 Bernburg 04636
 Wittenberg-Lutherstadt 05125
 Wittenberge 05126
Germany, Federal Republic
 Bad Mergentheim 05222
 Braubach 05336
 Höxter 05584
 Ingolstadt 05593
 Lüdinghausen 05716
 Lüneburg 05723
 Maulbronn 05748
 München 05796
 Murrhardt 05822
 Nürnberg 05837
 Saarbrücken 05902
India
 Baroda 06588
 Bijapur 06605
Italy
 Adrano 07152
 Asolo 07198
 Ciano d'Enza 07359
 Firenze 07472
 Venezia 08111
Japan
 Chikushi 08199
 Nagoya 08402
 Osaka 08462
 Shimonoseki 08499
 Takefu 08530
 Tokyo 08552
Netherlands
 Leiden 09229
 Rhenen 09296
 Rijnsburg 09312
Norway
 Bergen 09619, 09623
 Verdal 09913
Peru
 Lima 10007
Poland
 Giecz 10174
 Legnickie Pole 10266
 Ostrów Lednicki 10326
Romania
 Bran 10666
 Bucureşti 10679
 Călăraşi 10689
 Hunedoara 10727
 Iaşi 10730, 10737
 Tulcea 10793
Spain
 Aranjuez 11039
 Azpeitia (Véase Loyola) 11058
 Covarrubias 11170
 El Toboso 11184
 Gandía 11195
 Granada 11211
 Ibiza 11228
 Las Palmas 11250
 Madrid 11294, 11301, 11306
 Roncesvalles 11446
 Santa María de Huerta 11484
 Valladolid 11589
 Vitoria 11616
 Yuste 11625
Sweden
 Farösund 11691
 Stockholm 11840
 Varberg 11875
 Visby 11884
Switzerland
 Avenches 11916
United Kingdom
 Blair Atholl 12726

Bodiam 12729
Conwy 12878
Yugoslavia
Kruševac 17583
Požarevac 17665
Prilep 17671
Priština 17673
Škofja Loka 17718
Skopje 17721, 17722
History, Modern
Algeria
Alger 00026
Argentina
Buenos Aires 00073, 00077, 00082, 00127
Salta 00339
San Miguel de Tucumán 00365
Australia
Adelaide 00434
Armadale 00444
Armidale 00445
Campbell 00470
Cannington 00471
Parkville 00553
Vaucluse 00590
Austria
Forchtenstein 00653
Fresach 00655
Gloggnitz 00660
Peuerbach 00757
Schallaburg 00795
Wien 00828, 00829, 00847, 00852, 00858, 00860, 00864, 00877, 00895, 00896
Bahamas
Hope Town 00910
Belgium
Bellem 00963
Braine-l'Alleud 00979
Braine-le-Comte 00980
Brugge 00990
Bruxelles 01014, 01029
De Panne 01053
Diksmuide 01061, 01062
Ieper 01120
Ligny 01169
Mesen 01187
Mons 01195
Nieuwpoort 01214
Overmere 01233
Tournai 01278
Vieux-Genappe 01294
Wachtebeke 01303
Waterloo 01305
Wetteren 01309
Wijtschate 01312
Willebroek 01313
Zeebrugge 01317
Zillebeke 01319
Bermuda
Hamilton 01330
Brazil
Olinda 01409
Ouro Prêto 01411
Rio de Janeiro 01454, 01479
Salvador 01497
São Paulo 01513
Bulgaria
Asenovgrad 01547
Balčik 01549
Bansko 01550
Batak 01551
Belogradčik 01552
Bjala 01556
Blagoevgrad 01557
Bracigovo 01560
Časkovo 01565
Čurek 01568
Dimitrovgrad 01569
Drjanovo 01570, 01571
Elena 01573
Etropole 01575
Gabrovo 01576
Ichtiman 01579
Jambol 01580

Kalofer 01583
Kărdžali 01582
Karlovo 01584, 01585
Karnobat 01586
Kazanlăk 01589
Koprivštica 01594-01596
Kotel 01597
Kovačevci 01600
Lom 01601
Loveč 01602
Madan 01604
Melnik 01606
Michajlovgrad 01607
Nova Zagora 01609
Orjachovo 01610
Panagjurište 01611, 01612
Pazardžik 01613
Peruštica 01617
Pleven 01618, 01619, 01622
Plovdiv 01624, 01627, 01629
Pordim 01631, 01632
Razlog 01636
Ruse 01638
Sevlievo 01644
Sliven 01646, 01648
Sofija 01653, 01655, 01656, 01662, 01668, 01671, 01673
Stanke Dimitrov 01678
Ştara Zagora 01679
Šumen 01682, 01683
Svištov 01686
Targovište 01687
Teteven 01688
Tolbuchin 01689
Varna 01696, 01697
Veliko Tărnovo 01702, 01705
Velingrad 01706
Vraca 01710
Canada
Alexandria 01754
Alliston 01757
Amherstburg 01758
Atlin 01769
Baie Comeau 01775
Bancroft 01776
Belleville 01794
Borden 01803
Bruce Mines 01818
Burlington 01820
Burnaby 01822
Calgary 01829, 01836
Cayuga 01857
Cereal 01859
Colinton 01879
Collingwood 01881
Dalhousie 01897
Dawson City 01900
Dunvegan 01918
Edmonton 01928, 01936
Elk Point 01943
Evansburg 01950
Fort St. James 01964
Fort Steele 01967
Fredericton 01969
Golden 01985
Gow-Ganda 01988
Gravenhurst 02000
Halifax 02020
Hamilton 02023, 02024
Huntsville 02040
Innisville 02044
Jordan 02051
Kelowna 02055
Kitimat 02073
Knowlton 02075
Lang 02082
Lethbridge 02090
Liverpool 02095
London 02103
Louisbourg 02108
Maitland 02113
Melbourne 02128
Milton 02136
Montréal 02166, 02167
Oromocto 02216, 02217

Ottawa 02223, 02234
Pointe-au-Pic 02260
Reston 02302
St. Andrews 02323
Saint John 02333
St. John's 02338
St.-Hyacinthe 02352
Sherbrooke 02388
Sidney 02391
Sydney 02422
Tillsonburg 02432
Toronto 02449, 02453, 02460, 02461
Truro 02470
Upper Woodstock 02472
Welshpool 02522, 02523
Westport 02525
Willowdale 02535
Wingham 02540
Winnipeg 02545
Woodstock 02565
China, People's Republic
Beijing 02617
Guangzhou 02627, 02631
Lhasa 02640
Nanchang 02645, 02647
Nanjing 02650
Nanning 02651
Yanan 02674
China, Republic
Taipei 02683
Colombia
Bogotá 02692, 02693
Manizales 02746
Medellín 02756
Rionegro 02774
Santa Marta 02776
Cuba
La Habana 02808, 02814
Cyprus
Nicosia 02833
Czechoslovakia
1884 02838
Banská Bystrica 02841
Bojnice 02857
Bratislava 02867
Brno 02879, 02880
České Budějovice 02903
Chlum 02910
Chlumec nad Cidlinou 02911
Chlumec u Ústí nad Labem 02912
Dašice 02921
Děčin 02922
Dědice u Vyškova 02923
Dobruška 02927
Domažlice 02934
Dunajská Streda 02936
Fulnek 02943
Galanta 02944
Gelnica 02945
Habry 02949
Havířov 02951
Havýrov 02956
Hlohovec 02958
Horní Branná 02968
Jeseník 02993
Jindřichův Hradec 03001
Karlovy Vary 03010
Klatovy 03018
Kopřivnice 03026
Králův Dvůr 03037
Kravaře 03038
Kremnica 03040
Krupina 03043
Levoča 03057
Lidice 03061
Litoměřice 03068
Litvínov 03073
Maleč 03084
Mariánské Lázně 03086
Martin 03090
Mladá Vožice 03100
Olomučany 03134
Prace 03170

Praha 03193
Prešov 03215
Rousínov u Vyškova 03230
Rožmitál pod Třemšínem 03232
Rtyně v Podkrkonoši 03236
Ružomberok 03237
Sečovce 03243
Slavkov u Brna 03253
Terezín 03281
Vsetín 03322
Denmark
København 03468
Rønne 03536
Skørping 03552
Stege 03559
Ecuador
Quito 03600
Egypt
El-Alamein 03641
Port Said 03647
Finland
Kuopio 03774
France
Ajaccio 03907
Antibes 03935
Arbois 03940
Argenteuil 03942
Arromanches-les-Bains 03949
Auxonne 03961
Bayonne 03982
Besançon 03999
Bordeaux 04008
Brienne-le-Château 04026
Castres 04048
Chambéry 04055
Châteauroux 04066
Chauny 04069
Cherbourg 04071
Cholet 04074
Colmar 04083
Déols 04095
Lectoure 04178
Magny-les-Hameaux 04229
Morosaglia 04282
Paris 04337, 04345, 04357, 04365, 04373, 04388
Pau 04392
Richelieu 04423
Riquewihr 04426
Rueil-Malmaison 04439, 04440
Saint-Malo 04459
Sainte-Menehould 04473
Tarbes 04504
Thann 04508
Varennes-en-Argonne 04537
Verdun 04540
Versailles 04543
Wissembourg 04557
Yzeure 04559
Germany, Democratic Republic
Adorf 04564
Angermünde 04572
Anklam 04574
Annaberg-Buchholz 04575
Arendsee 04580
Aue 04587
Bad Sülze 04593
Bad Blankenburg 04594
Bad Lauchstädt 04602
Belgern 04612
Berlin 04631
Burg 04643
Crimmitschau 04653
Dippoldiswalde 04664
Dömitz 04666
Dresden 04676
Eilenburg 04702
Eisenach 04704
Ellrich 04716
Erfurt 04718
Finsterbergen 04728
Frankfurt/Oder 04732
Friedland 04740
Frohburg 04741
Gadebusch 04743

Gardelegen   04744, 04745
Gerstungen   04752
Goldberg   04758
Gotha   04765
Grabow   04770
Greiz   04774
Greussen   04775
Grimma   04776
Gröbzig   04778
Grossenhain   04781
Güstrow   04786
Haldensleben   04793
Halle   04796
Heldrungen   04804
Hiddensee   04808
Hildburghausen   04809
Hohnstein   04812
Hoyerswerda   04813
Jena   04822, 04827
Jüterbog   04829
Kapellendorf   04833
Karl-Marx-Stadt   04835, 04836,
04838, 04839
Kirchdorf auf Poel   04843
Kölleda   04848
Lancken-Granitz   04855
Landsberg   04856
Leipzig   04870
Lengenfeld   04878
Lenzen   04879
Liebstadt   04880
Löbau   04881, 04882
Lommatzsch   04883, 04884
Luckenwalde   04887
Lugau   04888
Lützen   04890
Markkleeberg   04896
Meerane   04900
Meissen   04906
Merseburg   04907
Mittweida   04908
Molchow-Stendenitz   04909
Mügeln   04913
Mühlberg   04914
Mühlhausen   04916, 04917
Mutzschen   04919
Neubrandenburg   04926
Neugersdorf   04928
Neukirch   04930
Neuruppin   04931
Neusalza-Spremberg   04932
Niedercunnersdorf   04934
Oederan   04941
Oelsnitz   04942
Oranienbaum   04946
Oranienburg   04947
Oschatz   04948
Osterburg   04950
Ostseebad Graal-Müritz   04952
Oybin   04953
Parchim   04954
Pegau   04955
Pirna   04957
Prieros   04980
Pritzwalk   04981
Pulsnitz   04982
Querfurt   04987
Rabenau   04988
Radeberg   04989
Radebeul   04990
Reichenau   04997
Reitzengeschwenda   04999
Rerik   05001
Römhild   05009
Rothenburg   05016
Schkeuditz   05030
Schöneck   05037
Schöneiche   05038
Schwedt   05041
Sperenberg   05058
Sternberg   05063
Strausberg   05069
Templin   05075
Triebsees   05080
Wandlitz   05086

Wehlen   05090
Weida   05091
Wittenberg-Lutherstadt   05125
Wolgast   05131
Wolkenstein   05132
Zittau   05148
Germany, Federal Republic
Bad Honnef   05218
Bad Karlshafen   05219
Berlin   05275, 05278, 05303
Düsseldorf   05406
Friedrichsruh   05484
Ingolstadt   05593
Karlsruhe   05609
Kaub   05622
Kelheim   05624
Lübeck   05711
Lüdenscheid   05715
Lüdinghausen   05716
Lüneburg   05723
Marktrodach   05744
Maulbronn   05748
München   05802
Oberammergau   05845
Offenburg   05856
Rastatt   05873
Regensburg   05884
Remscheid   05888
Rothenburg ob der Tauber
05893
Stuttgart   05930
Trier   05945
Worpswede   05992
Zwiesel   06010
Greece
Athens   06053, 06079
Lachanas   06164
Spetsai   06276
Zakinthos   06311
Guatemala
Antigua   06315
India
Calcutta   06637
Hooghly   06691
New Delhi   06800
Indonesia
Bandung   06874
Iran
Tabrīz   06967
Iraq
Baghdad   06996
Ireland
Galway   07019
Israel
Acre   07029
Jerusalem   07099
Kefar Gil'adi Kibbutz   07101
Lohame Hageta'ot Kibbutz
07106
Tel Aviv   07135
Tel Hay   07144
Yad Mordekhay Kibbutz   07146
Zikhron Ya'aqov   07150
Italy
Alessandria   07168, 07169
Asti   07205
Bergamo   07226
Bologna   07248
Borgosesia   07268
Brescia   07279
Caprera   07306
Cologna Veneta   07375
Como   07376
Cremona   07391
Diano d'Alba   07398
Ferrara   07429
Fidenza   07434
Forlì   07489
Gallarate   07502
Gavinana   07507
Genova   07523
Gorizia   07533
Gradara   07535
Imola   07550
Lecco   07571

Legnago   07573
Macerata   07596
Mantova   07603
Milano   07637, 07642
Modena   07658
Modigliani   07666
Napoli   07687
Palermo   07726
Parma   07741, 07746
Pavia   07749
Peschiera del Garda   07768
Piacenza   07773
Pieve di Cadore   07781
Portoferraio   07802
Redipuglia   07822
Roma   07854, 07879, 07893
San Martino della Battaglia
07937
Solferino   07987
Torino   08041
Torre del Lago Puccini   08048
Trento   08059
Trieste   08072
Varese   08096
Venezia   08113
Vicenza   08145
Vittorio Veneto   08155
Japan
Hamamatsu   08220
Hiroshima   08235
Kumamoto   08311
Mito   08378
Nagasaki   08396, 08397
Tokyo   08552
Ueno   08603
Korea, Democratic People's
Republic
P'yongyang   08655, 08659
Luxembourg
Esch   08761
Mexico
Campeche   08818
Hermosillo   08833
México City   08849, 08854
Nayarit   08870
Mongolia
Altanbulag   08905
Ulan Bator   08907, 08914, 08915
Namibia
Swakopmund   08938
Netherlands
Amsterdam   08963, 08970, 08971
Deventer   09084
Helmond   09183
Naarden   09263
Oosterbeek   09278
Sneek   09364
Netherlands Antilles
Curaçao   09463
New Zealand
Howick   09504
Shantytown   09548
Wanganui   09570
Norway
Eidsvoll Verk   09658
Fjøsanger   09669
Grimstad   09682
Hurdal   09710
Narvik   09765
Oslo   09779, 09786, 09793
Rjukan   09826
Stavanger   09866
Tromsø   09881, 09883
Trondheim   09884
Vanse   09907
Varteig   09910
Vigrestad   09914
Pakistan
Karachi   09938
Paraguay
Asunción   09982
Philippines
Badoc   10018
Batan   10023
Calamba   10028

Dapitan   10031
Kawit   10037
Malacañang   10041
Malolos   10043
Manila   10051, 10056, 10066
Quezon   10084
Santo Tomas   10091
Taal   10093, 10094
Tanauan   10097, 10098
Vinzons   10104
Poland
Łambinowice   10259
Leśnica   10267
Leszno   10268
Łódź   10274
Łuków   10287
Majdanek   10288
Miechów   10291
Moræg   10296
Olesno   10316
Opinogóra   10321
Oświęcim   10329
Police   10340
Polichno   10341
Poronin   10343
Poznań   10348, 10351, 10355
Szczecinek   10416
Sztutowo   10422
Warka-Winary   10441
Warszawa   10446, 10448, 10453,
10469
Września   10503
Wschowa   10504
Żagań   10505
Zyrardów   10529
Romania
Bucureşti   10678, 10679
Doftana   10713
Giurgiu   10724
Iaşi   10730, 10737
Tirgu Mureş   10791
San Marino
San Marino   10804
South Africa
Colesberg   10858
Durban   10866
Kimberley   10919
King William's Town   10921
Knysna   10924
Potgietersrus   10955
Pretoria   10965
Saxonwold   10985
Vryheid   11015
Windhoek   11017
Spain
Burgos   11121
Madrid   11310
Onda   11391
Pamplona   11418
San Lorenzo de El Escorial
11465
Santander   11487
Vitoria   11617
Sweden
Göteborg   11701
Kristinehamn   11738
Switzerland
Genève   12031
Grenchen   12050
Hilterfingen   12065
Rapperswil   12185, 12186
Solothurn   12242
Tanzania
Arusha   12343
Bagamoyo   12346
Tabora   12356
Tunisia
Ksar Hellal   12429
Téboursouk   12440
Tunis   12443, 12446, 12447
Turkey
Akşehir   12453
Alagoz   12456
Ankara   12460, 12462, 12464
Bursa   12479

History, Social see Social conditions
Horology see Clocks and watches
Horses

Weeping Water NE 16821
West Hartford CT 16839
Westfield NY 16853
Wilkes-Barre Pa 16875
Williamsburg VA 16879
Willmar MN 16887
Window Rock AZ 16904
Winona MN 16911
Woodward OK 16932
Wrangell AK 16940
Yuba City CA 16958
Yucca Valley CA 16960

Industrial arts (*see also* Technology;
Trades and guilds)
Argentina
Buenos Aires 00160
Paraná 00293
Australia
Brompton 00465
Whyalla Norrie 00596
Austria
Murau 00743
Belgium
Sprimont 01264
Canada
Barrington 01785
Bridgewater 01813
Freetown 01973
Guelph 02009
Longueuil 02105
Montréal 02149
Ottawa 02233
Valcout 02474
Czechoslovakia
Brno 02883
Denmark
Fjerritslev 03394
Frederiksværk 03400
Valby 03574
Finland
Nuutajärvi 03808
Ruotsinpyhtää 03846
France
Poitiers 04404
Saint-Etienne 04451
Germany, Democratic Republic
Gerstungen 04752
Landsberg 04856
Riesa 05004
Velten 05082
Germany, Federal Republic
Aalen 05164
Braunschweig 05340
Frankfurt 05466
Hagen 05524
Kümmersbruck 05680
Lüdenscheid 05715
Remscheid-Hasten 05889
Hungary
Budapest 06386
Herend 06423
Ózd 06462
Rudabánya 06480
Siófok 06488
Tatabánya 06528
India
Bangalore 06582
Bombay 06614
Calcutta 06624
Hooghly 06690
Pilani 06807
Simla 06840
Japan
Tokyo 08558
Mongolia
Darham 08906
Netherlands
Amsterdam 08983
Enschede 09127
Genemuiden 09138
Groningen 09153
Norway
Haugfoss 09694
Pakistan
Lahore 09941

Poland
Łódź 10275
Poznań 10346
Sielpia Wielka 10386
Wodzisław Śląski 10486
Spain
Barcelona 11085
Sweden
Eskilstuna 11683
Jönköping 11724
Uganda
Kampala 12598
United Kingdom
Birmingham 12717
Cardiff 12825
Dunfermline 12931
Dursley 12937
Havant 13048
Kendal 13099
Kirkcaldy 13116
London 13240
Sheffield 13450
United States
Alamo TX 13632
Albany NY 13641
Apalachicola FL 13713
Atlanta GA 13753
Beaumont TX 13845
Brainerd MN 13955
Colorado Springs CO 14249
Cornwall PA 14292
Corry PA 14297
Edgartown MA 14473
Elmira NY 14495
Elverson PA 14502
Exton PA 14532
Fairlee VT 14541
Hugoton KS 14923
Jamestown NY 14993
Juneau AK 15019
Kent CT 15044
Kokomo IN 15084
Liverpool NY 15214
Metamora IN 15377
New Britain CT 15554
North Andover Ma 15696
Oak Ridge TN 15724
Philadelphia PA 15867, 15870
Raleigh NC 16033
Richmond TX 16072
St James MO 16177
St Louis MO 16190
Seattle WA 16353
Tampa FL 16542
Tonanwanda NY 16591
Warehouse Point CT 16719
Washington DC 16733
Wilmington DE 16890
Windsor VT 16908

Inscriptions and epitaphs
Austria
Leibnitz 00723
Czechoslovakia
Poděbrady 03163
Denmark
Aarhus 03359
France
Avignon 03966
Carpentras 04044
Die 04096
Lyon 04219
Nice 04306
Toulouse 04518
Vienne 04547, 04549
Germany, Democratic Republic
Jena 04821
Germany, Federal Republic
Soest 05921
Greece
Amphiareion 06035
Athens 06058
Chora 06095, 06097
Epidaurus 06109
Farsala 06114
Ios 06131

Kalymnos 06139
Kastelli Kisamou 06148
Kos 06160
Lindos 06177
Loutra Aidhipsou 06182
Lykosoura 06183
Mandraki 06184
Maroneia 06185
Mavromation 06187
Navpaktos 06208
Nemea 06213
Paramythia 06222
Plaka 06233
Pythagoreion 06242
Salamis 06250
Sikinos 06267
Tanagra 06280
Telos 06282
Tenos 06283
Thespiae 06291
Traïanoupolis 06295
India
Ajmer 06564
Alampur 06565
Amaravati 06573
Bhubaneshwar 06603
Calcutta 06620
Dharwar 06659
Gulbarga 06677
Guntur 06679
Jamnagar 06707
Kakinada 06719
Kalpi 06720
Khajuraho 06727
Kittur 06730
Kolanupaka 06733
Kotah 06736
Mathura 06770
Padmanabhapuram 06803
Pondicherry 06809
Prabhas Patan 06815
Pudukottai 06816
Rajamundry 06819
Sagar 06825
Sanchi 06826
Shimoga 06835
Shirali 06836
Tirupati 06848
Udupi 06857
Ujjain 06858
Vallabh Vidyanagar 06862
Vidisha 06868
Israel
Tel Aviv 07138
Italy
Aquileia 07184, 07185
Bologna 07257
Bovino 07271
Brescello 07274
Brindisi 07284
Camerino 07298
Casamari 07314
Corfinio 07381
Fondi 07486
Pievebovigliana 07783
Spoleto 07995
Sutri 08004
Taormina 08006
Vercelli 08130
Japan
Tokyo 08539
Libya
Tripoli 08748
Norway
Steinkjer 09868
Romania
Sarmizegetusa 10772
Spain
Albacete 11020
Badajoz 11059
Tarragona 11540
Tortosa 11569
Tuy 11573
Xàtiva 11621

United States
Austin TX 13783
Ramah NM 16035
Vatican
Città del Vaticano 17371
Insects
Australia
Sydney 00582
Austria
Admont 00603
Belgium
Namur 01208
Brazil
Porto Alegre 01418
Canada
Calgary 01832
Osoyoos 02222
Saskatoon 02361
Vancouver 02484
Winnipeg 02554
Chile
Santiago 02591
Colombia
Popayán 02768
Tunja 02782
Czechoslovakia
Brno 02874
Praha 03174
Egypt
Cairo 03623, 03634
Ethiopia
Addis Ababa 03658
Finland
Forssa 03679
Helsinki 03701
France
Dijon 04102
Sérignan-du-Comtat 04490
Troyes 04525
Germany, Democratic Republic
Annaberg-Buchholz 04576
Auerbach 04588
Bernburg 04636
Dorfchemnitz 04668
Germany, Federal Republic
Aschaffenburg 05200
Bielefeld 05315
Bonn 05333
Düsseldorf 05412
Erlangen 05436
Heidelberg 05570
Karlsruhe 05607
India
Darjeeling 06650
Muzaffarnagar 06777
Tiruchirapalli 06847
Italy
Bordighera 07267
Brescia 07277
Cremona 07392
Japan
Asahikawa 08180
Chichibu 08197
Fujiyoshida 08205
Fukui 08206
Gifu 08212
Hiwa 08237
Kitami 08294
Minamishidara 08369
Kenya
Meru 08651
Madagascar
Nosy-Bé 08772
Mauritius
Port Louis 08813
Mexico
México City 08848
Tuxla Gutiérrez 08892
Netherlands
Asten 09023
Steyl 09371
New Zealand
Auckland 09469
Philippines
Pasay 10078

Evanston IL   14525
New Orleans LA   15590
Paramus NJ   15812
Philadelphia PA   15886
Santa Barbara CA   16296
Uruguay
Montevideo   16979
USSR
Moskva   17216
Yugoslavia
Split   17737
Lace *see* Needlework
Lacquerwork
China, People's Republic
Changsha   02621
Germany, Democratic Republic
Berlin   04627
Germany, Federal Republic
Berlin   05289
India
Gauhati   06668
Japan
Fujinomiya   08204
Fukui   08208
Hachinohe   08215
Hagi   08216
Imabari   08247
Iwakuni   08259
Kamakura   08267, 08271
Kaminoyama   08273
Kanazawa   08277, 08279, 08280
Kashima   08285
Kyoto   08343, 08344, 08351
Matsumoto   08360
Matsuyama   08366
Miyagi   08379
Nagano   08388
Nagaoka   08393
Nagoya   08405
Naha   08408
Nara   08416
Nikko   08431
Nishiiwai   08438
Osaka   08460
Tagajo   08514
Takayama   08524, 08526, 08527
Tokyo   08545, 08570, 08572, 08580
Tottori   08588
United States
Washington DC   16744
Viet Nam
Hanoi   17422
Lamps and lighting
Argentina
San Miguel de Tucumán   00369
Austria
Leibnitz   00723
Wenigzell   00825
Belgium
Wezemaal   01311
Brazil
São João Del-Rei   01507
Canada
Belleville   01794
Longueuil   02105
Czechoslovakia
Nový Jičín   03128
Denmark
Fredericia   03396
France
Bourg-en-Bresse   04018
Germany, Federal Republic
Arnsberg   05193
Bad Karlshafen   05219
Kiel   05631
Greece
Olimbos   06217
Poland
Bystrzyca Kłodzka   10134
Rozewie   10376
Spain
El Pardo   11183
Madrid   11331

Switzerland
Büren an der Aare   11982
Halten   12060
Mellingen   12142
United States
Albemarle NC   13645
Baltimore MD   13799, 13806
Burlington NJ   14016
Camden NJ   14041
Charleston WV   14132
Constantine MI   14279
Minneapolis MN   15423
Northborough MA   15710
Philadelphia PA   15887
Sayville NY   16337
Titusville PA   16582
Valley Forge PA   16671
Windsor NY   16907
Winter Park FL   16922
Wooster OH   16934
Language and literature
Argentina
Buenos Aires   00078, 00084, 00106, 00111, 00134, 00156
Florencio Varela   00212
La Plata   00234
Mendoza   00276
Temperley   00407
Villa Ballester   00424
Villa de María   00426
Australia
Hahndorf   00500
Iondaryan   00507
Austria
Bad Goisern   00618
Bad Wimsbach-Neydharting   00629
Bruck a.d.Lafnitz   00639
Drosendorf   00643
Krieglach   00716
Linz   00729
Salzburg   00781
Schärding   00796
Wien   00826, 00827, 00829, 00830, 00850
Belgium
Antwerpen   00928, 00930
Beloeil   00964
Boom   00973
Braine-le-Comte   00980
Brugge   00989
Bruxelles   01000
Damme   01047
Gent   01083
Ingooigem   01121
Nevele   01212
Roisin   01240
Sint-Amands   01254
Stavelot   01266
Zichem   01318
Bulgaria
Berkovica   01555
Elena   01573
Kalofer   01583
Koprivštica   01594, 01595
Kotel   01597
Plovdiv   01624
Sliven   01647
Sofija   01654, 01657-01661
Sopot   01676
Stara Zagora   01679
Švištov   01686
Žeravna   01713
Canada
Caledonia   01825
Grand Forks   01993
Guelph   02008
Oakville   02212
Orillia   02215
Winnipeg   02545
China, People's Republic
Beijing   02614
Guangzhou   02628
Shanghai   02654
Xian   02671

Colombia
Popayán   02766
Usiacurí   02785
Cuba
La Habana   02811, 02815, 02817
Czechoslovakia
Blovice   02855
Bratislava   02864
Čáslavice   02892
Červený Kostelec   02898
Česká Skalice   02900
Český Dub   02905
Chudenice   02919
Diváky   02925
Doksy   02928
Dolínek   02929
Dolný Kubín   02932
Domažlice   02934, 02935
Havlíčkova Borová   02952
Havlíčkův Brod   02954
Horní Planá   02969
Hronov   02979
Jur pri Bratislave   03003
Kelč   03014
Klenčí pod Čerchovem   03019
Kolín   03022
Kostelec na Hané   03031
Kutná Hora   03048
Lázně Bělohrad   03052
Letohrad   03055
Liptovský Mikuláš   03064
Liteň   03067
Lukavec u Pacova   03080
Malé Svatoňovice   03083
Martin   03088
Mělník   03091
Miletín   03096
Modra   03102
Nový Bydžov   03126
Obříství   03131
Opava   03137
Ostředek   03145
Pacov   03147
Paseky nad Jizerou   03150
Plzeň   03157
Počátky   03161, 03162
Poděbrady   03164
Potštejn   03169
Praha   03184, 03199
Proseč u Skutče   03220
Semily   03245
Sobotka   03256, 03257
Stará Huť u Dobříše   03262
Strakonice   03265
Teplice nad Metují   03280
Třebíz   03290
Uherský Brod   03301
Úpice   03304
Ústí nad Labem   03305
Vodňany   03317
Vysoké Mýto   03325, 03326
Zbiroh   03334
Žebrák   03340
Denmark
Ballerup   03369
Esbjerg   03384
Espergærde   03385
Farsø   03393
Herning   03419
Kjellerup   03449
København   03450, 03461, 03462, 03479
Lundby   03488
Odense   03514, 03515
Padborg   03523
Roslev   03539
Skagen   03544
Struer   03561
Svendborg   03563
Thisted   03568
Vesløs   03580
Viborg   03582
Finland
Porvoo   03826
Sammatti   03849

France
Aix-en-Provence   03903
Aix-les-Bains   03906
Amiens   03922
Andillac   03925
Bergues   03995
Camaret-sur-Mer   04035
Carcassonne   04039
Châlons-sur-Marne   04051
Chambéry   04054
Charleville-Mézières   04057
Château-Thierry   04061
Grenoble   04132
Illiers Combray   04141
La Châtre   04151
Langres   04158
Le Petit-Couronne   04190
Le Vigan   04197
Liré   04205
Mâcon   04227
Meudon   04254
Montmorency   04277
Nohant-Vic   04324
Paris   04339, 04340, 04343, 04389
Pézenas   04398
Saint-Denis   04447
Saint-Sauveur-le-Vicomte   04468, 04469
Sète   04492
Uzès   04531
Villequier   04552
Villers-Cotterêts   04553
Germany, Democratic Republic
Bad Saarow-Pieskow   04591
Bauerbach   04607
Bautzen   04608
Berlin   04620
Dresden   04677, 04679
Eisenach   04706
Erkner   04724
Frankfurt/Oder   04731
Garz auf Rügen   04746
Gotha   04766
Grimma   04776
Grosskochberg   04782
Halberstadt   04790
Hiddensee   04807
Ilmenau   04814, 04815
Jena   04820, 04826
Kamenz   04831
Leipzig   04875
Magdeburg   04892
Meiningen   04901
Molmerswende   04910
Neuruppin   04931
Ossmannstedt   04949
Quedlinburg   04983
Rammenau   04993
Reuterstadt Stavenhagen   05002
Seebad Heringsdorf   05048
Stützerbach   05070
Thale   05076
Weimar   05092-05096, 05100, 05104, 05108
Wöbbelin   05129
Wurzen   05136
Germany, Federal Republic
Achstetten   05167
Bad Driburg   05213
Bad Homburg v.d. Höhe   05216
Bad Nenndorf   05227
Bad Oeynhausen   05229
Bamberg   05246, 05250
Biberach a.d. Riß   05311
Bingen am Rhein   05316
Bodenwerder   05325
Bonn   05329
Braunschweig   05343
Düsseldorf   05405, 05407
Eschershausen   05437
Frankfurt   05457, 05459
Garding   05497
Hausen   05562
Karlsruhe   05608

Germany, Federal Republic
  München 05787
Israel
  Tiberias 07145
United States
  Shelby 16379
  Taunton MA 16554
  Wenatchee WA 16828
Majolica *see* Porcelain and ceramics
Mammals
Argentina
  La Plata 00236
Belgium
  Bruxelles 01006
  Gent 01090
Canada
  Brandon 01808
  Calgary 01827, 01832
  Wawa 02517
Finland
  Helsinki 03701
France
  Orleans 04331
Germany, Democratic Republic
  Halle 04799
Germany, Federal Republic
  Heidelberg 05570
Iceland
  Reykjavik 06551
India
  Bombay 06612
  Lucknow 06755
Ireland
  Dublin 07018
Israel
  Kiriat Tivon 07104
Italy
  Carmagnola 07309
  Roma 07872
  Udine 08086
Luxembourg
  Luxembourg 08764
Netherlands
  Amsterdam 08979
  Groningen 09149
  Leiden 09234
  Nunspeet 09268
  Rotterdam 09305
New Zealand
  Wellington 09573
Portugal
  Cascais 10547
  Porto 10609
South Africa
  Grahamstown 10882
  Johannesburg 10899, 10909
  King William's Town 10921
  Pietermaritzburg 10945
  Stellenbosch 10996
Spain
  Bañolas 11066
Sweden
  Göteborg 11703
Switzerland
  Schaffhausen 12219
  Solothurn 12246
  Zürich 12329
Tanzania
  Arusha 12345
  Serengeti 12355
Uganda
  Lake Katwe 12599
  Murchison Falls 12601
United States
  Austin TX 13779
  Baltimore MD 13797
  Bancroft ME 13812
  Browning MT 13999
  Cambridge MA 14037
  Cedar Falls IA 14089
  Chattanooga TN 14138
  Chicago IL 14170
  Detroit MI 14414
  Emporia KS 14504
  Gainesville FL 14691

Greenville DE 14787
Havre MT 14854
Iowa City IA 14965
Jackson MS 14978
Lafayette LA 15097
Madison WI 15299
Midland MI 15396
Oakland CA 15728
Portales NM 15968
San Jose CA 16279
San Mateo CA 16284
Sharon CT 16372
Tacoma WA 16530
Vernal UT 16683
Man, Prehistoric
Algeria
  Alger 00024
  Constantine 00032
  El-Oued 00034
  Ouargla 00038
Austria
  Arnfels 00610
  Asparn a.d.Zaya 00612
  Bad Ischl 00621
  Eggenburg 00644
  Eibiswald 00646
  Freistadt 00654
  Gleisdorf 00659
  Gobelsburg 00663
  Hallein 00683
  Hollabrunn 00690
  St. Pölten 00794
  Schärding 00796
  Siegendorf-Schuschenwald 00805
  Solbad Hall 00807
  Spital am Pyhrn 00808
  Wien 00847, 00868, 00871
  Wiener Neustadt 00904
  Wieselburg 00905
Belgium
  Ath 00956
  Aubechies 00957
  Brecht 00981
  Comblain-au-Pont 01042
  Gesves 01094
  Ivoz-Ramet 01122
  Kanne 01128
  Kontich 01134
  Liège 01154
  Lommel 01172
  Marche-en-Famenne 01174
  Rumes 01244
  Soignies 01261
  Tongeren 01274
  Visé 01299
  Zonhoven 01320
Brazil
  Curitiba 01371
  Paranaguá 01413
Bulgaria
  Madara 01605
  Vidin 01709
Canada
  Chicoutimi 01868
  La Sarre 02086
  St. John's 02339
  Trois-Rivières 02465
Chile
  Arica 02580
China, People's Republic
  Guangzhou 02629
  Xian 02670
  Xinhui 02673
  Zhengzhou 02676
Cuba
  Cardenas 02800
Czechoslovakia
  Břeclav-Pohansko 02871
  Opava 03138
  Praha 03172
  Unhošť 03303
  Žatec 03332
Denmark
  Aarhus 03359

Asnæs 03366
Ebeltoft 03378
Esbjerg 03382
Espergærde 03385
Faarevejle 03390
Gilleleje 03403
Grindsted 03409
Haderslev 03412
Hjørring 03426
Højbjerg 03428
Holstebro 03435
Holte 03437
Køge 03481
Mariager 03491
Maribo 03494
Nykøbing Sjælland 03507
Odense 03512
Randers 03525
Ribe 03529
Ringkøbing 03533
Rudkøbing 03540
Silkeborg 03543
Skanderborg 03548
Skive 03549
Sønderborg 03555
Sorø 03558
Stege 03560
Thisted 03568
Varde 03576
Viborg 03586
Vinderup 03587
Dominican Republic
  Santo Domingo 03590
Egypt
  Cairo 03630
El Salvador
  San Salvador 03651
Finland
  Maarianhamina 03791
  Siilinjärvi 03852
  Vanhalinna 03889
France
  Abbeville 03896
  Aix-les-Bains 03905
  Albertville 03909
  Alençon 03911
  Altkirch 03915
  Angoulême 03930
  Annecy 03932
  Annonay 03933
  Apt 03939
  Argenteuil 03942
  Aurignac 03952
  Aurillac 03954
  Auvillar 03957
  Auxonne 03961
  Avallon 03962
  Belfort 03993
  Bordeaux 04008
  Boulogne-sur-Mer 04015
  Bourbonne-les-Bains 04017
  Bourg-en-Bresse 04018
  Brantôme 04023
  Brive-la-Gaillarde 04028
  Carnac 04040
  Châlons-sur-Marne 04052
  Chambéry 04055
  Châteaudun 04063
  Châtillon-sur-Seine 04067
  Chelles 04070
  Clermont-Ferrand 04077
  Cordes 04091
  Die 04096
  Digne 04098
  Dijon 04099
  Dole 04105
  Epernay 04111
  Figeac 04118
  Foix 04120
  Gap 04124
  Hagenau 04135
  La Rochelle 04162, 04165
  Lascaux 04166
  Lavaur 04173
  Lectoure 04177

Le Grand-Pressigny 04179
Le Havre 04183
Le Mas-d'Azil 04187
Les Andelys 04193
Les Eyzies de Tayac 04195
Les Sables d'Olonne 04196
Libourne 04198
Lons-le-Saunier 04210
Loudun 04212
Marseille 04239
Meaux 04245
Melun 04247
Menton 04251
Metz 04252
Meudon 04254
Millau 04258
Minerve 04260
Mont-de-Marsan 04265
Montaigu 04268
Mulhouse 04290
Narbonne 04300, 04302
Nice 04307
Nogent-le-Rotrou 04321
Périgueux 04395
Provins 04413
Reims 04417
Rennes 04419
Rethel 04421
Rochechouart 04428
Rodez 04432
Rouen 04437
Saint-Amand-Montrond 04444
Saint-Germain-en-Laye 04453
Saintes 04474
Sarrebourg 04479
Sartène 04480
Senlis 04488
Soissons 04494
Strasbourg 04496
Tautavel 04507
Thonon-les-Bains 04510
Toulouse 04518
Tulle 04529
Vannes 04536
Vernon 04541
Villeneuve-sur-Lot 04551
Germany, Democratic Republic
  Allstedt 04566
  Angermünde 04573
  Anklam 04574
  Arendsee 04580
  Arneburg 04581
  Auerbach 04588
  Bad Freienwalde 04598
  Bad Langensalza 04601
  Bad Liebenwerda 04603
  Bad Sulza 04605
  Ballenstedt 04606
  Belgern 04612
  Belzig 04613
  Berlin 04622
  Bitterfeld 04638
  Borna 04640
  Coswig 04650
  Eberswalde 04698
  Finsterwalde 04729
  Frankfurt/Oder 04732
  Freyburg/Unstrut 04738
  Kyffhäuser 04854
  Pirna 04957
  Ranis 04994
  Wolmirstedt 05133
Germany, Federal Republic
  Aalen 05161
  Abensberg 05165
  Alfeld 05173
  Allensbach 05175
  Altmannstein 05181
  Altötting 05183
  Alzey 05184
  Amberg 05185
  Amorbach 05188
  Ansbach 05189
  Augsburg 05206
  Bad Berneck 05211

Bad Kreuznach 05220
Berlin 05292
Blankenheim 05317
Blaubeuren 05318, 05319
Bonn 05331
Breisach 05346
Bremen 05349
Dortmund 05398
Dreieich 05399
Ellwangen 05421
Emden 05422
Emmendingen 05424
Erkrath 05428
Erlangen 05434, 05435
Frankfurt 05468
Friedrichshafen 05483
Gießen 05504
Ingolstadt 05593
Itzehoe 05595
Jülich 05599
Kaiserslautern 05601
Karlsruhe 05605
Kassel 05617
Kellinghusen 05625
Kempten 05626
Kevelaer 05628
Lörrach 05703
Lübeck 05711
Ludwigsburg 05719
Lüneburg 05723
Mainz 05731, 05733
Memmingen 05758
Menden 05759
Mindelheim 05766
Minden 05768
Mühlacker 05773
Münnerstadt 05812
Münster 05818
Neuss 05827
Neuwied 05829
Nienburg 05830
Oldenburg 05859
Reinfeld 05887
Rheine 05891
Saarbrücken 05902
Salzgitter 05905
Schleswig 05908
Schweinfurt 05914
Siegen 05919
Sigmaringen 05920
Sögel 05923
Traben-Trarbach 05942
Villingen-Schwenningen 05965
Wadersloh 05967
Greece
  Aegina 06021
  Aiyani 06029
  Almiros 06032
  Apeiranthos 06039
  Astros 06046
  Athens 06048, 06078
  Chios 06093
  Chora 06095
  Filippi 06117
  Kalamata 06133
  Kalymnos 06139
  Kastoria 06150
  Komotini 06156
  Kos 06159
  Kozani 06163
  Larissa 06172
  Liknades 06175
  Maroneia 06185
  Mirina 06197
  Nauplia 06206
  Naxos 06209
  Neapolis 06212
  Paros 06224
  Plaka 06233
  Rethymnon 06243
  Siatista 06265
  Sparta 06274
  Tegea 06281
  Thira 06292
  Veroia 06300

Volos 06302, 06303
Guatemala
  Ciudad de Guatemala 06317
Guinea
  Conakry 06325
  Kissidougou 06326
  Youkounkoun 06329
Hungary
  Pécs 06473
  Vértesszőllős 06536
India
  Bhubaneshwar 06603
  Gwalior 06680
  Khariar 06728
  Lucknow 06751
  Pillalamari 06808
  Poona 06810
  Sagar 06825
  Udaipur 06855
Ireland
  Dublin 07015
  Kilkenny 07021
  Monaghan 07025
Israel
  Be'er Sheva 07038
  Deganya Alef Kibbutz 07045
  Jerusalem 07091
Italy
  Agrigento 07155
  Alba 07163
  Albenga 07164
  Allumiere 07171
  Ancona 07177
  Ascoli Piceno 07195
  Bazzano 07219
  Bergamo 07225
  Bitonto 07235
  Bologna 07247
  Bordighera 07267
  Cagliari 07289
  Cesena 07347
  Chieti 07356
  Como 07377
  Corbetta 07380
  Erba 07404
  Este 07408
  Finale Ligure 07439
  Firenze 07479
  Forlì 07488
  Forlimpopoli 07493
  L'Aquila 07560
  Lugagnano Val d'Arda 07593
  Maglie 07598
  Matera 07610
  Milano 07625
  Modena 07656
  Molina di Ledro 07668
  Montalcino 07669
  Perugia 07760
  Pinerolo 07785
  Reggio Calabria 07823
  Roma 07831, 07884
  Rovereto 07916
  Rovigo 07918
  San Severino Marche 07942
  Sarsina 07954
  Sibari 07976
  Siracusa 07985
  Susa 08003
  Taranto 08007
  Terni 08014
  Torino 08034
  Ugento 08087
  Venosa 08126
  Ventimiglia 08128
  Verucchio 08140
Japan
  Kokubun-ji 08306
  Kurashiki 08316
  Mitaki 08374
  Nishi Tsugaru 08434
  Okaya 08450
  Sendai 08492
  Suwa 08510
  Tokyo 08536

Kenya
  Gilgil 08647
  Hyrax Hill 08648
  Olorgesailie 08654
Korea, Republic
  Seoul 08701, 08719
Libya
  Tripoli 08751
Liechtenstein
  Vaduz 08754
Malta
  Valletta 08804
Mexico
  Mérida 08836, 08837
Morocco
  Rabat 08921
  Tanger 08924
Netherlands
  Aalten 08949
  Aardenburg 08950
  Amersfoort 08958
  Assen 09021
  Barneveld 09026
  Bellingwolde 09029
  Bergeyk 09035
  Deventer 09082
  Drachten 09098
  Emmen 09121
  Gramsbergen 09146
  Heerenveen 09175
  Hilvarenbeek 09187
  Lievelde 09240
  Nijmegen 09272
  's-Hertogenbosch 09353
  Stein 09369
  Vriezenveen 09423
  Weert 09429
New Zealand
  Christchurch 09475
  Stoke 09550
Norway
  Arendal 09610
  Åsestranda 09613
  Haugesund 09693
  Jaren 09712
  Oslo 09806
  Sarpsborg 09842
Philippines
  Dumaguete 10032
  Tacloban 10096
Poland
  Biskupin 10124
  Częstochowa 10152
  Gdańsk 10170
  Łowicz 10280
  Miechów 10291
  Olkusz 10318
  Sulmierzyce 10407
  Szamotuły 10414
Portugal
  Evora 10558
  Guimarães 10567
  Lisboa 10571
Solomon Islands
  Honiara 10827
South Africa
  Harrismith 10889
  Pretoria 10967
Spain
  Albacete 11020
  Alicante 11029
  Almería 11030
  Altamira 11033
  Ambrona 11034
  Amposta 11035
  Ampudia 11036
  Aroche 11046
  Bañolas 11065
  Barcelona 11076
  Calahorra 11130
  Carmona 11139
  Cartagena 11140
  Huelva 11225
  Ibiza 11228
  Jaén 11237

Jerez de la Frontera 11238
Jumilla 11241
La Guardia 11246
Las Palmas 11252
Lérida 11259, 11264
Madrid 11300, 11313, 11322
Málaga 11345
Manacor 11349
Manresa 11351
Montblanch 11373
Murcia 11381
Oviedo 11401
Palma de Mallorca 11409, 11412
Poblet 11430
Pontevedra 11432
Sabadell 11450
San Gines de Vilasar 11459
Santa Cruz de Tenerife 11480
Santander 11490
Santillana del Mar 11496
Sevilla 11517
Sierra de Yeguas 11527
Solsona 11533
Soria 11535
Tárrega 11547
Valencia 11579, 11585
Valladolid 11590
Vendrell 11599
Vitoria 11619
Zamora 11628
Sweden
  Alingsås 11653
  Lund 11753
  Stockholm 11837
Switzerland
  Appenzell 11905
  Biel 11961
  Bischofszell 11963
  Boudry 11969
  Dietikon 12003
  Ederswiler 12009
  Frauenfeld 12014
  Herzogenbuchsee 12064
  Hitzkirch 12068
  Horgen 12071
  La Neuveville 12089
  Lausanne 12096
  Meilen 12141
  Meride 12143
  Neuchâtel 12161
  Nyon 12166
  St. Gallen 12210
  St. Moritz 12214
  Vevey 12276
  Wohlen 12301
  Zofingen 12309
  Zug 12313
Syria
  Homs 12342
Thailand
  Bangkok 12378
  Kanchanaburi 12385
Turkey
  Bodrum 12474
  Bursa 12477
  Karain Cave 12539
  Karaman 12540
  Yassihoyuk 12588
United Kingdom
  Avebury 12640
  Barrow-in-Furness 12666
  Bath 12672
  Dartford 12897
  Harlyn Bay 13036
  Kingston upon Hull 13111
  Lewes 13147
  Oxford 13348
  Peebles 13353
  Sunderland 13519
United States
  Alamosa CO 13635
  Alpine TX 13673
  Arkadelphia AR 13722
  Attleboro MA 13756
  Beloit WI 13859

Toronto   02458
Czechoslovakia
  Kremnica   03040
Denmark
  Frederiksværk   03400
  København   03467
Finland
  Helsinki   03691
  Imatra   03737
  Riihimäki   03841
France
  Bayonne   03983
  Chambéry   04055
  Paris   04336, 04349, 04380
  Strasbourg   04495
Germany, Democratic Republic
  Dresden   04678
  Eisenach   04705
  Gotha   04769
  Kölleda   04848
Germany, Federal Republic
  Düsseldorf   05405
  Karlsruhe   05611
  Lübeck   05713
  Nürnberg   05832
Greece
  Apeiranthos   06039
India
  Calcutta   06637
  Jaunpur   06708
  Madras   06761
Indonesia
  Jakarta   06890
Italy
  Arezzo   07190
  Imola   07550
  Padova   07717
  Pistoia   07793
  Roma   07886
  Siena   07983
Netherlands
  Vlaardingen   09413
Norway
  Oslo   09805
Panama
  Ancon   09962
Poland
  Wrocław   10499
Spain
  Barcelona   11072
  La Rábida   11248
  Madrid   11307, 11311
  Vich   11604
Switzerland
  La Chaux-de-Fonds   12087
United Kingdom
  Aberdeen   12606
  Bagshot   12648
  Belfast   12688
  Berwick-upon-Tweed   12694
  Beverley   12696
  Blackburn   12721
  Brecon   12755
  Bury   12787
  Caernarvon   12796
  Camberley   12800
  Canterbury   12817
  Carlisle   12826
  Chichester   12853
  Chiddingstone   12858
  Dorchester   12913
  Durham   12935
  Edinburgh   12960
  Exeter   12972
  Fort George   12985
  King's Lynn   13108
  Norwich   13328
  Sheffield   13452
  Shrewsbury   13459
  Stirling   13492
United States
  Fort Lauderdale FL   14620
  Fort McClellan AL   14627
  Gulf Shores AL   14799
  Little Rock AR   15209

Montgomery AL   15462
Port Hueneme CA   15957
Washington DC   16773
Wright-Patterson AFB OH
16941
Medicine and hygiene
Argentina
  Buenos Aires   00104
  Corrientes   00203
Australia
  Alice Springs   00441
Austria
  Wien   00849, 00867, 00882,
  00896
Belgium
  Antwerpen   00951
  Gent   01089
  Villers-devant-Orval   01295
Brazil
  Rio de Janeiro   01447, 01468
  Salvador   01499
Burma
  Rangoon   01727
Canada
  Biggar   01797
  Brandon   01809
  Carlyle   01848
  Cumberland   01895
  Edmonton   01926
  Flesherton   01953
  Fort Qu'appelle   01963
  Lethbridge   02090
  London   02102
  Ponoka   02263
  Québec   02285
  St. Thomas   02346
  Toronto   02455
  Tracadie   02463
  Twillingate   02471
  Vancouver   02475
  Victoria   02502
Colombia
  Bogotá   02704
Cuba
  La Habana   02813
Czechoslovakia
  Františkovy Lázně   02939
  Piešťany   03153
  Praha   03173, 03180
Denmark
  Ærøskøbing   03364
  Hillerød   03421
  København   03465
  Nykøbing   03504
  Sæby   03541
Egypt
  Alexandria   03611
  Cairo   03633
Finland
  Helsinki   03703
France
  Kaysersberg   04146
  La Rochelle   04163
  Lyon   04221
  Troyes   04527
Germany, Democratic Republic
  Dresden   04672
Germany, Federal Republic
  Bad Brückenau   05212
  Bad Wörishofen   05239
  Düsseldorf   05415
  Heidelberg   05566
  Ingolstadt   05592
  Remscheid   05888
  Tübingen   05956, 05958
Hungary
  Budapest   06394
India
  Baroda   06586
  Bombay   06610
  Calcutta   06631, 06635
  Gauhati   06671
  Hyderabad   06697
  Lucknow   06752, 06753
  Madras   06757, 06758

Mysore   06781
Israel
  Petah Tiqwa   07116
Italy
  Bologna   07243
  Castiglione delle Stiviere   07329
  Firenze   07474
  Lodi   07582
  Pavia   07751, 07753
  Roma   07845, 07875, 07897,
  07904-07906
  Torino   08037
Japan
  Tokyo   08554
  Toyama   08591
Korea, Republic
  Seoul   08697
Netherlands
  Amsterdam   08968
  Deventer   09084
  Enkhuizen   09124
  Gouda   09145
  Leiden   09228
  Utrecht   09396
Norway
  Bergen   09628
  Trondheim   09887
Poland
  Warszawa   10452
South Africa
  Johannesburg   10906, 10912
  Pretoria   10970
Spain
  Llivia   11267
  Madrid   11279, 11297, 11303,
  11308
  Masnou   11360
  Peñaranda de Duero   11425
Sweden
  Stockholm   11823
Switzerland
  Basel   11922, 11937
  Fribourg   12018
  Genève   12031
  Zürich   12325
Thailand
  Bangkok   12363, 12365, 12372,
  12375
United Kingdom
  Birmingham   12716
  Liverpool   13159, 13160
  London   13174, 13195, 13209,
  13215, 13217, 13235, 13237,
  13238, 13248
  Middle Claydon   13291
United States
  Allen NE   13663
  Amarillo TX   13680
  Bailey NC   13787
  Baltimore MD   13808
  Barron WI   13819
  Battle Creek MI   13831
  Beatrice NE   13840
  Brooklyn NY   13994
  Brooks Air Force Base TX
  13995
  Carrollton OH   14072
  Celina OH   14094
  Charleston SC   14122, 14128
  Chicago IL   14165
  Cleveland OH   14212, 14219
  Columbus OH   14264
  Dallas TX   14331
  Durham NC   14448
  Eureka Springs AR   14521
  Grand Haven MI   14752
  Grand Marais MN   14756
  Halstead KS   14812
  Houston TX   14917
  Idaho Falls ID   14943
  Indianapolis IN   14954
  Jacksonville al   14983
  Jefferson GA   15000
  Junction City OR   15018
  Lexington OH   15179

Los Angeles CA   15237, 15245
Mexico City MO   15379
Millersburg OH   15406
Minneapolis MN   15422
Nampa ID   15519
Nashville IN   15525
New Brunswick NJ   15559
Orange CA   15759
Oswego NY   15783
Park Ridge IL   15814
Philadelphia PA   15865, 15869,
15880
Port Sanilac MI   15960
Portage WI   15964
Prairie du Chien WI   15995
Randolph VT   16036
Reading VT   16047
Red Cloud NE   16048
Rochester NY   16117
St Louis MO   16194
St. Petersburg FL   16212
Seattle WA   16359
Sioux Falls SD   16400
Sturbridge MA   16505
Taylorsville MS   16555
Tobias NE   16583
Toledo OH   16588
Washington DC   16732
Watseka IL   16803
Weeping Water NE   16821
Wilber NE   16873
Winterville GA   16924
Worthington MN   16937
USSR
  Leningrad   17137, 17142
  Riga   17268
Metals and metallurgy
Austria
  Döllach   00640
Belgium
  Saint-Hubert   01248
Canada
  Elliot Lake   01945
Colombia
  Belencito   02691
Czechoslovakia
  Ostrava   03143
  Rokycany   03227
Germany, Federal Republic
  Altenbeken   05178
  Biedenkopf   05312
  Köln   05654
Ghana
  Ho   06014
Hungary
  Budapest   06386
  Miskolc   06449
  Székesfehérvár   06504
India
  Sibsagar   06838
Japan
  Yasuki   08615
Netherlands
  Buren   09053
Poland
  Chlewiska   10139
  Głogów   10176
  Legnica   10265
  Ostrowiec Świętokrzyski   10327
  Samsonów   10379
  Sielpia Wielka   10386
  Tarnowskie Góry   10427
  Złoty Stok   10525
South Africa
  Dundee   10861
Spain
  Madrid   11323
United States
  Cornwall PA   14292
Yugoslavia
  Bor   17484
  Kropa   17582
Metalwork (see also Bronzes;
  Copper; Gold and silver)

Klagenfurt 00708
Mittersill 00738
Oberzeiring 00748
Salzburg 00773
Solbad Hall 00806
Villach 00819
Wien 00870
Belgium
Chaudfontaine 01041
Deurne 01057
Gent 01090
Han-sur-Lesse 01103
Ivoz-Ramet 01122
Liège 01163
Roly 01241
Schoten 01252
Sprimont 01264
Tournai 01279
Zonhoven 01320
Bolivia
La Paz 01340
Potosí 01343
Brazil
Diamantina 01373
Florianópolis 01375
Porto Alegre 01418
Recife 01429
Canada
Alberta Beach 01750
Ashcroft 01766
Ashville 01767
Barkerville 01782
Black Lake 01798
Chapleau 01861
Chatham 01864
Dryden 01912
Grand Manan 01994
Grande Prairie 01996
Grandview 01998
Hope 02036
Invermere 02045
Kamloops 02052
Kenora 02057
Massey 02125
Mission City 02142
Parrsboro 02243
Penticton 02249
St. Joseph 02341
The Pas 02428
Vancouver 02481
Victoria 02498
Winnipeg 02548
Chile
Osorno 02588
Santiago 02592, 02601
Valparaíso 02605
China, People's Republic
Dalian 02625
China, Republic
Taipei 02688
Colombia
Bogotá 02706, 02714
Cali 02725
Medellín 02748, 02749, 02757
Czechoslovakia
Bučovice 02886
Gelnica 02945
Nová Paka 03119
Radnice u Rokycan 03224
Rakovník 03225
Uherský Brod 03301
Velké Meziříčí 03312
Volyně 03318
Denmark
Fakse 03391
Frederiksværk 03401
Fur 03402
Gram 03407
København 03458
Lintrup 03487
Ecuador
Quito 03601, 03608
Finland
Espoo 03675
Forssa 03677

Porvoo 03827
Tankavaara 03867
Vaasa 03885
France
Laval 04170
Le Puy 04191
Paris 04360
Saint Dizier 04442
Germany, Democratic Republic
Annaberg-Buchholz 04576
Ansprung 04577
Auerbach 04588
Bad Sülze 04593
Bad Dürrenberg 04596
Camburg 04647
Dermbach 04659
Dresden 04691
Ebersbach 04697
Eibenstock 04701
Eisfeld 04711
Eisleben 04714
Erfurt 04723
Falkensee 04725
Freiberg 04734, 04735
Freital 04737
Freyburg/Unstrut 04738
Gera 04751
Geyer 04753
Glauchau 04755
Görlitz 04761
Gotha 04768
Greifswald 04771
Greussen 04775
Grimma 04777
Haldensleben 04793
Halle 04795
Hartenstein 04801
Heiligenstadt 04803
Hiddensee 04808
Hohenleuben 04811
Hoyerswerda 04813
Ilsenburg 04816
Kahla 04830
Kapellendorf 04833
Karl-Marx-Stadt 04837
Kölleda 04848
Kyffhäuser 04854
Lengenfeld 04878
Liebstadt 04880
Magdeburg 04894
Markranstädt 04899
Meerane 04900
Mügeln 04913
Mühlhausen 04915
Mylau 04920
Nordhausen 04937
Nossen 04938
Oderberg 04940
Ohrdruf 04943
Olbernau 04945
Osterburg 04950
Osterwieck/Harz 04951
Pegau 04955
Potsdam 04964
Prerow 04979
Quedlinburg 04985
Radeberg 04989
Radebeul 04990
Ranis 04994
Rochlitz 05006
Rodewisch 05008
Rübeland 05017
Ruhla 05020
Saalfeld 05021, 05023
Sangerhausen 05027
Scharfenberg 05028
Schirgiswalde 05029
Schneeberg 05034
Schönebeck 05036
Seifhennersdorf 05051
Sondershausen 05056
Stadtilm 05059
Stolberg 05065
Stralsund 05068
Taucha 05074

Thale 05076
Tharandt 05078
Ummendorf 05081
Wandlitz 05086
Weissenfels 05112
Werdau 05113
Wittenberge 05127
Worbis 05134
Wurzen 05136
Wusterhausen 05137
Zeitz 05140
Zella-Mehlis 05141
Zerbst 05142
Zittau 05147
Zwickau 05152
Germany, Federal Republic
Aalen 05160
Altenbeken 05178
Aschaffenburg 05200
Bad Brückenau 05212
Bielefeld 05315
Bonn 05330
Eichstätt 05419
Freiburg 05476
Langelsheim 05686
Marburg 05741
München 05789
Münster 05819
Murrhardt 05822
Nördlingen 05831
Oldenburg 05859
Regensburg 05883
Salzgitter 05905
Tübingen 05951, 05953
Ulm 05962
Wilhelmshaven 05983
Wunsiedel 05994
Würzburg 06001
Greece
Athens 06060, 06075
Hungary
Budapest 06398
India
Coimbatore 06645
Faizabad 06664
Jhalawar 06713
Lucknow 06746-06748
Narendrapur 06784
Purulia 06817
Roorkee 06823
Ireland
Dublin 07017
Israel
Jerusalem 07090
Italy
Bologna 07253
Caltanissetta 07296
Camerino 07300
Carmagnola 07309
Catania 07335
Cremona 07392
Firenze 07471
Genova 07518
Grosseto 07539
Iglesias 07547
Milano 07632
Modena 07659
Napoli 07684
Parma 07744
Pavia 07752
Perticara 07758
Predazzo 07811
Roma 07870
Sassari 07957
Siena 07982
Spello 07991
Termini Imerese 08012
Torino 08036
Udine 08083
Valdagno 08093
Varallo Sesia 08094
Verona 08134
Japan
Akita 08176
Kami 08272

Minamitsuru 08370
Tokyo 08557
Mozambique
Manica 08931
Netherlands
Aalten 08949
Amsterdam 08969
Bourtange 09043
Delft 09063
Dokkum 09089
Domburg 09091
Echt 09103
Enschede 09125
Gorredijk 09142
Groningen 09151, 09155
Hilversum 09188
Hulst 09196
Kerkrade 09204
Laren 09209
Leeuwarden 09218
Leiden 09234
Maastricht 09247, 09248
Ommen 09277
Schokland 09326
Schoonoord 09329
Sint Odiliënberg 09356
Sittard 09357
Valkenburg 09401
Winterwijk 09435
New Zealand
Dunedin 09484
Havelock 09498
Kerikeri 09510
Thames 09556
Waikouaiti 09564
Norway
Bergen 09625
Selbu 09843
Stjørdal 09870
Pakistan
Mangla 09948
Quetta 09955
Paraguay
Asunción 09983
Peru
Lima 10008
Poland
Lębork 10262
Portugal
Coimbra 10554
Lisboa 10585, 10588
Réunion
Saint-Denis 10644
Romania
Aiud 10648
Bucureşti 10680
Dorohoi 10714
Iaşi 10731
Rwanda
Kigali 10802
Saudi Arabia
Riyadh 10810
South Africa
Oudtshoorn 10939
Stellenbosch 10994
Spain
Aroche 11046
Avilés 11055
Barcelona 11082, 11083
Madrid 11305, 11323
Onda 11390
Pontevedra 11431
Vilajuiga 11607
Sweden
Stockholm 11811
Switzerland
Brig 11974
Fribourg 12021
Guttannen 12056
Heiden 12061
Isérables 12074
Laufen 12093
Lausanne 12101
Locarno 12118
Lugano 12123

United States
Anniston AL 13709
Minneapolis MN 15426
Vatican
Città del Vaticano 17366
Mural painting and decoration
(*see also* Mosaics)
Austria
Perchtoldsdorf 00753
St. Johann 00786
Wien 00863
Bulgaria
Sofija 01667
Canada
Montréal 02165
France
Lyon 04224
Marseille 04239
Nice 04316
Paris 04384
Tanlay 04503
Germany, Democratic Republic
Karl-Marx-Stadt 04834
Kriebstein 04852
Potsdam 04974
Germany, Federal Republic
Büdingen 05365
Kißlegg 05640
Konstanz 05664
Oberschleißheim 05851
Schwangau 05913
Würzburg 06002
Xanten 06008
Greece
Agios Andreas 06023
Corfu 06100
Delos 06106
Mistra 06198
Steiri 06278
Hungary
Tata 06527
India
Madanapalle 06756
Italy
Agrigento 07158
Angera 07179
Argenta 07191
Assisi 07202
Biella 07234
Bogliaco 07239
Camerino 07302
Ferrara 07427
Firenze 07457, 07467, 07477, 07483
Genova 07522
Mantova 07602
Milano 07619
Palermo 07723
Parma 07736
Perugia 07762
Pisa 07787
Prato 07809
Roma 07911
Sansepolcro 07943
Siena 07978
Spoleto 07997
Squinzano 07998
Teggiano 08009
Thiene 08016
Torino 08045
Urbania 08088
Urbino 08091
Venezia 08108
Viadana 08142
Japan
Kumamoto 08310
Nagoya 08401
Norway
Brevik 09642
Spain
Figueras 11189
La Rábida 11248
Madrid 11334
Pamplona 11417
Segovia 11510

Valladolid 11591
Switzerland
Müstair 12157
Turkey
Nevsehir 12564
Trabzon 12580
United Kingdom
Hemel Hempstead 13057
Llanfairpwll 13168
Worcester 13592
United States
Weston VT 16855
Vatican
Città del Vaticano 17363
Yugoslavia
Cetinje 17506
Kraljevo 17574
Zagreb 17818
Music and musical instruments
Angola
Dundo 00049
Sá da Bandeira 00056
Argentina
Alta Gracia 00059
Buenos Aires 00078, 00107
Córdoba 00188
La Plata 00237
Rio Cuarto 00318
Rosario 00326
San José 00351
San Martín de los Andes 00363
Australia
Lilydale 00519
Nedlands 00542
Oatlands 00551
Parkville 00552
Austria
Ansfelden 00609
Arnfels 00610
Bad Goisern 00618
Bad Ischl 00620, 00623
Eisbach 00647
Eisenstadt 00650
Innsbruck 00700
Oberndorf 00746
Perchtoldsdorf 00752
Raiding 00761
Rohrau 00769
Salzburg 00774, 00775
Wien 00828, 00845, 00853, 00860, 00879, 00889, 00894, 00895
Belgium
Aarschot 00925
Brugge 00988
Bruxelles 01028, 01032
Harelbeke 01104
Koksijde 01133
Liège 01163, 01164
Brazil
Caeté 01358
Campinas 01360
Rio de Janeiro 01437, 01474, 01475
Santa Leopoldina 01501
São Paulo 01527
Burundi
Gitega 01735
Canada
Bowmanville 01805
Imperial 02042
London 02098
Moncton 02148
Ste.-Foy 02351
Spy Hill 02400
Winnipeg 02553
China, People's Republic
Beijing 02618, 02619
Colombia
Bogotá 02719
Czechoslovakia
Brandýs nad Labem - Stará Boleslav 02861
Bratislava 02865
Brno 02876
Chropyně 02917

Domažlice 02935
Hudlice 02980
Jabkenice 02987
Jindřichův Hradec 03001
Kamenice nad Lipou 03006
Klenčí pod Čerchovem 03019
Křečovice u Sedlčan 03039
Kroměříž 03042
Litomyšl 03070
Nelahozeves 03112
Opava 03135
Polička 03167
Praha 03185, 03186, 03188, 03200
Skuteč 03249
Týn nad Vltavou 03297
Všebořice 03321
Vysoká u Příbrami 03324
Zlonice 03348
Denmark
Humlebæk 03443
København 03462, 03466, 03470
Nørre Søby 03501
Skørping 03553
Ecuador
Quito 03604
Finland
Pielavesi 03819
Turku 03875
France
La Côte Saint-André 04152, 04153
La Couture-Boussey 04154
Lourdes 04213
Montfort-l'Amaury 04275
Montluçon 04276
Paris 04372
Gabon
Libreville 04563
Germany, Democratic Republic
Arnstadt 04582
Bad Köstritz 04600
Dresden 04671
Eisenach 04703, 04706
Freiberg 04736
Halle 04797
Leipzig 04861, 04873
Weimar 05098
Weissenfels 05111
Zittau 05149
Zwickau 05151
Germany, Federal Republic
Augsburg 05205
Bad Krozingen 05221
Baden-Baden 05241, 05242
Bayreuth 05259
Berlin 05294
Bonn 05328
Braunschweig 05342
Düsseldorf 05407
Eutin 05446
Fuldatal 05489
Füssen 05494
Hamburg 05534
Köln 05653
Mittenwald 05770
Prien 05872
Rüdesheim 05899
Greece
Athens 06050, 06082
Hungary
Balassagyarmat 06348
Budapest 06361, 06384, 06402
Gyula 06418
Martonvásár 06443
Sopron 06492
India
Ahmedabad 06561
Alwar 06572
Dharampur 06658
Madurai 06766
Mysore 06778, 06779
Poona 06814
Purulia 06817

Israel
Haifa 07061
Jerusalem 07084
Italy
Bergamo 07228
Bologna 07241
BorgoVal di Taro 07269
Busseto 07286
Catania 07332
Cremona 07393
Firenze 07463
Maiolati Spontini 07599
Milano 07633, 07634
Parma 07737
Pesaro 07763, 07766
Roma 07881
Savio 07963
Treviso 08064
Trieste 08075
Japan
Hikone 08228
Tokyo 08540
Liberia
Monrovia 08738
Malaysia
Seremban 08794
Malta
Mdina 08801
Netherlands
Asten 09022
Bergeyk 09036
's-Gravenhage 09331
Utrecht 09389
New Zealand
Christchurch 09477
Wellington 09576
Norway
Fagernes 09665
Hop 09705
Rauland 09821
Tromsø 09883
Trondheim 09889
Peru
Lima 10003
Philippines
Manila 10065
Poland
Antonin 10106
Barczewo 10110
Istebna 10195
Odolanów 10314
Oliwa 10317
Poznań 10349
Służewo 10392
Szafarnia 10413
Szydłowiec 10424
Warszawa 10442, 10461
Wejherowo 10477
Zachełmie 10512
Zbąszyń 10520
Żelazowa Wola 10507
Portugal
Lisboa 10576, 10581, 10583
Romania
Dorohoi 10715
Iaşi 10733
South Africa
Bloemfontein 10839
Mariannhill 10927
Potgietersrus 10955
Stellenbosch 10993
Spain
Barcelona 11093
Gijón 11203
Granada 11209
Jerez de la Frontera 11239
Madrid 11282
Pamplona 11421
Sweden
Stockholm 11825, 11826
Switzerland
Appenzell 11906
Basel 11935
Brienz 11972
Ebnat-Kappel 12008

New Zealand
  Auckland 09467
  Christchurch 09478
  Dunedin 09483, 09485
  Timaru 09558
  Waihi 09563
Norway
  Eggedal 09655
  Holmsbu 09701
  Kristiansand S 09725
Philippines
  Cagayan de Oro 10027
Poland
  Gdańsk 10172
  Kórnik 10223
  Kraków 10249
  Łódź 10276
  Nieborów i Arkadia 10303
  Niedzica 10304
  Poznań 10352
  Puławy 10363
  Radom 10369
  Sanok 10383
Portugal
  Lisboa 10573, 10592, 10593
  Mafra 10595
  Sintra 10617
South Africa
  Cape Town 10845, 10847, 10853
  East London 10870
  Oudtshoorn 10939
  Pretoria 10958, 10959
  Riversdale 10982
  Worcester 11018
Spain
  Madrid 11287, 11288
  Palma de Mallorca 11407, 11415
  Vigo 11605
Sri Lanka
  Ratnapura 11636
Sweden
  Bålsta 11661
  Göteborg 11702
Switzerland
  Basel 11933
  Bern 11949
  Oron-le-Châtel 12176
  Zürich 12323, 12334
Tanzania
  Marangu 12352
Turkey
  Yalvac 12586
United Kingdom
  Arbroath 12630
  Aylesbury 12643
  Brodick 12777
  Chippenham 12859
  Hampton Court 13034
  Harrogate 13037
  Hastings 13045
  Inverness 13087
  Ipswich 13089
  Keighley 13096
  Kendal 13097
  Leamington Spa 13125
  Leeds 13132
  Leighton Buzzard 13144
  Lincoln 13155
  Liverpool 13163
  London 13185, 13190, 13206, 13221, 13230, 13231, 13241, 13243
  Maidenhead 13262
  St. Ives, Huntingdon 13418
  Sheffield 13448
  Southampton 13474
United States
  Abilene TX 13620
  Amherst MA 13685
  Anchorage KS 13695
  Anderson SC 13698
  Atchison KS 13745
  Bakersfield CA 13789
  Baltimore MD 13809
  Beloit WI 13860
  Binghamton NY 13895

Blue Hill ME 13916
Boston MA 13935, 13938
Brigham City UT 13972
Brooklyn NY 13991
Cedarburg WI 14093
Cherry Valley CA 14147
Cheyenne WY 14152
Clemson SC 14210
Columbia MO 14253
Columbia SC 14255
Columbus GA 14260
Columbus OH 14265
Corydon IA 14304
Danville VA 14343
Daytona Beach FL 14362
Deadwood SD 14364
Denton TX 14388
Denver CO 14398
Downey CA 14431
Duluth MN 14440
East Hampton NY 14458
Eureka Springs AR 14523
Evansville IN 14528
Flagstaff AZ 14571
Freehold NJ 14677
Glen Ellen CA 14724
Gorham ME 14741
Hartford CT 14844
Houston TX 14914
Hudson NY 14921
Hungtington NY 14925
Independence KS 14949
Jacksonville FL 14984
Jefferson City MO 14999
Jennings LA 15007
Jerome AZ 15009
Johnson City TN 15011
Kalispell MT 15025
Knoxville TN 15078, 15079
Lake George NY 15107
Leadville CO 15152
Lincoln NE 15191
Lindsborg KS 15200
Little Rock AR 15208
Liverpool NY 15214
Longview TX 15230
Los Angeles CA 15251
Macon GA 15287
Memphis TN 15358, 15361
Mexico City MO 15379
Miami FL 15381
Milwaukee WI 15414
Monterey CA 15455
Montgomery AL 15461
Mumford NY 15503
Nashville TN 15538, 15539
New Brunswick NJ 15558
New York NY 15607, 15648, 15653
Newark NJ 15655
North Miami Beach FL 15703
Oakland CA 15727
Omaha NE 15750
Palm Beach FL 15800
Palm Springs CA 15802
Paterson NJ 15824
Pensacola FL 15844, 15845
Philadelphia PA 15873
Phoenix AZ 15907
Pittsburgh PA 15928
Poughkeepsie NY 15992
Princeton NJ 15999
Providence RI 16003
Quincy IL 16025
Richmond IN 16067
Riverside CA 16097
Rock Springs WY 16123
Sacramento CA 16160
St. Helena CA 16174
St Louis MO 16193
St. Paul MN 16204
San Francisco CA 16259, 16264
Sarasota FL 16313
Saratoga CA 16314
Sewanee TN 16369

Snyder TX 16407
South Bend IN 16417
Stanford CA 16465
State University AR 16469
Stuart FL 16503
Terre Haute IN 16569
University AL 16649
Warehouse Point CT 16719
Washington Crossing PA 16727
Washington DC 16730, 16740, 16745, 16754, 16766, 16775, 16776
Waterville ME 16797
Wilmington NC 16894
USSR
  Alma-Ata 16989
  Archangel'sk 16993
  Čeboksary 17015
  Chabarovsk 17022
  Char'kov 17024
  Dnepropetrovsk 17029
  Erevan 17034
  Gor'kij 17042
  Ivanovo 17050
  Jakutsk 17053
  Kalinin 17057
  Kaluga 17061
  Kaunas 17066
  Kazan' 17072
  Kiev 17080
  Kirov 17083
  Kislovodsk 17087
  Komsomol'sk-na-Amure 17092
  Kostroma 17095
  Krasnodar 17096
  Krasnojarsk 17097
  Kujbyšev 17101
  Kursk 17105
  Leningrad 17113, 17120, 17123
  L'vov 17151
  Minsk 17162
  Moskva 17177
  Nižnij Tagil 17225
  Novokuzneck 17229
  Novosibirsk 17231
  Odessa 17235
  Omsk 17238
  Orel 17244
  Orenburg 17246
  Perm' 17250
  Petrozavodsk 17255
  Rjazan' 17273
  Rostov-na-Donu 17275
  Saransk 17280
  Saratov 17284
  Stavropol' 17296
  Strachovo 17298
  Sverdlovsk 17301
  Tallin 17307, 17308
  Tambov 17309
  Tartu 17314
  Tbilisi 17319
  Tjumen' 17329
  Tobol'sk 17330
  Tula 17333
  Ufa 17335
  Vil'njus 17343
  Vologda 17353
  Voronež 17356
  Vorošilovgrad 17357
Venezuela
  Barcelona 17377
Yugoslavia
  Beograd 17467, 17469
  Ečka kod Zrenjanina 17523
  Hvar 17536
  Karlovac 17552
  Ljubljana 17595
  Motovun 17617
  Nova Gorica 17626
  Split 17739
  Zadar 17805
  Zagreb 17813
Zimbabwe
  Bulawayo 17863
Painting, English

Australia
  Geelong 00497
Belgium
  Brugge 00984
Canada
  Fredericton 01968
Finland
  Vaasa 03886
Netherlands
  Bergeyk 09036
  Denekamp 09074
New Zealand
  Wellington 09572
United Kingdom
  Aberdeen 12604
  Barnsley 12663
  Bembridge 12692
  Blackheath 12724
  Bradford 12742
  Buscot 12792
  Chirk 12860
  Cockermouth 12869
  Darlington 12896
  Douglas 12915
  Driffield 12919
  Edinburgh 12964
  Egham 12967
  Falmouth 12978
  Guildford 13025
  Haverfordwest 13049
  Kettering 13102
  Kingston upon Hull 13110
  Kirkcaldy 13117
  Leeds 13128
  Leicester 13138
  Liverpool 13162, 13163
  London 13186, 13196, 13219, 13221, 13242-13244
  Melton Mowbray 13287
  Newcastle-upon-Tyne 13309
  Oldham 13340
  Perth 13358
  Port Sunlight 13370
  Preston 13378
  Rochdale 13397
  St. Ives, Cornwall 13416
  Scarborough 13439
  Sherborne 13454
  Shrewsbury 13461
  Stretford 13512
  Sudbury 13515
  Swindon 13526
  Torquay 13539
  Turriff 13543
  Wakefield 13546
  Wednesbury 13560
  Welshpool 13563
  Whitby 13571
  Wolverhampton 13591
United States
  Baton Rouge LA 13827
  Buffalo NY 14009
  Denver CO 14398
  New Haven CT 15574
  Owensboro KY 15789
  Syracuse NY 16526
  Wilmington DE 16889
Painting, European
Argentina
  Buenos Aires 00140
  Mar del Plata 00266
Australia
  New Norcia 00544
Austria
  Aigen i.M. 00604
  Innsbruck 00698
  Klagenfurt 00710
  Niederleis 00745
  Reichersberg 00762
  Riezlern 00767
  Rohrau 00768
  Salzburg 00778
  Sankt Florian 00784, 00785
  Villach 00819
  Wien 00839, 00887

Belgium
 Antwerpen 00931
 Brugge 00991
 Carnières-Morlanwelz 01036
 Deinze 01051
 Deurle 01054
 Diksmuide 01062
 Drogenbos 01063
 Hoogstraten 01112
 Mons 01192
 Nismes 01215
 Nivelles 01216
 Spa 01262
 Zulte 01322
Brazil
 Niteroi 01407
Bulgaria
 Berkovica 01554
 Burgas 01563
 Jambol 01581
 Kjustendil 01591
 Pazardžik 01613, 01615
 Razgrad 01635
 Ruse 01640
 Sliven 01650
 Sofija 01667, 01669, 01674
 Štara Zagora 01681
 Šumen 01685
 Veliko Tărnovo 01704
 Vidin 01708
Canada
 Belleville 01794
 Hamilton 02025
 Regina 02297
Czechoslovakia
 Betliar 02851
 Bratislava 02868
 Březnice 02872
 Brno 02877
 Čechy pod Kosířem 02893
 Chropyně 02917
 Havlíčkův Brod 02955
 Jaroměř 02990
 Kroměříž 03042
 Kutná Hora 03046
 Liberec 03059
 Litoměřice 03069
 Loštice 03076
 Malé Svatoňovice 03083
 Mirotice 03098
 Náchod 03109
 Nepomuk 03113
 Ostrava 03141
 Praha 03177
 Ronov nad Doubravkou 03228
 Šlapanice 03251
 Štará Huť u Dobříše 03262
 Úpice 03304
 Železnice 03342
 Železný Brod 03344
Denmark
 Aarhus 03358
 Auning 03368
 Charlottenlund 03372
 Dragør 03376
 Dronningmølle 03377
 Espergærde 03385
 Faaborg 03386
 Flauenskjold 03395
 Frederikssund 03399
 Holte 03437
 København 03475
 Lemvig 03486
 Maribo 03493
 Marstal 03495
 Randers 03527
 Ribe 03531
 Skagen 03544
 Torrig 03572
France
 Agen 03898
 Aix-en-Provence 03902
 Alès 03912
 Angoulême 03931
 Avignon 03964

Bergues 03995
Bordeaux 04011
Caen 04030
Calais 04034
Chantilly 04056
Cherbourg 04072
Dijon 04101
Douai 04106
Dunkerque 04108
Grenoble 04131
Honfleur 04140
Le Havre 04182
Lille 04200
Lons-le-Saunier 04210
Lyon 04220
Mâcon 04228
Marseille 04237, 04241
Menton 04249
Metz 04252
Montpellier 04280
Nancy 04293
Nantes 04296
Narbonne 04301
Nice 04308, 04311
Nîmes 04318
Orléans 04329
Paris 04378
Pau 04393
Périgueux 04395
Perpignan 04397
Riom 04424
Rochefort 04429
Rouen 04436
Saint-Omer 04462
Saintes 04475
Strasbourg 04500
Tarbes 04505
Tourcoing 04519
Tours 04521
Valence 04532
Germany, Democratic Republic
 Bautzen 04609
 Dresden 04683
 Meiningen 04903
 Schwerin 05045
Germany, Federal Republic
 Aschaffenburg 05201
 Bamberg 05252
 Bayreuth 05257, 05261
 Berlin 05276, 05300
 Braunschweig 05341
 Frankfurt 05471
 Füssen 05496
 Heidelberg 05567
 Kassel 05621
 Köln 05660
 Konstanz 05667
 Krefeld 05670
 Landshut 05685
 Langenargen 05687
 München 05774
 Siegen 05919
 Würzburg 06000
Greece
 Amfissa 06034
 Athens 06064, 06069, 06080
 Larissa 06171
Hungary
 Badacsony 06345
 Budapest 06392
 Szentes 06515
 Zala 06540
 Zebegény 06544
India
 Aundh 06578
 Burdwan 06618
Ireland
 Dublin 07013, 07014
Italy
 Piacenza 07771
 Reggio Emilia 07824
Japan
 Akita 08175
 Kurume 08322
 Tokyo 08559

Mexico
 México City 08845
 Puebla 08877
Netherlands
 Amsterdam 08987
 Otterlo 09285
 's-Heerenberg 09350
New Zealand
 Invercargill 09505
Norway
 Mandal 09746
 Oslo 09784
 Stavanger 09865
 Trondhjem 09894
Poland
 Białystok 10115
 Bielsko-Biała 10121
 Brzeg 10131
 Grudziædz 10188
 Kłdzko 10215
 Koryznówka 10224
 Kraków 10228-10230, 10248
 Krośniewice 10252
 Legnica 10265
 Mława 10294
 Nysa 10312
 Płock 10336
 Poznań 10345
 Rogalin 10373
 Rzeszów 10378
 Toruń 10431
 Warszawa 10450, 10463
Portugal
 Alpiarça 10532
 Lisboa 10586
 Viseu 10626
Puerto Rico
 Ponce 10630
Romania
 Bucureşti 10671
 Topalu 10792
South Africa
 Cape Town 10856
 Kimberley 10920
Spain
 Barcelona 11071
 Bilbao 11110
 Madrid 11309, 11317
 Málaga 11347
 Montserrat (Monistrol) 11374
Sweden
 Eldersberga 11678
 Eskilstuna 11681
 Ödeshög 11779
 Stockholm 11807, 11816, 11840
 Västerås 11876
Switzerland
 Ascona 11911
 Gruyères 12053
 Loco 12120
 Lugano 12124
 Moutier 12152
 Neuchâtel 12162
 Sion 12238
 Winterthur 12289, 12290, 12295
 Zurzach 12339
United Kingdom
 Aberford 12609
 Barnsley 12663
 Kingston-upon-Hull 13113
 London 13219
 Manchester 13270
 Newcastle-upon-Tyne 13309
 Oxford 13343, 13344
 York 13609
United States
 Anderson IN 13696
 Augusta GA 13768
 Birmingham AL 13897
 Bloomington IN 13912
 Casper WY 14079
 Charlottesville VA 14137
 Coral Gables FL 14285
 Dallas TX 14333
 Duxbury MS 14450

Elmira NY 14494
El Paso TX 14499
Greenwich CT 14792
Hanover NH 14825
Hempstead NY 14863
Honolulu HI 14902
Indianapolis IN 14959
Ithaca NY 14974
Lawrence KS 15145
Lexington KY 15172
Malibu CA 15305
Manchester NH 15310
Milwaukee WI 15416
Minneapolis MN 15427
Moraga CA 15475
Muskegon MI 15511
New Haven CT 15575
New London CT 15578
Norfolk VA 15688
Park Rapids MN 15813
Pasadena CA 15817
St Louis MO 16196
St. Petersburg FL 16210
San Diego CA 16254
Santa Barbara CA 16294
Sarasota FL 16312
Savannah GA 16334
Seattle WA 16350, 16352
Shreveport LA 16387
Springfield MO 16449
Tucson AZ 16618
Washington DC 16737, 16755, 16763
West Palm Beach FL 16844
Winter Park FL 16921
USSR
 Leningrad 17123
Venezuela
 Caracas 17389
Yugoslavia
 Osijek 17646
 Zagreb 17826
Painting, French
Denmark
 Charlottenlund 03372
Finland
 Helsinki 03712
 Lahti 03779
France
 Abbeville 03896
 Aix-en-Provence 03899
 Aix-les-Bains 03906
 Albi 03910
 Alès 03912
 Altkirch 03915
 Arles 03946
 Arras 03948
 Autun 03956
 Avignon 03965
 Bagnols-sur-Ceze 03972
 Bar-le-Duc 03975
 Béziers 04001
 Brest 04024
 Cagnes-sur-Mer 04032
 Carcassonne 04039
 Carpentras 04041
 Chambéry 04053
 Chartres 04058
 Clamecy 04075
 Dijon 04103
 Dole 04105
 Gordes 04127
 Hazebrouck 04136
 La Fère 04155
 Langres 04158
 La Rochelle 04161
 Laval 04168
 Le Cateau 04175
 Limoges 04204
 L'Isle-Adam 04208
 Maubeuge 04244
 Meaux 04245
 Meudon 04254
 Orléans 04329, 04330
 Ornans 04334

Cevio 11987
Chur 11989
Diessenhofen 12002
Ebnat-Kappel 12008
Genève 12035, 12037
Hilterfingen 12066
La Sarraz 12091
Ligornetto 12117
Locarno 12119
Muttenz 12158
Olten 12173
Payerne 12177
Pully 12182
St. Moritz 12215
Solothurn 12243
Winterthur 12295, 12296
United Kingdom
Aberdeen 12604
Accrington 12615
Blackpool 12725
Edinburgh 12949, 12963
Liverpool 13163
Maidstone 13263
Manchester 13273
Middlesborough 13293
Oxford 13345
Woburn 13589
United States
Baltimore MD 13798
Berkeley CA 13874
Bethlehem PA 13883
Cedar City UT 14086
Cedar Falls IA 14088
Charlottesville VA 14137
Chattanooga TN 14141
Cold Spring NY 14240
Davenport IA 14348
Dearborn MI 14367
Des Moines IA 14400
East Lansing MI 14461
Elmira NY 14494
Farmington CT 14551
Flushing NY 14588
Fort Lauderdale FL 14619
Fort Worth TX 14650
Hagerstown MD 14806
Hollywood FL 14893
Huntington WV 14931
Huntsville AL 14933
Jackson MS 14977
Jamestown NY 14994
Kingston NY 15070
Laurel MS 15141
Los Angeles CA 15247
Memphis TN 15360
Milwaukee WI 15415
Minneapolis MN 15427
Moraga CA 15475
Mountainville NY 15502
Nashville TN 15529
New Brighton PA 15553
New Orleans LA 15590
Newark OH 15657
Northampton MA 15709
Oshkosh WI 15778
Park Rapids MN 15813
Pasadena CA 15817
Pine Bluff AR 15913
Pittsburgh PA 15924, 15927
Portland ME 15973
St. Johnsbury VT 16179
St. Paul MN 16206
Salt Lake City UT 16232
San Francisco CA 16268
San Jose CA 16274
San Marino CA 16282
Seattle WA 16350, 16352
Springfield MO 16449
Springville UT 16455
Stockton CA 16488
Tacoma WA 16531
Tampa FL 16543
Tempe AZ 16561
Washington DC 16770
Wichita KS 16868

Williamstown MA 16881
Yugoslavia
Bački Petrovac 17442
Dubrovnik 17518
Maribor 17610
Osijek 17646
Rijeka 17686
Paleontology see Fossils
Paper
Australia
Manjimup 00524
Finland
Verla 03892
France
Ambert 03916
Japan
Osaka 08460
Tokyo 08564
Netherlands
Apeldoorn 09009
Poland
Duszniki Zdrój 10165
United States
Appleton WI 13714
Bethel ME 13880
Dalton MA 14339
Peasant life and traditions (see also
Farms and farming)
Argentina
Buenos Aires 00086
Chacabuco 00171
Ranchos 00311
Australia
Moe 00535
Williamstown 00599
Austria
Alpl 00606
Bad Goisern 00617
Bad Tatzmannsdorf 00625
Haag 00681
Hermagor 00688
Längenfeld 00719
Lienz 00728
Mariazell 00734
Mittersill 00738
Mondsee 00741
Pöchlarn 00759
St. Johann i.S. 00788
Schwarzenberg 00801
Stadl-Paura 00811
Stainz 00812
Wildschönau-Oberau 00906
Zwettl 00909
Belgium
Dampicourt 01049
Diksmuide 01061
Izenberge 01124
Lommel 01171
Saint-Hubert 01246
Bulgaria
Sofija 01666
Canada
Caraquet 01843
Carman 01849
College Bridge 01880
Kamloops 02053
Patricia 02244
Prince William 02279
Shandro 02379
Vernon 02493
Whitemouth 02533
Czechoslovakia
Rožnov pod Radhoštěm 03234
Denmark
Aabenraa 03353
Ærøskøbing 03364
Faaborg 03387
Faarevejle 03390
Gilleleje 03403
Glamsbjerg 03406
Hadsund 03413
Herning 03419
Højby 03429
Kalundborg 03447
Køge 03481

Lyngby 03490
Mariager 03491
Odder 03509
Odense 03513
Ølgod 03519
Randers 03526
Rønne 03535
Skørping 03552
Vaerløse 03573
Vinderup 03587
Finland
Arkkukari 03669
Hämeenlinna 03681
Helsinki 03705, 03717
Hollola 03731
Imatra 03738
Isokyrö 03741
Kaarlela 03752
Käkkäräniemi, Kuopio 03754
Kangasniemi 03756
Keuruu 03764
Kokemäki 03765
Kokimäki 03766
Kurikka 03776
Laukaa 03785
Lieksa 03787
Luopioinen 03790
Niemisjärvi 03804
Orimattila 03809
Parainen 03816
Pielavesi 03819
Porlammi 03824
Pyhäjoki 03832
Rajamäki 03834
Rovaniemi 03844
Ruovesi 03847
Rymättylä 03848
Seinäjoki 03850
Somero 03853
Tammisaari 03855
Urjalankylä 03881
Vaasa 03883
Valtimo 03887
Vasikka-aho 03891
Vihanti 03893
Yläne 03895
France
Ambierle 03917
Moulins 04283
Oltingue 04326
Germany, Democratic Republic
Bad Freienwalde 04598
Belzig 04613
Eisenach 04709
Erfurt 04721
Gerstungen 04752
Gnandstein 04756
Göhren 04757
Grossengottern 04780
Haldensleben 04793
Hinzdorf 04810
Kahla 04830
Lehde 04860
Lommatzsch 04883
Luckau 04886
Neukirch 04930
Nieder-Neundorf 04933
Perleberg 04956
Posterstein 04962
Rudolstadt 05019
Schmölln 05033
Schönebeck 05036
Schwedt 05041
Tangermünde 05073
Weimar 05107
Germany, Federal Republic
Altmannstein 05181
Amerang 05186
Bad Brückenau 05212
Bad Oeynhausen 05230
Bad Schussenried 05234
Bad Wimpfen 05238
Bad Zwischenahn 05240
Berchtesgaden 05264
Bielefeld 05313

Cloppenburg 05372
Dinkelsbühl 05394
Emmendingen 05424
Finsterau 05450
Fischbachtal 05451
Furth im Wald 05492
Geißen 05499
Grafenau 05512
Grefrath 05516
Großweil 05518
Gutach 05521
Hagen 05523
Hamburg 05538
Heidenheim 05571
Hersbruck 05575
Husum 05585
Illerbeuren 05590
Kiel 05634
Königsbrunn 05663
Korbach 05668
Loßburg 05705
Maihingen 05725
Massing 05747
Mechernich-Kommern 05750
Meldorf 05756
Melle 05757
Mittenwald 05770
Mühlacker 05773
Münnerstadt 05812
Wadersloh 05967
Wangen 05969
Hungary
Abony 06343
Balmazujváros 06352
Budapest 06391
Nyíregyháza 06459
Szenna 06507
Szentendre 06513
Szombathely 06524
Tihany 06529
Zalaegerszeg 06541
India
Trivandrum 06852, 06853
Wardha 06871
Ireland
Dublin 07008
Israel
Be'er Sheva 07038
Italy
Alagna Valsesia 07161
Cavalese 07339
Cesena 07346
Domodossola 07400
Forlì 07491
Gorizia 07534
Gravina di Puglia 07537
Lonato 07584
Monterosso Grana 07676
Nuoro 07704
Palazzolo Acreide 07721
Palmi 07735
Roma 07882
Rovigo 07918
San Michele all'Adige 07939
Torre Pellice 08049
Japan
Asahikawa 08182
Mito 08376
Naha 08407
Omiya 08457
Toyonaka 08592
Yokohama 08616
Norway
Aga 09602
Ål 09603
Ålen 09604
Alvdal 09606
Åndalsnes 09607
Årnes 09612
Askim 09615
Bagn 09617
Ballangen 09618
Bjerka 09635
Bodø 09638
Borkenes 09640

Petrolium industry and trade

Lima OH   15189
Lindenhurst NY   15199
McCook NE   15281
Montrose CO   15469
Mount Pleasant IA   15494
Nashua IA   15523
Nevada City CA   15547
Noblesville IN   15684
North East PA   15700
North Freedom WI   15701
Norwood NY   15718
Perris CA   15850
Phillips ME   15900
Pottsville PA   15990
Pueblo CO   16012
Raton NM   16042
Roanoke VA   16103
Rockhill Furnace PA   16128
Rugby ND   16152
W. Sacramento CA   16159
Seattle WA   16356
Selkirk NY   16365
Silverton CO   16394
South Carver MA   16422
South St. Paul MN   16427
Strasburg PA   16497, 16498
Teague TX   16556
Temple TX   16562
Union IL   16644
Warwick NY   16725
Washington PA   16782
Waycross GA   16812
West Henrietta NY   16841
Wilson NY   16897
Worthington OH   16938
USSR
  Leningrad   17138
Yugoslavia
  Beograd   17474
  Jesenice   17548
  Ravne na Koreškem   17684
Zimbabwe
  Bulawayo   17865
Rare books *see* Books
Religious art and symbolism
Argentina
  Buenos Aires   00123, 00130, 00131
  Córdoba   00184
  Corrientes   00199, 00202
  Jesús María   00229
  La Rioja   00249
  La Roja   00251
  Longchamps   00257
  Luján   00263
  Mendoza   00271
  Salta   00338
  San Ignacio   00345
  San Miguel de Tucumán   00367
  Santa Fé   00387, 00390
  Santiago del Estero   00398
  Vichigasta   00422
Australia
  Newtown   00545
Austria
  Bad Aussee   00614
  Bad Ischl   00621
  Breitenau   00638
  Haus   00686
  Klagenfurt   00709
  Klosterneuburg   00713
  Mariazell   00735
  Melk   00737
  St. Lambrecht   00789
  St. Martin   00790
  St. Paul   00791
  St. Pölten   00793
  Schlierbach   00800
  Seckau   00802
  Spittal   00809
  Stams   00813
  Wien   00834, 00848, 00858, 00866
  Wilhering   00907

Belgium
  Antwerpen   00942
  Beauraing   00962
  Bouvignes   00978
  Brugge   00985, 00993, 00995, 00996
  Damme   01045
  Gent   01081
  Gistel   01095
  Halle   01100
  Huy   01114, 01116
  Leuven   01146
  Liège   01158, 01165
  Mechelen   01182
  Mons   01194, 01197
  Namur   01206, 01209
  Oostende   01226
  Rekem   01236
  Saint-Vith   01249
  Schelle   01250
  Stavelot   01267
  Tienen   01272
  Tongeren   01275
  Tournai   01283
  Zoutleeuw   01321
Brazil
  Belo Horizonte   01353
  Cachoeira   01357
  Caeté   01358
  Carpina   01367
  Diamantina   01373
  João Pessoa   01389
  Maceió   01397
  Pôrto Alegre   01419
  Recife   01428, 01432
  Rio de Janeiro   01441, 01458, 01461
  Salvador   01490, 01494-01496
  São Paulo   01520
  Sobral   01533
  Vitória   01538, 01539, 01541
Bulgaria
  Bačkovo   01548
  Sofija   01665, 01667
  Varna   01697
Burma
  Pegu   01724
  Rangoon   01728
Cameroon
  Yaoundé   01747
Canada
  Berthierville   01795
  Caughnawaga   01856
  Chatham   01865
  Clemensport   01874
  Cooks Creek   01883
  Joliette   02048
  Montréal   02162, 02165
  Odanak   02213
  Québec   02284
  St. Albert   02321
  Toronto   02439
  Winnipeg   02551
Chile
  Santiago   02594
China, People's Republic
  Chengde   02622
  Chengdu   02624
  Jinan   02635
  Taiyuan   02663
Colombia
  Bogotá   02709, 02710, 02713
  Cartagena   02730
  Duitama   02735
  Popayán   02765, 02770
  Ráquira   02771
  Rionegro   02772
  Santa Fé   02775
  Sonsón   02780
  Tunja   02784
  Villa de Leiva   02788
Costa Rica
  San José   02798
Czechoslovakia
  Bardejov   02845

Červený Klástor-Kúpele   02897
Komárno   03023
Praha   03205
Stará L'ubovňa   03263
Svidník   03273
Denmark
  Esbjerg   03384
  Helsingør   03417
  København   03469
  Ribe   03529
  Rudkøbing   03540
  Stege   03560
  Vordingborg   03588
Ethiopia
  Addis Ababa   03655, 03656
Finland
  Kuopio   03775
  Mikkeli   03799
France
  Amboise   03920
  Auxerre   03958
  Avallon   03962
  Bordeaux   04012
  Brive-la-Gaillarde   04028
  Carpentras   04042
  Chalon-sur-Saône   04050
  Conques   04090
  Coulommiers   04092
  Crépy-en-Valois   04094
  Dijon   04100
  Issoudun   04142
  Lyon   04223
  Marseille   04240
  Nancy   04291
  Nice   04313
  Nissan-lez-Ensérune   04320
  Paray-le-Monial   04335
  Paris   04367
  Saulieu   04481
  Troyes   04528
  Ussel   04530
  Versailles   04544
  Vienne   04547
  Villeneuve-les-Avignon   04550
  Villeneuve-sur-Lot   04551
Germany, Democratic Republic
  Arnstadt   04583
  Berlin   04616, 04622
  Blankenburg   04639
  Frankfurt/Oder   04730
  Grossschönau   04784
  Halberstadt   04789
  Heiligenstadt   04803
  Köthen   04850
  Neuruppin   04931
  Senftenberg   05052
Germany, Federal Republic
  Aachen   05155
  Alsfeld   05176
  Altötting   05182, 05183
  Amberg   05185
  Arnsberg   05194
  Autenried   05209
  Bad Münstereifel   05224
  Baden-Baden   05244
  Bamberg   05247
  Beuron   05308
  Braunschweig   05339
  Eichstätt   05417
  Ellwangen   05421
  Essen   05439, 05442
  Fladungen   05452
  Freising   05480
  Fritzlar   05485
  Fulda   05487
  Hildesheim   05577
  Kalkar   05602
  Kassel   05618
  Köln   05649, 05650
  Limburg   05698
  Lörrach   05703
  Loßburg   05705
  Lübeck   05712
  Ludwigshafen   05721
  Mainz   05727

Münnerstadt   05812
Offenburg   05856
Osnabrück   05861
Ottobeuren   05865
Paderborn   05867
Passau   05868
Recklinghausen   05876
Regensburg   05879
Reichenau   05886
Rottweil   05897
Ruhpolding   05900
Soest   05921
Speyer   05926
Trier   05943, 05944
Tübingen   05954
Überlingen   05960
Xanten   06008, 06009
Greece
  Aigion   06028
  Apoikia   06040
  Athens   06055, 06068, 06076
  Batsi   06087
  Chora   06098
  Corfu   06101
  Falika   06113
  Herakleion   06127
  Kalamata   06135
  Kalavrita   06137
  Kalloni   06138
  Karditsa   06144
  Karpenision   06145, 06146
  Kavalla   06152
  Kissos   06154
  Kolymbary   06155
  Komotini   06157
  Kos   06161
  Kozani   06163
  Leukas   06174
  Meteora   06191-06193
  Parga   06223
  Paros   06225
  Patmos   06226
  Pyrgos   06239, 06241
  Rethymnon   06244, 06246
  Rhodos   06249
  Samos   06261
  Skiathos   06269
  Skopelos   06270
  Sparta   06273, 06275
  Tenos   06284
  Thira   06293
  Trikkala   06296, 06298
  Xanthe   06308
  Ypati   06309
Hungary
  Budapest   06364-06366, 06390
  Debrecen   06406
  Ópusztaszer   06460
  Pannonhalma   06463
  Pápa   06464
  Pécs   06468
  Sárospatak   06483, 06484
  Sopron   06490
  Szentendre   06511
India
  Ahmedabad   06561
  Allahabad   06568
  Amritsar   06576
  Bombay   06614
  Jhansi   06714
  New Delhi   06801
Indonesia
  Jakarta   06889
Israel
  Abu Gosh   07027
  Haifa   07063
  Jerusalem   07076, 07079, 07098
  Tel Aviv   07139
Italy
  Agrigento   07158
  Albenga   07165
  Anagni   07175
  Ancona   07176
  Aosta   07182, 07183
  Arezzo   07189

Asciano 07193
Ascoli Piceno 07196
Assisi 07201
Atri 07207
Avellino 07208
Bari 07215
Bitonto 07236
Bologna 07254, 07256, 07257
Brescia 07278
Bressanone 07283
Cagliari 07290
Caltanissetta 07295
Camaiore 07297
Camerino 07301
Campobasso 07304
Castel Sant'Elia 07318
Castell'Arquato 07323
Castiglion Fiorentino 07327
Chieri 07353
Chieti 07355
Città di Castello 07361
Cividale del Friuli 07364
Colle di Val d'Elsa 07373
Cortona 07386
Cremona 07391
Enna 07402
Ferrara 07428
Firenze 07446, 07447, 07449, 07457, 07467, 07468
Gaeta 07499
Gandino 07504
Genova 07521, 07525
Grosseto 07540
Grottaferrata 07541
Gubbio 07546
L'Aquila 07561
Macerata 07597
Matelica 07609
Messina 07616
Milano 07619, 07630, 07636, 07651
Modena 07657
Montalcino 07671
Montecatini Val di Nievole 07672
Monza 07679
Nonantola 07698
Orte 07709
Osimo 07713
Palermo 07724, 07728
Perugia 07761
Piacenza 07775
Pienza 07778
Pompei 07797
Roma 07901
Salerno 07925
San Gimignano 07930
San Miniato 07940
Santa Maria degli Angeli 07946
Savona 07964
Spello 07992
Sulmona 08002
Todi 08021
Trani 08051
Trento 08056
Urbino 08091
Varese 08097
Velletri 08100
Vicchio 08144
Vipiteno 08151
Volterra 08157
Japan
Ashigarashimo 08185
Biwa-ko 08192
Chikushi 08201
Enzan 08203
Hanamaki 08222
Higashimuro 08225
Hirado 08232
Hofu 08238, 08239
Ikoma 08243, 08244
Ise 08253
Ito 08257
Kakogawa 08266
Kasai 08283

Kashima 08285
Koganei 08305
Komatsu 08309
Kumamoto 08314
Kyoto 08327, 08329, 08330, 08345, 08347, 08349, 08352
Matsue 08356, 08358
Minamikoma 08368
Mishima 08372
Nagano 08392
Nagoya 08400
Nara 08418, 08421, 08423, 08424
Narita 08427
Nikko 08431
Nishiiwai 08435, 08437, 08438
Nishikanbara 08439
Ochi 08446
Otsu 08470
Saeki 08475
Saiki 08478
Sendai 08493
Shingu 08501
Shiogama 08502
Takayama 08529
Tokyo 08535, 08546, 08572
Toyota 08593
Uji 08604
Wakayama 08607
Korea, Republic
Seoul 08709
Mexico
México City 08858
Querétaro 08881
Tepotztlán 08888
Yuriria 08899
Mongolia
Ulan Bator 08909
Mozambique
Maputo 08934
Netherlands
Amsterdam 08972, 08975
Breda 09045
Culemborg 09058
Delft 09067
Eernewoude 09108
Etten-Leur 09129
Gouda 09144, 09145
Groenlo 09148
Haarlem 09160, 09161
Huijbergen 09197
Janum 09198
Maastricht 09249, 09250
Oirschot 09273
Oldenzaal 09275
's-Hertogenbosch 09351, 09353
Ter Apel 09373
Thorn 09375
Uden 09381
Valkenburg 09401
Vries 09422
Woerden 09436
Zutphen 09458
New Zealand
Reefton 09541
Norway
Drammen 09651
Kirkenes 09718
Oslo 09806
Pakistan
Banbhore 09923
Peru
Ayacucho 09992
Lima 10004
Philippines
Manila 10059, 10067, 10068
San Pablo 10090
Poland
Częstochowa 10153
Dobra 10161
Haczów 10190
Istebna na Kubalonce 10196
Kamień Pomorski 10205
Pelpin 10332
Płock 10336

Poznań 10345
Przemyśl 10359
Sandomierz 10381
Sanok 10383
Szczyrzyc 10418
Ulucz 10439
Wrocław 10494
Portugal
Aeouca 10530
Braga 10542
Coimbra 10551, 10556
Faro 10561
Guimarães 10565
Lamego 10569
Lisboa 10579
Óbidos 10598
Puerto Rico
San German 10633
São Tomé and Príncipe
São Tomé 10808
South Africa
Cape Town 10849
Johannesburg 10905
Spain
Agreda 11019
Albocácer 11022
Almería 11031
Alquezar 11032
Aranjuez 11041
Arcos de la Frontera 11042
Arenas de San Pedro 11043
Astorga 11049
Avila 11050, 11054
Badajoz 11060, 11061
Barbastro 11068
Barcelona 11075, 11077, 11090
Barco de Avila 11104
Belmonte 11106
Bilbao 11112
Bocairente 11114
Burgos 11119, 11123
Cáceres 11126
Cádiz 11127
Calahorra 11131
Castelló de Ampurias 11141
Celanova 11143
Chillon 11146
Ciudad Real 11150
Colmenar Viejo 11154
Córdoba 11166
Covadonga 11168, 11169
Covarrubias 11170
Cuenca 11173
Daroca 11175, 11176
El Escorial 11182
Gascueña 11196
Gerona 11199, 11201, 11202
Granada 11206, 11207, 11213, 11216
Guadix 11220
Ibiza 11229
Illescas 11233
Jaén 11236
Junquera de Ambia 11242
Las Palmas 11254
León 11256, 11257
Lérida 11260
Lugo 11273, 11275
Madrid 11281, 11294, 11295
Málaga 11346, 11348
Manresa 11352
Marchena 11354
Medina de Pomar 11363
Medina de Ríoseco 11364
Medinaceli 11365
Monforte de Lemos 11371
Morella 11375
Murcia 11378
Oncala 11389
Orense 11393
Orihuela 11395, 11396
Osuna 11397, 11399
Oviedo 11400
Padrón 11403
Palencia 11406

Palma de Mallorca 11410
Pamplona 11419
Paradas 11422
Paredes de Nava 11423
Pastrana 11424
Plasencia 11429
Roda de Isábena 11445
Sahagún 11452
Salamanca 11456
San Ildefonso o La Granja 11460
San Juan de las Abadesas 11462
San Lorenzo de El Escorial 11464, 11465
San Mateo 11467
San Millán de la Cogolla 11468
San Millán de Suso 11469
Santa Gadea del Cid 11483
Santa María del Campo 11485
Santa María del Puig 11486
Santiago de Compostela 11494
Santillana del Mar 11498
Santo Domingo de la Calzada 11500
Segorbe 11502
Segovia 11505, 11507
Seo de Urgel 11511
Sevilla 11512, 11513, 11518, 11521, 11524, 11525
Sigüenza 11528, 11529
Teruel 11550
Toledo 11555, 11561, 11564
Tordesillas 11567
Tortosa 11568
Traiguera 11571
Tudela 11572
Valencia 11582
Valladolid 11592
Verdú 11601
Villagarcía de Campos 11609
Villanueva de Lorenzana 11610
Zafra 11626
Zamora 11627
Zaragoza 11631
Sweden
Härnösand 11716
Lund 11753
Örebro 11780
Skellefteå 11795
Strängenäs 11850
Uppsala 11870
Västerås 11877
Växjö 11880
Switzerland
Altdorf 11900
Altstätten 11902
Appenzell 11905
Baden 11918
Basel 11926
Beromünster 11959
Bischofszell 11962
Bremgarten 11970
Chur 11991
Delémont 12001
Dornach 12005
Ernen 12011
Hitzkirch 12069
Küssnacht am Rigi 12083
Laufen 12093
Lausanne 12098
Le Grand-Saint-Bernard 12105
Loco 12120
Lugano 12125
Münster 12154
Muri 12155
Müstair 12157
Olivone 12171
Payerne 12177
Rapperswil 12185
Saint-Maurice 12207
San Vittore 12209
Schwyz 12229
Siebnen 12233
Sion 12237

Solothurn 12241
Stans 12251
Sursee 12257, 12258
Wettingen 12281
Wil 12284
Turkey
Nevsehir 12564
United Kingdom
Bagshot 12648
Barnstaple 12665
Beaulieu 12680
Canterbury 12818
Dundee 12929
Durham 12934
Hemel Hempstead 13057
Norwich 13329
St. Andrews 13412
United States
Baton Rouge LA 13828
Berkeley CA 13869
Bethlehem PA 13884
Chattanooga TN 14139
Cincinnati OH 14189
Cleveland OH 14223
Greenville SC 14790
Lincoln NE 15192
Los Angeles CA 15242
Milwaukee WI 15413
Montreat NC 15468
Nashville TN 15527, 15532, 15537
New York NY 15598, 15622, 15625, 15644, 15650
North Newton KS 15704
Oroville CA 15775
Philadelphia PA 15890
Ringoes NJ 16088
Rochester NY 16110
St Louis MO 16186
Santa Fe NM 16305, 16306
Staten Island NY 16471
Taos NM 16549
Washington DC 16734, 16743
USSR
Leningrad 17118, 17139
Moskva 17166, 17167, 17171, 17198, 17215, 17219, 17220
Vatican
Città del Vaticano 17364, 17373, 17375
Venezuela
Ciudad Bolívar 17401
Maracay 17408
Yugoslavia
Beograd 17456, 17463
Cetinje 17505
Dečane 17509
Dubrovnik 17514
Džakovo 17521
Fojnica 17525
Hvar 17534
Imotski 17540
Jajce 17543
Karlobag 17551
Korčula 17565-17568
Kotor 17571
Oplenac kod Topole 17644
Peć 17652
Perast 17654
Prčanj 17667
Raška 17683
Sarajevo 17701
Senj 17706
Šibenik 17711
Split 17744
Trogir 17775, 17776
Vršac 17799
Zadar 17805, 17807
Zagreb 17811, 17833
Zaostrog 17839

Religious history and traditions
Argentina
Buenos Aires 00123, 00130, 00131
La Paz 00233

Posadas 00301
Australia
New Norcia 00544
Newtown 00545
Austria
Bad Aussee 00614
Breitenau 00638
Forchtenstein 00653
Fresach 00655
Haus 00686
Lendorf 00725
Reichersberg 00762
Rosenau 00770
Wien 00851, 00861, 00887, 00888
Belgium
Antwerpen 00942
Arlon 00954
Beauraing 00962
Borgerhout 00974, 00975
Brugge 00999
Bruxelles 01002
Durbuy 01064
Gent 01080, 01082
Gistel 01095
Halle 01100
Hastière-par-delà 01105
Kontich 01134
Kortrijk 01135
Lembeke 01143
Liège 01165
Mesen 01187
Mons 01197
Namur 01206
Opheylissem 01228
Roeselare 01238
Tournai 01277, 01283
Tubize 01284
Turnhout 01287
Waasmunster 01302
Wetteren 01309, 01310
Brazil
Rio de Janeiro 01458, 01462
São Paulo 01512
Bulgaria
Bačkovo 01548
Drjanovo 01570
Elena 01573
Sofija 01665
Canada
Bothwell 01804
Chatham 01865
Clemensport 01874
Dunvegan 01918
Edmonton 01929
Esterhazy 01948
Kelowna 02055
Miscouche 02141
Moncton 02148
Nicolet 02203
Norwich 02210
Prelate 02275
Québec 02281, 02285, 02288
Rosthern 02318
St. Albert 02321
Saskatoon 02365
Sharon 02380
Tadoussac 02423
Tofield 02434
Toronto 02439
Trois-Rivières 02467
Uxbridge 02473
Winnipeg 02551
China, People's Republic
Quanzhou 02653
Colombia
Bogotá 02712
Czechoslovakia
Husinec 02983
Praha 03204, 03205
Tábor 03250
Tachov 03276
Denmark
København 03469

Finland
Hämeenlinna 03683
Helsinki 03710
Kuopio 03775
Mikkeli 03799
Naantali 03803
France
Conques 04090
La Rochelle 04164
Limoges 04204
Lyon 04223
Magny-les-Hameaux 04229
Monsireigne 04263
Paray-le-Monial 04335
Paris 04341
Germany, Democratic Republic
Berlin 04618
Eisleben 04712
Georgenthal 04748
Nossen 04939
Wittenberg-Lutherstadt 05122, 05124
Germany, Federal Republic
Autenried 05209
Bad Karlshafen 05219
Braunschweig 05345
Bremen 05348
Eichstätt 05417
Ellingen 05420
Göttingen 05510
Kalkar 05602
Kiedrich 05629
Köln 05649, 05650
Konstanz 05665, 05666
Lüdinghausen 05716
Mainz 05727
Marburg 05742
Münster 05814
Regensburg 05879
Reichenau 05886
Reinfeld 05887
Rothenburg ob der Tauber 05895
Stuttgart 05928
Trier 05943
Tübingen 05954
Überlingen 05960
Würzburg 05997
Xanten 06008
Greece
Aigion 06028
Apoikia 06040
Argostolion 06044
Athens 06076
Batsi 06087
Herakleion 06127
Kalavrita 06136
Karpenision 06145, 06146
Kolymbary 06155
Leukas 06174
Mavradzei 06186
Meteora 06193
Nea Moni 06211
Parga 06223
Skiathos 06269
Sparta 06273
Trikkala 06296
Hungary
Budapest 06366, 06390
Debrecen 06406
Sopron 06490
Szentendre 06511
India
Allahabad 06570
Amritsar 06576
Israel
Jerusalem 07070, 07074, 07079, 07093, 07094
Italy
Riese Pio X 07826
Roma 07848, 07874, 07877
Rossano 07912
San Gimignano 07930
San Miniato 07940
Sant'Angelo Lodigiano 07947

Santuario di Montevergine 07952
Savona 07964
Sulmona 08002
Torino 08046
Torre Pellice 08049
Venezia 08116
Japan
Hanamaki 08222
Higashimuro 08225
Hofu 08238, 08239
Ikoma 08244
Ito 08257
Izumo 08262
Kyoto 08326, 08327, 08329, 08345, 08347, 08349
Minamikoma 08368
Nagano 08392
Nagoya 08400
Nara 08423
Nikko 08431
Nishiiwai 08435
Ochi 08446
Osaka 08467
Saiki 08478
Sawara 08490
Toyota 08593
Uji 08604
Yoshida 08624
Mongolia
Ulan Bator 08911
Netherlands
Aarle-Rixtel 08951
Amsterdam 08972, 08986
Asselt 09019
Goirle 09140
Huijbergen 09197
Maastricht 09249, 09250
Naarden 09262
Nijmegen 09270
Oldenzaal 09275
Oudenbosch 09289
Sittard 09357
Ter Apel 09373
Thorn 09375
Uden 09381
Utrecht 09393
Valkenburg 09399
Zutphen 09458
Nigeria
Oshogbo 09599
Norway
Rolvsøy 09829
Trondheim 09887
Utstein Kloster 09901
Philippines
Manila 10067
Poland
Częstochowa 10153
Przemyśl 10359
Portugal
Aeouca 10530
Barganca 10540
Saudi Arabia
Riyadh 10811
South Africa
Genadendal 10877
King William's Town 10922
Pretoria 10958
Stellenbosch 10997
Spain
Agreda 11019
Aroche 11045
Azpeitia 11057
Azpeitia (Véase Loyola) 11058
Badajoz 11060, 11061
Belmonte 11106
Burgos 11119
Calahorra 11131
Chillon 11146
Ciudad Real 11150
Covadonga 11168
Covarrubias 11170
Guadelupe 11219
Lérida 11260

Madrid 11294, 11295
Málaga 11346
Manresa 11352
Morella 11375
Murcia 11378
Oviedo 11400
Palma de Mallorca 11410
Plasencia 11429
Ripoll 11443
Salamanca 11456
San Cugat del Valles 11457
San Ildefonso o La Granja 11460
San Juan de las Abadesas 11462
San Millán de Suso 11469
Santa Gadea del Cid 11483
Segorbe 11502
Sevilla 11518
Sigüenza 11528
Toledo 11561
Verdú 11600
Vich 11604
Vilafranca del Panades 11606
Vileña de Bureba 11608
Villanueva y Geltrú 11612
Vitoria 11616
Zamora 11629
Sweden
Nårunga 11769
Switzerland
Baden 11918
Basel 11927, 11929
Bremgarten 11970
Bubikon 11979
Ernen 12011
Immensee 12073
Lausanne 12098
Maur 12140
Münster 12154
Reinach 12189
Sachseln 12204
Steckborn 12254
Stein am Rhein 12255
Sursee 12257, 12258
Wildhaus 12286
Zurzach 12340
Turkey
Derinkuyu 12488
Kaymakli 12543
United Kingdom
Bagshot 12648
Dolwyddelan 12908
Glasgow 13000
United States
Altenburg MO 13674
Belvidere NE 13861
Berkeley CA 13869
Bethlehem PA 13884
Brenham TX 13961
Brookline MA 13989
Chappaqua NY 14111
Cleveland OH 14223
Clinton MS 14229
Dagsboro DE 14328
Fort Scott KS 14640
Frederica DE 14665
Liberty MO 15185
Lincoln NE 15192
Marquette MI 15337
Moccasin AZ 15444
Montague MI 15451
Montreat NC 15468
Nashville TN 15532
New York NY 15622, 15644, 15650, 15654
North Newton KS 15704
Oroville CA 15775
Philadelphia PA 15878, 15890, 15895
Phoenix AZ 15906
Princeton NJ 16002
Quincy IL 16024
Ringoes NJ 16088
Riverside CA 16095

Saint George UT 16173
St Louis MO 16186
St. Paul MN 16203
Salt Lake City UT 16234
Santa Fe NM 16305
Savannah GA 16326
Sitka AK 16402
Ventura CA 16678
Walla Walla WA 16712
Walterboro SC 16715
Waltham MA 16716
Washington DC 16734, 16743
Weaverville CA 16820
Woodbury CT 16926
Zion IL 16963
USSR
Leningrad 17118
Moskva 17215, 17219
Vil'njus 17345
Yugoslavia
Beograd 17463

Reptiles
Argentina
Posadas 00300
Austria
Admont 00603
Canada
Wawa 02517
Germany, Federal Republic
Bonn 05333
India
Bombay 06612
Darjeeling 06650
Israel
Kiriat Tivon 07104
Japan
Hiwa 08237
Kurayoshi 08321
Nishimuro 08441
Senboku 08491
Luxembourg
Luxembourg 08764
Namibia
Okaukuejo 08937
Netherlands
Amsterdam 09007
South Africa
Durban 10865
Pretoria 10967
Uganda
Lake Katwe 12599
Murchison Falls 12601
United States
Atlanta GA 13753
Baton Rouge IA 13826
Cambridge MA 14037
Carlsbad NM 14068
Chicago IL 14170
Dover NH 14428
Gatlinburg TN 14710
Lansing MI 15122
Lawrence KS 15147
Lincoln MA 15190
Lubbock TX 15265
McKinney TX 15284
Milton MS 15410
Minneapolis MN 15424
New Canaan CT 15561
Oakland CA 15728
Owensboro KY 15788
Paicines CA 15797
Portales NM 15968
Provo UT 16010
Richmond IN 16069
Rock Hill SC 16120
Savannah GA 16332
Sharon CT 16372
Stamford CT 16463
Tucson AZ 16616
Waco TX 16702
Rescue equipment see Fire fighting and rescue work
Rocks see Mineralogy
Rugs see Carpets
Sarcophagi see Tombs

Scientific apparatus and instruments
(see also Optics; Precision instruments)
Canada
Edmonton 01926
Vancouver 02476
Denmark
Aarhus 03362
Finland
Helsinki 03697
France
Paris 04359, 04388, 04391
Germany, Democratic Republic
Potsdam 04966
Germany, Federal Republic
Kassel 05617
Schweinfurt 05914
India
Bangalore 06582
Italy
Firenze 07474
Roma 07910
Japan
Asahikawa 08180
Ikoma 08245
Yama 08608
Netherlands
Groningen 09155
Leiden 09228
Utrecht 09394, 09395
New Zealand
Auckland 09471
Portugal
Coimbra 10552
Spain
Barcelona 11087
Madrid 11289
Peñaranda de Duero 11425
Switzerland
Genève 12031, 12033
United Kingdom
Glasgow 12992
Oxford 13347
Redcar 13390
Warley 13552
United States
Berkeley CA 13870
Chapel Hill NC 14109
Charleston SC 14122
Chicago IL 14154
Lexington KY 15176
Los Angeles CA 15245
Pittsburgh PA 15922
Washington DC 16732
Winterville GA 16924
Scientific expeditions
Australia
Adventure Bay 00437
Grange 00499
Belgium
Rupelmonde 01245
Brazil
Natal 01406
Rio de Janeiro 01466
Salvador 01498
São Leopoldo 01508
Canada
St. Andrews 02322
China, People's Republic
Nanchang 02646
Suzhou 02662
Denmark
Hundested 03445
Egypt
Cairo 03625
Germany, Democratic Republic
Leipzig 04864
India
Faizabad 06664
Roorkee 06824
Italy
Chiavenna 07352
Gran San Bernardo 07536
Roma 07862, 07907

Japan
Kyoto 08326
Netherlands
Breukelen 09048
Culemborg 09057
Zeist 09449
New Zealand
Russell 09547
Norway
Andenes 09608
Borge 09639
Larvik 09735
Morgedal 09757
Oslo 09780, 09797
Sandefjord 09840
Svartskog 09875
Tromsø 09881
Spain
Barcelona 11103
La Rábida 11248
Valladolid 11589
Zumárraga 11634
Sweden
Gränna 11710
Stockholm 11810
Uppsala 11866
Switzerland
Chur 11990
Dornach 12005
Fribourg 12021
Genève 12033, 12036
United Kingdom
Blantyre 12728
Cambridge 12811
Glasgow 12995
Oxford 13348
United States
Astoria OR 13742
Ilwaco WA 14947
Spokane WA 16439
Walla Walla WA 16712
Yugoslavia
Ljubljana 17602
Sculpture (see also Plaster casts; Wood carving)
Argentina
Avellaneda 00063
Bahía Blanca 00068
Buenos Aires 00089, 00091, 00093, 00095, 00135
Campana 00164
Chacabuco 00170
Concordia 00181
Córdoba 00190, 00192
Coronel Pringles 00197
Corrientes 00200
Gálvez 00213
Gualeguaychú 00222
Junín 00230
La Plata 00240
Las Heras 00252
Luján de Cuyo 00264
Mar del Plata 00266
Morón 00285
Paraná 00296
Pergamino 00299
Posadas 00304
Puerto Iguazú 00306
Quilmes 00308
Rafaela 00310
Rauch 00312
Resistencia 00313
Rio Cuarto 00317
Rosario 00330
San Francisco 00344
San Ignacio 00346
San Isidro 00347
San Juan 00356
San Martín 00362
San Miguel de Tucumán 00368, 00373
San Nicolás de los Arroyos 00376
San Rafael 00379
Santa Fé 00387, 00392

Santiago del Estero   00400
Tilcara   00412
Tres Arroyos   00417
Vicente López   00421
Villa Carlos Paz   00425
Villa María   00428
Australia
   Langwarrin   00515
   Melbourne   00528
   Sydney   00585
Austria
   Graz   00667
   Innsbruck   00698
   Klagenfurt   00710
   Langenzersdorf   00721
   Mödling   00739
   Niederleis   00745
   Reichersberg   00762
   Riezlern   00767
   Sankt Florian   00784, 00785
   Wien   00843, 00853
Belgium
   Antwerpen   00944
   Ath   00956
   Buzenol   01035
   Deinze   01051
   De Panne   01053
   Herentals   01108
   Koksijde   01132
   Leuven   01149
   Liège   01158, 01162
   Lokeren   01170
   Mechelen   01180
   Nivelles   01216
   Oudenaarde   01231
   Sint-Martens-Latem   01255
   Sint-Truiden   01260
   Uccle   01289
   Verviers   01292
Brazil
   Natal   01404
   Salvador   01496
   São Cristóvão   01505
   São Paulo   01518
Bulgaria
   Ruse   01640
   Sofija   01652
   Vidin   01708
Cameroon
   Dschang   01739
Canada
   Dorval   01906
   Jonquière   02049
   London   02099
   Montréal   02154, 02157, 02163,
   02171
   Saskatoon   02364
   Stratford   02410
   Toronto   02435, 02438, 02452
   Verdun   02491
   Whitby   02529
   Wolfville   02561
China, People's Republic
   Chengdu   02623
   Lintong   02641
   Shanghai   02656
   Taiyuan   02663
   Wuxi   02668
   Xian   02671
Czechoslovakia
   Český Krumlov   02906
   Cheb   02909
   Chomutov   02914
   Hostinné   02973
   Jaroměř   02990
   Litoměřice   03069
   Nová Paka   03120
   Opava   03136
   Plzeň   03159
   Stupava   03269
   Zbraslav nad Vltavou   03335
Denmark
   Aarhus   03358
   Faaborg   03386
   Flauenskjold   03395

Frederikssund   03399
Herning   03418
København   03472, 03477
Maribo   03493
Nykøbing Sjælland   03506
Præstø   03524
Randers   03527
Vejen   03578
Ecuador
   Quito   03600
Equatorial guinea
   Santa Isabel   03653
Finland
   Anjala   03668
   Koski Tl   03770
   Lapinlahti   03782
   Merstola   03798
   Mikkeli   03800
   Porvoo   03830
   Tampere   03860, 03865
   Tarttila   03868
   Turku   03878, 03880
France
   Aix-en-Provence   03902
   Aix-les-Bains   03905, 03906
   Alise-Sainte-Reine   03913
   Angers   03927
   Angoulême   03930
   Annecy   03932
   Apt   03939
   Arles   03944, 03945
   Arras   03948
   Auch   03951
   Avesnes-sur-Helpe   03963
   Avignon   03965, 03966
   Beaune   03988
   Beauvais   03991
   Bordeaux   04011
   Brest   04025
   Cahors   04033
   Calais   04034
   Carcassonne   04038
   Caudebec-en-Caux   04049
   Châlons-sur-Marne   04052
   Chartres   04058
   Châteaudun   04062
   Clermont-Ferrand   04077
   Compiègne   04085
   Die   04096
   Dijon   04100, 04101
   Epernay   04112
   Epinal   04114
   Langres   04159
   Laval   04169
   Le Havre   04180
   Le Mée-sur-Seine   04188
   Les Andelys   04193
   Libourne   04198
   Longwy   04209
   Lyon   04220
   Maisons-Laffitte   04230
   Marseille   04234, 04237, 04241
   Meaux   04245
   Melun   04247
   Metz   04252
   Meudon   04255
   Mont-de-Marsan   04264
   Montargis   04269
   Montpellier   04279, 04280
   Nantes   04295, 04296
   Narbonne   04301
   Nice   04308, 04310, 04312
   Nîmes   04318
   Nogent-le-Rotrou   04321
   Nogent-sur-Seine   04323
   Orleans   04330
   Paris   04342, 04381
   Provins   04413
   Rennes   04420
   Riom   04424
   Rodez   04431
   Rouen   04436
   Saint-Denis   04447
   Saint Dizier   04442
   Saint-Etienne   04450

Saint-Lô   04458
Saint-Rémy-de-Provence   04467
Saint-Sauveur-le-Vicomte   04468
Saint-Tropez   04471
Sarrebourg   04479
Saulieu   04481
Senlis   04488
Soissons   04494
Strasbourg   04496, 04498
Thann   04508
Toulouse   04515, 04516
Tours   04521
Valenciennes   04533
Vaucouleurs   04538
Vendôme   04539
Versailles   04545
Vienne   04547
Villeneuve-sur-Lot   04551
Germany, Democratic Republic
   Altenburg   04571
   Berlin   04616, 04626, 04632
   Dresden   04684, 04689
   Halberstadt   04789
   Karl-Marx-Stadt   04840
   Magdeburg   04893
   Potsdam   04968
   Rostock   05012
Germany, Federal Republic
   Aachen   05159
   Arolsen   05196
   Aschaffenburg   05199
   Augsburg   05204
   Bad Dürrheim   05215
   Bamberg   05247
   Berlin   05295
   Bielefeld   05314
   Bocholt   05320
   Duisburg   05401
   Erlangen   05433
   Frankfurt   05462, 05471
   Füssen   05496
   Garmisch-Partenkirchen   05498
   Gießen   05502
   Göttingen   05508
   Hannover   05549, 05550
   Heidelberg   05567
   Heidenheim   05571
   Kaiserslautern   05600
   Karlsruhe   05610
   Kassel   05620
   Kelheim   05624
   Marl   05745
   München   05781, 05792, 05803,
   05808
   Münster   05813
   Ratzeburg   05875
   Stuttgart   05938
   Trier   05946, 05947
   Tübingen   05949
   Villingen-Schwenningen   05966
   Willebadessen   05984
   Würzburg   05998, 06000, 06004
Greece
   Amphiareion   06035
   Arta   06045
   Athens   06047, 06054, 06063,
   06080
   Chalkis   06091
   Ermoupolis   06112
   Filiatra   06116
   Lamia   06165
   Leukas   06173
   Lindos   06177
   Loutra Aidhipsou   06182
   Megara   06189
   Monemvasia   06205
   Navpaktos   06208
   Paros   06225
   Patras   06227
   Piraeus   06231
   Salonika   06252, 06258
   Siphnos   06268
   Telos   06282
   Tenos   06283, 06286
   Thespiae   06291

Trikkala   06297
Guatemala
   Antigua   06313
Hungary
   Budapest   06381, 06395
   Turkeve   06531
   Zalaegerszeg   06542
Iceland
   Reykjavik   06548
India
   Ahmedabad   06560
   Banda   06580
   Bangalore   06581
   Baroda   06585
   Basavakalyan   06590
   Bhanpura   06593
   Bombay   06611
   Bratacharigram   06615
   Bulandshahar   06616
   Bundi   06617
   Chandigarh   06640, 06641
   Darjeeling   06648
   Etawah   06662
   Gorakhpur   06673, 06675
   Gulbarga   06677
   Guntur   06679
   Gwalior   06680
   Hooghly   06688
   Hyderabad   06695
   Jaunpur   06708
   Jeypore   06711
   Khajuraho   06727
   Kittur   06730
   Konarak   06735
   Krishnapuram   06737
   Mysore   06780
   Nalanda   06783
   Prabhas Patan   06815
   Rajamundry   06819
   Sagar   06825
   Satna   06832
   Shirali   06836
   Shivpuri   06837
   Sikar   06839
   Sonagir   06841
   Tamluk   06845
   Udaipur   06855
   Ujjain   06858
   Vaisali   06860
Iraq
   Baghdad   06998
Ireland
   Dublin   07013
Israel
   Haifa   07059, 07060
Italy
   Bari   07213
   Bomarzo   07266
   Caltanissetta   07294
   Caprese   07307
   Chieti   07356, 07357
   Città di Castello   07362
   Collodi   07374
   Feltre   07418
   Firenze   07448, 07450, 07453
   Genova   07512, 07524
   Milano   07633, 07645
   Modena   07654
   Napoli   07681, 07686
   Pavia   07749
   Pisa   07791
   Pordenone   07801
   Roma   07853, 07878
   Saluzzo   07927
   Santuario di Montevergine
   07952
   Sassoferrato   07959
   Savigliano   07961
   Sestino   07971
   Siena   07978, 07981
   Spoleto   07995
   Sulmona   08001
   Sutri   08004
   Teggiano   08009
   Torino   08031

Torre del Greco 08047
Treviso 08064
Urbino 08090
Valdagno 08092
Varese 08098
Venezia 08107, 08124
Verona 08136, 08137
Ivory Coast
Abidjan 08160
Japan
Ashigarashimo 08184, 08185
Fukushima 08210
Ikoma 08243
Kamakura 08268, 08270
Kawachi-Nagano 08287
Kobe 08296
Kochi 08301
Komatsu 08309
Kyoto 08325, 08332,
08339-08341, 08346
Matsuyama 08364
Nara 08419, 08421, 08424
Niigata 08430
Okawa 08449
Osaka 08465
Sendai 08493
Suwa 08511
Takaichi 08516
Tokyo 08537, 08538, 08559,
08575, 08579
Utsunomiya 08605
Wakayama 08606
Yoshida 08624
Korea, Republic
Kamiminochi 08674
Lebanon
Beirut 08733
Liechtenstein
Vaduz 08756
Mexico
México City 08865
Monterrey 08866
Toluca 08891
Mongolia
Ulan Bator 08908
Morocco
Volubilis 08928
Nepal
Bhaktapur 08943
Netherlands
Deurne 09080
Heino 09180
Leeuwarden 09222
Leiden 09236
Utrecht 09385
Woerden 09436
Zevenaar 09451
New Zealand
Christchurch 09478
Nigeria
Ife 09592
Oshogbo 09599
Norway
Dalen i Telemark 09647
Hornindal 09706
Høvikodden 09708
Kristiansand S 09725
Leirvik 09736
Oslo 09808, 09809
Stavanger 09865
Utne 09900
Vanse 09907
Paraguay
Asunción 09986
Peru
Lima 10005
Philippines
Cagayan de Oro 10027
Poland
Kraków 10229, 10248
Nieborów i Arkadia 10303
Poznań 10345
Warszawa 10450
Portugal
Faro 10559

Mafra 10595
Porto 10605
Puerto Rico
San Juan 10638
Réunion
Saint-Denis 10643
Romania
Bucureşti 10671, 10673
Craiova 10708
Hunedoara 10727
Topalu 10792
South Africa
Johannesburg 10908
Spain
Badajoz 11062
Baños de Cerrato 11067
Barcelona 11078, 11088, 11094
Béjar 11105
Bilbao 11110, 11111
Cáceres 11125
Crevillente 11171
Cuenca 11172, 11174
Fromista 11191
Granada 11207
La Coruna 11243
Lérida 11261
Madrid 11277, 11287, 11309,
11316
Málaga 11347
Murcia 11380, 11382
Orense 11393
Orihuela 11396
Paredes de Nava 11423
Salamanca 11454, 11455
San Juan de Vilasar 11463
Santander 11489
Sevilla 11516, 11517
Solsona 11533
Tarrasa 11544
Toledo 11551, 11553
Valencia 11577
Valladolid 11591, 11594
Vigo 11605
Yecla 11623
Zaragoza 11630
Sweden
Eskilstuna 11681
Göteborg 11702
Stockholm 11807
Switzerland
Basel 11930
Bern 11949
Chur 11989
Ligornetto 12117
Locarno 12119
Lugano 12124
Rüeggisberg 12201
Winterthur 12290, 12295
Zürich 12315, 12334
Tanzania
Marangu 12352
United Kingdom
Cambridge 12816
Compton 12874
Conway 12877
Dundee 12928
Huddersfield 13077
London 13196, 13231
Milngavie 13295
Newlyn 13316
St. Ives, Cornwall 13416
Stockport 13494
United States
Akron OH 13629
Albuquerque NM 13650
Amherst MA 13685
Anadarko OK 13692
Arlington TX 13724
Asheville NC 13731
Athens GA 13746
Atlantic City 13755
Augusta GA 13768
Austin TX 13774, 13775
Baltimore MD 13802
Bartlesville OK 13822

Big Horn WY 13888
Binghamton NY 13894
Bloomsfield Hills MI 13915
Boston MA 13935
Brookings SD 13987
Brunswick ME 14004
Buffalo NY 14009
Cedar Falls IA 14088
Charleston SC 14120
Cheyenne WY 14152
Claremore OK 14197
Columbus OH 14266
Corvallis OR 14302
Dallas TX 14336
Dayton OH 14358
Denton TX 14388
Des Moines IA 14400
Downey CA 14431
Duluth MN 14441
East Hampton NY 14458
Farmington CT 14551
Flagstaff AZ 14571
Florence SC 14584
Flushing NY 14588
Fort Wayne IN 14646
Fort Worth TX 14650
Gorham ME 14741
Hempstead NY 14863
Hollywood FL 14893
Houston TX 14914
Independence KS 14949
Indianapolis IN 14957
Ithaca NY 14974
Kalispell MT 15025
Lincoln NE 15191
Longview TX 15230
Los Angeles CA 15240
Memphis TN 15358
Menomonie WI 15366
Miami FL 15381
Milwaukee WI 15415
Mountainville NY 15502
Mumford NY 15503
Nashville TN 15528, 15538,
15539
New Britain CT 15555
New Brunswick NJ 15558
New York NY 15605, 15620,
15621, 15645, 15648, 15653
Newburgh NY 15659
Newport RI 15674
North Miami Beach FL 15703
Omaha NE 15750
Palm Beach FL 15800
Paterson NJ 15824
Philadelphia PA 15873, 15882,
15884, 15893
Pittsburgh PA 15928
Ponca City OK 15952
Portland ME 15973
Poughkeepsie NY 15992
Princeton NJ 15999
Quincy IL 16025
Redlands CA 16053
Richmond VA 16085
Riverside CA 16097
Rock Springs WY 16123
Saco ME 30 04072 16157
St. Paul MN 16204
San Antonio TX 16242
San Jose CA 16274
San Marino CA 16282
Sarasota FL 16313
Saratoga CA 16314
Springfield MA 16447
Tampa FL 16543
Terre Haute IN 16569
Topeka KS 16595
University AL 16649
Washington DC 16746, 16754,
16755, 16763
Uruguay
Montevideo 16975, 16976
San José de Mayo 16984

USSR
Leningrad 17116
Pavlovsk 17248
Venezuela
Barcelona 17377
Caracas 17388
Zaire
Kinshasa 17847
Mushenge 17854
Seals (Numismatics) *(see also*
Numismatics)
Germany, Democratic Republic
Berlin 04623
Germany, Federal Republic
Berlin 05303
Greece
Athens 06052, 06057
India
Allahabad 06567
Bhuj 06604
New Delhi 06786
Pondicherry 06809
Vaisali 06860
Vidisha 06868
Netherlands
Harderwijk 09167
Poland
Wrocław 10491
South Africa
Durban 10863
Spain
Lérida 11262
Switzerland
Burgdorf 11983
Luzern 12135
Wil 12284
Zug 12313
Shells *(see also* Mollusks)
Australia
Port Lincoln 00561
Austria
Wien 00844
Bahamas
Nassau 00912, 00913
Belgium
Lasne 01140
Nieuwpoort 01213
Sprimont 01264
Brazil
Rio Grande 01480
Canada
Gibsons 01980
Shoal Lake 02390
Chile
Viña del Mar 02607
Cuba
La Habana 02803
Ethiopia
Addis Ababa 03658
France
Dijon 04102
Germany, Federal Republic
Eichstätt 05419
Iceland
Akureyri 06546
India
Lucknow 06742
Israel
Nahariyya 07111
Italy
Torre del Greco 08047
Japan
Miyagi 08379
Mozambique
Beira 08929
Nampula 08935
Netherlands
Bourtange 09043
Denekamp 09073
Frederiksoord 09135
Groningen 09151
Meersen 09255
Noordwijk Aan Zee 09266
Ost-Vlieland 09283
Scheveningen 09322

Norway
  Oslo 09786
Philippines
  Cebu 10030
Portugal
  Lisboa 10571
  Tomar 10620
Spain
  Arenas de San Pedro 11043
  Burgos 11117
  Covadonga 11169
  Gerona 11198
  León 11258
  Pastrana 11424
  Quejana 11436
  San Millán de Suso 11469
  San Sebastián 11476
  Santes Creus 11491
  Tarragona 11542
  Vileña de Bureba 11608
  Villanueva de Lorenzana 11610
Switzerland
  Basel 11927
Turkey
  Ahlat 12452
  Akşehir 12454
  Konya 12546, 12550
  Sivas 12573
United States
  Lake of the Woods MN 15108
  Narrowsburg NY 15522
  Rome NY 16144
USSR
  Moskva 17166
Vatican
  Città del Vaticano 17366, 17371

Tools, carpentry
Australia
  Corrigin 00481
  Hahndorf 00500
  Landsborough 00514
  Snug 00571
Austria
  Fulpmes 00658
  St. Johann i.S. 00788
  Telfs 00818
Belgium
  Antwerpen 00946
  Borgerhout 00975
  Gesves 01094
  Marche-en-Famenne 01174
  Mons 01195
  Oostduinkerke 01222
Canada
  Ashcroft 01766
  Castlegar 01853
  Gow-Ganda 01988
  Grimsby 02006
  Hanna 02028
  Hudson's Hope 02039
  KIngston 02066
  Melbourne 02128
  Montréal 02150
  New Denmark 02192
  Pictou 02256
  Rocanville 02311
  Rock Island 02312
  Salvage 02357
  Souris 02397
  Strathroy 02412
  Toronto 02440
  Veregin 02492
Czechoslovakia
  Dobřiv 02926
  Nový Jičin 03128
Denmark
  Aabenraa 03353
  Aarhus 03363
  Faaborg 03388
  Faarevejle 03390
  Give 03404
  Glamsbjerg 03406
  Hadsund 03413
  Maribo 03494
  Sorø 03557

Finland
  Hartola 03689
  Helsinki 03717
  Kauhajoki 03759
  Mänttä 03796
  Riihimäki 03840
  Rovaniemi 03843
  Vammala 03888
  Vihanti 03893
France
  Les Arcs 04194
  Rouen 04438
  Tautavel 04507
Germany, Democratic Republic
  Belzig 04613
  Brand-Erbisdorf 04641
  Frohnau 04742
  Halberstadt 04792
  Ummendorf 05081
Germany, Federal Republic
  Achern 05166
  Adelsheim 05168
  Altenthann 05180
  Frankfurt 05460
  Kassel 05616
  Koblenz 05644
  Marktrodach 05744
  Marxzell 05746
  Remscheid-Hasten 05889
  Rothenburg ob der Tauber
  05892
  Schleswig 05907
  Westfehmarn 05976
Greece
  Volos 06303
Hungary
  Budapest 06386, 06388
  Miskolc 06449
India
  Deoria 06655
  Khiching 06729
  Tamluk 06845
Israel
  Tel Aviv 07137
Italy
  Firenze 07482
  Squinzano 07998
  Trieste 08078
Netherlands
  Allingawier 08953
  Almelo 08954
  Bellingwolde 09029
  Bourtange 09043
  Hilvarenbeek 09185
  Krimpen aan den IJssel 09208
  Leerdam 09215
  Lievelde 09240
  Ommen 09277
  Rijssen 09313
  Tilburg 09378
  Veenkloster 09403
  West-Terschelling 09434
  Wolvega 09437
  Workum 09438
New Zealand
  New Plymouth 09524
Norway
  Bleikvasslia 09636
  Egersund 09654
  Kaupanger 09716
  Kvernaland 09729
  Namsos 09764
  Selbu 09843
  Stjørdal 09870
Poland
  Duszniki Zdrój 10165
  Stara Kuźnica 10398
  Szczekociny 10417
Romania
  Bucureşti 10686
Switzerland
  Aarau 11891
  Aarburg 11892
  Aigle 11896, 11897
  Albisrieden 11898

  Allschwil 11899
  Altishofen 11901
  Attiswil 11912
  Aubonne 11914
  Bennwil 11942
  Berneck 11956
  Bex 11960
  Bottmingen 11967
  Brienz 11972
  Büren an der Aare 11982
  Davos Platz 12000
  Estavayer-le-Lac 12013
  Gontenschwil 12044
  Gränichen 12049
  Grindelwald 12051
  Grüningen 12052
  Güllen 12054
  Hinwil 12067
  Huttwil 12072
  Isérables 12074
  Klosters 12079
  Kreuzlingen 12081
  Küblis 12082
  Ligerz 12116
  Moudon 12150
  Rothrist 12199
  Sempach 12232
  Siebnen 12233
  Stampa 12249
  Utzenstorf 12269
  Wädenswil 12279
  Wiesendangen 12283
United Kingdom
  Abergavenny 12610
  Ashwell 12639
  Halifax 13031
  Hutton-le-Hole 13080
  Johnstown Castle 13095
United States
  Antigo WI 13711
  Barrington IL 13818
  Black River Falls WI 13902
  Burlington NJ 14016
  Cape May NJ 14062
  Cedar Falls IA 14087
  Charleston SC 14127
  Colorado Springs CO 14249
  Dillon CO 14417
  Douglass KS 14422
  Easton PA 14469
  Edwardsville IL 14478
  Eureka Springs AR 14521
  Fairfax VT 14535
  Fillmore UT 14565
  Harper KS 14830
  Harrison AR 14835
  High Point NC 14877
  Hot Springs SD 14908
  Ithaca NY 14975
  Kent CT 15044
  Keystone SD 15059, 15060
  La Crosse KS 15089
  La Fargeville NY 15092
  Lake George NY 15106
  Lemmon SD 15160
  Liverpool NY 15214
  Loachapoka AL 15216
  Long Beach CA 15227
  Mequon WI 15368
  Monroe NY 15449
  Montpelier VT 15467
  Montrose CO 15469
  New Canaan CT 15560
  Northport NY 15713
  Orlando FL 15769
  Ottumwa IA 15787
  Peacham VT 15830
  Peoria IL 15848
  Port Clinton OH 15955
  Portsmouth NH 15983
  Prairie du Rocher IL 15996
  Rhinelander WI 16062
  Rome NY 16144
  Salisbury NH 16227
  Schaefferstown PA 16339

  Shaftsbury VT 16371
  Simsbury CT 16395
  South Effingham NH 16424
  Springs PA 16453
  Staten Island NY 16474
  Sterling CO 16480
  Stockbridge MA 16486
  Sturbridge MA 16505
  Sussex NJ 16520
  Table Rock NE 16529
  Toledo IA 16585
  Topeka KS 16593
  Towanda PA 16599
  Troy NY 16609
  Tyler TX 16640
  Warren PA 16722
  Warsaw NY 16724
  Washington RI 16784
  Watertown CT 16793
  Watertown NY 16795
  Waterville ME 16798
  Weston CT 16854
  Wilson NY 16897
  Windsor VT 16908
  Zoar OH 16964
Zambia
  Livingstone 17855
Zimbabwe
  Bulawayo 17863
  Marandellas 17869

Toys and games (see also Dolls and
puppets)
Argentina
  Buenos Aires 00158
Australia
  Westbury 00595
Austria
  Salzburg 00780
  Vöcklamarkt 00820
Belgium
  Bruxelles 01024
  Keerbergen 01129
Canada
  Bowmanville 01805
  Dufresne 01914
  Dundas 01916
  Gananoque 01976
  London 02100
  Mooretown 02172
  Niagara Falls 02198
  Peterborough 02254
  Souris 02397
  Waterloo 02515
  Wolfville 02562
Denmark
  Randers 03526
  Roskilde 03537
France
  Mont-Saint-Aignan 04266
  Poissy 04402
Germany, Democratic Republic
  Seiffen 05050
  Sonneberg 05057
  Zittau 05149
Germany, Federal Republic
  Hersbruck 05575
  Kirchberg 05638
  Meldorf 05756
  Nürnberg 05840
  Rüdesheim 05899
  Tecklenburg 05941
India
  Bhopal 06600
  Calcutta 06632
  Dharampur 06658
  Lucknow 06750
  Nasik 06785
Japan
  Ashiya 08189
  Kyoto 08342
Netherlands
  Deventer 09081, 09083
  Dokkum 09090
  Roden 09297
  Vlaardingen 09414

Vught 09424
Switzerland
  Basel 11928
  Beromünster 11958
  Brugg 11976
  Donzhausen 12004
  Güttingen 12057
  Riehen 12195
  Zürich 12333
United Kingdom
  Bristol 12768
  Hartlebury 13041
  London 13173, 13197, 13228
  Rottingdean 13404
  Runbridge Wells 13407
  Warwick 13557
United States
  Burlington WI 14018
  Canton OH 14057
  Cape May NJ 14062
  Chillicothe OH 14178
  Danbury CT 14341
  Deming NM 14383
  Detroit Mi 14415
  Eastchester NY 14467
  Fairfield CT 14537
  Flemmington NJ 14576
  Fredonia KS 14674
  Greensburg PA 14785
  Honolulu HI 14904
  Ithaca NY 14975
  Las Cruces NM 15135
  Macon GA 15287
  Mason City IA 15346
  Morris IL 15479
  Morristown NJ 15480
  Nampa ID 15519
  Neptune NJ 15546
  New Brunswick NJ 15557
  New York NY 15606, 15642
  Old Lyme CT 15746
  Penn Yan NY 15838
  Philadelphia PA 15885
  Pittsburgh PA 15931
  Port Clinton OH 15955
  Portsmouth RI 15985
  Riverhead NY 16094
  Sandwich MA 16290
  Savannah GA 16329
  Springfield VT 16452
  Strasburg PA 16498
  Sumter SC 16512
  Troy NY 16609
  Ukiah CA 16642
  Wenham MA 16830
  West Allis WI 16831
  Westerly RI 16852
  Wethersfield CT 16857
Trades and guilds (see also Industrial arts)
Austria
  Wien 00902
Bahamas
  Hope Town 00910
Belgium
  Boom 00973
  Gent 01082
  Lessines 01144
  Marchienne-au-Pont 01175
  Terhagen 01269
Canada
  Arichat 01762
  Arnprior 01764
  Barkerville 01781
  Bowmanville 01805
  Burnaby 01822
  Dauphin 01899
  Emerson 01946
  Fort Langley 01960
  Goderich 01984
  Jordan 02050
  Kamloops 02052
  Kirkland Lake 02070
  Peace River 02245
  Rocky Mountain House 02315

Selkirk 02376
South Rawdon 02398
Thunder Bay 02429
Trinity 02464
Vaudreuil 02490
Finland
  Helsinki 03714
  Hirvihaara 03730
  Kristiinankaupunki 03773
  Kurikka 03776
  Loviisa 03789
  Maarianhamina 03794
  Pietarsaari 03820
  Rajamäki 03835
Germany, Democratic Republic
  Altenburg 04570
  Angermünde 04573
  Ansprung 04577
  Arneburg 04581
Germany, Federal Republic
  Bensberg 05263
  Bremen 05354
  Cloppenburg 05372
  Düsseldorf 05411
  München 05785
India
  Calcutta 06628
  Gauhati 06670
  Kanpur 06723
  Madras 06760
  Trichur 06850
Italy
  Roma 07892, 07908
Netherlands
  Hellendoorn 09181
  Rotterdam 09307
  Weert 09429
  West-Terschelling 09434
  Zaandijk 09446
  Zierikzee 09455
Norway
  Bergen 09626
  Bodø 09637
  Kvernaland 09729
  Lonevåg 09743
Pakistan
  Lahore 09941
Poland
  Świdnica 10410
Switzerland
  Arbon 11908
  Basel 11925
  Lenzburg 12111
  Lichtensteig 12113
  Näfels 12159
  Olten 12172
  Sainte-Croix 12205
  Winterthur 12288
United Kingdom
  Biggar 12702
  Gloucester 13005
  Leicester 13141
  London 13197
  Worcester 13592
United States
  Ambridge PA 13682
  Bath ME 13824
  Belvidere NE 13861
  Chadron NE 14102
  Ft. Bridger WY 14598
  Granville OH 14764
  Green River WY 14773
  Jackson WY 14981
  Moose WY 15474
  New York NY 15636
  Oconto WI 15731
  Philadelphia PA 15870
  Rockingham VT 16129
  Shaftsbury VT 16371
  South St. Paul MN 16427
  Vancouver WA 16677
  Watrous NM 16802
  Whitewater WI 16866
  Williamsport PA 16880
  Windsor NY 16907

Transportation (see also Boats and shipping; Railroads; Vehicles)
Argentina
  Buenos Aires 00108
  Longchamps 00256
Australia
  Broadway 00464
  Echuca 00489
  Ferny Grove 00493
  Melbourne 00532
  St. Kilda 00569
  Westbury 00595
Austria
  Graz 00675
  Wien 00836, 00874
Belgium
  Schepdaal 01251
Brazil
  Botafogo 01355
Bulgaria
  Ruse 01641
Canada
  Alida 01755
  Barrie 01784
  Bonshaw 01802
  Clinton 01875
  Cottonwood 01887
  Fort MacLeod 01962
  Fort Steele 01967
  Goderich 01984
  Melville 02129
  Moose Jaw 02174
  Readlyn 02291
  Saskatoon 02371
  Whitehorse 02532
Denmark
  Aalestrup 03357
  Valby 03575
  Vejby 03577
Egypt
  Cairo 03639
Finland
  Helsinki 03707
  Hyvinkää 03734
  Jokioinen 03747
  Pietarsaari 03820
France
  Compiègne 04086
  Le Mans 04185
  Mulhouse 04288
  Paris 04385
  Pithiviers 04399
  Versailles 04543
Germany, Democratic Republic
  Pegau 04955
  Riesa 05004
  Rittersgrün 05005
Germany, Federal Republic
  Bad Oeynhausen 05231
  Berlin 05290
  Bochum 05322
  Düsseldorf 05411
  Emmendingen 05423
  Frankfurt 05472
  Friedrichshafen 05482
  Gundelfingen 05520
  Hamburg 05526, 05528
  Isny 05594
  Karlsruhe 05613
  Langenburg 05688
  Marktrodach 05744
  München 05799
  Sehnde 05917
Hungary
  Budapest 06367, 06375
Japan
  Nagoya 08404
  Osaka 08461
  Tokyo 08581
Netherlands
  Leek 09212
  Utrecht 09390
New Zealand
  Gisborne 09492

Norway
  Hamar 09691
Portugal
  Caramulo 10545
South Africa
  Barkley East 10832
  Heidelberg 10891
  Johannesburg 10907, 10910
  Pretoria 10966
Sweden
  Dalarö 11670
  Gävle 11695
  Malmö 11758, 11759
  Stockholm 11815, 11836
Switzerland
  Bern 11954
United Kingdom
  Bristol 12770
  Cheddleton 12841
  Coventry 12881
  Eastney 12944
  Hamilton 13032
  Hartlebury 13041
  Holywood 13072
  Horsham 13074
  Leicester 13139
  Llandrindod Wells 13165
  London 13197, 13213, 13240
  Lutterworth 13259
  Maidstone 13265
  Matlock 13280
  Newcastle-upon-Tyne 13314
  Norwich 13330
  Portmadoc 13371
  Scarborough 13438
  Stockton-on-Tees 13496
  Sunderland 13518
  Weston-super-Mare 13568
  York 13608
United States
  Akron OH 13631
  Alpena MI 13672
  Ashburnham MA 13729
  Athens PA 13748
  Aurora IL 13772
  Bellows Falls VT 13856
  Beverly MA 13886
  Blue Mountain Lake NY 13918
  Boothbay ME 13929
  Boston MA 13939
  Boyertown PA 13949
  Brewerton NY 13962
  Bucksport ME 14007
  Canal Fulton OH 14047
  Chattanooga TN 14142
  Cincinnati OH 14191
  Cleveland OH 14216
  Clintonville WI 14232
  Colorado Springs CO 14244
  Conneaut OH 14276
  Corry PA 14297
  Cresson PA 14317
  Crookston MN 14321
  Dearborn Mi 14366
  DeKalb IL 14376
  Denver CO 14394
  East Troy WI 14465
  Elmira NY 14495
  Encampment WY 14505
  Eureka CA 14520
  Evansville IN 14528
  Fort Eustis VA 14610
  Fort Leavenworth KS 14621
  Geneso NY 14712
  Glencoe MO 14726
  Glenwood OR 14732
  Green Bay WI 14770
  Greenbush WI 14776
  Greensboro NC 14782
  Hastings MI 14846
  High Falls NY 14876
  Hinsdale IL 14886
  Indianapolis IN 14955
  Jacksonport AR 14982
  Jamestown RI 14995

Río Grande 00321
Rosario 00332
San Rafael 00380
Australia
Adelaide 00436
Fortitude Valley 00494
Hobart 00505
Perth 00558
Austria
Graz 00673
Wien 00870
Belgium
Liège 01151
Namur 01208
Tervuren 01270
Bolivia
La Paz 01341
Brazil
Macapá 01395
Porto Alegre 01424
Rio de Janeiro 01452, 01472
São Paulo 01524
Bulgaria
Kotel 01599
Canada
Calgary 01834
Claresholm 01873
Hamiota 02026
Morpeth 02178
Ottawa 02232
Prince Rupert 02278
Regina 02296
Vancouver 02478
Winnipeg 02560
Chile
Angol 02579
Viña del Mar 02607
China, People's Republic
Dalian 02625
Harbin 02633
Colombia
Bogotá 02705
Cali 02725
Duitama 02736
Medellín 02749, 02750
Pasto 02763
Tunja 02782
Cuba
La Habana 02809, 02819, 02820
Pinar del Rio 02823
Czechoslovakia
Hořovice 02971
Slatiňany 03252
Soběslav 03255
Zilina 03345
Denmark
Aarhus 03361
Frederiksværk 03401
Grindsted 03410
København 03480
Ølgod 03519
Sorø 03557
Svendborg 03565
Viborg 03584
Ecuador
Quito 03601
Egypt
Cairo 03638
Giza 03643
El Salvador
San Salvador 03652
Finland
Helsinki 03701
Oulu 03812
Porvoo 03827
Turku 03871
Vaasa 03885
France
Barcelonnette 03974
Biarritz 04003
Brignoles 04027
Dijon 04102
Gevrey-Chambertin 04125
Laval 04170
Le Havre 04183

Nantes 04297
French Guiana
Cayenne 04560
Germany, Democratic Republic
Freiberg 04735
Gera 04751
Görlitz 04761
Gotha 04768
Hoyerswerda 04813
Jena 04819
Kamenz 04832
Karl-Marx-Stadt 04837
Leipzig 04874
Magdeburg 04894
Mühlhausen 04915
Mylau 04920
Nossen 04938
Osterwieck/Harz 04951
Prenzlau 04978
Rabenau 04988
Renthendorf 05000
Rudolstadt 05018
Saalfeld 05022
Siebenlehn 05054
Stralsund 05068
Waldenburg 05083
Wittenberg-Lutherstadt 05123
Germany, Federal Republic
Alfeld 05173
Aschaffenburg 05200
Bonn 05333
Dortmund 05397
Düsseldorf 05412
Erlangen 05436
Karlsruhe 05607
Kassel 05619
Kiel 05637
Lübeck 05710
Lüneburg 05724
Münster 05821
Osnabrück 05863
Stuttgart 05936
Ulm 05962
Greece
Athens 06085
Guatemala
Ciudad de Guatemala 06319, 06321
Guinea
N'Zerekore 06328
Guyana
Georgetown 06331
Hungary
Budapest 06398
Gyöngyös 06417
India
Allahabad 06571
Annamalai Nagar 06577
Coimbatore 06645
Dehradun 06654
Deoria 06656
Ernakulam 06661
Faizabad 06666
Gorakhpur 06676
Hardwar 06686
Jaunpur 06710
Kanpur 06725
Lucknow 06755
Madras 06763
Mangalore 06768
Meerut 06772
Muzaffarnagar 06776, 06777
Pudukottai 06816
Tiruchirapalli 06847
Iran
Karaj 06956
Ireland
Cork 07007
Dublin 07018
Israel
'En Harod 07050
Kiriat Tivon 07104
Italy
Alassio 07162
Bologna 07251

Bra 07272
Carmagnola 07309
Catania 07337
Favara 07417
Firenze 07476
Genova 07518
Imola 07548
Messina 07617
Milano 07632
Modena 07660
Napoli 07684
Palermo 07727
Pavia 07756
Roma 07855
Siena 07982
Torino 08044
Trento 08060
Treviso 08065
Trieste 08076
Udine 08083, 08085
Verona 08134
Japan
Chichibu 08197
Fukui 08206
Kyoto 08335
Miyazaki 08381
Mukaishima 08386
Nagaoka 08395
Sendai 08494
Shima 08498
Tokyo 08557
Korea, Republic
Seoul 08711
Malaysia
Taiping 08795
Mali
Bamako 08797
Morocco
Rabat 08923
Nepal
Kathmandu 08945
Netherlands
Amsterdam 08981, 09007
Domburg 09091
Eindhoven 09115
Enschede 09125
Holten 09192
Rhenen 09295
Sint Odiliënberg 09356
Utrecht 09394, 09397
Zwartsluis 09461
New Zealand
Invercargill 09506
Lower Hutt 09512
Nigeria
Ibadan 09591
Norway
Bergen 09633
Oslo 09812
Pakistan
Peshawar 09950
Peru
Lima 10006
Philippines
Manila 10047
Poland
Białowieża 10113
Kraków 10240, 10241
Krościenko 10251
Łódź 10277
Lublin 10286
Warszawa 10445
Wrocław 10500
Portugal
Coimbra 10555
Porto 10609
Puerto Rico
Mayaguez 10629
Réunion
Saint-Denis 10644
Romania
Aiud 10648
Bacău 10657
Constanta 10702
Galaţi 10722

Iaşi 10731
Sibiu 10777
Senegal
Saint-Louis 10816
South Africa
Kimberley 10918
Spain
Amposta 11035
Barcelona 11086
Madrid 11321
Pontevedra 11431
Santiago de Compostela 11493
Valencia 11585
Zaragoza 11633
Sweden
Lund 11755
Uppsala 11871
Switzerland
Basel 11932
Bern 11950
Ebikon 12007
Fribourg 12021
Genève 12036
Glarus 12042
La Chaux-de-Fonds 12085
Lausanne 12103
Lugano 12123
Neuchâtel 12163
Sion 12239
Vevey 12273
Zofingen 12309
Zürich 12338
Uganda
Kampala 12594
United Kingdom
Bangor/Wales 12658
Belfast 12689, 12690
Birmingham 12714
Cambridge 12804, 12815
Cardiff 12823
Cheddar 12840
Downe 12918
Dumfries 12922
Edinburgh 12966
Glasgow 12995
London 13177, 13191
Oxford 13350
Reading 13386
United States
Albuquerque NM 13656
Ashland OR 13737
Athens GA 13747
Atlanta GA 13752
Austin TX 13781
Baker NE 13788
Berkeley CA 13870, 13872
Bloomfield Hills MI 13908
Brazosport TX 13958
Brewster MA 13963
Buffalo NY 14011
Canon City CO 14050
Charles City IA 14113
Charleston SC 14117
Charlotte NC 14133
Cincinnati OH 14186
Corvallis OR 14303
Dallas TX 14334
Durham NC 14447
Grand Forks ND 14751
Greenboro NC 14775
Hanford CA 14823
Houston TX 14913
Irvine CA 14971
Lebanon Mo 15153
Lincoln NE 15195
Los Angeles CA 15249
Madison WI 15299
Manchester CT 15309
Milton MS 15410
Milwaukee WI 15418
Niles MI 15680
Pacific Grove CA 15792
Palm Desert CA 15801
Pittsburgh PA 15923
Raleigh NC 16034

saur

Handbuch der Museen
Handbook of Museums

Deutschland (BRD, DDR), Österreich, Schweiz /
Germany, Austria, Switzerland
2. verbesserte Ausgabe 1981 / 2nd revised edition
1981. Ca. 750 Seiten / ca. 750 pages. Lin. DM 298, —
ISBN 3-598-10345-X

Das „Handbuch der Museen'' enthält in seiner 2. er-
gänzten und verbesserten Auflage Adresse und
spezifische Daten von über 3400 Museen aus der
Bundesrepublik Deutschland, der DDR, aus Österreich, der Schweiz und dem Fürstentum Liechtenstein.

Neben dem Namen des Museums mit Anschrift
und Telephonanschluß gibt ein Eintrag Auskunft
über folgende Besonderheiten:
Museumsträger, Museumsleiter und Stellvertreter,
Öffnungszeiten, Eintrittspreise, Ausstellungsfläche,
Sonderausstellungen, Führungen. Bei größeren
Museen finden sich auch Angaben zur Unterbrin-
gung der Sammlung und zur Sammlungsgeschichte;
über besondere wissenschaftliche Einrichtungen
und deren Leiter; über geplante Erweiterungen;
über die Publikationen seit 1970 und die Ausstel-
lungskataloge seit 1975. Das Handbuch ist nach
Ländern geordnet, innerhalb der Länder orts-
alphabetisch.

Die Register ermöglichen ein schnelles Auffinden
nach Orten und nach Museumsnamen. Das Stich-
wortregister ordnet und erschließt ca. 200 Sammel-
gebiete.

The 2nd revised and expanded edition of Handbook of Museums contains addresses and information on over 3400 museums from the Federal
Republic of Germany, the German Democratic
Republic, Austria, Switzerland and Liechtenstein.
Evaluation of questionnaires, press releases, and
trade publications provided the basis for detailed
and up-to-date information.

In addition to name, address, and telephone
number of the museum, each entry includes the
following additional data:
Museum sponsor, director and assistant director,
hours of operation, admission prices, exhibition
area, special exhibitions. Larger museums include
data on the organization and history of the collection, special facilities and their directors, planned
additions, publications since 1970, and catalogues
since 1975.

The handbook is arranged alphabetically by
country and subarranged by place. Subject, geographical, and institution indexes assure convenient, multiple access to the material.

K·G·Saur München·New York·London·Paris

K·G·Saur Verlag KG · Postfach 71 10 09 · 8000 München 71 · Tel. (0 89) 79 89 01 · Telex 05 212 067 saur d
K·G·Saur Publishing Inc.· 45 N. Broad St.· Ridgewood, N.J. 07450, USA· Tel. (609) 652-6360 · Telex 130596 kasp ur
K·G·Saur Ltd.· 1-19 New Oxford Street · London WC1A 1 NE · Telephone 01-404-4818 · Telex 24 902
K·G·Saur Editeur S.A.R.L. · 38, rue de Bassano · 75008 Paris · Téléphone 723 55-18 · Télex Iso Bur. 630144